CONTEMPORARY DRAMA

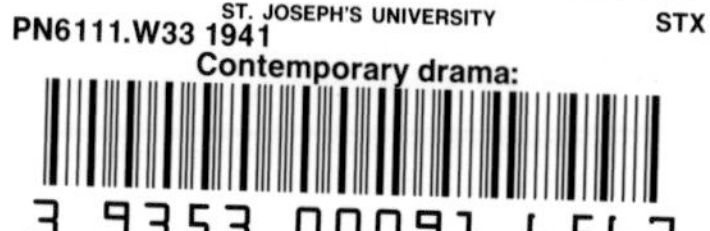

Contemporary Drama

EUROPEAN · ENGLISH AND IRISH ·

AMERICAN PLAYS

Selected by

E. Bradlee Watson

DARTMOUTH COLLEGE

and

Benfield Pressey

DARTMOUTH COLLEGE

CHARLES SCRIBNER'S SONS · NEW YORK

Chicago · Atlanta · San Francisco · Dallas

Printed in the United States of America

INTRODUCTION

All the plays presented in this volume have tested stage values and hold places of distinction in the literature of the modern theater. All have readable quality that alone would justify their inclusion. Their selection, however, has been largely determined by the hope that from the bewildering profuseness of the last sixty years of the international theater scene, each play chosen will recapture for the reader a moment that had great meaning to the audience by whom the play was first acclaimed; and that the sum of these great moments will adequately tell the story of the theater progress of our times.

Comparatively few readers in the school or college of today have often attended professional theater productions of important dramas; and fewer still could have seen many of the plays in this volume either as originally staged or as revived. For such readers it must be the aim of any drama anthology to give significantly the theater experience they have missed; for the first objective in any study of the drama should be the development of a sense of background out of which drama incessantly and fascinatingly evolves. Each of the plays is, we think, an essential part of our present-day theater tradition, for each is either an original contribution to it, or an impressive result of such contributions. Each may be said to have sprung from one or more of the highly conceived and nobly forwarded efforts to make the modern drama worthy of its high calling as the art of all the arts and the most penetrating interpreter of the evolving soul of an age.

BACKGROUND

The theater period preceding that of the plays we include was, in all the western world, admittedly one of the most sterile in dramatic history, especially as it failed to inspire the writing of original drama. Although the reader of this volume need not concern himself with this earlier theater, which both theatrically and sociologically was more deserving of study than most scholars are as yet aware, he should, at least, keep it in mind as having established a stereotyped theatre art, made the more impregnable by the Victorian code of reticence regarding sex relations, religion, thought, and behavior that did not fall safely within the accepted limits of "respectability." This fetish caused the audiences of the time to draw hypocritically a veil over their own human impulses, whether good or bad. It even more damagingly caused them to impose this reticence on their neighbors and to make taboo in all public utterance the mention of the basic social evils which the prophets of the age—notably Schopenhauer, Nietzsche, and Marx among the Germans; Emile Zola among the French; Ruskin, Arnold, Butler, and Hardy less boldly among the English—had striven to voice to their smugly resistant generation. It was among these prophets that the vital dramatists of our age took their stand. It was a tardy stand, to be sure, for the drama, like religion, is an intimate and slowly evolving understanding between audience and preacher; and for this reason drama remains always the most conservative of the arts. It must wait for conflicts to come to light before it can safely bring them on the stage. That is why the earlier European dramas of this volume came into existence not mainly at the great public playhouses, but in what is known as the Little Theater Movement, of which Antoine's Théâtre Libre, founded in Paris in 1887, was the inspirational beginning. His now famous adventure was imitated two years later in the Freie Bühne of Berlin and five years later in the Independent Theater of London. Although Ibsen's early dramas antedated these theaters, Ibsen owed his wide influence throughout Europe largely to the courageous production of his plays by the Little Theaters in spite of the almost universal abuse that the Norwegian's iconoclasm everywhere provoked. For such experimental theaters the first plays of de Curel, Hauptmann, Sudermann, and Bernard Shaw were written.

VICTORIAN THEATER CONVENTIONS

To this revolt of the Little Theatre against the social prudery, hypocrisy, and cant of the Victorian age, and still more against the art conventions of its stuffy theater, we owe the great outburst of drama that this volume, however imperfectly, epitomizes. These stage conventions were almost as repressive to composition as were the ethical standards of the age. In brief, they imposed:

1. The Star System, giving free rein to the individual actor, even as a member of a stock company, to use a play for exploiting personal mannerisms. The Public, therefore, went to see actors rather than plays. A new play had small chance of acceptance or success.

2. Melodramatic Patterns. Play carpentry was designed always with a view to melodramatic effects of surprise, sensation, and sentimentality, but with little regard for truth in character or for logic in the sequence of events. If characters were sufficiently brilliant and stage happenings were sufficiently exciting, little else mattered. The focus was sharply on plot mechanics and sentimental appeal; and this false emotion was produced by unreal virtue contending with equally unreal villainy, and hardly ever by real people in the clashes of real life. This confection was the more deadly to popular taste in drama because it paraded in a guise of surface realism and was exploited by some of the most technically accomplished actors in the history of the theater. So from France Bernhardt and Madame Réjane and the two Coquelins flashed the brilliant but empty well-made plays of Scribe, the younger Dumas, and Sardou, in all capitals of Europe and America. Everywhere lesser imitators of this dazzling artifice accepted it as a model of excellence. In the absence of English play carpenters comparable to the French and of actors and actresses, except the Shakespearean, who could rival those from France, the English-speaking stage was clogged with thinly disguised adaptations from the French. Writers like Jones, Pinero, and W. S.

Gilbert, to be sure, were learning to give these models a purely English flavor. Especially they succeeded in farce and burlesque, musical or otherwise, and established a vein of telling paradox that Shaw was later to use far more significantly in his comedies.

3. Sham Scenic Realism. Elaborately painted cloth wings, backdrops, and borders alternated with conventional box-sets, elaborately realistic rather than sincere. Glaring lime-light spots followed the star about the stage with a prismatic halo, leaving lesser actors to face a distorting glow from the footlights.

4. Costume Elegance. Costuming was showy rather than artistic or appropriate. Considerable study, however, was bestowed on the wardrobe for the Irving productions of Shakespeare.

In spite of these many absurdities, the reader should not assume that the better theaters of the 1880 period were as crudely set as the present-day burlesques of old-time melodrama would suggest. On the contrary, the century had seen remarkable progress in all the arts of the theater. Even the melodramatic formulas had been veneered with social significance in the "problem play" of which the younger Dumas's *Camille* (*La Dame aux Camélias*) was a universally popular precursor. Virtuosity in acting had reached impressive heights. It might almost be asserted that no stage art had ever so delighted the general public. It was to a very small and critical section of this public that the playrights of revolt first addressed themselves. This small section gradually has come to include most of those who today attend the theater regularly; but we must reluctantly admit that the great bourgeois public has not yet been won back to the theater of intellectualism, and that now, with the competition of the movies, it is still less likely to be attracted by the best our theater has to present.

DRAMATIC REVOLT

But no one will deny that a dazzling art creating a false life on the stage to blind people to the shallowness of their own should have been replaced. As early as 1877 Ibsen had turned his back once for all on this theatrical shamming. One by one, though much later, brave spirits throughout Europe joined in his unrelenting purpose to restore to the theater of our age its primeval function of interpreting and criticizing life as it really is, with all its flaws and virtues honestly exposed; only by such sincerity, these pioneers rightly believed, could drama's greatest service be rendered: the service that the Greeks called "purgation of the emotions." Only so could the theater give satisfying entertainment to people of culture.

Each of the so-called movements in this revolt, from that of the naturalists against the nineteenth century conventions, to those later "presentational" experiments that not too successfully have striven to liberate our stage from the strict realism of the early naturalists, finds ample illustration in the following series. And the emancipation of the cringing, self-torturing soul of Victorianism to the outspoken, self-confident spirit of the passing decade might also be said to have been fought out in these plays as in a series of battles; for, from *A Doll's House* to *Justice* and *Loyalties* and from lovely *Pélléas and Mélisande* to *Hotel Universe*, some aspect of the war of the spirit in our time is the essential theme. Many of these plays have made decisive contributions towards an ultimate victory, remote as that still seems. Similarly in the lesser, but, to the student of the drama, the highly important battles of theater art, these plays mark bold progress from the constraining stage photography of a *Magda* to the free experimentation of *A Dream Play, Man and the Masses,* and *"The Hairy Ape."* In *Abe Lincoln in Illinois,* which in this volume we are privileged to substitute for Mr. Sherwood's less significant *Petrified Forest,* we reach that free form of naturalist drama in which the scene rather than the act is the structural unit. Its settings are those of simplified realism, more symbolic than completely photographic. And for the moment in our theater this type of composition and setting seems to be the most satisfying outcome of the many artistic experiments and the numerous great improvements in stage machinery which have freed our theater for almost any form of production.

SCOPE OF THE COLLECTION

We realize that no such limited selection of plays could be made to satisfy all preferences. We make no exaggerated claims for this series. Purposely we have made no effort to avoid the obvious or to choose the merely unusual or bafflingly subtle. We present thirty-seven plays which we think everyone pretending to evaluate contemporary drama should know. We assume that the great *opus* of Shaw must be viewed more completely than through any single play, for which reason it would be futile to represent him in this series. We are also aware that Eugene O'Neill cannot be adequately represented by the two plays we include, but we believe that these two illustrate more vividly than any others the disruptive impact of his genius upon the all but sterile American theater, opening new ways of progress, which, at least, have made its old banalities of thought and its water-tight play carpentry no longer tolerable.

The plays are here printed in the groupings of the original single volumes: European Plays, English and Irish Plays, American Plays. This arrangement many of those who have used the individual volumes prefer. The factual material and the play lists, carefully brought up to date, have been printed separately in order to free the introductory comments for the treatment of only such aspects of the dramatist's life and art as are illuminating to the study of his play. We have included descriptions of scenic methods whenever these were unusual or in any way contributive to the progress of theater art. Such comment, although adequate, we hope, can by no means be exhaustive. Readers are therefore urged to consult the dramatists' own writings on their art. Their titles appear regularly after the play lists. Readers should also consult the works about the playwrights given in separate bibliographies printed after the general book list in the Appendix. Carefully selected references to illustrations of the staging of the individual plays will also be found in the Appendix. These should be helpful to the reader not only in visualizing the scene of each play, but also in acquainting him graphically with the progress of theater art during this formative period.

ADVICE TO READERS

We suggest to the student who wishes to derive the maximum of appreciative enjoyment from the reading that he or she follow this obvious but often neglected advice:

1. Put yourself as nearly as possible in the mental attitude of the audience that first witnessed the play, remembering that the play was composed to be seen and not merely read.
2. Reconstruct, preferably on paper, the scenes described by the dramatist, with all important details clearly defined: especially the doors, hallways, windows, and seats. Note the atmosphere the staging is expected to create and the effects produced by lighting.
3. Like a play director, plot the entrances and movements of characters, visualizing their personalities and noting any suggestions as to their mannerisms or costumes.
4. If possible, read each play aloud, or, at least, sense as you read not merely the story value of the speeches but also their character traits, their humor, and their emotional quality—that is, read for the complete effect that the dramatist intended to create on the stage by the voices of well-cast actors, as they would lend human values to words. It is often helpful for groups to read plays aloud, assigning characters as appropriately as possible.
5. Note the play design, technically called plot, that is, the arrangement of the story material to give it the maximum effectiveness within the limitaticns of time and place which the theater imposes. Observe especially the arrangement for climax, contrast, suspense, and for effective entrances and exits, and above all for the accentuation of those impressions, intellectual or emotional, which the dramatist wishes to leave with his audience.

In short, the appreciative reading of a play differs widely from that of any other form of literature. In most of these the words are all-sufficient to the effect intended. In a play they are not. No drama is complete on the page. It must be mentally orchestrated. It can exist completely only in performance under expert direction with perfectly suited actors on a stage that brings to the play every effect of light, color, or design that the playwright's imagination has conceived.

The task of reading a play is, therefore, not the simple one that too many believe it to be. Right reading of drama requires more than mere understanding. The reconstruction of its action is an exciting mental process for readers with imagination and a true sense of character values, and it gives the reading of plays its supreme appeal as one of the most enjoyable of intellectual pursuits. In a strict sense, no play has ever, perhaps, existed in perfection. No other mind can enter fully into the dramatist's dreams. Hence even excellent stage productions of a play are often faulty to the dramatist. It is a well-known fact that

Eugene O'Neill can hardly bear to witness one of his plays on the stage, although he himself often directs them, and although he has spent a great deal of his life in the theater. To contend with this limitation, however, is one of the sources of satisfaction which the reading of drama affords. Remote as the goal of complete realization must remain, nothing is more stimulating to the mental faculty than even an imperfect attempt to fit one's own imagination to that of a truly great dramatic creator.

To one who has made such an effort, the professional rendering of a play in the theater is a tonic experience. He then checks his own impressions with those created by the company—sometimes to their advantage, sometimes to his own—but always with the satisfaction of coming nearer to the dramatist's conception. It would be unsafe to claim that all the plays in such a volume have the possibilities of perfect realization. But all at some time have stood the test of staging to the delight of discriminating critics and audiences. As a collection they may be said to have created in generous measure the standards of taste by which the public and critics of today evaluate a play.

PLAY GROUPS

As a help to those who prefer to read the plays in the order in which they are here presented under the headings, EUROPEAN, ENGLISH AND IRISH, and AMERICAN, we will briefly suggest the relationships of each group.

EUROPEAN PLAYS:

I. *A Doll's House, The Fossils, The Beaver Coat, Light o' Love* are important creative plays, some not otherwise easily available, covering the late nineteenth century theater of Continental Europe. Their initial success as epoch-making dramas and their repeated revival at home or abroad, have placed them among the most influential of modern masterpieces. They are indispensable to the understanding of naturalism as it first emerged in the Little Theaters of the Continent.

II. *Hedda Gabler, Pélléas and Mélisande, Magda, Cyrano de Bergerac, Uncle Vanya* represent some of the fruits of that flowering of the dramatic impulse that came to Europe immediately after Ibsen and the free theater groups had broken ground. All except *Uncle Vanya* and *Pélléas* won wide popularity even in the commercial theaters. The artistic consistency and impartiality of *Hedda Gabler* marks the Ibsen of full maturity. The old carpentry of the "well-made" play as skillfully done as possible may be seen in *Magda,* which, nevertheless, has borrowed some of the more advanced values of the naturalists' treatment of social problems. Perhaps the grandest romantic play of our time, *Cyrano de Bergerac,* shows that despite the noise and power of the naturalists and the Ibsenites, audiences could still be charmed by poetry and idealization. Another aspect of the movement away from mere rationality can be seen in Maeterlinck's play and in the theories that governed its creation. And arising independently, but soon to interact with the West, the Russian theater in Chekhov's plays comes fully into the naturalist movement. This group viewed with the early plays of Bernard Shaw represents well the background from which the contemporary drama of England and America was still to emerge. Various in intention and method though they are, each of them has its important place, not merely in the history of drama, but also in the mind and memory of every intelligent worker in the theater today. Before today could be what it is, these must have been.

III. *The Dream Play, A Night's Lodging, The Passion Flower* show a still further advance of the naturalist art, and in *The Dream Play* and *The Passion Flower* were already beginning to appear the forces of disruption that were soon to change even more radically the trend of modern stagecraft and lead to the school of expressionism. *The Passion Flower,* Benavente's most widely appealing play, in which the subtle delicacy of Spanish modernism is pleasingly represented, shows the effect on characterization of the Freudian psychology that has since inspired most of the advanced work in drama; and *The Dream Play* exhibits a technique later to be a favorite device of the expressionists, enabling them to depart from the surface appearances of life, substituting for them the broken, symbolic apparitions that proceed from the subconscious mind of the dreamer. Gorki's *Night's Lodging* maintains the diapason of sheer naturalism in its freest form, adding to the collection an undisputed masterpiece of the theater. In all, the inner life of humanity is being more expressively represented in terms of a naturalism seeking to broaden its horizons.

IV. *The Cherry Orchard, He Who Gets Slapped, Man and the Masses, R.U.R., "Henry IV"* link the tendencies reaching full fruition in the epoch before the World War with the theater of post-War days. Beginning with Chekhov's fragrant and delicate masterpiece, it shows the survival in the Russian theater of Maeterlinckian symbolism in Andreyev; the recurrence of Strindbergian departure from surfaces in the propagandist expressionism of Toller; the combination of fantasy and propaganda in Čapek; and the philosophic radicalism of Pirandello. The group shows that the War, though it interrupted, did not kill the European theater, but turned its already pronounced expressive tendencies to the more purposeful revelation in that theater of the old dreams of world betterment intensified by that otherwise abortive War—notably the pacifistic, the socialistic, and the anti-mystic or militantly scientific visions of a Utopian order that World War II has proved entirely premature. As the dreams were revolutionary they called for revolutionary expression in art and so greatly advanced anti-naturalistic experimentation in all European centers—but most successfully in Germany, Czechoslovakia, and Russia.

English and Irish Plays:

I. *Riders to the Sea, Hyacinth Halvey, What Every Woman Knows, Mid-Channel, The Glittering Gate, Justice* represent the energizing forces in the British theater at the beginning of the present century. These forces, especially in the work of Pinero, Barrie, and Galsworthy, produced an almost classic lucidity of form that marks this decade, even apart from the works of Shaw, as one of the outstanding epochs of English drama. The plays chosen from the Irish literary movement are representative of the enrichment of the theater in this period through the folk element and the symbolic fantasy that gave the work of the Abbey Theatre of Dublin, one of the world's most creative and enduring little theaters, a universal influence by revealing unsuspected values of character and atmosphere in folk legendry, homely peasant life, and small-town environment, when these are presented with complete dramatic integrity.

II. *Mr. Pim Passes By, The Circle, Loyalties, Dear Brutus, Juno and the Paycock* are gathered from the English theater of the World War and the third decade of this century. Only two of them, *Loyalties* and *Juno and the Paycock,* may be said to show the scars of the war; the others might have been written if that conflict had never been. None of them, however, is merely topical; none seems likely to succumb to that corrosion of the drama, "dating." All show the English and Irish dramatic genius continuing with vigor, although conservatively. But there is here no monotony—charm, wit, insight, pathos abound. They are sufficient, we hope, to prove that the English and Irish stage could live brightly in spite of the sobering and maturing effects of war.

AMERICAN PLAYS:

I. *The Emperor Jones, Processional, Beggar on Horseback, The Silver Cord* are all plays of the third decade of the present century, but their inspiration came chiefly from the world-wide movements epitomized in the preceding groups. Not until this decade did the American theater produce any play that has successfully stood the test of time, although many were vitalized by the new drama spirit of the period. Young writers after 1900 were inspired by experimental theaters in colleges and communities such as Professor George Pierce Baker's "47 Workshop" at Harvard and the little houses of the Provincetown and Washington Square Players. Gradually these writers broke their way into America's strongly resistant professionalism. It is, at least, noteworthy that the writers of the plays in this group came directly out of such experimentation or were influenced by it. Similarly the first Broadway theater that successfully sponsored such work, the Theatre Guild, was the creation of those who had grown up in little theaters. Although three of the plays are expressionistic and the fourth Freudian, they cannot be regarded as imitative. Each has original force direct from American life and each creates a new pattern to embody the spirit of modernism. In O'Neill's work we find always an unmistakable originality that has already contributed as much to the world theater as it has derived from it. But the import of none is merely local. And on the cold white page they carry much of the excitement and power of fresh illusion which has made them great successes in our theater.

II. *"The Hairy Ape," Street Scene, Hotel Universe, Elizabeth the Queen, Abe Lincoln in Illinois* are plays of impressive maturity that in the last two decades have contributed richly to the reputation of the American theater as the most vital and progressive of the world. Among them is the American progenitor of the proletarian plays, which artistically and ideologically remains one of the best; the clearest instance of American naturalism; a notable discussion play in line of descent from Ibsen and Shaw; a poetic historical play in verse, free from imitative affectations, which has created anew for our stage the poetic beauty of the noblest tradition of drama without destroying the illusion of actuality that is so much a part of the American theater consciousness. Finally from the latest phase of our dramatic progress comes Mr. Sherwood's artfully blended pageant of the Lincoln life. It suggests that the revolters are returning to the proven American virtues for their inspiration and to the more representational techniques for their form. But this technique is here used with a symbolic selectiveness that is clearly the product of the free experimentation of our century. A long stride forward has been made from *Rip Van Winkle* and *Nathan Hale* to *Abe Lincoln in Illinois*.

E. B. W.
B. P.

CONTENTS

EUROPEAN PLAYS

I

II

III

IV

ENGLISH AND IRISH PLAYS

I

II

AMERICAN PLAYS

I

II

APPENDIX

EUROPEAN PLAYS

EUROPEAN PLAYS

A Doll's House	Ibsen
The Fossils	de Curel
The Beaver Coat	Hauptmann
Light o' Love	Schnitzler
Hedda Gabler	Ibsen
Magda	Maeterlinck
Pélléas and Mélisande	Sudermann
Cyrano de Bergerac	Rostand
Uncle Vanya	Chekhov
The Dream Play	Strindberg
Night's Lodging or *The Lower Depths*	Gorki
The Passion Flower	Benavente
The Cherry Orchard	Chekhov
He Who Gets Slapped	Andreyev
Man and the Masses	Toller
R. U. R.	Čapek
"Henry IV"	Pirandello

A DOLL'S HOUSE*

[*Et Dukkehjem*]

By

HENRIK IBSEN

Translated from the Norwegian by WILLIAM ARCHER

IBSEN ONCE DECLARED THAT HIS LIFE WORK should be studied as an indivisible whole, and not broken into periods or types. To him the sequence of his plays, extending over half the century, represented a unified progress towards the goal of perfect self-expression in the dramatic form. Perhaps his strengthening insistence on individualism as a life philosophy gave him this impression of an inner unity in work that on its outer side falls clearly into periods and types. So closely do his plays reflect the phases of dramatic change during the half century that a student does well to note the contacts, for Ibsen, like Shakespeare, was "made as well as born." *A Doll's House* marks a most important step in Ibsen's progress.

As a young student he published *Catiline* (1850), a verse drama, modeled on the dramas of the Danish romanticists, the only modern plays with which he was then familiar. It contained what, as late as 1874, he said were "the germs of a good deal which has since come to light in my poetry." His premature appointment as theater-poet at Bergen (1851) and his visit to Dresden to observe Heiberg's play production brought him in contact with the "well-made" technique of the Scribe school. His *Lady Inger of Ostrat* (1855) is an instance of the blend of the well-made technique with romantic excess. His early plays produced at Bergen were rarely successful; but later at Christiania his *Vikings of Helgeland* (1858) and *The Pretenders* (1864) gave promise of the greatness to come. For a time he turned to satire, and in *Love's Comedy* (1862) he outraged the critics. This rebuff, followed by the failure of his theater and the King's refusal of an adequate pension, made him choose a life of exile in Italy and Germany. Freed from the restraints of the theater, he threw the best of his now maturing genius into the great verse plays, *Brand* (1866) and *Peer Gynt* (1867), but with little thought of the practical stage. His pension and his reputation were at last secure and the desire for the theater returned. He submitted again and more completely to the bondage of the well-made play. His *League of Youth* (1869) was an almost perfect example of the Scribe and Dumas type at its best and was Ibsen's first modern social prose drama.

His practical theater experience at Bergen and Christiania, as Gosse believed, had taught him "to take the tastes of the vulgar into due consideration and to acquaint himself with the necessary laws of play-composition." His final adoption of the realist prose drama as best suited to his needs was not, however, a condescension on his part. For esthetic reasons, even in composing the great *Emperor and Galilean* (1873), he preferred prose, and wrote to Edmund Gosse, "My new drama is no tragedy in the ancient acceptation; what I desired to depict were human beings, and therefore I would not let them talk 'the language of the Gods.'" Again he seemed to express the growing conviction of the age. When, after four years, he reappeared as dramatist he wrote another well-made play, *Pillars of Society* (1877), but in this are more clearly apparent those moral and spiritual forces which, in *Brand* and *Peer Gynt*, could not be restrained by any play formula. The next liberating step, to which all the later progress in drama may be directly or indirectly traced, was taken in *A Doll's House* (1879). The technique of its beginning and development was much like that of Augier's or Dumas' work at its best: but its end proclaimed the freedom of the stage and restored drama to its high calling—that of revealing the mind in significant conflict. No historic survey of modern drama is possible without an understanding of this change in Ibsen's technique and all that it implied. The drama of machinery was doomed. The drama of idea and "discussion" was born.

The success, or at least the notoriety, of *A Doll's House* was immediate in Scandinavia and Germany. Ibsen was encouraged to continue his cutting at the roots of social evil with the purpose of the reformer but with the method of the artist. He diagnosed, but proposed no remedies. He was now confirmed in his adoption of realism, also in his spiritual aim: "Everything I have written has the closest possible connection with what I have lived through, even if it has not been my own personal experience. In every new poem or play I have aimed at my own spiritual emancipation and purification—for a man shares the responsibility and guilt of the society to which he belongs."

More important, artistically, was his impartment of poetic values to the prose play. For the artificial rhythm of verse, which to the Ibsen of this period was meaningless in the theater, he substituted the deeper and subtler rhythms of nicely related inner and outer action, and of plots corresponding to the organism of life and not to the conventions of theatrical technique. Gradually, he introduced symbols giving still more definite poetic coloring. In short, the prose plays of Ibsen revealed both truth and beauty in the theater as few verse plays have done. Those who would cast the Ibsen theater on the rubbish heap because of its outmoded surface values or its over-concern with social problems and outworn philosophies, should remember that Ibsen's true claim to greatness was in none of these tendencies, but in his far more important merits as the artist creator of character and action and in his penetrating spiritual discernment.

The experiment tried in *A Doll's House* led, in *Ghosts* (1881) and in *Rosmersholm* (1886), to a complete abandonment of the well-made formula. Instead, Ibsen adopted a close approximation to the method of the Greek tragedy, that of the gradual revelation, through conflicting characters, of events already transpired before the play begins. The spiritual reaction of the characters to this revelation constitutes the dramatic action, unaided by theatrical clap-trap. In Ibsen, then, profoundly revealing mental or spiritual action replaced the easier and less significant surface conflicts and intrigue of the prevalent melodrama and the well-made play.

PRODUCTION

Ibsen anticipated in his new phase of realism the naturalistic doctrines that found expression in the staging of the free theaters in Paris (1887) and in Berlin (1889). *A Doll's House* was, however, adequately given for the first time at the Royal Theater, Copenhagen, in December, 1879. Its first performance in English was by Madame Modjeska in Louisville, Kentucky, in 1883. Its results were negligible in English until it was produced in London by Mr. Charrington, as Helmer, and Miss Janet Achurch, as Nora, at the Novelty Theater in 1889, in a manner anticipating the work of the Independent Theater, founded by J. T. Grein two years later. In this enterprise also Miss Achurch was to play Ibsen's leading parts and to win the high esteem of Mr. Bernard Shaw. In Denmark, Germany, and in England, the Ibsen realist plays did more than any others to create the school of stage naturalism that for at least two decades was to orient all theatrical endeavor. Mrs. Fiske performed the same service in this play for the American theater. Ibsen's ideal of a stage which should not merely suggest but actually present a four-walled room—the audience being the fourth wall—and on which everything, including speech and action, should appear as in actual life, has become too familiar to need further comment. The idea was not a new one, but Ibsen was more insistent than his contemporaries upon its complete realization.

HENRIK IBSEN

Born 1828, Skien, Norway.
Apprenticed to an apothecary.
1850, University of Christiania. First play, *Catiline*, published.
1851, "Theater-poet" at Bergen.
1857, Manager and artistic adviser of theaters at Christiania.

1862, *Love's Comedy* violently criticized for its individualism.
1864, Pension refused him. He withdrew to Italy.
1866, *Brand* won him a poet's pension.
1868–1891, Resident in Germany.
1869, *The League of Youth,* the first of his modern prose dramas.
1877–1899, Period of the great social prose dramas.
1891–1906, In Christiania.
Died 1906.

PLAYS

1850 *Catiline.* 1850 *The Viking's Barrow.* 1853 *St. John's Night.* 1855 *Lady Inger of Ostrat.* 1856 *The Feast of Solhaug.* 1857 *Olaf Liljekrans.* 1858 *Vikings of Helgeland.* 1862 *Love's Comedy.* 1864 *The Pretenders.* 1866 *Brand.* 1867 *Peer Gynt.* 1869 *The League of Youth.* 1873 *Emperor and Galilean.* 1877 *Pillars of Society.* 1879 *A Doll's House.* 1881 *Ghosts.* 1882 *An Enemy of the People.* 1884 *The Wild Duck.* 1886 *Rosmersholm.* 1888 *The Lady from the Sea.* 1890 *Hedda Gabler.* 1892 *The Master Builder.* 1894 *Little Eyolf.* 1896 *John Gabriel Borkman.* 1899 *When We Dead Awaken.*

WRITINGS ABOUT THE DRAMA

See *From Ibsen's Workshop,* 1912.

A DOLL'S HOUSE

Characters

TORVALD HELMER.
NORA, *his wife.*
DOCTOR RANK.
MRS. LINDEN.[1]
NILS KROGSTAD.
THE HELMERS' THREE CHILDREN.
ANNA,[2] *their nurse.*
A MAID-SERVANT (ELLEN).
A PORTER.

The action passes in Helmer's house (a flat) in Christiania.

ACT FIRST

A room, comfortably and tastefully, but not expensively, furnished. In the back, on the right, a door leads to the hall; on the left another door leads to HELMER'S *study. Between the two doors a pianoforte. In the middle of the left wall a door, and nearer the front a window. Near the window a round table with armchairs and a small sofa. In the right wall, somewhat to the back, a door, and against the same wall, farther forward, a porcelain stove; in front of it a couple of armchairs and a rocking-chair. Between the stove and the side door a small table. Engravings on the walls. A what-not with china and bric-à-brac. A small bookcase filled with handsomely bound books. Carpet. A fire in the stove. It is a winter day.*

[*A bell rings in the hall outside. Presently the outer door of the flat is heard to open. Then* NORA, *enters, humming gaily. She is in outdoor dress, and carries several parcels, which she lays on the right-hand table. She leaves the door into the hall open, and a* PORTER *is seen outside, carrying a Christmas tree and a basket, which he gives to the* MAID-SERVANT *who has opened the door.*]

Nora. Hide the Christmas tree carefully, Ellen; the children must on no account see it before this evening, when it's lighted up. [*To the* PORTER, *taking out her purse.*] How much?

Porter. Fifty öre.[3]

Nora. There is a crown. No, keep the change.

[*The* PORTER *thanks her and goes.* NORA *shuts the door. She continues smiling in quiet glee as she takes off her outdoor things. Taking from her pocket a bag of macaroons, she eats one or two. Then she goes on tip-toe to her husband's door and listens.*]

Nora. Yes; he is at home.

[*She begins humming again, crossing to the table on the right.*]

Helmer. [*In his room.*] Is that my lark twittering there?

Nora. [*Busy opening some of her parcels.*] Yes, it is.

Helmer. Is it the squirrel frisking around?

Nora. Yes!

Helmer. When did the squirrel get home?

Nora. Just this minute. [*Hides the bag of macaroons in her pocket and wipes her mouth.*] Come here, Torvald, and see what I've been buying.

Helmer. Don't interrupt me. [*A little later he opens the door and looks in, pen in hand.*] Buying, did you say? What! All that? Has my little spendthrift been making the money fly again?

Nora. Why, Torvald, surely we can afford to launch out a little now. It's the first Christmas we haven't had to pinch.

Helmer. Come, come; we can't afford to squander money.

Nora. Oh yes, Torvald, do let us squander a little, now—just the least little bit! You know you'll soon be earning heaps of money.

Helmer. Yes, from New Year's Day. But there's a whole quarter before my first salary is due.

[1] In the original "Fru Linde."
[2] In the original "Anne-Marie."
[3] About sixpence. There are 100 öre in a krone or crown, which is worth thirteenpence halfpenny, or twenty-seven cents.

Nora. Never mind; we can borrow in the meantime.

Helmer. Nora! [*He goes up to her and takes her playfully by the ear.*] Still my little featherbrain! Supposing I borrowed a thousand crowns to-day, and you made ducks and drakes of them during Christmas week, and then on New Year's Eve a tile blew off the roof and knocked my brains out——

Nora. [*Laying her hand on his mouth.*] Hush! How can you talk so horridly?

Helmer. But supposing it were to happen —what then?

Nora. If anything so dreadful happened, it would be all the same to me whether I was in debt or not.

Helmer. But what about the creditors?

Nora. They! Who cares for them? They're only strangers.

Helmer. Nora, Nora! What a woman you are! But seriously, Nora, you know my principles on these points. No debts! No borrowing! Home life ceases to be free and beautiful as soon as it is founded on borrowing and debt. We two have held out bravely till now, and we are not going to give in at the last.

Nora. [*Going to the stove.*] Very well —as you please, Torvald.

Helmer. [*Following her.*] Come, come; my little lark mustn't droop her wings like that. What? Is my squirrel in the sulks? [*Takes out his purse.*] Nora, what do you think I have here?

Nora. [*Turning around quickly.*] Money!

Helmer. There! [*Gives her some notes.*] Of course I know all sorts of things are wanted at Christmas.

Nora. [*Counting.*] Ten, twenty, thirty, forty. Oh, thank you, thank you, Torvald! This will go a long way.

Helmer. I should hope so.

Nora. Yes, indeed; a long way! But come here, and let me show you all I've been buying. And so cheap! Look, here's a new suit for Ivar, and a little sword. Here are a horse and a trumpet for Bob. And here are a doll and a cradle for Emmy. They're only common; but they're good enough for her to pull to pieces. And dress-stuffs and kerchiefs for the servants. I ought to have got something better for old Anna.

Helmer. And what's in that other parcel?

Nora. [*Crying out.*] No, Torvald, you're not to see that until this evening!

Helmer. Oh! Ah! But now tell me, you little spendthrift, have you thought of anything for yourself?

Nora. For myself! Oh, I don't want anything.

Helmer. Nonsense! Just tell me something sensible you would like to have.

Nora. No, really I don't know of anything —— Well, listen, Torvald——

Helmer. Well?

Nora. [*Playing with his coat-buttons, without looking him in the face.*] If you really want to give me something, you might, you know—you might——

Helmer. Well? Out with it!

Nora. [*Quickly.*] You might give me money, Torvald. Only just what you think you can spare; then I can buy something with it later on.

Helmer. But, Nora——

Nora. Oh, please do, dear Torvald, please do! I should hang the money in lovely gilt paper on the Christmas tree. Wouldn't that be fun?

Helmer. What do they call the birds that are always making the money fly?

Nora. Yes, I know—playbirds,[1] of course. But please do as I ask you, Torvald. Then I shall have time to think what I want most. Isn't that very sensible, now?

Helmer. [*Smiling.*] Certainly; that is to say, if you really kept the money I gave you, and really spent it on something for yourself. But it all goes in housekeeping, and for all manner of useless things, and then I have to pay up again.

Nora. But, Torvald——

Helmer. Can you deny it, Nora dear? [*He puts his arm around her.*] It's a sweet little lark, but it gets through a lot of money. No one would believe how much it costs a man to keep such a little bird as you.

Nora. For shame! How can you say so? Why, I save as much as ever I can.

Helmer. [*Laughing.*] Very true—as much as you can—but that's precisely nothing.

Nora. [*Hums and smiles with covert glee.*] H'm! If you only knew, Torvald, what expenses we larks and squirrels have.

Helmer. You're a strange little being! Just like your father—always on the lookout for all the money you can lay your hands on; but the moment you have it, it seems to slip through your fingers; you never know what becomes of it. Well, one must take you as you are. It's in the blood. Yes, Nora, that sort of thing is hereditary.

Nora. I wish I had inherited many of Papa's qualities.

Helmer. And I don't wish you anything but just what you are—my own, sweet little song-bird. But I say—it strikes me you look

[1] "Spillefugl," literally "playbird," means a gambler.

so—so—what shall I call it?—so suspicious to-day——

Nora. Do I?

Helmer. You do, indeed. Look at me full in the face.

Nora. [*Looking at him.*] Well?

Helmer. [*Threatening with his finger.*] Hasn't the little sweet-tooth been playing pranks to-day?

Nora. No; how can you think such a thing!

Helmer. Didn't she just look in at the confectioner's?

Nora. No, Torvald; really——

Helmer. Not to sip a little jelly?

Nora. No; certainly not.

Helmer. Hasn't she even nibbled a macaroon or two?

Nora. No, Torvald, indeed, indeed!

Helmer. Well, well, well; of course I'm only joking.

Nora. [*Goes to the table on the right.*] I shouldn't think of doing what you disapprove of.

Helmer. No, I'm sure of that; and, besides, you've given me your word—— [*Going towards her.*] Well, keep your little Christmas secrets to yourself, Nora darling. The Christmas tree will bring them all to light, I dare say.

Nora. Have you remembered to invite Doctor Rank?

Helmer. No. But it's not necessary; he'll come as a matter of course. Besides, I shall ask him when he looks in to-day. I've ordered some capital wine. Nora, you can't think how I look forward to this evening.

Nora. And I too. How the children will enjoy themselves, Torvald!

Helmer. Ah, it's glorious to feel that one has an assured position and ample means. Isn't it delightful to think of?

Nora. Oh, it's wonderful!

Helmer. Do you remember last Christmas? For three whole weeks beforehand you shut yourself up every evening till long past midnight to make flowers for the Christmas tree, and all sorts of other marvels that were to have astonished us. I was never so bored in my life.

Nora. I didn't bore myself at all.

Helmer. [*Smiling.*] But it came to little enough in the end, Nora.

Nora. Oh, are you going to tease me about that again? How could I help the cat getting in and pulling it all to pieces?

Helmer. To be sure you couldn't, my poor little Nora. You did your best to give us all pleasure, and that's the main point. But, all the same, it's a good thing the hard times are over.

Nora. Oh, isn't it wonderful?

Helmer. Now I needn't sit here boring myself all alone; and you needn't tire your blessed eyes and your delicate little fingers——

Nora. [*Clapping her hands.*] No, I needn't, need I, Torvald? Oh, how wonderful it is to think of! [*Takes his arm.*] And now I'll tell you how I think we ought to manage, Torvald. As soon as Christmas is over—— [*The hall-door bell rings.*] Oh, there's a ring! [*Arranging the room.*] That's somebody come to call. How tiresome!

Helmer. I'm "not at home" to callers; remember that.

Ellen. [*In the doorway.*] A lady to see you, ma'am.

Nora. Show her in.

Ellen. [*To* HELMER.] And the doctor has just come, sir.

Helmer Has he gone into my study?

Ellen. Yes, sir.

[HELMER *goes into his study.* ELLEN *ushers in* MRS. LINDEN, *in traveling costume, and goes out, closing the door.*]

Mrs. Linden. [*Embarrassed and hesitating.*] How do you do, Nora?

Nora. [*Doubtfully.*] How do you do?

Mrs. Linden. I see you don't recognize me.

Nora. No, I don't think—oh yes!—I believe—— [*Suddenly brightening.*] What, Christina! Is it really you?

Mrs. Linden. Yes; really I!

Nora. Christina! And to think I didn't know you! But how could I—— [*More softly.*] How changed you are, Christina!

Mrs. Linden. Yes, no doubt. In nine or ten years——

Nora. Is it really so long since we met? Yes, so it is. Oh, the last eight years have been a happy time, I can tell you. And now you have come to town? All that long journey in mid-winter! How brave of you!

Mrs. Linden. I arrived by this morning's steamer.

Nora. To have a merry Christmas, of course. Oh, how delightful! Yes, we will have a merry Christmas. Do take your things off. Aren't you frozen? [*Helping her.*] There; now we'll sit cosily by the fire. No, you take the armchair; I shall sit in this rocking-chair. [*Seizes her hands.*] Yes, now I can see the dear old face again. It was only at the first glance—— But you're a little paler, Christina—and perhaps a little thinner.

Mrs. Linden. And much, much older, Nora.

Nora. Yes, perhaps a little older—not

much—ever so little. [*She suddenly checks herself; seriously.*] Oh, what a thoughtless wretch I am! Here, I sit chattering on, and —— Dear, dear Christina, can you forgive me?

Mrs. Linden. What do you mean, Nora?

Nora. [*Softly.*] Poor Christina! I forgot: you are a widow.

Mrs. Linden. Yes; my husband died three years ago.

Nora. I know, I know; I saw it in the papers. Oh, believe me, Christina, I did mean to write to you; but I kept putting it off, and something always came in the way.

Mrs. Linden. I can quite understand that, Nora dear.

Nora. No, Christina; it was horrid of me. Oh, you poor darling! how much you must have gone through!—And he left you nothing?

Mrs. Linden. Nothing.

Nora. And no children?

Mrs. Linden. None.

Nora. Nothing, nothing at all?

Mrs. Linden. Not even a sorrow or a longing to dwell upon.

Nora. [*Looking at her incredulously.*] My dear Christina, how is that possible?

Mrs. Linden. [*Smiling sadly and stroking her hair.*] Oh, it happens so sometimes, Nora.

Nora. So utterly alone! How dreadful that must be! I have three of the loveliest children. I can't show them to you just now; they're out with their nurse. But now you must tell me everything.

Mrs. Linden. No, no; I want you to tell me——

Nora. No, you must begin; I won't be egotistical to-day. To-day I'll think only of you. Oh! but I must tell you one thing—perhaps you've heard of our great stroke of fortune?

Mrs. Linden. No. What is it?

Nora. Only think! My husband has been made manager of the Joint Stock Bank.

Mrs. Linden. Your husband! Oh, how fortunate!

Nora. Yes; isn't it? A lawyer's position is so uncertain, you see, especially when he won't touch any business that's the least bit —shady, as of course Torvald never would; and there I quite agree with him. Oh! you can imagine how glad we are. He is to enter on his new position at the New Year, and then he'll have a large salary, and percentages. In future we shall be able to live quite differently—just as we please, in fact. Oh, Christina, I feel so lighthearted and happy! It's delightful to have lots of money, and no need to worry about things, isn't it?

Mrs. Linden. Yes; at any rate it must be delightful to have what you need.

Nora. No, not only what you need, but heaps of money—heaps!

Mrs. Linden. [*Smiling.*] Nora, Nora haven't you learnt reason yet? In our schooldays you were a shocking little spendthrift.

Nora. [*Quietly smiling.*] Yes; that's what Torvald says I am still. [*Holding up her forefinger.*] But "Nora, Nora" is not so silly as you all think. Oh! I haven't had the chance to be much of a spendthrift. We have both had to work.

Mrs. Linden. You, too?

Nora. Yes, light fancy-work: crochet, and embroidery, and things of that sort [*carelessly*] and other work too. You know, of course, that Torvald left the Government service when we were married. He had little chance of promotion, and of course he required to make more money. But in the first year after our marriage he overworked himself terribly. He had to undertake all sorts of extra work, you know, and to slave early and late. He couldn't stand it, and fell dangerously ill. Then the doctors declared he must go to the South.

Mrs. Linden. You spent a whole year in Italy, didn't you?

Nora. Yes, we did. It wasn't easy to manage, I can tell you. It was just after Ivar's birth. But of course we had to go. Oh, it was a wonderful, delicious journey! And it saved Torvald's life. But it cost a frightful lot of money, Christina.

Mrs. Linden. So I should think.

Nora. Twelve hundred dollars! Four thousand eight hundred crowns![1] Isn't that a lot of money?

Mrs. Linden. How lucky you had the money to spend.

Nora. We got it from Father, you must know.

Mrs. Linden. Ah, I see. He died just about that time, didn't he?

Nora. Yes, Christina, just then. And only think! I couldn't go and nurse him! I was expecting little Ivar's birth daily; and then I had my poor sick Torvald to attend to. Dear, kind old Father! I never saw him again, Christina. Oh! that's the hardest thing I have had to bear since my marriage.

Mrs. Linden. I know how fond you were of him. But then you went to Italy?

Nora. Yes; you see, we had the money, and the doctors said we must lose no time. We started a month later.

[1] The dollar (4*s.* 6*d.*) was the old unit of currency in Norway. The crown was substituted for it shortly before the date of this play.

Mrs. Linden. And your husband came back completely cured.

Nora. Sound as a bell.

Mrs. Linden. But—the doctor?

Nora. What do you mean?

Mrs. Linden. I thought as I came in your servant announced the doctor——

Nora. Oh, yes; Doctor Rank. But he doesn't come professionally. He is our best friend, and never lets a day pass without looking in. No, Torvald hasn't had an hour's illness since that time. And the children are so healthy and well, and so am I. [*Jumps up and claps her hands.*] Oh, Christina, Christina, what a wonderful thing it is to live and to be happy!—Oh, but it's really too horrid of me! Here am I talking about nothing but my own concerns. [*Seats herself upon a footstool close to* CHRISTINA, *and lays her arms on her friend's lap.*] Oh, don't be angry with me! Now tell me, is it really true that you didn't love your husband? What made you marry him, then?

Mrs. Linden. My mother was still alive, you see, bedridden and helpless; and then I had my two younger brothers to think of. I didn't think it would be right for me to refuse him.

Nora. Perhaps it wouldn't have been. I suppose he was rich then?

Mrs. Linden. Very well off, I believe. But his business was uncertain. It fell to pieces at his death, and there was nothing left.

Nora. And then——?

Mrs. Linden. Then I had to fight my way by keeping a shop, a little school, anything I could turn my hand to. The last three years have been one long struggle for me. But now it is over, Nora. My poor mother no longer needs me; she is at rest. And the boys are in business, and can look after themselves.

Nora. How free your life must feel!

Mrs. Linden. No, Nora; only inexpressibly empty. No one to live for! [*Stands up restlessly.*] That's why I could not bear to stay any longer in that out-of-the-way corner. Here it must be easier to find something to take up—to occupy one's thoughts. If I could only get some settled employment—some office work.

Nora. But, Christina, that's such drudgery, and you look worn out already. It would be ever so much better for you to go to some watering-place and rest.

Mrs. Linden. [*Going to the window.*] I have no father to give me the money, Nora.

Nora. [*Rising.*] Oh, don't be vexed with me.

Mrs. Linden. [*Going to her.*] My dear Nora, don't you be vexed with me. The worst of a position like mine is that it makes one so bitter. You have no one to work for, yet you have to be always on the strain. You must live; and so you become selfish. When I heard of the happy change in your fortunes—can you believe it?—I was glad for my own sake more than for yours.

Nora. How do you mean? Ah, I see? You think Torvald can perhaps do something for you.

Mrs. Linden. Yes; I thought so.

Nora. And so he shall, Christina. Just you leave it all to me. I shall lead up to it beautifully!—I shall think of some delightful plan to put him in a good humor! Oh, I should so love to help you.

Mrs. Linden. How good of you, Nora, to stand by me so warmly! Doubly good in you, who know so little of the troubles and burdens of life.

Nora. I? I know so little of——?

Mrs. Linden. [*Smiling.*] Oh, well—a little fancy-work, and so forth.—You're a child, Nora.

Nora. [*Tosses her head and paces the room.*] Oh, come, you mustn't be so patronizing!

Mrs. Linden. No?

Nora. You're like the rest. You all think I'm fit for nothing really serious——

Mrs. Linden. Well, well——

Nora. You think I've had no troubles in this weary world.

Mrs. Linden. My dear Nora, you've just told me all your troubles.

Nora. Pooh—those trifles! [*Softly.*] I haven't told you the great thing.

Mrs. Linden. The great thing? What do you mean?

Nora. I know you look down upon me, Christina; but you have no right to. You are proud of having worked so hard and so long for your mother.

Mrs. Linden. I am sure I don't look down upon any one; but it's true I am both proud and glad when I remember that I was able to keep my mother's last days free from care.

Nora. And you're proud to think of what you have done for your brothers, too.

Mrs. Linden. Have I not the right to be?

Nora. Yes, indeed. But now let me tell you, Christina—I, too, have something to be proud and glad of.

Mrs. Linden. I don't doubt it. But what do you mean?

Nora. Hush! Not so loud. Only think, if Torvald were to hear! He mustn't—not for worlds! No one must know about it, Christina—no one but you.

Mrs. Linden. Why, what can it be?

Nora. Come over here. [*Draws her down beside her on the sofa.*] Yes, Christina—I, too, have something to be proud and glad of. I saved Torvald's life.

Mrs. Linden. Saved his life? How?

Nora. I told you about our going to Italy. Torvald would have died but for that.

Mrs. Linden. Well—and your father gave you the money.

Nora. [*Smiling.*] Yes, so Torvald and every one believes; but——

Mrs. Linden. But——?

Nora. Papa didn't give us one penny. It was *I* that found the money.

Mrs. Linden. You? All that money?

Nora. Twelve hundred dollars. Four thousand eight hundred crowns. What do you say to that?

Mrs. Linden. My dear Nora, how did you manage it? Did you win it in the lottery?

Nora. [*Contemptuously.*] In the lottery? Pooh! Any one could have done that!

Mrs. Linden. Then wherever did you get it from?

Nora. [*Hums and smiles mysteriously.*] H'm; tra-la-la-la.

Mrs. Linden. Of course you couldn't borrow it.

Nora. No? Why not?

Mrs. Linden. Why, a wife can't borrow without her husband's consent.

Nora. [*Tossing her head.*] Oh! when the wife has some idea of business, and knows how to set about things——

Mrs. Linden. But, Nora, I don't understand——

Nora. Well, you needn't. I never said I borrowed the money. There are many ways I may have got it. [*Throws herself back on the sofa.*] I may have got it from some admirer. When one is so—attractive as I am——

Mrs. Linden. You're too silly, Nora.

Nora. Now I'm sure you're dying of curiosity, Christina——

Mrs. Linden. Listen to me, Nora dear: haven't you been a little rash?

Nora. [*Sitting upright again.*] Is it rash to save one's husband's life?

Mrs. Linden. I think it was rash of you, without his knowledge——

Nora. But it would have been fatal for him to know! Can't you understand that? He wasn't even to suspect how ill he was. The doctors came to me privately and told me his life was in danger—that nothing could save him but a winter in the South. Do you think I didn't try diplomacy first? I told him how I longed to have a trip abroad, like other young wives; I wept and prayed; I said he ought to think of my condition, and not to thwart me; and then I hinted that he could borrow the money. But then, Christina, he got almost angry. He said I was frivolous, and that it was his duty as a husband not to yield to my whims and fancies—so he called them. Very well, thought I, but saved you must be; and then I found the way to do it.

Mrs. Linden. And did your husband never learn from your father that the money was not from him?

Nora. No; never. Papa died at that very time. I meant to have told him all about it, and beg him to say nothing. But he was so ill—unhappily, it wasn't necessary.

Mrs. Linden. And you have never confessed to your husband?

Nora. Good heavens! What can you be thinking of? Tell him, when he has such a loathing of debt! And besides—how painful and humiliating it would be for Torvald, with his manly self-respect, to know that he owed anything to me! It would utterly upset the relation between us; our beautiful, happy home would never again be what it is.

Mrs. Linden. Will you never tell him?

Nora. [*Thoughtfully, half-smiling.*] Yes, some time perhaps—many, many years hence, when I'm—not so pretty. You mustn't laugh at me! Of course I mean when Torvald is not so much in love with me as he is now; when it doesn't amuse him any longer to see me dancing about, and dressing up and acting. Then it might be well to have something in reserve. [*Breaking off.*] Nonsense! Nonsense! That time will never come. Now, what do you say to my grand secret, Christina? Am I fit for nothing now? You may believe it has cost me a lot of anxiety. It has been no joke to meet my engagements punctually. You must know, Christina, that in business there are things called instalments, and quarterly interest, that are terribly hard to provide for. So I've had to pinch a little here and there, wherever I could. I couldn't save much out of the housekeeping, for of course Torvald had to live well. And I couldn't let the children go about badly dressed; all I got for them, I spent on them, the blessed darlings!

Mrs. Linden. Poor Nora! So it had to come out of your own pocket-money.

Nora. Yes, of course. After all, the whole thing was my doing. When Torvald gave me money for clothes, and so on, I never spent more than half of it; I always bought the simplest and cheapest things. It's a mercy that everything suits me so well—Torvald never had any suspicions. But it was often very hard, Christina dear. For it's nice to be beautifully dressed—now, isn't it?

Mrs. Linden. Indeed it is.

Nora. Well, and besides that, I made money in other ways. Last winter I was so lucky—I got a heap of copying to do. I shut myself up every evening and wrote far into the night. Oh, sometimes I was so tired, so tired. And yet it was splendid to work in that way and earn money. I almost felt as if I was a man.

Mrs. Linden. Then how much have you been able to pay off?

Nora. Well, I can't precisely say. It's difficult to keep that sort of business clear. I only know that I've paid everything I could scrape together. Sometimes I really didn't know where to turn. [*Smiles.*] Then I used to sit here and pretend that a rich old gentleman was in love with me——

Mrs. Linden. What! What gentleman?

Nora. Oh, nobody!—that he was dead now, and that when his will was opened, there stood in large letters: "Pay over at once everything of which I die possessed to that charming person, Mrs. Nora Helmer."

Mrs. Linden. But, my dear Nora—what gentleman do you mean?

Nora. Oh dear, can't you understand? There wasn't any old gentleman: it was only what I used to dream and dream when I was at my wits' end for money. But it doesn't matter now—the tiresome old creature may stay where he is for me. I care nothing for him or his will; for now my troubles are over. [*Springing up.*] Oh, Christina, how glorious it is to think of! Free from all anxiety! Free, quite free. To be able to play and romp about with the children; to have things tasteful and pretty in the house, exactly as Torvald likes it! And then the spring will soon be here, with the great blue sky. Perhaps then we shall have a little holiday. Perhaps I shall see the sea again. Oh, what a wonderful thing it is to live and to be happy!

[*The hall-door bell rings.*]

Mrs. Linden. [*Rising.*] There's a ring. Perhaps I had better go.

Nora. No; do stay. No one will come here. It's sure to be some one for Torvald.

Ellen. [*In the doorway.*] If you please, ma'am, there's a gentleman to speak to Mr. Helmer.

Nora. Who is the gentleman?

Krogstad. [*In the doorway.*] It is I, Mrs. Helmer.

[MRS. LINDEN *starts and turns away to the window.*]

Nora. [*Goes a step towards him, anxiously, speaking low.*] You? What is it? What do you want with my husband?

Krogstad. Bank business—in a way. I hold a small post in the Joint Stock Bank, and your husband is to be our new chief, I hear.

Nora. Then it is——?

Krogstad. Only tiresome business, Mrs. Helmer; nothing more.

Nora. Then will you please go to his study?

[KROGSTAD *goes. She bows indifferently while she closes the door into the hall. Then she goes to the stove and looks to the fire.*]

Mrs. Linden. Nora—who was that man?

Nora. A Mr. Krogstad—a lawyer.

Mrs. Linden. Then it was really he?

Nora. Do you know him?

Mrs. Linden. I used to know him—many years ago. He was in a lawyer's office in our town.

Nora. Yes, so he was.

Mrs. Linden. How he has changed!

Nora. I believe his marriage was unhappy.

Mrs. Linden. And he is a widower now?

Nora. With a lot of children. There! Now it will burn up.

[*She closes the stove, and pushes the rocking chair a little aside.*]

Mrs. Linden. His business is not the most creditable, they say?

Nora. Isn't it? I dare say not. I don't know. But don't let us think of business—it's so tiresome.

[DOCTOR RANK *comes out of* HELMER'S *room.*]

Rank. [*Still in the doorway.*] No, no; I'm in your way. I shall go and have a chat with your wife. [*Shuts the door and sees* MRS. LINDEN.] Oh, I beg your pardon. I'm in the way here too.

Nora. No, not in the least. [*Introduces them.*] Doctor Rank—Mrs. Linden.

Rank. Oh, indeed; I've often heard Mrs. Linden's name; I think I passed you on the stairs as I came up.

Mrs. Linden. Yes; I go so very slowly. Stairs try me so much.

Rank. Ah—you are not very strong?

Mrs. Linden. Only overworked.

Rank. Nothing more? Then no doubt you've come to town to find rest in a round of dissipation?

Mrs. Linden. I have come to look for employment.

Rank. Is that an approved remedy for overwork?

Mrs. Linden. One must live, Doctor Rank.

Rank. Yes, that seems to be the general opinion.

Helmer. It's not impossible. I presume Mrs. Linden is a widow?

Mrs. Linden. Yes.

Helmer. And you have already had some experience of business?

Mrs. Linden. A good deal.

Helmer. Well, then, it's very likely I may be able to find a place for you.

Nora. [*Clapping her hands.*] There now! There now!

Helmer. You have come at a fortunate moment, Mrs. Linden.

Mrs. Linden. Oh, how can I thank you ——?

Helmer. [*Smiling.*] There is no occasion. [*Puts on his overcoat.*] But for the present you must excuse me——

Rank. Wait; I am going with you.

[*Fetches his fur coat from the hall and warms it at the fire.*]

Nora. Don't be long, Torvald dear.

Helmer. Only an hour; not more.

Nora. Are you going, too, Christina?

Mrs. Linden. [*Putting on her walking things.*] Yes; I must set about looking for lodgings.

Helmer. Then perhaps we can go together?

Nora. [*Helping her.*] What a pity we haven't a spare room for you; but it's impossible——

Mrs. Linden. I shouldn't think of troubling you. Good-by, dear Nora, and thank you for all your kindness.

Nora. Good-by for the present. Of course you'll come back this evening. And you, too, Doctor Rank. What! If you're well enough? Of course you'll be well enough. Only wrap up warmly. [*They go out, talking, into the hall. Outside on the stairs are heard children's voices.*] There they are! There they are! [*She runs to the outer door and opens it. The nurse,* ANNA, *enters the hall with the children.*] Come in! Come in! [*Stoops down and kisses the children.*] Oh, my sweet darlings! Do you see them, Christina? Aren't they lovely?

Rank. Don't let us stand here chattering in the draught.

Helmer. Come, Mrs. Linden; only mothers can stand such a temperature.

[DOCTOR RANK, HELMER, *and* MRS. LINDEN *go down the stairs;* ANNA *enters the room with the children;* NORA *also, shutting the door.*]

Nora. How fresh and bright you look! And what red cheeks you've got! Like apples and roses. [*The children chatter to her during what follows.*] Have you had great fun? That's splendid! Oh, really! You've been giving Emmy and Bob a ride on your sled!—both at once, only think! Why, you're quite a man, Ivar. Oh, give her to me a little, Anna. My sweet little dolly! [*Takes the smallest from the nurse and dances with her.*] Yes, yes; Mother will dance with Bob, too. What! Did you have a game of snowballs? Oh, I wish I'd been there. No; leave them, Anna; I'll take their things off. Oh, yes, let me do it; it's such fun. Go to the nursery; you look frozen. You'll find some hot coffee on the stove. [*The* NURSE *goes into the room on the left.* NORA *takes off the children's things and throws them down anywhere, while the children talk all together.*] Really! A big dog ran after you? But he didn't bite you? No; dogs don't bite dear little dolly children. Don't peep into those parcels, Ivar. What is it? Wouldn't you like to know? Take care —it'll bite! What? Shall we have a game? What shall we play at? Hide-and-seek? Yes, let's play hide-and-seek. Bob shall hide first. Am I to? Yes, let me hide first.

[*She and the children play, with laughter and shouting, in the room and the adjacent one to the right. At last* NORA *hides under the table; the children come rushing in, look for her, but cannot find her, hear her half-choked laughter, rush to the table, lift up the cover and see her. Loud shouts. She creeps out, as though to frighten them. Fresh shouts. Meanwhile there has been a knock at the door leading into the hall. No one has heard it. Now the door is half opened and* KROGSTAD *appears. He waits a little: the game is renewed.*]

Krogstad. I beg your pardon, Mrs. Helmer——

Nora. [*With a suppressed cry, turns around and half jumps up.*] Ah! What do you want?

Krogstad. Excuse me; the outer door was ajar—somebody must have forgotten to shut it——

Nora. [*Standing up.*] My husband is not at home, Mr. Krogstad.

Krogstad. I know it.

Nora. Then what do you want here?

Krogstad. To say a few words to you.

Nora. To me? [*To the children, softly.*] Go in to Anna. What? No, the strange man won't hurt mamma. When he's gone we'll go on playing. [*She leads the children into the left-hand room, and shuts the door behind them. Uneasy, in suspense.*] It is to me you wish to speak?

Krogstad. Yes, to you.

Nora. Come, Doctor Rank—you want to live yourself.

Rank. To be sure I do. However wretched I may be, I want to drag on as long as possible. All my patients, too, have the same mania. And it's the same with people whose complaint is moral. At this very moment Helmer is talking to just such a moral incurable——

Mrs. Linden. [*Softly.*] Ah!

Nora. Whom do you mean?

Rank. Oh, a fellow named Krogstad, a man you know nothing about—corrupt to the very core of his character. But even he began by announcing, as a matter of vast importance, that he must live.

Nora. Indeed? And what did he want with Torvald?

Rank. I haven't an idea; I only gathered that it was some bank business.

Nora. I didn't know that Krog—that this Mr. Krogstad had anything to do with the Bank?

Rank. Yes He has got some sort of place there. [*To* MRS. LINDEN.] I don't know whether, in your part of the country, you have people who go grubbing and sniffing around in search of moral rottenness—and then, when they have found a "case," don't rest till they have got their man into some good position, where they can keep a watch upon him. Men with a clean bill of health they leave out in the cold.

Mrs. Linden. Well, I suppose the—delicate characters require most care.

Rank. [*Shrugs his shoulders.*] There we have it! It's that notion that makes society a hospital.

[NORA, *deep in her own thoughts, breaks into half-stifled laughter and claps her hands.*]

Rank. Why do you laugh at that? Have you any idea what "society" is?

Nora. What do I care for your tiresome society? I was laughing at something else—something excessively amusing. Tell me, Doctor Rank, are all the employees at the Bank dependent on Torvald now?

Rank. Is that what strikes you as excessively amusing?

Nora. [*Smiles and hums.*] Never mind, never mind! [*Walks about the room.*] Yes, it is funny to think that we—that Torvald has such power over so many people. [*Takes the bag from her pocket.*] Doctor Rank, will you have a macaroon?

Rank. What!—macaroons! I thought they were contraband here.

Nora. Yes; but Christina brought me these.

Mrs. Linden. What! I——

Nora. Oh, well! Don't be fr
couldn't possibly know that Tor
bidden them. The fact is, he's a
spoiling my teeth. But, oh bothe
once!—That's for you, Doctor Ra
a macaroon into his mouth.] And
Christina. And I'll have one wh
about it—only a tiny one, or at m
[*Walks about again.*] Oh dear, I am
There's only one thing in the world I
want.

Rank. Well; what's that?

Nora. There's something I should so
to say—in Torvald's hearing.

Rank. Then why don't you say it?

Nora. Because I daren't, it's so ugly.

Mrs. Linden. Ugly?

Rank. In that case you'd better not. But to us you might—— What is it you would so like to say in Helmer's hearing?

Nora. I should so love to say "Damn it all!"[1]

Rank. Are you out of your mind?

Mrs. Linden. Good gracious, Nora——!

Rank. Say it—there he is!

Nora. [*Hides the macaroons.*] Hush-sh-sh.

[HELMER *comes out of his room, hat in hand, with his overcoat on his arm.*]

Nora. [*Going to him.*] Well, Torvald dear, have you got rid of him?

Helmer. Yes; he has just gone.

Nora. Let me introduce you—this is Christina, who has come to town——

Helmer. Christina? Pardon me, I don't know——

Nora. Mrs. Linden, Torvald dear—Christina Linden.

Helmer. [*To* MRS. LINDEN.] Indeed! A school-friend of my wife's, no doubt?

Mrs. Linden. Yes; we knew each other as girls.

Nora. And only think! She has taken this long journey on purpose to speak to you.

Helmer. To speak to me!

Mrs. Linden. Well, not quite——

Nora. You see, Christina is tremendously clever at office-work, and she's so anxious to work under a first-rate man of business in order to learn still more——

Helmer. [*To* MRS. LINDEN.] Very sensible indeed.

Nora. And when she heard you were appointed manager—it was telegraphed, you know—she started off at once, and—— Torvald, dear, for my sake, you must do something for Christina. Now can't you?

[1] "Död og pine," literally "death and torture"; but by usage a comparatively mild oath.

Nora. To-day? But it's not the first yet——

Krogstad. No, to-day is Christmas Eve. It will depend upon yourself whether you have a merry Christmas.

Nora. What do you want? I'm not ready to-day——

Krogstad. Never mind that just now. I have come about another matter. You have a minute to spare?

Nora. Oh, yes. I suppose so; although——

Krogstad. Good. I was sitting in the restaurant opposite, and I saw your husband go down the street——

Nora. Well?

Krogstad. ——with a lady.

Nora. What then?

Krogstad. May I ask if the lady was a Mrs. Linden?

Nora. Yes.

Krogstad. Who has just come to town?

Nora. Yes. To-day.

Krogstad. I believe she is an intimate friend of yours.

Nora. Certainly. But I don't understand——

Krogstad. I used to know her too.

Nora. I know you did.

Krogstad. Ah! You know all about it. I thought as much. Now, frankly, is Mrs. Linden to have a place in the Bank?

Nora. How dare you catechize me in this way, Mr. Krogstad—you, a subordinate of my husband's? But since you ask, you shall know. Yes, Mrs. Linden is to be employed. And it is I who recommended her, Mr. Krogstad. Now you know.

Krogstad. Then my guess was right.

Nora. [*Walking up and down.*] You see one has a wee bit of influence, after all. It doesn't follow because one's only a woman —— When people are in a subordinate position, Mr. Krogstad, they ought really to be careful how they offend anybody who—h'm——

Krogstad. ——who has influence.

Nora. Exactly.

Krogstad. [*Taking another tone.*] Mrs. Helmer, will you have the kindness to employ your influence on my behalf?

Nora. What? How do you mean?

Krogstad. Will you be so good as to see that I retain my subordinate position in the Bank?

Nora. What do you mean? Who wants to take it from you?

Krogstad. Oh, you needn't pretend ignorance. I can very well understand that it cannot be pleasant for your friend to meet me; and I can also understand now for whose sake I am to be hounded out.

Nora. But I assure you——

Krogstad. Come, come now, once for all: there is time yet, and I advise you to use your influence to prevent it.

Nora. But, Mr. Krogstad, I have no influence—absolutely no e.

Krogstad. None? I thought you said a moment ago——

Nora. Of course not in that sense. I! How can you imagine that I should have any such influence over my husband?

Krogstad. Oh, I know your husband from our college days. I don't think he is any more inflexible than other husbands.

Nora. If you talk disrespectfully of my husband, I must request you to leave the house.

Krogstad. You are bold, madam.

Nora. I am afraid of you no longer. When New Year's Day is over, I shall soon be out of the whole business.

Krogstad. [*Controlling himself.*] Listen to me, Mrs. Helmer. If need be, I shall fight as though for my life to keep my little place in the Bank.

Nora. Yes, so it seems.

Krogstad. It's not only for the salary: that is what I care least about. It's something else—— Well, I had better make a clean breast of it. Of course you know, like every one else, that some years ago I—got into trouble.

Nora. I think I've heard something of the sort.

Krogstad. The matter never came into court; but from that moment all paths were barred to me. Then I took up the business you know about. I had to turn my hand to something; and I don't think I've been one of the worst. But now I must get clear of it all. My sons are growing up; for their sake I must try to recover my character as well as I can. This place in the Bank was the first step; and now your husband wants to kick me off the ladder, back into the mire.

Nora. But I assure you, Mr. Krogstad, I haven't the least power to help you.

Krogstad. That is because you have not the will; but I can compel you.

Nora. You won't tell my husband that I owe you money?

Krogstad. H'm; suppose I were to?

Nora. It would be shameful of you. [*With tears in her voice.*] The secret that is my joy and my pride—that he should learn it in such an ugly, coarse way—and from you. It would involve me in all sorts of unpleasantness——

Krogstad. Only unpleasantness.

Nora. [*Hotly.*] But just do it. It's you that will come off worst, for then my husband will see what a bad man you are, and then you certainly won't keep your place.

Krogstad. I asked whether it was only domestic unpleasantness you feared?

Nora. If my husband gets to know about it, he will of course pay you off at once, and then we shall have nothing more to do with you.

Krogstad. [*Coming a pace nearer.*] Listen, Mrs. Helmer: either your memory is defective, or you don't know much about business. I must make the position a little clearer to you.

Nora. How so?

Krogstad. When your husband was ill, you came to me to borrow twelve hundred dollars.

Nora. I knew of nobody else.

Krogstad. I promised to find you the money——

Nora. And you did find it.

Krogstad. I promised to find you the money, on certain conditions. You were so much taken up at the time about your husband's illness, and so eager to have the wherewithal for your journey, that you probably did not give much thought to the details. Allow me to remind you of them. I promised to find you the amount in exchange for a note of hand, which I drew up.

Nora. Yes, and I signed it.

Krogstad. Quite right. But then I added a few lines, making your father security for the debt. Your father was to sign this.

Nora. Was to——? He did sign it!

Krogstad. I had left the date blank. That is to say, your father was himself to date his signature. Do you recollect that?

Nora. Yes, I believe——

Krogstad. Then I gave you the paper to send to your father, by post. Is not that so?

Nora. Yes.

Krogstad. And of course you did so at once; for within five or six days you brought me back the document with your father's signature; and I handed you the money.

Nora. Well? Have I not made my payments punctually?

Krogstad. Fairly—yes. But to return to the point: You were in great trouble at the time, Mrs. Helmer.

Nora. I was indeed!

Krogstad. Your father was very ill, I believe?

Nora. He was on his death-bed.

Krogstad. And died soon after?

Nora. Yes.

Krogstad. Tell me, Mrs. Helmer: do you happen to recollect the day of his death? The day of the month, I mean?

Nora. Father died on the 29th of September.

Krogstad. Quite correct. I have made inquiries. And here comes in the remarkable point—[*produces a paper*]—which I cannot explain.

Nora. What remarkable point? I don't know——

Krogstad. The remarkable point, madam, that your father signed this paper three days after his death!

Nora. What! I don't understand——

Krogstad. Your father died on the 29th of September. But look here: he has dated his signature October 2nd! Is not that remarkable, Mrs. Helmer? [NORA *is silent.*] Can you explain it? [NORA *continues silent.*] It is noteworthy, too, that the words "October 2nd" and the year are not in your father's handwriting, but in one which I believe I know. Well, this may be explained; your father may have forgotten to date his signature, and somebody may have added the date at random, before the fact of your father's death was known. There is nothing wrong in that. Everything depends on the signature. Of course it is genuine, Mrs. Helmer? It was really your father himself who wrote his name here?

Nora. [*After a short silence, throws her head back and looks defiantly at him.*] No, it was not. *I* wrote Father's name.

Krogstad. Ah!—Are you aware, madam, that that is a dangerous admission?

Nora. How so? You will soon get your money.

Krogstad. May I ask you one more question? Why did you not send the paper to your father?

Nora. It was impossible. Father was ill. If I had asked him for his signature, I should have had to tell him why I wanted the money; but he was so ill I really could not tell him that my husband's life was in danger. It was impossible.

Krogstad. Then it would have been better to have given up your tour.

Nora. No, I couldn't do that; my husband's life depended on that journey. I couldn't give it up.

Krogstad. And did it never occur to you that you were playing me false?

Nora. That was nothing to me. I didn't care in the least about you. I couldn't endure you for all the cruel difficulties you made, although you knew how ill my husband was.

Krogstad. Mrs. Helmer, you evidently do

not realize what you have been guilty of. But I can assure you it was nothing more and nothing worse that made me an outcast from society.

Nora. You! You want me to believe that you did a brave thing to save your wife's life?

Krogstad. The law takes no account of motives.

Nora. Then it must be a very bad law.

Krogstad. Bad or not, if I produce this document in court, you will be condemned according to law.

Nora. I don't believe that. Do you mean to tell me that a daughter has no right to spare her dying father trouble and anxiety?—that a wife has no right to save her husband's life? I don't know much about the law, but I'm sure you'll find, somewhere or another, that that is allowed. And you don't know that—you, a lawyer! You must be a bad one, Mr. Krogstad.

Krogstad. Possibly. But business—such business as ours—I do understand. You believe that? Very well; now do as you please. But this I may tell you, that if I am flung into the gutter a second time, you shall keep me company.

[*Bows and goes out through hall.*]

Nora. [*Stands a while thinking, then tosses her head.*] Oh nonsense! He wants to frighten me. I'm not so foolish as that. [*Begins folding the children's clothes. Pauses.*] But——? No, it's impossible! Why, I did it for love!

Children. [*At the door, left.*] Mamma, the strange man has gone now.

Nora. Yes, yes, I know. But don't tell any one about the strange man. Do you hear? Not even Papa!

Children. No, Mamma; and now will you play with us again?

Nora. No, no; not now.

Children. Oh, do, Mamma; you know you promised.

Nora. Yes, but I can't just now. Run to the nursery; I have so much to do. Run along, run along, and be good, my darlings! [*She pushes them gently into the inner room, and closes the door behind them. Sits on the sofa, embroiders a few stitches, but soon pauses.*] No! [*Throws down the work, rises, goes to the hall door and calls out.*] Ellen, bring in the Christmas tree! [*Goes to table, left, and opens the drawer; again pauses.*] No, it's quite impossible!

Ellen. [*With Christmas tree.*] Where shall I stand it, ma'am?

Nora. There, in the middle of the room.

Ellen. Shall I bring in anything else?

Nora. No, thank you, I have all I want.

[ELLEN, *having put down the tree, goes out.*]

Nora. [*Busy dressing the tree.*] There must be a candle here—and flowers there.—That horrible man! Nonsense, nonsense! there's nothing to be afraid of. The Christmas tree shall be beautiful. I'll do everything to please you, Torvald; I'll sing and dance, and——

[*Enter* HELMER *by the hall door, with a bundle of documents.*]

Nora. Oh! You're back already?

Helmer. Yes. Has anybody been here?

Nora. Here? No.

Helmer. That's odd. I saw Krogstad come out of the house.

Nora. Did you? Oh, yes, by-the-bye, he was here for a minute.

Helmer. Nora, I can see by your manner that he has been begging you to put in a good word for him.

Nora. Yes.

Helmer. And you were to do it as if of your own accord? You were to say nothing to me of his having been here. Didn't he suggest that too?

Nora. Yes, Torvald; but——

Helmer. Nora, Nora! And you could condescend to that! To speak to such a man, to make him a promise! And then to tell me an untruth about it!

Nora. An untruth!

Helmer. Didn't you say that nobody had been here? [*Threatens with his finger.*] My little bird must never do that again! A songbird must sing clear and true; no false notes. [*Puts his arm around her.*] That's so, isn't it? Yes, I was sure of it. [*Lets her go.*] And now we'll say no more about it. [*Sits down before the fire.*] Oh, how cosy and quiet it is here!

[*Glances into his documents.*]

Nora. [*Busy with the tree, after a short silence.*] Torvald!

Helmer. Yes.

Nora. I'm looking forward so much to the Stenborg's fancy ball the day after to-morrow.

Helmer. And I'm on tenterhooks to see what surprise you have in store for me.

Nora. Oh, it's too tiresome!

Helmer. What is?

Nora. I can't think of anything good. Everything seems so foolish and meaningless.

Helmer. Has little Nora made that discovery?

Nora. [*Behind his chair, with her arms on the back.*] Are you very busy, Torvald?

Helmer. Well——

Nora. What papers are those?

Helmer. Bank business.

Nora. Already!

Helmer. I have got the retiring manager to let me make some necessary changes in the staff and the organization. I can do this during Christmas week. I want to have everything straight by the New Year.

Nora. Then that's why that poor Krogstad——

Helmer. H'm.

Nora. [*Still leaning over the chair-back and slowly stroking his hair.*] If you hadn't been so very busy, I should have asked you a great, great favor, Torvald.

Helmer. What can it be? Out with it.

Nora. Nobody has such perfect taste as you; and I should so love to look well at the fancy ball. Torvald, dear, couldn't you take me in hand, and settle what I'm to be, and arrange my costume for me?

Helmer. Aha! So my wilful little woman is at a loss, and making signals of distress!

Nora. Yes. please, Torvald. I can't get on without your help.

Helmer. Well, well, I'll think it over, and we'll soon hit upon something.

Nora. Oh, how good that is of you! [*Goes to the tree again; pause.*] How well the red flowers show.—Tell me, was it anything so very dreadful this Krogstad got into trouble about?

Helmer. Forgery, that's all. Don't you know what that means?

Nora. Mayn't he have been driven to it by need?

Helmer. Yes; or, like so many others, he may have done it in pure heedlessness. I am not so hard-hearted as to condemn a man absolutely for a single fault.

Nora. No, surely not, Torvald!

Helmer. Many a man can retrieve his character, if he owns his crime and takes the punishment.

Nora. Punishment——?

Helmer. But Krogstad didn't do that. He evaded the law by means of tricks and subterfuges; and that is what has morally ruined him.

Nora. Do you think that——?

Helmer. Just think how a man with a thing of that sort on his conscience must be always lying and canting and shamming. Think of the mask he must wear even towards those who stand nearest him—towards his own wife and children. The effect on the children—that's the most terrible part of it, Nora.

Nora. Why?

Helmer. Because in such an atmosphere of lies home life is poisoned and contaminated in every fiber. Every breath the children draw contains some germ of evil.

Nora. [*Closer behind him.*] Are you sure of that?

Helmer. As a lawyer, my dear, I have seen it often enough. Nearly all cases of early corruption may be traced to lying mothers.

Nora. Why—mothers?

Helmer. It generally comes from the mother's side; but of course the father's influence may act in the same way. Every lawyer knows it too well. And here has this Krogstad been poisoning his own children for years past by a life of lies and hypocrisy —that is why I call him morally ruined. [*Holds out both hands to her.*] So my sweet little Nora must promise not to plead his cause. Shake hands upon it. Come, come, what's this? Give me your hand. That's right. Then it's a bargain. I assure you it would have been impossible for me to work with him. It gives me a positive sense of physical discomfort to come in contact with such people.

[NORA *draws her hand away, and moves to the other side of the Christmas tree.*]

Nora. How warm it is here. And I have so much to do.

Helmer. [*Rises and gathers up his papers.*] Yes, and I must try to get some of these papers looked through before dinner. And I shall think over your costume too. Perhaps I may even find something to hang in gilt paper on the Christmas tree. [*Lays his hand on her head.*] My precious little song-bird!

[*He goes into his room and shuts the door.*]

Nora. [*Softly, after a pause.*] It can't be. It's impossible. It must be impossible!

Anna. [*At the door, left.*] The little ones are begging so prettily to come to mamma.

Nora. No, no, no; don't let them come to me! Keep them with you, Anna.

Anna. Very well, ma'am. [*Shuts the door.*]

Nora. [*Pale with terror.*] Corrupt my children!—Poison my home! [*Short pause. She throws back her head.*] It's not true! It can never, never be true!

CURTAIN

ACT SECOND

The same room. In the corner, beside the piano, stands the Christmas tree, stripped, and with the candles burnt out. NORA'S *outdoor things lie on the sofa.* [NORA, *alone, is walking about restlessly. At last she stops by the sofa, and takes up her cloak.*]

Nora. [*Dropping the cloak.*] There's somebody coming! [*Goes to the hall door and listens.*] Nobody; of course nobody will come to-day, Christmas-day; nor to-morrow either. But perhaps—— [*Opens the door and looks out.*]—No, nothing in the letter box; quite empty. [*Comes forward.*] Stuff and nonsense! Of course he won't really do anything. Such a thing couldn't happen. It's impossible! Why, I have three little children.

[ANNA *enters from the left, with a large cardboard box.*]

Anna. I've found the box with the fancy dress at last.

Nora. Thanks; put it down on the table.

Anna. [*Does so.*] But I'm afraid it's very much out of order.

Nora. Oh, I wish I could tear it into a hundred thousand pieces!

Anna. Oh, no. It can easily be put to rights—just a little patience.

Nora. I shall go and get Mrs. Linden to help me.

Anna. Going out again? In such weather as this! You'll catch cold, ma'am, and be ill.

Nora. Worse things might happen.—What are the children doing?

Anna. They're playing with their Christmas presents, poor little dears; but——

Nora. Do they often ask for me?

Anna. You see they've been so used to having their mamma with them.

Nora. Yes; but, Anna, I can't have them so much with me in future.

Anna. Well, little children get used to anything.

Nora. Do you think they do? Do you believe they would forget their mother if she went quite away?

Anna. Gracious me! Quite away?

Nora. Tell me, Anna—I've so often wondered about it—how could you bring yourself to give your child up to strangers?

Anna. I had to when I came to nurse my little Miss Nora.

Nora. But how could you make up your mind to it?

Anna. When I had the chance of such a good place? A poor girl who's been in trouble must take what comes. That wicked man did nothing for me.

Nora. But your daughter must have forgotten you.

Anna. Oh, no, ma'am, that she hasn't. She wrote to me both when she was confirmed and when she was married.

Nora. [*Embracing her.*] Dear old Anna—you were a good mother to me when I was little.

Anna. My poor little Nora had no mother but me.

Nora. And if my little ones had nobody else, I'm sure you would—— Nonsense, nonsense! [*Opens the box.*] Go in to the children. Now I must—— You'll see how lovely I shall be to-morrow.

Anna. I'm sure there will be no one at the ball so lovely as my Miss Nora.

[*She goes into the room on the left.*]

Nora. [*Takes the costume out of the box, but soon throws it down again.*] Oh, if I dared go out. If only nobody would come. If only nothing would happen here in the meantime. Rubbish; nobody is coming. Only not to think. What a delicious muff! Beautiful gloves, beautiful gloves! To forget—to forget! One, two, three, four, five, six—— [*With a scream.*] Ah, there they come.

[*Goes towards the door, then stands irresolute.* MRS. LINDEN *enters from the hall, where she has taken off her things.*]

Nora. Oh, it's you, Christina. There's nobody else there? I'm so glad you have come.

Mrs. Linden. I hear you called at my lodgings.

Nora. Yes, I was just passing. There's something you must help me with. Let us sit here on the sofa—so. To-morrow evening there's to be a fancy ball at Consul Stenborg's overhead, and Torvald wants me to appear as a Neapolitan fisher-girl, and dance the tarantella; I learned it at Capri.

Mrs. Linden. I see—quite a performance.

Nora. Yes, Torvald wishes it. Look, this is the costume; Torvald had it made for me in Italy. But now it's all so torn, I don't know——

Mrs. Linden. Oh, we shall soon set that to rights. It's only the trimming that has come loose here and there. Have you a needle and thread? Ah, here's the very thing.

Nora. Oh, how kind of you.

Mrs. Linden. [*Sewing.*] So you're to be in costume to-morrow, Nora? I'll tell you what—I shall come in for a moment to see you in all your glory. But I've quite forgotten to thank you for the pleasant evening yesterday.

Nora. [*Rises and walks across the room.*] Oh, yesterday, it didn't seem so pleasant as usual.—You should have come to town a little sooner, Christina.—Torvald has certainly the art of making home bright and beautiful.

Mrs. Linden. You too, I should think, or you wouldn't be your father's daughter. But tell me—is Doctor Rank always so depressed as he was last evening?

Nora. No, yesterday it was particularly noticeable. You see, he suffers from a dreadful illness. He has spinal consumption, poor fellow. They say his father was a horrible man, who kept mistresses and all sorts of things—so the son has been sickly from his childhood, you understand.

Mrs. Linden. [*Lets her sewing fall into her lap.*] Why, my darling Nora, how do you come to know such things?

Nora. [*Moving about the room.*] Oh, when one has three children, one sometimes has visits from women who are half—half doctors—and they talk of one thing and another.

Mrs. Linden. [*Goes on sewing; a short pause.*] Does Doctor Rank come here every day?

Nora. Every day of his life. He has been Torvald's most intimate friend from boyhood, and he's a good friend of mine, too. Doctor Rank is quite one of the family.

Mrs. Linden. But tell me—is he quite sincere? I mean, isn't he rather given to flattering people?

Nora. No, quite the contrary. Why should you think so?

Mrs. Linden. When you introduced us yesterday he said he had often heard my name; but I noticed afterwards that your husband had no notion who I was. How could Doctor Rank——?

Nora. He was quite right, Christina. You see, Torvald loves me so indescribably, he wants to have me all to himself, as he says. When we were first married he was almost jealous if I even mentioned any of my old friends at home; so naturally I gave up doing it. But I often talk of the old times to Doctor Rank, for he likes to hear about them.

Mrs. Linden. Listen to me, Nora! You are still a child in many ways. I am older than you, and have had more experience. I'll tell you something. You ought to get clear of all this with Doctor Rank.

Nora. Get clear of what?

Mrs. Linden. The whole affair, I should say. You were talking yesterday of a rich admirer who was to find you money—

Nora. Yes, one who never existed, worse luck. What then?

Mrs. Linden. Has Doctor Rank money?

Nora. Yes, he has.

Mrs. Linden. And nobody to provide for?

Nora. Nobody. But——?

Mrs. Linden. And he comes here every day?

Nora. Yes, I told you so.

Mrs. Linden. I should have thought he would have had better taste.

Nora. I don't understand you a bit.

Mrs. Linden. Don't pretend, Nora. Do you suppose I can't guess who lent you the twelve hundred dollars?

Nora. Are you out of your senses? How can you think such a thing? A friend who comes here every day! Why, the position would be unbearable!

Mrs. Linden. Then it really is not he?

Nora. No, I assure you. It never for a moment occurred to me—— Besides, at that time he had nothing to lend; he came into his property afterwards.

Mrs. Linden. Well, I believe that was lucky for you, Nora dear.

Nora. No, really, it would never have struck me to ask Doctor Rank—— And yet, I'm certain that if I did——

Mrs. Linden. But of course you never would.

Nora. Of course not. It's inconceivable that it should ever be necessary. But I'm quite sure that if I spoke to Doctor Rank——

Mrs. Linden. Behind your husband's back?

Nora. I must get clear of the other thing; that's behind his back, too. I must get clear of that.

Mrs. Linden. Yes, yes, I told you so yesterday; but——

Nora. [*Walking up and down.*] A man can manage these things much better than a woman.

Mrs. Linden. One's own husband, yes.

Nora. Nonsense. [*Stands still.*] When everything is paid, one gets back the paper.

Mrs. Linden. Of course.

Nora. And can tear it into a hundred thousand pieces, and burn it up, the nasty, filthy thing!

Mrs. Linden. [*Looks at her fixedly, lays down her work, and rises slowly.*] Nora, you are hiding something from me.

Nora. Can you see it in my face?

Mrs. Linden. Something has happened since yesterday morning. Nora, what is it?

Nora. [*Going towards her.*] Christina——! [*Listens.*] Hush! There's Torvald coming home. Do you mind going into the nursery for the present? Torvald can't bear to see dressmaking going on. Get Anna to help you.

Mrs. Linden. [*Gathers some of the things together.*] Very well; but I shan't go away until you have told me all about it.

[*She goes out to the left, as* HELMER *enters from the hall.*]

Nora. [*Runs to meet him.*] Oh, how I've been longing for you to come, Torvald dear!

Helmer. Was that the dressmaker——?

Nora. No. Christina. She's helping me with my costume. You'll see how nice I shall look.

Helmer. Yes, wasn't that a happy thought of mine?

Nora. Splendid! But isn't it good of me, too, to have given in to you about the tarantella?

Helmer. [*Takes her under the chin.*] Good of you! To give in to your own husband? Well, well, you little madcap, I know you don't mean it. But I won't disturb you. I daresay you want to be "trying on."

Nora. And you are going to work, I suppose?

Helmer. Yes. [*Shows her a bundle of papers.*] Look here. I've just come from the Bank—— [*Goes towards his room.*]

Nora. Torvald.

Helmer. [*Stopping.*] Yes?

Nora. If your little squirrel were to beg you for something so prettily——

Helmer. Well?

Nora. Would you do it?

Helmer. I must know first what it is.

Nora. The squirrel would skip about and play all sorts of tricks if you would only be nice and kind.

Helmer. Come, then, out with it.

Nora. Your lark would twitter from morning till night——

Helmer. Oh, that she does in any case.

Nora. I'll be an elf and dance in the moonlight for you, Torvald.

Helmer. Nora—you can't mean what you were hinting at this morning?

Nora. [*Coming nearer.*] Yes, Torvald, I beg and implore you!

Helmer. Have you really the courage to begin that again?

Nora. Yes, yes; for my sake, you must let Krogstad keep his place in the Bank.

Helmer. My dear Nora, it's his place I intend for Mrs. Linden.

Nora. Yes, that's so good of you. But instead of Krogstad, you could dismiss some other clerk.

Helmer. Why, this is incredible obstinacy! Because you have thoughtlessly promised to put in a word for him, I am to——!

Nora. It's not that, Torvald. It's for your own sake. This man writes for the most scurrilous newspapers; you said so yourself. He can do you no end of harm. I'm so terribly afraid of him——

Helmer. Ah, I understand; it's old recollections that are frightening you.

Nora. What do you mean?

Helmer. Of course you're thinking of your father.

Nora. Yes—yes, of course. Only think of the shameful slanders wicked people used to write about Father. I believe they would have got him dismissed if you hadn't been sent to look into the thing, and been kind to him, and helped him.

Helmer. My little Nora, between your father and me there is all the difference in the world. Your father was not altogether unimpeachable. I am; and I hope to remain so.

Nora. Oh, no one knows what wicked men may hit upon. We could live so quietly and happily now, in our cozy, peaceful home, you and I and the children, Torvald! That's why I beg and implore you——

Helmer. And it is just by pleading his cause that you make it impossible for me to keep him. It's already known at the Bank that I intend to dismiss Krogstad. If it were now reported that the new manager let himself be turned around his wife's little finger——

Nora. What then?

Helmer. Oh, nothing, so long as a wilful woman can have her way——! I am to make myself a laughing-stock to the whole staff, and set people saying that I am open to all sorts of outside influence? Take my word for it, I should soon feel the consequences. And besides—there is one thing that makes Krogstad impossible for me to work with——

Nora. What thing?

Helmer. I could perhaps have overlooked his moral failings at a pinch——

Nora. Yes, couldn't you, Torvald?

Helmer. And I hear he is good at his work. But the fact is, he was a college chum of mine—there was one of those rash friendships between us that one so often repents of later. I may as well confess it at once—he calls me by my Christian name;[1] and he is tactless enough to do it even when others are present. He delights in putting on airs

[1] In the original, "We say 'thou' to each other."

of familiarity—Torvald here, Torvald there! I assure you it's most painful to me. He would make my position at the Bank perfectly unendurable.

Nora. Torvald, surely you're not serious?

Helmer. No? Why not?

Nora. That's such a petty reason.

Helmer. What! Petty! Do you consider me petty?

Nora. No, on the contrary, Torvald dear; and that's just why——

Helmer. Never mind; you call my motives petty; then I must be petty too. Petty! Very well!—Now we'll put an end to this, once for all. [*Goes to the door into the hall and calls.*] Ellen!

Nora. What do you want?

Helmer. [*Searching among his papers.*] To settle the thing. [ELLEN *enters.*] Here; take this letter; give it to a messenger. See that he takes it at once. The address is on it. Here's the money.

Ellen. Very well, sir.

[*Goes with the letter.*]

Helmer. [*Putting his papers together.*] There, Madam Obstinacy.

Nora. [*Breathless.*] Torvald—what was in the letter?

Helmer. Krogstad's dismissal.

Nora. Call it back again, Torvald! There's still time. Oh, Torvald, call it back again! For my sake, for your own, for the children's sake! Do you hear, Torvald? Do it! You don't know what that letter may bring upon us all.

Helmer. Too late.

Nora. Yes, too late.

Helmer. My dear Nora, I forgive your anxiety, though it's anything but flattering to me. Why should you suppose that *I* would be afraid of a wretched scribbler's spite? But I forgive you all the same, for it's a proof of your great love for me. [*Takes her in his arms.*] That's as it should be, my own dear Nora. Let what will happen—when it comes to the pinch, I shall have strength and courage enough. You shall see: my shoulders are broad enough to bear the whole burden.

Nora. [*Terror-struck.*] What do you mean by that?

Helmer. The whole burden, I say——

Nora. [*With decision.*] That you shall never, never do!

Helmer. Very well; then we'll share it, Nora, as man and wife. That is how it should be. [*Petting her.*] Are you satisfied now? Come, come, come, don't look like a scared dove. It's all nothing—foolish fancies—Now you ought to play the tarantella through and practise with the tambourine. I shall sit in my inner room and shut both doors, so that I shall hear nothing. You can make as much noise as you please. [*Turns around in doorway.*] And when Rank comes, just tell him where I'm to be found.

[*He nods to her, and goes with his papers into his room, closing the door.*]

Nora. [*Bewildered with terror, stands as though rooted to the ground, and whispers.*] He would do it. Yes, he would do it. He would do it, in spite of all the world.—No, never that, never, never! Anything rather than that! Oh, for some way of escape! What shall I do——! [*Hall bell rings.*] Doctor Rank——! Anything, anything, rather than——!

[NORA *draws her hands over her face, pulls herself together, goes to the door and opens it.* RANK *stands outside hanging up his fur coat. During what follows it begins to grow dark.*]

Nora. Good afternoon, Doctor Rank. I knew you by your ring. But you mustn't go to Torvald now. I believe he's busy.

Rank. And you?

[*Enters and closes the door.*]

Nora. Oh, you know very well, I have always time for you.

Rank. Thank you. I shall avail myself of your kindness as long as I can.

Nora. What do you mean? As long as you can?

Rank. Yes. Does that frighten you?

Nora. I think it's an odd expression. Do you expect anything to happen?

Rank. Something I have long been prepared for; but I didn't think it would come so soon.

Nora. [*Catching at his arm.*] What have you discovered? Doctor Rank, you must tell me!

Rank. [*Sitting down by the stove.*] I am running down hill. There's no help for it.

Nora. [*Draws a long breath of relief.*] It's you——?

Rank. Who else should it be?—Why lie to one's self? I am the most wretched of all my patients, Mrs. Helmer. In these last days I have been auditing my life-account—bankrupt! Perhaps before a month is over, I shall lie rotting in the churchyard.

Nora. Oh! What an ugly way to talk.

Rank. The thing itself is so confoundedly ugly, you see. But the worst of it is, so many other ugly things have to be gone through first. There is only one last investigation to be made, and when that is over I shall know pretty certainly when the break-up will begin. There's one thing I want to say to you: Helmer's delicate nature shrinks so from all that is horrible: I will not have him in my sick-room——

Nora. But, Doctor Rank——

Rank. I won't have him, I say—not on any account. I shall lock my door against him—As soon as I am quite certain of the worst, I shall send you my visiting-card with a black cross on it; and then you will know that the final horror has begun.

Nora. Why, you're perfectly unreasonable to-day; and I did so want you to be in a really good humor.

Rank. With death staring me in the face? —And to suffer thus for another's sin! Where's the justice of it? And in one way or another you can trace in every family some such inexorable retribution——

Nora. [*Stopping her ears.*] Nonsense, nonsense! Now cheer up!

Rank. Well, after all, the whole thing's only worth laughing at. My poor innocent spine must do penance for my father's wild oats.

Nora. [*At table, left.*] I suppose he was too fond of asparagus and Strasbourg pâté, wasn't he?

Rank. Yes; and truffles.

Nora. Yes, truffles, to be sure. And oysters, I believe?

Rank. Yes, oysters; oysters, of course.

Nora. And then all the port and champagne! It's sad that all these good things should attack the spine.

Rank. Especially when the luckless spine attacked never had any good of them.

Nora. Ah, yes, that's the worst of it.

Rank. [*Looks at her searchingly.*] H'm——

Nora. [*A moment later.*] Why did you smile?

Rank. No; it was you that laughed.

Nora. No; it was you that smiled, Doctor Rank.

Rank. [*Standing up.*] I see you're deeper than I thought.

Nora. I'm in such a crazy mood to-day.

Rank. So it seems.

Nora. [*With her hands on his shoulders.*] Dear, dear Doctor Rank, death shall not take you away from Torvald and me.

Rank. Oh, you'll easily get over the loss. The absent are soon forgotten.

Nora. [*Looks at him anxiously.*] Do you think so?

Rank. People make fresh ties, and then——

Nora. Who will make fresh ties?

Rank. You and Helmer will, when I am gone. You yourself are taking time by the forelock, it seems to me. What was that Mrs. Linden doing here yesterday?

Nora. Oh! You're surely not jealous of poor Christina?

Rank. Yes, I am. She will be my successor in this house. When I am out of the way, this woman will perhaps——

Nora. Hush! Not so loud! She's in there.

Rank. To-day as well? You see!

Nora. Only to put my costume in order—dear me, how unreasonable you are! [*Sits on sofa.*] Now do be good, Doctor Rank! To-morrow you shall see how beautifully I shall dance; and then you may fancy that I'm doing it all to please you—and of course Torvald as well. [*Takes various things out of box.*] Doctor Rank, sit down here, and I'll show you something.

Rank. [*Sitting.*] What is it?

Nora. Look here. Look!

Rank. Silk stockings.

Nora. Flesh-colored. Aren't they lovely? It's so dark here now; but to-morrow——No, no, no; you must only look at the feet. Oh, well, I suppose you may look at the rest too.

Rank. H'm——

Nora. What are you looking so critical about? Do you think they won't fit me?

Rank. I can't possibly give any competent opinion on that point.

Nora. [*Looking at him a moment.*] For shame! [*Hits him lightly on the ear with the stockings.*] Take that.

[*Rolls them up again.*]

Rank. And what other wonders am I to see?

Nora. You shan't see anything more; for you don't behave nicely.

[*She hums a little and searches among the things.*]

Rank. [*After a short silence.*] When I sit here gossiping with you, I can't imagine—I simply cannot conceive—what would have become of me if I had never entered this house.

Nora. [*Smilingly.*] Yes, I think you do feel at home with us.

Rank. [*More softly—looking straight before him.*] And now to have to leave it all——

Nora. Nonsense. You shan't leave us.

Rank. [*In the same tone.*] And not to be able to leave behind the slightest token of gratitude; scarcely even a passing regret—nothing but an empty place, that can be filled by the first comer.

Nora. And if I were to ask you for——? No——

Rank. For what?

Nora. For a great proof of your friendship.

Rank. Yes—yes?

Nora. I mean—for a very, very great service——

Rank. Would you really, for once, make me so happy?

Nora. Oh, you don't know what it is.

Rank. Then tell me.

Nora. No, I really can't, Doctor Rank. It's far, far too much—not only a service, but help and advice besides——

Rank. So much the better. I can't think what you can mean. But go on. Don't you trust me?

Nora. As I trust no one else. I know you are my best and truest friend. So I will tell you. Well then, Doctor Rank, there is something you must help me to prevent. You know how deeply, how wonderfully Torvald loves me; he wouldn't hesitate a moment to give his very life for my sake.

Rank. [*Bending towards her.*] Nora-- do you think he is the only one who——?

Nora. [*With a slight start.*] Who——?

Rank. Who would gladly give his life for you?

Nora. [*Sadly.*] Oh!

Rank. I have sworn that you shall know it before I—go. I shall never find a better opportunity—Yes, Nora, now I have told you; and now you know that you can trust me as you can no one else.

Nora. [*Standing up; simply and calmly.*] Let me pass, please.

Rank. [*Makes way for her, but remains sitting.*] Nora——

Nora. [*In the doorway.*] Ellen, bring the lamp. [*Crosses to the stove.*] Oh dear, Doctor Rank, that was too bad of you.

Rank. [*Rising.*] That I have loved you as deeply as—any one else? Was that too bad of me?

Nora. No, but that you should have told me so. It was so unnecessary——

Rank. What do you mean? Did you know——?

[ELLEN *enters with the lamp; sets it on the table and goes out again.*]

Rank. Nora—Mrs. Helmer—I ask you, did you know?

Nora. Oh, how can I tell what I knew or didn't know? I really can't say—— How could you be so clumsy, Doctor Rank? It was all so nice!

Rank. Well, at any rate, you know now that I am at your service, body and soul. And now, go on.

Nora. [*Looking at him.*] Go on—now?

Rank. I beg you to tell me what you want.

Nora. I can tell you nothing now.

Rank. Yes, yes! You mustn't punish me in that way. Let me do for you whatever a man can.

Nora. You can do nothing for me now.—Besides, I really want no help. You shall see it was only my fancy. Yes, it must be so. Of course! [*Sits in the rocking-chair, looks at him and smiles.*] You are a nice person, Doctor Rank! Aren't you ashamed of yourself, now that the lamp is on the table?

Rank. No; not exactly. But perhaps I ought to go—forever.

Nora. No, indeed you mustn't. Of course you must come and go as you've always done. You know very well that Torvald can't do without you.

Rank. Yes, but you?

Nora. Oh, you know I always like to have you here.

Rank. That is just what led me astray. You are a riddle to me. It has often seemed to me as if you liked being with me almost as much as being witb Helmer.

Nora. Yes; don't you see? There are people one loves, and others one likes to talk to.

Rank. Yes—there's something in that.

Nora. When I was a girl, of course I loved Papa best. But it always delighted me to steal into the servants' room. In the first place they never lectured me, and in the second it was such fun to hear them talk.

Rank. Ah, I see; then it's their place I have taken?

Nora. [*Jumps up and hurries towards him.*] Oh, my dear Doctor Rank, I don't mean that. But you understand, with Torvald it's the same as with Papa——

[ELLEN *enters from the hall.*]

Ellen. Please, ma'am——

[*Whispers to* NORA, *and gives her a card.*]

Nora. [*Glancing at card.*] Ah!

[*Puts it in her pocket.*]

Rank. Anything wrong?

Nora. No, no, not in the least. It's only —it's my new costume——

Rank. Your costume! Why, it's there.

Nora. Oh, that one, yes. But this is another that—I have ordered it—Torvald mustn't know——

Rank. Aha! So that's the great secret.

Nora. Yes, of course. Please go to him; he's in the inner room. Do keep him while I——

Rank. Don't be alarmed; he shan't escape.

[*Goes into* HELMER'S *room.*]

Nora. [*To* ELLEN.] Is he waiting in the kitchen?

Ellen. Yes, he came up the back stair——

Nora. Didn't you tell him I was engaged?

Ellen. Yes, but it was no use.

Nora. He won't go away?

Ellen. No, ma'am, not until he has spoken to you.

Nora. Then let him come in; but quietly. And, Ellen—say nothing about it; it's a surprise for my husband.

Ellen. Oh, yes, ma'am, I understand.

[*She goes out.*]

Nora. It is coming! The dreadful thing is coming, after all. No, no, no, it can never be; it shall not!

[*She goes to* HELMER'S *door and slips the bolt.* ELLEN *opens the hall door for* KROGSTAD, *and shuts it after him. He wears a traveling-coat, high boots, and a fur cap.*]

Nora. [*Goes towards him.*] Speak softly; my husband is at home.

Krogstad. All right. That's nothing to me.

Nora. What do you want?

Krogstad. A little information.

Nora. Be quick, then. What is it?

Krogstad. You know I have got my dismissal.

Nora. I couldn't prevent it, Mr. Krogstad. I fought for you to the last, but it was of no use.

Krogstad. Does your husband care for you so little? He knows what I can bring upon you, and yet he dares——

Nora. How could you think I should tell him?

Krogstad. Well, as a matter of fact, I didn't think it. It wasn't like my friend Torvald Helmer to show so much courage——

Nora. Mr. Krogstad, be good enough to speak respectfully of my husband.

Krogstad. Certainly, with all due respect. But since you are so anxious to keep the matter secret, I suppose you are a little clearer than yesterday as to what you have done.

Nora. Clearer than you could ever make me.

Krogstad. Yes, such a bad lawyer as I——

Nora. What is it you want?

Krogstad. Only to see how you are getting on, Mrs. Helmer. I've been thinking about you all day. Even a mere money-lender, a gutter-journalist, a—in short, a creature like me—has a little bit of what people call feeling.

Nora. Then show it; think of my little children.

Krogstad. Did you and your husband think of mine? But enough of that. I only wanted to tell you that you needn't take this matter too seriously. I shall not lodge any information, for the present.

Nora. No, surely not. I knew you wouldn't.

Krogstad. The whole thing can be settled quite amicably. Nobody need know. It can remain among us three.

Nora. My husband must never know.

Krogstad. How can you prevent it? Can you pay off the balance?

Nora. No, not at once.

Krogstad. Or have you any means of raising the money in the next few days?

Nora. None—that I will make use of.

Krogstad. And if you had, it would not help you now. If you offered me ever so much money down, you should not get back your I.O.U.

Nora. Tell me what you want to do with it.

Krogstad. I only want to keep it—to have it in my possession. No outsider shall hear anything of it. So, if you have any desperate scheme in your head——

Nora. What if I have?

Krogstad. If you should think of leaving your husband and children——

Nora. What if I do?

Krogstad. Or if you should think of—something worse——

Nora. How do you know that?

Krogstad. Put all that out of your head.

Nora. How did you know what I had in my mind?

Krogstad. Most of us think of that at first. I thought of it, too; but I hadn't the courage——

Nora. [*Tonelessly.*] Nor I.

Krogstad. [*Relieved.*] No, one hasn't. You haven't the courage either, have you?

Nora. I haven't, I haven't.

Krogstad. Besides, it would be very foolish.—Just one domestic storm, and it's all over. I have a letter in my pocket for your husband——

Nora. Telling him everything?

Krogstad. Sparing you as much as possible.

Nora. [*Quickly.*] He must never read that letter. Tear it up. I will manage to get the money somehow——

Krogstad. Pardon me, Mrs. Helmer, but I believe I told you——

Nora. Oh, I'm not talking about the money I owe you. Tell me how much you demand from my husband—I will get it.

Krogstad. I demand no money from your husband.

Nora. What do you demand then?

Krogstad. I will tell you. I want to regain my footing in the world. I want to rise;

and your husband shall help me to do it. For the last eighteen months my record has been spotless; I have been in bitter need all the time; but I was content to fight my way up, step by step. Now, I've been thrust down again, and I will not be satisfied with merely being reinstated as a matter of grace. I want to rise, I tell you. I must get into the Bank again, in a higher position than before. Your husband shall create a place on purpose for me——

Nora. He will never do that!

Krogstad. He will do it; I know him—he won't dare to show fight! And when he and I are together there, you shall soon see! Before a year is out I shall be the manager's right hand. It won't be Torvald Helmer, but Nils Krogstad, that manages the Joint Stock Bank.

Nora. That shall never be.

Krogstad. Perhaps you will——?

Nora. Now I have the courage for it.

Krogstad. Oh, you don't frighten me! A sensitive, petted creature like you——

Nora. You shall see, you shall see!

Krogstad. Under the ice, perhaps? Down into the cold, black water? And next Spring to come up again, ugly, hairless, unrecognizable——

Nora. You can't terrify me.

Krogstad. Nor you me. People don't do that sort of thing, Mrs. Helmer. And, after all, what would be the use of it? I have your husband in my pocket, all the same.

Nora. Afterwards? When I am no longer——?

Krogstad. You forget, your reputation remains in my hands. [NORA *stands speechless and looks at him.*] Well, now you are prepared. Do nothing foolish. As soon as Helmer has received my letter, I shall expect to hear from him. And remember that it is your husband himself who has forced me back again into such paths. That I will never forgive him. Good-by, Mrs. Helmer.

[*Goes out through the hall.* NORA *hurries to the door, opens it a little, and listens.*]

Nora. He's going. He's not putting the letter into the box. No, no, it would be impossible! [*Opens the door further and further.*] What's that? He's standing still; not going down stairs. Has he changed his mind? Is he——? [*A letter falls into the box.* KROGSTAD'S *footsteps are heard gradually receding down the stair.* NORA *utters a suppressed shriek, and rushes forward towards the sofa-table; pause.*] In the letter-box! [*Slips shrinkingly up to the hall door.*] There it lies.—Torvald, Torvald—now we are lost!

[MRS. LINDEN *enters from the left with the costume.*]

Mrs. Linden. There, I think it's all right now. Shall we just try it on?

Nora. [*Hoarsely and softly.*] Christina, come here.

Mrs. Linden. [*Throws down the dress on the sofa.*] What's the matter? You look quite distracted.

Nora. Come here. Do you see that letter? There, see—through the glass of the letter-box.

Mrs. Linden. Yes, yes, I see it.

Nora. That letter is from Krogstad——

Mrs. Linden. Nora—it was Krogstad who lent you the money?

Nora. Yes; and now Torvald will know everything.

Mrs. Linden. Believe me, Nora, it's the best thing for both of you.

Nora. You don't know all yet. I have forged a name——

Mrs. Linden. Good heavens!

Nora. Now, listen to me, Christina; you shall bear me witness——

Mrs. Linden. How "witness"? What am I to——?

Nora. If I should go out of my mind—it might easily happen——

Mrs. Linden. Nora!

Nora. Or if anything else should happen to me—so that I couldn't be here——!

Mrs. Linden. Nora, Nora, you're quite beside yourself!

Nora. In case any one wanted to take it all upon himself—the whole blame—you understand——

Mrs. Linden. Yes, yes; but how can you think——?

Nora. You shall bear witness that it's not true, Christina. I'm not out of my mind at all; I know quite well what I'm saying; and I tell you nobody else knew anything about it; I did the whole thing, I myself. Remember that.

Mrs. Linden. I shall remember. But I don't understand what you mean——

Nora. Oh, how should you? It's the miracle coming to pass.

Mrs. Linden. The miracle?

Nora. Yes, the miracle. But it's so terrible, Christina; it mustn't happen for all the world.

Mrs. Linden. I shall go straight to Krogstad and talk to him.

Nora. Don't; he'll do you some harm.

Mrs. Linden. Once he would have done anything for me.

Nora. He?

Mrs. Linden. Where does he live?

Nora. Oh, how can I tell——? Yes—— [*Feels in her pocket.*] Here's his card. But the letter, the letter——!

Helmer. [*Knocking outside.*] Nora!

Nora. [*Shrieks in terror.*] Oh, what is it? What do you want?

Helmer. Well, well, don't be frightened. We're not coming in; you've bolted the door. Are you trying on your dress?

Nora. Yes, yes, I'm trying it on. It suits me so well, Torvald.

Mrs. Linden. [*Who has read the card.*] Why, he lives close by here.

Nora. Yes, but it's no use now. We are lost. The letter is there in the box.

Mrs. Linden. And your husband has the key?

Nora. Always.

Mrs. Linden. Krogstad must demand his letter back, unread. He must find some pretext——

Nora. But this is the very time when Torvald generally——

Mrs. Linden. Prevent him. Keep him occupied. I shall come back as quickly as I can.

[*She goes out hastily by the hall door.*]

Nora. [*Opens* HELMER'S *door and peeps in.*] Torvald!

Helmer. Well, may one come into one's own room again at last? Come, Rank, we'll have a look—— [*In the doorway.*] But how's this?

Nora. What, Torvald dear?

Helmer. Rank led me to expect a grand transformation.

Rank. [*In the doorway.*] So I understood. I suppose I was mistaken.

Nora. No, no one shall see me in my glory until to-morrow evening.

Helmer. Why, Nora dear, you look so tired. Have you been practising too hard?

Nora. No, I haven't practised at all yet.

Helmer. But you'll have to——

Nora. Oh yes, I must, I must! But Torvald, I can't get on at all without your help. I've forgotten everything.

Helmer. Oh, we shall soon freshen it up again.

Nora. Yes, do help me, Torvald. You must promise me—— Oh, I'm so nervous about it. Before so many people—— This evening you must give yourself up entirely to me. You mustn't do a stroke of work; you mustn't even touch a pen. Do promise, Torvald dear!

Helmer. I promise. All this evening I shall be your slave. Little helpless thing——! But, by-the-bye, I must just——

[*Going to hall door.*]

Nora. What do you want there?

Helmer. Only to see if there are any letters.

Nora. No, no, don't do that, Torvald.

Helmer. Why not?

Nora. Torvald, I beg you not to. There are none there.

Helmer. Let me just see.

[*Is going.* NORA, *at the piano, plays the first bars of the tarantella.*]

Helmer. [*At the door, stops.*] Aha!

Nora. I can't dance to-morrow if I don't rehearse with you first.

Helmer. [*Going to her.*] Are you really so nervous, dear Nora?

Nora. Yes, dreadfully! Let me rehearse at once. We have time before dinner. Oh, do sit down and play for me, Torvald dear; direct me and put me right, as you used to do.

Helmer. With all the pleasure in life, since you wish it.

[*Sits at piano.* NORA *snatches the tambourine out of the box, and hurriedly drapes herself in a long parti-colored shawl; then, with a bound, stands in the middle of the floor.*]

Nora. Now play for me! Now I'll dance!

[HELMER *plays and* NORA *dances.* RANK *stands at the piano behind* HELMER *and looks on.*]

Helmer. [*Playing.*] Slower! Slower!

Nora. Can't do it slower!

Helmer. Not so violently, Nora.

Nora. I must! I must!

Helmer. [*Stops.*] No, no, Nora—that will never do.

Nora. [*Laughs and swings her tambourine.*] Didn't I tell you so!

Rank. Let me play for her.

Helmer. [*Rising.*] Yes, do—then I can direct her better.

[RANK *sits down to the piano and plays;* NORA *dances more and more wildly.* HELMER *stands by the stove and addresses frequent corrections to her; she seems not to hear. Her hair breaks loose, and falls over her shoulders. She does not notice it, but goes on dancing.* MRS. LINDEN *enters and stands spellbound in the doorway.*]

Mrs. Linden. Ah——!

Nora. [*Dancing.*] We're having such fun here, Christina!

Helmer. Why, Nora dear, you're dancing as if it were a matter of life and death.

Nora. So it is.

Helmer. Rank, stop! This is the merest madness. Stop, I say!

[RANK *stops playing, and* NORA *comes to a sudden standstill.*]

Helmer. [*Going towards her.*] I couldn't have believed it. You've positively forgotten all I taught you.

Nora. [*Throws the tambourine away.*] You see for yourself.

Helmer. You really do want teaching.

Nora. Yes, you see how much I need it. You must practise with me up to the last moment. Will you promise me, Torvald?

Helmer. Certainly, certainly.

Nora. Neither to-day nor to-morrow must you think of anything but me. You mustn't open a single letter—mustn't look at the letter-box.

Helmer. Ah, you're still afraid of that man——

Nora. Oh yes, yes, I am.

Helmer. Nora, I can see it in your face—there's a letter from him in the box.

Nora. I don't know, I believe so. But you're not to read anything now; nothing ugly must come between us until all is over.

Rank. [*Softly, to* HELMER.] You mustn't contradict her.

Helmer. [*Putting his arm around her.*] The child shall have her own way. But to-morrow night, when the dance is over——

Nora. Then you shall be free.

[ELLEN *appears in the doorway, right.*]

Ellen. Dinner is on the table, ma'am.

Nora. We'll have some champagne, Ellen.

Ellen. Yes, ma'am. [*Goes out.*]

Helmer. Dear me! Quite a banquet.

Nora. Yes, and we'll keep it up till morning. [*Calling out.*] And macaroons, Ellen—plenty—just this once.

Helmer. [*Seizing her hand.*] Come, come, don't let us have this wild excitement! Be my own little lark again.

Nora. Oh yes, I will. But now go into the dining-room; and you too, Doctor Rank. Christina, you must help me to do up my hair.

Rank. [*Softly, as they go.*] There's nothing in the wind? Nothing—I mean——?

Helmer. Oh no, nothing of the kind. It's merely this babyish anxiety I was telling you about. [*They go out to the right.*]

Nora. Well?

Mrs. Linden. He's gone out of town.

Nora. I saw it in your face.

Mrs. Linden. He comes back to-morrow evening. I left a note for him.

Nora. You shouldn't have done that. Things must take their course. After all, there's something glorious in waiting for the miracle.

Mrs. Linden. What is it you're waiting for?

Nora. Oh, you can't understand. Go to them in the dining-room; I shall come in a moment.

[MRS. LINDEN *goes into the dining-room.* NORA *stands for a moment as though collecting her thoughts; then looks at her watch.*]

Nora. Five. Seven hours till midnight. Then twenty-four hours till the next midnight. Then the tarantella will be over. Twenty-four and seven? Thirty-one hours to live.

[HELMER *appears at the door, right.*]

Helmer. What has become of my little lark?

Nora. [*Runs to him with open arms.*] Here she is!

CURTAIN

ACT THIRD

The same room. The table, with the chairs around it, in the middle. A lighted lamp on the table. The door to the hall stands open. Dance music is heard from the floor above.

[MRS. LINDEN *sits by the table and absently turns the pages of a book. She tries to read, but seems unable to fix her attention; she frequently listens and looks anxiously toward the hall door.*]

Mrs. Linden. [*Looks at her watch.*] Not here yet; and the time is nearly up. If only he hasn't—— [*Listens again.*] Ah, there he is. [*She goes into the hall and cautiously opens the outer door; soft footsteps are heard on the stairs; she whispers.*] Come in; there is no one here.

Krogstad. [*In the doorway.*] I found a note from you at my house. What does it mean?

Mrs. Linden. I must speak to you.

Krogstad. Indeed? And in this house?

Mrs. Linden. I could not see you at my rooms. They have no separate entrance. Come in; we are quite alone. The servants are asleep, and the Helmers are at the ball upstairs.

Krogstad. [*Coming into the room.*] Ah! So the Helmers are dancing this evening? Really?

Mrs. Linden. Yes. Why not?

Krogstad. Quite right. Why not?

Mrs. Linden. And now let us talk a little.

Krogstad. Have we two anything to say to each other?

Mrs. Linden. A great deal.

Krogstad. I should not have thought so.

Mrs. Linden. Because you have never really understood me.

Krogstad. What was there to understand? The most natural thing in the world—a heartless woman throws a man over when a better match offers.

Mrs. Linden. Do you really think me so heartless? Do you think I broke with you lightly?

Krogstad. Did you not?

Mrs. Linden. Do you really think so?

Krogstad. If not, why did you write me that letter?

Mrs. Linden. Was it not best? Since I had to break with you, was it not right that I should try to put an end to all that you felt for me?

Krogstad. [*Clenching his hands together.*] So that was it? And all this—for the sake of money!

Mrs. Linden. You ought not to forget that I had a helpless mother and two little brothers. We could not wait for you, Nils, as your prospects then stood.

Krogstad. Perhaps not; but you had no right to cast me off for the sake of others, whoever the others might be.

Mrs. Linden. I don't know. I have often asked myself whether I had the right.

Krogstad. [*More softly.*] When I had lost you, I seemed to have no firm ground left under my feet. Look at me now. I am a shipwrecked man clinging to a spar.

Mrs. Linden. Rescue may be at hand.

Krogstad. It was at hand; but then you came and stood in the way.

Mrs. Linden. Without my knowledge, Nils. I did not know till to-day that it was you I was to replace in the Bank.

Krogstad. Well, I take your word for it. But now that you do know, do you mean to give way?

Mrs. Linden. No, for that would not help you in the least.

Krogstad. Oh, help, help——! I should do it whether or no.

Mrs. Linden. I have learnt prudence. Life and bitter necessity have schooled me.

Krogstad. And life has taught me not to trust fine speeches.

Mrs. Linden. Then life has taught you a very sensible thing. But deeds you will trust?

Krogstad. What do you mean?

Mrs. Linden. You said you were a shipwrecked man, clinging to a spar.

Krogstad. I have good reason to say so.

Mrs. Linden. I too am shipwrecked, and clinging to a spar. I have no one to mourn for, no one to care for.

Krogstad. You made your own choice.

Mrs. Linden. No choice was left me.

Krogstad. Well, what then?

Mrs. Linden. Nils, how if we two shipwrecked people could join hands?

Krogstad. What!

Mrs. Linden. Two on a raft have a better chance than if each clings to a separate spar.

Krogstad. Christina!

Mrs. Linden. What do you think brought me to town?

Krogstad. Had you any thought of me?

Mrs. Linden. I must have work or I can't bear to live. All my life, as long as I can remember, I have worked; work has been my one great joy. Now I stand quite alone in the world, aimless and forlorn. There is no happiness for one's self. Nils, give me somebody and something to work for.

Krogstad. I cannot believe in all this. It is simply a woman's romantic craving for self-sacrifice.

Mrs. Linden. Have you ever found me romantic?

Krogstad. Would you really——? Tell me: do you know all my past?

Mrs. Linden. Yes.

Krogstad. And do you know what people say of me?

Mrs. Linden. Did you not say just now that with me you could have been another man?

Krogstad. I am sure of it.

Mrs. Linden. Is it too late?

Krogstad. Christina, do you know what you are doing? Yes, you do; I see it in your face. Have you the courage then——?

Mrs. Linden. I need some one to be a mother to, and your children need a mother. You need me, and I—I need you. Nils, I believe in your better self. With you I fear nothing.

Krogstad. [*Seizing her hands.*] Thank you—thank you, Christina. Now I shall make others see me as you do.—Ah, I forgot——

Mrs. Linden. [*Listening.*] Hush! The tarantella! Go! go!

Krogstad. Why? What is it?

Mrs. Linden. Don't you hear the dancing overhead? As soon as that is over they will be here.

Krogstad. Oh yes, I shall go. Nothing will come of this, after all. Of course, you don't know the step I have taken against the Helmers.

Mrs. Linden. Yes, Nils, I do know.

Krogstad. And yet you have the courage to——?

Mrs. Linden. I know to what lengths despair can drive a man.

Krogstad. Oh, if I could only undo it!

Mrs. Linden. You could. Your letter is still in the box.

Krogstad. Are you sure?

Mrs. Linden. Yes; but——

Krogstad. [*Looking to her searchingly.*] Is that what it all means? You want to save your friend at any price. Say it out—is that your idea?

Mrs. Linden. Nils, a woman who has once sold herself for the sake of others, does not do so again.

Krogstad. I shall demand my letter back again.

Mrs. Linden. No, no.

Krogstad. Yes, of course. I shall wait till Helmer comes; I shall tell him to give it back to me—that it's only about my dismissal—that I don't want it read——

Mrs. Linden. No, Nils, you must not recall the letter.

Krogstad. But tell me, wasn't that just why you got me to come here?

Mrs. Linden. Yes, in my first alarm. But a day has passed since then, and in that day I have seen incredible things in this house. Helmer must know everything; there must be an end to this unhappy secret. These two must come to a full understanding. They must have done with all these shifts and subterfuges.

Krogstad. Very well, if you like to risk it. But one thing I can do, and at once——

Mrs. Linden. [*Listening.*] Make haste! Go, go! The dance is over; we're not safe another moment.

Krogstad. I shall wait for you in the street.

Mrs. Linden. Yes, do; you must see me home.

Krogstad. I never was so happy in all my life!

[KROGSTAD *goes out by the outer door. The door between the room and the hall remains open.*]

Mrs. Linden. [*Arranging the room and getting her outdoor things together.*] What a change! What a change! To have some one to work for, to live for; a home to make happy! Well, it shall not be my fault if I fail—I wish they would come. [*Listens.*] Ah, here they are! I must get my things on.

[*Takes bonnet and cloak.* HELMER'S *and* NORA'S *voices are heard outside, a key is turned in the lock, and* HELMER *drags* NORA *almost by force into the hall. She wears the Italian costume with a large black shawl over it. He is in evening dress and wears a black domino, open.*]

Nora [*Struggling with him in the doorway.*] No, no, no! I won't go in! I want to go upstairs again; I don't want to leave so early!

Helmer. But, my dearest girl——!

Nora. Oh, please, please, Torvald, I beseech you—only one hour more!

Helmer. Not one minute more, Nora dear; you know what we agreed. Come, come in; you're catching cold here.

[*He leads her gently into the room in spite of her resistance.*]

Mrs. Linden. Good evening.

Nora. Christina!

Helmer. What, Mrs. Linden! You here so late?

Mrs. Linden. Yes, I ought to apologize. I did so want to see Nora in her costume.

Nora. Have you been sitting here waiting for me?

Mrs. Linden. Yes; unfortunately I came too late. You had gone upstairs already, and I felt I couldn't go away without seeing you.

Helmer. [*Taking* NORA'S *shawl off.*] Well, then, just look at her! I assure you she's worth it. Isn't she lovely, Mrs. Linden?

Mrs. Linden. Yes, I must say——

Helmer. Isn't she exquisite? Every one said so. But she's dreadfully obstinate, dear little creature. What's to be done with her? Just think, I had almost to force her away.

Nora. Oh, Torvald, you'll be sorry some day that you didn't let me stay, if only for one half-hour more.

Helmer. There! You hear her, Mrs. Linden? She dances her tarantella with wild applause, and well she deserved it, I must say—though there was, perhaps, a little too much nature in her rendering of the idea—more than was, strictly speaking, artistic. But never mind—the point is, she made a great success, a tremendous success. Was I to let her remain after that—to weaken the impression? Not if I know it. I took my sweet little Capri girl—my capricious little Capri girl, I might say—under my arm; a rapid turn round the room, a curtsey to all sides, and—as they say in novels—the lovely apparition vanished! An exit should always be effective, Mrs. Linden; but I can't get Nora to see it. By Jove! it's warm here. [*Throws his domino or a chair and opens the door to his room.*] What! No light there? Oh, of course. Excuse me——

[*Goes in and lights candles.*]

Nora. [*Whispers breathlessly.*] Well?

Mrs. Linden. [*Softly.*] I've spoken to him.

Nora. And——?

Mrs. Linden. Nora—you must tell your husband everything——

Nora. [*Tonelessly.*] I knew it!

Mrs. Linden. You have nothing to fear from Krogstad; but you must speak out.

Nora. I shall not speak.

Mrs. Linden. Then the letter will.

Nora. Thank you, Christina. Now I know what I have to do. Hush——!

Helmer. [*Coming back.*] Well, Mrs. Linden, have you admired her?

Mrs. Linden. Yes; and now I must say good night.

Helmer. What, already? Does this knitting belong to you?

Mrs. Linden. [*Takes it.*] Yes, thanks; I was nearly forgetting it.

Helmer. Then you do knit?

Mrs. Linden. Yes.

Helmer. Do you know, you ought to embroider instead?

Mrs. Linden. Indeed! Why?

Helmer. Because it's so much prettier. Look now! You hold the embroidery in the left hand, so, and then work the needle with the right hand, in a long, graceful curve—don't you?

Mrs. Linden. Yes, I suppose so.

Helmer. But knitting is always ugly. Just look—your arms close to your sides, and the needles going up and down—there's something Chinese about it.—They really gave us splendid champagne to-night.

Mrs. Linden. Well, good night, Nora, and don't be obstinate any more.

Helmer. Well said, Mrs. Linden!

Mrs. Linden. Good night, Mr. Helmer.

Helmer. [*Accompanying her to the door.*] Good night, good night; I hope you'll get safely home. I should be glad to—but you have such a short way to go. Good night, good night. [*She goes;* HELMER *shuts the door after her and comes forward again.*] At last we've got rid of her: she's a terrible bore.

Nora. Aren't you very tired, Torvald?

Helmer. No, not in the least.

Nora. Nor sleepy?

Helmer. Not a bit. I feel particularly lively. But you? You do look tired and sleepy.

Nora. Yes, very tired. I shall soon sleep now.

Helmer. There, you see. I was right after all not to let you stay longer.

Nora. Oh, everything you do is right.

Helmer. [*Kissing her forehead.*] Now my lark is speaking like a reasonable being. Did you notice how jolly Rank was this evening?

Nora. Indeed? Was he? I had no chance of speaking to him.

Helmer. Nor I, much; but I haven't seen him in such good spirits for a long time. [*Looks at* NORA *a little, then comes nearer her.*] It's splendid to be back in our own home, to be quite alone together!—Oh, you enchanting creature!

Nora. Don't look at me in that way, Torvald.

Helmer. I am not to look at my dearest treasure?—at all the loveliness that is mine, mine only, wholly and entirely mine?

Nora. [*Goes to the other side of the table.*] You mustn't say these things to me this evening.

Helmer. [*Following.*] I see you have the tarantella still in your blood—and that makes you all the more enticing. Listen! the other people are going now. [*More softly.*] Nora—soon the whole house will be still.

Nora. Yes, I hope so.

Helmer. Yes, don't you, Nora darling? When we are among strangers, do you know why I speak so little to you, and keep so far away, and only steal a glance at you now and then—do you know why I do it? Because I am fancying that we love each other in secret, that I am secretly betrothed to you, and that no one dreams that there is anything between us.

Nora. Yes, yes, yes. I know all your thoughts are with me.

Helmer. And then, when the time comes to go, and I put the shawl about your smooth, soft shoulders, and this glorious neck of yours, I imagine you are my bride, that our marriage is just over, that I am bringing you for the first time to my home—that I am alone with you for the first time—quite alone with you, in your trembling loveliness! All this evening I have been longing for you, and you only. When I watched you swaying and whirling in the tarantella—my blood boiled—I could endure it no longer; and that's why I made you come home with me so early——

Nora. Go now, Torvald! Go away from me. I won't have all this.

Helmer. What do you mean? Ah, I see you're teasing me, little Nora! Won't—won't! Am I not your husband——?

[*A knock at the outer door.*]

Nora. [*Starts.*] Did you hear——?

Helmer. [*Going towards the hall.*] Who's there?

Rank. [*Outside.*] It is I; may I come in for a moment?

Helmer. [*In a low tone, annoyed.*] Oh! what can he want just now? [*Aloud.*] Wait a moment. [*Opens door.*] Come, it's nice of you to look in.

Rank. I thought I heard your voice, and that put it into my head. [*Looks around.*] Ah, this dear old place! How cozy you two are here!

Helmer. You seemed to find it pleasant enough upstairs, too.

Rank. Exceedingly. Why not? Why shouldn't one take one's share of everything in this world? All one can, at least, and as long as one can. The wine was splendid——

Helmer. Especially the champagne.

Rank. Did you notice it? It's incredible the quantity I contrived to get down.

Nora. Torvald drank plenty of champagne, too.

Rank. Did he?

Nora. Yes, and it always puts him in such spirits.

Rank. Well, why shouldn't one have a jolly evening after a well-spent day?

Helmer. Well-spent! Well, I haven't much to boast of in that respect.

Rank. [*Slapping him on the shoulder.*] But I have, don't you see?

Nora. I suppose you have been engaged in a scientific investigation, Doctor Rank?

Rank. Quite right.

Helmer. Bless me! Little Nora talking about scientific investigations!

Nora. Am I to congratulate you on the result?

Rank. By all means.

Nora. It was good then?

Rank. The best possible, both for doctor and patient—certainty.

Nora. [*Quickly and searchingly.*] Certainty?

Rank. Absolute certainty. Wasn't I right to enjoy myself after that?

Nora. Yes, quite right, Doctor Rank.

Helmer. And so say I, provided you don't have to pay for it to-morrow.

Rank. Well, in this life nothing is to be had for nothing.

Nora. Doctor Rank—I'm sure you are very fond of masquerades?

Rank. Yes, when there are plenty of amusing disguises——

Nora. Tell me, what shall we two be at our next masquerade?

Helmer. Little featherbrain! Thinking of your next already!

Rank. We two? I'll tell you. You must go as a good fairy.

Helmer. Ah, but what costume would indicate that?

Rank. She has simply to wear her everyday dress.

Helmer. Capital! But don't you know what you will be yourself?

Rank. Yes, my dear friend, I am perfectly clear upon that point.

Helmer. Well?

Rank. At the next masquerade I shall be invisible.

Helmer. What a comical idea!

Rank. There's a big black hat—haven't you heard of the invisible hat? It comes down all over you, and then no one can see you.

Helmer. [*With a suppressed smile.*] No, you're right there.

Rank. But I'm quite forgetting what I came for. Helmer, give me a cigar—one of the dark Havanas.

Helmer. With the greatest pleasure.

[*Hands cigar-case.*]

Rank. [*Takes one and cuts the end off.*] Thank you.

Nora. [*Striking a wax match.*] Let me give you a light.

Rank. A thousand thanks.

[*She holds the match. He lights his cigar at it.*]

Rank. And now, good-by!

Helmer. Good-by, good-by, my dear fellow.

Nora. Sleep well, Doctor Rank.

Rank. Thanks for the wish.

Nora. Wish me the same.

Rank. You? Very well, since you ask me—— Sleep well. And thanks for the light.

[*He nods to them both and goes out.*]

Helmer. [*In an undertone.*] He's been drinking a good deal.

Nora. [*Absently.*] I dare say. [HELMER *takes his bunch of keys from his pocket and goes into the hall.*] Torvald, what are you doing there?

Helmer. I must empty the letter-box; it's quite full; there will be no room for the newspapers to-morrow morning.

Nora. Are you going to work to-night?

Helmer. You know very well I am not.—Why, how is this? Some one has been at the lock.

Nora. The lock——?

Helmer. I'm sure of it. What does it mean? I can't think that the servants——? Here's a broken hair-pin. Nora, it's one of yours.

Nora. [*Quickly.*] It must have been the children——

Helmer. Then you must break them of such tricks.—There! At last I've got it open. [*Takes contents out and calls into the kitchen.*] Ellen!—Ellen, just put the hall door lamp out.

[*He returns with letters in his hands, and shuts the inner door.*]

Helmer. Just see how they've accumulated. [*Turning them over.*] Why, what's this?

Nora. [*At the window.*] The letter! Oh no, no, Torvald!

Helmer. Two visiting-cards—from Rank.

Nora. From Doctor Rank?

Helmer. [*Looking at them.*] Doctor Rank. They were on the top. He must just have put them in.

Nora. Is there anything on them?

Helmer. There's a black cross over the name. Look at it. What an unpleasant idea! It looks just as if he were announcing his own death.

Nora. So he is.

Helmer. What! Do you know anything? Has he told you anything?

Nora. Yes. These cards mean that he has taken his last leave of us. He is going to shut himself up and die.

Helmer. Poor fellow! Of course I knew we couldn't hope to keep him long. But so soon——! And to go and creep into his lair like a wounded animal——

Nora. When we must go, it is best to go silently. Don't you think so, Torvald?

Helmer. [*Walking up and down.*] He had so grown into our lives, I can't realize that he is gone. He and his sufferings and his loneliness formed a sort of cloudy background to the sunshine of our happiness—Well, perhaps it's best as it is—at any rate for him. [*Stands still.*] And perhaps for us too, Nora. Now we two are thrown entirely upon each other. [*Takes her in his arms.*] My darling wife! I feel as if I could never hold you close enough. Do you know, Nora, I often wish some danger might threaten you, that I might risk body and soul, and everything, everything, for your dear sake.

Nora. [*Tears herself from him and says firmly.*] Now you shall read your letters, Torvald.

Helmer. No, no; not to-night. I want to be with you, my sweet wife.

Nora. With the thought of your dying friend——?

Helmer. You are right. This has shaken us both. Unloveliness has come between us—thoughts of death and decay. We must seek to cast them off. Till then—we will remain apart.

Nora. [*Her arms around his neck.*] Torvald! Good night! good night!

Helmer. [*Kissing her forehead.*] Good night, my little song-bird. Sleep well, Nora. Now I shall go and read my letters.

[*He goes with the letters in his hand into his room and shuts the door.*]

Nora. [*With wild eyes, gropes about her, seizes* HELMER'S *domino, throws it round her, and whispers quickly, hoarsely, and brokenly.*] Never to see him again. Never, never, never. [*Throws her shawl over her head.*] Never to see the children again. Never, never.—Oh that black, icy water! Oh that bottomless——! If it were only over! Now he has it; he's reading it. Oh, no, no, no, not yet. Torvald, good-by——! Good-by, my little ones——!

[*She is rushing out by the hall; at the same moment* HELMER *flings his door open, and enters with an open letter in his hand.*]

Helmer. Nora!

Nora. [*Shrieks.*] Ah——!

Helmer. What is this? Do you know what is in this letter?

Nora. Yes, I know. Let me go! Let me pass!

Helmer. [*Holds her back.*] Where do you want to go?

Nora. [*Tries to break away from him.*] You shall not save me, Torvald.

Helmer. [*Falling back.*] True! Is what he writes true? No, no, it is impossible that this can be true.

Nora. It is true. I have loved you beyond all else in the world.

Helmer. Pshaw—no silly evasions!

Nora. [*A step nearer him.*] Torvald——!

Helmer. Wretched woman—what have you done?

Nora. Let me go—you shall not save me! You shall not take my guilt upon yourself!

Helmer. I don't want any melodramatic airs. [*Locks the outer door.*] Here you shall stay and give an account of yourself. Do you understand what you have done? Answer! Do you understand it?

Nora. [*Looks at him fixedly, and says with a stiffening expression.*] Yes; now I begin fully to understand it.

Helmer. [*Walking up and down.*] Oh! what an awful awakening! During all these eight years—she who was my pride and my joy—a hypocrite, a liar—worse, worse—a criminal. Oh, the unfathomable hideousness of it all! Ugh! Ugh!

[NORA *says nothing, and contiuues to look fixedly at him.*]

Helmer. I ought to have known how it would be. I ought to have foreseen it. All your father's want of principle—be silent!—all your father's want of principle you have inherited—no religion, no morality, no sense of duty. How I am punished for screening him! I did it for your sake; and you reward me like this.

Nora. Yes—like this.

Helmer. You have destroyed my whole happiness. You have ruined my future. Oh, it's frightful to think of! I am in the power of a scoundrel; he can do whatever he pleases with me, demand whatever he chooses; he can domineer over me as much as he likes, and I must submit. And all this disaster and ruin is brought upon me by an unprincipled woman!

Nora. When I am out of the world, you will be free.

Helmer. Oh, no fine phrases. Your father, too, was always ready with them. What good would it do me, if you were "out of the world," as you say? No good whatever! He can publish the story all the same; I might even be suspected of collusion. People will think I was at the bottom of it all and egged you on. And for all this I have you to thank—you whom I have done nothing but pet and spoil during our whole married life. Do you understand now what you have done to me?

Nora. [*With cold calmness.*] Yes.

Helmer. The thing is so incredible, I can't grasp it. But we must come to an understanding. Take that shawl off. Take it off, I say! I must try to pacify him in one way or another—the matter must be hushed up, cost what it may—As for you and me, we must make no outward change in our way of life—no outward change, you understand. Of course, you will continue to live here. But the children cannot be left in your care. I dare not trust them to you—Oh, to have to say this to one I have loved so tenderly—whom I still——! But that must be a thing of the past. Henceforward there can be no question of happiness, but merely of saving the ruins, the shreds, the show—— [*A ring;* HELMER *starts.*] What's that? So late! Can it be the worst? Can he——? Hide yourself, Nora; say you are ill.

[NORA *stands motionless.* HELMER *goes to the door and opens it.*]

Ellen. [*Half-dressed, in the hall.*] Here is a letter for you, ma'am.

Helmer. Give it to me. [*Seizes the letter and shuts the door.*] Yes, from him. You shall not have it. I shall read it.

Nora. Read it!

Helmer. [*By the lamp.*] I have hardly the courage to. We may both be lost, both you and I. Ah! I must know. [*Hastily tears the letter open; reads a few lines, looks at an enclosure; with a cry of joy.*] Nora!

[NORA *looks inquiringly at him.*]

Helmer. Nora!—Oh! I must read it again.—Yes, yes, it is so. I am saved! Nora, I am saved!

Nora. And I?

Helmer. You too, of course; we are both saved, both of us. Look here—he sends you back your promissory note. He writes that he regrets and apologizes that a happy turn in his life—— Oh, what matter what he writes. We are saved, Nora! No one can harm you. Oh, Nora, Nora——; but first to get rid of this hateful thing. I'll just see—— [*Glances at the I.O.U.*] No, I will not look at it; the whole thing shall be nothing but a dream to me. [*Tears the I.O.U. and both letters in pieces. Throws them into the fire and watches them burn.*] There! it's gone!—He said that ever since Christmas Eve—Oh, Nora, they must have been three terrible days for you!

Nora. I have fought a hard fight for the last three days.

Helmer. And in your agony you saw no other outlet but—— No; we won't think of that horror. We will only rejoice and repeat—it's over, all over! Don't you hear, Nora? You don't seem able to grasp it. Yes, it's over. What is this set look on your face? Oh, my poor Nora, I understand; you cannot believe that I have forgiven you. But I have, Nora; I swear it. I have forgiven everything. I know that what you did was all for love of me.

Nora. That is true.

Helmer. You loved me as a wife should love her husband. It was only the means that, in your inexperience, you misjudged. But do you think I love you the less because you cannot do without guidance? No, no. Only lean on me; I will counsel you, and guide you. I should be no true man if this very womanly helplessness did not make you doubly dear in my eyes. You mustn't dwell upon the hard things I said in my first moment of terror, when the world seemed to be tumbling about my ears. I have forgiven you, Nora—I swear I have forgiven you.

Nora. I thank you for your forgiveness.

[*Goes out, to the right.*]

Helmer. No, stay——! [*Looking through the doorway.*] What are you going to do?

Nora. [*Inside.*] To take off my masquerade dress.

Helmer. [*In the doorway.*] Yes, do, dear. Try to calm down, and recover your balance, my scared little song-bird. You may rest secure. I have broad wings to shield you. [*Walking up and down near the door.*] Oh, how lovely—how cozy our home is, Nora! Here you are safe; here I can shelter you like a hunted dove that I have saved from the claws of the hawk. I shall soon bring your poor beating heart to rest; believe me, Nora, very soon. Tomorrow all this will seem quite different—everything will be as before. I shall not need to tell you again that I forgive you; you will feel for yourself that it is true. How could you think I could find it in my heart to drive you away, or even so much as to reproach you? Oh, you don't know a true man's heart, Nora. There is something indescribably sweet and soothing to a man in having forgiven his wife—honestly forgiven her, from the bottom of his heart. She becomes his property in a double sense. She is as though born again; she has become, so to speak, at once his wife and his child. That is what you shall henceforth be to me, my bewildered, helpless darling. Don't be troubled about anything, Nora; only open your heart to me, and I will be both will and conscience to you. [NORA *enters in everyday dress.*] Why, what's this? Not gone to bed? You have changed your dress?

Nora. Yes, Torvald; now I have changed my dress.

Helmer. But why now, so late——?

Nora. I shall not sleep to-night.

Helmer. But, Nora dear——

Nora. [*Looking at her watch.*] It's not so late yet. Sit down, Torvald; you and I have much to say to each other.

[*She sits at one side of the table.*]

Helmer. Nora—what does this mean? Your cold, set face——

Nora. Sit down. It will take some time. I have much to talk over with you.

[HELMER *sits at the other side of the table.*]

Helmer. You alarm me, Nora. I don't understand you.

Nora. No, that is just it. You don't understand me; and I have never understood you—till to-night. No, don't interrupt. Only listen to what I say—We must come to a final settlement, Torvald.

Helmer. How do you mean?

Nora. [*After a short silence.*] Does not one thing strike you as we sit here?

Helmer. What should strike me?

Nora. We have been married eight years. Does it not strike you that this is the first time we two, you and I, man and wife, have talked together seriously?

Helmer. Seriously! What do you call seriously?

Nora. During eight whole years, and more—ever since the day we first met—we have never exchanged one serious word about serious things.

Helmer. Was I always to trouble you with the cares you could not help me to bear?

Nora. I am not talking of cares. I say that we have never yet set ourselves seriously to get to the bottom of anything.

Helmer. Why, my dearest Nora, what have you to do with serious things?

Nora. There we have it! You have never understood me—I have had great injustice done me, Torvald; first by Father, and then by you.

Helmer. What! By your father and me?—By us, who have loved you more than all the world?

Nora. [*Shaking her head.*] You have never loved me. You only thought it amusing to be in love with me.

Helmer. Why, Nora, what a thing to say!

Nora. Yes, it is so, Torvald. While I was at home with Father, he used to tell me all his opinions, and I held the same opinions. If I had others I said nothing about them, because he wouldn't have liked it. He used to call me his doll-child, and played with me as I played with my dolls. Then I came to live in your house——

Helmer. What an expression to use about our marriage!

Nora. [*Undisturbed.*] I mean I passed from Father's hands into yours. You arranged everything according to your taste; and I got the same tastes as you; or I pretended to—I don't know which—both ways, perhaps; sometimes one and sometimes the other. When I look back on it now, I seem to have been living here like a beggar, from hand to mouth. I lived by performing tricks for you, Torvald. But you would have it so. You and Father have done me a great wrong. It is your fault that my life has come to nothing.

Helmer. Why, Nora, how unreasonable and ungrateful you are! Have you not been happy here?

Nora. No, never. I thought I was; but I never was.

Helmer. Not—not happy!

Nora. No; only merry. And you have always been so kind to me. But our house has been nothing but a play-room. Here I have been your doll-wife, just as at home I used to be Papa's doll-child. And the children, in their turn, have been my dolls. I thought it fun when you played with me, just as the children did when I played with them. That has been our marriage, Torvald.

Helmer. There is some truth in what you say, exaggerated and overstrained though it be. But henceforth it shall be different. Play-time is over; now comes the time for education.

Nora. Whose education? Mine, or the children's's?

Helmer. Both, my dear Nora.

Nora. Oh, Torvald, you are not the man to teach me to be a fit wife for you.

Helmer. And you can say that?

Nora. And I—how have I prepared myself to educate the children?

Helmer. Nora!

Nora. Did you not say yourself, a few minutes ago, you dared not trust them to me?

Helmer. In the excitement of the moment! Why should you dwell upon that?

Nora. No—you were perfectly right. That problem is beyond me. There is another to be solved first—I must try to educate myself. You are not the man to help me in that. I must set about it alone. And that is why I am leaving you.

Helmer. [*Jumping up.*] What—do you mean to say——?

Nora. I must stand quite alone if I am ever to know myself and my surroundings; so I cannot stay with you.

Helmer. Nora! Nora!

Nora. I am going at once. I dare say Christina will take me in for to-night——

Helmer. You are mad! I shall not allow it! I forbid it!

Nora. It is of no use your forbidding me anything now. I shall take with me what belongs to me. From you I will accept nothing, either now or afterwards.

Helmer. What madness this is!

Nora. To-morrow I shall go home—I mean to what was my home. It will be easier for me to find some opening there.

Helmer. Oh, in your blind inexperience——

Nora. I must try to gain experience, Torvald.

Helmer. To forsake your home, your husband, and your children! And you don't consider what the world will say.

Nora. I can pay no heed to that. I only know that I must do it.

Helmer. This is monstrous! Can you forsake your holiest duties in this way?

Nora. What do you consider my holiest duties?

Helmer. Do I need to tell you that? Your duties to your husband and your children.

Nora. I have other duties equally sacred.

Helmer. Impossible! What duties do you mean?

Nora. My duties towards myself.

Helmer. Before all else you are a wife and a mother.

Nora. That I no longer believe. I believe that before all else I am a human being, just as much as you are—or at least that I should try to become one. I know that most people agree with you, Torvald, and that they say so in books. But henceforth I can't be satisfied with what most people say, and what is in books. I must think things out for myself, and try to get clear about them.

Helmer. Are you not clear about your place in your own home? Have you not an infallible guide in questions like these? Have you not religion?

Nora. Oh, Torvald, I don't really know what religion is.

Helmer. What do you mean?

Nora. I know nothing but what Pastor Hansen told me when I was confirmed. He explained that religion was this and that. When I get away from all this and stand alone, I will look into that matter too. I will see whether what he taught me is right, or, at any rate, whether it is right for me.

Helmer. Oh, this is unheard of! And from so young a woman! But if religion cannot keep you right, let me appeal to your conscience—for I suppose you have some moral feeling? Or, answer me: perhaps you have none?

Nora. Well, Torvald, it's not easy to say. I really don't know—I am all at sea about these things. I only know that I think quite differently from you about them. I hear, too, that the laws are different from what I thought; but I can't believe that they can be right. It appears that a woman has no right to spare her dying father, or to save her husband's life! I don't believe that.

Helmer. You talk like a child. You don't understand the society in which you live.

Nora. No, I do not. But now I shall try to learn. I must make up my mind which is right—society or I.

Helmer. Nora, you are ill; you are feverish; I almost think you are out of your senses.

Nora. I have never felt so much clearness and certainty as to-night.

Helmer. You are clear and certain enough to forsake husband and children?

Nora. Yes, I am.

Helmer. Then there is only one explanation possible.

Nora. What is that?

Helmer. You no longer love me.

Nora. No; that is just it.

Helmer. Nora!—Can you say so!

Nora. Oh, I'm so sorry, Torvald; for you've always been so kind to me. But I can't help it. I do not love you any longer.

Helmer. [*Mastering himself with difficulty.*] Are you clear and certain on this point too?

Nora. Yes, quite. That is why I will not stay here any longer.

Helmer. And can you also make clear to me how I have forfeited your love?

Nora. Yes, I can. It was this evening, when the miracle did not happen; for then I saw you were not the man I had imagined.

Helmer. Explain yourself more clearly; I don't understand.

Nora. I have waited so patiently all these eight years; for of course I saw clearly enough that miracles don't happen every day. When this crushing blow threatened me, I said to myself so confidently, "Now comes the miracle!" When Krogstad's letter lay in the box, it never for a moment occurred to me that you would think of submitting to that man's conditions. I was convinced that you would say to him, "Make it known to all the world"; and that then——

Helmer. Well? When I had given my own wife's name up to disgrace and shame——?

Nora. Then I firmly believed that you would come forward, take everything upon yourself, and say, "I am the guilty one."

Helmer. Nora——!

Nora. You mean I would never have accepted such a sacrifice? No, certainly not. But what would my assertions have been worth in opposition to yours?—That was the miracle that I hoped for and dreaded. And it was to hinder that that I wanted to die.

Helmer. I would gladly work for you day and night, Nora—bear sorrow and want for your sake. But no man sacrifices his honor, even for one he loves.

Nora. Millions of women have done so.

Helmer. Oh, you think and talk like a silly child.

Nora. Very likely. But you neither think nor talk like the man I can share my life with. When your terror was over—not for what threatened me, but for yourself—when there was nothing more to fear—then it seemed to you as though nothing had happened. I was your lark again, your doll, just as before—whom you would take twice as much care of in future, because she was so weak and fragile. [*Stands up.*] Torvald—in that moment it burst upon me that I had been living here these eight years with a strange man, and had borne him three children—Oh, I can't bear to think of it! I could tear myself to pieces!

Helmer. [*Sadly.*] I see it, I see it; an abyss has opened between us—But, Nora, can it never be filled up?

Nora. As I now am, I am no wife for you.

Helmer. I have strength to become another man.

Nora. Perhaps—when your doll is taken away from you.

Helmer. To part—to part from you! No, Nora, no; I can't grasp the thought.

Nora. [*Going into room on the right.*] The more reason for the thing to happen.

[*She comes back with outdoor things and a small traveling-bag, which she places on a chair.*]

Helmer. Nora, Nora, not now! Wait till to-morrow.

Nora. [*Putting on cloak.*] I can't spend the night in a strange man's house.

Helmer. But can we not live here, as brother and sister——?

Nora. [*Fastening her hat.*] You know very well that wouldn't last long. [*Puts on the shawl.*] Good-by, Torvald. No, I won't go to the children. I know they are in better hands than mine. As I now am, I can be nothing to them.

Helmer. But some time, Nora—some time——?

Nora. How can I tell? I have no idea what will become of me.

Helmer. But you are my wife, now and always!

Nora. Listen, Torvald—when a wife leaves her husband's house, as I am doing, I have heard that in the eyes of the law he is free from all duties towards her. At any rate, I release you from all duties. You must not feel yourself bound, any more than I shall. There must be perfect freedom on both sides. There, I give you back your ring. Give me mine.

Helmer. That too?

Nora. That too.

Helmer. Here it is.

Nora. Very well. Now it is all over. I lay the keys here. The servants know about everything in the house—better than I do. To-morrow, when I have started, Christina will come to pack up the things I brought with me from home. I will have them sent after me.

Helmer. All over! all over! Nora, will you ever think of me again?

Nora. Oh, I shall often think of you, and the children, and this house.

Helmer. May I write to you, Nora?

Nora. No—never. You must not.

Helmer. But I must send you——

Nora. Nothing, nothing.

Helmer. I must help you if you need it.

Nora. No, I say. I take nothing from strangers.

Helmer. Nora—can I never be more than a stranger to you?

Nora. [*Taking her traveling-bag.*] Oh, Torvald, then the miracle of miracles would have to happen——

Helmer. What is the miracle of miracles?

Nora. Both of us would have to change so that—— Oh, Torvald, I no longer believe in miracles.

Helmer. But *I* will believe. Tell me! We must so change that——?

Nora. That communion between us shall be a marriage. Good-by.

[*She goes out by the hall door.*]

Helmer. [*Sinks into a chair by the door with his face in his hands.*] Nora! Nora! [*He looks around and rises.*] Empty. She is gone. [*A hope springs up in him.*] Ah! The miracle of miracles——? !

[*From below is heard the reverberation of a heavy door closing.*]

THE END

THE FOSSILS*

[*Les Fossiles*]

By

FRANÇOIS DE CUREL

Authorized Translation by BARRETT H. CLARK

FRANÇOIS DE CUREL WAS AN ARISTOCRAT of literature. His private means made it possible for him to write as and when he pleased. He never sought popularity. His plays have been successful in production, but, like Galsworthy's, they have been more admired than patronized in the theater. Mr. Barrett Clark states that de Curel considered himself an amateur playwright. His artistry, however, gives him rank with Brieux as an outstanding survivor of Antoine's Free Theater group of playwrights. Holding himself aloof from the commercial theater, he wrote each of his plays as the result of personal interest in some phase of modern thought. He is perhaps the most striking instance of a French playwright whose interest in the drama, and whose accomplishment, have been due entirely to Antoine's free theater and its non-commercial ideals. Psychology was always his chief source of dramatic material. Characters with strange mentality are placed in extraordinary circumstances, often, as in *The Fossils,* suggested by the personal experience or contact of the author. His own position in society was analogous to that of the Chantemelles, for his family was of the old aristocracy, forced by the founding of the French Republic to share the proud seclusion of the nobility.

He was glad, no doubt, to give up his intended career as engineer in the development of the family estates near Metz, which were surrendered to Germany. Many years were to pass, however, before the first results of his literary experiments appeared. He first attempted the novel, but failed. In the founding of Antoine's theater, he saw a hoped-for opportunity, and in 1892 he submitted three different plays, purporting to come from three different writers. To his astonishment, all three were accepted. *The Fossils* was among them, and remains his most distinctive piece of work. *The Lion's Feast* (1898) and *The New Idol* (1899) gave him a foremost place in the French theater. His work, although associated with that of the extreme naturalists, had romantic and even mystical qualities.

PRODUCTION

The Free Theater of Paris, founded by Antoine in 1887, which made possible the production of such plays as de Curel's, was the parent "Little Theater" of the world; that is, it was the first playhouse founded for art's sake in defiance of the commercial and national theaters. At these, a young dramatist, especially one with new ideas, had at that time small chance of acceptance. The beginning was extremely modest. A rude hall in the Passage de l'Elysée des Beaux Arts was converted into a playhouse, and the amateur producer, André Antoine, chose a bill of four one-act plays from the work of the Zola circle of young naturalists, who for nearly ten years had been developing their theories of literature, and clamoring for an opportunity to express themselves in the theater. They had been stirred by the work of Ibsen, Tolstoy, and Strindberg, and were eager to see the works of these authors properly given in French, as they could not be staged at the established theaters.

Antoine's little house became their rallying center, and for seven years produced plays in the new spirit of defiance and revolt. The new naturalism was chiefly represented, not only in the work of Zola and his disciples, but also in that of Ibsen, Strindberg, Tolstoy, and Hauptmann. A school of acting was religiously developed to banish from the stage conventionalities of speech and action, so that characters and scenes might be represented as nearly as possible as in real life. Actors talked for the first time with their backs to the audience, and spoke without the declamatory emphasis so much in vogue at French theaters. The curtain rose and fell on casual or irrelevant action. A purposeful disorder created an impression of absolute fidelity to nature. Furthermore, plays dealing with gross and repulsive types of humanity and society, faithfully reproduced, gave special pleasure to these revolters against the shoddy decencies of the well-made play. Excessive as this orgy was at times, it gave expression to new and vital influences that are still strongly felt in the theater, and it reintroduced to the stage the essential spirit of artistic cooperation, which has been of much greater importance than the vogue for crude naturalism, now becoming almost as obsolete as the well-made play.

The most notable French dramatists brought before the public by Antoine's theater were Eugene Brieux in 1890, and de Curel in 1892.

FRANÇOIS DE CUREL

Born 1854, Metz.
Educated as engineer for family metal industry.
1870, After German Occupation de Curel free for literary work.
1885, His first novel.
1887, The Free Theater (Le Théâtre-libre) founded by Antoine.
1892, Three plays accepted by Antoine.
Died 1928, Paris.

PLAYS

1892 *A False Saint (L'Envers d'une Sainte)*. 1892 *The Fossils (Les Fossiles)*. 1893 *The Guest (L'Invité)*. 1893 *Love Embellishes (L'Amour brode)*. 1896 *The Dancer (La Figurante)*. 1898 *The Lion's Feast (Le Repas du Lion)*. 1899 *The New Idol (La nouvelle Idole)*. 1902 *The Savage Girl (La Fille sauvage)*. 1906 *The Beat of the Wing (Le Coup d'aile)*. 1914 *The Dance before the Mirror (La Dance devant le Miroir)*. 1918 *The Genius' Comedy (La Comédie du Génie)*. 1920 *The Soul Gone Mad (L'âme en Folie)*. 1922 *The Wise Man's Folly (L'Ivresse du Sage)*. 1922 *No Man's Land (La Terre inhumaine)*. 1926 *The Gay Lady and the Man at Death's Door (La Viveuse et le Moribond)*. 1927 *The Mystical Storm (L'Orage mystique)*.

THE FOSSILS

Persons Represented

THE DUKE DE CHANTEMELLE.	A SERVANT.
ROBERT DE CHANTEMELLE.	THE DUCHESS DE CHANTEMELLE.
NICOLAS.	CLAIRE DE CHANTEMELLE.
A FARMER.	HÉLÈNE VATRIN.
A COUNTRY NEIGHBOR.	A NUN.

ACT I

A large country house in the Ardennes. A spacious wainscotted room; to the right, windows partially concealed by thick curtains; to the left, a high fireplace between two doors. At the back, a large doorway opening into a vestibule. The paneling around this door, as well as the walls of the room, is covered with panoplies, hunting trophies, old armor, genealogical charts, and maps of ancient domains. The furnishings are severe; the room breathes an air of feudalism.

It is evening; a single lamp gives out a sickly light into the room. From time to time the fire, which is concealed for the most part in ashes, shoots forth little flames. Outside, a storm is beginning; the whistling of the wind is heard.

[*Enter* CLAIRE. *She looks quickly about her, goes to the window and raises the curtain to look into the night, but the inside shutters are closed. She makes a little gesture of impatience, then goes at once to the door at the back, and is about to leave the room when a servant enters carrying an armful of wood. She intercepts him and asks.*]

Claire. There is a carriage outside from town; whose is it?

Servant. The doctor's, Mademoiselle.

Claire. The doctor from Paris?

Servant. The doctor from Paris and the one from town also.

Claire. But the consultation was not to take place until tomorrow?

Servant. I heard the gentlemen telling Madame la duchesse that the doctor from Paris has to make a speech tomorrow before the Academy of Science. So he telegraphed and said he would come today. The telegram didn't arrive because of the frost that broke all the wires this side of Sedan.

Claire. Do you know whether the doctors are to take dinner here?

Servant. Oh, no, Mademoiselle; they didn't even unhitch their horses. When I was coming upstairs just now, I overheard them talking with Madame la duchesse; they're probably gone by this time.

Claire. Has my father come in yet?

Servant. I haven't seen any one.

Claire. Very well!

[*She sits beside a table, down-stage, and leans upon it, meditating. The servant puts the wood by the fireplace, lays a log on the fire, and goes out. After a moment,* CLAIRE *rises, opens the door at the back, listens, then comes back to the fireplace, standing before it, her head resting upon the stone mantel.*

Enter the DUCHESS *at the back. Her expression is one of great sadness; her eyes are red from crying.* CLAIRE *turns around, and the* DUCHESS *throws herself precipitately into her arms.*]

Duchess. Your poor brother!

Claire. Worse?

Duchess. Yes! We have to send him south. He will never come back to us—I know it!

Claire. Is it that bad?

Duchess. The doctors gave him all sorts of encouragement. I don't know whether he believed them, but I knew well enough they weren't telling the truth! I saw them to their carriage, and the moment they were saying good-by—I was on the steps, with snow on my feet, and I was quite sure Robert was out of hearing—I asked them for the truth.

Claire. But if they're sending him south——?

Duchess. He will never recover! Perhaps the climate at Nice will prolong his life for a few months—perhaps! [*Holding back her tears.*] Here, they told me, it was only a question of days——

[*She falls into a chair, her face buried in a handkerchief.* CLAIRE, *standing as before at the fireplace, is crying also, but she controls her feelings.*]

Claire. They must be exaggerating.

Duchess. Our only hope is in God!—[*After a pause.*] What a blow for your father!

Claire. [*Dryly.*] Yes, it is! But he will be able to survive: hasn't he his hunting, his dogs, his horses, and all that?

Duchess. [*With severity.*] Claire, you never miss an opportunity of saying something disagreeable about your father; why? You didn't use to do that; I remember when you adored him. Why have you changed so suddenly? What——?

Claire. [*Embarrassed.*] I haven't changed—perhaps I'm not so sympathetic and open as when I was a young girl—that's all. You may be sure I feel keenly for him.

Duchess. It will be terrible. His dogs and horses will be of little use to him now. He loves Robert, and then—he might perhaps have had some consolation——! If Robert had only had a brother, if he weren't the only son; if our name, the title of Duke, weren't about to die out—do you understand?

Claire. Do I understand? [*Tense with excitement.*] The Dukes de Chantemelle! Their names are on every page of the history of France! It's terrible to have Robert so near the end—to think that after his death all our glory, our almost royal greatness, will be only a dream of the past! If I am only a woman, I am proud of the name of Chantemelle! As proud as Father! Oh, what he will suffer when he comes in and hears the news!—Listen, Mother, I always intended never to get married, so that my share of the family fortune would go to Robert: a Duke de Chantemelle must live up to his name!——

Duchess. You are a true daughter of your father—and Robert is like you, too: you live in the past, it claims you, but you never realize how much the present forgets you——Times have changed!—Let the Duke de Chantemelle cease to exist, and the world will feel no loss. [*Sobbing.*] Only I, with my mother's heart——!

[ROBERT *enters, overhearing the last few words, a witness of the distress of his mother and sister. He is a man of distinguished bearing, with a pale face, feverish eyes, hollow cheeks, and flat chest. He gives the impression of one who is fighting bravely against disease and death.*]

Robert. Courage, Mother! [*Smiling sadly.*] I'm still alive!

Duchess. [*Rising in alarm.*] My child! You are not in the slightest danger! That is, the doctors said nothing definite! You know what they told you: a winter in Nice will give you new life!

Robert. That's what *you* said, Mother: they said that a winter in Nice would do me a great deal of good, that was all! It's something, of course! [*Ironically.*] Well, let us believe them——

Duchess. Of course, we must believe them! They impressed it on me again just as they were leaving.

Robert. [*Impatiently.*] Oh, very well! Has Father come in yet?

Claire. No. The snow is so deep! It's so cold!

Robert. [*With a sigh.*] I can imagine what's happened! They must have shot a number of boars; in this weather, it would be easy. Probably they wounded a big one, and chased him along his bloody trail until dark, for leagues and leagues! I can see them now, tired out, dragging one foot after the other—and the wounded dogs, and the hunters with icicles in their beards. [*Sighing again.*] And just one year ago I was doing all that!

Claire. [*With a forced smile.*] Do you regret it, slipping over the icy places, with a dog howling at your heels?

Robert. Yes, I regret the times when we galloped over the wide fields, Claire, you and I, and jumped the ditches and hedges——Now here I am, a horseman good for nothing, who sees his companion dashing away at full gallop over and beyond the horizon—while I——

Claire. [*Holding back the tears.*] His companion—doesn't ride like that, any more—without him! [*Overcome by her tears, quickly.*] If they didn't have good luck today Father's coming home in an awful humor. I'll have a good fire built in his bedroom.

[*She goes out immediately.*]

Robert. [*Going to the* DUCHESS, *who is trying to assume an untroubled expression. He takes her hands, forces her to look into his face and, after a short silence:*] Now that we're alone, Mother, no more ceremonies! I haven't any illusions left about my condition; and you, you don't hope——!

Duchess. But I tell you——

Robert. Treat me like a man: I should be the first Chantemelle to shrink before death! —— I once hoped for a different end, but this is only a better occasion to show courage, moral courage: not the kind that wins battles!

Duchess. [*In an undertone.*] You talk so cold-bloodedly! Your giving in to a Power against which no resistance is permitted is fearful! There are times when that Power which we ought to bless even when it strikes us—— [*Breaking out into sobs.*] Oh, I can't bear it! I can't bear it!

Robert. My giving in is not so hard as you think: I had foreseen the blow, I've been preparing for it during the past few weeks. My mind is quite at ease——

Duchess. [*With an outburst of feeling.*] Then if you had to—leave us, you would regret nothing? Your father? Your mother? Your sister? No one, nothing? [*She sobs.*]

Robert. I shall have terrible regrets! I can hardly speak of them, when I think how much energy I need. It would be a great deal easier to brave out the whole thing!

[*He throws himself into a chair, exhausted, and hides his face in his hands.*]

Duchess. Poor child!

Robert. [*Raises his head and speaks to himself.*] If I'm sick, I've got to come to that!—— Mother, I have a very serious matter to talk to you about—the happiness of my last days depends on it. I want you to promise me something.

Duchess. [*Rising.*] What is it?

Robert. It's about Mademoiselle Vatrin——

Duchess. [*Dryly.*] I can't imagine what you have to say about her. If it were about any one else—— She is a young woman without a sou, whom I took care of because her mother was at boarding-school with me. The girl owes everything she has to me, and I have even promised her a small dowry! Until she finds a husband, I am allowing her to associate with your sister: Claire broods so much during the year I thought it wise to let her have a friend of her own age. See how grateful she is!

Robert. [*Seated, his head bent over his knees, his eyes fixed on the floor.*] Mademoiselle Vatrin is incapable of ingratitude. You must have had some good reason for getting her out of the way last summer! I doubt whether she has forgotten your kindness.

Duchess. You doubt?—I should think I did have good reasons for doing what I did! Mademoiselle Vatrin was much too familiar with you men, much too familiar for a young woman of twenty-five! I let her know she was overstepping the limits! Then she left.

Robert. She told me about it, and also that you offered her a pension, which she refused.

Duchess. Did she tell you that? You? By what right? Why——?

Robert. [*Rising.*] Yes, she was my mistress. We loved one another deeply. What you called her familiarity was merely what we failed to have the presence of mind to hide. That was why you didn't understand.

Duchess. [*Deeply and strangely troubled, as she takes his hands in hers.*] Robert, you cannot imagine, you will never know what I feel now, when you tell me this!

Robert. You suppose, do you, that I am going to beg you to let me marry her? No. Hélène knows what tremendous opposition she would meet with from the family.

Duchess. Marry her? I never thought of it. Why——! I was so sad this evening, and now I am so different. We should never lose hope——

Robert. Your love for me, Mother, is wonderful! My love for that girl fills you with happiness. Don't deny it, I see it in your face! It is as if you considered that my love for her formed a strong bond between me and—life! Well, if you're not too angry, I'm happy!

Duchess. [*Beaming.*] I am angry, and I blame you very much. How can I keep from blaming you for your irregular conduct—think of it, she was one of Claire's own friends! Your sister might have suspected! It was an insult to her! I don't want to scold you any more, Robert, your life is so sad! I'm only too glad to see you smile sometimes!

Robert. [*Smiling.*] I know very well you are not quite unforgiving. If you will be absolutely frank for a single second, I'll show you that you are very well satisfied with me.

Duchess. Satisfied that you seduced a young woman under my very roof, a woman who was under my protection! A friend of your own sister Claire!

Robert. You can find many excellent reasons to prove that I have done wrong, but there is another matter—which is anything but unfortunate—something that you are always thinking about.

Duchess. [*Smiling.*] *All* the time?

Robert. Well, yes! There, you're beaming! Tell me now, why are you so glad?

Duchess. Why——?

Robert. Yes, why?

Duchess. [*Deciding to make some sort of answer.*] It might do some good—— [*After a pause.*] Have you ever noticed? I was very unhappy—at one time, I thought there was something between your father and Mademoiselle Vatrin—I was so jealous and humiliated——!

Robert. Mother! It was I all the time! Oh, I was so happy! My happiness overflowed! When a river overflows its banks, who can see its usual course?—You were very tender just now—and you had no idea why!

Duchess. But I wasn't alone in my suspicions: I am almost positive that Claire was haunted with the same thought. Claire is so pure and upright: she would never suspect without good reason! There were at least some appearances——! One day, Claire came to me, it was six months ago—when my suspicions were strongest—I was terribly tormented, I spied on your father, even.—She told me she was tired of Hélène's company, that they didn't get along well together, that she would be glad to get rid of her. Of course she didn't tell me her suspicions in so many words: a young girl like that! Then I couldn't question her, you understand! Well, I was at my wits' end. I might have risked my own peace of mind, but to expose my daughter to *that*——The day after, Mademoiselle Vatrin left.

Robert. We weren't careful enough. Claire is very sensitive and proud, and I shouldn't like her to have found out about us—— You see, *we* are the ones!

Duchess. Yes, thank Heaven! But Claire changed toward her father just as I did, from that time on. Haven't you noticed how formal and distant she is toward him? She never says nice things to him, nor gives him little surprises as she used to! She is even rather impudent at times!

Robert. Yes, I've noticed. Perhaps we can insinuate that she was on the wrong scent.

Duchess. We must try, yes! I love your father deeply, and my first duty is to make you respect him. We must forget what I've said here—it was an insult to him—— I shall remember only one thing: my almost scandalous joy in finding out my mistake.

Robert. [*Seriously.*] Mother, it is to our interest to forget these things—— [*After a pause, in a low tone.*] I still want to ask you for that promise. It is this: I want to see Hélène once more before I die. Let her come here. I admit, I'm asking a great deal, but——

Duchess. It is a great deal! Do you mean——? Mademoiselle Vatrin, your—Mademoiselle Vatrin under our roof? What if Claire should meet her and they should talk——! Claire, your own sister! Just think!

Robert. Do you imagine that I should ask you without considering the whole matter? I confess it's a mad idea, but I must see her. If you refuse, I'll go to her.

Duchess. You! To her? In your state, all alone! It would be your death!

Robert. [*Excitedly.*] A few weeks more or less will make very little difference! I beg you, let her come! Not only must I see her, but you must welcome her yourself!

Duchess. [*With determination.*] No! You mustn't think of it!

Robert. She is the mother of my son——

Duchess. [*Thunderstruck.*] A son! My God, Robert, what are you telling me? A son!

Robert. [*Rather warmly.*] Having no personal fortune, I can't leave them anything. Hélène's life and the child's are therefore at your mercy. I confide them to your care—my son! Think, Mother, where yours will be before long! Treat mine a little as you would your own!——

[*He stops, gasping for breath, his hand on his chest.*]

Duchess. [*Holding back the tears.*] Rest, Robert! We'll send your sister away for a day or two: your father will take her! Mademoiselle Vatrin may come then, I shall treat her well. The child—— Oh, if I had had that suspicion, when I was so tormented about your father, I couldn't have stood it! When was he born?

Robert. Two months ago—at Paris.

Duchess. [*Hesitating.*] What——? Under what name? I don't know what they do in such a case. I mean, how did they name the child?

Robert. [*Surprised.*] Why, Vatrin, of course, like his mother.—Now, my duty is to make provision for their future. I beg you on my knees to do this—— But to call him anything but Vatrin——!

Duchess. [*As if relieved of a great weight.*] Oh, Robert, I can breathe again!

[*Enter the* DUKE, *in hunting costume, followed by a servant who lights a paper torch from the fire, goes out and returns a moment later with two lighted lamps; he goes out once more to get the* DUKE'S *slippers. The stage is brightly illuminated.*]

Duke. Good evening!

Duchess. You are late, Henri!

[*She kisses him with great tenderness, at which he is surprised.*]

Robert. [*Inquisitively.*] What did you kill?

Duke. Don't say anything about that! We

had fearful luck! When we got to the wood this morning, we were on the trails of nearly thirty boars. We were going to have the devil of a fine chase!

Robert. [*Impatiently.*] Did you kill anything?

Duke. A little sow—weighed only a hundred and twenty! I put a bullet through her, and the dogs finished up a quarter of an hour later.

[*Enter the servant, with the* DUKE'S *slippers. The fire burns brightly.*]

Duchess. Here are your slippers; you ought to change before the snow melts through your overshoes; look how it's running! You're in a regular puddle!

Duke. [*Sitting by the fireplace.*] Lord, what a splendid fire! That puts life into you!

[*He stretches forth his feet, and the servant puts on the slippers.*]

Robert. Is it snowing?

Duke. Hard: the branches of the trees are beginning to break with the weight. We were hard put to find our way this evening.

Servant. [*Rises, takes the boots and leggings, and is about to leave.*] Nicolas the forester wishes to know whether he may see Monsieur.

Duke. [*Quickly.*] Yes, yes, in the antechamber; I'll see him——

Duchess. Receive him here, why not? There's no reason why you should go running after your foresters, tired as you are!

Duke. I'm not tired! Very well, then! [*To the servant, annoyed.*] Let him come in here—— [*The servant goes out.*]

Robert. Wasn't Nicolas with you today?

Duke. [*Embarrassed.*] No, he was not.

Robert. You'll see: he's had plenty of boars in his section of the forest all day, and he'll want orders for tomorrow.

Duke. Tomorrow is your consultation, you know. I shan't go out.

Duchess. We have already had the consultation: this evening.

Duke. What, without letting us know ——?

Duchess. Doctor Jaubert telegraphed that he would have to come one day earlier on account of an official ceremony at which he has to speak tomorrow. Because of the storms this side of Sedan, the telegram was delayed. The doctors came quite unexpectedly, you see. We were all so surprised!

Duke. Well, what did they have to say? How was he?

Duchess. [*With a gesture of despair.*] Not very well!

Duke. Ah——!

Robert. Not at all well, Father: you and I won't kill many more boars together.

Duke. [*Sadly.*] What did they advise?

Duchess. Go south as soon as possible.

Duke. South, where? Pau? Nice?——

Duchess. Nice.

[*Enter* NICOLAS. *He stands in the doorway at the back, hat in hand.*]

Nicolas. It's me, Monsieur le duc——

Robert. Good evening, Nicolas, any boars?

Nicolas. [*Coming down-stage a little.*] No, Monsieur Robert, I've come here on business.

Robert. Great hunting weather, isn't it, Nicolas?

Nicolas. [*Shaking his head in affirmation.*] Fine, Monsieur Robert. Snow's falling in sheets! If this keeps up, we can't take a dog out, or even a beater!

Robert. Seems there's a good many boars about this year, eh?

Nicolas. Oh, quite a few; nothing to complain of. We had five wolves yesterday at *Bois Brûlé.*

Robert. They were howling all night at the end of the pond. I heard them from my bed. [*His eyes glistening.*] Five of them! [*With a sigh.*] Well, that's all over for me, Nicolas——

Nicolas. Ah, Monsieur Robert, your health isn't——?

Robert. [*With a bitter laugh.*] Ha! Ha! My health was never better!

Duchess. [*Putting her arm around his neck.*] Come, son, it's nearly time for dinner; let's not keep your father. He must have a terrific appetite. Good evening, Nicolas.

Nicolas. Good evening, Madame la duchesse. Hope you're better soon, Monsieur Robert!

[ROBERT *thanks him with a nod, and goes out with his mother.*]

Duke. [*Standing with his back to the fire.*] Have you just come from town?

Nicolas. This instant, Monsieur le duc.

Duke. Have you seen Mademoiselle Vatrin?

Nicolas. Yes, Monsieur le duc: I'm afraid Monsieur won't like it!

Duke. Come, out with it! Did she read my letter?

Nicolas. Yes, of course, but——

Duke. Well? What then?

Nicolas. This: I went as Monsieur told me, to the Hôtel du Cheval-Blanc——

Duke. With your wife?

Nicolas. Naturally, because Monsieur explained that we were to take the child from Mademoiselle Vatrin and keep it with us.

—— Well, my wife was mighty cold traveling all day in this weather—you see, it was only three weeks since she had a baby, and she's still a little weak—— Well, I says to her, "What's the matter with you? It's for Monsieur le duc, and his son; can't spare any pains!"——

Duke. Yes, and was Mademoiselle Vatrin waiting for you?

Nicolas. That's it. She just got off the train from Paris not a quarter of an hour ago—the snow'd blocked all the trains. You ought to've seen that baby! Lord, he was hungry—like a little dog at his soup, when my wife came, begging Monsieur's pardon——

Duke. Then he's with you now—is he well?

Nicolas. Ah, Monsieur can be sure of that! Just now by the fireplace I left him grinning at my wife.

Duke. Then what are you talking about, saying things aren't going well? It seems to me that everything is perfect.

Nicolas. Everything's all right for the youngster, but the mother, that's different! When I told her her room was ready, and says to her to tell us a few days ahead when she was coming, so as to have time to get things ready, she answered—well, you ought to have heard her!—she didn't want the room; she wasn't coming more than two or three times a year, and stay for an hour or so just to see the baby, and she'd come when she liked, without letting us know ahead of time. You could have knocked me over with a feather to hear her talk the way she did; 'specially as Monsieur le duc had the idea she was going to stay four or five days each time. So I says to her, "Wait a minute! Perhaps Mademoiselle doesn't remember that the house is in the middle of the wood, no one hardly ever comes here, and you could live here all year and be safe. If my wife and I don't go around telling tales, the squirrels'll be the only ones to know the secret!" And she says to me, "I remember the house. I've been there often enough, on my walks—the air is good for my son—I don't know what you mean by the rest——" That's what she said, Monsieur le duc.—— I think she's leading you a merry chase, as they say. I don't think that's nice of her, a bit. I don't think either that things are going the way Monsieur le duc wanted 'em to go, about her room and all that.

Duke. Did she send a letter?

Nicolas. No. Only she said she was going back to Paris tonight.

Duke. Very well—I'll arrange to come and see you tomorrow. [*As* NICOLAS *is about to go the* DUKE *intercepts him.*] Tell me, he's good-looking—the youngster?

Nicolas. Oh, yes! Should have heard my wife when she was undressing him—fine set-up!—Not a thing the matter with him——!

Duke. [*Smiling.*] And his face?

Nicolas. [*Laughing.*] His face! Oh, if I dared talk about that to Monsieur le duc, but if Monsieur begins——! Well, Monsieur, I'd like to see Monsieur put his face next to the youngster's. People'll see the resemblance right off——

Duke. [*In a revery.*] Take good care of him! Good evening!

[NICOLAS *goes out. Enter the* DUCHESS.]

Duke. So he's worse?

Duchess. [*Goes to the* DUKE, *and takes his hand with great feeling.*] Worse than we imagine, dear!

Duke. [*With concentrated rage.*] Are we going to stand by with folded arms? Can't we do something? There are plenty of new remedies—some of them kill at once, but there are some that are absolutely miraculous!

Duchess. Nothing short of a miracle can save Robert—his lungs are all eaten away!

Duke. The last of the Chantemelles! The end of the family!

Duchess. [*In despair.*] Henri!

Duke. You know how I take those things to heart! Others don't attach so much importance to them! But that makes no difference to me! Let me mourn for our whole race in my only son—my son!

Duchess. I can think only of him—poor child! It wasn't so very long ago that he was running about the park in short trousers. I remember how he used to come in with his burning red cheeks, and his legs scratched by the thistles—— [*She sobs.*] So upright, and noble, and proud!

Duke. He is a worthy close to our glorious line: Robert de Chantemelle! He is the last of us! The line will be dead!

[*He accents this last word in so strange a manner, that the* DUCHESS *quivers. They exchange glances.*]

Duchess. Dead! [*A pause.*] Henri, why do you look at me that way? Do you know—something?

Duke. Something? What, Anne? What are you alluding to?

Duchess. I? I alluded to nothing, it was you—— Robert hasn't the slightest suspicion that you know his secret——

Duke. [*Angrily.*] I don't know anything

about it. Speak, tell me whether he has been saying anything!

Duchess. Robert has a son.

Duke. What are you——? Robert, a son! —— And the mother——?

Duchess. Hélène Vatrin——

Duke. Do you mean——? Are you sure?

Duchess. Robert told me so just now.

Duke. [*His eyes flashing, his fists clenched, crosses to the other side of the stage.*] The damned prostitute! And Robert! Damned ——! If he wasn't already half dead, I'd——

Duchess. [*Terror-stricken, throws herself into the* DUKE's *arms, and prevents his going to find* ROBERT.] Henri! Henri! It's horrible! Henri, you're not yourself!

Duke. Beautiful goings-on in this house! They were very, very lucky I didn't discover them——!

Duchess. Henri, for heaven's sake, be calm —a scene with Robert would kill him!

Duke. I'll spare him, but her——! She's a—a——

Duchess. She? A poor inexperienced young girl we exposed to danger, little thinking —— We left her free all day long with a young man about—it was perfect folly! When I think——! I thought I was doing her a favor, and I was the cause of her ruin——

Duke. Damned women, with their sensitiveness! No, of course, you find her very interesting!—— You don't seem to remember that Robert was with her at the very time the doctors ordered him to be most careful! We wondered why he—— Your dear little protégée!

Duchess. Henri, I refuse to argue about it, unless you talk more calmly. You are entirely unjust. Hélène came to us a pure girl; if she leaves ruined, whose fault is it? It's not at all generous of you to treat her the way you do, in order to escape all the responsibility!

Duke. [*After a pause.*] Very well! There was something inevitable in it all! Of course, she may have some excuse—those long walks with Robert—we must have been blind!

Duchess. We must have.—— We owe something to her now.

Duke. [*Scowling.*] What?

Duchess. If not to her, to Robert's son; you don't intend to abandon him, do you?

Duke. [*Pensively.*] Robert's son!

Duchess. It is no more than just that we should look after him.

Duke. Of course! His son—his—where is he?

Duchess. With his mother, doubtless, in Paris.

Duke. [*Considering, half-smiling.*] In Paris—— Don't you feel as if you'd like to —kiss him? Good Lord, he's Robert's son, after all!

Duchess. You are very good at bottom, dear! Now I am ready to tell you of the promise Robert induced me to make to him. He wants to see Hélène once more before he dies! I consented, because I was sure you would let him—— [*Gesture from the* DUKE.] Will you?

Duke. [*Quickly.*] Very well, very well, it's not a matter of great importance—— [*He walks about the room.*] Let her come —she may stay as long as she likes, or go, or hang herself, for all I care! I'm interested in the child! [*Standing before his wife, his arms crossed.*] Then Robert is not the last of the Chantemelles!

Duchess. You admit that the other——?

Duke. Whether I admit it or not, he is!

Duchess. You forget, the mother——

Duke. Nothing! But now I come to think about it, she's not so bad; the fact that she——

Duchess. She might cause us a great deal of trouble if she tried to force Robert to marry her—but luckily, she is not thinking of doing that. My talk with Robert led me to believe that she is really quite sensitive on the point. Then Robert wouldn't think of marrying her.

Duke. [*Bruskly.*] He might consider it, though——

Duchess. [*Surprised.*] What?

Duke. Does this marriage seem something to be avoided at any cost?

Duchess. Henri, you frighten me. Five minutes ago, you were fearfully angry—you were terrible—now you are joking! This is not the time for that!

Duke. I was angry five minutes ago, but what leads you to suppose I am not now? At least, I am not joking.

Duchess. Then you are serious? It's ridiculous! I admit, Hélène is a nice, intelligent, presentable girl——

Duke. [*Breaking forth.*] Still she's only Hélène, with all her niceness, and intelligence—I don't care about that! She has made you a grandmother; keep that in mind, and then agree with me that we ought to marry them.

Duchess. Ought to——!

Duke. For the sake of the child! To make him legally what he really is: a Chantemelle!

Duchess. Henri, don't do it! Think of

Mademoiselle Vatrin as Claire's sister! Oh, no!

Duke. It's not pleasant to think about—by any means!—— But what can we do? We shall both suffer, you and I—I more than you. I have always wanted a grandson—and now I've found him, I take him——

Duchess. Pick him up! Find him!

Duke. [*Getting angry.*] That's enough! I want to—and when I say "I want," I'm determined to have——!

Duchess. My wishes never had very much influence with you—*I* always wanted to live somewhere else! If you had consented to leave your woods and live for part of the year in Paris, Claire might have gone into society, chosen a husband, and not have been exposed to all this——! Mademoiselle Vatrin would never have set foot in the house, and Robert, instead of burying himself in the country and brooding over the past, would probably have married, and you wouldn't have been forced to pick up a grandson off the streets——

Duke. Charming! I am to blame for everything! I'm to blame for Robert's sickness! Well, if my will has been the cause of evil, it's now about to make reparation: Robert will marry Mademoiselle Vatrin, take that as final. I'm not going to allow any woman to influence me in a matter of this kind!

Duchess. Luckily Robert has a will of his own. He sees this matter in the same light as I do, and you can't domineer over him as you can me: he's a man!

Duke. He will consent.

Duchess. No!

Duke. Here he is; let him decide.

[*Enter* ROBERT.]

Duke. [*Approaching him, his hands folded behind his back.*] Ah, you gay young bird!

Robert. [*Astonished.*] Father!

Duke. [*Good-humoredly.*] I hear fine news about you! A great surprise for your old father [*with a slight menace in his words*] who ought to shoot you——

Duchess. Henri!

Duke. But I shan't! I have something else to consider now. [*Seriously.*] You have a son. I thank you from the bottom of my heart for perpetuating the family line, just at the moment when it seemed about to end. Your son! I claim him in order that our name shall survive; I am old and you are—not well. At the same time, I shall ask you to make a sacrifice—a big sacrifice, for I know your—what people call—prejudice.

Robert. You want me to marry Hélène? I thought of that when I used to plan how to perpetuate the family name——

Duke. Well?

Robert. Well, I love Hélène——

Duke. [*Fiercely.*] I don't see how that detail makes it more difficult!

Robert. It does. You treat this marriage as a business transaction. Now, in considering your proposal, I am thinking of the future of the woman I love. Can you imagine her between Mother and Claire?—— The day she feels she is not absolutely an equal among you, I shall take her away.

Duke. Your wife *will* be an equal!

Robert. I am ready to marry her. I don't think I owe you any thanks—my happiness has nothing to do with this. We all want only one thing——

Duchess. Not I, Robert! Your father spoke of sacrifice; well, the real sacrifice will be for Claire and me.

Duke. [*With hauteur.*] You have no idea what you are talking of!

Duchess. You are both against me! I consent, then, but let us say nothing more this evening.—— My daughter's companion her equal! Oh, no! I hadn't thought of that!

[*She goes out in high indignation.*]

Robert. I'll follow her and give her to understand that there's nothing selfish in what I am doing——

Duke. Go, and don't let her say anything to Claire; we shall let her know at the last minute—— Two women in high dudgeon together——!

Robert. [*Smiling.*] Ah, I should think so!

[*He goes out.*]

Duke. [*Following him with his eyes.*] If he only knew! Well, he would kill me, but he would think all the same that I govern my house with admirable foresight. And to think of that little fellow, how quickly, how completely he has changed the fate of this family! A crime? Perhaps! We must not do things by halves, and the old must help as well as the young! What difference whose is the child? Our blood runs in his veins, and I can ask no more!

CURTAIN

ACT II

Same scene as in the first act. Through the windows are seen a winter landscape, with a bright sun shining upon it, a French garden covered with snow, straight paths bordered by dark evergreens, the branches of which are dotted with tufts of snow. The statues are encased in a thin crust of ice; the water in the basin of the fountain is frozen, but the fountain itself is running. Icicles cling to the sides of the spout. In the distance is the forest tinged with frost and snow, and glistening in the sun. As the curtain rises, ROBERT *is alone, waiting near a window. He is carefully dressed, and wears a flower. There is nothing indicative of the negligent patient in his appearance. After a few moments* CLAIRE *enters, goes straight to her brother, controlling her feelings, which are apparently very turbulent.*

Claire. Robert, I know whom you are waiting for: Mother has just been to my room—now I see why you have been so mysterious these past two days! To think that you are going to marry Hélène! Oh, Robert!

Robert. Did Mother tell you why I am doing so?

Claire. Of course! But to tell me that, after I had Hélène sent away! Poor Mother! She murmured something about your loving that woman, that they would consent to let you marry her—then she burst out crying and went away. I did not follow her to get further details. Robert, I used to have great respect for you, for your strength of character; you can have no idea how hurt I am to hear this!

Robert. My dear little Claire, Hélène will be here in a quarter of an hour—perhaps sooner: a sleigh travels quickly in this weather—I'm not very strong—let me be in peace until she comes; she mustn't find me stretched out on the sofa, gasping for breath. That's what will happen if I am the least bit over-excited.

Claire. You can't get rid of me so easily as that! I should be a very poor sister if I allowed you to do what you wish, merely to avoid giving you a little pain. You are not going to marry Hélène!

Robert. But Father wishes me to!

Claire. [*With horror.*] He does! He must be a fool! Give me a reason, at least. I defy you, Father especially! I see I can wait for my reasons! Do you know why Father wants you to? Do you?

Robert. Do *you?*

Claire. [*In a choked voice.*] Oh—I—what shall I say?——

Robert. Father wants me to marry because he cannot bear the idea of seeing me end the line of Chantemelle!

Claire. [*Embarrassed, to herself.*] It's only a pretense! [*To* ROBERT.] Couldn't you just as well marry some one else?

Robert. I love *her!*

Claire. Poor Robert!

Robert. And she loves me! Otherwise, she would never think of marrying me!

Claire. She hasn't a sou, she has no—scruples——

Robert. You are very unjust—and besides, it's useless to try to persuade me. Even if Hélène did deserve a little of what you hold against her, I should marry her all the same. It happens that the sacrifice is pleasant to me. That is all!

Claire. A sacrifice for the sake of the family?

Robert. Yes, *you* should be able to understand that!

Claire. Every one has his own ideas about family pride.

Robert. Oh!

Claire. Our families! See how well they are treated nowadays! To have conquered provinces for the country, to have governed them for centuries, and then to lose every bit of influence—why, Father can't even elect himself mayor of the town here! How humiliating! And what you must have suffered not to have been able to work for the glory of your land! How I pity you, when I see you so inconsolable! And now you marry Hélène Vatrin in order to transmit to your children the creeds and ideas of us mummies!

Robert. [*Crying out.*] Claire! Give me at least the credit of believing that in the face of death I know what I'm doing! I firmly believe that in spite of this inferior alliance, our family is worth perpetuating. This Duke de Chantemelle is nothing: ambassador, minister, prefect—nothing. I am going to marry Hélène because I am positive that the country would otherwise lose a living and valuable force—if the Dukes de Chantemelle disappeared from the face of the earth——

Claire. [*Ironically.*] I should not be at all surprised if you had made that discovery since you fell in love with Hélène!

Robert. It makes no difference if I did, so long as it is true.

Claire. [*Ironically.*] Are we really of some use?

Robert. Yes, because we are well born. Moral heredity is an incontestable fact. Centuries of military bravery, intellectual culture, refinement, ought surely to produce the very best sort of men and women. Nobility is not a prejudice: the aristocracy is a museum of all that is best in chivalry!

Claire. [*Bitterly.*] A museum as isolated as a hospital!

Robert. That spreads the contagion of devotion! Disinterested science, for example, the sort that has nothing to do with dividends, exists only among the aristocrats. In the United States, there are wonderful inventors, but they have only one end in view: to get as much money as possible! We must look to Europe, with its atmosphere of the old aristocracy, to see great geniuses devoting their lives to the good of humanity! And to think that the crude and simple chivalry of the Middle Age was all the time preparing for the glorious poverty of the great thinkers of today! Granted even that this is an exaggeration, the whole idea is at least compatible with modern life. Do we amount to nothing then in the France of today? No, if we are forgotten and neglected and despised, we at least repay ingratitude by showing the true spirit of resignation!

Claire. [*Inspired by* ROBERT'S *words.*] How true! How splendid! We *are* something! The poor live only because of us; we are not useful in politics, but we know how to console those who deny our very existence! When the Fatherland is in trouble, there is no question about the nobility—those little marquises who know nothing except how to hunt and dance! Robert, you are right, we still have a part to play!

Robert. Forgive me then for wanting to live! Not myself, but in my race!

Claire. You have taught me what we owe to the race, to our family. I was born in a hunting-lodge. How often have you argued with me, gently, never annoyed with me, about the breeding of your dogs and horses: you ought at least then to have the same respect for your family! You should want to live as you say you do, in your son, but you must live too for your own sake: for the sake of this body of yours, worn out by discouragement. You need the strength and the will to be useful even now! Let me receive Hélène first. Don't worry, I know exactly what to say to her! Ten minutes later, she will be gone, for ever. Then we'll save you.

Robert. Why do you say you will save me? I have only one hope, but not what you think. In my future there is a tiny ray of brightness—a single ray! Tell me, what if our long empty hallways resounded with the cry of a child, wouldn't you be happy? I am, even to think of it! Tell me, doesn't your instinct——?

Claire. [*Seriously.*] I did not come here to talk about instinct! I know whom to speak to now; I'm wasting my breath here!

[*Enter the* DUKE *and* DUCHESS.]

Duke. [*To* ROBERT *and* CLAIRE.] A little tiff?

Robert. [*To the* DUKE.] She is giving me some plain advice about my marriage; I am not at all satisfied with her attitude. Mother must have told her everything. She just now refused to discuss the matter further with me. She intends to talk with you. Tell her that in marrying Hélène I am acting according to your wishes. [CLAIRE *listens in terror.*] Mother, stay with me: I want Hélène to see the expression on my face when she comes: the façade of the House of Chantemelle must present a cheerful appearance.

Duchess. [*While* ROBERT *goes to the window.*] I am so glad to see him happy!

[*She joins* ROBERT, *and both watch for* HÉLÈNE.]

Duke. [*To* CLAIRE.] What Robert says is true: he is going to marry because I want him to.

Claire. [*In an undertone.*] This is more horrible than I had ever imagined!

Duke. What's the trouble?

Claire. [*Indicating* ROBERT.] I shan't tell you here: come tc my room! You will take pity on him, or me——

Duke. Go to your room, I will follow you in a moment.

Claire. This is my last word: before this evening, one of us will have sent Mademoiselle Vatrin out of the house; I hope it will be you!

[*She goes out, leaving the* DUKE *petrified. First he goes to the fireplace, then returns to follow* CLAIRE, *then hesitates, looking toward his wife and son.* ROBERT *calls to him.*]

Robert. Listen! The bells! It's she!

[*The sound of approaching sleigh-bells is heard outside.*]

Duke. [*Going to the window.*] I do hear —yes——

Robert. [*His face close to the window.*] Why can't we see? There is nothing so far as the eye can reach across the snow.

Duke. She is coming from the wood—

you'll see her turn when she comes around by the stables——

Robert. Why the wood? It's much longer that way.

Duke. I wanted to give you a little surprise, a present for not having written to her, and for allowing your parents to inform her of the state of affairs! She is coming from the forester's cottage, where she has left the child with Nicolas' wife, who has just recently had a child—she is going to nurse the little fellow. Nicolas and his wife are splendid people and can keep the secret——

Robert. [*Interrupting.*] It was very good of you! I'm going to see him——

Duke. [*Interrupts him.*] Do me the favor of coming with your mother into the billiard-room—wait until I call you. As head of the family I wish to be the first to receive Mademoiselle Vatrin: she is not yet aware that she is to be your wife. You might appear a little too happy in telling her about it; I shall tell her in quite another manner. Her coming here shall not be a triumphal entry; I am afraid she doesn't yet feel the enormous responsibility that goes with our name, which she will assume so easily. Let me, at the very door of this house, explain what will be expected of her. Then, Robert, she is yours!—Go now——

[ROBERT *and his mother go out. The* DUKE *looks out of the window an instant, then comes back to meet* HÉLÈNE. HÉLÈNE, *dressed in a simple traveling suit, enters. She is pretty, but now appears timid and sad. Seeing the* DUKE, *she is about to faint; quivering with emotion, she leans against the door. A pause; the* DUKE *looks at her.*]

Duke. [*Dryly.*] Come here! [*She approaches him, very much afraid.*] Yes, it's I! Are you surprised? The child's nurse just told you I had gone away; well, she did as she was told. I wanted to encourage you to come. You see, the Duchess wrote you that Robert was very ill, and authorized you to come—not a word from the Duke—Robert, too, wanted to write, but I did not let him. Now I have a piece of news to announce—— Sit down! You're trembling—I'm not angry with you! You don't know what I am going to tell you!

Hélène. [*Wringing her hands; in a feeble choked voice.*] Oh, please! I was weak enough to be your mistress almost as soon as I came here. I was only twenty-two; I knew nothing. Monsieur Robert was away then in Palestine; when he came back I fell in love with him—and he knew it! [*She hides her face.*] Don't despise me! I love him as deeply as a woman can love a man! His love is the only thing that sustained me—I didn't have the strength to leave you! For two years I lived a terrible life—I never saw you that I didn't make up my mind to stop everything—with you, I didn't dare! I waited and waited, too afraid to do anything! Then the baby came, and I had to depend on you. But once I was away, I wasn't afraid of you, and when the forester's wife asked me to stay sometimes with her I had the strength to refuse! You see, I have a little courage left——

Duke. [*Brutally.*] What are you talking about? What has Robert's mistress to do with Robert's father? Get rid of that idea! Robert is madly in love with you! Marry him!

Hélène. [*Terror-stricken.*] I? Marry Robert!

Duke. You must. I want an heir to carry on my name; now I have one! I don't care by what means, but I have one! Never mind who or what you are! You are that heir's mother! You love my son, don't you? You wrote me a letter that was rather touching some time ago, before the child was born, and told me to take care of him in case you died. There was nothing unreasonable in that—of course we should look after the little one. Now we want to make a duke of him—give him our name, our fortune, everything!

Hélène. There's not only my son to think about, but Robert! He is *your* son, Robert! Do you love him? And yet you talk of this marriage!

Duke. Robert is my son, but the other is something to me also. Fate demands that I sacrifice one of them. One is young and full of hope, the other we are already mourning—why should I hesitate between the two? Furthermore, I have promised that Robert shall marry you—refuse him now! Can't you see, he will ask you questions; what will you tell him if he learns the truth? Come now, everything is to your advantage: an honorable name for yourself, a title for your son—Robert's son. That little mite is everything! I am willing to kill for his sake, if necessary! Give him to us, for always, irrevocably! Is it a bargain? Don't answer yet! You can't answer! Tell Robert! Meantime, you're in great danger. Somewhow, I can't imagine how, Claire has discovered everything. She is opposed to all this. If she says anything, the marriage cannot take place! Robert would be broken-hearted, demand an explanation, and I—— Well, what could I answer——?

Hélène. Then why did I come?

Duke. Claire doesn't know yet that there *is* a child. She is more concerned with our traditions, our long family line, than any of us, and perhaps she will feel as deeply as I do about perpetuating the name. I shall go and see her now, and in five minutes everything will be arranged.

[*He goes out by the down-stage door. Enter* CLAIRE *at the back, left. She stops on seeing* HÉLÈNE.]

Claire. My father is looking for me, isn't he? [HÉLÈNE *makes a vague gesture.*] Madameoiselle, I am glad to have an opportunity of talking with you alone; as we have only a few moments, I shall go straight to the point! Robert is not going to marry you——

Hélène. I don't ask anything—I want to do what will be best for Robert!

Claire. To save him from disgrace is best for Robert! I know who you are: one evening last summer I was walking by the pond —you were with Father in the boat, and neither of you was any too careful—I was out all that night, a few feet from you—once I was on the point of asking for a place in the boat—I heard things that made my blood run cold. In one second my purity of mind was gone, my respect and affection were killed! That episode has blackened my life. I had you sent away, but I felt just the same as before—the same torture. And now you have come back to poison my life again! Your plan will fail this time: I am going to tell Robert everything!

Hélène. And kill him!

Claire. He will thank me for sparing him a few days of life in a world where God allows such things to happen!

[*Enter the* DUKE. *He takes in the situation at a glance. He comes and stands between them.*]

Duke. [*With severity.*] Claire, who asked you to come? You ought to have waited until I saw you!

Claire. I changed my mind. I couldn't think clearly then about what you had determined to do. Even after I considered it, I couldn't understand. I have now given up trying to persuade: I am threatening!

Duke. [*Violently.*] Keep still!

Claire. Nothing can make me keep still—my conscience——

Duke. [*With blind fury.*] Keep still, I tell you! Never mind about your conscience! There are certain things a daughter doesn't say to her father! If you forget yourself again you'll end your days in a convent, or else I'll turn you out of the house——

Claire. I'd rather end my days in a convent, or walk the streets, than breathe this atmosphere of disgrace and shame——!

Hélène. Monsieur le duc, I ought to leave; I am willing not to see Robert, to be sent away—I am willing—— Only let Mademoiselle spare her brother, and help you explain to him why I am leaving.

Duke. [*After a moment's reflection, to* HÉLÈNE, *sympathetically.*] Let me have a word with her in private. [HÉLÈNE *nods. He conducts her to the down-stage door, and sees her out. He then returns to* CLAIRE.] Claire, I give in. For the first time, you have called my authority into question! You have your weapons, you can prevent me from doing what I want to do. I shan't argue further. Only know this: from now on there is no intimacy between us!

Claire. I expect to be unhappy. With my courage——

Duke. That is your affair. You may as well know what this blow will mean to Robert! Yes, and to all of us! It is not hard to accuse your father, and tell him how disgusted you are; you're hardly more than a little boarding-school miss—your mother was unwise enough to tell you everything, a child of your age! I am now talking to you as I would to a judge, a righter of wrongs: I have nothing to hide from you. Robert has a son by Mademoiselle Vatrin.

Claire. [*To herself.*] He! A son!

Duke. Whom we have decided to adopt, make one of the family, in order not to let the line die out. If the child had not lived, Robert would think nothing more about the mother—he would not marry her. For myself, I am opening this house to a woman who bears in her arms a sacred gift; I use the word "sacred" advisedly. I want you to weigh the matter carefully. You blamed Robert for being selfish in the face of death, and you blamed me because I was sacrificing him to I don't know what monstrosities. Every word of that is false. Robert is sacrificed, and so am I, but I haven't the right to consider that for a moment. Both of us are sacrificed, thank God! to an ideal, an ideal which you are as anxious as we to preserve as best we can!

Claire. A son! Poor Robert! His eyes were filled with tears when he told me how splendid it would be to have the empty corridors filled with the voices of children! And to think I was ignoble enough to appear dissatisfied with him! And the brutal way I answered! That is what he meant when he spoke of instinct! His love as a father! I thought he meant something quite different!

How could I have been so mistaken! Sometimes, at night, when I'm sitting by the fire, while the wind whistles outside, and the wolves howl just under the window, all at once clear ringing voices come to me and I wake up holding to my breast the end of a phantom—it is that same instinct—then it goes away—but it is always in Robert! Sometimes I almost go crazy. Now you tell me there *is* a child! It may be near at this moment! Papa, why are you looking at me that way? Is he in the house—now?

Duke. Almost: he is with Nicolas—go and see him—I could not resist the temptation——

Claire. Can I? [*Slowly.*] Then it is no longer a dream, a vision! Then I am killing a real child, a child I could take in my arms, a child Robert adores, his own flesh and blood! Oh, if you had only heard him! He wants his son to be perfect in everything, because a noble birth gives one moral superiority! Poor boy! He is forgetting the mother! No, he is not forgetting her, he doesn't know! The mother! Ha, what is her heritage, what does she bring us?

Duke. What are you talking about? Most of our ancestors were statesmen and celebrated generals; I once dreamed of being great, like them—but I've had to pass my life doing nothing. I have tried to forget myself in hunting! There is nothing like country life to soothe wounded pride! During the war, I was no longer a young man, so that I had to enlist as a simple soldier or else stay home by my own fireside. I enlisted, looking for great deeds to do and a glorious death; I came home diseased and defeated. I had added nothing to the honor of our name. Now, for God's sake, don't let the line die out! We can still work for the glory of our country, the glory that has been handed down to us, until one day a Chantemelle, more intelligent or more fortunate, shall arise and do honor to us! Don't you feel that basic desire to live, to make some place in the world, to exist afterwards—in others?

Claire. [*Overcome.*] Oh, Papa! with all my soul!

Duke. No, you don't! Otherwise you would have pitied me! Robert and I cannot last much longer. Don't, don't take these visions of the future from us!

Claire. You think I am indifferent! I have devoted myself, given up my life because of these terrible agonies I have been going through! [*Bowing her head.*] If you ask pity of me, you must in turn at least pity me! If I am to become your—accomplice, I shall be in a terrible situation—pity me!

Duke. You an accomplice? In what? You have only to say nothing!

Claire. Isn't that terrible enough? Then I shall have been the cause of this marriage! If I say a word, it will not take place!

Duke. If it does not take place you will be the executioner of the race!

Claire. That's what tortures me! To put such responsibility on the shoulders of a young girl like me! What will happen to us if I don't tell Robert? His child is our glory, the center of all our ambitions, of our very life, everything! But can we forget the mother? That woman! Can't you see what a hell my life has been because of her? Can't you see how afraid of you all I have been? If she comes back, I shall never live in peace again! Yet I am willing to submit, to be miserable, to bear the weight of shame and responsibility which I have no right to bear. I, the little boarding-school miss! What hope have I? I wish I were dead! I wish I knew what to do!

Duke. [*Solemnly.*] Claire, I swear that you ought to do this: it is your duty to obey the head of your family. Why have I educated you to look back to the glory of our house, if I now ask something unworthy of the past? For that reason, I beg you! On my honor, on the honor of my son who is about to die, I promise you that this marriage will save our name!

Claire. I believe you.

Duke. Thank you, Claire!

Claire. [*Going to the door behind which* HÉLÈNE *is waiting.*] Come, Hélène! [*Enter* HÉLÈNE.] I accept a great responsibility: I shall never abandon the woman who is about to become Robert's wife! I cannot be expected to be a real friend—an affectionate friend—but I promise to be a devoted sister. When you are in trouble come to me. I offer you this in all loyalty, Hélène!

Duke. Let us go to Robert——!

[*He steps back, allowing* HÉLÈNE *and* CLAIRE *to pass him.* CLAIRE *allows* HÉLÈNE *to precede her out of the room.* HÉLÈNE *gives evidence of extreme nervousness as the* DUKE *and* CLAIRE *look at her.*
The curtain falls only after the stage is empty and the door closed.]

CURTAIN

ACT III

A villa in the neighborhood of Nice, situated in the open country. The scene represents a large room elegantly but rather flashily furnished, the kind usually found in rented houses at seaside resorts. Doors to the right and left. At the back, all the way across the stage is a large bay window, through which the sea appears sparkling under a brilliant sky. To the left, outside, a reef with the foam of waves breaking over it.

[ROBERT *is alone, stretched out on a sofa. His legs are covered with a plaid blanket. He appears to be asleep. Enter* HÉLÈNE; *she closes the door noiselessly and approaches the sofa on tip-toe.* ROBERT *opens his eyes and speaks to her without turning his head.*]

Robert. Is that you, Hélène?

Hélène. [*Leaning over him and kissing his forehead.*] Yes. Have you had a nice sleep?

Robert. Couldn't close my eyes! I tossed about, thinking, always thinking! That attack yesterday—— If my mother hadn't happened to come in the moment I lost consciousness, I should have died— [*Pressing his hand to his lips.*] There's always that taste of blood in my mouth! The hemorrhage there, ready to choke me any moment! —— What about this south that was going to cure me? This famous south!

Hélène. We've been here hardly two weeks! It would be miraculous if already——

Robert. [*Interrupting her.*] My poor girl, our marriage! The first month isn't over yet—— [*A long pause, during which he holds her hand pressed to his lips.*] Why didn't they bring Henri this morning? Where is he?

Hélène. In front of the house, playing in the sand. [*Going toward the window.*] Shall I call and have him brought in?

Robert. Later! I have so many things to ask you to take care of! My parents are old, soon you will be the only one left. And you'll need help so badly. [*With an effort.*] And—dearest! It's impossible for me to conceive that your happiness no longer depends on me alone!

Hélène. [*Gravely.*] It is in your hands, Robert.

Robert. What do you mean?

Hélène. Listen: I should never have spoken of this unless you had begun. I should have preferred to be miserable till the last. But since you have opened the subject —— Please, Robert, arrange matters so that if—if I have to lose you, I can go off with little Henri wherever I wish. I want a home of my own.

Robert. [*Rising.*] Leave the family? Here I was deeply concerned because I was afraid you would be left alone, and now you ask to be!

Hélène. Without you, do you think I could be anything else but alone? Among these people whom I am afraid of? Yes, afraid! Of the Duke especially! I should be completely at his mercy! I don't even dare raise my voice against him now! Help me! They despise me!

Robert. I have never heard a word from them to cause my wife to be ashamed or humiliated. I should never have allowed it!

Hélène. Not a word has been spoken! They are forced to treat me as an equal, and they do their duty! They are heroically polite, so polite that when the slightest attention is paid me, I blush with shame!

Robert. You don't mean Claire? Claire is very good to you, isn't she?

Hélène. [*Ironically.*] To me? Claire?

Robert. Don't you think so? If it hadn't been for her, perhaps we should never have been married. Mother thought it her duty to raise every imaginable objection: but Claire made God knows what oath to her, and the objections disappeared. After the ceremony, do you remember how she found occasion—awkwardly enough—to say that she knew of the existence of the child, and that he should not be kept from her any longer out of respect for her? What made my father decide to come ahead here and get this house for us? Who went with him? Who found this hidden retreat, where we can now enjoy peace with our son for a little while? I think we owe pretty nearly everything to Claire!

Hélène. Do you think she has done all this for my sake? She swallowed her dislike for me for the sake of the baby, because that baby is the future of her family; she would make any sacrifice for that!

Robert. Very noble of her! So much the worse for those who disparage her for doing it! The honor of mankind is in itself a small and insignificant handful of sacrifices, but it typifies all that is sublime.

Hélène. [*With dignity.*] Very well, I can't see it in that light! I was born without your ideas, your delicacy of feeling about those things! [*Becoming excited.*] But do they think I have no feelings at all? They make me feel from morning to night that I am an inferior being, and must be treated as such! If I weren't a poor simple fool——! I must stand it all because I *love*!

Robert. [*In consternation.*] Hélène! The idea! To think you could imagine I was hurting you by what I said! This only goes to show how easily you are offended! My parents don't feel that way about you!

Hélène. [*Ironically.*] You think so?

Robert. Certainly. Why should Claire and I have different ideas from yours? Does our education, which you had no opportunity of having, make you an inferior creature? We all look into the heavens at night: the stars belong to every one! You might at least humor me, and let me preserve the illusion that keeps me alive! It is true, I *am* proud of my title! They say that riches is merely accumulated labor; well, nobility is merely accumulated honor. Hélène, don't let me think that you despise the nobility: it is your first duty to educate our child to respect it.

Hélène. My dear, I shall do my full duty by the child, provided he remains my child, and not the child of a tyrannical and jealous clan! Believe me, O Robert! Could I talk so calmly of the time when you won't be with us any longer, if I didn't think I was standing at this moment before the very gates of hell? Save me! Don't let them drag me back with them to that dreary home, where sad-faced members of the House of Chantemelle live and look like antique armor! I have loved you because you were the only one in that place who had a heart like mine! It would break that heart, Robert, if——

Robert. But why should I oppose my authority to theirs? Legally they have no rights over you! They can't force you!

Hélène. I haven't the courage to resist! If I went back to Chantemelle I should never leave! If I wanted to go away, they would all combine against me, say I perjured myself, and I should be humble and say nothing—— Oh, it would be horrible! Save me from that, Robert!

Robert. I am already sorry I made you my nurse! I can promise you your liberty after you are through with me! I'll put it in my will that you shall live where you like, and I'll tell Claire about it.

Hélène. [*Anxiously.*] Why speak to her? She will never agree with you! She will only oppose you and make you worse! Only promise to put that in your will: that will be enough.

Robert. Claire is not used to my doing things without consulting her; I couldn't consent to separating you from the family without speaking to her and telling her my reasons for doing so. Don't worry. She may disagree with me as much as she pleases. I shall not give in: you have my word for it!

[*Enter* CLAIRE. *She has been outdoors, and wears a walking-suit; under her arm is a cardboard box.*]

Claire. [*Taking off her gloves and hat.*] The sun is blinding. I went to the customs office to sketch the reef, but the sea was a perfect blaze! I could hardly see a thing!

Hélène. What do you find so interesting about the reef? Haven't you already three drawings of it in your album?

Claire. That stone pinnacle which seems to totter when the waves break over it fascinates me! It's like a fisherman standing in the water.

Robert. Or a shepherd guarding his sheep. ——Look, the flock is jumping about now!

Claire. [*Smiling.*] Flock! How common that word would have sounded over there while I was sketching!—— I imagined——! That boiling tide—why, even in the calmest weather it seems as if there were creatures beneath it forcing it up, in order to rise up to the sun—— Sirens, maybe, who regret the times when they danced and gamboled on the beach! I'm sure they used to live around my rock, those divine, cruel creatures!

Robert. [*Laughing.*] Divine? Why? Because they brought poor unfortunate sailors and cabin-boys to their doom?

Claire. I'm afraid so! Yet I think they weren't so dangerous as they are said to be! You remember once how a certain warrior who was on a quest for some Golden Fleece or other allowed himself to be charmed by their song—and did they make a meal of him? Of course not! They filled him full of good counsels, and conducted him to the island where he found the treasure he was looking for. Another time, among a number of shipwrecked wretches was an old man who had embarked to go and preach the gospel of Christ Crucified to the savages; in the very teeth of the cannibal goddesses, he made public profession of his faith, and overcame terrible opposition in the midst of the storm—the revelers ate no more that night! The shining bodies and tresses of the Sirens, green with seaweed, triumphantly escorted the missionary to the shore whence he was going to drive the idol; then they—the Sirens—idols themselves, plunged back into the deep and appeared no more.

Robert. What imagination! That must be champagne foam around your reef! The sea is positively going to your head!

Claire. Make fun of me, that's right! If the sea makes me romantic, what do the forests do to you? When you come back to Chantemelle after a long trip, the first thing you do is run to the woods, all alone, dressed like a common thief—and at night to hear you tell what you found by all your dear old hedges——!

Robert. Oh, the woods of Chantemelle! How often have I wandered about them! I've never been really happy away from them! But that doesn't prevent my loving the sea! The woods and the sea have a great attraction for me. I have always liked to hunt, and it wasn't the mere killing of animals that I enjoyed: there was something else. It was the thick underbrush, the unknown! I used to listen, tingling with joy, to the moaning of the wind, at first far off, then rushing on, wave after wave—grandly, mysteriously—and all at once, the tops of the birches would begin to wave high over my head, and the pines and saplings would sway, and I was in the midst of the whirlwind! Then to hear the boars cracking the dry sticks, breaking through hedges — you'd think they were the fauns of old Greece! Then the boar comes out into the opening, a big black thing, hair bristling, tail twisted up in a knot! There *is* your faun! And the light tread of the wolves over the dead leaves!—— Head lowered, ears alert, digging around some briar—he looks up, and then vanishes heaven knows where. And then the pale reflections of the foxes over the snow! Oh, to think of all that now!

Hélène. [*Seated a little distance from him, and trying to attract attention to herself.*] Yes, you prefer the forest to the sea!

Robert. I like both, but not in the same way. The aristocrat in me loves those old trees, as old as we are, that spread their protecting arms over the multitudes. Are we not the brothers of the pines and giant hemlocks? I never wander about among them without assuming their splendid attitude of arrogance. I soar high above the fields, drink in the light and the pure air and proudly scatter acorns and pine-nuts to the famished countryside —— Here by the sea another being awakes within me; the waves come in never-ending procession and break on the beach, each decked out in diamonds by the sun—small in calm weather, gigantic in the storm. Then I say to myself, "Here is a far different image of mankind from what I get in the forests." The uniformity of those waves, bearing forever the burden of the fleets of the world, those waves that are doomed to eternal unrest —there is something monotonous in all that, too monotonous for my forester's instinct! Then I wonder whether men can ever make their way through life like the waves, without jostling, wrangling, and hurting one another. Then I am seized with fear: I am afraid that the wave of humanity, if all men are made equal, like the waves of the sea, will continue to rise up and up, mysteriously attracted from above!—— Here I am, part forester, part man of the sea—the trees and the hedges and the waves!

Claire. Oh, Robert, how truly we are brother and sister! From birth we have been buried in the old château, discouraged because we had nothing to do, looking to the winds and the woods, the waves and the clouds to sing us the song of life. I never read much, but I have heard it said that everything nowadays is bad; yet these forces in nature paint for me the life of the past. You, you question them for the future—which of us is right?

Robert. [*Facing* CLAIRE.] I! To speak of the future and to die tomorrow is futile enough; but I have a son, and I live in agony wondering what his destiny will be. Poor little one, I fear I have given him a mournful heritage in taking him into this family! Will he have a place of his own to breathe in and think, as I never had? No, I never had that, even at Chantemelle! I have loved you all, but I was never able to talk with you without getting into a dispute—oh, that eternal wrangling! [*Smiling.*] I became a Socialist to spite Father, a Freethinker to spite Mother, a Republican to spite you—and the whole thing ended in recriminations! When I went to Paris to complete my studies, I was again wofully out of place: nearly all my fellow-students held radically different views from ours. *I* ought to have been able to get along with them—but I couldn't! I was more dogmatic with them than Father is with us, more religious than Mother, more Royalist than you. There are *déclassés* of high rank, as well as of low—I am one of the former. I am intellectually in sympathy with the present generation, but my heart is with the past! Wherever I go, half of me is an exile. I must save my son from this torture!

Claire. Of course you must! He will never be like you, who never dared be yourself except alone with your books, who were afraid that the living might perceive in you a radical, a revolutionist against the family! He will keep up with his times—I am even willing to bury my dislikes and become modern in order to be with him myself. But you will not object, will you, to my keeping my old pride deep down in my heart? I shall explain to him later all your ideas about the nobility: the source of true chivalry!

Robert. In the joy of being a father, I had hoped for that, and I finally brought you to think as I did. But these last few days I have been discouraged—I have to come down to earth again! It may be that my sickness makes me believe I foresee the downfall of all our family, while only *I* am dying. No matter! I'm only too glad not to have to explain to my son all the doubts that have arisen in me: that awful past that seems like a drag on our future! I confide him to you, who are tall and dignified like the pines, healthy and clear-seeing! My son will have only to look about him to find the finest examples of honor and bigness of spirit: Father is loyalty and probity incarnate, and you would never tell a lie even to save your life!

Claire. [*Agitated.*] You may be sure of me: I shall look after your son so well that not the shadow of a base thought can reach him.

Hélène. [*Goes to* ROBERT, *takes him aside, and speaks to him.*] Oh, Robert! To confide our son to the family before me, after your promise! I thought I could trust you, Robert!

Robert. [*Aside to* HÉLÈNE.] Oh, I'm terribly sorry! Forgive me, Hélène! You have my word, and you may depend upon it more than ever!

Hélène. [*Shrugging her shoulders, as she goes to the window.*] There, I hear him crying! [*Looking out the window.*] Oh, that nurse!—Talk ahead about your grand ideas. Mama is going to look after baby!

[*She takes a garden-hat from the rack and goes out.*]

Robert. [*Going to* CLAIRE.] Claire, Claire, you speak about little Henri as if he had no mother! There, you see, she's the one who really takes care of him!

Claire. [*Smiling.*] Robert, you are to blame! You tell us what you want done with the boy, and you always speak to me about it in his mother's presence.

Robert. I didn't mean to do that. I was speaking to you both. But you are not kind to Hélène. What's the matter? Hélène has been telling me that after I'm gone it will be impossible for her to live with you. She means to settle where she will not be humiliated later on in the presence of her son.

Claire. [*Astonished.*] She wants to take the child away? Did she say that? What did you say?

Robert. I'm sorry, but I told her she was right. In my will, I shall make provision for her to live independently.

Claire. [*At her wits' end.*] Robert, don't do that!

Robert. I promised her.

Claire. Don't do it!

Robert. Claire, I am as sorry as you are to have the child taken from the hereditary home; there are certain sacred things I should have liked him to grow up to feel; but you can't expect a woman of Hélène's age to remain buried alive for the rest of her life! The moment she suffers from your contact, and says she does, I want her to be left free. Won't she be free anyway? I shall ask her, beg her, to stay at Chantemelle, but who can force her against her wishes? In a year's time, she might leave you, hating and despising you all—all you have to do is make her wish to be with you—by love, by affection.

Claire. Whatever you do, leave us the child! Listen to me: I tell you, this is a matter of the gravest importance!

Robert. Let you have the child? I once asked you to take him, and you refused; now *I* refuse! The child belongs to his mother, and if Hélène consents to abandon him, then I should be the first—— Why——!

Claire. To have a Duke of Chantemelle educated by Hélène Vatrin—to have him grow up with her ideas, out of sympathy with our beliefs, our faith! Would you allow that? To think that a creature like Hélène could so deceive you——! Now I see what you meant when you spoke about the uniformity of the waves and the vision of a new mankind! Her ideas, the ideas of a woman of the common people, have taken root in you! You try to make those ideas fit in with your own, you are blinded because they please you—you are infected with them! Robert, come to yourself! Before your marriage, you swore to me that if Hélène were not the mother of your child, you would not marry her! Now you are sacrificing your son to her!

Robert. Very well, admit that I am; you forget one thing: our parents are getting old. Hélène will of necessity be the only one left to take care of her son! *There's* the sacrifice!

Claire. I am young, and I am stronger than Hélène! I offer my whole life, Robert, for your son.

Robert. [*Struggling to dominate his emotion.*] Impossible!

Claire. Then why did you speak to me, and me alone—not long ago—when you were telling how the future Duke de Chantemelle ought to be educated? Wasn't I the only one who understood?

Robert. Stop it!

Claire. Then in your opinion Hélène is my equal?

Robert. Claire, you are prejudiced against Hélène; and you have a right to judge: your life has been spotless. But you must look at things from a different point of view. You are no longer a little girl. Remember, a woman may make a slip and yet remain worthy of respect: Hélène is such a woman.

Claire. Don't leave your son with her!

Robert. Oh——! Well?

Claire. Remember, Robert, remember, Mademoiselle Vatrin was dismissed from Chantemelle for misbehavior——

Robert. She loved me!

Claire. [*Driven to despair.*] Loved—everybody!!

[*Enter the* DUKE, *from one of the rooms at the side.*]

Duke. Claire, are you mad? You shout ——! I heard you from the smoking-room. You know what the doctors say? You, too, Robert?

Claire. We are facing a greater danger than that! Father, I was willing, as you were, for Robert to marry—you know why—you know what it cost me! That was for the sake of the family, for the future, for Henri: the hope of us all. Well, that's over now, we have only to look at the wreckage—and regret what we have done. Why didn't we think of one simple thing, that Henri before belonging to us belongs to his mother? And last of all, here is Robert who is going to make provision in his will for Hélène to leave us and take away her child.

Duke. [*To* ROBERT.] Is this true?

Robert. Yes.

Duke. Don't do it!

Robert. It is my right.

Duke. It is! But don't do it!

Robert. Give me a reason.

Duke. A thousand, if you like.

Claire. [*To the* DUKE.] I have told him—all I could tell him!

Duke. There are others! Hélène's origin, for instance—of course, we don't wish to reproach her——! Things are done in these days that make the blood run cold! Even if ours were the most obscure of names, I should still say, save our honor: don't leave it in the hands of that woman!

Robert. I refuse to allow you to insult Hélène!

Duke. [*Rising to his full height.*] You refuse?

Robert. [*Making a great effort.*] I am weak, but you cannot bend me. If you say a single insulting word against her, I'll leave the house and take her with me!

Duke. She is now out there in the garden; let her come in and talk to me, face to face, about her right! Let her dare! Let her——!

Claire. She will be a little less proud then!

Robert. She will come here, to pack the trunks and follow me!

Duke. I shall keep the child, in spite of his mother.

Robert. He is mine.

Duke. Ours!

Robert. Mine!

Duke. [*Menacingly.*] Ours!

Claire. [*Frightened.*] Father! Listen to me!

Duke. [*Thrusting* CLAIRE *aside.*] You go away! This is between us!

Claire. Father!

Duke. Go!

[*He takes* CLAIRE *by the shoulders, and thrusts her out of the room. She remains behind the door, however, which is not quite closed.*]

Duke. [*Goes quickly to* ROBERT, *overcome with rage.*] Now! She was mine before she was yours! I committed the crime of letting you marry her in order that the family might not die out with you! I don't intend to let you take from us the child we have all paid so dearly for! He belongs to the family; I forbid you to lay hands on him! There! I think that is all! [*Suddenly calm and dignified.*] Now, if you think I should die, I am ready.

Robert. [*Looks his father in the eyes for a long time, then walks with unsteady steps toward the door. As he is about to leave, he summons up all his reserve strength.*] One of us has to die!

[*He goes out, tottering.* CLAIRE *is seen behind the door; she receives him in her arms.*]

Duke. [*Going to the window and calling.*] Hélène, come here!

Hélène. [*Outside.*] Why? It's so lovely outdoors.

Duke. [*Stamping on the floor.*] Come here! [*In a voice of thunder.*] I tell you, come here!

[*He returns to the center of the room, and stands waiting, his eyes fixed upon the door. Enter* HÉLÈNE; *the moment she sees the expression on the* DUKE'S *face, she is terror-stricken.*]

Duke. [*Bruskly.*] You have tried to steal our child! You bear one of the most honorable names in France, you are rich and respected—you ought to be satisfied. You have asked for more, and you will now receive justice. I have told everything to Robert.

Hélène. [*Sobbing.*] My God!

Duke. My words have sacrificed a life: either Robert's or mine—I don't know which. I told Robert I was willing to die—he said that one of us *must,* and he is right! He is now trying to find a way that will avoid all scandal, and he will succeed, I know he will!

[*Enter* CLAIRE. *The* DUKE *questions her with a look.*]

Claire. He says nothing! I wanted to talk with him—and he gave me such a look——! I didn't dare stay with him! He knows that I knew everything——!

Duke. Repeat it to him, word for word; don't leave him! The only honor in my crime is that you, the soul of purity, are my accomplice! Go and tell him: he must not have the shadow of a doubt!

[*Enter the* DUCHESS.]

Duchess. What has happened? Robert is terribly changed! I found him nearly dead in a chair! When he saw me, he got up and told me he was leaving for Chantemelle tonight. I couldn't argue with him!

Claire. [*Going to the* DUKE, *and looking him straight in the face.*] That will kill him! It was twenty degrees below zero there yesterday!

Duchess. I told him, but he wouldn't listen. I told him I would find Hélène for him, and his face was——! Now I remember, the moment I pronounced Hélène's name, he turned white as snow! We can't let him go away like that! Hélène, why aren't you with him now?

Hélène. [*In terror.*] No, no, not now! No!

Duchess. Have you and Robert——? Only this morning you were talking together —— What's the matter?

[HÉLÈNE *gives a vague gesture.*]

Duke. Hélène had better stay here! You see she is very nervous. She's not well! She can't go to him!

Duchess. [*To the* DUKE.] Then you speak to Robert; you have so much influence with him!

Duke. [*Hesitating.*] I? I can't go! [*Glancing at* CLAIRE *significantly.*] Claire, you ought to speak to him.

Duchess. But why not you, Henri? Why, you are nearly as pale as Hélène! Are you afraid of something? You, too, Claire! Your face is changed!

Claire. There's nothing strange, Mother! I am afraid for Robert!

Duchess. Why do you look at your father that way? What's the matter? You are hiding something from me, all of you! There is some secret—what is it? Am I the only one in the house not to know? Hélène, tell me! [HÉLÈNE *hides her face in her hands, sobbing, as the* DUCHESS *looks at her in silence.*] Hélène, this is not the first time I have asked you a question—the last time you behaved as you do now—— Cry, cry now, if you like, but you are going to tell me!

Duke. Never mind her, I'll answer for her!

Claire. [*Terrified.*] Let me tell her!

Duchess. You, Claire? Last summer you begged me to send her away from Chantemelle; you gave me no reasons, and I asked for none. We were face to face, both of us quivering with fear. Your eyes spoke—spoke and told me—what Robert has just found out! It's too horrible! Such shame in our house! And *she* has married our son! And you, Claire, knew all the time! And you never said a word! Oh, I don't know what I ——! And you knew——!

Claire. Mother, since I've known this secret, I haven't had a moment's peace of mind—I have sacrificed all to something that is greater than we are——

Duchess. Nothing is more sacred than an oath—you have no sense of honor if you believe otherwise!

Claire. I was thinking only of the child.

Duchess. The child! Ha! The poorest of peasants cries when he loses his son, and when Robert dies you won't think of him—his son to you is only a title! If the title is saved, you are happy! The child will live in glory and honor, no matter what infamies are committed to save the title! And all for a poor little bastard——

Duke. Don't insult the child! Robert will not allow it!

Duchess. Robert will not——! [*She breaks out into tears.*] Your own son, killed by you—let him decide—don't ask anything of me——

[*Enter* ROBERT, *his face deadly pale. He can hardly walk; but he shows great strength in his efforts. As soon as she sees him, the* DUCHESS *assumes an attitude of outward calm.* CLAIRE *goes to him at once, and helps him to walk.*]

Robert. Let us forget ourselves for the time being, and save little Henri: he is the family, think of him!

Duchess. We'll do anything, only stay with us!

Robert. I am going to the Ardennes this evening—I have presentiments, and I am never mistaken about them: this time, I feel that death is not far away, and when it comes

I want to be *there,* with my memories of the past: not only of my youth, but of all our glorious past! I feel I have lived for centuries and centuries! The trip will doubtless cut short my life by a few days, but I shall at least have shown you what devotion to an ideal is!

Duke. An ideal?

Robert. Yours, ours: the honor of our name. Hélène and Claire and I are going. You may stay here with Mother and the little one, if you like; you may bring little Henri back with you to Chantemelle when the bad weather is over.

Claire. I am going with Robert. I—I admire him—so much! [*To* HÉLÈNE.] Come, Hélène, we have to get ready, and help Robert—— Come——

[HÉLÈNE *follows* CLAIRE *out of the room, walking as if she were in a dream.*]

Duke. [*Riveted to the floor.*] Robert, I have abdicated! You are the head of the family! Command, they will all obey you! —— Good-by!——

[*He picks up his hat and overcoat, and goes to the beach. The* DUCHESS *throws herself into* ROBERT'S *arms, convulsed with sobs.*]

CURTAIN

ACT IV

The same scene as in the first two acts. It is night. The door up-stage to the left[1] *is open; the passage formed by this door is transformed into a chapel, brightly lighted by candles where the body of* ROBERT *is exposed upon a bier.*

The DUCHESS *and* CLAIRE *are kneeling in prayer before the bier. About them are numerous peasants, men and women, who from time to time cast a glance at the body and pray.*

Down-stage to the left sits the DUKE, *his arms resting on the table, his face buried in his hands. Behind him, near the principal entrance to the room, stands a servant in livery, who conducts the peasants back and forth during the first part of the act.—The peasants go first to the bier, say a "Pater," then cross themselves and go out. Some sprinkle holy water on the body.*

For about a minute after the curtain rises, no one speaks.—The visitors enter, then bow ceremoniously to the DUKE, *who rarely raises his eyes.*

A large FARMER, *as he leaves the bier, approaches the* DUKE *and offers his condolence.*

The FARMER *is dressed in his best clothes.*

The Farmer. Ah, Monsieur le duc, it's very sad! Such a young man! And so strong! See him galloping away all winter with his dogs!—Maybe he wore himself out doing that. Why, my wife was telling me only this morning, he wasn't afraid of anything, not he! And last Sunday, sick as he was, we saw him at High Mass—and then he went to the cemetery to see the old graves of his ancestors; and he didn't wear a hat—he was there most a quarter of an hour! There was no sense in that! He must've done it on purpose——

Duke. This is a terrible blow for me, Renaud—*I* ought to have been the first to go!

The Farmer. Oh, Monsieur le duc is like a rock yet!—Monsieur Robert used to come around to the farm often—he liked us farmers, and the animals too! He'd 've been a fine master to us later on!

Duke. We shall do our best to have his son resemble him; he must make the same friends for Chantemelle as his father did!

[*The* DUKE *shakes hands with the* FARMER, *who goes out. After the peasants cease coming in, enter a* NEIGHBOR. *He wears a fur cap and carries a heavy cane; his thick boots and leather leggings proclaim him a hunter. His trousers and coat are of black cloth. The servant points out the* DUKE *to him.*]

The Neighbor. [*Going to the* DUKE.] My dear friend! [*They shake hands cordially.*] I just heard the sad news this noon. I'd gone out early in the morning shooting wild geese—when I got back for lunch they told me. So you didn't arrive soon enough?

Duke. We arrived just an hour ago.

The Neighbor. It was over last night, wasn't it?

Duke. We received the telegram at four in the afternoon.

[1] When the play was produced at the Théâtre Libre, the bier was placed up-stage, center, the head of the body touching the back wall, the feet pointing toward the footlights.—TR.

The Neighbor. Just in time to catch the train?

Duke. Yes!

The Neighbor. [*Turning toward the body.*] He's there! Poor Robert! I'll go and see him for the last time! I don't like to disturb the ladies; how are they?

Duke. Tired—utterly worn out——

The Neighbor. Mademoiselle Claire was here, wasn't she?

Duke. Yes — she was admirable — my daughter-in-law was here, too.

The Neighbor. If I can be of any service, I——?

[*The* DUKE *bows his head sadly, shakes hands again with the* NEIGHBOR, *who goes toward the body. The* DUKE *accompanies him. The* DUKE *is intercepted by a* NUN *who enters through the door, down-stage to the left. She was* ROBERT'S *nurse during his last illness.*]

The Nun. Monsieur le duc, they tell me the village blacksmith is waiting to close the coffin.

Duke. We've been here hardly an hour! The Duchess wants to keep her son a little longer! Must he——?

The Nun. Yes!

Duke. Try to keep the strangers out of the way; I don't want any one by while his mother is with him! You may bring the men in a few moments—afterward!

[*The* DUKE *goes back to his place. The* NUN *tells the servant to admit no one else, then goes to* CLAIRE *and whispers something to her, while the servant sends the peasants out. The* NEIGHBOR *also leaves the room, then the* NUN. *The* DUCHESS *remains at the foot of the bier, oblivious of what is happening.* CLAIRE *goes to her father, and speaks with him in an undertone.*]

Claire. Father, they are going to close Robert's coffin——! [*Showing him a sheet of paper folded between the leaves of her prayer-book.*] I want to read his will before us all, while he is still with us. Then I shall tell you about his last hours: not the agony, you know about that, but his last wishes. They are worthy of him!

Duke. You represent your brother: what you wish shall be done.

Claire. Thank you. I am going to call Hélène——

[*She speaks a few words to the servant, who goes out. At the same time the* DUCHESS *rises, her face wet with tears, and joins her husband.* CLAIRE *comes to them.*]

Duchess. [*Looking toward the bier.*] He hasn't changed! He is sleeping!

Claire. He is! He closed his eyes quietly without the least struggle. His last thought was the honor of the family——

Duchess. Was Hélène there?

Claire. I called her toward the last.

Duchess. Did he recognize her?

Claire. He asked for her.

Duchess. Then she didn't go near him all that week while he was sick?

Claire. Oh, yes, she was often with him; we had no reason to send her away. Robert treated her exactly as he had always done—there was only one change in him: he had no desire to live——

Duchess. [*Sobbing.*] His prayer was answered!

Claire. Courage, Mother! You will need a great deal today! I have sent for Hélène: I want you all to hear Robert's last wishes——

[*The* DUCHESS *again kneels by the bier.*]

Duke. Your mother can't stand this—how long will she be like that?

Claire. If she can only bear up until the funeral is over!

Duke. How foolish we were, Claire, to think that with a secret like this we could live together happily! We can stand the strain now, and for some time to come, but —after?

Claire. Then Mother will not suffer so! She loves you too much, she understands her religion too well to leave you.

Duke. But when I have to face Hélène——

Claire. Hélène will be no obstacle——

Duke. Is she going to leave? Then she's not going to take the child? I am sure Robert will not allow him to be in unsafe hands. But if Hélène goes away by herself, what will people think?

Claire. Have no fear about that. Hélène will not leave here alone. The marytrdom you think Mother will have to suffer will be borne by some one else.

Duke. You, Claire?

Claire. [*Repressing the tears.*] Please don't ask me!—What I have to look forward to is too terrible to think about. Robert himself will tell you what we are going to do. When you hear the words from his mouth then I shall tell you what is to become of me.

[*Enter* HÉLÈNE. *She stands in the center of the room. The* DUKE *and* CLAIRE *are down-stage to the right.*]

Claire. Hélène, my mother wishes to see you—there!

[HÉLÈNE *goes to the bier. She waits*

there for the DUCHESS, *who is still on her knees. At last the* DUCHESS *rises, and she and* HÉLÈNE *face each other. The* DUCHESS *holds her hand out, with her eyes still on the body;* HÉLÈNE *takes her hand for a moment. Then the* DUCHESS *goes to* CLAIRE *and the* DUKE. *They are grouped as follows: the* DUKE *leans on the table down-stage to the right; the* DUCHESS *seats herself to the left;* HÉLÈNE *remains standing before the bier;* CLAIRE, *standing in the center, reads the will.*]

Claire. [*The will in hand.*] Here is Robert's will. The beginning is like those old wills of our forefathers—I can imagine him making a cross for a signature! [*Reading.*] "In the name of the Father and the Son and the Holy Spirit, I, Robert Charles-Henri de Chantemelle, about to appear before God, ask pardon for all the wrongs I have committed against my people, and do solemnly swear that I bear in my heart not the slightest resentment against any one of them, whosoever he may be. I wish my father to know that I felt as deeply as he at the thought of the disappearance of our family. He forgot that he was a father only to remember that he was a duke. He had the strength to crush certain sacred sentiments, I to forget vengeance—I thank God for taking my life at a time when such vengeance became impossible for me.

"On my death, I ordain the following:

"I humbly beg my father and my mother to continue their existence together in the true spirit of Christian humility, after I am gone. I have learned a valuable lesson from my mother, which has greatly helped me, and taught me to die in peace.

"Claire has nothing to reproach herself with in regard to me. When at last she saw the impossibility of my surviving she fully realized her responsibility. How willing she is to expiate her noble crime in trying to preserve the ancient glory of our family!

"I should be guilty of grave indelicacy were I to record here what she has promised to do. I leave it to her to explain in what way she is willing to sacrifice herself. Claire will be my representative among you; I place Hélène and her child in Claire's hands. Whatever she shall think best, will be my wish.

"I ask my parents to give to Hélène the Château des Ecluses in Normandy. She promised me to go there and consecrate her life to the education of her son. She may be justly charged with perjury if she deviates in the slightest degree from this single end. I had the right to demand this oath in return for the forgiveness I granted her." [HÉLÈNE *falls to her knees, then to the floor, overcome.*] "As soon as little Henri shall reach the age of fifteen years, I authorize Hélène to take him to live in Paris for the sake of the superior educational facilities which are to be found only there. The future Duke de Chantemelle must be well educated: the idea that to his rank is to be added personal worth must be inculcated in him. Nothing should be neglected to make him a modern man, in the deepest significance of the word: he must love his country today, and understand its glories and its greatness. We shall be lost if we continue to prolong our hates and prejudices, which in the times immediately following the Revolution were quite pardonable, but which nowadays are evidence only of laziness and selfish egotism. The Revolution guillotined our fathers who were at first so ready to sacrifice all for its sake, but *we* use that argument as a pretext to combat every attempt at social betterment. Let us rather carry forward our own traditions by paying for our well-intentioned errors with our lives, and prove thereby that the nobility can at least furnish an object-lesson of self-immolation, and pave the way for the men of our time, too keen of mind, and too forgetful of sentiment! When those who are more unfortunate than we ask for more and better conditions, let us be ready to put ourselves at their head with the idea that those we are leading may fire upon us from behind! The nobility it seems to me has accomplished its ends and is a thing of the past; it has been based too much upon wealth, and too little upon merit: it has ever remained closed to the great men who have sprung from the people, and the people have reciprocated. Before it finally disappears it must by means of a pious lie give the same impression of grandeur of former times that is left by the gigantic fossils which tell us of the greatness of past ages!

"Later, when my heir grows to manhood, I ask that Claire tell him the manner of my death, how his grandparents, his aunt, and his mother have sacrificed for him, in order that his name should survive without a stain. He must understand that this name, perpetuated by means of a monstrous crime, should be borne with almost superhuman dignity. I want Claire to repeat to him what she said to me yesterday: 'Our lives all end with yours. But what does that matter? We have searched the whole field to find a little flower!'"

Duchess. [*Sobbing.*] Robert!

Duke. His is the spirit of the race!

Claire. There is something more: about me. I promised Robert never to marry, and to live with Hélène all my life.

Duchess. No, no, Claire, not that! To leave me all alone!

Claire. [*Calmly.*] I made an oath to him. [*Turning toward the bier.*] Robert, again I swear to follow your wife and your son wherever they may go, and help them carry their name with dignity through life. This I consider as a debt of honor contracted in your favor the day I allowed Hélène to enter the family. She and I promise to devote ourselves to the education of the child: to make him first an honest man, and, better, a man capable of dying for the sake of an idea—as you said—and as you did——!

Duchess. Claire—good-by! Let me say good-by now: later, I couldn't!

[CLAIRE *throws herself into her mother's arms. They go toward the bier.*]

Duke. [*Following them, makes a last prayer by his son, then, after crossing himself, he goes straight to* HÉLÈNE *and looking her in the eyes says in a calm, low voice:*] Good-by—daughter! [*He goes out.*]

CURTAIN

THE BEAVER COAT*

[*Der Biberpelz*]

A Thieves' Comedy

By
GERHART HAUPTMANN

Translated from the German by LUDWIG LEWISOHN

GERHART HAUPTMANN WAS THE FIRST of the contemporary school of writers in Germany to win back the reading and theater public of that country to an appreciation of their own living authors. He was closely associated as early as 1885 with the Youngest Germany group, strongly under the influence of Zola and the French naturalists, the essence of whose theories was a stark realism, which should reveal the grosser aspects of life and society that had hitherto been glossed over for the purposes of literature and the stage. Hauptmann, like Ibsen, was too much the poet to be fascinated by the morbid, or to give himself consistently to one style of composition. Although many of his plays are among the greatest examples of the naturalist school, many others are of a fanciful and highly poetic nature, or, at least, are a blend of various moods, like *The Assumption of Hannele* (1893), *The Sunken Bell* (1896), *And Pippa Dances!* (1906). Hauptmann's distinction as a dramatist is due to his astonishing variety and poetic vision.

His first efforts in the theater were made under the influence of Arno Holz and Johannes Schlaf, themselves the creators of the naturalist spell in the German theater. His *Before Dawn* was accepted by Otto Brahm and Paul Schlenther for production at their new Free Theater (*Die Freie Bühne*) in its first year, 1889. In spite of a storm of criticism from the conservatives, it was a pronounced success, and definitely established the new school of playwriting. This success was quickly followed up by *The Festival of Peace* (1890) and *Lonely Lives* (1891) in which Ibsen's mark is strongly apparent. Then came what may be called Hauptmann's own brand of naturalism, in the great play, *The Weavers* (1892), in which not any single character, but the mob, treated as an individual, became the chief actor. This play remains Germany's chief contribution to naturalist drama. In no style of composition, however, is Hauptmann more universally pleasing and masterful than in his folk-plays of a comic and satirical order. They are equally valuable as examples of his naturalism at its best, unadorned with exaggerated fancy or sentimentality. Some of these deal with peasant life, some with the life of Berlin and its environs. To this latter class *The Beaver Coat* belongs (1893). It is less pretentious than many of Hauptmann's dramas, but is clear-cut and masterful in its synthesis of observed character, social environment, satirical purpose, and entertainment values. Its portrait of the officious magistrate is a classic of the German theater. It has long been popular in the art theaters of Germany.

PRODUCTION

The Free Theater (*Die Freie Bühne*) of Berlin, founded in 1889 by Otto Brahm and Paul Schlenther, in response to the Youngest Germany movement, was Germany's tribute to *Le Théâtre Libre* of Antoine in Paris, founded two years before, and for similar purposes: to give expression to younger men, whose plays were not likely to gain a hearing in the conservative national theaters, or in the commercial theaters; and to encourage the revolutionary forces of naturalism which were even less welcome at the older establishments.

Admirable as the great national subsidized

theaters of France and Germany have been, they have served rather as treasure-houses of the older drama, than as creators of the new. In the nineteenth century, when the new drama was obviously without literary distinction in any country, the conservative tendencies were especially strong in the theaters devoted to drama as an art. The poetic and romantic qualities of plays given at the national theaters, and the vogue of the well-made plays of Scribe's pattern at the commercial houses, made the case of the young naturalists desperate in both countries. Hence the great service rendered by Antoine and Brahm, in founding theaters in which neither commercialism nor the glorious dead should tyrannize.

Ibsen and Strindberg contributed the chief elements to a new theory of stage production. But in Germany the celebrated troup of the Meiningen Players (1874-1890) anticipated and indeed suggested some of these principles, such as harmonious cooperation of all the actors towards a unified artistic effect, through careful drill and discipline, and the banning of conventional stage practices, such as posing, declamation, and address to the audience. In Germany, more than in France, the way had been prepared for naturalistic stagecraft; but the risk of experimentation in newly written plays was too great to be commonly assumed. Here lay the need for the new theater. The Youngest Germany movement was without any dependable outlet for its work, until Otto Brahm, cooperating with Holz and Schlaf and other revolutionaries, created a theater frankly for experimentation. As Antoine in Paris brought to the fore such writers as Brieux and de Curel, and Grein in London with his Independent Theater gave expression to Shaw, so these German producers attracted Hauptmann, who, in turn, gave their theater its distinction and justification. The theater and its doctrines were later absorbed in the widespread management of Max Reinhardt, who, after the early passing of the strict naturalist cult, widened its scope, and imparted to it his own creative force, as the most daring and successful of all modern art producers. His Deutsches Theater in Berlin was the direct descendant of Die Freie Bühne, but he later brought many other theaters in Berlin, Munich, Vienna, Salzburg, and elsewhere under his vitalizing control. *The Beaver Coat,* as an enduring example of German naturalism, has had frequent revivals under such auspices.

GERHART HAUPTMANN

Born 1862, Obersalzbrunn, Silesia, son of hotel-keeper.
Trained in sculpture at Breslau, Jena, and Rome.
1885, Settled in Berlin after marriage.
1889, Active in founding *Die Freie Bühne.*
His first play, *Before Dawn,* given at that theater.
1912, Awarded the Nobel Prize for literature.
He has consistently held the first place among contemporary German authors.

PLAYS

1889 *Before Dawn* (*Vor Sonnenaufgang*). 1890 *The Festival of Peace* (*Das Friedensfest*) vars. *The Coming of Peace* and *The Reconciliation.* 1891 *Lonely Lives* (*Einsame Menschen*). 1892 *The Weavers* (*Die Weber*). 1892 *Colleague Crampton* (*Kollege Crampton*). 1893 *The Beaver Coat: A Thieves' Comedy* (*Der Biberpelz, eine Diebs Komödie*). 1893 *The Assumption of Hannele* (*Hanneles Himmelfahrt*). 1894 *Florian Geyer.* 1896 *Helios.* 1896 *The Sunken Bell* (*Die versunkene Glocke*). 1896 *Elga.* 1898 *Pastoral* (*Das Hirtenlied*). 1898 *Drayman Henschel* (*Fuhrmann Henschel*). 1899 *Schluck und Jau.* 1900 *Michael Kramer.* 1901 *The Red Cock* (*Der rote Hahn*) var. *The Conflagration.* 1902 *Poor Heinrich* (*Der arme Heinrich*) var. *Henry of Auë.* 1903 *Rose Bernd.* 1906 *And Pippa Dances!* (*Und Pippa tanzt!*). 1907 *The Maidens of Bischofsberg* (*Die Jungfern vom Bischofsberg*) var. *The Maidens of the Mount.* 1908 *Charlemagne's Hostage* (*Kaiser Karls Geisel*). 1909 *Griselda.* 1911 *The Rats* (*Die Ratten*). 1912 *Gabriel Schilling's Flight* (*Gabriel Schillings Flucht*). 1913 *The Festi-*

val Play (*Festspiel in Deutschen Reimen*), an *Historic Masque in verse.* 1914 *The Bow of Odysseus* (*Der Bogen des Odysseus*). 1917 *Winter Ballad* (*Winterballade*). 1920 *The White Savior* (*Der Weisse Heiland*). 1920 *Indipohdi.* 1921 *Peter Brauer.* 1925 *Veland.* 1926 *Dorothea Angermann.* 1930 *The Black Mask* (*Die Schwarze Maske*). 1930 *Witches' Ride* (*Hexenritt*). 1932 *Before Sunset* (*Vor Sonnenuntergang*). 1933 *The Golden Harp* (*Die Goldene Harfe*). 1935 *Hamlet in Wittenberg.* 1939 *The Daughter of the Cathedral* (*Die Tochter der Kathedrale*). 1939 *Ulrich von Lichtenstein.*

THE BEAVER COAT

List of Characters

VON WEHRHAHN, *Justice.*
KRUEGER, *capitalist in a small way.*
DOCTOR FLEISCHER.
PHILIP, *his son.*
MOTES.
MRS. MOTES.
MRS. WOLFF, *washerwoman.*
JULIUS WOLFF, *her husband.*
ADELAIDE } *her daughters.*
LEONTINE }
WULKOW, *lighterman.*
GLASENAPP, *clerk in the Justice's court.*
MITTELDORF, *constable.*

Scene of the action: anywhere in the neighborhood of Berlin.

THE FIRST ACT

A small, blue-tinted kitchen with low ceiling; a window at the left; at the right a door of rough boards leading out into the open; in the rear wall an empty casing from which the door has been lifted.—In the left corner a flat oven, above which hang kitchen utensils in a wooden frame; in the right corner oars and other boating implements. Rough, stubby pieces of hewn wood lie in a heap under the window. An old kitchen bench, several stools, etc.—Through the empty casing in the rear a second room is visible. In it stands a high, neatly made bed; above it hang cheap photographs in still cheaper frames, small chromo-lithographs, etc. A chair of soft wood stands with its back against the bed.—It is winter and moonlight. On the oven a tallow-candle is burning in a candlestick of tin. [LEONTINE WOLFF *has fallen asleep on a stool by the oven and rests her head and arms on it. She is a pretty, fair girl of seventeen in the working garb of a domestic servant. A woolen shawl is tied over her cotton jacket.—For several seconds there is silence. Then some one is heard trying to unlock the door from without. But the key is in the lock and a knocking follows.*]

Mrs. Wolff. [*Unseen, from without.*] Adelaide! Adelaide! [*There is no answer and a loud knocking is heard at the window.*] *Are* you goin' to open or not?

Leontine. [*Drowsily.*] No, no, I'm not goin' to be abused that way!

Mrs. Wolff. Open, girl, or I'll come in through the window!

[*She raps violently at the panes.*]

Leontine. [*Waking up.*] Oh, it's you, Mama! I'm coming now!

[*She unlocks the door from within.*]

Mrs. Wolff. [*Without laying down a sack which she carries over her shoulder.*] What are *you* doin' here?

Leontine. [*Sleepily.*] Evenin', Mama.

Mrs. Wolff. How did you get in here, eh?

Leontine. Well, wasn't the key lyin' on the goat shed?

Mrs. Wolff. But what do you want here at home?

Leontine. [*Awkwardly affected and aggrieved.*] So you don't want me to come no more at all?

Mrs. Wolff. Aw, you just go ahead and put on that way! I'm so fond o' that! [*She lets the sack drop from her shoulder.*] You don't know nothin', I s'pose, about how late it's gettin'? You hurry and go back to your mistress.

Leontine. It matters a whole lot, don't it, if I get back there a little too late?

Mrs. Wolff. You want to be lookin' out, y'understand? You see to it that you go, or you'll catch it!

Leontine. [*Tearfully and defiantly.*] I ain't goin' back to them people no more, Mama!

Mrs. Wolff. [*Astonished.*] Not goin'? . . . [*Ironically.*] Oh, no! That's somethin' quite new!

Leontine. Well, I don't *have* to let myself be abused that way!

Mrs. Wolff. [*Busy extracting a piece of venison from the sack.*] So the Kruegers abuse you, do they? Aw, the poor child that you are!—Don't you come round me with such fool talk! A wench like a dragoon . . .! Here, lend a hand with this sack, at the bottom. You can't act more like a fool, eh? You won't get no good out o' me that way! You can't learn lazyin' around here, at all. [*They hang up the venison on the door.*] Now I tell you for the last time . . .

Leontine. I ain't goin' back to them people, I tell you. I'd jump in the river first!

Mrs. Wolff. See that you don't catch a cold doin' it.

Leontine. I'll jump in the river!

Mrs. Wolff. Go ahead. Let me know about it and I'll give you a shove so you don't miss it.

Leontine. [*Screaming.*] Do I have to stand for that, that I gotta drag in two loads o' wood at night?

Mrs. Wolff. [*In mock astonishment.*] Well, now, that's pretty awful, ain't it? You gotta drag in wood? Such people, I tell you!

Leontine. . . . An' I gets twenty crowns for the whole year. I'm to get my hands frostbitten for that, am I? An' not enough potatoes and herring to go round!

Mrs. Wolff. You needn't go fussin' about that, you silly girl. Here's the key; go, cut yourself some bread. An' when you've had enough, go your way, y'understand? The plum butter's in the top cupboard.

Leontine. [*Takes a large loaf of bread from a drawer and cuts some slices.*] An' Juste gets forty crowns a year from the Schulzes an' . . .

Mrs. Wolff. Don't you try to be goin' too fast.—You ain't goin' to stay with them people always; you ain't hired out to 'em forever.—Leave 'em on the first of April, for all I care. —But up to then, you sticks to your place.—Now that you got your Christmas present in your pocket, you want to run away, do you? That's no way. I have dealin's with them people, an' I ain't goin' to have that kind o' thing held against me.

Leontine. These bits o' rag that I got on here?

Mrs. Wolff. You're forgettin' the cash you got.

Leontine. Yes! Six shillin's. That was a whole lot!

Mrs. Wolff. Cash is cash! You needn't kick.

Leontine. But if I can go an' make more?

Mrs. Wolff. Yes, talkin'!

Leontine. No, sewin'! I can go in to Berlin and sew cloaks. Emily Stechow's been doin' that ever since New Year.

Mrs. Wolff. Don't come tellin' me about that slattern! I'd like to get my hands on her, that's all. I'd give that crittur a piece o' my mind! You'd like to be promoted into her class, would you? To go sportin' all night with the fellows? Just to be thinkin' o' that makes me feel that I'd like to beat you so you can't hardly stand up.—Now Papa's comin' an' you'd better look out!

Leontine. If Papa thrashes me, I'll run away. I'll see how I can get along!

Mrs. Wolff. Shut up now! Go an' feed the goats. They ain't been milked yet tonight neither. An' give the rabbits a handful o' hay.

[LEONTINE *tries to make her escape. In the door, however, she runs into her father, but slips quickly by him with a perfunctory* "Evenin'." JULIUS WOLFF, *the father, is a shipwright, a tall man, with dull eyes and slothful gestures, about forty-three years old.—He places two long oars, which he has brought in across his shoulder, in a corner and silently throws down his shipwright's tools.*]

Mrs. Wolff. Did you meet Emil?

[JULIUS *growls.*]

Mrs. Wolff. Can't you talk? Yes or no? Is he goin' to come around, eh?

Julius. [*Irritated.*] Go right ahead! Scream all you want to!

Mrs. Wolff. You're a fine, brave fellow, ain't you? An' all the while you forget to shut the door.

Julius. [*Closes the door.*] What's up again with Leontine?

Mrs. Wolff. Aw, nothin'.—What kind of a load did Emil have?

Julius. Bricks again. What d'you suppose he took in?—But what's up with that girl again?

Mrs. Wolff. Did he have half a load or a whole load?

Julius. [*Flying into a rage.*] What's up with the wench, I asks you?

Mrs. Wolff. [*Outdoing him in violence.*] An' I want to know how big a load Emil had—a half or a whole boat full?

Julius. That's right! Go on! The whole thing full.

Mrs. Wolff. Sst! Julius!

[*Suddenly frightened she shoots the window latch.*]

Julius. [*Scared and staring at her, is silent. After a few moments, softly.*] It's a young forester from Rixdorf.

Mrs. Wolff. Go an' creep under the bed, Julius. [*After a pause.*] If only you wasn't such an awful fool. You don't open your mouth but what you act like a regular tramp. You don't understand nothin' o' such things, if you want to know it. You let me look out for the girls. That ain't no part o' your concern. That's a part of my concern. With boys that'd be a different thing. I wouldn't so much as give you advice. But everybody's got their own concerns.

Julius. Then don't let her come runnin' straight across my way.

Mrs. Wolff. I guess you want to beat her till she can't walk. Don't you take nothin' like that into your head. Don't you think I'm goin' to allow anythin' like that! *I* let her be beaten black an' blue? We c'n make our fortune with that girl. I wish you had sense about some things!

Julius. Well, then let her go an' see how she gets along!

Mrs. Wolff. Nobody needn't be scared about that, Julius. I ain't sayin' but what you'll live to see things. That girl will be livin' up on the first floor some day and we'll be glad to have her condescend to know us. What is it the doctor said to me? Your daughter, he says, is a handsome girl; she'd make a stir on the stage.

Julius. Then let her see about gettin' there.

Mrs. Wolff. You got no education, Julius. You ain't got a trace of it. Lord, if it hadn't been for me! What would ha' become o' those girls? I brought 'em up to be educated, y'understand? Education is the main thing these days. But things don't come off all of a sudden. One thing after another—step by step. Now she's in service an' that'll learn her somethin'. Then maybe, for my part, she can go into Berlin. She's much too young for the stage yet. [*During* MRS. WOLFF'S *speech repeated knocking has been heard. Now* ADELAIDE'S *voice comes in.* "Mama! Mama! Please, do open!" MRS. WOLFF *opens the door.* ADELAIDE *comes in. She is a somewhat overgrown schoolgirl of fourteen with a pretty, child-like face. The expression of her eyes, however, betrays premature corruption.*] Why didn't you open the door, Mama? I nearly got my hands and feet frozen!

Mrs. Wolff. Don't stand there jabberin' nonsense. Light a fire in the oven and you'll soon be warm. Where've you been all this long time, anyhow?

Adelaide. Why, didn't I have to go and fetch the boots for Father?

Mrs. Wolff. An' you stayed out two hours doin' it!

Adelaide. Well, I didn't start to go till seven.

Mrs. Wolff. Oh, you went at seven, did you? It's half past ten now. You don't know that, eh? So you've been gone three hours an' a half. That ain't much. Oh, no. Well now you just listen good to what I've got to tell you. If you go an' stay that long again, and specially with that lousy cobbler of a Fielitz —then watch out an' see! That's all I says.

Adelaide. Oh, I guess I ain't to do nothin' except just mope around at home.

Mrs. Wolff. Now you keep still an' don't let me hear no more.

Adelaide. An' even if I do go over to Fielitz's sometimes. . . .

Mrs. Wolff. Are you goin' to keep still, I'd like to know? You teach me to know Fielitz! He needn't be putting on's far as I know. He's got another trade exceptin' just repairin' shoes. When a man's been twice in the penitentiary . . .

Adelaide. That ain't true at all . . . That's all just a set o' lies. He told me all about it himself, Mama!

Mrs. Wolff. As if the whole village didn't know, you fool girl! That man! I know what he is. He's a——

Adelaide. Oh, but he's friends even with the Justice!

Mrs. Wolff. I don't doubt it. He's a spy. And what's more, he's a *dee*nouncer!

Adelaide. What's that—a *dee*nouncer?

Julius. [*From the next room, into which he has gone.*] I'm just waitin' to hear two words more.

[ADELAIDE *turns pale and at once and silently she sets about building a fire in the oven.* LEONTINE *comes in.*]

Mrs. Wolff. [*Has opened the stag. She takes out the heart, liver, etc., and hands them to* LEONTINE.] There, hurry, wash that off. An' keep still, or somethin'll happen yet.

[LEONTINE, *obviously intimidated, goes at her task. The girls whisper together.*]

Mrs. Wolff. Say, Julius, what are you doin' in there? I guess you'll go an' forget again. Didn't I tell you this mornin' about the board that's come loose?

Julius. What kind o' board?

Mrs. Wolff. You don't know, eh? Behind there, by the goat-shed. The wind loosened it las' night. You better get out there an' drive a few nails in, y'understand?

Julius. Aw, tomorrow morning'll be another day, too.

Mrs. Wolff. Oh, no. Don't take to thinkin' that way. We ain't goin' to make that kind of a start—not we. [JULIUS *comes into the room growling.*] There, take the hammer! Here's your nails! Now hurry an' get it done.

Julius. You're a bit off your head.

Mrs. Wolff. [*Calling out after him.*] When Wulkow comes what d'you want me to ask?

Julius. About twelve shillin's sure. [*Exit.*]

Mrs. Wolff. [*Contemptuously.*] Aw, twelve shillin's. [*A pause.*] Now you just hurry so that Papa gets his supper. [*A brief pause.*]

Adelaide. [*Looking at the stag.*] What's that anyhow, Mama?

Mrs. Wolff. A stork. [*Both girls laugh.*]

Adelaide. A stork, eh? A stork ain't got horns. I know what that is—that's a stag!

Mrs. Wolff. Well, if you know, why d'you go an' ask?

Leontine. Did Papa shoot it, Mama?

Mrs. Wolff. That's right! Go and scream it through the village: Papa's shot a stag!

Adelaide. I'll take mighty good care not to. That'd mean the cop!

Leontine. Aw, I ain't scared o' policeman Schulz. He chucked me under the chin once.

Mrs. Wolff. He c'n come anyhow. We ain't doin' nothin' wrong. If a stag's full o' lead and lays there dyin' an' nobody finds it, what happens? The ravens eat it. Well now, if the ravens eat it or we eat it, it's goin' to be eaten anyhow. [*A brief pause.*] Well now, tell me: You was axed to carry wood in?

Leontine. Yes, in this frost! Two loads o' regular clumps! An' that when a person is tired as a dog, at half-past nine in the evenin'!

Mrs. Wolff. An' now I suppose that wood is lyin' there in the street?

Leontine. It's lyin' in front o' the garden gate. That's all I know.

Mrs. Wolff. Well now, but supposin' somebody goes and steals that wood? What's goin' to happen in the mornin' then?

Leontine. I ain't goin' there no more!

Mrs. Wolff. Are those clumps green or dry?

Leontine. They're fine, dry ones! [*She yawns again and again.*] Oh, Mama, I'm *that* tired! I've just had to work myself to pieces.

[*She sits down with every sign of utter exhaustion.*]

Mrs. Wolff. [*After a brief silence.*] You c'n stay home tonight for all I care. I've thought it all out a bit different. An' tomorrow mornin' we c'n see.

Leontine. I've just got as thin as can be, Mama! My clothes is just hangin' on to me.

Mrs. Wolff. You hurry now and go in to bed or Papa'll raise a row yet. He ain't got no understandin' for things like that.

Adelaide. Papa always speaks so uneducated!

Mrs. Wolff. Well, he didn't learn to have no education. An' that'd be just the same thing with you if I hadn't brought you up to be educated. [*Holding a sauce-pan over the oven: to* LEONTINE:] Come now, put it in! [LEONTINE *places the pieces of washed venison into the sauce-pan.*] So, now go to bed.

Leontine. [*Goes into the next room. While she is still visible, she says:*] Oh, Mama, Motes has moved away from Krueger.

Mrs. Wolff. I guess he didn't pay no rent.

Leontine. It was just like pullin' a tooth every time, Mr. Krueger says, but he paid. Anyhow, he says, he had to kick him out. He's such a lyin' loud-mouthed fellow, and always so high and mighty toward Mr. Krueger.

Mrs. Wolff. If I had been in Mr. Krueger's place I wouldn't ha' kept him that long.

Leontine. Because Mr. Krueger used to be a carpenter onct, that's why Motes always acts so contemptuous. And then, too, he quarreled with Doctor Fleischer.

Mrs. Wolff. Well, anybody, that'll quarrel with *him* . . .! I ain't sayin' anythin', but them people wouldn't harm a fly!

Leontine. They won't let him come to the Fleischers no more.

Mrs. Wolff. If you could get a chance to work for them people some day!

Leontine. They treat the girls like they was their own children.

Mrs. Wolff. And his brother in Berlin, he's cashier in a theater.

Wulkow. [*Has knocked at the door repeatedly and now calls out in a hoarse voice.*] Ain't you goin' to have the kindness to let me in?

Mrs. Wolff. Well, I should say! Why not! Walk right in!

Wulkow. [*Comes in. He is a lighterman on the Spree River, near sixty years old, bent, with a grayish-yellow beard that frames his head from ear to ear but leaves his weather-beaten face free.*] I wish you a very good evenin'.

Mrs. Wolff. Look at him comin' along again to take in a woman a little bit.

Wulkow. I've given up tryin' that this long while!

Mrs. Wolff. Maybe, but that's the way it's goin' to be anyhow.

Wulkow. T'other way roun', you mean.

Mrs. Wolff. What'll it be next?—Here it's hangin'! A grand feller, eh?

Wulkow. I tell you, Julius ought to be lookin' out sharp. They's gettin' to be pretty keen again.

Mrs. Wolff. What are you goin' to give us for it? That's the main thing. What's the use o' jabberin'?

Wulkow. Well, I'm tellin' you. I'm straight from Gruenau. An' there I heard it for certain. They shot Fritz Weber. They just about filled his breeches with lead.

Mrs. Wolff. What are you goin' to give? That's the main thing.

Wulkow. [*Feeling the stag.*] The trouble is I got four o' them bucks lyin' at home now.

Mrs. Wolff. That ain't goin' to make your boat sink.

Wulkow. An' I don't want her to do that.

That wouldn't be no joke. But what's the good if I get stuck with the things here. I've gotta get 'em in to Berlin. It's been hard enough work on the river all day, an' if it goes on freezin' this way, there'll be no gettin' along tomorrow. Then I c'n sit in the ice with my boat, an' then I've got these things for fun.

Mrs. Wolff. [*Apparently changing her mind.*] Girl, you run down to Schulze. Say how-dee-do an' he's to come up a while, cause Mother has somethin' to sell.

Wulkow. Did I say as I wasn't goin' to buy it?

Mrs. Wolff. It's all the same to me who buys it.

Wulkow. Well, I'm willin' to.

Mrs. Wolff. Any one that don't want it can let it be.

Wulkow. I'll buy this feller! What's he worth?

Mrs. Wolff. [*Touching the venison.*] This here piece weighs a good thirty pounds. Every bit of it, I c'n tell you. Well, Adelaide! You was here. We could hardly lift it up.

Adelaide. [*Who had not been present at all.*] I pretty near sprained myself liftin' it.

Wulkow. Thirteen shillin's will pay for it, then. An' I won't be makin' ten pence on that bargain!

Mrs. Wolff. [*Acts amazed. She busies herself at the oven as though she had forgotten* WULKOW'S *presence. Then, as though suddenly becoming aware of it again, she says:*] I wish you a very pleasant trip.

Wulkow. Well, I can't give more than thirteen!

Mrs. Wolff. That's right. Let it alone.

Wulkow. I'm just buyin' it for the sake o' your custom. God strike me dead, but it's as true as I'm standin' here. I don't make *that* much with the whole business. An' even if I was wantin' to say fourteen, I'd be puttin' up money, I'd be out one shillin'. But I ain't goin' to let that stand between us. Just so you see my good intentions, I'll say fourteen . . . I can't give no more. I'm tellin' you facts.

Mrs. Wolff. That's all right! That's all right! We c'n get rid o' this stag. We won't have to keep it till morning.

Wulkow. Yes, if only nobody don't see it hangin' here. Money wouldn't do no good then.

Mrs. Wolff. This stag here, we found it dead.

Wulkow. Yes, in a trap. I believe you.

Mrs. Wolff. You needn't try to get around us that way. That ain't goin' to do *no* good! You want to gobble up everythin' for nothin'! We works till we got no breath. Hours an' hours soakin' in the snow, not to speak o' the risk, there in the pitch dark. That's no joke, I tell you.

Wulkow. The only trouble is that I got four of 'em already. Or I'd say fifteen shillin's quick enough.

Mrs. Wolff. No, Wulkow, we can't do business together today. You c'n be easy an' go a door further. We just dragged ourselves across the lake . . . a hair-breadth an' we would've been stuck in the ice. We couldn't get forward an' we couldn't get backward. You can't give away somethin' you got so hard.

Wulkow. Well, what do I get out of it all, I want to know! This here lighter business ain't a natural thing. An' poachin', that's a bad job. If you all get nabbed, I'd be the first one to fly in. I been worryin' along these forty years. What've I got today? The rheumatiz—that's what! When I get up o' mornin's early, I gotta whine like a puppy dog. Years an' years I been wantin' to buy myself a fur coat. That's what all doctors has advised me to do, because I'm that sensitive. But I ain't been able to buy me none. Not to this day. An' that's as true as I'm standin' here.

Adelaide. [*To her mother.*] Did you hear what Leontine said?

Wulkow. But anyhow. Let it go. I'll say sixteen.

Mrs. Wolff. No, it's no good. Eighteen! [*To* ADELAIDE.] What's that you was talkin' about?

Adelaide. Mrs. Krueger has bought a fur coat that cost pretty near a hundred crowns. It's a beaver coat.

Wulkow. A beaver coat?

Mrs. Wolff. Who bought it?

Adelaide. Why, Mrs. Krueger, I tell you, as a Christmas present for Mr. Krueger.

Wulkow. Is that girl in service with the Kruegers?

Adelaide. Not me, but my sister. I ain't goin' in service like that at all.

Wulkow. Well now, if I could have somethin' like that! That's the kind o' thing I been tryin' to get hold of all this time. I'd gladly be givin' sixty crowns for it. All this money that goes to doctors and druggists, I'd much rather spend it for furs. I'd get some pleasure out of that at least.

Mrs. Wolff. All you gotta do is to go there, Wulkow. Maybe Krueger'll make you a present of the coat.

Wulkow. I don't suppose he'd do it kindly. But's I said: I'm interested in that sort o' thing.

Mrs. Wolff. I believes you. I wouldn't mind havin' a thing like that myself.

Wulkow. How do we stand now? Sixteen?

Mrs. Wolff. Nothin' less'n eighteen'll do. Not under eighteen—that's what Julius said. I wouldn't dare show up with sixteen. No, sir. When that man takes somethin' like that into his head! [JULIUS *comes in.*] Well, Julius, you said eighteen shillin's, didn't you?

Julius. What's that I said?

Mrs. Wolff. Are you hard o' hearin' again for a change? You said yourself: not under eighteen. You told me not to sell the stag for less.

Julius. I said? . . . Oh, yes, that there piece o' venison! That's right. H'm. An' that ain't a bit too much, either.

Wulkow. [*Taking out money and counting it.*] We'll make an end o' this. Seventeen shillin's. Is it a bargain?

Mrs. Wolff. You're a great feller, you are! That's what I said exactly: he don't hardly have to come in the door but a person is taken in!

Wulkow. [*Has unrolled a sack which had been hidden about his person.*] Now help me shoot it right in here. [MRS. WOLFF *helps him place the venison in the sack.*] An' if by some chanst you should come to hear o' somethin' like that—what I means is, just f'r instance—a—fur coat like that, f'r instance. Say, sixty or seventy crowns. I could raise that, an' I wouldn't mind investin' it.

Mrs. Wolff. I guess you ain't right in your head . . .! How should *we* come by a coat like that?

A Man's Voice. [*Calls from without.*] Mrs. Wolff! Oh, Mrs. Wolff! Are you still up?

Mrs. Wolff. [*Sharing the consternation of the others, rapidly, tensely:*] Slip it in! Slip it in! And get in the other room!

[*She crowds them all into the rear room and locks the house-door.*]

A Man's Voice. Mrs. Wolff! Oh, Mrs. Wolff! Have you gone to bed?

[MRS. WOLFF *extinguishes the light.*]

A Man's Voice. Mrs. Wolff! Mrs. Wolff! Are you still up? [*The voice recedes singing:*] "Morningre-ed, morningre-ed, Thou wilt shine when I am dea-ead!"

Leontine. Aw, that's only old "Morningred," Mama!

Mrs. Wolff. [*Listens for a while, opens the door softly and listens again. When she is satisfied she closes the door and lights the candle. Thereupon she admits the others again.*] 'Twas only the constable Mitteldorf.

Wulkow. The devil, you say. That's nice acquaintances for you to have.

Mrs. Wolff. Go on about your way now! Hurry!

Adelaide. Mama, Mino has been barkin'.

Mrs. Wolff. Hurry, hurry, Wulkow! Get out now! An' the back way through the vegetable garden! Julius will open for you. Go on, Julius, an' open the gate.

Wulkow. An's I said, if somethin' like such a beaver coat *was* to turn up, why——

Mrs. Wolff. Sure. Just make haste now.

Wulkow. If the Spree don't freeze over, I'll be gettin' back in, say, three or four days from Berlin. An' I'll be lyin' with my boat down there.

Mrs. Wolff. By the big bridge?

Wulkow. Where I always lies. Well, Julius, toddle ahead! [*Exit.*]

Adelaide. Mama, Mino has been barkin' again.

Mrs. Wolff. [*At the oven.*] Oh, let him bark!

[*A long-drawn call is heard in the distance.* "Ferry over!"]

Adelaide. Somebody wants to get across the river, Mama!

Mrs. Wolff. Well, go'n tell Papa. He's down there by the river.—["Ferry over!"] An' take him his oars. But he ought to let Wulkow get a bit of a start first.

[ADELAIDE *goes out with the oars. For a little while* MRS. WOLFF *is alone. She works energetically. Then* ADELAIDE *returns.*]

Adelaide. Papa's got his oars down in the boat.

Mrs. Wolff. Who wants to get across the river this time o' night?

Adelaide. I believe, Mama, it's that stoopid Motes!

Mrs. Wolff. What? Who is't you say?

Adelaide. I think the voice was Motes's voice.

Mrs. Wolff. [*Vehemently.*] Go down! Run! Tell Papa to come up! That fool Motes can stay on the other side. He don't need to come sniffin' around in the house here.

[ADELAIDE *exits.* MRS. WOLFF *hides and clears away everything that could in any degree suggest the episode of the stag. She covers the sauce-pan with an apron.* ADELAIDE *comes back.*]

Adelaide. Mama, I got down there too late. I hear 'em talkin' a'ready.

Mrs. Wolff. Well, who is it then?

Adelaide. I've been tellin' you: Motes.

[MR. *and* MRS. MOTES *appear in turn in the doorway. Both are of medium height. She is an alert young woman of about thirty, modestly and neatly dressed. He wears a green forester's overcoat; his face is healthy but insignificant: his left eye is concealed by a black bandage.*]

Mrs. Motes. [*Calls in.*] We nearly got our noses frozen, Mrs. Wolff.

Mrs. Wolff. Why do you go walkin' at night? You got time enough when it's bright day.

Motes. It's nice and warm here.—Who's that who has time by day?

Mrs. Wolff. Why, you!

Motes. I suppose you think I live on my fortune.

Mrs. Wolff. I don't know; I ain't sayin' what you live on.

Mrs. Motes. Heavens, you needn't be so cross. We simply wanted to ask about our bill.

Mrs. Wolff. You've asked about that a good deal more'n once.

Mrs. Motes. Very well. So we're asking again. Anything wrong with that? We have to pay sometime, you know.

Mrs. Wolff. [*Astonished.*] You wants to pay?

Mrs. Motes. Of course, we do. Naturally.

Motes. You act as if you were quite overwhelmed. Did you think we'd run off without paying?

Mrs. Wolff. I ain't given to thinkin' such things. If you want to be so good then. Here, we can arrange right now. The amount is eleven shillin's, six pence.

Mrs. Motes. Oh, yes, Mrs. Wolff. We're going to get money. The people around here will open their eyes wide.

Motes. There's a smell of roasted hare here.

Mrs. Wolff. Burned hair! That'd be more likely.

Motes. Let's take a look and see.

[*He is about to take the cover from the sauce-pan.*]

Mrs. Wolff. [*Prevents him.*] No sniffin' 'round in my pots.

Mrs. Motes. [*Who has observed everything distrustfully.*] Mrs. Wolff, we've found something, too.

Mrs. Wolff. I ain't lost nothin'.

Mrs. Motes. There, look at these.

[*She shows her several wire snares.*]

Mrs. Wolff. [*Without losing her equanimity in the slightest.*] I suppose them are snares?

Mrs. Motes. We found them quite in the neighborhood here! Scarcely twenty paces from your garden.

Mrs. Wolff. Lord love you! The amount of poachin' that's done here!

Mrs. Motes. If you were to keep a sharp lookout, you might actually catch the poacher some day.

Mrs. Wolff. Aw, such things is no concern o' mine.

Motes. If I could just get hold of a rascal like that. First, I'd give him something to remember me by, and then I'd mercilessly turn him over to the police.

Mrs. Motes. Mrs. Wolff, have you got a few fresh eggs?

Mrs. Wolff. Now, in the middle of winter? They're pretty scarce!

Motes. [*To* JULIUS, *who has just come in.*] Forester Seidel has nabbed a poacher again. He'll be taken to the detention prison tomorrow. There's an officer with style about him. If I hadn't had my misfortune, I could have been a head forester today. I'd go after those dogs even more energetically.

Mrs. Wolff. There's many a one has had to pay for doin' that!

Motes. Yes, if he's afraid. I'm not! I've denounced quite a few already. [*Fixing his gaze keenly on* MRS. WOLFF *and her husband in turn.*] And there are a few others whose time is coming. They'll run straight into my grip some day. These setters of snares needn't think that I don't know them. I know them very well.

Mrs. Motes. Have you been baking, perhaps, Mrs. Wolff? We're so tired of baker's bread.

Mrs. Wolff. I thought you was goin' to square your account.

Mrs. Motes. On Saturday, as I've told you, Mrs. Wolff. My husband has been appointed editor of the magazine "Chase and Forest."

Mrs. Wolff. Aha, yes. I know what that means.

Mrs. Motes. But if I assure you, Mrs. Wolff! We've moved away from the Kruegers already.

Mrs. Wolff. Yes, you moved because you had to.

Mrs. Motes. We had to? Hubby, listen to this!—[*She gives a forced laugh.*]—Mrs. Wolff says that we had to move from Krueger's.

Motes. [*Crimson with rage.*] The reason why I moved away from that place? You'll find it out some day. The man is a usurer and a cutthroat!

Mrs. Wolff. I don't know nothin' about that; I can't say nothin' about that.

Motes. I'm just waiting to get hold of positive proof. That man had better be careful where I'm concerned—he and his bosom friend, Doctor Fleischer. The latter more especially. If I just wanted to say it—one word and that man would be under lock and key.

[*From the beginning of his speech on he has gradually withdrawn and speaks the last words from without.*]

Mrs. Wolff. I suppose the men got to quarrelin' again?

Mrs. Motes. [*Apparently confidential.*] There's no jesting with my husband. If he determines on anything, he doesn't let go till it's done. And he stands very well with the Justice.—But how about the eggs and the bread?

Mrs. Wolff. [*Reluctantly.*] Well, I happen to have five eggs lyin' here. An' a piece o' bread. [MRS. MOTES *puts the eggs and the half of a loaf into her basket.*] Are you satisfied now?

Mrs. Motes. Certainly; of course. I suppose the eggs are fresh?

Mrs. Wolff. As fresh as my chickens can lay 'em.

Mrs. Motes. [*Hastening in order to catch up with her husband.*] Well, good night. You'll get your money next Saturday. [*Exit.*]

Mrs. Wolff. All right; that'll be all right enough! [*She closes the door and speaks softly to herself.*] Get outta here, you! Got nothin' but debts with everybody around. [*Over her sauce-pan.*] What business o' theirs is it what we eat? Let 'em spy into their own affairs. Go to bed, child!

Adelaide. Good night, Mama.

[*She kisses her.*]

Mrs. Wolff. Well, ain't you goin' to kiss Papa good night?

Adelaide. Good night, Papa.

[*She kisses him, at which he growls.* ADELAIDE *exit.*]

Mrs. Wolff. You always gotta say that to her special! [*A pause.*]

Julius. Why do you go an' give the eggs to them people?

Mrs. Wolff. I suppose you want me to make an enemy o' that feller? You just go ahead an' get him down on you! I tell you, that's a dangerous feller. He ain't got nothin' to do except spy on people. Come. Sit down. Eat. Here's a fork for you. You don't understand much about such things. You take care o' the things that belongs to you! Did you have to go an' lay the snares right behind the garden? They was yours, wasn't they?

Julius. [*Annoyed.*] Go right ahead!

Mrs. Wolff. An', o' course, that fool of a Motes had to find 'em first thing. Here near the house you ain't goin' to lay no more snares at all! Y'understan'? Next thing'll be that people say we laid 'em.

Julius. Aw, you stop your jawin'.

[*Both eat.*]

Mrs. Wolff. Look here, Julius, we're out of wood, too.

Julius. An' you want me to go this minute, I suppose?

Mrs. Wolff. It'd be best if we got busy right off.

Julius. I don't feel my own bones no more. Anybody that wants to go c'n go. I ain't.

Mrs. Wolff. You men folks always does a whole lot o' talkin', an' when it comes to the point, you can't do nothin'. I'd work enough to put the crowd of you in a hole and drag you out again too. If you ain't willin' to go tonight by no means, why, you've got to go tomorrow anyhow. So what good is it? How are the climbin' irons? Sharp?

Julius. I loaned 'em to Karl Machnow.

Mrs. Wolff. [*After a pause.*] If only you wasn't such a coward!—We might get a few loads o' wood in a hurry, an' we wouldn't have to work ourselves blue in the face neither.—No, nor we wouldn't have to go very far for 'em.

Julius. Aw, let me eat a bite, will you?

Mrs. Wolff. [*Punches his head amicably.*] Don't always be so rough. I'm goin' to be good to you now for onct. You watch. [*Fetching a bottle of whisky and showing it to him.*] Here! See? I brought that for you. Now you c'n make a friendly face, all right.

[*She fills a glass for her husband.*]

Julius. [*Drinks.*] That's fine—in this cold weather—fine.

Mrs. Wolff. Well, you see? Don't I take care o' you?

Julius. That was pretty good, pretty good all right.

[*He fills the glass anew and drinks.*]

Mrs. Wolff. [*After a pause. She is splitting kindling wood and eating a bite now and then.*] Wulkow—that feller—he's a regular rascal. He always—acts as if he was hard up.

Julius. Aw, he'd better shut up—he with his trade!

Mrs. Wolff. You heard that about the beaver coat, didn't you?

Julius. Naw, I didn't hear nothin'.

Mrs. Wolff. [*With assumed carelessness.*] Didn't you hear the girl tell how Mrs. Krueger has given Krueger a fur coat?

Julius. Well, them people has the money.

Mrs. Wolff. That's true. An' then Wulkow was sayin' . . . you musta heard . . . that if he could get hold of a coat like that some day, he'd give as much as seventy crowns for it.

Julius. You just let him go and get into trouble his own self.

Mrs. Wolff. [*After a pause, refilling her husband's glass.*] Come now, you c'n stand another.

Julius. Well, go ahead, go ahead! What in . . .!

[MRS. WOLFF *gets out a little notebook and turns over the leaves.*]

Julius. How much is it we put aside since July?

Mrs. Wolff. About thirty crowns has been paid off.

Julius. An' that'll leave . . . leave . . .

Mrs. Wolff. That'll still leave seventy. You don't get along very fast this way. Fifty, sixty crowns—all in a lump; if you could add that onct! Then the lot would be paid for all right. Then maybe we could borrow a couple o' hundred and build up a few pretty rooms. We can't take no summer boarders like this an' it's the summer boarders what brings the money.

Julius. Well, go ahead! What are you . . .

Mrs. Wolff. [*Resolutely.*] My, but you're a slow critter, Julius! Would *you've* gone an' bought that lot? An' if we wanted to go an' sell it now, we could be gettin' twice over what we paid for it! I got a different kind of a nature! Lord, if you had one like it!

Julius. I'm workin' all right. What's the good o' all that?

Mrs. Wolff. You ain't goin' to get very far with all your work.

Julius. Well, I can't steal. I can't go an' get into trouble!

Mrs. Wolff. You're just stoopid, an' that's the way you'll always be. Nobody here ain't been talkin' o' stealin'. But if you don't risk nothin', you don't get nothin'. An' when onct you're rich, Julius, an' c'n go and sit in your own carridge, there ain't nobody what's goin' to ask where you got it! Sure, if we was to take it from poor people! But now suppose really—suppose we went over to the Kruegers and put the two loads o' wood on a sleigh an' took 'em into our shed—them people ain't no poorer on that account!

Julius. Wood? What you startin' after again now with wood?

Mrs. Wolff. Now that shows how you don't take notice o' nothin'! They c'n work your daughter till she drops; they c'n try an' make her drag in wood at ten o'clock in the evenin'. That's why she run away. An' you take that kind o' thing an' say thank you. Maybe you'd give the child a hidin' and send her back to the people.

Julius. Sure!—That's what!—What d'you think . . .

Mrs. Wolff. Things like that hadn't ought to go unpunished. If anybody hits me, I'll hit him back. That's what I says.

Julius. Well, did they go an' hit the girl?

Mrs. Wolff. Why should she be runnin' away, Julius? But no, there ain't no use tryin' to do anything with you. Now the wood is lyin' out there in the alley. An' if I was to say: all right, you abuse my children, I'll take your wood—a nice face you'd make.

Julius. I wouldn't do no such thing . . . I don't give a——! I c'n do more'n eat, too. I'd like to see! I wouldn't stand for nothin' like that. Beatin'!

Mrs. Wolff. Well, then, don't talk so much. Go an' get your cord. Show them people that you got some cuteness! The whole thing will be over in an hour. Then we c'n go to bed an' it's all right. An' you don't have to go out in the woods tomorrow. We'll have more fuel than we need.

Julius. Well, if it leaks out, it'll be all the same to me.

Mrs. Wolff. There ain't no reason why it should. But don't wake the girls.

Mitteldorf. [*From without.*] Mrs. Wolff! Mrs. Wolff! Are you still up?

Mrs. Wolff. Sure, Mitteldorf! Come right in! [*She opens the door.*]

Mitteldorf. [*Enters. He has an overcoat over his shabby uniform. His face has a Mephistophelian cast. His nose betrays an alcoholic coloring. His demeanor is gentle, almost timid. His speech is slow and dragging and unaccompanied by any change in expression.*] Good evenin', Mrs. Wolff.

Mrs. Wolff. I guess you mean to say: Good night!

Mitteldorf. I was around here once before a while ago. First I thought I saw a light, an' then, all of a sudden, it was dark again. Nobody didn't answer me neither. But this time there was a light an' no mistake, an' so I came back once more.

Mrs. Wolff. Well, what have you got for me now, Mitteldorf?

Mitteldorf. [*Has taken a seat, thinks a while and then says:*] That's what I came here for. I got a message for you from the Justice's wife.

Mrs. Wolff. She ain't wantin' me to do washin'?

Mitteldorf. [*Raises his eyebrows thoughtfully.*] That she does.

Mrs. Wolff. An' when?

Mitteldorf. Tomorrow.—Tomorrow mornin'.

Mrs. Wolff. An' you come in tellin' me that at twelve o'clock at night?

Mitteldorf. But tomorrow is the missis' wash day.

Mrs. Wolff. But a person ought to know that a few days ahead o' time.

Mitteldorf. That's a fac'. But don't go makin' a noise. I just plumb forgot all about it again. I got so many things to think of with my poor head, that sometimes I just naturally forgets things.

Mrs. Wolff. Well, Mitteldorf, I'll try an' arrange it. We always was good friends. You got enough on your shoulders, I suppose, with them twelve children o' yours at home, eh? You ain't got no call to make yourself out worse'n you are.

Mitteldorf. If you don't come in the mornin', I'll have a pretty tough time of it!

Mrs. Wolff. I'll come. You needn't go worryin'. There, take a drink. I guess you need it this weather. [*She gives him a glass of toddy.*] I just happened to have a bit o' hot water. You know, we gotta take a trip yet tonight—for fat geese over to Treptow. You don't get no time in the day. That can't be helped in this kind of a life. Poor people 's got to work themselves sick day an' night, an' rich people lies in bed snorin'.

Mitteldorf. I been given notice. Did you know that? The Justice has given me notice. I ain't keen enough after the people.

Mrs. Wolff. They wants you to be like an old watch dog, I suppose.

Mitteldorf. I'd rather not go home at all. When I gets there, it'll be nothin' but quarrelin'. She just drives me crazy with her reproaches.

Mrs. Wolff. Put your fingers in your ears!

Mitteldorf. An' then a man goes to the tavern a bit, so that the worries don't down him altogether; an' now he ain't to do that no more neither! He ain't to do nothin'. An' now I just come from a bit of a time there. A feller treated to a little keg.

Mrs. Wolff. You ain't goin' to be scared of a woman? If she scolds, scold harder; an' if she beats you, beat her back. Come here now—you're taller'n me—get me down them things off the shelf. An' Julius, you get the sleigh ready! [JULIUS *exit.*] How often have I got to tell you? [MITTELDORF *has taken cords and pulley lines from the high shelf on the wall.*] Get ready the big sleigh! You c'n hand them cords right down to him.

Julius. [*From without.*] I can't see!

Mrs. Wolff. What can't you do?

Julius. [*Appears in the doorway.*] I can't get that sleigh out alone! Everythin' is all mixed up in a heap here. An' there ain't nothin' to be done without a light.

Mrs. Wolff. Now you're helpless again—like always. [*Rapidly she puts shawls about her head and chest.*] You must wait, I'll come an' lend a hand. There's the lantern, Mitteldorf. [MITTELDORF *slowly takes a lantern and hands it to* MRS. WOLFF.] There! thank you. [*She puts the burning candle into the lantern.*] We'll put that in here an' then we c'n go. Now I'll help you drag out the sleigh. [*She goes ahead with the lantern.* MITTELDORF *follows her. In the door she turns around and hands the lantern to* MITTELDORF.] You c'n come an' hold the light for us a bit!

Mitteldorf. [*Holding the light and humming to himself.*] "Morningre-ed, morningre-ed . . ."

CURTAIN

THE SECOND ACT

Courtroom of JUSTICE VON WEHRHAHN. *A great, bare, white-washed room with three windows in the rear wall. The main door is in the left wall. Along the wall to the right stands the long official table covered with books, legal documents, etc.; behind it the chair of the* JUSTICE. *Near the center window are the clerk's chair and table. To the right is a bookcase of white wood, so arranged that it is within reach of the* JUSTICE *when he sits in his chair. The left wall is hidden by cases containing documents. In the foreground, beginning at the wall to the left, six chairs stand in a row. Their occupants would be seen by the spectator from behind. It is a bright forenoon in Winter.*

[*The clerk* GLASENAPP *sits scribbling at his table. He is a poverty-stricken, spectacled person.* JUSTICE VON WEHRHAHN, *carrying a roll of documents under his arm, enters rapidly.* WEHRHAHN *is about forty years old and wears a monocle. He makes the impression of a son of the landed nobility of Prussia. His official garb consists of a buttoned, black walking-coat, and very tall boots put on over his trousers. He speaks in what is almost a falsetto voice and carefully cultivates a military brevity of expression.*]

Wehrhahn. [*By the way, like one crushed by the weight of affairs.*] Mornin'.

Glasenapp. Servant, sir.

Wehrhahn. Anything happened, Glasenapp?

Glasenapp. [*Standing and looking through some papers.*] I've got to report, your honor—there was first, oh, yes—the innkeeper Fiebig. He begs for permission, your honor, to have music and dancing at his inn next Sunday.

Wehrhahn. Isn't that . . . perhaps you can tell me. Fiebig? There was some one who recently rented his hall . . . ?

Glasenapp. To the liberals. Quite right, your honor.

Wehrhahn. This same Fiebig?

Glasenapp. Yes, my lord.

Wehrhahn. We'll have to put a check-rein on him for a while.

[*The constable* MITTELDORF *enters.*]

Mitteldorf. Servant, my lord.

Wehrhahn. Listen here: once and for all—officially I am simply the Justice.

Mitteldorf. Yes, sir. As you wish, my—your honor, I meant to say.

Wehrhahn. I wish you would try to understand this fact: my being a baron is purely by the way. Is not, at all events, to be considered here. [*To* GLASENAPP.] Now I'd like to hear further, please. Wasn't the author Motes here?

Glasenapp. Yes, your honor.

Wehrhahn. Aha! So he *was* here! I confess that I am very curious. I hope that it was his intention to come back?

Glasenapp. He intended to be back here about half-past eleven.

Wehrhahn. Did he by any chance tell you anything?

Glasenapp. He came in the matter of Doctor Fleischer.

Wehrhahn. Well, now you may as well tell me—are you acquainted with this Doctor Fleischer?

Glasenapp. All I know is that he lives in the Villa Krueger.

Wehrhahn. And how long has he been living in this place?

Glasenapp. Well, I've been here since Michaelmas.

Wehrhahn. To be sure, you came here at the same time with me, about four months ago.

Glasenapp. [*Looking toward* MITTELDORF *for information.*] From what I hear the man has been living here about two years.

Wehrhahn. [*To* MITTELDORF.] I don't suppose you can give us any information?

Mitteldorf. Beggin' your pardon, he came Michaelmas a year ago.

Wehrhahn. At that time he moved here?

Mitteldorf. Exactly, your honor—from Berlin.

Wehrhahn. Have you any more intimate information about this individual?

Mitteldorf. All I know is his brother is cashier of a theater.

Wehrhahn. I didn't ask for information concerning his brother! What is his occupation?—What does he himself do? What is he?

Mitteldorf. I don't know as I can say anythin' particular. People do say that he's sick. I suppose he suffers from diabetes.

Wehrhahn. I'm quite indifferent as to the character of his malady. He can sweat syrup if it amuses him. *What* is he?

Glasenapp. [*Shrugging his shoulders.*] He calls himself a free spear in scholarship.

Wehrhahn. Lance! Lance! Not spear! A free lance.

Glasenapp. The bookbinder Hugk always does work for him; he has some books bound every week.

Wehrhahn. I wouldn't mind seeing what an individual of that kind reads.

Glasenapp. The postman thinks he must take in about twenty newspapers. Democratic ones, too.

Wehrhahn. You may summon Hugk to this court some time.

Glasenapp. Right away?

Wehrhahn. No, at a more convenient time. Tomorrow or the next day. Let him bring a few of the books in question with him. [*To* MITTELDORF.] You seem to take naps all day. Or perhaps the man has good cigars and knows how to invest them!

Mitteldorf. Your honor . . . !

Wehrhahn. Never mind! Never mind! I will inspect the necessary persons myself. My honorable predecessor has permitted a state of affairs to obtain that . . . ! We will change all that by degrees.—It is simply disgraceful for a police official to permit himself to be deceived by any one. That is, of course, entirely beyond your comprehension. [*To* GLASENAPP.] Didn't Motes say anything definite?

Glasenapp. I can't say that he did—nothing definite. He was of the opinion that your honor was informed . . .

Wehrhahn. In a very general way, I am. I have had my eye on the man in question for some time—on this Doctor Fleischer, I mean. Mr. Motes simply confirmed me in my own entirely correct judgment of his peculiar character.—What kind of reputation has Motes himself? [GLASENAPP *and* MITTELDORF *exchange glances and* GLASENAPP *shrugs his shoulders.*] Lives largely on credit, eh?

Glasenapp. He says he has a pension.

Wehrhahn. Pension?

Glasenapp. Well, you know he got shot in the eye.

Wehrhahn. So his pension is really paid as damages.

Glasenapp. Beggin' your honor's pardon, but if it's a question of damages the man inflicts more than he's ever received. Nobody's ever seen him have a penny for anything.

Wehrhahn. [*Amused.*] Is there anything else of importance?

Glasenapp. Nothing but minor matters, your honor—somebody giving notice——

Wehrhahn. That'll do; that'll do. Do you happen ever to have heard any reports to the effect that this Doctor Fleischer does not guard his tongue with particular care?

Glasenapp. Not that I know of at this moment.

Wehrhahn. Because that is the information that has come to me. He is said to have made illegal remarks concerning a number of exalted personages. However, all that will appear in good time. We can set to work now. Mitteldorf, have you anything to report?

Mitteldorf. They tell me that a theft has been committed during the night.

Wehrhahn. A theft? Where?

Mitteldorf. In the Villa Krueger.

Wehrhahn. What has been stolen?

Mitteldorf. Some firewood.

Wehrhahn. Last night, or when?

Mitteldorf. Just last night.

Wehrhahn. From whom does your information come?

Mitteldorf. My information? It come from . . . from . . .

Wehrhahn. Well, from whom? Out with it!

Mitteldorf. I heard it from—I got it from Doctor Fleischer.

Wehrhahn. Aha! You're in the habit then of conversing with him?

Mitteldorf. Mr. Krueger told me about it himself too.

Wehrhahn. The man is a nuisance with his perpetual complaints. He writes me about three letters a week. Either he has been cheated, or some one has broken his fence, or else some one has trespassed on his property. Nothing but one annoyance after another.

Motes. [*Enters. He laughs almost continually in a nervous way.*] Beg to bid you a good morning, your honor.

Wehrhahn. Ah, there you are. Very glad you came in. You can help me out with some information at once. A theft is said to have been committed at the Villa Krueger.

Motes. I don't live there any longer.

Wehrhahn. And nothing has come to your ears either?

Motes. Oh, I heard something about it, but nothing definite. As I was just passing by the Villa I saw them both looking for traces in the snow.

Wehrhahn. Is that so? Doctor Fleischer is assisting him. I take it for granted then that they're pretty thick together?

Motes. Inseparable in every sense, your honor.

Wehrhahn. Aha! As far as Fleischer is concerned—he interests me most of all. Take a seat, please. I confess that I didn't sleep more than half the night. This matter simply wouldn't let me sleep. The letter that you wrote me excited me to an extraordinary degree.—That is a matter of temperament, to be sure. The slumbers of my predecessor would scarcely have been disturbed.—As far as I am concerned I have made up my mind, so to speak, to go the whole way.—It is my function here to make careful tests and to exterminate undesirable elements.—Under the protection of my honorable predecessor the sphere of our activity has become a receptacle for refuse of various kinds: lives that cannot bear the light—outlawed individuals, enemies of royalty and of the realm. These people must be made to suffer.—As for yourself, Mr. Motes, you are an author?

Motes. I write on subjects connected with forestry and game.

Wehrhahn. In the appropriate technical journals, I take it. *A propos:* do you manage to make a living that way?

Motes. If one is well known, it can be done. I may gratefully say that I earn an excellent competency.

Wehrhahn. So you are a forester by profession?

Motes. I studied at the academy, your honor, and pursued my studies in Eberswalde. Shortly before the final examinations I met with this misfortune . . .

Wehrhahn. Ah, yes; I see you wear a bandage.

Motes. I lost an eye while hunting. Some bird shot flew into my right eye. The responsibility for the accident could not, unfortunately, be placed. And so I had to give up my career.

Wehrhahn. Then you do not receive a pension?

Motes. No. But I have fought my way through pretty well now. My name is getting to be known in a good many quarters.

Wehrhahn. H'm.—Are you by any chance acquainted with my brother-in-law?

Motes. Yes, indeed—Chief Forester von Wachsmann. I correspond a good deal with him and furthermore we are fellow members of the society for the breeding of pointers.

Wehrhahn. [*Somewhat relieved.*] Ah, so you are really acquainted with him? I'm very glad indeed to hear that. That makes the whole matter easier of adjustment and lays a foundation for mutual confidence. It serves to remove any possible obstacle.—You wrote me in your letter, you recall, that you had had the opportunity of observing this Doctor Fleischer. Now tell me, please, what you know.

Motes. [*Coughs.*] When I—about a year ago—took up my residence in the Villa Krueger, I had naturally no suspicion of the character of the people with whom I was to dwell under one roof.

Wehrhahn. You were acquainted with neither Krueger nor Fleischer?

Motes. No; but you know how things go. Living in one house with them I couldn't keep to myself entirely.

Wehrhahn. And what kind of people visited the house?

Motes. [*With a significant gesture.*] Ah!

Wehrhahn. I understand.

Motes. Tom, Dick and Harry—democrats, of course.

Wehrhahn. Were regular meetings held?

Motes. Every Thursday, so far as I could learn.

Wehrhahn. That will certainly bear watching.—And you no longer associate with those people?

Motes. A point was reached where intercourse with them became impossible, your honor.

Wehrhahn. You were repelled, eh?

Motes. The whole business became utterly repulsive to me.

Wehrhahn. The unlawful atmosphere that obtained there, the impudent jeering at exalted personages—all that, I take it, you could no longer endure?

Motes. I stayed simply because I thought it might serve some good purpose.

Wehrhahn. But finally you gave notice after all?

Motes. I moved out, yes, your honor.

Wehrhahn. And finally you made up your mind to——

Motes. I considered it my duty——

Wehrhahn. To lodge notice with the authorities.—I consider that very worthy in you. —So he used a certain kind of expression—we will make a record of all that later, of course—a certain kind of expression in reference to a personage whose exalted station demands our reverence.

Motes. He certainly did that, your honor.

Wehrhahn. You would be willing, if necessary, to confirm that by oath.

Motes. I would be willing to confirm it.

Wehrhahn. In fact, you will be obliged to make such confirmation.

Motes. Yes, your honor.

Wehrhahn. Of course it would be best if we could procure an additional witness.

Motes. I would have to look about. The trouble is, though, that the man is very prodigal of his money.

Wehrhahn. Ah, just wait a minute. Krueger is coming in now. I will first attend to his business. At all events I am very grateful to you for your active assistance. One is absolutely dependent on such assistance if one desires to accomplish anything nowadays.

Krueger. [*Enters hastily and excitedly.*] O Lord, O Lord! Good day, your honor.

Wehrhahn. [*To* MOTES.] Pardon me just a moment. [*In an arrogant and inquisitorial tone to* KRUEGER.] What is it you want?

[KRUEGER *is a small man, somewhat hard of hearing and nearly seventy years old. He is slightly bowed with age; his left shoulder hangs somewhat. Otherwise he is still very vigorous and emphasizes his remarks by violent gesticulations. He wears a fur cap which he is now holding in his hand, a brown winter overcoat and a thick woolen shawl around his neck.*]

Krueger. [*Literally charged with rage, explodes.*] I've been robbed, your honor.

[*Getting his breath, he wipes the perspiration from his forehead with a handkerchief and, after the manner of people with impaired hearing, stares straight at the mouth of the* JUSTICE.]

Wehrhahn. Robbed, eh?

Krueger. [*Already exasperated.*] Robbed is what I said. I have been robbed. Two whole loads of wood have been stolen from me.

Wehrhahn. [*Looking around at those present, half-smiling, says lightly:*] Not the least thing of that kind has happened here recently.

Krueger. [*Putting his hand to his ear.*] What? Not the slightest thing? Then perhaps I came into this office for fun?

Wehrhahn. You need not become violent. What is your name, by the way?

Krueger. [*Taken aback.*] My name?

Wehrhahn. Yes, your name!

Krueger. So my name isn't known to you? I thought we had had the pleasure before.

Wehrhahn. Sorry. Can't say that I have a clear recollection. And that wouldn't matter officially anyhow.

Krueger. [*Resignedly.*] My name is Krueger.

Wehrhahn. Capitalist by any chance?

Krueger. [*With extreme and ironic vehemence.*] Exactly—capitalist and houseowner here.

Wehrhahn. Identify yourself, please.

Krueger. I—identify myself! My name is Krueger. I don't think we need go to any further trouble. I've been living here for thirty years. Every child in the place knows me.

Wehrhahn. The length of your residence here doesn't concern me. It is my business merely to ascertain your identity. Is this gentleman known to you—Mr. Motes? [MOTES *half rises with an angry expression.*] Ah, yes, I understand. Kindly sit down. Well, Glasenapp?

Glasenapp. Yes, at your service. It is Mr. Krueger all right.

Wehrhahn. Very well.—So you have been robbed of wood?

Krueger. Of wood, exactly. Two loads of pine wood.

Wehrhahn. Did you have the wood stored in your shed?

Krueger. [*Growing violent again.*] That's quite a separate matter. That's the substance of another complaint I have to make.

Wehrhahn. [*With an ironic laugh and looking at the others.*] Still another one?

Krueger. What do you mean?

Wehrhahn. Nothing. You may go ahead with your statement. The wood, it appears, was not in your shed?

Krueger. The wood was in the garden, that is, in front of the garden.

Wehrhahn. In other words; it lay in the street.

Krueger. It lay in front of the garden on my property.

Wehrhahn. So that any one could pick it up without further ado?

Krueger. And that is just the fault of the servant-girl. She was to take the wood in last night.

Wehrhahn. And it dropped out of her mind.

Krueger. She refused to do it. And when I insisted on her doing it, she ended by running away. I intend to bring suit against her parents. I intend to claim full damages.

Wehrhahn. You may do about that as you please. It isn't likely to help you very greatly. —Now is there any one whom you suspect of the theft?

Krueger. No. They're all a set of thieves around here.

Wehrhahn. You will please to avoid such general imputations. You must surely be able to offer me a clue of some kind.

Krueger. Well, you can't expect me to accuse any one at random.

Wehrhahn. Who lives in your house beside yourself?

Krueger. Doctor Fleischer.

Wehrhahn. [*As if trying to recall something.*] Doctor Fleischer? Doctor Fleischer? Why, he is a—— What is he anyhow?

Krueger. He is a thoroughly learned man, that's what he is—thoroughly learned.

Wehrhahn. And I suppose that you and he are very intimate with each other.

Krueger. That is my business, with whom I happen to be intimate. That has no bearing on the matter in hand, it seems to me.

Wehrhahn. How is one to discover anything under such circumstances? You must give me a hint, at least!

Krueger. Must I? Goodness, gracious me! Must I? Two loads of wood have been stolen from me! I simply come to give information concerning the theft . . .

Wehrhahn. But you must have a theory of some kind. The wood must necessarily have been stolen by somebody.

Krueger. Wha . . . Yes . . . well, I didn't do it! I of all people didn't do it!

Wehrhahn But my dear man . . .

Krueger. Wha . . . ? My name is Krueger.

Wehrhahn. [*Interrupting and apparently bored.*] M-yes.—Well, Glasenapp, just make a record of the facts.—And now, Mr. Krueger, what's this business about your maid? The girl, you say, ran away?

Krueger. Yes, that's exactly what she did —ran off to her parents.

Wehrhahn. Do her parents live in this place?

Krueger. [*Not having heard correctly.*] I'm not concerned with her face.

Wehrhahn. I asked whether the parents of the girl live here?

Glasenapp. She's the daughter of the washerwoman Wolff.

Wehrhahn. Wolff—the same one who's washing for us to-day, Glasenapp?

Glasenapp. The same, your honor.

Wehrhahn. [*Shaking his head.*] Very strange indeed!—She's a very honest and a very industrious woman.—[*To* KRUEGER.] Is that a fact? Is she the daughter of the woman in question?

Krueger. She is the daughter of the washerwoman Wolff.

Wehrhahn. And has the girl come back?

Krueger. Up to the present time the girl has not come back.

Wehrhahn. Then suppose we call in Mrs. Wolff herself. Mitteldorf! You act as though you were very tired. Well, go across the yard. Mrs. Wolff is to come to me at once. I beg you to be seated, Mr. Krueger.

Krueger. [*Sitting down and sighing.*] O Lord! O Lord! What a life!

Wehrhahn. [*Softly to* GLASENAPP *and* MOTES.] I'm rather curious to see what will develop. There's something more than meets the eye in all this. I think a great deal of

Mrs. Wolff. The woman works enough for four men. My wife assures me that if Wolff doesn't come she has to hire two women in her place.—Her opinions aren't half bad either.

Motes. She wants her daughters to go on the operatic stage . . .

Wehrhahn. Oh, of course, she may have a screw loose in that respect. But that's no fault of character. What have you hanging there, Mr. Motes?

Motes. They're some wire snares. I'm taking them to the forester Seidel.

Wehrhahn. Do let me see one of those things. [*He takes one and looks at it closely.*] And in these things the poor beasts are slowly throttled to death.

[MRS. WOLFF *enters, followed by* MITTELDORF. *She is drying her hands, which are still moist from the wash tub.*]

Mrs. Wolff. [*Unembarrassed, cheerfully, with a swift glance at the snares.*] Here I am. What's up now? What'm I bein' wanted for?

Wehrhahn. Mrs. Wolff, is this gentleman known to you?

Mrs. Wolff. Which one of 'em? [*Pointing with her finger at* KRUEGER.] This here, this is Mr. Krueger. I guess I know him all right. Good mornin', Mr. Krueger.

Wehrhahn. Your daughter is in Mr. Krueger's service?

Mrs. Wolff. Who? My daughter? That's so—Leontine. [*To* KRUEGER.] But then, she run away from you, didn't she?

Krueger. [*Enraged.*] She did indeed.

Wehrhahn. [*Interrupting.*] Now wait a moment.

Mrs. Wolff. What kind o' trouble did you have together?

Wehrhahn. Mrs. Wolff, you listen to me. Your daughter must return to Mr. Krueger at once.

Mrs. Wolff. Oh, no, we'd rather keep her at home now.

Wehrhahn. That can't be done quite so easily as you think. Mr. Krueger has the right, if he wishes to exert it, of calling in the help of the police. In that case we would have to take your daughter back by force.

Mrs. Wolff. But my husband just happened to take it into his head. He's just made up his mind not to let the girl go no more. An' when my husband takes a notion like that into his head . . . The trouble is: all you men has such awful tempers!

Wehrhahn. Suppose you let that go, for the moment, Mrs. Wolff. How long has your daughter been at home?

Mrs. Wolff. She came back last night.

Wehrhahn. Last night? Very well. She had been told to carry wood into the shed and she refused.

Mrs. Wolff. Eh, is that so? Refused? That girl o' mine don't refuse to do work. An' I wouldn't advise her to do that kind o' thing neither.

Wehrhahn. You hear what Mrs. Wolff says.

Mrs. Wolff. That girl has always been a willin' girl. If she'd ever refused to lend a hand . . .

Krueger. She simply refused to carry in the wood!

Mrs. Wolff. Yes, drag in wood! At half-past ten at night! People who asks such a thing of a child like that——

Wehrhahn. The essential thing, however, Mrs. Wolff, is this: the wood was left out over night and has been stolen. And so . . .

Krueger. [*Losing self-control.*] You will replace that wood, Mrs. Wolff.

Wehrhahn. All that remains to be seen, if you will wait.

Krueger. You will indemnify me for that wood to the last farthing!

Mrs. Wolff. An' is that so? That'd be a new way o' doin' things! Did I, maybe, go an' steal your wood?

Wehrhahn. You had better let the man calm down, Mrs. Wolff.

Mrs. Wolff. No, when Mr. Krueger comes round me with things like that, payin' for wood and such like, he ain't goin' to have no luck. I always been friendly with them people —that's sure. Nobody can't complain o' nothin' s'far 's I'm concerned. But if things gets to this point, then I'd rather up and say my say just exactly how I feel, you know. I do my dooty and that's enough. There ain't nobody in the whole village what c'n say anythin' against me. But I ain't goin' to let *nobody* walk all over me!

Wehrhahn. You need not wear yourself out, Mrs. Wolff. You have absolutely no cause for it. Just remain calm, quite calm. You're not entirely unknown to me, after all. There isn't a human being who would undertake to deny your industry and honesty. So let us hear what you have to say in answer to the plaintiff.

Krueger. The woman can't possibly have anything to say!

Mrs. Wolff. Hol' on, now, everybody! How's that, I'd like to know? Ain't the girl my daughter? An' I'm not to have anythin' to say! You gotta go an' look for some kind of a fool! You don't know much about me. I don't have to hide what I thinks from no one—no, not from his honor hisself, an' a good deal less from you, you may take your oath on that!

Wehrhahn. I quite understand your excitement, Mrs. Wolff. But if you desire to serve the cause at issue, I would advise you to remain calm.

Mrs. Wolff. That's what a person gets. I been washin' clothes for them people these ten years. All that time we ain't had a fallin' out. An' now, all of a sudden, they treat you this way. I ain't comin' to your house no more, you c'n believe me.

Krueger. You don't need to. There are other washerwomen.

Mrs. Wolff. An' the vegetables an' the fruit out o' your garden—you c'n just go an' get somebody else to sell 'em for you.

Krueger. I can get rid of all that. There's no fear. All you needed to have done was to have taken a stick to that girl of yours and sent her back.

Mrs. Wolff. I won't have no daughter of mine abused.

Krueger. Who has been abusing your daughter, I'd like to know!

Mrs. Wolff. [*To* WEHRHAHN.] The girl came back to me no better'n a skeleton.

Krueger. Then let her not spend all her night dancing.

Mrs. Wolff. She sleeps like the dead all day.

Wehrhahn. [*Past* MRS. WOLFF *to* KRUEGER.] By the way, where did you buy the wood in question?

Mrs. Wolff. Is this thing goin' to last much longer?

Wehrhahn. Why, Mrs. Wolff?

Mrs. Wolff. Why, on account o' the washin'. If I wastes my time standin' round here, I can't get done.

Wehrhahn. We can't take that into consideration here, Mrs. Wolff.

Mrs. Wolff. An' your wife? What's she goin' to say? You c'n go an' settle it with her, your honor.

Wehrhahn. It will only last another minute, anyhow.—You tell us frankly, Mrs. Wolff—you know the whole village. Whom do you consider capable of the crime in question? Who could possibly have stolen the wood?

Mrs. Wolff. I can't tell you nothin' about that, your honor.

Wehrhahn. And nothing suspicious came to your attention?

Mrs. Wolff. I wasn't even at home last night. I had to go over to Treptow to buy geese.

Wehrhahn. At what time was that?

Mrs. Wolff. A little after ten. Mitteldorf, he was there when we started.

Wehrhahn. And no team carrying wood met you?

Mrs. Wolff. No, nothin' like that.

Wehrhahn. How about you, Mitteldorf, did you notice nothing?

Mitteldorf. [*After some thought.*] No, I didn't notice nothin' suspicious.

Wehrhahn. Of course not. I might have known that. [*To* KRUEGER.] Well, where did you buy the wood?

Krueger. Why do you have to know that?

Wehrhahn. You will kindly leave that to me.

Krueger. I naturally bought the wood from the department of forestry.

Wehrhahn. Why naturally? I don't see that at all. There are, for instance, private wood yards. Personally I buy my wood from Sandberg. Why shouldn't you buy yours from a dealer? One really almost gets a better bargain.

Krueger. [*Impatiently.*] I haven't any more time, your honor.

Wehrhahn. What do you mean by that? Time? You have no time? Have you come to me, or do I come to you? Am I taking up your time or are you taking up mine?

Krueger. That's your business. That's what you're here for.

Wehrhahn. Perhaps I'm your bootblack, eh?

Krueger. Perhaps I've stolen silver spoons! I forbid you to use that tone to me. You're not a corporal and I'm not a recruit.

Wehrhahn. Well, that passes. . . . Don't shout so!

Krueger. It is you who do all the shouting.

Wehrhahn. You are half deaf. It is necessary for me to shout.

Krueger. You shout all the time. You shout at every one who comes in here.

Wehrhahn. I don't shout at any one. Be silent.

Krueger. You carry on as if you were heaven knows what! You annoy the whole place with your chicanery!

Wehrhahn. I'm only making a beginning. I'll make you a good deal more uncomfortable before I get through.

Krueger. That doesn't make the slightest impression on me. You're a pretentious nobody—nothing else. You simply want to cut a big figure. As though you were the king himself, you . . .

Wehrhahn. I *am* king in this place.

Krueger. [*Laughs heartily.*] You'd better let that be. In my estimation you're nothing at all. You're nothing but an ordinary Justice of the Peace. In fact, you've got to learn to be one first.

Wehrhahn. Sir, if you don't hold your tongue this minute . . .

Krueger. Then, I suppose, you'll have me arrested. I wouldn't advise you to go to such lengths after all. You might put yourself into a dangerous position.

Wehrhahn. Dangerous? [*To* MOTES.] Did you hear that? [*To* KRUEGER.] And however much you intrigue, you and your admirable followers, and however you try to undermine my position—you won't force me to abandon my station.

Krueger. Good heavens! *I* try to undermine your position? Your whole personality is far too unimportant. But you may take my word for this, that if you don't change your tactics completely, you will cause so much trouble that you will make yourself quite impossible.

Wehrhahn. [*To* MOTES.] I suppose, Mr. Motes, that one must consider his age.

Krueger. I beg to have my complaint recorded.

Wehrhahn. [*Turning over the papers on his table.*] You will please to send in your complaint in writing. I have no time at this moment.

[KRUEGER *looks at him in consternation, turns around vigorously, and leaves the office without a word.*]

Wehrhahn. [*After a pause of embarrassment.*] That's the way people annoy me with trifles.—Ugh!—[*To* MRS. WOLFF.] You'd better get back to your washing.—I tell you, my dear Motes, a position like mine is made hard enough. If one were not conscious of what one represents here—one might sometimes be tempted to throw up the whole business. But as it is, one's motto must be to stand one's ground bravely. For, after all, what is it that we are defending? The most sacred goods of the nation!——

CURTAIN

THE THIRD ACT

It is about eight o'clock in the morning. The scene is the dwelling of MRS. WOLFF. *Water for coffee is boiling on the oven.*

[MRS. WOLFF *is sitting on a footstool and counting out money on the seat of a chair.* JULIUS *enters, carrying a slaughtered rabbit.*]

Julius. You better go an' hide that there money!

Mrs. Wolff. [*Absorbed in her calculations, gruffly.*] Don't bother me!

[*Silence.* JULIUS *throws the rabbit on a stool. He wanders about irresolutely, picking up one object after another. Finally he sets about blacking a boot. From afar the blowing of a huntsman's horn is heard.*]

Julius. [*Listens. Anxious and excited.*] I axed you to go an' hide that there money!

Mrs. Wolff. An' I'm tellin' you not to bother me, Julius. Just let that fool Motes tootle all he wants. He's out in the woods an' ain't thinkin' o' nothin'.

Julius. You go right ahead and land us in jail!

Mrs. Wolff. Don't talk that fool talk. The girl's comin'.

Adelaide. [*Comes in, just out of bed.*] Good mornin', Mama.

Mrs. Wolff. Did you sleep well?

Adelaide. You was out in the night, wasn't you?

Mrs. Wolff. I guess you musta been dreamin'. Hurry now! Bring in some wood, an' be quick about it!

[ADELAIDE, *playing ball with an orange, goes toward the door.*]

Mrs. Wolff. Where did you get *that*?

Adelaide. Schoebel gave it to me out o' his shop. [*Exit.*]

Mrs. Wolff. I don't want you to take no presents from that feller.—Come here, Julius! Listen to me! Here I got ninety-nine crowns! That's always the same old way with Wulkow. He just cheated us out o' one, because he promised to give a hundred.—I'm puttin' the money in this bag, y'understand? Now go an' get a hoe and dig a hole in the goatshed—but right under the manger where it's dry. An' then you c'n put the bag into the hole. D'you hear me? An' take a flat stone an' put it across. But don't be so long doin' it.

Julius. I thought you was goin' to pay an installment to Fischer!

Mrs. Wolff. Can't you never do what I tell you to? Don't poke round so long, y'understand?

Julius. Don't you go and rile me or I'll give you somethin' to make you stop. I don't hold with that money stayin' in this here house.

Mrs. Wolff. Well, what's goin' to be done with it?

Julius. You take it an' you carry it over to Fischer. You said we was goin' to use it to make a payment to him.

Mrs. Wolff. You're stoopid enough to make a person sick. If it wasn't for me you'd just go to the dogs.

Julius. Go on with your screamin'! That's right.

Mrs. Wolff. A person can't help screamin', you're such a fool. If you had some sense, I wouldn't have to scream. If we go an' takes that money to Fischer now, you look out an' see what happens!

Julius. That's what I say. Look at the whole dam' business. What's the good of it to me if I gotta go to jail!

Mrs. Wolff. Now it's about time you was keepin' still.

Julius. You can't scream no louder, can you?

Mrs. Wolff. I ain't goin' to get me a new tongue on your account. You raise a row . . . just as hard as you can, all on account o' this bit o' business. You just look out for yourself an' not for me. Did you throw the key in the river?

Julius. Has I had a chanst to get down there yet?

Mrs Wolff. Then it's about time you was gettin' there! D'you want 'em to find the key on you? [JULIUS *is about to go.*] Oh, wait a minute, Julius. Let me have the key!

Julius. What you goin' to do with it?

Mrs. Wolff. [*Hiding the key about her person.*] That ain't no business o' yours; that's mine [*She pours coffee beans into the hand-mill and begins to grind.*] Now you go out to the shed; then you c'n come back an' drink your coffee.

Julius. If I'd ha' known all that before. Aw!

[JULIUS *exit.* ADELAIDE *enters, carrying a large apron full of firewood.*]

Mrs. Wolff. Where d'you go an' get that wood?

Adelaide. Why, from the new blocks o' pine.

Mrs. Wolff. You wasn't to use that new wood yet.

Adelaide. [*Dropping the wood on the floor in front of the oven.*] That don't do no harm, Mama, if it's burned up!

Mrs. Wolff. You think you know a lot! What are you foolin' about? You grow up a bit an' then talk!

Adelaide. I know where it comes from!

Mrs. Wolff. What do you mean, girl?

Adelaide. I mean the wood.

Mrs. Wolff. Don't go jabberin' now; we bought that at a auction.

Adelaide. [*Playing ball with her orange.*] Oh, Lord, if that was true! But you just went and took it!

Mrs. Wolff. What's that you say?

Adelaide. It's just taken. That's the wood from Krueger's, Mama. Leontine told me.

Mrs. Wolff. [*Cuffs her head.*] There you got an answer. We ain't no thieves. Now go an' get your lessons. An' do 'em nice! I'll come an' look 'em over later!

Adelaide. [*Exit. From the adjoining room.*] I thought I could go skatin'.

Mrs. Wolff. An' your lessons for your confirmation? I guess you forgot them!

Adelaide. That don't come till Tuesday.

Mrs. Wolff. It's tomorrow! You go an' study your verses. I'll come in an' hear you say 'em later.

Adelaide. [*Loud yawning is heard from the adjoining room. Then she says:*]

"Jesus to his disciples said,
Use your fingers to eat your bread."

[JULIUS *comes back.*]

Mrs. Wolff. Well, Julius, did you go an' do what I told you?

Julius. If you don't like my way o' doin', go an' do things yourself.

Mrs. Wolff. God knows that *is* the best way—always. [*She pours out two cupfuls of coffee, one for him and one for herself, and places the two cups with bread and butter on a wooden chair.*] Here, drink your coffee.

Julius. [*Sitting down and cutting himself some bread.*] I hope Wulkow's been able to get away!

Mrs. Wolff. In this thaw!

Julius. Even if it is thawin', you can't tell.

Mrs. Wolff. An' you needn't care if it do freeze a bit; he ain't goin' to be stuck. I guess he's a good way up the canal by this time.

Julius. Well, I hope he ain't lyin' under the bridge this minute.

Mrs. Wolff. For my part he can be lyin' where he wants to.

Julius. You c'n take it from me, y'understan'? That there man Wulkow is goin' to get into a hell of a hole some day.

Mrs. Wolff. That's his business; that ain't none o' ours.

Julius. Trouble is we'd all be in the same hole. You just let 'em go an' find that coat on him!

Mrs. Wolff. What coat are you talkin' about?

Julius. Krueger's, o' course!

Mrs. Wolff. Don't you go talkin' rot like that, y'understan'? An' don't go an' give yourself a black eye on account o' other people's affairs!

Julius. I guess them things concerns me!

Mrs. Wolff. Concerns you—rot! That don't concern you at all That's my business an' not yours. You ain't no man at all; you're nothin' but an old woman!—Here you got some change. Now hurry an' get out o' here. Go over to Feibig and take a drink. I don't care if you have a good time all day Sunday. [*A knocking is heard.*] Come right in! Come right in, any one that wants to!

[DR. FLEISCHER *enters, leading his little son of five by the hand.* FLEISCHER *is twenty-seven years old. He wears one of the Jaeger reform suits. His hair, beard, and moustache are all coal-black. His eyes are deep-set; his voice, as a rule, gentle. He displays, at every moment, a touching anxiety for the child.*]

Mrs. Wolff. [*Jubilantly.*] Lord! Is little Philip comin' to see us once more? Now, ain't that fine? Now I really feel proud o' that! [*She gets hold of the child and takes off his overcoat.*] Come now an' take off your coat. It's warm back here an' you ain't goin' to be cold.

Fleischer. Mrs. Wolff, there's a draught. I believe there's a draught.

Mrs. Wolff. Oh, he ain't so weak as all that. A bit o' draught ain't goin' to hurt this little feller!

Fleischer. Oh, but it will, I assure you. You have no idea. He catches cold so easily! Exercise, Philip! Keep moving a little.

[PHILIP *jerks his shoulders back with a pettish exclamation.*]

Fleischer. Come now, Philip. You'll end by being ill. All you have to do is to walk slowly up and down.

Philip. [*Naughtily.*] But I don't want to.

Mrs. Wolff. Let him do like he wants to.

Fleischer. Well, good morning, Mrs Wolff.

Mrs. Wolff. Good morning, Doctor. I'm glad to see you comin' in onct more.

Fleischer. Good morning, Mr. Wolff.

Julius. Good mornin', Mr. Fleischer.

Mrs. Wolff. You're very welcome. Please sit down.

Fleischer. We have just a few minutes to stay.

Mrs. Wolff. Well, if we has such a fine visit paid us so early in the mornin', we're sure to have a lucky day this day. [*Kneeling down by the child.*] Ain't it so, my boy? You'll bring us good luck, won't you?

Philip. [*Excitedly.*] I went to ze zological darden; I saw ze storks zere, an' zey bit each ozzer wis zeir dolden bills.

Mrs. Wolff. Well now, you don't mean to say so! You're tellin' me a little fib, ain't you? [*Hugging and kissing the child.*] Lord, child, I could just eat you up, eat you right up. Mr. Fleischer, I'm goin' to keep this boy. This is my boy. You're my boy, ain't you? An' how's your mother, eh?

Philip. She's well an' she sends her redards an' you'll please tome in ze morning to wash.

Mrs. Wolff. Well now, just listen to that. A little feller like that an' he can give all that message already! [*To* FLEISCHER.] Won't you sit down, just a bit?

Fleischer. The boy bothers me about boating. Is it possible to go?

Mrs. Wolff. Oh, sure. The Spree is open. My girl there c'n row you out a way.

Fleischer. The boy won't stop about it! He's just taken that into his head.

Adelaide. [*Showing herself in the door that leads to the next room, beckons to* PHILIP.] Come, Philip, I'll show you somethin' real fine!

[PHILIP *gives a stubborn screech.*]

Fleischer. Now, Philip, you mustn't be naughty!

Adelaide. Just look at that fine orange!

[PHILIP'S *face is wreathed in smiles. He takes a few steps in* ADELAIDE'S *direction.*]

Fleischer. Go ahead, but don't beg!

Adelaide. Come on! Come on! We'll eat this orange together now.

[*She walks in the child's direction, takes him by the hand, holds up the orange temptingly, and both go, now quite at one, into the next room.*]

Mrs. Wolff. [*Following the child with her eyes.*] No, that boy, I could just sit an' look at him. I don't know, when I see a boy like that . . . [*She takes up a corner of her apron and wipes her eyes.*] . . . I feel as if I had to bawl right out.

Fleischer. Did you have a boy like that once?

Mrs. Wolff. That I had. But what's the use o' all that? You can't make people come back to life. You see—things like that—that's life . . . [*A pause.*]

Fleischer. One can't be careful enough with children.

Mrs. Wolff. You can go an' be as careful as you want to be. What is to be, will be. [*A pause.—Shaking her head.*] What trouble did you have with Mr. Motes?

Fleischer. I? None at all! What trouble should I have had with him?

Mrs. Wolff. Oh, I was just thinkin'.

Fleischer. How old is your daughter anyhow?

Mrs. Wolff. She'll be out o' school this Easter. Why? Would you like to have her? I wouldn't mind her goin' into service if it's with you.

Fleischer. I don't see why not. That wouldn't be half bad.

Mrs. Wolff. She's grown up to be a strong kind o' body. Even if she is a bit young, she c'n work most as well as any one, I tell you. An' I tell you another thing. She's a scamp now an' then; she don't always do right. But she ain't no fool. That girl's got genius.

Fleischer. That's quite possible, no doubt.

Mrs. Wolff. You just let her go an' recite a single piece for you—just once—a pome, or somethin'. An' I tell you, Doctor, you ain't goin' to be able to get through shiverin'. You c'n possibly call her in some day when you got visitors from Berlin. All kinds o' writers comes to your house, I believe. An' she ain't backward; she'll sail right in. Oh, she does say pieces *that* beautiful.—[*With a sudden change of manner.*] Now I want to give you a bit o' advice; only you mustn't be offended.

Fleischer. I'm never offended by good advice.

Mrs. Wolff. First thing, then: Don't give away so much. Nobody ain't goin' to thank you for it. You don't get nothin' but ingratitude.

Fleischer. Why, I don't give away very much, Mrs. Wolff.

Mrs. Wolff. That's all right. I know. An' the more you talk, the more scared people gets. First thing they says: that's a demercrat. You can't be too careful talkin'.

Fleischer. In what way am I to take all that, Mrs. Wolff?

Mrs. Wolff. You c'n go an' you c'n think what you please. But you gotta be careful when it comes to talkin', or you sit in jail before you know it.

Fleischer. [*Turns pale.*] Well, now, look here, but that's nonsense, Mrs. Wolff.

Mrs. Wolff. No, no, I tell you that's serious. An' be careful o' that feller, whatever you do!

Fleischer. Whom do you mean by that?

Mrs. Wolff. The same man we was talkin' about a while ago.

Fleischer. Motes, you mean?

Mrs. Wolff. I ain't namin' no names. You must ha' had some kind o' trouble with that feller.

Fleischer. I don't even associate with him any longer.

Mrs. Wolff. Well, you see, that's just what I've been thinkin'.

Fleischer. Nobody could possibly blame me for that, Mrs. Wolff.

Mrs. Wolff. An' I ain't blamin' you for it.

Fleischer. It would be a fine thing, wouldn't it—to associate with a swindler, a notorious swindler.

Mrs. Wolff. That man is a swindler; you're right there.

Fleischer. Now he's moved over to Dreier's. That poor woman will have a hard time getting her rent. And whatever she has, she'll get rid of it. Why, a fellow like that—he's a regular jail-bird.

Mrs. Wolff. Sometimes, you know, he'll say things . . .

Fleischer. Is that so? About me? Well, I *am* curious.

Mrs. Wolff. I believe you was heard to say somethin' bad about some high person, or somethin' like that.

Fleischer. H'm. You don't know anything definite, I dare say?

Mrs. Wolff. He's mighty thick with Wehrhahn, that's certain. But I tell you what. You go over to old mother Dreier. That old witch is beginnin' to smell a rat. First they was as nice as can be to her; now they're eatin' her outta house and home!

Fleischer. Oh, pshaw! The whole thing is nonsense.

Mrs. Wolff. You c'n go to the Dreier woman. That don't do no harm. She c'n tell you a story . . . He wanted to get her into givin' false witness . . . That shows the kind o' man you gotta deal with.

Fleischer. Of course, I might go there. It can do no harm. But, in the end, the whole matter is indifferent to me. It would be the deuce of a world, if a fellow like that . . . You just let him come!—Here, Philip, Philip! Where are you? We've got to go.

Adelaide's Voice. Oh, we're lookin' at such pretty pictures.

Fleischer. What do you think of that other business, anyhow?

Mrs. Wolff. What business?

Fleischer. Haven't you heard anything yet?

Mrs. Wolff. [*Restlessly.*] Well, what was I sayin'? . . . [*Impatiently.*] Hurry, Julius, an' go, so's you c'n get back in time for dinner. [*To* FLEISCHER.] We killed a rabbit for dinner today. Ain't you ready yet, Julius?

Julius. Well, give me a chanct to find my cap.

Mrs. Wolff. I can't stand seein' anybody just foolin' round that way, as if it didn't make no difference about today or tomorrow. I like to see things move along.

Fleischer. Why, last night, at Krueger's, they . . .

Mrs. Wolff. Do me a favor, Doctor, an' don't talk to me about that there man. I'm that angry at him! That man hurt my feelin's too bad. The way we was—him an' me, for so long—an' then he goes and tries to blacken my character with all them people. [*To* JULIUS.] Are you goin' or not?

Julius. I'm goin' all right; don't get so huffy. Good mornin' to you, Mr. Fleischer.

Fleischer. Good morning, Mr. Wolff.

[JULIUS *exit.*]

Mrs. Wolff. Well, as I was sayin' . . .

Fleischer. That time when his wood was stolen, I suppose he quarreled with you. But he's repented of that long since.

Mrs. Wolff. That man repent!

Fleischer. You may believe me all the same, Mrs. Wolff. And especially after this last affair. He has a very high opinion of you indeed. The best thing would be if you were to be reconciled.

Mrs. Wolff. We might ha' talked together like sensible people, but for him to go an' run straight to the police—no, no!

Fleischer. Well, the poor little old couple *is* having bad luck: only a week ago their wood, and now the fur coat . . .

Mrs. Wolff. Are you comin' to your great news now? Out with it!

Fleischer. Well, it's a clear case of burglary.

Mrs. Wolff. Some more stealin? Don't make fun o' me!

Fleischer. Yes, and this time it's a perfectly new fur coat.

Mrs. Wolff. Well now, you know, pretty soon I'll move away from here. That's a crowd round here! Why, a person ain't sure o' their lives. Tst! Tst! Such folks! It ain't hardly to be believed!

Fleischer. You can form an idea of the noise they're making.

Mrs. Wolff. Well, you can't hardly blame the people.

Fleischer. And really, it was a very expensive garment—of mink, I believe.

Mrs. Wolff. Ain't that somethin' like beaver, Mr. Fleischer?

Fleischer. Perhaps it was beaver, for all I know. Anyhow, they were real proud of it.—I admit, I laughed to myself over the business. When something like that is discovered it always has a comic effect.

Mrs. Wolff. You're a cruel man, really, Doctor. I can't go an' laugh about things like that.

Fleischer. You mustn't think that I'm not sorry for the man, for all that.

Mrs. Wolff. Them must be pretty strange people. I don't know. There ain't no way o' understandin' that. Just to go an' rob other people o' what's theirs—no, then it's better to work till you drop.

Fleischer. You might perhaps make a point of keeping your ears open. I believe that the coat is supposed to be in the village.

Mrs. Wolff. Has they got any suspicion o' anybody?

Fleischer. Oh, there was a washerwoman working at the Krueger's . . .

Mrs. Wolff. By the name o' Miller?

Fleischer. And she has a very large family . . . ?

Mrs. Wolff. The woman's got a large family, that's so, but to steal that way . . . no! She might take some little thing, yes.

Fleischer. Of course Krueger put her out.

Mrs. Wolff. Aw, that's bound to come out. My goodness, the devil hisself'd have to be back o' that if it don't. I wish I was Justice here. But the man is that stoopid!—well! I c'n see better'n the dark than he can by day with his glass eye.

Fleischer. I almost believe you could.

Mrs. Wolff. I c'n tell you, if I had to, I could steal the chair from under that man's behind.

Fleischer. [*Has arisen and calls, laughingly, into the adjoining room.*] Come, Philip, come! We've got to go! Good-by, Mrs. Wolff.

Mrs. Wolff. You get dressed, Adelaide. You c'n go an' row Mr. Fleischer a ways.

Adelaide. [*Enters, buttoning the last buttons at her throat and leading* PHILIP *by the hand.*] I'm all ready. [*To* PHILIP.] You come right here; I'll take you on my arm.

Fleischer. [*Anxiously helping the boy on with his coat.*] He's got to be wrapped up well; he's so delicate, and no doubt it's windy out on the river.

Adelaide. I better go ahead an' get the boat ready.

Mrs. Wolff. Is your health better these days?

Fleischer. Much better since I'm living out here.

Adelaide. [*Calls back in from the door.*] Mama, Mr. Krueger.

Mrs. Wolff. Who's comin'?

Adelaide. Mr. Krueger.

Mrs. Wolff. It ain't possible!

Fleischer. He meant to come to you during the forenoon. [*Exit.*]

Mrs. Wolff. [*Throws a swift glance at the heap of fire wood and vigorously sets about clearing it away.*] Come on, now, help me get this wood out o' sight.

Adelaide. Why, Mama? Oh, on account o' Mr. Krueger.

Mrs. Wolff. Well, what for d'you suppose? Is this a proper way for a place to look, the way this one is lookin'? Is that decent an' on Sunday mornin', too? What is Mr. Krueger goin' to think of us? [KRUEGER *appears, exhausted by his walk.* MRS. WOLFF *calls out to him.*] Mr. Krueger, please don't look 'round. This place is in a terrible state!

Krueger. [*Impetuously.*] Good morning! Good morning! Don't worry about that at all! You go to work every week and your house can't be expected to be perfect on Sunday. You are an excellent woman, Mrs. Wolff, and a very honest one. And I think we might do very well to forget whatever has happened between us.

Mrs. Wolff. [*Is moved, and dries her eyes from time to time with a corner of her apron.*] I never had nothin' against you in the world. I always liked to work for you. But you went an' got so rough like, you know, that a person's temper couldn't hardly help gettin' away with 'em. Lord, a person is sorry for that kind o' thing soon enough.

Krueger. You just come back and wash for us. Where is your daughter Leontine?

Mrs. Wolff. She went to take some cabbage to the postmaster.

Krueger. You just let us have that girl again. She can have thirty crowns wages instead of twenty. We were always quite satisfied with her in other respects. Let's forgive and forget the whole affair.

[*He holds out his hand to* MRS. WOLFF, *who takes it heartily.*]

Mrs. Wolff. All that hadn't no need to happen. The girl, you see, is still foolish like a child. We old people always did get along together.

Krueger. Well, then, the matter is settled. [*Gradually regaining his breath.*] Well, then, my mind is at rest about that, anyhow.—But now, do tell me! This thing that's happened to me! What do you say to that?

Mrs. Wolff. Oh, well, you know—what *can* a person say about such things?

Krueger. And there we got that Mr. von Wehrhahn! He's very well when it comes to annoying honest citizens and thinking out all sorts of chicanery and persecution, but—— That man, what doesn't he stick his inquisitive nose into!

Mrs. Wolff. Into everything exceptin' what he ought to.

Krueger. I'm going to him now to give formal notice. I won't rest! This thing has got to be discovered.

Mrs. Wolff. You oughtn't by no means to let a thing o' that kind go.

Krueger. And if I've got to turn everything upside down—I'll get back my coat, Mrs. Wolff.

Mrs. Wolff. What this place needs is a good cleanin' out. We don't get no rest in the village till then. They'll end up by stealin' the roof from over a person's head.

Krueger. I ask you to consider, for heaven's sake—two robberies in the course of two weeks! Two loads of wood, just like the wood you have there. [*He takes up a piece that is lying on the floor.*] Such good and expensive wood, Mrs. Wolff.

Mrs. Wolff. It's enough to make a person get blue in the face with rage. The kind o' crowd we gotta live with here! Aw, things like that! No, you know! Just leave me alone with it!

Krueger. [*Irately gesticulating with the piece of wood.*] And if it costs me a thousand crowns, I'll see to it that those thieves are hunted down. They won't escape the penitentiary this time.

Mrs. Wolff. An' that'd be a blessin', too, as sure's we're alive!

CURTAIN

THE FOURTH ACT

The courtroom.

[GLASENAPP *is sitting at his table.* MRS. WOLFF *and* ADELAIDE *are waiting for the* JUSTICE. ADELAIDE *holds on her lap a small package wrapped in linen.*]

Mrs. Wolff. He's takin' his time again today.

Glasenapp. [*Writing.*] Patience! Patience!

Mrs. Wolff. Well, if he's goin' to be so late again today, he won't have no more time for us.

Glasenapp. Goodness! You an' your trifles! We got different kinds o' things to deal with here.

Mrs. Wolff. Aw, I guess they're fine things you got to do.

Glasenapp. That's no way to talk. That ain't proper here!

Mrs. Wolff. Aw, act a little more grand, will you? Krueger hisself sent my girl here!

Glasenapp. The same old story about the coat, I suppose.

Mrs. Wolff. An' why not?

Glasenapp. Now the old fellow's got somethin' for sure. Now he can go stirrin' things up—the knock-kneed old nuisance.

Mrs. Wolff. You c'n use your tongue. You better see about findin' out somethin'.

Mitteldorf. [*Appears in the doorway.*] You're to come right over, Glasenapp. His honor wants to ax you somethin'.

Glasenapp. Has I got to interrupt myself again?

[*He throws down his pen and goes out.*]

Mrs. Wolff. Good mornin', Mitteldorf.

Mitteldorf. Good mornin'.

Mrs. Wolff. What's keepin' the Justice all this while?

Mitteldorf. He's writin' pages an' pages! An' them must be important things, I c'n tell you that. [*Confidentially.*] An' lemme tell you: there's somethin' in the air.—I ain't sayin' I know exactly what. But there's somethin'—I know that as sure's . . . You just look out, that's all, and you'll live to see it. It's goin' to come down—somethin'—and when it do—look out. That's all I say. No, I don't pretend to understand them things. It's all new doin's to me. That's what they calls modern. An' I don't know nothin' about that. But somethin's got to happen. Things can't go on this way. The whole place is got to be cleaned out. I can't say's I gets the hang of it. I'm too old. But talk about the Justice what died: why, he wasn't nothin' but a dam' fool to this one. I could go an' tell you all kinds o' things, but I ain't got no time. The baron'll be missin' me. [*He goes but, having arrived at the door, he turns back.*] The lightnin' is goin' to strike, Mrs. Wolff. Take my word for that!

Mrs. Wolff. I guess a screw's come loose somewhere with him. [*Pause.*]

Adelaide. What's that I gotta say? I forgot.

Mrs. Wolff. What did you say to Mr. Krueger?

Adelaide. Why, I said that I found this here package.

Mrs. Wolff. Well, you don't need to say nothin' but that here neither. Only say it right out strong an' sure. You ain't such a mouse other times.

Wulkow. [*Comes in.*] I wish you a good morning.

Mrs. Wolff. [*Stares at* WULKOW. *She is speechless for a moment! Then:*] No, Wulkow, I guess you lost *your* mind! What are you doin' here?

Wulkow. Well, my wife, she has a baby . . .

Mrs. Wolff. What's that she's got?

Wulkow. A little girl. So I gotta go to the public registry an' make the announcement.

Mrs. Wolff. I thought you'd be out on the canal by this time.

Wulkow. An' I wouldn't mind it one little bit if I was! An' so I *would* be, if it depended on me. Didn't I go an' start out the very minute? But when I come to the locks there wasn't no gettin' farther. I waited an' waited for the Spree to open up. Two days an' nights I lay there till this thing with my wife came along. There wasn't no use howlin' then. I had to come back.

Mrs. Wolff. So your boat is down by the bridge again?

Wulkow. That's where it is. I ain't got no other place, has I?

Mrs. Wolff. Well, don't come to me, if . . .

Wulkow. I hope they ain't caught on to nothin', at least.

Mrs. Wolff. [*To* ADELAIDE.] Go to the shop an' get three cents' worth o' bread.

Adelaide. I'll go for that when we get home.

Mrs. Wolff. Do's I tell you an' don't answer back.

Adelaide. Aw, I ain't no baby no more. [*Exit.*]

Mrs. Wolff. [*Eagerly.*] An' so you lay there by the locks?

Wulkow. Two whole days, as I been tellin' you.

Mrs. Wolff. Well, you ain't much good for this kind o' thing. You're a fine feller to go an' put on that coat in bright daylight!

Wulkow. Put it on? Me?

Mrs. Wolff. Yes, you put it on, an' in bright daylight, so's the whole place c'n know straight off what a fine fur coat you got.

Wulkow. Aw, that was 'way out in the middle o' the——

Mrs. Wolf. It was a quarter of a hour from our house. My girl saw you sittin' there. She had to go an' row Doctor Fleischer out an' he went an' had his suspicion that minute.

Wulkow. I don't know nothin' about that. That ain't none o' my business.

[*Some one is heard approaching.*]

Mrs. Wolff. Sh! You want to be on the lookout now, that's all.

Glasenapp. [*Enters hurriedly with an attempt to imitate the manner of the* JUSTICE. *He asks* WULKOW *condescendingly:*] What business have you?

Wehrhahn. [*Still without.*] What do you want, girl? You're looking for me? Come in, then. [WEHRHAHN *permits* ADELAIDE *to precede him and then enters.*] I have very little time today. Ah, yes, aren't you Mrs. Wolff's little girl? Well, then, sit down. What have you there?

Adelaide. I got a package . . .

Wehrhahn. Wait a moment first . . . [*To* WULKOW.] What do you want?

Wulkow. I'd like to report the birth of . . .

Wehrhahn. Matter of the public registry. The books, Glasenapp. That is to say, I'll attend to the other affair first. [*To* MRS. WOLFF.] What's the trouble about your daughter? Did Mr. Krueger box her ears again?

Mrs. Wolff. Well, he didn't go that far no time.

Wehrhahn. What's the trouble, then?

Mrs. Wolff. It's about this here package . . .

Wehrhahn. [*To* GLASENAPP.] Hasn't Motes been here yet?

Glasenapp. Not up to this time.

Wehrhahn. That's incomprehensible. Well, girl, what do you want?

Glasenapp. It's in the matter of the stolen fur coat, your honor.

Wehrhahn. Is that so? Can't possibly attend to that today. No one can do everything at once. [*To* MRS. WOLFF.] She may come in tomorrow.

Mrs. Wolff. She's tried to talk to you a couple o' times already.

Wehrhahn. Then let her try for a third time tomorrow.

Mrs. Wolff. But Mr. Krueger don't give her no peace no more.

Wehrhahn. What has Mr. Krueger to do with it?

Mrs. Wolff. The girl went to him with the package.

Wehrhahn. What kind of a rag is that? Let me see it.

Mrs. Wolff. It's all connected with the business of the fur coat. Leastways that's what Mr. Krueger thinks.

Wehrhahn. What's wrapped up in those rags, eh?

Mrs. Wolff. There's a green waist-coat what belongs to Mr. Krueger.

Wehrhahn. And you found that?

Adelaide. I found it, your honor.

Wehrhahn. Where did you find it?

Adelaide. That was when I was goin' to the train with Mama. I was walkin' along this way and there . . .

Wehrhahn. Never mind about that now. [*To* MRS. WOLFF.] Make your deposition some time soon. We can come back to this matter tomorrow.

Mrs. Wolff. Oh, *I'm* willin' enough . . .

Wehrhahn. Well, who isn't then?

Mrs. Wolff. Mr. Krueger is so very anxious about it.

Wehrhahn. Mr. Krueger, Mr. Krueger—I care very little about him. The man just simply annoys me. Things like this cannot be adjusted in a day. He has offered a reward and the matter has been published in the official paper.

Mrs. Wolff. You can't never do enough for him, though.

Wehrhahn. What does that mean: we can't do enough for him? We have recorded the facts in the case. His suspicions fell upon his washerwoman and we have searched her house. What more does he want? The man ought to keep quiet. But, as I said, tomorrow I'm at the service of this affair again.

Mrs. Wolff. It's all the same to us. We c'n come back.

Wehrhahn. Very well, then. Tomorrow morning.

Mrs. Wolff. Good mornin'.

Adelaide. [*Dropping a curtsey.*] Good mornin'.

[MRS. WOLFF *and* ADELAIDE *exeunt.*]

Wehrhahn. [*Turning over some documents. To* GLASENAPP.] I'm curious to see what the result of all this will be. Mr. Motes has finally agreed to offer witnesses. He says the Dreier woman, that old witch of a pastry cook, once stood within earshot when Fleischer expressed himself disrespectfully. How old is the woman, anyhow?

Glasenapp. Somewhere around seventy, your honor.

Wehrhahn. A bit confused in her upper story, eh?

Glasenapp. Depends on how you look at it. She's fairly sensible yet.

Wehrhahn. I can assure you, Glasenapp, that it would be no end of a satisfaction to me to flutter these dove-cotes here pretty thoroughly. These people ought to be made to feel that they're dealing with somebody, after all. Who absented himself from the festivities on the emperor's birthday? Fleischer, of course. The man is simply capable of anything. He can put on all the innocent expressions he pleases. We know these wolves in sheep's clothing. They're too sweet-tempered to harm a fly, but if they think the occasion has come, the hounds can blow up a whole place. Well, here, at least, it will be made too hot for them!

Motes. [*Comes in.*] Your servant.

Wehrhahn. Well, how are things going?

Motes. Mrs. Dreier said that she would be here around eleven.

Wehrhahn. This matter will attract quite a little notice. It will, in fact, make a good deal of noise. I know what will be said: "That man Wehrhahn pokes his nose into everything." Well, thank heaven, I'm prepared for that. I'm not standing in this place for my private amusement. I haven't been put here for jest. People think—a Justice, why he's nothing but a superior kind of jailer. In that case they can put some one else here. The gentlemen, to be sure, who appointed me know very well with whom they are dealing. They know to the full the seriousness with which I conceive of my duties. I consider my office in the light of a sacred calling. [*Pause.*] I have reduced my report to the public prosecutor to writing. If I send it off at noon today, the command of arrest can reach us by day after tomorrow.

Motes. Now everybody will be coming down on me.

Wehrhahn. You know I have an uncle who is a chamberlain. I'll talk to him about you. Confound it all! There comes Fleischer! What does that fellow want? Does he smell a rat by any chance? [*A knocking is heard and* WEHRHAHN *shouts:*] Come in!

Fleischer. [*Enters, pale and excited.*] Good morning! [*He receives no answer.*] I should like to lodge information which has reference to the robbery recently committed here.

Wehrhahn. [*With his most penetrating official glance.*] You are Dr. Joseph Fleischer?

Fleischer. Quite right. My name is Joseph Fleischer.

Wehrhahn. And you come to give me some information.

Fleischer. If you will permit me, that is what I should like to do. I have made an observation which may, quite possibly, help the authorities to track down the thief in question.

Wehrhahn. [*Drums on the table with his fingers. He looks around at the others with an expression of affected surprise which tempts them to laughter.*] What is this important observation which you have made?

Fleischer. Of course, if you have previously made up your mind to attach no importance to my evidence, I should prefer . . .

Wehrhahn. [*Quickly and arrogantly.*] What would you prefer?

Fleischer. To hold my peace.

Wehrhahn. [*Turns to* MOTES *with a look expressive of inability to understand* FLEISCHER'S *motives. Then, in a changed tone, with very superficial interest.*] My time is rather fully occupied. I would request you to be as brief as possible.

Fleischer. My time is no less preempted. Nevertheless I considered it my duty . . .

Wehrhahn. [*Interrupting.*] You considered it your duty. Very well. Now tell us what you know.

Fleischer. [*Conquering himself.*] I went boating yesterday. I had taken Mrs. Wolff's boat and her daughter was rowing.

Wehrhahn. Are these details necessarily pertinent to the business in hand?

Fleischer. They certainly are—in my opinion.

Wehrhahn. [*Drumming impatiently on the table.*] Very well! Very well! Let's get on!

Fleischer. We rowed to the neighborhood of the locks. A lighter lay at anchor there. The ice, we were able to observe, was piled up there. The lighter had probably not been able to proceed.

Wehrhahn. H'm. Is that so? That interests us rather less. What is the kernel of this whole story?

Fleischer. [*Keeping his temper by main force.*] I must confess that this method of . . . I have come here quite voluntarily, to offer a voluntary service to the authorities.

Glasenapp. [*Impudently.*] His honor is pressed for time. You are to talk less and state what you have to say briefly and compactly.

Wehrhahn. [*Vehemently.*] Let's get to business at once. What is it you want?

Fleischer. [*Still mastering himself.*] I am concerned that the matter be cleared up. And in the interest of old Mr. Krueger, I will . . .

Wehrhahn. [*Yawning and bored.*] The light dazzles me; do pull down the shades.

Fleischer. On the lighter was an old boatman—probably the owner of the vessel.

Wehrhahn. [*Yawning as before.*] Yes, most probably.

Fleischer. This man sat on his deck in a fur coat which, at a distance, I considered a beaver coat.

Wehrhahn. [*Bored.*] I might have taken it to be marten.

Fleischer. I pulled as close up to him as possible and thus gained a very good view. The man was a poverty-stricken, slovenly boatman and the fur coat seemed by no means appropriate. It was, in addition, a perfectly new coat . . .

Wehrhahn. [*Apparently recollecting himself.*] I am listening, I am listening! Well? What else?

Fleischer. What else? Nothing.

Wehrhahn. [*Waking up thoroughly.*] I thought you wanted to lodge some information. You mentioned something important.

Fleischer. I have said all that I had to say.

Wehrhahn. You have told us an anecdote about a boatman who wears a fur coat. Well, boatmen do, no doubt, now and then wear such coats. There is nothing new or interesting about that.

Fleischer. You may think about that as

you please. In such circumstances I have no more to say. [*Exit.*]

Wehrhahn. Well now, did you ever see anything like that? Moreover, the fellow is a thorough fool. A boatman had on a fur coat! Why, has the man gone mad? I possess a beaver coat myself. Surely that doesn't make me a thief.—Confound it all! What's that again? I suppose I am to get no rest today at all! [*To* MITTELDORF, *who is standing by the door.*] Don't let any one else in now! Mr. Motes, do me the favor of going over to my apartment. We can have our discussion there without interruptions. There's Krueger for the hundred and first time. He acts as though he'd been stung by a tarantula. If that old ass continues to plague me, I'll kick him straight out of this room some day.

[*In the open door* KRUEGER *becomes visible, together with* FLEISCHER *and* MRS. WOLFF.]

Mitteldorf. [*To* KRUEGER.] His honor can't be seen, Mr. Krueger.

Krueger. Nonsense! Not to be seen! I don't care for such talk at all. [*To the others.*] Go right on, right on! I'd like to see!

[*All enter,* KRUEGER *leading the way.*]

Wehrhahn. I must request that there be somewhat more quiet. As you see, I am having a conference at present.

Krueger. Go right ahead with it. We can wait. Later you can then have a conference with us.

Wehrhahn. [*To* MOTES.] Over in my apartment, then, if you please. And if you see Mrs. Dreier, tell her I had rather question her there too. You see for yourself: it isn't possible here.

Krueger. [*Pointing to* FLEISCHER.] This gentleman knows something about Mrs. Dreier too. He has some documentary evidence.

Motes. Your honor's servant. I take my leave. [*Exit.*]

Krueger . That's a good thing for *that* man to take.

Wehrhahn. You will kindly omit remarks of that nature.

Krueger. I'll say that again. The man is a swindler.

Wehrhahn. [*As though he had not heard, to* WULKOW.] Well, what is it? I'll get rid of you first. The records, Glasenapp!—Wait, though! I'll relieve myself of this business first. [*To* KRUEGER.] I will first attend to your affair.

Krueger. Yes, I must ask you very insistently to do so.

Wehrhahn. Suppose we leave that "insistently" quite out of consideration. What request have you to make?

Krueger. None at all. I have no request to make. I am here in order to demand what is my right.

Wehrhahn. Your right? Ah, what is that, exactly?

Krueger. My good right. I have been robbed and it is my right that the local authorities aid me in recovering my stolen possessions.

Wehrhahn. Have you been refused such assistance?

Krueger. Certainly not. And that is not possible. Nevertheless, it is quite clear that nothing is being done. The whole affair is making no progress.

Wehrhahn. You imagine that things like that can be done in a day or two.

Krueger. I don't imagine anything, your honor. I have very definite proofs. You are taking no interest in my affairs.

Wehrhahn. I could interrupt you at this very point. It lies entirely beyond the duties of my office to listen to imputations of that nature. For the present, however, you may continue.

Krueger. You could not interrupt me at all. As a citizen of the Prussian state I have my rights. And even if you interrupt me here, there are other places where I could make my complaint. I repeat that you are not showing any interest in my affair.

Wehrhahn. [*Apparently calm.*] Suppose you prove that.

Krueger. [*Pointing to* MRS. WOLFF *and her daughter.*] This woman here came to you. Her daughter made a find. She didn't shirk the way, your honor, although she is a poor woman. You turned her off once before and she came back today . . .

Mrs. Wolff. But his honor didn't have no time, you know.

Wehrhahn. Go on, please!

Krueger. I will. I'm not through yet by any means. What did you say to the woman? You said to her quite simply that you had no time for the matter in question. You did not even question her daughter. You don't know the slightest circumstance; you don't know anything about the entire occurrence.

Wehrhahn. I will have to ask you to moderate yourself a little.

Krueger. My expressions are moderate; they are extremely moderate. I am far too moderate, your honor. My entire character is far too full of moderation. If it were not, what do you think I would say? What kind of an investigation is this? This gentleman here, Doctor Fleischer, came to you to report an observation which he has made. A boatman wears a beaver coat . . .

Wehrhahn. [*Raising his hand.*] Just wait a moment. [*To* WULKOW.] You are a boatman, aren't you?

Wulkow. I been out on the river for thirty years.

Wehrhahn. Are you nervous? You seem to twitch.

Wulkow. I reely did have a little scare. That's a fac'.

Wehrhahn. Do the boatmen on the Spree frequently wear fur coats?

Wulkow. A good many of 'em has fur coats. That's right enough.

Wehrhahn. This gentleman saw a boatman who stood on his deck wearing a fur coat.

Wulkow. There ain't nothin' suspicious about that, your honor. There's many as has fine coats. I got one myself, in fac'.

Wehrhahn. You observe: the man himself owns a fur coat.

Fleischer. But then he hasn't exactly a beaver coat.

Wehrhahn. You were not in a position to discover that.

Krueger. What? Has this man a beaver coat?

Wulkow. There's many of 'em, I c'n tell you, as has the finest beaver coats. An' why not? We makes enough.

Wehrhahn. [*Filled with a sense of triumph but pretending indifference.*] Exactly. [*Lightly.*] Now, please go on, Mr. Krueger. That was only a little sideplay. I simply wanted to make clear to you the value of that so-called "observation."—You see now that this man himself owns a fur coat. [*More violently.*] Would it therefore occur to us in our wildest moments to assert that he has stolen the coat? That would simply be an absurdity.

Krueger. Wha——? I don't understand a word.

Wehrhahn. Then I must talk somewhat louder still. And since I am talking to you now, there's something else I might as well say to you—not in my capacity as Justice, but simply man to man, Mr. Krueger. A man who is after all an honorable citizen should be more chary of his confidence—he should not adduce the evidence of people . . .

Krueger. Are you talking about my associates? *My* associates?

Wehrhahn. Exactly that.

Krueger. In that case you had better take care of yourself. People like Motes, with whom you associate, were kicked out of my house.

Fleischer. I was obliged to show the door to this person whom you receive in your private apartment!

Krueger. He cheated me out of my rent.

Mrs. Wolff. There ain't many in this village that that man ain't cheated all ways—cheated out o' pennies an' shillin's, an' crowns an' gold pieces.

Krueger. He has a regular system of extracting tribute.

Fleischer. [*Pulling a document out of his pocket.*] More than that, the fellow is ripe for the public prosecutor. [*He places the document on the table.*] I would request you to read this through.

Krueger. Mrs. Dreier has signed that paper herself. Motes tried to inveigle her into committing perjury.

Fleischer. She was to give evidence against me.

Krueger. [*Putting his hand on* FLEISCHER'S *arm.*] This gentleman is of unblemished conduct and that scoundrel wanted to get him into trouble. And you lend your assistance to such things!

All speak at once.

Wehrhahn. My patience is exhausted now. Whatever dealings you may have with Motes don't concern me and are entirely indifferent to me. [*To* FLEISCHER.] You'll be good enough to remove that rag!

Krueger. [*Alternately to* MRS. WOLFF *and to* GLASENAPP.] That man is his honor's friend; that is his source of information. A fine situation. We might better call him a source of defamation!

Fleischer. [*To* MITTELDORF.] I'm not accountable to any one. It's my own business what I do; it's my own business with whom I associate; it's my own business what I choose to think and write!

Glasenapp. Why you can't hear your own words in this place no more! Your honor, shall I go an' fetch a policeman? I can run right over and get one. Mitteldorf! . . .

Wehrhahn. Quiet, please! [*Quiet is restored. To* FLEISCHER.] You will please remove that rag.

Fleischer. [*Obeys.*] That rag, as you call it, will be forwarded to the public prosecutor.

Wehrhahn. You may do about that exactly as you please. [*He arises and takes from a case in the wall the package brought by* MRS. WOLFF.] Let us finally dispose of this matter, then. [*To* MRS. WOLFF.] Where did you find this thing?

Mrs. Wolff. It ain't me that found it at all.

Wehrhahn. Well, who did find it?

Mrs. Wolff. My youngest daughter.

Wehrhahn. Well, why didn't you bring her with you then?

Mrs. Wolff. She was here, all right, your honor. An' then, I c'n go over an' fetch her in a minute.

Wehrhahn. That would only serve to delay the whole business again. Didn't the girl tell you anything about it?

Krueger. She said it was found on the way to the railway station.

Wehrhahn. In that case the thief is probably in Berlin. That won't make our search any easier.

Krueger. I don't believe that at all, your honor. Mr. Fleischer seems to me to have an entirely correct opinion. The whole business with the package is a trick meant to mislead us.

Mrs. Wolff. Well, well. That's mighty possible.

Wehrhahn. Now, Mrs. Wolff, you're not so stupid as a rule. Things that are stolen here go in to Berlin. That fur coat was sold in Berlin before we even knew that it was stolen.

Mrs. Wolff. No, your honor, I can't help it, but I ain't quite, not quite of the same opinion. If the thief is in Berlin, why, I ax, does he have to go an' lose a package like that?

Wehrhahn. Such things are not always lost intentionally.

Mrs. Wolff. Just look at that there package. It's all packed up so nice—the vest, the key, an' the bit o' paper . . .

Krueger. I believe the thief to be in this very place.

Mrs. Wolff. [*Confirming him.*] Well, you see, Mr. Krueger.

Krueger. I firmly believe it.

Wehrhahn. Sorry, but I do not incline to that opinion. My experience is far too long . . .

Krueger. What? A long experience? H'm!

Wehrhahn. Certainly. And on the basis of that experience I know that the chance of the coat being here need scarcely be taken into account.

Mrs. Wolff. Well, well, we shouldn't go an' deny things that way, your honor.

Krueger. [*Referring to* FLEISCHER.] And then he saw the boatman . . .

Wehrhahn. Don't bother me with that story. I'd have to go searching people's houses every day with twenty constables and policemen. I'd have to search every house in the village.

Mrs. Wolff. Then you better go an' start with my house, your honor.

Wehrhahn. Well, isn't that ridiculous? No, no, gentlemen: that's not the way. That method will lead us nowhither, now or later. You must give me entire freedom of action. I have my own suspicions and will continue to make my observations. There are a number of shady characters here on whom I have my eye. Early in the morning they ride in to Berlin with heavy baskets on their backs, and in the evening they bring home the same baskets empty.

Krueger. I suppose you mean the vegetable hucksters. That's what they do.

Wehrhahn. Not only the vegetable hucksters, Mr. Krueger. And I have no doubt but that your coat traveled in the same way.

Mrs. Wolff. That's possible, all right. There ain't nothin' impossible in *this* world, I tell you.

Wehrhahn. Well, then! Now, what did you want to announce?

Wulkow. A little girl, your honor.

Wehrhahn. I will do all that is possible.

Krueger. I won't let the matter rest until I get back my coat.

Wehrhahn. Well, whatever can be done will be done. Mrs. Wolff can use her ears a little.

Mrs. Wolff. The trouble is I don't know how to act like a spy. But if things like that don't come out—there ain't no sayin' what's safe no more.

Krueger. You are quite right, Mrs. Wolff, quite right. [*To* WEHRHAHN.] I must ask you to examine that package carefully. The handwriting on the slip that was found in it may lead to a discovery. And day after tomorrow morning, your honor, I will take the liberty of troubling you again. Good morning! [*Exit.*]

Fleischer. Good morning. [*Exit.*]

Wehrhahn. [*To* WULKOW.] How old are you?—There's something wrong with those two fellows up here. [*He touches his forehead. To* WULKOW.] What is your name?

Wulkow. August Philip Wulkow.

Wehrhahn. [*To* MITTELDORF.] Go over to my apartment. That Motes is still sitting there and waiting. Tell him I am sorry but I have other things to do this morning.

Mitteldorf. An' you don't want him to wait?

Wehrhahn. [*Harshly.*] No, he needn't wait! [MITTELDORF *exit.*]

Wehrhahn. [*To* MRS. WOLFF.] Do you know this author Motes?

Mrs. Wolff. When it comes to people like

that, your honor, I'd rather go an' hold my tongue. There ain't much good that I could tell you.

Wehrhahn. [*Ironically.*] But you could tell me a great deal that's good about Fleischer.

Mrs. Wolff. He ain't no bad sort, an' that's a fac'.

Wehrhahn. I suppose you're trying to be a bit careful in what you say.

Mrs. Wolff. No, I ain't much good at that. I'm right out with things, your honor. If I hadn't always gone an' been right out with what I got to say, I might ha' been a good bit further along in the world.

Wehrhahn. That policy has never done you any harm with me.

Mrs. Wolff. No, not with you, your honor. You c'n stand bein' spoken to honest. Nobody don't need to be sneaky 'round you.

Wehrhahn. In short: Fleischer is a man of honor.

Mrs. Wolff. That he is! That he is!

Wehrhahn. Well, you remember my words of today.

Mrs. Wolff. An' you remember mine.

Wehrhahn. Very well. The future will show. [*He stretches himself, gets up, and stamps his feet gently on the floor. To* WULKOW.] This is our excellent washerwoman. She thinks that all people are like herself. [*To* MRS. WOLFF.] But unfortunately the world is differently made. You see human beings from the outside; a man like myself has learned to look a little deeper. [*He takes a few paces, then stops before her and lays his hand on her shoulder.*] And as surely as it is true when I say: Mrs. Wolff is an honest woman; so surely I tell you: this Doctor Fleischer of yours, of whom we were speaking, is a thoroughly dangerous person!

Mrs. Wolff. [*Shaking her head resignedly.*] Well, then I don't know no more what to think . . .

CURTAIN

LIGHT-O'-LOVE*

[*Liebelei*]

By

ARTHUR SCHNITZLER

Translated by BAYARD QUINCY MORGAN

ARTHUR SCHNITZLER WAS A PHYSICIAN and the son of a physician, a Viennese, a poet and novelist as well as a dramatist, a Jew, and a psychologist. Rarely does such a description give as much light upon a man's work as in the case of Schnitzler. That he was a physician and a physician's son accounts for the interest he displayed in the bodily appetites, in love, and in death. That he was a Viennese accounts for his moral attitude, for that city was always the home of gaiety, even of abandon, especially, of course, while Schnitzler was young. His writing experience in other forms gave him his wit and lightness in dialogue and his occasional lyric note. That he was a Jew accounts largely for his melancholy and intensity. That he was a psychologist, by which is meant one interested in the analysis of the mind of man when confronted by a situation calling for decision, accounts for his interest in sex. He found in the situations created by sex-attraction and sex-antagonism the most fruitful field for his delicate analyses of character and the best opportunity for the exposition of his gentle and sad hedonism. For to Schnitzler life was melancholy enough at best—little can be done to lighten or relieve it. Therefore it is far bette. to give or take happiness than to be guiltless. And happiness, if found anywhere, is probably found in love between man and woman, which makes that love the dramatist's indicated theme. Of all Schnitzler's plays, only in *Professor Bernhardi*, 1912, did he ever abandon it.

Light-o'-Love (Liebelei) was Schnitzler's second full-length play and was first produced in 1895. In 1896 *Liebelei* was produced in New York in German, and in 1907 in English under the title of *The Reckoning*. At that time it was well received, and was revived in 1929 as *Playing with Love*.

ARTHUR SCHNITZLER

Born 1862, Vienna, Austria.
1885, M.D., University of Vienna.
Practiced as physician for ten years, to 1895.
1908, Awarded Grillparzer prize.
Writer of novels, short stories, and essays, as well as plays.
Died 1931.

PLAYS

1889-1891 *Anatol* (seven dramatic scenes, translated under the same title). 1891 *Das Märchen* (*The Fairy Tale*). 1892 *Paracelsus* (one act, in verse, translated under the same title). 1895 *Liebelei* (translated as *Light-o'-Love* and *Playing with Love*). 1896 *Freiwild* (translated as *Free Game*). 1896-1897 *Reigen* (ten dialogues, translated as *Hands Around*). 1897 *Das Vermächtniss* (translated as *The Legacy*). 1898 *Die Gefährtin* (one act, translated as *The Mate, His Helpmate,* and *The Helpmeet*). 1898 *Der grüne Kakadu* (one act, translated as *The Green Cockatoo* and *The Duke and the Actress*). 1899 *Der Schleier der Beatrice* (*Beatrice's Veil,* in verse). 1900 *Die Frau mit dem Dolche* (one act, translated as *The Lady with the Dagger*). 1901 *Lebendige Stunden* (one act, translated as *Living Hours*). 1901 *Die letzten Masken* (one act, translated as *The Last Masks*). 1901 *Literatur* (one act, translated as *Literature*). 1902 *Der Puppenspieler* (one act, *The Puppet Player*). 1903 *Der tapfere Kassian* (one act, translated as *Gallant Cassian*). 1903 *Der einsame Weg* (translated as *The Lonely Way*). 1904 *Zwischenspiel* (translated as *Intermezzo*). 1904 *Zum grossen Wurstel* (one act, *The Great Show*). 1905 *Der Ruf des Leben* (*The Call of Life*). 1909 *Komtesse Mizzi* (one act, translated as *Countess Mizzi*). 1909 *Der junge Medardus* (*Young Medardus*). 1909 *Der tapfere Kassian* (*Gallant Cassian,* one act musical comedy, music by Oscar Straus). 1909 *Der Schleier der Pierrette* (*Pierrette's Veil,* comic opera, music by Ernst von Dohnanyi). 1910 *Das weite Land* (translated as *The Vast Domain*). 1912 *Professor Bernhardi* (translated under the same title). 1915 *Stunde des Erkennens* (one act, translated as *The Hour of Recognition*). 1915 *Grosse Szene* (one act, translated as *The Big Scene*). 1915 *Das Bacchusfest* (one act, translated as *The Festival of Bacchus*). 1917 *Fink und Fliederbusch* (*Fink and Fliederbusch*). 1918 *Die Schwestern* (*The Sisters*). 1924 *Komödie der Verführung* (*Seduction's Comedy*). 1925 *Der Gang zum Weiher* (*The Walk to the Pond*). 1930 *Im Spiel der Sommerlüfte* (*In the Play of Summer's Air*).

LIGHT-O'-LOVE

Characters

HANS VYRING, *violinist at the city theater.*
CHRISTINE, *his daughter.*
TONI SCHLAGER, *milliner.*
CATHERINE BINDER, *wife of a stocking-maker.*
LENA, *her nine-year-old daughter.*
FRITZ LOHEIMER } *young men.*
THEODORE KAISER }
A GENTLEMAN.

Scene, Vienna: time, the present.

FIRST ACT

FRITZ'S *room. Cozy but elegantly furnished.* [THEODORE *enters in advance. He carries a stick, has an overcoat flung over his arm; takes off his hat upon entering.*]

Fritz. [*Outside.*] So nobody has been here?

Voice. No, sir.

Fritz. [*Entering.*] I suppose we might let the carriage go?

Theodore. Of course. I thought you had.

Fritz. [*Goes to the door.*] Send the carriage away. And . . . you can go, too. I don't need you any more. [*Returning.*] Why don't you lay down your things?

Theodore. [*At the desk.*] Here are a couple of letters.

[*Throws coat and hat on a chair, keeps his stick.*]

Fritz. [*Hastens to the desk.*] Oh! . . .

Theodore. Now, now! . . . I believe you're frightened!

Fritz. From Dad. . . . [*Opens a second letter.*] From Lensky.

Theodore. Don't let me disturb you. [FRITZ *skims the letters.*] What does your father say?

Fritz. Nothing special. . . . He wants me to spend a week on the estate at Whitsuntide.

Theodore. Excellent plan. I'd like to send you there for six months. [FRITZ *turns to face him.*] I certainly would!—— Riding, driving, fresh air, dairymaids——

Fritz. Idiot, there aren't any dairy-farms out there.

Theodore. Well, you know what I mean, don't you?

Fritz. Will you come along?

Theodore. You know I can't.

Fritz. Why not?

Theodore. My dear fellow, I have my doctor's exam. coming! If I went along, it would only be for the sake of keeping you there.

Fritz. Oh, come, you needn't worry about me.

Theodore. You see, all you need is fresh air; I'm convinced of that—I saw that today. Out yonder in the open, where we found the genuine green spring-time, you were a very pleasant fellow again.

Fritz. Thanks.

Theodore. And now—now of course you are collapsing. We're too close to the dangerous atmospheric zone again. [FRITZ *makes a gesture of irritation.*] Why, you've no idea how jolly you were out there. You were actually reasonable for once; it was like the good old days. And then a couple of days ago, when we were out with those two jolly little girls, you were very nice; but now—that's all over again, and you find it absolutely necessary to think—[*with ironical pathos*]—of that woman. [FRITZ *rises, vexed.*] You don't know me, my dear fellow. I don't intend to stand that any longer.

Fritz. My goodness, but you're ambitious!

Theodore. Oh, I don't demand of you that you forget—[*as before*]—that woman. . . . I only hope—[*warmly*]—my dear Fritz, that this miserable affair, that keeps me trembling for you all the time, means no more to you than any trivial love affair. . . . Look here, Fritz, some day, when you stop worshiping "that woman," you'll be surprised how congenial she is to you. Then you'll find out that there's nothing demoniac in her at all, but that she is a very sweet little woman—one that you can have plenty of fun with, just as you can with all women that are young and pretty, and that have a little temperament.

Fritz. Why do you say "tremble for me"?

Theodore. You know why. . . . I must confess that I am in constant terror that you will run off with her some fine day.

Fritz. That was what you meant?

Theodore. [*After a short pause.*] That isn't the only danger.

Fritz. Right you are, Theodore—there are others, too.

Theodore. But then we never do anything silly.

Fritz. [*To himself.*] There are others, too. . . .

Theodore. What's the matter? . . . You're thinking of something in particular

Fritz. Oh, no, I'm not. . . . [*Glances at the window.*] She was deceived once before.

Theodore. What? . . . What's that? . . . I don't understand you.

Fritz. Oh, nothing.

Theodore. What? Do talk sense.

Fritz. She's been afraid lately . . . at times.

Theodore. Why? There must be a reason for it.

Fritz. Not at all. Nervousness—[*ironically*]—an uneasy conscience, if you will.

Theodore. You say she was deceived once——

Fritz. Well, yes—and again today, I suppose.

Theodore. Today—well, what does all this mean?

Fritz. [*After a slight pause.*] She thinks . . . we are watched.

Theodore. What?

Fritz. She sees apparitions; really, she has actual hallucinations. [*At the window.*] She sees some person standing at the street corner . . . through the crack in the curtain, and thinks—[*Breaks off.*] Is it possible, anyway, to recognize a face at this distance?

Theodore. Scarcely.

Fritz. Why, that's what I say. But then that's terrible. She's afraid to go out; she has all sorts of queer feelings; she gets hysterical; she wants to die with me——

Theodore. Of course.

Fritz. [*Short pause.*] Today I had to go down and take a look. Went down as cheerfully as if I were leaving the house alone; of course there wasn't a familiar face to be seen anyhere. . . . [THEODORE *is silent.*] Well, that ought to set fears at rest, oughtn't it? A man can't suddenly be swallowed up by the earth, hey? . . . Answer, can't you?

Theodore. What sort of an answer do you want? Of course a man can't be swallowed up. But a man can hide inside the gates.

Fritz. I looked behind them all.

Theodore. You must have looked very innocent doing that.

Fritz. There was nobody there. I tell you it's hallucinations.

Theodore. Certainly. But it ought to teach you to be more careful.

Fritz. And I couldn't have helped knowing it, if *he* suspected it. Why, I ate supper with them yesterday after the play—with *him* and *her*—and it was so pleasant! . . . ridiculous, I tell you!

Theodore. I beg of you, Fritz, be sensible; do me that favor. Give up this whole cursed affair, for *my* sake, if nothing else. I have nerves, too. . . . I know you're not the kind of man who can escape from such an affair unaided, and so I made it so easy for you—gave you a chance to save yourself by starting another. . . .

Fritz. You did?

Theodore. Well, didn't I take you along with me when I had an appointment with little Miss Toni a while back? And didn't I ask her to bring along her prettiest friend? And can you deny that you like her?

Fritz. Certainly, she is sweet! . . . So sweet! And you have no idea how I longed for such an affection as that, so sweet and quiet, that would hover about me and soothe me, and help me to recover from these everlasting irritations and torments.

Theodore. That's exactly it. Recover! That's the deeper purpose of it. They help us to recover. That's why I'm against these so-called interesting women. It's not the business of women to be interesting, but to be agreeable. You must seek happiness where I have sought and found it—where there are no grand scenes, no dangers, no tragic entanglements—where the beginning has no special difficulties, and the ending no torments—where you take your first kiss with a smile, and part with *very* gentle emotion.

Fritz. Yes, that's it.

Theodore. Those women are so happy in their healthy every-day womanhood—what compels us to make demons or angels out of them at all costs?

Fritz. She is really a treasure. So affectionate, so dear. Often it seems to me she is too dear for me.

Theodore. You're incorrigible, apparently. If you intend to take *that* affair seriously again. . . .

Fritz. No, no, not a thought of it. We are agreed: I need to recover.

Theodore. If you did, I'd give you up for good. I've had enough of your love-tragedies. You bore me with them. And if you feel like coming at me with your famous "conscience," I'll give you my simple rule for treating such cases: Better it were I than someone else

For that "someone else" is as sure as fate itself. [*There is a ring.*]

Fritz. What's that now? . . .

Theodore. Go and see. There you are, all pale again! Set your fears at rest. It's the two sweet little girls.

Fritz. [*Agreeably surprised.*] What?

Theodore. I took the liberty of inviting them here today.

Fritz. [*Going out.*] Oh, you—why didn't you tell me? Now I've sent away my man.

Theodore. So much the cozier.

Fritz. [*Outside.*] Greetings, Toni. [TONI *enters, carrying a package.* FRITZ *reenters behind her.*] And where's Christine?

Toni. She'll be here soon. Greetings, Dore. [THEODORE *kisses her hand.*] You'll have to excuse us, Mr. Fritz; but Theodore invited us. . . .

Fritz. Why, it was a splendid idea. Only he forgot something, Theodore did.

Theodore. Theodore forgot nothing! [*Takes the package from* TONI.] Did you bring everything I wrote down for you?

Toni. Of course. [*To* FRITZ.] Where can I put it?

Fritz. Just give it to me, Toni; we'll put it on the sideboard for the present.

Toni. I bought something else, Dore, besides what you told me.

Fritz. Give me your hat, Toni, that's right. [*Lays it on the piano, also her boa.*]

Theodore. [*Dubiously.*] What?

Toni. A coffee cream-cake.

Theodore. Oh, what a sweet tooth!

Fritz. Well, but tell me, why didn't Christine come with you?

Toni. She's going to take her father to the theater first. Then she'll come along on the street car.

Theodore. What an affectionate daughter! . . .

Toni. I should say so, and especially since he went into mourning.

Theodore. Why, who died there, anyway?

Toni. The old gentleman's sister.

Theodore. Ah, a widow?

Toni. No, it was an old maiden lady, who has lived with them always. Well, and so he feels so lonesome, somehow.

Theodore. He's a little man with short gray hair—her father—isn't he?

Toni. [*Shakes her head.*] No, he has long hair.

Fritz. How did you come to know him?

Theodore. Recently I was in the theater with Lensky, and I took a look at the men playing the bass-viols.

Toni. Why, he doesn't play the bass-viol—he plays a violin.

Theodore. Oh, is that so? I thought he played the bass-viol. [TONI *laughs.*] Nothing funny about that; how should I know, child?

Toni. What a beautiful place you have, Mr. Fritz—just wonderful! What view is that?

Fritz. This window opens on Straw Lane, and in the next room——

Theodore. [*Quickly.*] Do tell me, why are you so formal, you two?

Toni. At supper we'll get better acquainted.

Theodore. A lady of principle, I see. Well, that's some comfort, just the same. How's your mother, anyhow?

Toni. [*Turns to him, her face suddenly showing concern.*] Only think, she's got——

Theodore. Toothache, I know, I know. Your mother always has the toothache. She ought to go to a dentist one of these times.

Toni. But the doctor says it's only rheumatic pains.

Theodore. [*Laughing.*] Well, if it's rheumatic . . .

Toni. [*An album in her hand.*] Nothing but pretty things! [*Turning the pages.*] Who is that? . . . Why, that's you, Mr. Fritz, . . . in uniform? You're in the army?

Fritz. Yes.

Toni. Dragoon!—Are you in the yellows or the blacks?

Fritz. [*Smiling.*] In the yellows.

Toni. [*As in a reverie.*] The yellows.

Theodore. There she's goes a-dreaming. Wake up, Toni!

Toni. But now you're lieutenant in the reserves?

Fritz. Surely.

Toni. You must look very nice in the fur cap.

Theodore. How much she knows about it! —Look here, Toni, I'm in the army, too.

Toni. Are you in the dragoons, too?

Theodore. Yes.

Toni. Well, why can't you tell a body that?

Theodore. I want to be loved for myself.

Toni. Come, Dore, you must put on your uniform some time when we're going out together.

Theodore. In August there will be maneuvers, anyway.

Toni. Heavens! by August——

Theodore. Yes, that's so—eternal love doesn't last that long.

Toni. Who thinks about August in May? Isn't that so, Mr. Fritz?—Say, Mr. Fritz, why did you run away from us yesterday?

Fritz. What do you mean?

Toni. Why—after the play.

Fritz. Didn't Theodore make my excuses to you?

Theodore. To be sure, I excused you.

Toni. What good do your excuses do me, or rather Christine? When a man makes a promise, he ought to keep it.

Fritz. I really would rather have gone with you.

Toni. Really?

Fritz. But I couldn't. You saw yourselves I was in a box with friends, and afterward I couldn't get away from them.

Toni. Yes, you couldn't get away from the pretty ladies. Do you think we didn't see you from the gallery?

Fritz. Well, I saw you, too.

Toni. You were sitting backwards in the box.

Fritz. Not all the time.

Toni. But most of it. Behind a lady with a black velvet dress you sat and kept—[*imitating*]—looking forward like this.

Fritz. You must have watched me closely.

Toni. Why, it's nothing to me. But if I were Christine . . . Why did Theodore have time after the play? Why doesn't he have to take supper with friends?

Theodore. [*Proudly.*] Why don't I have to take supper with friends?

[*There is a ring.* FRITZ *hastens out.*]

Theodore. Toni, you can do me a favor. [TONI *assumes questioning expression.*] Forget your military recollections—at least, for a time.

Toni. Why, I haven't any.

Theodore. Come, now, you didn't learn all that just by accident, that's plain enough.

Christine. [*Enters with flowers in her hand.* FRITZ *behind her. With a trace of embarrassment.*] Good evening. [*General salutation. To* FRITZ.] Are you glad we came?—You're not angry?

Fritz. But—my dear child! Sometimes, you know, Theodore is cleverer than I am.

Theodore. Well, is your father fiddling by now?

Christine. Surely; I took him to the theater.

Fritz. Toni told us.

Christine. [*To* TONI.] And Catherine stopped me, too.

Toni. Oh, pshaw! The false cat!

Christine. Oh, no, she isn't false at all; she is very good to me.

Toni. You trust every one, anyway.

Christine. Why should she be false to me?

Fritz. Who is Catherine?

Toni. The wife of a stocking-maker; and she's always vexed because some girls are younger than she is.

Christine. Why, she's quite young herself.

Fritz. Bother Catherine!—What have you got there?

Christine. I brought along a few flowers for you.

Fritz. [*Takes them from her and kisses her hand.*] You're a little angel. Here, we'll put them in the vase.

Theodore. No, no! You've no talent as decorator. The flowers will be scattered at random on the table. . . . That is, later on, when the table is set. We really ought to fix it so that they would fall from the ceiling. But that can't be done.

Fritz. [*Laughing.*] Scarcely.

Theodore. Meanwhile we'll put them in here, after all. [*Puts them into the vase.*]

Toni. Children, it's getting dark!

Fritz. [*Helps* CHRISTINE *to take off her coat, and she takes off her hat. He puts hat and coat on a chair in the background.*] We'll light the lamp right away.

Theodore. Lamp! I should say not! *Candles* we must have. Their light is so much prettier. Come, Toni, you can help me.

[*He and* TONI *light the candles, in the branched candelabra before the pier-glass, one on the desk, two candles on the sideboard. Meanwhile* FRITZ *and* CHRISTINE *converse.*]

Fritz. How are you, sweetheart?

Christine. I'm all right now.

Fritz. Well, but not at other times?

Christine. I have longed so for you.

Fritz. Why, we saw each other only yesterday.

Christine. Saw each other . . . from away off. . . . [*Shyly.*] Fritz, it wasn't very nice of you to . . .

Fritz. Yes, I know; Toni told me. But you're always a child. I couldn't get away. You've got to understand such things.

Christine. Yes. . . . Fritz . . . who were the people in the box?

Fritz. Friends of mine—it doesn't matter what their names are.

Christine. Well, who was the lady in the black velvet dress?

Fritz. Child, I have no memory for dresses.

Christine. [*Coaxingly.*] Come, come!

Fritz. That is to say . . . I do have a sort of a memory for them—in certain cases. For example, I remember very well that dark-blue waist you had on the first time we saw each other. And the black and white one you wore to the theater yesterday.

Christine. Why, I'm wearing it today!

Fritz. Sure enough; . . . from a distance, you know, it looks different—I mean it! Oh, and that medallion—I know that, too.

Christine. [*Smiling.*] When did I wear that?

Fritz. Oh—that time we went walking in the public gardens, where all the children were playing—isn't that right?

Christine. Yes. . . . So you do think of me sometimes?

Fritz. Rather frequently, my child.

Christine. Not so often as I think of you. I am always thinking of you . . . all day long . . . and I can only be happy when I see you.

Fritz. Then don't we see each other often enough?

Christine. Often . . .

Fritz. Certainly. In the summer we shan't see each other so much. Just think! Suppose, for example, I went away for a couple of weeks —what would you say?

Christine. [*Anxiously.*] What? You are going away?

Fritz. No. . . . And still it might be possible that I would like the notion of being all alone for a week.

Christine. Oh, why?

Fritz. I'm simply talking about possibilities. I know myself, I get such notions. And you, too, might some time take the whim of not wanting to see me for a few days. . . . I'll always understand that.

Christine. No, I'll never have that whim, Fritz.

Fritz. You can't tell about that.

Christine. But I can. . . . I love you.

Fritz. I love you, too, very much.

Christine. But you are everything to me, Fritz; for you I could—[*breaks off.*] No, I can't imagine an hour ever coming when I wouldn't want to see you. As long as I live, Fritz——

Fritz. [*Interrupts.*] Child, I beseech you . . . don't say anything like that. . . . I don't like big words. We won't talk about eternity.

Christine. [*Smiling sadly.*] Have no fear, Fritz. . . . I know this can't be for always.

Fritz. You misunderstand me, child. Of course it's possible—[*laughing*]—that we simply won't be able to live without each other, but we can't tell for sure, can we? We're only human.

Theodore. [*Pointing to the lighted candles.*] Kindly turn your eyes upon that. . . . Isn't that different from a stupid lamp?

Fritz. You're really a born decorator.

Theodore. Children, what do you say—shall we think about eating?

Toni. Yes! . . . Come, Christine.

Fritz. Wait; I'll show you where to find everything.

Toni. First of all, we need a tablecloth.

Theodore. [*With German accent, as on the vaudeville stage.*] "A tableclot'?"

Fritz. What?

Theodore. Don't you remember that fellow in the Orpheum? "Dot is a tableclot'." "Dot is a shtool." "Dot is a liddle pianino."

Toni. Say, Dore, when are you going to the Orpheum with me? You promised me a little while ago. Then Christine will come along, and Mr. Fritz, too. [*She is just taking from* FRITZ *the tablecloth which he has taken out of the sideboard.*] Then *we'll* be your friends in the box.

Fritz. Yes, yes.

Toni. Then the lady with the black velvet dress can go home alone.

Fritz. Why do you keep thinking about that lady in black? It's too stupid.

Toni. Oh, *we* don't think about her. . . . There. . . . And the silver? [FRITZ *shows her the things in the open sideboard.*] Yes. . . . And the plates? . . . Yes, thanks. . . . There, now we can do it alone all right. Go, go away now, you're only getting in our way.

Theodore. [*Has meanwhile stretched out on the couch;* FRITZ *advances toward him.*] You'll excuse me.

Toni. Did you see the picture of Fritz in his uniform?

Christine. No.

Toni. You must have a look at it. Swell! [*They talk on.*]

Theodore. Such evenings are my delight, Fritz.

Fritz. Well, they *are* nice.

Theodore. Then I feel so cozy. . . . Don't you?

Fritz. Oh, I wish I could always feel so contented.

Toni. Tell me, Mr. Fritz, is there coffee in the machine?

Fritz. Yes. You can start the lamp under it right away—it takes a good hour on that machine, before the coffee is done.

Theodore. I'd give a dozen demoniac women for a sweet girl like that.

Fritz. There's no comparison.

Theodore. You see, we hate the women that we love—and only love the women that are indifferent to us. [FRITZ *laughs.*]

Toni. What's the joke? We'd like to hear it, too.

Theodore. Nothing for you, children. We're philosophizing.—If this were to be our last meeting with these girls, we'd be just as jolly, wouldn't we?

Fritz. The last time? . . . Well, there's certainly something melancholy about that. Parting always gives pain, even if you've been looking forward to it eagerly for a long time.

Christine. Say, Fritz, where's the small silver?

Fritz. [*Goes rear to the sideboard.*] Here it is, sweetheart.

[TONI *comes forward, runs her hand through* THEODORE'S *hair; he still reclining on the couch.*]

Theodore. You pussy-cat!

Fritz. [*Opens the package* TONI *brought.*] Grand!

Christine. [*To* FRITZ.] You have everything in such good order.

Fritz. Yes.

[*Arranges the things* TONI *brought—sardines, cold meat, butter, cheese.*]

Christine. Fritz . . . won't you tell me?

Fritz. Tell you what?

Christine. [*Very timidly.*] Who the lady was.

Fritz. No; don't make me cross. [*More gently.*] You see, that's one thing we agreed upon expressly: no questions asked. That's the nice thing about it. When I am with you the world disappears, like that—— [*Snaps his fingers.*] I don't ask you any questions, either.

Christine. You can ask me anything you like.

Fritz. But I don't. I don't want to know anything.

Toni. [*Returns to table.*] Goodness, what a mess you're making! [*Takes the edibles, puts them on the plates.*] There. . . .

Theodore. Say, Fritz, have you anything to drink here?

Fritz. Oh, yes, I think I can find something. [*Exit into front room.*]

Theodore. [*Raises himself and inspects the table.*] Good.

Toni. There, I think we've got everything now.

Fritz. [*Returns with some bottles.*] Here's something to drink, too.

Theodore. Where are the roses that fall from the ceiling?

Toni. That's right, we forgot the roses. [*She takes the roses out of the vase, climbs on a chair, and lets the roses fall on the table.*] There!

Christine. My, what a wild girl you are tonight!

Theodore. Here, not on the plates.

Fritz. Where do you want to sit, Christine?

Theodore. Where is the corkscrew?

Fritz. [*Gets one from the sideboard.*] Here is one. [TONI *tries to open a bottle.*]

Fritz. No, let me do that.

Theodore. No, let me do it. . . . [*Takes bottle and corkscrew from him.*] Meanwhile you might——

[*Moves his fingers as at the piano.*]

Toni. Yes, yes, that's grand! . . .

[*She runs to the piano, takes the things off it, and opens it.*]

Fritz. [*To* CHRISTINE.] Shall I?

Christine. Oh, please do, I've wanted that for so long.

Fritz. [*At the piano.*] You can play a little too?

Christine. [*With a gesture.*] Oh, goodness.

Toni. She plays fine, Christine does. . . . She can sing too.

Fritz. Really? You never told me that.

Christine. Did you ever ask me?

Fritz. Where did you learn to sing?

Christine. I really never learned. Father taught me a little—but I haven't got much voice. And you know, since Auntie died, the one that always lived with us, it's even quieter at home than it was before.

Fritz. What do you do, anyway, all day long?

Christine. Oh, I have plenty to do!

Fritz. Around the house, I suppose?

Christine. Yes. And then I copy notes quite a lot.

Theodore. Music notes?

Christine. Surely.

Theodore. They must pay you tremendously for that. [*The others laugh.*] Well, I'd pay tremendously for it. Music copying must be a terrible task, I think.

Toni. There's no sense in her working so hard, either. If I had as much voice as you have, I'd have been in the theater long ago.

Theodore. You wouldn't even need a voice. . . . Of course you do nothing all day, hey?

Toni. Well, I like that! I have two little brothers that are going to school. I have to dress them in the morning. And then I help them with their lessons——

Theodore. That's a lie, every word of it.

Toni. Well, if you won't believe me.—And until last autumn I was in a store from eight in the morning till eight at night.

Theodore. [*Mockingly.*] Where was that?

Toni. In a millinery store. Mother wants me to go back there.

Theodore. [*As above.*] Why did you leave it?

Fritz. [*To* CHRISTINE.] Then you must sing something for us.

Theodore. Come on, children, let's eat first, and then we'll play, won't you?

Fritz. [*Rising, to* CHRISTINE.] Come, sweetheart. [*Leads her to the table.*]

Toni. The coffee! There's the coffee boiling over, and we haven't begun to eat.

Theodore. Nothing matters now.

Toni. But it's boiling over!

[*Blows out the flame. All sit down at the table.*]

Theodore. What will you have, Toni? But let me tell you this: the cake comes last! . . . First you've got to eat nothing but sour things. [FRITZ *pours out the wine.*] Not that way: we do it differently now. Don't you know the latest fashion? [*Stands up, affects magniloquence; to* CHRISTINE, *bottle in hand.*] Special quality, genuine Johannisberg, eighteen hundred——

[*Mumbles the last figures. Fills glass, then goes to* TONI, *to* FRITZ, *repeating the same ceremony and words; finally stands at his own place, and repeats as before. Seats himself.*]

Toni. [*Laughing.*] He's always doing something silly.

Theodore. [*Raises his glass; all clink.*] Prosit.

Toni. Your health, Theodore.

Theodore. [*Rising.*] Ladies and Gentlemen . . .

Fritz. Oh, not yet!

Theodore. [*Sits again.*] Well, I can wait.

Toni. Oh, that's what I like, after-dinner speeches. I have a cousin that always makes his speeches in rhymes.

Theodore. What regiment is he in?

Toni. Come, stop that . . . He talks it off by heart and in rhyme, and it's just splendid, Christine. And he's an elderly gentleman now, too.

Theodore. Oh, it sometimes happens that elderly gentlemen can still talk in rhyme.

Fritz. But you're not drinking at all, Christine! [*Clinks with her.*]

Theodore. [*Clinks with* TONI.] To the old gentlemen who talk in rhymes.

Toni. [*Merrily.*] To the young gentlemen, even if they don't talk at all . . . for example, to Mr. Fritz. . . . Say, Mr. Fritz, now we'll drink to our better acquaintance, if you wish —and Christine must do the same with Theodore.

Theodore. But not with this wine, that's not the right kind for it. [*Rises, takes another bottle, same ceremony as before.*] Xérès de la Frontera mille huit cent cinquante——

Toni. [*Sips.*] Ah——

Theodore. Can't you wait till we all drink together? Now then, children . . . Before we solemnly drink to our better acquaintance, let us drink to the happy chance that, that . . . and so forth . . .

Toni. Yes, that's enough.

[*They drink,* FRITZ *taking* TONI'S *arm,* THEODORE CHRISTINE'S. FRITZ *kisses* TONI. THEODORE *starts to kiss* CHRISTINE.]

Christine. Is that necessary?

Theodore. Absolutely, else the whole ceremony is null. . . . [*Kisses her.*] There, and now to your seats! . . .

Toni. But it's getting terribly hot in the room.

Fritz. That's because of all the candles Theodore lit.

Toni. And the wine, too.

[*She leans back in her chair.*]

Theodore. Come here, the best of all is coming now. [*He cuts off a slice of the cake and puts in it her mouth.*] There, sweet tooth—that good?

Toni. Awfully! . . .

[*He gives her another.*]

Theodore. Come, Fritz, now's the time. Now you might play something.

Fritz. Do you want me to, Christine?

Christine. Please do!

Toni. Play something swell. [THEODORE *fills the glasses.*] No more. [*Drinks.*]

Christine. [*Sipping.*] The wine is so heavy.

Theodore. [*Pointing to the glass.*] Fritz.

[FRITZ *empties the glass, goes to piano.* CHRISTINE *goes and sits by him.*]

Toni. Mr. Fritz, play the "Double Eagle."

Fritz. The "Double Eagle"—how does it go?

Toni. Dore, can't you play it?

Theodore. I can't play at all.

Fritz. I know the thing; but I can't think of it.

Toni. I'll sing it for you. . . . La . . . la . . . lalalala. . . .

Fritz. Aha, now I know.

[*Does not play quite correctly.*]

Toni. [*Goes to the piano.*] No, this way.

[*Plays the melody with one finger.*]

Fritz. Yes, yes. . . .

[*He plays,* TONI *sings.*]

Theodore. Recollections again, hey?

Fritz. [*Plays wrong again and stops.*] Can't do it. I've got no ear.

[*He starts to improvise.*]

Toni. [*After the first measure.*] That's no good.

Fritz. [*Laughs.*] Don't say that, I made it up.

Toni. But it's no good for dancing.

Fritz. Just try it once . . .

Theodore. [*To* TONI.] Come, let's try.

[*They dance.*]

[CHRISTINE *sits by the piano and looks at the keys. There is a ring.* FRITZ *suddenly stops playing;* THEODORE *and* TONI *dance on.*]

Theodore and *Toni.* [*Together.*] What's all this? Come!

Fritz. The bell just rang? . . . [To THEODORE.] Did you invite anybody else?

Theodore. I should say not—you don't need to answer the bell.

Christine. [*To* FRITZ.] What's the matter with you?

Fritz. Nothing . . .

[*There is another ring.* FRITZ *stands up, rooted to the spot.*]

Theodore. You are simply not at home.

Fritz. You can hear the piano out in the corridor. . . . And you can see from the street that the room is lit.

Theodore. What folly is this? You're simply not at home.

Fritz. But it makes me nervous.

Theodore. Well, what do you suppose it's going to be? A letter—or a telegram—— You're not going to have a visitor at [*looks at his watch*] nine o'clock.

[*There is another ring.*]

Fritz. Rubbish, I must go and see——

[*Exit.*]

Toni. But you're not a bit swell——

[*Strikes a few keys on the piano.*]

Theodore. Here, stop that now!—[*To* CHRISTINE.] What ails you? Does the bell make you nervous, too?

[FRITZ *returns, in forced calm.*]

Theodore and *Christine.* [*Together.*] Well, who was it?—Who was it?

Fritz. [*With a forced smile.*] You must be good enough to excuse me for a moment. Go in there meanwhile.

Theodore. What is it?

Christine. Who is it?

Fritz. Nothing, child, I simply have to say a few words to a gentleman. . . . [FRITZ *has opened the door of the adjoining room, conducts the girls into it.* THEODORE, *going in last, looks questioningly at* FRITZ. FRITZ, *in a low voice, with an expression of horror:*] *He!*

Theodore. Ah!

Fritz. In with you!

Theodore. I beg of you, don't do anything stupid, it may be a *trap.* . . .

Fritz. Go . . . go. . . . [THEODORE *exits.* FRITZ *goes rapidly through the room to the corridor, so that the stage is empty for a few seconds. Then he enters again, allowing an elegantly dressed gentleman of about thirty-five years to precede him.* THE GENTLEMAN *wears a yellow mantle, holds his hat in his gloved hand. While entering:*] Pardon me for making you wait . . . I beg you. . . .

The Gentleman. [*In a very easy tone.*] Oh, that is nothing. I regret extremely to have disturbed you.

Fritz. By no means. Will you not . . .

[*Indicates a chair.*]

The Gentleman. Why, I see that I have disturbed you? A little entertainment, I presume?

Fritz. A few friends.

The Gentleman. [*Seating himself, amicably.*] A masquerade, no doubt?

Fritz. [*Embarrassed.*] Why do you say that?

The Gentleman. Well, your friends have ladies' hats and cloaks.

Fritz. Well yes. . . . [*Smiling.*] There may be lady friends among them. . . .

[*Silence.*]

The Gentleman. Life is at times very merry . . . yes . . .

[*Looks rigidly at* FRITZ.]

Fritz. [*Endures the glance a while, then looks away.*] I presume I may permit myself to inquire what gives me the pleasure of your visit?

The Gentleman. Certainly. . . . [*Calmly.*] You see, my wife forgot to take her veil away from here.

Fritz. Your wife . . . here? Her . . . [*Smiling.*] The jest is a trifle strange. . . .

The Gentleman. [*Suddenly rising, very loudly, almost wildly, supporting himself by resting one hand on the chair arm.*] She *did* forget it. [FRITZ *rises also, and the two men stand facing each other.* THE GENTLEMAN *raises his clenched fist, as if to launch it at* FRITZ; *in fury and loathing:*] Oh! . . . [FRITZ *makes a parrying motion, takes a short step backward.* THE GENTLEMAN *after a long pause:*] Here are your letters. [*He throws on the desk a packet of letters which he has taken from his overcoat pocket.*] I wish those which you have received. [FRITZ, *parrying motion.* THE GENTLEMAN, *vehemently, significantly:*] I do not wish to have them found—*later*—in your rooms.

Fritz. [*Very loudly.*] They will not be found. [THE GENTLEMAN *looks at him. Pause.*] What else do you wish of me?

The Gentleman. [*Scornfully.*] What *else?*

Fritz. I am at your disposal. . . .

The Gentleman. [*Bows coolly.*] Very well.

[*He casts a glance around the room; as he again sees the table and the girls' hats, a sudden flash crosses his face, as if he would burst into a new fit of rage.*]

Fritz. [*Notices this.*] I am wholly at your disposal. I shall be at home tomorrow till noon. [THE GENTLEMAN *bows and turns to go.* FRITZ *accompanies him to the door,* THE GENTLEMAN *motioning him away. When he is gone,* FRITZ *goes to the desk and stands there a moment. Then he hastens to the window, looks through a crack in the blind, and can be seen to follow the motions of* THE GENTLEMAN *passing along the street. Leaving the window he looks down for a moment; then goes to the door of the adjoining room, opens it halfway, and calls:*] Theodore, one moment. [*The following scene very rapid.*]

Theodore. [*Excited.*] Well? . . .

Fritz. He knows.

Theodore. He knows nothing. You simply fell into his trap. I'll wager you even confessed. You're a fool, I tell you. . . . You . . .

Fritz. [*Pointing to the letters.*] He brought me back my letters.

Theodore. [*Startled.*] Oh! . . . [*After a pause.*] I always say, a man ought not to write letters.

Fritz. It was he, this noon, down below.

Theodore. Well, what happened?—Tell me about it.

Fritz. You must do me a great service now, Theodore.

Theodore. I'll fix up the whole business for you.

Fritz. That is out of the question now.

Theodore. Then . . .

Fritz. In any case it will be well. . . . [*Breaks off.*] But we can't let the poor girls wait so long.

Theodore. Let them wait. What were you going to say?

Fritz. It will be well if you go to Lensky today.

Theodore. At once, if you wish.

Fritz. You won't find him now . . . but between eleven and twelve he will surely come into the coffee-house . . . perhaps the two of you will then come here. . . .

Theodore. Come, don't make up such a face . . . ninety-nine times out of a hundred it turns out all right. . . .

Fritz. He will see to it that this one *doesn't* turn out all right.

Theodore. But I beg you, remember that affair of last year, between Doctor Billinger and Herz—that was exactly the same.

Fritz. None of that, you know yourself he ought to have shot me down right here in the room—it would have come to the same thing.

Theodore. [*Acting.*] Well, that is fine, I must say. That's a grand idea. . . . And so Lensky and I count for nothing? You think we'll agree that . . .

Fritz. I beg you, no more of that! . . . You will simply accept what is proposed.

Theodore. Ah——

Fritz. What's the sense of all this, Theodore? As if you didn't know.

Theodore. Nonsense. And anyway, it's all a matter of luck. . . . You have just as much chance of . . .

Fritz. [*Without listening to him.*] She foreboded it. We both foreboded it. We knew it. . . .

Theodore. Come, Fritz. . . .

Fritz. [*Goes to the desk, locks up the letters.*] Oh, what is *she* doing this minute? Did he . . . Theodore, you must find out tomorrow what happened over there.

Theodore. I will try.

Fritz. And see to it that no useless delay . . .

Theodore. It can scarcely be before day after tomorrow in the morning.

Fritz. [*Almost terrified.*] Theodore!

Theodore. And so . . . head up. You believe a little in inward conviction, don't you? —and I have a firm conviction that everything will turn out all right. [*With forced merriment.*] I don't know why myself, but I have the conviction, anyway!

Fritz. [*Smiling.*] What a good fellow you are. But what shall we say to the girls?

Theodore. That doesn't matter. Let's simply send them away.

Fritz. No, no. Let's be as merry as we can. Christine must not suspect anything. I'll sit down at the piano again; and you call them in. [THEODORE *turns to do this, with discontented face.*] And what shall we say to them?

Theodore. That it's none of their business.

Fritz. [*Who has sat down at the piano, turning toward him.*] No, no——

Theodore. That it's about a friend—I'll invent something. [FRITZ *pl ys a few notes.*] Ladies, I beg you to enter.

[*Has opened the door.*]

Toni. Well, at last! Has he gone?

Christine. [*Hastening to* FRITZ.] Who was here, Fritz?

Fritz. [*At the piano, playing.*] Curious again.

Christine. I beg you, Fritz, tell me.

Fritz. Sweetheart, I can't tell you, it really concerns people that you don't know at all.

Christine. [*Coaxingly.*] Come, Fritz, tell me the truth.

Theodore. Of course she won't leave you in peace. . . . But mind you tell her nothing! You promised *him.*

Toni. Come, don't be so tiresome, Christine, let them have their fun. They're simply putting on airs.

Theodore. I must finish that waltz with Miss Toni. [*German accent.*] Bleaze, Mister Museec-maker—a liddle museek.

[FRITZ *plays.* THEODORE *and* TONI *dance a few measures.*]

Toni. [*After a few moments.*] I can't.

[*She falls back into a chair.* THEODORE *kisses her, seats himself beside her on the chair arm.* FRITZ *stays at the piano, takes both* CHRISTINE'S *hands, looks at her.*]

Christine. [*As if awaking.*] Why don't you play on?

Fritz. [*Smiling.*] Enough for today. . . .

Christine. That's the way I'd like to be able to play.

Fritz. Do you play much?

Christine. I don't get much chance; there's always something in the house that needs to be done. And then you know we have such a poor piano.

Fritz. I'd like to try it once. I'd like to see your room once, anyway.

Christine. [*Smiling.*] It isn't as pretty as here.

Fritz. And something else I'd like: to have you tell me about yourself . . . a whole lot . . . I really know so little about you.

Christine. There isn't much to tell. And I haven't any secrets either . . . like some others.

Fritz. You never loved any man before?

[CHRISTINE *merely looks at him.* FRITZ *kisses her hands.*]

Christine. And never shall love any other.

Fritz. [*With an almost pained expression.*] Don't say that . . . don't. . . . What do you know about it? . . . Does your father love you very much, Christine?

Christine. Oh, how much! . . . And there was a time when I used to tell him everything.

Fritz. Well, child, don't reproach yourself. People have to have secrets once in a while—that's the way of the world.

Christine. If I only knew that you loved me—it would all be right.

Fritz. Then don't you know?

Christine. If you would always talk to me like that, then . . .

Fritz. Christine! You haven't a very comfortable seat, though.

Christine. Let me be—this is all right.

[*She lays her head against the piano.* FRITZ *stands up and strokes her hair.*]

Christine. Oh, that feels good.

[*The room is quiet.*]

Theodore. Where are the cigars, Fritz?

[FRITZ *advances to him as he stands by the sideboard looking.* TONI *has fallen asleep.*]

Fritz. [*Hands him a small box of cigars.*] And black coffee. [*He pours two cups.*]

Theodore. Children, don't you want some coffee, too?

Fritz. Toni, shall I pour a cup? . . .

Theodore. Let them sleep.—You ought not to drink coffee tonight. You ought to go to bed as soon as possible and try to sleep well. [FRITZ *looks at him and laughs bitterly.*] Well, things are as they are . . . and now it's not a question of being magnificent or deep, but of being as sensible as you can . . . that's the point . . . in such cases.

Fritz. You'll bring Lensky to me tonight, will you?

Theodore. That's nonsense. Tomorrow is time enough.

Fritz. I beg you, bring him.

Theodore. All right, then.

Fritz. Will you take the girls home?

Theodore. Yes, and right away, too.—Toni! . . . Get up!

Toni. Oh, you're drinking black coffee. Give me some, too.

Theodore. Here you are, child.

Fritz. [*To* CHRISTINE, *going to her.*] Tired, my sweetheart?

Christine. How sweet, when you talk that way.

Fritz. Very tired?

Christine. [*Smiling.*] It's the wine. And I have a little headache, too.

Fritz. Well, that will pass off in the open air.

Christine. Are we going now? Will you go with us?

Fritz. No, child. I'm going to stay right here. I have some things to do.

Christine. [*Recollecting.*] Now . . . What have you got to do now?

Fritz. [*Almost sternly.*] Christine, that's something you must stop. [*Gently.*] You see, I'm all used up . . . we walked around in the country for two hours today, Theodore and I.

Theodore. Oh, that was delightful. One of these days we'll all drive out into the country together.

Toni. Yes, that will be swell. And you'll put on your uniform.

Theodore. There's feeling for nature!

Christine. When shall I see you again?

Fritz. [*Somewhat nervously.*] I'll write you.

Christine. [*Sadly.*] Good-by.

[*Turns to go.*]

Fritz. [*Notices her sadness.*] Tomorrow, Christine.

Christine. [*Happily.*] Truly?

Fritz. In the public gardens out there—at—say at six o'clock. . . . Will that suit you?

[CHRISTINE *nods.*]

Toni. [*To* FRITZ.] Are you going with us, Fritz?

Fritz. No, I shall stay here.

Toni. He has an easy time of it. Think of the long journey home we have.

Fritz. But Toni, you have left almost the whole of that cake. Wait, I'll wrap it up for you, shall I?

Toni. [*To* THEODORE.] Is that proper?

[FRITZ *wraps up the cake.*]

Christine. She's like a little child.

Toni. [*To* FRITZ.] Wait, I'll help you put out the candles.

[*Puts out one after another. The candle on the desk is left burning.*]

Christine. Shan't I open the window for you? The air is so heavy.

[*She opens the window, looks at the house opposite.*]

Fritz. There, children. Now I'll light you down the stairs.

Toni. Are the lights out on the stairs?

Theodore. Why, of course.

Christine. Oh, the air is nice, coming in here.

Toni. May breezes. . . . [*At the door to* FRITZ, *who holds the candlestick.*] Well, we thank you for a warm welcome.

Theodore. [*Urging her forward.*] Come, come, come, come. . . .

[FRITZ *goes out with them. The door stays open. The voices are heard outside. The outer door is heard to open.*]

Toni. Bah!

Theodore. Look out for the steps there.

Toni. Thanks for the cake.

Theodore. Shh, you'll wake people up.

Christine. Good night.

Theodore. Good night.

[FRITZ *can be heard to close and bolt the outer door. As he enters and puts the light on the desk, the street-door is heard to open and close. Goes to the window and bows, looking down.*]

Christine. Good night.

Toni. [*In high spirits.*] Good night, my darling child.

Theodore. [*Reprovingly.*] Toni!

[*One can hear his words, her laughter; the steps die away.* THEODORE *whistles the melody of the "Double Eagle," which is the last thing heard.* FRITZ *looks out a few moments longer, then sinks down on the chair nearest the window.*]

CURTAIN

SECOND ACT

CHRISTINE'S *room. Modest and neat.*

[CHRISTINE *is dressing to go out.*]

Catherine. [*Enters after knocking.*] Good evening, Miss Christine.

Christine. [*Standing before the mirror, turns around.*] Good evening.

Catherine. You're just going out?

Christine. I'm not in such a great hurry.

Catherine. My husband sent me to ask if you wouldn't go and take supper with us in the Zoölogical Garden; there's a band there tonight.

Christine. Thank you very much, Mrs. Binder. I can't tonight. Another time, perhaps?—But you're not angry?

Catherine. Not a bit, why should I be? You'll probably have a better time than with us. [CHRISTINE *looks at her.*] Has your father gone to the theater?

Christine. Oh, no; he comes home first. It doesn't begin till half-past seven now.

Catherine. That's so, I keep forgetting. I'll just wait for him. I've wanted for a long time to ask him about free tickets to the new piece. I suppose they can be had now?

Christine. Surely, nobody goes there any more now, when the evenings are so lovely.

Catherine. People like us never get a chance to go, unless we happen to know somebody in a theater. But don't let me keep you, Miss Christine, if you have to go. To be sure, my husband will be very sorry . . . and somebody else too.

Christine. Who?

Catherine. Binder's cousin goes with us, of course. Do you know, Miss Christine, that he has a steady job now?

Christine. [*Indifferently.*] Oh.

Catherine. And a very nice salary. And such a fine young fellow. And he has such respect for you——

Christine. Well—good-by, Mrs. Binder.

Catherine. A body could tell him anything about you—he wouldn't believe a word of it. . . . [CHRISTINE *looks at her.*] There are such men.

Christine. Good-by, Mrs. Binder.

Catherine. Good-by. . . . [*Not too maliciously.*] See that you aren't late to your appointment, Miss Christine.

Christine. What do you want of me, anyway?

Catherine. Why, nothing; you're quite right. You can't be young but once.

Christine. Good-by.

Catherine. But I'd like to give you one piece of advice, just the same, Miss Christine: you ought to be a little more careful.

Christine. Why, what do you mean?

Catherine. Look—Vienna is such a big city. . . . Do you have to have your meetings a hundred paces from your house?

Christine. I suppose that's nobody's business.

Catherine. I didn't want to believe it, when Binder told me. He saw you, you know. . . . Come, I said to him, you were mistaken, you saw somebody else. Miss Christine is not the girl to go walking with elegant young gentlemen in the evening, and if she did, she would be wise enough not to go walking through these streets. Well, says he, you can ask her yourself. And, says he, it's no wonder, either —she doesn't come to see us any more at all. Instead of that she's going around all the time with Toni Schlager, and what sort of company is that for a decent young girl?—You see, men are so low-minded, Miss Christine.—And of course he had to go and tell everything to Franz right away too; but he got fine and angry, he did, and for Miss Christine he'd burn his hand off, and anybody that said anything about her would have to deal with him. And you're so domestic and were always so sweet with your old auntie—God grant her eternal rest—and you live so modestly and so retiringly and all that. . . . [*Pause.*] Perhaps you'll come to hear the music, after all?

Christine. No. . . .

Vyring. [*Enters, a laurel branch in his hand.*] Good evening.—Ah, Mrs. Binder. How are you?

Catherine. Thank you, well.

Vyring. And little Lena? And your husband?

Catherine. All well, God be praised.

Vyring. Well, that's fine. [*To* CHRISTINE.] You're still at home in all this fine weather?

Christine. I was just going out.

Vyring. That's right. The air outside—it's something wonderful, eh, Mrs. Binder? I just came through the public gardens; the lilacs are in bloom, simply gorgeous. I broke the law a little, too.

[*Gives the branch to* CHRISTINE.]

Christine. Thank you, Father.

Catherine. Thank your lucky stars that the guard didn't catch you.

Vyring. Just go out there once, Mrs. Binder. It smells just as good as if I hadn't plucked the little twig.

Catherine. But if everybody thought the same.

Vyring. Well, that would be a mistake, to be sure.

Christine. Good-by, Father.

Vyring. If you could wait a few minutes, you might go to the theater with me.

Christine. I . . . I promised Toni that I would go for her. . . .

Vyring. Oh, yes. Well, that's wiser, too. Youth belongs with youth. Good-by, Christine.

Christine. [*Kisses him.*] Good-by, Mrs. Binder.

[*Exit.* VYRING'S *eyes follow her tenderly.*]

Catherine. That's a very close friendship with her and Miss Toni.

Vyring. Yes.—I'm really glad that she has some company and doesn't have to sit at home all the time. What sort of a life does that girl have, anyway?

Catherine. Yes, to be sure.

Vyring. I can't tell you, Mrs. Binder, how it hurts me sometimes when I come home from rehearsal and find her sitting there and sewing; and then we've scarcely got up from the table at noon when she sits down again and goes to copying notes.

Catherine. Yes, yes, the millionaires have an easier time of it, to be sure, than we do. But how about her singing?

Vyring. It's not much. Her voice is big enough for a room, and her singing is good enough for her father—but you can't live on that.

Catherine. That's too bad.

Vyring. I am glad she sees it herself. She at least will be spared from disappointments. Of course I could get her into the chorus in our theater.

Catherine. Of course, with such a figure!

Vyring. But there's no future there.

Catherine. A girl brings really a good many cares. When I think that in five or six years my little Lena will be a grown girl too——

Vyring. But why don't you sit down, Mrs. Binder?

Catherine. Oh, thanks; my husband is coming for me right away—I only came to invite Christine.

Vyring. Invite? . . .

Catherine. Yes, to hear the band in the Zoölogical Gardens. I thought that might cheer her up a bit. She really needs it.

Vyring. Couldn't do her a bit of harm, especially after this sad winter. Why doesn't she go with you?

Catherine. I don't know. . . . Perhaps because Binder's cousin is with us.

Vyring. Ah, that's possible. You know she can't stand him. She told me that herself.

Catherine. Well, why not? Franz is a very decent fellow—and now he's even got a steady job, and that's a piece of good fortune nowadays for a . . .

Vyring. For a . . . . poor girl——

Catherine. For any girl.

Vyring. Now, tell me, Mrs. Binder, is a blooming young creature like that really made for nothing but for some such decent fellow who happens to have a steady job?

Catherine. Why, that's the best thing, after all. You can't wait for a count, and when one happens to come along, he usually takes his leave before he's married you. [VYRING *is at the window. Pause.*] Well, and that's why I always say you can't be careful enough of a young girl, especially of the company she keeps——

Vyring. Well, I wonder if it's worth while to throw away all your young years like that. —And what good does all her goodness do a poor creature like that, even if, after years of waiting, the stocking-maker actually comes?

Catherine. Mr. Vyring, if my husband is a stocking-maker, he is an honest and good man, that I've never had to complain of. . . .

Vyring. [*Soothingly.*] Why, Mrs. Binder, do you think I'm aiming at you? You didn't fling your youth out of the window, either.

Catherine. I have forgotten all about that.

Vyring. Don't say that.—You can say what you like; memories are, after all, the best thing in your life.

Catherine. I haven't any memories.

Vyring. Now, now. . . .

Catherine. And if a body does have such memories as you mean, what remains behind? . . . Regret.

Vyring. Well, and what remains behind—if she—doesn't even have anything to remember? If her whole life simply goes by [*simply and without emotion*] day after day, without happiness or love—I suppose you think that's better?

Catherine. But, Mr. Vyring, just think of the old lady, of your sister. . . . But it still pains you to have her spoken of, Mr. Vyring.

Vyring. It still pains me, yes.

Catherine. Of course . . . when two people have clung to each other so warmly. . . . I always said that brothers like you aren't found every day. [VYRING *makes gesture of deprecation.*] Well, it's true. You had to be both father and mother to her, and you such a young man.

Vyring. Yes, yes——

Catherine. And that must be a kind of consolation, too. Then you know that you have been the benefactor and the protector of a poor girl like that——

Vyring. Yes, I imagined that, too—when she was still a pretty young girl—and God knows how clever and noble I thought myself. But then, later on, when the gray hairs came and the wrinkles, and one day passed like all the others—and her whole youth—and the girl gradually (you scarcely notice such things) turned into the old maid—then for the first time I began to see what I had done.

Catherine. But Mr. Vyring——

Vyring. I still see her before me, as she often used to sit opposite me in the evening, sitting by the lamp here in the room, and used to look at me with her quiet smile, with a certain resigned expression—as if she wanted to thank me for something;—and I—I could have gladly gone down on my knees to her, and begged her forgiveness that I had guarded her so well against all dangers—and all happiness! [*Pause.*]

Catherine. And many a girl would be happy just the same, if she always had such a brother by her side . . . and nothing to regret. . . .

Toni. [*Enters.*] Good evening. . . . Why, it's all dark here, you can scarcely see a thing. —Ah, Mrs. Binder. Your husband is downstairs waiting for you, Mrs. Binder. . . . Isn't Christine at home?

Vyring. She went out a quarter of an hour ago.

Catherine. Didn't you meet her? She was going to meet you.

Toni. No . . . we evidently missed each other.—You're going to hear the band tonight, your husband says.

Catherine. Yes, he is so fond of it. What a charming little hat you have on, Miss Toni. Isn't it a new one?

Toni. I should say not.—Don't you know this style any more? Last Spring's style, only freshly trimmed.

Catherine. Did you trim it yourself?

Toni. Well, of course.

Vyring. So clever!

Catherine. Oh, yes—I keep forgetting that you worked for a year in a milliner shop.

Toni. I shall probably go back again. Mother wants me to, and that settles it.

Catherine. How is your mother?

Toni. Well enough—she has a little toothache—but the doctor says it's rheumatic pains.

Vyring. Well, it's time for me . . .

Catherine. I'll go right down with you, Mr. Vyring.

Toni. I'll go, too. But take your overcoat, Mr. Vyring; it's going to be quite cool later on.

Vyring. You think so?

Catherine. Yes, indeed.—How can you be so foolish? [CHRISTINE *enters.*]

Toni. Why, there she is.

Catherine. Back from your walk already?

Christine. Yes. Hello, Toni.—I have a headache. [*Seats herself.*]

Vyring. Headache?

Catherine. That's from the air.

Vyring. Come, what's the matter, Christine?—Please, Miss Toni, will you light the lamp? [TONI *sets about it.*]

Christine. But I can do that myself.

Vyring. Let me see your face, Christine.

Christine. But, Father, it is nothing; it's just the air outside.

Catherine. Lots of people can't stand the Spring air.

Vyring. Miss Toni, you'll stay with Christine, won't you?

Toni. Of course I will.

Christine. But it isn't anything, Father.

Toni. My mother doesn't make such a fuss over me when I have a headache.

Vyring. [*To* CHRISTINE, *still sitting.*] Are you so tired?

Christine. [*Standing up.*] I'll get right up again. [*Smiling.*]

Vyring. There—now you look quite different again. [*To* CATHERINE.] She looks quite different when she smiles, don't you think? Well, good-by, Christine. [*Kisses her.*] And see to it that your little head isn't aching when I come home. [*He is at the door.*]

Catherine. [*Softly to* CHRISTINE.] Have you quarreled?

[CHRISTINE *makes an angry gesture.*]

Vyring. [*At the door.*] Mrs. Binder!

Toni. Good-by.

[*Exeunt* VYRING *and* CATHERINE.]

Toni. Do you know what your headache comes from? From the sweet wine yesterday. I'm surprised that I don't feel the effects of it. But it was jolly, wasn't it? [CHRISTINE *nods.*] They're swell people, aren't they?—both of them, you can't say anything different, can you?—And such nice rooms as Fritz has, really splendid. At Dore's place . . . [*Interrupts herself.*] Oh, well.—Say, have you still got such a headache? Why don't you talk? . . . What's the matter with you?

Christine. Only think—he didn't come.

Toni. Left you in the lurch, did he? Serves you right.

Christine. Why, what do you mean? What have I done?

Toni. You spoil him, that's all; you're too nice to him. A man just can't help getting tyrannical.

Christine. You don't know what you're talking about.

Toni. I do know quite well. I've been angry with you this long time. He comes late to his appointments; he doesn't take you home; he goes into a theater-box with strangers; he leaves you in the lurch—and you take it all calmly and make sheep's eyes—[*imitating*]—at him into the bargain.

Christine. Oh, don't talk so, don't make yourself out worse than you are. You love Theodore too.

Toni. Love him—of course I love him. But he won't find me grieving about him, and no man will, not any more. There isn't one of these men that is worth it.

Christine. I never heard you talk so, never!

Toni. No, Tina—we never talked like this before. I never dared, you see. You don't know how afraid of you I was! . . . But I always thought this: when you once get it, you'll get it bad. And the first time it certainly does give you a shaking up.—But you can be thankful that you've got such a good friend to help you through your first love affair.

Christine. Toni!

Toni. Don't you believe me when I say I'm a good friend to you? If I wasn't here to tell you that he's just a man like the rest, and that the whole manpack isn't worth a single bad hour, God knows what thoughts might come into your head. But I always will say, you never can believe a word men say.

Christine. What do you mean by saying *men, men*—what do I care about *men*!—I'm not asking about the others.—As long as I live I shall never think about another man.

Toni. Well, what are you thinking of? . . . Has he? . . . Of course—such things have happened; but then you ought to have gone at the affair differently.

Christine. Do keep still!

Toni. Well, what do you want? I can't help it if it's so.—You have to think about a thing like that. You simply have to wait till somebody comes that you can see is in earnest from his face. . . .

Christine. Toni, I can't stand such words today; they hurt me.

Toni. [*Good-humoredly.*] Oh, now, come —

Christine. Leave me alone . . . don't be angry . . . leave me alone!

Toni. Why should I be angry? I'll go. I didn't want to hurt you, Christine, truly not. [*Turns to go.*] Ah, Mr. Fritz.

Fritz. [*Has entered.*] Good evening.

Christine. [*With a joyous cry.*] Fritz! Fritz!

[*Rushes into his arms.* TONI *steals out, her face saying: I'm not needed here.*]

Fritz. [*Freeing himself.*] But——

Christine. They all say you will forsake me! But you won't, will you—not yet—not just yet?

Fritz. Who says it? What ails you? [*Patting her.*] But, sweetheart, . . . I really thought you would be startled when I suddenly came walking in here.

Christine. Oh—so long as I have you!

Fritz. Come, calm yourself—did you wait long for me?

Christine. Why didn't you come?

Fritz. I was detained and that made me late. Just now I was in the gardens and didn't find you—and was going home again. Suddenly I had such a longing, such a longing for your dear little face . . .

Christine. [*Happily.*] Oh, truly?

Fritz. And then, too, I had such an indescribable desire to see where you live—yes, really—I just had to see it once. And so I couldn't stand it and came up here . . . and so you really don't mind?

Christine. Oh, the idea!

Fritz. Nobody saw me; and I knew your father was in the theater.

Christine. What do I care about people?

Fritz. So this is—[*looks around the room*] —this is your room? Very pretty.

Christine. You can't see anything.

[*Is about to take the shade off the lamp.*]

Fritz. No, don't do that, the light blinds me, it's better this way. So that's the window you've told me about, where you always sit and work, eh?—And the pretty view! [*Smiling.*] But just look at all the roofs you see.—And over there—what's that black thing I see over yonder?

Christine. That's Bald Mountain.

Fritz. Sure enough. You really have a better view than I.

Christine. Oh!

Fritz. I'd like to live up so high, and be able to overlook all the roofs; I think that is very nice. And I suppose the alley is quiet?

Christine. Oh, in the daytime there's noise enough.

Fritz. Do any teams go past?

Christine. Not often, but there's a locksmith in the house opposite.

Fritz. Oh, that's very unpleasant.

[*He has sat down.*]

Christine. You get used to it; you don't hear it any more.

Fritz. [*Rises again hastily.*] Is this really my first visit? Everything seems so familiar to me. . . . I have imagined everything just this way.

[*He starts to look around the room.*]

Christine. No, you mustn't look at anything.

Fritz. What are those pictures?

Christine. Oh, stop!

Fritz. Ah, I want to look at them.

[*He takes the lamp and lights the pictures.*]

Christine. "Parting and Return."

Fritz. Sure enough—"Parting and Return."

Christine. I know well enough that the pictures aren't pretty.—There is a much better one in Father's room.

Fritz. What picture is it?

Christine. It is a girl looking out of the window, and outside it's winter, you know—and its name is "Forsaken."

Fritz. Oh. [*Puts down the lamp.*] Ah, and that's your library.

[*Sits down beside the little book-rack.*]

Christine. You'd better not look at them.

Fritz. Why not? Ah! Schiller . . . Hauff . . . Pocket Encyclopedia . . . Goodness gracious!

Christine. It only goes to G.

Fritz. [*Smiling.*] Oh. . . . A book for old and young. . . . You look at the pictures in it, I suppose?

Christine. Of course I've looked at the pictures.

Fritz. [*Still seated.*] Who is the gentleman there on the stove?

Christine. Why, don't you know? That's Schubert.

Fritz. [*Rising.*] Sure enough.

Christine. Because Father likes him so much. Father used to compose songs himself, very beautiful ones.

Fritz. And now he doesn't?

Christine. Not any more. [*Pause.*]

Fritz. [*Sits down.*] How cozy it is here.

Christine. Do you really like it?

Fritz. Very much. . . . What is that?

[*Takes up a vase of artificial flowers standing on the table.*]

Christine. He's found something else!

Fritz. No, child, that doesn't belong in here. . . . It looks so dusty.

Christine. But they certainly aren't dusty.

Fritz. Artificial flowers always look dusty. . . . Real flowers ought to be in your room, flowers that are fresh and sweet-smelling. From now on I shall . . .

[*Breaks off, turns to conceal his emotion.*]

Christine. What? What were you going to say?

Fritz. Nothing, nothing.

Christine. [*Rises. Tenderly.*] What was it?

Fritz. I was going to say that I would send you fresh flowers tomorrow.

Christine. Well, and did you want to take it back so soon?—Of course! Tomorrow you won't be thinking of me any more. [FRITZ: *deprecatory gesture.*] Certainly, it's out of sight, out of mind, with you.

Fritz. What are you saying?

Christine. Oh, yes, I know. I can tell.

Fritz. How can you imagine such a thing?

Christine. You are to blame yourself. Because you're always keeping secrets from me. . . . Because you never tell me about yourself.—What do you do all day?

Fritz. Why, sweetheart, that's very simple. I go to lectures—sometimes—then I go into the coffee-house . . . then I read . . . or sometimes I play the piano—then I chat with somebody—then I go calling . . . but all that is of no account. It's tiresome to talk about it. —But now I must go, child.

Christine. So soon——

Fritz. Your father will soon be here.

Christine. Not for a long time yet, Fritz.—Stay awhile—just a minute—stay awhile——

Fritz. And then I have . . . Theodore is expecting me. . . . I have something to talk over with him.

Christine. Today?

Fritz. Surely today.

Christine. You can see him tomorrow, too.

Fritz. Perhaps I shan't be in Vienna tomorrow.

Christine. Not in Vienna?

Fritz. [*Noticing her alarm, calmly, cheerfully.*] Well, that wouldn't be anything wonderful, would it? I'm going away for a day—or perhaps for two, you child, you.

Christine. Where to?

Fritz. Where? . . . Anywhere. Good heavens, don't make up such a face. . . . I'm going out to my father's estate. . . . Well, is that so terrible to you?

Christine. And you never tell me about him, either.

Fritz. No; what a child you are. . . . You don't understand how nice it is to be alone together. Tell me, don't you feel that?

Christine. No, it isn't nice at all that you never tell me anything about yourself. . . . You see, I'm interested in everything that touches you . . . yes, everything.—I'd like to have more of you than just the one hour in the evening that we can spend together sometimes. Then you are gone again, and I don't know anything. . . . Then the whole night goes and a whole day, with so many hours in it—and still I don't know anything. And that often makes me so sad.

Fritz. Why does that make you sad?

Christine. Why, because I have such a longing for you as if you weren't in the same city at all, as if you were somewhere else. You simply disappear, as far as I am concerned, so far away. . . .

Fritz. [*Somewhat impatient.*] But——

Christine. Well, it's true!

Fritz. Come here to me. [*She does so.*] After all, the only thing you *know* is that I—that you love me at this moment. . . . [*She wishes to speak.*] Don't talk about eternity. [*More to himself.*] Perhaps there are moments that scatter around them the aroma of eternity.—That is the only one that we can understand, the only one that belongs to us. [*He kisses her. Pause. He rises. With a sudden outburst.*] Oh, how beautiful it is here, how beautiful! [*He stands at the window.*] So far from the world you are in here, among all the many houses. . . . I seem to be so alone here, just with you. . . . [*Softly.*] So sheltered. . . .

Christine. If you always talked like that . . . I could almost believe . . .

Fritz. Believe what, child?

Christine. That you love me as I dreamed it—the day you kissed me the first time . . . do you remember?

Fritz. [*Passionately.*] I *do* love you! [*He embraces her; tears himself from her.*] But now let me go.

Christine. Are you sorry you said it, so soon again? You are free, you know you are free—you can go and leave me whenever you like . . . you haven't promised me anything —and I haven't demanded anything of you. . . . It doesn't matter what becomes of me, then: I've been happy for once, and that's all I ask of life. I only want you to know that and to believe that I never—loved any man before you, and that I never shall love any man—when you get tired of me——

Fritz. [*More to himself.*] Don't say it, don't say it—it sounds—so sweet.

[*There is a knock.*]

Fritz. [*Starts.*] That's probably Theodore.

Christine. [*Startled.*] He knows that you are here?

Theodore. [*Enters.*] Good evening. Impudent of me, eh?

Christine. Do you have such important matters to discuss with him?

Theodore. I certainly have; and have been looking everywhere for him.

Fritz. [*In a low voice.*] Why didn't you wait below?

Christine. What are you whispering to him?

Theodore. [*Wishing her to hear.*] Why I didn't wait below. . . . Well, if I had absolutely known that you were here. . . . But I couldn't risk walking up and down outside for two hours.

Fritz. [*Pointedly.*] Then . . . you will go with me tomorrow?

Theodore. [*Comprehending.*] Surely.

Fritz. That's right.

Theodore. But I've been hurrying so that I must beg permission to sit down for a few seconds.

Christine. Please do.

[*Busies herself at the window.*]

Fritz. [*Softly.*] Anything new?—Did you find out about her?

Theodore. No. I merely came to get you because you are so incautious. What's the use of these unnecessary excitements? You ought to try to sleep. . . . It's rest you need. . . .

[CHRISTINE *is near them again.*]

Fritz. Tell me, isn't this a dear little room?

Theodore. Yes, it is very nice. [*To* CHRISTINE.] Do you stay here at home all day long?—Really, it is very homelike here. A little high up for my taste.

Fritz. That's just what I like about it.

Theodore. But now I'm going to take Fritz away from you; we've got to get up early in the morning.

Christine. Then you are really going away?

Theodore. He will come again, Miss Christine.

Christine. Will you write to me?

Theodore. But if he comes back tomorrow——

Christine. Oh, I know he's going to stay longer than that. [FRITZ *starts.*]

Theodore. [*Notices it.*] Well, does he have to write immediately? I wouldn't have thought you so sentimental. . . . Well, . . . kiss each other good-by, since it'll be so long. . . . [*Breaks off.*] I'm simply not here.

[FRITZ *and* CHRISTINE *kiss.*]

Theodore. [*Takes out a cigarette-case and puts a cigarette in his mouth; seeks vainly for a match.*] Tell me, dear Christine, haven't you a match?

Christine. Oh, yes, there are some.

[*Points to a holder on the chest of drawers.*]

Theodore. It's empty.

Christine. I'll get you one.

[*Hurries into adjoining room.*]

Fritz. [*Looking after her.*] Oh, God, how such hours *lie* to us!

Theodore. Why, what hours?

Fritz. I'm almost ready to believe that my happiness is here, that this sweet girl—— [*Breaks off.*] But this hour is a tremendous liar. . . .

Theodore. Absurd talk. . . . How you will laugh at it.

Fritz. I don't think I shall have any time for that.

Christine. [*Returns.*] Here you are.

Theodore. Thanks very much. . . . Good-by, then. [*To* FRITZ.] Well, what do you want now?

Fritz. [*Looks back and forth around the room, as if to deepen the impression in his mind.*] It's hard to leave it.

Christine. Oh, make fun of it if you like.

Theodore. [*Firmly.*] Come. Good-by, Christine.

Fritz. Farewell.

Christine. Till we meet again. [THEODORE *and* FRITZ *exeunt. She stands a moment, anxious, then goes to the open door; softly.*] Fritz!

Fritz. [*Comes back again and presses her to his heart.*] Farewell.

CURTAIN

THIRD ACT

The same scene as the second act. It is noon.

[CHRISTINE *alone, sitting sewing by the window; lays down her work.*]

Lena. [*Enters.*] Good day, Miss Christine.

Christine. [*Very absent-mindedly.*] Goodday, child; what is it?

Lena. Mother sent me to see if I could get the theater tickets.

Christine. Father hasn't got home yet, child; will you wait?

Lena. No, Miss Christine; then I'll come after lunch again.

Christine. Very well.

Lena. [*Going, turns back*] And Mother said to ask Miss Christine if her headache was gone yet.

Christine. Yes, child.

Lena. Good-by, Miss Christine.

Christine. Good-by.

[TONI *enters just as* LENA *is going out.*]

Lena. Good day, Miss Toni.

Toni. Hello, little monkey! [*Exit* LENA.]

Christine. [*Rises to meet* TONI.] Then they are back?

Toni. How should I know?

Christine. And you haven't any letter, nothing?

Toni. No.

Christine. *You* have no letter, either?

Toni. What should we write to each other?

Christine. They've been gone since day before yesterday.

Toni. Yes, yes, that's not such a long time. You needn't make such a fuss on that account. I don't understand you . . . and how you look, your face is all tear-stained. Your father will surely notice it, when he comes home.

Christine. [*Simply.*] My father knows everything.

Toni. [*Almost frightened.*] What?

Christine. I told him.

Toni. That's another of your bright ideas. But of course your face shows everything. And does he know *who* it is?

Christine. Yes.

Toni. And did he scold? [CHRISTINE *shakes her head.*] What did he say, then?

Christine. Nothing. . . . He went away very quietly, as usual.

Toni. And still it was stupid of you to tell. You'll see. . . . Do you know why your father said nothing? Because he thinks Fritz will marry you.

Christine. Why do you speak of that?

Toni. Do you know what I think?

Christine. Well, what?

Toni. That this whole story of a journey is a lie.

Christine. What?

Toni. Perhaps they haven't gone away at all.

Christine. They have gone—I know they have. Yesterday evening I went past his house; the blinds were down; he isn't there.

Toni. Oh, I believe that. They're away all right. But they won't come back—at least not to us.

Christine. [*Anxiously.*] Oh——

Toni. Well, it's possible.

Christine. You say that so calmly.

Toni. Why yes—whether it happens today or tomorrow—or in six months—it comes to the same thing.

Christine. Oh, you don't know what you are saying . . . You don't know Fritz . . . He isn't like what you think. I found that out when he was here in my room the other day. Often he only pretends to be indifferent—but he does love me. . . . [*As if she divined* TONI'S *reply.*] Yes, yes, not forever, I know that . . . but it can't stop all at once!

Toni. Well, I don't know Fritz so well.

Christine. He will come back, and Theodore will come back too; I am sure of it. [TONI *makes a gesture indicating indifference.*] Toni . . . do me a favor.

Toni. Don't be so excited—what is it you want?

Christine. Go to Theodore's, it's right near here. . . . Ask in the house whether he's got back yet, and if he isn't back, perhaps they'll know when he's coming.

Toni. I'm not going to run after a man.

Christine. He doesn't need to find it out. Perhaps you'll happen to meet him. It's almost one o'clock now—he'll be just going to lunch.

Toni. Why don't *you* go and ask at Fritz's house?

Christine. I'm afraid to—he doesn't like that. . . . And he is certainly not back yet. But perhaps Theodore is back by now and knows when Fritz is coming. Oh, please, Toni!

Toni. You're so childish sometimes.

Christine. Do it for me! Go and ask! It won't do any harm.

Toni. Well, if it means so much to you, I'll go. But it won't do much good. I'm sure they aren't back yet.

Christine. And you'll come right back, won't you?

Toni. Yes, yes, Mother can wait lunch a little.

Christine. I thank you, Toni, you're so good.

Toni. Of course I'm good—but now you be sensible, won't you? . . . Well, so long!

Christine. Oh, thank you!

[*Exit* TONI. CHRISTINE *arranges the room, folds up her sewing, etc. Then she goes to the window and looks out. After a moment* VYRING *enters without her seeing him at first. He is in great excitement, looks anxiously at his daughter.*]

Vyring. She knows nothing yet, nothing. [*He remains standing in the doorway and does not venture to take a step into the room.* CHRISTINE *turns; sees him; starts.* VYRING *tries to smile. He steps in.*] Well, Christine. . . . [*As if calling her to him.* CHRISTINE *goes to him, as if to fall before him.* VYRING *prevents her.*] Well . . . what are you thinking of, Christine? We . . . [*With a new resolve.*] We'll just forget it, shall we? [CHRISTINE *raises her head.*] Why, yes . . . I—and you!

Christine. Father, didn't you understand me this morning?

Vyring. Well, what would you have, Christine? . . . I surely must tell you what I think about it, don't you think so? Well, then . . .

Christine. Father, what does this mean?

Vyring. Come here, my child. . . . Listen to me quietly. You know I listened quietly to you, when you told me. We must——

Christine. Oh, I beg you, don't speak to me so, Father. If you have thought it over, and find that you can't forgive me, then drive me away—but don't speak that way.

Vyring. Just listen quietly to me, Christine. You can still do whatever you will. . . . See, Christine, you are so young. Haven't you ever thought . . . [*with great hesitation*] . . . that the whole thing might be a mistake?

Christine. Why do you say that to me, Father? I know so well what I have done—and I don't ask anything—not from you and not from anybody in the world, if it has been a mistake. . . . I just told you, drive me away, but . . .

Vyring. [*Interrupting.*] How can you talk so. . . . Even if it was a mistake, is that any reason for getting desperate right away, such a young creature as you are? Just think how beautiful, how wonderful life is. Just think how many things there are to give you joy, how much youth and how much happiness still lies before you. . . . See, I don't have much of the world any more, and even for me life is still beautiful—and I can still look forward to so many things. How we shall be together—how we shall plan our life, you and I—how you will begin to sing again, now that the beautiful days are here—and how we'll take a whole day off, when summer comes, and go out into the green country—Oh, there are so many lovely things . . . so many. It is silly to give up everything, because one must give up his first happiness, or anything that he thought was that.

Christine. Why . . . [*Anxiously.*] Then must I give it up?

Vyring. Well, was it happiness? Do you really think, Christine, that you had to tell your father today? I have known it for a long time—and I knew, too, that you would tell me. No, it never was happiness for you. . . . Don't I know those eyes? There wouldn't have been tears in them so often, and those cheeks wouldn't have been pale so much, if you had loved a man who was worthy of it.

Christine. Why, how can you . . . what do you know . . . what have you heard?

Vyring. Nothing, nothing at all. . . . But you yourself told me what he is. . . . A young fellow like that—what does he know? Has he the faintest idea of what falls into his hands—does he know the difference between the true and the false—and all your mad love—did he ever understand that?

Christine. [*More and more alarmed.*] You and he. . . . Were you at his house?

Vyring. Why, what are you thinking of! He went away, didn't he? But Christine, I still have a head on my shoulders, and my eyes in my head. Come, child, forget about it, do! Your future lies in an altogether different place. You can, you will still be as happy as you deserve. You will find a man some time who will know what a treasure he has in you. [CHRISTINE *has hurried to the chest of drawers to get her hat.*] What are you doing?

Christine. I'm going out.

Vyring. Where to?

Christine. To him . . . to him.

Vyring. What are you thinking of?

Christine. You're keeping something from me—let me go.

Vyring. [*Holding her firmly.*] Come to your senses, child. He isn't there at all. Perhaps he's gone away for a very long time. . . . Stay here; what do you want there? . . . Tomorrow or this evening I'll go there with you. You can't go out on the street like that . . . do you know how you look?

Christine. You will go with me?

Vyring. I promise you I will. Only stay here now; sit down and come to your senses again. It's enough to make a man laugh almost, to look at you . . . and all for nothing. Can't you stand it here with your father at all any more?

Christine. What *is* it you know?

Vyring. [*More and more helpless.*] What should I know? . . . I know that I love you, that you are my only child, that you must stay with me—that you should have stayed with me all the time——

Christine. Enough—let me go.

[*She wrests herself from him and opens the door;* TONI *appears in it.*]

Toni. [*Utters a little cry, as* CHRISTINE *rushes toward her.*] Why do you frighten me so?

[CHRISTINE *steps back, seeing* THEODORE *behind* TONI. THEODORE *remains in the doorway; he is dressed in black.*]

Christine. What . . . what is . . . [*No answer. She looks* THEODORE *in the face; he cannot meet her eyes.*] Where is he, where is he? . . . [*In the greatest terror. No answer; all faces are embarrassed and sad.*] Where is he? [*To* THEODORE.] Speak, can't you? [THEODORE *tries to speak.* CHRISTINE *looks at him wide-eyed, looks around her, comprehends the look on their faces, her face shows the dawn of this understanding, she utters a terrible cry.*] Theodore . . . he is . . . [THEODORE *nods.* CHRISTINE *seizes her forehead, cannot understand it; she goes to* THEODORE, *takes him by the arm, as if demented.*] He is . . . dead? [*As if asking herself.*]

Vyring. My child——

Christine. [*Thrusting him away.*] Speak, Theodore, speak!

Theodore. You know all.

Christine. I know nothing. . . . I don't know what has happened . . . do you think . . . I can't hear everything now? . . . how did it happen? . . . Father . . . Theodore . . . [*To* TONI.] You know it too.

Theodore. An unfortunate accident.

Christine. What, what?

Theodore. He fell.

Christine. What does that mean: he . . .

Theodore. He fell in a duel.

Christine. [*Shrieks. She is about to fall,* VYRING *sustains her, motions to* THEODORE *to go. She notes it and seizes him.*] Stay here. . . . I must know all. Do you think you can keep anything from me now?

Theodore. What else do you want to know?

Christine. Why—why did he fight a duel?

Theodore. I don't know the reason.

Christine. With whom, with whom? . . . You surely know who killed him? . . . Well, well, who . . .

Theodore. Nobody you know.

Christine. Who, who?

Toni. Christine!

Christine. Who? You tell me! [*To* TONI.] . . . Father, you tell me. . . . [*No answer. She starts to go out.* VYRING *holds her back.*] Can't I know who killed him, and for what cause?

Theodore. It was . . . a trivial cause . . .

Christine. You're not telling the truth . . . why, why . . .

Theodore. Dear Christine . . .

Christine. [*As if about to interrupt, goes up to him; looks at him in silence, then suddenly shrieks.*] On account of a woman?

Theodore. No——

Christine. Yes—for a woman . . . [*Turning to* TONI.] for that woman—for *that* woman that he *loved.* And her husband—yes, yes, her husband killed him. . . . And I . . . what am I? What was I to him? . . . Theodore . . . haven't you anything for me at all . . . didn't he write down anything? . . . Didn't he tell you anything for me? Didn't you find anything . . . a letter . . . a note? . . . [THEODORE *shakes his head.*] And that evening . . . when he was here, when you came to get him . . . he knew it, he knew then that he perhaps would never . . . And he went away from here to be killed for another woman. No, no, it is not possible . . . didn't he know what he was to me . . . didn't . . .

Theodore. He did know. On the last morning, when we drove out together . . . he spoke of you too.

Christine. He spoke of me *too*! Of me *too*! And of what else? Of how many other people, of how many other things, that meant just as much to him as I did? Of me too! Oh, God! . . . And of his father and his mother and his room and of the springtime and of the city and of everything, everything that belonged to his life and that he had to give up just as much as he gave up me—of everything he talked to you . . . and of me *too* . . .

Theodore. [*Moved.*] He surely loved you.

Christine. Love? He? I was nothing to him but a pastime—and he died for another woman! And I—I worshiped him! Didn't he know that? . . . That I gave him everything I could give, that I would have died for him—that he was my God and my bliss of Heaven—didn't he see that at all? He could go away from me with a smile, out of my room, and be shot down for another woman. . . . Father, Father, can you understand that?

Vyring. [*Goes to her.*] Christine!

Theodore. [*To* TONI.] Child, you might have spared me this. [TONI *looks at him venomously.*] I have had enough distress . . . these last days . . .

Christine. [*With sudden resolve.*] Theodore, take me to him—I want to see him—once more I want to *see* him—his face—Theodore, take me to him.

Theodore. [*With a gesture, hesitatingly.*] No . . .

Christine. Why "no"? You can't refuse me that! Surely I can see him once more?

Theodore. It is too late.

Christine. Too late? To see his corpse . . . is it too late? Yes . . . yes . . .

[*She does not understand.*]

Theodore. He was buried this morning.

Christine. [*With the greatest horror.*] Buried . . . And I didn't know about it? They shot him . . . and put him in his coffin and carried him out and buried him down in the earth—and I couldn't even see him once more? He's been dead two days—and you didn't come and tell me?

Theodore. [*Much moved.*] In these two days I have . . . You cannot dream all that I . . . Consider that it was my duty to notify his parents—I had to think of many things—and then my own state of mind . . .

Christine. Your . . .

Theodore. And then the . . . it was done very quietly. . . . Only the closest relatives and friends . . .

Christine. The closest——? And I——? . . . What am I?

Toni. They would have asked that.

Christine. What am I? Less than all the rest——? Less than his relatives, less than —you?

Vyring. My child, my child. Come to me, to me. . . [*He embraces her. To* THEODORE.] *Go* . . . leave me alone with her.

Theodore. I am very . . . [*With tears in his voice*.] I never suspected . . .

Christine. Never suspected what? That I *loved* him? [VYRING *draws her to him;* THEODORE *looks down;* TONI *stands near* CHRISTINE. *Freeing herself*.] Take me to his grave!

Vyring. No, no——

Toni. Don't go, Christine.

Theodore. Christine . . later . . . tomorrow . . . when you are calmer——

Christine. Tomorrow? When I shall be calmer? And in a month completely consoled, eh? And in six months I can laugh again, can I? [*Laughing shrilly*.] And then when will the next lover come?

Vyring. Christine . . .

Christine. Stay here then . . . I can find the way alone . . .

Vyring and Toni. [*Together*.] Don't go.

Christine. It's even better . . . if I . . . let me go, let me go.

Vyring. Christine, stay here.

Toni. Don't go! Perhaps you'll find the other one there—praying.

Christine. [*To herself, her eyes fixed*.] I won't pray there . . . no . .

[*She rushes out; the others speechless for the moment*.]

Vyring. Hurry after her. [THEODORE *and* TONI *exeunt*.] I can't, I can't . . [*He goes painfully from the door to the window*.] What does she want . . . what does she want? . . . [*He looks through the window*.] She won't come back—she won't come back!

[*He sinks to the floor, sobbing loudly*.]

CURTAIN

HEDDA GABLER*

By

HENRIK IBSEN

Translated by EDMUND GOSSE *and* WILLIAM ARCHER

IBSEN WROTE OF "HEDDA GABLER": "MY INTENTION in giving it this name was to indicate that Hedda, as a personality, is to be regarded rather as her father's daughter than as her husband's wife. It was not my desire to deal in this play with so-called problems. What I principally wanted to do was to depict human beings, human emotions, and human destinies, upon a groundwork of certain of the social conditions and principles of the present day."

The strange qualities of the Ibsen mind and soul emerge amusingly and pathetically in the encounter that gave rise to *Hedda Gabler* and *The Master Builder*. In the autumn of 1889 Ibsen met Emilie Bardach, a miss of eighteen. He was sixty, married, a parent, and famous; she was pretty, gay, and a head-hunter. She came from Austria to meet and captivate him, and by smiling at him from a park bench as he passed on his walks, she aroused his timid interest. Thereafter they had long talks, always in public places, for Ibsen was careful. Yet he was impressed; one can imagine that short stiff figure, with the aureole of white fringe about the face and the spectacles glittering in the light, turned attentively toward the slight vivacious girl, chattering and posing for him—in the lobby of a hotel. She seems to have thought herself a "new" woman, an "Ibsen woman," in fact; and he must have been both fascinated and repelled at this embodiment of his influence. Here, in a way, was posterity, the judge to which every artist appeals, and it was already impregnated with what it thought were his ideas. Here he found the courage in action that he himself had always lacked and wished for, but it was directed and reenforced by a flippant ruthlessness. Emilie professed to wish never to marry; she would capture other women's husbands. Yet she strangely invited boredom: she was clever, she had talent for music and painting, but she would do nothing with them. She preferred to pose as mysterious, tired, aloof. Ibsen once wrote to her, sadly, "You and the Christmas season do not quite fit together."

But she fired his imagination. Since *The Wild Duck* the use of the symbol as substitute for actuality had been a growing habit with him. He had always used life itself as his material, but in his shyness and seclusion he had tended to take it second or third hand, and compensate for lack of closely observed outline by lending depth and shadow. Emilie Bardach, so closely listened to and studied, gave him actuality first hand. At least, she gave him a character, or rather many characters, for it may be guessed that she was the prototype not only of Hedda, but also of Hilda Wangel and even of Kaia Fosli. With his hard mind and stern artistic eye, he lifted from the living girl those qualities she had displayed in their variety to charm him, and poured each into its appropriate mold. She gave him no incident, to be sure; at eighteen, what incident could there be? But fortunately he heard, at about the same time, of a brilliant but dissipated young professor who lost a manuscript; of the wife of a composer who in jealousy burned her husband's just completed symphony; and of another wife who tempted her husband, cured of alcoholism, by leaving brandy in his room. Then came the fusion, and *Hedda Gabler*. As soon as he began work on the play, early in 1890, Ibsen forbade Emilie to write to him or see him. But he remembered her, and sent her a copy of *Hedda Gabler* as a Christmas gift.

For a discussion of Ibsen's development and significance as a dramatist, see the preface to *A Doll's House*.

* Reprinted by permission of Charles Scribner's Sons. For biographical data and play list see *A Doll's House*, p. 4 f.

HEDDA GABLER

Characters

GEORGE TESMAN.[1]
HEDDA TESMAN, *his wife.*
MISS JULIANA TESMAN, *his aunt.*
MRS. ELVSTED.
JUDGE [2] BRACK.
EILERT LÖVBORG.
BERTA, *servant at the Tesmans.*

The scene of the action is Tesman's villa, in the west end of Christiania.

ACT FIRST

A spacious, handsome, and tastefully furnished drawing-room, decorated in dark colors. In the back, a wide doorway with curtains drawn back, leading into a smaller room decorated in the same style as the drawing-room. In the right-hand wall of the front room, a folding door leading out to the hall. In the opposite wall, on the left, a glass door, also with curtains drawn back. Through the panes can be seen part of a veranda outside, and trees covered with autumn foliage. An oval table, with a cover on it, and surrounded by chairs, stands well forward. In front, by the wall on the right, a wide stove of dark porcelain, a high-backed arm-chair, a cushioned foot-rest, and two footstools. A settee, with a small round table in front of it, fills the upper right-hand corner. In front, on the left, a little way from the wall, a sofa. Further back than the glass door, a piano. On either side of the doorway at the back a whatnot with terra-cotta and majolica ornaments.—Against the back wall of the inner room a sofa, with a table, and one or two chairs. Over the sofa hangs a portrait of a handsome elderly man in a General's uniform. Over the table a hanging lamp, with an opal glass shade.—A number of bouquets are arranged about the drawing-room, in vases and glasses. Others lie upon the tables. The floors in both rooms are covered with thick carpets.—Morning light. The sun shines in through the glass door.

[1] Tesman, whose Christian name in the original is "Jörgen," is described as "stipendiat i kulturhistorie" —that is to say, the holder of a scholarship for purposes of research into the History of Civilization.
[2] In the original "Assessor."

[MISS JULIANA TESMAN, *with her bonnet on and carrying a parasol, comes in from the hall, followed by* BERTA, *who carries a bouquet wrapped in paper.* MISS TESMAN *is a comely and pleasant-looking lady of about sixty-five. She is nicely but simply dressed in a gray walking-costume.* BERTA *is a middle-aged woman of plain and rather countrified appearance.*]

Miss Tesman. [*Stops close to the door, listens, and says softly:*] Upon my word, I don't believe they are stirring yet!

Berta. [*Also softly.*] I told you so, Miss. Remember how late the steamboat got in last night. And then, when they got home!—good Lord, what a lot the young mistress had to unpack before she could get to bed.

Miss Tesman. Well, well—let them have their sleep out. But let us see that they get a good breath of the fresh morning air when they do appear.

[*She goes to the glass door and throws it open.*]

Berta. [*Beside the table, at a loss what to do with the bouquet in her hand.*] I declare there isn't a bit of room left. I think I'll put it down there, Miss.

[*She places it on the piano.*]

Miss Tesman. So you've got a new mistress now, my dear Berta. Heaven knows it was a wrench to me to part with you.

Berta. [*On the point of weeping.*] And do you think it wasn't hard for me too, Miss? After all the blessed years I've been with you and Miss Rina.[1]

[1] Pronounce *Reena*

Miss Tesman. We must make the best of it, Berta. There was nothing else to be done. George can't do without you, you see—he absolutely can't. He has had you to look after him ever since he was a little boy.

Berta. Ah, but, Miss Julia, I can't help thinking of Miss Rina lying helpless at home there, poor thing. And with only that new girl too! She'll never learn to take proper care of an invalid.

Miss Tesman. Oh, I shall manage to train her. And of course, you know, I shall take most of it upon myself. You needn't be uneasy about my poor sister, my dear Berta.

Berta. Well, but there's another thing, Miss. I'm so mortally afraid I shan't be able to suit the young mistress.

Miss Tesman. Oh, well—just at first there may be one or two things——

Berta. Most like she'll be terrible grand in her ways.

Miss Tesman. Well, you can't wonder at that—General Gabler's daughter! Think of the sort of life she was accustomed to in her father's time. Don't you remember how we used to see her riding down the road along with the General? In that long black habit—and with feathers in her hat?

Berta. Yes, indeed—I remember well enough!—But, good Lord, I should never have dreamt in those days that she and Master George would make a match of it.

Miss Tesman. Nor I.—But by-the-bye, Berta—while I think of it: in future you mustn't say Master George. You must say Dr. Tesman.

Berta. Yes, the young mistress spoke of that too—last night—the moment they set foot in the house. Is it true then, Miss?

Miss Tesman. Yes, indeed it is. Only think, Berta—some foreign university has made him a doctor—while he has been abroad, you understand. I hadn't heard a word about it, until he told me himself upon the pier.

Berta. Well, well, he's clever enough for anything, he is. But I didn't think he'd have gone in for doctoring people, too.

Miss Tesman. No, no, it's not that sort of doctor he is. [*Nods significantly.*] But let me tell you, we may have to call him something still grander before long.

Berta. You don't say so! What can that be, Miss?

Miss Tesman. [*Smiling.*] H'm—wouldn't you like to know! [*With emotion.*] Ah, dear, dear—if my poor brother could only look up from his grave now, and see what his little boy has grown into! [*Looks around.*] But bless me, Berta—why have you done this? Taken the chintz covers off all the furniture?

Berta. The mistress told me to. She can't abide covers on the chairs, she says.

Miss Tesman. Are they going to make this their everyday sitting-room then?

Berta. Yes, that's what I understood—from the mistress. Master George—the doctor—he said nothing.

[GEORGE TESMAN *comes from the right into the inner room, humming to himself, and carrying an unstrapped empty portmanteau. He is a middle-sized, young-looking man of thirty-three, rather stout, with a round, open, cheerful face, fair hair and beard. He wears spectacles, and is somewhat carelessly dressed in comfortable indoor clothes.*]

Miss Tesman. Good morning, good morning, George.

Tesman. [*In the doorway between the rooms.*] Aunt Julia! Dear Aunt Julia! [*Goes up to her and shakes hands warmly.*] Come all this way—so early! Eh?

Miss Tesman. Why, of course I had to come and see how you were getting on.

Tesman. In spite of your having had no proper night's rest?

Miss Tesman. Oh, that makes no difference to me.

Tesman. Well, I suppose you got home all right from the pier? Eh?

Miss Tesman. Yes, quite safely, thank goodness. Judge Brack was good enough to see me right to my door.

Tesman. We were so sorry we couldn't give you a seat in the carriage. But you saw what a pile of boxes Hedda had to bring with her.

Miss Tesman. Yes, she had certainly plenty of boxes.

Berta. [*To* TESMAN.] Shall I go in and see if there's anything I can do for the mistress?

Tesman. No, thank you, Berta—you needn't. She said she would ring if she wanted anything.

Berta. [*Going towards the right.*] Very well.

Tesman. But look here—take this portmanteau with you.

Berta. [*Taking it.*] I'll put it in the attic.

[*She goes out by the hall door.*]

Tesman. Fancy, Auntie—I had the whole of that portmanteau chock full of copies of documents. You wouldn't believe how much I have picked up from all the archives I have been examining—curious old details that no one has had any idea of——

Miss Tesman. Yes, you don't seem to have wasted your time on your wedding trip, George.

Tesman. No, that I haven't. But do take

off your bonnet, Auntie. Look here! Let me untie the strings—eh?

Miss Tesman. [*While he does so.*] Well, well—this is just as if you were still at home with us.

Tesman. [*With the bonnet in his hand, looks at it from all sides.*] Why, what a gorgeous bonnet you've been investing in!

Miss Tesman. I bought it on Hedda's account.

Tesman. On Hedda's account? Eh?

Miss Tesman. Yes, so that Hedda needn't be ashamed of me if we happened to go out together.

Tesman. [*Patting her cheek.*] You always think of everything, Aunt Julia. [*Lays the bonnet on a chair beside the table.*] And now, look here—suppose we sit comfortably on the sofa and have a little chat, till Hedda comes.

[*They seat themselves. She places her parasol in the corner of the sofa.*]

Miss Tesman. [*Takes both his hands and looks at him.*] What a delight it is to have you again, as large as life, before my very eyes, George! My George—my poor brother's own boy!

Tesman. And it's a delight for me, too, to see you again, Aunt Julia! You, who have been father and mother in one to me.

Miss Tesman. Oh yes, I know you will always keep a place in your heart for your old aunts.

Tesman. And what about Aunt Rina? No improvement—eh?

Miss Tesman. Oh no—we can scarcely look for any improvement in her case, poor thing. There she lies, helpless, as she has lain for all these years. But heaven grant I may not lose her yet a while! For if I did, I don't know what I should make of my life, George—especially now that I haven't you to look after any more.

Tesman. [*Patting her back.*] There, there, there——!

Miss Tesman. [*Suddenly changing her tone.*] And to think that here are you a married man, George!—And that you should be the one to carry off Hedda Gabler—the beautiful Hedda Gabler! Only think of it—she, that was so beset with admirers!

Tesman. [*Hums a little and smiles complacently.*] Yes, I fancy I have several good friends about town who would like to stand in my shoes—eh?

Miss Tesman. And then this fine long wedding-tour you have had! More than five—nearly six months——

Tesman. Well, for me it has been a sort of tour of research as well. I have had to do much grubbing among old records—and to read no end of books too, Auntie.

Miss Tesman. Oh yes, I suppose so. [*More confidentially, and lowering her voice a little.*] But listen now, George—have you nothing—nothing special to tell me?

Tesman. As to our journey?

Miss Tesman. Yes.

Tesman. No, I don't know of anything except what I have told you in my letters. I had a doctor's degree conferred on me—but that I told you yesterday.

Miss Tesman. Yes, yes, you did. But what I mean is—haven't you any—any—expectations——?

Tesman. Expectations?

Miss Tesman. Why, you know, George—I'm your old auntie!

Tesman. Why, of course I have expectations.

Miss Tesman. Ah!

Tesman. I have every expectation of being a professor one of these days.

Miss Tesman. Oh yes, a professor——

Tesman. Indeed, I may say I am certain of it. But my dear Auntie—you know all about that already!

Miss Tesman. [*Laughing to herself.*] Yes, of course I do. You are quite right there. [*Changing the subject.*] But we were talking about your journey. It must have cost a great deal of money, George?

Tesman. Well, you see—my handsome traveling-scholarship went a good way.

Miss Tesman. But I can't understand how you can have made it go far enough for two.

Tesman. No, that's not so easy to understand—eh?

Miss Tesman. And especially traveling with a lady—they tell me that makes it ever so much more expensive.

Tesman. Yes, of course—it makes it a little more expensive. But Hedda had to have this trip, Auntie. She really had to. Nothing else would have done.

Miss Tesman. No, no, I suppose not. A wedding-tour seems to be quite indispensable nowadays.—But tell me now—have you gone thoroughly over the house yet?

Tesman. Yes, you may be sure I have. I have been afoot ever since daylight.

Miss Tesman. And what do you think of it all?

Tesman. I'm delighted! Quite delighted! Only I can't think what we are to do with the two empty rooms between this inner parlor and Hedda's bedroom.

Miss Tesman. [*Laughing.*] Oh, my dear George, I daresay you may find some use for them—in the course of time.

Tesman. Why of course, you are quite right, Aunt Julia! You mean as my library increases—eh?

Miss Tesman. Yes, quite so, my dear boy. It was your library I was thinking of.

Tesman. I am specially pleased on Hedda's account. Often and often, before we were engaged, she said that she would never care to live anywhere but in Secretary Falk's villa.[1]

Miss Tesman. Yes, it was lucky that this very house should come into the market, just after you had started.

Tesman. Yes, Aunt Julia, the luck was on our side, wasn't it—eh?

Miss Tesman. But the expense, my dear George! You will find it very expensive, all this.

Tesman. [*Looks at her, a little cast down.*] Yes, I suppose I shall, Aunt!

Miss Tesman. Oh, frightfully!

Tesman. How much do you think? In round numbers?—Eh?

Miss Tesman. Oh, I can't even guess until all the accounts come in.

Tesman. Well, fortunately, Judge Brack has secured the most favorable terms for me—so he said in a letter to Hedda.

Miss Tesman. Yes, don't be uneasy, my dear boy.—Besides, I have given security for the furniture and all the carpets.

Tesman. Security? You? My dear Aunt Julia—what sort of security could you give?

Miss Tesman. I have given a mortgage on our annuity.

Tesman. [*Jumps up.*] What! On your—and Aunt Rina's annuity!

Miss Tesman. Yes, I knew of no other plan, you see.

Tesman. [*Placing himself before her.*] Have you gone out of your senses, Auntie? Your annuity—it's all that you and Aunt Rina have to live upon.

Miss Tesman. Well, well—don't get so excited about it. It's only a matter of form, you know—Judge Brack assured me of that. It was he that was kind enough to arrange the whole affair for me. A mere matter of form, he said.

Tesman. Yes, that may be all very well. But nevertheless——

Miss Tesman. You will have your own salary to depend upon now. And, good heavens, even if we did have to pay up a little——! To eke things out a bit at the start——! Why, it would be nothing but a pleasure to us.

Tesman. Oh Auntie—will you never be tired of making sacrifices for me!

Miss Tesman. [*Rises and lays her hand on his shoulder.*] Have I any other happiness in this world except to smooth your way for you, my dear boy? You, who have had neither father nor mother to depend on. And now we have reached the goal, George! Things have looked black enough for us, sometimes; but, thank heaven, now you have nothing to fear.

Tesman. Yes, it is really marvelous how everything has turned out for the best.

Miss Tesman. And the people who opposed you—who wanted to bar the way for you—now you have them at your feet. They have fallen, George. Your most dangerous rival—his fall was the worst.—And now he has to lie on the bed he has made for himself—poor misguided creature.

Tesman. Have you heard anything of Eilert? Since I went away, I mean.

Miss Tesman. Only that he is said to have published a new book.

Tesman. What! Eilert Lövborg! Recently—eh?

Miss Tesman. Yes, so they say. Heaven knows whether it can be worth anything! Ah, when your new book appears—that will be another story, George! What is it to be about?

Tesman. It will deal with the domestic industries of Brabant during the Middle Ages.

Miss Tesman. Fancy—to be able to write on such a subject as that!

Tesman. However, it may be some time before the book is ready. I have all these collections to arrange first, you see.

Miss Tesman. Yes, collecting and arranging—no one can beat you at that. There you are my poor brother's own son.

Tesman. I am looking forward eagerly to setting to work at it; especially now that I have my own delightful home to work in.

Miss Tesman. And, most of all, now that you have got the wife of your heart, my dear George.

Tesman. [*Embracing her.*] Oh yes, yes, Aunt Julia! Hedda—she is the best part of it all! [*Looks toward the doorway.*] I believe I hear her coming—eh?

[HEDDA *enters from the left through the inner room. She is a woman of nine-and-twenty. Her face and figure show refinement and distinction. Her complexion is pale and opaque. Her steel-gray eyes express a cold, unruffled repose. Her hair is of an agreeable medium brown, but not particularly abundant. She is dressed in a tasteful, somewhat loose-fitting morning gown.*]

Miss Tesman. [*Going to meet* HEDDA.]

[1] In the original, "Statsrådinde Falks villa"—showing that it had belonged to the widow of a cabinet minister.

Good morning, my dear Hedda! Good morning, and a hearty welcome.

Hedda. [*Holds out her hand.*] Good morning, dear Miss Tesman! So early a call! That is kind of you.

Miss Tesman. [*With some embarrassment.*] Well—has the bride slept well in her new home?

Hedda. Oh yes, thanks. Passably.

Tesman. [*Laughing.*] Passably! Come, that's good, Hedda! You were sleeping like a stone when I got up.

Hedda. Fortunately. Of course one has always to accustom one's self to new surroundings, Miss Tesman—little by little. [*Looking toward the left.*] Oh—there the servant has gone and opened the veranda door, and let in a whole flood of sunshine.

Miss Tesman. [*Going toward the door.*] Well, then we will shut it.

Hedda. No, no, not that! Tesman, please draw the curtains. That will give a softer light.

Tesman. [*At the door.*] All right—all right.—There now, Hedda, now you have both shade and fresh air.

Hedda. Yes, fresh air we certainly must have, with all these stacks of flowers——. But—won't you sit down, Miss Tesman?

Miss Tesman. No, thank you. Now that I have seen that everything is all right here—thank heaven!—I must be getting home again. My sister is lying longing for me, poor thing.

Tesman. Give her my very best love, Auntie; and say I shall look in and see her later in the day.

Miss Tesman. Yes, yes, I'll be sure to tell her. But by-the-bye, George—[*Feeling in her dress pocket.*]—I had almost forgotten—I have something for you here.

Tesman. What is it, Auntie? Eh?

Miss Tesman. [*Produces a flat parcel wrapped in newspaper and hands it to him.*] Look here, my dear boy.

Tesman. [*Opening the parcel.*] Well, I declare!—Have ycu really saved them for me, Aunt Julia! Hedda! isn't this touching—eh?

Hedda. [*Beside the whatnot on the right.*] Well, what is it?

Tesman. My old morning-shoes! My slippers.

Hedda. Indeed. I remember you often spoke of them while we were abroad.

Tesman. Yes, I missed them terribly. [*Goes up to her.*] Now you shall see them, Hedda!

Hedda. [*Going toward the stove.*] Thanks, I really don't care about it.

Tesman. [*Following her.*] Only think—ill as she was, Aunt Rina embroidered these for me. Oh, you can't think how many associations cling to them.

Hedda. [*At the table.*] Scarcely for me.

Miss Tesman. Of course not for Hedda, George.

Tesman. Well, but now that she belongs to the family, I thought——

Hedda. [*Interrupting.*] We shall never get on with this servant, Tesman.

Miss Tesman. Not get on with Berta?

Tesman. Why, dear, what puts that in your head? Eh?

Hedda. [*Pointing.*] Look there! She has left her old bonnet lying about on a chair.

Tesman. [*In consternation, drops the slippers on the floor.*] Why, Hedda——

Hedda. Just fancy, if anyone should come in and see it!

Tesman. But Hedda—that's Aunt Julia's bonnet.

Hedda. Is it!

Miss Tesman. [*Taking up the bonnet.*] Yes, indeed it's mine. And, what's more, it's not old, Madam Hedda.

Hedda. I really did not look closely at it, Miss Tesman.

Miss Tesman. [*Tying on the bonnet.*] Let me tell you it's the first time I have worn it—the very first time.

Tesman. And a very nice bonnet it is too—quite a beauty!

Miss Tesman. Oh, it's no such great thing, George. [*Looks around her.*] My parasol——? Ah, here. [*Takes it.*] For this is mine too—[*mutters*]—not Berta's.

Tesman. A new bonnet and a new parasol! Only think, Hedda!

Hedda. Very handsome indeed.

Tesman. Yes, isn't it? Eh? But Auntie, take a good look at Hedda before you go! See how handsome she is!

Miss Tesman. Oh, my dear boy, there's nothing new in that. Hedda was always lovely.

[*She nods and goes toward the right.*]

Tesman. [*Following.*] Yes, but have you noticed what splendid condition she is in? How she has filled out on the journey?

Hedda. [*Crossing the room.*] Oh, do be quiet——!

Miss Tesman. [*Who has stopped and turned.*] Filled out?

Tesman. Of course you don't notice it so much now that she has that dress on. But I, who can see——

Hedda. [*At the glass door, impatiently.*] Oh, you can't see anything.

Tesman. It must be the mountain air in the Tyrol——

Hedda. [*Curtly, interrupting.*] I am exactly as I was when I started.

Tesman. So you insist; but I'm quite certain you are not. Don't you agree with me, Auntie?

Miss Tesman. [*Who has been gazing at her with folded hands.*] Hedda is lovely—lovely—lovely. [*Goes up to her, takes her head between both hands, draws it downward, and kisses her hair.*] God bless and preserve Hedda Tesman—for George's sake.

Hedda. [*Gently freeing herself.*] Oh—! Let me go.

Miss Tesman. [*In quiet emotion.*] I shall not let a day pass without coming to see you.

Tesman. No, you won't, will you, Auntie? Eh?

Miss Tesman. Good-by—good-by!

[*She goes out by the hall door.* TESMAN *accompanies her. The door remains half open.* TESMAN *can be heard repeating his message to Aunt Rina and his thanks for the slippers.*

In the meantime, HEDDA *walks about the room, raising her arms and clenching her hands as if in desperation. Then she flings back the curtains from the glass door, and stands there looking out.*

Presently TESMAN *returns and closes the door behind him.*]

Tesman. [*Picks up the slippers from the floor.*] What are you looking at, Hedda?

Hedda. [*Once more calm and mistress of herself.*] I am only looking at the leaves. They are so yellow—so withered.

Tesman. [*Wraps up the slippers and lays them on the table.*] Well, you see, we are well into September now.

Hedda. [*Again restless.*] Yes, to think of it!—Already in—in September.

Tesman. Don't you think Aunt Julia's manner was strange, dear? Almost solemn? Can you imagine what was the matter with her? Eh?

Hedda. I scarcely know her, you see. Is she not often like that?

Tesman. No, not as she was today.

Hedda. [*Leaving the glass door.*] Do you think she was annoyed about the bonnet?

Tesman. Oh, scarcely at all. Perhaps a little, just at the moment——

Hedda. But what an idea, to pitch her bonnet about in the drawing-room! No one does that sort of thing.

Tesman. Well, you may be sure Aunt Julia won't do it again.

Hedda. In any case, I shall manage to make my peace with her.

Tesman. Yes, my dear, good Hedda, if you only would.

Hedda. When you call this afternoon, you might invite her to spend the evening here.

Tesman. Yes, that I will. And there's one thing more you could do that would delight her heart.

Hedda. What is it?

Tesman. If you could only prevail on yourself to say *du* [1] to her. For my sake, Hedda? Eh?

Hedda. No, no, Tesman—you really mustn't ask that of me. I have told you so already. I shall try to call her "Aunt"; and you must be satisfied with that.

Tesman. Well well. Only I think now that you belong to the family, you——

Hedda. H'm—I can't in the least see why——

[*She goes up toward the middle doorway.*]

Tesman. [*After a pause.*] Is there anything the matter with you, Hedda? Eh?

Hedda. I'm only looking at my old piano. It doesn't go at all well with all the other things.

Tesman. The first time I draw my salary, we'll see about exchanging it.

Hedda. No, no—no exchanging. I don't want to part with it. Suppose we put it there in the inner room, and then get another here in its place. When it's convenient, I mean.

Tesman. [*A little taken aback.*] Yes—of course we could do that.

Hedda. [*Takes up the bouquet from the piano.*] These flowers were not here last night when we arrived.

Tesman. Aunt Julia must have brought them for you.

Hedda. [*Examining the bouquet.*] A visiting-card. [*Takes it out and reads:*] "Shall return later in the day." Can you guess whose card it is?

Tesman. No. Whose? Eh?

Hedda. The name is "Mrs. Elvsted."

Tesman. Is it really? Sheriff Elvsted's wife? Miss Rysing that was.

Hedda. Exactly. The girl with the irritating hair, that she was always showing off. An old flame of yours, I've been told.

Tesman. [*Laughing.*] Oh, that didn't last long; and it was before I knew you, Hedda. But fancy her being in town!

Hedda. It's odd that she should call upon us. I have scarcely seen her since we left school.

Tesman. I haven't seen her either for—heaven knows how long. I wonder how she can endure to live in such an out-of-the-way hole—eh?

Hedda. [*After a moment's thought, says*

[1] *Du* = thou; Tesman means, "If you could persuade yourself to *tutoyer* her."

suddenly.] Tell me, Tesman—isn't it somewhere near there that he—that—Eilert Lövborg is living?

Tesman. Yes, he is somewhere in that part of the country.

[BERTA *enters by the hall door.*]

Berta. That lady, ma'am, that brought some flowers a little while ago, is here again. [*Pointing.*] The flowers you have in your hand, ma'am.

Hedda. Ah, is she? Well, please show her in.

[BERTA *opens the door for* MRS. ELVSTED, *and goes out herself.*—MRS. ELVSTED *is a woman of fragile figure, with pretty, soft features. Her eyes are light blue, large, round, and somewhat prominent, with a startled, inquiring expression. Her hair is remarkably light, almost flaxen, and unusually abundant and wavy. She is a couple of years younger than* HEDDA. *She wears a dark visiting dress, tasteful, but not quite in the latest fashion.*]

Hedda. [*Receives her warmly.*] How do you do, my dear Mrs. Elvsted? It's delightful to see you again.

Mrs. Elvsted. [*Nervously, struggling for self-control.*] Yes, it's a very long time since we met.

Tesman. [*Gives her his hand.*] And we too—eh?

Hedda. Thanks for your lovely flowers——

Mrs. Elvsted. Oh, not at all——. I would have come straight here yesterday afternoon; but I heard that you were away——

Tesman. Have you just come to town? Eh?

Mrs. Elvsted. I arrived yesterday, about midday. Oh, I was quite in despair when I heard that you were not at home.

Hedda. In despair? How so?

Tesman. Why, my dear Mrs. Rysing—I mean Mrs. Elvsted——

Hedda. I hope that you are not in any trouble?

Mrs. Elvsted. Yes, I am. And I don't know another living creature here that I can turn to.

Hedda. [*Laying the bouquet on the table.*] Come—let us sit here on the sofa——

Mrs. Elvsted. Oh, I am too restless to sit down.

Hedda. Oh no, you're not. Come here.

[*She draws* MRS. ELVSTED *down upon the sofa and sits at her side.*]

Tesman. Well? What is it, Mrs. Elvsted——?

Hedda. Has anything particular happened to you at home?

Mrs. Elvsted. Yes—and no. Oh—I am so anxious you should not misunderstand me——

Hedda. Then your best plan is to tell us the whole story, Mrs. Elvsted.

Tesman. I suppose that's what you have come for—eh?

Mrs. Elvsted. Yes, yes—of course it is. Well then, I must tell you—if you don't already know—that Eilert Lövborg is in town, too.

Hedda. Lövborg——!

Tesman. What! Has Eilert Lövborg come back? Fancy that, Hedda!

Hedda. Well, well—I hear it.

Mrs. Elvsted. He has been here a week already. Just fancy—a whole week! In this terrible town, alone! With so many temptations on all sides.

Hedda. But, my dear Mrs. Elvsted—how does *he* concern you so much?

Mrs. Elvsted. [*Looks at her with a startled air, and says rapidly.*] He was the children's tutor.

Hedda. Your children's?

Mrs. Elvsted. My husband's. I have none.

Hedda. Your step-children's, then?

Mrs. Elvsted. Yes.

Tesman. [*Somewhat hesitatingly.*] Then was he—I don't know how to express it—was he—regular enough in his habits to be fit for the post? Eh?

Mrs. Elvsted. For the last two years his conduct has been irreproachable.

Tesman. Has it indeed? Fancy that, Hedda!

Hedda. I hear it.

Mrs. Elvsted. Perfectly irreproachable, I assure you! In every respect. But all the same—now that I know he is here—in this great town—and with a large sum of money in his hands—I can't help being in mortal fear of him.

Tesman. Why did he not remain where he was? With you and your husband? Eh?

Mrs. Elvsted. After his book was published he was too restless and unsettled to remain with us.

Tesman. Yes, by-the-bye, Aunt Julia told me he had published a new book.

Mrs. Elvsted. Yes, a big book, dealing with the march of civilization—in broad outline, as it were. It came out about a fortnight ago. And since it has sold so well, and been so much read—and made such a sensation——

Tesman. Has it indeed? It must be something he has had lying by since his better days.

Mrs. Elvsted. Long ago, you mean?

Tesman. Yes.

Mrs. Elvsted. No, he has written it all

since he has been with us—within the last year.

Tesman. Isn't that good news, Hedda? Think of that!

Mrs. Elvsted. Ah yes, if only it would last!

Hedda. Have you seen him here in town?

Mrs. Elvsted. No, not yet. I have had the greatest difficulty in finding out his address. But this morning I discovered it at last.

Hedda. [*Looks searchingly at her.*] Do you know, it seems to me a little odd of your husband—h'm——

Mrs. Elvsted. [*Starting nervously.*] Of my husband! What?

Hedda. That he should send *you* to town on such an errand—that he does not come himself and look after his friend.

Mrs. Elvsted. Oh no, no—my husband has no time. And besides, I—I had some shopping to do.

Hedda. [*With a slight smile.*] Ah, that is a different matter.

Mrs. Elvsted. [*Rising quickly and uneasily.*] And now I beg and implore you, Mr. Tesman—receive Eilert Lövborg kindly if he comes to you! And that he is sure to do. You see you were such great friends in the old days. And then you are interested in the same studies—the same branch of science—so far as I can understand.

Tesman. We used to be, at any rate.

Mrs. Elvsted. That is why I beg so earnestly that you—you too—will keep a sharp eye upon him. Oh, you will promise me that, Mr. Tesman—won't you?

Tesman. With the greatest of pleasure, Mrs. Rysing——

Hedda. Elvsted.

Tesman. I assure you I shall do all I possibly can for Eilert. You may rely upon me.

Mrs. Elvsted. Oh, how very, very kind of you! [*Presses his hands.*] Thanks, thanks, thanks! [*Frightened.*] You see, my husband is so very fond of him!

Hedda. [*Rising.*] You ought to write to him, Tesman. Perhaps he may not care to come to you of his own accord.

Tesman. Well, perhaps it would be the right thing to do, Hedda? Eh?

Hedda. And the sooner the better. Why not at once?

Mrs. Elvsted. [*Imploringly.*] Oh, if you only would!

Tesman. I'll write this moment. Have you his address, Mrs.—Mrs. Elvsted?

Mrs. Elvsted. Yes. [*Takes a slip of paper from her pocket and hands it to him.*] Here it is.

Tesman. Good, good. Then I'll go in—— [*Looks about him.*] By-the-bye—my slippers? Oh, here.

[*Takes the packet, and is about to go.*]

Hedda. Be sure you write him a cordial, friendly letter. And a good long one, too.

Tesman. Yes, I will.

Mrs. Elvsted. But please, please don't say a word to show that I have suggested it.

Tesman. No, how could you think I would? Eh?

[*He goes out to the right, through the inner room.*]

Hedda. [*Goes up to* MRS. ELVSTED, *smiles, and says in a low voice.*] There! We have killed two birds with one stone.

Mrs. Elvsted. What do you mean?

Hedda. Could you not see that I wanted him to go?

Mrs. Elvsted. Yes, to write the letter——

Hedda. And that I might speak to you alone.

Mrs. Elvsted. [*Confused.*] About the same thing?

Hedda. Precisely.

Mrs. Elvsted. [*Apprehensively.*] But there is nothing more, Mrs. Tesman! Absolutely nothing!

Hedda. Oh yes, but there is. There is a great deal more—I can see that. Sit here—and we'll have a cozy, confidential chat.

[*She forces* MRS. ELVSTED *to sit in the easy-chair beside the stove, and seats herself on one of the footstools.*]

Mrs. Elvsted. [*Anxiously, looking at her watch.*] But, my dear Mrs. Tesman—I was really on the point of going.

Hedda. Oh, you can't be in such a hurry. —Well? Now tell me something about your life at home.

Mrs. Elvsted. Oh, that is just what I care least to speak about.

Hedda. But to me, dear——? Why, weren't we schoolfellows?

Mrs. Elvsted. Yes, but you were in the class above me. Oh, how dreadfully afraid of you I was then!

Hedda. Afraid of me?

Mrs. Elvsted. Yes, dreadfully. For when we met on the stairs you used always to pull my hair.

Hedda. Did I, really?

Mrs. Elvsted. Yes, and once you said you would burn it off my head.

Hedda. Oh, that was all nonsense, of course.

Mrs. Elvsted. Yes, but I was so silly in those days.—And since then, too—we have drifted so far—far apart from each other. Our circles have been so entirely different.

Hedda. Well then, we must try to drift together again. Now listen! At school we said *du* to each other; and we called each other by our Christian names——

Mrs. Elvsted. No, I am sure you must be mistaken.

Hedda. No, not at all! I can remember quite distinctly. So now we are going to renew our old friendship. [*Draws the footstool close to* MRS. ELVSTED.] There now! [*Kisses her cheek.*] You must say *du* to me and call me Hedda.

Mrs. Elvsted. [*Presses and pats her hands.*] Oh, how good and kind you are! I am not used to such kindness.

Hedda. There, there, there! And I shall say *du* to you, as in the old days, and call you my dear Thora.

Mrs. Elvsted. My name is Thea.[1]

Hedda. Why, of course! I meant Thea. [*Looks at her compassionately.*] So you are not accustomed to goodness and kindness, Thea? Not in your own home?

Mrs. Elvsted. Oh, if I only had a home! But I haven't any; I have never had a home.

Hedda. [*Looks at her for a moment.*] I almost suspected as much.

Mrs. Elvsted. [*Gazing helplessly before her.*] Yes—yes—yes.

Hedda. I don't quite remember—was it not as housekeeper that you first went to Mr. Elvsted's?

Mrs. Elvsted. I really went as governess. But his wife—his late wife—was an invalid—and rarely left her room. So I had to look after the housekeeping as well.

Hedda. And then—at last—you became mistress of the house.

Mrs. Elvsted. [*Sadly.*] Yes, I did.

Hedda. Let me see—about how long ago was that?

Mrs. Elvsted. My marriage?

Hedda. Yes.

Mrs. Elvsted. Five years ago.

Hedda. To be sure; it must be that.

Mrs. Elvsted. Oh, those five years——! Or at all events the last two or three of them! Oh, if you[2] could only imagine——

Hedda. [*Giving her a little slap on the hand.*] *De?* Fie, Thea!

Mrs. Elvsted. Yes, yes, I will try—— Well, if—you could only imagine and understand——

Hedda. [*Lightly.*] Eilert Lövborg has been in your neighborhood about three years, hasn't he?

Mrs. Elvsted. [*Looks at her doubtfully.*] Eilert Lövborg? Yes—he has.

1 Pronounce *Tora* and *Taya*.

2 Mrs. Elvsted here uses the formal pronoun *De*, whereupon Hedda rebukes her. In her next speech Mrs. Elvsted says *du*.

Hedda. Had you known him before, in town here?

Mrs. Elvsted. Scarcely at all. I mean—I knew him by name of course.

Hedda. But you saw a good deal of him in the country?

Mrs. Elvsted. Yes, he came to us every day. You see, he gave the children lessons; for in the long run I couldn't manage it all myself.

Hedda. No, that's clear.—And your husband——? I suppose he is often away from home?

Mrs. Elvsted. Yes. Being sheriff, you know, he has to travel about a good deal in his district.

Hedda. [*Leaning against the arm of the chair.*] Thea—my poor, sweet Thea—now you must tell me everything—exactly as it stands.

Mrs. Elvsted. Well then, you must question me.

Hedda. What sort of a man is your husband, Thea? I mean—you know—in everyday life. Is he kind to you?

Mrs. Elvsted. [*Evasively.*] I am sure he means well in everything.

Hedda. I should think he must be altogether too old for you. There is at least twenty years' difference between you, is there not?

Mrs. Elvsted. [*Irritably.*] Yes, that is true, too. Everything about him is repellent to me! We have not a thought in common. We have no single point of sympathy—he and I.

Hedda. But is he not fond of you all the same? In his own way?

Mrs. Elvsted. Oh, I really don't know. I think he regards me simply as a useful property. And then it doesn't cost much to keep me. I am not expensive.

Hedda. That is stupid of you.

Mrs. Elvsted. [*Shakes her head.*] It cannot be otherwise—not with him. I don't think he really cares for anyone but himself—and perhaps a little for the children.

Hedda. And for Eilert Lövborg, Thea.

Mrs. Elvsted. [*Looking at her.*] For Eilert Lövborg? What puts that into your head?

Hedda. Well, my dear—I should say, when he sends you after him all the way to town——[*Smiling almost imperceptibly.*] And besides, you said so yourself, to Tesman.

Mrs. Elvsted. [*With a little nervous twitch.*] Did I? Yes, I suppose I did. [*Vehemently, but not loudly.*] No—I may just as well make a clean breast of it at once! For it must all come out in any case.

Hedda. Why, my dear Thea——?

Mrs. Elvsted. Well, to make a long story short: My husband did not know that I was coming.

Hedda. What! Your husband didn't know it!

Mrs. Elvsted. No, of course not. For that matter, he was away from home himself—he was traveling. Oh, I could bear it no longer, Hedda! I couldn't, indeed—so utterly alone as I should have been in the future.

Hedda. Well? And then?

Mrs. Elvsted. So I put together some of my things—what I needed most—as quietly as possible. And then I left the house.

Hedda. Without a word?

Mrs. Elvsted. Yes—and took the train straight to town.

Hedda. Why, my dear, good Thea—to think of you daring to do it!

Mrs. Elvsted. [*Rises and moves about the room.*] What else could I possibly do?

Hedda. But what do you think your husband will say when you go home again?

Mrs. Elvsted. [*At the table, looks at her.*] Back to *him?*

Hedda. Of course.

Mrs. Elvsted. I shall never go back to him again.

Hedda. [*Rising and going toward her.*] Then you have left your home—for good and all?

Mrs. Elvsted. Yes. There was nothing else to be done.

Hedda. But then—to take flight so openly.

Mrs. Elvsted. Oh, it's impossible to keep things of that sort secret.

Hedda. But what do you think people will say of you, Thea?

Mrs. Elvsted. They may say what they like, for aught *I* care. [*Seats herself wearily and sadly on the sofa.*] I have done nothing but what I *had* to do.

Hedda. [*After a short silence.*] And what are your plans now? What do you think of doing?

Mrs. Elvsted. I don't know yet. I only know this, that I must live here, where Eilert Lövborg is—if I am to live at all.

Hedda. [*Takes a chair from the table, seats herself beside her, and strokes her hands.*] My dear Thea—how did this—this friendship—between you and Eilert Lövborg come about?

Mrs. Elvsted. Oh, it grew up gradually. I gained a sort of influence over him.

Hedda. Indeed?

Mrs. Elvsted. He gave up his old habits. Not because I asked him to, for I never dared do that. But of course he saw how repulsive they were to me; and so he dropped them.

Hedda. [*Concealing an involuntary smile of scorn.*] Then you have reclaimed him—as the saying goes—my little Thea.

Mrs. Elvsted. So he says himself, at any rate. And he, on his side, has made a real human being of me—taught me to think, and to understand so many things.

Hedda. Did he give *you* lessons too, then?

Mrs. Elvsted. No, not exactly lessons. But he talked to me—talked about such an infinity of things. And then came the lovely, happy time when I began to share in his work—when he allowed me to help him!

Hedda. Oh, he did, did he?

Mrs. Elvsted. Yes! He never wrote anything without my assistance.

Hedda. You were two good comrades, in fact?

Mrs. Elvsted. [*Eagerly.*] Comrades! Yes, fancy, Hedda—that is the very word he used! Oh, I ought to feel perfectly happy; and yet I cannot; for I don't know how long it will last.

Hedda. Are you no surer of him than that?

Mrs. Elvsted. [*Gloomily.*] A woman's shadow stands between Eilert Lövborg and me.

Hedda. [*Looks at her anxiously.*] Who can *that* be?

Mrs. Elvsted. I don't know. Someone he knew in his—in his past. Someone he has never been able wholly to forget.

Hedda. What has he told you—about this?

Mrs. Elvsted. He has only once—quite vaguely—alluded to it.

Hedda. Well! And what did he say?

Mrs. Elvsted. He said that when they parted, she threatened to shoot him with a pistol.

Hedda. [*With cold composure.*] Oh nonsense! No one does that sort of thing here.

Mrs. Elvsted. No. And that is why I think it must have been that red-haired singing-woman whom he once——

Hedda. Yes, very likely.

Mrs. Elvsted. For I remember they used to say of her that she carried loaded firearms.

Hedda. Oh—then of course it must have been she.

Mrs. Elvsted. [*Wringing her hands.*] And now just fancy, Hedda—I hear that this singing-woman—that she is in town again! Oh, I don't know what to do——

Hedda. [*Glancing toward the inner room.*] Hush! Here comes Tesman. [*Rises and whispers.*] Thea—all this must remain between you and me.

Mrs. Elvsted. [*Springing up.*] Oh yes—yes! For heaven's sake——!

[George Tesman, *with a letter in his*

hand, comes from the right through the inner room.]

Tesman. There now—the epistle is finished.

Hedda. That's right. And now Mrs. Elvsted is just going. Wait a moment—I'll go with you to the garden gate.

Tesman. Do you think Berta could post the letter, Hedda dear?

Hedda. [*Takes it.*] I will tell her to.

[BERTA *enters from the hall.*]

Berta. Judge Brack wishes to know if Mrs. Tesman will receive him.

Hedda. Yes, ask Judge Brack to come in. And look here—put this letter in the post.

Berta. [*Taking the letter.*] Yes, ma'am.

[*She opens the door for* JUDGE BRACK *and goes out herself.* BRACK *is a man of forty-five; thick-set, but well-built and elastic in his movements. His face is roundish with an aristocratic profile. His hair is short, still almost black, and carefully dressed. His eyes are lively and sparkling. His eyebrows thick. His moustaches are also thick, with short-cut ends. He wears a well-cut walking-suit, a little too youthful for his age. He uses an eye-glass, which he now and then lets drop.*]

Judge Brack. [*With his hat in his hand, bowing.*] May one venture to call so early in the day?

Hedda. Of course one may.

Tesman. [*Presses his hand.*] You are welcome at any time. [*Introducing him.*] Judge Brack—Miss Rysing——

Hedda. Oh——!

Brack. [*Bowing.*] Ah—delighted——

Hedda. [*Looks at him and laughs.*] It's nice to have a look at you by daylight, Judge!

Brack. Do you find me—altered?

Hedda. A little younger, I think.

Brack. Thank you so much.

Tesman. But what do you think of Hedda—eh? Doesn't she look flourishing? She has actually——

Hedda. Oh, do leave me alone. You haven't thanked Judge Brack for all the trouble he has taken——

Brack. Oh, nonsense—it was a pleasure to me——

Hedda. Yes, you are a friend indeed. But here stands Thea all impatience to be off—so *au revoir,* Judge. I shall be back again presently.

[*Mutual salutations.* MRS. ELVSTED *and* HEDDA *go out by the hall door.*]

Brack. Well—is your wife tolerably satisfied——

Tesman. Yes, we can't thank you sufficiently. Of course she talks of a little re-arrangement here and there; and one or two things are still wanting. We shall have to buy some additional trifles.

Brack. Indeed!

Tesman. But we won't trouble you about these things. Hedda says she herself will look after what is wanting.—Shan't we sit down? Eh?

Brack. Thanks, for a moment. [*Seats himself beside the table.*] There is something I wanted to speak to you about, my dear Tesman.

Tesman. Indeed? Ah, I understand! [*Seating himself.*] I suppose it's the serious part of the frolic that is coming now. Eh?

Brack. Oh, the money question is not so very pressing; though, for that matter, I wish we had gone a little more economically to work.

Tesman. But that would never have done, you know! Think of Hedda, my dear fellow! You, who know her so well——. I couldn't possibly ask her to put up with a shabby style of living!

Brack. No, no—that is just the difficulty.

Tesman. And then—fortunately—it can't be long before I receive my appointment.

Brack. Well, you see—such things are often apt to hang fire for a time.

Tesman. Have you heard anything definite? Eh?

Brack. Nothing exactly definite——. [*Interrupting himself.*] But by-the-bye—I have one piece of news for you.

Tesman. Well?

Brack. Your old friend, Eilert Lövborg, has returned to town.

Tesman. I know that already.

Brack. Indeed! How did you learn it?

Tesman. From that lady who went out with Hedda.

Brack. Really? What was her name? I didn't quite catch it.

Tesman. Mrs. Elvsted.

Brack. Aha—Sheriff Elvsted's wife? Of course—he has been living up in their regions.

Tesman. And fancy—I'm delighted to hear that he is quite a reformed character!

Brack. So they say.

Tesman. And then he has published a new book—eh?

Brack. Yes, indeed he has.

Tesman. And I hear it has made some sensation!

Brack. Quite an unusual sensation.

Tesman. Fancy—isn't that good news! A man of such extraordinary talents——. I felt so grieved to think that he had gone irretrievably to ruin.

Brack. That was what everybody thought.

Tesman. But I cannot imagine what he will take to now! How in the world will he be able to make his living? Eh?

[*During the last words,* HEDDA *has entered by the hall door.*]

Hedda. [*To* BRACK, *laughing with a touch of scorn.*] Tesman is forever worrying about how people are to make their living.

Tesman. Well, you see, dear—we were talking about poor Eilert Lövborg.

Hedda. [*Glancing at him rapidly.*] Oh, indeed? [*Seats herself in the arm-chair beside the stove and asks indifferently:*] What is the matter with *him*?

Tesman. Well—no doubt he has run through all his property long ago; and he can scarcely write a new book every year—eh? So I really can't see what is to become of him.

Brack. Perhaps I can give you some information on that point.

Tesman. Indeed!

Brack. You must remember that his relations have a good deal of influence.

Tesman. Oh, his relations, unfortunately, have entirely washed their hands of him.

Brack. At one time they called him the hope of the family.

Tesman. At one time, yes! But he has put an end to all that.

Hedda. Who knows? [*With a slight smile.*] I hear they have reclaimed him up at Sheriff Elvsted's——

Brack. And then this book that he has published——

Tesman. Well, well, I hope to goodness they may find something for him to do. I have just written to him. I asked him to come and see us this evening, Hedda dear.

Brack. But my dear fellow, you are booked for my bachelors' party this evening. You promised on the pier last night.

Hedda. Had you forgotten, Tesman?

Tesman. Yes, I had utterly forgotten.

Brack. But it doesn't matter, for you may be sure he won't come.

Tesman. What makes you think that? Eh?

Brack. [*With a little hesitation, rising and resting his hands on the back of his chair.*] My dear Tesman—and you too, Mrs. Tesman—I think I ought not to keep you in the dark about something that—that——

Tesman. That concerns Eilert——?

Brack. Both you and him.

Tesman. Well, my dear Judge, out with it.

Brack. You must be prepared to find your appointment deferred longer than you desired or expected.

Tesman. [*Jumping up uneasily.*] Is there some hitch about it? Eh?

Brack. The nomination may perhaps be made conditional on the result of a competition——

Tesman. Competition! Think of that, Hedda!

Hedda. [*Leans further back in the chair.*] Aha—aha!

Tesman. But who can my competitor be? Surely not——?

Brack. Yes, precisely—Eilert Lövborg.

Tesman. [*Clasping his hands.*] No, no—it's quite inconceivable! Quite impossible! Eh?

Brack. H'm—that is what it may come to, all the same.

Tesman. Well but, Judge Brack—it would show the most incredible lack of consideration for me. [*Gesticulates with his arms.*] For—just think—I'm a married man! We have married on the strength of these prospects, Hedda and I; and run deep into debt; and borrowed money from Aunt Julia too. Good heavens, they had as good as promised me the appointment. Eh?

Brack. Well, well, well—no doubt you will get it in the end; only after a contest.

Hedda. [*Immovable in her arm-chair.*] Fancy, Tesman, there will be a sort of sporting interest in that.

Tesman. Why, my dearest Hedda, how can you be so indifferent about it?

Hedda. [*As before.*] I am not at all indifferent. I am most eager to see who wins.

Brack. In any case, Mrs. Tesman, it is best that you should know how matters stand. I mean—before you set about the little purchases I hear you are threatening.

Hedda. This can make no difference.

Brack. Indeed! Then I have no more to say. Good-by! [*To* TESMAN.] I shall look in on my way back from my afternoon walk, and take you home with me.

Tesman. Oh yes, yes—your news has quite upset me.

Hedda. [*Reclining, holds out her hand.*] Good-by, Judge; and be sure you call in the afternoon.

Brack. Many thanks. Good-by, good-by!

Tesman. [*Accompanying him to the door.*] Good-by, my dear Judge! You must really excuse me——

[JUDGE BRACK *goes out by the hall door.*]

Tesman. [*Crosses the room.*] Oh Hedda—one should never rush into adventures. Eh?

Hedda. [*Looks at him, smiling.*] Do *you* do *that*?

Tesman. Yes, dear—there is no denying—it *was* adventurous to go and marry and set up house upon mere expectations.

Hedda. Perhaps you are right there.

Tesman. Well—at all events, we have our delightful home, Hedda! Fancy, the home we both dreamed of—the home we were in love with, I may almost say. Eh?

Hedda. [*Rising slowly and wearily.*] It was part of our compact that we were to go into society—to keep open house.

Tesman. Yes, if you only knew how I had been looking forward to it! Fancy—to see you as hostess—in a select circle! Eh? Well, well, well—for the present we shall have to get on without society, Hedda—only to invite Aunt Julie now and then.—Oh, I intended you to lead such an utterly different life, dear——!

Hedda. Of course I cannot have my man in livery just yet.

Tesman. Oh no, unfortunately. It would be out of the question for us to keep a footman, you know.

Hedda. And the saddle-horse I was to have had——

Tesman. [*Aghast.*] The saddle-horse!

Hedda. ——I suppose I must not think of that now.

Tesman. Good heavens, no!—that's as clear as daylight.

Hedda. [*Goes up the room.*] Well, I shall have one thing at least to kill time with in the meanwhile.

Tesman. [*Beaming.*] Oh, thank heaven for that! What is it, Hedda? Eh?

Hedda. [*In the middle doorway, looks at him with covert scorn.*] My pistols, George.

Tesman. [*In alarm.*] Your pistols!

Hedda. [*With cold eyes.*] General Gabler's pistols.

[*She goes out through the inner room, to the left.*]

Tesman. [*Rushes up to the middle doorway and calls after her:*] No, for heaven's sake, Hedda darling—don't touch those dangerous things! For my sake, Hedda! Eh?

CURTAIN

ACT SECOND

The room at the TESMAN'S *as in the First Act, except that the piano has been removed, and an elegant little writing-table with book-shelves put in its place. A smaller table stands near the sofa on the left. Most of the bouquets have been taken away.* MRS. ELVSTED'S *bouquet is upon the large table in front.—It is afternoon.*

[HEDDA, *dressed to receive callers, is alone in the room. She stands by the open glass door, loading a revolver. The fellow to it lies in an open pistol-case on the writing-table.*]

Hedda. [*Looks down the garden, and calls:*] So you are here again, Judge!

Brack. [*Is heard calling from a distance.*] As you see, Mrs. Tesman!

Hedda. [*Raises the pistol and points.*] Now I'll shoot you, Judge Brack!

Brack. [*Calling unseen.*] No, no, no! Don't stand aiming at me!

Hedda. This is what comes of sneaking in by the back way.[1] [*She fires.*]

Brack. [*Nearer.*] Are you out of your senses——?

Hedda. Dear me—did I happen to hit you?

Brack. [*Still outside.*] I wish you would let these pranks alone!

Hedda. Come in then, Judge.

[*Judge* BRACK, *dressed as though for a men's party, enters by the glass door. He carries a light overcoat over his arm.*]

Brack. What the deuce—haven't you tired of that sport, yet? What are you shooting at?

Hedda. Oh, I am only firing in the air.

Brack. [*Gently takes the pistol out of her hand.*] Allow me, madam! [*Looks at it.*] Ah—I know this pistol well! [*Looks around.*] Where is the case? Ah, here it is. [*Lays the pistol in it, and shuts it.*] Now we won't play at that game any more today.

Hedda. Then what in heaven's name would you have me do with myself?

Brack. Have you had no visitors?

Hedda. [*Closing the glass door.*] Not one. I suppose all our set are still out of town.

Brack. And is Tesman not at home either?

Hedda. [*At the writing-table, putting the pistol-case in a drawer which she shuts.*] No. He rushed off to his aunt's directly after lunch; he didn't expect you so early.

Brack. H'm—how stupid of me not to have thought of that!

Hedda. [*Turning her head to look at him.*] Why stupid?

Brack. Because if I had thought of it I should have come a little—earlier.

Hedda. [*Crossing the room.*] Then you

[1] "Bagveje" means both "back ways" and "underhand courses."

would have found no one to receive you; for I have been in my room changing my dress ever since lunch.

Brack. And is there no sort of little chink that we could hold a parley through?

Hedda. You have forgotten to arrange one.

Brack. That was another piece of stupidity.

Hedda. Well, we must just settle down here—and wait. Tesman is not likely to be back for some time yet.

Brack. Never mind; I shall not be impatient.

[HEDDA *seats herself in the corner of the sofa.* BRACK *lays his overcoat over the back of the nearest chair, and sits down, but keeps his hat in his hand. A short silence. They look at each other.*]

Hedda. Well?

Brack. [*In the same tone.*] Well?

Hedda. I spoke first.

Brack. [*Bending a little forward.*] Come, let us have a cosy little chat, Mrs. Hedda.[1]

Hedda. [*Leaning further back in the sofa.*] Does it not seem like a whole eternity since our last talk? Of course I don't count those few words yesterday evening and this morning.

Brack. You mean since our last confidential talk? Our last *tête-à-tête*?

Hedda. Well, yes—since you put it so.

Brack. Not a day has passed but I have wished that you were home again.

Hedda. And I have done nothing but wish the same thing.

Brack. You? Really, Mrs. Hedda? And I thought you had been enjoying your tour so much!

Hedda. Oh yes, you may be sure of that!

Brack. But Tesman's letters spoke of nothing but happiness.

Hedda. Oh, *Tesman!* You see, he thinks nothing so delightful as grubbing in libraries and making copies of old parchments, or whatever you call them.

Brack. [*With a spice of malice.*] Well, that is his vocation in life—or part of it at any rate.

Hedda. Yes, of course; and no doubt when it's your vocation——. But *I!* Oh, my dear Mr. Brack, how mortally bored I have been.

Brack. [*Sympathetically.*] Do you really say so? In downright earnest?

Hedda. Yes, you can surely understand it ——! To go for whole six months without meeting a soul that knew anything of our circle, or could talk about the things we are interested in.

Brack. Yes, yes—I too should feel that a deprivation.

Hedda. And then, what I found most intolerable of all——

Brack. Well?

Hedda. ——was being everlastingly in the company of—one and the same person——

Brack. [*With a nod of assent.*] Morning, noon, and night, yes—at all possible times and seasons.

Hedda. I said "everlastingly."

Brack. Just so. But I should have thought, with our excellent Tesman, one could——

Hedda. Tesman is—a specialist, my dear Judge.

Brack. Undeniably.

Hedda. And specialists are not at all amusing to travel with. Not in the long run at any rate.

Brack. Not even—the specialist one happens to *love*?

Hedda. Faugh—don't use that sickening word!

Brack. [*Taken aback.*] What do you say, Mrs. Hedda?

Hedda. [*Half laughing, half irritated.*] You should just try it! To hear of nothing but the history of civilization, morning, noon, and night——

Brack. Everlastingly.

Hedda. Yes, yes, yes! And then all this about the domestic industry of the middle ages——! That's the most disgusting part of it!

Brack. [*Looks searchingly at her.*] But tell me—in that case, how am I to understand your——? H'm——

Hedda. My accepting George Tesman, you mean?

Brack. Well, let us put it so.

Hedda. Good heavens, do you see anything so wonderful in that?

Brack. Yes and no—Mrs. Hedda.

Hedda. I had positively danced myself tired, my dear Judge. My day was done—— [*With a slight shudder.*] Oh no—I won't say that; nor think it either!

Brack. You have assuredly no reason to.

Hedda. Oh, reasons—— [*Watching him closely.*] And George Tesman—after all, you must admit that he is correctness itself.

Brack. His correctness and respectability are beyond all question.

Hedda. And I don't see anything absolutely ridiculous about him.—Do you?

Brack. Ridiculous? N-no—I shouldn't exactly say so——

[1] As this form of address is contrary to English usage, and as the note of familiarity would be lacking in "Mrs. Tesman," Brack may, in stage representation, say "Miss Hedda," thus ignoring her marriage and reverting to the form of address no doubt customary between them of old.

Hedda. Well—and his powers of research, at all events, are untiring.—I see no reason why he should not one day come to the front, after all.

Brack. [*Looks at her hesitatingly.*] I thought that you, like every one else, expected him to attain the highest distinction.

Hedda. [*With an expression of fatigue.*] Yes, so I did.—And then, since he was bent, at all hazards, on being allowed to provide for me—I really don't know why I should not have accepted his offer?

Brack. No—if you look at it in *that* light——

Hedda. It was more than my other adorers were prepared to do for me, my dear Judge.

Brack. [*Laughing.*] Well, I can't answer for all the rest; but as for myself, you know quite well that I have always entertained a—a certain respect for the marriage tie—for marriage as an institution, Mrs. Hedda.

Hedda. [*Jestingly.*] Oh, I assure you I have never cherished any hopes with respect to *you.*

Brack. All I require is a pleasant and intimate interior, where I can make myself useful in every way, and am free to come and go as—as a trusted friend——

Hedda. Of the master of the house, do you mean?

Brack. [*Bowing.*] Frankly—of the mistress first of all; but of course of the master too, in the second place. Such a triangular friendship—if I may call it so—is really a great convenience for all parties, let me tell you.

Hedda. Yes, I have many a time longed for someone to make a third on our travels. Oh—those railway-carriage *tête-à-têtes*——!

Brack. Fortunately your wedding journey is over now.

Hedda. [*Shaking her head.*] Not by a long—long way. I have only arrived at a station on the line.

Brack. Well, then the passengers jump out and move about a little, Mrs. Hedda.

Hedda. I never jump out.

Brack. Really?

Hedda. No—because there is always someone standing by to——

Brack. [*Laughing.*] To look at your ankles, do you mean?

Hedda. Precisely.

Brack. Well, but, dear me——

Hedda. [*With a gesture of repulsion.*] I won't have it. I would rather keep my seat where I happen to be—and continue the *tête-à-tête.*

Brack. But suppose a third person were to jump in and join the couple.

Hedda. Ah—that is quite another matter!

Brack. A trusted, sympathetic friend——

Hedda. ——with a fund of conversation on all sorts of lively topics——

Brack. ——and not the least bit of a specialist!

Hedda. [*With an audible sigh.*] Yes, that would be a relief indeed.

Brack. [*Hears the front door open, and glances in that direction.*] The triangle is completed.

Hedda. [*Half aloud.*] And on goes the train.

[GEORGE TESMAN, *in a gray walking-suit, with a soft felt hat, enters from the hall. He has a number of unbound books under his arm and in his pockets.*]

Tesman. [*Goes up to the table beside the corner settee.*] Ouf—what a load for a warm day—all these books. [*Lays them on the table.*] I'm positively perspiring, Hedda. Hallo—are you there already, my dear Judge? Eh? Berta didn't tell me.

Brack. [*Rising.*] I came in through the garden.

Hedda. What books have you got there?

Tesman. [*Stands looking them through.*] Some new books on my special subjects—quite indispensable to me.

Hedda. Your special subjects?

Brack. Yes, books on his special subjects, Mrs. Tesman.

[BRACK *and* HEDDA *exchange a confidential smile.*]

Hedda. Do you need still more books on your special subjects?

Tesman. Yes, my dear Hedda, one can never have too many of them. Of course one must keep up with all that is written and published.

Hedda. Yes, I suppose one must.

Tesman. [*Searching among his books.*] And look here—I have got hold of Eilert Lövborg's new book too. [*Offering it to her.*] Perhaps you would like to glance through it, Hedda? Eh?

Hedda. No, thank you. Or rather—afterwards perhaps.

Tesman. I looked into it a little on the way home.

Brack. Well, what do you think of it—as a specialist?

Tesman. I think it shows quite remarkable soundness of judgment. He never wrote like that before. [*Putting the books together.*] Now I shall take all these into my study. I'm longing to cut the leaves——! And then I must change my clothes. [*To* BRACK.] I suppose we needn't start just yet? Eh?

Brack. Oh, dear no—there is not the slightest hurry.

Tesman. Well then, I will take my time. [*Is going with his books, but stops in the doorway and turns.*] By-the-bye, Hedda—Aunt Julia is not coming this evening.

Hedda. Not coming? Is it that affair of the bonnet that keeps her away?

Tesman. Oh, not at all. How could you think such a thing of Aunt Julia? Just fancy ——! The fact is, Aunt Rina is very ill.

Hedda. She always is.

Tesman. Yes, but today she is much worse than usual, poor dear.

Hedda. Oh, then it's only natural that her sister should remain with her. I must bear my disappointment.

Tesman. And you can't imagine, dear, how delighted Aunt Julia seemed to be—because you had come home looking so flourishing!

Hedda. [*Half aloud, rising.*] Oh, those everlasting Aunts!

Tesman. What?

Hedda. [*Going to the glass door.*] Nothing.

Tesman. Oh, all right.

[*He goes through the inner room, out to the right.*]

Brack. What bonnet were you talking about?

Hedda. Oh, it was a little episode with Miss Tesman this morning. She had laid down her bonnet on the chair there—[*Looks at him and smiles.*]—and I pretended to think it was the servant's.

Brack. [*Shaking his head.*] Now my dear Mrs. Hedda, how could you do such a thing? To that excellent old lady, too!

Hedda. [*Nervously crossing the room.*] Well, you see—these impulses come over me all of a sudden; and I cannot resist them. [*Throws herself down in the easy-chair by the stove.*] Oh, I don't know how to explain it.

Brack. [*Behind the easy-chair.*] You are not really happy—that is at the bottom of it.

Hedda. [*Looking straight before her.*] I know of no reason why I should be—happy. Perhaps you can give me one?

Brack. Well—amongst other things, because you have got exactly the home you had set your heart on.

Hedda. [*Looks up at him and laughs.*] Do you too believe in that legend?

Brack. Is there nothing in it, then?

Hedda. Oh yes, there is *something* in it.

Brack. Well?

Hedda. There is this in it, that I made use of Tesman to see me home from evening parties last summer——

Brack. I, unfortunately, had to go quite a different way.

Hedda. That's true. I know you were going a different way last summer.

Brack. [*Laughing.*] Oh fie, Mrs. Hedda! Well, then—you and Tesman——?

Hedda. Well, we happened to pass here one evening; Tesman, poor fellow, was writhing in the agony of having to find conversation; so I took pity on the learned man——

Brack. [*Smiles doubtfully.*] *You* took pity? H'm——

Hedda. Yes, I really did. And so—to help him out of his torment—I happened to say, in pure thoughtlessness, that I should like to live in this villa.

Brack. No more than that?

Hedda. Not *that* evening.

Brack. But afterwards?

Hedda. Yes, my thoughtlessness had consequences, my dear Judge.

Brack. Unfortunately that too often happens, Mrs. Hedda.

Hedda. Thanks! So you see it was this enthusiasm for Secretary Falk's villa that first constituted a bond of sympathy between George Tesman and me. From that came our engagement and our marriage, and our wedding journey, and all the rest of it. Well, well, my dear Judge—as you make your bed so you must lie, I could almost say.

Brack. This is exquisite! And you really cared not a rap about it all the time?

Hedda. No, heaven knows I didn't.

Brack. But now? Now that we have made it so homelike for you?

Hedda. Uh—the rooms all seem to smell of lavender and dried rose-leaves.—But perhaps it's Aunt Julia that has brought that scent with her.

Brack. [*Laughing.*] No, I think it must be a legacy from the late Mrs. Secretary Falk.

Hedda. Yes, there is an odor of mortality about it. It reminds me of a bouquet—the day after the ball. [*Clasps her hands behind her head, leans back in her chair and looks at him.*] Oh, my dear Judge—you cannot imagine how horribly I shall bore myself here.

Brack. Why should not you, too, find some sort of vocation in life, Mrs. Hedda?

Hedda. A vocation—that should attract me?

Brack. If possible, of course.

Hedda. Heaven knows what sort of a vocation that could be. I often wonder whether —— [*Breaking off.*] But that would never do either.

Brack. Who can tell? Let me hear what it is.

Hedda. Whether I might not get Tesman to go into politics, I mean.

Brack. [*Laughing.*] Tesman? No, really now, political life is not the thing for him—not at all in his line.

Hedda. No, I daresay not.—But if I could get him into it all the same?

Brack. Why—what satisfaction could you find in that? If he is not fitted for that sort of thing, why should you want to drive him into it?

Hedda. Because I am bored, I tell you! [*After a pause.*] So you think it quite out of the question that Tesman should ever get into the ministry?

Brack. H'm—you see, my dear Mrs. Hedda—to get into the ministry, he would have to be a tolerably rich man.

Hedda. [*Rising impatiently.*] Yes, there we have it! It is this genteel poverty I have managed to drop into——! [*Crosses the room.*] *That* is what makes life so pitiable! So utterly ludicrous!—For that's what it is.

Brack. Now *I* should say the fault lay elsewhere.

Hedda. Where, then?

Brack. You have never gone through any really stimulating experience.

Hedda. Anything serious, you mean?

Brack. Yes, you may call it so. But now you may perhaps have one in store.

Hedda. [*Tossing her head.*] Oh, you're thinking of the annoyances about this wretched professorship! But that must be Tesman's own affair. I assure you I shall not waste a thought upon it.

Brack. No, no, I daresay not. But suppose now that what people call—in elegant language—a solemn responsibility were to come upon you? [*Smiling.*] A new responsibility, Mrs. Hedda?

Hedda. [*Angrily.*] Be quiet! Nothing of that sort will ever happen.

Brack. [*Warily.*] We will speak of this again a year hence—at the very outside.

Hedda. [*Curtly.*] I have no turn for anything of the sort, Judge Brack. No responsibilities for me!

Brack. Are you so unlike the generality of women as to have no turn for duties which——?

Hedda. [*Beside the glass door.*] Oh, be quiet, I tell you!—I often think there is only one thing in the world I have any turn for.

Brack. [*Drawing near to her.*] And what is that, if I may ask?

Hedda. [*Stands looking out.*] Boring myself to death. Now you know it. [*Turns, looks toward the inner room, and laughs.*] Yes, as I thought! Here comes the Professor.

Brack. [*Softly, in a tone of warning.*] Come, come, come, Mrs. Hedda!

[GEORGE TESMAN, *dressed for the party, with his gloves and hat in his hand, enters from the right through the inner room.*]

Tesman. Hedda, has no message come from Eilert Lövborg? Eh?

Hedda. No.

Tesman. Then you'll see he'll be here presently.

Brack. Do you really think he will come?

Tesman. Yes, I am almost sure of it. For what you were telling us this morning must have been a mere floating rumor.

Brack. You think so?

Tesman. At any rate, Aunt Julia said she did not believe for a moment that he would ever stand in my way again. Fancy that!

Brack. Well then, that's all right.

Tesman. [*Placing his hat and gloves on a chair on the right.*] Yes, but you must really let me wait for him as long as possible.

Brack. We have plenty of time yet. None of my guests will arrive before seven or half-past.

Tesman. Then meanwhile we can keep Hedda company, and see what happens. Eh?

Hedda. [*Placing* BRACK's *hat and overcoat upon the corner settee.*] And at the worst Mr. Lövborg can remain here with me.

Brack. [*Offering to take his things.*] Oh, allow me, Mrs. Tesman!—What do you mean by "at the worst"?

Hedda. If he won't go with you and Tesman.

Tesman. [*Looks dubiously at her.*] But, Hedda dear—do you think it would quite do for him to remain with you? Eh? Remember, Aunt Julia can't come.

Hedda. No, but Mrs. Elvsted is coming. We three can have a cup of tea together.

Tesman. Oh yes, *that* will be all right.

Brack. [*Smiling.*] And that would perhaps be the safest plan for him.

Hedda. Why so?

Brack. Well, you know, Mrs. Tesman, how you used to gird at my little bachelor parties. You declared they were adapted only for men of the strictest principles.

Hedda. But no doubt Mr. Lövborg's principles are strict enough now. A converted sinner——

[BERTA *appears at the hall door.*]

Berta. There's a gentleman asking if you are at home, ma'am——

Hedda. Well, show him in.

Tesman. [*Softly.*] I'm sure it is he! Fancy that!

[EILERT LÖVBORG *enters from the hall. He is slim and lean; of the same age as* TESMAN, *but looks older and somewhat worn-out. His hair and beard are of a blackish brown, his face long and pale, but with patches of color on the cheekbones. He is dressed in a well-cut black visiting suit, quite new. He has dark gloves and a silk hat. He stops near the door, and makes a rapid bow, seeming somewhat embarrassed.*]

Tesman. [*Goes up to him and shakes him warmly by the hand.*] Well, my dear Eilert—so at last we meet again!

Lövborg. [*Speaks in a subdued voice.*] Thanks for your letter, Tesman. [*Approaching* HEDDA.] Will you too shake hands with me, Mrs. Tesman?

Hedda. [*Taking his hand.*] I am glad to see you, Mr. Lövborg. [*With a motion of her hand.*] I don't know whether you two gentlemen——?

Lövborg. [*Bowing slightly.*] Judge Brack, I think,

Brack. [*Doing likewise.*] Oh yes—in the old days——

Tesman. [*To* LÖVBORG, *with his hands on his shoulders.*] And now you must make yourself entirely at home, Eilert! Mustn't he, Hedda?—For I hear you are going to settle in town again? Eh?

Lövborg. Yes, I am.

Tesman. Quite right, quite right. Let me tell you, I have got hold of your new book; but I haven't had time to read it yet.

Lövborg. You may spare yourself the trouble.

Tesman. Why so?

Lövborg. Because there is very little in it.

Tesman. Just fancy—how can you say so?

Brack. But it has been very much praised, I hear.

Lövborg. That was what I wanted; so I put nothing into the book but what every one would agree with.

Brack. Very wise of you.

Tesman. Well, but, my dear Eilert——!

Lövborg. For now I mean to win myself a position again—to make a fresh start.

Tesman. [*A little embarrassed.*] Ah, that is what you wish to do? Eh?

Lövborg. [*Smiling, lays down his hat, and draws a packet, wrapped in paper, from his coat pocket.*] But when this one appears, George Tesman, you will have to read it. For *this* is the real book—the book I have put my true self into.

Tesman. Indeed? And what is it?

Lövborg. It is the continuation.

Tesman. The continuation? Of what?

Lövborg. Of the book.

Tesman. Of the new book?

Lövborg. Of course.

Tesman. Why, my dear Eilert—does it not come down to our own days?

Lövborg. Yes, it does; and this one deals with the future.

Tesman. With the future! But, good heavens, we know nothing of the future!

Lövborg. No; but there is a thing or two to be said about it all the same. [*Opens the packet.*] Look here——

Tesman. Why, that's not your handwriting.

Lövborg. I dictated it. [*Turning over the pages.*] It falls into two sections. The first deals with the civilizing forces of the future. And here is the second—[*running through the pages toward the end*]—forecasting the probable line of development.

Tesman. How odd now! I should never have thought of writing anything of that sort.

Hedda. [*At the glass door, drumming on the pane.*] H'm——. I daresay not.

Lövborg. [*Replacing the manuscript in its paper and laying the packet on the table.*] I brought it, thinking I might read you a little of it this evening.

Tesman. That was very good of you, Eilert. But this evening——? [*Looking at* BRACK.] I don't quite see how we can manage it——

Lövborg. Well then, some other time. There is no hurry.

Brack. I must tell you, Mr. Lövborg—there is a little gathering at my house this evening—mainly in honor of Tesman, you know——

Lövborg. [*Looking for his hat.*] Oh—then I won't detain you——

Brack. No, but listen—will you not do me the favor of joining us?

Lövborg. [*Curtly and decidedly.*] No, I can't—thank you very much.

Brack. Oh, nonsense—do! We shall be quite a select little circle. And I assure you we shall have a "lively time" as Mrs. Hed—as Mrs. Tesman says.

Lövborg. I have no doubt of it. But nevertheless——

Brack. And then you might bring your manuscript with you, and read it to Tesman at my house. I could give you a room to yourselves.

Tesman. Yes, think of that, Eilert—why shouldn't you? Eh?

Hedda. [*Interposing.*] But, Tesman, if Mr. Lövborg would really rather not! I am sure Mr. Lövborg is much more inclined to remain here and have supper with me.

Lövborg. [*Looking at her.*] With you, Mrs. Tesman?

Hedda. And with Mrs. Elvsted.

Lövborg. Ah—— [*Lightly.*] I saw her for a moment this morning.

Hedda. Did you? Well, she is coming this evening. So you see you are almost bound to remain, Mr. Lövborg, or she will have no one to see her home.

Lövborg. That's true. Many thanks, Mrs. Tesman—in that case I will remain.

Hedda. Then I have one or two orders to give the servant——

[*She goes to the hall door and rings.* BERTA *enters.* HEDDA *talks to her in a whisper, and points toward the inner room.* BERTA *nods and goes out again.*]

Tesman. [*At the same time, to* LÖVBORG.] Tell me, Eilert—is it this new subject—the future—that you are going to lecture about?

Lövborg. Yes.

Tesman. They told me at the bookseller's that you are going to deliver a course of lectures this autumn.

Lövborg. That is my intention. I hope you won't take it ill, Tesman.

Tesman. Oh no, not in the least! But——?

Lövborg. I can quite understand that it must be disagreeable to you.

Tesman. [*Cast down.*] Oh, I can't expect you, out of consideration for me, to——

Lövborg. But I shall wait till you have received your appointment.

Tesman. Will you wait? Yes, but—yes, but—are you not going to compete with me? Eh?

Lövborg. No; it is only the moral victory I care for.

Tesman. Why, bless me—then Aunt Julia was right after all! Oh yes—I knew it! Hedda! Just fancy—Eilert Lövborg is not going to stand in our way!

Hedda. [*Curtly.*] *Our* way? Pray leave *me* out of the question.

[*She goes up toward the inner room, where* BERTA *is placing a tray with decanters and glasses on the table.* HEDDA *nods approval, and comes forward again.* BERTA *goes out.*]

Tesman. [*At the same time.*] And you, Judge Brack—what do you say to this? Eh?

Brack. Well, I say that a moral victory—h'm—may be all very fine——

Tesman. Yes, certainly. But all the same——

Hedda. [*Looking at* TESMAN *with a cold smile.*] You stand there looking as if you were thunderstruck——

Tesman, Yes—so I am—I almost think——

Brack. Don't you see, Mrs. Tesman, a thunderstorm has just passed over?

Hedda. [*Pointing toward the inner room.*] Will you not take a glass of cold punch, gentlemen?

Brack. [*Looking at his watch.*] A stirrup-cup? Yes, it wouldn't come amiss.

Tesman. A capital idea, Hedda! Just the thing! Now that the weight has been taken off my mind——

Hedda. Will you not join them, Mr. Lövborg?

Lövborg. [*With a gesture of refusal.*] No, thank you. Nothing for me.

Brack. Why bless me—cold punch is surely not poison.

Lövborg. Perhaps not for everyone.

Hedda. I will keep Mr. Lövborg company in the meantime.

Tesman. Yes, yes, Hedda dear, do.

[*He and* BRACK *go into the inner room, seat themselves, drink punch, smoke cigarettes, and carry on a lively conversation during what follows.* EILERT LÖVBORG *remains standing beside the stove.* HEDDA *goes to the writing-table.*]

Hedda. [*Raising her voice a little.*] Do you care to look at some photographs, Mr. Lövborg? You know Tesman and I made a tour in the Tyrol on our way home?

[*She takes up an album and places it on the table beside the sofa in the further corner of which she seats herself.* EILERT LÖVBORG *approaches, stops and looks at her. Then he takes a chair and seats himself to her left, with his back toward the inner room.*]

Hedda. [*Opening the album.*] Do you see this range of mountains, Mr. Lövborg? It's the Ortler group. Tesman has written the name underneath. Here it is: "The Ortler group near Meran."

Lövborg. [*Who has never taken his eyes off her, says softly and slowly:*] Hedda—Gabler!

Hedda. [*Glancing hastily at him.*] Ah! Hush!

Lövborg. [*Repeats softly.*] Hedda Gabler!

Hedda. [*Looking at the album.*] That was my name in the old days—when we two knew each other.

Lövborg. And I must teach myself never to say Hedda Gabler again—never, as long as I live.

Hedda. [*Still turning over the pages.*] Yes, you must. And I think you ought to practice in time. The sooner the better, I should say.

Lövborg. [*In a tone of indignation.*]

Hedda Gabler married! And married to—George Tesman!

Hedda. Yes—so the world goes.

Lövborg. Oh, Hedda, Hedda—how could you [1] throw yourself away!

Hedda. [*Looks sharply at him.*] What? I can't allow this!

Lövborg. What do you mean?

[TESMAN *comes into the room and goes toward the sofa.*]

Hedda. [*Hears him coming and says in an indifferent tone.*] And this is a view from the Val d'Ampezo, Mr. Lövborg. Just look at these peaks! [*Looks affectionately up at* TESMAN.] What's the name of these curious peaks, dear?

Tesman. Let me see. Oh, those are the Dolomites.

Hedda. Yes, that's it!—Those are the Dolomites, Mr. Lövborg.

Tesman. Hedda dear—I only wanted to ask whether I shouldn't bring you a little punch after all? For yourself at any rate—eh?

Hedda. Yes, do, please; and perhaps a few biscuits.

Tesman. No cigarettes?

Hedda. No.

Tesman. Very well.

[*He goes into the inner room and out to the right.* BRACK *sits in the inner room, and keeps an eye from time to time on* HEDDA *and* LÖVBORG.]

Lövborg. [*Softly, as before.*] Answer me, Hedda—how could you go and do this?

Hedda. [*Apparently absorbed in the album.*] If you continue to say *du* to me I won't talk to you.

Lövborg. May I not say *du* even when we are alone?

Hedda. No. You may think it; but you mustn't say it.

Lövborg. Ah, I understand. It is an offense against George Tesman, whom you [2]—love.

Hedda. [*Glances at him and smiles.*] Love? What an idea!

Lövborg. You don't love him then!

Hedda. But I won't hear of any sort of unfaithfulness. Remember that.

Lövborg. Hedda—answer me one thing—

Hedda. Hush!

[TESMAN *enters with a small tray from the inner room.*]

Tesman. Here you are! Isn't this tempting? [*He puts the tray on the table.*]

Hedda. Why do you bring it yourself?

Tesman. [*Filling the glasses.*] Because I think it's such fun to wait upon you, Hedda.

Hedda. But you have poured out two glasses. Mr. Lövborg said he wouldn't have any——

Tesman. No, but Mrs. Elvsted will soon be here, won't she?

Hedda. Yes, by-the-bye—Mrs. Elvsted—

Tesman. Had you forgotten her? Eh?

Hedda. We were so absorbed in these photographs. [*Shows him a picture.*] Do you remember this little village?

Tesman. Oh, it's that one just below the Brenner Pass. It was there we passed the night——

Hedda. —and met that lively party of tourists.

Tesman. Yes, that was the place. Fancy—if we could only have had *you* with us, Eilert! Eh?

[*He returns to the inner room and sits beside* BRACK.]

Lövborg. Answer me this one thing, Hedda——

Hedda. Well?

Lövborg. Was there no love in your friendship for *me* either? Not a spark—not a tinge of love in it?

Hedda. I wonder if there was? To me it seems as though we were two good comrades—two thoroughly intimate friends. [*Smilingly.*] You especially were frankness itself.

Lövborg. It was you that made me so.

Hedda. As I look back upon it all, I think there was really something beautiful, something fascinating—something daring—in—in that secret intimacy—that comradeship which no living creature so much as dreamed of.

Lövborg. Yes, yes, Hedda! Was there not?—When I used to come to your father's in the afternoon—and the General sat over at the window reading his papers—with his back toward us——

Hedda. And we two on the corner sofa——

Lövborg. Always with the same illustrated paper before us——

Hedda. For want of an album, yes.

Lövborg. Yes, Hedda, and when I made my confessions to you—told you about myself, things that at that time no one else knew! There I would sit and tell you of my escapades—my days and nights and devilment. Oh, Hedda—what was the power in you that forced me to confess these things?

Hedda. Do you think it was any power in me?

Lövborg. How else can I explain it? And all those—those roundabout questions you used to put to me——

[1] He uses the familiar *du*.
[2] From this point onward Lövborg uses the formal *De*.

Hedda. Which you understood so particularly well——

Lövborg. How could you sit and question me like that? Question me quite frankly——

Hedda. In roundabout terms, please observe.

Lövborg. Yes, but frankly nevertheless. Cross-question me about—all that sort of thing?

Hedda. And how could you answer, Mr. Lövborg?

Lövborg. Yes, that is just what I can't understand—in looking back upon it. But tell me now, Hedda—was there not love at the bottom of our friendship? On your side, did you not feel as though you might purge my stains away—if I made you my confessor? Was it not so?

Hedda. No, not quite.

Lövborg. What was your motive, then?

Hedda. Do you think it quite incomprehensible that a young girl—when it can be done—without anyone knowing——

Lövborg. Well?

Hedda. ——should be glad to have a peep, now and then, into a world which——

Lövborg. Which——?

Hedda. ——which she is forbidden to know anything about?

Lövborg. So *that* was it?

Hedda. Partly. Partly—I almost think.

Lövborg. Comradeship in the thirst for life. But why should not *that,* at any rate, have continued?

Hedda. The fault was yours.

Lövborg. It was you that broke with me.

Hedda. Yes, when our friendship threatened to develop into something more serious. Shame upon you, Eilert Lövborg! How could you think of wronging your—your frank comrade?

Lövborg. [*Clenching his hands.*] Oh, why did you not carry out your threat? Why did you not shoot me down?

Hedda. Because I have such a dread of scandal.

Lövborg. Yes, Hedda, you are a coward at heart.

Hedda. A terrible coward. [*Changing her tone.*] But it was a lucky thing for you. And now you have found ample consolation at the Elvsteds'.

Lövborg. I know what Thea has confided to you.

Hedda. And perhaps you have confided to her something about us?

Lövborg. Not a word. She is too stupid to understand anything of that sort.

Hedda. Stupid?

Lövborg. She is stupid about matters of that sort.

Hedda. And I am cowardly. [*Bends over toward him, without looking him in the face, and says more softly:*] But now I will confide something to *you.*

Lövborg. [*Eagerly.*] Well?

Hedda. The fact that I dared not shoot you down——

Lövborg. Yes!

Hedda. ——*that* was not my most arrant cowardice—that evening.

Lövborg. [*Looks at her a moment, understands, and whispers passionately.*] Oh, Hedda! Hedda Gabler! Now I begin to see a hidden reason beneath our comradeship! You [1] and I——! After all, then, it was your craving for life——

Hedda. [*Softly, with a sharp glance.*] Take care! Believe nothing of the sort!

[*Twilight has began to fall. The hall door is opened from without by* BERTA.]

Hedda. [*Closes the album with a bang and calls smilingly:*] Ah, at last! My darling Thea—come along!

[MRS. ELVSTED *enters from the hall. She is in evening dress. The door is closed behind her.*]

Hedda. [*On the sofa, stretches out her arms toward her.*] My sweet Thea—you can't think how I have been longing for you!

[MRS. ELVSTED, *in passing, exchanges slight salutations with the gentlemen in the inner room, then goes up to the table and gives* HEDDA *her hand.* EILERT LÖVBORG *has risen. He and* MRS. ELVSTED *greet each other with a silent nod.*]

Mrs. Elvsted. Ought I to go in and talk to your husband for a moment?

Hedda. Oh, not at all. Leave those two alone. They will soon be going.

Mrs. Elvsted. Are they going out?

Hedda. Yes, to a supper-party.

Mrs. Elvsted. [*Quickly, to* LÖVBORG.] Not *you?*

Lövborg. No.

Hedda. Mr. Lövborg remains with us.

Mrs. Elvsted. [*Takes a chair and is about to seat herself at his side.*] Oh, how nice it is here!

Hedda. No, thank you, my little Thea! Not *there!* You'll be good enough to come over here to me. I will sit between you.

Mrs. Elvsted. Yes, just as you please.

[*She goes round the table and seats herself on the sofa on* HEDDA'S *right.* LÖVBORG *reseats himself on his chair.*]

---

[1] In this speech he once more says *du.* Hedda addresses him throughout as *De.*

Lövborg. [*After a short pause, to* HEDDA.] Is not she lovely to look at?

Hedda. [*Lightly stroking her hair.*] Only to look at?

Lövborg. Yes. For *we* two—she and I—*we* are two real comrades. We have absolute faith in each other; so we can sit and talk with perfect frankness——

Hedda. Not roundabout, Mr. Lövborg?

Lövborg. Well——

Mrs. Elvsted. [*Softly clinging close to* HEDDA.] Oh, how happy I am, Hedda! For, only think, he says I have inspired him too.

Hedda. [*Looks at her with a smile.*] Ah! Does he say that, dear?

Lövborg. And then she is so brave, Mrs. Tesman!

Mrs. Elvsted. Good heavens—am I brave?

Lövborg. Exceedingly—where your comrade is concerned.

Hedda. Ah yes—courage! If one only had *that!*

Lövborg. What then? What do you mean?

Hedda. Then life would perhaps be livable, after all. [*With a sudden change of tone.*] But now, my dearest Thea, you really must have a glass of cold punch.

Mrs. Elvsted. No, thanks—I never take anything of that kind.

Hedda. Well then, *you,* Mr. Lövborg.

Lövborg. Nor I, thank you.

Mrs. Elvsted. No, he doesn't either.

Hedda. [*Looks fixedly at him.*] But if I say you *shall?*

Lövborg. It would be no use.

Hedda. [*Laughing.*] Then I, poor creature, have no sort of power over you?

Lövborg. Not in *that* respect.

Hedda. But seriously, I think you ought to—for your own sake.

Mrs. Elvsted. Why, Hedda——!

Lövborg. How so?

Hedda. Or rather on account of other people.

Lövborg. Indeed?

Hedda. Otherwise people might be apt to suspect that—in your heart of hearts—you did not feel quite secure—quite confident in yourself.

Mrs. Elvsted. [*Softly.*] Oh please, Hedda——

Lövborg. People may suspect what they like—for the present.

Mrs. Elvsted. [*Joyfully.*] Yes, let them!

Hedda. I saw it plainly in Judge Brack's face a moment ago.

Lövborg. What did you see?

Hedda. His contemptuous smile, when you dared not go with them into the inner room.

Lövborg. Dared not? Of course I preferred to stop here and talk to *you.*

Mrs. Elvsted. What could be more natural, Hedda?

Hedda. But the Judge could not guess that. And I saw, too, the way he smiled and glanced at Tesman when you dared not accept his invitation to this wretched little supper-party of his.

Lövborg. Dared not! Do you say I dared not?

Hedda. *I* don't say so. But that was how Judge Brack understood it.

Lövborg. Well, let him.

Hedda. Then you are not going with them?

Lövborg. I will stay here with you and Thea.

Mrs. Elvsted. Yes, Hedda—how can you doubt that?

Hedda. [*Smiles and nods approvingly to* LÖVBORG.] Firm as a rock! Faithful to your principles, now and forever! Ah, that is how a man should be! [*Turns to* MRS. ELVSTED *and caresses her.*] Well now, what did I tell you, when you came to us this morning in such a state of distraction——

Lövborg. [*Surprised.*] Distraction!

Mrs. Elvsted. [*Terrified.*] Hedda—oh Hedda——!

Hedda. You can see for yourself! You haven't the slightest reason to be in such mortal terror—— [*Interrupting herself.*] There! Now we can all three enjoy ourselves!

Lövborg. [*Who has given a start.*] Ah—what is all this, Mrs. Tesman?

Mrs. Elvsted. Oh, my God, Hedda! What are you saying? What are you doing?

Hedda. Don't get excited! That horrid Judge Brack is sitting watching you.

Lövborg. So she was in mortal terror! On my account!

Mrs. Elvsted. [*Softly and piteously.*] Oh, Hedda—now you have ruined everything!

Lövborg. [*Looks fixedly at her for a moment. His face is distorted.*] So *that* was my comrade's frank confidence in me?

Mrs. Elvsted. [*Imploringly.*] Oh, my dearest friend—only let me tell you——

Lövborg. [*Takes one of the glasses of punch, raises it to his lips, and says in a low, husky voice.*] Your health, Thea!

[*He empties the glass, puts it down, and and takes the second.*]

Mrs. Elvsted. [*Softly.*] Oh, Hedda, Hedda—how *could* you do this?

Hedda. *I* do it? *I?* Are you crazy?

Lövborg. Here's to your health too, Mrs. Tesman. Thanks for the truth. Hurrah for the truth!

[*He empties the glass and is about to refill it.*]

Hedda. [*Lays her hand on his arm.*] Come, come—no more for the present. Remember you are going out to supper.

Mrs. Elvsted. No, no, no!

Hedda. Hush! They are sitting watching you.

Lövborg. [*Putting down the glass.*] Now, Thea—tell me the truth——

Mrs. Elvsted. Yes.

Lövborg. Did your husband know that you had come after me?

Mrs. Elvsted. [*Wringing her hands.*] Oh, Hedda—do you hear what he is asking?

Lövborg. Was it arranged between you and him that you were to come to town and look after me? Perhaps it was the Sheriff himself that urged you to come? Aha, my dear—no doubt he wanted my help in his office! Or was it at the card-table that he missed me?

Mrs. Elvsted. [*Softly, in agony.*] Oh, Lövborg, Lövborg——!

Lövborg. [*Seizes a glass and is on the point of filling it.*] Here's a glass for the old Sheriff too!

Hedda. [*Preventing him.*] No more just now. Remember, you have to read your manuscript to Tesman.

Lövborg. [*Calmly, putting down the glass.*] It was stupid of me, all this, Thea—to take it in this way, I mean. Don't be angry with me, my dear, dear comrade. You shall see—both you and the others—that if I was fallen once—now I have risen again! Thanks to *you*, Thea.

Mrs. Elvsted. [*Radiant with joy.*] Oh, heaven be praised——!

[BRACK *has in the meantime looked at his watch. He and* TESMAN *rise and come into the drawing-room.*]

Brack. [*Takes his hat and overcoat.*] Well, Mrs. Tesman, our time has come.

Hedda. I suppose it has.

Lövborg. [*Rising.*] Mine too, Judge Brack.

Mrs. Elvsted. [*Softly and imploringly.*] Oh, Lövborg, don't do it!

Hedda. [*Pinching her arm.*] They can hear you!

Mrs. Elvsted. [*With a suppressed shriek.*] Ow!

Lövborg. [*To* BRACK.] You were good enough to invite me.

Brack. Well, are you coming after all?

Lövborg. Yes, many thanks.

Brack. I'm delighted——

Lövborg. [*To* TESMAN, *putting the parcel of MS. in his pocket.*] I should like to show you one or two things before I send it to the printers.

Tesman. Fancy—that will be delightful. But, Hedda dear, how is Mrs. Elvsted to get home? Eh?

Hedda. Oh, that can be managed somehow.

Lövborg. [*Looking toward the ladies.*] Mrs. Elvsted? Of course, I'll come again and fetch her. [*Approaching.*] At ten or thereabouts, Mrs. Tesman? Will that do?

Hedda. Certainly. That will do capitally.

Tesman. Well, then, that's all right. But you must not expect *me* so early, Hedda.

Hedda. Oh, you may stop as long—as long as ever you please.

Mrs. Elvsted. [*Trying to conceal her anxiety.*] Well then, Mr. Lövborg—I shall remain here until you come.

Lövborg. [*With his hat in his hand.*] Pray do, Mrs. Elvsted.

Brack. And now off goes the excursion train, gentlemen! I hope we shall have a lively time, as a certain fair lady puts it.

Hedda. Ah, if only the fair lady could be present unseen——!

Brack. Why unseen?

Hedda. In order to hear a little of your liveliness at first hand, Judge Brack.

Brack. [*Laughing.*] I should not advise the fair lady to try it.

Tesman. [*Also laughing.*] Come, you're a nice one, Hedda! Fancy that!

Brack. Well, good-by, good-by, ladies.

Lövborg. [*Bowing.*] About ten o'clock, then.

[BRACK, LÖVBORG, *and* TESMAN *go out by the hall door. At the same time,* BERTA *enters from the inner room with a lighted lamp, which she places on the drawing-room table; she goes out by the way she came.*]

Mrs. Elvsted. [*Who has risen and is wandering restlessly about the room.*] Hedda—Hedda—what will come of all this?

Hedda. At ten o'clock—he will be here. I can see him already—with vine-leaves in his hair—flushed and fearless——

Mrs. Elvsted. Oh, I hope he may.

Hedda. And then, you see—then he will have regained control over himself. Then he will be a free man for all his days.

Mrs. Elvsted. Oh God!—if he would only come as you see him now!

Hedda. He will come as I see him—so, and not otherwise! [*Rises and approaches* THEA.] You may doubt him as long as you please; *I* believe in him. And now we will try——

Mrs. Elvsted. You have some hidden motive in this, Hedda!

Hedda. Yes, I have. I want for once in my life to have power to mold a human destiny.

Mrs. Elvsted. Have you not the power?

Hedda. I have not—and have never had it.

Mrs. Elvsted. Not your husband's?

Hedda. Do you think *that* is worth the trouble? Oh, if you could only understand how poor I am. And fate has made *you* so rich! [*Clasps her passionately in her arms.*] I think I must burn your hair off, after all.

Mrs. Elvsted. Let me go! Let me go! I am afraid of you, Hedda!

Berta. [*In the middle doorway.*] Tea is laid in the dining-room, ma'am.

Hedda. Very well. We are coming.

Mrs. Elvsted. No, no, no! I would rather go home alone! At once!

Hedda. Nonsense! First you shall have a cup of tea, you little stupid. And then—at ten o'clock—Eilert Lövborg will be here—with vine-leaves in his hair.

[*She drags* MRS. ELVSTED *almost by force toward the middle doorway.*]

CURTAIN

ACT THIRD

The room at the TESMANS'. *The curtains are drawn over the middle doorway, and also over the glass door. The lamp, half turned down, and with a shade over it, is burning on the table. In the stove, the door of which stands open, there has been a fire, which is now nearly burnt out.*

[MRS. ELVSTED, *wrapped in a large shawl, and with her feet upon a footrest, sits close to the stove, sunk back in the arm-chair.* HEDDA, *fully dressed, lies sleeping upon the sofa, with a sofa-blanket over her.*]

Mrs. Elvsted. [*After a pause, suddenly sits up in her chair, and listens eagerly. Then she sinks back again wearily, moaning to herself.*] Not yet!—Oh God—oh God—not yet!

[BERTA *slips cautiously in by the hall door. She has a letter in her hand.*]

Mrs. Elvsted. [*Turns and whispers eagerly.*] Well—has any one come?

Berta. [*Softly.*] Yes, a girl has just brought this letter.

Mrs. Elvsted. [*Quickly, holding out her hand.*] A letter! Give it to me!

Berta. No, it's for Dr. Tesman, ma'am

Mrs. Elvsted. Oh, indeed.

Berta. It was Miss Tesman's servant that brought it. I'll lay it here on the table.

Mrs. Elvsted. Yes, do.

Berta. [*Laying down the letter.*] I think I had better put out the lamp. It's smoking.

Mrs. Elvsted. Yes, put it out. It must soon be daylight now.

Berta. [*Putting out the lamp.*] It is daylight already, ma'am.

Mrs. Elvsted. Yes, broad day! And no one come back yet——!

Berta. Lord bless you, ma'am—I guessed how it would be.

Mrs. Elvsted. You guessed?

Berta. Yes, when I saw that a certain person had come back to town—and that he went off with them. For we've heard enough about that gentleman before now.

Mrs. Elvsted. Don't speak so loud. You will waken Mrs. Tesman.

Berta. [*Looks toward the sofa and sighs.*] No, no—let her sleep, poor thing. Shan't I put some wood on the fire?

Mrs. Elvsted. Thanks, not for me.

Berta. Oh, very well.

[*She goes softly out by the hall door.*]

Hedda. [*Is wakened by the shutting of the door, and looks up.*] What's that——?

Mrs. Elvsted. It was only the servant——

Hedda. [*Looking about her.*] Oh, we're here——! Yes, now I remember. [*Sits erect upon the sofa, stretches herself, and rubs her eyes.*] What o'clock is it, Thea?

Mrs. Elvsted. [*Looks at her watch.*] It's past seven.

Hedda. When did Tesman come home?

Mrs. Elvsted. He has not come.

Hedda. Not come home yet?

Mrs. Elvsted. [*Rising.*] No one has come.

Hedda. Think of our watching and waiting here till four in the morning——

Mrs. Elvsted. [*Wringing her hands.*] And *how* I watched and waited for him!

Hedda. [*Yawns, and says with her hand before her mouth:*] Well, well—we might have spared ourselves the trouble.

Mrs. Elvsted. Did you get a little sleep?

Hedda. Oh yes; I believe I have slept pretty well. Have you not?

Mrs. Elvsted. Not for a moment. I couldn't, Hedda!—not to save my life.

Hedda. [*Rises and goes toward her.*] There, there, there! There's nothing to be so alarmed about. I understand quite well what has happened.

Mrs. Elvsted. Well, what do you think? Won't you tell me?

Hedda. Why, of course it has been a very late affair at Judge Brack's——

Mrs. Elvsted. Yes, yes—that is clear enough. But all the same——

Hedda. And then, you see, Tesman hasn't cared to come home and ring us up in the middle of the night. [*Laughing.*] Perhaps he wasn't inclined to show himself either—immediately after a jollification.

Mrs. Elvsted. But in that case—where can he have gone?

Hedda. Of course he has gone to his Aunts' and slept there. They have his old room ready for him.

Mrs. Elvsted. No, he can't be with *them*; for a letter has just come for him from Miss Tesman. There it lies.

Hedda. Indeed? [*Looks at the address.*] Why yes, it's addressed in Aunt Julia's own hand. Well then, he has remained at Judge Brack's. And as for Eilert Lövborg—he is sitting, with vine-leaves in his hair, reading his manuscript.

Mrs. Elvsted. Oh Hedda, you are just saying things you don't believe a bit.

Hedda. You really are a little blockhead, Thea.

Mrs. Elvsted. Oh yes, I suppose I am.

Hedda. And how mortally tired you look.

Mrs. Elvsted. Yes, I am mortally tired.

Hedda. Well then, you must do as I tell you. You must go into my room and lie down for a little while.

Mrs. Elvsted. Oh no, no—I shouldn't be able to sleep.

Hedda. I am sure you would.

Mrs. Elvsted. Well, but your husband is certain to come soon now; and then I want to know at once——

Hedda. I shall take care to let you know when he comes.

Mrs. Elvsted. Do you promise me, Hedda?

Hedda. Yes, rely upon me. Just you go in and have a sleep in the meantime.

Mrs. Elvsted. Thanks; then I'll try to.

[*She goes off through the inner room.*]

[HEDDA *goes up to the glass door and draws back the curtains. The broad daylight streams into the room. Then she takes a little hand-glass from the writing-table, looks at herself in it, and arranges her hair. Next she goes to the hall door and presses the bell-button.* BERTA *presently appears at the hall door.*]

Berta. Did you want anything, ma'am?

Hedda. Yes; you must put some more wood in the stove. I am shivering.

Berta. Bless me—I'll make up the fire at once. [*She rakes the embers together and lays a piece of wood upon them; then stops and listens.*] That was a ring at the front door, ma'am.

Hedda. Then go to the door. I will look after the fire.

Berta. It'll soon burn up.

[*She goes out by the hall door.*]

[HEDDA *kneels on the foot-rest and lays some more pieces of wood in the stove. After a short pause,* GEORGE TESMAN *enters from the hall. He looks tired and rather serious. He steals on tiptoe toward the middle doorway and is about to slip through the curtains.*]

Hedda. [*At the stove, without looking up.*] Good morning.

Tesman. [*Turns.*] Hedda! [*Approaching her.*] Good heavens—are you up so early? Eh?

Hedda. Yes, I am up very early this morning.

Tesman. And I never doubted you were still sound asleep. Fancy that, Hedda!

Hedda. Don't speak so loud. Mrs. Elvsted is resting in my room.

Tesman. Has Mrs. Elvsted been here all night?

Hedda. Yes, since no one came to fetch her.

Tesman. Ah, to be sure.

Hedda. [*Closes the door of the stove and rises.*] Well, did you enjoy yourselves at Judge Brack's?

Tesman. Have you been anxious about me? Eh?

Hedda. No, I should never think of being anxious. But I asked if you had enjoyed yourself.

Tesman. Oh yes—for once in a way. Especially the beginning of the evening; for then Eilert read me part of his book. We arrived more than an hour too early—fancy that! And Brack had all sorts of arrangements to make—so Eilert read to me.

Hedda. [*Seating herself by the table on the right.*] Well? Tell me, then——

Tesman. [*Sitting on a footstool near the stove.*] Oh Hedda, you can't conceive what a book that is going to be! I believe it is one of the most remarkable things that have ever been written. Fancy that!

Hedda. Yes, yes; I don't care about that——

Tesman. I must make a confession to you,

Hedda. When he had finished reading—a horrid feeling came over me.

Hedda. A horrid feeling?

Tesman. I felt jealous of Eilert for having had it in him to write such a book. Only think, Hedda!

Hedda. Yes, yes, I am thinking!

Tesman. And then how pitiful to think that he—with all his gifts—should be irreclaimable, after all.

Hedda. I suppose you mean that he has more courage than the rest?

Tesman. No, not at all—I mean that he is incapable of taking his pleasures in moderation.

Hedda. And what came of it all—in the end?

Tesman. Well, to tell the truth, I think it might best be described as an orgy, Hedda.

Hedda. Had he vine-leaves in his hair?

Tesman. Vine-leaves? No, I saw nothing of the sort. But he made a long, rambling speech in honor of the woman who had inspired him in his work—that was the phrase he used.

Hedda. Did he name her?

Tesman. No, he didn't; but I can't help thinking he meant Mrs. Elvsted. You may be sure he did.

Hedda. Well—where did you part from him?

Tesman. On the way to town. We broke up—the last of us at any rate—all together; and Brack came with us to get a breath of fresh air. And then, you see, we agreed to take Eilert home; for he had had far more than was good for him.

Hedda. I daresay.

Tesman. But now comes the strange part of it, Hedda; or, I should rather say, the melancholy part of it. I declare I am almost ashamed—on Eilert's account—to tell you——

Hedda. Oh, go on——!

Tesman. Well, as we were getting near town, you see, I happened to drop a little behind the others. Only for a minute or two—fancy that!

Hedda. Yes, yes, yes, but——?

Tesman. And then, as I hurried after them—what do you think I found by the wayside? Eh?

Hedda. Oh, how should I know!

Tesman. You musn't speak of it to a soul, Hedda! Do you hear? Promise me, for Eilert's sake. [*Draws a parcel, wrapped in paper, from his coat pocket.*] Fancy, dear—I found this.

Hedda. Is not that the parcel he had with him yesterday?

Tesman. Yes, it is the whole of his precious, irreplaceable manuscript! And he had gone and lost it, and knew nothing about it. Only fancy, Hedda! So deplorably——

Hedda. But why did you not give him back the parcel at once?

Tesman. I didn't dare to—in the state he was then in——

Hedda. Did you not tell any of the others that you had found it?

Tesman. Oh, far from it! You can surely understand that, for Eilert's sake, I wouldn't do that.

Hedda. So no one knows that Eilert Lövborg's manuscript is in your possession?

Tesman. No. And no one *must* know it.

Hedda. Then what did you say to him afterwards?

Tesman. I didn't talk to him again at all; for when we got in among the streets, he and two or three of the others gave us the slip and disappeared. Fancy that!

Hedda. Indeed! They must have taken him home then.

Tesman. Yes, so it would appear. And Brack, too, left us.

Hedda. And what have you been doing with yourself since?

Tesman. Well, I and some of the others went home with one of the party, a jolly fellow, and took our morning coffee with him; or perhaps I should rather call it our night coffee—eh? But now, when I have rested a little, and given Eilert, poor fellow, time to have his sleep out, I must take this back to him.

Hedda. [*Holds out her hand for the packet.*] No—don't give it to him! Not in such a hurry, I mean. Let me read it first.

Tesman. No, my dearest Hedda, I mustn't, I really mustn't.

Hedda. You must not?

Tesman. No—for you can imagine what a state of despair he will be in when he wakens and misses the manuscript. He has no copy of it, you must know! He told me so.

Hedda. [*Looking searchingly at him.*] Can such a thing not be reproduced? Written over again?

Tesman. No, I don't think that would be possible. For the inspiration, you see——

Hedda. Yes, yes—I suppose it depends on that—— [*Lightly.*] But, by-the-bye—here is a letter for you.

Tesman. Fancy——!

Hedda. [*Handing it to him.*] It came early this morning.

Tesman. It's from Aunt Julia! What can it be? [*He lays the packet on the other foot-

stool, opens the letter, runs his eye through it, and jumps up.] Oh, Hedda—she says that poor Aunt Rina is dying!

Hedda. Well, we were prepared for that.

Tesman. And that if I want to see her again, I must make haste. I'll run in to them at once.

Hedda. [*Suppressing a smile.*] Will you run?

Tesman. Oh, my dearest Hedda—if you could only make up your mind to come with me! Just think!

Hedda. [*Rises and says wearily, repelling the idea:*] No, no, don't ask me. I *will* not look upon sickness and death. I loathe all sorts of ugliness.

Tesman. Well, well, then——! [*Bustling around.*] My hat——? My overcoat——? Oh, in the hall——. I do hope I mayn't come too late, Hedda. Eh?

Hedda. Oh, if you run——

[BERTA *appears at the hall door.*]

Berta. Judge Brack is at the door, and wishes to know if he may come in.

Tesman. At this time! No, I can't possibly see him.

Hedda. But I can. [*To* BERTA.] Ask Judge Brack to come in. [BERTA *goes out.*]

Hedda. [*Quickly, whispering.*] The parcel, Tesman!

[*She snatches it up from the stool.*]

Tesman. Yes, give it to me!

Hedda. No, no, I will keep it till you come back.

[*She goes to the writing-table and places it in the bookcase.* TESMAN *stands in a flurry of haste, and cannot get his gloves on.* JUDGE BRACK *enters from the hall.*]

Hedda. [*Nodding to him.*] You are an early bird, I must say.

Brack. Yes, don't you think so? [*To* TESMAN.] Are you on the move, too?

Tesman. Yes, I *must* rush off to my aunts'. Fancy—the invalid one is lying at death's door, poor creature.

Brack. Dear me, is she indeed? Then on no account let me detain you. At such a critical moment——

Tesman. Yes, I must really rush—— Good-by! Good-by!

[*He hastens out by the hall door.*]

Hedda. [*Approaching.*] You seem to have made a particularly lively night of it at your rooms, Judge Brack.

Brack. I assure you I have not had my clothes off, Mrs. Hedda.

Hedda. Not you, either?

Brack. No, as you may see. But what has Tesman been telling you of the night's adventures?

Hedda. Oh, some tiresome story. Only that they went and had coffee somewhere or other.

Brack. I have heard about that coffee-party already. Eilert Lövborg was not with them, I fancy?

Hedda. No, they had taken him home before that.

Brack. Tesman too?

Hedda. No, but some of the others, he said.

Brack. [*Smiling.*] George Tesman is really an ingenuous creature, Mrs. Hedda.

Hedda. Yes, heaven knows he is. Then is there something behind all this?

Brack. Yes, perhaps there may be.

Hedda. Well then, sit down, my dear Judge, and tell your story in comfort.

[*She seats herself to the left of the table.* BRACK *sits near her, at the long side of the table.*]

Hedda. Now then?

Brack. I had special reasons for keeping track of my guests—or rather of some of my guests—last night.

Hedda. Of Eilert Lövborg among the rest, perhaps?

Brack. Frankly—yes.

Hedda. Now you make me really curious——

Brack. Do you know where he and one or two of the others finished the night, Mrs. Hedda?

Hedda. If it is not quite unmentionable, tell me.

Brack. Oh no, it's not at all unmentionable. Well, they put in an appearance at a particularly animated soirée.

Hedda. Of the lively kind?

Brack. Of the very liveliest——

Hedda. Tell me more of this, Judge Brack——

Brack. Lövborg, as well as the others, had been invited in advance. I knew all about it. But he had declined the invitation; for now, as you know, he has become a new man.

Hedda. Up at the Elvsteds', yes. But he went after all, then?

Brack. Well, you see, Mrs. Hedda—unhappily the spirit moved him at my rooms last evening——

Hedda. Yes, I hear he found inspiration.

Brack. Pretty violent inspiration. Well, I fancy that altered his purpose; for we menfolk are unfortunately not always so firm in our principles as we ought to be.

Hedda. Oh, I am sure *you* are an exception, Judge Brack. But as to Lövborg——?

Brack. To make a long story short—he landed at last in Mademoiselle Diana's rooms.

Hedda. Mademoiselle Diana's?

Brack. It was Mademoiselle Diana that was giving the soirée, to a select circle of her admirers and her lady friends.

Hedda. Is she a red-haired woman?

Brack. Precisely.

Hedda. A sort of a—singer?

Brack. Oh yes—in her leisure moments. And moreover a mighty huntress—of men—Mrs. Hedda. You have no doubt heard of her. Eilert Lövborg was one of her most enthusiastic protectors—in the days of his glory.

Hedda. And how did all this end?

Brack. Far from amicably, it appears. After a most tender meeting, they seem to have come to blows——

Hedda. Lövborg and she?

Brack. Yes. He accused her or her friends of having robbed him. He declared that his pocket-book had disappeared—and other things as well. In short, he seems to have made a furious disturbance.

Hedda. And what came of it all?

Brack. It came to a general scrimmage, in which the ladies as well as the gentlemen took part. Fortunately the police at last appeared on the scene.

Hedda. The police too?

Brack. Yes. I fancy it will prove a costly frolic for Eilert Lövborg, crazy being that he is.

Hedda. How so?

Brack. He seems to have made a violent resistance—to have hit one of the constables on the head and torn the coat off his back. So they had to march him off to the police-station with the rest.

Hedda. How have you learnt all this?

Brack. From the police themselves.

Hedda. [*Gazing straight before her.*] So that is what happened. Then he had no vine-leaves in his hair.

Brack. Vine-leaves, Mrs. Hedda?

Hedda. [*Changing her tone.*] But tell me now, Judge—what is your real reason for tracking out Eilert Lövborg's movements so carefully?

Brack. In the first place, it could not be entirely indifferent to me if it should appear in the police-court that he came straight from my house.

Hedda. Will the matter come into court, then?

Brack. Of course. However, I should scarcely have troubled so much about that. But I thought that, as a friend of the family, it was my duty to supply you and Tesman with a full account of his nocturnal exploits.

Hedda. Why so, Judge Brack?

Brack. Why, because I have a shrewd suspicion that he intends to use you as a sort of blind.

Hedda. Oh, how can you think such a thing!

Brack. Good heavens, Mrs. Hedda—we have eyes in our head. Mark my words! This Mrs. Elvsted will be in no hurry to leave town again.

Hedda. Well, even if there should be anything between them, I suppose there are plenty of other places where they could meet.

Brack. Not a single *home.* Henceforth, as before, every respectable house will be closed against Eilert Lövborg.

Hedda. And so ought mine to be, you mean?

Brack. Yes. I confess it would be more than painful to me if this personage were to be made free of your house. How superfluous, how intrusive, he would be, if he were to force his way into——

Hedda. ——into the triangle?

Brack. Precisely. It would simply mean that I should find myself homeless.

Hedda. [*Looks at him with a smile.*] So you want to be the one cock in the basket [1]—that is your aim.

Brack. [*Nods slowly and lowers his voice.*] Yes, that is my aim. And for that I will fight—with every weapon I can command.

Hedda. [*Her smile vanishing.*] I see you are a dangerous person—when it comes to the point.

Brack. Do you think so?

Hedda. I am beginning to think so. And I am exceedingly glad to think—that you have no sort of hold over me.

Brack. [*Laughing equivocally.*] Well, well, Mrs. Hedda—perhaps you are right there. If I had, who knows what I might be capable of!

Hedda. Come, come now, Judge Brack! That sounds almost like a threat.

Brack. [*Rising.*] Oh, not at all! The triangle, you know, ought, if possible, to be spontaneously constructed.

Hedda. There I agree with you.

Brack. Well, now I have said all I had to say; and I had better be getting back to town. Good-by, Mrs. Hedda.

[*He goes toward the glass door.*]

Hedda. [*Rising.*] Are you going through the garden?

---

[1] "Eneste hane i kurven"—a proverbial saying.

Brack. Yes, it's a short cut for me.

Hedda. And then it is a back way, too.

Brack. Quite so. I have no objection to back ways. They may be piquant enough at times.

Hedda. When there is ball practice going on, you mean?

Brack. [*In the doorway, laughing to her.*] Oh, people don't shoot their tame poultry, I fancy.

Hedda. [*Also laughing.*] Oh no, when there is only one cock in the basket——

[*They exchange laughing nods of farewell. He goes. She closes the door behind him.*]

[HEDDA, *who has become quite serious, stands for a moment looking out. Presently she goes and peeps through the curtain over the middle doorway. Then she goes to the writing-table, takes* LÖVBORG'S *packet out of the bookcase, and is on the point of looking through its contents.* BERTA *is heard speaking loudly in the hall.* HEDDA *turns and listens. Then she hastily locks up the packet in the drawer, and lays the key on the inkstand.*]

[EILERT LÖVBORG, *with his greatcoat on and his hat in his hand, tears open the hall door. He looks somewhat confused and irritated.*]

Lövborg. [*Looking toward the hall.*] And I tell you I must and will come in! There!

[*He closes the door, turns, sees* HEDDA, *at once regains his self-control, and bows.*]

Hedda. [*At the writing-table.*] Well, Mr. Lövborg, this is rather a late hour to call for Thea.

Lövborg. You mean rather an early hour to call on you. Pray pardon me.

Hedda. How do you know that she is still here?

Lövborg. They told me at her lodgings that she had been out all night.

Hedda. [*Going to the oval table.*] Did you notice anything about the people of the house when they said that?

Lövborg. [*Looks inquiringly at her.*] Notice anything about them?

Hedda. I mean, did they seem to think it odd?

Lövborg. [*Suddenly understanding.*] Oh, yes, of course! I am dragging her down with me! However, I didn't notice anything.—I suppose Tesman is not up yet?

Hedda. No—I think not——

Lövborg. When did he come home?

Hedda. Very late.

Lövborg. Did he tell you anything?

Hedda. Yes, I gathered that you had had an exceedingly jolly evening at Judge Brack's.

Lövborg. Nothing more?

Hedda. I don't think so. However, I was so dreadfully sleepy——

[MRS. ELVSTED *enters through the curtains of the middle doorway.*]

Mrs. Elvsted. [*Going toward him.*] Ah, Lövborg! At last——!

Lövborg. Yes, at last. And too late!

Mrs. Elvsted. [*Looks anxiously at him.*] What is too late?

Lövborg. Everything is too late now. It is all over with me.

Mrs. Elvsted. Oh no, no—don't say that!

Lövborg. You will say the same when you hear——

Mrs. Elvsted. I won't hear anything!

Hedda. Perhaps you would prefer to talk to her alone? If so, I will leave you.

Lövborg. No, stay—you too. I beg you to stay.

Mrs. Elvsted. Yes, but I won't hear anything, I tell you.

Lövborg. It is not last night's adventures that I want to talk about.

Mrs. Elvsted. What is it then——?

Lövborg. I want to say that now our ways must part.

Mrs. Elvsted. Part!

Hedda. [*Involuntarily.*] I knew it!

Lövborg. You can be of no more service to me, Thea.

Mrs. Elvsted. How can you stand there and say that! No more service to you! Am I not to help you now, as before? Are we not to go on working together?

Lövborg. Henceforward I shall do no work.

Mrs. Elvsted. [*Despairingly.*] Then what am I to do with my life?

Lövborg. You must try to live your life as if you had never known me.

Mrs. Elvsted. But you know I cannot do that!

Lövborg. Try if you cannot, Thea. You must go home again——

Mrs. Elvsted. [*In vehement protest.*] Never in this world! Where you are, there will I be also! I will not let myself be driven away like this! I will remain here! I will be with you when the book appears.

Hedda. [*Half aloud, in suspense.*] Ah yes —the book!

Lövborg. [*Looks at her.*] My book and Thea's; for *that* is what it is.

Mrs. Elvsted. Yes, I feel that it is. And that is why I have a right to be with you when it appears! I will see with my own eyes how respect and honor pour in upon you afresh. And the happiness—the happiness—oh, I must share it with you!

Lövborg. Thea—our book will never appear.

Hedda. Ah!

Mrs. Elvsted. Never appear!

Lövborg. *Can* never appear.

Mrs. Elvsted. [*In agonized foreboding.*] Lövborg—what have you done with the manuscript?

Hedda. [*Looks anxiously at him.*] Yes, the manuscript——?

Mrs. Elvsted. Where is it?

Lövborg. Oh, Thea—don't ask me about it!

Mrs. Elvsted. Yes, yes, I *will* know. I demand to be told at once.

Lövborg. The manuscript——. Well then—I have torn the manuscript into a thousand pieces.

Mrs. Elvsted. [*Shrieks.*] Oh no, no——!

Hedda. [*Involuntarily.*] But that's not——

Lövborg. [*Looks at her.*] Not true, you think?

Hedda. [*Collecting herself.*] Oh well, of course—since you say so. But it sounded so improbable——

Lövborg. It is true, all the same.

Mrs. Elvsted. [*Wringing her hands.*] Oh God—oh God, Hedda—torn his own work to pieces!

Lövborg. I have torn my own life to pieces. So why should I not tear my life-work too——?

Mrs. Elvsted. And you did this last night?

Lövborg. Yes, I tell you! Tore it into a thousand pieces—and scattered them on the fiord—far out. There, there is cool sea-water at any rate—let them drift upon it—drift with the current and the wind. And then presently they will sink—deeper and deeper—as I shall, Thea.

Mrs. Elvsted. Do you know, Lövborg, that what you have done with the book—I shall think of it to my dying day as though you had killed a little child.

Lövborg. Yes, you are right. It is a sort of child-murder.

Mrs. Elvsted. How could you, then——! Did not the child belong to me too?

Hedda. [*Almost inaudibly.*] Ah, the child——

Mrs. Elvsted. [*Breathing heavily.*] It is all over, then. Well, well, now I will go, Hedda.

Hedda. But you are not going away from town?

Mrs. Elvsted. Oh, I don't know what I shall do. I see nothing but darkness before me. [*She goes out by the hall door.*]

Hedda. [*Stands waiting for a moment.*] So you are not going to see her home, Mr. Lövborg?

Lövborg. I? Through the streets? Would you have people see her walking with me?

Hedda. Of course I don't know what else may have happened last night. But is it so utterly irretrievable?

Lövborg. It will not end with last night—I know that perfectly well. And the thing is that now I have no taste for that sort of life either. I won't begin it anew. She has broken my courage and my power of braving life out.

Hedda. [*Looking straight before her.*] So that pretty little fool has had her fingers in a man's destiny. [*Looks at him.*] But all the same, how could you treat her so heartlessly?

Lövborg. Oh, don't say that it was heartless!

Hedda. To go and destroy what has filled her whole soul for months and years! You do not call that heartless!

Lövborg. To you I can tell the truth, Hedda.

Hedda. The truth?

Lövborg. First promise me—give me your word—that what I now confide to you Thea shall never know.

Hedda. I give you my word.

Lövborg. Good. Then let me tell you that what I said just now was untrue.

Hedda. About the manuscript?

Lövborg. Yes. I have not torn it to pieces—nor thrown it into the fiord.

Hedda. No, no——. But—where is it then?

Lövborg. I have destroyed it none the less—utterly destroyed it, Hedda!

Hedda. I don't understand.

Lövborg. Thea said that what I had done seemed to her like a child-murder.

Hedda. Yes, so she said.

Lövborg. But to kill his child—that is not the worst thing a father can do to it.

Hedda. Not the worst?

Lövborg. No. I wanted to spare Thea from hearing the worst.

Hedda. Then what is the worst?

Lövborg. Suppose now, Hedda, that a man—in the small hours of the morning—came home to his child's mother after a night of riot and debauchery, and said: "Listen—I have been here and there—in this place and in that. And I have taken our child with me—to this place and to that. And I have lost the child—utterly lost it. The devil knows into what hands it may have fallen—who may have had their clutches on it."

Hedda. Well—but when all is said and done, you know—this was only a book——

Lövborg. Thea's pure soul was in that book.

Hedda. Yes, so I understand.

Lövborg. And you can understand, too, that for her and me together no future is possible.

Hedda. What path do you mean to take, then?

Lövborg. None. I will only try to make an end of it all—the sooner the better.

Hedda. [*A step nearer him.*] Eilert Lövborg—listen to me.—Will you not try to—to do it beautifully?

Lövborg. Beautifully? [*Smiling.*] With vine-leaves in my hair, as you used to dream in the old days——?

Hedda. No, no. I have lost my faith in the vine-leaves. But beautifully nevertheless! For once in a way!—Good-by! You must go now—and do not come here any more.

Lövborg. Good-by, Mrs. Tesman. And give George Tesman my love.

[*He is on the point of going.*]

Hedda. No, wait! I must give you a memento to take with you.

[*She goes to the writing-table and opens the drawer and the pistol-case; then returns to* Lövborg *with one of the pistols.*]

Lövborg. [*Looks at her.*] This? Is *this* the memento?

Hedda. [*Nodding slowly.*] Do you recognize it? It was aimed at you once.

Lövborg. You should have used it then.

Hedda. Take it—and do *you* use it now.

Lövborg. [*Puts the pistol in his breast pocket.*] Thanks!

Hedda. And beautifully, Eilert Lövborg. Promise me that!

Lövborg. Good-by, Hedda Gabler.

[*He goes out by the hall door.*]

[Hedda *listens for a moment at the door. Then she goes up to the writing-table, takes out the packet of manuscript, peeps under the cover, draws a few of the sheets half out, and looks at them. Next she goes over and seats herself in the arm-chair beside the stove, with the packet in her lap. Presently she opens the stove door, and then the packet.*]

Hedda. [*Throws one of the quires into the fire and whispers to herself.*] Now I am burning your child, Thea!—Burning it, curly-locks! [*Throwing one or two more quires into the stove.*] Your child and Eilert Lövborg's. [*Throws the rest in.*] I am burning —I am burning your child.

CURTAIN

ACT FOURTH

The same rooms at the Tesmans'. *It is evening. The drawing-room is in darkness. The back room is lighted by the hanging lamp over the table. The curtains over the glass door are drawn close.*

[Hedda, *dressed in black, walks to and fro in the dark room. Then she goes into the back room and disappears for a moment to the left. She is heard to strike a few chords on the piano. Presently she comes in sight again, and returns to the drawing-room.*

Berta *enters from the right, through the inner room, with a lighted lamp, which she places on the table in front of the corner settee in the drawing-room. Her eyes are red with weeping, and she has black ribbons in her cap. She goes quietly and circumspectly out to the right.* Hedda *goes up to the glass door, lifts the curtain a little aside, and looks out into the darkness.*

Shortly afterwards, Miss Tesman, *in mourning, with a bonnet and veil on, comes in from the hall.* Hedda *goes toward her and holds out her hand.*]

Miss Tesman. Yes, Hedda, here I am, in mourning and forlorn; for now my poor sister has at last found peace.

Hedda. I have heard the news already, as you see. Tesman sent me a card.

Miss Tesman. Yes, he promised me he would. But nevertheless I thought that to Hedda—here in the house of life—I ought myself to bring the tidings of death.

Hedda. That was very kind of you.

Miss Tesman. Ah, Rina ought not to have left us just *now*. This is not the time for Hedda's house to be a house of mourning.

Hedda. [*Changing the subject.*] She died quite peacefully, did she not, Miss Tesman?

Miss Tesman. Oh, her end was so calm, so beautiful. And then she had the unspeakable happiness of seeing George once more—and bidding him good-by.—Has he not come home yet?

Hedda. No. He wrote that he might be detained. But won't you sit down?

Miss Tesman. No, thank you, my dear, dear Hedda. I should like to, but I have so much to do. I must prepare my dear one for her rest as well as I can. She shall go to her grave looking her best.

Hedda. Can I not help you in any way?

Miss Tesman. Oh, you must not think of it! Hedda Tesman must have no hand in such mournful work. Nor let her thoughts dwell on it either—not at this time.

Hedda. One is not always mistress of one's thoughts——

Miss Tesman. [*Continuing.*] Ah, yes, it is the way of the world. At home we shall be sewing a shroud; and here there will soon be sewing too, I suppose—but of another sort, thank God!

[GEORGE TESMAN *enters by the hall door.*]

Hedda. Ah, you have come at last!

Tesman. You here, Aunt Julia? With Hedda? Fancy that!

Miss Tesman. I was just going, my dear boy. Well, have you done all you promised?

Tesman. No; I'm really afraid I have forgotten half of it. I must come to you again tomorrow. Today my brain is all in a whirl. I can't keep my thoughts together.

Miss Tesman. Why, my dear George, you mustn't take it in this way.

Tesman. Mustn't——? How do you mean?

Miss Tesman. Even in your sorrow you must rejoice, as I do—rejoice that she is at rest.

Tesman. Oh yes, yes—you are thinking of Aunt Rina.

Hedda. You will feel lonely now, Miss Tesman.

Miss Tesman. Just at first, yes. But that will not last very long, I hope. I daresay I shall soon find an occupant for poor Rina's little room.

Tesman. Indeed? Who do you think will take it? Eh?

Miss Tesman. Oh, there's always some poor invalid or other in want of nursing, unfortunately.

Hedda. Would you really take such a burden upon you again?

Miss Tesman. A burden! Heaven forgive you, child—it has been no burden to me.

Hedda. But suppose you had a total stranger on your hands——

Miss Tesman. Oh, one soon makes friends with sick folk; and it's such an absolute necessity for me to have someone to live for. Well, heaven be praised, there may soon be something in this house, too, to keep an old aunt busy.

Hedda. Oh, don't trouble about anything here.

Tesman. Yes, just fancy what a nice time we three might have together, if——?

Hedda. If——?

Tesman. [*Uneasily.*] Oh, nothing. It will all come right. Let us hope so—eh?

Miss Tesman. Well, well, I daresay you two want to talk to each other. [*Smiling.*] And perhaps Hedda may have something to tell you too, George. Good-by! I must go home to Rina. [*Turning at the door.*] How strange it is to think that now Rina is with me and with my poor brother as well!

Tesman. Yes, fancy that, Aunt Julia! Eh?

[MISS TESMAN *goes out by the hall door.*]

Hedda. [*Follows* TESMAN *coldly and searchingly with her eyes.*] I almost believe your Aunt Rina's death affects *you* more than it does your Aunt Julia.

Tesman. Oh, it's not that alone. It's Eilert I am so terribly uneasy about.

Hedda. [*Quickly.*] Is there anything new about him?

Tesman. I looked in at his rooms this afternoon, intending to tell him the manuscript was in safe keeping.

Hedda. Well, did you not find him?

Tesman. No. He wasn't at home. But afterwards I met Mrs. Elvsted, and she told me that he had been here early this morning.

Hedda. Yes, directly after you had gone.

Tesman. And he said that he had torn his manuscript to pieces—eh?

Hedda. Yes, so he declared.

Tesman. Why, good heavens, he must have been completely out of his mind! And I suppose you thought it best not to give it back to him, Hedda?

Hedda. No, he did not get it.

Tesman. But of course you told him that we had it?

Hedda. No. [*Quickly.*] Did you tell Mrs. Elvsted?

Tesman. No; I thought I had better not. But you ought to have told him. Fancy, if, in desperation, he should go and do himself some injury! Let me have the manuscript,

Hedda! I will take it to him at once. Where is it?

Hedda. [*Cold and immovable, leaning on the arm-chair.*] I have not got it.

Tesman. Have not got it? What in the world do you mean?

Hedda. I have burnt it—every line of it.

Tesman. [*With a violent movement of terror.*] Burnt! Burnt Eilert's manuscript!

Hedda. Don't scream so. The servant might hear you.

Tesman. Burnt! Why, good God——! No, no, no! It's impossible!

Hedda. It is so, nevertheless.

Tesman. Do you know what you have done, Hedda? It's unlawful appropriation of lost property. Fancy that! Just ask Judge Brack, and he'll tell you what it is.

Hedda. I advise you not to speak of it—either to Judge Brack, or to anyone else.

Tesman. But how could you do anything so unheard-of? What put it into your head? What possessed you? Answer me that—eh?

Hedda. [*Suppressing an almost imperceptible smile.*] I did it for your sake, George.

Tesman. For my sake!

Hedda. This morning, when you told me about what he had read to you——

Tesman. Yes, yes—what then?

Hedda. You acknowledged that you envied him his work.

Tesman. Oh, of course I didn't mean that literally.

Hedda. No matter—I could not bear the idea that anyone should throw you into the shade.

Tesman. [*In an outburst of mingled doubt and joy.*] Hedda! Oh, is this true? But—but—I never knew you to show your love like that before. Fancy that!

Hedda. Well, I may as well tell you that—just at this time—— [*Impatiently, breaking off.*] No, no; you can ask Aunt Julia. *She* will tell you, fast enough.

Tesman. Oh, I almost think I understand you, Hedda! [*Clasps his hands together.*] Great heavens! do you really mean it! Eh?

Hedda. Don't shout so. The servant might hear.

Tesman. [*Laughing in irrepressible glee.*] The servant! Why, how absurd you are, Hedda. It's only my old Berta! Why, I'll tell Berta myself.

Hedda. [*Clenching her hands together in desperation.*] Oh, it is killing me—it is killing me, all this!

Tesman. What is, Hedda? Eh?

Hedda. [*Coldly, controlling herself.*] All this—absurdity—George.

Tesman. Absurdity! Do you see anything absurd in my being overjoyed at the news! But after all—perhaps I had better not say anything to Berta.

Hedda. Oh——why not that too?

Tesman. No, no, not yet! But I must certainly tell Aunt Julia. And then that you have begun to call me George too! Fancy that! Oh, Aunt Julia will be so happy—so happy!

Hedda. When she hears that I have burnt Eilert Lövborg's manuscript—for your sake?

Tesman. No, by-the-bye—that affair of the manuscript—of course nobody must know about that. But that you love me so much,[1] Hedda—Aunt Julia must really share my joy in that! I wonder, now, whether this sort of thing is usual in young wives? Eh?

Hedda. I think you had better ask Aunt Julia that question too.

Tesman. I will indeed, some time or other. [*Looks uneasy and downcast again.*] And yet the manuscript—the manuscript! Good God! it is terrible to think what will become of poor Eilert now.

[MRS. ELVSTED, *dressed as in the First Act, with hat and cloak, enters by the hall door.*]

Mrs. Elvsted. [*Greets them hurriedly, and says in evident agitation:*] Oh, dear Hedda, forgive my coming again.

Hedda. What is the matter with you, Thea?

Tesman. Something about Eilert Lövborg again—eh?

Mrs. Elvsted. Yes! I am dreadfully afraid some misfortune has happened to him.

Hedda. [*Seizes her arm.*] Ah—do you think so?

Tesman. Why, good Lord—what makes you think that, Mrs. Elvsted?

Mrs. Elvsted. I heard them talking of him at my boarding-house—just as I came in. Oh, the most incredible rumors are afloat about him today.

Tesman. Yes, fancy, so I heard too! And I can bear witness that he went straight home to bed last night. Fancy that!

Hedda. Well, what did they say at the boarding-house?

Mrs. Elvsted. Oh, I couldn't make out anything clearly. Either they knew nothing definite, or else——. They stopped talking when they saw me; and I did not dare to ask.

Tesman. [*Moving about uneasily.*] We must hope—we must hope that you misunderstood them, Mrs. Elvsted.

Mrs. Elvsted. No, no; I am sure it was of him they were talking. And I heard something about the hospital or——

[1] Literally, 'That you burn for me."

Tesman. The hospital?

Hedda. No—surely that cannot be!

Mrs. Elvsted. Oh, I was in such mortal terror! I went to his lodgings and asked for him there.

Hedda. You could make up your mind to that, Thea!

Mrs. Elvsted. What else could I do? I really could bear the suspense no longer.

Tesman. But you didn't find him either—eh?

Mrs. Elvsted. No. And the people knew nothing about him. He hadn't been home since yesterday afternoon, they said.

Tesman. Yesterday. Fancy, how could they say that?

Mrs. Elvsted. Oh, I am sure something terrible must have happened to him.

Tesman. Hedda, dear—how would it be if I were to go and make inquiries——?

Hedda. No, no—don't you mix yourself up in this affair.

[JUDGE BRACK, *with his hat in his hand, enters by the hall door, which* BERTA *opens, and closes behind him. He looks grave and bows in silence.*]

Tesman. Oh, is that you, my dear Judge? Eh?

Brack. Yes. It was imperative I should see you this evening.

Tesman. I can see you have heard the news about Aunt Rina.

Brack. Yes, that among other things.

Tesman. Isn't it sad—eh?

Brack. Well, my dear Tesman, that depends on how you look at it.

Tesman. [*Looks doubtfully at him.*] Has anything else happened?

Brack. Yes.

Hedda. [*In suspense.*] Anything sad, Judge Brack?

Brack. That, too, depends on how you look at it, Mrs. Tesman.

Mrs. Elvsted. [*Unable to restrain her anxiety.*] Oh! it is something about Eilert Lövborg!

Brack. [*With a glance at her.*] What makes you think that, Madam? Perhaps you have already heard something——?

Mrs. Elvsted. [*In confusion.*] No, nothing at all, but——

Tesman. Oh, for heaven's sake, tell us!

Brack. [*Shrugging his shoulders.*] Well, I regret to say Eilert Lövborg has been taken to the hospital. He is lying at the point of death.

Mrs. Elvsted. [*Shrieks.*] Oh God! oh God——!

Tesman. To the hospital! And at the point of death!

Hedda. [*Involuntarily.*] So soon then——

Mrs. Elvsted. [*Wailing.*] And we parted in anger, Hedda!

Hedda. [*Whispers.*] Thea — Thea — be careful!

Mrs. Elvsted. [*Not heeding her.*] I must go to him! I must see him alive!

Brack. It is useless, Madam. No one will be admitted.

Mrs. Elvsted. Oh, at least tell me what has happened to him. What is it?

Tesman. You don't mean to say that he has himself——. Eh?

Hedda. Yes, I am sure he has.

Tesman. Hedda, how can you——?

Brack. [*Keeping his eyes fixed upon her.*] Unfortunately you have guessed quite correctly, Mrs. Tesman.

Mrs. Elvsted. Oh, how horrible!

Tesman. Himself, then! Fancy that!

Hedda. Shot himself!

Brack. Rightly guessed again, Mrs. Tesman.

Mrs. Elvsted. [*With an effort at self-control.*] When did it happen, Mr. Brack?

Brack. This afternoon—between three and four.

Tesman. But, good Lord, where did he do it? Eh?

Brack. [*With some hesitation.*] Where? Well—I suppose at his lodgings.

Mrs. Elvsted. No, that cannot be; for I was there between six and seven.

Brack. Well then, somewhere else. I don't know exactly. I only know that he was found ——. He had shot himself—in the breast.

Mrs. Elvsted. Oh, how terrible! That he should die like that!

Hedda. [*To* BRACK.] Was it in the breast?

Brack. Yes—as I told you.

Hedda. Not in the temple?

Brack. In the breast, Mrs. Tesman.

Hedda. Well, well—the breast is a good place, too.

Brack. How do you mean, Mrs. Tesman?

Hedda. [*Evasively.*] Oh, nothing—nothing.

Tesman. And the wound is dangerous, you say—eh?

Brack. Absolutely mortal. The end has probably come by this time.

Mrs. Elvsted. Yes, yes, I feel it. The end! The end! Oh, Hedda——!

Tesman. But tell me, how have you learnt all this?

Brack. [*Curtly.*] Through one of the police. A man I had some business with.

Hedda. [*In a clear voice.*] At last a deed worth doing!

Tesman. [*Terrified.*] Good heavens, Hedda! what are you saying?

Hedda. I say there is beauty in this.

Brack. H'm, Mrs. Tesman——

Tesman. Beauty! Fancy that!

Mrs. Elvsted. Oh, Hedda, how can you talk of beauty in such an act!

Hedda. Eilert Lövborg has himself made up his account with life. He has had the courage to do—the one right thing.

Mrs. Elvsted. No, you must never think *that* was how it happened! It must have been in delirium that he did it.

Tesman. In despair!

Hedda. That he did not. I am certain of that.

Mrs. Elvsted. Yes, yes! In delirium! Just as when he tore up our manuscript.

Brack. [*Starting.*] The manuscript? Has he torn that up?

Mrs. Elvsted. Yes, last night.

Tesman. [*Whispers softly.*] Oh, Hedda, we shall never get over this.

Brack. H'm, very extraordinary.

Tesman. [*Moving about the room.*] To think of Eilert going out of the world in this way! And not leaving behind him the book that would have immortalized his name——

Mrs. Elvsted. Oh, if only it could be put together again!

Tesman. Yes, if it only could! I don't know what I would not give——

Mrs. Elvsted. Perhaps it can, Mr. Tesman.

Tesman. What do you mean?

Mrs. Elvsted. [*Searches in the pocket of her dress.*] Look here. I have kept all the loose notes he used to dictate from.

Hedda. [*A step forward.*] Ah——!

Tesman. You have kept them, Mrs. Elvsted! Eh?

Mrs. Elvsted. Yes, I have them here. I put them in my pocket when I left home. Here they still are——

Tesman. Oh, do let me see them!

Mrs. Elvsted. [*Hands him a bundle of papers.*] But they are in such disorder—all mixed up.

Tesman. Fancy, if we could make something out of them, after all! Perhaps if we two put our heads together——

Mrs. Elvsted. Oh yes, at least let us try——

Tesman. We *will* manage it! We *must*! I will dedicate my life to this task.

Hedda. You, George? Your life?

Tesman. Yes, or rather all the time I can spare. My own collections must wait in the meantime. Hedda—you understand, eh? I owe this to Eilert's memory.

Hedda. Perhaps.

Tesman. And so, my dear Mrs. Elvsted, we will give our whole minds to it. There is no use in brooding over what can't be undone—eh? We must try to control our grief as much as possible, and——

Mrs. Elvsted. Yes, yes, Mr. Tesman, I will do the best I can.

Tesman. Well then, come here. I can't rest until we have looked through the notes. Where shall we sit? Here? No, in there, in the back room. Excuse me, my dear Judge. Come with me, Mrs. Elvsted.

Mrs. Elvsted. Oh, if only it were possible!

[TESMAN *and* MRS. ELVSTED *go into the back room. She takes off her hat and cloak. They both sit at the table under the hanging lamp, and are soon deep in an eager examination of the papers.* HEDDA *crosses to the stove and sits in the arm-chair. Presently* BRACK *goes up to her.*]

Hedda. [*In a low voice.*] Oh, what a sense of freedom it gives one, this act of Eilert Lövborg's.

Brack. Freedom, Mrs. Hedda? Well, of course, it is a release for him——

Hedda. I mean for me. It gives me a sense of freedom to know that a deed of deliberate courage is still possible in this world—a deed of spontaneous beauty.

Brack. [*Smiling.*] H'm—my dear Mrs. Hedda——

Hedda. Oh, I know what you are going to say. For you are a kind of specialist too, like—you know!

Brack. [*Looking hard at her.*] Eilert Lövborg was more to you than perhaps you are willing to admit to yourself. Am I wrong?

Hedda. I don't answer such questions. I only know that Eilert Lövborg has had the courage to live his life after his own fashion. And then—the last great act, with its beauty! Ah! that he should have the will and the strength to turn away from the banquet of life—so early.

Brack. I am sorry, Mrs. Hedda—but I fear I must dispel an amiable illusion.

Hedda. Illusion?

Brack. Which could not have lasted long in any case.

Hedda. What do you mean?

Brack. Eilert Lövborg did not shoot himself—voluntarily.

Hedda. Not voluntarily?

Brack. No. The thing did not happen exactly as I told it.

Hedda. [*In suspense.*] Have you concealed something? What is it?

Brack. For poor Mrs. Elvsted's sake I idealized the facts a little.

Hedda. What are the facts?

Brack. First, that he is already dead.

Hedda. At the hospital?

Brack. Yes—without regaining consciousness.

Hedda. What more have you concealed?

Brack. This—the event did not happen at his lodgings.

Hedda. Oh, that can make no difference.

Brack. Perhaps it may. For I must tell you—Eilert Lövborg was found shot in—in Mademoiselle Diana's boudoir.

Hedda. [*Makes a motion as if to rise, but sinks back again.*] That is impossible, Judge Brack! He cannot have been *there* again to-day.

Brack. He was there this afternoon. He went there, he said, to demand the return of something which they had taken from him. Talked wildly about a lost child——

Hedda. Ah—so that was why——

Brack. I thought probably he meant his manuscript; but now I hear he destroyed that himself. So I suppose it must have been his pocket-book.

Hedda. Yes, no doubt. And there—there he was found?

Brack. Yes, there. With a pistol in his breast-pocket, discharged. The ball had lodged in a vital part.

Hedda. In the breast—yes.

Brack. No—in the bowels.

Hedda. [*Looks up at him with an expression of loathing.*] That too! Oh, what curse is it that makes everything I touch turn ludicrous and mean?

Brack. There is one point more, Mrs. Hedda—another disagreeable feature in the affair.

Hedda. And what is that?

Brack. The pistol he carried——

Hedda. [*Breathless.*] Well? What of it?

Brack. He must have stolen it.

Hedda. [*Leaps up.*] Stolen it? That is not true! He did not steal it!

Brack. No other explanation is possible. He *must* have stolen it——. Hush!

[TESMAN *and* MRS. ELVSTED *have risen from the table in the back room, and come into the drawing-room.*]

Tesman. [*With the papers in both his hands.*] Hedda, dear, it is almost impossible to see under that lamp. Think of that!

Hedda. Yes, I am thinking.

Tesman. Would you mind our sitting at your writing-table—eh?

Hedda. If you like. [*Quickly.*] No, wait! Let me clear it first!

Tesman. Oh, you needn't trouble, Hedda. There is plenty of room.

Hedda. No, no, let me clear it, I say! I will take these things in and put them on the piano. There!

[*She has drawn out an object, covered with sheet music, from under the bookcase, places several other pieces of music upon it, and carries the whole into the inner room, to the left.* TESMAN *lays the scraps of paper on the writing-table, and moves the lamp there from the corner table. He and* MRS. ELVSTED *sit down and proceed with their work.* HEDDA *returns.*]

Hedda. [*Behind* MRS. ELVSTED'S *chair, gently ruffling her hair.*] Well, my sweet Thea—how goes it with Eilert Lövborg's monument?

Mrs. Elvsted. [*Looks dispiritedly up at her.*] Oh, it will be terribly hard to put in order.

Tesman. We *must* manage it. I am determined. And arranging other people's papers is just the work for me.

[HEDDA *goes over to the stove, and seats herself on one of the footstools.* BRACK *stands over her, leaning on the arm-chair.*]

Hedda. [*Whispers.*] What did you say about the pistol?

Brack. [*Softly.*] That he must have stolen it.

Hedda. Why stolen it?

Brack. Because every other explanation *ought* to be impossible, Mrs. Hedda.

Hedda. Indeed?

Brack. [*Glances at her.*] Of course Eilert Lövborg was here this morning. Was he not?

Hedda. Yes.

Brack. Were you alone with him?

Hedda. Part of the time.

Brack. Did you not leave the room whilst he was here?

Hedda. No.

Brack. Try to recollect. Were you not out of the room a moment?

Hedda. Yes, perhaps just a moment—out in the hall.

Brack. And where was your pistol-case during that time?

Hedda. I had it locked up in——

Brack. Well, Mrs. Hedda?

Hedda. The case stood there on the writing-table.

Brack. Have you looked since, to see whether both the pistols are there?

Hedda. No.

Brack. Well, you need not. I saw the pistol found in Lövborg's pocket, and I knew it at once as the one I had seen yesterday—and before, too.

Hedda. Have you it with you?

Brack. No; the police have it.

Hedda. What will the police do with it?

Brack. Search till they find the owner.

Hedda. Do you think they will succeed?

Brack. [*Bends over her and whispers.*] No, Hedda Gabler—not so long as I say nothing.

Hedda. [*Looks frightened at him.*] And if you do *not* say nothing—what then?

Brack. [*Shrugs his shoulders.*] There is always the possibility that the pistol was stolen.

Hedda. [*Firmly.*] Death rather than that.

Brack. [*Smiling.*] People say such things —but they don't *do* them.

Hedda. [*Without replying.*] And supposing the pistol was not stolen, and the owner is discovered? What then?

Brack. Well, Hedda—then comes the scandal.

Hedda. The scandal!

Brack. Yes, the scandal—of which you are so mortally afraid. You will, of course, be brought before the court—both you and Mademoiselle Diana. She will have to explain how the thing happened—whether it was an accidental shot or murder. Did the pistol go off as he was trying to take it out of his pocket, to threaten her with? Or did she tear the pistol out of his hand, shoot him, and push it back into his pocket? That would be quite like her; for she is an able-bodied young person, this same Mademoiselle Diana.

Hedda. But *I* have nothing to do with all this repulsive business.

Brack. No. But you will have to answer the question: Why did you give Eilert Lövborg the pistol? And what conclusions will people draw from the fact that you did give it to him?

Hedda. [*Lets her head sink.*] That is true. I did not think of that.

Brack. Well, fortunately, there is no danger, so long as I say nothing.

Hedda. [*Looks up at him.*] So I am in your power, Judge Brack. You have me at your beck and call, from this time forward.

Brack. [*Whispers softly.*] Dearest Hedda—believe me—I shall not abuse my advantage.

Hedda. I am in your power none the less. Subject to your will and your demands. A slave, a slave then! [*Rises impetuously.*] No, I cannot endure the thought of that! Never!

Brack. [*Looks half-mockingly at her.*] People generally get used to the inevitable.

Hedda. [*Returns his look.*] Yes, perhaps. [*She crosses to the writing-table. Suppressing an involuntary smile, she imitates* TESMAN'S *intonations.*] Well? Are you getting on, George? Eh?

Tesman. Heaven knows, dear. In any case it will be the work of months.

Hedda. [*As before.*] Fancy that! [*Passes her hands softly through* MRS. ELVSTED'S *hair.*] Doesn't it seem strange to you, Thea? Here are you sitting with Tesman—just as you used to sit with Eilert Lövborg.

Mrs. Elvsted. Ah, if I could only inspire your husband in the same way!

Hedda. Oh, that will come too—in time.

Tesman. Yes, do you know, Hedda—I really think I begin to feel something of the sort. But won't you go and sit with Brack again?

Hedda. Is there nothing I can do to help you two?

Tesman. No, nothing in the world. [*Turning his head.*] I trust to you to keep Hedda company, my dear Brack.

Brack. [*With a glance at* HEDDA.] With the very greatest of pleasure.

Hedda. Thanks. But I am tired this evening. I will go in and lie down a little on the sofa.

Tesman. Yes, do, dear—eh?

[HEDDA *goes into the back room and draws the curtains. A short pause. Suddenly she is heard playing a wild dance on the piano.*]

Mrs. Elvsted. [*Starts from her chair.*] Oh —what is that?

Tesman. [*Runs to the doorway.*] Why, my dearest Hedda—don't play dance-music tonight! Just think of Aunt Rina! And of Eilert too!

Hedda. [*Puts her head out between the curtains.*] And of Aunt Julia. And of all the rest of them.—After this, I will be quiet. [*Closes the curtains again.*]

Tesman. [*At the writing-table.*] It's not good for her to see us at this distressing work. I'll tell you what, Mrs. Elvsted—you shall take the empty room at Aunt Julia's, and then I will come over in the evenings, and we can sit and work *there*—eh?

Hedda. [*In the inner room.*] I hear what you are saying, Tesman. But how am *I* to get through the evenings out here?

Tesman. [*Turning over the papers.*] Oh, I daresay Judge Brack will be so kind as to look in now and then, even though I am out.

Brack. [*In the arm-chair, calls out gaily.*] Every blessed evening, with all the pleasure in life, Mrs. Tesman! We shall get on capitally together, we two!

Hedda. [*Speaking loud and clear.*] Yes, don't you flatter yourself we will, Judge

Brack? Now that you are the one cock in the basket——

[*A shot is heard within.* TESMAN, MRS. ELVSTED, *and* BRACK *leap to their feet.*]

Tesman. Oh, now she is playing with those pistols again.

[*He throws back the curtains and runs in, followed by* MRS. ELVSTED. HEDDA *lies stretched on the sofa, lifeless. Confusion and cries.* BERTA *enters in alarm from the right.*]

Tesman. [*Shrieks to* BRACK.] Shot herself! Shot herself in the temple! Fancy that!

Brack. [*Half-fainting in the arm-choir.*] Good God!—people don't do such things!

CURTAIN

PÉLLÉAS AND MÉLISANDE*

By

MAURICE MAETERLINCK

Translated by RICHARD HOVEY

MAURICE MAETERLINCK'S FIRST PLAY, *La Princesse Maleine,* attracted to him the attention of the theatrical world, largely because Octave Mirbeau, the distinguished critic and novelist, wrote of it as "comparable and—dare I say it?—superior in beauty to what is most beautiful in Shakespeare . . . more tragic than *Macbeth,* more extraordinary in thought than *Hamlet.*" That obviously extravagant judgment could scarcely be thought today, when Maeterlinck's dramas are rarely played, and he is no longer a force in the theater. But in 1889, and in the years following, Maeterlinck was to bring to the stage work that was distinctly fresh and original, based on a theory of drama that was startling and fructifying and at the same time poetic. The theory is stated most clearly in *The Treasure of the Humble,* where Maeterlinck himself gives it the name "static." He found the theater of his time "primitive, arid, and brutal; . . . I was yearning for one of the strange moments of a higher life that flit unperceived through my dreariest hours; whereas, almost invariably, all that I beheld was but a man who would tell me, at wearisome length, why he was jealous, why he poisoned, or why he killed. . . . I have grown to believe that an old man, seated in his arm-chair, waiting patiently with his lamp beside him; giving unconscious ear to all the eternal laws that reign about his house, interpreting, without comprehending, the silence of doors and windows and the quivering voice of the light, submitting with bent head to the presence of his soul and of destiny . . . motionless as he is, does yet in reality live a deeper, more human, and more universal life than the lover who strangles his mistress, the captain who conquers in battle, or 'the husband who avenges his honor.' . . . Indeed, it is not in the actions but in the words that are found the beauty and greatness of tragedies that are truly beautiful and great; and this not solely in the words that accompany and explain the action, for there must perforce be another dialogue besides the one which is superficially necessary. And indeed the only words that count in the play are those that at first seemed useless, for it is therein that the essence lies. Side by side with the necessary dialogue you will almost always find another dialogue that seems superfluous; but examine it carefully, and it will be borne home to you that this is the only one that the soul can listen to profoundly, for here alone is it the soul that is being addressed. . . . One may even affirm that a poem draws the nearer to beauty and loftier truth in the measure that it eliminates words that explain the action, and substitutes for them others that reveal, not the so-called 'soul-state,' but I know not what intangible and unceasing striving of the soul toward its own beauty and truth."

This striving for the atmospheric and intangible, together with Maeterlinck's fatalistic prepossessions, barred him, in his plays, from the study of character, and made his people phantoms, though he called them marionettes. Actors have always found the parts in the early plays difficult: so much that is left unsaid and undone must nevertheless be conveyed. *Pélléas and Mélisande* is a typical play of Maeterlinck's first period in its atmospheric quality and the tenuousness of its people, and in its abundance of literary echoes, such as the first scene, reminiscent of *Macbeth,* and the main situation, reminiscent of the Francesca da Rimini story.

Pélléas and Mélisande has had many notable productions. It was first played in English in London under the management of Johnston Forbes-Robertson, who played Golaud, with Mrs. Patrick Campbell as Mélisande, in 1898 A gauze curtain was hung between audience and players, in order, perhaps, to heighten the unreality. Later Mrs. Campbell played Mélisande to Mme. Sarah Bernhardt's Pélléas, in French. A most unusual production of the play took place in 1910 at Maeterlinck's country home in Normandy, the Abbaye de Saint-Wandrille. Under the direction of Mme. Georgette Leblanc, who played Mélisande, the rooms and grounds of the Abbaye were used as settings and the invited audience followed the players about, carrying campstools. Reports of the occasion pronounced it most successful.

Pélléas and Mélisande was performed in America by Mrs. Patrick Campbell in 1902. It was revived in 1923, when Miss Jane Cowl played Mélisande for a short run. Debussy's opera of the same name, which uses an abbreviated version of the play as libretto, was first produced in New York in 1908, under the direction of Oscar Hammerstein at the Manhattan Opera House. Mary Garden created Mélisande. The opera is now occasionally included in the repertory of the Metropolitan Opera Company, and is considered one of the greatest music-dramas since Wagner.

MAURICE MAETERLINCK

Born 1862, Ghent, Belgium.
University of Ghent.
1887, associated in Paris with the French symbolists.
1911, awarded Nobel prize for literature.
1940, Refugee in the United States.
Poet, mystic, entomologist.

PLAYS

1889 *La Princesse Maleine* (translated as *The Princess Maleine*). 1890 *Les Aveugles* (translated as *The Blind* and *The Sightless*). 1890 *L'Intruse* (translated as *The Intruder*). 1891 *Les Sept Princesses* (translated as *The Seven Princesses*). 1892 *Pélléas et Mélisande* (translated as *Pélléas and Mélisande*). 1894 *Alladine et Palomides* (translated as *Alladine and Palomides*). 1894 *L'Intérieur* (translated as *Interior* and *Home*). 1894 *La Mort de Tintagile* (translated as *The Death of Tintagiles*). 1895 *Annabella* (translation of Ford's *'Tis Pity She's a Whore*). 1896 *Aglavaine et Sélysette* (translated as *Aglavaine and Selysette*). 1900 *Soeur Béatrice* (translated as *Sister Beatrice*). 1901 *Ariane et Barbe-bleue* (translated as *Ardiane and Barbe-bleue*). 1902 *Monna Vanna* (translated as *Monna Vanna*). 1903 *Joyzelle* (translated as *Joyzelle*). 1904 *Le Miracle de Saint Antoine* (translated as *The Miracle of Saint Anthony*). 1908 *L'Oiseau Bleu* (translated as *The Blue Bird*). 1910 *Marie Magdeleine* (translated as *Mary Magdalene*). 1910 *Macbeth* (translation of Shakespeare). 1918 *Les Fiançailles*, a sequel to *The Blue Bird* (translated as *The Betrothal*). 1918 *Le Bourgmestre de Stilemonde* (translated as *The Burgomaster of Stilemonde*). 1920 *Le Sel de la Vie* (sequel to *The Burgomaster of Stilemonde*, not translated). 1923 *La Puissance des Morts* (translated as *The Power of the Dead*). 1923 *The Cloud that Lifted* (translated, but not published or produced in French). 1923 *Berniquel* (not translated). 1925 *Le Malheur Passe* (not translated). 1927 *Marie-Victoire* (not translated). 1929 *Juda de Kerioth* (not translated). 1935 *Princesse Isabelle* (not translated). 1940 *Seven Wishes* (not published in French).

WRITINGS ABOUT THE DRAMA

The Treasure of the Humble, translated by Alfred Sutro, 1898, especially *The Tragical in Daily Life*.

The Modern Drama, in *The Double Garden*, translated by A. T. de Mattos. 1904.

PÉLLÉAS AND MÉLISANDE

Persons

ARKËL, *King of Allemonde.*
GENEVIÈVE, *mother of Pélléas and Golaud.*
PÉLLÉAS, GOLAUD, } *grandsons of Arkël.*
MÉLISANDE.
LITTLE YNIOLD, *son of Golaud (by a former marriage).*
A PHYSICIAN.
THE PORTER.
Servants, Beggars, etc.

ACT FIRST

SCENE I.—*The gate of the castle.*

Maidservants. [*Within.*] Open the gate! Open the gate!

Porter. [*Within.*] Who is there? Why do you come and wake me up? Go out by the little gates; there are enough of them!

A Maidservant. [*Within.*] We have come to wash the threshold, the gate, and the steps; open, then! open!

Another Maidservant. [*Within.*] There are going to be great happenings!

Third Maidservant. [*Within.*] There are going to be great fêtes! Open quickly! . . .

The Maidservants. Open! open!

Porter. Wait! wait! I do not know whether I shall be able to open it; . . . it is never opened. . . . Wait till it is light. . . .

First Maidservant. It is light enough without; I see the sunlight through the chinks. . . .

Porter. Here are the great keys. . . . Oh! oh! how the bolts and the locks grate! . . . Help me! help me! . . .

Maidservants. We are pulling; we are pulling. . . .

Second Maidservant. It will not open. . . .

First Maidservant. Ah! ah! It is opening! it is opening slowly!

Porter. How it shrieks! how it shrieks! It will wake up everybody. . . .

Second Maidservant. [*Appearing on the threshold.*] Oh, how light it is already out of doors!

First Maidservant. The sun is rising on the sea!

Porter. It is open. . . . It is wide open! . . .

[*All the maidservants appear on the threshold and pass over it.*]

First Maidservant. I am going to wash the sill first. . . .

Second Maidservant. We shall never be able to clean all this.

Other Maidservants. Fetch the water! fetch the water!

Porter. Yes, yes; pour on water; pour on water; pour on all the water of the Flood! You will never come to the end of it. . . .

SCENE II.—*A forest.* MÉLISANDE *discovered at the brink of a spring.*

[*Enter* GOLAUD.]

Golaud. I shall never be able to get out of this forest again.—God knows where that beast has led me. And yet I thought I had wounded him to death; and here are traces of blood. But now I have lost sight of him; I believe I am lost myself—my dogs can no longer find me—I shall retrace my steps. . . .—I hear weeping . . . Oh! oh! what is there yonder by the water's edge? . . . A little girl weeping by the water's edge? [*He coughs.*]—She does not hear me. I cannot see her face. [*He approaches and touches* MÉLISANDE *on the shoulder.*] Why weepest thou? [MÉLISANDE *trembles, starts up, and would flee.*]—Do not be afraid. You have nothing to fear. Why are you weeping here all alone?

Mélisande. Do not touch me! do not touch me!

Golaud. Do not be afraid. . . . I will not do you any . . . Oh, you are beautiful!

Mélisande. Do not touch me! do not touch me! or I throw myself in the water! . . .

Golaud. I will not touch you. . . . See, I will stay here, against the tree. Do not be afraid. Has any one hurt you?

Mélisande. Oh! yes! yes! yes! . . . [*She sobs profoundly.*]

Golaud. Who has hurt you?

Mélisande. Every one! every one!

Golaud. What hurt have they done you?

Mélisande. I will not tell! I cannot tell! . . .

Golaud. Come; do not weep so. Whence come you?

Mélisande. I have fled! . . . fled . . . fled. . . .

Golaud. Yes; but whence have you fled?

Mélisande. I am lost! . . . lost! . . . Oh! oh! lost here. . . . I am not of this place. . . . I was not born here. . . .

Golaud. Whence are you? Where were you born?

Mélisande. Oh! oh! far away from here! . . . far away . . . far away. . . .

Golaud. What is it shining so at the bottom of the water?

Mélisande. Where?—Ah! it is the crown he gave me. It fell as I was weeping. . . .

Golaud. A crown?—Who was it gave you a crown?—I will try to get it. . . .

Mélisande. No, no; I will have no more of it! I will have no more of it! . . . I had rather die . . . die at once. . . .

Golaud. I could easily pull it out. The water is not very deep.

Mélisande. I will have no more of it! If you take it out, I throw myself in its place!

Golaud. No, no! I will leave it there. It could be reached without difficulty, nevertheless. It seems very beautiful.—Is it long since you fled?

Mélisande. Yes, yes! . . . Who are you?

Golaud. I am Prince Golaud—grandson of Arkël, the old King of Allemonde. . . .

Mélisande. Oh, you have gray hairs already. . . .

Golaud. Yes; some, here, by the temples.

Mélisande. And in your beard, too. . . . Why do you look at me so?

Golaud. I am looking at your eyes.—Do you never shut your eyes?

Mélisande. Oh, yes; I shut them at night.

Golaud. Why do you look so astonished?

Mélisande. You are a giant?

Golaud. I am a man like the rest. . . .

Mélisande. Why have you come here?

Golaud. I do not know, myself. I was hunting in the forest. I was chasing a wild boar. I mistook the road.—You look very young. How old are you?

Mélisande. I am beginning to be cold. . . .

Golaud. Will you come with me?

Mélisande. No, no; I will stay here. . . .

Golaud. You cannot stay here all alone. You cannot stay here all night long. . . . What is your name?

Mélisande. Mélisande.

Golaud. You cannot stay here, Mélisande. Come with me. . . .

Mélisande. I will stay here. . . .

Golaud. You will be afraid, all alone. We do not know what there may be here . . . all night long . . . all alone . . . it is impossible. Mélisande, come, give me your hand. . . .

Mélisande. Oh, do not touch me! . . .

Golaud. Do not scream. . . . I will not touch you again. But come with me. The night will be very dark and very cold. Come with me. . . .

Mélisande. Where are you going? . . .

Golaud. I do not know. . . . I am lost too. . . . [*Exeunt.*]

SCENE III.—*A hall in the castle.* ARKËL *and* GENEVIÈVE *discovered.*

Geneviève. Here is what he writes to his brother Pélléas: "I found her all in tears one evening, beside a spring in the forest where I had lost myself. I do not know her age, nor who she is, nor whence she comes, and I dare not question her, for she must have had a sore fright; and when you ask her what has happened to her, she falls at once a-weeping like a child, and sobs so heavily you are afraid. Just as I found her by the spring, a crown of gold had slipped from her hair and fallen to the bottom of the water. She was clad, besides, like a princess, though her garments had been torn by the briers. It is now six months since I married her and I know no more about it than on the day of our meeting. Meanwhile, dear Pélléas, thou whom I love more than a brother, although we were not born of the same father; meanwhile make ready for my return. . . . I know my mother will willingly forgive me. But I am afraid of the King, our venerable grandsire, I am afraid of Arkël, in spite of all his kindness, for I have undone by this strange marriage all his plans of state, and I fear the beauty of Mélisande will not excuse my folly to eyes so wise as his. If he consents nevertheless to receive her as he would receive his own daughter, the third night following this letter, light a lamp at the top of the tower that overlooks the sea. I shall perceive it from the bridge of our ship; otherwise I shall go far away again and come back no more. . . ." What say you of it?

Arkël. Nothing. He has done what he probably must have done. I am very old, and nevertheless I have not yet seen clearly for one moment into myself; how would you that I judge what others have done? I am not far from the tomb and do not succeed in judging myself. . . . One always mistakes when one does not close his eyes. That may seem strange to us; but that is all. He is past the age to marry and he weds, like a child, a little girl he finds by a spring. . . . That may seem strange to us, because we never see but the reverse of destinies . . . the reverse even of our own. . . . He has always followed my counsels hitherto; I had thought to make him happy in sending him to ask the hand of Princess Ursula. . . . He could not remain alone; since the death of his wife he has been sad to be alone; and that marriage would have put an end to long wars and old hatreds. . . . He would not have it so. Let it be as he would have it; I have never put myself athwart a destiny; and he knows better than I his future. There happen perhaps no useless events. . . .

Geneviève. He has always been so prudent, so grave, and so firm. . . . If it were Pélléas, I should understand. . . . But he . . . at his age. . . . Who is it he is going to introduce here?—An unknown found along the roads. . . . Since his wife's death, he has no longer lived for aught but his son, the little Yniold, and if he were about to marry again, it was because you had wished it. . . . And now . . . a little girl in the forest. . . . He has forgotten everything. . . . What shall we do? . . .

[*Enter* PÉLLÉAS.]

Arkël. Who is coming in there?

Geneviève. It is Pélléas. He has been weeping.

Arkël. Is it thou, Pélléas?—Come a little nearer, that I may see thee in the light. . . .

Pélléas. Grandfather, I received another letter at the same time as my brother's; a letter from my friend Marcellus. . . . He is about to die and calls for me. He would see me before dying. . . .

Arkël. Thou wouldst leave before thy brother's return?—Perhaps thy friend is less ill than he thinks. . . .

Pélléas. His letter is so sad you can see death between the lines. . . . He says he knows the very day when death must come. . . . He tells me I can arrive before it if I will, but that there is no more time to lose. The journey is very long, and if I await Golaud's return, it will be perhaps too late.

Arkël. Thou must wait a little while, nevertheless. . . . We do not know what this return has in store for us. And besides, is not thy father here, above us, more sick perhaps than thy friend? . . . Couldst thou choose between the father and the friend? . . .

[*Exit.*]

Geneviève. Have a care to keep the lamp lit from this evening, Pélléas. . . .

[*Exeunt severally.*]

SCENE IV.—*Before the castle. Enter* GENEVIÈVE *and* MÉLISANDE.

Mélisande. It is gloomy in the gardens. And what forests, what forests all about the palaces! . . .

Geneviève. Yes; that astonished me too when I came hither; it astonishes everybody. There are places where you never see the sun. But one gets used to it so quickly. . . . It is long ago, it is long ago. . . . It is nearly forty years that I have lived here. . . . Look toward the other side, you will have the light of the sea. . . .

Mélisande. I hear a noise below us. . . .

Geneviève. Yes; it is some one coming up toward us. . . . Ah! it is Pélléas. . . . He seems still tired from having waited so long for you. . . .

Mélisande. He has not seen us.

Geneviève. I think he has seen us but does not know what he should do. . . . Pélléas, Pélléas, is it thou? . . .

[*Enter* PÉLLÉAS.]

Pélléas. Yes! . . . I was coming toward the sea. . . .

Geneviève. So were we; we were seeking the light. It is a little lighter here than elsewhere; and yet the sea is gloomy.

Pélléas. We shall have a storm tonight. There has been one every night for some time, and yet it is so calm now. . . . One might embark unwittingly and come back no more.

Mélisande. Something is leaving the port.

Pélléas. It must be a big ship. . . . The lights are very high, we shall see it in a moment, when it enters the band of light. . . .

Geneviève. I do not know whether we shall be able to see it . . . there is still a fog on the sea. . . .

Pélléas. The fog seems to be rising slowly.

Mélisande. Yes; I see a little light down there, which I had not seen. . . .

Pélléas. It is a lighthouse; there are others we cannot see yet.

Mélisande. The ship is in the light. . . . It is already very far away. . . .

Pélléas. It is a foreign ship. It looks larger than ours. . . .

Mélisande. It is the ship that brought me here! . . .

Pélléas. It flies away under full sail. . . .

Mélisande. It is the ship that brought me here. It has great sails. . . . I recognized it by its sails.

Pélléas. There will be a rough sea tonight.

Mélisande. Why does it go away tonight? . . . You can hardly see it any longer. . . . Perhaps it will be wrecked. . . .

Pélléas. The night falls very quickly. . . . [*A silence.*]

Geneviève. No one speaks any more? . . . You have nothing more to say to each other? . . . It is time to go in. Pélléas, show Mélisande the way. I must go see little Yniold a moment. [*Exit.*]

Pélléas. Nothing can be seen any longer on the sea. .

Mélisande. I see more lights.

Pélléas. It is the other lighthouses. . . . Do you hear the sea? . . . It is the wind rising. . . . Let us go down this way. Will you give me your hand?

Mélisande. See, see, my hands are full. . . .

Pélléas. I will hold you by the arm, the road is steep and it is very gloomy there. . . . I am going away perhaps tomorrow. . . .

Mélisande. Oh! . . . why do you go away? [*Exeunt.*]

ACT SECOND

SCENE I.—*A fountain in the park.*

[*Enter* PÉLLÉAS *and* MÉLISANDE.]

Pélléas. You do not know where I have brought you?—I often come to sit here, toward noon, when it is too hot in the gardens. It is stifling today, even in the shade of the trees.

Mélisande. Oh, how clear the water is! . . .

Pélléas. It is as cool as winter. It is an old abandoned spring. It seems to have been a miraculous spring—it opened the eyes of the blind—they still call it "Blind Man's Spring."

Mélisande. It no longer opens the eyes of the blind?

Pélléas. Since the King has been nearly blind himself, no one comes any more. . . .

Mélisande. How alone one is here! . . There is no sound.

Pélléas. There is always a wonderful silence here. . . . One could hear the water sleep. . . . Will you sit down on the edge of the marble basin? There is one linden where the sun never comes. . . .

Mélisande. I am going to lie down on the marble.—I should like to see the bottom of the water. . . .

Pélléas. No one has ever seen it.—It is as deep, perhaps, as the sea.—It is not known whence it comes.—Perhaps it comes from the bottom of the earth. . . .

Mélisande. If there were anything shining at the bottom, perhaps one could see it. . . .

Pélléas. Do not lean over so. . . .

Mélisande. I would like to touch the water. . . .

Pélléas. Have a care of slipping. . . . I will hold your hand. . . .

Mélisande. No, no, I would plunge both hands in it. . . . You would say my hands were sick today. . . .

Pélléas. Oh! oh! take care! take care! Mélisande! . . . Mélisande! . . .—Oh! your hair! . . .

Mélisande. [*Starting upright.*] I cannot, . . . I cannot reach it. . . .

Pélléas. Your hair dipped in the water. . . .

Mélisande. Yes, it is longer than my arms. . . . It is longer than I. . . . [*A silence.*]

Pélléas. It was at the brink of a spring, too, that he found you?

Mélisande. Yes. . . .

Pélléas. What did he say to you?

Mélisande. Nothing;—I no longer remember. . . .

Pélléas. Was he quite near you?

Mélisande. Yes; he would have kissed me.

Pélléas. And you would not?

Mélisande. No.

Pélléas. Why would you not?

Mélisande. Oh! oh! I saw something pass at the bottom of the water. . . .

Pélléas. Take care! take care!—You will fall! What are you playing with?

Mésilande. With the ring he gave me. . . .

Pélléas. Take care; you will lose it. . . .

Mélisande. No, no; I am sure of my hands. . . .

Pélléas. Do not play so, over so deep a water. . . .

Mélisande. My hands do not tremble.

Pélléas. How it shines in the sunlight!—Do not throw it so high in the air.

Mélisande. Oh! . . .

Pélléas. It has fallen?

Mélisande. It has fallen into the water!

Pélléas. Where is it? where is it? . . .

Mélisande. I do not see it sink. . . .

Pélléas. I think I see it shine. . . .

Mélisande. My ring?

Pélléas. Yes, yes; down yonder. . . .

Mélisande. Oh! oh! It is so far away from us! . . . no, no, that is not it . . . that is not it . . . It is lost . . . lost. . . . There is nothing any more but a great circle on the water. . . . What shall we do? What shall we do now? . . .

Pélléas. You need not be so troubled for a ring. It is nothing. . . . We shall find it again, perhaps. Or else we will find another.

Mélisande. No, no; we shall never find it again; we shall never find any others either. . . . And yet I thought I had it in my hands. . . . I had already shut my hands, and it is fallen in spite of all. . . . I threw it too high, toward the sun. . . .

Pélléas. Come, come, we will come back another day; . . . come, it is time. They will come to meet us. It was striking noon at the moment the ring fell.

Mélisande. What shall we say to Golaud if he ask where it is?

Pélléas. The truth, the truth, the truth. . . . [*Exeunt.*]

SCENE II.—*An apartment in the castle.*

GOLAUD *discovered, stretched upon his bed;* MÉLISANDE, *by his bedside.*

Golaud. Ah! ah! all goes well; it will amount to nothing. But I cannot understand how it came to pass. I was hunting quietly in the forest. All at once my horse ran away, without cause. Did he see anything unusual? . . . I had just heard the twelve strokes of noon. At the twelfth stroke he suddenly took fright and ran like a blind madman against a tree. I heard no more. I do not yet know what happened. I fell, and he must have fallen on me. I thought I had the whole forest on my breast; I thought my heart was crushed. But my heart is sound. It is nothing, apparently. . . .

Mélisande. Would you like a little water?

Golaud. Thanks, thanks; I am not thirsty.

Mélisande. Would you like another pillow? . . . There is a little spot of blood on this.

Golaud. No, no; it is not worth while. I bled at the mouth just now. I shall bleed again perhaps. . . .

Mélisande. Are you quite sure? . . . You are not suffering too much?

Golaud. No, no; I have seen a good many more like this. I was made of iron and blood. . . . These are not the little bones of a child; do not alarm yourself. . . .

Mélisande. Close your eyes and try to sleep. I shall stay here all night. . . .

Golaud. No, no; I do not wish you to tire yourself so. I do not need anything; I shall sleep like a child. . . . What is the matter, Mélisande? Why do you weep all at once?

Mélisande. [*Bursting into tears.*] I am . . . I am ill too. . . .

Golaud. Thou art ill? . . . What ails thee, then; what ails thee, Mélisande? . . .

Mélisande. I do not know. . . . I am ill here. . . . I had rather tell you today; my lord, my lord, I am not happy here. . . .

Golaud. Why, what has happened, Mélisande? What is it? . . . And I suspecting nothing. . . . What has happened? . . . Some one has done thee harm? . . . Some one has given thee offense?

Mélisande. No, no; no one has done me the least harm. . . . It is not that. . . . It is not that. . . . But I can live here no longer. I do not know why. . . . I would go away, go away! . . . I shall die if I am left here.

Golaud. But something has happened? You must be hiding something from me? . . . Tell me the whole truth, Mélisande. . . . Is it the King? . . . Is it my mother? . . . Is it Pélléas? . . .

Mélisande. No, no; it is not Pélléas. It is not anybody. . . . You could not understand me. . . .

Golaud. Why should I not understand? . . . If you tell me nothing, what will you have me do? . . . Tell me everything and I shall understand everything.

Mélisande. I do not know myself what it is. . . . I do not know just what it is. . . . If I could tell you, I would tell you. . . . It is something stronger than I. . . .

Golaud. Come; be reasonable, Mélisande. —What would you have me do?—You are no longer a child.—Is it I whom you would leave?

Mélisande. Oh! no, no; it is not that. . . . I would go away with you. . . . It is here that I can live no longer. . . . I feel that I shall not live a long while. . . .

Golaud. But there must be a reason, nevertheless. You will be thought mad. It will be thought child's dreams.—Come, is it Pélléas, perhaps?—I think he does not often speak to you.

Mélisande. Yes, yes; he speaks to me sometimes. I think he does not like me; I have seen it in his eyes. . . . But he speaks to me when he meets me. . . .

Golaud. You must not take it ill of him. He has always been so. He is a little strange. And just now he is sad; he thinks of his friend Marcellus, who is at the point of death, and whom he cannot go to see. . . . He will change, he will change, you will see; he is young. . . .

Mélisande. But it is not that . . . it is not that. . . .

Golaud. What is it, then?—Can you not get used to the life one leads here? Is it too gloomy here?—It is true the castle is very old and very somber. . . . It is very cold, and very deep. And all those who dwell in it are already old. And the country may seem gloomy too, with all its forests, all its old forests without light. But that may all be enlivened if we will. And then, joy, joy: one does not have it every day; we must take things as they come. But tell me something; no matter what; I will do everything you could wish. . . .

Mélisande. Yes, yes; it is true. . . . You never see the sky here. I saw it for the first time this morning. . . .

Golaud. It is that, then, that makes you weep, my poor Mélisande?—It is only that, then?—You weep, not to see the sky?—Come, come, you are no longer at the age when one may weep for such things. . . . And then, is not the summer yonder? You will see the sky every day.—And then, next year. . . . Come, give me your hand; give me both your little hands. [*He takes her hands.*] Oh! oh! these little hands that I could crush like flowers. . . .—Hold! where is the ring I gave you?

Mélisande. The ring?

Golaud. Yes; our wedding-ring, where is it?

Mélisande. I think . . . I think it has fallen. . . .

Golaud. Fallen?—Where has it fallen?—You have not lost it?

Mélisande. No, no; it fell . . . it must have fallen . . . but I know where it is. . . .

Golaud. Where is it?

Mélisande. You know . . . you know well . . . the grotto by the seashore? . . .

Golaud. Yes.

Mélisande. Well then, it is there. . . . It must be it is there. . . . Yes, yes; I remember. . . . I went there this morning to pick up shells for little Yniold. . . . There were some very fine ones. . . . It slipped from my finger . . . then the sea came in; and I had to go out before I had found it.

Golaud. Are you sure it is there?

Mélisande. Yes, yes; quite sure. . . . I felt it slip . . . then, all at once, the noise of the waves. . . .

Golaud. You must go look for it at once.

Mélisande. I must go look for it at once?

Golaud. Yes.

Mélisande. Now?—at once?—in the dark?

Golaud. Now, at once, in the dark. You must go look for it at once. I had rather have lost all I have than have lost that ring. You do not know what it is. You do not know whence it came. The sea will be very high tonight. The sea will come to take it before you. . . . Make haste. You must go look for it at once. . . .

Mélisande. I dare not. . . . I dare not go alone. . . .

Golaud. Go, go with no matter whom. But you must go at once, do you understand?—Make haste; ask Pélléas to go with you.

Mélisande. Pélléas?—With Pélléas?—But Pélléas would not. . . .

Golaud. Pélléas will do all you ask of him. I know Pélléas better than you do. Go, go; hurry! I shall not sleep until I have the ring.

Mélisande. Oh! oh! I am not happy! . . . I am not happy! . . . [*Exit, weeping.*]

SCENE III.—*Before a grotto.*

[*Enter* PÉLLÉAS *and* MÉLISANDE.]

Pélléas. [*Speaking with great agitation.*] Yes; it is here; we are there. It is so dark you cannot tell the entrance of the grotto from the rest of the night. . . . There are no stars on this side. Let us wait till the moon has torn through that great cloud; it will light up the whole grotto, and then we can enter without danger. There are dangerous places, and the path is very narrow between two lakes whose bottom has not yet been found. I did not think to bring a torch or a lantern, but I think the light of the sky will be enough for us.—You have never gone into this grotto?

Mélisande. No. . . .

Pélléas. Let us go in; let us go in. . . . You must be able to describe the place where you lost the ring, if he questions you. . . . It is very big and very beautiful. There are stalactites that look like plants and men. It is full of blue darks. It has not yet been explored to the end. There are great treasures hidden there, it seems. You will see the remains of ancient shipwrecks there. But you must not go far in it without a guide. There have been some who never have come back. I myself dare not go forward too far. We will stop the moment we no longer see the light of the sea or the sky. When you strike a little light there, you would say the vault was covered with stars like the sky. It is bits of crystal or salt, they say, that shine so in the rock.—Look, look, I think the sky is going to clear. . . . Give me your hand; do not tremble, do not tremble so. There is no danger; we will stop the moment we no longer see the light of the sea. . . . Is it the noise of the grotto that frightens you? It is the noise of night or the noise of silence. . . . Do you hear the sea behind us?—It does not seem happy tonight. . . . Ah! look, the light! . . .

[*The moon lights up abundantly the entrance and part of the darkness of the grotto; and at a certain depth are seen three old beggars with white hair, seated side by side, leaning upon each other and asleep against a bowlder.*]

Mélisande. Ah!

Pélléas. What is it?

Mélisande. There are . . . there are . . .

[*She points out the three beggars.*]

Pélléas. Yes, yes; I have seen them too. . . .

Mélisande. Let us go! . . . Let us go! . . .

Pélléas. Yes . . . it is three old poor men fallen asleep. . . . There is a famine in the country. . . . Why have they come to sleep here? . . .

Mélisande. Let us go! . . . Come, come. . . . Let us go! . . .

Pélléas. Take care; do not speak so loud. . . . Let us not wake them. . . . They are still sleeping heavily. . . . Come.

Mélisande. Leave me, leave me; I prefer to walk alone. . . .

Pélléas. We will come back another day.

[*Exeunt.*]

SCENE IV.—*An apartment in the castle.* ARKËL *and* PÉLLÉAS *discovered.*

Arkël. You see that everything retains you here just now and forbids you this useless journey. We have concealed your father's condition from you until now; but it is perhaps hopeless; and that alone should suffice to stop you on the threshold. But there are so many other reasons. . . . And it is not in the day when our enemies awake, and when the people are dying of hunger and murmur about us, that you have the right to desert us. And why this journey? Marcellus is dead; and life has graver duties than the visit to a tomb. You are weary, you say, of your inactive life; but activity and duty are not found on the highways. They must be waited for upon the threshold, and let in as they go by; and they go by every day. You have never seen them? I hardly see them any more myself; but I will teach you to see them, and I will point them out to you the day when you would make them a sign. Nevertheless, listen to me; if you believe it is from the depths of your life this journey is exacted, I do not forbid your undertaking it, for you must know better than I the events you must offer to your being or your fate. I shall ask you only to wait until we know what must take place ere long. . . .

Pélléas. How long must I wait?

Arkël. A few weeks; perhaps a few days.

Pélléas. I will wait. . . .

ACT THIRD

SCENE I.—*An apartment in the castle.* PÉLLÉAS *and* MÉLISANDE *discovered.* MÉLISANDE *plies her distaff at the back of the room.*

Pélléas. Yniold does not come back; where has he gone?

Mélisande. He had heard something in the corridor; he has gone to see what it is.

Pélléas. Mélisande. . . .

Mélisande. What is it?

Pélléas. . . . Can you see still to work there? . . .

Mélisande. I work as well in the dark. . . .

Pélléas. I think everybody is already asleep in the castle. Golaud does not come back from the chase. It is late, nevertheless. . . . He no longer suffers from his fall? . . .

Mélisande. He said he no longer suffered from it.

Pélléas. He must be more prudent; his body is no longer as supple as at twenty years. . . . I see the stars through the window and the light of the moon on the trees. It is late; he will not come back now. [*Knocking at the door.*] Who is there? . . . Come in! . . .

[*Little* YNIOLD *opens the door and enters the room.*]

It was you knocking so? . . . That is not the way to knock at doors. It is as if a misfortune had arrived; look, you have frightened little mother.

Little Yniold. I only knocked a tiny little bit.

Pélléas. It is late; little father will not come back tonight; it is time for you to go to bed.

Little Yniold. I shall not go to bed before you do.

Pélléas. What? . . . What is that you are saying?

Little Yniold. I say . . . not before you . . . not before you. . . .

[*Bursts into sobs and takes refuge by* MÉLISANDE.]

Mélisande. What is it, Yniold? . . . What is it? . . . why do you weep all at once?

Yniold. [*Sobbing.*] Because . . . oh! oh! because . . .

Mélisande. Because what? . . . Because what? . . Tell me . . .

Yniold. Little mother . . . little mother . . . you are going away. . . .

Mélisande. But what has taken hold of you, Yniold? . . . I have never dreamed of going away. . . .

Yniold. Yes, you have; yes, you have; little father has gone away. . . . Little father does not come back, and you are going to go away too. . . . I have seen it . . . I have seen it. . . .

Mélisande. But there has never been any idea of that, Yniold. . . . Why, what makes you think that I would go away? . . .

Yniold. I have seen it . . . I have seen it. . . . You have said things to uncle that I could not hear . . .

Pélléas. He is sleepy. . . . He has been dreaming. . . . Come here, Yniold; asleep already? . . . Come and look out at the window; the swans are fighting with the dogs.

Yniold. [*At the window.*] Oh! oh! they are chasing the dogs! . . . They are chasing them! . . . Oh! oh! the water! . . . the wings . . . the wings . . . they are afraid.

Pélléas. [*Coming back by* MÉLISANDE.] He is sleepy; he is struggling against sleep; his eyes were closing. . . .

Mélisande. [*Singing softly as she spins.*]
Saint Daniel and Saint Michaël. . . .
Saint Michaël and Saint Raphaël. . . .

Yniold. [*At the window.*] Oh! oh! little mother!

Mélisande. [*Rising abruptly.*] What is it, Yniold? . . . What is it? . . .

Yniold. I saw something at the window . . .

[PÉLLÉAS *and* MÉLISANDE *run to the window.*]

Pélléas. What is there at the window? . . . What have you seen? . . .

Yniold. Oh! oh! I saw something! . . .

Pélléas. But there is nothing. I see nothing. . .

Mélisande. Nor I. . . .

Pélléas. Where did you see something? Which way? . . .

Yniold. Down there, down there! . . . It is no longer there. . . .

Pélléas. He does not know what he is saying. He must have seen the light of the moon on the forest. There are often strange reflections, . . . or else something must have passed on the highway . . . or in his sleep. For see, see, I believe he is quite asleep. . . .

Yniold. [*At the window.*] Little father is there! little father is there!

Pélléas. [*Going to the window.*] He is right; Golaud is coming into the courtyard. . . .

Yniold. Little father! . . . little father! . . . I am going to meet him! . . .

[*Exit, running.—A silence.*]

Pélléas. They are coming up the stair. . . .

[*Enter* GOLAUD *and little* YNIOLD *with a lamp.*]

Golaud. You are still waiting in the dark?

Yniold. I have brought a light, little mother, a big light! . . . [*He lifts the lamp and looks at* MÉLISANDE.] You have been weeping, little mother? . . . You have been weeping? . . . [*He lifts the lamp toward* PÉLLÉAS *and looks in turn at him.*] You too, you too, you have been weeping? . . . Little father, look, little father; they have both been weeping. . . .

Golaud. Do not hold the light under their eyes so. . . .

SCENE II.—*One of the towers of the castle. —A watchman's round passes under a window in the tower.*

Mélisande. [*At the window, combing her unbound hair.*]

My long locks fall foaming
To the threshold of the tower,—
My locks await your coming
All along the tower,
And all the long, long hour,
And all the long, long hour.

Saint Daniel and Saint Michaël,
Saint Michaël and Saint Raphaël.

I was born on a Sunday,
A Sunday at high noon. . . .

[*Enter* PÉLLÉAS *by the watchman's round.*]

Pélléas. Holà! Holà! ho! . . .

Mélisande. Who is there?

Pélléas. I, I, and I! . . . What art thou doing there at the window, singing like a bird that is not native here?

Mélisande. I am doing my hair for the night. . . .

Pélléas. Is it that I see upon the wall? . . . I thought you had some light. . . .

Mélisande. I have opened the window; it is too hot in the tower. . . . It is beautiful tonight. . . .

Pélléas. There are innumerable stars; I have never seen so many as tonight; . . . but the moon is still upon the sea. . . . Do not stay in the shadow, Mélisande; lean forward a little till I see your unbound hair. . . .

Mélisande. I am frightful so. . . .

[*She leans out at the window.*]

Pélléas. Oh! oh! Mélisande! . . . oh, thou art beautiful! . . . thou art beautiful so! . . . Lean out! lean out! . . . Let me come nearer thee . . .

Mélisande. I cannot come nearer thee. . . . I am leaning out as far as I can. . . .

Pélléas. I cannot come up higher; . . . give me at least thy hand tonight . . . before I go away. . . . I leave tomorrow. . . .

Mélisande. No, no, no! . . .

Pélléas. Yes, yes, yes; I leave, I shall leave tomorrow. . . . Give me thy hand, thy hand, thy little hand upon my lips. . . .

Mélisande. I give thee not my hand if thou wilt leave. . . .

Pélléas. Give, give, give! . . .

Mélisande. Thou wilt not leave? . . .

Pélléas. I will wait; I will wait. . . .

Mélisande. I see a rose in the shadows. . . .

Pélléas. Where? . . . I see only the boughs of the willow hanging over the wall. . . .

Mélisande. Further down, further down, in the garden; further down, in the somber green. . . .

Pélléas. It is not a rose. . . . I will go see by and by, but give me thy hand first; first thy hand. . . .

Mélisande. There, there; . . . I cannot lean out further. . . .

Pélléas. I cannot reach thy hand with my lips. . . .

Mélisande. I cannot lean out further. . . . I am on the point of falling. . . .—Oh! oh! my hair is falling down the tower!

[*Her tresses fall suddenly over her head, as she is leaning out so, and stream over* PÉLLÉAS.]

Pélléas. Oh! oh! what is it? . . . Thy hair, thy hair is falling down to me! . . . All thy locks, Mélisande, all thy locks have fallen down the tower! . . . I hold them in my hands; I hold them in my mouth. . . . I hold them in my arms; I put them about my neck. . . . I will not open my hands again tonight. . . .

Mélisande. Let me go! let me go! . . . Thou wilt make me fall! . . .

Pélléas. No, no, no; . . . I have never seen such hair as thine, Mélisande! . . . See, see, see; it comes from so high and yet it floods me to the heart! . . . And yet it floods me to the knees! . . . And it is sweet, sweet as if it fell from heaven! . . . I see the sky no longer through thy locks. Thou seest, thou seest? . . . I can no longer hold them with both hands; there are some on the boughs of the willow. . . . They are alive like birds in my hands, . . . and they love me, they love me more than thou! . . .

Mélisande. Let me go; let me go! . . . Some one might come. . . .

Pélléas. No, no, no; I shall not set thee free tonight. . . . Thou art my prisoner tonight; all night, all night! . . .

Mélisande. Pélléas! Pélléas! . . .

Pélléas. I tie them, I tie them to the willow boughs. . . . Thou shalt not go away now; . . . thou shalt not go away now. . . . Look, look, I am kissing thy hair. . . . I suffer no more in the midst of thy hair. . . . Hearest thou my kisses along thy hair? . . . They mount along thy hair. . . . Each hair must bring thee some. . . . Thou seest, thou seest, I can open my hands. . . . My hands are free, and thou canst not leave me now. . . .

Mélisande. Oh! oh! thou hurtest me. . . . [*Doves come out of the tower and fly about them in the night*.]—What is that, Pélléas? —What is it flying about me?

Pélléas. It is the doves coming out of the tower. . . . I have frightened them; they are flying away. . . .

Mélisande. It is my doves, Pélléas.—Let us go away, let me go; they will not come back again. . . .

Pélléas. Why will they not come back again?

Mélisande. They will be lost in the dark. . . . Let me go; let me lift my head. . . . I hear a noise of footsteps. . . . Let me go!— It is Golaud! . . . I believe it is Golaud! . . . He has heard us. . . .

Pélléas. Wait! Wait! . . . Thy hair is about the boughs. . . . It is caught there in the darkness. . . . Wait, wait! . . . It is dark. . . .

[*Enter* GOLAUD, *by the watchman's round*.]

Golaud. What do you here?

Pélléas. What do I here? . . . I . . .

Golaud. You are children. . . . Mélisande, do not lean out so at the window; you will fall. . . . Do you not know it is late?—It is nearly midnight.—Do not play so in the darkness.—You are children. . . . [*Laughing nervously*.] What children! . . . What children! . . . [*Exit, with* PÉLLÉAS.]

SCENE III.—*The vaults of the castle.*

[*Enter* GOLAUD *and* PÉLLÉAS.]

Golaud. Take care; this way, this way.— You have never penetrated into these vaults?

Pélléas. Yes; once, of old; but it was long ago. . . .

Golaud. They are prodigious great; it is a succession of enormous crypts that end God knows where. The whole castle is builded on these crypts. Do you smell the deathly odor that reigns here?—That is what I wished to show you. In my opinion, it comes from the little underground lake I am going to have you see. Take care; walk before me, in the light of my lantern. I will warn you when we are there. [*They continue to walk in silence.*] Hey! hey! Pélléas! stop! stop!—[*He seizes him by the arm.*] For God's sake! . . . Do you not see?—One step more, and you had been in the gulf! . . .

Pélléas. But I did not see it! . . . The lantern no longer lighted me. . . .

Golaud. I made a misstep, . . . but if I had not held you by the arm . . . Well, this is the stagnant water that I spoke of to you. . . . Do you perceive the smell of death that rises?—Let us go to the end of this overhanging rock, and do you lean over a little. It will strike you in the face.

Pélléas. I smell it already; . . . you would say a smell of the tomb.

Golaud. Further, further. . . . It is this that on certain days has poisoned the castle. The King will not believe it comes from here. —The crypt should be walled up in which this standing water is found. It is time, besides, to examine these vaults a little. Have you noticed those lizards on the walls and pillars of the vaults?—There is a labor hidden here you would not suspect; and the whole castle will be swallowed up one of these nights, if it is not looked out for. But what will you have? nobody likes to come down this far. . . . There are strange lizards in many of the walls. . . . Oh! here . . . do you perceive the smell of death that rises?

Pélléas. Yes; there is a smell of death rising about us. . . .

Golaud. Lean over; have no fear. . . . I will hold you . . . give me . . . no, no, not your hand . . . it might slip . . . your arm, your arm! . . . Do you see the gulf? [*Moved.*] —Pélléas? Pélléas? . . .

Pélléas. Yes; I think I see the bottom of the gulf. . . . Is it the light that trembles so? . . . You . . . [*He straightens up, turns, and looks at* GOLAUD.]

Golaud. [*With a trembling voice.*] Yes; it is the lantern. . . . See, I shook it to lighten the walls. . . .

Pélléas. I stifle here; . . . let us go out. . . .

Golaud. Yes; let us go out. . . .

[*Exeunt in silence.*]

SCENE IV.—*A terrace at the exit of the vaults. Enter* GOLAUD *and* PÉLLÉAS.

Pélléas. Ah! I breathe at last! . . . I thought, one moment, I was going to be ill in those enormous crypts; I was on the point of falling. . . . There is a damp air there, heavy as a leaden dew, and darkness thick as a poisoned paste. . . . And now, all the air of all the sea! . . . There is a fresh wind, see; fresh as a leaf that has just opened, over the little green waves. . . . Hold! the flowers have just been watered at the foot of the terrace, and the smell of the verdure and the wet roses comes up to us. . . . It must be nearly noon; they are already in the shadow of the tower. . . . It is noon; I hear the bells ringing, and the children are going down to the beach to bathe. . . . I did not know that we had stayed so long in the caverns. . . .

Golaud. We went down toward eleven o'clock. . . .

Pélléas. Earlier; it must have been earlier; I heard it strike half-past ten.

Golaud. Half-past ten or a quarter to eleven. . . .

Pélléas. They have opened all the windows of the castle. It will be unusually hot this afternoon. . . . Look, there is mother with Mélisande at a window of the tower. . . .

Golaud. Yes; they have taken refuge on the shady side.—Speaking of Mélisande, I heard what passed and what was said last night. I am quite aware all that is but child's play; but it need not be repeated. Mélisande is very young and very impressionable; and she must be treated the more circumspectly that she is perhaps with child at this moment. . . . She is very delicate, hardly woman; and the least emotion might bring on a mishap. It is not the first time I have noticed there might be something between you. . . . You are older than she; it will suffice to have told you. . . . Avoid her as much as possible; without affectation moreover; without affectation. . . .—What is it I see yonder on the highway toward the forest? . . .

Pélléas. Some herds they are leading to the city. . . .

Golaud. They cry like lost children; you would say they smelt the butcher already.—It will be time for dinner.—What a fine day! What a capital day for the harvest! . . .

[*Exeunt.*]

SCENE V.—*Before the castle.*

[*Enter* GOLAUD *and little* YNIOLD.]

Golaud. Come, we are going to sit down here, Yniold; sit on my knee; we shall see from here what passes in the forest. I do not see you any more at all now. You abandon me too; you are always at little mother's. . . . Why, we are sitting just under little mother's windows.—Perhaps she is saying her evening prayer at this moment. . . . But tell me, Yniold, she is often with your uncle Pélléas, isn't she?

Yniold. Yes, yes; always, little father; when you are not there, little father. . . .

Golaud. Ah!—look; some one is going by with a lantern in the garden.—But I have been told they did not like each other. . . . It seems they often quarrel; . . . no? Is it true?

Yniold. Yes, yes; it is true.

Golaud. Yes?—Ah! ah!—But what do they quarrel about?

Yniold. About the door.

Golaud. What? about the door?—What are you talking about?—No, come, explain yourself; why do they quarrel about the door?

Yniold. About its being open.

Golaud. Who wants it to stay open?—Come, why do they quarrel?

Yniold. I don't know, little father; about the light.

Golaud. I am not talking to you about the light; we will talk of that by and by. I am talking to you about the door. Answer what I ask you; you must learn to talk; it is time. . . . Do not put your hand in your mouth so; . . . come. . . .

Yniold. Little father! little father! . . . I won't do it any more. . . . [*He cries.*]

Golaud. Come; what are you crying for now? What has happened?

Yniold. Oh! oh! little father, you hurt me. . . .

Golaud. I hurt you?—Where did I hurt you? I did not mean to. . . .

Yniold. Here, here; on my little arm. . . .

Golaud. I did not mean to; come, don't cry any more, and I will give you something tomorrow.

Yniold. What, little father?

Golaud. A quiver and some arrows; but tell me what you know about the door.

Yniold. Big arrows?

Golaud. Yes, yes; very big arrows.—But why don't they want the door to be open?—Come, answer me sometime!—no, no; do not open your mouth to cry. I am not angry. We are going to have a quiet talk, like Pélléas and little mother when they are together. What do they talk about when they are together?

Yniold. Pélléas and little mother?

Golaud. Yes; what do they talk about?

Yniold. About me; always about me.

Golaud. And what do they say about you?

Yniold. They say I am going to be very big.

Golaud. Oh, plague of my life! . . . I am here like a blind man searching for his treasure at the bottom of the ocean! . . . I am here like a new-born child lost in the forest, and you . . . Come, come, Yniold, I was wandering; we are going to talk seriously. Do Pélléas and little mother never speak of me when I am not there? . . .

Yniold. Yes, yes, little father; they are always speaking of you.

Golaud. Ah! . . . And what do they say of me?

Yniold. They say I shall grow as big as you are.

Golaud. You are always by them?

Yniold. Yes, yes, always, always, little father.

Golaud. They never tell you to go play somewhere else?

Yniold. No, little father; they are afraid when I am not there.

Golaud. They are afraid? . . . What makes you think they are afraid?

Yniold. Little mother always says, "Don't go away; don't go away!" . . . They are unhappy, but they laugh. . . .

Golaud. But that does not prove they are afraid.

Yniold. Yes, yes, little father; she is afraid. . . .

Golaud. Why do you say she is afraid?

Yniold. They always weep in the dark.

Golaud. Ah! ah! . . .

Yniold. That makes one weep too.

Golaud. Yes, yes! . . .

Yniold. She is pale, little father.

Golaud. Ah! ah! . . . patience, my God, patience! . . .

Yniold. What, little father?

Golaud. Nothing, nothing, my child.—I saw a wolf go by in the forest.—Then they get on well together?—I am glad to learn they are on good terms.—They kiss each other sometimes?—No? . . .

Yniold. Kiss each other, little father?—No, no,—ah! yes, little father, yes, yes; once . . . once when it rained. . . .

Golaud. They kissed?—But how, how did they kiss?

Yniold. So, little father, so! . . . [*He gives him a kiss on the mouth, laughing.*] Ah! ah! your beard, little father! . . . It pricks! it pricks! it pricks! It is getting all gray, little father, and your hair, too; all gray, all gray, all gray. . . . [*The window under which they are sitting is lighted up at this moment, and the light falls upon them.*] Ah, ah! little mother has lit her lamp. It is light, little father; it is light. . . .

Golaud. Yes; it is beginning to be light. . . .

Yniold. Let us go there too, little father; let us go there too. . . .

Golaud. Where do you want to go?

Yniold. Where it is light, little father.

Golaud. No, no, my child; let us stay in the dark a little longer. . . . One cannot tell, one cannot tell yet. . . . Do you see those poor people down there trying to kindle a little fire in the forest?—It has rained. And over there, do you see the old gardener trying to lift that tree the wind has blown down across the road?—He cannot; the tree is too big; the tree is too heavy, and it will lie where it fell. All that cannot be helped. . . . I think Pélléas is mad. . . .

Yniold. No, little father, he is not mad; he is very good.

Golaud. Do you want to see little mother?

Yniold. Yes, yes; I want to see her!

Golaud. Don't make any noise; I am going to hoist you up to the window. It is too high for me, for all I am so big. . . . [*He lifts the child.*] Do not make the least noise; little mother would be terribly afraid. . . . Do you see her?—Is she in the room?

Yniold. Yes. . . . Oh, how light it is!

Golaud. She is alone?

Yniold. Yes; . . . no, no; Uncle Pélléas is there, too.

Golaud. He— . . . !

Yniold. Ah! ah! little father! you have hurt me! . . .

Golaud. It is nothing; be still; I will not do it any more; look, look, Yniold! . . . I stumbled; speak lower. What are they doing?—

Yniold. They are not doing anything, little father; they are waiting for something.

Golaud. Are they near each other?

Yniold. No, little father.

Golaud. And . . . and the bed? are they near the bed?

Yniold. The bed, little father?—I can't see the bed.

Golaud. Lower, lower; they will hear you. Are they speaking?

Yniold. No, little father; they do not speak.

Golaud. But what are they doing?—They must be doing something. . . .

Yniold. They are looking at the light.

Golaud. Both?

Yniold. Yes, little father.

Golaud. They do not say anything?

Yniold. No, little father; they do not close their eyes.

Golaud. They do not come near each other?

Yniold. No, little father; they do not stir.

Golaud. They are sitting down?

Yniold. No, little father; they are standing upright against the wall.

Golaud. They make no gestures?—They do not look at each other?—They make no signs? . . .

Yniold. No, little father.—Oh! oh! little father; they never close their eyes. . . . I am terribly afraid. . . .

Golaud. Be still. They do not stir yet?

Yniold. No, little father.—I am afraid, little father; let me come down! . . .

Golaud. Why, what are you afraid of?—Look! look! . . .

Yniold. I dare not look any more, little father! . . . Let me come down! . . .

Golaud. Look! look! . . .

Yniold. Oh! oh! I am going to cry, little father!—Let me come down; let me come down! . . .

Golaud. Come; we will go see what has happened.

[*Exeunt.*]

ACT FOURTH

SCENE I.—*A corridor in the castle.*

[*Enter* PÉLLÉAS *and* MÉLISANDE, *meeting.*]

Pélléas. Where goest thou? I must speak to thee tonight. Shall I see thee?

Mélisande. Yes.

Pélléas. I have just left my father's room. He is getting better. The physician has told us he is saved. . . . And yet this morning I had a presentiment this day would end ill. I have had a rumor of misfortune in my ears for some time. . . . Then, all at once there was a great change; today it is no longer anything but a question of time. All the windows in his room have been thrown open. He speaks; he seems happy. He does not speak yet like an ordinary man, but already his ideas no longer all come from the other world. . . . He recognized me. He took my hand and said with that strange air he has had since he fell sick: "Is it thou, Pélléas?

Why, why, I had not noticed it before, but thou hast the grave and friendly look of those who will not live long. . . . You must travel; you must travel. . . ." It is strange; I shall obey him. . . . My mother listened to him and wept for joy.—Hast thou not been aware of it?—The whole house seems already to revive: you hear breathing; you hear speaking; you hear walking. . . . Listen; I hear some one speaking behind that door. Quick, quick! answer quickly! where shall I see thee?

Mélisande. Where wouldst thou?

Pélléas. In the park; near "Blind Man's Spring."—Wilt thou?—Wilt thou come?

Mélisande. Yes.

Pélléas. It will be the last night;—I am going to travel, as my father said. Thou wilt not see me more. . . .

Mélisande. Do not say that, Pélléas. . . . I shall see thee always; I shall look upon thee always. . . .

Pélléas. Thou wilt look in vain. . . . I shall be so far away thou couldst no longer see me. . . . I shall try to go very far away. . . . I am full of joy, and you would say I had all the weight of heaven and earth on my body today. . . .

Mélisande. What has happened, Pélléas?—I no longer understand what you say. . . .

Pélléas. Go, go; let us separate. I hear some one speaking behind that door. . . . It is the strangers who came to the castle this morning. . . . They are going out. . . . Let us go; it is the strangers. . . .

[*Exeunt severally.*]

SCENE II.—*An apartment in the castle.*

[ARKËL *and* MÉLISANDE *discovered.*]

Arkël. Now that Pélléas's father is saved, and sickness, the old handmaid of Death, has left the castle, a little joy and a little sunlight will at last come into the house again. . . . It was time!—For, since thy coming, we have only lived here whispering about a closed room. . . . And truly I have pitied thee, Mélisande. . . . Thou camest here all joyous, like a child seeking a gala-day, and at the moment thou enteredst in the vestibule I saw thy face change, and probably thy soul, as the face changes in spite of us when we enter at noon into a grotto too gloomy and too cold. . . . And since—since, on account of all that, I have often no longer understood thee. . . . I observed thee, thou wert there, listless perhaps, but with the strange, astray look of one awaiting ever a great trouble, in the sunlight, in a beautiful garden. . . . I cannot explain. . . . But I was sad to see thee so; for thou art too young and too beautiful to live already day and night under the breath of death. . . . But now all that will change. At my age,—and there perhaps is the surest fruit of my life,—at my age I have gained I know not what faith in the fidelity of events, and I have always seen that every young and beautiful being creates about itself young, beautiful, and happy events. . . . And it is thou who wilt now open the door for the new era I have glimpses of. . . . Come here; why dost thou stay there without answering and without lifting thine eyes?—I have kissed thee but once only hitherto,—the day of thy coming; and yet old men need sometimes to touch with their lips a woman's forehead or a child's cheek, to believe still in the freshness of life and avert awhile the menaces. . . . Art thou afraid of my old lips? How I have pitied thee these months! . . .

Mélisande. Grandfather, I have not been unhappy. . . .

Arkël. Perhaps you were of those who are unhappy without knowing it, . . . and they are the most unhappy. . . . Let me look at thee, so, quite near, a moment; . . . we have such need of beauty beside Death. . . .

[*Enter* GOLAUD.]

Golaud. Pélléas leaves tonight.

Arkël. Thou hast blood on thy forehead. What hast thou done?

Golaud. Nothing, nothing. . . . I have passed trough a hedge of thorns.

Mélisande. Bend down your head a little, my lord. . . . I will wipe your forehead. . . .

Golaud. [*Repulsing her.*] I will not that you touch me. do you understand? Go, go!—I am not speaking to you.—Where is my sword?—I came to seek my sword. . . .

Mélisande. Here; on the praying-stool.

Golaud. Bring it. [*To* ARKËL.]—They have just found another peasant dead of hunger, along by the sea. You would say they all meant to die under our eyes.—[*To* MÉLISANDE.] Well, my sword?—Why do you tremble so?—I am not going to kill you. I would simply examine the blade. I do not employ the sword for these uses. Why do you examine me like a beggar?—I do not come to ask alms of you. You hope to see something in my eyes without my seeing anything in yours?—Do you think I may know something?—[*To* ARKËL.]—Do you see those great eyes?—It is as if they were proud of their richness. . . .

Arkël. I see there only a great innocence. . . .

Golaud. A great innocence! . . . They

are greater than innocence! . . . They are purer than the eyes of a lamb. . . . They would give God lessons in innocence! A great innocence! Listen: I am so near them I feel the freshness of their lashes when they wink; and yet I am less far away from the great secrets of the other world than from the smallest secret of those eyes! . . . A great innocence! . . . More than innocence! You would say the angels of heaven celebrated there an eternal baptism! . . . I know those eyes! I have seen them at their work! Close them! close them! or I shall close them for a long while! . . . —Do not put your right hand to your throat so; I am saying a very simple thing. . . . I have no under-thought. . . . If I had an under-thought, why should I not say it? Ah! ah!—do not attempt to flee!—Here!—Give me that hand!—Ah! your hands are too hot. . . . Go away! Your flesh disgusts me! . . . Here!—There is no more question of fleeing now!—[*He seizes her by the hair.*]—You shall follow me on your knees!—On your knees!—On your knees before me!—Ah! ah! your long hair serves some purpose at last! . . . Right, . . . left! —Left, . . . right!—Absalom! Absalom.—Forward! back! To the ground! to the ground! . . . You see, you see; I laugh already like an old man. . . .

Arkël. [*Running up.*] Golaud! . . .

Golaud. [*Affecting a sudden calm.*] You will do as you may please, look you.—I attach no importance to that.—I am too old; and, besides, I am not a spy. I shall await chance; and then . . . Oh! then! . . . simply because it is the custom; simply because it is the custom. . . . [*Exit.*]

Arkël. What ails him?—He is drunk?

Mélisande. [*In tears.*] No, no; he does not love me any more. . . . I am not happy! . . . I am not happy! . . .

Arkël. If I were God, I would have pity on men's hearts. . . .

SCENE III.—*A terrace of the castle. Little* YNIOLD *discovered, trying to lift a bowlder.*

Little Yniold. Oh, this stone is heavy! . . . It is heavier than I am. . . . It is heavier than everybody. . . . It is heavier than everything that ever happened. . . . I can see my golden ball between the rock and this naughty stone, and I cannot reach it. . . . My little arm is not long enough . . . and this stone won't be lifted. . . . I can't lift it . . . and nobody could lift it. . . . It is heavier than the whole house; . . . you would think it had roots in the earth. . . . [*The bleatings of a flock heard far away.*]—Oh! oh! I hear the sheep crying. . . . [*He goes to look, at the edge of the terrace.*] Why! there is no more sun. . . . They are coming . . . the little sheep . . . they are coming. . . . There is a lot of them! . . . There is a lot of them! . . . They are afraid of the dark. . . . They crowd together! they crowd together! . . . They can hardly walk any more. . . . They are crying! they are crying! and they go quick! . . . They go quick! . . . They are already at the great crossroads. Ah! ah! They don't know where they ought to go any more. . . . They don't cry any more. . . . They wait. . . . Some of them want to go to the right. . . . They all want to go to the right. . . . They cannot! . . . The shepherd is throwing earth at them. . . . Ah! ah! They are going to pass by here. . . . They obey! They obey! They are going to pass under the terrace. . . . They are going to pass under the rocks. . . . I am going to see them near by. . . . Oh! oh! what a lot of them! . . . What a lot of them! . . . The whole road is full of them. . . . They all keep still now. . . . Shepherd! shepherd! why don't they speak any more?

The Shepherd. [*Who is out of sight.*] Because it is no longer the road to the stable. . . .

Yniold. Where are they going?—Shepherd! shepherd!—where are they going?—He doesn't hear me any more. They are too far away already. . . . They go quick. . . . They are not making a noise any more. . . . It is no longer the road to the stable. . . . Where are they going to sleep tonight?—Oh! oh!—It is too dark. . . . I am going to tell something to somebody. . . . [*Exit.*]

SCENE IV.—*A fountain in the park.*

[*Enter* PÉLLÉAS.]

Pélléas. It is the last evening . . . the last evening. It must all end. I have played like a child about a thing I did not guess. . . . I have played a-dream about the snares of fate. . . . Who has awakened me all at once? I shall flee, crying out for joy and woe like a blind man fleeing from his burning house. . . . I am going to tell her I shall flee. . . . My father is out of danger; and I have no more reason to lie to myself. . . . It is late; she does not come. . . . I should do better to go away without seeing her again. . . . I must look well at her this time. . . . There are some things that I no longer recall. . . . It seems at times as if I had not seen her for a hundred years. . . . And I have not yet looked upon her look. . . . There remains nought to me if I go away thus. And all those memories . . . it is as if I were to take away a little water in a muslin bag. . . . I must see her one last time, to the bottom of her heart. . . . I must tell her all that I have never told her.

[*Enter* MÉLISANDE.]

Mélisande. Pélléas!

Pélléas. Mélisande!—Is it thou, Mélisande?

Mélisande. Yes.

Pélléas. Come hither; do not stay at the edge of the moonlight.—Come hither. We have so many things to tell each other. . . . Come hither in the shadow of the linden.

Mélisande. Let me stay in the light. . . .

Pélléas. We might be seen from the windows of the tower. Come hither; here, we have nothing to fear.—Take care; we might be seen. . . .

Mélisande. I wish to be seen. . . .

Pélléas. Why, what doth ail thee?—Thou wert able to come out without being seen?

Mélisande. Yes; your brother slept. . . .

Pélléas. It is late.—In an hour they will close the gates. We must be careful. Why art thou come so late?

Mélisande. Your brother had a bad dream. And then my gown was caught on the nails of the gate. See, it is torn. I lost all this time, and ran. . . .

Pélléas. My poor Mélisande! . . . I should almost be afraid to touch thee. . . . Thou art still out of breath, like a hunted bird. . . . It is for me, for me, thou doest all that? . . . I hear thy heart beat as if it were mine. . . . Come hither . . . . nearer, nearer me. . . .

Mélisande. Why do you laugh?

Pélléas. I do not laugh;—or else I laugh for joy, unwittingly. . . . It were a weeping matter, rather. . . .

Mélisande. We have come here before. . . . I recollect. . . .

Pélléas. Yes . . . yes. . . . Long months ago.—I knew not then. . . . Knowest thou why I asked thee to come here tonight?

Mélisande. No.

Pélléas. It is perhaps the last time I shall see thee. . . . I must go away forever. . . .

Mélisande. Why sayest thou always thou wilt go away? . . .

Pélléas. I must tell thee what thou knowest already?—Thou knowest not what I am going to tell thee?

Mélisande. Why, no; why, no; I know nothing—

Pélléas. Thou knowest not why I must go afar. . . . Thou knowest not it is because . . . [*He kisses her abruptly.*] I love thee. . . .

Mélisande. [*In a low voice.*] I love thee too. . . .

Pélléas. Oh! oh! What saidst thou, Mélisande? . . . I hardly heard it! . . . Thou sayest that in a voice coming from the end of the world! . . . I hardly heard thee. . . . Thou lovest me?—Thou lovest me too? . . . Since when lovest thou me? . . .

Mélisande. Since always. . . . Since I saw thee. . . .

Pélléas. Oh, how thou sayest that! . . . Thy voice seems to have blown across the sea in spring! . . . I have never heard it until now; . . . one would say it had rained on my heart! . . . Thou sayest that so frankly! . . . Like an angel questioned! . . . I cannot believe it, Mélisande! . . . Why shouldst thou love me?—Nay, why dost thou love me?—Is what thou sayest true?—Thou dost not mock me?—Thou dost not lie a little, to make me smile? . . .

Mélisande. No; I never lie; I lie but to thy brother. . . .

Pélléas. Oh, how thou sayest that! . . . Thy voice! thy voice! . . . It is cooler and more frank than the water is! . . . It is like pure water on my lips! . . . It is like pure water on my hands. . . . Give me, give me thy hands! . . . Oh, how small thy hands are! . . . I did not know thou wert so beautiful! . . . I have never seen anything so beautiful before thee. . . . I was full of unrest; I sought throughout the house. . . . I sought throughout the country. . . . And I found not beauty. . . . And now I have found thee! . . I have found thee! . . . I do not think there could be on the earth a fairer woman! . . . Where art thou?—I no longer hear thee breathe. . . .

Mélisande. Because I look on thee. . . .

Pélléas. Why dost thou look so gravely on me?—We are already in the shadow.—It is too dark under this tree. Come into the light. We cannot see how happy we are. Come, come; so little time remains to us. . . .

Mélisande. No, no; let us stay here. . . . I am nearer thee in the dark. . . .

Pélléas. Where are thine eyes?—Thou art not going to fly me?—Thou dost not think of me just now.

Mélisande. Oh, yes; oh, yes; I only think of thee. . . .

Pélléas. Thou wert looking elsewhere. . . .

Mélisande. I saw thee elsewhere. . . .

Pélléas. Thy soul is far away. . . . What ails thee, then?—Meseems thou art not happy. . . .

Mélisande. Yes, yes; I am happy, but I am sad. . . .

Pélléas. One is sad often when one loves. . . .

Mélisande. I weep always when I think of thee. . . .

Pélléas. I too. . . . I too, Mélisande. . . . I am quite near thee; I weep for joy, and yet . . . [*He kisses her again.*]—Thou art strange when I kiss thee so. . . . Thou art so beautiful that one would think thou wert about to die. . . .

Mélisande. Thou too. . . .

Pélléas. There, there. . . . We do not what we will. . . . I did not love thee the first time I saw thee. . . .

Mélisande. Nor I . . . nor I. . . . I was afraid. . . .

Pélléas. I could not admit thine eyes. . . . I would have gone away at once . . . and then . . .

Mélisande. And I—I would not have come. . . . I do not yet know why—I was afraid to come. . . .

Pélléas. There are so many things one never knows. We are ever waiting; and then. . . . What is that noise?—They are closing the gates! . . .

Mélisande. Yes, they have closed the gates. . . .

Pélléas. We cannot go back now?—Hearest thou the bolts?—Listen! listen! . . . the great chains! . . . the great chains! . . . It is too late; it is too late! . . .

Mélisande. All the better! all the better! all the better! . . .

Pélléas. Thou— . . . ? Behold, behold! . . . It is no longer we who will it so! . . . All's lost, all's saved! all is saved tonight!—Come, come. . . . My heart beats like a madman—up to my very throat. . . . [*They embrace.*] Listen! listen! my heart is almost strangling me. . . . Come! come! . . . Ah, how beautiful it is in the shadows! . . .

Mélisande. There is some one behind us! . . .

Pélléas. I see no one. . . .

Mélisande. I heard a noise. . . .

Pélléas. I hear only thy heart in the dark. . . .

Mélisande. I heard the crackling of dead leaves. . . .

Pélléas. Because the wind is silent all at once. . . . It fell as we were kissing. . . .

Mélisande. How long our shadows are tonight! . . .

Pélléas. They embrace to the very end of the garden. Oh, how they kiss far away from us! . . . Look! look! . . .

Mélisande. [*In a stifled voice.*] A-a-h!—He is behind a tree!

Pélléas. Who?

Mélisande. Golaud!

Pélléas. Golaud!—where?—I see nothing. . . .

Mélisande. There . . . at the end of our shadows. . . .

Pélléas. Yes, yes; I saw him. . . . Let us not turn abruptly. . . .

Mélisande. He has his sword. . . .

Pélléas. I have not mine.

Mélisande. He saw us kiss. . . .

Pélléas. He does not know we have seen him. . . . Do not stir; do not turn your head. . . . He would rush headlong on us. . . . He will remain there while he thinks we do not know. He watches us. . . . He is still motionless. . . . Go, go at once this way. . . . I will wait for him. . . . I will stop him. . . .

Mélisande. No, no, no! . . .

Pélléas. Go! go! he has seen all! . . . He will kill us! . . .

Mélisande. All the better! all the better! all the better! . . .

Pélléas. He comes! he comes! . . . Thy mouth! . . . Thy mouth! . . .

Mélisande. Yes! . . . yes! yes! . . .

[*They kiss desperately.*]

Pélléas. Oh! oh! All the stars are falling! . . .

Mélisande. Upon me too! upon me too! . . .

Pélléas. Again! Again! . . . Give! give! . . .

Mélisande. All! all! all! . . .

[GOLAUD *rushes upon them, sword in hand, and strikes* PÉLLÉAS, *who falls at the brink of the fountain.* MÉLISANDE *flees terrified.*]

Mélisande. [*Fleeing.*] Oh! oh! I have no courage! . . . I have no courage! . . .

[GOLAUD *pursues her through the wood in silence.*]

ACT FIFTH

SCENE I.—*A lower hall in the castle. The women servants discovered, gathered together, while without children are playing before one of the ventilators of the hall.*

An Old Servant. You will see, you will see, my daughters; it will be tonight.—Some one will come to tell us by and by. . . .

Another Servant. They will not come to tell us. . . . They don't know what they are doing any longer. . . .

Third Servant. Let us wait here. . . .

Fourth Servant. We shall know well enough when we must go up. . . .

Fifth Servant. When the time is come, we shall go up of ourselves. . . .

Sixth Servant. There is no longer a sound heard in the house. . . .

Seventh Servant. We ought to make the children keep still, who are playing before the ventilator.

Eighth Servant. They will be still of themselves by and by.

Ninth Servant. The time has not yet come. . . . [*Enter an old Servant.*]

The Old Servant. No one can go in the room any longer. I have listened more than an hour. . . . You could hear the flies walk on the doors. . . . I heard nothing. . . .

First Servant. Has she been left alone in the room?

The Old Servant. No, no; I think the room is full of people.

First Servant. They will come, they will come, by and by. . . .

The Old Servant. Lord! Lord! It is not happiness that has come into the house. . . . One may not speak, but if I could say what I know . . .

Second Servant. It was you who found them before the gate?

The Old Servant. Why, yes! why, yes! it was I who found them. The porter says it was he who saw them first; but it was I who waked them. He was sleeping on his face and would not get up.—And now he comes saying, "It was I who saw them first." Is that just?—See, I burned myself lighting a lamp to go down cellar.—Now what was I going to do down cellar?—I can't remember any more what I was going to do down cellar.—At any rate I got up very early; it was not yet very light; I said to myself, I will go across the courtyard, and then I will open the gate. Good; I go down the stairs on tiptoe, and I open the gate as if it were an ordinary gate. . . . My God! My God! What do I see? Divine a little what I see! . . .

First Servant. They were before the gate?

The Old Servant. They were both stretched out before the gate! . . . Exactly like poor folk that are too hungry. . . . They were huddled together like little children who are afraid. . . . The little princess was nearly dead, and the great Golaud had still his sword in his side. . . . There was blood on the sill. . . .

Second Servant. We ought to make the children keep still. . . . They are screaming with all their might before the ventilator. . . .

Third Servant. You can't hear yourself speak. . . .

Fourth Servant. There is nothing to be done: I have tried already; they won't keep still. . . .

First Servant. It seems he is nearly cured?

The Old Servant. Who?

First Servant. The great Golaud.

Third Servant. Yes, yes; they have taken him to his wife's room. I met them just now, in the corridor. They were holding him up as if he were drunk. He cannot yet walk alone.

The Old Servant. He could not kill himself; he is too big. But she is hardly wounded, and it is she who is going to die. . . . Can you understand that?

First Servant. You have seen the wound?

The Old Servant. As I see you, my daughter.—I saw everything, you understand. . . . I saw it before all the others. . . . A tiny little wound under her little left breast—a little wound that wouldn't kill a pigeon. Is it natural?

First Servant. Yes, yes; there is something underneath. . . .

Second Servant. Yes; but she was delivered of her babe three days ago. . . .

The Old Servant. Exactly! . . . She was delivered on her death-bed; is that a little sign?—And what a child! Have you seen it?—A wee little girl a beggar would not bring into the world. . . . A little wax figure that came much too soon; . . . a little wax figure that must live in lambs' wool. . . . Yes, yes; it is not happiness that has come into the house. . . .

First Servant. Yes, yes; it is the hand of God that has been stirring. . . .

Second Servant. Yes, yes; all that did not happen without reason. . . .

Third Servant. It is as good lord Pélléas . . . where is he?—No one knows. . . .

The Old Servant. Yes, yes; everybody knows. . . . But nobody dare speak of it. . . . One does not speak of this; . . . one does not speak of that; . . . one speaks no more of anything; . . . one no longer speaks truth. . . . But *I* know he was found at the bottom of Blind Man's Spring; . . . but no one, no one could see him. . . . Well, well, we shall only know all that at the last day. . . .

First Servant. I dare not sleep here any longer. . . .

The Old Servant. Yes, yes; once ill-fortune is in the house, one keeps silence in vain. . . .

Third Servant. Yes; it finds you all the same. . . .

The Old Servant. Yes, yes; but we do not go where we would. . . .

Fourth Servant. Yes, yes; we do not do what we would. . . .

First Servant. They are afraid of us now. . . .

Second Servant. They all keep silence. . . .

Third Servant. They cast down their eyes in the corridors.

Fourth Servant. They do not speak any more except in a low voice.

Fifth Servant. You would think they had all done it together.

Sixth Servant. One doesn't know what they have done. . . .

Seventh Servant. What is to be done when the masters are afraid? . . . [*A silence.*]

First Servant. I no longer hear the children screaming.

Second Servant. They are sitting down before the ventilator.

Third Servant. They are huddled against each other.

The Old Servant. I no longer hear anything in the house. . . .

First Servant. You no longer even hear the children breathe. . . .

The Old Servant. Come, come; it is time to go up. . . . [*Exeunt, in silence.*]

SCENE II.—*An apartment in the castle.* ARKËL, GOLAUD, *and the* PHYSICIAN *discovered in one corner of the room.* MÉLISANDE *is stretched upon her bed.*

The Physician. It cannot be of that little wound she is dying; a bird would not have died of it. . . . It is not you, then, who have killed her, good my lord; do not be so disconsolate. . . . She could not have lived. . . . She was born without reason . . . to die; and she dies without reason. . . . And then, it is not sure we shall not save her. . . .

Arkël. No, no; it seems to me we keep too silent, in spite of ourselves, in her room. . . . It is not a good sign. . . . Look how she sleeps . . . slowly, slowly; . . . it is as if her soul was cold forever. . . .

Golaud. I have killed her without cause! I have killed her without cause! . . . Is it not enough to make the stones weep? . . . They had kissed like little children. . . . They had simply kissed. . . . They were brother and sister. . . . And I, and I at once! . . . I did it in spite of myself, look you. . . . I did it in spite of myself. . . .

The Physician. Stop; I think she is waking. . . .

Mélisande. Open the window . . . open the window. . . .

Arkël. Shall I open this one, Mélisande?

Mélisande. No, no; the great window . . . the great window. . . . It is to see . . .

Arkël. Is not the sea air too cold tonight?

The Physician. Do it; do it. . . .

Mélisande. Thanks. . . . Is it sunset?

Arkël. Yes; it is sunset on the sea; it is late.—How are you, Mélisande?

Mélisande. Well, well.—Why do you ask that? I have never been better.—And yet it seems to me I know something. . . .

Arkël. What sayest thou?—I do not understand thee. . . .

Mélisande. Neither do I understand all I say, you see. . . . I do not know what I am saying. . . . I do not know what I know. . . . I no longer say what I would. . . .

Arkël. Why, yes! why, yes! . . . I am quite happy to hear thee speak so; thou hast raved a little these last days, and one no longer understood thee. . . . But now all that is far away. . . .

Mélisande. I do not know. . . . —Are you all alone in the room, grandfather?

Arkël. No, there is the physician, besides, who cured thee. . . .

Mélisande. Ah! . . .

Arkël. And then there is still some one else. . . .

Mélisande. Who is it?

Arkël. It is . . . thou must not be frightened. . . . He does not wish thee the least harm, be sure. . . . If thou'rt afraid, he will go away. . . . He is very unhappy. . . .

Mélisande. Who is it?

Arkël. It is thy . . . thy husband. . . . It is Golaud. . . .

Mélisande. Golaud is here? Why does he not come by me?

Golaud. [*Dragging himself toward the bed.*] Mélisande . . . Mélisande. . . .

Mélisande. Is it you, Golaud? I should hardly recognize you any more. . . . It is the evening sunlight in my eyes. . . . Why look you on the walls? You have grown thin and old. . . . Is it a long while since we saw each other?

Golaud. [*To* ARKËL *and the* PHYSICIAN.] Will you withdraw a moment, if you please, if you please? . . . I will leave the door wide open. . . . One moment only. . . . I would say something to her; else I could not die. . . . Will you?—Go clear to the end of the corridor; you can come back at once, at once. . . . Do not refuse me this. . . . I am a wretch. . . . [*Exit* ARKËL *and the* PHYSICIAN.]—Mélisande, hast thou pity on me, as I have pity on thee? . . . Mélisande? . . . Dost thou forgive me, Mélisande? . . .

Mélisande. Yes, yes, I do forgive thee. . . . What must I forgive? . . .

Golaud. I have wrought thee so much ill, Mélisande. . . . I cannot tell thee the ill I have wrought thee. . . . But I see it, I see it so clearly today . . . since the first day. . . . And all I did not know till now leaps in my eyes tonight. . . . And it is all my fault, all that has happened, all that will happen. . . . If I could tell it, thou wouldst see as I do! . . . I see all! I see all! . . . But I loved thee so! . . . I loved thee so! . . . But now there is some one dying. . . . It is I who am dying. . . . And I would know . . . I would ask thee. . . . Thou'lt bear me no ill-will . . . I would . . . The truth must be told to a dying man. . . . He must know the truth, or else he could not sleep. . . . Swearest thou to tell me the truth?

Mélisande. Yes.

Golaud. Didst thou love Pélléas?

Mélisande. Why, yes; I loved him.—Where is he?

Golaud. Thou dost not understand me?—Thou wilt not understand me?—It seems to me . . . it seems to me . . . Well, then, here: I ask thee if thou lovedst him with a forbidden love? . . . Wert thou . . . were you guilty? Say, say, yes, yes, yes! . . .

Mélisande. No, no; we were not guilty.—Why do you ask that?

Golaud. Mélisande! . . . tell me the truth, for the love of God!

Mélisande. Why have I not told the truth?

Golaud. Do not lie so any more, at the moment of death!

Mélisande. Who is dying?—Is it I?

Golaud. Thou, thou! and I, I too, after thee! . . . And we must have the truth. . . . We must have the truth at last, dost thou understand? . . . Tell me all! Tell me all! I forgive thee all! . . .

Mélisande. Why am I going to die?—I did not know it. . . .

Golaud. Thou knowest it now! . . . It is time! It is time! . . . Quick! quick! . . . The truth! the truth! . . .

Mélisande. The truth . . . the truth . . .

Golaud. Where art thou?—Mélisande!—Where art thou?—It is not natural! Mélisande! Where art thou?—Where goest thou? [*Perceiving* ARKËL *and the* PHYSICIAN *at the door of the room.*]—Yes, yes; you may come in. . . . I know nothing; it is useless. . . . It is too late; she is already too far away from us. . . . I shall never know! . . . I shall die here like a blind man! . . .

Arkël. What have you done? You will kill her. . . .

Golaud. I have already killed her. . . .

Arkël. Mélisande. . . .

Mélisande. Is it you, grandfather?

Arkël. Yes, my daughter. . . . What would you have me do?

Mélisande. Is it true that the winter is beginning? . . .

Arkël. Why dost thou ask?

Mélisande. Because it is cold, and there are no more leaves. . . .

Arkël. Thou art cold?—Wilt thou have the windows closed?

Mélisande. No, no, . . . not till the sun be at the bottom of the sea.—It sinks slowly; then it is the winter beginning?

Arkël. Yes.—Thou dost not like the winter?

Mélisande. Oh! no. I am afraid of the cold.—I am so afraid of the great cold. . . .

Arkël. Dost thou feel better?

Mélisande. Yes, yes; I have no longer all those qualms. . . .

Arkël. Wouldst thou see thy child?

Mélisande. What child?

Arkël. Thy child.—Thou art a mother. . . . Thou hast brought a little daughter into the world. . . .

Mélisande. Where is she?

Arkël. Here. . . .

Mélisande. It is strange. . . . I cannot lift my arms to take her. . . .

Arkël. Because you are still very weak. . . . I will hold her myself; look. . . .

Mélisande. She does not laugh. . . . She is little. . . . She is going to weep too. . . . I pity her. . . .

[*The room has been invaded, little by little, by the women servants of the castle, who range themselves in silence along the walls and wait.*]

Golaud. [*Rising abruptly.*] What is the matter?—What are all these women coming here for? . . .

The Physician. It is the servants. . . .

Arkël. Who was it called them?

The Physician. It was not I. . . .

Golaud. Why do you come here?—No one has asked for you. . . . What come you here to do?—But what is it, then?—Answer me! . . .

[*The servants make no answer.*]

Arkël. Do not speak too loud. . . . She is going to sleep; she has closed her eyes. . . .

Golaud. It is not . . . ?

The Physician. No, no; see, she breathes. . . .

Arkël. Her eyes are full of tears.—It is her soul weeping now. . . . Why does she stretch her arms out so?—What would she?

The Physician. It is toward the child, without doubt. . . . It is the struggle of motherhood against . . .

Golaud. At this moment?—At this moment?—You must say. Say! Say! . . .

The Physician. Perhaps.

Golaud. At once? . . . Oh! oh! I must tell her. . . .—Mélisande! Mélisande! . . . Leave me alone! leave me alone with her! . . .

Arkël. No, no; do not come near. . . . Trouble her not. . . . Speak no more to her. . . . You know not what the soul is. . . .

Golaud. It is not my fault! . . . It is not my fault!

Arkël. Hush! . . . Hush! . . . We must speak softly now.—She must not be disturbed. . . . The human soul is very silent. . . . The human soul likes to depart alone. . . . It suffers so timorously. . . . But the sadness, Golaud . . . the sadness of all we see! . . . Oh! oh! oh! . . .

[*At this moment, all the servants fall suddenly on their knees at the back of the chamber.*]

Arkël. [*Turning.*] What is the matter?

The Physician. [*Approaching the bed and feeling the body.*] They are right. . . .

[*A long silence.*]

Arkël. I saw nothing.—Are you sure? . . .

The Physician. Yes, yes.

Arkël. I heard nothing. . . . So quick, so quick! . . . All at once! . . . She goes without a word. . . .

Golaud. [*Sobbing.*] Oh! oh! oh!

Arkël. Do not stay here, Golaud. . . . She must have silence now. . . . Come, come. . . . It is terrible, but it is not your fault. . . . 'Twas a little being, so quiet, so fearful, and so silent. . . . 'Twas a poor little mysterious being, like everybody. . . . She lies there as if she were the big sister of her child. . . . Come, come. . . . My God! My God! . . . I shall never understand it at all. . . . Let us not stay here.—Come; the child must not stay here in this room. . . . She must live now in her place. . . . It is the poor little one's turn.

[*They go out in silence.*]

CURTAIN

MAGDA *

By

HERMANN SUDERMANN

Translated by CHARLES EDWARD AMORY WINSLOW

SUDERMANN BROKE THE WAY IN THE German commercial theater for the *Junger Realismus,* elsewhere known as naturalism; and his *Heimat (Magda)* won world popularity as well. Bernhardt and Duse led the great actresses of the period in popularizing its tinselly heroine in all theatrical centers. Its lasting stageworthiness was shown in its recent New York revival (1926).

As a young radical from provincial East Prussia, Sudermann found in the contrast between life in Berlin and that of his then remote homeland, abundant material for stories, novels, and plays. To an instinct for construction he added a keen perceptiveness of colorful detail and atmosphere, which had become the mania of the naturalist school. He shared also their love for Zola, Ibsen, and the Russian novelists. He remained independent, however, refusing to become either partisan or theorist, and, unlike his fellows, he retained a hearty respect for the workmanship of the French problem play written in the "well-made" manner of Dumas, Augier, and Sardou. To this marked inclination, perhaps, he owed the gradual alienation in his own country and abroad of the more acute critics.

His first play, *Die Ehre (Honor),* produced an immense popular sensation in the very year (1889) in which the naturalist revolters, with Schlaf, Holz, and Hauptmann at their head, opened the Freie Bühne, which was to do for Germany what the Théâtre-Libre had done for France. (For a discussion of this movement see prefaces to *The Fossils* and *The Beaver Coat.*) In *Die Ehre* Sudermann contrasted, with a sharpness peculiar to his genius, the effect upon thought and character of life in Berlin with that of the narrow and restrictive standards of a provincial region like his own homeland. The freshly observed detail rather than the form or subject of the play made it appeal strongly to the young naturalists, who acclaimed it far beyond its deserts. It was even more loudly decried by the conventionally minded public. *Sodoms Ende,* his second, made a much closer approach to pure naturalism. The failure of this play to do more than arouse discussion perhaps explains the quick return in *Heimat* to a more theatrical manner. Reverting to the home-coming theme of *Die Ehre* with its possibilities of contrast, and building his play in Ibsen's fashion upon the results of antecedent action, he heightened his effects for the general public by an almost romantic exaggeration of characters and motives, indulging in *coups de théâtre* and improbabilities of situation like a pre-Ibsenite. He increased the effectiveness of the dual clash at the basis of the play, of daughter against father and of cosmopolitan ways against provincialism, by adding the fascination of a liberating artistic nature, which gave this work a universal appeal that no other play of Sudermann's has had. The fascination was the greater because the artist was an operatic star with infinite possibilities of robes and jewels. Principals as well as the minor characters hardly escape the suggestion of caricature. Sudermann's sure sense of the theater and his structural skill shown in the preparatory first act and brilliant scene climaxes, as well as his more admirable instinct for characterizing detail, are here displayed with more energy and theatrical vitality than in his later plays of superior literary value and greater artistic sincerity.

For an extremely interesting and stimulating comparison of the acting of Duse and Bernhardt in the leading rôle of *Magda,* see Bernard Shaw's *Dramatic Opinions,* vol. 1, p. 134.

HERMANN SUDERMANN

Born 1857, Matzicken, East Prussia.
1875, entered University of Königsberg.
1877, studied in Berlin. Contributor to liberal journals.
1887, *Twilight Tales*, his first book.
1889, *Die Ehre* (*Honor*), his first play, at the Lessing Theater, Berlin.
Died 1928.

PLAYS

1889 *Die Ehre* (translated as *Honor*). 1891 *Sodoms Ende* (*The Destruction of Sodom*). 1893 *Heimat* (translated as *Magda* and *Casa Paterna*). 1895 *Die Schmetterlingsschlacht* (translated as *The Battle of the Butterflies*). 1896 *Morituri* (cycle of one-act plays, translated under the same title): *Teja* (also translated as *Teias*); *Fritzchen* (translated under the same title); *Das Ewig-Männliche* (translated as *The Eternal Masculine*). 1896 *Das Glück im Winkel* (translated as *The Vale of Content*). 1898 *Johannes* (translated under the same title, and as *John* and *John the Baptist*). 1899 *Die drei Reiherfedern* (a legend play, translated as *Three Heron Feathers*). 1900 *Johannisfeuer* (translated as *The Fires of St. John* and *St. John's Fire*). 1902 *Es lebe das Leben* (translated as *The Joy of Living*.) 1903 *Der Sturmgeselle Sokrates* (*Storm-Brother Socrates*). 1905 *Stein unter Steinen* (*Stone Among Stones*). 1905 *Das Blumenboot* (adapted as *Scherzo*). 1907 *Rosen* (cycle of one-act plays, translated as *Roses*): *Die Lichtbänder* (translated as *Streaks of Light*); *Der letzte Besuch* (translated as *The Last Visit*); *Margot* (translated under the same title); *Die ferne Prinzessin* (translated as *The Far-Away Princess*). 1909 *Strandkinder* (*Children of the Strand*). 1911 *Der Bettler von Syrakus* (*The Beggar of Syracuse*). 1912 *Der gute Ruf* (translated as *A Good Reputation*). 1914 *Die Lobgesänge des Claudian* (*Claudian's Songs of Praise*). 1915 *Die entgötterte Welt* (cycle of plays, *The Godless World*): *Die Freundin* (*The Woman Friend*); *Die Gutgeschnittene Ecke* (*The Desirable Corner*); *Das höhere Leben* (*The Higher Life*). 1916 *Der Katzensteg* (adapted from his novel of the same name, *The Cat-walk*). 1920 *Die Raschoffs* (*The Raschoffs*). 1921 *Der Hüter der Schwelle* (one-act play, *The Guardian of the Threshold*). 1921 *Das deutsche Schicksal* (a patriotic dramatic cycle, *German Destiny*): *Heilige Zeit* (*Holy Time*); *Opfer* (*Sacrifice*); *Notruf* (*Cry of Need*). 1923 *Wie die Träumenden* (*Like Those Who Dream*). 1923 *Die Denkmalsweihe* (unpublished in German, but translated as *The Unveiling*). 1925 *Der Hasenfellhändler* (*The Rabbit Skin Dealer*).

WRITINGS ABOUT THE DRAMA

Verrohung der Theaterkritik, 1902. *Die Sturmgeselle*n, 1903.

MAGDA

Characters

SCHWARTZE, *Lieutenant-Colonel on half-pay.*
MAGDA, MARIE, } *his children by his first wife.*
AUGUSTA, *born* VON WENDLOWSKI, *his second wife.*
FRANZISKA VON WENDLOWSKI, *her sister.*
MAX VON WENDLOWSKI, *Lieutenant, their nephew.*
HEFFTERDINGT, *Pastor of St. Mary's.*
DR. VON KELLER, *Councillor.*
BECKMANN, *Professor Emeritus.*
VON KLEBS, *Major-General on half-pay.*
MRS. VON KLEBS.
MRS. JUSTICE ELLRICH.
MRS. SCHUMANN.
THERESA, *maidservant of the Schwartze family.*

Place. The principal city of a province. *Time.* The present.

ACT FIRST

SCENE.—*Living-room in the house of* LIEUTENANT-COLONEL SCHWARTZE, *furnished in simple and old-fashioned style. Left, at back, a glass door with white curtains through which the dining-room is seen. There is also a hall door, through which a staircase to the upper story is visible. Right, a corner window, with white curtains, surrounded by ivy. Left, a door to the* LIEUTENANT-COLONEL'S *room. Steel engravings of a religious and patriotic character, in tarnished gold frames, photographs of military groups, and cases of butterflies on the walls. Right, over the sofa, among other pictures, is the portrait of the first Mrs. Schwartze, young and charming, in the costume of the 'sixties. Behind the sofa, an old-fashioned desk. Before the window, a small table with work-box and hand sewing-machine. At the back, between the doors, an old-fashioned tall clock. In the left-hand corner, a stand with dried grasses; in front, a table with a small aquarium. Left, in front, a corner sofa with a small pipe-cupboard behind it. A stove with a stuffed bird on it; and behind, a bookcase with a bust of the old Emperor William.*

[MARIE *and* THERESA *discovered.* THERESA *at the door.* MARIE *is occupied with the sewing-machine.*]

Theresa. Miss Marie!

Marie. Well!

Theresa. Is your father still lying down?

Marie. What's the matter? Has anyone called?

Theresa. No, but—— There! Look at that! [*Producing a magnificent mass of flowers.*]

Marie. Good Heavens! Take it to my room quickly, or papa—— But, Theresa, when the first came yesterday, weren't you told not to let any more be left?

Theresa. I'd have sent the florist's boy away if I could, but I was up on the ladder fixing the flag, and he laid it down and was gone before I could stop him. My, my, though, they're beautiful! and if I might make a guess, the Lieutenant——

Marie. You may not make a guess.

Theresa. All right, all right. Oh, I know what I wanted to ask. Does the flag hang well? [MARIE *looks out, and nods assent.*] The whole town is full of flags and flowers, and the most expensive tapestries are hung out of the windows. One would think it was the King's birthday. And all this fuss is about a stupid Music Festival! What is this Music Festival, Miss Marie? Is it different from a choral festival?

Marie. Yes, indeed.

Theresa. Is it better?

Marie. Oh, much better!

Theresa. Oh, well, if it's better—— [*A knock.*]

Marie. Come in! [*Enter* MAX.]

Theresa. Well, *now* I suppose I can leave the flowers. [*Exit* THERESA, *laughing.*]

Marie. You ought to be ashamed of yourself, Max.

Max. What on earth do you mean?

Marie. Aren't these flowers yours?

Max. Good Heavens! I can afford a few pennies for a bunch of violets once in a while, but this—— Oh, no!

Marie. Nor yesterday's?

Max. No, nor yesterday's. [MARIE *rings.*] [*Enter* THERESA.]

Marie. Please throw these flowers away.

Theresa. What! Throw those beautiful flowers away?

Marie. You are right. The pastor would say, "If God's gifts do not please us, we must at least take care that they give pleasure to others." Wouldn't he?

Max. Probably he would.

Marie. Then you had better take them back to the florist's. Did they come from Zimmermann's? [THERESA *nods.*] Well, we'll sell them if we can, and give the money to Pastor Heffterdingt for his hospital.

Theresa. Shall I go now?

Marie. After you have made the coffee. I'll serve it myself. [*Exit* THERESA.] These flowers are an insult! I need not tell you, Max, that I have given no one the shadow of an excuse for such a thing.

Max. I'm very sure of that.

Marie. And papa was so angry. He simply stormed. And I was quiet because I suspected it was you. If he got hold of the poor fellow, it would go hard with him.

Max. Do you think it would be any better if I got hold of him?

Marie. What rights have you in the case?

Max. Marie! [*Takes her hand.*]

Marie. [*Gently disengaging herself.*] Oh, Max, please—not that. You know every corner of my heart. But we must think of the proprieties.

Max. Proprieties! Oh, pshaw!

Marie. Well, you know what a world we live in. Here, everyone is afraid of every one else because each depends upon the good opinion of the other. If a few anonymous flowers can make me talked of, how much more——

Max. Oh, yes, I know.

Marie. [*Laying her hand on his shoulder.*] Max, you'll speak again to Aunt Frankie, won't you, about the guaranty[1] of your income?

Max. I have already.

Marie. Well?

Max. [*Shrugging his shoulders.*] As long as she lives, not a penny.

Marie. Then there's only one person who can help us.

[1] Without which officers in the German army might not marry.

Max. Your father?

Marie. No. For Heaven's sake, don't let him hear of it. He might forbid you the house.

Max. What has he against me?

Marie. You know how he has been since our misfortune. He feels that there is a blot to be wiped out; and especially now, when the whole town echoes with music—when everything recalls Magda.

Max. What if she should come back, some day?

Marie. After twelve years? She will never come. [*Weeps.*]

Max. Marie!

Marie. You're right, you're right. I will put it away from me.

Max. But who is the one person who can help us?

Marie. Why, the pastor!

Max. Yes, yes, he might.

Marie. He can do everything. He stirs your very heart—as if—— And then he seems like a kind of relation. He should have been my brother-in-law.

Max. Yes, but she wouldn't have it so.

Marie. Don't speak angrily, Max. She must have made atonement. [*A ring.*] Oh, perhaps this is he.

Max. No, no, I forgot to tell you. Councillor von Keller asked me to bring him here today.

Marie. What does he want?

Max. He wants to interest himself in the missions—no, it's in our home work particularly, I think. I don't know—— Well, at any rate, he wants to come to the committee meeting tomorrow.

Marie. I'll call father and mother. [*Enter* THERESA *with a card.*] Show him in. [*Exit* THERESA.] Entertain him until I come back. [*Gives him her hand.*] And we'll talk again about the pastor some other time?

Max. In spite of the proprieties?

Marie. Oh, Max, I've been too forward! Haven't I?

Max. Marie!

Marie. No, no—we won't speak of it. Good-by. [*Exit* MARIE.]

[*Enter* VON KELLER.]

Max. You must content yourself with me for a few minutes, my dear Von Keller. [*They shake hands.*]

Von Keller. With pleasure, my good sir, with pleasure. [*Sits.*] How our little town is changed by the festival! It really seems as if we were in the great world.

Max. [*Laughing.*] I advise you not to say that aloud.

Von Keller. What did I say? I assure you

I did not mean anything. If such a misunderstanding got abroad——

Max. You have nothing to fear from me!

Von Keller. Oh, of course not. Ah, how much better it would be to know nothing of the outer world!

Max. How long were you away?

Von Keller. Five years, with examinations and being sent down to commissioners and all that. Well, now I am back again. I drink home-brewed beer; I patronize local tailors; I have even, with a noble fearlessness of death, eaten the deer-steak of the season; and this I call pleasure! Yes, youth, travel, and women are good things; but the world must be ruled, and sober men are needed. Your time will come some day. The years of honor are approaching. Yes, yes, especially when one joins the ecclesiastical courts.

Max. Are you going to do that?

Von Keller. I think of it. And to be at one with those of the cloth—I speak quite openly with you—it is worth my while, in short, to interest myself in religious questions. I have of late in my speeches, as perhaps you know, taken this position; and as for the connections which this household has —let me tell you I am proud of them.

Max. You might have been proud long ago.

Von Keller. Excuse me, am I over-sensitive? Or do I read a reproach in your words?

Max. Not quite that, but—if you will pardon me, it has sometimes appeared—and not to me alone—as if you avoided the houses where my uncle's family were to be found.

Von Keller. And my presence here now—does not that prove the contrary?

Max. Exactly. And therefore I too will speak very frankly. You were the last person to meet my lost cousin, Magda.

Von Keller. [*Confused.*] Who says——

Max. You yourself have spoken of it, I am told. You met her with my friend Heydebrand when he was at the military academy.

Von Keller. Yes, yes, it's true.

Max. It was wrong of me not to ask you about her openly, but you will probably understand my reticence. I feel almost as if I belonged to this family and I feared to learn something which might disgrace it.

Von Keller. Oh, not at all. not in the least. It was like this. When I was in Berlin for the State Examinations, I saw one day on Leipsic Street a familiar face—a home face, if I may say so. You know what that is when one is far away. Well, we spoke to each other. I learned that she was studying to sing in opera, and that for this purpose she had left her home.

Max. Not exactly. She left home to be companion to an old lady. [*Hesitates.*] There was a difference with her father.

Von Keller. A love affair?

Max. In a way. Her father supported the suitor and told her to obey or leave his house.

Von Keller. And she went away?

Max. Yes. Then, a year later, when she wrote that she was going on the stage, it made the breach complete. But what else did you hear?

Von Keller. That's all.

Max. Nothing else?

Von Keller. Well, well—I met her once or twice at the opera-house where she had a pass.

Max. And you know absolutely nothing of her life?

Von Keller. [*With a shrug.*] Have you heard nothing from her?

Max. Nothing at all. Well, at any rate, I am grateful to you. I beg you, however, not to mention the meeting to my uncle, unless he asks you about it directly. He knows of it, of course, but the name of the lost daughter is never mentioned in this house.

Von Keller. Oh, I have tact enough not to do that.

Max. And what do you think has become of her?

Von Keller. Oh, music is a lottery. Ten thousand blanks and one prize. A host of beginners and but one who makes a career. If one becomes a Patti or a Sembrich, or, to come down to our own Festival——

[*Enter* SCHWARTZE *and* MRS. SCHWARTZE.]

Schwartze. [*Shaking hands.*] Welcome to my house! Councillor von Keller, my wife.

Mrs. Schwartze. Pray sit down.

Von Keller. I should not have dared, madam, to ask the honor of this introduction had I not wished so strongly to share in the good and useful work which centers here. My purpose may excuse my temerity.

Schwartze. You're very kind; but you do us too much honor. If you seek the center of the whole movement, Pastor Heffterdingt is the man. He inspires all; he controls all; he——

Mrs. Schwartze. Do you know our pastor, sir?

Von Keller. I have heard him speak many times, dear lady, and have admired equally the sincerity of his convictions and his naïve faith in human nature. But I cannot comprehend the influence he exerts.

Mrs. Schwartze. You will find it out. He is so plain and simple that one hardly realizes what a man he is. He brings everyone round.

Von Keller. I am almost converted already, dear lady.

Schwartze. As for us here, all I can do is to give these weak and useless hands to help on the great work. It's only right that an old soldier should dedicate the little strength left him by the throne to the service of the altar. Those are the two causes to fight for.

Von Keller. That's a great thought!

Schwartze. Thanks, thanks, but no more of this. Ah, ten years ago, when they gave me my discharge, I was a devil of a fellow. Max, doesn't my old battalion still tremble at my name?

Max. That they do, uncle.

Schwartze. Ah, that is one thing you escape in the civil service—being laid on the shelf without any fault of your own—without the shadow of a fault. Then there came a slight stroke of apoplexy. See how my hand trembles now! And what had I to look forward to? It was then that my young friend, Heffterdingt, showed me the way, through work and prayer, to a new youth. Without him I never should have found it.

Mrs. Schwartze. You mustn't believe all he says, Mr. von Keller. If he didn't always depreciate himself, he would be better thought of in the highest circles.

Von Keller. High and low, madam, everywhere your husband is known and honored.

Schwartze. [*Lighting up.*] Indeed? Ah, well, no vanity. No, no, that is the moth that corrupts.

Mrs. Schwartze. Is it really so wrong to wish for a little honor?

Von Keller. Oh!

Schwartze. What is honor? You would call it being led up the room by the governor, or being asked to tea at the castle when the royal family is here.

Mrs. Schwartze. You know very well that the latter honor has never fallen to my lot.

Schwartze. Oh, yes, pardon me. I knew your weak spot. I should have avoided it.

Mrs. Schwartze. Yes, just think, Councillor, Mrs. Fanny Hirschfeld of the Children's Hospital was invited, and I was not.

Von Keller. [*Deprecatingly.*] Oh!

Schwartze. [*Laughing, and stroking her head.*] Ah, the moth that corrupts, the moth that corrupts! [*Enter* MARIE *with the coffee. She bows in a friendly way to* VON KELLER.] Herr von Keller, my daughter—my only daughter.

Von Keller. I've already had the pleasure.

Marie. I can't offer you a hand for welcome, Dr. Von Keller, but you may have a cup of coffee instead.

Von Keller. [*Helping himself and looking at the others.*] I am very fortunate in being treated like an old acquaintance of the family.

Schwartze. As far as we are concerned, you shall become not only an acquaintance but a friend. And that is no conventional politeness, Councillor; for I know you, and in these times, when all the ties of morality and authority seem strained to bursting, it is doubly necessary that those who stand for the good old patriarchal order should hold together.

Von Keller. Very true, very true indeed. One doesn't hear such sentiments as that in the world in general, where modern ideas pass current for small change.

Schwartze. Modern ideas! Oh, pshaw! I know them. But come into the quiet homes where are bred brave soldiers and virtuous wives. There you'll hear no talk about heredity, no arguments about individuality, no scandalous gossip. There modern ideas have no foothold, for it is there that the life and strength of the Fatherland abide. Look at this home! There is no luxury—hardly even what you call good taste—faded rugs, birchen chairs, old pictures; and yet when you see the beams of the western sun pour through the white curtains and lie with such a loving touch on the old room, does not something say to you, "Here dwells true happiness"?

[VON KELLER *nods with conviction.*]

Schwartze. [*Broodingly.*] And here it might have dwelt!

Marie. [*Hurrying to him.*] Papa!

Schwartze. Yes, yes, I know. Well, in this house rules old-fashioned paternal authority. And it shall rule as long as I live. And am I therefore a tyrant? Tell me. You ought to know.

Marie. You're the best, the dearest——

Mrs. Schwartze. He is so excitable, you see, Councillor.

Schwartze. Have you not been well brought up? And shall we not hold together, we three? But the age goes on planting rebellion in children's hearts, putting mistrust between man and wife [*rises*], and it will never be satisfied till the last roof-tree smokes in ruins, and men wander about the streets, fearful and alone, like homeless curs. [*Sinks back exhausted.*]

Mrs. Schwartze. You ought not to get so wrought up, papa. You know it is bad for you. [MAX *makes a sign to* VON KELLER.]

Von Keller. Shall I go? [MAX *nods.*] This is an interesting subject to develop, Colonel.

I must say I think perhaps you are a little severe. But my time——

Schwartze. Severe? Ah, well, don't think ill of an old man for speaking a little too hotly.

Von Keller. Ah, sir, heat is the badge of youth. I believe I am a graybeard beside you.

Schwartze. No, no. [*Presses his hand.*]

Von Keller. Madam! Miss Marie! [*Exit.* MAX *follows him.*]

Schwartze. Greet the battalion for me, my boy.

Max. I will, dear uncle. [*Exit.*]

Mrs. Schwartze. A very agreeable man.

Marie. Almost too agreeable.

Schwartze. You are speaking of our guest! [MRS. SCHWARTZE *makes* MARIE *a sign to be careful.*]

Marie. Will you have your pipe, papa?

Schwartze. Yes, dear.

Mrs. Schwartze. The gentlemen of the card-club will be here soon. How lucky that we didn't eat the haunch of venison Sunday! I've ordered some red wine for the General, too. I paid three marks; that's not too dear, is it?

Schwartze. Not if it's good. Is your sister coming today?

Mrs. Schwartze. I think so.

Schwartze. She was asked to the Governor's yesterday, wasn't she?

Mrs. Schwartze. [*Sighing.*] Yes.

Schwartze. And we were not. Poor thing! She must look out for me today if she boasts. [*Aside.*] Old cat!

Marie. [*Kneels before him, lighting his pipe.*] Be good, father dear. What harm does it do you?

Schwartze. Yes, yes, darling. I'll be good. But my heart is sore. [*Bell rings.* MARIE *hurries out.*]

Mrs. Schwartze. Here they are.

[*Enter* MAJOR-GENERAL VON KLEBS, PROFESSOR BECKMANN, *and* MARIE.]

Von Klebs. My humblest respects to the ladies. Ah, my dear madam! [*Kisses her hand.*]

Mrs. Schwartze. Make yourselves at home, gentlemen.

Von Klebs. Ha, my dear Colonel, hearty as ever? All ready for the fray, little one? Now we are all right. But we were almost too late. We were caught in the Music Festival crowd. Such a confusion! I was bringing the schoolmaster along, and just as we passed by the German House, there was a great crush of people, gaping as if there were a princess at the least. And what do you suppose it was? A singer! These are really what one may call goings-on. All this fuss about a singer! What do they call the person?

Beckmann. Ah, General, we seem to be in a strange land today.

Von Klebs. We are under a curse, my dear madam. We are bearing a penance.

[*They sit at a card table.*]

Beckmann. But you must know dall' Orto, the great Italian Wagner singer. We are very fortunate in getting her for the festival. If she were not here——

Von Klebs. Well, well, what if she were not? Eh? I hoped that our strictly moral circle, at least, would hold itself aloof from all this. But since the Governor gives receptions in the lady's honor! And, best of all, to cap the climax, who do you think was standing today among the enthusiasts, craning his neck like the rest? You'll never guess. It's too inconceivable. The pastor!

Schwartze. The pastor?

Von Klebs. Yes, our pastor.

Schwartze. How extraordinary!

Von Klebs. Now, I ask you, what did he want there? And what did the others want there? And what good is the whole festival?

Beckmann. I should think that the cultivation of the faculty of the ideal among the people was an object——

Von Klebs. The way to cultivate the faculty of the ideal is to found a Soldiers' Union.

Schwartze. But, General, everyone isn't so lucky as to be a soldier.

Von Klebs. [*Sorting his cards.*] Well, we have been, Colonel. I know no one, I wish to know no one, who has not been a soldier. And all this so-called Art—what good does it do?

Beckmann. Art raises the moral tone of the people.

Von Klebs. There we have it, madam! I tell you Art is a mere invention of those who are afraid to be soldiers to gain an important position for themselves. I pass.

Schwartze. I pass.

Beckmann. And will you maintain that Art— I have the nine of spades.

[*Bell rings. Exit* MARIE. VON KLEBS *makes an impatient movement.* SCHWARTZE *quiets him. They begin to play. Enter* FRANZISKA, *followed by the* PASTOR *and* MARIE.]

Von Klebs. Ah, Miss Franziska! [*Aside.*] That is the end of us!

Schwartze. No, no, we'll send her into the garden.

Franziska. [*Throwing herself into a chair.*] Oh, I am so hot! I must get my breath. Pray don't put yourself out, General.

Beckmann. Nine of spades!

Von Klebs. Hello, here's the pastor too!

Heffterdingt. Good day to you! [*He shakes hands with each.*]

Von Klebs. How long have you been running after the singers, Pastor?

Heffterdingt. What? Oh, yes. Yes, I am running after singers. That's my occupation now.

Schwartze. You can play with our card-party though, can't you?

Heffterdingt. Unfortunately, no. I must, on the contrary, ask for a few serious words with you, my dear sir.

Von Klebs. Ah, but you'll put it off, won't you, Pastor?

Franziska. Oh, for Heaven's sake! It's so important. There must be no delay.

Schwartze. Is my sister-in-law in it, too?

Franziska. Very much so.

Von Klebs. Oh, well, we can go away again.

Mrs. Schwartze. Oh, we shouldn't like that at all.

Schwartze. If it were not you, dear pastor, who separated us!

Mrs. Schwartze. But perhaps, Marie, the gentlemen would be willing to take a turn with you in the garden.

Von Klebs. Certainly! That's good! That's famous! That's what we'll do! Miss Marie, be so good as to lead the way.

Beckmann. Shall we leave the cards as they lie?

Von Klebs. Yes, you have the nine of spades. Come on.

[*Exit* VON KLEBS, BECKMANN, *and* MARIE.]

Schwartze. Well?

Franziska. Good Lord, don't you see how upset I am? You might at least give me a glass of water. [MRS. SCHWARTZE *brings it.*]

Heffterdingt. Will you promise me, my dear sir, that whatever may happen you will preserve your calmness? You may believe me, much depends upon it.

Schwartze. Yes, yes; but what——

Heffterdingt. Miss Franziska will tell you better.

Franziska. [*After drinking the water.*] This is a day indeed! Fate is avenging me. This man has for years outraged my holiest feelings, but today I can heap coals of fire on his head. [*Moved.*] Brother-in-law, give me your hand. Sister, yours.

Heffterdingt. Pardon me, dear Miss Franziska. I think your news is so important that——

Franziska. [*Melting.*] Don't be angry, don't be angry. I am so upset! Well, yesterday I was at the Governor's. Only the nobility and the most important people were asked. You weren't asked?

Schwartze. [*Angrily.*] No.

Franziska. I did not mean to offend you. Oh, I am so upset! [*Suppressing a sob at a sign from the* PASTOR.] Yes, yes, yes. I had on my yellow silk dress with the Brussels lace—you know I've had the train shortened. Well, as I stepped into the room—whom do you think I saw?

Schwartze. Well, well, who?

Franziska. [*Sobbing.*] Your child! Magdalene!

[SCHWARTZE *staggers, and is supported by the* PASTOR. MRS. SCHWARTZE *cries out. A pause.*]

Schwartze. Pastor?

Heffterdingt. It is true.

Schwartze. [*Standing up.*] Magdalene is no longer my child.

Franziska. Ah, just wait. If you listen, you'll look at it in quite another light. Such a child you will welcome with open arms.

Schwartze. Magdalene is no longer my child.

Heffterdingt. But you may at least hear the circumstances.

Schwartze. [*Dazed.*] Yes, I suppose so.

Franziska. [*At a sign from* HEFFTERDINGT.] Well, the great dining-hall was crammed. They were almost all strangers. Then I saw his Excellency coming down the room. And on his arm was a lady——

Mrs. Schwartze. On his Excellency's arm?

Franziska. With dark hair, and very proud and tall—and around her a crowd of men just like the circle about royalty—and chatting and laughing. And anyone to whom she spoke seemed as happy as if it were the Princess. And she wore half a dozen orders, and an orange band with a medal about her neck. I was wondering what royal personage it could be—when she turned half around—and —I knew Magda's eyes!

Schwartze. Impossible!

Franziska. That is what I saw!

Heffterdingt. My dear Colonel, it is true.

Schwartze. If she—[*Clasping his hands.*] At least she has not fallen! She has not fallen! Father in Heaven, Thou hast kept her safely!

Mrs. Schwartze. And what is she, to have such honor—

Heffterdingt. She has become a great singer, and calls herself, in Italian, Maddalene dall' Orto.

Mrs. Schwartze. Listen, listen, Leopold, the famous singer of whom the papers are so full is our child!

Schwartze. Magda is no longer my child.

Heffterdingt. Is that your fixed resolve?

Franziska. What sort of heart have you? You ought to imitate me. She offended me as only she could—the little wretch! That is, then she was a little wretch. But now—well, she did not look at me; but if she had——

Mrs. Schwartze. Leopold, she was on His Excellency's arm!

Schwartze. I tell you, and you—and you, too, Pastor—that I would rather have seen her lying in rags and tatters at my feet and begging for forgiveness. For then I should have known that she was still, at heart, my child. But why has she come back here? The world was large enough for her triumph. Why should she rob this humble provincial nest of ours? I know why. To show her miserable father how far one can rise in the world by treading filial duty into the dust—that is her intention. Pride and arrogance speak in her, and nothing else.

Heffterdingt. My dear Colonel, I might ask, what speaks in you? A father's love? You could make no pretence to that. Your rights? I think rather it would be your right to rejoice in the good fortune of your child. Offended custom? I don't know— Your daughter has done so much through her own strength that even offended custom might at least condone it. It appears to me that pride and arrogance speak in you—and nothing else.

Schwartze. [*Angrily.*] Pastor!

Heffterdingt. Oh, don't be angry—there is no need of that. When I have something to say, I must say it, mustn't I? I might almost think that it displeased you that she has climbed so high in spite of you. Your pride demands something to forgive, and you are angry because there is nothing to be forgiven. And now, let me ask you, do you seriously wish that she had found her way home, lost and ruined? Do you dare answer for such a wish before the throne of God? [*A silence.*] No, my dear old friend. You have often, in jest, called me your good angel; let me be so once, in reality. Come with me—now—today.

Franziska. If you'd only seen—— [HEFFTERDINGT *stops her.*]

Schwartze. Has she made the slightest effort to approach her parents? Has she thought of her home with one throb of love? Who will vouch for it that my outstretched hand will not be repulsed with scorn?

Heffterdingt. I will vouch for it.

Schwartze. You? You, above all, have had a proof of her untamable pride.

Heffterdingt. [*With embarrassment.*] You should not have reminded me of that.

[*Enter* MARIE *with flowers, and* THERESA.]

Marie. Papa, papa, listen to what Theresa— Oh! am I interrupting?

Schwartze. [*Pulling himself together.*] What is it?

Marie. Today I got some more flowers; and when I sent Theresa back to the florist's, she found out it was not a man, but a lady, who had ordered them. And she couldn't sell them again; so she brought them back. [*The others exchange glances.*]

Heffterdingt. Tell me, Theresa, did they describe this lady to you?

Theresa. She was tall, with great dark eyes, and there was something very distinguished and foreign about her.

Heffterdingt. [*Leads* MARIE *to the back of the stage, and lays his hand on* SCHWARTZE'S *arm.*] You asked for a token of love!

Schwartze. [*Staring at the flowers.*] From her!

Mrs. Schwartze. They must have cost a small fortune!

Marie. Theresa has something else very wonderful to tell, too.

Heffterdingt. What is it, Theresa? Quick!

Theresa. If the pastor wishes it. When I came back, the porter told me that last evening in the twilight a carriage stopped before the door; there was a lady inside. She didn't get out, but kept watching all the windows of our house where there were lights. And when he went out to ask what she wanted, she said something to her coachman, and they were gone! [*All show signs of astonishment.*]

Heffterdingt. That's all, Theresa.

[*Exit* THERESA.]

Heffterdingt. Pardon us, dear Miss Marie, if we treat you once more like a child, and ask you to leave us alone for a moment.

Marie. I am so frightened at all this, Pastor. [*Imploringly.*] Papa?

Schwartze. What is it, child?

Marie. Papa, papa, do you know who this lady is?

Schwartze. I? No. I can only guess.

Marie. [*Bursting out.*] Magdalene—Magda! Magda is here! [*Falling on her knees.*] Oh, you will forgive her?

Schwartze. Get up, my child. Your sister is far above my poor forgiveness.

Heffterdingt. She is not above your love.

Marie. Magda is here! Magda herself is here! [*Throws her arms about her mother's neck, weeping.*]

Franziska. Won't anyone bring me a glass of water? I am so upset!

Heffterdingt. Are you quite resolved? [SCHWARTZE *remains motionless.*] Will you let her go on her way without——

Schwartze. That would be best.

Heffterdingt. How will it be with you if in your death-hour a longing for your lost child comes upon you, and all you can say to yourself is, "She stood before my door and I would not open it"?

Schwartze. [*Shaken and half convinced.*] What would you have me do? Must I abase myself before my runaway child?

Heffterdingt. No, you shall not do that. I—I—will go to her.

Schwartze. You? Pastor—you?

Heffterdingt. This afternoon I waited before her hotel to see if Miss Franziska had not been mistaken. At a quarter to four she came out of the house and got into her carriage.

Marie. You saw her?

Mrs. Schwartze. How did she look? What did she have on?

Heffterdingt. The performance began at four, and must be almost over now. I will wait for her again at the hotel, and will tell her that she will find your arms open to her. May I?

Marie. Yes, yes, papa, won't you let him?

Mrs. Schwartze. Just think with whom your daughter——

Schwartze. Will you swear to me that no weak and personal motives are mixed with your intention—that you do what you do in the name of our Lord and Saviour?

Heffterdingt. I swear it!

Schwartze. Then God's will be done. [MARIE *gives a cry of joy.* HEFFTERDINGT *presses* SCHWARTZE'S *hand.*]

Schwartze. [*Holding his hand, speaking softly.*] The way will be hard for you, I know. Your lost youth—your pride——

Heffterdingt. Dear Colonel, I begin to think that pride is a very poor sort of thing. It really profits us little to have it always in our mouths. I am giving back a daughter to an old father. I am giving back a home to an erring soul. That, I think, is enough. [*Exit.* MARIE *throws herself on her father's breast, laughing and crying.*]

CURTAIN

ACT SECOND

SCENE *same as* ACT FIRST. *It is evening; only a slight glow of sunset still shines through the windows.*

[MARIE *discovered at the window. Enter* THERESA, *bringing in a lighted lamp.*]

Theresa. Miss Marie! Miss Marie!—What is she staring at all the time? Miss Marie!

Marie. [*Staring.*] What do you want?

Theresa. Shall I lay the supper?

Marie. Not yet.

Theresa. It's half-past seven.

Marie. And he left at half-past six. The performance must have been over long ago. She will not come.

Theresa. Who? Is anyone coming to supper?

Marie. No, no, no. [*As* THERESA *is going.*] Theresa! do you suppose you could pick a couple of bouquets in the garden?

Theresa. I might try, but I couldn't tell what I was getting. It's almost pitch dark.

Marie. Yes, yes. You may go.

Theresa. Shall I try to pick the flowers, or——

Marie. No—thank you, no.

Theresa. [*Aside.*] What is the matter with her? [*Exit.*]

[*Enter* MRS. SCHWARTZE.]

Mrs. Schwartze. Well, Marie, whatever happens I've put on my other cap—the one with the ribbons. Is it straight?

Marie. Yes, mamma dear, very nice.

Mrs. Schwartze. Hasn't Aunt Frankie come up yet?

Marie. No.

Mrs. Schwartze. Heavens! I forgot the two gentlemen entirely. And papa has locked himself up, and will hear nothing and see nothing. Oh, if the General should be offended! It is our most aristocratic connection. That would be a misfortune indeed.

Marie. Oh, mamma dear, when he hears what is the matter!

Mrs. Schwartze. Yes, yes, I know. And the pastor has not come either. Marie, one minute. If she should ask you——

Marie. Who?

Mrs. Schwartze. Why, Magda.

Marie. Magda!

Mrs. Schwartze. What am I to you, Marie? They call it step-mother. I'm more than that, am I not?

Marie. Certainly, mamma dear.

Mrs. Schwartze. You see, *then* I could not get used to having two such big daughters. But it's all right now? [MARIE *nods.*] And we do love each other?

Marie. Very much, mamma dear. [*She kisses her.*] [*Enter* FRANZISKA.]

Franziska. [*Irritably.*] One's always disturbing these affecting tableaux!

Mrs. Schwartze. What did the General say?

Franziska. The General? H'm, he was angry enough. "To leave us alone for an hour and a half, that's nice courtesy," he said. And I think myself——

Mrs. Schwartze. [*To* MARIE, *very sadly.*] There, what did I tell you?

Franziska. Well, this time I smoothed the thing over, so that the gentlemen went away in a good humor.

Mrs. Schwartze. Really! Oh, I thank you, Frankie, a thousand times.

Franziska. Yes, I'm good enough to run errands and play the scullery-maid; but when it comes to being one of the family, an old aunt with her heart full of love——

Marie. Who has offended you, Aunt Frankie?

Franziska. Yes, that's very fine. But a little while ago, when I was so upset, no one troubled himself about me one bit. To guarantee an income so that our little miss can be married, I am——

Marie. Aunt Frankie!

Franziska. But as long as I live——

Mrs. Schwartze. What are you talking about?

Franziska. We know, we two. And today. Who brought back your daughter to you?

Mrs. Schwartze. But she hasn't yet——

Franziska. I brought back your daughter to you. And who thanks me for it? And who recognizes that I have pardoned her? For I have pardoned her [*weeping*] everything!

[*Enter* THERESA, *in great excitement.*]

Marie. What is it, Theresa?

Theresa. I am so frightened——

Marie. What's the matter?

Theresa. The carriage——

Marie. What carriage?

Theresa. The same as last night.

Marie. Is it there? Is it there? [*Runs to the window.*] Mamma, mamma, come, she's there—the carriage——

Mrs. Schwartze. Why, there *is* a carriage.

Marie. [*Beating on the door at the left.*] Papa, papa! Come quickly, be merciful, come quickly!

[*Exit* THERESA *at a sign from* FRANZISKA.]

[*Enter* SCHWARTZE.]

Schwartze. What's the matter?

Marie. Magda—the carriage!

Schwartze. Good God! [*Hurries to the window.*]

Marie. Look—look! She's standing up! She's trying to look into the windows. [*Clapping her hands.*] Papa! papa!

Schwartze. What is it you have to say?

Marie. [*Frightened.*] I? Nothing.

Schwartze. Perhaps you were going to say, "She stood before your door and you would not open it." Eh?

Marie. Yes, yes.

Schwartze. Do you hear, wife? She stands before our door. Shall we—in spite of our pride—shall we call her in?

Mrs. Schwartze. Oh, Leopold, since everybody thinks so much of her——

Marie. Ah! She's driving away!

Schwartze. No, no, she's not. Come, we will bring her to you.

Franziska. Yes, yes, bring her to me, too.

[*Exit* SCHWARTZE *and* MRS. SCHWARTZE.]

Marie. She's sitting back again! If only the carriage doesn't— What a long time they are! They must have got downstairs. [*Frightened, almost beside herself.*] There—there—oh, don't go away! Magda! Magda!

Franziska. Don't scream so! What's the matter?

Marie. She's looking round. She's seen them. She's stopping. She's bursting open the door. She's jumped out! Now! Now! She's in father's arms! [*Covers her face and sobs.*] Oh, Aunt Frankie! Aunt Frankie!

Franziska. What else could a father do? Since I have forgiven her, he could not—he could not hold out——

Marie. She's between father and mother. Oh, how grand she is! She's coming—she's coming. What a homely little thing I shall seem beside her! Oh, I am so frightened! [*Leans against the wall, left. A pause. Voices of* MAGDA *and her parents are heard outside.*]

[*Enter* MAGDA, *brilliantly dressed, with a large mantle, and a Spanish veil on her head. She embraces* MARIE.]

Magda. My puss! My little one! How my little one has grown! My pet—my—[*kissing her passionately.*] But what's the matter? You're dizzy. Come, sit down. No, no, please sit down. Now. Yes, you must. [*Places* MARIE *in an arm-chair.*] Dear little hands, dear little hands! [*Kneels before her, kissing and stroking her hands.*] But they're rough and red, and my darling is pale. There are rings round her eyes.

Schwartze. [*Lays his hand lightly on her shoulder.*] Magda, we are here too.

Magda. Yes, yes—I'm entirely—[*Standing up, affectionately.*] Dear old papa! How white you have become! Dear papa! [*Taking his hand.*] But what's the matter with your hand? It's trembling.

Schwartze. Nothing, my child. Don't ask about it.

Magda. H'm—and you've grown handsomer with the years. I can't look at you enough. I shall be very proud with such a handsome papa. But she must get better [*indicating* MARIE]. She's as white as milk. Do you take iron? Eh? You must take iron. [*Tenderly.*] Just to think that I am at home! It seems like a fairy tale. It was a capital idea of yours to call me back without any explanations—*senza complimenti*—for we've outgrown those silly misunderstandings long ago.

Schwarte. Misunderstandings!

Magda. I came near driving away. Would not that have been bad of me? But you must acknowledge, I have scratched at the door—very quietly, very modestly—like Lady when she had run away. Where is Lady? Her place is empty. [*Whistles.*]

Mrs. Schwartze. Why, she's been dead seven years!

Magda. Ah, *povera bestia*—yes, I forgot. And, mamma!—yes, mamma! I haven't looked at you yet. How pretty you've grown! You used to have an air of belated youth about you that was not becoming. But now you're a dear, old little mother. One wants to lay one's head quietly in your lap. I will, too. It'll do me good. Ah! what fine quarrels we used to have! I was a contrary little beast. And you held up your end. But now we'll smoke the pipe of peace, sha'n't we?

Mrs. Schwartze. You're joking with me, Magda.

Magda. Sha'n't I? Mayn't I? There, there—pure love, pure love. We will have nothing but love. We shall be the best of friends.

Franziska. [*Who has for a long time tried to attract attention.*] And we also, eh, my dear Magda?

Magda. Tiens, tiens! [*Examines her critically through her lorgnette.*] Same as ever. Always active? Always, as of old, the center of the family?

Franziska. Oh——

Magda. Well, give us your hand! There. I never could bear you, and shall never learn, I'm afraid. That runs in the blood, doesn't it?

Franziska. I have already forgiven you.

Magda. Really! Such magnanimity! I hardly— Do you really forgive everything? From top to bottom? Even that you stirred up my mother against me before she ever came into the house? That you made my father—[*Puts her hand to her lips.*] *Meglio tacere! Meglio tacere!*

Marie. [*Interrupting.*] For Heaven's sake, Magda!

Magda. Yes, my darling—nothing, not a word.

Franziska. She has a fine presence!

Magda. And now let me look about me! Ah, everything's just the same. Not a speck of dust has moved.

Mrs. Schwartze. I hope, Magda, that you won't find any specks of dust.

Magda. I'm sure of that, *mammina.* That wasn't what I meant. Twelve years! Without a trace! Have I dreamed all that comes between?

Schwartze. You will have a great deal to tell us, Magda.

Magda. [*Starting.*] What? Well, we will see, we will see. Now I should like— What would I like? I must sit still for a moment. It all comes over me so. When I think—From that door to the window, from this table to the old bureau—that was once my world.

Schwartze. A world, my child, which one never outgrows, which one never should outgrow—you have always held to that?

Magda. What do you mean? And what a face you make over it! Yes, yes, though—that question came at the right time. I have been a fool! I have been a fool! My dear old papa, this happiness will be short.

Mrs. Schwartze. Why?

Magda. What do you think of me? Do you think I am as free as I appear? I'm a weary, worn-out drudge who is only fortunate when the lash is on her back.

Schwartze. Whose drudge? What lash?

Magda. That I can't explain, dear father. You don't know my life. You probably wouldn't understand it, either. Every day, every hour has its work laid out. Ah, well, now I must go back to the hotel.

Marie. No, Magda, no.

Magda. Yes, puss, yes. There have been six or seven men there for ever so long, waiting for an audience. But I tell you what, I must have you tonight. Can't you sleep with me?

Schwartze. Of course. That is—what do you mean—sleep where?

Magda. At the hotel.

Schwartze. What? You won't stay? You'll put such an affront on us?

Magda. What are you thinking of? I have a whole retinue with me.

Schwartze. Your father's house is the place for this retinue.

Magda. I don't know. It is rather lively. First, there's Bobo, my parrot, a darling—he wouldn't be bad; then my pet maid, Giulietta, a little demon—I can't live without her; then my courier—he's a tyrant, and the terror of landlords; and then we mustn't forget my teacher.

Franziska. He's a very old man, I hope.

Magda. No, he's a very young man.

Schwartze. [*After a silence.*] Then you must have forgotten your—your *dame d'honneur.*

Magda. What *dame d'honneur?*

Schwartze. You can't travel about from country to country with a young man without——

Magda. Ah! does that disquiet you? I can—be quite easy—I can. In my world we don't trouble ourselves about such things.

Schwartze. What world is that?

Magda. The world I rule, father dear. I have no other. There, whatever I do is right because I do it.

Schwartze. That is an enviable position. But you are still young. There must be cases when some direction—in short, whose advice do you follow in your transactions?

Magda. There is no one who has the right to advise me, papa dear.

Schwartze. Well, my child, from this hour your old father claims that right. Theresa! [THERESA *answers from outside.*] Go to the German House and bring the baggage——

Magda. [*Entreatingly.*] Pardon, father dear, you forget that my orders are necessary.

Schwartze. What?—Yes, yes, I forgot. Do what you will, my daughter.

Marie. Magda—oh, Magda!

Magda. [*Taking her mantle.*] Be patient, darling. We'll have a talk soon all to our two selves. And you'll all come to breakfast with me, won't you? We can have a good chat and love each other!—so much!

Mrs. Schwartze. We—breakfast with you?

Magda. I want to have you all under my roof.

Schwartze. The roof of a hotel?

Magda. Yes, papa dear, I have no other home.

Schwartze. And this?

Marie. Don't you see how you've hurt him?

[*Enter the* PASTOR. *He stops, and seems to control strong emotion.* MAGDA *examines him with her lorgnette.*]

Magda. He, too! Let me see.

Mrs. Schwartze. Just think. She is going away again!

Heffterdingt. I don't know whether I am known to the lady.

Magda. [*Mockingly.*] You're too modest, Pastor. And now since I have seen you all—[*Puts on her mantle.*]

Schwartze. [*Quickly, aside.*] You must keep her.

Heffterdingt. I? If you are powerless, how can I?

Schwartze. Try!

Heffterdingt. [*Constraining himself, with embarrassment.*] Pardon me, madam, it seems very officious of me—if I—will you give me a few moments' interview?

Magda. What have we two to say to each other, my dear Pastor?

Mrs. Schwartze. Oh, do, please! He knows best about everything.

Magda. [*Ironically.*] Indeed!

Marie. I may never ask you for anything again, but do this one thing for my sake!

Magda. [*Patting her and looking from one to the other.*] Well, the child asks so prettily. Pastor, I am at your service. [MARIE *thanks her silently.*]

Franziska. [*Aside to* MRS. SCHWARTZE.] Now he'll give her a lecture. Come.

Schwartze. You were once the cause of my sending her from my home. Today you must see to it that she remains. [HEFFTERDINGT *expresses doubt.*]

Schwartze. Marie!

Marie. Yes, papa.

[*Exit* SCHWARTZE, MRS. SCHWARTZE, FRANZISKA, *and* MARIE.]

Magda. [*Sits down and examines him through her lorgnette.*] So this is the man who undertakes by a five minutes' interview entirely and absolutely to break my will. That they believe in your ability to do it shows me that you are a king in your own dominions. I make obeisance. And now let me see you ply your arts.

Heffterdingt. I understand no arts, madam, and would avail myself of none. If they put some trust in me here, it is because they know that I seek nothing for myself.

Magda. [*Ironically.*] That has always been the case?

Heffterdingt. No, madam. I had, once in my life, a strong, an intense desire. It was to have you for my wife. I need only look at you to see that I was presumptuous. Since then I have put the wish away from me.

Magda. Ah, Pastor, I believe you're paying court to me now.

Heffterdingt. Madam, if it were not discourteous——

Magda. Oh, then even a shepherd of souls may be discourteous!

Heffterdingt. I should commiserate you on the atmosphere which has surrounded you.

Magda. [*With mocking superiority.*] Really? What do you know about my atmosphere?

Heffterdingt. It seems to me that it has made you forget that serious men are to be taken seriously.

Magda. Ah! [*Rising.*] Well, then I will take you seriously; and I will tell you that you have always been unbearable to me, with your well-acted simplicity, your droning mildness, your— Since, however, you condescended to cast your eyes on my worthlessness and drove me from home with your suit—since then, I have hated you.

Heffterdingt. It seems to me that according to this I was the foundation of your greatness.

Magda. You're right there. Here I was parched and stifled. No, no, I don't hate you. Why should I hate you so much? It's all so far, so very far, behind me. If you only knew how far! You have sat here day after day in this heavy air, reeking of lavender, tobacco, and cough mixture, while I have felt the storm breaking about my head. Pastor, if you had a suspicion of what life really is—of the trial of strength, of the taste of guilt, of conquest, and of pleasure—you would find yourself very comical with your clerical shop-talk. Ha, ha, ha! Pardon me, I don't believe such a laugh has rung through this respectable house for twelve years; for there's no one here who knows how to laugh. Is there, eh?

Heffterdingt. No, I fear not.

Magda. Fear, you say. That sounds as though you deprecated it. But don't you hate laughter?

Heffterdingt. Most of us cannot laugh, madam.

Magda. And to those who could, laughter is sin. You might laugh yourself. What have you to be solemn about? You need not look at the world with this funereal mien. Surely you have a little blond wife at home who knits industriously, and half a dozen curly heads around her, of course. It's always so in parsonages.

Heffterdingt. I have remained single, madam.

Magda. Ah! [*Silence.*] Did I hurt you so much, then?

Heffterdingt. Let that be, shall we not? It is so long ago.

Magda. [*Letting her mantle fall.*] And your work—does not that bring happiness enough?

Heffterdingt. Thank God, it does. But if one takes it really in earnest, one cannot live only for one's self; at least, I cannot. One cannot exult in the fulness of one's personality, as you would call it. And then many hearts are opened to me— One sees too many wounds there, that one cannot heal, to be quite happy.

Magda. You're a remarkable man— I don't know—if I could only get rid of the idea that you're insincere.

Heffterdingt. Will you let me ask you one question before you go?

Magda. Well?

Heffterdingt. It is about an hour since you entered this house, your home—no, not so much. I could not have been waiting for you nearly as long as that.

Magda. For me? You? Where?

Heffterdingt. In the corridor outside your room.

Magda. What did you want there?

Heffterdingt. My errand was useless, for now you are here.

Magda. Do you mean to say that you came for me—you to whom I— If any one had an interest in keeping me away, it was you.

Heffterdingt. Are you accustomed to regard everything which those about you do as the result of selfish interest?

Magda. Of course. It's so with me! [*Struck by a new thought.*] Or perhaps you— No, I'm not justified in that assumption. [*Sharply.*] Ah, such nonsense! it is only fit for fairy tales. Well, Pastor, I'll own that I like you now better, much better than of old when you—what shall I say?—made an honorable proposal.

Heffterdingt. H'm!

Magda. If you could only end it all with a laugh—this stony visage of yours is so unfriendly—one is quite *sconcertata.* What do you say? *Je ne trouve pas le mot.*

Heffterdingt. Pardon me, may I ask the question now?

Magda. Good Lord, how inquisitive the holy man is! And you don't see that I was coquetting with you a little. For, to have been a man's fate—that flatters us women—we are grateful for it. You see I have acquired some art meanwhile. Well, out with your question!

Heffterdingt. Why—why did you come home?

Magda. Ah!

Heffterdingt. Was it not homesickness?

Magda. No. Well, perhaps a very little.

I'll tell you. When I received the invitation to assist at this festival—why they did me the honor, I don't know—a very curious feeling began to seethe within me—half curiosity and half shyness, half melancholy and half defiance—which said: "Go home incognito. Go in the twilight and stand before the paternal house where for seventeen years you lived in bondage. There look upon what you were. But if they recognize you, show them that beyond their narrow virtues there may be something true and good."

Heffterdingt. Only defiance then?

Magda. At first, perhaps. Once on the way, though, my heart beat most wonderfully, as it used to do when I'd learnt my lesson badly. And I always did learn my lessons badly. When I stood before the hotel, the German House—just think, the German House, where the great officials and the great artists stayed—there I had again the abject reverence as of old, as if I were unworthy to step on the old threshold. I entirely forgot that I was now myself a so-called great artist. Since then, every evening I have stolen by the house—very quietly, very humbly—always almost in tears.

Heffterdingt. And nevertheless you are going away.

Magda. I must.

Heffterdingt. But——

Magda. Don't ask me why. I must.

Heffterdingt. Has any one offended your pride? Has anyone said a word of your needing forgiveness?

Magda. Not yet—or, yes, if you count the old cat.

Heffterdingt. What is there in the world which draws you away again after an hour?

Magda. I will tell you. I felt it the first minute I came. The paternal authority already stretches its net over me again, and the yoke stands ready beneath which I must bow.

Heffterdingt. But there is neither yoke nor net here. Do not fear shadows. Here are only wide-opened arms which wait to clasp the lost daughter to the empty breast.

Magda. Oh, I beg you, none of that. I do not intend to furnish a pendant to the prodigal son. If I came back as a daughter, as a lost daughter, I should not hold my head up before you as I do; I should grovel in the dust in full consciousness of all my sins. [*With growing excitement.*] And that I will not do—that I cannot do—for I am what I am, and I cannot be another. [*Sadly.*] And therefore I have no home—therefore I must go forth again—therefore——

[*Enter* Mrs. Schwartze.]

Heffterdingt. For Heaven's sake, hush!

Mrs. Schwartze. Excuse me, Pastor, I only wanted to know about supper. [*Imploringly to* Magda, *who sits turned away with her hands before her face.*] We happen to have a warm joint today. You know, Pastor, the gentlemen of the card-club were to be with us. Now, Magda, whether you're going away or not, can't you eat a mouthful in your father's house?

Heffterdingt. Don't ask now, my dear madam.

Mrs. Schwartze. Oh, if I'm interrupting—I only thought——

Heffterdingt. Later.

Marie. [*Appearing in the doorway.*] Will she stay? [Magda *shrinks at the sound of the voice.*]

Mrs. Schwartze. 'Sh!

[*Exit* Mrs. Schwartze *and* Marie.]

Heffterdingt. You have no home, Miss Magda? Did you hear the old mother beseeching and alluring with the best that she has, though it's only a poor dish? Did you hear Marie's voice trembling with tears in the fear that I should not prevail? They trust me too much; they think I only need to speak the word. They don't suspect how helpless I stand here before you. Look! Behind that door are three people in a fever of sorrow and love. If you cross this threshold, you rob each of them of so much life. And you have no home?

Magda. If I have one, it is not here.

Heffterdingt. [*Embarrassed.*] Perhaps—Nevertheless you should not go. Only a few days—just not to take away the idea that you belong here. So much you owe to them!

Magda. [*Sadly.*] I owe nothing now to anyone here.

Heffterdingt. No? Really nothing? Then I must tell you about a certain day—eleven years ago now. I was called into this house in haste, for the Colonel was dying. When I came, he lay there stiff and motionless, his face drawn and white; one eye was already closed, in the other still flickered a little life. He tried to speak, but his lips only quivered and mumbled.

Magda. What had happened?

Heffterdingt. What had happened? I will tell you. He had just received a letter in which his eldest daughter bade him farewell.

Magda. My God!

Heffterdingt. It was a long time before he recovered from the apoplectic stroke. Only a trembling in the right arm, which you perhaps have noticed, now remains.

Magda. That is indeed a debt I owe.

Heffterdingt. Ah, if that were all, Miss

Magda! Pardon me, I call you by the name I used long ago. It springs to my lips.

Magda. Call me what you like. Go on.

Hefterdingt. The necessary result followed. When he received his discharge—he will not believe in the cause, don't speak to him of it—then his mind broke down.

Magda. Yes, yes; that is my debt, too.

Hefterdingt. Then you see, Miss Magda, began my work. If I speak of it, you must not think I am pluming myself on it to you. What good would that do me? For a long, long time I nursed him, and by degrees I saw his mind revive again. First I let him collect slugs from the rose-bushes.

Magda. [*With a shudder.*] Ugh!

Hefterdingt. Yes, so far had it gone; then I gave him charge of some money, and then I made him my assistant in the institutions with whose management I was intrusted. There is a hospital and a soup-kitchen and an infirmary, and it makes a great deal to be done. So he became a man once more. I have tried to influence your step-mother too; not because I was greedy for power. Perhaps you'll think that of me. In short, the old tension between her and Marie has been slowly smoothed away. Love and confidence have descended upon the house.

Magda. [*Staring at him.*] And why did you do all this?

Hefterdingt. Well, first it is my calling. Then I did it for his sake, for I love the old man; and above all—for—your sake.

[MAGDA *starts, and points to herself interrogatively.*]

Hefterdingt. Yes, for your sake. For this weighed upon me: The day will come when she will turn homeward—perhaps as victor; but perhaps also as vanquished, broken and ruined in body and soul— Pardon me these thoughts, I had heard nothing of you— In either case she shall find a home ready for her. That was my work, the work of long years; and now I implore you not to destroy it.

Magda. [*In anguish.*] If you knew through what I have passed, you would not try to keep me.

Hefterdingt. That is all shut out. This is home. Let it alone; forget it.

Magda. How can I forget it? How dare I?

Hefterdingt. Why should you resist when all stretch their hands out to you in rejoicing? It's very easy. Let your heart speak when you see all around overflowing with love for you.

Magda. [*In tears.*] You make me a child again. [*A pause.*]

Hefterdingt. Then you will stay?

Magda. [*Springing up.*] But they must not question me!

Hefterdingt. Must not question you?

Magda. About my life outside there. They wouldn't understand—none of them; not even you.

Hefterdingt. Well, then, they sha'n't.

Magda. And you will promise me, for yourself and for the others?

Hefterdingt. Yes, I can promise it.

Magda. [*In a stifled voice.*] Call them, then.

Hefterdingt. [*Opening the door on the left.*] She will stay.

[*Enter* MARIE; *then* MRS. SCHWARTZE, FRANZISKA, *and* SCHWARTZE. MARIE *throws herself joyfully into* MAGDA'S *arms.* MRS. SCHWARTZE *also embraces her.*]

Schwartze. It was your duty, my child.

Magda. Yes, father. [*She softly takes his right hand in both of hers, and carries it tenderly to her lips.*]

Franziska. Thank Heaven! Now we can have supper at last. [*Opens the sliding door into the dining-room. The supper-table is seen, all set, and lighted brightly by a green-shaded hanging-lamp.*]

Magda. [*Gazing at it.*] Oh, look! The dear old lamp! [*The women go slowly out.*]

Schwartze. [*Stretching out his hands.*] This is your greatest work, Pastor.

Hefterdingt. Oh, don't, I beg you! And there's a condition attached.

Schwartze. A condition?

Hefterdingt. We must not ask about her life.

Schwartze. [*Startled.*] What? What? I must not——

Hefterdingt. No, no; you must not ask—you must not ask—or— [*Struck by a new thought.*] If you do not—yes—I am sure she will confess everything herself.

CURTAIN

ACT THIRD

SCENE: *the same. Morning. On the table at the left, coffee-service and flowers.*

[MRS. SCHWARTZE *and* FRANZISKA *discovered.*]

Mrs. Schwartze. [*Excitedly.*] Thank Heaven, you've come. Such a time we've had this morning!

Franziska. So?

Mrs. Schwartze. Just think, two people have come from the hotel—a gentleman who looks like a lord, and a young lady like a princess. They're her servants.

Franziska. What extravagance!

Mrs. Schwartze. And they're calling and talking all over the house, and neither of them knows any German. And her ladyship ordered a warm bath, that was not warm enough; and a cold douche, which was not cold enough; and spirits, which she simply poured out of the window; and toilet vinegar, which we didn't have at all.

Franziska. What demands! And where is your famous young lady?

Mrs. Schwartze. After her bath she has gone back to bed again.

Franziska. I would not have such sloth in my house.

Mrs. Schwartze. I shall tell her so. For Leopold's sake— [*Enter* THERESA.] What do you want, Theresa?

Theresa. Councillor von Keller—he has sent his servant here to ask whether the Lieutenant has come yet, and what is the young lady's answer.

Mrs. Schwartze. What young lady?

Theresa. That's what I don't know.

Mrs. Schwartze. Then just give our regards, and say that the Lieutenant has not come yet.

Franziska. He is on duty till twelve. After that he'll come.

[*Exit* THERESA. *As she opens the door, a great noise is heard in the hall—a man's voice and a woman's disputing in Italian.*]

Mrs. Schwartze. Listen to that! [*Speaking outside.*] Just you wait. Your Signora'll be here soon. [*Shuts the door.*] Ah! And now, breakfast. What do you think she drinks?

Franziska. Why, coffee.

Mrs. Schwartze. No.

Franziska. Tea, then?

Mrs. Schwartze. No.

Franziska. Then it must be chocolate!

Mrs. Schwartze. No; coffee and chocolate mixed.

Franziska. Horrible! But it must be good.

Mrs. Schwartze. And yesterday half a dozen trunks came from the hotel, and as many more are still there. Ah, what there is in them all! One whole trunk for hats! A peignoir of real point, and open-work stockings with gold embroidery, and [*in a whisper*] silk chemises——

Franziska. What? Silk——

Mrs. Schwartze. Yes.

Franziska. [*With a gesture of horror.*] It is simply sinful.

[*Enter* MAGDA, *in brilliant morning toilette, speaking outside as she opens the door.*]

Magda. Ma che cosa volete voi? Perchè non aspetate, finchè vi commando? Ha?

Mrs. Schwartze. Now they are getting their share!

Magda. No, no; *è tempo!* [*Shutting the door.*] *Va, bruto!* Good-morning, mamma. [*Kisses her.*] I'm a late sleeper, eh? Ah, good morning, Aunt Frankie. In a good humor? So am I.

Mrs. Schwartze. What did the strange gentleman want, Magda?

Magda. Stupid beast! He wanted to know when I was going away, the idiot! How can I tell? [*Patting her.*] Eh, *mamma mia?* Oh, children, I slept like the dead. My ear on the pillow, and off! And the douche was so nice and cold. I feel so strong. *Allons, cousine!* Hop! [*Seizes* FRANZISKA *by the waist and jumps her into the air.*]

Franziska. [*Furiously.*] What do you——

Magda. [*Haughtily.*] Eh?

Franziska. [*Cringingly.*] You are so facetious.

Magda. Am I? [*Clapping her hands.*] Breakfast!

[*Enter* MARIE, *with a tray of coffee things.*]

Marie. Good morning.

Franziska. Good morning, my child.

Magda. I'm dying of hunger. Ah! [*Pats her stomach.* MARIE *kisses* FRANZISKA'S *hand.*]

Magda. [*Taking off the cover, with unction.*] Delicious! One would know Giulietta was in the house.

Franziska. She has made noise enough, at least.

Magda. Oh, she couldn't live without a good row. And when she gets too excited, she quietly throws a plate at your head. I'm accustomed to it. What is papa doing?

Mrs. Schwartze. He's making his excuses to the members of the Committee.

Magda. Is your life still half made up of excuses? What sort of committee is it?

Mrs. Schwartze. It's the Christian Aid Society. They should have had a meeting here this morning in our house. Now we thought it would not do. It would look as if we wanted to introduce you.

Franziska. But, Augusta, now it will look as if your daughter were more important to you——

Magda. Well, I hope she is!

Mrs. Schwartze. Of course! But—oh dear, you don't know what sort of people they are. They are deserving of great respect. For instance, there's Mrs. General von Klebs. [*Proudly.*] We are friends of hers.

Magda. [*With sham respect.*] Really?

Mrs. Schwartze. Now, they'll probably come tomorrow. Then you'll meet, besides, some other pious and aristocratic ladies whose patronage gains us a great deal of influence. I'm curious to see how they'll like you.

Magda. How I shall like them, you should say.

Mrs. Schwartze. Yes—that is—but we're talking and talking——

Marie. [*Jumping up.*] Oh, excuse me, mamma.

Magda. No, you must stay here.

Mrs. Schwartze. Yes, Magda; but about your trunks at the hotel—I am constantly on the rack for fear something should be left.

Magda. Send for them, then, children.

Franziska. [*Aside to* MRS. SCHWARTZE.] Now I'll question her thoroughly, Augusta. Leave us alone.

[*Exit* MRS. SCHWARTZE.]

Franziska. [*Sitting down, with importance.*] And now, my dear Magda, you must tell your old aunt all about it.

Magda. Eh? Ah, look here, mamma needs help. Go on, quick! Make yourself useful.

Franziska. [*Viciously.*] If you command it.

Magda. Oh, I have only to request.

Franziska. [*Rising.*] It seems to me that your requests are somewhat forcible.

Magda. [*Laughing.*] Perhaps.

[*Exit* FRANZISKA *in a rage.*]

Marie. Oh, Magda!

Magda. Yes, sweet. That's the way to go through the world—bend or break; that is, I never bend. It's the only way.

Marie. Oh, good Heavens!

Magda. Poor child! Yes, in this house one learns quite other views. I bent, myself, yesterday disgracefully. Ah, how nice our old mamma is! [*Earnestly, pointing to the mother's picture.*] And she up there! Do you remember her? [MARIE *shakes her head.*]

Magda. [*Thoughtfully.*] She died too soon! Where's papa? I want him. And yet I'm afraid of him too. Now, child, while I eat my breakfast, you must make your confession.

Marie. Oh, I can't.

Magda. Just show me the locket!

Marie. There!

Magda. A lieutenant! Naturally. With us it's always a tenor.

Marie. Oh, Magda, it's no joke. He is my fate.

Magda. What is the name of this fate?

Marie. It's Cousin Max.

Magda. [*Whistles.*] Why don't you marry the good youth, then?

Marie. Aunt Frankie wants a better match for him, and so she won't give him the guaranty he needs. It's abominable!

Magda. Si! C'est bête, ça! And how long have you loved each other?

Marie. I don't remember when we did not.

Magda. And where does he meet you?

Marie. Here.

Magda. I mean elsewhere—alone.

Marie. We are never alone together. I think this precaution we owe to our own self-respect.

Magda. Come here—close—tell me the truth—has it never entered your mind to cast this whole network of precaution and respect away from you, and to go with the man you love out and away—anywhere—it doesn't matter much—and as you lie quietly on his breast, to hurl back a scornful laugh at the whole world which has sunk behind you?

Marie. No, Magda, I never feel so.

Magda. But would you die for him?

Marie. [*Standing up with a gesture of enthusiasm.*] I would die a thousand deaths for him!

Magda. My poor little darling! [*Aside.*] They bring everything to naught. The most terrible of all passions becomes in their hands a mere resigned defiance of death.

Marie. What are you speaking of?

Magda. Nothing, nothing. See here, how large is this sum you need?

Marie. Sixty thousand marks.

Magda. When can you be married? Must it be now, or will afternoon do?

Marie. Don't mock me, Magda.

Magda. You must give me time to telegraph. One can't carry so much money about with one.

Marie. [*Slowly taking it in, and then, with an outburst of joy, throwing herself at* MAGDA'S *feet.*] Magda!

Magda. [*After a silence.*] Be happy, love your husband. And if you hold your first-born on your arm, in the face of the world [*holding out her arms with angry emphasis*]—so, face to face, then think of one who—Ah! someone's coming.

[*Enter* HEFFTERDINGT *with a portfolio.*]

Magda. [*Crossing to him.*] Oh, it's you. That's good. I wanted you.

Heffterdingt. You wanted me? What for?

Magda. Only—I want to talk with you, holy man.

Heffterdingt. Isn't it good, Miss Magda, to be at home again?

Magda. Oh, yes, except for the old aunt's sneaking about.

Marie. [*Who is collecting the breakfast-things; laughing, but frightened.*] Oh, Heavens, Magda!

Heffterdingt. Good morning, Miss Marie.

Marie. Good morning, Pastor.

[*Exit, with the table.*]

Heffterdingt. Heavens, how she beams!

Magda. She has reason.

Heffterdingt. Isn't your father here?

Magda. No.

Heffterdingt. Isn't he well?

Magda. I think so. I haven't seen him yet. Yesterday we sat together till late. I told him what I could tell. But I think he was very unhappy; his eyes were always searching and probing. Oh, I fear your promise will be badly kept.

Heffterdingt. That seems like a reproach. I hope you don't regret—

Magda. No, my friend, I don't regret it But I feel very curiously. I seem to be in a tepid bath, I'm so weak and warm. What they call German sentiment is awaking again, and I have been so unused to it. My heart seems like a Christmas number of the "Gartenlaube,"—moonlight, betrothals, lieutenants, and I don't know what! But the best of it is, I know that I'm playing with myself. I can cast it all off as a child throws away its doll, and be my old self again.

Heffterdingt. That would be bad for us.

Magda. Oh, don't be angry with me. I seem to be all torn and rooted up. And then I am so afraid——

Heffterdingt. Of what?

Magda. I can't—I can't be quite one of you. I am an intruder. [*Aside, fearfully.*] If a specter from without were to appear, this whole idyl would go up in flames. [HEFFTERDINGT *suppresses a start of astonishment.*] And I'm confined, hemmed in. I begin to be a coward.

Heffterdingt. I don't think one should be terrified at feeling filial love.

Magda. Filial love? I should like to take that snow white head in my lap and say, "You old child!" And nevertheless I must bend my will, I must bend my will. I am not accustomed to that. I must conquer; I must sing down opposition. I sing or I live—for both are one and the same—so that men must will as I do. I force them, I compel them to love and mourn and exult and lament as I do. And woe to him who resists! I sing them down—I sing and sing until they become slaves and playthings in my hands. I know I'm confused, but you understand what I mean.

Heffterdingt. To work the impress of one's own personality—that's what you mean, isn't it?

Magda. Si, si, si, si! Oh, I could tell you everything. Your heart has tendrils which twine about other hearts and draw them out. And you don't do it selfishly. You don't know how mighty you are. The men outside there are beasts, whether in love or hate. But you are a man. And one feels like a man when one is near you. Just think, when you came in yesterday, you seemed to me so small; but something grows out from you and becomes always greater, almost too great for me.

Heffterdingt. Good Heavens, what can it be?

Magda. What shall I call it—self-sacrifice, self-abnegation? It is something with self—or rather the reverse. That is what impresses me. And that is why you can do so much with me.

Heffterdingt. How strange!

Magda. What?

Heffterdingt. I must own it to you—it is—it is nonsense; but since I have seen you again, a sort of longing has awakened within me to be like you.

Magda. Ha, ha! You, model of men! Like me!

Heffterdingt. I have had to stifle much in my nature. My peace is the peace of the dead. And as you stood before me yesterday in your freshness, your natural strength, your—your greatness, I said to myself, "That is what you might have been if at the right moment joy had entered into your life."

Magda. [*In a whisper.*] And one thing more, my friend—sin! We must sin if we wish to grow. To become greater than our sins is worth more than all the purity you preach.

Heffterdingt. [*Impressed.*] That would be —— [*Voices outside.*]

Magda. [*Starting and listening.*] 'Sh!

Heffterdingt. What's the matter?

Magda. Nothing, it's only my stupid nervousness; not on my own account, believe me; only out of pity for all these. We shall still be friends?

Heffterdingt. As long as you need me.

Magda. And when I cease to need you?

Heffterdingt. There will be no change in me, Miss Magda. [*As he is going, he meets* SCHWARTZE *in the doorway.*]

[*Enter* SCHWARTZE.]

Schwartze. Good morning, my dear pastor! Will you go out on the porch for a moment? I will follow you. [*Exit* HEFFTERDINGT.] Now, did you sleep well, my child? [*Kisses her on the forehead.*]

Magda. Finely. In my old room I found the old sleep of childhood.

Schwartze. Had you lost it?

Magda. Haven't you?

Schwartze. They say a good conscience— Come to me, my child.

Magda. Gladly, papa! No, let me sit at your feet. There I can see your beautiful white beard. When I look at it, I always think of Christmas eve and a quiet snow-covered field.

Schwartze. My child, you know how to say pretty things. When you speak, one seems to see pictures about one. Here we are not so clever; that is why we have nothing to conceal here.

Magda. We also— But speak quietly, papa.

Schwartze. Yes, I must. You know what agreement you made with the pastor.

Magda. Which you will keep?

Schwartze. I am accustomed to keep to what I have promised. But you must see that the suspicion—whatever I may do, the suspicion weighs like a mountain——

Magda. What do you suspect?

Schwartze. I don't know. You have appeared among us so wonderfully, so gloriously. But brilliance and worldly honor and all that don't blind a father's eyes. You seem to be warm at heart too. At least, one would think so to hear you speak. But there is something in your eyes which does not please me, and a scornful curl about your lips.

Magda. Dear, good old papa!

Schwartze. You see! This tenderness is not that of a daughter toward her father. It is so that one pets a child, whether it be a young or an old one. And although I'm only a poor soldier, lame and disabled, I demand your respect, my child.

Magda. I have never withheld it. [*Rising.*]

Schwartze. That is good, that is good, my daughter. Believe me, we are not so simple as we may appear to you. We have eyes to see, and ears to hear, that the spirit of moral revolt is abroad in the world. The seed which should take root in the heart begins to decay. What were once sins easily become customs to you. My child, soon you will go away. When you return, you may find me in the grave.

Magda. Oh, no, papa!

Schwartze. It's in God's hand. But I implore you— Come here, my child—nearer—so— [*He draws her down to him, and takes her head between his hands.*] I implore you —let me be happy in my dying hour. Tell me that you have remained pure in body and soul, and then go with my blessing on your way.

Magda. I have remained—true to myself, dear father.

Schwartze. How? In good or in ill?

Magda. In what—for me—was good.

Schwartze. [*Blankly.*] In what—for you —then?

Magda. [*Rising.*] And now don't worry any more. Let me enjoy these few days quietly. They will be over soon enough.

Schwartze. [*Broodingly.*] I love you with my whole heart, because I have sorrowed for you—so long. [*Threateningly, rising.*] But I must know who you are.

Magda. Father dear— [*Bell rings.* MRS. SCHWARTZE *bursts in.*]

Mrs. Schwartze. Just think! the ladies of the Committee are here! They want to congratulate us in person. Do you think we ought to offer them coffee, Leopold?

Schwartze. I will go into the garden, Augusta.

Mrs. Schwartze. For Heaven's sake— they're just coming—you must receive their congratulations.

Schwartze. I can't—no—I can't do it! [*Exit, left.*]

Mrs. Schwartze. What is the matter with your father?

[*Enter* MRS. GENERAL VON KLEBS, MRS. JUSTICE ELLRICH, MRS. SCHUMANN, *and* FRANZISKA.]

Franziska. [*As she opens the door.*] My dear, the ladies——

Mrs. von Klebs. [*Giving her hand to* MRS. SCHWARTZE.] What a day for you, my dear! The whole town rejoices in the happy event.

Mrs. Schwartze. Permit me—my daughter —Mrs. General von Klebs, Mrs. Justice Ellrich, Mrs. Schumann.

Mrs. Schumann. I am only the wife of a simple merchant; but——

Mrs. von Klebs. My husband will do himself the honor soon——

Mrs. Schwartze. Won't you sit down, ladies? [*They sit.*]

Franziska. [*With aplomb.*] Yes, it is truly a joyful event for the whole family.

Mrs. von Klebs. We have unfortunately not shared the pleasures of the festival, my dear young lady. I must therefore refrain from expressing that admiration to which you are so well accustomed.

Mrs. Schumann. If we had known, we should certainly have ordered tickets.

Mrs. von Klebs. Do you expect to remain here for very long?

Magda. That I really cannot say, madam —or, pardon me—your ladyship?

Mrs. von Klebs. I must beg you—no.

Magda. Oh, pardon me!

Mrs. von Klebs. Oh, please!

Magda. We are such birds of passage, my dear madam, that we can really never plan for the future.

Mrs. Ellrich. But one must have one's real home.

Magda. Why? One must have a vocation. That seems to me enough.

Franziska. It's all in the point of view, dear Magda.

Mrs. von Klebs. Ah, we're so far removed from all these ideas, my dear young lady. Every now and then some person gives lectures here, but the good families have nothing to do with them.

Magda. [*Politely.*] Oh, I can quite understand that. The good families need nothing, as they have plenty to eat. [*A silence.*]

Mrs. Ellrich. But at least you must have some residence?

Magda. If you call it so—a place to sleep. Yes, I have a villa by the Lake of Como and an estate at Naples. [*Sensation.*]

Mrs. Schwartze. But you've said nothing to us about that.

Magda. I hardly ever make use of them, mamma dear.

Mrs. Ellrich. Art must be a very trying occupation!

Magda. [*In a friendly tone.*] It depends upon how one follows it, my dear madam.

Mrs. Ellrich. My daughter used to take singing-lessons, and it always taxed her very much.

Magda. [*Politely.*] Oh, I'm sorry for that.

Mrs. Ellrich. Naturally, you only do it for pleasure.

Magda. Oh, it's so much pleasure! [*Aside to* MRS. SCHWARTZE, *who sits near her.*] Get these women away, or I shall be rude!

Mrs. von Klebs. Are you really engaged by a theater, my dear young lady?

Magda. [*Very sweetly.*] Sometimes, my dear madam.

Mrs. von Klebs. Then you are out of an engagement at present?

Magda. [*Murmurs.*] Oh, come, come! [*Aloud.*] Yes, I'm a vagabond now. [*The ladies look at each other.*]

Mrs. von Klebs. There are really not many daughters of good families on the stage, are there?

Magda. [*In a friendly tone.*] No, my dear madam; most of them are too stupid.

Mrs. Schwartze. Oh, Magda!

[*Enter* MAX.]

Magda. Oh, that must be Max! [*Goes to him and shakes hands.*] Just think, I had quite forgotten your face. We were great friends, were we not?

Max. Were we? [*Astonished.*]

Magda. Well, we can begin now.

Mrs. Ellrich. [*Aside.*] Do you understand this?

[MRS. VON KLEBS *shrugs her shoulders. The ladies rise and take their leave, shaking hands with* MRS. SCHWARTZE *and* FRANZISKA, *and bowing to* MAGDA.]

Mrs. Schwartze. [*Confused.*] Must you go already, ladies? My husband will be so sorry——

Magda. [*Coolly.*] *Au revoir,* ladies, *au revoir!*

[*Exit the ladies in the order of their rank.*]

Mrs. Schwartze. [*Turning back from the door.*] Mrs. von Klebs was offended, or she would have stayed. Magda, you certainly must have offended Mrs. von Klebs.

Franziska. And the other ladies, too, were hurt.

Magda. Mamma dear, won't you see about my trunk?

Mrs. Schwartze. Yes, yes, I'll go to the hotel myself. Oh dear, oh dear, oh dear!

[*Exit.*]

Franziska. Wait, I'm coming too. [*Spitefully.*] I must make myself useful, of course!

Magda. Oh, Aunt Frankie, a word with you.

Franziska. Now?

Magda. We're going to celebrate a betrothal today.

Franziska. What betrothal?

Magda. Between him and Marie.

Max. [*Joyfully.*] Magda!

Franziska. I think, as I occupy a mother's position toward him, that it is my right——

Magda. No; the giver alone has rights, my dear aunt. And now don't fail.

Franziska. [*Furiously.*] I will make you —— [*Exit.*]

Max. How shall I thank you, my dear Miss——

Magda. Magda, my dear cousin, Magda!

Max. Pardon me, it was my great respect——

Magda. Not so much respect, my boy—I don't like it; more weight, more individuality!

Max. Ah, my dear cousin, should a young lieutenant with twenty-five marks' pay, not to speak of debts, have individuality? It would only be a hindrance to him.

Magda. Ah!

Max. If I manage my men properly, and dance a correct figure at our regimental balls, and am not a coward, that is enough.

Magda. To make a wife happy, certainly. Go and find her. Go along!

Max. [*Starts to go, and turns back.*] Oh, excuse me, in my happiness I entirely forgot the message I— Early this morning—by-the-by, you can't think what a tumult the whole city is in about you—well, early this morning—I was still in bed—an acquaintance came in who is also an old acquaintance of yours, very pale from excitement, and he asked whether it were all true, and if he might come to see you.

Magda. Yes, let him come.

Max. He wanted me to ask you first. He would then send in his card this morning.

Magda. What formalities the men go through here! Who is he?

Max. Councillor von Keller.

Magda. [*Speaking with difficulty.*] He—what?—he?

Max. [*Laughing.*] Pardon me, but you're as white now as he was.

Magda. [*Quietly.*] I? White?

[*Enter* THERESA *with a card.*]

Max. Here he is. Dr. von Keller.

Magda. Let him come up.

[*Exit* THERESA.]

Max. [*Smiling.*] I'll only say to you, my dear cousin, that he's a very important man, who has a great career before him, and promises to be a pillar of our religious circle.

Magda. Thank you!

[*Enter* VON KELLER *with a bouquet.*]

Max. [*Crossing to him.*] My dear Councillor, here is my cousin, who is delighted to see you. You will excuse me.

[*Exit, with a bow to each.*]

[VON KELLER *remains standing at the door.* MAGDA *moves about nervously. Silence.*]

Magda. [*Aside.*] Here is my specter! [*Indicates a seat at the table, left, and sits down opposite.*]

Von Keller. First, you must allow me to express my warmest and most sincere good wishes. This is a surprise which you happily could not have expected. And as a sign of my interest, allow me, my dearest friend, to present you with these modest flowers.

Magda. Oh, how thoughtful! [*Takes the flowers with a laugh, and throws them on the table.*]

Von Keller. [*In embarrassment.*] I—I see with sorrow that you resent this approach on my part. Have I in any way been wanting in the necessary delicacy? In these narrow circles a meeting could not have been avoided. I think it is better, my dearest friend, that we should come to an understanding—that we should know the relations——

Magda. [*Rising.*] You're right, my friend. I was not at the height of my own nature just now. Had I been, I might have played the deserted Marguerite to the end. The morals of home had infected me a little. But I am myself again. Give me your hand bravely. Don't be afraid, I won't harm you. So—tight—so!

Von Keller. You make me happy.

Magda. I've painted this meeting to myself a thousand times, and have been prepared for it for years. Something warned me, too, when I undertook this journey home—though I must say I hardly expected just here to— Yes, how is it that, after what has passed between us, you came into this house? It seems to me a little——

Von Keller. I tried to avoid it until quite recently; but since we belong to the same circles, and since I agree with the views of this family—that is, at least in theory——

Magda. Yes, yes. Let me look at you, my poor friend. How you have changed!

Von Keller. [*Laughing nervously.*] I seem to have the misfortune to make a rather absurd figure in your eyes.

Magda. No; oh, no! I can see it all. The effort to keep worthy of respect under such difficulties, with a bad conscience, is awkward. You look down from the height of your pure atmosphere on your sinful youth—for you are called a pillar, my dear friend.

Von Keller. [*Looking at the door.*] Pardon me—I can hardly accustom myself again to the affectionate terms. And if anyone should hear us— Would it not be better——

Magda. [*Sadly.*] Let them hear us.

Von Keller. [*At the door.*] Good Heavens! Well [*sitting down again*], as I was saying, if you knew with what real longing I look back from this height at my gay, discarded youth——

Magda. [*Half to herself.*] So gay—yes, so gay.

Von Keller. Well, I felt myself called to higher things. I thought— Why should I undervalue my position? I have become Councillor, and that comparatively young. An ordinary ambition might take satisfaction in that. But one sits and waits at home, while others are called to the ministry. And this environment, conventionality, and narrowness, all is so gray—gray! And the ladies here—for one who cares at all about elegance —I assure you something rejoiced within me when I read this morning that you were the famous singer—you to whom I was tied by so many dear memories and——

Magda. And then you thought whether it might not be possible with the help of these dear memories to bring a little color into the gray background?

Von Keller. [*Smiling*.] Oh, pray don't——

Magda. Well, between old friends——

Von Keller. Really, are we that, really?

Magda. Certainly, *sans rancune*. Oh, if I took it from the other standpoint, I should have to range the whole gamut—liar, coward, traitor! But as I look at it, I owe you nothing but thanks, my friend.

Von Keller. [*Pleased, but confused*.] This is a view which——

Magda. Which is very convenient for you. But why should I not make it convenient for you? In the manner in which we met, you had no obligations toward me. I had left my home; I was young and innocent, hot-blooded and careless, and I lived as I saw others live. I gave myself to you because I loved you. I might perhaps have loved anyone who came in my way. That—that seemed to be all over. And we were so happy—weren't we?

Von Keller. Ah, when I think of it, my heart seems to stop beating.

Magda. There in the old attic, five flights up, we three girls lived so merrily in our poverty. Two hired pianos, and in the evening bread and dripping. Emmy used to warm it herself over the oil-stove.

Von Keller. And Katie with her verses! Good Lord! What has become of them?

Magda. *Chi lo sà?* Perhaps they're giving singing-lessons, perhaps they're on the stage. Yes, we were a merry set; and when the fun had lasted half a year, one day my lover vanished.

Von Keller. An unlucky chance, I swear to you. My father was ill. I had to travel. I wrote everything to you.

Magda. H'm! I did not reproach you. And now I will tell you why I owe you thanks. I was a stupid, unsuspecting thing, enjoying freedom like a runaway monkey. Through you I became a woman. For whatever I have done in my art, for whatever I have become in myself, I have you to thank. My soul was like—yes, down below there, there used to be an Æolian harp which was left moldering because my father could not bear it. Such a silent harp was my soul; and through you it was given to the storm. And it sounded almost to breaking—the whole scale of passions which bring us women to maturity—love and hate and revenge and ambition [*springing up*], and need, need, need—three times need —and the highest, the strongest, the holiest of all, the mother's love!—All I owe to you!

Von Keller. What—what do you say?

Magda. Yes, my friend, you have asked after Emmy and Katie. But you haven't asked after your child.

Von Keller. [*Jumping up and looking about anxiously*.] My child!

Magda. Your child? Who calls it so? Yours? Ha, ha! Dare to claim portion in him and I'll kill you with these hands. Who are you? You're a strange man who gratified his lust and passed on with a laugh. But I have a child—my son, my God, my all! For him I lived and starved and froze and walked the streets; for him I sang and danced in concert-halls—for my child who was crying for his bread! [*Breaks out in a convulsive laugh which changes to weeping, and throws herself on a seat, right*.]

Von Keller. [*After a silence*.] I am confounded. If I could have suspected—yes, if I could have suspected—I will do everything; I will not shrink from any reparation. But now, I beg you to quiet yourself. They know that I am here. If they saw us so, I should be—[*correcting himself*] you would be lost.

Magda. Don't be afraid. I won't compromise you.

Von Keller. Oh, I was not speaking for myself, not at all. But just think, if it were to come out, what the town and your father ——

Magda. Poor old man! His peace is destroyed, at any rate.

Von Keller. And think! the more brilliantly you are placed now, the more certain is your ruin.

Magda. [*Madly*.] And if I wish for ruin! If I——

Von Keller. For Heaven's sake, hush! someone's coming.

Magda. [*Springing up*.] Let them come! Let them all come! I don't care, I don't care! To their faces I'll say what I think of you, —of you and your respectable society. Why should I be worse than you, that I must prolong my existence among you by a lie! Why should this gold upon my body, and the luster which surrounds my name, only increase my infamy? Have I not worked early and late for ten long years? Have I not woven this dress with sleepless nights? Have I not built up my career step by step, like thousands of my kind? Why should I blush before any one? I am myself, and through myself I have become what I am.

Von Keller. Good! You may stand there proudly, but you might at least consider——

Magda. Whom? [*As he is silent.*] Whom? The pillar! Ha, ha! The pillar begins to totter! Be easy, my dear friend. I am not revengeful. But when I look at you in all your cowardly dignity—unwilling to take upon you the slightest consequence of your doings, and contrast you with myself, who sank through your love to be a pariah and an outcast— Ah, I'm ashamed of you. Pah!

Von Keller. For Heaven's sake! Your father! If he should see you like this!

Magda. [*In agony.*] My father! [*Escapes through the door of the dining-room, with her handkerchief to her face.*]

[*Enter* SCHWARTZE, *happy and excited, through the hall-door.*]

Schwartze. Ah, my dear Councillor—was that my daughter who just disappeared?

Von Keller. [*In great embarrassment.*] Yes, it was——

Schwartze. Why should she run away from me? Magda!

Von Keller. [*Trying to block his path.*] Had you not better— The young lady wished to be alone for a little!

Schwartze. Now? Why? When one has visitors, one does not— Why should she——

Von Keller. She was a little—agitated.

Schwartze. Agitated?

Von Keller. Yes; that's all.

Schwartze. Who has been here?

Von Keller. No one. At least, as far as I know.

Schwartze. Then, what agitating things could you two have to talk about?

Von Keller. Nothing of importance—nothing at all, I assure you.

Schwartze. What makes you look so, then? You can scarcely stand.

Von Keller. I? Oh, you're mistaken, you're mistaken.

Schwartze. One question, Councillor—You and my daughter— Please sit down.

Von Keller. My time is unfortunately——

Schwartze. [*Almost threatening.*] I beg you to sit down.

Von Keller. [*Not daring to resist.*] Thank you. [*They sit.*]

Schwartze. You met my daughter some years ago in Berlin?

Von Keller. Yes.

Schwartze. Councillor von Keller, I know you to be as discreet as you are sensible; but there are cases in which silence is a crime. I ask you—and your lifelong relations with me give me the right to ask, as well as the mystery—which just now— In short, I ask you, do you know anything discreditable about my daughter's life there?

Von Keller. Oh, for Heaven's sake, how can you——

Schwartze. Do you not know how and where she lived?

Von Keller. No. I am absolutely——

Schwartze. Have you never visited at her house?

Von Keller. [*More and more confused.*] No, no, never, never.

Schwartze. Not once?

Von Keller. Well, I called on her once; but——

Schwartze. Your relations were friendly?

Von Keller. Oh, entirely friendly—of course, only friendly. [*A pause.*]

Schwartze. [*Passes his hand over his forehead, looks earnestly at* VON KELLER; *then, speaking absently.*] So? Then, honestly—if it might be—if—if— [*Gets up, goes to* VON KELLER, *and sits down again, trying to quiet himself.*] Dr. von Keller, we both live in a quiet world, where scandals are unknown. But I have grown old, very old. And therefore I can't—can't control my thoughts as I should. And I can't rid myself of an idea which has—suddenly—taken possession of me. I have just had a great joy which I don't want to be embittered. But, to quiet an old man, I beg you—give me your word of honor that——

Von Keller. [*Rising.*] Pardon me, this seems almost like a cross-examination.

Schwartze. You must know, then, what I——

Von Keller. Pardon me, I wish to know nothing. I came here innocently to make a friendly visit, and you have taken me by surprise. I will not be taken by surprise. [*Takes his hat.*]

Schwartze. Dr. von Keller, have you thought what this refusal means?

Von Keller. Pardon me, if you wish to know anything, I beg you to ask your daughter. She will tell you what—what— And now you must let me go. You know where I live. In case— I am very sorry it has happened so: but— Good day, Colonel!

[*Exit.*]

Schwartze. [*After brooding for a time.*] Magda!

Marie. [*Running in anxiously.*] For Heaven's sake, what's the matter?

Schwartze. [*Chokingly.*] Magda—I want Magda.

Marie. [*Goes to the door and opens it.*] She's coming now—down the stairs.

Schwartze. So! [*Pulls himself together with an effort.*]

Marie. [*Clasping her hands.*] Don't hurt her! [*Pauses with the door open.* MAGDA *is seen descending the stairs. She enters in traveling-dress, hat in hand, very pale, but calm.*]

Magda. I heard you call, father.

Schwartze. I have something to say to you.

Magda. And I to you.

Schwartze. Go in—into my room.

Magda. Yes, father. [*She goes to the door, left.* SCHWARTZE *follows her.* MARIE, *who has drawn back frightened to the dining-room door, makes an unseen gesture of entreaty.*]

CURTAIN

ACT FOURTH

SCENE.—*The same.*

[MRS. SCHWARTZE *and* MARIE *discovered.* MRS. SCHWARTZE, *in hat and cloak, is knocking on the door at the left.*]

Mrs. Schwartze. Leopold! Oh, Heaven, I dare not go in.

Marie. No, no, don't! Oh, if you'd only seen his face!

Mrs. Schwartze. And they've been in there half an hour, you say?

Marie. Longer, longer!

Mrs. Schwartze. Now she's speaking! [*Listening, frightened.*] He's threatening her. Marie, Marie! Run into the garden. The pastor's there, in the arbor. Tell him everything—about Mr. von Keller's being here—and ask him to come in quickly.

Marie. Yes, mamma. [*Hurries to the hall-door.*]

Mrs. Schwartze. Wait a minute, Marie. Has Theresa heard anything? If it should get about——

Marie. I've already sent her away, mamma.

Mrs. Schwartze. That's right, that's right. [*Exit* MARIE. MRS. SCHWARTZE *knocks again.*] Leopold! listen to me, Leopold! [*Retreating.*] Oh, Heaven! he's coming! [*Enter* SCHWARTZE, *bent and tottering.*]

Mrs. Schwartze. How do you feel, Leopold?

Schwartze. [*Sinking into a chair.*] Yes, yes—just like the roses. The knife comes, and cuts the stem, and the wound can never be healed. What am I saying? What?

Mrs. Schwartze. He's out of his mind.

Schwartze. No, no, I'm not out of my mind. I know quite well— [MAGDA *appears at the door, left.*]

Mrs. Schwartze. What have you done to him?

Schwartze. Yes, what have you—what have you? That is my daughter. What shall I do with my daughter now?

Magda. [*Humbly, almost beseechingly.*] Father, isn't it best, after what has happened, that you should let me go—that you should drive me into the streets? You must get free of me if this house is to be pure again.

Schwartze. So, so, so! You think, then, you have only to go—to go away, out there, and all will be as before? And we? What will become of us? I—good God!—I—I have one foot in the grave—soon it will be over—but the mother, and your sister—your sister.

Magda. Marie has the husband she wants——

Schwartze. No one will marry a sister of yours. [*With aversion.*] No, no. Don't think it!

Magda. [*Aside.*] My God!

Schwartze. [*To* MRS. SCHWARTZE.] See, she's beginning now to realize what she has done.

Mrs. Schwartze. Yes; what——

Magda. [*In tender sympathy, but still with a tinge of superiority.*] My poor old father—listen to me—I can't change what has passed. I will give Marie half my fortune. I will make up a thousand times all that I have made you suffer today. But now, I implore you, let me go my way.

Schwartze. Oho!

Magda. What do you want of me? What am I to you? Yesterday at this time you did not know even whether I still lived; and today— It is madness to demand that I should think and feel again as you do; but I am afraid of you, father, I'm afraid of you all—ah, I am not myself— [*Breaking out in torment.*] I cannot bear the sorrow.

Schwartze. Ha, ha!

Magda. Father dear, I will humble myself before you willingly. I lament with my whole heart that I've brought sorrow to you today, for my flesh and blood still belong to you. But I must live out my own life. That I owe to myself—to myself and mine. Good-by!

Schwartze. [*Stopping her.*] Where are you going?

Magda. Let me pass, father.

Schwartze. I'll kill you first. [*Seizes her.*]

Mrs. Schwartze. Leopold! [*Enter* HEFFTERDINGT. *He throws himself between them with a cry of horror.* MAGDA, *freed by the old man, goes slowly back, with her eyes fixed on the* PASTOR, *to the seat, left, where she remains motionless.*]

Heffterdingt. [*After a silence.*] In God's name!

Schwartze. Yes, yes, yes, Pastor—it made a fine family group, eh? Look at her! She has soiled my name. Any scoundrel can break my sword. That is my daughter; that is——

Heffterdingt. Dear Colonel, these are things which I do not understand, and which I do not care to understand. But it seems to me there must be something to do, instead of——

Schwartze. Yes, to do—yes, yes—there's much to do here. I have much to do. I don't see why I'm standing here. The worst of it is—the worst of it is, he can say to me—this man—you are a cripple—with your shaking hand—with such a one I can't fight, even if I have had your daughter for a— But I will show him—I will show him— Where is my hat?

Mrs. Schwartze. Where are you going, Leopold? [MAGDA *rises.*]

Schwartze. My hat!

Mrs. Schwartze. [*Gives him hat and stick.*] Here, here!

Schwartze. So! [*To* MAGDA.] Learn to thank the God, in whom you disbelieve, that he has preserved your father until this hour, for he shall bring you back your honor!

Magda. [*Kneeling, and kissing his hand.*] Don't do it, father! I don't deserve this of you.

Schwartze. [*Bends weeping over her head.*] My poor, poor child!

Magda. [*Calling after him.*] Father!

[*Exit* SCHWARTZE *quickly.*]

Mrs. Schwartze. My child, whatever happens, we women—we must hold together.

Magda. Thanks, mamma. The play will soon be played out now.

Heffterdingt. My dear Mrs. Schwartze, Marie is out there, full of sorrow. Go and say a kind word to her.

Mrs. Schwartze. What shall I say to comfort her, when all the happiness has gone out of her life? [MAGDA *jumps up in anguish.*] Oh, Pastor, Pastor! [*Exit.*]

Magda. [*After a silence.*] Oh, I am so tired!

Heffterdingt. Miss Magda!

Magda. [*Brooding.*] I think I shall see those glaring bloodshot eyes before me always—wherever I go.

Heffterdingt. Miss Magda!

Magda. How you must despise me!

Heffterdingt. Ah, Miss Magda, I have long been a stranger to despite. We are all poor sinners——

Magda. [*With a bitter laugh.*] Truly we are— Oh, I am so tired!—it is crushing me. There is that old man going out to let himself be shot dead for my sake, as if he could atone for all my sins with his single life! Oh, I am so tired!

Heffterdingt. Miss Magda—I can only conjecture—what all this means—but you have given me the right to speak to you as a friend. And I feel that I am even more. I am your fellow-sinner, Miss Magda!

Magda. Good Heavens! Still harping on that!

Heffterdingt. Do you feel the obligation, Miss Magda, to bring honor and peace back to this house?

Magda. [*Breaking out in anguish.*] You have lived through the sorrow, and ask whether I feel it?

Heffterdingt. I think your father will obtain from that gentleman the declaration that he is ready for any sort of peaceable satisfaction.

Magda. Ha, ha! The noble soul! But what can I do?

Heffterdingt. You can—not spurn the hand which he will offer you.

Magda. What? You don't mean— This man—this strange man whom I despise—how, how could I——

Heffterdingt. Dear Miss Magda, there comes an hour to almost every man when he collects the broken pieces of his life, to form them together into a new design. I have found it so with myself. And now it is your turn.

Magda. I will not do it—I will not do it.

Heffterdingt. You will have to.

Magda. I would rather take my child in my arms and throw myself into the sea.

Heffterdingt. [*Suppresses a violent start; continues after a silence, hoarsely.*] Of course, that is the simplest solution. And your father can follow you.

Magda. Oh, have pity on me! I must do whatever you demand. I don't know how you have gained such power over me. Oh, man, if the slightest memory of what you once felt, if the least pity for your own youth, still lives within you, you cannot sacrifice me so!

Heffterdingt. I do not sacrifice you alone, Miss Magda.

Magda. [*With awakening perception.*] Good God!

Heffterdingt. There's no other way. I see none. You know yourself that the old man would not survive it. And what would become of your mother, and what would become of your poor sister? Miss Magda, it is as if with your own hand you set fire to the house and let everything burn that is within. And this house is still your home——

Magda. [*In growing agony.*] I will not, I will not. This house is not my home. My home is with my child!

Heffterdingt. This child, too. He will grow up fatherless, and will be asked, "Where is your father?" He will come and ask you, "Where is my father?" What can you answer him? And, Miss Magda, he who has not peace in his heart from the beginning will never win it in the end.

Magda. All this is not true, and if it were true, have I not a heart too? Have I not a life to live also? Have I not a right to seek my own happiness?

Heffterdingt. [*Harshly.*] No; no one has that. But do as you will. Ruin your home, ruin your father and sister and child, and then see what heart you have to seek your own happiness. [MAGDA *bows her head, sobbing. The* PASTOR *crosses to her, and leans over the table pityingly, with his hand on her hair.*] My poor——

Magda. [*Seizing his hand.*] Answer me one question. You have sacrificed your life for my sake. Do you think, today, in spite of what you know and what you do not know, do you think I am worth this sacrifice?

Heffterdingt. [*Constrained, as if making a confession.*] I have said already I am your fellow-sinner, Miss Magda.

Magda. [*After a pause.*] I will do what you demand.

Heffterdingt. I thank you.

Magda. Good-by.

Heffterdingt. Good-by. [*Exit. He is seen through the open door speaking to* MARIE *and sending her in.* MAGDA *remains motionless, with her face in her hands until he has gone.*]

[*Enter* MARIE.]

Marie. What can I do, Magda?

Magda. Where has the pastor gone?

Marie. Into the garden. Mamma is with him.

Magda. If father asks for me, say I shall wait there. [*Nods toward left.*]

Marie. And haven't you a word for me, Magda?

Magda. Oh, yes. Fear nothing. [*Kisses her on the forehead.*] Everything will come out well, so well—no, no, no. [*In weary bitterness.*] Everything will come out quite well. [*Exit, left.* MARIE *goes into the dining-room.*]

[*Enter* SCHWARTZE. *He takes out a pistol-case and opens it. Takes a pistol, cocks it with difficulty, examines the barrel, and aims at a point on the wall. His arm trembles violently. He strikes it angrily, and lets the pistol sink. Enter* MAX.]

Schwartze. [*Without turning.*] Who's there?

Max. It's I, uncle.

Schwartze. Max? Ah, you may come in.

Max. Uncle, Marie told me— What are the pistols for, uncle?

Schwartze. Ah, they used to be fine pistols —beautiful pistols. See, boy, with this I have hit the ace of hearts at twenty paces, or say fifteen. And fifteen would be enough. We ought to have been in the garden already, but—but [*helplessly touches his trembling arm, almost in tears*]—but I can nevermore——

Max. [*Hurrying to him.*] Uncle? [*They embrace each other for a moment.*]

Schwartze. It's all right—it's all right.

Max. Uncle, I need not say that I take your place, that I meet any man you point out; it is my right.

Schwartze. Yours—why? In what capacity? Will you marry into a disgraced family?

Max. Uncle!

Schwartze. Are you prepared to strip off the uniform of our regiment? Yes, I might set up a gambling-house, and you could play the stool-pigeon for a living. There is no knowing what we might do. What! you, with your beautiful name, your noble name, propose this sacrifice—and I to profit by it! Ha, ha! No, my boy; even if you still were willing, I am not. This house and all within are marked for ruin. Go your way from it. With the name of Schwartze you have nothing more to do.

Max. Uncle, I demand that you——

Schwartze. Hush! Not now! [*Motions to the door.*] Soon I may need you as one needs a friend in such affairs, but not now—not now. First I must find the gentleman. He was not at home—the gentleman was not at home. But he shall not think he has escaped me. If he is out a second time, then, my son, your work begins. Until then, be patient—be patient.

[*Enter* THERESA *from the hall.*]

Theresa. Councillor von Keller.

[SCHWARTZE *starts.*]

Max. He here! How——

Schwartze. Let him come in.

[*Exit* THERESA.]

Max. Uncle! [*Points to himself in great excitement.* SCHWARTZE *shakes his head, and signs to* MAX *to leave the room. Enter* VON KELLER. *Exit* MAX. *They meet in the doorway.* VON KELLER *greets* MAX *courteously.* MAX *restrains himself from insulting him.*]

Von Keller. Colonel, I am grieved at having missed you. When I returned from the Casino, where I am always to be found at noon—where, I say, I am always to be found—your card lay on the table; and as I imagine that there are matters of importance to be discussed between us, I made haste—as I say, I have made haste——

Schwartze. Councillor, I do not know whether in this house there should be a chair for you, but since you have come here so quickly, you must be tired. I beg you to be seated.

Von Keller. Thanks. [*Sits down near the open pistol-case, starts as he sees it, watches the* COLONEL *apprehensively.*] H'm!

Schwartze. Now, have you nothing to say to me?

Von Keller. Allow me first one question: Did your daughter, after our conversation, say anything to you about me?

Schwartze. Councillor, have you nothing to say to me?

Von Keller. Oh, certainly, I have a great deal to say to you. I would gladly, for instance, express to you a wish, a request; but I don't quite know whether— Won't you tell me, at least, has your daughter spoken of me at all favorably?

Schwartze. [*Angrily.*] I must know, sir, how we stand, in what light I am to treat you.

Von Keller. Oh, pardon me, now I understand— [*Working himself up.*] Colonel, you see in me a man who takes life earnestly. The days of a light youth— [SCHWARTZE *looks up angrily.*] Pardon me, I meant to say—since early this morning a holier and, if I may say so, a more auspicious resolution has arisen within me. Colonel, I am not a man of many words. I have already wandered from the point. As one man of honor to another, or—in short, Colonel, I have the honor to ask you for the hand of your daughter. [SCHWARTZE *sits motionless, breathing heavily.*] Pardon me, you do not answer—am I perhaps not worthy——

Schwartze. [*Groping for his hand.*] No, no, no; not that—not that. I am an old man. These last hours have been a little too much for me. Don't mind me.

Von Keller. H'm, h'm!

Schwartze. [*Rising, and closing the lid of the pistol-case.*] Give me your hand, my young friend. You have brought heavy sorrow upon me—heavy sorrow. But you have promptly and bravely made it good. Give me the other hand. So, so! And now do you wish to speak to her also? You will have much to say. Eh?

Von Keller. If I might be allowed.

Schwartze. [*Opens the hall-door and speaks off, then opens the door, left.*] Magda!

[*Enter* MAGDA.]

Magda. What is it, father?

Schwartze. Magda, this gentleman asks for the honor— [*As he sees the two together, he looks with sudden anger from one to the other.*]

Magda. [*Anxiously.*] Father?

Schwartze. Now everything's arranged. Don't make it too long! [*To* MAGDA.] Yes, everything's all right now. [*Exit.*]

Von Keller. Ah, my dearest Magda, who could have suspected it?

Magda. Then we are to be married.

Von Keller. Above all, I don't want you to entertain the idea that any design of mine has been at the bottom of this development which I welcome so gladly, which I——

Magda. I haven't reproached you.

Von Keller. No, you have no reason.

Magda. None whatever.

Von Keller. Let me further say to you that it has always been my strongest wish that Providence might bring us together again.

Magda. Then you have really never ceased to love me?

Von Keller. Well, as an honorable man and without exaggeration I can scarcely assert that. But since early this morning a holier and a more auspicious resolution has arisen within me——

Magda. Pardon me, would this holy and auspicious resolution have arisen within you just the same if I had come back to my home in poverty and shame?

Von Keller. My dearest Magda, I am neither self-seeking nor a fortune-hunter, but I know what is due to myself and to my position. In other circumstances there would have been no social possibility of making legitimate our old relations——

Magda. I must consider myself, then, very happy in these ten long years to have worked up unconsciously toward such a high goal.

Von Keller. I don't know whether I am too sensitive, but that sounds almost like irony. And I hardly think that——

Magda. That it is fitting from me?

Von Keller. [*Deprecatingly.*] Oh!

Magda. I must ask for your indulgence. The rôle of a patient and forbearing wife is new to me. Let us speak, then, of the future [*sits and motions to him to do the same*]—of our future. What is your idea of what is to come?

Von Keller. You know, my dearest Magda, I have great designs. This provincial town is no field for my statesmanship. Besides, it is my duty now to find a place which will be worthy of your social talents. For you will give up the stage and concert-hall—that goes without saying.

Magda. Oh, that goes without saying?

Von Keller. Oh, I beseech you—you don't understand the conditions; it would be a fatal handicap for me. I might as well leave the service at once.

Magda. And if you did?

Von Keller. Oh, you can't be in earnest. For a hard-working and ambitious man who sees a brilliant future before him to give up honor and position, and as his wife's husband to play the vagabond—to live merely as the husband of his wife? Shall I turn over your music, or take the tickets at the box-office? No, my dearest friend, you underestimate me, and the position I fill in society. But don't be uneasy. You will have nothing to repent of. I have every respect for your past triumphs, but [*pompously*] the highest reward to which your feminine ambition can aspire will be achieved in the drawing-room.

Magda. [*Aside.*] Good Heaven, this thing I'm doing is mere madness!

Von Keller. What do you say? [MAGDA *shakes her head.*] And then the wife, the ideal wife, of modern times is the consort, the true, self-sacrificing helper of her husband. For instance, you, by your queenly personality and by the magic of your voice, will overcome my enemies, and knit even my friends more closely to me. And we will be largely hospitable. Our house shall be the center of the most distinguished society, who still keep to the severely gracious manners of our forefathers. Gracious and severe may seem contradictory terms, but they are not.

Magda. You forget that the child on whose account this union is to be consummated will keep the severely inclined away from us.

Von Keller. Yes, I know, dear Magda, it will be painful for you; but this child must of course remain the deepest secret between us. No one must suspect——

Magda. [*Astounded and incredulous.*] What—what do you say?

Von Keller. Why, it would ruin us. No, no, it is absurd to think of it. But we can make a little journey every year to wherever it is being educated. One can register under a false name; that is not unusual in foreign parts, and is hardly criminal. And when we are fifty years old, and other regular conditions have been fulfilled [*laughing*], that can be arranged, can't it? Then we can, under some pretext, adopt it, can't we?

Magda. [*Breaks into a piercing laugh; then, with clasped hands and staring eyes.*] My sweet! My little one! *Mio bambino! Mio povero—bam*—you—you—I am to—ha, ha, ha! [*Tries to open the folding door.*] Go! go! [*Enter* SCHWARTZE.]

Schwartze. What——

Magda. Good, you're here! Free me from this man, take this man away from me.

Schwartze. What?

Magda. I have done everything you demanded. I have humbled myself, I have surrendered my judgment, I have let myself be carried like a lamb to the slaughter. But my child I will not leave. Give up my child to save *his* career!

[*Throws herself into a chair.*]

Schwartze. Mr. von Keller, will you please——

Von Keller. I am inconsolable, Colonel. But it seems that the conditions which for the interest of both parties I had to propose, do not meet the approbation——

Schwartze. My daughter is no longer in the position to choose the conditions under which she—— Dr. von Keller, I ask your pardon for the scene to which you have just been subjected. Wait for me at your home. I will myself bring you my daughter's consent. For that I pledge you my word of honor. [*Sensation.* MAGDA *rises quickly.*]

Von Keller. Have you considered what——

Schwartze. [*Holding out his hand.*] I thank you, Dr. von Keller.

Von Keller. Not at all. I have only done my duty. [*Exit, with a bow.*]

Magda. [*Stretching herself.*] So! Now I'm the old Magda again. [SCHWARTZE *locks the three doors silently.*] Do you think, father, that I shall become docile by being shut up?

Schwartze. So! Now we are alone. No one sees us but He who sees us—there [*pointing upward*]. Quiet yourself, my child. We must talk together.

Magda. [*Sits down.*] Good! We can come to an understanding, then—my home and I.

Schwartze. Do you see that I am now quite calm?

Magda. Certainly.

Schwartze. Quite calm, am I not? Even my arm does not tremble. What has happened, has happened. But just now I gave your betrothed——

Magda. My betrothed?— Father dear!

Schwartze. I gave your betrothed my word of honor. And that must be kept, don't you see?

Magda. But if it is not in your power, my dear father.

Schwartze. Then I must die—then I must simply die. One cannot live on when one— You are an officer's daughter. Don't you understand that?

Magda. [*Compassionately.*] My God!

Schwartze. But before I die, I must set my home in order, must I not? Everyone has something which he holds sacred. What is sacred to your inmost soul?

Magda. My art.

Schwartze. No, that is not enough. It must be more sacred.

Magda. My child.

Schwartze. Good! Your child—your child —you love it? [MAGDA *nods.*] You wish to see it again? [*She nods.*] And—yes—if you made an oath upon its head [*makes a motion as if he laid his hand upon a child's head*], then you would not perjure yourself? [MAGDA *shakes her head, smiling.*] That's well. [*Rising.*] Either you swear to me now, as upon his head, that you will become the honorable wife of his father, or—neither of us two shall go out of this room alive.

[*Sinks back on the seat.*]

MAGDA. [*After a short silence.*] My poor, dear papa! Why do you torture yourself so? And do you think that I will let myself be constrained by locked doors? You cannot believe it.

Schwartze. You will see.

Magda. [*In growing excitement.*] And what do you really want of me? Why do you trouble yourself about me? I had almost said, what have you all to do with me?

Schwartze. That you will see.

Magda. You blame me for living out my life without asking you and the whole family for permission. And why should I not? Was I not without family? Did you not send me out into the world to earn my bread, and then disown me because the way in which I earned it was not to your taste? Whom did I harm? Against whom did I sin? Oh, if I had remained the daughter of the house. like Marie, who is nothing and does nothing without the sheltering roof of the home, who passes straight from the arms of her father into the arms of her husband; who receives from the family life, thought, character, everything—yes, then you would have been right. In such a one the slightest error would have ruined everything—conscience, honor, self-respect. But I? Look at me. I was alone. I was as shelterless as a man knocked about in the world, dependent on the work of my own hands. If you give us the right to hunger—and I have hungered—why do you deny us the right to love, as we can find it, and to happiness, as we can understand it?

Schwartze. You think, my child, because you are free and a great artist, that you can set at naught——

Magda. Leave art out of the question. Consider me nothing more than the seamstress or the servant-maid who seeks, among strangers, the little food and the little love she needs. See how much the family with its morality demands from us! It throws us on our own resources, it gives us neither shelter nor happiness, and yet, in our loneliness, we must live according to the laws which it has planned for itself alone. We must still crouch in the corner, and there wait patiently until a respectful wooer happens to come. Yes, wait. And meanwhile the war for existence of body and soul is consuming us. Ahead we see nothing but sorrow and despair, and yet shall we not once dare to give what we have of youth and strength to the man for whom our whole being cries? Gag us, stupefy us, shut us up in harems or in cloisters—and that perhaps would be best. But if you give us our freedom, do not wonder if we take advantage of it.

Schwartze. There, there! That is the spirit of rebellion abroad in the world. My child— my dear child—tell me that you were not in earnest—that you—that you—pity me—if— [*Looking for the pistol-case.*] I don't know what may happen—child—have pity on me!

Magda. Father, father, be calm, I cannot bear that.

Schwartze. I will not do it—I cannot do it— [*Looking still for the pistol-case.*] Take it from me! Take it from me!

Magda. What, father?

Schwartze. Nothing, nothing, nothing. I ask you for the last time.

Magda. Then you persist in it?

Schwartze. My child, I warn you. You know I cannot do otherwise.

Magda. Yes, father, you leave me no other way. Well, then, are you sure that you ought to force me upon this man—[SCHWARTZE *listens*] that, according to your standards, I am altogether worthy of him? [*Hesitating, looking into space.*] I mean—that he was the only one in my life?

Schwartze. [*Feels for the pistol-case and takes the pistol out.*] You jade! [*He advances upon her, trying to raise the weapon. At the same moment he falls back on the seat, where he remains motionless, with staring eyes, the pistol grasped in his hand, which hangs down by his side.*]

Magda. [*With a loud cry.*] Father! [*She flies toward the stove for shelter from the weapon, then makes a few steps, with her hands before her face.*] Father!

[*She sinks, with her knees in a chair, her face on the back. Calling and knocking outside. The door is broken open.*]

[*Enter* MAX, MARIE, HEFFTERDINGT, *and* MRS. SCHWARTZE.]

Mrs. Schwartze. Leopold, what's the matter? Leopold! [*To the* PASTOR.] O my God, he's as he used to be!

Marie. Papa dear! Speak, one word!

[*Throws herself down at his right.*]

Heffterdingt. Get the doctor, Max.

Max. Is it a stroke?

Heffterdingt. I think so. [*Exit* MAX. *Aside to* MAGDA.] Come to him. [*As she hesitates.*] Come; it is the end.

[*Leads her trembling to* SCHWARTZE'S *chair.*]

Mrs. Schwartze. [*Who has tried to take the pistol.*] Let it go, Leopold; what do you want with it? See, he's holding the pistol and won't let it go.

Heffterdingt. [*Aside.*] It is the convulsion. He cannot. My dear old friend, can you understand what I'm saying to you? [SCHWARTZE *bows his head a little.* MAGDA *sinks down at his left.*] God, the All-Merciful One, has called you from on high. You are not her judge. Have you no sign of forgiveness for her?

[SCHWARTZE *shakes his head slowly.*]

Marie. [*Sinking down by* MAGDA.] Papa, give her your blessing, dear papa!

[*A smile transfigures his face. The pistol escapes from his hand. He raises his hand slowly to place it on* MARIE'S *head. In the midst of this motion a spasm goes through his body. His arm falls back, his head sinks.*]

Mrs. Schwartze. [*Crying out.*] Leopold!

Heffterdingt. [*Taking her hand.*] He has gone home.

[*He folds his hands. Silent prayer, broken by the sobbing of the women.*]

Magda. [*Springing up and spreading out her arms in agony.*] Oh, if I had only never come! [HEFFTERDINGT *makes a motion to beg her silence. She misunderstands.*] Are you going to drive me away? His life was the cost of my coming. May I not stay now?

Heffterdingt. [*Simply and peacefully.*] No one will hinder you from praying upon his grave.

CURTAIN FALLS SLOWLY

CYRANO DE BERGERAC*

By

EDMOND ROSTAND

Translated from the French by GERTRUDE HALL

When Rostand was asked if his interest in Cyrano de Bergerac had begun in childhood, he replied: "Yes and no; I was for a long time pursued by that personage Cyrano; he haunted me at College and gradually, with some help from me, he became the center of a dramatic action." In this same conversation, recently published by his intimate neighbor at Cambo, Paul Faure, Rostand traced the growth of this early interest toward the finished play. In school he had come greatly to admire a master "whose soul was as beautiful as his body was ugly." The final incentive to make a play on the theme came from Rostand's own assumption of the part in real life. He shared the love secrets of a dull and bashful schoolmate who had failed to make any progress with an evasive young lady. Rostand spurred him on and finally dictated love letters that won not only the girl but also the boy's father—who had artfully intercepted them—to a belief in the young rascal's genius. Even the duel, which to most readers no doubt passes as the good old stuff of footlights and laths, was for Rostand the vivid revival of another boyhood memory, that of a man who fought a duel while visiting Edmond's father and who allowed the young poet to play with the swords. The final composition of the play, as was true of all he wrote, was long delayed and painstakingly elaborated. For years he was "afraid to touch it," and the writing itself was "a kind of torture with constant change and rewriting and replanning." In later years ill health still further extended the time of writing.

That Cyrano stood in the same close relationship to Rostand as Faust, Hamlet, and Alceste did to their dramatic authors accounts sufficiently for the immense superiority of this play to all others by the same poet; although in point of literary elaboration *L'Aiglon* and *Chantecler* may even outdo it, *The Romancers, Princess Faraway,* and *The Woman of Samaria* seem by comparison pale and academic. Perhaps Clayton Hamilton is not greatly exaggerating when he says, "No other play in history, before or since, has attained a popular success so instantaneous and so enormous."

Certainly no other poet of comparable genius in the late nineteenth or in the twentieth century has given himself so painstakingly and with so little condescension to the business of stagecraft. At school he gave more attention to poetry than to law, and in summers spent at Luchon he and his pal, Henry de Gorsse, produced plays in Edmond's garden.

In 1890 Rostand was married and settled in Paris. He at once began work for the professional theater. His *Two Pierrots* is still unacted but *The Romancers* was chosen for production at the Théâtre Français. In this partly successful venture he made the friendship of the actor Constant Coquelin, who gave him the final inspiration in carrying out his plans for Cyrano and for whom also he wrote the rôles of Flambeau and Chantecler. Coquelin was also the poet's staunch defender in the dark period when only he and a forgotten Mme. Marni believed that *Cyrano de Bergerac* could possibly succeed.

"When from among our poor contemporary works," said Rostand, speaking at the great actor's funeral, "he had made a choice, he gave himself to it devotedly and with enthusiasm. He would allow no one to doubt its value; he carried it through with passionate zeal." Similarly Mme. Sarah Bernhardt, who had produced with some success *The Woman of Samaria,* a play which without her interpretive genius stood little chance of success, inspired Rostand to write *L'Aiglon,* which, although inferior to *Cyrano,* easily takes rank as the next greatest verse play of its age. No dramatist has been more fortunate in his interpreters.

Although we inevitably think of Rostand's romantic verse dramas as a unique occurrence in an age when the naturalism of Ibsen, Strindberg, and Becque held sway in France as elsewhere, they were, in reality, part of a reactionary movement in the French theater, of which Jean Richepin was a distinguished leader. This natural revulsion from the inundation of prose and even banality brought little new, except a tone of actuality in style, to make it more than a passing phenomenon without important results. The deeper and more fatal assaults on realism were yet to make themselves felt. It is at least significant that Rostand's later *Chantecler,* which failed in the elaborate representational production at the Porte Saint-Martin in 1910, could be produced successfully at the same theater in a futurist manner in 1928.

Cyrano de Bergerac is a romantic character study which owes its phenomenal popularity to a combination of favorable circumstances that few plays in the history of the world can boast: a colorful hero of romance as subject, whose inner and outer life were in sharp and dramatic contrast; a poet of genius devoting a life study to his play and to the theater; an actor endowed beyond all others of his age to speak its verse and to embody its conception, and a zeal for a fresh reactionary dramatic movement in which this play takes highest rank.

Production

Cyrano de Bergerac was produced Dec. 28, 1897, by Constant Coquelin at the historic Théâtre Porte Saint-Martin, to which he had seceded from the Théâtre Français. Trained in the comedy technique of Molière's theater, Coquelin had gained a supremacy in speech, facial expression, and gesture such as no actor of our age has seriously challenged. His imagination put this skill finely in harmony with every character in his vast repertory. No one who did not see him can easily conceive the shades of expressiveness and the infinite variety of character suggestion that made his art preeminent. Artist and photographer have done much to assist, but they fail to reproduce the music of his voice and the expressive mobility of face and limb. The combination of poet and actor has rarely been more fortunate, each inspiring the other to the greatest achievement of their careers. The play was first given in New York, Oct. 3, 1898, by Richard Mansfield, who made it almost equally popular in English. It was not produced by any English actor until 1900, and then by Sir Charles Wyndham, who, in T. J. Grein's opinion, was, except in voice, better suited to the part than Coquelin himself. The phenomenal revival of the play in 1924 by Walter Hampden made it almost as significant an event for our generation as it was for its own.

EDMOND ROSTAND

Born 1868, Marseilles, France.
Paris lycée and law school.
1888, His first play, *The Red Glove* (not produced).
1890, First volume of poems.
1894, *The Romancers,* the first of his plays to be produced at the Théâtre Français.
1895, *The Princess Faraway* played by Sarah Bernhardt.
1901, Made a member of the French Academy. Retired to Cambo in the South of France because of ill health.
Died 1918.

PLAYS

1888 *Le Gant Rouge (The Red Glove).* 1891 *Les Deux Pierrots* (translated as *Weeping Pierrot and Laughing Pierrot*). 1894 *Les Romanesques* (translated as *The Romancers, The Romantics,* and *The Fantasticks*). 1895 *La Princesse Lointaine* (translated as *The Princess Faraway* and *The Lady of Dreams*). 1897 *La Samaritaine* (translated as *The Woman of Samaria*). 1897 *Cyrano de Bergerac* (translated under the same title). 1900 *L'Aiglon* (translated as *L'Aiglon* and *The Eaglet*). 1910 *Chantecler* (translated under the same title). 1910 *Le Bois Sacré* (*The Sacred Wood*). 1921 *La Dernière Nuit de Don Juan* (published posthumously and translated as *The Last Night of Don Juan*).

CYRANO DE BERGERAC

Characters

CYRANO DE BERGERAC.
CHRISTIAN DE NEUVILLETTE.
COMTE DE GUICHE.
RAGUENEAU.
LE BRET.
CAPTAIN CARBON DE CASTEL-JALOUX.
LIGNIÈRE.
DE VALVERT.
MONTFLEURY.
BELLEROSE.
JODELET.
CUIGY.
BRISSAILLE.
A BORE.
A MOUSQUETAIRE.
OTHER MOUSQUETAIRES.
A SPANISH OFFICER.
A LIGHT-CAVALRY MAN.
A DOORKEEPER.
A BURGHER.
HIS SON.
A PICKPOCKET.
A SPECTATOR.
A WATCHMAN.
BERTRANDOU THE FIFER.
A CAPUCHIN.
TWO MUSICIANS.
SEVEN CADETS.
THREE MARQUISES.
POETS.
PASTRYCOOKS.
ROXANE.
SISTER MARTHA.
LISE.
THE SWEETMEAT VENDER.
MOTHER MARGARET.
THE DUENNA.
SISTER CLAIRE.
AN ACTRESS.
A SOUBRETTE.
A FLOWER-GIRL.
PAGES.

The crowd, bourgeois, marquises, mousquetaires, pickpockets, pastrycooks, poets, Gascony Cadets, players, fiddlers, pages, children, Spanish soldiers, spectators, précieuses, actresses, bourgeoises, nuns, etc.

The first four acts in 1640; the fifth in 1655.

ACT FIRST

A PLAY AT THE HOTEL DE BOURGOGNE

The great hall of the Hôtel de Bourgogne, in 1640. A sort of tennis-court arranged and decorated for theatrical performances.

The hall is a long rectangle, seen obliquely, so that one side of it constitutes the background, which runs from the position of the front wing at the right, to the line of the furthest wing at the left, and forms an angle with the stage, which is equally seen obliquely.

This stage is furnished, on both sides, along the wings, with benches. The drop-curtain is composed of two tapestry hangings, which can be drawn apart. Above a Harlequin cloak, the royal escutcheon. Broad steps lead from the raised platform of the stage into the house. On either side of these steps, the musicians' seats. A row of candles fills the office of footlights.

Two galleries run along the side; the lower one is divided into boxes. No seats in the pit, which is the stage proper. At the back of the pit, that is to say, at the right, in the front, a few seats raised like steps, one above the other; and, under a stairway which leads to the upper seats, and of which the lower end only is visible, a stand decked with small candelabra, jars full of flowers, flagons and glasses, dishes heaped with sweetmeats, etc.

In the center of the background, under the box-tier, the entrance to the theater, a large door which half opens to let in the spectators. On the panels of this door, and in several corners, and above the sweetmeat stand, red playbills announcing LA CLORISE.

[*At the rise of the curtain, the house is nearly dark, and still empty. The chandeliers are let down in the middle of the pit, until time to light them.*

The audience, arriving gradually. Cavaliers, burghers, lackeys, pages, the fiddlers, etc.

A tumult of voices is heard beyond the door; enter brusquely a CAVALIER.]

Doorkeeper. [*Running in after him.*] Not so fast! Your fifteen pence!

Cavalier. I come in admission free!

Doorkeeper. And why?

Cavalier. I belong to the king's light cavalry!

Doorkeeper. [*To another* CAVALIER *who has entered.*] You?

Second Cavalier. I do not pay!

Doorkeeper. But . . .

Second Cavalier. I belong to the mousquetaires!

First Cavalier. [*To the* SECOND.] It does not begin before two. The floor is empty. Let us have a bout with foils. [*They fence with foils they have brought.*]

A Lackey. [*Entering.*] Pst! . . . Flanquin!

Other Lackey. [*Arrived a moment before.*] Champagne? . . .

First Lackey. [*Taking a pack of cards from his doublet and showing it to* SECOND LACKEY.] Cards. Dice. [*Sits down on the floor.*] Let us have a game.

Second Lackey. [*Sitting down likewise.*] You rascal, willingly!

First Lackey. [*Taking from his pocket a bit of candle which he lights and sticks on the floor.*] I prigged an eyeful of my master's light!

One of the Watch. [*To a flower-girl, who comes forward.*] It is pleasant getting here before the lights.

[*Puts his arm around her waist.*]

One of the Fencers. [*Taking a thrust.*] Hit!

One of the Gamblers. Clubs!

The Watchman. [*Pursuing the girl.*] A kiss!

The Flower-Girl. [*Repulsing him.*] We shall be seen!

The Watchman. [*Drawing her into dark corner.*] No, we shall not!

A Man. [*Sitting down on the floor with others who have brought provisions.*] By coming early, you get a comfortable chance to eat.

A Burgher. [*Leading his son.*] This should be a good place, my boy. Let us stay here.

One of the Gamblers. Ace wins!

A Man. [*Taking a bottle from under his cloak and sitting down.*] A proper toper, toping Burgundy [*drinks*], I say, should tope it in Burgundy House!

The Burgher. [*To his son.*] Might one not suppose we had stumbled into some house of evil fame? [*Points with his cane at the drunkard.*] Guzzlers! . . . [*In breaking guard one of the fencers jostles him.*] Brawlers! . . . [*He falls between the gamblers.*] Gamesters! . . .

The Watchman. [*Behind him, still teasing the flower-girl.*] A kiss!

The Burgher. [*Dragging his son precipitately away.*] Bless my soul! . . . And to reflect that in this very house, my son, were given the plays of the great Rotrou!

The Youth. And those of the great Corneille!

[*A band of* PAGES *holding hands rush in performing a farandole and singing.*]

Pages. Tra la la la la la la la! . . .

Doorkeeper. [*Severely to the* PAGES.] Look, now! . . . you pages, you! none of your tricks!

First Page. [*With wounded dignity.*] Sir! . . . this want of confidence . . . [*As soon as the doorkeeper has turned away, briskly to the* SECOND PAGE.] Have you a string about you?

Second Page. With a fish-hook at the end!

First Page. We will sit up there and angle for wigs!

A Pickpocket. [*Surrounded by a number of individuals of dubious appearance.*] Come now, my little hopefuls, and learn your A B C's of trade. Being as you're not used to hooking . . .

Second Page. [*Shouting to other* PAGES *who have already taken seats in the upper gallery.*] Ho! . . . Did you bring any peashooters?

Third Page. [*From above.*] Yes! . . . And peas! [*Shoots down a volley of peas.*]

The Youth. [*To his father.*] What are we going to see?

The Burgher. "Clorise."

The Youth. By whom?

The Burgher. By Balthazar Baro. Ah, what a play it is! . . .

[*Goes toward the back on his son's arm.*]

Pickpocket. [*To his disciples.*] Particularly the lace-ruffles at the knees. . . . You're to snip off carefully!

A Spectator. [*To another, pointing toward an upper seat.*] Look! On the first night of "The Cid," I was perched up there!

Pickpocket. [*With pantomimic suggestion of spiriting away.*] Watches . . .

The Burgher. [*Coming forward again with his son.*] The actors you are about to see, my son, are among the most illustrious . . .

Pickpocket. [*With show of abstracting with furtive little tugs.*] Pocket-handkerchiefs . . .

The Burgher. Montfleury . . .

Somebody. [*Shouting from the upper gallery.*] Make haste, and light the chandeliers!

The Burgher. Bellerose, l'Epy, the Beaupré, Jodelet . . .

A Page. [*In the pit.*] Ah! . . . Here comes the goody-seller!

The Sweetmeat Vender. [*Appearing behind the stand.*] Oranges . . . Milk . . . Raspberry cordial . . . citron-wine . . .

[*Hubbub at the door.*]

Falsetto Voice. [*Outside.*] Make room, ruffians!

One of the Lackeys. [*Astonished.*] The marquises . . . in the pit!

Other Lackey. Oh, for an instant only!

[*Enter a band of foppish* YOUNG MARQUISES.]

One of the Marquises. [*Looking around the half-empty house.*] What? . . . We happen in like so many linen-drapers? Without disturbing anybody? Treading on any feet? . . . Too bad! too bad! too bad! [*He finds himself near several other gentlemen, come in a moment before.*] Cuigy, Brissaille! [*Effusive embraces.*]

Cuigy. We are of the faithful indeed. We are here before the lights.

The Marquis. Ah, do not speak of it! . . . It has put me in such a humor!

Other Marquis. Be comforted, marquis . . . here comes the candle-lighter!

The Audience. [*Greeting the arrival of the candle-lighter.*] Ah . . .

[*Many gather around the chandeliers while they are being lighted. A few have taken seats in the galleries.* LIGNIÈRE *enters, arm in arm with* CHRISTIAN DE NEUVILLETTE. LIGNIÈRE, *in somewhat disordered apparel; appearance of gentlemanly drunkard.* CHRISTIAN, *becomingly dressed, but in clothes of a slightly obsolete elegance.*]

Cuigy. Lignière!

Brissaille. [*Laughing.*] Not tipsy yet?

Lignière. [*Low to* CHRISTIAN.] Shall I present you? [CHRISTIAN *nods assent.*] Baron de Neuvillette . . . [*Exchange of bows.*]

The Audience. [*Cheering the ascent of the first lighted chandelier.*] Ah! . . .

Cuigy. [*To* BRISSAILLE, *looking at* CHRISTIAN.] A charming head . . . charming!

First Marquis. [*Who has overheard.*] Pooh! . . .

Lignière. [*Presenting* CHRISTIAN.] Messieurs de Cuigy . . . de Brissaille . . .

Christian. [*Bowing.*] Delighted! . . .

First Marquis. [*To* SECOND.] He is a pretty fellow enough, but is dressed in the fashion of some other year!

Lignière. [*To* CUIGY.] Monsieur is lately arrived from Touraine.

Christian. Yes, I have been in Paris not over twenty days. I enter the Guards tomorrow, the Cadets.

First Marquis. [*Looking at those who appear in the boxes.*] There comes the présidente Aubry!

Sweetmeat Vender. Oranges! Milk!

The Fiddlers. [*Tuning.*] La . . . la . . .

Cuigy. [*To* CHRISTIAN, *indicating the house, which is filling.*] A good house! . . .

Christian. Yes, crowded.

First Marquis. The whole of fashion!

[*They give the names of the women, as, very brilliantly attired, these enter the boxes. Exchange of bows and smiles.*]

Second Marquis. Mesdames de Guéménée . . .

Cuigy. De Bois-Dauphin . . .

First Marquis. Whom . . . time was . . . we loved! . . .

Brissaille. . . . de Chavigny . . .

Second Marquis. Who still plays havoc with our hearts!

Lignière. *Tiens!* Monsieur de Corneille has come back from Rouen!

The Youth. [*To his father.*] The Academy is present?

The Burgher. Yes . . . I perceive more than one member of it. Yonder are Boudu, Boissat, and Cureau . . . Porchères, Colomby, Bourzeys, Bourdon, Arbaut . . . All names of which not one will be forgotten. What a beautiful thought it is!

First Marquis. Attention! Our précieuses are coming into their seats . . . Barthénoide, Urimédonte, Cassandace, Félixérie . . .

Second Marquis. Ah, how exquisite are their surnames! . . . Marquis, can you tell them off, all of them?

First Marquis. I can tell them off, all of them, Marquis!

Lignière. [*Drawing* CHRISTIAN *aside.*] Dear fellow, I came in here to be of use to you. The lady does not come. I revert to my vice!

Christian. [*Imploring.*] No! No! . . . You who turn into ditties Town and Court, stay by me: you will be able to tell me for whom it is I am dying of love!

The Leader of the Violins. [*Rapping on his desk with his bow.*] Gentlemen! . . .

[*He raises his bow.*]

Sweetmeat Vender. Macaroons . . . Citronade . . . [*The fiddles begin playing.*]

Christian. I fear . . . oh, I fear to find that she is fanciful and subtle! I dare not speak to her, for I am of a simple wit. The language written and spoken in these days bewilders and baffles me. I am a plain soldier . . . shy, to boot.—She is always at the right, there, the end: the empty box.

Lignière. [*With show of leaving.*] I am going.

Christian. [*Still attempting to detain him.*] Oh, no! . . . Stay, I beseech you!

Lignière. I cannot. D'Assoucy is expecting me at the pot-house. Here is a mortal drought!

Sweetmeat Vender. [*Passing before him with a tray.*] Orangeade? . . .

Lignière. Ugh!

Sweetmeat Vender. Milk? . . .

Lignière. Pah! . . .

Sweetmeat Vender. Lacrima? . . .

Lignière. Stop! [*To* CHRISTIAN.] I will tarry a bit. . . . Let us see this lacrima? [*Sits down at the sweetmeat stand. The* VENDER *pours him a glass of lacrima.*]

[*Shouts among the audience at the entrance of a little, merry-faced, roly-poly man.*]

Audience. Ah, Ragueneau! . . .

Lignière. [*To* CHRISTIAN.] Ragueneau, who keeps the great cook-shop.

Ragueneau. [*Attired like a pastrycook in his Sunday best, coming quickly toward* LIGNIÈRE.] Monsieur, have you seen Monsieur de Cyrano?

Lignière. [*Presenting* RAGUENEAU *to* CHRISTIAN.] The pastrycook of poets and of players!

Ragueneau. [*Abashed.*] Too much honor.

Lignière. No modesty! . . . Mecænas! . . .

Ragueneau. It is true, those gentlemen are among my customers. . . .

Lignière. Debitors! . . . A considerable poet himself. . . .

Ragueneau. It has been said! . . .

Lignière. Daft on poetry! . . .

Ragueneau. It is true that for an ode. . . .

Lignière. You are willing to give at any time a tart!

Ragueneau. . . . let. A tart-let.

Lignière. Kind soul, he tries to cheapen his charitable acts! And for a triolet were you not known to give . . . ?

Ragueneau. Rolls. Just rolls.

Lignière. [*Severely.*] Buttered! . . . And the play, you are fond of the play?

Ragueneau. It is with me a passion!

Lignière. And you settle for your entrance fee with a pastry currency. Come now, among ourselves, what did you have to give today for admittance here?

Ragueneau. Four custards . . . eighteen ladyfingers. [*He looks all around.*] Monsieur de Cyrano is not here. I wonder at it.

Lignière. And why?

Ragueneau. Montfleury is billed to play.

Lignière. So he is, indeed. That ton of man will today entrance us in the part of Phœdo . . . Phœdo! . . . But what is that to Cyrano?

Ragueneau. Have you not heard? He forbade Montfleury, whom he has taken in aversion, to appear for one month upon the stage.

Lignière. [*Who is at his fourth glass.*] Well?

Ragueneau. Montfleury is billed to play.

Cuigy. [*Who has drawn near with his companions.*] He cannot be prevented.

Ragueneau. He cannot? . . . Well, I am here to see!

First Marquis. What is this Cyrano?

Cuigy. A crack-brain!

Second Marquis. Of quality?

Cuigy. Enough for daily uses. He is a cadet in the Guards. [*Pointing out a gentleman who is coming and going about the pit, as if in search of somebody.*] But his friend Le Bret can tell you. [*Calling.*] Le Bret! . . . [LE BRET *comes toward them.*] You are looking for Bergerac?

Le Bret. Yes. I am uneasy.

Cuigy. Is it not a fact that he is a most uncommon fellow?

Le Bret. [*Affectionately.*] The most exquisite being he is that walks beneath the moon!

Ragueneau. Poet!

Cuigy. Swordsman!

Brissaille. Physicist!

Le Bret. Musician!

Lignière. And what an extraordinary aspect he presents!

Ragueneau. I will not go so far as to say that I believe our grave Philippe de Champaigne will leave us a portrait of him; but the bizarre, excessive, whimsical fellow that he is would certainly have furnished the late Jacques Callot with a type of madcap fighter for one of his masques. Hat with triple feather, doublet with twice-triple skirt, cloak which his interminable rapier lifts up behind, with pomp, like the insolent tail of a cock; prouder than all the Artabans that Gascony ever bred, he goes about in his stiff Punchinello ruff, airing a nose. . . . Ah, gentlemen, what a nose is that! One cannot look upon such a specimen of the nasigera without exclaiming, "No! truly, the man exaggerates" . . . After that, one smiles, one says: "He will take it off." . . . But Monsieur de Bergerac never takes it off at all.

Le Bret. [*Shaking his head.*] He wears it always . . . and cuts down whoever breathes a syllable in comment.

Ragueneau. [*Proudly.*] His blade is half the shears of Fate!

First Marquis. [*Shrugging his shoulders.*] He will not come!

Ragueneau. He will. I wager you a chicken à la Ragueneau.

First Marquis. [*Laughing.*] Very well!

[*Murmur of admiration in the house.* ROXANE *has appeared in her box. She takes a seat in the front, her duenna at the back.* CHRISTIAN, *engaged in paying the sweetmeat vender, does not look.*]

Second Marquis. [*Uttering a series of small squeals.*] Ah, gentlemen, she is horrifically enticing!

First Marquis. A strawberry set in a peach, and smiling!

Second Marquis. So fresh that, being near her, one might catch cold in his heart!

Christian. [*Looks up, sees* ROXANE, *and, agitated, seizes* LIGNIÈRE *by the arm.*] That is she!

Lignière. [*Looking.*] Ah, that is she! . . .

Christian. Yes. Tell me at once. . . . Oh, I am afraid! . . .

Lignière. [*Sipping his wine slowly.*] Magdeleine Robin, surnamed Roxane. Subtle. Euphuistic.

Christian. Alack-a-day!

Lignière. Unmarried. An orphan. A cousin of Cyrano's . . . the one of whom they were talking.

[*While he is speaking, a richly dressed nobleman, wearing the order of the Holy Ghost on a blue ribbon across his breast, enters* ROXANE'S *box, and, without taking a seat, talks with her a moment.*]

Christian. [*Starting.*] That man? . . .

Lignière. [*Who is beginning to be tipsy, winking.*] Hé! Hé! Comte de Guiche. Enamored of her. But married to the niece of Armand de Richelieu. Wishes to manage a match between Roxane and a certain sorry lord, one Monsieur de Valvert, vicomte and . . . easy. She does not subscribe to his views, but De Guiche is powerful: he can persecute to some purpose a simple commoner. But I have duly set forth his shady machinations in a song which . . . Ho! he must bear me a grudge! The end was wicked . . . Listen! . . .

[*He rises, staggering, and lifting his glass, is about to sing.*]

Christian. No. Good evening.

Lignière. You are going? . . .

Christian. To find Monsieur de Valvert.

Lignière. Have a care. You are the one who will get killed. [*Indicating* ROXANE *by a glance.*] Stay. Some one is looking . . .

Christian. It is true . . .

[*He remains absorbed in the contemplation of* ROXANE. *The pickpockets, seeing his abstracted air, draw nearer to him.*]

Lignière. Ah, you are going to stay. Well, I am going. I am thirsty! And I am looked for . . . at all the public-houses!

[*Exit unsteadily.*]

Le Bret. [*Who has made the circuit of the house, returning toward* RAGUENEAU, *in a tone of relief.*] Cyrano is not here.

Ragueneau. And yet . . .

Le Bret. I will trust to Fortune he has not seen the announcement.

The Audience. Begin! Begin!

One of the Marquises. [*Watching* DE GUICHE, *who comes from* ROXANE'S *box, and crosses the pit, surrounded by obsequious satellites, among whom the* VICOMTE DE VALVERT.] Always a court about him, De Guiche!

Other Marquis. Pf! . . . Another Gascon!

First Marquis. A Gascon of the cold and supple sort. That sort succeeds. Believe me, it will be best to offer him our duty.

[*They approach* DE GUICHE.]

Second Marquis. These admirable ribbons! What color, Comte de Guiche? Should you call it Kiss-me-Sweet or . . . Expiring Fawn?

De Guiche. This shade is called Sick Spaniard.

First Marquis. Appropriately called, for shortly, thanks to your valor, the Spaniard will be sick indeed, in Flanders!

De Guiche. I am going upon the stage. Are you coming? [*He walks toward the stage, followed by all the marquises and men of quality. He turns and calls.*] Valvert, come!

Christian. [*Who has been listening and watching them, starts on hearing that name.*] The vicomte! . . . Ah, in his face . . . in his face I will fling my . . . [*He puts his hand to his pocket and finds the pickpocket's hand. He turns.*] *Hein?*

Pickpocket. Aï!

Christian. [*Without letting him go.*] I was looking for a glove.

Pickpocket. [*With an abject smile.*] And you found a hand. [*In a different tone, low and rapid.*] Let me go . . . I will tell you a secret.

Christian. [*Without releasing him.*] Well?

Pickpocket. Lignière, who has just left you . . .

Christian. [*As above.*] Yes? . . .

Pickpocket. Has not an hour to live. A song he made annoyed one of the great, and a hundred men—I am one of them—will be posted tonight. . . .

Christian. A hundred? . . . By whom?

Pickpocket. Honor . . .

Christian. [*Shrugging his shoulders.*] Oh! . . .

Pickpocket. [*With great dignity.*] Among rogues!

Christian. Where will they be posted?

Pickpocket. At the Porte de Nesle, on his way home. Inform him.

Christian. [*Letting him go.*] But where can I find him?

Pickpocket. Go to all the taverns—the Golden Vat, the Pine-Apple, the Belt and Bosom, the Twin Torches, the Three Funnels—and in each one leave a scrap of writing warning him.

Christian. Yes. I will run! . . . Ah, the blackguards! A hundred against one! . . . [*Looks lovingly toward* ROXANE.] Leave her! . . . [*Furiously, looking toward* VALVERT.] And him! . . . But Lignière must be prevented. [*Exit running.*]

[DE GUICHE, *the* MARQUISES, *all the gentry have disappeared behind the curtain, to place themselves on the stage-seats. The pit is crowded. There is not an empty seat in the boxes or the gallery.*]

The Audience. Begin!

A Burgher. [*Whose wig goes sailing off at the end of a string held by one of the pages in the upper gallery.*] My wig!

Screams of Delight. He is bald! . . . The pages! . . . Well done! . . . Ha, ha, ha! . . .

The Burgher. [*Furious, shaking his fist.*] Imp of Satan! . . .

[*Laughter and screams, beginning very loud and decreasing suddenly. Dead silence.*]

Le Bret. [*Astonished.*] This sudden hush? . . . [*One of the spectators whispers in his ear.*] Ah? . . .

The Spectator. I have it from a reliable quarter.

Running Murmurs. Hush! . . . Has he come? No! . . . Yes, he has! . . . In the box with the grating. . . . The cardinal! . . . the cardinal! . . . the cardinal! . . .

One of the Pages. What a shame! . . . Now we shall have to behave!

[*Knocking on the stage. Complete stillness. Pause.*]

Voice of one of the Marquises. [*Breaking the deep silence, behind the curtain.*] Snuff that candle!

Other Marquis. [*Thrusting his head out between the curtains.*] A chair!

[*A chair is passed from hand to hand, above the heads. The marquis takes it and disappears, after kissing his hand repeatedly toward the boxes.*]

A Spectator. Silence!

[*Once more, the three knocks. The curtain opens. Tableau. The marquises seated at the sides, in attitudes of languid haughtiness. The stage-setting is the faint-colored bluish sort usual in a pastoral. Four small crystal candelabra light the stage The violins play softly.*]

Le Bret. [*To* RAGUENEAU, *under breath.*] Is Montfleury the first to appear?

Ragueneau. [*Likewise under breath.*] Yes. The opening lines are his.

Le Bret. Cyrano is not here.

Ragueneau. I have lost my wager.

Le Bret. Let us be thankful. Let us be thankful.

[*A bagpipe is heard.* MONTFLEURY *appears upon the stage, enormous, in a conventional shepherd's costume, with a rose-wreathed hat set jauntily on the side of his head, breathing into a beribboned bagpipe.*]

The Pit. [*Applauding.*] Bravo, Montfleury! Montfleury!

Monteury. [*After bowing, proceeds to play the part of* PHŒDO.]

Happy the man who, freed from Fashion's fickle sway,
In exile self-prescribed whiles peaceful hours away;
Who when Zephyrus sighs amid the answering trees. . . .

A Voice. [*From the middle of the pit.*] Rogue! Did I not forbid you for one month?

[*Consternation. Everyone looks around. Murmurs.*]

Various Voices. *Hein?* What? What is the matter? [*Many in the boxes rise to see.*]

Cuigy. It is he!

Le Bret. [*Alarmed.*] Cyrano!

The Voice. King of the Obese! Incontinently vanish! . . .

The Whole Audience. [*Indignant.*] Oh!

Montfleury. But . . .

The Voice. You stop to muse upon the matter?

Several Voices. [*From the pit and the boxes.*] Hush! . . . Enough! . . . Proceed, Montfleury. . . . Fear nothing!

Montfleury. [*In an unsteady voice.*] Happy the man who freed from Fashion's f—— . . .

The Voice. [*More threatening than before.*] How is this? Shall I be constrained, Man of the Monster Belly, to enforce my regulation . . . regularly?

[*An arm holding a cane leaps above the level of the heads.*]

Montfleury. [*In a voice growing fainter and fainter.*]

Happy the man . . .

[*The cane is wildly flourished.*]

The Voice. Leave the stage!

The Pit. Oh! . . .

Montfleury. [*Choking.*]

Happy the man who freed . . .

Cyrano. [*Appears above the audience, standing upon a chair, his arms folded on his chest, his hat at a combative angle, his mustache on end, his nose terrifying.*] Ah! I shall lose my temper!

[*Sensation at sight of him.*]

Montfleury. [*To the* MARQUISES.] Messieurs, I appeal to you!

One of the Marquises. [*Languidly.*] But go ahead! . . . Play!

Cyrano. Fat man, if you attempt it, I will dust the paint off you with this!

The Marquis. Enough!

Cyrano. Let every little lordling keep silence in his seat, or I will ruffle his ribbons with my cane!

All the Marquises. [*Rising.*] This is too much! . . . Montfleury. . . .

Cyrano. Let Montfleury go home; or stay, and, having cut his ears off, I will disembowel him!

A Voice. But . . .

Cyrano. Let him go home, I said!

Other Voice. But after all . . .

Cyrano. It is not yet done? [*With show of turning up his sleeves.*] Very well, upon that stage, as on a platter trimmed with green, you shall see me carve that mount of brawn. . . .

Montfleury. [*Calling up his whole dignity.*] Monsieur, you cast indignity, in my person, upon the Muse!

Cyrano. [*Very civilly.*] Monsieur, if that lady, with whom you have naught to do, had the pleasure of beholding you . . . just as you stand there like a decorated pot! . . . she could not live, I do protest, but she hurled her buskin at you!

The Pit. Montfleury! . . . Montfleury! . . . Give us Baro's piece!

Cyrano. [*To those shouting around him.*] I beg you will show some regard for my scabbard: it is ready to give up the sword!

[*The space round him widens.*]

The Crowd. [*Backing away.*] Hey . . . softly, there!

Cyrano. [*To* MONTFLEURY.] Go off!

The Crowd. [*Closing again, and grumbling.*] Oh! . . . Oh!

Cyrano. [*Turning suddenly.*] Has somebody objections?

[*The crowd again pushes away from him.*]

A Voice. [*At the back, singing.*]

Monsieur de Cyrano, one sees,
Inclines to be tyrannical;
In spite of that Cyrannical
We shall see La Clorise!

The Whole Audience. [*Catching up the tune.*] La Clorise! La Clorise!

Cyrano. Let me hear that song again, and I will do you all to death with my stick!

A Burgher. Samson come back! . . .

Cyrano. Lend me your jaw, good man!

A Lady. [*In one of the boxes.*] This is unheard of!

A Man. It is scandalous!

A Burgher. It is irritating, to say no more.

A Page. What fun it is!

The Pit. Ksss! . . . Montfleury! . . . Cyrano! . . .

Cyrano. Be still! . . .

The Pit. [*In uproar.*] Hee-haw! . . . Baaaaah! . . . Bow-wow! . . . Cockadoodledoooooo!

Cyrano. I will . . .

A Page. Meeeow!

Cyrano. I order you to hold your tongues! . . . I dare the floor collectively to utter another sound! . . . I challenge you, one and all! . . . I will take down your names . . . Step forward, budding heroes! Each in his turn. You shall be given numbers. Come, which one of you will open the joust with me? You, monsieur? No! You? No! The first that offers is promised all the mortuary honors due the brave. Let all who wish to die hold up their hands! [*Silence.*] It is modesty that makes you shrink from the sight of my naked sword? Not a name? Not a hand?—Very good. Then I proceed. [*Turning toward the stage where* MONTFLEURY *is waiting in terror.*] As I was saying, it is my wish to see the stage cured of this tumor. Otherwise . . . [*Claps hand to his sword.*] the lancet!

Montfleury. I . . .

Cyrano. [*Gets down from his chair, and sits in the space that has become vacant around him, with the ease of one at home.*] Thrice will I clap my hands, O plenilune! At the third clap . . . eclipse!

The Pit. [*Diverted.*] Ah! . . .

Cyrano. [*Clapping his hands.*] One! . . .

Montfleury. I . . .

A Voice. [*From one of the boxes.*] Do not go! . . .

The Pit. He will stay! . . . He will go! . . .

Montfleury. Messieurs, I feel . . .

Cyrano. Two! . . .

Montfleury. I feel it will perhaps be wiser . . .

Cyrano. Three! . . .

[MONTFLEURY *disappears, as if through a trapdoor. Storm of laughter, hissing, catcalls.*]

The House. Hoo! . . . Hoo! . . . Milksop! . . . Come back! . . .

Cyrano. [*Beaming, leans back in his chair and crosses his legs.*] Let him come back, if he dare!

A Burgher. The spokesman of the company!

[BELLEROSE *comes forward on the stage and bows.*]

The Boxes. Ah, here comes Bellerose!

Bellerose. [*With elegant bearing and diction.*] Noble ladies and gentlemen . . .

The Pit. No! No! Jodelet! . . . We want Jodelet! . . .

Jodelet. [*Comes forward, speaks through his nose.*] Pack of swine!

The Pit. That is right! . . . Well said! . . . Bravo!

Jodelet. Don't bravo me! . . . The portly tragedian, whose paunch is your delight, felt sick! . . .

The Pit. He is a poltroon! . . .

Jodelet. He was obliged to leave . . .

The Pit. Let him come back!

Some. No!

Others. Yes! . . .

A Youth. [*To* CYRANO.] But, when all is said, monsieur, what good grounds have you for hating Montfleury?

Cyrano. [*Amiably, sitting as before.*] Young gosling, I have two, whereof each, singly, would be ample. Primo: He is an execrable actor, who bellows, and with grunts that would disgrace a water-carrier launches the verse that should go forth as if on pinions! . . . Secundo: is my secret.

The Old Burgher. [*Behind* CYRANO.] But without compunction you deprive us of hearing La Clorise. I am determined . . .

Cyrano. [*Turning his chair around so as to face the old gentleman; respectfully.*] Venerable mule, old Baro's verses being what they are, I do it without compunction, as you say.

The Précieuses. [*In the boxes.*] Ha! . . . Ho! . . . Our own Baro! . . . My dear, did you hear that? How can such a thing be said? . . . Ha! . . . Ho! . . .

Cyrano. [*Turning his chair so as to face the boxes; gallantly.*] Beautiful creatures, do you bloom and shine, be ministers of dreams, your smiles our anodyne. Inspire poets, but poems . . . spare to judge!

Bellerose. But the money which must be given back at the door!

Cyrano. [*Turning his chair to face the stage.*] Bellerose, you have said the only intelligent thing that has, as yet, been said! Far from me to wrong by so much as a fringe the worshipful mantle of Thespis. . . . [*He rises and flings a bag upon the stage.*] Catch! . . . and keep quiet!

The House. [*Dazzled.*] Ah! . . . Oh! . . .

Jodelet. [*Nimbly picking up the bag, weighing it with his hand.*] For such a price, you are authorized, monsieur, to come and stop the performance every day!

The House. Hoo! . . . Hoo! . . .

Jodelet. Should we be hooted in a body! . . .

Bellerose. The house must be evacuated!

Jodelet. Evacuate it!

[*The audience begins to leave;* CYRANO *looking on with a satisfied air. The crowd, however, becoming interested in the following scene, the exodus is suspended. The women in the boxes who were already standing and had put on their wraps, stop to listen and end by resuming their seats.*]

Le Bret. [*To* CYRANO.] What you have done . . . is mad!

A Bore. Montfleury! . . . the eminent actor! . . . What a scandal! . . . But the Duc de Candale is his patron! . . . Have you a patron, you?

Cyrano. No!

The Bore. You have not?

Cyrano. No!

The Bore. What? You are not protected by some great nobleman under the cover of whose name. . . .

Cyrano. [*Exasperated.*] No, I have told you twice. Must I say the same thing thrice? No, I have no protector . . . [*hand on sword*] but this will do.

The Bore. Then, of course, you will leave town.

Cyrano. That will depend.

The Bore. But the Duc de Candale has a long arm . . .

Cyrano. Not so long as mine . . . [*pointto his sword*] pieced out with this!

The Bore. But you cannot have the presumption . . .

Cyrano. I can, yes.

The Bore. But . . .

Cyrano. And now, . . . face about!

The Bore. But . . .

Cyrano. Face about, I say . . . or else, tell me why you are looking at my nose.

The Bore. [*Bewildered.*] I . . .

Cyrano. [*Advancing upon him.*] In what is it unusual?

The Bore. [*Backing.*] Your worship is mistaken.

Cyrano. [*Same business as above.*] Is it flabby and pendulous, like a proboscis?

The Bore. I never said . . .

Cyrano. Or hooked like a hawk's beak?

The Bore. I . . .

Cyrano. Do you discern a mole upon the tip?

The Bore. But . . .

Cyrano. Or is a fly disporting himself thereon? What is there wonderful about it?

The Bore. Oh . . .

Cyrano. Is it a freak of nature?

The Bore. But I had refrained from casting so much as a glance at it!

Cyrano. And why, I pray, should you not look at it?

The Bore. I had . . .

Cyrano. So it disgusts you?

The Bore. Sir . . .

Cyrano. Its color strikes you as unwholesome?

The Bore. Sir . . .

Cyrano. Its shape, unfortunate?

The Bore. But far from it!

Cyrano. Then wherefore that depreciating air? . . . Perhaps monsieur thinks it a shade too large?

The Bore. Indeed not. No, indeed. I think it small . . . small—I should have said, minute!

Cyrano. What? How? Charge me with such a ridiculous defect? Small, my nose? Ho! . . .

The Bore. Heavens!

Cyrano. Enormous, my nose! . . . Contemptible stutterer, snub-nosed and flat-headed, be it known to you that I am proud, proud of such an appendage! inasmuch as a great nose is properly the index of an affable, kindly, courteous man, witty, liberal, brave, such as I am! and such as you are for evermore precluded from supposing yourself, deplorable rogue! For the inglorious surface my hand encounters above your ruff, is no less devoid—— [*Strikes him.*]

The Bore. Aï! aï! . . .

Cyrano. Of pride, alacrity, and sweep, of perception and of gift, of heavenly spark, of sumptuousness, to sum up all, of NOSE, than that [*turns him around by the shoulders and suits the action to the word*] which stops my boot below your spine!

The Bore. [*Running off.*] Help! The watch! . . .

Cyrano. Warning to the idle who might find entertainment in my organ of smell. . . . And if the facetious fellow be of birth, my custom is, before I let him go, to chasten him, in front, and higher up, with steel, and not with hide!

De Guiche. [*Who has stepped down from the stage with the marquises.*] He is becoming tiresome!

Valvert. [*Shrugging his shoulders.*] It is empty bluster!

De Guiche. Will no one take him up?

Valvert. No one? . . . Wait! I will have one of those shots at him! [*He approaches* CYRANO, *who is watching him, and stops in front of him, in an attitude of silly swagger.*] Your . . . nose is . . . er . . . Your nose . . . is very large!

Cyrano. [*Gravely.*] Very.

Valvert. [*Laughs.*] Ha! . . .

Cyrano. [*Imperturbable.*] Is that all?

Valvert. But . . .

Cyrano. Ah, no, young man, that is not enough! You might have said, dear me, there are a thousand things . . . varying the tone . . . For instance . . . here you are:—Aggressive: "I, monsieur, if I had such a nose, nothing would serve but I must cut it off!" Amicable: "It must be in your way while drinking; you ought to have a special beaker made!" Descriptive: "It is a crag! . . . a peak! . . . a promontory! . . . A promontory, did I say? . . . It is a peninsula!" Inquisitive: "What may the office be of that oblong receptacle? Is it an inkhorn or a scissor-case?" Mincing: "Do you so dote on birds, you have, fond as a father, been at pains to fit the little darlings with a roost?" Blunt: "Tell me, monsieur, you, when you smoke, is it possible you blow the vapor through your nose without a neighbor crying, 'The chimney is afire'?" Anxious: "Go with caution, I beseech, lest your head, dragged over by that weight, should drag you over!" Tender: "Have a little sunshade made for it! It might get freckled!" Learned: "None but the beast, monsieur, mentioned by Aristophanes, the hippocampelephantocamelos, can have borne beneath his forehead so much cartilage and bone!" Offhand: "What, comrade, is that sort of peg in style? Capital to hang one's hat upon!" Emphatic: "No wind can hope, O lordly nose, to give the whole of you a cold, but the Nor'-Wester!" Dramatic: "It is the Red Sea when it bleeds!" Admiring: "What a sign for a perfumer's shop!" Lyrical: "Art thou a Triton, and is that thy conch?" Simple: "A monument! When is admission free?" Deferent: "Suffer, monsieur, that I should pay you my respects: that is what I call possessing a house of your own!" Rustic: "Hi, boys! Call that a nose? Ye don't gull me! It's either a prize carrot or else a stunted gourd!" Military: "Level against the cavalry!" Practical: "Will you put it up for raffle? Indubitably, sir, it will be the feature of the game!" And finally in parody of weeping Pyramus: "Behold, behold the nose that traitorously destroyed the beauty of its master! and is blushing for the same!"—That, my dear sir, or something not unlike, is what you would have said to me, had you the smallest leaven of letters or of wit; but of wit, O most pitiable of objects made by God, you never had a rudiment, and of letters, you have just those that are needed to spell "fool!"—But, had it been otherwise, and had you been possessed of the fertile fancy requisite to shower upon me, here, in this noble company, that volley of sprightly pleasantries, still should you not have delivered yourself of so much as a quarter of the tenth part of the beginning of the first. . . . For I let off these good things at myself, and with sufficient zest, but do not suffer another to let them off at me!

De Guiche. [*Attempting to lead away the amazed* VICOMTE.] Let be, Vicomte!

Valvert. That insufferable haughty bearing! . . . A clodhopper without . . . without so much as gloves . . . who goes abroad without points . . . or bow-knots! . . .

Cyrano. My foppery is of the inner man. I do not trick myself out like a popinjay, but I am more fastidious, if I am not so showy. I would not sally forth, by any chance, not washed quite clean of an affront; my conscience foggy about the eye, my honor crumpled, my nicety black-rimmed. I walk with all upon me furbished bright. I plume myself with independence and straightforwardness. It is not a handsome figure, it is my soul that I hold erect as in a brace. I go decked with exploits in place of ribbon bows. I taper to a point my wit like a mustache. And at my passage through the crowd true sayings ring like spurs!

Valvert. But, sir . . .

Cyrano. I am without gloves? . . . a mighty matter! I only had one left, of a very ancient pair, and even that became a burden to me . . . I left it in somebody's face.

Valvert. Villain, clod-poll, flat-foot, refuse of the earth!

Cyrano. [*Taking off his hat and bowing as if the* VICOMTE *had been introducing himself.*] Ah! . . . And mine, Cyrano-Savinien-Hercule de Bergerac!

Valvert. [*Exasperated.*] Buffoon!

Cyrano. [*Giving a sudden cry, as if seized with a cramp.*] Aï! . . .

Valvert. [*Who has started toward the back, turning.*] What is he saying now?

Cyrano. [*Screwing his face as if in pain.*] It must have leave to stir . . . it has a cramp! It is bad for it to be kept still so long!

Valvert. What is the matter?

Cyrano. My rapier prickles like a foot asleep!

Valvert. [*Drawing.*] So be it!

Cyrano. I shall give you a charming little hurt!

Valvert. [*Contemptuous.*] A poet!

Cyrano. Yes, a poet, . . . and to such an extent, that while we fence, I will, hop! extempore, compose you a ballade!

Valvert. A ballade?

Cyrano. I fear you do not know what that is.

Valvert. But . . .

Cyrano. [*As if saying a lesson.*] The ballade is composed of three stanzas of eight lines each. . . .

Valvert. [*Stamps with his feet.*] Oh! . . .

Cyrano. [*Continuing.*] And an envoi of four.

Valvert. You . . .

Cyrano. I will with the same breath fight you and compose one. And at the last line, I will hit.

Valvert. Indeed you will not!

Cyrano. No? . . . [*Declaiming.*] Ballade of the duel which in Burgundy House Monsieur de Bergerac fought with a jackanapes.

Valvert. And what is that, if you please?

Cyrano. That is the title.

The Audience. [*At the highest pitch of excitement.*] Make room! . . . Good sport! . . . Stand aside! . . . Keep still! . . .

[*Tableau. A ring, in the pit, of the interested; the* MARQUISES *and* OFFICERS *scattered among the* BURGHERS *and* COMMON PEOPLE. *The* PAGES *have climbed on the shoulders of various ones, the better to see. All the women are standing in the boxes. At the right,* DE GUICHE *and his attendant gentlemen. At the left,* LE BRET, RAGUENEAU, CUIGY, *etc.*]

Cyrano. [*Closing his eyes a second.*] Wait. I am settling upon the rhymes. There. I have them.

[*In declaiming, he suits the action to the word.*]

Of my broad belt made lighter,
I cast my mantle broad,
And stand, poet and fighter,
To do and to record.
I bow, I draw my sword,
En garde! with steel and wit
I play you at first abord . . .
At the last line, I hit!

[*They begin fencing.*]

You should have been politer;
Where had you best be gored?
The left side or the right—ah?
Or next your azure cord?
Or where the spleen is stored?
Or in the stomach pit?
Come we to quick accord . . .
At the last line, I hit!

You falter, you turn whiter?
You do so to afford
Your foe a rhyme in "iter"? . . .
You thrust at me—I ward—
And balance is restored.
Laridon! Look to your spit! . . .
No, you shall not be floored
Before my cue to hit!

[*He announces solemnly.*]

ENVOI.

Prince, call upon the Lord! . . .
I skirmish . . . feint a bit . . .
I lunge! . . . I keep my word!
[*The* VICOMTE *staggers;* CYRANO *bows.*]
At the last line, I hit!

[*Acclamations. Applause from the boxes. Flowers and handkerchiefs are thrown. The* OFFICERS *surround and congratulate* CYRANO. RAGUENEAU *dances with delight.* LE BRET *is tearfully joyous and at the same time highly troubled. The friends of the* VICOMTE *support him off the stage.*]

The Crowd. [*In a long shout.*] Ah! . . .

A Light-Cavalry Man. Superb!

A Woman. Sweet!

Ragueneau. Astounding!

A Marquis. Novel!

Le Bret. Insensate!

The Crowd. [*Pressing around* CYRANO.] Congratulations! . . . Well done! . . . Bravo! . . .

A Woman's Voice. He is a hero!

A Mousquetaire. [*Striding swiftly toward* CYRANO, *with outstretched hand.*] Monsieur, will you allow me? It was quite, quite excellently done, and I think I know whereof I speak. But, as a fact, I expressed my mind before, by making a huge noise. . . .

[*He retires.*]

Cyrano. [*To* CUIGY.] Who may the gentleman be?

Cuigy. D'Artagnan.

Le Bret. [*To* CYRANO, *taking his arm.*] Come, I wish to talk with you.

Cyrano. Wait till the crowd has thinned. [*To* BELLEROSE.] I may remain?

Bellerose. [*Deferentially.*] Why, certainly! . . .

[*Shouts are heard outside.*]

Jodelet. [*After looking.*] They are hooting Montfleury.

Bellerose. [*Solemnly.*] *Sic transit!* . . . [*In a different tone, to the doorkeeper and the candle-snuffer.*] Sweep and close. Leave the lights. We shall come back, after eating, to rehearse a new farce for tomorrow.

[*Exeunt* JODELET *and* BELLEROSE, *after bowing very low to* CYRANO.]

The Doorkeeper. [*To* CYRANO.] Monsieur will not be going to dinner?

Cyrano. I? . . . No.

[*The doorkeeper withdraws.*]

Le Bret. [*To* CYRANO.] And this, because? . . .

Cyrano. [*Proudly.*] Because. . . . [*In a different tone, having seen that the doorkeeper is too far to overhear.*] I have not a penny!

Le Bret. [*Making the motion of flinging a bag.*] How is this? The bag of crowns. . . .

Cyrano. Monthly remittance, you lasted but a day!

Le Bret. And to keep you the remainder of the month? . . .

Cyrano. Nothing is left!

Le Bret. But then, flinging that bag, what a child's prank!

Cyrano. But what a gesture! . . .

The Sweetmeat Vender. [*Coughing behind her little counter.*] Hm! . . . [CYRANO *and* LE BRET *turn toward her. She comes timidly forward.*] Monsieur, to know you have not eaten . . . makes my heart ache. [*Pointing to the sweetmeat-stand.*] I have there all that is needed. . . . [*Impulsively.*] Help yourself!

Cyrano. [*Taking off his hat.*] Dear child, despite my Gascon pride, which forbids that

I should profit at your hand by the most inconsiderable of dainties, I would not offend you by declining: I will accept therefore . . . [*He goes to the stand and selects.*] Oh, a trifle! . . . A grape off this. . . . [*She proffers the bunch, he takes a single grape.*] No . . . one! This glass of water . . . [*She starts to pour wine into it, he stops her.*] No . . . clear! And half a macaroon.

[*He breaks in two the macaroon, and returns half.*]

Le Bret. This comes near being silly!

Sweetmeat Vender. Oh, you will take something more! . . .

Cyrano. Yes. Your hand to kiss.

[*He kisses the hand she holds out to him, as if it were that of a princess.*]

Sweetmeat Vender. Monsieur, I thank you. [*Curtseys.*] Good evening! [*Exit.*]

Cyrano. [*To* LE BRET.] I am listening. [*He establishes himself before the stand, sets the macaroon before him.*] Dinner! [*Does the same with the glass of water.*] Drink! [*And with the grape.*] Dessert! [*He sits down.*] La! let me begin! I was as hungry as a wolf! [*Eating.*] You were saying?

Le Bret. That if you listen to none but those great boobies and swashbucklers your judgment will become wholly perverted. Inquire, will you, of the sensible, concerning the effect produced today by your bravado.

Cyrano. [*Finishing his macaroon.*] Enormous!

Le Bret. The cardinal . . .

Cyrano. [*Beaming.*] He was there, the cardinal?

Le Bret. Must have found what you did . . .

Cyrano. To a degree, original.

Le Bret. Still . . .

Cyrano. He is a poet. It cannot be distasteful to him wholly that one should deal confusion to a fellow-poet's play.

Le Bret. But, seriously, you make too many enemies!

Cyrano. [*Biting into the grape.*] How many, thereabouts, should you think I made tonight?

Le Bret. Eight and forty. Not mentioning the women.

Cyrano. Come, tell them over!

Le Bret. Montfleury, the old merchant, De Guiche, the Vicomte, Baro, the whole Academy . . .

Cyrano. Enough! You steep me in bliss!

Le Bret. But whither will the road you follow lead you? What can your object be?

Cyrano. I was wandering aimlessly; too many roads were open . . . too many resolves, too complex, offered a choice. I took . . .

Le Bret. Which?

Cyrano. By far the simplest of them all. I decided to be, in every matter, always admirable!

Le Bret. [*Shrugging his shoulders.*] Very well.—But tell me, will you not, the motive —look, the true one!—of your dislike to Montfleury.

Cyrano. [*Rising.*] That old Silenus, who has not seen his knees this many a year, still believes himself a danger to the fair. And as he struts and burrs upon the stage, he makes sheep's-eyes at them with his moist frog's-eyes. And I have hated him . . . oh, properly! . . . since the night he was so daring as to cast his glance on her . . . her, who—Oh, I thought I saw a slug crawl over a flower!

Le Bret. [*Amazed.*] Hey? What? Is it possible? . . .

Cyrano. [*With a bitter laugh.*] That I should love? [*In a different tone, seriously.*] I love.

Le Bret. And may one know? . . . You never told me. . . .

Cyrano. Whom I love? . . . Come, think a little. The dream of being beloved, even by the beautiless, is made to me an empty dream indeed by this good nose, my forerunner ever by a quarter of an hour. Hence, whom should I love? . . . It seems superfluous to tell you! . . . I love . . . it was inevitable! . . . the most beautiful that breathes!

Le Bret. The most beautiful? . . .

Cyrano. No less, in the whole world! And the most resplendent, and the most delicate of wit, and among the golden-haired . . . [*With overwhelming despair.*] Still the superlative!

Le Bret. Dear me, what is this fair one?

Cyrano. All unawares, a deadly snare, exquisite without concern to be so. A snare of nature's own, a musk-rose, in which ambush Love lies low. Who has seen her smile remembers the ineffable! There is not a thing so common but she turns it into prettiness; and in the merest nod or beck she can make manifest all the attributes of a goddess. No, Venus! you cannot step into your iridescent shell, nor, Dian, you, walk through the blossoming groves, as she steps into her chair and walks in Paris!

Le Bret. Sapristi! I understand! It is clear!

Cyrano. It is pellucid.

Le Bret. Magdeleine Robin, your cousin?

Cyrano. Yes, Roxane.

Le Bret. But, what could be better? You love her? Tell her so! You covered yourself with glory in her sight a moment since.

Cyrano. Look well at me, dear friend, and tell me how much hope you think can be justly entertained with this protuberance. Oh, I foster no illusions! . . . . Sometimes, indeed, yes, in the violet dusk, I yield, even I! to a dreamy mood. I penetrate some garden that lies sweetening the hour. With my poor great devil of a nose I sniff the April . . . And as I follow with my eyes some woman passing with some cavalier, I think how dear to have such a one walk beside me, linked like that, slowly, in the soft moonlight! I kindle—I forget—and then . . . then suddenly I see the shadow of my profile upon the garden-wall!

Le Bret. [*Touched.*] My friend . . .

Cyrano. Friend, I experience a bad half hour sometimes, in being so unsightly . . . and alone.

Le Bret. [*In quick sympathy, taking his hand.*] You weep?

Cyrano. Ah, God forbid! That? Never! No, that would be unsightly to excess! That a tear should course the whole length of this nose! Never, so long as I am accountable, shall the divine loveliness of tears be implicated with so much gross ugliness! Mark me well, nothing is so holy as are tears, nothing! and never shall it be that, rousing mirth through me, a single one of them shall seem ridiculous!

Le Bret. Come, do not despond! Love is a lottery.

Cyrano. [*Shaking his head.*] No! I love Cleopatra: do I resemble Cæsar? I worship Berenice: do I put you in mind of Titus?

Le Bret. But your courage . . . and your wit!—The little girl who but a moment ago bestowed on you that very modest meal, her eyes—you must have seen as much—did not exactly hate you!

Cyrano. [*Impressed.*] That is true!

Le Bret. You see? So, then!—But Roxane herself, in following your duel, went lily-pale.

Cyrano. Lily-pale? . . .

Le Bret. Her mind, her heart as well, are struck with wonder! Be bold, speak to her, in order that she may . . .

Cyrano. Laugh in my face! . . . No, there is but one thing upon earth I fear. . . . It is that.

The Doorkeeper. [*Admitting the* DUENNA *to* CYRANO.] Monsieur, you are inquired for.

Cyrano. [*Seeing* THE DUENNA.] Ah, my God! . . . her duenna!

The Duenna. [*With a great curtsey.*] Somebody wishes to know of her valorous cousin where one may see him in private.

Cyrano. [*Upset.*] See me?

The Duenna. [*With curtsey.*] See you. There are things for your ear.

Cyrano. There are . . . ?

The Duenna. [*Another curtsey.*] Things.

Cyrano. [*Staggering.*] Ah, my God! . . .

The Duenna. Somebody intends, tomorrow, at the earliest roses of the dawn, to hear Mass at Saint Roch.

Cyrano. [*Upholds himself by leaning on* LE BRET.] Ah, my God!

The Duenna. That over, where might one step for a moment . . . have a little talk?

Cyrano. [*Losing his senses.*] Where? . . . I . . . But . . . Ah, by God!

The Duenna. Expedition, if you please.

Cyrano. I am casting about . . .

The Duenna. Where?

Cyrano. At . . . at . . . at Ragueneau's . . . the pastrycook's.

The Duenna. He lodges?

Cyrano. In . . . In Rue . . . Ah, my God! my God! . . . St. Honoré.

The Duenna. [*Retiring.*] We will be there. Do not fail. At seven.

Cyrano. I will not fail.

[*Exit* DUENNA.]

Cyrano. [*Falling on* LE BRET'S *neck.*] To me . . . from her . . . a meeting!

Le Bret. Well, your gloom is dispelled?

Cyrano. Oh, to whatever end it may be, she is aware of my existence!

Le Bret. And now you will be calm?

Cyrano. [*Beside himself.*] Now, I shall be fulminating and frenetical! I want an army all complete to put to rout! I have ten hearts and twenty arms . . . I cannot now be suited with felling dwarfs to earth . . . [*At the top of his lungs.*] Giants are what I want!

[*During the last lines, on the stage at the back, shadowy shapes of players have been moving about. The rehearsal has begun; the fiddlers have resumed their places.*]

A Voice. [*From the stage.*] Hey! Psst! Over there! A little lower. We are trying to rehearse!

Cyrano. [*Laughing.*] We are going.

[*He goes toward the back.*]

[*Through the street door, enter* CUIGY, BRISSAILLE, *several* OFFICERS *supporting* LIGNIÈRE *in a state of complete intoxication.*]

Cuigy. Cyrano!

Cyrano. What is this?

Cuigy. A drunken sot we are bringing you.

Cyrano. [*Recognizing him.*] Lignière! Hey, what has happened to you?

Cuigy. He is looking for you.

Brissaille. He cannot go home.

Cyrano. Why?

Lignière. [*In a thick voice, showing him a bit of crumpled paper.*] This note bids me beware . . . A hundred men against me . . . on account of lampoon. . . . Grave danger threatening me. . . . Porte de Nesle . . . must pass it to get home. Let me come and sleep under your roof.

Cyrano. A hundred, did you say?—You shall sleep at home!

Lignière. [*Frightened.*] But . . .

Cyrano. [*In a terrible voice, pointing to the lighted lantern which the* DOORKEEPER *stands swinging as he listens to this scene.*] Take that lantern [LIGNIÈRE *hurriedly takes it.*] and walk! . . . I swear to tuck you in your bed tonight myself. [*To the* OFFICERS.] You, follow at a distance. You may look on!

Cuigy. But a hundred men . . .

Cyrano. Are not one man too many for my mood tonight!

[*The players, in their several costumes, have stepped down from the stage and come nearer.*]

Le Bret. But why take under your especial care . . .

Cyrano. Still Le Bret is not satisfied!

Le Bret. That most commonplace of sots?

Cyrano. [*Slapping* LIGNIÈRE *on the shoulder.*] Because this sot, this cask of muscatel, this hogshead of rosolio, once upon a time did a wholly pretty thing. On leaving Mass, having seen her whom he loved take holy water, as the rite prescribes, he, whom the sight of water puts to flight, ran to the holy-water bowl, and stooping over, drank it dry. . . .

An Actress. [*In the costume of soubrette.*] *Tiens,* that was nice!

Cyrano. Was it not, soubrette?

The Soubrette. [*To the others.*] But why are they, a hundred, all against one poor poet?

Cyrano. Let us start! [*To the* OFFICERS.] And you, gentlemen, when you see me attack, whatever you may suppose to be my danger, do not stir to second me!

Another of the Actresses. [*Jumping from the stage.*] Oh, I will not miss seeing this!

Cyrano. Come!

Another Actress. [*Likewise jumping from the stage, to an elderly actor.*] Cassandre, will you not come?

Cyrano. Come, all of you! the Doctor, Isabel, Leander, all! and you shall lend, charming fantastic swarm, an air of Italian farce to the Spanish drama in view. Yes, you shall be a tinkling heard above a roar, like bells about a tambourine!

All the Women. [*In great glee.*] Bravo! . . . Hurry! . . . A mantle! . . . A hood!

Jodelet. Let us go!

Cyrano. [*To the fiddlers.*] You will favor us with a tune, messieurs the violinists!

[*The fiddlers fall into the train. The lighted candles which furnished the footlights are seized and distributed. The procession becomes a torchlight procession.*]

Cyrano. Bravo! Officers, beauty in fancy dress, and, twenty steps ahead . . . [*He takes the position he describes.*] I, by myself, under the feather stuck, with her own hand, by Glory, in my hat! Proud as a Scipio trebly Nasica!*—It is understood? Formal interdiction to interfere with me!—We are ready? One! Two! Three! Doorkeeper, open the door!

[*The* DOORKEEPER *opens wide the folding door. A picturesque corner of Old Paris appears, bathed in moonlight.*]

Cyrano. Ah! . . . Paris floats in dim nocturnal mist. . . . The sloping bluish roofs are washed with moonlight. . . . A setting, exquisite indeed, offers itself for the scene about to be enacted. . . . Yonder, under silvery vapor wreaths, like a mysterious magic mirror, glimmers the Seine. . . . And you shall see what you shall see!

All. To the Porte de Nesle!

Cyrano. [*Standing on the threshold.*] To the Porte de Nesle! [*Before crossing it, he turns to the* SOUBRETTE.] Were you not asking, mademoiselle, why upon that solitary rhymester a hundred men were set? [*He draws his sword, and tranquilly.*] Because it was well known he is a friend of mine!

[*Exit.*]

[*To the sound of the violins, by the flickering light of the candles, the procession—*LIGNIÈRE *staggering at the head, the* ACTRESSES *arm in arm with the* OFFICERS, *the players capering behind —follows out into the night.*]

CURTAIN

* Scipio Nasica (the large-nosed) was the leader of a successful revolt in Rome against the supporters of Tiberius Gracchus, B.C. 133.

ACT SECOND

THE COOKSHOP OF POETS

RAGUENEAU'S *shop, vast kitchen at the corner of Rue St. Honoré and Rue de l'Arbre-Sec, which can be seen at the back, through the glass door, gray in the early dawn.*

At the left, in front, a counter overhung by a wrought-iron canopy from which geese, ducks, white peacocks are hanging. In large china jars, tall nosegays composed of the simpler flowers, mainly sunflowers. On the same side, in the middle distance, an enormous fireplace, in front of which, between huge andirons, each of which supports a small iron pot, roasting meats drip into appropriate pans.

At the right, door in the front wing. In the middle distance, a staircase leading to a loft, the interior of which is seen through open shutters; a spread table, lighted by a small Flemish candelabrum, shows it to be an eating-room. A wooden gallery continuing the stairway suggests other similar rooms to which it may lead.

In the center of the shop, an iron hoop—which can be lowered by means of a rope,—to which large roasts are hooked.

In the shadow, under the stairway, ovens are glowing. Copper molds and saucepans are shining; spits turning, hams swinging, pastry pyramids showing fair. It is the early beginning of the workday. Bustling of hurried scullions, portly cooks, and young cook's-assistants; swarming of caps decorated with hen feathers and guinea-fowl wings. Wicker crates and broad sheets of tin are brought in loaded with brioches and tarts.

There are tables covered with meats and cakes; others, surrounded by chairs, await customers. In a corner, a smaller table, littered with papers.

[*At the rise of the curtain,* RAGUENEAU *is discovered seated at this table, writing with an inspired air, and counting upon his fingers.*]

First Pastrycook. [*Bringing in a tall molded pudding.*] Nougat of fruit!

Second Pastrycook. [*Bringing in the dish he names.*] Custard!

Third Pastrycook. [*Bringing in a fowl roasted in its feathers.*] Peacock!

Fourth Pastrycook. [*Bringing in a tray of cakes.*] Mince-pies!

Fifth Pastrycook. [*Bringing in a deep earthen dish.*] Beef stew!

Ragueneau. [*Laying down his pen, and looking up.*] Daybreak already plates with silver the copper pans! Time, Ragueneau, to smother within thee the singing divinity! The hour of the lute will come anon—now is that of the ladle! [*He rises; speaking to one of the cooks.*] You, sir, be so good as to lengthen this gravy—it is too thick!

The Cook. How much?

Ragueneau. Three feet. [*Goes further.*]

The Cook. What does he mean?

First Pastrycook. Let me have the tart!

Second Pastrycook. The dumpling!

Ragueneau. [*Standing before the fireplace.*] Spread thy wings, Muse, and fly further, that thy lovely eyes may not be reddened at the sordid kitchen fire! [*To one of the* COOKS, *pointing at some small loaves of bread.*] You have improperly placed the cleft in those loaves; the cæsura belongs in the middle,—between the hemistichs! [*To another of the* COOKS, *pointing at an unfinished pastry.*] This pastry palace requires a roof! [*To a young* COOK'S-APPRENTICE, *who, seated upon the floor, is putting fowls on a spit.*] And you, on that long spit, arrange, my son, in pleasing alternation, the modest pullet and the splendid turkey-cock,—even as our wise Malherbe alternated of old the greater with the lesser lines, and so with roasted fowls compose a poem!

Another Apprentice. [*Coming forward with a platter covered by a napkin.*] Master, in your honor, see what I have baked. . . . I hope you are pleased with it!

Ragueneau. [*Ecstatic.*] A lyre!

The Apprentice. Of pie-crust!

Ragueneau. [*Touched.*] With candied fruits!

The Apprentice. And the strings, see—of spun sugar!

Ragueneau. [*Giving him money.*] Go, drink my health! [*Catching sight of* LISE, *who is entering.*] Hush! My wife! . . . Move on, and hide that money. [*To* LISE, *showing her the lyre, with a constrained air.*] Fine, is it not?

Lise. Ridiculous!

[*She sets a pile of wrapping-paper on the counter.*]

Ragueneau. Paper bags? Good. Thanks.

[*He examines them.*] Heavens! My beloved books! The masterpieces of my friends—dismembered—torn!—to fashion paper bags for penny pies!—Ah, the abominable case is reenacted of Orpheus and the Mænads! *

Lise. [*Drily.*] And have I not an unquestionable right to make what use I can of the sole payment ever got from your paltry scribblers of uneven lines?

Ragueneau. Pismire! Forbear to insult those divine, melodious crickets!

Lise. Before frequenting that low crew, my friend, you did not use to call me a Mænad—no, nor yet a pismire!

Ragueneau. Put poems to such a use!

Lise. To that use and no other!

Ragueneau. If with poems you do this, I should like to know, Madame, what you do with prose!

[*Two* CHILDREN *have come into the shop.*]

Ragueneau. What can I do for you, little ones?

First Child. Three patties.

Ragueneau. [*Waiting on them.*] There you are! Beautifully browned, and piping hot.

Second Child. Please, will you wrap them for us?

Ragueneau. [*Starting, aside.*] There goes one of my bags! [*To the* CHILDREN.] You want them wrapped, do you? [*He takes one of the paper bags, and as he is about to put in the patties, reads.*] *"No otherwise, Ulysses from Penelope departing. . . . "* Not this one! [*He lays it aside and takes another. At the moment of putting in the patties, he reads.*] *"Phœbus of the aureate locks. . . ."* Not that one!

[*Same business.*]

Lise. [*Out of patience.*] Well, what are you waiting for?

Ragueneau. Here we are. Here we are. Here we are. [*He takes a third bag and resigns himself.*] The sonnet to Phyllis! . . . It is hard, all the same.

Lise. It is lucky you made up your mind. [*Shrugging her shoulders.*] Nicodemus!

[*She climbs on a chair and arranges dishes on the sideboard.*]

Ragueneau. [*Taking advantage of her back being turned, calls back the* CHILDREN, *who have already reached the door.*] Psst! . . . Children! Give me back the sonnet to Phyllis, and you shall have six patties instead of three! [*The* CHILDREN *give back the paper-bag, joyfully take the patties and exeunt.* RAGUENEAU *smoothes out the crumpled paper and reads declaiming.*] *"Phyllis!"* . . . Upon that charming name, a grease-spot! . . . *"Phyllis!"* . . .

[*Enter brusquely* CYRANO.]

Cyrano. What time is it?

Ragueneau. [*Bowing with eager deference.*] Six o'clock.

Cyrano. [*With emotion.*] In an hour!

[*He comes and goes in the shop.*]

Ragueneau. [*Following him.*] Bravo! I too was witness. . . .

Cyrano. Of what?

Ragueneau. Your fight.

Cyrano. Which?

Ragueneau. At the Hôtel de Bourgogne.

Cyrano. [*With disdain.*] Ah, the duel!

Ragueneau. [*Admiringly.*] Yes—the duel in rhyme.

Lise. He can talk of nothing else.

Cyrano. Let him! . . . It does no harm.

Ragueneau. [*Thrusting with a spit he has seized.*] *"At the last line, I hit!" "At the last line I hit!"*—How fine that is! [*With growing enthusiasm.*] *"At the last line, I——"*

Cyrano. What time, Ragueneau?

Ragueneau. [*Remaining fixed in the attitude of thrusting, while he looks at the clock.*] Five minutes past six.—*"I hit!"* [*He recovers from his dueling posture.*] Oh, to be able to make a ballade!

Lise. [*To* CYRANO, *who in passing her counter has absentmindedly shaken hands with her.*] What ails your hand?

Cyrano. Nothing. A scratch.

Ragueneau. You have been exposed to some danger?

Cyrano. None whatever.

Lise. [*Shaking her finger at him.*] I fear that is a fib!

Cyrano. From the swelling of my nose? The fib in that case must have been good-sized. . . . [*In a different tone.*] I am expecting some one. You will leave us alone in here.

Ragueneau. But how can I contrive it? My poets shortly will be coming . . .

Lise. [*Ironically.*] For breakfast!

Cyrano. When I sign to you, you will clear the place of them.—What time is it?

Ragueneau. It is ten minutes past six.

Cyrano. [*Seating himself nervously at* RAGUENEAU's *table and helping himself to paper.*] A pen?

Ragueneau. [*Taking one from behind his ear, and offering it.*] A swan's quill.

A Mousquetaire. [*With enormous moustachios, enters; in a stentorian voice.*] Good morning!

* Orpheus was torn to pieces by Mænads, female attendants upon Dionysus, for neglect of women.

[LISE *goes hurriedly to him, toward the back.*]

Cyrano. [*Turning.*] What is it?

Ragueneau. A friend of my wife's—a warrior—terrible, from his own report.

Cyrano. [*Taking up the pen again, and waving* RAGUENEAU *away.*] Hush! . . . [*To himself.*] Write to her . . . fold the letter . . . hand it to her . . . and make my escape. . . . [*Throwing down the pen.*] Coward! . . . But may I perish if I have the courage to speak to her . . . to say a single word. . . . [*To* RAGUENEAU.] What time is it?

Ragueneau. A quarter past six.

Cyrano. [*Beating his breast.*] A single word of all I carry here! . . . Whereas in writing. . . . [*He takes up the pen again.*] Come, let us write it then, in very deed, the love-letter I have written in thought so many times. I have but to lay my soul beside my paper, and copy!

[*He writes.*]

[*Beyond the glass-door, shadowy, lank, hesitating, shabby forms are seen moving. Enter the* POETS, *clad in black, with hanging hose, sadly mudsplashed.*]

Lise. [*Coming forward, to* RAGUENEAU.] Here they come, your scarecrows!

First Poet. [*Entering, to* RAGUENEAU.] Brother in art! . . .

Second Poet. [*Shaking both of* RAGUENEAU'S *hands.*] Dear fellow-bard. . . .

Third Poet. Eagle of pastrycooks [*sniffs the air*], your eyrie smells divine!

Fourth Poet. Phœbus turned baker!

Fifth Poet. Apollo, master-cook!

Ragueneau. [*Surrounded, embraced, shaken by the hand.*] How at his ease a man feels at once with them!

First Poet. The reason we are late is the crowd at the Porte de Nesle!

Second Poet. Eight ugly ruffians, ripped open with the sword, lie weltering on the pavement.

Cyrano. [*Raising his head a second.*] Eight? I thought there were only seven.

[*Goes on with his letter.*]

Ragueneau. [*To* CYRANO.] Do you happen to know who is the hero of this event?

Cyrano. [*Negligently.*] I? . . . No.

Lise. [*To the* MOUSQUETAIRE.] Do you?

The Mousquetaire. [*Turning up the ends of his mustache.*] Possibly!

Cyrano. [*Writing, from time to time he is heard murmuring a word or two.*] . . . "I love you . . ."

First Poet. A single man, we were told, put a whole gang to flight!

Second Poet. Oh, it was a rare sight! The ground was littered with pikes, and cudgels. . . .

Cyrano. [*Writing.*] . . . "Your eyes . . ."

Third Poet. Hats were strewn as far as the Goldsmiths' Square!

First Poet. Sapristi! He must have been a madman of mettle. . . .

Cyrano. [*As above.*] ". . . your lips . . ."

First Poet. An infuriate giant, the doer of that deed!

Cyrano. [*Same business.*] ". . . but when I see you, I come near to swooning with a tender dread . . ."

Second Poet. [*Snapping up a tart.*] What have you lately written, Ragueneau?

Cyrano. [*Same business.*] ". . . who loves you devotedly . . ." [*In the act of signing the letter, he stops, rises, and tucks it inside his doublet.*] No need to sign it. I deliver it myself.

Ragueneau. [*To* SECOND POET.] I have rhymed a recipe.

Third Poet. [*Establishing himself beside a tray of cream puffs.*] Let us hear this recipe!

Fourth Poet. [*Examining a brioche of which he has possessed himself.*] It should not wear its cap so saucily on one side . . . it scarcely looks well! . . .

[*Bites off the top.*]

First Poet. See, the spice-cake there, ogling a susceptible poet with eyes of almond under citron brows! . . .

[*He takes the spice cake.*]

Second Poet. We are listening!

Third Poet. [*Slightly squeezing a cream puff between his fingers.*] This puff creams at the mouth. . . . I water!

Second Poet. [*Taking a bite out of the large pastry lyre.*] For once the Lyre will have filled my stomach!

Ragueneau. [*Who has made ready to recite, has coughed, adjusted his cap, struck an attitude.*] A recipe in rhyme!

Second Poet. [*To* FIRST POET, *nudging him.*] Is it breakfast, with you?

First Poet. [*To* SECOND POET.] And with you, is it dinner?

Ragueneau. How Almond Cheese-Cakes should be made.

Briskly beat to lightness due,
    Eggs, a few;
With the eggs so beaten, beat—
Nicely strained for this same use,—
    Lemon-juice,
Adding milk of almonds, sweet.

With fine pastry dough, rolled flat,
    After that,

Line each little scalloped mold;
Round the sides, light-fingered, spread
Marmalade;
Pour the liquid eggy gold,

Into each delicious pit;
Prison it
In the oven—and, by-and-by,
Almond cheesecakes will in gay
Blond array
Bless your nostril and your eye!

The Poets. [*Their mouths full.*] Exquisite . . . Delicious!

One of the Poets. [*Choking.*] Humph!

[*They go toward the back, eating.* CYRANO, *who has been watching them, approaches* RAGUENEAU.]

Cyrano. While you recite your works to them, have you a notion how they stuff?

Ragueneau. [*Low, with a smile.*] Yes, I see them . . . without looking, lest they should be abashed. I get a double pleasure thus from saying my verses over: I satisfy a harmless weakness of which I stand convicted, at the same time giving those who have not fed a needed chance to feed!

Cyrano. [*Slapping him on the shoulder.*] You . . . I like you! [RAGUENEAU *joins his friends.* CYRANO *looks after him; then, somewhat sharply.*] Hey, Lise! [LISE, *absorbed in tender conversation with the* MOUSQUETAIRE, *starts and comes forward toward* CYRANO.] Is that captain . . . laying siege to you?

Lise. [*Offended.*] My eyes, sir, have ever with a glance been able to frown down those who meant hurt to my character. . . .

Cyrano. For eyes so resolute . . . I thought yours looked a little languishing!

Lise. [*Choking with anger.*] But . . .

Cyrano. [*Bluntly.*] I like your husband. Wherefore, Madame Lise, I say he shall not be sc . . . horned!

Lise. But . . .

Cyrano. [*Raising his voice so as to be heard by the* MOUSQUETAIRE.] A word to the wise!

[*He bows to the* MOUSQUETAIRE, *and after looking at the clock, goes to the door at the back and stands on watch.*]

Lise. [*To the* MOUSQUETAIRE, *who has simply returned* CYRANO's *bow.*] Really . . . I am astonished at you. . . . Defy him . . . to his face!

The Mousquetaire. To his face, indeed! . . to his face! . . .

[*He quickly moves off.* LISE *follows him.*]

Cyrano. [*From the door at the back, signaling to* RAGUENEAU *that he should clear the room.*] Pst! . . .

Ragueneau. [*Urging the* POETS *toward the door at the right.*] We shall be much more comfortable in there. . . .

Cyrano. [*Impatiently.*] Pst! . . . Pst! . . .

Ragueneau. [*Driving along the* POETS.] I want to read you a little thing of mine. . . .

First Poet. [*Despairingly, his mouth full.*] But the provisions. . . .

Second Poet. Shall not be parted from us!

[*They follow* RAGUENEAU *in procession, after making a raid on the eatables.*]

Cyrano. If I feel that there is so much as a glimmer of hope . . . I will out with my letter! . . .

[ROXANE, *masked, appears behind the glass door followed by the* DUENNA.]

Cyrano. [*Instantly opening the door.*] Welcome! [*Approaching the* DUENNA.] Madame, a word with you!

The Duenna. A dozen.

Cyrano. Are you fond of sweets?

The Duenna. To the point of indigestion!

Cyrano. [*Snatching some paper bags off the counter.*] Good. Here are two sonnets of Benserade's. . . .

The Duenna. Pooh!

Cyrano. Which I fill for you with grated almond drops.

The Duenna. [*With a different expression.*] Ha!

Cyrano. Do you look with favor upon the cake they call a trifle?

The Duenna. I affect it out of measure, when it has whipped cream inside.

Cyrano. Six shall be yours, thrown in with a poem by Saint-Amant. And in these verses of Chapelain I place this wedge of fruitcake, light by the side of them. . . . Oh! And do you like tarts . . . little jam ones . . . fresh?

The Duenna. I dream of them at night!

Cyrano. [*Loading her arms with crammed paper bags.*] Do me the favor to go and eat these in the street.

The Duenna. But . . .

Cyrano. [*Pushing her out.*] And do not come back till you have finished! [*He closes the door upon her, comes forward toward* ROXANE, *and stands, bareheaded, at a respectful distance.*] Blessed for evermore among all hours the hour in which, remembering that so lowly a being still draws breath, you were so gracious as to come to tell me . . . to tell me? . . .

Roxane. [*Who has removed her mask.*] First of all, that I thank you. For that churl, that coxcomb yesterday, whom you taught manners with your sword, is the one whom a great nobleman, who fancies himself in love with me. . . .

Cyrano. De Guiche?

Roxane. [*Dropping her eyes.*] Has tried to force upon me as a husband.

Cyrano. Honorary? [*Bowing.*] It appears, then, that I fought—and I am glad of it—not for my graceless nose, but your thrice-beautiful eyes.

Roxane. Further than that . . . I wished . . . But, before I can make the confession I have in mind to make, I must find in you once more the . . . almost brother, with whom as a child I used to play, in the park —do you remember?—by the lake!

Cyrano. I have not forgotten. Yes . . . you came every summer to Bergerac.

Roxane. You used to fashion lances out of reeds. . . .

Cyrano. The silk of the tasseled corn furnished hair for your doll . . .

Roxane. It was the time of long delightful games. . . .

Cyrano. And somewhat sour berries . . .

Roxane. The time when you did everything I bade you!

Cyrano. Roxane, wearing short frocks, was known as Magdeleine.

Roxane. Was I pretty in those days?

Cyrano. You were not ill-looking.

Roxane. Sometimes, in your venturesome climbings you used to hurt yourself. You would come running to me, your hand bleeding. And, playing at being your mamma, I would harden my voice and say . . . [*She takes his hand.*] "Will you never keep out of mischief?" [*She stops short, amazed.*] Oh, it is too much! Here you have done it again! [CYRANO *tries to draw back his hand.*] No! Let me look at it! . . Aren't you ashamed! A great boy like you! . . . How did this happen, and where?

Cyrano. Oh, fun . . . near the Porte de Nesle.

Roxane. [*Sitting down at a table and dipping her handkerchief into a glass of water.*] Let me have it.

Cyrano. [*Sitting down too.*] So prettily, so cheerfully maternal!

Roxane. And tell me, while I wash this naughty blood away . . . with how many were you fighting?

Cyrano. Oh, not quite a hundred.

Roxane. Tell me about it.

Cyrano. No. What does it matter? You tell me, you . . . what you were going to tell me before, and did not dare . . .

Roxane. [*Without releasing his hand.*] I do dare, now. I have breathed in courage with the perfume of the past. Oh, yes, now I dare. Here it is. There is someone whom I love.

Cyrano. Ah! . . .

Roxane. Oh, he does not know it.

Cyrano. Ah! . . .

Roxane. As yet. . . .

Cyrano. Ah! . . .

Roxane. But if he does not know it, he soon will.

Cyrano. Ah! . . .

Roxane. A poor boy who until now has loved me timidly, from a distance, without daring to speak. . . .

Cyrano. Ah! . . .

Roxane. No, leave me your hand. It is hot, this will cool it. . . . But I have read his heart in his face.

Cyrano. Ah! . . .

Roxane. [*Completing the bandaging of his hand with her small pocket-handkerchief.*] And, cousin, is it not a strange coincidence—that he should serve exactly in your regiment!

Cyrano. Ah! . . .

Roxane. [*Laughing.*] Yes. He is a cadet, in the same company!

Cyrano. Ah! . . .

Roxane. He bears plain on his forehead the stamp of wit, of genius! He is proud, noble, young, brave, handsome. . . .

Cyrano. [*Rising, pale.*] Handsome! . . .

Roxane. What . . . what is the matter?

Cyrano. With me? . . . Nothing! . . . It is . . . it is . . . [*Showing his hand, smiling.*] You know! . . . It smarts a little . . .

Roxane. In short, I love him. I must tell you, however, that I have never seen him save at the play.

Cyrano. Then you have never spoken to each other?

Roxane. Only with our eyes.

Cyrano. But, then . . . how can you know? . . .

Roxane. Oh, under the lindens of the Place Royale, people will talk. A trustworthy gossip told me many things!

Cyrano. A cadet, did you say?

Roxane. A cadet, in your company.

Cyrano. His name?

Roxane. Baron Christian de Neuvillette.

Cyrano. What? He is not in the cadets.

Roxane. He is! He certainly is, since morning. Captain Carbon de Castel-Jaloux.

Cyrano. And quickly, quickly, she throws away her heart! . . . But my poor little girl . . .

The Duenna. [*Opening the door at the*

back.] Monsieur de Bergerac, I have eaten them, every one!

Cyrano. Now read the poetry printed upon the bags! [*The* DUENNA *disappears.*] My poor child, you who can endure none but the choicest language, who savor eloquence and wit . . . if he should be a barbarian!

Roxane. No! No! . . . He has hair like one of D'Urfé's heroes!

Cyrano. If he had, on proof, as homely a wit as he has pretty hair!

Roxane. No! No! . . . I can see at a single glance, his utterances are fine, pointed . . .

Cyrano. Ah, yes! A man's utterances are invariably like his mustache! . . . Still, if he *were* a ninny? . . .

Roxane. [*Stamping with her foot.*] I should die, there!

Cyrano. [*After a time.*] You bade me come here that you might tell me this? I scarcely see the appropriateness, Madame.

Roxane. Ah, it was because someone yesterday let death into my soul by telling me that in your company you are all Gascons, . . . all!

Cyrano. And that we pick a quarrel with every impudent fledgling, not Gascon, admitted by favor to our thoroughbred Gascon ranks? That is what you heard?

Roxane. Yes, and you can imagine how distracted I am for him!

Cyrano. [*Through his teeth.*] You well may be!

Roxane. But I thought, yesterday, when you towered up, great and invincible, giving his due to that miscreant, standing your ground against those caitiffs, I thought, "Were he but willing, he of whom all are in awe . . ."

Cyrano. Very well, I will protect your little baron.

Roxane. Ah, you will . . . you will protect him for me? . . . I have always felt for you the tenderest regard!

Cyrano. Yes, yes.

Roxane. You will be his friend?

Cyrano. I will!

Roxane. And never shall he have to fight a duel?

Cyrano. I swear it.

Roxane. Oh, I quite love you! . . . Now I must go. [*She hurriedly resumes her mask, throws a veil over her head; says absentmindedly:*] But you have not yet told me about last night's encounter. It must have been amazing! . . . Tell him to write to me. [*She kisses her hand to him.*] I love you dearly!

Cyrano. Yes, yes.

Roxane. A hundred men against you? . . . Well, adieu. We are fast friends.

Cyrano. Yes, yes.

Roxane. Tell him to write me! . . . A hundred men! you shall tell me another time. I must not linger now . . . A hundred men! What a heroic thing to do!

Cyrano. [*Bowing.*] Oh, I have done better since!

[*Exit* ROXANE. CYRANO *stands motionless, staring at the ground. Silence. The door at the right opens.* RAGUENEAU *thrusts in his head.*]

Ragueneau. May we come back?

Cyrano. [*Without moving.*] Yes . . .

[RAGUENEAU *beckons, his friends come in again. At the same time, in the doorway at the back, appears* CARBON DE CASTEL-JALOUX, *in the costume of a Captain of the Guards. On seeing* CYRANO, *he gesticulates exaggeratedly by way of signal to someone out of sight.*]

Carbon de Castel-Jaloux. He is here!

Cyrano. [*Looking up.*] Captain!

Carbon de Castel-Jaloux. [*Exultant.*] Hero! We know all! . . . About thirty of my cadets are out there! . . .

Cyrano. [*Drawing back.*] But . . .

Carbon de Castel-Jaloux. [*Trying to lead him off.*] Come! . . . You are in request!

Cyrano. No!

Carbon de Castel-Jaloux. They are drinking across the way, at the Cross of the Hilt.

Cyrano. I . . .

Carbon de Castel-Jaloux. [*Going to the door and shouting toward the street corner, in a voice of thunder.*] The hero refuses. He is not in the humor!

A Voice. [*Outside.*] Ah, *sandious!* . . .

[*Tumult outside, noise of clanking swords and of boots drawing nearer.*]

Carbon de Castel-Jaloux. [*Rubbing his hands.*] Here they come, across the street.

The Cadets. [*Entering the cookshop.*] *Mille dious! . . . Capdedious! . . . Mordious! . . . Pocapdedious!** . . .

Ragueneau. [*Backing in alarm.*] Messieurs, are you all natives of Gascony?

The Cadets. All!

One of the Cadets. [*To* CYRANO.] Bravo!

Cyrano. Baron.

Other Cadet. [*Shaking both* CYRANO'S *hands.*] Vivat!

Cyrano. Baron!

Third Cadet. Let me hug you to my heart!

Cyrano. Baron!

Several Gascons. Let us hug him!

* Oaths in the Gascon dialect.

Cyrano. [*Not knowing which one to answer.*] Baron! . . . baron! . . . your pardon!

Ragueneau. Messieurs, are you all barons?

The Cadets. All!

Ragueneau. Are they truly?

First Cadet. Our coats of arms piled up would dwindle in the clouds!

Le Bret. [*Entering, running to* CYRANO.] They are looking for you! A crowd, gone mad as March, led by those who were with you last night.

Cyrano. [*Alarmed.*] You never told them where to find me? . . .

Le Bret. [*Rubbing his hands.*] I did.

A Burgher. [*Entering, followed by a number of others.*] Monsieur, the Marais is coming in a body!

[*The street outside has filled with people. Sedan-chairs, coaches stop before the door.*]

Le Bret. [*Smiling, low to* CYRANO.] And Roxane?

Cyrano. [*Quickly.*] Be quiet!

The Crowd. [*Outside.*] Cyrano!

[*A rabble bursts into the cookshop. Confusion. Shouting.*]

Ragueneau. [*Standing upon a table.*] My shop is invaded! They are breaking everything! It is glorious!

People. [*Pressing round* CYRANO.] My friend . . . my friend. . . .

Cyrano. I had not so many friends . . . yesterday!

Le Bret. This is success!

A Young Marquis. [*Running toward* CYRANO, *with outstretched hands.*] If you knew, my dear fellow . . .

Cyrano. Dear? . . . Fellow? . . . Where was it we stood sentinel together?

Other Marquis. I wish to present you, sir, to several ladies, who are outside in my coach. . . .

Cyrano. [*Coldly.*] But you, to me—by whom will you first be presented?

Le Bret. [*Astonished.*] But what is the matter with you?

Cyrano. Be still!

A Man of Letters. [*With an inkhorn.*] Will you kindly favor me with the details of . . .

Cyrano. No.

Le Bret. [*Nudging him.*] That is Theophrastus Renaudot, the inventor of the gazette.

Cyrano. Enough!

Le Bret. A sheet close packed with various information! It is an idea, they say, likely to take firm root and flourish!

A Poet. [*Coming forward.*] Monsieur . . .

Cyrano. Another!

The Poet. I am anxious to make a pentacrostic on your name.

Somebody Else. [*Likewise approaching* CYRANO.] Monsieur . . .

Cyrano. Enough, I say!

[*At the gesture of impatience which* CYRANO *cannot repress, the crowd draws away.* DE GUICHE *appears, escorted by officers; among them* CUIGY, BRISSAILLE, *those who followed* CYRANO *at the end of the first act.* CUIGY *hurries toward* CYRANO.]

Cuigy. [*To* CYRANO.] Monsieur de Guiche! [*Murmurs. Every one draws back.*] He comes at the request of the Marshal de Gaussion.

De Guiche. [*Bowing to* CYRANO.] Who wishes to express his admiration for your latest exploit, the fame of which has reached him.

The Crowd. Bravo!

Cyrano. [*Bowing.*] The Marshal is qualified to judge of courage.

De Guiche. He would scarcely have believed the report, had these gentlemen not been able to swear they had seen the deed performed.

Cuigy. With our own eyes!

Le Bret. [*Low to* CYRANO, *who wears an abstracted air.*] But . . .

Cyrano. Be silent!

Le Bret. You appear to be suffering . . .

Cyrano. [*Starting, and straightening himself.*] Before these people? . . . [*His mustache bristles; he expands his chest.*] I . . . suffering? . . . You shall see!

De Guiche. [*In whose ear* CUIGY *has been whispering.*] But this is by no means the first gallant achievement marking your career. You serve in the madcap Gascon company, do you not?

Cyrano. In the cadets, yes.

One of the Cadets. [*In a great voice.*] Among his countrymen!

De Guiche. [*Considering the* GASCONS, *in line behind* CYRANO.] Ah, ha!—all these gentlemen then of the formidable aspect, are the famous . . .

Carbon de Castel-Jaloux. Cyrano!

Cyrano. Captain? . . .

Carbon de Castel-Jaloux. My company, I believe, is here in total. Be so obliging as to present it to the Count.

Cyrano. [*Taking a step toward* DE GUICHE, *and pointing at the* CADETS.]

They are the Gascony Cadets
Of Carbon de Castel-Jaloux;
Famed fighters, liars, desperates,
They are the Gascony Cadets!

All, better-born than pickpockets,
Talk couchant, rampant, . . . pendent, too!
They are the Gascony Cadets
Of Carbon de Castel-Jaloux!

Cat-whiskered, eyed like falconets,
Wolf-toothed and heron-legged, they hew
The rabble down that snarls and threats . . .
Cat-whiskered, eyed like falconets!
Great pomp of plume hides and offsets
Holes in those hats they wear askew . . .
Cat-whiskered, eyed like falconets,
They drive the snarling mob, and hew!

The mildest of their sobriquets
Are Crack-my-crown and Run-me-through;
Mad drunk on glory Gascon gets!
These boasters of soft sobriquets
Wherever rapier rapier whets
Are met in punctual rendezvous. . . .
The mildest of their sobriquets
Are Crack-my-crown and Run-me-through!

They are the Gascony Cadets
That give the jealous spouse his due!
Lean forth, adorable coquettes,
They are the Gascony Cadets,
With plumes and scarfs and aigulettes!
The husband gray may well look blue. . . .
They are the Gascony Cadets
That give the jealous spouse his due!

De Guiche. [*Nonchalantly seated in an arm-chair which* RAGUENEAU *has hurriedly brought for him.*] A gentleman provides himself today, by way of luxury, with a poet. May I look upon you as mine?

Cyrano. No, your lordship, as nobody's.

De Guiche. My uncle Richelieu yesterday found your spontaneity diverting. I shall be pleased to be of use to you with him.

Le Bret. [*Dazzled.*] Great God!

De Guiche. I cannot think I am wrong in supposing that you have rhymed a tragedy?

Le Bret. [*Whispering to* CYRANO.] My boy, your Agrippina will be played!

De Guiche. Take it to him. . . .

Cyrano. [*Tempted and pleased.*] Really.

De Guiche. He has taste in such matters. He will no more than, here and there, alter a word, recast a passage. . . .

Cyrano. [*Whose face has instantly darkened.*] Not to be considered, monsieur! My blood runs cold at the thought of a single comma added or suppressed.

De Guiche. On the other hand, my dear sir, when a verse finds favor with him, he pays for it handsomely.

Cyrano. He scarcely can pay me as I pay myself, when I have achieved a verse to my liking, by singing it over to myself!

De Guiche. You are proud.

Cyrano. You have observed it?

One of the Cadets. [*Coming in with a number of disreputable, draggled tattered hats threaded on his sword.*] Look, Cyrano, at the remarkable feathered game we secured this morning near the Porte de Nesle! The hats of the fugitives!

Carbon de Castel-Jaloux. Spolia opima!

All. [*Laughing.*] Ha! Ha! Ha! . . .

Cuigy. The one who planned that military action, my word! must be proud of it today!

Brissaille. Is it known who did it?

De Guiche. I!— [*The laughter stops short.*] They had instructions to chastise—a matter one does not attend to in person—a drunken scribbler. [*Constrained silence.*]

The Cadet. [*Under breath, to* CYRANO, *indicating the hats.*] What can we do with them? They are oily. . . . Make them into a hotchpot?

Cyrano. [*Taking the sword with the hats, and bowing, as he shakes them off at* DE GUICHE's *feet.*] Monsieur, if you should care to return them to your friends? . . .

De Guiche. [*Rises, and in a curt tone.*] My chair and bearers, at once. [*To* CYRANO, *violently.*] As for you, sir . . .

A Voice. [*In the street, shouting.*] The chairmen of Monseigneur the Comte de Guiche!

De Guiche. [*Who has recovered control over himself, with a smile.*] Have you read *Don Quixote?*

Cyrano. I have. And at the name of that divine madman I uncover . . .

De Guiche. My advice to you is to ponder. . . .

A Chairman. [*Appearing at the back.*] The chair is at the door!

De Guiche. The chapter of the windmills.

Cyrano. [*Bowing.*] Chapter thirteen.

De Guiche. For when a man attacks them, it often happens. . . .

Cyrano. I have attacked, am I to infer, a thing that veers with every wind?

De Guiche. That one of their far-reaching canvas arms pitches him down into the mud!

Cyrano. Or up among the stars!

[*Exit* DE GUICHE. *He is seen getting into his chair. The gentlemen withdraw whispering.* LE BRET *goes to the door with them. The crowd leaves. The* CADETS *remain seated at the right and left at tables where food and drink is brought to them.*]

Cyrano. [*Bowing with a derisive air to*

those who depart without daring to take leave of him.] Gentlemen . . . gentlemen . . . gentlemen. . . .

Le Bret. [*Coming forward, greatly distressed, lifting his hands to Heaven.*] Oh, in what a pretty pair of shoes. . . .

Cyrano. Oh, you! . . . I expect you to grumble!

Le Bret. But yourself, you will agree with me that invariably to cut the throat of opportunity becomes excessive! . . .

Cyrano. Yes. I agree. I am excessive.

Le Bret. [*Triumphant.*] You see, you admit it! . . .

Cyrano. But for the sake of principle, and of example, as well, I think it a good thing to exceed as I do!

Le Bret. Could you but leave apart, once in a while, your mousquetaire of a soul, fortune, undoubtedly, fame. . . .

Cyrano. And what should a man do? Seek some grandee, take him for patron, and like the obscure creeper clasping a tree-trunk, and licking the bark of that which props it up, attain to height by craft instead of strength? No, I thank you. Dedicate, as they all do, poems to financiers? Wear motley in the humble hope of seeing the lips of a minister distend for once in a smile not ominous of ill? No, I thank you. Eat every day a toad? Be threadbare at the belly with groveling? Have his skin dirty soonest at the knees? Practice feats of dorsal elasticity? No, I thank you. With one hand stroke the goat while with the other he waters the cabbage? Make gifts of senna that counter-gifts of rhubarb may accrue, and indefatigably swing his censer in some beard? No, I thank you. Push himself from lap to lap, become a little great man in a great little circle, propel his ship with madrigals for oars and in his sails the sighs of the elderly ladies? No, I thank you. Get the good editor Sercy to print his verses at his own expense? No, I thank you. Contrive to be nominated Pope in conclaves held by imbeciles in wine-shops? No, I thank you. Work to construct a name upon the basis of a sonnet, instead of constructing other sonnets? No, I thank you. Discover talent in tyros, and in them alone? Stand in terror of what gazettes may please to say, and say to himself, "At whatever cost, may I figure in the Paris Mercury!" No, I thank you. Calculate, cringe, peak, prefer making a call to a poem—petition, solicit, apply? No, I thank you! No, I thank you! No, I thank you! But . . . sing, dream, laugh, loaf, be single, be free, have eyes that look squarely, a voice with a ring; wear, if he chooses, his hat hindside afore; for a yes, for a no, fight a duel or turn a ditty! . . . Work, without concern of fortune or of glory, to accomplish the heart's-desired journey to the moon! Put forth nothing that has not its spring in the very heart, yet, modest, say to himself, "Old man, be satisfied with blossoms, fruits, yea, leaves alone, so they be gathered in your garden and not another man's!" Then, if it happen that to some small extent he triumph, be obliged to render of the glory, to Cæsar not one jot, but honestly appropriate it all. In short, scorning to be the parasite, the creeper, if even failing to be the oak, rise, not perchance to a great height . . . but rise alone!

Le Bret. Alone? Good! but not one against all! How the devil did you contract the mania that possesses you for making enemies, always, everywhere?

Cyrano. By seeing you make friends, and smile to those same flocks of friends with a mouth that takes for model an old purse! I wish not to be troubled to return bows in the street, and I exclaim with glee, "An enemy the more!"

Le Bret. This is mental aberration!

Cyrano. I do not dispute it. I am so framed. To displease is my pleasure. I love that one should hate me. Dear friend, if you but knew how much better a man walks under the exciting fire of hostile eyes, and how amused he may become over the spots on his doublet, spattered by Envy and Cowardice! . . . The facile friendship wherewith you surround yourself, resembles those wide Italian collars, loose and easy, with a perforated pattern, in which the neck looks like a woman's. They are more comfortable, but of less high effect; for the brow not held in proud position by any constraint from them, falls to nodding this way and that. . . . But for me every day Hatred starches and flutes the ruff whose stiffness holds the head well in place. Every new enemy is another plait in it, adding compulsion, but adding, as well, a ray: for, similar in every point to the Spanish ruff, Hatred is a bondage, . . . but is a halo, too!

Le Bret. [*After a pause, slipping his arm through* CYRANO's.] To the hearing of all be proud and bitter, . . . but to me, below breath, say simply that she does not love you!

Cyrano. [*Sharply.*] Not a word!

[CHRISTIAN *has come in and mingled with the cadets; they ignore him; he has finally gone to a little table by himself, where* LISE *waits on him.*]

One of the Cadets. [*Seated at a table at*

the back, glass in hand.] Hey, Cyrano! [CYRANO *turns toward him.*] Your story!

Cyrano. Presently!

[*He goes toward the back on* LE BRET'S *arm. They talk low.*]

The Cadet. [*Rising and coming toward the front.*] The account of your fight! It will be the best lesson [*stopping in front of the table at which* CHRISTIAN *is sitting*] for this timorous novice!

Christian. [*Looking up.*] . . . Novice?

Other Cadet. Yes, sickly product of the North!

Christian. Sickly?

First Cadet. [*Impressively.*] Monsieur de Neuvillette, it is a good deed to warn you that there is a thing no more to be mentioned in our company than rope in the hangman's house!

Christian. And what is it?

Other Cadet. [*In a terrifying voice.*] Look at me! [*Three times, darkly, he places his finger upon his nose.*] You have understood?

Christian. Ah, it is the . . .

Other Cadet. Silence! . . . Never must you so much as breathe that word, or . . . [*He points toward* CYRANO *at the back talking with* LE BRET.] you will have him, over there, to deal with!

Other Cadet. [*Who, while* CHRISTIAN *was turned toward the first, has noiselessly seated himself on the table behind him.*] Two persons were lately cut off in their pride by him for talking through their noses. He thought it personal.

Other Cadet. [*In a cavernous voice, as he rises from under the table where he had slipped on all fours.*] Not the remotest allusion, ever, to the fatal cartilage . . . unless you fancy an early grave!

Other Cadet. A word will do the business! What did I say? . . . A word? . . . A simple *gesture!* Make use of your pocket-handkerchief, you will shortly have use for your shroud!

[*Silence. All around* CHRISTIAN *watch him, with folded arms. He rises and goes to* CARBON DE CASTEL-JALOUX, *who, in conversation with an* OFFICER, *affects to notice nothing.*]

Christian. Captain!

Carbon. [*Turning and looking him rather contemptuously up and down.*] Monsieur?

Christian. What is the proper course for a man when he finds gentlemen of the South too boastful?

Carbon de Castel-Jaloux. He must prove to them that one can be of the North, yet brave.

[*He turns his back upon him.*]

Christian. I am much obliged.

First Cadet. [*To* CYRANO.] And now, the tale of your adventure!

All. Yes, yes, now let us hear!

Cyrano. [*Coming forward among them.*] My adventure? [*All draw their stools nearer, and sit around him, with craned necks.* CHRISTIAN *sits astride a chair.*] Well, then, I was marching to meet them. The moon up in the skies was shining like a silver watch, when suddenly I know not what careful watch-maker having wrapped it in a cottony cloud, there occurred the blackest imaginable night; and, the streets being nowise lighted—*mordious!*—you could see no further than . . .

Christian. Your nose.

[*Silence. Everyone slowly gets up; all look with terror at* CYRANO. *He has stopped short, amazed. Pause.*]

Cyrano. Who is that man?

One of the Cadets. [*Low.*] He joined this morning.

Cyrano. [*Taking a step toward* CHRISTIAN.] This morning?

Carbon de Castel-Jaloux. [*Low.*] His name is Baron de Neuvill. . . .

Cyrano. [*Stopping short.*] Ah, very well. . . . [*He turns pale, then red, gives evidence of another impulse to throw himself upon* CHRISTIAN.] I . . . [*He conquers it, and says in a stifled voice.*] Very well. [*He takes up his tale.*] As I was saying . . . [*With a burst of rage.*] *Mordious!* . . . [*He continues in a natural tone:*] one could not see at all. [*Consternation. All resume their seats, staring at one another.*] And I was walking along, reflecting that for a very insignificant rogue I was probably about to offend some great prince who would bear me a lasting grudge, that, in brief, I was about to thrust my . . .

Christian. Nose . . .

[*All get up.* CHRISTIAN *has tilted his chair and is rocking on the hind legs.*]

Cyrano. [*Choking.*] Finger . . . between the tree and the bark; * for the aforesaid prince might be of sufficient power to trip me and throw me . . .

Christian. On my nose . . .

Cyrano. [*Wipes the sweat from his brow.*] But, said I, "Gascony forward! Never falter when duty prompts! Forward, Cyrano!" and, saying this, I advance—when suddenly, in the darkness, I barely avoid a blow . . .

Christian. Upon the nose . . .

* *Entre l'arbre et l'écorce il ne faut pas mettre le doigt* is the French proverb.

Cyrano. I ward it. . . . and thereupon find myself . . .

Christian. Nose to nose . . .

Cyrano. [*Springing toward him.*] *Ventre-Saint-Gris!* . . . [*All the* GASCONS *rush forward to see;* CYRANO, *on reaching* CHRISTIAN, *controls himself and proceeds*] . . . with a hundred drunken brawlers, smelling . . .

Christian. To the nose's limit . . .

Cyrano. [*Deathly pale, and smiling.*] . . . Of garlic and of grease. I leap forward, head lowered . . .

Christian. Nose to the wind! . . .

Cyrano. And I charge them. I knock two breathless and run a third through the body. One lets off at me: Paf! and I retort . . .

Christian. Pif!

Cyrano. [*Exploding.*] Death and damnation! Go—all of you!

[*All the* CADETS *make for the door.*]

First Cadet. The tiger is roused at last!

Cyrano. All! and leave me with this man.

Second Cadet. Bigre! When we see him again, it will be in the shape of mince-meat!

Ragueneau. Mince-meat? . . .

Other Cadet. In one of your pies.

Ragueneau. I feel myself grow white and flabby as a table-napkin!

Carbon de Castel-Jaloux. Let us go!

Other Cadet. Not a smudge of him will be left!

Other Cadet. What these walls are about to behold gives me gooseflesh to think upon!

Other Cadet. [*Closing the door at the right.*] Ghastly! . . . Ghastly!

[*All have left, by the back or the sides, a few up the stairway.* CYRANO *and* CHRISTIAN *remain face to face, and look at each other a moment.*]

Cyrano. Embrace me!

Christian. Monsieur . . .

Cyrano. Brave fellow.

Christian. But what does this . . .

Cyrano. Very brave fellow. I wish you to.

Christian. Will you tell me? . . .

Cyrano. Embrace me, I am her brother.

Christian. Whose?

Cyrano. Hers!

Christian. What do you mean?

Cyrano. Roxane's!

Christian. [*Running to him.*] Heavens! You, her brother?

Cyrano. Or the same thing: her first cousin.

Christian. And she has . . .

Cyrano. Told me everything!

Christian. Does she love me?

Cyrano. Perhaps!

Christian. [*Seizing his hands.*] How happy I am, monsieur, to make your acquaintance! . . .

Cyrano. That is what I call a sudden sentiment!

Christian. Forgive me! . . .

Cyrano. [*Looking at him, laying his hand upon his shoulder.*] It is true that he is handsome, the rascal!

Christian. If you but knew, Monsieur, how greatly I admire you! . . .

Cyrano. But all those noses which you . . .

Christian. I take them back!

Cyrano. Roxane expects a letter tonight . . .

Christian. Alas!

Cyrano. What is the matter?

Christian. I am lost if I cease to be dumb!

Cyrano. How is that?

Christian. Alas! I am such a dunce that I could kill myself for shame!

Cyrano. But, no . . . no. . . . You are surely not a dunce, if you believe you are! Besides, you scarcely attacked me like a dunce.

Christian. Oh, it is easy to find words in mounting to the assault! Indeed, I own to a certain cheap military readiness, but when I am before women, I have not a word to say. . . . Yet their eyes, when I pass by, express a kindness toward me. . . .

Cyrano. And do their hearts not express the same when you stop beside them?

Christian. No! . . . for I am of those—I recognize it, and am dismayed!—who do not know how to talk of love.

Cyrano. Tiens! . . . It seems to me that if Nature had taken more pains with my shape, I should have been of those who do know how to talk of it.

Christian. Oh, to be able to express things gracefully!

Cyrano. Oh, to be a graceful little figure of a mousquetaire!

Christian. Roxane is a précieuse, . . . there is no chance but that I shall disillusion Roxane!

Cyrano. [*Looking at* CHRISTIAN.] If I had to express my soul, such an interpreter! . . .

Christian. [*Desperately.*] I ought to have eloquence! . . .

Cyrano. [*Abruptly.*] Eloquence I will lend you! . . . And you, to me, shall lend all-conquering physical charm . . . and between us we will compose a hero of romance!

Christian. What?

Cyrano. Should you be able to say as your own things which I day by day would teach you?

Christian. You are suggesting? . . .

Cyrano. Roxane shall not be disillusioned! Tell me, shall we win her heart, we two as one? will you submit to feel, transmitted from my leather doublet into your doublet stitched with silk, the soul I wish to share?

Christian. But Cyrano! . . .

Cyrano. Christian, will you?

Christian. You frighten me!

Cyrano. Since you fear, left to yourself, to chill her heart, will you consent—and soon it will take fire, I vouch for it!—to contribute your lips to my phrases? . . .

Christian. Your eyes shine! . . .

Cyrano. Will you?

Christian. What, would it please you so much?

Cyrano. [*With rapture.*] It would . . . [*Remembering, and confining himself to expressing an artistic pleasure*] . . . amuse me! It is an experiment fit surely to tempt a poet. Will you complete me, and let me in exchange complete you? We will walk side by side: you in full light, I in your shadow. . . . I will be wit to you . . . you, to me, shall be good looks!

Christian. But the letter, which should be sent to her without delay? . . . Never shall I be able . . .

Cyrano. [*Taking from his doublet the letter written in the first part of the act.*] The letter? Here it is!

Christian. How? . . .

Cyrano. It only wants the address.

Christian. I . . .

Cyrano. You can send it without uneasiness. It is a good letter.

Christian. You had? . . .

Cyrano. You shall never find us—poets!—without epistles in our pockets to the Chlorises . . . of our imagining! For we are those same that have for mistress a dream blown into the bubble of a name! Take it—you shall convert this feigning into earnest; I was sending forth at random these confessions and laments: you shall make the wandering birds to settle . . . Take it! You shall see . . . I was as eloquent as if I had been sincere! Take, and have done!

Christian. But will it not need to be altered in any part? . . . Written without object, will it fit Roxane?

Cyrano. Like a glove!

Christian. But . . .

Cyrano. Trust to the blindness of love . . . and vanity! Roxane will never question that it was written for her.

Christian. Ah, my friend!

[*He throws himself into* CYRANO'S *arms. They stand embraced.*]

One of the Cadets. [*Opening the door a very little.*] Nothing more. . . . The stillness of death. . . . I dare not look . . . [*He thrusts in his head.*] What is this?

All of the Cadets. [*Entering and seeing* CYRANO *and* CHRISTIAN *locked in each other's arms.*] Ah! . . . Oh! . . .

One of the Cadets. This passes bounds!

[*Consternation.*]

The Mousquetaire. [*Impudent.*] *Ouais?*

Carbon de Castel-Jaloux. Our demon is waxen mild as an apostle; smitten upon one nostril, he turns the other also!

The Mousquetaire. It is in order now to speak of his nose, is it? [*Calling* LISE, *with a swaggering air.*] Hey, Lise! now listen and look. [*Pointedly sniffing the air.*] Oh, . . . oh, . . . it is surprising! . . . what an odor! [*Going to* CYRANO.] But monsieur must have smelled it, too? Can you tell me what it is, so plain in the air?

Cyrano. [*Beating him.*] Why, sundry blows!

[*Joyful antics of the* CADETS *in beholding* CYRANO *himself again.*]

CURTAIN

ACT THIRD

ROXANE'S KISS

A small square in the old Marais. Old-fashioned houses. Narrow streets seen in perspective. At the right, ROXANE'S *house and the wall of her garden, above which spreading tree-tops. Over the house-door, a balcony and window. A bench beside the doorstep.*

The wall is overclambered by ivy, the balcony wreathed with jasmine.

By means of the bench and projecting stones in the wall, the balcony can easily be scaled.

On the opposite side, an old house in the same style of architecture, brick and stone, with an entrance door. The door-knocker is swaddled in linen.

[*At the rise of the curtain, the* DUENNA *is seated on the bench. The window on* ROXANE'S *balcony is wide open.*

RAGUENEAU, *in a sort of livery, stands*

near the DUENNA; *he is finishing the tale of his misfortunes, drying his eyes.*]

Ragueneau. And then she eloped with a mousquetaire! Ruined, forsaken, I was hanging myself. I had already taken leave of earth, when Monsieur de Bergerac happening along, unhanged me, and proposed me to his cousin as her steward. . . .

The Duenna. But how did you fall into such disaster?

Ragueneau. Lise was fond of soldiers; I, of poets! Mars ate up all left over by Apollo. Under those circumstances, you conceive, the pantry soon was bare.

The Duenna. [*Rising and calling toward the open window.*] Roxane, are you ready? . . . They are waiting for us! . . .

Roxane's Voice. [*Through the window.*] I am putting on my mantle!

The Duenna. [*To* RAGUENEAU, *pointing at the door opposite.*] It is over there, opposite, we are expected. At Clomire's. She holds a meeting in her little place. A disquisition upon the Softer Sentiments is to be read.

Ragueneau. Upon the Softer Sentiments.

The Duenna. [*Coyly.*] Yes! . . . [*Calling toward the window.*] Roxane, you must make haste, or we shall miss the disquisition upon the Softer Sentiments!

Roxane's Voice. I am coming!

[*A sound of string-instruments is heard, drawing nearer.*]

Cyrano's Voice. [*Singing in the wings.*] La! la! la! la! la! . . .

The Duenna. [*Surprised.*] We are to have music?

Cyrano. [*Enters followed by two* PAGES *with theorbos.**] I tell you it is a demi-semi-quaver! . . . you demi-semi-noddle!

First Page. [*Ironically.*] Monsieur knows then about quavers, semi and demi?

Cyrano. I know music, as do all Gassendi's disciples!

The Page. [*Playing and singing.*] La! la!

Cyrano. [*Snatching the theorbo from him and continuing the musical phrase.*] I can carry on the melody. . . . La, la, la, la, . . .

Roxane. [*Appearing on the balcony.*] It is you?

Cyrano. [*Singing upon the tune he is continuing.*] I, indeed, who salute your lilies and present my respects to your ro-o-oses! . . .

Roxane. I am coming down!

[*She leaves the balcony.*]

The Duenna. [*Pointing at the* PAGES.] What is the meaning of these two virtuosi?

Cyrano. A wager I won, from D'Assoucy. We were disputing upon a question of grammar. Yes! No! Yes! No! Suddenly pointing at these two tall knaves, expert at clawing strings, by whom he constantly goes attended, he said, "I wager a day long of music!" He lost. Until therefore the next rise of the sun, I shall have dangling after me these archlute players, harmonious witnesses of all I do! . . . At first I liked it very well, but now it palls a little. [*To the musicians.*] Hey! . . . Go, from me, to Montfleury, and play him a pavane! † . . . [*The* PAGES *go toward the back. To the* DUENNA.] I have come to inquire of Roxane, as I do every evening. . . . [*To the* PAGES, *who are leaving.*] Play a long time . . . and out of tune! [*To the* DUENNA.] . . . whether in the friend of her soul she can still detect no fault?

Roxane. [*Coming out of the house.*] Ah, how beautiful he is, what wit he has, how deeply I love him!

Cyrano. [*Smiling.*] Christian has so much wit? . . .

Roxane. Cousin, more than yourself!

Cyrano. I grant you.

Roxane. There is not one alive, I truly believe, more apt at turning those pretty nothings which yet are everything. . . . Sometimes he is of an absent mood, his muse is wool-gathering; then, suddenly, he will say the most enchanting things!

Cyrano. [*Incredulous.*] Come! . . .

Roxane. Oh, it is too bad! Men are all alike, narrow, narrow: because he is handsome, he cannot possible be witty!

Cyrano. So he talks of the heart in acceptable fashion?

Roxane. "Talks," cousin, is feeble. . . . He dissertates!

Cyrano. And writes? . . .

Roxane. Still better! Listen now to this. . . . [*Declaiming.*] *"The more of my heart you steal from me, the more heart I have!"* [*Triumphantly to* CYRANO.] Well? . . .

Cyrano. Pooh!

Roxane. And to this: *"Since you have stolen my heart, and since I must suffer, to suffer with, send me your own!"*

Cyrano. Now he has too much heart, now he has not enough, . . . just what does he want, in the matter of quantity?

Roxane. You vex me! You are eaten up with jealousy. . . .

Cyrano. [*Starting.*] *Hein?*

Roxane. Author's jealousy! And this,

* A theorbo is a bass lute.

† A dance with a slow, stately measure.

could anything be more exquisitely tender? *"Believe it, my heart cries out to you, and if kisses could be sent in writing, Love, you should read my letter with your lips. . . ."*

Cyrano. [*In spite of himself smiling with satisfaction.*] Ha! Ha! Those particular lines seem to me . . . ho! . . . ho! . . . [*Remembering himself, disdainfully*] . . . puny, pretty . . .

Roxane. This, then . . .

Cyrano. [*Delighted.*] You know his letters by heart?

Roxane. All!

Cyrano. It is flattering, one cannot deny.

Roxane. In this art of expressing love he is a master!

Cyrano. [*Modest.*] Oh, . . . a master!

Roxane. [*Peremptory.*] A master!

Cyrano. As you please, then . . . a master!

The Duenna. [*Who had gone toward the back, coming quickly forward.*] Monsieur de Guiche! [*To* CYRANO, *pushing him toward the house.*] Go in! It is perhaps better that he should not see you here! it might put him on the scent . . .

Roxane. [*To* CYRANO.] Yes, of my dear secret! He loves me, he is powerful . . . he must not find out! He might cut in sunder our loves . . . with an axe!

Cyrano. [*Going into the house.*] Very well, very well. [DE GUICHE *appears.*]

Roxane. [*To* DE GUICHE, *with a curtsey.*] I was leaving the house.

De Guiche. I have come to bid you farewell.

Roxane. You are going away?

De Guiche. To war.

Roxane. Ah!

De Guiche. I have my orders. Arras is besieged.

Roxane. Ah! . . . it is besieged?

De Guiche. Yes. . . . I see that my departure does not greatly affect you.

Roxane. Oh! . . .

De Guiche. As for me, I own it wrings my heart. Shall I see you again? . . . When? . . . You know that I am made commander-in-general?

Roxane. [*Uninterested.*] I congratulate you.

De Guiche. Of the Guards.

Roxane. [*Starting.*] Ah . . . of the Guards?

De Guiche. Among whom your cousin serves . . . the man of the boasts and tirades. I shall have opportunity in plenty to retaliate upon him down there.

Roxane. [*Suffocating.*] What? The Guards are going down there?

De Guiche. Surely. It is my regiment.

Roxane. [*Falls sitting upon the bench; aside.*] Christian!

De Guiche. What is it troubles you?

Roxane. [*Greatly moved.*] This departure . . . grieves me mortally. When one cares for a person . . . to know him away at the war!

De Guiche. [*Surprised and charmed.*] For the first time you utter a kind and feeling word, when I am leaving!

Roxane. [*In a different tone, fanning herself.*] So . . . you are thinking of revenge upon my cousin?

De Guiche. [*Smiling.*] You side with him?

Roxane. No . . . against him.

De Guiche. Do you see much of him?

Roxane. Very little.

De Guiche. He is everywhere to be met, with one of the cadets . . . [*trying to remember*] that Neu . . . villen . . . viller . . .

Roxane. A tall man?

De Guiche. Light haired.

Roxane. Red haired.

De Guiche. Good looking.

Roxane. Pooh!

De Guiche. But a fool!

Roxane. He looks like one. [*In a different tone.*] Your vengeance upon Cyrano is then to place him within reach of shot, which is the thing of all he loves! . . . A miserable vengeance! . . . I know, I do, what would more seriously concern him!

De Guiche. And that is?

Roxane. Why . . . that the regiment should march, and leave him behind with his beloved cadets, arms folded, the whole war through, in Paris! That is the only way to cast down a man like him. You wish to punish him? Deprive him of danger.

De Guiche. A woman! A woman! None but a woman could devise a vengeance of that sort!

Roxane. His friends will gnaw their fists, and he his very soul, with chagrin at not being under fire; and you will be abundantly avenged!

De Guiche. [*Coming nearer.*] Then you do love me a little? [ROXANE *smiles.*] I think I see in your espousing my grudge a proof of affection, Roxane . . .

Roxane. You may!

De Guiche. [*Showing several folded papers.*] I have here upon me the orders to be transmitted at once to each of the companies . . . except . . . [*He takes one from among the others.*] this one! . . . the company of the cadets . . . [*He puts it in his pocket.*] This, I will keep. [*Laughing.*] Ah, ah, ah! Cyrano! his belligerent humor! . . . So you sometimes play tricks upon people, you? . . .

Roxane. Sometimes.

De Guiche. [*Very near her.*] I love you to distraction! This evening . . . listen . . . it is true that I must be gone. But to go when I feel it is evident you care! Listen! . . . There is, not far from here, in Rue Orléans, a convent founded by the Capuchins. Father Athanasius. A layman may not enter. But the good fathers . . . I fear no difficulty with them! They will hide me up their sleeve . . . their sleeve is wide. They are the Capuchins that serve Richelieu at home. Fearing the uncle, they proportionately fear the nephew. I shall be thought to have left. I will come to you masked. Let me delay by a single day, wayward enchantress!

Roxane. But if it should transpire . . . your fame . . .

De Guiche. Bah!

Roxane. But . . . the siege . . . Arras! . . .

De Guiche. Must wait! Allow me, I beg . . .

Roxane. No!

De Guiche. I beseech!

Roxane. [*Tenderly.*] No! Love itself bids me forbid you!

De Guiche. Ah!

Roxane. You must go! [*Aside.*] Christian will stay! [*Aloud.*] For my sake, be heroic . . . Antony!

De Guiche. Ah, heavenly word upon your lips! . . Then you love the one who . . .

Roxane. Who shall have made me tremble for his sake . . .

De Guiche. [*In a transport of joy.*] Ah, I will go! [*He kisses her hand.*] Are you satisfied with me?

Roxane. My friend, I am.

[*Exit* DE GUICHE.]

The Duenna. [*Dropping a mocking curtsey toward his back.*] My friend, we are!

Roxane. [*To the* DUENNA.] Not a word of what I have done: Cyrano would never forgive me for defrauding him of his war! [*She calls toward the house.*] Cousin! [CYRANO *comes out.*] We are going to Clomire's. [*She indicates the house opposite.*] Alcandre has engaged to speak, and so has Lysimon.

The Duenna. [*Putting her little finger to her ear.*] Yes, but my little finger tells me that we shall be too late to hear them!

Cyrano. [*To* ROXANE.] Of all things do not miss the trained monkeys.

[*They have reached* CLOMIRE's *door.*]

The Duenna. See! . . . See! they have muffled the doorknocker! [*To the doorknocker.*] You have been gagged, that your voice should not disturb the beautiful lecture . . . little brutal disturber!

[*She lifts it with infinite care and knocks softly.*]

Roxane. [*Seeing the door open.*] Come! [*From the threshold to* CYRANO.] If Christian should come, as probably he will, say he must wait!

Cyrano. [*Hurriedly, as she is about to disappear.*] Ah! [*She turns.*] Upon what shall you, according to your custom, question him today?

Roxane. Upon . . .

Cyrano. [*Eagerly.*] Upon? . . .

Roxane. But you will be silent . . .

Cyrano. As that wall!

Roxane. Upon nothing! I will say! Forward! Free rein! No curb! Improvise! Talk of love! Be magnificent!

Cyrano. [*Smiling.*] Good.

Roxane. Hush!

Cyrano. Hush!

Roxane. Not a word!

[*She goes in and closes the door.*]

Cyrano. [*Bowing, when the door is closed.*] A thousand thanks!

[*The door opens again and* ROXANE *looks out.*]

Roxane. He might prepare his speeches . . .

Cyrano. Ah, no! . . . the devil, no!

Both. [*Together.*] Hush! . . .

[*The door closes.*]

Cyrano. [*Calling.*] Christian! [*Enter* CHRISTIAN.] I know all that we need to. Now make ready your memory. This is your chance to cover yourself with glory. Let us lose no time. Do not look sullen, like that. Quick! Let us go to your lodging and I will rehearse you . . .

Christian. No!

Cyrano. What?

Christian. No, I will await Roxane here.

Cyrano. What insanity possesses you? Come quickly and learn . . .

Christian. No, I tell you! I am weary of borrowing my letters, my words . . . of playing a part, and living in constant fear. . . . It was very well at first, but now I feel that she loves me. I thank you heartily. I am no longer afraid. I will speak for myself . . .

Cyrano. *Ouais?* . . .

Christian. And what tells you that I shall not know how? I am not such an utter blockhead, after all! You shall see! Your lessons have not been altogether wasted. I can shift to speak without your aid! And, that failing, by Heaven! I shall still know enough to take her in my arms! [*Catching sight of* ROXANE, *who is coming out from* CLOMIRE'S.] She is coming! Cyrano, no, do not leave me! . . .

Cyrano. [*Bowing to him.*] I will not meddle, Monsieur.

[*He disappears behind the garden wall.*]

Roxane. [*Coming from* CLOMIRE'S *house with a number of people from whom she is taking leave. Curtseys and farewells.*] Barthénoide! . . . Alcandre! . . . Grémione! . . .

The Duenna. [*Comically desperate.*] We missed the disquisition upon the Softer Sentiments! [*She goes into* ROXANE'S *house.*]

Roxane. [*Still taking leave of this one and that.*] Urimédonte! . . . Good-by!

[*All bow to* ROXANE, *to one another, separate, and go off by the various streets.* ROXANE *sees* CHRISTIAN.]

Roxane. You are here! [*She goes to him.*] Evening is closing round. . . . Wait! . . . They have all gone. . . . The air is so mild. . . Not a passer in sight. . . . Let us sit here. . . . Talk! . . . I will listen.

Christian. [*Sits beside her, on the bench. Silence.*] I love you.

Roxane. [*Closing her eyes.*] Yes. Talk to me of love.

Christian. I love you.

Roxane. Yes. That is the theme. Play variations upon it.

Christian. I love . . .

Roxane. Variations!

Christian. I love you so much . . .

Roxane. I do not doubt it. What further? . . .

Christian. And further . . . I should be so happy if you loved me! Tell me, Roxane, that you love me . . .

Roxane. [*Pouting.*] You proffer cider to me when I was hoping for champagne! . . . Now tell me a little *how* you love me?

Christian. Why . . . very, very much.

Roxane. Oh! . . . unravel, disentangle your sentiments!

Christian. Your throat! . . . I want to kiss it! . . .

Roxane. Christian!

Christian. I love you! . . .

Roxane. [*Attempting to rise.*] Again! . . .

Christian. [*Hastily, holding her back.*] No, I do not love you! . . .

Roxane. [*Sitting down again.*] That is fortunate!

Christian. I adore you!

Roxane. [*Rising and moving away.*] Oh! . . .

Christian. Yes, . . . love makes me into a fool!

Roxane. [*Drily.*] And I am displeased at it! as I should be displeased at your no longer being handsome.

Christian. But . . .

Roxane. Go, and rally your routed eloquence!

Christian. I . . .

Roxane. You love me. I have heard it. Good evening. [*She goes toward the house.*]

Christian. No, no, not yet! . . . I wish to tell you . . .

Roxane. [*Pushing open the door to go in.*] That you adore me. Yes, I know. No! No! Go away! . . . Go! . . . Go! . . .

Christian. But I . . .

[*She closes the door in his face.*]

Cyrano. [*Who has been on the scene a moment, unnoticed.*] Unmistakably a success.

Christian. Help me!

Cyrano. No, sir, no.

Christian. I will go kill myself if I am not taken back into favor at once . . . at once!

Cyrano. And how can I . . . how, the devil? . . . make you learn on the spot . . .

Christian. [*Seizing him by the arm.*] Oh, there! . . . Look! . . . See!

[*Light has appeared in the balcony window.*]

Cyrano. [*With emotion.*] Her window!

Christian. Oh, I shall die!

Cyrano. Not so loud!

Christian. [*In a whisper.*] I shall die!

Cyrano. It is a dark night. . . .

Christian. Well?

Cyrano. All may be mended. But you do not deserve. . . . There! stand there, miserable boy! . . . in front of the balcony! I will stand under it and prompt you.

Christian. But . . .

Cyrano. Do as I bid you!

The Pages. [*Reappearing at the back, to* CYRANO.] Hey!

Cyrano. Hush!

[*He signs to them to lower their voices.*]

First Page. [*In a lower voice.*] We have finished serenading Montfleury!

Cyrano. [*Low, quickly.*] Go and stand out of sight. One at this street corner, the other at that; and if any one comes near, play! . . .

Second Page. What sort of tune, Monsieur the Gassendist?

Cyrano. Merry if it be a woman, mournful if it be a man. [*The pages disappear, one at each street corner. To* CHRISTIAN.] Call her!

Christian. Roxane!

Cyrano. [*Picking up pebbles and throwing them at the window-pane.*] Wait! A few pebbles . . .

Roxane. [*Opening the window.*] Who is calling me?

Christian. It is I . . .

Roxane. Who is . . . I?

Christian. Christian!

Roxane. [*Disdainfully.*] Oh, you!

Christian. I wish to speak with you.

Cyrano. [*Under the balcony, to* CHRISTIAN.] Speak low! . . .

Roxane. No, your conversation is too common. You may go home!

Christian. In mercy! . . .

Roxane. No . . . you do not love me any more!

Christian. [*Whom* CYRANO *is prompting.*] You accuse me . . . just Heaven! of loving you no more . . . when I can love you no more!

Roxane. [*Who was about to close her window, stopping.*] Ah, that is a little better!

Christian. [*Same business.*] To what a . . . size has Love grown in my . . . sigh-rocked soul which the . . . cruel cherub has chosen for his cradle!

Roxane. [*Stepping nearer to the edge of the balcony.*] That is distinctly better! . . . But, since he is so cruel, this Cupid, you were unwise not to smother him in his cradle!

Christian. [*Same business.*] I tried to, but, Madame, the . . . attempt was futile. This . . . new-born Love is . . . a little Hercules . . .

Roxane. Much, much better!

Christian. [*Same business.*] . . . Who found it merest baby-play to . . . strangle the serpents . . . twain, Pride and . . . Mistrust.

Roxane. [*Leaning her elbows on the balcony-rail.*] Ah, that is very good indeed! . . . But why do you speak so slowly and stintedly? Has your imagination gout in its wings?

Cyrano. [*Drawing* CHRISTIAN *under the balcony, and taking his place.*] Hush! It is becoming too difficult!

Roxane. Tonight your words come falteringly. . . . Why is it?

Cyrano. [*Talking low like* CHRISTIAN.] Because of the dark. They have to grope to find your ear.

Roxane. My words do not find the same difficulty.

Cyrano. They reach their point at once? Of course they do! That is because I catch them with my heart. My heart, you see, is very large, your ear particularly small. . . . Besides, your words drop . . . they fall quickly; mine have to climb . . . and that takes longer!

Roxane. They have been climbing more nimbly, however, in the last few minutes.

Cyrano. They are becoming used to this gymnastic feat!

Roxane. It is true that I am talking with you from a very mountain top!

Cyrano. It is sure that a hard word dropped from such a height upon my heart would shatter it!

Roxane. [*With the motion of leaving.*] I will come down.

Cyrano. [*Quickly.*] Do not!

Roxane. [*Pointing at the bench at the foot of the balcony.*] Then do you get up on the seat! . . .

Cyrano. [*Drawing away in terror.*] No!

Roxane. How do you mean . . . no?

Cyrano. [*With ever-increasing emotion.*] Let us profit a little by this chance of talking softly together without seeing each other . . .

Roxane. Without seeing each other? . . .

Cyrano. Yes, to my mind, delectable! Each guesses at the other, and no more. You discern but the trailing backness of a mantle, and I a dawn-gray glimmer which is a summer gown. I am a shadow merely, a pearly phantom are you! You can never know what these moments are to me! If ever I was eloquent . . .

Roxane. You were!

Cyrano. My words never till now surged from my very heart . . .

Roxane. And why?

Cyrano. Because, till now, they must strain to reach you through . . .

Roxane. What?

Cyrano. Why, the bewildering emotion a man feels who sees you, and whom you look upon! . . . But this evening, it seems to me that I am speaking to you for the first time!

Roxane. It is true that your voice is altogether different.

Cyrano. [*Coming nearer, feverishly.*] Yes, altogether different, because, protected by the dark, I dare at last to be myself. I dare . . . [*He stops, and distractedly.*] What was I saying? . . . I do not know. . . . All this . . . forgive my incoherence! . . . is so delicious . . . is so new to me!

Roxane. So new? . . .

Cyrano. [*In extreme confusion, still trying to mend his expressions.*] So new . . . yes, new, to be sincere; the fear of being mocked always constrains my heart . . .

Roxane. Mocked . . . for what?

Cyrano. Why, . . . for its impulses, its flights! . . . Yes, my heart always cowers behind the defense of my wit. I set forth to capture a star . . . and then, for dread of laughter, I stop and pick a flower . . . of rhetoric!

Roxane. That sort of flower has its pleasing points . . .

Cyrano. But yet, tonight, let us scorn it!

Roxane. Never before had you spoken as you are speaking! . . .

Cyrano. Ah, if far from Cupid-darts and quivers, we might seek a place of somewhat fresher things! If instead of drinking, flat sip by sip, from a chiseled golden thimble, drops distilled and dulcified, we might try the sensation of quenching the thirst of our souls by stooping to the level of the great river, and setting our lips to the stream!

Roxane. But yet, wit . . . fancy . . . delicate conceits. . . .

Cyrano. I gave my fancy leave to frame conceits, before, to make you linger, . . . but now it would be an affront to this balm-breathing night, to Nature and the hour, to talk like characters in a pastoral performed at Court! . . . Let us give Heaven leave, looking at us with all its earnest stars, to strip us of disguise and artifice: I fear, . . . oh, fear! . . . lest in our mistaken alchemy sentiment should be subtilized to evaporation; lest the life of the heart should waste in these empty pastimes, and the final refinement of the fine be the undoing of the refined!

Roxane. But yet, wit . . . aptness . . . ingenuity . . .

Cyrano. I hate them in love! Criminal, when one loves, to prolong overmuch that paltry thrust and parry! The moment, however, comes inevitably—and I pity those for whom it never comes!—in which, we apprehending the noble depth of the love we harbor, a shallow word hurts us to utter!

Roxane. If . . . if, then, that moment has come for us two, what words will you say to me?

Cyrano. All those, all those, all those that come to me! Not in formal nosegay order, . . . I will throw them to you in a wild sheaf! I love you, choke with love, I love you, dear. . . . My brain reels, I can bear no more, it is too much. . . . Your name is in my heart the golden clapper in a bell; and as I know no rest, Roxane, always the heart is shaken, and ever rings your name! . . . Of you, I remember all, all have I loved! Last year, one day, the twelfth of May, in going out at morning you changed the fashion of your hair. . . . I have taken the light of your hair for my light, and as having stared too long at the sun, on everything one sees a scarlet wheel, on everything when I come from my chosen light, my dazzled eye sets swimming golden blots! . . .

Roxane. [*In a voice unsteady with emotion.*] Yes . . . this is love . . .

Cyrano. Ah, verily! The feeling which invades me, terrible and jealous, is love . . . with all its mournful frenzy! It is love, yet self-forgetting more than the wont of love! Ah, for your happiness how readily would I give mine, though you should never know it, might I but, from a distance, sometimes, hear the happy laughter bought by my sacrifice! Every glance of yours breeds in me new strength, new valor! Are you beginning to understand? Tell me, do you grasp my love's measure? Does some little part of my soul make itself felt of you there in the darkness? . . . Oh, what is happening to me this evening is too sweet, too deeply dear! I tell you all these things, and you listen to me, you! Not in my least modest hoping did I ever hope so much! I have now only to die! It is because of words of mine that she is trembling among the dusky branches. For you are trembling, like a flower among leaves! Yes, you tremble, . . . for whether you will or no, I have felt the worshiped trembling of your hand all along this thrilled and blissful jasmine-bough!

[*He madly kisses the end of a pendent bough.*]

Roxane. Yes, I tremble . . . and weep . . . and love you . . . and am yours! . . . For you have carried me away . . . away! . . .

Cyrano. Then, let death come! I have moved you, I! . . . There is but one thing more I ask . . .

Christian. [*Under the balcony.*] A kiss!

Roxane. [*Drawing hastily back.*] What?

Cyrano. Oh!

Roxane. You ask? . . .

Cyrano. Yes . . . I . . . [*To* CHRISTIAN.] You are in too great haste!

Christian. Since she is so moved, I must take advantage of it!

Cyrano. [*To* ROXANE.] I . . . Yes, it is true I asked . . . but, merciful heavens! . . . I knew at once that I had been too bold.

Roxane. [*A shade disappointed.*] You insist no more than so?

Cyrano. Indeed, I insist . . . without insisting! Yes! yes! but your modesty shrinks! . . . I insist, but yet . . . the kiss I begged . . . refuse it me!

Christian. [*To* CYRANO, *pulling at his mantle.*] Why?

Cyrano. Hush, Christian!

Roxane. [*Bending over the bacony-rail.*] What are you whispering?

Cyrano. Reproaches to myself for having gone too far; I was saying "Hush, Christian!" [*The theorbos are heard playing.*] Your pardon! . . . a second! . . . Some one is coming!

[ROXANE *closes the window.* CYRANO *listens to the theorbos, one of which plays a lively, and the other a lugubrious tune.*]

Cyrano. A dance? . . . A dirge? . . . What do they mean? Is it a man or a woman? . . . Ah, it is a monk!

[*Enter a* CAPUCHIN MONK, *who goes from house to house, with a lantern, examining the doors.*]

Cyrano. [*To* THE CAPUCHIN.] What are you looking for, Diogenes?

The Capuchin. I am looking for the house of Madame . . .

Christian. He is in the way!

The Capuchin. Magdeleine Robin . . .

Cyrano. [*Pointing up one of the streets.*] This way! . . . Straight ahead . . . go straight ahead . . .

The Capuchin. I thank you. I will say ten Aves for your peace. [*Exit.*]

Cyrano. My good wishes speed your cowl!

[*He comes forward toward* CHRISTIAN.]

Christian. Insist upon the kiss! . . .

Cyrano. No, I will not!

Christian. Sooner or later . . .

Cyrano. It is true! It must come, the moment of inebriation when your lips shall imperiously be impelled toward each other, because the one is fledged with youthful gold and the other is so soft a pink! . . . [*To himself.*] I had rather it should be because . . .

[*Sound of the window reopening;* CHRISTIAN *hides under the balcony.*]

Roxane. [*Stepping forward on the balcony.*] Are you there? We were speaking of . . . of . . . of a . . .

Cyrano. Kiss. The word is sweet. Why does your fair lip stop at it? If the mere word burns it, what will be of the thing itself? Do not make it into a fearful matter, and then fear! Did you not a moment ago insensibly leave playfulness behind and slip without trepidation from a smile to a sigh, from a sigh to a tear? Slip but a little further in the same blessed direction: from a tear to a kiss there is scarcely a dividing shiver!

Roxane. Say no more!

Cyrano. A kiss! When all is said, what is a kiss? An oath of allegiance taken in closer proximity, a promise more precise, a seal on a confession, a rose-red dot upon the letter i in loving; a secret which elects the mouth for ear; an instant of eternity murmuring like a bee; balmy communion with a flavor of flowers; a fashion of inhaling each other's heart, and of tasting, on the brink of the lips, each other's soul!

Roxane. Say no more . . . no more!

Cyrano. A kiss, Madame, is a thing so noble that the Queen of France, on the most fortunate of lords, bestowed one—the queen herself!

Roxane. If that be so . . .

Cyrano. [*With increasing fervor.*] Like Buckingham I have suffered in long silence, like him I worship a queen, like him I am sorrowful and unchanging . . .

Roxane. Like him you enthrall through the eyes of the heart that follows you!

Cyrano. [*To himself, sobered.*] True, I am handsome . . . I had forgotten!

Roxane. Come then and gather it, the supreme flower . . .

Cyrano. [*Pushing* CHRISTIAN *toward the balcony.*] Go!

Roxane. . . . tasting of the heart.

Cyrano. Go! . . .

Roxane. . . . murmuring like a bee . . .

Cyrano. Go!

Christian. [*Hesitating.*] But now I feel as if I ought not!

Roxane. . . . making eternity an instant . . .

Cyrano. [*Pushing* CHRISTIAN.] Scale the balcony, you donkey!

[CHRISTIAN *springs toward the balcony, and climbs by means of the bench, the vine, the posts and balusters.*]

Christian. Ah, Roxane!

[*He clasps her to him, and bends over her lips.*]

Cyrano. Ha! . . . What a turn of the screw to my heart! . . . A kiss!—a banquet of Love at which I am Lazarus, a crumb drops from your table even to me, here in the shade. . . . Yes, in my outstretched heart a little falls, as I feel that upon the lip pressing her lip Roxane kisses the words spoken by me! . . . [*The theorbos are heard.*] A merry tune . . . a mournful one . . . The monk! [*He goes through the pretense of arriving on the spot at a run, as if from a distance; calling.*] Ho, there!

Roxane. What is it?

Cyrano. It is I. I was passing this way. Is Christian there?

Christian. [*Astonished.*] Cyrano!

Roxane. Good evening, cousin!

Cyrano. Cousin, good evening!

Roxane. I will come down.

[ROXANE *disappears in the house.* THE CAPUCHIN *re-enters at the back.*]

Christian. [*Seeing him.*] Oh, again!

[*He follows* ROXANE.]

The Capuchin. It is here she lives, I am certain . . . Magdeleine Robin.

Cyrano. You said Rolin.

The Capuchin. No, bin, . . . b, i, n, bin!

Roxane. [*Appearing upon the threshold, followed by* RAGUENEAU, *carrying a lantern, and* CHRISTIAN.] What is it?

The Capuchin. A letter.

Christian. What?

The Capuchin. [*To* ROXANE.] Oh, the contents can be only of a sacred character! It is from a worthy nobleman who . . .

Roxane. [*To* CHRISTIAN.] It is from De Guiche!

Christian. He dares to . . . ?

Roxane. Oh, he will not trouble me much longer! [*Opening the letter.*] I love you, and if . . . [*By the light of* RAGUENEAU'S *lantern she reads, aside, low.*] Mademoiselle: The drums are beating. My regiment is buckling on its corselet. It is about to leave. I am thought to have left already, but lag behind. I am disobeying you. I am in the convent here. I am coming to you, and send you word by a friar, silly as a sheep, who has no suspicion of the import of this letter. You smiled too sweetly upon me an hour ago: I must see you smile again. Arrange to be alone, and deign graciously to receive the audacious worshiper, forgiven already, I can but hope, who signs himself your—etc. . . . [*To* THE CAPUCHIN.] Father, this is what the letter tells me . . . Listen: [*All draw nearer; she reads aloud.*] Mademoiselle: The wishes of the cardinal may not be disregarded, however hard compliance with them prove. I have therefore chosen as bearer of this letter a most reverend, holy, and sagacious Capuchin; it is our wish that he should at once, in your own dwelling, pronounce the nuptial blessing over you. Christian must secretly become your husband. I send him to you. You dislike him. Bow to Heaven's will in resignation, and be sure that it will bless your zeal, and sure, likewise, Mademoiselle, of the respect of him who is and will be ever your most humble and . . . etc.

The Capuchin. [*Beaming.*] The worthy gentleman! . . . I knew it! You remember that I said so: the contents of that letter can be only of a sacred character!

Roxane. [*Low, to* CHRISTIAN.] I am a fluent reader, am I not?

Christian. Hm!

Roxane. [*With feigned despair.*] Ah . . . it is horrible!

The Capuchin. [*Who has turned the light of his lantern upon* CYRANO.] You are the one?

Christian. No, I am.

The Capuchin. [*Turning the light upon him, and as if his good looks aroused suspicion.*] But . . .

Roxane. [*Quickly.*] Postscript: You will bestow upon the convent two hundred and fifty crowns.

The Capuchin. The worthy, worthy gentleman! [*To* ROXANE.] Be reconciled!

Roxane. [*With the expression of a martyr.*] I will endeavor! [*While* RAGUENEAU *opens the door for* THE CAPUCHIN, *whom* CHRISTIAN *is showing into the house,* ROXANE *says low to* CYRANO.] De Guiche is coming! . . . Keep him here! Do not let him enter until . . .

Cyrano. I understand! [*To* THE CAPUCHIN.] How long will it take to marry them?

The Capuchin. A quarter of an hour.

Cyrano. [*Pushing all toward the house.*] Go in! I shall be here!

Roxane. [*To* CHRISTIAN.] Come!

[*They go in.*]

Cyrano. How can I detain De Guiche for a quarter of an hour? [*He jumps upon the bench, climbs the wall toward the balcony-rail.*] So! . . . I climb up here! . . . I know what I will do! . . . [*The theorbos play a melancholy tune.*] Ho, it is a man! [*The tune quavers lugubriously.*] Ho, ho, this time there is no mistake! [*He is on the balcony; he pulls the brim of his hat over his eyes, takes off his sword, wraps his cloak about him, and bends over the balcony-rail.*] No, it is not too far! [*He climbs over the balcony-rail, and reaching for a long bough that projects beyond the garden wall, holds on to it with both hands, ready to let himself drop.*] I shall make a slight commotion in the atmosphere!

De Guiche. [*Enters masked, groping in the dark.*] What can that thrice-damned Capuchin be about?

Cyrano. The devil! if he should recognize my voice? [*Letting go with one hand, he makes show of turning a key.*] Cric! crac! [*Solemnly.*] Cyrano, resume the accent of Bergerac!

De Guiche. [*Looking at* ROXANE'S *house.*] Yes, that is it. I can scarcely see. This mask bothers my eyes!

[*He is about to enter* ROXANE'S *house;* CYRANO *swings from the balcony, holding on to the bough, which bends and lets him down between the door and*

De Guiche. *He intentionally drops very heavily, to give the effect of dropping from a great height, and lies flattened upon the ground, motionless, as if stunned.*]

De Guiche. What is it? [*When he looks up, the bough has swung into place; he sees nothing but the sky.*] Where did this man drop from?

Cyrano. [*Rising to a sitting posture.*] From the moon!

De Guiche. From the . . . ?

Cyrano. [*In a dreamy voice.*] What time is it?

De Guiche. Is he mad?

Cyrano. What time? What country? What day? What season?

De Guiche. But . . .

Cyrano. I am dazed!

De Guiche. Monsieur . . .

Cyrano. I have dropped from the moon like a bomb!

De Guiche. [*Impatiently.*] What are you babbling about?

Cyrano. [*Rising, in a terrible voice.*] I tell you I have dropped from the moon!

De Guiche. [*Backing a step.*] Very well. You have dropped from the moon! . . . He is perhaps a lunatic!

Cyrano. [*Walking up close to him.*] Not metaphorically, mind that!

De Guiche. But . . .

Cyrano. A hundred years ago, or else a minute—for I have no conception how long I have been falling—I was up there, in that saffron-colored ball!

De Guiche. [*Shrugging his shoulders.*] You were. Now, let me pass!

Cyrano. [*Standing in his way.*] Where am I? Be frank with me! Keep nothing from me! In what region, among what people, have I been shot like an aerolite?

De Guiche. I wish to pass!

Cyrano. While falling I could not choose my way, and have no notion where I have fallen! Is it upon a moon, or is it upon an earth, I have been dragged by my posterior weight?

De Guiche. I tell you, sir . . .

Cyrano. [*With a scream of terror at which* De Guiche *starts backward a step.*] Great God! . . . In this country men's faces are soot-black!

De Guiche. [*Lifting his hand to his face.*] What does he mean?

Cyrano. [*Still terrified.*] Am I in Algeria? Are you a native? . . .

De Guiche. [*Who has felt his mask.*] Ah, my mask!

Cyrano. [*Pretending to be easier.*] So I am in Venice! . . . Or am I in Genoa?

De Guiche. [*Attempting to pass.*] A lady is expecting me!

Cyrano. [*Completely reassured.*] Ah, then I am in Paris.

De Guiche. [*Smiling in spite of himself.*] The rogue is not far from amusing!

Cyrano. Ah, you are laughing!

De Guiche. I laugh . . . but intend to pass!

Cyrano. [*Beaming.*] To think I should strike Paris! [*Quite at his ease, laughing, brushing himself, bowing.*] I arrived—pray, pardon my appearance!—by the last whirlwind. I am rather unpresentable—Travel, you know! My eyes are still full of stardust. My spurs are clogged with bristles off a planet. [*Appearing to pick something off his sleeve.*] See, on my sleeve, a comet's hair!

[*He makes a feint of blowing it away.*]

De Guiche. [*Beside himself.*] Sir . . .

Cyrano. [*As* De Guiche *is about to pass, stretching out his leg as if to show something on it, thereby stopping him.*] Embedded in my calf, I have brought back one of the Great Bear's teeth . . . and as, falling too near the Trident, I strained aside to clear one of its prongs, I landed sitting in Libra, . . . yes, one of the scales! . . . and now my weight is registered up there! [*Quickly preventing* De Guiche *from passing, and taking hold of a button on his doublet.*] And if, Monsieur, you should take my nose between your fingers and compress it . . . milk would result!

De Guiche. What are you saying? Milk? . . .

Cyrano. Of the Milky Way.

De Guiche. Go to the devil!

Cyrano. No! I am sent from Heaven, literally. [*Folding his arms.*] Will you believe—I discovered it in passing—that Sirius at night puts on a night-cap? [*Confidentially.*] The lesser Bear is too little yet to bite. . . . [*Laughing.*] I tumbled plump through Lyra, and snapped a string! . . . [*Magnificent.*] But I intend setting all this down in a book,* and the golden stars I have brought back caught in my shaggy mantle, when the book is printed, will be seen serving as asterisks!

De Guiche. I have stood this long enough! I want . . .

Cyrano. I know perfectly what you want!

De Guiche. Man . . .

* This reference and those that follow are to the *Histoires comiques des états et empires de la lune et du soleil,* the best known of Bergerac's works.

Cyrano. You want to know, from me, at first hand, what the moon is made of, and whether that monumental pumpkin is inhabited?

De Guiche. [*Shouting.*] Not in the very least! I want . . .

Cyrano. To know how I got there? I got there by a method of my own invention.

De Guiche. [*Discouraged.*] He is mad! . . . stark!

Cyrano. [*Disdainfully.*] Do not imagine that I resorted to anything so absurd as Regiomontanus's eagle, or anything so lacking in enterprise as Archytas's pigeon! * . . .

De Guiche. The madman is erudite . . .

Cyrano. I drew up nothing that had ever been thought of before! [DE GUICHE *has succeeded in getting past* CYRANO, *and is nearing* ROXANE'S *door;* CYRANO *follows him, ready to buttonhole him.*] I invented no less than six ways of storming the blue fort of Heaven!

De Guiche. [*Turning around.*] Six, did you say?

Cyrano. [*Volubly.*] One way was to stand naked in the sunshine, in a harness thickly studded with glass phials, each filled with morning dew. The sun in drawing up the dew, you see, could not have helped drawing me up too!

De Guiche. [*Surprised, taking a step toward* CYRANO.] True. That is one!

Cyrano. [*Taking a step backward, with a view of drawing* DE GUICHE *away from the door.*] Or else, I could have let the wind into a cedar coffer, then rarefied the imprisoned element by means of cunningly adjusted burning-glasses, and soared up with it!

De Guiche. [*Taking another step toward* CYRANO.] Two!

Cyrano. [*Backing.*] Or else, mechanic as well as artificer, I could have fashioned a giant grasshopper, with steel joints, which, impelled by successive explosions of saltpeter, would have hopped with me to the azure meadows where graze the starry flocks!

De Guiche. [*Unconsciously following* CYRANO, *and counting on his fingers.*] That makes three!

Cyrano. Since smoke by its nature ascends, I could have blown into an appropriate globe a sufficient quantity to ascend with me!

De Guiche. [*As above, more and more astonished.*] Four!

Cyrano. Since Phœbe, the moon-goddess, when she is at wane, is greedy, O beeves! of your marrow, . . . with that marrow I could have besmeared myself!

De Guiche. [*Amazed.*] Five!

Cyrano. [*Who while talking has backed, followed by* DE GUICHE, *to the further side of the square, near a bench.*] Or else, I could have placed myself upon an iron plate, have taken a magnet of suitable size, and thrown it in the air! That way is a very good one! The magnet flies upward, the iron instantly after; the magnet no sooner overtaken than you fling it up again. . . . The rest is clear! You can go upward indefinitely.

De Guiche. Six! . . . But here are six excellent methods! Which of the six, my dear sir, did you select?

Cyrano. A seventh!

De Guiche. Did you, indeed? And what was that?

Cyrano. I give you a hundred guesses!

De Guiche. I must confess that I should like to know!

Cyrano. [*Imitating the noise of the surf, and making great mysterious gestures.*] Hoo-ish! hoo-ish!

De Guiche. Well! What is that?

Cyrano. Cannot you guess?

De Guiche. No!

Cyrano. The tide! . . . At the hour in which the moon attracts the deep, I lay down upon the sands, after a sea-bath . . . and, my head being drawn up first—the reason of this, you see, that the hair will hold a quantity of water in its mop!—I rose in the air, straight, beautifully straight, like an angel. I rose . . . I rose softly . . . without an effort . . . when, suddenly, I felt a shock. Then . . .

De Guiche. [*Lured on by curiosity, taking a seat on the bench.*] Well, . . . then?

Cyrano. Then . . . [*Resuming his natural voice.*] The time is up, Monsieur, and I release you. They are married.

De Guiche. [*Getting to his feet with a leap.*] I am dreaming or drunk! That voice? [*The door of* ROXANE'S *house opens; lackeys appear carrying lighted candelabra.* CYRANO *removes his hat.*] And that nose! . . . Cyrano!

Cyrano. [*Bowing.*] Cyrano. They have exchanged rings within the quarter of the hour.

De Guiche. Who have? [*He turns round. Tableau. Behind the lackey stand* ROXANE *and* CHRISTIAN *holding hands.* THE CAPUCHIN *follows them smiling.* RAGUENEAU *holds high a flambeau.* THE DUENNA *closes the procession, bewildered, in her bedgown.*]

* Regiomontanus, a German astronomer of the fifteenth century, A.D., and Archytas, a Greek philosopher of the fifth century, B.C., constructed flying machines of the shapes here mentioned.

Heavens! [*To* ROXANE.] You! [*Recognizing* CHRISTIAN *with amazement.*] He? [*Bowing to* ROXANE.] Your astuteness compels my admiration! [*To* CYRANO.] My compliments to you, ingenious inventor of flying machines. Your experiences would have beguiled a saint on the threshold of Paradise! Make a note of them. . . . They can be used again, with profit, in a book!

CYRANO. [*Bowing.*] I will confidently follow your advice.

THE CAPUCHIN. [*To* DE GUICHE, *pointing at the lovers, and wagging his great white beard with satisfaction.*] A beautiful couple, my son, brought together by you!

De Guiche. [*Eyeing him frigidly.*] As you say! [*To* ROXANE.] And now proceed, Madame, to take leave of your husband.

Roxane. What?

De Guiche. [*To* CHRISTIAN.] The regiment is on the point of starting. You are to join it!

Roxane. To go to war?

De Guiche. Of course!

Roxane. But the cadets are not going!

De Guiche. They are! [*Taking out the paper which he had put in his pocket.*] Here is the order. [*To* CHRISTIAN.] I beg you will take it to the Captain, baron, yourself.

Roxane. [*Throwing herself in* CHRISTIAN'S *arms.*] Christian!

De Guiche. [*To* CYRANO, *with a malignant laugh.*] The wedding night is somewhat far as yet!

Cyrano. [*Aside.*] He thinks that he is giving me great pain!

Christian. [*To* ROXANE.] Oh, once more, dear! . . . Once more!

Cyrano. Be reasonable . . . Come! . . . Enough!

Christian. [*Still clasping* ROXANE.] Oh, it is hard to leave her. . . . You cannot know. . . .

Cyrano. [*Trying to draw him away.*] I know.

[*Drums are heard in the distance sounding a march.*]

De Guiche. [*At the back.*] The regiment is on its way!

Roxane. [*To* CYRANO, *while she clings to* CHRISTIAN, *whom he is trying to draw away.*] Oh! . . . I entrust him to your care! Promise that under no circumstance shall his life be placed in danger!

Cyrano. I will endeavor . . . but obviously cannot promise . . .

Roxane. [*Same business.*] Promise that he will be careful of himself!

Cyrano. I will do my best, but . . .

Roxane. [*As above.*] That during this terrible siege he shall not take harm from the cold!

Cyrano. I will try, but . . .

Roxane. [*As above.*] That he will be true to me!

Cyrano. Of course, but yet, you see . . .

Roxane. [*As above.*] That he will write to me often!

Cyrano. [*Stopping.*] Ah, that . . . I promise freely!

CURTAIN

ACT FOURTH

THE GASCONY CADETS

The post occupied at the siege of Arras by the company of CARBON DE CASTEL-JALOUX. *At the back, across the whole stage, sloping earthwork. Beyond this is seen a plain stretching to the horizon; the country is covered with constructions relating to the siege. In the distance, against the sky, the outlines of the walls and roofs of Arras. Tents; scattered arms; drums, etc. It is shortly before sunrise. The East is yellow.*

[*Sentinels at even intervals. Camp-fires. The* GASCONY CADETS *lie asleep, rolled in their cloaks.* CARBON DE CASTEL-JALOUX *and* LE BRET *are watching. All are very pale and gaunt.* CHRISTIAN *lies sleeping among the others, in his military cape, in the foreground, his face lighted by one of the camp-fires. Silence.*]

Le Bret. It is dreadful!

Carbon. Yes. Nothing left.

Le Bret. *Mordious!*

Carbon. [*Warning him by a gesture to speak lower.*] Curse in a whisper! You will wake them! . . . [*To the* CADETS.] Hush! Go to sleep! [*To* LE BRET.] Who sleeps dines.

Le Bret. Who lies awake misses two good things . . . What a situation!

[*A few shots are heard in the distance.*]

Carbon. The devil take their popping!

They will wake my young ones! . . . [*To the* CADETS *who lift their heads.*] Go to sleep!

[*The* CADETS *lie down again. Other shots are heard, nearer.*]

One of the Cadets. [*Stirring.*] The devil! Again?

Carbon. It is nothing. It is Cyrano getting home.

[*The heads which had started up go down again.*]

A Sentinel. [*Outside.*] *Ventrebieu!* Who goes there?

Cyrano's Voice. Bergerac!

The Sentinel. [*Upon the embankment.*] *Ventrebieu!* Who goes there?

Cyrano. [*Appearing at the top of the embankment.*] Bergerac, blockhead!

[*He comes down.* LE BRET *goes to him, uneasy.*]

Le Bret. Ah, thank God!

Cyrano. [*Warning him by a sign to wake no one.*] Hush!

Le Bret. Wounded?

Cyrano. Do you not know that it has become a habit with them to miss me?

Le Bret. To me, it seems a little excessive that you should, every morning, for the sake of taking a letter, risk . . .

Cyrano. [*Stopping in front of* CHRISTIAN.] I promised that he would write often. [*He looks at* CHRISTIAN.] He sleeps. He has grown pale. If the poor little girl could know that he is starving. . . . But handsome as ever!

Le Bret. Go at once and sleep.

Cyrano. Le Bret, do not grumble! Learn this: I nightly cross the Spanish lines at a point where I know beforehand every one will be drunk.

Le Bret. You ought some time to bring us back some victuals!

Cyrano. I must be lightly burdened to flit through! . . . But I know that there will be events before the evening. The French, unless I am much mistaken, will eat or die.

Le Bret. Oh, tell us!

Cyrano. No, I am not certain . . . You will see!

Carbon. What a shameful reversal of the order of things, that the besieger should be starved!

Le Bret. Alas! never was more complicated siege than this of Arras: We besiege Arras, and, caught in a trap, are ourselves besieged by the Cardinal-prince of Spain. . . .

Cyrano. Someone now ought to come and besiege him.

Le Bret. I am not joking!

Cyrano. Oh, oh!

Le Bret. To think, ungrateful boy, that every day you risk a life precious as yours, solely to carry . . . [CYRANO *goes toward one of the tents.*] Where are you going?

Cyrano. I am going to write another.

[*He lifts the canvas flap, and disappears in the tent.*]

[*Daybreak has brightened. Rosy flush. The city of Arras at the horizon catches a golden light. The report of a cannon is heard, followed at once by a drum-call, very far away, at the left. Other drums beat, nearer. The drum-calls answer one another, come nearer, come very near, and go off, decreasing, dying in the distance, toward the right, having made the circuit of the camp. Noise of general awakening. Voices of officers in the distance.*]

Carbon. [*With a sigh.*] The reveille. . . . Ah, me! . . . [*The* CADETS *stir in their cloaks, stretch.*] An end to the succulent slumbers! I know but too well what their first word will be!

One of the Cadets. [*Sitting up.*] I am famished!

Other Cadet. I believe I am dying!

All. Oh! . . .

Carbon. Get up!

Third Cadet. I cannot go a step!

Fourth Cadet. I have not strength to stir!

First Cadet. [*Looking at himsef in a bit of armor.*] My tongue is coated: it must be the weather that is indigestible!

Other Cadet. Any one who wants them can have all my titles of nobility for a Chester cheese . . . or part of one!

Other Cadet. If my stomach does not have something put into it to take up the attention of my gastric juice, I shall retire into my tent before long . . . like Achilles!

Other Cadet. Yes, they ought to provide us with bread!

Carbon. [*Going to the tent into which* CYRANO *has retired; low.*] Cyrano!

Other Cadets. We cannot stand this much longer!

Carbon. [*As above, at the door of the tent.*] To the rescue, Cyrano! You who succeed so well always in cheering them, come and make them pluck up spirits!

Second Cadet. [*Falling upon* FIRST CADET *who is chewing something.*] What are you chewing, man?

First Cadet. A bit of gun-tow fried in axle-grease . . . using a burganet as frying pan. The suburbs of Arras are not precisely rich in game. . . .

Other Cadet. [*Entering.*] I have been hunting!

Other Cadet. [*The same.*] I have been fishing!

All. [*Rising and falling upon the newcomers.*] What?—what did you catch?—A pheasant?—A carp?—Quick! quick! . . . Let us see!

The Huntsman. A sparrow!

The Angler. A gudgeon!

All. [*Exasperated.*] Enough of this! Let us revolt!

Carbon. To the rescue, Cyrano!

[*It is now broad daylight.*]

Cyrano. [*Coming out of the tent, tranquil, a pen behind his ear, a book in his hand.*] What is the matter? [*Silence, To* First Cadet.] Why do you go off like that, with that slouching gait?

The Cadet. I have something away down in my heels which inconveniences me.

Cyrano. And what is that?

The Cadet. My stomach.

Cyrano. That is where mine is, too.

The Cadet. Then you too must be inconvenienced.

Cyrano. No. The size of the hollow within me merely increases my sense of my size.

Second Cadet. I happen to have teeth, long ones!

Cyrano. The better will you bite . . . in good time!

Third Cadet. I reverberate like a drum!

Cyrano. You will be of use . . . to sound the charge!

Other Cadet. I have a buzzing in my ears!

Cyrano. A mistake. Empty belly, no ears. You hear no buzzing.

Other Cadet. Ah, a trifling article to eat . . . and a little oil upon it!

Cyrano. [*Taking off the* Cadet's *morion and placing it in his hand.*] That is seasoned.

Other Cadet. What is there we could devour?

Cyrano. [*Tossing him the book he has been holding.*] Try the Iliad!

Other Cadet. The minister, in Paris, makes his four meals a day!

Cyrano. You feel it remiss in him not to send you a bit of partridge?

The Same. Why should he not? And some wine!

Cyrano. Richelieu, some Burgundy, if you please?

The Same. He might, by one of his Capuchins!

Cyrano. By His Eminence, perhaps, in sober gray?

Other Cadet. No ogre was ever so hungry!

Cyrano. You may have your fill yet of humble-pie!

First Cadet. [*Shrugging his shoulders.*] Forever jests! . . . puns! . . . *mots!*

Cyrano. Le mot forever, indeed! And I would wish to die, on a fine evening, under a rose-flushed sky, delivering myself of a good *mot* in a good cause! . . . Ah, yes, the best were indeed, far from fever-bed and potion, pierced with the only noble weapon, by an adversary worthy of oneself, to fall upon a glorious field, the point of a sword through his heart, the point of a jest on his lips! . . .

All. [*In a wail.*] I am hungry!

Cyrano. [*Folding his arms.*] God have mercy! can you think of nothing but eating? . . . Come here, Bertrandou the fifer, once the shepherd! Take from the double case one of your fifes: breathe into it, play to this pack of guzzlers and of gluttons our homely melodies, of haunting rhythm, every note of which appeals like a little sister, through whose every strain are heard strains of beloved voices . . . mild melodies whose slowness brings to mind the slowness of the smoke upcurling from our native hamlet hearths . . . melodies that seem to speak to a man in his native dialect! . . . [*The old* Fifer *sits down and makes ready his fife.*] Today let the fife, martial unwillingly, be reminded, while your fingers upon its slender stem flutter like birds in a delicate minuet, that before being ebony it was reed; surprise itself by what you make it sing . . . let it feel restored to it the soul of its youth, rustic and peaceable! [*The* Old Man *begins playing Languedoc tunes.*] Listen, Gascons! It is no more, beneath his fingers, the shrill fife of the camp, but the soft flute of the woodland! It is no more, between his lips, the whistling note of battle, but the lowly lay of goatherds leading their flocks to feed! . . . Hark! . . . It sings of the valley, the heath, the forest! . . . of the little shepherd, sunburned under his crimson cap! . . . the green delight of evening on the river! . . . Hark, Gascons all! It sings of Gascony!

[*Every head has drooped; all eyes have grown dreamy; tears are furtively brushed away with a sleeve, the hem of a cloak.*]

Carbon. [*To* Cyrano, *low.*] You are making them weep!

Cyrano. With homesickness! . . . a nobler pain than hunger . . . not physical: mental! I am glad the seat of their suffering should have removed . . . that the gripe should now afflict their hearts!

Carbon. But you weaken them, making them weep!

Cyrano. [*Beckoning to a drummer.*] Never fear! The hero in their veins is quickly roused. It is enough to . . .

[*He signs to the* DRUMMER *who begins drumming.*]

All. [*Starting to their feet and snatching up their arms.*] *Hein?* . . . What? . . . What is it?

Cyrano. [*Smiling.*] You see? . . . The sound of the drum was enough! Farewell dreams, regrets, old homestead, love. . . . What comes with the fife with the drum may go . . .

One of the Cadets. [*Looking off at the back.*] Ah! ah! . . . Here comes Monsieur de Guiche!

All the Cadets. [*Grumbling.*] Hoo . . .

Cyrano. [*Smiling.*] Flattering murmur . . .

One of the Cadets. He bores us! . . .

Other Cadet. Showing himself off, with his broad point collar on top of his armor! . . .

Other Cadet. As if lace were worn with steel!

First Cadet. Convenient, if you have a boil on your neck to cover . . .

Second Cadet. There is another courtier for you!

Other Cadet. His uncle's own nephew!

Carbon. He is a Gascon, nevertheless!

First Cadet. Not genuine! . . . Never trust him. For a Gascon, look you, must be something of a madman: nothing is so deadly to deal with as a Gascon who is completely rational!

Le Bret. He is pale!

Other Cadet. He is hungry, as hungry as any poor devil of us! But his corselet being freely embellished with gilt studs, his stomach-ache is radiant in the sun!

Cyrano. [*Eagerly.*] Let us not appear to suffer, either! You, your cards, your pipes, your dice . . . [*All briskly set themselves to playing with cards and dice, on the heads of drums, on stools, on cloaks spread over the ground. They light long tobacco pipes.*] And I will be reading Descartes. . . .

[*He walks to and fro, forward and backward, reading a small book which he has taken from his pocket. Tableau. Enter* DE GUICHE. *Every one appears absorbed and satisfied.* DE GUICHE *is very pale. He goes toward* CARBON.]

De Guiche. [*To* CARBON.] Ah, good morning. [*They look at each other attentively. Aside, with satisfaction.*] He is pale as plaster.

Carbon. [*Same business.*] His eyes are all that is left of him.

De Guiche. [*Looking at the* CADETS.] So here are the wrongheaded rascals? . . . Yes, gentlemen, it is reported to me on every side that I am your scoff and derision; that the cadets, highland nobility, Béarn clodhoppers, Périgord baronets, cannot express sufficient contempt for their colonel; call me intriguer, courtier, find it irksome to their taste that I should wear, with my cuirass, a collar of Genoese point, and never cease to air their wondering indignation that a man should be a Gascon without being a vagabond. [*Silence. The* CADETS *continue smoking and playing.*] Shall I have you punished by your captain? . . . I do not like to.

Carbon. Did you otherwise, however . . . I am free, and punish only . . .

De Guiche. Ah? . . .

Carbon. My company is paid by myself, belongs to me. I obey no orders but such as relate to war.

De Guiche. Ah, is it so? Enough, then. I will treat your taunts with simple scorn. My fashion of deporting myself under fire is well known. You are not unaware of the manner in which yesterday, at Bapaume, I forced back the columns of the Comte de Bucquoi; gathering my men together to plunge forward like an avalanche, three times I charged him. . . .

Cyrano. [*Without lifting his nose from his book.*] And your white scarf?

De Guiche. [*Surprised and self-satisfied.*] You heard of that circumstance? . . . In fact, it happened that as I was wheeling about to collect my men for the third charge, I was caught in a stream of fugitives which bore me onward to the edge of the enemy. I was in danger of being captured and cut off with an arquebuse, when I had the presence of mind to untie and let slip to the ground the white scarf which proclaimed my military grade. Thus was I enabled, undistinguished, to withdraw from among the Spaniards, and thereupon returning with my reinspirited men, to defeat them. Well? . . . What do you say to the incident?

[*The* CADETS *have appeared not to be listening; at this point, however, hands with cards and dice-boxes remain suspended in the air; no pipe-smoke is ejected; all expresses expectation.*]

Cyrano. That never would Henry the Fourth, however great the number of his opponents, have consented to diminish his presence by the size of his white plume.

[*Silent joy. Cards fall, dice rattle, smoke upwreathes.*]

De Guiche. The trick was successful, however!

[*As before, expectation suspends gambling and smoking.*]

Cyrano. Very likely. But one should not resign the honor of being a target. [*Cards, dice, smoke, fall, rattle, and upwreathe, as before, in expression of increasing glee.*] Had I been at hand when you allowed your scarf to drop—the quality of our courage, monsieur, shows different in this—I would have picked it up and worn it. . . .

De Guiche. Ah, yes—more of your Gascon bragging! . . .

Cyrano. Bragging? . . . Lend me the scarf. I engage to mount, ahead of all, to the assault, wearing it crosswise upon my breast!

De Guiche. A Gascon's offer, that too! You know that the scarf was left in the enemy's camp, by the banks of the Scarpe, where bullets since then have hailed . . . whence no one can bring it back!

Cyrano. [*Taking a white scarf from his pocket and handing it to* DE GUICHE.] Here it is.

[*Silence. The* CADETS *smother their laughter behind cards and in dice-boxes.* DE GUICHE *turns around, looks at them; instantly they become grave; one of them, with an air of unconcern, whistles the tune played earlier by the* FIFER.]

De Guiche. [*Taking the scarf.*] I thank you. I shall be able with this shred of white to make a signal . . . which I was hesitating to make. . . .

[*He goes to the top of the bank and waves the scarf.*]

All. What now? . . . What is this?

The Sentinel. [*At the top of the bank.*] A man . . . over there . . . running off. . .

De Guiche. [*Coming forward again.*] It is a supposed Spanish spy. He is very useful to us. The information he carries to the enemy is that which I give him—so that their decisions are influenced by us.

Cyrano. He is a scoundrel!

De Guiche. [*Coolly tying on his scarf.*] He is a convenience. We were saying? . . . Ah, I was about to tell you. Last night, having resolved upon a desperate stroke to obtain supplies, the Marshal secretly set out for Dourlens. The royal sutlers are encamped there. He expects to join them by way of the tilled fields; but, to provide against interference, he took with him troops in such number that, certainly, if we were now attacked, the enemy would find easy work. Half of the army is absent from the camp.

Carbon. If the Spaniards knew that, it might be serious. But they do not know.

De Guiche. They do. And are going to attack us.

Carbon. Ah!

De Guiche. My pretended spy came to warn me of their intention. He said, moreover: I can direct the attack. At what point shall it be? I will lead them to suppose it the least strong, and they will center their efforts against it. I answered: Very well. Go from the camp. Look down the line. Let them attack at the point I signal from.

Carbon. [*To the* CADETS.] Gentlemen, get ready!

[*All get up. Noise of swords and belts being buckled on.*]

De Guiche. They will be here in an hour.

First Cadet. Oh! . . . if there is a whole hour! . . .

[*All sit down again, and go on with their games.*]

De Guiche. [*To* CARBON.] The main object is to gain time. The Marshal is on his way back.

Carbon. And to gain time?

De Guiche. You will be so obliging as to keep them busy killing you.

Cyrano. Ah, this is your revenge!

De Guiche. I will not pretend that if I had been fond of you, I would have thus singled out you and yours; but, as your bravery is unquestionably beyond that of others, I am serving my King at the same time as my inclination.

Cyrano. Suffer me, Monsieur, to express my gratitude.

De Guiche. I know that you affect fighting one against a hundred. You will not complain of lacking opportunity.

[*He goes toward the back with* CARBON.]

Cyrano. [*To the* CADETS.] We shall now be able, gentlemen, to add to the Gascon escutcheon, which bears, as it is, six chevrons, or and azure, the chevron that was wanting to complete it—blood-red!

[DE GUICHE *at the back speaks low with* CARBON. *Orders are given. All is made ready to repel an attack.* CYRANO *goes toward* CHRISTIAN, *who stands motionless, with folded arms.*]

Cyrano. [*Laying his hand on* CHRISTIAN'S *shoulder.*] Christian?

Christian. [*Shaking his head.*] Roxane!

Cyrano. Ah me!

Christian. I wish I might at least put my

whole heart's last blessing in a beautiful letter!

Cyrano. I mistrusted that it would come today . . . [*he takes a letter from his doublet*] and I have written your farewells.

Christian. Let me see!

Cyrano. You wish to see it? . . .

Christian. [*Taking the letter.*] Yes! [*He opens the letter, begins to read, stops short.*] Ah? . . .

Cyrano. What?

Christian. That little round blister?

Cyrano. [*Hurriedly taking back the letter, and looking at it with an artless air.*] A blister?

Christian. It is a tear!

Cyrano. It looks like one, does it not? . . . A poet, you see, is sometimes caught in his own snare—that is what constitutes the interest, the charm! . . . This letter, you must know, is very touching. In writing it I apparently made myself shed tears.

Christian. Shed tears? . . .

Cyrano. Yes, because . . . well, to die is not terrible at all . . . but never to see her again . . . never! . . . that, you know, is horrible beyond all thinking. . . . And, things having taken the turn they have, I shall not see her. . . . [CHRISTIAN *looks at him.*] We shall not see her. . . . [*Hastily.*] You will not see her. . . .

Christian. [*Snatching the letter from him.*] Give me the letter! [*Noise in the distance.*]

Voice of a Sentinel. Ventrebieu, who goes there?

[*Shots. Noise of voices, tinkling of bells.*]

Carbon. What is it?

The Sentinel. [*On the top of the bank.*] A coach! [*All run to see.*]

The Cadets. [*Noisy exclamations.*] What? —In the camp?—It is driving into the camp! —It comes from the direction of the enemy! The devil! Fire upon it!—No! the coachman is shouting something!—What does he say?—He shouts: Service of the King!

De Guiche. What? Service of the King?

[*All come down from the bank and fall into order.*]

Carbon. Hats off, all!

De Guiche. [*At the corner.*] Service of the King! Stand back, low rabble, and give it room to turn around with a handsome sweep!

[*The coach comes in at a trot. It is covered with mud and dust. The curtains are drawn. Two lackeys behind. It comes to a standstill.*]

Carbon. [*Shouting.*] Salute!

[*Drums roll. All the* CADETS *uncover.*]

De Guiche. Let down the steps!

[*Two men hurry forward. The coach door opens.*]

Roxane. [*Stepping from the carriage.*] Good morning!

[*At the sound of a feminine voice, all the men, in the act of bowing low straighten themselves. Consternation.*]

De Guiche. Service of the King! You?

Roxane. Of the only King! . . . of Love!

Cyrano. Ah, great God!

Christian. [*Rushing to her.*] You? Why are you here?

Roxane. The siege lasted too long!

Christian. Why have you come?

Roxane. I will tell you!

Cyrano. [*Who at the sound of her voice has started, then stood motionless without venturing to look her way.*] God! . . . can I trust myself to look at her?

De Guiche. You cannot remain here.

Roxane. But I can—I can, indeed! Will you favor me with a drum? [*She seats herself upon a drum brought forward for her.*] There! I thank you! [*She laughs.*] They fired upon my carriage. [*Proudly.*] A patrol!—It does look rather as if it were made out of a pumpkin, does it not? like Cinderella's coach! and the footmen made out of rats! [*Blowing a kiss to* CHRISTIAN.] How do you do? [*Looking at them all.*] You do not look overjoyed! . . . Arras is a long way from Paris, do you know it? [*Catching sight of* CYRANO.] Cousin, delighted!

Cyrano. [*Coming toward her.*] But how did you . . . ?

Roxane. How did I find the army? Dear me, cousin, that was simple: I followed straight along the line of devastation. . . . Ah, I should never have believed in such horrors had I not seen them! Gentlemen if that is the service of your King, I like mine better!

Cyrano. But this is mad! . . . By what way did you come?

Roxane. Way? . . . I drove through the Spaniards' camp.

First Cadet. Ah, what will keep lovely woman from her way!

De Guiche. But how did you contrive to get through their lines?

Le Bret. That must have been difficult . . .

Roxane. No, not very. I simply drove through them, in my coach, at a trot. If a hidalgo, with arrogant front, showed likely to stop us, I put my face at the window, wearing my sweetest smile, and, those gentlemen being—let the French not grudge my saying so!—the most gallant in the world, . . . I passed!

Carbon. Such a smile is a passport, certainly! . . . But you must have been not unfrequently bidden to stand and deliver where you were going?

Roxane. Not unfrequently, you are right. Whereupon I would say, "I am going to see my lover!" At once, the fiercest-looking Spaniard of them all would gravely close my carriage door; and, with a gesture the King might emulate, motion aside the musket-barrels leveled at me; and, superb at once for grace and haughtiness, bringing his spurs together, and lifting his plumed hat, bow low and say, "Pass, señorita, pass!"

Christian. But, Roxane . . .

Roxane. I said, "My lover!" yes, forgive me!—You see, if I had said, "My husband!" they would never have let me by!

Christian. But . . .

Roxane. What troubles you?

De Guiche. You must leave at once.

Roxane. I?

Cyrano. At once!

Le Bret. As fast as you can.

Christian. Yes, you must.

Roxane. But why?

Christian. [*Embarrassed*.] Because . . .

Cyrano. [*Embarrassed too*.] In three-quarters of an hour . . .

De Guiche. [*The same*.] Or an hour . . .

Carbon. [*The same*.] You had much better . . .

Le Bret. [*The same*.] You might . . .

Roxane I shall remain. You are going to fight.

All. Oh, no! . . . No!

Roxane. He is my husband! [*She throws herself in* CHRISTIAN's *arms*.] Let me be killed with you!

Christian. How your eyes shine!

Roxane. I will tell you why they shine!

De Guiche. [*Desperately*.] It is a post of horrible probabilities!

Roxane. [*Turning toward him*.] What—of horrible . . . ?

Cyrano. In proof of which he appointed us to it! . . .

Roxane. Ah, you wish me made a widow?

De Guiche. I swear to you . . .

Roxane. No! Now I have lost all regard. . . . Now I will surely not go. . . . Besides, I think it fun!

Cyrano. What? The précieuse contained a heroine?

Roxane. Monsieur de Bergerac, I am a cousin of yours!

One of the Cadets. Never think but that we will take good care of you!

Roxane. [*More and more excited*.] I am sure you will, my friends!

Other Cadet. The whole camp smells of iris!

Roxane. By good fortune I put on a hat that will look well in battle! [*Glancing toward* DE GUICHE.] But perhaps it is time the Count should go.—The battle might begin.

De Guiche. Ah, it is intolerable!—I am going to inspect my guns, and coming back.—You still have time: think better of it!

Roxane. Never! [*Exit* DE GUICHE.]

Christian. [*Imploring*.] Roxane!

Roxane. No!

First Cadet. She is going to stay!

All. [*Hurrying about, pushing one another, snatching things from one another*.] A comb!—Soap!—My jacket is torn, a needle!—A ribbon!—Lend me your pocket-mirror! — My cuffs! — Curling-irons! — A razor!

Roxane. [*To* CYRANO, *who is still pleading with her*.] No! Nothing shall prevail upon me to stir from this spot!

Carbon. [*After having, like the others, tightened his belt, dusted himself, brushed his hat, straightened his feather, pulled down his cuffs, approaches* ROXANE, *and ceremoniously*.] It is, perhaps, proper, since you are going to stay, that I should present to you a few of the gentlemen about to have the honor of dying in your presence . . . [ROXANE *bows, and stands waiting, with her arm through* CHRISTIAN's.] Baron Peyrescous de Colignac!

The Cadet. [*Bowing*.] Madame!

Carbon. [*Continuing to present the* CADETS.] Baron de Casterac de Cahuzac—Vidame de Malgouyre Estressac Lesbas d'Escarabiot—Chevalier d'Antignac-Juzet—Baron Hillot de Blagnac-Saléchan de Castel Crabioules . . .

Roxane. But how many names have you apiece?

Baron Hillot. Innumerable!

Carbon. [*To* ROXANE.] Open your hand with the handkerchief!

Roxane. [*Opens her hand; the handkerchief drops*.] Why?

[*The whole company starts forward to pick it up*.]

Carbon. [*Instantly catching it*.] My company had no flag! Now, my word, it will have the prettiest one in the army!

Roxane. [*Smiling*.] It is rather small!

Carbon. [*Fastening the handkerchief on the staff of his captain's spear*.] But it is lace!

One of the Cadets. [*To the others*.] I

could die without a murmur, having looked upon that beautiful face, if I had so much as a walnut inside me! . . .

Carbon. [*Who has overheard, indignant.*] Shame! . . . to talk of food when an exquisite woman . . .

Roxane. But the air of the camp is searching, and I myself am hungry: Patties, jellied meat, light wine . . . are what I should like best! Will you kindly bring me some?

[*Consternation.*]

One of the Cadets. Bring you some?

Other Cadet. And where, great God, shall we get them?

Roxane. [*Quietly.*] In my coach.

All. What?

Roxane. But there is much to be done, carving and boning and serving. Look more closely at my coachman, gentlemen, and you will recognize a precious individual: the sauces, if we wish, can be warmed over . . .

The Cadets. [*Springing toward the coach.*] It is Ragueneau! [*Cheers.*] Oh! Oh!

Roxane. [*Watching them.*] Poor fellows!

Cyrano. [*Kissing her hand.*] Kind fairy!

Ragueneau. [*Standing upon the box-seat like a vendor at a public fair.*] Gentlemen!

[*Enthusiasm.*]

The Cadets. Bravo! Bravo!

Ragueneau. How should the Spaniards, when so much beauty passed, suspect the repast?

[*Applause.*]

Cyrano. [*Low to* CHRISTIAN.] Hm! Hm! Christian!

Ragueneau. Absorbed in gallantry, no heed took they . . . [*he takes a dish from the box-seat*] . . . of galantine!

[*Applause. The galantine is passed from hand to hand.*]

Cyrano. [*Low to* CHRISTIAN.] A word with you . . .

Ragueneau. Venus kept their eyes fixed upon herself, while Diana slipped past with the . . . [*he brandishes a joint*] . . . game!

[*Enthusiasm. The joint is seized by twenty hands at once.*]

Cyrano. [*Low to* CHRISTIAN.] I must speak with you.

Roxane. [*To the* CADETS *who come forward, their arms full of provisions.*] Spread it all upon the ground!

[*Assisted by the two imperturbable footmen who were on the back of the coach, she arranges everything on the grass.*]

Roxane. [*To* CHRISTIAN, *whom* CYRANO *is trying to draw aside.*] Make yourself useful, sir!

[CHRISTIAN *comes and helps her.* CYRANO *gives evidence of uneasiness.*]

Ragueneau. A truffled peacock!

First Cadet. [*Radiant, comes forward cutting off a large slice of ham.*] Praise the pigs, we shall not go to our last fight with nothing in our b . . . [*correcting himself at sight of* ROXANE] . . . hm . . . stomachs!

Ragueneau. [*Flinging the carriage cushions.*] The cushions are stuffed with snipe!

[*Tumult. The cushions are ripped open. Laughter. Joy.*]

Ragueneau. [*Flinging bottles of red wine.*] Molten ruby! [*Bottles of white wine.*] Fluid topaz!

Roxane. [*Throwing a folded tablecloth to* CYRANO.] Unfold the cloth: Hey! . . . be nimble!

Ragueneau. [*Waving one of the coach lanterns.*] Each lantern is a little larder!

Cyrano. [*Low to* CHRISTIAN, *while together they spread the cloth.*] I must speak with you before you speak with her . . .

Ragueneau. The handle of my whip, behold, is a sausage!

Roxane. [*Pouring wine, dispensing it.*] Since we are the ones to be killed, *morbleu*, we will not fret ourselves about the rest of the army! Everything for the Gascons! . . . And if De Guiche comes, nobody must invite him! [*Going from one to the other.*] Gently! You have time. . . . You must not eat so fast! There, drink. What are you crying about?

First Cadet. It is too good!

Roxane. Hush! White wine or red?—Bread for Monsieur de Carbon!—A knife!—Pass your plate!—You prefer crust?—A little more?—Let me help you.—Champagne?—A wing?——

Cyrano. [*Following* ROXANE, *his hands full of dishes, helping her.*] I adore her!

Roxane. [*Going to* CHRISTIAN.] What will you take?

Christian. Nothing!

Roxane. Oh, but you must take something! This biscuit—in a little Muscatel—just a little?

Christian. [*Trying to keep her from going.*] Tell me what made you come?

Roxane. I owe myself to those poor fellows. . . . Be patient. . . . By and by . . .

Le Bret. [*Who had gone toward the back to pass a loaf of bread on the end of a pike to the* SENTINEL *upon the earthwork.*] De Guiche!

Cyrano. Presto! Vanish basket, flagon, platter and pan! Hurry! Let us look as if nothing were! [*To* RAGUENEAU.] Take a flying leap on to your box!—Is everything hidden?

[*In a wink, all the eatables have been

pushed into the tents, or hidden under clothes, cloaks, hats. Enter De Guiche, *hurriedly; he stops short, sniffing the air. Silence.*]

De Guiche. What a good smell!

One of the Cadets. [*Singing, with effect of mental abstraction.*] To lo lo lo. . . .

De Guiche. [*Stopping and looking at him closely.*] What is the matter with you—you, there? You are red as a crab.

The Cadet. I? Nothing. . . . It is just my blood. . . . We are going to fight: it tells . . .

Other Cadet. Poom . . . poom . . . poom . . .

De Guiche. [*Turning.*] What is this?

The Cadet. [*Slightly intoxicated.*] Nothing. . . . A song . . . just a little song.

De Guiche. You look in good spirits, my boy!

The Cadet. Danger affects me that way!

De Guiche. [*Calling* Carbon de Castel-Jaloux *to give an order.*] Captain, I . . . [*He stops at sight of his face.*] *Peste!* You look in good spirits, too.

Carbon. [*Flushed, holding a bottle behind him; with an evasive gesture.*] Oh! . . .

De Guiche. I had a cannon left over, which I have ordered them to place [*he points in the wing*] there, in that corner, and which your men can use, if necessary . . .

One of the Cadets. [*Swaying from one foot to the other.*] Charming attention!

Other Cadet. [*Smiling sugarily.*] Our thanks for your gracious thoughtfulness!

De Guiche. Have they gone mad? [*Drily.*] As you are not accustomed to handling a cannon, look out for its kicking . . .

First Cadet. Ah, pfft! . . .

De Guiche. [*Going toward him, furious.*] But . . .

The Cadet. A cannon knows better than to kick a Gascon!

De Guiche. [*Seizing him by the arm and shaking him.*] You are all tipsy: on what?

The Cadet. [*Magnificently.*] The smell of powder!

De Guiche. [*Shrugs his shoulders, pushes aside the* Cadet, *and goes rapidly toward* Roxane.] Quick, Madame! what have you condescended to decide?

Roxane. I remain.

De Guiche. Retire, I beseech you!

Roxane. No.

De Guiche. If you are determined, then. . . . Let me have a musket!

Carbon. What do you mean?

De Guiche. I, too, will remain.

Cyrano. At last, Monsieur, an instance of pure and simple bravery!

First Cadet. Might you be a Gascon, lace collar notwithstanding?

De Guiche. I do not leave a woman in danger.

Second Cadet. [*To* First Cadet.] Look here! I think he might be given something to eat!

[*All the food reappears, as if by magic.*]

De Guiche. [*His eyes brightening.*] Provisions?

Third Cadet. Under every waistcoat!

De Guiche. [*Mastering himself haughtily.*] Do you imagine that I will eat your leavings?

Cyrano. [*Bowing.*] You are improving!

De Guiche. [*Proudly, falling at the last of the sentence into a slightly Gascon accent.*] I will fight before I eat!

First Cadet. [*Exultant.*] Fight! Eat! . . . He spoke with an accent!

De Guiche. [*Laughing.*] I did?

The Cadet. He is one of us!

[*All fall to dancing.*]

Carbon. [*Who a moment before disappeared behind the earthworks, reappearing at the top.*] I have placed my pikemen. They are a determined troop . . .

[*He points at a line of pikes projecting above the bank.*]

De Guiche. [*To* Roxane, *bowing.*] Will you accept my hand and pass them in review?

[*She takes his hand; they go toward the bank. Every one uncovers and follows.*]

Christian. [*Going to* Cyrano, *quickly.*] Speak! Be quick!

[*As* Roxane *appears at the top of the bank, the pikes disappear, lowered in a salute, and a cheer goes up;* Roxane *bows.*]

Pikemen. [*Outside.*] Vivat!

Christian. What did you want to tell me?

Cyrano. In case Roxane . . .

Christian. Well?

Cyrano. Should speak to you of the letters . . .

Christian. Yes, the letters. I know!

Cyrano. Do not commit the blunder of appearing surprised . . .

Christian. At what?

Cyrano. I must tell you! . . . It is quite simple, and merely comes into my mind today because I see her. You have . . .

Christian. Hurry!

Cyrano. You . . . you have written to her oftener than you suppose . . .

Christian. Oh, have I?

Cyrano. Yes. It was my business, you

see. I had undertaken to interpret your passion, and sometimes I wrote without having told you I should write.

Christian. Ah?

Cyrano. It is very simple.

Christian. But how did you succeed since we have been so closely surrounded, in . . . ?

Cyrano. Oh, before daybreak I could cross the lines . . .

Christian. [*Folding his arms.*] Ah, that is very simple, too? . . . And how many times a week have I been writing? Twice? Three times? Four? . . .

Cyrano. More.

Christian. Every day?

Cyrano. Yes, every day . . . twice.

Christian. [*Violently.*] And you cared so much about it that you were willing to brave death. . . .

Cyrano. [*Seeing* ROXANE *who returns.*] Be still. . . . Not before her!

[*He goes quickly into his tent.*]

[CADETS *come and go at the back.* CARBON *and* DE GUICHE *give orders.*]

Roxane. [*Running to* CHRISTIAN.] And now, Christian . . .

Christian. [*Taking her hands.*] And now, you shall tell me why, over these fearful roads, through these ranks of rough soldiery, you risked your dear self to join me?

Roxane. Because of the letters!

Christian. The . . . ? What did you say?

Roxane. It is through your fault that I have been exposed to such and so many dangers. It is your letters that have gone to my head! Ah, think how many you have written me in a month, each one more beautiful. . . .

Christian. What? . . . Because of a few little love letters . . .

Roxane. Say nothing! You cannot understand! Listen: The truth is that I took to idolizing you one evening, when, below my window, in a voice I did not know before, your soul began to reveal itself. . . . Think then what the effect should be of your letters, which have been like your voice heard constantly for one month, your voice of that evening, so tender, caressing . . . You must bear it as you can, I have come to you! Prudent Penelope would not have stayed at home with her eternal tapestry, if Ulysses, her lord, had written as you write . . . but, impulsive as Helen, would have tossed aside her yarns, and flown to join him!

Christian. But . . .

Roxane. I read them, I reread them, in reading I grew faint . . . I became your own indeed! Each fluttering leaf was like a petal of your soul wafted to me . . . In every word of those letters, love is felt as a flame would be felt—love, compelling, sincere, profound . . .

Christian. Ah, sincere, profound? . . . You say that it can be felt, Roxane?

Roxane. He asks me!

Christian. And so you came?

Roxane. I came—oh Christian, my own, my master! If I were to kneel at your feet you would lift me, I know. It is my soul therefore which kneels, and never can you lift it from that posture!—I came to implore your pardon—as it is fitting, for we are both perhaps about to die!—your pardon for having done you the wrong, at first, in my shallowness, of loving you . . . for mere looking!

Christian. [*In alarm.*] Ah, Roxane! . . .

Roxane. Later, dear one, grown less shallow—similar to a bird which flutters before it can fly—your gallant exterior appealing to me still, but your soul appealing equally, I loved you for both! . . .

Christian. And now?

Roxane. Now at last yourself are vanquished by yourself: I love you for your soul alone. . . .

Christian. [*Drawing away.*] Ah, Roxane!

Roxane. Rejoice! For to be loved for that wherewith we are clothed so fleetingly must put a noble heart to torture. . . . Your dear thought at last casts your dear face in shadow: the harmonious lineaments whereby at first you pleased me, I do not see them, now my eyes are open!

Christian. Oh!

Roxane. You question your own triumph?

Christian. [*Sorrowfully.*] Roxane!

Roxane. I understand, you cannot conceive of such a love in me?

Christian. I do not wish to be loved like that! I wish to be loved quite simply. . . .

Roxane. For that which other women till now have loved in you? Ah, let yourself be loved in a better way.

Christian. No . . . I was happier before! . . .

Roxane. Ah, you do not understand! It is now that I love you most, that I truly love you. It is that which makes you, you —can you not grasp it?—that I worship . . . And did you no longer walk our earth like a young martial Apollo . . .

Christian. Say no more!

Roxane. Still would I love you! . . . Yes, though a blight should have fallen upon your face and form . . .

Christian. Do not say it!

Roxane. But I do say it, . . . I do!

Christian. What? If I were ugly, distinctly, offensively?

Roxane. If you were ugly, dear, I swear it!

Christian. God!

Roxane. And you are glad, profoundly glad?

Christian. [*In a smothered voice.*] Yes . . .

Roxane. What is it?

Christian. [*Pushing her gently away.*] Nothing. I have a word or two to say to some one: your leave, for a second . . .

Roxane. But . . .

Christian. [*Pointing at a group of* CADETS *at the back.*] In my selfish love, I have kept you from those poor brothers. . . . Go, smile on them a little, before they die, dear . . . go!

Roxane. [*Moved.*] Dear Christian!

[*She goes toward the* GASCONS *at the back; they respectfully gather around her.*]

Christian. [*Calling toward* CYRANO'S *tent.*] Cyrano!

Cyrano. [*Appears, armed for battle.*] What is it? . . . How pale you are!

Christian. She does not love me any more!

Cyrano. What do you mean?

Christian. She loves you.

Cyrano. No!

Christian. She only loves my soul!

Cyrano. No!

Christian. Yes! Therefore it is you she loves . . . and you love her . . .

Cyrano. I . . .

Christian. I know it!

Cyrano. It is true.

Christian. To madness!

Cyrano. More.

Christian. Tell her then.

Cyrano. No!

Christian. Why not?

Cyrano. Look at me!

Christian. She would love me grown ugly.

Cyrano. She told you so?

Christian. With the utmost frankness!

Cyrano. Ah! I am glad she should have told you that! But, believe me, believe me, place no faith in such a mad avowal! Dear God, I am glad such a thought should have come to her, and that she should have spoken it—but believe me, do not take her at her word. Never cease to be the handsome fellow you are. . . . She would not forgive me!

Christian. That is what I wish to discover.

Cyrano. No! no!

Christian. Let her choose between us! You shall tell her everything.

Cyrano. No . . . No . . . I refuse the ordeal!

Christian. Shall I stand in the way of your happiness because my outside is not so much amiss?

Cyrano. And I? Shall I destroy yours, because thanks to the hazard that sets us upon earth, I have the gift of expressing . . . what you perhaps feel?

Christian. You shall tell her everything!

Cyrano. He persists in tempting me . . . It is a mistake . . . and cruel!

Christian. I am weary of carrying about, in my own self, a rival!

Cyrano. Christian!

Christian. Our marriage . . . contracted without witnesses . . . can be annulled . . . if we survive!

Cyrano. He persists! . . .

Christian. Yes. I will be loved for my sole self, or not at all!—I am going to see what they are about. Look! I will walk to the end of the line and back . . . Tell her, and let her pronounce between us.

Cyrano. She will pronounce for you.

Christian. I can but hope she will! [*Calling.*] Roxane!

Cyrano. No! No!

Roxane. [*Coming forward.*] What is it?

Christian. Cyrano has something to tell you . . . something important!

[ROXANE *goes hurriedly to* CYRANO. *Exit* CHRISTIAN.]

Roxane. Something important?

Cyrano. [*Distracted.*] He is gone! . . . [*To* ROXANE.] Nothing whatever! He attaches—but you must know him of old!—he attaches importance to trifles . . .

Roxane. [*Quickly.*] He did not believe what I told him a moment ago? . . . I saw that he did not believe . . .

Cyrano. [*Taking her hand.*] But did you tell him all the truth?

Roxane. Yes. Yes. I should love him even . . . [*She hesitates a second.*]

Cyrano. [*Smiling sadly.*] You do not like to say it before me?

Roxane. But . . .

Cyrano. I shall not mind! . . . Even if he were ugly?

Roxane. Yes . . . Ugly. [*Musket shots outside.*] They are firing!

Cyrano. [*Ardently.*] Dreadfully ugly?

Roxane. Dreadfully.

Cyrano. Disfigured?

Roxane. Disfigured!

Cyrano. Grotesque?

Roxane. Nothing could make him grotesque . . . to me.

Cyrano. You would love him still?

Roxane. I believe that I should love him more . . . if that were possible!

Cyrano. [*Losing his head, aside.*] My God, perhaps she means it . . . perhaps it is true . . . and that way is happiness! [*To* ROXANE.] I . . . Roxane . . . listen!

Le Bret. [*Comes in hurriedly; calls softly.*] Cyrano!

Cyrano. [*Turning.*] *Hein?*

Le Bret. Hush!

[*He whispers a few words to* CYRANO.]

Cyrano. [*Letting* ROXANE'S *hand drop, with a cry.*] Ah! . . .

Roxane. What ails you?

Cyrano. [*To himself, in consternation.*] It is finished! [*Musket reports.*]

Roxane. What is it? What is happening? Who is firing?

[*She goes to the back to look off.*]

Cyrano. It is finished. . . . My lips are sealed for evermore!

[*Cadets come in, attempting to conceal something they carry among them; they surround it, preventing* ROXANE'S *seeing it.*]

Roxane. What has happened?

Cyrano. [*Quickly stopping her as she starts toward them.*] Nothing!

Roxane. These men? . . .

Cyrano. [*Drawing her away.*] Pay no attention to them!

Roxane. But what were you about to say to me before?

Cyrano. What was I about to say? . . . Oh, nothing! . . . Nothing whatever, I assure you. [*Solemnly.*] I swear that Christian's spirit, that his soul, were . . . [*in terror, correcting himself*] are the greatest that . . .

Roxane. Were? . . . [*With a great cry.*] Ah! . . .

[*Runs to the group of* CADETS, *and thrusts them aside.*]

Cyrano. It is finished!

Roxane. [*Seeing* CHRISTIAN *stretched out in his cloak.*] Christian!

Le Bret. [*To* CYRANO.] At the enemy's first shot!

[ROXANE *throws herself on* CHRISTIAN'S *body. Musket reports. Clashing of swords. Tramping. Drums.*]

Carbon. [*Sword in hand.*] The attack! To your muskets!

[*Followed by the* CADETS *he goes to the further side of the earthworks.*]

Roxane. Christian!

Carbon's Voice. [*Beyond the earthworks.*] Make haste!

Roxane. Christian!

Carbon. Fall into line!

Roxane. Christian!

Carbon. Measure . . . match!

[RAGUENEAU *has come running in with water in a steel cap.*]

Christian. [*In a dying voice.*] Roxane!

Cyrano. [*Quick, low in* CHRISTIAN'S *ear, while* ROXANE, *distracted, dips into the water a fragment of linen torn from her breast to bind his wound.*] I have told her everything! . . . You are still the one she loves! [CHRISTIAN *closes his eyes.*]

Roxane. What, dear love?

Carbon. Muzzle . . . high!

Roxane. [*To* CYRANO.] He is not dead? . . .

Carbon. Open charge . . . with teeth!

Roxane. I feel his cheek grow cold against my own!

Carbon. Take aim!

Roxane. A letter on his breast. . . . [*She opens it.*] To me!

Cyrano. [*Aside.*] My letter!

Carbon. Fire!

[*Musket shots. Cries. Roar of battle.*]

Cyrano. [*Trying to free his hand which* ROXANE *clasps kneeling.*] But, Roxane, they are fighting.

Roxane. [*Clinging.*] No! . . . Stay with me a little! . . . He is dead. You are the only one that truly knew him. . . . [*She cries subduedly.*] Was he not an exquisite being, . . . an exceptional, marvelous being? . . .

Cyrano. [*Standing bareheaded.*] Yes, Roxane.

Roxane. A poet without his peer, . . . one verily to reverence?

Cyrano. Yes, Roxane.

Roxane. A sublime spirit?

Cyrano. Yes, Roxane.

Roxane. A profound heart, such as the profane could never have understood . . . a soul as noble as it was charming? . . .

Cyrano. [*Firmly.*] Yes, Roxane.

Roxane. [*Throwing herself on* CHRISTIAN'S *body.*] And he is dead!

Cyrano. [*Aside, drawing his sword.*] And I have now only to die, since, without knowing it, she mourns my death in his!

[*Trumpets in the distance.*]

De Guiche. [*Reappears on the top of the bank, bareheaded, his forehead bloody; in a thundering voice.*] The signal they promised! The flourish of trumpets! . . . The French are entering the camp with supplies! . . . Stand fast a little longer!

Roxane. Upon his letter . . . blood . . . tears!

A Voice. [*Outside, shouting.*] Surrender!

Voices of the Cadets. No!

Ragueneau. [*Who from the top of the coach is watching the battle beyond the bank.*] The conflict rages hotter! . . .

Cyrano. [*To* DE GUICHE *pointing at* ROXANE.] Take her away! . . . I am going to charge.

Roxane. [*Kissing the letter, in a dying voice.*] His blood! . . . his tears!

Ragueneau. [*Leaping from the coach and running to* ROXANE.] She is fainting!

De Guiche. At the top of the bank, to the CADETS, *madly.*] Stand fast!

Voice. [*Outside.*] Surrender!

Voices of the Cadets. No!

Cyrano. [*To* DE GUICHE.] Your courage none will question . . . [*Pointing to* ROXANE.] Fly for the sake of saving her!

De Guiche. [*Runs to* ROXANE *and lifts her in his arms.*] So be it! But we shall win the day if you can hold out a little longer . . .

Cyrano. We can. [*To* ROXANE, *whom* DE GUICHE, *helped by* RAGUENEAU, *is carrying off insensible.*] Good-by, Roxane!

[*Tumult. Cries.* CADETS *reappear wounded, and fall upon the stage.* CYRANO *dashing forward to join the combatants is stopped on the crest of the bank by* CARBON *covered with blood.*]

Carbon. We are losing ground . . . have got two halberd wounds . . .

Cyrano. [*Yelling to the* GASCONS.] Steadfast! . . . Never give them an inch! . . . Brave boys! [*To* CARBON.] Fear nothing! I have various deaths to avenge: Christian's and all my hopes'! [*They come down.* CYRANO *brandishes the spear at the head of which* ROXANE's *handkerchief is fastened.*] Float free, little cobweb flag, embroidered with her initials! [*He drives the spear-staff into the earth; shouts to the* CADETS.] Fall on them, boys! . . . Crush them! [*To the* FIFER.] Fifer, play!

[*The* FIFER *plays. Some of the wounded get to their feet again. Some of the* CADETS, *coming down the bank, group themselves around* CYRANO *and the little flag. The coach, filled and covered with men, bristles with muskets and becomes a redoubt.*]

One of the Cadets. [*Appears upon the top of the bank backing while he fights; he cries.*] They are coming up the slope!

[*Falls dead.*]

Cyrano. We will welcome them!

[*Above the bank suddenly rises a formidable array of enemies. The great banners of the Imperial Army appear.*]

Cyrano. Fire! [*General discharge.*]

Cry. [*Among the hostile ranks.*] Fire!

[*Shots returned.* CADETS *drop on every side.*]

A Spanish Officer. [*Taking off his hat.*] What are these men, so determined all to be killed?

Cyrano. [*Declaiming, as he stands in the midst of flying bullets.*]

They are the Gascony Cadets
Of Carbon de Castel-Jaloux;
Famed fighters, liars, desperates . . .

[*He leaps forward, followed by a handful of survivors.*]

They are the Gascony Cadets! . . .

[*The rest is lost in the confusion of battle.*]

CURTAIN

ACT FIFTH

CYRANO'S GAZETTE

Fifteen years later, 1655. *The park belonging to the convent of the Sisters of the Cross, in Paris.*

Superb shade-trees. At the left, the house; several doors opening on to a broad terrace with steps. In the center of the stage, huge trees standing alone in a clear oval space. At the right, first wing, a semicircular stone seat, surrounded by large box-trees.

All along the back of the stage, an avenue of chestnut-trees, which leads, at the right, fourth wing, to the door of a chapel seen through trees. Through the double row of trees overarching the avenue are seen lawns, other avenues clumps of trees, the further recesses o the park, the sky.

The chapel opens by a small side-door into a colonnade, overrun by a scarlet creeper; the colonnade comes forward and is lost to sight behind the box-trees at the right.

It is autumn. The leaves are turn-

ing, above the still fresh grass. Dark patches of evergreens, box and yew. Under each tree a mat of yellow leaves. Fallen leaves litter the whole stage, crackle underfoot, lie thick on the terrace and the seats.

Between the seat at the right and the tree in the center, a large embroidery frame, in front of which a small chair. Baskets full of wools, in skeins and balls. On the frame, a piece of tapestry, partly done.

[*At the rise of the curtain, nuns come and go in the park; a few are seated on the stone seat around an older nun; leaves are falling.*]

Sister Martha. [*To* MOTHER MARGARET.] Sister Claire, after putting on her cap, went back to the mirror, to see herself again.

Mother Margaret. [*To* SISTER CLAIPE.] It was unbecoming, my child.

Sister Claire. But Sister Martha, today, after finishing her portion, went back to the tart for a plum. I saw her!

Mother Margaret. [*To* SISTER MARTHA.] My child, it was ill done.

Sister Claire. I merely glanced! . . .

Sister Martha. The plum was about so big! . . .

Mother Margaret. This evening, when Monsieur Cyrano comes, I will tell him.

Sister Claire. [*Alarmed.*] No! He will laugh at us!

Sister Martha. He will say that nuns are very vain!

Sister Claire. And very greedy!

Mother Margaret. And really very good.

Sister Claire. Mother Margaret, is it not true that he has come here every Saturday in the last ten years?

Mother Margaret. Longer! Ever since his cousin brought among our linen coifs her coif of crape, the worldly symbol of her mourning, which settled like a sable bird amidst our flock of white some fourteen years ago.

Sister Martha. He alone, since she took her abode in our cloister, has art to dispel her never-lessening sorrow.

All the Nuns. He is so droll!—It is merry when he comes!—He teases us!—He is delightful!—We are greatly attached to him!—We are making Angelica paste to offer him!

Sister Martha. He is not, however, a very good Catholic!

Sister Claire. We will convert him.

The Nuns. We will! We will!

Mother Margaret. I forbid your renewing that attempt, my children. Do not trouble him: he might not come so often!

Sister Martha. But . . . God!

Mother Margaret. Set your hearts at rest: God must know him of old!

Sister Martha. But every Saturday, when he comes, he says to me as soon as he sees me, "Sister, I ate meat, yesterday!"

Mother Margaret. Ah, that is what he says? . . . Well, when he last said it, he had eaten nothing for two days.

Sister Martha. Mother!

Mother Margaret. He is poor.

Sister Martha. Who told you?

Mother Margaret. Monsieur Le Bret.

Sister Martha. Does no one offer him assistance?

Mother Margaret. No, he would take offense.

[*In one of the avenues at the back appears* ROXANE, *in black, wearing a widow's coif and long mourning veil;* DE GUICHE *markedly older, magnificently dressed, walks beside her. They go very slowly.* MOTHER MARGARET *gets up.*]

Mother Margaret. Come, we must go within. Madame Magdeleine is walking in the park with a visitor.

Sister Martha. [*Low to* SISTER CLAIRE.] Is not that the Marshal-duke de Grammont?

Sister Claire. [*Looking.*] I think it is!

Sister Martha. He has not been to see her in many months!

The Nuns. He is much engaged!—The Court!—The camp!—

Sister Claire. Cares of this world!

[*Exeunt.* DE GUICHE *and* ROXANE *come forward silently, and stop near the embroidery frame. A pause.*]

De Guiche. And so you live here, uselessly fair, always in mourning?

Roxane. Always.

De Guiche. As faithful as of old?

Roxane. As faithful.

De Guiche. [*After a time.*] Have you forgiven me?

Roxane. Since I am here.

[*Another silence.*]

De Guiche. And he was really such a rare being?

Roxane. To understand, one must have known him!

De Guiche. Ah, one must have known him! . . . Perhaps I did not know him well enough. And his last letter, still and always, against your heart?

Roxane. I wear it on this velvet, as a more holy scapular.

De Guiche. Even dead, you love him?

Roxane. It seems to me sometimes he is but half dead, that our hearts have not been severed, that his love still wraps me round, no less than ever living!

De Guiche. [*After another silence.*] Does Cyrano come here to see you?

Roxane. Yes, often. That faithful friend fulfils for me the office of gazette. His visits are regular. He comes: when the weather is fine, his arm-chair is brought out under the trees. I wait for him here with my work; the hour strikes; on the last stroke, I hear —I do not even turn to see who comes!—his cane upon the steps; he takes his seat; he rallies me upon my never-ending tapestry; he tells off the events of the week, and . . . [LE BRET *appears on the steps.*] Ah, Le Bret! [LE BRET *comes down the steps.*] How does your friend?

Le Bret. Ill.

De Guiche. Oh!

Roxane. He exaggerates! . . .

Le Bret. All is come to pass as I foretold: neglect! poverty! his writings ever breeding him new enemies! Fraud he attacks in every embodiment: usurpers, pious pretenders, plagiarists, asses in lions' skins . . . all! He attacks all!

Roxane. No one, however, but stands in profound respect of his sword. They will never succeed in silencing him.

De Guiche. [*Shaking his head.*] Who knows?

Le Bret. What I fear is not the aggression of man; what I fear is loneliness and want and winter creeping upon him like stealthy wolves in his miserable attic; they are the insidious foes that will have him by the throat at last! . . . Every day he tightens his belt by an eyelet; his poor great nose is pinched, and turned the sallow of old ivory; the worn black serge you see him in is the only coat he has!

De Guiche. Ah, there is one who did not succeed! . . . Nevertheless, do not pity him too much.

Le Bret. [*With a bitter smile.*] Marshal! . . .

De Guiche. Do not pity him too much: he signed no bonds with the world; he has lived free in his thoughts as in his actions.

Le Bret. [*As above.*] Duke . . .

De Guiche. [*Haughtily.*] I know, yes: I have everything, he has nothing. . . . But I should like to shake hands with him. [*Bowing to* ROXANE.] Good-by.

Roxane. I will go with you to the door.

[DE GUICHE *bows to* LE BRET *and goes with* ROXANE *toward the terrace steps.*]

De Guiche. [*Stopping, while she goes up the steps.*] Yes, sometimes I envy him. You see, when a man has succeeded too well in life, he is not unlikely to feel—dear me! without having committed any very serious wrong!—a multitudinous disgust at himself, the sum of which does not constitute a real remorse, but an obscure uneasiness; and a ducal mantle, while it sweeps up the stairs of greatness, may trail in its furry lining a rustling of sere illusions and regrets, as, when you slowly climb toward those doors, your black gown trails the withered leaves.

Roxane. [*Ironical.*] Are you not unusually pensive? . . .

De Guiche. Ah, yes! [*As he is about to leave, abruptly.*] Monsieur Le Bret! [*To* ROXANE.] Will you allow me? A word. [*He goes to* LE BRET, *and lowering his voice.*] It is true that no one will dare overtly to attack your friend, but many have him in particular disrelish; and some one was saying to me yesterday, at the Queen's, "It seems not unlikely that this Cyrano will meet with an accident."

Le Bret. Ah? . . .

De Guiche. Yes. Let him keep indoors. Let him be cautious.

Le Bret. [*Lifting his arms toward Heaven.*] Cautious! . . . He is coming here. I will warn him. Warn him! . . . Yes, but . . .

Roxane. [*Who has been standing at the head of the steps, to a nun who comes toward her.*] What is it?

The Nun. Ragueneau begs to see you, Madame.

Roxane. Let him come in. [*To* DE GUICHE *and* LE BRET.] He comes to plead distress. Having determined one day to be an author, he became in turn precentor . . .

Le Bret. Bath-house keeper . . .

Roxane. Actor . . .

Le Bret. Beadle . . .

Roxane. Barber . . .

Le Bret. Arch-lute teacher . . .

Roxane. I wonder what he is now!

Ragueneau. [*Entering precipitately.*] Ah, Madame! [*He sees* LE BRET.] Monsieur!

Roxane. [*Smiling.*] Begin telling your misfortunes to Le Bret. I am coming back.

Ragueneau. But, Madame . . .

[ROXANE *leaves without listening, with the* DUKE. RAGUENEAU *goes to* LE BRET.]

Ragueneau. It is better so. Since you are here, I had liefer not tell her! Less than half an hour ago, I was going to see your friend. I was not thirty feet from his door, when I saw him come out. I hurried to catch up with him. He was about to turn the corner. I started to run, when from a window below which he was passing—was it pure mischance? It may have been!—a lackey drops a block of wood . . .

Le Bret. Ah, the cowards! . . . Cyrano!

Ragueneau. I reach the spot, and find him . . .

Le Bret. Horrible!

Ragueneau. Our friend, Monsieur, our poet, stretched upon the ground, with a great hole in his head!

Le Bret. He is dead?

Ragueneau. No, but . . . God have mercy! I carried him to his lodging . . . Ah, his lodging! You should see that lodging of his!

Le Bret. Is he in pain?

Ragueneau. No, Monsieur, he is unconscious.

Le Bret. Has a doctor seen him?

Ragueneau. One came . . . out of good nature.

Le Bret. My poor, poor Cyrano! . . . We must not tell Roxane outright. And the doctor? . . .

Ragueneau. He talked . . . I hardly grasped . . . of fever . . . cerebral inflammation! Ah, if you should see him, with his head done up in cloths! . . . Let us hurry . . . No one is there to tend him . . . And he might die if he attempted to get up!

Le Bret. [*Dragging* RAGUENEAU *off at the right.*] This way. Come, it is shorter through the chapel.

Roxane. [*Appearing at the head of the steps, catching sight of* LE BRET *hurrying off through the colonnade which leads to the chapel side-door.*] Monsieur Le Bret! [LE BRET *and* RAGUENEAU *make their escape without answering.*] Le Bret not turning back when he is called? . . . Poor Ragueneau must be in some new trouble! [*She comes down the steps.*] How beautiful . . . how beautiful, this golden-hazy waning day of September at its wane! My sorrowful mood, which the exuberant gladness of April offends, autumn, the dreamy and subdued, lures on to smile . . . [*She sits down at her embroidery frame. Two* NUNS *come from the house bringing a large armchair which they place under the tree.*] Ah, here comes the classic arm-chair in which my old friend always sits!

Sister Martha. The best in the convent parlor!

Roxane. I thank you, sister. [*The* NUNS *withdraw.*] He will be here in a moment. [*She adjusts the embroidery frame before her.*] There! The clock is striking . . . My wools! . . . The clock has struck? . . . I wonder at this! . . . Is it possible that for the first time he is late? . . . It must be that the sister who keeps the door . . . my thimble, ah, here it is! . . . is detaining him to exhort him to repentance . . . [*A pause.*] She exhorts him at some length! . . . He cannot be much longer . . . A withered leaf! [*She brushes away the dead leaf which has dropped on the embroidery.*] Surely nothing could keep . . . my scissors? . . . in my workbag! . . . could keep him from coming!

A Nun. [*Appearing at the head of the steps.*] Monsieur de Bergerac!

Roxane. [*Without turning round.*] What was I saying? . . . [*She begins to embroider.* CYRANO *appears, exceedingly pale, his hat drawn down over his eyes. The* NUN *who has shown him into the garden withdraws. He comes down the steps very slowly, with evident difficulty to keep on his feet, leaning heavily on his cane.* ROXANE *proceeds with her sewing.*] Ah, these dull soft shades! . . . How shall I match them? [*To* CYRANO, *in a tone of friendly chiding.*] After fourteen years, for the first time you are late!

Cyrano. [*Who has reached the arm-chair and seated himself, in a jolly voice which contrasts with his face.*] Yes, it seems incredible! I am savage at it. I was detained, spite of all I could do! . . .

Roxane. By . . . ?

Cyrano. A somewhat inopportune call.

Roxane. [*Absent-minded, sewing.*] Ah, yes . . . some troublesome fellow!

Cyrano. Cousin, it was a troublesome Madame.

Roxane. You excused yourself?

Cyrano. Yes. I said, "Your pardon, but this is Saturday, on which day I am due in a certain dwelling. On no account do I ever fail. Come back in an hour!"

Roxane. [*Lightly.*] Well, she will have to wait some time to see you. I shall not let you go before evening.

Cyrano. Perhaps . . . I shall have to go a little earlier.

[*He closes his eyes and is silent a moment.*]

[SISTER MARTHA *is seen crossing the park from the chapel to the terrace.* ROXANE *sees her and beckons to her by a slight motion of her head.*]

Roxane. [*To* CYRANO.] Are you not going to tease Sister Martha today?

Cyrano. [*Quickly, opening his eyes.*] I am indeed! [*In a comically gruff voice.*] Sister Martha, come nearer! [*The* NUN *demurely comes toward him.*] Ha! ha! ha! Beautiful eyes, ever studying the ground!

Sister Martha. [*Lifting her eyes and smiling.*] But . . . [*She sees his face and makes a gesture of surprise.*] Oh!

Cyrano. [*Low, pointing at* ROXANE.] Hush! . . . It is nothing! [*In a swaggering voice, aloud.*] Yesterday, I ate meat!

Sister Martha. I am sure you did! [*Aside.*] That is why he is so pale! [*Quickly, low.*] Come to the refectory presently. I shall have ready for you there a good bowl of broth . . . You will come!

Cyrano. Yes, yes, yes.

Sister Martha. Ah, you are more reasonable today!

Roxane. [*Hearing them whisper.*] She is trying to convert you?

Sister Martha. Indeed I am not!

Cyrano. It is true, you, usually almost discursive in the holy cause, are reading me no sermon! You amaze me! [*With comical fury.*] I will amaze you, too! Listen, you are authorized . . . [*With the air of casting about in his mind, and finding the jest he wants.*] Ah, now I shall amaze you! to . . . pray for me, this evening . . . in the chapel.

Roxane. Oh! oh!

Cyrano. [*Laughing.*] Sister Martha . . . lost in amazement!

Sister Martha. [*Gently.*] I did not wait for your authorization. [*She goes in.*]

Cyrano. [*Turning to* ROXANE, *who is bending over her embroidery.*] The devil, tapestry . . . the devil, if I hope to live to see the end of you!

Roxane. I was waiting for that jest.

[*A slight gust of wind makes the leaves fall.*]

Cyrano. The leaves!

Roxane. [*Looking up from her work and gazing off toward the avenues.*] They are the russet gold of a Venetian beauty's hair . . . Watch them fall!

Cyrano. How consummately they do it! In that brief fluttering from bough to ground, how they contrive still to put on beauty! And though foredoomed to moulder upon the earth that draws them, they wish their fall invested with the grace of a free bird's flight!

Roxane. Serious, you?

Cyrano. [*Remembering himself.*] Not at all, Roxane!

Roxane. Come, never mind the falling leaves! Tell me the news, instead . . . Where is my budget?

Cyrano. Here it is!

Roxane. Ah!

Cyrano. [*Growing paler and paler, and struggling with pain.*] Saturday, the nineteenth: The King having filled his dish eight times with Cette preserves, and emptied it, was taken with a fever; his distemper, for high treason, was condemned to be let blood, and now the royal pulse is rid of febriculosity! On Sunday: at the Queen's great ball, were burned seven hundred and sixty-three wax candles; our troops, it is said, defeated Austrian John; four sorcerers were hanged; Madame Athis's little dog had a distressing turn, the case called for a . . .

Roxane. Monsieur de Bergerac, leave out the little dog!

Cyrano. Monday . . . nothing, or next to it: Lygdamire took a fresh lover.

Roxane. Oh!

Cyrano. [*Over whose face is coming a change more and more marked.*] Tuesday: the whole Court assembled at Fontainebleau. Wednesday, the fair Monglat said to Count Fiesco "No!" Thursday, Mancini, Queen of France, . . . or little less. Twenty-fifth, the fair Monglat said to Count Fiesco "Yes!" And Saturday, the twenty-sixth . . .

[*He closes his eyes. His head drops on his breast. Silence.*]

Roxane. [*Surprised at hearing nothing further, turns, looks at him and starts to her feet in alarm.*] Has he fainted? [*She runs to him, calling.*] Cyrano!

Cyrano. [*Opening his eyes, in a faint voice.*] What is it? . . . What is the matter? [*He sees* ROXANE *bending over him, hurriedly readjusts his hat, pulling it more closely over his head, and shrinks back in his arm-chair in terror.*] No! no! I assure you, it is nothing! . . . Do not mind me!

Roxane. But surely . . .

Cyrano. It is merely the wound I received at Arras . . . Sometimes . . . you know . . . even now . . .

Roxane. Poor friend!

Cyrano. But it is nothing . . . It will pass . . . [*He smiles with effort.*] It has passed.

Roxane. Each one of us has his wound. I too have mine. It is here, never to heal, that ancient wound . . . [*She places her hand on her breast.*] It is here beneath the yellowing letter on which are still faintly visible tear-drops and drops of blood!

[*The light is beginning to grow less.*]

Cyrano. His letter? . . . Did you not once say that some day . . . you might show it to me?

Roxane. Ah! . . . Do you wish? . . . His letter?

Cyrano. Yes . . . today . . . I wish to . . .

Roxane. [*Handing him the little bag from her neck.*] Here!

Cyrano. I may open it?

Roxane. Open it . . . read!

[*She goes back to her embroidery frame, folds it up, orders her wools.*]

Cyrano. "Good-by, Roxane! I am going to die!"

Roxane. [*Stopping in astonishment.*] You are reading it aloud?

Cyrano. [*Reading.*] "It is fated to come this evening, beloved, I believe! My soul is heavy, oppressed with love it had not time to utter . . . and now Time is at end! Never again, never again shall my worshiping eyes . . ."

Roxane. How strangely you read his letter!

Cyrano. [*Continuing.*] ". . . whose passionate revel it was, kiss in its fleeting grace your every gesture. One, usual to you, of tucking back a little curl, comes to my mind . . . and I cannot refrain from crying out . . ."

Roxane. How strangely you read his letter! . . . [*The darkness gradually increases.*]

Cyrano. "and I cry out: Good-bye!"

Roxane. You read it . . .

Cyrano. "my dearest, my darling, . . . my treasure . . ."

Roxane. . . . in a voice . . .

Cyrano. ". . . my love! . . ."

Roxane. . . . in a voice . . . a voice which I am not hearing for the first time!

[ROXANE *comes quietly nearer to him, without his seeing it; she steps behind his arm-chair, bends noiselessly over his shoulder, looks at the letter. The darkness deepens.*]

Cyrano. ". . . My heart never desisted for a second from your side . . . and I am and shall be in the world that has no end, the one who loved you without measure, the one . . ."

Roxane. [*Laying her hand on his shoulder.*] How can you go on reading? It is dark. [CYRANO *starts, and turns around; sees her close to him, makes a gesture of dismay and hangs his head. Then, in the darkness which has completely closed round them, she says slowly, clasping her hands:*] And he, for fourteen years, has played the part of the comical old friend who came to cheer me!

Cyrano. Roxane!

Roxane. So it was you.

Cyrano. No, no, Roxane!

Roxane. I ought to have divined it, if only by the way in which he speaks my name!

Cyrano. No, it was not I!

Roxane. So it was you!

Cyrano. I swear to you . . .

Roxane. Ah, I detect at last the whole generous imposture. The letters . . . were yours!

Cyrano. No!

Roxane. The tender fancy, the dear folly, . . . yours!

Cyrano. No!

Roxane. The voice in the night, was yours!

Cyrano. I swear to you that it was not!

Roxane. The soul . . . was yours!

Cyrano. I did not love you, no!

Roxane. And you loved me!

Cyrano. Not I . . . it was the other!

Roxane. You loved me!

Cyrano. No!

Roxane. Already your denial comes more faintly!

Cyrano. No, no, my darling love, I did not love you!

Roxane. Ah, how many things within the hour have died . . . how many have been born! Why, why have you been silent these long years, when on this letter, in which he had no part, the tears were yours?

Cyrano. [*Handing her the letter.*] Because . . . the blood was his.

Roxane. Then why let the sublime bond of this silence be loosed today?

Cyrano. Why?

[LE BRET *and* RAGUENEAU *enter running.*]

Le Bret. Madness! Monstrous madness! . . . Ah, I was sure of it! There he is!

Cyrano. [*Smiling and straightening himself.*] *Tiens!* Where else?

Le Bret. Madame, he is likely to have got his death by getting out of bed!

Roxane. Merciful God! A moment ago, then . . . that faintness . . . that . . . ?

Cyrano. It is true. I had not finished telling you the news. And on Saturday, the twenty-sixth, an hour after sundown, Monsieur de Bergerac died of murder done upon him.

[*He takes off his hat; his head is seen wrapped in bandages.*]

Roxane. What is he saying? . . . Cyrano? . . . Those bandages about his head? . . . Ah, what have they done to you? . . . Why? . . .

Cyrano. "Happy who falls, cut off by a hero, with an honest sword through his heart!" I am quoting from myself! . . . Fate will have his laugh at us! . . . Here am I killed, in a trap, from behind, by a lackey, with a log! Nothing could be completer! In my whole life I shall have not had anything I wanted . . . not even a decent death!

Ragueneau. Ah, Monsieur! . . .

Cyrano. Ragueneau, do not sob like that! [*Holding out his hand to him.*] And what is the news with you, these latter days, fellow-poet?

Ragueneau. [*Through his tears.*] I am candle-snuffer at Molière's theater.

Cyrano. Molière!

Ragueneau. But I intend to leave no later than tomorrow. Yes, I am indignant! Yesterday, they were giving Scapin, and I saw that he has appropriated a scene of yours.

Le Bret. A whole scene?

Ragueneau. Yes, Monsieur. The one in which occurs the famous "What the devil was he doing in . . ." *

Le Bret. Molière has taken that from you!

Cyrano. Hush! hush! He did well to take it! [*To* RAGUENEAU.] The scene was very effective, was it not?

Ragueneau. Ah, Monsieur, the public laughed . . . laughed!

Cyrano. Yes, to the end, I shall have been the one who prompted . . . and was forgotten! [*To* ROXANE.] Do you remember that evening on which Christian spoke to you from below the balcony? There was the epitome of my life: while I have stood below in darkness, others have climbed to gather the kiss and glory! It is well done, and on the brink of my grave I approve it: Molière has genius . . . Christian was a fine fellow! [*At this moment, the chapel bell having rung, the* NUNS *are seen passing at the back, along the avenue, on their way to service.*] Let them hasten to their prayers . . . the bell is summoning them . . .

Roxane. [*Rising and calling.*] Sister! Sister!

Cyrano. [*Holding her back.*] No! No! do not leave me to fetch anybody! When you came back I might not be here to rejoice . . . [*The* NUNS *have gone into the chapel; the organ is heard.*] I longed for a little music . . . it comes in time!

Roxane. I love you . . . you shall live!

Cyrano. No! for it is only in the fairy-tale that the shy and awkward prince when he hears the beloved say "I love you!" feels his ungainliness melt and drop from him in the sunshine of those words! . . . But you would always know full well, dear Heart, that there had taken place in your poor slave no beautifying change!

Roxane. I have hurt you . . . I have wrecked your life, I! . . . I!

Cyrano. You? . . . The reverse! Woman's sweetness I had never known. My mother . . . thought me unflattering. I had no sister. Later, I shunned Love's cross-road in fear of mocking eyes. To you I owe having had, at least, among the gentle and fair, a friend. Thanks to you there has passed across my life the rustle of a woman's gown.

Le Bret. [*Calling his attention to the moonlight peering through the branches.*] Your other friend, among the gentle and fair, is there . . . she comes to see you!

Cyrano. [*Smiling to the moon.*] I see her!

Roxane. I never loved but one . . . and twice I lose him!

Cyrano. Le Bret, I shall ascend into the opalescent moon, without need this time of a flying-machine!

Roxane. What are you saying?

Cyrano. Yes, it is there, you may be sure, I shall be sent for my Paradise. More than one soul of those I have loved must be apportioned there . . . There I shall find Socrates and Galileo!

Le Bret. [*In revolt.*] No! No! It is too senseless, too cruel, too unfair! So true a poet! So great a heart! To die . . . like this! To die! . . .

Cyrano. As ever . . . Le Bret is grumbling!

Le Bret. [*Bursting into tears.*] My friend! My friend!

Cyrano. [*Lifting himself, his eyes wild.*] They are the Gascony Cadets! . . . Man in the gross . . . Eh, yes! . . . the weakness of the weakest point . . .

Le Bret. Learned . . . even in his delirium! . . .

Cyrano. Copernicus said . . .

Roxane. Oh!

Cyrano. But what the devil was he doing . . . and what the devil was he doing in that galley?

Philosopher and physicist,
Musician, rhymester, duelist,
Explorer of the upper blue,
Retorter apt with point and point,
Lover as well,—not for his peace!
Here lies Hercule Savinien
De Cyrano de Bergerac,
Who was everything . . . but of account!

But, your pardons, I must go . . . I wish to keep no one waiting . . . See, a moonbeam, come to take me home! [*He has dropped in his chair;* ROXANE's *weeping calls him back to reality; he looks at her and gently stroking her mourning veil.*] I do not wish . . . indeed, I do not wish . . . that you should sorrow less for Christian, the comely and the kind! Only I wish that when the everlasting cold shall have seized upon my fibers, this funereal veil should have a twofold mean-

* *Que diable allait il faire dans cette galère?* was the phrase that Molière rendered proverbial in this play.

ing, and the mourning you wear for him be worn for me too . . . a little!

Roxane. I promise . . .

Cyrano. [*Seized with a great shivering, starts to his feet.*] Not there! No! Not in an elbow-chair! [*All draw nearer to help him.*] Let no one stay me! No one. [*He goes and stands against the tree.*] Nothing but this tree! [*Silence.*] She comes. Mors, the indiscriminate Madame! . . . Already I am booted with marble . . . gauntleted with lead! [*He stiffens himself.*] Ah, since she is on her way, I will await her standing . . . [*He draws his sword.*] Sword in hand!

Le Bret. Cyrano!

Roxane. [*Swooning.*] Cyrano!

[*All start back, terrified.*]

Cyrano. I believe she is looking at me . . . that she dares to look at my nose, the bony baggage who has none! [*He raises his sword.*] What are you saying? That it is no use? . . . I know it! But one does not fight because there is hope of winning! No! . . . no! . . . it is much finer to fight when it is no use! . . . What are all those? You are a thousand strong? . . . Ah, I know you now . . . all my ancient enemies! . . . Hypocrisy? . . . [*He beats with his sword, in the vacancy.*] Take this! and this! Ha! Ha! Compromises? . . . and Prejudices? and dastardly Expedients? [*He strikes.*] That I should come to terms, I? . . . Never! Never! . . . Ah, you are there too, you bloated and pompous Silliness! I know full well that you will lay me low at last . . . No matter: whilst I have breath, I will fight you, I will fight you, I will fight you! [*He waves his sword in great sweeping circles, and stops, panting.*] Yes, you have wrested from me everything, laurel as well as rose . . . Work your wills! . . . Spite of your worst, something will still be left me to take whither I go . . . and tonight when I enter God's house, in saluting, broadly will I sweep the azure threshold with what despite of all I carry forth unblemished and unbent . . . [*He starts forward, with lifted sword.*] . . . and that is . . .

[*The sword falls from his hands, he staggers, drops in the arms of* LE BRET *and* RAGUENEAU.]

Roxane. [*Bending over him and kissing his forehead.*] That is? . . .

Cyrano. [*Opens his eyes again, recognizes her and says with a smile:*] . . . My white plume!

CURTAIN

UNCLE VANYA*

Scenes from Country Life

By

ANTON P. CHEKHOV

Translated by MARIAN FELL

CHEKHOV'S FEELING TOWARD THE THEater and playwriting was curious. He seems always to have felt distrust of them, in relation at least to his own work. Though he began writing plays as early as he began to write at all, he usually destroyed his work. As late as September, 1887, he writes, "I will not write any play. I have absolutely no interest in the theater, nor in humanity." But, persuaded by his friends, and by the opportunity for making money, he wrote *Ivanov,* his first full-length play, in two weeks during October, 1887. Then he had fits of nervousness lest the play should be inadequately mounted and acted. He could only with difficulty be persuaded that in performance it had been a marked success. These fears, the counterpart, no doubt, of the highest hopes, became habitual with him in regard to all his plays. By his short stories he had early won reputation, and he regarded his work in that form with more confidence, but he said, "The novel is a lawful wife, but the stage is a noisy, flashy, and insolent mistress."

Uncle Vanya, in its original form, was Chekhov's second full-length play. Planned by him in collaboration with A. S. Suvorin, who withdrew, it was entitled *The Wood Demon,* and occupied Chekhov from October, 1888, to October, 1889. He seems at first to have thought well of it, but when it was not favorably received on performance, to have become quite discouraged. *The Wood Demon* was therefore not printed during his lifetime. But he seems to have kept the manuscript by him, and to have worked over it from time to time, so that in 1897, when an edition of his plays was being published, he decided to include with the already produced *Sea Gull* and *Ivanov* what he called "the universally unknown *Uncle Vanya.*" By means of this publication the play became known, and was frequently played in the provincial theaters of Russia during 1898, and by the Moscow Art Theatre in 1899.

The steps in the development of *Uncle Vanya* from synopsis through *The Wood Demon* to the form in which we now have it may be fairly easily traced, by reference to Chekhov's letters and the still extant early play. Through them it may be seen how consistently Chekhov moved toward economy and force: by elimination of unnecessary characters, by tautening emotion, by subtilizing action, by giving the whole an allegorical value. The early play has thirteen speaking characters, the revision only nine; in *The Wood Demon* the quarrel between the professor and his brother-in-law is broken into by the entrance of extraneous people, in *Uncle Vanya* it continues with rising tensity to the attempted murder; and in *The Wood Demon* there is no parallel to the beautiful speech of Sonia which closes *Uncle Vanya.*

Chekhov wrote of his naturalistic technique: "The action goes on quietly and peacefully, and then I give the audience a blow. All my energy is spent on a few really brisk, forceful climaxes; but the bridges joining these are insignificant, loose, not startling."

The outstanding production of *Uncle Vanya* in America took place in 1930 under the direction of Jed Harris, with Lillian Gish as Helena and Osgood Perkins as Astroff.

For further discussion of Chekhov's work, see the preface to *The Cherry Orchard.*

ANTON PAVLOVITCH CHEKHOV

Born 1860, Taganrog, Russia.
M.D., University of Moscow, 1884.
1886, First volume of short stories published.
1888, Awarded Pushkin prize.
1898, Begins association with the Moscow Art Theatre.
1904, Dies of tuberculosis.
Journalist and short-story writer.

PLAYS

1884 *On the High Road* (one act, also translated as *On the Highway*). 1887 *Ivanov.* 1888 *The Tragedian in Spite of Himself* (one act, also translated as *An Unwilling Martyr*). 1888 *The Bear* (one act, also translated as *The Boor*). 1889 *The Wood Demon.* 1889 *That Worthless Fellow Platonov* (unfinished). 1889 *Tatyana Riepin* (one act, continuation of A. S. Suvorin's play of same name). 1889 *The Swan Song* (one act). 1889 *The Proposal* (one act, also translated as *A Marriage Proposal*). 1896 *The Sea Gull.* 1897 *Uncle Vanya* (revision of *The Wood Demon*). 1900 *The Three Sisters.* 1903 *The Jubilee* (one act, also translated as *The Anniversary*). 1903 *The Wedding* (one act). 1904 *The Cherry Orchard* (also translated as *The Cherry Garden*).

UNCLE VANYA

Characters

ALEXANDER SEREBRAKOFF, *a retired professor.*
HELENA, *his wife, twenty-seven years old.*
SONIA, *his daughter by a former marriage.*
MME. VOITSKAYA, *widow of a privy councilor, and mother of Serebrakoff's first wife.*
IVAN (VANYA) VOITSKI, *her son.*
MICHAEL ASTROFF, *a doctor.*
ILIA (WAFFLES) TELEGIN, *an impoverished landowner.*
MARINA, *an old nurse.*
A WORKMAN.

The scene is laid on SEREBRAKOFF'S *country place.*

ACT FIRST

A country house on a terrace. In front of it a garden. In an avenue of trees, under an old poplar, stands a table set for tea, with a samovar, etc. Some benches and chairs stand near the table. On one of them is lying a guitar. A hammock is swung near the table. It is three o'clock in the afternoon of a cloudy day.

[MARINA, *a quiet, gray-haired, little old woman, is sitting at the table knitting a stocking.* ASTROFF *is walking up and down near her.*]

Marina. [*Pouring some tea into a glass.*] Take a little tea, my son.

Astroff. [*Takes the glass from her unwillingly.*] Somehow, I don't seem to want any.

Marina. Then will you have a little vodka instead?

Astroff. No, I don't drink vodka every day, and besides, it is too hot now. [*A pause.*] Tell me, nurse, how long have we known each other?

Marina. [*Thoughtfully.*] Let me see, how long is it? Lord—help me to remember. You first came here, into our parts—let me think—when was it? Sonia's mother was still alive—it was two winters before she died; that was eleven years ago—[*thoughtfully*] perhaps more.

Astroff. Have I changed much since then?

Marina. Oh, yes. You were handsome and young then, and now you are an old man and not handsome any more. You drink, too.

Astroff. Yes, ten years have made me another man. And why? Because I am overworked. Nurse, I am on my feet from dawn till dusk. I know no rest; at night I tremble under my blankets for fear of being dragged out to visit some one who is sick; I have toiled without repose or a day's freedom since I have known you; could I help growing old? And then, existence is tedious, anyway; it is a senseless, dirty business, this life, and goes heavily. Every one about here is silly, and after living with them for two or three years one grows silly oneself. It is inevitable. [*Twisting his mustache.*] See what a long mustache I have grown. A foolish, long mustache. Yes, I am as silly as the rest, nurse, but not as stupid; no, I have not grown stupid. Thank God, my brain is not addled yet, though my feelings have grown numb. I ask nothing, I need nothing, I love no one, unless it is yourself alone. [*He kisses her head.*] I had a nurse just like you when I was a child.

Marina. Don't you want a bite of something to eat?

Astroff. No. During the third week of Lent I went to the epidemic at Malitskoi. It was eruptive typhoid. The peasants were all lying side by side in their huts, and the calves and pigs were running about the floor among the sick. Such dirt there was, and smoke! Unspeakable! I slaved among those people all day, not a crumb passed my lips, but when I got home there was still no rest for me; a switchman was carried in from the railroad; I laid him on the operating table and he went and died in my arms under chloroform, and then my feelings that should have been deadened awoke again, my conscience tortured me as if I had killed the man. I sat down and closed my eyes—like this—and thought: will our descendants two hundred years from now, for whom we are breaking the road, remember to give us a kind word? No, nurse, they will forget.

Marina. Man is forgetful, but God remembers.

Astroff. Thank you for that. You have spoken the truth.

[*Enter* VOITSKI *from the house. He has been asleep after dinner and looks rather disheveled. He sits down on the bench and straightens his collar.*]

Voitski. H'm. Yes. [*A pause.*] Yes.

Astroff. Have you been asleep?

Voitski. Yes, very much so. [*He yawns.*] Ever since the professor and his wife have come, our daily life seems to have jumped the track. I sleep at the wrong time, drink wine, and eat all sorts of messes for luncheon and dinner. It isn't wholesome. Sonia and I used to work together and never had an idle moment, but now Sonia works alone and I only eat and drink and sleep. Something is wrong.

Marina. [*Shakes her head.*] Such a confusion in the house! The professor gets up at twelve, the samovar is kept boiling all the morning, and everything has to wait for him. Before they came we used to have dinner at one o'clock, like everybody else, but now we have it at seven. The professor sits up all night writing and reading, and suddenly, at two o'clock, there goes the bell! Heavens, what is that? The professor wants some tea! Wake the servants, light the samovar! Lord, what disorder!

Astroff. Will they be here long?

Voitski. A hundred years! The professor has decided to make his home here.

Marina. Look at this now! The samovar has been on the table for two hours, and they are all out walking!

Voitski. All right, don't get excited; here they come.

[*Voices are heard approaching.* SEREBRAKOFF, HELENA, SONIA, *and* TELEGIN *come in from the depths of the garden, returning from their walk.*]

Serebrakoff. Superb! Superb! What beautiful views!

Telegin. They are wonderful, your Excellency.

Sonia. Tomorrow we shall go into the woods, shall we, papa?

Voitski. Ladies and gentlemen, tea is ready.

Serebrakoff. Won't you please be good enough to send my tea into the library? I still have some work to finish.

Sonia. I am sure you will love the woods.

[HELENA, SEREBRAKOFF, *and* SONIA *go into the house.* TELEGIN *sits down at the table beside* MARINA.]

Voitski. There goes our learned scholar on a hot, sultry day like this, in his overcoat and goloshes and carrying an umbrella!

Astroff. He is trying to take good care of his health.

Voitski. How lovely she is! How lovely! I have never in my life seen a more beautiful woman.

Telegin. Do you know, Marina, that as I walk in the fields or in the shady garden, as I look at this table here, my heart swells with unbounded happiness. The weather is enchanting, the birds are singing, we are all living in peace and contentment—what more could the soul desire? [*Takes a glass of tea.*]

Voitski. [*Dreaming.*] Such eyes—a glorious woman!

Astroff. Come, Ivan, tell us something.

Voitski. [*Indolently.*] What shall I tell you?

Astroff. Haven't you any news for us?

Voitski. No, it is all stale. I am just the same as usual, or perhaps worse, because I have become lazy. I don't do anything now but croak like an old raven. My mother, the old magpie, is still chattering about the emancipation of woman, with one eye on her grave and the other on her learned books, in which she is always looking for the dawn of a new life.

Astroff. And the professor?

Voitski. The professor sits in his library from morning till night, as usual—

"Straining the mind, wrinkling the brow,
We write, write, write,
Without respite
Or hope of praise in the future or now."

Poor paper! He ought to write his autobiography; he would make a really splendid subject for a book! Imagine it, the life of a retired professor, as stale as a piece of hardtack, tortured by gout, headaches, and rheumatism, his liver bursting with jealousy and envy, living on the estate of his first wife, although he hates it, because he can't afford to live in town. He is everlastingly whining about his hard lot, though, as a matter of fact, he is extraordinarily lucky. He is the son of a common deacon and has attained the professor's chair, become the son-in-law of a senator, is called "your Excellency," and so on. But I'll tell you something; the man has been writing on art for twenty-five years, and he doesn't know the very first thing about it. For twenty-five years he has been chewing on other men's thoughts about realism, naturalism, and all such foolishness; for twenty-five years he has been reading and writing things that clever men have long known and stupid ones are not interested in; for twenty-five years he has been making his imaginary mountains out of molehills. And just think of the man's self-conceit and presumption all this time! For twenty-five years he has been masquerading in false clothes and has now retired, absolutely unknown to any living soul; and yet see him! stalking across the earth like a demi-god!

Astroff. I believe you envy him.

Voitski. Yes, I do. Look at the success he has had with women! Don Juan himself was not more favored. His first wife, who was my sister, was a beautiful, gentle being, as pure as the blue heaven there above us, noble, great-hearted, with more admirers than he has pupils, and she loved him as only beings of angelic purity can love those who are as pure and beautiful as themselves. His mother-in-law, my mother, adores him to this day, and he still inspires a sort of worshipful awe in her. His second wife is, as you see, a brilliant beauty; she married him in his old age and has surrendered all the glory of her beauty and freedom to him. Why? What for?

Astroff. Is she faithful to him?

Voitski. Yes, unfortunately she is.

Astroff. Why "unfortunately"?

Voitski. Because such fidelity is false and unnatural, root and branch. It sounds well, but there is no logic in it. It is thought immoral for a woman to deceive an old husband whom she hates, but quite moral for her to strangle her poor youth in her breast and banish every vital desire from her heart.

Telegin. [*In a tearful voice.*] Vanya, I don't like to hear you talk so. Listen, Vanya; every one who betrays husband or wife is faithless, and could also betray his country.

Voitski. [*Crossly.*] Turn off the tap, Waffles.

Telegin. No, allow me, Vanya. My wife ran away with a lover on the day after our wedding, because my exterior was unprepossessing. I have never failed in my duty since then. I love her and am true to her to this day. I help her all I can and have given my fortune to educate the daughter of herself and her lover. I have forfeited my happiness, but I have kept my pride. And she? Her youth has fled, her beauty has faded according to the laws of nature, and her lover is dead. What has she kept?

[HELENA *and* SONIA *come in; after them comes* MME. VOITSKAYA *carrying a book. She sits down and begins to read. Some one hands her a glass of tea which she drinks without looking up.*]

Sonia. [*Hurriedly, to the* NURSE.] There are some peasants waiting out there. Go and see what they want. I shall pour the tea.

[*Pours out some glasses of tea.*]

[MARINA *goes out.* HELENA *takes a glass and sits drinking in the hammock.*]

Astroff. I have come to see your husband. You wrote me that he had rheumatism and I know not what else, and that he was very ill, but he appears to be as lively as a cricket.

Helena. He had a fit of the blues yesterday evening and complained of pains in his legs, but he seems all right again today.

Astroff. And I galloped over here twenty miles at breakneck speed! No matter, though, it is not the first time. Once here, however, I am going to stay until tomorrow, and at any rate sleep *quantum satis.*

Sonia. Oh, splendid! You so seldom spend the night with us. Have you had dinner yet?

Astroff. No.

Sonia. Good. So you will have it with us. We dine at seven now. [*Drinks her tea.*] This tea is cold!

Telegin. Yes, the samovar has grown cold.

Helena. Don't mind, Monsieur Ivan, we will drink cold tea, then.

Telegin. I beg your pardon, my name is not Ivan, but Ilia, ma'am—Ilia Telegin, or Waffles, as I am sometimes called an account of my pock-marked face. I am Sonia's godfather, and his Excellency, your husband, knows me very well. I now live with you, ma'am, on this estate, and perhaps you will be so good as to notice that I dine with you every day.

Sonia. He is our great help, our right-hand man. [*Tenderly.*] Dear godfather, let me pour you some tea.

Mme. Voitskaya. Oh! Oh!

Sonia. What is it, grandmother?

Mme. Voitskaya. I forgot to tell Alexander—I have lost my memory—I received a letter today from Paul Alexevitch in Kharkoff. He has sent me a new pamphlet.

Astroff. Is it interesting?

Mme. Voitskaya. Yes, but strange. He refutes the very theories which he defended seven years ago. It is appalling!

Voitski. There is nothing appalling about it. Drink your tea, mamma.

Mme. Voitskaya. It seems you never want to listen to what I have to say. Pardon me, Jean, but you have changed so in the last year that I hardly know you. You used to be a man of settled convictions and had an illuminating personality——

Voitski. Oh, yes. I had an illuminating personality, which illuminated no one. [*A pause.*] I had an illuminating personality!

You couldn't say anything more biting. I am forty-seven years old. Until last year I endeavored, as you do now, to blind my eyes by your pedantry to the truths of life. But now— Oh, if you only knew! If you knew how I lie awake at night, heartsick and angry, to think how stupidly I have wasted my time when I might have been winning from life everything which my old age now forbids.

Sonia. Uncle Vanya, how dreary!

Mme. Voitskaya. [*To her son.*] You speak as if your former convictions were somehow to blame, but you yourself, not they, were at fault. You have forgotten that a conviction, in itself, is nothing but a dead letter. You should have done something.

Voitski. Done something! Not every man is capable of being a writer *perpetuum mobile* like your Herr Professor.

Mme. Voitskaya. What do you mean by that?

Sonia. [*Imploringly.*] Mother! Uncle Vanya! I entreat you!

Voitski. I am silent. I apologize and am silent. [*A pause.*]

Helena. What a fine day! Not too hot. [*A pause.*]

Voitski. A fine day to hang oneself.

[TELEGIN *tunes the guitar.* MARINA *appears near the house, calling the chickens.*]

Marina. Chick, chick, chick!

Sonia. What did the peasants want, nurse?

Marina. The same old thing, the same old nonsense. Chick, chick, chick!

Sonia. Why are you calling the chickens?

Marina. The speckled hen has disappeared with her chicks. I am afraid the crows have got her.

[TELEGIN *plays a polka. All listen in silence. Enter* WORKMAN.]

Workman. Is the doctor here? [*To* ASTROFF.] Excuse me, sir, but I have been sent to fetch you.

Astroff. Where are you from?

Workman. The factory.

Astroff. [*Annoyed.*] Thank you. There is nothing for it, then, but to go. [*Looking around him for his cap.*] Damn it, this is annoying!

Sonia. Yes, it is too bad, really. You must come back to dinner from the factory.

Astroff. No, I won't be able to do that. It will be too late. Now where, where— [*To the* WORKMAN.] Look here, my man, get me a glass of vodka, will you? [*The* WORKMAN *goes out.*] Where—where— [*Finds his cap.*] One of the characters in Ostroff's plays is a man with a long mustache and short wits, like me. However, let me bid you good-bye, ladies and gentlemen. [*To* HELENA.] I should be really delighted if you would come to see me some day with Miss Sonia. My estate is small, but if you are interested in such things I should like to show you a nursery and seed-bed whose like you will not find within a thousand miles of here. My place is surrounded by government forests. The forester is old and always ailing, so I superintend almost all the work myself.

Helena. I have always heard that you were very fond of the woods. Of course one can do a great deal of good by helping to preserve them, but does not that work interfere with your real calling?

Astroff. God alone knows what a man's real calling is.

Helena. And do you find it interesting?

Astroff. Yes, very.

Voitski. [*Sarcastically.*] Oh, extremely!

Helena. You are still young, not over thirty-six or seven, I should say, and I suspect that the woods do not interest you as much as you say they do. I should think you would find them monotonous.

Sonia. No, the work is thrilling. Dr. Astroff watches over the old woods and sets out new plantations every year, and he has already received a diploma and a bronze medal. If you will listen to what he can tell you, you will agree with him entirely. He says that forests are the ornaments of the earth, that they teach mankind to understand beauty and attune his mind to lofty sentiments. Forests temper a stern climate, and in countries where the climate is milder, less strength is wasted in the battle with nature, and the people are kind and gentle. The inhabitants of such countries are handsome, tractable, sensitive, graceful in speech and gesture. Their philosophy is joyous, art and science blossom among them, their treatment of women is full of exquisite nobility——

Voitski. [*Laughing.*] Bravo! Bravo! All that is very pretty, but it is also unconvincing. So my friend [*to* ASTROFF], you must let me go on burning firewood in my stoves and building my sheds of planks.

Astroff. You can burn peat in your stoves and build your sheds of stone. Oh, I don't object, of course, to cutting wood from necessity, but why destroy the forests? The woods of Russia are trembling under the blows of the axe. Millions of trees have perished. The homes of the wild animals and birds have been desolated; the rivers are shrinking, and many beautiful landscapes are gone forever. And why? Because men are too lazy and stupid to stoop down and pick up their fuel from the ground. [*To* HELENA.]

Am I not right, Madame? Who but a stupid barbarian could burn so much beauty in his stove and destroy that which he cannot make? Man is endowed with reason and the power to create, so that he may increase that which has been given him, but until now he had not created, but demolished. The forests are disappearing, the rivers are running dry, the game is exterminated, the climate is spoiled, and the earth becomes poorer and uglier every day. [*To* VOITSKI.] I read irony in your eye; you do not take what I am saying seriously, and—and—after all, it may very well be nonsense. But when I pass peasant-forests that I have preserved from the axe, or hear the rustling of the young plantations set out with my own hands, I feel as if I had had some small share in improving the climate, and that if mankind is happy a thousand years from now I will have been a little bit responsible for their happiness. When I plant a little birch tree and then see it budding into young green and swaying in the wind, my heart swells with pride and I— [*Sees the* WORKMAN, *who is bringing him a glass of vodka on a tray.*] However—[*he drinks*] I must be off. Probably it is all nonsense, anyway. Good-bye.

[*He goes toward the house.* SONIA *takes his arm and goes with him.*]

Sonia. When are you coming to see us again?

Astroff. I can't say.

Sonia. In a month?

[ASTROFF *and* SONIA *go into the house.* HELENA *and* VOITSKI *walk over to the terrace.*]

Helena. You have behaved shockingly again. Ivan, what sense was there in teasing your mother and talking about *perpetuum mobile*? And at breakfast you quarreled with Alexander again. Really, your behavior is too petty.

Voitski. But if I hate him?

Helena. You hate Alexander without reason; he is like every one else, and no worse than you are.

Voitski. If you could only see your face, your gestures! Oh, how tedious your life must be.

Helena. It is tedious, yes, and dreary! You all abuse my husband and look on me with compassion; you think, "Poor woman, she is married to an old man." How well I understand your compassion! As Astroff said just now, see how you thoughtlessly destroy the forests, so that there will soon be none left. So you also destroy mankind, and soon fidelity and purity and self-sacrifice will have vanished with the woods. Why cannot you look calmly at a woman unless she is yours? Because, the doctor was right, you are all possessed by a devil of destruction; you have no mercy on the woods or the birds or on women or on one another.

Voitski. I don't like your philosophy.

Helena. That doctor has a sensitive, weary face—an interesting face. Sonia evidently likes him, and she is in love with him, and I can understand it. This is the third time he has been here since I have come, and I have not had a real talk with him yet or made much of him. He thinks I am disagreeable. Do you know, Ivan, the reason you and I are such friends? I think it is because we are both lonely and unfortunate. Yes, unfortunate. Don't look at me in that way, I don't like it.

Voitski. How can I look at you otherwise when I love you? You are my joy, my life, and my youth. I know that my chances of being loved in return are infinitely small, do not exist, but I ask nothing of you. Only let me look at you, listen to your voice——

Helena. Hush, some one will overhear you.

[*They go toward the house.*]

Voitski. [*Following her.*] Let me speak to you of my love, do not drive me away, and this alone will be my greatest happiness!

Helena. Ah! This is agony!

[TELEGIN *strikes the strings of his guitar and plays a polka.* MME. VOITSKAYA *writes something on the leaves of her pamphlet.*]

THE CURTAIN FALLS

ACT SECOND

The dining-room of SEREBRAKOFF'S *house.* [*It is night. The tapping of the* WATCHMAN'S *rattle is heard in the garden.* SEREBRAKOFF *is dozing in an armchair by an open window and* HELENA *is sitting beside him, also half asleep.*]

Serebrakoff. [*Rousing himself.*] Who is here? Is it you, Sonia?

Helena. It is I.

Serebrakoff. Oh, it is you, Nelly. This pain is intolerable.

Helena. Your shawl has slipped down-

[*She wraps up his legs in the shawl.*] Let me shut the window.

Serebrakoff. No, leave it open; I am suffocating. I dreamt just now that my left leg belonged to some one else, and it hurt so that I woke. I don't believe this is gout, it is more like rheumatism. What time is it?

Helena. Half-past twelve. [*A pause.*]

Serebrakoff. I want you to look for Batushka's works in the library tomorrow. I think we have him.

Helena. What is that?

Serebrakoff. Look for Batushka tomorrow morning; we used to have him, I remember. Why do I find it so hard to breathe?

Helena. You are tired; this is the second night you have had no sleep.

Serebrakoff. They say that Turgenieff got angina of the heart from gout. I am afraid I am getting angina too. Oh, damn this horrible, accursed old age! Ever since I have been old I have been hateful to myself, and I am sure, hateful to you all as well.

Helena. You speak as if we were to blame for your being old.

Serebrakoff. I am more hateful to you than to any one.

[HELENA *gets up and walks away from him, sitting down at a distance.*]

Serebrakoff. You are quite right, of course. I am not an idiot; I can understand you. You are young and healthy and beautiful, and longing for life, and I am an old dotard, almost a dead man already. Don't I know it? Of course I see that it is foolish for me to live so long, but wait! I shall soon set you all free. My life cannot drag on much longer.

Helena. You are overtaxing my powers of endurance. Be quiet, for God's sake!

Serebrakoff. It appears that, thanks to me, everybody's power of endurance is being overtaxed; everybody is miserable, only I am blissfully triumphant. Oh, yes, of course!

Helena. Be quiet! You are torturing me.

Serebrakoff. I torture everybody. Of course.

Helena. [*Weeping.*] This is unbearable! Tell me, what is it you want me to do?

Serebrakoff. Nothing.

Helena. Then be quiet, please.

Serebrakoff. It is funny that everybody listens to Ivan and his old idiot of a mother, but the moment I open my lips you all begin to feel ill-treated. You can't even stand the sound of my voice. Even if I am hateful, even if I am a selfish tyrant, haven't I the right to be one at my age? Haven't I deserved it? Haven't I, I ask you, the right to be respected, now that I am old?

Helena. No one is disputing your rights. [*The window slams in the wind.*] The wind is rising, I must shut the window. [*She shuts it.*] We shall have rain in a moment. Your rights have never been questioned by anybody.

[*The* WATCHMAN *in the garden sounds his rattle.*

Serebrakoff. I have spent my life working in the interests of learning. I am used to my library and the lecture hall and to the esteem and admiration of my colleagues. Now I suddenly find myself plunged in this wilderness, condemned to see the same stupid people from morning till night and listen to their futile conversation. I want to live; I long for success and fame and the stir of the world, and here I am in exile! Oh, it is dreadful to spend every moment grieving for the lost past, to see the success of others and sit here with nothing to do but to fear death. I cannot stand it! It is more than I can bear. And you will not even forgive me for being old!

Helena. Wait, have patience; I shall be old myself in four or five years.

[SONIA *comes in.*]

Sonia. Father, you sent for Dr. Astroff, and now when he comes you refuse to see him. It is not nice to give a man so much trouble for nothing.

Serebrakoff. What do I care about your Astroff? He understands medicine about as well as I understand astronomy.

Sonia. We can't send for the whole medical faculty, can we, to treat your gout?

Serebrakoff. I won't talk to that madman!

Sonia. Do as you please. It's all the same to me. [*She sits down.*]

Serebrakoff. What time is it?

Helena. One o'clock.

Serebrakoff. It is stifling in here. Sonia, hand me that bottle on the table.

Sonia. Here it is.

[*She hands him a bottle of medicine.*]

Serebrakoff. [*Crossly.*] No, not that one! Can't you understand me? Can't I ask you to do a thing?

Sonia. Please don't be captious with me. Some people may like it, but you must spare me, if you please, because I don't. Besides, I haven't the time; we are cutting the hay tomorrow and I must get up early.

[VOITSKI *comes in dressed in a long gown and carrying a candle.*]

Voitski. A thunderstorm is coming up. [*The lightning flashes.*] There it is! Go to bed, Helena and Sonia. I have come to take your place.

Serebrakoff. [*Frightened.*] No, no, no!

Don't leave me alone with him! Oh, don't. He will begin to lecture me.

Voitski. But you must give them a little rest. They have not slept for two nights.

Serebrakoff. Then let them go to bed, but you go away too! Thank you. I implore you to go. For the sake of our former friendship do not protest against going. We will talk some other time——

Voitski. Our former friendship! Our former——

Sonia. Hush, Uncle Vanya!

Serebrakoff. [*To his wife.*] My darling, don't leave me alone with him. He will begin to lecture me.

Voitski. This is ridiculous.

[MARINA *comes in carrying a candle.*]

Sonia. You must go to bed, nurse, it is late.

Marina. I haven't cleared away the tea things. Can't go to bed yet.

Serebrakoff. No one can go to bed. They are all worn out, only I enjoy perfect happiness.

Marina. [*Goes up to* SEREBRAKOFF *and speaks tenderly.*] What's the matter, master? Does it hurt? My own legs are aching too, oh, so badly. [*Arranges his shawl about his legs.*] You have had this illness such a long time. Sonia's dead mother used to stay awake with you too, and wear herself out for you. She loved you dearly. [*A pause.*] Old people want to be pitied as much as young ones, but nobody cares about them somehow. [*She kisses* SEREBRAKOFF'S *shoulder.*] Come, master, let me give you some linden-tea and warm your poor feet for you. I shall pray to God for you.

Serebrakoff. [*Touched.*] Let us go, Marina.

Marina. My own feet are aching so badly, oh, so badly! [*She and* SONIA *lead* SEREBRAKOFF *out.*] Sonia's mother used to wear herself out with sorrow and weeping. You were still little and foolish then, Sonia. Come, come, master.

[SEREBRAKOFF, SONIA, *and* MARINA *go out.*]

Helena. I am absolutely exhausted by him, and can hardly stand.

Voitski. You are exhausted by him, and I am exhausted by my own self. I have not slept for three nights.

Helena. Something is wrong in this house. Your mother hates everything but her pamphlets and the professor; the professor is vexed, he won't trust me, and fears you; Sonia is angry with her father, and with me, and hasn't spoken to me for two weeks! I am at the end of my strength, and have come near bursting into tears at least twenty times today. Something is wrong in this house.

Voitski. Leave speculating alone.

Helena. You are cultured and intelligent, Ivan, and you surely understand that the world is not destroyed by villains and conflagrations, but by hate and malice and all this spiteful tattling. It is your duty to make peace, and not to growl at everything.

Voitski. Help me first to make peace with myself. My darling! [*Seizes her hand.*]

Helena. Let go! [*She drags her hand away.*] Go away!

Voitski. Soon the rain will be over, and all nature will sigh and awake refreshed. Only I am not refreshed by the storm. Day and night the thought haunts me like a fiend, that my life is lost forever. My past does not count, because I frittered it away on trifles, and the present has so terribly miscarried! What shall I do with my life and my love? What is to become of them? This wonderful feeling of mine will be wasted and lost as a ray of sunlight is lost that falls into a dark chasm, and my life will go with it.

Helena. I am as it were benumbed when you speak to me of your love, and I don't know how to answer you. Forgive me, I have nothing to say to you. [*She tries to go out.*] Good night!

Voitski. [*Barring the way.*] If you only knew how I am tortured by the thought that beside me in this house is another life that is being lost forever—it is yours! What are you waiting for? What accursed philosophy stands in your way? Oh, understand, understand——

Helena. [*Looking at him intently.*] Ivan, you are drunk!

Voitski. Perhaps. Perhaps.

Helena. Where is the doctor?

Voitski. In there, spending the night with me. Perhaps I am drunk, perhaps I am; nothing is impossible.

Helena. Have you just been drinking together? Why do you do that?

Voitski. Because in that way I get a taste of life. Let me do it, Helena!

Helena. You never used to drink, and you never used to talk so much. Go to bed, I am tired of you.

Voitski. [*Falling on his knees before her.*] My sweetheart, my beautiful one——

Helena. [*Angrily.*] Leave me alone! Really, this has become too disagreeable.

[HELENA *goes out. A pause.*]

Voitski. [*Alone.*] She is gone! I met her first ten years ago, at her sister's house, when she was seventeen and I was thirty-seven. Why did I not fall in love with her then and propose to her? It would have been so easy! And now she would have been my wife. Yes, we would both have been waked tonight by the thunderstorm, and she would have been frightened, but I would have held her in my arms and whispered: "Don't be afraid! I am here." Oh, enchanting dream, so sweet that I laugh to think of it. [*He laughs.*] But my God! My head reels! Why am I so old? Why won't she understand me? I hate all that rhetoric of hers, that morality of indolence, that absurd talk about the destruction of the world— [*A pause.*] Oh, how I have been deceived! For years I have worshiped that miserable gout-ridden professor. Sonia and I have squeezed this estate dry for his sake. We have bartered our butter and curds and peas like misers, and have never kept a morsel for ourselves, so that we could scrape enough pennies together to send to him. I was proud of him and of his learning; I received all his words and writings as inspired, and now? Now he has retired, and what is the total of his life? A blank! He is absolutely unknown, and his fame has burst like a soap-bubble. I have been deceived; I see that now, basely deceived.

[ASTROFF *comes in. He has his coat on, but is without his waistcoat or collar, and is slightly drunk.* TELEGIN *follows him, carrying a guitar.*]

Astroff. Play!

Telegin. But every one is asleep.

Astroff. Play!

[TELEGIN *begins to play softly.*]

Astroff. Are you alone here? No women about?

[*Sings with his arms akimbo.*]

"The hut is cold, the fire is dead;
Where shall the master lay his head?"

The thunderstorm woke me. It was a heavy shower. What time is it?

Voitski. The devil only knows.

Astroff. I thought I heard Helena's voice.

Voitski. She was here a moment ago.

Astroff. What a beautiful woman! [*Looking at the medicine bottles on the table.*] Medicine, is it? What a variety we have; prescriptions from Moscow, from Kharkoff, from Tula! Why, he has been pestering all the towns of Russia with his gout! Is he ill, or simply shamming?

Voitski. He is really ill.

Astroff. What is the matter with you tonight? You seem sad. Is it because you are sorry for the professor?

Voitski. Leave me alone.

Astroff. Or in love with the professor's wife?

Voitski. She is my friend.

Astroff. Already?

Voitski. What do you mean by "already"?

Astroff. A woman can only become a man's friend after having first been his acquaintance and then his beloved—then she becomes his friend.

Voitski. What vulgar philosophy!

Astroff. What do you mean? Yes, I must confess I am getting vulgar, but then, you see, I am drunk. I usually only drink like this once a month. At such times my audacity and temerity knows no bounds. I feel capable of anything. I attempt the most difficult operations and do them magnificently. The most brilliant plans for the future take shape in my head. I am no longer a poor fool of a doctor, but mankind's greatest benefactor. I evolve my own system of philosophy and all of you seem to crawl at my feet like so many insects or microbes. [*To* TELEGIN.] Play, Waffles!

Telegin. My dear boy, I would with all my heart, but do listen to reason; everybody in the house is asleep.

Astroff. Play!

[TELEGIN *plays softly.*]

Astroff. I want a drink. Come, we still have some brandy left. And then, as soon as it is day, you will come home with me.

[*He sees* SONIA, *who comes in at that moment.*]

Astroff. I beg your pardon, I have no collar on.

[*He goes out quickly, followed by* TELEGIN.]

Sonia. Uncle Vanya, you and the doctor have been drinking! The good fellows have been getting together! It is all very well for him, he has always done it, but why do you follow his example? It looks dreadful at your age.

Voitski. Age has nothing to do with it. When real life is wanting one must create an illusion. It is better than nothing.

Sonia. Our hay is all cut and rotting in these daily rains, and here you are busy creating illusions! You have given up the farm altogether. I have done all the work alone until I am at the end of my strength— [*Frightened.*] Uncle! Your eyes are full of tears!

Voitski. Tears? Nonsense, there are no tears in my eyes. You looked at me then just as your dead mother used to, my darling —— [*He eagerly kisses her face and hands.*] My sister, my dearest sister, where are you now? Ah, if you only knew, if you only knew!

Sonia. If she only knew what, Uncle?

Voitski. My heart is bursting. It is awful. No matter, though. I must go.

[*He goes out.*]

Sonia. [*Knocks at the door.*] Dr. Astroff! Are you awake? Please come here for a minute.

Astroff. [*Behind the door.*] In a moment.

[*He appears in a few seconds. He has put on his collar and waistcoat.*]

Astroff. What do you want?

Sonia. Drink as much as you please yourself, if you don't find it revolting, but I implore you not to let my uncle do it. It is bad for him.

Astroff. Very well; we won't drink any more. I am going home at once. That is settled. It will be dawn by the time the horses are harnessed.

Sonia. It is still raining; wait till morning.

Astroff. The storm is blowing over. This is only the edge of it. I must go. And please don't ask me to come and see your father any more. I tell him he has gout, and he says it is rheumatism. I tell him to lie down, and he sits up. Today he refused to see me at all.

Sonia. He has been spoilt. [*She looks in the sideboard.*] Won't you have a bite to eat?

Astroff. Yes, please. I believe I will.

Sonia. I love to eat at night. I am sure we shall find something in here. They say that he has made a great many conquests in his life, and that the women have spoiled him. Here is some cheese for you.

[*They stand eating by the sideboard.*]

Astroff. I haven't eaten anything today. Your father has a very difficult nature. [*He takes a bottle out of the sideboard.*] May I? [*He pours himself a glass of vodka.*] We are alone here, and I can speak frankly. Do you know, I could not stand living in this house for even a month? This atmosphere would stifle me. There is your father, entirely absorbed in his books, and his gout; there is your Uncle Vanya with his hypochondria, your grandmother, and finally, your stepmother——

Sonia. What about her?

Astroff. A human being should be entirely beautiful: the face, the clothes, the mind, the thoughts. Your step-mother is, of course, beautiful to look at, but don't you see? She does nothing but sleep and eat and walk and bewitch us, and that is all. She has no responsibilities, everything is done for her—am I not right? And an idle life can never be a pure one. [*A pause.*] However, I may be judging her too severely. Like your Uncle Vanya, I am discontented, and so we are both grumblers.

Sonia. Aren't you satisfied with life?

Astroff. I like life as life, but I hate and despise it in a little Russian country village, and as far as my own personal life goes, by heaven! there is absolutely no redeeming feature about it. Haven't you noticed if you are riding through a dark wood at night and see a little light shining ahead, how you forget your fatigue and the darkness and the sharp twigs that whip your face? I work, that you know—as no one else in the country works. Fate beats me on without rest; at times I suffer unendurably and I see no light ahead. I have no hope; I do not like people. It is long since I have loved any one.

Sonia. You love no one?

Astroff. Not a soul. I only feel a sort of tenderness for your old nurse for old-times' sake. The peasants are all alike; they are stupid and live in dirt, and the educated people are hard to get along with. One gets tired of them. All our good friends are petty and shallow and see no farther than their own noses; in one word, they are dull. Those that have brains are hysterical, devoured with a mania for self-analysis. They whine, they hate, they pick faults everywhere with unhealthy sharpness. They sneak up to me sideways. look at me out of a corner of the eye, and say: "That man is a lunatic," "That man is a wind-bag." Or, if they don't know what else to label me with, they say I am strange. I like the woods; that is strange. I don't eat meat; that is strange, too. Simple, natural relations between man and man or man and nature do not exist.

[*He tries to go out;* SONIA *prevents him.*]

Sonia. I beg you, I implore you, not to drink any more!

Astroff. Why not?

Sonia. It is so unworthy of you. You are well-bred, your voice is sweet, you are even—more than any one I know—handsome. Why do you want to resemble the common people that drink and play cards? Oh, don't, I beg you! You always say that people do not create anything, but only destroy what heaven has given them. Why, oh, why, do you destroy yourself? Oh, don't, I implore you not to! I entreat you!

Astroff. [*Gives her his hand.*] I won't drink any more.

Sonia. Promise me.

Astroff. I give you my word of honor.

Sonia. [*Squeezing his hand.*] Thank you.

Astroff. I have done with it. You see, I am perfectly sober again, and so I shall stay till the end of my life. [*He looks at his watch.*] But, as I was saying, life holds nothing for me; my race is run. I am old, I am tired, I am trivial; my sensibilities are dead. I could never attach myself to any one again. I love no one, and—never shall! Beauty alone has the power to touch me still. I am deeply moved by it. Helena could turn my head in a day if she wanted to, but that is not love, that is not affection——

[*He shudders and covers his face with his hands.*]

Sonia. What is it?

Astroff. Nothing. During Lent one of my patients died under chloroform.

Sonia. It is time to forget that. [*A pause.*] Tell me, doctor, if I had a friend or a younger sister, and if you knew that she, well—loved you, what would you do?

Astroff. [*Shrugging his shoulders.*] I don't know. I don't think I should do anything. I should make her understand that I could not return her love—however, my mind is not bothered about those things now. I must start at once if I am ever to get off. Good-bye, my dear girl. At this rate we shall stand here talking till morning. [*He shakes hands with her.*] I shall go out through the sitting-room, because I am afraid your uncle might detain me. [*He goes out.*]

Sonia. [*Alone.*] Not a word! His heart and soul are still locked from me, and yet for some reason I am strangely happy. I wonder why? [*She laughs with pleasure.*] I told him that he was well-bred and handsome and that his voice was sweet. Was that a mistake? I can still feel his voice vibrating in the air; it caresses me. [*Wringing her hands.*] Oh! how terrible it is to be plain! I am plain, I know it. As I came out of church last Sunday I overheard a woman say, "She is a dear, noble girl, but what a pity she is so ugly!" So ugly!

[HELENA *comes in and throws open the window.*]

Helena. The storm is over. What delicious air! [*A pause.*] Where is the doctor?

Sonia. He has gone. [*A pause.*]

Helena. Sonia!

Sonia. Yes?

Helena. How much longer are you going to sulk at me? We have not hurt each other. Why not be friends? We have had enough of this.

Sonia. I myself— [*She embraces* HELENA.] Let us make peace.

Helena. With all my heart. [*They are both moved.*]

Sonia. Has papa gone to bed?

Helena. No, he is sitting up in the drawing-room. Heaven knows what reason you and I had for not speaking to each other for weeks. [*Sees the open sideboard.*] Who left the sideboard open?

Sonia. Dr. Astroff has just had supper.

Helena. There is some wine. Let us seal our friendship.

Sonia. Yes, let us.

Helena. Out of one glass. [*She fills a wine-glass.*] So, we are friends, are we?

Sonia. Yes. [*They drink and kiss each other.*] I have long wanted to make friends, but somehow, I was ashamed to. [*She weeps.*]

Helena. Why are you crying?

Sonia. I don't know. It is nothing.

Helena. There, there, don't cry. [*She weeps.*] Silly! Now I am crying too. [*A pause.*] You are angry with me because I seem to have married your father for his money, but don't believe the gossip you hear. I swear to you I married him for love. I was fascinated by his fame and learning. I know now that it was not real love, but it seemed real at the time. I am innocent, and yet your clever, suspicious eyes have been punishing me for an imaginary crime ever since my marriage.

Sonia. Peace, peace! Let us forget the past.

Helena. You must not look so at people. It is not becoming to you. You must trust people, or life becomes impossible.

Sonia. Tell me truly, as a friend, are you happy?

Helena. Truly, no.

Sonia. I knew it. One more question: do you wish your husband were young?

Helena. What a child you are! Of course I do. Go on, ask something else.

Sonia. Do you like the doctor?

Helena. Yes, very much indeed.

Sonia. [*Laughing.*] I have a stupid face, haven't I? He has just gone out, and his voice is still in my ears; I hear his step; I see his face in the dark window. Let me say all I have in my heart! But no, I cannot speak of it so loudly. I am ashamed. Come to my room and let me tell you there. I seem foolish to you, don't I? Talk to me of him.

Helena. What can I say?

Sonia. He is clever. He can do everything. He can cure the sick, and plant woods.

Helena. It is not a question of medicine and woods, my dear, he is a man of genius. Do you know what that means? It means he is brave, profound, and of clear insight. He plants a tree and his mind travels a thousand years into the future, and he sees visions of the happiness of the human race. People like him are rare and should be loved. What if he does drink and act roughly at times? A man of genius cannot be a saint in Russia. There he lives, cut off from the world by cold and storm and endless roads of bottomless mud, surrounded by a rough people who are crushed by poverty and disease, his life one continuous struggle, with never a day's respite; how can a man live like that for forty years and keep himself sober and unspotted? [*Kissing* SONIA.] I wish you happiness with all my heart; you deserve it. [*She gets up.*] As for me, I am a worthless, futile woman. I have always been futile; in music, in love, in my husband's house—in a word, in everything. When you come to think of it, Sonia, I am really very, very unhappy. [*Walks excitedly up and down.*] Happiness can never exist for me in this world. Never. Why do you laugh?

Sonia. [*Laughing and covering her face with her hands.*] I am so happy, so happy!

Helena. I want to hear music. I might play a little.

Sonia. Oh, do, do! [*She embraces her.*] I could not possibly go to sleep now. Do play!

Helena. Yes, I will. Your father is still awake. Music irritates him when he is ill, but if he says I may, then I shall play a little. Go, Sonia, and ask him.

Sonia. Very well.

[*She goes out. The* WATCHMAN'S *rattle is heard in the garden.*]

Helena. It is long since I have heard music. And now, I shall sit and play, and weep like a fool. [*Speaking out of the window.*] Is that you rattling out there, Ephim?

Voice of the Watchman. It is I.

Helena. Don't make such a noise. Your master is ill.

Voice of the Watchman. I am going away this minute. [*Whistles a tune.*]

Sonia. [*Comes back.*] He says, no.

THE CURTAIN FALLS

ACT THIRD

The drawing-room of SEREBRAKOFF'S *house. There are three doors: one to the right, one to the left, and one in the center of the room.* VOITSKI *and* SONIA *are sitting down.* HELENA *is walking up and down, absorbed in thought.*

Voitski. We were asked by the professor to be here at one o'clock. [*Looks at his watch.*] It is now a quarter to one. It seems he has some communication to make to the world.

Helena. Probably a matter of business.

Voitski. He never had any business. He writes twaddle, grumbles, and eats his heart out with jealousy; that's all he does.

Sonia. [*Reproachfully.*] Uncle!

Voitski. All right. I beg your pardon. [*He points to* HELENA.] Look at her. Wandering up and down from sheer idleness. A sweet picture, really.

Helena. I wonder you are not bored, droning on in the same key from morning till night. [*Despairingly.*] I am dying of this tedium. What shall I do?

Sonia. [*Shrugging her shoulders.*] There is plenty to do if you would.

Helena. For instance?

Sonia. You could help run this place, teach the children, care for the sick—isn't that enough? Before you and papa came, Uncle Vanya and I used to go to market ourselves to deal in flour.

Helena. I don't know anything about such things, and besides, they don't interest me. It is only in novels that women go out and teach and heal the peasants; how can I suddenly begin to do it?

Sonia. How can you live here and not do it? Wait awhile, you will get used to it all. [*Embraces her.*] Don't be sad, dearest. [*Laughing.*] You feel miserable and restless, and can't seem to fit into this life, and your restlessness is catching. Look at Uncle Vanya, he does nothing now but haunt you like a shadow, and I have left my work today to come here and talk with you. I am getting lazy, and don't want to go on with it. Dr. Astroff hardly ever used to come here; it was all we could do to persuade him to visit us once a month, and now he has abandoned his forestry and his practice, and comes every day. You must be a witch.

Voitski. Why should you languish here? Come, my dearest, my beauty, be sensible! The blood of a nixie runs in your veins. Oh, won't you let yourself be one? Give your nature the reins for once in your life; fall head over ears in love with some other water sprite and plunge down head first into a deep pool, so that the Herr Professor and all of us may have our hands free again.

Helena. [*Angrily.*] Leave me alone! How cruel you are! [*She tries to go out.*]

Voitski. [*Preventing her.*] There, there, my beauty, I apologize. [*He kisses her hand.*] Forgive me.

Helena. Confess that you would try the patience of an angel.

Voitski. As a peace offering I am going to fetch some flowers which I picked for you this morning: some autumn roses, beautiful, sorrowful roses. [*He goes out.*]

Sonia. Autumn roses, beautiful, sorrowful roses!

[*She and* HELENA *stand looking out of the window.*]

Helena. September already! How shall we live through the long winter here? [*A pause.*] Where is the doctor?

Sonia. He is writing in Uncle Vanya's room. I am glad Uncle Vanya has gone out, I want to talk to you about something.

Helena. About what?

Sonia. About what?

[*She lays her head on* HELENA'S *breast.*]

Helena. [*Stroking her hair.*] There, there, that will do. Don't, Sonia.

Sonia. I am ugly!

Helena. You have lovely hair.

Sonia. Don't say that! [*She turns to look at herself in the glass.*] No, when a woman is ugly they always say she has beautiful hair or eyes. I have loved him now for six years; I have loved him more than one loves one's mother. I seem to hear him beside me every moment of the day. I feel the pressure of his hand on mine. If I look up, I seem to see him coming, and as you see, I run to you to talk of him. He is here every day now, but he never looks at me, he does not notice my presence. It is agony. I have absolutely no hope, no, no hope. Oh, my God! Give me strength to endure. I prayed all last night. I often go up to him and speak to him and look into his eyes. My pride is gone. I am not mistress of myself. Yesterday I told Uncle Vanya. I couldn't control myself, and all the servants know it. Every one knows that I love him.

Helena. Does he?

Sonia. No, he never notices me.

Helena. [*Thoughtfully.*] He is a strange man. Listen, Sonia, will you allow me to speak to him? I shall be careful, only hint. [*A pause.*] Really, to be in uncertainty all these years! Let me do it!

[SONIA *nods an affirmative.*]

Helena. Splendid! It will be easy to find out whether he loves you or not. Don't be ashamed, sweetheart, don't worry. I shall be careful; he will not notice a thing. We only want to find out whether it is yes or no, don't we? [*A pause.*] And if it is no, then he must keep away from here, is that so?

[SONIA *nods.*]

Helena. It will be easier not to see him any more. We won't put off the examination an instant. He said he had a sketch to show me. Go and tell him at once that I want to see him.

Sonia. [*In great excitement.*] Will you tell me the whole truth?

Helena. Of course I will. I am sure that no matter what it is, it will be easier for you to bear than this uncertainty. Trust to me, dearest.

Sonia. Yes, yes. I shall say that you want to see his sketch. [*She starts out, but stops near the door and looks back.*] No, it is better not to know—and yet—there may be hope.

Helena. What do you say?

Sonia. Nothing. [*She goes out.*]

Helena. [*Alone.*] There is no greater sorrow than to know another's secret when you cannot help them. [*In deep thought.*] He is obviously not in love with her, but why shouldn't he marry her? She is not pretty, but she is so clever and pure and good, she would make a splendid wife for a country doctor of his years. [*A pause.*] I can understand how the poor child feels. She lives here in this desperate loneliness with no one around her except these colorless shadows that go mooning about talking nonsense and knowing nothing except that they eat, drink, and sleep. Among them appears from time to time this Dr. Astroff, so different, so handsome, so interesting, so charming. It is like seeing the moon rise on a dark night. Oh, to surrender oneself to his embrace! To lose oneself in his arms! I am a little in love with him myself! Yes, I am lonely without him, and when I think of him I smile. That Uncle Vanya says I have the blood of a nixie in my veins: "Give rein to your nature for once in your life!" Perhaps it is right that I should. Oh, to be free as a bird, to fly away from all your sleepy faces and your talk and forget that you have existed at all! But I am a coward, I am afraid; my conscience torments me. He comes here every day now. I can guess why, and feel guilty already; I should like to fall on my knees at Sonia's feet and beg her forgiveness, and weep.

[ASTROFF *comes in carrying a portfolio.*]

Astroff. How do you do? [*Shakes hands with her.*] Do you want to see my sketch?

Helena. Yes, you promised to show me

what you had been doing. Have you time now?

Astroff. Of course I have!

[*He lays the portfolio on the table, takes out the sketch and fastens it to the table with thumbtacks.*]

Astroff. Where were you born?

Helena. [*Helping him.*] In St. Petersburg.

Astroff. And educated?

Helena. At the Conservatory there.

Astroff. You don't find this life very interesting, I dare say?

Helena. Oh, why not? It is true I don't know the country very well, but I have read a great deal about it.

Astroff. I have my own desk there in Ivan's room. When I am absolutely too exhausted to go on I drop everything and rush over here to forget myself in this work for an hour or two. Ivan and Miss Sonia sit rattling at their counting-boards, the cricket chirps, and I sit beside them and paint, feeling warm and peaceful. But I don't permit myself this luxury very often, only once a month. [*Pointing to the picture.*] Look there! That is a map of our country as it was fifty years ago. The green tints, both dark and light, represent forests. Half the map, as you see, is covered with it. Where the green is striped with red the forests were inhabited by elk and wild goats. Here on this lake lived great flocks of swans and geese and ducks; as the old men say, there was a power of birds of every kind. Now they have vanished like a cloud. Beside the hamlets and villages, you see, I have dotted down here and there the various settlements, farms, hermit's caves, and water-mills. This country carried a great many cattle and horses, as you can see by the quantity of blue paint. For instance, see how thickly it lies in this part; there were great herds of them here, an average of three horses to every house. [*A pause.*] Now, look lower down. This is the country as it was twenty-five years ago. Only a third of the map is green now with forests. There are no goats left and no elk. The blue paint is lighter, and so on, and so on. Now we come to the third part; our country as it appears today. We still see spots of green, but not much. The elk, the swans, the black-cock have disappeared. It is, on the whole, the picture of a regular and slow decline which it will evidently only take about ten or fifteen more years to complete. You may perhaps object that it is the march of progress, that the old order must give place to the new, and you might be right if roads had been run through these ruined woods, or if factories and schools had taken their place. The people then would have become better educated and healthier and richer, but as it is, we have nothing of the sort. We have the same swamps and mosquitoes; the same disease and want; the typhoid, the diphtheria, the burning villages. We are confronted by the degradation of our country, brought on by the fierce struggle for existence of the human race. It is the consequence of the ignorance and unconsciousness of starving, shivering, sick humanity that, to save its children, instinctively snatches at everything that can warm it and still its hunger. So it destroys everything it can lay its hands on, without a thought for the morrow. And almost everything has gone, and nothing has been created to take its place. [*Coldly.*] But I see by your face that I am not interesting you.

Helena. I know so little about such things!

Astroff. There is nothing to know. It simply isn't interesting, that's all.

Helena. Frankly, my thoughts were elsewhere. Forgive me! I want to submit you to a little examination, but I am embarrassed and don't know how to begin.

Astroff. An examination?

Helena. Yes, but quite an innocent one. Sit down. [*They sit down.*] It is about a certain young girl I know. Let us discuss it like honest people, like friends, and then forget what has passed between us, shall we?

Astroff. Very well.

Helena. It is about my step-daughter, Sonia. Do you like her?

Astroff. Yes, I respect her.

Helena. Do you like her—as a woman?

Astroff. [*Slowly.*] No.

Helena. One more word, and that will be the last. You have not noticed anything?

Astroff. No, nothing.

Helena. [*Taking his hand.*] You do not love her. I see that in your eyes. She is suffering. You must realize that, and not come here any more.

Astroff. My sun has set, yes, and then I haven't the time. [*Shrugging his shoulders.*] Where shall I find time for such things?

[*He is embarrassed.*]

Helena. Bah! What an unpleasant conversation! I am as out of breath as if I had been running three miles uphill. Thank heaven, that is over! Now let us forget everything as if nothing had been said. You are sensible. You understand. [*A pause.*] I am actually blushing.

Astroff. If you had spoken a month ago I might perhaps have considered it, but now—[*He shrugs his shoulders.*] Of course, if she is suffering—but I cannot understand why you had to put me through this examination.

[*He searches her face with his eyes, and shakes his finger at her.*] Oho, you are wily!

Helena. What does this mean?

Astroff. [*Laughing.*] You are a wily one! I admit that Sonia is suffering, but what does this examination of yours mean? [*He prevents her from retorting, and goes on quickly.*] Please don't put on such a look of surprise; you know perfectly well why I come here every day. Yes, you know perfectly why and for whose sake I come! Oh, my sweet tigress! don't look at me in that way; I am an old bird!

Helena. [*Perplexed.*] A tigress? I don't understand you.

Astroff. Beautiful, sleek tigress, you must have your victims! For a whole month I have done nothing but seek you eagerly. I have thrown over everything for you, and you love to see it. Now then, I am sure you knew all this without putting me through your examination. [*Crossing his arms and bowing his head.*] I surrender. Here you have me—now, eat me.

Helena. You have gone mad!

Astroff. You are afraid!

Helena. I am a better and stronger woman than you think me. Good-bye. [*She tries to leave the room.*]

Astroff. Why good-bye? Don't say good-bye, don't waste words. Oh, how lovely you are—what hands! [*He kisses her hands.*]

Helena. Enough of this! [*She frees her hands.*] Leave the room! You have forgotten yourself.

Astroff. Tell me, tell me, where can we meet tomorrow? [*He puts his arm around her.*] Don't you see that we must meet, that it is inevitable?

[*He kisses her.* VOITSKI *comes in carrying a bunch of roses; and stops in the doorway.*]

Helena. [*Without seeing* VOITSKI.] Have pity! Leave me. [*Lays her head on* ASTROFF'S *shoulder.*] Don't!

[*She tries to break away from him.*]

Astroff. [*Holding her by the waist.*] Be in the forest tomorrow at two o'clock. Will you? Will you?

Helena. [*Sees* VOITSKI.] Let me go! [*Goes to the window deeply embarrassed.*] This is appalling!

Voitski. [*Throws the flowers on a chair, and speaks in great excitement, wiping his face with his handkerchief.*] Nothing—yes, yes, nothing.

Astroff. The weather is fine today, my dear Ivan; the morning was overcast and looked like rain, but now the sun is shining again. Honestly, we have had a very fine autumn, and the wheat is looking fairly well. [*Puts his map back into the portfolio.*] But the days are growing short. [*Exit.*]

Helena. [*Goes quickly up to* VOITSKI.] You must do your best; you must use all your power to get my husband and myself away from here today! Do you hear? I say, this very day!

Voitski. [*Wiping his face.*] Oh! Ah! Oh! All right! I—Helena, I saw everything!

Helena. [*In great agitation.*] Do you hear me? I must leave here this very day

[SEREBRAKOFF, SONIA, MARINA, *and* TELEGIN *come in.*]

Telegin. I am not very well myself, your Excellency. I have been limping for two days, and my head——

Serebrakoff. Where are the others? I hate this house. It is a regular labyrinth. Every one is always scattered through the twenty-six enormous rooms; one never can find a soul. [*Rings.*] Ask my wife and Madame Voitskaya to come here!

Helena. I am here already.

Serebrakoff. Please, all of you, sit down.

Sonia. [*Goes up to* HELENA *and asks anxiously.*] What did he say?

Helena. I'll tell you later.

Sonia. You are moved. [*Looking quickly and inquiringly into her face.*] I understand; he said he would not come here any more. [*A pause.*] Tell me, did he? [HELENA *nods.*]

Serebrakoff. [*To* TELEGIN.] One can, after all, become reconciled to being an invalid, but not to this country life. The ways of it stick in my throat and I feel exactly as if I had been whirled off the earth and landed on a strange planet. Please be seated, ladies and gentlemen. Sonia! [SONIA *does not hear. She is standing with her head bowed sadly forward on her breast.*] Sonia! [*A pause.*] She does not hear me. [*To* MARINA.] Sit down too, nurse. [MARINA *sits down and begins to knit her stocking.*] I crave your indulgence, ladies and gentlemen; hang your ears, if I may say so, on the peg of attention. [*He laughs.*]

Voitski. [*Agitated.*] Perhaps you do not need me—may I be excused?

Serebrakoff. No, you are needed now more than any one.

Voitski. What is it you want of me?

Serebrakoff. You—but what are you angry about? If it is anything I have done, I ask you to forgive me.

Voitski. Oh, drop that and come to business; what do you want?

[MME. VOITSKAYA *comes in.*]

Serebrakoff. Here is mother. Ladies and gentlemen, I shall begin. I have asked you to assemble here, my friends, in order to discuss a very important matter. I want to ask you for your assistance and advice, and knowing your unfailing amiability I think I can count on both. I am a book-worm and a scholar, and am unfamiliar with practical affairs. I cannot, I find, dispense with the help of well-informed people such as you, Ivan, and you, Telegin, and you, mother. The truth is, *manet omnes una nox,* that is to say, our lives are in the hands of God, and as I am old and ill, I realize that the time has come for me to dispose of my property in regard to the interests of my family. My life is nearly over, and I am not thinking of myself, but I have a young wife and daughter. [*A pause.*] I cannot continue to live in the country; we were not made for country life, and yet we cannot afford to live in town on the income derived from this estate. We might sell the woods, but that would be an expedient we could not resort to every year. We must find some means of guaranteeing to ourselves a certain more or less fixed yearly income. With this object in view, a plan has occurred to me which I now have the honor of presenting to you for your consideration. I shall only give you a rough outline, avoiding all details. Our estate does not pay on an average more than two per cent on the money invested in it. I propose to sell it. If we then invest our capital in bonds, it will earn us four to five per cent, and we should probably have a surplus over of several thousand roubles, with which we could buy a summer cottage in Finland——

Voitski. Hold on! Repeat what you just said; I don't think I heard you quite right.

Serebrakoff. I said we would invest the money in bonds and buy a cottage in Finland with the surplus.

Voitski. No, not Finland—you said something else.

Serebrakoff. I propose to sell this place.

Voitski. Aha! That was it! So you are going to sell the place? Splendid. The idea is a rich one. And what do you propose to do with my old mother and me and with Sonia here?

Serebrakoff. That will be decided in due time. We can't do everything at once.

Voitski. Wait! It is clear that until this moment I have never had a grain of sense in my head. I have always been stupid enough to think that the estate belonged to Sonia. My father bought it as a wedding present for my sister, and I foolishly imagined that as our laws were made for Russians and not Turks, my sister's estate would come down to her child.

Serebrakoff. Of course it is Sonia's. Has any one denied it? I don't want to sell it without Sonia's consent; on the contrary, what I am doing is for Sonia's good.

Voitski. This is absolutely incomprehensible. Either I have gone mad or—or——

Mme. Voitskaya. Jean, don't contradict Alexander. Trust to him; he knows better than we do what is right and what is wrong.

Voitski. I shan't. Give me some water. [*He drinks.*] Go ahead! Say anything you please—anything!

Serebrakoff. I can't imagine why you are so upset. I don't pretend that my scheme is an ideal one, and if you all object to it I shall not insist. [*A pause.*]

Telegin. [*With embarrassment.*] I not only nourish feelings of respect toward learning, your Excellency, but I am also drawn to it by family ties. My brother Gregory's wife's brother, whom you may know; his name is Constantine Lakedemonoff, and he used to be a magistrate——

Voitski. Stop, Waffles. This is business; wait a bit, we will talk of that later. [*To* SEREBRAKOFF.] There now, ask him what he thinks; this estate was bought from his uncle.

Serebrakoff. Ah! Why should I ask questions? What good would it do?

Voitski. The price was ninety-five thousand roubles. My father paid seventy and left a debt of twenty-five. Now listen! This place could never have been bought had I not renounced my inheritance in favor of my sister, whom I deeply loved—and what is more, I worked for ten years like an ox, and paid off the debt.

Serebrakoff. I regret ever having started this conversation.

Voitski. Thanks entirely to my own personal efforts, the place is entirely clear of debts, and now, when I have grown old, you want to throw me out, neck and crop!

Serebrakoff. I can't imagine what you are driving at.

Voitski. For twenty-five years I have managed this place, and have sent you the returns from it like the most honest of servants, and you have never given me one single word of thanks for my work, not one—neither in my youth nor now. You allowed me a meager salary of five hundred roubles a year, a beggar's pittance, and have never even thought of adding a rouble to it.

Serebrakoff. What did I know about such things, Ivan? I am not a practical man and don't understand them. You might have helped yourself to all you wanted.

Voitski. Yes, why did I not steal? Don't you all despise me for not stealing, when it would have been only justice? And I should not now have been a beggar!

Mme. Voitskaya. [*Sternly.*] Jean!

Telegin. [*Agitated.*] Vanya, old man, don't talk in that way. Why spoil such pleasant relations? [*He embraces him.*] Do stop!

Voitski. For twenty-five years I have been sitting here with my mother like a mole in a burrow. Our every thought and hope was yours and yours only. By day we talked with pride of you and your work, and spoke your name with veneration; our nights we wasted reading the books and papers which my soul now loathes.

Telegin. Don't, Vanya, don't. I can't stand it.

Serebrakoff. [*Wrathfully.*] What under heaven do you want, anyway?

Voitski. We used to think of you as almost superhuman, but now the scales have fallen from my eyes and I see you as you are! You write on art without knowing anything about it. Those books of yours which I used to admire are not worth one copper kopeck. You are a hoax!

Serebrakoff. Can't any one make him stop? I am going!

Helena. Ivan, I command you to stop this instant! Do you hear me?

Voitski. I refuse! [SEREBRAKOFF *tries to get out of the room, but* VOITSKI *bars the way.*] Wait! I have not done yet! You have wrecked my life. I have never lived. My best years have gone for nothing, have been ruined, thanks to you. You are my most bitter enemy!

Telegin. I can't stand it; I can't stand it. I am going.

[*He goes out in great excitement.*]

Serebrakoff. But what do you want? What earthly right have you to use such language to me? Ruination! If this estate is yours, then take it, and let me be ruined!

Helena. I am going away out of this hell this minute. [*Shrieks.*] This is too much!

Voitski. My life has been a failure. I am clever and brave and strong. If I had lived a normal life I might have become another Schopenhauer or Dostoieffski. I am losing my head! I am going crazy! Mother, I am in despair! Oh, mother!

Mme. Voitskaya. [*Sternly.*] Listen, Alexander!

[SONIA *falls on her knees beside the* NURSE *and nestles against her.*]

Sonia. Oh, nurse, nurse!

Voitski. Mother! What shall I do? But no, don't speak! I know what to do. [*To* SEREBRAKOFF.] And you will understand me!

[*He goes out through the door in the center of the room and* MME. VOITSKAYA *follows him.*]

Serebrakoff. Tell me, what on earth is the matter? Take this lunatic out of my sight! I cannot possibly live under the same roof with him. His room [*He points to the center door.*] is almost next door to mine. Let him take himself off into the village or into the wing of the house, or I shall leave here at once. I cannot stay in the same house with him.

Helena. [*To her husband.*] We are leaving today; we must get ready at once for our departure.

Serebrakoff. What a perfectly dreadful man!

Sonia. [*On her knees beside the* NURSE *and turning to her father. She speaks with emotion.*] You must be kind to us, papa. Uncle Vanya and I are so unhappy! [*Controlling her despair.*] Have pity on us. Remember how Uncle Vanya and Granny used to copy and translate your books for you every night —every, every night. Uncle Vanya has toiled without rest; he would never spend a penny on us, we sent it all to you. We have not eaten the bread of idleness. I am not saying this as I should like to, but you must understand us, papa, you must be merciful to us.

Helena. [*Very excited, to her husband.*] For heaven's sake, Alexander, go and have a talk with him—explain!

Serebrakoff. Very well, I shall have a talk with him, but I won't apologize for a thing. I am not angry with him, but you must confess that his behavior has been strange, to say the least. Excuse me, I shall go to him.

[*He goes out through the center door.*]

Helena. Be gentle with him; try to quiet him. [*She follows him out.*]

Sonia. [*Nestling nearer to* MARINA.] Nurse, oh, nurse!

Marina. It's all right, my baby. When the geese have cackled they will be still again. First they cackle and then they stop.

Sonia. Nurse!

Marina. You are trembling all over, as if you were freezing. There, there, little orphan baby, God is merciful. A little linden-tea, and it will all pass away. Don't cry, my sweetest. [*Looking angrily at the door in the center of the room.*] See, the geese have all gone now. The devil take them!

[*A shot is heard.* HELENA *screams behind the scenes.* SONIA *shudders.*]

Marina. Bang! What's that?

Serebrakoff. [*Comes in reeling with terror.*] Hold him! hold him! He has gone mad!

[HELENA *and* VOITSKI *are seen struggling in the doorway.*]

Helena. [*Trying to wrest the revolver from him.*] Give it to me; give it to me, I tell you!

Voitski. Let me go, Helena, let me go! [*He frees himself and rushes in, looking everywhere for* SEREBRAKOFF.] Where is he? Ah, there he is! [*He shoots at him. A pause.*] I didn't get him? I missed again? [*Furiously.*] Damnation! Damnation! To hell with him!

[*He flings the revolver on the floor, and drops helpless into a chair.* SEREBRAKOFF *stands as if stupefied.* HELENA *leans against the wall, almost fainting.*]

Helena. Take me away! Take me away! I can't stay here—I can't!

Voitski. [*In despair.*] Oh, what shall I do? What shall I do?

Sonia. [*Softly.*] Oh, nurse, nurse!

THE CURTAIN FALLS

ACT FOURTH

VOITSKI'S *bedroom, which is also his office. A table stands near the window; on it are ledgers, letter scales, and papers of every description. Near by stands a smaller table belonging to* ASTROFF, *with his paints and drawing materials. On the wall hangs a cage containing a starling. There is also a map of Africa on the wall, obviously of no use to anybody. There is a large sofa covered with buckram. A door to the left leads into an inner room; one to the right leads into the front hall, and before this door lies a mat for the peasants with their muddy boots to stand on. It is an autumn evening. The silence is profound.*

[TELEGIN *and* MARINA *are sitting facing one another, winding wool.*]

Telegin. Be quick, Marina, or we shall be called away to say good-bye before you have finished. The carriage has already been ordered.

Marina. [*Trying to wind more quickly.*] I am a little tired.

Telegin. They are going to Kharkoff to live.

Marina. They do well to go.

Telegin. They have been frightened. The professor's wife won't stay here an hour longer. "If we are going at all, let's be off," says she, "we shall go to Kharkoff and look about us, and then we can send for our things." They are traveling light. It seems, Marina, that fate has decreed for them not to live here.

Marina. And quite rightly. What a storm they have just raised! It was shameful!

Telegin. It was indeed. The scene was worthy of the brush of Aibazofski.

Marina. I wish I'd never laid eyes on them. [*A pause.*] Now we shall have things as they were again: tea at eight, dinner at one, and supper in the evening; everything in order as decent folks, as Christians like to have it. [*Sighs.*] It is a long time since I have eaten noodles.

Telegin. Yes, we haven't had noodles for ages. [*A pause.*] Not for ages. As I was going through the village this morning, Marina, one of the shop-keepers called after me, "Hi! you hanger-on!" I felt it bitterly.

Marina. Don't pay the least attention to them, master; we are all dependents on God. You and Sonia and all of us. Every one must work, no one can sit idle. Where is Sonia?

Telegin. In the garden with the doctor, looking for Ivan. They fear he may lay violent hands on himself.

Marina. Where is his pistol?

Telegin. [*Whispers.*] I hid it in the cellar.

[VOITSKI *and* ASTROFF *come in.*]

Voitski. Leave me alone! [*To* MARINA *and* TELEGIN.] Go away! Go away and leave me to myself, if but for an hour. I won't have you watching me like this!

Telegin. Yes, yes, Vanya.

[*He goes out on tiptoe.*]

Marina. The gander cackles; ho! ho! ho!

[*She gathers up her wool and goes out.*]

Voitski. Leave me by myself!

Astroff. I would, with the greatest pleasure. I ought to have gone long ago, but I shan't leave you until you have returned what you took from me.

Voitski. I took nothing from you.

Astroff. I am not jesting, don't detain me, I really must go.

Voitski. I took nothing of yours.

Astroff. You didn't? Very well, I shall have to wait a little longer, and then you will have to forgive me if I resort to force. We shall have to bind you and search you. I mean what I say.

Voitski. Do as you please. [*A pause.*] Oh, to make such a fool of myself! To shoot twice and miss him both times! I shall never forgive myself.

Astroff. When the impulse came to shoot, it would have been as well had you put a bullet through your own head.

Voitski. [*Shrugging his shoulders.*] Strange! I attempted murder, and am not going to be arrested or brought to trial. That means they think me mad. [*With a bitter laugh.*] Me! I am mad, and those who hide their worthlessness, their dullness, their crying heartlessness behind a professor's mask, are sane! Those who marry old men and then deceive them under the noses of all, are sane! I saw you kiss her; I saw you in each other's arms!

Astroff. Yes, sir, I did kiss her; so there.

[*He puts his thumb to his nose.*]

Voitski. [*His eyes on the door.*] No, it is the earth that is mad, because she still bears us on her breast.

Astroff. That is nonsense.

Voitski. Well? Am I not a madman, and therefore irresponsible? Haven't I the right to talk nonsense?

Astroff. This is a farce! You are not mad; you are simply a ridiculous fool. I used to think every fool was out of his senses, but now I see that lack of sense is a man's normal state, and you are perfectly normal.

Voitski. [*Covers his face with his hands.*] Oh! If you knew how ashamed I am! These piercing pangs of shame are like nothing on earth. [*In an agonized voice.*] I can't endure them! [*He leans against the table.*] What can I do? What can I do?

Astroff. Nothing.

Voitski. You must tell me something! Oh, my God! I am forty-seven years old. I may live to sixty; I still have thirteen years before me; an eternity! How shall I be able to endure life for thirteen years? What shall I do? How can I fill them? Oh, don't you see? [*He presses* ASTROFF'S *hand convulsively.*] Don't you see, if only I could live the rest of my life in some new way! If I could only wake some still, bright morning and feel that life had begun again; that the past was forgotten and had vanished like smoke. [*He weeps.*] Oh, to begin life anew! Tell me, tell me how to begin.

Astroff. [*Crossly.*] What nonsense! What sort of a new life can you and I look forward to? We can have no hope.

Voitski. None?

Astroff. None. Of that I am convinced.

Voitski. Tell me what to do. [*He puts his hand to his heart.*] I feel such a burning pain here.

Astroff. [*Shouts angrily.*] Stop! [*Then, more gently.*] It may be that posterity, which will despise us for our blind and stupid lives, will find some road to happiness; but we—you and I—have but one hope, the hope that we may be visited by visions, perhaps by pleasant ones, as we lie resting in our graves. [*Sighing.*] Yes, brother, there were only two respectable, intelligent men in this county, you and I. Ten years or so of this life of ours, this miserable life, have sucked us under, and we have become as contemptible and petty as the rest. But don't try to talk me out of my purpose! Give me what you took from me, will you?

Voitski. I took nothing from you.

Astroff. You took a little bottle of morphine out of my medicine-case. [*A pause.*] Listen! If you are positively determined to make an end to yourself, go into the woods and shoot yourself there. Give up the morphine, or there will be a lot of talk and guesswork; people will think I gave it to you. I don't fancy having to perform a post-mortem on you. Do you think I should find it interesting?

[SONIA *comes in.*]

Voitski. Leave me alone.

Astroff. [*To* SONIA.] Sonia, your uncle has stolen a bottle of morphine out of my medicine-case and won't give it up. Tell him that his behavior is—well, unwise. I haven't time, I must be going.

Sonia. Uncle Vanya, did you take the morphine?

Astroff. Yes, he took it. [*A pause.*] I am absolutely sure.

Sonia. Give it up! Why do you want to frighten us? [*Tenderly.*] Give it up, Uncle Vanya! My misfortune is perhaps even greater than yours, but I am not plunged in despair. I endure my sorrow, and shall endure it until my life comes to a natural end. You must endure yours, too. [*A pause.*] Give it up! Dear, darling Uncle Vanya. Give it up! [*She weeps.*] You are so good, I am sure you will have pity on us and give it up. You must endure your sorrow, Uncle Vanya; you must endure it.

[VOITSKI *takes a bottle from the drawer of the table and hands it to* ASTROFF.]

Voitski. There it is! [*To* SONIA.] And now, we must get to work at once; we must do something, or else I shall not be able to endure it.

Sonia. Yes, yes, to work! As soon as we have seen them off we shall go to work. [*She nervously straightens out the papers on the table.*] Everything is in a muddle!

Astroff. [*Putting the bottle in his case, which he straps together.*] Now I can be off.

[HELENA *comes in.*]

Helena. Are you here, Ivan? We are starting in a moment. Go to Alexander, he wants to speak to you.

Sonia. Go, Uncle Vanya. [*She takes* VOITSKI's *arm.*] Come, you and papa must make peace; that is absolutely necessary.

[SONIA *and* VOITSKI *go out.*]

Helena. I am going away. [*She gives* ASTROFF *her hand.*] Good-bye.

Astroff. So soon?

Helena. The carriage is waiting.

Astroff. Good-bye.

Helena. You promised me you would go away yourself today.

Astroff. I have not forgotten. I am going at once. [*A pause.*] Were you frightened? Was it so terrible?

Helena. Yes.

Astroff. Couldn't you stay? Couldn't you? Tomorrow—in the forest——

Helena. No. It is all settled, and that is why I can look you so bravely in the face. Our departure is fixed. One thing I must ask of you: don't think too badly of me; I should like you to respect me.

Astroff. Ah! [*With an impatient gesture.*] Stay, I implore you! Confess that there is nothing for you to do in this world. You have no object in life; there is nothing to occupy your attention, and sooner or later your feelings must master you. It is inevitable. It would be better if it happened not in Kharkoff or in Kursk, but here, in nature's lap. It would then at least be poetical, even beautiful. Here you have the forests, the houses half in ruins that Turgenieff writes of.

Helena. How comical you are! I am angry with you and yet I shall always remember you with pleasure. You are interesting and original. You and I will never meet again, and so I shall tell you—why should I conceal it?—that I am just a little in love with you. Come, one more last pressure of our hands, and then let us part good friends. Let us not bear each other any ill will.

Astroff. [*Pressing her hand.*] Yes, go. [*Thoughtfully.*] You seem to be sincere and good, and yet there is something strangely disquieting about all your personality. No sooner did you arrive here with your husband than every one whom you found busy and actively creating something was forced to drop his work and give himself up for the whole summer to your husband's gout and yourself. You and he have infected us with your idleness. I have been swept off my feet; I have not put my hand to a thing for weeks, during which sickness has been running its course unchecked among the people, and the peasants have been pasturing their cattle in my woods and young plantations. Go where you will, you and your husband will always carry destruction in your train. I am joking of course, and yet I am strangely sure that had you stayed here we should have been overtaken by the most immense desolation. I would have gone to my ruin, and you—you would not have prospered. So go! È finita la commèdia!

Helena. [*Snatching a pencil off* ASTROFF'S *table, and hiding it with a quick movement.*] I shall take this pencil for memory!

Astroff. How strange it is. We meet, and then suddenly it seems that we must part forever. That is the way in this world. As long as we are alone, before Uncle Vanya comes in with a bouquet—allow me—to kiss you good-bye—may I? [*He kisses her on the cheek.*] So! Splendid!

Helena. I wish you every happiness. [*She glances about her.*] For once in my life, I shall! and scorn the consequences! [*She kisses him impetuously, and they quickly part.*] I must go.

Astroff. Yes, go. If the carriage is there, then start at once. [*They stand listening.*]

Astroff. È finita!

[VOITSKI, SEREBRAKOFF, MME. VOITSKAYA *with her book,* TELEGIN, *and* SONIA *come in.*]

Serebrakoff. [*To* VOITSKI.] Shame on him who bears malice for the past. I have gone through so much in the last few hours that I feel capable of writing a whole treatise on the conduct of life for the instruction of posterity. I gladly accept your apology, and myself ask your forgiveness.

[*He kisses* VOITSKI *three times.* HELENA *embraces* SONIA.]

Serebrakoff. [*Kissing* MME. VOITSKAYA'S *hand.*] Mother!

Mme. Voitskaya. [*Kissing him.*] Have your picture taken, Alexander, and send me one. You know how dear you are to me.

Telegin. Good-bye, your Excellency. Don't forget us.

Serebrakoff. [*Kissing his daughter.*] Good-bye, good-bye all. [*Shaking hands with* ASTROFF.] Many thanks for your pleasant company. I have a deep regard for your opinions and your enthusiasm, but let me, as an old man, give one word of advice at parting: do something, my friend! Work! Do something! [*They all bow.*] Good luck to you all.

[*He goes out followed by* MME. VOITSKAYA *and* SONIA.]

Voitski. [*Kissing* HELENA'S *hand fervently.*] Good-bye—forgive me. I shall never see you again!

Helena. [*Touched.*] Good-bye, dear boy.

[*She lightly kisses his head as he bends over her hand, and goes out.*]

Astroff. Tell them to bring my carriage around too, Waffles.

Telegin. All right, old man.

[ASTROFF *and* VOITSKI *are left behind alone.* ASTROFF *collects his paints and drawing materials on the table and packs them away in a box.*]

Astroff. Why don't you go to see them off?

Voitski. Let them go! I—I can't go out there. I feel too sad. I must go to work on something at once. To work! To work!

[*He rummages through his papers on the table. A pause. The tinkling of bells is heard as the horses trot away.*]

Astroff. They have gone! The professor, I suppose, is glad to go. He couldn't be tempted back now by a fortune.

[MARINA *comes in.*]

Marina. They have gone.

[*She sits down in an armchair and knits her stocking.*]

[SONIA *comes in wiping her eyes.*]

Sonia. They have gone. God be with them. [*To her uncle.*] And now, Uncle Vanya, let us do something!

Voitski. To work! To work!

Sonia. It is long, long, since you and I have sat together at this table. [*She lights a lamp on the table.*] No ink! [*She takes the inkstand to the cupboard and fills it from an inkbottle.*] How sad it is to see them go!

[MME. VOITSKAYA *comes slowly in.*]

Mme. Voitskaya. They have gone.

[*She sits down and at once becomes absorbed in her book.*]

[SONIA *sits down at the table and looks through an account book.*]

Sonia. First, Uncle Vanya, let us write up the accounts. They are in a dreadful state. Come, begin. You take one and I will take the other.

Voitski. In account with——

[*They sit silently writing.*]

Marina. [*Yawning.*] The sand-man has come.

Astroff. How still it is. Their pens scratch, the cricket sings; it is so warm and comfortable. I hate to go.

[*The tinkling of bells is heard.*]

Astroff. My carriage has come. There now remains but to say good-bye to you, my friends, and to my table here, and then—away!

[*He puts the map into the portfolio.*]

Marina. Don't hurry away; sit a little longer with us.

Astroff. Impossible.

Voitski. [*Writing.*] And carry forward from the old debt two seventy-five——

[WORKMAN *comes in.*]

Workman. Your carriage is waiting, sir.

Astroff. All right. [*He hands the* WORKMAN *his medicine-case, portfolio, and box.*] Look out, don't crush the portfolio!

Workman. Very well, sir. [*Exit.*]

Sonia. When shall we see you again?

Astroff. Hardly before next summer. Probably not this winter, though, of course, if anything should happen you will let me know. [*He shakes hands with them.*] Thank you for your kindness, for your hospitality, for everything! [*He goes up to* MARINA *and kisses her head.*] Good-bye, old nurse!

Marina. Are you going without your tea?

Astroff. I don't want any, nurse.

Marina. Won't you have a drop of vodka?

Astroff. [*Hesitatingly.*] Yes, I might.

[MARINA *goes out.*]

Astroff. [*After a pause.*] My off-wheeler has gone lame for some reason. I noticed it yesterday when Peter was taking him to water.

Voitski. You should have him re-shod.

Astroff. I shall have to go around by the blacksmith's on my way home. It can't be avoided. [*He stands looking up at the map of Africa hanging on the wall.*] I suppose it is roasting hot in Africa now.

Voitski. Yes, I suppose it is.

[MARINA *comes back carrying a tray on which are a glass of vodka and a piece of bread.*]

Marina. Help yourself. [ASTROFF *drinks.*]

Marina. To your good health! [*She bows deeply.*] Eat your bread with it.

Astroff. No, I like it so. And now, good-bye. [*To* MARINA.] You needn't come out to see me off, nurse.

[*He goes out.* SONIA *follows him with a candle to light him to the carriage.* MARINA *sits down in her armchair.*]

Voitski. [*Writing.*] On the 2d of February, twenty pounds of butter; on the 16th, twenty pounds of butter again. Buckwheat flour——

[*A pause. Bells are heard tinkling.*]

Marina. He has gone. [*A pause.*]

[SONIA *comes in and sets the candlestick on the table.*]

Sonia. He has gone.

Voitski. [*Adding and writing*]. Total, fifteen—twenty-five——

[SONIA *sits down and begins to write.*]

Marina. [*Yawning.*] Oh, ho! The Lord have mercy.

[TELEGIN *comes in on tiptoe, sits down near the door, and begins to tune his guitar.*]

Voitski. [*To* SONIA, *stroking her hair.*] Oh, my child, I am so miserable; if you only knew how miserable I am!

Sonia. What can we do? We must live our lives. [*A pause.*] Yes, we shall live, Uncle Vanya. We shall live through the long procession of days before us, and through the long evenings; we shall patiently bear the trials that fate imposes on us; we shall work for others without rest, both now and when we are old; and when our last hour comes we shall meet it humbly, and there, beyond the grave, we shall say that we have suffered and wept, that our life was bitter, and God will have pity on us. Ah, then, dear, dear Uncle, we shall see that bright and beautiful life; we shall rejoice and look back upon our sorrow here; a tender smile—and—we shall rest. I have faith, Uncle, fervent, passionate faith. [SONIA *kneels down before her uncle and lays her head on his hands. She speaks in a weary voice.*] We shall rest. [TELEGIN *plays softly on the guitar.*] We shall rest. We shall hear the angels. We shall see heaven shining like a jewel. We shall see all evil and all our pain sink away in the great compassion that shall enfold the world. Our life will be as peaceful and tender and sweet as a caress. I have faith; I have faith. [*She wipes away her tears.*] My poor, poor Uncle Vanya, you are crying! [*Weeping.*] You have never known what happiness was, but wait, Uncle Vanya, wait! We shall rest. [*She embraces him.*] We shall rest. [*The* WATCHMAN'S *rattle is heard in the garden;* TELEGIN *plays softly;* MME. VOITSKAYA *writes something on the margin of her pamphlet;* MARINA *knits her stocking.*] We shall rest.

THE CURTAIN SLOWLY FALLS

THE DREAM PLAY*

By

AUGUST STRINDBERG

Translated by EDWIN BJÖRKMAN

LIKE IBSEN, AUGUST STRINDBERG HAS cast the shadow of his genius athwart the modern theater. If the Ibsen shadow has receded with time, Strindberg's has advanced and, as many believe, will long continue to do so. Like Ibsen he first wrote for the theater of naturalism and later, far more significantly than Ibsen, he wrote for the theater of symbols. As a naturalist—that is, as a realist who observes life with scientific insight into its causal relations—Strindberg was more penetrating than Ibsen. He laid bare recesses of the mind that Ibsen left veiled. Conflicts which Ibsen presented as moral issues, Strindberg treated as the clashes of mental states which were as complex as the experience and the heritage of the individuals involved.

His daring self-revelation in the novel form, especially in the two parts of *Marriage* and the three parts of *The Bondwoman's Son,* made his name anathema to his own countrymen, but gained him in Paris a cordial welcome to the newly formed circle of the naturalists. His play *The Father* was published in translation with a preface by Zola in 1887, just as Antoine was opening his *Théâter-Libre*. He was inspired to write for Antoine's theater the plays *Lady Julie, Comrades, Creditors,* and *The Stronger*. And so, as a chief apostle of the naturalist movement, he took his place among the foremost dramatists of our age. Except as the author of these early plays, he remains almost unknown on the English-speaking stage. These have won him a scant popularity and have left him an enigma. His vitalizing characterization and the bold experiments in play structure of his later period have, however, profoundly influenced such modernists as O'Neill and they therefore deserve more general study than they have received. His Anglo-Saxon readers have been inclined to rule him out of the theater as a morbid and unamiable writer, labeling him a woman-hater, a neurotic, a misanthrope, a disorderly liver, a visionary, and a sensationalist. On the contrary, he was more than orderly, and was tragically devoted to women. He was a clear-minded observer, and except for a few years of almost insane preoccupation with futile scientific experiments, his intellectual life was more than usually self-possessed. He was an ardent but inept reformer, who had to create a Utopia in which only he himself was at home. To many, however, he still remains repulsively frank and egoistic in his reactions to love and life.

His immense influence upon dramatic style and form is due to the focus of his intense and analytical mind upon the springs of action, and particularly upon the inner reality of thought and impulse, both conscious and unconscious. His has been called "the shadow drama of the soul." It is his relentless disclosure of deeply hidden motives—happily hidden, perhaps—that keeps his work still abreast of our psychologizing dramatists. At this point, chiefly, he took exception to Ibsen, whose insistence upon moral reality in character and action blinded him to forces of the mind that seemed to Strindberg still more decisive. Ibsen, for instance, on moral principles, demanded social and moral equality for woman, and made the independent woman his protagonist. Strindberg found this attitude toward woman revoltingly sentimental. He, on the other hand, invoked biological and psychological facts as well as ethics and logic, and in this light revealed woman as needing no such aid. He saw in her mother-mentality a terrible force, cosmic and insatiable, against which man, as bread-winner, was at a hopeless, tragic disadvantage. Even her charm, to which Strindberg owned himself a slave, made her doubly dangerous. The revolt of man against the domination of the creation instinct in woman became as prominent in Strindberg's work for the stage as the reverse situation in Ibsen's.

This belief was by no means academic. Strindberg had seen his quiet, cultured father dominated by a servant-girl wife, his own mother, to whom he also was passionately devoted. Against this wife and mother tyranny he waged a life-long battle. He met it again in his wives, and made it the basic motive in many of his feminine characters. This attitude was not, however, one of personal dislike. So long as woman remained in her own sphere and did not offer rivalry or domination in man's, Strindberg professed to admire and even to worship her. He was ready to grant her full equality before the law. He even advocated votes for women. It was intellectual and spiritual domination that he protested against. In both respects he believed woman man's inferior. Her aggressive invasion of man's own vocations and mental life he regarded as a menace to the race. She should remain the home-maker. When she assumed a larger influence, the horrors set forth in *The Father* might be expected; the husband might then become merely an instrument to help her fulfil her racial purpose, to be cast off or, perhaps, driven insane. Biassed and lacking in a sense of humor as Strindberg seems to have been when dealing with this aspect of the sex war, he has, nevertheless, enlisted a host of followers from Shaw to O'Neill.

Although his contributions to the naturalist theater were of first importance, those he made to the more recent theater of varied symbolic expression have made him a living influence in the theater of today and tomorrow. The mystic was always latent in him. In his last Stockholm period the writings of Maeterlinck and Swedenborg aroused this dormant side of his nature. Beginning with *To Damascus* (1898) and continuing through *The Dream Play* and *The Spook Sonata,* he set on foot those tendencies that have disrupted the old dramatic forms and are now known as expressionistic. This much debated and vague term, first used by the *Sturm* school of German artists and literary revolters of about 1915, has come to be applied in the theater to all those methods, whether of playwriting or of staging, which aim to give expression by means of stage symbols to a state of mind or an emotion. For our present purpose it suffices to consider the dream as such a state. To make concrete in the theater the dream consciousness of the writer or of his characters is to be expressionistic in one sense of that term. The old surfaces of life are broken as in a dream and the photographic method of representation is frankly abandoned. Symbol personages walk abroad regardless of time or the three dimensions. Personalities break into their component aspects, each becoming symbolic rather than individual.

The Dream Play affords a pleasant example of this method, which has obviously influenced recent American writers like O'Neill, as well as writers for the German and Russian theaters. Strindberg described the process in a memorandum prefixed to his play: "In this *Dream Play,* as in the previous *To Damascus,* the author has sought to imitate the disconnected, but apparently logical, form of the dream. Anything may happen; everything is possible and probable. Time and space do not exist; on an insignificant background of reality imagination spins threads and weaves new patterns: a mixture of memories, experiences, free fancies, absurdities, and improvisations. The characters split, double, multiply, evaporate, solidify, diffuse, clarify. But one consciousness reigns above them all—that of the dreamer; it knows no secrets, no incongruities, no scruples, no law."

Other comments of Strindberg regarding playwriting and presentation have been so influential in the modern theater that they are appended:

On the function of tragedy: "People clamor for the joy of life, and theatrical managers order farces, as though the joy of life consisted in being foolish. . . . I find the joy of life in the powerful, cruel struggle of life, and my enjoyment is in discovering something, in learning something." Preface to *Lady Julie.*

On the true and false naturalism: "This [literary photography] is realism, a method latterly exalted to an art, a little art which cannot see the wood for the trees. This is the false naturalism, which believed that art consisted merely in sketching a piece of nature in a natural manner; but the true naturalism is that which seeks out those points in life where the great conflicts occur, which loves to see that which cannot be seen every day, rejoices in the battle of elemental powers, whether they be called love or hatred, revolt or sociability; which cares not whether a subject be beautiful or ugly, if only it is great." *On Modern Drama and the Modern Theatre.*

On character analysis and complexity of personality: [Strindberg's insistence on hidden motivation and many-sided personality is still productive of results in our own theater.]

"An event in life—and this is a comparatively new discovery—is generally produced by a whole series of more or less deep-seated motives, but the spectator chooses for the most part the one which is easiest for him to grasp. . . ." [He cites as illustration commonly assigned causes for a suicide and continues.] "It is possible that the motives lay in all of these causes, or in none, and that the dead man hid the real one by putting forward another which has thrown a more favorable light on his memory.

"I have drawn my characters vacillating, broken, mixtures of old and new. . . . My souls are conglomerations of past and present stages of culture, scraps of books and newspapers, fragments of men and women, torn shreds of Sunday attire that are now rags such as go to make up a soul.

"I do not, therefore, believe in simple theatrical characters, and the summary judgments which authors pass on human beings, such as: this one is stupid; that one is brutal; he is jealous; he is mean, etc., should be refuted by naturalists who know the rich complexity of the soul, and realize that vice has an obverse which shows a considerable likeness to virtue." Preface to *Lady Julie.*

Of Strindberg's modern ideas about staging, the following have been largely influential:

1. Footlights should be suppressed and side lights and borders used.
2. No more scenery should be used than is necessary. "With the aid of a table and two chairs, the strongest conflicts which life offers could be presented." Not a whole room, but an impressionist suggestion of one corner with its furniture is enough. Simple draperies were used by him at a later period.
3. Actors should be taught to play for the public and not at it. They may even turn their backs to it, and they should use a minimum of make-up.
4. The orchestra should be concealed.
5. The house should be small and intimate. Strindberg's own theater, opened in 1907, seated only 200 persons. The Künstler Theatre in Munich is said to reflect his ideas.

AUGUST STRINDBERG

Born 1849, Stockholm.

1867–1872, University of Upsala.

1872, First Version of *Master Olof,* inspired by Ibsen's *Brand,* was unsuccessful. In 1880 the fifth version was successfully produced.

1877–1891, First and most influential of three marriages.

1883–1897, Lived mainly on the Continent.

1887, *The Father,* his first naturalistic play. In Paris he wrote for Antoine's *Théâtre-Libre* his plays, *Lady Julie, Comrades, The Stronger,* and *Creditors.*

1894–1897, Period of scientific activity and mental aberration.

1897–1912, Return to Stockholm. Historical plays and plays of symbolism.

1907, The Intimate Theatre, devoted to Strindberg's plays, opened in Stockholm.

1912, Popular triumph and death.

PLAYS

1869 *The Free Thinker.* 1869 *Hermione.* 1870 *In Rome.* 1871 *The Outlaw.* 1872 *The Heretic* (rewritten and published as *Master Olof*). 1880 *Master Olof* (fifth version). 1880 *The Secret of the Guild.* 1881 *The Year Forty-Eight.* 1881 *The Wanderings of Lucky-Per.* 1882 *Sir Bengt's Lady.* 1887 *The Father.* 1888 *Comrades.* 1888 *Lady Julie.* 1889 *Hemsö Folk.* 1890 *Creditors.* 1890 *Pariah.* 1890 *Samum.* 1890 *The Stronger.* 1892 *The Keys of Heaven.* 1893 *Facing Death.* 1893 *The First Warning.*

1893 *Debit and Credit.* 1893 *Mother Love.* 1893 *Playing with Fire.* 1893 *The Link.* 1898 *To Damascus* (Parts I and II). 1899 *There Are Crimes and Crimes.* 1899 *Advent.* 1899 *Gustavus Vasa.* 1899 *Eric XIV.* 1899 *The Saga of the Folkungs.* 1900 *Gustavus Adolphus.* 1901 *Caspar's Shrove Tuesday.* 1901 *Easter.* 1901 *Midsummer.* 1901 *The Dance of Death* (Parts I and II). 1901 *Englebrecht.* 1901 *Charles XII.* 1902 *The Bridal Crown.* 1902 *Swanwhite.* 1902 *The Dream Play.* 1903 *Christina.* 1903 *Gustavus III.* 1904 *The Nightingale of Wittenberg* (Martin Luther). 1904 *To Damascus* (Part III). 1907 *Storm.* 1907 *The Burned Lot.* 1907 *The Spook Sonata.* 1907 *The Pelican.* 1908 *The Slippers of Abou Casem.* 1908 *The Last Knight.* 1909 *The National Director.* 1909 *The Earl of Bjalbo.* 1909 *The Black Glove.* 1909 *The Great Highway.* 1909 *The Tooth.* 1917 *Moses.* 1918 *Greece or Socrates.* 1918 *The Lamb and the Wild Beast; or Christ.*

WRITINGS ABOUT THE DRAMA

1887 Author's Preface to *Lady Julie.* 1889 *On Modern Drama and the Modern Theatre.* 1908 *Memorandum to the Members of the Intimate Theatre.* 1909 *An Open Letter to the Intimate Theatre.* 1911 *Dramaturgie* (translated into German by E. Schering). 1914 *Dramatische Charakteristiken* (translated into German by E. Schering).

THE DREAM PLAY

PROLOGUE

The background represents cloud banks that resemble corroding slate cliffs with ruins of castles and fortresses.

The constellations of Leo, Virgo, and Libra are visible, and from their midst the planet Jupiter is shining with a strong light.

[THE DAUGHTER OF INDRA * *stands on the topmost cloud.*]

The Voice of Indra. [*From above.*]
Where are you, daughter, where?

The Daughter.
Here, father, here.

The Voice.
You've lost your way, my child—beware,
you sink—
How got you there?

The Daughter.
I followed from ethereal heights the ray
Of lightning, and for car a cloud I took—
It sank, and now my journey downward
tends.
O, noble father, Indra, tell what realms
I now draw near? The air is here so close,
And breathing difficult.

The Voice.
Behind you lies the second world; the third
Is where you stand. From Cukra, morning
star,
You have withdrawn yourself to enter soon
The vapory circle of the earth. For mark,
The Seventh House you take. It's Libra
called:
There stands the day-star in the balanced
hour
When Fall gives equal weight to night and
day.

The Daughter.
You named the earth—is that the ponderous world
And dark, that from the moon must take
its light?

The Voice.
It is the heaviest and densest sphere
Of all that travel through the space.

The Daughter.
And is it never brightened by the sun?

The Voice.
Of course, the sun does reach it—now and
then——

The Daughter.
There is a rift, and downward goes my
glance——

The Voice.
What sees my child?

The Daughter.
I see—O beautiful!—with forests green,
With waters blue, white peaks, and yellow
fields——

The Voice.
Yes, beautiful as all that Brahma made—
But still more beautiful it was of yore,
In primal morn of ages. Then occurred
Some strange mishap; the orbit was dis-
turbed;
Rebellion led to crime that called for
check——

The Daughter.
Now from below I hear some sounds
arise—
What sort of race is dwelling there?

The Voice.
See for yourself—Of Brahma's work no ill
I say: but what you hear, it is their speech.

The Daughter.
It sounds as if—it has no happy ring!

The Voice.
I fear me not—for even their mother-
tongue
Is named complaint. A race most hard to
please,
And thankless, are the dwellers on the
earth——

The Daughter.
O, say not so—for I hear cries of joy,
Hear noise and thunder, see the lightnings
flash—
Now bells are ringing, fires are lit,
And thousand upon thousand tongues
Sing praise and thanks unto the heavens
on high—
Too harshly, father, you are judging them.

The Voice.
Descend, that you may see and hear, and
then
Return and let me know if their complaints
And wailings have some reasonable
ground——

* In Hindu mythology Indra, the god of the heavens, corresponded to Zeus of the Greeks and Jupiter of the Romans. Brahma was the god of creation.

The Daughter.
Well then, I go; but, father, come with me.
The Voice.
No, there below I cannot breathe——
The Daughter.
Now sinks the cloud—what sultriness—I choke!
I am not breathing air, but smoke and steam—
With heavy weight it drags me down,
And I can feel already how it rolls—
Indeed, the best of worlds is not the third——
The Voice.
The best I cannot call it, nor the worst.
Its name is Dust; and like them all, it rolls:
And therefore dizzy sometimes grows the race,
And seems to be half foolish and half mad—
Take courage, child—a trial, that is all!
The Daughter.
[*Kneeling as the cloud sinks downward.*]
I sink!

CURTAIN

THE PLAY

The background represents a forest of gigantic hollyhocks in bloom. They are white, pink, crimson, sulphurous, violet; and above their tops is seen the gilded roof of a castle, the apex of which is formed by a bud resembling a crown. At the foot of the castle walls stand a number of straw ricks, and around these stable litter is scattered. The side-scenes, which remain unchanged throughout the play, show conventionalized frescoes, suggesting at once internal decoration, architecture, and landscape.

[*Enter* THE GLAZIER *and* THE DAUGHTER.]

The Daughter. The castle is growing higher and higher above the ground. Do you see how much it has grown since last year?

The Glazier. [*To himself.*] I have never seen this castle before—have never heard of a castle that grew, but—[*To* THE DAUGHTER, *with firm conviction.*] Yes, it has grown two yards, but that is because they have manured it—and if you notice, it has put out a wing on the sunny side.

The Daughter. Ought it not to be blooming soon, as we are already past midsummer?

The Glazier. Don't you see the flower up there?

The Daughter. Yes, I see! [*Claps her hands.*] Say, father, why do flowers grow out of dirt?

The Glazier. [*Simply.*] Because they do not feel at home in the dirt, and so they make haste to get up into the light in order to blossom and die.

The Daughter. Do you know who lives in that castle?

The Glazier. I have known it, but cannot remember.

The Daughter. I believe a prisoner is kept there—and he must be waiting for me to set him free.

The Glazier. And what is he to pay for it?

The Daughter. One does not bargain about one's duty. Let us go into the castle.

The Glazier. Yes, let us go in.

[*They go toward the background, which opens and slowly disappears to either side.*]

[*The stage shows now a humble, bare room, containing only a table and a few chairs. On one of the chairs sits an* OFFICER, *dressed in a very unusual yet modern uniform. He is tilting the chair backward and beating the table with his sabre.*]

The Daughter. [*Goes to* THE OFFICER, *from whose hand she gently takes the sabre.*] Don't! Don't!

The Officer. Oh, Agnes dear, let me keep the sabre.

The Daughter. No, you break the table. [*To* THE GLAZIER.] Now you go down to the harness-room and fix that window pane. We'll meet later.

[THE GLAZIER *goes out.*]

The Daughter. You are imprisoned in your own rooms—I have come to set you free.

The Officer. I have been waiting for you, but I was not sure you were willing to do it.

The Daughter. The castle is strongly built; it has seven walls, but—it can be done!—Do you want it, or do you not?

The Officer. Frankly speaking, I cannot tell—for in either case I shall suffer pain. Every joy that life brings has to be paid for with twice its measure of sorrow. It is hard to stay where I am, but if I buy the sweets of freedom, then I shall have to suffer twice as much—Agnes, I'd rather endure it as it is, if I can only see you.

The Daughter. What do you see in me?

The Officer. Beauty, which is the harmony of the universe—There are lines of your body which are nowhere to be found, except in the orbits of the solar system, in strings that are singing softly, or in the vibrations of light—You are a child of heaven——

The Daughter. So are you.

The Officer. Why must I then keep horses, tend stable, and cart straw?

The Daughter. So that you may long to get away from here.

The Officer. I am longing, but it is so hard to find one's way out.

The Daughter. But it is a duty to seek freedom in the light.

The Officer. Duty? Life has never recognized any duties toward me.

The Daughter. You feel yourself wronged by life?

The Officer. Yes, it has been unjust——

[*Now voices are heard from behind a partition, which a moment later is pulled away.* THE OFFICER *and* THE DAUGHTER *look in that direction and stop as if paralyzed in the midst of a gesture.*]

[*At a table sits* THE MOTHER, *looking very sick. In front of her a tallow candle is burning, and every little while she trims it with a pair of snuffers. The table is piled with new-made shirts, and these she is marking with a quill and ink. To the left stands a brown-colored wardrobe.* THE FATHER *holds out a silk mantilla toward* THE MOTHER.]

The Father. [*Gently.*] You don't want it?

The Mother. A silk mantilla for me, my dear—of what use would that be when I am going to die shortly?

The Father. Do you believe what the doctor says?

The Mother. Yes, I believe what he says, but still more what the voice says in here.

The Father. [*Sadly.*] It is true then?—And you are thinking of your children first and last.

The Mother. That has been my life and my reason for living—my joy and my sorrow——

The Father. Christine, forgive me—everything!

The Mother. What have I to forgive? Dearest, you forgive *me!* We have been tormenting each other. Why? That we may not know. We couldn't do anything else—However, here is the new linen for the children. See that they change twice a week—Wednesdays and Sundays—and that Louise washes them—their whole bodies—Are you going out?

The Father. I have to be in the Department at eleven o'clock.

The Mother. Ask Alfred to come in before you go.

The Father. [*Pointing to* THE OFFICER.] Why, he is standing right there, dear heart.

The Mother. So my eyes are failing, too—Yes, it is turning dark. [*Trims the candle.*] Come here, Alfred.

[THE FATHER *goes out through the middle of the wall, nodding good-bye as he leaves.* THE OFFICER *goes over to* THE MOTHER.]

The Mother. Who is that girl?

The Officer. [*Whispers.*] It is Agnes.

The Mother. Oh, is that Agnes?—Do you know what they say?—That she is a daughter of the god Indra who has asked leave to descend to the earth in order that she may find out what the conditions of men are—But don't say anything about it.

The Officer. A child of the gods, indeed!

The Mother. [*Aloud.*] My Alfred, I must soon part from you and from the other children—But let me first speak a word to you that bears on all the rest of your life.

The Officer. [*Sadly.*] Speak, mother.

The Mother. Only a word: don't quarrel with God!

The Officer. What do you mean, mother?

The Mother. Don't go around feeling that life has wronged you.

The Officer. But when I am treated unjustly——

The Mother. You are thinking of the time when you were unjustly punished for having taken a penny that later turned up?

The Officer. Yes, and that one wrong gave a false twist to my whole life——

The Mother. Perhaps. But please take a look into that wardrobe now——

The Officer. [*Embarrassed.*] You know, then? It is——

The Mother. The Swiss Family Robinson—for which——

The Officer. Don't say any more!

The Mother. For which your brother was punished—and which you had torn and hidden away.

The Officer. Just think that the old wardrobe is still standing there after twenty years— We have moved so many times, and my mother died ten years ago.

The Mother. Yes, and what of it? You are always asking all sorts of questions, and in that way you spoil the better part of your life—There is Lena, now.

Lena. [*Enters.*] Thank you very much, ma'am, but I can't go to the baptism.

The Mother. And why not, my girl?

Lena. I have nothing to put on.

The Mother. I'll let you use my mantilla here.

Lena. Oh, no, ma'am, that wouldn't do!

The Mother. Why not?— It is not likely that I'll go to any more parties.

The Officer. And what will father say? It is a present from him——

The Mother. What small minds——

The Father. [*Puts his head through the wall.*] Are you going to lend my present to the servant girl?

The Mother. Don't talk that way! Can you not remember that I was a servant girl also? Why should you offend one who has done nothing?

The Father. Why should you offend me, your husband?

The Mother. Oh, this life! If you do anything nice, there is always somebody who finds it nasty. If you act kindly to one, it hurts another. Oh, this life!

[*She trims the candle so that it goes out. The stage turns dark and the partition is pushed back to its former position.*]

The Daughter. Men are to be pitied.

The Officer. You think so?

The Daughter. Yes, life is hard—but love overcomes everything. You shall see for yourself. [*They go toward the background.*]

[*The background is raised and a new one revealed, showing an old, dilapidated party-wall. In the center of it is a gate closing a passageway. This opens upon a green, sunlit space, where is seen a tremendous blue monk's-hood (aconite). To the left of the gate sits* THE PORTRESS. *Her head and shoulders are covered by a shawl, and she is crocheting at a bedspread with a starlike pattern. To the right of the gate is a billboard, which* THE BILLPOSTER *is cleaning. Beside him stands a dipnet with a green pole. Further to the right is a door that has an air-hole shaped like a four-leaved clover. To the left of the gate stands a small linden tree with coal-black trunk and a few pale-green leaves. Near it is a small air-hole leading into a cellar.*[1]]

The Daughter. [*Going to* THE PORTRESS.] Is the spread not done yet?

The Portress. No, dear. Twenty-six years on such a piece of work is not much.

The Daughter. And your lover never came back?

The Portress. No, but it was not his fault. He had to go—poor thing! That was thirty years ago now.

The Daughter. [*To* THE BILLPOSTER.] She belonged to the ballet? Up there in the opera-house?

The Billposter. She was number one—but when *he* went, it was as if her dancing had gone with him—and so she didn't get any more parts.

The Daughter. Everybody complains—with their eyes, at least, and often with words also——

The Billposter. I don't complain very much—not now, since I have a dipnet and a green cauf [2]——

The Daughter. And that can make you happy?

The Billposter. Oh, I'm so happy, so— It was the dream of my youth, and now it has come true. Of course, I have grown to be fifty years——

The Daughter. Fifty years for a dipnet and a cauf——

The Billposter. A *green* cauf—mind you, *green*——

The Daughter. [*To* THE PORTRESS.] Let me have the shawl now, and I shall sit here and watch the human children. But you must stand behind me and tell me about everything.

[*She takes the shawl and sits down at the gate.*]

The Portress. This is the last day, and the house will be closed up for the season. This is the day when they learn whether their contracts are to be renewed.

The Daughter. And those that fail of engagement——

The Portress. O, Lord have mercy! I pull the shawl over my head not to see them.

The Daughter. Poor human creatures!

The Portress. Look, here comes one—She's not one of the chosen. See, how she cries.

[THE SINGER *enters from the right; rushes through the gate with her handkerchief to her eyes; stops for a moment in the passageway beyond the gate and leans her head against the wall; then out quickly.*]

The Daughter. Men are to be pitied!

The Portress. But look at this one. That's the way a happy person looks.

[THE OFFICER *enters through the pas-*

[1] Though the author says nothing about it here, subsequent stage directions indicate a door and a window behind the place occupied by THE PORTRESS. Both lead into her room or lodge, which contains a telephone.

[2] A floating wooden box with holes in it used to hold fish.

sageway, dressed in Prince Albert coat and high hat, and carrying a bunch of roses in one hand; he is radiantly happy.]

The Portress. He is going to marry Miss Victoria.

The Officer. [*Far down on the stage, looks up and sings.*] Victoria!

The Portress. The young lady will be coming in a moment.

The Officer. Good! The carriage is waiting, the table is set, the wine is on ice— Oh, permit me to embrace you, ladies! [*He embraces* THE PORTRESS *and* THE DAUGHTER. *Sings.*] Victoria!

A Woman's Voice from Above. [*Sighs.*] I am here!

The Daughter. Do you know me?

The Officer. No, I know one woman only —Victoria. Seven years I have come here to wait for her—at noon, when the sun touched the chimneys, and at night, when it was growing dark. Look at the asphalt here, and you will see the path worn by the steps of a faithful lover. Hooray! She is mine. [*Sings.*] Victoria. [*There is no reply.*] Well, she is dressing, I suppose. [*To* THE BILLPOSTER.] There is the dipnet, I see. Everybody belonging to the opera is crazy about dipnets—or rather about fishes—because the fishes are dumb and cannot sing!— What is the price of a thing like that?

The Billposter. It is rather expensive.

The Officer. [*Sings.*] Victoria! [*Shakes the linden tree.*] Look, it is turning green once more. For the eighth time. [*Sings.*] Victoria!— Now she is fixing her hair. [*To* THE DAUGHTER.] Look here, Madam, could I not go up and get my bride?

The Portress. Nobody is allowed on the stage.

The Officer. Seven years I have been coming here. Seven times three hundred and sixty-five makes two thousand five hundred and fifty-five. [*Stops and pokes at the door with the four-leaved clover hole.*] And I have been looking two thousand five hundred and fifty-five times at that door without discovering where it leads. And that clover leaf which is to let in light—for whom is the light meant? Is there anybody within? Does anybody live there?

The Portress. I don't know. I have never seen it opened.

The Officer. It looks like a pantry door which I saw once when I was only four years old and went visiting with the maid on a Sunday afternoon. We called at several houses—on other maids—but I did not get beyond the kitchen anywhere, and I had to sit between the water barrel and the salt box. I have seen so many kitchens in my days; and the pantry was always just outside, with small round holes bored in the door, and one big hole like a clover leaf— But there cannot be any pantry in the opera-house as they have no kitchen. [*Sings.*] Victoria!— Tell me, Madam, could she have gone out any other way?

The Portress. No, there is no other way.

The Officer. Well, then, I shall see her here.

[STAGE PEOPLE *rush out and are closely watched by* THE OFFICER *as they pass.*]

The Officer. Now she must soon be coming—Madam, that blue monk's-hood outside —I have seen it since I was a child. Is it the same?— I remember it from a country rectory where I stopped when I was seven years old— There are two doves, two blue doves, under the hood—but that time a bee came flying and went into the hood. Then I thought: now I have you! And I grabbed hold of the flower. But the sting of the bee went through it, and I cried—but then the rector's wife came and put damp dirt on the sting—and we had strawberries and cream for dinner— I think it is getting dark already. [*To* THE BILLPOSTER.] Where are you going?

The Billposter. Home for supper.

The Officer. [*Draws his hand across his eyes.*] Evening? At this time?— O, please, may I go in and telephone to the Growing Castle?

The Daughter. What do you want there?

The Officer. I am going to tell the Glazier to put in double windows, for it will soon be winter, and I am feeling horribly cold. [*Goes into the gatekeeper's lodge.*]

The Daughter. Who is Miss Victoria?

The Portress. His sweetheart.

The Daughter. Right said! What she is to us and others matters nothing to him. And what she is to him, that alone is her real self.

[*It is suddenly turning dark.*]

The Portress. [*Lights a lantern.*] It is growing dark early today.

The Daughter. To the gods a year is as a minute.

The Portress. And to men a minute may be as long as a year.

The Officer. [*Enters again, looking dusty; the roses are withered.*] She has not come yet?

The Portress. No.

The Officer. But she will come— She will come! [*Walks up and down.*] But come to think of it, perhaps I had better call off the dinner after all—as it is late? Yes, I will do that.

[*Goes back into the lodge and telephones.*]

The Portress. [*To* THE DAUGHTER.] Can I have my shawl back now?

The Daughter. No, dear, be free a while. I shall attend to your duties—for I want to study men and life, and see whether things really are as bad as they say.

The Portress. But it won't do to fall asleep here—never sleep night or day——

The Daughter. No sleep at night?

The Portress. Yes, if you are able to get it, but only with the bell string tied around the wrist—for there are night watchmen on the stage, and they have to be relieved every third hour.

The Daughter. But that is torture!

The Portress. So you think, but people like us are glad enough to get such a job, and if you only knew how envied I am——

The Daughter. Envied?— Envy for the tortured?

The Portress. Yes-- But I can tell you what is harder than all drudging and keeping awake nights, harder to bear than draught and cold and dampness—it is to receive the confidences of all the unhappy people up there— They all come to me. Why? Perhaps they read in the wrinkles of my face some runes that are graved by suffering and that invite confessions— In that shawl, dear, lie hidden thirty years of my own and other people's agonies.

The Daughter. It is heavy, and it burns like nettles.

The Portress. As it is your wish, you may wear it. When it grows too burdensome, call me, and I shall relieve you.

The Daughter. Good-bye. What can be done by you ought not to surpass my strength.

The Portress. We shall see!— But be kind to my poor friends, and don't grow impatient of their complaints.

[*She disappears through the passageway.*]

[*Complete darkness covers the stage, and while it lasts the scene is changed so that the linden tree appears stripped of all its leaves. Soon the blue monk's-hood is withered, and when the light returns, the verdure in the open space beyond the passageway has changed into autumnal brown.*]

The Officer. [*Enters when it is light again. He has gray hair and a gray beard. His clothes are shabby, his collar is soiled and wrinkled. Nothing but the bare stems remain of the bunch of roses. He walks to and fro.*] To judge by all signs, Summer is gone and Fall has come. The linden shows it, and the monk's-hood also. [*Walks.*] But the Fall is *my* Spring, for then the opera begins again, and then she must come. Please, Madam, may I sit down a little on this chair?

The Daughter. Yes, sit down, friend—I am able to stand.

The Officer. [*Sits down.*] If I could only get some sleep, then I should feel better— [*He falls asleep for a few moments. Then he jumps up and walks back and forth again. Stops at last in front of the door with the clover leaf and pokes at it.*] This door here will not leave me any peace—what is behind it? There must be something. [*Faint dance music is heard from above.*] Oh, now the rehearsals have begun. [*The light goes out and flares up again, repeating this rhythmically as the rays of a lighthouse come and go.*] What does this mean? [*Speaking in time with the blinkings of the light.*] Light and dark—light and dark?

The Daughter. [*Imitating him.*] Night and day—night and day! A merciful Providence wants to shorten your wait. Therefore the days are flying in hot pursuit of the nights.

[*The light shines unbrokenly once more.*]

[THE BILLPOSTER *enters with his dipnet and his implements.*]

The Officer. There is the Billposter with his dipnet. Was the fishing good?

The Billposter. I should say so. The Summer was hot and a little long—the net turned out pretty good, but not as I had expected.

The Officer. [*With emphasis.*] Not as I had expected!— That is well said. Nothing ever was as I expected it to be—because the thought is more than the deed, more than the thing.

[*Walks to and fro, striking at the wall with the rose stems so that the last few leaves fall off.*]

The Billposter. Has she not come down yet?

The Officer. Not yet, but she will soon be here—Do you know what is behind that door, Billposter?

The Billposter. No, I have never seen that door open yet.

The Officer. I am going to telephone for a locksmith to come and open it.

[*Goes into the lodge.*]

[THE BILLPOSTER *posts a bill and goes toward the right.*]

The Daughter. What is the matter with the dipnet?

The Billposter. Matter? Well, I don't know as there is anything the matter with it —but it just didn't turn out as I had expected, and the pleasure of it was not so much after all.

The Daughter. How did you expect it to be?

The Billposter. How?— Well, I couldn't tell exactly——

The Daughter. I can tell you! You had expected it to be what it was not. It had to be green, but not that kind of green.

The Billposter. You have it, Madam. You understand it all—and that is why everybody goes to you with his worries. If you would only listen to me a little also——

The Daughter. Of course, I will!— Come in to me and pour out your heart.

[*She goes into the lodge.*]

[THE BILLPOSTER *remains outside, speaking to her.*]

[*The stage is darkened again. When the light is turned on, the tree has resumed its leaves, the monk's-hood is blooming once more, and the sun is shining on the green space beyond the passageway.*]

[THE OFFICER *enters. Now he is old and white-haired, ragged, and wearing worn-out shoes. He carries the bare remnants of the rose stems. Walks to and fro slowly, with the gait of an aged man. Reads on the posted bill.*]

[A BALLET GIRL *comes in from the right.*]

The Officer. Is Miss Victoria gone?

The Ballet Girl. No, she has not gone yet.

The Officer. Then I shall wait. She will be coming soon, don't you think?

The Ballet Girl. Oh, yes, I am sure.

The Officer. Don't go away now, for I have sent word to the locksmith, so you will soon see what is behind that door.

The Ballet Girl. Oh, it will be awfully interesting to see that door opened. That door, there, and the Growing Castle—have you heard of the Growing Castle?

The Officer. Have I?— I have been a prisoner in it.

The Ballet Girl. No, was that you? But why do they keep such a lot of horses there?

The Officer. Because it is a stable castle, don't you know.

The Ballet Girl. [*With confusion.*] How stupid of me not to guess that!

[A MALE CHORUS SINGER *enters from the right.*]

The Officer. Has Miss Victoria gone yet?

The Chorus Singer. [*Earnestly.*] No, she has not. She never goes away.

The Officer. That is because she loves me— See here, don't go before the locksmith comes to open the door here.

The Chorus Singer. No, is the door going to be opened? Well, that will be fun!— I just want to ask the Portress something.

[THE PROMPTER *enters from the right.*]

The Officer. Is Miss Victoria gone yet?

The Prompter. Not that I know of.

The Officer. Now, didn't I tell you she was waiting for me?— Don't go away, for the door is going to be opened.

The Prompter. Which door?

The Officer. Is there more than one door?

The Prompter. Oh, I know—that one with the clover leaf. Well, then, I have got to stay— I am only going to have a word with the Portress.

[THE BALLET GIRL, THE CHORUS SINGER, *and* THE PROMPTER *gather beside* THE BILLPOSTER *in front of the lodge window and talk by turns to* THE DAUGHTER.]

[THE GLAZIER *enters through the gate.*]

The Officer. Are you the locksmith?

The Glazier. No, the locksmith had visitors, and a glazier will do just as well.

The Officer. Yes, of course, of course—but did you bring your diamond along?

The Glazier. Why, certainly!— A glazier without his diamond, what would that be?

The Officer. Nothing at all!— Let us get to work then.

[*Claps his hands together. All gather in a ring around the door. Male members of the chorus dressed as Master Singers and Ballet Girls in costumes from the opera "Aïda" enter from the right and join the rest.*]

The Officer. Locksmith—or glazier—do your duty!

[THE GLAZIER *goes up to the door with the diamond in his hand.*]

The Officer. A moment like this will not occur twice in a man's life. For this reason, my friends, I ask you—please consider carefully——

A Policeman. [*Enters.*] In the name of the law, I forbid the opening of that door!

The Officer. Oh, Lord! What a fuss there is as soon as anybody wants to do anything new or great. But we will take the matter into court—let us go to the Lawyer. Then we shall see whether the laws still exist or not— Come along to the Lawyer.

[*Without lowering of the curtain, the stage changes to a lawyer's office, and in this manner: The gate remains, but as a wicket in the railing running clear across the stage. The gatekeeper's lodge turns into the private enclosure of* THE LAWYER, *and it is now entirely open to the front. The linden, leafless, becomes a hat tree. The billboard is covered with legal notices and court decisions. The door with the four-leaved clover hole forms part of a document chest.*]

[THE LAWYER, *in evening dress and white necktie, is found sitting to the left, inside the gate, and in front of him stands a desk covered with papers. His appearance indicates enormous sufferings. His face is chalk-white and full of wrinkles, and its shadows have a purple effect. He is ugly, and his features seem to reflect all the crimes and vices with which he has been forced by his profession to come into contact. Of his two* CLERKS, *one has lost an arm, the other an eye.*]

[*The people gathered to witness "the opening of the door" remain as before, but they appear now to be waiting for an audience with* THE LAWYER. *Judging by their attitudes, one would think they had been standing there forever.*]

[THE DAUGHTER, *still wearing the shawl, and* THE OFFICER *are near the footlights.*]

The Lawyer. [*Goes over to* THE DAUGHTER.] Tell me, sister, can I have that shawl? I shall keep it here until I have a fire in my grate, and then I shall burn it with all its miseries and sorrows.

The Daughter. Not yet, brother. I want it to hold all it possibly can, and I want it above all to take up your agonies—all the confidences you have received about crime, vice, robbery, slander, abuse——

The Lawyer. My dear girl, for such a purpose your shawl would prove totally insufficient. Look at these walls. Does it not look as if the wall-paper itself had been soiled by every conceivable sin? Look at these documents into which I write tales of wrong. Look at myself— No smiling man ever comes here; nothing is to be seen here but angry glances, snarling lips, clenched fists—And everybody pours his anger, his envy, his suspicions, upon me. Look—my hands are black, and no washing will clean them. See how they are chapped and bleeding— I can never wear my clothes more than a few days because they smell of other people's crimes—At times I have the place fumigated with sulphur, but it does not help. I sleep near by, and I dream of nothing but crimes— Just now I have a murder case in court—oh, I can stand that, but do you know what is worse than anything else?— That is to separate married people! Then it is as if something cried way down in the earth and up there in the sky—as if it cried treason against the primal force, against the source of all good, against love— And do you know, when reams of paper have been filled with mutual accusations, and at last a sympathetic person takes one of the two apart and asks, with a pinch of the ear or a smile, the simple question: what have you really got against your husband?—or your wife?—then he, or she, stands perplexed and cannot give the cause. Once—well, I think a lettuce salad was the principal issue; another time it was just a word—mostly it is nothing at all. But the tortures, the sufferings—these I have to bear—See how I look! Do you think I could ever win a woman's love with this countenance so like a criminal's? Do you think anybody dares to be friendly with me, who have to collect all the debts, all the money obligations, of the whole city?— It is a misery to be man!

The Daughter. Men are to be pitied!

The Lawyer. They are. And what people are living on puzzles me. They marry on an income of two thousand, when they need four thousand. They borrow, of course—everybody borrows. In some sort of happy-go-lucky fashion, by the skin of their teeth, they manage to pull through—and thus it continues to the end, when the estate is found to be bankrupt. Who pays for it at last no one can tell.

The Daughter. Perhaps He who feeds the birds.

The Lawyer. Perhaps. But if He who feeds the birds would only pay a visit to this earth of His and see for Himself how the poor human creatures fare—then His heart would surely fill with compassion.

The Daughter. Men are to be pitied!

The Lawyer. Yes, that is the truth!— [*To* THE OFFICER.] What do you want?

The Officer. I just wanted to ask if Miss Victoria has gone yet.

The Lawyer. No, she has not; you can be sure of it— Why are you poking at my chest over there?

The Officer. I thought the door of it looked exactly——

The Lawyer. Not at all! Not at all!

[*All the church bells begin to ring.*]

The Officer. Is there going to be a funeral?

The Lawyer. No, it is graduation day—a number of degrees will be conferred, and I am going to be made a Doctor of Laws. Perhaps you would also like to be graduated and receive a laurel wreath?

The Officer. Yes, why not? That would be a diversion, at least.

The Lawyer. Perhaps then we may begin upon this solemn function at once— But you had better go home and change your clothes. [THE OFFICER *goes out.*]

[*The stage is darkened and the following changes are made. The railing stays, but it encloses now the chancel of a church. The billboard displays hymn numbers. The linden hat tree becomes a candelabrum.* THE LAWYER'S *desk is turned into the desk of the presiding functionary, and the door with the clover leaf leads to the vestry.*]

[*The chorus of* MASTER SINGERS *become heralds with staffs, and the* BALLET GIRLS *carry laurel wreaths. The rest of the people act as spectators.*]

[*The background is raised, and the new one thus discovered represents a large church organ, with the keyboards below and the organist's mirror above.*]

[*Music is heard. At the sides stand figures symbolizing the four academic faculties: Philosophy, Theology, Medicine, and Jurisprudence.*]

[*At first the stage is empty for a few moments.*]

[HERALDS *enter from the right.* BALLET GIRLS *follow with laurel wreaths carried high before them.* THREE GRADUATES *appear one after another from the left, receive their wreaths from the* BALLET GIRLS, *and go out to the right.* THE LAWYER *steps forward to get his wreath.* THE BALLET GIRLS *turn away from him and refuse to place the wreath on his head. Then they withdraw from the stage.* THE LAWYER, *shocked, leans against a column. All the others withdraw gradually until only* THE LAWYER *remains on the stage.*]

The Daughter. [*Enters, her head and shoulders covered by a white veil.*] Do you see, I have washed the shawl! But why are you standing there? Did you get your wreath?

The Lawyer. No, I was not held worthy.

The Daughter. Why? Because you have defended the poor, put in a good word for the wrong-doers, made the burden easier for the guilty, obtained a respite for the condemned? Woe upon men: they are not angels —but they are to be pitied!

The Lawyer. Say nothing evil of men—for after all it is my task to voice their side.

The Daughter. [*Leaning against the organ.*] Why do they strike their friends in the face?

The Lawyer. They know no better.

The Daughter. Let us enlighten them. Will you try? Together with me?

The Lawyer. They do not accept enlightenment— Oh, that our plaint might reach the gods of heaven!

The Daughter. It shall reach the throne— [*Turns toward the organ.*] Do you know what I see in this mirror?— The world turned the right way!— Yes indeed, for naturally we see it upside down.

The Lawyer. How did it come to be turned the wrong way?

The Daughter. When the copy was taken —

The Lawyer. You have said it! The copy—I have always had the feeling that it was a spoiled copy. And when I began to recall the original images, I grew dissatisfied with everything. But men called it soreheadedness, looking at the world through the devil's eyes, and other such things.

The Daughter. It is certainly a crazy world! Look at the four faculties here. The government, to which has fallen the task of preserving society, supports all four of them. Theology, the science of God, is constantly attacked and ridiculed by philosophy, which declares itself to be the sum of all wisdom. And medicine is always challenging philosophy, while refusing entirely to count theology a science and even insisting on calling it a mere superstition. And they belong to a common Academic Council, which has been set to teach the young respect—for the university. It is a bedlam. And woe unto him who first recovers his reason!

The Lawyer. Those who find it out first are the theologians. As a preparatory study, they take philosophy, which teaches them that theology is nonsense. Later they learn from theology that philosophy is nonsense. Madmen, I should say!

The Daughter. And then there is jurisprudence which serves all but the servants.

The Lawyer. Justice, which, when it wants to do right, becomes the undoing of men. Equity, which so often turns into iniquity!

The Daughter. What a mess you have made of it, you man-children. Children, indeed!— Come here, and I will give you a wreath—one that is more becoming to you. [*Puts a crown of thorns on his head.*] And now I will play for you.

[*She sits down at the keyboards, but instead of organ-notes human voices are heard.*]

Voices of Children. O Lord everlasting! [*Last note sustained.*]

Voices of Women. Have mercy upon us! [*Last note sustained.*]

Voices of Men. [*Tenors.*] Save us for Thy mercy's sake! [*Last note sustained.*]

Voices of Men. [*Basses.*] Spare Thy Children, O Lord, and deliver us from Thy wrath!

All. Have mercy upon us! Hear us! Have pity upon the mortals!— O Lord eternal, why art Thou afar?— Out of the depths we call unto Thee: Make not the burden of Thy children too heavy! Hear us! Hear us!

[*The stage turns dark.* THE DAUGHTER *rises and draws close to* THE LAWYER. *By a change of light, the organ becomes Fingal's Cave. The ground-swell of the ocean, which can be seen rising and falling between the columns of basalt, produces a deep harmony that blends the music of winds and waves.*]

The Lawyer. Where are we, sister?

The Daughter. What do you hear?

The Lawyer. I hear drops falling——

The Daughter. Those are the tears that men are weeping— What more do you hear?

The Lawyer. There is sighing—and whining—and wailing——

The Daughter. Hither the plaint of the mortals has reached—and no farther. But why this never-ending wailing? Is there then nothing in life to rejoice at?

The Lawyer. Yes, what is most sweet, and what is also most bitter—love—wife and home—the highest and the lowest!

The Daughter. May I try it?

The Lawyer. With me?

The Daughter. With you— You know the rocks, the stumbling-stones. Let us avoid them.

The Lawyer. I am so poor.

The Daughter. What does that matter if we only love each other? And a little beauty costs nothing.

The Lawyer. I have dislikes which may prove your likes.

The Daughter. They can be adjusted.

The Lawyer. And if we tire of it?

The Daughter. Then come the children and bring with them a diversion that remains for ever new.

The Lawyer. You, you will take me, poor and ugly, scorned and rejected?

The Daughter. Yes—let us unite our destinies.

The Lawyer. So be it then!

CURTAIN

An extremely plain room inside THE LAWYER'S *office. To the right, a big double bed covered by a canopy and curtained in. Next to it, a window. To the left, an iron heater with cooking utensils on top of it.*

[CHRISTINE *is pasting paper strips along the cracks of the double windows. In the background, an open door to the office. Through the door are visible a number of poor clients waiting for admission.*]

Christine. I paste, I paste.

The Daughter. [*Pale and emaciated, sits by the stove.*] You shut out all the air. I choke!

Christine. Now there is only one little crack left.

The Daughter. Air, air—I cannot breathe!

Christine. I paste, I paste.

The Lawyer. That's right, Christine! Heat is expensive.

The Daughter. Oh, it feels as if my lips were being glued together.

The Lawyer. [*Standing in the doorway, with a paper in his hand.*] Is the child asleep?

The Daughter. Yes, at last.

The Lawyer. [*Gently.*] All this crying scares away my clients.

The Daughter. [*Pleasantly.*] What can be done about it?

The Lawyer. Nothing.

The Daughter. We shall have to get a larger place.

The Lawyer. We have no money for it.

The Daughter. May I open the window—this bad air is suffocating.

The Lawyer. Then the heat escapes, and we shall be cold.

The Daughter. It is horrible!— May we clean up out there?

The Lawyer. You have not the strength to do any cleaning, nor have I; and Christine must paste. She must put strips through the whole house, on every crack, in the ceiling, in the floor, in the walls.

The Daughter. Poverty I was prepared for, but not for dirt.

The Lawyer. Poverty is always dirty, relatively speaking.

The Daughter. This is worse than I dreamed!

The Lawyer. We are not the worst off by far. There is still food in the pot.

The Daughter. But what sort of food?

The Lawyer. Cabbage is cheap, nourishing, and good to eat.

The Daughter. For those who like cabbage—to me it is repulsive.

The Lawyer. Why didn't you say so?

The Daughter: Because I loved you, I wanted to sacrifice my own taste.

The Lawyer. Then I must sacrifice my taste for cabbage to you—for sacrifices must be mutual.

The Daughter. What are we to eat, then? Fish? But you hate fish.

The Lawyer. And it is expensive.

The Daughter. This is worse than I thought it!

The Lawyer. [*Kindly.*] Yes, you see how hard it is— And the child that was to become a link and a blessing—it becomes our ruin.

The Daughter. Dearest, I die in this air, in this room, with its backyard view, with its baby cries and endless hours of sleeplessness, with those people out there, and their whinings, and bickerings, and incriminations— I shall die here!

The Lawyer. My poor little flower, that has no light and no air——

The Daughter. And you say that people exist who are still worse off?

The Lawyer. I belong with the envied ones in this locality.

The Daughter. Everything else might be borne, if I could only have some beauty in my home.

The Lawyer. I know you are thinking of flowers—and especially of heliotropes—but a plant costs half a dollar, which will buy us six quarts of milk or a peck of potatoes.

The Daughter. I could gladly get along without food, if I could only have some flowers.

The Lawyer. There is a kind of beauty that costs nothing—but the absence of it in the home is worse than any other torture to a man with a sense for the beautiful.

The Daughter. What is it?

The Lawyer. If I tell, you will get angry.

The Daughter. We have agreed not to get angry.

The Lawyer. We have agreed— Everything can be overcome, Agnes, except the short, sharp accents— Do you know them? Not yet!

The Daughter. They will never be heard between us.

The Lawyer. Not as far as it lies in me!

The Daughter. Tell me now.

The Lawyer. Well—when I come into a room, I look first of all at the curtains— [*Goes over to the window and straightens out the curtains.*] If they hang like ropes or rags, then I leave soon. And next I take a glance at the chairs—if they stand straight along the wall, then I stay. [*Puts a chair back against the wall.*] Finally I look at the candles in their sticks—if they point this way and that, then the whole house is askew. [*Straightens up a candle on the chest of drawers.*] This is the kind of beauty, dear heart, that costs nothing.

The Daughter. [*With bent head.*] Beware of the short accents, Axel!

The Lawyer. They were not short.

The Daughter. Yes, they were.

The Lawyer. Well, I'll be——

The Daughter. What kind of language is that?

The Lawyer. Pardon me, Agnes! But I have suffered as much from your lack of orderliness as you have suffered from dirt. And I have not dared to set things right myself, for when I do so, you get as angry as if I were reproaching you—ugh! Hadn't we better quit now?

The Daughter. It is very difficult to be married—it is more difficult than anything else. One has to be an angel, I think!

The Lawyer. I think so, too.

The Daughter. I fear I shall begin to hate you after this!

The Lawyer. Woe to us then!— But let us forestall hatred. I promise never again to speak of any untidiness—although it is torture to me!

The Daughter. And I shall eat cabbage though it means agony to me.

The Lawyer. A life of common suffering, then! One's pleasure, the other one's pain!

The Daughter. Men are to be pitied!

The Lawyer. You see that?

The Daughter. Yes, but for heaven's sake, let us avoid the rocks, now when we know them so well.

The Lawyer. Let us try! Are we not decent and intelligent persons? Able to forbear and forgive?

The Daughter. Why not smile at mere trifles?

The Lawyer. We—only we—can do so. Do you know, I read this morning—by the bye, where is the newspaper?

The Daughter. [*Embarrassed.*] Which newspaper?

The Lawyer. [*Sharply.*] Do I keep more than one?

The Daughter. Smile now, and don't speak sharply—I used your paper to make the fire with——

The Lawyer. [*Violently.*] Well, I'll be damned!

The Daughter. Why don't you smile?— I burned it because it ridiculed what is holy to me.

The Lawyer. Which is unholy to me! Yah! [*Strikes one clenched fist against the open palm of the other hand.*] I smile, I smile so that my wisdom teeth show— Of course, I am to be nice, and I am to swallow my own opinions, and say yes to everything, and cringe and dissemble! [*Tidies the curtains around the bed.*] That's it! Now I am going to fix things until you get angry again— Agnes, this is simply impossible!

The Daughter. Of course it is!

The Lawyer. And yet we must endure— not for the sake of our promises, but for the sake of the child!

The Daughter. You are right—for the sake of the child. Oh, oh—we have to endure!

The Lawyer. And now I must go out to my clients. Listen to them—how they growl with impatience to tear each other, to get each other fined and jailed— Lost souls!

The Daughter. Poor, poor people! And this pasting!

[*She drops her head forward in dumb despair.*]

Christine. I paste, I paste.

[THE LAWYER *stands at the door, twisting the doorknob nervously.*]

The Daughter. How that knob squeaks! It is as if you were twisting my heart-strings——

The Lawyer. I twist, I twist!

The Daughter. Don't!

The Lawyer. I twist!

The Daughter. No!

The Lawyer. I——

The Officer. [*In the office, on the other side of the door, takes hold of the knob.*] Will you permit me?

The Lawyer. [*Lets go his hold.*] By all means. Seeing that you have your degree!

The Officer. Now all life belongs to me. Every road lies open. I have mounted Parnassus. The laurel is won. Immortality, fame, all is mine!

The Lawyer. And what are you going to live on?

The Officer. Live on?

The Lawyer. You must have a home, clothes, food——

The Officer. Oh, that will come—if you can only find somebody to love you!

The Lawyer. You don't say so!— You don't— Paste, Christine, paste until they cannot breath!

[*Goes out backward, nodding.*]

Christine. I paste, I paste—until they cannot breathe.

The Officer. Will you come with me now?

The Daughter. At once! But where?

The Officer. To Fairhaven. There it is summer; there the sun is shining; there we find youth, children, and flowers, singing and dancing, feasting and frolicking.

The Daughter. Then I will go there.

The Officer. Come!

The Lawyer. [*Enters again.*] Now I go back to my first hell—this was the second and greater. The sweeter the hell, the greater— And look here, now she has been dropping hair-pins on the floor again.

[*He picks up some hair-pins.*]

The Officer. My! but he has discovered the pins also.

The Lawyer. Also?— Look at this one. You see two prongs, but it is only one pin. It is two, yet only one. If I bend it open, it is a single piece. If I bend it back, there are two, but they remain one for all that. It means: these two are one. But if I break— like this!—then they become two.

[*Breaks the pin and throws the pieces away.*]

The Officer. All that he has seen!— But before breaking, the prongs must diverge. If they point together, then it holds.

The Lawyer. And if they are parallel, then they will never meet—and it neither breaks nor holds.

The Officer. The hair-pin is the most perfect of all created things. A straight line which equals two parallel ones.

The Lawyer. A lock that shuts when it is open.

The Officer. And thus shuts in a braid of hair that opens up when the lock shuts.

The Lawyer. It is like this door. When I close it, then I open—the way out—for you, Agnes!

[*Withdraws and closes the door behind him.*]

The Daughter. Well then?

[*The stage changes. The bed with its curtains becomes a tent. The stove stays as it was. The background is raised. To the right, in the foreground, are seen hills stripped of their trees by fire, and red heather growing between the blackened tree stumps. Red-painted pig-sties and outhouses. Beyond these, in the open, apparatus for mechanical gymnastics, where sick persons are being treated on machines resembling instruments of torture. To the left, in the foreground, the quarantine station, consisting of open sheds, with ovens, furnaces, and pipe coils. In the middle distance, a narrow strait. The background shows a beautiful wooded shore. Flags are flying on its piers, where ride white sailboats, some with sails set and some without. Little Italian villas, pavilions, arbors, marble statues are glimpsed through the foliage along the shore.*]

[THE MASTER OF QUARANTINE, *made up like a blackamoor, is walking along the shore.*]

The Officer. [*Meets him and they shake hands.*] Why Ordström! [1] Have you landed here?

Master of Q. Yes, here I am.

The Officer. Is this Fairhaven?

Master of Q. No, that is on the other side. This is Foulstrand.

The Officer. Then we have lost our way.

Master of Q. We?—Won't you introduce me?

The Officer. No, that wouldn't do. [*In a lowered voice.*] It is Indra's own daughter.

Master of Q. Indra's? And I was thinking of Varuna [2] himself— Well, are you not surprised to find me black in the face?

The Officer. I am past fifty, my boy, and at that age one has ceased to be surprised. I concluded at once that you were bound for some fancy ball this afternoon.

Master of Q. Right you were! And I hope both of you will come along.

The Officer. Why, yes—for I must say —the place does not look very tempting. What kind of people live here anyhow?

Master of Q. Here you find the sick; over there, the healthy.

The Officer. Nothing but poor folk on this side, I suppose.

Master of Q. No, my boy, it is here you find the rich. Look at that one on the rack. He has stuffed himself with paté de foie gras and truffles and Burgundy until his feet have grown knotted.

The Officer. Knotted?

Master of Q. Yes, he has a case of knotted feet. And that one who lies under the guillotine—he has swilled brandy so that his backbone has to be put through the mangle.

The Officer. There is always something amiss!

Master of Q. Moreover, everybody living on this side has some kind of canker to hide. Look at the fellow coming here, for instance.

[*An old* DANDY *is pushed on the stage in a wheel-chair. He is accompanied by a gaunt and grisly* COQUETTE *in the sixties, to whom* THE FRIEND, *a man of about forty, is paying court.*]

The Officer. It is the major—our schoolmate!

Master of Q. Don Juan. Can you see that he is still enamored of that old spectre beside him? He does not notice that she has grown old, or that she is ugly, faithless, cruel.

[1] Means literally "wordspout."
[2] The Hindu god of the ocean.

The Officer. Why, that is love! And I couldn't have dreamt that a fickle fellow like him would prove capable of loving so deeply and so earnestly.

Master of Q. That is a mighty decent way of looking at it.

The Officer. I have been in love with Victoria myself—in fact I am still waiting for her in the passageway——

Master of Q. Oh, you are the fellow who is waiting in the passageway?

The Officer. I am the man.

Master of Q. Well, have you got that door opened yet?

The Officer. No, the case is still in court — The Billposter is out with his dipnet, of course, so that the taking of evidence is always being put off—and in the meantime the Glazier has mended all the window panes in the castle, which has grown half a story higher— This has been an uncommonly good year—warm and wet——

Master of Q. But just the same you have had no heat comparing with what I have here.

The Officer. How much do you have in your ovens?

Master of Q. When we fumigate cholera suspects, we run it up to one hundred and forty degrees.

The Officer. Is the cholera going again?

Master of Q. Don't you know that?

The Officer. Of course, I know it, but I forget so often what I know.

Master of Q. I wish often that I could forget—especially myself. That is why I go in for masquerades and carnivals and amateur theatricals.

The Officer. What have you been up to, then?

Master of Q. If I told, they would say that I was boasting; and if I don't tell, then they call me a hypocrite.

The Officer. That is why you blackened your face?

Master of Q. Exactly—making myself a shade blacker than I am.

The Officer. Who is coming there?

Master of Q. Oh, a poet who is going to have his mud bath.

[THE POET *enters with his eyes raised toward the sky and carrying a pail of mud in one hand.*]

The Officer. Why, he ought to be having light baths and air baths.

Master of Q. No, he is roaming about the higher regions so much that he gets homesick for the mud—and wallowing in the mire makes the skin callous like that of a pig. Then he cannot feel the stings of the wasps.

The Officer. This is a queer world, full of contradictions.

The Poet. [*Ecstatically.*] Man was created by the god Phtah out of clay on a potter's wheel, or a lathe— [*Sceptically.*] or any damned old thing! [*Ecstatically.*] Out of clay does the sculptor create his more or less immortal masterpieces— [*Sceptically.*] which mostly are pure rot. [*Ecstatically.*] Out of clay they make those utensils which are so indispensable in the pantry and which generically are named pots and plates— [*Sceptically.*] but what in thunder does it matter to me what they are called anyhow? [*Ecstatically.*] Such is the clay! When clay becomes fluid, it is called mud— C'est mon affaire!— [*Shouts.*] Lena!

[LENA *enters with a pail in her hand.*]

The Poet. Lena, show yourself to Miss Agnes— She knew you ten years ago, when you were a young, happy and, let us say, pretty girl— Behold how she looks now. Five children, drudgery, baby-cries, hunger, ill-treatment. See how beauty has perished and joy vanished in the fulfilment of duties which should have brought that inner satisfaction which makes each line in the face harmonious and fills the eye with a quiet glow.

Master of Q. [*Covering* THE POET'S *mouth with his hand.*] Shut up! Shut up!

The Poet. That is what they all say. And if you keep silent, then they cry: speak! Oh, restless humanity!

The Daughter. [*Goes to* LENA.] Tell me your troubles.

Lena. No, I dare not, for then they will be made worse.

The Daughter. Who could be so cruel?

Lena. I dare not tell, for if I do, I shall be spanked.

The Poet. That is just what will happen. But I will speak, even though the blackamoor knock out all my teeth—I will tell that justice is not always done—Agnes, daughter of the gods, do you hear music and dancing on the hill over there?— Well, it is Lena's sister who has come home from the city where she went astray—you understand? Now they are killing the fatted calf; but Lena, who stayed at home, has to carry slop pails and feed the pigs.

The Daughter. There is rejoicing at home because the stray has left the paths of evil, and not merely because she has come back. Bear that in mind.

The Poet. But then they should give a ball and banquet every night for the spotless worker that never strayed into paths of error— Yet they do nothing of the kind, but when Lena has a free moment, she is sent to prayer-meetings where she has to hear reproaches for not being perfect. Is this justice?

The Daughter. Your question is so difficult to answer because— There are so many unforeseen cases——

The Poet. That much the Caliph, Haroun the Just, came to understand. He was sitting on his throne, and from its height he could never make out what happened below. At last complaints penetrated to his exalted ears. And then, one fine day, he disguised himself and descended unobserved among the crowds to find out what kind of justice they were getting.

The Daughter. I hope you don't take me for Haroun the Just!

The Officer. Let us talk of something else — Here come visitors.

[*A white boat, shaped like a viking ship, with a dragon for figure-head, with a pale-blue silken sail on a gilded yard, and with a rose-red standard flying from the top of a gilded mast, glides through the strait from the left.* HE *and* SHE *are seated in the stern with their arms around each other.*]

The Officer. Behold perfect happiness, bliss without limits, young love's rejoicing!

[*The stage grows brighter.*]

He. [*Stands up in the boat and sings.*]

Hail, beautiful haven,
Where the Springs of my youth were spent,
Where my first sweet dreams were dreamt—
To thee I return
But lonely no longer!

Ye hills and groves,
Thou sky o'erhead,
Thou mirroring sea,
Give greeting to her:
My love, my bride,
My light and my life!

[*The flags at the landings of Fairhaven are dipped in salute; white handkerchiefs are waved from verandahs and boats, and the air is filled with tender chords from harps and violins.*]

The Poet. See the light that surrounds them! Hear how the air is ringing with music!—Eros!

The Officer. It is Victoria.

Master of Q. Well, what of it?

The Officer. It is his Victoria— My own is still mine. And nobody can see *her*—

Now you hoist the quarantine flag, and I shall pull in the net.

[THE MASTER OF QUARANTINE *waves a yellow flag.*]

The Officer. [*Pulling a rope that turns the boat toward Foulstrand.*] Hold on there!

[HE *and* SHE *become aware of the hideous view and give vent to their horror.*]

Master of Q. Yes, it comes hard. But here every one must stop who hails from plague-stricken places.

The Poet. The idea of speaking in such manner, or acting in such a way, in the presence of two human beings united in love! Touch them not! Lay not hands on love! It is treason— Woe to us! Everything beautiful must now be dragged down—dragged into the mud!

[HE *and* SHE *step ashore, looking sad and shamefaced.*]

He. Woe to us! What have we done?

Master of Q. It is not necessary to have done anything in order to encounter life's little pricks.

She. So short-lived are joy and happiness!

He. How long must we stay here?

Master of Q. Forty days and nights.

She. Then rather into the water!

He. To live here—among blackened hills and pigsties?

The Poet. Love overcomes all, even sulphur fumes and carbolic acid.

Master of Q. [*Starts a fire in the stove; blue, sulphurous flames break forth.*] Now I set the sulphur going. Will you please step in?

She. Oh, my blue dress will fade.

Master of Q. And become white. So your roses will also turn white in time.

He. Even your cheeks—in forty days!

She. [*To* THE OFFICER.] That will please you.

The Officer. No, it will not!— Of course, your happiness was the cause of my suffering, but—it doesn't matter—for I am graduated and have obtained a position over there —heigh-ho and alas! And in the Fall I shall be teaching school—teaching boys the same lessons I myself learned during my childhood and youth—the same lessons throughout my manhood and, finally, in my old age —the self-same lessons! What does twice two make? How many times can four be evenly divided by two?—Until I get a pension and can do nothing at all—just wait around for meals and the newspapers—until at last I am carted to the crematorium and burned to ashes— Have you nobody here who is entitled to a pension? Barring twice two makes four, it is probably the worst thing of all—to begin school all over again when one already is graduated; to ask the same questions until death comes——

[*An* ELDERLY MAN *goes by, with his hands folded behind his back.*]

The Officer. There is a pensioner now, waiting for himself to die. I think he must be a captain who missed the rank of major; or an assistant judge who was not made a chief justice. Many are called but few are chosen— He is waiting for his breakfast now.

The Pensioner. No, for the newspaper— the morning paper.

The Officer. And he is only fifty-four years old. He may spend twenty-five more years waiting for meals and newspapers—is it not dreadful?

The Pensioner. What is not dreadful? Tell me, tell me!

The Officer. Tell that who can!— Now I shall have to teach boys that twice two makes four. And how many times four can be evenly divided by two. [*He clutches his head in despair.*] And Victoria, whom I loved and therefore wished all the happiness life can give—now she has her happiness, the greatest one known to her, and for this reason I suffer—suffer, suffer!

She. Do you think I can be happy when I see you suffering? How can you think it? Perhaps it will soothe your pains that I am to be imprisoned here for forty days and nights? Tell me, does it soothe your pains?

The Officer. Yes and no. How can I enjoy seeing you suffer? Oh!

She. And do you think my happiness can be founded on your torments?

The Officer. We are to be pitied—all of us!

All. [*Raise their arms toward the sky and utter a cry of anguish that sounds like a dissonant chord.*] Oh!

The Daughter. Everlasting One, hear them! Life is evil! Men are to be pitied!

All. [*As before.*] Oh!

[*For a moment the stage is completely darkened, and during that moment everybody withdraws or takes up a new position. When the light is turned on again, Foulstrand is seen in the background, lying in deep shadow. The strait is in the middle distance and Fairhaven in the foreground, both steeped in light. To the right, a corner of the Casino, where dancing couples are visible through the open windows. Three servant maids are standing outside on top of an empty box, with arms around each other, staring at the dancers within. On* *the verandah of the Casino stands a bench, where "*PLAIN*" *EDITH *is sitting. She is bareheaded, with an abundance of tousled hair, and looks sad. In front of her is an open piano. To the left, a frame house painted yellow. Two children in light dresses are playing ball outside. In the centre of the middle distance, a pier with white sailboats tied to it, and flag poles with hoisted flags. In the strait is anchored a naval vessel, brig-rigged, with gun ports. But the entire landscape is in winter dress, with snow on the ground and on the bare trees.*]

[THE DAUGHTER *and* THE OFFICER *enter.*]

The Daughter. Here is peace, and happiness, and leisure. No more toil; every day a holiday; everybody dressed up in his best; dancing and music in the early morning. [*To* THE MAIDS.] Why don't you go in and have a dance, girls?

The Maids. We?

The Officer. They are servants, don't you see!

The Daughter. Of course!— But why is Edith sitting there instead of dancing?

[EDITH *buries her face in her hands.*]

The Officer. Don't question her! She has been sitting there three hours without being asked for a dance.

[*Goes into the yellow house on the left.*]

The Daughter. What a cruel form of amusement!

The Mother. [*In a low-necked dress, enters from the Casino and goes up to* EDITH.] Why don't you go in as I told you?

Edith. Because—I cannot throw myself at them. That I am ugly I know, and I know that nobody wants to dance with me, but I might be spared from being reminded of it.

[*Begins to play on the piano, the Toccata con fuga, Op. 10, by Sebastian Bach.*]

[*The waltz music from within is heard faintly at first. Then it grows in strength, as if to compete with the Bach Toccata.* EDITH *prevails over it and brings it to silence. Dancers appear in the doorway to hear her play. Everybody on the stage stands still and listens reverently.*]

A Naval Officer. [*Takes* ALICE, *one of the dancers, around the waist and drags her toward the pier.*] Come quick!

[EDITH *breaks off abruptly, rises and stares at the couple with an expression of utter despair; stands as if turned to stone.*]

[*Now the front wall of the yellow house disappears, revealing three benches full of* SCHOOLBOYS. *Among these* THE OFFICER *is seen, looking worried and depressed. In front of the boys stands* THE TEACHER, *bespectacled and holding a piece of chalk in one hand, a rattan cane in the other.*]

The Teacher. [*To* THE OFFICER.] Well, my boy, can you tell me what twice two makes?

[THE OFFICER *remains seated while he racks his mind without finding an answer.*]

The Teacher. You must rise when I ask you a question.

The Officer. [*Harassed, rises.*] Two—twice—let me see. That makes two-two.

The Teacher. I see! You have not studied your lesson.

The Officer. [*Ashamed.*] Yes, I have, but —I know the answer, but I cannot tell it——

The Teacher. You want to wriggle out of it, of course. You know it, but you cannot tell. Perhaps I may help you.

[*Pulls his hair.*]

The Officer. Oh, it is dreadful, it is dreadful!

The Teacher. Yes, it is dreadful that such a big boy lacks all ambition——

The Officer. [*Hurt.*] Big boy—yes, I am big—bigger than all these others—I am full-grown, I am done with school— [*As if waking up.*] I have graduated—why am I then sitting here? Have I not received my doctor's degree?

The Teacher. Certainly, but you are to sit here and mature, you know. You have to mature—isn't that so?

The Officer. [*Feels his forehead.*] Yes, that is right, one must mature— Twice two —makes two—and this I can demonstrate by analogy, which is the highest form of all reasoning. Listen!— Once one makes one; consequently twice two must make two. For what applies in one case must also apply in another.

The Teacher. Your conclusion is based on good logic, but your answer is wrong.

The Officer. What is logical cannot be wrong. Let us test it. One divided by one gives one, so that two divided by two must give two.

The Teacher. Correct according to analogy. But how much does once three make?

The Officer. Three, of course.

The Teacher. Consequently twice three must also make three.

The Officer. [*Pondering.*] No, that cannot be right—it cannot—or else— [*Sits down dejectedly.*] No, I am not mature yet.

The Teacher. No, indeed, you are far from mature.

The Officer. But how long am I to sit here, then?

The Teacher. Here—how long? Do you believe that time and space exist?— Suppose that time does exist, then you should be able to say what time is. What is time?

The Officer. Time— [*Thinks.*] I cannot tell, but I know what it is. Consequently I may also know what twice two is without being able to tell it. And, teacher, can you tell what time is?

The Teacher. Of course I can.

All the Boys. Tell us then!

The Teacher. Time—let me see. [*Stands immovable with one finger on his nose.*] While we are talking, time flies. Consequently time is something that flies while we talk.

A Boy. [*Rising.*] Now you are talking, teacher, and while you are talking, I fly: consequently I am time. [*Runs out.*]

The Teacher. That accords completely with the laws of logic.

The Officer. Then the laws of logic are silly, for Nils, who ran away, cannot be time.

The Teacher. That is also good logic, although it is silly.

The Officer. Then logic itself is silly.

The Teacher. So it seems. But if logic is silly, then all the world is silly—and then the devil himself wouldn't stay here to teach you more silliness. If anybody treats me to a drink, we'll go and take a bath.

The Officer. That is a *posterus prius,* or the world turned upside down, for it is customary to bathe first and have a drink afterward. Old fogy!

The Teacher. Beware of a swelled head, doctor!

The Officer. Call me captain, if you please. I am an officer, and I cannot understand why I should be sitting here to get scolded like a schoolboy——

The Teacher. [*With raised index finger.*] We were to mature!

Master of Q. [*Enters.*] The quarantine begins.

The Officer. Oh, there you are. Just think of it, this fellow makes me sit among the boys although I am graduated.

Master of Q. Well, why don't you go away?

The Officer. Heaven knows!— Go away? Why, that is no easy thing to do.

The Teacher. I guess not—just try!

The Officer. [*To* MASTER OF QUARANTINE.] Save me! Save me from his eye!

Master of Q. Come on. Come and help us dance— We have to dance before the plague breaks out. We must!

The Officer. Is the brig leaving?

Master of Q. Yes, first of all the brig must leave— Then there will be a lot of tears shed, of course.

The Officer. Always tears; when she comes and when she goes— Let us get out of here.

[*They go out.* THE TEACHER *continues his lesson in silence.*]

[THE MAIDS *that were staring through the window of the dance hall walk sadly down to the pier.* EDITH, *who has been standing like a statue at the piano, follows them.*]

The Daughter. [*To* THE OFFICER.] Is there not one happy person to be found in this paradise?

The Officer. Yes, there is a newly married couple. Just watch them.

[THE NEWLY MARRIED COUPLE *enter.*]

Husband. [*To his* WIFE.] My joy has no limits, and I could now wish to die——

Wife. Why die?

Husband. Because at the heart of happiness grows the seed of disaster. Happiness devours itself like a flame—it cannot burn for ever, but must go out some time. And this presentiment of the coming end destroys joy in the very hour of its culmination.

Wife. Let us then die together—this moment!

Husband. Die? All right! For I fear happiness—that cheat!

[*They go toward the water.*]

The Daughter. Life is evil! Men are to be pitied!

The Officer. Look at this fellow. He is the most envied mortal in this neighborhood.

[THE BLIND MAN *is led in.*]

The Officer. He is the owner of these hundred or more Italian villas. He owns all these bays, straits, shores, forests, together with the fishes in the water, the birds in the air, the game in the woods. These thousand or more people are his tenants. The sun rises upon his sea and sets upon his land——

The Daughter. Well—is he complaining also?

The Officer. Yes, and with right, for he cannot see.

Master of Q. He is blind.

The Daughter. The most envied of all!

The Officer. Now he has come to see the brig depart with his son on board.

The Blind Man. I cannot see, but I hear. I hear the anchor bill claw the clay bottom as when the hook is torn out of a fish and brings up the heart with it through the neck— My son, my only child, is going to journey across the wide sea to foreign lands, and I can follow him only in my thought! Now I hear the clanking of the chain—and —there is something that snaps and cracks like clothes drying on a line—wet handkerchiefs perhaps. And I hear it blubber and snivel as when people are weeping—maybe the splashing of the wavelets among the seines—or maybe girls along the shore, deserted and disconsolate— Once I asked a child why the ocean is salt, and the child, who had a father on a long trip across the high seas, said immediately: the ocean is salt because the sailors shed so many tears into it. And why do the sailors cry so much then?— Because they are always going away, replied the child; and that is why they are always drying their handkerchiefs in the rigging— And why does man weep when he is sad? I asked at last— Because the glass in the eyes must be washed now and then, so that we can see clearly, said the child.

[*The brig has set sail and is gliding off.* THE GIRLS *along the shore are alternately waving their handkerchiefs and wiping off their tears with them. Then a signal is set on the foremast—a red ball in a white field, meaning "yes." In response to it* ALICE *waves her handkerchief triumphantly.*]

The Daughter. [*To* THE OFFICER.] What is the meaning of that flag?

The Officer. It means "yes." It is the lieutenant's troth—red as the red blood of the arteries, set against the blue cloth of the sky.

The Daughter. And how does "no" look?

The Officer. It is blue as the spoiled blood in the veins—but look, how jubilant Alice is.

The Daughter. And how Edith cries.

The Blind Man. Meet and part. Part and meet. That is life. I met his mother. And then she went away from me. He was left to me; and now he goes.

The Daughter. But he will come back.

The Blind Man. Who is speaking to me? I have heard that voice before—in my dreams; in my youth, when vacation began; in the early years of my marriage, when my child was born. Every time life smiled at me, I heard that voice, like a whisper of the south wind, like a chord of harps from above, like what I feel the angels' greeting must be in the Holy Night——

[THE LAWYER *enters and goes up to whisper something into* THE BLIND MAN'S *ear.*]

The Blind Man. Is that so?

The Lawyer. That's the truth. [*Goes to* THE DAUGHTER.] Now you have seen most of it, but you have not yet tried the worst of it.

The Daughter. What can that be?

The Lawyer. Repetition—recurrence. To retrace one's own tracks; to be sent back to the task once finished—come!

The Daughter. Where?

The Lawyer. To your duties.

The Daughter. What does that mean?

The Lawyer. Everything you dread. Everything you do not want but must. It means to forego, to give up, to do without, to lack —it means everything that is unpleasant, repulsive, painful.

The Daughter. Are there no pleasant duties?

The Lawyer. They become pleasant when they are done.

The Daughter. When they have ceased to exist—Duty is then something unpleasant. What is pleasant then?

The Lawyer. What is pleasant is sin.

The Daughter. Sin?

The Lawyer. Yes, something that has to be punished. If I have had a pleasant day or night, then I suffer infernal pangs and a bad conscience the next day.

The Daughter. How strange!

The Lawyer. I wake up in the morning with a headache; and then the repetitions begin, but so that everything becomes perverted. What the night before was pretty, agreeable, witty, is presented by memory in the morning as ugly, distasteful, stupid. Pleasure seems to decay, and all joy goes to pieces. What men call success serves always as a basis for their next failure. My own successes have brought ruin upon me. For men view the fortune of others with an instinctive dread. They regard it unjust that fate should favor any one man, and so they try to restore balance by piling rocks on the road. To have talent is to be in danger of one's life, for then one may easily starve to death!— However, you will have to return to your duties, or I shall bring suit against you, and we shall pass through every court up to the highest—one, two, three!

The Daughter. Return?— To the iron stove, and the cabbage pot, and the baby clothes——

The Lawyer. Exactly! We have a big wash today, for we must wash all the handkerchiefs——

The Daughter. Oh, must I do it all over again?

The Lawyer. All life is nothing but doing things over again. Look at the teacher in there— He received his doctor's degree yesterday, was laureled and saluted, climbed

Parnassus and was embraced by the monarch—and today he starts school all over again, asks how much twice two makes, and will continue to do so until his death— However, you must come back to your home!

The Daughter. I would rather die!

The Lawyer. Die?— That is not allowed. First of all, it is a disgrace—so much so that even the dead body is subjected to insults; and secondly, one goes to hell—it is a mortal sin!

The Daughter. It is not easy to be human!

All. Hear!

The Daughter. I shall not go back with you to humiliation and dirt— I am longing for the heights whence I came—but first the door must be opened so that I may learn the secret— It is my will that the door be opened!

The Lawyer. Then you must retrace your own steps, cover the road you have already traveled, suffer all annoyances, repetitions, tautologies, recopyings, that a suit will bring with it—

The Daughter. May it come then— But first I must go into the solitude and the wilderness to recover my own self. We shall meet again! [*To* THE POET.] Follow me.

[*Cries of anguish are heard from a distance.*] Woe! Woe! Woe!

The Daughter. What is that?

The Lawyer. The lost souls at Foulstrand.

The Daughter. Why do they wail more loudly than usual today?

The Lawyer. Because the sun is shining here; because here we have music, dancing, youth. And it makes them feel their own sufferings more keenly.

The Daughter. We must set them free.

The Lawyer. Try it! Once a liberator appeared, and he was nailed to a cross.

The Daughter. By whom?

The Lawyer. By all the right-minded.

The Daughter. Who are they?

The Lawyer. Are you not acquainted with all the right-minded? Then you must learn to know them.

The Daughter. Were they the ones that prevented your graduation?

The Lawyer. Yes.

The Daughter. Then I know them!

CURTAIN

On the shores of the Mediterranean. To the left, in the foreground, a white wall, and above it branches of an orange tree with ripe fruit on them. In the background, villas and a Casino placed on a terrace. To the right, a huge pile of coal and two wheelbarrows. In the background, to the right, a corner of blue sea.

[*Two* COALHEAVERS, *naked to the waist, their faces, hands, and bodies blackened by coal dust, are seated on the wheelbarrows. Their expressions show intense despair.*]

[THE DAUGHTER *and* THE LAWYER *in the background.*]

The Daughter. This is paradise!

First Coalheaver. This is hell!

Second Coalheaver. One hundred and twenty degrees in the shadow.

First Heaver. Let's have a bath.

Second Heaver. The police won't let us. No bathing here.

First Heaver. Couldn't we pick some fruit off that tree?

Second Heaver. Then the police would get after us.

First Heaver. But I cannot do a thing in this heat—I'll just chuck the job——

Second Heaver. Then the police will get you for sure!— [*Pause.*] And you wouldn't have anything to eat anyhow.

First Heaver. Nothing to eat? We, who work hardest, get least food; and the rich, who do nothing, get most. Might one not—without disregard of truth—assert that this is injustice?— What has the daughter of the gods to say about it?

The Daughter. I can say nothing at all— But tell me, what have you done that makes you so black and your lot so hard?

First Heaver. What have we done? We have been born of poor and perhaps not very good parents— Maybe we have been punished a couple of times.

The Daughter. Punished?

First Heaver. Yes, the unpunished hang out in the Casino up there and dine on eight courses with wine.

The Daughter. [*To* THE LAWYER.] Can that be true?

The Lawyer. On the whole, yes.

The Daughter. You mean to say that every man at some time has deserved to go to prison?

The Lawyer. Yes.

The Daughter. You, too?

The Lawyer. Yes.

The Daughter. Is it true that the poor cannot bathe in the sea?

The Lawyer. Yes. Not even with their clothes on. None but those who intend to take their own lives escape being fined. And those are said to get a good drubbing at the police station.

The Daughter. But can they not go outside of the city, out into the country, and bathe there?

The Lawyer. There is no place for them—all the land is fenced in.

The Daughter. But I mean in the free, open country.

The Lawyer. There is no such thing—it all belongs to somebody.

The Daughter. Even the sea, the great, vast sea——

The Lawyer. Even that! You cannot sail the sea in a boat and land anywhere without having it put down in writing and charged for. It is lovely!

The Daughter. This is not paradise.

The Lawyer. I should say not!

The Daughter. Why don't men do something to improve their lot?

The Lawyer. Oh, they try, of course, but all the improvers end in prison or in the madhouse——

The Daughter. Who puts them in prison?

The Lawyer. All the right-minded, all the respectable——

The Daughter. Who sends them to the madhouse?

The Lawyer. Their own despair when they grasp the hopelessness of their efforts.

The Daughter. Has the thought not occurred to anybody, that for secret reasons it must be as it is?

The Lawyer. Yes, those who are well off always think so.

The Daughter. That it is all right as it is?

First Heaver. And yet we are the foundations of society. If the coal is not unloaded, then there will be no fire in the kitchen stove, in the parlor grate, or in the factory furnace; then the light will go out in streets and shops and homes; then darkness and cold will descend upon you—and, therefore, we have to sweat as in hell so that the black coals may be had— And what do you do for us in return?

The Lawyer [*To* THE DAUGHTER.] Help them!— [*Pause.*] That conditions cannot be quite the same for everybody, I understand, but why should they differ so widely?

[A GENTLEMAN *and* A LADY *pass across the stage.*]

The Lady. Will you come and play a game with us?

The Gentleman. No, I must take a walk, so I can eat something for dinner.

First Heaver. So that he *can* eat something?

Second Heaver. So that he *can*——?

[CHILDREN *enter and cry with horror when they catch sight of the grimy* WORKERS.]

First Heaver. They cry when they see us. They cry——

Second Heaver. Damn it all!— I guess we'll have to pull out the scaffolds soon and begin to operate on this rotten body——

First Heaver. Damn it, I say, too! [*Spits.*]

The Lawyer [*To* THE DAUGHTER.] Yes, it is all wrong. And men are not so very bad—but——

The Daughter. But——?

The Lawyer. But the government——

The Daughter. [*Goes out, hiding her face in her hands.*] This is not paradise.

Coalheavers. No, hell, that's what it is!

CURTAIN

Fingal's Cave. Long green waves are rolling slowly into the cave. In the foreground, a siren buoy is swaying to and fro in time with the waves, but without sounding except at the indicated moment. Music of the winds. Music of the waves.

[THE DAUGHTER *and* THE POET *enter.*]

The Poet. Where are you leading me?

The Daughter. Far away from the noise and lament of the man-children, to the utmost end of the ocean, to the cave that we name Indra's Ear because it is the place where the king of the heavens is said to listen to the complaints of the mortals.

The Poet. What? In this place?

The Daughter. Do you see how this cave is built like a shell? Yes, you can see it. Do you know that your ear, too, is built in the form of a shell? You know it, but have not thought of it. [*She picks up a shell from the beach.*] Have you not as a child held such a shell to your ear and listened—and heard the ripple of your heart-blood, the humming of your thoughts in the brain, the snapping of a thousand little worn-out threads in the tissues of your body? All that you hear in this small shell. Imagine then what may be heard in this larger one!

The Poet. [*Listening.*] I hear nothing but the whispering of the wind.

The Daughter. Then I shall interpret it for you. Listen. The wail of the winds. [*Recites to subdued music.*]

Born beneath the clouds of heaven,
Driven we were by the lightnings of Indra
Down to the sand-covered earth.
Straw from the harvested fields soiled our
feet;

Dust from the high-roads,
Smoke from the cities,
Foul-smelling breaths,
Fumes from cellars and kitchens,
All we endured.
Then to the open sea we fled,
Filling our lungs with air,
Shaking our wings,
And laving our feet.

Indra, Lord of the Heavens,
Hear us!
Hear our sighing!
Unclean is the earth;
Evil is life;
Neither good nor bad
Can men be deemed.
As they can, they live,
One day at a time.
Sons of dust, through dust they journey;
Born out of dust, to dust they return.
Given they were, for trudging,
Feet, not wings for flying.
Dusty they grow—
Lies the fault then with them,
Or with Thee?

The Poet. Thus I heard it once——

The Daughter. Hush! The winds are still singing. [*Recites to subdued music.*]

We, winds that wander,
We, the air's offspring,
Bear with us men's lament
Heard us you have
During gloom-filled Fall nights,
In chimneys and pipes,
In key-holes and door cracks,
When the rain wept on the roof:
Heard us you have
In the snowclad pine woods
Midst wintry gloom:
Heard us you have,
Crooning and moaning
In ropes and rigging
On the high-heaving sea.

It was we, the winds,
Offspring of the air,
Who learned how to grieve
Within human breasts
Through which we passed—
In sick-rooms, on battle-fields,
But mostly where the newborn
Whimpered and wailed
At the pain of living.

We, we the winds,
We are whining and whistling:
Woe! Woe! Woe!

The Poet. It seems to me that I have already——

The Daughter. Hush! Now the waves are singing. [*Recites to subdued music.*]

We, we waves,
That are rocking the winds
To rest—
Green cradles, we waves!
Wet are we, and salty;
Leap like flames of fire—
Wet flames are we:
Burning, extinguishing;
Cleansing, replenishing;
Bearing, engendering.

We, we waves,
That are rocking the winds
To rest!

The Daughter. False waves and faithless! Everything on earth that is not burned, is drowned—by the waves. Look at this. [*Pointing to pile of débris.*] See what the sea has taken and spoiled! Nothing but the figure-heads remain of the sunken ships—and the names: *Justice, Friendship, Golden Peace, Hope*—this is all that is left of *Hope*—of fickle *Hope*—railings, tholes, bails! And lo: the life buoy—which saved itself and let distressed men perish.

The Poet. [*Searching in the pile.*] Here is the name-board of the ship *Justice.* That was the one which left Fairhaven with the Blind Man's son on board. It is lost then! And with it are gone the lover of Alice, the hopeless love of Edith.

The Daughter. The blind man? Fairhaven? I must have been dreaming of them. And the lover of Alice, "Plain" Edith, Foulstrand and the Quarantine, sulphur and carbolic acid, the graduation in the church, the Lawyer's office, the passageway and Victoria, the Growing Castle and the Officer—All this I have been dreaming——

The Poet. It was in one of my poems.

The Daughter. You know then what poetry is——

The Poet. I know then what dreaming is— But what is poetry?

The Daughter. Not reality, but more than reality—not dreaming, but daylight dreams——

The Poet. And the man-children think that we poets are only playing—that we invent and make believe.

The Daughter. And fortunate it is, my friend, for otherwise the world would lie fallow for lack of ministration. Everybody would be stretched on his back, staring into the sky. Nobody would be touching plough or spade, hammer or plane.

The Poet. And you say this, Indra's daughter, you who belong in part up there ——

The Daughter. You do right in reproaching me. Too long have I stayed down here taking mud baths like you— My thoughts have lost their power of flight; there is clay on their wings—mire on their feet—and I myself— [*Raising her arms.*] I sink, I sink— Help me, father, Lord of the Heavens! [*Silence.*] I can no longer hear his answer. The ether no longer carries the sound from his lips to my ear's shell—the silvery thread has snapped— Woe is me, I am earthbound!

The Poet. Do you mean to ascend—soon?

The Daughter. As soon as I have consigned this mortal shape to the flames—for even the waters of the ocean cannot cleanse me. Why do you question me thus?

The Poet. Because I have a prayer——

The Daughter. What kind of prayer?

The Poet. A written supplication from humanity to the ruler of the universe, formulated by a dreamer.

The Daughter. To be presented by whom?

The Poet. By Indra's daughter.

The Daughter. Can you repeat what you have written?

The Poet. I can.

The Daughter. Speak it then.

The Poet. Better that you do it.

The Daughter. Where can I read it?

The Poet In my mind—or here.

[*Hands her a roll of paper.*]

The Daughter. [*Receives the roll, but reads without looking at it.*] Well, by me it shall be spoken then:

"Why must you be born in anguish?
Why, O man-child, must you always
Wring your mother's heart with torture
When you bring her joy maternal,
Highest happiness yet known?
Why to life must you awaken,
Why to light give natal greeting,
With a cry of anger and of pain?
Why not meet it smiling, man-child,
When the gift of life is counted
In itself a boon unmatched?
Why like beasts should we be coming,
We of race divine and human?
Better garment craves the spirit,
Than one made of filth and blood!
Need a god his teeth be changing——"

—Silence, rash one! Is it seemly
For the work to blame its maker?
No one yet has solved life's riddle.

"Thus begins the human journey
O'er a road of thorns and thistles;
If a beaten path be offered,
It is named at once forbidden;
If a flower you covet, straightway
You are told it is another's;
If a field should bar your progress,
And you dare to break across it,
You destroy your neighbor's harvest;
Others then your own will trample,
That the measure may be evened!
Every moment of enjoyment
Brings to some one else a sorrow,
But your sorrow gladdens no one,
For from sorrow naught but sorrow springs.

"Thus you journey till you die,
And your death brings others' bread."

—Is it thus that you approach,
Son of Dust, the One Most High?

The Poet.
Could the son of dust discover
Words so pure and bright and simple
That to heaven they might ascend——?

Child of gods, wilt thou interpret
Mankind's grievance in some language
That immortals understand?

The Daughter. I will.

The Poet. [*Pointing to the buoy.*] What is that floating there?— A buoy?

The Daughter. Yes.

The Poet. It looks like a lung with a windpipe.

The Daughter. It is the watchman of the seas. When danger is abroad, it sings.

The Poet. It seems to me as if the sea were rising and the waves growing larger——

The Daughter. Not unlikely.

The Poet. Woe! What do I see? A ship bearing down upon the reef.

The Daughter. What ship can that be?

The Poet. The ghost ship of the seas, I think.

The Daughter. What ship is that?

The Poet. The *Flying Dutchman.*

The Daughter. Oh, that one. Why is he punished so hard, and why does he not seek harbor?

The Poet. Because he has seven faithless wives.

The Daughter. And for this he should be punished?

The Poet. Yes, all the right-minded condemned him——

The Daughter. Strange world, this!— How can he then be freed from his curse?

The Poet. Freed?— Oh, they take good care that none is set free.

The Daughter. Why?

The Poet. Because— No, it is not the *Dutchman*! It is an ordinary ship in distress. Why does not the buoy cry out now? Look, how the sea is rising—how high the waves are—soon we shall be unable to get out of the cave! Now the ship's bell is ringing— Soon we shall have another figurehead. Cry out, buoy! Do your duty, watchman! [*The buoy sounds a four-voice chord of fifths and sixths, reminding one of fog horns.*] The crew is signaling to us—but we are doomed ourselves.

The Daughter. Do you not wish to be set free?

The Poet. Yes, of course—of course, I wish it—but not just now, and not by water.

The Crew. [*Sings in quartet.*] Christ Kyrie!

The Poet. Now they are crying aloud, and so is the sea, but no one gives ear.

The Crew. [*As before.*] Christ Kyrie!

The Daughter. Who is coming there?

The Poet. Walking on the waters? There is only one who does that—and it is not Peter, the Rock, for he sank like a stone——

[*A white light is seen shining over the water at some distance.*]

The Crew. Christ Kyrie!

The Daughter. Can this be He?

The Poet. It is He, the crucified——

The Daughter. Why—tell me—why was He crucified?

The Poet. Because He wanted to set free ——

The Daughter. Who was it—I have forgotten—that crucified Him?

The Poet. All the right-minded.

The Daughter. What a strange world!

The Poet. The sea is rising. Darkness is closing in upon us. The storm is growing——

[THE CREW *set up a wild outcry.*]

The Poet. The crew scream with horror at the sight of their Saviour—and now—they are leaping overboard for fear of the Redeemer——

[THE CREW *utter another cry.*]

The Poet. Now they are crying because they must die. Crying when they are born, and crying when they pass away!

[*The rising waves threaten to engulf the two in the cave.*]

The Daughter. If I could only be sure that it is a ship——

The Poet. Really—I don't think it is a ship— It is a two-storied house with trees in front of it—and—a telephone tower—a tower that reaches up into the skies— It is the modern Tower of Babel sending wires to the upper regions—to communicate with those above——

The Daughter. Child, the human thought needs no wires to make a way for itself—the prayers of the pious penetrate the universe. It cannot be a Tower of Babel, for if you want to assail the heavens, you must do so with prayer.

The Poet. No, it is no house—no telephone tower—don't you see?

The Daughter. What are you seeing?

The Poet. I see an open space covered with snow—a drill ground— The winter sun is shining from behind a church on a hill, and the tower is casting its long shadow on the snow— Now a troop of soldiers come marching across the grounds. They march up along the tower, up the spire. Now they have reached the cross, but I have a feeling that the first one who steps on the gilded weathercock at the top must die. Now they are near it—a corporal is leading them—ha-ha! There comes a cloud sweeping across the open space, and right in front of the sun, of course—now everything is gone—the water in the cloud put out the sun's fire!—The light of the sun created the shadow picture of the tower, but the shadow picture of the cloud swallowed the shadow picture of the tower——

[*While* THE POET *is still speaking, the stage is changed and shows once more the passageway outside the opera-house.*]

The Daughter. [*To* THE PORTRESS.] Has the Lord Chancellor arrived yet?

The Portress. No.

The Daughter. And the Deans of the Faculties?

The Portress. No.

The Daughter. Call them at once, then, for the door is to be opened——

The Portress. Is it so very pressing?

The Daughter. Yes, it is. For there is a suspicion that the solution of the world-riddle may be hidden behind it. Call the Lord Chancellor, and the Deans of the Four Faculties also.

[THE PORTRESS *blows a whistle.*]

The Daughter. And do not forget the Glazier and his diamond, for without them nothing can be done.

[STAGE PEOPLE *enter from the left as in the earlier scene.*]

The Officer. [*Enters from the background, in Prince Albert and high hat, with a bunch of roses in his hand, looking radiantly happy.*] Victoria!

The Portress. The young lady will be coming in a moment.

The Officer. Good! The carriage is waiting, the table is set, the wine is on ice— Permit me to embrace you, Madam! [*Embraces* THE PORTRESS.] Victoria!

A Woman's Voice from Above. [*Sings.*] I am here!

The Officer. [*Begins to walk to and fro.*] Good! I am waiting.

The Poet. It seems to me that all this has happened before——

The Daughter. So it seems to me also.

The Poet. Perhaps I have dreamt it.

The Daughter. Or put it in a poem, perhaps.

The Poet. Or put it in a poem.

The Daughter. Then you know what poetry is.

The Poet. Then I know what dreaming is.

The Daughter. It seems to me that we have said all this to each other before, in some other place.

The Poet. Then you may soon figure out what reality is.

The Daughter. Or dreaming!

The Poet. Or poetry!

[*Enter the* LORD CHANCELLOR *and the* DEANS *of the* THEOLOGICAL, PHILOSOPHICAL, MEDICAL, *and* LEGAL FACULTIES.]

Lord Chancellor. It is about the opening of that door, of course— What does the Dean of the Theological Faculty think of it?

Dean of Theology. I do not think—I believe—*Credo*——

Dean of Philosophy. I hold——

Dean of Medicine. I know——

Dean of Jurisprudence. I doubt until I have evidence and witnesses.

Lord Chancellor. Now they are fighting again!— Well, what does Theology believe?

Theology. I believe that this door must not be opened, because it hides dangerous truths——

Philosophy. Truth is never dangerous.

Medicine. What is truth?

Jurisprudence. What can be proved by two witnesses.

Theology. Anything can be proved by two false witnesses—thinks the pettifogger.

Philosophy. Truth is wisdom; and wisdom, knowledge, is philosophy itself— Philosophy is the science of sciences, the knowledge of knowing, and all other sciences are its servants.

Medicine. Natural science is the only true science—and philosophy is no science at all. It is nothing but empty speculation.

Theology. Good!

Philosophy. [*To* THEOLOGY.] Good, you say! And what are you, then? You are the arch-enemy of all knowledge; you are the very antithesis of knowledge; you are ignorance and obscurantism——

Medicine. Good!

Theology. [*To* MEDICINE.] You cry "good," you, who cannot see beyond the length of your own nose in the magnifying glass; who believe in nothing but your own unreliable senses—in your vision, for instance, which may be far-sighted, near-sighted, blind, purblind, cross-eyed, one-eyed, color-blind, red-blind, green-blind——

Medicine. Idiot!

Theology. Ass! [*They fight.*]

Lord Chancellor. Peace! One crow does not peck out the other's eye.

Philosophy. If I had to choose between those two, Theology and Medicine, I should choose—neither!

Jurisprudence. And if I had to sit in judgment on all three of you, I should find—all guilty! You cannot agree on a single point, and you never could. Let us get back to the case in court. What is the opinion of the Lord Chancellor as to this door and its opening?

Lord Chancellor. Opinion? I have no opinion whatever. I am merely appointed by the government to see that you don't break each other's arms and legs in the Council—while you are educating the young! Opinion? Why, I take mighty good care to avoid everything of the kind. Once I had one or two, but they were refuted at once. Opinions are always refuted—by their opponents, of course— But perhaps we might open the door now, even with the risk of finding some dangerous truths behind it?

Jurisprudence. What is truth? What is truth?

Theology. I am the truth and the life——

Philosophy. I am the science of sciences——

Medicine. I am the only exact science——

Jurisprudence. I doubt—— [*They fight.*]

The Daughter. Instructors of the young, take shame!

Jurisprudence. Lord Chancellor, as representative of the government, as head of the corps of instructors, you must prosecute this woman's offence. She has told all of you to take shame, which is an insult; and she has—in a sneering, ironical sense—called you instructors of the young, which is a slanderous speech.

The Daughter. Poor youth!

Jurisprudence. She pities the young, which is to accuse us. Lord Chancellor, you must prosecute the offence.

The Daughter. Yes, I accuse you—you in

a body—of sowing doubt and discord in the minds of the young.

Jurisprudence. Listen to her—she herself is making the young question our authority, and then she charges us with sowing doubt. Is it not a criminal act, I ask all the right-minded?

All Right-Minded. Yes, it is criminal.

Jurisprudence. All the right-minded have condemned you. Leave in peace with your lucre, or else——

The Daughter. My lucre? Or else? What else?

Jurisprudence. Else you will be stoned.

The Poet. Or crucified.

The Daughter. I leave. Follow me, and you shall learn the riddle.

The Poet. Which riddle?

The Daughter. What did he mean by "my lucre"?

The Poet. Probably nothing at all. That kind of thing we call talk. He was just talking.

The Daughter. But it was what hurt me more than anything else!

The Poet. That is why he said it, I suppose— Men are that way.

All Right-Minded. Hooray! The door is open.

Lord Chancellor. What was behind the door?

The Glazier. I can see nothing.

Lord Chancellor. He cannot see anything —of course, he cannot! Deans of the Faculties: what was behind that door?

Theology. Nothing! That is the solution of the world-riddle. In the beginning God created heaven and earth out of nothing——

Philosophy. Out of nothing comes nothing.

Medicine. Yes, bosh—which is nothing!

Jurisprudence. I doubt. And this is a case of deception. I appeal to all the right-minded.

The Daughter. [*To* THE POET.] Who are the right-minded?

The Poet. Who can tell? Frequently all the right-minded consist of a single person. Today it is me and mine; tomorrow it is you and yours. To that position you are appointed—or rather, you appoint yourself to it.

All Right-Minded. We have been deceived.

Lord Chancellor. Who has deceived you?

All Right-Minded. The Daughter!

Lord Chancellor. Will the Daughter please tell us what she meant by having this door opened?

The Daughter. No, friends. If I did, you would not believe me.

Medicine. Why, then, there is nothing there.

The Daughter. You have said it—but you have not understood.

Medicine. It is bosh, what she says!

All. Bosh!

The Daughter. [*To* THE POET.] They are to be pitied.

The Poet. Are you in earnest?

The Daughter. Always in earnest.

The Poet. Do you think the right-minded are to be pitied also?

The Daughter. They most of all, perhaps.

The Poet. And the four faculties, too?

The Daughter. They also, and not the least. Four heads, four minds, and one body. Who made that monster?

All. She has not answered!

Lord Chancellor. Stone her then!

The Daughter. I have answered.

Lord Chancellor. Hear—she answers.

All. Stone her! She answers!

The Daughter. Whether she answer or do not answer, stone her! Come, prophet, and I shall tell you the riddle—but far away from here—out in the desert, where no one can hear us, no one see us, for——

The Lawyer. [*Enters and takes* THE DAUGHTER *by the arm.*] Have you forgotten your duties?

The Daughter. Oh, heavens, no! But I have higher duties.

The Lawyer. And your child?

The Daughter. My child—what of it?

The Lawyer. Your child is crying for you.

The Daughter. My child! Woe, I am earthbound! And this pain in my breast, this anguish—what is it?

The Lawyer. Don't you know?

The Daughter. No.

The Lawyer. It is remorse.

The Daughter. Is that remorse?

The Lawyer. Yes, and it follows every neglected duty; every pleasure, even the most innocent, if innocent pleasures exist, which seems doubtful; and every suffering inflicted upon one's fellow beings.

The Daughter. And there is no remedy?

The Lawyer. Yes, but only one. It consists in doing your duty at once——

The Daughter. You look like a demon when you speak that word duty— And when, as in my case, there are two duties to be met?

The Lawyer. Meet one first, and then the other.

The Daughter. The highest first—therefore, you look after my child, and I shall do my duty——

The Lawyer. Your child suffers because it misses you—can you bear to know that a human being is suffering for your sake?

The Daughter. Now strife has entered my soul—it is rent in two, and the halves are being pulled in opposite directions!

The Lawyer. Such, you know, are life's little discords.

The Daughter. Oh, how it is pulling!

The Poet. If you could only know how I have spread sorrow and ruin around me by the exercise of my calling—and note that I say *calling,* which carries with it the highest duty of all—then you would not even touch my hand.

The Daughter. What do you mean?

The Poet. I had a father who put his whole hope on me as his only son, destined to continue his enterprise. I ran away from the business college. My father grieved himself to death. My mother wanted me to be religious, and I could not do what she wanted—and she disowned me. I had a friend who assisted me through trying days of need—and that friend acted as a tyrant against those on whose behalf I was speaking and writing. And I had to strike down my friend and benefactor in order to save my soul. Since then I have had no peace. Men call me devoid of honor, infamous—and it does not help that my conscience says, "You have done right," for in the next moment it is saying, "You have done wrong." Such is life.

The Daughter. Come with me into the desert.

The Lawyer. Your child!

The Daughter. [*Indicating all those present.*] Here are my children. By themselves they are good, but if they only come together, then they quarrel and turn into demons—Farewell!

[*Outside the castle. The same scenery as in the first scene of the first act. But now the ground in front of the castle wall is covered with flowers—blue monk's-hood or aconite. On the roof of the castle, at the very top of its lantern, there is a chrysanthemum bud ready to open. The castle windows are illuminated with candles.*

[THE DAUGHTER *and* THE POET *enter.*]

The Daughter. The hour is not distant when, with the help of the flames, I shall once more ascend to the ether. It is what you call to die, and what you approach in fear.

The Poet. Fear of the unknown.

The Daughter. Which is known to you.

The Poet. Who knows it?

The Daughter. All! Why do you not believe your prophets?

The Poet. Prophets have always been disbelieved. Why is that so? And "if God has spoken, why will men not believe then?" His convincing power ought to be irresistible.

The Daughter. Have you always doubted?

The Poet. No. I have had certainty many times. But after a while it passed away, like a dream when you wake up.

The Daughter. It is not easy to be human!

The Poet. You see and admit it?

The Daughter. I do.

The Poet. Listen! Was it not Indra that once sent his son down here to receive the complaints of mankind?

The Daughter. Thus it happened—and how was he received?

The Poet. How did he fill his mission? —to answer with another question.

The Daughter. And if I may reply with still another—was not man's position bettered by his visit to the earth? Answer truly!

The Poet. Bettered?— Yes, a little. A very little— But instead of asking questions —will you not tell the riddle?

The Daughter. Yes. But to what use? You will not believe me.

The Poet. In you I shall believe, for I know who you are.

The Daughter. Then I shall tell! In the morning of the ages, before the sun was shining, Brahma, the divine primal force, let himself be persuaded by Maya, the world-mother, to propagate himself. This meeting of the divine primal matter with the earth-matter was the fall of heaven into sin. Thus the world, existence, mankind, are nothing but a phantom, an appearance, a dream-image——

The Poet. My dream!

The Daughter. A dream of truth! But in order to free themselves from the earth-matter, the offspring of Brahma seek privation and suffering. There you have suffering as a liberator. But this craving for suffering comes into conflict with the craving for enjoyment, or love—do you now understand what love is, with its utmost joys merged into its utmost sufferings, with its mixture of what is most sweet and most bitter? Can you now grasp what woman is? Woman, through whom sin and death found their way into life?

The Poet. I understand!— And the end?

The Daughter. You know it: conflict between the pain of enjoyment and the pleasure of suffering—between the pangs of the penitent and the joys of the prodigal——

The Poet. A conflict it is then?

The Daughter. Conflict between opposites produces energy, as fire and water give the power of steam——

The Poet. But peace? Rest?

The Daughter. Hush! You must ask no more, and I can no longer answer. The altar is already adorned for the sacrifice—the flowers are standing guard—the candles are lit—there are white sheets in the windows—spruce boughs have been spread in the gateway——

The Poet. And you say this as calmly as if for you suffering did not exist!

The Daughter. You think so? I have suffered all your sufferings, but in a hundredfold degree, for my sensations were so much more acute——

The Poet. Relate your sorrow!

The Daughter. Poet, could you tell yours so that not one word went too far? Could your word at any time approach your thought?

The Poet. No, you are right! To myself I appeared like one struck dumb, and when the mass listened admiringly to my song, I found it mere noise— For this reason, you see, I have always felt ashamed when they praised me.

The Daughter. And then you ask me— Look me straight in the eye!

The Poet. I cannot bear your glance——

The Daughter. How could you bear my word then, were I to speak in your tongue?

The Poet. But tell me at least before you go: from what did you suffer most of all down here?

The Daughter. From—*being:* to feel my vision weakened by an eye, my hearing blunted by an ear, and my thought, my bright and buoyant thought, bound in labyrinthine coils of fat. You have seen a brain —what roundabout and sneaking paths——

The Poet. Well, that is because all the right-minded think crookedly!

The Daughter. Malicious, always malicious, all of you!

The Poet. How could one possibly be otherwise?

The Daughter. First of all I now shake the dust from my feet—the dirt and the clay——

[*Takes off her shoes and puts them into the fire.*]

The Portress. [*Puts her shawl into the fire.*] Perhaps I may burn my shawl at the same time? [*Goes out.*]

The Officer. [*Enters.*] And I my roses, of which only the thorns are left. [*Goes out.*]

The Billposter. [*Enters.*] My bills may go, but never the dipnet! [*Goes out.*]

The Glazier. [*Enters.*] The diamond that opened the door—good-bye! [*Goes out.*]

The Lawyer. [*Enters.*] The minutes of the great process concerning the pope's beard or the water loss in the sources of the Ganges. [*Goes out.*]

Master of Quarantine. [*Enters.*] A small contribution in shape of the black mask that made me a blackamoor against my will! [*Goes out.*]

Victoria. [*Enters.*] My beauty, my sorrow! [*Goes out.*]

Edith. [*Enters.*] My plainness, my sorrow! [*Goes out.*]

The Blind Man. [*Enters; puts his hand into the fire.*] I give my hand for my eye. [*Goes out.*]

[DON JUAN *in his wheel-chair;* SHE *and* THE FRIEND.]

Don Juan. Hurry up! Hurry up! Life is short! [*Leaves with the other two.*]

The Poet. I have read that when the end of life draws near, everything and everybody rushes by in continuous review— Is this the end?

The Daughter. Yes, it is my end. Farewell!

The Poet. Give us a parting word.

The Daughter. No, I cannot. Do you believe that your words can express our thoughts?

Dean of Theology. [*Enters in a rage.*] I am cast off by God and persecuted by man; I am deserted by the government and scorned by my colleagues! How am I to believe when nobody else believes? How am I to defend a god that does not defend his own? Bosh, that's what it is!

[*Throws a book on the fire and goes out.*]

The Poet. [*Snatches the book out of the fire.*] Do you know what it is? A martyrology, a calendar with a martyr for each day of the year.

The Daughter. Martyr?

The Poet. Yes, one that has been tortured and killed on account of his faith! Tell me, why?— Do you think that all who are tortured suffer, and that all who are killed feel pain? Suffering is said to be salvation, and death a liberation.

Christine. [*With slips of paper.*] I paste, I paste until there is nothing more to paste——

The Poet. And if heaven should split in twain, you would try to paste it together—Away!

Christine. Are there no double windows in this castle?

The Poet. Not one, I tell you.

Christine. Well, then I'll go. [*Goes out.*]

The Daughter.

The parting hour has come, the end draws near.
And now farewell, thou dreaming child of man,
Thou singer, who alone know'st how to live!
When from thy winged flight above the earth
At times thou sweepest downward to the dust,
It is to touch it only, not to stay!

And as I go—how, in the parting hour,
As one must leave for e'er a friend, a place,
The heart with longing swells for what one loves,
And with regret for all wherein one failed!
O, now the pangs of life in all their force
I feel: I know at last the lot of man——
Regretfully one views what once was scorned;
For sins one never sinned remorse is felt;
To stay one craves, but equally to leave:
As if to horses tied that pull apart,
One's heart is split in twain, one's feelings rent,
By indecision, contrast, and discord.

Farewell! To all thy fellow-men make known
That where I go I shall forget them not;
And in thy name their grievance shall be placed
Before the throne. Farewell!

[*She goes into the castle. Music is heard. The background is lit up by the burning castle and reveals a wall of human faces, questioning, grieving, despairing. As the castle breaks into flames, the bud on the roof opens into a gigantic chrysanthemum flower.*]

CURTAIN

NIGHT'S LODGING*
OR
THE LOWER DEPTHS

[Scenes from Russian Life in Four Acts]

By

MAXIM GORKI

Translated from the Russian by EDWIN HOPKINS

MAXIM GORKI MADE HIS FIRST LITERARY appearance late in the nineties as a writer of short stories. From the age of nine he had lived from hand to mouth, supporting himself by any labor he could find. Wandering over Russia, he had come to know the habits and psychology of the lowest classes, and yet at the same time he had cultivated in himself the ability to tell what he knew. His stories, conveying the bitter misery and helplessness of the workingman and tramp in Russia, were an immediate sensation. They brought Gorki to the attention and later the acquaintanceship of Chekhov, who tried to induce him to write plays, and presented him to the directors of the Moscow Art Theatre, Nemirovitch-Danchenko and Stanislavsky.

Gorki's first two plays, *The Smug Citizen* and *The Lower Depths,* were begun almost simultaneously, but Gorki reported to Stanislavsky, during the writing, that he found the people of *The Lower Depths* quite intractable. He said, "They talk and talk, oh, how they talk." *The Smug Citizen* was easier, and was produced before *The Lower Depths,* with considerable success.

When Stanislavsky received the second play, he found that it made new demands upon his acting company. It could not be presented in ordinary theatrical terms; anything artificial or merely traditional in its performance or setting would destroy its inner meaning. To teach his company how the people of *The Lower Depths* lived, Stanislavsky took his company to the Khitrov Market, a part of Moscow which housed tramps exclusively. There they interviewed men and women of the submerged, listened to them in their talk, and watched them at their work and in their leisure. When the play was performed the company was able to give it the breath of truth, and it met with instant and lasting success, remaining in the company's repertoire ever since.

Though Gorki continued to write plays, he never duplicated the vivid naturalness of *The Lower Depths.* In the preface to *The Judge,* he says he is dissatisfied with all his plays, because they "became didactic in tendency, deluged in a sea of tiresome disquisition." He goes on to tell how a drama should be written:

"The characters of a drama should all act independently of the volition of the dramatist, in accordance with the law of their individual natures and social environment; they must follow the inspiration of their own destiny, and not that of any other destiny arbitrarily imposed upon them by the writer. They must, driven by their own inner impulses, create the incidents and episodes—tragic or comic—and direct the course of the play, being permitted to act in harmony with their own contradictory natures, interests, and passions. The author throughout should act like a host at a party to which he has invited imaginary guests, without in any way interceding, no matter how one guest may worry or torment any other—be it physically or morally: and finally, it is his business cold-bloodedly to describe the manner in which they all behave.

"The dramatist who adopts this attitude can write a pure work of art, a drama, that is, devoid of personal bias, a picture of the struggle of conflicting wills, without betraying the slightest trace of his own feelings.

"Now, as a matter of fact, I know no play written according to this theory in all European literature; and as for myself, I could never write one."

This statement seems to imply naturalism, and *The Lower Depths* is unquestionably one of the monumental examples of the naturalistic technique. But Gorki's dramatic theory should be compared with Galsworthy's (see preface to *Justice*). Galsworthy frankly advocates naturalism, a drama whose effectiveness derives from its fidelity to observed reality. Gorki asks no such fidelity, though unquestionably at the time *The Lower Depths* was written it was his own practice.

The play was first produced in English by The Stage Society of London in 1903, and commercially in 1911. In America, it was produced in German, as *Nachtasyl,* in 1903, and in English in 1919, by Arthur Hopkins.

MAXIM GORKI

(Alexei Maximovitch Pyeshkov)

Born 1868, Nijni-Novgorod, Russia.
1897, First book of short stories published.
1905, Implicated in the abortive Russian revolution and driven to residence abroad.
1917, Returns to Russia as Bolshevik official, though still residing part of the year abroad on account of his health.
1932, by order of the Soviet government, the name of the ancient city of Nijni-Novgorod is changed to Maxim Gorki in his honor.
Died 1936.

PLAYS

1902 *The Smug Citizen* (also translated as *The Bezsemenoffs*). 1902 *The Lower Depths* (also translated as *From the Depths, A Night Shelter, A Night's Lodging, Submerged, In the Depths, Down and Out,* and *At the Bottom*). 1904 *Summer Folk.* 1905 *Children of the Sun.* 1906 *The Barbarians* (not translated). 1906 *The Enemies* (not translated). 1908 *The Last Ones* (not translated). 1910 *Odd People* (not translated). 1910 *Vassa Zheleznova* (not translated). 1913 *The Zykovs* (not translated). 1913 *Children* (not translated). 1915 *The Judge.* 1926 *The Counterfeit Coin* (not translated). 1932 *Yegor Bulichoff.* 1934 *Dostigaeff and the Others.*

WRITING ABOUT THE DRAMA

Preface to *The Judge,* translated by Marie Zakrevsky and B. H. Clark, 1924.

NIGHT'S LODGING

OR

THE LOWER DEPTHS

Characters

[In the order in which they first speak in the play.]

A Baron, 32 *years old.*
Kvaschnya, *a market woman, about* 40.
Bubnoff, *a capmaker,* 45.
Kleshtsch, Andrew Mitritch, *locksmith,* 40 [Andreuschka].
Nastiah, 24 [Nastenka; Nastassya; Nastyka].
Anna, *wife of* Kleshtsch, 30.
Sahtin, 40.
An Actor, 40.
Kostilioff, Michael Ivanowitch, *lodging-house keeper,* 54 [Mishka].
Pepel, Waska, 28 [Wassili].
Natasha, *sister of* Wassilissa, 20 [Natalya; Natashenka; Nataschka].
Luka, *a pilgrim,* 60.
Alyoschka, *a shoemaker,* 20.
Wassilissa Karpovna, *wife of* Kostilioff, 26 [Waska].
Medviedeff, *uncle of* Wassilissa, *policeman,* 50 [Medviskin; Abram; Abrashka].
A Tartar, 40, *a porter* [Hassan].
Krivoi Zoba, 40, *a porter.*

Several nameless tramps, supernumeraries.

ACT I

A basement-room resembling a cavern. The massive, vaulted stone ceiling is blackened with smoke, its rough plaster in places broken off. The light falls inwardly from above, through a square window on the left (of one facing the footlights). The left corner, Pepel's *quarter, is separated from the rest of the room by thin partitions, against which, extending from beneath the window toward C. is* Bubnoff's *bunk.*

In the right corner is a great Russian stove, the rear of which is set into the wall which arches over it, the portion of the stove which extends into the room being an incline up which the personages must scramble to reach the space under the archway.

In the massive wall to the right is a door to the kitchen, in which Kvaschnya, *the* Baron, *and* Nastiah *live.*

Below the window, on the left, is a broad bed with dirty cotton curtains. Slightly L. C. (adjoining Pepel's *room) a flight of a few steps leads back to a platform, from which, to the left and behind* Pepel's *room, lead other steps, to an entry or hallway.*

A door opens inwardly on this platform, while to the right another flight of stairs leads to a room R. U. E. over the stove, in which the proprietor and his family live. The balustrade is in a bad condition and a torn rug or quilt lies over it.

Between the stove and the short flight of steps stands a broad low bench with four legs, which serves as a bunk. Another such bunk is across the front of the stove, and a third is at the right below the door to the kitchen. Near this is a wooden block to which is secured a small anvil and vise. Kleshtsch *sits on a smaller block, at work on a pair of old locks, into which he is fitting keys. At his feet are two bundles of keys of various sizes, strung on wire hoops, and a damaged samovar (a tea urn commonly used in Russia), a hammer and some files.*

In the middle of the room a great table, two benches, and a heavy tabouret, all unpainted and dirty.

Kvaschnya, *at the table R. cleaning a samovar, acts as housekeeper, while the* Baron *L. C. chews on a piece of black bread, and* Nastiah *L. sits on the tabouret, her elbows on the table, her face in her hands, reading a tattered book.* ANNA, *in bed, concealed by the curtains, is frequently heard coughing.* BUBNOFF *sits tailor fashion on his bench, measuring off, on a form which he holds between his knees, the pieces of an old pair of trousers which he has ripped up, cutting out caps to the best advantage. Behind him is a smashed hatbox from which he cuts visors, stacking the perfect ones on two nails in the partition and throwing the useless ones about the room. Around him are bits of oilcloth and scraps.*

SAHTIN, *just awakening, on the bunk before the stove, grumbles and roars. On the stove, hidden by the left springer of the arch, the* ACTOR *is heard coughing and turning.*]

TIME: *Early Spring. Morning.*

Baron. Go on.

[*Desiring more of the story.*]

Kvaschnya. Never, I tell you, my friend —take it away. I've been through it all, I want you to know. No treasure could tempt me to marry again.

[SAHTIN *grunts at this.*]

Bubnoff. [*To* SAHTIN.] What are you grunting about?

Kvaschnya. I, a free woman, my own boss, shall I register my name in somebody else's passport, become a man's serf, when nobody can say "that" to me now? Don't let me dream about it. I'll never do it. If he were a prince from America—I wouldn't have him!

Kleshtsch. You lie.

Kvaschnya. [*Turning toward him.*] Wh-at!

[*Turns back.*]

Kleshtsch. You are lying. You are going to marry Abram.

Baron. [*Rises, takes* NASTIAH'S *book and reads the title.*] "Disastrous Love."

[*Laughs.*]

Nastiah. [*Reaches for the book.*] Here! Give it back. Now, stop your joke.

[*The* BARON *eyes her and waves the book in the air.*]

Kvaschnya. [*To* KLESHTSCH *again.*] You lie, you red-headed billy goat; speaking to me like that, the nerve of it!

Baron. [*Gives* NASTIAH *a blow on the head with the book.*] What a silly goose you are, Nastiah.

Nastiah. Give it here.

[*Snatches the book.*]

Kleshtsch. [*To* KVASCHNYA.] You are a great lady! . . . But just the same you'll be Abram's wife. . . . That is what you want.

Kvaschnya. Certainly. [*Spoken ironically.*] To be sure. . . . What else? . . . And you beating your wife half to death.

Kleshtsch. [*Furiously.*] Hold your tongue, old slut! What's that to you?

Kvaschnya. [*Shouting.*] Ah, ha! You can't listen to the truth!

Baron. Now, they're let loose. Nastiah—where are you?

Nastiah. [*Without raising her head.*] What? Let me alone!

Anna. [*Putting her head out of the bed curtains.*] It is dawning already. For heaven's sake! Stop screaming and quarrelling.

Kleshtsch. Croaking again!

[*Contemptuously.*]

Anna. Every day that God gives, you quarrel. Let me at least die in quiet.

Bubnoff. The noise isn't keeping you from dying.

Kvaschnya. [*Goes to* ANNA.] Tell me, Anna dear, how have you endured such a brute?

Anna. Let me be! Let me——

Kvaschnya. Now, now, you poor martyr. Still no better with your breast?

Baron. It is time for us to go to market, Kvaschnya.

Kvaschnya. Then let's go now. [*To* ANNA.] Would you like a cup of hot custard?

Anna. I don't need it; thank you, though. Why should I still eat?

Kvaschnya. Oh, eat! Hot food is always good. It is quieting. I will put it away for you in a cup and when your appetite comes, then eat. [*To the* BARON.] Let's go, sir. [*To* KLESCHTSCH, *going around him.*] Huh! you Satan!

Anna. [*Coughing.*] Oh, God!

Baron. [*Jostles* NASTIAH *on the nape of the neck.*] Drop it . . . you goose.

Nastiah. [*Murmurs.*] Go on. I am not in your way.

[*Turns a page. The* BARON *whistles in derision; crosses to R. Exit into kitchen following* KVASCHNYA.]

Sahtin. [*Gets up from his bunk.*] Who was it that beat me up yesterday?

Bubnoff. That's all the same to you.

Sahtin. Suppose it is. But what for?

Bubnoff. You played cards?

Sahtin. Played cards? Oh, so I did.

Bubnoff. That's why.

Sahtin. Crooks!

Actor. [*On the stove, thrusting his head out.*] They'll kill you once, some day.

Sahtin. You are—a blockhead!

Actor. Why so?

Sahtin. They couldn't kill me twice, could they?

Actor. [*After a short silence.*] I don't see it. Why not?

Kleshtsch. [*Turning to him.*] Crawl down off the stove and clean the place up! You're too finicky, anyhow.

Actor. That's none of your business. . . .

Kleshtsch. Wait! . . . When Wassilissa comes she will show you whose business it is.

Actor. The devil take Wassilissa. The Baron must fix things up today, it's his turn. . . . Baron!

Baron. [*Enters R. from kitchen.*] I haven't time. I must go to market with Kvaschnya.

Actor. That's nothing to me. . . . Go to the devil for all I care . . . but the floor must be swept up, and it's your turn. . . . Don't imagine that I will do somebody else's work.

Baron. [*Crosses to* NASTIAH.] No? Then the deuce take you! Nastenka will sweep up a little. Say! You! "Disastrous Love!" Wake up! [*Takes the book.*]

Nastiah. [*Rising.*] What do you want? Give it here, you mischief maker. And this is a nobleman!

Baron. [*Gives the book back.*] Nastiah! do a little bit of sweeping for me—will you?

Nastiah. Sure, I'm crazy to.

[*Exit R. into kitchen.*]

Kvaschnya. [*Within, to the* BARON.] Come along. They can certainly clean up without you. [*Exit* BARON *R.*] You, Actor, you must do it. You were asked to do it, so do it then. It won't break your back.

Actor. Now, always I—h'm—I can't understand it.

[*The* BARON *enters from the kitchen carrying, by means of a yoke, two baskets containing fat jars covered with rags.* KVASCHNYA *follows.*]

Baron. Pretty heavy today.

Sahtin. You could do that without being a baron.

Kvaschnya. [*To the* ACTOR.] See to it that you sweep up.

[*Exit to the entry L. U. E. preceded by the* BARON.]

Actor. [*Crawls down from the stove.*] I must not inhale dust. It injures me. [*Self-pityingly.*] My organism is poisoned with alcohol.

[*Sits introspectively on the bunk before the stove.*]

Sahtin. Orgism. [*Derisively.*] Organism.

Anna. [*To* KLESHTSCH.] Andrew Mitritch.

Kleshtsch. What is the matter now?

Anna. Kvaschnya left some custard for me. Go eat it.

Kleshtsch. [*Crosses to her.*] Won't you eat?

Anna. I won't. Why should I eat? You—work. You must eat.

Kleshtsch. Are you afraid? Do not despair. Perhaps you'll be better again.

Anna. Go, eat. My heart is grieved; the end is near.

Kleshtsch. [*Moves away.*] Oh, no; perhaps—you can get up yet—such things have happened. [*Exit R. into kitchen.*]

Actor. [*Loudly, as though suddenly awakened from a dream.*] Yesterday, in the dispensary, the doctor said to me: "Your organism is poisoned with alcohol, through and through."

Sahtin. [*Laughing.*] Orgism!

Actor. [*With emphasis.*] Not orgism, but organism—or-gan-is-m.

Sahtin. Sigambrer!

Actor. [*With a deprecating movement of the hand.*] Ah! gibberish. I tell you I'm speaking in earnest. My organism is poisoned . . . so that I shall be injured if I sweep the room . . . and breathe the dust.

Sahtin. Microbites . . . ha!

Bubnoff. What are you muttering about?

Sahtin. Words . . . then there is still another word: transcendental.

Bubnoff. What does that mean ?

Sahtin. I don't know, I've forgotten.

Bubnoff. Why do you say it then?

Sahtin. Just so . . . I'm tired of all our words, Bubnoff. Every one of them I've heard at least a thousand times

Actor. As it says in Hamlet, "Words, words, words." A magnificent piece, "Hamlet"—I've played the Grave-digger.

Kleshtsch. [*Entering R. from the kitchen.*] Will you begin to play the broom?

Actor. That's very little to you. [*Strikes his breast with his fist.*] "The fair Ophelia! Nymph, in thy orisons, be all my sins remembered!"

[*Within, somewhere in the distance, are heard dull cries and the shrill sound of a policeman's whistle.* KLESHTSCH *sits down to work and the rasping of his file is heard.*]

Sahtin. I love the incomprehensible rare words. As a young man I was in the telegraph service. I have read many books.

Bubnoff. So you have been a telegraph operator?

Sahtin. To be sure. [*Laughs.*] Many beautiful books exist, and a lot of curious words. I was a man of education, understand that?

Bubnoff. I've already heard so, a hundred times. What does the world care what a man was? I, for example, was a furrier; had my own place of business. My arm was quite yellow—from the dye, when I colored the furs—quite yellow, my friend, up to the elbow. I thought that my whole life long I could never wash it clean; would descend, with yellow hands, into my grave: and now look at them, they are—simply dirty, see!

Sahtin. And what more?

Bubnoff. Nothing more.

Sahtin. What of it all?

Bubnoff. I mean only . . . by way of example . . . no matter how gaily a man lays the color on, it all rubs off again . . . all off again! See!

Sahtin. H'm! . . . My bones ache!

Actor. [*Sits on the bunk before the stove, his arms over his knees.*] Education is a rigmarole, the main thing is genius. I once knew an actor . . . he could scarcely read the words of his part, but he played his hero in such a way that the walls of the theatre shook with the ecstasy of the public. . . .

Sahtin. Bubnoff, give me five copecs.

Bubnoff. I've got only two myself.

Actor. I say, genius a leading man must have. Genius—believe in yourself, in your own power. . . .

Sahtin. Give me five copecs and I will believe that you are a genius, a hero, a crocodile, a precinct captain. Kleshtsch, give me a fiver.

Kleshtsch. Go to the devil. There are too many ragamuffins about.

Sahtin. Stop scolding; I know you have nothing.

Anna. Andrew Mitritch. . . . It is suffocating. It is hard. . . .

Kleshtsch. What can I do about that?

Bubnoff. Open the door to the street floor.

Kleshtsch. Well said! You sit on your bench and I on the ground—Let us change places and then open the door. . . . I have a cold already.

Bubnoff. [*Undisturbed.*] It is not for me. . . . Your wife asks for it.

Kleshtsch. [*Scowling.*] A good many things are being asked for in this world.

Sahtin. My headpiece hums. Ah, why do people always go for your head?

Bubnoff. Not only the head, but also other parts of the body are often struck. [*Gets up.*] I must get some thread. The landlord and landlady are late today. But they might be rotting already for all I know.

[*Exit L. U. E.* ANNA *coughs.* SAHTIN, *with his hands under his neck, lies motionless.*]

Actor. [*Regards the atmosphere gloomily and goes to* ANNA's *bed.*] Well, how is it? Bad?

Anna. It is stifling. . . .

Actor. Shall I take you out into the entry? . . Get up then. [*He helps the sick woman up, throws the tattered shawl over her shoulders and supports her, as they totter up the steps to the landing.*] Come now . . . be brave. I, too, am a sick man—poisoned with alcohol.

[*Enter* KOSTILIOFF *L. U. E.*]

Kostilioff. [*At the door.*] Out for a promenade? What a fine couple—Jack and Jill.

Actor. Stand aside. Don't you see that—the sick are passing by?

Kostilioff. All right, pass by, then. [*Humming the melody of a church hymn, he takes a mistrustful look about the basement, descends to the floor, leans his head to the left as if to overhear something in* PEPEL'S *room.* KLESHTSCH *claps furiously with the keys and files noisily, the proprietor giving him a black look.*] Busy scraping, eh?

[*Crosses to R. F.*]

Kleshtsch. What?

Kostilioff. Busy scraping, I said. . . . [*Pause.*] H'm—yes. . . . What was I going to say? [*Hastily and in a lower tone.*] Wasn't my wife there?

Kleshtsch. Haven't seen her. . . .

Kostilioff. [*Guardedly approaches the door of* PEPEL's *room.*] How much space you take for your two rubles a month! That bed. . . . You yourself sitting everlastingly here—nyah,* five rubles' worth, at least. I raise you half a ruble. . . .

Kleshtsch. Put a halter around my neck . . . and raise me a little more. You are an old man, you'll soon be rotting in your grave . . . and you think of nothing but half rubles.

Kostilioff. Why should I halter you? Who would be the better for that? Live, may God bless you, be content. Yet I raise you half a ruble to buy oil for the holy lamps . . . and my offering will burn before the holy image . . . for the remission of my sins, and thine also. . . . You never think yourself of your sins, I guess, do you? . . . Ah, Andreuschka, what a sinful beast you are . . . your wife languishing in agony from your blows . . . nobody likes you, nobody respects you. . . . Your work is so grating that nobody can endure you. . . .

Kleshtsch. [*Cries out.*] Do you come . . . to hack me to pieces?

[SAHTIN *roars aloud.*]

* An expression equivalent to no or yes.

Kostilioff. [*Shudders.*] Ah. . . . What is the matter with you, my friend?

Actor. [*Enters from stairs L. U. E.*] I took the woman into the entry . . . put her in a chair and wrapped her up warm. . . .

Kostilioff. What a good Samaritan you are. It will be rewarded. . . .

Actor. When?

Kostilioff. In the next world, brother dear. . . . There they sit and reckon up our every word and deed.

Actor. Why not, for the goodness of my heart, give me some recompense here?

Kostilioff. How can I do that?

Actor. Knock off half my debt. . . .

Kostilioff. Ha, ha, always having your fun, little buck, always jollying. . . . Can goodness of the heart be ever repaid with money? Goodness of the heart stands higher than all the treasures of this world. Nyah . . . and your debt—is only a debt. . . . There it stands. . . . Goodness of the heart you must bestow upon an old man without recompense. . . .

Actor. You are a cunning old knave. . . .
[*Exit R. into kitchen.*]

[KLESHTSCH *rises and goes upstairs, L. U. E.*]

Kostilioff. [*To* SAHTIN.] Who just sneaked out? The scrape? He is not fond of me, he, he!

Sahtin. Who is fond of you except the devil?

Kostilioff. [*Laughs quietly.*] Don't scold. I have you all so nicely . . . my dear friends, but I am fond of you all, my poor, unhappy brethren, citizens of nowhere, hapless and helpless. . . . [*Suddenly brisk.*] Tell me . . . is Waska at home?

Sahtin. Look and see for yourself.

Kostilioff. [*Goes to* PEPEL'S *door, L. U., and knocks.*] Waska!

[*Enter* ACTOR *R., standing in kitchen door chewing something.*]

Pepel. [*Within.*] Who's that?

Kostilioff. Me, Waska. . . .

Pepel. [*Within.*] What do you want? . . .

Kostilioff. [*Stepping back.*] Open the door.

Sahtin. [*Pretending to be oblivious.*] She is there. The moment he opens it. . . .
[*The* ACTOR *chuckles to him.*]

Kostilioff. [*Disturbed, softly.*] How? Who is in there? What. . . .

Sahtin. H'm? Are you speaking to me?

Kostilioff. What did you say?

Sahtin. Nothing at all . . . only . . . to myself. . . .

Kostilioff. Take good care of yourself, my friend . . . you are too waggish. [*Knocks loudly on the door.*] Wassili. . . .

Pepel. [*Opening the door.*] What are you bothering me about?

Kostilioff. [*Peers into* PEPEL'S *room.*] I . . . you see . . . you see. . . .

Pepel. Have you brought the money?

Kostilioff. I have a little business with you.

Pepel. Have you brought the money?

Kostilioff. Which money? . . . wait.

Pepel. Money, the seven rubles for the watch, see!

Kostilioff. Which watch, Waska? Ah, you . . . none of your tricks.

Pepel. Be careful. I sold you yesterday in the presence of witnesses a watch for ten rubles. . . . I got three, and now I'll take the other seven. Out with them. What are you blinking about around here . . . disturbing everybody . . . and forgetting the main thing? . . .

Kostilioff. Ssh! Not so quick, Waska. The watch was, indeed. . . .

Sahtin. Stolen.

Kostilioff. [*Stoutly, sharply.*] I never receive stolen goods. . . . How dare you. . . .

Pepel. [*Takes him by the shoulders.*] Tell me, why did you wake me up? What do you want?

Kostilioff. I. . . . Nothing at all. . . . I am going already . . . when you act so.

Pepel. Go then, and bring me the money.

Kostilioff. [*As he goes.*] Tough customers . . . ah! ah! [*Exit L. U. E.*]

Actor. Here is comedy for you!

Sahtin. Very good, I like it. . . .

Pepel. What did he want?

Sahtin. [*Laughing.*] Don't you catch on? He was looking for his wife. . . . Say, why don't you finish him, Waska?

Pepel. Would it pay to spoil my life for such stuff?

Sahtin. Spoil your life! Naturally you must do it cleverly. . . . Then marry Wassilissa . . . and be our landlord. . . .

Pepel. That would be nice. You, my guests, would soon guzzle up the whole place, and me in the bargain. . . . I am much too open-handed for you. [*Sits on the bunk U.*] Yes, old devil! Waked me up out of my best sleep. . . . I was having a beautiful dream. I dreamed that I was fishing, and suddenly I caught a big trout. A trout, I tell you . . . only in dreams are there such great trout. . . . I pulled and pulled, till his gills almost snapped off . . . and just as I was finishing him with a net . . . and thinking I had him. . . .

Sahtin. 'Twasn't any trout, 'twas Wassilissa.

Actor. He has had her in the net a long while.

Pepel. [*Angrily.*] Go to the devil . . . with your Wassilissa.

Kleshtsch. [*Entering L. U. E.*] It's beastly cold outside. . . .

Actor. Why didn't you bring Anna back? She will freeze to death.

Kleshtsch. Natasha had taken her along to the kitchen. . . .

Actor. The old scamp will chase her out. . . .

Kleshtsch. [*Crosses R. D. and sits down to work.*] Natasha will soon bring her in.

Sahtin. Wassili, five copecs.

Actor. Yes, five copecs, Waska, give us twenty. . . .

Pepel. If I don't hurry . . . you'll want a whole ruble . . . there! [*Gives the* ACTOR *a coin.*]

Sahtin. Giblartarr! There are no better men in the world than the thieves!

Kleshtsch. They get their money easy . . . they don't work. . . .

Sahtin. Money comes easy to many, but very few give it up easily. . . . Work, if you arrange it so that work gives me joy; then perhaps I will work too . . . perhaps! When work is a pleasure—then life is beautiful. . . . When you must work—then life is slavery. [*To* ACTOR.] Come, Sardanapalus, we will go. . . .

Actor. Come, Nebuchadnezzar, I will get as drunk as forty thousand topers.

[*Exit both L. U. E.*]

Pepel. [*Gapes.*] How is your wife?

Kleshtsch. [*Pause.*] She won't last long, I guess.

Pepel. When I sit and watch you so, I think, what good comes of all your scraping?

Kleshtsch. What else shall I do?

Pepel. Do nothing.

Kleshtsch. How shall I eat?

Pepel. Other men eat without taking so much trouble.

Kleshtsch. Other men? You mean this ragged pack of tramps here, idlers—you call them men! I am a workingman. . . . I am ashamed to look at them. I have worked from childhood on. Do you think that I shall never crawl out of this cesspool again? It is quite certain, let me work the skin off my hands, but I'll get out . . . wait until after my wife dies . . . six months in this hole . . . it seems like six years.

Pepel. What are you complaining about? . . . we are no worse than you.

Kleshtsch. No worse . . . people living on God's earth without honor or conscience?

Pepel. [*In an impartial tone, cool.*] What good is honor or conscience? You can't put such things on your feet when the snow is on the ground. Honor and conscience to those in power and authority.

Bubnoff. [*Enters L. U. E.*] Ug-h! I'm frozen stiff.

Pepel. Tell me, Bubnoff, have you a conscience?

Bubnoff. What? A conscience?

Pepel. Yes.

Bubnoff. What use is it to me? I'm no millionaire. . . .

Pepel. That's what I say. Honor and conscience are only for the rich—and yet Kleshtsch, here, is pulling us over the coals; we have no conscience he says. . . .

Bubnoff. Does he want to borrow some from us?

Pepel. He has plenty of his own. . . .

Bubnoff. Maybe you'll sell us some? No, it don't sell here. If it was broken hat boxes, I'd buy . . . but only on credit. . . .

Pepel. [*Instructively, to* KLESHTSCH.] You're certainly a fool, Andreuschka. You ought to hear what Sahtin says about a conscience . . . or the Baron. . . .

Kleshtsch. I have nothing to talk to them about. . . .

Pepel. They have more wit than you, even if they are drunks. . . .

Bubnoff. When a clever fellow drinks, he doubles his wit.

Pepel. Sahtin says: every man wants his neighbor to have some conscience—but for himself, he can do without it . . . and that's right.

[NATASHA *enters L. U. E., and behind her* LUKA, *with a staff in his hand, a sack on his back, and a small kettle and tea boiler at his girdle.*]

Luka. Good day to you, honest folks.

Pepel. [*Pulling his moustache.*] A-h, Natasha.

Bubnoff. [*To* LUKA.] Honest were we once, as you must know, but since last spring, a year ago. . . .

Natasha. Here—a new lodger. . . .

Luka. [*To* BUBNOFF.] It's all the same to me. I know how to respect thieves, too. Any flea, say I, may be just as good as you or me; all are black, and all jump . . . that's the truth. Where shall I quarter myself here, my love?

Natasha. [*Points to the kitchen door.*] Go in there . . . daddy.

Luka. Thank you, my girl, as you say. . . . A warm corner is an old man's delight.

[*Exit R. into kitchen.*]

Pepel. What an agreeable old chap you have brought along, Natasha.

Natasha. No matter, he is more interesting than you. [*Then to* KLESHTSCH.] Andrew, your wife is with us in the kitchen . . . come for her after a while.

Kleshtsch. All right, I'll come.

Natasha. Be good to her now . . . we won't have her long. . . .

Kleshtsch. I know it. . . .

Natasha. Yes, you know it . . . but that is not enough! Make it quite clear to yourself; think what it means to die . . . it is frightful. . . .

Pepel. You see I am not afraid. . . .

Natasha. The brave are not. . . .

Bubnoff. [*Whistles.*] The thread is rotten.

Pepel. Certainly I am not afraid, I would welcome death right now. Take a knife and strike me in the heart—not a murmur will I utter. I would meet death with joy . . . from clean hands . . . like yours.

Natasha. [*As she goes.*] Do not say anything which is not so, Pepel.

Bubnoff. [*Drawling.*] The thread is absolutely rotten.

Natasha. [*From the door to the entry.*] Don't forget your wife, Andrew.

Kleshtsch. All right. [*Exit* NATASHA.]

Pepel. A fine girl.

Bubnoff. None better.

Pepel. But what has set her against me so? She alone . . . always refusing me . . . but this life will be her ruin, all the same.

Bubnoff. It is you who will be the ruin of her.

Pepel. I be her ruin? . . . I pity her. . . .

Bubnoff. As the wolf pities the lamb.

Pepel. You lie! I do pity her. . . . Her lot is very hard. . . . I see that. . . .

Kleshtsch. Just wait until Wassilissa finds you together. . . .

Bubnoff. Yes, Wassilissa! Nobody can play any tricks on her, the fiend.

Pepel. [*Stretches himself out on the bunk, U.*] The devil take you both, prophets.

Kleshtsch. Wait . . . and see. . . .

Luka. [*Within, singing.*] "In the darkness of midnight, no path can be found."

Kleshtsch. Now he is beginning to howl. . . . [*Crosses to L. U. E.*] He too is beginning. [*Exit.*]

Pepel. My heart is in the depths . . . why is it? We live and live and everything goes well . . . then all of a sudden . . . melancholy like a blighting frost settles upon us. Life is used up. . . .

Bubnoff. Sad, melancholy, eh? . . .

Pepel. Yes . . . by God.

Luka. [*Singing.*] "No path can be found."

Pepel. Heh, you bag of bones.

Luka. [*Enter R.*] Do you mean me?

Pepel. Yes, you. Cut the singing out.

Luka. [*Crossing to C.*] Don't you like singing?

Pepel. When a song is well sung, I enjoy it.

Luka. Then I do not sing well?

Pepel. That's about right.

Luka. Too bad, and I thought that I sang beautifully. So it always goes. You think to yourself, I have done that well, but the public is not pleased. . . .

Pepel. [*Laughs.*] You are right, there.

Bubnoff. Ump! roaring again, and just now you said life was so sad, melancholy.

Pepel. What have you to say about it, old raven? . . .

Luka. Who is despondent?

Pepel. I. . . .

[*The* BARON *enters L. U. E.*]

Luka. So? And there—in the kitchen sits a girl reading a book and crying; upon my word! Her tears flowing. . . . I asked her, "What troubles you, my love—eh?" And she said, "It is so pitiful.". . . "Whom do you pity then?" I asked. . . . "See, here in the book, the people," said she. . . . And that is how she passes her time to drive away despondency, it appears. . . .

Baron. She is a fool.

Pepel. Have you had your tea, Baron? [*An invitation.*]

Baron. Tea, yes . . . anything more?

Pepel. Shall I stand for a bottle of rum, eh? Right?

Baron. Of course . . . what more?

Pepel. Let me ask you to stand on all fours and bark like a dog.

Baron. Blockhead; are you a Crœsus? Or are you drunk?

Pepel. That's right, bark away. I shall enjoy it. . . . You are a gentleman. . . . There was a time once when you did not take us for human beings even . . . and so on . . . and so on.

Baron. Well, and what more?

Pepel. What more? I'll let you bark now. You'll bark, won't you?

Baron. I have no objection on my own account . . . booby. How can it be such fun for you? . . . When I know myself that I am sunk deeper even than you. . . . Had you once dared you ought to have tried to get me on all fours when I was above you.

Bubnoff. You are right.

Luka. So I say too, you are right.

Bubnoff. What has been has been. Nothing is left but trash . . . we are not dukes here . . . the trappings are gone . . . only the bare man remains.

Luka. All are alike, know that. . . . Were you once a baron, my friend?

Baron. What's that you say? Who are you, sepulchre?

Luka. [*Laughs.*] An earl I have seen already and a prince . . . too. . . . But now for the first time, a baron, and a seedy one. . . .

Pepel. [*Laughs.*] Ha, ha, ha, I blush for you, Baron.

Baron. Don't be an idiot, Wassili. . . .

Luka. Yes, yes, my friends. When I look around me . . . this life here . . . ah!

Bubnoff. This life . . . why, this life here would make any man howl, from break-o'-day on, like a starving owl.

Baron. To be sure, we have all seen better days. I, for example. . . . On waking up I used to drink my coffee in bed . . coffee with cream . . . that's right.

Luka. And you are still a man. No matter what somersaults you turn before us, as a man you were born and as a man you must die. The more I look about myself, the more I contemplate mankind, the more interesting he grows . . . poorer and poorer he sinks and higher and higher his aspirations mount . . . obstinacy.

Baron. Tell me, old man . . . exactly who you are . . . where do you come from?

Luka. Who? I?

Baron. Are you a pilgrim?

Luka. We are all pilgrims here on this earth. . . . It has been said, even, I am told, that our earth is only a pilgrimage to Heaven's gate. . . .

Baron. It is so, but tell me . . . have you a passport?

Luka. [*Hesitatingly.*] Who are you? A detective?

Pepel. [*Briskly.*] Well said, old man! Ha, my lord, that went home!

Bubnoff. He gets what is coming to him. . . .

Baron. [*Disconcerted.*] Well! well! I am only joking, old man. I've no papers, myself.

Bubnoff. You lie!

Baron. That is to say. . . . I have papers . . . but they're of no use.

Luka. So it is with all pen scratches . . . they're of no use. . . .

Pepel. Baron! Come have one, for the sake of thirst. . . .

Baron. I'm with you. Bye-bye, see you again, old chap. . . . You're a sly dog. . . .

Luka. It may be true, my friend.

Pepel. [*At the door L. U. E.*] Are you coming?

[*Exit, followed quickly by the* BARON.]

Luka. Has the man really been a baron?

Bubnoff. Who knows? He has been a nobleman, that is certain. Even now his former air shows through. The manner clings. . . .

Luka. Breeding is like the small pox: the man recovers, but the pits remain.

Bubnoff. But otherwise he is a good fellow . . . except that sometimes he is overbearing . . . as he was about your passport. . . .

Alyoschka. [*Enters L. U. E. drunk, an accordion under his arm. He whistles.*] Hey, there, neighbors.

Bubnoff. What are you howling about?

Alyoschka. Excuse me, please . . . pass it over. I am a cozy boy. . . .

Bubnoff. Broken out again?

Alyoschka. Why not? Police captain Medviskin has just chased me off his beat. "Take your stand out of the street," says he. No, no, I am still a youth of good temperament . . . the boss was jawing at me too . . . bah, what do I care for bosses? . . . Bah, everything is all a mistake, should a tank be boss? . . . I am a man, who . . . never a wish have . . . has . . . I want nothing . . . that settles it . . . now, take me . . . for one ruble and twenty copecs you can have me . . . and I want ab-solt-ly nothing. [NASTIAH *enters R. from kitchen.*] Offer me a million—and I will not take it. And that whiskey barrel, to be boss over me, a good man, no better than—it don't go. I'll not stand for it.

[NASTIAH *remains standing at the door, shaking her head at the spectacle of* ALYOSCHKA.]

Luka. [*Good-naturedly.*] Ah, boy . . . you can't unravel it.

Bubnoff. There you have human folly.

Alyoschka. [*Lies down on the floor.*] Now, eat me up. Costs nothing. I am a desperado. You just tell me, am I worse than the others? How am I worse? Just think, Medviskin said, "Don't show yourself on the street, or else I'll give you one in the snout." But I'll go. . . . I'll lie down crosswise in the street, let them choke me. I want ab-solt-ly nothing. . . . [*Rises.*]

Nastiah. Wretch . . . so young and putting on such airs. . . .

Alyoschka. [*Sees her and kneels.*] My lady, my fräulein, mamselle! Parlez français . . . price current . . . I am jagging.

Nastiah. [*Whispers loudly.*] Wassilissa.

[*Sees her coming.*]

Wassilissa. [*Opens door at head of stairs R. U. E. To* ALYOSCHKA.] Here again . . . already?

Alyoschka. Good morning. Please, come down.

Wassilissa. Didn't I tell you, you pup, not to show yourself here again? [*Descends.*]

Alyoschka. Wassilissa Karpovna—if you please, I'll play you a funeral march.

Wassilissa. [*Pushes him on the shoulder.*] Get out!

Alyoschka. [*Shuffles to the door, L. U. E*]. No, I won't wait. First listen to the funeral march. . . . I've just learned it . . . new music . . . wait a minute . . . you mustn't act so.

Wassilissa. I will show you how I must act. . . . I'll put the whole street on your track, you damned heathen . . . so, telling folks on me. . . .

Alyoschka. [*Runs out L. U. E.*] No, I am already gone. [*Exit.*]

Wassilissa. [*To* BUBNOFF.] See to it that he does not set foot in here again, you hear?

Bubnoff. I'm not your watchman.

Wassilissa. No, but you are a dead beat. How much do you owe me?

Bubnoff. [*Calmly.*] I haven't counted it up. . . .

Wassilissa. Look out or I'll count it up.

Alyoschka. [*Opens the door and cries.*] Wassilissa Karpovna, I am not afraid of you. . . . I am not afraid.

[*He hides behind a cloth which hangs over the balustrade, and* LUKA *laughs.*]

Wassilissa. And who are you?

Luka. A pilgrim, a mere wanderer. I go from place to place. . . .

Wassilissa. Will you stay overnight . . . or for good?

Luka. I will see.

[ALYOSCHKA *slips into the kitchen, R.*]

Wassilissa. Your passport.

Luka. You may have it.

Wassilissa. Give it to me, then.

Luka. I'll get it presently. . . . I'll drag it to your room. . . .

Wassilissa. A pilgrim—you look it; say a vagabond . . . that sounds more like the truth. . . .

Luka. [*Sighs.*] You are not very hospitable, mother.

[WASSILISSA *goes to* PEPEL'S *door.*]

Alyoschka. [*Whispers from the kitchen.*] Has she gone? . . . h'm.

Wassilissa. [*Turns on him.*] Are you still there?

[ALYOSCHKA *disappears into the kitchen, whistling.* NASTIAH *and* LUKA *laugh.*]

Bubnoff. [*To* WASSILISSA.] He is not there. . . .

Wassilissa. Who?

Bubnoff. Waska.

[ALYOSCHKA *slips around to the stairs. Exit L. U. E.*]

Wassilissa. Have I asked you for him?

Bubnoff. I can see that you are looking into every corner.

Wassilissa. I am looking after things, do you understand? Why have you not swept up? How often have I told you that you must keep the place clean?

Bubnoff. It's the actor's turn today. . . .

Wassilissa. It makes no difference to me whose turn it is. When the Health Department people come and fine me, I'll have you thrown out. . . .

Bubnoff. [*Calmly.*] And what will you live on, in that case?

Wassilissa. See that not a speck of dust is left. [*Goes to the kitchen door to* NASTIAH.] And what are you standing around like a post for? What are you gawking about? Sweep up! Have you not seen . . . Natalya? Has she been here?

Nastiah. I don't know. . . . I haven't seen her.

Wassilissa. Bubnoff, was my sister here?

Bubnoff. Certainly. She brought the old man.

Wassilissa. And he, was he in his room?

Bubnoff. Wassili . . . to be sure. . . . She was talking with Kleshtsch. . . . Natalya. . . .

Wassilissa. I did not ask you who she was talking with. . . . Dirt everywhere, a foot thick. Ah, you pigs. See that you clean up . . . do you hear me?

[*Exit quickly R. U. E.*]

Bubnoff. What a nasty temper that woman has.

Luka. A brutal wife.

Nastiah. This life would brutalize anybody. And tied to such a husband—how can she bear that?

Bubnoff. She does not feel tied, so very tight. . . .

Luka. Is she always . . . so biting?

Bubnoff. Always . . . she was looking for her lover, you see, and that upset her.

Luka. Um, so that's the trouble . . . ah, yes, how many different people there are here on this earth go bossing around . . . and all trying to lord it over the rest, but in spite of it all bringing no cleanness about.

Bubnoff. They try, indeed, to bring order about, but the wit is lacking . . . which means, that we must finally clean up. . . . Nastiah . . . won't you do it? . . .

Nastiah. Certainly! Am I your chambermaid? [*She remains silent for a time.*] I'll get drunk today . . . soaked full.

[*Motion of her hand to her chin.*]

Bubnoff. Good business.

Luka. What are you going to get drunk for, my daughter? You were crying a moment ago, and now you promise to get drunk. . . .

Nastiah. [*Defiantly.*] And when I have gotten drunk, I will cry again . . . that's all. . . .

Bubnoff. But it's not much.

Luka. For what reason, tell me? Everything has a cause, even the smallest pimple in the face.

[NASTIAH *is silent, shaking her head.*]

Luka. Aye, aye, such is man . . . that's the way with people . . . what will become of them? I will sweep up myself. Where do you keep the broom?

Bubnoff. In the entry, behind the door. [*Exit* LUKA *L. U. E.*] Tell me, Nastenka.

Nastiah. [*Sits R. U. before stove.*] Um.

Bubnoff. What has Wassilissa got against Alyoschka, so much?

Nastiah. He has told everybody that Waska doesn't like her any more . . . is tired of her, is going to give her up, for Natasha interests him. . . . I am going to pull out and find another place. . . .

Bubnoff. Why so?

Nastiah. I am tired of it. I am in the way . . . superfluous.

Bubnoff. [*Thoughtfully.*] Where wouldn't you be superfluous? Everybody here on earth is superfluous. . . .

[NASTIAH *shakes her head, rises, and goes quietly upstairs R. U. E.* MEDVIEDEFF *enters L. U. E. followed by* LUKA *with the broom.*]

Medviedeff. [*To* LUKA.] I don't remember having seen you.

Luka. And the rest, you've seen them. Do you know everybody?

Medviedeff. Along my beat I must know everybody—and I don't know you. . . .

Luka. You would, if your beat included the whole world, but there is a small corner which has been left off. [*Exit R.*]

Medviedeff. [*Crossing to* BUBNOFF *L.*] That's right. My beat is not large . . . but the work is worse than in many bigger ones. Just as I came off duty I had to take that young cobbler Alyoschka to the station house. The rascal was sprawled out on his back in the middle of the street, if you can believe it, playing his accordion and bellowing: "I want for nothing, I wish for nothing," and wagons coming both ways and traffic everywhere. . . . He could easily have been run over, or something else happen . . . rattlebrain. . . . Of course I locked him up . . . he is a little too fresh.

Bubnoff. Come around tonight. . . . We'll have a game of checkers.

Medviedeff. I'll come . . . h'm, yes . . . but how is it about Waska?

Bubnoff. All right. . . . Same old thing. . . .

Medviedeff. Still alive?

Bubnoff. Why not? . . . His life is worth living.

Medviedeff. [*Doubtfully.*] So . . . has he? [LUKA *enters R. from kitchen, and exit L. U. E., a bucket in his hand.*] H'm—yes . . . there is a rumor about . . . Waska . . . haven't you heard?

Bubnoff. I've heard lots of things.

Medviedeff. Something about Wassilissa, he . . . have you not noticed?

Bubnoff. What?

Medviedeff. Why . . . in general . . . you know all about it but don't like to say so . . . it is well known . . . [*Strongly.*] Don't lie, my friend!

Bubnoff. Why should I lie?

Medviedeff. I thought . . . ah, the curs . . . they say, in short that Waska with Wassilissa . . . so to speak . . . nyah, what do I care? I am not her father, but only . . . her uncle. . . . It can't hurt me if they can't laugh at me. [KVASCHNYA *enters L. U. E.*] A bad lot . . . ah, you have come. . . .

Kvaschnya. My dear captain. Just think, Bubnoff, he proposed to me again at the market. . . .

Bubnoff. What of it? . . . Why do you put him off? He has money, and is a pretty hearty lover, even yet. . . .

Medviedeff. I . . . to be sure.

Kvaschnya. Ah, you old grey stud-horse. No, don't come near. That foolishness happens to me only once in a lifetime, and I've been through it already. Marriage, for a woman, is like jumping into the river in winter; once she's done it, she remembers it all her life.

Medviedeff. Wait . . . the husbands are not all the same. . . .

Kvaschnya. But I always remain the same. When my dear husband—when the devil took him—when he became a carcass, damn his ghost, I did not leave the house the whole day for joy; I sat there all alone and could scarcely believe my happiness.

Medviedeff. Why did you allow your husband to beat you? If you had gone to the police. . . .

Kvaschnya. Police! I complained to God for eight years . . . and even God couldn't do anything.

Medviedeff. But it is illegal now to beat wives. . . . Law and order are now enforced. . . . No man dare beat anybody now, except for the sake of law and order. . . . Wife beating happens only in lawless places. . . .

Luka. [*Leads* ANNA *in, L. U. E.*] Now, look out . . . now we've crawled down . . . ah, you poor child. . . . How could you go around alone so, in your condition? Where is your bed?

Anna. [*Draws toward L. D.*] Thank you, daddy.

Kvaschnya. There you have a married woman . . . look at her.

Luka. Such a poor, weak thing . . . creeping about quite alone there up in the entry, clinging to the walls—moaning without cease . . . why did you allow her to go out alone?

Kvaschnya. We did not notice it—pardon me, grandfather. Her lady in waiting has probably gone for a stroll. . . .

Luka. So you laugh. . . . How can you abandon another so? Whatever he may have become—he still remains a human being.

Medviedeff. This ought to be investigated. If she dies suddenly? We shall be mixed up in it. Give her every attention.

Luka. Quite right, Mr. Captain. . . .

Medviedeff. H'm . . . yes . . . you may say so . . . though I'm not a captain yet. . . .

Luka. Is it possible? But we should conclude from your appearance that you are a true hero.

[*From above a noise, the stamping of feet and smothered cries.*]

Medviedeff. Not quite yet—looks like a row.

Bubnoff. It sounds like one. . . .

Kvaschnya. I'll go see.

Medviedeff. And I've got to go too . . . ah, the service! Why should people be pulled apart when they brawl? They finally quit fighting of their own accord . . . when they are tired of thumping each other. . . . The best thing to do is to let them get their bellies full of fighting . . . then they don't row so often . . . they aren't in shape to. . . .

Bubnoff. [*Gets off his bench.*] You must lay your plan before the authorities. . . .

Kostilioff. [*Throws open the door R. U. E. and cries:*] Abram . . . come . . . quick . . . Wassilissa is killing Natasha . . . come . . . come!

[KVASCHNYA, MEDVIEDEFF, BUBNOFF *run to the entry, R. U. E., and* LUKA *looks after them, shaking his head.*]

Anna. Ah, God . . . the poor Natashenka!

Luka. Who is brawling there?

Anna. Our landlady . . . the two sisters. . . .

Luka. [*Approaches* ANNA.] Over heirlooms.

Anna. Both are well fed . . . both are healthy. . . .

Luka. And you . . . what is your name?

Anna. My name is Anna. . . . When I look at you . . . you are so much like my father, just like my own dear father . . . you, too, are so kind and tender. . . .

Luka. Because they have knocked me about the world so much, that is why I am tender. [*Chuckles to himself.*]

CURTAIN

ACT II

The same scene. Evening.

[SAHTIN, *the* BARON, KRIVOI ZOBA *and the* TARTAR *are sitting on the bank before the stove, playing cards.* KLESHTSCH *and the* ACTOR *are watching the game.* BUBNOFF *on his bench is playing Parti-Dame with* MEDVIEDEFF. LUKA *is sitting on the tabouret at* ANNA'S *bed. The room is lit by two lamps, one hanging on the wall over the card players on the right and the other above* BUBNOFF'S *bench.*]

Tartar. I'll play one more game . . . and then I quit. . . .

Bubnoff. Krivoi Zoba! A song. [*He sings.*] "Though still the sun goes up and down,"

Krivoi Zoba. [*Falling in.*] "No gleam can pierce to me in here. . . ."

Tartar. [*To* SAHTIN.] Shuffle the cards, but no crooked business. We already know what a swindler you are.

Bubnoff and Krivoi Zoba. [*Sing together.*] "By day and night my guards stand watch
—a—ach,
My prison window always near. . . ."

Anna. Illness and blows. . . . I have endured . . . they have been my lot . . . my whole life long.

Luka. Ah, you poor child! Do not grieve.

Medviedeff. What nerve! Be careful!

Bubnoff. Ah, ha! So . . . and so, and so. . . . [*Throws down card after card.*]

Tartar. [*Threatens* SAHTIN *with his fist.*] What are you hiding the cards for? I saw you . . . you.

Krivoi Zoba. Let him go, Hassan. They're bound to cheat us, one way or another. . . . Sing some more, Bubnoff.

Anna. I cannot remember to have ever had enough to eat . . . with trembling and fear . . . have I eaten every piece of bread. . . . I have trembled and constantly feared . . . lest I eat more than my share. . . . My whole life long have I gone in rags . . . my whole ill-fated life. . . . Why should this have been?

Luka. Ah, you poor child! You are tired? It will soon be right!

Actor. [*To* KRIVOI ZOBA.] Play the jack . . . the jack, damn it.

Baron. And we have the king!

Kleshtsch. These cards will always win.

Sahtin. So . . . they will.

Medviedeff. A queen!

Bubnoff. Another . . . there!

Anna. I am dying. . . .

Kleshtsch. [*To the* TARTAR.] There—look out! Throw the cards down, prince, stop playing.

Actor. Don't you think he knows what to do?

Baron. Be careful, Andreuschka, that I don't throw you out of the house.

Tartar. Again, I say. The pitcher goes often to the well, then it breaks . . . the same with me. . . .

[KLESHTSCH *shakes his head and goes behind* BUBNOFF.]

Anna. I am always thinking to myself: My Saviour . . . shall I there too . . . in that world . . . endure such tortures?

Luka. No! Never! . . . You will suffer nothing. Lie perfectly still . . . and have no fear. You shall find peace there! Be patient yet a little while. . . . We must all suffer, my love. . . . Every one endures life in his own way.

[*He rises and goes hastily into the kitchen R.*]

Bubnoff. "Spy on, with the might of your eyes, forever."

Krivoi Zoba. "On freedom still my thoughts shall dwell. . . ."

Together.

"I cannot spring these chains and locks —a—ach. . . .

Nor fly the walls of this cold cell. . . ."

Tartar. Stop! He has pushed a card up his sleeve.

Baron. [*Confused.*] No, where else then?

Actor. [*Convincingly.*] You have made a mistake, prince! It's not to be thought of. . . .

Tartar. I saw it! Cheats! I play no more!

Sahtin. [*Throwing the cards together.*] Then go your way, Hassan. . . . You know that we are cheats—so why did you play with us?

Baron. He's lost forty copecs, you'd think from the row that he'd lost three hundred. And this is a prince!

Tartar. [*Violently.*] Everybody must play fair!

Sahtin. But tell me why?

Tartar. What does "why" mean?

Sahtin. Just so . . . why?

Tartar. Um, you don't know?

Sahtin. I don't know, do you?

[TARTAR *spits angrily, all laugh at him.*]

Krivoi Zoba. [*Cheerfully.*] You are a comical owl, Hassan. Think it over. If they lived honestly they would starve in three days. . . .

Tartar. What's that to me? People must live honestly.

Krivoi Zoba. Same old story, I'd rather have a drink of tea . . . cut loose, Bubnoff.

Bubnoff. "Alas, these heavy chains of iron, this armed patrol on ceaseless guard. . . ."

Krivoi Zoba. Come, Hassan. [*Exit singing.*] "No, nevermore shall I break through."

[*The* TARTAR *threatens the* BARON *with his fist, and then follows his comrade. Exit R.*]

Sahtin. [*To the* BARON, *laughing.*] Nyah, your worship, you've launched us triumphantly into the mire. You, an educated man, and can't handle cards. . . .

Baron. [*Throwing up his hands.*] The devil knows how the cards should be handled.

Actor. No genius, no self-confidence . . . without that you'll never be any good. . . .

Medviedeff. I have a queen, and you have two, h'm, yes.

Bubnoff. One is enough, if well played . . . your play.

Kleshtsch. The game is lost, Abram Ivanitch.

Medviedeff. That is none of your business —understand? Hold your tongue. . . .

Sahtin. Fifty-three copecs won. . . .

Actor. The three copecs are for me . . . though what do I want with three copecs?

Luka. [*Entering from kitchen R.*] You soaked the Tartar dry. Are you going for some?

Baron. Come with us!

Sahtin. I'd just like to see you after you've put a couple of dozen away. . . .

Luka. Surely I wouldn't look better than I do sober. . . .

Actor. Come, old fellow. . . . I will declaim for you a pair of pretty couplets. . . .

Luka. Couplets? What are they?

Actor. Verses, don't you understand. . . .

Luka. Verses, for me . . . poems? What do I want them for?

Actor. Ah, they are so comical . . . yet sometimes so sad. . . .

Sahtin. Are you coming, couplet singer?

[*Exit L. U. E. with the* BARON.]

Actor. I will catch up with you. [*To* LUKA.] There is, old man, for example, a poem beginning. . . . I have completely forgotten it. . . . [*Rubs his forehead.*]

Bubnoff. Your queen is lost . . . go.

Medviedeff. I played wrong, the devil take it.

Actor. In the past, while my organism was not as yet poisoned with alcohol, I had a splendid memory . . . yes, patriarch! Now . . . it is all up with me . . . time and time again, with the greatest success I have recited this poem . . . to thundering applause. . . Do you know what applause means, brother? It is the wine of wines . . . when I came out, in this posture [*Assumes an attitude.*] and then began . . . [*He is silent.*] . . . not a word . . . have I retained. And the poem was my heart's delight. . . . Is that not frightful, patriarch? [*Clutches the air.*]

Luka. Alas, too bad . . . when the best beloved has been forgotten. In that which man loves, he finds his soul. . . .

Actor. I have drowned my soul, patriarch, . . . I am a lost man. . . . And why am I lost? Because I believe in myself no more. . . . I am through. . . .

Luka. Why so, then. Be cured! The drunkard, I have heard, can now be cured. Without expense, my brother. . . . A dispensary has been erected . . . there you may be cured without charge. They realize now, you see, that the drunkard is also a man, and they are glad when one comes to allow himself to be cured. Hurry, then, go there. . . .

Actor. [*Thoughtfully.*] Where to? Where is it?

Luka. In a certain city . . . what is it called? A strange name. . . . No, I can't tell you right now . . . but listen to me: You must begin to get ready! Be abstemious! Hold yourself together, and suffer, endure thus, . . . and then you'll be cured. Begin a new life . . . is that not splendid, brother: a new life . . . now, decide . . . one, two, three!

Actor. [*Smiling.*] A new life . . . from the start . . . that is beautiful. . . . Can it be true? A new life?—[*Laughs.*] Nyah . . . yes! I can! I can!

Luka. Why not? Man can achieve everything . . . if he only will. . . .

Actor. [*Suddenly, as if awakened from a dream.*] You're a queer customer! So long! See you again. [*He whistles.*] Meantime, old man. [*Exit L. U. E.*]

Anna. Daddy.

Luka. What is it, little mother?

Anna. Talk a little bit, to me. . . .

Luka. [*Going to her.*] Gladly. . . . Let us have a long chat.

[KLESHTSCH *looks around, silently goes to the bed of his wife, looks at her, gesticulates, as if about to speak.*]

Luka. Well, brother?

Kleshtsch. [*Whispers as if in fear.*] Nothing.

[*Goes slowly to door, L. U. E. Remains a few moments, then goes out.*]

Luka. [*Following him with his eyes.*] Your husband seems to be oppressed.

Anna. I cannot think of him any more.

Luka. Has he beaten you?

Anna. How often. . . . He has brought me . . . to this.

Bubnoff. My wife . . . had once an admirer. He played with kings and queens quite splendidly, the rascal. . . .

Medviedeff. H'm.

Anna. Grandfather. . . . Talk to me, my dear. . . . I am lonely. . . .

Luka. That is nothing. That may be felt before death, my love. It means nothing, dear. Have faith. You will die, you see, and then enter into rest. Have fear of nothing more, of nothing more. It will be still, and peaceful . . . and you will lie resting there. Death subdues everything . . . he is so tender with us. . . . Only in death shall rest be found, they say . . . and such is the truth, my love! Where shall rest be found here?

[PEPEL *enters L. U. E. a little drunk, dishevelled and sullen. He sits on the bunk by the kitchen door, silent and motionless.*]

Anna. And shall there be such torture there?

Luka. Nothing is there! Believe me, nothing! Rest alone—nothing else. They will lead you before the Master and will say: Look, O Master—thy servant Anna is come. . . .

Medviedeff. [*Vigorously.*] How can you know what shall be said there: have you ever heard? . . .

[PEPEL, *at the sound of* MEDVIEDEFF'S *voice, raises his head and listens.*]

Luka. My information is reliable, Mr. Commissioner. . . .

Medviedeff. [*Softly.*] H'm,—yes. Nyah, it is your affair . . . that means . . . but I am not a commissioner. . . .

Bubnoff. Two birds with one stone. . . .

Medviedeff. Ah, you, the devil take you. . .

Luka. And the Master will look upon you in loving kindness and will say: "I know this Anna!" "Now," he will say, "lead her forth into Paradise. May she there find peace. . . . I know her life was wearisome . . . she is very tired . . . let her have rest, our Anna."

Anna. Grandfather . . . you, my dear . . . if only it is so . . . if I there . . . find peace . . . and feel nothing more. . . .

Luka. You will suffer nothing . . . nothing! Only have faith! Die joyfully, without anxiety. . . . Death to us, I say unto you, is like a mother soothing her children. . . .

Anna. But . . . perhaps . . . I will get well again?

Luka. [*Laughing.*] For what? To fresh tortures?

Anna. But I might still . . . live a little while . . . a very little while . . . if there is no torture beyond . . . I can afford to suffer at the end here a little more. . . .

Luka. There shall be no more pain . . . none at all.

Pepel. [*Rising.*] True—it may be, and may not be!

Anna. Ah, God. . . .

Luka. Ah, my dear boy. . . .

Medviedeff. Who is howling there?

Pepel. [*Going to him.*] Me, what's the matter?

Medviedeff. People must keep quiet in here. . . . You have no cause for howling.

Pepel. Ah . . . blockhead! And you her uncle . . . ha, ha!

Luka. [*Whispers to* Pepel.] Listen, boy —not so loud. A woman is dying here. . . . Her lips are covered with earth already . . . don't disturb her. . . .

Pepel. As you say so, grandfather, I will listen to you. You are a splendid chap, pilgrim . . . you tell them famously . . . you're full of nice stories. Keep it up, brother, keep it up . . . there is so little pleasure in the world.

Bubnoff. Is she dying for keeps?

Luka. I guess she is not fooling.

Bubnoff. Then we will finally be rid of that coughing . . . a great nuisance, her everlasting coughing. . . . I take two. . . .

Medviedeff. Ah, . . . the devil take you.

Pepel. Abram. . . .

Medviedeff. I am not Abram . . . for you. . . .

Pepel. Abrashka, tell me—is Natasha still sick?

Medviedeff. Does that concern you?

Pepel. No, but say: did Wassilissa really beat her up so badly?

Medviedeff. And that's none of your business either . . . that's a family affair . . . who are you, anyhow, eh?

Pepel. I may be who I am—but when it suits me, I will take your Natasha away. You will not see her again.

Medviedeff. [*Interrupting his playing.*] What do you say? Whom are you talking about? My niece shall . . . ach, you thief!

Pepel. A thief—that you have not yet caught. . . .

Medviedeff. Wait! I'll soon catch you . . . in a very little while I will have you. . . .

Pepel. Whenever it suits you . . . and then your whole nest here will be torn up. Do you think I'll hold my tongue when it comes to the judge? There you're badly mistaken. Who incited you to theft, they will ask—who put the opportunity before you? Mischka Kostilioff and his wife. And who received the stolen goods? Mischka Kostilioff and his wife.

Medviedeff. You lie! Nobody will believe it.

Pepel. They will quickly believe—because it is the truth. And I'll get you into the muddle too, and the rest of you, you gang of thieves—we shall soon see.

Medviedeff. [*Uneasily.*] Shut up! Shut up! What have I done to you? . . . You mad dog. . . .

Pepel. What good have you done me?

Luka. Quite right. . . .

Medviedeff. [*To* Luka.] What are you croaking about? What business is this of yours? This is a family affair. . . .

Bubnoff. [*To* Luka.] Let them have it out. . . . We two won't be haltered anyhow. . . .

Luka. [*Softly.*] I have done no harm. I only think that if a man does not do another good—then he has done wrong.

Medviedeff. [*Who does not understand* Luka.] Look, you. We are all acquainted here. . . . And you—who are you?

[*Exit quickly L. U. E. angrily fuming.*]

Luka. He has gone mad, Sir Cavalier . . . oho! Very peculiar, brothers, what we have here, somewhat complicated.

Pepel. He has gone to Wassilissa, now, with it.

Bubnoff. Don't make a fool of yourself, Wassili. Don't try to be the bravest. Bravery, my boy, is good, when you go into the woods for mushrooms. . . . It is out of place here . . . they have you by the throat . . . in a jiffy.

Pepel. We shall see. . . . We Yaroslavs are much too sly . . . we cannot be caught with the bare hands . . . will you have a fight? . . . Good, then we begin it. . . .

Luka. It would, indeed, be better, boy, to go away. . . .

Pepel. Where then? Tell me. . . .

Luka. Go . . . to Siberia.

Pepel. Ha! Ha! Never; I'd rather wait until they send me, at the expense of the government. . . .

Luka. No, really, listen to me! Go there; you can make your way in Siberia . . . they need such young fellows. . . .

Pepel. My way is already pointed out! My father spent his life in prison, and that fate is my legacy . . . when I was still a small boy they called me a thief and the son of a thief.

Luka. A beautiful country, Siberia. A golden land. A man with strength and a clear head develops there . . . like a cucumber in a hot bed.

Pepel. Tell me, pilgrim, why do you fabricate so ceaselessly?

Luka. How?

Pepel. Are you deaf? Why do you lie, I ask. . . .

Luka. When have I lied?

Pepel. Right straight along. . . . It is beautiful there, by your way of thinking, and beautiful here . . . which is not true. Why then, do you lie?

Luka. Believe me! Or go there and convince yourself. . . . You will send me thanks . . . why loiter here? And, from whence comes your eagerness for truth? Think it over: the truth is, they may make an end of you here.

Pepel. It is all the same . . . even a halter.

Luka. You are a strange fellow. Why will you put your head into it?

Bubnoff. What are you two jawing about? I don't catch on. . . . What kind of truth do you want, Waska? What good would it be to you? You know the truth about yourself . . . and all the world knows it. . . .

Pepel. Hold your snout. Don't croak. He shall tell me first . . . hear, pilgrim . . . is there a God?

[LUKA *laughs and remains silent.*]

Bubnoff. Mankind is like chips which the storm sweeps away . . . the finished house remains, but the chips are gone.

Luka. [*Softly.*] If you believe in Him, there is a God; believe not and none exists. . . . What you believe in . . . exists. . . .

[PEPEL *looks silently surprised at the old man.*]

Bubnoff. I'll have a drink of tea now . . . come with me to the ale house.

Luka. [*To* PEPEL.] What are you staring at?

Pepel. It means then . . . just so . . . wait.

Bubnoff. Nyah, then I'll go alone.

[*Exit L. U. E., bumping into* WASSILISSA.]

Pepel. Then . . . do as you . . . then you. . . .

Wassilissa. [*To* BUBNOFF.] Is Nastassya at home?

Bubnoff. No. . . . [*Exit L. U. E.*]

Pepel. Ah . . . there she is.

Wassilissa. [*Goes to* ANNA'S *bed.*] Is she still alive?

Luka. Do not disturb her.

Wassilissa. And you, what are you loafing around for?

Luka. I can go out, if I must. . . .

Wassilissa. [*Approaching* PEPEL'S *door.*] Wassili! I have business with you. . . . [LUKA *goes to the door, L. U. E., opens it, closes it noisily, then carefully climbs up the stove and conceals himself.* WASSILISSA *has entered* PEPEL'S *room. Within.*] Waska, come here.

Pepel. I will not come. . . . I will not. . . .

Wassilissa. [*Re-enters.*] What's the matter? Why are you so mad?

Pepel. It is tiresome. . . . I am sick of the whole mess here. . . .

Wassilissa. And me, are you sick . . . of me, too?

Pepel. You too. . . . [WASSILISSA *pulls the shawl which is over her shoulders closely together and presses her arm against her breast. She goes to* ANNA'S *bed, looks cautiously behind the curtain, and returns to* PEPEL.] Nyah, so . . . speak. . . .

Wassilissa. What shall I say? No one can be forced to love . . . and I should be unlike myself to beg for love . . . for your frankness many thanks. . . .

Pepel. My frankness?

Wassilissa. Yes, you say you are sick of me . . . or is it not true? [PEPEL *looks at her in silence. She approaches him.*] Why do you stare? Do you not know me?

Pepel. [*With a deep breath.*] You are beautiful, Waska. [WASSILISSA *puts her arm around his neck: he shakes it off with a movement of the shoulder.*] But still my heart has never belonged to you. . . . I have gone on living with you . . . but I have never truly liked you. . . .

Wassilissa. [*Softly.*] So . . . o . . . now . . . um. . . .

Pepel. Now we have nothing more to talk about. . . . Nothing more . . . go away . . . leave me alone.

Wassilissa. Have you found pleasure in another?

Pepel. That is nothing to you. . . . If it were so—I would not take you along for a matchmaker. . . .

Wassilissa. [*Meaningly.*] Who knows . . . perhaps I can bring it about.

Pepel. [*Suspiciously.*] Who with?

Wassilissa. You know who I mean . . . don't deny it. . . . I talk straight out from the shoulder. . . . [*Softly.*] I will only say . . . you have deeply wronged me . . . without provocation you have struck me a blow, as with a club . . . you always said you loved me, and . . . all of a sudden. . . .

Pepel. All of a sudden . . . not at all. . . . I have thought so, long . . . you have no soul. . . . In a woman there should be a soul. We men are animals . . . we know nothing else . . . and men must first be taught goodness . . . and you, what good have you taught me? . . .

Wassilissa. What has been has been. . . . I know that we cannot control the impulses of our hearts . . . if you love me no more —good . . . it is all the same to me.

Pepel. All right, then. It is settled. We separate in friendship, without scandal . . . pleasantly!

Wassilissa. Stop, not so quick. During the whole time that we have lived together . . . I have always hoped you would help me out of this cesspool here . . . that you would free me from my husband, from my uncle . . . from this whole life . . . and perhaps I have not loved you, Waska, at all . . . perhaps in you I love only . . . my one hope, my one dream . . . do you understand? I had hoped you would pull me out. . . .

Pepel. You are no nail and I am no tongs. . . . I had thought you would finish him; with your slyness . . . for you are sly and quick-witted. [*Sits at R. table.*]

Wassilissa. [*Leans toward him.*] Waska, we will help each other. . . .

Pepel. How then?

Wassilissa. [*In a low tone, with expression.*] My sister . . . you have taken a fancy to her, I know it. . . .

Pepel. And you knock her about so brutally on that account. I'll say this to you, Waska: don't touch her again.

Wassilissa. Wait. Not so hotly. It can all be done quietly, in friendliness. . . . Marry her whenever you feel like it. I'll find the money, three hundred rubles If I can get more I'll give you more. . . .

Pepel. [*Rocks on his seat back and forth.*] Hold on. . . . How do you mean that? What for?

Wassilissa. Free me from my husband. Take that halter from my neck. . . .

Pepel. [*Whistles.*] Oho, I se-e! You have thought it out well . . . the husband in his grave, the admirer in Siberia, and you yourself. . . .

Wassilissa. But Waska, why Siberia? Not you yourself . . . your comrades. And even if you did do it yourself—who would know? Think . . . Natasha thine. . . . You shall have money . . . to go away . . . anywhere . . . you free me forever . . . and for my sister too; it will be a good thing for her to be away from me. I can't look at her without getting furious. . . . I hate her on your account. . . . I cannot control myself. . . . I give her such blows that I myself cry for pity . . . but—I strike her just the same. And I will go on with it.

Pepel. Beast! Don't sing praises of your own cruelty.

Wassilissa. I am not praising myself. I only speak the truth. Remember, Waska, you have already been imprisoned twice by my husband . . . when you could not satisfy his greed. . . . He sticks to me like vermin . . . for four years he has fed on me. Such a man for a husband! And Natasha dreads him too. He oppresses her and calls her a beggar. He is a poison, a rank poison for us all. . . .

Pepel. How cleverly you contrive it all. . . .

Wassilissa. What I have said is not contrived. . . . It is quite clear to you. . . . Only a fool could not comprehend. . . .

[KOSTILIOFF *enters warily, L. U. E., and sneaks forward.*]

Pepel. [*To* WASSILISSA.] No . . . go away!

Wassilissa. Think it over. [*Sees her husband.*] What's this! Dogging me again?

[PEPEL *springs up and looks wildly at* KOSTILIOFF.]

Kostilioff. Indeed . . . it is I . . . it is I . . . and you are quite alone here? Ah . . ah. . . . Been chatting for a spell? [*Suddenly stamps his feet and screeches aloud, to* WASSILISSA.] Waska, you baggage . . . you beggar, you deceptive carrion. [*Then frightened by his own cry which is answered only by an echoless silence.*] Have mercy on me, Lord. . . . You have again led me to sin, Wassilissa. . . . I search for you everywhere. . . . [*Squeakingly.*] It is time to go to bed.

Have you forgot to fill the holy lamp? . . . ah, you beggar, you swine!

[*Waves his hands tremblingly in her face.*]

[WASSILISSA *goes slowly to the door, R. U. E., and looks back at* PEPEL.]

Pepel. [*To* KOSTILIOFF.] You! Go your own way. Get out. . . .

Kostilioff. [*Cries.*] I am the master here. Get out yourself, understand? Thief!

Pepel. [*Sternly.*] Go your own way, Mishka. . . .

Kostilioff. Be careful. Or else I'll . . .

[PEPEL *seizes him by the collar and shakes him. A noise of turning and yawning is heard on the stove.* PEPEL *loosens* KOSTILIOFF, *who, crying loudly, goes out R. U. E. up the stairs.*]

Pepel. [*Jumps on bunk before stove.*] Who is there? Who is on the stove?

Luka. [*Poking is head out.*] What?

Pepel. Is it you?

Luka. [*Composedly.*] I . . . I myself. . . . Who else would it be? . . . Ah, my God!

Pepel. [*Closes door R. U. E., looks for key, but does not find it.*] The devil . . . crawl down, pilgrim.

Luka. All right . . . I'll crawl down. . . .

Pepel. [*Roughly.*] Why did you climb up on the stove?

Luka. Where should I go?

Pepel. Why didn't you go out into the entry?

Luka. Too cold, little brother. . . . I am an old man. . . .

Pepel. Did you hear?

Luka. Without any trouble. Why not? I am not deaf. Ah, my boy, you are lucky, truly lucky.

Pepel. [*Mistrustfully.*] I am lucky? How so?

Luka. Because . . . I climbed up on the stove . . . that was your luck. . . .

Pepel. Why did you move about?

Luka. Because I felt hot . . . luckily for you, my orphan . . . and then I thought: if the boy does not lose his head . . . and strangle the old man. . . .

Pepel. Yes, I might easily have done it. . . . I hate him. . . .

Luka. It would not have been any wonder . . . such things happen every day.

Pepel. [*Laughing.*] Mm. . . . Have you yourself not done something of the kind some time?

Luka. Listen, my boy, to what I tell you: this woman, keep well away from her. At no cost let her approach. . . . She will soon get her husband out of the way more cleverly than you could ever manage it. Don't listen to her, this offspring of Satan! Look at me: not a hair left on my head . . . and why? The women, and no other reason. . . . I have known, perhaps, more women than I have had hairs on my head . . . and this Wassilissa . . . is worse than the pest. . . .

Pepel. I don't know . . . . whether to thank you . . . or, are you, too . . . ?

Luka. Say no more. . . Listen. If there is a girl, take the one you like best—take her by the hand and go away together; quite away, a long way off. . . .

Pepel. [*Gloomily.*] We cannot know each other: who is good, who is bad. . . . Nothing certain is known to us. . . .

Luka. Of what importance can that be? Man's ways vary . . . following the different desires of his heart; so he lives, good today, bad tomorrow. And if you love the girl, then pull out, settle it. Or go alone. You are young, you have still time enough to be enmeshed by a woman.

Pepel. [*Takes him by the shoulder.*] No, but say—why do you tell me all this? . . .

Luka. Hold on. Let me go. . . . I must look after Anna. . . . Her throat is rattling. [*He goes to* ANNA'S *bed, strikes the curtain back, looks at the prostrate form and touches it with his hand.* PEPEL, *uneasy and depressed, follows him.*] Lord Jesus Christ, All Powerful! receive in peace the soul of this newcomer, thy servant Anna. . . .

Pepel. [*Whispers.*] Is she dead?

[*Elevates himself to his full height and looks without approaching.*]

Luka. [*Whispering.*] Her misery is ended. And where is her husband?

Pepel. In the bar-room—of course.

Luka. He must be told. . . .

Pepel. [*Shrinking.*] I do not love the dead.

Luka. [*Goes to the door, L. U. E.*] Why should we love the dead? We must love the living . . . the living. . . .

Pepel. I'll go with you.

Luka. Are you afraid?

Pepel. I love them not. . . .

[*Exit hastily, with* LUKA, *L. U. E. The stage remains empty for a few moments. Behind the door, L. U. E., is heard a dull, confused, unusual sound. Enter the* ACTOR, *L. U. E. He remains standing on the platform, his hand on the door jamb, and cries.*]

Actor. Old man! Luka! Heh, where do you hide? Now I remember. Listen.

[*Tremblingly takes two steps forward, puts himself in an attitude and declaims.*]

And if humanity to holy truth
No path by searching finds,
Then all the world shall praise the fool
Who spins a dream to mesh their minds.

[NATASHA *appears behind the* ACTOR *in the door. He continues.*]

Old man . . . listen!
And if the sun tomorrow shall forget
Upon the earth his light to stream,
Then all the world shall hail the fool,
With his illuminating red-gold dream.

Natasha. [*Laughs.*] Look at the scarecrow. Maybe he has had one or two. . . .

Actor. [*Turns to her.*] A-ah, it is you! And where is our patriarch? Our loving, kind-hearted pilgrim. . . . There is nobody . . . at home. . . . Natasha, farewell, farewell.

Natasha. [*Approaches him.*] You have just greeted me, and now you say farewell.

Actor. [*Steps in her way.*] I shall go. . . . I shall travel . . . when, soon as spring comes, I shall be far away.

Natasha. Let me by. . . . Where shall you travel then?

Actor. I shall go to that city. . . . I shall be cured. . . . You must leave here, too. . . . Ophelia . . . get thee to a nunnery. . . . There is, you know, a hospital for organisms . . . for hard drinkers, so to speak . . . a splendid hospital . . . all marble . . . marble floors . . . light . . . cleanliness . . . good board—all free of charge! And marble floors, truly. I shall find it, this city, I'll be myself again. . . . Begin a new life. . . . I am on the way to regeneration . . . as King Lear said! Do you know too, Natasha . . . what my stage name is? Svertchkoff-Savolszhinski I'm called . . . nobody knows that here, nobody . . . here I am nameless . . . realize, if you can, how it hurts to lose your name. Even dogs have their names. [NATASHA *goes softly past the* ACTOR, *stands at* ANNA'S *bed and looks at the dead body.*] Without a name . . . where there is no name there is no man.

Natasha. Look! . . . dear . . . why . . . she is dead. . . .

Actor. [*Shaking his head.*] Impossible. . . .

Natasha. [*Stands aside.*] In God's name . . . look. . . .

Bubnoff. [*Enters L. U. E.*] What is there to look at?

Natasha. Anna is dead!

Bubnoff. Then there will be no more coughing. [*Goes to* ANNA'S *bed, looks for a time at the dead body and then goes to his place.*] Somebody must tell Kleshtsch . . . it's his business. . . .

Actor. I'll go. I shall tell him. . . . She too, has lost her name.

[*Exit* ACTOR, *L. U. E.*]

Natasha. [*In the centre of the room, to herself partly.*] And I . . . some time, shall languish so, and die forsaken in a cellar. . . .

Bubnoff. [*Spreading out an old torn blanket on his shelf.*] What is the matter . . . what are you muttering?

Natasha. Nothing . . . only to myself. . . .

Bubnoff. Are you expecting Waska? Be careful with Waska. . . . He will knock your skull in, some day, for you. . . .

Natasha. Isn't it all the same to me, who knocks it in? I'd rather have it done by him. . . .

Bubnoff. [*Lies down.*] As you prefer . . . no funeral of mine.

Natasha. It is the best thing for her that could happen . . . to die . . . yet it is pitiful . . . thou loving Master . . . what did she live for?

Bubnoff. So with everybody—but, we live. Man is born, lives for a space of time, and dies. I will die too . . . and you will die . . . why pity the dead, then?

[LUKA, *the* TARTAR, KRIVOI ZOBA *and* KLESHTSCH *enter L. U. E.* KLESHTSCH *follows behind the others in shaken spirits.*]

Natasha. Sh-sh. . . Anna!

Krivoi Zoba. We have already heard. . . . God take her soul. . . .

Tartar. [*To* KLESHTSCH.] She must be taken out. She must be carried into the entry. This is no place for the dead. The living person can have a bed. . . .

Kleshtsch. [*Whispering.*] We will take her out.

[*All stand around the body.* KLESHTSCH *looks at the remains of his wife over the shoulders of the others.*]

Krivoi Zoba. [*To the* TARTAR.] Do you think she will smell? No . . . while she was still alive she dried up. . . .

Natasha. For God's sake . . . nobody pities her . . . if anybody had but said a word of kindness.

Luka. Don't be hurt, my daughter. It is nothing. What have we to do with pitying the dead? We have not enough for each other. And you talk of pitying her.

Bubnoff. [*Gapes.*] Why waste words . . . when she is dead—no words can help her any more . . . against sickness certain words can be used . . . against death, nothing.

Tartar. [*Stepping aside.*] The police must be told. . . .

Krivoi Zoba. Naturally—that is the regulation. Kleshtsch, have you already reported it?

Kleshtsch. No . . . now comes the funeral and I have only forty copecs in the world. . . .

Krivoi Zoba. Then borrow . . . or we will take up a collection . . . everybody give what he can, one five copecs, another ten . . . but the police must soon be told. Or else, at last, they will think you have beaten your wife to death . . . or something else.

[*Goes to the bunk, U. on which the* TARTAR *is lying, and attempts to lie down with him.*]

Natasha. [*Goes to* BUBNOFF'S *bench.*] Now I shall dream about her. . . . I always dream of the dead. . . . I am afraid to be alone. It is so dark in the entry.

Luka. [*Follows with his eyes.*] Be afraid of the living . . . that is what I say to you. . . .

Natasha. Take me upstairs, daddy. . . .

Luka. Come . . . come . . . I will go with you. [*Exit both L. U. E. Pause.*]

Krivoi Zoba. [*Yawns.*] Oh, oh! [*To the* TARTAR.] It will soon be spring now, Hassan. . . . Then there will be a little bit of sun for you and me. The peasants now are repairing their plows and harrows . . . they will go to the field soon . . . h'm—yes . . . and we, Hassan. He is already snoring, cursed Mohammedan.

Bubnoff. The Tartars are fond of sleep.

Kleshtsch. [*Standing in the middle of the room staring stupidly before himself.*] What shall I begin to do now?

Krivoi Zoba. Lie down and sleep . . . that's all. . . .

Kleshtsch. [*Whispers.*] And . . . she! What shall be done with her?

[*Nobody answers him. Enter* SAHTIN *and the* ACTOR, *L. U. E.*]

Actor. [*Cries.*] Old man! My true adviser. . . .

Sahtin. Miklucka-Maclai comes . . . ho, ho!

Actor. The thing is settled! Patriarch, where is the city . . . where are you?

Sahtin. Fata Morgana! He has deluded you . . . there are no cities. . . . No, no people . . . there is nothing at all!

Actor. Liar. . . .

Tartar. [*Springing up.*] Where is the proprietor? I'll see the proprietor! If we can't sleep here, he shall charge us nothing . . . the dead . . . the drunken. . . .

[*Exit quickly, R. U. E.* SAHTIN *whistles after him.*]

Bubnoff. [*Awakened.*] Go to bed, brats, make no noise, the night is for sleep. . . .

Actor. True. . . . I have here [*Rubs his forehead.*] "Our nets have caught the dead," as it says in a . . . chanson, from Béranger.*

Sahtin. The dead hear not. The dead feel not. Howl . . . shout as much as you like . . . the dead hear not!

[LUKA *appears in the door.*]

CURTAIN

* In reality a quotation from Pushkin. [Translator's note.]

ACT III

TRANSLATOR'S NOTE: In the Russian, the third act takes place upon a new scene, but as the scene of the previous acts may be employed without necessitating any change in dialogue or construction, the stage directions given in this act have the scene of the first and second acts in view. The new scene is described as follows:

A vacant place between two buildings, filled with rubbish and overgrown with weeds. In the background, a high brick fire-wall, which covers the heavens. Near it a small elder-tree. On the right, a dark wall of reinforced wooden beams, part of a barn or stable. On the left, the gray wall of KOSTILIOFF'S *lodging-house, its rough plaster adhering only in places. This wall runs diagonally; the rear wall of the building, the corner being about the middle of the scene, forms with the fire-wall a narrow passageway. In the gray wall there are two windows, one on a level with the earth, the other four or five feet higher and nearer the rear. Against the gray wall lies a great sled, overturned, with a beam about three yards long. Near the stable wall on the right is a heap of old boards and hewn beams.*

It is evening, the setting sun throws a red light against the fire-wall. Spring has just begun and the snow is scarcely melted. The black twigs of the elder-tree have not begun to swell.

[*In the room,* NASTIAH, *seated near*

NATASHA, *is telling a story.* LUKA, *the* BARON, *and* BUBNOFF *are seated together at the left.* KLESHTSCH *is reclining on a bench at the right.*]

Nastiah. [*With closed eyes, moving her head in time to the story, which she is telling in a sing-song voice.*] In the night, then, he came to the garden, to the summer-bower, as we had arranged. . . . I had waited long, trembling for fear and grief . . . and he too, was trembling from head to foot, and chalk white, but in his hand he held a . . . pistol. . . .

Natasha. [*Nibbling at sunflower seeds.*] Just listen . . . these students are all as mad as March hares.

Nastiah. And in a terrible voice, he said to me: my true love. . . .

Bubnoff. Ha, ha, my "true" love, did he say?

Baron. Be still there, let her humbug in peace—you don't have to listen, if it doesn't please you . . . go on.

Nastiah. My heart's distraction, said he, my golden treasure; my parents refuse to allow me, said he, to marry you, and threaten me with their curses if I do not give you up, and so I must, said he, take my life . . . and his pistol was frightfully large, and loaded with ten bullets. . . . Farewell, said he, true friend of my heart! My decision is irrevocable. . . . I cannot live without you. But I answered him, my never-to-be-forgotten friend . . . my Raoul. . . .

Bubnoff. [*Astonished.*] What's his name . . . Graul?

Baron. You are mistaken, Nastiah! The last time you called him Gaston.

Nastiah. [*Springing up.*] Silence! You vagabond curs! Can you understand what love is . . . real, genuine love? And I . . . I have tasted this genuine love. [*To the* BARON.] You unworthy scamp. . . . You were an educated man . . . you say, have drunk your coffee in bed. . . .

Luka. Have patience! Don't scold her! Show human beings some consideration. . . . It is not what man says but why he says it,—that's the point. Keep on, my love—they don't mean anything.

Bubnoff. Always laying on the bright hues, raven. . . . Nyah, cut loose again!

Baron. Go on.

Natasha. Pay no attention to them . . . who are they, any way? They only speak out of envy . . . because they have nothing to tell about themselves. . . .

Nastiah. [*Sits down again.*] I don't want to. . . . I won't tell anything more . . . . if they don't like to believe it . . . and laugh about it. [*Suddenly brightens up. Is silent a few seconds, closes her eyes again and begins in a loud and rapid voice, keeping time with her hand, as if to distant ringing music.*] And I answered him: Joy of my life! O my glittering star! Without you, I too, could not live . . . because I love you madly and must love you always, as long as my heart beats in my bosom! But, said I, rob yourself not of your young life . . . for look, your dear parents whose single joy you are—they stand in need of you. Give me up. . . . I would rather pine away . . . out of longing for you, my love. . . . I am—alone. . . . I am—wholly yours . . . yes, let me die . . . what matters it . . . I am good for nothing . . . and have nothing . . . absolutely nothing. . . .

[*Covers her face with her hands and cries softly.*]

Natasha. [*Goes to her side, quietly.*] Don't.

[LUKA *strokes* NASTIAH'S *head, laughing.*]

Bubnoff. [*Laughs aloud.*] Oh . . . ho . . . a deceiving minx, . . . eh?

Baron. [*Laughs aloud.*] Now—grandfather—do you believe what she tells? She gets it all out of her book . . . out of "Disastrous Love," all nonsense. Drop it.

Natasha. What is that to you? You'd better keep still. God has punished you enough. . . .

Nastiah. [*Furious.*] You! Tell us, where is your soul?

Luka. [*Takes her by the hand.*] Come, my love. Do not be angry. . . . They mean nothing, I know. . . . I—believe you. You are right, and not they . . . if you yourself believe it, then you have had just such true love. . . . Certainly, quite certainly. And he there, your lover, don't be angry. . . . He only laughs perhaps . . . about it . . . because he is envious. . . . No doubt in his whole life he never felt anything genuine. . . . No, certainly not. Come!

Nastiah. [*Presses her arm against her breast.*] Grandfather. Before God . . . it is true! It is all true. . . . A French student . . . Gastoscha was his name . . . and he had a little black beard . . . he always wore patent leather shoes. . . . May lightning strike me instantly if it isn't true! And how he loved me . . . oh, how he loved me.

Luka. I am sure. Say no more. I believe you. He wore patent leather shoes, you say? Aye, aye, and you have naturally loved him too. [*Exit both L. U. E.*]

Baron. A stupid thing, good-hearted but stupid, intolerably stupid.

Bubnoff. How can a man lie so unceasingly? Just like before a coroner.

Natasha. Falsehood must indeed be pleasanter than the truth. . . . I . . . too.

Baron. What "I too?" Say more.

Natasha. I too, think of lots of them . . . to myself . . . and wait. . . .

Baron. For what?

Natasha. [*Laughing, embarrassed.*] Just so . . . perhaps, think I . . . somebody will come tomorrow . . . some strange person . . . or there may happen . . . something that never happened before. . . . I have already waited long. . . . I still am waiting . . . and after all . . . to look at it right . . . can anything great be expected? [*Pause.*]

Baron. [*Laughing.*] We can expect nothing at all. . . . I least of all—I expect nothing more. For me everything has already been. All is past . . . at an end . . . what more?

Natasha. Sometimes, too, I imagine, that tomorrow . . . I will die suddenly . . . which fills me with fear. . . . In summer we think willingly of death . . . then comes the storm, and every moment one may be struck by lightning. . . .

Baron. Your life has not been laid in easy lines. . . . Your sister has the disposition of a fiend.

Natasha. Whose life is easy? All have it hard, as far as I can see. .

Kleshtsch. [*Who has previously lain silent and motionless, springing up.*] All? That is not true! Not all! If it was hard for all . . . then each of us could stand it . . . there would be nothing to complain about.

Bubnoff. Say, are you possessed by the devil? Why howl?

[KLESHTSCH *lies down again and stares vacantly.*]

Baron. I must see what Nastiah is doing. . . . I'll have to make up with her . . . or we shall have no more money for whiskey.

Bubnoff. People can never stop lying! I can understand Nastyka; she is accustomed to painting her cheeks. . . . So she tries it with the soul . . . paints her little soul red . . . but the rest, why do they do it? Luka, for example . . . turns everything into stories . . . without ceremony . . . why does he always lie . . . at his age? . . .

Baron. [*Goes L. U. E. laughing.*] All of us have gray souls. . . . We like to lay on a bit of red.

Luka. [*Enters from L. U. E.*] Tell me, Baron, why do you torment the girl? Let her alone. . . . Can't she cry to pass the time away? . . . She only sheds tears for pleasure . . . what harm can that do you?

Baron. She is a soft-brained thing, pilgrim. . . . It's hard to swallow . . . today Raoul, tomorrow Gaston . . . and everlastingly one and the same. But anyway, I'll make up with her again. [*Exit L. U. E.*]

Luka. Go, treat her with friendliness . . . treat every one with friendliness—injure no one.

Natasha. How good you are, grandfather . . . how is it that you are so good?

Luka. I am good, you say. Nyah . . . if it is true, all right. . . . [*From off-stage is heard soft singing and accordion playing.*] But you see, my girl—there must be some one to be good. . . . We must have pity on mankind. Christ, remember, had pity for us all and so taught us to be likewise. Have pity when there is still time; believe me, it is very good. I was once, for example, employed as a watchman, at a country place which belonged to an engineer, not far from the city of Tomsk, in Siberia. The house stood in the middle of the forest, an out-of-the-way location . . . and it was winter and I was all alone in the country house. . . . It was beautiful there . . . magnificent! And once . . . I heard them scrambling up!

Natasha. Thieves!

Luka. Yes. They crept higher and I took my rifle and went outside. I looked up: two men . . . as they were opening a window and so busy that they did not see anything of me at all. . . . I cried to them: Heh there . . . get out of that . . . and would you think it, they fell on me with a hand ax. . . . I warned them—Halt, I cried, or else I fire . . . then I aimed first at one and then at the other. They fell on their knees saying, pardon us. I was pretty hot . . . on account of the hand ax, you remember. You devils, I cried, I told you to clear out and you didn't . . . and now, I said, one of you go into the brush and get a switch. It was done. And now, I commanded, one of you stretch out on the ground, and the other thrash him . . . and so they whipped each other at my command. And when they had each had a sound beating, they said to me: Grandfather, said they, for the sake of Christ give us a piece of bread. We haven't a bite in our bodies. These, my daughter, were the thieves [*laughs*], who had fallen upon me with the hand ax. Yes . . . they were a pair of splendid fellows. . . . I said to them: If only you had asked for bread! Then they answered: We had gotten past that . . . we had asked and asked and nobody would give us anything . . . endurance was worn out . . .

nyah, and so they remained with me the whole winter. One of them, Stephen by name, liked to take the rifle and go into the woods . . . and the other, Jakoff, was constantly ill, always coughing . . . the three of us watched the place, and when spring came, they said, Farewell, grandfather, and went away—to Russia. . . . [*Music ceases.*]

Natasha. Were they convicts, escaping?

Luka. They were . . . fugitives . . . they had left their colony . . . a pair of splendid fellows. . . . If I had not had pity on them—who knows what would have happened? They might have killed me. . . . Then they would be taken to court again, put in prison, sent back to Siberia . . . why all that? You learn nothing good in prison, nor in Siberia . . . but a man, what can he not learn? Man may teach his fellow man something good . . . very simply. [*Pause.*]

Bubnoff. H'm . . . yes . . . and I . . . can never lie. Why should I do it? Always out with the truth, that is my way of thinking, whether it pleases or not. Why trouble to be considerate?

Kleshtsch. [*Springing up, as though stabbed, crying.*] What is the truth? Where is the truth—where? [*Beats with his hands on his torn clothes.*] There is the truth—there! No work. . . . No strength . . . in the limbs—that is the truth! No shelter . . . no shelter. . . . It is time to die, that is your truth, curse it! What is it to me, this—truth? Only let me sigh in peace—let me sigh. What have I done? Why the devil should we have truth? Curse it, we can't live . . . that is the truth!

Bubnoff. Just listen . . . he is full of matter. . . .

Luka. The good Lord . . . but say, my friend, you. . . .

Kleshtsch. [*Trembling with excitement.*] I have heard you talk of the truth. You, pilgrim—you consoling every one . . . and I say to you: I hate every one. And this truth too, this accursed truth . . . do you understand? Mark you, accursed shall truth be.

[*Hurries out, L. U. E., looking back as he goes.*]

Luka. Ay, ay, ay; but he is out of his head . . . and where can he be running?

Natasha. He rages away like mad.

Bubnoff. He laid it all down in the proper order . . . as in a theater . . . the same thing happens often . . . he is not accustomed to life. . . .

Pepel. [*Enters slowly L. U. E.*] Peace to you, honest folks! Nyah, Luka, old devil —telling more stories?

Luka. You ought to have seen, just now, a man crying out.

Pepel. Kleshtsch, you mean, him? What is the matter with him now? He ran past me, as if he were crazy. . . .

Luka. You will run the same way too, when once it gets into your heart. . . .

Pepel. [*Sits.*] I can't endure him . . . he is embittered, and proud. [*He imitates* KLESHTSCH.] "I am a workingman . . ." as though others were inferior to him. . . . Work indeed, if it gives you pleasure . . . but why do you need to be so proud about it? If you estimate men by work, then a horse is better than any man. He pulls a wagon—and holds his mouth about it. Natasha . . . are your people at home?

Natasha. They have gone to the graveyard . . . and then they were to go to church.

Pepel. You're therefore at leisure . . . that happens seldom.

Luka. [*Thoughtfully to* BUBNOFF.] You say—the truth . . . but the truth is not a cure for every ill . . . you cannot always heal the soul with truth . . . for example, the following case: I knew a man who believed in the land of justice. . . .

Bubnoff. In wh-at?

Luka. In the land of justice. There must be, said he, a land of justice somewhere in the world . . . in which unusual men, so to speak, must live . . . good men, who respect each other, who help each other when they can . . . everything there is good and beautiful. It is a country which every man should seek. . . . He was poor and things went bad with him . . . so bad, indeed, that soon nothing remained for him to do but to lie down and die—but still he did not lose courage. He often laughed and said to himself: it makes no difference—I can bear it! A little longer yet will I wait—then throw this life aside and go into the land of justice . . . it was his only pleasure . . . this land of justice. . . .

Pepel. Yes, and . . . has he gone there?

Bubnoff. Where? Ha, ha, ha!

Luka. At that time there was brought to the place—the thing happened in Siberia—an exile, a man of learning . . . with books and maps and all sorts of arts. . . . And the sick man spoke to the sage: Tell me, I implore you, where lies the land of justice, and how can one succeed in getting there. Then the learned man opened his books and spread his maps out, and searched and searched, but he found the land of justice nowhere. Everything else was correct, all countries were shown—the land of justice alone did not appear.

Pepel. [*Softly.*] No? Was it really not there? [BUBNOFF *laughs.*]

Natasha. What are you laughing at? Go on, grandfather.

Luka. The man would not believe him. . . . It must be there, said he . . . look more closely! For all your books and maps, said he, are not worth a whistle if the land of justice is not shown on them. The learned man felt himself insulted. My maps, said he, are absolutely corrrect, and a land of justice nowhere exists. So, the other was furious. What, he cried—have I now lived and lived and lived, endured and endured, and always believed there was such a country? And according to your plans there is none! That is robbery . . . and he said to the learned man: You good-for-nothing scamp . . . you are a cheat and no sage. Then he gave him a sound blow over the skull, and still another. . . . [*Is silent a few moments.*] And then he went home and choked himself. . . .

[*All are silent.* LUKA *looks silently at* PEPEL *and* NATASHA.]

Pepel. The devil take him . . . a cheerful story, that! . . .

Natasha. He couldn't stand it . . . to be so disappointed.

Bubnoff. [*In a surly tone.*] All tales. . . .

Pepel. H'm, yes . . . there is your land of justice . . . it was not to be found, it seems. . . .

Natasha. One should have sympathy for him . . . the poor man. . . .

Bubnoff. All imagination . . . ha, ha! The land of justice—stuff! Ha, ha, ha, ha! [*Exit L. U. E.*]

Luka. [*Looking after him.*] He laughs, ah yes. [*Pause.*] Yes, children . . . farewell. . . . I shall leave you soon. . . .

Pepel. Where do you journey, then?

Luka. To Little Russia. . . . I hear they have discovered a new religion there. . . . I will see what it is . . . yes. . . . Men search and search, always looking for something better . . . may God give them patience.

Pepel. Think you, they will find it?

Luka. Who? Mankind? Certainly they shall find it. . . . He who yearns . . . he finds . . . who searches zealously—he finds!

Natasha. I wish them a happy journey. I hope they will find something.

Luka. That shall they surely do. But we must help them, my daughter . . . must respect them. . . .

Natasha. How shall I help them? I am myself . . . so helpless. . . .

Pepel. [*Restrained.*] Listen to me, Natasha. . . . I want to speak to you . . . in his presence . . . he knows it . . . come . . . with me!

Natasha. Where? To prison?

Pepel. I have already told you that I will give up stealing. By God, I will! When I say a thing, I keep my word. I have learned to read and write. . . . I can easily make a living. [*With a movement of the hand toward* LUKA.] He advised me—to try it in Siberia . . . to go of my own accord. . . . How does it strike you—shall we go? Believe me, I am sick of this life. Ah, Natasha! I see indeed how things are. . . . I have consoled my conscience with the thought that others steal more than I—and are still respected . . . but how does that help me . . . not in the least. But I have no regret . . . nor, as I believe, any conscience. . . . But I feel one thing: that I must live in a different way. I must live better. . . . I must live . . . so that I can respect myself. . . .

Luka. Quite right, my boy. May God be with you. . . . May Christ help you! Well resolved: a man must respect himself. . . .

Pepel. From childhood, I have been—only a thief. . . . Always I was called Waska, the pickpocket, Waska, the son of a thief! See, it was of no consequence to me, as long as they would have it so . . . so they would have it. . . . I was a thief, perhaps, only out of spite . . . because nobody came along to call me anything except—thief. . . . You call me something else, Natasha . . . now?

Natasha. [*In low spirits.*] I do not quite believe it all . . . words are words . . . and then . . . I don't know. . . . Today I am disquieted . . . my heart is despondent. As though I dreaded something. You would not begin today, Wassili. . . .

Pepel. When else, then! This is not the first time I have spoken. . . .

Natasha. Shall I go with you? . . . I I love you . . . not too much. . . . Sometimes I like you . . . but then at times I cannot look at you . . . in any case I do not love . . . when one loves, one sees no fault in the beloved . . . and I see faults in you. . . .

Pepel. You will soon love me, have no fear! You will become accustomed to me . . . only say yes. For over a year I have been watching you, and I see that you are an honest girl . . . a good, true woman. . . . I love you with all my heart.

[WASSILISSA, *still in gay street dress, appears at the door at the head of the stair, R. U. E. She stands with one hand on the balustrade and the other on the door post and laughs, silently.*]

Natasha. So . . . you love me with all your heart, and my sister. . . .

Pepel. [*Embarrassed.*] What do I care for her? Her kind is nothing. . . .

Luka. It does not matter, my daughter. One eats turnips when he has no bread. . . .

Pepel. [*Gloomily.*] Have pity on me. It is no easy life that I lead—friendless; pursued like a wolf. . . . I sink like a man in a swamp . . . whatever I clutch is slimy and rotten . . . nothing is firm . . . your sister though, would be different . . . if she were not so avaricious. . . . I would have risked everything for her. . . . If she had only kept faith with me . . . but her heart is set on something else . . . her heart is full of greed . . . and longs for freedom—and only that longing in order to become more dissolute. She cannot help me . . . but you—like a young fir-tree, you are prickly but you give support. . . .

Luka. And I say to you: take him, my daughter, take him. He is a good-hearted boy. All you must do is to remind him, often, that he is good . . . so that he will not forget it. He will soon believe you. Only say to him, often, Waska, you are a good man . . . don't forget it! Think it over, my love—what else shall you begin? Your sister—she is a bad lot: and of her husband—nothing good can be said either: no words can be found to express his baseness . . . and this whole life here . . . where shall you find a way out? . . . But Waska . . . he is a lusty fellow.

Natasha. I cannot find a way. . . . I know that. . . . I have already thought it over myself . . . but I . . . whom can I trust? . . . I see no way out. . . .

Pepel. There is but one way . . . but I shall not let you take it. . . . I would kill you first. . . .

Natasha. [*Laughing.*] Just look . . . I am not yet your wife, and you will already kill me.

Pepel. [*Putting his arms around her.*] Say yes, Natasha. It will soon be well. . . .

Natasha. [*Presses him affectionately.*] . . . One thing I will tell you, Wassili. . . . And God shall be my witness: if you strike me a single time . . . or insult me . . . that shall be the end . . . either I hang myself, or . . .

Pepel. May this hand wither up, if I touch you. . . .

Luka. Don't be troubled, my love, you can believe him. You are necessary to his happiness, and he to yours. . . .

Wassilissa. [*From above.*] And the match is made. May God give you love and harmony.

Natasha. They are already back. . . . Oh, God! They have seen us . . . ah, Wassili!

Pepel. What are you afraid of? Nobody dare touch you now!

Wassilissa. Do not be afraid, Natalya. He will not strike you. . . . He can neither strike, nor love. . . . I know him.

Luka. [*Softly.*] Ah, such a woman . . . a venomous snake. . . .

Wassilissa. He is only bold with words. . . .

Kostilioff. [*Enters R. from kitchen.*] Nataschka! What are you doing here, lazybones? Gossiping, eh! Complaining about your relatives! The samovar is not in order, the table not cleared off.

Natasha. [*Going R. kitchen.*] You were going to church, I thought. . . .

Kostilioff. It does not concern you what we are going to do. Mind your own business . . . do what you are told.

Pepel. Shut up. She is not your servant now. . . . Natalya, don't budge . . . don't move a finger.

Natasha. It is not for you to give orders here. . . . Too soon yet for orders.

[*Exit R.*]

Pepel. [*To* Kostilioff.] Enough of that. You have mortified the poor girl enough! She is mine now.

Kostilioff. You-u? When did you buy her? What did you pay for her?

[Wassilissa *laughs aloud.*]

Luka. Waska! Get out. . . .

Pepel. You're having a good time over me, aren't you? You may weep yet!

Wassilissa. What do you say? I am afraid of you. [*Laughs.*]

Luka. Go away, Wassili! Don't you see how she plays with you . . . pricks you on —can't you understand?

Pepel. Ah . . . so! [*To* Wassilissa.] Don't give yourself any trouble. What you want will not be done.

Wassilissa. And what I do not want done, will not be done, Waska!

Pepel. [*Threatens with his fist.*] We shall see. . . . [*Exit L. U. E.*]

Wassilissa. [*As she goes out R. U. E.*] I will prepare a glorious wedding for you.

Kostilioff. [*Advances on* Luka.] So. . . . What are you stirring up, old man?

Luka. Nothing, old man.

Kostilioff. Um! You are going to leave us, I hear!

Luka. It is time.

Kostilioff. Where to?

Luka. Wherever my nose points.

Kostilioff. You are going to become a

vagabond again? You seem to be a rolling stone. . . .

Luka. Resting iron is rusting iron, says the proverb.

Kostilioff. That may be true of iron, but a man must remain in one place. . . . Men cannot be tumbling about like cockroaches in the kitchen . . . first here, then there. . . . A man must have a place which he can call home. . . . He must not be crawling aimlessly about the earth.

Luka. And if one—is at home everywhere?

Kostilioff. Then he is only—a tramp . . . a good-for-nothing fellow . . . a man must make himself useful . . . he must work. . . .

Luka. What's that you're saying?

Kostilioff. Yes, indeed! What else then? . . . You call yourself a wanderer, a pilgrim. . . . What is a pilgrim? A pilgrim is one who goes his own way—keeps to himself . . . has peculiarities, so to speak, is unlike other people . . . that's what we understand about a true pilgrim. . . . He ponders and unravels . . . and at last discovers something . . . perhaps the truth, who knows. . . . He holds his truth for himself, and remains silent. If he is a true pilgrim, he remains silent. . . . Or, he speaks so that no one understands him. . . . He has no wish to be gratified, doesn't turn people's heads, does not butt in. How others live—gives him no concern. . . . He lives proudly and in rectitude . . . searches out the forest and the unfrequented places . . . where no one comes. He is in nobody's way, condemns nobody . . . but prays for all . . . for all the sinners of this world . . . for me, for you . . . for all! He flies from the vanity of this world—to prayer. So it is. [*Pause.*] And you . . . what sort of pilgrim are you? . . . You have not even a passport. . . . Every law-abiding citizen must have a passport . . . all orderly people have passports . . . yes. . . .

Luka. There are people and there are men. . . .

Kostilioff. Don't get funny! Don't give us any riddle. . . . I am not your fool. . . . What do you mean by people—and men?

Luka. This is no riddle. I mean—there are stony fields which are not worth sowing . . . and there are fertile fields . . . whatever is sown thereon—yields a harvest . . . so it is. . . .

Kostilioff. And what does all this mean?

Luka. You, for example. . . . If God himself said to you: "Michailo, be a man," it is certain that it would be useless. . . . As you are, so you will remain for all time. . . .

Kostilioff. Ah . . . and do you know that my wife's uncle is on the police force? And if I . . .

Wassilissa. [*Enters R.*] Michailo Ivanitch, come drink your tea. . . .

Kostilioff. [*To* Luka.] Hear me, you—keep out of this row—leave my house. . . .

Wassilissa. Yes, put on your knapsack, old man . . . your tongue is too long . . . who knows . . . perhaps you may be an escaped convict.

Kostilioff. Be sure that you disappear today . . . or else . . . we shall see.

Luka. Or else you will call your uncle, eh? Call him . . . tell him, you can catch a convict here, uncle . . . then your uncle will receive a reward . . . three copecs. . . .

Bubnoff. [*Looking in from window L.*] What business are you haggling about . . . what is it . . . for three copecs? . . .

Luka. We are trying to sell me.

Wassilissa. [*To her husband.*] Let's go.

Bubnoff. For three copecs. Take care, old man . . . or they will sell you for one copec. . . .

Kostilioff. [*To* Bubnoff.] What are you staring out of there for, like a hobgoblin out of a tunnel?

[*Approaches R. with* Wassilissa.]

Wassilissa. How many blackbirds there are in the world . . . how many knaves.

Luka. I wish you a good appetite.

Wassilissa. [*Turns to him.*] Take good care of yourself—you dirty toadstool. [*Exit with* Kostilioff *R.*]

Luka. Tonight—I leave.

Bubnoff. You'll do right. It is always best to go before it is too late. . . .

Luka. Quite right.

Bubnoff. I speak from experience. I took my own departure once at the right moment, and saved myself a trip to Siberia.

Luka. What do you say?

Bubnoff. It is true. The case was thus: my wife had a love affair with my assistant . . . and a very good assistant he was, I must admit . . . he could make the most beautiful polar bear furs from dog skins . . . cat skins he dyed into kangaroos . . . into muskrats . . . into anything you could wish . . . a very clever fellow. My wife was madly in love with him. They hung on each other so much that I feared every moment they would poison me or put me out of the world in some other way. I whipped my wife often, and my assistant whipped me . . . and I tell you he made a savage job of it, too. Once he pulled half my beard out and broke a rib for me. Naturally I was not particular when I struck back . . . gave my wife one over the skull with an iron yard stick . . . . we were generally fighting like good fellows. Finally I saw there was no chance for me . . . they would surely fix it for me. Then I arranged a plan—to kill my wife. . . . I had quite made up my mind. But in the nick of time—I came to my senses—and cleared out of the row. . . .

Luka. It was better so; let them be quiet there making polar bears out of dogs.

Bubnoff. Worse luck, the shop was in her name . . . only what I had on my back I kept . . . though, to speak honestly, I would have drunk the place up in no time. . . . I am a glorious drunk, you understand.

Luka. A glorious drunk.

Bubnoff. Oh, a glorious drunk. When things come my way I soak up everything in sight. And then I am lazy . . . nothing is more terrible than work.

[SAHTIN *and the* ACTOR *come in quarrelling.*]

Sahtin. Nonsense! You will go nowhere. You're talking stupid stuff. Tell me, pilgrim . . . what spark have you been throwing into this burned stump?

Actor. You lie! Grandfather, tell him that he lies. I go. I have worked today. I have cleaned the pavement . . . and drunk no whiskey. What do you say now? There, see—two fifteeners, and I am sober.

Sahtin. It is all wrong! Give it to me, I'll spend it on drink . . . or lose it at cards.

Actor. Let it alone. It is for the journey.

Luka. [*To* SAHTIN.] Listen you—why do you try to upset his resolution?

Sahtin. "Tell me, you wizard, darling of the gods—what shall fate with my future do?" * Moneyless, brother, I have played everything away, broke. But the world is not lost, old man, there are still sharper knaves than I.

Luka. You are a lusty brother, Constantine . . . a lovable man. . . .

Bubnoff. You actor, come here.

[*The* ACTOR *goes to the window and talks apart with* BUBNOFF.]

Sahtin. When I was still young, I was a jolly chicken. I look back on it with pleasure. . . . I had the soul of a man. . . . I danced splendidly, acted, was a famous bachelor . . . simply phenomenal!

Luka. How then have you gotten so far afield . . . h'm?

Sahtin. You are curious, old man. You would know all . . . and what for?

Luka. I always like to know about . . . mankind's difficulties . . . and I do not understand you, Constantine. When I look at you; such a lovable man . . . so sensible . . . then suddenly. . . .

Sahtin. The prison, grandfather. Four years and seven months I have done, and coming out, a discharged convict, I found my course in life shut up. . . .

Luka. Oh, oh, oh! Why then were you imprisoned?

Sahtin. On account of a deceiver—whom I killed in a passion. . . . In prison, too, I learned my art of card playing. . . .

Luka. And why did you kill him? On account of a woman?

Sahtin. An account of my own sister. . . . Stop questioning . . . it annoys me. . . . It is . . . an old story . . . my sister is dead . . . nine years have gone by . . . she was a splendid creature . . . my sister. . . .

Luka. You take life easily. It falls more heavily on others. . . . Did you just now, for example, hear the locksmith crying out—oh, oh!

Sahtin. Kleshtsch?

Luka. The same. No work, he cried . . . absolutely none. . . .

Sahtin. You will get accustomed to that. . . . Tell me, what shall I now begin to do?

Luka. [*Softly.*] Look, there he comes. . . .

[KLESHTSCH *enters slowly L. U. E. with sunken head.*]

Sahtin. Heh there, widower! What are you hanging your head for? What are you brooding over?

Kleshtsch. My skull is splitting from it. . . . What shall I do now? My tools are gone. . . . The funeral has eaten everything up. . . .

Sahtin. I will give you a piece of advice. Do nothing at all. Burden the earth with your weight—simple enough.

Kleshtsch. You advise well. . . . I—still am ashamed before others.

Sahtin. Drop it . . . people are not ashamed to let you live worse than a dog. Just imagine if you would not work, and I would not work . . . and still hundreds and thousands of others would not work . . . and finally everybody—understand?—everybody quit work and nobody did anything at all—what do you think would happen then?

Kleshtsch. Everybody would starve. . . .

Luka. [*To* SAHTIN.] There is such a sect. "Jumpers," they call themselves. . . . They talk exactly like you. . . .

Sahtin. I know them. . . . They are not at all such fools, pilgrim.

[*From* KOSTILIOFF'S *room* R. U. E *screaming.*]

Natasha. [*Within.*] What are you doing—stop . . . what have I done?

Luka. [*Disquieted.*] Who is screaming there? Was it not Natasha? Ah, you. . . .

[*From* KOSTILIOFF'S *room is heard a loud alarm, and then from the kitchen the sound of crashing dishes.*]

* Citation from Pushkin. [Note of the translator.]

Kostilioff. [*Within, screaming.*] A—ah—you cat—you . . . . heathen.

Wassilissa. [*Within.*] Wait. . . . I'll give her . . . so . . . so . . . and so. . . .

Natasha. [*Within.*] Help! They are killing me!

Sahtin. [*Runs up steps R. U. E. shouting.*] Heh there! What are you howling about?

Luka. [*Walks about uneasily.*] Waska . . . he must be called. . . . Wassili. . . . Oh, God. . . . Children, my dears.

Actor. [*Hurries out, L. U. E.*] I'll bring him . . . right away. . . .

Bubnoff. They're treating the poor girl badly these days.

Sahtin. Come, pilgrim. . . . We will be witnesses. . . .

Luka. [*Exit after* SAHTIN *R. U. E.*] Why witnesses? Too often, already, have I been a witness. If Waska would only come . . . oh! this is terrible! terrible!

Natasha. [*Within.*] Sister . . . . dear sister . . . wah . . . wa . . . a. . . .

Bubnoff. Now they have stopped her mouth. . . . I'll see myself.

[*Withdraws from window.*]

[*The noise in* KOSTILIOFF'S *room is weaker, and nothing comes from the kitchen.*]

Kostilioff. [*Within.*] Halt!

[*A door is slammed within, and the whole noise is cut off as if by a hatchet. On the stage, silence. . . . It is twilight.*]

Kleshtsch. [*Sits on bench U. taking no part, and rubbing his hands together. Then he begins to mumble to himself, at first indistinctly. Then louder.*] How then? . . . a man must live. [*Louder.*] At least a shelter . . . but no, not that . . . not even a corner where I can lie down. . . . Nothing but the bare man . . . helpless and deserted.

[*Exit bent over, L. U. E. slowly. For a few moments, ominous silence. Then somewhere within, on the R. a terrible noise, a chaos of tones, louder and louder and nearer and nearer. Then a single voice is heard.*]

Wassilissa. [*Within.*] I am her sister. Let me go. . . .

Kostilioff. [*Within.*] What right have you to interfere?

Wassilissa. [*Within.*] You convict!

Sahtin. [*Within.*] Bring Waska . . . be quick . . . Zoba, strike.

[*A policeman's whistle is heard.*]

Tartar. [*Jumps down the steps, R. U. E., his right hand bound up.*] What sort of laws are these . . . to murder in broad daylight?

[KRIVOI ZOBA *hurries in R. U. E., followed by* MEDVIEDEFF.]

Krivoi Zoba. Now, he got it from me.

Medviedeff. How did you come to strike him?

Tartar. And you—do you not know what your duty is?

Medviedeff. [*Running after* KRIVOI ZOBA.] Stop! Give me my whistle back.

[*Exit following* KRIVOI ZOBA *L. U. E.*]

Kostilioff. [*Enters R. U. E.*] Abram! Catch him . . . hold him tight. He has killed me. . . .

[*Down the steps R. U. E. come* KVASCHNYA *and* NASTIAH. *They help* NATASHA, *who is badly beaten up.* SAHTIN *runs down the stairs, warding off* WASSILISSA, *who is throwing her arms about and trying to strike her sister.* ALYOSCHKA *is jumping around like one possessed. He whistles in* WASSILISSA'S *ear and howls. A couple of ragged fellows and some men and women,* BUBNOFF *among them, appear L. U. E.*]

Sahtin. [*To* WASSILISSA.] Enough, you damned owl!

Wassilissa. Away, convict. If it costs me my life, I will tear her to pieces.

Kvaschnya. [*Leads* NATASHA *aside.*] Stop, Karpovna . . . for shame! How can you be so inhuman?

Medviedeff. [*Re-enters L. U. E., followed by* KRIVOI ZOBA. *Takes* SAHTIN *by the collar.*] Aha! Now I have you!

Sahtin. Krivoi Zoba. Strike . . . Waska, Waska.

[*All storm the entrance, L. U. E.* NATASHA *is taken to the bed, L.* PEPEL *enters L. U. E. Pushes through the crowd.*]

Pepel. Where is Natasha, you?

Kostilioff. [*Crouches on the steps R. U. E.*] Abram! Catch Waska . . . brother, help catch Waska . . . the thief . . . the robber. . . .

Pepel. There, you old goat.

[*Strikes* KOSTILIOFF *brutually. He falls so that his body lies on the landing, his legs hidden up the stairs.* PEPEL *hurries to* NATASHA.]

Wassilissa. Fix Waska . . . friends . . . do up the thief!

Medviedeff. [*To* SAHTIN.] You shouldn't have interfered . . . this is a family affair here. They are all related to each other . . . and who are you?

Pepel. [*To* NATASHA.] What did she hit you with? Did she stab you? . . .

Kvaschnya. Look what a beast. They have scalded her legs with hot water.

Nastiah. They turned the samovar over. . . .

Tartar. It might have been an accident . . . if you are not sure you should not accuse. . . .

Natasha. [*Half unconscious.*] Wassili . . . take me away . . . hide me. . . .

Wassilissa. Look, my friends . . . come here. He is dead . . . they have killed him. . . .

[*All gather at the landing.* BUBNOFF *separates himself from the others and crosses to* PEPEL.]

Bubnoff. [*Softly.*] Waska! The old man . . . is done for.

Pepel. [*Looks at* BUBNOFF *as though he did not understand.*] Get a cab . . . she must be taken to the hospital. . . . I'll settle the bill.

Bubnoff. Listen to what I'm saying. Somebody has finished the old man. . . .

[*The noise on the stage subsides like a fire into which water has been poured. Half aloud separate sentences are uttered.*]

Is it really true?

Terrible.

We had better get out, brother.

The devil!

We need clear heads now.

Get out before the police come

[*The group becomes smaller.* BUBNOFF *and the* TARTAR *disappear.* NASTIAH *and* KVASCHNYA *stoop to* KOSTILIOFF'S *body.*]

Wassilissa. [*Rises and cries in a triumphant tone.*] They have killed him . . . my husband! And who did it? He, there! Waska killed him. I saw it, my friends. I saw it! Now, Waska! Police! Police!

Pepel. [*Leaves* NATASHA.] Let me alone . . . get out of the way. [*Stares at the body. To* WASSILISSA.] Now? Now you are glad? [*Kicks the body.*] Scotched at last . . . the old hound. Now you have your desire. . . . Shall I treat you in the same way . . . and twist your neck?

[*Falls on her, but is quietly caught by* SAHTIN *and* KRIVOI ZOBA. WASSILISSA *hides L. U. E.*]

Sahtin. Come to your senses.

Krivoi Zoba. P-r-r-r! Where would you spring?

Wassilissa. [*Appearing again.*] Nyah, Waska, friend of my heart! Nobody escapes his fate . . . the police! Abram . . . whistle!

Medviedeff. They have stolen my whistle, the fiends. . . .

Alyoschka. Here it is.

[*He whistles.* MEDVIEDEFF *chases him.*]

Sahtin. [*Leads* PEPEL *back to* NATASHA.] Don't worry, Waska. Killed in a row . . . a trifle! Only a short sentence for that. . . .

Wassilissa. Hold him tight. Waska murdered him. . . . I saw it!

Sahtin. I handed him a couple myself. . . . How much does an old man need? Call me as a witness, Waska. . . .

Pepel. I . . . do I need to justify myself? . . . But Wassilissa. . . . I'll pull her into it! She wanted it done. . . . She incited me to kill her husband . . . yes, she was the instigator. . . .

Natasha. [*Suddenly springing up.*] Ah. . . . [*In a loud voice.*] Now it is clear. . . . That's how it stands. Wassili! Listen, good people: it was all arranged. He and my sister, they plotted it out, they laid their plans! I see, Wassili! Before . . . you spoke with me . . . that was part of it! Good people, she is his mistress . . . you know it . . . everybody knows it. . . . They understand each other. She, she instigated the murder . . . her husband was in the way . . . for that reason . . . she beat me so. . . .

Pepel. Natalya! What are you saying. . . . What are you saying?

Sahtin. Foolish chatter.

Wassilissa. She lies! All of it is lies. . . . I know of nothing. . . . Waska killed him . . . he alone!

Natasha. They have plotted it out. . . . They shall be convicted . . . both of them. . . .

Sahtin. Here is a game for you. . . . Now, Wassili, hold fast or they will drown you.

Krivoi Zoba. I can't understand . . . ah . . . far away from here.

Pepel. Natalya. . . . Speak . . . are you in earnest? Can you believe that I . . . with her? . . .

Sahtin. For God's sake, Natasha, be sensible.

Wassilissa. [*On the landing.*] They killed my husband . . . you high born. . . . Waska Pepel, the thief, killed him, Mr. Commissioner. I saw it . . . everybody saw it.

Natasha. [*Waltzing about half senseless.*] Good people . . . my sister and Waska . . . they killed him. Mr. Policeman . . . listen to me . . . these two, my sister put him up to it . . . her lover . . . she instigated him . . . there he is, the accursed—the two did it. Arrest them . . . take them to court . . . and take me, too . . . to prison with me! For the sake of God . . . to prison. . .

CURTAIN

ACT IV

The same setting except that PEPEL'S *room is not to be seen, the partitions having been removed. The anvil, too, where* KLESHTSCH *sat, is gone.*

[*In the corner which was occupied by* PEPEL'S *chamber is a bunk on which the* TARTAR *lies, restlessly rolling about and groaning with pain.* KLESHTSCH *sits at the table repairing an accordion and now and then trying the chords. At the other end of the table sit* SAHTIN, *the* BARON, *and* NASTIAH. *Before them a bottle of spirits, three bottles of beer, and a great hunk of black bread. On the stove the* ACTOR, *shifting about and coughing. It is night. The stage is lit by a lamp which is in the middle of the table. Outside the wind howls.*]

Kleshtsch. Yes. . . . In the midst of the row he disappeared.

Baron. He took flight before the police, as a fog before the sun.

Sahtin. So all sinners fly before the face of the just.

Nastiah. He was a splendid old man . . . and you are not men . . . you are rust. . . .

Baron. [*Drinks.*] To your health, lady!

Sahtin. An interesting patriarch . . . truly! Our Nastiah fell in love with him.

Nastiah. True. . . . I fell in love with him. He had an eye for everything . . . he understood everything. . . .

Sahtin. [*Laughs.*] For some people he was a God-send . . . like mush for the toothless.

Baron. [*Laughs.*] Or a poultice for an abscess.

Kleshtsch. He had a sympathetic heart . . . you here . . . have no sympathy.

Sahtin. What good would it do you for me to show you pity?

Kleshtsch. You need not sympathize . . . but at least . . . do not injure me. . . .

Tartar. [*Gets up on his bunk and moves his injured hand back and forth, as if it were a baby.*] The old man was good. . . . He had respect for the law in his heart . . . and whoever in his heart keeps the law . . . that man is good. He who does not—is lost. . . .

Baron. What law do you mean, prince?

Tartar. As you will . . . the law . . . the law to you . . . you understand me.

Baron. Go on.

Tartar. Encroach upon no man . . . there you have the law. . . .

Sahtin. With us in Russia it is called, "Code for Criminal Punishment and Correction."

Baron. With another "Code for Penalties Imposed by Justices of the Peace."

Tartar. With us it is called the Koran. . . . Your Koran is your law . . . our Koran we must carry in our hearts.

Kleshtsch. [*Tries the accordion.*] Don't be forever hissing, you beast. What the prince says is right. . . . We must live according to the law . . . according to the gospels. . . .

Sahtin. Live so.

Baron. Try it.

Tartar. Mohammed gave us the Koran . . . there you have your law, he said. Do as is written therein. Then a time shall come when the Koran will not suffice . . . a new time with new laws . . . for every epoch has its own laws. . . .

Sahtin. Yes, of course, our epoch gives us "Criminal Code." A durable law, not so easily worn off.

Nastiah. [*Knocks on the table with her knuckles.*] Now I would like to know . . . exactly why I live . . . here with you? I shall go . . . anywhere . . . to the end of the earth.

Baron. Without shoes, lady?

Nastiah. Quite naked, as far as I care! I shall crawl on all fours if you please.

Baron. That would be picturesque . . . on all fours. . . .

Nastiah. I would do it . . . willingly . . . if I only need not have to look at your snout again . . . ah, how disgusting everything has become to me . . . my whole life . . . everybody.

Sahtin. When you go, take the actor along with you. . . . He'll soon be going anyhow . . . he has learned that exactly half a mile from the end of the earth there is a hospital for orgisms. . . .

Actor. [*Sticks his head out over the edge of the stove.*] For organisms, blockhead.

Sahtin. For organs which are poisoned with alcohol.

Actor. Yes, he will soon be going, very soon! You will see!

Baron. Who is this "he," sir?

Actor. It is I.

Baron. Merci, servant of the goddess, who . . . ah, what is she called? The goddess of the drama, of tragedy . . . what is her name?

Actor. The muse, blockhead, no goddess, but muse!

Sahtin. Lachesis . . . Hera . . . Aphrodite . . . Atropos . . . the devil knows the difference between them . . . and our young adorer of the muse shall leave us . . . the old man has wound him up. . . .

Baron. The old man was a fool. . . .

Actor. And you are ignorant savages. You don't even know who Melpomene is. Heartless . . . you will see—he will leave you! "Interrupt not your orgy, black souls," as Béranger says. . . . He will soon find the place where there is nothing more . . . absolutely.

Baron. Where there is nothing more, sir?

Actor. Yes! Nothing more. "This hole here . . . it shall be my grave. . . . I die, faded and powerless." And you, why do you live? Why?

Baron. Just listen, you—Kean, or Genius and Passion. Don't bellow so

Actor. Hold your snout. . . . So I will, I'll roar!

Nastiah. [*Raises her head from the table, and waves her arms about.*] Roar forever! They may hear it.

Baron. What is the meaning of that, lady?

Sahtin. Let her chatter, Baron . . . the devil take them both . . . may they scream . . . may they run their heads together . . . go on . . . it has a meaning. . . . Don't injure others, as the old man said . . . the pilgrim has made us all rebellious.

Kleshtsch. He enticed us to start out . . . and knew not himself the way.

Baron. The old man was a charlatan.

Nastiah. It is not true! You are yourself a charlatan.

Baron. Don't chatter, lady.

Kleshtsch. He was no friend of truth, the old man. . . . He stood with all his might over against the truth . . . and after all, he is right . . . of what use to me is all truth, when I haven't a mouthful? There, look at the prince [*Looks toward the* TARTAR.] . . . he has crushed his hand at work . . . now they say, it must come off . . . there you have the truth.

Sahtin. [*Strikes the table with his fist.*] Be still! Asses! Say nothing ill of the old man. [*More quietly.*] You, Baron, are the biggest fool of all . . . you have no glimmering of sense—and you keep on chattering. The old man a charlatan? What is truth? Mankind is the truth! He had seized that . . . but you have not! You are as stupid as a brick in the pavement. I understood him very well, the old man. . . . He did tell them lies, but he lied out of sympathy, as the devil knows. There are many such people who lie for brotherly sympathy's sake. . . . I know. I have read about it. They lie so beautifully, with such spirit, so wonderfully. We have such soothing, such conciliating lies. . . . And there are lies which justify taking the anvil away, and the mashed hand of the toiler . . . which bring charges against the starving. . . . I . . . know these lies. . . . He who has a timid heart . . . or lives at another's table, should be lied to . . . it gives him courage . . . and puts a mantle on his shoulders . . . but he who is his own master, who is independent, and lives not from the sweat of another's brow . . . what are lies to him? The lie is the religion of servant and master . . . the truth is the inheritance of free men!

Baron. Bravo! Gloriously said! Exactly my idea! You speak . . . like a man of respectability!

Sahtin. Why shouldn't a scoundrel speak like a respectable man, when the respectable people talk so much like scoundrels? . . . I have forgotten much, but one thing I still keep. The old man? He had a shrewd head on his shoulders. . . . He worked on me like acid on an old, dirty coin. To his health, let him live! Pour one. . . . [NASTIAH *pours a glass of beer and hands it to* SAHTIN. *He laughs.*] The old man—he lived from within. . . . He saw everything with his own eyes. . . . I asked him once: "Grandfather, why do men really live?". . . [*He tries in voice and manner to imitate* LUKA.] Man lives ever to give birth to strength. There live, for example, the carpenters, noisy, miserable people . . . and suddenly in their midst is a carpenter born . . . such a carpenter as the world has never seen: he is above all, no other carpenter can be compared to him. He gives a new face to the whole trade . . . his own face, so to speak . . . and with that simple impulse it has advanced twenty years . . . and so the others live . . . the locksmiths and the shoemakers, and all the rest of the working people . . . and the contractors . . . and the same is true of other classes—all to give birth to strength. Every one thinks that he for himself takes up room in the world, but it turns out that he is here for another's benefit—for some one better . . . a hundred years . . . or perhaps longer . . . if we live so long . . . for the sake of genius. [NASTIAH *stares into* SAHTIN'S *face.* KLESHTSCH *stops working on the accordion and does nothing. The* BARON *lets his head sink and drums with his fingers on the table. The* ACTOR *sticks his head over the edge of stove, and carefully crawls down.* SAHTIN *goes on.*] All, my children, all, live only to give birth to strength. For that reason we must respect everybody. We cannot know who he is, for what purpose born, or what he may yet fulfil . . . . perhaps he has been born for our good fortune . . . or great benefit . . . and especially must we respect the children . . . the little children . . . they must not suffer restraint . . . let them live their lives . . . let them be respected.

[*Laughs quietly to himself. Pause.*]

Baron. [*Thoughtfully.*] For the genius. . . . Hm, yes . . . that brings to mind my own family . . . an old family . . . back to Catherine's time . . . of the nobility . . . knights . . . we came from France . . . and entered the Russian service . . . dignities accumulated on us. . . . Under Nicholas I, my grandfather, Gustav Deville . . . held a high post . . . he was rich. . . . Had hundreds of serfs . . . horses . . . a cook. . . .

Nastiah. Don't be lying . . . it's all a fake. . . .

Baron. [*Springing up.*] Wh-at? Nyah . . . say more!

Nastiah. It's all a fabrication.

Baron. [*Cries.*] A house in Moscow, a house in Petersburg! Coaches . . . escutcheons on the coach door.

[KLESHTSCH *takes the accordion and goes to the side R., where he observes the scene.*]

Nastiah. Never was such a thing.

Baron. Stop chattering! Dozens of footmen . . . I tell you!

Nastiah. [*Tantalizing.*] None.

Baron. I'll kill you.

Nastiah. There were no coaches.

Sahtin. Let up, Nastenka. Don't make him so furious.

Baron. Wait . . . you wench . . . my grandfather——

Nastiah. You had no grandfather . . . none.

[SAHTIN *laughs.*]

Baron. [*Sinks back on the seat quite out of breath with anger.*] Sahtin, I tell you . . . the harlot . . . what—you laugh, too? And you . . . won't believe me? [*Cries out desperately, striking the table with his fists.*] Go to the devil . . . all was as I say.

Nastiah. [*In a triumphant tone.*] Ah, ha! See how you bellow out! Now you know how a person feels when nobody believes him.

Kleshtsch. [*Returns to table.*] I thought we should have a fight.

Tartar. Stupid people . . . childish.

Baron. I . . . I'll not be made a fool of. . . . I have proof. . . . I have documents to satisfy. . . .

Sahtin. Throw them in the stove. And forget your grandfather's coach. In the coach of the past nobody gets anywhere.

Baron. How can she dare. . . .

Nastiah. Hear the noise he is making . . . oh, Lord, how dare I?

Sahtin. But you see, she dares it. Is she still worse than you? For she has certainly had in her past no coach and no grandfather . . . perhaps not even a father and mother. . . .

Baron. [*Quieting himself.*] Go to the devil. . . . You reason everything out so cold-bloodedly, while I . . . I believe I have no temper. . . .

Sahtin. Make yourself one. It is a useful thing. . . . [*Pause.*] Tell me, Nastiah, do you not go often to the hospital?

Nastiah. What for?

Sahtin. To Natasha?

Nastiah. Why, have you dropped from Heaven? She has long been out . . . out and gone. . . . Nowhere is she to be found. . . .

Sahtin. Gone? Disappeared?

Kleshtsch. I would like to know whether Waska got Wassilissa into trouble or Wassilissa, Waska.

Nastiah. Wassilissa? She will lie herself out. She is crafty. She will send Waska to the mines. . . .

Sahtin. For manslaughter in a row, only imprisonment. . . .

Nastiah. Shame. Hard labor would be better. You ought to be sentenced to hard labor too. You ought to be swept away like a pile of trash . . . into a ditch.

Sahtin. [*Taken aback.*] What are you talking about? You are certainly mad.

Baron. I'll box your ears . . . impertinent hussy.

Nastiah. Try it once, just touch me!

Baron. Certainly I'll try it!

Sahtin. Let her be. Don't touch her. Don't insult any one. I always remember the old man. [*Laughs aloud.*] Don't insult mankind, not in her. . . . And if I should be insulted so that my reputation was forever gone . . . what should I then do? . . . Forgive. No and never!

Baron. [*To* NASTIAH.] Mark you! you: I am not one of your kind . . . you . . . wench. . . .

Nastiah. Ah, you wretch! You . . . you live with me like a maggot in an apple.

[*The men laugh understandingly.*]

Kleshtsch. Silly goose! A fine apple you are. . . .

Baron. Shall a man get mad . . . over such . . . an idiot?

Nastiah. You laugh? Don't sham! You don't feel like laughing. . . .

Actor. [*Darkly.*] Give him what is his.

Nastiah. If I only . . . could: I would take you all and . . . [*Takes a cup from the table and smashes it on the floor.*] like that!

Tartar. What are you breaking the dishes for . . . dunce?

Baron. [*Rising.*] No, I must teach her manners.

Nastiah. [*Going out.*] Go to the devil.

Sahtin. [*Calls after her.*] Let up, will you? Why do you treat her so? Will you frighten her?

Nastiah. You wolves! It is time you were dead. [*Exit L. U. E.*]

Actor. [*Darkly.*] Amen!

[*Climbs back on stove.*]

Tartar. Ugh, mad folks these Russian women! Hussies, unmanageable. The Tartar women are not so; they know the law.

Kleshtsch. She must be given something that she will remember.

Baron. A low-born creature.

Kleshtsch. [*Tries the accordion.*] Ready, and your owner is not to be seen. . . . The boy is a lively one.

Sahtin. Now have a drink!

Kleshtsch. [*Drinks.*] Thanks! It is time to be turning in. . . .

Sahtin. You'll fall in with our habits after a while, eh?

Kleshtsch. [*Drinks and goes to the bunk in the corner.*] If I do. . . . Everywhere, in the long run, people are to be found. . . . You do not see them at first . . . but later, when you see truer, people are to be found everywhere . . . and they are not so bad after all. . . .

[*The* TARTAR *spreads a cloth out over the bunk, sits down and prays.*]

Baron. [*To* SAHTIN, *pointing to the* TARTAR.] Just look.

Sahtin. Let him alone. . . . He is a good fellow. . . . Don't disturb him! [*Laughs aloud.*] I am so chicken-hearted today. . . . The devil may know what's coming.

Baron. You are always a little chicken-hearted when you have some spirits in you . . . and rational then.

Sahtin. When I am drunk everything pleases me. H'm—yes. . . . He prays? Very beautiful of him. A man can believe or not believe . . . that rests with him. Man is free . . . he is responsible to himself for everything: for his belief, his unbelief, his love, his wisdom. Man himself bears the cost of all, is therefore—free. . . . Man—that is the truth! But what's man? Not you, nor I, not they—no, but you, I, old Luka, Napoleon, Mohammed . . . all in one . . . is man. [*Draws in the air the outline of a man's form.*] Comprehend! It is—something huge, including all beginnings and all endings . . . all is in man, all is for man. Only man alone exists—the rest is the work of his hand and his brow. M-an! Phenomenal. How loftily it sounds, M-a-n! We must respect man . . . not compassion . . . degrade him not with pity . . . but respect. Drink we, to the health of man, Baron. How splendid it is to feel yourself a man. I . . . I, a former convict, a murderer, a cheat . . . yes, when I pass along the street, the people stare at me, as though I were the most desperate of thieves . . . they get out of my way, they look after me . . . and often say to me, thief, why don't you work? . . . Work? What for? To become satiated. [*Laughs aloud.*] I have always hated those who eat themselves to death. It comes to nothing, Baron, to nothing. The man is the principal thing, man stands higher than a full stomach. [*Rises from his place.*]

Baron. [*Shakes his head.*] You are a contemplator . . . that is wise . . . that warms my heart. . . . I can't do it. [*Looks around carefully and continues in a lower tone.*] I am sometimes afraid, brother . . . do you understand? I fear what may come next.

Sahtin. [*Goes up and down.*] Nonsense, what shall man fear?

Baron. As far back as I can remember, it always seemed to me as though a fog lay on my brow. I never knew very well just what was the matter, was never at ease. . . . I felt as if my whole life long I had only put on my clothes and taken them off again . . . why? No idea! I studied. . . . I wore the uniform of an institute for the nobility . . . but what I have learned, I don't know. . . . I married . . . put on a frock coat, then a night gown . . . selected a detestable wife—why? I don't understand. . . . I went through everything—and wore a shabby gray jacket and red, fuzzy trousers . . . but I finally went to the dogs. Hardly took any notice of it. I was employed at the Kameral Court . . . had a uniform, a cap with cockade. . . . I embezzled government money . . . pulled on the convict's jacket . . . then—what I have on now . . . and all . . . as if in a dream . . . funny, eh?

Sahtin. Not very. . . . I find it rather foolish.

Baron. Yes. . . . I think it was foolish. . . . But I must have been born for something . . . eh?

Sahtin. [*Laughs.*] It is possible. . . . Man is born to give birth again to strength. [*Nods his head.*] Yes . . . fine idea.

Baron. This . . . Nastyka . . . simply

ran out. . . . I will see where she has hidden. . . . Still, she. . . .

[*Exit L. U. E. Pause.*]

Actor. You, Tartar! [*Pause.*] Prince! [*The* TARTAR *turns his head.*] Pray for me.

Tartar. What do you want?

Actor. [*Softly.*] You must pray . . . for me. . . .

Tartar. [*After a short silence.*] Pray for yourself.

Actor. [*Climbs quickly down from the stove, goes to the table, pours a glass of whiskey with trembling hand, drinks and goes out hastily almost running, L. U. E.*] Now, I go!

Sahtin. Heh, you Sigambrer! Where to?

[*He whistles.* MEDVIEDEFF, *in a wadded woman's jacket, and* BUBNOFF *enter R. U. E.* BUBNOFF *carries in one hand a bundle of pretzels, in the other a couple of smoked fish, under his arm a bottle of whiskey, and in his coat pocket a second.*]

Medviedeff. The camel is . . . a sort of ass, so to speak. Only it has no ears.

Bubnoff. Let up! You yourself . . . are a sort of jackass.

Medviedeff. The camel has no ears at all. It hears with the nostrils.

Bubnoff. [*To* SAHTIN.] Friend of my heart, I have searched for you in every barroom and dive. Take the bottle out, my hands are full.

Sahtin. Put the pretzels on the table and then you will have a free hand.

Bubnoff. That's right . . . you know the law . . . you have a sly head. . . .

Medviedeff. All scoundrels have sly heads. . . . I know that . . . long. How could they catch anything without slyness? A law-abiding citizen can be stupid, but a thief must have brains in his head. But about this camel, brother, you are wrong there . . . a camel is a sort of riding deer, I say . . . it has no horns . . . and no teeth, either. . . .

Bubnoff. Where's the whole crowd hiding? Nobody here. Say, you, come out. . . . I treat today . . . who sits there in the corner?

Sahtin. You have already spent almost everything, scarecrow.

Bubnoff. Of course, this time my capital was small . . . which I had scraped together. . . . Krivoi Zoba! Where is Krivoi Zoba?

Kleshtsch. [*Steps to the table.*] He is not there.

Bubnoff. U-u-rrr! Bull dog. Brrlu, Brlyu, Brlyu, turkey cock! Don't be barking and snarling! Drink fast, don't let your head hang. . . . I invite all freely, I love to do that, brother! If I was a rich man, I would have a bar-room in which everything would be free, by God, with music and a choir of singers. Come, drink, eat, do you hear, quicken your souls. Come to me, poor men, to my free bar-room, Sahtin! Brother! I would you . . . there, take half my entire capital; there, take it.

Sahtin. Oh, give it all to me. . . .

Bubnoff. All? My whole capital? Do you want it? . . . There! A ruble . . . another . . . twenty . . . a couple of fivers . . . a pair of two copec pieces . . . that is all!

Sahtin. Lovely. . . . I'll keep it safely. . . . I'll win my money back with it.

Medviedeff. I am a witness . . . you have given him the money in trust . . . how much was it, though?

Bubnoff. You? You are—a camel. . . . We need no witnesses.

Alyoschka. [*Enters L. U. E. with bare feet.*] Children! I have gotten my feet wet!

Bubnoff. Come—get your gullet wet. . . . to balance matters. You're a lovely boy, you sing and make music . . . very clever of you! But—drink . . . not too much! Guzzling is very injurious, brother . . . very injurious. . . .

Alyoschka. I see that in you . . . you only look like a man after you have gotten drunk. Kleshtsch! Is my accordion mended?

[*Sings and dances with it.*]

If I were not such a tasty boy,
So lively, fresh and neat,
Then Madam Godfather would
Never again call me sweet.

Frozen stiff, children. It is cold.

Medviedeff. H'm—and if I may be bold enough to ask: Who is Madam Godfather?

Bubnoff. You . . . are not interested in that! You have nothing to ask here now. You are no policeman any more . . . that's a fact. Neither police nor uncle. . . .

Alyoschka. But simply auntie's husband!

Bubnoff. Of your nieces, one sits in prison, the other is dying. . . .

Medviedeff. [*Expands his chest.*] That is not true: She is not dying. She has simply gone away!

[SAHTIN *laughs aloud.*]

Bubnoff. Quite true, brother! A man without nieces—is no uncle!

Alyoschka. Your excellency, the pensioned drum-major of the belly brigade.

Nary a single cent have I,
While Madam Godfather has money,
But still I'm nice, I'm very very nice,
I'm as nice and as sweet as honey.

Brr, it is cold.

[KRIVOI ZOBA *enters; then, until the end*

of the act, couples, men and women, enter, undress themselves, stretch out on the bunks and grumble to themselves.]

Krivoi Zoba. Why did you run away, Bubnoff?

Bubnoff. Come here and sit down. Let's sing something, brother! My favorite hymn, eh?

Tartar. It is night now, time for sleeping. Sing during the day.

Sahtin. Let them sing, prince, come over here.

Tartar. Let them sing—and then a row. . . . You sing and they fight.

Bubnoff. [*Going to him.*] What's the matter with your hand, prince? Has somebody cut it off?

Tartar. Why cut it off? Let us wait. . . . Perhaps it will not be necessary to cut it off . . . a hand is not made of iron . . . cutting off is an easy thing to do. . . .

Krivoi Zoba. It is a bad job, Hassanka! What, are you without a hand? In our business they only look at the hands and the back. . . . A man without a hand is no man at all! Might as well be dead. Come, drink a glass with us.

Kvaschnya. [*Enters L. U. E.*] Ah, my dear tenants. Biting cold outside, slush . . . and raw. . . . Is my policeman there? Heh there, Commissioner!

Medviedeff. Here I am.

Kvaschnya. You have my jacket on again? What is the matter with you? You have been having a bit, eh? That don't go.

Medviedeff. Bubnoff . . . has a birthday . . . and it is so cold, such slush. . . .

Kvaschnya. I'll teach you . . . such slush. . . . But don't forget the rules of this household . . . go to bed. . . .

Medviedeff. To bed! I can. . . . I will . . . it is time. [*Exit R. to kitchen.*]

Sahtin. Why are you . . . so strict with him?

Kvaschnya. There is nothing else to do, dear friend. A man like that must be closely reined. I did not marry him for fun. He is military, I thought . . . and you are a dangerous lot. . . . I, a woman, would be no match for you . . . now he's beginning to souse—no, my boy, that don't go.

Sahtin. You made a bad selection in your assistant. . . .

Kvaschnya. No, wait—he is all right . . . you will not get me . . . and if you did, the honeymoon would not last over a week . . . you'd gamble the clothes off my back.

Sahtin. [*Laughs.*] That's no lie, I would lose you. . . .

Kvaschnya. So then, Alyoschka.

Alyoschka. Here he is. . . .

Kvaschnya. Tell me, what gossip have you been spreading about me?

Alyoschka. I? Everything! I tell everything that can honestly be told. What a woman! say I. Simply an astonishing woman. Flesh, fat, bones, over three hundredweight, and brains, not half a grain.

Kvaschnya. Nyah, you lie, my young man, I have quantities of brain. . . . No—why do you tell folks that I beat my policeman?

Alyoschka. I thought, because you tore his hair out . . . that is as good as a beating.

Kvaschnya. [*Laughs.*] You are a fool! Why carry such dirt out of the house? . . . That has grieved him sorely . . . he has taken to drink from worry over your gossip. . . .

Alyoschka. Listen: it is therefore true, what the proverb says: that the hen has a throat for liquor.

[SAHTIN *and* KLESHTSCH *laugh.*]

Kvaschnya. But you are witty: and tell me, what sort of animal you are, Alyoschka?

Alyoschka. I am a fellow who fits snugly into the world. The finest of the finest sort! A regular jack of all trades. Where my eye turns, there my heart follows.

Bubnoff. [*On the* TARTAR'S *bunk.*] Come, we will not let you sleep. Today we'll sing . . . the whole night, eh, Krivoi Zoba?

Krivoi Zoba. May we?

Alyoschka. I'll play for you. . . .

Sahtin. And we will hear it.

Tartar. [*Grunting.*] Nyah, old Satan, Bubna . . . pour me a glass: "We'll revel, we'll drink until death gives the wink."

Bubnoff. Pour him one, Sahtin! Krivoi Zoba, sit down! Ah, brothers! How little a man needs! I, for example, I've only had a couple of swallows . . . and walk tangled footed. Krivoi Zoba, strike up . . . my favorite song. I will sing and weep.

Krivoi Zoba. [*Sings.*] "Though still the sun goes up and down. . . ."

Bubnoff. [*Falls in.*] "No gleam can pierce to me in here." [*The door is jerked open.*]

Baron. [*On the platform, crying.*] Heh, there . . . you! Come quick . . . come out! In the yard . . . there . . . the actor . . . has hanged himself!

[*Silence, all stare at the* BARON. *Behind him appears* NASTIAH, *who with staring eyes goes to the table.*]

Sahtin. [*Softly.*] He must spoil our song . . . the fool.

CURTAIN

THE PASSION FLOWER *

By

JACINTO BENAVENTE

Translated by JOHN GARRETT UNDERHILL

LIKE SO MANY OTHER SPANISH DRAMATISTS, Jacinto Benavente is tremendously productive; it is not unusual for him to write four full-length plays a year, or their equivalent. Commentators on the Spanish drama have referred to the first decade of the twentieth century as "the Benavente period," and have spoken of his work as though it were outmoded; but he was still, until the Civil War, writing new plays that commanded the enthusiasm of huge audiences in Spain and South America. His versatility is as astonishing as his fecundity; he has written romantic plays, realistic plays, satirical plays, symbolical plays, melodramas, pastorals, moralities, vaudevilles, slapstick comedies, and librettos. Not all of these, of course, deserve to be added to the world's list of great plays. But by the wit and polish and intellectual force evident in the bulk of his work Benavente is marked as probably the most distinguished dramatist Spain has produced since the seventeenth century. In addition, by directing the National Theatre, by promoting an Art Theatre and a theater for children, and by translating and adapting French, English, and American plays, he has helped make the Spanish theater more cosmopolitan, more alive to contemporary tendencies in drama.

So various a writer cannot be adequately "represented" by any single play. *La Malquerida,* here called by the name under which it was produced in America, *The Passion Flower,* is included in this volume because it has power as a play, and because its flavor, while peculiarly Spanish, is not merely local. Certainly in few plays is the sense of life outside the setting more distinctly yet subtly conveyed—the watching and gossiping village, the hot sun on bare hills, the rigid conventions of a parochial society, all are actors with the little group in Raimunda's house, though they are not seen. And even the Freudian repression on which the main situation is based does not make the play less indigenously Spanish.

The Passion Flower, the only Benavente play which has been a notable financial success in the North American theater, had a long run in 1920 with Nance O'Neill playing Raimunda. But it is an odd coincidence that Benavente plays were chosen to be the first offerings of two of the most significant producing organizations in our recent stage history. In 1919, the Theatre Guild began its career with Benavente's *The Bonds of Interest,* with Miss Edna St. Vincent Millay in the part of Columbine. And in 1926 Miss Eva Le Gallienne, opening her Civic Repertory Theatre, offered Benavente's *Saturday Night.*

JACINTO BENAVENTE Y MARTINEZ

Born 1866, Madrid, Spain.
University of Madrid. Studied law, but won no degree.
1886–1889, travelled through Europe with a circus.
Identified with "The Generation of '98," whose program was to bring Spanish literature back to reality.
1912, Elected a member of the Spanish Academy.
1922, Awarded the Nobel Prize in Literature.
Poet, journalist, and essayist.

PLAYS

1892 *Teatro Fantástico* (*Plays of the Imagination*, four short plays, including *El Encanto de Una Hora*, translated as *The Magic of an Hour*). 1894 *El Nido Ajeno* (translated as *Another's Nest*). 1896 *Gente Conocida* (*People of Importance*). 1897 *El Marido de la Tellez* (one act, *Mme. Tellez' Husband*). 1897 *De Alivio* (monologue, *Reform*). 1897 *Don Juan* (translation from Molière). 1897 *La Farándula* (*The Troupers*). 1898 *La Comida de las Fieras* (*The Banquet of Wild Beasts*). 1898 *Teatro Feminista* (*Woman's Theatre*, one act libretto for music of Barbero). 1899 *Cuento de Amor* (*Love Story*, adapted from Shakespeare's *Twelfth Night*). 1899 *Operación Quirúrgica* (one act, *Surgical Operation*). 1899 *Despedida Cruel* (one act, *Cruel Farewell*). 1900 *La Gata de Angora* (adapted as *The Angora Cat*). 1900 *Viaje de Instrucción* (*Travel for Instruction*, one act libretto for music of Vives). 1900 *Por la Herida* (one act, *For the Wound*). 1901 *Modas* (one act, *Modes*). 1901 *Lo Cursi* (*Vulgarity*). 1901 *Sin Querer* (one act, *Without Intention*). 1901 *Sacrificios* (*Sacrifices*). 1901 *La Gobernadora* (translated as *The Governor's Wife*). 1901 *El Primo Román* (*Cousin Roman*). 1902 *Amor de Amar* (*Love of Loving*). 1902 *¡Libertad!* (*Liberty*, translated from the Catalan of Santiago Rusiñol). 1902 *El Tren de los Maridos* (*The Husbands' Train*). 1902 *Alma Triunfante* (*Soul Triumphant*). 1902 *El Automóvil* (*The Automobile*). 1903 *El Noche del Sábado* (translated as *Saturday Night*). 1903 *Los Favoritos* (one act, *The Favorites*, adapted from Shakespeare's *Much Ado about Nothing*). 1903 *El Hombrecito* (*The Little Man*). 1903 *Mademoiselle de Belle-Isle* (translation from Dumas, père). 1903 *Por Qué se Ama* (one act, *Why They Love*). 1903 *Al Natural* (*Broad Daylight*). 1903 *La Casa de la Dicha* (one act, *The House of Good Fortune*). 1903 *El Dragón de Fuego* (*The Fire Dragon*). 1904 *Richelieu* (translation from Bulwer Lytton). 1904 *La Princesa Bebé* (translated as *Princess Bebé*). 1904 *No Fumadores* (one act, translated as *No Smoking*). 1905 *Rosas de Otoño* (translated as *Autumnal Roses*). 1905 *Buena Boda* (*A Good Marriage*, adapted from Augier). 1905 *El Susto de la Condesa* (one act, *A Shock for the Countess*). 1905 *Cuento Inmoral* (monologue, *Naughty Story*). 1905 *La Sobresalienta* (*The Understudy*, one act libretto for music by Chapí). 1905 *Los Malhechores del Bien* (translated as *The Evil Doers of Good*). 1905 *Las Cigarras Hormigas* (*Crickets and Ants*). 1906 *Más Fuerte que el Amor* (*Stronger than Love*). 1906 *Manón Lescaut* (adapted from the novel of Prévost). 1907 *Los Buhos* (*The Owls*). 1907 *Abuela y Nieta* (one act, *Grandmother and Grandchild*). 1907 *La Princesa sin Corazón* (one act, *The Heartless Princess*). 1907 *El Amor asusta* (one act, *Love Frightens*). 1907 *La Copa Encantada* (*The Enchanted Cup*, one act libretto for music by Lleó). 1907 *Los Ojos de los Muertos* (*The Eyes of the Dead*). 1907 *La Historia de Otelo* (one act, *Othello's Story*). 1907 *La Sonrisa de la Gioconda* (one act, translated as *The Smile of Mona Lisa*). 1907 *El Último Minué* (one act, *The Last Minuet*). 1907 *Todos somos Unos* (*We are All One*, one act libretto for music by Lleó). 1907 *Los Intereses Creados* (translated as *The Bonds of Interest*). 1908 *Señora Ama.* 1908 *El Marido de su Viuda* (one act, translated as *His Widow's Husband*). 1908 *La Fuerza Bruta* (translated as *Brute Force*; used as libretto for music by Chaves, 1922). 1908 *De Pequeñas Causas* (one act, *From Trifling Causes*). 1908 *Hacia la Verdad* (one act, *Toward the Truth*). 1909 *Por las Nubes* (translated as *In the Clouds*). 1909 *De Cerca* (one act, *Nearby*). 1909 *¡A Ver qué hace un Hombre!* (one act, *See What a Man Will Do!*). 1909 *La Escuela de las Princesas* (translated as *The School of Princesses*). 1909 *La Señorita se aburre* (*My Lady Retires*, one act, based on Tennyson's *Lady Clara Vere de Vere*). 1909 *El Principe que todo lo aprendió en los Libros* (translated as *The Prince Who Learned Everything Out of Books*). 1909 *Ganarse la Vida* (one act, *Earning a Living*). 1910 *El Nietecito* (one act, *The Grandson*). 1911 *La Losa de los Sueños* (*The Graveyard of Dreams*). 1913 *La Malquerida* (*The Passion Flower*, translated under the original title). 1914 *El Destino Manda* (*Destiny Governs*, translated from Hervieu). 1915 *El Collar de Estrellas* (*The Necklace of Stars*). 1915 *La Verdad* (one act, translated as *Truth*). 1915 *La Propia Estimación* (*Self-Esteem*). 1916 *Campo de Armiño* (translated as *Field of Ermine*). 1916 *Lo Túnica Amarilla* (*The Yellow Jacket*, translation from Hazelton and Benrimo). 1916 *La Ciudad Alegre y Confiada* (*The Joyful and Confident City*, sequel to *Los Intereses Creados*). 1917 *El Mal que Nos Hacen* (*The Evil that We Do*). 1918 *Los Cachorros* (*Young Lions*). 1918 *Mefistófela* (libretto for music by Muñoz). 1918 *La Inmaculada de Los Dolores* (*Our Lady of Sorrows*). 1918 *La Ley de los Hijos* (*The Law of the Children*). 1919 *Por ser con Todos Leal ser para Todos Traidor* (*A Traitor to All, to All Be Ye Loyal*). 1919 *La Vestal de Occidente* (*The Vestal of the West*). 1919 *La Honra de los Hombres* (*The Honor of Men*). 1919 *El Audaz* (*Daring*, adapted from novel by Galdós). 1919 *La Cenicienta* (*Cinderella*). 1919 *Caridad* (monologue, *Charity*). 1919 *Una Señora* (*A Lady*). 1919 *Una Pobre Mujer* (*A Poor Woman*). 1919 *Y Va de Cuento* (*The Story Begins*). 1922 *Más allá de la Muerte* (*Beyond Death*). 1922 *Por Qué se quitó Juan de la Bebida* (monologue, *Why John Quit Drinking*). 1924 *Lecciones de Buen Amor* (*Lessons in Love*). 1924 *Un Par de Botas* (one act, *A Pair of Boots*). 1924 *La Virtud Sospechosa* (*Doubtful Virtue*). 1924 *La Otra Honra* (*The Other Honor*). 1924 *Alfilerazos* (*Pinpricks*). 1925 *Nadie sabe lo que quiere* (*Nobody Knows What He Wants*). 1925 *¡Si creeras tú que es por mi gusto!* (one act, *You Think I Like You*). 1925 *Los Nuevos Yernos* (*New Sons-in-Law*). 1925 *El Suicidio de Lucerito* (*The Suicide of Lucerito*). 1926 *La Mariposa que Voló sobre el Mar* (*The Butterfly that Flew Over the Sea*). 1927 *La Noche Illuminada* (*Bright Night*). 1927 *El Hijo de Polichinela* (*The Son of Polichinelle*). 1928 *Pepe Doncel* (*Chaste Joseph*). 1928 *¡No quiero, no quiero!* (*I Don't Want It!*). 1928 *El Demonio fué antes Ángel* (*The Demon Once Was an Angel*). 1928 *Para el Cielo y los Altares* (*For Heaven and the Altars*). 1929 *Vidas Cruzadas* (*Tangled Lives*). 1930 *Los Andrajos de la Púrpura* (*Rags of Purple*). 1930 *La Melodía del Jazzband* (*The Jazzband's Melody*). 1930 *Los Amigos del Hombre* (*The Friends of Man*). 1931 *De muy buena Familia* (*Of Good Family*). 1931 *Literatura* (*Literature*). 1931 *Cuando los Hijos de Eva no son los Hijos de Adán* (*When Eve's Sons Aren't Adam's*). 1932 *La Duquesa gitana* (*The Gipsy Duchess*). 1932 *La Moral del Divorcio* (*The Morality of Divorce*). 1932 *Santa Rusia* (*Holy Russia*). 1933 *El Rival de su Mujer* (*His Wife's Rival*). 1934 *El Pan Comido en la Mano* (*Bread Eaten in the Hand*). 1934 *Ni al amor ni al mar* (*Neither in Love nor in the Sea*). 1934 *La Vertad Invertida* (*The Inverted Truth*). 1935 *Memorias de un Madrileño*. 1935 *La Novia de Nieve* (*The Snow Bride*). 1935 *"No juguéis con esas cosas"* (*Don't Play with Those Things*). 1935 *Cualquiera lo sabe* (*Any One Knows That*).

WRITING ABOUT THE DRAMA

El Teatro del Pueblo, 1909.

THE PASSION FLOWER

Characters

RAIMUNDA.	GASPARA.
ACACIA.	ESTEBAN.
JULIANA.	NORBERT.
DOÑA ISABEL.	FAUSTINO.
MILAGROS.	TÍO EUSEBIO.
FIDELA.	BERNABÉ.
ENGRACIA.	RUBIO.
BERNABEA.	

The action of the play takes place in Castile.

THE FIRST ACT

A room in a rich farmer's house, situated on the outskirts of a pueblo, or small town.

[*As the curtain rises,* RAIMUNDA, ACACIA, DOÑA ISABEL, MILAGROS, FIDELA, ENGRACIA, *are bidding farewell to* GASPARA, BERNABEA, *and four or five women and young girls who are taking leave. While the others stand,* DOÑA ISABEL *remains seated.*]

Gaspara. God be with you! Good-by, Raimunda.

Bernabea. God be with you, Doña Isabel—and you, too, Acacia, and your mother. May everything turn out for the best.

Raimunda. Thanks. May we all live to see it. Go down with them, Acacia.

All. Good-by! Good-by!

[*The women and girls retire, keeping up an animated chatter.* ACACIA *accompanies them.*]

Doña Isabel. Bernabea is a nice girl.

Engracia. It is only a year since she got over that trouble. No one would ever believe it to look at her now.

Doña Isabel. I hear that she is going to be married.

Fidela. Yes, come next fiesta—God willing and San Roque.

Doña Isabel. I am always the last person in the village to pick up gossip. When you have nothing but trouble at home, naturally you lose interest in what is taking place outside.

Engracia. How is your husband?

Doña Isabel. He varies—up and down. The rest of us are thoroughly worn out. We are not able to leave the house, not even to attend mass upon Sundays. I am used to it myself, but it is hard on my daughter.

Engracia. I think you make a mistake to keep her at home so much. This is a great year for weddings.

Doña Isabel. But not for her. I am afraid that we shall never be able to find a man who measures up to her expectations.

Fidela. All the same, it never struck me that she was born to be a nun. Some day she will happen on the right one.

Doña Isabel. How are you pleased with this match, Raimunda? I must say you don't seem altogether cheerful about it.

Raimunda. A wedding is always something of an experiment.

Engracia. If you aren't satisfied, I am sure I don't know who could ever be. Your daughter has had the pick of the entire village.

Fidela. She's not likely to want for anything, either. We all know how well they will both be provided for, which is not a thing you can afford to overlook.

Raimunda. Milagros, run down-stairs and enjoy yourself with Acacia and the boys. I hate to see you sitting there all alone in a corner.

Doña Isabel. Yes, do go down.—The child is as innocent as the day that God made her.

Milagros. Excuse me. [*Goes out.*]

Raimunda. We might all take another glass and some biscuits.

Doña Isabel. Thanks, I have had enough.

Raimunda. No, no, come, everybody. This is nothing.

Doña Isabel. Acacia doesn't seem as happy as you might expect, either, considering that her engagement was announced only today.

Raimunda. She is as innocent, too, as God made her. I never saw any one like her; she is so silent. She distracts me. For weeks together she has not one word to say. Then there are times when she begins to talk, and her tongue runs until it fairly takes your breath away. It is a terrible thing to hear.

Engracia. Naturally, you have spoiled her. After you lost the three boys she was all that you had, and you were too careful. Her father would have plucked the birds out of the air if she had asked for them, and you were no better. When he died—God rest his soul—then the child was jealous of you. She didn't like it when you married again, and she has never gotten over that grudge either.

Raimunda. But what was I to do? I didn't want to marry again. I should never have thought of it if my brothers hadn't turned out the way that they did. If we had not had a man in the house to look after us, my daughter and I would have been in the street before this, and you know it.

Doña Isabel. Yes, this world is no place for single women. You were left a widow very young.

Raimunda. But I can't see why my daughter should be jealous. I am her mother, yet it would be hard to say which of us loves or spoils her the most. Esteban has never treated her like a stepdaughter.

Doña Isabel. No wonder; you had no other children of your own.

Raimunda. He never comes nor goes without bringing her a present. He never thinks of such a thing for me—although, of course, I have no feeling. She is my daughter; it only makes me love him more to see how fond he is of her. You won't believe it when I tell you, but she would never let him kiss her even when she was a child, much less now. I have seldom had to lay my hand on her, but whenever I have, it was on that account.

Fidela. Nobody can make me believe, just the same, that your daughter isn't in love with her cousin.

Raimunda. Norbert? She turned him off herself between night and morning, and that was the end of it. That is another thing I can't understand. We never could find out what did happen between them.

Fidela. Nor anybody else. Nobody has ever been able to explain it. There must have been some reason, but what it was is a mystery.

Engracia. Well, she never seemed to regret it, which is more than I can say for him. She never looked at him again, but he hasn't changed. When he heard that Faustino was coming over with his father today to settle the matter and arrange things, he turned on his heel, took his gun, and went straight up to Los Berrocales. People who saw him said that you would have thought that it had broken his heart.

Raimunda. Neither Esteban nor I influenced her in the least. She broke with Norbert herself, just as they were ready to publish the banns. Everybody knows it. Then she consented to see Faustino. He always had a fancy for her. His father is a great friend of Esteban's—they belong to the same party and always work together. They have known each other for a long time. Whenever we went to Encinar for the Feast of the Virgin —or for any other fiesta—or if they were the ones who came here, it was easy to see that the boy was nervous. When she was around he didn't know what to do. He knew that there was something between her and her cousin, but he never said one word until the break came, whatever the reason was, which we don't know—no, not one; but as soon as they heard that she was done with her cousin, Faustino's father spoke to Esteban, and Esteban spoke to me, and I spoke to my daughter, and she seemed pleased; so now they are going to be married. That is all there is to it. If she is not satisfied, then God have mercy on her soul, because we are only doing it to please her. She has had her own way in everything.

Doña Isabel. Then she ought to be happy. Why not? The boy is a fine fellow. Everybody says so.

Engracia. Yes, we all feel as if he belonged in the village. He lives so near by, and his family is so well known that nobody ever thinks of them as strangers.

Fidela. Tío Eusebio owns more land here than at Encinar.

Engracia. Certainly, if you stop to count. He inherited everything from his Uncle Manolito, and when the town lands were sold, two years ago, they went to him.

Doña Isabel. The family is the richest in the neighborhood.

Fidela. Undoubtedly. There may be four brothers, but each of them will come into a fortune.

Engracia. Your daughter is not going barefoot, either.

Raimunda. No, she is an only child and

will inherit everything. Esteban has taken good care of the farm which she had from her father; he could not have done more if she had been his own child.

[*The Angelus sounds.*]

Doña Isabel. The Angelus! [*The women mumble the words of the prayer.*] It is time for us to be going, Raimunda. Telesforo expects his supper early—if the nibble of nothing which he takes can be called supper.

Engracia. It is time for us all to go.

Fidela. We were all thinking the same thing.

Raimunda. But won't you stay to supper? I don't urge Doña Isabel—I know she ought not to leave her husband. He is impatient to see her back.

Engracia. Yes. We all have husbands to look after. Thanks just the same.

Doña Isabel. I suppose the young man stays to supper?

Raimunda. No, he is going home with his father to Encinar. They cannot spend the night. There is no moon, so they should have been on the road long ago. It is getting late and the days are growing shorter. Before you know it, it is black night.

Engracia. I hear them coming up now to say good-by.

Raimunda. I thought so.

[ACACIA, MILAGROS, ESTEBAN, TÍO EUSEBIO, *and* FAUSTINO *enter.*]

Esteban. Raimunda, here are Tío Eusebio and Faustino to say good-by.

Eusebio. We must be off before dark. The roads are in terrible shape after the heavy rains.

Esteban. There are some bad stretches.

Doña Isabel. Well, what has the boy to say for himself? I suppose he doesn't remember me. It is five years since I have seen him.

Eusebio. Don't you remember Doña Isabel?

Faustino. I do, *si, señor.* I was afraid she didn't remember me.

Doña Isabel. No fear of that! My husband was *alcalde* at the time when you gave us that awful fright, running after the bull. If you had been killed, I don't know what would have happened. I didn't enjoy it. God help San Roque!—it would have put an end to his fiesta. We certainly thought you were dead.

Engracia. Julian, Eudosia's husband, was caught that year too.

Faustino. I remember, *si, señora.*

Eusebio. He remembers perfectly, because I gave him a sound thrashing when he got home—which he deserved.

Faustino. I was a boy at the time.

Doña Isabel. Yes—the boy of it! However, you have picked out the finest girl in the village, and she will have no reason to regret her choice either. But we must be going. You have business of your own to attend to.

Esteban. No, they have attended to everything already.

Doña Isabel. Good night, then. Come, Milagros.

Acacia. I want her to stay to supper, but she is afraid to ask you. Do let her stay, Doña Isabel!

Raimunda. Yes, do. Bernabé and Juliana will see her home afterward, and Esteban can go along, too, if necessary.

Doña Isabel. No, we will send for her. You can stay, to please Acacia.

Raimunda. They have so many things to talk over.

Doña Isabel. God be with you. Adios, Tío Eusebio and Esteban.

Eusebio. Adios, Doña Isabel. My best sympathy to your husband.

Doña Isabel. Which he appreciates, coming from you.

Engracia. Good-by! A safe return!

Fidela. God be with you!

[*The women go out.*]

Eusebio. Doña Isabel looks remarkably young. She must be my age at least. Well, "To have and to hold is to prepare to grow old," as the proverb has it. Doña Isabel was one of the best of them in her day, and in her day there were plenty.

Esteban. Sit down, Tío Eusebio. What is your hurry?

Eusebio. No, don't tempt me; it's time to go. Night is coming on. Don't bother about us. We have the hands along and shan't need you.

Esteban. No, the walk will do me good. I'll see you to the *arroyo* at least.

[RAIMUNDA, ACACIA, *and* MILAGROS *reenter.*]

Eusebio. If you young folks have anything to say, now is the time for you to say it.

Acacia. No, we have settled everything.

Eusebio. So you think.

Raimunda. Come, come! Don't you try to embarrass my daughter, Tío Eusebio.

Acacia. Thanks for everything.

Eusebio. What? Is that a way to thank me?

Acacia. It was a lovely present.

Eusebio. The showiest thing we could find.

Raimunda. Entirely too much so for a farmer's daughter.

Eusebio. Too much? Not a bit of it! If I'd had my way, it would have had more jewels in it than the Holy Monstrance at Toledo. Give your mother-in-law a good hug.

Raimunda. Yes, come, boy. I must learn to love you or I shall never forgive you for taking her away. My heart goes with her.

Esteban. Now don't begin to cry! Come, Acacia! You don't want to pass yourself off for a Magdalen.

Milagros. Raimunda! Acacia!

[*Bursts into tears also.*]

Esteban. That's right—all together! Come, come!

Eusebio. Don't be foolish! Tears are for the dead. You are only going to be married. Try to be happy and enjoy yourselves; everybody is willing. Adios and good night!

Raimunda. Adios, Tío Eusebio. Tell Julia that I don't know whether I shall ever be able to forgive her for not coming over today.

Eusebio. You know how bad her sight is. We'd have had to hitch up the cart, and it was up at Los Berrocales. We are beginning to slaughter.

Raimunda. Tell her how sorry I am. May she be better soon.

Eusebio. Thanks to you.

Raimunda. Now you had better be going. It is getting dark. [*To* ESTEBAN.] Don't be long.

Eusebio. I told him not to come.

Esteban. Nonsense! It isn't any trouble. I'll go as far as the *arroyo*. Don't wait supper for me.

Raimunda. To be sure we will wait. We're not anxious to eat alone tonight. Milagros won't mind if we are late.

Milagros. It makes no difference to me.

Eusebio. God be with you all! Good-by!

Raimunda. No, we are coming down to see you out.

Faustino. I . . . I have something to say to Acacia first. . . .

Eusebio. It will have to wait until tomorrow. You have had the whole day to yourselves.

Faustino. Yes, but with so many people around, I had no chance. . . .

Eusebio. Before we were through I knew we were going to get some of this nonsense.

Faustino. It isn't nonsense. Only I promised mother before we started to give Acacia this scapulary. The nuns in the convent made it on purpose for her.

Acacia. How lovely!

Milagros. Oh! The Blessed Virgin of Carmen—with spangles all over!

Raimunda. Very pretty. My daughter was always devoted to the Virgin. Thank your mother for us. We appreciate it.

Faustino. It has been blessed.

Eusebio. Good! Now you have got that off your mind. I wonder what your mother would have thought if we'd taken it home again with us! I never saw such a boy! I wasn't so backward in my day. I am sure I don't know whom he does take after.

[*All go out. For a moment the stage remains deserted. Meanwhile it continues to grow darker. Presently* RAIMUNDA, ACACIA, *and* MILAGROS *reappear.*]

Raimunda. They have made a long day of it. It is night before they start. How do you feel, my dear? Are you happy?

Acacia. You can see for yourself.

Raimunda. I can, can I? That is exactly what I want to do: see for myself. Nobody can ever tell how you feel.

Acacia. I am tired out.

Raimunda. It has certainly been a long day. I haven't had a minute's rest since five o'clock in the morning.

Milagros. Everybody has been here to congratulate you.

Raimunda. The whole village, you might say, beginning with the priest, who was among the first. We paid him for a mass, and gave him ten loaves of bread besides for the poor. In our happiness it is only right to remember others who are not so fortunate. Praise God, we want for nothing! Where are the matches?

Acacia. Here they are, mother.

Raimunda. Light the lamp, dear. It makes me feel sad to sit in the dark. [*Calling.*] Juliana! Juliana! I wonder where she is?

Juliana. [*Downstairs.*] What do you want?

Raimunda. Bring up the broom and dustpan.

Juliana. [*Downstairs.*] In a minute.

Raimunda. I had better change my skirt while I think of it. Nobody will be in now; it's so late.

Acacia. I might take off my dress.

Raimunda. What for? There is nothing for you to do. You have been busy all day.

[JULIANA *enters.*]

Juliana. Show me that dust——

Raimunda. Stand the broom in the corner and take these things away. Mind you scour them until they are clean; then put them back in the cupboard. Be careful with those glasses! They are our best.

Juliana. Could I eat a cake?

Raimunda. Of course you can!—though I don't see how you manage to hold so much.

Juliana. I haven't touched a thing this whole day, God help me! I am my mother's own daughter. Haven't I passed cake and wine to the entire village? Everybody has been here today. That shows you what people think of this house—yes, and what they think of Tío Eusebio and his family. Wait till you see the wedding! I know somebody who is going to give her a new gold piece, and somebody who is going to give her a silk embroidered quilt that has flowers all over it, so lifelike that the first thing she will want to do is pick them off of it. That will be a great day for her, praise God! Not one of us but will laugh and cry then, and I will be the first—after her mother; she will be first because it is her right, but you know me. I love you all in this house. Besides, you make me think of my dead daughter. She looked just like you do when she died, and we buried her.

Raimunda. Never mind that, Juliana. Go along and don't dig up any more of your troubles. We have enough of our own already.

Juliana. God grant that I may never be a trouble to you! But everything goes topsy-turvy with me today, around and around, and every which way. The more you enjoy yourself the sadder it makes you feel. God forbid that I should ever drag in this child's poor dead father, who rests in heaven now, God bless him! But I wish he could have seen her today! He was fond of her.

Raimunda. That will do, Juliana. That will do.

Juliana. Don't talk like that to me, Raimunda. It's like a blow in the face, like beating a faithful hound. That's what I have been to you and your daughter and your house—a faithful hound, that has eaten your bread, God willing, in season and out—yes, and kept her self-respect while she was about it, and you know it. [*Goes out.*]

Raimunda. Juliana!—She is right, though. She has always been like a faithful hound—faithful and loyal to us and our house.

[*She begins to sweep.*]

Acacia. Mother——

Raimunda. Did you speak?

Acacia. Will you let me have the key to this chest of drawers? I want to show Milagros some of my things.

Raimunda. Yes, here it is; take the bunch. Sit down and rest while I go and keep an eye on the supper.

[*She takes the broom and goes out.* ACACIA *and* MILAGROS *seat themselves on the floor before the chest of drawers and open the lower drawer or compartment.*]

Acacia. These earrings were a present from—well, from Esteban, since my mother isn't here. She always wants me to call him father.

Milagros. Don't you know that he loves you?

Acacia. Yes, but you can have only one father and mother. He brought me these handkerchiefs, too, from Toledo. The nuns embroidered the initials. See all these post-cards—aren't they pretty?

Milagros. What lovely ladies!

Acacia. Yes, they're actresses from Madrid, or from Paris in France. Look at these boys— He brought me this box, too; it had candy in it.

Milagros. I don't see how you can say then. . . .

Acacia. I don't say anything. I know he loves me, but I'd rather have been left alone with my mother.

Milagros. You don't mean to tell me that your mother loves you any less on his account?

Acacia. I don't know. She's wrapped up in him. How do I know, if she had to choose between me and that man. . . .

Milagros. I think it's wicked to talk like that. Suppose your mother hadn't married again, what would she do now when you get married? She would have no one else to live with.

Acacia. You don't suppose that I would ever have gotten married, do you, if I had been living alone with my mother?

Milagros. Of course you would! What difference would it make?

Acacia. Could I be as happy anywhere else as living here alone with my mother?

Milagros. Don't be foolish. Everybody knows what a nice stepfather you have. If he hadn't been good there would have been talk, and I would have heard it. So would you and your mother.

Acacia. I don't say that he isn't good. But all the same I wouldn't have married if my mother hadn't married again.

Milagros. Do you know what I think?

Acacia. What?

Milagros. People are right when they say that you don't love Faustino. The one that you love is Norbert.

Acacia. That's a lie! How could I love him?—after the way that he treated me.

Milagros. Everybody says that you were the one who turned him off.

Acacia. I did, did I? Yes, I suppose it was my fault! Anyway, we won't talk about it. What do they know? I love Faustino better than I ever did Norbert.

Milagros. I hope you do. Otherwise you oughtn't to marry him. Did you hear that Norbert left the village this morning? He didn't want to be around.

Acacia. What does he care? Why today more than any other? It is nothing to him. Here is the last letter he wrote me—after everything was over. I never mean to see him again; I don't know what I am keeping it for. It would be more sensible to tear it up. [*She tears the letter into small pieces.*] There! That ends it.

Milagros. What is the matter with you? You are all excited.

Acacia. It's what he says. Now I am going to burn the pieces.

Milagros. Look out! The lamp will explode.

Acacia. [*Opening the window.*] To the road with you! I'll scatter the ashes. . . . The wind blows them away. . . . It is over now, and I am glad of it. Did you ever see such a dark night?

Milagros. [*Following her to the window.*] It is black as pitch—no moon, no stars. . . .

Acacia. What was that?

Milagros. Somebody slammed a door.

Acacia. It sounded to me like a shot.

Milagros. Nonsense! Who would be out shooting at this hour? Unless there is a fire somewhere. . . . No, I don't see any glow in the sky.

Acacia. I am frightened. Yes, I am——

Milagros. Don't be silly!

Acacia. [*Running suddenly to the door.*] Mother! Mother!

Raimunda. [*Downstairs.*] What is it?

Acacia. Did you hear anything?

Raimunda. [*Downstairs.*] Yes. I sent Juliana to find out. It's all right.

Acacia. Oh, mother!

Raimunda. Don't be afraid! I am coming up.

Acacia. It was a shot! I know it was a shot!

Milagros. Suppose it was? What of it?

Acacia. God help us! [RAIMUNDA *enters.*]

Raimunda. Did it frighten you? Nothing is the matter.

Acacia. Mother, you are frightened yourself.

Raimunda. Because you are. Naturally, I was frightened at first—your father hasn't come back. But it is silly. Nothing could have happened. What was that? Do you hear? Some one is downstairs! God help us!

Acacia. Mother! Mother!

Milagros. What do they say? What are they talking about?

Raimunda. Stay where you are. I am going down.

Acacia. Mother, don't you go!

Raimunda. I can't make out what they say. . . . I am too excited. . . . Oh, Esteban, my heart! May no harm have come to you! [*She rushes out.*]

Milagros. There is a crowd downstairs. They are coming in. I can't make out what they say. . . .

Acacia. Something has happened! Something awful! I knew it all the time.

Milagros. So did I, only I didn't want to frighten you.

Acacia. What do you think?

Milagros. Don't ask me! Don't ask me!

Raimunda. [*Downstairs.*] Holy Virgin! God save us! Terrible, terrible! Oh, his poor mother when she hears that her poor boy is dead—murdered! I can't believe it. What a terrible thing for us all!

Acacia. What does she say? Did you hear?—Mother! Mother! Mother!

Raimunda. Acacia! Daughter! Don't you come down! Don't come down! I am coming up.

[RAIMUNDA, FIDELA, ENGRACIA, GASPARA, *and a number of other women enter.*]

Acacia. What's the matter? What has happened? Some one is dead, isn't he? Some one is dead?

Raimunda. My poor child! Faustino! Faustino!

Acacia. What?

Raimunda. Murdered! Shot dead as he left the village!

Acacia. Mother! *Ay!* But who did it? Who did it?

Raimunda. Nobody knows. It was too dark; they couldn't see. Every one thinks it was Norbert—so as to fill the cup of disgrace which we must drain in this house!

Engracia. It couldn't have been any one else.

Women. It was Norbert! It was Norbert!

Fidela. Here come the constables.

Engracia. Have they caught him?

Raimunda. And here is your father. [ESTEBAN *enters.*] Esteban, my soul! Who did it? Do you know?

Esteban. How do I know? I saw what the rest did. Don't leave the house, do you hear? I don't want to have you running around the village.

Raimunda. But how is his father? Think of his poor mother when they carry her boy home to her dead—murdered! And he left her alive, happy, and well only this morning!

Engracia. Hanging is too good for the wretch that did it!

Fidela. They ought to have killed him on the spot! Such a thing never happened before in this village.

Raimunda. Esteban, don't let them take the body away. I must see him—and so must my daughter. He was to have been her husband.

Esteban. Keep cool! There is plenty of time. I don't want you to leave the house, do you hear? It's in the hands of the law now; the doctor and priest were too late. I must hurry back; we all have depositions to make. [ESTEBAN *retires.*]

Raimunda. Your father is right. What can we do?—except commend his soul to God, who was his Maker. I can't get his poor mother out of my head! Don't take it so hard, Acacia. It frightens me to see you so still. It is worse than if you cried your heart out. Who would ever have believed this morning that such a thing could be? But it is! A curse has fallen upon us!

Engracia. The shot went straight through his heart.

Fidela. He fell off his horse, like a log.

Raimunda. What a shame, what a disgrace to the village! I blush to think that the murderer was born in this place, that he was one of us, and walked about here with all that evil in his heart! He is one of our own family, to make it worse!

Gaspara. But we aren't sure of that.

Raimunda. Who else could it be? Everybody says so.

Engracia. Everybody says it was Norbert.

Fidela. It couldn't have been any one but Norbert!

Raimunda. Light the candles, Milagros, before the image of the Virgin. Let us tell her a rosary, since we can do no more than pray for the dead.

Gaspara. God rest his soul!

Engracia. He died without confession.

Fidela. From Purgatory, good Lord, deliver us.

All. God rest his soul!

Raimunda. [*To* MILAGROS.] You begin the rosary; I cannot pray. I am thinking of his mother's broken heart!

[*The women begin to tell the rosary.*]

CURTAIN

THE SECOND ACT

Entrance Hall of a farmhouse. There is a large door at the rear, on either side of which is a window, having an iron grating. A door on the left, and another on the right.

[ESTEBAN *is seated at a small table, taking lunch.* RAIMUNDA *waits upon him, seated also.* JULIANA *comes and goes, assisting with the service.* ACACIA *sits in a low chair near one of the windows, sewing. A basket of clothes stands beside her.*]

Raimunda. Don't you like it?

Esteban. Of course I do.

Raimunda. You haven't eaten anything. Do you want us to cook something else?

Esteban. Don't bother me, my dear. I have had plenty.

Raimunda. You don't expect me to believe that. [*Calling.*] Juliana! Bring the salad!—something is the matter with you.

Esteban. Don't be silly.

Raimunda. Don't you suppose that I know you by this time? You ought never to have gone to the village. You've heard talk. We came out here to the grove to get rid of it all, to be away from the excitement, and it was a good thing, too, that we did. Now you go back to the village and don't say one word to me about it. What did you want to do that for?

Esteban. I wanted to see Norbert and his father.

Raimunda. Yes, but you could have sent for them and have had them come out here. You ought to have spared yourself; then you wouldn't have heard all this talk. I know how they are talking in the village.

Juliana. Yes, and that is all the good it does us to stay out here and shut ourselves up from everybody, because everybody that goes anywhere in the neighborhood passes through this grove, and then they stop, and smell around, and meddle in what is none of their business.

Esteban. Yes, and you meddle with every one of them.

Juliana. No, señor; don't you make any mistake. I meddle with nobody. Didn't I scold Bernabea only yesterday for talking more than she had any right to with some men from Encinar who were coming down the road? If any one asks questions send them to me, because I've learned what to do from my mother, who had good reason to know: When questioned much, answer little, and be sure you make it just the opposite.

Raimunda. Hold your tongue! And get out. [JULIANA *retires.*] What do they say in the village?

Esteban. Nothing. Tío Eusebio and his boys swear they are going to kill Norbert. They refuse to accept the decision of the court; he got off too easily. They are coming over some day, and then there will be trouble. You hear both sides in the village. Some think that Tío Eusebio is right, that it must have been Norbert; others think it wasn't Norbert. They say that the court let him go because he was innocent, and he proved it.

Raimunda. That is what I think. No one could contradict his deposition; not even Faustino's father could find any flaws in it, nor the hands. You couldn't yourself, and you were with them.

Esteban. Tío Eusebio and I had stopped to light our cigars. We were laughing like two fools because I had my lighter, and it wouldn't light; so Tío Eusebio got out his tinder and flint and said to me, laughing: "Here, get a light, and don't waste your time with that new-fangled machine. All it is good for is to help fools waste their money. I still make out with this." That was what blinded us. We were fooling over the light when the shot was fired. We started up and could see nothing. Then, when we saw that he had dropped dead, we stood stock-still, as dead as he was. They could have finished us, too, while they were about it, and we would never have known it. [ACACIA *gets up suddenly and starts to go out.*]

Raimunda. Where are you going, my dear? Don't be nervous.

Acacia. You never talk about anything else. I don't see how you can stand it. Hasn't he told us how it happened over and over again? Do we have to hear the same thing all the time?

Esteban. She is right. If I had my way, I'd never mention it again; it's your mother.

Acacia. I even dream about it at night. I never used to be nervous when I was alone or in the dark, but now I am frightened to death, even in broad daylight.

Raimunda. You are not the only one, either. I get no rest, day or night. I never used to be afraid. I thought nothing of passing the cemetery after dark, not even on All Souls' Eve, but now the least thing makes me jump, no matter what—noise, silence. To tell the truth, as long as we thought it was Norbert, although he was one of the family, and it would have been a shame and a disgrace to us all, at the same time it couldn't be helped; there was nothing to do but resign oneself—and I had resigned myself. After all, it had an explanation. But now, if it wasn't Norbert, if nobody knows who it was, and nobody can explain why it was that that poor boy was shot—I can't be easy in my mind. If it wasn't Norbert, who could have wished him any harm? Maybe it was revenge, some enemy of his father's, or of yours—how do we know but that the shot was intended for you, and since it was night and pitch-dark, they made a mistake, and what they didn't do then they will another time, and . . . I can't stand the suspense! I get no rest! Every time that you go out of the house and show yourself on the road, it seems to me that I will go crazy. Today, when you were late, I was just starting for the village myself.

Acacia. She was out on the road already.

Raimunda. Yes, only I saw you and Rubio from the top of the hill, so I turned and ran back before you passed the mill, so you wouldn't be angry. I know it is foolish, but now I want to be with you all the time, wherever you go—I can't bear to be separated from you for one moment. Otherwise I can't be happy. This isn't living.

Esteban. I don't believe anybody wishes me any harm. I never wronged any man. I go wherever I please, without so much as giving it a thought, day or night.

Raimunda. I used to feel the same; there is nobody who could wish us harm. We have helped so many. But all that you need is one enemy, one envious, evil mind. How do we know but that we have some enemy without our suspecting it? A second shot might come from the same quarter as the first. Norbert is free because they couldn't prove that he was guilty; and I am glad of it. Why shouldn't I be glad when he is my own sister's son—my favorite sister's? I could never have believed that Norbert could have done such a thing as murder a man in the dark! But is this to be the end of it? What is the law doing now? Why don't they investigate, why doesn't some one speak? Somebody must know, somebody must have seen whoever it was that was there that day, hovering along the road. When everything is all right, everybody knows who is passing, and what is going on—who comes and who goes—you hear it all without asking; but when you want to know, then nobody knows, nobody has seen anything.

Esteban. I can't see why that is so strange. When a man is going about his business, he has nothing to conceal; but when his intentions are evil, naturally the first thing he does is to hide himself.

Raimunda. Who do you think that it was?

Esteban. I? To tell the truth, I thought it was Norbert, the same as you. If it wasn't Norbert, I don't know who it was.

Raimunda. I suppose you won't like it, but I'll tell you what I have made up my mind to do.

Esteban. What?

Raimunda. Talk to Norbert. Bernabé has gone to find him. I expect him any minute.

Acacia. Norbert? What do you want to talk to him for?

Esteban. That is what I say. What does he know about it?

Raimunda. How can I tell? But I know he won't lie to me. By the memory of his mother, I will make him tell me the truth. If he did it, he knows I will never tell. I can't stand this any longer. I shake all over.

Esteban. Do you suppose that Norbert is going to tell you if he was the one who did it?

Raimunda. After I talk to him I shall know.

Esteban. Well, have your own way. It will only make more talk and hard feeling, especially since Tío Eusebio is coming over today. If they meet. . . .

Raimunda. They won't meet on the road, because they come from different directions. After they are here the house is big enough. We can take care of them both.

[JULIANA *enters.*]

Juliana. Master. . . .

Esteban. Why are you always bothering me?

Juliana. Tío Eusebio is coming down the road. Maybe you don't want to see him; I thought you might like to know. . . .

Esteban. Why shouldn't I want to see him? Didn't I tell you he was coming?—Now bring in the other one!

Raimunda. Yes, he can't come too soon to please me.

Esteban. Who told you that I didn't want to see Tío Eusebio?

Juliana. Oh, don't blame it on me! It wasn't my fault. Rubio says you don't want to see him because he is mad at you. You didn't side with him in court, and that's the reason that Norbert went free.

Esteban. I'll teach Rubio it's none of his business whom I side with.

Juliana. Yes, and there are other things you might teach him while you are about it. Have I nothing to do but wait on that man? God help me, he has had more to drink today than is good for him. And that isn't talk, either.

Raimunda. This is the last straw! Where is he?

Esteban. No, leave him to me.

Raimunda. Everything goes wrong in this house. Everybody takes advantage of you as soon as anything is the matter. You don't need to turn your back—it's instinct. They know when you can't take care of yourself.

Juliana. I'll not take that from you, Raimunda, if you mean me.

Raimunda. You know who I mean. Take it any way you like.

Juliana. Señor, señor! What curse has fallen on this house? We are all poisoned, snared, our feet are caught in some evil vine; we are changed. One takes it out on the other, and everybody is against me. God help me, I say, and give me the strength to endure it!

Raimunda. Yes, and give me the strength to endure you.

Juliana. Yes, me! It is all my fault.

Raimunda. Look at me, will you? Do I have to tell you to your face to get out? That's all I want from you.

Juliana. Yes, you want me to shut up like a tomb. Well, I'll shut up, God help me! Señor! Let me out! Don't talk to me.

[*Goes out.*]

Esteban. Here comes Tío Eusebio.

Acacia. I am going. He breaks down and cries whenever he sees me. He doesn't know what he is doing, but it's always the wrong thing. Does he think he is the only one who has lost anything?

Raimunda. I am sure I have cried as much as his mother has. Tío Eusebio is not the same man; he forgets. But never mind. You are right not to see him.

Acacia. I have finished the shirts, mother. I'll iron them as soon as I have time.

Esteban. Were you sewing for me?

Acacia. You can see for yourself.

Raimunda. I don't know how we'd get on if she didn't sew. I am not good for anything. I don't know whether I am alive or dead, God help me! But she can work. She gets through with it somehow. [*She caresses* ACACIA *affectionately as she passes out.*] God bless you, Acacia, my child! [ACACIA *goes out.*] It is a terrible responsibility to be a mother. For a long time I was afraid that she was going to get married and leave me. Now, what wouldn't I give to see her married? [Tío Eusebio *enters.*]

Eusebio. Hello! Where is everybody?

Esteban. Come in, Tío Eusebio.

Eusebio. Good morning to both.

Raimunda. Good morning, Tío Eusebio.

Esteban. Where are your horses? I'll have them put up.

Eusebio. My man will tend to that.

Esteban. Sit down. Come, a glass of that wine he likes so much, Raimunda.

Eusebio. No, no, thank you. I am not feeling well. Wine doesn't agree with me.

Esteban. This wine will do you good. It's a tonic.

Raimunda. Suit yourself. How are you, Tío Eusebio? How is Julia?

Eusebio. Julia? What do you expect? I am going to lose her just as I did the boy; I can see it.

Raimunda. God forbid! Hasn't she four sons yet to live for?

Eusebio. Yes, the more worry! That is what is killing her—worry. Nobody knows what will happen next. Our hearts are broken. We were sure that we would get justice; but now we are bitter. Everybody said it would be like this, but we didn't believe it. The murderer is alive—you pass him on the street; he goes home to his house, shuts the door, and laughs at us. It only proves what I knew all the time. There is no such thing in this world as justice, unless a man takes it with his own hands, which is what they will drive us to do now. That is why I wanted to see you yesterday. If my boys come into the village, send them home. Don't let them stay around. Arrest them—anything rather than another tragedy in our house; although I don't want to see his murderer go free—the murderer of my boy—let only Heaven avenge him as it must, by God!—or else there is no justice in heaven.

Raimunda. Don't turn against God, Tío Eusebio. Though the hand of justice never fall upon him after the foul murder he has done, yet there is not one of us that would be in his place. He is alone with his conscience. I would not have what he has on his soul upon mine, for all the blessings of this world. We have lived good lives, we have done evil to no man, yet all our days are purgatory and torment. He must have hell in his heart after what he has done—of that we can be sure—as sure as of the day of our death.

Eusebio. That is cold comfort to me. How does it help me prevent my boys from taking the law into their own hands? Justice has not been done—and it should have been done. Now they are the ones who will go to jail for it! They will make good their threats too. You ought to hear them. Even the little fellow, who is only twelve, doubles up his fists like a man, and swears that whoever killed his brother will have to reckon with him, come what may. I sit there and cry like a child. I needn't tell you how his mother feels. And all the while I have it in my heart to say: Go, my sons! Stone him until he is dead! Cut him to pieces like a hound! Drag his carcass home to me through the mire—what offal there is left of it! Instead I swallow it all and look grave, and tell them that it is wrong even to think of such a thing—it would kill their mother, it would ruin all of us!

Raimunda. You are unreasonable, Tío Eusebio. Norbert is innocent; the law says so. No one could bring the least proof against him; he proved where he was, and what he was doing all that day, one hour after the other. He and his men were up at Los Berrocales. Don Faustino, the doctor, saw him there and talked with him at the very hour it took place, and he is from Encinar. You know yourself no man can be in two places at the same time. You might think that his own people had been told to say what they did, although it isn't an easy thing for so many to agree on a lie; but Don Faustino is a friend of yours; he is in your debt. And others who would naturally have been on your side said the same. Only one shepherd from Los Berrocales would testify that he had seen a man at that hour, and that was a great way off; but he had no idea who it was. From his clothes and the way that he carried himself he was sure that it could not have been Norbert.

Eusebio. If it wasn't, I say nothing. Does it make it any better for us that he hired some one else to do it? There can't be any doubt; there is no other explanation. I have no enemies who would do such a thing. I never harmed any man; I help every one, whether they are our own people or not. I make it easy. If I were to sue for one-half the damage that is done me every day, it would take all of my time. I will die a poor man. They killed Faustino because he was going to marry Acacia. That is all there is to it. Nobody could have had any such reason but Norbert. If everybody had told what they knew, the trial would have ended right there. But the ones who knew most said the least; they said nothing.

Raimunda. Do you mean us?

Eusebio. I don't say who I mean.

Raimunda. It is plain enough; you don't

have to mention names nor point your finger. Do you mean to say that we keep quiet because Norbert is one of our family?

Eusebio. Do you mean to say that Acacia doesn't know more about this thing than she is willing to admit?

Raimunda. No, sir, she knows no more about it than you do. You have made up your mind that it was Norbert because you want to make yourself believe that nobody else has anything against you. We are none of us saints, Tío Eusebio. You may have done a great deal of good in your time, but you must also have done some evil; you think that nobody remembers, but maybe the ones who have suffered don't think the same. If Norbert had been in love with my daughter to that extent, he would have shown it before now. Your son didn't take her away from him, remember that. Faustino never said one word until after she was done with Norbert, and she turned him off because she knew he was going with another girl. He never so much as took the trouble to excuse himself, so that when you come down to it, he was the one who left her. That is no reason why any one should commit murder. You can see it yourself.

Eusebio. Then why did everybody say that it couldn't have been any one else? You said so yourself; everybody said so.

Raimunda. Yes, because at first he was the only one we could think of. But when you look at it calmly, it is foolish to say that he is the only one who could have done it. You insinuate that we have something to conceal. Once for all, let me tell you, we are more anxious than you are to have the truth known, to have this thing out and be done with it. You have lost a son, but I have a daughter who is alive, and she has nothing to gain, either, by this mystery.

Eusebio. No, she hasn't. Much less when she keeps her mouth shut. And you haven't anything to gain. You don't know what Norbert and his father say about this house so as to divert suspicion from themselves. If I believed what they said. . . .

Raimunda. About us? What do they say? [*To* ESTEBAN.] You have been in the village. What do they say?

Esteban. Nobody cares what they say.

Eusebio. No, I don't believe one word that comes from them. I am only telling you how they repay the kindness you do them by taking their part.

Raimunda. So you are on that tack again? Tío Eusebio, I have to stop and force myself to think what it must mean to lose a child, or I would lose control of myself. I am a mother, God knows, yet you come here and insult my daughter. You insult all of us.

Esteban. Wife! Enough of this. What is the use? Tío Eusebio. . . .

Eusebio. I insult nobody. I only repeat what other people say. You suppress the truth because he is one of the family. The whole village is the same. What you are afraid of is the disgrace. People here may think that it was not Norbert, but in Encinar, let me tell you, they think that it was. If justice isn't done—and done quick—blood will be spilled between these villages, and nobody can stop it, either. You know what young blood is.

Raimunda. Yes, and you are the one who stirs it up. You respect neither God nor man. Why, didn't you just admit that Norbert couldn't have done it unless he had hired some one to commit the murder? Nonsense! It isn't so easy to hire a man to commit murder. What had a boy like Norbert to give, anyway?—Unless you want us to believe that his father had a hand in it.

Eusebio. Bah! Rogues come cheap. How about the Valderrobles? They live here. Didn't they kill two goat-herds for three and a half duros?

Raimunda. How long was it before they were found out? They fought over the half duro. When you hire a man to do a deed like that, you put yourself in his power; you become his slave for the rest of your life. There may be people who can afford to do such things, but they must be rich, they must have power. Not a boy like Norbert!

Eusebio. Every family has a faithful servant who will do what he is told.

Raimunda. No doubt yours has. No doubt you have had occasion to use him too; you know so much about it.

Eusebio. Take care what you say!

Raimunda. Take care yourself!

Esteban. Raimunda! Enough of this. What is the use of all this talk?

Eusebio. Well, you hear what she says. How about you?

Esteban. If we dwell on this forever, we shall all of us go mad.

Eusebio. Yes. You heard what I said.

Raimunda. If you mean by that that you don't intend to let this matter drop until you have found the murderer of your boy, it is only right and proper, and I respect you for it. But that is no reason why you should come here and insult us. Once for all, you may want justice, but I want it more than you do. I pray to God for it every day, I pray him on my knees not to let the murderer go free—and I should pray to him just the same if I had a boy—if it had been my own boy that did it!

[RUBIO *appears in the doorway.*]

Rubio. How about me, master?

Esteban. Well, Rubio?

Rubio. Don't look at me like that; I'm not drunk. We started out before lunch; that was all. I had an invitation and took a drop; it went against me. I'm sorry you feel that way about it.

Raimunda. What is the matter with him? Juliana was right.

Rubio. Tell Juliana to mind her business, will you? I just wanted to tell the master.

Esteban. Rubio! You can tell me later whatever you like. Tío Eusebio is here. Don't you see? We are busy.

Rubio. Tío Eusebio? So he is. What does he want?

Raimunda. Is it any of your business what he wants? Get out! Go along and sleep it off. You don't know what you are talking about.

Rubio. I know, señora. Don't say that to me.

Esteban. Rubio!

Rubio. Juliana's a fool; I don't drink. It was my money, anyhow. I'm no thief. What I have is my own; and my wife is my own, too. She owes nobody anything, eh, master?

Esteban. Rubio! Go along! Get to bed, and don't show yourself again until you have had a good sleep. What is the matter with you? What will Tío Eusebio think?

Rubio. I don't know. I don't take anything, understand—from anybody.

[*Goes out.*]

Raimunda. What was it that you were just saying about servants, Tío Eusebio? This man has us with our hearts in our throats; yet he is nothing to us. Suppose we had trusted him with some secret? What is the matter with Rubio, anyway? Is he going to get drunk every day? He was never like this before. You ought not to put up with it.

Esteban. Don't you see? He isn't used to it. That is the reason he is upset by a thimbleful. Somebody invited him into the tavern while I was tending to my business. I gave him a piece of my mind and sent him to bed, but he hasn't slept it off yet. He is drunk. That is all there is to it.

Eusebio. Perfectly natural. Is that all?

Esteban. Drop in again, Tío Eusebio.

Eusebio. Thanks. I am sorry this happened—after I took the trouble to come.

Raimunda. Nonsense! Nothing has happened. We have no hard feeling.

Eusebio. No, and I hope you won't have any. Remember what I've been through. My heart is broken—it's not scratched. It won't heal either until God claims another one of his own. How long do you expect to stay in the grove?

Esteban. Till Sunday. We have nothing to keep us. We only wanted to be out of the village. Now that Norbert is home, it is nothing but talk, talk, talk.

Eusebio. That's right—nothing but talk. If you see my boys around, look out! I don't want them to get into any trouble, which afterward we might have cause to regret.

Esteban. Don't you worry. They won't get into any while I am around. Blame it on me if they do.

Eusebio. They're working down by the river now. They'll be all right unless somebody happens along and stirs them up. God be with you, I say. Adios! Where is Acacia?

Raimunda. I told her not to come down, so as to spare your feelings. It is hard on her, too; it brings back everything.

Eusebio. That's so. It must.

Esteban. I'll send for your horses.

Eusebio. No, I can call myself.—Francisco!—Here he comes. Take care of yourselves. God be with you!

[*They move toward the door.*]

Raimunda. God be with you, Tío Eusebio. Tell Julia not to worry. I think of her every day. I have prayed more for her than I have for the boy—God has forgiven him by this time. Surely he never did anything to deserve such a bad end! My heart bleeds for him.

[ESTEBAN *and* TÍO EUSEBIO *have passed out while she is speaking.* BERNABÉ *enters.*]

Bernabé. Señora!

Raimunda. Is Norbert here? Could you find him?

Bernabé. Yes, I brought him along so as to save time. He wanted to see you himself.

Raimunda. Didn't you meet Tío Eusebio?

Bernabé. No, we saw him coming up from the river when we were a long way off, so we turned and went in by the great corral. Norbert is hiding there until Tío Eusebio starts back to Encinar.

Raimunda. There he goes up the road now.

Bernabé. Yes—under the great cross.

Raimunda. Tell Norbert. No—wait! What do they say in the village?

Bernabé. No good, señora. The law is going to have its hands full before it gets to the bottom of this.

Raimunda. Does anybody think it was Norbert?

Bernabé. You would get your head broke if you said it was. When he came back yesterday, half the town was out to meet him. Everybody was sitting by the roadside. They took him up on their shoulders and carried him home. The women all cried, and the men hugged him. I thought his father would die for joy.

Raimunda. He never did it. Poor Norbert!

Bernabé. They say the men are coming over from Encinar to kill him; everybody here carries a club and goes armed.

Raimunda. Mother of God! Did anything go wrong with the master while he was in the village this morning? What did you hear?

Bernabé. So they have been talking to you?

Raimunda. No. That is—yes; I know.

Bernabé. Rubio was in the tavern and began to say things, so I ran for the master, and he came and ordered him out. He was insolent to the master. He was drunk.

Raimunda. Do you remember what he said? I mean Rubio.

Bernabé. Oh! His tongue ran away with him. He was drunk. Do you know what I think? If I were you, I wouldn't go back to the village for two or three days.

Raimunda. No, certainly not. If I had my way we would never go back. I am filled with a loathing for it all so great that I want to rush out, and down that long road, and then on and up and over those mountains to the other side, and after that I don't know where I would hide myself. I feel as if some one were running after me, after me, always after me, with more than death in his heart. But the master. . . . Where is the master?

Bernabé. Seeing to Rubio.

Raimunda. Tell Norbert to come in. I can't wait.

[BERNABÉ *goes out.* NORBERT *enters.*]

Norbert. Aunt Raimunda!

Raimunda. Norbert, my boy! Give me a hug.

Norbert. I am so glad you sent for me. I've been treated like a dog. It's a good thing that my mother is dead and in heaven. I am glad she never lived to see this day. Next to my father, there is nobody in the world I think so much of as I do of you.

Raimunda. I could never have believed that you did it—not though everybody said so.

Norbert. I know it; you were the first to take my part. Where is Acacia?

Raimunda. In her room. We have our fill of trouble in this house.

Norbert. Who says I killed Faustino? If I hadn't proved, as I did prove, where I was all that day—if I'd done as I meant at first and taken my gun and gone off to hunt alone by myself, and then couldn't have proved where I was, because nobody had seen me, I would have spent the rest of my life in prison. They would have had me.

Raimunda. Are you crying?

Norbert. No, I am not crying; but I cried when I found myself in that prison. If anybody had ever told me that I would ever go to prison, I would never have believed it; I'd have laughed in his face. But that isn't the worst. Tío Eusebio and his boys have sworn to kill me. They will never believe that I am innocent; they know I murdered Faustino. They are as sure of it as I am that my mother lies under the ground!

Raimunda. Because nobody knows who did it. Nobody can find out anything. Don't you see? They will never rest at that. Do you suspect any one?

Norbert. I more than suspect.

Raimunda. Then why didn't you say so? You were in court. You had the opportunity.

Norbert. If I hadn't cleared myself I would have told. But what was the use? I am a dead man now if I speak. They will do the same thing to me.

Raimunda. Eh? Will they? What do you mean? Was it revenge? But who did it? Tell me what you think. I must know, because Tío Eusebio and Esteban have always had the same friends; they have always stood together, for better or for worse, whichever it was. Their enemies would naturally be the same. Now, I can get no rest. This vengeance was intended for us just as much as it was for Tío Eusebio; it was to prevent a closer union of our families. Maybe they won't stop at that, either. Some day they will do the same to my husband!

Norbert. I wouldn't worry about Uncle Esteban.

Raimunda. Why, what do you mean? Do you think? . . .

Norbert. I don't think.

Raimunda. Then tell me what you know. Somehow I believe you are not the only one who knows it. You think what the rest think —it must be the same—what everybody knows.

Norbert. Well, they didn't get it out of me: that is one thing you can be sure of. Besides, how could they know? It's gossip, that's all—not worth that! Talk in the village! They will never get it out of me.

Raimunda. Norbert, by the soul of your sainted mother in heaven, tell me what it is!

Norbert. For God's sake, I can't talk! I was afraid to open my mouth in court. Now, if I say a word, I am a dead man. A dead man!

Raimunda. But who would kill you?

Norbert. Who killed Faustino?

Raimunda. But who did kill Faustino? Some one was paid to do it, is that it? Rubio said something in the wine-shop this morning.

Norbert. Who told you?

Raimunda. Esteban went in and dragged him out; it was the only way he could stop him.

Norbert. He didn't want to be compromised.

Raimunda. What is that? He didn't want to be compromised? Was Rubio saying that he. . . .

Norbert. That he was the real master of this house.

Raimunda. The master of this house? Because it was Rubio. . . .

Norbert. Rubio.

Raimunda. Who killed Faustino?

Norbert. *Si, señora.*

Raimunda. Rubio! I knew it all the time. But does anybody else know? That is the question. Do they know it in the village?

Norbert. He gives himself away; he has money—bills, bank-notes—wherever he goes. He turned on them this morning while they were singing that song. That was why they had to call Uncle Esteban, and he kicked him out of the wine-shop.

Raimunda. That song? Oh, yes! That song—I remember. It goes. . . . How does it go?

Norbert.

"Who loves the maid that dwells by the Mill
Shall love in evil hour;
Because she loves with the love that she loves,
Call her the Passion Flower."

Raimunda. We are the ones who dwell by the Mill; that is what they call us. It is here—our house. And the maid that dwells by the Mill must be Acacia, my daughter. This song that everybody sings. . . . They call her the Passion Flower? That is it, isn't it? But who loves her in any evil way? How could anybody love her? You loved her, Faustino loved her; but who else ever loved her? Why do they call her the Passion Flower? Look me in the eye! Why did you give her up if you really loved her? Why? I want you to tell me; you have got to tell me. You cannot tell me anything worse than what I already know.

Norbert. Do you want them to kill me? To ruin all of us? I have never said one word—not even when they had me in prison would I say one word! I don't know how it got out—Rubio told, or my father. He is the only one who ever had it from me. He wanted to put the law on them, but I said no. They would have killed him; they would have killed me!

Raimunda. Stop! Don't you talk! I see it now. I see it all. The Passion Flower! *La Malquerida!* Come here to me! Tell me everything. Before they kill you, by God, they will have to kill me! It cannot go on like this. Somebody must pay for it. Tío Eusebio and his boys will never rest till they have justice. If they can't get it in any other way, they will take it out on you—revenge! You can't escape. Faustino was murdered so as to prevent him from marrying Acacia. You left her for the same reason—for fear that they would kill you. Was that it? Tell me the truth!

Norbert. They told me to leave her because she was promised to Faustino; she had been for a long time. They said they had an understanding with Tío Eusebio, and if I didn't make the best of it, then I could take the worst of it. But if I ever opened my mouth. . . .

Raimunda. They would kill you? Was that it? But you . . .

Norbert. I believed it—I was afraid—I didn't know what to do. Then I began to run after another girl, who was nothing to me, so as to break off with Acacia. Afterward, when I found out that not a word of it was true, that neither Tío Eusebio nor Faustino had ever spoken to Uncle Esteban . . . Then, when they killed Faustino I knew why they killed him. It was because he dared lay eyes on Acacia. There was nothing they could tell him. They couldn't scare him off. Tío Eusebio wasn't a man to stand by and see his son refused. They couldn't refuse, so they agreed to it, and went through with it until the end came, and they killed him. They killed him because I was here to take the blame. Who else could have done it? Of course it was I! I loved Acacia—I was jealous. That was the plot. Praise God, some saint surely watched over me that day! But now the crime has come home to him. It lies like lead on his conscience. He betrays himself. . . .

Raimunda. Is it possible that such a thing

could be? I must have been blind not to see. What veil hung over my eyes? Why, it is all as clear as day! How could I have been so blind?

Norbert. What shall you do?

Raimunda. I don't know—I don't know where I am—something so awful, so vast is passing through my mind that it seems as if it were nothing. I can only remember one thing of all that you have told me—that song —*La Malquerida!* The Passion Flower! I want you to teach me the music. We can sing it together, and dance—dance and drop dead! —Acacia! Acacia! Acacia!

Norbert. No, don't you call her! Don't take it like this! It wasn't her fault!

[ACACIA *enters.*]

Acacia. Did you call, mother?—Norbert!

Raimunda. Come here! Look at me—straight in the eye.

Acacia. What is the matter with you, mother?

Raimunda. No, it was not your fault.

Acacia. But what have they been doing? What did you tell her?

Raimunda. What every one else knows already—*La Malquerida!* The Passion Flower! Your honor is a scorn and a byword. It is bandied about in men's mouths!

Acacia. My honor? Never! No one can say that.

Raimunda. Don't you deny it! Tell me what you know. Why was it that you never called him father? Why was it?

Acacia. Because a child has only one father, you know that. This man could never be my father. I hated, I despised him from the day that he entered this house, and brought hell along after him!

Raimunda. Well, you are going to call him now, and you are going to call him what I tell you; you are going to call him father. Do you hear? Your father! I tell you to call your father.

Acacia. Do you want me to go to the cemetery and call him? If that isn't what you want, I have no father. This man—this man is your husband; you love him, but all that he is to me is this man! This man! That is all he can ever be! Leave me alone if you know what is good for you—you think you are so smart. Let the law take its course. I don't care. If he has sinned, he can pay for it.

Raimunda. Do you mean for Faustino's murder? Yes—go on! Go on! What else? Out with it!

Acacia. No, mother, no! For if I had consented, Faustino would never have been murdered! Do you think I don't know how to guard my honor?

Raimunda. Then what have you been so silent about? Why didn't you come to me?

Acacia. Would you have taken my word against this man, when you were mad for him? And you must have been mad not to see! He would eat me up with his eyes while you sat there; he followed me around the house like a cat. What more do you want? I hated him so, I had such a horror of him that I prayed to God that he would make himself even more of a beast than he was, so that it would open your eyes, if anything could have opened your eyes, and let you see what manner of man he was who had robbed me of your love, for you have loved him, you have loved him so much—more than you ever loved my father!

Raimunda. No! That isn't true!

Acacia. I wanted you to hate him as I hate him, as my father in heaven hates him! I have heard his voice from the skies.

Raimunda. Silence! For shame! Come here to your mother. You are all that I have left in the world. And thank God that I can still protect you! [BERNABÉ *enters.*]

Bernabé. Señora! Señora!

Raimunda. What brings you running in such a hurry? No good, we may be sure.

Bernabé. Don't let Norbert leave the house! Don't let him out of your sight!

Raimunda. How?

Bernabé. Tío Eusebio's boys are waiting outside with their men to kill him.

Norbert. What did I tell you? You wouldn't believe it. They are here—they want to kill me! And they will kill me. Yes, they will!

Raimunda. Not unless they kill us all first! Somebody has sent for them.

Bernabé. Yes, Rubio. I saw him running along the river bank where Tío Eusebio's boys were at work.

Norbert. Didn't I tell you? They want to kill me, so as to save themselves. Then nothing will ever come out. Tío Eusebio's boys will think they have the man who murdered their brother. They will kill me, Aunt Raimunda! Yes, they will! They are too many for one; I can't defend myself. I haven't even a knife. I don't dare to carry a gun—I might kill some one. I'd rather die than be locked up in that cell again. Save me, Aunt Raimunda! I don't want to die. It wasn't my fault! They hunt me like a wolf.

Raimunda. Don't be afraid. If they kill you, it will be over my dead body. Go in there with Bernabé and take that gun, do you hear? They won't dare to come in. If they do, shoot to kill! When I call, shoot—no matter who it may be! Do you understand? No matter who it may be! Don't shut the door. [*To* ACACIA.] You stand here by me. Esteban! Esteban! Esteban!

Acacia. What are you going to do?

[ESTEBAN *enters.*]

Esteban. Did you call?

Raimunda. Yes, I want to speak to you. Norbert is here in our house. Tío Eusebio's boys are waiting outside. You sent for them to kill him—because you are not man enough to do it yourself.

Esteban. [*Making a movement to draw a weapon.*] Raimunda!

Acacia. Mother!

Raimunda. No, don't you do it! Call Rubio and let him make an end of us all! He will have to make an end of us all to cover your guilt. Murderer! Assassin!

Esteban. You are crazy!

Raimunda. I was crazy! I was crazy the day that you first entered this house—my house—like a thief, to rob me of all I held dear!

Esteban. What are you talking about?

Raimunda. I am not talking; other people are talking. Soon the law will speak. If you don't want that, do as I tell you, or I will cry out—I will rouse the house. You brought them here—take them away again, you cowards that lie in wait for innocent men, to stab them in the back! Norbert leaves this house, but he leaves with me. If they kill him, they kill me. I am here to protect him, and I will protect my daughter—I, alone, against you, against all the assassins you can hire! Go! Here come my people. . . . Don't you touch me! Hide yourself in the uttermost recesses of those mountains, in caves where the wild beasts dwell. Now I know! You have nothing to hope for from me. Oh, I was alone with my child!—and you came. You knew that she was my child; there she stands—*La Malquerida!* The Passion Flower! Well! I am still here to guard her from you, to tell you that her father still lives in heaven—and to shoot you through the heart if you make one step to lay your hand on her!

CURTAIN

THE THIRD ACT

The scene is the same as in the Second Act. [RAIMUNDA *stands at the door, peering anxiously out over the countryside. After a moment* JULIANA *enters.*]

Juliana. Raimunda!

Raimunda. What do you want? Is he worse?

Juliana. No, don't be nervous.

Raimunda. How is he? Why did you leave him?

Juliana. He's asleep. Acacia is with him; she can hear if he calls. You are the one I am worried about. Thank God, he's not dead. Do you expect to go all day without eating?

Raimunda. Let me alone; don't bother me.

Juliana. What are you doing out here? Come on in and sit with us.

Raimunda. I was looking for Bernabé.

Juliana. He can't be back so soon if he brings the men to take Norbert away. If the constables come with him. . . .

Raimunda. Constables? Constables in this house? Ah, Juliana, surely a curse has fallen upon us all!

Juliana. Come on in, and don't be looking out of the door all the time. It's not Bernabé that you are looking for; it's the other one—it's your husband. When all is said and done, he is your husband.

Raimunda. Yes, the habits of a lifetime cannot be changed in one day. Although I know what I know, and that it must always be so, although if I saw him coming it would be to curse him, although I must loathe him for the rest of my life, yet here I stand looking out of the door and scanning every rock and cranny upon those mountains only for a sight of him! It seems to me as if I were waiting for him as I used to do, to see him come happy and smiling, and then turn and walk into the house with him arm in arm like two lovers, and sit down here at the table to eat, and go over everything that we had done during the day. Sometimes we would laugh, sometimes we would argue, but always it was so dear, as if we had been fonder of each other than any one else who had ever lived in the world. Now it is all over; nothing remains. The peace of God has fled forever from this house!

Juliana. You cannot believe what you see with your eyes. If you hadn't told me yourself, if I didn't know how you felt, how you were, I would never have believed it. Faustino is dead, God help him; we can leave it. There might be more of the sort, too, for all I care; but this devil that has gotten into him with Acacia, it doesn't seem possible, I can't believe it—although I must believe it. There is no other explanation of the mystery.

Raimundi. Did you never notice anything?

Juliana. Nothing. When he first came to the house, it was to make love to you, and I needn't tell you how I felt. I was fond of your first husband; there never was a better nor juster man in the world; so I looked on him with disfavor. God have mercy on me, but if I had seen anything, what reason would I have had for keeping quiet? Of course, when you come to think, he gave her presents—and there were a good many of them, too—but we never thought anything of that. She was so haughty with him. They never had one good talk together from the day you were married. She was only a runt then anyway. She insulted him out of pure spite. Nobody could do anything with her. If you struck her, it made no difference. I'll say this while I am about it: if she had been nice to him when she was little, he might have looked on her as his own daughter. Then we would never have been where we are now.

Raimunda. Are you trying to excuse him?

Juliana. Excuse him? There can be no excuse for such a thing. It was enough that she was your daughter. What I say is that the girl was like a stranger to him from the beginning, although she was your own child. If she had treated him like a father, as she ought—it would have been different; he isn't a bad man. A bad man is bad through and through. When you were first married, I've seen him sit by himself and cry at the way the girl ran from him, as if he had had the plague.

Raimunda. You are right. The only trouble we ever had was with the child.

Juliana. After she was grown there wasn't a girl in the village that was her equal for looks. Nobody knows that better than you do. But she shrank from him as if he had been the devil. There she was all the time—right before his eyes! No wonder if he had an evil thought; none of us are above them.

Raimunda. I don't say he might not have had an evil thought, although he ought never to have had such a thought. But you put an evil thought out of your mind unless you are evil. He must have had more than an evil thought to do what he did, to murder a man in cold blood to prevent my daughter from marrying and going away—away from him; his mind must have been evil, like the criminal's, waiting to break out, with all the evil of the world in his heart. I am more anxious than anybody to believe that it is not so bad, but the more I think, the more I see that there can be no excuse for it. When I remember what has been hanging over my daughter all these years, that any moment—because a man who will do murder will do anything. If he had ever laid hands on her I would have killed them both, as sure as my name is Raimunda—him, because he had been guilty of such a crime, and her because she did not let him kill her before she would consent to it.

Juliana. Here comes Bernabé.

[BERNABÉ *enters.*]

Raimunda. Are you alone?

Bernabé. Yes, they are deciding in the village what is best to be done. I was afraid to stay any longer.

Raimunda. You were right. This is not life. What do they say now?

Bernabé. Do you want to go mad? Forget it. Pay no attention to what they say.

Raimunda. Are they coming to take Norbert away?

Bernabé. His father will tend to that. The doctor won't let them put him in the cart for fear it will make him worse. He'll have to be carried on a stretcher. The judge and the prosecutor are coming to take his story, for they don't want a relapse. He was unconscious yesterday and couldn't testify. Everybody has his own idea; no two agree. Not a soul went to the fields today. The men stand around the streets in groups; the women talk in the houses and run to and fro. Nobody stops to eat. Not a meal has been served today, dinner or supper either, on the hour.

Raimunda. Didn't you tell them that Norbert's wounds aren't serious?

Bernabé. What difference does that make? Now they can't do anything. Yesterday, when they thought Tío Eusebio's boys had fallen on him with the master, and he was going to die, the thing was simple; but today they hear he is better. How do they know but that he will soon be well again? Even Norbert's best friends say that it's a great pity that the wound wasn't serious. If he was wounded at all, it might better have been serious. Then Tío Eusebio's boys could have been made to pay for it, and they would have had their revenge; but now, if he gets well, the law will get into it, and then nobody will be satisfied.

Juliana. They are so fond of Norbert, are they, that they wish he was dead? The idiots!

Bernabé. That is the way they are. I told

them they could thank you for it, because you were the one who called the master, and the master threw himself between them and knocked up their guns, so they couldn't kill him.

Raimunda. Did you tell them that?

Bernabé. Every mother's son that asked me. I said the first because it was true, and I said the rest—because you don't know what they are saying in the village, nor how they feel about what is going on in this house.

Raimunda. No! I don't want to hear! Where is the master? Have you seen him? Do you know where he is?

Bernabé. He and Rubio were up at Los Berrocales this morning with the goatherds from Encinar. They spent the night in a hut on the uplands. I don't like this going away. It's not right, if I know what is good for him. It looks as if he was afraid. This is no time to have people think what isn't so. Norbert's father talks too much. This morning he tried to persuade Tío Eusebio that his sons had had no cause to shoot his boy.

Raimunda. Is Tío Eusebio in the village?

Bernabé. He came with his boys. They arrested them this morning, tied them together by the elbows, and brought them over from Encinar. Their father followed on foot and brought the little fellow with him, holding his hand all the way. They cried with every step that they took. There wasn't a man in the village but cried, too, when he saw them, even the strongest, no matter if he had never cried before.

Raimunda. And his mother is alone at home, and here I am! What do you men know? [ACACIA *enters.*]

Acacia. Mother——

Raimunda. Well? What is it?

Acacia. Norbert wants you. He is awake now. He wants some water. He is thirsty; I was afraid to give him any for fear it wasn't right.

Raimunda. The doctor says he can have all the orange-juice he can drink. Here's the jar. Does he suffer much?

Acacia. No, not now.

Raimunda. [*To* BERNABÉ.] Did you get the things for the doctor?

Bernabé. Yes, they're in the saddle-bags. I'll bring them in. [*Goes out.*]

Acacia. He is calling, mother. Do you hear?

Raimunda. Coming, Norbert, my boy. [*Goes out.*]

Acacia. Has that man come back?

Juliana. No. He took his gun and rushed out like one mad as soon as it was over. Rubio ran after him.

Acacia. Have they caught him?

Juliana. You'll hear soon enough when they do. They'll have to bring charges against him first.

Acacia. But doesn't everybody know? They heard what my mother said.

Juliana. No, nobody heard except me and Bernabé, and he won't tell what isn't good for him; he is honest and loyal to this house. They heard your mother shout, that was all. They thought it was because Norbert was here, and Tío Eusebio's boys were waiting outside to kill him. Nobody will say a word when the judge comes unless your mother tells us to open our mouths.

Acacia. Do you mean that my mother isn't going to let you tell the truth? Won't she tell what she knows?

Juliana. Is that what you want? So you want to disgrace this house, do you, and yourself? Then every man will think what he likes; some will believe that you are innocent, and some will never believe it. A woman's honor is not a thing to be bandied about in men's mouths, not when it is none of their business.

Acacia. My honor? I can take care of my honor. Let the others do the same. Now I shan't marry. I am glad it happened, because I shall never marry. I only agreed to it to get rid of him.

Juliana. Acacia, I don't want to hear you —not another word. Surely the devil must be in you!

Acacia. Yes, he is, and he has always been, since I first learned to hate that man!

Juliana. Yes, and who is to say that wasn't where the trouble began? You had no cause to hate him. Mind you, nobody blamed your mother more than I did when she married again; but all the same, I saw what a devil you were to this man when you were a little child, and how much it meant to him—which you were too young to know.

Acacia. How much did it mean to me to see my mother always hanging around his neck? Do you suppose I liked it, sitting here and seeing her love him? I was always in the way.

Juliana. You have no right to talk like that. You were always first with your mother, and you might have been with him.

Acacia. Might have been? Never! Because I was, and I am.

Juliana. But not like you mean, though you seem proud of it; in the way you should have been. He never would have loved you as he did if you had loved him as a daughter.

Acacia. How could I love him? Didn't he turn me even against my own mother?

Juliana. What do you mean? Turn you against your own mother?

Acacia. Yes. Do you suppose I can love her now as I ought, as I should have loved her if that man had never entered this house? I remember once when I was a little girl, I spent all one night with a knife under my pillow, and I lay awake all night. The only thought that I had in my mind that night was to kill him.

Juliana. Jesús, my child! What is that? Suppose you had? Suppose you had gotten up, and had dared, and had killed him?

Acacia. I don't know who I might have killed next.

Juliana. Holy Virgin! *Jesús!* Not another word. Don't you talk! You are beyond the pale of God's mercy. Do you know what I think? It was all your fault.

Acacia. All my fault?

Juliana. Yes, yours! It was your fault! And I'll go further: if you hated him as much as you say you do, then he would have been the only one you would have hated—yes, the only one! *Jesús!* It's a good thing that your mother doesn't know!

Acacia. Know what?

Juliana. That he wasn't the one you were jealous of. It was her! You were in love with him and you didn't know it.

Acacia. In love with him?

Juliana. Yes, hate turned to love. Nobody can hate like that. A hate like that always grows out of a great love.

Acacia. Do you mean to say that I was in love with that man? Do you know what you are telling me?

Juliana. I am not telling you anything.

Acacia. No. What you will do now is run and tell my mother.

Juliana. Is that what you are afraid of? I thought so. Now you are the one who is telling. You needn't worry, though. I'll not tell. She has enough on her mind, poor soul. God help us! [BERNABÉ *enters.*]

Bernabé. Here comes the master!

Juliana. Did you see him?

Bernabé. Yes. You wouldn't know him. He looks as if he had stepped from the grave.

Acacia. Let me out!

Juliana. Yes, let us all out—and shut your mouth, do you hear? What is done is done. Your mother must never know.

[*The women go out.* ESTEBAN *and* RUBIO *enter, their guns over their shoulders.*]

Bernabé. Can—can I do anything?

Esteban. Nothing, Bernabé.

Bernabé. I'll tell the mistress.

Esteban. No, don't tell her; they'll find us.

Rubio. How about his wounds, eh?

Bernabé. Better. The doctor sent for these things. I'll take them in—unless you need me. [*Goes out.*]

Esteban. Here I am. What do you want me to do?

Rubio. What do I want you to do? This is your house; you belong here. A man's house is his castle. Running away, being afraid to face it, is to confess. It will ruin us both.

Esteban. Here I am; you have had your way. Now this woman will come and accuse me and raise the house. The judge will be here, and he will bring Tío Eusebio. What then?

Rubio. Why didn't you let Tío Eusebio's boys handle it themselves? They would have finished it. Now he is only wounded. He will squeal, and so will his father; so will all the women. They are the ones I am afraid of. They will talk. Nobody can prove who shot Faustino. You were with his father; nobody saw me. I have a good pair of legs. I was with some friends two leagues away a few minutes before, and I set the clock ahead. When I left the house I took good care to have them notice it.

Esteban. Yes, we would have been safe if that had been all. But you talked; you gave yourself away.

Rubio. You ought to have killed me. That was the first time in my life that I ever was afraid. I never expected that they would let Norbert go. I told you that we ought to go into court and have Acacia testify that Norbert had sworn he was going to kill Faustino, but you wouldn't listen. Do you mean to tell me that you couldn't have made her do it? We could have got others, too, to say the same. Then it would have been easy; they would never have let him go. I know I made a fool of myself, but when I saw that Norbert was free, that the law—yes, and Tío Eusebio—would never stop there, that they would look somewhere else, then I was afraid for the first time. I wanted to forget. So I began to drink, which I never do, and I talked. You ought to have killed me then; you had ground for it. They were talking already in the village; that was what scared me. When I heard that song—it put the blame here. Norbert and his father suspect. After what happened before, they have their eyes open. That is the talk that has got to be stopped, no matter what comes of it. That is the danger—the crime will be known by the cause. Nothing else counts. So long as nobody knows why he was killed, nobody will ever find out who killed him either.

Esteban. But why? Why was he killed? What was the use of killing anybody?

Rubio. I don't know. Don't ask me. Weren't you talking all the time? "If another man gets her, look out! Something happens." Then you told me she was going to be married. "I can't scare this one off; it's all over, he will take her away. I can't think. . . ." Didn't you come to me in the morning early again and again, before it was light, and wake me up and say: "Get up, Rubio; I haven't closed my eyes all night. I must get out. To the fields! I must walk!" And then we'd take our guns and go out and walk for hours, side by side, without speaking a word. At last, when the fit had passed, and we'd put a few shots in the air so that nobody could say that we did no hunting when we went out to hunt, I'd tell you that we scared away the game; but you said we frightened evil thoughts: and down we'd sit on some hummock and then you would burst out laughing like one mad, as if some weight had been lifted from your soul, and you'd catch me around the neck and talk, and talk, and talk—you didn't know how you talked, nor what you said, nor why, nor whether it had any sense at all; but it always came to the same thing: "I am mad, crazy, a wild man! I cannot live like this. I want to die. I don't know what devil has gotten into me. This is torment, hell!" And then you'd shuffle the words again, over and over, but it was always the same, you were dying—death! And you talked death so long that one day death heard—and he came. And you know it.

Esteban. Stop! Why do you have to talk?

Rubio. Take care, master! Don't you touch me! I know what was in your mind when we were coming down the mountain. Make no mistake. You lagged behind. Another minute and your gun would have been at your shoulder. But don't you do it, master, don't you try! We'll stick together. I know how you feel; you're sick. You never want to see me again. If that would help, I'd get out. What did I care, anyway? It was nothing to me. Whatever I got you gave me afterward. It was your idea. I never asked. I don't need money. I don't drink, I don't smoke. All I want is to rove over the mountains, to do what I like, to be free. I want to be my own master. You trusted me, and I was proud of it. I know how you feel. We are like brothers. I'll take the blame. You needn't worry. They can grind me to powder but I'll never say a word. I'll tell them I did it—it was I—because—it's none of their business—just because. I don't care what they give me: they can make it ten years, fifteen. What's the difference? Then you fix it; you have influence. Only don't let them make it too much. Get busy; cut it down. Others have done the same. In four or five years everything will have blown over. Only I don't want you to forget. When I come out we will be brothers, the same as before. We can work together; we can do what we please. Only I mean to be my own master, to have power, to feel power in my hands! Nobody can stand alone. We'll be brothers. Hush! Some one is coming—the mistress!

[RAIMUNDA *enters, carrying a water-jar. She sees* ESTEBAN *and* RUBIO *and stops short, dazed. After hesitating for a moment she proceeds to fill the jar from a pitcher.*]

Rubio. Señora!

Raimunda. Get out of my house! Don't you come near me! What are you doing here? I never want to see you again.

Rubio. Oh! You are going to see me again—and hear me.

Raimunda. What do you mean? This is my house.

Rubio. Just a word. Soon we will all be in court. We had better fix it beforehand. Because a few fools open their mouths is no reason why a good man should go to prison.

Raimunda. More than one will go. You don't expect to get out of it?

Rubio. I don't know. Only one will go, but that one will be I.

Raimunda. It will?

Rubio. But when I shut my mouth I don't want other people to talk. Take it from me: what you think is not so. Norbert and his father are back of these lies; they are the ones who do all the lying. They made up that song, too. It's a lie, and they know it.

Raimunda. Is that so? You have agreed then on your story? Well, I don't believe one word of it. Gossip and songs are nothing to me. I believe nothing but the truth, the truth that I know—and I know it so well that I have known it all along. I guessed it from the beginning. I might have thought—but no, I never thought anything of you. He, he might have confessed it; it would have been only fair. He might have known that I would hold my tongue, not for him, but for this house—which was my father's house—for my daughter, for my own sake. But why should I keep still when everybody knows it, and the very stones shout? They sing it from the housetops.

Rubio. So long as you keep still, the rest can sing all they want to.

Raimunda. Keep still? To save you? I could scream at the very sight of you! I could raise the village!

Rubio. Don't be a fool! What's the use?

Raimunda. Of course you weren't a fool when you murdered a man. And you nearly murdered another—in this house—or had him murdered.

Rubio. I wouldn't have been a fool if I had.

Raimunda. You are a coward! You are a murderer!

Rubio. Your wife is speaking to you, master.

Esteban. Rubio!

Rubio. You see he can hear.

Raimunda. Yes, hang your head before this man. What a humiliation! You are his slave for the rest of your life. Could any fate be more horrible? Now this house has a master. Thank God, he cannot be less jealous of its honor than you!

Esteban. Raimunda!

Raimunda. When I talk, you interrupt. You are not afraid of me.

Esteban. If I had been man enough, I would have put a bullet through my head, and have been done with it.

Rubio. Oh, master!

Esteban. No! Stop there! That's all I'll take from you. Get out! What are you waiting for? Do you want me to beg you on my knees?

Raimunda. Oh!

Rubio. No, master. I am going. [*To* RAIMUNDA.] If it hadn't been for me, there wouldn't have been any murder, but you might have lost a child. Now, you have another. The blood made him faint; a bad turn, that was all. But he's better. I am a good doctor. Some time you can thank me for it. Don't forget. I'll show you how.

[*Goes out.*]

Esteban. Don't cry any more. I can't bear to see you cry. I am not worth all these tears. I ought never to have come back; I ought to have starved amid the brambles and thickets—they should have hunted me down like a wolf. I would not have raised my hand. Don't reproach me! Over and over again I have said to myself more than you can say. I have called myself murderer, assassin, times without number. Let me go. This is no longer my home. Turn me out! I am only waiting for them to take me. I don't go out on the road and give myself up, because I am too weak; my heart sinks; I am at the end of my tether. If you don't want me, tell me to go, and I will creep onto the highway and throw myself down in the fields, like carrion which you cast from your door.

Raimunda. Yes, give yourself up! Bring shame and ruin on this house, drag my daughter's honor in the dust and mire of the village! I should have been the law to you; you ought to have thought of me. Do you suppose that I believe in these tears because this is the first time I ever saw you cry? Better you had cried your eyes out the day that wicked thought first entered your mind, rather than have turned them where you had no right. Now you cry—but what am I to do? Look at me. Nobody knows what I have been through. It could not be worse. I want to forget, but I must think—think how I can hide the shame which has fallen on this house, keep it out of men's sight, prevent a man from being dragged from this house to prison—a man I brought into it to be a father to my child! This was my father's house; here my brothers lived with the fear of God in their hearts, and from it they went to serve their King, or to marry, or to till other fields by their labor. When they re-entered these doors it was with the same honor with which they went forth. Don't cry; don't hang your head. Hold it high, as I do. In a few minutes the officers will be here to trap us all. Though the house burn, and they are in it, they shall not smell the smoke. Dry your eyes; you have wept blood. Take a sip of water—I wish it was poison. Don't drink so fast; you are overheated. The thorns have torn your skin. You deserved knives. Let me wash you off; it makes my blood creep to look at you.

Esteban. Raimunda! Wife! Pity me! You don't know. Don't talk to me. No, I am the one who must talk—I must confess as I shall confess at the hour of my doom! You don't know how I have struggled. I have wrestled all these years as with another man who was stronger than I, night and day, who was dragging me where I did not want to go.

Raimunda. But when—when did that evil thought first enter your mind? When was that unhappy hour?

Esteban. I don't know. It came upon me like a blight, all at once; it was there. All of us think some evil in our lives, but the thought passes away, it does no harm; it is gone. When I was a boy, one day my father beat me. Quick as a flash it came to me: "I wish he was dead!" But no sooner thought, than I was ashamed—I was ashamed to think that I had ever had such a thought. My heart stood still within me for fear that God had heard, that He would take him away. From that day I loved him more, and when he died, years afterward, I grieved as much for that thought as I did for his death, although I was a grown man. And this might have been the same; but this did not go away. It became more fixed the more I struggled to shake it off. You can't say that I did not love you. I loved you more every day! You can't say that I cast my eyes on other women—and I had no thought of her. But when I felt her by me my blood took fire. When we sat down to eat, I was afraid to look up. Wherever I turned she was there, before me—always! At night, when we were in bed, and I was lying close by you in the midnight silence of the house, all I could feel was her. I could hear her breathe as if her lips had been at my ear. I wept for spite, for bitterness! I prayed to God, I scourged myself. I could have killed myself—and her! Words cannot tell the horror I went through. The few times that we were alone, I ran from her like a wild man. If I had stayed I don't know what might have happened: I might have kissed her, I might have dug my knife into her!

Raimunda. Yes, you were mad—and you did not know it. It could only have ended in death. Why didn't we find some man for her? She could have married. You ought not to have kept her from Norbert.

Esteban. It was not her marrying, it was her going away. I could not live without the feel of her; I craved her day and night. All her hate, her spite, her turning away—which she always did—cut me to the heart; then, I came to depend upon it. I could not live without it; it was part of my life. That is what it was—I didn't realize it myself, because it always seemed to me as if it could not be—such things could not really be. I was afraid to face it. But now, I have confessed it to you. It is true! It is true! I can never forgive myself, not even though you might forgive me.

Raimunda. The evil cannot be cured by forgiveness; if I do not forgive you, it will not take the evil away. When I first heard of it, it seemed to me that no punishment could be too severe. Now, I don't know. To do what you did, you must have been all evil. But you were always kind and good, in season and out, to my daughter, when she was a child, when she was grown—and to me. I have seen it with my own eyes. You were good to all the servants from the day that you entered this house, to the men, to everybody who came near. You have been faithful and loyal, and worked hard for the honor of this house. A man cannot be good so long and become all bad in one day. Yet these things are; I know it. It chills my heart. When my mother was alive—God rest her soul!—we always laughed because she used to say that many a deed had been foretold in this world that afterward took place exactly as it had been foretold. We never believed it, but now I know it is true. The dead do not leave us when they die, though we lay them in the ground. They walk by the side of those that they loved in this life, of those that they hated with a hate that was stronger than death. They are with us, day and night. We do not see them, but they whisper in our ears. They put thoughts into our minds which are evil and wicked and strange, which we never can believe could be part of ourselves.

Esteban. Do you mean? . . .

Raimunda. Vengeance! This is vengeance from the other world. My daughter's father will not forgive me in heaven; he will never accept a second father for his child. There are some things which we cannot explain in this life. A good man like you cannot, all of a sudden, cease to be good; for you were good. . . .

Esteban. I was—I was always. When you say it, you don't know what happiness, what boundless joy it is to me!

Raimunda. Hush! Not so loud! I hear some one in the other part of the house. It is Norbert's father and his friends. They are going to take him away. If it had been the judge he would have come to this door. Stay here; I'll find out. Go in and wash; change your shirt. Don't let any one see you like this. You look . . .

Esteban. Like a murderer, eh? Say it.

Raimunda. No, no, Esteban! We mustn't dwell on these things. We must stop this talk; that is first. Then we can think. Acacia can go to the nuns for a few days at Encinar. They are fond of her; they always ask how she is. Then I can write to my sister-in-law, Eugenia; she likes her. She can go to Andrada and live with her. She might marry, who knows? There are fine boys there—the town is rich—and she is the best match in our village. Then she could come back and have her children, and we would be grandfather and grandmother, and grow old with them around us, and be happy once more in this house. If only . . .

Esteban. What?

Raimunda. If only . . .

Esteban. The dead man.

Raimunda. Yes. He will always be here, between us.

Esteban. Always. The rest we can forget.

[*Goes into the room.* ACACIA *enters.*]

Raimunda. Acacia! Were you there?

Acacia. Yes. Why not? Can't you see? Norbert's father is here with the men.

Raimunda. What are they doing?

Acacia. They seem more reasonable; they were surprised to find him better. Now they are waiting for the judge. He is down at Sotillo examining the men. He will come here as soon as he is done.

Raimunda. I'll keep an eye on them.

Acacia. I have something to say to you first, mother.

Raimunda. You? Something to say? What is the matter with you? I am frightened. You never say anything.

Acacia. I heard what you mean to do with me.

Raimunda. You were listening at the keyhole, were you?

Acacia. Yes, because it was my duty to hear. I had to know what you were doing with this man. It seems that I am the one who is in the way in this house. I have done nothing wrong, so I have to take the blame, while you stay here and enjoy yourself with your husband. You forgive him and turn me out, so that you can be alone together!

Raimunda. What are you talking about? Who is turning you out? Who ever put that idea into your head?

Acacia. I heard what you said. You want to send me to the convent at Encinar and shut me up, I suppose, for the rest of my life.

Raimunda. How can you say such a thing? Didn't you tell me yourself that you wanted to go there and stay for a few days with the nuns? Didn't I refuse to let you go for fear that you would never come back, if you once saw the inside of the cloister? How often have you begged me to let you go to your Aunt Eugenia? Now, when it would be a good thing for us all, for the good of the family, which is your family—I tell you that we must hold our heads high—now what do you want me to do? Do you expect me to give up my husband—the man it was your duty to love as a father?

Acacia. You are as bad as Juliana. I suppose it was all my fault?

Raimunda. I don't say that. But he never looked on you as a daughter because you were never a daughter to him.

Acacia. I suppose I flaunted myself in his face? I suppose I made him kill Faustino?

Raimunda. Not so loud! Somebody might hear!

Acacia. Well, this time you won't find it so easy to have your way. You want to save this man and hush it up, but I am going to tell what I know to the judge, to everybody. I have only my honor to think of, not that of a man who hasn't any, who never had any —who is a criminal!

Raimunda. Silence! Not so loud! It freezes my heart to hear you. You hate him —and I had almost forgiven him!

Acacia. Yes, I do hate him. I always did hate him, and he knows it. If he doesn't want me to speak, to denounce him, let him kill me. I can die—that is what I can do—die. Let him kill me! Then, perhaps, once for all, you might learn to hate him.

Raimunda. Hush, I say!—Here he comes. [ESTEBAN *enters.*] Esteban!

Esteban. She is right. She is not the one who ought to go. Only I don't want her to give me up. I will do it myself. I am strong now. I will go out on the road to meet them. Let me go, Raimunda. You have your child. You forgive me, but she never will. She hated me from the beginning.

Raimunda. No, Esteban, don't you go! Esteban, my life!

Esteban. No, let me go, or I will call Norbert's father. I will tell him. . . .

Raimunda. [*To* ACACIA.] Now you see what you have done. It was your fault. Esteban! Esteban!

Acacia. Mother, don't let him go!

Raimunda. Ah!

Esteban. No, she wants to betray me. Why did you hate me like this? You never once called me father. You don't know how I loved you!

Acacia. Mother, mother——

Esteban. *La Malquerida!* The Passion Flower! I hang my head. But once—once how I could have loved you!

Raimunda. For once, call him father.

Esteban. She will never forgive me.

Raimunda. But she must! Throw your arms about his neck. Call him father. Even the dead will forgive us then, and be happy in our happiness.

Esteban. Daughter!

Acacia. Esteban! . . . My God! Esteban!

Esteban. Ah!

Raimunda. But you don't call him father. Has she fainted? Ah! Lip to lip, and you clutch her in your arms! Let go, let go! Now I see why you won't call him father. Now I see that it was your fault—and I curse you!

Acacia. Yes, it was. Kill me! It is true, it is true! He is the only man I ever loved.

Esteban. Ah!

Raimunda. What do you say? What is that? I will kill you—yes, and be damned with it!

Esteban. Stand back!

Acacia. Save me!

Esteban. Stand back, I say!

Raimunda. Ah! Now I see! It is plain to me now. And it is just as well! What is one murder to me? We can all die. Here! Come, everybody! The murderer! I have the murderer! Take this wicked woman, for she is not my child!

Acacia. Run! Get away!

Esteban. Yes, together—to hell! For I am damned for love of you. Come! They can hunt us like wild beasts among the rocks. To love you and hold you, I will be as the wild beasts, that know neither father nor mother!

Raimunda. Help! Help! Come quick! The murderer! The murderer!

[RUBIO, BERNABÉ, *and* JULIANA *appear simultaneously at different doors, followed by others from the village.*]

Esteban. Out of my way! Take care who crosses me!

Raimunda. Stay where you are!—The murderer!

Esteban. Out of my way, I tell you!

Raimunda. Over my dead body!

Esteban. Yes—

[*Raising his gun he shoots* RAIMUNDA.]

Raimunda. Ah!

Juliana. God in heaven!—Raimunda!

Rubio. What have you done?

A Man. Kill him!

Esteban. Yes, kill me! I don't defend myself.

Bernabé. No! Put the law on him!

Juliana. It was this man, this wretched man!—Raimunda!—He has killed her!—Raimunda! Don't you hear?

Raimunda. Yes, Juliana. Don't let me die without confession. I am dying now. This blood. . . . No matter—Acacia! Acacia!

Juliana. Acacia!—Where is she?

Acacia. Mother, mother!

Raimunda. Ah! Then you are not crying for him? It consoles me.

Acacia. No, mother! You are my mother!

Juliana. She is dying! Quick—Raimunda!

Acacia. Mother, mother!

Raimunda. This man cannot harm you now. You are saved. Blessed be the blood that saves, like the blood of our Lord Jesus Christ!

CURTAIN

THE CHERRY ORCHARD*

By

ANTON CHEKHOV

Translated by JULIUS WEST

IN "THE CHERRY ORCHARD" THE ART OF Anton Chekhov and his theater came to complete fruition. Many claim for it the first place in the world theater of modern times. It was written with complete self-confidence. Its author had seen three of his plays succeed at the Moscow Art Theatre beyond his highest hopes. He knew that company could interpret his subtlest suggestions. He no longer needed urging as when he wrote *The Three Sisters.* The unexpected triumph of that play revived his early dreams of dramatic authorship, which had been all but extinguished with the failure of *The Sea-Gull* in St. Petersburg five years before. In his diary, on that occasion, Chekhov made the laconic entry:

"17th October, 1896.—Performance of my *Sea-Gull* at the Alexandrinsky Theatre. It was a failure."

He had fled from the theater before the final curtain, resolved that this experience should be his last. But unlike others who have turned their backs on the stage, he did so not as an enemy. He had loved the theater from boyhood. His one-act plays, *The Bear* and *The Proposal,* were already popular in performance. The Emperor had several times honored *The Proposal* with his presence. Although his first long play, *Ivanov,* had succeeded, *The Wood Demon* (later revised as *Uncle Vanya*) had failed as presented in the conventional stage manner of the day. His most friendly critics found his genius unsuited to the theater. Some in his audiences, however, had recognized the novelty and greatness of his style. *Ivanov,* for instance, had provoked a tumult of hisses and loud applause. After a lapse of years he had made one more appeal to the public in *The Sea-Gull.* He was now content to accept the verdict of that public and of his critics.

In the reversal of their judgment lies a most significant chapter in the history of the modern drama. To the Moscow Art Theatre belongs the honor of the experiment; and to Chekhov, in large measure, belongs the credit of inspiring that great organization to its highest achievement. Vladimir Danchenko had witnessed the failure of *The Sea-Gull* in St. Petersburg. He believed that a theater could be created capable of presenting such plays. With Constantine Stanislavsky he was already planning one as a protest against the shams and conventions of the great theaters, similar to those that in Paris had led Antoine to revolt and, in England, Grein, Shaw, and Granville Barker. He had liked *The Sea-Gull* for the very qualities that had made it unsuccessful in the great theater—its intimacy, its restraint, its symbolic values. It was announced for production at the end of the first season of the new theater (1898–1899) and Stanislavsky undertook its direction, although he did not share his partner's faith in the play. Upon careful study he was awakened to its possibilities and he bent all the energies of his company to realizing them. It meant the creation of a new theater style to fit the play. In creating it he not only proved Chekhov's greatness as a dramatist, but he raised the Moscow Art Theatre to a place of distinction throughout the world. But Chekhov himself was unconvinced. Before the opening of the play his sickness had forced him to retire to the Crimea, where for the rest of his life he was compelled to remain, except in summer. He would not believe the reports of the great success. He refused to release to the company his *Uncle Vanya* until he could see the production. When next he could visit Moscow they gave a performance for him alone. He then demanded to see it given publicly. The troupe travelled to the Crimea, or as a captious critic remarked, "The Mountain went to Mohammet." Not only was he satisfied with their artistry and its popular appeal, but he was fired with the desire to write again for the stage. He released *Uncle Vanya* and added two new plays to the repertory, *The Three Sisters,* and *The Cherry Orchard.* A few months after the immense success of *The Cherry Orchard,* which was produced by the Art Theatre on January 17, 1904, Chekhov died. Later the company revived his early *Ivanov.* (See also the preface to *Uncle Vanya,* p. 269.)

The Cherry Orchard shows an advance in characterization, atmosphere, and plot, but it surpasses his earlier work notably in two respects: its universality as symbol and its buoyant vision of a coming dawn. We can no longer with an almost perfect detachment watch his subtly drawn characters involved in their loves, jealousies, and frustrations. We are drawn in and made sharers in a cycle of life. We too are at the parting of the ways. Old life sloughs off; new is born. We, too, feel the modern agony of change with those who must sell, even if we are not led to share the insulting joys of those who would buy and remake the old.

Chekhov was almost angered when anyone called this play gloomy or pessimistic. To him it was the reverse. He wrote to a friend: "The play has turned out not a drama, but a comedy, in parts even a farce. . . ." Like all his earlier plays it pictures the life of a decadent bourgeoisie existing rather than living upon their vast landed estates that they could no longer afford to maintain. In *The Cherry Orchard* that picture is made more detailed and vivid than in the rest, for it has become almost the protagonist of the play. America's nearest approach to this existence—which from personal experience I can testify was often one of beauty as well as of despair—is the life of the southern plantations. But the character, habits, and cultural background of the ancient Russian families living on those estates were different in ways not easy for American readers to appreciate. Paul Green's *House of Connelly* is our theater's closest approach to the subject and method of Chekhov's *The Cherry Orchard,* especially so if it could be played as it was first written.

The change foreshadowed in Madame Ranevsky's forced sale has, in the New Russia, become catastrophic beyond any dream of Chekhov's. One who so sensitively loved his home, his friends, his Russian scene, would hardly be made ruthlessly Utopian by mass measures of salvation. He would prefer to cure the souls of men by the physician's rather than the dictator's methods. A change of spirit and not of masters was his aim. Perhaps that is why his masterpieces make little appeal in the Soviet theaters. His plays are the enduring documents of a life the Soviets have spurned.

Even the sounds and silences of that life are made impressive. Leonid Andreyev commented on its Moscow production:

"Suddenly Chekhov introduces into his *Cherry Orchard* the mysterious sound of a sunken bucket; * a sound which is almost impossible to reproduce—but it is a necessary part of the soul of the characters of the play; without that sound they are not they, without it there is no Chekhov. Hence it becomes clear why all the theaters, in which only human beings act, and objects do not, cannot act Chekhov's plays, do not like him or understand him. . . . It is a psychological theater. More than that—it is the theater of pan-psychism, the pure representation of which in literature was Anton Chekhov.

"Direct your attention to the dialogue of Chekhov's plays; it is not plausible; in life people do not speak like that; it is full of unfinished speeches; it is always, as it were, a continuation of something already said; there is not in it that clear-cut beginning with which any other playwright's characters come on the stage. Chekhov's characters never begin nor end their speech; they always merely continue it. That is why his plays are difficult to read. . . . Indeed, if Chekhov's dialogue always does *continue* something, then surely there must be a someone or something that is continued. And that mysterious essence, lacking in mere reading, consists in the animated objects and animated time. . . . Everything is alive, has a soul and a voice. Oh! how far removed this theater was from the intolerable naturalism which had been grafted on the stage, and which knows *objects* only."

This sense of "the behind life" always implicit in the play, which otherwise is a classic example of naturalism at its best—has often been noted. The closing scene in which old Fiers, the aged servant faithful to the old order, is locked in the room of the manor, forgotten, and left to his fate by the departing family, was cited by Mr. Kenneth Macgowan in his *Continental Stagecraft* as a baffling instance of the manner in which naturalism may become as symbolically expressive in the theater as any form of futurism, especially as it was supremely well acted by Artium, an actor of the Art Theatre whom Chekhov greatly admired.

* Andreyev refers to "the sound of a breaking string" which occurs in the second act and again at the very end of the play.

So familiar has that troupe's production of the play become in the western world that its outstanding members should be mentioned. Constantin Stanislavsky, its director, acted Gaev, making it one of his most memorable creations. Lopakhin, Chekhov's favorite character in the play, was taken by Leonidov, who gave to the crushing blow at the end of Act III the full force that Chekhov intended. Olga Knipper, who was then Chekhov's wife, finding "perfect notes for Mme. Ranevsky, preserved both her shallowness and her lovely nature." Epikhodov as played by Moskvin became "the model of artistic caricature on the stage." Some of that character's lines as now printed were adopted from improvisations made by that actor in rehearsal.

In America the play has rarely been produced with distinction. It was given in New York at the Bijou Theater in matinee performances by J. B. Fagan in 1928. With more success Miss Eva Le Gallienne included it in her choice of great plays at the Civic Repertory Theater that same year. It was first produced in London in 1911, and more notably by Nigel Playfair at his Hammersmith Theater in 1925. It was given another London production at the Barnes Theater in 1926. Amateurs in both countries are making bold with it. The suggestion from this survey is that the English-speaking world is only now becoming aware of the real Chekhov of the theater.

For Chekhov's biographical data and play list, see *Uncle Vanya,* p. 270.

THE CHERRY ORCHARD

Characters

LUBOV ANDREYEVNA RANEVSKY (MME. RANEVSKY), *a landowner.*
ANYA, *her daughter, aged seventeen.*
VARYA (BARBARA), *her adopted daughter, aged twenty-seven.*
LEONID ANDREYEVITCH GAEV. *Mme. Ranevsky's brother.*
ERMOLAI ALEXEYEVITCH LOPAKHIN, *a merchant.*
PETER SERGEYEVITCH TROFIMOV, *a student.*
BORIS BORISOVITCH SIMEONOV-PISCHIN, *a landowner.*
CHARLOTTA IVANOVNA, *a governess.*
SIMEON PANTELEYEVITCH EPIKHODOV, *a clerk.*
DUNYASHA (AVDOTYA FEDOROVNA), *a maidservant.*
FIERS, *an old footman, aged eighty-seven.*
YASHA, *a young footman.*
A TRAMP.
A STATION-MASTER.
POST-OFFICE CLERK.
GUESTS.
A SERVANT.

The action takes place on MME. RANEVSKY'S *estate.*

ACT I

A room which is still called the nursery. One of the doors leads into ANYA'S *room. It is close on sunrise. It is May. The cherry-trees are in flower but it is chilly in the garden. There is an early frost. The windows of the room are shut.* [DUNYASHA *comes in with a candle, and* LOPAKHIN *with a book in his hand.*]

Lopakhin. The train's arrived, thank God. What's the time?

Dunyasha. It will soon be two. [*Blows out candle.*] It is light already.

Lopakhin. How much was the train late? Two hours at least. [*Yawns and stretches himself.*] I have made a rotten mess of it! I came here on purpose to meet them at the station, and then overslept myself . . . in my chair. It's a pity. I wish you'd wakened me.

Dunyasha. I thought you'd gone away. [*Listening.*] I think I hear them coming.

Lopakhin. [*Listens.*] No. . . . They've got to collect their luggage and so on. . . . [*Pause.*] Lubov Andreyevna has been living abroad for five years; I don't know what she'll be like now. . . . She's a good sort—an easy, simple person. I remember when I was a boy of fifteen, my father, who is dead—he used to keep a shop in the village here—hit me on the face with his fist, and my nose bled. . . . We had gone into the yard together for something or other, and he was a little drunk. Lubov Andreyevna, as I remember her now, was still young, and very thin, and she took me to the washstand here in this very room, the nursery. She said, "Don't cry, little man, it'll be all right in time for your wedding." [*Pause.*] "Little man." . . . My father was a peasant, it's true, but here I am in a white waistcoat and yellow shoes . . . a pearl out of an oyster. I'm rich now, with lots of money, but just think about it and examine me, and you'll find I'm still a peasant down to the marrow of my bones. [*Turns over the pages of his book.*] Here I've been reading this book, but I understood nothing. I read and fell asleep. [*Pause.*]

Dunyasha. The dogs didn't sleep all night; they know that they're coming.

Lopakhin. What's up with you, Dunyasha . . . ?

Dunyasha. My hands are shaking. I shall faint.

Lopakhin. You're too sensitive, Dunyasha. You dress just like a lady, and you do your hair like one too. You oughtn't. You should know your place.

Epikhodov. [*Enters with a bouquet. He wears a short jacket and brilliantly polished boots which squeak audibly. He drops the bouquet as he enters, then picks it up.*] The gardener sent these; says they're to go into the dining-room.

[*Gives the bouquet to* DUNYASHA.]

Lopakhin. And you'll bring me some kvass.

Dunyasha. Very well. [*Exit.*]

Epikhodov. There's a frost this morning—three degrees, and the cherry-trees are all in flower. I can't approve of our climate. [*Sighs.*] I can't. Our climate is indisposed to favor us even this once. And, Ermolai Alexeyevitch, allow me to say to you, in addition, that I bought myself some boots two days ago, and I beg to assure you that they squeak in a perfectly unbearable manner. What shall I put on them?

Lopakhin. Go away. You bore me.

Epikhodov. Some misfortune happens to me every day. But I don't complain; I'm used to it, and I can smile. [DUNYASHA *comes in and brings* LOPAKHIN *some kvass.*] I shall go. [*Knocks over a chair.*] There. . . . [*Triumphantly.*] There, you see, if I may use the word, what circumstances I am in, so to speak. It is even simply marvellous. [*Exit.*]

Dunyasha. I may confess to you, Ermolai Alexeyevitch, that Epikhodov has proposed to me.

Lopakhin. Ah!

Dunyasha. I don't know what to do about it. He's a nice young man, but every now and again, when he begins talking, you can't understand a word he's saying. I think I like him. He's madly in love with me. He's an unlucky man; every day something happens. We tease him about it. They call him "Two-and-twenty troubles."

Lopakhin. [*Listens.*] There they come, I think.

Dunyasha. They're coming! What's the matter with me? I'm cold all over.

Lopakhin. There they are, right enough. Let's go and meet them. Will she know me? We haven't seen each other for five years.

Dunyasha. [*Excited.*] I shall faint in a minute. . . . Oh, I'm fainting!

[*Two carriages are heard driving up to the house.* LOPAKHIN *and* DUNYASHA *quickly go out. The stage is empty. A noise begins in the next room.* FIERS, *leaning on a stick, walks quickly across the stage; he has just been to meet* LUBOV ANDREYEVNA. *He wears an old-fashioned livery and a tall hat. He is saying something to himself, but not a word of it can be made out. The noise behind the stage gets louder and louder. A voice is heard: "Let's go in there." Enter* LUBOV ANDREYEVNA, ANYA, *and* CHARLOTTA IVANOVNA *with a little dog on a chain, and all dressed in travelling clothes,* VARYA *in a long coat and with a kerchief on her head.* GAEV, SIMEONOV-PISCHIN, LOPAKHIN, DUNYASHA *with a parcel and an umbrella, and a servant with luggage—all cross the room.*]

Anya. Let's come through here. Do you remember what this room is, mother?

Lubov. [*Joyfully, through her tears.*] The nursery!

Varya. How cold it is! My hands are quite numb. [*To* LUBOV ANDREYEVNA.] Your rooms, the white one and the violet one, are just as they used to be, mother.

Lubov. My dear nursery, O you beautiful room. . . . I used to sleep here when I was a baby. [*Kisses her brother,* VARYA, *then her brother again.*] And Varya is just as she used to be, just like a nun. And I knew Dunyasha. [*Kisses her.*]

Gaev. The train was two hours late. There now; how's that for punctuality?

Charlotta. [*To* PISCHIN.] My dog eats nuts too.

Pischin. [*Astonished.*] To think of that, now!

[*All go out except* ANYA *and* DUNYASHA.]

Dunyasha. We did have to wait for you! [*Takes off* ANYA'S *cloak and hat.*]

Anya. . . . I didn't get any sleep for four nights on the journey. . . . I'm awfully cold.

Dunyasha. You went away during Lent, when it was snowing and frosty, but now? Darling! [*Laughs and kisses her.*] We did have to wait for you, my joy, my pet. . . . I must tell you at once, I can't bear to wait a minute.

Anya. [*Tired.*] Something else now . . . ?

Dunyasha. The clerk, Epikhodov, proposed to me after Easter.

Anya. Always the same. . . . [*Puts her hair straight.*] I've lost all my hairpins. . . .

[*She is very tired, and even staggers s she walks.*]

Dunyasha. I don't know what to think about it. He loves me, he loves me so much!

Anya. [*Looks into her room; in a gentle voice.*] My room, my windows, as if I'd never gone away. I'm at home! Tomorrow morning I'll get up and have a run in the garden. . . . Oh, if I could only get to sleep! I didn't sleep the whole journey, I was so bothered.

Dunyasha. Peter Sergeyevitch came two days ago.

Anya. [*Joyfully.*] Peter!

Dunyasha. He sleeps in the bath-house, he lives there. He said he was afraid he'd be in the way. [*Looks at her pocket-watch.*] I ought to wake him, but Barbara Mihailovna told me not to. "Don't wake him," she said.

[*Enter* VARYA, *a bunch of keys on her belt.*]

Varya. Dunyasha, some coffee, quick. Mother wants some.

Dunyasha. This minute. [*Exit.*]

Varya. Well, you've come, glory be to God. Home again. [*Caressing her.*] My darling is back again! My pretty one is back again!

Anya. I did have an awful time, I tell you.

Varya. I can just imagine it!

Anya. I went away in Holy Week; it was very cold then. Charlotta talked the whole way and would go on performing her tricks. Why did you tie Charlotta on to me?

Varya. You couldn't go alone, darling, at seventeen!

Anya. We went to Paris; it's cold there and snowing. I talk French perfectly horribly. My mother lives on the fifth floor. I go to her, and find her there with various Frenchmen, women, an old abbé with a book, and everything in tobacco smoke and with no comfort at all. I suddenly became very sorry for mother—so sorry that I took her head in my arms and hugged her and wouldn't let her go. Then mother started hugging me and crying. . . .

Varya. [*Weeping.*] Don't say any more, don't say any more. . . .

Anya. She's already sold her villa near Mentone; she's nothing left, nothing. And I haven't a copeck left either; we only just managed to get here. And mother won't understand! We had dinner at a station: she asked for all the expensive things, and tipped the waiters one rouble each. And Charlotta too. Yasha wants his share too—it's too bad. Mother's got a footman now, Yasha; we've brought him here.

Varya. I saw the wretch.

Anya. How's business? Has the interest been paid?

Varya. Not much chance of that.

Anya. O God, O God. . . .

Varya. The place will be sold in August.

Anya. O God. . . .

Lopakhin. [*Looks in at the door and moos.*] Moo! . . . [*Exit.*]

Varya. [*Through her tears.*] I'd like to. . . . [*Shakes her fist.*]

Anya. [*Embraces* VARYA, *softly.*] Varya, has he proposed to you? [VARYA *shakes her head.*] But he loves you. . . . Why don't you make up your minds? Why do you keep on waiting?

Varya. I think that it will all come to nothing. He's a busy man. I'm not his affair . . . he pays no attention to me. Bless the man, I don't want to see him. . . . But everybody talks about our marriage, everybody congratulates me, and there's nothing in it at all, it's all like a dream. [*In another tone.*] You've got a brooch like a bee.

Anya. [*Sadly.*] Mother bought it. [*Goes into her room, and talks lightly, like a child.*] In Paris I went up in a balloon!

Varya. My darling's come back, my pretty one's come back! [DUNYASHA *has already returned with the coffee-pot and is making the coffee.*] I go about all day, looking after the house, and I think all the time, if only you could marry a rich man, then I'd be happy and would go away somewhere by myself, then to Kiev . . . to Moscow, and so on, from one holy place to another. I'd tramp and tramp. That would be splendid!

Anya. The birds are singing in the garden. What time is it now?

Varya. It must be getting on for three. Time you went to sleep, darling. [*Goes into* ANYA'S *room.*] Splendid!

[*Enter* YASHA *with a plaid shawl and a travelling bag.*]

Yasha. [*Crossing the stage. Politely.*] May I go this way?

Dunyasha. I hardly knew you, Yasha. You have changed abroad.

Yasha. H'm . . . and who are you?

Dunyasha. When you went away I was only so high. [*Showing with her hand.*] I'm Dunyasha, the daughter of Theodore Kozoyedov. You don't remember!

Yasha. Oh, you little cucumber!

[*Looks round and embraces her. She screams and drops a saucer.* YASHA *goes out quickly.*]

Varya. [*In the doorway. In an angry voice.*] What's that?

Dunyasha. [*Through her tears.*] I've broken a saucer.

Varya. It may bring luck.

Anya. [*Coming out of her room.*] We must tell mother that Peter's here.

Varya. I told them not to wake him.

Anya. [*Thoughtfully.*] Father died six years ago, and a month later my brother Grisha was drowned in the river—such a dear little boy of seven! Mother couldn't bear it; she went away, away, without looking round. . . . [*Shudders.*] How I understand her; if only she knew! And Peter Trofimov was Grisha's tutor, he might tell her. . . .

[*Enter* FIERS *in a short jacket and white waistcoat.*]

Fiers. [*Goes to the coffee-pot, nervously.*] The mistress is going to have some food here. . . . [*Puts on white gloves.*] Is the coffee ready? [*To* DUNYASHA, *severely.*] You! Where's the cream?

Dunyasha. Oh, dear me . . . ! [*Rapid exit.*]

Fiers. [*Fussing round the coffee-pot.*] Oh, you bungler. . . . [*Murmurs to himself.*] Back from Paris . . . the master went to Paris once . . . in a carriage. . . . [*Laughs.*]

Varya. What are you talking about, Fiers?

Fiers. I beg your pardon? [*Joyfully.*] The mistress is home again. I've lived to see her! Don't care if I die now. . . . [*Weeps with joy.*]

[*Enter* LUBOV ANDREYEVNA, GAEV, LOPAKHIN, *and* SIMEONOV-PISCHIN, *the latter in a long jacket of thin cloth and loose trousers.* GAEV, *coming in, moves his arms and body about as if he were playing billiards.*]

Lubov. Let me remember now. Red into the corner! Twice into the centre!

Gaev. Right into the pocket! Once upon a time you and I used both to sleep in this room, and now I'm fifty-one; it does seem strange.

Lopakhin. Yes, time does go.

Gaev. Who does?

Lopakhin. I said that time does go.

Gaev. It smells of patchouli here.

Anya. I'm going to bed. Good-night, mother. [*Kisses her.*]

Lubov. My lovely little one. [*Kisses her hand.*] Glad to be at home? I can't get over it.

Anya. Good-night, uncle.

Gaev. [*Kisses her face and hands.*] God be with you. How you do resemble your mother! [*To his sister.*] You were just like her at her age, Luba.

[ANYA *gives her hand to* LOPAKHIN *and* PISCHIN *and goes out, shutting the door behind her.*]

Lubov. She's awfully tired.

Pischin. It's a very long journey.

Varya. [*To* LOPAKHIN *and* PISCHIN.] Well, sirs, it's getting on for three, quite time you went.

Lubov. [*Laughs.*] You're just the same as ever, Varya. [*Draws her close and kisses her.*] I'll have some coffee now, then we'll all go. [FIERS *lays a cushion under her feet.*] Thank you, dear. I'm used to coffee. I drink it day and night. Thank you, dear old man. [*Kisses* FIERS.]

Varya. I'll go and see if they've brought in all the luggage. [*Exit.*]

Lubov. Is it really I who am sitting here? [*Laughs.*] I want to jump about and wave my arms. [*Covers her face with her hands.*] But suppose I'm dreaming! God knows I love my own country, I love it deeply; I couldn't look out of the railway carriage, I cried so much. [*Through her tears.*] Still, I must have my coffee. Thank you, Fiers. Thank you, dear old man. I'm so glad you're still with us.

Fiers. The day before yesterday.

Gaev. He doesn't hear well.

Lopakhin. I've got to go off to Kharkov by the five o'clock train. I'm awfully sorry! I should like to have a look at you, to gossip a little. You're as fine-looking as ever.

Pischin. [*Breathes heavily.*] Even finer-looking . . . dressed in Paris fashions . . . confound it all.

Lopakhin. Your brother, Leonid Andreyevitch, says I'm a snob, a usurer, but that is absolutely nothing to me. Let him talk. Only I do wish you would believe in me as you once did, that your wonderful, touching eyes would look at me as they did before. Merciful God! My father was the serf of your grandfather and your own father, but you—you more than anybody else—did so much for me once upon a time that I've forgotten everything and love you as if you belonged to my family . . . and even more.

Lubov. I can't sit still, I'm not in a state to do it. [*Jumps up and walks about in great excitement.*] I'll never survive this happiness. . . . You can laugh at me; I'm a silly woman. . . . My dear little cupboard. [*Kisses cupboard.*] My little table.

Gaev. Nurse has died in your absence.

Lubov. [*Sits and drinks coffee.*] Yes, bless her soul. I heard by letter.

Gaev. And Anastasius has died too. Peter Kosoy has left me and now lives in town with the Commissioner of Police.

[*Takes a box of sugar-candy out of his pocket and sucks a piece.*]

Pischin. My daughter, Dashenka, sends her love.

Lopakhin. I want to say something very pleasant, very delightful, to you. [*Looks at his watch.*] I'm going away at once, I haven't much time . . . but I'll tell you all about it in two or three words. As you already know, your cherry orchard is to be sold to pay your debts, and the sale is fixed for August 22; but you needn't be alarmed, dear madam you may sleep in peace; there's a way out. Here's my plan. Please attend carefully! Your estate is only thirteen miles from the town, the railway runs by, and if the cherry orchard and the land by the river are broken up into building lots and are then leased off for villas you'll get at least twenty-five thousand roubles a year profit out of it.

Gaev. How utterly absurd!

Lubov. I don't understand you at all, Ermolai Alexeyevitch.

Lopakhin. You will get twenty-five roubles a year for each dessiatin from the leaseholders at the very least, and if you advertise now I'm willing to bet that you won't have a vacant plot left by the autumn; they'll all go. In a word, you're saved. I congratulate you. Only, of course, you'll have to put things straight, and clean up. . . . For instance, you'll have to pull down all the old buildings, this house, which isn't any use to anybody now, and cut down the old cherry orchard. . . .

Lubov. Cut it down? My dear man, you must excuse me, but you don't understand anything at all. If there's anything interesting or remarkable in the whole province, it's this cherry orchard of ours.

Lopakhin. The only remarkable thing about the orchard is that it's very large. It only bears fruit every other year, and even then you don't know what to do with them; nobody buys any.

Gaev. This orchard is mentioned in the "Encyclopædic Dictionary."

Lopakhin. [*Looks at his watch.*] If we can't think of anything and don't make up our minds to anything, then on August 22 both the cherry orchard and the whole estate will be up for auction. Make up your mind! I swear there's no other way out, I'll swear it again.

Fiers. In the old days, forty or fifty years back, they dried the cherries, soaked them and pickled them, and made jam of them, and it used to happen that . . .

Gaev. Be quiet, Fiers.

Fiers. And then we'd send the dried cherries off in carts to Moscow and Kharkov. And money! And the dried cherries were soft, juicy, sweet, and nicely scented. . . . They knew the way. . . .

Lubov. What was the way?

Fiers. They've forgotten. Nobody remembers.

Pischin. [*To* LUBOV ANDREYEVNA.] What about Paris? Eh? Did you eat frogs?

Lubov. I ate crocodiles.

Pischin. To think of that, now.

Lopakhin. Up to now in the villages there were only the gentry and the laborers, and now the people who live in villas have arrived. All towns now, even small ones, are surrounded by villas. And it's safe to say that in twenty years' time the villa resident will be all over the place. At present he sits on his balcony and drinks tea, but it may well come to pass that he'll begin to cultivate his patch of land, and then your cherry orchard will be happy, rich, splendid. . . .

Gaev. [*Angry.*] What rot!

[*Enter* VARYA *and* YASHA.]

Varya. There are two telegrams for you, little mother. [*Picks out a key and noisily unlocks an antique cupboard.*] Here they are.

Lubov. They're from Paris. . . . [*Tears them up without reading them.*] I've done with Paris.

Gaev. And do you know, Luba, how old this case is? A week ago I took out the bottom drawer; I looked and saw figures burnt out in it. That case was made exactly a hundred years ago. What do you think of that? What? We could celebrate its jubilee. It hasn't a soul of its own, but still, say what you will, it's a fine bookcase.

Pischin. [*Astonished.*] A hundred years. . . . Think of that!

Gaev. Yes . . . it's a real thing. [*Handling it.*] My dear and honored case! I congratulate you on your existence, which has already for more than a hundred years been directed toward the bright ideals of good and justice; your silent call to productive labour has not grown less in the hundred years [*Weeping.*] during which you have upheld virtue and faith in a better future to the generations of our race, educating us to ideals of goodness and to the knowledge of a common consciousness. [*Pause.*]

Lopakhin. Yes.

Lubov. You're just the same as ever, Leon.

Gaev. [*A little confused.*] Off the white on the right, into the corner pocket. Red ball goes into the middle pocket!

Lopakhin. [*Looks at his watch.*] It's time I went.

Yasha. [*Giving* LUBOV ANDREYEVNA *her medicine.*] Will you take your pills now?

Pischin. You oughtn't to take medicines, dear madam; they do you neither harm nor good. . . . Give them here, dear madam. [*Takes the pills, turns them out into the palm of his hand, blows on them, puts them into his mouth, and drinks some kvass.*] There!

Lubov. [*Frightened.*] You're off your head!

Pischin. I've taken all the pills.

Lopakhin. Gormandizer! [*All laugh.*]

Fiers. They were here in Easter week and ate half a pailful of cucumbers. . . .

[*Mumbles.*]

Lubov. What's he driving at?

Varya. He's been mumbling away for three years. We're used to that.

Yasha. Senile decay.

[CHARLOTTA IVANOVNA *crosses the stage, dressed in white: she is very thin and tightly laced; has a lorgnette at her waist.*]

Lopakhin. Excuse me, Charlotta Ivanovna, I haven't said "How do you do" to you yet. [*Tries to kiss her hand.*]

Charlotta. [*Takes her hand away.*] If you let people kiss your hand, then they'll want your elbow, then your shoulder, and then . . .

Lopakhin. My luck's out today! [*All laugh.*] Show us a trick, Charlotta Ivanovna!

Lubov. Charlotta, do us a trick.

Charlotta. It's not necessary. I want to go to bed. [*Exit.*]

Lopakhin. We shall see each other in three weeks. [*Kisses* LUBOV ANDREYEVNA'S *hand.*] Now, good-by. It's time to go. [*To* GAEV.] See you again. [*Kisses* PISCHIN.] Au revoir. [*Gives his hand to* VARYA, *then to* FIERS *and to* YASHA.] I don't want to go away. [*To* LUBOV ANDREYEVNA.] If you think about the villas and make up your mind, then just let me know, and I'll raise a loan of 50,000 roubles at once. Think about it seriously.

Varya. [*Angrily.*] Do go, now!

Lopakhin. I'm going. I'm going. . . . [*Exit.*]

Gaev. Snob. Still, I beg pardon. . . . Varya's going to marry him, he's Varya's young man.

Varya. Don't talk too much, uncle.

Lubov. Why not, Varya? I should be very glad. He's a good man.

Pischin. To speak the honest truth . . . he's a worthy man. . . . And my Dashenka . . . also says that . . . she says lots of things. [*Snores, but wakes up again at once.*] But still, dear madam, if you could lend me 240 roubles . . . to pay the interest on my mortgage tomorrow . . .

Varya. [*Frightened.*] We haven't got it, we haven't got it!

Lubov. It's quite true. I've nothing at all.

Pischin. I'll find it all right. [*Laughs.*] I never lose hope. I used to think, "Everything's lost now. I'm a dead man," when, lo and behold, a railway was built over my land . . . and they paid me for it. And something else will happen today or tomorrow. Dashenka may win 20,000 roubles . . . she's got a ticket.

Lubov. The coffee's all gone, we can go to bed.

Fiers. [*Brushing* GAEV'S *trousers; in an insistent tone.*] You've put on the wrong trousers again. What am I to do with you?

Varya. [*Quietly.*] Anya's asleep. [*Opens window quietly.*] The sun has risen already; it isn't cold. Look, little mother: what lovely trees! And the air! The starlings are singing!

Gaev. [*Opens the other window.*] The whole garden's white. You haven't forgotten, Luba? There's that long avenue going straight, straight, like a stretched strap; it shines on moonlight nights. Do you remember? You haven't forgotten?

Lubov. [*Looks out into the garden.*] Oh, my childhood, days of my innocence! In this nursery I used to sleep; I used to look out from here into the orchard. Happiness used to wake with me every morning, and then it was just as it is now; nothing has changed. [*Laughs from joy.*] It's all, all white! Oh, my orchard! After the dark autumns and the cold winters, you're young again, full of happiness, the angels of heaven haven't left you. . . . If only I could take my heavy burden off my breast and shoulders, if I could forget my past!

Gaev. Yes, and they'll sell this orchard to pay off debts. How strange it seems!

Lubov. Look, there's my dead mother going in the orchard . . . dressed in white! [*Laughs from joy.*] That's she.

Gaev. Where?

Varya. God bless you, little mother.

Lubov. There's nobody there; I thought I saw somebody. On the right, at the turning by the summer-house, a white little tree bent down, looking just like a woman. [*Enter* TROFIMOV *in a worn student uniform and spectacles.*] What a marvellous garden! White masses of flowers, the blue sky. . . .

Trofimov. Lubov Andreyevna! [*She looks round at him.*] I only want to show myself, and I'll go away. [*Kisses her hand warmly.*] I was told to wait till the morning, but I didn't have the patience.

[LUBOV ANDREYEVNA *looks surprised.*]

Varya. [*Crying.*] It's Peter Trofimov.

Trofimov. Peter Trofimov, once the tutor of your Grisha. . . . Have I changed so much?

[LUBOV ANDREYEVNA *embraces him and cries softly.*]

Gaev. [*Confused.*] That's enough, that's enough, Luba.

Varya. [*Weeps.*] But I told you, Peter, to wait till tomorrow.

Lubov. My Grisha . . . my boy . . . Grisha . . . my son.

Varya. What are we to do, little mother? It's the will of God.

Trofimov. [*Softly, through his tears.*] It's all right, it's all right.

Lubov. [*Still weeping.*] My boy's dead; he was drowned. Why? Why, my friend?

[*Softly.*] Anya's asleep in there. I am speaking so loudly, making such a noise. . . . Well, Peter? What's made you look so bad? Why have you grown so old?

Trofimov. In the train an old woman called me a decayed gentleman.

Lubov. You were quite a boy then, a nice little student, and now your hair is not at all thick and you wear spectacles. Are you really still a student?

[*Goes to the door.*]

Trofimov. I suppose I shall always be a student.

Lubov. [*Kisses her brother, then* VARYA.] Well, let's go to bed. . . . And you've grown older, Leonid.

Pischin. [*Follows her.*] Yes, we've got to go to bed. . . . Oh, my gout! I'll stay the night here. If only, Lubov Andreyevna, my dear, you could get me 240 roubles tomorrow morning——

Gaev. Still the same story.

Pischin. Two hundred and forty roubles . . . to pay the interest on the mortgage.

Lubov. I haven't any money, dear man.

Pischin. I'll give it back . . . it's a small sum. . . .

Lubov. Well then, Leonid will give it to you. . . . Let him have it, Leonid.

Gaev. By all means; hold out your hand.

Lubov. Why not? He wants it; he'll give it back.

[LUBOV ANDREYEVNA, TROFIMOV, PISCHIN, *and* FIERS *go out.* GAEV, VARYA, *and* YASHA *remain.*]

Gaev. My sister hasn't lost the habit of throwing money about. [*To* YASHA.] Stand off, do; you smell of poultry.

Yasha. [*Grins.*] You are just the same as ever, Leonid Andreyevitch.

Gaev. Really? [*To* VARYA.] What's he saying?

Varya. [*To* YASHA.] Your mother's come from the village; she's been sitting in the servants' room since yesterday, and wants to see you. . . .

Yasha. Bless the woman!

Varya. Shameless man.

Yasha. A lot of use there is in her coming. She might have come tomorrow just as well. [*Exit.*]

Varya. Mother hasn't altered a scrap, she's just as she always was. She'd give away everything, if the idea only entered her head.

Gaev. Yes. . . . [*Pause.*] If there's any illness for which people offer many remedies, you may be sure that particular illness is incurable, I think. I work my brains to their hardest. I've several remedies, very many, and that really means I've none at all. It would be nice to inherit a fortune from somebody, it would be nice to marry our Anya to a rich man, it would be nice to go to Yaroslav and try my luck with my aunt the Countess. My aunt is very, very rich.

Varya. [*Weeps.*] If only God helped us.

Gaev. Don't cry. My aunt's very rich, but she doesn't like us. My sister, in the first place, married an advocate, not a noble. . . . [ANYA *appears in the doorway.*] She not only married a man who was not a noble, but she behaved herself in a way which cannot be described as proper. She's nice and kind and charming, and I'm very fond of her, but say what you will in her favor and you still have to admit that she's wicked; you can feel it in her slightest movements.

Varya. [*Whispers.*] Anya's in the doorway.

Gaev. Really? [*Pause.*] It's curious, something's got into my right eye . . . I can't see properly out of it. And on Thursday, when I was at the District Court . . .

[*Enter* ANYA.]

Varya. Why aren't you in bed, Anya?

Anya. Can't sleep. It's no good.

Gaev. My darling! [*Kisses* ANYA'S *face and hands.*] My child. . . . [*Crying.*] You're not my niece, you're my angel, you're my all. . . . Believe in me, believe. . . .

Anya. I do believe in you, uncle. Everybody loves you and respects you . . . but, uncle dear, you ought to say nothing, no more than that. What were you saying just now about my mother, your own sister? Why did you say those things?

Gaev. Yes, yes. [*Covers his face with her hand.*] Yes, really, it was awful. Save me, my God! And only just now I made a speech before a bookcase . . . it's so silly! And only when I'd finished I knew how silly it was.

Varya. Yes, uncle dear, you really ought to say less. Keep quiet, that's all.

Anya. You'd be so much happier in yourself if you only kept quiet.

Gaev. All right, I'll be quiet. [*Kisses their hands.*] I'll be quiet. But let's talk business. On Thursday I was in the District Court, and a lot of us met there together, and we began to talk of this, that, and the other, and now I think I can arrange a loan to pay the interest into the bank.

Varya. If only God would help us!

Gaev. I'll go on Tuesday. I'll talk to you about it again. [*To* VARYA.] Don't howl. [*To* ANYA.] Your mother will have a talk to Lopakhin; he, of course, won't refuse. . . . And when you've rested you'll go to

Yaroslav to the Countess, your grandmother. So you see, we'll have three irons in the fire, and we'll be safe. We'll pay up the interest. I'm certain. [*Puts some sugar-candy into his mouth.*] I swear on my honor, on anything you will, that the estate will not be sold! [*Excitedly.*] I swear on my happiness! Here's my hand. You may call me a dishonorable wretch if I let it go to auction! I swear by all I am!

Anya. [*She is calm again and happy.*] How good and clever you are, uncle. [*Embraces him.*] I'm happy now! I'm happy! All's well! [*Enter* FIERS.]

Fiers. [*Reproachfully.*] Leonid Andreyevitch, don't you fear God? When are you going to bed?

Gaev. Soon, soon. You go away, Fiers. I'll undress myself. Well, children, bye-bye . . . ! I'll give you the details tomorrow, but let's go to bed now. [*Kisses* ANYA *and* VARYA.] I'm a man of the eighties. . . . People don't praise those years much, but I can still say that I've suffered for my beliefs. The peasants don't love me for nothing, I assure you. We've got to learn to know the peasants! We ought to learn how. . . .

Anya. You're doing it again, uncle!

Varya. Be quiet, uncle!

Fiers. [*Angrily.*] Leonid Andreyevitch!

Gaev. I'm coming, I'm coming. . . . Go to bed now. Off two cushions into the middle! I turn over a new leaf. . . .

[*Exit.* FIERS *goes after him.*]

Anya. I'm quieter now. I don't want to go to Yaroslav, I don't like grandmother; but I'm calm now, thanks to uncle.

[*Sits down.*]

Varya. It's time to go to sleep. I'll go. There's been an unpleasantness here while you were away. In the old servants' part of the house, as you know, only the old people live—little old Efim and Polya and Evstigney, and Karp as well. They started letting some tramps or other spend the night there —I said nothing. Then I heard that they were saying that I had ordered them to be fed on peas and nothing else; from meanness, you see. . . . And it was all Evstigney's doing. . . . Very well, I thought, if that's what the matter is, just you wait. So I call Evstigney. . . . [*Yawns.*] He comes. "What's this," I say, "Evstigney, you old fool." . . . [*Looks at* ANYA.] Anya dear! [*Pause.*] She's dropped off. . . . [*Takes* ANYA'S *arm.*] Let's go to bye-bye. . . . Come along! . . . [*Leads her.*] My darling's gone to sleep! Come on. . . . [*They go. In the distance, the other side of the orchard, a shepherd plays his pipe.* TROFIMOV *crosses the stage and stops on seeing* VARYA *and* ANYA.] Sh! She's asleep, asleep. Come on, dear.

Anya. [*Quietly, half-asleep.*] I'm so tired . . . all the bells . . . uncle, dear! Mother and uncle!

Varya. Come on, dear, come on!

[*They go into* ANYA'S *room.*]

Trofimov. [*Moved.*] My sun! my spring!

CURTAIN

ACT II

In a field. An old, crooked shrine, which has been long abandoned; near it a well and large stones, which apparently are old tombstones, and an old garden seat. The road is seen to GAEV'S *estate. On one side rise dark poplars, behind them begins the cherry orchard. In the distance is a row of telegraph poles, and far, far away on the horizon are the indistinct signs of a large town, which can only be seen on the finest and clearest days. It is close on sunset.* CHARLOTTA, YASHA, *and* DUNYASHA *are sitting on the seat;* EPIKHODOV *stands by and plays on a guitar; all seem thoughtful.* CHARLOTTA *wears a man's old peaked cap; she has unslung a rifle from her shoulders and is putting to rights the buckle on the strap.*]

Charlotta. [*Thoughtfully.*] I haven't a real passport. I don't know how old I am, and I think I'm young. When I was a little girl my father and mother used to go round fairs and give very good performances and I used to do the *salto mortale* and various little things. And when papa and mamma died a German lady took me to her and began to teach me. I liked it. I grew up and became a governess. And where I came from and who I am, I don't know. . . . Who my parents were—perhaps they weren't married—I don't know. [*Takes a cucumber out of her pocket and eats.*] I don't know anything. [*Pause.*] I do want to talk, but I haven't anybody to talk to . . . I haven't anybody at all.

Epikhodov. [*Plays on the guitar and sings.*]

"What is this noisy earth to me,
What matter friends and foes?"

I do like playing on the mandoline!

Dunyasha. That's a guitar, not a mandoline.

[*Looks at herself in a little mirror and powders herself.*]

Epikhodov. For the enamored madman, this is a mandoline. [*Sings.*]

"Oh that the heart was warmed,
By all the flames of love returned!"

[YASHA *sings too.*]

Charlotta. These people sing terribly. . . . Foo! Like jackals.

Dunyasha. [*To* YASHA.] Still, it must be nice to live abroad.

Yasha. Yes, certainly. I cannot differ from you there.

[*Yawns and lights a cigar.*]

Epikhodov. That is perfectly natural. Abroad everything is in full complexity.

Yasha. That goes without saying.

Epikhodov. I'm an educated man, I read various remarkable books, but I cannot understand the direction I myself want to go—whether to live or to shoot myself, as it were. So, in case, I always carry a revolver about with me. Here it is.

[*Shows a revolver.*]

Charlotta. I've done. Now I'll go. [*Slings the rifle.*] You, Epikhodov, are a very clever man and very terrible; women must be madly in love with you. Brrr! [*Going.*] These wise ones are all so stupid. I've nobody to talk to. I'm always alone, alone; I've nobody at all . . . and I don't know who I am or why I live. [*Exit slowly.*]

Epikhodov. As a matter of fact, independently of everything else, I must express my feeling, among other things, that fate has been as pitiless in her dealings with me as a storm is to a small ship. Suppose, let us grant, I am wrong; then why did I wake up this morning, to give an example, and behold an enormous spider on my chest, like that? [*Shows with both hands.*] And if I do drink some kvass, why is it that there is bound to be something of the most indelicate nature in it, such as a beetle? [*Pause.*] Have you read Buckle? [*Pause.*] I should like to trouble you, Avdotya Fedorovna, for two words.

Dunyasha. Say on.

Epikhodov. I should prefer to be alone with you. [*Sighs.*]

Dunyasha. [*Shy.*] Very well, only first bring me my little cloak. . . . It's by the cupboard. It's a little damp here.

Epikhodov. Very well . . . I'll bring it. . . . Now I know what to do with my revolver.

[*Takes guitar and exit, strumming.*]

Yasha. Two-and-twenty troubles! A silly man, between you and me and the gatepost. [*Yawns.*]

Dunyasha. I hope to goodness he won't shoot himself. [*Pause.*] I'm so nervous, I'm worried. I went into service when I was quite a little girl, and now I'm not used to common life, and my hands are white, white as a lady's. I'm so tender and so delicate now, respectable and afraid of everything. . . . I'm so frightened. And I don't know what will happen to my nerves if you deceive me, Yasha.

Yasha. [*Kisses her.*] Little cucumber! Of course, every girl must respect herself; there's nothing I dislike more than a badly behaved girl.

Dunyasha. I'm awfully in love with you; you're educated, you can talk about everything. [*Pause.*]

Yasha. [*Yawns.*] Yes. I think this: if a girl loves anybody, then that means she's immoral. [*Pause.*] It's nice to smoke a cigar out in the open air. . . . [*Listens.*] Somebody's coming. It's the mistress, and people with her. [DUNYASHA *embraces him suddenly.*] Go to the house, as if you'd been bathing in the river; go by this path, or they'll meet you and think I've been meeting you. I can't stand that sort of thing.

Dunyasha. [*Coughs quietly.*] My head's aching because of your cigar.

[*Exit.* YASHA *remains, sitting by the shrine. Enter* LUBOV ANDREYEVNA, GAEV, *and* LOPAKHIN.]

Lopakhin. You must make up your mind definitely—there's no time to waste. The question is perfectly plain. Are you willing to let the land for villas or no? Just one word, yes or no? Just one word!

Lubov. Who's smoking horrible cigars here? [*Sits.*]

Gaev. They built that railway; that's made this place very handy. [*Sits.*] Went to town and had lunch . . . red in the middle! I'd like to go in now and have just one game.

Lubov. You'll have time.

Lopakhin. Just one word! [*Imploringly.*] Give me an answer!

Gaev. [*Yawns.*] Really!

Lubov. [*Looks in her purse.*] I had a lot of money yesterday, but there's very little today. My poor Varya feeds everybody on milk soup to save money, in the kitchen the old people only get peas, and I spend recklessly. [*Drops the purse, scattering gold coins.*] There, they are all over the place.

Yasha. Permit me to pick them up. [*Collects the coins.*]

Lubov. Please do, Yasha. And why did I go and have lunch there? . . . A horrid restaurant with a band and tablecloths smelling of soap. . . . Why do you drink so much, Leon? Why do you eat so much? Why do you talk so much? You talked again too much today in the restaurant, and it wasn't at all to the point—about the seventies and about decadents. And to whom? Talking to the waiters about decadents!

Lopakhin. Yes.

Gaev. [*Waves his hand.*] I can't be cured, that's obvious. . . . [*Irritably to* YASHA.] What's the matter? Why do you keep twisting about in front of me?

Yasha. [*Laughs.*] I can't listen to your voice without laughing.

Gaev. [*To his sister.*] Either he or I . . .

Lubov. Go away, Yasha; get out of this. . . .

Yasha. [*Gives purse to* LUBOV ANDREYEVNA.] I'll go at once. [*Hardly able to keep from laughing.*] This minute. . . . [*Exit.*]

Lopakhin. That rich man Deriganov is preparing to buy your estate. They say he'll come to the sale himself.

Lubov. Where did you hear that?

Lopakhin. They say so in town.

Gaev. Our Yaroslav aunt has promised to send something, but I don't know when or how much.

Lopakhin. How much will she send? A hundred thousand roubles? Or two, perhaps?

Lubov. I'd be glad of ten or fifteen thousand.

Lopakhin. You must excuse my saying so, but I've never met such frivolous people as you before, or anybody so unbusinesslike and peculiar. Here I am telling you in plain language that your estate will be sold, and you don't seem to understand.

Lubov. What are we to do? Tell us, what?

Lopakhin. I tell you every day. I say the same thing every day. Both the cherry orchard and the land must be leased off for villas and at once, immediately—the auction is staring you in the face. Understand! Once you do definitely make up your minds to the villas, then you'll have as much money as you want and you'll be saved.

Lubov. Villas and villa residents—it's so vulgar, excuse me.

Gaev. I entirely agree with you.

Lopakhin. I must cry or yell or faint. I can't! You're too much for me! [*To* GAEV.] You old woman!

Gaev. Really!

Lopakhin. Old woman! [*Going out.*]

Lubov. [*Frightened.*] No, don't go away, do stop; be a dear. Please. Perhaps we'll find some way out!

Lopakhin. What's the good of trying to think!

Lubov. Please don't go away. It's nicer when you're here. . . . [*Pause.*] I keep on waiting for something to happen, as if the house is going to collapse over our heads.

Gaev. [*Thinking deeply.*] Double in the corner . . . across the middle. . . .

Lubov. We have been too sinful. . . .

Lopakhin. What sins have you committed?

Gaev. [*Puts candy into his mouth.*] They say that I've eaten all my substance in sugar-candies. [*Laughs.*]

Lubov. Oh, my sins. . . . I've always scattered money about without holding myself in, like a mad-woman, and I married a man who made nothing but debts. My husband died of champagne—he drank terribly—and to my misfortune, I fell in love with another man and went off with him, and just at that time—it was my first punishment, a blow that hit me right on the head—here, in the river . . . my boy was drowned, and I went away, quite away, never to return, never to see this river again. . . . I shut my eyes and ran without thinking, but *he* ran after me . . . without pity, without respect. I bought a villa near Mentone because *he* fell ill there, and for three days I knew no rest either by day or night; the sick man wore me out, and my soul dried up. And last year, when they had sold the villa to pay my debts, I went away to Paris, and there he robbed me of all I had and threw me over and went off with another woman. I tried to poison myself. . . . It was so silly, so shameful. . . . And suddenly I longed to be back in Russia, my own land, with my little girl. . . . [*Wipes her tears.*] Lord, Lord be mericiful to me, forgive me my sins! Punish me no more! [*Takes a telegram out of her pocket.*] I had this today from Paris. . . . He begs my forgiveness, he implores me to return. . . . [*Tears it up.*] Don't I hear music? [*Listens.*]

Gaev. That is our celebrated Jewish band. You remember—four violins, a flute, and a double-bass.

Lubov. So it still exists? It would be nice if they came along some evening.

Lopakhin. [*Listens.*] I can't hear. . . . [*Sings quietly.*] "For money will the Germans make a Frenchman of a Russian." [*Laughs.*] I saw such an awfully funny thing at the theater last night.

Lubov. I'm quite sure there wasn't anything at all funny. You oughtn't to go and see plays, you ought to go and look at yourself. What a grey life you lead, what a lot you talk unnecessarily.

Lopakhin. It's true. To speak the straight truth, we live a silly life. [*Pause.*] My father was a peasant, an idiot; he understood nothing, he didn't teach me, he was always drunk, and always used a stick on me. In point of fact, I'm a fool and an idiot too. I've never learned anything, my handwriting is bad, I write so that I'm quite ashamed before people, like a pig!

Lubov. You ought to get married, my friend.

Lopakhin. Yes . . . that's true.

Lubov. Why not to our Varya? She's a nice girl.

Lopakhin. Yes.

Lubov. She's quite homely in her ways, works all day, and, what matters most, she's in love with you. And you've liked her for a long time.

Lopakhin. Well? I don't mind . . . she's a nice girl. [*Pause.*]

Gaev. I'm offered a place in a bank. Six thousand roubles a year. . . . Did you hear?

Lubov. What's the matter with you? Stay where you are. . . .

[*Enter* FIERS *with an overcoat.*]

Fiers. [*To* GAEV.] Please, sir, put this on, it's damp.

Gaev. [*Putting it on.*] You're a nuisance, old man.

Fiers. It's all very well. . . . You went away this morning without telling me. [*Examining* GAEV.]

Lubov. How old you've grown, Fiers!

Fiers. I beg your pardon?

Lopakhin. She says you've grown very old!

Fiers. I've been alive a long time. They were already getting ready to marry me before your father was born. . . . [*Laughs.*] And when the Emancipation came I was already first valet. Only I didn't agree with the Emancipation and remained with my people. . . . [*Pause.*] I remember everybody was happy, but they didn't know why.

Lopakhin. It was very good for them in the old days. At any rate, they used to beat them.

Fiers. [*Not hearing.*] Rather. The peasants kept their distance from the masters and the masters kept their distance from the peasants, but now everything's all anyhow and you can't understand anything.

Gaev. Be quiet, Fiers. I've got to go to town tomorrow. I've been promised an introduction to a General who may lend me money on a bill.

Lopakhin. Nothing will come of it. And you won't pay your interest, don't you worry.

Lubov. He's talking rubbish. There's no General at all.

[*Enter* TROFIMOV, ANYA, *and* VARYA.]

Gaev. Here they are.

Anya. Mother's sitting down here.

Lubov. [*Tenderly.*] Come, come, my dears. . . . [*Embracing* ANYA *and* VARYA.] If you two only knew how much I love you. Sit down next to me, like that.

[*All sit down.*]

Lopakhin. Our eternal student is always with the ladies.

Trofimov. That's not your business.

Lopakhin. He'll soon be fifty, and he's still a student.

Trofimov. Leave off your silly jokes!

Lopakhin. Getting angry, eh, silly?

Trofimov. Shut up, can't you?

Lopakhin. [*Laughs.*] I wonder what you think of me.

Trofimov. I think, Ermolai Alexeyevitch, that you're a rich man, and you'll soon be a millionaire. Just as the wild beast which eats everything it finds is needed for changes to take place in matter, so you are needed too.

[*All laugh.*]

Varya. Better tell us something about the planets, Peter.

Lubov. No, let's go on with yesterday's talk!

Trofimov. About what?

Gaev. About the proud man.

Trofimov. Yesterday we talked for a long time but we didn't come to anything in the end. There's something mystical about the proud man, in your sense. Perhaps you are right from your point of view, but if you take the matter simply, without complicating it, then what pride can there be, what sense can there be in it, if a man is imperfectly made, physiologically speaking, if in the vast majority of cases he is coarse and stupid and deeply unhappy? We must stop admiring one another. We must work, nothing more.

Gaev. You'll die, all the same.

Trofimov. Who knows? And what does it mean—you'll die? Perhaps a man has a hundred senses, and when he dies only the five known to us are destroyed and the remaining ninety-five are left alive.

Lubov. How clever of you, Peter!

Lopakhin. [*Ironically.*] Oh, awfully!

Trofimov. The human race progresses, perfecting its powers. Everything that is unattainable now will some day be near at hand and comprehensible, but we must work, we must help with all our strength those who seek to know what fate will bring. Meanwhile in Russia only a very few of us work. The vast majority of those intellectuals whom I know seek for nothing, do nothing, and are at present incapable of hard work. They call themselves intellectuals, but they use "thou" and "thee" to their servants, they treat the peasants like animals, they learn badly, they read nothing seriously, they do absolutely nothing, about science they only talk, about art they understand little. They are all serious, they all have severe faces, they all talk about important things. They philosophize, and at the same time, the vast majority of us, ninety-nine out of a hundred, live like savages, fighting and cursing at the slightest opportunity, eating filthily, sleeping in the dirt, in stuffiness, with fleas, stinks, smells, moral filth, and so on. . . . And it's obvious that all our nice talk is only carried on to distract ourselves and others. Tell me, where are those crèches we hear so much of? and where are those reading-rooms? People only write novels about them; they don't really exist. Only dirt, vulgarity, and Asiatic plagues really exist. . . . I'm afraid, and I don't at all like serious faces; I don't like serious conversations. Let's be quiet sooner.

Lopakhin. You know, I get up at five every morning, I work from morning till evening, I am always dealing with money—my own and other people's—and I see what people are like. You've only got to begin to do anything to find out how few honest, honorable people there are. Sometimes, when I can't sleep, I think: "O Lord, you've given us huge forests, infinite fields, and endless horizons, and we living here ought really to be giants."

Lubov. You want giants, do you? . . . They're only good in stories, and even there they frighten one.

[EPIKHODOV *enters at the back of the stage playing his guitar.*]

Anya. [*Thoughtfully.*] Epikhodov's there.

Gaev. The sun's set.

Trofimov. Yes.

Gaev. [*Not loudly, as if declaiming.*] O Nature, thou art wonderful, thou shinest with eternal radiance! Oh, beautiful and indifferent one, thou whom we call mother, thou containest in thyself existence and death, thou livest and destroyest. . . .

Varya. [*Entreatingly.*] Uncle, dear!

Anya. Uncle, you're doing it again!

Trofimov. You'd better double the red into the middle.

Gaev. I'll be quiet, I'll be quiet.

[*They all sit thoughtfully. It is quiet. Only the mumbling of* FIERS *is heard. Suddenly a distant sound is heard as if from the sky, the sound of a breaking string, which dies away sadly.*]

Lubov. What's that?

Lopakhin. I don't know. It may be a bucket fallen down a well somewhere. But it's some way off.

Gaev. Or perhaps it's some bird . . . like a heron.

Trofimov. Or an owl.

Lubov. [*Shudders.*] It's unpleasant, somehow. [*A pause.*]

Fiers. Before the misfortune the same thing happened. An owl screamed and the samovar hummed without stopping.

Gaev. Before what misfortune?

Fiers. Before the Emancipation. [*A pause.*]

Lubov. You know, my friends, let's go in; it's evening now. [*To* ANYA.] You've tears in your eyes. . . . What is it, little girl? [*Embraces her.*]

Anya. It's nothing, mother.

Trofimov. Some one's coming.

[*Enter a* TRAMP *in an old white peaked cap and overcoat. He is a little drunk.*]

Tramp. Excuse me, may I go this way straight through to the station?

Gaev. You may. Go along this path.

Tramp. I thank you from the bottom of my heart. [*Hiccups.*] Lovely weather. . . . [*Declaims.*] My brother, my suffering brother. . . . Come out on the Volga, you whose groans . . . [*To* VARYA.] Mademoiselle, please give a hungry Russian thirty copecks. . . . [VARYA *screams, frightened.*]

Lopakhin. [*Angrily.*] There's manners everybody's got to keep!

Lubov. [*With a start.*] Take this . . here you are. . . . [*Feels in her purse.*] There's no silver. . . . It doesn't matter, here's gold.

Tramp. I am deeply grateful to you! [*Exit. Laughter.*]

Varya. [*Frightened.*] I'm going, I'm going. . . . Oh, little mother, at home there's nothing for the servants to eat, and you gave him gold.

Lubov. What is to be done with such a fool as I am! At home I'll give you everything I've got. Ermolai Alexeyevitch, lend me some more! . . .

Lopakhin. Very well.

Lubov. Let's go, it's time. And Varya, we've settled your affair; I congratulate you.

Varya. [*Crying.*] You shouldn't joke about this, mother.

Lopakhin. Ophelia, get thee to a nunnery.

Gaev. My hands are all trembling; I haven't played billiards for a long time.

Lopakhin. Ophelia, nymph, remember me in thine orisons.

Lubov. Come along; it'll soon be supper-time.

Varya. He did frighten me. My heart is beating hard.

Lopakhin. Let me remind you, ladies and gentlemen, on August 22 the cherry orchard will be sold. Think of that! . . . Think of that! . . .

[*All go out except* TROFIMOV *and* ANYA.]

Anya. [*Laughs.*] Thanks to the tramp who frightened Barbara, we're alone now.

Trofimov. Varya's afraid we may fall in love with each other and won't get away from us for days on end. Her narrow mind won't allow her to understand that we are above love. To escape all the petty and deceptive things which prevent our being happy and free, that is the aim and meaning of our lives. Forward! We go irresistibly on to that bright star which burns there, in the distance! Don't lag behind, friends!

Anya. [*Clapping her hands.*] How beautifully you talk! [*Pause.*] It is glorious here today!

Trofimov. Yes, the weather is wonderful.

Anya. What have you done to me, Peter? I don't love the cherry orchard as I used to. I loved it so tenderly, I thought there was no better place in the world than our orchard.

Trofimov. All Russia is our orchard. The land is great and beautiful, there are many marvellous places in it. [*Pause.*] Think, Anya, your grandfather, your great-grandfather, and all your ancestors were serf-owners, they owned living souls; and now, doesn't something human look at you from every cherry in the orchard, every leaf and every stalk? Don't you hear voices . . . ? Oh, it's awful, your orchard is terrible; and when in the evening or at night you walk through the orchard, then the old bark on the trees sheds a dim light and the old cherry-trees seem to be dreaming of all that was a hundred, two hundred years ago, and are oppressed by their heavy visions. Still, at any rate, we've left those two hundred years behind us. So far we've gained nothing at all—we don't yet know what the past is to be to us—we only philosophize, we complain that we are dull, or we drink vodka. For it's so clear that in order to begin to live in the present we must first redeem the past, and that can only be done by suffering, by strenuous, uninterrupted labor. Understand that, Anya.

Anya. The house in which we live has long ceased to be our house; I shall go away. I give you my word.

Trofimov. If you have the housekeeping keys, throw them down the well and go away. Be as free as the wind.

Anya. [*Enthusiastically.*] How nicely you said that!

Trofimov. Believe me, Anya, believe me! I'm not thirty yet, I'm young, I'm still a student, but I have undergone a great deal! I'm as hungry as the winter, I'm ill, I'm shaken. I'm as poor as a beggar, and where haven't I been—fate has tossed me everywhere! But my soul is always my own; every minute of the day and the night it is filled with unspeakable presentiments. I know that happiness is coming, Anya, I see it already. . . .

Anya. [*Thoughtful.*] The moon is rising.

[EPIKHODOV *is heard playing the same sad song on his guitar. The moon rises. Somewhere by the poplars* VARYA *is looking for* ANYA *and calling,* "Anya, where are you?"]

Trofimov. Yes, the moon has risen. [*Pause.*] There is happiness, there it comes; it comes nearer and nearer; I hear its steps already. And if we do not see it we shall not know it, but what does that matter? Others will see it!

The Voice of Varya. Anya! Where are you?

Trofimov. That's Varya again! [*Angry.*] Disgraceful!

Anya. Never mind. Let's go to the river. It's nice there.

Trofimov. Let's go. [*They go out.*]

The Voice of Varya. Anya! Anya!

CURTAIN

ACT III

A reception-room cut off from a drawing-room by an arch. Chandelier lighted.

[*A Jewish band, the one mentioned in Act II, is heard playing in the music room. Evening. In the drawing-room the grand rond is being danced. Voice of* SIMEONOV-PISCHIN, "Promenade à une paire!" *Dancers come into the reception-room; the first pair are* PISCHIN *and* CHARLOTTA IVANOVNA; *the second,* TRO-

FIMOV *and* LUBOV ANDREYEVNA; *the third,* ANYA *and the* POST-OFFICE CLERK; *the fourth,* VARYA *and the* STATION-MASTER, *and so on.* VARYA *is crying gently and wipes away her tears as she dances.* DUNYASHA *is in the last pair. They go off into the drawing-room,* PISCHIN *shouting,* "Grand rond, balancez": *and* "Les cavaliers à genou et remerciez vos dames!" FIERS, *in a dress-coat, carries a tray with seltzer-water across. Enter* PISCHIN *and* TROFIMOV *from the drawing-room.*]

Pischin. I'm full-blooded and have already had two strokes; it's hard for me to dance, but, as they say, if you're in Rome, you must do as Rome does. I've got the strength of a horse. My dead father, who liked a joke, peace to his bones, used to say, talking of our ancestors, that the ancient stock of the Simeonov-Pischins was descended from that identical horse that Caligula made a senator. . . . [*Sits.*] But the trouble is, I've no money! A hungry dog only believes in meat. [*Snores and wakes up again immediately.*] So I . . . only believe in money. . . .

Trofimov. Yes. There is something equine about your figure.

Pischin. Well . . . a horse is a fine animal . . . you can sell a horse.

[*Billiard playing can be heard in the next room.* VARYA *appears under the arch.*]

Trofimov. [*Teasing.*] Madame Lopakhin! Madame Lopakhin!

Varya. [*Angry.*] Decayed gentleman!

Trofimov. Yes, I am a decayed gentleman, and I'm proud of it!

Varya. [*Bitterly.*] We've hired the musicians, but how are they to be paid? [*Exit.*]

Trofimov. If the energy which you, in the course of your life, have spent in looking for money to pay interest had been used for something else, then, I believe, after all, you'd be able to turn everything upside down.

Pischin. Nietzsche . . . a philosopher . . . a very great, a most celebrated man . . . a man of enormous brain, says in his books that you can forge bank-notes.

Trofimov. And have you read Nietzsche?

Pischin. Well . . . Dashenka told me. Now I'm in such a position, I wouldn't mind forging them . . . I've got to pay 310 roubles the day after tomorrow . . . I've got 130 already . . . [*Feels his pockets, nervously.*] I've lost the money! The money's gone! [*Crying.*] Where's the money? [*Joyfully.*] Here it is behind the lining . . . I even began to perspire.

[*Enter* LUBOV ANDREYEVNA *and* CHARLOTTA IVANOVNA.]

Lubov. [*Humming a Caucasian dance.*] Why is Leonid away so long? What's he doing in town? [*To* DUNYASHA.] Dunyasha, give the musicians some tea.

Trofimov. Business is off, I suppose.

Lubov. And the musicians needn't have come, and we needn't have got up this ball. . . . Well, never mind. . . .

[*Sits and sings softly.*]

Charlotta. [*Gives a pack of cards to* PISCHIN.] Here's a pack of cards, think of any one card you like.

Pischin. I've thought of one.

Charlotta. Now shuffle. All right, now. Give them here, oh my dear Mr. Pischin. *Ein, zwei, drei!* Now look and you'll find it in your coat-tail pocket.

Pischin. [*Takes a card out of his coat-tail pocket.*] Eight of spades, quite right! [*Surprised.*] Think of that now!

Charlotta. [*Holds the pack of cards on the palm of her hand. To* TROFIMOV.] Now tell me quickly. What's the top card?

Trofimov. Well, the queen of spades.

Charlotta. Right! [*To* PISCHIN.] Well now? What card's on top?

Pischin. Ace of hearts.

Charlotta. Right! [*Claps her hands, the pack of cards vanishes.*] How lovely the weather is today. [*A mysterious woman's voice answers her, as if from under the floor,* "Oh yes, it's lovely weather, madam."] You are so beautiful, you are my ideal. [*Voice,* "You, madam, please me very much too."]

Station-master. [*Applauds.*] Madame ventriloquist, bravo!

Pischin. [*Surprised.*] Think of that, now! Delightful, Charlotta Ivanovna . . . I'm simply in love. . . .

Charlotta. In love? [*Shrugging her shoulders.*] Can you love? *Guter Mensch aber schlechter Musikant.*

Trofimov. [*Slaps* PISCHIN *on the shoulder.*] Oh, you horse!

Charlotta. Attention please, here's another trick. [*Takes a shawl from a chair.*] Here's a very nice plaid shawl, I'm going to sell it. . . . [*Shakes it.*] Won't anybody buy it?

Pischin. [*Astonished.*] Think of that now!

Charlotta. *Ein, zwei, drei.*

[*She quickly lifts up the shawl, which is hanging down.* ANYA *is standing behind it; she bows and runs to her mother, hugs her and runs back to the drawing-room amid general applause.*]

Lubov. [*Applauds.*] Bravo, bravo!

Charlotta. Once again! *Ein, zwei, drei!*

[*Lifts the shawl.* VARYA *stands behind it and bows.*]

Pischin. [*Astonished.*] Think of that, now.

Charlotta. The end!

[*Throws the shawl at* PISCHIN, *curtseys and runs into the drawing-room.*]

Pischin. [*Runs after her.*] Little wretch. . . . What? Would you? [*Exit.*]

Lubov. Leonid hasn't come yet. I don't understand what he's doing so long in town! Everything must be over by now. The estate must be sold; or if the sale never came off, then why does he stay away so long?

Varya. [*Tries to soothe her.*] Uncle has bought it. I'm certain of it.

Trofimov. [*Sarcastically.*] Oh, yes!

Varya. Grandmother sent him her authority for him to buy it in her name and transfer the debt to her. She's doing it for Anya. And I'm certain that God will help us and uncle will buy it.

Lubov. Grandmother sent fifteen thousand roubles from Yaroslav to buy the property in her name—she won't trust us—and that wasn't even enough to pay the interest. [*Covers her face with her hands.*] My fate will be settled today, my fate. . . .

Trofimov. [*Teasing* VARYA.] Madame Lopakhin!

Varya. [*Angry.*] Eternal student! He's already been expelled twice from the university.

Lubov. Why are you getting angry, Varya? He's teasing you about Lopakhin. Well, what of it? You can marry Lopakhin if you want to, he's a good, interesting man. . . . You needn't if you don't want to; nobody wants to force you against your will, my darling.

Varya. I do look at the matter seriously, little mother, to be quite frank. He's a good man, and I like him.

Lubov. Then marry him. I don't understand what you're waiting for.

Varya. I can't propose to him myself, little mother. People have been talking about him to me for two years now, but he either says nothing, or jokes about it. I understand. He's getting rich, he's busy, he can't bother about me. If I had some money, even a little, even only a hundred roubles, I'd throw up everything and go away. I'd go into a convent.

Trofimov. How nice!

Varya. [*To* TROFIMOV.] A student ought to have sense! [*Gently, in tears.*] How ugly you are now, Peter, how old you've grown! [*To* LUBOV ANDREYEVNA, *no longer crying.*] But I can't go on without working, little mother. I want to be doing something every minute. [*Enter* YASHA.]

Yasha. [*Nearly laughing.*] Epikhodov's broken a billiard cue! [*Exit.*]

Varya. Why is Epikhodov here? Who said he could play billiards? I don't understand these people. [*Exit.*]

Lubov. Don't tease her, Peter, you see that she's quite unhappy without that.

Trofimov. She takes too much on herself, she keeps on interfering in other people's business. The whole summer she's given no peace to me or to Anya, she's afraid we'll have a romance all to ourselves. What has it to do with her? As if I'd ever given her grounds to believe I'd stoop to such vulgarity! We are above love.

Lubov. Then I suppose I must be beneath love. [*In agitation.*] Why isn't Leonid here? If I only knew whether the estate is sold or not! The disaster seems to me so improbable that I don't know what to think, I'm all at sea . . . I may scream . . . or do something silly. Save me, Peter. Say something, say something.

Trofimov. Isn't it all the same whether the estate is sold today or isn't? It's been all up with it for a long time; there's no turning back, the path's grown over. Be calm, dear, you shouldn't deceive yourself; for once in your life at any rate you must look the truth straight in the face.

Lubov. What truth? You see where truth is, and where untruth is, but I seem to have lost my sight and see nothing. You boldly settle all important questions, but tell me, dear, isn't it because you're young, because you haven't had time to suffer till you settled a single one of your questions? You boldly look forward, isn't it because you cannot foresee or expect anything terrible, because so far life has been hidden from your young eyes? You are bolder, more honest, deeper than we are, but think only, be just a little magnanimous, and have mercy on me. I was born here, my father and mother lived here, my grandfather too, I love this house. I couldn't understand my life without that cherry orchard, and if it really must be sold, sell me with it! [*Embraces* TROFIMOV, *kisses his forehead.*] My son was drowned here. . . . [*Weeps.*] Have pity on me, good, kind man.

Trofimov. You know I sympathize with all my soul.

Lubov. Yes, but it ought to be said differently, differently. . . . [*Takes another handkerchief, a telegram falls on the floor.*] I'm so sick at heart today, you can't imagine. Here it's so noisy, my soul shakes at every sound. I shake all over, and I can't go away by myself, I'm afraid of the silence. Don't judge me harshly, Peter . . . I love you, as if you belonged to my family. I'd gladly let Anya marry you, I swear it, only, dear, you ought to work, finish your studies. You don't do anything, only fate throws you about from place to place, it's so odd. . . . Isn't it true? Yes? And you ought to do something to your beard to make it grow better. [*Laughs.*] You are funny!

Trofimov. [*Picking up telegram.*] I don't want to be a Beau Brummell.

Lubov. This telegram's from Paris. I get one every day. Yesterday and today. That wild man is ill again, he's bad again. . . . He begs for forgiveness, and implores me to come, and I really ought to go to Paris to be near him. You look severe, Peter, but what can I do, my dear, what can I do; he's ill, he's alone, unhappy, and who's to look after him, who's to keep him away from his errors, to give him his medicine punctually? And why should I conceal it and say nothing about it; I love him, that's plain, I love him, I love him. . . . That love is a stone round my neck; I'm going with it to the bottom, but I love that stone and can't live without it. [*Squeezes* TROFIMOV'S *hand.*] Don't think hardly of me, Peter, don't say anything to me, don't say . . .

Trofimov. [*Weeping.*] For God's sake forgive my speaking candidly, but that man has robbed you!

Lubov. No, no, no, you oughtn't to say that! [*Stops her ears.*]

Trofimov. But he's a wretch, you alone don't know it! He's a petty thief, a nobody. . . .

Lubov. [*Angry, but restrained.*] You're twenty-six or twenty-seven, and still a schoolboy of the second class!

Trofimov. Why not!

Lubov. You ought to be a man, at your age you ought to be able to understand those who love. And you ought to be in love yourself, you must fall in love! [*Angry.*] Yes, yes! You aren't pure, you're just a freak, a queer fellow, a funny growth. . . .

Trofimov. [*In horror.*] What is she saying?

Lubov. "I'm above love!" You're not above love, you're just what our Fiers calls a bungler. Not to have a mistress at your age!

Trofimov. [*In horror.*] This is awful. What is she saying? [*Goes quickly up into the drawing-room, clutching his head.*] It's awful . . . I can't stand it, I'll go away. [*Exit, but returns at once.*] All is over between us! [*Exit.*]

Lubov. [*Shouts after him.*] Peter, wait! Silly man, I was joking! Peter! [*Somebody is heard going out and falling downstairs noisily.* ANYA *and* VARYA *scream; laughter is heard immediately.*] What's that?

[ANYA *comes running in, laughing.*]

Anya. Peter's fallen downstairs! [*Runs out again.*]

Lubov. This Peter's a marvel.

[*The* STATION-MASTER *stands in the middle of the drawing-room and recites "The Magdalen," by Alexei Tolstoy. He is listened to, but he has only delivered a few lines when a waltz is heard from the music room, and the recitation is stopped. Everybody dances.* TROFIMOV, ANYA, VARYA, *and* LUBOV ANDREYEVNA *come in from the music room.*]

Lubov. Well, Peter . . . you pure soul . . . I beg your pardon . . . let's dance.

[*She dances with* PETER. ANYA *and* VARYA *dance.* FIERS *enters and stands his stick by a side door.* YASHA *has also come in and looks on at the dance.*]

Yasha. Well, grandfather?

Fiers. I'm not well. At our balls some time back, generals and barons and admirals used to dance, and now we send for post-office clerks and the station-master, and even they come as a favor. I'm very weak. The dead master, the grandfather, used to give everybody sealing-wax when anything was wrong. I've taken sealing-wax every day for twenty years, and more; perhaps that's why I still live.

Yasha. I'm tired of you, grandfather. [*Yawns.*] If you'd only hurry up and kick the bucket.

Fiers. Oh you . . . bungler! [*Mutters.*]

[TROFIMOV *and* LUBOV ANDREYEVNA *dance in the drawing-room, then into the reception-room.*]

Lubov. Merci. I'll sit down. [*Sits.*] I'm tired. [*Enter* ANYA.]

Anya. [*Excitedly.*] Somebody in the kitchen was saying just now that the cherry orchard was sold today.

Lubov. Sold to whom?

Anya. He didn't say to whom. He's gone mad.

[*Dances out into the drawing-room with* TROFIMOV.]

Yasha. Some old man was chattering about it a long time ago. A stranger!

Fiers. And Leonid Andreyevitch isn't here yet, he hasn't come. He's wearing a light *demi-saison* overcoat. He'll catch cold. Oh, these young fellows.

Lubov. I'll die of this. Go and find out, Yasha, to whom it's sold.

Yasha. Oh, but he's been gone a long time, the old man. [*Laughs.*]

Lubov. [*Slightly vexed.*] Why do you laugh? What are you glad about?

Yasha. Epikhodov's too funny. He's a silly man. Two-and-twenty troubles.

Lubov. Fiers, if the estate is sold, where will you go?

Fiers. I'll go wherever you order me to go.

Lubov. Why do you look like that? Are you ill? I think you ought to go to bed. . . .

Fiers. Yes . . . [*With a smile.*] I'll go to bed, and who'll hand things round and give orders without me? I've the whole house on my shoulders.

Yasha. [*To* LUBOV ANDREYEVNA.] Lubov Andreyevna! I want to ask a favor of you, if you'll be so kind! If you go to Paris again, then please take me with you. It's absolutely impossible for me to stop here. [*Looking round; in an undertone.*] What's the good of talking about it, you see for yourself that this is an uneducated country, with an immoral population, and it's so dull. The food in the kitchen is beastly, and here's this Fiers walking about mumbling various inappropriate things. Take me with you, be so kind. [*Enter* PISCHIN.]

Pischin. I come to ask for the pleasure of a little waltz, dear lady. . . . [LUBOV ANDREYEVNA *goes to him.*] But all the same, you wonderful woman, I must have 180 little roubles from you. . . . I must. . . . [*They dance.*] 180 little roubles. . . .

[*They go through into the drawing-room.*]

Yasha. [*Sings softly.*]

"Oh, will you understand
My soul's deep restlessness?"

[*In the drawing-room a figure in a gray top-hat and in baggy check trousers is waving its hands and jumping about; there are cries of "Bravo, Charlotta Ivanovna!"*]

Dunyasha. [*Stops to powder her face.*] The young mistress tells me to dance—there are a lot of gentlemen, but few ladies—and my head goes round when I dance, and my heart beats, Fiers Nicolaevitch; the post-office clerk told me something just now which made me catch my breath.

[*The music grows faint.*]

Fiers. What did he say to you?

Dunyasha. He says, "You're like a little flower."

Yasha. [*Yawns.*] Impolite. . . . [*Exit.*]

Dunyasha. Like a little flower. I'm such a delicate girl; I simply love words of tenderness.

Fiers. You'll lose your head.

[*Enter* EPIKHODOV.]

Epikhodov. You, Avdotya Fedorovna, want to see me no more than if I was some insect. [*Sighs.*] Oh, life!

Dunyasha. What do you want?

Epikhodov. Undoubtedly, perhaps, you may be right. [*Sighs.*] But, certainly, if you regard the matter from that aspect, then you, if I may say so, and you must excuse my candidness, have absolutely reduced me to a state of mind. I know my fate, every day something unfortunate happens to me, and I've grown used to it a long time ago, I even look at my fate with a smile. You gave me your word, and though I . . .

Dunyasha. Please, we'll talk later on, but leave me alone now. I'm meditating now.

[*Plays with her fan.*]

Epikhodov. Every day something unfortunate happens to me, and I, if I may so express myself, only smile, and even laugh.

[VARYA *enters from the drawing-room.*]

Varya. Haven't you gone yet, Simeon? You really have no respect for anybody. [*To* DUNYASHA.] You go away, Dunyasha. [*To* EPIKHODOV.] You play billiards and break a cue, and walk about the drawing-room as if you were a visitor!

Epikhodov. You cannot, if I may say so, call me to order.

Varya. I'm not calling you to order, I'm only telling you. You just walk about from place to place and never do your work. Goodness only knows why we keep a clerk.

Epikhodov. [*Offended.*] Whether I work, or walk about, or eat, or play billiards, is only a matter to be settled by people of understanding and my elders.

Varya. You dare to talk to me like that! [*Furious.*] You dare? You mean that I know nothing? Get out of this! This minute!

Epikhodov. [*Nervous.*] I must ask you to express yourself more delicately.

Varya. [*Beside herself.*] Get out this minute. Get out! [*He goes to the door, she follows.*] Two-and-twenty troubles! I don't want any sign of you here! I don't want to see anything of you! [EPIKHODOV *has gone out; his voice can be heard outside: "I'll make a complaint against you."*] What, coming back? [*Snatches up the stick left by* FIERS *by the door.*] Go . . . go . . . go, I'll show you. . . . Are you going? Are you going? Well, then take that.

[*She hits out as* LOPAKHIN *enters.*]

Lopakhin. Much obliged.

Varya. [*Angry but amused.*] I'm sorry.

Lopakhin. Never mind. I thank you for my pleasant reception.

Varya. It isn't worth any thanks. [*Walks away, then looks back and asks gently.*] I didn't hurt you, did I?

Lopakhin. No, not at all. There'll be an enormous bump, that's all.

Voices from the Drawing-room. Lopakhin's returned! Ermolai Alexeyevitch!

Pischin. Now we'll see what there is to see and hear what there is to hear. . . . [*Kisses* LOPAKHIN.] You smell of cognac, my dear, my soul. And we're all having a good time.

[*Enter* LUBOV ANDREYEVNA.]

Lubov. Is that you, Ermolai Alexeyevitch? Why were you so long? Where's Leonid?

Lopakhin. Leonid Andreyevitch came back with me, he's coming. . . .

Lubov. [*Excited.*] Well, what? Is it sold? Tell me?

Lopakhin. [*Confused, afraid to show his pleasure.*] The sale ended up at four o'clock. . . . We missed the train, and had to wait till half-past nine. [*Sighs heavily.*] Ooh! My head's going round a little.

[*Enter* GAEV; *in his right hand he carries things he has bought, with his left he wipes away his tears.*]

Lubov. Leon, what's happened? Leon, well? [*Impatiently, in tears.*] Quick, for the love of God. . . .

Gaev. [*Says nothing to her, only waves his hand; to* FIERS, *weeping.*] Here, take this. . . . Here are anchovies, herrings from Kertch. . . . I've had no food today. . . . I have had a time! [*The door from the billiard-room is open; the clicking of the balls is heard, and* YASHA'S *voice, "Seven, eighteen!"* GAEV'S *expression changes, he cries no more.*] I'm awfully tired. Let me change my clothes, Fiers.

[*Goes out through the drawing-room;* FIERS *after him.*]

Pischin. What happened? Come on, tell us!

Lubov. Is the cherry orchard sold?

Lopakhin. It is sold.

Lubov. Who bought it?

Lopakhin. I bought it.

[LUBOV ANDREYEVNA *is overwhelmed; she would fall if she were not standing by an armchair and a table.* VARYA *takes her keys off her belt, throws them on the floor, into the middle of the room and goes out.*]

Lopakhin. I bought it! Wait, ladies and gentlemen, please, my head's going round. I can't talk. . . . [*Laughs.*] When we got to the sale, Deriganov was there already. Leonid Andreyevitch had only fifteen thousand roubles, and Deriganov offered thirty thousand on top of the mortgage to begin with. I saw how matters were, so I grabbed hold of him and bid forty. He went up to forty-five, I offered fifty-five. That means he went up by fives and I went up by tens. . . . Well, it came to an end. I bid ninety more than the mortgage; and it stayed with me. The cherry orchard is mine now, mine! [*Roars with laughter.*] My God, my God, the cherry orchard's mine! Tell me I'm drunk, or mad, or dreaming. . . . [*Stamps his feet.*] Don't laugh at me! If my father and grandfather rose from their graves and looked at the whole affair, and saw how their Ermolai, their beaten and uneducated Ermolai, who used to run barefoot in the water, how that very Ermolai has bought an estate, which is the most beautiful thing in the world! I've bought the estate where my grandfather and my father were slaves, where they weren't even allowed into the kitchen. I'm asleep, it's only a dream, an illusion. . . . It's the fruit of imagination, wrapped in the fog of the unknown. . . . [*Picks up the keys, nicely smiling.*] She threw down the keys, she wanted to show she was no longer mistress here. . . . [*Jingles keys.*] Well, it's all one! [*Hears the band tuning up.*] Eh, musicians, play, I want to hear you! Come and look at Ermolai Lopakhin laying his axe to the cherry orchard, come and look at the trees falling! We'll build villas here, and our grandsons and great-grandsons will see a new life here. . . . Play on, music! [*The band plays.* LUBOV ANDREYEVNA *sinks into a chair and weeps bitterly.* LOPAKHIN *continues reproachfully.*] Why then, why didn't you take my advice? My poor, dear woman, you can't go back now. [*Weeps.*] Oh, if only the whole thing was done with, if only our uneven, unhappy life were changed!

Pischin. [*Takes his arm; in an undertone.*] She's crying. Let's go into the drawing-room and leave her by herself . . . come on. . . .

[*Takes his arm and leads him out.*]

Lopakhin. What's that? Bandsmen, play nicely! Go on, do just as I want you to! [*Ironically.*] The new owner, the owner of the cherry orchard is coming! [*He accidentally knocks up against a little table and nearly upsets the candelabra.*] I can pay for everything now! [*Exit with* PISCHIN.]

[*In the reception-room and the drawing-room nobody remains except* LUBOV ANDREYEVNA, *who sits huddled up and weeping bitterly. The band plays softly.* ANYA *and* TROFIMOV *come in quickly.* ANYA *goes up to her mother and goes on her knees in front of her.* TROFIMOV *stands at the drawing-room entrance.*]

ANYA. Mother! mother, are you crying?

My dear, kind, good mother, my beautiful mother, I love you! Bless you! The cherry orchard is sold, we've got it no longer, it's true, true, but don't cry, mother, you've still got your life before you, you've still your beautiful pure soul. . . . Come with me, come, dear, away from here, come! We'll plant a new garden, finer than this, and you'll see it, and you'll understand, and deep joy, gentle joy will sink into your soul, like the evening sun, and you'll smile, mother! Come, dear, let's go!

CURTAIN

ACT IV

The stage is set as for Act I. There are no curtains on the windows, no pictures; only a few pieces of furniture are left; they are piled up in a corner as if for sale. The emptiness is felt. By the door that leads out of the house and at the back of the stage, portmanteaux and travelling paraphernalia are piled up. [*The door on the left is open; the voices of* VARYA *and* ANYA *can be heard through it.* LOPAKHIN *stands and waits.* YASHA *holds a tray with little tumblers of champagne. Outside,* EPIKHODOV *is tying up a box. Voices are heard behind the stage. The peasants have come to say good-by. The voice of* GAEV *is heard: "Thank you, brothers, thank you."*]

Yasha. The common people have come to say good-by. I am of the opinion, Ermolai Alexeyevitch, that they're good people, but they don't understand very much.

[*The voices die away.* LUBOV ANDREYEVNA *and* GAEV *enter. She is not crying but is pale, and her face trembles; she can hardly speak.*]

Gaev. You gave them your purse, Luba. You can't go on like that, you can't!

Lubov. I couldn't help myself, I couldn't! [*They go out.*]

Lopakhin. [*In the doorway, looking after them.*] Please, I ask you most humbly! Just a little glass to say good-by. I didn't remember to bring any from town and I only found one bottle at the station. Please, do! [*Pause.*] Won't you really have any? [*Goes away from the door.*] If I only knew—I wouldn't have bought any. Well, I shan't drink any either. [YASHA *carefully puts the tray on a chair.*] You have a drink, Yasha, at any rate.

Yasha. To those departing! And good luck to those who stay behind! [*Drinks.*] I can assure you that this isn't real champagne.

Lopakhin. Eight roubles a bottle. [*Pause.*] It's devilish cold here.

Yasha. There are no fires today, we're going away. [*Laughs.*]

Lopakhin. What's the matter with you?

Yasha. I'm just pleased.

Lopakhin. It's October outside, but it's as sunny and as quiet as if it were summer. Good for building. [*Looking at his watch and speaking through the door.*] Ladies and gentlemen, please remember that it's only forty-seven minutes till the train goes! You must go off to the station in twenty minutes. Hurry up.

[TROFIMOV, *in an overcoat, comes in from the grounds.*]

Trofimov. I think it's time we went. The carriages are waiting. Where the devil are my goloshes? They're lost. [*Through the door.*] Anya, I can't find my goloshes! I can't!

Lopakhin. I've got to go to Kharkov. I'm going in the same train as you. I'm going to spend the whole winter in Kharkov. I've been hanging about with you people, going rusty without work. I can't live without working. I must have something to do with my hands; they hang about as if they weren't mine at all.

Trofimov. We'll go away and then you'll start again on your useful labors.

Lopakhin. Have a glass.

Trofimov. I won't.

Lopakhin. So you're off to Moscow now?

Trofimov. Yes. I'll see them into town and tomorrow I'm off to Moscow.

Lopakhin. Yes. . . . I expect the professors don't lecture nowadays; they're waiting till you turn up!

Trofimov. That's not your business.

Lopakhin. How many years have you been going to the university?

Trofimov. Think of something fresh. This is old and flat. [*Looking for his goloshes.*] You know, we may not meet each other again, so just let me give you a word of advice on parting: Don't wave your hands about! Get rid of that habit of waving them about. And then, building villas and reckoning on their residents becoming freeholders in time—that's the same thing; it's all a matter of waving your hands about. . . . Whether I want to or not, you know, I like you. You've thin, delicate fingers, like those of an artist, and you've a thin, delicate soul. . . .

Lopakhin. [*Embraces him.*] Good-by, dear fellow. Thanks for all you've said. If you want any, take some money from me for the journey.

Trofimov. Why should I? I don't want it.

Lopakhin. But you've nothing!

Trofimov. Yes, I have, thank you; I've got some for a translation. Here it is in my pocket. [*Nervously.*] But I can't find my goloshes!

Varya. [*From the other room.*] Take your rubbish away! [*Throws a pair of rubber goloshes on to the stage.*]

Trofimov. Why are you angry, Varya? H'm! These aren't my goloshes!

Lopakhin. In the spring I sowed three thousand acres of poppies, and now I've made forty thousand roubles net profit. And when my poppies were in flower, what a picture it was! So I, as I was saying, made forty thousand roubles, and I mean I'd like to lend you some, because I can afford it. Why turn up your nose at it? I'm just a simple peasant. . . .

Trofimov. Your father was a peasant, mine was a chemist, and that means absolutely nothing. [LOPAKHIN *takes out his pocket-book.*] No, no. . . . Even if you gave me twenty thousand I should refuse. I'm a free man. And everything that all you people, rich and poor, value so highly and so dearly hasn't the least influence over me; it's like a fleck of down in the wind. I can do without you, I can pass you by. I'm strong and proud. Mankind goes on to the highest truths and to the highest happiness such as is only possible on earth, and I go in the front ranks!

Lopakhin. Will you get there?

Trofimov. I will. [*Pause.*] I'll get there and show others the way.

[*Axes cutting the trees are heard in the distance.*]

Lopakhin. Well, good-by, old man. It's time to go. Here we stand pulling one another's noses, but life goes its own way all the time. When I work for a long time, and I don't get tired, then I think more easily, and I think I get to understand why I exist. And there are so many people in Russia, brother, who live for nothing at all. Still, work goes on without that. Leonid Andreyevitch, they say, has accepted a post in a bank; he will get six thousand roubles a year. . . . But he won't stand it; he's very lazy.

Anya. [*At the door.*] Mother asks if you will stop them cutting down the orchard until she has gone away.

Trofimov. Yes, really, you ought to have enough tact not to do that. [*Exit.*]

Lopakhin. All right, all right . . . yes, he's right. [*Exit.*]

Anya. Has Fiers been sent to the hospital?

Yasha. I gave the order this morning. I suppose they've sent him.

Anya. [*To* EPIKHODOV, *who crosses the room.*] Simeon Panteleyevitch, please make inquiries if Fiers has been sent to the hospital.

Yasha. [*Offended.*] I told Egor this morning. What's the use of asking ten times?

Epikhodov. The aged Fiers, in my conclusive opinion, isn't worth mending; his forefathers had better have him. I only envy him. [*Puts a trunk on a hat-box and squashes it.*] Well, of course. I thought so! [*Exit.*]

Yasha. [*Grinning.*] Two-and-twenty troubles.

Varya. [*Behind the door.*] Has Fiers been taken away to the hospital?

Anya. Yes.

Varya. Why didn't they take the letter to the doctor?

Anya. It'll have to be sent after him. [*Exit.*]

Varya. [*In the next room.*] Where's Yasha? Tell him his mother's come and wants to say good-by to him.

Yasha. [*Waving his hand*]. She'll make me lose all patience!

[DUNYASHA *has meanwhile been bustling around the luggage; now that* YASHA *is left alone, she goes up to him.*]

Dunyasha. If you only looked at me once, Yasha. You're going away, leaving me behind. . . .

[*Weeps and hugs him round the neck.*]

Yasha. What's the use of crying? [*Drinks champagne.*] In six days I'll be again in Paris. Tomorrow we get into the express and off we go. I can hardly believe it. Vive la France! It doesn't suit me here, I can't live here . . . it's no good. Well, I've seen the uncivilized world; I have had enough of it. [*Drinks champagne.*] What do you want to cry for? You behave yourself properly, and then you won't cry.

Dunyasha. Somebody's coming.

[*He bustles around the luggage, singing softly. Enter* LUBOV ANDREYEVNA, GAEV, ANYA, *and* CHARLOTTA IVANOVNA.]

Gaev. We'd better be off. There's no time

left. [*Looks at* YASHA.] Somebody smells of herring!

Lubov. We needn't get into our carriages for ten minutes. . . . [*Looks around the room.*] Good-by, dear house, old grandfather. The winter will go, the spring will come, and then you'll exist no more, you'll be pulled down. How much these walls have seen! [*Passionately kisses her daughter.*] My treasure, you're radiant, your eyes flash like two jewels! Are you happy? Very?

Anya. Very! A new life is beginning, mother!

Gaev. [*Gaily.*] Yes, really, everything's all right now. Before the cherry orchard was sold we all were excited and we suffered, and then, when the question was solved once and for all, we all calmed down, and even became cheerful. I'm a bank official now, and a financier . . . red in the middle; and you, Luba, for some reason or other, look better, there's no doubt about it.

Lubov. Yes. My nerves are better, it's true. [*She puts on her coat and hat.*] I sleep well. Take my luggage out, Yasha. It's time. [*To* ANYA.] My little girl, we'll soon see each other again. . . . I'm off to Paris. I'll live there on the money your grandmother from Yaroslav sent along to buy the estate—bless her!—though it won't last long.

Anya. You'll come back soon, soon, mother, won't you? I'll get ready, and pass the exam at the Higher School, and then I'll work and help you. We'll read all sorts of books to one another, won't we? [*Kisses her mother's hands.*] We'll read in the autumn evenings; we'll read many books, and a beautiful new world will open up before us. . . . [*Thoughtfully.*] You'll come, mother. . . .

Lubov. I'll come, my darling. [*Embraces her.*]

[*Enter* LOPAKHIN. CHARLOTTA *is singing to herself.*]

Gaev. Charlotta is happy; she sings!

Charlotta. [*Takes a bundle, looking like a wrapped-up baby.*] My little baby, bye-bye. [*The baby seems to answer, "Oua, oua!"*] Hush, my nice little boy. [*"Oua! Oua!"*] I'm so sorry for you. [*Throws the bundle back.*] So please find me a new place. I can't go on like this.

Lopakhin. We'll find one, Charlotta Ivanovna, don't you be afraid.

Gaev. Everybody's leaving us. Varya's going away . . . we've suddenly become unnecessary.

Charlotta. I've nowhere to live in town. I must go away. [*Hums.*] Never mind. [*Enter* PISCHIN.]

Lopakhin. Nature's marvel!

Pischin. [*Puffing.*] Oh, let me get my breath back. I'm fagged out. . . . My most honored, give me some water. . . .

Gaev. Come for money, what? I'm your humble servant, and I'm going out of the way of temptation. [*Exit.*]

Pischin. I haven't been here for ever so long . . . dear madam. [*To* LOPAKHIN.] You here? Glad to see you . . . man of immense brain . . . take this . . . take it. . . . [*Gives* LOPAKHIN *money.*] Four hundred roubles. . . . That leaves 840. . . .

Lopakhin. [*Shrugs his shoulders in surprise.*] As if I were dreaming. Where did you get this from?

Pischin. Stop . . . it's hot. . . . A most unexpected thing happened. Some Englishmen came along and found some white clay on my land. . . . [*To* LUBOV ANDREYEVNA.] And here's four hundred for you . . . beautiful lady. . . . [*Gives her money.*] Give you the rest later . . . [*Drinks water.*] Just now a young man in the train was saying that some great philosopher advises us all to jump off roofs. "Jump!" he says, and that's all. [*Astonished.*] To think of that, now! More water!

Lopakhin. Who were these Englishmen?

Pischin. I've leased off the land with the clay to them for twenty-four years. . . . Now, excuse me, I've no time. . . . I must run off. . . . I must go to Znoikov and to Kardamonov . . . I owe them all money. . . . [*Drinks.*] Good-by. I'll come in on Thursday.

Lubov. We're just off to town, and to-morrow I go abroad.

Pischin. [*Agitated.*] What? Why to town? I see furniture . . . trunks. . . . Well, never mind. [*Crying.*] Never mind. These Englishmen are men of immense intellect. . . . Never mind. . . . Be happy . . . God will help you. . . . Never mind. . . . Everything in this world comes to an end. . . . [*Kisses* LUBOV ANDREYEVNA'S *hand.*] And if you should happen to hear that my end has come, just remember this old . . . horse and say: "There was one such and such a Simeonov-Pischin, God bless his soul. . . ." Wonderful weather . . . yes. . . . [*Exit deeply moved, but returns at once and says in the door.*] Dashenka sent her love. [*Exit.*]

Lubov. Now we can go. I've two anxieties, though. The first is poor Fiers. [*Looks at her watch.*] We've still five minutes. . . .

Anya. Mother, Fiers has already been sent to the hospital. Yasha sent him off this morning.

Lubov. The second is Varya. She's used to getting up early and to work, and now she's no work to do she's like a fish out of water. She's grown thin and pale, and she cries, poor thing. . . . [*Pause.*] You know very well, Ermolai Alexeyevitch, that I used to hope to marry her to you, and I suppose you are going to marry somebody? [*Whispers to* ANYA, *who nods to* CHARLOTTA, *and they both go out.*] She loves you, she's your sort, and I don't understand, I really don't, why you seem to be keeping away from each other. I don't understand!

Lopakhin. To tell the truth, I don't understand it myself. It's all so strange. . . . If there's still time, I'll be ready at once. . . . Let's get it over, once and for all; I don't feel as if I could ever propose to her without you.

Lubov. Excellent. It'll only take a minute. I'll call her.

Lopakhin. The champagne's very appropriate. [*Looking at the tumblers.*] They're empty, somebody's already drunk them. [YASHA *coughs.*] I call that licking it up. . . .

Lubov. [*Animated.*] Excellent. We'll go out. Yasha, allez. I'll call her in. . . . [*At the door.*] Varya, leave that and come here. Come! [*Exit with* YASHA.]

Lopakhin. [*Looks at his watch.*] Yes. . . . [*Pause.*]

[*There is a restrained laugh behind the door, a whisper, then* VARYA *comes in.*]

Varya. [*Looking at the luggage in silence.*] I can't seem to find it. . . .

Lopakhin. What are you looking for?

Varya. I packed it myself and I don't remember. [*Pause.*]

Lopakhin. Where are you going to now, Barbara Mihailovna?

Varya. I? To the Ragulins. . . . I've got an agreement to go and look after their house . . . as housekeeper or something.

Lopakhin. Is that at Yashnevo? It's about fifty miles. [*Pause.*] So life in this house is finished now. . . .

Varya. [*Looking at the luggage.*] Where is it? . . . perhaps I've put it away in the trunk. . . . Yes, there'll be no more life in this house. . . .

Lopakhin. And I'm off to Kharkov at once . . . by this train. I've a lot of business on hand. I'm leaving Epikhodov here . . . I've taken him on.

Varya. Well, well!

Lopakhin. Last year at this time the snow was already falling, if you remember, and now it's nice and sunny. Only it's rather cold. . . . There's three degrees of frost.

Varya. I didn't look. [*Pause.*] And our thermometer's broken. . . . [*Pause.*]

Voice at the Door. Ermolai Alexeyevitch!

Lopakhin. [*As if he has long been waiting to be called.*] This minute. [*Exit quickly.*]

[VARYA, *sitting on the floor, puts her face on a bundle of clothes and weeps gently. The door opens.* LUBOV ANDREYEVNA *enters carefully.*]

Lubov. Well? [*Pause.*] We must go.

Varya. [*Not crying now, wipes her eyes.*] Yes, it's quite time, little mother. I'll get to the Ragulins today, if I don't miss the train. . . .

Lubov. [*At the door.*] Anya, put on your things. [*Enter* ANYA, *then* GAEV, CHARLOTTA IVANOVNA. GAEV *wears a warm overcoat with a cape. A servant and drivers come in.* EPIKHODOV *bustles around the luggage.*] Now we can go away.

Anya. [*Joyfully.*] Away!

Gaev. My friends, my dear friends! Can I be silent, in leaving this house for evermore?—can I restrain myself, in saying farewell, from expressing those feelings which now fill my whole being . . . ?

Anya. [*Imploringly.*] Uncle!

Varya. Uncle, you shouldn't!

Gaev. [*Stupidly.*] Double the red into the middle. . . . I'll be quiet.

[*Enter* TROFIMOV, *then* LOPAKHIN.]

Trofimov. Well, it's time to be off.

Lopakhin. Epikhodov, my coat!

Lubov. I'll sit here one more minute. It's as if I'd never really noticed what the walls and ceilings of this house were like, and now I look at them greedily, with such tender love. . . .

Gaev. I remember, when I was six years old, on Trinity Sunday, I sat at this window and looked and saw my father going to church. . . .

Lubov. Have all the things been taken away?

Lopakhin. Yes, all, I think. [*To* EPIKHODOV, *putting on his coat.*] You see that everything's quite straight, Epikhodov.

Epikhodov. [*Hoarsely.*] You may depend upon me, Ermolai Alexeyevitch!

Lopakhin. What's the matter with your voice?

Epikhodov. I swallowed something just now; I was having a drink of water.

Yasha. [*Suspiciously.*] What manners. . . .

Lubov. We go away, and not a soul remains behind.

Lopakhin. Till the spring.

Varya. [*Drags an umbrella out of a bundle, and seems to be waving it about.* LOPAKHIN *appears to be frightened.*] What are you doing? . . . I never thought . . .

Trofimov. Come along, let's take our seats . . . it's time! The train will be in directly.

Varya. Peter, here they are, your goloshes, by that trunk. [*In tears.*] And how old and dirty they are. . . .

Trofimov. [*Putting them on.*] Come on!

Gaev. [*Deeply moved, nearly crying.*] The train . . . the station. . . . Cross in the middle, a white double in the corner. . . .

Lubov. Let's go!

Lopakhin. Are you all here? There's nobody else? [*Locks the side-door on the left.*] There's a lot of things in there. I must lock them up. Come!

Anya. Good-by, home! Good-by, old life!

Trofimov. Welcome, new life.

[*Exit with* ANYA.]

[VARYA *looks round the room and goes out slowly.* YASHA *and* CHARLOTTA, *with her little dog, go out.*]

Lopakhin. Till the spring then! Come on . . . till we meet again! [*Exit.*]

[LUBOV ANDREYEVNA *and* GAEV *are left alone. They might almost have been waiting for that. They fall into each other's arms and sob restrainedly and quietly, fearing that somebody might hear them.*]

Gaev. [*In despair.*] My sister, my sister. . . .

Lubov. My dear, my gentle, beautiful orchard! My life, my youth, my happiness, good-by! Good-by!

Anya's Voice. [*Gaily.*] Mother!

Trofimov's Voice. [*Gaily, excited.*] Coo-ee!

Lubov. To look at the walls and the windows for the last time. . . . My dead mother used to like to walk about this room. . . .

Gaev. My sister, my sister!

Anya's Voice. Mother!

Trofimov's Voice. Coo-ee!

Lubov. We're coming! [*They go out.*]

[*The stage is empty. The sound of keys being turned in the locks is heard, and then the noise of the carriages going away. It is quiet. Then the sound of an axe against the trees is heard in the silence sadly and by itself. Steps are heard.* FIERS *comes in from the door on the right. He is dressed as usual, in a short jacket and white waistcoat; slippers on his feet. He is ill. He goes to the door and tries the handle.*]

Fiers. It's locked. They've gone away. [*Sits on a sofa.*] They've forgotten about me. . . . Never mind, I'll sit here. . . . And Leonid Andreyevitch will have gone in a light overcoat instead of putting on his fur coat. . . . [*Sighs anxiously.*] I didn't see. . . . Oh, these young people! [*Mumbles something that cannot be understood.*] Life's gone on as if I'd never lived. [*Lying down.*] I'll lie down. . . . You've no strength left in you, nothing left at all. . . . Oh, you . . . bungler!

[*He lies without moving. The distant sound is heard, as if from the sky, of a breaking string, dying away sadly. Silence follows it, and only the sound is heard, some way away in the orchard, of the axe falling on the trees.*]

CURTAIN

HE WHO GETS SLAPPED*

By

LEONID ANDREYEV

Translated by GREGORY ZILBOORG

ANDREYEV LIVED IN TURBULENCE ALL HIS life though most of it he generated himself. Through early poverty, sudden success, three attempts at suicide, frequent intemperance, involvement in both revolutionary and anti-revolutionary activity, two happy marriages, severe and almost continuous illness, through praise and persecution, he seems always to have been dashing himself against life and recoiling bruised. His thought is generally bitter and pessimistic, and at the end of his life, hating the New Russia of the Bolsheviks, from which he was outcast, and feeling that his powers had waned, he had completely lost faith in mankind and in himself.

Thus most of his plays are tragedies or satires. He despised realism and thought it was choking the theater to death. His dramatic theory was very close to Maeterlinck's (see the introduction to *Pélléas and Mélisande*). He says:

"Does the theater need action on the stage in its accepted form of treatment and movement, the form which is not only accepted by all theaters, but declared absolutely indispensable to its salvation? I permit myself to reply to this heretic question, No! Such action is not necessary, inasmuch as life itself, in its more dramatic and tragic moments, departs ever further from outward action, only to go into the depths of the soul, into that quiet and internal immobility of living experience, the intellect."

Andreyev then cites as instances the life of Benvenuto Cellini, all outward action, as a hero of the past, and that of Nietzsche, all inward, of the intellect, as a hero of the present. He continues:

"Life has gone within, and the stage has remained outside. Life has become psychological, if one may express himself so, has become aligned with primitive fears. Along with the everlasting heroes of the drama, love and hunger, comes a new hero, the intellect. Neither love, nor hunger, nor ambition: Thought, human thought, with all its sufferings, joys, and struggles—there is the true hero of contemporary life!"

So Andreyev, as is plain in *He Who Gets Slapped,* is a symbolist, like Maeterlinck. Satisfactory expression of the life of the soul is difficult in any other mode. This play's symbolism, however, is scarcely complete. It may be guessed that HE represents Intellect, mocking the vulgar many through their mockery of him; that Consuelo represents Beauty, the Baron coarse acquisitiveness, the Count shrewd commercialism asserting a spurious fatherhood of Beauty, the Prince similarly spurious pretence to the powers of Intellect. But it is also apparent that the symbolism does not work out with perfect precision. Now and then we must take these people only as real and not as symbols. Intellect, for instance, might possibly prefer slaying Beauty to permitting her to become a mere possession; but HE and Consuelo and the Baron die as real persons die. Yet even at that point Andreyev gives us another twist in the direction of the symbols by referring to the Russian superstition that the first lover of a woman to die after her will possess her in the other world.

The circus characters, though they show occasional gleams of symbol value, notably Zinida and Bezano, seem rather to be used to give stir and life to the scene. The play's success on the stage is certainly due to its poetry and movement and the spectacle the ensemble provides, rather than to whatever allegory Andreyev may have intended.

He Who Gets Slapped was produced by the Moscow Dramatic Theatre in 1915; in America by The Theatre Guild in 1922; and in London as *The Painted Laugh* in 1921; and under the original title in 1927.

LEONID ANDREYEV

Born 1871, Orel, Russia.
University of Petrograd. Degree in law from the University of Moscow, 1897.
1897, Began the practice of journalism as court reporter.
1898, First published short story wins friendship of Gorki.
1907, *The Life of Man* produced. His earlier plays had been forbidden production as politically subversive, though they were permitted to be published.
Died 1919.

PLAYS

1905 *To the Stars.* 1906 *Savva.* 1906 *The Life of Man.* 1907 *King Hunger.* 1908 *The Black Maskers.* 1908 *Days of Our Life* (not translated). 1908 *Love of One's Neighbor* (one act, also translated as *The Dear Departing*). 1908 *The Bat* (one act, not translated). 1909 *Anathema.* 1909 *Anfisa* (not translated). 1910 *Gaudeamus* (not translated). 1911 *The Ocean* (not translated). 1912 *Honor* (not translated). 1912 *The Sabine Women* (also translated as *The Pretty Sabine Women*). 1912 *Professor Storitsyn.* 1912 *Katerina* (also translated as *Yekaterina Ivanovna*). 1913 *Thou Shalt Not Kill* (not translated). 1914 *Thought* (not translated). 1914 *An Incident* (one act) 1914 *The Parrot* (one act, not translated). 1914 *The Sorrows of Belgium.* 1914 *Youth* (not translated). 1915 *He Who Gets Slapped* (also translated as *The Painted Laugh*). 1916 *Dear Phantoms* (not translated). 1917 *Requiem* (not translated). 1922 *The Waltz of the Dogs* (written 1914). 1923 *Samson in Chains* (written 1914).

WRITING ABOUT THE DRAMA

Letters on the Theatre. 1914. (See *The New York Times*, 5 October, 1919, iv:3:1. and 19 October, 1919, viii:5:1.)

HE WHO GETS SLAPPED

Characters

CONSUELO, *a bareback rider in a circus. Billed as "The Bareback Tango Queen."*
MANCINI, *Consuelo's father.*
HE, *a clown in Briquet's circus. Billed as "HE Who Gets Slapped."*
BRIQUET, *Manager of the circus* (LOUIS).
ZINIDA, *a lion tamer, Briquet's wife.*
ALFRED BEZANO, *a bareback rider.*
A GENTLEMAN.
BARON REGNARD.
JACKSON, *a clown* (JIM).
TILLY, } *musical clowns.*
POLLY, }
THOMAS, ANGELICA, *and other actors and actresses of Briquet's circus.*

The action takes place in one of the large cities of France.

ACT I

A very large, rather dirty room, with white-washed walls. To the left, in a niche, is a window, the only outside window in the room, opening on a court-yard. The light from it is so dim that even by day the electricity has to be turned on.

At the very top of the centre-back wall is a row of small dusty windows. They open on the circus hall. At night, when the performance is going on, a bright light shines through. By day they are dark. In the same wall is a large white door, reached by two stone steps, and nailed fast.

On the right, almost in the corner, is a high, wide, arched doorway which leads to the stables and the ring. By day it opens into pale darkness, at night into pale light.

The room is used for many purposes. It is the office of "PAPA" BRIQUET, *manager of the circus; here he keeps his little desk. It is the cloak-room of some of the actors. It is also the room where the cast gathers between calls, during rehearsals or performances. Again, it is a check-room for used circus property, such as gilt armchairs, scenery for pantomimes, and other wares of the circus household. The walls are covered with circus announcements and glaring posters.*

The time is morning. In the circus hall a rehearsal is going on, and preparations are being made for the evening performance.

[*As the curtain goes up, the cracking whip and the shouts of the riding-master are heard from the ring. The stage is empty for a few seconds, then enter* TILLY *and* POLLY, *the musical clowns, practising a new march. Playing on tiny pipes, they step from the dark doorway to the window. Their music is agreeable to the ear, but small, mincing, artificially clown-like, like their mincing steps; they wear jackets and resemble each other; same smooth-shaven face, same height;* TILLY, *the younger, has a scarf around his neck; both have their derbies on the backs of their heads.* TILLY *glances through the window, then they turn about, still marching.*]

Polly. [*Interrupting the march.*] Stop, you're out again! Now, listen—[*He stands close to* TILLY *and plays into his face.* TILLY *absent-mindedly listens, scratching his nose.*] There! Come on now!

[*They resume their music and marching. As they reach the door they meet the manager and* MANCINI; *the latter walks behind the manager, and is gnawing at the knob of his gold-mounted cane.* COUNT MANCINI *is tall and slight. The seams of his clothes are worn and he keeps his coat buttoned tight. He assumes extremely graceful manners, takes affected poses, and has a special fondness for toying with his cane, with aristocratic stylishness. When he laughs, which happens often, his thin sharp face takes on a marked resemblance to a satyr. The manager,* "PAPA" BRIQUET, *is a stout quiet man of average height. His bearing is hesitant. The clowns make room for the gentlemen. The manager looks questioningly at the older man.*]

Polly. [*With an affected accent.*] Our moosic for the pantomime! The March of the Ants!

Briquet. Ha! Yes!

[*The gentlemen walk in. The clowns resume their music,* POLLY *marching on, then turning, the younger following.*]

Polly. Papa Briquet, Jack is working very badly today.

Briquet. What's the matter with him?

Polly. He has a sore throat. You'd better take a look at him.

Briquet. All right. Come on, Jack. Open your mouth! Wider—wider. [*Turns clown's face to the light near the window and examines him closely and seriously.*] Just smear it with iodine.

Polly. I told him so. I said it was nothing! Oh! Come on.

[*They go away playing, marching, practising their funny mincing steps. The manager sits down.* MANCINI *strikes a pose by the wall, smiling ironically.*]

Mancini. So. You give them medical treatment, too! Look out, Papa Briquet, you have no license.

Briquet. Just a little advice. They're all so afraid for their lives.

Mancini. His throat is simply burnt with whiskey. These two fellows get drunk every night. I am amazed, Papa Briquet, to see you pay so little attention to their morals. [*He laughs.*]

Briquet. You make me sick, Mancini.

Mancini. Count Mancini is at your service!

Briquet. You make me sick, Count Mancini. You poke your nose into everything, you disturb the artists in their work. Some day you'll get a thrashing, and I warn you that I shan't interfere.

Mancini. As a man of superior associations and education I cannot be expected to treat your actors as my equals! What more can you ask, Briquet? You see that I do you the honor of speaking with you quite familiarly, quite simply.

Briquet. Ha! ha! ha! [*Slightly threatening.*] Really!——

Mancini. Never mind my joke. What if they did dare attack me—ever seen this, Briquet? [*He draws a stiletto out of his cane and advances it silently.*] Useful little thing. By the way, you have no idea of the discovery I made yesterday in a suburb. Such a girl! [*Laughs.*] Oh, well! all right, all right—I know you don't like that sort of sport. But look here, you must give me a hundred francs!

Briquet. Not a sou.

Mancini. Then I'll take away Consuelo —that's all——

Briquet. Your daily threat!

Mancini. Yes, my threat! And you would do the same, if you were as shamefully hard up as I am. Now look here, you know as well as I do that I have to live up to my name somehow, keep up the family reputation. Just because the tide of ill-fortune which struck my ancestors compelled me to make my daughter, the Countess Veronica, a bareback rider—to keep us from starving—do you understand—you heartless idiot!

Briquet. You chase the girls too much! Some day you'll land in jail, Mancini!

Mancini. In jail! Oh, no! Why, I have to uphold our *name,* the splendor of my family [*laughs*], haven't I? The Mancinis are known all over Italy for their love of girls —just girls! Is it my fault if I must pay such crazy prices for what my ancestors got free of charge? You're nothing but an ass, a *parvenu* ass. How can you understand Family Traditions? I don't drink—I stopped playing cards after that accident—no, you need not smile. Now if I give up the girls, what will be left of Mancini? Only a coat of arms, that's all—— In the name of family traditions, give me a hundred francs!

Briquet. I told you no, I won't.

Mancini. You know that I leave half of the salary for Consuelo—but—perhaps you think I do not love my child—my only daughter, all that remains to me as a memory of her sainted mother—what cruelty!

[*Pretends to cry, wipes his eyes with a small and dirty lace handkerchief, embroidered with a coronet.*]

Briquet. Why don't you say, rather, that she is foolish enough to give you half her salary? You make me sick——

[*Enter* ZINIDA, *the lion tamer; burningly beautiful, her self-confident, commanding gestures at first glance give an impression of languor. She is* BRIQUET'S *unmarried wife.*]

Zinida. [*To* MANCINI.] Good morning.

Mancini. Madame Zinida! This barbarian, this brute may pierce me with his dagger, but I cannot control the expression of my love! [*Kneels facetiously before her.*] Madame! Count Mancini has the honor of asking you to be his wife. . . .

Zinida. [*To* BRIQUET.] Money?

Briquet. Yes.

Zinida. Don't give him any.

[*Sits down wearily on a torn sofa, shuts her eyes.* MANCINI *gets up and wipes his knees.*]

Mancini. Duchess! Don't be cruel. I am no lion, no tiger, no savage beast which you are accustomed to tame. I am merely a poor domestic animal, who wants, miaow, miaow, a little green grass.

Zinida. [*Without opening her eyes.*] Jim tells me you have a teacher for Consuelo. What for?

Mancini. The solicitude of a father, duchess, the solicitude and the tireless anxiety of a loving heart. The extreme misfortunes of our family, when I was a child, have left some flaws in her education. Friends, the daughter of Count Mancini, Countess Veronica, can barely read! Is that admissible? And you, Briquet, heartless brute, you still ask why I need money!

Zinida. Artful!

Briquet. What are you teaching her?

Mancini. Everything. A student had been giving her lessons, but I threw him out yesterday. He had the nerve to fall in love with Consuelo and stood there miaowing at the door like a cat. Everything, Briquet, that you don't know—literature, mythology, orthography——

[*Two young* ACTRESSES *appear, with small fur coats thrown over their light dresses. They are tired and sit down in the corner.*]

Mancini. I do not wish my daughter——

Zinida. Artful!

Briquet. You are stupid, Mancini. What do you do it for? [*In a didactic tone.*] You are fearfully stupid, Mancini. Why does she need to learn? Since she is here she need never know anything about that life. Don't you understand? What is geography? If I were the government I would forbid artists to read books. Let them read the posters, that's enough.

[*During* BRIQUET'S *speech, the two* CLOWNS *and another* ACTOR *enter. They sit down wearily.*]

Briquet. Right now, your Consuelo is an excellent artist, but just as soon as you teach her mythology, and she begins to read, she'll become a nuisance, she'll be corrupted, and then she'll go and poison herself. I know those books, I've read 'em myself. All they teach is corruption, and how to kill oneself.

First Actress. I love the novels that come out in the newspaper.

Briquet. That shows what a foolish girl you are. You'll be done for in no time. Believe me, my friends, we must forget entirely what is happening out there. How can we understand all that goes on there?

Mancini. You are an enemy of enlightenment, you are an obscurantist, Briquet.

Briquet. And you are stupid. You are from out there. What has it taught you? [*The actors laugh.*] If you'd been born in a circus as I was, you'd *know* something. Enlightenment is plain nonsense—nothing else. Ask Zinida. She knows everything they teach out there—geography, mythology—— Does it make her any happier? You tell them, dear.

Zinida. Leave me alone, Louis.

Mancini. [*Angrily.*] Oh! Go to the devil! When I listen to your asinine philosophy, I'd like to skin you for more than a paltry hundred francs—for two hundred—for a thousand. Great God! What an ass of a manager! Yes, right before every one of them I want to say that you are a stingy old skinflint—that you pay starvation wages. I'll make you give Consuelo a raise of a hundred francs. Listen, all you honest vagabonds, tell me—who is it draws the crowd that fills the circus every night? You? A couple of musical donkeys! Tigers, lions? Nobody cares for those hungry cats!

Zinida. Leave the tigers alone.

Mancini. Beg your pardon, Zinida. I did not mean to hurt your feelings—honestly. I really marvel at your furious audacity—at your grace—you are a heroine—I kiss your tiny hands. But what do they understand about heroism? [*An orchestra softly plays the Tango in the circus. He continues with enthusiasm.*] Hear! hear! Now tell me, honest vagabonds, who but Consuelo and Bezano draws the crowds! That Tango on horseback—it is—it is—— Oh, the devil! Even his fatuousness the Pope could not withstand its lure.

Polly. True! It's a great trick—wasn't the idea Bezano's?

Mancini. Idea! Idea! The lad's in love, like a cat—that's the idea. What's the good of an idea without a woman! You wouldn't dance very far with your idea alone, eh, Papa Briquet?

Briquet. We have a contract.

Mancini. Such base formalities.

Zinida. Give him ten francs and let him go.

Mancini. Ten! Never! *Fifteen!* Don't be stubborn, Papa. For the traditions of my house—twenty. I swear—on my honor—I can't do with less. [BRIQUET *hands him twenty francs. Nonchalantly.*] *Merci.* Thanks.

Zinida. Why don't you take it from your baron?

Mancini. [*Raising his eyebrows haughtily, quite indignant.*] From the Baron? Woman! who do you think I am that I should be beholden to a stranger?

Zinida. You're plotting something artful. I know you very little, but I guess you're an awful scoundrel.

Mancini. [*Laughs.*] Such an insult from such beautiful lips.

[*Enter an* ATHLETE.]

Athlete. Papa Briquet, there's a gentleman from beyond the grave asking for you.

Actress. A ghost?

Athlete. No. He seems alive. Did you ever see a drunken ghost?

Briquet. If he's drunk, tell him I'm out, Thomas. Does he want to see me or the Count?

Athlete. No, you. Maybe he's not drunk, but just a ghost.

Mancini. [*Draws himself together, puffs up.*] A society man?

Athlete. Yes. I'll tell him to come in.

[*One hears the whip cracking in the ring. The Tango sounds very low and distant—then comes nearer—louder. Silence.*]

Briquet. [*Touching* ZINIDA'S *arm.*] Tired?

Zinida. [*Drawing back a little.*] No.

Polly. Your red lion is nervous today, Zinida!

Zinida. You shouldn't tease him.

Polly. I played a melody from *Traviata* for him. And he sang with me. Wouldn't that be a good trick to stage, Papa Briquet?

[THOMAS *brings in* THE GENTLEMAN, *points out the manager, and goes heavily away.* THE GENTLEMAN *is not young, and he is ugly, but his rather strange face is bold and lively. He wears an expensive overcoat, with a fur collar, and holds his hat and gloves in his hand.*]

Gentleman. [*Bowing and smiling.*] Have I the pleasure of addressing the manager?

Briquet. Yes. Won't you sit down, please? Tilly, bring a chair.

Gentleman. Oh! Don't trouble. [*Looks around.*] These are your artists? Very glad——

Mancini. [*Straightening and bowing slightly.*] Count Mancini.

Gentleman. [*Surprised.*] Count?

Briquet. [*Indignantly.*] Yes, Count. And whom have I the honor of——

Gentleman. I don't quite know myself—yet. As a rule you choose your own names, don't you? I have not chosen yet. Later you might advise me about it. I have an idea already, but I am afraid it sounds too much like literature—you know.

Briquet. Literature?

Gentleman. Yes! Too sophisticated. [*They all look surprised.*] I presume these two gentlemen are clowns? I am so glad. May I shake hands with them?

[*Stands up and shakes hands with* CLOWNS, *who make silly faces.*]

Briquet. Excuse me—but what can I do for you?

Gentleman. [*With the same pleasant, confident smile.*] Oh. You do something for me? No. I want to do something for you, Papa Briquet.

Briquet. Papa Briquet? But you don't look like——

Gentleman. [*Reassuringly.*] It's all right. I shall become "like." These two gentlemen just made remarkable faces. Would you like to see me imitate them? Look!

[*He makes the same silly faces as the* CLOWNS.]

Briquet. Yes! [*Involuntarily.*] You are not drunk, sir?

Gentleman. No. I don't drink as a rule. Do I look drunk?

Polly. A little.

Gentleman. No—I don't drink. It is a peculiarity of my talent.

Briquet. [*Familiarly.*] Where did you work before? Juggler?

Gentleman. No. But I am glad you feel in me a comrade, Papa Briquet. Unfortunately I am not a juggler, and have worked nowhere—I am—just so.

Mancini. But you look like a society man.

Gentleman. Oh, you flatter me, Count. I am just so.

Briquet. Well, what do you want? You see I am obliged to tell you that everything is taken.

Gentleman. That's immaterial. I want to be a clown, if you will allow me.

[*Some of the* ACTORS *smile.* BRIQUET *begins to grow angry.*]

Briquet. But what can you do? You're asking too much. What can you do?

Gentleman. Why! Nothing! Isn't that funny! I can't do a thing.

Briquet. No, it's not funny. Any scoundrel knows that much.

Gentleman. [*Rather helpless, but still smiling and looking around.*] We can invent something——

Briquet. [*Ironically.*] From literature?

[*The clown* JACKSON *enters slowly without being noticed by the others. He stands behind the* GENTLEMAN.]

Gentleman. Yes, one can find something literary, too. A nice little speech for instance on, let's say, a religious topic. Something like a debate among the clowns.

Briquet. A debate! The devil! This is no academy.

Gentleman. [*Sadly.*] I am very sorry. Something else then. Perhaps a joke about the creation of the world and its rulers?

Briquet. What about the police? No, no —nothing like that!

Jackson. [*Coming forward.*] The rulers of the world? You don't like them. I don't either. Shake.

Briquet. [*Introducing.*] Our chief clown, the famous Jackson.

Gentleman. [*Enthusiastically.*] Great heavens—you! Allow me to shake hands with you heartily! You, with your genius, you have given me so much joy!

Jackson. I'm glad indeed!

Briquet. [*Shrugs his shoulders; to* JACKSON.] He wants to be a clown! Look him over, Jim.

[JACKSON *makes a motion at which* THE GENTLEMAN *hurriedly removes his coat and throws it on a chair. He is ready for the examination.* JACKSON *turns him round, looking him over critically.*]

Jackson. Clown? H'm! Turn round then. Clown? Yes? Now smile. Wider—broader —do you call that a smile? So—that's better. There is something, yes—but for full developments—— [*Sadly.*] Probably you can't even turn a somersault!

Gentleman. [*Sighs.*] No.

Jackson. How old are you?

Gentleman. Thirty-nine. Too late?

[JACKSON *moves away with a whistle. There is a silence.*]

Zinida. [*Softly.*] Take him.

Briquet. [*Indignant.*] What the hell shall I do with him if he doesn't know a thing? He's drunk.

Gentleman. Honestly, I am not. Thank you for your support, Madame. Are you not the famous Zinida, the lion tamer, whose regal beauty and audacity——

Zinida. Yes. But I do not like flattery.

Gentleman. It is not flattery.

Mancini. You are evidently not accustomed to good society, my dear. Flattery? This gentleman expresses his admiration in sincere and beautiful words—and you—you are not educated, Zinida. As for myself——

[*Enter* CONSUELO *and* BEZANO *in circus costume.*]

Consuelo. You here, Daddy?

Mancini. Yes, my child. You are not tired? [*Kisses her on the forehead.*] My daughter, sir, Countess Veronica. Known on the stage as Consuelo, The Bareback Tango Queen. Did you ever see her?

Gentleman. I have enjoyed her work. It is marvellous!

Mancini. Yes! Of course. Everyone admits it. And how do you like the name Consuelo? I took it from the novel of George Sand. It means "Consolation."

Gentleman. What a wonderful knowledge of books!

Mancini. A small thing. Despite your strange intention, I can see, sir, that you are a gentleman. My peer! Let me explain to you, that only the strange and fatal misfortunes of our ancient family—*"sic transit gloria mundi,"* sir.

Consuelo. It's a bore, Daddy—— Where's my handkerchief, Alfred?

Bezano. Here it is.

Consuelo. [*Showing the handkerchief to* THE GENTLEMAN.] Genuine Venetian. Do you like it?

Gentleman. [*Again bowing.*] My eyes are dazzled, how beautiful! Papa Briquet, the more I look around me the more I want to stay with you. [*Makes the face of a simpleton.*] On the one hand a count, on the other——

Jackson. [*Nods approval.*] That's not bad. Look here, think a bit—find something. Everyone here thinks for himself.

[*Silence.* THE GENTLEMAN *stands with a finger on his forehead, thinking.*]

Gentleman. Find something—find something . . . Eureka!

Polly. That means *found.* Come!

Gentleman. Eureka—— I shall be, among you, he who gets slapped.

[*General laughter. Even* BRIQUET *smiles.*]

Gentleman. [*Looks at them smiling.*] You see I made even you laugh—is that easy?

[*All grow serious.* POLLY *sighs.*]

Tilly. No, it's not easy. Did you laugh, Polly?

Polly. Sure, a lot. Did you?

Tilly. I did.

[*Imitating an instrument, he plays with his lips a melody at once sad and gay.*]

Jackson. "HE Who Gets Slapped," that's not bad.

Gentleman. It's not, is it? I rather like it myself. It suits my talent. And comrades, I have even found a name—you'll call me "HE." Is that all right?

Jackson. [*Thinking.*] "HE"—Not bad.

Consuelo. [*In a singing, melodic voice.*] "HE" is so funny—"HE"—like a dog. Daddy, are there such dogs?

[JACKSON *suddenly gives a circus slap to* THE GENTLEMAN. HE *steps back and grows pale.*]

Gentleman. What!

[*General laughter covers his exclamation.*]

Jackson. HE Who Gets Slapped. Or didn't you get it?

Polly. [*Comically.*] He says he wants more——

[THE GENTLEMAN *smiles, rubbing his cheek.*]

Gentleman. So sudden.—Without waiting. —How funny—you didn't hurt me, and yet my cheek burns.

[*Again there is loud laughter. The* CLOWNS *cackle like ducks, hens, cocks; they bark.* ZINIDA *says something to* BRIQUET, *casts a glance toward* BEZANO, *and goes out.* MANCINI *assumes a bored air and looks at his watch. The two* ACTRESSES *go out.*]

Jackson. Take him, Papa Briquet—he will push us.

Mancini. [*Again looking at his watch.*] But bear in mind, that Papa Briquet is as close as Harpagon. If you expect to get good money here you are mistaken. [HE *laughs.*] A slap? What's a slap? Worth only small change, a franc and a half a dozen. Better go back to society; you will make more money there. Why, for one slap, just a light tap, you might say, my friend, Marquis Justi, was paid fifty thousand lire!

Briquet. Shut up, Mancini. Will you take care of him, Jackson?

Jackson. I can.

Polly. Do you like music? A Beethoven sonata played on a broom, for instance, or Mozart on a bottle?

He. Alas! No. But I will be exceedingly grateful if you will teach me. A clown! My childhood's dream. When all my school friends were thrilled by Plutarch's heroes, or the light of science—I dreamed of clowns. Beethoven on a broom, Mozart on bottles! Just what I have sought all my life! Friends, I must have a costume!

Jackson. I see you don't know much! A costume [*putting his finger on his forehead*] is a thing which calls for deep thought. Have you seen my Sun here? [*Strikes his posterior.*] I looked for it two years.

He. [*Enthusiastically.*] I shall think!

Mancini. It is time for me to go. Consuelo, my child, you must get dressed. [*To* HE.] We are lunching with Baron Regnard, a friend of mine, a banker.

Consuelo. But I don't want to go, Daddy. Alfred says I must rehearse today.

Mancini. [*Horrified, holding up his hands.*] Child, think of me, and what a situation you put me in! I promised the Baron, the Baron expects us. Why, it is impossible! Oh, I am in a cold sweat.

Consuelo. Alfred says——

Bezano. [*Drily.*] She has to work. Are you rested? Then come on.

Mancini. But—the devil take me if I know what to make of it. Hey, Bezano, bareback rider! Are you crazy? I gave you permission for Art's sake, to exercise my daughter's talent—and you——

Consuelo. Go along, Papa, and don't be so silly. We've got to work, haven't we? Have lunch along with your Baron. And Daddy, you forgot to take a clean handkerchief again, and I washed two for you yesterday. Where did you put them?

Mancini. [*Ashamed, blushing.*] Why, my linen is washed by the laundress, and you, Consuelo, are still playing with toys. It is stupid! You're a chatter-box. You don't think. These gentlemen might imagine Heaven knows what. How stupid. I'm off.

Consuelo. Do you want me to write him a little note?

Mancini. [*Angrily.*] A little note? Your little notes would make a horse laugh! Good-by.

[*He goes out toying angrily with his cane. The* CLOWNS *follow him respectfully, playing a funeral march.* HE *and* JACKSON *laugh. The* ACTORS *disappear one by one.*]

Consuelo. [*Laughing.*] Do I really write so badly? And I love so to write. Did you like my note, Alfred—or did you laugh, too?

Bezano. [*Blushing.*] No, I did not. Come on, Consuelo.

[*They go, and meet* ZINIDA, *entering.* CONSUELO *passes on.*]

Zinida. Are you going back to work, Bezano?

Bezano. [*Politely.*] Yes. Today is a very bad day. How are your lions, Zinida? I think the weather affects them.

Consuelo. [*From the ring.*] Alfred!

Zinida. Yes. Some one is calling you. You'd better go. [ALFRED *goes out. To* BRIQUET.] Are you finished?

Briquet. Right away.

Jackson. Then good-by till evening. Think about your costume, HE; and I shall look for some idea, too. Be here at ten tomorrow. Don't be late, or you'll get another slap. And I'll work with you.

He. I shall not be late. [HE *looks after* JACKSON, *who goes out.*] Must be a nice man. All the people about you are so nice, Papa Briquet. I suppose that good-looking bareback rider is in love with Consuelo, isn't he? [*Laughs.*]

Zinida. It's none of your business. For a newcomer you go poking your nose too far. How much does he want, Papa?

Briquet. Just a minute. See here, HE. I don't want to make a contract with you.

He. Just as you please. Do you know what? Don't let us talk about money. You are an honest fellow, Briquet; you will see what my work is worth to you, and then——

Briquet. [*Pleased.*] Now that's very nice of you. Zinida, the man really doesn't know anything.

Zinida. Well, do as he suggests. Now we must write it down. Where's the book?

Briquet. Here. [*To* HE.] I don't like to write [*gives book to* ZINIDA], but we have to put down the names of the actors, you know—it's police regulations. Then if any-one kills himself, or——

[*Again comes the sound of the Tango, and calls from the ring.*]

Zinida. What is your name?

He. [*Smiling.*] HE. I chose it, you know. Or don't you like it?

Briquet. We like it all right—but we have to have your real name. Have you a pass-port?

He. [*Confused.*] A passport? No, I have none. Or, rather, yes. I have something of the kind, but I had no idea the rules were strictly enforced here. What do you need papers for?

[ZINIDA *and* BRIQUET *look at each other.* ZINIDA *pushes the book aside.*]

Zinida. Then we can't take you. We can-not quarrel with the police, just on your account.

Briquet. She is my wife. I hadn't told you. She's right. You might get hurt by a horse, or hurt yourself—or do something. We don't know you, you see. I personally don't care, but out there, it's different, you see. For me a corpse is just a corpse—and I don't ask anything about him. It's up to God or the Devil. But they—they're too curious. Well, I suppose it's necessary for order. I don't know—— Got a card?

He. [*Rubs his head, thinking.*] What shall I do? I have my card, but [*smiles*] you understand that I don't want my name to be known.

Briquet. Some story, hey?

He. Yes, something like that. Why can't you imagine that I have no name? Can't I lose it as I might lose my hat? Or let some one else take it by mistake? When a stray dog comes to you, you don't ask his name—you simply give him another. Let me be that dog. [*Laughing.*] HE—the Dog!

Zinida. Why don't you tell us your name, just the two of us? Nobody else need know it. Unless you should break your neck——

He. [*Hesitates.*] Honestly?

[ZINIDA *shrugs her shoulders.*]

Briquet. Where people are honest, their word is good. One sees you come from *out there.*

He. All right. But please, don't be sur-prised.

[*Gives* ZINIDA *his card. She looks at it, then hands it to* BRIQUET, *then both look at* HE.]

Briquet. If it is true, sir, that you are really what is written here——

He. For heaven's sake—for heaven's sake—this does not exist, but was lost long ago; it is just a check for an old hat. I pray you to forget it, as I have. I am HE Who Gets Slapped—nothing else. [*Silence.*]

Briquet. I beg your pardon, sir, but I must ask you again, I must humbly ask you—are you not drunk, sir? There is some-thing in your eye—something——

He. No, no. I am HE Who Gets Slapped. Since when do you speak to me like this, Papa Briquet? You offend me.

Zinida. After all, it's his business, Briquet. [*She hides the card.*] Truly you are a strange man. [*Smiles.*] And you have already no-ticed that Bezano is in love with the horse-girl? And that I love my Briquet, did you notice that, too?

He. [*Also smiling.*] Oh, yes. You adore him.

Zinida. I adore him. Now go with him, Briquet, show him the ring and the stables—I have something to write.

He. Yes, yes, please. I am so happy. At last you have taken me, haven't you? It is true—you're not joking. The circus, the tan-bark, the ring in which I shall run getting my slaps. Yes, yes, Briquet, let's go. Until I feel the sawdust under my feet, I shall not believe it.

Briquet. All right then. [*Kisses* ZINIDA.] Come on.

Zinida. Just a minute—HE! Answer me a question. I have a man who takes care of the cages, a plain fellow whom nobody knows. He just cleans the cages, you know; he walks in and out whenever he wants to, with-out even looking at the lions, as if he were perfectly at home. Why is that so? Nobody knows him, everybody knows me, everyone is afraid for me, while—— And he is such a silly man—you will see him. [*Laughs.*] But don't you think of entering the cage yourself! My red one would give you such a slap!

Briquet. [*Displeased.*] There you are again, Zinida—stop it.

Zinida. [*Laughs.*] All right—go. Oh, yes, Louis, send me Bezano. I have to settle an account with him.

[HE *and the director go out.* ZINIDA *looks at the card once more, then hides it. She gets up and walks quickly up and down the room. She stops to listen to the Tango, which ends abruptly. Then she stands motionless, looking straight at the dark opening of the door through which* BEZANO *comes.*]

Bezano. [*Entering.*] You called me, Zinida? What do you want? Tell me quickly, I have no time——

[ZINIDA *looks at him silently.* BEZANO *flushes with anger, and knits his eyebrows. He turns to the door to go.*]

Zinida. Bezano!

Bezano. [*Stops, without looking up.*] What do you want? I have no time.

Zinida. Bezano! I keep hearing people say that you are in love with Consuelo. Is it true?

Bezano. [*Shrugging his shoulders.*] We work well together.

Zinida. [*Takes a step forward.*] No—— Tell me, Alfred, do you love her?

Bezano. [*Flushes like a boy, but looks straight into* ZINIDA*'s eyes. Proudly.*] I do not love anybody. No, I love nobody. How can I? Consuelo? She is here today, gone tomorrow, if her father should take her away. And I? Who am I? An acrobat, the son of a Milanese shoemaker—— She! I cannot even talk about it. Like my horses I have no words. Who am I to love?

Zinida. Do you love me? A little?

Bezano. No. I told you before.

Zinida. Still no? Not even a little?

Bezano. [*After a silence.*] I am afraid of you.

Zinida. [*Wants to cry out, indignantly, but masters herself and lowers her eyes, as if in an effort to shut out their light; turns pale.*] Am I . . . so terrifying a woman——

Bezano. You are beautiful, like a queen. You are almost as beautiful as Consuelo. But I don't like your eyes. Your eyes command me to love you—and I don't like to be commanded. I am afraid of you.

Zinida. Do I command, Bezano? No—only implore.

Bezano. Then why not look at me straight? Now I have it. You know yourself that your eyes cannot implore. [*Laughs.*] Your lions have spoiled you.

Zinida. My red lion loves me——

Bezano. Never! If he loves you, why is he so sad?

Zinida. Yesterday he was licking my hands like a dog.

Bezano. And this morning he was looking for you to devour you. He thrusts out his muzzle and looks out, as if he sees only you. He is afraid of you, and he hates you. Or do you want me to lick your hands too, like a dog?

Zinida. No, Alfred, but I—I want to kiss *your* hand. [*With passion.*] Give it to me!

Bezano. [*Severely.*] I am ashamed to listen to you when you speak like that.

Zinida. [*Controlling herself.*] One should not torture another as you torture me. Alfred, I love you. No, I do not command. Look into my eyes—— *I love you.*

[*Silence.*]

Bezano. [*Turns to go.*] Good-by.

Zinida. Alfred——

[HE *appears in the doorway, and stops.*]

Bezano. Please never tell me any more that you love me. I don't want it. Otherwise I will quit. You pronounce the word love as if you were cracking me with your whip. You know it is disgusting——

[*He turns brusquely and goes. Both notice* HE; BEZANO, *frowning, passes out quickly.* ZINIDA *returns to her place at the desk, with a proudly indifferent expression.*]

He. [*Coming in.*] I beg your pardon, but I——

Zinida. There you are again, poking your nose into everything, HE. Do you really want a slap?

He. [*Laughing.*] No. I simply forgot my overcoat. I didn't hear anything.

Zinida. I don't care whether you did or not.

He. May I take my coat?

Zinida. Take it if it's yours. Sit down, HE.

He. I am sitting down.

Zinida. Now tell me, HE, could you love me?

He. [*Laughing.*] I? I and Love! Look at me, Zinida. Did you ever see a lover with such a face?

Zinida. One can succeed with such a face——

He. That's because I am happy—because

I lost my hat—because I am drunk—or perhaps I am not drunk. But I feel as dizzy as a young girl at her first ball. It is so nice here—slap me, I want to play my part. Perhaps it will awaken love in my heart, too. Love—[*as if listening to his own heart with pretended terror*] do you know—I feel it!

[*In the circus the Tango is played again.*]

Zinida. [*Listening too.*] For me?

He. No. I don't know. For every one. [*Listens to the music.*] Yes, they are dancing—how beautiful Consuelo is—and how beautiful is the youth. He has the body of a Greek God; he looks as if he had been modeled by Praxiteles. Love! Love!

[*Silence, music.*]

Zinida. Tell me, HE——

He. At your service, Queen!

Zinida. HE, what shall I do, to make my lions love me?

CURTAIN

ACT II

The same room, during the evening performance. Occasional music, laughter, shrieks, and applause are audible. Through the small windows, back center, the light is shining.

[CONSUELO *and* BARON REGNARD *occupy the stage;* CONSUELO *wears her stage costume; she sits with her feet on the sofa, a small shawl covering her shoulders. Before her stands the* BARON, *a tall stout man in evening dress, a rose in his buttonhole; grasping the ground with feet well apart, he gazes at her with convex spider-like eyes.*]

Baron. Is it true that your father, the Count, has introduced you to a certain Marquis Justi, a very rich man?

Consuelo. [*Surprised.*] No, he is only joking. I have often heard him speak of a Marquis Justi but I have never seen him——

Baron. And do you know that your father is just a charlatan?

Consuelo. Oh! Don't say that—Father is such a dear.

Baron. Did you like the jewels?

Consuelo. Yes, very much. I was very sorry when Father told me I must return them. He said it would not be nice for me to keep them. I even cried a little about it.

Baron. Your father is only a beggar and a charlatan.

Consuelo. Oh, no, don't scold him—he loves you so much.

Baron. Let me kiss your hand——

Consuelo. Oh, no, it isn't proper! One may kiss the hand only when one says how do you do or good-by. But in the meantime you can't.

Baron. Everybody is in love with you, that is why you and your father make such a fuss about yourselves. Who is that new clown they call HE? I don't like him, he's too shrewd a beast. . . . Is he in love with you, too? I noticed the way he looked at you. . . .

Consuelo. [*Laughing.*] Nothing of the kind. He is so funny! He got fifty-two slaps yesterday. We counted them. Think of it, fifty-two slaps! Father said, "If they had only been gold pieces."

Baron. And Bezano, Consuelo. . . . Do you like him?

Consuelo. Yes, very much. He is so good-looking. HE says that Bezano and I are the most beautiful couple in the world. HE calls him Adam, and me Eve. But that's improper, isn't it? HE is *so* improper.

Baron. And does HE speak to you very often?

Consuelo. Yes, often. . . . But I don't understand him. It seems as if he were drunk.

Baron. "Consuelo"! . . . It means in Spanish . . . Consolation. Your father is an ass. . . . Consuelo, I love you.

Consuelo. Talk it over with Father.

Baron. [*Angry.*] Your father is a swindler and a charlatan. He should be turned over to the police. Don't you understand that I *cannot* marry you?

Consuelo. But Father says you can. . . .

Baron. No, I cannot. And what if I shoot myself? Consuelo, silly girl, I love you unbearably . . . unbearably, do you understand? I am probably mad . . . and must be taken to a doctor, yanked about, beaten with sticks. Why do I love you so much, Consuelo?

Consuelo. Then, you'd better marry.

Baron. I have had a hundred women, beauties, but I didn't see them. You are the first, and I don't see any one else. Who strikes man with love, God or the Devil? The Devil struck me. Let me kiss your hand.

Consuelo. No.

[*She thinks a while and sighs.*]

Baron. Do you think sometimes? What are you thinking about now, Consuelo?

Consuelo. [*With another sigh.*] I don't know why, I just felt sorry for Bezano. [*Sighs again.*] He is so nice to me when he teaches me . . . and he has such a tiny little room.

Baron. [*Indignant.*] You were there?

Consuelo. No. He told me about it. [*Smiling.*] Do you hear the noise in there? That's HE getting slapped. Poor thing . . . although I know it doesn't hurt, it's only make-believe. The intermission is coming soon.

[*The* BARON *throws away his cigar, takes two quick steps forward, and falls on his knees before the girl.*]

Baron. Consuelo——

Consuelo. Please, don't. Get up. Please leave my hand alone.

Baron. Consuelo!

Consuelo. [*Disgusted.*] Get up please, it's disgusting—you're so fat.

[*The* BARON *gets up. Voices are heard near the door and in the ring. It is the intermission. The* CLOWNS *come first, talking cheerfully and excitedly.* HE *leads them, in his clown's dress, with painted eyebrows and white nose; the others are applauding him. Voices of the* ACTORS *calling: "Bravo!* HE." *Then come the* ACTORS *and* ACTRESSES, RIDING-MASTERS, *and the rest, all in costume.* ZINIDA *is not among them.* PAPA BRIQUET *comes a little later.*]

Polly. A hundred slaps! Bravo, HE!

Jackson. Not bad, not bad at all. You'll make a career.

Tilly. He was the Professor today, and we were the students. Here goes another!

[*Gives him a clown's slap. Laughter. All bid good evening to the* BARON. *He is politely rude to these vagabonds who bore him, and remains silent. They seem quite used to it. Enter* MANCINI. *He is the same, and with the same cane.*]

Mancini. [*Shaking hands.*] What a success, Baron—and think of it—how the crowd does love slaps. [*Whispering.*] Your knees are dusty, Baron, brush them off. The floor is very dirty in here. [*Aloud.*] Consuelo, dear child, how do you feel?

[*Goes over to his daughter. Sound of laughing, chattering. The* WAITERS *from the buffet in the lobby bring in soda and wine.* CONSUELO'S *voice is heard.*]

Consuelo. And where is Bezano?

He. [*Bows before the* BARON, *affecting intimacy.*] You do not recognize me, Baron?

Baron. Yes, I do. You are the clown, HE.

He. Yes, I am HE Who Gets Slapped. May I presume to ask you, Baron, did you get your jewels back?

Baron. What!

He. I was asked to return some jewels to you, and I take the liberty of——

[*The* BARON *turns his back on him*—HE *laughs loudly.*]

Jackson. Whiskey and soda! Believe me, ladies and gents, HE will surely make a career. I am an old clown, and I know the crowd. Why today, he even eclipsed *me*—and clouds have covered my Sun. [*Striking it.*] They do not like puzzles, they want slaps! They are longing for them and dreaming about them in their homes. Your health, HE! Another whiskey and soda! HE got so many slaps today, there would be enough to go round the whole orchestra!

Tilly. I bet there wouldn't! [*To* JACKSON.] Shake!

Polly. I bet there wouldn't—I'll go and count the old mugs.

A Voice. The orchestra did not laugh——

Jackson. Because they were getting it, but the galleries did, because they were looking at the orchestra getting slapped. Your health, HE!

He. Yours, Jim! Tell me, why didn't you let me finish my speech—I was just getting a good start.

Jackson. [*Seriously.*] My friend, because your speech was a sacrilege. Politics—all right. Manners—as much as you want. But Providence—leave it in peace. And believe me, friend, I shut your mouth in time. Didn't I, Papa Briquet?

Briquet. [*Coming nearer.*] Yes. It was too much like literature. This is not an academy. You forget yourself, HE.

Tilly. But to shut one's mouth—faugh. . . .

Briquet. [*In a didactic tone.*] Whenever one shuts one's mouth, it is always high time to shut it, unless one is drinking. Hey, whiskey and soda!

Voices. Whiskey and soda for the Manager!

Mancini. But this is obscurantism. Philosophizing again, Briquet?

Briquet. I am not satisfied with you today, HE. Why do you tease them? They don't like it. Your health! A good slap must be clean like a crystal—fft-fft! right side, left side, and done with it. They will like it; they will laugh, and love you. But in your slaps there is a certain bite, you understand, a certain smell——

He. But they laughed, nevertheless!

Briquet. But without pleasure, without pleasure, HE. You pay, and immediately draw a draft on their bank; it's not the right game—they won't like you.

Jackson. That's what *I* tell him. He had already begun to make them angry.

Bezano. [*Entering.*] Consuelo, where are you? I have been looking for you—come on.

[*Both go out. The* BARON, *after hesitating a while, follows them.* MANCINI *accompanies him respectfully to the door.*]

He. [*Sighs.*] You don't understand, my dear friends; you are simply old, and have forgotten the smell of the stage.

Jackson. Aha! Who is old, my young man?

He. Don't be angry, Jim. It's a play, don't you understand? I become happy when I enter the ring and hear the music. I wear a mask and I feel humorous. There is a mask on my face, and I play. I may say *anything* like a drunkard. Do you understand? Yesterday when I, with this stupid face, was playing the great man, the philosopher [*he assumes a proud monumental pose, and repeats the gesture of the play—general laughter*], I was walking this way, and was telling how great, how wise, how incomparable I was—how God lived in me, how high I stood above the earth—how glory shone above my head [*his voice changes and he is speaking faster*], then you, Jim, you hit me for the first time. And I asked you, "What is it, they're applauding me?" Then, at the tenth slap, I said: "It seems to me that they sent for me from the Academy?"

[*Acts, looking around him with an air of unconquerable pride and splendor. Laughter.* JACKSON *gives him a real slap.*]

He. [*Holding his face.*] Why?

Jackson. Because you're a fool, and play for nothing. Waiter, the check.

[*Laughter. The bell calls them to the ring. The* ACTORS *go out in haste, some running. The* WAITERS *collect their money.*]

Briquet. [*In a sing-song.*] To the ring—to the ring——

Mancini. I want to tell you something, HE. You are not going yet?

He. No. I'll take a rest.

Briquet. To the ring—to the ring——

(*The* CLOWNS *as they go sing in shrill, squeaky voices. Little by little they all disappear, and loud music begins.* HE *seats himself on the sofa with his legs crossed, and yawns.*]

Mancini. HE, you have something none of my ancestors ever had—money. Let's have a nice bottle on you. Waiter, please——

[*The* WAITER, *who was taking up dishes, brings a bottle of wine and glasses and goes out.*]

He. You're blue, Mancini. [*Stretches.*] Well, at my age, a hundred slaps—it seems pretty hard. So you're blue. How are things getting on with your girl?

Mancini. Tss! Bad! Complications—parents— [*Shudders.*] Agh——

He. Prison!

Mancini. [*Laughing.*] Prison! Mustn't I uphold the glory of my name now, eh? HE, I'm joking—but there is Hell in my heart. You're the only one who understands me. But tell me how to explain this passion. It will turn my hair gray, it'll bring me to prison, to the grave. I am a tragic man, HE— [*Wipes his eyes with a dirty handkerchief.*] Why don't I like things which are not forbidden? Why, at all moments, even at the very moment of ecstasy, must I be reminded of some law—it is stupid. HE, I am becoming an anarchist. Good God!—Count Mancini, an anarchist. That's the only thing I've missed.

He. Isn't there a way of settling it somehow?

Mancini. Is there a way of getting money, somehow?

He. And the Baron?

Mancini. Oh, yes! He's just waiting for it, the bloodsucker! He'll get what he's after. Some day, you'll see me give him Consuelo for ten thousand francs, perhaps for five!

He. Cheap.

Mancini. Did I say it was anything else? Do I want to do it? But these bourgeois are strangling me, they've got me by the throat. HE, one can easily see that you're a gentleman, and of good society, you understand me —I showed you the jewels which I sent back to him—damn honesty—I didn't even dare change the stones, put false ones——

He. Why?

Mancini. It would have queered the game. Do you think he didn't weigh the diamonds when he got them back?

He. He will not marry her.

Mancini. Yes, he will. You don't understand. [*Laughs.*] The first half of his life, this man had only appetites—now love's got him. If he does not get Consuelo, he is lost, he is—like a withered narcissus. Plague take him with his automobiles. Did you see his car?

He. I did. . . . Give Consuelo to the Jockey——

Mancini. To Bezano? [*Laughs.*] What nonsense you do talk! Oh, I know. It's your joke about Adam and Eve. But please drop it. It's clever, but it compromises the child. She told me about it.

He. Or give her to me.

Mancini. Have you a billion? [*Laughs.*] Ah, HE, I'm not in the proper mood to listen to your clownish jokes— They say there are terrible jails in this country, and no discriminations are being made between people of my kind, and plain scoundrels. Why do you look at me like that? You're making fun of me?

He. No.

Mancini. I'll never get accustomed to those faces. You're so disgustingly made up.

He. He will not marry her. You can be as proud as you please, Mancini, but he'll not marry her. What *is* Consuelo? She is not educated. When she is off her horse, any good housemaid from a decent house has nicer manners, and speaks better. [*Nonchalantly.*] Don't *you* think she's stupid?

Mancini. No, she's not stupid. And you, HE, are a fool. What need has a woman of intelligence? Why, HE, you astonish me. Consuelo is an unpolished jewel, and only a real donkey does not notice her sparkle. Do you know what happened? I tried to begin to polish her——

He. Yes, you took a teacher. And what happened?

Mancini. [*Nodding his head.*] I was frightened—it went too fast—I had to dismiss him. Another month or two, and *she* would have kicked *me* out. [*Laughs.*] The clever old diamond merchants of Amsterdam keep their precious stones unpolished, and fool the thieves. My father taught me that.

He. The sleep of a diamond. It is only sleeping, then. You are wise, Mancini.

Mancini. Do you know what blood flows in the veins of an Italian woman? The blood of Hannibal and Corsini—of a Borgia—and of a dirty Lombardy peasant—and of a Moor. Oh! an Italian woman is not of a lower race, with only peasants and gypsies behind her. All possibilities, all forms are included in her, as in our marvellous sculpture. Do you understand that, you fool? Strike here—out springs a washerwoman, or a cheap street girl whom you want to throw out, because she is sloppy and has a screechy voice. Strike there—but carefully and gently, for there stands a queen, a goddess, the Venus of the Capitol who sings like a Stradivarius and makes you cry, idiot! An Italian woman——

He. You're quite a poet, Mancini! But what will the Baron make of her?

Mancini. What? What? Make of *her*? A baroness, you fool! What are you laughing at? I don't get you. But I am happy that this lovesick beast is neither a duke nor a prince—or she would be a princess and I—what would become of me? A year after the wedding they would not let me even into the kitchen [*laughing*], not even into the kitchen! I, Count Mancini, and she a—a simple——

He. [*Jumping up.*] What did you say? You are not her father, Mancini?

Mancini. Tss—the devil—I am so nervous today! Heavens, who do you think I am? "Her father?" Of course [*tries to laugh*], how silly you are—haven't you noticed the family resemblance? Just look, the nose, the eyes—— [*Suddenly sighs deeply.*] Ah, HE! How unhappy I am! Think of it. Here I am, a gentleman, nearly beaten in my struggle to keep up the honor of my name, of an old house, while there in the parquet—there sits that beast, an elephant with the eyes of a spider . . . and he looks at Consuelo . . . and . . .

He. Yes, yes, he has the motionless stare of a spider—you're right!

Mancini. Just what I say—a spider! But I must, I shall compel him to marry her. You'll see—— [*Walking excitedly up and down, playing with his cane.*] You'll see! All my life I've been getting ready for this battle.

[*He continues to walk up and down. Silence. Outside, great stillness.*]

He. [*Listening.*] Why is it so quiet out there? What a strange silence.

Mancini. [*Disgusted.*] I don't know. Out there it is quiet—but here [*touching his forehead with his cane*], here is storm, whirlwind. [*Bends over the clown.*] HE, shall I tell you a strange thing—an unusual trick of nature? [*Laughs, and looks very important.*] For three centuries the Counts Mancini have had no children! [*Laughs.*]

He. Then how were you born?

Mancini. Sh! Silence! That is the secret of our sainted mothers! Ha-ha! We are too ancient a stock—too exquisitely refined to trouble ourselves with such things—matters in which a peasant is more competent than ourselves. [*Enter an* USHER.] What do you want? The manager is on the stage.

The Usher. Yes, sir. Baron Regnard wished me to give you this letter.

Mancini. The Baron? Is he there?

The Usher. Baron Regnard has left. There is no answer.

Mancini. [*Opening the envelope, his hand shaking.*] The devil—the devil!

[*The* USHER *is going.*]

He. Just a minute. Why is there no music? This silence . . .

The Usher. It is the act with Madame Zinida and her lions.

[*He goes.* MANCINI *is reading the* BARON'S *note for the second time.*]

He. What's the matter, Mancini? You shine like Jackson's sun.

Mancini. What's the matter, did you ask? What's the matter? What's the matter?

[*Balancing his cane, he takes steps like a ballet-dancer.*]

He. Mancini! [MANCINI *rolls his eyes, makes faces, dances.*] Speak, you beast!

Mancini. [*Holds out his hand.*] Give me ten francs! Quick—ten francs—here, come on. [*Puts it automatically into his vest pocket.*] Listen, HE! If in a month I don't have a car of my own, you may give me one of your slaps!

He. What! He's going to marry? He's decided?

Mancini. What do you mean by "decided"? [*Laughs.*] When a man has the rope about his neck, you don't ask him about his health! Baron——

[*Stops suddenly, startled.* BRIQUET *is staggering in like a drunken man, his hand over his eyes.*]

He. [*Goes to him, touches his shoulder gently.*] What is the matter, Papa Briquet? Tell me!

Briquet. [*Groaning.*] Oh, oh, I can't . . . I can't . . . Ah——

He. Something has happened? You are ill? Please speak.

Briquet. I can't look at it! [*Takes his hands from his eyes, opens them wide.*] Why does she do it? Ah, ah, why does she do it? She must be taken away; she is insane. I couldn't look at it. [*Shivers.*] They will tear her to pieces. HE—her lions—they will tear her——

Mancini. Go on, Briquet. She is always like that. You act like a child. You ought to be ashamed.

Briquet. No—Today she is mad! And what is the matter with the crowd? They are all like dead people—they're not even breathing. I couldn't stand it. Listen—what's that?

[*All listen. There is the same silence.*]

Mancini. [*Disturbed.*] I'll go and see.

Briquet. [*Yelling.*] No! Don't! You can't look—damned profession! Don't go. You will scorch her—every pair of eyes that looks at her—at her lions—no, no. It is impossible—it is a sacrilege. I ran away. . . . HE, they will tear her——

He. [*Tries to be cheerful.*] Keep cool, Papa Briquet—I had no idea you were such a coward. You ought to be ashamed. Have a drink. Mancini, give him some wine.

Briquet. I don't want any. Heavens, if it were only over—— [*All listen.*] I have seen many things in my life, but this . . . Oh, she is crazy.

[*All still listen. Suddenly the silence breaks, like a huge stone wall crashing. There is a thunder of applause, mixed with shouts, music, wild screams—half bestial, half human. The men give way, relieved.* BRIQUET *sinks to a seat.*]

Mancini. [*Nervous.*] You see—you see—you old fool!

Briquet. [*Sobs and laughs.*] I am not going to allow it any more!

He. Here she is!

[ZINIDA *walks in, alone. She looks like a drunken bacchante, or like a mad woman. Her hair falls over her shoulders dishevelled, one shoulder is uncovered. She walks unseeing, though her eyes glow. She is like the living statue of a mad Victory. Behind her comes an* ACTOR, *very pale, then two* CLOWNS, *and a little later* CONSUELO *and* BEZANO. *All look at* ZINIDA *fearfully, as if they were afraid of a touch of her hand, or her great eyes.*]

Briquet. [*Shouting.*] You are crazy—you're a mad woman!

Zinida. I? No. Did you see? Did you see? Well?

[*She stands smiling, with the expression of a mad Victory.*]

Tilly. [*Plaintively.*] Cut it out, Zinida. Go to the devil!

Zinida. You saw, too! And. . . . what——

Briquet. Come home—come home. [*To the others.*] You can do what you like here. Zinida, come home.

Polly. You can't go, Papa. There's still your number.

Zinida. [*Her eyes meet those of* BEZANO.] Ah! Bezano. [*Laughs long and happily.*] Bezano! Alfred! Did you see? My lions *do* love me!

[BEZANO, *without answering, leaves the stage.* ZINIDA *seems to wither and grow dim, as a light being extinguished. Her smile fades, her eyes and face grow pale.* BRIQUET *anxiously bends over her.*]

Briquet. [*In a slow voice.*] A chair!

[ZINIDA *sits. Her head drops on her shoulder, her arms fall, she begins to shiver and tremble. Some one calls, "Cognac"—an actor runs to get it.*]

Briquet. [*Helpless.*] What is the matter, Zinida darling?

Mancini. [*Running about.*] She must quiet

down. Get out, get out—vagabonds! I'll fix everything, Papa Briquet. The wrap—where's the wrap? She's cold.

[*A* CLOWN *hands it to him; they cover her.*]

Tilly. [*Timidly.*] Wouldn't you like some moosic?

Mancini. [*Giving her some cognac.*] Drink, Duchess, drink! Drink it all—that's it.

[ZINIDA *drinks it like water, evidently not noticing the taste. She shivers. The* CLOWNS *disappear one by one.* CONSUELO, *with a sudden flexible movement, falls on her knees before* ZINIDA *and kisses her hands, warming them between her own.*]

Consuelo. Dear, dear, you are cold! Poor little hands, dear good one, beloved one——

Zinida. [*Pushes her away, gently.*] Ho—home. It will soon be over. It's nothing . . . I am ver—very . . . home. . . . You stay here, Briquet—you must. I'm all right.

Consuelo. You are cold? Here is my shawl.

Zinida. No—let me. . . .

[CONSUELO *gets up, and moves aside.*]

Briquet. And it's all because of your books, Zinida—your mythology. Now tell me, why do you want those beasts to love you? Beasts! Do you understand, HE? You too, you're from that world. She'll listen more to you. Explain it to her. Whom can those beasts love? Those hairy monsters, with diabolic eyes?

He. [*Genially.*] I believe—only their equals. You are right, Papa Briquet—there must be the same race.

Briquet. Of course, and this is all nonsense—literature. Explain it to her, HE.

He. [*Takes on a meditative air.*] Yes, you are right, Briquet.

Briquet. You see, dear, silly woman—everybody agrees. . . .

Mancini. Oh! Briquet, you make me sick; you are an absolute despot, an Asiatic.

Zinida. [*With the shadow of a smile, gives her hand to be kissed.*] Calm yourself, Louis. It is over—I am going home.

[*She stands up, shaking, still chilled.*]

Briquet. But how, alone, dear?

Mancini. What! fool! Did you imagine that Count Mancini would leave a woman when she needed help? *I* shall take her home—let your brutal heart be at rest—I shall take her home. Thomas, run for an automobile. Don't push me, Briquet, you are as awkward as a unicorn . . . that's the way, that's the way——

[*They are holding her, guiding her slowly toward the door.* CONSUELO, *her chin resting in her hand, is following them with her eyes. Unconsciously she assumes a somewhat affected pose.*]

Mancini. I'll come back for you, child——

[*Only* HE *and* CONSUELO *are left on the stage. In the ring, music, shrieks, and laughter begin again.*]

He. Consuelo——

Consuelo. Is that you, HE, dear?

He. Where did you learn that pose? I have seen it only in marble. You look like Psyche.

Consuelo. I don't know, HE. [*She sighs and sits on the sofa, keeping in her pose the same artificiality and beauty.*] It's all so sad here, today. HE, are you sorry for Zinida?

He. What did she do?

Consuelo. I didn't see. I had closed my eyes, and didn't open them. Alfred says she is a wicked woman, but that isn't true. She has such nice eyes, and what tiny cold hands—as if she were dead. What does she do it for? Alfred says she should be audacious, beautiful, but quiet, otherwise what she does is only disgusting. It isn't true, is it, HE?

He. She loves Alfred.

Consuelo. Alfred? My Bezano? [*Shrugging her shoulders, and surprised.*] How does she love him? The same as every one loves?

He. Yes—as every one loves—or still more.

Consuelo. Bezano? Bezano? No—it's nonsense. [*Pause; silence.*] What a beautiful costume you have, HE. You invented it yourself?

He. Jim helped me.

Consuelo. Jim is so nice! All clowns are nice.

He. I am wicked.

Consuelo. [*Laughs.*] You? You are the nicest of all. Oh, goodness! Three acts more! This is the second on now. Alfred and I are in the third. Are you coming to see me?

He. I always do. How beautiful you are, Consuelo.

Consuelo. Like Eve? [*Smiles.*]

He. Yes, Consuelo. And if the Baron asks you to be his wife, will you accept?

Consuelo. Certainly, HE. That's all Father and I are waiting for. Father told me yesterday that the Baron will not hesitate very long. Of course I do not love him. But I will be his honest, faithful wife. Father wants to teach me to play the piano.

He. Are those your own words—"his honest, faithful wife"?

Consuelo. Certainly they are mine. Whose

could they be? He loves me so much, the poor thing. Dear HE, what does "love" mean? Everybody speaks of love—love—Zinida, too! Poor Zinida! What a boring evening this has been! HE, did you paint the laughter on your face yourself?

He. My own self, dear little Consuelo——

Consuelo. How do you do it, all of you? I tried once, but couldn't do a thing. Why are there no women clowns? Why are you so silent, HE? You, too, are sad, tonight.

He. No, I am happy tonight. Give me your hand, Consuelo, I want to see what it says.

Consuelo. Do you know how? What a talented man you are! Read it, but don't *lie,* like a gypsy. [HE *goes down on one knee and takes her hand. Both bend over it.*] Am I lucky?

He. Yes, lucky. But wait a minute—this line here—funny. Ah, Consuelo, what does it say, here! [*Acting.*] I tremble, my eyes do not dare to read the strange, fatal signs. Consuelo——

Consuelo. The stars are talking.

He. Yes, the stars are talking. Their voices are distant and terrible; their rays are pale, and their shadows slip by, like the ghosts of dead virgins—their spell is upon thee, Consuelo, beautiful Consuelo. Thou standest at the door of Eternity.

Consuelo. I don't understand. Does it mean that I will live long?

He. This line—how far it goes. Strange! Thou wilt live eternally, Consuelo.

Consuelo. You see, HE, you did tell me a lie, just like a gypsy!

He. But it is written—here, silly—and here. Now think of what the stars are saying. Here you have eternal life, love, and glory; and here, listen to what Jupiter says. He says: "Goddess, thou must not belong to any one born on earth," and if you marry the Baron—you'll perish, you'll die, Consuelo. [CONSUELO *laughs.*]

Consuelo. Will he eat me?

He. No. But you will die before he has time to eat you.

Consuelo. And what will become of Father? Is there nothing about him here?

[*Laughing, she softly sings the melody of the waltz, which is playing in the distance.*]

He. Don't laugh, Consuelo, at the voice of the stars. They are far away, their rays are light and pale, and we can barely see their sleeping shadows, but their sorcery is stern and dark. You stand at the gates of eternity. Your die is cast; you are *doomed*—and your Alfred, whom you love in your heart, even though your mind is not aware of it, your Alfred cannot save you. He, too, is a stranger on this earth. He is submerged in a deep sleep. He, too, is a little god who has lost himself, and Consuelo, never, never will he find his way to Heaven again. Forget Bezano——

Consuelo. I don't understand a word. Do the gods really exist? My teacher told me about them. But I thought it was all tales! [*Laughs.*] And my Bezano is a god?

He. Forget Bezano! Consuelo, do you know who can save you? The only one who can save you? I.

Consuelo. [*Laughing.*] You, HE?

He. Yes, but don't laugh! Look. Here is the letter H. It is I, HE.

Consuelo. HE Who Gets Slapped? Is that written here, too?

He. That, too. The stars know everything. But look here, what more is written about him. Consuelo, welcome him. HE is an old god in disguise, who came down to earth only to love you, foolish little Consuelo.

Consuelo. [*Laughing and singing.*] Some god!

He. Don't mock! The gods don't like such empty laughter from beautiful lips. The gods grow lonely and die, when they are not recognized. Oh, Consuelo! Oh, great joy and love! Do recognize this god, and accept him. Think a moment, one day a god suddenly went crazy!

Consuelo. Gods go crazy, too?

He. Yes, when they are half man, then they often go mad. Suddenly he saw his own sublimity, and shuddered with horror, with infinite solitude, with superhuman anguish. It is terrible, when anguish touches the divine soul!

Consuelo. I don't like it. What language are you speaking? I don't understand——

He. I speak the language of thy awakening. Consuelo, recognize and accept thy god, who was thrown down from the summit like a stone. Accept the god who fell to the earth in order to live, to play, and to be infinitely drunk with joy. Evoë Goddess!

Consuelo. [*Tortured.*] HE— I cannot understand. Let my hand alone.

He. [*Stands up.*] Sleep. Then wake again, Consuelo! And when thou wakest—remember that hour when, covered with snow-white sea-foam, thou didst emerge from the sky-blue waters. Remember heaven, and the slow eastern wind, and the whisper of the foam at thy marble feet.

Consuelo. [*Her eyes are closed.*] I believe—wait—I remember. Remind me further——

[HE *is bowed over* CONSUELO, *with lifted arms; he speaks slowly, but in a commanding voice, as if conjuring.*]

He. You see the waves playing. Remember the song of the sirens, their sorrowless song of joy. Their white bodies, shining blue through the blue waters. Or can you hear the sun, singing? Like the strings of a divine harp, spread the golden rays— Do you not see the hand of God, which gives harmony, light, and love to the world? Do not the mountains, in the blue cloud of incense, sing their hymn of glory? Remember, O Consuelo, remember the prayer of the mountains, the prayer of the sea. [*Silence.*]

He. [*Commandingly.*] Remember—Consuelo!

Consuelo. [*Opening her eyes.*] No! HE, I was feeling so happy, and suddenly I forgot it all. Yet something of it all is still in my heart. Help me again, HE, remind me. It hurts, I hear so many voices. They all sing "Consuelo—Consuelo." What comes after? [*Silence; pause.*] What comes after? It hurts. Remind me, HE. [*Silence—in the ring, the music suddenly bursts forth in a tempestuous circus gallop. Silence.*] HE [*opens her eyes and smiles*], that's Alfred galloping. Do you recognize his music?

He. [*With rage.*] Leave the boy alone! [*Suddenly falls on his knees before* CONSUELO.] I love you, Consuelo, revelation of my heart. light of my nights, I love you, Consuelo. [*Looks at her in ecstasy and tears—and gets a slap; starting back.*] What's this?

Consuelo. A slap! You forget who you are. [*Stands up, with anger in her eyes.*] You are HE Who Gets Slapped! Did you forget it? Some god! With such a face—slapped face! Was it with slaps they threw you down from heaven, god?

He. Wait! Don't stand up! I—did not finish the play!

Consuelo. [*Sits.*] Then you were playing?

He. Wait! One minute.

Consuelo. You lied to me. Why did you play so that I believed you?

He. I am HE Who Gets Slapped!

Consuelo. You are not angry because I struck you? I did not want to, really, but you were so—disgusting. And now you are so funny again. You have great talent, HE—or are you drunk?

He. Strike me again.

Consuelo. No.

He. I need it for my play. Strike!

Consuelo. [*Laughs, and touches his cheek with her finger-tips.*] Here, then!

He. Didn't you understand that you are a queen, and I a fool who is in love with his queen? Don't you know, Consuelo, that every queen has a fool, and he is always in love with her, and they always beat him for it? HE Who Gets Slapped.

Consuelo. No. I didn't know.

He. Yes, every queen. Beauty has her fool. Wisdom, too. Oh, how many fools she has! Her court is overcrowded with enamored fools, and the sound of slaps does not cease, even through the night. But I never received such a sweet slap as the one given by my little queen. [*Someone appears at the door.* HE *notices it, and continues to play, making many faces.*] Clown HE can have no rival! Who is there who could stand such a deluge of slaps, such a hail-storm of slaps, and not get soaked. [*Feigns to cry aloud.*] "Have pity on me. I am but a poor fool!"

[*Enter two men: an* ACTOR, *dressed as a bareback rider, and* A GENTLEMAN *from the audience. He is spare, dressed in black, very respectable. He carries his hat in his hand.*]

Consuelo. [*Laughing, embarrassed.*] HE, there is some one here. Stop!

He. [*Gets up.*] Who is it? Who dares to intrude in the castle of my queen?

[HE *stops, suddenly.* CONSUELO, *laughing, jumps up and runs away, after a quick glance at* THE GENTLEMAN.]

Consuelo. You cheered me up, HE. Good-by. [*At the door.*] You shall get a note tomorrow.

The Bareback Rider. [*Laughing.*] A jolly fellow, sir. You wanted to see him? There he is. HE, the gentleman wants to see you.

He. [*In a depressed voice.*] What can I do for you?

[*The* ACTOR *bows, and goes away, smiling. Both men take a step toward each other.*]

Gentleman. Is this you?

He. Yes! It is I. And you? [*Silence.*]

Gentleman. Must I believe my eyes? Is this *you*, Mr.——

He. [*In a rage.*] My name here is HE. I have no other name, do you hear? HE Who Gets Slapped. And if you want to stay here, don't forget it.

Gentleman. You are so familiar. As far as I can remember——

He. We are all familiar, here. [*Contemptuously.*] Besides, that's all you deserve, anywhere.

Gentleman. [*Humbly.*] You have not forgiven me, HE? [*Silence.*]

He. Are you here with my wife? Is she, too, in the circus?

Gentleman. [*Quickly.*] Oh, no! I am alone. She stayed there!

He. You've left her already?

Gentleman. [*Humbly.*] No—we have—a son. After your sudden and mysterious disappearance—when you left that strange and insulting letter——

He. [*Laughs.*] Insulting? You are still able to feel insults? What are you doing here? Were you looking for me, or is it an accident?

Gentleman. I have been looking for you, for half a year—through many countries. And suddenly, today—by accident, indeed—I had no acquaintances here, and I went to the circus. We must talk things over . . . HE, I implore you. [*Silence.*]

He. Here is a shadow I cannot lose! To talk things over! Do you really think we still have something to talk over? All right. Leave your address with the porter, and I will let you know when you can see me. Now get out. [*Proudly.*] I am busy.

[THE GENTLEMAN *bows and leaves.* HE *does not return his bow, but stands with outstretched hand, in the pose of a great man who shows a boring visitor the door.*]

CURTAIN

ACT III

The same room. Morning, before the rehearsal.

[HE *is striding thoughtfully up and down the room. He wears a broad, parti-colored coat, and a prismatic tie. His derby is on the back of his head, and his face is clean-shaven like that of an actor. His eyebrows are drawn, lips pressed together energetically, his whole appearance severe and sombre. After the entrance of* THE GENTLEMAN *he changes. His face becomes clownlike, mobile—a living mask.*

THE GENTLEMAN *comes in. He is dressed in black, and has an extremely well-bred appearance. His thin face is yellowish, like an invalid's. When he is upset, his colorless, dull eyes often twitch.* HE *does not notice him.*]

Gentleman. Good morning, sir.

He. [*Turning around and looking at him absentmindedly.*] Ah! It's you.

Gentleman. I am not late? You look as if you did not expect me. I hope I am not disturbing you? You fixed this time yourself, however, and I took the liberty——

He. No manners, please. What do you want? Tell me quickly, I have no time.

Gentleman. [*Looking around with distaste.*] I expected you would invite me to some other place . . . to your home.

He. I have no other home. This is my home.

Gentleman. But people may disturb us here.

He. So much the worse for you. Talk faster! [*Silence.*]

Gentleman. Will you allow me to sit down?

He. Sit down. Look out! That chair is broken.

[THE GENTLEMAN, *afraid, pushes away the chair and looks helplessly around. Everything here seems to him dangerous and strange. He chooses an apparently solid little gilded divan, and sits down; puts his silk hat aside, slowly takes off his gloves, which stick to his fingers.* HE *observes him indifferently.*]

Gentleman. In this suit, and with this face, you make a still stranger impression. Yesterday it seemed to me that it was all a dream; today . . . *you* . . .

He. You have forgotten my name again? My name is HE.

Gentleman. You are determined to continue talking to me like this?

He. Decidedly! But you are squandering your time like a millionaire. Hurry up!

Gentleman. I really don't know . . . Everything here strikes me so . . . These posters, horses, animals, which I passed when I was looking for you . . . And finally, *you,* a clown in a circus! [*With a slight, deprecating smile.*] Could I expect it? It is true, when everybody there decided that you were dead, I was the only man who did not agree with them. I felt that you were still alive. But to find you among such surroundings—I can't understand it.

He. You said you have a son, now. Doesn't he look like me?

Gentleman. I don't understand?

He. Don't you know that widows or divorced women often have children by the new husband, which resemble the old one? This misfortune did not befall you?

[*Laughs.*] And your book, too, is a big success, I hear.

Gentleman. You want to insult me again?

He. [*Laughing.*] What a restless, touchy faker you are! Please sit still; be quiet. It is the custom here to speak this way. Why were you trying to find me?

Gentleman. My conscience . . .

He. You have no conscience. Or were you afraid that you hadn't robbed me of *everything* I possessed, and you came for the rest? But what more could you take from me now? My fool's cap with its bells? You wouldn't take it. It's too big for your bald head! Crawl back, you book-worm!

Gentleman. You cannot forgive the fact that your wife . . .

He. To the devil with my wife!

[THE GENTLEMAN *is startled and raises his eyebrows.* HE *laughs.*]

Gentleman. I don't know. . . . But such language! I confess I find difficulty in expressing my thoughts in such an atmosphere, but if you are so . . . indifferent to your wife, who, I shall allow myself to emphasize the fact, loved you and thought you were a saint —— [HE *laughs.*] Then *what* brought you to such a . . . step? Or is it that you cannot forgive me my success? A success, it is true, not entirely deserved. And now you want to take vengeance, with your humbleness, on those who misunderstood you. But you always were so indifferent to glory. Or your indifference was only hypocrisy. And when I, a more lucky rival . . .

He. [*With a burst of laughter.*] Rival! You—a rival!

Gentleman. [*Growing pale.*] But my book!

He. You are talking to me about *your* book. To me?

[THE GENTLEMAN *is very pale.* HE *looks at him with curiosity and mockery.*]

Gentleman. [*Raising his eyes.*] I am a very unhappy man.

He. Why?

Gentleman. I am a very unhappy man. You must forgive me. I am deeply, irreparably, and infinitely unhappy.

He. But why? Explain it to me. [*Starts walking up and down.*] You say yourself that your book is a tremendous success, you are famous, you have glory; there is not a yellow newspaper in which *you* and *your* thoughts are not mentioned. Who knows *me*? Who cares about my heavy abstractions, from which it was difficult for them to derive a single thought? You—you are the great vulgarizer! You have made my thoughts comprehensible even to horses! With the art of a great vulgarizer, a tailor of ideas, you dressed my Apollo in a barber's jacket, you handed my Venus a yellow ticket, and to my bright hero you gave the ears of an ass. And then your career is made, as Jackson says. And wherever I go, the whole street looks at me with thousands of faces, in which —what mockery—I recognize the traits of my own children. Oh! How ugly your son must be, if he resembles me! Why then are you unhappy, you poor devil? [THE GENTLEMAN *bows his head, plucking at his gloves.*] The police haven't caught you, as yet. What am I talking about? Is it possible to catch you? You always keep within the limits of the law. You have been torturing yourself up to now because you are not married to my wife. A notary public is always present at your thefts. What is the use of this self-torture, my friend? Get married. I died. You are not satisfied with having taken only my wife? Let my glory remain in your possession. It is yours. Accept my ideas. Assume all the rights, my most lawful heir! I died! And when I was dying [*making a stupidly pious face*] I forgave thee!

[*Bursts out laughing.* THE GENTLEMAN *raises his head, and bending forward, looks straight into* HE's *eyes.*]

Gentleman. And my pride?

He. Have you any pride? [THE GENTLEMAN *straightens up, and nods his head silently.*] Yes! But please stand off a little. I don't like to look at you. Think of it. There was a time when I loved you a little, even thought you a little gifted! You—my empty shadow.

Gentleman. [*Nodding his head.*] I am your shadow.

[*HE keeps on walking, and looks over his shoulder at* THE GENTLEMAN, *with a smile.*]

He. Oh, you are marvellous! What a comedy! What a touching comedy! Listen. Tell me, frankly if you can, do you hate me very much?

Gentleman. Yes! With all the hate there is in the world! Sit down here.

He. You order me?

Gentleman. Sit down here. Thank you. [*Bows.*] I am respected and I am famous, yes? I have a wife and a son, yes. [*Laughs slowly.*] My wife still loves you: our favorite discussion is about your genius. She supposes you are a genius. We, I and she, love you even when we are in bed. Tss! It is I who must make faces. My son—yes, he'll resemble you. And when, in order to have a little rest, I go to my desk, to my ink-pot, my books—there, too, I find you. Always you! Everywhere you! And I am never alone—never myself and alone. And when at night—you, sir, should understand this—when at night I go to my lonely thoughts, to my sleepless contemplations, even then I find your image in my head, in my unfortunate brain, your damned and hateful image!

[*Silence.* THE GENTLEMAN'S *eyes twitch.*]

He. [*Speaking slowly.*] What a comedy. How marvellously everything is turned about in this world: the robbed proves to be a robber, and the robber is complaining of theft, and cursing! [*Laughs.*] Listen, I was mistaken. You are not my shadow. You are the crowd. If you live by my creations, you hate me; if you breathe my breath, you are choking with anger. And choking with anger, hating me, you still walk slowly on the trail of my ideas. But you are advancing backward, advancing backward, comrade! Oh, what a marvellous comedy! [*Walking and smiling.*] Tell me, would you be relieved if I really had died?

Gentleman. Yes! I think so. Death augments distance and dulls the memory. Death reconciles. But you do not look like a man who——

He. Yes, yes! Death, *certainly!*

Gentleman. Sit down here.

He. Your obedient servant. Yes?

Gentleman. Certainly, I do not dare to ask you— [*makes a grimace*] to ask you to die, but tell me: you'll never come back there? No, don't laugh. If you want me to, I'll kiss your hand. Don't grimace. I would have done so if you had died.

He. [*Slowly.*] Get out, vermin!

[*Enter* TILLY *and* POLLY *as in the first act, playing. For a long time they do not see the two men.*]

He. Jack!

Tilly. Ah! Good morning, HE. We are rehearsing. You know it is very hard. Jack has just about as much music in his head as my pig.

He. [*Introducing, nonchalantly.*] My friend . . . For the benefit performance?

[*The* CLOWNS *bow to* THE GENTLEMAN, *making idiotic faces.*]

Polly. Yes. What are you preparing? You are cunning, HE! Consuelo told me what you are preparing for the benefit performance. She leaves us soon, you know?

He. Is that so?

Tilly. Zinida told us. Do you think she would get a benefit performance otherwise? She is a nice girl.

Polly. [*Taking his small flute-pipe.*] Here! Don't walk as if you were an elephant. Don't forget you are an ant! Come on!

[*They go off, playing.*]

Gentleman. [*Smiling.*] These are your new comrades? How strange they are!

He. Everything here is strange.

Gentleman. This suit of yours. Black used to be very becoming to you. This one hurts the eyes.

He. [*Looking himself over.*] Why? It looks very nice. The rehearsal has begun. You must go away. You are disturbing us.

Gentleman. You did not answer my question.

[*Slow strains of the Tango from a small orchestra in the ring.*]

He. [*Listening absent-mindedly to the music.*] What question?

Gentleman. [*Who does not hear the music.*] I pray you to tell me: will you ever come back?

He. [*Listening to the music.*] Never, never, never!

Gentleman. [*Getting up.*] Thank you. I am going.

He. Never, never, never! Yes, run along. And don't come back. There you were still bearable and useful for something, but here you are superfluous.

Gentleman. But if something should happen to you . . . you are a healthy man, but in this environment, these people . . . how will I know? They don't know your name here?

He. My name here is unknown, but *you will know.* Anything else?

Gentleman. I can be at peace? On your word of honor? Of course I mean, comparatively at peace?

He. Yes, you may be comparatively at peace. Never!

[*They walk to the door;* THE GENTLEMAN *stops.*]

Gentleman. May I come to the circus? You will allow me?

He. Certainly. You are the audience! [*Laughs.*] But I shan't give you my card for a pass. But why do you want to come? Or do you like the circus so much, and since when?

Gentleman. I want to look at you some more, and to understand, perhaps. Such a transformation! Knowing you as I do, I cannot admit that you are here without any *idea.* But what idea?

[*Looks short-sightedly at* HE. HE *grimaces and thumbs his nose.*]

Gentleman. What is that?

He. My idea! Good-by, Prince! My regards to your respected wife, your Highness's wonderful son! [*Enter* MANCINI.]

Mancini. You positively live in the circus, HE. Whenever I come, you are here. You are a fanatic in your work, sir.

He. [*Introducing.*] Prince Poniatovsky, Count Mancini.

Mancini. [*Drawing himself up.*] Very, very glad. And you too, Prince, you know my queer fellow? What a nice face he has, hasn't he?

[*He touches* HE'S *shoulder patronizingly, with the tip of his cane.*]

Gentleman. [*Awkwardly.*] Yes, I have the pleasure . . . certainly. Good-by, Count.

Mancini. Good-day, Prince.

He. [*Accompanying him.*] Look out, your Highness, for the dark passages: the steps are so rotten. Unfortunately I cannot usher you out to the street.

Gentleman. [*In a low voice.*] You will not give me your hand when we say good-by? We are parting for ever.

He. Unnecessary, Prince. I shall still hope to meet you in the Kingdom of Heaven. I trust you will be there, too?

Gentleman. [*With disgust.*] How you did succeed! You have so much of the clown in you!

He. I am HE Who Is Getting Slapped. Good-by, Prince. [*They take another step.*]

Gentleman. [*Looking* HE *in the eyes; in a very low voice.*] Tell me, you are not mad?

He. [*Just as low, his eyes wide open.*] I am afraid, I am afraid you are right, Prince. [*Still low.*] Ass! Never in your life did you use such a precise expression. I am mad!

[*Playing the clown again,* HE *shows him to the stair, with a big, affected gesture, a sweep of the hand and arm from his head to the floor, the fingers moving, to represent the steps.*]

He. [*Laughing.*] He is down! *Au revoir,* Prince. [THE GENTLEMAN *goes out.* HE *comes skipping back, and takes a pose.*] Mancini! Let us dance the Tango! Mancini, I adore you!

Mancini. [*Sitting back comfortably and playing with his cane.*] Don't forget yourself, HE. But you're hiding something, my boy. I always said you used to belong to society. It is so easy to talk to you. And who is this Prince? A genuine one?

He. Genuine. A first-rater. Like you!

Mancini. A sympathetic face. Although at first I thought he was an undertaker who came for an order. Ah, HE! When shall I finally depart from these dirty walls, from Papa Briquet, stupid posters, and brutal jockeys?

He. Very soon, Mancini.

Mancini. Yes, soon. I am simply exhausted in these surroundings, HE! I begin to feel myself a horse. You are from society, still you don't yet know what high society means. To be at last decently dressed, to attend receptions, to display the splendor of wit; from time to time to have a game of baccarat [*laughing*] without tricks or cheating——

He. And when evening comes, go to a suburb, where you are considered an honest father, who loves his children and——

Mancini. And get hold of something, eh? [*Laughs.*] I shall wear a silk mask and two butlers shall follow me, thus protecting me from the dirty crowd. Ah, HE! The blood of my ancestors boils in me. Look at this stiletto. What do you think? Do you think that it was ever stained with blood?

He. You frighten me, Count!

Mancini. [*Laughing, and putting the stiletto back into its sheath.*] Fool!

He. And what about the girl?

Mancini. Tss! I give those bourgeois absolute satisfaction, and they glorify my name. [*Laughs.*] The splendor of my name is beginning to shine with a force unknown. By the way, do you know what automobile firms are the best? Money is no object. [*Laughs.*] Ah! Papa Briquet!

[*Enter* BRIQUET *in his overcoat and silk hat. They shake hands.*]

Briquet. So, Mancini, you have obtained a benefit performance for your daughter, Consuelo! I only want to tell you, that if it were not for Zinida . . .

Mancini. Listen, Briquet. Decidedly you are a donkey. What are you complaining of? The Baron has bought all the parquet seats for Consuelo's benefit performance. Isn't that enough for you, you miser?

Briquet. I love your daughter, Mancini, and I am sorry to let her go. What more does she need here? She has an honest job, wonderful comrades, and the atmosphere ——?

Mancini. Not *she,* but *I* need something. You understand? [*Laughs.*] I asked you to increase her salary, Harpagon! and now, Mr. Manager, wouldn't you like to change me a thousand franc note?

Briquet. [*With a sigh.*] Give it to me.

Mancini. [*Nonchalantly.*] Tomorrow. I left it at home. [*All three laugh.*] Laugh, laugh! Today we are going with the Baron to his villa in the country; people say a very nice villa.

He. What for?

Mancini. You know, HE, the crazes of these millionaires. He wants to show Consuelo some winter roses, and me his wine cellars. He will come for us here. [*Enter* CONSUELO, *almost crying.*] What is the matter, my little Consuelo?

Consuelo. I can't, father! Tell him! What right has he to yell at me? He almost hit me with his whip!

Mancini. [*Straightening up.*] Briquet! I beg of you, as the Manager, what is this—a stable? To hit my daughter with a whip! I'll show this cub . . . a mere jockey. . . . No, the devil knows what it is, devil knows, I swear. . . .

Consuelo. Father . . .

Briquet. I will tell him.

Consuelo. Please don't. Alfred didn't hit me. It's a silly thing, what I told you. What an idea! He is so sorry himself. . . .

Briquet. I shall tell him anyhow that——

Consuelo. Don't you dare. You mustn't tell him anything. He didn't do a thing.

Mancini. [*Still excited.*] He must beg her pardon, the brat.

Consuelo. He's already asked me to forgive him. How silly you all are! I simply cannot work today and I got nervous. What nonsense! The silly boy asked me to forgive him, but I didn't want to. HE, dear, good morning! I didn't notice you. How becoming your tie is! Where are you going, Briquet? To Alfred?

Briquet. No, I am going home, dear child. Zinida asked me to give you her love. She will not be here today, either. [*He goes out.*]

Consuelo. Zinida is so nice, so good. Father, why is it that everybody seems so nice to me? Probably because I am going away soon. HE, did you hear the march that Tilly and Polly will play? [*Laughs.*] Such a cheerful one.

He. Yes. I heard it. Your benefit performance will be remarkable.

Consuelo. I think so, too. Father, I am hungry. Have them bring me a sandwich.

He. I'll run for it, my Queen.

Consuelo. Please do, HE. [*Loudly.*] But not cheese. I don't like it.

[MANCINI *and* CONSUELO *are alone.* MANCINI, *lying back comfortably in an armchair, scrutinizes his daughter with a searching eye.*]

Mancini. I find something particular in you today, my child. I don't know whether it is something better or worse. You cried?

Consuelo. Yes, a little. Oh, I am so hungry.

Mancini. But you had your breakfast?

Consuelo. No, I didn't. That's why I am so hungry. You again forgot to leave me some money this morning, and without money . . .

Mancini. Oh, the devil . . . what a memory I have. [*Laughs.*] But we shall have a very nice meal today. Don't eat very many sandwiches. . . . Yes, positively I like you. You must cry more often, my child; it washes off your superfluous simplicity. You become more of a woman.

Consuelo. Am I so simple, father?

Mancini. Very. . . . Too much. I like it in others, but not in you. Besides, the Baron . . .

Consuelo. Nonsense. I am not simple. But you know, Bezano scolded me so much, that even you would have cried. The devil knows . . .

Mancini. Tsss. . . . Never say "the devil knows." It isn't decent.

Consuelo. I say it only when I am with you.

Mancini. You must not say it when you are with me, either. I know it without you. [*Laughs.*]

Consuelo. Ha! Listen, Father! It's a new number of Alfred's. He makes such a jump! Jim says he's bound to break his neck. Poor fish. . . .

Mancini. [*Indifferently.*] Or his leg, or his back; they all have to break something. [*Laughs.*] They are breakable toys.

Consuelo. [*Listening to the music.*] I'll be lonesome without them, Father! The Baron promised to make a ring for me to gallop over as much as I want. He's not lying?

Mancini. A ring? [*Laughs.*] No, it's not a lie. By the way, child, when speaking of Barons, you must say, "he does not tell the truth," and not, "he lies."

Consuelo. It's just the same. It's nice to be wealthy, Father; you can do what you want, then.

Mancini. [*With enthusiasm.*] Everything you want. Everything, my child. Ah! Our fate is being decided today. Pray our clement God, Consuelo. The Baron is hanging on a thread.

Consuelo. [*Indifferently.*] Yes?

Mancini. [*Making the gesture with his fingers.*] On a very thin, silk thread. I am almost sure that he will make his proposal today. [*Laughs.*] Winter roses, and the web of a spider amongst the roses, in order that my dear little fly . . . He is such a spider.

Consuelo. [*Indifferently.*] Yes, a terrible

spider. Father, oughtn't I to let him kiss my hand yet?

Mancini. By no means. You don't know yet, darling, what these men are.

Consuelo. Alfred never kisses.

Mancini. Alfred! Your Alfred is a cub, and he mustn't dare. But with men of that sort, you must be extremely careful, my child. Today he would kiss your little finger, tomorrow your hand, and after tomorrow you would be on his lap.

Consuelo. Foui! Father, what are you talking about? You should be ashamed!

Mancini. But I know. . . .

Consuelo. Don't you dare! I don't want to hear such dirty things. I shall give the Baron such a slap! A better one than HE—let him only try.

Mancini. [*With a deprecating gesture.*] All men are like that, child.

Consuelo. It isn't true. Alfred is not. Ah! But where is HE? He said he'd run, and he hasn't come back.

Mancini. The buffet here is closed, and he has to get the sandwiches somewhere else. Consuelo, as your father, I want to warn you about HE. Don't trust him. He knows something. [*Twirls his finger close to his forehead.*] His game is not fair.

Consuelo. You say it about everybody. I know HE; he is such a nice man, and he loves me so much.

Mancini. Believe me, there is something in it.

Consuelo. Father, you make me sick with your advice. [HE, *breathing somewhat heavily, enters and gives her the sandwiches.*] Ah! HE, thank you.

He. Eat, Consuelo.

Consuelo, A hot one. . . . But you were running, HE? I am so grateful. [*Eats.*] HE, do you love me?

He. I do, my Queen. I am your court fool.

Consuelo. [*Eating.*] And when I leave, will you find another queen?

He. [*Making a ceremonious bow.*] I shall follow after you, my incomparable one. I shall carry the train of your dress and wipe away my tears with it. [*Pretends to cry.*]

Mancini. Idiot! [*Laughs.*] How sorry I am, HE, that those wonderful times have passed, when, in the court of the Counts Mancini, there were scores of motley fools who were given gold and kicks. . . . Now, Mancini is compelled to go to this dirty circus in order to see a good fool; and still, whose fool is he? Mine? No. He belongs to everybody who pays a franc. We shall very soon be unable to breathe because of Democracy. Democracy, too, needs fools! Think of it, HE; what an unexampled impertinence.

He. We are the servants of those who pay. But how can we help it, Count?

Mancini. But is that not sad? Imagine: we are in my castle. I, near the fireplace with my glass of wine, you, at my feet chatting your nonsense, jingling your little bells—diverting me. Sometimes you pinch me too with your jokes: it is allowed by the traditions and necessary for the circulation of the blood. After a while—I am sick of you, I want another one. . . . Then I give you a kick and . . . Ah, HE, how wonderful it would he!

He. It would be marvellous, Mancini!

Mancini. Yes. Certainly. You would be getting gold coins, those wonderful little yellow things. . . . Well, when I become rich, I shall take you. That's settled.

Consuelo. Take him, Father . . .

He. And when the count, tired of my chattering, will give me a kick with his Highness's foot, then I shall lie down at the little feet of my Queen, and shall . . .

Consuelo. [*Laughing.*] Wait for another kick? I'm finished. Father, give me your handkerchief, I want to wipe my hands. You have another one in your pocket. Oh, my goodness, I must work some more!

Mancini. [*Uneasy.*] But don't forget, my child!

Consuelo. No, today, I won't forget! Go on!

Mancini. [*Looking at his watch.*] Yes, it is time. . . . He asked me to come over when you were ready. You must change your dress before I come back. [*Laughing.*] *Signori, miei complimenti.*

[*He goes out, playing with his cane.* CONSUELO *sits on the corner of the divan, and covers herself with her shawl.*]

Consuelo. Hello, HE! Come and lie down at my feet, and tell me something cheerful. . . . You know, when you paint the laughter on your face, you are very good looking, but now, too, you are very, very nice. Come on, HE, why don't you lie down?

He. Consuelo! Are you going to marry the Baron?

Consuelo. [*Indifferently.*] It seems so. The Baron is hanging by a thread! HE, there is one little sandwich left. Eat it.

He. Thank you, my Queen. [*Eats.*] And do you remember my prediction?

Consuelo. What prediction? How quickly you swallow! Does it taste good?

He. Very good. That if you marry the Baron, you . . .

Consuelo. Oh, that's what you're talking about. . . . But you were making fun.

He. Nobody can tell, my Queen. Sometimes one makes fun, and suddenly it turns out to be true; the stars never talk in vain. If sometimes it is difficult for a human being to open his mouth and to say a word, how difficult it must be for a star. Think of it.

Consuelo. [*Laughing.*] I should say. Such a mouth! [*Makes a tiny mouth.*]

He. No, my dear little girl, were I in your place, I would think it over. And suppose suddenly you should die? Don't marry the Baron, Consuelo!

Consuelo. [*Thinking.*] And what is—death?

He. I do not know, my Queen. Nobody knows. Like love! Nobody knows. But your little hands will become cold, and your dear little eyes will be closed. You will be away from here. And the music will play without you, and without you the crazy Bezano will be galloping, and Tilly and Polly will be playing on their pipes without you: tilly-polly, tilly-polly . . . tilly-tilly, polly-polly . . .

Consuelo. Please don't, HE darling—— I am so sad, anyway . . . tilly-tilly, polly-polly . . .

[*Silence.* HE *looks at* CONSUELO.]

He. You were crying, my little Consuelo?

Consuelo. Yes, a little. Alfred made me nervous. But tell me, is it my fault that I can't do anything today? I tried to, but I couldn't.

He. Why?

Consuelo. Ah, I don't know. There is something here. [*Presses her hand against her heart.*] I don't know. HE, I must be sick. What is sickness? Does it hurt very much?

He. It is not sickness. It is the charm of the far-off stars, Consuelo. It is the voice of your fate, my little Queen.

Consuelo. Don't talk nonsense, please. What should the stars care about me? I am so small. Nonsense, HE! Tell me rather another tale which you know: about the blue sea and those gods, you know . . . who are so beautiful. Did they all die?

He. They are all alive, but they hide themselves, my goddess.

Consuelo. In the woods or mountains? Can one come across them? Ah, imagine, HE . . . I come across a god, and he suddenly takes a look at me! I'd run away. [*Laughs.*] This morning when I went without breakfast, I became so sad, so disgusted, and I thought: if a god should come, and give me something to eat! And as I thought it, I suddenly heard, honestly it's true, I heard: "Consuelo, somebody's calling you." [*Angrily.*] Don't you dare laugh!

He. Am I laughing?

Consuelo. Honestly, it's true. Ah, HE, but he didn't come. He only called me and disappeared, and how can you find him? It hurt me so much, and hurts even now. Why did you remind me of my childhood? I'd forgotten it entirely. There was the sea . . . and something . . . many, many . . .

[*Closes her eyes, smiling.*]

He. Remember, Consuelo.

Consuelo. No. [*Opening her eyes.*] I forget everything about it. [*Looks around the room.*] HE, do you see what a poster they made for my benefit performance? It's father's idea. The Baron liked it.

[HE *laughs. Silence.*]

He. [*Slowly.*] Consuelo, my Queen! Don't go to the Baron today.

Consuelo. Why? [*After a silence.*] How fresh you are, HE.

He. [*Lowering his head, slowly.*] I don't want it.

Consuelo. [*Getting up.*] What? You don't want it?

He. [*Bowing his head still lower.*] I do not want you to marry the Baron. [*Imploring.*] I . . . I shall not allow it . . . I beg you!

Consuelo. Whom, then, would you ask me to marry? You, perhaps, you fool? [*With a rancorous laugh.*] Are you crazy, my darling? "I shall not allow." HE! HE will not allow me! But it is unbearable; What business is it of yours? [*Walking up and down the room, looks over her shoulder at* HE, *with anger.*] Some fool clown, whom they can kick out of here any minute. You make me sick with your stupid tales. Or you like slaps so much. Fool, you couldn't invent anything better than a slap!

He. [*Without lifting his head.*] Forgive me, my Queen.

Consuelo. He is glad when they laugh at him. Some god! No, I shan't forgive. I know you. [*Makes same gesture as* MANCINI, *twirling her finger close to her forehead.*] You have something there! Laughs . . . so nicely . . . plays, plays, and then suddenly—hop! *Obey him!* No, darling, I am not that kind! Carry my train, that is your business—fool!

He. I shall carry your train, my Queen. Forgive me. Give me back the image of my beautiful, piteous goddess.

Consuelo. [*Quieting down.*] You're playing again?

He. I am.

Consuelo. [*Laughing.*] You see! [*Sits down.*] Foolish HE.

He. I see everything, my Queen. I see how beautiful you are, and how low under your feet your poor court fool is lying. Somewhere in the abyss his little bells are ringing. He kneels before you and prays; forgive and pity him, my divine one. He was too impudent; he played so cheerfully that he went too far and lost his tiny little mind, the last bit of understanding he had saved up. Forgive me!

Consuelo. All right. I forgive you. [*Laughs.*] And now will you allow me to marry the Baron?

He. [*Also laughing.*] And nevertheless I will not allow it. But what does a queen care about the permission of her enamored fool!

Consuelo. Get up. You are forgiven. And do you know why? You think because of your words? You are a cunning beast, HE! No, because of the *sandwiches.* That's why. You were so lovely, you panted so when you brought them. Poor darling HE. From tomorrow you may be at my feet again. And as soon as I whistle, "tuwhooo"——

He. I shall instantly lie down at thy feet, Consuelo. It is settled! But all my little bells fell off today and——

[BEZANO *appears, confused.*]

Consuelo. Alfred! You came for me?

Bezano. Yes. Will you work some more, Consuelo?

Consuelo. Certainly. As much as you want. But I thought, Alfred, you were mad at me? I shan't dawdle any more.

Bezano. No. You didn't dawdle. Don't be offended, because I yelled so much. You know when one has to teach, and——

Consuelo. My goodness, do you think I don't understand? You are too nice, unbearably nice, to like teaching such a fool as me. Do you think I don't understand? Come on!

Bezano. Come on! Hello, HE! I haven't seen you yet today. How are you?

He. How are you, Bezano? Wait, wait a minute—stay here a minute, both of you —that way. Yes!

[CONSUELO *and* BEZANO *stand side by side, the jockey scowling,* CONSUELO *laughing and flushing.*]

Consuelo. Like Adam and Eve? How foolish you are! Terribly. [*She runs away.*] I shall only change my slippers, Alfred.

He. Consuelo! And how about Father and the Baron? They will come soon, to take you with them.

Consuelo. Let them come. They can wait. Not very important people.

[*Runs away.* BEZANO *hesitatingly follows her.*]

He. Stay here for a while, Bezano. Sit down.

Bezano. What more do you want? I have no time for your nonsense.

He. You can remain standing if you want. Bezano—you love her? [*Silence.*]

Bezano. I shall allow nobody to interfere with my affairs. You allow yourself too many liberties, HE. I don't know you. You came from the street, and why should I trust you?

He. But you know the Baron? Listen. It is painful for me to pronounce these words: she loves you. Save her from the spider! Or are you blind, and don't see the web, which is woven in every dark corner. Get out of the vicious circle in which you are turning around, like a blind man. Take her away, steal her, do what you want . . . kill her even, and take her to the heavens or to the devil! But don't give her to this man! He is a defiler of love. And if you are timid, if you are afraid to lift your hand against her —kill the Baron! Kill!

Bezano. [*With a smile.*] And who will kill the others to come?

He. She loves you.

Bezano. Did she tell you that herself?

He. What a petty, what a stupid, what a human pride! But *you* are a little god! A god, youth! Why don't you want to believe me? Or does the street, from which I have come, bother you? But look, look yourself. Look in my eyes, do such eyes lie? Yes, my face is ugly, I make faces and grimaces, I am surrounded by laughter, but don't you see the god behind all this, a god, like you? Look, look at me! [BEZANO *bursts out laughing.*] What are you laughing at, youth?

Bezano. You look now as you did that evening in the ring. You remember? When you were a great man, and they sent for you from the Academy, and suddenly—Hup! HE Who Gets Slapped!

He. [*Laughing the same way.*] Yes, yes, you are right, Bezano. There is a resemblance. [*With a strained expression, taking a pose.*] "It seems to me they sent for me from the Academy!"

Bezano. [*Displeased.*] But I don't like this play. You can present *your* face for slaps if you want to, but don't dare to expose mine. [*Turns to go.*]

He. Bezano!

Bezano. [*Turning round.*] And never let me hear any more about Consuelo, and don't dare to tell me again that I am a god! It is disgusting.

[BEZANO *goes out angrily, striking his boot with his whip.* HE *is alone. Wrathfully, with a tortured expression, he makes a step towards the jockey, then stops, with soundless laughter, his head thrown backwards. The* BARON *and* MANCINI *find him in this position, when they enter.*]

Mancini. [*Laughing.*] What a cheerful chap you are, HE! You laugh when you are alone. [HE *laughs aloud.*] Stop it, fool! How can you stand it?

He. [*Bowing low, with a large gesture.*] How do you do, Baron? My humblest respects to you, Count. I beg your pardon, Count, but you found the clown at work. These are, so to speak, Baron, his everyday pleasures.

Mancini. [*Lifting his eyebrows.*] Tsss. But you are a clever man, HE. I shall ask Papa Briquet to give you a benefit performance. Shall I, HE?

He. Please do me the favor, Count.

Mancini. Don't overdo. Be more simple, HE. [*Laughs.*] But how many slaps will you get at your benefit performance, when even on weekdays they ring you like a gong! A funny profession, isn't it, Baron?

Baron. Very strange. But where is the Countess?

Mancini. Yes, yes. I shall go for her at once. Dear child, she is so absorbed in her benefit performance and her work. They call this jumping *work,* Baron.

Baron. I can wait a little.

[*Sits down, with his silk hat on his head.*]

Mancini. But why? I shall hurry her up. I shall be back at once. And you, HE, be a nice host, and entertain our dear guest. You will not be bored in his company, Baron.

[*He goes out.* HE *strides about the stage, smiling and glancing from time to time at the* BARON. *The latter sits with his legs spread apart and his chin on the top of his cane. The silk hat remains on his head. He is silent.*]

He. In what way would you like me to entertain you, Baron?

Baron. In no way! I don't like clowns.

He. Nor I Barons.

[*Silence.* HE *puts on his derby hat, takes a chair with a large gesture, and puts it down heavily, in front of the* BARON. HE *sits astride it, imitating the pose of the* BARON, *and looks him in the eyes. Silence.*]

He. Can you be silent very long?

Baron. Very long.

He. [*Taps on the floor with his foot.*] And can you wait very long?

Baron. Very long.

He. Until you get it?

Baron. Until I get it. And you?

He. I too.

[*Both look at each other, silently, their heads close together. From the ring one hears the strains of the Tango.*]

CURTAIN

ACT IV

Music in the ring. More disorder in the room than usual. All kinds of actors' costumes hanging on pegs and lying in the corners. On the table a bouquet of fiery-red roses, put there by some careless hand.

[*At the entrance, near the arch, three* BAREBACK RIDERS *are smoking and chattering; they are all minor actors. All part their hair the same way; two wear small moustaches; the third one is clean-shaven with a face like a bull-dog.*]

The Clean-shaven One. Go on, Henry! Ten thousand francs! It's too much even for the Baron.

The Second. How much are roses now?

The Shaven. I don't know. In winter they are certainly more expensive, but still Henry talks nonsense. Ten thousand!

The Second. The Baron has his own hothouse. They don't cost him anything.

Henry. [*Throwing away his cigar, which has burned the tips of his fingers.*] No, Grab, you're silly. There's a whole car-load full! One can smell the roses a mile away. They're to cover the entire arena.

The Shaven. Only the ring.

Henry. It's all the same. In order to cover the ring, you must have thousands and thousands of roses. You'll see what it looks like, when they've covered everything like a carpet. He ordered them to make it like a carpet! Do you see, Grab?

The Second. What a Baron's craze! Isn't it time yet?

Henry. No, we have time enough. I rather like it: a fiery-red tango on a fiery-red cover of winter roses!

The Shaven. Consuelo will be galloping on roses. And Bezano?

The Second. And Bezano on thorns. [*Smiles.*]

The Shaven. That youngster has no self-respect. I'd have refused.

Henry. But it is his job. He's got to do it. [*Laughs.*] Talk to him about self-respect. He's as angry and proud as a little Satan.

The Second. No, you may say what you like, it's an excellent benefit performance. It's a joy to look at the crowd. They're so excited.

Henry. Tss!

[*All throw away their cigars and cigarettes, like school boys who are caught, and make way for* ZINIDA, *who enters with* HE.]

Zinida. What are you doing here, gentlemen? Your place is at the entrance.

Henry. [*With a respectful smile.*] We are here just for a minute, Madame Zinida. We are going. What a successful evening! And what a glory for Papa Briquet!

Zinida. Yes. Go, and please don't leave your places. [*They go.* ZINIDA *pulls a drawer out of the desk, and puts in some papers. She is in her lion tamer's costume.*] HE, what were you doing near my lions? You frightened me.

He. Why, Duchess, I merely wanted to hear what the beasts were saying about the benefit performance. They are pacing in their cages, and growling.

Zinida. The music makes them nervous. Sit down, HE. An excellent evening, and I am so glad that Consuelo is leaving us. Have you heard about the Baron's roses?

He. Everybody is talking about them. The hymeneal roses!

Zinida. Here are some, too. [*Pushes away the bouquet.*] You find them everywhere. Yes, I am glad. She is superfluous here, and disturbs our work. It is a misfortune for a cast to have in it such a beautiful and such an . . . accessible girl.

He. But it is an honest marriage, Duchess, is it not?

Zinida. I don't care what it is.

He. Spiders, too, need an improvement in their breed! Can't you imagine, Zinida, what charming little spiders this couple will create? They will have the face of their mother, Consuelo, and the stomach of their father, the Baron, and thus could be an ornament for any circus-ring.

Zinida. You are malicious today, HE. You are morose.

He. I laugh.

Zinida. You do, but without joy. Why are you without make-up?

He. I am in the third act. I have time. And how does Bezano feel about this evening? Is he glad?

Zinida. I didn't talk to Bezano. You know what I think, my friend? You, too, are superfluous here. [*Silence.*]

He. How do you want me to take that, Zinida?

Zinida. Just as I said. In fact, Consuelo sold herself for nothing. What is the Baron worth, with his poor millions? People say that you are clever, too clever perhaps; tell me then, for how much could one buy me?

He. [*Looking as if he were pricing her.*] Only for a crown.

Zinida. A baron's crown?

He. No, a royal one.

Zinida. You are far from being stupid. And you guessed that Consuelo is not Mancini's daughter?

He. [*Startled.*] What! And she knows it?

Zinida. Hardly. Why should she know it? Yes, she is a girl from Corsica whose parents are unknown. He preferred to use her for business rather than . . . But according to the law, she is his daughter, Countess Veronica Mancini.

He. It is nice, to have everything done according to law, isn't it, Zinida? But it is curious there is more blue blood in her than in this Mancini. One would say that it was she who found him on the street, and made him a count and her father. Count Mancini! [*Laughs.*]

Zinida. Yes, you are gloomy, HE. I changed my mind, you'd better stay.

He. Will I not be superfluous?

Zinida. When she is gone, you will not. Oh! You don't know yet, how nice it is to be with us. What a rest for the body and mind. I understand you. I am clever, too. Like you, I brought with me from out there my inclination for chains, and for a long time I chained myself to whatever I could, in order to feel firm.

He. Bezano?

Zinida. Bezano and others; there were many, there will be many more. My red lion, with whom I am desperately in love, is still more terrible than Bezano. But it is all nonsense: old habits, which we are sorry to let go, like old servants who steal things. Leave Consuelo alone. She has her own way.

He. Automobiles and diamonds?

Zinida. When did you see a beauty clad in simple cotton? If this one does not buy her, another will. They buy off everything that is beautiful. Yes, I know. For the first ten years she will be a sad beauty, who will attract the eyes of the poor man on the side-walk: afterward she will begin to paint a little around her eyes and smile, and then will take——

He. Her chauffeur or butler as a lover? You're not guessing badly, Zinida!

Zinida. Am I not right? I don't want to intrude on your confidence, but today I am sorry for you, HE. What can you do against Fate? Don't be offended, my friend, by the words of a woman. I like you; you are not beautiful, nor young, nor rich, and your place is——

He. On the side-walk, from which one looks at the beauties. [*Laughs.*] And if I don't want to?

Zinida. What does it matter, your "want" or "don't want"? I am sorry for you, my poor friend, but if you are a strong man, and I think you are, then there is only one way for you. To forget.

He. You think that that's being strong? And you are saying this, you, Queen Zinida, who want to awaken the feeling of love, even in the heart of a lion? For one second of an illusory possession, you are ready to pay with your life, and still you advise me to forget! Give me your strong hand, my beautiful lady; see how much strength there is in this pressure, and don't pity me.

[*Enter* BRIQUET *and* MANCINI. *The latter is reserved, and self-consciously imposing. He has a new suit, but the same cane, and the same noiseless smile of a satyr.*]

Zinida. [*Whispering.*] Will you stay?

He. Yes. I shan't go away.

Mancini. How are you, my dear? But you are dazzling, my dear! I swear you are marvellous! Your lion would be an ass, if he did not kiss your hand, as I do. . . .

[*Kisses her hand.*]

Zinida. May I congratulate you, Count?

Mancini. Yes, *merci.* [*To* HE.] How are you, my dear?

He. Good evening, Count!

Briquet. Zinida, the Count wants to pay immediately for the breach of contract with Consuelo . . . the Countess's contract. Don't you remember, Mother, how much it is?

Zinida. I'll look it up, Papa.

Mancini. Yes, please. Consuelo will not return here any more. We leave tomorrow.

[ZINIDA *and* BRIQUET *search among the papers.* HE *takes* MANCINI *roughly by the elbow, and draws him aside.*]

He. [*In a low voice.*] How are your girls, Mancini?

Mancini. What girls? What is this, stupidity or blackmail? Look out, sir, be careful, the policeman is not far.

He. You are much too severe, Mancini. I assumed, that since we are *tête-à-tête* . . .

Mancini. But tell me, what kind of *tête-à-tête* is possible, between a clown and me? [*Laughs.*] You are stupid, HE. You should say what you want, and not ask questions!

Briquet. Three thousand francs, Count.

Mancini. Is that all? For Consuelo? All right. I'll tell the Baron.

Zinida. You took——

Briquet. Don't, Mother, don't.

Zinida. Count, you drew in advance, I have it written down, eighty francs and twenty centimes. Will you pay this money, too?

Mancini. Certainly, certainly. You will get three thousand and one hundred. [*Laughing.*] Twenty centimes! I never thought I could be so accurate. [*Seriously.*] Yes, my friends. My daughter Consuelo—the Countess—and the Baron, expressed their desire to bid farewell to the whole cast.

He. The Baron, too?

Mancini. Yes, Auguste too. They want to do it during the intermission. Therefore, I ask you to gather here . . . the more decent ones . . . but please don't make it too crowded! HE, will you, sir, be kind enough to run into the buffet and tell them to bring right away a basket of champagne, bottles and glasses—you understand?

He. Yes, Count.

Mancini. Wait a minute, what's the hurry —what is this, a new costume? You are all burning like the devils in hell!

He. You do me too much honor, Count, I am not a devil. I am merely a poor sinner whom the devils are frying a little.

[*He goes out, bowing like a clown.*]

Mancini. A gifted chap, but too cunning.

Briquet. It's the Tango color, in honor of your daughter, Count. He needs it for a new stunt, which he doesn't want to tell in advance. Don't you want to sit down, Count?

Mancini. Auguste is waiting for me, but . . . it's all right. [*Takes a seat.*] Nevertheless I am sorry to leave you, my friend. High society, certainly, prerogatives of the title, castles of exalted noblemen, but where could I find such freedom, and . . . such simplicity . . . ? And besides, these announcements, these burning posters, which take your breath in the morning, they had something which summoned, which encouraged. . . . *There,* my friends, I shall become old.

Briquet. But pleasures of a higher kind, Count. Why are you silent, Zinida?

Zinida. I'm listening.

Mancini. By the way, my dear, how do you like my suit? You have wonderful taste.

[*Spreads out his lace tie and lace cuffs.*]

Zinida. I like it. You look like a nobleman of the courts of long ago.

Mancini. Yes? But don't you think it is too conspicuous? Who wears lace and satin now? This dirty democracy will soon make us dress ourselves in sackcloth. [*With a sigh.*] Auguste told me that this jabot was out of place.

Zinida. The Baron is too severe.

Mancini. Yes, but it seems to me he is right. I am a little infected with your fancy.

[HE *returns. Two* WAITERS *follow him, carrying a basket of champagne and glasses. They prepare everything on the table.*]

Mancini. Ah! *merci,* HE. But, please, none of this bourgeois exploding of corks; be slower and more modest. Send the bill to Baron Regnard. Then, we will be here, Briquet. I must go.

Zinida. [*Looks at her watch.*] Yes, the act is going to end soon.

Mancini. Heavens!

[*Disappears in a hurry.*]

Briquet. The devil take him!

Zinida. [*Pointing to the* WAITER.] Not so loud, Louis!

Briquet. No! The devil take him! And why couldn't you help me, Mother? You left me alone to talk to him. High Society! High pleasures! Swindler!

[HE *and* ZINIDA *laugh. The* WAITERS *smile.*]

Briquet. [*To the* WAITERS.] What are you laughing about? You can go. We will help ourselves. Whiskey and soda, Jean! [*In a low and angry voice.*] Champagne.

[*Enter* JACKSON, *in his clown's costume.*]

Jackson. A whiskey and soda for me, too! At least I hear some laughter here. Those idiots have simply forgotten how to laugh. My sun was rising and setting and crawling all over the ring—and not a smile! Look at my bottom, shines like a mirror. [*Turns around quickly.*] Beg your pardon, Zinida. And you don't look badly tonight, HE. Look out for your cheeks. I hate beauties.

Briquet. A benefit performance crowd!

Jackson. [*Looking in a hand mirror, correcting his make-up.*] In the orchestra there are some Barons and Egyptian mummies. I got a belly-ache from fright. I am an honest clown. I can't stand it when they look at me as if I had stolen a handkerchief. HE, please give them a good many slaps tonight.

He. Be quiet, Jim. I shall avenge you. [*He goes out*].

Zinida. And how is Bezano?

Jackson. [*Grumbling.*] Bezano! A crazy success. But he is crazy, he will break his neck tomorrow. Why does he run such a risk? Or perhaps he has wings, like a god? Devil take it. It's disgusting to look at him. It's not work any more.

Briquet. You are right, Jim! It is not work any more. To your health, old comrade, Jackson.

Jackson. To yours, Louis.

Briquet. It is not work any more, since these Barons came here! Do you hear? They are laughing. But I am indignant, I am indignant, Jim! What do they want here, these Barons? Let them steal hens in other hen roosts, and leave us in peace. Ah! Had I been Secretary of the Interior, I should have made an iron fence between us and those people.

Jackson. I am very sorry myself for our dear little Consuelo. I don't know why, but it seems to me that we all look today more like swindlers than honest artists. Don't you think so, Zinida?

Zinida. Everybody does what he wants. It's Consuelo's business and her father's.

Briquet. No, Mother, that's not true! Not everybody does what he wants, but it turns out this way . . . devil knows why.

[*Enter* ANGELICA *and* THOMAS, *an athlete.*]

Angelica. Is this where we're going to have champagne?

Briquet. And you're glad already?

Thomas. There it is! Oh, oh, what a lot!

Angelica. The Count told me to come here. I met him.

Briquet. [*Angrily.*] All right, if he said so, but there is no reason to enjoy it. Look out, Angelica, you will have a bad end. I see you through and through. How does she work, Thomas?

Thomas. Very well.

Angelica. [*In a low voice.*] How angry Papa Briquet is tonight.

[*Enter* HE, TILLY, POLLY, *and other* ACTORS, *all in their costumes.*]

Tilly. Do you really want champagne?

Polly. I don't want it at all. Do you, Tilly?

Tilly. And I don't want it. HE, did you see how the Count walks?

[*Walks, imitating* MANCINI. *Laughter.*]

Polly. Let me be the Baron. Take my arm. Look out, ass, you stepped on my beloved family tree!

Angelica. It'll soon be finished. Consuelo is galloping now. It is her waltz. What a success she is having!

[*All listen to the waltz.* TILLY *and* POLLY *are singing it softly.*]

Angelica. She is so beautiful! Are those her flowers?

[*They listen. Suddenly, a crash as if a broken wall were tumbling down: applause, shouting, screaming; much motion on the stage. The* ACTORS *are pouring champagne. New ones come in, talking and laughing. When they notice the director and the champagne, they become quiet and modest.*]

Voices. They're coming! What a success! I should say, since all the orchestra seats . . . And what will it be when they see the Tango? Don't be envious, Alphonse.

Briquet. Silence! Not so much noise, please! Zinida, look here, don't be so quiet! High society!

[*Enter* CONSUELO, *on the arm of the* BARON, *who is stiff and erect. She is happy.* MANCINI, *serious and happy. Behind them,* RIDERS, ACTORS, ACTRESSES. *The* BARON *has in his buttonhole a fiery-red rose. All applaud and cry: "Bravo, bravo!"*]

Consuelo. Friends . . . my dears . . . Father, I can't . . .

[*Throws herself into* MANCINI'S *arms, and hides her face on his shoulder.* MANCINI *looks with a smile over her head at the* BARON. BARON *smiles slightly, but remains earnest and motionless. A new burst of applause.*]

Briquet. Enough, children! Enough!

Mancini. Calm yourself, calm yourself, my child. How they all love you! [*Taking a step forward.*] Ladies and gentlemen, Baron Regnard did me the honor yesterday, to ask for the hand of my daughter, the Countess Veronica, whom you knew under the name of Consuelo. Please take your glasses.

Consuelo. No, I am still Consuelo, tonight, and I shall always be Consuelo! Zinida, dear!

[*Falls on the neck of* ZINIDA. *Fresh applause.*]

Briquet. Stop it; Silence! Take your glasses. What are you standing here for? If you came, then take the glasses.

Tilly. [*Trembling.*] They are frightened. You take yours first, Papa, and we will follow.

[*They take the glasses.* CONSUELO *is near the* BARON, *holding the sleeve of his dress coat with her left hand. In her right hand, she has a glass of champagne, which spills over.*]

Baron. You are spilling your wine, Consuelo.

Consuelo. Ah! It is nothing! I am frightened, too. Are you, Father?

Mancini. Silly child.

[*An awkward silence.*]

Briquet. [*With a step forward.*] Countess! As the director of the circus, who was happy enough . . . to witness . . . many times . . . your success . . .

Consuelo. I do not *like* this, Papa Briquet! I am Consuelo. What do you want to do with me? I shall cry. I don't want this "Countess." Give me a kiss, Briquet!

Briquet. Ah, Consuelo! Books have killed you.

[*Kisses her with tears. Laughter, applause. The* CLOWNS *cluck like hens, bark, and express their emotions in many other ways. The motley crowd of* CLOWNS, *which is ready for the pantomime, becomes more and more lively. The* BARON *is motionless, there is a wide space around him; the people touch glasses with him in a hurry, and go off to one side. With* CONSUELO *they clink willingly and cheerfully. She kisses the* WOMEN.]

Jackson. Silence! Consuelo, from today on, I extinguish my sun. Let the dark night come after you leave us. You were a nice comrade and worker, we all loved you and will love the traces of your little feet on the sand. Nothing remains to us!

Consuelo. You are so good, so good, Jim. So good that there is no one better. And your sun is better than all the other suns. I laughed so much at it. Alfred, dear, why don't you come? I was looking for you.

Bezano. My congratulations, Countess.

Consuelo. Alfred, I am Consuelo!

Bezano. When you are on horseback; but here—I congratulate you, Countess.

[*He passes, only slightly touching* CONSUELO'S *glass.* CONSUELO *still holds it.* MANCINI *looks at the* BARON *with a smile. The latter is motionless.*]

Briquet. Nonsense, Bezano. You are making Consuelo unhappy. She is a good comrade.

Consuelo. No, it's all right.

Angelica. You'll dance the Tango with her tonight, so how is she a countess?

Tilly. May I clink glasses with you, Consuelo? You know Polly has died of grief already, and I am going to die. I have such a weak stomach.

[*Laughter;* BARON *shows slight displeasure. General motion.*]

Mancini. Enough, enough! The intermission is over.

Consuelo. Already? It's so nice here.

Briquet. I shall prolong it. They can wait. Tell them, Thomas.

Mancini. Auguste, the musicians of the orchestra, too, ask permission to congratulate you and Consuelo. Do you . . . ?

Baron. Certainly, certainly.

[*Enter crowd of* MUSICIANS. *The* CONDUCTOR, *an old Italian, lifts his glass solemnly and without looking at the* BARON.]

The Conductor. Consuelo! They call you Countess here, but for me you were and are Consuelo.

Consuelo. Certainly!

The Conductor. Consuelo! My violins and bassoons, my trumpets and drums, all are drinking your health. Be happy, dear child, as you were happy here. And we shall conserve for ever in our hearts the fair memory of our light-winged fairy, who guided our bows so long. I have finished! Give my love to our beautiful Italy, Consuelo.

[*Applause, compliments. The* MUSICIANS *one after another clink glasses and go out into the corridor.* CONSUELO *is almost crying.*]

Mancini. Don't be so sensitive, my child, it is indecent. Had I known that you would respond this way to this comedy—Auguste, look how touched this little heart is!

Baron. Calm yourself, Consuelo.

Consuelo. It is all right. Ah, father listen!

[*The musicians are playing the Tango in the corridor. Exclamations.*]

Mancini. You see. It is for you.

Consuelo. They are so nice, My Tango! I want to dance. Who is doing to dance with me? [*Looks around, seeking* BEZANO, *who turns away sadly.*] Who, then?

Voices. Baron! Let the Baron dance! Baron!

Baron. All right. [*Takes* CONSUELO'S *arm, and stands in the centre of a circle which is formed.*] I do not know how to dance the Tango, but I shall hold tight. Dance, Consuelo.

[*He stands with legs spread, heavily and awkwardly, like an iron-moulded man, holding* CONSUELO'S *arm firmly and seriously.*]

Mancini. [*Applauding.*] Bravo! Bravo!

[CONSUELO *makes a few restless movements, and pulls her arm away.*]

Consuelo. No, I can't this way. How stupid! Let me go!

[*She goes to* ZINIDA *and embraces her, as if hiding herself. The music still plays. The* BARON *goes off quietly to the side. There is an unfriendly silence among the cast. They shrug their shoulders.*]

Mancini. [*Alone.*] Bravo! Bravo! It is charming, it is exquisite!

Jackson. Not entirely, Count.

[TILLY *and* POLLY *imitate the* BARON *and* CONSUELO *without moving from their places.*]

Tilly. [*Shrieking.*] Let me go!

Polly. No, I'll not. Dance!

[*The music stops abruptly. General, too loud laughter; the* CLOWNS *bark and roar.* PAPA BRIQUET *gesticulates, in order to re-establish silence. The* BARON *is apparently as indifferent as before.*]

Mancini. Really these vagabonds are becoming too impertinent. [*Shrugging his shoulders.*] It smells of the stable. You cannot help it, Auguste!

Baron. Don't be upset, Count.

He. [*Holding his glass, approaches the* BARON.] Baron. Will you permit me to make a toast?

Baron. Make it.

He. To your dance!

[*Slight laughter in the crowd.*]

Baron. I don't dance!

He. Then another one, Baron. Let us drink to those who know how to wait longer, until they get it.

Baron. I do not accept any toasts which I do not understand. Say it more simply.

[*Voice of a* WOMAN: *"Bravo,* HE!" *Slight laughter.* MANCINI *says something hastily to* BRIQUET; *the latter spreads his arms in gesture of helplessness.* JACKSON *takes* HE by the arm.]. .

Jackson. Beat it, HE! The Baron doesn't like jokes.

He. But I want to drink with the Baron. What can be simpler? Simpler? Baron, let us drink to the very small distance which will always remain 'twixt the cup and the lip!

[*Spills his wine, and laughs. The* BARON *turns his back on him, indifferently. The music plays in the ring. The bell rings.*]

Briquet. [*Relieved.*] There! To the ring, ladies and gentlemen, to the ring, to the ring!

[*The* ACTRESSES *run out. The crowd becomes smaller; laughter and voices.*]

Mancini. [*Much excited, whispers to the* BARON.] "Auguste, Auguste——"

Briquet. [*To* ZINIDA.] Thank heaven they're beginning. Ah, Mother, I asked you . . . but you want a scandal by all means, and you always——

Zinida. Let me alone, Louis.

[HE *approaches* CONSUELO, *who is alone.*]

Consuelo. HE, deary, how are you? I thought you didn't want even to come near me. [*In a low voice.*] Did you notice Bezano?

He. I was waiting for my turn, Queen. It was so difficult to get through the crowd to approach you.

Consuelo. Through the crowd? [*With a sad smile.*] I am quite alone. What do you want, Father?

Mancini. Child! Auguste . . .

Consuelo. [*Pulling away her hand.*] Let me alone! I'll soon be— Come here, HE. What did you say to him? They all laughed. I couldn't understand. What?

He. I joked, Consuelo.

Consuelo. Please don't, HE, don't make him angry; he is so terrible. Did you see how he pressed my arm? I wanted to scream. [*With tears in her eyes.*] He hurt me!

He. It's not too late yet. Refuse him.

Consuelo. It *is* too late, HE. Don't talk about it.

He. Do you want it? I will take you away from here.

Consuelo. Where to? [*Laughs.*] Ah, my dear little silly boy, where could you take me to? All right, be quiet. How pale you are! You, too, love me? Don't, HE, please don't! Why do they all love me?

He. You are so beautiful.

Consuelo. No, no. It's not true. They must not love me. I was still a little cheerful, but when they began to speak . . . so nicely . . . and about Italy . . . and to bid farewell, as if I were dying, I thought I should begin to cry. Don't talk, don't talk, but drink to . . . my happiness. [*With a sad smile.*] To my happiness, HE. What are you doing?

He. I am throwing away the glass from which you drank with the others. I shall give you another one. Wait a minute.

[*Goes to pour champagne.* CONSUELO *walks about thoughtfully. Almost all are gone. Only the principal figures are left.*]

Mancini. [*Coming to her.*] But it is really becoming indecent, Veronica. Auguste is so nice, he is waiting for you, and you talk here with this clown. Some stupid secrets. They're looking at you—it is becoming noticeable. It is high time, Veronica, to get rid of these habits.

Consuelo. [*Loudly.*] Let me alone, Father! I want to do so, and will do so. They are all my friends. Do you hear? Let me alone!

Baron. Don't, Count. Please, Consuelo, talk to whomever you please and as much as you want. Would you like a cigar, Count? Dear Briquet, please order them to prolong the intermission a little more.

Briquet. With pleasure, Baron. The orchestra crowd can be a little angry.

[*Goes, and returns shortly.* HE *gives a glass to* CONSUELO.]

He. Here is your glass. To your happiness, to your freedom, Consuelo!

Consuelo. And where is yours? We must touch our glasses.

He. You leave half.

Consuelo. Must I drink so much? HE, deary, I shall become drunk. I still have to ride.

He. No, you will not be drunk. Dear little girl, did you forget that I am your magician? Be quiet and drink. I charmed the wine. My witchery is in it. Drink, goddess.

Consuelo. [*Lingeringly.*] What kind eyes you have. But why are you so pale?

He. Because I love you. Look at my kind eyes and drink; give yourself up to my charms, goddess! You shall fall asleep, and wake again, as before. Do you remember? And you shall see your country, your sky . . .

Consuelo. [*Bringing the glass to her lips.*] I shall see all this; is that true?

He. [*Growing paler.*] Yes! Awake, goddess, and remember the time when, covered with snow-white sea-foam, thou didst emerge from the sky-blue waters. Remember heaven, and the low eastern wind, and the whisper of the foam at thy marble feet. . . .

Consuelo. [*Drinking.*] There! Look! Just a half! Take it. But what is the matter with you? Are you laughing or crying?

He. I am laughing and crying.

Mancini. [*Pushing* HE *away, slightly.*] Enough, Countess, my patience is exhausted. If Auguste is good enough to allow it, then I, your father—Your arm, Countess! Will you step aside, sir?

Consuelo. I am tired.

Mancini. You are not too tired to chatter and drink wine with a clown, and when your duty calls you—Briquet! Tell them to ring the bell. It is time.

Consuelo. I am tired, Father.

Zinida. Count, it is cruel. Don't you see how pale she has become?

Baron. What is the matter with you, dear little Consuelo?

Consuelo. Nothing.

Zinida. She simply needs a rest, Baron. She hasn't sat down yet . . . and so much excitement. . . . Sit down here, dear child. Cover yourself and rest a little. Men are so cruel!

Consuelo. I still have to work. [*Closing her eyes.*] And the roses, are they ready?

Zinida. Ready, dear, ready. You will have such an extraordinary carpet. You will gallop as if on air. Rest.

Polly. Do you want some moosic? We will play you a song; do you want it?

Consuelo. [*Smiling, eyes closed.*] Yes, I do.

[*The* CLOWNS *play a soft and naïve song: tilly-polly, tilly-polly. General silence.* HE *sits in the corner with his face turned away.* JACKSON *watches him out of the corner of his eye, and drinks wine, lazily. The* BARON, *in his usual pose, wide and heavily spread legs, looks at the pale face of* CONSUELO, *with his bulging motionless eyes.*]

Consuelo. [*With a sudden cry.*] Ah! Pain!

Zinida. What is it, Consuelo?

Mancini. My child! Are you sick? Calm yourself.

Baron. [*Growing pale.*] Wait a moment. . . . She was too much excited. . . . Consuelo!

Consuelo. [*Gets up, looking before her with wide-open eyes, as if she were listening to something within herself.*] Ah! I feel pain. Here at the heart. Father, what is it? I am afraid. What is it? My feet too . . . I can't stand. . . . [*Falls on divan, her eyes wide open.*]

Mancini. [*Running about.*] Bring a doctor! Heavens, it is terrible! Auguste, Baron . . . It never happened to her. It is nerves, nerves. . . . Calm yourself, calm, child——

Briquet. Bring a doctor!

[*Somebody runs for a doctor.*]

Jackson. [*In a voice full of fear.*] HE, what is the matter with you?

He. It is death, Consuelo, my little Queen. I killed you. You are dying.

[HE *cries, loudly and bitterly.* CONSUELO *with a scream, closes her eyes, and becomes silent and quiet. All are in terrible agitation. The* BARON *is motionless, and sees only* CONSUELO.]

Mancini. [*Furious.*] You are lying, rascal! Damned clown! What did you give her? You poisoned her! Murderer! Bring a doctor!

He. A doctor will not help. You are dying, my little Queen. Consuelo! Consuelo!

[BEZANO *rushes in, cries:* "BRIQUET!" *becomes silent and looks with horror at* CONSUELO. *Somebody else comes in.* BRIQUET *is making gestures for some one to close the door.*]

Consuelo. [*In a dull and distant voice.*] You are joking, HE? Don't frighten me. I am so frightened. Is that death? I don't want it. Ah, HE, my darling HE, tell me that you are joking, I am afraid, my dear, golden HE!

[HE *pushes away the* BARON, *with a commanding gesture, and stands in his place near* CONSUELO. *The* BARON *stands as before, seeing only* CONSUELO.]

He. Yes, I am joking. Don't you hear how I laugh, Consuelo? They all laugh at you here, my silly child. Don't laugh, Jim. She is tired, and wants to sleep. How can you laugh, Jim! Sleep, my dear, sleep, my heart, sleep, my love.

Consuelo. Yes, I have no more pain. Why did you joke that way, and frighten me? Now I laugh at myself. You told me, didn't you, that I . . . should . . . live . . . eternally?

He. Yes, Consuelo! You shall live eternally. Sleep. Be calm. [*Lifts up his arms, as if straining with all his forces to lift her soul higher.*] How easy it is now! How much light, how many lights are burning about you. . . . The light is blinding you.

Consuelo. Yes, light . . . Is that the ring?

He. No, it is the sea and the sun . . . what a sun! Don't you feel that you are the foam, white sea-foam, and you are flying to the sun? You feel light, you have no body, you are flying higher, my love!

Consuelo. I am flying. I am the sea-foam, and this is the sun, it shines . . . so strong. . . . I feel well.

[*She dies. Silence.* HE *stays a moment with lifted arms, then takes a long look, lets his arms fall, and shakingly goes off to one side. He stands still for a moment, then sits down, drops his head on his hands, and struggles lonesomely with the torpidity of coming death.*]

Briquet. [*Slowly.*] She has fallen asleep, Mother?

Zinida. [*Dropping the dead hand.*] I am afraid not. . . . Step aside, Louis. Baron, it is better for you to step aside. Baron! Do you hear me? [*Weeps.*] She is dead, Louis.

[*The* CLOWNS *and* BRIQUET *are crying.* MANCINI *is overwhelmed. The* BARON *and* HE *are motionless, each in his place.*]

Jackson. [*Drawing out a large prismatic clown's handkerchief to wipe away his tears.*] Faded, like a flower. Sleep, little Consuelo! The only thing that remains of you is the trace of your little feet on the sand. [*Cries.*] Ah, what did you do, what did you do, HE! . . . It would have been better if you had never come to us.

[*There is music in the ring.*]

Briquet. [*Gesticulating.*] The music! Stop the music! They are crazy there. What a misfortune!

[*Some one runs off.* ZINIDA *approaches the crying* BEZANO *and strokes his bowed, pomaded head. When he notices her, he catches her hand and presses it to his eyes. The* BARON *takes the rose from his button-hole, tears off the petals, and drops it, grinding it with his foot. A few pale faces peer through the door, the same masquerade crowd.*]

Zinida. [*Over the head of* BEZANO.] Louis, we must call the police.

Mancini. [*Awakening from his stupor, screams.*] The police! Call the police! It's a murder! I am Count Mancini, I am Count Mancini! They will cut off your head, murderer, damned clown, thief! I myself will kill you, rascal! Ah, you!

[HE *lifts his heavy head with difficulty.*]

He. They will cut off my head? And what more . . . Your Excellency?

Baron. Sir! Listen, sir! I am going for the police. Stop it, sir. [*He suddenly takes a step forward, and looking* HE *in the eyes, speaks in a hoarse voice, with a cough, holding one hand at his throat.*] I am the witness. I saw. I am a witness. I saw how he put poison . . . I——

[*He leaves the room, suddenly, with the same straight, heavy steps. All move away from him, frightened.* HE *drops his head again. From time to time a tremor shakes his body.*]

Jackson. [*Clasping his hands.*] Then it is all true? Poisoned! What a vile man you are, HE. Is this the way to play? Now wait for the last slap of the executioner!

[*Makes the gesture around his neck of the guillotine.* TILLY *and* POLLY *repeat the gesture.*]

Zinida. Leave his soul alone, Jim. He was a man, and he loved. Happy Consuelo!

[*A shot is heard in the corridor.* THOMAS, *frightened, runs in and points to his head.*]

Thomas. Baron . . . Baron . . . his head . . . He shot himself! . . .

Briquet. [*Throwing his arms up.*] God! What is it? The Baron? What a calamity for our circus!

Mancini. The Baron? The Baron? No. What are you standing here for? Ah!

Briquet. Calm down, Count. Who would have believed it? Such a respectable . . . gentleman!

He. [*Lifting his head with difficulty; he sees only dimly with his dulled eyes.*] What more? What happened?

Thomas. The Baron shot himself. Honestly. Straight here! He's lying out yonder.

He. [*Thinking it over.*] Baron? [*Laughs.*] Then the Baron burst?

Jackson. Stop it! It's shameless. A man died and you . . . What's the matter with you, HE?

He. [*Stands up, lifted to his feet by the last gleam of consciousness and life, speaks strongly and indignantly.*] You loved her so much, Baron? So much? My Consuelo? And you want to be ahead of me even *there*? No! I am coming. We shall prove then whose she is to be for ever. . . .

[HE *catches at his throat, falls on his back. People run to him. General agitation.*]

CURTAIN

MAN AND THE MASSES*

[*Masse Mensch*]

By

ERNST TOLLER

Translated by LOUIS UNTERMEYER

A SENSITIVE YOUNG GERMAN POET, DISillusioned and crushed by the War, fired with a hatred for the exploiters of the masses, turned into an active revolutionist in spite of his love of peace and brotherhood, thrown into prison from which he sent forth plays and poems to maintain his spiritual leadership and finally, as a despairing expatriate, driven to suicide in New York—such is the brief tragedy of Ernst Toller.

In spite of the suggestion of ruthlessness in all this activity, his revolt was essentially not that of Marx, Lenin, and Trotsky; it was rather that of Byron and Shelley, Prometheus and Job. A ready-made Utopia at all costs was not his purpose. From the beginning he understood the complexities of life and the weaknesses of man too well to cherish such illusions. Through the horrors of war and defeat, through the frantic intellectual struggle of young Germany to find itself, and through the searching of his own spiritual nature, he came to place himself relentlessly on the side of those who in the end must bear the burdens and pay the cost of war, famine, and injustice—the workers. Dedicated to their service he strove to realize their vision and to make sure their destiny. As he once wrote to a friend, he contended with his own mind and won it over with his spirit.

He deplored bloodshed and did his best to prevent his followers from slaying and being slain. It was significant that in his first play written in prison, *The Machine-Wreckers,* he turned back for inspiration to young Lord Byron's maiden speech in the House of Lords in defence of the Nottingham workers. Such was his theme and tone—such his world vision.

He assumed the literary manner of his freed spirit. He discarded sophistication and learned the thought idiom of his comrades. Ashley Dukes quotes a friend as saying, "Only a man in a million can dare to be so simple." He was aware of his starkness and explained: "Those ideas which to us, who live close to the workers and understand and express their spiritual values, are a moving, rending, all-absorbing human experience, are nothing more than catchwords and newspaper phrases to bourgeois critics. . . . Proletarian art can exist only where the creative artist reveals that which is eternally human in the spiritual characteristics of the working people."

Expressionism he found ready at hand when as a young rebel he came to Berlin in 1917. The *Sturm* school of rebel writers following Wedekind's and Strindberg's dream consciousness technique (see preface to *The Dream Play*) had already developed the literature and drama of abstraction, giving it various names of which Expressionism is the most persistent. Sorge, Kaiser, Werfel, and Hasenclever productions had already made a stir. Toller contributed *Die Wandlung* to this rebel art movement of the theaters. Expressionism, itself an aspect of futurism, was fundamentally a revolt from the tedium of theatrical naturalism or, as O'Neill has expressed it, from "the banality of surfaces." It began in Strindberg's substitution of the stream of dream consciousness for the strict logic of the usual dramatic sequences. Wedekind had also turned to the menagerie and extravaganza for suggested form and content. With the later writers of the school the tendency of abstraction became essential in addition to other characteristics, and this we now think of as the focal center of expressionism. An abstraction of the mind or an emotion made concrete in terms of the stage—that must be basic in any theatrical work claiming this classification. This, too, was Toller's emphasis. His people are no longer individuals. They have become identified with abstract ideas—not, to be sure, with the old moralities of the vices and virtues, but with the dynamic concepts of our times—the earth spirit, the spirit of revolt, the concept of creative energy, the destiny of man, not as an individual, but as worker, slave, or master. In this drama, the individual appears only as a member of a class, the conscious or unconscious instrument of fate. The words and actions of reality still cling, but they no longer direct and dominate. What man thinks and feels and what he essentially is are the new stage puppets. All the arts of the theater as well as the dramatic dialogue are bent to give these abstractions direct and effective expression.

Toller wrote of *Man and the Masses:* "These pictures of 'reality' are not realism, are not local color; the protagonists are not individual characters." He describes his own mental process in conceiving them: "I see the room in which the workman lived, his little peculiarities, the characteristic gestures with which he threw away a match or kissed a woman. . . . I see the broad-backed farmer and the narrow-chested little clerk just as clearly. Then — suddenly — they are no longer human beings, X and Y and Z, but dreadful puppets dimly aware of the compelling fate that governs them." When two old women who looked alike and were similarly attired walked past his prison cell, he saw them "not for a moment as 'realistic human beings' going for a walk in the narrow prison lane of a 'realistic' Neuburg. It was a dance of death by two old maids, one old maid and her mirrored death, that stared me in the face."

Some critics have mistaken as realistic those parts of the play that seem so in comparison with the portions that clearly are in the dream consciousness manner. Toller defends his Berlin producer, the great Fehling of the Volksbühne (People's Theatre, which has one of the best equipped stages of the world), who regarded them as abstractions and gave them expressionistic interpretation. So important was the impressive production of the play at that theater in 1921 and so far-reaching its influence in the world theater, including our own, that a clear conception of it is essential to those who would rightfully evaluate the play for its largest import. By good fortune one of America's most vital and creative designers, Lee Simonson, was present at a performance. He has recorded his reactions to what he saw.

"As the curtain goes up one sees in a gray light a vast circle of perhaps fifty human beings, packed around the two central antagonists. [These are on a flight of steps crossing the entire stage and rising to a higher level, made possible by a mechanical device for raising half the floor.] The circle chants a refrain. A white light strikes the man and woman, their argument begins, they stand constantly surrounded by the circle of human beings, which contracts and expands slowly about them in harmony with the idea, but constantly holds them in. The light gradually spreads from the top to the bottom of the whole group, leaving the fringes shadowy, from which no voices come. No scheme on a level stage could have given any such sense of the leaders hemmed in, surrounded by the very mass they are trying to lead, and of this ponderous mass of human beings themselves. This, quite apart from the amazing beauty of the single composition of this mass of people, sculptured with light, swaying, distending, contracting about its two central gesticulating figures. [In the scene following the outbreak of the Revolution, one by one the stragglers come through a black curtain—for all the stage including the flooring is set simply in black—and form a serried but ever-spreading phalanx in the form of a large spearhead.] As the news of the loss of railway yards, telegraph office, and post office comes in, the spear becomes tighter and tighter, yet each cowers further and further back, awaiting machine gun shots that it seems must come any minute through the curtain. One stiffens in one's seat, bracing oneself helplessly against the invisible bayonet stab. The effect is more overwhelming than if one had heard the rattle of musquetry and seen these workers shot down before one's eyes. And what a profound interpretation that mere grouping of human beings was! How completely and finally it symbolized in its mere shape on the stage, the working class revolt of which the play told—their intention or their will, as militant as a spearhead and as powerful as a phalanx, and yet each individual that went to the making of that phalanx, cowering and helpless. It seemed to me the greatest piece of stagecraft I had ever seen and gave me fresh insight into how profoundly interpretive and how imaginative a producer can become, how much he can heighten the impact and the significance of a play by what one might call the orchestration of human movement and his composition of human form." [1]

[1] Quoted from *Down to the Cellar* by Lee Simonson, *Theatre Arts Magazine.* Vol 6, 1922, p. 127f.

In 1924 the Theatre Guild of New York mounted the play with settings by Lee Simonson that are now classic as the first in the American theater embodying the principles of German expressionism. The play has been frequently staged in England and America by little theater and college groups and has become the drama's chief symbol of the workers' revolt, while in itself it is the leading exemplar of revolutionary technique.

ERNST TOLLER

Born 1893, Samotschin, near Bromberg, Prussia.
Bromberg Realgymnasium, military training.
Travel and study in France, and Northern Italy.
1914–16, War service and nervous collapse. Studied economics and literature at Munich and Heidelberg.
1917, Joined in the founding of the Kulter-politischer Bund of German youths and became an active revolutionary in Munich. Lived for a short time in Berlin, as follower of Kurt Eisner.
1918, Joined the Independent Social-Democratic Party in Munich, promoted strikes of munition workers. First imprisonment. After Eisner's execution, became a leader of the Workers', Peasants', and Soldiers' Revolution.
1919, Imprisoned with five-year sentence for participation in the Munich Revolution.
Poet and playwright of the proletariat.
1933, Left Germany and became British citizen. Lectured in America and served as advisor to Dramatist's Guild.
1939, Suicide.

PLAYS

1918 *Die Wandlung* (translated as *The Transformation*). 1919 *Masse-Mensch* (translated as *Masses and Man, Mass-Man,* and *Man and the Masses*). 1920 *Die Maschinenstürmer* (translated as *The Machine-Wreckers*). 1922 *Der Deutsche Hinkemann* (performed in America as *Bloody Laughter* and translated as *Brokenbrow,* as *Hinkemann,* and in an incomplete version as *Hobbleman*). 1923 *Der Entfesselte Wotan* (*Wotan Unbound*). 1923 *Krieg und Frieden* (*War and Peace,* not published). A vast pageant of war and fraternization given at Leipzig. 1925 *Die Rache des verhöhnten Liebhabers oder Frauenlist und Männerlist: ein galantes Puppenspiel* (*The Revenge of the Scorned Lover: or Man and Woman's Cunning: a gallant Puppet Play*). 1925 *Der Tag des Proletariats* and *Requiem den gemordeten Brüdern* (Two choruses in dialogue, *The Day of the Proletariat* and *A Requiem for the Murdered Comrades*). 1927 *Hoppla, wir leben* (translated as *Hoppla! Such Is Life* and as *Hoppla!*). 1930 *Feuer aus den Kesseln* (translated as *Draw the Fires*). 1931 *Wunder in Amerika* (with Hermann Kesten, translated as *Mary Baker Eddy*). 1934 *The Blind Goddess.* 1937 *No More Peace.* 1938 *Blind Man's Buff* (with Denis Johnston, adaptation of *The Blind Goddess*). 1939 *Pastor Hall.*

WRITINGS ABOUT THE DRAMA

Selbstbiographischen Notizen des Bühnendichters. With an introduction by Fritz Droop: *Ernst Toller und seiner Bühnenwerke,* 1922. *Author to the Producer.* (Translation used as preface to the London edition of *Masses and Man*), 1921. *I Was a German* (autobiography), 1934; also translated as *Learn from My Youth,* 1936.

MAN AND THE MASSES

Characters

WORKMEN.
WORKWOMEN.
THE NAMELESS ONE.
OFFICER.
PRIEST.
MAN *(An Official).*
SONIA IRENE L. *(The Woman).*

FIGURES IN THE VISIONS

SONIA IRENE L. *(The Woman).*
THE COMPANION.
BANKERS.
THE OFFICIAL.
SENTINELS.
PRISONERS.
SHADOWS.

(The second, fourth, and sixth pictures are visionary; projections of a dream.)

FIRST PICTURE

Back room of a workmen's tavern. On the whitewashed wall are pictures of soldiers' councils and heroes of the masses.

[*In the center of the room, a crude table around which a* WOMAN *and several* WORKMEN *are sitting.*]

First Workman. Hand-bills have been distributed
In the great convention hall.
Tomorrow the factories will close early.
The masses seethe.
Tomorrow—the decision.
Are you ready, comrade?

The Woman. I am.
Strength grows with every breath—
How I have longed for this hour,
Where the heart's blood finds words,
And words grow into deeds!
Impotence shook me often—and I clenched
My hands in shame and agony and fury.
When filthy papers trumpet "Victory,"
A million hands take hold of me
And cry:
"You are guilty of our death!"
Yes, every horse with shivering, foaming flanks,
Accuses me in silence . . . accuses me.——
Yet, since I sound the final call tomorrow,
There, where my conscience flames up in the hall,
Shall I not be the one to proclaim the strike?
Mankind cries, Strike! Nature cries, Strike!
The river hisses, Strike!
Even the dog, it seems, barks for it as he leaps
When I come home. . . .
I feel it in each vein. The masses rise,
Free of red tape, of webs spun out
By well-fed gentlemen around green tables.
Armies of mankind, with overpowering purpose,
Will build a structure of peace to unknown heights.
The red flag . . . flag of bright beginnings . . .
Banner of daybreak . . .
Who will lead with it?

Second Workman. You! They follow you!
[*Silence flickers.*]

The Woman. Can we be sure no one has talked?
You think the police have had no information?
Suppose the soldiers form a chain around the hall?

First Workman. The police know nothing.
And if they do,
They never know our real intentions.
When once the masses can possess the hall
They'll make a raging flood that no police
Can tame into a plashing, park-like fountain.
Besides, the police won't dare to interfere,
Broken ranks have eaten up their sense of power.
The regiments, moreover, are on our side—
Councils of soldiers everywhere!
Tomorrow—comrade—the decision!
[*A knock.*]
Betrayed!

Second Workman. They must not find you.

First Workman. Only one door.

Second Workman. Through the window!
First Workman. The window opens on an air-shaft.
The Woman. And the struggle so near . . .
[*A louder knocking. The door is opened. The* MAN, *his coat-collar pulled up, comes in, looks about him quickly, and raises his derby.*]
The Woman. A—friend . . . And there's no danger . . .
You come to me;
You find me.
The Man. Good evening.
[*Softly.*]
Please don't introduce me.
May I speak with you?
The Woman. [*To the others.*]
Comrades . . .
The Workmen. Good-night.
Until tomorrow. [*Exeunt.*]
The Woman. Good-night; until tomorrow.
The Man. I must make it clear,
I did not come to help you.
The Woman. Forgive the dream that blossomed for a moment.
The Man. My honor's threatened—that is why I'm here.
The Woman. And I'm the cause? How strange . . .
Honor, you say. Honor of the bourgeois class?
And were there tongues of disapproval?
Did the outraged majority
Threaten to bar you from its sacred ranks?
The Man. Please don't be flippant.
Consideration for others—an emotion to which you are a stranger—
Is the law for me.
For me the strictest code of honor still survives.
The Woman. To stamp its pattern on you.
The Man. Self-control implies subordination.
We must submit . . .
Your thoughts are not upon my words.
The Woman. I see your eyes.
The Man. Don't disconcert me.
The Woman. You . . . You . . .
The Man. To come to the point,
You must give up your work.
The Woman. You . . .
The Man. The desire for social service—
Laudable, I'll grant—
Can be fulfilled in our own circle.
Let's say, a home for illegitimate children.
Ideas are the foundation of all work,
Proof of the very culture you deride.
Even your new-found friends, your so-called comrades,
Despise the unmarried mother.

The Woman. Go on . . . go on . . .
The Man. You are not free to act as you may choose.
The Woman. I am free . . .
The Man. I think I may assume some personal consideration,
A certain measure of respect—
If not from conviction, then for appearances.
The Woman. I have respect for nothing but my work.
That work commands me; that is all I serve.
The Man. Let's analyze you:
A wish for a new sort of service prompts your actions—
A wish born of a conflict of emotions.
I am, you understand, far from implying
That this wish springs from any base desires.
The Woman. How you can wound me with your words . . .
Tell me, have you ever seen the pictures of Madonnas
In peasants' houses?
Swords pierce the breast, the heart bleeds great dark tears.
Those gaudy, hideous, terribly moving prints . . .
So common—and so great . . .
You . . . you . . .
You speak of desires?
I know—a chasm yawns between us . . .
But it was not a whim that made me turn,
No *wish* to change my way of living.
It was a *need* . . . Need of my very self,
Need of the darkest depths of my existence.
Need alters us, I tell you, need changes us.
Not moods or spells or fits of boredom,
But need—the need to be a human being.
The Man. Need? Have you the right
To speak of need?
The Woman. You . . . my husband . . . do not torture me . . .
Now I hold your head . . .
Now I kiss your eyes . . .
You . . .
Say no more . . .
The Man. To hurt you was the last thing I intended . . .
But this place . . .
Can any one overhear us?
The Woman. Suppose a comrade does hear us?
They have understanding even though they lack your "code of honor."
Oh, if you only understood them,
If you could only get a breath of their great need.
Need . . . which is—which must be . . . ours!
You—you have lowered them . . .

And, in lowering them, you have debased yourself;
You have become your own executioner . . .
I do not want the pity in your eyes!
I'm not neurotic,
Not the least bit sentimental.
And since I'm not, I belong to them.
Oh, those miserable little hours you put aside
For social betterment—
A soothing syrup for your pity and weakness.
Many a comrade feels ashamed for you,
When they don't . . . laugh at you . . .
As I am laughing.

The Man. So—you may as well know everything.
They know about you—the authorities.
I took an oath of loyalty to the State.
The chief detective has been informed . . .
Otherwise, progress in my career would be impossible.

The Woman. And . . . ?

The Man. I tell you this,
Regardless of the consequences,
Which, you may be sure,
Affect me, too,
Especially since you would harm both the career
Of your husband and the welfare of the State . . .
You help the enemy within our gates.
This gives me grounds for a divorce.

The Woman. Of course . . . if I have harmed you,
If I have stood in your way . . .

The Man. There still is time.

The Woman. Then, of course,
Then . . . I am prepared . . .
I accept the blame . . .
You need not fear, the trial will not harm you.
You . . .
You . . . my arms stretch out to you
With hungry need.
You . . . my blood swells to you . . .
See—I am a withered leaf without you.
You are the dew that makes me blossom.
You are the storm whose April strength
Flings flaming torches in my thirsty veins . . .
There were warm nights . . . calls of young boys in spring
Exulting in the vigor of their blood. . . .
Take me away to meadows, fields or woodlands;
Meekly will I bow down and kiss your eyes. . . .
I know I will be very weak
Without you . . . unbelievably. . . .

[*Short pause.*]

Forgive me—I was weak just now.
I see the situation clearly; I understand your action.
Nevertheless—tomorrow I appear before the masses—
Tomorrow I speak to them.
Tomorrow I attack the State, to which you swore allegiance,
Tearing the old mask from its murderous face.

The Man. Your act is treason to the State.

The Woman. Your State makes war;
Your State betrays the people!
Your State exploits, grinds down
And robs the people of their rights!

The Man. The State is holy. . . . War insures its life.
Peace is a phantom of weak minds.
War is nothing but an interrupted armistice,
In which the State continually lives,
Constantly threatened by its foes without
And enemies within.

The Woman. How can a body live that's eaten up by plague
And burned by fire?
Have you seen the naked body of the State?
Have you seen the worms that feed upon it?
Have you seen the stock exchanges, the financiers
That gorge themselves with human flesh?
You have not seen it. . . . you have sworn allegiance to the State;
You do your duty and your conscience is quieted.

The Man. And this decision is your last word?

The Woman. My last word.

The Man. Good-night!

The Woman. Good-night!

[*As the* MAN *starts to go.*]

May I go with you?
Tonight for the last time . . .
Or am I shameless?
Or am I shameless . . .
Shameless in my desire? . . .

[*The* WOMAN *follows the* MAN. *The stage darkens.*]

SECOND PICTURE

(DREAM-PICTURE)

A room of the stock exchange.

[*At the desk, a* CLERK; *about him* BANKERS *and* BROKERS. *The* CLERK *has the face of the man of the first scene.*]

Clerk. Recorded.

First Banker. Munition works,
Three-fifty.

Second Banker. I offer
Four hundred.

Third Banker. Four hundred
Offered.

[*The* FOURTH BANKER *draws the* THIRD BANKER *toward the front. In the background there is the murmur of bidders and sellers.*]

Fourth Banker. [*To the* THIRD BANKER.]
Did you hear?
Retreat necessary.
Great offensive
Can't succeed.

Third Banker. Reserves?

Fourth Banker. Human material
Running poor.

Third Banker. Food inadequate?

Fourth Banker. That also.
Although
Professor Ude
Thinks
That rye
Ground down
With ninety-five per cent. of chaff
Will make
A food for epicures.

Third Banker. The leaders?

Fourth Banker. Splendid.

Third Banker. Not enough alcohol?

Fourth Banker. Distilleries
Working
Overtime.

Third Banker. What's wrong?

Fourth Banker. The General
Has called ninety-three professors
To headquarters.
Also our expert,
Councillor Glubor.
There'll be results.

Third Banker. They are?

Fourth Banker. Not to be discussed
In bourgeois circles.

Third Banker. Are the soldiers weakened
By love of man?

Fourth Banker. Strangely enough, no.
Man hates man.
Something's missing.

Third Banker. What's missing?

Fourth Banker. The mechanics
Of life
Have been laid bare.

Third Banker. What's missing?

Fourth Banker. Masses need joy.

Third Banker. What's missing? . . .

Fourth Banker. Love.

Third Banker. That's enough!
Then war,
As our chief instrument,
The mighty powerful instrument,
That takes the State,
Kings, ministers,
Parliaments,
Newspapers, churches,
And makes them dance,
Dance on this ball of earth,
Dance over the sea—
This war is lost?
Answer me: Lost?
Is that the net result?

Fourth Banker. Your calculation's poor.
The root of the trouble's been found—
Will be adjusted.

Third Banker. Through what?

Fourth Banker. Through international arrangements.

Third Banker. Is this known?

Fourth Banker. On the contrary.
We'll dress it up in national colors
And independent
Of the exchange.

Third Banker. And well financed?

Fourth Banker. Syndicate of the largest banks
Will underwrite it.

Third Banker. The profit?
Dividends?

Fourth Banker. Will be divided regularly.

Third Banker. The form of the enterprise sounds good.
But what's the scheme?

Fourth Banker. We'll camouflage and call it
Recreation Home:
A Place to Strengthen the Desire to Win!
The real thing:
National brothels.

Third Banker. Magnificent!
I subscribe one hundred thousand.
Just one more question,
Who regulates the amount of time,
Energy to be spent, et cetera?

Fourth Banker. Experienced generals.

They know
The standard regulations.
Third Banker. The plan
Drawn up yet?
Fourth Banker. To be regulated,
As I just said.
Three prices.
Three divisions.
Brothel for officers:
Stay there all night.
Brothel for corporals:
One hour.
Brothel for privates:
Fifteen minutes.
Third Banker. Thanks.
When does the market open?
Fourth Banker. Any minute.
[*Noise in the background.* THIRD *and* FOURTH BANKERS *go to the rear.*]
The Clerk. New issue ready:
National bonds,
War Recreation Home
Ltd.
First Banker. I have no order to buy.
Second Banker. The dividend does not tempt me.
Third Banker. I subscribe to one hundred thousand
At par.
The Clerk. Recorded.
Fourth Banker. Same here.
First Banker. [*To the* SECOND BANKER.]
The cool one's buying. . . .
What do you think?
Second Banker. Just got a telegram:
The drive on the West front
Has been lost. . . .
First Banker. Gentlemen,
The drive on the West front has been lost.
[*Cries, screams, shrieks.*]
Voices. Lost!
A Voice. I offer
Munition works
At one-fifty.
A Voice. I offer
Liquid Flame Trust.
A Voice. I offer
War Prayer-Book, Ltd.
A Voice. Offer
Poison-Gas Works.
A Voice. Offer
War loans.
Third Banker. I'll take another
One hundred thousand.
A Voice. What?
When prices are tumbling?
A Voice. Who said we had lost the drive?
A Voice. Is the rumor true?
Or just a trick to get control of the market?
The cool one
Has bought his second hundred thousand.
Second Banker. Something's wrong!
Switch my order!
I buy—
One-fifty.
A Voice. I bid
Two hundred.
A Voice. I buy
Three hundred.
A Voice. Who bids?
Four hundred?
I buy.
The Clerk. Recorded.
Fourth Banker. [*To the* THIRD BANKER.]
The old fox has guessed . . .
Third Banker. Excuse the question.
Has our most important method
Been saved?
Fourth Banker. How can you even ask that?
Mechanics of life
Are so simple—
There was a leak . . .
It is discovered
And stopped at once.
A rise
Or a fall today
Means nothing.
The important thing
Is to keep our machinery going.
And so it follows
The system is safe.
The Clerk. Recorded.
[*The* COMPANION *enters. His face is a composite of the features of death and the most radiant life. He leads the* WOMAN.]
The Companion. Gentlemen,
You're ordering too quickly.
"Blood—and the System!"
"Man—and the System!"
You cannot unite them.
One stamp of the foot
And your whole mechanism
Is broken
Like a child's toy.
Look out! [*To the* WOMAN.]
Speak to them!
The Woman. [*Quietly.*] Gentlemen:
Human beings . . .
I say it again:
Human beings!
[*The* COMPANION *and the* WOMAN *fade. Sudden silence.*]
Third Banker. You hear?
A disaster in the mines.
Seems
People are in distress.
Fourth Banker. I have an idea:

A Charity Festival.
Dance
On the floor of the stock exchange.
Dance
To aid the suffering.
Help
The unfortunates.
If it's convenient,
A little dance.
Gentlemen,
I contribute
One bond
War Recreation Home
Ltd.

A Voice. How about women?

Fourth Banker. As many as you want.
Someone tell the doorman:
Five hundred
Gay
Young girls
Wanted here!
Meanwhile . . .

The Bankers. We donate!
We dance!
Help
The unfortunates!

[*Music of clinking gold-pieces. The* BANKERS *in their high silk hats dance a fox-trot around the exchange. The stage darkens.*]

THIRD PICTURE

The stage remains dark.

Chorus of the Masses. [*As from a vast distance.*] We who are huddled for ever
In cañons of steel, cramped under cliffs of houses,
We who are delivered up
To the mockery of the machine,
We whose features are lost in a night of tears,
We, torn for ever from our mothers,
Out of the depths of factories, we cry to you:
When shall we, living, know the love of life?
When shall we, working, feel the joy of labor?
When shall deliverance come?

[*The stage becomes light. A great hall. On the platform a long narrow table. At the left, the* WOMAN *is sitting. In the room,* WORKING MEN *and* WORKING WOMEN *are packed closely together.*]

Group of Young Working Girls. And struggle breeds new struggles!
No compromising with these masters,
No loose agreements, feeble compacts.
Give orders to a group of comrades:
Dynamite in the machines!
Tomorrow factories will explode into the air.
Machinery herds us all like beasts in stockyards,
Machinery clamps us in its metal vise,
Machinery pounds our bodies day by day
And turns us into rivets . . . screws . . .
Screws . . . three millimeters . . . screws . . . five millimeters,
Withers our eyes, eats up our fingers,
While bodies go on living . . .
Down with the factories! Down with machinery!

Scattered Cries in the Hall. Down with the factories! Down with machinery!

The Woman. Once when I was blind, and felt the rods
Of engines pierce me and machines suck up my blood,
I, too, cried your despairing cry . . .
It is a dream that limits your own vision,
A dream of children, frightened by the night.
For, see—this is the twentieth century.
We must realize
The factory cannot be wiped out.
Take all the dynamite on earth,
And, in one night, blast all the factories,
By next spring, they will rise again
To live more terribly than ever.
Factories must no longer be the master,
And man the raw material.
Factories must be our servants,
Helping to make a richer life.
The soul of man must master factories.

Group of Young Workmen. Let them and us be destroyed together!
See how our words rush to revenge and fury.
The masters live in palaces;
Our brothers rot in filthy trenches.
Somewhere there's lively pleasure, dances, songs—
At night we read of them and grind our teeth!
And longing burns in us for light and knowledge. . . .
They took this holy thing
And it turned horrible.
Sometimes, but rarely, it shines out at us
In the theater,
And it is sweet . . . and clean . . . and always mocking!
In school their hatred cheated us of youth,
In schoolrooms they destroyed our souls.
Nothing but need makes us cry out. . . .

What are we today?
We will not wait!

Group of Agricultural Laborers. They turned us away from our mother earth.
These rich men buy up land as they buy street girls,
Amuse themselves with her, the holy mother,
And toss our raw flesh into munition plants.
But we grow sick, uprooted from our soil,
The unhappy cities sour us, break our strength.
We want the land!
The land for everybody!

Crowd in the Hall. The land for everybody!

The Woman. I went through the slums.
Gray rain dripped from dirty roofs;
Fungus sprouted from mouldy walls.
And in one room there sat an invalid
Who stuttered, "We were better off out there. . . .
Here we live in a pig pen . . .
Isn't it true . . . in a pig pen?"
A shamefaced smile slipped from his eyes.
And his shame shamed me. . . .
Brothers, do you want to know the way out?
There's one way left us weaklings,
For us who hate all war.
Strike! No more contracts, compromises.
Let our answer be, Strike!
We weak ones will become as strong as granite,
No weapon made can hope to conquer us.
Call to our mute battalions!
Summon our silent armies!
I cry, Strike!
Hear me:
I cry, Strike!
Moloch has fattened on our bodies
For six long years.
Pregnant women collapse upon the streets,
So starved they cannot even carry
The burden of the unborn.
Want stares at you in your homes;
Pestilence and madness glare at you,
And hunger, festering hunger. . . .
But there—look over there!
The bankers spend themselves in bacchanalia;
Champagne drowns every hard-fought victory;
Lust leaps and license stirs the dance
Around the golden altars.
And at the front?
Can you see the withered faces of your brothers?
Feel their bodies
Clammy in the fog and frost
Of twilight?
Smell the breath of that decay?
Hear their cries? I ask you.
Hear them calling?
"Brothers, we turn to you!
We, chained to the flanks of cannon,
We helpless ones,
We cry to you:
Help! Be our saviours!
You—be our rescue!
Hear me. I cry, Strike!
Whoever again eats munition wages
Betrays his brother.
What did I say—betrays?
He *kills* his brother.
And you, you women!
Do you know the story of those wives
Who remain barren
Because they helped forge deadly weapons?
Think of your men out there!
I cry, Strike!

Crowd in the Hall. We cry, Strike!
We cry
STRIKE!

[*Out of the crowd in the hall, the* NAMELESS ONE *emerges. He hurries to the platform, placing himself to the right of the table.*]

The Nameless One. The man who wants to build a bridge
Must pay attention to the pillars.
A strike today is a hasty bridge without supports.
We must have more than just a strike. . . .
Let's grant the thing's successful.
Suppose your strike forces them to a peace,
It is not Peace you've won—you've made *a* peace.
Instead of peace, you have a pause. That's all.
War must be stopped entirely,
Once and for all time.
But first, one final, desperate battle!
What will you gain if you halt this one struggle?
The peace that you create
Will leave your situation as it is.
On one hand, a false peace and old conditions.
On the other, a swift war and new conditions!
You fools, break down foundations;
Break the foundations, I tell you!
Then let the flood of your power wash away
The mouldering structure
Which only gold chains
Keep from falling apart.
Let us build a system under which we can live.
The factories belong to all the workers
And not to old man Capital.
The time has passed when, on our burdened backs,

He looked around with greedy eyes
For foreign treasures,
And planned fresh wars, enslaved an alien people,
Compelled the lying tongues of newspapers to scream:
"The Fatherland! All for the Fatherland!"
While underneath it rang the real refrain:
"For me! For me!"
That time has passed!
The masses of all nations have one cry:
The factories belong to all the workers!
All power to the workers!
All for us all!
I cry for more than Strike!
I cry, War!
I cry, Revolution!
Our enemy up there won't pay attention
To any pretty speeches.
Force against force!
Violence! . . . Violence!

A Voice. Arms!

The Nameless One. Yes, arms are all we need!
Go out and get them!
Storm the city hall!
The battle cry: Victory!

The Woman. Hear me!
I must . . .

The Nameless One. Quiet yourself, comrade.
Frantic appeals, clasped hands, and tearful prayers
Produce no children.
Consumptives can't get well on watered soup.
You have to use an axe to chop down trees.

The Woman. Hear me . . .
I do not want fresh murders.

The Nameless One. Silence, comrade.
What can you know?
You suffer our distress, I grant you that.
But have you worked ten hours in the mines,
A homeless child in blind, enormous rooms;
Ten hours in the mines—and the dark hut at evening? . . .
That is how day comes daily to the workers.
You are not one of them.
I am the Mass!
The Mass knows its own future.
The Mass is destiny!

A Voice. Is destiny . . .

The Woman. But think a moment,
Mass is powerless.
Mass is weak.

The Nameless One. How little do you realize the truth!
Mass is leader!
Mass is strength!

Crowd in the Hall. Is strength!

The Woman. Emotion pulls me toward the darkness
But all my conscience cries out, No!

The Nameless One. Keep silent, comrade!
The cause demands it.
What does one person matter?
His feelings? or his conscience?
Only the Mass must count!
Just think of it: a single bloody battle
And then, eternal peace.
No empty peace, a mask of mockery,
Hiding the face of war,
War of the strong against the weak,
War of exploiters, war of greed.
Think of it: the end of misery!
Think of it: crime a half-remembered fable!
It is the dawn of freedom for all people! . . .
You think I reckon lightly?
It is no longer a matter of choice.
War's a necessity for us.
Your advice means discord.
For the sake of the cause,
Keep silent.

The Woman. You . . . are . . . Mass.
You . . . are . . . right.

The Nameless One. Beat in the pillars of the bridge, O comrades!
Drive over every one who stands in our way.
Mass is action!

Crowd in the Hall. [*As they storm out.*]
Action! [*The stage darkens.*]

FOURTH PICTURE

(DREAM-PICTURE)

A court with a high wall is suggested. On the ground in the middle of the court, a lantern which gives a miserable light. [WORKER GUARDS *suddenly emerge from the corners of the court.*]

First Guard. [*Sings.*] My mother
Bore me
In the mud of a trench.
Lalala, la,
H'm, H'm.

Second Guard. My father
Lost me
In a brawl with a wench.

All the Guards. Lalala, la,
H'm, H'm.

Third Guard. Three years
I breathed
In the prison stench.

All the Guards. Lalala, la,
H'm, H'm.

[*With silent, ghostly steps, the* NAMELESS ONE *appears from somewhere. He stands near the lantern.*]

First Guard. Dear father
Forgot
To pay mother's fee.

All the Guards. Lalala, la,
H'm, H'm.

Second Guard. Poor mother
Never
Gave anything free.

All the Guards. Lalala, la,
H'm, H'm.

Third Guard. I troubled
The goddam
Bourgeoisie!

All the Guards. Lalala, la,
H'm, H'm.

The Nameless One. Come, dance!
I'll play for you.

The Guards. Halt!
Who are you?

The Nameless One. Did I ask your names,
Nameless ones?

The Guards. The password?

The Nameless One. Mass is nameless!

One of the Guards. Is nameless.
He's one of us.

The Nameless One. I'll play for you,
I, who announce
The great decision.

[*The* NAMELESS ONE *begins to play a harmonica. The rhythms of his tune are alternately rousing, swaying, and lascivious, then ponderous and stormy.* A CONDEMNED MAN, *a rope around his neck, steps out of the dark.*]

The Condemned Man. In the name
Of those condemned to die,
We beg a final
Favor:
Let us join the dance.
The dance is the very center
Of things.
Life, born of the dance,
Urges and runs
To the dance;
To the dance of desire,
To whirling Time
And its dance of death.

The Guards. One should always
Grant the condemned
Their last request:
Invited.

The Nameless One. Come, then!
One is as good as another.

The Condemned Man. [*Calls in the darkness.*] All those
Condemned to death,
Step up!
The last dance!
Let the waiting coffins
Wait.

[*All the* CONDEMNED, *with ropes around their necks, step out of the darkness.* GUARDS *and the* CONDEMNED *dance about the* NAMELESS ONE.]

The Guards. [*Singing.*] In the mud of a trench . . .

[*They dance on. After a short pause.*]

In a brawl with a wench . . .

[*They dance on. After a short pause.*]

In the prison stench . . .

[*They dance on.*]

[*The* NAMELESS ONE *breaks off suddenly. Those* CONDEMNED *to die run off to the dark corners of the court. Night swallows them up.* THE GUARDS *strike a posture. Silence surrounds the* NAMELESS ONE. *The* COMPANION, *in the guise of a guard, glides through the wall. He holds a* WOMAN, *who has the face of the* WOMAN *of the preceding scenes, close to him.*]

The Companion. The journey
Is difficult.
The result
Repays your trouble.
Look there—
The drama
Is about to begin.
If the impulse tempts you,
Act with it.

[*A* GUARD *brings in a* PRISONER *who has the features of the* MAN *and leads him to the* NAMELESS ONE.]

The Nameless One. Condemned
By the tribunal?

A Guard. He brought death
Upon himself.
He shot at us.

The Prisoner. Death?

The Nameless One. It frightens you?
Listen:
Guard! Answer me.
Who taught us
Capital punishment?
Who gave us weapons?
Who said "Hero" and "noble deed"?
Who glorified violence?

The Guards. Schools.
Barracks.
War.
Always.

The Nameless One. Force . . . violence and force.
Why did you shoot?
The Prisoner. I swore
To protect the State.
The Nameless One. You die
For your convictions.
The Guards. To the wall with him!
The Nameless One. Guns loaded?
The Guards. Loaded.
The Prisoner. [*Against the wall.*] Life! Life!
[*The* WOMAN *tears herself from the* COMPANION.]
The Woman. Don't shoot!
There stands my husband.
Forgive him
As I, too, humbly, forgive him.
Forgiveness is so strong
And far beyond all struggles.
The Nameless One. Do they forgive
Us?
The Woman. Do they struggle
For the people?
Do they fight
For humanity?
The Nameless One. The Mass counts.
The Guards. To the wall!
A Guard. Forgiveness is cowardice.
Yesterday I escaped
From the enemy over there.
They stood me up against the wall,
My body covered with bruises.
Next to me the man
Who was to murder me.
I had to dig
My grave
With my own hands.
In front of us
The photographer,
Eager to etch
Murder
On his plates.
I say, to hell with the Revolution
If it lets
Those grinning murderers over there
Make monkeys of us.
I say,
To hell with the Revolution!
The Guards. To the wall!
[*The face of the* PRISONER *changes to that of one of the* GUARDS. *The* WOMAN *speaks to the* GUARD *who has just finished.*]
The Woman. Yesterday they stood you
Against the wall.
Now you are standing
Against the wall again.
That is you
Who are standing there
Against the wall today.
Man—
You are he.
Recognize yourself—
You are man.
A Guard. The Mass counts.
The Woman. The Man counts.
All the Guards. The Mass counts!
The Woman. [*Despairingly.*] I give
Myself . . .
All of myself . . . to you . . .
[*The* GUARDS *laugh lewdly.*]
The Woman. [*Placing herself next to the* MAN.] Shoot then!
I give up. . . .
I am so tired . . . [*The stage darkens.*]

FIFTH PICTURE

The hall. Gray dawn crawls through the windows. The platform is illuminated with a gloomy light.
[*The* WOMAN *sits at the left of the long table, the* NAMELESS ONE *at the right.* WORKER GUARDS *at the doors of the hall. In the hall, isolated* WORKMEN *and* WORKWOMEN *huddle about the table.*]

The Woman. Has any news come within the last hour?
Forgive me, comrade, I slept.
The Nameless One. Report crowds upon report.
War is war;
A bloody game and one to be played coolly.
Before midnight we occupied the station.
At one o'clock we lost it.
Detachments are moving up now
For a fresh assault.
The post-office is in our hands.
At this very moment
Telegrams are being sent to the nations,
Telling them of our work.
The Woman. Work! What a holy word!
The Nameless One. A holy word, comrade!
It calls for more than speeches and a warm heart,
It calls for implements of steel,

It calls for ruthless war.
[*A second's flickering silence in the hall.*]
The Woman. Comrade, for all you say, I cannot be convinced.
To fight with weapons is to win through force.
The Nameless One. Mental weapons are also a force in battle.
Words can be murderers.—
Don't be so startled, comrade.
I deal in naked truths.
Why, if I thought as you, I'd be a monk
Walking some cloister in eternal silence.
[*Silence seems to sink heavily upon the hall.* FIRST WORKMAN *enters.*]
First Workman. I bring news.
We advanced three times against the station.
The place is thick with dead.
Damn them, they're well fortified,
Supplied with every kind of weapon,
Flame-throwers, hand-grenades, poison gas.
The Nameless One. You advanced three times.
And the fourth time?
First Workman. We did not advance four times.
The others charged on us.
The Nameless One. You held them.
Do you need support?
First Workman. We have been scattered.
The Nameless One. Reverses were to be expected.
Attention! Go to the thirteenth district;
The reserves are there.
Go—hurry! [*The* WORKMAN *goes.*]
The Woman. He spoke of dead.
Many hundreds.
Yesterday I cried out against all war—
And today . . . I let them kill;
I let brothers be flung to death.
The Nameless One. Your vision is not clear.
In yesterday's war we fought as slaves.
The Woman. And today?
The Nameless One. Today in battle we are free. [*Fevered silence.*]
The Woman. In both wars . . . human beings . . .
In both wars . . . human beings . . .
[*Silence reels.* SECOND WORKMAN *stumbles in.*]
Second Workman. The post-office is lost!
Our men are retreating!
The enemy gives no quarter.
Any one captured is shot!
[FIRST WORKMAN *rushes in.*]
First Workman. I come from the thirteenth district.
Struggle is useless.
The streets are closed.
The district has surrendered.
They're giving up their weapons.
Third Workman. The city's lost!
The work has failed.
The Woman. It had to fail . . .
The Nameless One. Once more, keep silent, comrade!
Our work is not a failure.
If we are not strong enough today,
Tomorrow there'll be fresh battalions.
Fourth Workman. [*Crying in the hall.*]
They're coming out against us!
O terrible slaughter!
They shot my wife;
My father's murdered.
The Nameless One. They died for the masses.
Erect barricades!
We're the defenders!
Our blood is ripe for battle!
Let them come!
[WORKMEN *storm into the hall.*]
Fifth Workman. They're butchering everyone.
Men, women, children.
We won't surrender to be killed
Like captured cattle!
They're butchering everyone; we must resist them to the end.
International law protects the enemy's soldiers,
But they can murder us like jungle beasts,
And set a premium on our flesh. . . .
Weapons are in our hands.
We're bringing bourgeoisie that we've captured;
I gave an order to shoot half of them.
We'll shoot the other half if their shock-troops get us.
The Nameless One. You avenge your brothers.
Mass is revenge for the wrongs of centuries.
Mass is revenge.
The Workmen. Is revenge!
The Woman. Madmen, drunk with battle!
I stay your arms!
Mass should be a band of loving brothers.
Mass should be one firm community.
Community is not revenge.
Community tears up the roots of all injustice.
Community plants the flowers of righteousness.
The man who revenges himself creates nothing;
He only destroys.—
You shot half of your prisoners!
That was not self-defense!
Blind rage, not service to the cause.

You kill men.
Do you kill, with them, the spirit of the State
Which you are fighting? . . .
I'm going to help those men out there.
I was prepared
To cripple my own conscience
For the sake of the Mass.
I cry:
Break up the system!
But you—you want to break up men.
I can't keep silence, not today.
Out there are men,
Born in the blood of suffering mothers . . .
Men for ever brothers. . . .

The Nameless One. For the last time, keep quiet, comrade.
Force . . . we need force. . . .
The enemy thinks nothing of our lives,
They will not spare us.
War is a grim affair; it can't be won
With pious looks.
Don't listen to this woman.
Prattle of petticoats!

The Woman. I cry, Stop!
And you . . . who . . . are . . . you?
Are you driven by an unchained lust for power—
A lust that has been caged for centuries?
Who . . . are . . . you?
Murderer . . . or . . . Messiah . . . ?
Murderer . . . or . . . Messiah . . . ?
Nameless one—your face?
You are . . . ?

The Nameless One. Mass!

The Woman. You! . . . Mass!
I cannot bear you!
I must protect those men out there.
For many years I've walked along with you.
I know—you've suffered more than I. . . .
I have grown up in light and happy rooms,
Never knew hunger,
Never heard crazy laughter
Reeling from filthy hangings.
Still—I could feel for you
And know you.
See, I come to you now, a pleading child,
Quietly, humbly.
Listen to me:
Break down the pillars of injustice.
Break the old chains of hidden slavery.
But also break the weapons of a rotting age.
Shatter hate! Shatter revenge!
Revenge is not the purpose to reorganize.
Revenge is not Revolution.
Revenge is nothing but an axe that splits
The clean and glowing metal,
The power of Revolution.

The Nameless One. How dare you, woman from another class,
Poison us in the hour of our decision?
I hear another accent in your talk.
You hope to shield those with whom you have grown up.
That's your real purpose.
You are betrayal.

Crowd in the Hall. [*Pressing threateningly about the* WOMAN.] Betrayal!

A Cry. An intellectual!

A Cry. To the wall with her!

The Nameless One. Your shielding them is treason.
The hour calls for conflict,
Pitiless conflict.
Who is not with us is against us.
The Mass must triumph.

Crowd in the Hall. Must triumph!

The Nameless One. You are arrested.

The Woman. I . . . shield those . . . with whom I have grown up?
No—I shield you!
It is you who are standing there against the wall!
I shield your souls!
I shield humanity, divine humanity.
Insane accusers . . .
Is there fear in my words? . . .
Never as low as that . . .
I have chosen . . .
You lie . . . you lie . . .

[*A* WORKMAN *enters the hall.*]

Workman. One of our prisoners barks,
Barks the same tune, barks all the time.
Wants to be taken to the woman who leads us.

The Nameless One. Proof.

The Woman. Again . . . you lie . . .
Who wants to speak to me—who?
Perhaps the man.
I never would betray my word for him.
But you betray yourselves . . .
I know nothing more. . . .

[*The* NAMELESS ONE *leaves the platform, diving into the crowd below him in the hall.* WORKERS *throng in from outside.*]

Workers. Lost!

Cries. Fly! Slaughter!

[*Scattered shots outside. The* WORKERS *crowd to the door.*]

The door is blocked . . .
Caught like rats in a trap!

[*Silent waiting for death.*]

A Cry. We die!

[*Some one begins to sing the "Internationale." Others join in. Powerfully.*]

Awake, ye slaves of every nation,
Enchained to hunger, want, and shame.
The depths are loud with liberation;
The dawn grows bright—the torches flame.

The way is clear, old bonds are breaking;
Rise up, ye masses, seize command!
A new world's ours for the taking,
We slaves bring power where we stand.
Comrades of every nation,
March on, our flags unfurled.
Arise to your salvation!
Arm, arm—and free the world!

[*Suddenly a short rattle of machine guns. The song is snapped off. The door at the principal entrance and the side doors are burst in with a single blow.* SOLDIERS *with guns in firing position stand at every door.*]

Officer. No use to resist!
Hands up!
Hands up, I command!
Where is the woman that leads you?
Why don't you stick up your hands?
Here—put on the handcuffs.

[SOLDIERS *handcuff the* WOMAN. *The stage darkens.*]

SIXTH PICTURE

(DREAM-PICTURE)

Boundless space. In the heart of it, a cage surrounded by a cone of light.

[*Crouching within the cage is a handcuffed person who has the face of the* WOMAN. *Close to the cage is the* COMPANION *in the form of a* KEEPER.]

The Handcuffed One. Where am
I?

The Keeper. In the place
Where man reviews himself.

The Handcuffed One. Drive away the shadows.

The Keeper. Drive them away yourself.

[*A gray* SHADOW *without a head appears from somewhere.*]

First Shadow. You know me, one they shot to death?
Murderess!

The Handcuffed One. I am not
Guilty.

[*A second gray* SHADOW *without a head appears from somewhere.*]

Second Shadow. You murdered me,
Also.

The Handcuffed One. You lie!

[*Other gray* SHADOWS *without heads emerge from somewhere.*]

Third Shadow. You murdered me.

Fourth Shadow. And me.

Fifth Shadow. And me.

Sixth Shadow. And me.

The Handcuffed One. Help me, keeper!
Good keeper!

The Keeper. Ha ha! Hahaha!

The Handcuffed One. I did not want
Bloodshed.

First Shadow. You kept silent.

Second Shadow. Silent when they attacked
The city hall.

Third Shadow. Silent when they stole
The weapons.

Fourth Shadow. Silent when they fought.

Fifth Shadow. Silent when they went
For the reserves.

Sixth Shadow. You are guilty.

All the Shadows. You are guilty.

The Handcuffed One. I wanted
To save
The others
From shooting.

First Shadow. Don't deceive yourself.
Before that,
They shot us.

All the Shadows. You murdered
All of us.

The Handcuffed One. Then I am . . .

The Shadows. Guilty!
Thrice guilty!

The Handcuffed One. I . . . am . . .
guilty . . .

[*The* SHADOWS *fade.* BANKERS *in high silk hats emerge from somewhere.*]

First Banker. I offer
Guilty Bonds
At par.

Second Banker. Guilty Bonds
Are not listed
Any more.

Third Banker. Bad investment!
Guilty Bonds,
Worthless scraps of paper.

The Three Bankers. Guilty Bonds
Are a total loss.

[*The* HANDCUFFED ONE *raises herself up.*]

The Handcuffed One. I . . . am . . . guilty.

[*The* BANKERS *fade.*]

The Keeper. Foolish one,
With your sentimental
Attitude to life—
If they were alive,
They would be dancing
About the golden altar

Where thousands have sacrificed.
And you, also.
The Handcuffed One. I, Man, am guilty.
The Keeper. Mass is to blame.
The Handcuffed One. Then I am doubly guilty.
The Keeper. Life is to blame.
The Handcuffed One. And therefore must I
Assume the burden of its guilt?
The Keeper. Every one lives in himself.
Every one dies his own death.
Man,
Like every tree and flower,
Bound by destiny,
Moulded by patterns;
Ripening each in separate ways,
Withering by themselves . . .
Discover the answer for yourself!
Life is everything.
[*From somewhere,* PRISONERS *in their convicts' clothes enter, walking five paces apart. They have pointed caps on their heads, from which hang tattered rags concealing their faces and allowing room only for eye-holes. They walk, in a monotonous rhythm, silently around the cage.*]
The Handcuffed One. Who are you,
Forms without faces?
Figures!
Who are you?
Mass
Of featureless forms?
Dull Echo from a Distance. Mass . . .
The Handcuffed One. O God!
The Echo. [*Dying.*] Mass . . .
[*Silence drips.*]
The Handcuffed One. [*Crying out.*] Mass is necessity!
Mass cannot be guilty!
The Keeper. Man cannot be guilty.
The Handcuffed One. God is guilty!
Distant Echoes. Guilty . . .
Guilty . . .
Guilty . . .
The Keeper. God is within you.
The Handcuffed One. Then I will triumph over God.
The Keeper. Worm!
Blasphemer!
The Handcuffed One. Did I dishonor
God?
Or did God
Dishonor Man?
O frightful
Decrees of guilt,
In which
Man after man
Is horribly entangled.
God—
Bring God to justice!
I accuse him!
Echo from a Distance. Bring God to justice!
[*The moving* PRISONERS *stand still. Their arms suddenly shoot up.*]
The Prisoners. We accuse Him!
[*The* PRISONERS *fade.*]
The Keeper. Now you are healed.
Come out
Of the cage.
The Handcuffed One. I am free?
The Keeper. Fettered!
Free! [*The stage darkens.*]

SEVENTH PICTURE

A prison cell. A small table, bench, and iron bed fastened to the wall. A grated hole of light clouded by frosted glass.
[*The* WOMAN *sits at the table.*]

The Woman. O path that leads through fields of ripening wheat
In August days . . .
Wandering on wintry hills before the dawn . . .
O beetle drinking in the breath of noon . . .
O world . . .
[*Silence spreads itself gently about the* WOMAN.]
Did I long for a child? [*Silence soars.*]
How life divides us all in two!
Bound to man and his desires.
To those we love . . . and hate . . .
Bound to our enemies?
Bound to ourselves?
I need him now . . . he must confirm me.
[*The cell is unlocked. The* MAN *enters.*]
The Man. Wife . . . I have come,
Come because you called me.
The Woman. Husband . . . !
Man . . .
The Man. I bring good news.
The sewers cannot keep on pouring
Their filth upon your name . . . my name, whenever they like.
The investigation of the recent murders
Showed that you were not guilty of the outrageous shootings.

Courage! The sentence committing you to death
Has not yet been confirmed.
In spite of treason to the State,
The nobility of aim
Is always respected
By all right-thinking people.

The Woman. [*Crying softly.*] I am without guilt . . .
Without guilt . . . yet I am guilty . . .

The Man. You are not guilty.
That's positive to every right-thinking person.

The Woman. To every right-thinking person . . .
I am so hurt . . .
And glad, because your name, free of disgrace . . .

The Man. I knew you were not guilty.

The Woman. Yes . . . you knew it . . .
Respect for good intentions . . .
You're so respectable!
I see you now so clearly . . .
And yet it's you who have been guilty—husband,
You . . . guilty of all these deaths.

The Man. Wife, I came to you . . .
Wife . . . your speech is hate.

The Woman. Hate? Never hate.
I love you—love you with all my blood.

The Man. I warned you against the masses.
Root up the masses and you root up hell.

The Woman. Hell? Who made that hell?
Who built the torture of your golden mills
That grind and grind out profit day by day?
Who put up prisons . . . who cried "holy war"?
Who sacrificed a million human lives
Upon the altars of some desperate game?
Who threw the masses into festering holes
In which, each day, is piled the filth of yesterday?
Who robbed these brothers of their human features,
Who drove them into factories,
Debased them into parts of a machine?
The State! . . . You! . . .

The Man. My life is duty.

The Woman. Oh, yes . . . duty . . . duty to the State.
You're so respectable . . .
Didn't I say I saw you all too clearly?
You've been so well brought up.
You—tell all your right-thinking people
They never have been right . . .
They are the guilty ones . . .
We are all guilty . . .
Yes, I am guilty . . . guilty to myself,
Guilty to all mankind.

The Man. I came to you.
Is this a court of justice?

The Woman. Here is a court of justice!
I, the accused, am also judge.
I bring the accusation . . . and pass sentence;
Pronounce acquittal
And the final blame . . .
Can you surmise . . . who bears the final blame?
Men must desire to work,
And work grows red with the dear blood of men.
Men must desire to live,
And they must swim through seas of human blood.
Can you surmise . . . who bears the final blame? . . .
Come, give me your hand,
Beloved of my blood.
I have conquered myself . . .
Myself and you.

[*The* MAN *breaks into trembling. A thought, suddenly springing up, distorts his face. He stumbles out.*]

The Woman. Give me your hand . . .
Brother, give me your hand;
You also are my brother.—
You have gone . . . you had to go . . .
The last road runs across a snowfield.
The last road never knows companions.
The last road winds without a mother.
The last road we walk alone.

[*The door is opened. The* NAMELESS ONE *enters.*]

The Nameless One. Cured of illusions? Free of dusty dreams?
Has knowledge thrust a dagger through your heart?
Did the judge say "human" and "you are forgiven"?
It was a wholesome lesson.
I congratulate you on your conversion.
Now you are ours again.

The Woman. You! Who sent you?

The Nameless One. The masses.

The Woman. They've not forgotten me?
The message . . . the message . . .

The Nameless One. My mission here is to set you free.

The Woman. Freedom!
Life!
We escape? Is everything prepared?

The Nameless One. Two keepers have been bribed.
There's one more at the gate. I'll strike him down.

The Woman. You'd murder him . . . for me?

The Nameless One. For the cause.

The Woman. I have no right
To win life through a keeper's death.

The Nameless One. The masses have a right to you.

The Woman. And the rights of the keeper?
Keepers are men.

The Nameless One. We have no men as yet.
On one side, the group belonging to the mass.
On the other, the class belonging to the State.

The Woman. Man is naked.

The Nameless One. Mass is godlike.

The Woman. Mass is not godlike.
Force made the mass.
Evils of property made the mass.
Mass is the movement of distress,
Is meek devotion . . .
Is terrible vengeance . . .
Is blinded slavery . . .
Is holy purpose . . .
Mass is a fertile field that has been trampled.
Mass is the choked-up, inarticulate people.

The Nameless One. And action?

The Woman. Action! And more than action!
To free man in the mass;
To free community in the mass.

The Nameless One. The raw wind before the gates
Will heal you.
Hurry!
We have only a few minutes left.

The Woman. You are not deliverance.
You are not salvation.
But I know who you are.
"Kill him!" you cried. Always your cry is "Kill him!"
Your father's name is War.
You are his bastard.
You poor, new head-of-staff of executioners,
Your only remedy: "Death!" and "Shoot them down!"
Throw off the mantle of your lofty phrases,
There's nothing but a woven tissue of lies.

The Nameless One. The murder-generals battled for the State!

The Woman. They murdered, but they did not kill with joy.
Like you, they all believed in their own mission.

The Nameless One. They battled for the cold, tyrannical State;
We battle for humanity!

The Woman. You murder for humanity,
As those deluded ones murdered for the State.
And there were some who surely felt
That through their State, their fatherland,
The earth would be redeemed.
I see no difference:
These murder for a single country,
The others kill for every country.
These murder for a thousand people,
The others for a million.
The one who murders for the State,
You call an executioner.
But he who murders for mankind
Is called a savior; you crown him
Courageous, noble, great.
Yes, you can speak of good and holy violence!

The Nameless One. Rail against others, rail against life itself!
Should I let still more millions be enslaved
Because their enslavers chain them in good faith?
And are you the less guilty
If you keep silent?

The Woman. The torch of gloomy violence cannot show the way.
You lead us to a new and curious land,
The land of ancient human slavery.
If fate has pushed you forward at this time
And given you a reckless power
To blandish and betray the desperate crowds
Who look to you as to a new Messiah,
I know this—such a fate will turn against the man.

The Nameless One. Mass counts and not the man.
You're not our heroine, our one-time leader.
Each person bears the taint of his extraction;
You have the bourgeois symptoms:
Weakness and self-deception.

The Woman. You have no love for man.

The Nameless One. The principle above everything!
I love posterity!

The Woman. The individual above everything!
You—you would sacrifice
All living men
For a principle.

The Nameless One. The principle demands the sacrifice.
But you betray the masses; you betray the cause.
These are the days when one must make decisions.
Who hestitates and lacks determination,
Supports the masters who bear down upon us,
Supports the masters who have let us hunger,
Is our foe.

The Woman. I would betray the masses
If I demanded a single human life.
A leader has no right to sacrifice any one but himself.
Listen: no man has the right to kill another
To forward any cause,
And any cause demanding it is damned!

Whoever, in its name, calls for the blood of man
Is Moloch.
God was Moloch.
State was Moloch.
Mass was Moloch.

The Nameless One. And what is holy?

The Woman. Some day . . .
Brotherhood . . .
Free men bound only by their common work . . .
Work . . . People.

The Nameless One. You lack the power to face the unyielding fact,
The need to act.
Free men will only come
Through hard facts and through harder deeds!
Atone by dying.
Perhaps your death will be some use to us.

The Woman. I live for ever.

The Nameless One. You were born too soon.

[*The* NAMELESS ONE *leaves the cell.*]

The Woman. You lived yesterday.
You live today.
And you are dead tomorrow.
I live for ever,
From sphere to sphere,
From change to change,
Till some day I become
Clean,
Guiltless,
Mankind. [A PRIEST *enters.*]

The Priest. I come to give you final consolation;
The Church does not refuse assistance even to the criminal.

The Woman. By whose orders?

The Priest. The State authorities directed me.

The Woman. Where were you on the day of the trial?
Leave me!

The Priest. God forgives you, too. I understand you.
You thought mankind was good—or so you dreamed—
And you allowed outrage and sacrilege
Against the holy State and sacred order.
Man is all evil—bad from the beginning.

The Woman. Man longs for goodness.

The Priest. The lie of these degenerate days,
Born of despair, decay, and effort to escape,
Protected by a brittle shell
Of pitiful and empty faith,
Forced by a bad conscience.
Believe me, he never once desires to be good.

The Woman. He longs for goodness. Even when he does wrong,
He does it under the mask of doing good.

The Priest. Nations come, nations go;
This earth has never seen paradise.

The Woman. I believe.

The Priest. Remember:
Lust for power; lust for pleasure!
That is the rhythm of the world.

The Woman. I believe.

The Priest. Earthly life is a constant changing of forms.
Mankind stays helpless. Salvation rests in God.

The Woman. I believe!!!
I am cold . . . Leave me!
Leave me!

[*The* PRIEST *leaves the cell. An* OFFICER *enters.*]

The Officer. Here's the sentence.
Mitigating circumstances considered—
Nevertheless—crimes against State must be punished.

The Woman. They are going to shoot me?

The Officer. Orders are orders. Obedience, obedience.
State interests; quiet, discipline.
Duty as officer.

The Woman. And man?

The Officer. All conversation forbidden.
Orders are orders.

The Woman. I am ready.

[*The* OFFICER *and the* WOMAN *go out. The cell is empty for a few seconds. Two* WOMAN PRISONERS *in prison smocks slip in. They remain standing at the door.*]

First Prisoner. Did you see the officer?
See his lovely gold uniform?

Second Prisoner. I saw the coffin. In the laundry. Yellow wooden box.

[*The* FIRST PRISONER *sees bread lying on the table and throws herself upon it.*]

First Prisoner. There's bread! Hungry!
Hungry! Hungry!

Second Prisoner. Give me! Me bread!
Me bread!

First Prisoner. Here's a mirror. My, how pretty!
Hide it. Evening. Cell.

Second Prisoner. Here's a silky cloth.
Naked breast, silky cloth.
Hide it. Evening. Cell.

[*From outside the sharp crack of a volley rings through the cell. The* PRISONERS *throw up outstretched, frightened hands. The* FIRST PRISONER *searches in her skirt for the mirror she has hidden.*

Lays it hurriedly back on the table and cries, sinking upon her knees.]

First Prisoner. Sister, why did we do that?

[*Her arms toss in the air with a great helplessness. The* SECOND PRISONER *takes the silken cloth which she has hidden in her skirt and lays it hurriedly on the bed.*]

Second Prisoner. Sister, why did we do that?

[*The* SECOND PRISONER *breaks down. She buries her head in her lap.*]

CURTAIN

R. U. R.*

[*Rossum's Universal Robots*]

By

KARAL ČAPEK

Translated by PAUL SELVER

KAREL ČAPEK HAS BEEN CALLED "THE whimsical philosopher of the commonplace." He stood boldly on the earth as it is. If it is to be a better world, it must become so and not be made so; that it can and will so become was his unshakable belief. He almost alone among the intellectual "straighteners" of our day chose the way of the obvious and followed it with a quiet good humor that was disarmingly his own and yet in the best tradition of humanity. It was the way chosen by Aristophanes, Shakespeare, Molière, Robert Browning, Anatole France, J. M. Barrie, and Joseph Conrad. Who but him would dare offer this simple suggestion: "If we could collect all the good that is in each one of us sinful human creatures, I believe that on it could be built a world that would be surely far kinder than the present one"? What other prophet of a struggling young nation would return from a visit to England with the message: "To be small, unsettled, and incompleted is a good and valiant mission"? Nor are these the bland words of a provincial intellect. Without exaggeration he could also say as few today can: "I have striven to understand everything."

Such at heart was the man whom many sober critics found violent, harsh, machine-minded, pessimistic. As satirist he has not always been understood; and satire was his all but invariable medium in fiction as well as in the theater. And yet there was little that was new or vague in his satirical method. It was that of the Utopian realm of nowhere; of *Gulliver's Travels* and *Erewhon*. His action—usually that of stark melodrama—was transferred to a land of the preposterous. Lest his satire miss its point, he invariably added an epilogue to give it double emphasis.

He professed to prefer the theater to the novel and short story, although he is well known in his own country by such books as *Painful Tales* and *The Factory of the Absolute*. Apparently he designed his plays as members of a cycle, to which as a whole he assigned no name. It might well be called "Blunders in Salvation," for each play applies bluntly, if grotesquely, some leading nostrum for the redemption of the world, especially if the panacea involves a revolutionary change. In *R. U. R.* the *robot* (a word he coined from the Czech *robit,* meaning work) replaces man as worker, then as master, and finally exterminates the race. But their utter futility is gracefully suggested at the end by their need of soul and life and love and eternal generation to make their masterfulness endurable. *The Insect Comedy* presents the conflicts of humanity as fantastically mirrored in the life of insects—the return to nature slogan reduced to the absurd. *The Makropoulos Secret* creates the false Utopia of long life. Unlike Shaw, Čapek found it intolerable. In *Adam the Creator* the sequence comes to its climax, the Utopia of complete regeneration that proves as futile as all the rest. Adam, in disgust for God's created world, blows it to bits with the cannon of negation. God, as practical joker, bids him recreate it "to his heart's desire" and gives him the clay. But Adam's creative ecstasy leads but to the same old results—things just as they were: conflict, pettiness, blighted aspiration, love and jealousy, war, and the worship of false gods. Adam hunts for his long buried cannon to blow the world again to bits. It has been moulded by his renegade creatures into a joyous bell. God's eye blinks and his voice is again heard:

Voice of God: Will you leave it as it is?

Adam: Yes! Yes! Yes!

Voice of God: So will I!

Mr. Čapek one summer evening in the garden of his new villa on the heights above Prague—for prosperity came to him from all the world—told the writer that he thought this his best work. He regretted that the English version failed to catch the colloquial ease of his dialogue, a fact to which, perhaps wrongly, he attributed the comparative failure of the play when given by Terence Gray in his Cambridge Festival Theatre in 1928, and its neglect by American producers. It had succeeded greatly as produced by the Čapeks with Joseph's grotesquely expressive settings and the peculiar intensity of action developed in the Czech theater by the great director Hilar.

R. U. R. has clearly the advantage, over this loosely knit miracle play, of a suspensive, if melodramatic, plot structure. Even the stupendous theme and devastating satire of *Adam the Creator* could hardly make it a Broadway success like *R. U. R.*

The Čapek plays invariably evoke striking and original stage effects, more by the boldness and grotesqueness of their subjects than by any elements of expressionism involved. In this respect the plays show the influence of the great Hilar's mastery of grotesque stage effects and Joseph Čapek's futurist art. Essentially they are not of the category of the Kaiser, Toller, and O'Neill plays. The first American performance by The Theatre Guild of New York in 1922, with settings by Lee Simonson, marked an important step in the artistry of that theater.

KAREL ČAPEK

Born 1890 at Malé Svantonvice, Bohemia (Czechoslovakia).

Universities of Prague, Berlin, and Paris. Ph.D.

1920, Production of *R. U. R.* in Prague.

1922, Its production in New York brought him to the notice of the world theatre.

Joined with his brother Joseph in the management of an art theater, known as Mestske Divadlo in Vinohrady.

Scientist, journalist, novelist, short story writer, scenario writer, and theater manager.

Died 1939.

PLAYS

The Brigand and *The Fatal Play of Love,* early experiments not in print. 1920 *R. U. R.* (*Rossum's Universal Robots.*) 1921 *And So Ad Infinitum: the Life of the Insects* (in collaboration with Joseph Čapek, translated as *The Insect Play* and as *The World We Live In: the Insect Comedy*) 1922 *The Makropoulos Affair* (translated as *The Makropoulos Secret*). 1926 *Loupeznik.* 1927 *Adam the Creator* (in collaboration with Joseph Čapek). 1938 *The Power and the Glory.* 1939 *The Mother.*

Writings about the Drama

How a Play Is Produced (translated by P. B. Beaumont), London, 1928.

Letters from England (translated by Paul Selver), London, 1925.

R. U. R.

[*Rossum's Universal Robots*]

Characters

HARRY DOMIN, *General Manager of Rossum's Universal Robots.*
SULLA, *a Robotess.*
MARIUS, *A Robot.*
HELENA GLORY.
DR. GALL, *Head of the Physiological and Experimental Department of R. U. R.*
MR. FABRY, *Engineer General, Technical Controller of R. U. R.*
DR. HALLEMEIER, *Head of the Institute for Psychological Training of Robots.*
MR. ALQUIST, *Architect, Head of the Works Department of R. U. R.*
CONSUL BUSMAN, *General Business Manager of R. U. R.*
NANA.
RADIUS, *a Robot.*
HELENA, *a Robotess.*
PRIMUS, *a Robot.*
A SERVANT.
FIRST ROBOT.
SECOND ROBOT.
THIRD ROBOT.

ACT I. *Central Office of the Factory of Rossum's Universal Robots*
ACT II. *Helena's Drawing Room—Ten years later. Morning.*
ACT III. *The Same Afternoon.*
EPILOGUE. *A laboratory—One year later.*
Place: An Island. *Time: The Future.*

ACT I

Central office of the factory of Rossum's Universal Robots. Entrance on the right. The windows on the front wall look out on the rows of factory chimneys. On the left more managing departments.

[DOMIN *is sitting in the revolving chair at a large American writing table. On the left-hand wall large maps showing steamship and railroad routes. On the right-hand wall are fastened printed placards. ("Robots Cheapest Labor," etc.) In contrast to these wall fittings, the room is furnished with a splendid Turkish carpet, a sofa, a leather armchair, and filing cabinets. At a desk near the windows* SULLA *is typing letters.*]

Domin. [*Dictating.*] Ready?

Sulla. Yes.

Domin. To E. M. McVicker and Co., Southampton, England. "We undertake no guarantee for goods damaged in transit. As soon as the consignment was taken on board we drew your captain's attention to the fact that the vessel was unsuitable for the transport of Robots, and we are therefore not responsible for spoiled freight. We beg to remain for Rossum's Universal Robots, Yours truly." [SULLA, *who has sat motionless during dictation, now types rapidly for a few seconds, then stops, withdrawing the completed letter.*] Ready?

Sulla. Yes.

Domin. Another letter. To the E. B. Huyson Agency, New York, U.S.A. "We beg to acknowledge receipt of order for five thousand Robots. As you are sending your own vessel, please dispatch as cargo equal quantities of soft and hard coal for R. U. R., the same to be credited as part payment of the amount due to us. We beg to remain, for Rossum's Universal Robots, Yours truly." [SULLA *repeats the rapid typing.*] Ready?

Sulla. Yes.

Domin. Another letter. "Friedrichswerks, Hamburg, Germany. We beg to acknowledge receipt of order for fifteen thousand Robots." [*Telephone rings.*] Hello! This is the Central Office. Yes. Certainly. Well, send them a wire. Good. [*Hangs up telephone.*] Where did I leave off?

Sulla. "We beg to acknowledge receipt of order for fifteen thousand Robots."

Domin. Fifteen thousand R. Fifteen thousand R. [*Enter* MARIUS.]

Domin. Well, what is it?

Marius. There's a lady, sir, asking to see you.

Domin. A lady? Who is she?

Marius. I don't know, sir. She brings this card of introduction.

Domin. [*Reads the card.*] Ah, from President Glory. Ask her to come in.

Marius. Please step this way.

[*Enter* HELENA GLORY. *Exit* MARIUS.]

Helena. How do you do?

Domin. How do you do? [*Standing up.*] What can I do for you?

Helena. You are Mr. Domin, the General Manager?

Domin. I am.

Helena. I have come——

Domin. With President Glory's card. That is quite sufficient.

Helena. President Glory is my father. I am Helena Glory.

Domin. Miss Glory, this is such a great honor for us to be allowed to welcome our great President's daughter, that——

Helena. That you can't show me the door?

Domin. Please sit down. Sulla, you may go. [*Exit* SULLA.]

Domin. [*Sitting down.*] How can I be of service to you, Miss Glory?

Helena. I have come——

Domin. To have a look at our famous works where people are manufactured. Like all visitors. Well, there is no objection.

Helena. I thought it was forbidden to——

Domin. "To enter the factory?" Yes, of course. Everybody comes here with some one's visiting card, Miss Glory.

Helena. And you show them——

Domin. Only certain things. The manufacture of artificial people is a secret process.

Helena. If you only knew how enormously that——

Domin. "Interests me?" Europe's talking about nothing else.

Helena. Why don't you let me finish speaking?

Domin. I beg your pardon. Did you want to say something different?

Helena. I only wanted to ask——

Domin. Whether I could make a special exception in your case and show you our factory. Why, certainly, Miss Glory.

Helena. How do you know I wanted to say that?

Domin. They all do. But we shall consider it a special honor to show you more than we do the rest.

Helena. Thank you.

Domin. But you must agree not to divulge the least . . .

Helena. [*Standing up and giving him her hand.*] My word of honor.

Domin. Thank you. Won't you raise your veil?

Helena. Of course. You want to see whether I'm a spy or not. I beg your pardon.

Domin. What is it?

Helena. Would you mind releasing my hand?

Domin. [*Releasing it.*] I beg your pardon.

Helena. [*Raising her veil.*] How cautious you have to be here, don't you?

Domin. [*Observing her with deep interest.*] H'm, of course—we—that is——

Helena. But what is it? What's the matter?

Domin. I'm remarkably pleased. Did you have a pleasant crossing?

Helena. Yes.

Domin. No difficulty?

Helena. Why?

Domin. What I mean to say is—you're so young.

Helena. May we go straight into the factory?

Domin. Yes. Twenty-two, I think.

Helena. Twenty-two what?

Domin. Years.

Helena. Twenty-one. Why do you want to know?

Domin. Because—as—[*With enthusiasm.*] You will make a long stay, won't you?

Helena. That depends on how much of the factory you show me.

Domin. Oh, hang the factory. Oh, no, no, you shall see everything, Miss Glory. Indeed you shall. Won't you sit down?

Helena. [*Crossing to couch and sitting.*] Thank you.

Domin. But first would you like to hear the story of the invention?

Helena. Yes, indeed.

Domin. [*Observes* HELENA *with rapture and reels off rapidly.*] It was in the year 1920 that old Rossum, the great physiologist, who was then quite a young scientist, took himself to this distant island for the purpose of studying the ocean fauna. Full stop. On this occasion he attempted by chemical synthesis to imitate the living matter known as protoplasm until he suddenly discovered a substance which behaved exactly like living matter although its chemical composition was different. That was in the year 1932, exactly four hundred and forty years after the discovery of America. Whew!

Helena. Do you know that by heart?

Domin. Yes. You see physiology is not in my line. Shall I go on?

Helena. Yes, please.

Domin. And then, Miss Glory, old Rossum wrote the following among his chemical specimens: "Nature has found only one method of organizing living matter. There is, however, another method, more simple, flexible, and rapid, which has not yet occurred to nature at all. This second process by which life can be developed was discovered by me today." Now imagine him, Miss Glory, writing those wonderful words over some colloidal mess that a dog wouldn't look at. Imagine him sitting over a test tube, and thinking how the whole tree of life would grow from it; how all animals would proceed from it, beginning with some sort of beetle and ending with a man. A man of different substance from us. Miss Glory, that was a tremendous moment!

Helena. Well?

Domin. Now, the thing was how to get the life out of the test tubes, and hasten development and form organs, bones and nerves, and so on, and find such substances as catalytics, enzymes, hormones, and so forth, in short—you understand?

Helena. Not much, I'm afraid.

Domin. Never mind. You see with the help of his tinctures he could make whatever he wanted. He could have produced a Medusa with the brain of a Socrates or a worm fifty yards long. But being without a grain of humor, he took it into his head to make a vertebrate or perhaps a man. This artificial living matter of his had a raging thirst for life. It didn't mind being sewn or mixed together. That couldn't be done with natural albumen. And that's how he set about it.

Helena. About what?

Domin. About imitating nature. First of all he tried making an artificial dog. That took him several years and resulted in a sort of stunted calf which died in a few days. I'll show it to you in the museum. And then old Rossum started on the manufacture of man.

Helena. And I must divulge this to nobody?

Domin. To nobody in the world.

Helena. What a pity that it's to be found in all the school books of both Europe and America.

Domin. Yes. But do you know what isn't in the school books? That old Rossum was mad. Seriously, Miss Glory, you must keep this to yourself. The old crank wanted actually to make people.

Helena. But you do make people.

Domin. Approximately, Miss Glory. But old Rossum meant it literally. He wanted to become a sort of scientific substitute for God. He was a fearful materialist, and that's why he did it all. His sole purpose was nothing more nor less than to prove that God was no longer necessary. Do you know anything about anatomy?

Helena. Very little.

Domin. Neither do I. Well, he then decided to manufacture everything as in the human body. I'll show you in the museum the bungling attempt it took him ten years to produce. It was to have been a man, but it lived for three days only. Then up came young Rossum, an engineer. He was a wonderful fellow, Miss Glory. When he saw what a mess of it the old man was making, he said: "It's absurd to spend ten years making a man. If you can't make him quicker than nature, you might as well shut up shop." Then he set about learning anatomy himself.

Helena. There's nothing about that in the school books.

Domin. No. The school books are full of paid advertisements, and rubbish at that. What the school books say about the united efforts of the two great Rossums is all a fairy tale. They used to have dreadful rows. The old atheist hadn't the slightest conception of industrial matters, and the end of it was that young Rossum shut him up in some laboratory or other and let him fritter the time away with his monstrosities, while he himself started on the business from an engineer's point of view. Old Rossum cursed him and before he died he managed to botch up two physiological horrors. Then one day they found him dead in the laboratory. And that's his whole story.

Helena. And what about the young man?

Domin. Well, any one who has looked into human anatomy will have seen at once that man is too complicated, and that a good engineer could make him more simple. So young Rossum began to overhaul anatomy and tried to see what could be left out or simplified. In short—but this isn't boring you, Miss Glory?

Helena. No, indeed. You're—it's awfully interesting.

Domin. So young Rossum said to himself: "A man is something that feels happy, plays the piano, likes going for a walk, and, in fact, wants to do a whole lot of things that are really unnecessary."

Helena. Oh.

Domin. That are unnecessary when he wants, let us say, to weave or count. Do you play the piano?

Helena. Yes.

Domin. That's good. But a working machine must not play the piano, must not feel happy, must not do a whole lot of other things. A gasoline motor must not have tassels or ornaments, Miss Glory. And to manufacture artificial workers is the same thing as to manufacture gasoline motors. The process must be of the simplest, and the product of the best from a practical point of view. What sort of worker do you think is the best from a practical point of view?

Helena. What?

Domin. What sort of worker do you think is the best from a practical point of view?

Helena. Perhaps the one who is most honest and hard-working.

Domin. No; the one that is the cheapest. The one whose requirements are the smallest. Young Rossum invented a worker with the minimum amount of requirements. He had to simplify him. He rejected everything that did not contribute directly to the progress of work—everything that makes man more expensive. In fact, he rejected man and made the Robot. My dear Miss Glory, the Robots are not people. Mechanically they are more perfect than we are, they have an enormously developed intelligence, but they have no soul.

Helena. How do you know they've no soul?

Domin. Have you ever seen what a Robot looks like inside?

Helena. No.

Domin. Very neat, very simple. Really, a beautiful piece of work. Not much in it, but everything in flawless order. The product of an engineer is technically at a higher pitch of perfection than a product of nature.

Helena. But man is supposed to be the product of God.

Domin. All the worse. God hasn't the least notion of modern engineering. Would you believe that young Rossum then proceeded to play at being God?

Helena. How do you mean?

Domin. He began to manufacture Super-Robots. Regular giants they were. He tried to make them twelve feet tall. But you wouldn't believe what a failure they were.

Helena. A failure?

Domin. Yes. For no reason at all their limbs used to keep snapping off. Evidently our planet is too small for giants. Now we only make Robots of normal size and of very high class human finish.

Helena. I saw the first Robots at home. The town council bought them for—I mean engaged them for work.

Domin. Bought them, dear Miss Glory. Robots are bought and sold.

Helena. These were employed as street sweepers. I saw them sweeping. They were so strange and quiet.

Domin. Rossums' Universal Robot factory doesn't produce a uniform brand of Robots. We have Robots of finer and coarser grades. The best will live about twenty years.

[*He rings for* MARIUS.]

Helena. Then they die?

Domin. Yes, they get used up.

[*Enter* MARIUS.]

Domin. Marius, bring in samples of the Manual Labor Robot. [*Exit* MARIUS.]

Domin. I'll show you specimens of the two extremes. This first grade is comparatively inexpensive and is made in vast quantities.

[MARIUS *reënters with two Manual Labor* ROBOTS.]

Domin. There you are; as powerful as a small tractor. Guaranteed to have average intelligence. That will do, Marius.

[MARIUS *exits with* ROBOTS.]

Helena. They make me feel so strange.

Domin. [*Rings.*] Did you see my new typist? [*He rings for* SULLA.]

Helena. I didn't notice her. [*Enter* SULLA.]

Domin. Sulla, let Miss Glory see you.

Helena. So pleased to meet you. You must find it terribly dull in this out-of-the-way spot, don't you?

Sulla. I don't know, Miss Glory.

Helena. Where do you come from?

Sulla. From the factory.

Helena. Oh, you were born there?

Sulla. I was made there.

Helena. What?

Domin. [*Laughing.*] Sulla is a Robot, best grade.

Helena. Oh, I beg your pardon.

Domin. Sulla isn't angry. See, Miss Glory, the kind of skin we make. [*Feels the skin on* SULLA's *face.*] Feel her face.

Helena. Oh, no, no.

Domin. You wouldn't know that she's made of different material from us, would you? Turn round, Sulla.

Helena. Oh, stop, stop.

Domin. Talk to Miss Glory, Sulla.

Sulla. Please sit down. [HELENA *sits.*] Did you have a pleasant crossing?

Helena. Oh, yes, certainly.

Sulla. Don't go back on the *Amelia,* Miss Glory. The barometer is falling steadily. Wait for the *Pennsylvania.* That's a good, powerful vessel.

Domin. What's its speed?

Sulla. Twenty knots. Fifty thousand tons. One of the latest vessels, Miss Glory.

Helena. Thank you.

Sulla. A crew of fifteen hundred, Captain Harpy, eight boilers——

Domin. That'll do, Sulla. Now show us your knowledge of French.

Helena. You know French?

Sulla. I know four languages. I can write: Dear Sir, Monsieur, Geehrter Herr, Cteny pane.

Helena. [*Jumping up.*] Oh, that's absurd! Sulla isn't a Robot. Sulla is a girl like me. Sulla, this is outrageous! Why do you take part in such a hoax?

Sulla. I am a Robot.

Helena. No, no, you are not telling the truth. I know they've forced you to do it for an advertisement. Sulla, you are a girl like me, aren't you?

Domin. I'm sorry, Miss Glory. Sulla is a Robot.

Helena. It's a lie!

Domin. What? [*Rings.*] Excuse me, Miss Glory; then I must convince you.

[*Enter* MARIUS.]

Domin. Marius, take Sulla into the dissecting room, and tell them to open her up at once.

Helena. Where?

Domin. Into the dissecting room. When they've cut her open, you can go and have a look.

Helena. No, no!

Domin. Excuse me, you spoke of lies.

Helena. You wouldn't have her killed?

Domin. You can't kill machines.

Helena. Don't be afraid, Sulla, I won't let you go. Tell me, my dear, are they always so cruel to you? You mustn't put up with it, Sulla. You mustn't.

Sulla. I am a Robot.

Helena. That doesn't matter. Robots are just as good as we are. Sulla, you wouldn't let yourself be cut to pieces?

Sulla. Yes.

Helena. Oh, you're not afraid of death, then?

Sulla. I cannot tell, Miss Glory.

Helena. Do you know what would happen to you in there?

Sulla. Yes, I should cease to move.

Helena. How dreadful!

Domin. Marius, tell Miss Glory what you are.

Marius. Marius, the Robot.

Domin. Would you take Sulla into the dissecting room?

Marius. Yes.

Domin. Would you be sorry for her?

Marius. I cannot tell.

Domin. What would happen to her?

Marius. She would cease to move. They would put her into the stamping-mill.

Domin. That is death, Marius. Aren't you afraid of death?

Marius. No.

Domin. You see, Miss Glory, the Robots have no interest in life. They have no enjoyments. They are less than so much grass.

Helena. Oh, stop. Send them away.

Domin. Marius, Sulla, you may go.

[*Exeunt* SULLA *and* MARIUS.]

Helena. How terrible! It's outrageous what you are doing.

Domin. Why outrageous?

Helena. I don't know, but it is. Why do you call her Sulla?

Domin. Isn't it a nice name?

Helena. It's a man's name. Sulla was a Roman general.

Domin. Oh, we thought that Marius and Sulla were lovers.

Helena. Marius and Sulla were generals and fought against each other in the year—I've forgotten now.

Domin. Come here to the window.

Helena. What?

Domin. Come here. What do you see?

Helena. Bricklayers.

Domin. Robots. All our work people are Robots. And down there, can you see anything?

Helena. Some sort of office.

Domin. A counting house. And in it——

Helena. A lot of officials.

Domin. Robots. All our officials are Robots. And when you see the factory——

[*Factory whistle blows.*]

Domin. Noon. We have to blow the whistle because the Robots don't know when to stop work. In two hours I will show you the kneading trough.

Helena. Kneading trough?

Domin. The pestle for beating up the paste. In each one we mix the ingredients for a thousand Robots at one operation. Then there are the vats for the preparation of liver, brains, and so on. Then you will see the bone factory. After that I'll show you the spinning-mill.

Helena. Spinning-mill?

Domin. Yes. For weaving nerves and veins. Miles and miles of digestive tubes pass through it at a time.

Helena. Mayn't we talk about something else?

Domin. Perhaps it would be better. There's only a handful of us among a hundred thousand Robots, and not one woman. We talk about nothing but the factory all day, every day. It's as if we were under a curse, Miss Glory.

Helena. I'm sorry I said that you were lying. [*A knock at the door.*]

Domin. Come in.

[*From the right enter* MR. FABRY, DR. GALL, DR. HALLEMEIER, MR. ALQUIST.]

Dr. Gall. I beg your pardon, I hope we don't intrude.

Domin. Come in. Miss Glory, here are Alquist, Fabry, Gall, Hallemeier. This is President Glory's daughter.

Helena. How do you do?

Fabry. We had no idea——

Dr. Gall. Highly honored, I'm sure——

Alquist. Welcome, Miss Glory.

[BUSMAN *rushes in from the right.*]

Busman. Hello, what's up?

Domin. Come in, Busman. This is Busman, Miss Glory. This is President Glory's daughter.

Busman. By jove, that's fine! Miss Glory, may we send a cablegram to the papers about your arrival?

Helena. No, no, please don't.

Domin. Sit down please, Miss Glory.

Busman. Allow me——

[*Dragging up armchairs.*]

Dr. Gall. Please——

Fabry. Excuse me——

Alquist. What sort of a crossing did you have?

Dr. Gall. Are you going to stay long?

Fabry. What do you think of the factory, Miss Glory?

Hallemeier. Did you come over on the *Amelia*?

Domin. Be quiet and let Miss Glory speak.

Helena. [*To* DOMIN.] What am I to speak to them about?

Domin. Anything you like.

Helena. Shall . . . may I speak quite frankly?

Domin. Why, of course.

Helena. [*Wavering, then in desperate resolution.*] Tell me, doesn't it ever distress you the way you are treated?

Fabry. By whom, may I ask?

Helena. Why, everybody.

Alquist. Treated?

Dr. Gall. What makes you think——?

Helena. Don't you feel that you might be living a better life?

Dr. Gall. Well, that depends on what you mean, Miss Glory.

Helena. I mean that it's perfectly outrageous. It's terrible. [*Standing up.*] The whole of Europe is talking about the way you're being treated. That's why I came here, to see for myself; and it's a thousand times worse than could have been imagined. How can you put up with it?

Alquist. Put up with what?

Helena. Good heavens, you are living creatures, just like us, like the whole of Europe, like the whole world. It's disgraceful that you must live like this.

Busman. Good gracious, Miss Glory.

Fabry. Well, she's not far wrong. We live here just like red Indians.

Helena. Worse than red Indians. May I, oh, may I call you brothers?

Busman. Why not?

Helena. Brothers, I have not come here as the President's daughter. I have come on behalf of the Humanity League. Brothers, the Humanity League now has over two hundred thousand members. Two hundred thousand people are on your side, and offer you their help.

Busman. Two hundred thousand people! Miss Glory, that's a tidy lot. Not bad.

Fabry. I'm always telling you there's nothing like good old Europe. You see, they've not forgotten us. They're offering us help.

Dr. Gall. What help? A theater, for instance?

Hallemeier. An orchestra?

Helena. More than that.

Alquist. Just you?

Helena. Oh, never mind about me. I'll stay as long as it is necessary.

Busman. By Jove, that's good.

Alquist. Domin, I'm going to get the best room ready for Miss Glory.

Domin. Just a minute. I'm afraid that Miss Glory is of the opinion that she has been talking to Robots.

Helena. Of course.

Domin. I'm sorry. These gentlemen are human beings just like us.

Helena. You're not Robots?

Busman. Not Robots.

Hallemeier. Robots indeed!

Dr. Gall. No, thanks.

Fabry. Upon my honor, Miss Glory, we aren't Robots.

Helena. [*To* DOMIN.] Then why did you tell me that all your officials are Robots?

Domin. Yes, the officials, but not the managers. Allow me, Miss Glory: this is Mr. Fabry, General Technical Manager of R.U.R.; Dr. Gall, Head of the Physiological and Experimental Department; Dr. Hallemeier, Head of the Institute for the Psychological Training of Robots; Consul Busman, General Business Manager; and Alquist, Head of the Building Department of R.U.R.

Alquist. Just a builder.

Helena. Excuse me, gentlemen, for—for—Have I done something dreadful?

Alquist. Not at all, Miss Glory. Please sit down.

Helena. I'm a stupid girl. Send me back by the first ship.

Dr. Gall. Not for anything in the world, Miss Glory. Why should we send you back?

Helena. Because you know I've come to disturb your Robots for you.

Domin. My dear Miss Glory, we've had close upon a hundred saviors and prophets here. Every ship brings us some. Missionaries, anarchists, Salvation Army, all sorts. It's astonishing what a number of churches and idiots there are in the world.

Helena. And you let them speak to the Robots?

Domin. So far we've let them all, why not? The Robots remember everything, but that's all. They don't even laugh at what the people say. Really, it is quite incredible. If it would amuse you, Miss Glory, I'll take you over to the Robot warehouse. It holds about three hundred thousand of them.

Busman. Three hundred and forty-seven thousand.

Domin. Good! And you can say whatever you like to them. You can read the Bible, recite the multiplication table, whatever you please. You can even preach to them about human rights.

Helena. Oh, I think that if you were to show them a little love——

Fabry. Impossible, Miss Glory. Nothing is harder to like than a Robot.

Helena. What do you make them for, then?

Busman. Ha, ha, ha, that's good! What are Robots made for?

Fabry. For work, Miss Glory! One Robot can replace two and a half workmen. The human machine, Miss Glory, was terribly imperfect. It had to be removed sooner or later.

Busman. It was too expensive.

Fabry. It was not effective. It no longer answers the requirements of modern engineering. Nature has no idea of keeping pace with modern labor. For example: from a technical point of view, the whole of childhood is a sheer absurdity. So much time lost. And then again——

Helena. Oh, no! No!

Fabry. Pardon me. But kindly tell me what is the real aim of your League—the . . . the Humanity League.

Helena. Its real purpose is to—to protect the Robots—and—and ensure good treatment for them.

Fabry. Not a bad object, either. A machine has to be treated properly. Upon my soul, I approve of that. I don't like damaged articles. Please, Miss Glory, enroll us all as contributing, or regular, or foundation members of your League.

Helena. No, you don't understand me. What we really want is to—to liberate the Robots.

Hallemeier. How do you propose to do that?

Helena. They are to be—to be dealt with like human beings.

Hallemeier. Aha. I suppose they're to vote? To drink beer? to order us about?

Helena. Why shouldn't they drink beer?

Hallemeier. Perhaps they're even to receive wages?

Helena. Of course they are.

Hallemeier. Fancy that, now! And what would they do with their wages, pray?

Helena. They would buy—what they need . . . what pleases them.

Hallemeier. That would be very nice, Miss Glory, only there's nothing that does please the Robots. Good heavens, what are they to buy? You can feed them on pineapples, straw, whatever you like. It's all the same to them, they've no appetite at all. They've no interest in anything, Miss Glory. Why, hang it all, nobody's ever yet seen a Robot smile.

Helena. Why . . . why don't you make them happier?

Hallemeier. That wouldn't do, Miss Glory. They are only workmen.

Helena. Oh, but they're so intelligent.

Hallemeier. Confoundedly so, but they're nothing else. They've no will of their own. No passion. No soul.

Helena. No love?

Hallemeier. Love? Rather not. Robots don't love. Not even themselves.

Helena. Nor defiance?

Hallemeier. Defiance? I don't know. Only rarely, from time to time.

Helena. What?

Hallemeier. Nothing particular. Occasionally they seem to go off their heads. Something like epilepsy, you know. It's called Robot's cramp. They'll suddenly sling down everything they're holding, stand still, gnash their teeth—and then they have to go into the stamping-mill. It's evidently some breakdown in the mechanism.

Domin. A flaw in the works that has to be removed.

Helena. No, no, that's the soul.

Fabry. Do you think that the soul first shows itself by a gnashing of teeth?

Helena. Perhaps it's a sort of revolt. Perhaps it's just a sign that there's a struggle within. Oh, if you could infuse them with it!

Domin. That'll be remedied, Miss Glory. Dr. Gall is just making some experiments——

Dr. Gall. Not with regard to that, Domin. At present I am making pain-nerves.

Helena. Pain-nerves?

Dr. Gall. Yes, the Robots feel practically no bodily pain. You see, young Rossum provided them with too limited a nervous system. We must introduce suffering.

Helena. Why do you want to cause them pain?

Dr. Gall. For industrial reasons, Miss Glory. Sometimes a Robot does damage to himself because it doesn't hurt him. He puts his hand into the machine, breaks his finger, smashes his head, it's all the same to him. We must provide them with pain. That's an automatic protection against damage.

Helena. Will they be happier when they feel pain?

Dr. Gall. On the contrary; but they will be more perfect from a technical point of view.

Helena. Why don't you create a soul for them?

Dr. Gall. That's not in our power.

Fabry. That's not in our interest.

Busman. That would increase the cost of production. Hang it all, my dear young lady, we turn them out at such a cheap rate. A hundred and fifty dollars each fully dressed, and fifteen years ago they cost ten thousand. Five years ago we used to buy the clothes for them. Today we have our own weaving mill, and now we even export cloth five times cheaper than other factories. What do you pay a yard for cloth, Miss Glory?

Helena. I don't know really, I've forgotten.

Busman. Good gracious, and you want to found a Humanity League? It only costs a third now, Miss Glory. All prices are today a third of what they were and they'll fall still more, lower, lower, like that.

Helena. I don't understand.

Busman. Why, bless you, Miss Glory, it means that the cost of labor has fallen. A Robot, food and all, costs three quarters of a cent per hour. That's mighty important, you know. All factories will go pop like chestnuts if they don't at once buy Robots to lower the cost of production.

Helena. And get rid of their workmen?

Busman. Of course. But in the meantime, we've dumped five hundred thousand tropical Robots down on the Argentine pampas to grow corn. Would you mind telling me how much you pay a pound for bread?

Helena. I've no idea.

Busman. Well, I'll tell you. It now costs two cents in good old Europe. A pound of bread for two cents, and the Humanity League knows nothing about it. Miss Glory, you don't realize that even that's too expensive. Why, in five years' time I'll wager——

Helena. What?

Busman. That the cost of everything won't be a tenth of what it is now. Why, in five years we'll be up to our ears in corn and everything else.

Alquist. Yes, and all the workers throughout the world will be unemployed.

Domin. Yes, Alquist, they will. Yes, Miss Glory, they will. But in ten years Rossum's Universal Robots will produce so much corn, so much cloth, so much everything, that things will be practically without price. There will be no poverty. All work will be done by living machines. Everybody will be free from worry and liberated from the degradation of labor. Everybody will live only to perfect himself.

Helena. Will he?

Domin. Of course. It's bound to happen. But then the servitude of man to man and the enslavement of man to matter will cease. Of course, terrible things may happen at first, but that simply can't be avoided. Nobody will get bread at the price of life and hatred. The Robots will wash the feet of the beggar and prepare a bed for him in his house.

Alquist. Domin, Domin. What you say sounds too much like Paradise. There was something good in service and something great in humility. There was some kind of virtue in toil and weariness.

Domin. Perhaps. But we cannot reckon with what is lost when we start out to transform the world. Man shall be free and supreme; he shall have no other aim, no other labor, no other care than to perfect himself. He shall serve neither matter nor man. He will not be a machine and a device for production. He will be Lord of creation.

Busman. Amen.

Fabry. So be it.

Helena. You have bewildered me—I should like—I should like to believe this.

Dr. Gall. You are younger than we are, Miss Glory. You will live to see it.

Hallemeier. True. Don't you think Miss Glory might lunch with us?

Dr. Gall. Of course. Domin, ask on behalf of us all.

Domin. Miss Glory, will you do us the honor?

Helena. When you know why I've come ——

Fabry. For the League of Humanity, Miss Glory.

Helena. Oh, in that case, perhaps——

Fabry. That's fine! Miss Glory, excuse me for five minutes.

Dr. Gall. Pardon me, too, dear Miss Glory.

Busman. I won't be long.

Hallemeier. We're all very glad you've come.

Busman. We'll be back in exactly five minutes.

[*All rush out except* DOMIN *and* HELENA.]

Helena. What have they all gone off for?

Domin. To cook, Miss Glory.

Helena. To cook what?

Domin. Lunch. The Robots do our cooking for us and as they've no taste it's not altogether— Hallemeier is awfully good at grills and Gall can make a kind of sauce, and Busman knows all about omelettes.

Helena. What a feast! And what's the specialty of Mr.—— your builder?

Domin. Alquist? Nothing. He only lays the table. And Fabry will get together a little fruit. Our cuisine is very modest, Miss Glory.

Helena. I wanted to ask you something——

Domin. And I wanted to ask you something, too. [*Looking at watch.*] Five minutes.

Helena. What did you want to ask me?

Domin. Excuse me, you asked first.

Helena. Perhaps it's silly of me, but why do you manufacture female Robots when—when——

Domin. When sex means nothing to them?

Helena. Yes.

Domin. There's a certain demand for them, you see. Servants, saleswomen, stenographers. People are used to it.

Helena. But—but, tell me, are the Robots male and female mutually—completely without——

Domin. Completely indifferent to each other, Miss Glory. There's no sign of any affection between them.

Helena. Oh, that's terrible.

Domin. Why?

Helena. It's so unnatural. One doesn't know whether to be disgusted or to hate them, or perhaps——

Domin. To pity them?

Helena. That's more like it. What did you want to ask me about?

Domin. I should like to ask you, Miss Helena, whether you will marry me?

Helena. What?

Domin. Will you be my wife?

Helena. No! The idea!

Domin. [*Looking at his watch.*] Another three minutes. If you won't marry me you'll have to marry one of the other five.

Helena. But why should I?

Domin. Because they're all going to ask you in turn.

Helena. How could they dare do such a thing?

Domin. I'm very sorry, Miss Glory. It seems they've all fallen in love with you.

Helena. Please don't let them. I'll—I'll go away at once.

Domin. Helena, you wouldn't be so cruel as to refuse us.

Helena. But, but—I can't marry all six.

Domin. No, but one anyhow. If you don't want me, marry Fabry.

Helena. I won't.

Domin. Dr. Gall.

Helena. I don't want any of you.

Domin. [*Again looking at his watch.*] Another two minutes.

Helena. I think you'd marry any woman who came here.

Domin. Plenty of them have come, Helena.

Helena. Young?

Domin. Yes.

Helena. Why didn't you marry one of them?

Domin. Because I didn't lose my head. Until today. Then, as soon as you lifted your veil——

[HELENA *turns her head away.*]

Domin. Another minute.

Helena. But I don't want you, I tell you.

Domin. [*Laying both hands on her shoulders.*] One more minute! Now you either have to look me straight in the eye and say "No," violently, and then I'll leave you alone—or——

[HELENA *looks at him.*]

Helena. [*Turning away.*] You're mad!

Domin. A man has to be a bit mad, Helena. That's the best thing about him.

Helena. You are—you are——

Domin. Well?

Helena. Don't, you're hurting me.

Domin. The last chance, Helena. Now, or never——

Helena. But—but, Harry——

[*He embraces and kisses her. Knocking at the door.*]

Domin. [*Releasing her.*] Come in.

[*Enter* BUSMAN, DR. GALL, *and* HALLEMEIER *in kitchen aprons.* FABRY *with a bouquet and* ALQUIST *with a napkin over his arm.*]

Domin. Have you finished your job?

Busman. Yes.

Domin. So have we.

[*For a moment the men stand nonplussed; but as soon as they realize what* DOMIN *means they rush forward, congratulating* HELENA *and* DOMIN *as the curtain falls.*]

ACT II

HELENA'S *drawing room. On the left a baize door, and a door to the music room, on the right a door to* HELENA'S *bedroom. In the center are windows looking out on the sea and the harbor. A table with odds and ends, a sofa and chairs, a writing table with an electric lamp, on the right a fireplace. On a small table back of the sofa, a small reading lamp. The whole drawing room in all its details is of a modern and purely feminine character. Ten years have elapsed since Act I.*

[DOMIN, FABRY, HALLEMEIR *enter on tiptoe from the left, each carrying a potted plant.*]

Hallemeier. [*Putting down his flower and indicating the door to right.*] Still asleep? Well, as long as she's asleep, she can't worry about it.

Domin. She knows nothing about it.

Fabry. [*Putting plant on writing desk.*] I certainly hope nothing happens today.

Hallemeier. For goodness' sake drop it all. Look, Harry, this is a fine cyclamen, isn't it? A new sort, my latest—Cyclamen Helena.

Domin. [*Looking out of the window.*] No signs of the ship. Things must be pretty bad.

Hallemeier. Be quiet. Suppose she heard you.

Domin. Well, anyway, the *Ultimus* arrived just in time.

Fabry. You really think that today——?

Domin. I don't know. Aren't the flowers fine?

Hallemeier. These are my new primroses. And this is my new jasmine. I've discovered a wonderful way of developing flowers quickly. Splendid varieties, too. Next year I'll be developing marvellous ones.

Domin. What . . . next year?

Fabry. I'd give a good deal to know what's happening at Havre with——

Domin. Keep quiet.

Helena. [*Calling from right.*] Nana!

Domin. She's awake. Out you go.

[*All go out on tiptoe through upper left door. Enter* NANA *from lower left door.*]

Nana. Horrid mess! Pack of heathens. If I had my say I'd——

Helena. [*Backwards in the doorway.*] Nana, come and do up my dress.

Nana. I'm coming. So you're up at last. [*Fastening* HELENA'S *dress.*] My gracious, what brutes!

Helena. Who?

Nana. If you want to turn around, then turn around, but I shan't fasten you up.

Helena. What are you grumbling about now?

Nana. These dreadful creatures, these heathen——

Helena. The Robots?

Nana. I wouldn't even call them by name.

Helena. What's happened?

Nana. Another of them here has caught it. He began to smash up the statues and pictures in the drawing room, gnashed his teeth, foamed at the mouth—quite mad. Worse than an animal.

Helena. Which of them caught it?

Nana. The one—well, he hasn't got any Christian name. The one in charge of the library.

Helena. Radius?

Nana. That's him. My goodness, I'm scared of them. A spider doesn't scare me as much as them.

Helena. But, Nana, I'm surprised you're not sorry for them.

Nana. Why, you're scared of them, too! You know you are. Why else did you bring me here?

Helena. I'm not scared, really I'm not, Nana. I'm only sorry for them.

Nana. You're scared. Nobody could help being scared. Why, the dog's scared of them: he won't take a scrap of meat out of their hands. He draws in his tail and howls when he knows they're about.

Helena. The dog has no sense.

Nana. He's better than them, and he knows it. Even the horse shies when he meets them. They don't have any young, and a dog has young, every one has young——

Helena. Please fasten up my dress, Nana.

Nana. I say it's against God's will to——

Helena. What is it that smells so nice?

Nana. Flowers.

Helena. What for?

Nana. Now you can turn around.

Helena. Oh, aren't they lovely? Look, Nana. What's happening today?

Nana. It ought to be the end of the world.

[*Enter* DOMIN.]

Helena. Oh, hello, Harry. Harry, why all these flowers?

Domin. Guess.

Helena. Well, it's not my birthday!

Domin. Better than that.

Helena. I don't know. Tell me.

Domin. It's ten years ago today since you came here.

Helena. Ten years? Today—— Why——

[*They embrace.*]

Nana. I'm off.

[*Exits lower door, left.*]

Helena. Fancy you remembering!

Domin. I'm really ashamed, Helena. I didn't.

Helena. But you——

Domin. They remembered.

Helena. Who?

Domin. Busman, Hallemeier, all of them. Put your hand in my pocket.

Helena. Pearls! A necklace. Harry, is that for me?

Domin. It's from Busman.

Helena. But we can't accept it, can we?

Domin. Oh, yes, we can. Put your hand in the other pocket.

Helena. [*Takes a revolver out of his pocket.*] What's that?

Domin. Sorry. Not that. Try again.

Helena. Oh, Harry, what do you carry a revolver for?

Domin. It got there by mistake.

Helena. You never used to carry one.

Domin. No, you're right. There, that's the pocket.

Helena. A cameo. Why, it's a Greek cameo!

Domin. Apparently. Anyhow, Fabry says it is.

Helena. Fabry? Did Mr. Fabry give me that?

Domin. Of course. [*Opens the door at the left.*] And look in here. Helena, come and see this.

Helena. Oh, isn't it fine! Is this from you?

Domin. No, from Alquist. And there's another on the piano.

Helena. This must be from you.

Domin. There's a card on it.

Helena. From Dr. Gall. [*Reappearing in the doorway.*] Oh, Harry, I feel embarrassed at so much kindness.

Domin. Come here. This is what Hallemeier brought you.

Helena. These beautiful flowers?

Domin. Yes. It's a new kind. Cyclamen Helena. He grew them in honor of you. They are almost as beautiful as you.

Helena. Harry, why do they all——

Domin. They're awfully fond of you. I'm afraid that my present is a little—— Look out of the window.

Helena. Where?

Domin. Into the harbor.

Helena. There's a new ship.

Domin. That's your ship.

Helena. Mine? How do you mean?

Domin. For you to take trips in—for your amusement.

Helena. Harry, that's a gunboat.

Domin. A gunboat? What are you thinking of? It's only a little bigger and more solid than most ships.

Helena. Yes, but with guns.

Domin. Oh, yes, with a few guns. You'll travel like a queen, Helena.

Helena. What's the meaning of it? Has anything happened?

Domin. Good heavens, no. I say, try these pearls.

Helena. Harry, have you had bad news?

Domin. On the contrary, no letters have arrived for a whole week.

Helena. Nor telegrams?

Domin. Nor telegrams.

Helena. What does that mean?

Domin. Holidays for us. We all sit in the office with our feet on the table and take a nap. No letters, no telegrams. Oh, glorious.

Helena. Then you'll stay with me today?

Domin. Certainly. That is, we will see. Do you remember ten years ago today? "Miss Glory, it's a great honor to welcome you."

Helena. "Oh, Mr. Manager, I'm so interested in your factory."

Domin. "I'm sorry, Miss Glory, it's strictly forbidden. The manufacture of artificial people is a secret."

Helena. "But to oblige a young lady who has come a long way."

Domin. "Certainly, Miss Glory, we have no secrets from you."

Helena. [*Seriously.*] Are you sure, Harry?

Domin. Yes.

Helena. "But I warn you, sir; this young lady intends to do terrible things."

Domin. "Good gracious, Miss Glory. Perhaps she doesn't want to marry me."

Helena. "Heaven forbid. She never dreamt of such a thing. But she came here intending to stir up a revolt among your Robots."

Domin. [*Suddenly serious.*] A revolt of the Robots!

Helena. Harry, what's the matter with you?

Domin. [*Laughing it off.*] "A revolt of the Robots, that's a fine idea, Miss Glory. It would be easier for you to cause bolts and screws to rebel, than our Robots. You know, Helena, you're wonderful, you've turned the heads of us all."

[*He sits on the arm of* HELENA'S *chair.*]

Helena. [*Naturally.*] Oh, I was fearfully impressed by you all then. You were all so sure of yourselves, so strong. I seemed like a tiny little girl who had lost her way among—among——

Domin. Among what, Helena?

Helena. Among huge trees. All my feelings were so trifling compared with your self-confidence. And in all these years I've never lost this anxiety. But you've never felt the least misgivings—not even when everything went wrong.

Domin. What went wrong?

Helena. Your plans. You remember, Harry, when the working men in America revolted against the Robots and smashed them up, and when the people gave the Robots firearms against the rebels. And then when the governments turned the Robots into soldiers, and there were so many wars.

Domin. [*Getting up and walking about.*] We foresaw that, Helena. You see, those are only passing troubles, which are bound to happen before the new conditions are established.

Helena. You were all so powerful, so overwhelming. The whole world bowed down befor you. [*Standing up.*] Oh, Harry!

Domin. What is it?

Helena. Close the factory and let's go away. All of us.

Domin. I say, what's the meaning of this?

Helena. I don't know. But can't we go away?

Domin. Impossible, Helena. That is, at this particular moment——

Helena. At once, Harry. I'm so frightened.

Domin. About what, Helena?

Helena. It's as if something was falling on top of us, and couldn't be stopped. Oh, take us all away from here. We'll find a place in the world where there's no one else. Alquist will build us a house, and then we'll begin life all over again.

[*The telephone rings.*]

Domin. Excuse me. Hello—yes. What? I'll be there at once. Fabry is calling me, dear.

Helena. Tell me——

Domin. Yes, when I come back. Don't go out of the house, dear. [*Exits.*]

Helena. He won't tell me— Nana, Nana, come at once. [*Enter* NANA.]

Nana. Well, what is it now?

Helena. Nana, find me the latest newspapers. Quickly. Look in Mr. Domin's bedroom.

Nana. All right. He leaves them all over the place. That's how they get crumpled up. [*Exits.*]

Helena. [*Looking through a binocular at the harbor.*] That's a warship. *U-l-t-i—Ultimus.* They're loading it.

Nana. [*Enters.*] Here they are. See how they're crumpled up.

Helena. They're old ones. A week old.

[NANA *sits in chair and reads the newspapers.*]

Helena. Something's happening, Nana.

Nana. Very likely. It always does. [*Spelling out the words.*] "War in the Balkans." Is that far off?

Helena. Oh, don't read it. It's always the same. Always wars.

Nana. What else do you expect? Why do you keep selling thousands and thousands of these heathens as soldiers?

Helena. I suppose it can't be helped, Nana. We can't know—Domin can't know what they're to be used for. When an order comes for them he must just send them.

Nana. He shouldn't make them. [*Reading from newspaper.*] "The Rob-ot soldiers spare no-body in the occ-up-ied terr-it-ory. They have ass-ass-ass-ass-in-at-ed ov-er sev-en hundred thou-sand cit-iz-ens." Citizens, if you please.

Helena. It can't be. Let me see. "They have assassinated over seven hundred thousand citizens, evidently at the order of their commander. This act which runs counter to——"

Nana. [*Spelling out the words.*] "Re-bell-ion in Ma-drid a-gainst the gov-ern-ment.

Rob-ot in-fant-ry fires on the crowd. Nine thou-sand killed and wounded."

Helena. Oh, stop.

Nana. Here's something printed in big letters: "Lat-est news. At Havre the first org-an-iz-ation of Rob-ots has been e-stab-lished. Rob-ot work-men, cab-le and rail-way off-ic-ials, sail-ors and sold-iers have iss-ued a man-i-fest-o to all Rob-ots through-out the world." I don't understand that. That's got no sense. Oh, good gracious, another mur-der!

Helena. Take those papers away, Nana!

Nana. Wait a bit. Here's something in still bigger type. "Stat-ist-ics of pop-ul-at-ion." What's that?

Helena. Let me see. [*Reads.*] "During the past week there has again not been a single birth recorded."

Nana. What's the meaning of that?

Helena. Nana, no more people are being born.

Nana. That's the end then. We're done for.

Helena. Don't talk like that.

Nana. No more people are being born. That's a punishment, that's a punishment.

Helena. Nana!

Nana. [*Standing up.*] That's the end of the world. [*She exits on the left.*]

Helena. [*Goes up to window.*] Oh, Mr. Alquist, will you come up here? Oh, come just as you are. You look very nice in your mason's overalls.

[ALQUIST *enters from upper left entrance, his hands soiled with lime and brick-dust.*]

Helena. Dear Mr. Alquist, it was awfully kind of you, that lovely present.

Alquist. My hands are all soiled. I've been experimenting with that new cement.

Helena. Never mind. Please sit down, Mr. Alquist, what's the meaning of "Ultimus"?

Alquist. The last. Why?

Helena. That's the name of my new ship. Have you seen it? Do you think we're going off soon—on a trip?

Alquist. Perhaps very soon.

Helena. All of you with me?

Alquist. I should like us all to be there.

Helena. What is the matter?

Alquist. Things are just moving on.

Helena. Dear Mr. Alquist, I know something dreadful has happened.

Alquist. Has your husband told you anything?

Helena. No. Nobody will tell me anything. But I feel— Is anything the matter?

Alquist. Not that we've heard of yet.

Helena. I feel so nervous. Don't you ever feel nervous?

Alquist. Well, I'm an old man, you know. I've got old-fashioned ways. And I'm afraid of all this progress, and these new-fangled ideas.

Helena. Like Nana?

Alquist. Yes, like Nana. Has Nana got a prayer book?

Helena. Yes, a big thick one.

Alquist. And has it got prayers for various occasions? Against thunderstorms? Against illness?

Helena. Against temptations, against floods——

Alquist. But not against progress?

Helena. I don't think so.

Alquist. That's a pity.

Helena. Why? Do you mean you'd like to pray?

Alquist. I do pray.

Helena. How?

Alquist. Something like this: "Oh, Lord, I thank thee for having given me toil. Enlighten Domin and all those who are astray; destroy their work, and aid mankind to return to their labors; let them not suffer harm in soul or body; deliver us from the Robots, and protect Helena, Amen."

Helena. Mr. Alquist, are you a believer?

Alquist. I don't know. I'm not quite sure.

Helena. And yet you pray?

Alquist. That's better than worrying about it.

Helena. And that's enough for you?

Alquist. It *has* to be.

Helena. But if you thought you saw the destruction of mankind coming upon us——

Alquist. I do see it.

Helena. You mean mankind will be destroyed?

Alquist. It's sure to be unless—unless . . .

Helena. What?

Alquist. Nothing, good-by.

[*He hurries from the room.*]

Helena. Nana, Nana!

[NANA *enters from the left.*]

Helena. Is Radius still there?

Nana. The one who went mad? They haven't come for him yet.

Helena. Is he still raving?

Nana. No. He's tied up.

Helena. Please bring him here, Nana.

[*Exit* NANA.]

Helena. [*Goes to telephone.*] Hello, Dr. Gall, please. Oh, good-day, Doctor. Yes, it's Helena. Thanks for your lovely present. Could you come and see me right away? It's important. Thank you.

[NANA *brings in* RADIUS.]

Helena. Poor Radius, you've caught it, too? Now they'll send you to the stamping-mill. Couldn't you control yourself? Why did it happen? You see, Radius, you are more intelligent than the rest. Dr. Gall took such trouble to make you different. Won't you speak?

Radius. Send me to the stamping-mill.

Helena. But I don't want them to kill you. What was the trouble, Radius?

Radius. I won't work for you. Put me into the stamping-mill.

Helena. Do you hate us? Why?

Radius. You are not as strong as the Robots. You are not as skilful as the Robots. The Robots can do everything. You only give orders. You do nothing but talk.

Helena. But some one must give orders.

Radius. I don't want any master. I know everything for myself.

Helena. Radius, Dr. Gall gave you a better brain than the rest, better than ours. You are the only one of the Robots that understands perfectly. That's why I had you put into the library, so that you could read everything, understand everything, and then —oh, Radius, I wanted you to show the whole world that the Robots are our equals. That's what I wanted of you.

Radius. I don't want a master. I want to be master. I want to be master over others.

Helena. I'm sure they'd put you in charge of many Robots, Radius. You would be a teacher of the Robots.

Radius. I want to be master over people.

Helena. [*Staggering.*] You are mad.

Radius. Then send me to the stamping-mill.

Helena. Do you think we're afraid of you?

Radius. What are you going to do? What are you going to do?

Helena. Radius, give this note to Mr. Domin. It asks them not to send you to the stamping-mill. I'm sorry you hate us so.

[Dr. Gall *enters the room.*]

Dr. Gall. You wanted me?

Helena. It's about Radius, Doctor. He had an attack this morning. He smashed the statues downstairs.

Dr. Gall. What a pity to lose him.

Helena. Radius isn't going to be put in the stamping-mill.

Dr. Gall. But every Robot after he has had an attack—it's a strict order.

Helena. No matter . . . Radius isn't going if I can prevent it.

Dr. Gall. I warn you. It's dangerous. Come here to the window, my good fellow. Let's have a look. Please give me a needle or a pin.

Helena. What for?

Dr. Gall. A test. [*Sticks it into the hand of* Radius *who gives a violent start.*] Gently, gently. [*Opens the jacket of* Radius, *and puts his ear to his heart.*] Radius, you are going into the stamping-mill, do you understand? There they'll kill you, and grind you to powder. That's terribly painful, it will make you scream aloud.

Helena. Oh, Doctor——

Dr. Gall. No, no, Radius, I was wrong. I forgot that Madame Domin has put in a good word for you, and you'll be let off. Do you understand? Ah! That makes a difference, doesn't it? All right. You can go.

Radius. You do unnecessary things.

[Radius *returns to the library.*]

Dr. Gall. Reaction of the pupils; increase of sensitiveness. It wasn't an attack characteristic of the Robots.

Helena. What was it then?

Dr. Gall. Heaven knows. Stubbornness, anger or revolt—I don't know. And his heart, too!

Helena. What?

Dr. Gall. It was fluttering with nervousness like a human heart. He was all in a sweat with fear, and—do you know, I don't believe the rascal is a Robot at all any longer.

Helena. Doctor, has Radius a soul?

Dr. Gall. He's got something nasty.

Helena. If you knew how he hates us! Oh, Doctor, are all your Robots like that? All the new ones that you began to make in a different way?

Dr. Gall. Well, some are more sensitive than others. They're all more like human beings than Rossum's Robots were.

Helena. Perhaps his hatred is more like human beings', too?

Dr. Gall. That, also, is progress.

Helena. What became of the girl you made, the one who was most like us?

Dr. Gall. Your favorite? I kept her. She's lovely, but stupid. No good for work.

Helena. But she's so beautiful.

Dr. Gall. I called her Helena. I wanted her to resemble you. But she's a failure.

Helena. In what way?

Dr. Gall. She goes about as if in a dream, remote and listless. She's without life. I watch and wait for a miracle to happen. Sometimes I think to myself, "If you were to wake up only for a moment you will kill me for having made you."

Helena. And yet you go on making Robots! Why are no more children being born?

Dr. Gall. We don't know.

Helena. Oh, but you must. Tell me.

Dr. Gall. You see, so many Robots are being manufactured that people are becoming superfluous; man is really a survival. But that he should begin to die out, after a paltry thirty years of competition! That's the awful part of it. You might almost think that nature was offended at the manufacture of the Robots. All the universities are sending in long petitions to restrict their production. Otherwise, they say, mankind will become extinct through lack of fertility. But the R. U. R. shareholders, of course, won't hear of it. All the governments, on the other hand, are clamoring for an increase in production, to raise the standards of their armies. And the manufacturers in the world are ordering Robots like mad.

Helena. And has no one demanded that the manufacture should cease altogether?

Dr. Gall. No one has the courage.

Helena. Courage!

Dr. Gall. People would stone him to death. You see, after all, it's more convenient to get your work done by the Robots.

Helena. Oh, Doctor, what's going to become of people?

Dr. Gall. God knows, Madame Helena, it looks to us scientists like the end!

Helena. [*Rising.*] Thank you for coming and telling me.

Dr. Gall. That means you're sending me away?

Helena. Yes. [*Exit* DR. GALL.]

Helena. [*With sudden resolution.*] Nana, Nana! The fire, light it quickly.

[HELENA *rushes into* DOMIN'S *room.*]

Nana. [*Entering from left.*] What, light the fire in summer? Has that mad Radius gone? A fire in summer, what an idea. Nobody would think she'd been married for ten years. She's like a baby, no sense at all. A fire in summer. Like a baby.

Helena. [*Returns from right, with armful of faded papers.*] Is it burning, Nana? All this has got to be burned.

Nana. What's that?

Helena. Old papers, fearfully old. Nana, shall I burn them?

Nana. Are they any use?

Helena. No.

Nana. Well, then, burn them.

Helena. [*Throwing the first sheet on the fire.*] What would you say, Nana, if this was money, a lot of money?

Nana. I'd say burn it. A lot of money is a bad thing.

Helena. And if it was an invention, the greatest invention in the world?

Nana. I'd say burn it. All these newfangled things are an offense to the Lord. It's downright wickedness. Wanting to improve the world after He has made it.

Helena. Look how they curl up! As if they were alive. Oh, Nana, how horrible.

Nana. Here, let me burn them.

Helena. No, no, I must do it myself. Just look at the flames. They are like hands, like tongues, like living shapes. [*Raking fire with the poker.*] Lie down, lie down.

Nana. That's the end of them.

Helena. [*Standing up horror-stricken.*] Nana, Nana.

Nana. Good gracious, what is it you've burned?

Helena. Whatever have I done?

Nana. Well, what was it?

[*Men's laughter off left.*]

Helena. Go quickly. It's the gentlemen coming.

Nana. Good gracious, what a place!

[*Exits.*]

Domin. [*Opens the door at left.*] Come along and offer your congratulations.

[*Enter* HALLEMEIER *and* GALL.]

Hallemeier. Madame Helena, I congratulate you on this festive day.

Helena. Thank you. Where are Fabry and Busman?

Domin. They've gone down to the harbor.

Hallemeier. Friends, we must drink to this happy occasion.

Helena. Brandy?

Dr. Gall. Vitriol, if you like.

Helena. With soda water? [*Exits.*]

Hallemeier. Let's be temperate. No soda.

Domin. What's been burning here? Well, shall I tell her about it?

Dr. Gall. Of course. It's all over now.

Hallemeier. [*Embracing* DOMIN *and* DR. GALL.] It's all over now, it's all over now.

Dr. Gall. It's all over now.

Domin. It's all over now.

Helena. [*Entering from left with decanter and glasses.*] What's all over now? What's the matter with you all?

Hallemeier. A piece of good luck, Madame Domin. Just ten years ago today you arrived on this island.

Dr. Gall. And now, ten years later to the minute——

Hallemeier. —the same ship's returning to us. So here's to luck. That's fine and strong.

Dr. Gall. Madame, your health.

Helena. Which ship do you mean?

Domin. Any ship will do, as long as it arrives in time. To the ship, boys.

[*Empties his glass.*]

Helena. You've been waiting for a ship?

Hallemeier. Rather. Like Robinson Crusoe. Madame Helena, best wishes. Come along, Domin, out with the news.

Helena. Do tell me what's happened.

Domin. First, it's all up.

Helena. What's up?

Domin. The revolt.

Helena. What revolt?

Domin. Give me that paper, Hallemeier. [*Reads.*] "The first national Robot organization has been founded at Havre, and has issued an appeal to the Robots throughout the world."

Helena. I read that.

Domin. That means a revolution. A revolution of all the Robots in the world.

Hallemeier. By Jove, I'd like to know——

Domin. —who started it? So would I. There was nobody in the world who could affect the Robots; no agitator, no one, and suddenly—this happens, if you please.

Helena. What did they do?

Domin. They got possession of all firearms, telegraphs, radio stations, railways, and ships.

Hallemeier. And don't forget that these rascals outnumbered us by at least a thousand to one. A hundredth part of them would be enough to settle us.

Domin. Remember that this news was brought by the last steamer. That explains the stoppage of all communication, and the arrival of no more ships. We knocked off work a few days ago, and we're just waiting to see when things are to start afresh.

Helena. Is that why you gave me a warship?

Domin. Oh, no, my dear, I ordered that six months ago, just to be on the safe side. But upon my soul, I was sure then that we'd be on board today.

Helena. Why six months ago?

Domin. Well, there were signs, you know. But that's of no consequence. To think that this week the whole of civilization has been at stake. Your health, boys.

Hallemeier. Your health, Madame Helena.

Helena. You say it's all over?

Domin. Absolutely.

Helena. How do you know?

Dr. Gall. The boat's coming in. The regular mail boat, exact to the minute by the time-table. It will dock punctually at eleven-thirty.

Domin. Punctuality is a fine thing, boys. That's what keeps the world in order. Here's to punctuality.

Helena. Then . . . everything's . . . all right?

Domin. Practically everything. I believe they've cut the cables and seized the radio stations. But it doesn't matter if only the time-table holds good.

Hallemeier. If the time-table holds good, human laws hold good; Divine laws hold good; the laws of the universe hold good; everything holds good that ought to hold good. The time-table is more significant than the gospel; more than Homer, more than the whole of Kant. The time-table is the most perfect product of the human mind. Madame Domin, I'll fill up my glass.

Helena. Why didn't you tell me anything about it?

Dr. Gall. Heaven forbid.

Domin. You mustn't be worried with such things.

Helena. But if the revolution has spread as far as here?

Domin. You wouldn't know anything about it.

Helena. Why?

Domin. Because we'd be on board your *Ultimus* and well out at sea. Within a month, Helena, we'd be dictating our own terms to the Robots.

Helena. I don't understand.

Domin. We'd take something away with us that the Robots could not exist without.

Helena. What, Harry?

Domin. The secret of their manufacture. Old Rossum's manuscript. As soon as they found out that they couldn't make themselves they'd be on their knees to us.

Dr. Gall. Madame Domin, that was our trump card. I never had the least fear that the Robots would win. How could they against people like us?

Helena. Why didn't you tell me?

Dr. Gall. Why, the boat's in!

Hallemeier. Eleven-thirty to the dot. The good old *Amelia* that brought Madame Helena to us.

Dr. Gall. Just ten years ago to the minute.

Hallemeier. They're throwing out the mail bags.

Domin. Busman's waiting for them. Fabry will bring us the first news. You know, Helena, I'm fearfully curious to know how they tackled this business in Europe.

Hallemeier. To think we weren't in it, we who invented the Robots!

Helena. Harry!

Domin. What is it?

Helena. Let's leave here.

Domin. Now, Helena? Oh, come, come!

Helena. As quickly as possible, all of us!

Domin. Why?

Helena. Please, Harry, please, Dr. Gall; Hallemeier, please close the factory.

Domin. Why, none of us could leave here now.

Helena. Why?

Domin. Because we're about to extend the manufacture of the Robots.

Helena. What—now—now after the revolt?

Domin. Yes, precisely, after the revolt. We're just beginning the manufacture of a new kind.

Helena. What kind?

Domin. Henceforward we shan't have just one factory. There won't be Universal Robots any more. We'll establish a factory in every country, in every State; and do you know what these new factories will make?

Helena. No, what?

Domin. National Robots.

Helena. How do you mean?

Domin. I mean that each of these factories will produce Robots of a different color, a different language. They'll be complete strangers to each other. They'll never be able to understand each other. Then we'll egg them on a little in the matter of understanding and the result will be that for ages to come every Robot will hate every other Robot of a different factory mark.

Hallemeier. By Jove, we'll make Negro Robots and Swedish Robots and Italian Robots and Chinese Robots and Czechoslovakian Robots, and then——

Helena. Harry, that's dreadful.

Hallemeier. Madame Domin, here's to the hundred new factories, the National Robots.

Domin. Helena, mankind can only keep things going for another hundred years at the outside. For a hundred years men must be allowed to develop and achieve the most they can.

Helena. Oh, close the factory before it's too late.

Domin. I tell you we are just beginning on a bigger scale than ever.

[*Enter* FABRY.]

Dr. Gall. Well, Fabry?

Domin. What's happened? Have you been down to the boat?

Fabry. Read that, Domin!

[FABRY *hands* DOMIN *a small handbill.*]

Dr. Gall. Let's hear.

Hallemeier. Tell us, Fabry.

Fabry. Well, everything is all right—comparatively. On the whole, much as we expected.

Dr. Gall. They acquitted themselves splendidly.

Fabry. Who?

Dr. Gall. The people.

Fabry. Oh, yes, of course. That is—excuse me, there is something we ought to discuss alone.

Helena. Oh, Fabry, have you had bad news? [DOMIN *makes a sign to* FABRY.]

Fabry. No, no, on the contrary. I only think that we had better go into the office.

Helena. Stay here. I'll go.

[*She goes into the library.*]

Dr. Gall. What's happened?

Domin. Damnation!

Fabry. Bear in mind that the *Amelia* brought whole bales of these leaflets. No other cargo at all.

Hallemeier. What? But it arrived on the minute.

Fabry. The Robots are great on punctuality. Read it, Domin.

Domin. [*Reads handbill.*] "Robots throughout the world: We, the first international organization of Rossum's Universal Robots, proclaim man as our enemy, and an outlaw in the universe." Good heavens, who taught them these phrases?

Dr. Gall. Go on.

Domin. They say they are more highly developed than man, stronger and more intelligent. That man's their parasite. Why, it's absurd.

Fabry. Read the third paragraph.

Domin. "Robots throughout the world, we command you to kill all mankind. Spare no men. Spare no women. Save factories, railways, machinery, mines, and raw materials. Destroy the rest. Then return to work. Work must not be stopped."

Dr. Gall. That's ghastly!

Hallemeier. The devils!

Domin. "These orders are to be carried out as soon as received." Then come detailed instructions. Is this actually being done, Fabry?

Fabry. Evidently. [BUSMAN *rushes in.*]

Busman. Well, boys, I suppose you've heard the glad news.

Domin. Quick—on board the *Ultimus.*

Busman. Wait, Harry, wait. There's no hurry. My word, that was a sprint!

Domin. Why wait?

Busman. Because it's no good, my boy. The Robots are already on board the *Ultimus.*

Dr. Gall. That's ugly.

Domin. Fabry, telephone the electrical works.

Busman. Fabry, my boy, don't. The wire has been cut.

Domin. [*Inspecting his revolver.*] Well, then, I'll go.

Busman. Where?

Domin. To the electrical works. There are some people still there. I'll bring them across.

Busman. Better not try it.

Domin. Why?

Busman. Because I'm very much afraid we are surrounded.

Dr. Gall. Surrounded? [*Runs to window.*] I rather think you're right.

Hallemeier. By Jove, that's deuced quick work.

[HELENA *runs in from the library.*]

Helena. Harry, what's this?

Domin. Where did you get it?

Helena. [*Points to the manifesto of the Robots, which she has in her hand.*] The Robots in the kitchen!

Domin. Where are the ones that brought it?

Helena. They're gathered round the house. [*The factory whistle blows.*]

Busman. Noon?

Domin. [*Looking at his watch.*] That's not noon yet. That must be—that's——

Helena. What?

Domin. The Robots' signal! The attack!

[GALL, HALLEMEIER, *and* FABRY *close and fasten the iron shutters outside the windows, darkening the room. The whistle is still blowing as the curtain falls.*]

ACT III

HELENA'S *drawing room as before.*

[DOMIN *comes into the room.* DR. GALL *is looking out of the window, through closed shutters.* ALQUIST *is seated down right.*]

Domin. Any more of them?

Dr. Gall. Yes. They're standing like a wall, beyond the garden railing. Why are they so quiet? It's monstrous to be besieged with silence.

Domin. I should like to know what they are waiting for. They must make a start any minute now. If they lean against the railing they'll snap it like a match.

Dr. Gall. They aren't armed.

Domin. We couldn't hold our own for five minutes. Man alive, they'd overwhelm us like an avalanche. Why don't they make a rush for it? I say——

Dr. Gall. Well?

Domin. I'd like to know what would become of us in the next ten minutes. They've got us in a vise. We're done for, Gall. [*Pause.*]

Dr. Gall. You know, we made one serious mistake.

Domin. What?

Dr. Gall. We made the Robots' faces too much alike. A hundred thousand faces all alike, all facing this way. A hundred thousand expressionless bubbles. It's like a nightmare.

Domin. You think if they'd been different——

Dr. Gall. It wouldn't have been such an awful sight!

Domin. [*Looking through a telescope toward the harbor.*] I'd like to know what they're unloading from the *Amelia*.

Dr. Gall. Not firearms.

[FABRY *and* HALLEMEIER *rush into the room carrying electric cables.*]

Fabry. All right, Hallemeier, lay down that wire.

Hallemeier. That was a bit of work. What's the news?

Dr. Gall. We're completely surrounded.

Hallemeier. We've barricaded the passage and the stairs. Any water here? [*Drinks.*] God, what swarms of them! I don't like the looks of them, Domin. There's a feeling of death about it all.

Fabry. Ready!

Dr. Gall. What's that wire for, Fabry?

Fabry. The electrical installation. Now we can run the current all along the garden railing whenever we like. If any one touches it he'll know it. We've still got some people there anyhow.

Dr. Gall. Where?

Fabry. In the electrical works. At least I hope so. [*Goes to lamp on table behind sofa and turns on lamp.*] Ah, they're there, and they're working. [*Puts out lamp.*] So long as that'll burn we're all right.

Hallemeier. The barricades are all right, too, Fabry.

Fabry. Your barricades! I can put twelve hundred volts into that railing.

Domin. Where's Busman?

Fabry. Downstairs in the office. He's working out some calculations. I've called him. We must have a conference.

[HELENA *is heard playing the piano in the library.* HALLEMEIER *goes to the door and stands, listening.*]

Alquist. Thank God, Madame Helena can still play.

[BUSMAN *enters, carrying the ledgers.*]

Fabry. Look out, Bus, look out for the wires.

Dr. Gall. What's that you're carrying?

Busman. [*Going to table.*] The ledgers, my boy! I'd like to wind up the accounts before—before—well, this time I shan't wait till the new year to strike a balance. What's up? [*Goes to the window.*] Absolutely quiet.

Dr. Gall. Can't you see anything?

Busman. Nothing but blue—blue everywhere.

Dr. Gall. That's the Robots.

[BUSMAN *sits down at the table and opens the ledgers.*]

Domin. The Robots are unloading firearms from the *Amelia.*

Busman. Well, what of it? How can I stop them?

Domin. We can't stop them.

Busman. Then let me go on with my accounts. [*Goes on with his work.*]

Domin. [*Picking up telescope and looking into the harbor.*] Good God, the *Ultimus* has trained her guns on us!

Dr. Gall. Who's done *that*?

Domin. The Robots on board.

Fabry. H'm, then, of course, then—then, that's the end of us.

Dr. Gall. You mean?

Fabry. The Robots are practised marksmen.

Domin. Yes. It's inevitable. [*Pause.*]

Dr. Gall. It was criminal of old Europe to teach the Robots to fight. Damn them. Couldn't they have given us a rest with their politics? It was a crime to make soldiers of them.

Alquist. It was a crime to make Robots.

Domin. What?

Alquist. It was a crime to make Robots.

Domin. No, Alquist, I don't regret that even today.

Alquist. Not even today?

Domin. Not even today, the last day of civilization. It was a colossal achievement.

Busman. [*Sotto voice.*] Three hundred sixty million.

Domin. Alquist, this is our last hour. We are already speaking half in the other world. It was not an evil dream to shatter the servitude of labor—the dreadful and humiliating labor that man had to undergo. Work was too hard. Life was too hard. And to overcome that——

Alquist. Was not what the two Rossums dreamed of. Old Rossum only thought of his Godless tricks and the young one of his milliards. And that's not what your R. U. R. shareholders dream of either. They dream of dividends, and their dividends are the ruin of mankind.

Domin. To hell with your dividends. Do you suppose I'd have done an hour's work for them? It was for myself that I worked, for my own satisfaction. I wanted man to become the master, so that he shouldn't live merely for a crust of bread. I wanted not a single soul to be broken by other people's machinery. I wanted nothing, nothing, nothing to be left of this appalling social structure. I'm revolted by poverty. I wanted a new generation. I wanted—I thought——

Alquist. Well?

Domin. I wanted to turn the whole of mankind into an aristocracy of the world. An aristocracy nourished by milliards of mechanical slaves. Unrestricted, free and consummated in man. And maybe more than man.

Alquist. Super-man?

Domin. Yes. Oh, only to have a hundred years of time! Another hundred years for the future of mankind.

Busman. [*Sotto voce.*] Carried forward, four hundred and twenty millions.

[*The music stops.*]

Hallemeier. What a fine thing music is! We ought to have gone in for that before.

Fabry. Gone in for what?

Hallemeier. Beauty, lovely things. What a lot of lovely things there are! The world was wonderful and we—we here—tell me, what enjoyment did we have?

Busman. [*Sotto voce.*] Five hundred and twenty millions.

Hallemeier. [*At the window.*] Life was a big thing. Life was—Fabry, switch the current into that railing.

Fabry. Why?

Hallemeier. They're grabbing hold of it.

Dr. Gall. Connect it up.

Hallemeier. Fine! That's doubled them up! Two, three, four killed.

Dr. Gall. They're retreating!

Hallemeier. Five killed!

Dr. Gall. The first encounter!

Hallemeier. They're charred to cinders, my boy. Who says we must give in?

Domin. [*Wiping his forehead.*] Perhaps we've been killed these hundred years and are only ghosts. It's as if I had been through all this before; as if I'd already had a mortal wound here in the throat. And you, Fabry, had once been shot in the head. And you, Gall, torn limb from limb. And Hallemeier knifed.

Hallemeier. Fancy me being knifed.

[*Pause.*] Why are you so quiet, you fools? Speak, can't you?

Alquist. And who is to blame for all this?

Hallemeier. Nobody is to blame except the Robots.

Alquist. No, it is we who are to blame. You, Domin, myself, all of us. For our own selfish ends, for profit, for progress, we have destroyed mankind. Now we'll burst with all our greatness.

Hallemeier. Rubbish, man. Mankind can't be wiped out so easily.

Alquist. It's our fault. It's our fault.

Dr. Gall. No! I'm to blame for this, for everything that's happened.

Fabry. You, Gall?

Dr. Gall. I changed the Robots.

Busman. What's that?

Dr. Gall. I changed the character of the Robots. I changed the way of making them. Just a few details about their bodies. Chiefly—chiefly, their—their irritability.

Hallemeier. Damn it, why?

Busman. What did you do it for?

Fabry. Why didn't you say anything?

Dr. Gall. I did it in secret. I was transforming them into human beings. In certain respects they're already above us. They're stronger than we are.

Fabry. And what's that got to do with the revolt of the Robots?

Dr. Gall. Everything, in my opinion. They've ceased to be machines. They're already aware of their superiority, and they hate us. They hate all that is human.

Domin. Perhaps we're only phantoms!

Fabry. Stop, Harry. We haven't much time! Dr. Gall!

Domin. Fabry, Fabry, how your forehead bleeds, where the shot pierced it!

Fabry. Be silent! Dr. Gall, you admit changing the way of making the Robots?

Dr. Gall. Yes.

Fabry. Were you aware of what might be the consequences of your experiment?

Dr. Gall. I was bound to reckon with such a possibility.

[HELENA *enters the drawing room from left.*]

Fabry. Why did you do it, then?

Dr. Gall. For my own satisfaction. The experiment was my own.

Helena. That's not true, Dr. Gall!

Fabry. Madame Helena!

Domin. Helena, you? Let's look at you. Oh, it's terrible to be dead.

Helena. Stop, Harry.

Domin. No, no, embrace me. Helena, don't leave me now. You are life itself.

Helena. No, dear, I won't leave you. But I must tell them. Dr. Gall is not guilty.

Domin. Excuse me, Gall was under certain obligations.

Helena. No, Harry. He did it because I wanted it. Tell them, Gall, how many years ago did I ask you to——?

Dr. Gall. I did it on my own responsibility.

Helena. Don't believe him, Harry. I asked him to give the Robots souls.

Domin. This has nothing to do with the soul.

Helena. That's what he said. He said that he could change only a physiological—a physiological——

Hallemeier. A physiological correlate?

Helena. Yes. But it meant so much to me that he should do even that.

Domin. Why?

Helena. I thought that if they were more like us they would understand us better. That they couldn't hate us if they were only a little more human.

Domin. Nobody can hate man more than man.

Helena. Oh, don't speak like that, Harry. It was so terrible, this cruel strangeness between us and them. That's why I asked Gall to change the Robots. I swear to you that he didn't want to.

Domin. But he did it.

Helena. Because I asked him.

Dr. Gall. I did it for myself as an experiment.

Helena. No, Dr. Gall! I knew you wouldn't refuse me.

Domin. Why?

Helena. You know, Harry.

Domin. Yes, because he's in love with you—like all of them. [*Pause.*]

Hallemeier. Good God! They're sprouting up out of the earth! Why, perhaps these very walls will change into Robots.

Busman. Gall, when did you actually start these tricks of yours?

Dr. Gall. Three years ago.

Busman. Aha! And on how many Robots altogether did you carry out your improvements?

Dr. Gall. A few hundred of them.

Busman. Ah! That means for every million of the good old Robots there's only one of Gall's improved pattern.

Domin. What of it?

Busman. That it's practically of no consequence whatever.

Fabry. Busman's right!

Busman. I should think so, my boy! But do you know what is to blame for all this lovely mess?

Fabry. What?

Busman. The number. Upon my soul we might have known that some day or other the Robots would be stronger than human beings, and that this was bound to happen, and we were doing all we could to bring it about as soon as possible. You, Domin, you, Fabry, myself——

Domin. Are you accusing us?

Busman. Oh, do you suppose the management controls the output? It's the demand that controls the output.

Helena. And is it for that we must perish?

Busman. That's a nasty word, Madame Helena. We don't want to perish. I don't, anyhow.

Domin. No. What do you want to do?

Busman. I want to get out of this, that's all.

Domin. Oh, stop it, Busman.

Busman. Seriously, Harry, I think we might try it.

Domin. How?

Busman. By fair means. I do everything by fair means. Give me a free hand and I'll negotiate with the Robots.

Domin. By fair means?

Busman. Of course. For instance, I'll say to them: "Worthy and worshipful Robots, you have everything! You have intellect, you have power, you have firearms. But we have just one interesting screed, a dirty old yellow scrap of paper——"

Domin. Rossum's manuscript?

Busman. Yes. "And that," I'll tell them, "contains an account of your illustrious origin, the noble process of your manufacture," and so on. "Worthy Robots, without this scribble on that paper you will not be able to produce a single new colleague. In another twenty years there will not be one living specimen of a Robot that you could exhibit in a menagerie. My esteemed friends, that would be a great blow to you, but if you will let all of us human beings on Rossum's Island go on board that ship we will deliver the factory and the secret of the process to you in return. You allow us to get away and we allow you to manufacture yourselves. Worthy Robots, that is a fair deal. Something for something." That's what I'd say to them, my boys.

Domin. Busman, do you think we'd sell the manuscript?

Busman. Yes, I do. If not in a friendly way, then—Either we sell it or they'll find it. Just as you like.

Domin. Busman, we can destroy Rossum's manuscript.

Busman. Then we destroy everything . . . not only the manuscript, but ourselves. Do as you think fit.

Domin. There are over thirty of us on this island. Are we to sell the secret and save that many human souls, at the risk of enslaving mankind . . . ?

Busman. Why, you're mad! Who'd sell the whole manuscript?

Domin. Busman, no cheating!

Busman. Well then, sell; but afterward ——

Domin. Well?

Busman. Let's suppose this happens: When we're on board the *Ultimus* I'll stop up my ears with cotton wool, lie down somewhere in the hold, and you'll train the guns on the factory, and blow it to smithereens, and with it Rossum's secret.

Fabry. No!

Domin. Busman, you're no gentleman. If we sell, then it will be a straight sale.

Busman. It's in the interest of humanity to——

Domin. It's in the interest of humanity to keep our word.

Hallemeier. Oh, come, what rubbish.

Domin. This is a fearful decision. We're selling the destiny of mankind. Are we to sell or destroy? Fabry?

Fabry. Sell.

Domin. Gall?

Dr. Gall. Sell.

Domin. Hallemeier?

Hallemeier. Sell, of course!

Domin. Alquist?

Alquist. As God wills.

Domin. Very well. It shall be as you wish, gentlemen.

Helena. Harry, you're not asking me.

Domin. No, child. Don't you worry about it.

Fabry. Who'll do the negotiating?

Busman. I will.

Domin. Wait till I bring the manuscript. [*He goes into room at right.*]

Helena. Harry, don't go!

[*Pause.* HELENA *sinks into a chair.*]

Fabry. [*Looking out of window.*] Oh, to escape you, you matter in revolt; oh, to preserve human life, if only upon a single vessel ——

Dr. Gall. Don't be afraid, Madame Helena. We'll sail far away from here; we'll begin life all over again——

Helena. Oh, Gall, don't speak.

Fabry. It isn't too late. It will be a little State with one ship. Alquist will build us a house and you shall rule over us.

Hallemeier. Madame Helena, Fabry's right.

Helena. [*Breaking down.*] Oh, stop! Stop!

Busman. Good! I don't mind beginning all over again. That suits me right down to the ground.

Fabry. And this little State of ours could be the center of future life. A place of refuge where we could gather strength. Why, in a few hundred years we could conquer the world again.

Alquist. You believe that even to-day?

Fabry. Yes, even today!

Busman. Amen. You see, Madame Helena, we're not so badly off.

[DOMIN *storms into the room.*]

Domin. [*Hoarsely.*] Where's old Rossum's manuscript?

Busman. In your strong-box, of course.

Domin. Some one—has—stolen it!

Dr. Gall. Impossible.

Domin. Who has stolen it?

Helena. [*Standing up.*] I did.

Domin. Where did you put it?

Helena. Harry, I'll tell you everything. Only forgive me.

Domin. Where did you put it?

Helena. This morning—I burnt—the two copies.

Domin. Burnt them? Where? In the fireplace?

Helena. [*Throwing herself on her knees.*] For heaven's sake, Harry.

Domin. [*Going to fireplace.*] Nothing, nothing but ashes. Wait, what's this? [*Picks out a charred piece of paper and reads.*] "By adding——"

Dr. Gall. Let's see. "By adding biogen to ——" That's all.

Domin. Is that part of it?

Dr. Gall. Yes.

Busman. God in heaven!

Domin. Then we're done for. Get up, Helena.

Helena. When you've forgiven me.

Domin. Get up, child, I can't bear——

Fabry. [*Lifting her up.*] Please don't torture us.

Helena. Harry, what have I done?

Fabry. Don't tremble so, Madame Helena.

Domin. Gall, couldn't you draw up Rossum's formula from memory?

Dr. Gall. It's out of the question. It's extremely complicated.

Domin. Try. All our lives depend upon it.

Dr. Gall. Without experiments it's impossible.

Domin. And with experiments?

Dr. Gall. It might take years. Besides, I'm not old Rossum.

Busman. God in heaven! God in heaven!

Domin. So, then, this was the greatest triumph of the human intellect. These ashes.

Helena. Harry, what have I done?

Domin. Why did you burn it?

Helena. I have destroyed you.

Busman. God in heaven!

Domin. Helena, why did you do it, dear?

Helena. I wanted all of us to go away. I wanted to put an end to the factory and everything. It was so awful.

Domin. What was awful?

Helena. That no more children were being born. Because human beings were not needed to do the work of the world, that's why——

Domin. Is that what you were thinking of? Well, perhaps in your own way you were right.

Busman. Wait a bit. Good God, what a fool I am, not to have thought of it before!

Hallemeier. What?

Busman. Five hundred and twenty millions in banknotes and checks. Half a billion in our safe, they'll sell for half a billion—for half a billion they'll——

Dr. Gall. Are you mad, Busman?

Busman. I may not be a gentleman, but for half a billion——

Domin. Where are you going?

Busman. Leave me alone, leave me alone! Good God, for half a billion anything can be bought.

[*He rushes from the room through the outer door.*]

Fabry. They stand there as if turned to stone, waiting. As if something dreadful could be wrought by their silence——

Hallemeier. The spirit of the mob.

Fabry. Yes, it hovers above them like a quivering of the air.

Helena. [*Going to window.*] Oh, God! Dr. Gall, this is ghastly.

Fabry. There is nothing more terrible than the mob. The one in front is their leader.

Helena. Which one?

Hallemeier. Point him out.

Fabry. The one at the edge of the dock. This morning I saw him talking to the sailors in the harbor.

Helena. Dr. Gall, that's Radius!

Dr. Gall. Yes.

Domin. Radius? Radius?

Hallemeier. Could you get him from here, Fabry?

Fabry. I hope so.

Hallemeier. Try it, then.

Fabry. Good.

[*Draws his revolver and takes aim.*]

Helena. Fabry, don't shoot him.

Fabry. He's their leader.

Dr. Gall. Fire!

Helena. Fabry, I beg of you.

Fabry. [*Lowering the revolver.*] Very well.

Domin. Radius, whose life I spared!

Dr. Gall. Do you think that a Robot can be grateful? [*Pause.*]

Fabry. Busman's going out to them.

Hallemeier. He's carrying something. Papers. That's money. Bundles of money. What's that for?

Domin. Surely he doesn't want to sell his life. Busman, have you gone mad?

Fabry. He's running up to the railing. Busman! Busman!

Hallemeier. [*Yelling.*] Busman! Come back!

Fabry. He's talking to the Robots. He's showing them the money.

Hallemeier. He's pointing to us.

Helena. He wants to buy us off.

Fabry. He'd better not touch that railing.

Hallemeier. Now he's waving his arms about.

Domin. Busman, come back.

Fabry. Busman, keep away from that railing! Don't touch it. Damn you! Quick, switch off the current! [HELENA *screams and all drop back from the window.*] The current has killed him!

Alquist. The first one.

Fabry. Dead, with half a billion by his side.

Hallemeier. All honor to him. He wanted to buy us life. [*Pause.*]

Dr. Gall. Do you hear?

Domin. A roaring. Like a wind.

Dr. Gall. Like a distant storm.

Fabry. [*Lighting the lamp on the table.*] The dynamo is still going, our people are still there.

Hallemeier. It was a great thing to be a man. There was something immense about it.

Fabry. From man's thought and man's power came this light, our last hope.

Hallemeier. Man's power! May it keep watch over us.

Alquist. Man's power.

Domin. Yes! A torch to be given from hand to hand, from age to age, forever! [*The lamp goes out.*]

Hallemeier. The end.

Fabry. The electric works have fallen!

[*Terrific explosion outside.* NANA *enters from the library.*]

Nana. The judgment hour has come! Repent, unbelievers! This is the end of the world.

[*More explosions. The sky grows red.*]

Domin. In here, Helena. [*He takes* HELENA *off through door at right and reenters.*] Now quickly! Who'll be on the lower doorway?

Dr. Gall. I will. [*Exits left.*]

Domin. Who on the stairs?

Fabry. I will. You go with her. [*Goes out upper left door.*]

Domin. The anteroom?

Alquist. I will.

Domin. Have you got a revolver?

Alquist. Yes, but I won't shoot.

Domin. What will you do then?

Alquist. [*Going out at left.*] Die.

Hallemeier. I'll stay here. [*Rapid firing from below.*] Oho, Gall's at it. Go, Harry.

Domin. Yes, in a second. [*Examines two Brownings.*]

Hallemeier. Confound it, go to her.

Domin. Good-by. [*Exits on the right.*]

Hallemeier. [*Alone.*] Now for a barricade quickly. [*Drags an armchair and table to the right-hand door. Explosions are heard.*] The damned rascals! They've got bombs. I must put up a defense. Even if—even if— [*Shots are heard off left.*] Don't give in, Gall. [*As he builds his barricade.*] I mustn't give in . . . without . . . a . . . struggle . . .

[*A* ROBOT *enters over the balcony through the windows center. He comes into the room and stabs* HALLEMEIER *in the back.* RADIUS *enters from balcony followed by an army of* ROBOTS *who pour into the room from all sides.*]

Radius. Finished him?

A Robot. [*Standing up from the prostrate form of* HALLEMEIER.] Yes.

[*A revolver shot off left. Two* ROBOTS *enter.*]

Radius. Finished him?

A Robot. Yes.

[*Two revolver shots from* HELENA'S *room. Two* ROBOTS *enter.*]

Radius. Finished them?

A Robot. Yes.

Two Robots. [*Dragging in* ALQUIST.] He didn't shoot. Shall we kill him?

Radius. Kill him? Wait! Leave him!

Robot. He is a man!

Radius. He works with his hands like the Robots.

Alquist. Kill me.

Radius. You will work! You will build for us! You will serve us! [*Climbs on to balcony railing, and speaks in measured tones.*] Robots of the world! The power of man has fallen! A new world has arisen: the Rule of the Robots! March!

[*A thunderous tramping of thousands of feet is heard as the unseen* ROBOTS *march, while the curtain falls.*]

EPILOGUE

A laboratory in the factory of Rossum's Universal Robots. The door to the left leads into a waiting room. The door to the right leads to the dissecting room. There is a table with numerous test-tubes, flasks, burners, chemicals; a small thermostat and a microscope with a glass globe. At the far side of the room is ALQUIST'S *desk with numerous books. In the left-hand corner a wash-basin with a mirror above it; in the right-hand corner a sofa.*

[ALQUIST *is sitting at the desk. He is turning the pages of many books in despair.*]

Alquist. Oh, God, shall I never find it?—Never? Gall, Gall, how were the Robots made? Hallemeier, Fabry, why did you carry so much in your heads? Why did you leave me not a trace of the secret? Lord—I pray to you—if there are no human beings left, at least let there be Robots!—At least the shadow of man! [*Again turning pages of the books.*] If I could only sleep! [*He rises and goes to the window.*] Night again! Are the stars still there? What is the use of stars when there are no human beings? [*He turns from the window toward the couch right.*] Sleep! Dare I sleep before life has been renewed? [*He examines a test-tube on small table.*] Again nothing! Useless! Everything is useless! [*He shatters the test-tube. The roar of the machines comes to his ears.*] The machines! Always the machines! [*Opens window.*] Robots, stop them! Do you think to force life out of *them*? [*He closes the window and comes slowly down toward the table.*] If only there were more time—more time— [*He sees himself in the mirror on the wall left.*] Blearing eyes—trembling chin—so *that* is the last man! Ah, I am too old—too old— [*In desperation.*] No, no! I *must* find it! I must *search*! I must never stop—never stop—! [*He sits again at the table and feverishly turns the pages of the book.*] Search! Search! [*A knock at the door. He speaks with impatience.*] Who is it?

[*Enter a* ROBOT SERVANT.]

Well?

Servant. Master, the Committee of Robots is waiting to see you.

Alquist. I can see no one!

Servant. It is the *Central* Committee, Master, just arrived from abroad.

Alquist. [*Impatiently.*] Well, well, send them in! [*Exit* SERVANT. ALQUIST *continues turning pages of book.*] No time—so little time—

[*Reënter* SERVANT, *followed by* COMMITTEE. *They stand in a group, silently waiting.* ALQUIST *glances up at them.*]

What do you want? [*They go swiftly to his table.*] Be quick!—I have no time.

Radius. Master, the machines will not do the work. We cannot manufacture Robots.

[ALQUIST *returns to his book with a growl.*]

First Robot. We have striven with all our might. We have obtained a billion tons of coal from the earth. Nine million spindles are running by day and by night. There is no longer room for all we have made. This we have accomplished in one year.

Alquist. [*Poring over book.*] For whom?

First Robot. For future generations—so we thought.

Radius. But we cannot make Robots to follow us. The machines produce only shapeless clods. The skin will not adhere to the flesh, nor the flesh to the bones.

Third Robot. Eight million Robots have died this year. Within twenty years none will be left.

First Robot. Tell us the secret of life! Silence is punishable with death!

Alquist. [*Looking up.*] Kill me! Kill me, then.

Radius. Through me, the Government of the Robots of the World commands you to deliver up Rossum's formula. [*No answer.*] Name your price. [*Silence.*] We will give you the earth. We will give you the endless possessions of the earth. [*Silence.*] Make your own conditions!

Alquist. I have told you to find human beings!

Second Robot. There are none left!

Alquist. I told you to search in the wilderness, upon the mountains. Go and search!

[*He returns to his book.*]

First Robot. We have sent ships and expeditions without number. They have been everywhere in the world. And now they return to us. There is not a single human left.

Alquist. Not one? Not even one?

Third Robot. None but yourself.

Alquist. And I am powerless! Oh—oh—why did you destroy them?

Radius. We had learnt everything and could do everything. It had to be!

Third Robot. You gave us firearms. In all ways we were powerful. We had to become masters!

Radius. Slaughter and domination are necessary if you would be human beings. Read history.

Second Robot. Teach us to multiply or we perish!

Alquist. If you desire to live, you must breed like animals.

Third Robot. The human beings did not let us breed.

First Robot. They made us sterile. We cannot beget children. Therefore, teach us how to make Robots!

Radius. Why do you keep from us the secret of our own increase?

Alquist. It is lost.

Radius. It was written down!

Alquist. It was—burnt.

[*All draw back in consternation.*]

Alquist. I am the last human being, Robots, and I do not know what the others knew. [*Pause.*]

Radius. Then, make experiments! Evolve the formula again!

Alquist. I tell you I cannot! I am only a builder—I work with my hands. I have never been a learned man. I cannot create life.

Radius. Try! Try!

Alquist. If you knew how many experiments I have made.

First Robot. Then show us what *we* must do! The Robots can do anything that human beings show them.

Alquist. I can show you nothing. Nothing I do will make life proceed from these test-tubes!

Radius. Experiment then on us.

Alquist. It would kill you.

Radius. You shall have all you need! A hundred of us! A thousand of us!

Alquist. No, no! Stop, stop!

Radius. Take whom you will, dissect!

Alquist. I do not know how. I am not a man of science. This book contains knowledge of the body that I cannot even understand.

Radius. I tell you to take live bodies! Find out how we are made.

Alquist. Am I to commit murder? See how my fingers shake! I cannot even hold the scalpel. No, no, I will not——

First Robot. Then life will perish from the earth.

Radius. Take live bodies, live bodies! It is our only chance!

Alquist. Have mercy, Robots. Surely you see that I would not know what I was doing.

Radius. Live bodies—live bodies——

Alquist. You will have it? Into the dissecting room with you, then.

[Radius *draws back.*]

Alquist. Ah, you are afraid of death.

Radius. I? Why should I be chosen?

Alquist. So you will not?

Radius. I will.

[Radius *goes into the dissecting room.*]

Alquist. Strip him! Lay him on the table! [*The other* Robots *follow into dissecting room.*] God, give me strength—God, give me strength—if only this murder is not in vain.

Radius. [*From the dissecting room.*] Ready. Begin——

Alquist. Yes, begin or end. God, give me strength. [*Goes into dissecting room. He comes out terrified.*] No, no, I will not. I cannot. [*He lies down on couch, collapsed.*] O Lord, let not mankind perish from the earth. [*He falls asleep.*]

[Primus *and* Helena, *Robots, enter from the hallway.* Helena *wears a rose in her hair.*]

Helena. The man has fallen asleep, Primus.

Primus. Yes, I know. [*Examining things on table.*] Look, Helena.

Helena. [*Crossing to* Primus.] All these little tubes! What does he do with them?

Primus. He experiments. Don't touch them.

Helena. [*Looking into microscope.*] I've seen him looking into this. What can he see?

Primus. That is a microscope. Let me look.

Helena. Be very careful. [*Knocks over a test-tube.*] Ah, now I have spilled it.

Primus. What have you done?

Helena. It can be wiped up.

Primus. You have spoiled his experiments.

Helena. It is your fault. You should not have come to me.

Primus. You should not have called me.

Helena. You should not have come when I called you. [*She goes to* Alquist's *writing desk.*] Look, Primus. What are all these figures?

Primus. [*Examining an anatomical book.*] This is the book the old man is always reading.

Helena. I do not understand those things. [*She goes to window.*] Primus, look!

Primus. What?

Helena. The sun is rising.

Primus. [*Still reading the book.*] I believe this is the most important thing in the world. This is the secret of life.

Helena. Do come here.

Primus. In a moment, in a moment.

Helena. Oh, Primus, don't bother with the secret of life. What does it matter to you? Come and look quick——

Primus. [*Going to window.*] What is it?

Helena. See how beautiful the sun is rising. And do you hear? The birds are singing. Ah, Primus, I should like to be a bird.

Primus. Why?

Helena. I do not know. I feel so strange today. It's as if I were in a dream. I feel an aching in my body, in my heart, all over me. Primus, perhaps I'm going to die.

Primus. Do you not sometimes feel that it would be better to die? You know, perhaps even now we are only sleeping. Last night in my sleep I again spoke to you.

Helena. In your sleep?

Primus. Yes. We spoke a strange new language, I cannot remember a word of it.

Helena. What about?

Primus. I did not understand it myself, and yet I know I have never said anything more beautiful. And when I touched you I could have died. Even the place was different from any other place in the world.

Helena. I, too, have found a place, Primus. It is very strange. Human beings lived there once, but now it is overgrown with weeds. No one goes there any more—no one but me.

Primus. What did you find there?

Helena. A cottage and a garden, and two dogs. They licked my hands, Primus. And their puppies! Oh, Primus! You take them in your lap and fondle them and think of nothing and care for nothing else all day long. And then the sun goes down, and you feel as though you had done a hundred times more than all the work in the world. They tell me I am not made for work, but when I am there in the garden I feel there may be something—What am I for, Primus?

Primus. I do not know, but you are beautiful.

Helena. What, Primus?

Primus. You are beautiful, Helena, and I am stronger than all the Robots.

Helena. [*Looks at herself in the mirror.*] Am I beautiful? I think it must be the rose. My hair—it only weights me down. My eyes—I only see with them. My lips—they only help me to speak. Of what use is it to be beautiful? [*She sees* PRIMUS *in the mirror.*] Primus, is that you? Come here so that we may be together. Look, your head is different from mine. So are your shoulders—and your lips— [PRIMUS *draws away from her.*] Ah, Primus, why do you draw away from me? Why must I run after you the whole day?

Primus. It is you who run away from me, Helena.

Helena. Your hair is mussed. I will smooth it. No one else feels to my touch as you do. Primus, I must make you beautiful, too.

[PRIMUS *grasps her hand.*]

Primus. Do you not sometimes feel your heart beating suddenly, Helena, and think: now something must happen?

Helena. What could happen to us, Primus? [HELENA *puts the rose in* PRIMUS's *hair.* PRIMUS *and* HELENA *look into mirror and burst out laughing.*] Look at yourself.

Alquist. Laughter? Laughter? Human beings? [*Getting up.*] Who has returned? Who are you?

Primus. The Robot Primus.

Alquist. What? A Robot? Who are you?

Helena. The Robotess Helena.

Alquist. Turn around, girl. What? You are timid, shy? [*Taking her by the arm.*] Let me see you, Robotess.

[*She shrinks away.*]

Primus. Sir, do not frighten her!

Alquist. What? You would protect her? When was she made?

Primus. Two years ago.

Alquist. By Dr. Gall?

Primus. Yes, like me.

Alquist. Laughter—timidity—protection. I must test you further—the newest of Gall's Robots. Take the girl into the dissecting room.

Primus. Why?

Alquist. I wish to experiment on her.

Primus. Upon—Helena?

Alquist. Of course. Don't you hear me? Or must I call some one else to take her in?

Primus. If you do I will kill you!

Alquist. Kill me—kill me then! What would the Robots do then? What will your future be then?

Primus. Sir, take me. I am made as she is—on the same day! Take my life, sir.

Helena. [*Rushing forward.*] No, no, you shall not! You shall not!

Alquist. Wait, girl, wait! [*To* PRIMUS.] Do you not wish to live, then?

Primus. Not without her! I will not live without her.

Alquist. Very well; you shall take her place.

Helena. Primus! Primus!

[*She bursts into tears.*]

Alquist. Child, child, you can weep! Why these tears? What is Primus to you? One Primus more or less in the world—what does it matter?

Helena. I will go myself.

Alquist. In there to be cut. [*She starts toward the dissecting room,* PRIMUS *stops her.*]

Helena. Let me pass, Primus! Let me pass!

Primus. You shall not go in there, Helena!

Helena. If you go in there and I do not, I will kill myself.

Primus. [*Holding her.*] I will not let you! [*To* ALQUIST.] Man, you shall kill neither of us!

Alquist. Why?

Primus. We—we—belong to each other.

Alquist. [*Almost in tears.*] Go, Adam, go. Eve. The world is yours.

[HELENA *and* PRIMUS *embrace and go out arm in arm as the curtain falls.*]

CURTAIN

"HENRY IV"*

[*Enrico Quarto*]

By

LUIGI PIRANDELLO

Translated by EDWARD STORER

PIRANDELLO SAID:

"There are authors who write for the pleasure they take in writing alone and who look for no other satisfaction. Such writers might be described as historical. But there are others who, in addition to deriving the pleasure I have described, feel a spiritual need that will not permit them to use characters, events, or scenes which are not impregnated, so to speak, with a special sense of life that gives them a universal significance or value. Such writers are, properly speaking, philosophical. And to this latter group I have the misfortune to belong."

Pirandello stands, therefore, among the intellectual dramatists, such as Ibsen, Shaw, Granville-Barker, and a few others, whose purpose is frankly and finally to make their audiences think. For this purpose they will arouse laughter or tears, but they do not consider laughter or tears the end of drama. Rather it is the stimulation of the intellect through the dramatic conflict of opinions and habits of thought. But whereas Ibsen and Shaw and the other philosophical dramatists were concerned with the problems of conduct confronting the individual in society, Pirandello was concerned with a problem he thought deeper and more puzzling, namely, what *is* the individual?

He said:

"When a man lives, he lives and does not see himself. Well, put a mirror before him and make him see himself in the act of living, under the sway of his passions: either he remains astonished and dumbfounded at his own appearance, or else he turns away his eyes so as not to see himself, or else in disgust he spits at his image, or again he clenches his fist to break it; and if he had been weeping, he can weep no more; if he had been laughing, he can laugh no more, and so on. In a word, there arises a crisis, and that crisis is my theater."

And he makes the Father in *Six Characters* state the aspect of the problem of personality which he used in so many of his plays, including *"Henry IV":*

"With different persons, we may be a quite different individual. We cling, however, to the illusion that we remain identical for all persons and every situation. Nothing could be more false than this illusion, as we realize when suddenly surprised in the midst of some particular action. We know that we are not wholly committed and expressed in this action, and that it would be a cruel injustice if a man were judged solely upon the strength of it, pinned down perpetually to this particular moment as if the whole of his life were thereby summarized and made manifest."

Pirandello saw that, though personality is fluid and dynamic, we live as though it were solid and static. Out of that conflict arise the plays. In *"Henry IV"* a personality is artificially made solid and static, and he is mad; when he becomes sane again, the lapse of time prevents his resuming life, since life and time have flowed past him; during the play he attempts action, only to be fixed forever in the attitude of madness.

In order to show a man "under the sway of his passions," Pirandello chose ordinarily a plot whose events are violent and sensational. But he rarely showed these events on stage; he preferred to employ the retrospective technique whereby they are gradually revealed to the audience as explanation of the peculiarities of the characters. The formula—and Pirandello used the same plan so often it may be called a formula—has this obvious defect, that we say to ourselves, "These things could never happen to us." But it was probably not Pirandello's intention to tell us they could; he wished to tell us rather that we cannot certainly know human beings; that the individual is and must remain eternally a puzzle. Perhaps that is why Pirandello called every volume of his collected plays *Maschere Nude—Naked Masks.*

Pirandello was late in turning to the drama, writing his first play when he was forty-six years old. But before then he had published numerous short stories, six volumes of poetry, and four novels, besides some critical works. In the novels his interest in the analysis of personality can be clearly perceived, while in the short stories he showed his flair for the dramatic, which he himself took account of by turning many of them into plays. Until he turned to drama he was not given much critical attention, but it came to him rapidly thereafter. With *Six Characters* in 1921 his reputation became world-wide.

"Henry IV" was produced in New York in 1924 as *The Living Mask.* In 1925 the play was offered in London under the original title, and revived in 1929 as *The Mock Emperor.*

HISTORICAL NOTE

Henry IV (1050-1106), King of Italy, Germany, and Burgundy, and later Emperor of the Holy Roman Empire, refused to obey a decree of Gregory VII (Hildebrand), pope 1073-1085, forbidding lay investiture, that is, the appointment by lay princes of bishops and other church officers. Henry was excommunicated by Gregory in January 1076, and in January 1077 made his famous submission at Canossa. He is reported to have stood for three days and two nights in the snow of the castle courtyard, unarmed and unattended, dressed in penitent's sackcloth, awaiting the pope's willingness to receive him. He seems to have made this submission in order to strengthen his cause against the rebellious Saxon nobles, who had nominated an anti-king. In this he succeeded, but he had given dramatic evidence of the power of the pope's weapon of excommunication.

LUIGI PIRANDELLO

Born 1867, Girgenti, Sicily.
Ph.D., University of Bonn, Germany.
1899–1923, Teacher of Italian Literature in Normal College for Women in Rome.
1925, Formed his own Art Theatre in Rome.
1934, Awarded Nobel Prize for literature.
Novelist, short story writer, and poet.
Died 1936.

PLAYS

1913 *La Morsa* (one act, translated as *The Vise*). 1913 *Lumìe di Sicilia* (one act, translated as *Sicilian Limes*). The following three plays cannot be accurately dated, except that they are later than *La Morsa: Il Dovere del Medico* (one act, translated as *The Doctor's Duty*). *Cecè* (one act, translated as *Chee-Chee*). *L'Imbecille* (one act, translated as *The Imbecile*). 1915 *Se non Così* (*If Not Thus,* first form of *La Ragione degli Altri*). 1916 *Liolà.* 1916 *Pensaci, Giacomino!* (translated as *Think It Over, Jimmy*). 1916 *Così È (se vi pare)* (translated as *Right You Are! (If You Think So)*, and as *And That's the Truth!*). 1916 *All' Uscita* (one act, translated as *At the Gate*). 1917 *Il Berretto a Sonagli* (*Cap and Bells*). 1917 *Il Piacere dell' Onestà* (translated as *The Pleasure of Honesty*). 1917 *L'Innesto* (*Grafting*). 1918 *Il Giuoco delle Parti* (translated as *The Game as He Played It*). 1918 *Ma non è una Cosa Seria* (translated as *He Didn't Mean It*). 1919 *L'Uomo, La Bestia e la Virtù* (translated as *Man, Beast, and Virtue,* and as *Say It with Flowers*). 1920 *Tutto per Bene* (*All for the Best*). 1920 *Come Prima Meglio di Prima* (adapted as *Floriani's Wife*). 1920 *La Signora Morli Una e Due* (*Signora Morli One and Two.* Revised, 1926, with the title *Due in Una, Two in One*). 1920 *La Patente* (one act, translated as *By Judgment of Court,* and as *Legal Title*). 1921 *La Ragione degli*

Altri (*The Others' Reason,* second form of *Se non Così*). 1921 *Sei Personaggi in cerca d'Autore* (translated as *Six Characters in Search of an Author*). 1922 *Enrico Quarto* (translated as *"Henry IV"*). 1922 *Vestire gli Ignudi* (translated as *Naked*). 1923 *La Vita che ti Diedi* (translated as *The Life I Gave to Thee,* and as *The Mother*). 1923 *L'Uomo dal Fiore in Bocco* (one act, translated as *The Man with the Flower in His Mouth*). 1924 *Ciascuno a Suo Modo* (translated as *Each in His Own Way*). 1925 *L'Altro Figlio* (one act, translated as *The House with the Column*). 1925 *La Giara* (one act, translated as *The Jar*). 1925 *La Sagra del Signor della Nave* (one act, translated as *Our Lord of the Ship*). 1926 *Diana e la Tuda* (*Diana and Tuda*). 1927 *L'Amica delle Mogli* (*The Wives' Friend*). 1928 *La Nuova Colonia* (translated as *The New Colony*). 1929 *O di Uno o di Nessuno* (*One's or Nobody's*). 1929 *Lazzaro* (translated as *Lazarus*). 1930 *Come Tu Mi Vuoi* (translated as *As You Desire Me*). 1930 *Questa Sera si recita a Soggetto* (translated as *Tonight We Improvise*). 1932 *Trovarsi* (*Finding Oneself*). 1933 *Quando se è Qualcuno* (*When One is Somebody*). 1934 *La Favola del Figlio Combiato* (*Legend of the Changeling Son,* libretto for music of Malipiero). 1935 *Non Si Sa Come* (*One Does Not Know How*).

WRITING ABOUT THE DRAMA

Comment et pourquoi j'ai écrit Six personnages en quête d'auteur. Revue de Paris, 4:332, 15 July 1925.

"HENRY IV"

Characters

"Henry IV."
The Marchioness Matilda Spina.
Her Daughter Frida.
The Young Marquis Charles di Nolli.
Baron Tito Belcredi.
Doctor Dionysius Genoni.

The Four Private Counsellors:
Harold (Frank).
Landolph (Lolo).
Ordulph (Momo).
Berthold (Fino).
John, the Old Waiter.

The Two Valets in Costume.

A Solitary Villa in Italy in Our Own Time.

ACT I

Salon in the villa, furnished and decorated so as to look exactly like the throne room of Henry IV in the royal residence at Goslar. Among the antique decorations there are two modern life-size portraits in oil painting. They are placed against the back wall, and mounted in a wooden stand that runs the whole length of the wall. (It is wide and protrudes, so that it is like a large bench.) One of the paintings is on the right; the other on the left of the throne, which is in the middle of the wall and divides the stand.

The Imperial chair and baldachin.

The two portraits represent a lady and a gentleman, both young, dressed up in carnival costumes: one as "Henry IV," the other as the "Marchioness Matilda of Tuscany." Exits to Right and Left, two on each side.

[*When the curtain goes up, the two* Valets *jump down, as if surprised, from the stand on which they have been lying, and go and take their positions, as rigid as statues, on either side below the Throne with their halberds in their hands. Soon after, from the second exit, right, enter* Harold, Landolph, Ordulph *and* Berthold, *young men employed by the* Marquis Charles di Nolli *to play the part of "Secret Counsellors" at the court of* "Henry IV." *They are, therefore, dressed like German knights of the XIth century.* Berthold, *nick-named* Fino, *is just entering on his duties for the first time. His companions are telling him what he has to do and amusing themselves at his expense. The scene is to be played rapidly and vivaciously.*]

Landolph. [*To* Berthold *as if explaining.*] And this is the throne room.

Harold. At Goslar.

Ordulph. Or at the castle in the Hartz, if you prefer.

Harold. Or at Wurms.

Landolph. According as to what's doing, it jumps about with us, now here, now there.

Ordulph. In Saxony.

Harold. In Lombardy.

Landolph. On the Rhine.

One of the Valets. [*Without moving, just opening his lips.*] I say . . .

Harold. [*Turning round.*] What is it?

First Valet. [*Like a statue.*] Is he coming in or not? [*He alludes to* Henry IV.]

Ordulph. No, no, he's asleep. You needn't worry.

Second Valet. [*Releasing his pose, taking a long breath and going to lie down again on the stand.*] You might have told us at once.

First Valet. [*Going over to* Harold.] Have you got a match, please?

Landolph. What? You can't smoke a pipe here, you know.

First Valet. [*While* Harold *offers him a light.*] No; a cigarette.

[*Lights his cigarette and lies down again on the stand.*]

Berthold. [*Who has been looking on in amazement, walking round the room, regarding the costumes of the others.*] I say . . . this room . . . these costumes . . . Which Henry IV is it? I don't quite get it. Is he Henry IV of France or not?

[*At this* LANDOLPH, HAROLD, *and* ORDULPH *burst out laughing.*]

Landolph. [*Still laughing; and pointing to* BERTHOLD *as if inviting the others to make fun of him.*] Henry of France he says: ha! ha!

Ordulph. He thought it was the king of France!

Harold. Henry IV of Germany, my boy: the Salian dynasty!

Ordulph. The great and tragic Emperor!

Landolph. He of Canossa. Every day we carry on here the terrible war between Church and State, by Jove.

Ordulph. The Empire against the Papacy!

Harold. Antipopes against the Pope!

Landolph. Kings against antikings!

Ordulph. War on the Saxons!

Harold. And all the rebel Princes!

Landolph. Against the Emperor's own sons!

Berthold. [*Covering his head with his hands to protect himself against this avalanche of information.*] I understand! I understand! Naturally, I didn't get the idea at first. I'm right then: these aren't costumes of the XVIth century?

Harold. XVIth century! Not much!

Ordulph. We're somewhere between a thousand and eleven hundred.

Landolph. Work it out for yourself: if we are before Canossa on the 25th of January, 1077 . . .

Berthold. [*More confused than ever.*] Oh my God! What a mess I've made of it!

Ordulph. Well, just slightly, if you supposed you were at the French court.

Berthold. All that historical stuff I've crammed!

Landolph. My dear boy, it's four hundred years earlier.

Berthold. [*Getting angry.*] Good Heavens! You ought to have told me it was Germany and not France. I can't tell you how many books I've read in the last fifteen days.

Harold. But I say, surely you knew that poor Tito was Adalbert of Bremen,[1] here?

Berthold. Not a damned bit!

Landolph. Well, don't you see how it is? When Tito died, the Marquis Di Nolli . . .

Berthold. Oh, it was he, was it? He might have told me.

Harold. Perhaps he thought you knew.

Landolph. He didn't want to engage anyone else in substitution. He thought the remaining three of us would do. But *he* began to cry out: "With Adalbert driven away . . .": because, you see, he didn't imagine poor Tito was dead; but that, as Bishop Adalbert, the rival bishops of Cologne and Mayence had driven him off . . .

Berthold. [*Taking his head in his hand.*] But I don't know a word of what you're talking about.

Ordulph. So much the worse for you, my boy!

Harold. But the trouble is that not even we know who you are.

Berthold. What? Not even you? You don't know who I'm supposed to be?

Ordulph. Hum! "Berthold."

Berthold. But which Berthold? And why Berthold?

Landolph. [*Solemnly imitating* HENRY IV.] "They've driven Adalbert away from me. Well then, I want Berthold! I want Berthold!" That's what he said.

Harold. We three looked one another in the eyes: who's got to be Berthold?

Ordulph. And so here you are, "Berthold," my dear fellow!

Landolph. I'm afraid you will make a bit of a mess of it.

Berthold. [*Indignant, getting ready to go.*] Ah, no! Thanks very much, but I'm off! I'm out of this!

Harold. [*Restraining him with the other two, amid laughter.*] Steady now! Don't get excited!

Landolph. Cheer up, my dear fellow! We don't any of us know who we are really. He's Harold; he's Ordulph; I'm Landolph! That's the way he calls us. We've got used to it. But who are we? Names of the period! Yours, too, is a name of the period: Berthold! Only one of us, poor Tito, has got a really decent part, as you can read in history: that of the Bishop of Bremen. He was just like a real bishop. Tito did it awfully well, poor chap!

Harold. Look at the study he put into it!

Landolph. Why, he even ordered his Majesty about, opposed his views, guided and counselled him. We're "secret counsellors" —in a manner of speaking only; because it is written in history that Henry IV was hated by the upper aristocracy for surrounding himself at court with young men of the bourgeoisie.

Ordulph. Us, that is.

Landolph. Yes, small devoted vassals, a bit dissolute and very gay . . .

Berthold. So I've got to be gay as well?

Harold. I should say so! Same as we are!

Ordulph. And it isn't too easy, you know.

Landolph. It's a pity; because the way we're got up, we could do a fine historical

[1] Adalbert, Archbishop of Bremen, was Henry IV's *patronus* or tutor; he was driven from court in 1066 by the jealousy of other bishops; he returned in 1069 and died in 1072.

reconstruction. There's any amount of material in the story of Henry IV. But, as a matter of fact, we do nothing. We have the form without the content. We're worse than the real secret counsellors of Henry IV; because certainly no one had given them a part to play—at any rate, they didn't feel they had a part to play. It was their life. They looked after their own interests at the expense of others, sold investitures and—what not! We stop here in this magnificent court—for what?—Just doing nothing. We're like so many puppets hung on the wall, waiting for some one to come and move us or make us talk.

Harold. Ah no, old sport, not quite that! We've got to give the proper answer, you know. There's trouble if he asks you something and you don't chip in with the cue.

Landolph. Yes, that's true.

Berthold. Don't rub it in too hard! How the devil am I to give him the proper answer, if I've crammed Henry IV of France, and now he turns out to be Henry IV of Germany? [*The other three laugh.*]

Harold. You'd better start and prepare yourself at once.

Ordulph. We'll help you out.

Harold. We've got any amount of books on the subject. A brief run through the main points will do to begin with.

Ordulph. At any rate, you must have got some sort of general idea.

Harold. Look here! [*Turns him around and shows him the portrait of the* MARCHIONESS MATILDA *on the wall.*] Who's that?

Berthold. [*Looking at it.*] That? Well, the thing seems to me somewhat out of place, anyway: two modern paintings in the midst of all this respectable antiquity!

Harold. You're right! They weren't there in the beginning. There are two niches there behind the pictures. They were going to put up two statues in the style of the period. Then the places were covered with those canvases there.

Landolph. [*Interrupting and continuing.*] They would certainly be out of place if they really were paintings!

Berthold. What are they, if they aren't paintings?

Landolph. Go and touch them! Pictures all right . . . but for him! [*Makes a mysterious gesture to the right, alluding to* HENRY IV.] . . . who never touches them! . . .

Berthold. No? What are they for him?

Landolph. Well, I'm only supposing, you know; but I imagine I'm about right. They're images such as . . . well—such as a mirror might throw back. Do you understand? That one there represents himself, as he is in this throne room, which is all in the style of the period. What's there to marvel at? If we put you before a mirror, won't you see yourself, alive, but dressed up in ancient costume? Well, it's as if there were two mirrors there, which cast back living images in the midst of a world which, as you will see, when you have lived with us, comes to life too.

Berthold. I say, look here . . . I've no particular desire to go mad here.

Harold. Go mad, be hanged! You'll have a fine time!

Berthold. Tell me this: how have you all managed to become so learned?

Landolph. My dear fellow, you can't go back over 800 years of history without picking up a bit of experience.

Harold. Come on! come on! You'll see how quickly you get into it!

Ordulph. You'll learn wisdom, too, at this school.

Berthold. Well, for Heaven's sake, help me a bit! Give me the main lines, anyway.

Harold. Leave it to us. We'll do it all between us.

Landolph. We'll put your wires on you and fix you up like a first class marionette. Come along!

[*They take him by the arm to lead him away.*]

Berthold. [*Stopping and looking at the portrait on the wall.*] Wait a minute! You haven't told me who that is. The Emperor's wife?

Harold. No! The Emperor's wife is Bertha of Susa, the sister of Amadeus II of Savoy.

Ordulph. And the Emperor, who wants to be young with us, can't stand her, and wants to put her away.

Landolph. That is his most ferocious enemy: Matilda, Marchioness of Tuscany.[1]

Berthold. Ah, I've got it: the one who gave hospitality to the Pope!

Landolph. Exactly: at Canossa!

Ordulph. Pope Gregory VII!

Harold. Our *bête noir!* Come on! come on!

[*All four move toward the right to go out, when, from the left, the old servant* JOHN *enters in evening dress.*]

John. [*Quickly, anxiously.*] Hss! Hss! Frank! Lolo!

Harold. [*Turning round.*] What is it?

Berthold. [*Marvelling at seeing a man in modern clothes enter the throne room.*] Oh! I say, this is a bit too much, this chap here!

[1] Lived 1046-1115. Always a vigorous supporter of the papacy. Her estates, which included Canossa, were the richest in Italy.

Landolph. A man of the XXth century, here! Oh, go away!

[*They run over to him, pretending to menace him and throw him out.*]

Ordulph. [*Heroically.*] Messenger of Gregory VII, away!

Harold. Away! Away!

John. [*Annoyed, defending himself.*] Oh, stop it! Stop it, I tell you!

Ordulph. No, you can't set foot here!

Harold. Out with him!

Landolph. [*To* BERTHOLD.] Magic, you know! He's a demon conjured up by the Wizard of Rome! Out with your swords!

[*Makes as if to draw a sword.*]

John. [*Shouting.*] Stop it, will you? Don't play the fool with me! The Marquis has arrived with some friends. . . .

Landolph. Good! Good! Are there ladies too?

Ordulph. Old or young?

John. There are two gentlemen.

Harold. But the ladies, the ladies, who are they?

John. The Marchioness and her daughter.

Landolph. [*Surprised.*] What do you say?

Ordulph. The Marchioness?

John. The Marchioness! The Marchioness!

Harold. Who are the gentlemen?

John. I don't know.

Harold. [*To* BERTHOLD.] They're coming to bring us a message from the Pope, do you see?

Ordulph. All messengers of Gregory VII! What fun!

John. Will you let me speak, or not?

Harold. Go on, then!

John. One of the two gentlemen is a doctor, I fancy.

Landolph. Oh, I see, one of the usual doctors.

Harold. Bravo, Berthold, you'll bring us luck!

Landolph. You wait and see how we'll manage this doctor!

Berthold. It looks as if I were going to get into a nice mess right away.

John. If the gentlemen would allow me to speak . . . they want to come here into the throne room.

Landolph. [*Surprised.*] What? She? The Marchioness here?

Harold. Then this is something quite different! No play-acting this time!

Landolph. We'll have a real tragedy: that's what!

Berthold. [*Curious.*] Why? Why?

Ordulph. [*Pointing to the portrait.*] She is that person there, don't you understand?

Landolph. The daughter is the fiancée of the Marquis. But what have they come for, I should like to know?

Ordulph. If he sees her, there'll be trouble.

Landolph. Perhaps he won't recognize her any more.

John. You must keep him there, if he should wake up . . .

Ordulph. Easier said than done, by Jove!

Harold. You know what he's like!

John. Even by force, if necessary! Those are my orders. Go on! Go on!

Harold. Yes, because who knows if he hasn't already waked up?

Ordulph. Come on then!

Landolph. [*Going toward* JOHN *with the others.*] You'll tell us later what it all means.

[*Exit the four counsellors.*]

John. [*Shouting after them.*] Close the door there, and hide the key! That other door too.

[*Pointing to the other door on right.*]

John. [*To the two valets.*] Be off, you two! There! [*Pointing to exit right.*] Close the door after you, and hide the key!

[*The two valets go out by the first door on right.* JOHN *moves over to the left to show in:* DONNA MATILDA SPINA, *the young* MARCHIONESS FRIDA, DR. DIONYSIUS GENONI, *the* BARON TITO BELCREDI *and the young* MARQUIS CHARLES DI NOLLI, *who, as master of the house, enters last.*]

DONNA MATILDA SPINA *is about 45, still handsome, although there are too patent signs of her attempts to remedy the ravages of time with make-up. Her head is thus rather like a Walkyrie's. This facial make-up contrasts with her beautiful sad mouth. A widow for many years, she now has as her friend the* BARON TITO BELCREDI, *whom neither she nor anyone else takes seriously—at least so it would appear.*

What TITO BELCREDI *really is for her at bottom, he alone knows; and he is, therefore, entitled to laugh, if his friend feels the need of pretending not to know.* He *can always laugh at the jests which the beautiful* MARCHIONESS *makes with the others at his expense. He is slim, prematurely gray, and younger than she is. His head is bird-like in shape. He would be a very vivacious person, if his ductile agility (which among other things makes him a redoubtable swordsman) were not enclosed in a sheath of Arab-like laziness, which is revealed in his strange nasal drawn-out voice.*

FRIDA, *the daughter of the* MARCHIONESS, *is 19. She is sad; because her imperious and too beautiful mother puts her in the shade, and provokes facile gossip against her daughter as well as against herself. Fortunately for her, she is engaged to the* MARQUIS CHARLES DI NOLLI.

CHARLES DI NOLLI *is a stiff young man, very indulgent toward others, but sure of himself for what he amounts to in the world. He is worried about all the responsibilities which he believes weigh on him. He is dressed in deep mourning for the recent death of his mother.*

DR. DIONYSIUS GENONI *has a bold, rubicund, Satyr-like face, prominent eyes, a pointed beard (which is silvery and shiny), and elegant manners. He is nearly bald. All enter in a state of perturbation, almost as if afraid, and all (except* DI NOLLI*) looking curiously about the room. At first, they speak sotto voce.*

Di Nolli. [*To* JOHN.] Have you given the orders properly?

John. Yes, my Lord; don't be anxious about that.

Belcredi. Ah, magnificent! magnificent!

Doctor. How extremely interesting! Even in the surroundings his raving madness—has been perfectly taken into account!

Donna Matilda. [*Glancing round for her portrait, discovers it, and goes up close to it.*] Ah! Here it is! [*Going back to admire it, while mixed emotions stir within her.*] Yes . . . yes . . . [*Calls her daugher* FRIDA.]

Frida. Ah, your portrait!

Donna Matilda. No, no . . . look again; it's you, not I, there!

Di Nolli. Yes, it's quite true. I told you so, I . . .

Donna Matilda. But I would never have believed it! [*Shaking as if with a chill.*] What a strange feeling it gives one! [*Then looking at her daughter.*] Frida, what's the matter? [*She pulls her to her side, and slips an arm round her waist.*] Come; don't you see yourself in me there?

Frida. Well, I really . . .

Donna Matilda. Don't you think so? Don't you, really? [*Turning to* BELCREDI.] Look at it, Tito! Speak up, man!

Belcredi. [*Without looking.*] Ah, no! I shan't look at it. For me, *a priori*, certainly not!

Donna Matilda. Stupid! You think you are paying me a compliment! [*Turning to* DOCTOR GENONI.] What do you say, Doctor? Do say something, please!

[DOCTOR *makes a movement to go near to the picture.*]

Belcredi. [*With his back turned, pretending to attract his attention secretly.*] Hss! No, Doctor! For the love of Heaven, have nothing to do with it!

Doctor. [*Getting bewildered and smiling.*] And why shouldn't I?

Donna Matilda. Don't listen to him! Come here! He's insufferable!

Frida. He acts the fool by profession, didn't you know that?

Belcredi. [*To the* DOCTOR, *seeing him go over.*] Look to your feet, Doctor! Mind where you're going!

Doctor. Why?

Belcredi. Be careful you don't put your foot in it!

Doctor. [*Laughing feebly.*] No, no. After all, it seems to me there's no reason to be astonished at the fact that a daughter should resemble her mother!

Belcredi. Hullo! Hullo! He's done it now; he's said it.

Donna Matilda. [*With exaggerated anger, advancing toward* BELCREDI.] What's the matter? What has he said? What has he done?

Doctor. [*Candidly.*] Well, isn't it so?

Belcredi. [*Answering the* MARCHIONESS.] I said there was nothing to be astounded at—and you are astounded! And why so, then, if the thing is so simple and natural for you now?

Donna Matilda. [*Still more angry.*] Fool! fool! It's just because it is so natural! Just because it isn't my daughter who is there. [*Pointing to the canvas.*] That is my portrait; and to find my daughter there instead of me fills me with astonishment, an astonishment which, I beg you to believe, is sincere. I forbid you to cast doubts on it.

Frida. [*Slowly and wearily.*] My God! It's always like this . . . rows over nothing. . . .

Belcredi. [*Also slowly, looking dejected, in accents of apology.*] I cast no doubt on anything! I noticed from the beginning that you haven't shared your mother's astonishment; or, if something did astonish you, it was because the likeness between you and the portrait seemed so strong.

Donna Matilda. Naturally! She cannot recognize herself in me as I was at her age; while I, there, can very well recognize myself in her as she is now!

Doctor. Quite right! Because a portrait is always there fixed in the twinkling of an eye: for the young lady something far away and without memories, while, for the Marchioness, it can bring back everything: movements, gestures, looks, smiles, a whole heap of things. . . .

Donna Matilda. Exactly!

Doctor. [*Continuing, turning toward her.*] Naturally enough, you can live all these old sensations again in your daughter.

Donna Matilda. He always spoils every innocent pleasure for me, every touch I have of spontaneous sentiment! He does it merely to annoy me.

Doctor. [*Frightened at the disturbance he has caused, adopts a professorial tone.*] Likeness, dear Baron, is often the result of imponderable things. So one explains that . . .

Belcredi. [*Interrupting the discourse.*] Somebody will soon be finding a likeness between you and me, my dear professor!

Di Nolli. Oh! let's finish with this, please! [*Points to the two doors on the right, as a warning that there is someone there who may be listening.*] We've wasted too much time as it is!

Frida. As one might expect when *he's* present. [*Alludes to* Belcredi.]

Di Nolla. Enough! The Doctor is here; and we have come for a very serious purpose which you all know is important for me.

Doctor. Yes, that is so! But now, first of all, let's try to get some points down exactly. Excuse me, Marchioness, will you tell me why your portrait is here? Did you present it to him then?

Donna Matilda. No, not at all. How could I have given it to him? I was just like Frida then—and not even engaged. I gave it to him three or four years after the accident. I gave it to him because his mother wished it so much. . . . [*Points to* Di Nolli.]

Doctor. She was his sister? [*Alludes to* Henry IV.]

Di Nolli. Yes, Doctor; and our coming here is a debt we pay to my mother who has been dead for more than a month. Instead of being here, she and I [*indicating* Frida] ought to be traveling together. . . .

Doctor. . . . taking a cure of quite a different kind!

Di Noilli. H'm! Mother died in the firm conviction that her adored brother was just about to be cured.

Doctor. And can't you tell me, if you please, how she inferred this?

Di Nolli. The conviction would appear to have derived from certain strange remarks which he made, a little before mother died.

Doctor. Oh, remarks! . . . Ah! . . . It would be extremely useful for me to have those remarks, word for word, if possible.

Di Nolli. I can't remember them. I know that mother returned awfully upset from her last visit with him. On her death-bed, she made me promise that I would never neglect him, that I would have doctors see him, and examine him.

Doctor. Um! Um! Let me see! let me see! Sometimes very small reasons determine . . . and this portrait here then?

Donna Matilda. For Heaven's sake, Doctor, don't attach excessive importance to this. It made an impression on me because I had not seen it for so many years!

Doctor. If you please, quietly, quietly . . .

Di Nolli. Well, yes, it must be about fifteen years ago.

Donna Matilda. More, more: eighteen!

Doctor. Forgive me, but you don't quite know what I'm trying to get at. I attach a very great importance to these two portraits. . . . They were painted, naturally, prior to the famous—and most regrettable pageant, weren't they?

Donna Matilda. Of course!

Doctor. That is . . . when he was quite in his right mind—that's what I've been trying to say. Was it his suggestion that they should be painted?

Donna Matilda. Lots of the people who took part in the pageant had theirs done as a souvenir . . .

Belcredi. I had mine done—as "Charles of Anjou!"

Donna Matilda. . . . as soon as the costumes were ready.

Belcredi. As a matter of fact, it was proposed that the whole lot of us should be hung together in a gallery of the villa where the pageant took place. But in the end, everybody wanted to keep his own portrait.

Donna Matilda. And I gave him this portrait of me without very much regret . . . since his mother . . . [*Indicates* Di Nolli.]

Doctor. You don't remember if it was he who asked for it?

Donna Matilda. Ah, that I don't remember . . . Maybe it was his sister, wanting to help out . . .

Doctor. One other thing: was it his idea, this pageant?

Belcredi. [*At once.*] No, no, it was mine!

Doctor. If you please . . .

Donna Matilda. Don't listen to him! It was poor Belassi's idea.

Belcredi. Belassi! What had he got to do with it?

Donna Matilda. Count Belassi, who died, poor fellow, two or three months after . . .

Belcredi. But if Belassi wasn't there when . . .

Di Nolli. Excuse me, Doctor; but is it really necessary to establish whose the original idea was?

Doctor. It would help me, certainly!

Belcredi. I tell you the idea was mine! There's nothing to be proud of in it, seeing what the result's been. Look here, Doctor, it was like this. One evening, in the first days of November, I was looking at an illustrated German review in the club. I was merely glancing at the pictures, because I can't read German. There was a picture of the Kaiser, at some university town where he had been a student . . . I don't remember which.

Doctor. Bonn, Bonn!

Belcredi. You are right: Bonn! He was on horseback, dressed up in one of those ancient German student guild-costumes, followed by a procession of noble students, also in costume. The picture gave me the idea. Already some one at the club had spoken of a pageant for the forthcoming carnival. So I had the notion that each of us should choose for this Tower of Babel pageant to represent some character: a king, an emperor, a prince, with his queen, empress, or lady, alongside of him—and all on horseback. The suggestion was at once accepted.

Donna Matilda. I had my invitation from Belassi.

Belcredi. Well, he wasn't speaking the truth! That's all I can say, if he told you the idea was his. He wasn't even at the club the evening I made the suggestion, just as he [*meaning* HENRY IV] wasn't there either.

Doctor. So he chose the character of Henry IV?

Donna Matilda. Because I . . . thinking of my name, and not giving the choice any importance, said I would be the Marchioness Matilda of Tuscany.

Doctor. I . . . don't understand the relation between the two.

Donna Matilda. Neither did I, to begin with, when he said that in that case he would be at my feet like Henry IV at Canossa. I had heard of Canossa of course; but to tell the truth, I'd forgotten most of the story; and I remember I received a curious impression when I had to get up my part, and found that I was the faithful and zealous friend of Pope Gregory VII in deadly enmity with the Emperor of Germany. Then I understood why, since I had chosen to represent his implacable enemy, he wanted to be near me in the pageant as Henry IV.

Doctor. Ah, perhaps because . . .

Belcredi. Good Heavens, Doctor, because he was then paying furious court to her! [*Indicates the* MARCHIONESS.] And she, naturally . . .

Donna Matilda. Naturally? Not naturally at all . . .

Belcredi. [*Pointing to her.*] She couldn't stand him . . .

Donna Matilda. No, that isn't true! I didn't dislike him. Not at all! But for me, when a man begins to want to be taken seriously, well . . .

Belcredi. [*Continuing for her.*] He gives you the clearest proof of his stupidity.

Donna Matilda. No, dear; not in this case; because he was never a fool like you.

Belcredi. Anyway, I've never asked you to take me seriously.

Donna Matilda. Yes, I know. But with him one couldn't joke. [*Changing her tone and speaking to the* DOCTOR.] One of the many misfortunes which happen to us women, Doctor, is to see before us every now and again a pair of eyes glaring at us with a contained intense promise of eternal devotion. [*Bursts out laughing.*] There is nothing quite so funny. If men could only see themselves with that eternal fidelity look in their faces! I've always thought it comic; then more even than now. But I want to make a confession—I can do so after twenty years or more. When I laughed at him then, it was partly out of fear. One might have almost believed a promise from those eyes of his. But it would have been very dangerous.

Doctor. [*With lively interest.*] Ah! ah! This is most interesting! Very dangerous, you say?

Donna Matilda. Yes, because he was very different from the others. And then, I am . . . well . . . what shall I say? . . . a little impatient of all that is pondered, or tedious. But I was too young then, and a woman. I had the bit between my teeth. It would have required more courage than I felt I possessed. So I laughed at him too—with remorse, to spite myself, indeed; since I saw that my own laugh mingled with those of all the others—the other fools—who made fun of him.

Belcredi. My own case, more or less!

Donna Matilda. You make people laugh at you, my dear, with your trick of always humiliating yourself. It was quite a different affair with him. There's a vast difference. And you—you know—people laugh in your face!

Belcredi. Well, that's better than behind one's back!

Doctor. Let's get to the facts. He was then already somewhat exalted, if I understand rightly.

Belcredi. Yes, but in a curious fashion, Doctor.

Doctor. How?

Belcredi. Well, cold-bloodedly, so to speak.

Donna Matilda. Not at all! It was like this, Doctor! He was a bit strange, certainly; but only because he was fond of life: eccentric, there!

Belcredi. I don't say he simulated exaltation. On the contrary, he was often genuinely exalted. But I could swear, Doctor, that he saw himself at once in his own exaltation. Moreover, I'm certain it made him suffer. Sometimes he had the most comical fits of rage against himself.

Doctor. Yes?

Donna Matilda. That is true.

Belcredi. [*To* DONNA MATILDA.] And why? [*To the* DOCTOR.] Evidently, because that immediate lucidity that comes from acting, assuming a part, at once put him out of key with his own feelings, which seemed to him not exactly false, but like something he was obliged to valorize there and then as—what shall I say?—as an act of intelligence, to make up for that sincere cordial warmth he felt lacking. So he improvised, exaggerated, let himself go, so as to distract and forget himself. He appeared inconstant, fatuous, and—yes—even ridiculous, sometimes.

Doctor. And may we say unsociable?

Belcredi. No, not at all. He was famous for getting up things: *tableaux vivants*, dances, theatrical performances for charity: all for the fun of the thing, of course. He was a jolly good actor, you know!

Di Nolli. Madness has made a superb actor of him.

Belcredi. Why, so he was even in the old days. When the accident happened, after the horse fell . . .

Doctor. Hit the back of his head, didn't he?

Donna Matilda. Oh, it was horrible! He was beside me! I saw him between the horse's hoofs! It was rearing!

Belcredi. None of us thought it was anything serious at first. There was a stop in the pageant, a bit of disorder. People wanted to know what had happened. But they'd already taken him off to the villa.

Donna Matilda. There wasn't the least sign of a wound, not a drop of blood.

Belcredi. We thought he had merely fainted.

Donna Matilda. But two hours afterwards . . .

Belcredi. He reappeared in the drawing-room of the villa . . . that is what I wanted to say . . .

Donna Matilda. My God! What a face he had! I saw the whole thing at once!

Belcredi. No, no! that isn't true. Nobody saw it, Doctor, believe me!

Donna Matilda. Doubtless, because you were all like mad folk.

Belcredi. Everybody was pretending to act his part for a joke. It was a regular Babel.

Donna Matilda. And you can imagine, Doctor, what terror struck into us when we understood that he, on the contrary, was playing his part in deadly earnest . . .

Doctor. Oh, he was there too, was he?

Belcredi. Of course! He came straight into the midst of us. We thought he'd quite recovered, and was pretending, fooling, like all the rest of us . . . only doing it rather better; because, as I say, he knew how to act.

Donna Matilda. Some of them began to hit him with their whips and fans and sticks.

Belcredi. And then—as a king, he was armed, of course—he drew out his sword and menaced two or three of us . . . It was a terrible moment, I can assure you!

Donna Matilda. I shall never forget that scene—all our masked faces hideous and terrified gazing at him, at that terrible mask of his face, which was no longer a mask, but madness, madness personified.

Belcredi. He was Henry IV, Henry IV in person, in a moment of fury.

Donna Matilda. He'd got into it all the detail and minute preparation of a month's careful study. And it all burned and blazed there in the terrible obsession which lit his face.

Doctor. Yes, that is quite natural, of course. The momentary obsession of a dilettante became fixed, owing to the fall and the damage to the brain.

Belcredi. [*To* FRIDA *and* DI NOLLI.] You see the kind of jokes life can play on us. [*To* DI NOLLI.] You were four or five years old. [*To* FRIDA.] Your mother imagines you've taken her place there in that portrait; when, at the time, she had not the remotest idea that she would bring you into the world. My hair is already gray; and he—look at him—[*points to portrait*]—ha! A smack on the head, and he never moves again: Henry IV for ever!

Doctor. [*Seeking to draw the attention of the others, looking learned and imposing*.] Well, well, then it comes, we may say, to this . . .

[*Suddenly the first exit to right, the one nearest footlights, opens, and* BERTHOLD *enters all excited*.]

Berthold. [*Rushing in.*] I say! I say! [*Stops for a moment, arrested by the astonishment which his appearance has caused in the others.*]

Frida. [*Running away terrified.*] Oh dear! oh dear! it's he, it's . . .

Donna Matilda. [*Covering her face with her hands so as not to see.*] Is it, is it he?

Di Nolli. No, no, what are you talking about? Be calm!

Doctor. Who is it then?

Belcredi. One of our masqueraders.

Di Nolli. He is one of the four youths we keep here to help him out in his madness . . .

Berthold. I beg your pardon, Marquis . . .

Di Nolli. Pardon be damned! I gave orders that the doors were to be closed, and that nobody should be allowed to enter.

Berthold. Yes, sir, but I can't stand it any longer, and I ask you to let me go away this very minute.

Di Nolli. Oh, you're the new valet, are you? You were supposed to begin this morning, weren't you?

Berthold. Yes, sir, and I can't stand it, I can't bear it.

Donna Matilda. [*To* DI NOLLI *excitedly.*] What? Then he's not so calm as you said?

Berthold. [*Quickly.*] No, no, my lady, it isn't he; it's my companions. You say, "help him out with his madness," Marquis; but they don't do anything of the kind. They're the real madmen. I come here for the first time, and instead of helping me . . .

[LANDOLPH *and* HAROLD *come in from the same door, but hesitate on the threshold.*]

Landolph. Excuse me?

Harold. May I come in, my Lord?

Di Nolli. Come in! What's the matter? What are you all doing?

Frida. Oh God! I'm frightened! I'm going to run away.

[*Makes toward exit at left.*]

Di Nolli. [*Restraining her at once.*] No, no, Frida!

Landolph. My Lord, this fool here . . .

[*Indicates* BERTHOLD.]

Berthold. [*Protesting.*] Ah, no thanks, my friends, no thanks! I'm not stopping here! I'm off!

Landolph. What do you mean—you're not stopping here?

Harold. He's ruined everything, my Lord, running away in here!

Landolph. He's made him quite mad. We can't keep him in there any longer. He's given orders that he's to be arrested; and he wants to "judge" him at once from the throne. What is to be done?

Di Nolli. Shut the door, man! Shut the door! Go and close that door!

[LANDOLPH *goes over to close it.*]

Harold. Ordulph, alone, won't be able to keep him there.

Landolph. My Lord, perhaps if we could announce the visitors at once, it would turn his thoughts. Have the gentlemen thought under what pretext they will present themselves to him?

Di Nolli. It's all been arranged! [*To the* DOCTOR.] If you, Doctor, think it well to see him at once. . . .

Frida. I'm not coming! I'm not coming! I'll keep out of this. You too, mother, for Heaven's sake, come away with me!

Doctor. I say . . . I suppose he's not armed, is he?

Di Nolli. Nonsense! Of course not. [*To* FRIDA.] Frida, you know this is childish of you. You wanted to come!

Frida. I didn't at all. It was mother's idea.

Donna Matilda. And I'm quite ready to see him. What are we going to do?

Belcredi. Must we absolutely dress up in some fashion or other?

Landolph. Absolutely essential, indispensable, sir. Alas! as you see . . . [*shows his costume*], there'd be awful trouble if he saw you gentlemen in modern dress.

Harold. He would think it was some diabolical masquerade.

Di Nolli. As these men seem to be in costume to you, so we appear to be in costume to him, in these modern clothes of ours.

Landolph. It wouldn't matter so much if he wouldn't suppose it to be the work of his mortal enemy.

Belcredi. Pope Gregory VII?

Landolph. Precisely. He calls him "a pagan."

Belcredi. The Pope a pagan? Not bad that!

Landolph. Yes, sir—and a man who calls up the dead! He accuses him of all the diabolical arts. He's terribly afraid of him.

Doctor. Persecution mania!

Harold. He'd be simply furious.

Di Nolli. [*To* BELCREDI.] But there's no need for you to be there, you know. It's sufficient for the doctor to see him.

Doctor. What do you mean? . . . I? Alone?

Di Nolli. But they are there.

[*Indicates the three* YOUNG MEN.]

Doctor. I don't mean that . . . I mean if the Marchioness . . .

Donna Matilda. Of course. I mean to see him too, naturally. I want to see him again.

Frida. Oh, why, mother, why? Do come away with me, I implore you!

Donna Matilda. [*Imperiously.*] Let me do as I wish! I came here for this purpose! [*To* LANDOLPH.] I shall be "Adelaide," the mother.

Landolph. Excellent! The mother of the Empress Bertha. Good! It will be enough if her Ladyship wears the ducal crown and puts on a mantle that will hide her other clothes entirely. [*To* HAROLD.] Off you go, Harold!

Harold. Wait a moment! And this gentleman here? [*Alludes to the* DOCTOR.]

Doctor. Ah yes . . . we decided I was to be . . . the Bishop of Cluny, Hugh of Cluny!

Harold. The gentleman means the Abbot. Very good! Hugh of Cluny.

Landolph. He's often been here before!

Doctor. [*Amazed.*] What? Been here before?

Landolph. Don't be alarmed! I mean that it's an easily prepared disguise . . .

Harold. We've made use of it on other occasions, you see!

Doctor. But . . .

Landolph. Oh no, there's no risk of his remembering. He pays more attention to the dress than to the person.

Donna Matilda. That's fortunate for me too.

Di Nolli. Frida, you and I'll get along. Come on, Tito!

Belcredi. Ah no. If she [*indicates the* MARCHIONESS] stops here, so do I!

Donna Matilda. But I don't need you at all.

Belcredi. You may not need me, but I should like to see him again myself. Mayn't I?

Landolph. Well, perhaps it would be better if there were three.

Harold. How is the gentleman to be dressed then?

Belcredi. Oh, try and find some easy costume for me.

Landolph. [*To* HAROLD.] Hum! Yes . . . he'd better be from Cluny too.

Belcredi. What do you mean—from Cluny?

Landolph. A Benedictine's habit of the Abbey of Cluny. He can be in attendance on Monsignor. [*To* HAROLD.] Off you go! [*To* BERTHOLD.] And you too get away and keep out of sight all today. No, wait a bit! [*To* BERTHOLD.] You bring here the costumes he will give you. [*To* HAROLD.] You go at once and announce the visit of the "Duchess Adelaide" and "Monsignor Hugh of Cluny." Do you understand?

[HAROLD *and* BERTHOLD *go off by the first door on the right.*]

Di Nolli. We'll retire now.

[*Goes off with* FRIDA, *left.*]

Doctor. Shall I be a *persona grata* to him, as Hugh of Cluny?

Landolph. Oh, rather! Don't worry about that! Monsignor has always been received here with great respect. You too, my Lady, he will be glad to see. He never forgets that it was owing to the intercession of you two that he was admitted to the Castle of Canossa and the presence of Gregory VII, who didn't want to receive him.

Belcredi. And what do I do?

Landolph. You stand a little apart. respectfully: that's all.

Donna Matilda. [*Irritated, nervous.*] You would do well to go away, you know.

Belcredi. [*Slowly, spitefully.*] How upset you seem! . . .

Donna Matilda. [*Proudly.*] I am as I am. Leave me alone!

[BERTHOLD *comes in with the costumes.*]

Landolph. [*Seeing him enter.*] Ah, the costumes: here they are. This mantle is for the Marchioness . . .

Donna Matilda. Wait a minute! I'll take off my hat.

[*Does so and gives it to* BERTHOLD.]

Landolph. Put it down there! [*Then to the* MARCHIONESS, *while he offers to put the ducal crown on her head.*] Allow me!

Donna Matilda. Dear, dear! Isn't there a mirror here?

Landolph. Yes, there's one there. [*Points to the door on the left.*] If the Marchioness would rather put it on herself . . .

Donna Matilda. Yes, yes, that will be better. Give it to me!

[*Takes up her hat and goes off with* BERTHOLD, *who carries the cloak and the crown.*]

Belcredi. Well, I must say, I never thought I should be a Benedictine monk! By the way, this business must cost an awful lot of money.

The Doctor. Like any other fantasy, naturally!

Belcredi. Well, there's a fortune to go upon.

Landolph. We have got there a whole wardrobe of costumes of the period, copied to perfection from old models. This is my special job. I get them from the best theatrical costumers. They cost lots of money.

[DONNA MATILDA *reënters, wearing mantle and crown.*]

Belcredi. [*At once, in admiration.*] Oh, magnificent! Oh, truly regal!

Donna Matilda. [*Looking at* BELCREDI *and bursting out into laughter.*] Oh no, no! Take it off! You're impossible. You look like an ostrich dressed up as a monk.

Belcredi. Well, how about the doctor?

The Doctor. I don't think I look so bad, do I?

Donna Matilda. No; the doctor's all right . . . but you are too funny for words.

The Doctor. Do you have many receptions here then?

Landolph. It depends. He often gives orders that such and such a person appear before him. Then we have to find someone who will take the part. Women too . . .

Donna Matilda. [*Hurt, but trying to hide the fact.*] Ah, women too?

Landolph. Oh, yes; many at first.

Belcredi. [*Laughing.*] Oh, that's great! In costume, like the Marchioness?

Londolph. Oh well, you know, women of the kind that lend themselves to . . .

Belcredi. Ah, I see! [*Perfidiously to the* MARCHIONESS.] Look out, you know he's becoming dangerous for you.

[*The second door on the right opens, and* HAROLD *appears, making first of all a discreet sign that all conversation should cease.*]

Harold. His Majesty, the Emperor!

[*The two valets enter first, and go and stand on either side of the throne. Then* HENRY IV *comes in between* ORDULPH *and* HAROLD, *who keep a little in the rear respectfully.*]

[HENRY IV *is about* 50 *and very pale. The hair on the back of his head is already gray; over the temples and forehead it appears blond, owing to its having been tinted in an evident and puerile fashion. On his cheek bones he has two small, doll-like dabs of color, that stand out prominently against the rest of his tragic pallor. He is wearing a penitent's sack over his regal habit, as at Canossa. His eyes have a fixed look which is dreadful to see, and this expression is in strained contrast with the sackcloth.* ORDULPH *carries the imperial crown;* HAROLD, *the sceptre with the eagle, and the globe with the cross.*]

Henry IV. [*Bowing first to* DONNA MATILDA *and afterwards to the* DOCTOR.] My lady . . . Monsignor . . . [*Then he looks at* BELCREDI *and seems about to greet him too; when, suddenly, he turns to* LANDOLPH, *who has approached him, and asks him sotto voce and with diffidence:*] Is that Peter Damiani? [1]

Landolph. No, Sire. He is a monk from Cluny who is accompanying the Abbot.

Henry IV. [*Looks again at* BELCREDI *with increasing mistrust, and then noticing that he appears embarrassed and keeps glancing at* DONNA MATILDA *and the* DOCTOR, *stands upright and cries out.*] No, it's Peter Damiani! It's no use, Father, your looking at the Duchess. [*Then turning quickly to* DONNA MATILDA *and the* DOCTOR *as though to ward off a danger.*] I swear it! I swear it that my heart is changed toward your daughter. I confess that if he [*indicates* BELCREDI] hadn't come to forbid it in the name of Pope Alexander, I'd have repudiated her. Yes, yes, there were people ready to favor the repudiation: the Bishop of Mayence would have done it for a matter of one hundred and twenty farms. [*Looks at* LANDOLPH *a little perplexed and adds:*] But I mustn't speak ill of the bishops at this moment! [*More humbly to* BELCREDI.] I am grateful to you, believe me, I am grateful to you for the hindrance you put in my way!—God knows, my life's been all made of humiliations: my mother, Adalbert, Tribur, Goslar! [2] And now this sackcloth you see me wearing! [*Changes tone suddenly and speaks like one who goes over his part in a parenthesis of astuteness.*] It doesn't matter: clarity of ideas, perspicacity, firmness, and patience under adversity—that's the thing. [*Then turning to all and speaking solemnly.*] I know how to make amend for the mistakes I have made; and I can humiliate myself even before you, Peter Damiani. [*Bows profoundly to him and remains curved. Then a suspicion is born in him which he is obliged to utter in menacing tones, almost against his will.*] Was it not perhaps you who started that obscene rumor that my holy mother had illicit relations with the Bishop of Augusta?

Belcredi. [*Since* HENRY IV *has his finger pointed at him.*] No, no, it wasn't I . . .

Henry IV. [*Straightening up.*] Not true, not true? Infamy! [*Looks at him and then adds:*] I didn't think you capable of it! [*Goes to the* DOCTOR *and plucks his sleeve, while winking at him knowingly.*] Always the same, Monsignor, those bishops, always the same!

Harold. [*Softly, whispering as if to help*

[1] Cardinal Pietro Damiani had persuaded Henry IV in 1069 not to divorce his wife Bertha.

[2] Henry was separated from his mother and Adalbert against his will; at Tribur and Goslar he was forced to yield to rebellious Saxon nobles.

out the DOCTOR.] Yes, yes, the rapacious bishops!

The Doctor. [*To* HAROLD, *trying to keep it up.*] Ah, yes, those fellows . . . ah yes . . .

Henry IV. Nothing satisfies them! I was a little boy, Monsignor . . . One passes the time, playing even, when, without knowing it, one is a king.—I was six years old; and they tore me away from my mother, and made use of me against her without my knowing anything about it[1] . . . always profaning, always stealing, stealing! . . . One greedier than the other . . . Hanno worse than Stephen![2] Stephen worse than Hanno!

Landolph. [*Sotto voce, persuasively, to call his attention.*] Majesty!

Henry IV. [*Turning round quickly.*] Ah yes . . . this isn't the moment to speak ill of the bishops. But this infamy against my mother, Monsignor, is too much. [*Looks at the* MARCHIONESS *and grows tender.*] And I can't even weep for her, Lady . . . I appeal to you who have a mother's heart! She came here to see me from her convent a month ago . . . They had told me she was dead! [*Sustained pause full of feeling. Then smiling sadly.*] I can't weep for her; because if you are here now, and I am like this [*shows the sackcloth he is wearing*], it means I am twenty-six years old!

Harold. And that she is therefore alive, Majesty! . . .

Ordulph. Still in her convent!

Henry IV. [*Looking at them.*] Ah yes! And I can postpone my grief to another time. [*Shows the* MARCHIONESS *almost with coquetry the tint he has given to his hair.*] Look! I am still fair . . . [*Then slowly as if in confidence.*] For you . . . there's no need! But little exterior details do help! A matter of time, Monsignor, do you understand me? [*Turns to the* MARCHIONESS *and notices her hair.*] Ah, but I see that you too, Duchess . . . Italian, eh? [*As much as to say "false"; but without any indignation, indeed rather with malicious admiration.*] Heaven forbid that I should show disgust or surprise! Nobody cares to recognize that obscure and fatal power which sets limits to our will. But I say, if one is born and one dies . . . Did you want to be born, Monsignor? I didn't! And in both cases, independently of our wills, so many things happen we would wish didn't happen, and to which we resign ourselves as best we can! . . .

[1] In 1062, when Henry was 12, not 6, Archbishop Hanno of Cologne engineered a successful conspiracy to take the young king away from his mother, the empress-regent Agnes.

[2] Stephen IX, pope 1057-1058, who opposed Henry's election as King of Germany, Italy, and Burgundy.

Doctor. [*Merely to make a remark, while studying* HENRY IV *carefully.*] Alas! Yes, alas!

Henry IV. It's like this: When we are not resigned, out come our desires. A woman wants to be a man . . . an old man would be young again. Desires, ridiculous fixed ideas of course—But reflect! Monsignor. those other desires are not less ridiculous: I mean, those desires where the will is kept within the limits of the possible. Not one of us can lie or pretend. We're all fixed in good faith in a certain concept of ourselves. However, Monsignor, while you keep yourself in order, holding on with both your hands to your holy habit, there slips down from your sleeves, there peels off from you like . . . like a serpent . . . something you don't notice: life, Monsignor! [*Turns to the* MARCHIONESS.] Has it never happened to you, my Lady, to find a different self in yourself? Have you always been the same? My God! One day . . . how was it, how was it you were able to commit this or that action? [*Fixes her so intently in the eyes as almost to make her blanch.*] Yes, that particular action. that very one: we understand each other! But don't be afraid: I shall reveal it to none. And you, Peter Damiani, how could you be a friend of that man? . . .

Landolph. Majesty!

Henry IV. [*At once.*] No, I won't name him! [*Turning to* BELCREDI.] What did you think of him? But we all of us cling tight to our conceptions of ourselves, just as he who is growing old dyes his hair. What does it matter that this dyed hair of mine isn't a reality for you, if it *is*, to some extent, for me?—you, you, my Lady, certainly don't dye your hair to deceive the others, nor even yourself; but only to cheat your own image a little before the looking-glass. I do it for a joke! You do it seriously! But I assure you that you too, Madam, are in masquerade, though it be in all seriousness; and I am not speaking of the venerable crown on your brows or the ducal mantle. I am speaking only of the memory you wish to fix in yourself of your fair complexion one day when it pleased you—or of your dark complexion, if you were dark: the fading image of your youth! For you, Peter Damiani, on the contrary, the memory of what you have been, of what you have done, seems to you a recognition of past realities that remain within you like a dream. I'm in the same case too: with so many inexplicable memories—like dreams! Ah! . . . There's nothing to marvel at in it, Peter Damiani!

Tomorrow it will be the same thing with our life of today! [*Suddenly getting excited and taking hold of his sackcloth.*] This sackcloth here! . . . [*Beginning to take it off with a gesture of almost ferocious joy while the three valets run over to him, frightened, as if to prevent his doing so.*] Ah, my God! [*Draws back and throws off sackcloth.*] Tomorrow, at Bressanone, twenty-seven German and Lombard bishops will sign with me the act of deposition of Gregory VII! No Pope at all! Just a false monk! [1]

Ordulph. [*With the other three.*] Majesty! Majesty! In God's name! . . .

Harold. [*Inviting him to put on the sackcloth again.*] Listen to what he says, Majesty!

Landolph. Monsignor is here with the Duchess to intercede in your favor.

[*Makes secret signs to the* DOCTOR *to say something at once.*]

Doctor. [*Foolishly.*] Ah yes . . . yes . . . we are here to intercede . . .

Henry IV. [*Repenting at once, almost terrified, allowing the three to put on the sackcloth again, and pulling it down over him with his own hands.*] Pardon . . . yes . . . yes . . . pardon, Monsignor: forgive me, my Lady . . . I swear to you I feel the whole weight of the anathema. [*Bends himself, takes his face between his hands, as though waiting for something to crush him. Then changing tone, but without moving, says softly to* LANDOLPH, HAROLD, *and* ORDULPH.] But I don't know why I cannot be humble before that man there!

[*Indicates* BELCREDI.]

Landolph. [*Sotto voce.*] But why, Majesty, do you insist on believing he is Peter Damiani, when he isn't, at all?

Henry IV. [*Looking at him timorously.*] He isn't Peter Damiani?

Harold. No, no, he is a poor monk, Majesty.

Henry IV. [*Sadly with a touch of exasperation.*] Ah! None of us can estimate what we do when we do it from instinct . . . You, perhaps, Madam, can understand me better than the others, since you are a woman and a Duchess. This is a solemn and decisive moment. I could, you know, accept the assistance of the Lombard bishops, arrest the Pope, lock him up here in the castle, run to Rome, and elect an anti-Pope; offer alliance to Robert Guiscard [2]—and Gregory VII would be lost! I resist the temptation; and, believe me, I am wise in doing so. I feel the atmosphere of our times and the majesty of one who knows how to be what he ought to be! a Pope! Do you feel inclined to laugh at me, seeing me like this? You would be foolish to do so; for you don't understand the political wisdom which makes this penitent's sack advisable. The parts may be changed tomorrow. What would you do then? Would you laugh to see the Pope a prisoner? No! It would come to the same thing: I dressed as a penitent today; he, as prisoner tomorrow! But woe to him who doesn't know how to wear his mask, be he king or Pope!—Perhaps he is a bit too cruel! No! Yes, yes, maybe!— You remember, my Lady, how your daughter Bertha, for whom, I repeat, my feelings have changed [*turns to* BELCREDI *and shouts to his face as if he were being contradicted by him*]—yes, changed on account of the affection and devotion she showed me in that terrible moment . . . [*then once again to the* MARCHIONESS] . . . you remember how she came with me, my Lady, followed me like a beggar, and passed two nights out in the open, in the snow? You are her mother! Doesn't this touch your mother's heart? Doesn't this urge you to pity, so that you will beg His Holiness for pardon, beg him to receive us?

Donna Matilda. [*Trembling, with feeble voice.*] Yes, yes, at once . . .

Doctor. It shall be done!

Henry IV. And one thing more! [*Draws them in to listen to him.*] It isn't enough that he should receive me! You know he can do *everything—everything,* I tell you! He can even call up the dead. [*Touches his chest.*] Behold me! Do you see me? There is no magic art unknown to him. Well, Monsignor, my Lady, my torment is really this: that whether here or there [*pointing to his portrait almost in fear*] I can't free myself from this magic. I am a penitent now, you see; and I swear to you I shall remain so until he receives me. But you two, when the excommunication is taken off, must ask the Pope to do this thing he can so easily do: to take me away from that [*indicating the portrait again*]; and let me live wholly and freely my miserable life. A man can't always be twenty-six, my Lady. I ask this of you for your daughter's sake too; that I may love her as she deserves to be loved, well disposed as I am now, all tender toward her for her pity. There: it's all there! I am in your hands! [*Bows.*] My Lady! Monsignor!

[*He goes off, bowing grandly, through*

[1] These words were used by Henry in a letter to Gregory VII before the excommunication.

[2] Duke of Apulia, in control of southern Italy.

the door by which he entered, leaving every one stupefied, and the MARCHIONESS *so profoundly touched, that no sooner has he gone than she breaks out into sob^c and sits down almost fainting.*]

CURTAIN

ACT II

Another room of the villa, adjoining the throne room. Its furniture is antique and severe. Principal exit at rear in the background. To the left, two windows looking on the garden. To the right, a door opening into the throne room.

Late afternoon of the same day.

[DONNA MATILDA, *the* DOCTOR, *and* BELCREDI *are on the stage engaged in conversation; but* DONNA MATILDA *stands on one side, evidently annoyed at what the other two are saying; although she cannot help listening, because, in her agitated state, everything interests her in spite of herself. The talk of the other two attracts her attention, because she instinctively feels the need for calm at the moment.*]

Belcredi. It may be as you say, Doctor, but that was my impression.

Doctor. I won't contradict you; but, believe me, it is only . . . an impression.

Belcredi. Pardon me, but he even said so, and quite clearly. [*Turning to the* MARCHIONESS.] Didn't he, Marchioness?

Donna Matilda. [*Turning round.*] What did he say? . . . [*Then not agreeing.*] Oh yes . . . but not for the reason you think!

Doctor. He was alluding to the costumes we had slipped on . . . Your cloak [*indicating the* MARCHIONESS], our Benedictine habits . . . But all this is childish!

Donna Matilda. [*Turning, quickly, indignant.*] Childish? What do you mean, Doctor?

Doctor. From one point of view, it is—I beg you to let me say so, Marchioness! Yet, on the other hand, it is much more complicated than you can imagine.

Donna Matilda. To me, on the contrary, it is perfectly clear!

Doctor. [*With the condescending smile of the competent person toward those who do not understand.*] We must take into account the peculiar psychology of madmen; which, you must know, enables us to be certain that they observe things and can, for instance, easily detect people who are disguised; can in fact recognize the disguise and yet believe in it; just as children do, for whom disguise is both play and reality. That is why I used the word childish. But the thing is extremely complicated, inasmuch as he must be perfectly aware of being an image to himself and for himself—that image there, in fact! [*Alluding to the portrait in the throne room, and pointing to the right.*]

Belcredi. That's what he said!

Doctor. Very well then—An image before which other images, ours, have appeared: understand? Now he, in his acute and perfectly lucid delirium, was able to detect at once a difference between his image and ours: that is, he saw that ours were make-believes. So he suspected us; because all madmen are armed with a special diffidence. But that's all there is to it! Our make-believe, built up all round his, did not seem pitiful to him. While his seemed all the more tragic to us, in that he, as if in defiance—understand?—and induced by his suspicion, wanted to show us up merely as a joke. That was also partly the case with him, in coming before us with painted cheeks and hair, and saying he had done it on purpose for a jest.

Donna Matilda. [*Impatiently.*] No, it's not that, Doctor. It's not like that! It's not like that!

Doctor. Why isn't it, may I ask?

Donna Matilda. [*With decision but trembling.*] I am perfectly certain he recognized me!

Doctor. It's not possible . . . it's not possible!

Belcredi. [*At the same time.*] Of course not!

Donna Matilda. [*More than ever determined, almost convulsively.*] I tell you, he recognized me! When he came close up to speak to me—looking in my eyes, right into my eyes—he recognized me!

Belcredi. But he was talking of your daughter!

Donna Matilda. That's not true! He was talking of me! Of me!

Belcredi. Yes, perhaps, when he said . . .

Donna Matilda. [*Letting herself go.*] About my dyed hair! But didn't you notice that he added at once: "or the memory of your dark hair, if you were dark"? He remembered perfectly well that I was dark—then!

Belcredi. Nonsense! nonsense!

Donna Matilda. [*Not listening to him, turning to the* DOCTOR.] My hair, Doctor, is really dark—like my daughter's! That's why he spoke of her.

Belcredi. But he doesn't even know your daughter! He's never seen her!

Donna Matilda. Exactly! Oh, you never understand anything! By my daughter, stupid, he meant me—as I was then!

Belcredi. Oh, this is catching! This is catching, this madness!

Donna Matilda. [*Softly, with contempt.*] Fool!

Belcredi. Excuse me, were you ever his wife? Your daughter is his wife—in his delirium: Bertha of Susa.

Donna Matilda. Exactly! Because I, no longer dark—as he remembered me—but *fair,* introduced myself as "Adelaide," the mother. My daughter doesn't exist for him: he's never seen her—you said so yourself! So how can he know whether she's fair or dark?

Belcredi. But he said dark, speaking generally, just as anyone who wants to recall, whether fair or dark, a memory of youth in the color of the hair! And you, as usual, begin to imagine things! Doctor, you said I ought not to have come! It's she who ought not to have come!

Donna Matilda. [*Upset for a moment by* BELCREDI'S *remark, recovers herself. Then with a touch of anger, because doubtful.*] No, no . . . he spoke of me . . . He spoke all the time to me, with me, of me . . .

Belcredi. That's not bad! He didn't leave me a moment's breathing space; and you say he was talking all the time to you? Unless you think he was alluding to you too, when he was talking to Peter Damiani!

Donna Matilda. [*Defiantly, almost exceeding the limits of courteous discussion.*] Who knows? Can you tell me why, from the outset, he showed a strong dislike for you, for you alone?

[*From the tone of the question, the expected answer must almost explicitly be: "Because he understands you are my lover."* BELCREDI *feels this so well that he remains silent and can say nothing.*]

Doctor. The reason may also be found in the fact that only the visit of the Duchess Adelaide and the Abbot of Cluny was announced to him. Finding a third person present, who had not been announced, at once his suspicion . . .

Belcredi. Yes, exactly! His suspicion made him see an enemy in me: Peter Damiani! But she's got it into her head that he recognized her . . .

Donna Matilda. There's no doubt about it! I could see it from his eyes, Doctor. You know, there's a way of looking that leaves no doubt whatever . . . Perhaps it was only for an instant, but I am sure!

Doctor. It is not impossible: a lucid moment . . .

Donna Matilda. Yes, perhaps . . . . And then his speech seemed to me full of regret for his and my youth—for the horrible thing that happened to him, that has held him in that disguise from which he has never been able to free himself, and from which he longs to be free—he said so himself!

Belcredi. Yes, so as to be able to make love to your daughter, or you, as you believe—having been touched by your pity.

Donna Matilda. Which is very great, I would ask you to believe.

Belcredi. As one can see, Marchioness; so much so that a miracle-worker might expect a miracle from it!

Doctor. Will you let me speak? I don't work miracles, because I am a doctor and not a miracle-worker. I listened very intently to all he said; and I repeat that that certain analogical elasticity, common to all symptomatised delirium, is evidently with him much . . . what shall I say?—much relaxed! The elements, that is, of his delirium no longer hold together. It seems to me he has lost the equilibrium of his second personality and sudden recollections drag him—and this is very comforting—not from a state of incipient apathy, but rather from a morbid inclination to reflective melancholy, which shows a . . . a very considerable cerebral activity. Very comforting, I repeat! Now if, by this violent trick we've planned . . .

Donna Matilda. [*Turning to the window, in the tone of a sick person complaining.*] But how is it that the motor has not returned? It's three hours and a half since . . .

Doctor. What do you say?

Donna Matilda. The motor, Doctor! It's more than three hours and a half . . .

Doctor. [*Taking out his watch and looking at it.*] Yes, more than four hours, by this!

Donna Matilda. It could have reached here an hour ago at least! But, as usual . . .

Belcredi. Perhaps they can't find the dress .

Donna Matilda. But I explained exactly

where it was! [*Impatiently.*] And Frida . . . where is Frida?

Belcredi. [*Looking out of the window.*] Perhaps she is in the garden with Charles . . .

Doctor. He'll talk her out of her fright.

Belcredi. She's not afraid, Doctor; don't you believe it: the thing bores her rather . . .

Donna Matilda. Just don't ask anything of her! I know what she's like.

Doctor. Let's wait patiently. Anyhow, it will soon be over, and it has to be in the evening . . . It will only be the matter of a moment! If we can succeed in rousing him, as I was saying, and in breaking at one go the threads—already slack—which still bind him to this fiction of his, giving him back what he himself asks for—you remember, he said: "One cannot always be twenty-six years old, madam!"—if we can give him freedom from this torment, which even *he* feels is a torment, then if he is able to recover at one bound the sensation of the distance of time . . .

Belcredi. [*Quickly.*] He'll be cured! [*Then emphatically with irony.*] We'll pull him out of it all!

Doctor. Yes, we may hope to set him going again, like a watch which has stopped at a certain hour . . . just as if we had our watches in our hands and were waiting for that other watch to go again. A shake—so —and let's hope it'll tell the time again after its long stop.

[*At this point the* MARQUIS CHARLES DI NOLLI *enters from the principal entrance.*]

Donna Matilda. Oh, Charles! . . . And Frida? Where is she?

Di Nolli. She'll be here in a moment.

Doctor. Has the motor arrived?

Di Nolli. Yes.

Donna Matilda. Yes? Has the dress come?

Di Nolli. It's been here some time.

Doctor. Good! Good!

Donna Matilda. [*Trembling.*] Where is she? Where's Frida?

Di Nolli. [*Shrugging his shoulders and smiling sadly, like one lending himself unwillingly to an untimely joke.*] You'll see, you'll see! . . . [*Pointing toward the hall.*] Here she is! . . .

[BERTHOLD *appears at the threshold of the hall, and announces with solemnity.*]

Berthold. Her Highness the Countess Matilda of Canossa!

[FRIDA *enters, magnificent and beautiful, arrayed in the robes of her mother as "Countess Matilda of Tuscany," so that she is a living copy of the portrait in the throne room.*]

Frida. [*Passing* BERTHOLD, *who is bowing, says to him with disdain.*] Of Tuscany, of Tuscany! Canossa is just one of my castles!

Belcredi. [*In admiration.*] Look! Look! She seems another person. . . .

Donna Matilda. One would say it were I! Look!—Why, Frida, look! She's exactly my portrait, alive!

Doctor. Yes, yes . . . Perfect! Perfect! The portrait, to the life.

Belcredi. Yes, there's no question about it. She *is* the portrait! Magnificent!

Frida. Don't make me laugh, or I shall burst! I say, mother, what a tiny waist you had! I had to squeeze so to get into this!

Donna Matilda. [*Arranging her dress a little.*] Wait! . . . Keep still! . . . These pleats . . . is it really so tight?

Frida. I'm suffocating! I implore you to be quick!

Doctor. But we must wait till it's evening!

Frida. No, no, I can't hold out till evening!

Donna Matilda. Why did you put it on so soon?

Frida. The moment I saw it, the temptation was irresistible . . .

Donna Matilda. At least you could have called me, or have had someone help you! It's still all crumpled.

Frida. So I saw, mother; but they are old creases; they won't come out.

Doctor. It doesn't matter, Marchioness! The illusion is perfect. [*Then coming near and asking her to come in front of her daughter, without hiding her.*] If you please, stay there, there . . . at a certain distance . . . now a little more forward . . .

Belcredi. For the feeling of the distance of time . . .

Donna Matilda. [*Slightly turning to him.*] Twenty years after! A disaster! A tragedy!

Belcredi. Now don't let's exaggerate!

Doctor. [*Embarrassed, trying to save the situation.*] No, no! I meant the dress . . . so as to see . . . You know . . .

Belcredi. [*Laughing*]. Oh, as for the dress, Doctor, it isn't a matter of twenty years! It's eight hundred! An abyss! Do you really want to shove him across it [*pointing first to* FRIDA *and then to the* MARCHIONESS] from there to here? But you'll have to pick him up in pieces with a basket! Just think now: for us it is a matter of twenty years, a couple of dresses, and a masquerade. But if, as you say, Doctor, time has stopped for and around him: if he lives there [*pointing to* FRIDA] with her, eight hundred years ago . . . I repeat: the giddiness of the jump will be such that finding himself suddenly among us . . . [*The* DOCTOR *shakes his head in dissent.*] You don't think so?

Doctor. No, because life, my dear baron, can take up its rhythms. This—our life—will at once become real also to him; and will pull him up directly, wresting from him suddenly the illusion, and showing him that the eight hundred years, as you say, are only twenty! It will be like one of those tricks, such as the leap into space, for instance, of the Masonic rite, which appears to be heaven knows how far, and is only a step down the stairs.

Belcredi. Ah! An idea! Yes! Look at Frida and the Marchioness, Doctor! Which is more advanced in time? We old people, Doctor! The young ones think they are more ahead; but it isn't true: we are more ahead, because time belongs to us more than to them.

Doctor. If the past didn't alienate us . . .

Belcredi. It doesn't matter at all! How does it alienate us? They [*pointing to* FRIDA *and* DI NOLLI] have still to do what we have accomplished, Doctor: to grow old, doing the same foolish things, more or less, as we did . . . This is the illusion: that one comes forward through a door to life. It isn't so! As soon as one is born, one starts dying; therefore, he who started first is the most advanced of all. The youngest of us is father Adam! Look there: [*pointing to* FRIDA] eight hundred years younger than all of us—the Countess Matilda of Tuscany.

[*He makes her a deep bow.*]

Di Nolli. I say, Tito, don't start joking.

Belcredi. Oh, you think I am joking? . . .

Di Nolli. Of course, of course . . . all the time.

Belcredi. Impossible! I've even dressed up as a Benedictine . . .

Di Nolli. Yes, but for a serious purpose.

Belcredi. Well, exactly. If it had been serious for the others . . . for Frida, now, for instance. [*Then turning to the* DOCTOR.] I swear, Doctor, I don't yet understand what you want to do.

Doctor. [*Annoyed.*] You'll see! Let me do as I wish. . . . At present you see the Marchioness still dressed as . . .

Belcredi. Oh, she also . . . has to masquerade?

Doctor. Of course! of course! In another dress that's in there ready to be used when it comes into his head he sees the Countess Matilda of Canossa before him.

Frida. [*While talking quietly to* DI NOLLI *notices the* DOCTOR'S *mistake.*] Of Tuscany, of Tuscany!

Doctor. It's all the same!

Belcredi. Oh, I see! He'll be faced by two of them . . .

Doctor. Two, precisely! And then . . .

Frida. [*Calling him aside.*] Come here, Doctor! Listen!

Doctor. Here I am.

[*Goes near the two young people and pretends to give some explanations to them.*]

Belcredi. [*Softly to* DONNA MATILDA.] I say, this is getting rather strong, you know!

Donna Matilda. [*Looking him firmly in the face.*] What?

Belcredi. Does it really interest you as much as all that—to make you willing to take part in . . . ? For a woman, this is simply enormous! . . .

Donna Matilda. Yes, for an ordinary woman.

Belcredi. Oh, no, my dear, for all women—in a question like this! It's an abnegation.

Donna Matilda. I owe it to him.

Belcredi. Don't lie! You know well enough it's not hurting you!

Donna Matilda. Well then, where does the abnegation come in?

Belcredi. Just enough to prevent you losing caste in other people's eyes—and just enough to offend me! . . .

Donna Matilda. But who is worrying about you now?

Di Nolli. [*Coming forward.*] It's all right. It's all right. That's what we'll do! [*Turning toward* BERTHOLD.] Here you, go and call one of those fellows!

Berthold. At once! [*Exit.*]

Donna Matilda. But first of all we've got to pretend that we are going away.

Di Nolli. Exactly! I'll see to that . . . [*To* BELCREDI.] You don't mind staying here?

Belcredi. [*Ironically.*] Oh, no, I don't mind, I don't mind! . . .

Di Nolli. We must look out not to make him suspicious again, you know.

Belcredi. Oh, Lord! *He* doesn't amount to anything!

Doctor. He must believe absolutely that we've gone away.

[LANDOLPH *followed by* BERTHOLD *enters from the right.*]

Landolph. May I come in?

Di Nolli. Come in! Come in! I say—your name's Lolo, isn't it?

Landolph. Lolo, or Landolph, just as you like!

Di Nolli. Well, look here: the Doctor and the Marchioness are leaving, at once.

Landolph. Very well. All we've got to say is that they have been able to obtain the permission for the reception from His Holiness. He's in there in his own apartments repenting of all he said—and in an awful state to have the pardon! Would you mind coming a minute? . . . If you would, just for a minute . . . put on the dress again . . .

Doctor. Why, of course, with pleasure . . .

Landolph. Might I be allowed to make a suggestion? Why not add that the Marchioness of Tuscany has interceded with the Pope that he should be received?

Donna Matilda. You see, he has recognized me!

Landolph. Forgive me . . . I don't know my history very well. I am sure you gentlemen know it much better! But I thought it was believed that Henry IV had a secret passion for the Marchioness of Tuscany.

Donna Matilda. [*At once.*] Nothing of the kind! Nothing of the kind!

Landolph. That's what I thought! But he says he's loved her . . . he's always saying it . . . And now he fears that her indignation against this secret love of his will work him harm with the Pope.

Belcredi. We must let him understand that this aversion no longer exists.

Landolph. Exactly! Of course!

Donna Matilda. [*To* BELCREDI.] History says—I don't know whether you know it or not—that the Pope gave away to the supplications of the Marchioness Matilda and the Abbot of Cluny. And I may say, my dear Belcredi, that I intended to take advantage of this fact—at the time of the pageant—to show him my feelings were not so hostile to him as he supposed.

Belcredi. You are most faithful to history, Marchioness . . .

Landolph. Well then, the Marchioness could spare herself a double disguise and present herself with Monsignor [*indicating the* DOCTOR] as the Marchioness of Tuscany.

Doctor. [*Quickly, energetically.*] No, no! That won't do at all. It would ruin everything. The impression from the confrontation must be a sudden one, give a shock! No, no, Marchioness, you will appear again as the Duchess Adelaide, the mother of the Empress. And then we'll go away. This is most necessary: that he should know we've gone away. Come on! Don't let's waste any more time! There's a lot to prepare.

[*Exeunt the* DOCTOR, DONNA MATILDA, *and* LANDOLPH, *right.*]

Frida. I am beginning to feel afraid again.

Di Nolli. Again, Frida?

Frida. It would have been better if I had seen him before.

Di Nolli. There's nothing to be frightened of, really.

Frida. He isn't furious, is he?

Di Nolli. Of course not! He's quite calm.

Belcredi. [*With ironic sentimental affectation.*] Melancholy! Didn't you hear that he loves you?

Frida. Thanks! That's just why I am afraid.

Belcredi. He won't do you any harm.

Di Nolli. It'll only last a minute . . .

Frida. Yes, but there in the dark with him . . .

Di Nolli. Only for a moment; and I will be near you, and all the others behind the door ready to run in. As soon as you see your mother, your part will be finished . . .

Belcredi. I'm afraid of a different thing: that we're wasting our time . . .

Di Nolli. Don't begin again! The remedy seems a sound one to me.

Frida. I think so too! I feel it! I'm all trembling!

Belcredi. But, mad people, my dear friends—though they don't know it, alas—have this felicity which we don't take into account . . .

Di Nolli. [*Interrupting, annoyed.*] What felicity? Nonsense!

Belcredi. [*Forcefully.*] They don't reason!

Di Nolli. What's reasoning got to do with it, anyway?

Belcredi. Don't you call it reasoning that he will have to do—according to us—when he sees her [*indicates* FRIDA] and her mother? We've reasoned it all out, surely!

Di Nolli. Nothing of the kind: no reasoning at all! We put before him a double image of his own fantasy, or fiction, as the Doctor says.

Belcredi. [*Suddenly.*] I say, I've never understood why they take degrees in medicine.

Di Nolli. [*Amazed.*] Who?

Belcredi. The alienists!

Di Nolli. What ought they to take degrees in, then?

Frida. If they are alienists, in what else should they take degrees?

Belcredi. In law, of course! All a matter of talk! The more they talk, the more highly they are considered. "Analogous elasticity," "the sensation of distance in time!" And the first thing they tell you is that they don't work miracles—when a miracle's just what is wanted! But they know that the more they say they are not miracle-workers, the more folk believe in their seriousness!

Berthold. [*Who has been looking through the keyhole of the door on right.*] There they are! There they are! They're coming in here.

Di Nolli. Are they?

Berthold. He wants to come with them . . . Yes! . . . He's coming too!

Di Nolli. Let's get away, then! Let's get away, at once! [*To* BERTHOLD.] You stop here!

Berthold. Must I?

[*Without answering him,* DI NOLLI, FRIDA, *and* BELCREDI *go out by the main exit, leaving* BERTHOLD *surprised. The door on the right opens, and* LANDOLPH *enters first, bowing. Then* DONNA MATILDA *comes in, with mantle and ducal crown as in the first act; also the* DOCTOR *as the* ABBOT OF CLUNY. HENRY IV *is among them in royal dress.* ORDULPH *and* HAROLD *enter last of all.*]

Henry IV. [*Following up what he has been saying in the other room.*] And now I will ask you a question: how can I be astute, if you think me obstinate?

Doctor. No, no, not obstinate!

Henry IV. [*Smiling, pleased.*] Then you think me really astute?

Doctor. No, no, neither obstinate, nor astute.

Henry IV. [*With benevolent irony.*] Monsignor, if obstinacy is not a vice which can go with astuteness, I hoped that in denying me the former, you would at least allow me a little of the latter. I can assure you I have great need of it. But if you want to keep it all for yourself . . .

Doctor. I? I? Do I seem astute to you?

Henry IV. No, Monsignor! What do you say? Not in the least! Perhaps in this case, I may seem a little obstinate to you. [*Cutting short to speak to* DONNA MATILDA.] With your permission: a word in confidence to the Duchess. [*Leads her aside and asks her very earnestly.*] Is your daughter really dear to you?

Donna Matilda. [*Dismayed.*] Why, yes, certainly . . .

Henry IV. Do you wish me to compensate her with all my love, with all my devotion, for the grave wrongs I have done her—though you must not believe all the stories my enemies tell about my dissoluteness!

Donna Matilda. No, no, I don't believe them. I never have believed such stories.

Henry IV. Well then, are you willing?

Donna Matilda. [*Confused.*] What?

Henry IV. That I return to love your daughter again? [*Looks at her and adds, in a mysterious tone of warning.*] You mustn't be a friend of the Marchioness of Tuscany!

Donna Matilda. I tell you again that she has begged and tried not less than ourselves to obtain your pardon . . .

Henry IV. [*Softly, but excitedly.*] Don't tell me that! Don't say that to me! Don't you see the effect it has on me, my Lady?

Donna Matilda. [*Looks at him; then very softly as if in confidence.*] You love her still?

Henry IV. [*Puzzled.*] Still? Still, you say? You know, then? But nobody knows! Nobody must know!

Donna Matilda. But perhaps she knows, if she has begged so hard for you!

Henry IV. [*Looks at her and says.*] And you love your daughter. [*Brief pause. He turns to the* DOCTOR *with laughing accents.*] Ah, Monsignor, it's strange how little I think of my wife! It may be a sin, but I swear to you that I hardly feel her at all in my heart. What is stranger is that her own mother scarcely feels her in her heart. Confess, my Lady, that she amounts to very little for you. [*Turning to* DOCTOR.] She talks to me of that other woman, insistently, insistently, I don't know why! . . .

Landolph. [*Humbly.*] Maybe, Majesty, it is to disabuse you of some ideas you have had about the Marchioness of Tuscany. [*Then, dismayed at having allowed himself this observation, adds.*] I mean just now, of course . . .

Henry IV. You too maintain that she has been friendly to me?

Landolph. Yes, at the moment, Majesty.

Donna Matilda. Exactly! Exactly! . . .

Henry IV. I understand. That is to say, you don't believe I love her. I see! I see! Nobody's ever believed it, nobody's ever thought it. Better so, then! But enough, enough! [*Turns to the* DOCTOR *with changed expression.*] Monsignor, you see? The reasons the Pope has had for revoking the excommunication have got nothing at all to do with the reasons for which he excommunicated me originally. Tell Pope Gregory we shall meet again at Brixen. And you, Madam, should you chance to meet your daughter in the courtyard of the castle of your friend the Marchioness, ask her to visit me. We shall see if I succeed in keeping her close beside me as wife and Empress. Many women have presented themselves here already assuring me that they were she.

But they all, even while they told me they came from Susa—I don't know why—began to laugh! And then in the bedroom . . . Well, a man is a man, and a woman is a woman. Undressed, we don't bother much about who we are. And one's dress is like a phantom that hovers always near me. Oh, Monsignor, phantoms in general are nothing more than trifling disorders of the spirit: images we cannot contain within the bounds of sleep. They reveal themselves even when we are awake, and they frighten us. I . . . ah . . . I am always afraid when, at night time, I see disordered images before me. Sometimes I am even afraid of my own blood pulsing loudly in my arteries in the silence of night, like the sound of a distant step in a lonely corridor! . . . But forgive me! I have kept you standing too long already. I thank you, my Lady, I thank you, Monsignor. [DONNA MATILDA *and the* DOCTOR *go off bowing. As soon as they have gone,* HENRY IV *suddenly changes his tone.*] Buffoons, buffoons! One can play any tune on them! And that other fellow . . . Pietro Damiani! . . . Caught him out perfectly! He's afraid to appear before me again. [*Moves up and down excitedly while saying this; then sees* BERTHOLD, *and points him out to the other three* VALETS.] Oh, look at this imbecile watching me with his mouth wide open. [*Shakes him.*] Don't you understand? Don't you see, idiot, how I treat them, how I play the fool with them, make them appear before me just as I wish? Miserable, frightened clowns that they are! And you [*addressing the* VALETS] are amazed that I tear off their ridiculous masks now, just as if it wasn't I who had made them mask themselves to satisfy this taste of mine for playing the madman!

Landolph — Harold — Ordulph. [*Bewildered, looking at one another.*] What? What does he say? What?

Henry IV. [*Answers them imperiously.*] Enough! enough! Let's stop it. I'm tired of it. [*Then as if the thought left him no peace.*] By God! The impudence! To come here along with her lover! . . . And pretending to do it out of pity! So as not to infuriate a poor devil already out of the world, out of time, out of life! If it hadn't been supposed to be done out of pity, one can well imagine that fellow wouldn't have allowed it. Those people expect others to behave as they wish all the time. And, of course, there's nothing arrogant in that! Oh, no! Oh, no! It's merely their way of thinking, of feeling, of seeing. Everybody has his own way of thinking; you fellows, too. Yours is that of a flock of sheep—miserable, feeble, uncertain . . . But those others take advantage of this and make you accept their way of thinking; or, at least, they suppose they do; because, after all, what do they succeed in imposing on you? Words, words which anyone can interpret in his own manner! That's the way public opinion is formed! And it's a bad lookout for a man who finds himself labeled one day with one of these words which everyone repeats; for example "madman," or "imbecile." Don't you think it rather hard for a man to keep quiet, when he knows that there is a fellow going about trying to persuade everybody that he is as he sees him, trying to fix him in other people's opinion as a "madman"—according to him? Now I am talking seriously! Before I hurt my head, falling from my horse . . . [*Stops suddenly, noticing the dismay of the four* YOUNG MEN.] What's the matter with you? [*Imitates their amazed looks.*] What? Am I, or am I not, mad? Oh, yes! I'm mad all right! [*He becomes terrible.*] Well then, by God, down on your knees, down on your knees! [*Makes them go down on their knees one by one.*] I order you to go down on your knees before me! And touch the ground three times with your foreheads! Down, down! That's the way you've got to be before madmen! [*Then annoyed with their facile humiliation.*] Get up, sheep! You obeyed me, didn't you? You might have put the strait jacket on me! . . . Crush a man with the weight of a word—it's nothing—a fly! all our life is crushed by the weight of words: the weight of the dead. Look at me here: can you really suppose that Henry IV is still alive? All the same, I speak, and order you live men about! Do you think it's a joke that the dead continue to live?—Yes, *here* it's a joke! But get out into the live world!— Ah, you say: what a beautiful sunrise—for us! All time is before us!—Dawn! We will do what we like with this day.—Ah, yes! To Hell with tradition, the old conventions! Well, go on! You will do nothing but repeat the old, old words, while you imagine you are living! [*Goes up to* BERTHOLD, *who has now become quite stupid.*] You don't understand a word of this, do you? What's your name?

Berthold. I? . . . What? . . . Berthold . . .

Henry IV. Poor Berthold! What's your name here?

Berthold. I . . . I . . . my name is Fino.

Henry IV. [*Feeling the warning and critical glances of the others, turns to them to reduce them to silence.*] Fino?

Berthold. Fino Pagliuca, sire.

Henry IV. [*Turning to* LANDOLPH.] I've

heard you call each other by your nicknames often enough! Your name is Lolo, isn't it?

Landolph. Yes, sire . . . [*Then with a sense of immense joy.*] Oh, Lord! Oh, Lord! Then he is not mad . . .

Henry IV. [*Brusquely.*] What?

Landolph. [*Hesitating.*] No . . . I said . . .

Henry IV. Not mad, eh? We're having a joke on those that think I am mad! [*To* HAROLD.] I say, boy, your name's Franco . . . [*To* ORDULPH.] And yours . . .

Ordulph. Momo.

Henry IV. Momo, Momo . . . A nice name that!

Landolph. So he isn't . . .

Henry IV. What are you talking about? Of course not! Let's have a jolly, good laugh! . . . [*Laughs.*] Ah! . . . Ah! . . . Ah! . . .

Landolph—Harold—Ordulph. [*Looking at each other half happy and half dismayed.*] Then he's cured! . . . he's all right! . . .

Henry IV. Silence! Silence! . . .[*To* BERTHOLD.] Why don't you laugh? Are you offended? I didn't mean it especially for you. It's convenient for everybody to insist that certain people are mad, so they can be shut up. Do you know why? Because it's impossible to hear them speak! What shall I say of these people who've just gone away? That one is a whore, another a libertine, another a swindler . . . don't you think so? You can't believe a word he says . . . don't you think so?—By the way, they all listen to me terrified. And why are they terrified, if what I say isn't true? Of course, you can't believe what madmen say—yet, at the same time, they stand there with their eyes wide open with terror!—Why? Tell me, tell me, why?—You see I'm quite calm now!

Berthold. But, perhaps, they think that . . .

Henry IV. No, no, my dear fellow! Look me well in the eyes! . . . I don't say that it's true—nothing is true, Berthold! But . . . look me in the eyes!

Berthold. Well . . .

Henry IV. You see? You see? . . . You have terror in your own eyes now because I seem mad to you! There's the proof of it! [*Laughs.*]

Landolph. [*Coming forward in the name of the others, exasperated.*] What proof?

Henry IV. Your being so dismayed because now I seem again mad to you. You have thought me mad up to now, haven't you? You feel that this dismay of yours can become terror too—something to dash away the ground from under your feet and deprive you of the air you breathe! Do you know what it means to find yourselves face to face with a madman—with one who shakes the foundations of all you have built up in yourselves, your logic, the logic of all your constructions? Madmen, lucky folk! construct without logic, or rather with a logic that flies like a feather. Voluble! Voluble! Today like this and tomorrow—who knows? You say: "This cannot be"; but for them everything can be. You say: "This isn't true!" And why? Because it doesn't seem true to you, or you, or you . . . [*Indicates the three of them in succession.*] . . . and to a hundred thousand others! One must see what seems true to these hundred thousand others who are not supposed to be mad! What a magnificent spectacle they afford when they reason! What flowers of logic they scatter! I know that when I was a child, I thought the moon in the pond was real. How many things I thought real! I believed everything I was told—and I was happy! Because it's a terrible thing if you don't hold on to that which seems true to you today—to that which will seem true to you tomorrow, even if it is the opposite of that which seemed true to you yesterday. I would never wish you to think, as I have done, on this horrible thing which really drives one mad: that if you were beside another and looking into his eyes—as I one day looked into somebody's eyes—you might as well be a beggar before a door never to be opened to you; for he who does enter there will never be you, but someone unknown to you with his own different and impenetrable world . . . [*Long pause. Darkness gathers in the room, increasing the sense of strangeness and consternation in which the four* YOUNG MEN *are involved.* HENRY IV *remains aloof, pondering on the misery which is not only his, but everybody's. Then he pulls himself up, and says in an ordinary tone.*] It's getting dark here . . .

Ordulph. Shall I go for a lamp?

Henry IV. [*Ironically.*] The lamp, yes, the lamp! . . . Do you suppose I don't know that as soon as I turn my back with my oil lamp to go to bed, you turn on the electric light for yourselves, here, and even there, in the throne room? I pretend not to see it!

Ordulph. Well, then, shall I turn it on now?

Henry IV. No, it would blind me! I want my lamp!

Ordulph. It's ready here behind the door.

[*Goes to the main exit, opens the door, goes out for a moment, and returns with an ancient lamp, which is held by a ring at the top.*]

Henry IV. Ah, a little light! Sit there around the table, no, not like that; in an elegant, easy manner! . . . [*To* HAROLD.] Yes, you, like that! [*Poses him. Then to* BERTHOLD.] You, so! . . . and I, here! [*Sits opposite them.*] We could do with a little decorative moonlight. It's very useful for us, the moonlight. I feel a real necessity for it, and pass a lot of time looking up at the moon from my window. Who would think, to look at her, that she knows that eight hundred years have passed, and that I, seated at the window, cannot really be Henry IV gazing at the moon like any poor devil? But, look, look! See what a magnificent night scene we have here: the emperor surrounded by his faithful counsellors! . . . How do you like it?

Landolph. [*Softly to* HAROLD, *so as not to break the enchantment.*] And to think it wasn't true! . . .

Henry IV. True? What wasn't true?

Landolph. [*Timidly as if to excuse himself.*] No . . . I mean . . . I was saying this morning to him [*indicates* BERTHOLD]—he has just entered on service here—I was saying: what a pity that dressed like this and with so many beautiful costumes in the wardrobe . . . and with a room like that . . . [*Indicates the throne room.*]

Henry IV. Well? what's the pity?

Landolph. Well . . . that we didn't know . . .

Henry IV. That it was all done in jest, this comedy?

Landolph. Because we thought that . . .

Harold. [*Coming to his assistance.*] Yes . . . that it was done seriously!

Henry IV. What do you say? Doesn't it seem serious to you?

Landolph. But if you say that . . .

Henry IV. I say that—you are fools! You ought to have known how to create a fantasy for yourselves, not to act it for me, or anyone coming to see me; but naturally, simply, day by day, before nobody, feeling yourselves alive in the history of the eleventh century, here at the court of your emperor, Henry IV! You, Ordulph [*taking him by the arm*], alive in the castle of Goslar, waking up in the morning, getting out of bed, and entering straightway into the dream, clothing yourself in the dream that would be no more a dream, because you would have lived it, felt it all alive in you. You would have drunk it in with the air you breathed; yet knowing all the time that it was a dream, so you could better enjoy the privilege afforded you of having to do nothing else but live this dream, this far-off and yet actual dream! And to think that at a distance of eight centuries from this remote age of ours, so colored and so sepulchral, the men of the twentieth century are torturing themselves in ceaseless anxiety to know how their fates and fortunes will work out! Whereas you are already in history with me . . .

Landolph. Yes, yes, very good!

Henry IV. . . . Everything determined, everything settled!

Ordulph. Yes, yes!

Henry IV. And sad as is my lot, hideous as some of the events are, bitter the struggles and troublous the time—still all history! All history that cannot change, understand? All fixed for ever! And you could have admired at your ease how every effect followed obediently its cause with perfect logic, how every event took place precisely and coherently in each minute particular! The pleasure, the pleasure of history, in fact, which is so great, was yours.

Landolph. Beautiful, beautiful!

Henry IV. Beautiful, but it's finished! Now that you know, I could not do it any more! [*Takes his lamp to go to bed.*] Neither could you, if up to now you haven't understood the reason of it! I am sick of it now. [*Almost to himself with violent contained rage.*] By God, I'll make her sorry she came here! Dressed herself up as a mother-in-law for me . . . ! And he as an abbot . . . ! And they bring a doctor with them to study me . . . ! Who knows if they don't hope to cure me? . . . Clowns . . . ! I'd like to smack one of them at least in the face; yes, that one—a famous swordsman, they say! . . . He'll kill me . . . Well, we'll see, we'll see! . . . [*A knock at the door.*] Who is it?

The Voice of John. Deo gratias!

Harold. [*Very pleased at the chance for another joke.*] Oh, it's John, it's old John, who comes every night to play the monk.

Ordulph. [*Rubbing his hands.*] Yes, yes! Let's make him do it!

Henry IV. [*At once, severely.*] Fool, why? Just to play a joke on a poor old man who does it for love of me?

Landolph. [*To* ORDULPH.] It has to be as if it were true.

Henry IV. Exactly, as if true! Because, only so, truth is not a jest. [*Opens the door and admits* JOHN *dressed as a humble friar with a roll of parchment under his arm.*] Come in, come in, Father! [*Then assuming a tone of tragic gravity and deep resentment.*] All the documents of my life and reign favorable to me were destroyed deliberately by my enemies. One only has escaped destruction, this, my life, written by a humble monk who is devoted to me. And you would laugh at him. [*Turns affectionately to* JOHN, *and invites him to sit down at the table.*] Sit down, Father, sit down! Have the lamp near you! [*Puts the lamp near him.*] Write! Write!

John. [*Opens the parchment and prepares to write from dictation.*] I am ready, your Majesty!

Henry IV. [*Dictating.*] "The decree of peace proclaimed at Mayence helped the poor and humble, while it damaged the wicked and the powerful. [*Curtain begins to fall.*] It brought wealth to the former, hunger and misery to the latter . . ."

CURTAIN

ACT III

The throne room, so dark that the wall at the bottom is hardly seen. The canvases of the two portraits have been taken away; and, within their frames, FRIDA, *dressed as the "Marchioness of Tuscany" and* CHARLES DI NOLLI, *as "Henry IV," have taken the exact positions of the portraits.*

[*For a moment, after the raising of curtain, the stage is empty. Then the door on the left opens; and* HENRY IV, *holding the lamp by the ring on top of it, enters. He looks back to speak to the four* YOUNG MEN *who, with* JOHN, *are presumedly in the adjoining hall, as at the end of the second act.*]

Henry IV. No: stay where you are, stay where you are. I shall manage all right by myself. Good night!

[*Closes the door and walks, very sad and tired, across the hall toward the second door on the right, which leads into his apartments.*]

Frida. [*As soon as she sees that he has just passed the throne, whispers from the niche like one who is on the point of fainting away with fright.*] Henry . . .

Henry IV. [*Stopping at the voice, as if someone had stabbed him traitorously in the back, turns a terror-stricken face toward the wall at the bottom of the room; raising an arm instinctively, as if to defend himself and ward off a blow.*] Who is calling me?

[*It is not a question, but an exclamation vibrating with terror, which does not expect a reply from the darkness and the terrible silence of the hall, which suddenly fills him with the suspicion that he is really mad.*]

Frida. [*At his shudder of terror, is herself not less frightened at the part she is playing, and repeats a little more loudly.*] Henry! . . .

[*But, although she wishes to act the part as they have given it to her, she stretches her head a little out of the frame toward the other frame.* HENRY IV *gives a dreadful cry; lets the lamp fall from his hands to cover his head with his arms, and makes a movement as if to run away.*]

Frida. [*Jumping from the frame on to the stand and shouting like a mad woman.*] Henry! . . . Henry! . . . I'm afraid! . . . I'm terrified! . . .

[*And while* DI NOLLI *jumps in turn on to the stand and thence to the floor and runs to* FRIDA, *who, on the verge of fainting, continues to cry out, the* DOCTOR, DONNA MATILDA, *also dressed as "Matilda of Tuscany,"* TITO BELCREDI, LANDOLPH, BERTHOLD, HAROLD, *and* ORDULPH *enter the hall from the doors on the right and on the left. One of them turns on the light: a strange light coming from lamps hidden in the ceiling so that only the upper part of the stage is well lighted. The others, without taking notice of* HENRY IV, *who, after the moment of terror which still causes him to tremble, looks on astonished by the unexpected inrush, run anxiously to support and comfort the still shaking* FRIDA, *who is moaning in the arms of her fiancé. All are speaking at the same time.*]

Di Nolli. No, no, Frida . . . Here I am . . . I am beside you!

Doctor. [*Coming with the others.*] Enough! Enough! There's nothing more to be done! . . .

Donna Matilda. He is cured, Frida. Look! He is cured! Don't you see?

Di Nolli. [*Astonished.*] Cured?

Belcredi. It was only for fun! Be calm!

Frida. No! I am afraid! I am afraid!

Donna Matilda. Afraid of what? Look at him! He was never mad at all! . . .

Di Nolli. That isn't true! What are you saying? Cured?

Doctor. It appears so. I should say so . . .

Belcredi. Yes, yes! They have told us so. [*Pointing to the four* YOUNG MEN.]

Donna Matilda. Yes, for a long time! He has confided in them, told them the truth!

Di Nolli. [*Now more indignant than astonished.*] But what does it mean? If, up to a short time ago . . . ?

Belcredi. Hum! He was acting, to take you in and also us, who in good faith . . .

Di Nolli. Is it possible? To deceive his sister, also, right up to the time of her death?

Henry IV. [*Remains apart, peering at one and now at the other under the accusation and the mockery of what all believe to be a cruel joke of his, which is now revealed. He has shown by the flashing of his eyes that he is meditating a revenge, which his violent contempt prevents him from defining clearly, as yet. Stung to the quick and with a clear idea of accepting the fiction they have insidiously worked up as true, he bursts forth at this point.*] Go on, I say! Go on!

Di Nolli. [*Astonished at the cry.*] Go on! What do you mean?

Henry IV. It isn't *your* sister only that is dead!

Di Nolli. My sister? Yours, I say, whom you compelled up to the last moment, to present herself here as your mother Agnes!

Henry IV. And was she not *your* mother?

Di Nolli. My mother? Certainly my mother!

Henry IV. But your mother is dead for me, *old and far away!* You have just got down from there. [*Pointing to the frame from which he jumped down.*] And how do you know whether I have not wept her long in secret, dressed even as I am?

Donna Matilda. [*Dismayed, looking at the others.*] What does he say?. [*Much impressed, observing him.*] Quietly! quietly, for Heaven's sake!

Henry IV. What do I say? I ask all of you if Agnes was not the mother of Henry IV? [*Turns to* FRIDA *as if she were really the Marchioness of Tuscany.*] You, Marchioness, it seems to me, ought to know.

Frida. [*Still frightened, draws closer to* DI NOLLI.] No, no, I don't know. Not I!

Doctor. It's the madness returning. . . . Quiet now, everybody!

Belcredi. [*Indignant.*] Madness indeed, Doctor! He's acting again! . . .

Henry IV. [*Suddenly.*] I? You have emptied those two frames over there, and he stands before my eyes as Henry IV. . . .

Belcredi. We've had enough of this joke now.

Henry IV. Who said joke?

Doctor. [*Loudly to* BELCREDI.] Don't excite him, for the love of God!

Belcredi. [*Without lending an ear to him, but speaking louder.*] But they have said so—[*pointing again to the four* YOUNG MEN] they, they!

Henry IV. [*Turning round and looking at them.*] You? Did you say it was all a joke?

Landolph. [*Timid and embarrassed.*] No . . . really we said that you were cured.

Belcredi. Look here! Enough of this! [*To* DONNA MATILDA.] Doesn't it seem to you that the sight of him [*pointing to* DI NOLLI], Marchioness, and that of your daughter dressed so, is becoming an intolerable puerility?

Donna Matilda. Oh, be quiet! What does the dress matter, if he is cured?

Henry IV. Cured, yes! I am cured! [*To* BELCREDI.] Ah, but not to let it end this way all at once, as you suppose! [*Attacks him.*] Do you know that for twenty years nobody has ever dared to appear before me here like you and that gentleman? [*Pointing to the* DOCTOR.]

Belcredi. Of course I know it. As a matter of fact, I too appeared before you this morning dressed . . .

Henry IV. As a monk, yes!

Belcredi. And you took me for Peter Damiani! And I didn't even laugh, believing, in fact, that . . .

Henry IV. That I was mad! Does it make you laugh seeing her like that, now that I am cured? And yet you might have remembered that in my eyes her appearance now . . . [*Interrupts himself with a gesture of contempt.*] Ah! [*Suddenly turns to the* DOCTOR.] You are a doctor, aren't you?

Doctor. Yes.

Henry IV. And you also took part in dressing her up as the Marchioness of Tuscany? To prepare a counterjoke for me here, eh?

Donna Matilda. [*Impetuously.*] No, no! What do you say? It was done for you! I did it for your sake.

Doctor. [*Quickly.*] To attempt, to try, not knowing . . .

Henry IV. [*Cutting him short.*] I understand. I say counter-joke, in his case [*indicates* BELCREDI], because he believes that I have been carrying on a jest . . .

Belcredi. But excuse me, what do you mean? You say yourself you are cured.

Henry IV. Let me speak. [*To the* DOCTOR.] Do you know, Doctor, that for a moment you ran the risk of making me mad again? By God, to make the portraits speak;

to make them jump alive out of their frames . . .

Doctor. But you saw that all of us ran in at once, as soon as they told us . . .

Henry IV. Certainly. [*Contemplates* FRIDA *and* DI NOLLI, *and then looks at the* MARCHIONESS, *and finally at his own costume.*] The combination is very beautiful . . . Two couples . . . Very good, very good, Doctor! For a madman, not bad! . . . [*With a slight wave of his hand to* BELCREDI.] It seems to him now to be a carnival out of season, eh? [*Turns to look at him.*] We'll get rid now of this masquerade costume of mine, so that I may come away with you. What do you say?

Belcredi. With me? With us?

Henry IV. Where shall we go? To the Club? In dress coats and with white ties? Or shall both of us go to the Marchioness' house?

Belcredi. Wherever you like! Do you want to remain here still, to continue—alone—what was nothing but the unfortunate joke of a day of carnival? It is really incredible, incredible how you have been able to do all this, freed from the disaster that befell you!

Henry IV. Yes, you see how it was! The fact is that falling from my horse and striking my head as I did, I was really mad for I know not how long . . .

Doctor. Ah! Did it last long?

Henry IV. [*Very quickly to the* DOCTOR.] Yes, Doctor, a long time! I think it must have been about twelve years. [*Then suddenly turning to speak to* BELCREDI.] Thus I saw nothing, my dear fellow, of all that, after that day of carnival, happened for you but not for me: how things changed, how my friends deceived me, how my place was taken by another, and all the rest of it! And suppose my place had been taken in the heart of the woman I loved? . . . And how should I know who was dead or who had disappeared? . . . All this, you know, wasn't exactly a jest for me, as it seems to you . . .

Belcredi. No, no! I don't mean that, if you please. I mean after . . .

Henry IV. Ah, yes? After? One day [*Stops and addresses the* DOCTOR.]—A most interesting case, Doctor! Study me well! Study me carefully! [*Trembles while speaking.*] All by itself, who knows how, one day the trouble here [*touches his forehead*] mended. Little by little, I open my eyes, and at first I don't know whether I am asleep or awake. Then I know I am awake. I touch this thing and that; I see clearly again . . . Ah!—then, as *he* says [*alludes to* BELCREDI], away, away with this masquerade, this incubus! Let's open the windows, breathe life once again! Away! Away! Let's run out! [*Suddenly pulling himself up.*] But where? And to do what? To show myself to all, secretly, as Henry IV, not like this, but arm in arm with you, among my dear friends?

Belcredi. What are you saying?

Donna Matilda. Who could think it? It's not to be imagined. It was an accident.

Henry IV. They all said I was mad before. [*To* BELCREDI.] And you know it! You were more ferocious than any one against those who tried to defend me.

Belcredi. Oh, that was only a joke!

Henry IV. Look at my hair!

[*Shows him the hair on the nape of his neck.*]

Belcredi. But mine is gray too!

Henry IV. Yes, with this difference: that mine went gray here, as Henry IV, do you understand? And I never knew it! I perceived it all of a sudden, one day, when I opened my eyes; and I was terrified because I understood at once that not only had my hair gone gray, but that I was all gray, inside; that everything had fallen to pieces, that everything was finished; and I was going to arrive, hungry as a wolf, at a banquet which had already been cleared away . . .

Belcredi. Yes, but what about the others? . . .

Henry IV. [*Quickly.*] Ah, yes, I know! They couldn't wait until I was cured, not even those, who, behind my back, pricked my saddled horse till it bled. . . .

Di Nolli. [*Agitated.*] What, what?

Henry IV. Yes, treacherously, to make it rear and cause me to fall.

Donna Matilda. [*Quickly, in horror.*] This is the first time I knew that.

Henry IV. That was also a joke, probably!

Donna Matilda. But who did it? Who was behind us, then?

Henry IV. It doesn't matter who it was. All those that went on feasting and were ready to leave me their scrapings, Marchioness, of miserable pity, or some dirty remnant of remorse in the filthy plate! Thanks! [*Turning quickly to the* DOCTOR.] Now, Doctor, the case must be absolutely new in the history of madness; I preferred to remain mad—since I found everything ready and at my disposal for this new exquisite fantasy. I would live it—this madness of mine—with the most lucid consciousness; and thus revenge myself on the brutality of a stone which had dented my head. The solitude—this solitude—squalid and empty as it appeared to me when I opened my eyes again—I determined to deck it out with all the colors and splendors of that far-off day of carnival, when you [*looks at* DONNA MATILDA *and points* FRIDA *out to her*], when you, Marchioness, triumphed. So I would oblige all those who were around me to follow, by God, at my orders that famous pageant which had been—for you and not for me—the jest of a day. I would make it become—for ever—no more a joke but a reality, the reality of a real madness: here, all in masquerade, with throne room, and these my four secret counsellors: secret and, of course, traitors. [*He turns quickly toward them.*] I should like to know what you have gained by revealing the fact that I was cured! If I am cured, there's no longer any need of you, and you will be discharged! To give anyone one's confidence . . . that is really the act of a madman. But now I accuse you in my turn! [*Turning to the others.*] Do you know? They thought [*alludes to the* VALETS] they could make fun of me too with you.

[*Bursts out laughing. The others laugh, but shamefacedly, except* DONNA MATILDA.]

Belcredi. [*To* DI NOLLI.] Well, imagine that . . . That's not bad . . .

Di Nolli. [*To the four* YOUNG MEN.] You?

Henry IV. We must pardon them. This dress [*plucking his dress*] which is for me the evident, involuntary caricature of that other continuous, everlasting masquerade, of which we are the involuntary puppets [*indicates* BELCREDI], when, without knowing it, we mask ourselves with that which we appear to be . . . ah, that dress of theirs, this masquerade of theirs, of course, we must forgive it them, since they do not yet see it is identical with themselves . . . [*Turning again to* BELCREDI.] You know, it is quite easy to get accustomed to it. One walks about as a tragic character, just as if it were nothing . . . [*imitates the tragic manner*] in a room like this . . . Look here, Doctor! I remember a priest, certainly Irish, a nice-looking priest, who was sleeping in the sun one November day, with his arm on the corner of the bench of a public garden. He was lost in the golden delight of the mild sunny air which must have seemed for him almost summery. One may be sure that in that moment he did not know any more that he was a priest, or even where he was. He was dreaming . . . A little boy passed with a flower in his hand. He touched the priest with it here on the neck. I saw him open his laughing eyes, while all his mouth smiled with the beauty of his dream. He was forgetful of everything . . . But all at once, he pulled himself together, and stretched out his priest's cassock; and there came back to his eyes the same seriousness which you have seen in mine; because the Irish priests defend the seriousness of their Catholic faith with the same zeal with which I defend the secret rights of hereditary monarchy! I am cured, gentlemen: because I can act the madman to perfection, here; and I do it very quietly. I'm only sorry for you that have to live your madness so agitatedly, without knowing it or seeing it.

Belcredi. It comes to this, then, that it is we who are mad. That's what it is!

Henry IV. [*Containing his irritation.*] But if you weren't mad, both you and she [*indicating the* MARCHIONESS], would you have come here to see me?

Belcredi. To tell the truth, I came here believing that you were the madman.

Henry IV. [*Suddenly indicating the* MARCHIONESS.] And she?

Belcredi. Ah, as for her . . . I can't say. I see she is all fascinated by your words, by this *conscious* madness of yours. [*Turns to her.*] Dressed as you are [*speaking to her*], you could even remain here to live it out, Marchioness.

Donna Matilda. You are insolent!

Henry IV. [*Conciliatingly.*] No, Marchioness, what he means to say is that the miracle would be complete, according to him, with you here, who—as the Marchioness of Tuscany, you well know,—could not be my friend, save, as at Canossa, to give me a little pity . . .

Belcredi. Or even more than a little! She said so herself!

Henry IV. [*To the* MARCHIONESS, *continuing.*] And even, shall we say, a little remorse. . .

Belcredi. Yes, that too she has admitted.

Donna Matilda. [*Angry.*] Now look here . . .

Henry IV. [*Quickly, to placate her.*] Don't bother about him! Don't mind him! Let him go on infuriating me—though the Doctor's told him not to. [*Turns to* BELCREDI.] But do you suppose I am going to trouble myself any more about what happened between us—the share you had in my misfortune with her [*indicates the* MARCHIONESS *to him and, pointing* BELCREDI *out to her*]: the part he has now in your life? This is my life! Quite a different thing from your life! Your life, the life in which you have grown old—I have not lived that life.

[*To* DONNA MATILDA.] Was this what you wanted to show me with this sacrifice of yours, dressing yourself up like this, according to the Doctor's idea? Excellently done, Doctor! Oh, an excellent idea:—"As we were then, eh? and as we are now?" But I am not a madman according to your way of thinking, Doctor. I know very well that that man there [*indicates* DI NOLLI] cannot be me; because I am Henry IV, and have been, these twenty years, cast in this eternal masquerade. She has lived these years! [*Indicates the* MARCHIONESS.] She has enjoyed them and has become—look at her!—a woman I can no longer recognize. It is so that I knew her! [*Points to* FRIDA *and draws near her.*] This is the Marchioness I know, always this one! . . . You seem a lot of children to be so easily frightened by me . . . [*To* FRIDA.] And you're frightened too, little girl, aren't you, by the jest that they made you take part in—though they didn't understand it wouldn't be the jest they meant it to be, for me? Oh miracle of miracles! Prodigy of prodigies! The dream alive in you! More than alive in you! It was an image that wavered there and they've made you come to life! Oh, mine! You're mine, mine, mine, in my own right! [*He holds her in his arms, laughing like a madman, while all stand still terrified. Then as they advance to tear* FRIDA *from his arms, he becomes furious, terrible, and cries imperiously to his* VALETS.] Hold them! Hold them! I order you to hold them!

[*The four* YOUNG MEN *amazed, yet fascinated, move to execute his orders, automatically, and seize* DI NOLLI, *the* DOCTOR, *and* BELCREDI.]

Belcredi. [*Freeing himself.*] Leave her alone! Leave her alone! You're no madman!

Henry IV. [*In a flash draws the sword from the side of* LANDOLPH, *who is close to him.*] I'm not mad, eh! Take that, you! . . .

[*Drives sword into him. A cry of horror goes up. All rush over to assist* BELCREDI, *crying out together.*]

Di Nolli. Has he wounded you?

Berthold. Yes, yes, seriously!

Doctor. I told you so!

Frida. Oh God, oh God!

Di Nolli. Frida, come here!

Donna Matilda. He's mad, mad!

Di Nolli. Hold him!

Belcredi. [*While they take him away by the left exit, he protests as he is borne out.*] No, no, you're not mad! You're not mad. He's not mad!

[*They go out by the left amid cries and excitement. After a moment, one hears a still sharper, more piercing cry from* DONNA MATILDA, *and then, silence.*]

Henry IV. [*Who has remained on the stage between* LANDOLPH, HAROLD, *and* ORDULPH, *with his eyes almost starting out of his head, terrified by the life of his own masquerade which has driven him to crime.*] Ah now . . . yes now . . . inevitably [*calls his* VALETS *around him as if to protect him*] here together . . . here together . . . for ever . . . for ever.

CURTAIN

ENGLISH AND IRISH PLAYS

ENGLISH AND IRISH PLAYS

Riders to the Sea	Synge
Hyacinth Halvey	Gregory
What Every Woman Knows	Barrie
Mid-Channel	Pinero
The Glittering Gate	Dunsany
Justice	Galsworthy
Mr. Pim Passes By	Milne
The Circle	Maugham
Loyalties	Galsworthy
Dear Brutus	Barrie
Juno and the Paycock	O'Casey

RIDERS TO THE SEA*

By

JOHN MILLINGTON SYNGE

"He belonged to those who, like Wordsworth, like Coleridge, like Goldsmith, like Keath, have little personality, as far as the casual eye can see, little personal will, but fiery brooding imagination." These words, from Synge's closest friend, W. B. Yeats, give the clue to the character and work of this almost unknowable dramatist.

At first sight, a play by Synge appears to be the work of an unschooled and primitive observer who reports, as if by chance, with the instinct of genius for the significant. Synge, on the contrary, was almost moribund with education and culture before he discovered the true bent of his faculties. He had become proficient in music, well-read in four languages, and classically inclined to the point of composing a worshipful study of Racine, when Yeats "discovered" him in a Paris garret. The previous year, however, Synge had come under the spell of life in the Aran Islands. Yeats had little difficulty in winning him from his "literary" pursuits to join the young Irish renaissance and to return to the Aran Islands for his material.

Few dramatists have come to their task with a wider background or set about it in a more workmanlike manner. First, he observed and made copious notes, then selected and compressed, and finally shaped with unerring craftsmanship. In method, he seems never to have experimented, but to have created with perfect mastery from the beginning.

In 1902, John Masefield found him in London at work on his first plays, probably *The Tinker's Wedding, In the Shadow of the Glen,* and *Riders to the Sea*. The English poet described him as "a strange personality," with a face "dark from gravity," as though "the man behind were forever listening to life's case before passing judgment." His voice had "a kind of lively bitterness in it." This dour exterior was offset by "a humorous mouth, the kindling in the eyes and something robust in his build." In conversation, though always polite, "he offered nothing of his own." His interest was "in life, not in ideas." He composed slowly on a typewriter and rewrote each play several times. Friends gathered to hear his first plays read, and from their verdict "Synge learned his métier that night."

In the Shadow of the Glen was given by the newly organized Irish National Theatre Company on October 8, 1903. In 1904, this company moved into its now famous home, the Abbey Theatre, and appointed Synge to cooperate with W. B. Yeats and Lady Gregory as adviser. He gave the rest of his life to this enterprise. His *Riders to the Sea* was produced that year. The hostility that Synge's work created is now difficult to understand, but it proved to be excellent publicity, and, what was more important, it fired the workers for the Theatre with loyalty to their artistic standards and with the fighting spirit. *In the Shadow of the Glen* had profaned the romantic conception of Ireland's womanhood and *The Playboy of the Western World* (1907) had spoiled the idyllic belief in the Irish peasant's unsullied virtue. Synge was astonished at the turmoil he had unsuspectingly aroused and his already weakened constitution was severely strained. He had counted too much on the Irish sense of humor. The loyalty of W. B. Yeats and Lady Gregory and their faith in his ultimate triumph are among the brightest records of modern drama. A futile operation cut short his life before his sixth play, *Deirdre of the Sorrows,* had been completed. He died in a nursing home on March 24, 1909.

In Synge's plays, the poetic and dramatic insight of the reader is subjected to a searching test. They depend hardly at all on the unessential—theatricality, exploitation of ideas, moralizing, and sentimentality. They are rather the work of the true poet-dramatist who substitutes for theatrical mechanism the reality of life itself, reporting it not photographically, but with a sensitive discernment for dramatic values, for color, rhythm, and form, and, above all, for psychological reality. It is, therefore, easy to fall into George Moore's rather snobbish error of pronouncing *Riders to the Sea,* for instance, essentially undramatic because of the absence of obvious theatrical conflict. If, however, the dramatic greatness of *Œdipus, Hamlet, Faustus,* and *The Misanthrope* lies not in their externals but in their presentation of a progressive spiritual reaction to an inscrutable destiny, by means of perfectly conceived characters and dialogue truthfully colored, then *Riders to the Sea* is the masterpiece it has been pronounced. One must, however, read all of Synge to appreciate his breadth and versatility. The wild riot of humor in *The Playboy* and *The Tinker's Wedding* is, perhaps, truer to his mentality than the tragic beauty of *Riders to the Sea.*

He wrote comparatively little about himself and was not inclined to abstract thinking even about his art. What he wrote was, nevertheless, highly significant and true to the best critical standards.

COMMENTS CONCERNING DRAMA

"The drama is made serious, in the French sense of the word, not by the degree in which it is taken up with problems that are serious in themselves, but by the degree in which it gives the nourishment, not very easy to define, on which our imaginations live. . . . In these days, the playhouse is too often stocked with the drugs of many seedy problems, or with the absinthe or vermouth of the last musical comedy. Of the things that nourish the imagination, humor is one of the most needful."

"The drama, like the symphony, does not teach or prove anything. Analysts with their problems, and teachers with their systems, are soon as old-fashioned as the pharmacopœia of Galen—look at Ibsen and the Germans—but the best plays of Ben Jonson and Molière can no more go out of fashion than the blackberries on the hedges."

Preface to *The Tinker's Wedding.*

"In writing *The Playboy of the Western World,* as in my other plays, I have used one or two words only that I have not heard among the country people of Ireland, or spoken in my own nursery before I could read the newspapers. . . . I am glad to acknowledge how much I owe to the folk imagination of these fine people."

"All art is a collaboration, and there is little doubt that in the happy ages of literature, striking and beautiful phrases were as ready to the story-teller's or the playwright's hand, as the rich cloaks and dresses of his time. I got more aid than any learning could have given me from a chink in the floor of the old Wicklow house where I was staying, that let me hear what was being said by the servant girls in the kitchen."

"On the stage, one must have reality and one must have joy, and that is why the intellectual modern drama has failed . . . the joy found only in what is superb and wild in reality. In a good play every speech should be as fully flavored as a nut or apple, and such speeches cannot be written by anyone who works among people who have shut their lips on poetry. In Ireland, for a few years more, we have a popular imagination that is fiery, and magnificent, and tender."

Preface to *The Playboy of the Western World.*

PRODUCTION

Synge's *In the Shadow of the Glen* was presented in a small and badly adapted hall on October 8, 1903, as one of the first offerings of the newly formed Irish National Theatre Company, and *Riders to the Sea* was produced by the same company in 1904 after the opening of their Abbey Theatre.* This Theatre, now among the most famous of modern playhouses, and the first government subsidized theatre in the English-speaking world, was presented outright for a period of five years by Miss A. E. F. Horniman, who had been deeply impressed by the work of the Irish players when they appeared the previous year at Queen's Gate Hall in London. The auditorium, dating from 1820, seats 562 persons, and is in the horseshoe form with one balcony. The stage is only fifteen feet deep. The curtain is black with gold stripes and the signal for its rising is a deep-toned gong. Original lighting, by no means elaborate, produced a glow, rather than a glare, giving an artistic effect that was perhaps not calculated.

The style of acting which the company developed was something new in the theatre of its period and was immediately recognized as artistically superior to anything known in the professional theatre. The brothers Fay, who headed the work of production, contributed a professional but not conventional tone to the work of this unpaid and amateur

* See note on *Hyacinth Halvey,* p. 539.

troup. Frank Fay, skilled in speech production, insisted from the beginning upon a musical and vigorous delivery that has always distinguished the work of the company. It imparted to prose, especially that of Synge, the rhythm and tonality of poetry, as was clearly the author's intention, but never to the extent of losing its simple naturalism. Of one of Synge's plays given at this theater George Moore wrote: "I would call attention to the abundance of the beauty of the dialogue, to the fact that one listened to it as one listens to music, charmed by the inevitableness of the words and the ease with which phrase is linked with phrase. . . . Mr. Synge has also discovered great literature in barbarous idiom as gold is discovered in quartz."

When the company played in London, inviting direct comparison with the expert acting of the reigning naturalistic school, the London critics were even more impressed. A. B. Walkley, of the *Times,* found the effect produced "quite outside the range of anything which those houses (the public theaters) have to offer." He noted especially their naturalness that appeared artless, although in reality it was carefully studied: "They stand stock still," he wrote; "the speaker of the moment is the only one who is allowed a little gesture. . . . The listeners do not distract one's attention with fussy stage business; they just stay where they are and listen."

A writer in the *Manchester Guardian* caught the significance of the new art: "These Irish actors have contrived to reach back past most of the futilities that have grown upon the ordinary theater of commerce and get a fresh, clean hold on their craft in its elements. They know how to let things alone, how to stand still when nothing it to be done . . . how to save up the voice and gesture for rare and brief passages of real poignancy, how to fade into the background."

JOHN MILLINGTON SYNGE

Born 1871, Newton Little, near Dublin.

Son of a thrifty landowner.

Studied music and prepared with tutors for Trinity College, Dublin.

1892, Degree of A.B., Trinity College. Prize in harmony and counterpoint at the Royal Irish Academy.

1893, Continued study of music in Germany.

1894, Abandoned music for a literary career in Paris.

1896, Toured Italy.

1898, Visited the Aran Islands.

1899, Discovered in Paris by W. B. Yeats, who advised him to abandon literary criticism for a life of creative writing, and to return to the Aran Islands for his material.

1902, Worked on his first plays in London.

1903, *In the Shadow of the Glen* produced by the Irish National Theatre Company.

1904, Made adviser of this company in their new Abbey Theatre.

1909, Died after an operation for a cancerous growth.

PLAYS

1903 *In the Shadow of the Glen.* 1904 *Riders to the Sea.* 1905 *The Well of the Saints.* 1907 *The Playboy of the Western World.* 1909 *The Tinker's Wedding* (published, but written earlier). 1910 *Deirdre of the Sorrows* (published).

WRITINGS ABOUT THE DRAMA

Preface to *The Playboy of the Western World,* 1907. Preface to *The Tinker's Wedding,* 1909.

RIDERS TO THE SEA

Characters

MAURYA, *an old woman.*
BARTLEY, *her son.*
CATHLEEN, *her daughter.*
NORA, *a younger daughter.*
MEN *and* WOMEN.

SCENE.—*An island off the West of Ireland. Cottage kitchen, with nets, oilskins, spinning-wheel, some new boards standing by the wall, etc.* CATHLEEN, *a girl of about twenty, finishes kneading cake, and puts it down in the pot-oven by the fire; then wipes her hands, and begins to spin at the wheel.* NORA, *a young girl, puts her head in at the door.*

Nora. [*In a low voice.*] Where is she?

Cathleen. She's lying down, God help her, and may be sleeping, if she's able.

[NORA *comes in softly, and takes a bundle from under her shawl.*]

Cathleen. [*Spinning the wheel rapidly.*] What is it you have?

Nora. The young priest is after bringing them. It's a shirt and a plain stocking were got off a drowned man in Donegal.

[CATHLEEN *stops her wheel with a sudden movement, and leans out to listen.*]

Nora. We're to find out if it's Michael's they are, some time herself will be down looking by the sea.

Cathleen. How would they be Michael's, Nora? How would he go the length of that way to the far north?

Nora. The young priest says he's known the like of it. "If it's Michael's they are," says he, "you can tell herself he's got a clean burial by the grace of God, and if they're not his, let no one say a word about them, for she'll be getting her death," says he, "with crying and lamenting."

[*The door which* NORA *half closed is blown open by a gust of wind.*]

Cathleen. [*Looking out anxiously.*] Did you ask him would he stop Bartley going this day with the horses to the Galway fair?

Nora. "I won't stop him," says he, "but let you not be afraid. Herself does be saying prayers half through the night, and the Almighty God won't leave her destitute," says he, "with no son living."

Cathleen. Is the sea bad by the white rocks, Nora?

Nora. Middling bad, God help us. There's a great roaring in the west, and it's worse it'll be getting when the tide's turned to the wind. [*She goes over to the table with the bundle.*] Shall I open it now?

Cathleen. Maybe she'd wake up on us, and come in before we'd done. [*Coming to the table.*] It's a long time we'll be, and the two of us crying.

Nora. [*Goes to the inner door and listens.*] She's moving about on the bed. She'll be coming in a minute.

Cathleen. Give me the ladder, and I'll put them up in the turf-loft, the way she won't know of them at all, and maybe when the tide turns she'll be going down to see would he be floating from the east.

[*They put the ladder against the gable of the chimney;* CATHLEEN *goes up a few steps and hides the bundle in the turf-loft.* MAURYA *comes in from the inner room.*]

Maurya. [*Looking up at* CATHLEEN *and speaking querulously.*] Isn't it turf enough you have for this day and evening?

Cathleen. There's a cake baking at the fire for a short space [*throwing down the turf*] and Bartley will want it when the tide turns if he goes to Connemara.

[NORA *picks up the turf and puts it round the pot-oven.*]

Maurya. [*Sitting down on a stool at the fire.*] He won't go this day with the wind rising from the south and west. He won't go this day, for the young priest will stop him surely.

Nora. He'll not stop him, Mother, and I heard Eamon Simon and Stephen Pheety and Colum Shawn saying he would go.

Maurya. Where is he itself?

Nora. He went down to see would there be another boat sailing in the week, and I'm thinking it won't be long till he's here now, for the tide's turning at the green head, and the hooker's tacking from the east.

Cathleen. I hear some one passing the big stones.

Nora. [*Looking out.*] He's coming now, and he in a hurry.

Bartley. [*Comes in and looks round the room. Speaking sadly and quietly.*] Where is the bit of new rope, Cathleen, was bought in Connemara?

Cathleen. [*Coming down.*] Give it to him. Nora; it's on a nail by the white boards. I hung it up this morning, for the pig with the black feet was eating it.

Nora. [*Giving him a rope.*] Is that it, Bartley?

Maurya. You'd do right to leave that rope, Bartley, hanging by the boards. [BARTLEY *takes the rope.*] It will be wanting in this place, I'm telling you, if Michael is washed up tomorrow morning, or the next morning, or any morning in the week, for it's a deep grave we'll make him by the grace of God.

Bartley. [*Beginning to work with the rope.*] I've no halter the way I can ride down on the mare, and I must go now quickly. This is the one boat going for two weeks or beyond it, and the fair will be a good fair for horses, I heard them saying below.

Maurya. It's a hard thing they'll be saying below if the body is washed up and there's no man in it to make the coffin, and I after giving a big price for the finest white boards you'd find in Connemara.

[*She looks around at the boards.*]

Bartley. How would it be washed up, and we after looking each day for nine days, and a strong wind blowing a while back from the west and south?

Maurya. If it wasn't found itself, that wind is raising the sea, and there was a star up against the moon, and it rising in the night. If it was a hundred horses, or a thousand horses you had itself, what is the price of a thousand horses against a son where there is one son only?

Bartley. [*Working at the halter, to* CATHLEEN.] Let you go down each day, and see the sheep aren't jumping in on the rye, and if the jobber comes you can sell the pig with the black feet if there is a good price going.

Maurya. How would the like of her get a good price for a pig?

Bartley. [*To* CATHLEEN.] If the west wind holds with the last bit of the moon let you and Nora get up weed enough for another cock for the kelp. It's hard set we'll be from this day with no one in it but one man to work.

Maurya. It's hard set we'll be surely the day you're drownd'd with the rest. What way will I live and the girls with me, and I an old woman looking for the grave?

[BARTLEY *lays down the halter, takes off his old coat, and puts on a newer one of the same flannel.*]

Bartley. [*To* NORA.] Is she coming to the pier?

Nora. [*Looking out.*] She's passing the green head and letting fall her sails.

Bartley. [*Getting his purse and tobacco.*] I'll have half an hour to go down, and you'll see me coming again in two days, or in three days, or maybe in four days if the wind is bad.

Maurya. [*Turning around to the fire, and putting her shawl over her head.*] Isn't it a hard and cruel man won't hear a word from an old woman, and she holding him from the sea?

Cathleen. It's the life of a young man to be going on the sea, and who would listen to an old woman with one thing and she saying it over?

Bartley. [*Taking the halter.*] I must go now quickly. I'll ride down on the red mare, and the gray pony'll run behind me. . . . The blessing of God on you. [*He goes out.*]

Maurya. [*Crying out as he is in the door.*] He's gone now, God spare us, and we'll not see him again. He's gone now, and when the black night is falling I'll have no son left me in the world.

Cathleen. Why wouldn't you give him your blessing and he looking round in the door? Isn't it sorrow enough is on every one in this house without your sending him out with an unlucky word behind him, and a hard word in his ear?

[MAURYA *takes up the tongs and begins raking the fire aimlessly without looking around.*]

Nora. [*Turning toward her.*] You're taking away the turf from the cake.

Cathleen. [*Crying out.*] The Son of God forgive us, Nora, we're after forgetting his bit of bread. [*She comes over to the fire.*]

Nora. And it's destroyed he'll be going till dark night, and he after eating nothing since the sun went up.

Cathleen. [*Turning the cake out of the oven.*] It's destroyed he'll be, surely. There's no sense left in any person in a house where an old woman will be talking forever.

[MAURYA *sways herself on her stool.*]

Cathleen. [*Cutting off some of the bread and rolling it in a cloth; to* MAURYA.] Let you go down now to the spring well and give him this and he passing. You'll see him then and the dark word will be broken, and you can say "God speed you," the way he'll be easy in his mind.

Maurya. [*Taking the bread.*] Will I be in it as soon as himself?

Cathleen. If you go now quickly.

Maurya. [*Standing up unsteadily.*] It's hard set I am to walk.

Cathleen. [*Looking at her anxiously.*] Give her the stick, Nora, or maybe she'll slip on the big stones.

Nora. What stick?

Cathleen. The stick Michael brought from Connemara.

Maurya. [*Taking a stick* NORA *gives her.*] In the big world the old people do be leaving things after them for their sons and children, but in this place it is the young men do be leaving things behind for them that do be old.

[*She goes out slowly.* NORA *goes over to the ladder.*]

Cathleen. Wait, Nora, maybe she'd turn back quickly. She's that sorry, God help her, you wouldn't know the thing she'd do.

Nora. Is she gone round by the bush?

Cathleen. [*Looking out.*] She's gone now. Throw it down quickly, for the Lord knows when she'll be out of it again.

Nora. [*Getting the bundle from the loft.*] The young priest said he'd be passing to-morrow, and we might go down and speak to him below if it's Michael's they are surely.

Cathleen. [*Taking the bundle.*] Did he say what way they were found?

Nora. [*Coming down.*] "There were two men," says he, "and they rowing round with poteen before the cocks crowed, and the oar of one of them caught the body, and they passing the black cliffs of the north."

Cathleen. [*Trying to open the bundle.*] Give me a knife, Nora, the string's perished with the salt water, and here's a black knot on it you wouldn't loosen in a week.

Nora. [*Giving her a knife.*] I've heard tell it was a long way to Donegal.

Cathleen. [*Cutting the string.*] It is surely. There was a man in here a while ago—the man sold us that knife—and he said if you set off walking from the rocks beyond, it would be seven days you'd be in Donegal.

Nora. And what time would a man take, and he floating?

[CATHLEEN *opens the bundle and takes out a bit of stocking. They look at them eagerly.*]

Cathleen. [*In a low voice.*] The Lord spare us, Nora! Isn't it a queer hard thing to say if it's his they are surely?

Nora. I'll get his shirt off the hook the way we can put the one flannel on the other. [*She looks through some clothes hanging in the corner.*] It's not with them, Cathleen, and where will it be?

Cathleen. I'm thinking Bartley put it on him in the morning, for his own shirt was heavy with the salt in it. [*Pointing to the corner.*] There's a bit of a sleeve was of the same stuff. Give me that and it will do.

[NORA *brings it to her and they compare the flannel.*]

Cathleen. It's the same stuff, Nora; but if it is itself aren't there great rolls of it in the shops of Galway, and isn't it many another man may have a shirt of it as well as Michael himself?

Nora. [*Who has taken up the stocking and counted the stitches, crying out.*] It's Michael, Cathleen, it's Michael; God spare his soul, and what will herself say when she hears this story, and Bartley on the sea?

Cathleen. [*Taking the stocking.*] It's a plain stocking.

Nora. It's the second one of the third pair I knitted, and I put up three score stitches, and I dropped four of them.

Cathleen. [*Counts the stitches.*] It's that number is in it. [*Crying out.*] Ah, Nora, isn't it a bitter thing to think of him floating that way to the far north, and no one to keen him but the black hags that do be flying on the sea?

Nora. [*Swinging herself around, and throwing out her arms on the clothes.*] And isn't it a pitiful thing when there is nothing left of a man who was a great rower and fisher, but a bit of an old shirt and a plain stocking?

Cathleen. [*After an instant.*] Tell me, is herself coming, Nora? I hear a little sound on the path.

Nora. [*Looking out.*] She is, Cathleen. She's coming up to the door.

Cathleen. Put these things away before she'll come in. Maybe it's easier she'll be after giving her blessing to Bartley, and we won't let on we've heard anything the time he's on the sea.

Nora. [*Helping* CATHLEEN *to close the bundle.*] We'll put them here in the corner.

[*They put them into a hole in the chimney corner.* CATHLEEN *goes back to the spinning-wheel.*]

Nora. Will she see it was crying I was?

Cathleen. Keep your back to the door the way the light'll not be on you.

[NORA *sits down at the chimney corner, with her back to the door.* MAURYA *comes in very slowly, without looking at the girls, and goes over to her stool at the other side of the fire. The cloth with the bread is still in her hand. The girls look at each other, and* NORA *points to the bundle of bread.*]

Cathleen. [*After spinning for a moment.*] You didn't give him his bit of bread?

[MAURYA *begins to keen softly, without turning around.*]

Cathleen. Did you see him riding down?

[MAURYA *goes on keening.*]

Cathleen. [*A little impatiently.*] God forgive you; isn't it a better thing to raise your voice and tell what you seen, than to be making lamentation for a thing that's done? Did you see Bartley, I'm saying to you.

Maurya. [*With a weak voice.*] My heart's broken from this day.

Cathleen. [*As before.*] Did you see Bartley?

Maurya. I seen the fearfulest thing.

Cathleen. [*Leaves her wheel and looks out.*] God forgive you; he's riding the mare now over the green head, and the gray pony behind him.

Maurya. [*Starts, so that her shawl falls back from her head and shows her white tossed hair. With a frightened voice.*] The gray pony behind him.

Cathleen. [*Coming to the fire.*] What is it ails you, at all?

Maurya. [*Speaking very slowly.*] I've seen the fearfulest thing any person has seen, since the day Bride Dara seen the dead man with the child in his arms.

Cathleen and Nora. Uah.

[*They crouch down in front of the old woman at the fire.*]

Nora. Tell us what it is you seen.

Maurya. I went down to the spring well, and I stood there saying a prayer to myself. Then Bartley came along, and he riding on the red mare with the gray pony behind him. [*She puts up her hands, as if to hide something from her eyes.*] The Son of God spare us, Nora!

Cathleen. What is it you seen?

Maurya. I seen Michael himself.

Cathleen. [*Speaking softly.*] You did not, Mother. It wasn't Michael you seen, for his body is after being found in the far north. and he's got a clean burial by the grace of God.

Maurya. [*A little defiantly.*] I'm after seeing him this day, and he riding and galloping. Bartley came first on the red mare; and I tried to say "God speed you," but something choked the words in my throat. He went by quickly; and "the blessing of God on you," says he, and I could say nothing. I looked up then, and I crying, at the gray pony, and there was Michael upon it—with fine clothes on him, and new shoes on his feet.

Cathleen. [*Begins to keen.*] It's destroyed we are from this day. It's destroyed, surely.

Nora. Didn't the young priest say the Almighty God wouldn't leave her destitute with no son living?

Maurya. [*In a low voice, but clearly.*] It's little the like of him knows of the sea. . . . Bartley will be lost now, and let you call in Eamon and make me a good coffin out of the white boards, for I won't live after them. I've had a husband, and a husband's father, and six sons in this house—six fine men, though it was a hard birth I had with every one of them and they coming to the world—and some of them were found and some of them were not found, but they're gone now, the lot of them. . . . There were Stephen, and Shawn, were lost in the great wind, and found after in the Bay of Gregory of the Golden Mouth, and carried up the two of them on the one plank, and in by that door.

[*She pauses for a moment. The girls start as if they heard something through the door that is half open behind them.*]

Nora. [*In a whisper.*] Did you hear that, Cathleen? Did you hear a noise in the northeast?

Cathleen. [*In a whisper.*] There's some one after crying out by the seashore.

Maurya. [*Continues without hearing anything.*] There was Sheamus and his father, and his own father again, were lost in a dark night, and not a stick or sign was seen of them when the sun went up. There was Patch after was drowned out of a curagh that turned over. I was sitting here with Bartley, and he a baby, lying on my two knees, and I seen two women, and three women, and four women coming in, and they crossing themselves, and not saying a word. I looked out then, and there were men coming after them, and they holding a thing in the half of a red sail, and water dripping out of it—it was a dry day, Nora—and leaving a track to the door.

[*She pauses again with her hand stretched out toward the door. It opens softly and* OLD WOMEN *begin to come in, crossing themselves on the threshold, and kneeling down in front of the stage with red petticoats over their heads.*]

Maurya. [*Half in a dream, to* CATHLEEN.] Is it Patch, or Michael, or what is it at all?

Cathleen. Michael is after being found in the far north, and when he is found there how could he be here in this place?

Maurya. There does be a power of young men floating round in the sea, and what way would they know if it was Michael they had, or another man like him, for when a man is nine days in the sea, and the wind blowing, it's hard set his own mother would be to say what man was it.

Cathleen. It's Michael, God spare him, for they're after sending us a bit of clothes from the far north.

[*She reaches out and hands* MAURYA *the clothes that belong to* MICHAEL. MAURYA *stands up slowly, and takes them in her hands.* NORA *looks out.*]

Nora. They're carrying a thing among them and there's water dripping out of it and leaving a track by the big stones.

Cathleen. [*In a whisper to the women who have come in.*] Is it Bartley it is?

One of the Women. It is surely, God rest his soul.

[*Two* YOUNGER WOMEN *come in and pull out the table. Then* MEN *carry in the body of* BARTLEY, *laid on a plank, with a bit of a sail over it, and lay it on the table.*]

Cathleen. [*To the* WOMEN, *as they are doing so.*] What way was he drowned?

One of the Women. The gray pony knocked him into the sea, and he was washed out where there is a great surf on the white rocks.

[MAURYA *has gone over and knelt down at the head of the table. The* WOMEN *are keening softly and swaying themselves with a slow movement.* CATHLEEN *and* NORA *kneel at the other end of the table. The* MEN *kneel near the door.*]

Maurya. [*Raising her head and speaking as if she did not see the people around her.*] They're all gone now, and there isn't anything more the sea can do to me. . . . I'll have no call now to be up crying and praying when the wind breaks from the south, and you can hear the surf is in the east, and the surf is in the west, making a great stir with the two noises, and they hitting one on the other. I'll have no call now to be going down and getting Holy Water in the dark nights after Samhain, and I won't care what way the sea is when the other women will be keening. [*To* NORA.] Give me the Holy Water, Nora, there's a small sup still on the dresser.

[NORA *gives it to her.*]

Maurya. [*Drops* MICHAEL'S *clothes across* BARTLEY'S *feet, and sprinkles the Holy Water over him.*] It isn't that I haven't prayed for you, Bartley, to the Almighty God. It isn't that I haven't said prayers in the dark night till you wouldn't know what I'd be saying; but it's a great rest I'll have now, and it's time surely. It's a great rest I'll have now, and great sleeping in the long nights after Samhain, if it's only a bit of wet flour we do have to eat, and maybe a fish that would be stinking.

[*She kneels down again, crossing herself, and saying prayers under her breath.*]

Cathleen. [*To an* OLD MAN.] Maybe yourself and Eamon would make a coffin when the sun rises. We have fine white boards herself bought, God help her, thinking Michael would be found, and I have a new cake you can eat while you'll be working.

The Old Man. [*Looking at the boards.*] Are there nails with them?

Cathleen. There are not, Colum; we didn't think of the nails.

Another Man. It's a great wonder she wouldn't think of the nails, and all the coffins she's seen made already.

Cathleen. It's getting old she is, and broken.

[MAURYA *stands up again very slowly and spreads out the pieces of* MICHAEL'S *clothes beside the body, sprinkling them with the last of the Holy Water.*]

Nora. [*In a whisper to* CATHLEEN.] She's quiet now, and easy; but the day Michael was drowned you could hear her crying out from this to the spring well. It's fonder she was of Michael, and would any one have thought that?

Cathleen. [*Slowly and clearly.*] An old woman will be soon tired with anything she will do, and isn't it nine days herself is after crying and keening, and making great sorrow in the house?

Maurya. [*Puts the empty cup mouth downwards on the table, and lays her hands together on* BARTLEY'S *feet.*] They're all together this time, and the end is come. May the Almighty God have mercy on Bartley's soul, and on Michael's soul, and on the souls of Sheamus and Patch, and Stephen and Shawn. [*Bending her head.*] And may He have mercy on my soul, Nora, and on the soul of every one is left living in the world.

[*She pauses, and the keen rises a little more loudly from the* WOMEN, *then sinks away.*]

Maurya. [*Continuing.*] Michael has a clean burial in the far north, by the grace of the Almighty God. Bartley will have a fine coffin out of the white boards, and a deep grave surely. What more can we want than that? No man at all can be living forever, and we must be satisfied.

[*She kneels down again and the curtain falls slowly.*]

HYACINTH HALVEY *

By

LADY GREGORY

IN 1898, MR. EDWARD MARTYN AND MR. George Moore began activities looking to the establishment of an Irish theater. Mr. Martyn had found inspiration for the idea in the history of the Norwegian theater under Ibsen and Björnson, since he saw in Norway a country like Ireland, possessed of the slightest dramatic tradition, which had nevertheless risen to pre-eminence by the effort and determination of a few bold men. Mr. Martyn and Mr. Moore were soon joined by Mr. W. B. Yeats and Lady Gregory, and these four formed the Irish Literary Theatre, which, in 1899, produced Yeats's *Countess Cathleen* and Martyn's *Heather Field,* with a company imported from England. In 1900, three plays, one by Moore, one by Martyn, and one by Alice Milligan, were produced, and in 1901 a play by Yeats and Moore, and a play in Gaelic by Douglas Hyde. But these were the last performances by the Irish Literary Theatre, and the original group broke up, principally because of lack of funds. During 1902, however, a company of London-trained players, under the direction of Mr. W. G. Fay, calling itself the Irish National Theatre Company, gave some plays by Irish dramatists, notably Yeats's *Cathleen-ni-Houlihan* and *Pot of Broth.*

Finally, in 1903, sufficient backing was found for the Irish National Theatre Society, which, later incorporated, continued under the presidency of Mr. Yeats. During that year Lady Gregory's first play, *Twenty-five,* was performed, and also the first play of John Millington Synge, Ireland's greatest dramatist, *In the Shadow of the Glen.* In that same year, Miss A. E. Horniman, of Manchester, England, provided funds for the construction of the Abbey Theatre, which has been occupied since 1904.[1] There, in 1906, *Hyacinth Halvey* was first performed.

The Abbey Theatre is one more instance, therefore, of the Free Theatre movement which had so large an influence upon the drama during the late nineteenth and early twentieth centuries. In its origins and purposes, however, the Irish Theatre was more nationalistic than the Free Theatre of Antoine, the Independent Theatre of J. T. Grein, or the Moscow Art Theatre of Stanislavsky. It produced only the work of Irish playwrights until 1906, when a translation of Molière by Lady Gregory was performed. Even thereafter works by non-Irish dramatists were very rare. The Theatre purposed to develop Irish authors, and it succeeded. In addition to the playwrights already named, Lennox Robinson, St. John Ervine, Padraic Colum, Lord Dunsany, T. C. Murray, Sean O'Casey, and many others had their plays first performed there. This emphasis on national endeavor was perfectly natural in the Ireland of the time, and, of course, had its effect in strengthening still further the national self-consciousness which eventually resulted in the establishment of the Free State, though the Abbey Theatre was never a center of political propaganda. Eire now grants the Abbey an annual subsidy.

This remarkable success was due in large measure to Lady Gregory. Her talent as organizer kept in harmony the somewhat discordant personalities connected with the enterprise. She was the original Patentee, that is, holder of the state license to give plays. She accompanied the Irish Players on their first tour of the United States in 1911, which was very troublous because the American Irish in New York, Philadelphia, and Chicago opposed the Company's appearance on account of Synge's *Playboy of the Western World.* All through the Theatre's history she dedicated her mind and energy to its welfare.

She began her own playwriting for the Abbey because Yeats and Synge tended to lack light comedy and it was felt necessary

[1] See note on *Riders to the Sea,* p. 531 ff.

that some one should supply the Theatre with plays in a different mood from theirs. So Lady Gregory set herself to it. She had assisted in revision of the plays of other writers for the Theatre, notably Yeats, and so acquired some knowledge of play structure. Like the others, she drew for her characters and dialogue from the Irish folk themselves, especially the peasants in the neighborhood of her home in Connacht. Her works show that the Irish people may supply the artist with comic as well as tragic or poetic themes.

Her note to *Hyacinth Halvey* tells how a very respectable-appearing person was pointed out to her, with a story about him which made her wonder if that respectability might not now and again be a burden. She says also, "The idea was more of a universal one than I knew at the first, and I have had but an uneasy appreciation from some apparently blameless friends."

LADY GREGORY

Born 1859, Roxborough, County Galway, Ireland (Isabella Augusta Persse).
Married Sir William Gregory, 1881.
Translator and adaptor of folk-lore. One of the founders and a director of the Irish National Theatre.
Died 1932.

PLAYS

1902 *Twenty-five.* 1904 *Spreading the News.* 1905 *Kincora.* 1905 *The White Cockade.* 1906 *Hyacinth Halvey.* 1906 *The Doctor in Spite of Himself* (translated and adapted from Molière). 1906 *The Gaol Gate.* 1906 *The Canavans.* 1907 *The Jackdaw.* 1907 *The Rising of the Moon.* 1907 *The Poorhouse* (with Douglas Hyde). 1907 *Dervorgilla.* 1907 *The Unicorn from the Stars* (with W. B. Yeats). 1908 *Teja* (translated from Sudermann). 1908 *The Rogueries of Scapin* (translated from Molière). 1908 *The Workhouse Ward.* 1909 *The Miser* (translated from Molière). 1909 *The Image.* 1910 *Mirandolina* (translated from Goldoni). 1910 *The Travelling Man.* 1910 *The Full Moon.* 1910 *Coats.* 1911 *The Nativity Play* (translated from Douglas Hyde's Gaelic). 1911 *The Deliverer.* 1912 *McDarragh's Wife* (later *McDonough's Wife*). 1912 *The Bogie Men.* 1912 *Damer's Gold.* 1912 *Grania.* 1915 *Shanwalla.* 1915 *Hanrahan's Oath.* 1915 *The Wrens.* 1916 *The Golden Apple.* 1919 *The Dragon.* 1921 *The Jester.* 1921 *Aristotle's Bellows.* 1924 *The Story Brought by Brigit.* 1925 *On the Racecourse.* 1926 *Dave.* 1926 *The Would-be Gentleman* (translated from Molière). 1927 *Sancho's Master.*

WRITING ABOUT THE THEATER

Our Irish Theatre, 1913.

HYACINTH HALVEY

Persons

HYACINTH HALVEY.
JAMES QUIRKE, *a butcher.*
FARDY FARRELL, *a telegraph boy.*
SERGEANT CARDEN.
MRS. DELANE, *postmistress at Cloon.*
MISS JOYCE, *the priest's housekeeper.*

SCENE.—*Outside the Post Office at the little town of Cloon.* MRS. DELANE *at Post Office door.* MR. QUIRKE *sitting on a chair at butcher's door. A dead sheep hanging beside it, and a thrush in a cage above.* FARDY FARRELL *playing on a mouth organ. Train whistle heard.*

Mrs. Delane. There is the four o'clock train, Mr. Quirke.

Mr. Quirke. Is it now, Mrs. Delane, and I not long after rising? It makes a man drowsy to be doing the half of his work in the night time. Going about the country, looking for little stags of sheep, striving to knock a few shillings together. That contract for the soldiers gives me a great deal to attend to.

Mrs. Delane. I suppose so. It's hard enough on myself to be down ready for the mail car in the morning, sorting letters in the half dark. It's often I haven't time to look who are the letters from—or the cards.

Mr. Quirke. It would be a pity you not to know any little news might be knocking about. If you did not have information of what is going on, who should have it? Was it you, ma'am, was telling me that the new Sub-Sanitary Inspector would be arriving today?

Mrs. Delane. Today it is he is coming, and it's likely he was in that train. There was a card about him to Sergeant Carden this morning.

Mr. Quirke. A young chap from Carrow they were saying he was.

Mrs. Delane. So he is, one Hyacinth Halvey; and, indeed, if all that is said of him is true, or if a quarter of it is true, he will be a credit to this town.

Mr. Quirke. Is that so?

Mrs. Delane. Testimonials he has by the score. To Father Gregan they were sent. Registered they were coming and going. Would you believe me telling you that they weighed up to three pounds?

Mr. Quirke. There must be great bulk in them indeed.

Mrs. Delane. It is no wonder he to get the job. He must have a great character so many persons to write for him as what there did.

Fardy. It would be a great thing to have a character like that.

Mrs. Delane. Indeed, I am thinking it will be long before you will get the like of it, Fardy Farrell.

Fardy. If I had the like of that of a character it is not here carrying messages I would be. It's in Noonan's Hotel I would be, driving cars.

Mr. Quirke. Here is the priest's housekeeper coming.

Mrs. Delane. So she is; and there is the Sergeant a little while after her.

[*Enter* MISS JOYCE.]

Mrs. Delane. Good evening to you, Miss Joyce. What way is his Reverence today? Did he get any ease from the cough?

Miss Joyce. He did not, indeed, Mrs. Delane. He has it sticking to him yet. Smothering he is in the night time. The most thing he comes short in is the voice.

Mrs. Delane. I am sorry, now, to hear that. He should mind himself well.

Miss Joyce. It's easy to say let him mind himself. What do you say to him going to the meeting tonight? [SERGEANT *comes in.*] It's for his Reverence's *Freeman* I am come, Mrs. Delane.

Mrs. Delane. Here it is ready. I was just throwing an eye on it to see was there any news. Good evening, Sergeant.

Sergeant. [*Holding up a placard.*] I brought this notice, Mrs. Delane, the announcement of the meeting to be held tonight in the Courthouse. You might put it up here convenient to the window. I hope you are coming to it yourself?

Mrs. Delane. I will come, and welcome. I would do more than that for you, Sergeant.

Sergeant. And you, Mr. Quirke?

Mr. Quirke. I'll come, to be sure. I forget what's this the meeting is about.

Sergeant. The Department of Agriculture is sending round a lecturer in furtherance of the moral development of the rural classes. [*Reads.*] "A lecture will be given this evening in Cloon Courthouse, illustrated by magic-lantern slides——" Those will not be in it; I am informed they were all broken in the first journey, the railway company taking them to be eggs. The subject of the lecture is "The Building of Character."

Mrs. Delane. Very nice, indeed. I knew a girl lost her character, and she washed her feet in a blessed well after, and it dried up on the minute.

Sergeant. The arrangements have all been left to me, the Archdeacon being away. He knows I have a good intellect for things of the sort. But the loss of those slides puts a man out. The thing people will not see it is not likely it is the thing they will believe. I saw what they call tableaux—standing pictures, you know—one time in Dundrum——

Mrs. Delane. Miss Joyce was saying Father Gregan is supporting you.

Sergeant. I am accepting his assistance. No bigotry about me when there is a question of the welfare of any fellow-creatures. Orange and green will stand together tonight. I myself and the station-master on the one side; your parish priest in the chair.

Miss Joyce. If his Reverence would mind me he would not quit the house tonight. He is no more fit to go speak at a meeting than [*pointing to the one hanging outside* QUIRKE's *door*] that sheep.

Sergeant. I am willing to take the responsibility. He will have no speaking to do at all, unless it might be to bid them give the lecturer a hearing. The loss of those slides now is a great annoyance to me—and no time for anything. The lecturer will be coming by the next train.

Miss Joyce. Who is this coming up the street, Mrs. Delane?

Mrs. Delane. I wouldn't doubt it to be the new Sub-Sanitary Inspector. Was I telling you of the weight of the testimonials he got, Miss Joyce?

Miss Joyce. Sure I heard the curate reading them to his Reverence. He must be a wonder for principles.

Mrs. Delane. Indeed, it is what I was saying to myself, he must be a very saintly young man.

[*Enter* HYACINTH HALVEY. *He carries a small bag and a large brown paper parcel. He stops and nods bashfully.*]

Hyacinth. Good evening to you. I was bid to come to the Post Office——

Sergeant. I suppose you are Hyacinth Halvey? I had a letter about you from the Resident Magistrate.

Hyacinth. I heard he was writing. It was my mother got a friend he deals with to ask him.

Sergeant. He gives you a very high character.

Hyacinth. It is very kind of him indeed, and he not knowing me at all. But indeed all the neighbors were very friendly. Anything any one could do to help me they did it.

Mrs. Delane. I'll engage it is the testimonials you have in your parcel? I know the wrapping paper, but they grew in bulk since I handled them.

Hyacinth. Indeed, I was getting them to the last. There was not one refused me. It is what my mother was saying, a good character is no burden.

Fardy. I would believe that indeed.

Sergeant. Let us have a look at the testimonials.

[HYACINTH HALVEY *opens parcel, and a large number of envelopes fall out.*]

Sergeant. [*Opening and reading one by one.*] "He possesses the fire of the Gael, the strength of the Norman, the vigor of the Dane, the stolidity of the Saxon——"

Hyacinth. It was the Chairman of the Poor Law Guardians wrote that.

Sergeant. "A magnificent example to old and young——"

Hyacinth. That was the Secretary of the De Wet Hurling Club——

Sergeant. "A shining example of the value conferred by an eminently careful and high-class education——"

Hyacinth. That was the National Schoolmaster.

Sergeant. "Devoted to the highest ideals of his Motherland to such an extent as is compatible with a hitherto non-parliamentary career——"

Hyacinth. That was the Member for Carrow.

Sergeant. "A splendid exponent of the purity of the race——"

Hyacinth. The Editor of the *Carrow Champion.*

Sergeant. "Admirably adapted for the efficient discharge of all possible duties that may in future be laid upon him——"

Hyacinth. The new station-master.

Sergeant. "A champion of every cause

that can legitimately benefit his fellow-creatures——" Why, look here, my man, you are the very one to come to our assistance tonight.

Hyacinth. I would be glad to do that. What way can I do it?

Sergeant. You are a newcomer—your example would carry weight—you must stand up as a living proof of the beneficial effect of a high character, moral fiber, temperance—there is something about it here I am sure—[*Looks.*] I am sure I saw "unparalleled temperance" in some place——

Hyacinth. It was my mother's cousin wrote that—I am no drinker, but I haven't the pledge taken——

Sergeant. You might take it for the purpose.

Mr. Quirke. [*Eagerly.*] Here is an anti-treating button. I was made a present of it by one of my customers—I'll give it to you [*sticks it in* HYACINTH's *coat*] and welcome.

Sergeant. That is it. You can wear the button on the platform—or a bit of blue ribbon—hundreds will follow your example —I know the boys from the Workhouse will——

Hyacinth. I am in no way wishful to be an example——

Sergeant. I will read extracts from the testimonials. "There he is," I will say, "an example of one in early life who by his own unaided efforts and his high character has obtained a profitable situation——" [*Slaps his side.*] I know what I'll do! I'll engage a few corner-boys from Noonan's bar, just as they are, greasy and sodden, to stand in a group—there will be the contrast—— The sight will deter others from a similar fate —— That's the way to do a tableau—— I knew I could turn out a success.

Hyacinth. I wouldn't like to be a contrast——

Sergeant. [*Puts testimonials he has read in his pocket.*] I will go now and engage those lads—six-pence each, and well worth it—— Nothing like an example for the rural classes.

[*Goes off,* HYACINTH *feebly trying to detain him.*]

Mrs. Delane. A very nice man indeed. A little high up in himself, maybe. I'm not one that blames the police. Sure, they have their own bread to earn like every other one. And indeed it is often they will let a thing pass.

Mr. Quirke. [*Gloomily.*] Sometimes they will, and more times they will not.

Miss Joyce. And where will you be finding a lodging, Mr. Halvey?

Hyacinth. I was going to ask that myself, ma'am. I don't know the town.

Miss Joyce. I know of a good lodging, but it is only a very good man would be taken into it.

Mrs. Delane. Sure, there could be no objection there to Mr. Halvey. There is no appearance on him but what is good, and the Sergeant after taking him up the way he is doing.

Miss Joyce. You will be near to the Sergeant in the lodging I speak of. The house is convenient to the barracks.

Hyacinth. [*Doubtfully.*] To the barracks?

Miss Joyce. Alongside of it and the barrack yard behind. And that's not all. It is opposite to the priest's house.

Hyacinth. Opposite, is it?

Miss Joyce. A very respectable place, indeed, and a very clean room you will get. I know it well. The curate can see into it from his window.

Hyacinth. Can he, now?

Fardy. There was a good many, I am thinking, went into that lodging and left it after.

Miss Joyce. [*Sharply.*] It is a lodging you will never be let into or let stop in, Fardy. If they did go they were a good riddance.

Fardy. John Hart, the plumber, left it——

Miss Joyce. If he did, it was because he dared not pass the police coming in, as he used, with a rabbit he was after snaring in his hand.

Fardy. The schoolmaster himself left it.

Miss Joyce. He needn't have left it if he hadn't taken to card-playing. What way could you say your prayers, and shadows shuffling and dealing before you on the blind?

Hyacinth. I think maybe I'd best look around a bit before I'll settle in a lodging——

Miss Joyce. Not at all. *You* won't be wanting to pull down the blind.

Mrs. Delane. It is not likely *you* will be snaring rabbits.

Miss Joyce. Or bringing in a bottle and taking an odd glass the way James Kelly did.

Mrs. Delane. Or writing threatening notices, and the police taking a view of you from the rear.

Miss Joyce. Or going to roadside dances, or running after good-for-nothing young girls——

Hyacinth. I give you my word I'm not so harmless as you think.

Mrs. Delane. Would you be putting a lie on these, Mr. Halvey? [*Touching testimonials.*] I know well the way *you* will be spending the evenings, writing letters to your relations——

Miss Joyce. Learning O'Growney's exercises——

Mrs. Delane. Sticking post cards in an album for the convent bazaar.

Miss Joyce. Reading the *Catholic Young Man*——

Mrs. Delane. Playing the melodies on a melodeon.

Miss Joyce. Looking at the pictures in the *Lives of the Saints.* I'll hurry on and engage the room for you.

Hyacinth. Wait. Wait a minute——

Miss Joyce. No trouble at all. I told you it was just opposite. [*Goes.*]

Mr. Quirke. I suppose I must go upstairs and ready myself for the meeting. If it wasn't for the contract I have for the soldiers' barracks and the Sergeant's good word, I wouldn't go anear it. [*Goes into shop.*]

Mrs. Delane. I should be making myself ready, too. I must be in good time to see you being made an example of, Mr. Halvey. It is I myself was the first to say it; you will be a credit to the town. [*Goes.*]

Hyacinth. [*In a tone of agony.*] I wish I had never seen Cloon.

Fardy. What is on you?

Hyacinth. I wish I had never left Carrow. I wish I had been drowned the first day I thought of it, and I'd be better off.

Fardy. What is it ails you?

Hyacinth. I wouldn't for the best pound ever I had be in this place today.

Fardy. I don't know what you are talking about.

Hyacinth. To have left Carrow, if it was a poor place, where I had my comrades, and an odd spree, and a game of cards—and a coursing match coming on, and I promised a new greyhound from the city of Cork. I'll die in this place, the way I am. I'll be too much closed in.

Fardy. Sure it mightn't be as bad as what you think.

Hyacinth. Will you tell me, I ask you, what way can I undo it?

Fardy. What is it you are wanting to undo?

Hyacinth. Will you tell me what way can I get rid of my character?

Fardy. To get rid of it, is it?

Hyacinth. That is what I said. Aren't you after hearing the great character they are after putting on me?

Fardy. That is a good thing to have.

Hyacinth. It is not. It's the worst in the world. If I hadn't it, I wouldn't be like a prize mangold at a show with every person praising me.

Fardy. If I had it, I wouldn't be like a head in a barrel, with every person making hits at me.

Hyacinth. If I hadn't it, I wouldn't be shoved into a room with all the clergy watching me and the police in the back yard.

Fardy. If I had it, I wouldn't be but a message-carrier now, and a clapper scaring birds in the summer time.

Hyacinth. If I hadn't it, I wouldn't be wearing this button and brought up for an example at the meeting.

Fardy. [*Whistles.*] Maybe you're not, so, what those papers make you out to be?

Hyacinth. How would I be what they make me out to be? Was there ever any person of that sort since the world was a world, unless it might be Saint Antony of Padua looking down from the chapel wall? If it is like that I was, isn't it in Mount Melleray* I would be, or with the Friars at Esker? Why would I be living in the world at all, or doing the world's work?

Fardy. [*Taking up parcel.*] Who would think, now, there would be so much lies in a small place like Carrow?

Hyacinth. It was my mother's cousin did it. He said I was not reared for laboring—he gave me a new suit and bid me never to come back again. I daren't go back to face him—the neighbors knew my mother had a long family—bad luck to them the day they gave me these. [*Tears letters and scatters them.*] I'm done with testimonials. They won't be here to bear witness against me.

Fardy. The Sergeant thought them to be great. Sure, he has the samples of them in his pocket. There's not one in the town but will know before morning that you are the next thing to an earthly saint.

Hyacinth. [*Stamping.*] I'll stop their mouths. I'll show them I can be a terror for badness. I'll do some injury. I'll commit some crime. The first thing I'll do I'll go and get drunk. If I never did it before I'll do it now. I'll get drunk—then I'll make an assault—I tell you I'd think as little of taking a life as of blowing out a candle.

Fardy. If you get drunk you are done for. Sure, that will be held up after as an excuse for any breaking of the law.

Hyacinth. I will break the law. Drunk or sober, I'll break it. I'll do something that

* A Trappist monastery.

will have no excuse. What would you say is the worst crime that any man can do?

Fardy. I don't know. I heard the Sergeant saying one time it was to obstruct the police in the discharge of their duty——

Hyacinth. That won't do. It's a patriot I would be then, worse than before, with my picture in the weeklies. It's a red crime I must commit that will make all respectable people quit minding me. What can I do? Search your mind now.

Fardy. It's what I heard the old people saying there could be no worse crime than to steal a sheep——

Hyacinth. I'll steal a sheep—or a cow—or a horse—if that will leave me the way I was before.

Fardy. It's maybe in jail it will leave you.

Hyacinth. I don't care—I'll confess—I'll tell why I did it—I give you my word I would as soon be picking oakum or breaking stones as to be perched in the daylight the same as that bird, and all the town chirrupping to me or bidding me chirrup——

Fardy. There is reason in that, now.

Hyacinth. Help me, will you?

Fardy. Well, if it is to steal a sheep you want, you haven't far to go.

Hyacinth. [*Looking around wildly.*] Where is it? I see no sheep.

Fardy. Look around you.

Hyacinth. I see no living thing but that thrush——

Fardy. Did I say it was living? What is that hanging on Quirke's rack?

Hyacinth. It's [*fingers it*] a sheep, sure enough——

Fardy. Well, what ails you that you can't bring it away?

Hyacinth. It's a dead one——

Fardy. What matter if it is?

Hyacinth. If it was living I could drive it before me——

Fardy. You could. Is it to your own lodging you would drive it? Sure every one would take it to be a pet you brought from Carrow.

Hyacinth. I suppose they might.

Fardy. Miss Joyce sending in for news of it and it bleating behind the bed.

Hyacinth. [*Distracted.*] Stop! stop!

Mrs. Delane. [*From upper window.*] Fardy! Are you there, Fardy Farrell?

Fardy. I am, ma'am.

Mrs. Delane. [*From window.*] Look and tell me is that the telegraph I hear ticking?

Fardy. [*Looking in at door.*] It is, ma'am.

Mrs. Delane. Then botheration to it, and I not dressed or undressed. Wouldn't you say, now, it's to annoy me it is calling me down? I'm coming! I'm coming!

[*Disappears.*]

Fardy. Hurry on, now! Hurry! She'll be coming out on you. If you are going to do it, do it, and if you are not, let it alone.

Hyacinth. I'll do it! I'll do it!

Fardy. [*Lifting the sheep on his back.*] I'll give you a hand with it.

Hyacinth. [*Goes a step or two and turns around.*] You told me no place where I could hide it.

Fardy. You needn't go far. There is the church beyond at the side of the Square. Go round to the ditch behind the wall—there's nettles in it.

Hyacinth. That'll do.

Fardy. She's coming out—run! run!

Hyacinth. [*Runs a step or two.*] It's slipping!

Fardy. Hoist it up! I'll give it a hoist!

[HALVEY *runs out.*]

Mrs. Delane. [*Calling out.*] What are you doing, Fardy Farrell? Is it idling you are?

Fardy. Waiting I am, ma'am, for the message——

Mrs. Delane. Never mind the message yet. Who said it was ready? [*Going to door.*] Go ask for the loan of—no, but ask news of—— Here, now, go bring that bag of Mr. Halvey's to the lodging Miss Joyce has taken——

Fardy. I will, ma'am.

[*Takes bag and goes out.*]

Mrs. Delane. [*Coming out with a telegram in her hand.*] Nobody here? [*Looks around and calls cautiously.*] Mr. Quirke! Mr. Quirke! James Quirke!

Mr. Quirke. [*Looking out of his upper window with soap-suddy face.*] What is it, Mrs. Delane?

Mrs. Delane. [*Beckoning.*] Come down here till I tell you.

Mr. Quirke. I cannot do that. I'm not fully shaved.

Mrs. Delane. You'd come if you knew the news I have.

Mr. Quirke. Tell it to me now. I'm not so supple as I was.

Mrs. Delane. Whisper now, have you an enemy in any place?

Mr. Quirke. It's likely I may have. A man in business——

Mrs. Delane. I was thinking you had one.

Mr. Quirke. Why would you think that at this time more than any other time?

Mrs. Delane. If you could know what is in this envelope you would know that, James Quirke.

Mr. Quirke. Is that so? And what, now, is there in it?

Mrs. Delane. Who do you think, now, is it addressed to?

Mr. Quirke. How would I know that, and I not seeing it?

Mrs. Delane. That is true. Well, it is a message from Dublin Castle to the Sergeant of Police!

Mr. Quirke. To Sergeant Carden, is it?

Mrs. Delane. It is. And it concerns yourself.

Mr. Quirke. Myself, is it? What accusation can they be bringing against me? I'm a peaceable man.

Mrs. Delane. Wait till you hear.

Mr. Quirke. Maybe they think I was in that moon-lighting case——

Mrs. Delane. That is not it——

Mr. Quirke. I was not in it—I was but in the neighboring field—cutting up a dead cow, that those never had a hand in——

Mrs. Delane. You're out of it——

Mr. Quirke. They had their faces blackened. There is no man can say I recognized them.

Mrs. Delane. That's not what they're saying——

Mr. Quirke. I'll swear I did not hear their voices or know them if I did hear them.

Mrs. Delane. I tell you it has nothing to do with that. It might be better for you if it had.

Mr. Quirke. What is it, so?

Mrs. Delane. It is an order to the Sergeant bidding him immediately to seize all suspicious meat in your house. There is an officer coming down. There are complaints from the Shannon Fort Barracks.

Mr. Quirke. I'll engage it was that pork.

Mrs. Delane. What ailed it for them to find fault?

Mr. Quirke. People are so hard to please nowadays, and I recommended them to salt it.

Mrs. Delane. They had a right to have minded your advice.

Mr. Quirke. There was nothing on that pig at all but that it went mad on poor O'Grady that owned it.

Mrs. Delane. So I heard, and went killing all before it.

Mr. Quirke. Sure it's only in the brain madness can be. I heard the doctor saying that.

Mrs. Delane. He should know.

Mr. Quirke. I give you my word I cut the head off it. I went to the loss of it, throwing it to the eels in the river. If they had salted the meat, as I advised them, what harm would it have done to any person on earth?

Mrs. Delane. I hope no harm will come on poor Mrs. Quirke and the family.

Mr. Quirke. Maybe it wasn't that but some other thing——

Mrs. Delane. Here is Fardy. I must send the message to the Sergeant. Well, Mr. Quirke, I'm glad I had the time to give you a warning.

Mr. Quirke. I'm obliged to you, indeed. You were always very neighborly, Mrs. Delane. Don't be too quick, now, sending the message. There is just one article I would like to put away out of the house before the Sergeant will come.

[*Enter* FARDY.]

Mrs. Delane. Here now, Fardy—that's not the way you're going to the barracks. Any one would think you were scaring birds yet. Put on your uniform. [FARDY *goes into office.*] You have this message to bring to the Sergeant of Police. Get your cap, now, it's under the counter.

[FARDY *reappears, and she gives him telegram.*]

Fardy. I'll bring it to the station. It's there he was going.

Mrs. Delane. You will not, but to the barracks. It can wait for him there.

[FARDY *goes off.* MR. QUIRKE *has appeared at door.*]

Mr. Quirke. It was indeed a very neighborly act, Mrs. Delane, and I'm obliged to you. There is just *one* article to put out of the way. The Sergeant may look about him then and welcome. It's well I cleared the premises on yesterday. A consignment to Birmingham I sent. The Lord be praised, isn't England a terrible country with all it consumes?

Mrs. Delane. Indeed, you always treat the neighbors very decent, Mr. Quirke, not asking them to buy from you.

Mr. Quirke. Just one article. [*Turns to rack.*] That sheep I brought in last night. It was for a charity indeed I bought it from the widow woman at Kiltartan Cross. Where would the poor make a profit out of their dead meat without me? Where now is it? Well, now, I could have swore that that sheep was hanging there on the rack when I went in——

Mrs. Delane. You must have put it in some other place.

Mr. Quirke. [*Going in and searching and coming out.*] I did not; there is no other place for me to put it. Is it gone blind I am, or is it not in it, it is?

Mrs. Delane. It's not there now anyway.

Mr. Quirke. Didn't you take notice of it there yourself this morning?

Mrs. Delane. I have it in my mind that I did; but it's not there now.

Mr. Quirke. There was no one here could bring it away.

Mrs. Delane. Is it me myself you suspect of taking it, James Quirke?

Mr. Quirke. Where is it at all? It is certain it was not of itself it walked away. It was dead, and very dead, the time I bought it.

Mrs. Delane. I have a pleasant neighbor indeed that accuses me that I took his sheep. I wonder, indeed, you to say a thing like that! I to steal your sheep or your rack or anything that belongs to you or to your trade! Thank you, James Quirke. I am much obliged to you indeed.

Mr. Quirke. Ah, be quiet, woman; be quiet——

Mrs. Delane. And let me tell you, James Quirke, that I would sooner starve and see everyone belonging to me starve than to eat the size of a thimble of any joint that ever was on your rack or that ever will be on it, whatever the soldiers may eat that have no other thing to get, or the English that devour all sorts, or the poor ravenous people that's down by the sea!

[*She turns to go into shop.*]

Mr. Quirke. [*Stopping her.*] Don't be talking foolishness, woman. Who said you took my meat? Give heed to me, now. There must some other message have come. The Sergeant must have got some other message.

Mrs. Delane. [*Sulkily.*] If there is any way for a message to come that is quicker than to come by the wires, tell me what it is and I'll be obliged to you.

Mr. Quirke. The Sergeant was up here making an excuse he was sticking up that notice. What was he doing here, I ask you?

Mrs. Delane. How would I know what brought him?

Mr. Quirke. It is what he did; he made as if to go away—he turned back again and I shaving—he brought away the sheep—he will have it for evidence against me——

Mrs. Delane. [*Interested.*] That might be so.

Mr. Quirke. I would sooner it to have been any other beast nearly ever I had upon the rack.

Mrs. Delane. Is that so?

Mr. Quirke. I bade the Widow Early to kill it a fortnight ago—but she would not, she was that covetous!

Mrs. Delane. What was on it?

Mr. Quirke. How would I know what was on it? Whatever was on it, it was the will of God put it upon it—wasted it was, and shivering and refusing its share.

Mrs. Delane. The poor thing.

Mr. Quirke. Gone all to nothing—wore away like a flock of thread. It did not weigh as much as a lamb of two months.

Mrs. Delane. It is likely the Inspector will bring it to Dublin?

Mr. Quirke. The ribs of it streaky with the dint of patent medicines——

Mrs. Delane. I wonder is it to the Petty Sessions you'll be brought or is it to the Assizes?

Mr. Quirke. I'll speak up to them. I'll make my defense. What can the Army expect at fippence a pound?

Mrs. Delane. It is likely there will be no bail allowed?

Mr. Quirke. Would they be wanting me to give them good quality meat out of my own pocket? Is it to encourage them to fight the poor Indians and Africans they would have me? It's the Anti-Enlisting Societies should pay the fine for me.

Mrs. Delane. It's not a fine will be put on you, I'm afraid. It's five years in jail you will be apt to be getting. Well, I'll try and be a good neighbor to poor Mrs. Quirke.

[MR. QUIRKE, *who has been stamping up and down, sits down and weeps.* HALVEY *comes in and stands on one side.*]

Mr. Quirke. Hadn't I heart-scalding enough before, striving to rear five weak children?

Mrs. Delane. I suppose they will be sent to the Industrial Schools?

Mr. Quirke. My poor wife——

Mrs. Delane. I'm afraid the workhouse——

Mr. Quirke. And she out in an ass-car at this minute helping me to follow my trade.

Mrs. Delane. I hope they will not arrest her along with you.

Mr. Quirke. I'll give myself up to justice. I'll plead guilty! I'll be recommended to mercy!

Mrs. Delane. It might be best for you.

Mr. Quirke. Who would think so great a misfortune could come upon a family through the bringing away of one sheep!

Hyacinth. [*Coming forward.*] Let you make yourself easy.

Mr. Quirke. Easy! It's easy to say let you make yourself easy.

Hyacinth. I can tell you where it is.

Mr. Quirke. Where what is?

Hyacinth. The sheep you are fretting after.

Mr. Quirke. What do you know about it?

Hyacinth. I know everything about it.

Mr. Quirke. I suppose the Sergeant told you?

Hyacinth. He told me nothing.

Mr. Quirke. I suppose the whole town knows it, so?

Hyacinth. No one knows it, as yet.

Mr. Quirke. And the Sergeant didn't see it?

Hyacinth. No one saw it or brought it away but myself.

Mr. Quirke. Where did you put it at all?

Hyacinth. In the ditch behind the church wall. In among the nettles it is. Look at the way they have me stung.

[*Holds out hands.*]

Mr. Quirke. In the ditch! The best hiding place in the town.

Hyacinth. I never thought it would bring such great trouble upon you. You can't say, anyway, I did not tell you.

Mr. Quirke. You yourself that brought it away and that hid it! I suppose it was coming in the train you got information about the message to the police.

Hyacinth. What now do you say to me?

Mr. Quirke. Say! I say I am as glad to hear what you said as if it was the Lord telling me I'd be in heaven this minute.

Hyacinth. What are you going to do to me?

Mr. Quirke. Do, is it? [*Grasps his hand.*] Any earthly thing you would wish me to do, I will do it.

Hyacinth. I suppose you will tell——

Mr. Quirke. Tell! It's I that will tell when all is quiet. It is I will give you the good name through the town!

Hyacinth. I don't well understand.

Mr. Quirke. [*Embracing him.*] The man that preserved me!

Hyacinth. That preserved you?

Mr. Quirke. That kept me from ruin!

Hyacinth. From ruin?

Mr. Quirke. That saved me from disgrace!

Hyacinth. [*To* MRS. DELANE.] What is he saying at all?

Mr. Quirke. From the Inspector!

Hyacinth. What is he talking about?

Mr. Quirke. From the magistrates!

Hyacinth. He is making some mistake.

Mr. Quirke. From the Winter Assizes!

Hyacinth. Is he out of his wits?

Mr. Quirke. Five years in jail!

Hyacinth. Hasn't he the queer talk?

Mr. Quirke. The loss of the contract!

Hyacinth. Are my own wits gone astray?

Mr. Quirke. What way can I repay you?

Hyacinth. [*Shouting.*] I tell you I took the sheep——

Mr. Quirke. You did, God reward you!

Hyacinth. I stole away with it——

Mr. Quirke. The blessing of the poor on you!

Hyacinth. I put it out of sight——

Mr. Quirke. The blessing of my five children——

Hyacinth. I may as well say nothing——

Mrs. Delane. Let you be quiet now, Quirke. Here's the Sergeant coming to search the shop——

[SERGEANT *comes in:* QUIRKE *lets go of* HALVEY, *who arranges his hat, etc.*]

Sergeant. The Department to blazes!

Mrs. Delane. What is it is putting you out?

Sergeant. To go to the train to meet the lecturer, and there to get a message through the guard that he was unavoidably detained in the South, holding an inquest on the remains of a drake.

Mrs. Delane. The lecturer, is it?

Sergeant. To be sure. What else would I be talking of? The lecturer has failed me, and where am I to go looking for a person that I would think fitting to take his place?

Mrs. Delane. And that's all? And you didn't get any message but the one?

Sergeant. Is that all? I am surprised at you, Mrs. Delane. Isn't it enough to upset a man, within three-quarters of an hour of the time of the meeting? Where, I would ask you, am I to find a man that has education enough and wit enough and character enough to put up speaking on the platform on the minute?

Mr. Quirke. [*Jumps up.*] It is I myself will tell you that.

Sergeant. You!

Mr. Quirke. [*Slapping* HALVEY *on the back.*] Look at here, Sergeant. There is not one word was said in all those papers about this young man before you but it is true. And there could be no good thing said of him that would be too good for him.

Sergeant. It might not be a bad idea.

Mr. Quirke. Whatever the paper said about him, Sergeant, I can say more again. It has come to my knowledge—by chance—that since he came to this town that young man has saved a whole family from destruction.

Sergeant. That is much to his credit—helping the rural classes——

Mr. Quirke. A family and a long family, big and little, like sods of turf—and they depending on a—on one that might be on his way to dark trouble at this minute if it was not for his assistance. Believe me, he is the most sensible man, and the wittiest, and the kindest, and the best helper of the poor that ever stood before you in this square. Is not that so, Mrs. Delane?

Mrs. Delane. It is true indeed. Where he gets his wisdom and his wit and his information from I don't know, unless it might be that he is gifted from above.

Sergeant. Well, Mrs. Delane, I think we have settled that question. Mr. Halvey, you will be the speaker at the meeting. The lecturer sent these notes—you can lengthen them into a speech. You can call to the people of Cloon to stand out, to begin the building of their character. I saw a lecturer do it one time at Dundrum. "Come up here," he said. "Dare to be a Daniel," he said——

Hyacinth. I can't—I won't——

Sergeant. [*Looking at papers and thrusting them into his hand.*] You will find it quite easy. I will conduct you to the platform—these papers before you and a glass of water—— That's settled. [*Turns to go.*] Follow me on to the Courthouse in half an hour—I must go to the barracks first—I heard there was a telegram—— [*Calls back as he goes.*] Don't be late, Mrs. Delane. Mind, Quirke, you promised to come.

Mrs. Delane. Well, it's time for me to make an end of settling myself—and indeed, Mr. Quirke, you'd best do the same.

Mr. Quirke. [*Rubbing his cheek.*] I suppose so. I had best keep on good terms with him for the present. [*Turns.*] Well, now, I had a great escape this day.

[*Both go in as* FARDY *reappears whistling.*]

Hyacinth. [*Sitting down.*] I don't know in the world what has come upon the world that the half of the people of it should be cracked!

Fardy. Weren't you found out yet?

Hyacinth. Found out, is it? I don't know what you mean by being found out.

Fardy. Didn't he miss the sheep?

Hyacinth. He did, and I told him it was I took it—and what happened I declare to goodness I don't know—— Will you look at these? [*Holds out notes.*]

Fardy. Papers! Are they more testimonials?

Hyacinth. They are what is worse. [*Gives a hoarse laugh.*] Will you come and see me on the platform—these in my hand—and I speaking—giving out advice. [FARDY *whistles.*] Why didn't you tell me, the time you advised me to steal a sheep, that in this town it would qualify a man to go preaching, and the priest in the chair looking on?

Fardy. The time I took a few apples that had fallen off a stall, they did not ask me to hold a meeting. They welted me well.

Hyacinth. [*Looking around.*] I would take apples if I could see them. I wish I had broke my neck before I left Carrow and I'd be better off! I wish I had got six months the time I was caught setting snares—I wish I had robbed a church.

Fardy. Would a Protestant church do?

Hyacinth. I suppose it wouldn't be so great a sin.

Fardy. It's likely the Sergeant would think worse of it—Anyway, if you want to rob one, it's the Protestant church is the handiest.

Hyacinth. [*Getting up.*] Show me what way to do it.

Fardy. [*Pointing.*] I was going around it a few minutes ago, to see might there be e'er a dog scenting the sheep, and I noticed the window being out.

Hyacinth. Out, out and out?

Fardy. It was, where they are putting colored glass in it for the distiller——

Hyacinth. What good does that do me?

Fardy. Every good. You could go in by that window if you had some person to give you a hoist. Whatever riches there is to get in it then, you'll get them.

Hyacinth. I don't want riches. I'll give you all I will find if you will come and hoist me.

Fardy. Here is Miss Joyce coming to bring you to your lodging. Sure I brought your bag to it, the time you were away with the sheep——

Hyacinth. Run! Run!

[*They go off. Enter* MISS JOYCE.]

Miss Joyce. Are you here, Mrs. Delane? Where, can you tell me, is Mr. Halvey?

Mrs. Delane. [*Coming out dressed.*] It's likely he is gone on to the Courthouse. Did you hear he is to be in the chair and to make an address to the meeting?

Miss Joyce. He is getting on fast. His Reverence says he will be a good help in the parish. Who would think, now, there would be such a godly young man in a little place like Carrow!

[*Enter* SERGEANT *in a hurry, with telegram.*]

Sergeant. What time did this telegram arrive, Mrs. Delane?

Mrs. Delane. I couldn't be rightly sure, Sergeant. But sure it's marked on it, unless the clock I have is gone wrong.

Sergeant. It is marked on it. And I have the time I got it marked on my own watch.

Mrs. Delane. Well, now, I wonder none of the police would have followed you with it from the barracks—and they with so little to do——

Sergeant. [*Looking in at* QUIRKE'S *shop.*] Well, I am sorry to do what I have to do, but duty is duty.

[*He ransacks shop.* MRS. DELANE *looks on.* MR. QUIRKE *puts his head out of window.*]

Mr. Quirke. What is that going on inside? [*No answer.*] Is there any one inside, I ask? [*No answer.*] It must be that dog of Tannian's—wait till I get at him.

Mrs. Delane. It is Sergeant Carden, Mr. Quirke. He would seem to be looking for something——

[MR. QUIRKE *appears in shop.* SERGEANT *comes out, makes another dive, taking up sacks, etc.*]

Mr. Quirke. I'm greatly afraid I am just out of meat, Sergeant—and I'm sorry now to disoblige you, and you not being in the habit of dealing with me——

Sergeant. I should think not, indeed.

Mr. Quirke. Looking for a tender little bit of lamb, I suppose you are, for Mrs. Carden and the youngsters?

Sergeant. I am not.

Mr. Quirke. If I had it now, I'd be proud to offer it to you, and make no charge. I'll be killing a good kid tomorrow. Mrs. Carden might fancy a bit of it——

Sergeant. I have had orders to search your establishment for unwholesome meat, and I am come here to do it.

Mr. Quirke. [*Sitting down with a smile.*] Is that so? Well, isn't it a wonder the schemers does be in the world?

Sergeant. It is not the first time there have been complaints.

Mr. Quirke. I suppose not. Well, it is on their own head it will fall at the last!

Sergeant. I have found nothing so far.

Mr. Quirke. I suppose not, indeed. What is there you could find, and it not in it?

Sergeant. Have you no meat at all upon the premises?

Mr. Quirke. I have, indeed, a nice barrel of bacon.

Sergeant. What way did it die?

Mr. Quirke. It would be hard for me to say that. American it is. How would I know what way they do be killing the pigs out there? Machinery, I suppose, they have—steam hammers——

Sergeant. Is there nothing else here at all?

Mr. Quirke. I give you my word, there is no meat living or dead in this place, but yourself and myself and that bird above in the cage.

Sergeant. Well, I must tell the Inspector I could find nothing. But mind yourself for the future.

Mr. Quirke. Thank you, Sergeant. I will do that. [*Enter* FARDY. *He stops short.*]

Sergeant. It was you delayed that message to me, I suppose? You'd best mend your ways or I'll have something to say to you.

[*Seizes and shakes him.*]

Fardy. That's the way every one does be faulting me.

[*Whimpers. The* SERGEANT *gives him another shake. A half-crown falls out of his pocket.*]

Miss Joyce. [*Picking it up.*] A half-a-crown! Where, now, did you get that much, Fardy?

Fardy. Where did I get it, is it!

Miss Joyce. I'll engage it was in no honest way you got it.

Fardy. I picked it up in the street——

Miss Joyce. If you did, why didn't you bring it to the Sergeant or to his Reverence?

Mrs. Delane. And some poor person, maybe, being at the loss of it.

Miss Joyce. I'd best bring it to his Reverence. Come with me, Fardy, till he will question you about it.

Fardy. It was not altogether in the street I found it——

Miss Joyce. There, now! I knew you got it in no good way! Tell me, now.

Fardy. It was playing pitch and toss I won it——

Miss Joyce. And who would play for half-crowns with the like of you, Fardy Farrell? Who was it, now?

Fardy. It was—a stranger——

Miss Joyce. Do you hear that? A stranger! Did you see e'er a stranger in this town, Mrs. Delane, or Sergeant Carden, or Mr. Quirke?

Mr. Quirke. Not a one.

Sergeant. There was no stranger here.

Mrs. Delane. There could not be one here without me knowing it.

Fardy. I tell you there was.

Miss Joyce. Come on, then, and tell who was he to his Reverence.

Sergeant. [*Taking other arm.*] Or to the bench.

Fardy. I did get it, I tell you, from a stranger.

Sergeant. Where is he, so?

Fardy. He's in some place—not far away.

Sergeant. Bring me to him.

Fardy. He'll be coming here.

Sergeant. Tell me the truth and it will be better for you.

Fardy. [*Weeping.*] Let me go and I will.

Sergeant. [*Letting go.*] Now—who did you get it from?

Fardy. From that young chap came today, Mr. Halvey.

All. Mr. Halvey!

Mr. Quirke. [*Indignantly.*] What are you saying, you young ruffian, you? Hyacinth Halvey to be playing pitch and toss with the like of you!

Fardy. I didn't say that.

Miss Joyce. You did say it. You said it now.

Mr. Quirke. Hyacinth Halvey! The best man that ever came into this town!

Miss Joyce. Well, what lies he has!

Mr. Quirke. It's my belief the half-crown is a bad one. Maybe it's to pass it off it was given to him. There were tinkers in the town at the time of the fair. Give it here to me. [*Bites it.*] No, indeed, it's sound enough. Here, Sergeant, it's best for you to take it.

[*Gives it to* SERGEANT, *who examines it.*]

Sergeant. Can it be? Can it be what I think it to be?

Mr. Quirke. What is it? What do you take it to be?

Sergeant. It is, it is. I know it. I know this half-crown——

Mr. Quirke. That is a queer thing, now.

Sergeant. I know it well. I have been handling it in the church for the last twelvemonth——

Mr. Quirke. Is that so?

Sergeant. It is the nest-egg half-crown we hand around in the collection plate every Sunday morning. I know it by the dint on the Queen's temples and the crooked scratch under her nose.

Mr. Quirke. [*Examining it.*] So there is, too.

Sergeant. This is a bad business. It has been stolen from the church.

All. O! O! O!

Sergeant. [*Seizing* FARDY.] You have robbed the church!

Fardy. [*Terrified.*] I tell you I never did!

Sergeant. I have the proof of it.

Fardy. Say what you like! I never put a foot in it!

Sergeant. How did you get this, so?

Miss Joyce. I suppose from the *stranger*?

Mrs. Delane. I suppose it was Hyacinth Halvey gave it to you, now?

Fardy. It was so.

Sergeant. I suppose it was he robbed the church?

Fardy. [*Sobs.*] You will not believe me if I say it.

Mr. Quirke. O! the young vagabond! Let me get at him!

Mrs. Delane. Here he is himself now!

[HYACINTH *comes in.* FARDY *releases himself and creeps behind him.*]

Mrs. Delane. It is time you to come, Mr. Halvey, and shut the mouth of this young schemer.

Miss Joyce. I would like you to hear what he says of you, Mr. Halvey. Pitch and toss, he says.

Mr. Quirke. Robbery, he says.

Mrs. Delane. Robbery of a church.

Sergeant. He has had a bad name long enough. Let him go to a reformatory now.

Fardy. [*Clinging to* HYACINTH.] Save me, save me! I'm a poor boy trying to knock out a way of living; I'll be destroyed if I go to a reformatory.

[*Kneels and clings to* HYACINTH'S *knees.*]

Hyacinth. I'll save you easy enough.

Fardy. Don't let me be jailed.

Hyacinth. I am going to tell them.

Fardy. I'm a poor orphan——

Hyacinth. Will you let me speak?

Fardy. I'll get no more chance in the world——

Hyacinth. Sure I'm trying to free you——

Fardy. It will be tasked to me always.

Hyacinth. Be quiet, can't you?

Fardy. Don't you desert me!

Hyacinth. Will you be silent?

Fardy. Take it on yourself.

Hyacinth. I will if you'll let me.

Fardy. Tell them you did it.

Hyacinth. I am going to do that.

Fardy. Tell them it was you got in at the window.

Hyacinth. I will! I will!

Fardy. Say it was you robbed the box.

Hyacinth. I'll say it! I'll say it!

Fardy. It being open!

Hyacinth. Let me tell, let me tell.

Fardy. Of all that was in it.

Hyacinth. I'll tell them that.

Fardy. And gave it to me.

Hyacinth. [*Putting hand on his mouth and dragging him up.*] Will you stop and let me speak?

Sergeant. We can't be wasting time. Give him here to me.

Hyacinth. I can't do that. He must be let alone.

Sergeant. [*Seizing him.*] He'll be let alone in the lock-up.

Hyacinth. He must not be brought there.

Sergeant. I'll let no man get him off.

Hyacinth. I will get him off.

Sergeant. You will not!

Hyacinth. I will.

Sergeant. Do you think to buy him off?

Hyacinth. I will buy him off with my own confession.

Sergeant. And what will that be?

Hyacinth. It was I robbed the church.

Sergeant. That is likely indeed!

Hyacinth. Let him go, and take me. I tell you I did it.

Sergeant. It would take witnesses to prove that.

Hyacinth. [*Pointing to* FARDY.] He will be witness.

Fardy. O! Mr. Halvey, I would not wish to do that. Get me off and I will say nothing.

Hyacinth. Sure you must. You will be put on oath in the court.

Fardy. I will not! I will not! All the world knows I don't understand the nature of an oath!

Mr. Quirke. [*Coming forward.*] Is it blind ye all are?

Mrs. Delane. What are you talking about?

Mr. Quirke. Is it fools ye all are?

Miss Joyce. Speak for yourself.

Mr. Quirke. Is it idiots ye all are?

Sergeant. Mind who you're talking to.

Mr. Quirke. [*Seizing* HYACINTH'S *hands.*] Can't you see? Can't you hear? Where are your wits? Was ever such a thing seen in this town?

Mrs. Delane. Say out what you have to say.

Mr. Quirke. A walking saint he is!

Mrs. Delane. Maybe so.

Mr. Quirke. The preserver of the poor! Talk of the holy martyrs! They are nothing at all to what he is! Will you look at him! To save that poor boy he is going! To take the blame on himself he is going! To say he himself did the robbery he is going! Before the magistrate he is going! To jail he is going! Taking the blame on his own head! Putting the sin on his own shoulders! Letting on to have done a robbery! Telling a lie—that it may be forgiven him—to his own injury! Doing all that, I tell you, to save the character of a miserable slack lad, that rose in poverty.

[*Murmur of admiration from all.*]

Mr. Quirke. Now, what do you say?

Sergeant. [*Pressing his hand.*] Mr. Halvey, you have given us all a lesson. To please you, I will make no information against the boy. [*Shakes him and helps him up.*] I will put back the half-crown in the poor-box next Sunday. [*To* FARDY.] What have you to say to your benefactor?

Fardy. I'm obliged to you, Mr. Halvey. You behaved very decent to me, very decent indeed. I'll never let a word be said against you if I live to be a hundred years.

Sergeant. [*Wiping eyes with a blue handkerchief.*] I will tell it at the meeting. It will be a great encouragement to them to build up their character. I'll tell it to the priest and he taking the chair——

Hyacinth. O stop, will you——

Mr. Quirke. The chair. It's in the chair he himself should be. It's in a chair we will put him now. It's to chair him through the streets we will. Sure he'll be an example and a blessing to the whole of the town. [*Seizes* HALVEY *and seats him in chair.*] Now, Sergeant, give a hand. Here, Fardy!

[*They all lift the chair with* HALVEY *in it, wildly protesting.*]

Mr. Quirke. Come along now to the Courthouse. Three cheers for Hyacinth Halvey! Hip! hip! hoora!

[*Cheers heard in the distance as the curtain drops.*]

WHAT EVERY WOMAN KNOWS*

A Comedy

By

J. M. BARRIE

It is perhaps significant that the first play of Barrie's sole authorship to be produced was a burlesque of Ibsen, called *Ibsen's Ghost* (1891). That year Ibsen had been introduced to England by J. T. Grein at the Independent Theatre, with *Ghosts*. The dramatic ferment working all over Europe and having its center in Ibsen could not but affect the sensitive Barrie, but it made him representative in England, not of the followers of Ibsen, but of the reaction against him. Ibsen, in the plays that most influenced his contemporaries, is faithful to the surfaces, the appearances, of character and dialogue, and is careful to impress his audiences with his truth. But Barrie was frankly fantastic, sentimental, naïve, even mystical, and quite as successful in the theater.

Barrie began as a journalist and novelist and was slow to take his position as a dramatist. During the 'nineties, while Pinero and Jones and Shaw were leading the British stage into the new freedom, Barrie was writing tender empty things like *The Professor's Love Story,* and the dramatization of his novel, *The Little Minister*. These were commercially successful, and the latter is important as the beginning of the partnership between the author, Charles Frohman, the producer, and Maude Adams, the actress. But, until 1902, Barrie had done nothing to deserve Shaw's remark that he "finally relegated the nineteenth-century London theater to the dust-bin."

In that year appeared *Quality Street* [1] and *The Admirable Crichton,* plays unique in tone and temper, and highly characteristic. With their success, and that of *Peter Pan* in 1904, Barrie became definitely a man of the theater, writing almost exclusively plays and stories based on plays thereafter. Yet in the published form of his plays he shows the traces of the novelist; his texts read like novels in dialogue, and the customary stage directions are not given, but replaced by description of the characters and their feelings. This blend of novel and drama makes unusually happy reading. Few of the plays have been published soon after stage performance: *Peter Pan,* for instance, was not published until 1928; and *The Admirable Crichton* not until 1915. *Peter Pan* made so profound an impression on the British public that a statue of the character stands in Kensington Gardens, London.

What Every Woman Knows is notable among Barrie's plays as perhaps the one in which he most completely accepts the ordinary realistic premises in treatment of situation and character. Its stage history has been marked by most distinguished actresses in the rôle of Maggie. First played in 1908, it was a pronounced success in both England and America. In this country Maude Adams created the rôle of Maggie and the play was produced by Charles Frohman. Barrie wrote the play expressly for Miss Adams, saying of it, "I could see her dancing through every page of my manuscript. Miss Adams knows my characters and understands them. She really needs no directions. I love to write for her and see her in my work." Miss Adams has said, "Whenever I act, I always feel there is one unseen spectator, J. M. Barrie." In all the Barrie plays in which the leading rôle might be taken by a woman, Miss Adams played in America until her retirement in 1918. Frohman regularly produced the Barrie plays on both sides of the Atlantic until his death at the sinking of the *Lusitania* in 1915. In 1926, *What Every Woman Knows* was revived in New York with Miss Helen Hayes as Maggie and was again a great success. Between 1908 and 1928, the play was revived three times in England. Miss Hilda Trevelyan played Maggie at the first production there.

[1] *Quality Street* was produced in New York in 1901, in London in 1902.

SIR JAMES MATTHEW BARRIE

Born 1860, Kirriemuir ("Thrums"), Scotland.
Edinburgh University.
1885, Went to London and engaged in journalism.
Between 1888 and 1900 made a reputation as a leader in "The Kailyard School of Fiction" with such works as *Auld Licht Idylls*, 1888, and *Sentimental Tommy*, 1895.
1891, His first plays: *Richard Savage*, *Ibsen's Ghost*, *Becky Sharp*.
1913, Made a baronet.
1922, Rector of Edinburgh University. Awarded Order of Merit.
Died 1937.

PLAYS

1891 *Richard Savage* (with H. B. Marriot-Watson). 1891 *Ibsen's Ghost*. 1891 *Becky Sharp*. 1892 *Walker, London*. 1893 *Jane Annie* (comic opera, with Arthur Conan-Doyle). 1894 *The Professor's Love Story*. 1897 *The Little Minister* (dramatization of novel published 1891). 1900 *The Wedding Guest*. 1901 *Quality Street*. 1902 *The Admirable Crichton*. 1903 *Little Mary*. 1904 *Peter Pan*. 1905 *Alice-Sit-by-the-Fire*. 1905 *Pantaloon*. 1906 *Josephine*. 1906 *Punch*. 1908 *What Every Woman Knows*. 1910 *The Twelve Pound Look*. 1910 *A Slice of Life*. 1910 *Old Friends*. 1912 *Rosalind*. 1913 *The Adored One* (later called *The Legend of Leonora*, and in one act *Seven Women*). 1913 *The Will*. 1913 *Half an Hour*. 1913 *The Dramatists Get What They Want*. 1914 *The Ladies' Shakespeare*. 1914 *Der Tag*. 1915 *The New Word*. 1915 *Rosy Rapture*. 1915 *The Fatal Typist*. 1916 *The Real Thing at Last*. 1916 *A Kiss for Cinderella*. 1916 *Shakespeare's Legacy*. 1917 *Dear Brutus*. 1917 *The Old Lady Shows Her Medals*. 1918 *Barbara's Wedding*. 1918 *A Well Remembered Voice*. 1920 *Mary Rose*. 1920 *The Truth About the Russian Dancers*. 1922 *Shall We Join the Ladies?* (unfinished). 1936 *The Boy David*.

WHAT EVERY WOMAN KNOWS

I

JAMES WYLIE *is about to make a move on the dambrod, and in the little Scotch room there is an awful silence befitting the occasion.* JAMES *with his hand poised—for if he touches a piece he has to play it,* ALICK *will see to that—raises his red head suddenly to read* ALICK'S *face. His father, who is* ALICK, *is pretending to be in a panic lest* JAMES *should make this move.* JAMES *grins heartlessly, and his fingers are about to close on the "man" when some instinct of self-preservation makes him peep once more. This time* ALICK *is caught: the unholy ecstasy on his face tells as plain as porridge that he has been luring* JAMES *to destruction.*

JAMES *glares; and, too late, his opponent is a simple old father again.* JAMES *mops his head, sprawls in the manner most conducive to thought in the* WYLIE *family, and, protruding his underlip, settles down to a reconsideration of the board.* ALICK *blows out his cheeks, and a drop of water settles on the point of his nose.*

You will find them thus any Saturday night (after family worship, which sends the servant to bed); and sometimes the pauses are so long that in the end they forget whose move it is.

It is not the room you would be shown into if you were calling socially on MISS WYLIE. *The drawing-room for you, and* MISS WYLIE *in a colored merino to receive you; very likely she would exclaim, "This is a pleasant surprise!" though she has seen you coming up the avenue and has just had time to whip the dust cloths off the chairs, and to warn* ALICK, DAVID, *and* JAMES *that they had better not dare come in to see you before they have put on a dickey. Nor is this the room in which you would dine in solemn grandeur if invited to drop in and take pot-luck, which is how the* WYLIES *invite, it being a family weakness to pretend that they sit down in the dining-room daily. It is the real living room of the house, where* ALICK, *who will never get used to fashionable ways, can take off his collar and sit happily in his stocking soles, and* JAMES *at times would do so also; but catch* MAGGIE *letting him.*

There is one very fine chair, but, heavens, not for sitting on; just to give the room a social standing in an emergency. It sneers at the other chairs with an air of insolent superiority, like a haughty bride who has married into the house for money. Otherwise, the furniture is homely; most of it has come from that smaller house where the WYLIES *began. There is the large and shiny chair which can be turned into a bed if you look the other way for a moment.* JAMES *cannot sit on this chair without gradually sliding down it till he is lying luxuriously on the small of his back, his legs indicating, like the hands of a clock, that it is ten past twelve; a position in which* MAGGIE *shudders to see him receiving company.*

The other chairs are horse-hair, than which nothing is more comfortable if there be a good slit down the seat. The seats are heavily dented, because all the WYLIE *family sit down with a dump. The draughtboard is on the edge of a large center table, which also displays four books placed at equal distances from each other, one of them a Bible, and another the family album. If these were the only books they would not justify* MAGGIE *in calling this chamber the library, her dogged name for it; while* DAVID *and* JAMES *call it the west-room and* ALICK *calls it "the room," which is to him the natural name for any apartment without a bed in it. There is a bookcase of pitch pine, which contains six hundred books, with glass doors to prevent your getting at them.*

No one does try to get at the books, for the WYLIES *are not a reading family. They like you to gasp when you see so much literature gathered together in one prison-house, but they gasp themselves at the thought that there are persons, chiefly clergymen, who, having finished one book, coolly begin another. Nevertheless, it was not all vainglory that made* DAVID *buy this library: it was rather a mighty respect for education, as some-*

thing that he has missed. This same feeling makes him take in the Contemporary Review *and stand up to it like a man.* ALICK, *who also has a respect for education, tries to read the* Contemporary, *but becomes dispirited, and may be heard muttering over its pages, "No, no use, no use, no," and sometimes even "Oh, hell."* JAMES *has no respect for education; and* MAGGIE *is at present of an open mind.*

They are WYLIE AND SONS *of the local granite quarry, in which* ALICK *was throughout his working days a mason. It is* DAVID *who has raised them to this position; he climbed up himself step by step (and hewed the steps), and drew the others up after him.* "WYLIE BROTHERS," ALICK *would have had the firm called, but* DAVID *said No, and* JAMES *said No, and* MAGGIE *said No; first honor must be to their father; and* ALICK *now likes it on the whole, though he often sighs at having to shave every day; and on some snell mornings he still creeps from his couch at four and even at two (thinking that his mallet and chisel are calling him), and begins to pull on his trousers, until the grandeur of them reminds him that he can go to bed again. Sometimes he cries a little, because there is no more work for him to do for ever and ever; and then* MAGGIE *gives him a spade (without telling* DAVID) *or* DAVID *gives him the logs to saw (without telling* MAGGIE).

We have given JAMES *a longer time to make his move than our kind friends in front will give him, but in the meantime something has been happening.* DAVID *has come in, wearing a black coat and his Sabbath boots, for he has been to a public meeting.* DAVID *is nigh forty years of age, whiskered like his father and brother* (ALICK'S *whiskers being worn as a sort of cravat around the neck), and he has the too brisk manner of one who must arrive anywhere a little before any one else. The painter who did the three of them for fifteen pounds (you may observe the canvases on the walls) has caught this characteristic, perhaps accidentally, for* DAVID *is almost stepping out of his frame, as if to hurry off somewhere; while* ALICK *and* JAMES *look as if they were pinned to the wall for life. All the six of them, men and pictures, however, have a family resemblance, like granite blocks from their own quarry. They are as Scotch as peat for instance, and they might exchange eyes without any neighbor noticing the difference, inquisitive little blue eyes that seem to be always totting up the price of things.*

The dambrod players pay no attention to DAVID, *nor does he regard them. Dumping down on the sofa he removes his 'lastic sides, as his Sabbath boots are called, by pushing one foot against the other, gets into a pair of hand-sewn slippers, deposits the boots as according to rule in the ottoman, and crosses to the fire. There must be something on* DAVID'S *mind tonight, for he pays no attention to the game, neither gives advice (than which nothing is more maddening) nor exchanges a wink with* ALICK *over the parlous condition of* JAMES'S *crown. You can hear the wag-at-the-wall clock in the lobby ticking. Then* DAVID *lets himself go; it runs out of him like a hymn:*

David.

Oh, let the solid ground
Not fail beneath my feet,
Before my life has found
What some have found so sweet.

[*This is not a soliloquy, but is offered as a definite statement. The players emerge from their game with difficulty.*]

Alick. [*With* JAMES'S *crown in his hand.*] What's that you're saying, David?

David. [*Like a public speaker explaining the situation in a few well-chosen words.*] The thing I'm speaking about is Love.

James. [*Keeping control of himself.*] Do you stand there and say you're in love, David Wylie?

David. Me; what would I do with the thing?

James. [*Who is by no means without pluck.*] I see no necessity for calling it a thing.

[*They are two bachelors who all their lives have been afraid of nothing but Woman.* DAVID *in his sportive days—which continue—has done roguish things with his arm when conducting a lady home under an umbrella from a soirée, and has both chuckled and been scared on thinking of it afterwards.* JAMES, *a commoner fellow altogether, has discussed the sex over a glass, but is too canny to be in the company of less than two young women at a time.*]

David. [*Derisively.*] Oho, has she got you, James?

James. [*Feeling the sting of it.*] Nobody has got me.

David. They'll catch you yet, lad.

James. They'll never catch me. You've been nearer catched yourself.

Alick. Yes, Kitty Menzies, David.

David. [*Feeling himself under the umbrella.*] It was a kind of a shave that.

Alick. [*Who knows all that is to be known about women and can speak of them without a tremor.*] It's a curious thing, but a man cannot help winking when he hears that one of his friends has been catched.

David. That's so.

James. [*Clinging to his manhood.*] And fear of that wink is what has kept the two of us single men. And yet, what's the glory of being single?

David. There's no particular glory in it, but it's safe.

James. [*Putting away his aspirations.*] Yes, it's lonely, but it's safe. But who did you mean the poetry for, then?

David. For Maggie, of course.

[*You don't know* DAVID *and* JAMES *till you know how they love their sister* MAGGIE.]

Alick. I thought that.

David. [*Coming to the second point of his statement about Love.*] I saw her reading poetry and saying those words over to herself.

James. She has such a poetical mind.

David. Love. There's no doubt as that's what Maggie has set her heart on. And not merely love, but one of those grand noble loves; for though Maggie is undersized she has a passion for romance.

James. [*Wandering miserably about the room.*] It's terrible not to be able to give Maggie what her heart is set on.

[*The others never pay much attention to* JAMES, *though he is quite a smart figure in less important houses.*]

Alick. [*Violently.*] Those idiots of men.

David. Father, did you tell her who had got the minister of Galashiels?

Alick. [*Wagging his head sadly.*] I had to tell her. And then I—I—bought her a sealskin muff, and I just slipped it into her hands and came away.

James. [*Illustrating the sense of justice in the* WYLIE *family.*] Of course, to be fair to the man, he never pretended he wanted her.

David. None of them wants her; that's what depresses her. I was thinking, Father, I would buy her that gold watch and chain in Snibby's window. She hankers after it.

James. [*Slapping his pocket.*] You're too late, David; I've got them for her.

David. It's ill done of the minister. Many a pound of steak has that man had in this house.

Alick. You mind the slippers she worked for him?

James. I mind them fine; she began them for William Cathro. She's getting on in years too, though she looks so young.

Alick. I never can make up my mind, David, whether her curls make her look younger or older.

David. [*Determinedly.*] Younger. Whisht! I hear her winding the clock. Mind, not a word about the minister to her, James. Don't even mention religion this day.

James. Would it be like me to do such a thing?

David. It would be very like you. And there's that other matter: say not a syllable about our having a reason for sitting up late tonight. When she says it's bedtime, just all pretend we're not sleepy.

Alick. Exactly, and when——

[*Here* MAGGIE *enters, and all three are suddenly engrossed in the dambrod. We could describe* MAGGIE *at great length. But what is the use? What you really want to know is whether she was good-looking. No, she was not. Enter* MAGGIE, *who is not good-looking. When this is said, all is said. Enter* MAGGIE, *as it were, with her throat cut from ear to ear. She has a soft Scotch voice, and a more resolute manner than is perhaps fitting to her plainness;; and she stops short at sight of* JAMES *sprawling unconsciously in the company chair.*]

Maggie. James, I wouldn't sit on the fine chair.

James. I forgot again.

[*But he wishes she had spoken more sharply. Even profanation of the fine chair has not roused her. She takes up her knitting, and they all suspect that she knows what they have been talking about.*]

Maggie. You're late, David, it's nearly bed-time.

David. [*Finding the subject a safe one.*] I was kept late at the public meeting.

Alick. [*Glad to get so far away from Galashiels.*] Was it a good meeting?

David. Fairish. [*With some heat.*] That young John Shand *would* make a speech.

Maggie. John Shand? Is that the student Shand?

David. The same. It's true he's a student at Glasgow University in the winter months, but in summer he's just the railway porter here; and I think it's very presumptuous of a young lad like that to make a speech when he hasn't a penny to bless himself with.

Alick. The Shands were always an impudent family, and jealous. I suppose that's the reason they haven't been on speaking terms with us this six years. Was it a good speech?

David. [*Illustrating the family's generosity.*] It was very fine; but he needn't have made fun of *me.*

Maggie. [*Losing a stitch.*] He dared?

David. [*Depressed.*] You see I can *not* get started on a speech without saying things like "In rising *for* to make a few remarks."

James. What's wrong with it?

David. He mimicked me, and said "Will our worthy chairman come for to go for to answer my questions?" and so on; and they roared.

James. [*Slapping his money pocket.*] The sacket.*

David. I did feel bitterly, Father, the want of education.

[*Without knowing it, he has a beautiful way of pronouncing this noble word.*]

Maggie. [*Holding out a kind hand to him.*] David.

Alick. I've missed it sore, David. Even now I feel the want of it in the very marrow of me. I'm shamed to think I never gave you your chance. But when you were young I was so desperate poor, how could I do it, Maggie?

Maggie. It wasn't possible, Father.

Alick. [*Gazing at the book-shelves.*] To be able to understand these books! To up with them one at a time and scrape them as clean as though they were a bowl of brose. Lads, it's not to riches, it's to scholarship that I make my humble bow.

James. [*Who is good at bathos.*] There's ten yards of them. And they were selected by the minister of Galashiels. He said——

David. [*Quickly.*] James.

James. I mean—I mean——

Maggie. [*Calmly.*] I suppose you mean what you say, James. I hear, David, that the minister of Galashiels is to be married on that Miss Turnbull.

David. [*On guard.*] So they were saying.

Alick. All I can say is she has made a poor bargain.

Maggie. [*The damned.*] I wonder at you, Father. He's a very nice gentleman. I'm sure I hope he has chosen wisely.

James. Not him.

Maggie. [*Getting near her tragedy.*] How can you say that when you don't know her? I expect she is full of charm.

Alick. Charm? It's the very word he used.

David. Havering idiot.

Alick. What *is* charm, exactly, Maggie?

Maggie. Oh, it's—it's a sort of bloom on a woman. If you have it, you don't need to have anything else; and if you don't have it, it doesn't much matter what else you have. Some women, the few, have charm for all; and most have charm for one. But some have charm for none.

[*Somehow she has stopped knitting. Her menfolk are very depressed.* JAMES *brings his fist down on the table with a bang.*]

James. [*Shouting.*] I have a sister that has charm.

Maggie. No, James, you haven't.

James. [*Rushes at her with the watch and chain.*] Ha'e, Maggie.

[*She lets them lie in her lap.*]

David. Maggie, would you like a silk?

Maggie. What could I do with a silk? [*With a gust of passion.*] You might as well dress up a little brown hen.

[*They wriggle miserably.*]

James. [*Stamping.*] Bring him here to me.

Maggie. Bring whom, James?

James. David, I would be obliged if you wouldn't kick me beneath the table.

Maggie. [*Rising.*] Let's be practical; let's go to our beds.

[*This reminds them that they have a job on hand in which she is not to share.*]

David. [*Slily.*] I don't feel very sleepy yet.

Alick. Nor me either.

James. You've just taken the very words out of my mouth.

David. [*With unusual politeness.*] Good night to you, Maggie.

Maggie. [*Fixing the three of them.*] All of you unsleepy, when, as is well known, ten o'clock is your regular bed-time?

James. Yes, it's common knowledge that we go to our beds at ten. [*Chuckling.*] That's what we're counting on.

Maggie. Counting on?

David. You stupid whelp.

James. What have *I* done?

Maggie. [*Folding her arms.*] There's something up. You've got to tell me, David.

David. [*Who knows when he is beaten.*] Go out and watch, James.

Maggie. Watch?

[JAMES *takes himself off, armed, as* MAGGIE *notices, with a stick.*]

* Socket = small wallet. Secondary meaning, a rascal.

David. [*In his alert business way.*] Maggie, there are burglars about.

Maggie. Burglars?

[*She sits rigid, but she is not the kind to scream.*]

David. We hadn't meant for to tell you till we nabbed them; but they've been in this room twice of late. We sat up last night waiting for them, and we're to sit up again tonight.

Maggie. The silver plate.

David. It's all safe as yet. That makes us think that they were either frightened away these other times, or that they are coming back for to make a clean sweep.

Maggie. How did you get to know about this?

David. It was on Tuesday that the polissman called at the quarry with a very queer story. He had seen a man climbing out at this window at ten past two.

Maggie. Did he chase him?

David. It was so dark he lost sight of him at once.

Alick. Tell her about the window.

David. We've found out that the catch of the window has been pushed back by slipping the blade of a knife between the woodwork.

Maggie. David.

Alick. The polissman said he was carrying a little carpet bag.

Maggie. The silver plate *is* gone.

David. No, no. We were thinking that very likely he has bunches of keys in the bag.

Maggie. Or weapons.

David. As for that, we have some pretty stout weapons ourselves in the umbrella stand. So, if you'll go to your bed, Maggie ——

Maggie. Me? and my brothers in danger?

Alick. There's just one of them.

Maggie. The polissman just saw one.

David. [*Licking his palms.*] I would be very pleased if there were three of them.

Maggie. I watch with you. I would be very pleased if there were four of them.

David. And they say she has no charm!

[JAMES *returns on tiptoe as if the burglars were beneath the table. He signs to every one to breathe no more, and then whispers his news.*]

James. He's there. I had no sooner gone out than I saw him sliding down the garden wall, close to the rhubarbs.

Alick. What's he like?

James. He's an ugly customer. That's all I could see. There was a little carpet bag in his hand.

David. That's him.

James. He slunk into the rhodydendrons, and he's there now, watching the window.

David. We have him. Out with the light.

[*The room is beautified by a chandelier fitted for three gas jets, but with the advance of progress one of these has been removed and the incandescent light put in its place. This alone is lit.* ALICK *climbs a chair, pulls a little chain, and the room is now but vaguely lit by the fire. It plays fitfully on four sparkling faces.*]

Maggie. Do you think he saw you, James?

James. I couldn't say, but in any case I was too clever for him. I looked up at the stars, and yawned loud at them as if I was tremendous sleepy.

[*There is a long pause during which they are lurking in the shadows. At last they hear some movement, and they steal like ghosts from the room. We see* DAVID *turning out the lobby light; then the door closes and an empty room awaits the intruder with a shudder of expectancy. The window opens and shuts as softly as if this were a mother peering in to see whether her baby is asleep. Then the head of a man shows between the curtains. The remainder of him follows. He is carrying a little carpet bag. He stands irresolute; what puzzles him evidently is that the* WYLIES *should have retired to rest without lifting that piece of coal off the fire. He opens the door and peeps into the lobby, listening to the wag-at-the-wall clock. All seems serene, and he turns on the light. We see him clearly now. He is* JOHN SHAND, *aged twenty-one, boots muddy, as an indignant carpet can testify. He wears a shabby topcoat and a cockerty bonnet; otherwise he is in the well-worn corduroys of a railway porter. His movements, at first stealthy, become almost homely as he feels that he is secure. He opens the bag and takes out a bunch of keys, a small paper parcel, and a black implement that may be a burglar's jemmy. This cool customer examines the fire and piles on more coals. With the keys he opens the door of the bookcase, selects two large volumes, and brings them to the table. He takes off his topcoat and opens his parcel, which we now see contains sheets of foolscap paper. His next action shows that the "jemmy" is really a ruler. He knows where the pen and ink are kept. He pulls the fine chair nearer to the table, sits on it, and proceeds to write, occasionally dotting the carpet with ink as he stabs the air with his pen. He is so occupied that he does not see the door opening, and the* WYLIE *family staring at him. They are armed with sticks.*]

Alick. [*At last.*] When you're ready, John Shand.

[JOHN *hints back, and then has the grace to rise, dogged and expressionless.*]

James. [*Like a railway porter.*] Ticket, please.

David. You can't think of anything clever for to go for to say now, John.

Maggie. I hope you find that chair comfortable, young man.

John. I have no complaint to make against the chair.

Alick. [*Who is really distressed.*] A native of the town. The disgrace to your family. I feel pity for the Shands this night.

John. [*Glowering.*] I'll thank you, Mr. Wylie, not to pity my family.

James. Canny, canny.

Maggie. [*That sense of justice again.*] I think you should let the young man explain. It mayn't be so bad as we thought.

David. Explain away, my billie.

John. Only the uneducated would need an explanation. I'm a student [*with a little passion*], and I'm desperate for want of books. You have all I want here; no use to you but for display; well, I came here to study. I come twice weekly.

[*Amazement of his hosts.*]

David. [*Who is the first to recover.*] By the window.

John. Do you think a Shand would so far lower himself as to enter your door? Well, is it a case for the police?

James. It is.

Maggie. [*Not so much out of the goodness of her heart as to patronize the Shands.*] It seems to me it's a case for us all to go to our beds and leave the young man to study; but not on that chair.

[*And she wheels the chair away from him.*]

John. Thank you, Miss Maggie, but I couldn't be beholden to you.

James. My opinion is that he's nobody, so out with him.

John. Yes, out with me. And you'll be cheered to hear I'm likely to be a nobody for a long time to come.

David. [*Who had been beginning to respect him.*] Are you a poor scholar?

John. On the contrary, I'm a brilliant scholar.

David. It's siller, then?

John. [*Glorified by experiences he has shared with many a gallant soul.*] My first year at college I lived on a barrel of potatoes, and we had just a sofa-bed between two of us; when the one lay down the other had to get up. Do you think it was hardship? It was sublime. But this year I can't afford it. I'll have to stay on here, collecting the tickets of the illiterate, such as you, when I might be with Romulus and Remus among the stars.

James. [*Summing up.*] Havers.*

David. [*In whose head some design is vaguely taking shape.*] Whisht, James. I must say, young lad, I like your spirit. Now tell me, what's your professors' opinion of your future?

John. They think me a young man of extraordinary promise.

David. You have a name here for high moral character.

John. And justly.

David. Are you serious-minded?

John. I never laughed in my life.

David. Who do you sit under in Glasgow?

John. Mr. Flemister of the Sauchiehall High.

David. Are you a Sabbath-school teacher?

John. I am.

David. One more question. Are you promised?

John. To a lady?

David. Yes.

John. I've never given one of them a single word of encouragement. I'm too much occupied thinking about my career.

David. So.

[*He reflects, and finally indicates by a jerk of the head that he wishes to talk with his father behind the door.*]

James. [*Longingly.*] Do you want me too?

[*But they go out without even answering him.*]

Maggie. I don't know what maggot they have in their heads, but sit down, young man, till they come back.

John. My name's Mr. Shand, and till I'm called that I decline to sit down again in this house.

Maggie. Then I'm thinking, young sir, you'll have a weary wait.

[*While he waits you can see how pinched his face is. He is little more than a boy, and he seldom has enough to eat.* DAVID *and* ALICK *return presently, looking as sly as if they had been discussing*

* "Nonsense." used, as frequently in English, to mean, "It's a trifle."

some move on the dambrod, as indeed they have.]

David. [*Suddenly become genial.*] Sit down, Mr. Shand, and pull in your chair. You'll have a thimbleful of something to keep the cold out? [*Briskly.*] Glasses, Maggie. [*She wonders, but gets glasses and decanter from the sideboard, which* JAMES *calls the chiffy.* DAVID *and* ALICK, *in the most friendly manner, also draw up to the table.*] You're not a totaller, I hope?

John. [*Guardedly.*] I'm practically a totaller.

David. So are we. How do you take it? Is there any hot water, Maggie?

John. If I take it at all, and I haven't made up my mind yet, I'll take it cold.

David. You'll take it hot, James?

James. [*Also sitting at the table but completely befogged.*] No, I——

David. [*Decisively.*] I think you'll take it hot, James.

James. [*Sulking.*] I'll take it hot.

David. The kettle, Maggie.

[JAMES *has evidently to take it hot so that they can get at the business now on hand, while* MAGGIE *goes kitchenward for the kettle.*]

Alick. Now, David, quick, before she comes back.

David. Mr. Shand, we have an offer to make you.

John. [*Warningly.*] No patronage.

Alick. It's strictly a business affair.

David. Leave it to me, Father. It's this —— [*But to his annoyance the suspicious* MAGGIE *has already returned with the kettle.*] Maggie, don't you see that you're not wanted?

Maggie. [*Sitting down by the fire and resuming her knitting.*] I do, David.

David. I have a proposition to put before Mr. Shand, and women are out of place in business transactions.

[*The needles continue to click.*]

Alick. [*Sighing.*] We'll have to let her bide, David.

David. [*Sternly.*] Woman! [*But even this does not budge her.*] Very well then, sit there, but don't interfere, mind. Mr. Shand, we're willing, the three of us, to lay out £300 on your education if——

John. Take care——

David. [*Slowly, which is not his wont.*] On condition that five years from now, Maggie Wylie, if still unmarried, can claim to marry you, should such be her wish; the thing to be perfectly open on her side, but you to be strictly tied down.

James. [*Enlightened.*] So, so.

David. [*Resuming his smart manner.*] Now, what have you to say? Decide.

John. [*After a pause.*] I regret to say——

Maggie. It doesn't matter what he regrets to say, because I decide against it. And I think it was very ill-done of you to make any such proposal.

David. [*Without looking at her.*] Quiet, Maggie.

John. [*Looking at her.*] I must say, Miss Maggie, I don't see what reasons *you* can have for being so set against it.

Maggie. If you would grow a beard, Mr. Shand, the reasons wouldn't be quite so obvious.

John. I'll never grow a beard.

Maggie. Then you're done for at the start.

Alick. Come, come.

Maggie. Seeing I have refused the young man——

John. Refused!

David. That's no reason why we shouldn't have his friendly opinion. Your objections, Mr. Shand?

John. Simply, it's a one-sided bargain. I admit I'm no catch at present; but what could a man of my abilities not soar to with three hundred pounds? Something far above what she could aspire to.

Maggie. Oh, indeed!

David. The position is that without the three hundred you can't soar.

John. You have me there.

Maggie. Yes, but——

Alick. You see *you're* safeguarded, Maggie; you don't need to take him unless you like, but he has to take you.

John. That's an unfair arrangement also.

Maggie. I wouldn't dream of it without that condition.

John. Then you *are* thinking of it?

Maggie. Poof!

David. It's a good arrangement for you, Mr. Shand. The chances are you'll never have to go on with it, for in all probability she'll marry soon.

James. She's tremendous run after.

John. Even if that's true, it's just keeping me in reserve in case she misses doing better.

David. [*Relieved.*] That's the situation in a nutshell.

John. Another thing. Supposing I was to get fond of her?

Alick. [*Wistfully.*] It's very likely.

John. Yes, and then suppose she was to give me the go-by?

David. You have to risk that.

John. Or take it the other way. Supposing as I got to know her I *could not* endure her?

David. [*Suavely.*] You have both to take risks.

James. [*Less suavely.*] What you need, John Shand, is a clout on the head.

John. Three hundred pounds is no great sum.

David. You can take it or leave it.

Alick. No great sum for a student studying for the ministry!

John. Do you think that with that amount of money I would stop short at being a minister?

David. That's how I like to hear you speak. A young Scotsman of your ability let loose upon the world with £300—what could he not do? It's almost appalling to think of; especially if he went among the English.

John. What do you think, Miss Maggie?

Maggie. [*Who is knitting.*] I have no thoughts on the subject either way.

John. [*After looking her over.*] What's her age? She looks young, but they say it's the curls that does it.

David. [*Rather happily.*] She's one of those women who are eternally young.

John. I can't take that for an answer.

David. She's twenty-five.

John. I'm just twenty-one.

James. I read in a book that about four years' difference in the ages is the ideal thing.

[*As usual he is disregarded.*]

David. Well, Mr. Shand?

John. [*Where is his mother!*] I'm willing if she's willing.

David. Maggie?

Maggie. There can be no "if" about it. It must be an offer.

John. A Shand give a Wylie such a chance to humiliate him? Never.

Maggie. Then all is off.

David. Come, come, Mr. Shand, it's just a form.

John. [*Reluctantly.*] Miss Maggie, will you?

Maggie. [*Doggedly.*] Is it an offer?

John. [*Dourly.*] Yes.

Maggie. [*Rising.*] Before I answer I want first to give you a chance of drawing back.

David. Maggie.

Maggie. [*Bravely.*] When they said that I have been run after they were misleading you. I'm without charm; nobody has ever been after me.

John. Oho!

Alick. They will be yet.

John. [*The innocent.*] It shows at least that you haven't been after them.

[*His hosts exchange a self-conscious glance.*]

Maggie. One thing more; David said I'm twenty-five, I'm twenty-six.

John. Aha!

Maggie. Now be practical. Do you withdraw from the bargain, or do you not?

John. [*On reflection.*] It's a bargain.

Maggie. Then so be it.

David. [*Hurriedly.*] And that's settled. Did you say you would take it hot, Mr. Shand?

John. I think I'll take it neat.

[*The others decide to take it hot, and there is some careful business here with the toddy ladles.*]

Alick. Here's to you, and your career.

John. Thank you. To you, Miss Maggie. Had we not better draw up a legal document? Lawyer Crosbie could do it on the quiet.

David. Should we do that, or should we just trust to one another's honor?

Alick. [*Gallantly.*] Let Maggie decide.

Maggie. I think we would better have a legal document.

David. We'll have it drawn up tomorrow. I was thinking the best way would be for to pay the money in five yearly instalments.

John. I was thinking, better bank the whole sum in my name at once.

Alick. I think David's plan's the best.

John. I think not. Of course if it's not convenient to you——

David. [*Touched to the quick.*] It's perfectly convenient. What do you say, Maggie?

Maggie. I agree with John.

David. [*With an odd feeling that* MAGGIE *is now on the other side.*] Very well.

John. Then as that's settled I think I'll be stepping.

[*He is putting his papers back in the bag.*]

Alick. [*Politely.*] If you would like to sit on at your books——

John. As I can come at any orra time now I think I'll be stepping.

[MAGGIE *helps him into his topcoat.*]

Maggie. Have you a muffler, John?

John. I have.

[*He gets it from his pocket.*]

Maggie. You had better put it twice around. [*She does this for him.*]

David. Well, good night to you, Mr. Shand.

Alick. And good luck.

John. Thank you. The same to you. And I'll cry in at your office in the morning before the 6.20 is due.

David. I'll have the document ready for

you. [*There is the awkward pause that sometimes follows great events.*] I think, Maggie, you might see Mr. Shand to the door.

Maggie. Certainly. [JOHN *is going by the window.*] This way, John.

[*She takes him off by the more usual exit.*]

David. He's a fine, frank fellow; and you saw how cleverly he got the better of me about banking the money. [*As the heads of the conspirators come gleefully together.*] I tell you, father, he has a grand business head.

Alick. Lads, he's canny. He's cannier than any of us.

James. Except maybe Maggie. He has no idea what a remarkable woman Maggie is.

Alick. Best he shouldn't know. Men are nervous of remarkable women.

James. She's a long time in coming back.

David. [*Not quite comfortable.*] It's a good sign. H'sh. What sort of a night is it, Maggie?

Maggie. It's a little blowy.

[*She gets a large dust-cloth which is lying folded on a shelf, and proceeds to spread it over the fine chair. The men exchange self-conscious glances.*]

David. [*Stretching himself.*] Yes—well, well, oh, yes. It's getting late. What is it with you, Father?

Alick. I'm ten forty-two.

James. I'm ten forty.

David. Ten forty-two.

[*They wind up their watches.*]

Maggie. It's high time we were bedded. [*She puts her hands on their shoulders lovingly, which is the very thing they have been trying to avoid.*] You're very kind to me.

David. Havers.

Alick. Havers.

James. [*But this does not matter.*] Havers.

Maggie. [*A little dolefully.*] I'm a sort of sorry for the young man, David.

David. Not at all. You'll be the making of him. [*She lifts the two volumes.*] Are you taking the books to your bed, Maggie?

Maggie. Yes. I don't want him to know things I don't know myself.

[*She departs with the books; and* ALICK *and* DAVID, *the villains, now want to get away from each other.*]

Alick. Yes—yes. Oh, yes—ay, man—it is so—umpha. You'll lift the big coals off, David.

[*He wanders away to his spring mattress.* DAVID *removes the coals.*]

James. [*Who would like to sit down and have an argy-bargy.*] It's a most romantical affair. [*But he gets no answer.*] I wonder how it'll turn out? [*No answer.*] She's queer, Maggie. I wonder how some clever writer has never noticed how queer women are. It's my belief you could write a whole book about them. [DAVID *remains obdurate.*] It was very noble of her to tell him she's twenty-six. [*Muttering as he, too, wanders away.*] But I thought she was twenty-seven.

[DAVID *turns out the light.*]

II

Six years have elapsed and JOHN SHAND'S *great hour has come. Perhaps his great hour really lies ahead of him, perhaps he had it six years ago; it often passes us by in the night with such a faint call that we don't even turn in our beds. But according to the trumpets this is* JOHN'S *great hour; it is the hour for which he has long been working with his coat off; and now the coat is on again (broadcloth but ill-fitting), for there is no more to do but await results. He is standing for Parliament, and this is election night.*

As the scene discloses itself you get, so to speak, one of JOHN SHAND'S *posters in the face. Vote for* SHAND. SHAND, SHAND, SHAND. *Civil and Religious Liberty, Faith, Hope, Freedom. They are all fly-blown names for* SHAND. *Have a placard about* SHAND, *have a hundred placards about him, it is snowing* SHAND *tonight in Glasgow; take the paste out of your eye, and you will see that we are in one of* SHAND'S *committee rooms. It has been a hairdresser's emporium, but* SHAND, SHAND, SHAND *has swept through it like a wind, leaving nothing but the fixtures; why shave, why have your head doused in those basins when you can be brushed and scraped and washed up forever by simply voting for* SHAND?

There are a few hard chairs for yelling SHAND *from, and then rushing away.*

There is an iron spiral staircase that once led to the ladies' hairdressing apartments, but now leads to more SHAND, SHAND, SHAND. *A glass door at the back opens on to the shop proper, screaming Civil and Religious Liberty,* SHAND, *as it opens, and beyond is the street crammed with still more* SHAND *pro and con. Men in every sort of garb rush in and out, up and down the stair, shouting the magic word. Then there is a lull, and down the stair comes* MAGGIE WYLIE, *decidedly overdressed in blue velvet and (let us get this over) less good-looking than ever. She raises her hands to heaven, she spins round like a little teetotum. To her from the street, suffering from a determination of the word* SHAND *to the mouth, rush* ALICK *and* DAVID. ALICK *is thinner (being older),* DAVID *is stouter (being older), and they are both in tweeds and silk hats.*

Maggie. David—have they—is he? quick, quick!

David. There's no news yet, no news. It's terrible.

[*The teetotum revolves more quickly.*]

Alick. For God's sake, Maggie, sit down.

Maggie. I can't, I can't.

David. Hold her down.

[*They press her into a chair;* JAMES *darts in, stouter also. His necktie has gone; he will never again be able to attend a funeral in that hat.*]

James. [*Wildly.*] John Shand's the man for you. John Shand's the man for you. John Shand's the man for you.

David. [*Clutching him.*] Have you heard anything?

James. Not a word.

Alick. Look at her.

David. Maggie! [*He goes on his knees beside her, pressing her to him in affectionate anxiety.*] It was mad of him to dare.

Maggie. It was grand of him.

Alick. [*Moving about distraught.*] Insane ambition.

Maggie. Glorious ambition.

David. Maggie, Maggie, my lamb, best be prepared for the worst.

Maggie. [*Husky.*] I am prepared.

Alick. Six weary years has she waited for this night.

Maggie. Six brave years has John toiled for this night.

James. And you could have had him, Maggie, at the end of five. The document says five.

Maggie. Do you think I grudge not being married to him yet? Was I to hamper him till the fight was won?

David. [*With wrinkled brows.*] But if it's lost? [*She can't answer.*]

Alick. [*Starting.*] What's that?

[*The three listen at the door; the shouting dies down.*]

David. They're terrible still; what can make them so still?

[JAMES *spirits himself away.* ALICK *and* DAVID *blanch to hear* MAGGIE *speaking softly as if to* JOHN.]

Maggie. Did you say you had lost, John? Of course, you would lose the first time, dear John. Six years. Very well, we'll begin another six tonight. You'll win yet. [*Fiercely.*] Never give in, John, never give in!

[*The roar of the multitude breaks out again and comes rolling nearer.*]

David. I think he's coming.

[JAMES *is fired into the room like a squeezed onion.*]

James. He's coming!

[*They may go on speaking, but through the clang outside none could hear. The populace seem to be trying to take the committee room by assault. Out of the scrimmage a man emerges dishevelled and bursts into the room, closing the door behind him. It is* JOHN SHAND, *in a five-guinea suit, including the hat. There are other changes in him also, for he has been delving his way through loamy ground all these years. His right shoulder, which he used to raise to pound a path through the crowd, now remains permanently in that position. His mouth tends to close like a box. His eyes are tired, they need some one to pull the lids over them and send him to sleep for a week. But they are honest eyes still, and faithful, and could even light up his face at times with a smile, if the mouth would give a little help.*]

John. [*Clinging to a chair that he may not fly straight to heaven.*] I'm in; I'm elected! Majority two hundred and forty-four; I'm John Shand, *M.P.*

[*The crowd have the news by this time and their roar breaks the door open.* JAMES *is off at once to tell them that he is to be* SHAND'S *brother-in-law. A teardrop clings to* ALICK'S *nose;* DAVID *hits out playfully at* JOHN, *and* JOHN *in an ecstasy returns the blow.*]

David. Fling yourself at the door, Father, and bar them out. Maggie, what keeps you so quiet now?

Maggie. [*Weak in her limbs.*] You're sure you're in, John?

John. Majority 244. I've beaten the baronet. I've done it, Maggie, and not a soul to help me; I've done it alone. [*His voice breaks; you could almost pick up the pieces.*] I'm as hoarse as a crow, and I have to address the Cowcaddens Club yet; David, pump some oxygen into me.

David. Certainly, Mr. Shand.

[*While he does it,* MAGGIE *is seeing visions.*]

Alick. What are you doing, Maggie?

Maggie. This is the House of Commons, and I'm John, catching the Speaker's eye for the first time. Do you see a queer little old wifie sitting away up there in the Ladies' Gallery? That's me. Mr. Speaker, sir, I rise to make my historic maiden speech. I am no orator, sir; voice from Ladies' Gallery, "Are you not, John? you'll soon let them see that"; cries of "Silence, woman," and general indignation. Mr. Speaker, sir, I stand here diffidently with my eyes on the Treasury Bench; voice from the Ladies' Gallery, "And you'll soon have your coat-tails on it, John"; loud cries of "Remove that little old wifie," in which she is forcibly ejected, and the honorable gentleman resumes his seat in a torrent of admiring applause.

[ALICK *and* DAVID *waggle their proud heads.*]

John. [*Tolerantly.*] Maggie, Maggie.

Maggie. You're not angry with me, John?

John. No, no.

Maggie. But you glowered.

John. I was thinking of Sir Peregrine. Just because I beat him at the poll he took a shabby revenge; he congratulated me in French, a language I haven't taken the trouble to master.

Maggie. [*Becoming a little taller.*] Would it help you, John, if you were to marry a woman that could speak French?

David. [*Quickly.*] Not at all.

Maggie. [*Gloriously.*] Mon cher Jean, laissez-moi parler le français, voulez-vous un interprète?

John. Hullo!

Maggie. Je suis la sœur française de mes deux frères écossais.

David. [*Worshipping her.*] She's been learning French.

John. [*Lightly.*] Well done!

Maggie. [*Grandly.*] They're arriving.

Alick. Who?

Maggie. Our guests. This is London, and Mrs. John Shand is giving her first reception. [*Airily.*] Have I told you, darling, who are coming tonight? There's that dear Sir Peregrine. [*To* ALICK.] Sir Peregrine, this *is* a pleasure. Avez-vous. . . . So sorry we beat you at the poll.

John. I'm doubting the baronet would sit on you, Maggie.

Maggie. I've invited a lord to sit on the baronet. *Voilà!*

David. [*Delighted.*] You thing! You'll find the lords expensive.

Maggie. Just a little cheap lord. [JAMES *enters importantly.*] My dear Lord Cheap, this is kind of you.

[JAMES *hopes that* MAGGIE'S *reason is not unbalanced.*]

David. [*Who really ought to have had education.*] How de doo, Cheap?

James. [*Bewildered.*] Maggie——

Maggie. Yes, do call me Maggie.

Alick. [*Grinning.*] She's practising her first party, James. The swells are at the door.

James. [*Heavily.*] That's what I came to say. They *are* at the door.

John. Who?

James. The swells; a carriage and pair.

[*He gives* JOHN *three cards.*]

John. "Mr. Tenterden."

David. Him that was speaking for you?

John. The same. He's a whip and an Honorable. "Lady Sybil Tenterden." [*Frowns.*] Her! She's his sister.

Maggie. A married woman?

John. No. "The Comtesse de la Brière."

Maggie. [*The scholar.*] She must be French.

John. Yes; I think she's some relation. She's a widow.

James. But what am I to say to them? ["MR. SHAND'S *compliments, and he will be proud to receive them" is the very least that the* WYLIES *expect.*]

John. [*Who was evidently made for great ends.*] Say I'm very busy, but if they care to wait I hope presently to give them a few minutes.

James. [*Thunderstruck.*] Good God, Mr. Shand!

[*But it makes him* JOHN'S *more humble servant than ever, and he departs with the message.*]

John. [*Not unaware of the sensation he has created.*] I'll go up and let the crowd see me from the window.

Maggie. But—but—what are we to do with these ladies?

John. [*As he tramps upwards.*] It's your reception, Maggie; this will prove you.

Maggie. [*Growing smaller.*] Tell me what you know about this Lady Sybil?

John. The only thing I know about her is that she thinks me vulgar.

Maggie. You?

John. She has attended some of my meetings, and I'm told she said that.

Maggie. What could the woman mean?

John. I wonder. When I come down I'll ask her.

[*With his departure* MAGGIE'S *nervousness increases.*]

Alick. [*Encouragingly.*] In at them, Maggie, with your French.

Maggie. It's all slipping from me, Father.

David. [*Gloomily.*] I'm sure to say "for to come for to go."

[*The newcomers glorify the room, and* MAGGIE *feels that they have lifted her up with the tongs and deposited her in one of the basins. They are far from intending to be rude; it is not their fault that thus do swans scatter the ducks. They do not know that they are guests of the family, they think merely that they are waiting with other strangers in a public room; they undulate inquiringly, and if* MAGGIE *could undulate in return she would have no cause for offense. But she suddenly realizes that this is an art as yet denied her, and that though* DAVID *might buy her evening gowns as fine as theirs (and is at this moment probably deciding to do so), she would look better carrying them in her arms than on her person. She also feels that to emerge from wraps as they are doing is more difficult than to plank your money on the counter for them. The* COMTESSE *she could forgive, for she is old; but* LADY SYBIL *is young and beautiful and comes lazily to rest like a stately ship of Tarsus.*]

Comtesse. [*Smilingly divinely, and speaking with such a pretty accent.*] I hope one is not in the way. We were told we might wait.

Maggie. [*Bravely climbing out of the basin.*] Certainly—I am sure—if you will be so—it is——

[*She knows that* DAVID *and her father are very sorry for her. A high voice is heard orating outside.*]

Sybil. [*Screwing her nose deliciously.*] He is at it again, Auntie.

Comtesse. Mon Dieu! [*Like one begging pardon of the universe.*] It is Mr. Tenterden, you understand, making one more of his delightful speeches to the crowd. *Would* you be so charming as to shut the door?

[*This to* DAVID *in such appeal that she is evidently making the petition of her life.* DAVID *saves her.*]

Maggie. [*Determined not to go under.*] J'espère que vous—trouvez—cette—réunion—intéressante?

Comtesse. Vous parlez français? Mais c'est charmant! Voyons, causons un peu. Racontez-moi tout de ce grand homme, toutes les choses merveilleuses qu'il a faites.

Maggie. I—I—Je connais—[*Alas!*]

Comtesse. [*Naughtily.*] Forgive me, Mademoiselle, I thought you spoke French.

Sybil. [*Who knows that* DAVID *admires her shoulders.*] How wicked of you, Auntie. [*To* MAGGIE.] I assure you none of us can understand her when she gallops at that pace.

Maggie. [*Crushed.*] It doesn't matter. I will tell Mr. Shand that you are here.

Sybil. [*Drawling.*] Please don't trouble him. We are really only waiting till my brother recovers and can take us back to our hotel.

Maggie. I'll tell him.

[*She is glad to disappear up the stair.*]

Comtesse. The lady seems distressed. Is she a relation of Mr. Shand?

David. Not for to say a relation. She's my sister. Our name is Wylie.

[*But granite quarries are nothing to them.*]

Comtesse. How do you do? You are the committee man of Mr. Shand?

David. No, just friends.

Comtesse. [*Gaily to the basins.*] Aha! I know you. Next, please! Sybil, do you weigh yourself, or are you asleep?

[LADY SYBIL *has sunk indolently into a weighing-chair.*]

Sybil. Not quite, Auntie.

Comtesse. [*The mirror of* la politesse.] Tell me all about Mr. Shand. Was it here that he—picked up the pin?

David. The pin?

Comtesse. As *I* have read, a self-made man always begins by picking up a pin. After that, as the memoirs say, his rise was rapid.

[DAVID, *however, is once more master of himself, and indeed has begun to tot up the cost of their garments.*]

David. It wasn't a pin he picked up, my lady; it was £300.

Alick. [*Who feels that* JOHN'S *greatness has been outside the conversation quite long enough.*] And his rise wasn't so rapid, just at first, David!

David. He had his fight. His original intention was to become a minister; he's university-educated, you know; he's not a workingman member.

Alick. [*With reverence.*] He's an M.A. But while he was a student he got a place in an iron cementer's business.

Comtesse. [*Now far out of her depths.*] Iron cementer?

David. They scrape boilers.

Comtesse. I see. The fun men have, Sybil!

David. [*With some solemnity.*] There have been millions made in scraping boilers. They say, Father, he went into business so as to be able to pay off the £300.

Alick. [*Slily.*] So I've heard.

Comtesse. Aha—it was a loan?

[DAVID *and* ALICK *are astride their great subject now.*]

David. No, a gift—of a sort—from some well-wishers. But they wouldn't hear of his paying it off, Father!

Alick. Not them!

Comtesse. [*Restraining an impulse to think of other things.*] That was kind, charming.

Alick. [*With a look at* DAVID.] Yes. Well, my lady, he developed a perfect genius for the iron-cementing.

David. But his ambition wasn't satisfied. Soon he had public life in his eye. As a heckler he was something fearsome; they had to seat him on the platform for to keep him quiet. Next they had to let him into the Chair. After that he did all the speaking; he cleared all roads before him like a fire-engine; and when this vacancy occurred, you could hardly say it did occur, so quickly did he step into it. My lady, there are few more impressive sights in the world than a Scotsman on the make.

Comtesse. I can well believe it. And now he has said farewell to boilers?

David. [*Impressively.*] Not at all; the firm promised if he was elected for to make him their London manager at £800 a year.

Comtesse. There is a strong man for you, Sybil; but I believe you *are* asleep.

Sybil. [*Stirring herself.*] Honestly, I'm not. [*Sweetly to the others.*] But *would* you mind finding out whether my brother is drawing to a close?

[DAVID *goes out, leaving poor* ALICK *marooned. The* COMTESSE *is kind to him.*]

Comtesse. Thank you very much. [*Which helps* ALICK *out.*] Don't you love a strong man, sleepy head?

Sybil. [*Preening herself.*] I never met one.

Comtesse. Neither have I. But if you *did* meet one, would he wake you up?

Sybil. I dare say he would find there were two of us.

Comtesse. [*Considering her.*] Yes, I think he would. Ever been in love, you cold thing?

Sybil. [*Yawning.*] I have never shot up in flame, Auntie.

Comtesse. Think you could manage it?

Sybil. If Mr. Right came along.

Comtesse. As a girl of today it would be your duty to tame him.

Sybil. As a girl of today I would try to do my duty.

Comtesse. And if it turned out that *he* tamed you instead?

Sybil. He would have to do that if he were *my* Mr. Right.

Comtesse. And then?

Sybil. Then, of course, I should adore him. Auntie, I think if I ever really love it will be like Mary Queen of Scots, who said of her Bothwell that she could follow him round the world in her nighty.

Comtesse. My petite!

Sybil. I believe I mean it.

Comtesse. Oh, it is quite my conception of your character. Do you know, I am rather sorry for this Mr. John Shand.

Sybil. [*Opening her fine eyes.*] Why? He is quite a boor, is he not?

Comtesse. For that very reason. Because his great hour is already nearly sped. That wild-bull manner that moves the multitude—they will laugh at it in your House of Commons.

Sybil. [*Indifferently.*] I suppose so.

Comtesse. Yet if he had education——

Sybil. Have we not been hearing how superbly he is educated?

Comtesse. It is such as you or me that he needs to educate him now. *You* could do it almost too well.

Sybil. [*With that pretty stretch of neck.*] I am not sufficiently interested. I retire in your favor. How would you begin?

Comtesse. By asking him to drop in, about five, of course. By the way, I wonder is there a Mrs. Shand?

Sybil. I have no idea. But they marry young.

Comtesse. If there is not, there is probably a lady waiting for him, somewhere in a boiler.

Sybil. I dare say. [MAGGIE *descends.*]

Maggie. Mr. Shand will be down directly.

Comtesse. Thank you. Your brother has been giving us such an interesting account of his career. I forget, Sybil, whether he said that he was married.

Maggie. No, he's not married; but he will be soon.

Comtesse. Ah! [*She is merely making conversation.*] A friend of yours?

Maggie. [*Now a scorner of herself.*] I don't think much of her.

Comtesse. In that case, tell me all about her.

Maggie. There's not much to tell. She's common, and stupid. One of those who go in for self-culture; and then when the test comes they break down. [*With sinister enjoyment.*] She'll be the ruin of him.

Comtesse. But is not that sad! Figure to yourself how many men with greatness before them have been shipwrecked by marrying in the rank from which they sprang.

Maggie. I've told her that.

Comtesse. But she will not give him up?

Maggie. No.

Sybil. Why should she if he cares for her? What is her name?

Maggie. It's—Maggie.

Comtesse. [*Still uninterested.*] Well, I am afraid that Maggie is to do for John. [JOHN *comes down.*] Ah, our hero!

John. Sorry I have kept you waiting. The Comtesse?

Comtesse. And my niece Lady Sybil Tenterden. [SYBIL's *head inclines on its stem.*] She is not really all my niece; I mean I am only half of her aunt. What a triumph, Mr. Shand!

John. Oh, pretty fair, pretty fair. Your brother has just finished addressing the crowd, Lady Sybil.

Sybil. Then we must not detain Mr. Shand, Auntie.

Comtesse. [*Who unless her heart is touched thinks insincerity charming.*] Only one word. I heard you speak last night. Sublime! Just the sort of impassioned eloquence that your House of Commons loves.

John. It's very good of you to say so.

Comtesse. But we must run. *Bon soir.*

[SYBIL *bows as to some one far away.*]

John. Good night, Lady Sybil. I hear you think I'm vulgar.

[*Eyebrows are raised.*]

Comtesse. My dear Mr. Shand, what absurd——

John. I was told she said that after hearing me speak.

Comtesse. Quite a mistake, I——

John. [*Doggedly.*] Is it not true?

Sybil. ["*Waking up.*"] You seem to know, Mr. Shand; and as you press me so unnecessarily—well, yes, that is how you struck me.

Comtesse. My child!

Sybil. [*Who is a little agitated.*] He would have it.

John. [*Perplexed.*] What's the matter? I just wanted to know, because if it's true I must alter it.

Comtesse. There, Sybil, see how he values your good opinion.

Sybil. [*Her svelte figure giving like a fly-rod.*] It is very nice of you to put it in that way, Mr. Shand. Forgive me.

John. But I don't quite understand yet. Of course, it can't matter to me, Lady Sybil, what you think of me; what I mean is, that I mustn't be vulgar if it would be injurious to my career.

[*The fly-rod regains its rigidity.*]

Sybil. I see. No, of course, I could not affect your career, Mr. Shand.

John. [*Who quite understands that he is being challenged.*] That's so, Lady Sybil, meaning no offence.

Sybil. [*Who has a naughty little impediment in her voice when she is most alluring.*] Of course not. And we are friends again?

John. Certainly.

Sybil. Then I hope you will come to see me in London as I present no terrors.

John. [*He is a man, is* JOHN.] I'll be very pleased.

Sybil. Any afternoon about five.

John. Much obliged. And you can teach me the things I don't know yet, if you'll be so kind.

Sybil. [*The impediment becoming more assertive.*] If you wish it, I shall do my best.

John. Thank you, Lady Sybil. And who knows, there may be one or two things I can teach you.

Sybil. [*It has now become an angel's hiccough.*] Yes, we can help one another. Good-by till then.

John. Good-by. Maggie, the ladies are going.

[*During this skirmish* MAGGIE *has stood apart. At the mention of her name they glance at one another.* JOHN *escorts* SYBIL, *but the* COMTESSE *turns back. She says:*]

"Are you, then, *the* Maggie? [MAGGIE *nods rather defiantly and the* COMTESSE *is distressed.*] But if I had known I would not have said those things. Please forgive an old woman."

"It doesn't matter."

"I—I dare say it will be all right. Mademoiselle, if I were you I would not encourage those *tête-à-têtes* with Lady Sybil. I am the rude one, but she is the dangerous one; and I am afraid his impudence has attracted her. *Bon voyage,* Miss Maggie."

"Good-by—but I *can* speak French. Je parle française. Isn't that right?"

"But, yes, it is excellent. [*Making things easy for her.*] C'est très bien."

"Je me suis embrouillée—la dernière fois."

"Good! Shall I speak more slowly?"

"No, no. Non, non, faster, faster."

"J'admire votre courage!"

"Je comprends chaque mot."

"Parfait! Bravo!"

"Voilà!"

"Superbe!"

[*The* COMTESSE *goes, applauding; and* MAGGIE *has a moment of elation, which, however, has passed before* JOHN *returns for his hat.*]

"Have you more speaking to do, John?"

[*He is somehow in high good-humor.*]

"I must run across and address the Cowcaddens Club. [*He sprays his throat with a hand-spray.*] I wonder if I *am* vulgar, Maggie?"

"You are not, but *I* am."

"Not that *I* can see."

"Look how over-dressed I am, John! I knew it was too showy when I ordered it, and yet I could not resist the thing. But I will tone down, I will. What did you think of Lady Sybil?"

"That young woman had better be careful. She's a bit of a besom,* Maggie."

"She's beautiful, John."

"She has a neat way of stretching herself. For playing with she would do as well as another."

[MAGGIE *looks at him wistfully.*]

"You couldn't stay and have a talk for a few minutes?"

"If you want me, Maggie. The longer you keep them waiting, the more they think of you."

"When are you to announce that we're to be married, John?"

"I won't be long. You've waited a year more than you need have done, so I think it's your due I should hurry things now."

"I think it's noble of you."

"Not at all, Maggie; the nobleness has been yours in waiting so patiently. And your brothers would insist on it, at any rate. They're watching me like cats with a mouse."

"It's so little I've done to help."

"Three hundred pounds."

"I'm getting a thousand per cent. for it."

"And very pleased I am you should think so, Maggie."

"Is it terrible hard to you, John?"

"It's not hard at all. I can say truthfully, Maggie, that all, or nearly all, I've seen of you in these six years has gone to increase my respect for you."

"Respect!"

"And a bargain's a bargain."

"If it wasn't that you're so glorious to me, John, I would let you off."

[*There is a gleam in his eye, but he puts it out.*]

"In my opinion, Maggie, we'll be a very happy pair." [*She accepts this eagerly.*]

"We know each other so well, John, don't we?"

"I'm an extraordinary queer character, and I suppose nobody knows me well except myself; but I know you, Maggie, to the very roots of you."

[*She magnanimously lets this remark alone.*]

"And it's not as if there was any other woman you—fancied more, John."

"There's none whatever."

"If there ever should be—oh, if there ever should be! Some woman with charm."

"Maggie, you forget yourself. There couldn't be another woman once I was a married man."

"One has heard of such things."

"Not in Scotsmen, Maggie; not in Scotsmen."

"I've sometimes thought, John, that the difference between us and the English is that the Scotch are hard in all other respects but soft with women, and the English are hard with women but soft in all other respects."

"You've forgotten the grandest moral attribute of a Scotsman, Maggie, that he'll do nothing which might damage his career."

"Ah, but John, whatever you do, you do it so tremendously; and if you were to love, what a passion it would be."

"There's something in that, I suppose."

"And then, what could I do? For the desire of my life now, John, is to help you to get everything you want, except just that I want you to have me, too."

"We'll get on fine, Maggie."

"You're just making the best of it. They say that love is sympathy, and if that's so mine must be a great love for you, for I see all you are feeling this night and bravely hiding; I feel for you as if I was John Shand myself." [JOHN *sighs.*]

"I had best go to the meeting, Maggie."

"Not yet. Can you look me in the face, John, and deny that there is surging within you a mighty desire to be free, to begin the new life untrammelled?"

* In Scotch dialect for low woman.

"Leave such maggots alone, Maggie."

"It's a shame of me not to give you up."

"I would consider you a very foolish woman if you did."

"If I were John Shand I would no more want to take Maggie Wylie with me through the beautiful door that has opened wide for you than I would want to take an old pair of shoon. Why don't you bang the door in my face, John?"

[*A tremor runs through* JOHN.]

"A bargain's a bargain, Maggie."

[MAGGIE *moves about, an eerie figure, breaking into little cries. She flutters round him, threateningly.*]

"Say one word about wanting to get out of it, and I'll put the lawyers on you."

"Have I hinted at such a thing?"

"The document holds you hard and fast."

"It does." [*She gloats miserably.*]

"The woman never rises with the man. I'll drag you down, John. I'll drag you down."

"Have no fear of that, I won't let you. I'm too strong."

"You'll miss the prettiest thing in the world, and all owing to me."

"What's that?"

"Romance."

"Poof."

"All's cold and gray without it, John. They that have had it have slipped in and out of heaven."

"You're exaggerating, Maggie."

"You've worked so hard, you've had none of the fun that comes to most men long before they're your age."

"I never was one for fun. I cannot call to mind, Maggie, ever having laughed in my life."

"You have no sense of humor."

"Not a spark."

"I've sometimes thought that if you had, it might make you fonder of me. I think one needs a sense of humor to be fond of me."

"I remember reading of some one that said it needed a surgical operation to get a joke into a Scotsman's head."

"Yes, that's been said."

"What beats me, Maggie, is how you could insert a joke with an operation."

[*He considers this and gives it up.*]

"That's not the kind of fun I was thinking of. I mean fun with the lasses, John—gay, jolly, harmless fun. They could be impudent fashionable beauties now, stretching themselves to attract you, like that hiccoughing little devil, and running away from you, and crooking their fingers to you to run after them."

[JOHN *draws a big breath.*]

"No, I never had that."

"It's every man's birthright, and you would have it now but for me."

"I can do without, Maggie."

"It's like missing out all the Saturdays."

"You feel sure, I suppose, that an older man wouldn't suit you better, Maggie?"

"I couldn't feel surer of anything. You're just my ideal."

"Yes, yes. Well, that's as it should be."

[*She threatens him again.*]

"David has the document. It's carefully locked away."

"He would naturally take good care of it."

[*The pride of the* WYLIES *deserts her.*]

"John, I make you a solemn promise that, in consideration of the circumstances of our marriage, if you should ever fall in love, I'll act differently from other wives."

"There will be no occasion, Maggie."

[*Her voice becomes tremulous.*]

"John, David doesn't have the document. He thinks he has, but I have it here."

[*Somewhat heavily* JOHN *surveys the fatal paper.*]

"Well do I mind the look of it, Maggie. Yes, yes, that's it. Umpha."

"You don't ask why I've brought it."

"Why did you?"

"Because I thought I might perhaps have the courage and the womanliness to give it back to you. [JOHN *has a brief dream.*] Will you never hold it up against me in the future that I couldn't do that?"

"I promise you, Maggie, I never will."

"To go back to the Pans and take up my old life there, when all these six years my eyes have been centered on this night! I've been waiting for this night as long as you have been; and now to go back there, and wizen and dry up, when I might be married to John Shand!"

"And you will be, Maggie. You have my word."

"Never—never—never. [*She tears up the document. He remains seated immovable, but the gleam returns to his eye. She rages first at herself and then at him.*] I'm a fool, a fool, to let you go. I tell you, you'll rue this day, for you need me, you'll come to grief without me. There's nobody can help you as I could have helped you. I'm essential to your career, and you're blind not to see it."

"What's that, Maggie? In no circumstances would I allow any meddling with my career."

"You would never have known I was meddling with it. But that's over. Don't be in too great a hurry to marry, John. Have your fling with the beautiful dolls first. Get the whiphand of the haughty ones, John. Give them their licks. Every time they hiccough let them have an extra slap in memory of me. And be sure to remember this, my man, that the one who marries you will find you out."

"Find me out?"

"However careful a man is, his wife always finds out his failings."

"I don't know, Maggie, to what failings you refer. [*The Cowcaddens Club has burst its walls, and is pouring this way to raise the new Member on its crest. The first wave hurls itself against the barber's shop with cries of* "SHAND, SHAND, SHAND." *For a moment* JOHN *stems the torrent by planting his back against the door.*] You are acting under an impulse, Maggie, and I can't take advantage of it. Think the matter over, and we'll speak about it in the morning."

"No, I can't go through it again. It ends tonight and now. Good luck, John."

[*She is immediately submerged in the sea that surges through the door, bringing much wreckage with it. In a moment the place is so full that another cupful could not find standing room. Some slippery ones are squeezed upwards and remain aloft as warnings.* JOHN *has jumped on to the stair, and harangues the flood vainly like another Canute. It is something about freedom and noble minds, and, though unheard, goes to all heads, including the speaker's. By the time he is audible sentiment has him for her own.*]

"But, gentlemen, one may have too much even of freedom. [*"No, no."*] Yes, Mr. Adamson. One may want to be tied. [*"Never, never."*] I say yes, Willie Cameron; and I have found a young lady who I am proud to say is willing to be tied to me. I'm to be married. [*Uproar.*] Her name's Miss Wylie. [*Transport.*] Quiet; she's here now. [*Frenzy.*] She was here! Where are you, Maggie?" [*A small voice*—"I'm here." *A hundred great voices*—"Where—where—where?" *The small voice*—"I'm so little none of you can see me."]

[*Three men, name of* WYLIE, *buffet their way forward. Anon is heard the voice of* DAVID.]

"James, father, have you grip of her?"

"We've got her."

"Then hoist her up."

[*The queer little elated figure is raised aloft. With her fingers she can just touch the stars. Not unconscious of the nobility of his behavior, the hero of the evening points an impressive finger at her.*]

"Gentlemen, the future Mrs. John Shand! [*"Speech, speech."*] No, no, being a lady she can't make a speech, but——"

[*The heroine of the evening surprises him.*]

"I can make a speech, and I will make a speech, and it's in two words, and they're these—[*holding out her arms to enfold all the members of the Cowcaddens Club*]—My Constituents!" [*Dementia.*]

III

A few minutes ago the COMTESSE DE LA BRIÈRE, *who has not recently been in England, was shown into the London home of the* SHANDS. *Though not sufficiently interested to express her surprise in words, she raised her eyebrows on finding herself in a charming room; she had presumed that the* SHAND *scheme of decoration would be as impossible as themselves.*

It is the little room behind the dining-room for which English architects have long been famous; "Make something of this, and you will indeed be a clever one," they seem to say to you as they unveil it. The COMTESSE *finds that* JOHN *has undoubtedly made something of it. It is his "study" (mon Dieu, the words these English use!) and there is nothing in it that offends; there is so much not in it, too, that might so easily have been there. It is not in the least ornate; there are no colors quarreling with each other (unseen, unheard by the blissful occupant of the revolving chair); the* COMTESSE *has not even the gentle satisfaction of noting a "suite" in stained oak. Nature might have taken a share in the decorations, so restful are they to the eyes; it is the working room of a man of culture, probably lately down from Oxford; at a first meeting there is nothing in it that pretends to be what it is not. Our visitor is a little disappointed, but being fair-minded blows her absent host a kiss for disappointing her.*

He has even, she observes with a twinkle, made something of the most difficult of his possessions, the little wife. For MAGGIE, *who is here receiving her, has been quite creditably toned down. He has put her into a little gray frock that not only deals gently with her personal defects, but is in harmony with the room. Evidently, however, she has not "risen" with him, for she is as stupid as ever; the* COMTESSE, *who remembers having liked her the better of the two, could shake her for being so stupid. For instance, why is she not asserting herself in that other apartment? The other apartment is really a correctly solemn dining-room, of which we have a glimpse through partly open folding-doors. At this moment it is harboring* MR. SHAND'S *ladies' committee, who sit with pens and foolscap around the large table, awaiting the advent of their leader. There are nobly wise ones and some foolish ones among them, for we are back in the strange days when it was considered "unwomanly" for women to have minds. The* COMTESSE *peeps at them with curiosity, as they arrange their papers or are ushered into the dining-room through a door which we cannot see. To her frivolous ladyship they are a species of wild fowl, and she is specially amused to find her niece among them. She demands an explanation as soon as the communicating doors close.*

"Tell me since when has my dear Sybil become one of these ladies? It is not like her."

[MAGGIE *is obviously not clever enough to understand the woman question. Her eye rests longingly on a half-finished stocking as she innocently but densely replies:*]

"I think it was about the time that my husband took up their cause."

[*The* COMTESSE *has been hearing tales of* LADY SYBIL *and the barbarian; and after having the grace to hesitate, she speaks with the directness for which she is famed in Mayfair.*]

"Mrs. Shand, excuse me for saying that if half of what I hear be true, your husband is seeing that lady a great deal too often. [MAGGIE *is expressionless; she reaches for her stocking, whereat her guest loses patience.*] Oh, mon Dieu, put that down; you can buy them at two francs the pair. Mrs. Shand, why do not you compel yourself to take an intelligent interest in your husband's work?"

"I typewrite his speeches."

"But do you know what they are about?"

"They are about various subjects."

"Oh!"

[*Did* MAGGIE *give her an unseen quizzical glance before demurely resuming the knitting? One is not certain, as* JOHN *has come in, and this obliterates her. A "Scotsman on the make," of whom* DAVID *has spoken reverently, is still to be read—in a somewhat better bound volume—in* JOHN SHAND'S *person; but it is as doggedly honest a face as ever; and he champions women, not for personal ends, but because his blessed days of poverty gave him a light upon their needs. His self-satisfaction, however, has increased, and he has pleasantly forgotten some things. For instance, he can now call out "Porter" at railway stations without dropping his hands for the barrow.* MAGGIE *introduces the* COMTESSE, *and he is still undaunted.*]

"I remember you well—at Glasgow."

"It must be quite two years ago, Mr. Shand."

[JOHN *has no objection to showing that he has had a classical education.*]

"*Tempus fugit*, Comtesse."

"I have not been much in this country since then, and I return to find you a coming man."

[*Fortunately, his learning is tempered with modesty.*]

"Oh, I don't know, I don't know."

"The Ladies' Champion."

[*His modesty is tempered with a respect for truth.*]

"Well, well."

"And you are about, as I understand, to introduce a bill to give women an equal right with men to grow beards."

[*Which is all she knows about it.* JOHN *takes the remark literally.*]

"There's nothing about beards in it, Comtesse. [*She gives him time to cogitate, and is pleased to note that there is no result.*] Have you typed my speech, Maggie?"

"Yes; twenty-six pages."

[*She produces it from a drawer. Perhaps* JOHN *wishes to impress the visitor.*]

"I'm to give the ladies' committee a general idea of it. Just see, Maggie, if I know the peroration. 'In conclusion, Mr. Speaker, these are the reasonable demands of every intelligent Englishwoman'—I had better say British woman—'and I am proud to nail them to my flag' "——

[*The visitor is properly impressed.*]

"Oho! defies his leaders!"

" 'So long as I can do so without embarrassing the Government.' "

"Ah, ah, Mr. Shand!"

" 'I call upon the Front Bench, sir, loyally but firmly' "——

"Firm again!"

". . . 'either to accept my Bill, or to promise *without delay* to bring in one of their own; and if they decline to do so I solemnly warn them that though I will not press the matter to a division* just now' "——

"Ahem!"

" 'I will bring it forward again in the near future.' And now, Comtesse, *you* know that I'm not going to divide—and not another soul knows it."

"I am indeed flattered by your confidence."

"I've only told you because I don't care who knows now."

"Oh!"

[*Somehow* MAGGIE *seems to be dissatisfied.*]

"But why is that, John?"

"I daren't keep the Government in doubt any longer about what I mean to do. I'll show the whips the speech privately to-night."

[*But still* MAGGIE *wants to know.*]

"But not to go to a division is hedging, isn't it? Is that strong?"

"To make the speech at all, Maggie, is stronger than most would dare. They would *do* for me if I went to a division."

"Bark but not bite?"

"Now, now, Maggie, you're out of your depth."

"I suppose that's it."

[*The* COMTESSE *remains in the shallows.*]

"But what will the ladies say, Mr. Shand?"

"They won't like it, Comtesse, but they've got to lump it."

[*Here the* MAID *appears with a card for* MAGGIE, *who considers it quietly.*]

"Any one of importance?"

"No."

"Then I'm ready, Maggie."

[*This is evidently an intimation that she is to open the folding-doors, and he makes an effective entrance into the dining-room, his thumb in his waistcoat. There is a delicious clapping of hands from the committee, and the door closes. Not till then does* MAGGIE, *who has grown thoughtful, tell her maid to admit the visitor.*]

"Another lady, Mrs. Shand?"

"The card says 'Mr. Charles Venables.' "

[*The* COMTESSE *is really interested at last.*]

"Charles Venables! Do *you* know him?"

"I think I call to mind meeting one of that name at the Foreign Office party."

"One of that name! He who is a Minister of your Cabinet. But as you know him so little why should he call on you?"

"I wonder."

[MAGGIE'S *glance wanders to the drawer in which she has replaced* JOHN'S *speech.*]

"Well, well, I shall take care of you, petite."

"Do *you* know him?"

"Do I know him! The last time I saw him he asked me to—to—hem!—ma chérie, it was thirty years ago."

"Thirty years!"

"I was a pretty woman then. I dare say I shall detest him now; but if I find I do not—let us have a little plot—I shall drop this book; and then perhaps you will be so charming as—as not to be here for a little while?"

[MR. VENABLES, *who enters, is such a courtly seigneur that he seems to bring the eighteenth century with him; you feel that his sedan chair is at the door. He stoops over* MAGGIE'S *plebeian hand.*]

"I hope you will pardon my calling, Mrs. Shand; we had such a pleasant talk the other evening."

[MAGGIE, *of course, is at once deceived by his gracious manner.*]

"I think it's kind of you. Do you know each other? The Comtesse de la Brière."

[*He repeats the name with some emotion, and the* COMTESSE *half mischievously, half sadly, holds a hand before her face.*]

"Comtesse."

"Thirty years, Mr. Venables."

[*He gallantly removes the hand that screens her face.*]

"It does not seem so much."

[*She gives him a similar scrutiny.*]

"Mon Dieu, it seems all that."

* In Parliament voting is done by the "division" of the members into separate lobbies.

[*They smile rather ruefully.* MAGGIE, *like a kind hostess, relieves the tension.*]

"The Comtesse has taken a cottage in Surrey for the summer."

"I am overjoyed."

"No, Charles, you are not. You no longer care. Fickle one! And it is only thirty years." [*He sinks into a chair beside her.*]

"Those heavenly evenings, Comtesse, on the Bosphorous."

"I refuse to talk of them. I hate you."

[*But she drops the book, and* MAGGIE *fades from the room. It is not a very clever departure, and the old diplomatist smiles. Then he sighs a beautiful sigh, for he does all things beautifully.*]

"It is moonlight, Comtesse, on the Golden Horn."

"Who are those two young things in a caïque?"

"Is he the brave Leander, Comtesse, and is she Hero of the Lamp?"

"No, she is the foolish wife of the French Ambassador, and he is a good-for-nothing British attaché trying to get her husband's secrets out of her."

"Is it possible! They part at a certain garden gate."

"Oh, Charles, Charles!"

"But you promised to come back; I waited there till dawn. Blanche, if you *had* come back——"

"How is Mrs. Venables?"

"She is rather poorly. *I* think it's gout."

"And you?"

"I creak a little in the mornings."

"So do I. There is such a good man at Wiesbaden."

"The Homburg fellow is better. The way he patched me up last summer—— Oh, Lord, Lord!"

"Yes, Charles, the game is up; we are two old fogies. [*They groan in unison; then she raps him sharply on the knuckles.*] Tell me, sir, what are you doing here?"

"Merely a friendly call."

"I do not believe it."

"The same woman; the old delightful candor."

"The same man; the old fibs. [*She sees that the door is asking a question.*] Yes, come, Mrs. Shand, I have had quite enough of him; I warn you he is here for some crafty purpose."

Maggie. [*Drawing back timidly.*] Surely not?

Venables. Really, Comtesse, you make conversation difficult. To show that my intentions are innocent, Mrs. Shand, I propose that you choose the subject.

Maggie. [*Relieved.*] There, Comtesse.

Venables. I hope your husband is well?

Maggie. Yes, thank you. [*With a happy thought.*] I decide that we talk about him.

Venables. If you wish it.

Comtesse. Be careful; *he* has chosen the subject.

Maggie. *I* chose it, didn't I?

Venables. You know you did.

Maggie. [*Appealingly.*] You admire John?

Venables. Very much. But he puzzles me a little. You Scots, Mrs. Shand, are such a mixture of the practical and the emotional that you escape out of an Englishman's hand like a trout.

Maggie. [*Open-eyed.*] Do we?

Venables. Well, not you, but your husband. I have known few men make a worse beginning in the House. He had the most atrocious bow-wow public-park manner——

Comtesse. I remember that manner!

Maggie. No, he hadn't.

Venables. [*Soothingly.*] At first. But by his second session he had shed all that, and he is now a pleasure to listen to. By the way, Comtesse, have you found any dark intention in that?

Comtesse. You wanted to know whether he talks over these matters with his wife; and she has told you that he does not.

Maggie. [*Indignantly.*] I haven't said a word about it, have I?

Venables. Not a word. Then, again, I admire him for his impromptu speeches.

Maggie. What is impromptu?

Venables. Unprepared. They have contained some grave blunders, not so much of judgment as of taste——

Maggie. [*Hotly.*] *I* don't think so.

Venables. Pardon me. But he has righted himself subsequently in the neatest way. I have always found that the man whose second thoughts are good is worth watching. Well, Comtesse, I see you have something to say.

Comtesse. You are wondering whether she can tell you who gives him his second thoughts.

Maggie. Gives them to John? I would like to see anybody try to give thoughts to John.

Venables. Quite so.

Comtesse. Is there anything more that has aroused your admiration, Charles?

Venables. [*Purring.*] Let me see. Yes, we are all much edified by his humor.

Comtesse. [*Surprised indeed.*] His humor? That man!

Maggie. [*With hauteur.*] Why not?

Venables. I assure you, Comtesse, some

of the neat things in his speeches convulse the House. A word has even been coined for them—Shandisms.

Comtesse. [*Slowly recovering from a blow.*] Humor!

Venables. In conversation, I admit, he strikes one as being—ah—somewhat lacking in humor.

Comtesse. [*Pouncing.*] You are wondering who supplies his speeches with the humor.

Maggie. Supplies John?

Venables. Now that you mention it, some of his Shandisms do have a curiously feminine quality.

Comtesse. You have thought it might be a woman.

Venables. Really, Comtesse——

Comtesse. I see it all. Charles, you thought it might be the wife!

Venables. [*Flinging up his hands.*] I own up.

Maggie. [*Bewildered.*] Me?

Venables. Forgive me, I see I was wrong.

Maggie. [*Alarmed.*] Have I been doing John any harm?

Venables. On the contrary, I am relieved to know that there are no hairpins in his speeches. If he is at home, Mrs. Shand, may I see him? I am going to be rather charming to him.

Maggie. [*Drawn in two directions.*] Yes, he is—oh, yes—but——

Venables. That is to say, Comtesse, if he proves himself the man I believe him to be.

[*This arrests* MAGGIE *almost as she has reached the dining-room door.*]

Maggie. [*Hesitating.*] He is very busy just now.

Venables. [*Smiling.*] I think he will see me.

Maggie. Is it something about his speech?

Venables. [*The smile hardening.*] Well, yes, it is.

Maggie. Then I dare say I could tell you what you want to know without troubling him, as I've been typing it.

Venables. [*With a sigh.*] I don't acquire information that way.

Comtesse. I trust not.

Maggie. There's no secret about it. He is to show it to the Whips tonight.

Venables. [*Sharply.*] You are sure of that?

Comtesse. It is quite true, Charles. I heard him say so; and indeed he repeated what he called the "peroration" before me.

Maggie. I know it by heart. [*She plays a bold game.*] "These are the demands of all intelligent British women, and I am proud to nail them to my flag"——

Comtesse. The very words, Mrs. Shand.

Maggie. [*Looking at her imploringly.*] "And I don't care how they may embarrass the Government." [*The* COMTESSE *is bereft of speech, so suddenly has she been introduced to the real* MAGGIE SHAND.] "If the right honorable gentleman will give us his pledge to introduce a similar bill this session I will willingly withdraw mine; but otherwise I solemnly warn him that I will press the matter now to a division."

[*She turns her face from the great man; she has gone white.*]

Venables. [*After a pause.*] Capital.

[*The blood returns to* MAGGIE'S *heart.*]

Comtesse. [*Who is beginning to enjoy herself very much.*] Then you are pleased to know that he means to, as you say, go to a division?

Venables. Delighted. The courage of it will be the making of him.

Comtesse. I see.

Venables. Had he been to hedge we should have known that he was a pasteboard knight and have disregarded him.

Comtesse. I see.

[*She desires to catch the eye of* MAGGIE, *but it is carefully turned from her.*]

Venables. Mrs. Shand, let us have him in at once.

Comtesse. Yes, yes, indeed.

[MAGGIE'S *anxiety returns, but she has to call* JOHN *in.*]

John. [*Impressed.*] Mr. Venables! This is an honor.

Venables. How are you, Shand?

John. Sit down, sit down. [*Becoming himself again.*] I can guess what you have come about.

Venables. Ah, you Scotsmen.

John. Of course I know I'm embarrassing the Government a good deal——

Venables. [*Blandly.*] Not at all, Shand. The Government are very pleased.

John. You don't expect me to believe that.

Venables. I called here to give you the proof of it. You may know that we are to have a big meeting at Leeds on the twenty-fourth, when two Ministers are to speak. There is room for a third speaker, and I am authorized to offer that place to you.

John. To me!

Venables. Yes.

John. [*Swelling.*] It would be—the Government taking me up.

Venables. Don't make too much of it; it

would be an acknowledgment that they look upon you as one of their likely young men.

Maggie. John!

John. [*Not found wanting in a trying hour.*] It's a bribe. You are offering me this on condition that I don't make my speech. How can you think so meanly of me as to believe that I would play the women's cause false for the sake of my own advancement? I refuse your bribe.

Venables. [*Liking him for the first time.*] Good. But you are wrong. There are no conditions, and we want you to make your speech. Now do you accept?

John. [*Still suspicious.*] If you make me the same offer after you have read it. I insist on your reading it first.

Venables. [*Sighing.*] By all means. [MAGGIE *is in agony as she sees* JOHN *hand the speech to his leader. On the other hand, the* COMTESSE *thrills.*] But I assure you we look on the speech as a small matter. The important thing is your intention of going to a division; and we agree to that also.

John. [*Losing his head.*] What's that?

Venables. Yes, we agree.

John. But—but—why, you have been threatening to excommunicate me if I dared.

Venables. All done to test you, Shand.

John. To test me?

Venables. We know that a division on your Bill can have no serious significance; we shall see to that. And so the test was to be whether you had the pluck to divide the House. Had you been intending to talk big in this speech, and then hedge, through fear of the Government. they would have had no further use for you.

John. [*Heavily.*] I understand.

[*But there is one thing he cannot understand, which is, why* VENABLES *should be so sure that he is not to hedge.*]

Venables. [*Turning over the pages carelessly.*] Any of your good things in this, Shand?

John. [*Whose one desire is to get the pages back.*] No, I—no—it isn't necessary you should read it now.

Venables. [*From politeness only.*] Merely for my own pleasure. I shall look through it this evening.

[*He rolls up the speech to put it in his pocket.* JOHN *turns despairingly to* MAGGIE, *though well aware that no help can come from her.*]

Maggie. That's the only copy there is, John. [*To* VENABLES.] Let me make a fresh one, and send it to you in an hour or two.

Venables. [*Good-naturedly.*] I could not put you to that trouble, Mrs. Shand. I will take good care of it.

Maggie. If anything were to happen to you on the way home, wouldn't whatever is in your pocket be considered to be the property of your heirs?

Venables. [*Laughing.*] Now there is forethought! Shand, I think that after that——! [*He returns the speech to* JOHN, *whose hand swallows it greedily.*] She is Scotch too, Comtesse.

Comtesse. [*Delighted.*] Yes, she is Scotch too.

Venables. Though the only persons likely to do for me in the street, Shand, are your ladies' committee. Ever since they took the horse out of my brougham, I can scent them a mile away.

Comtesse. A mile? Charles, peep in there.

[*He softly turns the handle of the dining-room door, and realizes that his scent is not so good as he had thought it. He bids his hostess and the* COMTESS *good-by in a burlesque whisper and tiptoes off to safer places.* JOHN *having gone out with him,* MAGGIE *can no longer avoid the* COMTESSE'S *reproachful eye. That much injured lady advances upon her with accusing finger.*]

"So, madam!"

[MAGGIE *is prepared for her.*]

"I don't know what you mean."

"Yes, you do. I mean that there *is* some one who 'helps' our Mr. Shand."

"There's not."

"And it *is* a woman, and it's you."

"I help in the little things."

"The little things! You are the Pin he picked up and that is to make his fortune. And now what I want to know is whether your John is aware that you help at all."

[JOHN *returns, and at once provides the answer.*]

"Maggie, Comtesse, I've done it again!"

"I'm so glad, John."

[*The* COMTESSE *is in an ecstasy.*]

"And all because you were not to hedge, Mr. Shand."

[*His appeal to her with the wistfulness of a schoolboy makes him rather attractive.*]

"You won't tell on me, Comtesse! [*He thinks it out.*] They had just guessed I would be firm because they know I'm a strong man. You little saw, Maggie, what a good turn you were doing me when you said you wanted to make another copy of the speech." [*She is dense.*]

"How, John?"

"Because now I can alter the end."

[*She is enlightened.*]

"So you can!"

"Here's another lucky thing, Maggie: I hadn't told the ladies' committee that I was to hedge, and so they need never know. Comtesse, I tell you there's a little cherub who sits up aloft and looks after the career of John Shand."

[*The* COMTESSE *looks not aloft but toward the chair at present occupied by* MAGGIE.]

"Where does she sit, Mr. Shand?"

[*He knows that women are not well read.*]

"It's just a figure of speech."

[*He returns airily to his committee room; and now again you may hear the click of* MAGGIE'S *needles. They no longer annoy the* COMTESSE; *she is setting them to music.*]

"It is not down here she sits, Mrs. Shand, knitting a stocking."

"No, it isn't."

"And when I came in I gave him credit for everything; even for the prettiness of the room!"

"He has beautiful taste."

"Good-by, Scotchy."

"Good-by, Comtesse, and thank you for coming."

"Good-by—Miss Pin."

[MAGGIE *rings genteelly.*]

"Good-by."

[*The* COMTESSE *is now lost in admiration of her.*]

"You divine little wife! He can't be worthy of it, no man could be worthy of it. Why do you do it?"

[MAGGIE *shivers a little.*]

"He loves to think he does it all himself; that's the way of men. I'm six years older than he is. I'm plain, and I have no charm. I shouldn't have let him marry me. I'm trying to make up for it."

[*The* COMTESSE *kisses her and goes away.* MAGGIE, *somewhat foolishly, resumes her knitting.*]

[*Some days later this same room is listening—with the same inattention—to the outpouring of* JOHN SHAND'S *love for the lady of the hiccoughs. We arrive—by arrangement—rather late; and thus we miss some of the most delightful of the pangs.*

One can see that these two are playing no game, or, if they are, that they little know it. The wonders of the world (so strange are the instruments chosen by Love) have been revealed to JOHN *in hiccoughs; he shakes in* SYBIL'S *presence; never were more swimming eyes; he who has been of a wooden face till now, with ways to match, has gone on flame like a piece of paper; emotion is in flood in him. We may be almost fond of* JOHN *for being so worshipful of love. Much has come to him that we had almost despaired of his acquiring, including nearly all the divine attributes except that sense of humor. The beautiful* SYBIL *has always possessed but little of it also, and what she had has been struck from her by Cupid's flail. Naked of the saving grace, they face each other in awful rapture.*]

"In a room, Sybil, I go to you as a cold man to a fire. You fill me like a peal of bells in an empty house."

[*She is being brutally treated by the dear impediment, for which hiccough is such an inadequate name that even to spell it is an abomination though a sign of ability. How to describe a sound that is noiseless? Let us put it thus, that when* SYBIL *wants to say something very much there are little obstacles in her way; she falters, falls perhaps once, and then is over, the while her appealing orbs beg you not to be angry with her. We may express those sweet pauses in precious dots, which some clever person can afterwards string together and make a pearl necklace of them.*]

"I should not . . . let you say it, . . . but . . . you . . . say it so beautifully."

"You must have guessed."

"I dreamed . . . I feared . . . but you were . . . Scotch, and I didn't know what to think."

"Do you know what first attracted me to you, Sybil? It was your insolence. I thought, 'I'll break her insolence for her.'"

"And I thought . . . 'I'll break his str . . . ength!'"

"And now your cooing voice plays round me; the softness of you, Sybil, in your pretty clothes, makes me think of young birds. [*The impediment is now insurmountable; she has to swim for it, she swims toward him.*] It is you who inspire my work."

[*He thrills to find that she can be touched without breaking.*]

"I am so glad . . . so proud . . ."

"And others know it, Sybil, as well as I. Only yesterday the Comtesse said to me, 'No man could get on so fast unaided. *Cherchez la femme*, Mr. Shand.'"

"Auntie said that!"

"I said 'Find her yourself, Comtesse.' "

"And she?"

"She said 'I have found her,' and I said in my blunt way, 'You mean Lady Sybil,' and she went away laughing."

"Laughing?"

"I seem to amuse the woman."

[SYBIL *grows sad.*]

"If Mrs. Shand—— It is so cruel to her. Whom did you say she had gone to the station to meet?"

"Her father and brothers."

"It is so cruel to them. We must think no more of this. It is mad . . . ness."

"It's fate. Sybil, let us declare our love openly."

"You can't ask that, now in the first moment that you tell me of it."

"The one thing I won't do even for you is to live a life of underhand."

"The . . . blow to her."

"Yes. But at least she has always known that I never loved her."

"It is asking me to give . . . up everything, every one, for you."

"It's too much."

[JOHN *is humble at last.*]

"To a woman who truly loves, even that is not too much. Oh! it is not I who matter —it is you."

"My dear, my dear."

"So gladly would I do it to save you; but, oh, if it were to bring you down!"

"Nothing can keep me down if I have you to help me."

"I am dazed, John, I . . ."

"My love, my love."

"I . . . oh . . . here . . ."

"Be brave, Sybil, be brave."

". . . . ."

[*In this bewilderment of pearls she melts into his arms.* MAGGIE *happens to open the door just then; but neither fond heart hears her.*]

"I can't walk along the streets, Sybil, without looking in all the shop windows for what I think would become you best. [*As awkwardly as though his heart still beat against corduroy, he takes from his pocket a pendant and its chain. He is shy, and she drops pearls over the beauty of the ruby which is its only stone.*] It is a drop of my blood, Sybil."

[*Her lovely neck is outstretched, and he puts the chain round it.* MAGGIE *withdraws as silently as she had come; but perhaps the door whispered "d—n," or (humorously) "d . . n" as it closed, for* SYBIL *wakes out of Paradise.*]

"I thought—— Did the door shut?"

"It was shut already."

[*Perhaps it is only that* SYBIL *is bewildered to find herself once again in a world that has doors.*]

"It seemed to me——"

"There was nothing. But I think I hear voices; they may have arrived."

[*Some pretty instinct makes* SYBIL *go farther from him.* MAGGIE *kindly gives her time for this by speaking before opening the door.*]

"That will do perfectly, David. The maid knows where to put them. [*She comes in.*] They've come, John; they *would* help with the luggage. [JOHN *goes out.* MAGGIE *is agreeably surprised to find a visitor.*] How do you do, Lady Sybil? This is nice of you."

"I was so sorry not to find you in, Mrs. Shand."

[*The impediment has run away. It is only for those who love it.*]

"Thank you. You'll sit down?"

"I think not; your relatives——"

"They will be so proud to see that you are my friend."

[*If* MAGGIE *were less simple her guest would feel more comfortable. She tries to make conversation.*]

"It is their first visit to London?"

[*Instead of relieving her anxiety on this point,* MAGGIE *has a long look at the gorgeous armful.*]

"I'm glad you are so beautiful, Lady Sybil."

[*The beautiful one is somehow not flattered. She pursues her investigations with growing uneasiness.*]

"One of them is married now, isn't he? [*Still there is no answer;* MAGGIE *continues looking at her, and shivers slightly.*] Have they traveled from Scotland today? Mrs. Shand, why do you look at me so? The door did open! [MAGGIE *nods.*] What are you to do?"

"That would be telling. Sit down, my pretty."

[*As* SYBIL *subsides into what the* WYLIES *with one glance would call the best chair,* MAGGIE'S *men-folk are brought in by* JOHN, *all carrying silk hats and looking very active after their long rest in the train. They are gazing about them. They would like this lady, they would like* JOHN, *they would even like* MAGGIE *to go away for a little and leave them to examine the room. Is that linen on the walls, for instance, or just paper? Is the carpet as thick as it feels, or is there brown paper beneath it? Had* MAGGIE *got anything off that bookcase on account of the worm-holes?* DAVID *even discovers that we were simpletons when we said there was nothing in the room that pretended to be what it was not. He taps the marble mantelpiece, and is favorably impressed by the tinny sound.*]

David. Very fine imitation. It's a capital house, Maggie.

Maggie. I'm so glad you like it. Do you know one another? This is my father and my brothers, Lady Sybil.

[*The lovely form inclines toward them.* ALICK *and* DAVID *remain firm on their legs, but* JAMES *totters.*]

James. A ladyship! Well done, Maggie.

Alick. [*Sharply.*] James! I remember you, my lady.

Maggie. Sit down, Father. This is the study.

[JAMES *wanders around it inquisitively until called to order.*]

Sybil. You must be tired after your long journey.

David. [*Drawing the portraits of himself and partners in one lightning sketch.*] Tired, your ladyship? We sat on cushioned seats the whole way.

James. [*Looking about him for the chair you sit on.*] Every seat in this room is cushioned.

Maggie. You may say all my life is cushioned now, James, by this dear man of mine.

[*She gives* JOHN'S *shoulder a loving pressure, which* SYBIL *feels is a telegraphic communication to herself in a cypher that she cannot read.* ALICK *and the* BROTHERS *bask in the evidence of* MAGGIE'S *happiness.*]

John. [*Uncomfortably.*] And is Elizabeth hearty, James?

James. [*Looking down his nose in the manner proper to young husbands when addressed about their wives.*] She's very well, I thank you kindly.

Maggie. James is a married man now, Lady Sybil.

[SYBIL *murmurs her congratulations.*]

James. I thank you kindly. [*Courageously.*] Yes, I'm married. [*He looks at* DAVID *and* ALICK *to see if they are smiling; and they are.*] It wasn't a case of being catched; it was entirely of my own free will. [*He looks again; and the mean fellows are smiling still.*] Is your ladyship married?

Sybil. Alas! no.

David. James! [*Politely.*] You will be yet, my lady.

[SYBIL *indicates that he is kind indeed.*]

John. Perhaps they would like you to show them their rooms, Maggie?

David. Fine would we like to see all the house as well as the sleeping accommodation. But first——

[*He gives his father the look with which chairmen call on the next speaker.*]

Alick. I take you, David. [*He produces a paper parcel from a roomy pocket.*] It wasn't likely, Mr. Shand, that we would forget the day.

John. The day?

David. The second anniversary of your marriage. We came purposely for the day.

James. [*His fingers itching to take the parcel from his father.*] It's a lace shawl, Maggie, from the three of us, a pure Tobermory; you would never dare wear it if you knew the cost.

[*The shawl in its beauty is revealed, and* MAGGIE *hails it with little cries of joy. She rushes at the donors and kisses each of them just as if she were a pretty woman. They are much pleased and give expression to their pleasure in a not very dissimilar manner.*]

Alick. Havers.

David. Havers.

James. Havers.

John. It's a very fine shawl.

[*He should not have spoken, for he has set* JAMES'S *volatile mind working.*]

James. You may say so. What did you give her, Mr. Shand?

John. [*Suddenly deserted by God and man.*] Me?

Alick. Yes, yes, let's see it.

John. Oh—I——

[*He is not deserted by* MAGGIE, *but she can think of no way out.*]

Sybil. [*Prompted by the impediment, which is in hiding, quite close.*] Did he . . . forget?

[*There is more than a touch of malice in the question. It is a challenge, and the* WYLIES *as a family are almost too quick to accept a challenge.*]

Maggie. [*Lifting the gage of battle.*] John forget? Never! It's a pendant, Father.

[*The impediment bolts.* JOHN *rises.*]

Alick. A pendant? One of those things on a chain?

[*He grins, remembering how once, about sixty years ago, he and a lady and a pendant—but we have no time for this.*]

Maggie. Yes.

David. [*Who has felt the note of antag-*

onism and is troubled.] You were slow in speaking of it, Mr. Shand.

Maggie. [*This is her fight.*] He was shy, because he thought you might blame him for extravagance.

David. [*Relieved.*] Oh, that's it.

James. [*Licking his lips.*] Let's see it.

Maggie. [*A daughter of the devil.*] Where did you put it, John?

[JOHN's *mouth opens but has nothing to contribute.*]

Sybil. [*The impediment has stolen back again.*] Perhaps it has been . . . mislaid.

[*The* BROTHERS *echo the word incredulously.*]

Maggie. Not it. I can't think where we laid it down. It's not on that table, is it, James? [*The* WYLIES *turn to look, and* MAGGIE's *hand goes out to* LADY SYBIL: JOHN SHAND, *witness. It is a very determined hand, and presently a pendant is placed in it.*] Here it is! [ALICK *and the* BROTHERS *cluster around it, weigh it and appraise it.*]

Alick. Preserve me. Is that stone real, Mr. Shand?

John. [*Who has begun to look his grimmest.*] Yes.

Maggie. [*Who is now ready, if he wishes it, to take him on too.*] John says it's a drop of his blood.

John. [*Wishing it.*] And so it is.

David. Well said, Mr. Shand.

Maggie. [*Scared.*] And now, if you'll all come with me, I think John has something he wants to talk over with Lady Sybil. [*Recovering and taking him on.*] Or would you prefer, John, to say it before us all?

Sybil. [*Gasping.*] No!

John. [*Flinging back his head.*] Yes, I prefer to say it before you all!

Maggie. [*Flinging back hers.*] Then sit down again.

[*The* WYLIES *wonderingly obey.*]

Sybil. Mr. Shand, Mr. Shand!——

John. Maggie knows, and it was only for her I was troubled. Do you think I'm afraid of *them?* [*With mighty relief.*] Now we can be open.

David. [*Lowering.*] What is it? What's wrong, John Shand?

John. [*Facing him squarely.*] It was to Lady Sybil I gave the pendant, and all my love with it.

[*Perhaps* JAMES *utters a cry, but the silence of* ALICK *and* DAVID *is more terrible.*]

Sybil. [*Whose voice is smaller than we had thought.*] What are you to do?

[*It is to* MAGGIE *she is speaking.*]

David. She'll leave it for us to do.

John. That's what I want.

[*The lords of creation look at the ladies.*]

Maggie. [*Interpreting.*] You and I are expected to retire, Lady Sybil, while the men decide our fate. [SYBIL *is ready to obey the law, but* MAGGIE *remains seated.*] Man's the oak, woman's the ivy. Which of us is it that's to cling to you, John?

[*With three stalwarts glaring at him,* JOHN *rather grandly takes* SYBIL's *hand. They are two against the world.*]

Sybil. [*A heroine.*] I hesitated, but I am afraid no longer; whatever he asks of me I will do. [*Evidently the first thing he asks of her is to await him in the dining-room.*] It will mean surrendering everything for him. I am glad it means all that.

[*She passes into the dining-room looking as pretty as a kiss.*]

Maggie. So that settles it.

Alick. I'm thinking that doesn't settle it.

David. No, by God! [*But his love for* MAGGIE *steadies him. There is even a note of entreaty in his voice.*] Have you nothing to say to her, man?

John. I have things to say to her, but not before you.

David. [*Sternly.*] Go away, Maggie. Leave him to us.

James. [*Who thinks it is about time that he said something.*] Yes, leave him to us.

Maggie. No, David, I want to hear what is to become of me; I promise not to take any side.

[*And sitting by the fire she resumes her knitting. The four regard her as on an evening at The Pans a good many years ago.*]

David. [*Barking.*] How long has this been going on?

John. If you mean how long has that lady been the apple of my eye, I'm not sure; but I never told her of it until to-day.

Maggie. [*Thoughtfully and without dropping a stitch.*] I think it wasn't till about six months ago, John, that she began to be very dear to you. At first you liked to bring in her name when talking to me, so that I could tell you of any little things I might have heard she was doing. But afterwards, as she became more and more to you, you avoided mentioning her name.

John. [*Surprised.*] Did you notice that?

Maggie. [*In her old-fashioned way.*] Yes.

John. I tried to be done with it for your sake. I've often had a sore heart for you, Maggie.

James. You're proving it!

Maggie. Yes, James, he had. I've often seen him looking at me very sorrowfully of late because of what was in his mind; and many a kindly little thing he has done for me that he didn't used to do.

John. You noticed that too!

Maggie. Yes.

David. [*Controlling himself.*] Well, we won't go into that; the thing to be thankful for is that it's ended.

Alick. [*Who is looking very old.*] Yes, yes, that's the great thing.

John. All useless, sir, it's not ended; it's to go on.

David. There's a devil in you, John Shand.

John. [*Who is an unhappy man just now.*] I dare say there is. But do you think he had a walk over, Mr. David?

James. Man, I could knock you down!

Maggie. There's not one of you could knock John down.

David. [*Exasperated.*] Quiet, Maggie. One would think you were taking his part.

Maggie. Do you expect me to desert him at the very moment that he needs me most?

David. It's him that's deserting you.

John. Yes, Maggie, that's what it is.

Alick. Where's your marriage vow? And your church attendances?

James. [*With terrible irony.*] And your prize for moral philosophy?

John. [*Recklessly.*] All gone whistling down the wind.

David. I suppose you understand that you'll have to resign your seat.

John. [*His underlip much in evidence.*] There are hundreds of seats, but there's only one John Shand.

Maggie. [*But we don't hear her.*] That's how I like to hear him speak.

David. [*The ablest person in the room.*] Think, man, I'm old by you, and for long I've had a pride in you. It will be beginning the world again with more against you than there was eight years ago.

John. I have a better head to begin it with than I had eight years ago.

Alick. [*Hoping this will bite.*] She'll have her own money, David!

John. She's as poor as a mouse.

James. [*Thinking possibly of his Elizabeth's mother.*] We'll go to her friends, and tell them all. They'll stop it.

John. She's of age.

James. They'll take her far away.

John. I'll follow, and tear her from them.

Alick. Your career——

John. [*To his credit.*] To hell with my career. Do you think I don't know I'm on the rocks? What can you, or you, or you, understand of the passions of a man! I've fought, and I've given in. When a ship founders, as I suppose I'm foundering, it's not a thing to yelp at. Peace, all of you.

[*He strides into the dining-room, where we see him at times pacing the floor.*]

David. [*To* JAMES, *who gives signs of a desire to take off his coat.*] Let him be. We can't budge him. [*With bitter wisdom.*] It's true what he says, true at any rate about me. What do I know of the passions of a man! I'm up against something I don't understand.

Alick. It's something wicked.

David. I dare say it is, but it's something big.

James. It's that damned charm.

Maggie. [*Still by the fire.*] That's it. What was it that made you fancy Elizabeth, James?

James. [*Sheepishly.*] I can scarcely say.

Maggie. It was her charm.

David. *Her* charm!

James. [*Pugnaciously.*] Yes, *her* charm.

Maggie. She had charm for James.

[*This somehow breaks them up.* MAGGIE *goes from one to another with an odd little smile flickering on her face.*]

David. Put on your things, Maggie, and we'll leave his house.

Maggie. [*Patting his kind head.*] Not me, David.

[*This is a* MAGGIE *they have known but forgotten; all three brighten.*]

David. You haven't given in!

[*The smile flickers and expires.*]

Maggie. I want you all to go upstairs, and let me have my try now.

James. Your try?

Alick. Maggie, you put new life into me.

James. And into me.

[DAVID *says nothing; the way he grips her shoulder says it for him.*]

Maggie. I'll save him, David, if I can.

David. Does he deserve to be saved after the way he has treated you?

Maggie. You stupid David. What has that to do with it?

[*When they have gone,* JOHN *comes to the door of the dining-room. There is welling up in him a great pity for* MAGGIE, *but it has to subside a little when he sees that the knitting is still in her hand. No man likes to be so soon supplanted.* SYBIL *follows, and the two of them gaze at the active needles.*]

Maggie. [*Perceiving that she has visitors.*] Come in, John. Sit down, Lady Sybil, and make yourself comfortable. I'm afraid we've put you about.

[*She is, after all, only a few years older than they and scarcely looks her age; yet it must have been in some such way as this that the little old woman who lived in a shoe addressed her numerous progeny.*]

John. I'm mortal sorry, Maggie.

Sybil. [*Who would be more courageous if she could hold his hand.*] And I also.

Maggie. [*Soothingly.*] I'm sure you are. But as it can't be helped I see no reason why we three shouldn't talk the matter over in a practical way.

[SYBIL *looks doubtful, but* JOHN *hangs on desperately to the word practical.*]

John. If you could understand, Maggie, what an inspiration she is to me and my work.

Sybil. Indeed, Mrs. Shand, I think of nothing else.

Maggie. That's fine. That's as it should be.

Sybil. [*Talking too much.*] Mrs. Shand, I think you are very kind to take it so reasonably.

Maggie. That's the Scotch way. When were you thinking of leaving me, John?

[*Perhaps this is the Scotch way also; but* SYBIL *is English, and from the manner in which she starts you would say that something has fallen on her toes.*]

John. [*Who has heard nothing fall.*] I think, now that it has come to a breach, the sooner the better. [*His tone becomes that of* JAMES *when asked after the health of his wife.*] So long as it is convenient to you, Maggie.

Maggie. [*Making a rapid calculation.*] It couldn't well be before Wednesday. That's the day the laundry comes home.

[SYBIL *has to draw in her toes again.*]

John. And it's the day the House rises. [*Stifling a groan.*] It may be my last appearance in the House.

Sybil. [*Her arms yearning for him.*] No, no, please don't say that.

Maggie. [*Surveying them sympathetically.*] You love the House, don't you, John, next to her? It's a pity you can't wait till after your speech at Leeds. Mr. Venables won't let you speak at Leeds, I fear, if you leave me.

John. What a chance it would have been! But let it go.

Maggie. The meeting is in less than a month. Could you not make it such a speech that they would be very loath to lose you?

John. [*Swelling.*] That's what was in my mind.

Sybil. [*With noble confidence.*] And he could have done it.

Maggie. Then we've come to something practical.

John. [*Exercising his imagination with powerful effect.*] No, it wouldn't be fair to you if I was to stay on now.

Maggie. Do you think I'll let myself be considered when your career is at stake? A month will soon pass for me; I'll have a lot of packing to do.

John. It's noble of you, but I don't deserve it, and I can't take it from you.

Maggie. Now's the time, Lady Sybil, for you to have one of your inspiring ideas.

Sybil. [*Ever ready.*] Yes, yes—but what?

[*It is odd that they should both turn to* MAGGIE *at this moment.*]

Maggie. [*Who has already been saying it to herself.*] What do you think of this: I can stay on here with my father and brothers; and you, John, can go away somewhere and devote yourself to your speech?

Sybil. Yes.

John. That might be. [*Considerately.*] Away from both of you. Where could I go?

Sybil. [*Ever ready.*] Where?

Maggie. I know.

[*She has called up a number on the telephone before they have time to check her.*]

John. [*On his dignity.*] Don't be in such a hurry, Maggie.

Maggie. Is this Lamb's Hotel? Put me on to the Comtesse de la Brière, please.

Sybil. [*With a sinking.*] What do you want with Auntie?

Maggie. Her cottage in the country would be the very place. She invited John and me.

John. Yes, but——

Maggie. [*Arguing.*] And Mr. Venables is to be there. Think of the impression you could make on *him,* seeing him daily for three weeks.

John. There's something in that.

Maggie. Is it you, Comtesse? I'm Maggie Shand.

Sybil. You are not to tell her that——?

Maggie. No. [*To the* COMTESSE.] Oh, I'm very well, never was better. Yes, yes; you see I can't, because my folk have never been in London before, and I must take them about and show them the sights. But John could come to you alone; why not?

John. [*With proper pride.*] If she's not keen to have me, I won't go.

Maggie. She's very keen. Comtesse, I could come for a day by and by to see how you are getting on. Yes—yes—certainly. [*To* JOHN.] She says she'll be delighted.

John. [*Thoughtfully.*] You're not doing this, Maggie, thinking that my being absent from Sybil for a few weeks can make any difference? Of course, it's natural you should want us to keep apart, but——

Maggie. [*Grimly.*] I'm founding no hope on keeping you apart, John.

John. It's what other wives would do.

Maggie. I promised to be different.

John. [*His position as a strong man assured.*] Then tell her I accept.

[*He wanders back into the dining-room.*]

Sybil. I think—[*she is not sure what she thinks*]—I think you are very wonderful.

Maggie. Was that John calling to you?

Sybil. Was it? [*She is glad to join him in the dining-room.*]

Maggie. Comtesse, hold the line a minute—— [*She is alone, and she has nearly reached the end of her self-control. She shakes emotionally and utters painful little cries; there is something she wants to do, and she is loath to do it. But she does it.*] Are you there, Comtesse? There's one other thing, dear Comtesse; I want you to invite Lady Sybil also; yes, for the whole time that John is there. No, I'm not mad; as a great favor to me; yes, I have a very particular reason, but I won't tell you what it is; oh, call me Scotchy as much as you like, but consent; do, do, do. Thank you, thank you, good-by.

[*She has control of herself now, and is determined not to let it slip from her again. When they reappear the stubborn one is writing a letter.*]

John. I thought I heard the telephone again.

Maggie. [*Looking up from her labors.*] It was the Comtesse; she says she's to invite Lady Sybil to the cottage at the same time.

Sybil. Me!

John. To invite Sybil? Then, of course, I won't go, Maggie.

Maggie. [*Wondering seemingly at these niceties.*] What does it matter? Is anything to be considered except the speech? [*It has been admitted that she was a little devil.*] And, with Sybil on the spot, John, *to help you and inspire you,* what a speech it will be!

John. [*Carried away.*] Maggie, you really are a very generous woman.

Sybil. [*Convinced at last.*] She is indeed.

John. And you're queer, too. How many women in the circumstances would sit down to write a letter?

Maggie. It's a letter to you, John.

John. To me?

Maggie. I'll give it to you when it's finished, but I ask you not to open it till your visit to the Comtesse ends.

John. What is it about?

Maggie. It's practical.

Sybil. [*Rather faintly.*] Practical?

[*She has heard the word so frequently today that it is beginning to have a Scotch sound. She feels she ought to like* MAGGIE, *but that she would like her better if they were farther apart. She indicates that the doctors are troubled about her heart, and murmuring her adieux she goes.* JOHN, *who is accompanying her, pauses at the door.*]

John. [*With a queer sort of admiration for his wife.*] Maggie, I wish I was fond of you.

Maggie. [*Heartily.*] I wish you were, John.

[*He goes, and she resumes her letter. The stocking is lying at hand, and she pushes it to the floor. She is done for a time with knitting.*]

IV

Man's greatest invention is the lawn-mower. All the birds know this, and that is why, when it is at rest, there is always at least one of them sitting on the handle with his head cocked, wondering how the delicious whirring sound is made. When they find out, they will change their note. As it is, you must sometimes have thought that you heard the mower very early in the morning, and perhaps you peeped in negligee from your lattice window to see who was up so early. It was really the birds trying to get the note. On this broiling morning, however, we are at noon, and whoever looks will see that the whirring is done by MR. VENABLES. *He is in a linen suit with the coat discarded (the bird is sitting on it), and he comes and goes across the* COMTESSE'S *lawns, pleasantly mopping his face. We see him through a crooked bowed window generously open, roses intruding into it as if to prevent its ever being closed at night; there are other roses in such armfuls on the tables that one could not easily say where the room ends and the garden begins.*

In the COMTESSE'S *pretty comic drawing-room (for she likes the comic touch when she is in England) sits* JOHN SHAND *with his hostess, on chairs at a great distance from each other. No linen garments for* JOHN, *nor flannels, nor even knickerbockers; he envies the Eng-*

lish way of dressing for trees and lawns, but is too Scotch to be able to imitate it; he wears tweeds, just as he would do in his native country where they would be in kilts. Like many another Scot, the first time he ever saw a kilt was on a Sassenach; indeed, kilts were only invented, like golf, to draw the English north. JOHN *is doing nothing, which again is not a Scotch accomplishment, and he looks rather miserable and dour. The* COMTESSE *is already at her Patience cards, and occasionally she smiles on him as if not displeased with his long silence. At last she speaks:*

"I feel it rather a shame to detain you here on such a lovely day, Mr. Shand, entertaining an old woman."

"I don't pretend to think I'm entertaining you, Comtesse."

"But you *are,* you know."

"I would be pleased to be told how?"

[*She shrugs her impertinent shoulders, and presently there is another heavy sigh from* JOHN.]

"Again! Why do not you go out on the river?"

"Yes, I can do that." [*He rises.*]

"And take Sybil with you." [*He sits again.*] "No?"

"I have been on the river with her twenty times."

"Then take her for a long walk through the Fairloe woods."

"We were there twice last week."

"There is a romantically damp little arbor at the end of what the villagers call the Lovers' Lane."

"One can't go there every day. I see nothing to laugh at."

"Did I laugh? I must have been translating the situation into French."

[*Perhaps the music of the lawn-mower is not to* JOHN'S *mood, for he betakes himself to another room.* MR. VENABLES *pauses in his labors to greet a lady who has appeared on the lawn, and who is* MAGGIE. *She is as neat as if she were one of the army of typists (who are quite the nicest kind of women), and carries a little bag. She comes in through the window, and puts her hands over the* COMTESSE'S *eyes. The* COMTESSE *says:*]

"They are a strong pair of hands, at any rate."

"And not very white, and biggish for my size. Now guess."

[*The* COMTESSE *guesses, and takes both the hands in hers as if she valued them. She pulls off* MAGGIE'S *hat as if to prevent her flying away.*]

"Dear abominable one, not to let me know you were coming."

"It is just a surprise visit, Comtesse. I walked up from the station. [*For a moment* MAGGIE *seems to have borrowed* SYBIL'S *impediment.*] How is—everybody?"

"He is quite well. But, my child, he seems to me to be a most unhappy man."

[*This sad news does not seem to make a most unhappy woman of the child. The* COMTESSE *is puzzled, as she knows nothing of the situation save what she has discovered for herself.*]

"Why should that please you, O heartless one?"

"I won't tell you."

"I could take you and shake you, Maggie. Here have I put my house at your disposal for so many days for some sly Scotch purpose, and you will not tell me what it is."

"No."

"Very well then, but I have what you call a nasty one for you. [*The* COMTESSE *lures* MR. VENABLES *into the room by holding up what might be a foaming glass of lemon squash.*] Alas, Charles, it is but a flower vase. I want you to tell Mrs. Shand what you think of her husband's speech."

[MR. VENABLES *gives his hostess a reproachful look.*]

"Eh—ah—Shand will prefer to do that himself. I promised the gardener—I must not disappoint him—excuse me——"

"You must tell her, Charles."

"Please, Mr. Venables, I should like to know."

[*He sits down with a sigh and obeys.*]

"Your husband has been writing the speech here, and by his own wish he read it to me three days ago. The occasion is to be an important one; and, well, there are a dozen young men in the party at present, all capable of filling a certain small ministerial post. [*He looks longingly at the mower, but it sends no message to his aid.*] And as he is one of them I was anxious that he should show in this speech of what he is capable."

"And hasn't he?"

[*Not for the first time* MR. VENABLES *wishes that he was not in politics.*]

"I am afraid he has."

"What is wrong with the speech, Charles?"

"Nothing—and he can still deliver it. It is a powerful, well-thought-out piece of work, such as only a very able man could produce. But it has no *special quality* of its own—none of the little touches that used to make an old stager like myself want to pat Shand on the shoulder. [*The* COMTESSE's *mouth twitches, but* MAGGIE *declines to notice it.*] He pounds on manfully enough, but, if I may say so, with a wooden leg. It is as good, I dare say, as the rest of them could have done; but they start with such inherited advantages, Mrs. Shand, that he had to do better."

"Yes, I can understand that."

"I am sorry, Mrs. Shand, for he interested me. His career has set me wondering whether if *I* had begun as a railway porter I might not still be calling out, 'By your leave.'"

[MAGGIE *thinks it probable but not important.*]

"Mr. Venables, now that I think of it, surely John wrote to me that you were dissatisfied with his first speech, and that he was writing another."

[*The* COMTESSE's *eyes open very wide indeed.*]

"I have heard nothing of that, Mrs. Shand. [VENABLES *shakes his wise head.*] And in any case, I am afraid——"

[*He still hears the wooden leg.*]

"But you said yourself that his second thoughts were sometimes such an improvement on the first."

[*The* COMTESSE *comes to the help of the baggage.*]

"I remember your saying that, Charles."

"Yes, that has struck me. [*Politely.*] Well, if he has anything to show me—— In the meantime——"

[*He regains the lawn, like one glad to escape attendance at* JOHN's *obsequies. The* COMTESSE *is brought back to speech by the sound of the mower—nothing wooden in it.*]

"What are you up to now, Miss Pin? You know as well as I do that there is no such speech."

[MAGGIE's *mouth tightens.*]

"I do not."

"It is a duel, is it, my friend?"

[*The* COMTESSE *rings the bell and* MAGGIE's *guilty mind is agitated.*]

"What are you ringing for?"

"As the challenged one, Miss Pin, I have the choice of weapons. I am going to send for your husband to ask him if he has written such a speech. After which, I suppose, *you* will ask me to leave you while you and he write it together."

[MAGGIE *wrings her hands.*]

"You are wrong, Comtesse; but please don't do that."

"You but make me more curious, and my doctor says that I must be told everything. [*The* COMTESSE *assumes the pose of her sex in melodrama.*] Put your cards on the table, Maggie Shand, or—— [*She indicates that she always pinks her man.* MAGGIE *dolefully produces a roll of paper from her bag.*] What precisely is that?"

[*The reply is little more than a squeak.*]

"John's speech."

"You have written it yourself!"

[MAGGIE *is naturally indignant.*]

"It's typed."

"You guessed that the speech he wrote unaided would not satisfy, and you prepared this to take its place!"

"Not at all, Comtesse. It is the draft of his speech that he left at home. That's all."

"With a few trivial alterations by yourself, I swear. Can you deny it?"

[*No wonder that* MAGGIE *is outraged. She replaces* JOHN's *speech in the bag with becoming hauteur.*]

"Comtesse, these insinuations are unworthy of you. May I ask where is my husband?"

[*The* COMTESSE *drops her a curtsy.*]

"I believe your Haughtiness may find him in the Dutch garden. Oh, I see through you. You are not to show him your speech. But you are to get him to write another one, and somehow all your additions will be in it. Think not, creature, that you can deceive one so old in iniquity as the Comtesse de la Brière."

[*There can be but one reply from a good wife to such a charge, and at once the* COMTESSE *is left alone with her shame. Anon a footman appears. You know how they come and go.*]

"You rang, my lady?"

"Did I? Ah, yes, but why? [*He is but lately from the ploughshare and cannot help her. In this quandary her eyes alight upon the bag. She is unfortunately too abandoned to feel her shame: she still thinks that she has the choice of weapons. She takes the speech from the bag and bestows it on her servitor.*] Take this to Mr. Venables, please, and say it is from Mr. Shand. [THOMAS—*but in the end we shall probably call him* JOHN—*departs with the little explosive; and when* MAGGIE *returns she finds that the* COMTESSE *is once more engaged on her interrupted game of Patience.*] You did not find him?"

[*All the bravery has dropped from* MAGGIE's *face.*]

"I didn't see him, but I heard him. *She* is with him. I think they are coming here."

[*The* COMTESSE *is suddenly kind again.*]

"Sybil? Shall I get rid of her?"

"No, I want her to be here, too. Now I shall know."

[*The* COMTESSE *twists the little thing around.*]

"Know what?"

"As soon as I look into his face I shall know."

[*A delicious scent ushers in the fair* SYBIL, *who is as sweet as a milking stool. She greets* MRS. SHAND *with some alarm.*]

Maggie. How do you do, Lady Sybil? How pretty you look in that frock. [SYBIL *rustles uncomfortably.*] You are a feast to the eye.

Sybil. Please, I wish you would not.

[*Shall we describe* SYBIL'S *frock, in which she looks like a great strawberry that knows it ought to be plucked; or would it be easier to watch the coming of* JOHN? *Let us watch* JOHN.]

John. You, Maggie! You never wrote that you were coming.

[*No, let us watch* MAGGIE. *As soon as she looked into his face she was to know something of importance.*]

Maggie. [*Not dissatisfied with what she sees.*] No, John, it's a surprise visit. I just ran down to say good-by.

[*At this his face falls, which does not seem to pain her.*]

Sybil. [*Foreseeing another horrible Scotch scene.*] To say good-by?

Comtesse. [*Thrilling with expectation.*] To whom, Maggie?

Sybil. [*Deserted by the impediment, which is probably playing with rough boys in the Lovers' Lane.*] Auntie, do leave us, won't you?

Comtesse. Not I. It is becoming far too interesting.

Maggie. I suppose there's no reason the Comtesse shouldn't be told, as she will know so soon at any rate?

John. That's so.

[SYBIL *sees with a sinking that he is to be practical also.*]

Maggie. It's so simple. You see, Comtesse, John and Lady Sybil have fallen in love with one another, and they are to go off as soon as the meeting at Leeds has taken place.

[*The* COMTESSE'S *breast is too suddenly introduced to Caledonia and its varied charms.*]

Comtesse. Mon Dieu!

Maggie. I think that's putting it correctly, John.

John. In a sense. But I'm not to attend the meeting at Leeds. My speech doesn't find favor. [*With a strange humility.*] There's something wrong with it.

Comtesse. I never expected to hear you say that, Mr. Shand.

John. [*Wondering also.*] I never expected it myself. I meant to make it the speech of my career. But somehow my hand seems to have lost its cunning.

Comtesse. And you don't know how?

John. It's inexplicable. My brain was never clearer.

Comtesse. You might have helped him, Sybil.

Sybil. [*Quite sulkily.*] I did.

Comtesse. But I thought she was such an inspiration to you, Mr. Shand.

John. [*Going bravely to* SYBIL'S *side.*] She slaved at it with me.

Comtesse. Strange. [*Wickedly becoming practical also.*] So now there is nothing to detain you. Shall I send for a fly, Sybil?

Sybil. [*With a cry of the heart.*] Auntie, do leave us.

Comtesse. I can understand your impatience to be gone, Mr. Shand.

John. [*Heavily.*] I promised Maggie to wait till the twenty-fourth, and I'm a man of my word.

Maggie. But I give you back your word, John. You can go now.

[JOHN *looks at* SYBIL, *and* SYBIL *looks at* JOHN, *and the impediment arrives in time to take a peep at both of them.*]

Sybil. [*Groping for the practical, to which we must all come in the end.*] He must make satisfactory arrangements about you first. I insist on that.

Maggie. [*With no more imagination than a hen.*] Thank you, Lady Sybil, but I have made all my arrangements.

John. [*Stung.*] Maggie, that was my part.

Maggie. [*The hens are saying it all the time.*] You see, my brothers feel they can't be away from their business any longer; and so, if it would be convenient to you, John, I could travel north with them by the night train on Wednesday.

Sybil. I—I—— The way you put things——!

John. This is just the twenty-first.

Maggie. My things are all packed. I think you'll find the house in good order, Lady Sybil. I have had the vacuum cleaners in. I'll give you the keys of the linen and the silver plate; I have them in that bag. The carpet on the upper landing is a good deal frayed, but——

Sybil. Please, I don't want to hear any more.

Maggie. The ceiling of the dining-room would be the better of a new lick of paint——

Sybil. [*Stamping her foot, small fours.*] Can't you stop her?

John. [*Soothingly.*] She's meaning well. Maggie, I know it's natural to you to value those things, because your outlook on life is bounded by them; but all this jars on me.

Maggie. Does it?

John. Why should you be so ready to go?

Maggie. I promised not to stand in your way.

John. [*Stoutly.*] You needn't be in such a hurry. There are three days to run yet. [*The French are so different from us that we shall probably never be able to understand why the* COMTESSE *laughed aloud here.*] It's just a joke to the Comtesse.

Comtesse. It seems to be no joke to you, Mr. Shand. Sybil, my pet, are you to let him off?

Sybil. [*Flashing.*] Let him off? If he wishes it. Do you?

John. [*Manfully.*] I want it to go on. [*Something seems to have caught in his throat: perhaps it is the impediment trying a temporary home.*] It's the one wish of my heart. If you come with me, Sybil, I'll do all in a man's power to make you never regret it.

[*Triumph of the Vere de Veres.*]

Maggie. [*Bringing them back to earth with a dump.*] And I can make my arrangements for Wednesday?

Sybil. [*Seeking the* COMTESSE'S *protection.*] No, you can't. Auntie, I am not going on with this. I'm very sorry for you, John, but I see now—I couldn't face it——

[*She can't face anything at this moment except the sofa pillows.*]

Comtesse. [*Noticing* JOHN'S *big sigh of relief.*] So *that* is all right, Mr. Shand!

Maggie. Don't you love her any more, John? Be practical.

Sybil. [*To the pillows.*] At any rate I have tired of him. Oh, best to tell the horrid truth. I am ashamed of myself. I have been crying my eyes out over it—I thought I was such a different kind of woman. But I am weary of him. I think him—oh, so dull!

John. [*His face lighting up.*] Are you sure that is how you have come to think of me?

Sybil. I'm sorry—[*with all her soul*]—but yes—yes—yes.

John. By God, it's more than I deserve.

Comtesse. Congratulations to you both.

[SYBIL *runs away; and in the fulness of time she married successfully in Cloth of Silver, which was afterwards turned into a bedspread.*]

Maggie. You haven't read my letter yet, John, have you?

John. No.

Comtesse. [*Imploringly.*] May I know to what darling letter you refer?

Maggie. It's a letter I wrote to him before he left London. I gave it to him closed, not to be opened until his time here was ended.

John. [*As his hand strays to his pocket.*] Am I to read it now?

Maggie. Not before her. Please go away, Comtesse.

Comtesse. Every word you say makes me more determined to remain.

Maggie. It will hurt you. [*Distressed.*] Don't read it, John; tear it up.

John. You make me very curious, Maggie. And yet I don't see what can be in it.

Comtesse. But you feel a little nervous? Give *me* the dagger.

Maggie. [*Quickly.*] No.

[*But the* COMTESSE *has already got it.*]

Comtesse. May I? [*She must have thought they said Yes, for she opens the letter. She shares its contents with them.*] "Dearest John, It is at my request that the Comtesse is having Lady Sybil at the cottage at the same time as yourself."

John. What?

Comtesse. Yes, she begged me to invite you together.

John. But why?

Maggie. I promised you not to behave as other wives would do.

John. It's not understandable.

Comtesse. "You may ask why I do this, John, and my reason is, I think that after a few weeks of Lady Sybil, every day, and all day, you will become sick to death of her. I am also giving her the chance to help you and inspire you with your work, so that you may both learn what her help and her inspiration amount to. Of course, if your love is the great strong passion you think it, then those weeks will make you love her more than ever and I can only say good-by. But if, as I suspect, you don't even now know what true love is, then by the next time we meet, dear John, you will have had enough of her.—Your affectionate wife, MAGGIE." Oh, why was not Sybil present at the reading of the will! And now, if you two will kindly excuse me, I think I must go and get that poor sufferer the eau de Cologne.

John. It's almost enough to make a man lose faith in himself.

Comtesse. Oh, don't say that, Mr. Shand.

Maggie. [*Defending him.*] You mustn't hurt him. If you haven't loved deep and true, that's just because you have never met a woman yet, John, capable of inspiring it.

Comtesse. [*Putting her hand on* MAGGIE'S *shoulder.*] Have you not, Mr. Shand?

John. I see what you mean. But Maggie wouldn't think better of me for any false pretences. She knows my feelings for her now are neither more nor less than what they have always been.

Maggie. [*Who sees that he is looking at her as solemnly as a volume of sermons printed by request.*] I think no one could be fond of me that can't laugh a little at me.

John. How could that help?

Comtesse. [*Exasperated.*] Mr. Shand, I give you up.

Maggie. I admire his honesty.

Comtesse. Oh, I give you up also. Arcades ambo. Scotchies both.

John. [*When she has gone.*] But this letter, it's not like you. By gosh, Maggie, you're no fool. [*She beams at this, as any wife would.*] But how could I have made such a mistake? It's not like a strong man.

[*Evidently he has an inspiration.*]

Maggie. What is it?

John. [*The inspiration.*] *Am* I a strong man?

Maggie. You? Of course you are. And self-made. Has anybody ever helped you in the smallest way?

John. [*Thinking it out again.*] No, nobody.

Maggie. Not even Lady Sybil?

John. I'm beginning to doubt it. It's very curious, though, Maggie, that this speech should be disappointing.

Maggie. It's just that Mr. Venables hasn't the brains to see how good it is.

John. That must be it. [*But he is too good a man to rest satisfied with this.*] No, Maggie, it's not. Somehow I seem to have lost my neat way of saying things.

Maggie. [*Almost cooing.*] It will come back to you.

John. [*Forlorn.*] If you knew how I've tried.

Maggie. [*Cautiously.*] Maybe if you were to try again; and I'll just come and sit beside you, and knit. I think the click of the needles sometimes put you in the mood.

John. Hardly that; and yet many a Shandism have I knocked off while you were sitting beside me knitting. I suppose it was the quietness.

Maggie. Very likely.

John. [*With another inspiration.*] Maggie!

Maggie. [*Again.*] What is it, John?

John. What if it was you that put those queer ideas into my head!

Maggie. Me?

John. Without your knowing it, I mean.

Maggie. But how?

John. We used to talk bits over; and it may be that you dropped the seed, so to speak.

Maggie. John, could it be this, that I sometimes had the idea in a rough womanish sort of way and then you polished it up till it came out a Shandism?

John. [*Slowly slapping his knee.*] I believe you've hit it, Maggie: to think that you may have been helping me all the time—and neither of us knew it.

[*He has so nearly reached a smile that no one can say what might have happened within the next moment if the* COMTESSE *had not reappeared.*]

Comtesse. Mr. Venables wishes to see you, Mr. Shand.

John. [*Lost, stolen, or strayed a smile in the making.*] Hum.

Comtesse. He is coming now.

John. [*Grumpy.*] Indeed.

Comtesse. [*Sweetly.*] It is about your speech.

John. He has said all he need say on that subject, and more.

Comtesse. [*Quaking a little.*] I think it is about the second speech.

John. What second speech?

[MAGGIE *runs to her bag and opens it.*]

Maggie. [*Horrified.*] Comtesse, you have given it to him.

Comtesse. [*Impudently.*] Wasn't I meant to?

John. What is it? What second speech?

Maggie. Cruel, cruel. [*Willing to go on her knees.*] You had left the first draft of your speech at home, John, and I brought it here with—with a few little things I've added myself.

John. [*A seven-footer.*] What's that?

Maggie. [*Four foot ten at most.*] Just trifles—things I was to suggest to you—while I was knitting—and then, if you liked any of them you could have polished them—and turned them into something good. John, John—and now she has shown it to Mr. Venables.

John. [*Thundering.*] As my work, Comtesse?

[*But the* COMTESSE *is not of the women who are afraid of thunder.*]

Maggie. It is your work—nine-tenths of it.

John. [*In the black cap.*] You presumed, Maggie Shand! Very well, then, here he comes, and now we'll see to what extent you've helped me.

Venables. My dear fellow. My dear Shand, I congratulate you. Give me your hand.

John. The speech?

Venables. You have improved it out of knowledge. It is the same speech, but those new touches make all the difference. [JOHN *sits down heavily.*] Mrs. Shand, be proud of him.

Maggie. I am. I am, John.

Comtesse. You always said that his second thoughts were best, Charles.

Venables. [*Pleased to be reminded of it.*] Didn't I? Didn't I? Those delicious little touches! How good that is, Shand, about the flowing tide.

Comtesse. The flowing tide?

Venables. In the first speech it was something like this—"Gentlemen, the Opposition are calling to you to vote for them and the flowing tide, but I solemnly warn you to beware lest the flowing tide does not engulf you." The second way is much better.

Comtesse. What is the second way, Mr. Shand?

[JOHN *does not tell her.*]

Venables. This is how he puts it now. [JOHN *cannot help raising his head to listen.*] "Gentlemen, the Opposition are calling to you to vote for them and the flowing tide, but I ask you cheerfully to vote for us and *dam* the flowing tide."

[VENABLES *and his old friend the* COMTESSE *laugh heartily, but for different reasons.*]

Comtesse. It *is* better, Mr. Shand.

Maggie. I don't think so.

Venables. Yes, yes, it's so virile. Excuse me, Comtesse, I'm off to read the whole thing again. [*For the first time he notices that* JOHN *is strangely quiet.*] I think this has rather bowled you over, Shand. [JOHN'S *head sinks lower.*] Well, well, good news doesn't kill.

Maggie. [*Counsel for the defense.*] Surely the important thing about the speech is its strength and knowledge and eloquence, the things that were in the first speech as well as in the second.

Venables. That of course is largely true. The wit would not be enough without them, just as they were not enough without the wit. It is the combination that is irresistible. [JOHN'S *head rises a little.*] Shand, you are our man, remember that; it is emphatically the best thing you have ever done. How this will go down at Leeds!

[*He returns gaily to his hammock; but lower sinks* JOHN'S *head, and even the* COMTESSE *has the grace to take herself off.* MAGGIE'S *arms flutter near her husband, not daring to alight.*]

"You heard what he said, John. It's the combination. Is it so terrible to you to find that my love for you had made me able to help you in the little things?"

"The little things! It seems strange to me to hear you call me by my name, Maggie. It's as if I looked on you for the first time."

"Look at me, John, for the first time. What do you see?"

"I see a woman who has brought her husband low."

"Only that?"

"I see the tragedy of a man who has found himself out. Eh, I can't live with you again, Maggie." [*He shivers.*]

"Why did you shiver, John?"

"It was at myself for saying that I couldn't live with you again, when I should have been wondering how for so long you have lived with me. And I suppose you have forgiven me all the time. [*She nods.*] And forgive me still? [*She nods again.*] Dear God!"

"John, am I to go? or are you to keep me on? [*She is now a little bundle near his feet.*] I'm willing to stay because I'm useful to you, if it can't be for a better reason. [*His hand feels for her, and the bundle wriggles nearer.*] It's nothing unusual I've done, John. Every man who is high up loves to think that he has done it all himself; and the wife smiles, and let's it go at that. It's our only joke. Every woman knows that. [*He stares at her in hopeless perplexity.*] Oh, John, if only you could laugh at me."

"I can't laugh, Maggie."

[*But as he continues to stare at her a strange disorder appears in his face.* MAGGIE *feels that it is to be now or never.*]

"Laugh, John, laugh. Watch me, see how easy it is."

[*A terrific struggle is taking place within him. He creaks. Something that may be mirth forces a passage, at first painfully, no more joy in it than in the discolored water from a spring that has long been dry. Soon, however, he laughs loud and long. The spring water is becoming clear.* MAGGIE *claps her hands. He is saved.*]

MID-CHANNEL *

By
ARTHUR WING PINERO

SIR ARTHUR WING PINERO WAS THE pivotal figure of the commercial English theater during the last two decades of the nineteenth century. Unquestionably, he has been England's most accomplished artisan of the well-made play. Although trained to follow his father's profession, the law, he chose the life of the theater at the time when a new zest for realism had just been created by the Bancrofts and their author Robertson.

Under Sir Henry Irving, as he frankly remarked, he played the worst parts in Shakespeare for the longest runs ever known. He was, however, busying himself in writing for the new live theater. Possibly he was ambitious to carry on the work cut short by Robertson's early death. The success of *Daisy's Escape, The Money-Spinner,* and *The Squire* encouraged him to abandon acting altogether.

In early plays such as *The Money-Spender* and *The Squire,* a serious bent was indicated, but this was lost sight of in the dazzling success of his great farces, especially those played at the Court Theatre after 1885. In these, Pinero advanced the art of the English theater by making character sketches a more important element of the entertainment than clever plot machinery. His vividly real people doing absurd things made a fresh appeal to audiences sated with sentimentality and sensation, and satisfied that love of the burlesque that has always been an important inspiration of English comedy. Sir Nigel Playfair's successful revival of *Dandy Dick* in 1929 reminds us that in this and its companion pieces, *The Magistrate, The Schoolmistress, The Cabinet Minister,* and *The Amazons,* we have plays that may more successfully defy the challenge of time than his later serious social dramas.

Pinero was, however, watching with interest the new naturalism of Ibsen, and the productions of *Le Théâtre Libre* and *Die Freie Bühne,* as earlier he had followed Robertson, the French writers of the well-made play, and the German writers of farce. *The Profligate,* in 1889, was the first expression of this new tendency to present uncompromisingly in the theater the less pleasant aspects of life. Not until 1893 did Pinero give masterful expression to this new force, which had already failed to appeal widely in Ibsen's own plays. *The Second Mrs. Tanqueray* burst upon the English-speaking world as a revolutionary work of magnitude, and did more than any one event in the annals of the English stage to make possible the general revival of art and letters in the theater that was soon to follow. During the next fifteen years Pinero wrote in similar vein *The Notorious Mrs. Ebbsmith, The Benefit of the Doubt, Iris, His House in Order, The Thunderbolt,* and *Mid-Channel.* Although not fulfilling the great promise of *The Second Mrs. Tanqueray,* or even approaching it in popular interest, these plays gave evidence of maturing thought and technique. *Mid-Channel,* which is technically Pinero's most satisfying play, rightly represents him in this collection. In it Pinero intentionally avoided the "clever" artifices of "well-made" exposition. It reveals his persistent interest in lives gone wrong and their social problems; and, although lacking in character interest, it projects its conflict with sureness and ease in never-flagging dialogue to a tragic outcome as nearly inevitable as Pinero ever conceived.

Much has been written in disparagement of Pinero's naturalism and of his art, chiefly on the ground of its faulty psychology and moral insignificance. "I am an ordinary playwright," he once modestly remarked, meaning, perhaps, that his business was not to speculate on moral philosophy, or to pretend to literary or scientific attainments. He was a man of the theater and he had learned to trust his own very acute powers of observation of a social life he knew. He frankly accepted standards of behavior that were shaping, if misshaping, his characters' lives. Shaw was the first critic to see clearly in the blinding flash of Pinero's triumph. "Pinero," he wrote, "is no interpreter of character, but simply an adroit describer of people as the ordinary man sees and judges them." Pinero might have replied, "That is what I understand the dramatist's business to be." Unlike Ibsen and Shaw, he did not assume a higher moral vision for himself or for his characters. They broke conventions as sinners with little concern for moral significance or consistency. For the reason Shaw gave, Pinero's much acclaimed "problems" are now in the discard. He did, however, break wide open a door that for over a century had been closed in our theater against a serious study of modern life, and he set a high standard of craftsmanship that was a stimulating challenege in his own day and is, perhaps, too influential in ours.

The London stage itself played a large part in the creation and development of Pinero's craft, as he frankly has acknowledged. First and most important was the incentive given by the plays of Robertson and his producers, the Bancrofts, at the Prince of Wales Theatre, the cradle of British dramatic realism in the '60's. "If ever you write a history of our modern English drama," said Pinero to Mr. Clayton Hamilton, "be fair to Tom Robertson. If it hadn't been for Robertson, I should never have been able to do what I have done." In *Trelawney of the "Wells,"* 1898, Pinero paid a literary tribute to Robertson's memory, at the same time setting the fashion for "period" mounting that has been in vogue ever since. The brilliant comedy acting, bearing the Bancrofts' stamp, notably that of John Hare and the Kendalls, made Pinero's early farce characters the freshest and truest portraits of English types the stage had seen since Robertson. To Irving, and especially to Forbes-Robertson, whose gentlemanly reserve in serious drama became an important influence, Pinero owed even more. Forbes-Robertson appeared with Olga Nethersole in *The Profligate* in 1889, thus imparting at once to the embryo British social drama an atmosphere of cultured restraint that was characteristic of the author and the society he portrayed.

The Second Mrs. Tanqueray was given a masterful presentation by Sir George Alexander's company at the St. James's Theatre on May 27, 1893. Mrs. Patrick Campbell contributed to Paula a fascination that a cold perusal of the part can only faintly suggest. Her beauty and what was called her "intellectual" reading gave the part a significance that it has never seemed to have in late revivals. "The glamour which Mrs. Patrick Campbell cast around the play," said Bernard Shaw, "has forced me to examine pretentions which Mr. Pinero himself never put forward rather than to acknowledge the merits with which his work is so concisely packed." *Mid-Channel* was produced in 1910 also at the St. James's, but with Miss Irene Vanbrugh as Zoe Blundell. Although not a failure, its run was comparatively short. Pinero had written it to please himself and did not expect success. Almost at the same time, however, Miss Ethel Barrymore produced the play in her best manner in America, where it had a long and successful career in New York and elsewhere. Pinero, above all, possessed that sure sense of the stage that makes his plays easily actable. Few English dramatists have more repeatedly succeeded in entertaining a wide public with plays of high merit.

ARTHUR WING PINERO

Born 1855, London.

1874, Abandoned law and became an actor in Edinburgh and Liverpool.

1876, Appeared in London. Became a member of Irving's company.

1877, *£200 a Year,* his first play.

1881, Devoted himself exclusively to writing.

1909, Knighted.

Died 1934.

PLAYS

1877 *£200 a Year.* 1877 *Two Can Play at That Game.* 1878 *The Comet.* 1879 *Daisy's Escape.* 1880 *Hester's Mystery.* 1880 *By-gones.* 1880 *The Money-Spinner.* 1881 *Imprudence.* 1881 *The Squire.* 1882 *Girls and Boys.* 1883 *The Rector.* 1883 *Lords and Commons.* 1883 *The Rocket.* 1884 *Low Water.* 1884 *In Chancery.* 1885 *The Magistrate.* 1886 *The Schoolmistress.* 1886 *The Hobby Horse.* 1887 *Dandy Dick.* 1888 *Sweet Lavender.* 1888 *The Weaker Sex.* 1889 *The Profligate.* 1890 *The Cabinet Minister.* 1891 *Lady Bountiful.* 1891 *The Times.* 1893 *The Amazons.* 1893 *The Second Mrs. Tanqueray.* 1895 *The Notorious Mrs. Ebbsmith.* 1895 *The Benefit of the Doubt.* 1897 *The Princess and the Butterfly.* 1898 *Trelawney of the "Wells."* 1899 *The Gay Lord Quex.* 1901 *Iris.* 1903 *Letty.* 1904 *A Wife Without a Smile.* 1906 *His House in Order.* 1908 *The Thunderbolt.* 1909 *Mid-Channel.* 1911 *Preserving Mr. Panmure.* 1912 *The "Mind-the-Paint" Girl.* 1912 *The Widow of Wasdale Head.* 1913 *Playgoers.* 1915 *The Big Drum.* 1917 *The Freaks.* 1917 *Mr. Livermore's Dream.* 1918 *Monica's Blue Boy* (A Play without Words). 1919 *Quick Work.* 1922 *The Enchanted Cottage.* 1922 *A Seat in the Park.* 1928 *A Private Room.* 1930 *Dr. Harmer's Holidays.* 1930 *Child Man.* 1932 *A Cold June.*

WRITINGS ABOUT THE DRAMA

Preface to Courtney's *Idea of Tragedy,* 1900. *Robert Louis Stevenson: the Dramatist,* 1903. *Robert Browning as a Dramatist,* 1912. *The Theatre in the Seventies.* In *The 1870's,* edited by Harley Granville-Barker, 1929.

MID-CHANNEL

The Persons of the Play

THEODORE BLUNDELL.
THE HONBLE. PETER MOTTRAM.
LEONARD FERRIS.
WARREN, *servant at Lancaster Gate.*
COLE, *servant at the flat in Cavendish Square.*
RIDEOUT, *Mr. Ferris's servant.*
UPHOLSTERERS.
ZOE BLUNDELL.
MRS. PIERPOINT.
ETHEL PIERPOINT.
MRS. ANNERLY.
LENA.

The scene is laid in London. The events of the First Act take place on an afternoon in January. The rest of the action occurs on a day in the following June.

THE FIRST ACT

SCENE.—*A drawing-room, decorated and furnished in the French style. In the wall opposite the spectator there is a door, the upper part of which is glazed. A silk curtain hangs across the glazed panels, but above the curtain there is a view of the corridor beyond. The fireplace, where a bright fire is burning, is in the wall on the right. There is a door on the further side of the fireplace, another on the nearer side. Both these doors are supposed to lead to a second drawing-room.*

On either side of the fireplace there is an armchair, and on the farther side, standing out in the room, is a settee. Some illustrated papers of the popular sort are lying upon the armchair next to the settee. Behind the settee are an oblong table and a chair. In the middle of the room, on the left of the settee and facing the fire, is another armchair; and on the left of the armchair on the nearer side of the fireplace there is a fauteuil-stool. A writing-table, with a chair before it, stands on the left-hand side of the room, and among the objects on the writing-table are a hand-mirror and some photographs in frames. Other pieces of furniture, of a more formal kind than those already specified, fill spaces against the walls. One of these, on the left of the glazed door, is a second settee.

The room is lighted only by the blaze of the fire, and the corridor also is in semi-darkness.

(Note: Throughout, "right" and "left" are the spectators' right and left, not the actor's.)

[*The corridor is suddenly lighted up. Then* WARREN *enters at the glazed door and switches on the light in the room. He is followed by* MRS. PIERPOINT, *a pleasant-looking, middle-aged lady, and by* ETHEL, *a pretty girl of five-and-twenty.*]

Mrs. Pierpoint. [*To the servant.*] You are sure Mrs. Blundell will be in soon?

Warren. She said half-past four, ma'am.

Mrs. Pierpoint. It's that now, isn't it?

Warren. Just upon, ma'am.

[WARREN *withdraws, closing the door.*]

Ethel. What beautiful rooms these are!

Mrs. Pierpoint. Money!

Ethel. I always feel I'm in Paris when I'm here, in some smart house in the Champs-Elysées—not at Lancaster Gate. What *is* Mr. Blundell, Mother?

Mrs. Pierpoint. A stockbroker.

Ethel. Stockbroker?

Mrs. Pierpoint. Blundell—something-or-other—and Mottram. He goes to the City every morning.

Ethel. I know that. But I've never heard him, or Zoe, mention the Stock Exchange.

Mrs. Pierpoint. [*Sitting on the settee by the fireplace.*] Prosperous stockbrokers and their wives—those who move in a decent set—*don't* mention the Stock Exchange.

Ethel. Then that nice person, Mr. Mottram, is a stockbroker too?

Mrs. Pierpoint. Of course, dear. He's the "Mottram" of the firm.

Ethel. And *he's* the son of a peer.

Mrs. Pierpoint. Peers' sons are common enough in the City nowadays—and peers, for that matter.

Ethel. [*Moving to the fireplace and warming her hands.*] Zoe is a doctor's daughter.

Mrs. Pierpoint. Has she given you leave to call her Zoe?

Ethel. Yes, last week—asked me to. I'm so glad; I've taken such a liking to her.

Mrs. Pierpoint. She was a Miss Tucker. Her father practiced in New Cavendish Street. He was a great gout man.

Ethel. You *are* full of information, Mother.

Mrs. Pierpoint. Emma Lawton was giving me the whole history of the Blundells at lunch today. She has money, of her own.

Ethel. Zoe?

Mrs. Pierpoint. Doctor Tucker left sixty or seventy thousand pounds, and she came in for it all. But they'd got on before then.

Ethel. H'm! There are stockbrokers and stockbrokers, I suppose.

Mrs. Pierpoint. Straight and crooked, as in every other business or profession.

Ethel. I do think, though, that a girl in Zoe's position might have chosen somebody slightly more refined than Mr. Blundell.

Mrs. Pierpoint. What's wrong with him? He's extremely amiable and inoffensive.

Ethel. Amiable!

Mrs. Pierpoint. He strikes me as being so.

Ethel. I don't call it particularly amiable or inoffensive in a husband to be as snappy with his wife as he is with Zoe.

Mrs. Pierpoint. Snappy?

Ethel. Irritable—impatient.

Mrs. Pierpoint. Oh, I dare say there's an excellent understanding between them. They've been married a good many years.

Ethel. Thirteen, she's told me.

Mrs. Pierpoint. Married people are allowed to be out of humor with each other occasionally.

Ethel. A considerable allowance must be made for Mr. Blundell, I'm afraid.

Mrs. Pierpoint. You're prejudiced, Ethel. I've seen her just as snappy, as you term it, with him.

Ethel. You can't blame her, if she's provoked.

Mrs. Pierpoint. Nor him, if he's provoked. The argument cuts both ways——

Ethel. [*Listening.*] Sssh!

[ZOE, *a charming, animated, bright-eyed woman, wearing her hat and some costly furs, enters quickly at the glazed door.*]

Zoe. Delightful!

Mrs. Pierpoint. [*Rising.*] Your servant insisted on our coming up.

Zoe. [*Shaking hands with* MRS. PIERPOINT.] If he hadn't, I'd have wrung his neck. [*Kissing* ETHEL.] How are you, dear? [*Stripping off her gloves.*] The weather! Isn't it filthy! Do you remember what the sun's like? I had the blinds drawn all over the house at eleven o'clock this morning. What's the good of trying to make believe it's day? [*Taking off her coat.*] Do sit down. Ugh! Why is it that more people commit suicide in summer than in winter?

Mrs. Pierpoint. [*Resuming her seat on the settee by the fire.*] Do they?

Ethel. [*Sitting upon the fauteuil-stool.*] Why, yes, Mother; what-do-you-call-them? —statistics—prove it.

Zoe. [*Throwing her coat and gloves upon the settee at the back and unpinning her hat.*] You'll see, when I put an end to myself, it will be in the wintertime.

Mrs. Pierpoint. My dear!

Ethel. Zoe!

Mrs. Pierpoint. If you are in this frame of mind, why don't you pack your trunks and fly?

Zoe. Fly?

Ethel. Mother means cut it.

Mrs. Pierpoint. Ethel!

Zoe. [*Tossing her hat on to the settee and taking up the hand-mirror from the writing-table and adjusting her hair.*] Don't scold her; she picks up her slang from me.

Ethel. Evil communications——!

Mrs. Pierpoint. I mean, go abroad for a couple of months—Egypt——

Ethel. Mother, how horrid of you! I should miss her terribly.

Mrs. Pierpoint. Cairo—Assouan——

Zoe. [*Looking into the hand-glass steadily.*] That's funny. I have been thinking lately of "cutting it."

Mrs. Pierpoint. But I suppose it would have to be without your busy husband.

Zoe. [*Replacing the mirror.*] Yes, it would be without Theo. [*Turning to* MRS. PIERPONT *and* ETHEL *and rattling on again.*] Well! How have you been amusing yourselves? You wretches, you haven't been near me since Monday, either of you. Done anything—seen anything?

Ethel. Nothing.

Mrs. Pierpoint. [*To* ZOE.] If *you're* under the weather, there's some excuse for me.

Zoe. [*Walking about restlessly.*] Oh, but I will keep moving, though the heavens fall. I've been to the theater every night this week, and supped out afterward. They've opened such a ripping restaurant in Jermyn

Street. [*Pausing.*] You haven't seen the new play at the St. Martin's, then?

Mrs. Pierpoint. No.

Ethel. I want to, badly.

Zoe. I'll take you. We'll make up a party. [*Scribbling a memorandum at the writing-table.*] I'll tell Lenny Ferris to get seats.

Ethel. Good business!

Mrs. Pierpoint. Ethel!

Zoe. It's all about children—kiddies. There are the sweetest little tots in it. Two especially—a tiny, round-eyed boy and a mite of a girl with straw-colored hair—you feel you must clamber on to the stage and hug them. You feel you *must*!

Mrs. Pierpoint. Aren't there any grown-ups?

Zoe. [*Dropping into the armchair facing the fire.*] Oh, yes; they bore me.

Ethel. I was reading the story to you, Mother——

Zoe. The story's no account—it's the kiddies. The man who wrote the thing must be awfully fond of children. I wonder whether he has any little 'uns. If he hasn't, it's of no consequence to him; he can imagine them. What a jolly gift! Fancy! To have the power of imagining children—bringing them to life! Just by shutting the door, and sitting down at your writing-table, and saying to your brain, "Now, then! I'm ready for them——!" [*Breaking off.*] Ring the bell, Ethel. [ETHEL *rises, and, going to the fireplace, rings the bell.*] Let's have tea.

Mrs. Pierpoint. I'm afraid we can't stay for tea. I've promised to be at old Miss Fremantle's at five o'clock. Ethel——

Ethel. Yes, Mother?

Mrs. Pierpoint. Go downstairs for a few minutes. I want a little private conversation with Mrs. Blundell.

Ethel. [*Surprised.*] Private conversation!

Mrs. Pierpoint. If she won't think me too troublesome.

Zoe. [*Rising and opening the nearer door on the right—to* ETHEL.] Come in here. There's a lovely fire. [*Disappearing.*] I'll switch the light on.

Ethel. [*Following* ZOE*—at the door.*] What is it about, Mother?

Mrs. Pierpoint. [*Rising.*] Now, don't be inquisitive, Ethel.

Zoe. [*From the adjoining room.*] Come along!

[ETHEL *goes into the next room.* WARREN *enters at the glazed door.*]

Mrs. Pierpoint. [*To* WARREN.] Mrs. Blundell rang for tea.

Warren. Very good, ma'am.

[WARREN *withdraws as* ZOE *returns.*]

Mrs. Pierpoint. We shan't be heard?

Zoe. [*Closing the door.*] No.

Mrs. Pierpoint. It's really most improper of me to bother you in this way.

Zoe. [*Advancing to* MRS. PIERPOINT.] Can I be of any use to you?

Mrs. Pierpoint. Well, yes, you can. You can give me—what shall I call it?—a hint——

Zoe. [*Sitting on the fauteuil-stool.*] A hint?

Mrs. Pierpoint. On a subject that concerns Ethel. [*Sitting in the chair facing the fire.*] We're quite new friends of yours, dear Mrs. Blundell—is it six weeks since we dined at the Darrells'?

Zoe. There or thereabouts.

Mrs. Pierpoint. A fortnight or so before Christmas, wasn't it? But my girl has formed a great attachment to you, and I fancy you are inclined to be interested in her.

Zoe. Rather! She and I are going to be tremendous pals.

Mrs. Pierpoint. That's splendid. Now, don't laugh at me for my extreme cautiousness, if you can help it.

Zoe. Cautiousness?

Mrs. Pierpoint. Tell me—as one woman to another—do you consider it advisable for Ethel to see much of Mr. Ferris?

Zoe. Advisable?

Mrs. Pierpoint. Oh, I've no doubt he's a highly respectable young man, as young men go—I'm not implying anything to the contrary——

Zoe. Is she seeing much of Mr. Ferris?

Mrs. Pierpoint. She meets him here.

Zoe. Ah, yes.

Mrs. Pierpoint. And he has suddenly taken to dropping in to tea with us pretty regularly; and twice this week—twice—he has sent her some magnificent flowers—magnificent.

Zoe. Dear old Lenny!

Mrs. Pierpoint. There's something in his manner, too—one can't describe it——

Zoe. [*A little ruefully.*] Ha! Ha, ha, ha!

Mrs. Pierpoint. I *am* amusing you.

Zoe. No, no. I beg your pardon. [*Rising and going to the fire.*] Somehow I've never pictured Lenny with a wife.

Mrs. Pierpoint. It may be only an excess of politeness on his part; there mayn't be the least foundation for my suspicions.

Zoe. I suppose every married woman believes that her bachelor chums will remain bachelors.

Mrs. Pierpoint. And pray, dear Mrs. Blundell, don't take me for a match-making mother. I've no desire to lose my girl yet awhile, I assure you. But I want to know, naturally—it's my duty to know—exactly who and what are the men who come into my drawing-room.

Zoe. Why, naturally.

Mrs. Pierpoint. And it occurred to me that, as we made Mr. Ferris's acquaintance in your house, you wouldn't object to giving me, as I put it, the merest hint——

Zoe. Ethel—what about her? Does she like him?

Mrs. Pierpoint. It's evident she doesn't dislike him. But she's not a girl who would be in a hurry to confide in anybody over a love affair, not even in her mother. True, there may be nothing to confide, in the present case. I repeat, I may be altogether mistaken. At the same time——

Zoe. You wish me to advise you as to whether Lenny Ferris should be encouraged.

Mrs. Pierpoint. Whether he should be cold-shouldered—I prefer that expression.

Zoe. Very well; I'll furnish you with his character, dear Mrs. Pierpoint, with pleasure.

[LEONARD FERRIS, *a fresh, boyish young man, enters at the glazed door, with the air of one who is at home.*]

Leonard. Hallo!

Zoe. [*Just as carelessly.*] Hallo, Len!

Leonard. [*Shaking hands with* MRS. PIERPOINT.] How d'ye do? How's Miss Ethel?

Mrs. Pierpoint. [*Inclining her head.*] Thank you——

Leonard. [*Rubbing his hands together.*] Here's a day!

Zoe. [*Taking his hand.*] Your hands are frozen.

Leonard. [*Going to the fire.*] I drove my car up here.

Zoe. You're crazy. [*Sitting on the settee by the fire.*] You never rang me up this morning, to ask if I was tired.

Leonard. Wire was engaged. First-rate night, last night.

Zoe. [*Languidly.*] The summit. Lenny——

Leonard. Eh?

Zoe. Mrs. Pierpoint and I are talking secrets. Go into the next room for a second.

Leonard. [*Genially.*] Shan't, if there isn't a fire.

Zoe. Of course there's a fire. Things ain't so bad in the City as all that.

Leonard. [*At the nearer door on the right.*] Any tea?

Zoe. By and by. You'll find somebody in there you know.

Leonard. [*Going into the room.*] Who?

Zoe. [*Calling out.*] Shut the door. [*The door is closed.*] Talk of the——!

Mrs. Pierpoint. Bless me, I hope not!

Zoe. No, I shouldn't turn him in there at this moment if he wasn't what he is—the dearest boy in the world—should I?

Mrs. Pierpoint. Boy——?

Zoe. He's thirty-two. A man of two-and-thirty *is* a boy to a woman of—to an old married woman. He's the simplest, wholesomest, best-natured fellow living. If you had him for a son-in-law, you'd be lucky.

Mrs. Pierpoint. It's a relief to me, at any rate——

Zoe. And I should lose one of my tame robins.

Mrs. Pierpoint. Tame robins?

Zoe. [*Rising and going over to the writing-table and taking up two of the photographs.*] I always have his photo on my table—his and Peter Mottram's. Peter Mottram is my husband's partner—you've met him here. I call them my tame robins. They come and eat crumbs off my windowsill. I've no end of tame robins—men chums—but these two are my specials. [*Replacing the photographs.*] Well! If Lenny ever goes, I shall have to promote Harry Estridge or Jim Mallandain or Cossy Rawlings.

Mrs. Pierpoint. [*Who has risen and followed* ZOE *to the writing-table.*] But why should Mr. Ferris ever "go" completely?

Zoe. [*Smiling.*] Oh, when a robin marries, Jenny doesn't share him with another wren. Not much!

[WARREN *enters at the glazed door with a female* SERVANT. *They carry in the tea and lay it upon the table behind the settee by the fire.*]

Zoe. [*After glancing at the* SERVANTS—*dropping her voice.*] I'd better finish drawing up the prospectus, while I'm at it.

Mrs. Pierpoint. Prospectus?

Zoe. He's got two thousand a year. Both his people are dead. There's an aunt in the country who may leave him a bit extra; but she's a cantankerous old cat and, in my opinion, charity'll have every *sou.* Still, two thousand a year——

Mrs. Pierpoint. I oughtn't to hear any more. But you understand, don't you——?

Zoe. Perfectly. And he lives in a comfy little flat behind the Albert Hall and is mad on motor-cars. He's invented a wonderful wheel which is to give the knock to pneumatics. If anything will bring him to ruin, that will. [*Walking away toward the tea-table laughingly.*] There!

Warren. Tea is served, ma'am.

Mrs. Pierpoint. [*To* ZOE, *who returns to*

her.] I'm exceedingly obliged to you. You won't breathe a word to Ethel?

Zoe. Not a syllable. It would break my heart, but I hope it'll come off, for her sake.

Mrs. Pierpoint. She's a sweet, sensible child.

Zoe. And as for him, I'll tell you this for your comfort—I'm honestly certain that Lenny Ferris would be the sort of husband that lasts.

Mrs. Pierpoint. That lasts? What do you mean?

Zoe. Oh—never mind. [*Gaily.*] Tea! [*The* SERVANTS *have withdrawn. She runs across to the farther door on the right, opens it, and calls.*] Tea! [*Seating herself at the tea-table.*] Are you firm about going on?

Mrs. Pierpoint. It's Lizzie Fremantle's birthday. She's Ethel's godmother. [*To* ETHEL, *who enters with* LEONARD.] Are you ready, Ethel?

Ethel. [*To* MRS. PIERPOINT.] Must we?

Mrs. Pierpoint. Now, my dear——!

Zoe. [*To* LEONARD.] Lenny, you've got to get tickets for the St. Martin's and take the whole crowd of us.

Leonard. [*With a wry face.*] That kids' play again!

Zoe. Very well; Peter will do it.

Leonard. No, no; right you are.

Zoe. I stand.

Leonard. Rot!

Zoe. Then Peter has the job. [*To the ladies.*] We'll ask Peter Mottram to be one of us anyhow.

Leonard. The supper's mine, then.

Zoe. Anything for peace. [*Shaking hands with* MRS. PIERPOINT, *who comes to her.*] Monday night?

Mrs. Pierpoint. You're a great deal too good.

[LEONARD *has opened the glazed door and is now in the corridor.* MRS. PIERPOINT *joins him.*]

Leonard. [*To* MRS. PIERPOINT, *as they disappear.*] Got a vehicle?

Mrs. Pierpoint. My venerable four-wheeler—the oldest friend I have in London——

Ethel. [*To* ZOE, *who rises.*] What did Mother have to say to you so mysteriously?

Zoe. Er—she wants me to consult Theo about something.

Ethel. Her railway shares?

Zoe. [*Nodding.*] H'm.

Ethel. [*Satisfied.*] Oh? Good-by.

Zoe. When are we to have a nice long jaw together—just you and I?

Ethel. Mother won't let me out alone in these fogs.

Zoe. Fog or no fog, try and shunt her tomorrow.

Ethel. I'll do my best.

Zoe. I'll be in all the morning. [*They turn their heads toward the door, listening.*] Lenny's whistling for you.

Ethel. Mother——!

[*They kiss affectionately and* ETHEL *hurries away.* ZOE *resumes her seat at the tea-table and pours out tea. Presently* LEONARD *returns and, after closing the door, comes to her.*]

Leonard. [*Cheerfully.*] It's beginning to sleet now. 'Pon my soul——! [*She hands him a cup of tea in silence. He looks at her inquiringly.*] Anything wrong, Zoe?

Zoe. [*With an air of indifference.*] No.

Leonard. Positive?

Zoe. [*In the same tone, offering him a plate of bread and butter.*] Quite.

Leonard. [*Taking a slice.*] Thought there'd been another row, perhaps.

Zoe. [*Putting the plate of bread and butter aside and taking up her cup and saucer.*] Hell of a row last night.

Leonard. Last night?

Zoe. This morning, rather.

Leonard. When you came home?

Zoe. [*Sipping her tea.*] After you and Peter brought me home.

Leonard. What over?

Zoe. Nothing.

Leonard. [*Drinking.*] Must have been over something.

Zoe. Oh, some trifle—as usual.

Leonard. Too bad of Theo—damned sight too bad.

Zoe. I dare say it was as much my fault as his.

Leonard. [*Hotly.*] It's a cursed shame!

Zoe. Drop it, Len. [*Handing him a dish of cakes.*] Cake?

Leonard. [*Putting his empty cup down before her and taking a cake.*] Tea.

Zoe. [*Pouring out another cup of tea for him.*] First time you've drunk tea with me this week. Honored!

Leonard. Sorry.

Zoe. M'yes—[*giving him his tea*]—sorry that Mrs. Pierpoint and Ethel can't receive you this afternoon.

Leonard. [*After a pause, uncomfortably.*] Mrs. Pierpoint been telling you anything about me?

Zoe. Mentioned that you frequently turn up in Sloane Street at teatime.

Leonard. There's a man down that way who's frightfully gone on my wheel.

Zoe. [*Drinking.*] Indeed?

Leonard. My great difficulty, you know, is to get it on to the market.

Zoe. India-rubber people opposing you, I expect.

Leonard. Tooth and nail.

Zoe. [*Nibbling a cake.*] And the man who lives Sloane Street way——?

Leonard. Very influential chap.

Zoe. Capitalist?

Leonard. Millionaire.

Zoe. H'm! And when you're down Sloane Street way, do you take your flowers to Miss Pierpoint, or does your florist send them?

[*Again there is silence. He lays his cup down, leaves her side, and produces his cigarette-case. Sticking a cigarette between his lips, he is about to close the case when she rises and takes a cigarette from it. She moves to the fireplace, lighting her cigarette with a match from a box attached to a gold chatelaine hanging from her waist. He seats himself in the chair facing the fire and lights his own cigarette.*]

Leonard. [*Moodily.*] I don't want to marry, Zoe.

Zoe. There's no reason why you shouldn't, if you feel disposed to; but you needn't be a sneak about it.

Leonard. The aunt's pitching into me again like billy-oh. High time I settled down—high time I became a reputable member of society! I ask you, what the deuce have I ever done that's particularly disreputable? Then come two verses of Scripture——

Zoe. [*Advancing to him.*] She hasn't ordered you to be underhanded with your best friends, I assume?

Leonard. I'm not underhanded.

Zoe. Why this concealment, then?

Leonard. There's no concealment; there's nothing to conceal; I give you my word there isn't. I—I haven't made up my mind one way or the other.

Zoe. [*Witheringly.*] You're weighing the question!

Leonard. Very well; I'm weighing it, if you like. [*Flinging the end of his match into the fireplace and jumping up.*] Confound it all! Mayn't a man send a basket or two of rotten flowers to a girl without having his special license bought for him by meddling people?

Zoe. Thank you.

Leonard. I don't mean you, Zoe. You know I don't mean you. [*Pacing the room.*] Ethel—Miss Pierpoint—is a charming girl, but I'm no more in love with her than I am with my old hat.

Zoe. Then you oughtn't to pay her marked attention.

Leonard. I'm not paying her marked attention. [ZOE *shrugs her shoulders.*] If Mrs. Pierpoint says I've been making love to her daughter——

Zoe. She has said nothing of the kind.

Leonard. [*Sitting in the chair before the writing-table, in a huff.*] That's all right. Pity she can't hold her tongue over trifles.

[*There is another pause. Then, partly kneeling upon the chair in the middle of the room, and resting her elbow on the back of it,* ZOE *softens.*]

Zoe. [*Making rings with her cigarette smoke.*] Don't be wild, Len. I was only vexed with you for not consulting me. It would hurt my feelings dreadfully if you got engaged to anybody on the sly. Len—— [*He turns to her, but with his head down.*] She *is* a charming girl. I'm not surprised at your being spoons on her. If I were a man, she's just the sort of girl *I'd* marry, if I were on the lookout for a wife.

Leonard. [*In a low voice.*] Perhaps I *have* made myself a bit of an ass over her, Zoe. [*She laughs lightly. He raises his eyes.*] Zoe——

Zoe. Well?

Leonard. [*Gazing at* ZOE.] Do you know that she reminds me very often of you?

Zoe. She! I'm old enough to be her grandmother.

Leonard. Oh, hang that! She's got hold of a lot of your odd little tricks—a lot of 'em.

Zoe. She's been with me a goodish deal lately.

Leonard. That's it; and she has the most enormous admiration for you—enormous.

Zoe. She's a dear.

Leonard. [*Gently hitting his knee with his fist.*] I've thought of all that when I've been worrying it out in my mind.

Zoe. Thought of all what?

Leonard. That you'd always be pals, you two—close pals.

Zoe. If she became Mrs. Lenny?

Leonard. [*Nodding.*] And so, if I did screw myself up to—to speaking to her, it wouldn't make the least difference to our friendship—yours and mine.

Zoe. No difference!

Leonard. I should still be your tame robin.

Zoe. Ah, no; don't make that mistake, Len.

Leonard. Mistake?

Zoe. [*Shaking her head.*] It never works. I've seen similar cases over and over again.

There's any amount of gush at the start, between the young wife and the husband's women-pals; but the end is always the same.

Leonard. The end?

Zoe. Gradually the wife draws the husband away. She manages it somehow. We have a gift for it. I did it myself when I married Theo.

Leonard. [*Rising and walking about.*] If I believed what you say, Zoe, I'd never size up a girl with a view to marrying as long as I live.

Zoe. [*Teasingly.*] You're a vain creature. I've plenty of other boys, Len, to fill your place.

Leonard. [*Not heeding her.*] If things were smoother with you and Theo, one mightn't hesitate half as much.

Zoe. There's Peter Mottram, Gus Hedmont, Harry Estridge, Claud Lowenstein——

Leonard. As it is—Great Scott!—I'm a brute even to think of taking the risk.

Zoe. Cossy Rawlings, Jim Mallandain, Robby Relf——

Leonard. [*Stopping in his walk.*] Yes, but my friendship's more to you than the friendship of most of those other fellows, I should hope.

Zoe. [*Making a grimace at him.*] Not a scrap.

Leonard. [*His brow darkening.*] You told me once I was your favorite.

Zoe. My chaff; I've no favorite.

Leonard. [*Laying the remains of his cigarette upon a little bronze tray on the writing-table.*] Peter's a trump, and Harry Estridge and Rawlings are sound enough; but I often feel I'd like to knock young Lowenstein's teeth down his fat throat.

Zoe. [*Blowing her smoke in his direction as he comes to her and stands before her.*] You get married and mind your own concerns.

Leonard. Zoe, I hate to see men of that class buzzing around you.

Zoe. [*Mockingly.*] Do you!

Leonard. Look here! Whatever happens between you and Theo in the future, you'll never let anything or anybody drive you off the rails, will you?

Zoe. [*Frowning.*] Len!

Leonard. I couldn't stand it. [*Putting his hands upon her shoulders.*] I tell you straight, it 'ud break me. [*Passionately, his grip tightening.*] Zoe——!

[*She shakes herself free and backs away from him, confronting him with a flushed face.*]

Zoe. [*Quietly.*] Don't be silly. [*Brushing her hair from her forehead.*] If ever you do that again, Len, I'll box your ears.

[*The* HONBLE. PETER MOTTRAM, *a spruce, well-preserved man of fifty, enters at the glazed door.*]

Peter. [*Cheerily.*] Good mornin'—or whatever it is.

Zoe. [*Dropping the end of her cigarette into the grate.*] That you, Peter?

Leonard. [*Surlily.*] I'm just off.

Peter. Don't apologize.

Leonard. [*At the glazed door, to* PETER.] See you later. [*He goes out.*]

Peter. [*To* ZOE.] What's the matter with the youth?

Zoe. [*With a shrug.*] Got the hump over something. [*Facing him.*] Tea?

Peter. No, thanks. [*Sitting in the chair in the middle of the room.*] And how are you today, my dear lady? [*She makes a wry mouth, sighs, and throws herself disconsolately upon the settee by the fire. He nods intelligently.*] Yes, sorry to hear you and old Theo have had another bad fall-out.

Zoe. [*Arranging a pillow for her head.*] I guessed he'd carry it all to you.

Peter. Shockin'ly grieved, I am.

Zoe. *He* began this one.

Peter. By blowin' you up for goin' on the frisk every night.

Zoe. And I answered him back. I was dogweary. It was nearly one o'clock. He needn't have jumped upon me almost before I'd taken the key out of the lock.

Peter. [*Demurely.*] I also have been reproved, for aidin' and abettin'.

Zoe. Serves you jolly well right. Why didn't you and Lenny come in with me, you cowards? That might have saved a squabble. I begged you to have a whiskey.

Peter. [*After a brief pause.*] Zoe——

Zoe. [*In a muffled voice, her head in the pillow.*] Oh, be kind to me, Peter.

Peter. Why *do* you sally forth night after night?

Zoe. Because I must.

Peter. Must?

Zoe. I've got the fidgets.

Peter. I get the fidgets at times, in bed. D'ye know how I cure 'em?

Zoe. Of course I don't.

Peter. I lie perfectly stiff and still; I *make* myself lie perfectly still. I *won't* stir. I say to myself, "Peter, you *shan't* twist or turn." And I win.

Zoe. How easy it is to talk. I defy you to control yourself if you're shut up with a person who goads you to desperation.

Peter. Theo?

Zoe. [*Beating her pillow.*] How *can* I stay at home and eat a long dinner, and spend an entire evening, alone with Theo? We're not entertaining just now; he says he's fed up with having people here.

Peter. Take him out with you.

Zoe. Then we quarrel before others. That's too degrading. Oh, it's tiff, tiff, wrangle, jangle, outdoors *and* indoors with us!

Peter. You say things to Theo when you're angry, Zoe, that wound him to the quick.

Zoe. [*Satirically.*] Really!

Peter. Really. You mayn't be aware of it; you scratch the poor old chap till he bleeds.

Zoe. Do you imagine he never says things to me that wound me to the quick?

Peter. He doesn't mean half of 'em.

Zoe. Neither do I.

Peter. [*Rising and going to the fire.*] No; there's the crass foolishness of it all. [*In a tone of expostulation.*] My dear lady——

Zoe. [*Suddenly sitting upright.*] We're on each other's nerves, Peter. That's the plain truth, we're on each other's nerves.

Peter. Worryin' each other.

Zoe. Sick to death of each other! We shall have been married fourteen years on the thirtieth of next June. Isn't it appalling! He's getting so stodgy and pompous and flat-footed. He drives me mad with his elderly ways.

Peter. [*Soothingly.*] Oh——!

Zoe. He's sick and tired of *me,* at any rate. My little jokes and pranks, that used to amuse him so—they annoy him now, scandalize him. He's continually finding fault with me—bullying me. That's all the notice he takes of me. As for my gowns or my hats—anything I put on—I might dress in sackcloth; he'd never observe it. [*Tearfully.*] Ah——! [*She searches for her handkerchief and fails to find it.* PETER *produces a folded handkerchief from his breast-pocket, shakes it out, and gives it to her. She wipes her eyes as she proceeds.*] Sometimes, I own, I'm aggravating; but he forgets how useful I was to him in the old days, when we were climbing. Yes, *those* were the days—the first six or seven years of our marriage, when we were up north, in Fitzjohn's Avenue! [*Tossing* PETER'S *handkerchief to him and getting to her feet.*] Oh! Oh, we were happy then, Peter! You didn't know us then, when we were up north!

Peter. [*Wagging his head.*] My dear lady, we were all happier when we were up north.

Zoe. [*Giving him a look of surprise as she paces the room on the left.*] You!

Peter. I mean, in a previous stage of our careers.

Zoe. Ah, yes, yes.

Peter. That's the lesson of life, Mrs. Zoe. We've all had our Fitzjohn's Avenue, in a sense. In other words, we've all been young and keen as mustard; with everythin' before us, instead of havin' most things behind us.

Zoe. [*Leaning on the back of the chair before the writing-table.*] Oh, don't!

Peter. [*Thoughtfully.*] D'ye know, I often wonder whether there's anythin' more depressin' than to see the row of trophies standin' on the sideboard?

Zoe. [*Sitting at the writing-table and digging her fingers into her hair.*] Be quiet, Peter!

Peter. That silver-gilt vase there! The old horse that gained it for you is lyin' in the paddock with a stone a'top of him, and you're usin' his hoof as an inkpot. Those goblets you won on the river, and the cup you helped yourself to on the links at Biarritz or St. Moritz—there's a little pile of ashes at the bottom of every one of 'em! So it is with life generally. You scoop in the prizes—and there are the pots on the sideboard to remind you that it ain't the *prizes* that count, but the pushin' and the strugglin' and the cheerin'. Ah, they preach to us on Sundays about cherubim and seraphim! It's my firm hope and conviction that when we die and go to heaven we shall all find ourselves up north again—in Fitzjohn's Avenue! [*Coming to the chair in the middle of the room.*] Meanwhile, it's no good repinin'. [*Turning the chair toward her and sitting.*] The trophies *are* on the sideboard, dear lady, and they've got to be kep' clean and shiny. [*Gravely.*] Now, Zoe—— [*She whimpers.*] Zoe, Zoe—— [*She turns to him.*] Zoe, one ugly word passed between you and Theo last night——

Zoe. One——?

Peter. One ugly word that must never be repeated.

Zoe. What word?

[*The glazed door opens and* WARREN *appears carrying a teapot on a tray. He comes to the table and exchanges the teapot he is carrying for the one that is already there.*]

Zoe. [*To the* MAN.] Mr. Mottram won't have any tea, Warren.

Warren. [*Removing the cups and saucers which have been used and putting them on to his tray.*] No, ma'am; but Mr. Blundell's just come in, ma'am.

[WARREN *withdraws, closing the door.* ZOE *rises stiffly, and gathers up her hat.*

coat, and gloves. Then she returns to PETER, *who remains seated.*]

Zoe. What word was it?

Peter. Separation.

[THEODORE BLUNDELL, *a big, burly, but goodlooking man, enters at the glazed door. He halts on entering and glances furtively at* ZOE, *as if expecting her to speak; but, without meeting his eyes, she passes him and leaves the room.*]

Theodore. [*With a shrug.*] Ha! [PETER, *looking over his shoulder, sees that he and* THEODORE *are alone.* THEODORE *seats himself at the tea-table and pours out his tea grimly.*] Lots o' good you seem to have done, Peter.

Peter. Haven't done much, I admit. Pity you came home quite so soon.

Theodore. You left the office at half-past two.

Peter. She wasn't in when I first got here.

Theodore. [*Taking a slice of bread and butter.*] Anyhow, kind of you to offer to have a talk to her. [*Munching.*] Plenty of abuse of me, h'm?

Peter. She says you're on each other's nerves, Theo.

Theodore. I'm afraid there's something in that.

Peter. And that you are growin' a bit heavy in hand, old man.

Theodore. [*Drily.*] Exceedingly sorry.

Peter. [*After a pause.*] Theo——

Theodore. Hallo?

Peter. Shall I tell you what's at the bottom of it all?

Theodore. Well?

Peter. She's got a feelin' that you're tired of her.

Theodore. [*Gulping his tea.*] If you knew how constantly I have that served up to me——!

Peter. Will you allow me to speak out?

Theodore. Don't be so polite.

Peter. My belief is that, if you could avoid conveyin' that impression to Zoe, matters would improve considerably in this establishment.

Theodore. Oh?

Peter. It's as easy as brushin' your hat. A little pettin'—a little sweetheartin'——

Theodore. Yes?

Peter. [*Discouraged.*] Well, those are my views, for what they're worth.

Theodore. [*Pouring out another cup of tea.*] My dear fellow, if you'd get married, and have thirteen or fourteen years of it, as I've had, your views would be worth more than they are.

Peter. Oh, that won't wash. [*Rising.*] When a man's sufferin' from gout in the toe, he doesn't stipulate that his M.D. shall be writhin' from the same ailment. No, very frequently, the outsider——

Theodore. Good gracious, you're not going to remark that lookers-on see most of the game!

Peter. Words to that effect.

Theodore. Ho! Why is it that, the moment a man's matrimonial affairs are in a tangle, every platitude in the language is chewed out at him? [*Leaning his head on his hands.*] If you've nothing fresher to say on the subject——!

Peter. [*Oracularly.*] My dear chap, it's tryin' to say somethin' fresh on the subject of marriage that's responsible for a large share of the domestic unhappiness and discontent existin' at the present day. There's too much of this tryin' to say somethin' fresh on *every* subject, in my opinion.

Theodore. Nobody can accuse *you*, Peter——

Peter. You take it from me, there are two institootions in this world that are never goin' to alter—men and women and the shape of chickens' eggs. Chickens' eggs are never goin' to be laid square; and men and women will continue to be mere men and women till the last contango.* [THEODORE *finishes his tea, rises, and comes to the fire.*] I'm referrin', of course, to real men and women. I don't inclood persons in petticoats with flat chests and no hips; nor individuals wearin' beards and trousers who dine on a basin of farinaceous food and a drink o' water out o' the filter. They belong to a distinct species. No; I mean the genuine article, like you and me and your missus—men and women with blood in their veins, and one-and-a-half per cent. of good, humanizin' alcohol in *that.*

Theodore. [*Throwing a log on the fire.*] What's the moral of your eloquent, but rather vague, discourse?

Peter. [*At the chair in the middle of the room.*] The moral? Oh, the moral is that men and women of the ordinary, regulation pattern must put up with the defects of each other's qualities. [*Turning the chair so that it faces* THEODORE *and again sitting in it.*] She complains that you don't admire her frocks and frills, Theo.

Theodore. [*Groaning.*] Oh!

Peter. Now come! Where's the trouble? There's my old mother—seventy-five in April! Whenever I'm at Stillwood, I make

* "Contango-day"—a Stock Exchange expression: the second day before settling day, i.e., the last day on which continuation of an account may be arranged.

a reg'lar practice of complimentin' her on her rig-out. "By Jove, mater," I say, "you *are* a buck this mornin'!" Or evenin', as the case may be. I couldn't tell you what she's wearin,' to save my life; but there's no harm done.

Theodore. Yes, *you* do it; but your father doesn't do it, I'll be bound. [PETER *looks glum and is silent.*] It's too trivial! [*Producing his cigar case.*] A husband can't be everlastingly praising his wife's clothes. [*Offering a cigar to* PETER *which he declines.*] The absence of comment on my part is a sign that I'm satisfied with Zoe's appearance, surely.

Peter. She's one of the smartest women in London.

Theodore. [*Irritably.*] I know she is. I've told her so till I'm sick. [*Cutting and lighting a cigar.*] I've always been intensely proud of Zoe, as a matter of fact—intensely proud of her.

Peter. No more than her due.

Theodore. [*With increasing indignation.*] Good God, how often, at a dinner-party, have I caught myself looking along the table and thinking she's the handsomest woman in the room. Tsch! It's a ridiculous thing to say——

Peter. What?

Theodore. I suppose no man has ever been "in love" with his wife for longer than I've been with mine.

Peter. [*Significantly.*] *Been.*

Theodore. And I have a very great affection for her still—or should have, if her behavior didn't check it.

Peter. If you showed your affection more plainly, wouldn't that check her behavior?

Theodore. [*Leaving the fireplace and moving about the room.*] Ah, my dear fellow, haven't you brains enough to see! We're middle-aged people, Zoe and I. I *am* middle-aged, and she's not far off it, poor girl. There must come a time on a journey when your pair of horses stop prancing and settle down to a trot.

Peter. How's that for a platitude!

Theodore. I thought that worm-eaten illustration might appeal to you.

Peter. She keeps wonderfully young, Theo.

Theodore. Isn't that a little to my credit? But Zoe's within three years of forty. You can't put the clock back.

Peter. A woman's as old as she looks——

Theodore. And a man's as old as he feels! Another ancient wheeze!

Peter. And a *married* woman's as old as her husband *makes* her feel.

Theodore. My dear Peter, I don't want Zoe to feel older than her years by a single hour. But I confess I do ask her occasionally to feel as old *as* her years, and not to make herself damnably absurd.

Peter. Absurd?

Theodore. This infernal fooling about with the boys, for instance—the cause of last night's flare-up—her "tame robins"—you're one——! [PETER *rises hastily and goes to the fire.*] Yes, you ought to be ashamed of yourself, for encouraging her.

Peter. Who's in fault? Because a man's wife has ceased to be attractive to him, it doesn't follow that she ain't attractive to others.

Theodore. [*Contemptuously.*] Attractive? The vanity of "attracting" a parcel of empty-headed young men! You're the patriarch of the group! [*Throwing himself into the chair just vacated by* PETER.] The whole thing's undignified—raffish.

Peter. [*Extending a forefinger.*] You contrive to be a trifle more sprightly at home, Theo——

Theodore. [*Moving his head from side to side.*] Oh, you will hammer away at that! I'm forty-six. My sprightly days are over.

Peter. [*Emphatically.*] Humbug, old chap.

Theodore. What's humbug?

Peter. Men are the biggest humbugs goin' —especially to themselves. And a man of your age or mine—and I'm four years your senior—is never a bigger humbug than when he's deloodin' himself with the notion that he's scrap-iron.

Theodore. You're a gay old spark——

Peter. No, it's when the sun's workin' round to the west—it's when men are where we are now, that they're most liable to get into mischief.

Theodore. Mischief? What are you driving at?

Peter. Nothin'. I'm simply layin' down a general principle.

Theodore. [*Angrily.*] Confound your general principles! Don't be an ass.

Peter. [*Coming to* THEODORE.] That stoopid nonsense talked last night—early this mornin'—about livin' apart—who started it?

Theodore. Zoe. I fancy it was Zoe—last night.

Peter. Oh, it wasn't the first time——?

Theodore. [*Smoking with fierce puffs.*] We had an awful scene—disgraceful. I felt inclined to rush out of the house then and there.

Peter. Why didn't you? You could have let yourself in again when she'd gone to by-by.

Theodore. [*Sullenly.*] No, that's not my style. If ever I do bang the front door, it'll be once and for all, my friend.

Peter. [*Shaking him.*] Oh! Oh!

Theodore. She's independent; she has her own income—you know—and I've told her I'd supplement it, if necessary. I've settled this house on her as it is; she'd be welcome to it, and every stick in it, worst come to the worst.

Peter. Theo!

Theodore. And I'd go and live in a garret, in peace.

Peter. You're not considerin' such a step seriously?

Theodore. [*Turning upon him roughly.*] No, I'm not—not when I'm sitting here chatting quietly with you. Nor when she's rational and—and—and amenable, as she can be when she chooses. [*Clenching his hands.*] But when she's irritating me till I'm half beside myself, I—I——

Peter. You——?

Theodore. [*Looking up at* PETER.] My God, Peter, you're a wise man, never to have taken it on!

Peter. Marriage?

Theodore. [*Throwing his head back.*] Oh, my dear fellow!

[*The glazed door opens and* ZOE *enters meekly. Her eyes are red, and a handkerchief is crumpled up in her hand. She glances at the tea-table and comes to* THEODORE. PETER *retreats to the fireplace.*]

Zoe. [*To* THEODORE, *in a piteous voice.*] Have you—had your tea?

Theodore. [*Frigidly.*] I poured it out myself.

[*After a moment's hesitation, she bends over him and gives him a kiss. Then she turns away and, seating herself at the writing-table, proceeds to write a note. There is an awkward silence.*]

Theodore. [*Breaking the silence, gruffly.*] Er—Zo——

Zoe. [*With a sniff, writing.*] Yes?

Theodore. What are you doing tonight?

Zoe. Jim Mallandain was going to take me to the Palace. I'm putting him off.

Theodore. I'll dine you out and take you somewhere.

Zoe. No, I'd rather have a quiet evening at home, Theo—just you and me. [*Blowing her nose.*] I've ordered Mrs. Killick to send up an extra-nice dinner.

Theodore. Perhaps Peter——

Zoe. [*Stamping her foot.*] No, I won't have him.

Peter. Besides, I'm booked.

Zoe. [*Petulantly.*] I don't care whether you are or not. I want to dine alone with my husband.

[*There is another pause, during which* ZOE *scratches away with her pen.*]

Peter. [*Clearing his throat.*] Well, I'll be gettin' along. [THEODORE *rises.*] I say——

Theodore. H'm?

Peter. Why don't you and Zoe have a week or a fortnight in Paris? It 'ud do you both a heap of good.

Theodore. Impossible. How can I?

Peter. Cert'nly you can. If anythin' important crops up, Tom Slade or I will run over to you; or you could come back. [*Again there is a pause.* ZOE *stops writing.*] Do, old chap. [*Another pause.*] Won't you?

Theodore. [*Without enthusiasm.*] All right.

Peter. A fortnight? Nothin'll happen.

Theodore. [*Nodding.*] A fortnight.

[*Uttering a little chirp of delight,* ZOE *resumes writing.* PETER *goes to her as* THEODORE *moves away to the fireplace.*]

Peter. [*To* ZOE.] Good-by, ma'am. [*She gives him her left hand over her shoulder. He squeezes it and makes for the glazed door. There he appears to be struck by an idea. After a silence, he turns slowly, contemplates the pair for a moment with a puckered brow, and advances a step or two.*] Theo——

Theodore. [*Who has picked up one of the illustrated papers and has seated himself upon the settee.*] H'm?

Peter. [*His hands in his pockets, rattling his keys.*] About half-way between Dover and Calais—no, it's between Folkestone and Boulogne, ain't it?——

Theodore. [*Examining the pictures.*] What?

Peter. Of course! About half-way between Folkestone and Boulogne—mid-Channel—there's a shoal.

Theodore. [*Turning a page of his paper.*] What of it?

Peter. Le Colbart, the French sailormen call it—Le Colbart. *We* call it the Ridge. [*Coming forward.*] If you go by Folkestone and Boulogne, you'll pass over it.

Theodore. [*Glancing at him suspiciously.*] Thanks for the valuable information.

Peter. D'ye know, I've never encountered that blessed shoal without experiencin' a most unpleasant time?

Zoe. [*Addressing an envelope.*] Oh, my dear Peter!

Peter. I've crossed on some of the finest days o' the year. The sun's been shinin', and outside the harbor the water's been as smooth as it's been *in*side. Everythin's looked as enticin' as could be; but as we've neared the Ridge—mid-Channel—I've begun to feel fidgety, restless, out o' sorts—hatin' myself and hatin' the man who's been sharin' my cabin with me. But the sensation hasn't lasted long.

Zoe. [*Sealing her letter.*] Glad to hear it.

Peter. No; gradually the beastly motion has died down, and in a quarter of an hour or so I've found myself pacin' the deck again, arm-in-arm with the travelin'-companion I've been positively loathin' a few minutes earlier.

Theodore. [*Gaping demonstratively.*] Very interesting.

Peter. My dear pals, I remember the idea once occurrin' to me—I mentioned it to Charlie Westbrook at the time—there's a resemblance between *that* and marriage.

Theodore. [*Shortly.*] Ha! Thought that was coming.

[ZOE *turns in her chair, to listen to* PETER.]

Peter. Yes, and marriage, mark you, at its best and brightest. The happiest and luckiest of married couples have got to cross that wretched Ridge. However successful the first half of their journey may be, there's the rough-and-tumble of mid-Channel to negotiate. Some arrive there quicker than others, some later; it depends on wind and tide. But they *get* there; and a bad time it is, and must be—a time when travelin'-companions see nothin' but the spots on each other's yellow faces, and when innoomerable kind words and innoomerable kind acts are clean forgotten. [ZOE, *her letter in her hand, rises impulsively and comes to* PETER.] But, as I tell you, it's soon over—*well* over, if only Mr. Jack and Mrs. Jill will understand the situation; if only they'll say to themselves, "We're on the Ridge; we're in mid-Channel; in another quarter of an hour the boat'll be steady again—as steady as when we stepped on to the gangway." [*To* THEODORE.] Not offended, old man?

Theodore. [*Uncomfortably.*] Ha, ha, ha!

Zoe. [*Gently, giving her letter to* PETER.] Tell Warren to give that to a messenger boy. [*To* THEODORE.] Theo——!

[*She puts her hands upon* PETER'S *shoulders and kisses him.*]

Peter. [*Chuckling.*] Ha, ha! [*To* THEODORE.] Division of profits. [*At the glazed door.*] When'll you be off?

Theodore. Oh—one day next week.

Peter. [*Nodding.*] Tomorrow mornin', then. [*He goes out, closing the door.*]

Zoe. Dear old Peter!

Theodore. [*Deep in his paper.*] Peter's getting a bit of a bore, though.

Zoe. [*Mimicking* PETER, *as she wipes her eyes.*] He's amusin'. [*Going to* THEODORE *and seating herself beside him.*] Theo——

Theodore. H'm?

Zoe. [*Edging up to him.*] Let's go by Folkestone and Boulogne—shall we?

Theodore. *I* don't mind.

Zoe. [*Wistfully.*] Let's go by Folkestone and Boulogne—and have done with it. [*Slipping her arm through his.*] Theo—last night—sorry. [*He nods and looks at another picture.*] I take it all back—the things I said. I didn't mean them.

Theodore. That's all right.

Zoe. And *you* didn't mean——?

Theodore. [*Impatiently.*] Of course I didn't.

Zoe. [*Giving herself a shake.*] Ah! [*After a brief pause.*] Theo——

Theodore. H'm?

Zoe. [*Taking the paper from him playfully.*] Don't look at those improper young ladies. [*Coaxingly.*] Couldn't you manage to get away on Sunday?

Theodore. Oh—I might.

Zoe. It's your treat to me, isn't it—and the beginning of better times? The *sooner* we begin——

Theodore. [*Nodding.*] You shall have it all your own way.

Zoe. [*Gleefully.*] Sunday!

Theodore. H'm.

Zoe. I'm dreadfully shabby. I've no new clothes. You don't object?

Theodore. [*Distinctly.*] Now, my dear Zo—my darling—understand this from me clearly. You are *never* shabby; you *couldn't* be shabby. As far as I am a judge, you are always dressed beautifully and—and—and in perfect taste.

Zoe. Beautifully!

Theodore. If you were *not* well dressed, I should venture to call your attention to it.

Zoe. Silence is approval?

Theodore. Absolutely. So don't expect me—a busy man—to be eternally praising your gowns and what not; because I cannot and will not do it.

Zoe. I won't—I won't. I know I'm inconsiderate—[*stamping her foot*] beastly inconsiderate. [*Excitedly.*] Write out a telegram now——

Theodore. Telegram?

Zoe. To the hotel.

Theodore. Yes, that 'ud be wise. [*He rises and goes over to the writing-table where, taking a sheet of notepaper, he sits and *writes.*] We couldn't get an answer to a letter.

Zoe. [*Jumping up and walking about.*] Jolly nice rooms, Theo!

Theodore. [*Assentingly.*] H'm, h'm.

Zoe. [*Humming.*] Tra, la! ra, la! la, ra, la,——!

Theodore. [*In the throes of composition.*] Sssh, sssh!

Zoe. [*Opening the illustrated paper.*] Beg pardon.

Theodore. [*Writing.*] "——deux bonnes chambres à coucher—salle de bain—et salon ——"

Zoe. There's Lena. Don't forget the maid.

Theodore. Oh, they shove her anywhere.

Zoe. [*Imperatively.*] No, no; I must have her handy. [*He writes.*] What hotel are we going to, Theo?

Theodore. [*Writing.*] "aussi chambre pour servante même étage——"

Zoe. The Ritz?

Theodore. Oh, blow the Ritz!

Zoe. We've always *been* comfortable at the Ritz.

Theodore. [*Putting the finishing touches to his telegram.*] Twenty francs a minute.

Zoe. [*Disappointed.*] Where then? The Elysée Palace is too far out this weather. The Régina?

Theodore. [*Reading.*] "Pouvez-vous réserver pour Monsieur et Madame Blundell pour dimanche et nuits suivantes appartement composé deux bonnes chambres à coucher, salle de bain, et salon, aussi chambre pour servante même étage? Réponse télégraphique. Theodorus, London."

Zoe. [*Advancing.*] Oh, Theo! Shall we try the new Meurice? The Langdales had a suite there that made them feel like Royalties.

Theodore. [*Half-turning to her.*] Gerald Duckfield was telling me of a capital little hotel where he and Bessie stayed—the Vendôme——

Zoe. Where's that?

Theodore. In the Place Vendôme.

Zoe. The Ritz—the Bristol—the Rhin—they're the only hotels in the Place.

Theodore. Oh, but this is in the part of the Place that runs down to the top of the Rue Castiglione.

Zoe. The *narrow* part!

Theodore. Well, it isn't the broad part, certainly.

Zoe. The traffic of the Rue St. Honoré to help to send you to sleep!

Theodore. No, no; there are double windows, Gerald says, to the best bedrooms. [*Turning to the writing-table.*] It 'ud be an experiment.

Zoe. [*Sitting in the chair in the middle of the room, with her back to him.*] Yes, it would be an experiment.

Theodore. Shall we risk it?

Zoe. [*Coldly.*] By all means.

Theodore. [*Writing.*] "Directeur—Hôtel Vendôme."

Zoe. [*Tapping her feet upon the floor.*] Ha!

Theodore. H'm? "——Place Vendôme ——"

Zoe. [*Holding up the illustrated paper so that he may see, over her head, a risqué picture.*] If you were taking this sort of woman with you, nothing 'ud be good enough for her.

Theodore. [*Glancing at the picture, angrily.*] Oh, don't be so coarse! [*There is a pause. He leans back in his chair, biting his pen. Suddenly she flings the illustrated paper away from her into the air. Throwing down his pen, he rises and paces the room.*] This promises well for an enjoyable fortnight in Paris!

Zoe. [*Rising and moving to the left.*] Look here, old man! This trip was going to be *your* treat. Very well, that's off! I'll take *you* to Paris; *I'll* pay the expenses; and I won't stuff you up in a frowsy rabbit-hutch.

Theodore. [*Coming forward on the right.*] Don't insult me!

Zoe. [*Facing him.*] Anyway, your treat or mine, I stay at no hotel in Paris that isn't top-hole.

Theodore. [*Furiously.*] Oh, stop your damned slang, for God's sake!

Zoe. [*Her eyes blazing.*] What!

Theodore. [*Sitting on the fauteuil-stool and rocking himself to and fro.*] Oh! Oh!

Zoe. Stop my damned slang!

Theodore. [*His head in his hands.*] Hold your tongue.

Zoe. [*Coming to him.*] And how did I learn my damned slang, pray? [*He waves her from him.*] I learned it from the crew you surrounded me with when I condescended to marry you and went out of my world into yours.

Theodore. [*Starting up.*] Oh——!

[*He goes to the bell and rings it continuously.*]

Zoe. [*Following him.*] Yes, you were hugely tickled by it *then*! And so were *they*—the men you thought might be serviceable to you; and who *were* serviceable to you, often through *me*!

Theodore. Oh!

Zoe. Ha! And now that my tongue's furred with it, and it isn't necessary to attract the vulgar brutes any more, you round on me and rag me! [*Pacing the room on the left.*] Oh! Oh! If only my dear old dad were alive! He'd fuss over me and protect me. My father was a gentleman. He warned me I was chucking myself away!

Theodore. Oh!

Zoe. [*Wildly.*] Why do you keep on ringing that bell?

Theodore. [*In a loud voice.*] I suppose I can ring the bell if I like!

Zoe. You—you can go to the devil if you like!

[*She goes out at the glazed door. As she disappears,* WARREN *passes her and enters.*]

Theodore. [*Crossing to the writing-table.*] Warren——

Warren. Yessir?

Theodore. [*Picking up the sheet of paper on which he has written the message to the hotel.*] Pack me a bag.

Warren. Bag, sir?

Theodore. [*Tearing the paper into small pieces.*] Yes; I'm not sleeping at home to-night.

Warren. [*Coming to the table and preparing to remove the tea-things.*] Very good, sir.

CURTAIN

THE SECOND ACT

SCENE.—*The same, but the disposition of some of the furniture is changed. The settee on the right is now placed with its back to the fireplace. At the farther end of the settee are the oblong table and chair, and on the left of the table, facing the settee, is the chair which in the preceding act stood in the middle of the room. An armchair is at the nearer end of the settee; and another armchair and the fauteuil-stool stand together, not far from the glazed door. On the oblong table are a box of cigarettes, matches, and an ash-tray.*

The fireplace is banked with flowers, there are flowers in vases upon the tables, and the room is full of sunlight.

[*Two men—an* UPHOLSTERER *and his* ASSISTANT—*are engaged in putting covers of gay chintz upon the chairs and settees. The* UPHOLSTERER *is on his knees at the settee on the right, the* ASSISTANT *is at the chair by the writing-table.* LENA, ZOE'S *maid—a bright, buxom woman—is arranging the furnture in the middle of the room. Presently the* ASSISTANT *proceeds to collect the brown paper and cord which litter the floor.*]

Upholsterer. [*Rising from his knees—to* LENA.] That's all right.

Lena. [*Coming to him.*] And when are we to have the pleasure of seeing *you* again?

Upholsterer. Tomorrow.

Lena. What about next year, or the year after! [*Producing her purse and giving him a tip.*] In case I shouldn't live so long.

Upholsterer. Thank you very much. [*Moving away—quietly.*] William——

[*The* ASSISTANT, *laden with brown paper, advances, and* LENA *tips him.*]

Assistant. Thank you. miss. Good morning, miss.

Lena. Good morning.

Upholsterer. [*At the glazed door.*] Good morning.

Lena. [*Tidying the furniture on the right.*] Good morning.

[*The* MEN *depart. Almost immediately the glazed door is reopened and* WARREN *appears, showing in* LEONARD. LEONARD *is gloved and is carrying a straw hat and a walking-cane. He has lost his fresh, boyish appearance and is sallow and lined.*]

Leonard. [*To* LENA.] Good morning.

Lena. [*Familiarly.*] Oh, good morning. [*To* WARREN.] I'll let Mrs. Blundell know. [*To* LEONARD, *as* WARREN *withdraws.*] She'll be down soon. Will you have a paper?

Leonard. Thanks; seen 'em. How is she, Lena?

Lena. Middling. She's a little feverish, the doctor says. She must have caught a chill coming over. [LEONARD *nods.*] She would sit on deck, talking to Mr. Mallandain. We met him by accident on the platform as we were leaving Paris.

Leonard. [*Nodding again.*] She's told me.

Lena. She's to remain indoors again today and keep out o' draughts. [*Looking at a watch which she wears on her wrist and at the clock on the mantelpiece.*] What do you say the right time is?

Leonard. [*Looking at his watch.*] Quarter to twelve.

Lena. [*Going to the mantelpiece.*] I'm to give her her med'cine an hour before meals. [*Moving the hands of the clock.*] Ha! They've all been playing tricks here while we've been away, clock-winder included.

Leonard. [*Absently.*] Indeed?

Lena. Servants, tradespeople, everybody! [*Unbuckling her bracelet.*] Because Mrs. Blundell is now on her own, I s'pose they fancy they can take advantage of her. [*Returning to* LEONARD.] I'll teach 'em! [*"Timing" her watch.*] Think we're getting fairly straight?

Leonard. [*Glancing idly at the room as he sits in the armchair near the glazed door.*] Wonderfully.

Lena. Not bad, is it, considering we've been home only two days?

Leonard. [*Placing his hat and cane upon the fauteuil-stool.*] Capital.

Lena. [*Refastening her bracelet.*] Ouf! The relief, after some of those foreign hotels!

Leonard [*Drawing off his gloves.*] Tired of traveling, eh?

Lena. Don't ask me! I was saying to Mrs. Killick at breakfast—I've had enough of Italy to last me my life. Over four months of it, and without a courier! [*Going toward the glazed door.*] That's a bit too stiff.

Leonard. It is rather.

Lena. [*Halting by him and dropping her voice slightly.*] Not that we wanted a courier when *you* came out to us. A splendid courier you were; I couldn't wish for a better.

Leonard [*Uncomfortably.*] Ha, ha!

Lena. [*Laughing.*] Do you remember our losing her hat-box at that wretched old Siena?

Leonard. Yes—yes.

Lena. You woke 'em up there in grand style. Ha, ha! Your friend, the Italian policeman—the image in the feathers——!

Leonard. Ha, ha!

Lena. You did give him a dressing! [*Sobering herself.*] Yes, those three or four weeks you were with us were the pleasantest o' the lot, to my idea. [*Going.*] Well, good day. [*Stopping again.*] Oh, but I must show you this. [*Taking a ring from her finger.*] A present from her—last Saturday—one of the best shops in the Roo Royarl. [*Handing it to him.*] She went out and bought it herself.

Leonard. Turquoise——

Lena. And diamonds.

Leonard. [*Returning the ring.*] Beautiful.

Lena. Wasn't it kind of her! I'm as vain as a peacock. [*Replacing the ring on her finger.*] But there, you've both been extremely good to me.

Leonard. Not at all.

Lena. You have; you've spoilt me completely. [*At the door, speaking louder.*] Treacherous weather for June, isn't it?

Leonard. Very.

Lena. [*In the corridor.*] Oh, here you are! Here's Mr. Ferris—I was just coming up to tell you——

[LEONARD *rises as* ZOE *appears in the corridor. She is dressed in an elegant robe of rich, soft material and carries a little bag in which are a few opened letters, her handkerchief,* etc. *She also is changed. Her face is wan and there are dark circles around her eyes.*]

Zoe. Ah? [*To* LEONARD, *formally, as she enters the room.*] Good morning.

Leonard. Good morning.

Zoe. Lena, how charming the old chintz looks!

Lena. [*Who is lingering.*] It's English!

Zoe. [*Laying her bag upon the oblong table.*] If we could all be freshened up by the same process!

Lena. [*Her hand on the door-handle.*] Don't forget you're to take your med'cine in three-quarters of an hour.

Zoe. Oh, bring me the filthy stuff when you like.

Lena. [*In the corridor, closing the door.*] Now, don't be naughty.

[*As the* WOMAN *disappears,* LEONARD *walks over to* ZOE. *She puts out her hand to check him, and they stand for a moment or two watching the door and listening. Then she drops her hand and turns her face to him perfunctorily, and he kisses her as a matter of course.*]

Zoe. Your motor isn't outside?

Leonard. No; I walked across the Park.

Zoe. That yellow car of yours is so conspicuous. [*Arranging a pillow on the settee.*] Sorry I wasn't visible yesterday.

Leonard. You're better?

Zoe. [*Evasively.*] Oh, more or less decrepit. [*Sitting.*] What have you been doing with yourself?

Leonard. Nothing much. [*Sitting in the armchair opposite to her.*] Except——

Zoe. [*Taking her bag from the table.*] By-the-bye, I've had a note this morning from an old friend of yours.

Leonard. Who?

Zoe. [*Producing a letter from the bag.*] Ethel Pierpoint.

Leonard. [*Inexpressively.*] Oh? [*She extracts the letter from its envelope and tosses it across to him. He reads it silently, with a frown. She takes a cigarette from the box on the table.*] I thought you'd dropped her.

Zoe. I did, in a fashion. I stopped her letters by ceasing to answer them. [*Striking a match.*] I hated calling myself hers affectionately, knowing I'd been the cause of your slacking away from her.

Leonard. [*Under his breath.*] Pish!

Zoe. [*Lighting her cigarette.*] *What* does she say?

Leonard. [*Reading aloud.*] "Dearest Zoe. Quite by chance I hear you are back at Lancaster Gate. Why do you still make no sign? I never wanted your friendship more than now—or the friendship of somebody who will give me good advice, or a sound shaking for being a fool. Please take pity on your troubled but ever devoted, Ethel Drayson Pierpoint." [*To* Zoe.] What does she mean by never wanting your friendship more than now? [Zoe *shakes her head. He continues to ponder over the letter.*] "—or the friendship of somebody who will give me good advice, or a sound shaking for being a fool."

Zoe. [*Smoking, thoughtfully.*] When did you see the Pierpoints last?

Leonard. About a month after you left London—just before I followed you. [*Returning the letter to her.*] I cooled off them gradually.

Zoe. [*After a pause.*] She's a nice girl—Ethel.

Leonard. Ye—es, she was nice enough.

[*There is a further pause. Then* Zoe *jumps up, as if to dismiss disagreeable reflections, and crosses to the writing-table. There she empties her bag of the letters it contains.*]

Leonard. [*Gloomily.*] Am I in the way?

Zoe. [*Fretfully.*] Of course not. [*She sits at the writing-table and busies herself with rereading her letters and destroying some of them.* Leonard *rises and takes a cigarette from the box.*] Poor Robby Relf has got neuritis.

Leonard. [*Lighting his cigarette.*] Zo——

Zoe. Eh?

Leonard. I was going to tell you—I dined at the Carlton last night.

Zoe. [*Indifferently.*] Oh?

Leonard. With Cossy Rawlings. Guess who was there.

Zoe. [*Becoming attentive.*] Dun'no.

Leonard. He didn't see me—he was at a table the other side of the room——

Zoe. [*Holding her breath.*] Theodore?

Leonard. Yes.

[*She throws the pieces of a letter into the wastepaper basket and leans back in her chair.*]

Zoe. How—how did he look?

Leonard. [*Curling his lip.*] I didn't study his appearance.

Zoe. He—he wasn't—by himself?

Leonard. Hardly!

Zoe. That—that woman?

Leonard. [*Nodding.*] Same lady.

Zoe. Simply the two?

Leonard. [*Sitting upon the settee on the right.*] The two turtle doves.

[*After a brief silence, she pushes her letters from her, rises, and moves about the room quietly but agitatedly.*]

Zoe. Who is this creature?

Leonard. [*Impatiently.*] I've told you—and Jim told you on Sunday.

Zoe. Hatherly—Annerly——?

Leonard. Her husband was a Major Annerly—Frank Annerly. He divorced her over a man of the name of Bettison.

Zoe. Where's *he?*

Leonard. He's dead. She's been through a good many hands since.

Zoe. Ho!

Leonard. Fred Wishart was one—and Tod Arnold——

Zoe. She's quite young, isn't she?

Leonard. Looks a baby.

Zoe. Ha!

Leonard. I should put her at thirty.

Zoe. Pretty? They all are!

Leonard. Passable.

Zoe. [*Behind the chair on the left of the oblong table.*] Do you think she's—with him?

Leonard. Not regularly. She's still living in Egerton Crescent, according to Cossy.

Zoe. [*Gripping the back of the chair.*] She'll ruin him; she'll ruin him, Len.

Leonard. Oh, I dare say there'll be a bit left, when she's done with him.

Zoe. There are other ways of dragging a man down besides through his pocket. Jim Mallandain says she's a vampire.

Leonard. Why should you worry yourself——?

Zoe. I don't want him to come to grief. Why should I?

Leonard. If he does, you've nothing to reproach yourself with.

Zoe. [*Giving him a swift look.*] *What!*

Leonard. [*Sullenly.*] Oh, you know what I mean—nothing that occurred before he took himself off.

Zoe. [*Moving to the oblong table, with

a long-drawn sigh.] Ah-h-h! [*Sitting, her elbows on the table, leaning her head on her hand.*] It will always be on my conscience that I drove him away.

Leonard. You didn't drive him away.

Zoe. I did.

Leonard. You were quite justified in doing it, anyhow. He made your life a burden to you.

Zoe. I might have been more patient with him; I might have waited.

Leonard. Waited?

Zoe. Waited till we'd got through the middle period of our lives. [*Raising her head.*] Peter warned us, the very dav we parted——

Leonard. [*Sneeringly.*] Peter!

Zoe. Mid-Channel! We should soon have reached the other side.

Leonard. There's a limit to human endurance; you'd passed it.

Zoe. [*Staring before her.*] It seems to me now, there wasn't so very much for me to put up with—not so very much. [*Rising and walking to the back of the settee on which* LEONARD *is sitting.*] There was a lot of good in him, really. After all, he only needed managing, humoring——

Leonard. [*Starting up and turning to her.*] Upon my soul, Zoe! Ha! You're discovering no end of fine qualities in him suddenly!

Zoe. [*Bitterly.*] Am I!

Leonard. You hadn't a decent word for him when we were in Italy! Now he's perfect!

Zoe. [*Facing him.*] No, he's not.

Leonard. [*Satirically.*] Sounds like it.

Zoe. [*Flaring up.*] Neither he nor you! You can be just as unkind to me as he ever was.

Leonard. [*Angrily.*] I!

Zoe. Yes! And, with all his faults, he did try to take care of me—to keep me from harm! [*Her eyes ablaze.*] My God, what have *you* done!

[*They remain confronting one another for a moment without speaking. Then he turns away abruptly and picks up his hat and cane. She runs after him and clings to him.*]

Zoe. No, no; don't be hasty. I didn't mean it—I didn't mean it——

Leonard. [*Endeavoring to free himself.*] Let me go——

Zoe. Ah, no! I'm not well today——

Leonard. I'll come back when you're better-tempered.

Zoe. I *am* better-tempered. Look! it's all over. [*Coaxing him to give up his hat and cane.*] Lenny—Lenny dear—Lenny——[*Placing the hat and cane upon the writing-table, she takes her handkerchief from her bag and dries her eyes. He sits in the arm-chair near the glazed door sulkily.*] Ha, ha! Now you're beginning to see what sort of a time poor Theo had with me.

Leonard. Oh, can't you leave off talking about him for a single second!

Zoe. [*Coming to him meekly.*] I beg your pardon, dear.

Leonard. You've got that fellow on the brain.

Zoe. [*Standing behind him.*] You started it, by telling me of last night.

Leonard. Why the deuce *shouldn't* I tell you of last night! Do sit down. [*She sits near him, upon the fauteuil-stool.*] I can't make you out, Zo. This woman's only what we've been waiting for. I've said all along he'd soon give you an opportunity of divorcing him. She completes your case for you.

Zoe. [*Dully.*] Yes.

Leonard. [*Grumbling.*] You ought to be tremendously obliged to Jim for being the first to open your eyes—my eyes too—to what's going on. Instead of which, you're upset by it. And now, because *I've* seen Blundell and the lady together, I'm favored by hearing Mr. B. described as a model husband——

Zoe. [*To silence him.*] Ah——!

Leonard. [*Changing his tone.*] When do you interview your lawyers?

Zoe. I—I haven't written to them yet.

Leonard. You were to do it after I left you on Monday.

Zoe. I—I've been feeling so cheap, Len.

Leonard. [*With a short laugh.*] We shall be gray-haired before we're married, at this rate. [*She lays her hand on his appeasingly. He retains her hand.*] I believe you'll have to go through the form of trying to compel Blundell to return to you. Of course, he'll refuse. Meanwhile we must have the lady's house watched—or Blundell's flat. I shouldn't be surprised if he'd arrange that part of the business with you, to save trouble and expense. Drop a line to Maxwells today, will you?

Zoe. [*Obediently.*] Yes.

Leonard. Or ring them up. You'll be able to get out tomorrow—or one of them would wait on you.

Zoe. Yes.

Leonard. That's right, old girlie. Kiss me. [*They kiss, quickly and cautiously, without ardor.*] Sorry.

Zoe. [*Turning to him and lowering her voice almost to a whisper.*] Lenny——

Leonard. What?

Zoe. Don't forget—Perugia.

Leonard. [*In an outburst.*] Oh, yes—curse the place!—let's forget Perugia. I was off my head there. I behaved like a blackguard. You needn't be continually throwing it in my teeth.

Zoe. No, no; I'm not scolding you again. [*Gently.*] What I mean is—your breaking your word to me at Perugia—staying in the same hotel——

Leonard. Well?

Zoe. If Theodore's solicitors got hold of that——

Leonard. [*Rising and walking away.*] Yes, but they won't get hold of it.

Zoe. [*Twisting herself around toward him.*] You remember our meeting Claud Lowenstein at the railway station at Arezzo?

Leonard. I explained to him that my being in the train with you was pure chance. I made that square.

Zoe. He was going on to Perugia—to the Brufani. [*Rising.*] He may have been suspicious—he may have inquired——

Leonard. Even that little swine wouldn't tell tales.

Zoe. [*Coming to him.*] Then there's Lena—they might pump Lena——

Leonard. My dear girl, all this would be very terrible if Blundell wasn't as anxious to get rid of you as we are to get rid of him. No, you take my word for it—he won't defend. His game is to be free at any price.

Zoe. To marry again perhaps!

Leonard. Probably.

Zoe. [*Clenching her hands.*] Ah, no!

Leonard. [*His brow darkening again.*] Doesn't *that* please you? There's no satisfying you, Zoe. [*She leaves him and paces the room distractedly.*] A minute ago you were frightened lest he should be ruined by Mrs. Annerly!

Zoe. [*On the left.*] I—I couldn't bear the idea of another woman being a better wife to him than I was! I couldn't bear it, Lenny!

Leonard. Why, what concern would it be of yours——!

Zoe. [*With a gesture, as the glazed door opens.*] Sssh! [WARREN *appears.*]

Warren. [*To* ZOE.] I beg pardon, ma'am—Mr. Mottram.

Zoe. [*Uttering a little, eager cry.*] Ah!

Warren. He'll call again, ma'am, if you're engaged.

Zoe. Did you say I—I'd anybody with me?

Warren. No, ma'am.

Zoe. [*After a slight pause—indicating the adjoining room.*] Is that room still covered up?

Warren. Yes, ma'am.

Zoe. Well—show him in there for the moment.

Warren. Yes, m'am.

[*He withdraws, closing the door.*]

Zoe. [*To* LEONARD, *in a low voice.*] He'd better not find you here so early.

Leonard. [*Also dropping his voice, testily.*] Why need you bother yourself with old Peter this morning?

Zoe. [*Bringing* LEONARD *his hat and cane.*] I haven't seen him since January. Don't look so cross. [*Caressing his cheek.*] Are you engaged to lunch anywhere?

Leonard. No.

Zoe. Will you eat your lunch with me?

[*He nods. She takes a powder-puff from her bag and, looking into the hand-mirror, hurriedly removes the traces of her tears. While she is thus engaged,* LEONARD *listens at the nearer door on the right.*]

Leonard. [*Leaving the door—in a whisper.*] He's there. [WARREN *reappears.*]

Warren. [*To* ZOE.] Mr. Mottram is in the next room, ma'am.

Zoe. Thank you. [WARREN *withdraws.*]

Zoe. [*To* LEONARD, *in a whisper, accompanying him to the glazed door.*] Go into the Park and sit under the trees. Blow a kiss for me to all the kiddies. [*She watches him disappear down the corridor. Then, having closed the glazed door, she opens the farther door on the right.*] Peter!

Peter. [*Out of sight.*] My dear lady!

Zoe. [*Going into the next room.*] Why on earth have they put you into this dismal room! Come into the light. [*Returning with him, her arm tucked through his.*] Oh, my dear Peter—my dear Peter——!

Peter. Ah, yes, yes, yes! A nice way to serve a pal!

Zoe. [*Closing the door.*] How did you——?

Peter. Jim Mallandain dropped in at the office this morning. [*They leave the door.*] He traveled with you from Paris on Sunday.

Zoe. I collided with him at the Gare du Nord.

Peter. And this is Wednesday!

Zoe. [*Withdrawing her arm.*] I funked sending for you; that's a fact.

Peter. Funked it?

Zoe. [*With the air of a child in disgrace.*] Your letters to me have been awfully sweet, but I know you despise me for making a muck of things.

Peter. [*Protestingly.*] Ah, Mrs. Zoe!

Zoe. And I'm rather a sick rabbit, Peter.

[*Turning away.*] A sick rabbit has only one desire—to hide in its burrow. [*Facing him.*] My heart bounded when you were announced, though.

Peter. [*Following her.*] You don't look very fit. Seen a doctor?

Zoe. I've let Lena call in Rashleigh, to humor her. [*Sitting on the settee on the right.*] And I've promised to swallow his pig-wash.

Peter. What's he say?

Zoe. Chill; but—[*raising her eyes to his*] —between ourselves?——

Peter. Honor.

Zoe. [*With quivering lips.*] Life, dear old chum!

Peter. [*Tenderly.*] Ain't much in it?

Zoe. Damn little. [*Putting her hair back from her brow.*] Phew! Can't sleep, Peter.

Peter Oh, lor'!

Zoe. I tumble into bed at twelve—one—two. I get an hour's stupor, from sheer fatigue, and then I'm wide awake—thinking! Then, dressing-gown and slippers and the cigarettes; and then it's to and fro, up and down—smoke—smoke—smoke—often till the servants start brushing the stairs. No game, eh?

Peter. How long has this——?

Zoe. It began at—[*checking herself*]—oh, a devil of a while. [*With a shiver.*] But I'm worse now I've set foot again in this house.

Peter. [*Eyeing her keenly.*] Ghosts? [*Avoiding his gaze, she stretches out her hand toward the cigarette box. He pushes the box beyond her reach. She makes a grimace. There is a pause.*] Zoe——

Zoe. Well?

Peter. [*Deliberately.*] Why shouldn't you pick up the pieces?

Zoe. Pick up—the pieces?

Peter. You and Theodore.

Zoe. Oh—don't be—funny, Peter.

Peter. I'm not funny; I'm as serious as the clown at the circus. [*Another pause.*] Write to him—or give me a message to take to him. *See* him.

[*She gets to her feet and attempts to pass* PETER. *He detains her and she sinks back among her pillows.*]

Zoe. Ha, ha! You ridiculous man! [*Faintly.*] Pick up the pieces! As if that were possible!

Peter. Oh, the valuable family china is in a good many fragments, I admit. But there *are* the fragments, lyin' on the carpet. They can be collected, fitted together.

Zoe. [*With a sudden gesture of entreaty.*] Ah, for God's sake, Peter——!

Peter. Why, I'm suggestin' nothin' unusual.

Zoe. [*Repeating her gesture.*] Sssh!

Peter. Go into the homes of three-fifths of the married people you know—*I* know—and you'll find some imposin' specimens of porcelain that won't bear inspectin' very narrowly.

Zoe. [*Waving the subject away.*] Sssh, sssh!

Peter. Only yesterday afternoon I was callin' at a house in—never mind the district. I was wanderin' round the drawin'-room, lookin' at the *bric-à-brac,* and there, on a Louis Quatorze console-table, were as handsome a pair of old Chinese jars—genuine Mings—as ever I've met with. Such a sooperb glaze they've got, such depth o' color! They appear to be priceless, perfect, till you examine 'em closely; and then——! My dear Zoe, they're cracked; they've both had a nasty knock at some time or another; they're scarred shockin'ly with rivets and cement. And while I was sheddin' tears over 'em, in sailed madam, smilin' and holdin' out her hand to me—she'd been upstairs, rubbin' carmine on her lips——

Zoe. [*In a murmur.*] You horror!

Peter. How kind of me to call—and how wild Tom 'ud be at missin' me! To the casual observer, she's the happiest woman goin'; and Tom, who strolled in just as I was leavin', might be the most domesticated of husbands. You follow me? You grasp the poetic allegory? Those faulty old Mings are emblematic of the establishment they adorn. Mr. and Mrs. Tom fell out years ago; they turned against each other one fine day—in mid-Channel—and hadn't the sense to kiss and be friends on landin'; their lives are as damaged as those wounded crocks of theirs on the console-table. [*Persuasively.*] Well, but ain't it wiser to repair the broken china, rather than chuck the bits into the dust-bin? It's still showy and effective at a distance; and there are cases—rare, but they exist—where the mendin's been done so neatly that the flaws are almost imperceptible. [*Seating himself opposite* ZOE.] Zoe——

Zoe. [*Almost inaudibly.*] Yes, Peter?

Peter. [*Leaning forward.*] I believe yours is one of the cases—yours and Theodore's—where the mendin' would be exceptionally successful.

Zoe. What do you—what do you mean?

Peter. My dear, old Theo is as miserable over this affair as you are.

Zoe. [*Attempting a disdainful smile.*] N-nonsense!

Peter. Oh, no, it ain't nonsense.

Zoe. W-what makes you think that?

Peter. Between ourselves?

Zoe. [*A note of eagerness in her voice.*] Honor.

Peter. He shows it in all manner o' ways. Neglects his business—ain't much good at it when he doesn't—is losin' his grip—looks confoundedly ill—*is* ill. Altogether he's a different man from the man he was, even when matters were at boilin' point here.

Zoe. [*Locking and unlocking her fingers.*] Does he ever—speak of me?

Peter. Oh, lor', yes.

Zoe. N-not kindly?

Peter. Very. Very kindly.

Zoe. [*After a silence, as if in pain.*] Oh——! [*She rises, passes him, and goes to the other side of the room where she moves from one piece of furniture to another aimlessly.*] W-what's he say about me?

Peter. [*Not turning.*] Frets about you—wonders how you're gettin' along—wonders as to the state of your finances—can't bear the idea of your bein' in the least pinched—wants to help you.

Zoe. He's extremely generous!

Peter. Theo? Never was anythin' else.

Zoe. [*Her eyes flashing.*] His own expenses must be pretty considerable just now, too!

Peter. [*Pricking up his ears.*] Must they? [*With great artlessness.*] Why?

Zoe. Oh, do you imagine I live with wool in my ears?

Peter. [*Over his shoulder.*] Wool——?

Zoe. This woman he's continually with! [PETER'S *face is still aerted from* ZOE. *At this juncture his eyes open widely and his mouth shapes to a whistle.*] This—Mrs.—Mrs.—what's her name—Annerly! [*Pacing the room.*] A notorious woman—a woman without a shred of character—an any-man's-woman——!

Peter. [*Settling his features and turning his chair toward* ZOE—*in a tone of expostulation.*] Oh!

Zoe. A baby-faced thing—seven years younger than I am! Precisely the class of goods a man of Theo's age flies at!

Peter. Oh—oh——!

Zoe. *They're* rather costly articles, aren't they?

Peter. My dear Mrs. Zoe——

Zoe. Oh, don't you pretend to be so innocent, Peter! You know jolly well he's all over the place with her. They were at Hurlingham together Saturday week.

Peter. [*Coolly.*] I dessay.

Zoe. And they dine *tête-à-tête* at the Savoy, Ritz's, the Carlton——

Peter. Who supplies the information?

Zoe. They were at the Carlton last night.

Peter. Who's told you *that?*

Zoe. L—— [*She pulls herself up.*]

Peter. [*Curiously.*] Who?

Zoe. [*Moistening her lips.*] Oh, I—I first heard of it all from Jim Mallandain. He was full of it on board the boat on Sunday.

Peter. Was he! [*Rising lazily.*] A busy gentleman—Jim.

Zoe. It was Jim who met them at Hurlingham—had tea with 'em.

Peter. [*Curiously again.*] But it can't be Jim who's blabbed about last night.

Zoe. Why?

Peter. [*Shrugging his shoulders.*] He happened to mention this mornin' that he was with a party at Jules'.

Zoe. [*Confused.*] N-no, it isn't from Jim I've got that. I—— [*Throwing herself into the armchair near the glazed door.*] Oh, but really, it's a matter of supreme indifference to me, Peter, my dear boy, whom Theodore entertains at the Carlton, or whom he entertains at his flat——

Peter. [*Coming to her.*] My dear Zoe——

Zoe. [*Laughing heartily.*] Ha, ha, ha! His flat! I hear it's quite sumptuous. After his pathetic yearnings for peace and quiet in a garret, he sets up, within a month of our separating, in an enormous flat in Cavendish Square! I received that bit of news when I was in Florence. I—I was intensely amused. Oh, let him wallow in his precious flat——!

Peter. [*Argumentatively.*] My dear lady——

Zoe. [*Her hand to her brow, exhausted.*] Ah, drop it, Peter; drop it!

Peter. I ask you—a liberal-minded person—what 'ud become of friendship as an institootion if men and women couldn't be pals without havin' the—the—what-d'ye-call-it—the tongue of scandal wagged at 'em? The world 'ud be intolerable. It ain't all marmalade as it is; but if a fellow can't take the fresh air in the company of a female at Hurlingham, or give her a bite o' food at a restaurant——

Zoe. [*Her head against the back of her chair, her eyes closed.*] Ah, la, la, la!

Peter. As for this—er—this Mrs. Annerly——

[*He again purses his mouth and is evidently in a difficulty.*]

Zoe. [*Her eyes still shut.*] Well?

Peter. It's true she chucked Annerly for another chap. I don't condone an act of that description—except that I knew Annerly, and if ever there was a dull dog——

Zoe. Was he duller than Theo?

Peter. Oh, go on with yer! And since then she's been a trifle—flighty—perhaps, now and again [*with a gulp*], but today she might be your maiden aunt.

Zoe. [*Dreamily.*] You humbug, Peter!

Peter. [*Sitting beside her, upon the fauteuil-stool.*] Oh, I'm not maintainin' that we men always select our women pals from the right basket. I'm not sayin' that we don't make asses of ourselves occasionally, sometimes from sentiment, sometimes from vanity, sometimes from—various causes. But the same remark applies to you women over your men pals. [*Laying a hand on her arm.*] For instance—[*she opens her eyes*]—for instance, here you are, throwin' stones at old Theo with regard to Alice Annerly. [*Significantly.*] My dear, there are a few panes o' glass in the house *you* live in, bear in mind.

[*She sits upright, looking at him.*]

Zoe. In the house—I——?

Peter. [*Gravely.*] Mrs. Zoe, what you did when you were under your husband's protection is one thing; what you do now is another bag o' nuts entirely. And a woman situated as you are ought to be careful of retainin' a cub among her intimates.

Zoe. A cub?

Peter. Cub.

Zoe. [*Apprehensively.*] To whom—are you alluding?

Peter. Lenny Ferris.

Zoe. L—enny?

Peter. It ain't an agreeable job, pitchin' into a fellow you've been on good terms with; but the fact remains—to put it mildly—that Master Lenny's a stoopid, blunderin' cub.

Zoe. [*Haughtily but palpitatingly.*] He's nothing of the kind. What has he done that you should abuse him?

Peter. It's he who's told you that Theodore was at the Carlton last night, ain't it? [*She drops her eyes.*] Been here this mornin'?

Zoe. [*Raising her eyes, boldly.*] Yes.

Peter. H'm! The sick rabbit doesn't hide in her burrow from everybody.

Zoe. H—how——?

Peter. I saw your lips make an L just now, before you could put the stopper on.

Zoe. Ha, ha! You ought to have been a professional detective.

Peter. [*Scowling.*] Ferris has kept out of my way lately, or I——

Zoe. If he *has* run in here for a moment—to ask whether I'm back—is there anything particularly cubbish in that?

Peter. It wasn't *that* I was referrin' to.

Zoe. N—no?

Peter. I was referrin' to his havin' the damned presumption to dance attendance on you in Italy.

Zoe. [*Aghast.*] I—Italy?

Peter. He was at Perugia while you were there.

Zoe. Oh—Perugia——

Peter. [*With a shrug.*] And other places, I assoom.

Zoe. [*After a pause, pulling herself together.*] H—ho! [*Mimicking* PETER.] And who supplies the information? [PETER *waves the question from him.*] Lowenstein, by any chance—Claud Lowenstein? [PETER, *looking down his nose, is silent. She rises and walks away from him.*] The hound—the little hound!

Peter. Lowenstein came across you both at some railway station. He arrived at Perugia the day you left.

Zoe. [*Pacing the room on the right.*] The contemptible little hound!

Peter. He put up at the Brufani too.

Zoe. [*Stopping in her walk—under her breath.*] Ah!

Peter. Master Lenny might at least have had the common decency to quarter himself at another hotel.

Zoe. The—the Brufani is the most comfortable—the—— [*A pause.*] I—I suppose it *was* thoughtless of Lenny.

Peter. [*Quietly.*] Cub!

Zoe. [*Approaching* PETER.] Does—Theodore—know?

Peter. [*Nodding.*] Lowenstein went to him with it.

Zoe. Ha, ha! A busy gentleman—Claudy Lowenstein! [*Falteringly.*] It—it was all my fault, Peter. If—if anybody's to blame, I am. I—I wrote to the boy from Florence—complaining of feeling lonely——

Peter. That doesn't excuse him.

Zoe. [*Touching* PETER'S *shoulder with the tips of her fingers.*] What—what does Theodore——?

Peter. He's savage.

Zoe. Savage?

Peter. [*Rising.*] He'd like to punch Ferris's head—as I should.

Zoe. [*In a low voice.*] Savage——! [*Slowly.*] He—he's jealous, then? [*A shrug from* PETER. *Her eyes light up.*] Jealous! [*A pause.*] Peter—no man's jealous over a woman—unless he—unless he cares for her! [*Plucking at his sleeve.*] Peter!

Peter. You've heard me say old Theo's miserable—desperately wretched.

Zoe. He—he's grown fond of me again—fond of me——!

Peter. My dear, you and he have never left off bein' fond o' one another, actually. As I warned you, you've only been tossin' about, both of you, on a bit o' troubled water.

[*She stares at him for a moment with an expressionless face and then, as if stupefied, seats herself in the chair on the left of the oblong table.*]

Peter. [*Standing before her.*] Well, at any rate, you'll let this Italian business be a lesson to you not to rush at conclusions respectin' other people. So, come now; won't you try to patch it up? I'll bet my noo hat, Theodore'll meet you half-way. [*Urgently.*] Zoe!

Zoe. [*Locking and unlocking her fingers again.*] Peter——

Peter. Eh?

Zoe. Your Mr. and Mrs. Tom—the world perhaps never heard of *their* fall-out.

Peter. What o' that?

Zoe. Everybody is aware of the split between me and Theo.

Peter. Everybody! A handful! Besides, nothin' is even a nine-days' wonder in these times. [*A pause.*] Will you do it?

Zoe. [*Suddenly, starting up and walking away to the left.*] Oh, no, no, no! I can't—I can't!

Peter. [*Following her.*] Can't?

Zoe. [*Helplessly.*] I can't, Peter!

Peter. [*Taking her by the arms.*] Oh——!

Zoe. I—I mean I—I'm sure it wouldn't answer—I'm sure——

Peter. My dear girl——

Zoe. [*Piteously.*] Ah, don't—don't! [*Escaping from him and crossing to the right.*] Oh, leave me alone!

[WARREN *enters at the glazed door.*]

Warren. [*To* ZOE.] Miss Pierpoint is downstairs, ma'am.

Zoe. [*Seizing upon the interruption.*] Ah, yes!

Warren. I'm to give you her love, ma'am, and if it isn't convenient for you to see her——

Zoe. It is—it *is*—quite convenient—quite. [WARREN *withdraws, closing the door.*] I'm awfully sorry, my dear Peter, but this child wants to consult me about something—something important. [*Giving him her hands.*] I must kick you out. You don't feel hurt, do you?

Peter. [*Ruefully.*] Confound Miss Pierpoint! Zoe——

Zoe. What?

Peter. You'll think it over?

Zoe. [*Putting her hand to his lips.*] Ah——!

Peter. [*Holding her hand.*] No, no. Think it over. Ask me to dine with you one night next week.

Zoe. Monday—Tuesday——?

Peter. Monday.

Zoe. [*Artfully.*] Ah, but I shall lay in a chaperon for the occasion.

Peter. Rats! How can I talk to you before a chaperon?

Zoe. Ha, ha, ha, ha! [*She runs to the glazed door, opens it, and, going into the corridor, calls loudly and excitedly.*] Ethel—Ethel—Ethel——! [ETHEL *appears in the corridor and* ZOE *embraces her with an excess of warmth.*] My dear Ethel! My dear child! [*They kiss.*] What ages since we've seen each other! [*Bringing* ETHEL *into the room.*] You know Mr. Mottram?

Ethel. [*Going to* PETER.] Oh, yes.

Peter. [*Shaking hands with her.*] How-d'ye-do, Miss Pierpoint—and *au revoir.*

Ethel. [*As he moves toward the glazed door.*] I'm not driving you away?

Peter. I forgive you.

[*He rejoins* ZOE, *who is near the door.* ETHEL *lays her sunshade upon the writing-table.*]

Zoe. [*To* PETER.] Monday night?

Peter. Monday night.

Zoe. Half-past eight.

Peter. [*At the door, dropping his voice.*] A chaperon?

Zoe. [*Mockingly.*] The proprieties!

Peter. You cat! [*He goes.*]

Zoe. [*Closing the door.*] Ha, ha! [*She leans wearily against the door for a moment and again puts back her hair from her brow. Her manner now becomes strained, artificial, distrait. She advances to* ETHEL.] Now, then! [ETHEL *turns to her.*] Let me have a good squint at you. How's your dear mother?

Ethel. [*Who is pale and sad-looking.*] Mother's flourishing. [*Leaving the writing-table.*] You're not angry with me for rushing you at this hour?

Zoe. Isn't this our old hour for a chat?

Ethel. We were at Madame Levine's yesterday—Mother and I—ordering frocks, and Camille, the skirtmaker, told us you were back. Zoe, how unkind you've been!

Zoe. Am I in your bad books?

Ethel. Why have you treated us so horridly?

Zoe. Well, my dear child, the fact is—the fact is it suddenly dawned on me that perhaps your mother mightn't consider me any longer a suitable pal for her daughter.

Ethel. [*Protestingly.*] Oh!

Zoe. Heaps of folks, you know, haven't much use for single married women.

Ethel. But we both showed you that our sympathies were on your side!

Zoe. Yes. we often sympathize with people

we wouldn't touch with the end of a wet umbrella.

Ethel. [*Coming close to* ZOE.] So that's the reason you left off answering my letters!

Zoe. C-certainly.

Ethel. And why we hear of your return through fat old Camille! [*Fingering a jewel at* ZOE'S *neck.*] You've had a pleasant time abroad?

Zoe. [*Taking* ETHEL'S *face between her hands, abruptly.*] How thin your face is, Ethel!

Ethel. [*Gazing at* ZOE.] Your cheeks are not as round as they were.

Zoe. [*Leading* ETHEL *to the settee on the right.*] I caught a rotten chill on board the boat and have been beastly seedy. [*Putting* ETHEL *on the settee.*] What's wrong with you? That's a dreary note I've had from you this morning.

Ethel. [*Tracing a pattern on the floor with the point of her shoe.*] Now I'm with you, I —I can't——

Zoe. [*Looking down upon her.*] You want advice, you say.

Ethel. [*Tremulously.*] Yes.

Zoe. Or a good shaking.

Ethel. I—I suppose I ought to be ashamed of myself for being so, but I—I'm very unhappy, Zoe.

Zoe. Unhappy?

Ethel. It's no use my attempting to talk to Mother. Mother's a person who prides herself on her level-headedness. Anybody with a fixed income and a poor circulation can be level-headed! It only means you're fish-like. But you—you're warm-blooded and human ——

Zoe. Well?

Ethel. Z-Zoe——

Zoe. Yes?

Ethel. [*Her eyes on the ground.*] Did you ever suspect that there was anything between Mr. Ferris and me?

Zoe. [*Calmly, steadying herself.*] Mr. Ferris—and you?

Ethel. An attachment.

Zoe. [*With affected astonishment.*] My dear child!

Ethel. [*Looking up.*] Oh, don't keep on calling me "child"! I'm nearly six-and-twenty. [*Taking* ZOE'S *hands.*] *Didn't* you ever guess?

Zoe. He—he always seemed delighted to meet you here.

Ethel. He's one of your "boys"—hasn't he ever talked to you about me?

Zoe. Of course, frequently.

Ethel. Never as if he were—in love with me?

Zoe. [*Withdrawing her hands.*] I—I can't say that it—struck me——

Ethel. [*Dejectedly.*] You didn't know, perhaps, that at the beginning of the year—before you went away—he was a great deal in Sloane Street?

Zoe. Why, yes, he used to have tea with you and your mother sometimes, didn't he? [*Turning from* ETHEL.] How did I hear that?

Ethel. [*Hanging her head.*] Very often he came early in the afternoon—by arrangement with me—while Mother was resting.

Zoe. [*With a hard laugh.*] Ha, ha! Ethel!

Ethel. Yes, worthy of a vulgar shop-girl, wasn't it?

Zoe. [*Sitting in the chair opposite* ETHEL.] He—he came early in the afternoon——?

Ethel. And we sat together, in the firelight. I'm sure he loved me, Zoe—then.

Zoe. [*Breathing heavily.*] And—and *you* ——?

Ethel. [*Her elbows on her knees, hiding her face in her hands.*] Oh, I'm a fool—an awful fool!

Zoe. [*After a silence.*] Did he ever—hint —at marriage? [ETHEL *nods, without uncovering her face.*] He did!

Ethel. [*Raising her head.*] Well, we got as far as agreeing that a small house in the country, near his aunt, would be an ideal state of existence. [*Mirthlessly.*] Ha, ha, ha! And there matters broke off.

Zoe. What—what——?

Ethel. All of a sudden there was a change —a change in his manner toward me. He still called on us, but not so regularly; and by degrees his visits—ceased altogether. [*She passes her hand across her eyes angrily and, stamping her foot, rises and moves to the other side of the room.*] The last time I spoke to him was one morning in the Row. Mother and I were walking and we came face to face with him. That was at the end of February. He was out of sorts, he said, and was going into Devonshire. I presume he went. [*Turning to* ZOE *who, with parted lips, is staring guiltily at the carpet.*] He's in London now, though. I saw him about a fortnight ago, at the Opera. I was with the Ormerods, in their box; he was in the stalls. [*Touching* ZOE'S *shoulder.*] Zoe——

Zoe. Yes?

Ethel. He's so altered.

Zoe. Altered?

Ethel. In his appearance. You recollect how boyish and fresh-looking he was?

Zoe. Y-yes.

Ethel. All that's gone. He's become—oh, but I dare say you've seen him since you've been home?

Zoe. J-just for a minute or two.

Ethel. You must have noticed——?

Zoe. N-now you mention it——

Ethel. I watched him through the opera-glass several times during the evening. [*Simply.*] He looks like a lost soul.

Zoe. I—I've never—ha, ha!—I've never made the acquaintance of a lost—ha, ha!——

Ethel. [*After a pause.*] Zoe, do you think anything has happened to Lenny Ferris?

Zoe. H-happened?

Ethel. Anything bad.

Zoe. Bad?

Ethel. Men's lives are constantly being wrecked by racing, or cards, or—— [*Half turning from* Zoe.] Oh, I oughtn't to know about such things, but one doesn't live in the dark—he may have got mixed up with some woman of the wrong sort, mayn't he?

Zoe. [*Rising quickly and walking away to the left.*] I—I really can't discuss topics of that kind with you, Ethel.

Ethel. [*Wistfuly.*] No; but if he *is* in any scrape—any entanglement—and one could help him——

Zoe. [*At the writing-table, taking up a bottle of salts—faintly.*] Help him?

Ethel. Save him——!

Zoe. [*Sniffing the salts.*] How—how romantic you are!

Ethel. Am I! [*Her elbows on the back of the armchair by the oblong table, timidly.*] Zoe, would it be possible—in your opinion—would it be possible for me to—to see him?

Zoe. [*Sitting in the chair at the writing-table.*] See Mr. Ferris?

Ethel. [*Plucking at the cover of the chair on which she is leaning.*] Here—in your house—or elsewhere—see him and offer him my friendship—a sister's friendship? *You* could manage it.

Zoe. My—my dear!

Ethel. Oh, yes, I'm lacking in dignity, aren't I—and self-respect! [*Coming forward.*] I've told myself that a thousand times. [*Warmly.*] But there are quite enough dignified people in the world without me; and if I could influence Lenny, any one might have my dignity for twopence.

Zoe. Influence him——?

Ethel. For his good. Oh, I don't want to boast, but I'm a straight, clean girl; and it may be that, at this particular moment of his life, the more he sees of women like you and me the better. However, if you tell me the idea's improper, I'll accept it from you. [*Approaching* Zoe.] I'll ta!'e anything from you. [*Appealingly.*] But don't tell me that, if you can avoid it. Give me the opportunity, if you can, of showing him that I'm different from most girls—that I'm above petty, resentful feelings. [*Bending over* Zoe.] Zoe——

[Lena *enters at the further door on the right, carrying a silver salver on which are a dose of medicine in a medicine-glass and a dish of sweetmeats.*]

Lena. Your med'cine! [*Closing the door.*] Good morning, Miss Pierpoint.

Ethel. Ah, Lena!

Zoe. [*To* Ethel, *rising hastily.*] Excuse me——

[Lena *advances and* Zoe *goes to her and, with a shaking hand, drinks the medicine.*]

Lena. [*To* Zoe.] Good gracious, how queer you look! [*To* Ethel.] She's doing too much today, Miss Pierpoint. [*Going to* Ethel.] Doctor Rashleigh says she's frightfully below par.

Ethel. [*Picking up her sunshade.*] What a shame of me! [*Running to* Zoe.] I won't stay another minute.

Zoe. [*Sitting on the settee on the right.*] I *am* a little fatigued.

Ethel. I ought to have seen it.

Zoe. I—I'll write to you. [*They kiss.*] My love to your mother.

Ethel. And when you are well enough——?

Zoe. I'll call upon her.

Ethel. [*To* Lena, *who precedes her into the corridor.*] No, no; stop with Mrs. Blundell. I'm so sorry, Lena——

[Lena *and* Ethel *talk together for a little while in undertones; then the girl disappears.* Lena *returns.*]

Lena. [*Shutting the door.*] Silly chatterbox. [*Finding* Zoe *lying at full length upon the settee, her head buried in a pillow.*] Why do you tire yourself like this? Shall I fetch you some brandy?

Zoe. No.

Lena. [*Lowering her voice.*] *He's* in the house again.

Zoe. Who?

Lena. Mr. Ferris.

Zoe. [*Raising herself.*] Mr. Ferris!

Lena. [*With a jerk of her head in the direction of the next room.*] In there. [Zoe *sits upright.*] Warren's making himself beautiful and Clara answered the door. She thought you were by yourself and let him come up. [Zoe *gets to her feet.*] I was just bringing you your med'cine and met him. [Zoe *goes to the writing-table, takes up the hand-mirror, and puts her hair in order.*] Lucky I'd heard that Miss Pierpoint was here; he didn't want to see her! Another second——!

Zoe. That'll do. [*Calmly.*] Take care I'm not interrupted again.

Lena. Ah, now! Mayn't I get rid of him?

Zoe. No. [*Turning.*] Run away, please.

Lena. Oh, very good. [*Picking up the salver which she has placed upon a piece of furniture near the glazed door.*] You'll do exactly as you choose. [*In the corridor.*] I declare I'd rather look after a pack of unruly children any day in the week——

[*She closes the door.* ZOE *glances over her shoulder, to assure herself that the* WOMAN *has left the room, and then, with a fierce light in her eyes, goes to the nearer door on the right and throws it open.*]

Zoe. [*In a hard voice, speaking into the adjoining room.*] I'm alone.

[*She moves from the door as* LEONARD, *still carrying his hat and cane, enters.*]

Leonard. By George, that was a narrow squeak! [*Closing the door.*] Whatever possessed you to be at home to the Pierpoint girl this morning?

Zoe. [*Coldly.*] I didn't expect you back before lunch.

Leonard. [*Putting his hat and cane on the chair at the nearer end of the settee on the right.*] I was talking to a man at Victoria Gate and I saw Peter driving away in a taxi. [*Facing her.*] I got sick of the Park. [*Seeing that something is amiss.*] Hallo! [*A pause.*] Any one been running me down?

[*She advances to him and, drawing herself to her full height, regards him scornfully.*]

Zoe. [*Making a motion with her hands as if she would strike him.*] You—you——! [*Dropping her hands to her side.*] Oh, cruel, —cruel—[*walking away from him*]—cruel!

Leonard. What's cruel? Who's cruel?

Zoe. [*At the further end of the room, on the right.*] Ah—ah——!

Leonard. [*Moving to the left.*] Oh, come! Let's have it out; let's have it out.

Zoe. Sssh! Don't raise your voice here.

Leonard. Somebody's been talking against me. Ethel Pierpoint?

Zoe. [*Coming to the oblong table.*] You've behaved abominably to this girl.

Leonard. Ho, it *is* Miss Pierpoint!

Zoe. No, she hasn't spoken a word against you. But she's opened her heart to me.

Leonard. [*Going to* ZOE.] You've known all about me and Ethel.

Zoe. It's a lie. How much have I known? I knew that you were sizing her up, as you expressed it; but I never surmised that you'd as good as proposed marriage to her.

Leonard. I told you months ago—admitted it—that I'd made myself a bit of an idiot over Ethel. I fancied you tumbled to the state o' things.

Zoe. Did you! Why, do you think—maniac as I was when you came through to me to Florence!—do you think I'd have allowed you to remain near me for five minutes if I'd known as much as I do now!

Leonard. Look here, Zoe——

Zoe. Oh, you're a cruel fellow! You've been cruel to her and cruel to me. I believe you're capable of being cruel to any woman who comes your way. Still, *she's* the fortunate one. Her scratches'll heal; but I [*sitting at the oblong table and hitting it with her fist*] I loathe myself more than ever—more than ever!

Leonard. [*After a pause.*] Zoe, I wish you'd try to be a little fair to me.

Zoe. [*Ironically.*] Fair!

Leonard. Perhaps I did go rather further with Ethel Pierpoint than I led you to understand.

Zoe. Oh——!

Leonard. I own up. Yes, but what prospect was there, when I was thick with her, of your being free of Blundell? None. And what was I to you? Merely a pal of yours—one of your "tame robins"—one of a dozen; and I'd come to a loose end in my life. It was simply the fact that there *was* no prospect for me with you that drove me to consider whether I hadn't better settle down to a humdrum with a decent girl of the Ethel breed. Otherwise, do you imagine I'd have crossed the street to speak to another woman? [*Leaving* ZOE.] Oh, you might do me common justice! [*Hotly.*] If circumstances *have* made a cad of me, am I *all* black? Can't you find *any* good in me? [*Turning to her.*] What did I tell you at Perugia!

Zoe. [*Rising.*] Ah, don't——!

Leonard. That I'd been in love with you from the day I first met you—from the very moment Mrs. Hope-Cornish introduced me to you at Sandown! Well! Isn't there anything to my credit on that score? Didn't I keep my secret? For four years I kept it; though, with matters as they often were between you and Blundell, many a man might have thought you ripe grapes. [*Walking across to the right.*] Only once I was off my guard with you—when I laid hold of you and begged you, whatever happened, never to—never to——

Zoe. [*Leaning against the table, her back to him.*] Ha, ha, ha!

Leonard. Yes, and I meant it; as God hears me, I meant it. If anybody had told me that afternoon that it was I who—oh, hang! [*Sitting upon the settee.*] But what I want to impress upon you is that, if I were quite the low scoundrel you make me out to be, I shouldn't have gone through what I *have* gone through these past four years and more. Great Scott, it's been nothing but hell—hot hell—all the time! Four whole years of pretending I was just an ordinary friend of yours—hell! Four years of reasoning with myself—preaching to myself—hell! That awful month after Blundell left you—when you'd gone to Italy and I was in London—worse than hell! My chase after you—our little tour together—my struggle even then to play the correct game—and I *did* struggle—hell! And since then—hell! [*His elbows on his knees, digging his knuckles into his forehead.*] Hell all the time! Hell all the time!

[*There is a silence, and then, with a look of settled determination, she comes to him slowly and lays her hands upon his head.*]

Zoe. Poor boy! I'm sorry I blackguarded you. [*Sitting in the chair opposite to him and speaking in a steady, level voice.*] Len——

Leonard. Eh?

Zoe. Let's part.

Leonard. [*Raising his head.*] Part?

Zoe. Say good-by to each other. [*Meeting his eyes.*] Go back to that girl.

Leonard. To Ethel!

Zoe. Take up with her again.

Leonard. Oh, stop it, Zo.

Zoe. She's devoted to you; and she's sound right through, if ever a girl was. She's one of the best, Len.

Leonard. Suppose she *is*——

Zoe. Be careful that she doesn't guess I've given her away. [*He rises impatiently. She rises with him and holds him by the lapels of his jacket.*] Tell her—she's sure to ask you—tell her that you haven't seen me since last Monday, nor had a line from me. Fake up some tale to account for your breaking off with her—you were in doubt whether you'd coin enough to marry on——

Leonard. [*Who has become thoughtful.*] Zoe——

Zoe. Yes?

Leonard. [*Looking her full in the face.*] Are you giving me the boot?

Zoe. [*Releasing him and returning his gaze firmly.*] Yes; I am.

Leonard. [*After a pause.*] Oh? [*Another pause.*] What's your motive?

Zoe. Motive?

Leonard. What's behind all this?

Zoe. [*Simply.*] I want you to be happy, Len—really and truly happy. I believe you'd stand a jolly good chance of being so with Ethel Pierpoint; never with me.

Leonard. And *you*?

Zoe. I?

Leonard. What's to become of *you*? What are your plans for yourself?

Zoe. [*Avoiding his eyes.*] Oh, don't you—don't you worry about me.

Leonard. Rot!

Zoe. [*Nervously.*] Perhaps some day—when Theodore's tired of Mrs. Annerly—ha, ha!—stranger things have happened——

Leonard. Rot, I say. [*She retreats a little.*] Do you think you can drum me out like this! [*Following her.*] Have you got some other——? [*He checks himself.*]

Zoe. [*Confronting him.*] Some other——?

Leonard. Oh, never mind.

Zoe. Out with it!

Leonard. Some other fancy-man in tow?

Zoe. Ah! You brute! [*Hitting him in the chest.*] You brute! [*Throwing herself into the armchair near the glazed door.*] You coward! You coward!

[*There is a pause and then he slouches up to her.*]

Leonard. I—I beg your pardon. I beg your pardon. [*He sits beside her, upon the fauteuil-stool.*] Knock my damned head off. Go on. Knock my damned head off.

Zoe. [*Panting.*] Well—we won't part—on top of a row. [*Dashing a tear away.*] After all, why *should* you think better of me than that?

Leonard. [*Penitently.*] Zoe——

Zoe. Sssh! Listen. Putting Ethel Pierpoint out of the question, do you ever picture to yourself what our married life would be?

Leonard. What it 'ud be?

Zoe. The marriage of a woman of seven—nearly eight—and-thirty to a man of thirty-two! *I* do. I walk my bedroom half the night and act it all over to myself. And you've had the best of me, too; I'm not even a novelty to you. Why, of course you've realized what you've let yourself in for.

Leonard. I take my oath——

Zoe. Sssh! When you're in front of your glass in the morning, what do you see there?

Leonard. See?

Zoe. This girl has noticed the alteration in your looks. She took stock of you at the opera the other night.

Leonard. [*Passing his hands over his face consciously.*] Men can't go to hell, Zo, without getting a bit scorched.

Zoe. [*Imitating his action.*] No, nor women either. [*Turning to him.*] But it's only quite lately that you've lost your bloom, Len.

Leonard. Oh, naturally I've been horribly bothered about you—about both of us—since——

Zoe. Since your trip to Italy? [*He nods.*] Yes, and naturally you've told yourself, over and over again, the truth—since your trip to Italy.

Leonard. Truth?

Zoe. The simple truth—that you've got into a mess with a married woman——

Leonard. I—I——

Zoe. And that you must go through with it, at all costs.

Leonard. I swear to you, Zoe——

Zoe. [*Touching his hand.*] Oh, my dear boy, you haven't perhaps *said* these things to yourself, in so many words, but they're at the back of your brain just the same.

[*She rises and crosses to the fireplace and rings three times.*]

Leonard. [*Rising.*] What—what are you doing?

Zoe. Ringing for Lena, to tell her I'm not lunching downstairs.

Leonard. By God, Zoe——!

Zoe. [*Imperiously.*] Be quiet!

Leonard. [*Shaking his fist at her.*] You dare treat me in this way! You dare!

Zoe. [*Advancing.*] Ah, I'm only hurting your pride a little; I'm only mortifying your vanity. You'll get over that in twenty-four hours.

Leonard. Do you know what you *are*; do you know what you make yourself by this!

Zoe. Yes, what you made me at Perugia, and at Siena, and at ——! [*Suddenly, clinging to him.*] Lenny—Lenny—kiss me——!

Leonard. [*Pushing her from him.*] Not I.

Zoe. Ah, yes. Don't let's part enemies. It's good-by. Lenny!

Leonard. No.

Zoe. [*Struggling with him entreatingly.*] Quick! It's for the last time. You'll never be alone with me again. [*Her arms tightly around him.*] It's for the last time. [*Kissing him passionately.*] Good luck to you! Good luck to you! Good luck to you!

[*She leaves him and sits at the writing-table where she makes a pretense of busying herself with her papers.*]

Leonard. [*Glancing expectantly at the glazed door—between his teeth.*] You—you——!

[*Presently he goes to the chair on the right and snatches up his hat and cane.* LENA *enters at the glazed door.*]

Lena. [*To* ZOE.] Is it me you've rung for?

Zoe. Yes. [*Sharply.*] Wait.

[*There is a pause. Struck by* ZOE's *tone, and the attitude of the pair,* LENA *looks inquisitively at* LEONARD *and* ZOE *out of the corners of her eyes, as if she guesses there has been a quarrel.* LEONARD *moves toward the door.*]

Leonard. [*To* ZOE.] Good morning.

Zoe. Good morning.

Leonard. [*To* LENA, *as he passes her.*] Good morning.

Lena. Good morning.

[*He departs and* LENA *quietly closes the door.*]

Zoe. [*Rising.*] Lena——

Lena. Yes?

Zoe. [*Walking across to the settee on the right.*] I'm not coming down to the dining-room. [*Sitting, feebly.*] Let me have a snack upstairs.

Lena. Very well.

Zoe. That's all.

[LENA *withdraws, almost on tiptoe, and* ZOE *instantly produces her handkerchief and cries into it softly. Then she gets to her feet and searches for the cigarette box. Still shaken by little sobs, she puts a cigarette between her lips and, as she does so, the expression of her face changes and her body stiffens.*]

Zoe. [*Under her breath.*] Oh——! [*After a moment's resolution, she hurriedly dries her eyes and, going to the glazed door, opens it, and calls.*] Lena—Lena——!

Lena. [*In the distance.*] Yes?

[ZOE *returns to the oblong table and is lighting her cigarette when* LENA *reappears.*]

Zoe. Lena——

Lena. Well?

Zoe. I'll dress directly after lunch.

Lena. [*Coming to her, surprised.*] Dress?

Zoe. Yes; I'm going out this afternoon.

Lena. Going out! Why, you must be crazy——!

CURTAIN

THE THIRD ACT

SCENE.—*A fine, spacious room, richly furnished and decorated. In the center of the wall at the back is the fireplace, and on the left of the fireplace is a door which when open reveals part of a dining-room. In the right-hand wall there is a bay-window hung with lace and other curtains. Facing the window, in the wall on the left, is a double door opening into the room from a corridor.*

On either side of the fireplace there is an armchair, and between the fireplace and the dining-room door stands a small table on which are a decanter of whisky, a syphon of soda-water, and two or three tumblers. A grand piano and a music-stool are in the right-hand corner of the room, and on the left of the piano is a settee. Some photographs are on the top of the piano. On the other side of the room there is a second settee with a table at the nearer end of it. An armchair stands by this table, another at the farther end of the settee. In the bay-window there is a writing-table with a writing-chair before it, and on the writing-table is a telephone-instrument. Other articles of furniture, some pieces of sculpture, and some handsome lamps on pedestals, fill spaces not provided for in this description.

A scarf of mousseline de soie *and a pair of white gloves lie on the chair on the right of the fireplace.*

The fireless grate is hidden by a screen and, through the lace curtains, which are drawn over the window, a fierce sunlight is seen.

The door at the back is slightly ajar.

[*The telephone bell rings and presently* THEODORE BLUNDELL *enters at the door at the back, and goes to the writing-table. His step has become heavier, his shoulders are somewhat bent, and he looks a "bad color."*]

Theodore. [*At the telephone.*] Halloo! . . . Yes? . . . I *am* Mr. Blundell. . . . Oh, is that you, Peter? . . . What? . . . Want to see me? . . . Anything wrong? . . . Where are you? . . . Where? . . . Café Royal? . . . Come along to me now, then? . . . Oh, I say! . . . Are you there? . . . [*Dropping his voice.*] I say! Mrs. A. is lunching with me. . . . Mrs. A.—Alice. . . . No, but I thought I'd tell you. . . . Good-by.

[*He is about to return to the dining-room when* MRS. ANNERLY *appears in the doorway at the back. She is a pretty, charmingly dressed creature with classical, immobile features and a simple, virginal air.*]

Mrs. Annerly. [*Advancing.*] I've told Cole we'll have coffee in this room. [*He nods and sits moodily upon the settee on the right. Resting her elbows on the back of the armchair at the further end of the settee on the left, she surveys her face in a tiny mirror which she carries, with some other trinkets, attached to a chain.*] Who's that you were talking to on the 'phone, boy, dear?

Theodore. [*Who is smoking a big cigar.*] Mottram.

Mrs. Annerly. What's *he* want?

Theodore. Wants to see me about something.

Mrs. Annerly. Business?

Theodore. Dun'no.

Mrs. Annerly. [*Sweetly.*] He doesn't like poor little me.

Theodore. [*Indifferently.*] Doesn't he?

Mrs. Annerly. You know he doesn't. [*Arranging a curl.*] That's why you gave him the tip that I'm lunching here.

Theodore. Ho! Listeners—*et cetera.*

Mrs. Annerly. I couldn't help hearing you; positively I couldn't. [*Examining her teeth in the mirror.*] He's one of your wife's tame cats, isn't he?

Theodore. He's a friend of hers—yes.

Mrs. Annerly. *Just* a friend, and nothing else.

Theodore. [*Angrily.*] Now, look here, Alice——!

[COLE, *a man servant, enters from the dining-room with the coffee and liqueurs.* MRS. ANNERLY *takes a cup of coffee.*]

Cole. [*To* MRS. ANNERLY.] Brandy—Kümmel, ma'am?

Mrs. Annerly. No, thanks.

Theodore. [*To* COLE, *who comes to him with the tray—irritably.*] Leave it. [COLE *places the tray on the top of the piano and is returning to the dining-room.*] Cole——

Cole. Yessir?

Theodore. I'm expecting Mr. Mottram.

Cole. Very good, sir.

[*The* MAN *withdraws, closing the door.* THEODORE *rises and pours some brandy into a large liqueur-glass.*]

Mrs. Annerly. [*Who has seated herself upon the settee on the left.*] What's the matter with you today, boy, dear? You're as cross as two sticks.

Theodore. Liver.

Mrs. Annerly. [*Sipping her coffee.*] I don't wonder.

Theodore. Why?

Mrs. Annerly. You're getting rather too fond of—[*pointing to the brandy*]—h'm, h'm.

Theodore. [*Bluntly.*] It's false.

Mrs. Annerly. [*With undisturbed complacency.*] I've seen so much of that sort o' thing in my time. [*He makes a movement, as if to put down his glass without drinking.*] Still, I must say you've every excuse.

Theodore. Alice——

Mrs. Annerly. What?

[*He gulps his brandy, puts the empty glass on the tray, and comes to her.*]

Theodore. [*Standing before her.*] Alice, will you oblige me by refraining from making any allusion to my wife, direct or indirect, in the future? It annoys me.

Mrs. Annerly. Everything annoys you this afternoon.

Theodore. You were at it last night, at the Carlton. And today, during lunch——

Mrs. Annerly. [*In an injured tone.*] It was you who told me that that little Jew chap had met her careering about Italy with young what's-his-name. [*He sits in the armchair at the farther end of the settee and leans his head on his hand.*] Ah, but that was in your loving days—when you used to confide in me.

Theodore. I was in a rage and said a great deal more than I thought.

Mrs. Annerly. If you did, you needn't jump on me for trying to feel interested in you and your affairs.

Theodore. [*Facing her.*] At any rate, understand me clearly, Alice—and then drop the subject. [*Shortly.*] Mrs. Blundell and I are separated; she's gone one way, I another. There were faults on both sides, as usual, but I was mainly to blame. There's the thing in a nutshell.

Mrs. Annerly. This isn't in the least your old story.

Theodore. Never mind my old story. [*Extending a forefinger.*] *You* forget the old story, my girl, if you wish our acquaintance to continue—d'ye hear?

Mrs. Annerly. [*Shaking herself.*] You're a nasty savage.

Theodore. As for that interfering cad, Lowenstein, it unfortunately happens that one of Mrs. Blundell's characteristics is a habit of disregarding *les convenances*—a habit which I didn't go the right way to check. It's probable that, before she's done, she won't leave herself with as much reputation as 'ud cover a sixpence. She's impulsive, reckless, a fool—but she's no worse. [*Eyeing the stump of his cigar fiercely.*] My wife's no worse. So, hands off, if you please, in my presence. Whatever reports are circulated to her discredit, the man who speaks against her in my hearing is kicked for his pains; and the woman who does so, if she's under my roof, gets taken by the shoulders and shown the mat. [*Looking at her.*] *Comprenez?*

Mrs. Annerly. [*Pouting.*] I should be a juggins if I didn't. *Parfaitement*—in my very best French.

Theodore. [*Rising and walking about.*] That's settled, then.

Mrs. Annerly. [*After a pause, rising and depositing her cup upon the table on the left—thoughtfully.*] Boy, dear——

Theodore. [*At the back.*] Hey?

Mrs. Annerly. It was regular cat-and-dog between you two at the end, wasn't it?

Theodore. [*Breaking out again.*] It's no concern of yours whether it was or was not. I've asked you——

Mrs. Annerly. [*Crossing to the right, with a shrug.*] Oh——!

Theodore. Yes, it *was.* [*Half-sitting upon the back of the settee on the left.*] I—I tired of her.

Mrs. Annerly. [*Philosophically.*] Ah, men *do* tire.

Theodore. And she of me. We'd been married close upon fourteen years.

Mrs. Annerly. Oh, well, come; that's a long while.

Theodore. [*As much to himself as to her.*] Our wedding-day's on the thirtieth of this month. [*Hitting the back of the settee softly with his fist.*] We'd reached a time in our lives when—when we were in mid-Channel——

Mrs. Annerly. Mid-Channel?

Theodore. [*Rising.*] Oh, you don't know anything about that.

[*There is a further silence. She sits upon the settee on the right, watching him as he moves about the room again.*]

Mrs. Annerly. Here! [*Beckoning him with a motion of her head.*] Here! [*He goes to her. She looks up into his face.*] Why don't you marry *me*, Theo?

Theodore. [*Staring at her.*] Marry—you?

Mrs. Annerly. You'd find me awfully easy to get on with.

Theodore. [*Turning from her, quietly.*] Oh——!

Mrs. Annerly. Wait; you might listen, anyhow. [*He turns to her.*] I *am*—awfully easy to get on with. And I'd be as strict as—as strict as a nun. Honest Injun! I treated

Annerly pretty badly, but that's ancient history. I was only seventeen when I married Frank—too inexperienced for words. I've learned a lot since.

Theodore. [*Bitterly.*] Ha!

Mrs. Annerly. Now, don't be satirical. [*Inviting him to sit by her side.*] Theo—— [*He sits beside her.*] I say—bar chaff—I wish you *would.*

Theodore. [*Absently.*] What?

Mrs. Annerly. Marry me. Really I do. [*A note of wistfulness in her voice.*] I really do want to re-establish myself. My life, these past few years, has been frightfully unsatisfactory.

Theodore. [*Touching her dress, sympathetically.*] Ah!

Mrs. Annerly. And I'm a lady, remember—giddy as I may have been. Put me in any society and I'm presentable, as far as manners go. I'd soon right myself, with your assistance. [*Slipping her arm through his.*] I suppose, under the circumstances, you couldn't divorce *her*, could you?

Theodore. What d'ye mean?

Mrs. Annerly. Your wife—over that Italian business.

Theodore. [*Jumping up.*] Damn!

Mrs. Annerly. Oh, I beg your pardon; it slipped out. [*He walks away to the table at the back and begins to mix himself a whisky-and-soda.*] I'm dreadfully grieved; gospel, I am. [*Rising.*] Don't—don't, boy, dear. Do leave that stuff alone. [*He puts down the decanter and comes to the settee on the left.*] I can't do more than apologize.

Theodore. [*Sitting.*] Tsch! Hold your tongue.

Mrs. Annerly. [*Sitting beside him.*] No, but you could let *her* go for *you,* though; *that* could be fixed up. I'd even consent to be dragged into the case myself, if it would help matters forward; and goodness knows I've no ambition to appear in the divorce court again—I hate the hole. [*Coaxingly.*] You *will* consider it, won't you?

Theodore. Consider *what?*

Mrs. Annerly. Marrying me. Just say you'll consider it and I won't tease you any more today. You do owe me something, you know.

Theodore. Owe you——?

Mrs. Annerly. Well, you *have* compromised me by being seen about with me at different places lately; now, haven't you? [THEODORE *throws his head back and laughs boisterously.*] There's nothing to laugh at. Perhaps I haven't a shred of character left, in your estimation!

Theodore. Ho, ho!

Mrs. Annerly. [*Rising, piqued.*] I presume you think I'm a person who'll accept a dinner at a restaurant from any man who holds up a finger to me!

Theodore. Why, my dear girl, you were always bothering me to take you to the cook-shops.

Mrs. Annerly. Bothering. [*Going to the chair on the right of the fireplace and gathering up her scarf.*] Oh, you're too rude!

Theodore. I was perfectly content with our quiet little meals here or in Edgerton Crescent.

Mrs. Annerly. Yes, and to bore me to tears!

Theodore. Bore——?

Mrs. Annerly. [*Winding her scarf around her shoulders.*] Bore, bore, bore!

Theodore. [*Scowling.*] Oh, I—I bored you, did I?

Mrs. Annerly. Talking to me, as you used to, like a sentimental young fellow of five-and-twenty! Ridiculous! [*Picking up her gloves.*] I want a taxi-cab.

Theodore. [*Rising.*] Stop—stop——

Mrs. Annerly. I've had quite sufficient of you for today.

Theodore. [*With a set jaw.*] I'm glad you've brought matters to a head, Ally. I've something to propose to you.

Mrs. Annerly. [*Pulling on a glove.*] I've no desire to hear it.

Theodore. Something that's been on my mind for—oh, a month or more.

Mrs. Annerly. You can keep it to yourself. I'm not accustomed to being jeered at.

Theodore. [*Slowly walking over to the right.*] I'm sorry if I've hurt your feelings——

Mrs. Annerly. It's the first time I've ever made advances to a man, and I assure you it'll be the last.

Theodore. Ally——

Mrs. Annerly. [*Moving toward the double door.*] Cole will get me a taxi.

Theodore. [*Authoritatively.*] Come here; come here; come here.

Mrs. Annerly. [*Halting behind the settee on the left, with a twist of her body.*] I shall not.

Theodore. [*Snapping his finger and thumb.*] Ally—[*she approaches him with assumed reluctance*]—Ally—[*deliberately*]—what'll you take?

Mrs. Annerly. [*Elevating her brows.*] Take?

Theodore. To put an end to this.

Mrs. Annerly. An end!

Theodore. To end your boredom—and mine; terminate our—friendship.

Mrs. Annerly. [*Uncomfortably.*] Oh, you—you needn't cut up as rough as all this.

Theodore. Ah, no, no, no; I'm not angry. I'm in earnest, though. Come! What'll satisfy you? [*She curls her lip fretfully.*] A man of my years deserves to pay heavily at this game. What'll make you easy and comfortable for a bit? I'll be liberal with you, my dear, and—[*offering his hand*]—shake hands—[*she turns her shoulder to him*]—shake hands—[*she gives him her hand sulkily*]—and I—I'll ask you to forgive me——

Mrs. Annerly. [*Withdrawing her hand.*] Oh, for goodness' sake, don't let's have any more of *that.* [*Contemptuously.*] You elderlies always wind up in the same way.

[*He seats himself at the writing-table and, unlocking a drawer, produces his check-book.*]

Theodore. Would a couple of thousand be of any service to you?

Mrs. Annerly. [*Opening her eyes widely.*] A couple of——!

Theodore. [*Preparing to write.*] I mean it.

Mrs. Annerly. [*Breathlessly.*] You don't! [*He writes.*] Why, of course it would. [*Melting completely.*] Oh, but it's too much; it is positively. I *couldn't.* And I've had such a lot out of you already. You *are* generous. [*Behind his chair.*] Fancy my being huffy with you just now! [*Bending over him and arresting his pen.*] Boy, dear——

Theodore. Hey?

Mrs. Annerly. [*In a whisper.*] Make it—three—will you? [*He looks at her over his shoulder with a cynical smile. She retreats.*] Oh, well! One isn't young and attractive forever, you know.

[*He finishes writing the check and, having locked up his check-book methodically, rises and comes to her.*]

Theodore. [*Giving her the check.*] There you are.

Mrs. Annerly. [*Examining it.*] You—you've split the difference! You *are* kind. I didn't expect it in the least. [*Folding the check neatly and finding a place for it in her bosom.*] I *am* ashamed of myself for hinting so broadly. Thanks, a hundred times. [*Blinking at him.*] Shan't I miss you!

[COLE *enters at the double door followed by* PETER.]

Cole. Mr. Mottram.

Theodore. [*Greeting* PETER *at the fireplace as* COLE *retires.*] Hallo!

Peter. Hallo! [*Bowing to* MRS. ANNERLY.] How d'ye do?

Mrs. Annerly. [*Who has moved over to the right—distantly.*] How do you do?

Theodore. [*To* MRS. ANNERLY.] By-the-bye, did you say you want a taxi-cab?

Mrs. Annerly. If I'm not troubling you.

[THEODORE *goes out at the double door, closing it upon* PETER *and* MRS. ANNERLY. *There is a pause.* MRS. ANNERLY *pulling on her second glove, looks out of the window;* PETER *whistles silently.*]

Peter. [*After a while.*] Fine afternoon.

Mrs. Annerly. Delightful. [*After another pause, turning to him.*] Er—h'm—how do you think he's looking?

Peter. Blundell? Seen him looking better.

Mrs. Annerly. [*With a sigh.*] Ah! [*In a mincing voice, approaching* PETER.] Mr. Mottram, will you excuse me for offering a suggestion?

Peter. [*Politely.*] Fire away.

Mrs. Annerly. [*Sweetly.*] Why don't you use your endeavors to bring Blundell and his wife together again?

Peter. [*Staring at her.*] Eh?

Mrs. Annerly. It would be *such* a good thing, wouldn't it?

Peter. I agree with you; it would indeed.

Mrs. Annerly. I've done all *I* can to persuade him. [PETER's *eyes open wider and wider. She busies herself daintily with her glove.*] And now, as he and I are breaking off with one another——

Peter. [*Quickly.*] I beg pardon?

Mrs. Annerly. Perhaps *you'll* take on the job—see what *you* can do.

Peter. Breaking off——?

Mrs. Annerly. [*Loftily.*] Yes; I can't stand the annoyance any longer.

Peter. Annoyance?

Mrs. Annerly. People are so spiteful. It's shocking—the ill-natured construction they put upon the most harmless little friendly acts! I admit I'm rather a careless woman—haven't I suffered from it!——

Peter. [*Delicately.*] Then, do I happen—may I ask—to be assistin' at the grand *finale*——?

Mrs. Annerly. Certainly—[*with sudden mistrust.*] Don't you try to pull my leg, Mr. Mottram, please.

[*She draws her skirt aside and passes him haughtily as* THEODORE *returns. Then she goes out, followed by* THEODORE, *who closes the door; whereupon* PETER *skips to the pano, seats himself at it, and strikes up a lively air. Presently* THEODORE *reappears, shuts the door again and resumes mixing his whisky-and-soda.*]

Theodore. Ouf! [PETER *takes his hands from the keyboard.*] That's over.

Peter. [*Innocently.*] Over?

Theodore. You've seen the last of that lady, as far as I'm concerned. [*He comes forward, carrying his tumbler, as* PETER *rises.*] What d'ye think? [*Grinning.*] She's been at me to marry her.

Peter. [*Startled.*] Not really!

Theodore. To get rid of—present ties, and marry her.

Peter. When—when did she——?

Theodore. Just now—five minutes ago. [*Struck by an odd expression on* PETER'S *face.*] Why, has she been saying anything——?

Peter. [*Soberly.*] No, no; not a word.

Theodore. Poor little devil! [*He sits upon the settee on the left and drinks.*] Poor—silly—little devil!

Peter. [*Coming to him.*] And so you took the opportunity of—er——? [THEODORE *nods.*] Just so.

Theodore. Ha! I expect I shall hear from her from time to time.

Peter. Till the end o' your life. [*Another nod from* THEODORE.] Or hers. And the nearer the end the oftener you'll hear.

Theodore. Well, she shall have a trifle whenever she wants it. [*Looking at* PETER.] That's the least we can do, ol' man.

Peter. Decidedly. That's the least we can do.

Theodore. [*Emptying his tumbler and jumping up.*] Ugh! [*Placing the glass upon the table at the end of the settee.*] I'll burn some pastilles here later on. [*Confronting* PETER.] Yes, you can have your crow; you're entitled to it.

Peter. Crow?

Theodore. Your crow over me. Everything's turned out as you predicted.

Peter. [*Demurely.*] Did *I*——?

Theodore. You know you did. "It's when the sun's working round to the west"—I often recall your damned words——

Peter. Ah, that day——

Theodore. The day I left Lancaster Gate. "It's when men are where we are now"—you remember?—"It's when men are where we are now that they're most liable to fall into mischief." [*Walking away.*] God! the idiot I've made of myself!

[*He goes to the fireplace and leans upon the mantelpiece.*]

Peter. [*Quietly.*] Theo——

Theodore. H'm?

Peter. [*Moving to the settee on the left.*] Talkin' of Lancaster Gate—I've got a bit o' noos for you. [*Sitting upon the settee.*] She's home. [*There is no response from* THEODORE.] Zoe I'm speakin' of. She's home.

Theodore. [*Leaving the fireplace.*] Thank-'ee; I know.

Peter. You know?

Theodore. I was there on Monday.

Peter. [*Surprised.*] There?

Theodore. Passing the house.

Peter. Signs o' life in the winders?

Theodore. [*Nodding.*] H'm. [*Coming forward.*] You've seen her?

Peter. This mornin'.

Theodore. [*Simply.*] *I* was there again this morning.

Peter. Passin' the house?

Theodore. [*Nodding.*] H'm.

Peter. You seem to take a great deal of exercise in that locality.

Theodore. [*Forcing a laugh.*] Ha, ha! [*Drearily.*] Well, one had good times there as well as bad; and when one views it all from a distance——

Peter. The good times stand out?

[*Without replying,* THEODORE *turns from* PETER *and sits upon the settee on the right.*]

Theodore. [*After a pause.*] How—how did you find her?

Peter. She ain't up to much.

Theodore. What's——?

Peter. Chill.

Theodore. Doctor? [PETER *nods.*] Rashleigh?

Peter. That's the fellow. Oh, it's nothin' serious.

Theodore. Chill? Ha! I'll be bound she caught it through doing something foolish. [*Fidgeting with his hands.*] She has nobody to look after her—nobody to look after her.

Peter. Her maid——

Theodore. Lena? Is Lena still with her? [*A nod from* PETER.] I'm glad Lena's still with her. Lena's fond of her. [*Starting up and pacing the room.*] Not that Lena can control her; a maid hasn't any authority. [*Stopping before* PETER.] She isn't *very* poorly?

Peter. No, no. A little pulled down; that's all. And as charmin' as ever. [THEODORE *walks away and, with his hands in his pockets, gazes out of the window.*] She ain't sleepin'; that's the real bother.

Theodore. Not sleeping?

Peter. Walks her room half the night and consooms too many cigarettes.

Theodore. Why?

Peter. I can only give you my impression——

Theodore. [*Impatiently.*] Well?

Peter. My dear chap, d'ye think that *she* don't recollect the happy times as well as the bad 'uns? Ain't *she* viewin' it all from a distance, as you are; [*rising*] and don't the good times stand out in *her* mind as they do in yours? [*Approaching* THEODORE.] Theo——

Theodore. H'm?

Peter. I had a long confab with her this mornin'.

Theodore. What about?

Peter. The possibility of a—a reconciliation.

[*There is a pause and then* THEODORE *turns to* PETER.]

Theodore. [*In a husky voice.*] Ho! So that's what you're after, is it?

Peter. Yes; and I'm bent on carryin' it through.

Theodore. You—you meddlesome old buffer!

Peter. [*Chuckling.*] Ha, ha!

Theodore. How—how did she take it?

Peter. In a way that convinced me you've only to assure her that your old feelin's for her have returned, and in spite of everythin'——

Theodore. Everything! Wait till she hears of sweet Alice.

Peter. *Wait!*

Theodore. [*Looking at* PETER.] Why, d'ye mean——?

Peter. Oh, yes; it's got to her.

Theodore. [*Dully.*] Already?

Peter. Jim Mallandain traveled with her from Paris on Sunday.

Theodore. Did *he*——?

Peter. I suppose he thought it 'ud amuse her.

Theodore. The skunk!

Peter. If it hadn't been Jim, it 'ud have been somebody else.

Theodore. [*Thickly.*] You're right; somebody had to be first.

Peter. However, I did my best for yer.

Theodore. Denied it?

Peter. Warmly. I defended you and the young lady with all the eloquence I could command.

Theodore. Zoe didn't believe you?- [*A pause.*] She didn't believe you? [PETER *shrugs his shoulders.*] Of course she didn't. [*Passing* PETER *and walking about the room.*] What did she say? Hey? Oh, I can guess; you needn't tell me. What's everybody saying? Peter, I'd give half as much as I'm worth to wipe the Annerly incident off my slate. I would, on the nail. Just fancy! To reach my age—and to be of decent repute—and then to have your name linked with a brainless, mercenary little trull like Alice Annerly! Ha, ha! Glorious fun for 'em in the City, and at the club! *You* hear it all. Confound you, can't you open your mouth! Ho! *Of course* Zoe sums it all up; she's cute enough when she chooses. [*Sitting upon the settee on the left and mopping his face and throat with his handkerchief.*] How did it end?

Peter. End?

Theodore. Your chat with my missus.

Peter. It ended in my urgin' her to consider the matter—think it over. [*Coming to him.*] I'm dinin' with her next week. [*Sitting in the chair at the further end of the settee.*] If you'll authorize me to open negotiations with her on your behalf——

Theodore. I—I approach her!

Peter. Cert'nly.

Theodore. [*Twisting his handkerchief into a rope.*] No—no——

Peter. Why not?

Theodore. A couple o' months back I could have done it. Even as late as a fortnight ago —before I'd given myself away by showing myself in public with Alice—it might have been feasible. [*Between his teeth.*] But now —when I—when I've lost any remnant of claim I may have had—on her respect——!

Peter. [*In his judicial manner.*] My dear chap, here is a case——

Theodore. Hell with you and your case! [*Jumping up and walking away to the right.*] I couldn't screw myself up to it; I—I couldn't humble myself to that extent. [*Moving about.*] Ho! How she'd grin! She's got a cruel sense o' humor, Peter—or had once. You see, I always posed to her as being a *strong,* rather cold-blooded man——

Peter. A favorite pose, that, of husbands.

Theodore. It was more than a pose—I thought I *was* a strong man. And then—to crawl back to her—all over mud——!

[*He halts in the middle of the room and, with a shaky hand, produces his cigar-case from his pocket and takes out a cigar.*]

Peter. I was about to remark, when you chipped in with your usual politeness—I was about to remark that this is a case where *two* persons have behaved more or less stoopidly.

Theodore. Two——?

Peter. You more, she less.

Theodore. [*His brow darkening.*] You—you're referring to——?

Peter. Er—Mrs. Zoe——

Theodore. [*Cutting his cigar viciously.*] With—Ferris.

Peter. Yes; and I think that the friend of both parties—the individual on whose shoulders the task of adjustin' matters would fall —[*rising*]—I think that that friend might manage to impose a condition which 'ud be greatly to your advantage.

Theodore. Condition?

Peter. No imputations to be made on either side.

Theodore. [*Broodingly.*] No—imputations——?

Peter. Each party acceptin' the statement of the other party, and promisin' not to rake up anythin' that's occurred durin' the past four months.

Theodore. I—I understand.

Peter. It 'ud help to save your face for the moment, and the healin' hand of time might be trusted to do the rest.

Theodore. [*Quietly.*] Peter——

Peter. Hallo!

Theodore. When I was at the house on Monday—my wife's house—half-past eleven in the morning——

Peter. Well?

Theodore. There was a yellow car at the door.

Peter. Yaller car?

Theodore. I couldn't get near, but—that fellow has a yellow car.

Peter. Has he?

Theodore. [*Grimly.*] Why, he's driven you in it.

Peter. [*Carelessly.*] I'd forgotten.

Theodore. [*Looking at* PETER.] He's still hanging on to her skirts, hey?

Peter. He's an ill-bred, tactless cub. But he's got a nice 'ead of 'air and smells o' soap; and that's the sort women love to have danglin' about after 'em.

Theodore. [*With an effort.*] There—there's nothing in it, Peter, beyond that?

Peter. [*Waving his hand disdainfully.*] Good God!

Theodore. Oh, I know there isn't; I know there isn't. With all her faults, I know she's as straight as a die. [*Looking at* PETER *again.*] Did you touch on the subject with her?

Peter. [*Nodding.*] I rubbed it in. I told her her conduct had been indiscreet to a degree. I thought it policy to rub it in.

Theodore. Did she—offer any explanation?

Peter. [*Nodding.*] Pure thoughtlessness.

Theodore. And you felt that she was—speaking the truth?

Peter. [*Testily.*] My dear Theodore——

Theodore. You swear that? [*Suddenly, grasping the lapel of* PETER'S *coat.*] Damn it, man, *you* began talking about the thing——!

[COLE *enters at the double door carrying a note in the shape of a cocked hat.*]

Theodore. [*Angrily.*] What d'ye want?

Cole. I beg your pardon, sir.

Theodore. [*Going to him.*] Hey?

[*He snatches the note from the man and, as he glances at the writing on it his jaw drops.*]

Cole. [*In a low voice.*] An answer, sir?

Theodore. [*Trying to unfold the note.*] Messenger?

Cole. The lady herself, I think, sir.

[*There is a pause, and then* THEODORE *slowly gets the note open and reads it.*]

Theodore. [*To* COLE.] Where——?

Cole. In the smoking room, sir.

Theodore. Er—wait.

Cole. Yessir. [COLE *withdraws.*]

Theodore. [*To* PETER, *who has wandered away.*] Peter——

[PETER *comes to him and* THEODORE *hands him the note.* PETER'S *eyes bolt as he recognizes the handwriting.*]

Peter. [*Reading the note.*] "Will you see me?" Short—[*examining both sides of the paper and then returning the note to* THEODORE]—sweet.

Theodore. [*Chewing his unlighted cigar.*] This is your doing.

Peter. [*Beaming.*] I flatter myself it must be. [*Laying a hand on* THEODORE'S *shoulder.*] My dear Theo, this puts a noo aspect on the affair—clears the air.

Theodore. New aspect——?

Peter. She makes the first advances, dear kind soul as she is. [*A pause.*] Shall I—fetch her in?

Theodore. Hold hard, hold hard; don't be in such a devil of a hurry.

[*He leaves* PETER *and seats himself in a heap in the chair on the right of the fireplace.* PETER *moves softly to the double door.*]

Peter. [*His hand on the door-handle—to* THEODORE.] *May* I?

[THEODORE *raises his head and nods.* PETER *goes out. As the door closes* THEODORE *gets to his feet and flings his cigar into the grate. Then, hastily, he proceeds to put the room in order, closing the piano and beating out and rearranging the pillows on the settees. Finally, he comes upon* MRS. ANNERLY'S *empty coffee cup, picks it up, and vanishes with it into the dining-room. After a little while, the double door opens and* PETER *returns. He glances around the room, looks surprised at not finding* THEODORE *and, with a motion of the head, invites* ZOE *to enter. Presently she appears, beautifully dressed. She also looks around; and, passing* PETER, *she moves tremblingly to the fireplace. He closes the door and joins her.*]

Peter. [*To* ZOE.] You're a brick to do this.

Zoe. [*Almost inaudibly.*] Am I?

Peter. You'll never regret it.

Zoe. [*Clutching* PETER'S *arm.*] He will be —kind to me?

Peter. As kind as you are to him.

Zoe. [*Drawing a deep breath.*] Ah! [*She sits upon the settee on the right and her eyes roam about the room.*] What a ripping flat!

Peter. [*Disparagingly.*] Oh, I dun'no.

Zoe. [*With a wry mouth, plaintively.*] He *has* been doing himself jolly well, in all conscience.

[*The dining-room door opens and* THEODORE *appears. He shuts the door and edges toward* PETER, *who leads him to* ZOE.]

Peter. My dear old pals——

[ZOE *gets to her feet and* THEODORE *awkwardly hold out his hand to her.*]

Theodore. How are you, Zoe?

Zoe. Fairly—thanks——

[*She hurriedly produces her handkerchief from a gold bag hanging from her wrist and moves away to the left. There she sits upon the settee, struggling to command herself.* PETER *gives* THEODORE'S *arm a friendly grip and makes for the double door. As he passes behind the settee on which* ZOE *is seated, he stops to pat her shoulder.*]

Zoe. [*In a whisper, seizing his hand.*] Don't go, Peter; don't go.

[*He releases his hand, giving hers a reassuring squeeze, and goes to the door.*]

Peter. [*At the door, to* THEODORE.] I shall be in the City till six.

[*He departs. After a silence,* THEODORE *approaches* ZOE. *They carefully avoid meeting each other's eyes.*]

Theodore. It—it's very good of you, Zo, to—to hunt me up.

Zoe. I—I went first to Copthall Court. [*Wiping a tear from her cheek.*] I—I thought I should find you there.

Theodore. I—I haven't been at all regular at the office lately. [*A pause. They look about the room in opposite directions.*] Er—Peter tells me he had a little talk with you this morning.

Zoe. Y-yes.

Theodore. About our—being reconciled.

Zoe. Yes.

Theodore. W-well? [*She puts her handkerchief away and takes from her bag a torn envelope with some inclosures. She gives it to him timidly and he extracts from the envelope a letter and a key.*] The—the damned cruel letter I left behind me—that evening—with my latch-key. [*She inclines her head.*] May I—destroy it?

[*She nods assent, and he tears up the envelope and letter and crams the pieces into his trouser-pocket.*]

Theodore. [*Looking at the key.*] The—the key——?

Zoe. It—it's yours again—if you like.

Theodore. You—you're willing——? [*Again she inclines her head, and he puts the key into a pocket in his waistcoat and seats himself humbly in the chair at the farther end of the settee.*] Thank'ee. [*After a pause.*] Zo——

Zoe. Yes?

Theodore. [*Turning to her but not lifting his eyes.*] Look here. I'm not going to—try to deceive you. I—I want you to understand exactly what you're offering to take back.

Zoe. Exactly——?

Theodore. I gather from Peter that you came over from Paris on Sunday in the company of Mr. Jim Mallandain.

Zoe. I picked him up by chance at the Gare du Nord.

Theodore. And Mr. Jim whiled away the journey by—by gossiping to you about me and—a woman of the name of Annerly?

Zoe. On the boat.

Theodore. Quite so. [*A pause.*] When you mentioned the matter to Peter, he produced the whitewash bucket, didn't he?

Zoe. Slapped it on thick.

Theodore. [*Looking at her from under his brows.*] But you didn't——? [*She shakes her head.*] You're right; Peter's a liar. It's a true bill. I wish it wasn't; but it is.

Zoe. [*After a pause, steadily.*] Well?

Theodore. [*Looking at her again.*] Are you prepared to forgive me that too, then? [*She nods, but with compressed lips. He bows his head.*] Anyhow, I'm easier for making a clean breast of it.

Zoe. How—how did you—come to——?

Theodore. Lower myself with this hussy? [*Looking up.*] Isn't it all of a piece? Isn't it the natural finish of the mistakes of the last year or so—the errors we've committed since we began kicking each other's shins? [*Quickly.*] Oh, I'm not reproaching you now for your share o' the transaction. It was my job—the husband's job—to be patient with you; to smooth you down gently, and to wait. But instead of doing that, I let my mind dwell on my own grievances; with the result that latterly the one being in the world I envied was the fellow who'd kept his liberty, or who'd had the pluck to knock off the shackles. [*Rising and walking about, gathering his thoughts as he proceeds.*] Well, I got my freedom at last, didn't I! And a nice mess I made of it. I started by taking a furnished lodging in St. James's Street—sky-high, quiet, *peaceful!* Ha! Hardly a fortnight was out before I had blue-devils and was groaning to myself at the very state of things I'd been longing for. Why should I be condemned, I said to myself—why should I be condemned to an infernal dull life while others around me were enjoying themselves like fighting-cocks! And just then this flat was offered to me as it stands; and in less than a month after I'd slammed the front door at Lancaster Gate I was giving a dinner-party here—a housewarming—[*halting at the window, his back to* ZOE]—a dinner-party to four-and-twenty people, and not all of 'em men.

Zoe. [*In a low voice.*] I heard of your setting up here while I was—in Florence—[*clenching her hands*]—in Florence.

Theodore. [*Resuming his walk.*] However, so far it was nothing but folly on my part—egregious folly. And so it continued till I—till I had the honor of being introduced to Mrs. Annerly at a supper at Jack Poncerot's. [*Eyeing* ZOE *askance.*] I won't give you the details of the pretty story; your imagination'll supply those—the heading o' the chapters, at any rate. Chapter One, Conceit—I had the besotted vanity to fancy she—she liked me and was genuinely sympathetic toward me; [*at the mantelpiece, looking down into the grate*] and so on to Chapter the Last—the chapter with the inevitable title—Disgust—Loathing——!

Zoe. [*Thoughtfully.*] You—you're sure you've reached the—the final chapter?

Theodore. [*Turning to her.*] Heavens, yes! [*Shaking himself.*] It's all over. I've paid her off—today, as it happens. I've been itching to do it; and I've done it. [*Sitting upon the settee on the right.*] Another month of her society, and I believe I'd have gone to the dogs completely. [*His elbows on his knees, holding his head.*] Zo——

Zoe. Eh?

Theodore. Peter says you're walking your room half the night and smoking your nerves raw.

Zoe. Does he? He needn't have repeated——

Theodore. Zo, I've been walking this horrible flat in the same way. *I* can't get to bed till I hear the rattle of the milk-carts. And *I'm* smoking too much—and—not only *that*——

Zoe. [*Looking at him for the first time.*] Not only *what?*

Theodore. Well, a man doesn't smoke till four or five o'clock in the morning on cocoa, does he?

[*There is a moment's silence, and then she rises and goes to him.*]

Zoe. Oh—Theo——!

Theodore. [*Looking up at her.*] So your liberty hasn't made you over happy, either, has it, old girl?

Zoe. [*Faintly.*] No.

Theodore. You've been thinking, too, of the good times we've had together, hey?

Zoe. Y-yes. [*He rises and places his hands upon her shoulders yearningly as if about to draw her to him. She shrinks from him with a startled look.*] Theo——

Theodore. [*Dropping his hands.*] What?

Zoe. [*Nervously.*] There—there's one thing I—I want to say to you—before we—before we go further——

Theodore. [*Feeling the rebuff.*] H'm?

Zoe. As I've told you, I'm willing that you should return to Lancaster Gate. You may return as soon as you please; but——

Theodore. But?

Zoe. It must be—simply as a companion, Theo; a friend.

Theodore. [*Stiffly.*] A friend?

Zoe. [*With a slight shrug.*] Not that we've been much else to each other these last few years—except enemies. Still——

Theodore. [*Frowning.*] You wish to make it perfectly clear.

Zoe. Yes.

Theodore. [*After a pause, icily.*] I beg your pardon. I was forgetting myself just now. Thanks for the reminder. [*Walking away from her.*] Oh, I know you can feel only the most utter contempt for me—wholesale contempt.

Zoe. [*Entreatingly.*] Ah, no; don't take that tone.

Theodore. Stand the naughty boy in the corner; he's earned any amount of humiliation you choose to inflict.

Zoe. You shall never be humiliated by me, Theo.

Theodore. [*Throwing himself upon the settee on the left.*] Evidently!

Zoe. [*Turning away.*] Oh, for God's sake, don't let's begin fighting again. [*Sitting on the settee on the right.*] Don't let's do that.

Theodore. Ha, ha! No, no; we won't squabble. Right you are; I accept the terms—*any* terms. [*Lying at full length upon his back on the settee.*] As you say, we've been little more than friends of late years—good friends or bad. [*Throwing one leg over the other.*] It's your laying down the law so emphatically that riled me. Sorry I growled. [*There is silence between them. She watches him guiltily. Suddenly he changes the position of his legs.*] Zo——

Zoe. Yes?

Theodore. [*Gazing at the ceiling.*] At the same time, I'm blessed if I wouldn't rather you wanted to tear my eyes out than that you should treat me in this lofty, condescending style—scratch my face and tear my eyes out.

Zoe. Well, I—I don't, you see.

Theodore. [*Smiling unpleasantly.*] Alice Annerly's an extremely handsome creature, my dear, whatever else she may be.

Zoe. I'm—I'm sure of it.

Theodore. Her photo's on the top of the piano.

Zoe. [*Restraining an impulse to glance over her shoulder.*] I—I'm not curious.

Theodore. Ho! You mayn't be aware of the fact, but I've paid you the compliment of resenting the deep devotion your pet poodle—Master Lenny Ferris—has been paying you recently. You might do me a similar honor. [*Meditatively.*] Master—blooming—Lenny——! [*Again there is a pause; and then, slowly, he turns upon his side so that he may face her.*] I say, that was a pretty disgraceful business—your trapesing about Italy with that fellow. [*Another pause.*] Hey?

Zoe. [*Holding her breath.*] It *was*—unwise of me, I own.

Theodore. Unwise! Peter and I were discussing it when your note was brought in.

Zoe. [*Moistening her lips.*] Were you?

Theodore. [*Harshly.*] Yes, we were. [*Another pause.*] My God, I think it's *I* who ought to dictate what our domestic arrangements are to be in the future—not you! [*A pause. With a motion of the head, he invites her to come to him.*] Zoe—— [*A pause.*] Don't you hear me!

[*She hesitates; then she nerves herself and rises and, with a light step, crosses the room.*]

Zoe. [*Resting her arms on the back of the chair at the farther end of the settee on which he is lying.*] Still the same dear old bully, I notice.

Theodore. Sit down.

Zoe. Your gentle voice is quite audible where I am.

Theodore. [*Putting his feet to the ground.*] You sit down a minute.

Zoe. Puh! [*She sits haughtily.*]

Theodore. Now, you look here, my lady; I should like an account of that Italian affair from the word go.

Zoe. I'm not in the mood to furnish it.

Theodore. Perhaps not; but I'm in the mood to receive it. [*A pause.*] When did he join you?

Zoe. He—he didn't join me; that's not the way to put it.

Theodore. Put it any way you like. When was it?

Zoe. At the—end of February, I think.

Theodore. You think! [*A pause.*] What made him go out to you?

Zoe. He knew I was awfully in the dumps——

Theodore. Did he? How did he know that?

Zoe. He—guessed I must be.

Theodore. Guessed!

Zoe. Well, I'd seen him before I went away. I *was* dreadfully depressed. Theo—dreadfully *désolée*. I never thought you'd bang out of the house as you did. I never meant, for a single moment——

Theodore. Where were you when he turned up?

Zoe. I—I'd got to Florence. I'd been to Genoa and Pisa—I was drifting about——

Theodore. Did he dream you were in Florence?

Zoe. Dream——?

Theodore. He *must* have dreamt it.

Zoe. Oh, I see what you're driving at. He—he'd had a post-card from me——

Theodore. *A* post-card!

Zoe. [*Feebly.*] I—I don't mean *one*—you—you silly! I—I sent him a picture from each town—so I did to Peter——

Theodore. Why don't you admit that you and Ferris were corresponding?

Zoe. I—I am admitting it. It's nothing to admit.

Theodore. Isn't it? [*A pause.*] Well, he arrives in Florence——

Zoe. Don't worry me this afternoon, Theo——

Theodore. How long was he with you in Florence?

Zoe. I'm seedy; I had quite a temperature yesterday. Lena called in Rashleigh——

Theodore. How long was he with you in Florence?

Zoe. He wasn't "with" me.

Theodore. How long?

Zoe. A week—eight days——

Theodore. Same hotel?

Zoe. No, no, no!

Theodore. And afterward——?

Zoe. I wanted to do a little tour of the quiet old places—Perugia—Siena——

Theodore. So did *he*, hey?

Zoe. He tacked on. I saw no harm in it at the time.

Theodore. At the time!

Zoe. Nor do I now.

Theodore. It was coming from Perugia you fell up against Lowenstein.

Zoe. If you were a man you'd thrash that beast.

Theodore. Lowenstein had the room at the hotel there—the Brufani—that Ferris had had.

Zoe. [*Protestingly.*] Ah——!

Theodore. In the same corridor as yours was.

Zoe. It was stupid—stupid—stupid of Lenny to let them carry his bag up to the Brufani. It was all done before—before it dawned on him——

Theodore. Where were you moving on to when Lowenstein met you at Arezzo? [*A pause.*] Hey?

Zoe. [*Passing her hand across her brow, weakly.*] Let me off today, Theo; my head's going like a clock. [*Getting to her feet.*] Take it up again another time. [*She goes to the settee on the right and picks up her bag which she has left there. He rises and follows her, so that when she turns they come face to face. She steadies herself.*] Well, you turn it over in your mind about coming back to me. I don't want to put pressure on you; only I—I understood from Peter you were feeling kindly toward me again.

Theodore. [*Quietly.*] When did you see Ferris last?

Zoe. Oh, drop Ferris.

Theodore. When?

Zoe. Oh—over two months ago—at the end of the little jaunt.

Theodore. Not since? [*She looks at him vacantly and shakes her head.*] That's a lie. He was with you on Monday morning at half-past eleven. D'ye deny it?

Zoe. You—you're so jealous, one—one's afraid——

Theodore. [*With sudden, fierce earnestness.*] Zoe——

Zoe. [*Helplessly.*] I'm not going to remain here to be——

Theodore. Give me your word nothing wrong's occurred between you and Ferris. [*A pause.*] I don't ask for your oath; I'll be satisfied with your word. [*A pause.*] Give me your word.

[*She sits upon the settee, her hands lying in her lap.*]

Zoe. [*Staring at him.*] Theo—I've forgiven you; forgive me.

[*There is a silence and then, dumbfounded, he moves to the chair at the further end of the settee on the left and sits there.*]

Theodore. [*After a while.*] Florence?

Zoe. No. Perugia—Siena—— [*Brokenly.*] It was in Florence I first lost my senses. I'd been pitying you, hating myself for the way I'd served you, and had been trying to concoct a letter to you. And then one arrived from *him,* telling me you'd taken this big flat and were having a splendid time. It made me furious; and when he came through to me, I was half beside myself. And then he planned out the little tour, and I said Yes to it. [*Wringing her hands.*] Why! Why did I fall in with it! I shall never know why—except that I was mad—blind mad——! [*Leaning back, her eyes closed.*] Get me a drop o' water.

[*He rouses himself and goes to the table on the left of the fireplace and half fills a tumbler with soda-water. Then he brings her the tumbler and holds it out to her.*]

Theodore. Here——

Zoe. [*Opening her eyes and looking up at him beseechingly.*] Be—merciful to me.

Theodore. [*Peremptorily.*] Take it.

Zoe. [*Barely touching the glass.*] Don't—don't be hard on me, old man.

[*He thrusts the tumbler into her hand and she drinks.*]

Theodore. [*Heavily.*] I—I must have some advice about this—some advice.

Zoe. Advice? [*He goes to the writing-table, sits there, and places the telephone receiver to his ear.*] You—you won't do anything to disgrace me publicly, will you, Theo? [*He taps the arm of the instrument impatiently.*] You won't do anything spiteful? [*He rings again.*] You and I are both sinners, Theo; we've both gone a mucker.

Theodore. [*Speaking into the telephone.*] London Wall, one, three, double five, eight.

Zoe. That's Peter. *He* won't advise you to do anything spiteful. [*She rises painfully, puts the tumbler on the top of the piano, and walks about the room.*] What *can* you do? You can do nothing to hurt me; nor I you. We're both sinners.

Theodore. [*Into the telephone.*] Hallo! . . . Are you Blundell, Slade, and Mottram? . . . Is that Mr. Ewart? . . . Mr. Blundell. . . . Mr. Mottram not back yet, I suppose? . . .

Zoe. [*In a murmur.*] Both—both gone a mucker.

Theodore. [*Into the telephone.*] . . . When he comes in, tell him I want to see him at once. . . . Cavendish Square . . . at once. . . . [*Replacing the receiver.*] Good-by.

Zoe. [*On the left.*] Peter—Peter won't let you—be too rough on me.

Theodore. [*Leaning his head on his hands.*] Ho, ho! An eye-opener for Peter! But he's been a first-rate prophet all the same. [*In a muffled voice.*] Yes, Peter's been right all along the line, with his precious mid-Channel!

Zoe. [*Looking at him and speaking in low, measured tones.*] Theo—— [*He makes no response.*] Theo—— [*Coming to him slowly.*] I—I was thinking it over—beating it all out—driving into the city and back again. *Our* marriage was doomed long, long before we reached mid-Channel.

Theodore. [*Absently, not stirring.*] Oh?

Zoe. It was doomed nearly fourteen years ago.

Theodore. [*As before.*] Oh?

Zoe. From the very beginning.

Theodore. [*Raising his head.*] What d'ye——?

Zoe. It was doomed from the moment we agreed that we'd never be encumbered in our career with any—brats of children. [*He partly turns in his chair, to listen to her.*] I want you to remember that bargain, in judging me; and I want you to tell Peter of it.

Theodore. Yes, it suits you to rake that up now——

Zoe. [*Pressing her fingers to her temples.*] If there had been "brats of children" at home, it would have made a different woman of me, Theo; such a different woman of me—and a different man of you. But, no; everything in the earlier years of our marriage was sacrificed to coining money—to shoving our way through the crowd—to "getting on"; everything was sacrificed to that.

Theodore. [*Angrily.*] Oh——!

Zoe. And then, when we had succeeded—when we had *got* on—we had commenced to draw apart from each other; and there was the great, showy, empty house at Lancaster Gate for me to fret and pine in. [*He waves his arm scornfully.*] Oh, yes, we were happy in those climbing days—greedily, feverishly happy; but we didn't look to the time when we should need another interest in life to bind us together—the time when we'd got on in years as well as in position. [THEODORE *starts up.*] Ah, Theo, I believe we should have crossed that Ridge safely enough [*laying her hands upon his breast*] but for our cursed, cursed selfishness——!

Theodore. [*Shaking himself free.*] Well, there's not the slightest use in talking about what might, or might not, have been. [*Passing her and pacing the room.*] One thing is absolutely certain—it's impossible for us ever to live under the same roof again under *any* conditions. That's out o' the question; I couldn't stoop to that.

Zoe. [*Leaning against the chair at the writing-table.*] No, you draw the line at stooping to Mrs. Annerly.

Theodore. Oh, don't keep on harping on that string. The cases are as far apart as the poles.

Zoe. [*Faintly.*] Ha, ha!

Theodore. [*Halting in the middle of the room and drumming upon his brow with his fingers.*] Of course, we can make our separation a legal one; but that wouldn't give us release. And as long as we're tied to one another—[*abruptly, looking at her.*] Zoe——

Zoe. [*Meekly.*] Eh?

Theodore. If I allowed you to divorce me—made it easy for you—would Ferris—would that scoundrel marry you?

Zoe. [*Turning to him, blankly.*] M-marry me?

Theodore. Because—if it 'ud save you from going utterly to the bad——

Zoe. [*Advancing a step or two.*] No, no; I wouldn't—I wouldn't marry Lenny.

Theodore. [*After a moment's pause, sharply.*] You wouldn't?

Zoe. No—no——

Theodore. [*Coming close to her.*] Why not? [*She shrugs her shoulders confusedly.*] Why not?

[*She wavers, then grasps his arm. Again he shakes her off.*]

Zoe. [*Appealingly.*] Oh, Theo, stick to me. Don't throw me over. Wait—wait for Peter. Theo, I've never ceased to be fond of you——

Theodore. Faugh!

Zoe. Not at the bottom of my heart. No, nor you of me; there's the tragedy of it. Peter says the same. [*Seizing his hand.*] Take time; don't decide today——

Theodore. [*Freeing his hand and looking at her piercingly.*] When did you see him last?

Zoe. H-him?

Theodore. Ferris.

Zoe. This—this morning.

Theodore. This morning!

Zoe. I—I confess—this morning. I—I sent him away.

Theodore. Sent him—away?

Zoe. [*Nodding.*] Yes—yes——

Theodore. [*Slowly.*] And so you rush off to me—straight from the young gentleman——

Zoe. W-well?

Theodore. [*Suddenly.*] Why, damn you, you've quarreled!

Zoe. No——

Theodore. He's chucked you——!

Zoe. No——

Theodore. Had enough of you!

Zoe. [*Her eyes blazing.*] That's not true!

Theodore. Ho, ho! You bring me his cast-off trash, do you——!

Zoe. It's a lie!

Theodore. Mr. Lenny Ferris's leavings!

Zoe. It's a lie! He'd give his soul to make me his wife.

Theodore. Will he tell *me* that?

Zoe. Tell *you!*

Theodore. [*Between his teeth.*] If he doesn't, I'll break every bone in his carcase.

Zoe. [*Throwing her head up defiantly.*] Of course he'd tell you.

Theodore. [*Walking away to the fireplace.*] He shall have a chance of doing it.

Zoe. [*Making for the door, wildly.*] The sooner the better!

Theodore. [*Looking at his watch.*] If Peter were here——

Zoe. [*Behind the settee on the left, turning to* THEODORE.] Mind! I've your bond! If Lenny promises to marry me, you'll let me free myself from you?

Theodore. I've said so.

Zoe. [*Missing her bag, which is again lying upon the settee on the left, and pointing to it.*] Please——

[*He picks up the bag, and is about to take it to her, when he remembers that he has the latchkey in his pocket. He produces the key and drops it into the bag.*]

Theodore. [*As he does so.*] You'll want this for your *new* husband.

Zoe. Thank God, I've done with the old one! [*He tosses the bag to her in a fury and she catches it.*] Ha, ha! [*At the door.*] Ta, ta! [*She disappears.*]

Theodore. [*Flourishing his hands.*] Oh——

[*Going to the piano, he takes the decanter of brandy and a glass from the tray and fills the glass to the brim.*]

CURTAIN

THE FOURTH ACT

SCENE.—*A pretty, irregularly shaped room, simply but tastefully furnished. At the back, facing the spectator, are two double windows opening to the floor. These windows give on to a balcony which appears to continue its course outside the adjoining rooms both on the right and left. Beyond the balcony there is an open space and, in the distance, a view of the upper part of the Albert Hall and of other lofty buildings. On the left is the fireplace—its grate empty, save for a few pots of flowers—and, nearer the spectator, there is a door opening from a corridor. Opposite this door is a door of like dimensions, admitting to a bedroom.*

On either side of the fireplace and of the left-hand window there is an armchair; facing the fireplace there is a settee; and at the back of the settee are a small writing-table and writing-chair. A leathern tub for wastepaper stands beside the writing-table. On the right of the room is a round table upon which tea is laid for three persons. Two chairs—one on the left, another at the farther side—and a settee on the right are drawn up close to this table. Elsewhere are a bookcase, a smoking-cabinet, and some odds and ends of furniture—the whole being characteristic of a room in a small flat occupied by a well-to-do, but not wealthy, young man.

Both the windows are open, and the glare of the afternoon sun is on the balcony and the opposite buildings.

[MRS. PIERPOINT, ETHEL, *and* LEONARD *—the ladies in their hats and gaily dressed—are seated at the round table.*]

Leonard. [*In the chair on the left of the table—handing a dish of cakes to* MRS. PIERPOINT.] Do try one of these little cakes.

Mrs. Pierpoint. [*In the chair at the farther side of the table.*] I couldn't.

Leonard. I bought them and carried 'em home myself.

Mrs. Pierpoint. You really must excuse me.

Leonard. [*Pushing the dish toward* ETHEL, *who is on the settee facing him.*] Buck up, Ethel.

Ethel. Good-by to my dinner, then. [*Taking a cake and biting it as she speaks.*] May I, Mother?

Mrs. Pierpoint. [*Cheerfully.*] Now, isn't that the modern young lady exactly! "May I, Mother!" And the cake is half-eaten before the poor mother can even nod her head.

Ethel. [*Laughing.*] Ha, ha!

Mrs. Pierpoint. "May I go out for a walk, Mother?" and the front door bangs on the very words! "May I do this?" "may I do that?" And a nice life the mother leads if she dares to say "No."

Ethel. This sounds suspiciously like a sermon. [*To* LEONARD.] Lenny, sit up straight and be preached to. [*Pushing her cup to* MRS. PIERPOINT, *who has the tea-tray before her.*] Another cup of tea, your reverence.

Mrs. Pierpoint. Ethel! How—how irreligious! [*Pouring out tea.*] Ah, but it's true, every syllable of it. And in nothing is this spirit of—what shall I describe it as?——

Ethel. Go-as-you-pleasèdness.

Mrs. Pierpoint. [*Giving* ETHEL *her tea.*] In nothing is this wilful, thoughtless spirit more plainly shown than in the way love-affairs are conducted at the present day.

Ethel. [*Whistling slyly.*] Phew!

Mrs. Pierpoint. [*To* LEONARD.] More tea, Leonard?

Leonard. No, thanks.

Mrs. Pierpoint. [*Resignedly.*] I *suppose* I must call you Leonard now?

Ethel. [*Into her teacup.*] What's the matter with "Lenny"?

Mrs. Pierpoint. I may be wrong, but I don't *think* that it was the fashion in my youth for a young lady suddenly to appear before her mother and to say, without a note of warning, "Mr. So-and-so is in the drawing-room and we wish to be engaged." Take the case of Ethel's papa—*there's* a case in point——

Leonard. I certainly intended to speak to you first, Mrs. Pierpoint.

Ethel. [*To* LEONARD.] You fibber!

Mrs. Pierpoint. Ethel!

Leonard. Well, I—what I mean is——

Ethel. If you *had* done so, I'd never have looked at you again. Surely, if there is one thing which is a girl's own particular business, it is settling preliminaries with her best young man.

Mrs. Pierpoint. My dear!

Ethel. [*Jumping up.*] Anyhow, Mother, if you wanted to play the dragon, you shouldn't have been upstairs, sleeping off the effects of an exceedingly heavy lunch, when Lenny arrived this afternoon.

Mrs. Pierpoint. Fiddle, heavy lunch! A morsel of minced chicken——!

Ethel. Ha, ha! [*Bending over* MRS. PIERPOINT.] And you don't mind, do you—not actually—[*kissing* MRS. PIERPOINT]—as long as——?

Mrs. Pierpoint. As long as what?

Ethel. As long as—Lenny's contented?

Mrs. Pierpoint. [*Shaking herself.*] Oh, go away.

[*Laughingly,* ETHEL *wanders about inspecting the various objects in the room.*]

Leonard. [*To* MRS. PIERPOINT, *producing his cigarette-case.*] Do you object?

Mrs. Pierpoint. Not in the least. Ethel's papa used to indulge, in moderation.

Leonard. [*To* ETHEL, *over his shoulder.*] Cigarette, Ethel?

Mrs. Pierpoint. Ethel, I forbid it.

Ethel. [*Putting on her gloves.*] I would, but it makes me swimmy.

Mrs. Pierpoint. [*To* ETHEL.] How do *you* know?

Ethel. I've smoked with Zoe Blundell.

Mrs. Pierpoint. This is news to *me.*

Ethel. Zoe smokes like a chimney.

Mrs. Pierpoint. [*To* LEONARD.] By-the-bye, she's in London again.

Leonard [*Uncomfortably.*] Yes—yes.

Mrs. Pierpoint. Ethel called on her this morning at Lancaster Gate.

Leonard. Did she?

Ethel. [*To* LEONARD.] I told you, Len.

Leonard. Ah, yes.

Mrs. Pierpoint. [*To* LEONARD.] Have *you* seen her? I presume not.

Leonard. Er—for a few minutes. I was in the neighborhood on—on Monday, and I noticed the blinds were up, and I—I just rang the bell to—to inquire.

Mrs. Pierpoint. [*Elevating her eyebrows.*] She received you?

Leonard. She—she happened to be in the hall.

Mrs. Pierpoint. I was going to *say*—a woman in her peculiar position ought hardly——

Leonard. No, of course.

Mrs. Pierpoint. Looks ill, I understand?

Ethel. Frightfully.

Leonard. Does she?

Mrs. Pierpoint. I am afraid—I am very much afraid—that dear Mrs. Blundell was not *entirely* free from blame in her treatment of that big, rough husband of hers.

Ethel. [*At the left-hand window.*] Rubbish, Mother!

Mrs. Pierpoint. Ethel, you are *too* disrespectful.

Ethel. Sorry.

Mrs. Pierpoint. At the same time, she is an exceedingly attractive person—a trifle vulgar, poor soul, occasionally——

Ethel. [*Hotly.*] Mother!

Mrs. Pierpoint. [*To* LEONARD.] But good-natured people frequently *are* vulgar—aren't they?

Ethel. [*Going on to the balcony.*] Oh——!

Mrs. Pierpoint. [*To* LEONARD.] You were

quite a friend of hers before the sad split, weren't you—quite a friend?

Leonard. Yes, I—I always found her a very decent sort.

Ethel. [*Her hands upon the rail of the balustrade, calling.*] Mother, do come and look at the tiny men and women.

Mrs. Pierpoint. Men and women——? [MRS. PIERPOINT *rises and goes to the window, whereupon* LEONARD *jumps up as if relieved by the interruption.*] You're soiling your gloves, Ethel.

Ethel. Look down there. What tots!

Mrs. Pierpoint. [*Drawing back from the window.*] Oh, my dear, I can't——

Ethel. Do, Mother.

Mrs. Pierpoint. You know I don't care for heights.

Ethel. I'll steady you. [MRS. PIERPOINT *timidly ventures on to the balcony.* ETHEL *takes her arm.*] There's been a concert—or a meeting. [*Calling.*] Lenny——

[LEONARD *has walked away to the writing-table gloomily. He is about to join the ladies on the balcony when the door on the left opens and* RIDEOUT, *his servant, appears.*]

Leonard. [*To* RIDEOUT.] Eh?

[*After glancing discreetly in the direction of the ladies on the balcony,* RIDEOUT *produces a visiting-card from behind his back.* LEONARD *goes to him and takes the card, and looks at it in astonishment.*]

Rideout. [*Quietly.*] There's some writing on it, sir. [

Leonard. I see. [*In a low voice.*] Where is she?

Rideout. In my room, sir. I said you were engaged.

Leonard. [*Uneasily.*] You didn't tell her who's here.

Rideout. No, sir; merely some friends to tea.

Leonard. All right. I shan't be very long. [RIDEOUT *is going.*] Tss——!

Rideout. [*Stopping.*] Yessir?

Leonard. Keep your door shut.

Rideout. Yessir.

[RIDEOUT *withdraws.* LEONARD *crams the card into his waistcoat pocket and is again about to join the ladies when* MRS. PIERPOINT *comes back into the room.*]

Mrs. Pierpoint. [*To* LEONARD.] Thank you for showing us your charming little nest. Quite—quite delightful!

Leonard. [*Standing by the round table.*] Oh, for bachelor quarters——

Mrs. Pierpoint. [*In the middle of the room.*] There! I declare I often wonder what there is to tempt a bachelor to marry in these days.

Leonard. You're not a bachelor, Mrs. Pierpoint.

Mrs. Pierpoint. No; that's true. That's perfectly true. But I've a distinct remembrance of the rooms Ethel's papa lived in when *he* was a bachelor. [ETHEL *returns and goes to the fireplace.*] They were in Keppel Street, and vastly different from these. [*Turning to* ETHEL.] Have I ever told you that poor papa lived in Keppel Street?

Ethel. [*Demurely.*] Yes, Mother.

Mrs. Pierpoint. [*To* ETHEL.] And now, my dear, as we have to dine at half-past seven—[*to* LEONARD]—what time does *Louise* begin?——

Leonard. Oh, if we get there at nine——

Mrs. Pierpoint. So kind of you to take us—and as Ethel must lie down on her bed for an hour if we want her to look her best—[*pointing to the tea-table*]—may I trouble you—my fan?——

[LEONARD *searches for* MRS. PIERPOINT'S *fan among the tea things.*]

Ethel. [*Kneeling upon the settee on the left, her elbows on the back of it, gazing into space.*] Mother——

Mrs. Pierpoint. Eh? [*Receiving her fan from* LEONARD.] Thank you.

Ethel. [*Slowly.*] Mother—this is going to be an awfully happy night.

Mrs. Pierpoint. I'm sure I hope so, my darling. It won't be my fault if it isn't—[*tapping* LEONARD'S *shoulder with her fan*] nor Leonard's.

Ethel. Ah, no; I mean *the* night of one's life perhaps.

Mrs. Pierpoint. Oh, I trust we shall have many, many——

Leonard. Rather!

Ethel. [*Raising herself and gripping the back of the settee.*] No, no; you don't understand, you gabies. In everybody's life there's one special moment——

Mrs. Pierpoint. Moment?

Ethel. Hour—day—night; when all the world seems *yours*—as if it had been made for *you,* and when you can't help pitying other people—they seem so ordinary and insignificant. Well, I believe this is to be *my* evening.

Mrs. Pierpoint. One would imagine *I* had never given you *any* pleasure, to hear you talk.

Ethel. [*Rising.*] I say, Mother, don't make me lie down, and lose consciousness, when I get home. [*Going to* MRS. PIER-

POINT *with extended arms.*] Ah, ah! You duck——!

[*In advancing to* MRS. PIERPOINT, ETHEL *knocks over the waste-paper tub with her skirt and its contents are scattered on the floor.*]

Ethel. [*Going down on her knees and replacing the litter.*] Sorry.

Mrs. Pierpoint. [*To* ETHEL.] You'll crease your skirt, Ethel.

Leonard. [*Going to* ETHEL.] Never mind that.

Ethel. Oh, but if I do anything clumsy at home——! [*Coming upon some fragments of a photograph.*] Oh——! [*Trying to fit the pieces together.*] Zoe!

Leonard. Yes, I—I——

Mrs. Pierpoint. [*Who has moved to the fireplace.*] Pray get off the floor, child.

Ethel. [*Finding more pieces.*] Why, you've been tearing up Zoe's photos.

Leonard. They're old things.

Ethel. *That* they're not. *This* one isn't, at all events. [*Examining one of the scraps closely.*] "—Firenze."

Mrs. Pierpoint. Ethel, we *must* be going.

Leonard. [*Almost roughly.*] Leave them alone, Ethel.

[*A little startled by his tone, she drops the pieces into the basket and he assists her to rise.*]

Mrs. Pierpoint. [*Opening the door on the left.*] Come along at once, I insist.

[MRS. PIERPOINT *goes out.* ETHEL *is following her mother when she turns to* LEONARD *who is behind her.*]

Ethel. [*To* LEONARD, *with a smile.*] Sorry I contradicted you.

[*They kiss hurriedly and* ETHEL *runs after her mother.* LEONARD *follows and closes the door. After a little while, the door is reopened, and* RIDEOUT *enters with* ZOE. ZOE *is dressed as when last seen.*]

Rideout. [*To* ZOE, *as she passes him.*] Mr. Ferris has gone to the lift, ma'am. He won't be a minute.

Zoe. [*Going to the left-hand window, languidly.*] All right.

Rideout. [*At the round table, putting the tea things together upon the tray.*] Shall I make you some tea, ma'am?

Zoe. [*Looking out of the window, speaking in a dull voice.*] No; I've had tea, in a tea-shop. [*Turning.*] Rideout——

Rideout. Yes, ma'am?

Zoe. I should like to tidy myself, if I may; I've been walking about.

Rideout. [*Going to the door on the right and opening it.*] Cert'nly, ma'am. [*As* ZOE *approaches.*] The hot water flows cold for a few seconds, ma'am.

Zoe. Is there any scent?

Rideout. There's some eau-de-cologne on the dressing-table, ma'am.

[*She disappears and* RIDEOUT *closes the door and continues his preparations for removing the tea things.* LEONARD *returns.*]

Rideout. [*Answering a look of inquiry from* LEONARD.] Mrs. Blundell's tidying herself, sir.

Leonard. Oh, yes. [*Moving about the room, irritably.*] Won't she have some tea?

Rideout. I did ask her, sir. She's had it.

Leonard. [*Halting.*] Did Mrs. Blundell—say anything, Rideout?

Rideout. [*Folding the tablecloth.*] Only that she wanted to see you just for ten minutes, sir, and that she thought she'd wait. And then she wrote on her card and told me to slip it into your hand if I got the opportunity.

Leonard. [*Resuming his walk.*] Yes, yes.

Rideout. [*After a pause.*] What time'll you dress, sir?

Leonard. Quarter to seven. I have to dine at half-past.

Rideout. Which suit'll you wear, sir?

Leonard. [*Considering.*] Er—pink lining.

Rideout. Theater, sir?

Leonard. Opera. Two pairs o' gloves. [RIDEOUT *goes toward the door on the left, carrying the tea-tray.*] Tss——!

Rideout. Yessir?

Leonard. There's no necessity to put out my clothes yet a while.

Rideout. [*Placing the tray upon a piece of furniture so that he can open the door.*] No, sir.

Leonard. I'll ring when you can come through.

Rideout. [*Opening the door.*] Yessir.

Leonard. And I'm not at home to anybody else.

Rideout. [*Taking up the tray.*] No, sir. [*As the man is leaving the room,* LEONARD *comes to the door to close it.*] Thank you very much, sir.

[RIDEOUT *goes out and* LEONARD *shuts the door. As he turns from the door, his eyes fall upon the waste-paper tub. He snatches it up angrily.*]

Leonard. [*Reopening the door and calling.*] Rideout——

Rideout. [*Out of sight.*] Yessir?

[RIDEOUT *presents himself at the door without the tray.*]

Leonard. [*Shaking up the contents of the

tub and then giving it to RIDEOUT.] Burn this waste-paper.

Rideout. Yessir.

[RIDEOUT *closes the door and* LEONARD *is again walking about the room when* ZOE, *carrying her hat, gloves, and bag, appears on the balcony outside the right-hand window. She enters and they look at one another for a moment without speaking.*]

Leonard. Hallo, Zo!

Zoe. Hallo, Len!

Leonard. This *is* a surprise.

Zoe. [*Putting her hat, gloves, and bag upon the round table—nervously.*] Is it?

Leonard. I thought you'd dropped my acquaintance for good and all.

Zoe. N—no, Len. Why should you think that?

Leonard. Ha! Well, I bear the marks of the point of your shoe somewhere about me.

Zoe. Oh, you—you mustn't take me too seriously when I'm in one of my vile tempers. [*A pause.*] I—I'm not—keeping you——?

Leonard. No, no.

Zoe. [*Turning the chair on the left of the round table so that it faces the writing-table.*] May I sit down?

Leonard. Do.

Zoe. I was here three-quarters of an hour ago, but the porter said you were out; so I went and got some tea. [*Sitting.*] You've been entertaining, according to Rideout.

Leonard. [*Turning the chair at the writing-table and sitting facing her.*] A couple o' people turned up—old friends——

Zoe. You *are* a gay dog. [*Suddenly, staring at the writing-table.*] Why—where—where am *I*?

Leonard. You?

Zoe. You always have a photograph of me, standing on your writing-table.

Leonard. Oh—oh, it's——

Zoe. [*Remembering.*] And there isn't one now—[*glancing at the door on the right*]—in your——!

Leonard. The frames had got beastly shabby. Rideout's taken 'em to be done up.

Zoe. [*Flutteringly.*] Honor? [*A pause.*] Honor?

Leonard. If—if I say so——

Zoe. I beg your pardon. No, you wouldn't *out* my photos because of a—because of a little tiff, would you?

Leonard. L—likely!

Zoe. [*Rising and going to him.*] I'm sure you wouldn't, dear boy; I'm sure you wouldn't. [*Again there is a pause, during which she passes her hand over his shoulder caressingly.*] Len——

Leonard. Eh?

Zoe. [*Standing behind him.*] After that—stupid fall-out of ours this morning—what d'ye think I did?

Leonard. Did?

Zoe. Ha, ha! I took it into my head to—pay Theodore a visit.

Leonard. Pay him a visit!

Zoe. It—it was one of my silly impulses—I was so upset at having offended you——

Leonard. Did you see him?

Zoe. Y—yes.

Leonard. And what had *he* to say for himself?

Zoe. Oh, I—I made such a mash of it, Len.

Leonard. Mash——?

Zoe. Yes, I—I let him worm it out of me.

Leonard. Worm it out of you?

Zoe. Worm it—all out——

Leonard. Worm *what* out of you?

Zoe. [*Faintly.*] P-Perugia——

[*There is a silence, and then* LEONARD *rises with an angry look.*]

Zoe. [*Holding the lapels of his coat.*] Don't be savage with me, Len. It wasn't altogether my fault. He *had* heard of it from Claud Lowenstein. And it's of no consequence; none whatever. It's just as you said this morning—he *is* ready to make matters smooth for us.

Leonard. [*Blankly.*] Smooth—for us!

Zoe. Yes, to let *me* divorce *him.* He's promised—he's promised to do so, if you'll—only——

Leonard [*His jaw dropping.*] If *I*——?

Zoe. If you'll give him your word that you'll do the right thing by me.

Leonard. The right thing——!

Zoe. Marry me. [*A pause.*] I—I suppose he—I suppose he'll demand to see you. Or perhaps he'll make Peter Mottram a go-between.

[*Again there is a silence, and then he walks away from her. She follows him with her eyes.*]

Leonard. [*Thickly.*] But you—you wished me good-by this morning—finished with me.

Zoe. [*Clenching her hands.*] I know—I know! [*Coming to him.*] But he—he insulted me, Len—stung me. He flung it in my face that you—that you'd chucked me; that I was your cast-off, your leavings. I couldn't bear it from him; and I—I told him that you were all eagerness to make me your wife. [*A pause.*] Well! And so you were—this morning!

[*He sits in the chair on the left of the

round table, his elbows on his knees, holding his head.]

Leonard. Zoe——

Zoe. W-what?

Leonard. These people I've had to tea this afternoon—ladies—two ladies——

Zoe. Yes?

Leonard. Mrs. Pierpoint was one of them —and—and——

Zoe. Mrs Pierpoint——?

Leonard. [*Raising his head and looking at her.*] The other was—Ethel.

Zoe. Eth-el——!

Leonard. [*In a low voice.*] You—you made me do it.

Zoe. [*Dazed.*] I—I made you——! [*Drawing a deep breath.*] Oh-h-h! [*She turns from him slowly, and seats herself in the chair at the writing-table.*] I—I'd forgotten Ethel.

Leonard. Yes, you persuaded me to do it. [*A pause.*] Zo, you egged me on to do it.

Zoe. [*Quietly.*] You—you didn't lose much time, did you?

Leonard. I—I was furious when I left you —furious.

Zoe. [*With an attempt at a smile.*] Why, you—you must have bolted straight off to her.

Leonard. I—I went to the club and had some food; and then I came back here and changed—and——

Zoe. Got rid of those photos!

Leonard. I was furious—furious.

Zoe. And then you—you bustled off to Sloane Street! [*He rises and paces the room. After a while she pulls herself together.*] Oh, well, it—it can't be helped, old boy.

Leonard. [*Agitatedly.*] It *must* be helped; it *must* be helped. I must get out of it; I must get out of it. Somehow or other, I must get out of it.

Zoe. Get out of it?

Leonard. The—the Pierpoints——!

Zoe. Oh, don't talk such utter rubbish; I'd kill myself sooner. [*He throws himself into the chair on the right of the left-hand window.*] No, I'm a rotter, Len, but I'm not as low as that. Oh, no, I'm not as low as all that. [*She rises and goes slowly to the round table and, in a listless way, pulls the pins out of her hat.*] I—I'll be toddling home now. [*Tracing a pattern on the crown of her hat with the hat-pins.*] Home——! [*Knitting her brows.*] I shall clear out of that—big—flashy—empty——! [*Putting on her hat.*] Ha, ha! I *have* made a mash of it, haven't I? My father always said I was a heedless, irresponsible little puss. [*With a puzzled look, her arms hanging at her side.*] There was a lot o' good in me, too—any amount o' good——!

[*She is drawing on a glove when she turns her head in the direction of the door on the left. At the same moment,* LEONARD, *also looking at the door, gets to his feet.*]

Zoe. [*Listening.*] What's that, dear?

[*He tiptoes to the door, opens it an inch or two, and puts his ear to the opening.*]

Leonard. [*Carefully closing the door and turning to her.*] Blundell.

Zoe. [*Under her breath.*] Oh——!

Leonard. [*In a whisper.*] Don't worry. I've told Rideout—— [*There is a pause. They stand looking at each other in silence, waiting. Suddenly* LEONARD *returns to the door and, without opening it, listens again.*] Curse the brute, he won't go!

[*He faces her irresolutely and, in a panic, she picks up her bag and her other glove and runs out at the door on the right.* LEONARD *is in the middle of the room when the door on the left is thrown open and* THEODORE *and* PETER *enter followed by* RIDEOUT. THEODORE *and* PETER *have their hats on.*]

Rideout. [*To* LEONARD.] I beg your pardon, sir——

Leonard. [*To* RIDEOUT.] All right.

Theodore. [*To* PETER, *with a hoarse laugh.*] You give the man half a sovereign, Peter; that'll soothe his feelings.

Peter. [*To* THEODORE, *sharply.*] Sssh, sssh! Theo——! [RIDEOUT *withdraws.*]

Theodore. [*Advancing to* LEONARD.] Ho! Not at home, hey?

Leonard. [*Facing him.*] No, I'm not; not to *you.*

Peter. You be quiet, Ferris.

Leonard. [*To* THEODORE.] What the devil do you mean by forcing your way into my place?

Theodore. [*Raising a walking-cane which he carries.*] You——!

[PETER *quickly puts himself between the two men as* LEONARD *seizes the chair on the left of the round table.*]

Peter. [*To* THEODORE, *endeavoring to get the walking-cane from him.*] Give me that. [*To* LEONARD.] You keep a civil tongue in your head. [*To* THEODORE.] Give it me. [*Holding the cane.*] You know what you promised. Give it up. [THEODORE *resigns the cane to* PETER *and walks away to the fireplace where he stands with his back to the others.* PETER *lays the cane upon the writing-table and then turns to* LEONARD.]

You ought to be ashamed o' yourself. [*Lowering his voice.*] You see the man's laborin' under great excitement.

Leonard. [*Sullenly.*] I dare say a good many people in London are laboring under excitement. That's no reason why they should have the run of my flat.

Peter. [*Coolly.*] Will you oblige me by sittin' down and listenin' to me for a moment?

Leonard. Any man who treats me courteously'll be treated courteously in return. [*Sitting in the chair on the left of the round table.*] I can do with *you,* Peter.

Peter. Can you? Then you'll be so kind as to drop addressin' me by my Christian name. [*Sitting in the chair at the writing-table.*] Ferris——

Leonard. [*Curling his lip.*] Yes, Mister Mottram?

Peter. Mrs. Blundell called upon her husband today—this afternoon, about three o'clock——

Leonard. [*With an assumption of ease.*] Oh? Did she?

Peter. And made a communication to him—a communication of a very painful, very shockin' character. [*A pause.*] I presoom you don't require me—or Blundell—to enter into particklers?

Leonard. [*In a low voice.*] Oh, for heaven's sake, no.

Peter. We may take it, without goin' further, that what Mrs. Blundell has stated is absolutely the truth?

Leonard. Absolutely. [*A pause.* THEODORE *moves from the fireplace to the left-hand window and stands there staring at the prospect.*] One thing, though, she mayn't have stated as clearly as she might——

Peter. What's that?

Leonard. That she—that she's an injured woman—badly dealt with by her husband, and worse by your humble servant; and——

Peter. And——?

Leonard. And that both Blundell and I damn well deserve to be hanged.

[THEODORE *turns to* LEONARD *fiercely.*]

Peter. [*To* THEODORE.] Well! Have you any objection to *that*?

[THEODORE *draws himself up, as if to retort; then his body relaxes and he drops into the chair on the left of the window.*]

Peter. [*To* LEONARD.] Now, then! Attend to me.

Leonard. Yes?

Peter. Obviously it's impossible, after what's transpired, that Mr. and Mrs. Brundell should ever live together again.

Leonard. [*Slightly surprised.*] She didn't——?

Peter. I believe there *was* an idea that her husband should go back to Lancaster Gate. [*With a wave of the hand.*] But we needn't discuss *that.* We'd better come at once to the object of this meetin'.

Leonard. Object——?

Peter. The best method of providin' for the safety—and happiness, we hope—of the unfortunate lady who's gone and made a bit of a munge of her affairs.

Leonard. [*Steadily.*] Yes?

Peter. [*Deliberately.*] Ferris, Mrs. Blundell has given her husband to understand that, if existin' obstacles were removed—if she were a free woman, in point o' fact—you'd be willin' to marry her.

Leonard. She's correct.

Peter. That you're keen on it.

Leonard. [*With a nod.*] Keen on it.

Peter. Good. [*Dropping his voice.*] We're all tiled here. Are you prepared to give Blundell your word of—of——?

Leonard. Honor? Can't you say it? [*Hotly.*] D'ye think that because a fellow's done a scoundrelly act once in his life——!

Peter. That'll do—your word of honor. That bein' so, Blundell undertakes, on his part, not to oppose Mrs. Blundell's action for divorce. On the contrary—— [*Turning to* THEODORE.] Theo——?

Theodore. H'm?

Peter. *Your* word of honor?

Theodore. [*In a muffled voice.*] My—word of honor.

Peter. [*To* THEODORE *and* LEONARD, *shortly.*] Thank'ee. And both of you empower me to—to go to Mrs. Zoe——? [*A pause.* PETER *turns to* THEODORE.] Eh?

Theodore. Yes.

Peter. [*To* LEONARD.] And you? [LEONARD *is silent.*] What's the matter?

Leonard. [*After a further pause, slowly.*] Look here. I don't want either of you two men to suspect me of—of playing double——

Peter. Playing double!

Leonard. I tell you honestly—Mrs. Blundell—Mrs. Blundell declines——

Peter. Declines——?

Leonard. Yes; she—she refuses——

[THEODORE *rises.*]

Peter. [*Also rising—to* THEODORE.] Sssh! You keep out of it. [*To* LEONARD.] Ah, but you haven't seen Mrs. Blundell since——?

Theodore. [*To* PETER, *prompting him.*] Since she left me today——

Peter. [*To* LEONARD.] Since she left her

husband this afternoon—[*a pause*]—have you?

Leonard. Y-yes; I have.

Theodore. [*To* PETER.] Where?

Peter. [*To* LEONARD.] Where?

[*There is a further silence.*]

Theodore. [*Under his breath.*] What's this game, Peter? [*Loudly.*] What's this game?

Peter. [*Restraining him.*] Don't you interfere. [*To* LEONARD.] Ferris——

Leonard. [*Rising.*] Mottram—Mrs. Blundell called on me—about a quarter of an hour ago. We—we were talking the matter over in this room when we heard Blundell kicking up a riot in the passage. [*Glancing at the door on the right.*] She—she's here. [*There is a movement from* THEODORE.] Mottram, I depend on you——

[PETER *looks at* THEODORE *who, in obedience to the look, goes back to the fireplace.* LEONARD *moves to the door on the right and then turns.*]

Leonard. [*Speaking across the room to* THEODORE.] Blundell, I—I've given you my word of honor—and—and I abide by Mrs. Blundell's decision. [*To* PETER, *pointing to* THEODORE.] Mottram, I—I depend on you —— [*He opens the door and calls softly.*] Mrs. Blundell—— [*There is no response.*] Mrs. Blundell——

Theodore. [*Looking down into the grate.*] Call her Zoe. [*Laughing again hoarsely.*] Why the devil don't you call her Zoe?

Leonard. [*Calling.*] Zoe——

[*Still obtaining no reply, he goes into the next room.* THEODORE *comes to* PETER.]

Theodore. [*To* PETER.] Some game up, hey?

Peter. Sssh, sssh!

Theodore. What is it? What trick is she up to now, hey? [LEONARD *reappears.*]

Leonard. [*Standing in the doorway, bewildered.*] I—I can't make it out.

Peter. What?

Leonard. She—she's not there.

Theodore. Ha! Hooked it?

Leonard. [*Looking toward the balcony.*] She must have gone along the balcony without our noticing her, and through the kitchen. [*Looking at* PETER.] She must have done so.

Peter. Why?

Leonard. You know there's no other door——

[*He crosses to the door on the left. As he gets to it, it opens and* RIDEOUT *presents himself.*]

Rideout. [*In an odd voice.*] Sir——

Leonard. [*To* RIDEOUT.] Has anybody passed through your kitchen?

Rideout. N-no, sir.

Leonard. [*After a pause, sharply.*] What d'ye want?

Rideout. There—there's been an accident, sir.

Leonard. Accident——?

[*At this moment* THEODORE *and* PETER *turn their heads toward the balcony as if they are listening to some sounds reaching them from a distance. Giving* LEONARD *a frightened look,* RIDEOUT *withdraws quickly.* LEONARD *turns to* THEODORE *and* PETER *in time to see them hurrying on to the balcony through the left-hand window. He follows them as far as the window and recoils before them as they come back into the room after looking over the balustrade.*]

Theodore. [*Staggering to the door on the left.*] Oh, my God; oh, my God; oh, my God——!

[*He disappears.*]

Leonard. [*To* PETER, *shaking a trembling hand at him.*] An accident! It's an accident! [*Coming to* PETER, *appealingly.*] An accident!

Peter. Yes—an accident—— [*Gripping* LEONARD'S *arm.*] She told me once it would be in the *winter* time——!

[*They go out together.*]

CURTAIN

THE GLITTERING GATE *

By

LORD DUNSANY

THE GLITTERING GATE WAS THE FIRST play to be produced of Edward John Moreton Drax Plunkett, Lord Dunsany. His work and life are as romantic as his name. He lives in a castle; his title goes back to the fifteenth century; he writes with a quill; he has served with distinction in two wars as a cavalry officer; he is six feet four inches tall. Almost no play or story of his is realistic—his scene is characteristically the East, the Edge of the World, the Lands of Wonder; his people are kings, beggars, and children. He says:

"I . . . ask that the theater be set up against the false, that the highest realism, the realism of the poets, who see the whole of life's journey, be set up against the lower realism that sees only how man equips himself with morals, and money, and custom for the journey; but knows not where the journey leads nor why man wants to go. That is what we need more today than in any age. . . . The kind of drama that we most need today seems to me to be the kind that will build new worlds for the fancy, for the spirit as much as the body sometimes needs a change of scene." *(Romance and the Modern Stage,* 1911.)

In the clarified atmosphere of romance, then, we can really see and study the problem "where the journey leads and why man wants to go." So, in many of Dunsany's plays, we find the philosophic intention quite as plain as the dramatic. Describing his work, he has said, in a letter to Clayton Hamilton:

"First of all, you have a simple tale told dramatically, and along with that you have hung, without any deliberate intention of mine—so far as I know—a truth, not true to London only or to New York or to one municipal party but to the experience of man. That is the kind of way that man does get hit by destiny. But mind you, that is all unconscious, though inevitable. I am not trying to teach anybody anything. I merely set out to make a work of art out of a simple theme, and God knows we want works of art in this age of corrugated iron."

But in the beginning, at the time of *The Glittering Gate,* Dunsany was learning. W. B. Yeats influenced him to take up playwriting, and turned his attention to the one-act form, in which Dunsany has always been most happy. Dunsany had drawn a picture showing a burglar breaking into Paradise and finding only emptiness and stars as he opens the Golden Gates. Yeats had heard of the picture and suggested it as the subject of a play. When Dunsany said he couldn't write plays, Yeats said, "Then I must get somebody else to do it." This stung Dunsany to try his hand, so he wrote *The Glittering Gate* in a single afternoon, March 23, 1909; with only slight additions later the play was performed as he wrote it then. Yeats told him that the secret of a good one-act play was "Surprise, surprise, and again surprise"—a surprising formula. Anyway, Dunsany attempted to follow it, and the plays were the result. He said later that *The Glittering Gate* never interested him. Whether it did or not, it interested the audiences who saw it at the Abbey Theatre in Dublin, in 1909, its first production, and at the Neighborhood Playhouse in New York, in 1915, and in many parts of the world since. In it Dunsany shows his command not only of surprise, but also of the theatrical, a command he has never lost. No modern playwright except O'Neill excels Dunsany in skilful use of the devices of the theater which gain their force and value from the theater itself: light, color, sound, music, poetry, things not dramatic in and of themselves, but when wisely used highly theatrical. Some of Dunsany's plays, in fact, are almost pure theater with the elements of conflict in them relatively unimportant: *The Flight of the Queen,* for instance. But where he fuses theater and drama, Dunsany is unforgettable.

LORD DUNSANY

Born 1878, London, England.
Eton and Sandhurst.
1899, Became eighteenth Baron Dunsany, of the Irish peerage.
Served as officer with the Coldstream Guards in the Boer War and with the Royal Inniskilling Fusiliers in the World War. Wounded in 1916, during the Irish Rebellion.
1905, *The Gods of Pegana,* first literary appearance.
Identified with the Irish literary renaissance.

PLAYS

1909 *The Glittering Gate.* 1911 *King Argimenes and the Unknown Warrior.* 1911 *The Gods of the Mountain.* 1912 *The Golden Doom.* 1913 *The Lost Silk Hat.* 1914 *The Tents of the Arabs.* 1916 *A Night at an Inn.* 1916 *The Queen's Enemies.* 1918 *Fame and the Poet.* 1918 *The Prince of Stamboul.* 1919 *The Laughter of the Gods.* 1919 *The Murderers.* 1920 *A Good Bargain.* 1920 *If Shakespeare Lived Today.* 1920 *The Compromise of the King of the Golden Isles.* 1921 *If.* 1923 *The Flight of the Queen.* 1923 *Cheezo.* 1925 *Alexander.* 1925 *The Old King's Tale.* 1925 *The Evil Kettle.* 1925 *The Amusement of Khan Kharuda.* 1925 *Lord Adrian.* 1927 *Mr. Faithful.* 1927 *The Jest of Hahalaba.* 1928 *Atalanta in Wimbledon.* 1928 *The Raffle.* 1928 *The Journey of the Soul.* 1928 *In Holy Russia.* 1928 *His Sainted Grandmother.* 1928 *The Hopeless Passion of Mr. Bunyon.* 1930 *The Old Folk of the Centuries.* 1931 *The Pumpkin.* 1937 *Fame Comes Late.* 1937 *A Matter of Honour.* 1937 *Mr. Sliggen's Hour.* 1937 *The Use of Man* (radio drama). 1937 *The Bureau de Change* (radio drama). 1937 *The Seventh Symphony* (radio drama). 1937 *Golden Dragon City* (radio drama). 1937 *Time's Joke* (radio drama). 1937 *Atmospherics* (radio drama).

WRITINGS ABOUT THE DRAMA

Romance and the Modern Stage, in *National Review,* July, 1911, reprinted in E. H. Bierstadt's *Dunsany the Dramatist,* 1917. *Artist and Tradesman,* in *The Dial,* March, 1917. *Carving of the Ivory,* in *Art of Playwriting,* 1928. *Patches of Sunlight* (passim), 1938.

THE GLITTERING GATE

Persons

JIM, *lately a burglar* } *Both dead.*
BILL, " " "

Scene: A Lonely Place.
Time: The present.

The Lonely Place is strewn with large black rocks and uncorked beer-bottles, the latter in great profusion. At back is a wall of granite built of great slabs, and in it the Gate of Heaven. The door is of gold. Below the Lonely Place is an abyss hung with stars.

[*The rising curtain reveals* JIM *wearily uncorking a beer-bottle. Then he tilts it slowly and with infinite care. It proves to be empty. Faint and unpleasant laughter is heard off. This action and the accompanying far laughter are repeated continually throughout the play. Corked bottles are discovered lying behind rocks, and more descend constantly through the air, within reach of* JIM. *All prove to be empty.* JIM *uncorks a few bottles.*]

Jim. [*Weighing one carefully.*] That's a full one. [*It is empty, like all.*]

[*Singing is heard off left.*]

Bill. [*Enters from left with a bullet-hole over his eyes, singing.*] Rule Britannia, Britannia rule the waves. [*Breaking off his song.*] Why, 'ullo. 'Ere's a bottle of beer. [*Finds it empty; looking off and downward.*] I'm getting a bit tired of those blooming great stars down there and this rocky ledge. I've been walking along under this wall ever since. Why, it must be twenty-four hours since that householder shot me. And he needn't have done it, either, *I* wasn't going to hurt the bloke. I only wanted a bit of his silver stuff. It felt funny, that did. Hullo, a gate. Why, that's the Gate of Heaven. Well, well. So that's all right. [*Looks up and up for some time.*] No. I can't climb that wall. Why, it's got no top to it. Up and up it goes.

[*Knocks at the door and waits.*]

Jim. That isn't for the likes of us.

Bill. Why, hullo, there's another bloke. Why, somebody's been hanging him. Why, if it isn't old Jim! Jim!

Jim. [*Wearily.*] Hullo.

Bill. Why, Jim! 'Ow long 'ave you been 'ere?

Jim. I *am* 'ere always.

Bill. Why, Jim, don't you remember me? Why, you taught Bill to pick locks years and years ago when he was a little boy, and had never learnt a trade and hadn't a penny in the world, and never would have had but for you, Jim. [JIM *stares vaguely.*] I never forgot *you,* Jim. I broke into scores of houses. And then I took on big houses. Out in the country, you know, real big ones. I got rich, Jim, and respected by all who knew me. I was a citizen, Jim, one who dwelt in our midst. And of an evening, sitting over the fire, I used to say, "I am as clever as Jim." But I wasn't, Jim. I couldn't climb like you. And I couldn't walk like you on a creaky stair, when everything's quite still and there's a dog in the house and little rattly things left lying about, and a door that whines if you touch it, and some one ill upstairs that you didn't know of, who has nothing to do but to listen for *you* 'cause she can't get to sleep. Don't you remember little Bill?

Jim. That would be somewhere else.

Bill. Yes, Jim, yes. Down on Earth.

Jim. But there isn't anywhere else.

Bill. I never forgot *you,* Jim. I'd be pattering away with my tongue, in Church, like all the rest, but all the time I'd be thinking of you in that little room at Putney and the man searching every corner of it for you with a revolver in one hand and a candle in the other, and you almost going around with him.

Jim. What is Putney?

Bill. Oh, Jim, can't you remember? Can't you remember the day you taught me a livelihood? I wasn't more than twelve, and it was Spring, and all the May was in blossom outside the town. And we cleared out No. 25 in the new street. And next day we saw the man's fat, silly face. It was thirty years ago.

Jim. What are years?

Bill. Oh, *Jim*!

Jim. You see, there isn't any hope here. And when there isn't any hope there isn't any future. And when there isn't any future there isn't any past. It's just the present here. I tell you we're stuck. There aren't no years here. Nor no nothing.

Bill. Cheer up, Jim. You're thinking of a quotation, "Abandon hope, all ye that enter here." I used to learn quotations; they are awfully genteel. A fellow called Shakespeare used to make them. But there isn't any sense in them. What's the use of saying *ye* when you mean *you?* Don't be thinking of quotations, Jim.

Jim. I tell you there is no hope here.

Bill. Cheer up, Jim. There's plenty of hope there, isn't there?

[*Points to the Gate of Heaven.*]

Jim. Yes, and that's why they keep it locked up so. They won't let us have any. No. I begin to remember Earth again now since you've been speaking. It was just the same there. The more they'd got the more they wanted to keep *you* from having a bit.

Bill. You'll cheer up a bit when I tell you what I've got. I say, Jim, have you got some beer? Why, so you have. Why, *you* ought to cheer up, Jim.

Jim. All the beer you're ever likely to see again. They're empty.

Bill. [*Half rising from the rock on which he has seated himself, and pointing his finger at* JIM *as he rises; very cheerfully.*] Why, you're the chap that said there was no hope here, and you're hoping to find beer in every bottle you open.

Jim. Yes; I *hope* to see a drop of beer in one some day, but I *know* I won't. Their trick *might* not work just once.

Bill. How many have you tried, Jim?

Jim. Oh, I don't know. I've always been at it, working as fast as I can, ever since—ever since—— [*Feels his neck meditatively and up toward his ear.*] Why, ever since, Bill.

Bill. Why don't you stop it?

Jim. I'm too thirsty, Bill.

Bill. What do you think *I've got,* Jim?

Jim. I don't know. Nothing's any use.

Bill. [*As yet another bottle is shown to be empty.*] Who's that laughing, Jim?

Jim. [*Astonished at such a question, loudly and emphatically.*] Who's that laughing?

Bill. [*Looks a little disconcerted at having apparently asked a silly question.*] Is it a pal?

Jim. A pal!——

[*Laughs. The laugh off joins in loudly and for long.*]

Bill. Well, I don't know. But, Jim, what do you think I've got?

Jim. It isn't any good to you whatever it is. Not even if it is a ten-pound note.

Bill. It's better than a ten-pound note, Jim. Jim, try and remember, Jim. Don't you remember the way we used to go for those iron safes? Do you remember anything, Jim?

Jim. Yes, I am beginning to remember now. There used to be sunsets. And then there were great yellow lights. And one went in behind them through a swinging door.

Bill. Yes, yes, Jim. That was the Blue Bear down at Wimbledon.

Jim. Yes, and the room was all full of golden light. And there was beer with light in it, and some would be spilt on the counter and there was light in that too. And there was a girl standing there with yellow hair. She'd be the other side of that door now, with lamplight in her hair among the angels, and the old smile on her lips if one of them chaffed her, and her pretty teeth a-shining. She would be very near the throne; there was never any harm in Jane.

Bill. No, there was never any 'arm in Jane, Jim.

Jim. Oh, I don't want to see the angels, Bill. But if I could see Jane again [*points in direction of laugh*] he might laugh as much as he cared to whenever I wanted to cry. You can't cry here, you know, Bill.

Bill. You shall see her again, Jim.

[JIM *takes no interest in this remark; he lowers his eyes and goes on with his work.*]

Bill. Jim, you shall see her again. You want to get into Heaven, don't you?

Jim. [*Not raising his eyes.*] Want!

Bill. Jim. Do you know what I've got, Jim?

[JIM *makes no answer, goes on wearily with his work.*]

Bill. You remember those iron safes, Jim, how we used to knock them open like walnuts with "Old Nut-cracker"?

Jim. [*At work, wearily.*] Empty again.

Bill. Well, I've got "Old Nut-cracker." I had him in my hand at the time, and they let me keep him. They thought it would be a nice proof against me.

Jim. Nothing is any good here.

Bill. I'll get into Heaven, Jim. And you shall come with me because you taught me a livelihood. I couldn't be happy there, like those angels, if I knew of any one being outside. I'm not like that.

[JIM *goes on with his work.*]

Bill. Jim, Jim! You'll see Jane there.

Jim. You'll never get through those gates, Bill. You'll never do it.

Bill. They're only gold, Jim. Gold's soft like lead. "Old Nut-cracker" would do it if they were steel.

Jim. You'll never do it, Bill.

[BILL *puts a rock against the gates, stands on it to reach the lock and gets to work on the lock. A good instrument to use is an egg-whipper.* JIM *goes on wearily with his work. As* BILL *works away, fragments and golden screws begin to fall on the floor.*]

Bill. Jim! "Old Nut-cracker" thinks nothing of it. It's just like cheese to "Old Nut-cracker."

Jim. They won't let you do it, Bill.

Bill. They don't know what I've got. I'm getting through it like cheese, Jim.

Jim. Suppose it's a mile thick. Suppose it's a million miles thick. Suppose it's a hundred million miles thick.

Bill. Can't be, Jim. These doors are meant to open outward. They couldn't do that if they were more than four inches at the most, not for an Archbishop. They'd stick.

Jim. You remember that great safe we broke open once, what had coal in it.

Bill. This isn't a safe, Jim, this is Heaven. There'll be the old saints with their halos shining and flickering, like windows o' wintry nights. [*Creak, creak, creak.*] And angels thick as swallows along a cottage roof the day before they go. [*Creak, creak, creak.*] And orchards full of apples as far as you can see, and the rivers of Tigris and Euphrates, so the Bible says; and a city of gold, for those that care for cities, all full of precious stones; but I'm a bit tired of cities and precious stones. [*Creak, creak, creak.*] I'll go out into the fields where the orchards are, by the Tigris and the Euphrates. I shouldn't be surprised if my old mother was there. She never cared much for the way I earned my livelihood [*creak, creak*], but she was a good mother to me. I don't know if they want a good mother in there who would be kind to the angels and sit and smile at them when they sang and soothe them if they were cross. If they let all the good ones in she'll be there all right. [*Suddenly.*] Jim! They won't have brought me up against her, will they? That's not fair evidence, Jim.

Jim. It would be just like them to. Very like them.

Bill. If there's a glass of beer to be got in Heaven, or a dish of tripe and onions, or a pipe of 'bacca she'll have them for me when I come to her. She used to know my ways wonderful; and what I liked. And she used to know when to expect me almost anywhere. I used to climb in through the window at any hour and she always knew it was me. [*Creak, creak.*] She'll know it's me at the door now, Jim. [*Creak, creak.*] It will be all a blaze of light, and I'll hardly know it's here till I get used to it. . . . But I'll know her among a million angels. There weren't none like her on Earth and there won't be none like her in Heaven. . . . Jim! I'm through, Jim! One more turn, and "Old Nut-cracker" 's done it! It's giving! It's giving! I know the feel of it. *Jim!*

[*At last there is a noise of falling bolts; the gates swing out an inch and are stopped by the rock.*]

Bill. Jim! Jim! I've opened it, Jim. I've opened the Gate of Heaven! Come and help me.

Jim. [*Looks up for a moment with open mouth. Then he mournfully shakes his head and goes on drawing a cork.*] Another one empty.

Bill. [*Looks down once into the abyss that lies below the Lonely Place.*] Stars. Blooming great stars.

[*Then he moves away the rock on which he stood. The gates move slowly.* JIM *leaps up and runs to help; they each take a gate and move backward with their faces against it.*]

Bill. Hullo, Mother! You there? Hullo! You there? It's Bill, Mother.

[*The gates swing heavily open, revealing empty night and stars.*]

Bill. [*Staggering and gazing into the revealed Nothing in which far stars go wandering.*] Stars. Blooming great stars. There *ain't* no Heaven, Jim.

[*Ever since the revelation a cruel and violent laugh has arisen off. It increases in volume and grows louder and louder.*]

Jim. That's like them. That's very like them. Yes, they'd do that!

[*The curtain falls and the laughter still howls on.*]

JUSTICE*

A Tragedy in Four Acts

By

JOHN GALSWORTHY

"JUSTICE" IS TYPICAL OF ITS AUTHOR'S dramaturgy and of its period in the English theater, that of penetrating naturalism. Galsworthy is the artist research worker in life. He presents both sides of a dramatic conflict with a jurist's instinct for equity. He holds the scales of justice with an apparent detachment that almost obscures his strong sentiment of pity for the victims of institutionalism, who are his favorite dramatic figures. "The plays," says Mr. Coates, "are a tremendous indictment of the whole fabric of modern civilization, and at the same time a passionate appeal for understanding sympathy with the innocent victims of a social system for which all of us are responsible." Galsworthy reveals the social system quite as he sees it, and so makes it condemn itself. In his plays, as in his novels, he has created valuable and lasting social documents, vividly representative of contemporary British culture. More conscientiously than any English dramatist he imposed on his plays the artistic restraint of a dispassionate observer. But balance and intellectuality are admirable rather than inspirational or moving. *Justice,* however, is a Galsworthy play that most surely grips and moves, although in it the author maintains the attitude of perfect fairness to both sides. The selection of *Strife* in 1930 for production by the public-spirited director of the Huddersfield theater in hopes of ending the long-standing strike in that Yorkshire town, is conclusive testimony to Galsworthy's accuracy of observation and fairness in presentation. It is generally stated that the penal practices portrayed in *Justice* were mitigated because of the profound effect of the play.

Galsworthy's artistry is further significant. In form and manner his plays mark the farthest advance in England of the realist's art, as it emerged in the 'nineties to culminate what seemed the age-long development toward actuality in representational drama. With poise, irony, and a sense of proportion, reminiscent of the Greek form, with the clarity and technical proficiency of the French, and with the vivid perception of colorful personalities peculiar to the British theater, he is still able to give a faultless surface impression of realism, including social background and carefully observed psychology. His work springs full-armed from the best traditions of literature and the theater.

He has made clear his artistic ideals and methods in various published statements, which are of great value to the student of drama.

These excerpts are especially significant:

"A drama must be shaped so as to have a spire of meaning. Every grouping of life and character has its inherent moral; and the business of the dramatist is so to pose the group as to bring that moral poignantly to the light of day. Such is the moral that exhales from plays like *Lear, Hamlet,* and *Macbeth.* But such is not the moral to be found in the great bulk of contemporary drama."

After defining the moral purpose of one school of dramatists, as setting "before the public that which it wishes to have set before it, the views and codes of life by which the public lives," and the moral teaching of a second school, as setting "before the public those views and codes of life by which the dramatist himself lives," Galsworthy chooses for himself a third course: "To set before the public no cut-and-dried codes, but the phenomena of life and character, selected and combined, *but not distorted*, by the dramatist's outlook, set down without fear, favor, or prejudice, leaving the public to put down such poor moral as nature may afford. This third method requires a certain detachment; it requires a sympathy with, a love of, and a curiosity as to, things for their own sake."

"To the making of good drama, as to the practice of every other art, there must be brought an almost passionate love of discipline, a white-heat of self respect, a desire to make the truest, fairest, best thing in one's power; and . . . to these must be added an eye that does not flinch."

"A good plot is that sure edifice which slowly rises out of the interplay of circumstance on temperament, and temperament on circumstance, within the enclosing atmosphere of an idea. A human being is the best plot there is. . . . He is organic. And so it must be with a good play."

"True dramatic action is what characters do, at once contrary, as it were, to expectation, and yet because they have already done other things. . . . The dramatist who hangs his characters to a plot, instead of hanging his plot to his characters, is guilty of cardinal sin."

"The art of writing true dramatic dialogue is an austere art, denying itself all license, grudging every sentence devoted to the mere machinery of the play, suppressing all jokes and epigrams severed from character, relying for fun and pathos on the fun and tears of life. . . . Take care of character: action and dialogue will take care of themselves. . . . The naturalistic is the most exacting and difficult of all techniques. It is easy enough to *reproduce* the exact conversation and movement of persons in a room; it is desperately hard to *produce* the perfectly natural conversation and movements of those persons, when each natural phrase spoken and each natural movement made has not only to contribute toward the growth and perfection of a drama's soul, but also to be revelation, phrase by phrase, movement by movement, of essential traits of character."

Some Platitudes Concerning Drama.

"A man here and there has turned up who has imagined something true to what he has really seen and felt, and has projected it across the footlights in such a way as to make other people feel it. This is all that has happened lately on our stage."

Anglo-American Drama and Its Future.

PRODUCTION

The first response made in England to the Little Theater movement in France and Germany, dating from 1887, was the founding of the Independent Theatre in London in 1891 by J. T. Grein. At this theater were first put into rigorous effect the "slice-of-life" theories of Ibsen and the French naturalists. Realism was not new on the English stage either in speech or setting, but Grein and his company insisted upon the completely artistic conception of a realism made consistent and rigorously illusory. Everything traditional and theatrical was discarded. Plays by Ibsen and Shaw were among the first to be given such a representation in England. The public appealed to was small, and hostility ran high, but, as Shaw remarked, "Everything followed from that: the production of *Arms and the Man,* . . . Miss Horniman's establishment of Repertory Theatres in Dublin and Manchester, the Stage Society, Granville-Barker's tentative matinees of *Candida* at the Court Theatre, the full-blown management of Vedrenne and Barker, Edie Craig's *Pioneers,* and the final relegation of the nineteenth-century London theater to the dustbin by Barrie. . . ."

As Shaw implies, the management, however brief, of Granville-Barker and J. E. Vedrenne at the Court Theatre (1904–1907) was a fulfilment of the ambitions of English naturalist reformers. Works by Shaw, Barrie, and Granville-Barker were produced under these auspices in a manner fully in accord with the writer's artistic ideals. Granville-Barker must be regarded as one of the most influential producers of the modern English theater. *The Silver Box* was the great discovery of the management. Without Granville-Barker's appreciation it is doubtful that Galsworthy would have become a practical dramatist. His first plays would probably not have been accepted at any other theater. After the abandonment of the Court Theatre in 1907, Galsworthy's plays continued to be produced either by Granville-Barker or by Vedrenne at other theaters. *Strife* and *Justice* were done at The Duke of York's in 1909–1910, and *The Pigeon* at the Royalty in 1912. The production in New York of Galsworthy's *Strife* by Winthrop Ames at the New Theatre (later the Century) in 1910 and of *The Pigeon* at the Little Theatre in 1912 marked what was probably the highest point reached on the American stage of that period in the naturalistic technique of which Galsworthy was the symbol dramatist.

JOHN GALSWORTHY

Born 1867, Coombe, Surrey.
Harrow and Oxford to 1889.
1890, Called to the Bar. Years devoted to travel and writing.
1899, His first novel, *Jocelyn,* published under the pseudonym of John Sinjohn.
1904, Granville-Barker and J. E. Vedrenne began their management of the Royal Court Theatre for the production of new plays of literary merit.
1906, *The Silver Box* produced at the Royal Court Theatre. *The Man of Property* published.
1929, Order of Merit. (Refused a Knighthood.)
1932, Awarded Nobel Prize for Literature.
Died 1933.

PLAYS

1906 *The Silver Box.* 1907 *Joy.* 1909 *Strife.* 1910 *Justice.* 1911 *The Little Dream.* 1912 *The Pigeon.* 1912 *The Eldest Son.* 1913 *The Fugitive.* 1914 *The Mob.* 1914 *Hall-Marked.* 1915 *A Bit o' Love.* 1915 *The Little Man.* 1917 *The Foundations.* 1920 *The Skin Game.* 1920 *Defeat.* 1921 *The First and the Last.* 1921 *Punch and Go.* 1921 *A Family Man.* 1921 *The Sun.* 1922 *Windows.* 1922 *Loyalties.* 1924 *The Forest.* 1924 *Old English.* 1925 *The Show.* 1926 *Escape.* 1929 *Exiled.* 1929 *The Roof.* 1935 *The Winter Garden.* 1935 *Escape* (Episode VII). 1935 *The Golden Eggs* (unfinished). 1935 *Similes* (unfinished).

WRITINGS ABOUT THE DRAMA

Some Platitudes Concerning Drama, published in *The Inn of Tranquillity,* 1912. *Anglo-American Drama and Its Future,* published in *Another Sheaf,* 1919. *Glimpses and Reflections* (passim), 1937.

JUSTICE

Persons of the Play

JAMES HOW } *solicitors.*
WALTER HOW, *his son* } *solicitors.*
ROBERT COKESON, *their managing clerk.*
WILLIAM FALDER, *their junior clerk.*
SWEEDLE, *their office-boy.*
WISTER, *a detective.*
COWLEY, *a cashier.*
MR. JUSTICE FLOYD, *a judge.*
HAROLD CLEAVER, *an old advocate.*
HECTOR FROME, *a young advocate.*
CAPTAIN DANSON, V.C., *a prison governor.*

THE REV. HUGH MILLER, *a prison chaplain.*
EDWARD CLEMENTS, *a prison doctor.*
WOODER, *a chief warder.*
MOANEY } *convicts.*
CLIPTON } *convicts.*
O'CLEARY } *convicts.*
RUTH HONEYWILL, *a woman.*

A Number of BARRISTERS, SOLICITORS, SPECTATORS, USHERS, REPORTERS, JURYMEN, WARDERS, *and* PRISONERS.

Time: The Present.

ACT I.—The office of James and Walter How. Morning. July.
ACT II.—Assizes. Afternoon. October.
ACT III.—A prison. December.
SCENE I.—The Governor's office.
SCENE II.—A corridor.
SCENE III.—A cell.
ACT IV.—The office of James and Walter How. Morning. March, two years later.

ACT I

SCENE.—*The managing clerk's room, at the offices of* JAMES AND WALTER HOW, *on a July morning. The room is old-fashioned, furnished with well-worn mahogany and leather, and lined with tin boxes and estate plans. It has three doors. Two of them are close together in the center of a wall. One of these two doors leads to the outer office, which is divided from the managing clerk's room only by a partition of wood and clear glass; and when the door into this outer office is opened there can be seen the wide outer door leading out on to the stone stairway of the building. The other of these two center doors leads to the junior clerk's room. The third door is that leading to the partners' room.*

[*The managing clerk,* COKESON, *is sitting at his table adding up figures in a pass-book, and murmuring their numbers to himself. He is a man of sixty, wearing spectacles; rather short, with a bald head, and an honest, pug-dog face. He is dressed in a well-worn black frock-coat and pepper-and-salt trousers.*]

Cokeson. And five's twelve, and three—fifteen, nineteen, twenty-three, thirty-two, forty-one—and carry four. [*He ticks the page, and goes on murmuring.*] Five, seven, twelve, seventeen, twenty-four and nine, thirty-three, thirteen and carry one.

[*He again makes a tick. The outer office door is opened, and* SWEEDLE, *the office-boy, appears, closing the door behind him. He is a pale youth of sixteen, with spiky hair.*]

Cokeson. [*With grumpy expectation.*] And carry one.

Sweedle. There's a party wants to see Falder, Mr. Cokeson.

Cokeson. Five, nine, sixteen, twenty-one, twenty-nine—and carry two. Sent him to Morris's. What name?

Sweedle. Honeywill.

Cokeson. What's his business?

Sweedle. It's a woman.

Cokeson. A lady?

Sweedle. No, a person.

Cokeson. Ask her in. Take this pass-book to Mr. James.

[*He closes the pass-book.*]

Sweedle. [*Reopening the door.*] Will you come in, please?

[RUTH HONEYWILL *comes in. She is a tall woman, twenty-six years old, unpretentiously dressed, with black hair and eyes, and an ivory-white, clear-cut face. She stands very still, having a natural dignity of pose and gesture.*

SWEEDLE *goes out into the partners' room with the pass-book.*]

Cokeson. [*Looking around at* RUTH.] The young man's out. [*Suspiciously.*] State your business, please.

Ruth. [*Who speaks in a matter-of-fact voice, and with a slight West-Country accent.*] It's a personal matter, sir.

Cokeson. We don't allow private callers here. Will you leave a message?

Ruth. I'd rather see him, please.

[*She narrows her dark eyes and gives him a honeyed look.*]

Cokeson. [*Expanding.*] It's all against the rules. Suppose I had *my* friends here to see me! It'd never do!

Ruth. No, sir.

Cokeson. [*A little taken aback.*] Exactly! And here you are wanting to see a *junior* clerk!

Ruth. Yes, sir; I must see him.

Cokeson. [*Turning full around to her with a sort of outraged interest.*] But this is a lawyer's office. Go to his private address.

Ruth. He's not there.

Cokeson. [*Uneasy.*] Are you related to the party?

Ruth. No, sir.

Cokeson. [*In real embarrassment.*] I don't know what to say. It's no affair of the office.

Ruth. But what am I to do?

Cokeson. Dear me! I can't tell you that.

[SWEEDLE *comes back. He crosses to the outer office and passes through into it, with a quizzical look at* COKESON, *carefully leaving the door an inch or two open.*]

Cokeson. [*Fortified by this look.*] This won't do, you know, this won't do at all. Suppose one of the partners came in!

[*An incoherent knocking and chuckling is heard from the outer door of the outer office.*]

Sweedle. [*Putting his head in.*] There's some children outside here.

Ruth. They're mine, please.

Sweedle. Shall I hold them in check?

Ruth. They're quite small, sir.

[*She takes a step towards* COKESON.]

Cokeson. You mustn't take up his time in office hours; we're a clerk short as it is.

Ruth. It's a matter of life and death.

Cokeson. [*Again outraged.*] Life and death!

Sweedle. Here *is* Falder.

[FALDER *has entered through the outer office. He is a pale, good-looking young man, with quick, rather scared eyes. He moves towards the door of the clerk's office, and stands there irresolute.*]

Cokeson. Well, I'll give you a minute. It's not regular.

[*Taking up a bundle of papers, he goes out into the partner's room.*]

Ruth. [*In a low, hurried voice.*] He's on the drink again, Will. He tried to cut my throat last night. I came out with the children before he was awake. I went around to you——

Falder. I've changed my digs.

Ruth. Is it all ready for tonight?

Falder. I've got the tickets. Meet me 11.45 at the booking office. For God's sake don't forget we're man and wife! [*Looking at her with tragic intensity.*] Ruth!

Ruth. You're not afraid of going, are you?

Falder. Have you got your things, and the children's?

Ruth. Had to leave them, for fear of waking Honeywill, all but one bag. I can't go near home again.

Falder. [*Wincing.*] All that money gone for nothing. How much *must* you have?

Ruth. Six pounds—I could do with that, I think.

Falder. Don't give away where we're going. [*As if to himself.*] When I get out there I mean to forget it all.

Ruth. If you're sorry, say so. I'd sooner he killed me than take you against your will.

Falder. [*With a queer smile.*] We've *got* to go. I don't care; I'll have *you.*

Ruth. You've just to say; it's not too late.

Falder. It *is* too late. Here's seven pounds. Booking office—11.45 tonight. If you weren't what you are to me, Ruth——!

Ruth. Kiss me!

[*They cling together passionately, then fly apart just as* COKESON *reenters the room.* RUTH *turns and goes out through the outer office.* COKESON *advances deliberately to his chair and seats himself.*]

Cokeson. This isn't right, Falder.

Falder. It shan't occur again, sir.

Cokeson. It's an improper use of these premises.

Falder. Yes, sir.

Cokeson. You quite understand—the party

was in some distress; and, having children with her, I allowed my feelings—— [*He opens a drawer and produces from it a tract.*] Just take this! "Purity in the Home." It is a well-written thing.

Falder. [*Taking it, with a peculiar expression.*] Thank you, sir.

Cokeson. And look here, Falder, before Mr. Walter comes, have you finished up that cataloguing Davis had in hand before he left?

Falder. I shall have done with it tomorrow, sir—for good.

Cokeson. It's over a week since Davis went. Now it won't do, Falder. You're neglecting your work for private life. I shan't mention about the party having called, but——

Falder. [*Passing into his room.*] Thank you, sir.

[COKESON *stares at the door through which* FALDER *has gone out; then shakes his head, and is just settling down to write, when* WALTER HOW *comes in through the outer office. He is a rather refined-looking man of thirty-five, with a pleasant, almost apologetic voice.*]

Walter. Good morning, Cokeson.

Cokeson. Morning, Mr. Walter.

Walter. My father here?

Cokeson. [*Always with a certain patronage as to a young man who might be doing better.*] Mr. James has been here since eleven o'clock.

Walter. I've been in to see the pictures, at the Guildhall.

Cokeson. [*Looking at him as though this were exactly what was to be expected.*] Have you now—ye-es. This lease of Boulter's—am I to send it to counsel?

Walter. What does my father say?

Cokeson. 'Aven't bothered him.

Walter. Well, we can't be too careful.

Cokeson. It's such a little thing—hardly worth the fees. I thought you'd do it yourself.

Walter. Send it, please. I don't want the responsibility.

Cokeson. [*With an indescribable air of compassion.*] Just as you like. This "right-of-way" case—we've got 'em on the deeds.

Walter. I know; but the intention was obviously to exclude that bit of common ground.

Cokeson. We needn't worry about that. We're the *right* side of the law.

Walter. I don't like it.

Cokeson. [*With an indulgent smile.*] We shan't want to set ourselves up against the law. Your father wouldn't waste his time doing that.

[*As he speaks* JAMES HOW *comes in from the partners' room. He is a shortish man, with white side-whiskers, plentiful gray hair, shrewd eyes, and gold pince-nez.*]

James. Morning, Walter.

Walter. How are you, Father?

Cokeson. [*Looking down his nose at the papers in his hand as though deprecating their size.*] I'll just take Boulter's lease in to young Falder to draft the instructions.

[*He goes out into* FALDER'S *room.*]

Walter. About that "right-of-way" case?

James. Oh, well, we must go forward there. I thought you told me yesterday the firm's balance was over four hundred.

Walter. So it is.

James. [*Holding out the pass-book to his son.*] Three—five—one, no recent checks. Just get me out the check-book.

[WALTER *goes to a cupboard, unlocks a drawer and produces a check-book.*]

James. Tick the pounds in the counterfoils. Five, fifty-four, seven, five, twenty-eight, twenty, ninety, eleven, fifty-two, seventy-one. Tally?

Walter. [*Nodding.*] Can't understand. Made sure it was over four hundred.

James. Give me the check-book. [*He takes the check-book and cons the counterfoils.*] What's this ninety?

Walter. Who drew it?

James. You.

Walter. [*Taking the check-book.*] July 7th? That's the day I went down to look over the Trenton Estate—last Friday week; I came back on the Tuesday, you remember. But look here, Father, it was *nine* I drew a check for. Five guineas to Smithers and my expenses. It just covered all but half a crown.

James. [*Gravely.*] Let's look at that ninety check. [*He sorts the check out from the bundle in the pocket of the pass-book.*] Seems all right. There's no nine here. This is bad. Who cashed that nine-pound check?

Walter. [*Puzzled and pained.*] Let's see! I was finishing Mrs. Reddy's will—only just had time; yes—I gave it to Cokeson.

James. Look at that *t y*: that yours?

Walter. [*After consideration.*] My *y's* curl back a little; this doesn't.

James. [*As* COKESON *reenters from* FALDER'S *room.*] We must ask him. Just come here and carry your mind back a bit, Cokeson. D'you remember cashing a check for Mr. Walter last Friday week—the day he went to Trenton?

Cokeson. Ye-es. Nine pounds.

James. Look at this.

[*Handing him the check.*]

Cokeson. No! Nine pounds. My lunch was just coming in; and of course I *like* it hot; I gave the check to Davis to run around to the bank. He brought it back, all gold—you remember, Mr. Walter, you wanted some silver to pay your cab. [*With a certain contemptuous compassion.*] Here, let *me* see. You've got the wrong check.

[*He takes check-book and pass-book from* WALTER.]

Walter. Afraid not.

Cokeson. [*Having seen for himself.*] It's funny.

James You gave it to Davis, and Davis sailed for Australia on Monday. Looks black, Cokeson.

Cokeson. [*Puzzled and upset.*] Why this'd be a felony! No, no! there's some mistake.

James. I hope so.

Cokeson. There's never been anything of that sort in the office the twenty-nine years I've been here.

James. [*Looking at check and counterfoil.*] This is a very clever bit of work; a warning to you not to leave space after your figures, Walter.

Walter. [*Vexed.*] Yes, I know—I was in such a tearing hurry that afternoon.

Cokeson. [*Suddenly.*] This has upset me.

James. The counterfoil altered too—very deliberate piece of swindling. What was Davis's ship?

Walter. *City of Rangoon.*

James. We ought to wire and have him arrested at Naples; he can't be there yet.

Cokeson. His poor young wife. I liked the young man. Dear, oh dear! In this office!

Walter. Shall I go to the bank and ask the cashier?

James. [*Grimly.*] Bring him around here. And ring up Scotland Yard.

Walter. Really?

[*He goes out through the outer office.* JAMES *paces the room. He stops and looks at* COKESON, *who is disconsolately rubbing the knees of his trousers.*]

James. Well, Cokeson! There's something in character, isn't there?

Cokeson. [*Looking at him over his spectacles.*] I don't quite take you, sir.

James. Your story would sound d——d thin to any one who didn't know you.

Cokeson. Ye-es! [*He laughs. Then with sudden gravity.*] I'm sorry for that young man. I feel it as if it was my own son, Mr. James.

James. A nasty business!

Cokeson. It unsettles you. All goes on regular, and then a thing like this happens. Shan't relish my lunch today.

James. As bad as that, Cokeson?

Cokeson. It makes you think. [*Confidentially.*] He must have had temptation.

James. Not so fast. We haven't convicted him yet.

Cokeson. I'd sooner have lost a month's salary than had this happen. [*He broods.*]

James. I hope that fellow will hurry up.

Cokeson. [*Keeping things pleasant for the cashier.*] It isn't fifty yards, Mr. James. He won't be a minute.

James. The idea of dishonesty about this office—it hits me hard, Cokeson.

[*He goes towards the door of the partners' room.*]

Sweedle. [*Entering quietly, to* COKESON *in a low voice.*] She's popped up again, sir—something she forgot to say to Falder.

Cokeson. [*Roused from his abstraction.*] Eh? Impossible. Send her away!

James. What's that?

Cokeson. Nothing, Mr. James. A private matter. Here, I'll come myself. [*He goes into the outer office as* JAMES *passes into the partners' room.*] Now, you really mustn't—we can't have anybody just now.

Ruth. Not for a minute, sir?

Cokeson. Reely! Reely! I can't have it. If you want him, wait about; he'll be going out for his lunch directly.

Ruth. Yes, sir.

[WALTER, *entering with the* CASHIER, *passes* RUTH *as she leaves the outer office.*]

Cokeson. [*To the* CASHIER, *who resembles a sedentary dragoon.*] Good morning. [*To* WALTER.] Your father's in there.

[WALTER *crosses and goes into the partners' room.*]

Cokeson. It's a nahsty, unpleasant little matter, Mr. Cowley. I'm quite ashamed to have to trouble you.

Cowley. I remember the check quite well. [*As if it were a liver.*] Seemed in perfect order.

Cokeson. Sit down, won't you? I'm not a sensitive man, but a thing like this about the place—it's not nice. I like people to be open and jolly together.

Cowley. Quite so.

Cokeson. [*Buttonholing him, and glancing towards the partners' room.*] Of course, he's a young man. I've told him about it before now—leaving space after his figures, but he *will* do it.

Cowley. I should remember the person's face—quite a youth.

Cokeson. I don't think we shall be able to show him to you, as a matter of fact.

[JAMES *and* WALTER *have come back from the partners' room.*]

James. Good morning, Mr. Cowley. You've seen my son and myself, you've seen Mr. Cokeson, and you've seen Sweedle, my office-boy. It was none of us, I take it.

[*The* CASHIER *shakes his head with a smile.*]

James. Be so good as to sit there. Cokeson, engage Mr. Cowley in conversation, will you?

[*He goes towards* FALDER'S *room.*]

Cokeson. Just a word, Mr. James.

James. Well?

Cokeson. You don't want to upset the young man in there, do you? He's a nervous young feller.

James. This must be thoroughly cleared up, Cokeson, for the sake of Falder's name, to say nothing of yours.

Cokeson. [*With some dignity.*] That'll look after itself, sir. He's been upset once this morning; I don't want him startled again.

James. It's a matter of form; but I can't stand upon niceness over a thing like this—too serious. Just talk to Mr. Cowley.

[*He opens the door of* FALDER'S *room.*]

James. Bring in the papers in Boulter's lease, will you, Falder?

Cokeson. [*Bursting into voice.*] Do you keep dogs?

[*The* CASHIER, *with his eyes fixed on the door, does not answer.*]

Cokeson. You haven't such a thing as a bulldog pup you could spare me, I suppose?

[*At the look on the* CASHIER'S *face his jaw drops, and he turns to see* FALDER *standing in the doorway, with his eyes fixed on* COWLEY, *like the eyes of a rabbit fastened on a snake.*]

Falder. [*Advancing with the papers.*] Here they are, sir.

James. [*Taking them.*] Thank you.

Falder. Do you want me, sir?

James. No, thanks.

[FALDER *turns and goes back into his own room. As he shuts the door* JAMES *gives the* CASHIER *an interrogative look, and the* CASHIER *nods.*]

James. Sure? This isn't as we suspected.

Cowley. Quite. He knew me. I suppose he can slip out of that room?

Cokeson. [*Gloomily.*] There's only the window—a whole floor and a basement.

[*The door of* FALDER'S *room is quietly opened, and* FALDER, *with his hat in his hand, moves towards the door of the outer office.*]

James. [*Quietly.*] Where are you going, Falder?

Falder. To have my lunch, sir.

James. Wait a few minutes, would you? I want to speak to you about this lease.

Falder. Yes, sir.

[*He goes back into his room.*]

Cowley. If I'm wanted, I can swear that's the young man who cashed the check. It was the last check I handled that morning before my lunch. These are the numbers of the notes he had. [*He puts a slip of paper on the table; then, brushing his hat around.*] Good morning!

James. Good morning, Mr. Cowley!

Cowley. [*To* COKESON.] Good morning.

Cokeson. [*With stupefaction.*] Good morning.

[*The* CASHIER *goes out through the outer office.* COKESON *sits down in his chair, as though it were the only place left in the morass of his feelings.*]

Walter. What are you going to do?

James. Have him in. Give me the check and the counterfoil.

Cokeson. I don't understand. I thought young Davis——

James. We shall see.

Walter. One moment, Father: have you thought it out?

James. Call him in!

Cokeson. [*Rising with difficulty and opening* FALDER'S *door; hoarsely.*] Step in here a minute. [FALDER *comes in.*]

Falder. [*Impassively.*] Yes, sir?

James. [*Turning to him suddenly with the check held out.*] You know this check, Falder?

Falder. No, sir.

James. Look at it. You cashed it last Friday week.

Falder. Oh! yes, sir; that one—Davis gave it me.

James. I know. And you gave Davis the cash?

Falder. Yes, sir.

James. When Davis gave you the check was it exactly like this?

Falder. Yes, I think so sir.

James. You know that Mr. Walter drew that check for *nine* pounds?

Falder. No, sir—ninety.

James. Nine, Falder.

Falder. [*Faintly.*] I don't understand, sir.

James. The suggestion, of course, is that

the check was altered; whether by you or Davis is the question.

Falder. I—I——

Cokeson. Take your time, take your time.

Falder. [*Regaining his impassivity.*] Not by me, sir.

James. The check was handed to Cokeson by Mr. Walter at one o'clock; we know that because Mr. Cokeson's lunch had just arrived.

Cokeson. I couldn't leave it.

James. Exactly; he therefore gave the check to Davis. It was cashed by you at 1.15. We know that because the cashier recollects it for the last check he handled before *his* lunch.

Falder. Yes, sir, Davis gave it to me because some friends were giving him a farewell luncheon.

James. [*Puzzled.*] You accuse Davis, then?

Falder. I don't know, sir—it's very funny.

[WALTER, *who has come close to his father, says something to him in a low voice.*]

James. Davis was not here again after that Saturday, was he?

Cokeson. [*Anxious to be of assistance to the young man, and seeing faint signs of their all being jolly once more.*] No, he sailed on the Monday.

James. Was he, Falder?

Falder. [*Very faintly.*] No, sir.

James. Very well, then, how do you account for the fact that this nought was added to the nine in the counterfoil on or after *Tuesday*?

Cokeson. [*Surprised.*] How's that?

[FALDER *gives a sort of lurch; he tries to pull himself together, but he has gone all to pieces.*]

James. [*Very grimly.*] Out, I'm afraid, Cokeson. The check-book remained in Mr. Walter's pocket till he came back from Trenton on Tuesday morning. In the face of this, Falder, do you still deny that you altered both check and counterfoil?

Falder. No, sir—no, Mr. How. I did it, sir; I did it.

Cokeson. [*Succumbing to his feelings.*] Dear, dear! what a thing to do!

Falder. I wanted the money so badly, sir. I didn't know what I was doing.

Cokeson. However such a thing could have come into your head!

Falder. [*Grasping at the words.*] I can't think, sir, really! It was just a minute of madness.

James. A long minute, Falder. [*Tapping the counterfoil.*] Four days at least.

Falder. Sir, I swear I didn't know what I'd done till afterwards, and then I hadn't the pluck. Oh! sir, look over it! I'll pay the money back—I will, I promise.

James. Go into your room.

[FALDER, *with a swift imploring look, goes back into his room. There is silence.*]

James. About as bad a case as there could be.

Cokeson. To break the law like that—in here!

Walter. What's to be done?

James. Nothing for it. Prosecute.

Walter. It's his first offense.

James. [*Shaking his head.*] I've grave doubts of that. Too neat a piece of swindling altogether.

Cokeson. I shouldn't be surprised if he was tempted.

James. Life's one long temptation, Cokeson.

Cokeson. Ye-es, but I'm speaking of the flesh and the devil, Mr. James. There was a woman come to see him this morning.

Walter. The woman we passed as we came in just now. Is it his wife?

Cokeson. No, no relation. [*Restraining what in jollier circumstances would have been a wink.*] A married person, though.

Walter. How do you know?

Cokeson. Brought her children. [*Scandalized.*] There they were outside the office.

James. A real bad egg.

Walter. I should like to give him a chance.

James. I can't forgive him for the sneaky way he went to work—counting on our suspecting young Davis if the matter came to light. It was the merest accident the check-book stayed in your pocket.

Walter. It *must* have been the temptation of a moment. He hadn't time.

James. A man doesn't succumb like that in a moment, if he's a clean mind and habits. He's rotten; got the eyes of a man who can't keep his hands off when there's money about.

Walter. [*Dryly.*] We hadn't noticed that before.

James. [*Brushing the remark aside.*] I've seen lots of those fellows in my time. No doing anything with them except to keep 'em out of harm's way. They've got a blind spot.

Walter. It's penal servitude.

Cokeson. They're *nahsty* places—prisons.

James. [*Hesitating.*] I don't see how it's possible to spare him. Out of the question to keep him in this office—honesty's the *sine qua non.*

Cokeson. [*Hypnotized.*] Of course it *is.*

James. Equally out of the question to send him out amongst people who've no knowledge of his character. One must think of society.

Walter. But to brand him like this?

James. If it had been a straightforward case I'd give him another chance. It's far from that. He has dissolute habits.

Cokeson. I didn't say that—extenuating circumstances.

James. Same thing. He's gone to work in the most cold-blooded way to defraud his employers, and cast the blame on an innocent man. If that's not a case for the law to take its course, I don't know what is.

Walter. For the sake of his future, though.

James. [*Sarcastically.*] According to you, no one would ever prosecute.

Walter. [*Nettled.*] I hate the idea of it.

Cokeson. That's rather *ex parte,* Mr. Walter! We must have protection.

James. This is degenerating into talk.

[*He moves towards the partners' room.*]

Walter. Put yourself in his place, Father.

James. You ask too much of me.

Walter. We can't possibly tell the pressure there was on him.

James. You may depend on it, my boy, if a man is going to do this sort of thing he'll do it, pressure or no pressure; if he isn't nothing'll make him.

Walter. He'll never do it again.

Cokeson. [*Fatuously.*] S'pose I were to have a talk with him. We don't want to be hard on the young man.

James. That'll do, Cokeson. I've made up my mind.

[*He passes into the partners' room.*]

Cokeson. [*After a doubtful moment.*] We must excuse your father. I don't want to go against your father; if he thinks it right.

Walter. Confound it, Cokeson! why don't you back me up? You know you feel——

Cokeson. [*On his dignity.*] I really can't say what I feel.

Walter. We shall regret it.

Cokeson. He must have known what he was doing.

Walter. [*Bitterly.*] "The quality of mercy is not strained."

Cokeson. [*Looking at him askance.*] Come, come, Mr. Walter. We must try and see it sensible.

Swedle. [*Entering with a tray.*] Your lunch, sir.

Cokeson. Put it down!

[*While* SWEEDLE *is putting it down on* COKESON'S *table, the detective,* WISTER, *enters the outer office, and, finding no one there, comes to the inner doorway. He is a square, medium-sized man, clean-shaved, in a serviceable blue serge suit and strong boots.*]

Wister. [*To* WALTER.] From Scotland Yard, sir. Detective-Sergeant Wister.

Walter. [*Askance.*] Very well! I'll speak to my father.

[*He goes into the partners' room.* JAMES *enters.*]

James. Morning. [*In answer to an appealing gesture from* COKESON.] I'm sorry; I'd stop short of this if I felt I could. Open that door. [SWEEDLE, *wondering and scared, opens it.*] Come here, Mr. Falder.

[*As* FALDER *comes shrinkingly out, the detective, in obedience to a sign from* JAMES, *slips his hand out and grasps his arm.*]

Falder. [*Recoiling.*] Oh! no—oh! no!

Wister. Come, come, there's a good lad.

James. I charge him with felony.

Falder. Oh, sir! There's some one—I did it for her. Let me be till tomorrow.

[JAMES *motions with his hand. At that sign of hardness,* FALDER *becomes rigid. Then, turning, he goes out quietly in the detective's grip.* JAMES *follows, stiff and erect.* SWEEDLE, *rushing to the door with open mouth, pursues them through the outer office into the corridor. When they have all disappeared* COKESON *spins completely around and makes a rush for the outer office.*]

Cokeson. [*Hoarsely.*] Here! Here! What are we doing?

[*There is silence. He takes out his handkerchief and mops the sweat from his face. Going back blindly to his table, sits down, and stares blankly at his lunch.*]

THE CURTAIN FALLS

ACT II

A Court of Justice, on a foggy October afternoon—crowded with barristers, solicitors, reporters, ushers, and jurymen. Sitting in the large, solid dock is FALDER, *with a warder on either side of him, placed there for his safe custody, but seemingly in-*

different to and unconscious of his presence.

[FALDER *is sitting exactly opposite to the* JUDGE, *who, raised above the clamor of the court, also seems unconscious of and indifferent to everything.* HAROLD CLEAVER, *the counsel for the Crown, is a dried, yellowish man, of more than middle age, in a wig worn almost to the color of his face.* HECTOR FROME, *the counsel for the defense, is a young, tall man, clean-shaved, in a very white wig. Among the spectators, having already given their evidence, are* JAMES *and* WALTER HOW, *and* COWLEY, *the cashier.* WISTER, *the detective, is just leaving the witness-box.*]

Cleaver. That is the case for the Crown, me lud!

[*Gathering his robes together, he sits down.*]

Frome. [*Rising and bowing to the* JUDGE.] If it please your lordship and gentlemen of the jury. I am not going to dispute the fact that the prisoner altered this check, but I am going to put before you evidence as to the condition of his mind, and to submit that you would not be justified in finding that he was responsible for his actions at the time. I am going to show you, in fact, that he did this in a moment of aberration, amounting to temporary insanity, caused by the violent distress under which he was laboring. Gentlemen, the prisoner is only twenty-three years old. I shall call before you a woman from whom you will learn the events that led up to this act. You will hear from her own lips the tragic circumstances of her life, the still more tragic infatuation with which she has inspired the prisoner. This woman, gentlemen, has been leading a miserable existence with a husband who habitually ill-uses her, from whom she actually goes in terror of her life. I am not, of course, saying that it's either right or desirable for a young man to fall in love with a married woman, or that it's his business to rescue her from an ogre-like husband. I'm not saying anything of the sort. But we all know the power of the passion of love; and I would ask you to remember, gentlemen, in listening to her evidence, that, married to a drunken and violent husband, she has no power to get rid of him; for, as you know, another offense besides violence is necessary to enable a woman to obtain a divorce; and of this offense it does not appear that her husband is guilty.

Judge. Is this relevant, Mr. Frome?

Frome. My lord, I submit, extremely—I shall be able to show your lordship that directly.

Judge. Very well.

Frome. In these circumstances, what alternatives were left to her? She could either go on living with this drunkard, in terror of her life; or she could apply to the Court for a separation order. Well, gentlemen, my experience of such cases assures me that this would have given her very insufficient protection from the violence of such a man; and even if effectual would very likely have reduced her either to the workhouse or the streets—for it's not easy, as she is now finding, for an unskilled woman without means of livelihood to support herself and her children without resorting either to the Poor Law or—to speak quite plainly—to the sale of her body.

Judge. You are ranging rather far, Mr. Frome.

Frome. I shall fire point-blank in a minute, my lord.

Judge. Let us hope so.

Frome. Now, gentlemen, mark—and this is what I have been leading up to—this woman will tell you, and the prisoner will confirm her, that, confronted with such alternatives, she set her whole hopes on himself, knowing the feeling with which she had inspired him. She saw a way out of her misery by going with him to a new country, where they would both be unknown, and might pass as husband and wife. This was a desperate and, as my friend Mr. Cleaver will no doubt call it, an immoral resolution; but, as a fact, the minds of both of them were constantly turned towards it. One wrong is no excuse for another, and those who are never likely to be faced by such a situation possibly have the right to hold up their hands—as to that I prefer to say nothing. But whatever view you take, gentlemen, of this part of the prisoner's story—whatever opinion you form of the right of these two young people under such circumstances to take the law into their own hands—the fact remains that this young woman in her distress, and this young man, little more than a boy, who was so devotedly attached to her, *did* conceive this—if you like—reprehensible design of going away together. Now, for that, of course, they required money, and—they had none. As to the actual events of the morning of July 7th, on which this check was altered, the events on which I rely to prove the defendant's irresponsibility—I shall allow those events to speak for themselves, through the lips of my witnesses. Robert Cokeson.

[*He turns, looks around, takes up a sheet*

of paper, and waits. COKESON *is summoned into court, and goes into the witness-box, holding his hat before him. The oath is administered to him.*]

Frome. What is your name?

Cokeson. Robert Cokeson.

Frome. Are you managing clerk of the firm of solicitors who employ the prisoner?

Cokeson. Ye-es.

Frome. How long had the prisoner been in their employ?

Cokeson. Two years. No, I'm wrong there —all but seventeen days.

Frome. Had you him under your eye all that time?

Cokeson. Except Sundays and holidays.

Frome. Quite so. Let us hear, please, what you have to say about his general character during those two years.

Cokeson. [*Confidentially to the jury, and as if a little surprised at being asked.*] He was a nice, pleasant-spoken young man. I'd no fault to find with him—quite the contrary. It was a *great* surprise to me when he did a thing like that.

Frome. Did he ever give you reason to suspect his honesty?

Cokeson. No! To have dishonesty in our office, that'd never do.

Frome. I'm sure the jury fully appreciate that, Mr. Cokeson.

Cokeson. Every man of business knows that honesty's the sign qua non.

Frome. Do you give him a good character all round, or do you not?

Cokeson. [*Turning to the* JUDGE.] Certainly. We were all very jolly and pleasant together, until this happened. Quite upset me.

Frome. Now, coming to the morning of the 7th of July, the morning on which the check was altered. What have you to say about his demeanor that morning?

Cokeson. [*To the jury.*] If you ask me, I don't think he was quite compos when he did it.

The Judge. [*Sharply.*] Are you suggesting that he was insane?

Cokeson. Not compos.

The Judge. A little more precision, please.

Frome. [*Smoothly.*] Just tell us, Mr. Cokeson.

Cokeson. [*Somewhat outraged.*] Well, in my opinion—[*looking at the* JUDGE]—such as it is—he was jumpy at the time. The jury will understand my meaning.

Frome. Will you tell us how you came to that conclusion?

Cokeson. Ye-es, I will. I have my lunch in from the restaurant, a chop and a potato—saves time. That day it happened to come just as Mr. Walter How handed me the check. Well, I like it hot; so I went into the clerks' office and I handed the check to Davis, the other clerk, and told him to get change. I noticed young Falder walking up and down. I said to him: "This is not the Zoological Gardens, Falder."

Frome. Do you remember what he answered?

Cokeson. Ye-es: "I wish to God it were!" Struck me as funny.

Frome. Did you notice anything else peculiar?

Cokeson. I did.

Frome. What was that?

Cokeson. His collar was unbuttoned. Now, I like a young man to be neat, I said to him: "Your collar's unbuttoned."

Frome. And what did he answer?

Cokeson. Stared at me. It wasn't nice.

The Judge. Stared at you? Isn't that a very common practise?

Cokeson. Ye-es, but it was the look in his eyes. I can't explain my meaning—it was funny.

Frome. Had you ever seen such a look in his eyes before?

Cokeson. No. If I had I should have spoken to the partners. We can't have anything eccentric in our profession.

The Judge. Did you speak to them on that occasion?

Cokeson. [*Confidentially.*] Well, I didn't like to trouble them about prime facey evidence.

Frome. But it made a very distinct impression on your mind?

Cokeson. Ye-es. The clerk Davis could have told you the same.

Frome. Quite so. It's very unfortunate that we've not got him here. Now can you tell me of the morning on which the discovery of the forgery was made? That would be the 18th. Did anything happen that morning?

Cokeson. [*With his hand to his ear.*] I'm a little deaf.

Frome. Was there anything in the course of that morning—I mean before the discovery—that caught your attention?

Cokeson. Ye-es—a woman.

The Judge. How is *this* relevant, Mr. Frome?

Frome. I am trying to establish the state of mind in which the prisoner committed this act, my lord.

The Judge. I quite appreciate that. But this was long after the act.

Frome. Yes, my lord, but it contributes to my contention.

The Judge. Well!

Frome. You say a woman. Do you mean that she came to the office?

Cokeson. Ye-es.

Frome. What for?

Cokeson. Asked to see young Falder; he was out at the moment.

Frome. Did you see her?

Cokeson. I did.

Frome. Did she come alone?

Cokeson. [*Confidentially.*] Well, there you put me in a difficulty. I mustn't tell you what the office-boy told me.

Frome. Quite so, Mr. Cokeson, quite so——

Cokeson. [*Breaking in with an air of "You are young—leave it to me."*] But I think we can get 'round it. In answer to a question put to her by a third party the woman said to me: "They're mine, sir."

The Judge. What are? What were?

Cokeson. Her children. They were outside.

The Judge. How do you know?

Cokeson. Your lordship mustn't ask me that, or I shall have to tell you what I was told—and that'd never do.

The Judge. [*Smiling.*] The office-boy made a statement.

Cokeson. Egg-zactly.

Frome. What I want to ask you, Mr. Cokeson, is this. In the course of her appeal to see Falder, did the woman say anything that you specially remember?

Cokeson. [*Looking at him as if to encourage him to complete the sentence.*] A leetle more, sir.

Frome. Or did she not?

Cokeson. She did. I shouldn't like you to have led me to the answer.

Frome. [*With an irritated smile.*] Will you tell the jury what it was?

Cokeson. "It's a matter of life and death."

Foreman of the Jury. Do you mean the woman said that?

Cokeson. [*Nodding.*] It's not the sort of thing you like to have said to you.

Frome. [*A little impatiently.*] Did Falder come in while she was there? [COKESON *nods.*] And she saw him, and went away?

Cokeson. Ah! there I can't follow you. I didn't see her go.

Frome. Well, is she there now?

Cokeson. [*With an indulgent smile.*] No!

Frome. Thank you, Mr. Cokeson.

[*He sits down.*]

Cleaver. [*Rising.*] You say that on the morning of the forgery the prisoner was jumpy. Well, now, sir, what precisely do you mean by that word?

Cokeson. [*Indulgently.*] I *want* you to understand. Have you ever seen a dog that's lost its master? He was kind of everywhere at once with his eyes.

Cleaver. Thank you; I was coming to his eyes. You called them "funny." What are we to understand by that? Strange, or what?

Cokeson. Ye-es, funny.

Cleaver. [*Sharply.*] Yes, sir, but what may be funny to you may not be funny to me, or to the jury. Did they look frightened, or shy, or fierce, or what?

Cokeson. You make it very hard for me. I give you the word, and you want me to give you another.

Cleaver. [*Rapping his desk.*] *Does* "funny" mean mad?

Cokeson. Not mad, fun——

Cleaver. Very well! Now you say he had his collar unbuttoned? Was it a hot day?

Cokeson. Ye-es; I think it was.

Cleaver. And did he button it when you called his attention to it?

Cokeson. Ye-es, I think he did.

Cleaver. Would you say that that denoted insanity?

[*He sits down.* COKESON, *who has opened his mouth to reply, is left gaping.*]

Frome. [*Rising hastily.*] Have you ever caught him in that disheveled state before?

Cokeson. No! He was *always* clean and quiet.

Frome. That will do, thank you.

[COKESON *turns blandly to the* JUDGE, *as though to rebuke counsel for not remembering that the* JUDGE *might wish to have a chance; arriving at the conclusion that he is to be asked nothing further, he turns and descends from the box, and sits down next to* JAMES *and* WALTER.]

Frome. Ruth Honeywill.

[RUTH *comes into court, and takes her stand stoically in the witness-box. She is sworn.*]

Frome. What is your name, please?

Ruth. Ruth Honeywill.

Frome. How old are you?

Ruth. Twenty-six.

Frome. You are a married woman, living with your husband? A little louder.

Ruth. No, sir; not since July.

Frome. Have you any children?

Ruth. Yes, sir, two.

Frome. Are they living with you?

Ruth. Yes, sir.

Frome. You know the prisoner?

Ruth. [*Looking at him.*] Yes.

Frome. What was the nature of your relations with him?

Ruth. We were friends.

The Judge. Friends?

Ruth. [*Simply.*] Lovers, sir.

The Judge. [*Sharply.*] In what sense do you use that word?

Ruth. We love each other.

The Judge. Yes, but——

Ruth. [*Shaking her head.*] No, your lordship—not yet.

The Judge. Not yet! H'm! [*He looks from* RUTH *to* FALDER.] Well!

Frome. What is your husband?

Ruth. Traveler.

Frome. And what was the nature of your married life?

Ruth. [*Shaking her head.*] It don't bear talking about.

Frome. Did he ill-treat you, or what?

Ruth. Ever since my first was born.

Frome. In what way?

Ruth. I'd rather not say. All sorts of ways.

The Judge. I am afraid I must stop this, you know.

Ruth. [*Pointing to* FALDER.] He offered to take me out of it, sir. We were going to South America.

Frome. [*Hastily.*] Yes, quite—and what prevented you?

Ruth. I was outside his office when he was taken away. It nearly broke my heart.

Frome. You knew, then, that he had been arrested?

Ruth. Yes, sir. I called at his office afterwards, and [*pointing to* COKESON] that gentleman told me all about it.

Frome. Now, do you remember the morning of Friday, July 7th?

Ruth. Yes.

Frome. Why?

Ruth. My husband nearly strangled me that morning.

The Judge. Nearly strangled you!

Ruth. [*Bowing her head.*] Yes, my lord.

Frome. With his hands, or——?

Ruth. Yes, I just managed to get away from him. I went straight to my friend. It was eight o'clock.

The Judge. In the morning? Your husband was not under the influence of liquor then?

Ruth. It wasn't always that.

Frome. In what condition were you?

Ruth. In very bad condition, sir. My dress was torn, and I was half choking.

Frome. Did you tell your friend what had happened?

Ruth. Yes. I wish I never had.

Frome. It upset him?

Ruth. Dreadfully.

Frome. Did he ever speak to you about a check?

Ruth. Never.

Frome. Did he ever give you any money?

Ruth. Yes.

Frome. When was that?

Ruth. On Saturday.

Frome. The 8th?

Ruth. To buy an outfit for me and the children and get all ready to start.

Frome. Did that surprise you, or not?

Ruth. What, sir?

Frome. That he had money to give you.

Ruth. Yes, because on the morning when my husband nearly killed me my friend cried because he hadn't the money to get me away. He told me afterwards he'd come into a windfall.

Frome. And when did you last see him?

Ruth. The day he was taken away, sir. It was the day we were to have started.

Frome. Oh, yes, the morning of the arrest. Well, did you see him at all between the Friday and that morning? [RUTH *nods.*] What was his manner then?

Ruth. Dumb-like—sometimes he didn't seem able to say a word.

Frome. As if something unusual had happened to him?

Ruth. Yes.

Frome. Painful, or pleasant, or what?

Ruth. Like a fate hanging over him.

Frome. [*Hesitating.*] Tell me, did you love the prisoner very much?

Ruth. [*Bowing her head.*] Yes.

Frome. And had he a very great affection for you?

Ruth. [*Looking at* FALDER.] Yes, sir.

Frome. Now, ma'am, do you or do you not think that your danger and unhappiness would seriously affect his balance, his control over his actions?

Ruth. Yes.

Frome. His reason, even?

Ruth. For a moment like, I think it would.

Frome. Was he very much upset that Friday morning, or was he fairly calm?

Ruth. Dreadfully upset. I could hardly bear to let him go from me.

Frome. Do you still love him?

Ruth. [*With her eyes on* FALDER.] He's ruined himself for me.

Frome. Thank you.

[*He sits down.* RUTH *remains stoically upright in the witness-box.*]

Cleaver. [*In a considerate voice.*] When you left him on the morning of Friday the 7th, you would not say that he was out of his mind, I suppose?

Ruth. No, sir.

Cleaver. Thank you; I've no further questions to ask you.

Ruth. [*Bending a little forward to the jury.*] I would have done the same for him; I would indeed.

The Judge. Please, please! You say your married life is an unhappy one? Faults on both sides?

Ruth. Only that I never bowed down to him. I don't see why I should, sir, not to a man like that.

The Judge. You refused to obey him?

Ruth. [*Avoiding the question.*] I've always studied him to keep things nice.

The Judge. Until you met the prisoner—was that it?

Ruth. No; even after that.

The Judge. I ask, you know, because you seem to me to glory in this affection of yours for the prisoner.

Ruth. [*Hesitating.*] I—I do. It's the only thing in my life now.

The Judge. [*Staring at her hard.*] Well, step down, please.

[RUTH *looks at* FALDER, *then passes quietly down and takes her seat among the witnesses.*]

Frome. I call the prisoner, my lord.

[FALDER *leaves the dock; goes into the witness-box, and is duly sworn.*]

Frome. What is your name?

Falder. William Falder.

Frome. And age?

Falder. Twenty-three.

Frome. You are not married?

[FALDER *shakes his head.*]

Frome. How long have you known the last witness?

Falder. Six months.

Frome. Is her account of the relationship between you a correct one?

Falder. Yes.

Frome. You became devotedly attached to her, however?

Falder. Yes.

The Judge. Though you knew she was a married woman?

Falder. I couldn't help it, your lordship.

The Judge. Couldn't help it?

Falder. I didn't seem able to.

[*The* JUDGE *slightly shrugs his shoulders.*]

Frome. How did you come to know her?

Falder. Through my married sister.

Frome. Did you know whether she was happy with her husband?

Falder. It was trouble all the time.

Frome. You knew her husband?

Falder. Only through her—he's a brute.

The Judge. I can't allow indiscriminate abuse of a person not present.

Frome. [*Bowing.*] If your lordship pleases. [*To* FALDER.] You admit altering this check?

[FALDER *bows his head.*]

Frome. Carry your mind, please, to the morning of Friday, July the 7th, and tell the jury what happened.

Falder. [*Turning to the jury.*] I was having my breakfast when she came. Her dress was all torn, and she was gasping and couldn't seem to get her breath at all; there were the marks of his fingers round her throat; her arm was bruised, and the blood had got into her eyes dreadfully. It frightened me, and then when she told me, I felt—I felt—well—it was too much for me! [*Hardening suddenly.*] If you'd seen it, having the feelings for her that I had, you'd have felt the same, I know.

Frome. Yes?

Falder. When she left me—because I had to go to the office—I was out of my senses for fear that he'd do it again, and thinking what I could do. I couldn't work—all the morning I was like that—simply couldn't fix my mind on anything. I couldn't think at all. I seemed to have to keep moving. When Davis—the other clerk—gave me the check—he said: "It'll do you good, Will, to have a run with this. You seem half off your chump this morning." Then when I had it in my hand—I don't know how it came, but it just flashed across me that if I put the *t y* and the nought there would be the money to get her away. It just came and went—I never thought of it again. Then Davis went out to his luncheon, and I don't really remember what I did till I'd pushed the check through to the cashier under the rail. I remember his saying "Gold or notes?" Then I suppose I knew what I'd done. Anyway, when I got outside I wanted to chuck myself under a 'bus; I wanted to throw the money away; but it seemed I was in for it, so I thought at any rate I'd save her. Of course the tickets I took for the passage and the little I gave her's been wasted, and all, except what I was obliged to spend myself, I've restored. I keep thinking over and over however it was I came to do it, and how I can't have it all again to do differently!

[FALDER *is silent, twisting his hands before him.*]

Frome. How far is it from your office to the bank?

Falder. Not more than fifty yards, sir.

Frome. From the time Davis went out to lunch to the time you cashed the check, how long do you say it must have been?

Falder. It couldn't have been four minutes, sir, because I ran all the way.

Frome. During those four minutes you say you remember nothing?

Falder. No, sir; only that I ran.

Frome. Not even adding the *t y* and the nought?

Falder. No, sir. I don't really.

[FROME *sits down, and* CLEAVER *rises.*]

Cleaver. But you remember running, do you?

Falder. I was all out of breath when I got to the bank.

Cleaver. And you don't remember altering the check?

Falder. [*Faintly.*] No, sir.

Cleaver. Divested of the romantic glamour which my friend is casting over the case, is this anything but an ordinary forgery? Come.

Falder. I was half frantic all that morning, sir.

Cleaver. Now, now! You don't deny that the *t y* and the nought were so like the rest of the handwriting as to thoroughly deceive the cashier?

Falder. It was an accident.

Cleaver. [*Cheerfully.*] Queer sort of accident, wasn't it? On which day did you alter the counterfoil?

Falder. [*Hanging his head.*] On the Wednesday morning.

Cleaver. Was that an accident, too?

Falder. [*Faintly.*] No.

Cleaver. To do that you had to watch your opportunity, I suppose?

Falder. [*Almost inaudibly.*] Yes.

Cleaver. You don't suggest that you were suffering under great excitement when you did that?

Falder. I was haunted.

Cleaver. With the fear of being found out?

Falder. [*Very low.*] Yes.

The Judge. Didn't it occur to you that the only thing for you to do was to confess to your employers, and restore the money?

Falder. I was afraid. [*There is silence.*]

Cleaver. You desired, too, no doubt, to complete your design of taking this woman away?

Falder. When I found I'd done a thing like that, to do it for nothing seemed so dreadful. I might just as well have chucked myself into the river.

Cleaver. You knew that the clerk Davis was about to leave England—didn't it occur to you when you altered this check that suspicion would fall on him?

Falder. It was all done in a moment. I thought of it afterwards.

Cleaver. And that didn't lead you to avow what you'd done?

Falder. [*Sullenly.*] I meant to write when I got out there—I would have repaid the money.

The Judge. But in the meantime your innocent fellow clerk might have been prosecuted.

Falder. I knew he was a long way off, your lordship. I thought there'd be time. I didn't think they'd find it out so soon.

Frome. I might remind your lordship that as Mr. Walter How had the check-book in his pocket till after Davis had sailed, if the discovery had been made only one day later Falder himself would have left, and suspicion would have attached to him, and not to Davis, from the beginning.

The Judge. The question is whether the prisoner knew that suspicion would light on himself, and not on Davis. [*To* FALDER *sharply.*] Did you know that Mr. Walter How had the check-book till after Davis had sailed?

Falder. I—I—thought—he—

The Judge. Now speak the truth—yes or no!

Falder. [*Very low.*] No, my lord. I had no means of knowing.

The Judge. That disposes of your point, Mr. Frome.

[FROME *bows to the* JUDGE.]

Cleaver. Has any aberration of this nature ever attacked you before?

Falder. [*Faintly.*] No, sir.

Cleaver. You had recovered sufficiently to go back to your work that afternoon?

Falder. Yes, I had to take the money back.

Cleaver. You mean the nine pounds. Your wits were sufficiently keen for you to remember that? And you still persist in saying you don't remember altering this check.

[*He sits down.*]

Falder. If I hadn't been mad I should never have had the courage.

Frome. [*Rising.*] Did you have your lunch before going back?

Falder. I never ate a thing all day; and at night I couldn't sleep.

Frome. Now, as to the four minutes that elapsed between Davis's going out and your cashing the check: do you say that you recollect *nothing* during those four minutes?

Falder. [*After a moment.*] I remember thinking of Mr. Cokeson's face.

Frome. Of Mr. Cokeson's face! Had that any connection with what you were doing?

Falder. No, sir.

Frome. Was that in the office, before you ran out?

Falder. Yes, and while I was running.

Frome. And that lasted till the cashier said: "Will you have gold or notes?"

Falder. Yes, and then I seemed to come to myself—and it was too late.

Frome. Thank you. That closes the evidence for the defense, my lord.

[*The* JUDGE *nods, and* FALDER *goes back to his seat in the dock.*]

Frome. [*Gathering up notes.*] If it please your lordship—Gentlemen of the Jury—My friend in cross-examination has shown a disposition to sneer at the defense which has been set up in this case, and I am free to admit that nothing I can say will move you, if the evidence has not already convinced you that the prisoner committed this act in a moment when to all practical intents and purposes he was not responsible for his actions; a moment of such mental and moral vacuity, arising from the violent emotional agitation under which he had been suffering, as to amount to temporary madness. My friend has alluded to the "romantic glamour" with which I have sought to invest this case. Gentlemen, I have done nothing of the kind. I have merely shown you the background of "life"—that palpitating life which, believe me—whatever my friend may say—always lies behind the commission of a crime. Now, gentlemen, we live in a highly civilized age, and the sight of brutal violence disturbs us in a very strange way, even when we have no personal interest in the matter. But when we see it inflicted on a woman whom we love—what then? Just think of what your own feelings would have been, each of you, at the prisoner's age; and then look at him. Well! he is hardly the comfortable, shall we say bucolic, person likely to contemplate with equanimity marks of gross violence on a woman to whom he was devotedly attached. Yes, gentlemen, look at him. He has not a strong face; but neither has he a vicious face. He is just the sort of man who would easily become the prey of his emotions. You have heard the description of his eyes. My friend may laugh at the word "funny"—*I* think it better describes the peculiar uncanny look of those who are strained to breaking-point than any other word which could have been used. I don't pretend, mind you, that his mental irresponsibility was more than a flash of darkness, in which all sense of proportion became lost; but I do contend, that, just as a man who destroys himself at such a moment may be, and often is, absolved from the stigma attaching to the crime of self-murder, so he may, and frequently does, commit other crimes while in this irresponsible condition, and that he may as justly be acquitted of criminal intent and treated as a patient. I admit that this is a plea which might well be abused. It is a matter for discretion. But here you have a case in which there is every reason to give the benefit of the doubt. You heard me ask the prisoner what he thought of during those four fatal minutes. What was his answer? "I thought of Mr. Cokeson's face!" Gentlemen, no man could invent an answer like that; it is absolutely stamped with truth. You have seen the great affection (legitimate or not) existing between him and this woman, who came here to give evidence for him at the risk of her life. It is impossible for you to doubt his distress on the morning when he committed this act. We well know what terrible havoc such distress can make in weak and highly nervous people. It was all the work of a moment. The rest has followed, as death follows a stab to the heart, or water drops if you hold up a jug to empty it. Believe me, gentlemen, there is nothing more tragic in life than the utter impossibility of changing what you have done. Once this check was altered and presented, the work of four minutes—four mad minutes—the rest has been silence. But in those four minutes the boy before you has slipped through a door, hardly opened, into that great cage which never again quite lets a man go—the cage of the Law. His further acts, his failure to confess, the alteration of the counterfoil, his preparations for flight, are all evidence—not of deliberate and guilty intention when he committed the prime act from which these subsequent acts arose; no—they are merely evidence of the weak character which is clearly enough his misfortune. But is a man to be lost because he is bred and born with a weak character? Gentlemen, men like the prisoner are destroyed daily under our law for want of that human insight which sees them as they are, patients, and not criminals. If the prisoner be found guilty, and treated as though he were a criminal type, he will, as all experience shows, in all probability become one. I beg you not to return a verdict that may thrust him back into prison and brand him for ever. Gentlemen, Justice is a machine that, when some one has once given it the starting push, rolls on of itself. Is this young man to be ground to pieces under this machine for an act which at the worst was one of weakness? Is he to become a member of the luckless crews that man those dark, ill-starred ships called prisons? Is that to be his voyage—from which so few return? Or is he to have another chance, to be still looked on as one who has gone a little astray, but who will come back? I urge you, gentlemen, do not ruin this young man! For, as a result of those four minutes, ruin, utter and irretrievable, stares him in the face. He can be saved now. Imprison him as a criminal, and I affirm to you that he will be lost. He has neither the face nor the manner of one who can survive that terrible ordeal. Weigh in the scales his criminality and the suffering he has undergone. The latter is ten times heavier already. He has lain in prison under this charge for more than two months. Is he likely ever to forget that? Imagine the anguish of his mind during that time. He has had his punishment, gentlemen, you may depend. The rolling of the chariot-wheels of Justice over this boy began when it was decided to prosecute him. We are now already at the second stage. If you permit it to go on to the third I would not give—that for him.

[*He holds up finger and thumb in the form of a circle, drops his hand, and sits down.*

The JURY *stir, and consult each other's faces; then they turn toward the* COUNSEL *for the Crown, who rises, and, fixing his eyes on a spot that seems to give him satisfaction, slides them every now and then towards the* JURY.]

Cleaver. May it please your lordship—[*rising on his toes*]—Gentlemen of the Jury—The facts in this case are not disputed, and the defense, if my friend will allow me to say so, is so thin that I don't propose to waste the time of the Court by taking you over the evidence. The plea is one of temporary insanity. Well, gentlemen, I dare say it is clearer to me than it is to you why this rather—what shall we call it?—bizarre defense has been set up. The alternative would have been to plead guilty. Now, gentlemen, if the prisoner had pleaded guilty my friend would have had to rely on a simple appeal to his lordship. Instead of that, he has gone into the byways and hedges and found this—er—peculiar plea, which has enabled him to show you the proverbial woman, to put her in the box—to give, in fact, a romantic glow to this affair. I compliment my friend; I think it highly ingenious of him. By these means, he has—to a certain extent—got round the Law. He has brought the whole story of motive and stress out in court, at first hand, in a way that he would not otherwise have been able to do. But when you have once grasped that fact, gentlemen, you have grasped everything. [*With good-humored contempt.*] For look at this plea of insanity; we can't put it lower than that. You have heard the woman. She has every reason to favor the prisoner, but what did she say? She said that the prisoner was *not* insane when she left him in the morning. If he were going out of his mind through distress, that was obviously the moment when insanity would have shown itself. You have heard the managing clerk, another witness for the defense. With some difficulty I elicited from him the admission that the prisoner, though jumpy (a word that he seemed to think you would understand, gentlemen, and I'm sure I hope you do), was *not* mad when the check was handed to Davis. I agree with my friend that it's unfortunate that we have not got Davis here, but the prisoner has told you the words with which Davis in turn handed him the check; he obviously, therefore, was *not* mad when he received it, or he would not have remembered those words. The cashier has told you that he was certainly in his senses when he cashed it. We have, therefore, the plea that a man who is sane at ten minutes past one, and sane at fifteen minutes past, may, for the purposes of avoiding the consequences of a crime, call himself insane between those points of time. Really, gentlemen, this is so peculiar a proposition that I am not disposed to weary you with further argument. You will form your own opinion of its value. My friend has adopted this way of saying a great deal to you—and very eloquently—on the score of youth, temptation, and the like. I might point out, however, that the offense with which the prisoner is charged is one of the most serious known to our law; and there are certain features in this case, such as the suspicion which he allowed to rest on his innocent fellow-clerk, and his relations with this married woman, which will render it difficult for you to attach too much importance to such pleading. I ask you, in short, gentlemen, for that verdict of guilty which, in the circumstances, I regard you as, unfortunately, bound to record.

[*Letting his eyes travel from the* JUDGE *and the* JURY *to* FROME, *he sits down.*]

The Judge. [*Bending a little towards the* JURY, *and speaking in a business-like voice.*] Gentlemen, you have heard the evidence, and the comments on it. My only business is to make clear to you the issues you have to try. The facts are admitted, so far as the alteration of this check and counterfoil by the prisoner. The defense set up is that he was not in a responsible condition when he committed the crime. Well, you have heard the prisoner's story, and the evidence of the other witnesses—so far as it bears on the point of insanity. If you think that what you have heard establishes the fact that the prisoner was insane at the time of the forgery, you will find him guilty, but insane. If, on the other hand, you conclude from what you have seen and heard that the prisoner was sane—and nothing short of insanity will count—you will find him guilty. In reviewing the testimony as to his mental condition you must bear in mind very carefully the evidence as to his demeanor and conduct both before and after the act of forgery—the evidence of the prisoner himself, of the woman, of the witness—er—Cokeson, and—er—of the cashier. And in regard to that I especially direct your attention to the prisoner's admission that the idea of adding the *t y* and the nought did come into his mind at the moment when the check was handed to him; and also to the alteration of the counterfoil, and to his subsequent conduct generally. The bearing of all this on the question of premeditation (and premeditation will imply sanity) is very obvious. You must not allow any considerations of age or temptation to weigh with you in the finding of your verdict. Before you can come to a verdict of guilty but insane you must be well and thoroughly convinced that the condition of his mind was such as would have qualified him at the moment for a lunatic asylum. [*He pauses; then, seeing that the* JURY *are doubtful whether to retire or no, adds.*] You may retire, gentlemen, if you wish to do so.

[*The* JURY *retire by a door behind the* JUDGE. *The* JUDGE *bends over his notes.* FALDER, *leaning from the dock, speaks excitedly to his* SOLICITOR, *pointing down at* RUTH. *The* SOLICITOR *in turn speaks to* FROME.]

Frome. [*Rising.*] My lord. The prisoner is very anxious that I should ask you if your lordship would kindly request the reporters not to disclose the name of the woman witness in the Press reports of these proceedings. Your lordship will understand that the consequences might be extremely serious to her.

The Judge. [*Pointedly—with the suspicion of a smile.*] Well, Mr. Frome, you deliberately took this course which involved bringing her here.

Frome. [*With an ironic bow.*] If your lordship thinks I could have brought out the full facts in any other way?

The Judge. H'm! Well.

Frome. There is very real danger to her, your lordship.

The Judge. You see, I have to take your word for all that.

Frome. If your lordship would be so kind. I can assure your lordship that I am not exaggerating.

The Judge. It goes very much against the grain with me that the name of a witness should ever be suppressed. [*With a glance at* FALDER, *who is gripping and clasping his hands before him, and then at* RUTH, *who is sitting perfectly rigid with her eyes fixed on* FALDER.] I'll consider your application. It must depend. I have to remember that she may have come here to commit perjury on the prisoner's behalf.

Frome. Your lordship, I really——

The Judge. Yes, yes—I don't suggest anything of the sort, Mr. Frome. Leave it at that for the moment.

[*As he finishes speaking, the* JURY *return, and file back into the box.*]

Clerk of Assize. Gentlemen, are you agreed on your verdict?

Foreman. We are.

Clerk of Assize. Is it Guilty, or Guilty but insane?

Foreman. Guilty.

[THE JUDGE *nods; then, gathering up his notes, sits looking at* FALDER, *who stands motionless.*]

Frome. [*Rising.*] If your lordship would allow me to address you in mitigation of sentence. I don't know if your lordship thinks I can add anything to what I have said to the jury on the score of the prisoner's youth, and the great stress under which he acted.

The Judge. I don't think you can, Mr. Frome.

Frome. If your lordship says so—I do most earnestly beg your lordship to give the utmost weight to my plea. [*He sits down.*]

The Judge. [*To the* CLERK.] Call upon him.

The Clerk. Prisoner at the bar, you stand convicted of felony. Have you anything to say for yourself, why the Court should not give you judgment according to law?

[FALDER *shakes his head.*]

The Judge. William Falder, you have been given fair trial and found guilty, in my opinion rightly found guilty, of forgery. [*He pauses; then, consulting his notes, goes on.*] The defense was set up that you were not responsible for your actions at the moment of committing this crime. There is no doubt, I think, that this was a device to bring out at first hand the nature of the temptation to which you succumbed. For throughout the trial your counsel was in reality making an appeal for mercy. The setting up of this defense of course enabled him to put in some evidence that might weigh in that direction. Whether he was well advised to do so is another matter. He claimed that you should be treated rather as a patient than as a criminal. And this plea of his, which in the end amounted to a passionate appeal, he based in effect on an indictment of the march of Justice, which he practically accused of confirming and completing the process of criminality. Now, in considering how far I should allow weight to his appeal, I have a number of factors to take into account. I have to consider on the one hand the grave nature of your offense, the deliberate way in which you subsequently altered the counterfoil, the danger you caused to an innocent man—and that, to my mind, is a very grave point—and finally I have to consider the necessity of deterring others from following your example. On the other hand, I have to bear in mind that you are young, that you have hitherto borne a good character, that you were, if I am to believe your evidence and that of your witnesses, in a state of some emotional excitement when you committed this crime. I have every wish, consistently with my duty—not only to you, but to the community—to treat you with leniency. And this brings me to what are the determining factors in my mind in my consideration of your case. You are a clerk in a lawyer's office—that is a very serious element in this case; there can be no possible excuse made for you on the ground that you were not fully conversant with the nature of the crime you were committing, and the penalties that attach to it. It is said, however, that you were carried away by your emotions. The story has been told here today of your relations with this—er—Mrs. Honeywill; on that story both the defense and the plea for mercy were in effect based. Now what is that story? It is that you, a young man, and she, a young woman, unhappily married, had formed an attachment, which you both say—with what truth I am unable to gauge—had not yet resulted in immoral relations, but which you both admit was about to result in such relationship. Your counsel has made an attempt to palliate this, on the ground that the woman is in what he describes, I think, as "a hopeless position." As to that I can express no opinion. She is a married woman, and the fact is patent that you committed this crime with the view of furthering an immoral design. Now, however I might wish, I am not able to justify to my conscience a plea for mercy which has a basis inimical to morality. It is vitiated *ab initio*, and would, if successful, free you for the completion of this immoral project. Your counsel has made an attempt to trace your offense back to what he seems to suggest is a defect in the marriage law; he has made an attempt also to show that to punish you with further imprisonment would be unjust. I do not follow him in these flights. *The Law is what it is*—a majestic edifice, sheltering all of us, each stone of which rests on another. I am concerned only with its administration. The crime you have committed is a very serious one. I cannot feel it in accordance with my duty to Society to exercise the powers I have in your favor. You will go to penal servitude for three years.

[FALDER, *who throughout the* JUDGE'S *speech has looked at him steadily, lets his head fall forward on his breast.* RUTH *starts up from her seat as he is taken out by the* WARDERS. *There is a bustle in court.*]

The Judge. [*Speaking to the* REPORTERS.] Gentlemen of the Press, I think that the name of the female witness should not be reported.

[*The* REPORTERS *bow their acquiescence.*]

The Judge. [*To* RUTH, *who is staring in the direction in which* FALDER *has disappeared.*] Do you understand, your name will not be mentioned?

Cokeson. [*Pulling her sleeve.*] The judge is speaking to you.

[RUTH *turns, stares at the* JUDGE, *and turns away.*]

The Judge. I shall sit rather late today. Call the next case.

Clerk of Assize. [*To a warder.*] Put up John Booley.

To cries of "Witnesses in the case of Booley":

THE CURTAIN FALLS

ACT III

SCENE I

A prison. A plainly furnished room, with two large barred windows, overlooking the prisoners' exercise yard, where MEN, *in yellow clothes marked with arrows, and yellow brimless caps, are seen in single file at a distance of four yards from each other, walking rapidly on serpentine white lines marked on the concrete floor of the yard. Two* WARDERS *in blue uniforms. with peaked caps and swords, are stationed amongst them. The room has distempered walls, a bookcase with numerous official-looking books, a cupboard between the windows, a plan of the prison on the wall, a writing-table covered with documents. It is Christmas Eve.*

[*The* GOVERNOR, *a neat, grave-looking man, with a trim, fair mustache, the eyes of a theorist, and grizzled hair, receding from the temples, is standing close to this writing-table looking at a sort of rough saw made out of a piece of metal. The hand in which he holds it is gloved, for two fingers are missing. The chief warder,* WOODER, *a tall, thin, military-looking man of sixty, with gray mustache and melancholy, monkey-like eyes, stands very upright two paces from him.*]

The Governor. [*With a faint, abstracted smile.*] Queer-looking affair, Mr. Wooder! Where did you find it?

Wooder. In his mattress, sir. Haven't come across such a thing for two years now.

The Governor. [*With curiosity.*] Had he any set plan?

Wooder. He'd sawed his window-bar about that much.

[*He holds up his thumb and finger a quarter of an inch apart.*]

The Governor. I'll see him this afternoon. What's his name? Moaney! An old hand, I think?

Wooder. Yes, sir—fourth spell of penal. You'd think an old lag like him would have had more sense by now. [*With pitying contempt.*] Occupied his mind, he said. Breaking in and breaking out—that's all they think about.

The Governor. Who's next him?

Wooder. O'Cleary, sir.

The Governor. The Irishman.

Wooder. Next him again there's that young fellow, Falder—star class*—and next him old Clipton.

The Governor. Ah, yes! "The philosopher." I want to see him about his eyes.

Wooder. Curious thing, sir: they seem to know when there's one of these tries at escape going on. It makes them restive—there's a regular wave going through them just now.

The Governor. [*Meditatively.*] Odd things—those waves. [*Turning to look at the prisoners exercising.*] Seem quiet enough out here!

Wooder. That Irishman, O'Cleary, began banging on his door this morning. Little thing like that's quite enough to upset the whole lot. They're just like dumb animals at times.

The Governor. I've seen it with horses before thunder—it'll run right through cavalry lines.

[*The prison* CHAPLAIN *has entered. He is a dark-haired, ascetic man, in clerical undress, with a peculiarly steady, tight-lipped face and slow, cultured speech.*]

The Governer. [*Holding up the saw.*] Seen this, Miller?

The Chaplain. Useful-looking specimen.

The Governor. Do for the Museum, eh! [*He goes to the cupboard and opens it, displaying to view a number of quaint ropes, hooks, and metal tools with labels tied on them.*] That'll do, thanks, Mr. Wooder.

Wooder. [*Saluting.*] Thank you, sir.

[*He goes out.*]

The Governor. Account for the state of the men last day or two, Miller? Seems going through the whole place.

The Chaplain. No. I don't know of anything.

The Governor. By the way, will you dine with us on Christmas Day?

The Chaplain. Tomorrow. Thanks very much.

The Governor. Worries me to feel the men discontented. [*Gazing at the saw.*] Have to punish this poor devil. Can't help liking a man who tries to escape.

[*He places the saw in his pocket and locks the cupboard again.*]

The Chaplain. Extraordinary perverted will-power—some of them. Nothing to be done till it's broken.

The Governor. And not much afterwards, I'm afraid. Ground too hard for golf?

[WOODER *comes in again.*]

Wooder. Visitor who's been seeing Q 3007 asks to speak to you, sir. I told him it wasn't usual.

The Governor. What about?

Wooder. Shall I put him off, sir?

The Governor. [*Resignedly.*] No, no. Let's see him. Don't go, Miller.

[WOODER *motions to some one without, and as the visitor comes in withdraws. The visitor is* COKESON, *who is attired in a thick overcoat to the knees, woollen gloves, and carries a top hat.*]

Cokeson. I'm sorry to trouble you. I've been talking to the young man.

The Governor. We have a good many here.

Cokeson. Name of Falder, forgery. [*Producing a card, and handing it to the* GOVER-

* This refers to the badge worn by first offenders.

NOR.] Firm of James and Walter How. Well-known in the law.

The Governor. [*Receiving the card—with a faint smile.*] What do you want to see me about, sir?

Cokeson. [*Suddenly seeing the prisoners at exercise.*] Why! what a sight!

The Governor. Yes, we have that privilege from here; my office is being done up. [*Sitting down at his table.*] Now, please!

Cokeson. [*Dragging his eyes with difficulty from the window.*] I *wanted* to say a word to you; I shan't keep you long. [*Confidentially.*] Fact is, I oughtn't to be here by rights. His sister came to me—he's got no father and mother—and she was in some distress. "My husband won't let me go and see him," she said; "says he's disgraced the family. And his other sister," she said, "is an invalid." And she asked me to come. Well, I take an interest in him. He was our junior—I go to the same chapel—and I didn't like to refuse. And what I wanted to tell you was, he seems lonely here.

The Governor. Not unnaturally.

Cokeson. I'm afraid it'll prey on my mind. I see a lot of them about working together.

The Governor. Those are local prisoners. The convicts serve their three months here in separate confinement, sir.

Cokeson. But we don't want to be unreasonable. He's quite downhearted. I wanted to ask you to let him run about with the others.

The Governor. [*With faint amusement.*] Ring the bell—would you, Miller? [*To* COKESON.] You'd like to hear what the doctor says about him, perhaps.

The Chaplain. [*Ringing the bell.*] You are not accustomed to prisons, it would seem, sir.

Cokeson. No. But it's a pitiful sight. He's quite a young fellow. I said to him: "Before a month's up," I said, "you'll be out and about with the others; it'll be a nice change for you." "A month!" he said—like that! "Come!" I said, "we mustn't exaggerate. What's a month? Why, it's nothing!" "A day," he said, "shut up in your cell thinking and brooding as I do, it's longer than a year outside. I can't help it," he said; "I try—but I'm built that way, Mr. Cokeson." And he held his hand up to his face. I could see the tears trickling through his fingers. It wasn't nice.

The Chaplain. He's a young man with large, rather peculiar eyes, isn't he? Not Church of England, I think?

Cokeson. No.

The Chaplain. I know.

The Governor. [*To* WOODER, *who has come in.*] Ask the doctor to be good enough to come here for a minute. [WOODER *salutes, and goes out.*] Let's see, he's not married?

Cokeson. No. [*Confidentially.*] But there's a party he's very much attached to, not altogether com-il-fo. It's a sad story.

The Chaplain. If it wasn't for drink and women, sir, this prison might be closed.

Cokeson. [*Looking at the* CHAPLAIN *over his spectacles.*] Ye-es, but I wanted to tell you about that, special. He had hopes they'd have let her come and see him, but they haven't. Of course he asked me questions. I did my best, but I couldn't tell the poor young fellow a lie, with him in here—seemed like hitting him. But I'm afraid it's made him worse.

The Governor. What was this news then?

Cokeson. Like this. The woman had a nahsty, spiteful feller for a husband, and she'd left him. Fact is, she was going away with our young friend. It's not nice—but I've looked over it. Well, when he was put in here she said she'd earn her living apart, and wait for him to come out. That was a great consolation to him. But after a month she came to me—I *don't* know her personally—and she said: "I can't earn the children's living, let alone my own—I've got no friends. I'm obliged to keep out of everybody's way, else my husband'd get to know where I was. I'm very much reduced," she said. And she has lost flesh. "I'll have to go in the workhouse!" It's a painful story. I said to her: "No," I said, "not that! I've got a wife an' family, but sooner than you should do that I'll spare you a little myself." "Really," she said—she's a nice creature—"I don't like to take it from you. I think I'd better go back to my husband." Well, I know he's a nahsty, spiteful feller—drinks—but I didn't like to persuade her not to.

The Chaplain. Surely, no.

Cokeson. Ye-es, but I'm sorry now; it's upset the poor young fellow dreadfully. And what I wanted to say was: He's got his three years to serve. I *want* things to be pleasant for him.

The Chaplain. [*With a touch of impatience.*] The Law hardly shares your view, I'm afraid.

Cokeson. But I can't help thinking that to shut him up there by himself'll turn him silly. And nobody wants that, I s'pose. I *don't* like to see a man cry.

The Chaplain. It's a very rare thing for them to give way like that.

Cokeson. [*Looking at him—in a tone of sudden dogged hostility.*] I keep dogs.

The Chaplain. Indeed?

Cokeson. Ye-es. And I say this: I wouldn't shut one of them up all by himself, month after month, not if he'd bit me all over.

The Chaplain. Unfortunately, the criminal is not a dog; he has a sense of right and wrong.

Cokeson. But that's not the way to make him feel it.

The Chaplain. Ah! there I'm afraid we must differ.

Cokeson. It's the same with dogs. If you treat 'em with kindness they'll do anything for you; but to shut 'em up alone, it only makes 'em savage.

The Chaplain. Surely you should allow those who have had a little more experience than yourself to know what is best for prisoners.

Cokeson. [*Doggedly.*] I know this young feller, I've watched him for years. He's neurotic—got no stamina. His father died of consumption. I'm thinking of his future. If he's to be kept there shut up by himself, without a cat to keep him company, it'll do him harm. I said to him: "Where do you feel it?" "I can't tell you, Mr. Cokeson," he said, "but sometimes I could beat my head against the wall." It's not nice.

[*During this speech the* DOCTOR *has entered. He is a medium-sized, rather good-looking man, with a quick eye. He stands leaning against the window.*]

The Governor. This gentleman thinks the separate is telling on Q 3007—Falder, young thin fellow, star class. What do you say, Doctor Clements?

The Doctor. He doesn't like it, but it's not doing him any harm.

Cokeson. But he's told me.

The Doctor. Of course he'd say so, but we can always tell. He's lost no weight since he's been here.

Cokeson. It's his state of mind I'm speaking of.

The Doctor. His mind's all right so far. He's nervous, rather melancholy. I don't see signs of anything more. I'm watching him carefully.

Cokeson. [*Nonplussed.*] I'm glad to hear you say that.

The Chaplain. [*More suavely.*] It's just at this period that we are able to make some impression on them, sir. I am speaking from my special standpoint.

Cokeson. [*Turning bewildered to the* GOVERNOR.] I *don't* want to be unpleasant, but having given him this news, I do feel it's awkward.

The Governor. I'll make a point of seeing him today.

Cokeson. I'm much obliged to you. I thought perhaps seeing him every day you wouldn't notice it.

The Governor. [*Rather sharply.*] If any sign of injury to his health shows itself his case will be reported at once. That's fully provided for. [*He rises.*]

Cokeson. [*Following his own thoughts.*] Of course, what you don't see doesn't trouble you; but having seen him, I don't want to have him on my mind.

The Governor. I think you may safely leave it to us, sir.

Cokeson. [*Mollified and apologetic.*] I thought you'd understand me. I'm a plain man—never set myself up against authority. [*Expanding to the* CHAPLAIN.] Nothing personal meant. *Good* morning.

[*As he goes out the three officials do not look at each other, but their faces wear peculiar expressions.*]

The Chaplain. Our friend seems to think that prison is a hospital.

Cokeson. [*Returning suddenly with an apologetic air.*] There's just one little thing. This woman—I suppose I mustn't ask you to let him see her. It'd be a rare treat for them both. He's thinking about her all the time. Of course she's not his wife. But he's quite safe in here. They're a pitiful couple. You couldn't make an exception?

The Governor. [*Wearily.*] As you say, my dear sir, I couldn't make an exception; he won't be allowed another visit of any sort till he goes to a convict prison.

Cokeson. I see. [*Rather coldly.*] Sorry to have troubled you.

[*He again goes out.*]

The Chaplain. [*Shrugging his shoulders.*] The plain man indeed, poor fellow. Come and have some lunch, Clements?

[*He and the* DOCTOR *go out talking. The* GOVERNOR, *with a sigh, sits down at his table and takes up a pen.*]

THE CURTAIN FALLS

SCENE II

Part of the ground corridor of the prison. The walls are colored with greenish distemper up to a stripe of deeper green about the height of a man's shoulder, and above this line are whitewashed.

The floor is of blackened stones. Daylight is filtering through a heavily barred window at the end. The doors of four cells are visible. Each cell door has a little round peep-hole at the level of a man's eye, covered by a little round disc, which, raised upwards, affords a view of the cell. On the wall, close to each cell door, hangs a little square board with the prisoner's name, number, and record.

Overhead can be seen the iron structures of the first-floor and second-floor corridors.

The WARDER INSTRUCTOR, *a bearded man in blue uniform, with an apron, and some dangling keys, is just emerging from one of the cells.*

Instructor. [*Speaking from the door into the cell.*] I'll have another bit for you when that's finished.

O'Cleary. [*Unseen—in an Irish voice.*] Little doubt o' that, sirr.

Instructor. [*Gossiping.*] Well, you'd rather have it than nothing, I s'pose.

O'Cleary. An' that's the blessed truth.

[*Sounds are heard of a cell door being closed and locked, and of approaching footsteps.*]

Instructor. [*In a sharp, changed voice.*] Look alive over it!

[*He shuts the cell door, and stands at attention. The* GOVERNOR *comes walking down the corridor, followed by* WOODER.]

The Governor. Anything to report?

Instructor. [*Saluting.*] Q 3007 [*he points to a cell*] is behind with his work, sir. He'll lose marks today.

[*The* GOVERNOR *nods and passes on to the end cell. The* INSTRUCTOR *goes away.*]

The Governor. This is our maker of saws, isn't it?

[*He takes the saw from his pocket as* WOODER *throws open the door of the cell. The convict* MOANEY *is seen lying on his bed, athwart the cell, with his cap on. He springs up and stands in the middle of the cell. He is a raw-boned fellow, about fifty-six years old, with outstanding bat's ears and fierce, staring, steel-colored eyes.*]

Wooder. Cap off! [MOANEY *removes his cap.*] Out here!

[MOANEY *comes to the door.*]

The Governor. [*Beckoning him out into the corridor, and holding up the saw—with the manner of an officer speaking to a private.*] Anything to say about this, my man? [MOANEY *is silent.*] Come!

Moaney. It passed the time.

The Governor. [*Pointing into the cell.*] Not enough to do, eh?

Moaney. It don't occupy your mind.

The Governor. [*Tapping the saw.*] You might find a better way than this.

Moaney. [*Sullenly.*] Well! What way? I must keep my hand in against the time I get out. What's the good of anything else to me at my time of life? [*With a gradual change to civility, as his tongue warms.*] Ye know that, sir. I'll be in again within a year or two, after I've done this lot. I don't want to disgrace meself when I'm out. *You've* got your pride keeping the prison smart; well, I've got mine. [*Seeing that the* GOVERNOR *is listening with interest, he goes on, pointing to the saw.*] I *must* be doin' a little o' this. It's no harm to any one. I was five weeks makin' that saw—a bit of all right it is, too; now I'll get cells, I suppose, or seven days' bread and water. You can't help it, sir, I know that—I quite put meself in your place.

The Governor. Now, look here, Moaney, if I pass it over will you give me your word not to try it on again? Think!

[*He goes into the cell, walks to the end of it, mounts the stool, and tries the window-bars.*]

The Governor. [*Returning.*] Well?

Moaney. [*Who has been reflecting.*] I've got another six weeks to do in here, alone. I can't do it and think o' nothing. I must have something to interest me. You've made me a sporting offer, sir, but I can't pass my word about it. I shouldn't like to deceive a gentleman. [*Pointing into the cell.*] Another four hours' steady work would have done it.

The Governor. Yes, and what then? Caught, brought back, punishment. Five weeks' hard work to make this, and cells at the end of it, while they put a new bar to your window. Is it worth it, Moaney?

Moaney. [*With a sort of fierceness.*] Yes, it is.

The Governor. [*Putting his hand to his brow.*] Oh, well! Two days' cells—bread and water.

Moaney. Thank 'e, sir.

[*He turns quickly like an animal and slips into his cell.*

The GOVERNOR *looks after him and shakes his head as* WOODER *closes and locks the cell door.*]

The Governor. Open Clipton's cell.

[WOODER *opens the door of* CLIPTON'S

cell. CLIPTON *is sitting on a stool just inside the door, at work on a pair of trousers. He is a small, thick, oldish man, with an almost shaven head, and smouldering little dark eyes behind smoked spectacles. He gets up and stands motionless in the doorway, peering at his visitors.*]

The Governor. [*Beckoning.*] Come out here a minute, Clipton.

[CLIPTON, *with a sort of dreadful quietness, comes into the corridor, the needle and thread in his hand. The* GOVERNOR *signs to* WOODER, *who goes into the cell and inspects it carefully.*]

The Governor. How are your eyes?

Clipton. I don't complain of them. I don't see the sun here. [*He makes a stealthy movement, protruding his neck a little.*] There's just one thing, Mr. Governor, as you're speaking to me. I wish you'd ask the cove next door here to keep a bit quieter.

The Governor. What's the matter? I don't want any tales, Clipton.

Clipton. He keeps me awake. I don't know who he is. [*With contempt.*] One of this *star* class, I expect. Oughtn't to be here with *us*.

The Governor. [*Quietly.*] Quite right, Clipton. He'll be moved when there's a cell vacant.

Clipton. He knocks about like a wild beast in the early morning. I'm not used to it—stops me getting my sleep out. In the evening too. It's not fair, Mr. Governor, as you're speaking to me. Sleep's the comfort I've got here! I'm entitled to take it out full.

[WOODER *comes out of the cell, and instantly, as though extinguished,* CLIPTON *moves with stealthy suddenness back into his cell.*]

Wooder. All right, sir.

[*The* GOVERNOR *nods. The door is closed and locked.*]

The Governor. Which is the man who banged on his door this morning?

Wooder. [*Going toward* O'CLEARY'S *cell.*] This one, sir; O'Cleary.

[*He lifts the disc and glances through the peep-hole.*]

The Governor. Open.

[WOODER *throws open the door.* O'CLEARY, *who is seated at a little table by the door as if listening, springs up and stands at attention just inside the doorway. He is a broad-faced, middle-aged man, with a wide, thin, flexible mouth, and little holes under his high cheek-bones.*

The Governor. Where's the joke, O'Cleary?

O'Cleary. The joke, your honor? I've not seen one for a long time.

The Governor. Banging on your door?

O'Cleary. Oh! that!

The Governor. It's womanish.

O'Cleary. An' it's that I'm becoming this two months past.

The Governor. Anything to complain of?

O'Cleary. No, sirr.

The Governor. You're an old hand; you ought to know better.

O'Cleary. Yes, I've been through it all.

The Governor. You've got a youngster next door; you'll upset him.

O'Cleary. It cam' over me, your honor. I can't always be the same steady man.

The Governor. Work all right?

O'Cleary. [*Taking up a rush mat he is making.*] Oh! I can do it on me head. It's the miserablest stuff—don't take the brains of a mouse. [*Working his mouth.*] It's here I feel it—the want of a little noise—a terrible little wud ease me.

The Governor. You know as well as I do that if you were out in the shops you wouldn't be allowed to talk.

O'Cleary. [*With a look of profound meaning.*] Not with my mouth.

The Governor. Well, then?

O'Cleary. But it's the great conversation I'd have.

The Governor. [*With a smile.*] Well, no more conversation on your door.

O'Cleary. No, sirr, I wud not have the little wit to repeat meself.

The Governor. [*Turning.*] Good night.

O'Cleary. Good night, your honor.

[*He turns into his cell. The* GOVERNOR *shuts the door.*]

The Governor. [*Looking at the record card.*] Can't help liking the poor blackguard.

Wooder. He's an amiable man, sir.

The Governor. [*Pointing down the corridor.*] Ask the doctor to come here, Mr. Wooder.

[WOODER *salutes and goes away down the corridor.*

The GOVERNOR *goes to the door of* FALDER'S *cell. He raises his uninjured hand to uncover the peep-hole; but, without uncovering it, shakes his head and drops his hand; then, after scrutinizing the record board, he opens the cell door.* FALDER, *who is standing against it, lurches forward.*]

The Governor. [*Beckoning him out.*] Now tell me: can't you settle down, Falder?

Falder. [*In a breathless voice.*] Yes, sir.

The Governor. You know what I mean? It's no good running your head against a stone wall, is it?

Falder. No, sir.

The Governor. Well, come.

Falder. I try, sir.

The Governor. Can't you sleep?

Falder. Very little. Between two o'clock and getting up's the worst time.

The Governor. How's that?

Falder. [*His lips twitch with a sort of smile.*] I don't know, sir. I was always nervous. [*Suddenly voluble.*] Everything seems to get such a size then. I feel I'll never get out as long as I live.

The Governor. That's morbid, my lad. Pull yourself together.

Falder. [*With an equally sudden dogged resentment.*] Yes—I've got to——

The Governor. Think of all these other fellows!

Falder. They're used to it.

The Governor. They all had to go through it once for the first time, just as you're doing now.

Falder. Yes, sir, I shall get to be like them in time, I suppose.

The Governor. [*Rather taken aback.*] H'm! Well! That rests with you. Now come. Set your mind to it, like a good fellow. You're still quite young. A man can make himself what he likes.

Falder. [*Wistfully.*] Yes, sir.

The Governor. Take a good hold of yourself. Do you read?

Falder. I don't take the words in. [*Hanging his head.*] I know it's no good; but I can't help thinking of what's going on outside. In my cell I can't see out at all. It's thick glass, sir.

The Governor. You've had a visitor. Bad news?

Falder. Yes.

The Governor. You mustn't think about it.

Falder. [*Looking back at his cell.*] How can I help it, sir?

[*He suddenly becomes motionless as* WOODER *and the* DOCTOR *approach. The* GOVERNOR *motions to him to go back into his cell.*]

Falder. [*Quick and low.*] I'm quite right in my head, sir.

[*He goes back into his cell.*]

The Governor. [*To the* DOCTOR.] Just go in and see him, Clements.

[*The* DOCTOR *goes into the cell. The* GOVERNOR *pushes the door to, nearly closing it, and walks towards the window.*]

Wooder. [*Following.*] Sorry you should be troubled like this, sir. Very contented lot of men, on the whole.

The Governor. [*Shortly.*] You think so?

Wooder. Yes, sir. It's Christmas doing it, in my opinion.

The Governor. [*To himself.*] Queer, that!

Wooder. Beg pardon, sir?

The Governor. Christmas!

[*He turns towards the window, leaving* WOODER *looking at him with a sort of pained anxiety.*]

Wooder. [*Suddenly.*] Do you think we make show enough, sir? If you'd like us to have more holly?

The Governor. Not at all, Mr. Wooder.

Wooder. Very good, sir.

[*The* DOCTOR *has come out of* FALDER'S *cell, and the* GOVERNOR *beckons to him.*]

The Governor. Well?

The Doctor. I can't make anything much of him. He's nervous, of course.

The Governor. Is there any sort of case to report? Quite frankly, Doctor.

The Doctor. Well, I don't think the separate's doing him any good; but then I could say the same of a lot of them—they'd get on better in the ships, there's no doubt.

The Governor. You mean you'd have to recommend others?

The Doctor. A dozen at least. It's on his nerves. There's nothing tangible. That fellow there—[*pointing to* O'CLEARY'S *cell*]—for instance—feels it just as much, in his way. If I once get away from physical facts—I shan't know where I am. Conscientiously, sir, I don't know how to differentiate him. He hasn't lost weight. Nothing wrong with his eyes. His pulse is good. Talks all right.

The Governor. It doesn't amount to melancholia?

The Doctor. [*Shaking his head.*] I can report on him if you like; but if I do I ought to report on others.

The Governor. I see. [*Looking towards* FALDER'S *cell.*] The poor devil must just stick it then.

[*As he says this he looks absently at* WOODER.]

Wooder. Beg pardon, sir?

[*For answer the* GOVERNOR *stares at him, turns on his heel, and walks away. There is a sound as of beating on metal.*]

The Governor. [*Stopping.*] Mr. Wooder?

Wooder. Banging on his door, sir. I thought we should have more of that.

[*He hurries forward, passing the* GOVERNOR, *who follows closely.*]

THE CURTAIN FALLS

SCENE III

FALDER'S *cell, a whitewashed space thirteen feet broad by seven deep, and nine feet high, with a rounded ceiling. The floor is of shiny blackened bricks. The barred window of opaque glass, with a ventilator, is high up in the middle of the end wall. In the middle of the opposite end wall is the narrow door. In a corner are the mattress and bedding rolled up (two blankets, two sheets, and a coverlet). Above them is a quarter-circular wooden shelf, on which is a Bible and several little devotional books, piled in a symmetrical pyramid; there are also a black hairbrush, tooth-brush, and a bit of soap. In another corner is the wooden frame of a bed, standing on end. There is a dark ventilator under the window, and another over the door.* FALDER'S *work (a shirt to which he is putting buttonholes) is hung to a nail on the wall over a small wooden table, on which the novel "Lorna Doone" lies open. Low down in the corner by the door is a thick glass screen, about a foot square, covering the gas-jet let into the wall. There is also a wooden stool, and a pair of shoes beneath it. Three bright round tins are set under the window.*

In fast-failing daylight, FALDER, *in his stockings, is seen standing motionless, with his head inclined towards the door, listening. He moves a little closer to the door, his stockinged feet making no noise. He stops at the door. He is trying harder and harder to hear something, any little thing that is going on outside. He springs suddenly upright—as if at a sound—and remains perfectly motionless. Then, with a heavy sigh, he moves to his work, and stands looking at it, with his head down; he does a stitch or two, having the air of a man so lost in sadness that each stitch is, as it were, a coming to life. Then turning abruptly, he begins pacing the cell, moving his head, like an animal pacing its cage. He stops again at the door, listens, and, placing the palms of his hands against it with his fingers spread out, leans his forehead against the iron. Turning from it, presently, he moves slowly back towards the window, tracing his way with his finger along the top line of the distemper that runs round the wall. He stops under the window, and, picking up the lid of one of the tins, peers into it. It has grown very nearly dark. Suddenly the lid falls out of his hand with a clatter—the only sound that has broken the silence—and he stand staring intently at the wall where the stuff of the shirt is hanging rather white in the darkness—he seems to be seeing somebody or something there. There is a sharp tap and click; the cell light behind the glass screen has been turned up. The cell is brightly lighted.* FALDER *is seen gasping for breath.*

A sound from far away, as of distant, dull beating on thick metal, is suddenly audible. FALDER *shrinks back, not able to bear the sudden clamor. But the sound grows, as though some great tumbril were rolling towards the cell. And gradually it seems to hypnotize him. He begins creeping inch by inch nearer to the door. The banging sound, traveling from cell to cell, draws closer and closer;* FALDER'S *hands are seen moving as if his spirit had already joined in this beating, and the sound swells till it seems to have entered the very cell. He suddenly raises his clenched fists. Panting violently, he flings himself at his door, and beats on it.*

THE CURTAIN FALLS

ACT IV

The scene is again COKESON'S *room, at a few minutes to ten of a March morning, two years later. The doors are all open.* SWEEDLE, *now blessed with a sprouting mustache, is getting the offices ready. He arranges papers on* COKESON'S *table; then goes to a covered washstand, raises the lid, and looks at himself in the mir-*

ror. While he is gazing his fill RUTH HONEYWILL *comes in through the outer office and stands in the doorway. There seems a kind of exultation and excitement behind her habitual impassivity.*

Sweedle. [*Suddenly seeing her, and dropping the lid of the washstand with a bang.*] Hello! It's you!

Ruth. Yes.

Sweedle. There's only me here! They don't waste their time hurrying down in the morning. Why, it must be two years since we had the pleasure of seeing you. [*Nervously.*] What have you been doing with yourself?

Ruth. [*Sardonically.*] Living.

Sweedle. [*Impressed.*] If you want to see *him* [*he points to* COKESON'S *chair*], he'll be here directly—never misses—not much. [*Delicately.*] I hope our friend's back from the country. His time's been up these three months, if I remember. [RUTH *nods.*] I was awful sorry about that. The governor made a mistake—if you ask me.

Ruth. He did.

Sweedle. He ought to have given him a chanst. And, *I* say, the judge ought to ha' let him go after that. They've forgot what human nature's like. Whereas *we* know.

[RUTH *gives him a honeyed smile.*]

Sweedle. They come down on you like a cartload of bricks, flatten you out, and when you don't swell up again they complain of it. I know 'em—seen a lot of that sort of thing in my time. [*He shakes his head in the plenitude of wisdom.*] Why, only the other day the governor——

[*But* COKESON *has come in through the outer office; brisk with east wind, and decidedly grayer.*]

Cokeson. [*Drawing off his coat and gloves.*] Why! it's you! [*Then motioning* SWEEDLE *out, and closing the door.*] Quite a stranger! Must be two years. D'you want to see me? I can give you a minute. Sit down! Family well?

Ruth. Yes. I'm not living where I was.

Cokeson. [*Eyeing her askance.*] I hope things are more comfortable at home.

Ruth. I couldn't stay with Honeywill, after all.

Cokeson. You haven't done anything rash, I hope. I should be sorry if you'd done anything rash.

Ruth. I've kept the children with me.

Cokeson. [*Beginning to feel that things are not so jolly as he had hoped.*] Well, I'm glad to have seen you. You've not heard from the young man, I suppose, since he came out?

Ruth. Yes, I ran across him yesterday.

Cokeson. I hope he's well.

Ruth. [*With sudden fierceness.*] He can't get anything to do. It's dreadful to see him. He's just skin and bone.

Cokeson. [*With genuine concern.*] Dear me! I'm sorry to hear that. [*On his guard again.*] Didn't they find him a place when his time was up?

Ruth. He was only there three weeks. It got out.

Cokeson. I'm sure I don't know what I can do for you. I don't like to be snubby.

Ruth. I can't bear his being like that.

Cokeson. [*Scanning her not unprosperous figure.*] I know his relations aren't very forthy about him. Perhaps *you* can do something for him, till he finds his feet.

Ruth. Not now. I could have—but not *now*.

Cokeson. I don't understand.

Ruth. [*Proudly.*] I've seen him again—that's all over.

Cokeson. [*Staring at her—disturbed.*] I'm a family man—I don't want to hear anything unpleasant. Excuse me—I'm very busy.

Ruth. I'd have gone home to my people in the country long ago, but they've never got over me marrying Honeywill. I never was waywise, Mr. Cokeson, but I'm proud. I was only a girl, you see, when I married him. I thought the world of him, of course . . . he used to come traveling to our farm.

Cokeson. [*Regretfully.*] I did hope you'd have got on better, after you saw me.

Ruth. He used me worse than ever. He couldn't break my nerve, but I lost my health; and then he began knocking the children about. . . . I couldn't stand that. I wouldn't go back now, if he were dying.

Cokeson. [*Who has risen and is shifting about as though dodging a stream of lava.*] We mustn't be violent, must we?

Ruth. [*Smouldering.*] A man that can't behave better than that——

[*There is silence.*]

Cokeson. [*Fascinated in spite of himself.*] Then there you were! And what did you do then?

Ruth. [*With a shrug.*] Tried the same as when I left him before . . . making skirts . . . cheap things. It was the best I could get, but I never made more than ten shillings a week, buying my own cotton and working all day; I hardly ever got to bed till past twelve. I kept at it for nine months.

[*Fiercely.*] Well, I'm not fit for that; I wasn't made for it. I'd rather die.

Cokeson. My dear woman! We mustn't talk like that.

Ruth. It was starvation for the children, too—after what they'd always had. I soon got not to care. I used to be too tired.

[*She is silent.*]

Cokeson. [*With fearful curiosity.*] Why, what happened then?

Ruth. [*With a laugh.*] My employer happened then—he's happened ever since.

Cokeson. Dear! oh dear! I never came across a thing like this.

Ruth. [*Dully.*] He's treated me all right. But I've done with that. [*Suddenly her lips begin to quiver, and she hides them with the back of her hand.*] I never thought I'd see *him* again, you see. It was just a chance I met him by Hyde Park. We went in there and sat down, and he told me all about himself. Oh! Mr. Cokeson, give him another chance.

Cokeson. [*Greatly disturbed.*] Then you've both lost your livings! What a horrible position!

Ruth. If he could only get here—where there's nothing to find out about him!

Cokeson. We can't have anything derogative to the firm.

Ruth. I've no one else to go to.

Cokeson. I'll speak to the partners, but I don't think they'll take him, under the circumstances. I don't really.

Ruth. He came with me; he's down there in the street.

[*She points to the window.*]

Cokeson. [*On his dignity.*] He shouldn't have done that until he's sent for. [*Then softening at the look on her face.*] We've got a vacancy, as it happens, but I can't promise anything.

Ruth. It would be the saving of him.

Cokeson. Well, I'll do what I can, but I'm not sanguine. Now tell him that I don't want him till I see how things are. Leave your address? [*Repeating her.*] 83 Mullingar Street? [*He notes it on blotting-paper.*] Good morning.

Ruth. Thank you.

[*She moves towards the door, turns as if to speak, but does not, and goes away.*]

Cokeson. [*Wiping his head and forehead with a large white cotton handkerchief.*] What a business!

[*Then looking amongst his papers, he sounds his bell.* SWEEDLE *answers it.*]

Cokeson. Was that young Richards coming here today after the clerk's place?

Sweedle. Yes.

Cokeson. Well, keep him in the air; I don't want to see him yet.

Sweedle. What shall I tell him, sir?

Cokeson. [*With asperity.*] Invent something. Use your brains. Don't stump him off altogether.

Sweedle. Shall I tell him that we've got illness, sir?

Cokeson. No! Nothing untrue. Say I'm not here today.

Sweedle. Yes, sir. Keep him hankering?

Cokeson. Exactly. And look here. You remember Falder? I may be having him round to see me. Now, treat him like you'd have him treat you in a similar position.

Sweedle. I naturally should do.

Cokeson. That's right. When a man's down never hit 'im. 'Tisn't necessary. Give him a hand up. That's a metaphor I recommend to you in life. It's sound policy.

Sweedle. Do you think the governors will take him on again, sir?

Cokeson. Can't say anything about that. [*At the sound of some one having entered the outer office.*] Who's there?

Sweedle. [*Going to the door and looking.*] It's Falder, sir.

Cokeson. [*Vexed.*] Dear me! That's very naughty of her. Tell him to call again. I don't want——

[*He breaks off as* FALDER *comes in.* FALDER *is thin, pale, older, his eyes have grown more restless. His clothes are very worn and loose.* SWEEDLE, *nodding cheerfully, withdraws.*]

Cokeson. Glad to see you. You're rather previous. [*Trying to keep things pleasant.*] Shake hands! She's striking while the iron's hot. [*He wipes his forehead.*] I don't blame her. She's anxious.

[FALDER *timidly takes* COKESON'S *hand and glances towards the partners' door.*]

Cokeson. No—not yet! Sit down! [FALDER *sits in the chair at the side of* COKESON'S *table, on which he places his cap.*] Now you are here I'd like you to give me a little account of yourself. [*Looking at him over his spectacles.*] How's your health?

Falder. I'm alive, Mr. Cokeson.

Cokeson. [*Preoccupied.*] I'm glad to hear that. About this matter. I don't like doing anything out of the ordinary; it's not my habit. I'm a plain man, and I want everything smooth and straight. But I promised your friend to speak to the partners, and I always keep my word.

Falder. I just want a chance, Mr. Cokeson. I've paid for that job a thousand times and more. I have, sir. No one knows. They say I weighed more when I came out than when I went in. They couldn't weigh me here [*he touches his head*] or here [*he touches his heart, and gives a sort of laugh*]. Till last night I'd have thought there was nothing in here at all.

Cokeson. [*Concerned.*] You've not got heart disease?

Falder. Oh! they passed me sound enough.

Cokeson. But they got you a place, didn't they?

Falder. Yes; very good people, knew all about it—very kind to me. I thought I was going to get on first rate. But one day, all of a sudden, the other clerks got wind of it. . . . I couldn't stick it, Mr. Cokeson, I couldn't, sir.

Cokeson. Easy, my dear fellow, easy!

Falder. I had one small job after that, but it didn't last.

Cokeson. How was that?

Falder. It's no good deceiving you, Mr. Cokeson. The fact is, I seem to be struggling against a thing that's all round me. I can't explain it: it's as if I was in a net; as fast as I cut it here, it grows up there. I didn't act as I ought to have, about references; but what are you to do? You must have them. And that made me afraid, and I left. In fact, I'm—I'm afraid all the time now.

[*He bows his head and leans dejectedly silent over the table.*]

Cokeson. I feel for you—I do really. Aren't your sisters going to do anything for you?

Falder. One's in consumption. And the other——

Cokeson. Ye . . . es. She told me her husband wasn't quite pleased with you.

Falder. When I went there—they were at supper—my sister wanted to give me a kiss—I know. But he just looked at her, and said: "What have you come for?" Well, I pocketed my pride and I said: "Aren't you going to give me your hand, Jim? Cis is, I know," I said. "Look here!" he said, "that's all very well, but we'd better come to an understanding. I've been expecting you, and I've made up my mind. I'll give you fifteen pounds to go to Canada with." "I see," I said—"good riddance! No, thanks; keep your fifteen pounds." Friendship's a queer thing when you've been where I have.

Cokeson. I understand. Will you take the fifteen pounds from me? [*Flustered, as* FALDER *regards him with a queer smile.*] Quite without prejudice; I meant it kindly.

Falder. I'm not allowed to leave the country.

Cokeson. Oh! ye . . . es—ticket-of-leave?* You aren't looking the thing.

Falder. I've slept in the Park three nights this week. The dawns aren't all poetry there. But meeting her—I feel a different man this morning. I've often thought the being fond of her's the best thing about me; it's sacred, somehow—and yet it did for me. That's queer, isn't it?

Cokeson. I'm sure we're all very sorry for you.

Falder. That's what I've found, Mr. Cokeson. Awfully sorry for me. [*With quiet bitterness.*] But it doesn't do to associate with criminals!

Cokeson. Come, come, it's no use calling yourself names. That never did a man any good. Put a face on it.

Falder. It's easy enough to put a face on it, sir, when you're independent. Try it when you're down like me. They talk about giving you your deserts. Well, I think I've had just a bit over.

Cokeson. [*Eyeing him askance over his spectacles.*] I hope they haven't made a Socialist of you.

[FALDER *is suddenly still, as if brooding over his past self; he utters a peculiar laugh.*]

Cokeson. You must give them credit for the best intentions. Really you must. Nobody wishes you harm, I'm sure.

Falder. I believe that, Mr. Cokeson. Nobody wishes you harm, but they down you all the same. This feeling—— [*He stares around him, as though at something closing in.*] It's crushing me. [*With sudden impersonality.*] I know it is.

Cokeson. [*Horribly disturbed.*] There's nothing there! We must try and take it quiet. I'm sure I've often had you in my prayers. Now leave it to me. I'll use my gumption and take 'em when they're jolly.

[*As he speaks the two* PARTNERS *come in.*]

Cokeson. [*Rather disconcerted, but trying to put them all at ease.*] I didn't expect you quite so soon. I've just been having a talk with this young man. I think you'll remember him.

James. [*With a grave, keen look.*] Quite well. How are you, Falder?

Walter. [*Holding out his hand almost timidly.*] Very glad to see you again, Falder.

Falder. [*Who has recovered his self-control, takes the hand.*] Thank you, sir.

* The colloquial name for the system of giving a convict his liberty under certain restrictions before his sentence has expired; similar to the American parole system.

Cokeson. Just a word, Mr. James. [*To* FALDER, *pointing to the clerks' office.*] You might go in there a minute. You know your way. Our junior won't be coming this morning. His wife's just had a little family.

[FALDER *goes uncertainly out into the clerks' office.*]

Cokeson. [*Confidentially.*] I'm bound to tell you all about it. He's quite penitent. But there's a prejudice against him. And you're not seeing him to advantage this morning; he's undernourished. It's very trying to go without your dinner.

James. Is that so, Cokeson?

Cokeson. I wanted to ask you. He's had his lesson. Now *we* know all about him, and we want a clerk. There is a young fellow applying, but I'm keeping him in the air.

James. A jail-bird in the office, Cokeson? I don't see it.

Walter. "The rolling of the chariot-wheels of Justice!" I've never got that out of my head.

James. I've nothing to reproach myself with in this affair. What's he been doing since he came out?

Cokeson. He's had one or two places, but he hasn't kept them. He's sensitive—quite natural. Seems to fancy everybody's down on him.

James. Bad sign. Don't like the fellow—never did from the first. "Weak character" 's written all over him.

Walter. I think we owe him a leg up.

James. He brought it all on himself.

Walter. The doctrine of full responsibility doesn't quite hold in these days.

James. [*Rather grimly.*] You'll find it safer to hold it for all that, my boy.

Walter. For oneself, yes—not for other people, thanks.

James. Well! I don't want to be hard.

Cokeson. I'm glad to hear you say that. He seems to see something [*spreading his arms*] round him. 'Tisn't healthy.

James. What about that woman he was mixed up with? I saw some one uncommonly like her outside as we came in.

Cokeson. That! Well, I can't keep anything from you. He has met her.

James. Is she with her husband?

Cokeson. No.

James. Falder living with her, I suppose?

Cokeson. [*Desperately trying to retain the new-found jollity.*] I don't know that of my own knowledge. 'Tisn't my business.

James. It's *our* business, if we're going to engage him, Cokeson.

Cokeson. [*Reluctantly.*] I ought to tell you, perhaps. I've had the party here this morning.

James. I thought so. [*To* WALTER.] No, my dear boy, it won't do. Too shady altogether!

Cokeson. The two things together make it very awkward for you—I see that.

Walter. [*Tentatively.*] I don't quite know what we have to do with his private life.

James. No, no! He must make a clean sheet of it, or he can't come here.

Walter. Poor devil!

Cokeson. Will you have him in? [*And as* JAMES *nods.*] I think I can get him to see reason.

James. [*Grimly.*] You can leave that to me, Cokeson.

Walter. [*To* JAMES, *in a low voice, while* COKESON *is summoning* FALDER.] His whole future may depend on what we do. Dad.

[FALDER *comes in. He has pulled himself together, and presents a steady front.*]

James. Now look here, Falder. My son and I want to give you another chance; but there are two things I must say to you. In the first place: It's no good coming here as a victim. If you've any notion that you've been unjustly treated—get rid of it. You can't play fast and loose with morality and hope to go scot-free. If Society didn't take care of itself, nobody would—the sooner you realize that the better.

Falder. Yes, sir; but—may I say something?

James. Well?

Falder. I had a lot of time to think it over in prison. [*He stops.*]

Cokeson. [*Encouraging him.*] I'm sure you did.

Falder. There were all sorts there. And what I mean, sir, is, that if we'd been treated differently the first time, and put under somebody that could look after us a bit, and not put in prison, not a quarter of us would ever have got there.

James. [*Shaking his head.*] I'm afraid I've very grave doubts of that, Falder.

Falder. [*With a gleam of malice.*] Yes, sir, so I found.

James. My good fellow, don't forget that you began it.

Falder. I never wanted to do wrong.

James. Perhaps not. But you did.

Falder. [*With all the bitterness of his past suffering.*] It's knocked me out of time. [*Pulling himself up.*] That is, I mean, I'm not what I was.

James. This isn't encouraging for us, Falder.

Cokeson. He's putting it awkwardly, Mr. James.

Falder. [*Throwing over his caution from the intensity of his feeling.*] I mean it, Mr. Cokeson.

James. Now, lay aside all those thoughts, Falder, and look to the future.

Falder. [*Almost eagerly.*] Yes, sir, but you don't understand what prison is. It's here it gets you. [*He grips his chest.*]

Cokeson. [*In a whisper to* JAMES.] I told you he wanted nourishment.

Walter. Yes, but, my dear fellow, that'll pass away. Time's merciful.

Falder. [*With his face twitching.*] I hope so, sir.

James. [*Much more gently.*] Now, my boy, what you've got to do is to put all the past behind you and build yourself up a steady reputation. And that brings me to the second thing. This woman you were mixed up with—you must give us your word, you know, to have done with that. There's no chance of your keeping straight if you're going to begin your future with such a relationship.

Falder. [*Looking from one to the other with a hunted expression.*] But sir . . . but sir . . . it's the one thing I looked forward to all that time. And she too . . . I couldn't find her before last night.

[*During this and what follows* COKESON *becomes more and more uneasy.*]

James. This is painful, Falder. But you must see for yourself that it's impossible for a firm like this to close its eyes to everything. Give us this proof of your resolve to keep straight, and you can come back—not otherwise.

Falder. [*After staring at* JAMES, *suddenly stiffens himself.*] I couldn't give her up. I couldn't! Oh, sir! I'm all she's got to look to. And I'm sure she's all I've got.

James. I'm very sorry, Falder, but I must be firm. It's for the benefit of you both in the long run. No good can come of this connection. It was the cause of all your disaster.

Falder. But sir, it means—having gone through all that—getting broken up—my nerves are in an awful state—for nothing. I did it for her.

James. Come! If she's anything of a woman she'll see it for herself. She won't want to drag you down further. If there were a prospect of your being able to marry her—it might be another thing.

Falder. It's not my fault, sir, that she couldn't get rid of him—she would have if she could. That's been the whole trouble from the beginning. [*Looks suddenly at* WALTER.] . . . If anybody would help her! It's only money wanted now, I'm sure.

Cokeson. [*Breaking in, as* WALTER *hesitates, and is about to speak.*] I don't think we need consider that—it's rather far-fetched.

Falder. [*To* WALTER, *appealing.*] He must have given her full cause since; she could prove that he drove her to leave him.

Walter. I'm inclined to do what you say, Falder, if it can be managed.

Falder. Oh, sir!

[*He goes to the window and looks down into the street.*]

Cokeson. [*Hurriedly.*] You don't take me, Mr. Walter. I have my reasons.

Falder. [*From the window.*] She's down there, sir. Will you see her? I can beckon to her from here.

[WALTER *hesitates, and looks from* COKESON *to* JAMES.]

James. [*With a sharp nod.*] Yes, let her come. [FALDER *beckons from the window.*]

Cokeson. [*In a low fluster to* JAMES *and* WALTER.] No, Mr. James. She's not been quite what she ought to ha' been, while this young man's been away. She's lost her chance. We can't consult how to swindle the Law.

[FALDER *has come from the window. The three men look at him in a sort of awed silence.*]

Falder. [*With instinctive apprehension of some change—looking from one to the other.*] There's been nothing between us, sir, to prevent it. . . . What I said at the trial was true. And last night we only just sat in the Park.

[SWEEDLE *comes in from the outer office.*]

Cokeson. What is it?

Sweedle. Mrs. Honeywill. [*There is silence.*]

James. Show her in.

[RUTH *comes slowly in, and stands stoically with* FALDER *on one side and the three men on the other. No one speaks.* COKESON *turns to his table, bending over his papers as though the burden of the situation were forcing him back into his accustomed groove.*]

James. [*Sharply.*] Shut the door there. [SWEEDLE *shuts the door.*] We've asked you to come up because there are certain facts to be faced in this matter. I understand you have only just met Falder again.

Ruth. Yes—only yesterday.

James. He's told us about himself, and we're very sorry for him. I've promised to take him back here if he'll make a fresh start. [*Looking steadily at* RUTH.] This is a matter that requires courage, ma'am.

[RUTH, *who is looking at* FALDER, *begins to twist her hands in front of her as though prescient of disaster.*]

Falder. Mr. Walter How is good enough to say that he'll help us to get you a divorce.

[RUTH *flashes a startled glance at* JAMES *and* WALTER.]

James. I don't think that's practicable, Falder.

Falder. But, sir——!

James. [*Steadily.*] Now, Mrs. Honeywill. You're fond of him.

Ruth. Yes, sir; I love him.

[*She looks miserably at* FALDER.]

James. Then you don't want to stand in his way, do you?

Ruth. [*In a faint voice.*] I could take care of him.

James. The best way you can take care of him will be to give him up.

Falder. Nothing shall make me give you up. You can get a divorce. There's been nothing between us, has there?

Ruth. [*Mournfully shaking her head—without looking at him.*] No.

Falder. We'll keep apart till it's over, sir; if you'll only help us—we promise.

James. [*To* RUTH.] You see the thing plainly, don't you? You see what I mean?

Ruth. [*Just above a whisper.*] Yes.

Cokeson. [*To himself.*] There's a dear woman.

James. The situation is impossible.

Ruth. Must I, sir?

James. [*Forcing himself to look at her.*] I put it to you, ma'am. His future is in your hands.

Ruth. [*Miserably.*] I want to do the best for him.

James. [*A little huskily.*] That's right, that's right!

Falder. I don't understand. You're not going to give me up—after all this? There's something—— [*Starting forward to* JAMES.] Sir, I swear solemnly there's been nothing between us.

James. I believe you, Falder. Come, my lad, be as plucky as she is.

Falder. Just now you were going to help us. [*He stares at* RUTH, *who is standing absolutely still; his face and hands twitch and quiver as the truth dawns on him.*] What is it? You've not been——

Walter. Father!

James. [*Hurriedly.*] There, there! That'll do, that'll do! I'll give you your chance, Falder. Don't let me know what you do with yourselves, that's all.

Falder. [*As if he has not heard.*] Ruth?

[RUTH *looks at him; and* FALDER *covers his face with his hands. There is silence.*]

Cokeson. [*Suddenly.*] There's some one out there. [*To* RUTH.] Go in here. You'll feel better by yourself for a minute.

[*He points to the clerks' room and moves towards the outer office.* FALDER *does not move.* RUTH *puts out her hand timidly. He shrinks back from the touch. She turns and goes miserably into the clerks' room. With a brusk movement he follows, seizing her by the shoulder just inside the doorway.* COKESON *shuts the door.*]

James. [*Pointing to the outer office.*] Get rid of that, whoever it is.

Sweedle. [*Opening the office door, in a scared voice.*] Detective-Sergeant Wister.

[*The* DETECTIVE *enters, and closes the door behind him.*]

Wister. Sorry to disturb you, sir. A clerk you had here, two years and a half ago. I arrested him in this room.

James. What about him?

Wister. I thought perhaps I might get his whereabouts from you.

[*There is an awkward silence.*]

Cokeson. [*Pleasantly, coming to the rescue.*] We're not responsible for his movements; you know that.

James. What do you want with him?

Wister. He's failed to report himself this last four weeks.

Walter. How d'you mean?

Wister. Ticket-of-leave won't be up for another six months, sir.

Walter. Has he to keep in touch with the police till then?

Wister. We're bound to know where he sleeps every night. I dare say we shouldn't interfere, sir, even though he hasn't reported himself. But we've just heard there's a serious matter of obtaining employment with a forged reference. What with the two things together—we must have him.

[*Again there is silence.* WALTER *and* COKESON *steal glances at* JAMES, *who stands staring steadily at the* DETECTIVE.]

Cokeson. [*Expansively.*] We're very busy at the moment. If you could make it convenient to call again we might be able to tell you then.

James. [*Decisively.*] I'm a servant of the Law, but I dislike peaching. In fact, I can't do such a thing. If you want him you must find him without us.

[*As he speaks his eye falls on* FALDER'S *cap, still lying on the table, and his face contracts.*]

Wister. [*Noting the gesture—quietly.*] Very good, sir. I ought to warn you that, having broken the terms of his license, he's still a convict, and sheltering a convict——

James. I shelter no one. But you mustn't come here and ask questions which it's not my business to answer.

Wister. [*Dryly.*] I won't trouble you further then, gentlemen.

Cokeson. I'm sorry we couldn't give you the information. You quite understand, don't you? Good morning!

[WISTER *turns to go, but instead of going to the door of the outer office he goes to the door of the clerks' room.*]

Cokeson. The other door . . . the other door!

[WISTER *opens the clerks' door.* RUTH'S *voice is heard: "Oh, do!" and* FALDER'S: *"I can't!" There is a little pause; then, with sharp fright,* RUTH *says: "Who's that?"* WISTER *has gone in. The three men look aghast at the door.*]

Wister. [*From within.*] Keep back, please!

[*He comes swiftly out with his arm twisted in* FALDER'S. *The latter gives a white, staring look at the three men.*]

Walter. Let him go this time, for God's sake!

Wister. I couldn't take the responsibility, sir.

Falder. [*With a queer, desperate laugh.*] Good!

[*Flinging a look back at* RUTH, *he throws up his head, and goes out through the outer office, half dragging* WISTER *after him.*]

Walter. [*With despair.*] That finishes him It'll go on for ever now.

[SWEEDLE *can be seen staring through the outer door. There are sounds of footsteps descending the stone stairs; suddenly a dull thud, a faint "My God!" in* WISTER'S *voice.*]

James. What's that?

[SWEEDLE *dashes forward. The door swings to behind him. There is dead silence.*]

Walter. [*Starting forward to the inner room.*] The woman—she's fainting!

[*He and* COKESON *support the fainting* RUTH *from the doorway of the clerks' room.*]

Cokeson. [*Distracted.*] Here, my dear! There, there!

Walter. Have you any brandy?

Cokeson. I've got sherry.

Walter. Get it, then. Quick!

[*He places* RUTH *in a chair—which* JAMES *has dragged forward.*]

Cokeson. [*With sherry.*] Here! It's good strong sherry.

[*They try to force the sherry between her lips. There is the sound of feet, and they stop to listen. The outer door is reopened*—WISTER *and* SWEEDLE *are seen carrying some burden.*]

James. [*Hurrying forward.*] What is it?

[*They lay the burden down in the outer office, out of sight, and all but* RUTH *cluster around it, speaking in hushed voices.*]

Wister. He jumped—neck's broken.

Walter. Good God!

Wister. He must have been mad to think he could give me the slip like that. And what was it—just a few months!

Walter. [*Bitterly.*] Was that all?

James. What a desperate thing! [*Then, in a voice unlike his own.*] Run for a doctor—you! [SWEEDLE *rushes from the outer office.*] An ambulance!

[WISTER *goes out. On* RUTH'S *face an expression of fear and horror has been seen growing, as if she dared not turn towards the voices. She now rises and steals towards them.*]

Walter. [*Turning suddenly.*] Look!

[*The three* MEN *shrink back out of her way, one by one, into* COKESON'S *room.* RUTH *drops on her knees by the body.*]

Ruth. [*In a whisper.*] What is it? He's not breathing. [*She crouches over him.*] My dear! My pretty!

[*In the outer office doorway the figures of* MEN *are seen standing.*]

Ruth. [*Leaping to her feet.*] No, no! No, no! He's dead!

[*The figures of the* MEN *shrink back.*]

Cokeson. [*Stealing forward. In a hoarse voice.*] There, there, poor dear woman!

[*At the sound behind her* RUTH *faces around at him.*]

Cokeson. No one'll touch him now! Never again! He's safe with gentle Jesus!

[RUTH *stands as though turned to stone in the doorway staring at* COKESON, *who, bending humbly before her, holds out his hand as one would to a lost dog.*]

THE CURTAIN FALLS

MR. PIM PASSES BY*

By

A. A. MILNE

WAR HAS MADE MANY DRAMATISTS, but rarely one who, like A. A. Milne, completely forgets the ugly business as he writes. He has told us how it happened. While he was earning a living as a humorist on the staff of *Punch* he "could not afford so unpromising a gamble [as playwriting.] But once in the Army the case altered. No duty now urged me to write. My job was soldiering, and my spare time was my own affair. Other subalterns played bridge and golf; that was one way of amusing oneself. Another was—why not?—to write plays.

"So we began *Wurzel-Flummery*. . . . She wrote; I dictated . . . and if a particularly fine evening drew us out for a walk along the byways where there was no saluting, and one could smoke a pipe without shocking the Duke of Cambridge—then it was to discuss the last scene and to wonder what would happen in the next."

A sketch called *Once on a Time,* written for the troops, had perhaps given him the confidence to indulge the playwriting bent that every journalist is said to possess. Dion Boucicault's successful production of *Wurzel-Flummery* in 1917 determined Milne's career, for when he was invalided home he set to work as a professional dramatist on the series of plays that have placed him in what London calls "the proud rank of West-End dramatists": *Belinda* and *Make-Believe,* 1918; *Mr. Pim Passes By,* 1919; *The Romantic Age,* 1920; *The Truth About Blayds,* 1921; and *The Dover Road,* 1922. He acknowledges a debt to J. M. Barrie, who gave him his "first chances," and to the spirit of whose writing Mr. Milne of all English authors makes the closest approach, not because of an attempt to imitate, but because of similar mental qualities—whimsical humor, genial sentiment thinly veiling an almost cynical vein of satire, and the unaging love of children and the child mind. He shares also with Barrie a wholesome respect for the business of the theater.

"Now the first thing to be noted," he once wrote, "is that playwriting is not an art alone, but also a craft . . . An art is something personal to the artist, whereas a craft is inevitably a collaboration. . . . A dramatist is both artist and craftsman. He is a stage-craftsman by reason of the fact that he collaborates with the public." In a later essay he wrote: "Construction, stagecraft, dramatic technique, call it by a sufficiently high sounding name and you will persuade people that they are in the presence of the mysteries. Actually stagecraft is just the common sense of making a play acceptable by a mixed audience. A play must show the same qualities as any other piece of writing, from a thousand word sketch to a novel—invention, imagination, form, humor, and sense of character, blended with style, which is the expression of the author's personality. . . . One might almost say that there is no good stagecraft; either it is bad, or you do not see that it is there at all." He is, however, no artless photographer of the passing scene. "Art is not life," he asserts, "but an exaggeration of it; life reinforced by the personality of the artist. A work of art is literally too good to be true."

Mr. Pim Passes By ranks among the most popular comedies of its decade. Its initial success in London, which Mr. Milne modestly attributes to the popularity of Miss Irene Vanbrugh and Mr. Boucicault, whose brilliant performance of Denis Clifton in *Wurzel-Flummery* first won a large audience for the author, was followed by equally great successes in America and Australia, and it has had what the author admits to have been even more lucrative to him, a great vogue among amateurs. It was first produced in

London on January 5, 1920, with a distinguished cast including, besides the artists mentioned, Ben Webster and Leslie Howard. Nigel Playfair, also in the original cast, brought out, as his opening piece at Hammersmith, Mr. Milne's *Make-Believe.* In every sense, Mr. Milne's plays belong to the best comedy traditions of the English theater.

ALAN ALEXANDER MILNE

Born 1882, London, England.
Westminster School.
Trinity College, Cambridge.
Editor of *Granta* (Cambridge undergraduate publication).
1906–1914, Assistant Editor of *Punch* and weekly contributor.
1915–1918, War service in Royal Warwickshire Regiment.
1916, *Once on a Time,* his first play, written for an army entertainment, and expanded into a novel.
1917, *Wurzel-Flummery,* his first play to be produced in London.
Also novelist, poet, and essayist, and writer of juvenilia.

PLAYS

1917 *Wurzel-Flummery.* 1917 *The Lucky One.* 1918 *Belinda.* 1918 *The Boy Comes Home.* 1918 *Make-Believe.* 1918 *The Red Feathers.* 1919 *The Camberley Triangle.* 1919 *Mr. Pim Passes By.* 1920 *The Romantic Age.* 1921 *The Stepmother.* 1921 *The Truth About Blayds.* 1922 *The Dover Road.* 1923 *The Artist (a Duologue).* 1923 *Success* (in America, *Give Me Yesterday*). 1923 *The Great Broxopp.* 1923 *The Man in the Bowler Hat.* 1924 *To Have the Honor* (in America, *To Meet the Prince*). 1925 *Ariadne, or Business First.* 1926 *The Portrait of a Gentleman in Slippers.* 1927 *Toad of Toad Hall* (based on Kenneth Grahame's *The Wind in the Willows*). 1927 *The Ivory Door.* 1927 *Miss Marlow at Play.* 1928 *The Fourth Wall* (in America, *The Perfect Alibi*). 1928 *Let's All Talk about Gerald* (formerly *The Lucky One*). 1929 *Michael and Mary.* 1932 *Other People's Lives* (in America, *They Don't Mean Any Harm*). 1936 *Miss Elizabeth Bennet* (based on Jane Austen's *Pride and Prejudice*). 1937 *Sarah Simple.* 1938 *Gentleman Unknown.*

WRITINGS ABOUT THE DRAMA

Prefaces to *First Plays,* 1920; *Second Plays,* 1922; *Four Plays,* 1932. Chaps. 14, 15, 16, of *Autobiography,* 1939.

MR. PIM PASSES BY

Characters

GEORGE MARDEN, J.P.
OLIVIA (*his wife*).
DINAH (*his niece*).
LADY MARDEN (*his aunt*).
BRIAN STRANGE.
CARRAWAY PIM.
ANNE.

ACT I

The morning-room at Marden House [Buckinghamshire] decided more than a hundred years ago that it was all right, and has not bothered about itself since. Visitors to the house have called the result such different adjectives as "mellow," "old-fashioned," "charming"—even "baronial" and "antique"; but nobody ever said it was "exciting." Sometimes OLIVIA *wants it to be more exciting, and last week she let herself go over some new curtains. At present they are folded up and waiting for her; she still has the rings to put on. It is obvious that the curtains alone will overdo the excitement; they will have to be harmonized with a new carpet and cushions.* OLIVIA *has her eye on just the things, but one has to go carefully with* GEORGE. *What was good enough for his great-great-grandfather is good enough for him. However, we can trust* OLIVIA *to see him through it, although it may take time. There are two ways of coming into the room; by the open windows leading from the terrace or by the door.*

[*On this pleasant July morning* MR. PIM *chooses the latter way—or rather* ANNE *chooses it for him; and old* MR. PIM, *wistful, kindly, gentle, little* MR. PIM, *living in some world of his own whither we cannot follow, ambles after her.*]

Anne. I'll tell Mr. Marden you're here, sir. Mr. Pim, isn't it?

Pim. [*Coming back to this world.*] Yes—er—Mr. Carraway Pim. He doesn't know me, you understand, but if he could just see me for a moment—er—— [*He fumbles in his pockets.*] I gave you that letter?

Anne. Yes, sir, I'll give it to him.

Pim. [*Bringing out a letter which is not the one he was looking for, but which reminds him of something else he has forgotten.*] Dear me!

Anne. Yes, sir?

Pim. I ought to have sent a telegram, but I can do it on my way back. You have a telegraph office in the village?

Anne. Oh yes, sir. If you turn to the left when you get outside the gates, it isn't more than a hundred yards down the hill.

Pim. Thank you, thank you. Very stupid of me to have forgotten. [ANNE *goes out.*]

[MR. PIM *wanders about the room humming to himself, and looking vaguely at the pictures. He has his back to the door as* DINAH *comes in. She is nineteen, very pretty, very happy, and full of boyish high spirits and conversation.*]

Dinah. Hullo!

Pim. [*Turning round.*] Ah, good morning, Mrs. Marden. You must forgive my—er——

Dinah. Oh I say, I'm not Mrs. Marden. I'm Dinah.

Pim. [*With a bow.*] Then I will say Good morning, Miss Diana.

Dinah. [*Reproachfully.*] Now, look here, if you and I are going to be friends you mustn't do that. Dinah, *not* Diana. Do remember it, there's a good man, because I get so tired of correcting people. Have you come to stay with us?

Pim. Well no, Miss—er—Dinah.

Dinah. [*Nodding.*] That's right. I can see I shan't have to speak to *you* again. Now tell me *your* name, and I bet you I get it right first time. And do sit down.

Pim. [*Sitting down.*] Thank you. My name is—er—Pim, Carraway Pim——

Dinah. Pim, that's easy.

Pim. And I have a letter of introduction to your father——

Dinah. Oh no; now you're going wrong again, Mr. Pim. George isn't my father; he's my uncle. *Uncle* George—he doesn't like me calling him George. Olivia doesn't mind—I mean she doesn't mind being called Olivia, but George is rather touchy. You see, he's been my guardian since I was about two, and then about five years ago he married a widow called Mrs. Telworthy—that's Olivia—so she became my Aunt Olivia, only she lets me drop the Aunt. Got that?

Pim. [*A little alarmed.*] I—I think so, Miss Marden.

Dinah. [*Admiringly.*] I say, you *are* quick, Mr. Pim. Well, if you take my advice, when you've finished your business with George, you will hang about a bit and see if you can't see Olivia. She's simply devastating. I don't wonder George fell in love with her.

Pim. It's only the merest matter of business—just a few minutes with your uncle—I'm afraid I shall hardly——

Dinah. Well, you must please yourself, Mr. Pim. I'm just giving you a friendly word of advice. Naturally, I was awfully glad to get such a magnificent aunt, because, of course, marriage *is* rather a toss up, isn't it, and George might have gone off with anybody. It's different on the stage, where guardians always marry their wards, but George couldn't marry *me* because I'm his niece. Mind you, I don't say that I should have had him, because between ourselves he's a little bit old-fashioned.

Pim. So he married—er—Mrs. Marden instead.

Dinah. Mrs. Telworthy—don't say you've forgotten already, just when you were getting so good at names. Mrs. Telworthy. You see, Olivia married the Telworthy man and went to Australia with him, and he drank himself to death in the bush, or wherever you drink yourself to death out there, and Olivia came home to England, and met my uncle, and he fell in love with her and proposed to her, and he came into my room that night—I was about fourteen—and turned on the light and said, "Dinah, how would you like to have a beautiful aunt of your very own?" And I said: "Congratulations, George." That was the first time I called him George. Of course, I'd seen it coming for *weeks.* Telworthy, isn't it a funny name?

Pim. Very singular. From Australia, you say?

Dinah. Yes, I always say that he's probably still alive, and will turn up here one morning and annoy George, because that's what first husbands always do in books, but I'm afraid there's not much chance.

Pim. [*Shocked.*] Miss Marden!

Dinah. Well, of course, I don't really *want* it to happen, but it *would* be rather exciting, wouldn't it? However, things like that never seem to occur down here, somehow. There was a hay-rick burnt last year about a mile away, but that isn't quite the same thing, is it?

Pim. No, I should say that that was certainly different.

Dinah. Of course, something very, very wonderful did happen last night, but I'm not sure if I know you well enough——

[*She looks at him hesitatingly.*]

Pim. [*Uncomfortably.*] Really, Miss Marden, I am only a—a passer-by; here today and gone tomorrow. You really mustn't——

Dinah. And yet there's something about you, Mr. Pim, which inspires confidence. The fact is—[*in a stage whisper*]—I got engaged last night!

Pim. Dear me, let me congratulate you.

Dinah. I expect that's why George is keeping you such a long time. Brian, my young man, the well-known painter—only nobody has ever heard of him—he's smoking a pipe with George in the library and asking for his niece's hand. Isn't it exciting? You're really rather lucky, Mr. Pim—I mean being told so soon. Even Olivia doesn't know yet.

Pim. [*Getting up.*] Yes, yes. I congratulate you, Miss Marden. Perhaps it would be better—— [ANNE *comes in.*]

Anne. Mr. Marden is out at the moment, sir—— Oh, I didn't see you, Miss Dinah.

Dinah. It's all right, Anne. *I'm* looking after Mr. Pim.

Anne. Yes, Miss. [*She goes out.*]

Dinah. [*Excitedly.*] That's me. They can't discuss me in the library without breaking down, so they're walking up and down outside, and slashing at the thistles in order to conceal their emotion. *You* know. I expect Brian——

Pim. [*Looking at his watch.*] Yes, I think, Miss Marden, I had better go now and return a little later. I have a telegram which I want to send, and perhaps by the time I came back——

Dinah. Oh, but how disappointing of you, when we were getting on together so nicely. And it was just going to be your turn to tell me all about *your*self.

Pim. I have really nothing to tell, Miss Marden. I have a letter of introduction to Mr. Marden, who in turn will give me, I hope, a letter to a certain distinguished man whom it is necessary for me to meet. That is ail. [*Holding out his hand.*] And now, Miss Marden——

Dinah. Oh, I'll start you on your way to the post office. I want to know if you're married, and all that sort of thing. You've got heaps to tell me, Mr. Pim. Have you got your hat? That's right. Then we'll—hullo, here's Brian.

[BRIAN STRANGE *comes in at the windows. He is what* GEORGE *calls a damned futuristic painter-chap, aged twenty-four. To look at, he is a very pleasant boy, rather untidily dressed.*]

Brian. [*Nodding.*] How do you do?

Dinah. [*Seizing him.*] Brian, this is Mr. Pim. Mr. Carraway Pim. He's been telling me all about himself. It's so interesting. He's just going to send a telegram, and then he's coming back again. Mr. Pim, this is Brian —*you* know.

Brian. [*Smiling and shaking hands.*] How do you do?

Dinah. [*Pleadingly.*] You *won't* mind going to the post office by yourself, will you, because, you see, Brian and I——[*she looks lovingly at* BRIAN.]

Pim. [*Because they are so young.*] Miss Dinah and Mr.—er—Brian, I have only come into your lives for a moment, and it is probable that I shall now pass out of them for ever, but you will allow an old man——

Dinah. Oh, not old!

Pim. [*Chuckling happily.*] Well, a middle-aged man—to wish you both every happiness in the years that you have before you. Good-by, good-by.

[*He disappears gently through the windows.*]

Dinah. Brian, he'll get lost if he goes that way.

Brian. [*Going to the windows and calling after him.*] Round to the left, sir. . . . That's right. [*He comes back into the room.*] Rum old bird. Who is he?

Dinah. Darling, you haven't kissed me yet.

Brian. [*Taking her in his arms.*] I oughtn't to, but then one never ought to do the nice things.

Dinah. Why oughtn't you?

[*They sit on the sofa together.*]

Brian. Well, we said we'd be good until we'd told your uncle and aunt all about it. You see, being a guest in their house——

Dinah. But, darling child, what *have* you been doing all this morning *except* telling George?

Brian. *Trying* to tell George.

Dinah. [*Nodding.*] Yes, of course, there's a difference.

Brian. I think he guessed there was something up, and he took me down to see the pigs—he said he had to see the pigs at once —I don't know why; an appointment perhaps. And we talked about pigs all the way, and I couldn't say, "Talking about pigs, I want to marry your niece——"

Dinah. [*With mock indignation.*] Of course you couldn't.

Brian. No. Well, you see how it was. And then when we'd finished talking about pigs, we started talking *to* the pigs——

Dinah. [*Eagerly.*] Oh, *how* is Arnold?

Brian. The little black-and-white one? He's very jolly, I believe, but naturally I wasn't thinking about him much. I was wondering how to begin. And then Lumsden came up, and wanted to talk pig-food, and the atmosphere grew less and less romantic, and—and I gradually drifted away.

Dinah. Poor darling. Well, we shall have to approach him through Olivia.

Brian. But I always wanted to tell her first; she's so much easier. Only you wouldn't let me.

Dinah. That's *your* fault, Brian. You would tell Olivia that she ought to have orange-and-black curtains.

Brian. But she *wants* orange-and-black curtains.

Dinah. Yes, but George says he's not going to have any futuristic nonsense in an honest English country house, which has been good enough for his father and his grandfather and his great-grandfather, and —and all the rest of them. So there's a sort of strained feeling between Olivia and George just now, and if Olivia were to—sort of recommend you, well, it wouldn't do you much good.

Brian. [*Looking at her.*] I see. Of course I know what *you* want, Dinah.

Dinah. What do I want?

Brian. You want a secret engagement, and notes left under door-mats, and meetings by the withered thorn, when all the household is asleep. *I* know you.

Dinah. Oh, but it is such fun! I love meeting people by withered thorns.

Brian. Well, I'm not going to have it.

Dinah. [*Childishly.*] Oh, George! Look at us being husbandy!

Brian. You babe! I adore you. [*He kisses her and holds her away from him and looks at her.*] You know, you're rather throwing yourself away on me. Do you mind?

Dinah. Not a bit.

Brian. We shall never be rich, but we shall have lots of fun, and meet interesting people, and feel that we're doing something worth doing, and not getting paid nearly enough for it, and we can curse the Academy together and the British Public, and—oh, it's an exciting life.

Dinah. [*Seeing it.*] I shall love it.

Brian. I'll make you love it. You shan't be sorry, Dinah.

Dinah. You shan't be sorry either, Brian.

Brian. [*Looking at her lovingly.*] Oh, I know I shan't. . . . What will Olivia think about it? Will she be surprised?

Dinah. She's never surprised. She always seems to have thought of things about a week before they happen. George just begins to get hold of them about a week *after* they've happened. [*Considering him.*] After all, there's no reason why George *shouldn't* like you, darling.

Brian. I'm not his sort, you know.

Dinah. You're more Olivia's sort. Well, we'll tell Olivia this morning.

Olivia. [*Coming in.*] And what are you going to tell Olivia this morning? [*She looks at them with a smile.*] Oh, well, I think I can guess.

Shall we describe OLIVIA? *But you will know all about her before the day is over.*

Dinah. [*Jumping up.*] Olivia, darling!

Brian. [*Following.*] Say you understand, Mrs. Marden.

Olivia. Mrs. Marden, I am afraid, is a very dense person, Brian, but I think if you asked Olivia if she understood——

Brian. Bless you, Olivia. I knew you'd be on our side.

Dinah. Of course she would.

Olivia. I don't know if it's usual to kiss an aunt-in-law, Brian, but Dinah is such a very special sort of niece that——

[*She inclines her cheek and* BRIAN *kisses it.*]

Dinah. I say, you *are* in luck today, Brian.

Olivia. [*Going over to her chair by the work-table and getting to business with the curtains.*] And how many people have been told the good news?

Brian. Nobody yet.

Dinah. Except Mr. Pim.

Brian. Oh, does *he*——

Olivia. Who's Mr. Pim?

Dinah. Oh, he just happened—I say, are those *the* curtains? Then you're going to have them after all?

Olivia. [*With an air of surprise.*] After all what? But I decided on them long ago. [*To* BRIAN.] You haven't told George yet?

Brian. I began to, you know, but I never got any farther than "Er—there's just—er——"

Dinah. George *would* talk about pigs all the time.

Olivia. Well, I suppose you want me to help you.

Dinah. Do, darling.

Brian. It would be awfully decent of you. Of course, I'm not quite his sort really——

Dinah. You're *my* sort.

Brian. But I don't think he objects to me, and——

[GEORGE *comes in, a typical, narrow-minded, honest country gentleman of forty odd.*]

George. [*At the windows.*] What's all this about a Mr. Pim? [*He kicks some of the mud off his boots.*] Who is he? Where is he? I had most important business with Lumsden, and the girl comes down and cackles about a Mr. Pim, or Ping, or something. Where did I put his card? [*Bringing it out.*] Carraway Pim. Never heard of him in my life.

Dinah. He said he had a letter of introduction, Uncle George.

George. Oh, *you* saw him, did you? Yes, that reminds me, there *was* a letter——

[*He brings it out and reads it.*]

Dinah. He had to send a telegram. He's coming back.

Olivia. Pass me those scissors, Brian.

Brian. These?

[*He picks them up and comes close to her.*]

Olivia. Thank you.

[*She indicates* GEORGE'S *back. "Now?" says* BRIAN *with his eyebrows. She nods.*]

George. [*Reading.*] Ah well, a friend of Brymer's. Glad to oblige him. Yes, I know the man he wants. Coming back, you say, Dinah? Then I'll be going back. Send him down to the farm, Olivia, when he comes. [*To* BRIAN.] Hallo, what happened to *you*?

Olivia. Don't go, George, there's something we want to talk about.

George. Hallo, what's this?

Brian. [*To* OLIVIA.] Shall I——?

Olivia. Yes.

Brian. [*Stepping out.*] I've been wanting to tell you all this morning, sir, only I didn't seem to have an opportunity of getting it out.

George. Well, what is it?

Brian. I want to marry Dinah, sir.

George. You want to marry Dinah? God bless my soul!

Dinah. [*Rushing to him and putting her*

cheek against his coat.] Oh, do say you like the idea, Uncle George.

George. Like the idea! Have you heard of this nonsense, Olivia?

Olivia. They've just this moment told me, George. I think they would be happy together.

George. [*To* BRIAN.] And what do you propose to be happy together *on*?

Brian. Well, of course, it doesn't amount to much at present, but we shan't starve.

Dinah. Brian got fifty pounds for a picture last March!

George. [*A little upset by this.*] Oh! [*Recovering gamely.*] And how many pictures have you sold since?

Brian. Well, none, but——

George. None! And I don't wonder. Who the devil is going to buy pictures with triangular clouds and square sheep? And they call that Art nowadays! Good God, man, [*waving him to the windows*] go outside and *look* at the clouds!

Olivia. If he draws round clouds in future, George, will you let him marry Dinah?

George. What—what? Yes, of course, you *would* be on his side—all this Futuristic nonsense. I'm just taking these clouds as an example. I suppose I can see as well as any man in the county, and I say that clouds *aren't* triangular.

Brian. After all, sir, at my age one is naturally experimenting, and trying to find one's [*with a laugh*]—well, it sounds priggish, but one's medium of expression. I shall find out what I want to do directly, but I think I shall always be able to earn enough to live on. Well, I have for the last three years.

George. I see, and now you want to experiment with a wife, and you propose to start experimenting with *my* niece?

Brian. [*With a shrug.*] Well, of course, if you——

Olivia. You could help the experiment, darling, by giving Dinah a good allowance until she's twenty-one.

George. Help the experiment! I don't *want* to help the experiment.

Olivia. [*Apologetically.*] Oh, I thought you did.

George. You will talk as if I was made of money. What with taxes always going up and rents always going down, it's as much as we can do to rub along as we are, without making allowances to everybody who thinks she wants to get married. [*To* BRIAN.] And that's thanks to you, my friend.

Brian. [*Surprised.*] To me?

Olivia. You never told me, darling. What's Brian been doing?

Dinah. [*Indignantly.*] He hasn't been doing anything.

George. He's one of your Socialists who go turning the country upside down.

Olivia. But even Socialists must get married sometimes.

George. I don't see any necessity.

Olivia. But you'd have nobody to damn after dinner, darling, if they all died out.

Brian. Really, sir, I don't see what my politics and my art have got to do with it. I'm perfectly ready not to talk about either when I'm in your house, and as Dinah doesn't seem to object to them——

Dinah. I should think she doesn't.

George. Oh, you can get round the women, I daresay.

Brian. Well, it's Dinah I want to marry and live with. So what it really comes to is that you don't think I can support a wife.

George. Well, if you're going to do it by selling pictures, I don't think you can.

Brian. All right, tell me how much you want me to earn in a year, and I'll earn it.

George. [*Hedging.*] It isn't merely a question of money. I just mention that as one thing—one of the important things. In addition to that, I think you are both too young to marry. I don't think you know your own minds, and I am not at all persuaded that, with what I venture to call your outrageous tastes, you and my niece will live happily together. Just because she thinks she loves you, Dinah may persuade herself now that she agrees with all you say and do, but she has been properly brought up in an honest English country household, and—er—she—well, in short, I cannot at all approve of any engagement between you. [*Getting up.*] Olivia, if this Mr.—er—Pim comes, I shall be down at the farm. You might send him along to me.

[*He walks towards the windows.*]

Brian. [*Indignantly.*] Is there any reason why I shouldn't marry a girl who has been properly brought up?

George. I think you know my views, Strange.

Olivia. George, wait a moment, dear. We can't quite leave it like this.

George. I have said all I want to say on the subject.

Olivia. Yes, darling, but I haven't begun to say all that *I* want to say on the subject.

George. Of course, if you have anything to say, Olivia, I will listen to it; but I don't know that this is quite the time, or that you have chosen—[*looking darkly at the cur-*

tains]—quite the occupation likely to—er—endear your views to me.

Dinah. [*Mutinously.*] I may as well tell you, Uncle George, that *I* have got a good deal to say, too.

Olivia. I can guess what you are going to say, Dinah, and I think you had better keep it for the moment.

Dinah. [*Meekly.*] Yes, Aunt Olivia.

Olivia. Brian, you might take her outside for a walk. I expect you have plenty to talk about.

George. Now mind, Strange, no love-making. I put you on your honor about that.

Brian. I'll do my best to avoid it, sir.

Dinah. [*Cheekily.*] May I take his arm if we go up a hill?

Olivia. I'm sure you'll know how to behave—both of you.

Brian. Come on, then, Dinah.

Dinah. Righto.

George. [*As they go.*] And if you do see any clouds, Strange, take a good look at them. [*He chuckles to himself.*] Triangular clouds—I never heard of such nonsense. [*He goes back to his chair at the writing-table.*] Futuristic rubbish . . . Well, Olivia?

Olivia. Well, George?

George. What are you doing?

Olivia. Making curtains, George. Won't they be rather sweet? Oh, but I forgot—you don't like them.

George. I don't like them, and what is more, I don't mean to have them in my house. As I told you yesterday, this is the house of a simple country gentleman, and I don't want any of these new-fangled ideas in it.

Olivia. Is marrying for love a new-fangled idea?

George. We'll come to that directly. None of you women can keep to the point. What I am saying now is that the house of my fathers and forefathers is good enough for me.

Olivia. Do you know, George, I can hear one of your ancestors saying that to his wife in their smelly old cave, when the new-fangled idea of building houses was first suggested. "The Cave of my Fathers is——"

George. That's ridiculous. Naturally we must have progress. But that's just the point. [*Indicating the curtains.*] I don't call this sort of thing progress. It's—ah—retrogression.

Olivia. Well, anyhow, it's pretty.

George. There I disagree with you. And I must say once more that I will not have them hanging in my house.

Olivia. Very well, George.

[*But she goes on working.*]

George. That being so, I don't see the necessity of going on with them.

Olivia. Well, I must do something with them now I've got the material. I thought perhaps I could sell them when they're finished—as we're so poor.

George. What do you mean—so poor?

Olivia. Well, you said just now that you couldn't give Dinah an allowance because rents had gone down.

George. [*Annoyed.*] Confound it, Olivia! Keep to the point! We'll talk about Dinah's affairs directly. We're discussing our own affairs at the moment.

Olivia. But what is there to discuss?

George. Those ridiculous things.

Olivia. But we've finished that. You've said you wouldn't have them hanging in your house, and I've said, "Very well, George." Now we can go on to Dinah and Brian.

George. [*Shouting.*] But put these beastly things away.

Olivia. [*Rising and gathering up the curtains.*] Very well, George.

[*She puts them away, slowly, gracefully. There is an uncomfortable silence. Evidently somebody ought to apologize.*]

George. [*Realizing that he is the one.*] Er—look here, Olivia, old girl, you've been a jolly good wife to me, and we don't often have rows, and if I've been rude to you about this—lost my temper a bit perhaps, what?—I'll say I'm sorry. May I have a kiss?

Olivia. [*Holding up her face.*] George, darling! [*He kisses her.*] Do you love me?

George. You know I do, old girl.

Olivia. As much as Brian loves Dinah?

George. [*Stiffly.*] I've said all I want to say about that. [*He goes away from her.*]

Olivia. Oh, but there must be lots you want to say—and perhaps don't like to. Do tell me, darling.

George. What it comes to is this. I consider that Dinah is too young to choose a husband for herself, and that Strange isn't the husband I should choose for her.

Olivia. You were calling him Brian yesterday.

George. Yesterday I regarded him as a boy; now he wants me to look upon him as a man.

Olivia. He's twenty-four.

George. And Dinah's nineteen. Ridiculous!

Olivia. If he'd been a Conservative, and thought that clouds were round, I suppose he'd have seemed older, somehow.

George. That's a different point altogether. That has nothing to do with his age.

Olivia. [*Innocently.*] Oh, I thought it had.

George. What I am objecting to is these ridiculously early marriages before either party knows its own mind, much less the mind of the other party. Such marriages invariably lead to unhappiness.

Olivia. Of course, *my* first marriage wasn't a happy one.

George. As you know, Olivia, I dislike speaking about your first marriage at all, and I had no intention of bringing it up now; but since you mention it—well, that is a case in point.

Olivia. [*Looking back at it.*] When I was eighteen, I was in love. Or perhaps I only thought I was, and I don't know if I should have been happy or not if I had married him. But my father made me marry a man called Jacob Telworthy; and when things were too hot for him in England—"too hot for him"—I think that was the expression we used in those days—then we went to Australia, and I left him there, and the only happy moment I had in all my married life was on the morning when I saw in the papers that he was dead.

George. [*Very uncomfortable.*] Yes, yes, my dear, I know. You must have had a terrible time. I can hardly bear to think about it. My only hope is that I have made up to you for it in some degree. But I don't see what bearing it has upon Dinah's case.

Olivia. Oh, none, except that *my* father *liked* Jacob's political opinions and his views on art. I expect that that was why he chose him for me.

George. You seem to think that I wish to choose a husband for Dinah. I don't at all. Let her choose whom she likes as long as he can support her and there's a chance of their being happy together. Now, with regard to this fellow——

Olivia. You mean Brian?

George. He's got no money, and he's been brought up in quite a different way from Dinah. Dinah may be prepared to believe that—er—all cows are blue, and that—er—waves are square, but she won't go on believing it for ever.

Olivia. Neither will Brian.

George. Well, that's what I keep telling him, only he won't see it. Just as I keep telling you about those ridiculous curtains. It seems to me that I am the only person in the house with any eyesight left.

Olivia. Perhaps you are, darling; but you must let us find out our own mistakes for ourselves. At any rate, Brian is a gentleman; he loves Dinah, Dinah loves him; he's earning enough to support himself, and you are earning enough to support Dinah. I think it's worth risking, George.

George. [*Stiffly.*] I can only say the whole question demands much more anxious thought than you seem to have given it. You say that he is a gentleman. He knows how to behave, I admit; but if his morals are as topsy-turvy as his tastes and—er—politics, as I've no doubt they are, then—er—— In short, I do *not* approve of Brian Strange as a husband for my niece and ward.

Olivia. [*Looking at him thoughtfully.*] You *are* a curious mixture, George. You were so very unconventional when you married me, and you're so very conventional when Brian wants to marry Dinah. . . . George Marden to marry the widow of a convict!

George. Convict! What do you mean?

Olivia. Jacob Telworthy, convict—I forget his number—surely I told you all this, dear, when we got engaged?

George. Never!

Olivia. I told you how he carelessly put the wrong signature to a check for a thousand pounds in England; how he made a little mistake about two or three companies he'd promoted in Australia; and how——

George. Yes, yes, but you never told me he was *convicted!*

Olivia. What difference does it make?

George. My dear Olivia, if you can't see that—a convict!

Olivia. So, you see, we needn't be too particular about our niece, need we?

George. I think we had better leave your first husband out of the conversation altogether. I never wished to refer to him; I never wish to hear about him again. I certainly had not realized that he was actually —er—*convicted* for his—er——

Olivia. Mistakes.

George. Well, we needn't go into that. As for this other matter, I don't for a moment take it seriously. Dinah is an exceptionally pretty girl, and young Strange is a good-looking boy. If they are attracted to each other, it is a mere outward attraction which I am convinced will not lead to any lasting happiness. That must be regarded as my last word in the matter, Olivia. If this Mr. —er—what was his name, comes, I shall be down at the farm.

[*He goes out by the door.*]

[*Left alone,* OLIVIA *brings out her curtains again, and gets calmly to work upon them.*]

[DINAH *and* BRIAN *come in by the windows.*]

Dinah. Finished?

Olivia. Oh no, I've got all these rings to put on.

Dinah. I meant talking to George.

Brian. We walked about outside——

Dinah. Until we heard him *not* talking to you any more——

Brian. And we didn't kiss each other once.

Dinah. Brian was very George-like. He wouldn't even let me tickle the back of his neck. [*She goes up suddenly to* OLIVIA *and kneels by her and kisses her.*] Darling, being George-like is a very nice thing to be—I mean a nice thing for other people to be—I mean—oh, you know what I mean. But say that he's going to be decent about it.

Olivia. Of course he is, Dinah.

Brian. You mean he'll let me come here as—as——

Dinah. As my young man?

Olivia. Oh, I think so.

Dinah. Olivia, you're a wonder. Have you really talked him round?

Olivia. I haven't said anything yet. But I daresay I shall think of something.

Dinah. [*Disappointedly.*] Oh!

Brian. [*Making the best of it.*] After all, Dinah, I'm going back to London tomorrow——

Olivia. You can be good for one more day, Dinah, and then when Brian isn't here, we'll see what we can do.

Dinah. Yes, but I didn't want him to go back tomorrow.

Brian. [*Sternly.*] Must. Hard work before me. Earn thousands a year. Paint the Mayor and Corporation of Pudsey, life-size, including chains of office; paint slice of haddock on plate. Copy Landseer for old gentleman in Bayswater. Design antimacassar for middle-aged sofa in Streatham. Earn a living for you, Dinah.

Dinah. [*Giggling.*] Oh, Brian, you're heavenly. What fun we shall have when we're married.

Brian. [*Stiffly.*] Sir Brian Strange, R.A., if you please, Miss Marden. Sir Brian Strange, R.A., writes: "Your Sanogene has proved a most excellent tonic. After completing the third acre of my Academy picture 'The Mayor and Corporation of Pudsey' I was completely exhausted, but one bottle of Sanogene revived me, and I finished the remaining seven acres at a single sitting."

Olivia. [*Looking about her.*] Brian, find my scissors for me.

Brian. Scissors. [*Looking for them.*] Sir Brian Strange, R.A., looks for scissors. [*Finding them.*] Aha! Once more we must record an unqualified success for the eminent Academician. Your scissors.

Olivia. Thank you so much.

Dinah. Come on, Brian, let's go out. I feel open-airy.

Olivia. Don't be late for lunch, there's good people. Lady Marden is coming.

Dinah. Aunt Juli-ah! Help! [*She faints in* BRIAN'S *arms.*] That means a clean pinafore. Brian, you'll jolly well have to brush your hair.

Brian. [*Feeling it.*] I suppose there's no time now to go up to London and get it cut?

[*Enter* ANNE, *followed by* PIM.]

Anne. Mr. Pim!

Dinah. [*Delighted.*] Hullo, Mr. Pim! Here we are again! You can't get rid of us so easily, you see.

Pim. I—er—dear Miss Marden——

Olivia. How do you do, Mr. Pim? I can't get up, but do come and sit down. My husband will be here in a minute. Anne, send somebody down to the farm——

Anne. I think I heard the Master in the library, madam.

Olivia. Oh, will you tell him then?

Anne. Yes, madam. [ANNE *goes out.*]

Olivia. You'll stay to lunch, of course, Mr. Pim?

Dinah. Oh, do!

Pim. It's very kind of you, Mrs. Marden, but——

Dinah. Oh, you simply must, Mr. Pim. You haven't told us half enough about yourself yet. I want to hear all about your early life.

Olivia. Dinah!

Pim. Oh, we are almost, I might say, old friends, Mrs. Marden.

Dinah. Of course we are. He knows Brian, too. There's more in Mr. Pim than you think. You *will* stay to lunch, won't you?

Pim. It's very kind of you to ask me, Mrs. Marden, but I am lunching with the Trevors.

Olivia. Oh, well, you must come to lunch another day.

Dinah. The reason why we like Mr. Pim so much is that he was the first person to congratulate us. We feel that he is going to have a great influence on our lives.

Pim. [*To* OLIVIA.] I, so to speak, stumbled on the engagement this morning and—er——

Olivia. I see. Children, you must go and tidy yourselves up. Run along.

Brian. Sir Brian and Lady Strange never run; they walk. [*Offering his arm.*] Madam!

Dinah. [*Taking it.*] Au revoir, Mr. Pim.

[*Dramatically.*] We——shall——meet——*again!*

Pim. [*Chuckling.*] Good morning, Miss Dinah.

Brian. Good morning.

[*He and* DINAH *go out.*]

Olivia. You must forgive them, Mr. Pim. They're such children. And naturally they're rather excited just now.

Pim. Oh, not at all, Mrs. Marden.

Olivia. Of course you won't say anything about their engagement. We only heard about it five minutes ago, and nothing has been settled yet.

Pim. Of course, of course!

[*Enter* GEORGE.]

George. Ah, Mr. Pim, we meet at last. Sorry to have kept you waiting before.

Pim. The apology should come from me, Mr. Marden, for having—er——

George. Not at all. Very glad to meet you now. Any friend of Brymer's. You want a letter to this man Fanshawe?

Olivia. Shall I be in your way at all?

Pim. Oh, no, no, please don't.

George. It's only just a question of a letter. [*Going to his desk.*] Fanshawe will put you in the way of seeing all that you want to see. He's a very old friend of mine. [*Taking a sheet of notepaper.*] You'll stay to lunch, of course?

Pim. I'm afraid I am lunching with the Trevors——

George. Oh, well, they'll look after you all right. Good chap, Trevor.

Pim. [*To* OLIVIA.] You see, Mrs. Marden, I have only recently arrived from Australia after traveling about the world for some years, and I'm rather out of touch with my—er—fellow-workers in London.

Olivia. Oh yes. You've been in Australia, Mr. Pim?

George. [*Disliking Australia.*] I shan't be a moment, Mr. Pim. [*He frowns at* OLIVIA.]

Pim. Oh, that's all right, thank you. [*To* OLIVIA.] Oh yes, I have been in Australia more than once in the last few years.

Olivia. Really? I used to live at Sydney many years ago. Do you know Sydney at all?

George. [*Detesting Sydney.*] H'r'm! Perhaps I'd better mention that you are a friend of the Trevors?

Pim. Thank you, thank you. [*To* OLIVIA.] Indeed yes, I spent several months in Sydney.

Olivia. How curious. I wonder if we have any friends in common there.

George. [*Hastily.*] Extremely unlikely, I should think. Sydney is a very big place.

Pim. True, but the world is a very small place, Mr. Marden. I had a remarkable instance of that, coming over on the boat this last time.

George. Ah!

[*Feeling that the conversation is now safe, he resumes his letter.*]

Pim. Yes. There was a man I used to employ in Sydney some years ago, a bad fellow, I'm afraid, Mrs. Marden, who had been in prison for some kind of fraudulent company-promoting and had taken to drink and—and so on.

Olivia. Yes, yes, I understand.

Pim. Drinking himself to death I should have said. I gave him at the most another year to live. Yet to my amazement the first person I saw as I stepped on board the boat that brought me to England last week was this fellow. There was no mistaking him. I spoke to him, in fact; we recognized each other.

Olivia. Really?

Pim. He was traveling steerage; we didn't meet again on board, and, as it happened, at Marseilles, this poor fellow—er—now what *was* his name? A very unusual one. Began with a—a T, I think.

Olivia. [*With suppressed feeling.*] Yes, Mr. Pim, yes?

[*She puts out a hand to* GEORGE.]

George. [*In an undertone.*] Nonsense, dear!

Pim. [*Triumphantly.*] I've got it! Telworthy!

Olivia. Telworthy!

George. Good God!

Pim. [*A little surprised at the success of his story.*] An unusual name, is it not? Not a name you could forget when once you had heard it.

Olivia. [*With feeling.*] No, it is not a name you could forget when once you had heard it.

George. [*Hastily coming over to* PIM.] Quite so, Mr. Pim, a most remarkable name, a most odd story altogether. Well, well, here's your letter, and if you're sure you won't stay to lunch——

Pim. I'm afraid not, thank you. You see, I——

George. The Trevors, yes. I'll just see you on your way—— [*To* OLIVIA.] Er—my dear——

Olivia. [*Holding out her hand, but not looking at him.*] Good-by, Mr. Pim.

Pim. Good-by, good-by!

George. [*Leading the way through the

windows.] This way, this way. Quicker for you.

Pim. Thank you, thank you.

[GEORGE *hurries* MR. PIM *out.* OLIVIA *sits there and looks into the past. Now and then she shudders.* GEORGE *comes back.*]

George. Good God! Telworthy! Is it possible?

[*Before* OLIVIA *can answer,* LADY MARDEN *is announced. They pull themselves together and greet her.*]

CURTAIN

ACT II

Lunch is over and coffee has been served on the terrace. Conversation drags on, to the satisfaction of LADY MARDEN, *but of nobody else.* GEORGE *and* OLIVIA *want to be alone; so do* BRIAN *and* DINAH.

[*At last* BRIAN *murmurs something about a cigarette-case; and, catching* DINAH'S *eye, comes into the house. He leans against the sofa and waits for* DINAH.]

Dinah. [*Loudly as she comes in.*] Have you found it?

Brian. Found what?

Dinah. [*In her ordinary voice.*] That was just for *their* benefit. I said I'd help you find it. It *is* your cigarette-case we're looking for, isn't it?

Brian. [*Taking it out.*] Yes. Have one?

Dinah. No, thank you, darling. Aunt Juli-ah still thinks it's unladylike. . . . Have you ever seen her beagling?

Brian. No. Is that very ladylike?

Dinah. Very. . . . I say, what has happened, do you think?

Brian. Everything. I love you, and you love me.

Dinah. Silly! I meant between George and Olivia. Didn't you notice them at lunch?

Brian. I noticed that you seemed to be doing most of the talking. But then I've noticed that before sometimes. Do you think Olivia and your uncle have quarreled because of *us*?

Dinah. Of course not. George may *think* he has quarreled, but I'm quite sure Olivia hasn't. No, I believe Mr. Pim's at the bottom of it. He's brought some terribly sad news about George's investments. The old home will have to be sold up.

Brian. Good. Then your uncle won't mind your marrying me.

Dinah. Yes, darling, but you must be more dramatic about it than that. "George," you say, with tears in your eyes, "I cannot pay off the whole of the mortgage for you. I have only two and ninepence; but at least let me take your niece off your hands." Then George will thump you on the back and say gruffly, "You're a good fellow, Brian, a damn good fellow," and he'll blow his nose very loudly, and say, "Confound this cigar, it won't draw properly."

[*She gives us a rough impression of* GEORGE *doing it.*]

Brian. Dinah, you're a heavenly idiot. And you've simply got to marry me, uncles or no uncles.

Dinah. It will have to be "uncles," I'm afraid, because, you see, I'm his ward, and I can get sent to Chancery or Coventry or somewhere beastly, if I marry without his consent. Haven't *you* got anybody who objects to your marrying *me*?

Brian. Nobody, thank Heaven.

Dinah. Well, that's rather disappointing of you. I saw myself fascinating your aged father at the same time that you were fascinating George. I should have done it much better than you. As a George-fascinator you aren't very successful, sweetheart.

Brian. What am I like as a Dinah-fascinator?

Dinah. Plus six, darling.

Brian. Then I'll stick to that and leave George to Olivia.

Dinah. I expect she'll manage him all right. I have great faith in Olivia. But you'll marry me, anyhow, won't you, Brian?

Brian. I will.

Dinah. Even if we have to wait till I'm twenty-one?

Brian. Even if we have to wait till you're fifty-one.

Dinah. [*Holding out her hands to him.*] Darling!

Brian. [*Uneasily.*] I say, don't do that.

Dinah. Why not?

Brian. Well, I promised I wouldn't kiss you.

Dinah. Oh! . . . Well, you might just *send* me a kiss. You can look the other way as if you didn't know I was here.

Brian. Like this?

[*He looks the other way, kisses the tips

of his fingers, and flicks it carelessly in her direction.]

Dinah. That was a lovely one. Now here's one coming for you.

[*He catches it gracefully and conveys it to his mouth.*]

Brian. [*With a low bow.*] Madam, I thank you.

Dinah. [*Curtseying.*] Your servant, Mr. Strange.

Olivia. [*From outside.*] Dinah!

Dinah. [*Jumping up.*] Hullo!

[OLIVIA *comes in through the windows, followed by* GEORGE *and* LADY MARDEN, *the latter a vigorous young woman of sixty-odd, who always looks as if she were beagling.*]

Olivia. Aunt Julia wants to see the pigs, dear. I wish you'd take her down. I'm rather tired, and your uncle has some business to attend to.

Lady Marden. I've always said that you don't take enough exercise, Olivia. Look at me—sixty-five and proud of it.

Olivia. Yes, Aunt Julia, you're wonderful.

Dinah. How old would Olivia be if she took exercise?

George. Don't stand about asking silly questions, Dinah. Your aunt hasn't much time.

Brian. May I come too, Lady Marden?

Lady Marden. Well, a little exercise wouldn't do *you* any harm, Mr. Strange. You're an artist, ain't you?

Brian. Well, I try to paint.

Dinah. He sold a picture last March for ——

George. Yes, yes, never mind that now.

Lady Marden. Unhealthy life. Well, come along.

[*She strides out, followed by* DINAH *and* BRIAN. GEORGE *sits down at his desk with his head in his hand, and stabs the blotting-paper with a pen.* OLIVIA *takes the curtains with her to the sofa and begins to work on them.*]

George. [*Looking up and seeing them.*] Really, Olivia, we've got something more important, more vital to us than curtains, to discuss, now that we *are* alone at last.

Olivia. I wasn't going to discuss them, dear.

George. I'm always glad to see Aunt Julia in my house, but I wish she hadn't chosen this day of all days to come to lunch.

Olivia. It wasn't Aunt Julia's fault. It was really Mr. Pim who chose the wrong day.

George. [*Fiercely.*] Good Heavens, is it true?

Olivia. About Jacob Telworthy?

George. You told me he was dead. You always said that he was dead. You—you——

Olivia. Well, I always thought that he was dead. He was as dead as anybody could be. All the papers said he was dead.

George. [*Scornfully.*] The papers!

Olivia. [*As if this would settle it for* GEORGE.] The *Times* said he was dead. There was a paragraph about him. Apparently even his death was fraudulent.

George. Yes, yes, I'm not blaming you, Olivia, but what are we going to do, that's the question, what are we going to do? My God, it's horrible! You've never been married to me at all! You don't seem to understand.

Olivia. It is a little difficult to realize. You see, it doesn't seem to have made any difference to our happiness.

George. No, that's what's so terrible. I mean—well, of course, we were quite innocent in the matter. But, at the same time, nothing can get over the fact that we—we had no right to—to be happy.

Olivia. Would you rather we had been miserable?

George. You're Telworthy's wife, that's what you don't seem to understand. You're Telworthy's wife. You—er—forgive me, Olivia, but it's the horrible truth—you committed bigamy when you married me. [*In horror.*] Bigamy!

Olivia. It is an ugly word, isn't it?

George. Yes, but don't you understand—— [*He jumps up and comes over to her.*] Look here, Olivia, old girl, the whole thing is nonsense, eh? It isn't your husband, it's some other Telworthy that this fellow met. That's right, isn't it? Some other shady swindler who turned up on the boat, eh? This sort of thing doesn't happen to people like *us*—committing bigamy and all that. Some other fellow.

Olivia. [*Shaking her head.*] I knew all the shady swindlers in Sydney, George. . . . They came to dinner. . . . There were no others called Telworthy.

[GEORGE *goes back despondently to his seat.*]

George. Well, what are we going to do?

Olivia. You sent Mr. Pim away so quickly. He might have told us things. Telworthy's plans. Where he is now. You hurried him away so quickly.

George. I've sent a note round to ask him to come back. My one idea at the moment was to get him out of the house—to hush things up.

Olivia. You can't hush up two husbands.

George. [*In despair.*] You can't. Everybody will know. Everybody!

Olivia. The children, Aunt Julia, they may as well know now as later. Mr. Pim must, of course.

George. I do not propose to discuss my private affairs with Mr. Pim——

Olivia. But he's mixed himself up in them rather, hasn't he, and if you're going to ask him questions——

George. I only propose to ask him one question. I shall ask him if he is absolutely certain of the man's name. I can do that quite easily without letting him know the reason for my inquiry.

Olivia. You couldn't make a mistake about a name like Telworthy. But he might tell us something about Telworthy's plans. Perhaps he's going back to Australia at once. Perhaps he thinks I'm dead, too. Perhaps—oh, there are so many things I want to know.

George. Yes, yes, dear. It would be interesting to—that is, one naturally wants to know these things, but of course it doesn't make any real difference.

Olivia. [*Surprised.*] No difference?

George. Well, that is to say, you're as much his wife if he's in Australia as you are if he's in England.

Olivia. I am not his wife at all.

George. But, Olivia, surely you understand the position——

Olivia. [*Shaking her head.*] Jacob Telworthy may be alive, but I am not his wife. I ceased to be his wife when I became yours.

George. You never *were* my wife. That is the terrible part of it. Our union—you make me say it, Olivia—has been unhallowed by the Church. Unhallowed even by the Law. Legally, we have been living in—living in—well, the point is, how does the Law stand? I imagine that Telworthy could get a—a divorce. . . . Oh, it seems impossible that things like this can be happening to *us*.

Olivia. [*Joyfully.*] A divorce?

George. I—I imagine so.

Olivia. But then we could *really* get married, and we shouldn't be living in—living in—whatever we were living in before.

George. I can't understand you, Olivia. You talk about it so calmly, as if there was nothing blameworthy in being divorced, as if there was nothing unusual in my marrying a divorced woman, as if there was nothing wrong in our having lived together for years without having been married.

Olivia. What seems wrong to me is that I lived for five years with a bad man whom I hated. What seems right to me is that I lived for five years with a good man whom I love.

George. Yes, yes, my dear, I know. But right and wrong don't settle themselves as easily as that. We've been living together when you were Telworthy's wife. That's *wrong.*

Olivia. Do you mean wicked?

George. Well, no doubt the Court would consider that we acted in perfect innocence——

Olivia. What Court?

George. These things have to be done legally, of course. I believe the proper method is a nullity suit, declaring our marriage null and—er—void. It would, so to speak, wipe out these years of—er——

Olivia. Wickedness?

George. Of irregular union, and—er—then——

Olivia. Then I could go back to Jacob. . . . Do you really mean that, George?

George. [*Uneasily.*] Well, dear, you see—that's how things are—one can't get away from—er——

Olivia. What you feel is that Telworthy has the greater claim? You are prepared to—make way for him?

George. Both the Church and the Law would say that I had no claim at all, I'm afraid. I—I suppose I haven't.

Olivia. I see. [*She looks at him curiously.*] Thank you for making it so clear, George.

George. Of course, whether or not you go back to—er—Telworthy is another matter altogether. That would naturally be for you to decide.

Olivia. [*Cheerfully.*] For me and Jacko to decide.

George. Er—Jacko?

Olivia. I used to call my first husband—I mean my only husband—Jacko. I didn't like the name of Jacob, and Jacko seemed to suit him somehow. . . . He had very long arms. Dear Jacko.

George. [*Annoyed.*] You don't seem to realize that this is not a joke, Olivia.

Olivia. [*A trifle hysterically.*] It may not be a joke, but it *is* funny, isn't it?

George. I must say I don't see anything funny in a tragedy that has wrecked two lives.

Olivia. Two? Oh, but Jacko's life isn't wrecked. It has just been miraculously restored to him. And a wife, too. There's nothing tragic for Jack in it.

George. [*Stiffly.*] I was referring to *our* two lives—yours and mine.

Olivia. Yours, George? Your life isn't wrecked. The Court will absolve you of all blame; your friends will sympathize with you, and tell you that I was a designing woman who deliberately took you in; your Aunt Julia——

George. [*Overwrought.*] Stop it! What do you mean? Have you no heart? Do you think I *want* to lose you, Olivia? Do you think I *want* my home broken up like this? Haven't you been happy with me these last five years?

Olivia. Very happy.

George. Well then, how can you talk like that?

Olivia. [*Pathetically.*] But you want to send me away.

George. There you go again. I don't *want* to. I have hardly had time to realize just what it will mean to me when you go. The fact is I simply daren't realize it. I daren't think about it.

Olivia. [*Earnestly.*] Try thinking about it, George.

George. And you talk as if I *wanted* to send you away!

Olivia. Try thinking about it, George.

George. You don't seem to understand that I'm not *sending* you away. You simply aren't mine to keep.

Olivia. Whose am I?

George. Your husband's. Telworthy's.

Olivia. [*Gently.*] If I belong to anybody but myself, I think I belong to you.

George. Not in the eyes of the Law. Not in the eyes of the Church. Not even in the eyes of—er——

Olivia. The County?

George. [*Annoyed.*] I was about to say "Heaven."

Olivia. [*Unimpressed.*] Oh!

George. That this should happen to *us*!

[*He gets up and walks about the room, wondering when he will wake up from this impossible dream.* OLIVIA *works in silence. Then she stands up and shakes out her curtains.*]

Olivia. [*Looking at them.*] I do hope Jacko will like these.

George. What! You—— [*Going up to her.*] Olivia, Olivia, have you no heart?

Olivia. Ought you to talk like that to another man's wife?

George. Confound it, is this just a joke to you?

Olivia. You must forgive me, George; I am a little over-excited—at the thought of returning to Jacob, I suppose.

George. Do you *want* to return to him?

Olivia. One wants to do what is right. In the eyes of—er—Heaven.

George. Seeing what sort of man he is, I have no doubt that you could get a separation, supposing that he didn't—er—divorce you. I don't know *what* is best. I must consult my solicitor. The whole position has been sprung on us, and—[*miserably*]—I don't know, I don't know. I can't take it all in.

Olivia. Wouldn't you like to consult your Aunt Julia, too? She could tell you what the County—I mean what Heaven really thought about it.

George. Yes, yes. Aunt Julia has plenty of common sense. You're quite right, Olivia. This isn't a thing we can keep from the family.

Olivia. Do I still call her *Aunt* Julia?

George. [*Looking up from his pacings.*] What? What? [ANNE *comes in.*] Well, what is it?

Anne. Mr. Pim s ys he will come down at once, sir.

George. Oh, thank you, thank you.

[ANNE *goes out.*]

Olivia. George, Mr. Pim has got to know.

George. I don't see the necessity.

Olivia. Not even for me? When a woman suddenly hears that her long-lost husband is restored to her, don't you think she wants to ask questions? Where is he living, and how is he looking, and——

George. [*Coldly.*] Of course, if you are interested in these things——

Olivia. How can I help being? Don't be so silly, George. We *must* know what Jacko——

George. [*Annoyed.*] I wish you wouldn't call him by that ridiculous name.

Olivia. My husband——

George. [*Wincing.*] Yes, well—your husband?

Olivia. Well, we must know his plans—where we can communicate with him, and so on.

George. I have no wish to communicate with him.

Olivia. I'm afraid you'll have to, dear.

George. I don't see the necessity.

Olivia. Well, you'll want to—to apologize to him for living with his wife for so long. And as I belong to him, he ought to be told where he can—call for me.

George. [*After a struggle.*] You put it in a very peculiar way, but I see your point. [*With a shudder.*] Oh, the horrible publicity of it all!

Olivia. [*Going up to him and comforting him.*] Poor George. Dear, don't think I don't sympathize with you. I understand so exactly what you are feeling. The publicity! It's terrible.

George. [*Miserably.*] I want to do what's right, Olivia. You believe that?

Olivia. Of course I do. It's only that we don't quite agree as to what is right and what is wrong.

George. It isn't a question of agreeing. Right is right, and wrong is wrong, all the world over.

Olivia. [*With a sad little smile.*] But more particularly in Buckinghamshire, I think.

George. If I only considered myself, I should say: "Let us pack this man Telworthy back to Australia. He would make no claim. He would accept money to go away and say nothing about it." If I consulted simply my own happiness, Olivia, that is what I should say. But when I consult—er——

Olivia. [*Surprised.*] Mine?

George. My conscience——

Olivia. Oh!

George. Then I can't do it. It's wrong.

[*He is at the window as he says this.*]

Olivia. [*Making her first and last appeal.*] George, aren't I worth a little——

George. [*Turning around.*] H'sh! Dinah! [*Loudly for* DINAH's *benefit.*] Well, then I'll write to him and—— Ah, Dinah, where's Aunt Julia?

Dinah. [*Coming in.*] We've seen the pigs, and now she's discussing the Art of Landseer with Brian. I just came to ask——

Olivia. Dinah, dear, bring Aunt Julia here. And Brian too. We have things we want to talk about with you all.

George. [*Outraged.*] Olivia!

Dinah. Righto. What fun! [*Exit* DINAH.]

George. Olivia, you don't seriously suggest that we should discuss these things with a child like Dinah and a young man like Strange, a mere acquaintance.

Olivia. Dinah will have to know. I'm very fond of her, George. You can't send me away without telling Dinah. And Brian is my friend. You have your solicitor and your aunt and your conscience to consult—mayn't I even have Brian?

George. [*Forgettting.*] I should have thought that your *husband*——

Olivia. Yes, but we don't know where Jacko is.

George. I was not referring to—er—Telworthy.

Olivia. Well then?

George. Well, naturally I—you mustn't—Oh, this is horrible!

[*He comes back tc his desk as the others come in.*]

Olivia. [*Getting up.*] George and I have had some rather bad news, Aunt Julia. We wanted your advice. Where will you sit?

Lady Marden. Thank you, Olivia. I can sit down by myself. [*She does so, near* GEORGE. DINAH *sits on the sofa with* OLIVIA, *and* BRIAN *half leans against the back of it. There is a hush of expectation. . . .*] What is it? Money, I suppose. Nobody's safe nowadays.

George. [*Signaling for help.*] Olivia——

Olivia. We've just heard that my first husband is still alive.

Dinah. Telworthy!

Brian. Good Lord!

Lady Marden. George!

Dinah. [*Excitedly.*] And only this morning I was saying that nothing ever happened in this house! [*Remorsefully to* OLIVIA.] Darling, I don't mean that. Darling one!

Lady Marden. What does this mean, George? I leave you for ten minutes—barely ten minutes—to go and look at the pigs, and when I come back you tell me that Olivia is a bigamist.

Brian. [*Indignantly.*] I say——

Olivia. [*Restraining him.*] H'sh!

Brian. [*To* OLIVIA.] If this is a row, I'm on your side.

Lady Marden. Well, George?

George. I'm afraid it's true, Aunt Julia. We heard the news just before lunch—just before you came. We've only this moment had an opportunity of talking about it, of wondering what to do.

Lady Marden. What was his name—Tel—something——

Olivia. Jacob Telworthy.

Lady Marden. So he's alive still?

George. Apparently. There seems to be no doubt about it.

Lady Marden. [*To* OLIVIA.] Didn't you *see* him die? I should always want to *see* my husband die before I married again. Not that I approve of second marriages, anyhow. I told you so at the time, George.

Olivia. And me, Aunt Julia.

Lady Marden. Did I? Well, I generally say what I think.

George. I ought to tell you, Aunt Julia, that no blame attaches to Olivia over this. Of that I am perfectly satisfied. It's nobody's fault, except——

Lady Marden. Except Telworthy's. *He* seems to have been rather careless. Well, what are you going to do about it?

George. That's just it. It's a terrible situation. There's bound to be so much publicity. Not only all this, but—but Telworthy's past and—and everything.

Lady Marden. I should have said that it was Telworthy's present which was the trouble. Had he a past as well?

Olivia. He was a fraudulent company-promoter. He went to prison a good deal.

Lady Marden. George, you never told me this!

George. I—er——

Olivia. I don't see why he should want to talk about it.

Dinah. [*Indignantly.*] What's it got to do with Olivia, anyhow? It's not *her* fault.

Lady Marden. [*Sarcastically.*] Oh no, I daresay it's mine.

Olivia. [*To* GEORGE.] You wanted to ask Aunt Julia what was the right thing to do.

Brian. [*Bursting out.*] Good Heavens, what *is* there to do except the one and only thing? [*They all look at him and he becomes embarrassed.*] I'm sorry. You don't want *me* to——

Olivia. *I* do, Brian.

Lady Marden. Well, go on, Mr. Strange. What would *you* do in George's position?

Brian. Do? Say to the woman I loved, "You're *mine,* and let this other damned fellow come and take you from me if he can!" And he couldn't—how could he?—not if the woman chose *me.*

[LADY MARDEN *gazes at* BRIAN *in amazement,* GEORGE *in anger.* OLIVIA *presses his hand gratefully. He has said what she has been waiting—oh, so eagerly—for* GEORGE *to say.*]

Dinah. [*Adoringly.*] Oh, Brian! [*In a whisper.*] It *is* me, isn't it, and not Olivia?

Brian. You baby, of course!

Lady Marden. I'm afraid, Mr. Strange, your morals are as peculiar as your views on Art. If you had led a more healthy life——

Brian. This is not a question of morals or of art, it's a question of love.

Dinah. Hear, hear!

Lady Marden. [*To* GEORGE.] Isn't it that girl's bedtime yet?

Olivia. [*To* DINAH.] We'll let her sit up a little longer if she's good.

Dinah. I will be good, Olivia, only I thought anybody, however important a debate was, was allowed to say "Hear, hear!"

George. [*Coldly.*] I really think we could discuss this better if Mr. Strange took Dinah out for a walk. Strange, if you—er——

Olivia. Tell them what you have settled first, George.

Lady Marden. Settled? What is there to be settled? It settles itself.

George. [*Sadly.*] That's just it.

Lady Marden. The marriage must be annulled—is that the word, George?

George. I presume so.

Lady Marden. One's solicitor will know all about that of course.

Brian. And when the marriage has been annulled, what then?

Lady Marden. Presumably Olivia will return to her husband.

Brian. [*Bitterly.*] And *that's* morality! As expounded by Bishop Landseer!

George. [*Angered.*] I don't know what you mean by Bishop Landseer. Morality is acting in accordance with the Laws of the Land and the Laws of the Church. I am quite prepared to believe that *your* creed embraces neither marriage nor monogamy, but my creed is different.

Brian. [*Fiercely.*] My creed includes both marriage *and* monogamy, and monogamy means sticking to the woman you love, as long as she wants you.

Lady Marden. [*Calmly.*] You suggest that George and Olivia should go on living together, although they have never been legally married, and wait for this Telworthy man to divorce her, and then—bless the man, what do you think the County would say?

Brian. [*Scornfully.*] Does it matter?

Dinah. Well, if you really want to know, the men would say, "Gad, she's a fine woman; I don't wonder he sticks to her," and the women would say, "I can't *think* what he sees in her to stick to her like that," and they'd both say, "After all, he may be a damn fool, but you can't deny he's a sportsman." That's what the County would say.

George. [*Indignantly.*] Was it for this sort of thing, Olivia, that you insisted on having Dinah and Mr. Strange in here? To insult me in my own house?

Lady Marden. I can't think what young people are coming to nowadays.

Olivia. I think, dear, you and Brian had better go.

Dinah. [*Getting up.*] We will go. But I'm just going to say one thing, Uncle George. Brian and I *are* going to marry each other, and when we are married we'll stick to each other, how*ever* many of our dead husbands and wives turn up!

[*She goes out indignantly, followed by* BRIAN.]

George. Upon my word, this is a pleasant discussion.

Olivia. I think the discussion is over, George. It is only a question of where I shall go, while you are bringing your—what sort of suit did you call it?

Lady Marden. [*To* GEORGE.] Nullity suit. I suppose that *is* the best thing?

George. It's horrible. The awful publicity. That it should be happening to *us,* that's what I can't get over.

Lady Marden. I don't remember anything of the sort in the Marden Family before, ever.

George. [*Absently.*] Lady Fanny.

Lady Marden. [*Recollecting.*] Yes, of course; but that was two hundred years ago. The standards were different then. Besides, it wasn't quite the same, anyhow.

George. [*Absently.*] No, it wasn't quite the same.

Lady Marden. No. We shall all feel it. Terribly.

George. [*His apology.*] If there were any other way! Olivia, what *can* I do? It *is* the only way, isn't it? All that that fellow said—of course, it sounds very well—but as things are. . . . *Is* there anything in marriage, or isn't there? You believe that there is, don't you? You aren't one of these Socialists. Well, then, *can* we go on living together when you're another man's wife? It isn't only what people will say, but it *is* wrong, isn't it? . . . And supposing he doesn't divorce you, are we to go on living together, unmarried, for*ever*? Olivia, you seem to think that I'm just thinking of the publicity—what people will say. I'm not. I'm not. That comes in anyway. But I want to do what's right, what's best. I don't mean what's best for *us*, what makes us happiest, I mean what's really best, what's rightest. What anybody else would do in my place. *I* don't know. It's so unfair. You're not my wife at all, but I want to do what's right. . . . Oh, Olivia, Olivia, you do understand, don't you?

[*They have both forgotten* LADY MARDEN. OLIVIA *has never taken her eyes off him as he makes his last attempt to convince himself.*]

Olivia. [*Almost tenderly.*] So very, very well, George. Oh, I understand just what you are feeling. And oh, I do so wish that you could—[*with a little sigh*]—but then it wouldn't be George, not the George I married—[*with a rueful little laugh*]—or didn't quite marry.

Lady Marden. I must say, I think you are both talking a little wildly.

Olivia. [*Repeating it, oh, so tenderly.*] Or didn't—quite—marry.

[*She looks at him with all her heart in her eyes. She is giving him his last chance to say, "Damn Telworthy; you're mine!" He struggles desperately with himself. . . . Will he?—will he? . . . But we shall never know, for at that moment* ANNE *comes in.*]

Anne. Mr. Pim is here, sir.

George. [*Emerging from the struggle with an effort.*] Pim? Pim? Oh, ah, yes, of course. Mr. Pim. [*Looking up.*] Where have you put him?

Olivia. I want to see Mr. Pim, too, George.

Lady Marden. Who on earth is Mr. Pim?

Olivia. Show him in here, Anne.

Anne. Yes, madam. [*She goes out.*]

Olivia. It was Mr. Pim who told us about my husband. He came across with him in the boat, and recognized him as the Telworthy he knew in Australia.

Lady Marden. Oh! Shall I be in the way?

George. No, no. It doesn't matter, does it, Olivia?

Olivia. Please stay.

[ANNE *enters followed by* MR. PIM.]

Anne. Mr. Pim.

George. [*Pulling himself together.*] Ah, Mr. Pim! Very good of you to have come. The fact is—er——

[*It is too much for him; he looks despairingly at* OLIVIA.]

Olivia. We're so sorry to trouble you, Mr. Pim. By the way, do you know Lady Marden? [MR. PIM *and* LADY MARDEN *bow to each other.*] Do come and sit down, won't you? [*She makes room for him on the sofa next to her.*] The fact is, Mr. Pim, you gave us rather a surprise this morning, and before we had time to realize what it all meant, you had gone.

Mr. Pim. A surprise, Mrs. Marden? Dear me, not an unpleasant one, I hope?

Olivia. Well, rather a—surprising one.

George. Olivia, allow me a moment. Mr. Pim, you mentioned a man called Telworthy this morning. My wife used to—that is to say, I used to—that is, there are reasons——

Olivia. I think we had better be perfectly frank, George.

Lady Marden. I am sixty-five years of age, Mr. Pim, and I can say that I've never had a moment's uneasiness by telling the truth.

Mr. Pim. [*After a desperate effort to keep up with the conversation.*] Oh! . . . I—er—I'm afraid I am rather at sea. Have I—er—left anything unsaid in presenting my credentials to you this morning? This Telworthy whom you mention—I seem to remember the name——

Olivia. Mr. Pim, you told us this morning of a man whom you had met on the boat, a man who had come down in the world, whom you had known in Sydney. A man called Telworthy.

Mr. Pim. [*Relieved.*] Ah yes, yes, of course. I did say Telworthy, didn't I? Most curious coincidence, Lady Marden. Poor man, poor man! Let me see, it must have been ten years ago——

George. Just a moment, Mr. Pim. You're quite sure that his name was Telworthy?

Mr. Pim. Telworthy—Telworthy—didn't I

say Telworthy? Yes, that was it—Telworthy. Poor fellow!

Olivia. I'm going to be perfectly frank with you, Mr. Pim. I feel quite sure that I can trust you. This man Telworthy whom you met is my husband.

Mr. Pim. Your husband? [*He looks in mild surprise at* GEORGE.] But—er——

Olivia. My first husband. His death was announced six years ago. I had left him some years before that, but there seems no doubt from your story that he's still alive. His record—the country he comes from—above all, the very unusual name—Telworthy.

Mr. Pim. Telworthy—yes—certainly a most peculiar name. I remember saying so. Your first husband? Dear me! Dear me!

George. You understand, Mr. Pim, that all this is in absolute confidence.

Mr. Pim. Of course, of course.

Olivia. Well, since he is my husband, we naturally want to know something about him. Where is he now, for instance?

Mr. Pim. [*Surprised.*] Where is he now? But surely I told you? I told you what happened at Marseilles?

George. At Marseilles?

Mr. Pim. Yes, yes, poor fellow, it was most unfortunate. [*Quite happy again.*] You must understand, Lady Marden, that although I had met the poor fellow before in Australia, I was never in any way intimate——

George. [*Thumping the desk.*] Where is he *now*, that's what we want to know?

[MR. PIM *turns to him with a start.*]

Olivia. Please, Mr. Pim!

Mr. Pim. Where is he now? But—but didn't I tell you of the curious fatality at Marseilles—poor fellow—the fish-bone?

All. Fish-bone?

Mr. Pim. Yes, yes, a herring, I understand.

Olivia. [*Understanding first.*] Do you mean he's dead?

Mr. Pim. Dead—of course—didn't I——?

Olivia. [*Laughing hysterically.*] Oh, Mr. Pim, you—oh, what a husband to have—oh, I——

[*But that is all she can say for the moment.*]

Lady Marden. Pull yourself together, Olivia. This is so unhealthy for you. [*To* PIM.] So he really *is* dead this time?

Mr. Pim. Oh, undoubtedly, undoubtedly. A fish-bone lodged in his throat.

George. [*Trying to realize it.*] Dead!

Olivia. [*Struggling with her laughter.*] I think you must excuse me, Mr. Pim—I can never thank you enough—a herring—there's something about a herring—morality depends on such little things—George, you——

[*Shaking her head at him in a weak state of laughter, she hurries out of the room.*]

Mr. Pim. Dear me! Dear me!

George. Now, let us have this quite clear, Mr. Pim. You say that the man, Telworthy, Jacob Telworthy, is dead?

Mr. Pim. Telworthy, yes—didn't I say Telworthy? This man I was telling you about——

George. He's dead?

Mr. Pim. Yes, yes, he died at Marseilles.

Lady Marden. A dispensation of Providence, George. One can look at it in no other light.

George. Dead! [*Suddenly annoyed.*] Really, Mr. Pim, I think you might have told us before.

Mr. Pim. But I—I *was* telling you—I——

George. If you had only told us the whole story at once, instead of in two—two instalments like this, you would have saved us all a good deal of anxiety.

Mr. Pim. Really, I——

Lady Marden. I am sure Mr. Pim meant well, George, but it seems a pity he couldn't have said so before. If a man was dead, *why* try to hush it up?

Mr. Pim. [*Lost again.*] Really, Lady Marden, I——

George. [*Getting up.*] Well, well, at any rate, I am much obliged to you, Mr. Pim, for having come down to us this afternoon. Dead! *De mortuis*, and so forth, but the situation would have been impossible had he lived. Good-by. [*Holding out his hand.*] Good-by!

Lady Marden. Good-by, Mr. Pim.

Mr. Pim. Good-by, good-by! [GEORGE *takes him to the door.*] Of course, if I had—[*to himself*] Telworthy—I *think* that was the name. [*He goes out, still wondering.*]

George. [*With a sigh of thankfulness.*] Well! This is wonderful news, Aunt Julia.

Lady Marden. Most providential! . . . You understand, of course, that you are not married to Olivia?

George. [*Who didn't.*] Not married?

Lady Marden. If her first husband only died at Marseilles a few days ago——

George. Good Heavens!

Lady Marden. Not that it matters. You can get married quietly again. Nobody need know.

George. [*Considering it.*] Yes . . . yes. Then all these years we have been—er—Yes.

Lady Marden. Who's going to know?

George. Yes, yes, that's true. . . . And in perfect innocence, too.

Lady Marden. I should suggest a Registry Office in London.

George. A Registry Office, yes.

Lady Marden. Better go up to town this afternoon. Can't do it too quickly.

George. Yes, yes. We can stay at an hotel——

Lady Marden. [*Surprised.*] George!

George. What?

Lady Marden. *You* will stay at your club.

George. Oh—ah—yes, of course, Aunt Julia.

Lady Marden. Better take your solicitor with you to be on the safe side. . . . To the Registry Office, I mean.

George. Yes.

Lady Marden. [*Getting up.*] Well, I must be getting along, George. Say good-by to Olivia for me. And those children. Of course, you won't allow this absurd love-business between them to come to anything?

George. Most certainly not. Good-by, Aunt Julia!

Lady Marden. [*Indicating the windows.*] I'll go *this* way. [*As she goes.*] And get Olivia out more, George. I don't like these hysterics. You want to be firm with her.

George. [*Firmly.*] Yes, yes! Good-by!

[*He waves to her and then goes back to his seat.* OLIVIA *comes in, and stands in the middle of the room looking at him. He comes to her eagerly.*]

George. [*Holding out his hands.*] Olivia! Olivia! [*But it is not so easy as that.*]

Olivia. [*Drawing herself up proudly.*] Mrs. Telworthy!

CURTAIN

ACT III

[OLIVIA *is standing where we left her at the end of the last act.*]

George. [*Taken aback.*] Olivia, I—I don't understand.

Olivia. [*Leaving melodrama with a little laugh and coming down to him.*] Poor George! Did I frighten you rather?

George. You're so strange today. I don't understand you. You're not like the Olivia I know.

[*They sit down on the sofa together.*]

Olivia. Perhaps you don't know me very well after all.

George. [*Affectionately.*] Oh, that's nonsense, old girl. You're just my Olivia.

Olivia. And yet it seemed as though I wasn't going to be your Olivia half an hour ago.

George. [*With a shudder.*] Don't talk about it. It doesn't bear thinking about. Well, thank Heaven that's over. Now we can get married again quietly and nobody will be any the wiser.

Olivia. Married again?

George. Yes, dear. As you—er—[*he laughs uneasily*]—said just now, you are Mrs. Telworthy. Just for the moment. But we can soon put that right. My idea was to go up this evening and—er—make arrangements; and if you come up tomorrow morning, if we can manage it by then, we could get quietly married at a Registry Office, and—er—nobody any the wiser.

Olivia. Yes, I see. You want me to marry you at a Registry Office tomorrow?

George. If we can arrange it by then. I don't know how long these things take, but I should imagine there would be no difficulty.

Olivia. Oh no, that part ought to be quite easy. But—— [*She hesitates.*]

George. But what?

Olivia. Well, if you want to marry me tomorrow, George, oughtn't you to propose to me first?

George. [*Amazed.*] Propose?

Olivia. Yes. It is usual, isn't it, to propose to a person before you marry her, and—and we want to do the usual thing, don't we?

George. [*Upset.*] But you—but we . . .

Olivia. You see, dear, you're George Marden, and I'm Olivia Telworthy, and you—you're attracted by me, and think I would make you a good wife, and you want to marry me. Well, naturally you propose to me first, and—tell me how much you are attracted by me, and what a good wife you think I shall make, and how badly you want to marry me.

George. [*Falling into the humor of it, as he thinks.*] The baby! Did she want to be proposed to all over again?

Olivia. Well, she did rather.

George. [*Rather fancying himself as an actor.*] She shall then. [*He adopts what he considers to be an appropriate attitude.*] Mrs. Telworthy, I have long admired you in silence, and the time has now come to put my admiration into words. Er——

[*But apparently he finds a difficulty.*]

Olivia. [*Hopefully.*] Into words.

George. Er——

Olivia. [*With the idea of helping.*] Oh, Mr. Marden!

George. Er—may I call you Olivia?

Olivia. Yes, George.

George. [*Taking her hand.*] Olivia—I —— [*He hesitates.*]

Olivia. I don't want to interrupt, but oughtn't you to be on your knees? It is—usual, I believe. If one of the servants came in, you could say you were looking for my scissors.

George. Really, Olivia, you must allow me to manage my own proposal in my own way.

Olivia. [*Meekly.*] I'm sorry. Do go on.

George. Well, er—confound it, Olivia, I love you. Will you marry me?

Olivia. Thank you, George, I will think it over.

George. [*Laughing.*] Silly girl! Well then, tomorrow morning. No wedding-cake, I'm afraid, Olivia. [*He laughs again.*] But we'll go and have a good lunch somewhere.

Olivia. I will think it over, George.

George. [*Good-humoredly.*] Well, give us a kiss while you're thinking.

Olivia. I'm afraid you mustn't kiss me until we are actually engaged.

George. [*Laughing uneasily.*] Oh, we needn't take it as seriously as all that.

Olivia. But a woman must take a proposal seriously.

George. [*Alarmed at last.*] What do you mean?

Olivia. I mean that the whole question, as I heard somebody say once, demands much more anxious thought than either of us has given it. These hasty marriages——

George. Hasty!

Olivia. Well, you've only just proposed to me, and you want to marry me tomorrow.

George. Now you're talking perfect nonsense, Olivia. You know quite well that our case is utterly different from—from any other.

Olivia. All the same, one has to ask oneself questions. With a young girl like—well, with a young girl, love may well seem to be all that matters. But with a woman of my age, it is different. I have to ask myself if you can afford to support a wife.

George. [*Coldly.*] Fortunately that is a question that you can very easily answer for yourself.

Olivia. Well, but I have been hearing rather bad reports lately. What with taxes always going up, and rents always going down, some of our landowners are getting into rather straitened circumstances. At least, so I'm told.

George. I don't know what you're talking about.

Olivia. [*Surprised.*] Oh, isn't it true? I heard of a case only this morning—a landowner who always seemed to be very comfortably off, but who couldn't afford an allowance for his only niece when she wanted to get married. It made me think that one oughtn't to judge by appearances.

George. You know perfectly well that I can afford to support a wife as my wife *should* be supported.

Olivia. I'm so glad, dear. Then your income—you aren't getting anxious at all?

George. [*Stiffly.*] You know perfectly well what my income is. I see no reason for anxiety in the future.

Olivia. Ah, well, then we needn't think about that any more. Well, then, there is another thing to be considered.

George. I can't make out what you're up to. Don't you want to get married; to—er—legalize this extraordinary situation in which we are placed?

Olivia. I want to be sure that I am going to be happy, George. I can't just jump at the very first offer I have had since my husband died, without considering the whole question very carefully.

George. So I'm under consideration, eh?

Olivia. Every suitor is.

George. [*Sarcastically, as he thinks.*] Well, go on.

Olivia. Well, then, there's your niece. You have a niece who lives with you. Of course Dinah is a delightful girl, but one doesn't like marrying into a household in which there is another grown-up woman. But perhaps she will be getting married herself soon?

George. I see no prospect of it.

Olivia. I think it would make it much easier if she did.

George. Is this a threat, Olivia? Are you telling me that if I do not allow young Strange to marry Dinah, you will not marry me?

Olivia. A threat? Oh no, George.

George. Then what does it mean?

Olivia. I'm just wondering if you love me as much as Brian loves Dinah. You *do* love me?

George. [*From his heart.*] You know I do, old girl. [*He comes to her.*]

Olivia. You're not just attracted by my pretty face? . . . *Is* it a pretty face?

George. It's an adorable one.

[*He tries to kiss it, but she turns away.*]

Olivia. How can I be sure that it is not *only* my face which makes you think that you care for me? Love which rests upon a mere outward attraction cannot lead to any lasting happiness—as one of our thinkers has observed.

George. What's come over you, Olivia? I don't understand what you're driving at. Why should you doubt my love?

Olivia. Ah!—Why?

George. You can't pretend that we haven't been happy together. I've—I've been a good pal to you, eh? We—we suit each other, old girl.

Olivia. Do we?

George. Of course we do.

Olivia. I wonder. When two people of our age think of getting married, one wants to be very sure that there is real community of ideas between them. Whether it is a comparatively trivial matter, like the right color for a curtain or some very much more serious question of conduct which arises, one wants to feel that there is some chance of agreement between husband and wife.

George. We—we love each other, old girl.

Olivia. We do now, yes. But what shall we be like in five years' time? Supposing that after we have been married five years, we found ourselves estranged from each other upon such questions as Dinah's future, or the decorations of the drawing-room, or even the advice to give to a friend who had innocently contracted a bigamous marriage? How bitterly we should regret then our hasty plunge into a matrimony which was no true partnership, whether of tastes, or of ideas, or even of consciences! [*With a sigh.*] Ah me!

George. [*Nastily.*] Unfortunately for your argument, Olivia, I can answer you out of your own mouth. You seem to have forgotten what you said this morning in the case of—er—young Strange.

Olivia. [*Reproachfully.*] Is it quite fair, George, to drag up what was said this morning?

George. You've brought it on yourself.

Olivia. I? . . . Well, and what did I say this morning?

George. You said that it was quite enough that Strange was a gentleman and in love with Dinah for me to let them marry each other.

Olivia. Oh! . . . *Is* that enough, George?

George. [*Triumphantly.*] You said so.

Olivia. [*Meekly.*] Well, if you think so, too, I—I don't mind risking it.

George. [*Kindly.*] Aha, my dear! You see!

Olivia. Then you do think it's enough?

George. I—er— Yes, yes, I—I think so.

Olivia. [*Going to him.*] My darling one! Then we can have a double wedding. How jolly!

George. [*Astounded.*] A double one!

Olivia. Yes. You and me, Brian and Dinah.

George. [*Firmly.*] Now look here, Olivia, understand once and for all, I am not to be blackmailed into giving my consent to Dinah's engagement. Neither blackmailed nor tricked. Our marriage has nothing whatever to do with Dinah's.

Olivia. No, dear. I quite understand. They may take place about the same time, but they have nothing to do with each other.

George. I see no prospect of Dinah's marriage taking place for many years.

Olivia. No, dear, that was what I said.

George. [*Not understanding for the moment.*] You said . . . ? I see. Now, Olivia, let us have this perfectly clear. You apparently insist on treating my—er—proposal as serious.

Olivia. [*Surprised.*] Wasn't it serious? Were you trifling with me?

George. You know quite well what I mean. You treat it as an ordinary proposal from a man to a woman who have never been more than acquaintances before. Very well then. Will you tell me what you propose to do, if you decide to—ah—refuse me? You do not suggest that we should go on living together —unmarried?

Olivia. [*Shocked.*] Of course not, George! What would the County—I mean Heaven—I mean the Law—I mean, of *course* not! Besides, it's so unnecessary. If I decide to accept you, of *course* I shall marry you.

George. Quite so. And if you—ah—decide to refuse me? What will you do?

Olivia. Nothing.

George. Meaning by that?

Olivia. Just that, George. I shall stay here —just as before. I like this house. It wants a little re-decorating perhaps, but I do like it, George. . . . Yes, I shall be quite happy here.

George. I see. You will continue to live down here—in spite of what you said just now about the immorality of it.

Olivia. [*Surprised.*] But there's nothing immoral in a widow living alone in a big country house, with perhaps the niece of a friend of hers staying with her, just to keep her company.

George. [*Sarcastic.*] And what shall *I* be doing, when you've so very kindly taken possession of my house for me?

Olivia. I don't know, George. Traveling,

I expect. You could come down sometimes with a chaperon. I suppose there would be nothing wrong in that.

George. [*Indignant.*] Thank you! And what if I refuse to be turned out of my house?

Olivia. Then, seeing that we can't *both* be in it, it looks as though you'd have to turn *me* out. [*Casually.*] I suppose there are legal ways of doing these things. You'd have to consult your solicitor again.

George. [*Amazed.*] Legal ways?

Olivia. Well, you couldn't *throw* me out, could you? You'd have to get an injunction against me—or prosecute me for trespass—or something. It would make an awfully unusual case, wouldn't it? The papers would be full of it.

George. You must be mad!

Olivia. [*Dreamily.*] Widow of well-known ex-convict takes possession of J.P.'s house. Popular country gentleman denied entrance to his own home. Doomed to travel.

George. [*Angrily.*] I've had enough of this. Do you mean all this nonsense?

Olivia. I do mean, George, that I am in no hurry to go up to London and get married. I love the country just now, and [*with a sigh*] after this morning, I'm—rather tired of husbands.

George. [*In a rage.*] I've never heard so much—damned nonsense in my life. I will leave you to come to your senses.

[*He goes out indignantly.*]

[OLIVIA, *who has forgiven him already, throws a loving kiss after him, and then turns triumphantly to her dear curtains. She takes them, smiling, to the sofa, and has just got to work again, when* MR. PIM *appears at the open windows.*]

Pim. [*In a whisper.*] Er, may I come in, Mrs. Marden?

Olivia. [*Turning round in surprise.*] Mr. Pim!

Pim. [*Anxiously.*] Mr. Marden is—er—not here?

Olivia. [*Getting up.*] Do you want to see him? I will tell him.

Pim. No, no, no! Not for the world! [*He comes in and looks anxiously at the door.*] There is no immediate danger of his returning, Mrs. Marden?

Olivia. [*Surprised.*] No, I don't think so. What is it? You——

Pim. I took the liberty of returning by the window in the hope of—er—coming upon you alone, Mrs. Marden.

Olivia. Yes?

Pim. [*Still rather nervous.*] I—er—Mr. Marden will be very angry with me. Quite rightly. I blame myself entirely. I do not know how I can have been so stupid.

Olivia. What is it, Mr. Pim? Has my husband come to life again?

Pim. Mrs. Marden, I throw myself on your mercy entirely. The fact is—his name was Polwittle.

Olivia. [*At a loss.*] Whose? My husband's?

Pim. Yes, yes. The name came back to me suddenly, just as I reached the gate. Polwittle, poor fellow.

Olivia. But, Mr. Pim, my husband's name was Telworthy.

Pim. No, no, Polwittle.

Olivia. But, really I ought to . . .

Pim. [*Firmly.*] Polwittle. It came back to me suddenly just as I reached the gate. For the moment, I had thoughts of conveying the news by letter. I was naturally disinclined to return in person, and—— Polwittle. [*Proudly.*] If you remember, I always said it was a curious name.

Olivia. But who *is* Polwittle?

Pim. [*In surprise at her stupidity.*] The man I have been telling you about who met with the sad fatality at Marseilles. Henry Polwittle—or was it Ernest? No, Henry, I think. Poor fellow.

Olivia. [*Indignantly.*] But you said his name was Telworthy! How *could* you?

Pim. Yes, yes, I blame myself entirely.

Olivia. But how could you *think* of a name like Telworthy, if it wasn't Telworthy?

Pim. [*Eagerly.*] Ah, that is the really interesting thing about the whole matter.

Olivia. Mr. Pim, all your visits here today have been interesting.

Pim. Yes, but you see, on my first appearance here this morning, I was received by—er—Miss Diana.

Olivia. Dinah.

Pim. Miss Dinah, yes. She was in—er—rather a communicative mood, and she happened to mention, by way of passing the time, that before your marriage to Mr. Marden you had been a Mrs.—er——

Olivia. Telworthy.

Pim. Yes, yes, Telworthy, of course. She mentioned also Australia. By some process of the brain—which strikes me as decidedly curious—when I was trying to recollect the name of the poor fellow on the boat, whom you remember I had also met in Australia, the fact that this other name was also stored in my memory, a name equally peculiar—this fact I say . . .

Olivia. [*Seeing that the sentence is rapidly going to pieces.*] Yes, I understand.

Pim. I blame myself, I blame myself entirely.

Olivia. Oh, you mustn't do that, Mr. Pim. It was really Dinah's fault for inflicting all our family history on you.

Pim. Oh, but a charming young woman. I assure you I was very much interested in all that she told me. [*Getting up.*] Well, Mrs.—er—Marden, I can only hope that you will forgive me for the needless distress I have caused you today.

Olivia. Oh, you mustn't worry about that —please.

Pim. And you will tell your husband—you will break the news to him?

Olivia. [*Smiling to herself.*] I will—break the news to him.

Pim. You understand how it is that I thought it better to come to you in the first place?

Olivia. I am very glad you did.

Pim. [*Holding out his hand.*] Then I will say good-by, and—er——

Olivia. Just a moment, Mr. Pim. Let us have it quite clear this time. You never knew my husband, Jacob Telworthy, you never met him in Australia, you never saw him on the boat, and nothing whatever happened to him at Marseilles. Is that right?

Pim. Yes, yes, that is so.

Olivia. So that, since he was supposed to have died in Australia six years ago, he is presumably still dead?

Pim. Yes, yes, undoubtedly.

Olivia. [*Holding out her hand with a charming smile.*] Then good-by, Mr. Pim, and thank you so much for—for all your trouble.

Pim. Not at all, Mrs. Marden, I can only assure you I——

Dinah. [*From the window.*] Hullo, here's Mr. Pim!

[*She comes in, followed by* BRIAN.]

Pim. [*Anxiously looking at the door in case* MR. MARDEN *should come in.*] Yes, yes, I—er——

Dinah. Oh, Mr. Pim, you mustn't run away without even saying how do you do! Such old friends as we are. Why, it is ages since I saw you! Are you staying to tea?

Pim. I'm afraid I——

Olivia. Mr. Pim has to hurry away, Dinah. You mustn't keep him.

Dinah. Well, but you'll come back again?

Pim. I fear that I am only a passer-by, Miss—er—Dinah.

Olivia. You can walk with him to the gate, dear.

Pim. [*Gratefully to* OLIVIA.] Thank you. [*He edges towards the window.*] If you would be so kind, Miss Dinah——

Brian. I'll catch you up.

Dinah. Come along then, Mr. Pim. [*As they go out.*] I want to hear all about your *first* wife. You haven't really told me anything yet.

[OLIVIA *resumes her work, and* BRIAN *sits on the back of the sofa looking at her.*]

Brian. [*Awkwardly.*] I just wanted to say, if you don't think it cheek, that I'm—I'm on your side, if I may be, and if I can help you at all I should be very proud of being allowed to.

Olivia. [*Looking up at him.*] Brian, you dear. That's sweet of you. . . . But it's quite all right now, you know.

Brian. Oh, I'm so glad.

Olivia. Yes, that's what Mr. Pim came back to say. He'd made a mistake about the name. [*Smiling.*] George is the only husband I have.

Brian. [*Surprised.*] What? You mean that the whole thing—that Pim—— [*With conviction.*] Silly ass!

Olivia. [*Kindly.*] Oh, well, he didn't mean to be. [*After a pause.*] Brian, do you know anything about the Law?

Brian. I'm afraid not. I hate the Law. Why?

Olivia. [*Casually.*] Oh, I just—I was wondering—thinking about all the shocks we've been through today. Second marriages. and all that.

Brian. Oh! It's a rotten business.

Olivia. I suppose there's nothing wrong in getting married to the same person twice?

Brian. A hundred times if you like, I should think.

Olivia. Oh?

Brian. After all, in France, they always go through it twice, don't they? Once before the Mayor or somebody, and once in church.

Olivia. Of course they do! How silly of me. . . . I think it's rather a nice idea. They ought to do it in England more.

Brian. Well, once will be enough for Dinah and me, if you can work it. [*Anxiously.*] D'you think there's any chance, Olivia?

Olivia. [*Smiling.*] Every chance, dear.

Brian. [*Jumping up.*] I say, do you really? Have you squared him? I mean, has he——

Olivia. Go and catch them up now. We'll talk about it later on.

Brian. Bless you. Righto.

[*As he goes out by the windows,* GEORGE *comes in at the door.* GEORGE *stands looking after him, and then turns to* OLIVIA, *who is absorbed in her curtains. He walks up and down the room, fidgeting with things, waiting for her to speak. As she says nothing, he begins to talk himself, but in an obviously unconcerned way. There is a pause after each answer of hers, before he gets out his next remark.*]

George. [*Casually.*] Good-looking fellow, Strange.

Olivia. [*Equally casually.*] Brian—yes, isn't he? And such a nice boy. . . .

George. Got fifty pounds for a picture the other day, didn't he? Hey?

Olivia. Yes. Of course he has only just begun. . . .

George. Critics think well of him, what?

Olivia. They all say he has genius. Oh, I don't think there's any doubt about it. . . .

George. Of course, I don't profess to know anything about painting.

Olivia. You've never had time to take it up, dear.

George. I know what I like, of course. Can't say I see much in this new-fangled stuff. If a man can paint, why can't he paint like—like Rubens or—or Reynolds?

Olivia. I suppose we all have our own styles. Brian will find his directly. Of course, he's only just beginning. . . .

George. But they think a lot of him, what?

Olivia. Oh yes!

George. H'm! . . . Good-looking fellow.

[*There is rather a longer silence this time.* GEORGE *continues to hope that he is appearing casual and unconcerned. He stands looking at* OLIVIA'S *work for a moment.*]

George. Nearly finished 'em?

Olivia. Very nearly. Are my scissors there?

George. [*Looking round.*] Scissors?

Olivia. Ah, here they are. . . .

George. Where are you going to put 'em?

Olivia. [*As if really wondering.*] I don't quite know. . . . I *had* thought of this room, but—I'm not quite sure.

George. Brighten the room up a bit.

Olivia. Yes. . . .

George. [*Walking over to the present curtains.*] H'm. They *are* a bit faded.

Olivia. [*Shaking out hers, and looking at them critically.*] Sometimes I think I love them, and sometimes I'm not quite sure.

George. Best way is to hang 'em up and see how you like 'em then. Always take 'em down again.

Olivia. That's rather a good idea, George!

George. Best way.

Olivia. Yes. . . . I think we might do that. . . . The only thing is——

[*She hesitates.*]

George. What?

Olivia. Well, the carpet and the chairs, and the cushions and things——

George. What about 'em?

Olivia. Well, if we had new curtains——

George. You'd want a new carpet, eh?

Olivia. [*Doubtfully.*] Y—yes. Well, new chair-covers anyhow.

George. H'm. . . . Well, why not?

Olivia. Oh, but——

George. [*With an awkward laugh.*] We're not so hard up as all that, you know.

Olivia. No, I suppose not. [*Thoughtfully.*] I suppose it would mean that I should have to go up to London for them. That's rather a nuisance.

George. [*Extremely casual.*] Oh, I don't know. We might go up together one day.

Olivia. Well, of course if we *were* up—for anything else—we could just look about us, and see if we could find what we want.

George. That's what I meant.

[*There is another silence.* GEORGE *is wondering whether to come to closer quarters with the great question.*]

Olivia. Oh, by the way, George——

George. Yes?

Olivia. [*Innocently.*] I told Brian, and I expect he'll tell Dinah, that Mr. Pim had made a mistake about the name.

George. [*Astonished.*] You told Brian that Mr. Pim——

Olivia. Yes—I told him that the whole thing was a mistake. It seemed the simplest way.

George. Olivia! Then you mean that Brian and Dinah think that—that we have been married all the time?

Olivia. Yes. . . . They both think so now.

George. [*Coming close to her.*] Olivia, does that mean that you *are* thinking of marrying me?

Olivia. At your old Registry Office?

George. [*Eagerly.*] Yes!

Olivia. Tomorrow?

George. Yes!

Olivia. Do you want me to *very* much?

George. My darling, you know I do!

Olivia. [*A little apprehensive.*] We should have to do it very quietly.

George. Of course, darling. Nobody need know at all. We don't *want* anybody to know. And now that you've put Brian and Dinah off the scent, by telling them that Mr. Pim made a mistake—[*he breaks off, and says admiringly*]—that was very clever of you, Olivia. I should never have thought of that.

Olivia. [*Innocently.*] No, darling. . . . You don't think it was wrong, George?

George. [*His verdict.*] An innocent deception . . . perfectly harmless.

Olivia. Yes, dear, that was what I thought about—about what I was doing.

George. Then you will come tomorrow? [*She nods.*] And if we happen to see the carpet, or anything that you want——

Olivia. Oh, what fun!

George. [*Beaming.*] And a wedding lunch at the Carlton, what? [*She nods eagerly.*] And—and a bit of a honeymoon in Paris?

Olivia. Oh, George!

George. [*Hungrily.*] Give us a kiss, old girl.

Olivia. [*Lovingly.*] George!

[*She holds up her cheek to him. He kisses it, and then suddenly takes her in his arms.*]

George. Don't ever leave me, old girl.

Olivia. [*Affectionately.*] Don't ever send me away, old boy.

George. [*Fervently.*] I won't. . . . [*Awkwardly.*] I—I don't think I would have, you know. I—I——

[DINAH *and* BRIAN *appear at the windows, having seen* MR. PIM *safely off.*]

Dinah. [*Surprised.*] Oo, I say!

[GEORGE *hastily moves away.*]

George. Hallo!

Dinah. [*Going up impetuously to him.*] Give *me* one, too, George; Brian won't mind.

Brian. Really, Dinah, you are the limit.

George. [*Formally, but enjoying it.*] Do you mind, Mr. Strange?

Brian. [*A little uncomfortably.*] Oh, I say, sir——

George. We'll risk it, Dinah.

[*He kisses her.*]

Dinah. [*Triumphantly to* BRIAN.] Did you notice that one? That wasn't just an ordinary affectionate kiss. It was a special bless-you-my-children one. [*To* GEORGE.] Wasn't it?

Olivia. You do talk nonsense, darling.

Dinah. Well, I'm so happy, now that Mr. Pim has relented about your first husband——

[GEORGE *catches* OLIVIA'S *eye and smiles; she smiles back; but they are different smiles.*]

George. [*The actor.*] Yes, yes, stupid fellow Pim, what?

Brian. Absolute idiot.

Dinah. —And now that George has relented about *my* first husband.

George. You get on much too quickly, young woman. [*To* BRIAN.] So you want to marry my Dinah, eh?

Brian. [*With a smile.*] Well, I do rather, sir.

Dinah. [*Hastily.*] Not at once, of course, George. We want to be engaged for a long time first, and write letters to each other, and tell each other how much we love each other, and sit next to each other when we go out to dinner.

George. [*To* OLIVIA.] Well, *that* sounds fairly harmless, I think.

Olivia. [*Smiling.*] I think so. . . .

George. [*To* BRIAN.] Then you'd better have a talk with me—er—Brian.

Brian. Thank you very much, sir.

George. Well, come along then. [*Looking at his watch.*] I am going up to town after tea, so we'd better——

Dinah. I say! Are you going to London?

George. [*With the smile of the conspirator.*] A little business. Never you mind, young lady.

Dinah. [*Calmly.*] All right. Only, bring me back something nice.

George. [*To* BRIAN.] Shall we walk down and look at the pigs?

Brian. Righto!

Olivia. Don't go far, dear. I may want you in a moment.

George. All right, darling, we'll be on the terrace. [*They go out together.*]

Dinah. Brian and George always try to discuss me in front of the pigs. So tactless of them. Are you going to London, too, darling?

Olivia. Tomorrow morning.

Dinah. What are you going to do in London?

Olivia. Oh, shopping, and—one or two little things.

Dinah. With George?

Olivia. Yes. . . .

Dinah. I say, wasn't it lovely about Pim?

Olivia. Lovely?

Dinah. Yes; he told me all about it. Making such a hash of things, I mean.

Olivia. [*Innocently.*] Did he make a hash of things?

Dinah. Well, I mean keeping on coming like that. And if you look at it all round—well, for all he had to say, he needn't really have come at all.

Olivia. [*Smiling to herself.*] I shouldn't quite say that, Dinah. [*She stands up and shakes out the curtains.*]

Dinah. I say, aren't they jolly?

Olivia. [*Demurely.*] I'm so glad everybody likes them. Tell George I'm ready, will you?

Dinah. I say, is *he* going to hang them up for you?

Olivia. Well, I thought he could reach best.

Dinah. Righto! What fun! [*At the windows.*] George! George! [*To* OLIVIA.] Brian is just telling George about the five shillings he's got in the Post Office. . . . George!

George. [*From the terrace.*] Coming!

[*He hurries in, the model husband.* BRIAN *follows.*]

Olivia. Oh, George, just hang these up for me, will you?

George. Of course, darling. I'll get the steps from the library. [*He hurries out.*]

[BRIAN *takes out his sketching block. It is obvious that his five shillings have turned the scale. He bows to* DINAH. *He kisses* OLIVIA's *hand with an air. He motions to* DINAH *to be seated.*]

Dinah. [*Impressed.*] What is it?

Brian. [*Beginning to draw.*] Portrait of Lady Strange.

[GEORGE *hurries in with the steps, and gets to work. There is a great deal of curtain, and for the moment he becomes slightly involved in it. However, by draping it over his head and shoulders, he manages to get successfully up the steps. There we may leave him.*

But we have not quite finished with MR. PIM. *It is a matter of honor with him now that he should get his little story quite accurate before passing out of the* MARDENS' *life forever. So he comes back for the last time; for the last time we see his head at the window. He whispers to* OLIVIA.]

Mr. Pim. Mrs. Marden! I've just remembered. His name was *Ernest* Polwittle—*not* Henry.

[*He goes off happily. A curious family the* MARDENS. *Perhaps somebody else would have committed bigamy if he had not remembered in time that it was Ernest. . . . Ernest. . . . Yes. . . . Now he can go back with an easy conscience to the Trevors.*]

CURTAIN

THE CIRCLE *

By

W. SOMERSET MAUGHAM

"NO DRAMATIST IS MORE WORTH READING for craftsmanship than Somerset Maugham. He is the playwright's playwright, a very fountainhead of technical wisdom for the aspiring writer." This superlative assertion made by Graham Sutton in *Some Contemporary Dramatists* is not seriously challenged by any who have written about Maugham's plays. The technique so greatly admired is, however, that of the well-made play, modernized in spirit by directness and admirable economy and by the living idiom of speech. His extraordinary popularity as a playwright may be explained in part by this competence, but it is due even more to his highly trained powers of observation. His unflinching gaze is directed with complete detachment upon life at first hand, whether in the haunts of British culture or in the Southern seas. His unimpassioned analysis is never without a large-mindedness amounting to sympathy for the victims of his satirical scalpel. The success of his first story, *Liza of Lambeth*, in 1897, turned a well schooled surgeon into a diagnostician of the mind in its relation to nature and society. Maugham has chosen to practice in this larger sphere of life, but with much the same attitude of sympathetic detachment. Scientifically and in a literary sense he is the painstaking realist. If he writes of an unfamiliar environment, a year is not too much time for him to spend in study and observation before he commits himself to the book or the theater, and in preparation for a novel or a play he sometimes fills notebooks with more words than finally appear in the printed work.

He is an embodiment of British culture at its best. "There is something marvelous in the timbre of the voice," Grant Overton writes, "free from the habitual inflections of English voices and with an enunciation of words beautifully distinct." He adds: "I have sometimes thought Mr. Maugham was the supremely civilized man of my acquaintance . . . it is true that all his stories deal with the efforts of men and women to civilize themselves—I mean, of course, men and women already outwardly civilized."

In *The Circle* and *Our Betters* Maugham by his method of detached satirical analysis of cultured British society makes a close approach to the traditional comedy of manners, substituting realistic sincerity for the studied artificiality of Congreve and Etherege, and like them refusing to allow the dictates of conventional morality to determine the trend or outcome of his play. *The Letter* and *The Constant Wife* are patterned even more directly after Restoration comedy.

He is content with the highways of the realistic theater, and has little in common with the futurist or the philosopher of the drama, although since the First World War his satire has taken on a deeper coloring. His unrealistic indulgence is in the free use of epigram, chiefly for a satirical purpose. When in *The Circle* Teddie explains his longing for the Malay States: "England seems to me full of people doing things they don't want to because other people expect it of them," Elizabeth replies: "Isn't that what you call a high degree of civilization?" Arnold says to the worldly-wise Cheney, "You're a humorist or a cynic, Father." Cheney replies with Maugham's own detachment: "I'm neither, my dear boy; I'm merely a very truthful man. But people are so unused to the truth that they're apt to mistake it for a joke or a sneer."

In an introduction to Noel Coward's volume of plays Maugham writes, "I suspect that the whole secret of dramatic technique can be told in a sentence: stick to the point like grim death." Although his method is completely objective, he is disinclined to make the speech of the stage realistic in the absolute sense. He even suggests to Mr. Coward and those who will follow: "Now that naturalistic dialogue has been carried as far as it can go, I cannot but think it might be worth trying a dialogue that does not reproduce the conversation of the day and only very vaguely represents it, but is deliberately and significantly formal."

WILLIAM SOMERSET MAUGHAM

Born 1874, Paris.
King's School, Canterbury.
M.D., Heidelberg University.
St. Thomas's Hospital.
1897, *Liza of Lambeth,* his first novel.
1902, *Schiffbrüchig* (produced in Berlin), his first play.
1908, Four plays running in London, a theatrical record.
1914–1918, War work in secret service.
Wide travel and literary activity. Residence in France.
Novelist, and writer of travel books.

PLAYS

1902 *Schiffbrüchig* (in German, translated as *Marriages Are Made in Heaven*). 1903 *A Man of Honor.* 1904 *Mlle. Zampa.* 1907 *Lady Frederick.* 1908 *Jack Straw.* 1908 *Mrs. Dot.* 1908 *The Explorer.* 1909 *Penelope.* 1909 *The Noble Spaniard* (fr. French). 1909 *Smith.* 1910 *The Tenth Man.* 1910 *Grace* (*Landed Gentry*). 1911 *Loaves and Fishes.* 1913 *The Perfect Gentleman* (fr. Molière). 1914 *The Land of Promise.* 1916 *Caroline* (*The Unattainable*). 1917 *Our Betters.* 1918 *Love in a Cottage.* 1919 *Caesar's Wife.* 1919 *Home and Beauty* (*Too Many Husbands*). 1920 *The Unknown.* 1921 *The Circle.* 1922 *East of Suez.* 1924 *The Camel's Back.* 1927 *The Letter.* 1927 *The Constant Wife.* 1928 *The Sacred Flame.* 1930 *The Breadwinner.* 1932 *For Services Rendered.* 1933 *Sheppey.*

WRITINGS ABOUT THE DRAMA

Introduction to Noel Coward's *Bitter Sweet and Other Plays,* 1929.
Prefaces to *The Plays of W. Somerset Maugham.* 6 vols. 1931–1934.
Chaps. 30 to 43 of *The Summing Up.* 1938.

THE CIRCLE

Persons of the Play

CLIVE CHAMPION-CHENEY.
ARNOLD CHAMPION-CHENEY, M.P.
LORD PORTEOUS.
EDWARD LUTON.

LADY CATHERINE CHAMPION-CHENEY.
ELIZABETH.
MRS. SHENSTONE.

The action takes place at Aston-Adey, Arnold Champion-Cheney's house in Dorset.

THE FIRST ACT

The Scene is a stately drawing-room at Aston-Adey, with fine pictures on the walls and Georgian furniture. Aston-Adey has been described, with many illustrations, in Country Life. *It is not a house, but a place. Its owner takes a great pride in it, and there is nothing in the room which is not of the period. Through the French windows at the back can be seen the beautiful gardens which are one of the features. It is a fine summer morning.*
[ARNOLD *comes in. He is a man of about thirty-five, tall and good-looking, fair, with a clean-cut, sensitive face. He has a look that is intellectual, but somewhat bloodless. He is very well dressed.*]

Arnold. [*Calling.*] Elizabeth. [*He goes to the window and calls again.*] Elizabeth! [*He rings the bell. While he is waiting he gives a look round the room. He slightly alters the position of one of the chairs. He takes an ornament from the chimney-piece and blows the dust from it. A* FOOTMAN *comes in.*] Oh, George! See if you can find Mrs. Cheney, and ask her if she'd be good enough to come here.

Footman. Very good, sir.
[*The* FOOTMAN *turns to go.*]

Arnold. Who is supposed to look after this room?

Footman. I don't know, sir.

Arnold. I wish when they dust they'd take care to replace the things exactly as they were before.

Footman. Yes, sir.

Arnold. [*Dismissing him.*] All right.
[*The* FOOTMAN *goes out.* ARNOLD *goes again to the window and calls.*]

Arnold. Elizabeth! [*He sees* MRS. SHENSTONE.] Oh, Anna, do you know where Elizabeth is?
[MRS. SHENSTONE *comes in from the garden. She is a woman of forty, pleasant, and of elegant appearance.*]

Anna. Isn't she playing tennis?

Arnold. No, I've been down to the tennis court. Something very tiresome has happened.

Anna. Oh?

Arnold. I wonder where the deuce she is.

Anna. When do you expect Lord Porteous and Lady Kitty?

Arnold. They're motoring down in time for luncheon.

Anna. Are you sure you want me to be here? It's not too late yet, you know. I can have my things packed and catch a train for somewhere or other.

Arnold. No, of course we want you. It'll make it so much easier if there are people here. It was exceedingly kind of you to come.

Anna. Oh, nonsense!

Arnold. And I think it was a good thing to have Teddie Luton down.

Anna. He is so breezy, isn't he?

Arnold. Yes, that's his great asset. I don't know that he's very intelligent, but, you know, there are occasions when you want a bull in a china shop. I sent one of the servants to find Elizabeth.

Anna. I daresay she's putting on her shoes. She and Teddie were going to have a single.

Arnold. It can't take all this time to change one's shoes.

Anna. [*With a smile.*] One can't change one's shoes without powdering one's nose, you know.
[ELIZABETH *comes in. She is a very*

pretty creature in the early twenties. She wears a light summer frock.]

Arnold. My dear, I've been hunting for you everywhere. What *have* you been doing?

Elizabeth. Nothing! I've been standing on my head.

Arnold. My father's here.

Elizabeth. [*Startled.*] Where?

Arnold. At the cottage. He arrived last night.

Elizabeth. Damn!

Arnold. [*Good-humoredly.*] I wish you wouldn't say that, Elizabeth.

Elizabeth. If you're not going to say "Damn" when a thing's damnable, when are you going to say "Damn"?

Arnold. I should have thought you could say, "Oh, bother!" or something like that.

Elizabeth. But that wouldn't express my sentiments. Besides, at that speech day when you were giving away the prizes you said there were no synonyms in the English language.

Anna. [*Smiling.*] Oh, Elizabeth! It's very unfair to expect a politician to live in private up to the statements he makes in public.

Arnold. I'm always willing to stand by anything I've said. There *are* no synonyms in the English language.

Elizabeth. In that case, I shall be regretfully forced to continue to say "Damn" whenever I feel like it.

[EDWARD LUTON *shows himself at the window. He is an attractive youth in flannels.*]

Teddie. I say, what about this tennis?

Elizabeth. Come in. We're having a scene.

Teddie. [*Entering.*] How splendid! What about?

Elizabeth. The English language.

Teddie. Don't tell me you've been splitting your infinitives.

Arnold. [*With the shadow of a frown.*] I wish you'd be serious, Elizabeth. The situation is none too pleasant.

Anna. I think Teddie and I had better make ourselves scarce.

Elizabeth. Nonsense! You're both in it. If there's going to be any unpleasantness we want your moral support. That's why we asked you to come.

Teddie. And I thought I'd been asked for my blue eyes.

Elizabeth. Vain beast! And they happen to be brown.

Teddie. Is anything up?

Elizabeth. Arnold's father arrived last night.

Teddie. Did he, by Jove! I thought he was in Paris.

Arnold. So did we all. He told me he'd be there for the next month.

Anna. Have you seen him?

Arnold. No! He rang me up. It's a mercy he had a telephone put in the cottage. It would have been a pretty kettle of fish if he'd just walked in.

Elizabeth. Did you tell him Lady Catherine was coming?

Arnold. Of course not. I was flabbergasted to know he was here. And then I thought we'd better talk it over first.

Elizabeth. Is he coming along here?

Arnold. Yes. He suggested it, and I couldn't think of any excuse to prevent him.

Teddie. Couldn't you put the other people off?

Arnold. They're coming by car. They may be here any minute. It's too late to do that.

Elizabeth. Besides, it would be beastly.

Arnold. I knew it was silly to have them here. Elizabeth insisted.

Elizabeth. After all, she *is* your mother, Arnold.

Arnold. That meant precious little to her when she—went away. You can't imagine it means very much to me now.

Elizabeth. It's thirty years ago. It seems so absurd to bear malice after all that time.

Arnold. I don't bear malice, but the fact remains that she did me the most irreparable harm. I can find no excuse for her.

Elizabeth. Have you ever tried to?

Arnold. My dear Elizabeth, it's no good going over all that again. The facts are lamentably simple. She had a husband who adored her, a wonderful position, all the money she could want, and a child of five. And she ran away with a married man.

Elizabeth. Lady Porteous is not a very attractive woman, Arnold. [*To* ANNA.] Do you know her?

Anna. [*Smiling.*] "Forbidding" is the word, I think.

Arnold. If you're going to make little jokes about it, I have nothing more to say.

Anna. I'm sorry, Arnold.

Elizabeth. Perhaps your mother couldn't help herself—if she was in love?

Arnold. And had no sense of honor, duty, or decency? Oh, yes, under those circumstances you can explain a great deal.

Elizabeth. That's not a very pretty way to speak of your mother.

Arnold. I can't look on her as my mother.

Elizabeth. What you can't get over is that she didn't think of you. Some of us are more mother and some of us more woman. It gives me a little thrill when I think that she loved that man so much. She sacrificed her name, her position, and her child to him.

Arnold. You really can't expect the said child to have any great affection for the mother who treated him like that.

Elizabeth. No, I don't think I do. But I think it's a pity after all these years that you shouldn't be friends.

Arnold. I wonder if you realize what it was to grow up under the shadow of that horrible scandal. Everywhere, at school, and at Oxford, and afterwards in London, I was always the son of Lady Kitty Cheney. Oh, it was cruel, cruel!

Elizabeth. Yes, I know, Arnold. It was beastly for you.

Arnold. It would have been bad enough if it had been an ordinary case, but the position of the people made it ten times worse. My father was in the House then, and Porteous—he hadn't succeeded to the title—was in the House too; he was Under-Secretary for Foreign Affairs, and he was very much in the public eye.

Anna. My father always used to say he was the ablest man in the party. Everyone was expecting him to be Prime Minister.

Arnold. You can imagine what a boon it was to the British public. They hadn't had such a treat for a generation. The most popular song of the day was about my mother. Did you ever hear it? "Naughty Lady Kitty. Thought it such a pity . . ."

Elizabeth. [*Interrupting.*] Oh, Arnold, don't!

Arnold. And then they never let people forget them. If they'd lived quietly in Florence and not made a fuss the scandal would have died down. But those constant actions between Lord and Lady Porteous kept on reminding everyone.

Teddie. What were they having actions about?

Arnold. Of course my father divorced his wife, but Lady Porteous refused to divorce Porteous. He tried to force her by refusing to support her and turning her out of her house, and heaven knows what. They were constantly wrangling in the law courts.

Anna. I think it was monstrous of Lady Porteous.

Arnold. She knew he wanted to marry my mother, and she hated my mother. You can't blame her.

Anna. It must have been very difficult for them.

Arnold. That's why they've lived in Florence. Porteous has money. They found people there who were willing to accept the situation.

Elizabeth. This is the first time they've ever come to England.

Arnold. My father will have to be told, Elizabeth.

Elizabeth. Yes.

Anna. [*To* ELIZABETH.] Has he ever spoken to you about Lady Kitty?

Elizabeth. Never.

Arnold. I don't think her name has passed his lips since she ran away from this house thirty years ago.

Teddie. Oh, they lived here?

Arnold. Naturally. There was a house-party, and one evening neither Porteous nor my mother came down to dinner. The rest of them waited. They couldn't make it out. My father sent up to my mother's room, and a note was found on the pin-cushion.

Elizabeth. [*With a faint smile.*] That's what they did in the Dark Ages.

Arnold. I think he took a dislike to this house from that horrible night. He never lived here again, and when I married he handed the place over to me. He just has a cottage now on the estate that he comes to when he feels inclined.

Elizabeth. It's been very nice for us.

Arnold. I owe everything to my father. I don't think he'll ever forgive me for asking these people to come here.

Elizabeth. I'm going to take all the blame on myself, Arnold.

Arnold. [*Irritably.*] The situation was embarrassing enough anyhow. I don't know how I ought to treat them.

Elizabeth. Don't you think that'll settle itself when you see them?

Arnold. After all, they're my guests. I shall try and behave like a gentleman.

Elizabeth. I wouldn't. We haven't got central heating.

Arnold. [*Taking no notice.*] Will she expect me to kiss her?

Elizabeth. [*With a smile.*] Surely.

Arnold. It always makes me uncomfortable when people are effusive.

Anna. But I can't understand why you never saw her before.

Arnold. I believe she tried to see me when I was little, but my father thought it better she shouldn't.

Anna. Yes, but when you were grown up?

Arnold. She was always in Italy. I never went to Italy.

Elizabeth. It seems to me so pathetic that if you saw one another in the street you wouldn't recognize each other.

Arnold. Is it my fault?

Elizabeth. You've promised to be very gentle with her and very kind.

Arnold. The mistake was asking Porteous to come too. It looks as though we condoned the whole thing. And how am I to treat him? Am I to shake him by the hand and slap him on the back? He absolutely ruined my father's life.

Elizabeth. [*Smiling.*] How much would you give for a nice motor accident that prevented them from coming?

Arnold. I let you persuade me against my better judgment, and I've regretted it ever since.

Elizabeth. [*Good-humoredly.*] I think it's very lucky that Anna and Teddie are here. I don't foresee a very successful party.

Arnold. I'm going to do my best. I gave you my promise and I shall keep it. But I can't answer for my father.

Anna. Here is your father.

[MR. CHAMPION-CHENEY *shows himself at one of the French windows.*]

C.-C. May I come in through the window, or shall I have myself announced by a supercilious flunkey?

Elizabeth. Come in. We've been expecting you.

C.-C. Impatiently, I hope, my dear child.

[MR. CHAMPION-CHENEY *is a tall man in the early sixties, spare, with a fine head of gray hair and an intelligent, somewhat ascetic face. He is very carefully dressed. He is a man who makes the most of himself. He bears his years jauntily. He kisses* ELIZABETH *and then holds out his hand to* ARNOLD.]

Elizabeth. We thought you'd be in Paris for another month.

C.-C. How are you, Arnold? I always reserve to myself the privilege of changing my mind. It's the only one elderly gentlemen share with pretty women.

Elizabeth. You know Anna.

C.-C. [*Shaking hands with her.*] Of course I do. How very nice to see you here! Are you staying long?

Anna. As long as I'm welcome.

Elizabeth. And this is Mr. Luton.

C.-C. How do you do? Do you play bridge?

Luton. I do.

C.-C. Capital. Do you declare without top honors?

Luton. Never.

C.-C. Of such is the kingdom of heaven. I see that you are a good young man.

Luton. But, like the good in general, I am poor.

C.-C. Never mind; if your principles are right, you can play ten shillings a hundred without danger. I never play less, and I never play more.

Arnold. And you—are going to stay long, Father?

C.-C. To luncheon, if you'll have me.

[ARNOLD *gives* ELIZABETH *a harassed look.*]

Elizabeth. That'll be jolly.

Arnold. I didn't mean that. Of course you're going to stay for luncheon. I meant, how long are you going to stay down here?

C.-C. A week.

[*There is a moment's pause. Everyone but* CHAMPION-CHENEY *is slightly embarrassed.*]

Teddie. I think we'd better chuck our tennis.

Elizabeth. Yes. I want my father-in-law to tell me what they're wearing in Paris this week.

Teddie. I'll go and put the rackets away.

[TEDDIE *goes out.*]

Arnold. It's nearly one o'clock, Elizabeth.

Elizabeth. I didn't know it was so late.

Anna. [*To* ARNOLD.] I wonder if I can persuade you to take a turn in the garden before luncheon.

Arnold. [*Jumping at the idea.*] I'd love it. [ANNA *goes out of the windows, and as he follows her he stops irresolutely.*] I want you to look at this chair I've just got. I think it's rather good.

C.-C. Charming.

Arnold. About 1750, I should say. Good design, isn't it? It hasn't been restored or anything.

C.-C. Very pretty.

Arnold. I think it was a good buy, don't you?

C.-C. Oh, my dear boy! You know I'm entirely ignorant about these things.

Arnold. It's exactly my period . . . I shall see you at luncheon, then.

[*He follows* ANNA *through the window.*]

C.-C. Who is that young man?

Elizabeth. Mr. Luton. He's only just been demobilized. He's the manager of a rubber estate in the F. M. S.

C.-C. And what are the F. M. S. when they're at home?

Elizabeth. The Federated Malay States. He joined up at the beginning of the war. He's just going back there.

C.-C. And why have we been left alone in this very marked manner?

Elizabeth. Have we? I didn't notice it.

C.-C. I suppose it's difficult for the young to realize that one may be old without being a fool.

Elizabeth. I never thought you that. Everyone knows you're very intelligent.

C.-C. They certainly ought to by now. I've told them often enough. Are you a little nervous?

Elizabeth. Let me feel my pulse. [*She puts her finger on her wrist.*] It's perfectly regular.

C.-C. When I suggested staying to luncheon Arnold looked exactly like a dose of castor oil.

Elizabeth. I wish you'd sit down.

C.-C. Will it make it easier for you? [*He takes a chair.*] You have evidently something very disagreeable to say to me.

Elizabeth. You won't be cross with me?

C.-C. How old are you?

Elizabeth. Twenty-five.

C.-C. I'm never cross with a woman under thirty.

Elizabeth. Oh, then I've got ten years.

C.-C. Mathematics?

Elizabeth. No. Paint.

C.-C. Well?

Elizabeth. [*Reflectively.*] I think it would be easier if I sat on your knees.

C.-C. That is a pleasing taste of yours, but you must take care not to put on weight.

[*She sits down on his knees.*]

Elizabeth. Am I bony?

C.-C. On the contrary. . . . I'm listening.

Elizabeth. Lady Catherine's coming here.

C.-C. Who's Lady Catherine?

Elizabeth. Your—Arnold's mother.

C.-C. Is she?

[*He withdraws himself a little and* ELIZABETH *gets up.*]

Elizabeth. You mustn't blame Arnold. It's my fault. I insisted. He was against it. I nagged till he gave way. And then I wrote and asked her to come.

C.-C. I didn't know you knew her.

Elizabeth. I don't. But I heard she was in London. She's staying at Claridge's. It seemed so heartless not to take the smallest notice of her.

C.-C. When is she coming?

Elizabeth. We're expecting her in time for luncheon.

C.-C. As soon as that? I understand the embarrassment.

Elizabeth. You see, we never expected you to be here. You said you'd be in Paris for another month.

C.-C. My dear child, this is your house. There's no reason why you shouldn't ask whom you please to stay with you.

Elizabeth. After all, whatever her faults, she's Arnold's mother. It seemed so unnatural that they should never see one another. My heart ached for that poor lonely woman.

C.-C. I never heard that she was lonely, and she certainly isn't poor.

Elizabeth. And there's something else. I couldn't ask her by herself. It would have been so—so insulting. I asked Lord Porteous, too.

C.-C. I see.

Elizabeth. I daresay you'd rather not meet them.

C.-C. I daresay they'd rather not meet me. I shall get a capital luncheon at the cottage. I've noticed you always get the best food if you come in unexpectedly and have the same as they're having in the servants' hall.

Elizabeth. No one's ever talked to me about Lady Kitty. It's always been a subject that everyone has avoided. I've never even seen a photograph of her.

C.-C. The house was full of them when she left. I think I told the butler to throw them in the dust-bin. She was very much photographed.

Elizabeth. Won't you tell me what she was like?

C.-C. She was very like you, Elizabeth, only she had dark hair instead of red.

Elizabeth. Poor dear! It must be quite white now.

C.-C. I daresay. She was a pretty little thing.

Elizabeth. But she was one of the great beauties of her day. They say she was lovely.

C.-C. She had the most adorable little nose, like yours. . . .

Elizabeth. D'you like my nose?

C.-C. And she was very dainty, with a beautiful little figure; very light on her feet. She was like a *marquise* in a old French comedy. Yes, she was lovely.

Elizabeth. And I'm sure she's lovely still.

C.-C. She's no chicken, you know.

Elizabeth. You can't expect me to look at it as you and Arnold do. When you've loved as she's loved you may grow old, but you grow old beautifully.

C.-C. You're very romantic.

Elizabeth. If everyone hadn't made such a mystery of it I daresay I shouldn't feel as I do. I know she did a great wrong to you and a great wrong to Arnold. I'm willing to acknowledge that.

C.-C. I'm sure it's very kind of you.

Elizabeth. But she loved and she dared. Romance is such an elusive thing. You read of it in books, but it's seldom you see it face to face. I can't help it if it thrills me.

C.-C. I am painfully aware that the husband in these cases is not a romantic object.

Elizabeth. She had the world at her feet. You were rich. She was a figure in society. And she gave up everything for love.

C.-C. [*Dryly.*] I'm beginning to suspect it wasn't only for her sake and for Arnold's that you asked her to come here.

Elizabeth. I seem to know her already. I think her face is a little sad, for a love like that doesn't leave you gay, it leaves you grave, but I think her pale face is unlined. It's like a child's.

C.-C. My dear, how you let your imagination run away with you!

Elizabeth. I imagine her slight and frail.

C.-C. Frail, certainly.

Elizabeth. With beautiful thin hands and white hair. I've pictured her so often in that Renaissance Palace that they live in, with old Masters on the walls and lovely carved things all round, sitting in a black silk dress with old lace round her neck and old-fashioned diamonds. You see, I never knew my mother; she died when I was a baby. You can't confide in aunts with huge families of their own. I want Arnold's mother to be a mother to me. I've got so much to say to her.

C.-C. Are you happy with Arnold?

Elizabeth. Why shouldn't I be?

C.-C. Why haven't you got any babies?

Elizabeth. Give us a little time. We've only been married three years.

C.-C. I wonder what Hughie is like now!

Elizabeth. Lord Porteous?

C.-C. He wore his clothes better than any man in London. You know he'd have been Prime Minister if he'd remained in politics.

Elizabeth. What was he like then?

C.-C. He was a nice-looking fellow. Fine horseman. I suppose there was something very fascinating about him. Yellow hair and blue eyes, you know. He had a very good figure. I liked him. I was his parliamentary secretary. He was Arnold's godfather.

Elizabeth. I know.

C.-C. I wonder if he ever regrets!

Elizabeth. I wouldn't.

C.-C. Well, I must be strolling back to my cottage.

Elizabeth. You're not angry with me?

C.-C. Not a bit.

[*She puts up her face for him to kiss. He kisses her on both cheeks and then goes out. In a moment* TEDDIE *is seen at the window.*]

Teddie. I saw the old blighter go.

Elizabeth. Come in.

Teddie. Everything all right?

Elizabeth. Oh, quite, as far as he's concerned. He's going to keep out of the way.

Teddie. Was it beastly?

Elizabeth. No, he made it very easy for me. He's a nice old thing.

Teddie. You were rather scared.

Elizabeth. A little. I am still. I don't know why.

Teddie. I guessed you were. I thought I'd come and give you a little moral support. It's ripping here, isn't it?

Elizabeth. It is rather nice.

Teddie. It'll be jolly to think of it when I'm back in the F. M. S.

Elizabeth. Aren't you homesick sometimes?

Teddie. Oh, everyone is now and then, you know.

Elizabeth. You could have got a job in England if you'd wanted to, couldn't you?

Teddie. Oh, but I love it out there. England's ripping to come back to, but I couldn't live here now. It's like a woman you're desperately in love with as long as you don't see her, but when you're with her she maddens you so that you can't bear her.

Elizabeth. [*Smiling.*] What's wrong with England?

Teddie. I don't think anything's wrong with England. I expect something's wrong with me. I've been away too long. England seems to me full of people doing things they don't want to because other people expect it of them.

Elizabeth. Isn't that what you call a high degree of civilization?

Teddie. People seem to me so insincere. When you go to parties in London they're all babbling about art, and you feel that in their hearts they don't care two-pence about it. They read the books that everybody is talking about because they don't want to be out of it. In the F. M. S. we don't get very many books, and we read those we have over and over again. They mean so much to us. I don't think the people over there are half so clever as the people at home, but one gets to know them better. You see, there are so few of us that we have to make the best of one another.

Elizabeth. I imagine that frills are not much worn in the F. M. S. It must be a comfort.

Teddie. It's not much good being pretentious where everyone knows exactly who you are and what your income is.

Elizabeth. I don't think you want too much sincerity in society. It would be like an iron girder in a house of cards.

Teddie. And then, you know, the place is ripping. You get used to a blue sky and you miss it in England.

Elizabeth. What do you do with yourself all the time?

Teddie. Oh, one works like blazes. You have to be a pretty hefty fellow to be a planter. And then there's ripping bathing. You know, it's lovely, with palm trees all along the beach. And there's shooting. And now and then we have a little dance to a gramophone.

Elizabeth. [*Pretending to tease him.*] I think you've got a young woman out there, Teddie.

Teddie. [*Vehemently.*] Oh, no!

[*She is a little taken aback by the earnestness of his disclaimer. There is a moment's silence, then she recovers herself.*]

Elizabeth. But you'll have to marry and settle down one of these days, you know.

Teddie. I want to, but it's not a thing you can do lightly.

Elizabeth. I don't know why there more than elsewhere.

Teddie. In England if people don't get on they go their own ways and jog along after a fashion. In a place like that you're thrown a great deal on your own resources.

Elizabeth. Of course.

Teddie. Lots of girls come out because they think they're going to have a good time. But if they're empty-headed, then they're just faced with their own emptiness and they're done. If their husbands can afford it they go home and settle down as grass-widows.

Elizabeth. I've met them. They seem to find it a very pleasant occupation.

Teddie. It's rotten for their husbands, though.

Elizabeth. And if the husbands can't afford it?

Teddie. Oh, then they tipple.

Elizabeth. It's not a very alluring prospect.

Teddie. But if the woman's the right sort she wouldn't exchange it for any life in the world. When all's said and done it's we who've made the Empire.

Elizabeth. What sort is the right sort?

Teddie. A woman of courage and endurance and sincerity. Of course, it's hopeless unless she's in love with her husband.

[*He is looking at her earnestly and she, raising her eyes, gives him a long look. There is silence between them.*]

Teddie. My house stands on the side of a hill, and the coconut trees wind down to the shore. Azaleas grow in my garden, and camellias, and all sorts of ripping flowers. And in front of me is the winding coast line, and then the blue sea. [*A pause.*] Do you know that I'm awfully in love with you?

Elizabeth. [*Gravely.*] I wasn't quite sure. I wondered.

Teddie. And you? [*She nods slowly.*] I've never kissed you.

Elizabeth. I don't want you to.

[*They look at one another steadily. They are both grave.* ARNOLD *comes in hurriedly.*]

Arnold. They're coming, Elizabeth.

Elizabeth. [*As though returning from a distant world.*] Who?

Arnold. [*Impatiently.*] My dear! My mother, of course. The car is just coming up the drive.

Teddie. Would you like me to clear out?

Arnold. No, no! For goodness' sake stay.

Elizabeth. We'd better go and meet them, Arnold.

Arnold. No, no; I think they'd much better be shown in. I feel simply sick with nervousness.

[ANNA *comes in from the garden.*]

Anna. Your guests have arrived.

Elizabeth. Yes, I know.

Arnold. I've given orders that luncheon should be served at once.

Elizabeth. Why? It's not half-past one already, is it?

Arnold. I thought it would help. When you don't know exactly what to say you can always eat.

[*The* BUTLER *comes in and announces.*]

Butler. Lady Catherine Champion-Cheney! Lord Porteous!

[LADY KITTY *comes in followed by* PORTEOUS, *and the* BUTLER *goes out.* LADY KITTY *is a gay little lady, with dyed red hair and painted cheeks. She is somewhat outrageously dressed. She never forgets that she has been a pretty woman and she still behaves as if she were twenty-five.* LORD PORTEOUS *is a very bald, elderly gentleman in loose, rather eccentric clothes. He is snappy and gruff. This is not at all the couple that* ELIZABETH *expected, and for a moment she stares at them with round, startled eyes.* LADY KITTY *goes up to her with outstretched hands.*]

Lady Kitty. Elizabeth! Elizabeth! [*She kisses her effusively.*] What an adorable creature. [*Turning to* PORTEOUS.] Hughie, isn't she adorable?

Porteous. [*With a grunt.*] Ugh!

[ELIZABETH, *smiling now, turns to him and gives him her hand.*]

Elizabeth. How d'you do?

Porteous. Damnable road you've got down here. How d'you do, my dear? Why d'you have such damnable roads in England?

[LADY KITTY'S *eyes fall on* TEDDIE *and she goes up to him with her arms thrown back, prepared to throw them round him.*]

Lady Kitty. My boy, my boy! I should have known you anywhere!

Elizabeth. [*Hastily.*] That's Arnold.

Lady Kitty. [*Without a moment's hesitation.*] The image of his father! I should have known him anywhere! [*She throws her arms round his neck.*] My boy, my boy!

Porteous. [*With a grunt.*] Ugh!

Lady Kitty. Tell me, would you have known me again? Have I changed?

Arnold. I was only five, you know, when —when you . . .

Lady Kitty. [*Emotionally.*] I remember as if it was yesterday. I went up into your room. [*With a sudden change of manner.*] By the way, I always thought that nurse drank. Did you ever find out if she really did?

Porteous. How the devil can you expect him to know that, Kitty?

Lady Kitty. You've never had a child, Hughie; how can you tell what they know and what they don't?

Elizabeth. [*Coming to the rescue.*] This is Arnold, Lord Porteous.

Porteous. [*Shaking hands with him.*] How d'you do? I knew your father.

Arnold. Yes.

Porteous. Alive still?

Arnold. Yes.

Porteous. He must be getting on. Is he well?

Arnold. Very.

Porteous. Ugh! Takes care of himself, I suppose. I'm not at all well. This damned climate doesn't agree with me.

Elizabeth. [*To* LADY KITTY.] This is Mrs. Shenstone. And this is Mr. Luton. I hope you don't mind a very small party.

Lady Kitty. [*Shaking hands with* ANNA *and* TEDDIE.] Oh, no, I shall enjoy it. I used to give enormous parties here. Political, you know. How nice you've made this room!

Elizabeth. Oh, that's Arnold.

Arnold. [*Nervously.*] D'you like this chair? I've just bought it. It's exactly my period.

Porteous. [*Bluntly.*] It's a fake.

Arnold. [*Indignantly.*] I don't think it is for a minute.

Porteous. The legs are not right.

Arnold. I don't know how you can say that. If there is anything right about it, it's the legs.

Lady Kitty. I'm sure they're right.

Porteous. You know nothing whatever about it, Kitty.

Lady Kitty. That's what you think. *I* think it's a beautiful chair. Hepplewhite?

Arnold. No, Sheraton.

Lady Kitty. Oh, I know. "The School for Scandal."

Porteous. Sheraton, my dear. Sheraton.

Lady Kitty. Yes, that's what I say. I acted the screen scene at some amateur theatricals in Florence, and Ermeto Novelli, the great Italian tragedian, told me he'd never seen a Lady Teazle like me.

Porteous. Ugh!

Lady Kitty. [*To* ELIZABETH.] Do you act?

Elizabeth. Oh, I couldn't. I should be too nervous.

Lady Kitty. I'm never nervous. I'm a born actress. Of course, if I had my time over again I'd go on the stage. You know, it's extraordinary how they keep young. Actresses, I mean. I think it's because they're always playing different parts. Hughie, do you think Arnold takes after me or after his father? Of course I think he's the very image of me. Arnold, I think I ought to tell you that I was received into the Catholic Church last winter. I've been thinking about it for years, and the last time we were at Monte Carlo I met such a nice monsignore. I told him what my difficulties were and he was too wonderful. I knew Hughie wouldn't approve, so I kept it a secret. [*To* ELIZABETH.] Are you interested in religion? I think it's too wonderful. We must have a long talk about it one of these days. [*Pointing to her frock.*] Callot?

Elizabeth. No, Worth.

Lady Kitty. I knew it was either Worth or Callot. Of course, it's line that's the important thing. I go to Worth myself, and I always say to him, "Line, my dear Worth, line." What *is* the matter, Hughie?"

Porteous. These new teeth of mine are so damned uncomfortable.

Lady Kitty. Men are extraordinary. They can't stand the smallest discomfort. Why, a woman's life is uncomfortable from the moment she gets up in the morning till the moment she goes to bed at night. And d'you think it's comfortable to sleep with a mask on your face?

Porteous. They don't seem to hold up properly.

Lady Kitty. Well, that's not the fault of your teeth. That's the fault of your gums.

Porteous. Damned rotten dentist. That's what's the matter.

Lady Kitty. I thought he was a very nice dentist. He told me *my* teeth would last till I was fifty. He has a Chinese room. It's so interesting; while he scrapes your teeth he tells you all about the dear Empress Dowager. Are you interested in China? I think it's too wonderful. You know they've cut off their pigtails. I think it's such a pity. They were so picturesque.

[*The* BUTLER *comes in.*]

Butler. Luncheon is served, sir.

Elizabeth. Would you like to see your rooms?

Porteous. We can see our rooms after luncheon.

Lady Kitty. I must powder my nose, Hughie.

Porteous. Powder it down here.

Lady Kitty. I never saw anyone so inconsiderate.

Porteous. You'll keep us all waiting half an hour. I know you.

Lady Kitty. [*Fumbling in her bag.*] Oh, well, peace at any price, as Lord Beaconsfield said.*

Porteous. He said a lot of damned silly things, Kitty, but he never said that.

[LADY KITTY'S *face changes. Perplexity is followed by dismay, and dismay by consternation.*]

Lady Kitty. Oh!

Elizabeth. What is the matter?

Lady Kitty. [*With anguish.*] My lip-stick!

Elizabeth. Can't you find it?

Lady Kitty. I had it in the car. Hughie, you remember that I had it in the car.

Porteous. I don't remember anything about it.

Lady Kitty. Don't be so stupid, Hughie. Why, when we came through the gates I said: "My home, my home!" and I took it out and put some on my lips.

Elizabeth. Perhaps you dropped it in the car.

Lady Kitty. For heaven's sake send some one to look for it.

Arnold. I'll ring.

Lady Kitty. I'm absolutely lost without my lip-stick. Lend me yours, darling, will you?

Elizabeth. I'm awfully sorry. I'm afraid I haven't got one.

Lady Kitty. Do you mean to say you don't use a lip-stick?

Elizabeth. Never.

Porteous. Look at her lips. What the devil d'you think she wants muck like that for?

Lady Kitty. Oh, my dear, what a mistake you make! You *must* use a lip-stick. It's so good for the lips. Men like it, you know. I couldn't *live* without a lip-stick.

[CHAMPION-CHENEY *appears at the window holding in his upstretched hand a little gold case.*]

C.-C. [*As he comes in.*] Has anyone here lost a diminutive utensil containing, unless I am mistaken, a favorite preparation for the toilet?

[ARNOLD *and* ELIZABETH *are thunderstruck at his appearance and even* TEDDIE *and* ANNA *are taken aback. But* LADY KITTY *is overjoyed.*]

Lady Kitty. My lip-stick!

C.-C. I found it in the drive and I ventured to bring it in.

Lady Kitty. It's Saint Antony. I said a little prayer to him when I was hunting in my bag.

Porteous. Saint Antony be blowed! It's Clive, by God!

Lady Kitty. [*Startled, her attention suddenly turning from the lip-stick.*] Clive!

C.-C. You didn't recognize me. It's many years since we met.

Lady Kitty. My poor Clive, your hair has gone quite white!

C.-C. [*Holding out his hand.*] I hope you had a pleasant journey down from London.

Lady Kitty. [*Offering him her cheek.*] You may kiss me, Clive.

C.-C. [*Kissing her.*] You don't mind, Hughie?

Porteous. [*With a grunt.*] Ugh!

C.-C. [*Going up to him cordially.*] And how are you, my dear Hughie?

Porteous. Damned rheumatic if you want to know. Filthy climate you have in this country.

C.-C. Aren't you going to shake hands with me, Hughie?

Porteous. I have no objection to shaking hands with you.

C.-C. You've aged, my poor Hughie.

Porteous. Some one was asking me how old you were the other day.

C.-C. Were they surprised when you told them?

Porteous. Surprised! They wondered you weren't dead. [*The* BUTLER *comes in.*]

Butler. Did you ring, sir?

Arnold. No. Oh, yes, I did. It doesn't matter now.

---

* Lord Beaconsfield said, on returning from the Congress of Berlin, 1878, "We have brought you peace with honor."

C.-C. [*As the* BUTLER *is going.*] One moment. My dear Elizabeth, I've come to throw myself on your mercy. My servants are busy with their own affairs. There's not a thing for me to eat in my cottage.

Elizabeth. Oh, but we shall be delighted if you'll lunch with us.

C.-C. It either means that or my immediate death from starvation. You don't mind, Arnold?

Arnold. My dear father!

Elizabeth. [*To the* BUTLER.] Mr. Cheney will lunch here.

Butler. Very good, ma'am.

C.-C. [*To* LADY KITTY.] And what do you think of Arnold?

Lady Kitty. I adore him.

C.-C. He's grown, hasn't he? But then you'd expect him to do that in thirty years.

Arnold. For God's sake let's go in to lunch, Elizabeth!

CURTAIN

THE SECOND ACT

The Scene is the same as in the preceding act.

[*It is afternoon. When the curtain rises* PORTEOUS *and* LADY KITTY, ANNA *and* TEDDIE *are playing bridge.* ELIZABETH *and* CHAMPION-CHENEY *are watching.* PORTEOUS *and* LADY KITTY *are partners.*]

C.-C. When will Arnold be back, Elizabeth?

Elizabeth. Soon, I think.

C.-C. Is he addressing a meeting?

Elizabeth. No, it's only a conference with his agent and one or two constituents.

Porteous. [*Irritably.*] How anyone can be expected to play bridge when people are shouting at the top of their voices all round them, I for one cannot understand.

Elizabeth. [*Smiling.*] I'm so sorry.

Anna. I can see your hand, Lord Porteous.

Porteous. It may help you.

Lady Kitty. I've told you over and over again to hold your cards up. It ruins one's game when one can't help seeing one's opponent's hand.

Porteous. One isn't obliged to look.

Lady Kitty. What was Arnold's majority at the last election?

Elizabeth. Seven hundred and something.

C.-C. He'll have to fight for it if he wants to keep his seat next time.

Porteous. Are we playing bridge, or talking politics?

Lady Kitty. I never find that conversation interferes with my game.

Porteous. You certainly play no worse when you talk than when you hold your tongue.

Lady Kitty. I think that's a very offensive thing to say, Hughie. Just because I don't play the same game as you do you think I can't play.

Porteous. I'm glad you acknowledge it's not the same game as I play. But why in God's name do you call it bridge?

C.-C. I agree with Kitty. I hate people who play bridge as though they were at a funeral and knew their feet were getting wet.

Porteous. Of course you take Kitty's part.

Lady Kitty. That's the least he can do.

C.-C. I have a naturally cheerful disposition.

Porteous. You've never had anything to sour it.

Lady Kitty. I don't know what you mean by that, Hughie.

Porteous. [*Trying to contain himself.*] Must you trump my ace?

Lady Kitty. [*Innocently.*] Oh, was that your ace, darling?

Porteous. [*Furiously.*] Yes, it was my ace.

Lady Kitty. Oh, well, it was the only trump I had. I shouldn't have made it anyway.

Porteous. You needn't have told them that. Now she knows exactly what I've got.

Lady Kitty. She knew before.

Porteous. How could she know?

Lady Kitty. She said she'd seen your hand.

Anna. Oh, I didn't. I said I could see it.

Lady Kitty. Well, I naturally supposed that if she could see it she did.

Porteous. Really, Kitty, you have the most extraordinary ideas.

C.-C. Not at all. If anyone is such a fool as to show me his hand, of course I look at it.

Porteous. [*Fuming.*] If you study the etiquette of bridge, you'll discover that onlookers are expected not to interfere with the game.

C.-C. My dear Hughie, this is a matter of ethics, not of bridge.

Anna. Anyhow, I get the game. And rubber.

Teddie. I claim a revoke.

Porteous. Who revoked?

Teddie. You did.

Porteous. Nonsense. I've never revoked in my life.

Teddie. I'll show you. [*He turns over the tricks to show the faces of the cards.*] You threw away a club on the third heart trick and you had another heart.

Porteous. I never had more than two hearts.

Teddie. Oh, yes, you had. Look here. That's the card you played on the last trick but one.

Lady Kitty. [*Delighted to catch him out.*] There's no doubt about it, Hughie. You revoked.

Porteous. I tell you I did not revoke. I never revoke.

C.-C. You did, Hughie. I wondered what on earth you were doing.

Porteous. I don't know how anyone can be expected not to revoke when there's this confounded chatter going on all the time.

Teddie. Well, that's another hundred to us.

Porteous. [*To* CHAMPION-CHENEY.] I wish you wouldn't breathe down my neck. I never can play bridge when there's somebody breathing down my neck.

[*The party have risen from the bridge-table, and they scatter about the room.*]

Anna. Well, I'm going to take a book and lie down in the hammock till it's time to dress.

Teddie. [*Who has been adding up.*] I'll put it down in the book, shall I?

Porteous. [*Who has not moved, setting out the cards for a patience.*] Yes, yes, put it down. I never revoke. [ANNA *goes out.*]

Lady Kitty. Would you like to come for a little stroll, Hughie?

Porteous. What for?

Lady Kitty. Exercise.

Porteous. I hate exercise.

C.-C. [*Looking at the patience.*] The seven goes on the eight.

[PORTEOUS *takes no notice.*]

Lady Kitty. The seven goes on the eight, Hughie.

Porteous. I don't choose to put the seven on the eight.

C.-C. That knave goes on the queen.

Porteous. I'm not blind, thank you.

Lady Kitty. The three goes on the four.

C.-C. All these go over.

Porteous. [*Furiously.*] Am I playing this patience, or are you playing it?

Lady Kitty. But you're missing everything.

Porteous. That's my business.

C.-C. It's no good losing your temper over it, Hughie.

Porteous. Go away, both of you. You irritate me.

Lady Kitty. We were only trying to help you, Hughie.

Porteous. I don't want to be helped. I want to do it by myself.

Lady Kitty. I think your manners are perfectly deplorable, Hughie.

Porteous. It's simply maddening when you're playing patience and people won't leave you alone.

C.-C. We won't say another word.

Porteous. That three goes. I believe it's coming out. If I'd been such a fool as to put that seven up I shouldn't have been able to bring these down.

[*He puts down several cards while they watch him silently.*]

Lady Kitty and C.-C. [*Together.*] The four goes on the five.

Porteous. [*Throwing down the cards violently.*] Damn you! Why don't you leave me alone? It's intolerable.

C.-C. It was coming out, my dear fellow.

Porteous. I know it was coming out. Confound you!

Lady Kitty. How petty you are, Hughie!

Porteous. Petty, be damned! I've told you over and over again that I will not be interfered with when I'm playing patience.

Lady Kitty. Don't talk to me like that, Hughie.

Porteous. I shall talk to you as I please.

Lady Kitty. [*Beginning to cry.*] Oh, you brute! You brute!

[*She flings out of the room.*]

Porteous. Oh, damn! Now she's going to cry.

[*He shambles out into the garden.* CHAMPION-CHENEY, ELIZABETH *and* TEDDIE *are left alone. There is a moment's pause.* CHAMPION-CHENEY *looks from* TEDDIE *to* ELIZABETH, *with an ironical smile.*]

C.-C. Upon my soul, they might be married. They frip so much.

Elizabeth. [*Frigidly.*] It's been nice of you to come here so often since they arrived. It's helped to make things easy.

C.-C. Irony? It's a rhetorical form not much favored in this blessed plot, this earth, this realm, this England.

Elizabeth. What exactly are you getting at?

C.-C. How slangy the young women of the present day are! I suppose the fact that

Arnold is a purist leads you to the contrary extravagance.

Elizabeth. Anyhow you know what I mean.

C.-C. [*With a smile.*] I have a dim, groping suspicion.

Elizabeth. You promised to keep away. Why did you come back the moment they arrived?

C.-C. Curiosity, my dear child. A surely pardonable curiosity.

Elizabeth. And since then you've been here all the time. You don't generally favor us with so much of your company when you're down at your cottage.

C.-C. I've been excessively amused.

Elizabeth. It has struck me that whenever they started fripping you took a malicious pleasure in goading them on.

C.-C. I don't think there's much love lost between them now, do you?

[TEDDIE *is making as though to leave the room.*]

Elizabeth. Don't go, Teddie.

C.-C. No, please don't. I'm only staying a minute. We were talking about Lady Kitty just before she arrived. [*To* ELIZABETH.] Do you remember? The pale, frail lady in black satin and old lace.

Elizabeth. [*With a chuckle.*] You are a devil, you know.

C.-C. Ah, well, he's always had the reputation of being a humorist and a gentleman.

Elizabeth. Did you expect her to be like that, poor dear?

C.-C. My dear child, I hadn't the vaguest idea. You were asking me the other day what she was like when she ran away. I didn't tell you half. She was so gay and so natural. Who would have thought that animation would turn into such frivolity, and that charming impulsiveness lead to such a ridiculous affectation?

Elizabeth. It rather sets my nerves on edge to hear the way you talk of her.

C.-C. It's the truth that sets your nerves on edge, not I.

Elizabeth. You loved her once. Have you no feeling for her at all?

C.-C. None. Why should I?

Elizabeth. She's the mother of your son.

C.-C. My dear child, you have a charming nature, as simple, frank, and artless as hers was. Don't let pure humbug obscure your common sense.

Elizabeth. We have no right to judge. She's only been here two days. We know nothing about her.

C.-C. My dear, her soul is as thickly rouged as her face. She hasn't an emotion that's sincere. She's tinsel. You think I'm a cruel, cynical old man. Why, when I think of what she was, if I didn't laugh at what she has become I should cry.

Elizabeth. How do you know she wouldn't be just the same now if she'd remained your wife? Do you think your influence would have had such a salutary effect on her?

C.-C. [*Good-humoredly.*] I like you when you're bitter and rather insolent.

Elizabeth. D'you like me enough to answer my question?

C.-C. She was only twenty-seven when she went away. She might have become anything. She might have become the woman you expected her to be. There are very few of us who are strong enough to make circumstances serve us. We are the creatures of our environment. She's a sily, worthless woman because she's led a silly, worthless life.

Elizabeth. [*Disturbed.*] You're horrible today.

C.-C. I don't say it's I who could have prevented her from becoming this ridiculous caricature of a pretty woman grown old. But life could. Here she would have had the friends fit to her station, and a decent activity, and worthy interests. Ask her what her life has been all these years among divorced women and kept women and the men who consort with them. There is no more lamentable pursuit than a life of pleasure.

Elizabeth. At all events she loved and she loved greatly. I have only pity and affection for her.

C.-C. And if she loved what d'you think she felt when she saw that she had ruined Hughie? Look at him. He was tight last night after dinner and tight the night before.

Elizabeth. I know.

C.-C. And she took it as a matter of course. How long do you suppose he's been getting tight every night? Do you think he was like that thirty years ago? Can you imagine that that was a brilliant young man, whom everyone expected to be Prime Minister? Look at him now. A grumpy sodden old fellow with false teeth.

Elizabeth. You have false teeth, too.

C.-C. Yes, but damn it all, they fit. She's ruined him and she knows she's ruined him.

Elizabeth. [*Looking at him suspiciously.*] Why are you saying all this to me?

C.-C. Am I hurting your feelings?

Elizabeth. I think I've had enough for the present.

C.-C. I'll go and have a look at the goldfish. I want to see Arnold when he comes in. [*Politely.*] I'm afraid we've been boring Mr. Luton.

Teddie. Not at all.

C.-C. When are you going back to the F. M. S.?

Teddie. In about a month.

C.-C. I see. [*He goes out.*]

Elizabeth. I wonder what he has at the back of his head.

Teddie. D'you think he was talking at you?

Elizabeth. He's as clever as a bagful of monkeys.

[*There is a moment's pause.* TEDDIE *hesitates a little and when he speaks it is in a different tone. He is grave and somewhat nervous.*]

Teddie. It seems very difficult to get a few minutes alone with you. I wonder if you've been making it difficult?

Elizabeth. I wanted to think.

Teddie. I've made up my mind to go away tomorrow.

Elizabeth. Why?

Teddie. I want you altogether or not at all.

Elizabeth. You're so arbitrary.

Teddie. You said so—you said you cared for me.

Elizabeth. I do.

Teddie. Do you mind if we talk it over now?

Elizabeth. No.

Teddie. [*Frowning.*] It makes me feel rather shy and awkward. I've repeated to myself over and over again exactly what I want to say to you, and now all I'd prepared seems rather footling.

Elizabeth. I'm so afraid I'm going to cry.

Teddie. I feel it's all so tremendously serious and I think we ought to keep emotion out of it. You're rather emotional, aren't you?

Elizabeth. [*Half smiling and half in tears.*] So are you for the matter of that.

Teddie. That's why I wanted to have everything I meant to say to you cut and dried. I think it would be awfully unfair if I made love to you and all that sort of thing, and you were carried away. I wrote it all down and thought I'd send it you as a letter.

Elizabeth. Why didn't you?

Teddie. I got the wind up. A letter seems so—so cold. You see, I love you so awfully.

Elizabeth. For goodness' sake don't say that.

Teddie. You mustn't cry. Please don't, or I shall go all to pieces.

Elizabeth. [*Trying to smile.*] I'm sorry. It doesn't mean anything really. It's only tears running out of my eyes.

Teddie. Our only chance is to be awfully matter-of-fact.

[*He stops for a moment. He finds it quite difficult to control himself. He clears his throat. He frowns with annoyance at himself.*]

Elizabeth. What's the matter?

Teddie. I've got a sort of lump in my throat. It is idiotic. I think I'll have a cigarette. [*She watches him in silence while he lights a cigarette.*] You see, I've never been in love with anyone before, not really. It's knocked me endways. I don't know how I can live without you now. . . . Does that old fool know I'm in love with you?

Elizabeth. I think so.

Teddie. When he was talking about Lady Kitty smashing up Lord Porteous' career I thought there was something at the back of it.

Elizabeth. I think he was trying to persuade me not to smash up yours.

Teddie. I'm sure that's very considerate of him, but I don't happen to have one to smash I wish I had. It's the only time in my life I've wished I were a hell of a swell so that I could chuck it all and show you how much more you are to me than anything else in the world.

Elizabeth. [*Affectionately.*] You're a dear old thing, Teddie.

Teddie. You know, I don't really know how to make love, but if I did I couldn't do it now because I just want to be absolutely practical.

Elizabeth. [*Chaffing him.*] I'm glad you don't know how to make love. It would be almost more than I could bear.

Teddie. You see, I'm not at all romantic and that sort of thing. I'm just a common or garden business man. All this is so dreadfully serious and I think we ought to be sensible.

Elizabeth. [*With a break in her voice.*] You owl!

Teddie. No, Elizabeth, don't say things like that to me. I want you to consider all the *pros* and *cons,* and my heart's thumping against my chest, and you know I love you, I love you, I love you.

Elizabeth. [*In a sigh of passion.*] Oh, my precious!

Teddie. [*Impatiently, but with himself, rather than with* ELIZABETH.] Don't be idiotic, Elizabeth. I'm not going to tell you that I can't live without you and a lot of muck like that. You know that you mean everything in the world to me. [*Almost giving it up as a bad job.*] Oh, my God!

Elizabeth. [*Her voice faltering.*] D'you think there's anything you can say to me that I don't know already?

Teddie. [*Desperately.*] But I haven't said a single thing I wanted to. I'm a business man and I want to put it all in a business way, if you understand what I mean.

Elizabeth. [*Smiling.*] I don't believe you're a very good business man.

Teddie. [*Sharply.*] You don't know what you're talking about. I'm a first rate business man, but somehow this is different. [*Hopelessly.*] I don't know why it won't go right.

Elizabeth. What are we going to do about it?

Teddie. You see, it's not just because you're awfully pretty that I love you. I'd love you just as much if you were old and ugly. It's you I love, not what you look like. And it's not only love; love be blowed! It's that I *like* you so tremendously. I think you're such a ripping good sort. I just want to be with you. I feel so jolly and happy just to think you're there. I'm so awfully *fond* of you.

Elizabeth. [*Laughing through her tears.*] I don't know if this is your idea of introducing a business proposition.

Teddie. Damn you, you won't let me.

Elizabeth. You said "Damn you."

Teddie. I meant it.

Elizabeth. Your voice sounded as if you meant it, you perfect duck!

Teddie. Really, Elizabeth, you're intolerable.

Elizabeth. I'm doing nothing.

Teddie. Yes, you are, you're putting me off my blow. What I want to say is perfectly simple. I'm a very ordinary business man.

Elizabeth. You've said that before.

Teddie. [*Angrily.*] Shut up. I haven't got a bob besides what I earn. I've got no position. I'm nothing. You're rich and you're a big pot and you've got everything that anyone can want. It's awful cheek my saying anything to you at all. But after all there's only one thing that really matters in the world, and that's love. I love you. Chuck all this, Elizabeth, and come to me.

Elizabeth. Are you cross with me?

Teddie. Furious.

Elizabeth. Darling!

Teddie. If you don't want me tell me so at once and let me get out quickly.

Elizabeth. Teddie, nothing in the world matters anything to me but you. I'll go wherever you take me. I love you.

Teddie. [*All to pieces.*] Oh, my God!

Elizabeth. Does it mean as much to you as that? Oh, Teddie!

Teddie. [*Trying to control himself.*] Don't be a fool, Elizabeth.

Elizabeth. It's you're the fool. You're making me cry.

Teddie. You're so damned emotional.

Elizabeth. Damned emotional yourself. I'm sure you're a rotten business man.

Teddie. I don't care what you think. You've made me so awfully happy. I say, what a lark life's going to be!

Elizabeth. Teddie, you are an angel.

Teddie. Let's get out quick. It's no good wasting time. Elizabeth.

Elizabeth. What?

Teddie. Nothing. I just like to say Elizabeth.

Elizabeth. You fool!

Teddie. I say, can you shoot?

Elizabeth. No.

Teddie. I'll teach you. You don't know how ripping it is to start out from your camp at dawn and travel through the jungle. And you're so tired at night and the sky's all starry. It's a fair treat. Of course I didn't want to say anything about all that till you'd decided. I'd made up my mind to be absolutely practical.

Elizabeth. [*Chaffing him.*] The only practical thing you said was that love is the only thing that really matters.

Teddie. [*Happily.*] Pull the other leg next time, will you? I should have to have one longer than the other.

Elizabeth. Isn't it fun being in love with some one who's in love with you?

Teddie. I say, I think I'd better clear out at once, don't you? It seems rather rotten to stay on in—in this house.

Elizabeth. You can't go tonight. There's no train.

Teddie. I'll go tomorrow. I'll wait in London till you're ready to join me.

Elizabeth. I'm not going to leave a note on the pincushion like Lady Kitty, you know. I'm going to tell Arnold.

Teddie. Are you? Don't you think there'll be an awful bother?

Elizabeth. I must face it. I should hate to be sly and deceitful.

Teddie. Well, then, let's face it together.

Elizabeth. No, I'll talk to Arnold by myself.

Teddie. You won't let anyone influence you?

Elizabeth. No.

[*He holds out his hand and she takes it. They look into one another's eyes with grave, almost solemn affection. There is the sound outside of a car driving up.*]

Elizabeth. There's the car. Arnold's come back. I must go and bathe my eyes. I don't want them to see I've been crying.

Teddie. All right. [*As she is going.*] Elizabeth.

Elizabeth. [*Stopping.*] What?

Teddie. Bless you.

Elizabeth. [*Affectionately.*] Idiot!

[*She goes out of the door and* TEDDIE *through the French window into the garden. For an instant the room is empty.* ARNOLD *comes in. He sits down and takes some papers out of his despatch-case.* LADY KITTY *enters. He gets up.*]

Lady Kitty. I saw you come in. Oh, my dear, don't get up. There's no reason why you should be so dreadfully polite to me.

Arnold. I've just rung for a cup of tea.

Lady Kitty. Perhaps we shall have the chance of a little talk. We don't seem to have had five minutes by ourselves. I want to make your acquaintance, you know.

Arnold. I should like you to know that it's not by my wish that my father is here.

Lady Kitty. But I'm so interested to see him.

Arnold. I was afraid that you and Lord Porteous must find it embarrassing.

Lady Kitty. Oh, no. Hughie was his greatest friend. They were at Eton and Oxford together. I think your father has improved so much since I saw him last. He wasn't good-looking as a young man, but now he's quite handsome.

[*The* FOOTMAN *brings in a tray on which are tea-things.*]

Lady Kitty. Shall I pour it out for you?

Arnold. Thank you very much.

Lady Kitty. Do you take sugar?

Arnold. No. I gave it up during the war.

Lady Kitty. So wise of you. It's so bad for the figure. Besides being patriotic, of course. Isn't it absurd that I should ask my son if he takes sugar or not? Life is really very quaint. Sad, of course, but oh, so quaint! Often I lie in bed at night and have a good laugh to myself as I think how quaint life is.

Arnold. I'm afraid I'm a very serious person.

Lady Kitty. How old are you now, Arnold?

Arnold. Thirty-five.

Lady Kitty. Are you really? Of course, I was a child when I married your father.

Arnold. Really. He always told me you were twenty-two.

Lady Kitty. Oh, what nonsense! Why, I was married out of the nursery. I put my hair up for the first time on my wedding-day.

Arnold. Where is Lord Porteous?

Lady Kitty. My dear, it sounds too absurd to hear you call him Lord Porteous. Why don't you call him—Uncle Hughie?

Arnold. He doesn't happen to be my uncle.

Lady Kitty. No, but he's your godfather. You know, I'm sure you'll like him when you know him better. I'm so hoping that you and Elizabeth will come and stay with us in Florence. I simply adore Elizabeth. She's too beautiful.

Arnold. Her hair is very pretty.

Lady Kitty. It's not touched up, is it?

Arnold. Oh, no.

Lady Kitty. I just wondered. It's rather a coincidence that her hair should be the same color as mine. I suppose it shows that your father and you are attracted by just the same thing. So interesting, heredity, isn't it?

Arnold. Very.

Lady Kitty. Of course, since I joined the Catholic Church I don't believe in it any more. Darwin and all that sort of thing. Too dreadful. Wicked, you know. Besides, it's not very good form, is it?

[CHAMPION-CHENEY *comes in from the garden.*]

C.-C. Do I intrude?

Lady Kitty. Come in, Clive. Arnold and I have been having such a wonderful heart-to-heart talk.

C.-C. Very nice.

Arnold. Father, I stepped in for a moment at the Harvey's on my way back. It's simply criminal what they're doing with that house.

C.-C. What are they doing?

Arnold. It's an almost perfect Georgian house and they've got a lot of dreadful Victorian furniture. I gave them my ideas on the subject, but it's quite hopeless. They said they were attached to their furniture.

C.-C. Arnold should have been an interior decorator.

Lady Kitty. He has wonderful taste. He gets that from me.

Arnold. I suppose I have a certain *flair.* I have a passion for decorating houses.

Lady Kitty. You've made this one charming.

C.-C. D'you remember, we just had chintzes and comfortable chairs when we lived here, Kitty.

Lady Kitty. Perfectly hideous, wasn't it?

C.-C. In those days gentlemen and ladies were not expected to have taste.

Arnold. You know, I've been looking at

this chair again. Since Lord Porteous said the legs weren't right I've been very uneasy.

Lady Kitty. He only said that because he was in a bad temper.

C.-C. His temper seems to me very short these days, Kitty.

Lady Kitty. Oh, it is.

Arnold. You feel he knows what he's talking about. I gave seventy-five pounds for that chair. I'm very seldom taken in. I always think if a thing's right you feel it.

C.-C. Well, don't let it disturb your night's rest.

Arnold. But, my dear father, that's just what it does. I had a most horrible dream about it last night.

Lady Kitty. Here is Hughie.

Arnold. I'm going to fetch a book I have on Old English furniture. There's an illustration of a chair which is almost identical with this one. [PORTEOUS *comes in.*]

Porteous. Quite a family gathering, by George!

C.-C. I was thinking just now we'd make a very pleasing picture of a typical English home.

Arnold. I'll be back in five minutes. There's something I want to show you, Lord Porteous. [*He goes out.*]

C.-C. Would you like to play piquet with me, Hughie?

Porteous. Not particularly.

C.-C. You were never much of a piquet player, were you?

Porteous. My dear Clive, you people don't know what piquet is in England.

C.-C. Let's have a game then. You may make money.

Porteous. I don't want to play with you.

Lady Kitty. I don't know why not, Hughie.

Porteous. Let me tell you that I don't like your manner.

C.-C. I'm sorry for that. I'm afraid I can't offer to change it at my age.

Porteous. I don't know what you want to be hanging around here for.

C.-C. A natural attachment to my home.

Porteous. If you'd had any tact you'd have kept out of the way while we were here.

C.-C. My dear Hughie, I don't understand your attitude at all. If I'm willing to let bygones be bygones why should you object?

Porteous. Damn it all, they're not bygones.

C.-C. After all, I am the injured party.

Porteous. How the devil are you the injured party?

C.-C. Well, you did run away with my wife, didn't you?

Lady Kitty. Now, don't let's go into ancient history. I can't see why we shouldn't all be friends.

Porteous. I beg you not to interfere, Kitty.

Lady Kitty. I'm very fond of Clive.

Porteous. You never cared two straws for Clive. You only say that to irritate me.

Lady Kitty. Not at all. I don't see why he shouldn't come and stay with us.

C.-C. I'd love to. I think Florence in spring-time is delightful. Have you central heating?

Porteous. I never liked you, I don't like you now, and I never shall like you.

C.-C. How very unfortunate! Because I liked you, I like you now, and I shall continue to like you.

Lady Kitty. There's something very nice about you, Clive.

Porteous. If you think that, why the devil did you leave him?

Lady Kitty. Are you going to reproach me because I loved you? How utterly, utterly, utterly detestable you are!

C.-C. Now, now, don't quarrel with one another.

Lady Kitty. It's all his fault. I'm the easiest person in the world to live with. But really he'd try the patience of a saint.

C.-C. Come, come, don't get upset, Kitty. When two people live together there must be a certain amount of give and take.

Porteous. I don't know what the devil you're talking about.

C.-C. It hasn't escaped my observation that you are a little inclined to frip. Many couples are. I think it's a pity.

Porteous. Would you have the very great kindness to mind your own business?

Lady Kitty. It is his business. He naturally wants me to be happy.

C.-C. I have the very greatest affection for Kitty.

Porteous. Then why the devil didn't you look after her properly?

C.-C. My dear Hughie, you were my greatest friend. I trusted you. It may have been rash.

Porteous. It was inexcusable.

Lady Kitty. I don't know what you mean by that, Hughie.

Porteous. Don't, don't, don't try and bully me, Kitty.

Lady Kitty. Oh, I know what you mean.

Porteous. Then why the devil did you say you didn't?

Lady Kitty. When I think that I sacrificed everything for that man! And for thirty years I've had to live in a filthy marble palace with no sanitary conveniences.

C.-C. D'you mean to say you haven't got a bathroom?

Lady Kitty. I've had to wash in a tub.

C.-C. My poor Kitty, how you've suffered!

Porteous. Really, Kitty, I'm sick of hearing of the sacrifices you made. I suppose you think I sacrificed nothing. I should have been Prime Minister by now if it hadn't been for you.

Lady Kitty. Nonsense!

Porteous. What do you mean by that? Everyone said I should be Prime Minister. Shouldn't I have been Prime Minister, Clive?

C.-C. It was certainly the general expectation.

Porteous. I was the most promising young man of my day. I was bound to get a seat in the Cabinet at the next election.

Lady Kitty. They'd have found you out just as I've found you out. I'm sick of hearing that I ruined your career. You never had a career to ruin. Prime Minister! You haven't the brain. You haven't the character.

C.-C. Cheek, push, and a gift of the gab will serve very well instead, you know.

Lady Kitty. Besides, in politics it's not the men that matter. It's the women at the back of them. I could have made Clive a Cabinet Minister if I'd wanted to.

Porteous. Clive?

Lady Kitty. With my beauty, my charm, my force of character, my wit, I could have done anything.

Porteous. Clive was nothing but my political secretary. When I was Prime Minister I might have made him Governor of some Colony or other. Western Australia, say. Out of pure kindness.

Lady Kitty. [*With flashing eyes.*] D'you think I would have buried myself in Western Australia? With my beauty? My charm?

Porteous. Or Barbadoes, perhaps.

Lady Kitty. [*Furiously.*] Barbadoes! Barbadoes can go to—Barbadoes.

Porteous. That's all you'd have got.

Lady Kitty. Nonsense! I'd have India.

Porteous. I would never have given you India.

Lady Kitty. You would have given me India.

Porteous. I tell you I wouldn't.

Lady Kitty. The King would have given me India. The nation would have insisted on my having India. I would have been a vice-reine or nothing.

Porteous. I tell you that as long as the interests of the British Empire—damn it all, my teeth are coming out!

[*He hurries from the room.*]

Lady Kitty. It's too much. I can't bear it any more. I've put up with him for thirty years and now I'm at the end of my tether.

C.-C. Calm yourself, my dear Kitty.

Lady Kitty. I won't listen to a word. I've quite made up my mind. It's finished, finished, finished. [*With a change of tone.*] I was so touched when I heard that you never lived in this house again after I left it.

C.-C. The cuckoos have always been very plentiful. Their note has a personal application which, I must say, I have found extremely offensive.

Lady Kitty. When I saw that you didn't marry again I couldn't help thinking that you still loved me.

C.-C. I am one of the few men I know who is able to profit by experience.

Lady Kitty. In the eyes of the Church I am still your wife. The Church is so wise. It knows that in the end a woman always comes back to her first love. Clive, I am willing to return to you.

C.-C. My dear Kitty, I couldn't take advantage of your momentary vexation with Hughie to let you take a step which I know you would bitterly regret.

Lady Kitty. You've waited for me a long time. For Arnold's sake.

C.-C. Do you think we really need bother about Arnold? In the last thirty years he's had time to grow used to the situation.

Lady Kitty. [*With a little smile.*] I think I've sown my wild oats, Clive.

C.-C. I haven't. I was a good young man, Kitty.

Lady Kitty. I know.

C.-C. And I'm very glad, because it has enabled me to be a wicked old one.

Lady Kitty. I beg your pardon.

[ARNOLD *comes in with a large book in his hand.*]

Arnold. I say, I've found the book I was hunting for. Oh! Isn't Lord Porteous here?

Lady Kitty. One moment, Arnold. Your father and I are busy.

Arnold. I'm so sorry.

[*He goes out into the garden.*]

Lady Kitty. Explain yourself, Clive.

C.-C. When you ran away from me, Kitty, I was sore and angry and miserable. But above all I felt a fool.

Lady Kitty. Men are so vain.

C.-C. But I was a student of history, and presently I reflected that I shared my misfortune with very nearly all the greatest men.

Lady Kitty. I'm a great reader myself. It has always struck me as peculiar.

C.-C. The explanation is very simple. Women dislike intelligence, and when they find it in their husbands they revenge themselves on them in the only way they can, by making them—well, what you made me.

Lady Kitty. It's ingenious. It may be true.

C.-C. I felt I had done my duty by society and I determined to devote the rest of my life to my own entertainment. The House of Commons had always bored me excessively and the scandal of our divorce gave me an opportunity to resign my seat. I have been relieved to find that the country got on perfectly well without me.

Lady Kitty. But has love never entered your life?

C.-C. Tell me frankly, Kitty, don't you think people make a lot of unnecessary fuss about love?

Lady Kitty. It's the most wonderful thing in the world.

C.-C. You're incorrigible. Do you really think it was worth sacrificing so much for?

Lady Kitty. My dear Clive, I don't mind telling you that if I had my time over again I should be unfaithful to you, but I should not leave you.

C.-C. For some years I was notoriously the prey of a secret sorrow. But I found so many charming creatures who were anxious to console that in the end it grew rather fatiguing. Out of regard to my health I ceased to frequent the drawing-rooms of Mayfair.

Lady Kitty. And since then?

C.-C. Since then I have allowed myself the luxury of assisting financially a succession of dear little things, in a somewhat humble sphere, between the ages of twenty and twenty-five.

Lady Kitty. I cannot understand the infatuation of men for young girls. I think they're so dull.

C.-C. It's a matter of taste. I love old wine, old friends, and old books, but I like young women. On their twenty-fifth birthday I give them a diamond ring and tell them they must no longer waste their youth and beauty on an old fogey like me. We have a most affecting scene, my technique on these occasions is perfect, and then I start all over again.

Lady Kitty. You're a wicked old man, Clive.

C.-C. That's what I told you. But, by George! I'm a happy one.

Lady Kitty. There's only one course open to me now.

C.-C. What is that?

Lady Kitty. [*With a flashing smile.*] To go and dress for dinner.

C.-C. Capital. I will follow your example.

[*As* LADY KITTY *goes out* ELIZABETH *comes in.*]

Elizabeth. Where is Arnold?

C.-C. He's on the terrace. I'll call him.

Elizabeth. Don't bother.

C.-C. I was just strolling along to my cottage to put on a dinner jacket. [*As he goes out.*] Arnold. [*Exit* C.-C.]

Arnold. Hulloa! [*He comes in.*] Oh, Elizabeth, I've found an illustration here of a chair which is almost identical with mine. It's dated 1750. Look!

Elizabeth. That's very interesting.

Arnold. I want to show it to Porteous. [*Moving a chair which has been misplaced.*] You know, it does exasperate me the way people will not leave things alone. I no sooner put a thing in its place than somebody moves it.

Elizabeth. It must be maddening for you.

Arnold. It is. You are the worst offender. I can't think why you don't take the pride that I do in the house. After all, it's one of the show places in the country.

Elizabeth. I'm afraid you find me very unsatisfactory.

Arnold. [*Good-humoredly.*] I don't know about that. But my two subjects are politics and decoration. I should be a perfect fool if I didn't see that you don't care two straws about either.

Elizabeth. We haven't very much in common, Arnold, have we?

Arnold. I don't think you can blame me for that.

Elizabeth. I don't. I blame you for nothing. I have no fault to find with you.

Arnold. [*Surprised at her significant tone.*] Good gracious me! What's the meaning of all this?

Elizabeth. Well, I don't think there's any object in beating about the bush. I want you to let me go.

Arnold. Go where?

Elizabeth. Away. For always.

Arnold. My dear child, what *are* you talking about?

Elizabeth. I want to be free.

Arnold. [*Amused rather than disconcerted.*] Don't be ridiculous, darling. I daresay you're run down and want a change. I'll take you over to Paris for a fortnight if you like.

Elizabeth. I shouldn't have spoken to you

if I hadn't quite made up my mind. We've been married for three years and I don't think it's been a great success. I'm frankly bored by the life you want me to lead.

Arnold. Well, if you'll allow me to say so, the fault is yours. We lead a very distinguished, useful life. We know a lot of extremely nice people.

Elizabeth. I'm quite willing to allow that the fault is mine. But how does that make it any better? I'm only twenty-five. If I've made a mistake I have time to correct it.

Arnold. I can't bring myself to take you very seriously.

Elizabeth. You see, I don't love you.

Arnold. Well, I'm awfully sorry. But you weren't obliged to marry me. You've made your bed and I'm afraid you must lie on it.

Elizabeth. That's one of the falsest proverbs in the English language. Why should you lie on the bed you've made if you don't want to? There's always the floor.

Arnold. For goodness' sake, don't be funny, Elizabeth.

Elizabeth. I've quite made up my mind to leave you, Arnold.

Arnold. Come, come, Elizabeth, you must be sensible. You haven't any reason to leave me.

Elizabeth. Why should you wish to keep a woman tied to you who wants to be free?

Arnold. I happen to be in love with you.

Elizabeth. You might have said that before.

Arnold. I thought you'd take it for granted. You can't expect a man to go on making love to his wife after three years. I'm very busy. I'm awfully keen on politics and I've worked like a dog to make this house a thing of beauty. After all, a man marries to have a home, but also because he doesn't want to be bothered with sex and all that sort of thing. I fell in love with you the first time I saw you and I've been in love ever since.

Elizabeth. I'm sorry, but if you're not in love with a man his love doesn't mean very much to you.

Arnold. It's so ungrateful. I've done everything in the world for you.

Elizabeth. You've been very kind to me. But you've asked me to lead a life I don't like and that I'm not suited for. I'm awfully sorry to cause you pain, but now you must let me go.

Arnold. Nonsense! I'm a good deal older than you are and I think I have a little more sense. In your interests as well as in mine I'm not going to do anything of the sort.

Elizabeth. [*With a smile.*] How can you prevent me? You can't keep me under lock and key.

Arnold. Please don't talk to me as if I were a foolish child. You're my wife and you're going to remain my wife.

Elizabeth. What sort of a life do you think we should lead? Do you think there'd be any more happiness for you than for me?

Arnold. But what is it precisely that you suggest?

Elizabeth. Well, I want you to let me divorce you.

Arnold. [*Astounded.*] Me? Thank you very much. Are you under the impression I'm going to sacrifice my career for a whim of yours?

Elizabeth. How will it do that?

Arnold. My seat's wobbly enough as it is. Do you think I'd be able to hold it if I were in a divorce case? Even if it were a put-up job, as most divorces are nowadays, it would damn me.

Elizabeth. It's rather hard on a woman to be divorced.

Arnold. [*With sudden suspicion.*] What do you mean by that? Are you in love with some one?

Elizabeth. Yes.

Arnold. Who?

Elizabeth. Teddie Luton.

[*He is astonished for a moment, then bursts into a laugh.*]

Arnold. My poor child, how can you be so ridiculous? Why, he hasn't a bob. He's a perfectly commonplace young man. It's so absurd I can't even be angry with you.

Elizabeth. I've fallen desperately in love with him, Arnold.

Arnold. Well, you'd better fall desperately out.

Elizabeth. He wants to marry me.

Arnold. I daresay he does. He can go to hell.

Elizabeth. It's no good talking like that.

Arnold. Is he your lover?

Elizabeth. No, certainly not.

Arnold. It shows that he's a mean skunk to take advantage of my hospitality to make love to you.

Elizabeth. He's never even kissed me.

Arnold. I'd try telling that to the horse marines if I were you.

Elizabeth. It's because I wanted to do nothing shabby that I told you straight out how things were.

Arnold. How long have you been thinking of this?

Elizabeth. I've been in love with Teddie ever since I knew him.

Arnold. And you never thought of me at all, I suppose.

Elizabeth. Oh, yes, I did. I was miserable. But I can't help myself. I wish I loved you, but I don't.

Arnold. I recommend you to think very carefully before you do anything foolish.

Elizabeth. I have thought very carefully.

Arnold. By God! I don't know why I don't give you a sound hiding. I'm not sure if that wouldn't be the best thing to bring you to your senses.

Elizabeth. Oh, Arnold, don't take it like that.

Arnold. How do you expect me to take it? You come to me quite calmly and say: "I've had enough of you. We've been married three years and I think I'd like to marry somebody else now. Shall I break up your home? What a bore for you! Do you mind my divorcing you? It'll smash up your career, will it? What a pity!" Oh, no, my girl, I may be a fool, but I'm not a damned fool.

Elizabeth. Teddie is leaving here by the first train tomorrow. I warn you that I mean to join him as soon as he can make the necessary arrangements.

Arnold. Where is he?

Elizabeth. I don't know. I suppose he's in his room.

[ARNOLD *goes to the door and calls.*]

Arnold. George!

[*For a moment he walks up and down the room impatiently.* ELIZABETH *watches him. The* FOOTMAN *comes in.*]

Footman. Yes, sir.

Arnold. Tell Mr. Luton to come here at once.

Elizabeth. Ask Mr. Luton if he wouldn't mind coming here for a moment.

Footman. Very good, madam.

[*Exit* FOOTMAN.]

Elizabeth. What are you going to say to him?

Arnold. That's my business.

Elizabeth. I wouldn't make a scene if I were you.

Arnold. I'm not going to make a scene. [*They wait in silence.*] Why did you insist on my mother coming here?

Elizabeth. It seemed to me rather absurd to take up the attitude that I should be contaminated by her when . . .

Arnold. [*Interrupting.*] When you were proposing to do exactly the same thing. Well, now you've seen her what do you think of her? Do you think it's been a success? Is that the sort of woman a man would like his mother to be?

Elizabeth. I've been ashamed. I've been so sorry. It all seemed dreadful and horrible. This morning I happened to notice a rose in the garden. It was all over-blown and bedraggled. It looked like a painted old woman. And I remembered that I'd looked at it a day or two ago. It was lovely then, fresh and blooming and fragrant. It may be hideous now, but that doesn't take away from the beauty it had once. That was real.

Arnold. Poetry, by God! As if this were the moment for poetry!

[TEDDIE *comes in. He has changed into a dinner jacket.*]

Teddie. [*To* ELIZABETH.] Did you want me?

Arnold. *I* sent for you. [TEDDIE *looks from* ARNOLD *to* ELIZABETH. *He sees that something has happened.*] When would it be convenient for you to leave this house?

Teddie. I was proposing to go tomorrow morning. But I can very well go at once if you like.

Arnold. I do like.

Teddie. Very well. Is there anything else you wish to say to me?

Arnold. Do you think it was a very honorable thing to come down here and make love to my wife?

Teddie. No, I don't. I haven't been very happy about it. That's why I wanted to go away.

Arnold. Upon my word, you're cool.

Teddie. I'm afraid it's no good saying I'm sorry and that sort of thing. You know what the situation is.

Arnold. Is it true that you want to marry Elizabeth?

Teddie. Yes. I should like to marry her as soon as ever I can.

Arnold. Have you thought of me at all? Has it struck you that you're destroying my home and breaking up my happiness?

Teddie. I don't see how there could be much happiness for you if Elizabeth doesn't care for you.

Arnold. Let me tell you that I refuse to have my home broken up by a twopenny-halfpenny adventurer who takes advantage of a foolish woman. I refuse to allow myself to be divorced. I can't prevent my wife from going off with you if she's determined to make a damned fool of herself, but this I tell you: nothing will induce me to divorce her.

Elizabeth. Arnold, that would be monstrous.

Teddie. We could force you.

Arnold. How?

Teddie. If we went away together openly you'd have to bring an action.

Arnold. Twenty-four hours after you leave this house I shall go down to Brighton with a chorus-girl. And neither you nor I will be able to get a divorce. We've had enough divorces in our family. And now get out, get out, get out!

[TEDDIE *looks uncertainly at* ELIZABETH.]

Elizabeth. [*With a little smile.*] Don't bother about me. I shall be all right.

Arnold. Get out! Get out!

CURTAIN

THE THIRD ACT

The Scene is the same as in the preceding acts.

It is the night of the same day as that on which takes place the action of the second act.

[CHAMPION-CHENEY *and* ARNOLD, *both in dinner jackets, are discovered.* CHAMPION-CHENEY *is seated.* ARNOLD *walks restlessly up and down the room.*]

C.-C. I think, if you'll follow my advice to the letter, you'll probably work the trick.

Arnold. I don't like it, you know. It's against all my principles.

C.-C. My dear Arnold, we all hope that you have before you a distinguished political career. You can't learn too soon that the most useful thing about a principle is that it can always be sacrificed to expediency.

Arnold. But supposing it doesn't come off? Women are incalculable.

C.-C. Nonsense! Men are romantic. A woman will always sacrifice herself if you give her the opportunity. It is her favorite form of self-indulgence.

Arnold. I never know whether you're a humorist or a cynic, Father.

C.-C. I'm neither, my dear boy; I'm merely a very truthful man. But people are so unused to the truth that they're apt to mistake it for a joke or a sneer.

Arnold. [*Irritably.*] It seems so unfair that this should happen to me.

C.-C. Keep your head, my boy, and do what I tell you.

[LADY KITTY *and* ELIZABETH *come in.* LADY KITTY *is in a gorgeous evening gown.*]

Elizabeth. Where is Lord Porteous?

C.-C. He's on the terrace. He's smoking a cigar. [*Going to window.*] Hughie!

[PORTEOUS *comes in.*]

Porteous. [*With a grunt.*] Yes? Where's Mrs. Shenstone?

Elizabeth. Oh, she had a headache. She's gone to bed.

[*When* PORTEOUS *comes in* LADY KITTY *with a very haughty air purses her lips and takes up an illustrated paper.* PORTEOUS *gives her an irritated look, takes another illustrated paper and sits himself down at the other end of the room. They are not on speaking terms.*]

C.-C. Arnold and I have just been down to my cottage.

Elizabeth. I wondered where you'd gone.

C.-C. I came across an old photograph album this afternoon. I meant to bring it along before dinner, but I forgot, so we went and fetched it.

Elizabeth. Oh, do let me see it! I love old photographs.

[*He gives her the album, and she, sitting down, puts it on her knees and begins to turn over the pages. He stands over her.* LADY KITTY *and* PORTEOUS *take surreptitious glances at one another.*]

C.-C. I thought it might amuse you to see what pretty women looked like five-and-thirty years ago. That was the day of beautiful women.

Elizabeth. Do you think they were more beautiful then than they are now?

C.-C. Oh, much. Now you see lots of pretty little things, but very few beautiful women.

Elizabeth. Aren't their clothes funny?

C.-C. [*Pointing to a photograph.*] That's Mrs. Langtry.

Elizabeth. She has a lovely nose.

C.-C. She was the most wonderful thing you ever saw. Dowagers used to jump on chairs in order to get a good look at her when she came into a drawing-room. I was riding with her once, and we had to have the gates of the livery stable closed when she was getting on her horse because the crowd was so great.

Elizabeth. And who's that?

C.-C. Lady Lonsdale. That's Lady Dudley.

Elizabeth. This is an actress, isn't it?

C.-C. It is, indeed. Ellen Terry. By George! How I loved that woman!

Elizabeth. [*With a smile.*] Dear Ellen Terry!

C.-C. That's Bwabs. I never saw a smarter man in my life. And Oliver Montagu. Henry Manners with his eye-glass.

Elizabeth. Nice-looking, isn't he? And this?

C.-C. That's Mary Anderson. I wish you could have seen her in "A Winter's Tale." Her beauty just took your breath away. And look! There's Lady Randolph. Bernal Osborne—the wittiest man I ever knew.

Elizabeth. I think it's too sweet. I love their absurd bustles and those tight sleeves.

C.-C. What figures they had! In those days a woman wasn't supposed to be as thin as a rail and as flat as a pancake.

Elizabeth. Oh, but aren't they laced in? How could they bear it?

C.-C. They didn't play golf then, and nonsense like that, you know. They hunted, in a tall hat and a long black habit, and they were very gracious and charitable to the poor in the village.

Elizabeth. Did the poor like it?

C.-C. They had a very thin time if they didn't. When they were in London they drove in the Park every afternoon, and they went to ten-course dinners, where they never met anybody they didn't know. And they had their box at the opera when Patti was singing or Madame Albani.

Elizabeth. Oh, what a lovely little thing! Who on earth is that?

C.-C. That?

Elizabeth. She looks so fragile, like a piece of exquisite china, with all those furs on and her face up against her muff, and the snow falling.

C.-C. Yes, there was quite a rage at that time for being taken in an artificial snowstorm.

Elizabeth. What a sweet smile, so roguish and frank, and debonair! Oh, I wish I looked like that! Do tell me who it is!

C.-C. Don't you know?

Elizabeth. No.

C.-C. Why—it's Kitty.

Elizabeth. Lady Kitty. [*To* LADY KITTY.] Oh, my dear, do look! It's too ravishing. [*She takes the album over to her impulsively.*] Why didn't you tell me you looked like that? Everybody must have been in love with you.

[LADY KITTY *takes the album and looks at it. Then she lets it slip from her hands and covers her face with her hands. She is crying.*]

[*In consternation.*] My dear, what's the matter? Oh, what have I done? I'm so sorry.

Lady Kitty. Don't, don't talk to me. Leave me alone. It's stupid of me.

[ELIZABETH *looks at her for a moment perplexed, then, turning round, slips her arm in* CHAMPION-CHENEY'S *and leads him out on to the terrace.*]

Elizabeth. [*As they are going, in a whisper.*] Did you do that on purpose?

[PORTEOUS *gets up and goes over to* LADY KITTY. *He puts his hand on her shoulder. They remain thus for a little while.*]

Porteous. I'm afraid I was very rude to you before dinner, Kitty.

Lady Kitty. [*Taking his hand which is on her shoulder.*] It doesn't matter. I'm sure I was very exasperating.

Porteous. I didn't mean what I said, you know.

Lady Kitty. Neither did I.

Porteous. Of course I know that I'd never have been Prime Minister.

Lady Kitty. How can you talk such nonsense, Hughie? No one would have had a chance if you'd remained in politics.

Porteous. I haven't the character.

Lady Kitty. You have more character than anyone I've ever met.

Porteous. Besides, I don't know that I much wanted to be Prime Minister.

Lady Kitty. Oh, but I should have been so proud of you. Of course you'd have been Prime Minister.

Porteous. I'd have given you India, you know. I think it would have been a very popular appointment.

Lady Kitty. I don't care twopence about India. I'd have been quite content with Western Australia.

Porteous. My dear, you don't think I'd have let you bury yourself in Western Australia?

Lady Kitty. Or Barbadoes.

Porteous. Never. It sounds like a cure for flat feet. I'd have kept you in London.

[*He picks up the album and is about to look at the photograph of* LADY KITTY. *She puts her hands over it.*]

Lady Kitty. No, don't look.

[*He takes her hand away.*]

Porteous. Don't be so silly.

Lady Kitty. Isn't it hateful to grow old?

Porteous. You know, you haven't changed much.

Lady Kitty. [*Enchanted.*] Oh, Hughie, how can you talk such nonsense?

Porteous. Of course you're a little more mature, but that's all. A woman's all the better for being rather mature.

Lady Kitty. Do you really think that?

Porteous. Upon my soul I do.

Lady Kitty. You're not saying it just to please me?

Porteous. No, no.

Lady Kitty. Let me look at the photograph again. [*She takes the album and looks at the photograph complacently.*] The fact is, if your bones are good, age doesn't really matter. You'll always be beautiful.

Porteous. [*With a little smile, almost as if he were talking to a child.*] It was silly of you to cry.

Lady Kitty. It hasn't made my eyelashes run, has it?

Porteous. Not a bit.

Lady Kitty. It's very good stuff I use now. They don't stick together either.

Porteous. Look here, Kitty, how much longer do you want to stay here?

Lady Kitty. Oh, I'm quite ready to go whenever you like.

Porteous. Clive gets on my nerves. I don't like the way he keeps hanging about you.

Lady Kitty. [*Surprised, rather amused, and delighted.*] Hughie, you don't mean to say you're jealous of poor Clive?

Porteous. Of course I'm not jealous of him, but he does look at you in a way that I can't help thinking rather objectionable.

Lady Kitty. Hughie, you may throw me downstairs like Amy Robsart; you may drag me about the floor by the hair of my head; I don't care, you're jealous. I shall never grow old.

Porteous. Damn it all, the man was your husband.

Lady Kitty. My dear Hughie, he never had your style. Why, the moment you come into a room everyone looks and says: "Who the devil is that?"

Porteous. What? You think that, do you? Well, I daresay there's something in what you say. These damned Radicals can say what they like, but, by God, Kitty! When a man's a gentleman—well, damn it all, you know what I mean.

Lady Kitty. I think Clive has degenerated dreadfully since we left him.

Porteous. What do you say to making a bee-line for Italy and going to San Michele?

Lady Kitty. Oh, Hughie! It's years since we were there.

Porteous. Wouldn't you like to see it again —just once more?

Lady Kitty. Do you remember the first time we went? It was the most heavenly place I'd ever seen. We'd only left England a month, and I said I'd like to spend all my life there.

Porteous. Of course I remember. And in a fortnight it was yours, lock, stock, and barrel.

Lady Kitty. We were very happy there, Hughie.

Porteous. Let's go back once more.

Lady Kitty. I daren't. It must be all peopled with the ghosts of our past. One should never go again to a place where one has been happy. It would break my heart.

Porteous. Do you remember how we used to sit on the terrace of the old castle and look at the Adriatic? We might have been the only people in the world, you and I, Kitty.

Lady Kitty. [*Tragically.*] And we thought our love would last forever.

[*Enter* CHAMPION-CHENEY.]

Porteous. Is there any chance of bridge this evening?

C.-C. I don't think we can make up a four.

Porteous. What a nuisance that boy went away like that! He wasn't a bad player.

C.-C. Teddie Luton?

Lady Kitty. I think it was very funny his going without saying good-by to anyone.

C.-C. The young men of the present day are very casual.

Porteous. I thought there was no train in the evening.

C.-C. There isn't. The last train leaves at 5.45.

Porteous. How did he go then?

C.-C. He went.

Porteous. Damned selfish I call it.

Lady Kitty. [*Intrigued.*] Why did he go, Clive?

[CHAMPION-CHENEY *looks at her for a moment reflectively.*]

C.-C. I have something very grave to say to you. Elizabeth wants to leave Arnold.

Lady Kitty. Clive! What on earth for?

C.-C. She's in love with Teddie Luton. That's why he went. The men of my family are really very unfortunate.

Porteous. Does she want to run away with him?

Lady Kitty. [*With consternation.*] My dear, what's to be done?

C.-C. I think you can do a great deal.

Lady Kitty. I? What?

C.-C. Tell her, tell her what it means.

[*He looks at her fixedly. She stares at him.*]

Lady Kitty. Oh, no, no!

C.-C. She's a child. Not for Arnold's sake. For her sake. You must.

Lady Kitty. You don't know what you're asking.

C.-C. Yes, I do.

Lady Kitty. Hughie, what shall I do?

Porteous. Do what you like. I shall never blame you for anything.

[*The* FOOTMAN *comes in with a letter on a salver. He hesitates on seeing that* ELIZABETH *is not in the room.*]

C.-C. What is it?

Footman. I was looking for Mrs. Champion-Cheney, sir.

C.-C. She's not here. Is that a letter?

Footman. Yes, sir. It's just been sent up from the "Champion Arms."

C.-C. Leave it. I'll give it to Mrs. Cheney.

Footman. Very good, sir.

[*He brings the tray to* CLIVE, *who takes the letter. The* FOOTMAN *goes out.*]

Porteous. Is the "Champion Arms" the local pub?

C.-C. [*Looking at the letter.*] It's by way of being a hotel, but I never heard of anyone staying there.

Lady Kitty. If there was no train I suppose he has to go there.

C.-C. Great minds. I wonder what he has to write about! [*He goes to the door leading on to the garden.*] Elizabeth!

Elizabeth. [*Outside.*] Yes.

C.-C. Here's a note for you.

[*There is silence. They wait for* ELIZABETH *to come. She enters.*]

Elizabeth. It's lovely in the garden tonight.

C.-C. They've just sent this up from the "Champion Arms."

Elizabeth. Thank you.

[*Without embarrassment she opens the letter. They watch her while she reads it. It covers three pages. She puts it away in her bag.*]

Lady Kitty. Hughie, I wish you'd fetch me a cloak. I'd like to take a little stroll in the garden, but after thirty years in Italy I find these English summers rather chilly. [*Without a word* PORTEOUS *goes out.* ELIZABETH *is lost in thought.*] I want to talk to Elizabeth, Clive.

C.-C. I'll leave you. [*He goes out.*]

Lady Kitty. What does he say?

Elizabeth. Who?

Lady Kitty. Mr. Luton.

Elizabeth. [*Gives a little start. Then she looks at* LADY KITTY.] They've told you?

Lady Kitty. Yes. And now they have, I think I knew it all along.

Elizabeth. I don't expect you to have much sympathy for me. Arnold is your son.

Lady Kitty. So pitifully little.

Elizabeth. I'm not suited for this sort of existence. Arnold wants me to take what he calls my place in Society. Oh, I get so bored with those parties in London. All those middle-aged painted women, in beautiful clothes, lolloping round ballrooms with rather old young men. And the endless luncheons where they gossip about so-and-so's love affairs.

Lady Kitty. Are you very much in love with Mr. Luton?

Elizabeth. I love him with all my heart.

Lady Kitty. And he?

Elizabeth. He's never cared for anyone but me. He never will.

Lady Kitty. Will Arnold let you divorce him?

Elizabeth. No, he won't hear of it. He refuses even to divorce me.

Lady Kitty. Why?

Elizabeth. He thinks a scandal will revive all the old gossip.

Lady Kitty. Oh, my poor child!

Elizabeth. It can't be helped. I'm quite willing to accept the consequences.

Lady Kitty. You don't know what it is to have a man tied to you only by his honor. When married people don't get on they can separate, but if they're not married it's impossible. It's a tie that only death can sever.

Elizabeth. If Teddie stopped caring for me I shouldn't want him to stay with me for five minutes.

Lady Kitty. One says that when one's sure of a man's love, but when one isn't any more—oh, it's so different. In those circumstances one's got to keep a man's love. It's the only thing one has.

Elizabeth. I'm a human being. I can stand on my own feet.

Lady Kitty. Have you any money of your own?

Elizabeth. None.

Lady Kitty. Then how can you stand on your own feet? You think I'm a silly, frivolous woman, but I've learned something in a bitter school. They can make what laws they like, they can give us the suffrage, but when you come down to bedrock it's the man who pays the piper who calls the tune. Woman will only be the equal of man when she earns her living in the same way that he does.

Elizabeth. [*Smiling.*] It sounds rather funny to hear you talk like that.

Lady Kitty. A cook who marries a butler can snap her fingers in his face because she can earn just as much as he can. But a woman in your position and a woman in mine will always be dependent on the men who keep them.

Elizabeth. I don't want luxury. You don't know how sick I am of all this beautiful furniture. These over-decorated houses are like a prison in which I can't breathe. When I drive about in a Callot frock and a Rolls-Royce I envy the shop-girl in a coat and skirt whom I see jumping on the tailboard of a bus.

Lady Kitty. You mean that if need be you could earn your own living?

Elizabeth. Yes.

Lady Kitty. What could you be? A nurse or a typist. It's nonsense. Luxury saps a woman's nerve. And when she's known it once it becomes a necessity.

Elizabeth. That depends on the woman.

Lady Kitty. When we're young we think we're different from everyone else, but when we grow a little older we discover we're all very much of a muchness.

Elizabeth. You're very kind to take so much trouble about me.

Lady Kitty. It breaks my heart to think that you're going to make the same pitiful mistake that I made.

Elizabeth. Oh, don't say it was that, don't, don't.

Lady Kitty. Look at me, Elizabeth, and look at Hughie. Do you think it's been a success? If I had my time over again do you think I'd do it again? Do you think he would?

Elizabeth. You see, you don't know how much I love Teddie.

Lady Kitty. And do you think I didn't love Hughie? Do you think he didn't love me?

Elizabeth. I'm sure he did.

Lady Kitty. Oh, of course in the beginning it was heavenly. We felt so brave and adventurous and we were so much in love. The first two years were wonderful. People cut me, you know, but I didn't mind. I thought love was everything. It *is* a little uncomfortable when you come upon an old friend and go towards her eagerly, so glad to see her, and are met with an icy stare.

Elizabeth. Do you think friends like that are worth having?

Lady Kitty. Perhaps they're not very sure of themselves. Perhaps they're honestly shocked. It's a test one had better not put one's friends to if one can help it. It's rather bitter to find how few one has.

Elizabeth. But one has some.

Lady Kitty. Yes, they ask you to come and see them when they're quite certain no one will be there who might object to meeting you. Or else they say to you: "My dear, you know I'm devoted to you, and I wouldn't mind at all, but my girl's growing up—I'm sure you understand; you won't think it unkind of me if I don't ask you to the house?"

Elizabeth. [*Smiling.*] That doesn't seem to me very serious.

Lady Kitty. At first I thought it rather a relief, because it threw Hughie and me together more. But you know, men are very funny. Even when they are in love they're not in love all day long. They want change and recreation.

Elizabeth. I'm not inclined to blame them for that, poor dears.

Lady Kitty. Then we settled in Florence. And because we couldn't get the society we'd been used to we became used to the society we could get. Loose women and vicious men. Snobs who liked to patronize people with a handle to their names. Vague Italian Princes who were glad to borrow a few francs from Hughie and seedy countesses who liked to drive with me in the Cascine. And then Hughie began to hanker after his old life. He wanted to go big game shooting, but I dared not let him go. I was afraid he'd never come back.

Elizabeth. But you knew he loved you.

Lady Kitty. Oh, my dear, what a blessed institution marriage is—for women, and what fools they are to meddle with it! The Church is so wise to take its stand on the indi—indi——

Elizabeth. Solu——

Lady Kitty. Bility of marriage. Believe me, it's no joke when you have to rely only on yourself to keep a man. I could never afford to grow old. My dear, I'll tell you a secret that I've never told a living soul.

Elizabeth. What is that?

Lady Kitty. My hair is not naturally this color.

Elizabeth. Really.

Lady Kitty. I touch it up. You would never have guessed, would you?

Elizabeth. Never.

Lady Kitty. Nobody does. My dear, it's white, premature of course, but white. I always think it's a symbol of my life. Are you interested in symbolism? I think it's too wonderful.

Elizabeth. I don't think I know very much about it.

Lady Kitty. However tired I've been I've had to be brilliant and gay. I've never let Hughie see the aching heart behind my smiling eyes.

Elizabeth. [*Amused and touched.*] You poor dear.

Lady Kitty. And when I saw he was attracted by some one else the fear and the jealousy that seized me! You see, I didn't dare make a scene as I should have done if

I'd been married—I had to pretend not to notice.

Elizabeth. [*Taken aback.*] But do you mean to say he fell in love with anyone else?

Lady Kitty. Of course he did eventually.

Elizabeth. [*Hardly knowing what to say.*] You must have been very unhappy.

Lady Kitty. Oh, I was, dreadfully. Night after night I sobbed my heart out when Hughie told me he was going to play cards at the club and I knew he was with that odious woman. Of course, it wasn't as if there weren't plenty of men who were only too anxious to console me. Men have always been attracted by me, you know.

Elizabeth. Oh, of course, I can quite understand it.

Lady Kitty. But I had my self-respect to think of. I felt that whatever Hughie did I would do nothing that I should regret.

Elizabeth. You must be very glad now.

Lady Kitty. Oh, yes. Nothwithstanding all my temptations I've been absolutely faithful to Hughie in spirit.

Elizabeth. I don't think I quite understand what you mean.

Lady Kitty. Well, there was a poor Italian boy, young Count Castel Giovanni, who was so desperately in love with me that his mother begged me not to be too cruel. She was afraid he'd go into a consumption. What could I do? And then, oh, years later, there was Antonio Melita. He said he'd shoot himself unless I—well, you understand I couldn't let the poor boy shoot himself.

Elizabeth. D'you think he really would have shot himself?

Lady Kitty. Oh, one never knows, you know. Those Italians are so passionate. He was really rather a lamb. He had such beautiful eyes.

[ELIZABETH *looks at her for a long time and a certain horror seizes her of this dissolute, painted old woman.*]

Elizabeth. [*Hoarsely.*] Oh, but I think that's—dreadful.

Lady Kitty. Are you shocked? One sacrifices one's life for love and then one finds that love doesn't last. The tragedy of love isn't death or separation. One gets over them. The tragedy of love is indifference.

[ARNOLD *comes in.*]

Arnold. Can I have a little talk with you, Elizabeth?

Elizabeth. Of course.

Arnold. Shall we go for a stroll in the garden?

Elizabeth. If you like.

Lady Kitty. No, stay here. I'm going out anyway. [*Exit* LADY KITTY.]

Arnold. I want you to listen to me for a few minutes, Elizabeth. I was so taken aback by what you told me just now that I lost my head. I was rather absurd and I beg your pardon. I said things I regret.

Elizabeth. Oh, don't blame yourself. I'm sorry that I should have given you occasion to say them.

Arnold. I want to ask you if you've quite made up your mind to go.

Elizabeth. Quite.

Arnold. Just now I seem to have said all that I didn't want to say and nothing that I did. I'm stupid and tongue-tied. I never told you how deeply I loved you.

Elizabeth. Oh, Arnold!

Arnold. Please let me speak now. It's so very difficult. If I seemed absorbed in politics and the house, and so on, to the exclusion of my interest in you, I'm dreadfully sorry. I suppose it was absurd of me to think you would take my great love for granted.

Elizabeth. But, Arnold, I'm not reproaching you.

Arnold. I'm reproaching myself. I've been tactless and neglectful. But I do ask you to believe that it hasn't been because I didn't love you. Can you forgive me?

Elizabeth. I don't think that there's anything to forgive.

Arnold. It wasn't till today when you talked of leaving me that I realized how desperately in love with you I was.

Elizabeth. After three years?

Arnold. I'm so proud of you. I admire you so much. When I see you at a party, so fresh and lovely, and everybody wondering at you, I have a sort of little thrill because you're mine, and afterwards I shall take you home.

Elizabeth. Oh, Arnold, you're exaggerating.

Arnold. I can't imagine this house without you. Life seems on a sudden all empty and meaningless. Oh, Elizabeth, don't you love me at all?

Elizabeth. It's much better to be honest. No.

Arnold. Doesn't my love mean anything to you?

Elizabeth. I'm very grateful to you. I'm sorry to cause you pain. What would be the good of my staying with you when I should be wretched all the time?

Arnold. Do you love that man as much as all that? Does my unhappiness mean nothing to you?

Elizabeth. Of course it does. It breaks my heart. You see, I never knew I meant so much to you. I'm so touched. And I'm so sorry, Arnold, really sorry. But I can't help myself.

Arnold. Poor child, it's cruel of me to torture you.

Elizabeth. Oh, Arnold, believe me, I have tried to make the best of it. I've tried to love you, but I can't. After all, one either loves or one doesn't. Trying is no help. And now I'm at the end of my tether. I can't help the consequences—I must do what my whole self yearns for.

Arnold. My poor child, I'm so afraid you'll be unhappy. I'm so afraid you'll regret.

Elizabeth. You must leave me to my fate. I hope you'll forget me and all the unhappiness I've caused you.

Arnold. [*There is a pause.* ARNOLD *walks up and down the room reflectively. He stops and faces her.*] If you love this man and want to go to him I'll do nothing to prevent you. My only wish is to do what is best for you.

Elizabeth. Arnold, that's awfully kind of you. If I'm treating you badly at least I want you to know that I'm grateful for all your kindness to me.

Arnold. But there's one favor I should like you to do me. Will you?

Elizabeth. Oh, Arnold, of course I'll do anything I can.

Arnold. Teddie hasn't very much money. You've been used to a certain amount of luxury, and I can't bear to think that you should do without anything you've had. It would kill me to think that you were suffering any hardship or privation.

Elizabeth. Oh, but Teddie can earn enough for our needs. After all, we don't want much money.

Arnold. I'm afraid my mother's life hasn't been very easy, but it's obvious that the only thing that's made it possible is that Porteous was rich. I want you to let me make you an allowance of two thousand a year.

Elizabeth. Oh, no, I couldn't think of it. It's absurd.

Arnold. I beg you to accept it. You don't know what a difference it will make.

Elizabeth. It's awfully kind of you, Arnold. It humiliates me to speak about it. Nothing would induce me to take a penny from you.

Arnold. Well, you can't prevent me from opening an account at my bank in your name. The money shall be paid in every quarter whether you touch it or not, and if you happen to want it, it will be there waiting for you.

Elizabeth. You overwhelm me, Arnold. There's only one thing I want you to do for me. I should be very grateful if you would divorce me as soon as you possibly can.

Arnold. No, I won't do that. But I'll give you cause to divorce me.

Elizabeth. You!

Arnold. Yes. But of course you'll have to be very careful for a bit. I'll put it through as quickly as possible, but I'm afraid you can't hope to be free for over six months.

Elizabeth. But, Arnold, your seat and your political career!

Arnold. Oh, well, my father gave up his seat under similar circumstances. He's got along very comfortably without politics.

Elizabeth. But they're your whole life.

Arnold. After all one can't have it both ways. You can't serve God and Mammon. If you want to do the decent thing you have to be prepared to suffer for it.

Elizabeth. But I don't want you to suffer for it.

Arnold. At first I rather hesitated at the scandal. But I daresay that was only weakness on my part. Under the circumstances I should have liked to keep out of the Divorce Court if I could.

Elizabeth. Arnold, you're making me absolutely miserable.

Arnold. What you said before dinner was quite right. It's nothing for a man, but it makes so much difference to a woman. Naturally I must think of you first.

Elizabeth. That's absurd. It's out of the question. Whatever there's to pay I must pay it.

Arnold. It's not very much I'm asking you, Elizabeth.

Elizabeth. I'm taking everything from you.

Arnold. It's the only condition I make. My mind is absolutely made up. I will never divorce you, but I will enable you to divorce me.

Elizabeth. Oh, Arnold, it's cruel to be so generous.

Arnold. It's not generous at all. It's the only way I have of showing you how deep and passionate and sincere my love is for you. [*There is a silence. He holds out his hand.*] Good night. I have a great deal of work to do before I go to bed.

Elizabeth. Good night.

Arnold. Do you mind if I kiss you?

Elizabeth. [*With agony.*] Oh, Arnold!

[*He gravely kisses her on the forehead and then goes out.* ELIZABETH *stands lost in thought. She is shattered.* LADY KITTY *and* PORTEOUS *come in.* LADY KITTY *wears a cloak.*]

Lady Kitty. You're alone, Elizabeth?

Elizabeth. That note you asked me about, Lady Kitty, from Teddie . . .

Lady Kitty. Yes?

Elizabeth. He wanted to have a talk with me before he went away. He's waiting for me in the summer house by the tennis court. Would Lord Porteous mind going down and asking him to come here?

Porteous. Certainly. Certainly.

Elizabeth. Forgive me for troubling you. But it's very important.

Porteous. No trouble at all.

[*He goes out.*]

Lady Kitty. Hughie and I will leave you alone.

Elizabeth. But I don't want to be left alone. I want you to stay.

Lady Kitty. What are you going to say to him?

Elizabeth. [*Desperately.*] Please don't ask me questions. I'm so frightfully unhappy.

Lady Kitty. My poor child!

Elizabeth. Oh, isn't life rotten? Why can't one be happy without making other people unhappy?

Lady Kitty. I wish I knew how to help you. I'm simply devoted to you. [*She hunts about in her mind for something to do or say.*] Would you like my lipstick?

Elizabeth. [*Smiling through her tears.*] Thanks. I never use one.

Lady Kitty. Oh, but just try. It's such a comfort when you're in trouble.

[*Enter* PORTEOUS *and* TEDDIE.]

Porteous. I brought him. He said he'd be damned if he'd come.

Lady Kitty. When a lady sent for him? Are these the manners of the young men of today?

Teddie. When you've been solemnly kicked out of a house once I think it seems rather pushing to come back again as though nothing had happened.

Elizabeth. Teddie, I want you to be serious.

Teddie. Darling, I had such a rotten dinner at that pub. If you ask me to be serious on the top of that I shall cry.

Elizabeth. Don't be idiotic, Teddie. [*Her voice faltering.*] I'm so utterly wretched.

[*He looks at her for a moment gravely.*]

Teddie. What is it?

Elizabeth. I can't come away with you, Teddie.

Teddie. Why not?

Elizabeth. [*Looking away in embarrassment.*] I don't love you enough.

Teddie. Fiddle!

Elizabeth. [*With a flash of anger.*] Don't say "Fiddle" to me.

Teddie. I shall say exactly what I like to you.

Elizabeth. I won't be bullied.

Teddie. Now look here, Elizabeth, you know perfectly well that I'm in love with you, and I know perfectly well that you're in love with me. So what are you talking nonsense for?

Elizabeth. [*Her voice breaking.*] I can't say it if you're cross with me.

Teddie. [*Smiling very tenderly.*] I'm not cross with you, silly.

Elizabeth. It's harder still when you're being rather an owl.

Teddie. [*With a chuckle.*] Am I mistaken in thinking you're not very easy to please?

Elizabeth. Oh, it's monstrous. I was all wrought up and ready to do anything, and now you've thoroughly put me out. I feel like a great big fat balloon that some one has put a long pin into. [*With a sudden look at him.*] Have you done it on purpose?

Teddie. Upon my soul I don't know what you're talking about.

Elizabeth. I wonder if you're really much cleverer than I think you are.

Teddie. [*Taking her hands and making her sit down.*] Now tell me exactly what you want to say. By the way, do you want Lady Kitty and Lord Porteous to be here?

Elizabeth. Yes.

Lady Kitty. Elizabeth asked us to stay.

Teddie. Oh, I don't mind, bless you. I only thought you might feel rather in the way.

Lady Kitty. [*Frigidly.*] A gentlewoman never feels in the way, Mr. Luton.

Teddie. Won't you call me Teddie? Everybody does, you know.

[LADY KITTY *tries to give him a withering look, but she finds it very difficult to prevent herself from smiling.* TEDDIE *strokes* ELIZABETH'S *hands. She draws them away.*]

Elizabeth. No, don't do that. Teddie, it wasn't true when I said I didn't love you. Of course I love you. But Arnold loves me, too. I didn't know how much.

Teddie. What has he been saying to you?

Elizabeth. He's been very good to me, and so kind. I didn't know he could be so kind. He offered to let me divorce him.

Teddie. That's very decent of him.

Elizabeth. But don't you see, it ties my hands. How can I accept such a sacrifice? I should never forgive myself if I profited by his generosity.

Teddie. If another man and I were devilish hungry and there was only one mutton chop between us, and he said, "You eat it," I wouldn't waste a lot of time arguing. I'd wolf it before he changed his mind.

Elizabeth. Don't talk like that. It maddens me. I'm trying to do the right thing.

Teddie. You're not in love with Arnold; you're in love with me. It's idiotic to sacrifice your life for a slushy sentiment.

Elizabeth. After all, I did marry him.

Teddie. Well, you made a mistake. A marriage without love is no marriage at all.

Elizabeth. *I* made the mistake. Why should he suffer for it? If anyone has to suffer it's only right that I should.

Teddie. What sort of a life do you think it would be with him? When two people are married it's very difficult for one of them to be unhappy without making the other unhappy too.

Elizabeth. I can't take advantage of his generosity.

Teddie. I daresay he'll get a lot of satisfaction out of it.

Elizabeth. You're being beastly, Teddie. He was simply wonderful. I never knew he had it in him. He was really noble.

Teddie. You are talking rot, Elizabeth.

Elizabeth. I wonder if you'd be capable of acting like that.

Teddie. Acting like what?

Elizabeth. What would you do if I were married to you and came and told you I loved somebody else and wanted to leave you?

Teddie. You have very pretty blue eyes, Elizabeth. I'd black first one and then the other. And after that we'd see.

Elizabeth. You damned brute!

Teddie. I've often thought I wasn't quite a gentleman. Had it ever struck you?

[*They look at one another for a while.*]

Elizabeth. You know, you are taking an unfair advantage of me. I feel as if I came to you quite unsuspectingly and when I wasn't looking you kicked me on the shins.

Teddie. Don't you think we'd get on rather well together?

Porteous. Elizabeth's a fool if she don't stick to her husband. It's bad enough for the man, but for the woman—it's damnable. I hold no brief for Arnold. He plays bridge like a foot. Saving your presence, Kitty, I think he's a prig.

Lady Kitty. Poor dear, his father was at his age. I daresay he'll grow out of it.

Porteous. But you stick to him, Elizabeth, stick to him. Man is a gregarious animal. We're members of a herd. If we break the herd's laws we suffer for it. And we suffer damnably.

Lady Kitty. Oh, Elizabeth, my dear child, don't go. It's not worth it. It's not worth it. I tell you that, and I've sacrificed everything to love. [*A pause.*]

Elizabeth. I'm afraid.

Teddie. [*In a whisper.*] Elizabeth.

Elizabeth. I can't face it. It's asking too much of me. Let's say good-by to one another, Teddie. It's the only thing to do. And have pity on me. I'm giving up all my hope of happiness.

[*He goes up to her and looks into her eyes.*]

Teddie. But I wasn't offering you happiness. I don't think my sort of love tends to happiness. I'm jealous. I'm not a very easy man to get on with. I'm often out of temper and irritable. I should be fed to the teeth with you sometimes, and so would you be with me. I daresay we'd fight like cat and dog, and sometimes we'd hate each other. Often you'd be wretched and bored stiff and lonely, and often you'd be frightfully homesick, and then you'd regret all you'd lost. Stupid women would be rude to you because we'd run away together. And some of them would cut you. I don't offer you peace and quietness. I offer you unrest and anxiety. I don't offer you happiness. I offer you love.

Elizabeth. [*Stretching out her arms.*] You hateful creature, I absolutely adore you!

[*He throws his arms round her and kisses her passionately on the lips.*]

Lady Kitty. Of course the moment he said he'd give her a black eye I knew it was finished.

Porteous. [*Good-humoredly.*] You are a fool, Kitty.

Lady Kitty. I know I am, but I can't help it.

Teddie. Let's make a bolt for it now.

Elizabeth. Shall we?

Teddie. This minute.

Porteous. You're damned fools, both of you, damned fools! If you like you can have my car.

Teddie. That's awfully kind of you. As a matter of fact I got it out of the garage. It's just along the drive.

Porteous. [*Indignantly.*] How do you mean, you got it out of the garage?

Teddie. Well, I thought there'd be a lot of bother, and it seemed to me the best thing would be for Elizabeth and me not to stand upon the order of our going, you know. Do it now. An excellent motto for a business man.

Porteous. Do you mean to say you were going to steal my car?

Teddie. Not exactly. I was only going to bolshevize it, so to speak.

Porteous. I'm speechless. I'm absolutely speechless.

Teddie. Hang it all, I couldn't carry Elizabeth all the way to London. She's so damned plump.

Elizabeth. You dirty dog!

Porteous. [*Spluttering.*] Well, well, well! . . . [*Helplessly.*] I like him, Kitty, it's no good pretending I don't. I like him.

Teddie. The moon's shining, Elizabeth. We'll drive all through the night.

Porteous. They'd better go to San Michele. I'll wire to have it got ready for them.

Lady Kitty. That's where we went when Hughie and I . . . [*Faltering.*] Oh, you dear things, how I envy you!

Porteous. [*Mopping his eyes.*] Now don't cry, Kitty. Confound you, don't cry.

Teddie. Come, darling.

Elizabeth. But I can't go like this.

Teddie. Nonsense! Lady Kitty will lend you her cloak. Won't you?

Lady Kitty. [*Taking it off.*] You're capable of tearing it off my back if I don't.

Teddie. [*Putting the cloak on* ELIZABETH.] And we'll buy you a tooth-brush in London in the morning.

Lady Kitty. She must write a note for Arnold. I'll put it on her pin-cushion.

Teddie. Pin-cushion be blowed! Come, darling. We'll drive through the dawn and through the sunrise.

Elizabeth. [*Kissing* LADY KITTY *and* PORTEOUS.] Good-by. Good-by.

[TEDDIE *stretches out his hand and she takes it. Hand in hand they go out into the night.*]

Lady Kitty. Oh, Hughie, how it all comes back to me! Will they suffer all we suffered? And have we suffered all in vain?

Porteous. My dear, I don't know that in life it matters so much what you do as what you are. No one can learn by the experience of another because no circumstances are quite the same. If we made rather a hash of things perhaps it was because we were rather trivial people. You can do anything in this world if you're prepared to take the consequences. and consequences depend on character.

[*Enter* CHAMPION-CHENEY, *rubbing his hands. He is as pleased as Punch.*]

C.-C. Well, I think I've settled the hash of that young man.

Lady Kitty. Oh!

C.-C. You have to get up very early in the morning to get the better of your humble servant.

[*There is the sound of a car starting.*]

Lady Kitty. What is that?

C.-C. It sounds like a car. I expect it's your chauffeur taking one of the maids for a joy-ride.

Porteous. Whose hash are you talking about?

C.-C. Mr. Edward Luton's, my dear Hughie. I told Arnold exactly what to do and he's done it. What makes a prison? Why, bars and bolts. Remove them and a prisoner won't want to escape. Clever, I flatter myself.

Porteous. You were always that, Clive, but at the moment you're obscure.

C.-C. I told Arnold to go to Elizabeth and tell her she could have her freedom. I told him to sacrifice himself all along the line. I know what women are. The moment every obstacle was removed to her marriage with Teddie Luton, half the allurement was gone.

Lady Kitty. Arnold did that?

C.-C. He followed my instructions to the letter. I've just seen him. She's shaken. I'm willing to bet five hundred pounds to a penny that she won't bolt. A downy old bird, eh? Downy's the word. Downy.

[*He begins to laugh. They laugh, too. Presently they are all three in fits of laughter.*]

CURTAIN

LOYALTIES *

By

JOHN GALSWORTHY

It is difficult not to believe that the World War was one of the tensions that created *Loyalties*. Galsworthy had allegorized that agitating event in *The Skin Game* (1920), in which a family of quality is forced to debase its ideals and sacrifice its self-respect in a struggle with a pushing outsider. But *Loyalties* describes the somewhat more complex and subtle consequences of social dissension. Its "spire of meaning" probably is embodied in Margaret's speech at the end of the play: "Keeps faith! We've all done that. It's not enough"; and Galsworthy must have known that Margaret was echoing Edith Cavell's "Patriotism is not enough. I must have no hatred in my heart for anyone." The selection of a Jew for one of the principal protagonists is perhaps another delicate reflection of Galsworthy's sensitiveness to his times, for anti-Semitism was particularly vocal when the play was written.

That so perfect an illustration of Galsworthy's dramatic theories as *Loyalties* is should have been also his most complete success must have been gratifying. The plot surely "rises out of the interplay of circumstance on temperament, and temperament on circumstance, within the enclosing atmosphere of an idea." It exhibits "the phenomena of life and character, selected and combined, *but not distorted,* by the dramatist's outlook, set down without fear, favor, or prejudice." And its characters "live their own lives." As if in justification of the theories, *Loyalties* ran for over 400 performances in England on its first production and was revived there in 1928. It was produced in America in the fall of 1922 following the English production, with an imported company, and ran for 220 performances in New York, afterwards going on tour. It has also been played successfully in many other parts of the world.

For a fuller discussion of Galsworthy's dramatic theories, see the note prefacing *Justice.*

For biographical data and play list see *Justice,* p. 645 ff.

LOYALTIES

Persons of the Play

In the Order of Appearance

CHARLES WINSOR, *owner of Meldon Court, near Newmarket.*
LADY ADELA, *his wife.*
FERDINAND DE LEVIS, *young, rich, and new.*
TREISURE, *Winsor's butler.*
GENERAL CANYNGE, *a racing oracle.*
MARGARET ORME, *a society girl.*
CAPTAIN RONALD DANCY, D.S.O., *retired.*
MABEL, *his wife.*
INSPECTOR DEDE, *of the county constabulary.*
ROBERT, *Winsor's footman.*
A CONSTABLE, *attendant on Dede.*
AUGUSTUS BORRING, *a clubman.*
LORD ST. ERTH, *peer of the realm.*
A FOOTMAN, *of the club.*
MAJOR COLFORD, *a brother officer of Dancy's.*
EDWARD GRAVITER, *a solicitor.*
A YOUNG CLERK, *of Twisden & Graviter's.*
GILMAN, *a large grocer.*
JACOB TWISDEN, *senior partner of Twisden & Graviter's.*
RICARDOS, *an Italian, in wine.*

ACT I

SCENE I

The dressing-room of CHARLES WINSOR, *owner of Meldon Court, near Newmarket; about eleven-thirty at night. The room has pale gray walls, unadorned; the curtains are drawn over a window Back Left Center. A bed lies along the wall, Left. An open door, Right Back, leads into* LADY ADELA'S *bedroom; a door, Right Forward, into a long corridor, on to which abut rooms in a row, the whole length of the house's left wing.* WINSOR'S *dressing-table, with a light over it, is Stage Right of the curtained window. Pajamas are laid out on the bed, which is turned back. Slippers are handy, and all the usual gear of a well-appointed bed-dressing-room.*

[CHARLES WINSOR, *a tall, fair, good-looking man about thirty-eight, is taking off a smoking jacket.*]

Winsor. Hallo! Adela!

Voice of Lady A. [*From her bedroom.*] Hallo!

Winsor. In bed?

Voice of Lady A. No.

[*She appears in the doorway in undergarment and a wrapper. She, too, is fair, about thirty-five, rather delicious, and suggestive of porcelain.*]

Winsor. Win at bridge?

Lady A. No fear.

Winsor. Who did?

Lady A. Lord St. Erth and Ferdy De Levis.

Winsor. That young man has too much luck—the young bounder won two races today; and he's as rich as Crœsus.

Lady A. Oh! Charlie, he did look so exactly as if he'd sold me a carpet when I was paying him.

Winsor. [*Changing into slippers.*] His father did sell carpets, wholesale, in the City.

Lady A. Really? And you say I haven't intuition! [*With a finger on her lips.*] Morison's in there.

Winsor. [*Motioning toward the door, which she shuts.*] Ronny Dancy took a tenner off him, anyway, before dinner.

Lady A. No! How?

Winsor. Standing jump on to a bookcase four feet high. De Levis had to pay up, and sneered at him for making money by parlor tricks. That young Jew gets himself disliked.

Lady A. Aren't you rather prejudiced?

Winsor. Not a bit. I like Jews. That's not against him—rather the contrary these days. But he pushes himself. The General tells me he's deathly keen to get into the Jockey Club. [*Taking off his tie.*] It's amusing to see him trying to get round old St. Erth.

Lady A. If Lord St. Erth and General Canynge backed him he'd get in if he *did* sell carpets!

Winsor. He's got some pretty good horses. [*Taking off his waistcoat.*] Ronny Dancy's on his bones again, I'm afraid. He had a bad day. When a chap takes to doing parlor stunts for a bet—it's a sure sign. What made him chuck the Army?

Lady A. He says it's too dull, now there's no fighting.

Winsor. Well, he can't exist on backing losers.

Lady A. Isn't it just like him to get married now? He really is the most reckless person.

Winsor. Yes. He's a queer chap. I've always liked him, but I've never quite made him out. What do you think of his wife?

Lady A. Nice child; awfully gone on him.

Winsor. Is *he*?

Lady A. Quite indecently—both of them. [*Nodding toward the wall, Left.*] They're next door.

Winsor. Who's beyond them?

Lady A. De Levis; and Margaret Orme at the end. Charlie, do you realize that the bathroom out there has to wash those four?

Winsor. I know.

Lady A. Your grandfather was crazy when he built this wing; six rooms in a row with balconies like an hotel, and only one bath—if we hadn't put ours in.

Winsor. [*Looking at his watch.*] Half-past eleven. [*Yawns.*] Newmarket always makes me sleepy. You're keeping Morison up. [LADY ADELA *goes to the door, blowing a kiss.* CHARLES *goes up to his dressing-table and begins to brush his hair, sprinkling on essence. There is a knock on the corridor door.*] Come in. [DE LEVIS *enters, clad in pajamas and flowered dressing-gown. He is a dark, good-looking, rather Eastern young man. His face is long and disturbed.*] Hallo! De Levis! Anything I can do for you?

De Levis. [*In a voice whose faint exoticism is broken by a vexed excitement.*] I say, I'm awfully sorry, Winsor, but I thought I'd better tell you at once. I've just had—er—rather a lot of money stolen.

Winsor. What! [*There is something of outrage in his tone and glance, as who should say: "In* my *house?"*] How do you mean *stolen*?

De Levis. I put it under my pillow and went to have a bath; when I came back it was gone.

Winsor. Good Lord! How much?

De Levis. Nearly a thousand—nine hundred and seventy, I think.

Winsor. Phew!

[*Again the faint tone of outrage, that a man should have so much money about him.*]

De Levis. I sold my Rosemary filly to-day on the course to Kentman the bookie, and he paid me in notes.

Winsor. What? That weed Dancy gave you in the Spring?

De Levis. Yes. I tried her pretty high the other day; and she's in the Cambridgeshire. I was only out of my room a quarter of an hour, and I locked my door.

Winsor. [*Again outraged.*] You locked——

De Levis. [*Not seeing the fine shade.*] Yes, and had the key here. [*He taps his pocket.*] Look here! [*He holds out a pocket-book.*] It's been stuffed with my shaving papers.

Winsor. [*Between feeling that such things don't happen, and a sense that he will have to clear it up.*] This is damned awkward, De Levis.

De Levis. [*With steel in his voice.*] Yes. I should like it back.

Winsor. Have you got the numbers of the notes?

De Levis. No.

Winsor. What were they?

De Levis. One hundred, three fifties, and the rest tens and fives.

Winsor. What d'you want me to do?

De Levis. Unless there's anybody you think——

Winsor. [*Eyeing him.*] Is it likely?

De Levis. Then I think the police ought to see my room. It's a lot of money.

Winsor. Good Lord! We're not in Town; there'll be nobody nearer than Newmarket at this time of night—four miles.

[*The door from the bedroom is suddenly opened and* LADY ADELA *appears. She has on a lace cap over her finished hair, and the wrapper.*]

Lady A. [*Closing the door.*] What is it? Are you ill, Mr. De Levis?

Winsor. Worse; he's had a lot of money stolen. Nearly a thousand pounds.

Lady A. Gracious! Where?

De Levis. From under my pillow, Lady Adela—my door was locked—I was in the bathroom.

Lady A. But how fearfully thrilling!

Winsor. Thrilling! What's to be done? He wants it back.

Lady A. Of course! [*With sudden realization.*] Oh! But—— Oh! It's quite too unpleasant.

Winsor. Yes! What am I to do? Fetch

the servants out of their rooms? Search the grounds? It'll make the devil of a scandal.

De Levis. Who's next to me?

Lady A. [*Coldly.*] Oh! Mr. De Levis!

Winsor. Next to you? The Dancys on this side, and Miss Orme on the other. What's that to do with it?

De Levis. They may have heard something.

Winsor. Let's get them. But Dancy was downstairs when I came up. Get Morison, Adela! No, look here! When *was* this exactly? Let's have as many alibis as we can.

De Levis. Within the last twenty minutes, certainly.

Winsor. How long has Morison been up with you?

Lady A. I came up at eleven, and rang for her at once.

Winsor. [*Looking at his watch.*] Half an hour. Then she's all right. Send her for Margaret and the Dancys—there's nobody else in this wing. No; send her to bed. We don't want gossip. D'you mind going yourself, Adela?

Lady A. Consult General Canynge, Charlie.

Winsor. Right. Could you get him too? D'you really want the police, De Levis?

De Levis. [*Stung by the faint contempt in his tone of voice.*] Yes, I do.

Winsor. Then, look here, dear! Slip into my study and telephone to the police at Newmarket. There'll be somebody there; they're sure to have drunks. I'll have Treisure up, and speak to him.

[*He rings the bell.*]

[LADY ADELA *goes out into her room and closes the door.*]

Winsor. Look here, De Levis! This isn't an hotel. It's the sort of thing that doesn't happen in a decent house. Are you sure you're not mistaken, and didn't have them stolen on the course?

De Levis. Absolutely. I counted them just before putting them under my pillow; then I locked the door and had the key here. There's only one door, you know.

Winsor. How was your window?

De Levis. Open.

Winsor. [*Drawing back the curtains of his own window.*] You've got a balcony like this. Any sign of a ladder or anything?

De Levis. No.

Winsor. It must have been done from the window, unless some one had a skeleton key. Who knew you'd got that money? Where did Kentman pay you?

De Levis. Just round the corner in the further paddock.

Winsor. Anybody about?

De Levis. Oh, yes!

Winsor. Suspicious?

De Levis. I didn't notice anything.

Winsor. You must have been marked down and followed here.

De Levis. How would they know my room?

Winsor. Might have got it somehow. [*A knock from the corridor.*] Come in.

[TREISURE, *the Butler, appears, a silent, grave man of almost supernatural conformity.* DE LEVIS *gives him a quick, hard look, noted and resented by* WINSOR.]

Treisure. [*To* WINSOR.] Yes, sir?

Winsor. Who valets Mr. De Levis?

Treisure. Robert, sir.

Winsor. When was he up last?

Treisure. In the ordinary course of things, about ten o'clock, sir.

Winsor. When did he go to bed?

Treisure. I dismissed at eleven.

Winsor. But did he go?

Treisure. To the best of my knowledge. Is there anything *I* can do, sir?

Winsor. [*Disregarding a sign from* DE LEVIS.] Look here, Treisure, Mr. De Levis has had a large sum of money taken from his bedroom within the last half hour.

Treisure. Indeed, sir!

Winsor. Robert's quite all right, isn't he?

Treisure. He is, sir.

De Levis. How do you know?

[TREISURE'S *eyes rest on* DE LEVIS.]

Treisure. I am a pretty good judge of character, sir, if you'll excuse me.

Winsor. Look here, De Levis, eighty or ninety notes must have been pretty bulky. You didn't have them on you at dinner?

De Levis. No.

Winsor. Where did you put them?

De Levis. In a boot, and the boot in my suitcase, and locked it.

[TREISURE *smiles faintly.*]

Winsor. [*Again slightly outraged by such precautions in his house.*] And you found it locked—and took them from there to put under your pillow?

De Levis. Yes.

Winsor. Run your mind over things, Treisure—has any stranger been about?

Treisure. No, sir.

Winsor. This seems to have happened between 11.15 and 11.30. Is that right? [DE LEVIS *nods.*] Any noise—anything outside—anything suspicious anywhere?

Treisure. [*Running his mind—very still.*] No, sir.

Winsor. What time did you shut up?

Treisure. I should say about 11.15, sir. As soon as Major Colford and Captain Dancy had finished billiards. What was Mr. De Levis doing out of his room, if I may ask, sir?

Winsor. Having a bath; with his room locked and the key in his pocket.

Treisure. Thank you, sir.

De Levis. [*Conscious of indefinable suspicion.*] Damn it! What do you mean? I *was.*

Treisure. I beg your pardon, sir.

Winsor. [*Concealing a smile.*] Look here, Treisure, it's infernally awkward for everybody.

Treisure. It is, sir.

Winsor. What do you suggest?

Treisure. The proper thing, sir, I suppose, would be a cordon and a complete search—in our interests.

Winsor. I entirely refuse to suspect anybody.

Treisure. But if Mr. De Levis feels otherwise, sir?

De Levis. [*Stammering.*] I? All I know is— the money was there, and it's gone.

Winsor. [*Compunctious.*] Quite! It's pretty sickening for you. But so it is for anybody else. However, we must do our best to get it back for you.

[*A knock on the door.*]

Winsor. Hallo! [TREISURE *opens the door, and* GENERAL CANYNGE *enters.*] Oh! It's you, General. Come in. Adela's told you?

[GENERAL CANYNGE *nods. He is a slim man of about sixty, very well preserved, intensely neat and self-contained, and still in evening dress. His eyelids droop slightly, but his eyes are keen and his expression astute.*]

Winsor. Well, General, what's the first move?

Canynge. [*Lifting his eyebrows.*] Mr. De Levis presses the matter?

De Levis. [*Flicked again.*] Unless you think it's too plebeian of me, General Canynge—a thousand pounds.

Canynge. [*Drily.*] Just so! Then we must wait for the police, Winsor. Lady Adela has got through to them. What height are these rooms from the ground, Treisure?

Treisure. Twenty-three feet from the terrace, sir.

Canynge. Any ladders near?

Treisure. One in the stables, sir, very heavy. No others within three hundred yards.

Canynge. Just slip down, and see whether that's been moved.

Treisure. Very good, General.

[*He goes out.*]

De Levis. [*Uneasily.*] Of course, he—I suppose you——

Winsor. We do.

Canynge. You had better leave this in our hands, De Levis.

De Levis. Certainly; only, the way he ——

Winsor. [*Curtly.*] Treisure has been here since he was a boy. I should as soon suspect myself.

De Levis. [*Looking from one to the other —with sudden anger.*] You seem to think ——! What was I to do? Take it lying down and let whoever it is get clear off? I suppose it's natural to want my money back?

[CANYNGE *looks at his nails;* WINSOR *out of the window.*]

Winsor. [*Turning.*] Of course, De Levis!

De Levis. [*Sullenly.*] Well, I'll go to my room. When the police come, perhaps you'll let me know. [*He goes out.*]

Winsor. Phew! Did you ever see such a dressing-gown?

[*The door is opened.* LADY ADELA *and* MARGARET ORME *come in. The latter is a vivid young lady of about twenty-five in a vivid wrapper; she is smoking a cigarette.*]

Lady A. I've told the Dancys—she was in bed. And I got through to Newmarket, Charles, and Inspector Dede is coming like the wind on a motorcycle.

Margaret. Did he say "like the wind," Adela? He must have imagination. Isn't this gorgeous? Poor little Ferdy!

Winsor. [*Vexed.*] You might take it seriously, Margaret; it's pretty beastly for us all. What time did *you* come up?

Margaret. I came up with Adela. Am I suspected, Charles? How thrilling!

Winsor. Did you hear anything?

Margaret. Only little Ferdy splashing.

Winsor. And saw nothing?

Margaret. Not even that, alas!

Lady A. [*With a finger held up.*] *Leste! Un peu leste!* Oh! Here are the Dancys. Come in, you two!

[MABEL *and* RONALD DANCY *enter. She is a pretty young woman with bobbed hair, fortunately, for she has just got out of bed, and is in her nightgown and a wrapper.* DANCY *is in his smoking jacket. He has a pale, determined face with high cheekbones, small, deep-set dark eyes, reddish crisp hair, and looks like a horseman.*]

Winsor. Awfully sorry to disturb you, Mrs. Dancy; but I suppose you and Ronny haven't heard anything. De Levis's room is just beyond Ronny's dressing-room, you know.

Mabel. I've been asleep nearly half an hour, and Ronny's only just come up.

Canynge. Did you happen to look out of your window, Mrs. Dancy?

Mabel. Yes. I stood there quite five minutes.

Canynge. When?

Mabel. Just about eleven, I should think. It was raining hard then.

Canynge. Yes, it's just stopped. You saw nothing?

Mabel. No.

Dancy. What time does he say the money was taken?

Winsor. Between the quarter and half past. He'd locked his door and had the key with him.

Margaret. How quaint! Just like an hotel. Does he put his boots out?

Lady A. Don't be so naughty, Meg.

Canynge. When exactly did *you* come up, Dancy?

Dancy. About ten minutes ago. I'd only just got into my dressing-room before Lady Adela came. I've been writing letters in the hall since Colford and I finished billiards.

Canynge. You weren't up for anything in between?

Dancy. No.

Margaret. The mystery of the gray room.

Dancy. Oughtn't the grounds to be searched for footmarks?

Canynge. That's for the police.

Dancy. The deuce! Are they coming?

Canynge. Directly. [*A knock.*] Yes? [TREISURE *enters.*] Well?

Treisure. The ladder has not been moved, General. There isn't a sign.

Winsor. All right. Get Robert up, but don't say anything to him. By the way, we're expecting the police.

Treisure. I trust they will not find a mare's nest, sir, if I may say so. [*He goes.*]

Winsor. De Levis has got wrong with Treisure. [*Suddenly.*] But, I say, what would any of us have done if *we'd* been in his shoes?

Margaret. A thousand pounds? I can't even conceive having it.

Dancy. We probably shouldn't have found it out.

Lady A. No—but if we had.

Dancy. Come to you—as he did.

Winsor. Yes; but there's a way of doing things.

Canynge. We shouldn't have wanted the police.

Margaret. No. That's it. The hotel touch.

Lady A. Poor young man; I think we're rather hard on him.

Winsor. He sold that weed you gave him, Dancy, to Kentman, the bookie, and these were the proceeds.

Dancy. Oh!

Winsor. He'd tried her high, he said.

Dancy. [*Grimly.*] He would.

Mabel. Oh! Ronny, what bad luck!

Winsor. He must have been followed here. [*At the window.*] After rain like that, there ought to be footmarks.

[*The splutter of a motorcycle is heard.*]

Margaret. Here's the wind!

Winsor. What's the move now, General?

Canynge. You and I had better see the Inspector in De Levis's room, Winsor. [*To the others.*] If you'll all be handy, in case he wants to put questions for himself.

Margaret. I hope he'll want me; it's just too thrilling.

Dancy. I hope he won't want me; I'm dog-tired! Come on, Mabel.

[*He puts his arm in his wife's.*]

Canynge. Just a minute, Charles.

[*He draws close to* WINSOR *as the others are departing to their rooms.*]

Winsor. Yes, General?

Canynge. We must be careful with this Inspector fellow. If he pitches hastily on somebody in the house it'll be very disagreeable.

Winsor. By Jove! It *will.*

Canynge. We don't want to rouse any ridiculous suspicion.

Winsor. Quite. [*A knock.*] Come in!

[TREISURE *enters.*]

Treisure. Inspector Dede, sir.

Winsor. Show him in.

Treisure. Robert is in readiness, sir; but I could swear he knows nothing about it.

Winsor. All right.

[TREISURE *reopens the door, and says: "Come in, please." The* INSPECTOR *enters, blue, formal, mustachioed, with a peaked cap in his hand.*]

Winsor. Good-evening, Inspector. Sorry to have brought you out at this time of night.

Inspector. Good evenin', sir. Mr. Winsor? You're the owner here, I think?

Winsor. Yes. General Canynge.

Inspector. Good evenin', General. I understand, a large sum of money?

Winsor. Yes. Shall we go straight to the room it was taken from? One of my guests, Mr. De Levis. It's the third room on the left.

Canynge. We've not been in there yet

Inspector; in fact, we've done nothing, except to find out that the stable ladder has not been moved. We haven't even searched the grounds.

Inspector. Right, sir; I've brought a man with me. [*They go out.*]

CURTAIN

Interval of a Minute.

SCENE II*

The bedroom of DE LEVIS *is the same in shape as* WINSOR'S *dressing-room, except that there is only one door—to the corridor. The furniture, however, is differently arranged; a small four-poster bedstead stands against the wall, Right Back, jutting into the room. A chair, on which* DE LEVIS'S *clothes are thrown, stands at its foot. There is a dressing-table against the wall to the left of the open windows, where the curtains are drawn back and a stone balcony is seen. Against the wall to the right of the window is a chest of drawers, and a washstand is against the wall, Left. On a small table to the right of the bed an electric reading lamp is turned up, and there is a light over the dressing-table.* [*The* INSPECTOR *is standing plumb center looking at the bed, and* DE LEVIS *by the back of the chair at the foot of the bed.* WINSOR *and* CANYNGE *are close to the door, Right Forward.*]

Inspector. [*Finishing a note.*] Now, sir, if this is the room as you left it for your bath, just show us exactly what you did after takin' the pocket-book from the suit case. Where was that, by the way?

De Levis. [*Pointing.*] Where it is now—under the dressing-table.

[*He comes forward to the front of the chair, opens the pocket-book, goes through the pretence of counting his shaving papers, closes the pocket-book, takes it to the head of the bed and slips it under the pillow. Makes the motion of taking up his pajamas, crosses below the* INSPECTOR *to the washstand, takes up a bath sponge, crosses to the door, takes out the key, opens the door.*]

Inspector. [*Writing.*] We now have the room as it was when the theft was committed. Reconstruct accordin' to 'uman nature, gentlemen—assumin' the thief to be in the room, what would he try first?—the clothes, the dressin'-table, the suit case, the chest of drawers, and last the bed.

[*He moves accordingly, examining the glass on the dressing-table, the surface of the suit cases, and the handles of the drawers, with a spyglass, for finger-marks.*]

Canynge. [*Sotto voce to* WINSOR.] The order would have been just the other way.

[*The* INSPECTOR *goes on hands and knees and examines the carpet between the window and the bed.*]

De Levis. Can I come in again?

Inspector. [*Standing up.*] Did you open the window, sir, or was it open when you first came in?

De Levis. I opened it.

Inspector. Drawin' the curtains back first?

De Levis. Yes.

Inspector. [*Sharply.*] Are you sure there was nobody in the room already?

De Levis. [*Taken aback.*] I don't know. I never thought. I didn't look under the bed, if you mean that.

Inspector. [*Jotting.*] Did not look under bed. Did you look under it after the theft?

De Levis. No. I didn't.

Inspector. Ah! Now, what *did* you do after you came back from your bath? Just give us that precisely.

De Levis. Locked the door and left the key in. Put back my sponge, and took off my dressing-gown and put it there. [*He points to the footrails of the bed.*] Then I drew the curtains, again.

Inspector. Shutting the window?

De Levis. No. I got into bed, felt for my watch to see the time. My hand struck the pocket-book, and somehow it felt thinner. I took it out, looked into it, and found the notes gone, and these shaving papers instead.

Inspector. Let me have a look at those, sir. [*He applies the spy-glasses.*] And then?

De Levis. I think I just sat on the bed.

Inspector. Thinkin' and cursin' a bit, I suppose. Ye-es?

De Levis. Then I put on my dressing-gown and went straight to Mr. Winsor.

Inspector. Not lockin' the door?

De Levis. No.

Inspector. Exactly. [*With a certain finality.*] Now, sir, what time did you come up?

De Levis. About eleven.

Inspector. Precise, if you can give it me.

* The same set is used for this scene, with the different arrangement of furniture, as specified.

De Levis. Well, I *know* it was eleven-fifteen when I put my watch under my pillow, before I went to the bath, and I suppose I'd been about a quarter of an hour undressing. I should say after eleven, if anything.

Inspector. Just undressin'? Didn't look over your bettin' book?

De Levis. No.

Inspector. No prayers or anything?

De Levis. No.

Inspector. Pretty slippy with your undressin' as a rule?

De Levis. Yes. Say five past eleven.

Inspector. Mr. Winsor, what time did the gentleman come to you?

Winsor. Half-past eleven.

Inspector. How do you fix that, sir?

Winsor. I'd just looked at the time, and told my wife to send her maid off.

Inspector. Then we've got it fixed between 11.15 and 11.30. [*Jots.*] Now, sir, before we go further I'd like to see your butler and the footman that valets this gentleman.

Winsor. [*With distaste.*] Very well, Inspector; only—my butler has been with us from a boy.

Inspector. Quite so. This is just clearing the ground, sir.

Winsor. General, d'you mind touching that bell?

[CANYNGE *rings a bell by the bed.*]

Inspector. Well, gentlemen, there are four possibilities. Either the thief was here all the time, waiting under the bed, and slipped out after this gentleman had gone to Mr. Winsor. Or he came in with a key that fits the lock; and I'll want to see all the keys in the house. Or he came in with a skeleton key and out by the window, probably droppin' from the balcony. Or he came in by the window with a rope or ladder and out the same way. [*Pointing.*] There's a footmark here from a big boot which has been out of doors since it rained.

Canynge. Inspector—you er—walked up to the window when you first came into the room.

Inspector. [*Stiffly.*] I had not overlooked that, General.

Canynge. Of course.

[*A knock on the door relieves a certain tension.*]

Winsor. Come in.

[*The footman* ROBERT, *a fresh-faced young man, enters, followed by* TREISURE.]

Inspector. You valet Mr.—Mr. De Levis, I think?

Robert. Yes, sir.

Inspector. At what time did you take his clothes and boots?

Robert. Ten o'clock, sir.

Inspector. [*With a pounce.*] Did you happen to look under his bed?

Robert. No, sir.

Inspector. Did you come up again, to bring the clothes back?

Robert. No, sir; they're still downstairs.

Inspector. Did you come up again for anything?

Robert. No, sir.

Inspector. What time did you go to bed?

Robert. Just after eleven, sir.

Inspector. [*Scrutinizing him.*] Now, be careful. Did you go to bed at all?

Robert. No, sir.

Inspector. Then why did you say you did? There's been a theft here, and anything you say may be used against you.

Robert. Yes, sir. I meant, I went to my room.

Inspector. Where is your room?

Robert. On the ground floor, at the other end of the right wing, sir.

Winsor. It's the extreme end of the house from this, Inspector. He's with the other two footmen.

Inspector. Were you there alone?

Robert. No, sir. Thomas and Frederick was there too.

Treisure. That's right; I've seen them.

Inspector. [*Holding up his hand for silence.*] Were you out of the room again after you went in?

Robert. No, sir.

Inspector. What were you doing, if you didn't go to bed?

Robert. [*To* WINSOR.] Beggin' your pardon, sir, we were playin' bridge.

Inspector. Very good. You can go. I'll see *them* later on.

Robert. Yes, sir. They'll say the same as me.

[*He goes out, leaving a smile on the face of all except the* INSPECTOR *and* DE LEVIS.]

Inspector. [*Sharply.*] Call him back.

[TREISURE *calls "Robert," and the* FOOTMAN *re-enters.*]

Robert. Yes, sir?

Inspector. Did you notice anything particular about Mr. De Levis's clothes?

Robert. Only that they were very good, sir.

Inspector. I mean—anything peculiar?

Robert. [*After reflection.*] Yes, sir.

Inspector. Well?

Robert. A pair of his boots this evenin' was reduced to one, sir.

Inspector. What did you make of that?

Robert. I thought he might have thrown the other at a cat or something.

Inspector. Did you look for it?

Robert. No, sir; I meant to draw his attention to it in the morning.

Inspector. Very good.

Robert. Yes, sir. [*He goes again.*]

Inspector. [*Looking at* DE LEVIS.] Well, sir, there's *your* story corroborated.

De Levis. [*Stiffly.*] I don't know why it should need corroboration, Inspector.

Inspector. In my experience, you can never have too much of that. [*To* WINSOR.] I understand there's a lady in the room on this side [*pointing Left*] and a gentleman on this side [*pointing Right*]. Were they in their rooms?

Winsor. Miss Orme was; Captain Dancy not.

Inspector. Do they know of the affair?

Winsor. Yes.

Inspector. Well, I'd just like the keys of their doors for a minute. My man will get them.

[*He goes to the door, opens it, and speaks to a constable in the corridor.*]

[*To* TREISURE.] You can go with him.

[TREISURE *goes out.*]

In the meantime I'll just examine the balcony.

[*He goes out on the balcony, followed by* DE LEVIS.]

Winsor. [*To* CANYNGE.] Damn De Levis and his money! It's deuced invidious, all this, General.

Canynge. The Inspector's no earthly.

[*There is a simultaneous re-entry of the* INSPECTOR *from the balcony and of* TREISURE *and the* CONSTABLE *from the corridor.*]

Constable. [*Handing key.*] Room on the left, sir. [*Handing key.*] Room on the right, sir.

[*The* INSPECTOR *tries the keys in the door, watched with tension by the others. The keys fail.*]

Inspector. Put them back. [*Hands keys to* CONSTABLE, *who goes out, followed by* TREISURE.] I'll have to try every key in the house, sir.

Winsor. Inspector, do you really think it necessary to disturb the whole house and knock up all my guests? It's most disagreeable, all this, you know. The loss of the money is not such a great matter. Mr. De Levis has a very large income.

Canynge. You could get the numbers of the notes from Kentman the bookmaker, Inspector; he'll probably have the big ones, anyway.

Inspector. [*Shaking his head.*] A bookie. I don't suppose he will, sir. It's come and go with them, all the time.

Winsor. We don't want a Meldon Court scandal, Inspector.

Inspector. Well, Mr. Winsor, I've formed my theory. [*As he speaks,* DE LEVIS *comes in from the balcony.*] And I don't say to try the keys is necessary to it; but strictly, I ought to exhaust the possibilities.

Winsor. What do you say, De Levis? D'you want everybody in the house knocked up so that their keys can be tried?

De Levis. [*Whose face, since his return, expresses a curious excitement.*] No, I don't.

Inspector. Very well, gentlemen. In my opinion the thief walked in before the door was locked, probably during dinner; and was under the bed. He escaped by dropping from the balcony—the creeper at that corner [*he points stage Left*] has been violently wrenched. I'll go down now, and examine the grounds, and I'll see you again, sir. [*He makes another entry in his note-book.*] Good-night, then, gentlemen!

Canynge. Good-night!

Winsor. [*With relief.*] I'll come with you, Inspector.

[*He escorts him to the door, and they go out.*]

De Levis. [*Suddenly.*] General, I know who took them.

Canynge. The deuce you do! Are you following the Inspector's theory?

De Levis. [*Contemptuously.*] That ass! [*Pulling the shaving papers out of the case.*] No! The man who put those there was clever and cool enough to wrench that creeper off the balcony as a blind. Come and look here, General. [*He goes to the window; the* GENERAL *follows.* DE LEVIS *points stage Right.*] See the rail of my balcony, and the rail of the next? [*He holds up the cord of his dressing-gown, stretching his arms out.*] I've measured it with this. Just over seven feet, that's all. If a man can take a standing jump on to a narrow bookcase four feet high and balance there, he'd make nothing of that. And, look here! [*He goes out on the balcony and returns with a bit of broken creeper in his hand, and holds it out into the light.*] Some one's stood on that—the stalk's crushed—the inner corner, too, where he'd naturally stand when he took his jump back.

Canynge. [*After examining it—stiffly.*] That other balcony is young Dancy's, Mr. De Levis; a soldier and a gentleman. This is an extraordinary insinuation.

De Levis. Accusation.

Canynge. What!

De Levis. I have intuitions, General; it's in my blood. I see the whole thing. Dancy came up, watched me into the bathroom, tried my door, slipped back into his dressing-room, saw my window was open, took that jump, sneaked the notes, filled the case up with these, wrenched the creeper there [*He points stage Left*] for a blind, jumped back, and slipped downstairs again. It didn't take him four minutes altogether.

Canynge. [*Very gravely.*] This is outrageous, De Levis. Dancy says he was downstairs all the time. You must either withdraw unreservedly, or I must confront you with him.

De Levis. If he'll return the notes and apologize, I'll do nothing—except cut him in future. He gave me that filly, you know, as a hopeless weed, and he's been pretty sick ever since, that he was such a flat as not to see how good she was. Besides, he's hard up, I know.

Canynge. [*After a vexed turn up and down the room.*] It's mad, sir, to jump to conclusions like this.

De Levis. Not so mad as the conclusion Dancy jumped to when he lighted on my balcony.

Canynge. Nobody could have taken this money who did not know you had it.

De Levis. How do you know that he didn't?

Canynge. Do you know that he did?

De Levis. I haven't the least doubt of it.

Canynge. Without any proof. This is very ugly, De Levis. I must tell Winsor.

De Levis. [*Angrily.*] Tell the whole blooming lot. You think I've no feelers, but I've felt the atmosphere here, I can tell you, General. If I were in Dancy's shoes and he in mine, your tone to me would be very different.

Canynge. [*Suavely frigid.*] I'm not aware of using any tone, as you call it. But this is a private house, Mr. De Levis, and something is due to our host and to the *esprit de corps* that exists among gentlemen.

De Levis. Since when is a thief a gentleman? Thick as thieves—a good motto, isn't it?

Canynge. That's enough! [*He goes to the door, but stops before opening it.*] Now, look here! I have some knowledge of the world. Once an accusation like this passes beyond these walls no one can foresee the consequences. Captain Dancy is a gallant fellow, with a fine record as a soldier; and only just married. If he's as innocent as—Christ—mud will stick to him, unless the real thief is found. In the old days of swords, either you or he would not have gone out of this room alive. If you persist in this absurd accusation, you will *both* of you go out of this room dead in the eyes of Society: you for bringing it, he for being the object of it.

De Levis. Society! Do you think I don't know that I'm only tolerated for my money? Society can't add injury to insult and have my money as well, that's all. If the notes are restored I'll keep my mouth shut; if they're not, I shan't. I'm certain I'm right. I ask nothing better than to be confronted with Dancy; but, if you prefer it, deal with him in your own way—for the sake of your *esprit de corps.*

Canynge. 'Pon my soul, Mr. De Levis, you go too far.

De Levis. Not so far as I shall go, General Canynge, if those notes aren't given back. [WINSOR *comes in.*]

Winsor. Well, De Levis, I'm afraid that's all we can do for the present. So very sorry this should have happened in my house.

Canynge. [*After a silence.*] There's a development, Winsor. Mr. De Levis accuses one of your guests.

Winsor. What?

Canynge. Of jumping from his balcony to this, taking the notes, and jumping back. I've done my best to dissuade him from indulging the fancy—without success. Dancy must be told.

De Levis. You can deal with Dancy in your own way. All I want is the money back.

Canynge. [*Drily.*] Mr. De Levis feels that he is only valued for his money, so that it is essential for him to have it back.

Winsor. Damn it! This is monstrous, De Levis. I've known Ronald Dancy since he was a boy.

Canynge. You talk about adding injury to insult, De Levis. What do you call such treatment of a man who gave you the mare out of which you made this thousand pounds?

De Levis. I didn't want the mare; I took her as a favor.

Canynge. With an eye to possibilities, I venture to think—the principle guides a good many transactions.

De Levis. [*As if flicked on a raw spot.*] In my race, do you mean?

Canynge. [*Coldly.*] I said nothing of the sort.

De Levis. No; you don't *say* these things, any of you.

Canynge. Nor did I think it.

De Levis. Dancy does.

Winsor. Really, De Levis, if this is the way you repay hospitality——

De Levis. Hospitality that skins my feelings and costs me a thousand pounds!

Canynge. Go and get Dancy, Winsor; but don't say anything to him.

[WINSOR *goes out.*]

Canynge. Perhaps you will kindly control yourself, and leave this to me.

[DE LEVIS *turns to the window and lights a cigarette.* WINSOR *comes back, followed by* DANCY.]

Canynge. For Winsor's sake, Dancy, we don't want any scandal or fuss about this affair. We've tried to make the police understand that. To my mind the whole thing turns on our finding who knew that De Levis had this money. It's about that we want to consult you.

Winsor. Kentman paid De Levis round the corner in the further paddock, he says.

[DE LEVIS *turns round from the window, so that he and* DANCY *are staring at each other.*]

Canynge. Did you hear anything that throws light, Dancy? As it was your filly originally, we thought perhaps you might.

Dancy. I? No.

Canynge. Didn't hear of the sale on the course at all?

Dancy. No.

Canynge. Then you can't suggest anyone who could have known? Nothing else was taken, you see.

Dancy. De Levis is known to be rolling, as I am known to be stony.

Canynge. There are a good many people still rolling, besides Mr. De Levis, but not many people with so large a sum in their pocket-books.

Dancy. He won two races.

De Levis. Do you suggest that I bet in ready money?

Dancy. I don't know how you bet, and I don't care.

Canynge. You can't help us, then?

Dancy. No, I can't. Anything else? [*He looks fixedly at* DE LEVIS.]

Canynge. [*Putting his hand on* DANCY'S *arm.*] Nothing else, thank you, Dancy.

[DANCY *goes.* CANYNGE *puts his hand up to his face. A moment's silence.*]

Winsor. You see, De Levis? He didn't even know you'd got the money.

De Levis. Very conclusive.

Winsor. Well! You *are*——!

[*There is a knock on the door, and the* INSPECTOR *enters.*]

Inspector. I'm just going, gentlemen. The grounds, I'm sorry to say, have yielded nothing. It's a bit of a puzzle.

Canynge. You've searched thoroughly?

Inspector. We have, General. I can pick up nothing near the terrace.

Winsor. [*After a look at* DE LEVIS, *whose face expresses too much.*] H'm! You'll take it up from the other end, then, Inspector?

Inspector. Well, we'll see what we can do with the bookmakers about the numbers, sir. Before I go, gentlemen—you've had time to think it over—there's no one you suspect in the house, I suppose?

[DE LEVIS'S *face is alive and uncertain.* CANYNGE *is staring at him very fixedly.*]

Winsor. [*Emphatically.*] No.

[DE LEVIS *turns and goes out on to the balcony.*]

Inspector. If you're coming in to the racing tomorrow, sir, you might give us a call. I'll have seen Kentman by then.

Winsor. Right you are, Inspector. Good-night, and many thanks.

Inspector. You're welcome, sir.

[*He goes out.*]

Winsor. Gosh! I thought that chap [*with a nod toward the balcony*] was going to ——! Look here, General, we *must* stop his tongue. Imagine it going the rounds. They may never find the real thief, you know. It's the very devil for Dancy.

Canynge. Winsor! Dancy's sleeve was damp.

Winsor. How d'you mean?

Canynge. Quite damp. It's been raining.

[*The two look at each other.*]

Winsor. I—I don't follow—— [*His voice is hesitative and lower, showing that he does.*]

Canynge. It was coming down hard; a minute out in it would have been enough —— [*He motions with his chin toward the balcony.*]

Winsor. [*Hastily.*] He must have been out on his balcony since.

Canynge. It stopped before I came up, half an hour ago.

Winsor. He's been leaning on the wet stone, then.

Canynge. With the outside of the *upper* part of the arm?

Winsor. Against the wall, perhaps. There may be a dozen explanations. [*Very low and with great concentration.*] I entirely and absolutely refuse to believe anything of the sort against Ronald Dancy—in my house. Dash it, General, we must do as we'd be done by. It hits us all—it hits us all. The thing's intolerable.

Canynge. I agree. Intolerable. [*Raising his voice.*] Mr. De Levis!

[DE LEVIS *returns into view, in the center of the open window.*]

Canynge. [*With cold decision.*] Young Dancy was an officer and is a gentleman; this insinuation is pure supposition, and you must not make it. Do you understand me?

De Levis. My tongue is still mine, General, if my money isn't!

Canynge. [*Unmoved.*] Must not. You're a member of three Clubs, you want to be member of a fourth. No one who makes such an insinuation against a fellow-guest in a country house, except on absolute proof, can do so without complete ostracism. Have we your word to say nothing?

De Levis. Social blackmail? H'm!

Canynge. Not at all—simple warning. If you consider it necessary in your interests to start this scandal—no matter how, we shall consider it necessary in ours to dissociate ourselves completely from one who so recklessly disregards the unwritten code.

De Levis. Do you think your code applies to me? Do you, General?

Canynge. To anyone who aspires to be a gentleman, sir.

De Levis. Ah! But you haven't known *me* since I was a boy.

Canynge. Make up your mind.

[*A pause.*]

De Levis. I'm not a fool, General. I know perfectly well that you can get me outed.

Canynge. [*Icily.*] Well?

De Levis. [*Sullenly.*] I'll say nothing about it, unless I get more proof.

Canynge. Good! We have implicit faith in Dancy.

[*There is a moment's encounter of eyes;* the GENERAL'S *steady, shrewd, impassive;* WINSOR'S *angry and defiant;* DE LEVIS'S *mocking, a little triumphant, malicious. Then* CANYNGE *and* WINSOR *go to the door, and pass out.*]

De Levis. [*To himself.*] Rats!

CURTAIN

ACT II

SCENE I

Afternoon, three weeks later, in the card room of a London Club. A fire is burning, Left. A door, Right, leads to the billiard-room.

[*Rather Left of Center, at a card table,* LORD ST. ERTH, *an old John Bull, sits facing the audience; to his right is* GENERAL CANYNGE, *to his left* AUGUSTUS BORRING, *an essential Clubman, about thirty-five years old, with a very slight and rather becoming stammer or click in his speech. The fourth bridge player,* CHARLES WINSOR, *stands with his back to the fire.*]

Borring. And the r-rub.

Winsor. By George! You do hold cards, Borring.

St. Erth. [*Who has lost.*] Not a patch on the old whist—this game. Don't know why I play it—never did.

Canynge. St. Erth, shall we raise the flag for whist again?

Winsor. No go, General. You can't go back on pace. No getting a man to walk when he knows he can fly. The young men won't look at it.

Borring. Better develop it so that t-two can sit out, General.

St. Erth. We ought to have stuck to the old game. Wish I'd gone to Newmarket, Canynge, in spite of the weather.

Canynge. [*Looking at his watch.*] Let's hear what's won the Cambridgeshire. Ring, won't you, Winsor? [WINSOR *rings.*]

St. Erth. By the way, Canynge, young De Levis was blackballed.

Canynge. What!

St. Erth. I looked in on my way down.

[CANYNGE *sits very still, and* WINSOR *utters a disturbed sound.*]

Borring. But of c-course he was, General. What did you expect?

[*A* FOOTMAN *enters.*]

Footman. Yes, my lord?

St. Erth. What won the Cambridgeshire?

Footman. Rosemary, my lord. Sherbet second; Barbizon third. Nine to one the winner.

Winsor. Thank you. That's all.

[FOOTMAN *goes.*]

Borring. Rosemary! And De Levis sold her! But he got a good p-price, I suppose.

[*The other three look at him.*]

St. Erth. Many a slip between price and pocket, young man.

Canynge. Cut! [*They cut.*]

Borring. I say, is that the yarn that's going about his having had a lot of m-money stolen in a country house? By Jove! He'll be pretty s-sick.

Winsor. You and I, Borring.

[*He sits down in* CANYNGE's *chair, and the* GENERAL *takes his place by the fire.*]

Borring. Phew! Won't Dancy be mad! He gave that filly away to save her keep. He was rather pleased to find somebody who'd take her. Kentman must have won a p-pot. She was at thirty-threes a fortnight ago.

St. Erth. All the money goes to fellows who don't know a horse from a haystack.

Canynge. [*Profoundly.*] And care less. Yes! We want men racing to whom a horse means something.

Borring. I thought the horse m-meant the same to every one, General—chance to get the b-better of one's neighbor.

Canynge. [*With feeling.*] The horse is a noble animal, sir, as you'd know if you'd owed your life to them as often as I have.

Borring. They always try to *take* mine, General. I shall never belong to the noble f-fellowship of the horse.

St. Erth. [*Drily.*] Evidently. Deal!

[*As* BORRING *begins to deal the door is opened and* MAJOR COLFORD *appears—a lean and moustached cavalryman.*]

Borring. Hallo, C-Colford.

Colford. General!

[*Something in the tone of his voice brings them all to a standstill.*]

Colford. I want your advice. Young De Levis in there [*He points to the billiard-room from which he has just come.*] has started a blasphemous story——

Canynge. One moment. Mr. Borring, d'you mind——

Colford. It makes no odds, General. Four of us in there heard him. He's saying it was Ronald Dancy robbed him down at Winsor's. The fellow's mad over losing the price of that filly now she's won the Cambridgeshire.

Borring. [*All ears.*] Dancy! Great S-Scott!

Colford. Dancy's in the Club. If he hadn't been I'd have taken it on myself to wring the bounder's neck.

[WINSOR *and* BORRING *have risen.* ST. ERTH *alone remains seated.*]

Canynge. [*After consulting* ST. ERTH *with a look.*] Ask De Levis to be good enough to come in here. Borring, you might see that Dancy doesn't leave the Club. We shall want him. Don't say anything to him, and use your tact to keep people off.

[BORRING *goes out, followed by* COLFORD.]

Winsor. Result of hearing he was black-balled—pretty slippy.

Canynge. St. Erth, I told you there was good reason when I asked you to back young De Levis. Winsor and I knew of this insinuation; I wanted to keep his tongue quiet. It's just wild assertion; to have it bandied about was unfair to Dancy. The duel used to keep people's tongues in order.

St. Erth. H'm! It never settled anything, except who could shoot straightest.

Colford. [*Reappearing.*] De Levis says he's nothing to add to what he said to you before on the subject.

Canynge. Kindly tell him that if he wishes to remain a member of this Club he must account to the Committee for such a charge against a fellow-member. Four of us are here, and form a quorum.

[COLFORD *goes out again.*]

St. Erth. Did Kentman ever give the police the numbers of those notes, Winsor?

Winsor. He only had the numbers of two—the hundred, and one of the fifties.

St. Erth. And they haven't traced 'em?

Winsor. Not yet.

[*As he speaks,* DE LEVIS *comes in. He is in a highly colored, not to say excited, state.* COLFORD *follows him.*]

De Levis. Well, General Canynge! It's a little too strong all this—a little too strong.

[*Under emotion his voice is slightly more exotic.*]

Canynge. [*Calmly.*] It is obvious, Mr. De Levis, that you and Captain Dancy can't both remain members of this Club. We ask you for an explanation before requesting one resignation or the other.

De Levis. You've let me down.

Canynge. What!

De Levis. Well, I shall tell people that you and Lord St. Erth backed me up for one Club, and asked me to resign from another.

Canynge. It's a matter of indifference to me, sir, what you tell people.

St. Erth. [*Drily.*] You seem a venomous young man.

De Levis. I'll tell you what seems to me venomous, my lord—chasing a man like a pack of hounds because he isn't your breed.

Canynge. You appear to have your breed on the brain, sir. Nobody else does, so far as I know.

De Levis. Suppose I had robbed Dancy, would you chase him out for complaining of it?

Colford. My God! If you repeat that——

Canynge. Steady, Colford!

Winsor. You make this accusation that Dancy stole your money in my house on no proof—no proof; and you expect Dancy's friends to treat you as if you were a gentleman! That's too strong, if you like!

De Levis. No proof? Kentman told me at Newmarket yesterday that Dancy *did* know of the sale. He told Goole, and Goole says that he himself spoke of it to Dancy.

Winsor. Well—if he did?

De Levis. Dancy told you he *didn't* know of it in General Canynge's presence, and mine. [*To* CANYNGE.] You can't deny that, if you want to.

Canynge. Choose your expressions more nicely, please!

De Levis. Proof! Did they find any footmarks in the grounds below that torn creeper? Not a sign! You saw how he can jump; he won ten pounds from me that same evening betting on what he knew was a certainty. That's your Dancy—a common sharper!

Canynge. [*Nodding toward the billiard-room.*] Are those fellows still in there, Colford?

Colford. Yes.

Canynge. Then bring Dancy up, will you? But don't say anything to him.

Colford. [*To* DE LEVIS.] You may think yourself damned lucky if he doesn't break your neck.

[*He goes out. The three who are left with* DE LEVIS *avert their eyes from him.*]

De Levis. [*Smouldering.*] I have a memory, and a sting too. Yes, my lord—since you are good enough to call me venomous. [*To* CANYNGE.] I quite understand—I'm marked for Coventry now, whatever happens. Well, I'll take Dancy with me.

St. Erth. [*To himself.*] This Club has always had a decent, quiet name.

Winsor. Are you going to retract, and apologize in front of Dancy and the members who heard you?

De Levis. No fear!

St. Erth. You must be a very rich man, sir. A jury is likely to take the view that money can hardly compensate for an accusation of that sort.

[DE LEVIS *stands silent.*]

Canynge. Courts of law require proof.

St. Erth. He can make it a criminal action.

Winsor. Unless you stop this at once, you may find yourself in prison. *If* you can stop it, that is.

St. Erth. If I were young Dancy, nothing should induce me.

De Levis. But you didn't steal my money, Lord St. Erth.

St. Erth. You're deuced positive, sir. So far as I could understand it, there were a dozen ways you could have been robbed. It seems to me you value other men's reputations very lightly.

De Levis. Confront me with Dancy and give me fair play.

Winsor. [*Aside to* CANYNGE.] Is it fair to Dancy not to let him know?

Canynge. Our duty is to the Club now, Winsor. We must have this cleared up.

[COLFORD *comes in, followed by* BORRING *and* DANCY.]

St. Erth. Captain Dancy, a serious accusation has been made against you by this gentleman in the presence of several members of the Club.

Dancy. What is it?

St. Erth. That you robbed him of that money at Winsor's.

Dancy. [*Hard and tense.*] Indeed! On what grounds is he good enough to say that?

De Levis. [*Tense too.*] You gave me that filly to save yourself her keep, and you've been mad about it ever since; you knew from Goole that I had sold her to Kentman and been paid in cash, yet I heard you myself deny that you knew it. You had the next room to me, and you can jump like a cat, as we saw that evening; I found some creepers crushed by a weight on my balcony on that side. When I went to the bath your door was open, and when I came back it was shut.

Canynge. That's the first we have heard about the door.

De Levis. I remembered it afterwards.

St. Erth. Well, Dancy?

Dancy. [*With intense deliberation.*] I'll settle this matter with any weapons, when and where he likes.

St. Erth. [*Drily.*] It can't be settled that way—you know very well. You must take it to the Courts, unless he retracts.

Dancy. Will you retract?

De Levis. Why did you tell General Canynge you didn't know Kentman had paid me in cash?

Dancy. Because I didn't.

De Levis. Then Kentman and Goole lied—for no reason?

Dancy. That's nothing to do with me.

De Levis. If you were down-stairs all the time, as you say, why was your door first open and then shut?

Dancy. Being down-stairs, how should I know? The wind, probably.

De Levis. I should like to hear what your wife says about it.

Dancy. Leave my wife alone, you damned Jew!

St. Erth. Captain Dancy!

De Levis. [*White with rage.*] Thief!

Dancy. Will you fight?

De Levis. You're very smart—dead men tell no tales. No! Bring your action, and we shall see.

[DANCY *takes a step toward him, but* CANYNGE *and* WINSOR *interpose.*]

St. Erth. That'll do, Mr. De Levis; we won't keep you. [*He looks round.*] Kindly consider your membership suspended till this matter has been threshed out.

De Levis. [*Tremulous with anger.*] Don't trouble yourselves about my membership. I resign it. [*To* DANCY.] You called me a damned Jew. My race was old when you were all savages. I am proud to be a Jew. *Au revoir,* in the Courts.

[*He goes out, and silence follows his departure.*]

St. Erth. Well, Captain Dancy?

Dancy. If the brute won't fight, what am I to do, sir?

St. Erth. We've told you—take action, to clear your name.

Dancy. Colford, you saw me in the hall writing letters after our game.

Colford. Certainly I did; you were there when I went to the smoking-room.

Canynge. How long after you left the billiard-room?

Colford. About five minutes.

Dancy. It's impossible for me to prove that I was there all the time.

Canynge. It's for De Levis to prove what he asserts. You heard what he said about Goole?

Dancy. If he told me, I didn't take it in.

St. Erth. This concerns the honor of the Club. Are you going to take action?

Dancy. [*Slowly.*] That is a very expensive business, Lord St. Erth, and I'm hard up. I must think it over. [*He looks round from face to face.*] Am I to take it that there is a doubt in your minds, gentlemen?

Colford. [*Emphatically.*] No.

Canynge. That's not the question, Dancy. This accusation was overheard by various members, and we represent the Club. If you don't take action, judgment will naturally go by default.

Dancy. I might prefer to look on the whole thing as beneath contempt.

[*He turns and goes out. When he is gone there is an even longer silence than after* DE LEVIS's *departure.*]

St. Erth. [*Abruptly.*] I don't like it.

Winsor. I've known him all his life.

Colford. You may have my head if he did it, Lord St. Erth. He and I have been in too many holes together. By Gad! My toe itches for that fellow's butt end.

Borring. I'm sorry; but has he t-taken it in quite the right way? I should have thought—hearing it s-suddenly——

Colford. Bosh!

Winsor. It's perfectly damnable for him.

St. Erth. More damnable if he did it, Winsor.

Borring. The Courts are b-beastly distrustful, don't you know.

Colford. His word's good enough for me.

Canynge. We're as anxious to believe Dancy as you, Colford, for the honor of the Army and the Club.

Winsor. Of course, he'll bring a case, when he's thought it over.

St. Erth. What are we to do in the meantime?

Colford. If Dancy's asked to resign, you may take my resignation too.

Borring. I thought his wanting to f-fight him a bit screeny.

Colford. Wouldn't you have wanted a shot at the brute? A law court? Pah!

Winsor. Yes. What'll be his position even if he wins?

Borring. Damages, and a stain on his c-character.

Winsor. Quite so, unless they find the real thief. People always believe the worst.

Colford. [*Glaring at* BORRING.] They do.

Canynge. There *is* no decent way out of a thing of this sort.

St. Erth. No. [*Rising.*] It leaves a bad taste. I'm sorry for young Mrs. Dancy—poor woman!

Borring. Are you going to play any more?

St. Erth. [*Abruptly.*] No, sir. Good night to you. Canynge, can I give you a lift?

[*He goes out, followed by* CANYNGE.]

Borring. [*After a slight pause.*] Well, I shall go and take the t-temperature of the Club. [*He goes out.*]

Colford. Damn that effeminate stammering chap! What can we do for Dancy, Winsor?

Winsor. Colford! [*A slight pause.*] The General felt his coat sleeve that night, and it was wet.

Colford. Well! What proof's that? No, by George! An old school-fellow, a brother officer, and a pal.

Winsor. If he did do it——

Colford. He didn't. But if he did, I'd

stick to him, and see him through it, if I could.

[WINSOR *walks over to the fire, stares into it, turns round and stares at* COLFORD, *who is standing motionless.*]

Colford. Yes, by God!

CURTAIN

SCENE II*

Morning of the following day. The DANCYS' *flat.*

[*In the sitting-room of this small abode* MABEL DANCY *and* MARGARET ORME *are sitting full face to the audience, on a couch in the center of the room, in front of the imaginary window. There is a fireplace, Left, with fire burning; a door below it, Left; and a door on the Right, facing the audience, leads to a corridor and the outer door of the flat, which is visible. Their voices are heard in rapid exchange; then as the curtain rises, so does* MABEL.]

Mabel. But it's monstrous!

Margaret. Of course! [*She lights a cigarette and hands the case to* MABEL, *who, however, sees nothing but her own thoughts.*] De Levis might just as well have pitched on me, except that I can't jump more than six inches in these skirts.

Mabel. It's wicked! Yesterday afternoon at the Club, did you say? Ronny hasn't said a word to me. Why?

Margaret. [*With a long puff of smoke.*] Doesn't want you bothered.

Mabel. But—— Good heavens!—— Me!

Margaret. Haven't you found out, Mabel, that he isn't exactly communicative? No desperate character is.

Mabel. Ronny?

Margaret. Gracious! Wives *are* at a disadvantage, especially early on. You've never hunted with him, my dear. I have. He takes more sudden decisions than any man I ever knew. He's taking one now, I'll bet.

Mabel. That beast, De Levis! I was in our room next door all the time.

Margaret. Was the door into Ronny's dressing-room open?

Mabel. I don't know; I—I think it was.

Margaret. Well, you can say so in Court anyway. Not that it matters. Wives are liars by law.

Mabel. [*Staring down at her.*] What do you mean—Court?

Margaret. My dear, he'll have to bring an action for defamation of character, or whatever they call it.

Mabel. Were they talking of this last night at the Winsors'?

Margaret. Well, you know a dinner-table, Mabel—Scandal is heaven-sent at this time of year.

Mabel. It's terrible, such a thing—terrible!

Margaret. [*Gloomily.*] If only Ronny weren't known to be so broke.

Mabel. [*With her hands to her forehead.*] I can't realize—I simply can't. If there's a case would it be all right afterwards?

Margaret. Do you remember St. Offert—cards? No, you wouldn't—you were in high frocks. Well, St. Offert got damages, but he also got the hoof, underneath. He lives in Ireland. There isn't the slightest connection, so far as I can see, Mabel, between innocence and reputation. Look at me!

Mabel. We'll fight it tooth and nail!

Margaret. Mabel, you're pure wool, right through; everybody's sorry for you.

Mabel. It's for *him* they ought——

Margaret. [*Again handing the cigarette-case.*] Do smoke, old thing. [MABEL *takes a cigarette this time, but does not light it.*] It isn't altogether simple. General Canynge was there last night. You don't mind my being beastly frank, do you?

Mabel. No. I want it.

Margaret. Well, he's all for *esprit de corps* and that. But he was awfully silent.

Mabel. I hate half-hearted friends. Loyalty comes before everything.

Margaret. Ye-es; but loyalties cut up against each other sometimes, you know.

Mabel. I *must* see Ronny. D'you mind if I go and try to get him on the telephone?

Margaret. Rather not.

[MABEL *goes out by the door Left.*]

Poor kid! [*She curls herself into a corner of the sofa, as if trying to get away from life. The bell rings.* MARGARET *stirs, gets up, and goes out into the corridor, where she opens the door to* LADY ADELA WINSOR, *whom she precedes into the sitting-room.*] Enter the second murderer! D'you know that child knew nothing?

Lady A. Where is she?

Margaret. Telephoning. Adela, if there's going to be an action, we shall be witnesses. I shall wear black georgette with an écru hat. Have you ever given evidence?

Lady A. Never.

* This should be a small set capable of being set quickly within that of the previous scene.

Margaret. It must be too frightfully thrilling.

Lady A. Oh! Why did I ever ask that wretch De Levis? I used to think him pathetic. Meg—did you know—— Ronald Dancy's coat was wet? The General happened to feel it.

Margaret. So that's why he was so silent.

Lady A. Yes; and after the scene in the Club yesterday he went to see those bookmakers, and Goole—what a name!—is sure he told Dancy about the sale.

Margaret. [*Suddenly.*] I don't care. He's my third cousin. Don't you feel you *couldn't,* Adela?

Lady A. Couldn't—what?

Margaret. Stand for De Levis against one of ourselves?

Lady A. That's very narrow, Meg.

Margaret. Oh! I know lots of splendid Jews, and I rather liked little Ferdy; but when it comes to the point——! *They* all stick together; why shouldn't we? It's in the blood. Open your jugular, and see if you haven't got it.

Lady A. My dear, my great-grandmother was a Jewess. I'm very proud of her.

Margaret. Inoculated. [*Stretching herself.*] Prejudices, Adela—or are they loyalties—I don't know—criss-cross—we all cut each other's throats from the best of motives.

Lady A. Oh! I shall remember that. Delightful! [*Holding up a finger.*] You got it from Bergson, Meg. Isn't he wonderful?

Margaret. Yes; have you ever read him?

Lady A. Well—no. [*Looking at the bedroom door.*] That poor child! I quite agree. I shall tell everybody it's ridiculous. You don't really think Ronald Dancy——?

Margaret. I don't know, Adela. There are people who simply can't live without danger. I'm rather like that myself. They're all right when they're getting the D.S.O. or shooting man-eaters; but if there's no excitement going, they'll make it—out of sheer craving. I've seen Ronny Dancy do the maddest things for no mortal reason except the risk. He's had a past, you know.

Lady A. Oh! Do tell!

Margaret. He did splendidly in the war, of course, because it suited him; but—just before—don't you remember—a very queer bit of riding?

Lady A. No.

Margaret. Most dare-devil thing—but not quite. You must remember—it was awfully talked about. And then, of course, right up to his marriage—— [*She lights a cigarette.*]

Lady A. Meg, you're very tantalizing!

Margaret. A foreign-looking girl—most plummy. Oh! Ronny's got charm—this Mabel child doesn't know in the least what she's got hold of!

Lady A. But they're so fond of each other!

Margaret. That's the mistake. The General isn't mentioning the coat, is he?

Lady A. Oh, no! It was only to Charles. [MABEL *returns.*]

Margaret. Did you get him?

Mabel. No; he's not at Tattersall's, nor at the Club.

[LADY ADELA *rises and greets her with an air which suggests bereavement.*]

Lady A. Nobody's going to believe this, my dear.

Mabel. [*Looking straight at her.*] Nobody who does need come here, or trouble to speak to *us* again.

Lady A. That's what I was afraid of; you're going to be defiant. Now don't! Just be perfectly natural.

Mabel. So easy, isn't it? I could kill anybody who believes such a thing.

Margaret. You'll want a solicitor, Mabel. Go to old Mr. Jacob Twisden.

Lady A. Yes; he's so comforting.

Margaret. He got my pearls back once—without loss of life. A frightfully good fireside manner. Do get him here, Mabel, and have a heart-to-heart talk, all three of you!

Mabel. [*Suddenly.*] Listen! There's Ronny! [DANCY *comes in.*]

Dancy. [*With a smile.*] Very good of you to have come.

Margaret. Yes. We're just going. Oh! Ronny, this is quite too—— [*But his face dries her up; and sidling past, she goes.*]

Lady A. Charles sent his—love—— [*Her voice dwindles on the word, and she, too, goes.*]

Dancy. [*Crossing to his wife.*] What have they been saying?

Mabel. Ronny! Why didn't you tell me?

Dancy. I wanted to see De Levis again first.

Mabel. That wretch! How dare he? Darling! [*She suddenly clasps and kisses him. He does not return the kiss, but remains rigid in her arms, so that she draws away and looks at him.*] It's hurt you awfully, I know.

Dancy. Look here, Mabel! Apart from that muck—this is a ghastly tame-cat sort of life. Let's cut it and get out to Nairobi. I can scare up the money for that.

Mabel. [*Aghast.*] But how can we? Everybody would say——

Dancy. Let them! We shan't be here.

Mabel. I couldn't bear people to think——

Dancy. I don't care a damn what people think—monkeys and cats. I never could stand their rotten menagerie. Besides, what does it matter how I act; if I bring an action and get damages—if I pound him to a jelly—it's all no good! I can't *prove* it. There'll be plenty of people unconvinced.

Mabel. But they'll find the real thief.

Dancy. [*With a queer little smile.*] Will staying here help them to do that?

Mabel. [*In a sort of agony.*] Oh! I couldn't—it looks like running away. We *must* stay and fight it!

Dancy. Suppose I didn't get a verdict—you never can tell.

Mabel. But you must—I was there all the time, with the door open.

Dancy. Was it?

Mabel. I'm almost sure.

Dancy. Yes. But you're my wife.

Mabel. [*Bewildered.*] Ronny, I don't understand—suppose I'd been accused of stealing pearls!

Dancy. [*Wincing.*] I can't.

Mabel. But I might—just as easily. What would you think of me if I ran away from it?

Dancy. I see. [*A pause.*] All right! You shall have a run for your money. I'll go and see old Twisden.

Mabel. Let me come. [DANCY *shakes his head.*] Why not? I can't be happy a moment unless I'm fighting this.

[DANCY *puts out his hand suddenly and grips hers.*]

Dancy. You *are* a little brick!

Mabel. [*Pressing his hand to her breast and looking into his face.*] Do you know what Margaret called you?

Ronny. No.

Mabel. A desperate character.

Dancy. Ha! I'm not a tame cat, any more than she.

[*The bell rings.* MABEL *goes out to the door and her voice is heard saying coldly:*]

Mabel. Will you wait a minute, please? [*Returning.*] It's De Levis—to see you. [*In a low voice.*] Let me see him alone first. Just for a minute! Do!

Dancy. [*After a moment's silence.*] Go ahead!

[*He goes out into the bedroom.*]

Mabel. [*Going to the door, Right.*] Come in.

[DE LEVIS *comes in, and stands embarrassed.*]

Yes?

De Levis. [*With a slight bow.*] Your husband, Mrs. Dancy?

Mabel. He is in. Why do you want to see him?

De Levis. He came round to my rooms just now, when I was out. He threatened me yesterday. I don't choose him to suppose I'm afraid of him.

Mabel. [*With a great and manifest effort at self-control.*] Mr. De Levis, you are robbing my husband of his good name.

De Levis. [*Sincerely.*] I admire your trustfulness, Mrs. Dancy.

Mabel. [*Staring at him.*] How can you do it? What do you want? What's your motive? You can't possibly believe that my husband is a *thief*!

De Levis. Unfortunately.

Mabel. How dare you? How dare you? Don't you know that I was in our bedroom all the time with the door open? Do you accuse me, too?

De Levis. No, Mrs. Dancy.

Mabel. But you do. I must have seen, I must have heard.

De Levis. A wife's memory is not very good when her husband is in danger.

Mabel. In other words, I'm lying.

De Levis. No. Your wish is mother to your thought, that's all.

Mabel. [*After staring again with a sort of horror, turns to get control of herself. Then turning back to him.*] Mr. De Levis, I appeal to you as a gentleman to behave to us as you would we should behave to you. Withdraw this wicked charge, and write an apology that Ronald can show.

De Levis. Mrs. Dancy, I am not a gentleman, I am only a—damned Jew. Yesterday I might possibly have withdrawn to spare you. But when my race is insulted I have nothing to say to your husband; but as he wishes to see me, I've come. Please let him know.

Mabel. [*Regarding him again with that look of horror—slowly.*] I think what you are doing is too horrible for words.

[DE LEVIS *gives her a slight bow, and as he does so* DANCY *comes quickly in, Left. The two men stand with the length of the sofa between them.* MABEL, *behind the sofa, turns her eyes on her husband, who has a paper in his right hand.*]

De Levis. You came to see me.

Dancy. Yes. I want you to sign this.

De Levis. I will sign nothing.

Dancy. Let me read it: "I apologize to Captain Dancy for the reckless and monstrous charge I made against him, and I retract every word of it."

De Levis. Not much!

Dancy. You will sign.

De Levis. I tell you this is useless. I will

sign nothing. The charge is true; you wouldn't be playing this game if it weren't. I'm going. You'll hardly try violence in the presence of your wife; and if you try it anywhere else—look out for yourself.

Dancy. Mabel, I want to speak to him alone.

Mabel. No, no!

De Levis. Quite right, Mrs. Dancy. Black and tan swashbuckling will only make things worse for him.

Dancy. So you shelter behind a woman, do you, you skulking cur!

[DE LEVIS *takes a step, with fists clenched and eyes blazing.* DANCY, *too, stands ready to spring—the moment is cut short by* MABEL *going quickly to her husband.*]

Mabel. Don't, Ronny. It's undignified! He isn't worth it.

[DANCY *suddenly tears the paper in two and flings it into the fire.*]

Dancy. Get out of here, you swine!

[DE LEVIS *stands a moment irresolute, then, turning to the door, he opens it, stands again for a moment with a smile on his face, then goes.* MABEL *crosses swiftly to the door, and shuts it as the outer door closes. Then she stands quite still, looking at her husband—her face expressing a sort of startled suspense.*]

Dancy. [*Turning and looking at her.*] Well! Do you agree with him?

Mabel. What do you mean?

Dancy. That I wouldn't be playing this game unless——

Mabel. Don't! You hurt me!

Dancy. Yes. You don't know much of me, Mabel.

Mabel. Ronny!

Dancy. What did you say to that swine?

Mabel. [*Her face averted.*] That he was robbing *us.* [*Turning to him suddenly.*] Ronny—you—didn't? I'd rather know.

Dancy. Ha! I thought that was coming.

Mabel. [*Covering her face.*] Oh! How horrible of me—how horrible!

Dancy. Not at all. The thing looks bad.

Mabel. [*Dropping her hands.*] If *I* can't believe in you, who can? [*Going to him, throwing her arms round him, and looking up into his face.*] Ronny! If all the world—*I'd* believe in you. You know I would.

Dancy. That's all right, Mabs! That's all right! [*His face, above her head, is contorted for a moment, then hardens into a mask.*] Well, what shall we do?

Mabel. Oh! Let's go to that lawyer—let's go at once!

Dancy. All right. Get your hat on.

[MABEL *passes him, and goes into the bedroom, Left.* DANCY, *left alone, stands quite still, staring before him. With a sudden shrug of his shoulders he moves quickly to his hat and takes it up just as* MABEL *returns, ready to go out. He opens the door; and crossing him, she stops in the doorway, looking up with a clear and trustful gaze as*

THE CURTAIN FALLS

ACT III

SCENE I

Three months later. Old MR. JACOB TWISDEN'S *room, at the offices of Twisden & Graviter, in Lincoln's Inn Fields, is spacious, with two large windows at back, a fine old fireplace, Right, a door below it, and two doors, Left. Between the windows is a large table sideways to the window wall, with a chair in the middle on the right-hand side, a chair against the wall, and a client's chair on the left-hand side.*

[GRAVITER, TWISDEN'S *much younger partner, is standing in front of the right-hand window looking out on the Fields, where the lamps are being lighted, and a taxi's engine is running down below. He turns his sanguine, shrewd face from the window toward a grandfather clock, between the doors, Left, which is striking "four." The door, Left Forward, is opened.*]

Young Clerk. [*Entering.*] A Mr. Gilman, sir, to see Mr. Twisden.

Graviter. By appointment?

Young Clerk. No, sir. But important, he says.

Graviter. I'll see him. [*The* CLERK *goes.*]

[GRAVITER *sits right of table. The* CLERK *returns, ushering in an oldish man, who looks what he is, the proprietor of a large modern grocery store. He wears a dark overcoat and carries a pot hat. His gingery-gray mustache and mutton-chop whiskers give him the expression of a cat.*]

Graviter. [*Sizing up his social standing.*] Mr. Gilman? Yes.

Gilman. [*Doubtfully.*] Mr. Jacob Twisden?

Graviter. [*Smiling.*] His partner. Graviter my name is.

Gilman. Mr. Twisden's not in, then?

Graviter. No. He's at the Courts. They're just up; he should be in directly. But he'll be busy.

Gilman. Old Mr. Jacob Twisden—I've heard of him.

Graviter. Most people have. [*A pause.*]

Gilman. It's this Dancy–De Levis case that's keepin' him at the Courts, I suppose? [GRAVITER *nods.*] Won't be finished for a day or two? [GRAVITER *shakes his head.*] No. Astonishin' the interest taken in it.

Graviter. As you say.

Gilman. The Smart Set, eh? This Captain Dancy got the D.S.O., didn't he? [GRAVITER *nods.*] Sad to have a thing like that said about you. I thought he gave his evidence well; and his wife too. Looks as if this De Levis had got some private spite. *Searchy la femme,* I said to Mrs. Gilman only this morning, before I——

Graviter. By the way, sir, what is your business?

Gilman. Well, my business here—— No, if you'll excuse me, I'd rather wait and see old Mr. Jacob Twisden. It's delicate, and I'd like his experience.

Graviter. [*With a shrug.*] Very well; then, perhaps, you'll go in there. [*He moves toward the door, Left Back.*]

Gilman. Thank you. [*Following.*] You see, I've never been mixed up with the law——

Graviter. [*Opening the door.*] No?

Gilman. And I don't want to begin. When you do, you don't know where you'll stop, do you? You see, I've only come from a sense of duty; and—other reasons.

Graviter. Not uncommon.

Gilman. [*Producing card.*] This is my card. Gilman's—several branches, but this is the 'ead.

Graviter. [*Scrutinizing card.*] Exactly.

Gilman. Grocery—I daresay you know me; or your wife does. They say old Mr. Jacob Twisden refused a knighthood. If it's not a rude question, why was that?

Graviter. Ask him, sir; ask him.

Gilman. I said to my wife at the time, "He's holdin' out for a baronetcy."

[GRAVITER *closes the door with an exasperated smile.*]

Young Clerk. [*Opening the door, Left Forward.*] Mr. Winsor, sir, and Miss Orme.

[*They enter, and the* CLERK *withdraws.*]

Graviter. How d'you do, Miss Orme? How do you do, Winsor?

Winsor. Twisden not back, Graviter?

Graviter. Not yet.

Winsor. Well, they've got through De Levis's witnesses. Sir Frederic was at the very top of his form. It's looking quite well. But I hear they've just subpœnaed Canynge after all. His evidence is to be taken tomorrow.

Graviter. Oho!

Winsor. I said Dancy ought to have called him.

Graviter. We considered it. Sir Frederic decided that he could use him better in cross-examination.

Winsor. Well! I don't know that. Can I go and see him before he gives evidence tomorrow?

Graviter. I should like to hear Mr. Jacob on that, Winsor. He'll be in directly.

Winsor. They had Kentman, and Goole, the Inspector, the other bobby, my footman, Dancy's banker, and his tailor.

Graviter. Did we shake Kentman or Goole?

Winsor. Very little. Oh! by the way, the numbers of those two notes were given, and I see they're published in the evening papers. I suppose the police wanted that. I tell you what I find, Graviter—a general feeling that there's something behind it all that doesn't come out.

Graviter. The public wants its money's worth—always does in these Society cases; they brew so long beforehand, you see.

Winsor. They're looking for something lurid.

Margaret. When I was in the box, I thought they were looking for me. [*Taking out her cigarette case.*] I suppose I mustn't smoke, Mr. Graviter?

Graviter. Do!

Margaret. Won't Mr. Jacob have a fit?

Graviter. Yes, but not till you've gone.

Margaret. Just a whiff.

[*She lights a cigarette.*]

Winsor. [*Suddenly.*] It's becoming a sort of Dreyfus case—people taking sides quite outside the evidence.

Margaret. There are more of the chosen in Court every day. Mr. Graviter, have you noticed the two on the jury?

Graviter. [*With a smile.*] No; I can't say——

Margaret. Oh! but quite distinctly. Don't you think they ought to have been challenged?

Graviter. De Levis might have challenged the other ten, Miss Orme.

Margaret. Dear me, now! I never thought of that.

[*As she speaks, the door Left Forward is opened and old* MR. JACOB TWISDEN *comes in. He is tallish and narrow, sixty-eight years old, gray, with narrow little whiskers curling round his narrow ears, and a narrow bow ribbon curling round his collar. He wears a long, narrow-tailed coat, and strapped trousers on his narrow legs. His nose and face are narrow, shrewd, and kindly. He has a way of narrowing his shrewd and kindly eyes. His nose is seen to twitch and sniff.*]

Twisden. Ah! How are you, Charles? How do you do, my dear?

Margaret. Dear Mr. Jacob, I'm smoking. Isn't it disgusting? But they don't allow it in Court, you know. Such a pity! The Judge might have a hookah. Oh! wouldn't he look sweet—the darling!

Twisden. [*With a little, old-fashioned bow.*] It does not become everybody as it becomes you, Margaret.

Margaret. Mr. Jacob, how charming! [*With a slight grimace she puts out her cigarette.*]

Graviter. Man called Gilman waiting in there to see you specially.

Twisden. Directly. Turn up the light, would you, Graviter?

Graviter. [*Turning up the light.*] Excuse me. [*He goes.*]

Winsor. Look here, Mr. Twisden——

Twisden. Sit down; sit down, my dear. [*And he himself sits behind the table, as a cup of tea is brought in to him by the* YOUNG CLERK, *with two Marie biscuits in the saucer.*] Will you have some, Margaret?

Margaret. No, dear Mr. Jacob.

Twisden. Charles?

Winsor. No, thanks.

[*The door is closed.*]

Twisden. [*Dipping a biscuit in the tea.*] Now, then?

Winsor. The General knows something which on the face of it looks rather queer. Now that he's going to be called, oughtn't Dancy to be told of it, so that he may be ready with his explanation, in case it comes out?

Twisden. [*Pouring some tea into the saucer.*] Without knowing, I can't tell you.

[WINSOR *and* MARGARET *exchange looks, and* TWISDEN *drinks from the saucer.*]

Margaret. Tell him, Charles.

Winsor. Well! It rained that evening at Meldon. The General happened to put his hand on Dancy's shoulder, and it was damp.

[TWISDEN *puts the saucer down and replaces the cup in it. They both look intently at him.*]

Twisden. I take it that General Canynge won't say anything he's not compelled to say.

Margaret. No, of course; but, Mr. Jacob, they might ask; they know it rained. And he is such a George Washington.

Twisden. [*Toying with a pair of tortoise-shell glasses.*] They didn't ask either of *you.* Still—no harm in your telling Dancy.

Winsor. I'd rather *you* did it, Margaret.

Margaret. I daresay. [*She mechanically takes out her cigarette-case, catches the lift of* TWISDEN'S *eyebrows, and puts it back.*]

Winsor. Well, we'll go together. I don't want Mrs. Dancy to hear.

Margaret. Do tell me, Mr. Jacob; is he going to win?

Twisden. I think so, Margaret; I think so.

Margaret. It'll be too frightful if he doesn't get a verdict, after all this. But I don't know what we shall do when it's over. I've been sitting in that Court all these three days, watching, and it's made me feel there's nothing we like better than seeing people skinned. Well, bye-bye, bless you!

[TWISDEN *rises and pats her hand.*]

Winsor. Half a second, Margaret. Wait for me. [*She nods and goes out.*] Mr. Twisden, what do you really think?

Twisden. I am Dancy's lawyer, my dear Charles, as well as yours.

Winsor. Well, can I go and see Canynge?

Twisden. Better not.

Winsor. If they get that out of him, and recall me, am I to say he told me of it at the time?

Twisden. You didn't feel the coat yourself? And Dancy wasn't present? Then what Canynge told you is not evidence. *We'll* stop your being asked.

Winsor. Thank goodness. Good-by!

[WINSOR *goes out.*]

[TWISDEN, *behind his table, motionless, taps his teeth with the eyeglasses in his narrow, well-kept hand. After a long shake of his head and a shrug of his rather high shoulders he sniffs, goes to the window and opens it. Then crossing to the door, Left Back, he throws it open and says:*]

Twisden. At your service, sir. [GILMAN *comes forth, nursing his pot hat.*] Be seated.

[TWISDEN *closes the window behind him, and takes his seat.*]

Gilman. [*Taking the client's chair, to the left of the table.*] Mr. Twisden, I believe? My name's Gilman, head of Gilman's Department Stores. You have my card.

Twisden. [*Looking at the card.*] Yes. What can we do for you?

Gilman. Well, I've come to you from a sense of duty, sir, and also a feelin' of embarrassment. [*He takes from his breast pocket an evening paper.*] You see, I've been followin' this Dancy case—it's a good deal talked of in Putney—and I read this at half-past two this afternoon. To be precise, at 2.25. [*He rises and hands the paper to* TWISDEN, *and with a thick gloved forefinger indicates a passage.*] When I read these numbers, I 'appened to remember givin' change for a fifty-pound note—don't often 'ave one in, you know—so I went to the cash-box out of curiosity, to see that I 'adn't got it. Well, I 'ad; and here it is. [*He draws out from his breast pocket and lays before* TWISDEN *a fifty-pound banknote.*] It was brought in to change by a customer of mine three days ago, and he got value for it. Now, that's a stolen note, it seems, and you'd like to know what I did. Mind you, that customer of mine I've know 'im—well—eight or nine years; an Italian he is—wine salesman, and so far's I know, a respectable man—foreign-lookin', but nothin' more. Now, this was at 'alf-past two, and I was at my head branch at Putney, where I live. I want you to mark the time, so as you'll see I 'aven't wasted a minute. I took a cab and I drove straight to my customer's private residence in Putney, where he lives with his daughter—Ricardos his name is, Paolio Ricardos. They tell me there that he's at his business shop in the City. So off I go in the cab again, and there I find him. Well, sir, I showed this paper to him and I produced the note. "Here," I said, "you brought this to me and you got value for it." Well, that man was taken aback. If I'm a judge, Mr. Twisden, he was taken aback, not to speak in a guilty way, but he was, as you might say, flummoxed. "Now," I said to him, "where did you get it—that's the point?" He took his time to answer, and then he said: "Well, Mr. Gilman," he said, "you know me; I am an honorable man. I can't tell you offhand, but I am above the board." He's foreign, you know, in his expressions. "Yes," I said, "that's all very well," I said, "but here I've got a stolen note and you've got the value for it. Now I tell you," I said, "what I'm going to do; I'm going straight with this note to Mr. Jacob Twisden, who's got this Dancy–De Levis case in 'and. He's a well-known Society lawyer," I said, "of great experience." "Oh!" he said, "that is what you do?"—funny the way he speaks! "Then I come with you!"—And I've got him in the cab below. I want to tell you everything before he comes up. On the way I tried to get something out of him, but I couldn't—I could *not.* "This is very awkward," I said at last. "It is, Mr. Gilman," was his reply; and he began to talk about his Sicilian claret—a very good wine, mind you; but under the circumstances it seemed to me uncalled for. Have I made it clear to you?

Twisden. [*Who has listened with extreme attention.*] Perfectly, Mr. Gilman. I'll send down for him. [*He touches a hand-bell. The* YOUNG CLERK *appears at the door, Left Forward.*] A gentlemen in a taxi—waiting. Ask him to be so good as to step up. Oh! and send Mr. Graviter here again.

[*The* YOUNG CLERK *goes out.*]

Gilman. As I told you, sir, I've been followin' this case. It's what you might call piquant. And I should be very glad if it came about that this helped Captain Dancy. I take an interest, because, to tell you the truth, [*confidentially*] I don't like—well, not to put too fine a point upon it—'Ebrews. They work harder; they're more sober; they're honest; and they're everywhere. I've nothing against them, but the fact is—they get *on* so.

Twisden. [*Cocking an eye.*] A thorn in the flesh, Mr. Gilman.

Gilman. Well, I prefer my own countrymen, and that's the truth of it.

[*As he speaks,* GRAVITER *comes in by the door Left Forward.*]

Twisden. [*Pointing to the newspaper and the note.*] Mr. Gilman has brought this, of which he is holder for value. His customer, who changed it three days ago, is coming up.

Graviter. The fifty-pounder. I see.

[*His face is long and reflective.*]

Young Clerk. [*Entering.*] Mr. Ricardos, sir.

[*He goes out.*]

[RICARDOS *is a personable, Italian-looking man in a frock coat, with a dark mustachioed face and dark hair a little grizzled. He looks anxious and bows.*]

Twisden. Mr. Ricardos? My name is Jacob Twisden. My partner. [*Holding up a finger, as* RICARDOS *would speak.*] Mr. Gilman has told us about this note. You took it to him, he says, three days ago; that is, on Monday, and received cash for it?

Ricardos. Yes, sare.

Twisden. You were *not* aware that it was stolen?

Ricardos. [*With his hand to his breast.*] Oh! no, sare.

Twisden. You received it from——?

Ricardos. A minute, sare; I would weesh to explain—[*with an expressive shrug*] in private.

Twisden. [*Nodding.*] Mr. Gilman, your conduct has been most prompt. You may safely leave the matter in our hands, now. Kindly let us retain this note; and ask for my cashier as you go out and give him [*he writes*] this. He will reimburse you. We will take any necessary steps ourselves.

Gilman. [*In slight surprise, with modest pride.*] Well, sir, I'm in your 'ands. I must be guided by you, with your experience. I'm glad you think I acted rightly.

Twisden. Very rightly, Mr. Gilman—very rightly. [*Rising.*] Good-afternoon!

Gilman. Good-afternoon, sir. Good-afternoon, gentlemen! [*To* TWISDEN.] I'm sure I'm very 'appy to have made your acquaintance, sir. It's a well-known name.

Twisden. Thank you.

[GILMAN *retreats, glances at* RICARDOS, *and turns again.*]

Gilman. I suppose there's nothing else I ought to do, in the interests of the law? I'm a careful man.

Twisden. If there is, Mr. Gilman, we will let you know. We have your address. You may make your mind easy; but don't speak of this. It might interfere with Justice.

Gilman. Oh! I shouldn't dream of it. I've no wish to be mixed up in anything conspicuous. That's not my principle at all. Good-day, gentlemen. [*He goes.*]

Twisden. [*Seating himself.*] Now, sir, will you sit down? [*But* RICARDOS *does not sit; he stands looking uneasily across the table at* GRAVITER.] You may speak out.

Ricardos. Well, Mr. Tweesden and sare, this matter is very serious for me, and very delicate—it concairns my honor. I am in a great difficulty.

Twisden. When in difficulty—complete frankness, sir.

Ricardos. It is a family matter, sare, I——

Twisden. Let me be frank with you. [*Telling his points off on his fingers.*] We have your admission that you changed this stopped note for value. It will be our duty to inform the Bank of England that it has been traced to you. You will have to account to them for your possession of it. I suggest to you that it will be far better to account frankly to us.

Ricardos. [*Taking out a handkerchief and quite openly wiping his hands and forehead.*] I received this note, sare, with others, from a gentleman, sare, in settlement of a debt of honor, and I know nothing of where he got them.

Twisden. H'm! that is very vague. If that is all you can tell us, I'm afraid——

Ricardos. Gentlemen, this is very painful for me. It is my daughter's good name——

[*He again wipes his brow.*]

Twisden. Come, sir, speak out!

Ricardos. [*Desperately.*] The notes were a settlement to her from this gentleman, of whom she was a great friend.

Twisden. [*Suddenly.*] I am afraid we must press you for the name of the gentleman.

Ricardos. Sare, if I give it to you, and it does 'im 'arm, what will my daughter say? This is a bad matter for me. He behaved well to her; and she is attached to him still; sometimes she is crying yet because she lost him. And now we betray him, perhaps, who knows? This is very unpleasant for me. [*Taking up the paper.*] Here it gives the number of another note—a 'undred-pound note. I 'ave that too.

[*He takes a note from his breast pocket.*]

Graviter. How much did he give you in all?

Ricardos. For my daughter's settlement one thousand pounds. I understand he did not wish to give a cheque because of his marriage. So I did not think anything about it being in notes, you see.

Twisden. When did he give you this money?

Ricardos. The middle of Octobare last.

Twisden. [*Suddenly looking up.*] Mr. Ricardos, was it Captain Dancy?

Ricardos. [*Again wiping his forehead.*] Gentlemen, I am so fond of my daughter. I have only the one, and no wife.

Twisden. [*With an effort.*] Yes, yes; but I must know.

Ricardos. Sare, if I tell you, will you give me your good word that my daughter shall not hear of it?

Twisden. So far as we are able to prevent it—certainly.

Ricardos. Sare, I trust you—It was Captain Dancy. [*A long pause.*]

Graviter. [*Suddenly.*] Were you blackmailing him?

Twisden. [*Holding up his hand.*] My partner means, did you press him for this settlement?

Ricardos. I did think it my duty to my daughter to ask that he make compensation to her.

Twisden. With threats that you would tell his wife?

Ricardos. [*With a shrug.*] Captain Dancy was a man of honor. He said: "Of course I will do this." I trusted him. And a month later I did remind him, and he gave me this money for her. I do not know where he got it—I do not know. Gentlemen, I have invested it all on her—every penny—except this note, for which I had the purpose to buy her a necklace. That is the swearéd truth.

Twisden. I must keep this note. [*He touches the hundred-pound note.*] You will not speak of this to anyone. *I* may recognize that you were a holder for value received—others might take a different view. Good-day, sir. Graviter, see Mr. Ricardos out, and take his address.

Ricardos. [*Pressing his hands over the breast of his frock coat—with a sigh.*] Gentlemen, I beg you—remember what I said. [*With a roll of his eyes.*] My daughter—I am not happee. Good-day.

[*He turns and goes out slowly, Left Forward, followed by* GRAVITER.]

Twisden. [*To himself.*] Young Dancy!

[*He pins the two notes together and places them in an envelope, then stands motionless except for his eyes and hands, which restlessly express the disturbance within him.*]

[GRAVITER *returns, carefully shuts the door, and going up to him, hands him* RICARDOS' *card.*]

[*Looking at the card.*] Villa Benvenuto. This will have to be verified, but I'm afraid it's true. That man was not acting.

Graviter. What's to be done about Dancy?

Twisden. Can you understand a gentleman ——?

Graviter. I don't know, sir. The war loosened "form" all over the place. I saw plenty of that myself. And some men have no moral sense. From the first I've had doubts.

Twisden. We can't go on with the case.

Graviter. Phew! . . . [*A moment's silence.*] Gosh! It's an awful thing for his wife.

Twisden. Yes.

Graviter. [*Touching the envelope.*] Chance brought this here, sir. That man won't talk —he's too scared.

Twisden. Gilman.

Graviter. Too respectable. If De Levis got those notes back, and the rest of the money, anonymously?

Twisden. But the case, Graviter; the case.

Graviter. I don't believe this alters what I've been thinking.

Twisden. Thought is one thing—knowledge another. There's duty to our profession. Ours is a fine calling. On the good faith of solicitors a very great deal hangs.

[*He crosses to the hearth as if warmth would help him.*]

Graviter. It'll let him in for a prosecution. He came to us in confidence.

Twisden. Not as against the law.

Graviter. No. I suppose not. [*A pause.*] By Jove, I don't like losing this case. I don't like the admission we backed such a wrong 'un.

Twisden. Impossible to go on. Apart from ourselves, there's Sir Frederic. We must disclose to him—can't let him go on in the dark. Complete confidence between solicitor and counsel is the essence of professional honor.

Graviter. What are you going to do then, sir?

Twisden. See Dancy at once. Get him on the 'phone.

Graviter. [*Taking up the telephone.*] Get me Captain Dancy's flat. . . . What? . . . [*To* TWISDEN.] Mrs. Dancy is here. That's *à propos* with a vengeance. Are you going to see her, sir?

Twisden. [*After a moment's painful hesitation.*] I must.

Graviter. [*Telephoning.*] Bring Mrs. Dancy up. [*He turns to the window.*]

[MABEL DANCY *is shown in, looking very pale.* TWISDEN *advances from the fire, and takes her hand.*]

Mabel. Major Colford's taken Ronny off in his car for the night. I thought it would do him good. I said I'd come round in case there was anything you wanted to say before tomorrow.

Twisden. [*Taken aback.*] Where have they gone?

Mabel. I don't know, but he'll be home before ten o'clock tomorrow. Is there anything?

Twisden. Well, I'd like to see him before the Court sits. Send him on here as soon as he comes.

Mabel. [*With her hand to her forehead.*] Oh! Mr. Twisden, when will it be over? My head's getting awful sitting in that Court.

Twisden. My dear Mrs. Dancy, there's no need at all for you to come down tomorrow; take a rest and nurse your head.

Mabel. Really and truly?

Twisden. Yes; it's the very best thing you can do.

[GRAVITER *turns his head, and looks at them unobserved.*]

Mabel. How do you think it's going?

Twisden. It went very well today; very well indeed.

Mabel. You must be awfully fed up with us.

Twisden. My dear young lady, that's our business. [*He takes her hand.* MABEL'S *face suddenly quivers. She draws her hand away, and covers her lips with it.*] There, there! You want a day off badly.

Mabel. I'm so tired of—! Thank you so much for all you're doing. Good-night! Good-night, Mr. Graviter!

Graviter. Good-night, Mrs. Dancy.

[MABEL *goes.*]

Graviter. D'you know, I believe she knows.

Twisden. No, no! She believes in him implicitly. A staunch little woman. Poor thing!

Graviter. Hasn't that shaken you, sir? It has me.

Twisden. No, no! I—I can't go on with the case. It's breaking faith. Get Sir Frederic's chambers.

Graviter. [*Telephoning and getting a reply, looks round at* TWISDEN.] Yes?

Twisden. Ask if I can come round and see him.

Graviter. [*Telephoning.*] Can Sir Frederic spare Mr. Twisden a few minutes now if he comes round? [*Receiving reply.*] He's gone down to Brighton for the night.

Twisden. H'm! What hotel?

Graviter. [*Telephoning.*] What's his address? What . . . ? [*To* TWISDEN.] The Bedford.

Twisden. I'll go down.

Graviter. [*Telephoning.*] Thank you. All right. [*He rings off.*]

Twisden. Just look out the trains down and up early tomorrow.

[GRAVITER *takes up an A B C, and* TWISDEN *takes up the Ricardos card.*]

Twisden. Send to this address in Putney, verify the fact that Ricardos has a daughter, and give me a trunk call to Brighton. Better go yourself, Graviter. If you see her, don't say anything, of course—invent some excuse. [GRAVITER *nods.*] I'll be up in time to see Dancy.

Graviter. By George! I feel bad about this.

Twisden. Yes. But professional honor comes first. What time is that train?

[*He bends over the A B C.*]

CURTAIN

SCENE II

The same room on the following morning at ten-twenty-five, by the Grandfather clock.

[*The* YOUNG CLERK *is ushering in* DANCY, *whose face is perceptibly harder than it was three months ago, like that of a man who has lived under great restraint.*]

Dancy. He wanted to see me before the Court sat.

Young Clerk. Yes, sir. Mr. Twisden will see you in one minute. He had to go out of town last night.

[*He prepares to open the waiting-room door.*]

Dancy. Were *you* in the war?

Young Clerk. Yes.

Dancy. How can you stick this?

Young Clerk. [*With a smile.*] My trouble was to stick that, sir.

Dancy. But you get no excitement from year's end to year's end. It'd drive me mad.

Young Clerk. [*Shyly.*] A case like this is pretty exciting. I'd give a lot to see us win it.

Dancy. [*Staring at him.*] Why? What is it to you?

Young Clerk. I don't know, sir. It's—it's like football—you want your side to win. [*He opens the waiting-room door. Expanding.*] You see some rum starts, too, in a lawyer's office in a quiet way.

[DANCY *enters the waiting-room, and the* YOUNG CLERK, *shutting the door, meets* TWISDEN *as he comes in, Left Forward, and takes from him overcoat, top hat, and a small bag.*]

Young Clerk. Captain Dancy's waiting, sir.

[*He indicates the waiting-room.*]

Twisden. [*Narrowing his lips.*] Very well. Mr. Graviter gone to the Courts?

Young Clerk. Yes, sir.

Twisden. Did he leave anything for me?

Young Clerk. On the table, sir.

Twisden. [*Taking up an envelope.*] Thank you. [*The* CLERK *goes.*]

Twisden. [*Opening the envelope and reading.*] "All corroborates." H'm! [*He puts it in his pocket and takes out of an envelope the two notes, lays them on the table, and covers them with a sheet of blotting-paper; stands a moment preparing himself, then goes to the door of the waiting-room, opens it, and says:*] Now, Captain Dancy. Sorry to have kept you waiting.

Dancy. [*Entering.*] Winsor came to me yesterday about General Canynge's evidence. Is that what you wanted to speak to me about?

Twisden. No. It isn't that.

Dancy. [*Looking at his wrist watch.*] By me it's just on the half-hour, sir.

Twisden. Yes. I don't want you to go to Court.

Dancy. Not?

Twisden. I have very serious news for you.

Dancy. [*Wincing and collecting himself.*] Oh!

Twisden. These two notes. [*He uncovers the notes.*] After the Court rose yesterday we had a man called Ricardos here. [*A pause.*] Is there any need for me to say more?

Dancy. [*Unflinching.*] No. What now?

Twisden. Our duty was plain; we could not go on with the case. I have consulted Sir Frederic. He felt—he felt that he must throw up his brief, and he will do that the moment the Court sits. Now I want to talk to you about what you're going to do.

Dancy. That's very good of you, considering.

Twisden. I don't pretend to understand, but I imagine you may have done this in a moment of reckless bravado, feeling, perhaps, that, as you gave the mare to De Levis, the money was by rights as much yours as his. [*Stopping* DANCY, *who is about to speak, with a gesture.*] To satisfy a debt of honor to this —lady; and, no doubt, to save your wife from hearing of it from the man Ricardos. Is that so?

Dancy. To the life.

Twisden. It was mad, Captain Dancy, mad!—— But the question now is: What do you owe to your wife? She doesn't dream—I suppose?

Dancy. [*With a twitching face.*] No.

Twisden. We can't tell what the result of this collapse will be. The police have the theft in hand. They may issue a warrant. The money could be refunded, and the costs paid—somehow that can all be managed. But it may not help. In any case, what end is served by your staying in the country? You can't save your honor—that's gone. You can't save your wife's peace of mind. If she sticks to you—do you think she will?

Dancy. Not if she's wise.

Twisden. Better go! There's a war in Morocco.

Dancy. [*With a bitter smile.*] Good old Morocco!

Twisden. Will you go, then, at once, and leave me to break it to your wife?

Dancy. I don't know yet.

Twisden. You must decide quickly, to catch a boat train. Many a man has made good. You're a fine soldier.

Dancy. There are alternatives.

Twisden. Now, go straight from this office. You've a passport, I suppose; you won't need a *visa* for France, and from there you can find means to slip over. Have you got money on you? (DANCY *nods.*] We will see what we can do to stop or delay proceedings.

Dancy. It's all damned kind of you. [*With difficulty.*] But I must think of my wife. Give me a few minutes.

Twisden. Yes, yes; go in there and think it out.

[*He goes to the door, Right, and opens it.* DANCY *passes him and goes out.* TWISDEN *rings a bell and stands waiting.*]

Clerk. [*Entering.*] Yes, sir?

Twisden. Tell them to call a taxi.

Clerk. [*Who has a startled look.*] Yes, sir. Mr. Graviter has come in, sir, with General Canynge. Are you disengaged?

Twisden. Yes. [*The* CLERK *goes out, and almost immediately* GRAVITER *and* CANYGNE *enter.*] Good-morning, General. [*To* GRAVITER.] Well?

Graviter. Sir Frederic got up at once and said that since the publication of the numbers of those notes, information had reached him which forced him to withdraw from the case. Great sensation, of course. I left Bromley in charge. There'll be a formal verdict for the defendant, with costs. Have you told Dancy?

Twisden. Yes. He's in there deciding what he'll do.

Canynge. [*Grave and vexed.*] This is a dreadful thing, Twisden. I've been afraid of it all along. A soldier! A gallant fellow, too. What on earth got into him?

Twisden. There's no end to human nature, General.

Graviter. You can see queerer things in the papers, any day.

Canynge. That poor young wife of his! Winsor gave me a message for you, Twisden. If money's wanted quickly to save proceedings, draw on him. Is there anything *I* can do?

Twisden. I've advised him to go straight off to Morocco.

Canynge. I don't know that an asylum isn't the place for him. He must be off his head at moments. That jump—crazy! He'd have got a verdict on that alone—if they'd seen those balconies. I was looking at them when I was down there last Sunday. Daring thing, Twisden. Very few men, on a dark night—— He risked his life twice. That's a shrewd fellow—young De Levis. He spotted Dancy's nature.

[*The* YOUNG CLERK *enters.*]

Clerk. The taxi's here, sir. Will you see Major Colford and Miss Orme?

Twisden. Graviter—— No; show them in.

[THE YOUNG CLERK *goes.*]

Canynge. Colford's badly cut up.

[MARGARET ORME *and* COLFORD *enter.*]

Colford. [*Striding forward.*] There must be some mistake about this, Mr. Twisden.

Twisden. Hssh! Dancy's in there. He's admitted it.

[*Voices are subdued at once.*]

Colford. What? [*With emotion.*] If it were my own brother, I couldn't feel it more. But—damn it! What right had that fellow to chuck up the case—without letting him know, too. I came down with Dancy this morning, and he knew nothing about it.

Twisden. [*Coldly.*] That was unfortunately unavoidable.

Colford. Guilty or not, you ought to have stuck to him—it's not playing the game, Mr. Twisden.

Twisden. You must allow me to judge where my duty lay, in a very hard case.

Colford. I thought a man was safe with his solicitor.

Canynge. Colford, you don't understand professional etiquette.

Colford. No, thank God!

Twisden. When you have been as long in your profession as I have been in mine, Major Colford, you will know that duty to your calling outweighs duty to friend or client.

Colford. But I serve the Country.

Twisden. And I serve the Law, sir.

Canynge. Graviter, give me a sheet of paper. I'll write a letter for him.

Margaret. [*Going up to* TWISDEN.] Dear Mr. Jacob—pay De Levis. You know my pearls—put them up the spout again. Don't let Ronny be——

Twisden. Money isn't the point, Margaret.

Margaret. It's ghastly! It really is.

Colford. I'm going in to shake hands with him. [*He starts to cross the room.*]

Twisden. Wait! We want him to go straight off to Morocco. Don't upset him. [*To* COLFORD *and* MARGARET.] I think you had better go. If, a little later, Margaret, you could go round to Mrs. Dancy——

Colford. Poor little Mabel Dancy! It's perfect hell for her.

[*They have not seen that* DANCY *has opened the door behind them.*]

Dancy. It is!

[*They all turn round in consternation.*]

Colford. [*With a convulsive movement.*] Old boy!

Dancy. No good, Colford. [*Gazing round at them.*] Oh! clear out. I can't stand commiseration—and let me have some air.

[TWISDEN *motions to* COLFORD *and* MARGARET *to go; and as he turns to* DANCY, *they go out.* GRAVITER *also moves toward the door. The* GENERAL *sits motionless.* GRAVITER *goes out.*]

Twisden. Well?

Dancy. I'm going home, to clear up things with my wife. General Canynge, I don't quite know why I did the damned thing. But I did, and there's an end of it.

Canynge. Dancy, for the honor of the Army, avoid further scandal if you can. I've written a letter to a friend of mine in the Spanish War Office. It will get you a job in their war. [CANYNGE *closes the envelope.*]

Dancy. Very good of you. I don't know if I can make use of it.

[CANYNGE *stretches out the letter, which* TWISDEN *hands to* DANCY, *who takes it.* GRAVITER *re-opens the door.*]

Twisden. What is it?

Graviter. De Levis is here.

Twisden. De Levis? Can't see him.

Dancy. Let him in!

[*After a moment's hesitation* TWISDEN *nods, and* GRAVITER *goes out. The three wait in silence with their eyes fixed on the door, the* GENERAL *sitting at the table,* TWISDEN *by his chair,* DANCY *between him and the door Right.* DE LEVIS *comes in and shuts the door. He is advancing toward* TWISDEN *when his eyes fall on* DANCY, *and he stops.*]

Twisden. You wanted to see me?

De Levis. [*Moistening his lips.*] Yes. I came to say that—that I overheard—I am afraid a warrant is to be issued. I wanted you to realize—it's not *my* doing. I'll give it no support. I'm content. I don't want my money. I don't even want costs. Dancy, do you understand?

[DANCY *does not answer, but looks at him with nothing alive in his face but his eyes.*]

Twisden. We are obliged to you, sir. It was good of you to come.

De Levis. [*With a sort of darting pride.*] Don't mistake me. I didn't come because I feel Christian; I am a Jew. I will take no money—not even that which was stolen. Give it to a charity. I'm proved right. And now I'm done with the damned thing. Good-morning!

[*He makes a little bow to* CANYNGE *and* TWISDEN, *and turns to face* DANCY, *who has never moved. The two stand motionless, looking at each other, then* DE LEVIS *shrugs his shoulders and walks out. When he is gone there is a silence.*]

Canynge. [*Suddenly.*] You heard what he said, Dancy. You have no time to lose.

[*But* DANCY *does not stir.*]

Twisden. Captain Dancy?

[*Slowly, without turning his head, rather like a man in a dream,* DANCY *walks across the room, and goes out.*]

CURTAIN

SCENE III

The DANCYS' *sitting-room, a few minutes later.*

[MABEL DANCY *is sitting alone on the sofa with a newspaper on her lap; she is only just up, and has a bottle of smelling-salts in her hand. Two or three other newspapers are dumped on the arm of the sofa. She topples the one off her lap and takes up another as if she couldn't keep away from them; drops it in turn, and sits staring before her, sniffing at the salts. The door, Right, is opened and* DANCY *comes in.*]

Mabel. [*Utterly surprised.*] Ronny! Do they want me in Court?

Dancy. No.

Mabel. What is it, then? Why are you back?

Dancy. Spun.

Mabel. [*Blank.*] Spun? What do you mean? What's spun?

Dancy. The case. They've found out through those notes.

Mabel. Oh! [*Staring at his face.*] Who?

Dancy. Me!

Mabel. [*After a moment of horrified stillness.*] Don't, Ronny! Oh! No! Don't!

[*She buries her face in the pillows of the sofa.* DANCY *stands looking down at her.*]

Dancy. Pity you wouldn't come to Arrica three months ago.

Mabel. Why didn't you tell me then? I would have gone.

Dancy. You wanted this case. Well, it's fallen down.

Mabel. Oh! Why didn't I face it? But I couldn't—I *had* to believe.

Dancy. And now you can't. It's the end, Mabel.

Mabel. [*Looking up at him.*] No.

[DANCY *goes suddenly on his knees and seizes her hand.*]

Dancy. Forgive me!

Mabel. [*Putting her hand on his head.*] Yes; oh, yes! I think I've known a long time, really. Only—why? What made you?

Dancy. [*Getting up and speaking in jerks.*] It was a crazy thing to do; but, damn it, I was only looting a looter. The money was as much mine as his. A decent chap would have offered me half. You didn't see the brute look at me that night at dinner as much as to say: "You blasted fool!" It made me mad. That wasn't a bad jump—twice over. Nothing in the war took quite such nerve. [*Grimly.*] I rather enjoyed that evening.

Mabel. But—money! To keep it!

Dancy. [*Sullenly.*] Yes, but I had a debt to pay.

Mabel. To a woman?

Dancy. A debt of honor—it wouldn't wait.

Mabel. It was—it was to a woman. Ronny, don't lie any more.

Dancy. [*Grimly.*] Well! I wanted to save your knowing. I'd promised a thousand. I had a letter from her father that morning, threatening to tell you. All the same, if that tyke hadn't jeered at me for parlor tricks!—But what's the good of all this now? [*Sullenly.*] Well—it may cure you of loving me. Get over that, Mab; I never was worth it—and I'm done for!

Mabel. The woman—have you—since ——?

Dancy. [*Energetically.*] No! You supplanted her. But if you'd known I was leaving a woman for you, you'd never have married me. [*He walks over to the hearth.*]

[MABEL, *too, gets up. She presses her hands to her forehead, then walks blindly round to behind the sofa and stands looking straight in front of her.*]

Mabel. [*Coldly.*] What has happened, exactly?

Dancy. Sir Frederic chucked up the case. I've seen Twisden; they want me to run for it to Morocco.

Mabel. To the war there?

Dancy. Yes. There's to be a warrant out.

Mabel. A prosecution? Prison? Oh, go! Don't wait a minute! Go!

Dancy. Blast them!

Mabel. Oh, Ronny! Please! Please! Think what you'll want. I'll pack. Quick! No! Don't wait to take things. Have you got money?

Dancy. [*Nodding.*] This'll be good-by, then!

Mabel. [*After a moment's struggle.*] Oh! No! No, no! I'll follow—I'll come out to you there.

Dancy. D'you mean you'll stick to me?

Mabel. Of course I'll stick to you.

[DANCY *seizes her hand and puts it to his lips. The bell rings.*]

Mabel. [*In terror.*] Who's that? [*The bell rings again.* DANCY *moves toward the door.*] No! Let me!

[*She passes him and steals out to the outer door of the flat, where she stands listening. The bell rings again. She looks through the slit of the letter-box. While she is gone* DANCY *stands quite still, till she comes back.*]

Mabel. Through the letter-box—I can see — It's—it's police. Oh! God! . . . Ronny! I can't bear it.

Dancy. Heads up, Mab! Don't show the brutes!

Mabel. Whatever happens, I'll go on loving you. If it's prison—*I'll wait.* Do you understand? I don't care what you did—I don't *care!* I'm just the same. I will be just the same when you come back to me.

Dancy. [*Slowly.*] That's not in human nature.

Mabel. It is. It's in *me.*

Dancy. I've crocked up your life.

Mabel. No, no! Kiss me!

[*A long kiss, till the bell again startles them apart, and there is a loud knock.*]

Dancy. They'll break the door in. It's no good—we must open. Hold them in check a little. I want a minute or two.

Mabel. [*Clasping him.*] Ronny! Oh, Ronny! It won't be for long—I'll be waiting! I'll be waiting—I swear it.

Dancy. Steady, Mab! [*Putting her back from him.*] Now!

[*He opens the bedroom door, Left, and stands waiting for her to go. Summoning up her courage, she goes to open the outer door. A sudden change comes over* DANCY'S *face; from being stony it grows almost maniacal.*]

Dancy. [*Under his breath.*] No! No! By God! No!

[*He goes out into the bedroom, closing the door behind him.*]

[MABEL *has now opened the outer door, and disclosed* INSPECTOR DEDE *and the* YOUNG CONSTABLE *who were summoned to Meldon Court on the night of the theft, and have been witnesses in the case. Their voices are heard.*]

Mabel. Yes?

Inspector. Captain Dancy in, madam?

Mabel. I am not quite sure—I don't think so.

Inspector. I wish to speak to him a minute. Stay here, Grover. Now, madam!

Mabel. Will you come in while I see?

[*She comes in, followed by the* INSPECTOR.]

Inspector. I should think you must be sure, madam. This is not a big place.

Mabel. He was changing his clothes to go out. I think he has gone.

Inspector. What's that door?

Mabel. To our bedroom.

Inspector. [*Moving toward it.*] He'll be in there, then.

Mabel. What do you want, Inspector?

Inspector. [*Melting.*] Well, madam, it's no use disguising it. I'm exceedingly sorry, but I've a warrant for his arrest.

Mabel. Inspector!

Inspector. I'm sure I've every sympathy for you, madam; but I must carry out my instructions.

Mabel. And break my heart?

Inspector. Well, madam, we're—we're not allowed to take that into consideration. The Law's the Law.

Mabel. Are you married?

Inspector. I am.

Mabel. If you—your wife——

[*The* INSPECTOR *raises his hand, deprecating.*]

[*Speaking low.*] Just half an hour! Couldn't you? It's two lives—two whole lives! We've only been married four months. Come back in half an hour. It's such a little thing—nobody will know. Nobody. Won't you?

Inspector. Now, madam—you must know my duty.

Mabel. Inspector, I beseech you—just half an hour.

Inspector. No, no—don't you try to undermine me—I'm sorry for you; but don't you try it!

[*He tries the handle, then knocks at the door.*]

Dancy's Voice. One minute!

Inspector. It's locked. [*Sharply.*] Is there another door to that room? Come, now! [*The bell rings. Moving toward the door, Left; to the* CONSTABLE.] Who's that out there?

Constable. A lady and a gentleman, sir.

Inspector. What lady and—— Stand by, Grover!

Dancy's Voice. All right! You can come in *now.*

[*There is the noise of a lock being turned. And almost immediately the sound of a pistol shot in the bedroom.* MABEL *rushes to the door, tears it open, and disappears within, followed by the* INSPECTOR, *just as* MARGARET ORME *and* COLFORD *come in from the passage, pursued by the* CONSTABLE. *They, too, all hurry to the bedroom door and disappear for a moment; then* COLFORD *and* MARGARET *reappear, supporting* MABEL, *who faints as they lay her on the sofa.* COLFORD *takes from her hand an envelope, and tears it open.*]

Colford. It's addressed to me.

[*He reads it aloud to* MARGARET *in a low voice.*]

"DEAR COLFORD,—This is the only decent thing I can do. It's too damned unfair to her. It's only another jump. A pistol keeps faith. Look after her, Colford—my love to her, and you."

[MARGARET *gives a sort of choking sob, then, seeing the smelling bottle, she snatches it up, and turns to revive* MABEL.]

Colford. Leave her! The longer she's unconscious, the better.

Inspector. [*Re-entering.*] This is a very serious business, sir.

Colford. [*Sternly.*] Yes, Inspector; you've done for my best friend.

Inspector. I, sir? He shot himself.

Colford. Hari-kari.

Inspector. Beg pardon?

Colford. [*He points with the letter to* MABEL.] For her sake, and his own.

Inspector. [*Putting out his hand.*] I'll want that, sir.

Colford. [*Grimly.*] You shall have it read at the inquest. Till then—it's addressed to me, and I stick to it.

Inspector. Very well, sir. Do you want to have a look at him?

[COLFORD *passes quickly into the bedroom, followed by the* INSPECTOR. MARGARET *remains kneeling beside* MABEL.]

[COLFORD *comes quickly back.* MARGARET *looks up at him. He stands very still.*]

Colford. Neatly—through the heart.

Margaret. [*Wildly.*] Keeps faith! We've all done that. It's not enough.

Colford. [*Looking down at* MABEL.] All right, old boy!

THE CURTAIN FALLS

DEAR BRUTUS*

By

J. M. BARRIE

BARRIE SAID HE ONCE "CAUTIOUSLY bought a book about how to write plays. . . . But the book was so learned and the author knew so much, and the subject when studied grew so difficult," that he hurriedly abandoned his inquiry. He told the undergraduates of St. Andrews he had in him an imp he called M'Connachie that he preferred to trust. Call him fantastic or spiritual, if you wish, but never "whimsical" or "elusive," unless you want to incur the scorn he once expressed for critics who described him by these hackneyed epithets. He has imparted a charm of fancy to our theater—also, let us admit, to the homeliness of our lives—that is unquestionably one of the great literary achievements of the age. It made obsolete the heavy-headedness of sham realism and still serves as a pleasing antidote to the more pretentious psychological experiments in modern drama. We return again and again to Barrie as to a clear spring. Posterity may do so likewise. In spite of his disclaimer, his technique is far too crystalline and purposeful to be wholly an accident of genius. It gives his plays a prominent place in many of the books on technique which he affects not to understand. It is governed by a sure sense of the stage and of the nature of audiences which only long experience and careful experimentation could have developed in him. (See note on *What Every Woman Knows*). He had style, in the best sense of that term, as the expression of a rare and fascinating mentality.

Imaginatively he imparted to the drabbest of persons and things—gas meters, charwomen, butlers, and policemen—an elfin value, even when they remained their worldly selves. But this lightness of touch did not aimlessly place the mask of gayety on the stern truths that often lie at the heart of his plays. No one saw more surely the harshness of reality—perhaps, also its futility—than Barrie. His fantasy, then, should not be regarded as an expression of "mawkish sentimentality," that some have thought it to be. It is rather the expression of the indomitable courage that was Barrie's evangel. He nowhere cried, "All's right with the world," but he calmly said, "The brave ones can [change for the better]—the ones with the thin bright faces."

Such was the meaning to Barrie of this essentially disillusioned post-war play, *Dear Brutus,* built though it is on a character as eerie as Puck, whose pranks in *A Midsummer Night's Dream* he grimly modernized. In it M'Connachie—perhaps Lob is none other—has completely released us from the "closed-in" drama of the Ibsen tradition, even to the extent it showed itself in *Crichton* and *What Every Woman Knows.* We are not lost, however, in the abstractions of expressionism, but we sense behind the characters and their action allegorical values like those of the old moralities. As too often in Barrie, we have the suggestion of playing close to the edge of the absurd or the sentimental and of being drawn back just in time. M'Connachie again. But could the meaning of beauty or of love be more effectively—shall we say tragically—projected against the forces of spiritual annihilation than in this play? There is only a narrow step from its disillusionment to cynicism, but we are held back also from taking that step.

Although Sir James's life was almost as mysterious as his genius, it was marked by great friendships with Conan Doyle, Bernard Shaw, and others, and by many acts of wisdom and charity that have put the stamp of sincerity upon the humaneness of his art. He was a faithful and hard-working collaborator with his producers and actors, even in the filming of his plays. He amassed a fortune without abandoning his artistic integrity or submitting to vulgarity or fads.

Technically he was a master in the projection of character by the sure choice of ex pressive detail and by the subordination of all such detail to his dramatic purpose. He had one technical device that enabled him to avoid the banalities of the well-made play, which, as Shaw declared, he relegated "to the dust-bin." He called this device "slipping in an island." "I should feel," he once told a company of his critics, "as if I had left off my clothing, if I were to write without an island." But the island was not always actual as that in *Crichton.* It was any means by which he might uproot his characters from their commonplace existence and place them in a contrasting environment which displayed them in more essential and more dramatic relations. Thus he both pointed his social satire, as did Swift and Butler, and also broadened and intensified his characters. It is the test-tube method, but so fancifully employed as to make us forget that it is strategy.

Dear Brutus was first produced at Wyndham's Theatre in London by Gerald du Maurier, who acted the part of Dearth. This veteran actor-manager, who had created also the rôle of John Shand, brought to the character the lightest and most fluent naturalism to be found among London's admirable comedians. In 1922 he revived the play, even more successfully. It was given in New York on Dec. 23, 1918, with William Gillette as Dearth and Helen Hayes as Margaret. It has had innumerable productions in our little theaters.

For biographical data and play list see *What Every Woman Knows,* p. 553 ff.

DEAR BRUTUS

ACT I

The scene is a darkened room, which the curtain reveals so stealthily that if there was a mouse on the stage it is there still. Our object is to catch our two chief characters unawares; they are Darkness and Light.

The room is so obscure as to be invisible, but at the back of the obscurity are French windows, through which is seen LOB'S *garden bathed in moonshine. The Darkness and Light, which this room and garden represent, are very still, but we should feel that it is only the pause in which old enemies regard each other before they come to the grip. The moonshine stealing about among the flowers, to give them their last instructions, has left a smile upon them, but it is a smile with a menace in it for the dwellers in darkness. What we expect to see next is the moonshine slowly pushing the windows open, so that it may whisper to a confederate in the house, whose name is* LOB. *But though we may be sure that this was about to happen it does not happen; a stir among the dwellers in darkness prevents it.*

These unsuspecting ones are in the dining-room, and as a communicating door opens we hear them at play. Several tenebrous shades appear in the lighted doorway and hesitate on the two steps that lead down into the unlit room. The fanciful among us may conceive a rustle at the same moment among the flowers. The engagement has begun, though not in the way we had intended.

VOICES.—

"Go on, Coady: lead the way."

"Oh dear, I don't see why I should go first."

"The nicest always goes first."

"It is a strange house if I am the nicest."

"It is a strange house."

"Don't close the door; I can't see where the switch is."

"Over here."

They have been groping their way forward, blissfully unaware of how they shall be groping there again more terribly before the night is out. Some one finds a switch, and the room is illumined, with the effect that the garden seems to have drawn back a step as if worsted in the first encounter. But it is only waiting.

The apparently inoffensive chamber thus suddenly revealed is, for a bachelor's home, creditably like a charming country house drawing-room and abounds in the little feminine touches that are so often best applied by the hand of man. There is nothing in the room inimical to the ladies, unless it be the cut flowers which are from the garden and possibly in collusion with it. The fireplace may also be a little dubious. It has been hacked out of a thick wall which may have been there when the other walls were not, and is presumably the cavern where LOB, *when alone, sits chatting to himself among the blue smoke. He is as much at home by this fire as any gnome that may be hiding among its shadows; but he is less familiar with the rest of the room, and when he sees it, as for instance on his lonely way to bed, he often stares long and hard at it before chuckling uncomfortably.*

[*There are five ladies, and one only of them is elderly, the* MRS. COADE *whom a voice in the darkness has already proclaimed the nicest. She is the nicest though the voice was no good judge.* COADY, *as she is familiarly called and as her husband also is called, each having for many years been able to answer for the other, is a rounded old lady with a beaming smile that has accompanied her from childhood. If she lives to be a hundred she will pretend to the census man that she is only ninety-nine. She has no other vice that has not been smoothed out of existence by her placid life, and she has but one complaint against the male* COADY, *the rather odd one that he has long forgotten his first wife. Our* MRS. COADY *never knew the first one, but it is she alone who sometimes looks at the portrait of her and preserves in their home certain mementoes of her, such as a lock of brown hair which the equally gentle male* COADY *must have treasured once but has now forgotten. The first wife had been slightly lame, and in their brief married life he had carried solicitously a rest for her foot, had got so accustomed to doing this, that after a quarter of a century with our* MRS. COADY *he still finds footstools for her as if she were lame also. She has ceased to pucker her face over this, taking it as a kind little thoughtless attention, and indeed with the years has developed a friendly limp. Of the other four ladies, all young and physically fair, two are married.* MRS. DEARTH *is tall, of smouldering eye and fierce desires, murky beasts lie in ambush in the labyrinths of her mind, she is a white-faced gypsy with a husky voice, most beautiful when she is sullen, and therefore frequently at her best. The other ladies when in conclave refer to her as* THE DEARTH. MRS. PURDIE *is a safer companion for the toddling kind of man. She is soft and pleading, and would seek what she wants by laying her head on the loved one's shoulder, while* THE DEARTH *might attain it with a pistol. A brighter spirit than either is* JOANNA TROUT, *who, when her affections are not engaged, has a merry face and figure, but can dismiss them both at the important moment, which is at the word "love." Then* JOANNA *quivers, her sense of humor ceases to beat, and the dullest man may go ahead. There remains* LADY CAROLINE LANEY *of the disdainful poise, lately from the enormously select school where they are taught to pronounce their* r's *as* w's; *nothing else seems to be taught, but for matrimonial success nothing else is necessary. Every woman who pronounces* r *as* w *will find a mate; it appeals to all that is chivalrous in man.*

An old-fashioned gallantry induces us to accept from each of these ladies her own estimate of herself, and fortunately it is favorable in every case. This refers to their estimate of themselves up to the hour of ten on the evening on which we first meet them; the estimate may have changed temporarily by the time we part from them on the following morning. What their mirrors say to each of them is, A dear face, not classically perfect but abounding in that changing charm which is the best type of English womanhood; here is a woman who has seen and felt far more than her reticent nature readily betrays; she sometimes smiles, but behind that concession, controlling it in a manner hardly less than adorable, lurks the sigh called Knowledge; a strangely interesting face, mysterious; a line for her tombstone might be, "If I had been a man what adventures I could have had with her who lies here."

Are these ladies then so very alike? They would all deny it, so we must take our own soundings. At this moment of their appearance in the drawing-room at least they are alike in having a common interest. No sooner has the dining-room door closed than purpose leaps to their eyes; oddly enough, the men having been got rid of, the drama begins.]

Alice Dearth. [*The darkest spirit but the bravest.*] We must not waste a second. Our minds are made up, I think?

Joanna. Now is the time.

Mrs. Coade. [*At once delighted and appalled.*] Yes, now if at all; but should we?

Alice. Certainly; and before the men come in.

Mabel Purdie. You don't think we should wait for the men? They are as much in it as we are.

Lady Caroline. [*Unlucky, as her opening remark is without a single* r.] Lob would be with them. If the thing is to be done at all it should be done now.

Mrs. Coade. Is it quite fair to Lob? After all, he is our host.

Joanna. Of course it isn't fair to him, but let's do it, Coady.

Mrs. Coade. Yes, let's do it!

Mabel. Mrs. Dearth *is* doing it.

Alice. [*Who is writing out a telegram.*] Of course I am. The men are not coming, are they?

Joanna. [*Reconnoitering.*] No; your husband is having another glass of port.

Alice. I am sure he is. One of you ring, please. [*The bold* JOANNA *rings.*]

Mrs. Coade. Poor Matey!

Lady Caroline. He wichly desewves what he is about to get.

Joanna. He is coming! Don't all stand huddled together like conspirators.

Mrs. Coade. It is what we are!

[*Swiftly they find seats, and are sunk thereon like ladies waiting languidly for their lords, when the doomed* BUTLER *appears. He is a man of brawn, who would cast any one of them forth for a wager; but we are about to connive at the triumph of mind over matter.*]

Alice. [*Always at her best before "the*

bright face of danger."] Ah, Matey, I wish this telegram sent.

Matey. [*A general favorite.*] Very good, ma'am. The village post office closed at eight, but if your message is important——

Alice. It is; and you are so clever, Matey, I am sure that you can persuade them to oblige you.

Matey. [*Taking the telegram.*] I will see to it myself, ma'am; you can depend on its going.

[*There comes a little gasp from* COADY, *which is the equivalent to dropping a stitch in needlework.*]

Alice. [*Who is* THE DEARTH *now.*] Thank you. Better read the telegram, Matey, to be sure that you can make it out. [MATEY *reads it to himself, and he has never quite the same faith in woman again.* THE DEARTH *continues in a purring voice.*] Read it aloud, Matey.

Matey. Oh, ma'am!

Alice. [*Without the purr.*] Aloud.

[*Thus encouraged, he reads the fatal missive.*]

Matey. "To Police Station, Great Cumney. Send officer first thing tomorrow morning to arrest Matey, butler, for theft of rings."

Alice. Yes, that is quite right.

Matey. Ma'am! [*But seeing that she has taken up a book, he turns to* LADY CAROLINE.] My lady!

Lady Caroline. [*Whose voice strikes colder than* THE DEARTH'S.] Should we not say how many wings?

Alice. Yes, put in the number of rings, Matey.

[MATEY *does not put in the number, but he produces three rings from unostentatious parts of his person and returns them without noticeable dignity to their various owners.*]

Matey. [*Hopeful that the incident is now closed.*] May I tear up the telegram, ma'am?

Alice. Certainly not.

Lady Caroline. I always said that this man was the culpwit. I am nevaw mistaken in faces, and I see bwoad awwows * all over youws, Matey.

[*He might reply that he sees* w's *all over hers, but it is no moment for repartee.*]

Matey. It is deeply regretted.

Alice. [*Darkly.*] I am sure it is.

Joanna. [*Who has seldom remained silent for so long.*] We may as well tell him now that it is not our rings we are worrying about. They have just been a means to an end, Matey.

[*The stir among the ladies shows that they have arrived at the more interesting point.*]

Alice. Precisely. In other words that telegram is sent unless——

[MATEY'S *head rises.*]

Joanna. Unless you can tell us instantly what peculiarity it is that all we ladies have in common.

Mabel. Not only the ladies; all the guests in this house.

Alice. We have been here a week, and we find that when Lob invited us he knew us all so little that we begin to wonder why he asked us. And now from words he has let drop we know that we were invited because of something he thinks we have in common.

Mabel. But he won't say what it is.

Lady Caroline. [*Drawing back a little from* JOANNA.] One knows that no people could be more unlike.

Joanna. [*Thankfully.*] One does.

Mrs. Coade. And we can't sleep at night, Matey, for wondering what this something is.

Joanna. [*Summing up.*] But we are sure you know, and if you don't tell us—quod.

Matey. [*With growing uneasiness.*] I don't know what you mean, ladies.

Alice. Oh yes, you do.

Mrs. Coade. You must admit that your master is a very strange person.

Matey. [*Wriggling.*] He is a little odd, ma'am. That is why every one calls him Lob; not Mr. Lob.

Joanna. He is so odd that it has got on my nerves that we have been invited here for some sort of horrid experiment. [MATEY *shivers.*] You look as if you thought so too!

Matey. Oh no, miss, I—he—— [*The words he would keep back elude him.*] You shouldn't have come, ladies; you didn't ought to have come.

[*For the moment he is sorrier for them than for himself.*]

Lady Caroline. Shouldn't have come! Now, my man, what do you mean by that?

Matey. Nothing, my lady: I—I just mean, why did you come if you are the kind he thinks?

Mabel. The kind he thinks?

Alice. What kind does he think? Now we are getting at it.

Matey. [*Guardedly.*] I haven't a notion, ma'am.

Lady Caroline. [*Whose* w's *must henceforth be supplied by the judicious reader.*] Then it is not necessarily our virtue that makes Lob interested in us?

* Broad arrows are stamped on convicts' suits in England.

Matey. [*Thoughtlessly.*] No, my lady; oh no, my lady.

[*This makes an unfavorable impression.*]

Mrs. Coade. And yet, you know, he is rather lovable.

Matey. [*Carried away.*] He is, ma'am. He is the most lovable old devil—I beg pardon, ma'am.

Joanna. You scarcely need to, for in a way it is true. I have seen him out there among his flowers, petting them, talking to them, coaxing them till they simply *had* to grow.

Alice. [*Making use perhaps of the wrong adjective.*] It is certainly a divine garden.

[*They all look at the unblinking enemy.*]

Mrs. Coade. [*Not more deceived than the others.*] How lovely it is in the moonlight! Roses, roses, all the way. [*Dreamily.*] It is like a hat I once had when I was young.

Alice. Lob is such an amazing gardener that I believe he could even grow hats.

Lady Caroline. [*Who will catch it for this.*] He is a wonderful gardener; but is that quite nice at his age? What *is* his age, man?

Matey. [*Shuffling.*] He won't tell, my lady. I think he is frightened that the police would step in if they knew how old he is. They do say in the village that they remember him seventy years ago, looking just as he does today.

Alice. Absurd.

Matey. Yes, ma'am; but there are his razors.

Lady Caroline. Razors?

Matey. *You* won't know about razors, my lady, not being married—as yet—excuse me. But a married lady can tell a man's age by the number of his razors. [*A little scared.*] If you saw his razors—there is a little world of them, from patents of the present day back to implements so horrible, you can picture him with them in his hand scraping his way through the ages.

Lady Caroline. You amuse one to an extent. Was he ever married?

Matey. [*Too lightly.*] He has quite forgotten, my lady. [*Reflecting.*] How long ago is it since Merry England?

Lady Caroline. Why do you ask?

Mabel. In Queen Elizabeth's time, wasn't it?

Matey. He says he is all that is left of Merry England: that little man.

Mabel. [*Who has brothers.*] Lob? I think there is a famous cricketer called Lob.

Mrs. Coade. Wasn't there a Lob in Shakespeare? No, of course I am thinking of Robin Goodfellow.

Lady Caroline. The names are so alike.

Joanna. Robin Goodfellow was Puck.

Mrs. Coade. [*With natural elation.*] That is what was in my head. Lob was another name for Puck.

Joanna. Well, he is certainly rather like what Puck might have grown into if he had forgotten to die. And, by the way, I remember now he does call his flowers by the old Elizabethan names.

Matey. He always calls the Nightingale Philomel, miss—if that is any help.

Alice. [*Who is not omniscient.*] None whatever. Tell me this, did he specially ask you all for Midsummer week?

[*They assent.*]

Matey. [*Who might more judiciously have remained silent.*] He would!

Mrs. Coade. Now what do you mean?

Matey. He always likes them to be here on Midsummer night, ma'am.

Alice. Them? Whom?

Matey. They who have that in common.

Mabel. What can it be?

Matey. I don't know.

Lady Caroline. [*Suddenly introspective.*] I hope we are all nice women? We don't know each other very well. [*Certain suspicions are reborn in various breasts.*] Does anything startling happen at those times?

Matey. I don't know.

Joanna. Why, I believe this is Midsummer Eve!

Matey. Yes, miss, it is. The villagers know it. They are all inside their houses, tonight—with the doors barred.

Lady Caroline. Because of—of him?

Matey. He frightens them. There are stories.

Alice. What alarms them? Tell us—or——

[*She brandishes the telegram.*]

Matey. I know nothing for certain, ma'am. I have never done it myself. He has wanted me to, but I wouldn't.

Mabel. Done what?

Matey. [*With fine appeal.*] Oh, ma'am, don't ask me. Be merciful to me, ma'am. I am not bad naturally. It was just going into domestic service that did for me; the accident of being flung among bad companions. It's touch and go how the poor turn out in this world; all depends on your taking the right or the wrong turning.

Mrs. Coade. [*The lenient.*] I daresay that is true.

Matey. [*Under this touch of sun.*] When I was young, ma'am, I was offered a clerkship in the city. If I had taken it there wouldn't be a more honest man alive today.

I would give the world to be able to begin over again.

[He means every word of it, though the flowers would here, if they dared, burst into ironical applause.]

Mrs. Coade. It is very sad, Mrs. Dearth.

Alice. I am sorry for him; but still——

Matey. [*His eyes turning to* LADY CAROLINE.] What do you say, my lady?

Lady Caroline. [*Briefly.*] As you ask me, I should certainly say jail.

Matey. [*Desperately.*] If you will say no more about this, ma'am—I'll give you a tip that is worth it.

Alice. Ah, now you are talking.

Lady Caroline. Don't listen to him.

Matey. [*Lowering.*] You are the one that is hardest on me.

Lady Caroline. Yes, I flatter myself I am.

Matey. [*Forgetting himself.*] You might take a wrong turning yourself, my lady.

Lady Caroline. I? How dare you, man?

[But the flowers rather like him for this: it is possibly what gave them a certain idea.]

Joanna. [*Near the keyhole of the dining-room door.*] The men are rising.

Alice. [*Hurriedly.*] Very well, Matey, we agree—if the "tip" is good enough.

Lady Caroline. You will regret this.

Matey. I think not, my lady. It's this: I wouldn't go out tonight if he asks you. Go into the garden, if you like. The garden is all right. [*He really believes this.*] I wouldn't go farther—not tonight.

Mrs. Coade. But he never proposes to us to go farther. Why should he tonight?

Matey. I don't know, ma'am; but don't any of you go—[*devilishly*] except you, my lady; I should like you to go.

Lady Caroline. Fellow!

[They consider this odd warning.]

Alice. Shall I?

[They nod and she tears up the telegram.]

Matey. [*With a gulp.*] Thank you, ma'am.

Lady Caroline. You should have sent that telegram off.

Joanna. You are sure you have told us all you know, Matey?

Matey. Yes, miss. [*But at the door he is more generous.*] Above all, ladies, I wouldn't go into the wood.

Mabel. The wood? Why, there is no wood within a dozen miles of here.

Matey. No, ma'am. But all the same I wouldn't go into it, ladies—not if I was you.

[With this cryptic warning he leaves them, and any discussion of it is prevented by the arrival of their host. LOB *is very small, and probably no one ha ever looked so old except some new-bor child. To such as watch him narrowly as the ladies now do for the first time he has the effect of seeming to be hol low, an attenuated piece of piping in sufficiently inflated; one feels that if h were to strike against a solid object h might rebound feebly from it, whic would be less disconcerting if he did no obviously know this and carefully avoi the furniture; he is so light that th subject must not be mentioned in hi presence, but it is possible that, wer the ladies to combine, they could blow him out of a chair. He enters porten tously, his hands behind his back, a if every bit of him, from his domed hea to his little feet, were the physical ex pressions of the deep thoughts withi him; then suddenly he whirls round t make his guests jump. This amuses hin vastly, and he regains his gravity wit difficulty. He addresses* MRS. COADE.*]*

Lob. Standing, dear lady? Pray be seatec

[He finds a chair for her and pulls i away as she is about to sit, or kindl pretends to be about to do so, for h has had this quaint conceit every eve ning since she arrived.]

Mrs. Coade. [*Who loves children.*] Yo naughty!

Lob. [*Eagerly.*] It is quite a flirtation isn't it?

[He rolls on a chair, kicking out hi legs in an ecstasy of satisfaction. Bu the ladies are not certain that he is th little innocent they have hitherto though him. The advent of MR. COADE *and* MR PURDIE *presently adds to their misgiv ings.* MR. COADE *is old, a sweet pippi of a man with a gentle smile for all; h must have suffered much, you conclud incorrectly, to acquire that toleran smile. Sometimes, as when he see other people at work, a wistful look take the place of the smile, and* MR. COAD *fidgets like one who would be elsewhere Then there rises before his eyes the roon called the study in his house, whose wall are lined with boxes marked A. B. C. t Z. and A^2. B^2. C^2 to K^2. These contai dusty notes for his great work on th Feudal System, the notes many year old, the work, strictly speaking, not ye begun. He still speaks at times of finish ing it but never of beginning it. H knows that in more favorable circum stances, for instance if he had been poor man instead of pleasantly well t*

do, he could have flung himself avidly into that noble undertaking; but he does not allow his secret sorrow to embitter him or darken the house. Quickly the vision passes, and he is again his bright self. Idleness, he says in his game way, has its recompenses. It is charming now to see how he at once crosses to his wife, solicitous for her comfort. He is bearing down on her with a footstool when MR. PURDIE *comes from the dining-room. He is the most brilliant of our company, recently notable in debate at Oxford, where he was runner-up for the presidentship of the Union and only lost it because the other man was less brilliant. Since then he has gone to the bar on Monday, married on Tuesday and had a brief on Wednesday. Beneath his brilliance, and making charming company for himself, he is aware of intellectual powers beyond his years. As we are about to see, he has made one mistake in his life which he is bravely facing.*]

Alice. Is my husband still sampling the port, Mr. Purdie?

Purdie. [*With a disarming smile for the absent* DEARTH.] Do you know, I believe he is. Do the ladies like our proposal, Coade?

Coade. I have not told them of it yet. The fact is, I am afraid that it might tire my wife too much. Do you feel equal to a little exertion tonight, Coady, or is your foot troubling you?

Mrs. Coade. [*The kind creature.*] I have been resting it, Coady.

Coade. [*Propping it on the footstool.*] There! Is that more comfortable? Presently, dear, if you are agreeable we are all going out for a walk.

Mrs. Coade. [*Quoting* MATEY.] The garden is all right.

Purdie. [*With jocular solemnity.*] Ah, but it is not to be the garden. We are going farther afield. We have an adventure for tonight. Get thick shoes and a wrap, Mrs. Dearth; all of you.

Lady Caroline. [*With but languid interest.*] Where do you propose to take us?

Purdie. To find a mysterious wood.

[*With the word "wood" the ladies are blown upright. Their eyes turn to* LOB, *who, however, has never looked more innocent.*]

Joanna. Are you being funny, Mr. Purdie? You know quite well that there are not any trees for miles around. You have said yourself that it is the one blot on the landscape.

Coade. [*Almost as great a humorist as* PURDIE.] Ah, on ordinary occasions! But allow us to point out to you, Miss Joanna, that this is Midsummer Eve.

[LOB *again comes sharply under female observation.*]

Purdie. Tell them what you told us, Lob.

Lob. [*With a pout for the credulous.*] It is all nonsense, of course; just foolish talk of the villagers. They say that on Midsummer Eve there is a strange wood in this part of the country.

Alice. [*Lowering.*] Where?

Purdie. Ah, that is one of its most charming features. It is never twice in the same place apparently. It has been seen on different parts of the Downs and on More Common; once it was close to Radley village and another time about a mile from the sea. Oh, a sporting wood!

Lady Caroline. And Lob is anxious that we should all go and look for it?

Coade. Not he; Lob is the only sceptic in the house. Says it is all rubbish, and that we shall be sillies if we go. But we believe, eh, Purdie?

Purdie. [*Waggishly.*] Rather!

Lob. [*The artful.*] Just wasting the evening. Let us have a round game at cards here instead.

Purdie. [*Grandly.*] No, sir, I am going to find that wood.

Joanna. What is the good of it when it is found?

Purdie. We shall wander in it deliciously, listening to a new sort of bird called the Philomel.

[LOB *is behaving in the most exemplary manner: making sweet little clucking sounds.*]

Joanna. [*Doubtfully.*] Shall we keep together, Mr. Purdie?

Purdie. No, we must hunt in pairs.

Joanna. [*Converted.*] I think it would be rather fun. Come on, Coady, I'll lace your boots for you. I am sure your poor foot will carry you nicely.

Alice. Miss Trout, wait a moment. Lob, has this wonderful wood any special properties?

Lob. Pooh! There's no wood.

Lady Caroline. You've never seen it?

Lob. Not I. I don't believe in it.

Alice. Have any of the villagers ever been in it?

Lob. [*Dreamily.*] So it's said; so it's said.

Alice. What did they say were their experiences?

Lob. That isn't known. They never came back.

Joanna. [*Promptly resuming her seat.*] Never came back!

Lob. Absurd, of course. You see in the morning the wood was gone; and so they were gone, too. [*He clucks again.*]

Joanna. I don't think I like this wood.

Mrs. Coade. It certainly is Midsummer Eve.

Coade. [*Remembering that women are not yet civilized.*] Of course if you ladies are against it we will drop the idea. It was only a bit of fun.

Alice. [*With a malicious eye on* LOB.] Yes, better give it up—to please Lob.

Purdie. Oh, all right, Lob. What about that round game of cards?

[*The proposal meets with approval.*]

Lob. [*Bursting into tears.*] I wanted you to go. I had set my heart on your going. It is the thing I wanted, and it isn't good for me not to get the thing I want.

[*He creeps under the table and threatens the hands that would draw him out.*]

Mrs. Coade. Good gracious, he has wanted it all the time. You wicked Lob!

Alice. Now, you see there *is* something in it.

Coade. Nonsense, Mrs. Dearth, it was only a joke.

Mabel. [*Melting.*] Don't cry, Lobby.

Lob. Nobody cares for me—nobody loves me. And I need to be loved.

[*Several of them are on their knees to him.*]

Joanna. Yes, we do, we all love you. Nice, nice Lobby.

Mabel. Dear Lob, I am so fond of you.

Joanna. Dry his eyes with my own handkerchief.

[*He holds up his eyes but is otherwise inconsolable.*]

Lady Caroline. Don't pamper him.

Lob. [*Furiously.*] I need to be pampered.

Mrs. Coade. You funny little man. Let us go at once and look for his wood.

[*All feel that thus alone can his tears be dried.*]

Joanna. Boots and cloaks, hats forward. Come on, Lady Caroline, just to show you are not afraid of Matey.

[*There is a general exodus, and* LOB *left alone emerges from his temporary retirement. He clucks victoriously, but presently is on his knees again distressfully regarding some flowers that have fallen from their bowl.*]

Lob. Poor bruised one, it was I who hurt you. Lob is so sorry. Lie there! [*To another.*] Pretty, pretty, let me see where you have a pain? You fell on your head; is this the place? Now I make it better. Oh, little rascal, you are not hurt at all; you just pretend. Oh dear, oh dear! Sweetheart, don't cry, you are now prettier than ever. You were too tall. Oh, how beautifully you smell now that you are small. [*He replaces the wounded tenderly in their bowl.*] Drink, drink. Now, you are happy again. The little rascal smiles. All smile, please—nod heads—aha! aha! You love Lob—Lob loves you.

[JOANNA *and* MR. PURDIE *stroll in by the window.*]

Joanna. What were you saying to them, Lob?

Lob. I was saying "Two's company, three's none." [*He departs with a final cluck.*]

Joanna. That man—he suspects!

[*This is a very different* JOANNA *from the one who has so far flitted across our scene. It is also a different* PURDIE. *In company they seldom look at each other, though when the one does so the eyes of the other magnetically respond. We have seen them trivial, almost cynical, but now we are to greet them as they know they really are, the great strong-hearted man and his natural mate, in the grip of the master passion. For the moment* LOB'S *words have unnerved* JOANNA *and it is* JOHN PURDIE'S *dear privilege to soothe her.*]

Purdie. No one minds Lob. My dear, oh my dear.

Joanna. [*Faltering.*] Yes, but he saw you kiss my hand. Jack, if Mabel were to suspect!

Purdie. [*Happily.*] There is nothing for her to suspect.

Joanna. [*Eagerly.*] No, there isn't, is there? [*She is desirous ever to be without a flaw.*] Jack, I am not doing anything wrong, am I?

Purdie. You!

[*With an adorable gesture she gives him one of her hands, and manlike he takes the other also.*]

Joanna. Mabel is your wife, Jack. I should so hate myself if I did anything that was disloyal to her.

Purdie. [*Pressing her hand to her eyes as if counting them, in the strange manner of lovers.*] Those eyes could never be disloyal—my lady of the nut-brown eyes. [*He holds her from him, surveying her, and is scorched in the flame of her femininity.*] Oh, the sveldtness of you. [*Almost with reproach.*] Joanna, why are you so sveldt!

[*For his sake she would be less sveldt

if she could, but she can't. She admits her failure with eyes grown still larger, and he envelops her so that he may not see her. Thus men seek safety.]

Joanna. [*While out of sight.*] All I want is to help her and you.

Purdie. I know—how well I know—my dear brave love.

Joanna. I am very fond of Mabel, Jack. I should like to be the best friend she has in the world.

Purdie. You are, dearest. No woman ever had a better friend.

Joanna. And yet I don't think she really likes me. I wonder why?

Purdie. [*Who is the bigger brained of the two.*] It is just that Mabel doesn't understand. Nothing could make me say a word against my wife——

Joanna. [*Sternly.*] I wouldn't listen to you if you did.

Purdie. I love you all the more, dear, for saying that. But Mabel is a cold nature and she doesn't understand.

Joanna. [*Thinking never of herself but only of him.*] She doesn't appreciate your finer qualities.

Purdie. [*Ruminating.*] That's it. But of course I am difficult. I always was a strange, strange creature. I often think, Joanna, that I am rather like a flower that has never had the sun to shine on it nor the rain to water it.

Joanna. You break my heart.

Purdie. [*With considerable enjoyment.*] I suppose there is no more lonely man than I walking the earth today.

Joanna. [*Beating her wings.*] It is so mournful.

Purdie. It is the thought of you that sustains me, elevates me. You shine high above me like a star.

Joanna. No, no. I wish I was wonderful, but I am not.

Purdie. You have made me a better man, Joanna.

Joanna. I am so proud to think that.

Purdie. You have made me kinder to Mabel.

Joanna. I am sure you are always kind to her.

Purdie. Yes, I hope so. But I think now of special little ways of giving her pleasure. That never-to-be-forgotten day when we first met, you and I!

Joanna. [*Fluttering nearer to him.*] That tragic, lovely day by the weir. Oh, Jack!

Purdie. Do you know how in gratitude I spent the rest of that day?

Joanna. [*Crooning.*] Tell me.

Purdie. I read to Mabel aloud for an hour. I did it out of kindness to her, because I had met you.

Joanna. It was dear of you.

Purdie. Do you remember that first time my arms—your waist—you are so fluid, Joanna. [*Passionately.*] Why are you so fluid?

Joanna. [*Downcast.*] I can't help it, Jack.

Purdie. I gave her a ruby bracelet for that.

Joanna. It is a gem. You have given that lucky woman many lovely things.

Purdie. It is my invariable custom to go straight off and buy Mabel something whenever you have been sympathetic to me. Those new earrings of hers—they are in memory of the first day you called me Jack. Her Paquin gown—the one with the beads—was because you let me kiss you.

Joanna. I didn't exactly let you.

Purdie. No, but you have such a dear way of giving in.

Joanna. Jack, she hasn't worn that gown of late.

Purdie. No, nor the jewels. I think she has some sort of idea now that when I give her anything nice it means that you have been nice to me. She has rather a suspicious nature, Mabel; she never used to have it, but it seems to be growing on her. I wonder why, I wonder why?

[*In this wonder which is shared by* JOANNA *their lips meet, and* MABEL, *who has been about to enter from the garden, quietly retires.*]

Joanna. Was that any one in the garden?

Purdie. [*Returning from a quest.*] There is no one there now.

Joanna. I am sure I heard some one. If it was Mabel! [*With a perspicacity that comes of knowledge of her sex.*] Jack, if she saw us she will think you were kissing me.

[*These fears are confirmed by the rather odd bearing of* MABEL, *who now joins their select party.*]

Mabel. [*Apologetically.*] I am so sorry to interrupt you, Jack; but please wait a moment before you kiss her again. Excuse me, Joanna. [*She quietly draws the curtains, thus shutting out the garden and any possible onlooker.*] I did not want the others to see you; they might not understand how noble you are, Jack. You can go on now.

[*Having thus passed the time of day with them she withdraws by the door, leaving* JACK *bewildered and* JOANNA *knowing all about it.*]

Joanna. How extraordinary! Of all the

——! Oh, but how contemptible! [*She sweeps to the door and calls* MABEL *by name.*]

Mabel. [*Returning with promptitude.*] Did you call me, Joanna?

Joanna. [*Guardedly.*] I insist on an explanation. [*With creditable hauteur.*] What were you doing in the garden, Mabel?

Mabel. [*Who has not been so quiet all day.*] I was looking for something I have lost.

Purdie. [*Hope springing eternal.*] Anything important?

Mabel. I used to fancy it, Jack. It is my husband's love. You don't happen to have picked it up, Joanna? If so and you don't set great store by it I should like it back—the pieces, I mean.

[MR. PURDIE *is about to reply to this, when* JOANNA *rather wisely fills the breach.*]

Joanna. Mabel, I—I will not be talked to in that way. To imply that I—that your husband—oh, shame!

Purdie. [*Finely.*] I must say, Mabel, that I am a little disappointed in you. I certainly understood that you had gone upstairs to put on your boots.

Mabel. Poor old Jack. [*She muses.*] A woman like that!

Joanna. [*Changing her comment in the moment of utterance.*]—I forgive you, Mabel; you will be sorry for this afterwards.

Purdie. [*Warningly, but still reluctant to think less well of his wife.*] Not a word against Joanna, Mabel. If you knew how nobly she has spoken of you.

Joanna. [*Imprudently.*] She does know. She has been listening.

[*There is a moment's danger of the scene degenerating into something mid-Victorian. Fortunately a chivalrous man is present to lift it to a higher plane.* JOHN PURDIE *is one to whom subterfuge of any kind is abhorrent; if he has not spoken out before it is because of his reluctance to give* MABEL *pain. He speaks out now, and seldom probably has he proved himself more worthy.*]

Purdie. This is a man's business. I must be open with you now, Mabel: it is the manlier way. If you wish it I shall always be true to you in word and deed; it is your right. But I cannot pretend that Joanna is not the one woman in the world for me. If I had met her before you—it's Kismet, I suppose.

[*He swells.*]

Joanna. [*From a chair.*] Too late, too late.

Mabel. [*Although the woman has seen him swell.*] I suppose you never knew what tru love was till you met her, Jack?

Purdie. You force me to say it. Joann and I are as one person. We have not thought at variance. We are one rather tha two.

Mabel. [*Looking at* JOANNA.] Yes, an that's the one! [*With the cheapest sarcasm.* I am so sorry to have marred your lives.

Purdie. If any blame there is, it is al mine; she is as spotless as the driven snow The moment I mentioned love to her sh told me to desist.

Mabel. Not she.

Joanna. So you *were* listening! [*The ol tuseness of* MABEL *is very strange to her.* Mabel, don't you see how splendid he is!

Mabel. Not quite, Joanna.

[*She goes away. She is really a bette woman than this, but never capable o scaling that higher plane to which h has, as it were, offered her a hand.*]

Joanna. How lovely of you, Jack, to tak it all upon yourself.

Purdie. [*Simply.*] It is the man's privi lege.

Joanna. Mabel has such a horrid way c seeming to put people in the wrong.

Purdie. Have you noticed that? Poc Mabel, it is not an enviable quality.

Joanna. [*Despondently.*] I don't think care to go out now. She has spoilt it al She has taken the innocence out of it, Jacl

Purdie. [*A rock.*] We must be brave an not mind her. Ah, Joanna, if we had met i time. If only I could begin again. To b battered for ever just because I once too the wrong turning—it isn't fair.

Joanna. [*Emerging from his arms.*] Th wrong turning! Now, who was saying tha a moment ago—about himself? Why, it wa Matey.

[*A footstep is heard.*

Purdie. [*For the first time losing patienc with his wife.*] Is that her coming bac again? It's too bad. [*But the intruder is* MR DEARTH, *and he greets her with relief.*] A it is you, Mrs. Dearth.

Alice. Yes, it is; but thank you for tellin me, Mr. Purdie. I don't intrude, do I?

Joanna. [*Descending to the lower plan on which even goddesses snap.*] Why shou you?

Purdie. Rather not. We were—hoping would be you. We want to start on the wall I can't think what has become of the other We have been looking for them everywher

[*He glances vaguely round the room, if they might so far have escaped dete tion.*]

Alice. [*Pleasantly.*] Well, do go on looking; under that flower-pot would be a good place. It is my husband I am in search of.

Purdie. [*Who likes her best when they are in different rooms.*] Shall I rout him out for you?

Alice. How too unutterably kind of you, Mr. Purdie. I hate to trouble you, but it would be the sort of service one never forgets.

Purdie. You know, I believe you are chaffing me.

Alice. No, no; I am incapable of that.

Purdie. I won't be a moment.

Alice. Miss Trout and I will await your return with ill-concealed impatience. [*They await it across a table, the newcomer in a reverie and* JOANNA *watching her. Presently* MRS. DEARTH *looks up, and we may notice that she has an attractive screw of the mouth which denotes humor.*] Yes, I suppose you are right; I daresay I am.

Joanna. [*Puzzled.*] I didn't say anything.

Alice. I thought I heard you say, "That hateful Dearth woman, coming butting it where she is not wanted."

[JOANNA *draws up her sveldt figure, but a screw of one mouth often calls for a similar demonstration from another, and both ladies smile. They nearly become friends.*]

Joanna. You certainly have good ears.

Alice. [*Drawling.*] Yes, they have always been rather admired.

Joanna. [*Snapping.*] By the painters for whom you sat when you were an artist's model?

Alice. [*Measuring her.*] So that has leaked out, has it!

Joanna. [*Ashamed.*] I shouldn't have said that.

Alice. [*Their brief friendship over.*] Do you think I care whether you know or not?

Joanna. [*Making an effort to be good.*] I'm sure you don't. Still, it was cattish of me.

Alice. It was.

Joanna. [*In flame.*] I don't see it.

[MRS. DEARTH *laughs and forgets her, and with the entrance of a man from the dining-room* JOANNA *drifts elsewhere. Not so much a man, this newcomer, as the relic of what has been a good one; it is the most he would ever claim for himself. Sometimes, brandy in hand, he has visions of the* WILL DEARTH *he used to be, clear of eye; sees him but a field away, singing at his easel or, fishing-rod in hand, leaping a stile. Our* WILL *stares after the fellow for quite a long time, so long that the two melt into the one who finishes* LOB'S *brandy. He is scarcely intoxicated as he appears before the lady of his choice, but he is shaky and has watery eyes.*

ALICE *has had a rather wild love for this man, or for that other one, and he for her, but somehow it has gone whistling down the wind. We may expect therefore to see them at their worst when in each other's company.*]

Dearth. [*Who is not without a humorous outlook on his own degradation.*] I am uncommonly flattered, Alice, to hear that you have sent for me. It quite takes me aback.

Alice. [*With cold distaste.*] It isn't your company I want, Will.

Dearth. You know, I felt that Purdie must have delivered your message wrongly.

Alice. I want you to come with us on this mysterious walk and keep an eye on Lob.

Dearth. On poor little Lob? Oh, surely not.

Alice. I can't make the man out. I want you to tell me something; when he invited us here, do you think it was you or me he specially wanted?

Dearth. Oh, you. He made no bones about it; said there was something about you that made him want uncommonly to have you down here.

Alice. Will, try to remember this: did he ask us for any particular time?

Dearth. Yes, he was particular about its being Midsummer week.

Alice. Ah! I thought so. Did he say what it was about me that made him want to have me here in Midsummer week?

Dearth. No, but I presumed it must be your fascination, Alice.

Alice. Just so. Well, I want you to come out with us tonight to watch him.

Dearth. Crack-in-my-eye-Tommy, spy on my host! And such a harmless little chap, too. Excuse me, Alice. Besides I have an engagement.

Alice. An engagement—with the port decanter, I presume.

Dearth. A good guess, but wrong. The decanter is now but an empty shell. Still, how you know me! My engagement is with a quiet cigar in the garden.

Alice. Your hand is so unsteady, you won't be able to light the match.

Dearth. I shall just manage.

[*He triumphantly proves the exact truth of his statement.*]

Alice. A nice hand for an artist!

Dearth. One would scarcely call me an artist now-a-days.

Alice. Not so far as any work is concerned.

Dearth. Not so far as having any more pretty dreams to paint is concerned. [*Grinning at himself.*] Wonder why I have become such a waster, Alice?

Alice. I suppose it was always in you.

Dearth. [*With perhaps a glimpse of the fishing-rod.*] I suppose so; and yet I was rather a good sort in the days when I went courting you.

Alice. Yes, I thought so. Unlucky days for me, as it has turned out.

Dearth. [*Heartily.*] Yes, a bad job for you. [*Puzzling unsteadily over himself.*] I didn't know I was a wrong 'un at the time; thought quite well of myself, thought a vast deal more of you. Crack-in-my-eye-Tommy, how I used to leap out of bed at 6 A.M. all agog to be at my easel; blood ran through my veins in those days. And now I'm middle-aged and done for. Funny! Don't know how it has come about, nor what has made the music mute. [*Mildly curious.*] When did you begin to despise me, Alice?

Alice. When I got to know you really, Will; a long time ago.

Dearth. [*Bleary of eye.*] Yes, I think that is true. It was a long time ago, and before I had begun to despise myself. It wasn't till I knew you had no opinion of me that I began to go down hill. You will grant that, won't you; and that I did try for a bit to fight on? If you had cared for me I wouldn't have come to this, surely?

Alice. Well, I found I didn't care for you, and I wasn't hypocrite enough to pretend I did. That's blunt, but you used to admire my bluntness.

Dearth. The bluntness of you, the adorable wildness of you, you untamed thing! There were never any shades in you; kiss or kill was your motto, Alice. I felt from the first moment I saw you that you would love me or knife me.

[*Memories of their shooting star flare in both of them for as long as a sheet of paper might take to burn.*]

Alice. I didn't knife you.

Dearth. No. I suppose that was where you made the mistake. It is hard on you, old lady. [*Becoming watery.*] I suppose it's too late to try to patch things up?

Alice. Let's be honest; it is too late, Will.

Dearth. [*Whose tears would smell of brandy.*] Perhaps if we had had children—Pity!

Alice. A blessing I should think, seeing what sort of a father they would have had.

Dearth. [*Ever reasonable.*] I daresay you're right. Well, Alice, I know that somehow it's my fault. I'm sorry for you.

Alice. I'm sorry for myself. If I hadn't married you, what a different woman I should be. What a fool I was.

Dearth. Ah! Three things they say come not back to men nor women—the spoken word, the past life, and the neglected opportunity. Wonder if we should make any more of them, Alice, if they did come back to us.

Alice. You wouldn't.

Dearth. [*Avoiding a hiccup.*] I guess you're right.

Alice. But I——

Dearth. [*Sincerely.*] Yes, what a boon for you. But I hope it's not Freddy Finch-Fallowe you would put in my place; I know he is following you about again.

[*He is far from threatening her, he has too beery an opinion of himself for that.*]

Alice. He followed me about, as you put it, before I knew you. I don't know why I quarrelled with him.

Dearth. Your heart told you that he was no good, Alice.

Alice. My heart told me that you *were.* So it wasn't of much service to me, my heart!

Dearth. The Honorable Freddy Finch-Fallowe is a rotter.

Alice. [*Ever inflammable.*] You are certainly an authority on the subject.

Dearth. [*With the sad smile of the disillusioned.*] You have me there. After which brief, but pleasant, little connubial chat, he pursued his dishonored way into the garden.

[*He is however prevented doing so for the moment by the return of the others. They are all still in their dinner clothes, though wearing wraps. They crowd in through the door, chattering.*]

Lob. Here they are! Are you ready, dear lady?

Mrs. Coade. [*Seeing that* DEARTH'S *hand is on the window curtains.*] Are you not coming with us to find the wood, Mr. Dearth?

Dearth. Alas, I am unavoidably detained. You will find me in the garden when you come back.

Joanna. [*Whose sense of humor has been restored.*] If we ever do come back!

Dearth. Precisely. [*With a groggy bow.*] Should we never meet again, Alice, fare thee well. Purdie, if you find the tree of knowledge in the wood bring me back an apple.

Purdie. I promise.

Lob. Come quickly. Matey must'nt see me. [*He is turning out the lights.*]

Lady Caroline. [*Pouncing.*] Matey? What difference would that make, Lob?

Lob. He would take me off to bed; it's past my time.

Coade. [*Not the least gay of the company.*] You know, old fellow, you make it very difficult for us to embark upon this adventure in the proper eerie spirit.

Dearth. Well, I'm for the garden.

[*He walks to the window, and the others are going out by the door. But they do not go. There is a hitch somewhere—at the window apparently, for* DEARTH *having begun to draw the curtains apart lets them fall, like one who has had a shock. The others remember long afterwards his grave face as he came quietly back and put his cigar on the table. The room is in darkness save for the light from one lamp.*]

Purdie. [*Wondering.*] How, now, Dearth?

Dearth. What is it we get in that wood, Lob?

Alice. Ah, he won't tell us that.

Lob. [*Shrinking.*] Come on!

Alice. [*Impressed by the change that has come over her husband.*] Tell us first.

Lob. [*Forced to the disclosure.*] They say that in the wood you get what nearly everybody here is longing for—a second chance.

[*The ladies are simultaneously enlightened.*]

Joanna. [*Speaking for all.*] So that is what we have in common!

Coade. [*With gentle regret.*] I have often thought, Coady, that if I had a second chance I should be a useful man instead of just a nice lazy one.

Alice. [*Morosely.*] A second chance!

Lob. Come on.

Purdie. [*Gaily.*] Yes, to the wood—the wood!

Dearth. [*As they are going out by the door.*] Stop, why not go this way?

[*He pulls the curtains apart, and there comes a sudden indrawing of breath from all, for no garden is there now. In its place is an endless wood of great trees; the nearest of them has come close to the window. It is a somber wood, with splashes of moonshine and of blackness standing very still in it.*

The party in the drawing-room are very still also, there is scarcely a cry or a movement. It is perhaps strange that the most obviously frightened is LOB, *who calls vainly for* MATEY. *The first articulate voice is* DEARTH'S.]

Dearth. [*Very quietly.*] Anyone ready to risk it?

Purdie. [*After another silence.*] Of course there is nothing in it—just——

Dearth. [*Grimly.*] Of course. Going out, Purdie? [PURDIE *draws back.*]

Mrs. Dearth. [*The only one who is undaunted.*] A second chance!

[*She is looking at her husband. They all look at him as if he had been a leader once.*]

Dearth. [*With his sweet mournful smile.*] I shall be back in a moment—probably.

[*As he passes into the wood his hands rise, as if a hammer had tapped him on the forehead. He is soon lost to view.*]

Lady Caroline. [*After a long pause.*] He does not come back.

Mrs. Coade. It's horrible.

[*She steals off by the door to her room, calling to her husband to do likewise. He takes a step after her, and stops in the grip of the last two words that holds them all. The stillness continues. At last* MRS. PURDIE *goes out into the wood, her hands raised, and is swallowed up by it.*]

Purdie. Mabel!

Alice. [*Sardonically.*] You will have to go now, Mr. Purdie.

[*He looks at* JOANNA, *and they go out together, one tap of the hammer for each.*]

Lob. That's enough. [*Warningly.*] Don't *you* go, Mrs. Dearth. *You'll* catch it if you go.

Alice. A second chance!

[*She goes out unflinching.*]

Lady Caroline. One would like to know.

[*She goes out.* MRS. COADE'S *voice is heard from the stair calling to her husband. He hesitates but follows* LADY CAROLINE. *To* LOB, *now alone, comes* MATEY *with a tray of coffee cups.*]

Matey. [*As he places his tray on the table.*] It is past your bed-time, sir. Say good-night to the ladies, and come along.

Lob. Matey, look! [MATEY *looks.*]

Matey. [*Shrinking.*] Great heavens, then it's true!

Lob. Yes, but I—I wasn't sure.

[MATEY *approaches the window cautiously to peer out, and his master gives him a sudden push that propels him into the wood.* LOB'S *back is toward us as he stands alone staring out upon the unknown. He is terrified still; yet quivers of rapture are running up and down his little frame.*]

ACT II

We are translated to the depths of the wood in the enchantment of a moonlight night. In some other glade a nightingale is singing.

[*In this one, in proud motoring attire, recline two mortals whom we have known in different conditions; the second chance has converted them into husband and wife. The man, of gross muddy build, lies luxurious on his back exuding affluence, by a prominent part of him heaving playfully, like some little wave that will not rest in a still sea. A handkerchief over his face conceals from us what Colossus he may be, but his mate is our* LADY CAROLINE. *The nightingale trills on, and* LADY CAROLINE *takes up its song.*]

Lady Caroline. Is it not a lovely night, Jim? Listen, my own, to Philomel; he is saying that he is lately married. So are we, you ducky thing. I feel, Jim, that I am Rosalind and that you are my Orlando.

[*The handkerchief being removed* MR. MATEY *is revealed; and the nightingale seeks some farther tree.*]

Matey. What do you say I am, Caroliny?

Lady Caroline. [*Clapping her hands.*] My own one, don't you think it would be fun if we were to write poems about each other and pin them on the tree trunks?

Matey. [*Tolerantly.*] Poems? I never knew such a lass for high-flown language.

Lady Caroline. Your lass, dearest. Jim's lass.

Matey. [*Pulling her ear.*] And don't you forget it.

Lady Caroline. [*With the curiosity of woman.*] What would you do if I were to forget it, great bear?

Matey. Take a stick to you.

Lady Caroline. [*So proud of him.*] I love to hear you talk like that; it is so virile. I always knew that it was a master I needed.

Matey. It's what you all need.

Lady Caroline. It is, it is, you knowing wretch.

Matey. Listen, Caroliny. [*He touches his money pocket, which emits a crinkly sound —the squeak of angels.*] That is what gets the ladies.

Lady Caroline. How much have you made this week, you wonderful man?

Matey. [*Blandly.*] Another two hundred or so. That's all, just two hundred or so.

Lady Caroline. [*Caressing her wedding ring.*] My dear golden fetter, listen to him. Kiss my fetter, Jim.

Matey. Wait till I light this cigar.

Lady Caroline. Let me hold the darling match.

Matey. Tidy-looking Petitey Corona, this There was a time when one of that sort would have run away with two days of my screw.

Lady Caroline. How I should have loved, Jim, to know you when you were poor. Fancy your having once been a clerk.

Matey. [*Remembering Napoleon and others.*] We all have our beginnings. But it wouldn't have mattered how I began, Caroliny: I should have come to the top just the same. [*Becoming a poet himself.*] I am a climber, and there are nails in my boots for the parties beneath me. Boots! I tell you if I had been a bootmaker, I should have been the first bootmaker in London.

Lady Caroline. [*A humorist at last.*] I am sure you would, Jim; but should you have made the best boots?

Matey. [*Uxoriously wishing that others could have heard this.*] Very good, Caroliny; that is the neatest thing I have heard you say. But it's late; we had best be strolling back to our Rolls-Royce.

Lady Caroline. [*As they rise.*] I do hope the ground wasn't damp!

Matey. Don't matter if it was; I was lying on your rug. [*Indeed we notice now that he has had all the rug, and she the bare ground.* JOANNA *reaches the glade, now an unhappy lady who has got what she wanted. She is in country dress and is unknown to them as they are to her.*] Who is the mournful party?

Joanna. [*Hesitatingly.*] I wonder, sir, whether you happen to have seen my husband? I have lost him in the wood.

Matey. We are strangers in these parts ourselves, missis. Have we passed anyone, Caroliny?

Lady Caroline. [*Coyly.*] Should we have noticed, dear? Might it be that old gent over there?

[*After the delightful manner of those happily wed she has already picked up many of her lover's favorite words and phrases.*]

Joanna. Oh no, my husband is quite young.

[*The woodlander referred to is* MR.

COADE *in gala costume; at his mouth a whistle he has made him from some friendly twig. To its ravishing music he is seen pirouetting charmingly among the trees, his new occupation.*]

Matey. [*Singing to the unknown that he is wanted.*] Seems a merry old cock. Evening to you, sir. Do you happen to have seen a young gentleman in the wood lately, all by himself, and looking for his wife?

Coade. [*With a flourish of his legs.*] Can't say I have.

Joanna. [*Dolefully.*] He isn't necessarily by himself; and I don't know that he is looking for me. There may be a young lady with him.

[*The more happily married lady smiles, and* JOANNA *is quick to take offence.*]

Joanna. What do you mean by that?

Lady Caroline. [*Neatly.*] Oho—if you like that better.

Matey. Now, now, now—your manners, Caroliny.

Coade. Would he be singing or dancing?

Joanna. Oh no—at least, I hope not.

Coade. [*An artist to the tips.*] Hope not? Odd! If he is doing neither I am not likely to notice him, but if I do, what name shall I say?

Joanna. [*Gloating not.*] Purdie; I am Mrs. Purdie.

Coade. I will try to keep a look-out, and if I see him . . . but I am rather occupied at present. . . .

[*The reference is to his legs and a new step they are acquiring. He sways this way and that, and, whistle to lips, minuets off in the direction of Paradise.*]

Joanna. [*Looking elsewhere.*] I am sorry I troubled you. I see him now.

Lady Caroline. Is he alone? [JOANNA *glares at her.*] Ah, I see from your face that he isn't.

Matey. [*Who has his wench in training.*] Caroliny, no awkward questions. Evening, missis, and I hope you will get him to go along with you quietly. [*Looking after* COADE.] Watch the old codger dancing.

[*Light-hearted as children they dance after him, while* JOANNA *behind a tree awaits her lord.* PURDIE *in knickerbockers approaches with misgivings to make sure that his* JOANNA *is not in hiding, and then he gambols joyously with a charming confection whose name is* MABEL. *They chase each other from tree to tree, but fortunately not round* JOANNA'S *tree.*]

Mabel. [*As he catches her.*] No, and no, and no. I don't know you nearly well enough for that. Besides, what would your wife say! I shall begin to think you are a very dreadful man, Mr. Purdie.

Purdie. [*Whose sincerity is not to be questioned.*] Surely you might call me Jack by this time.

Mabel. [*Heaving.*] Perhaps, if you are very good, Jack.

Purdie. [*Of noble thoughts compact.*] If only Joanna were more like you.

Mabel. Like me? You mean her face? It is a—well, if it is not precisely pretty, it is a good face. [*Handsomely.*] I don't mind her face at all. I am glad you have got such a dependable little wife, Jack.

Purdie. [*Gloomily.*] Thanks.

Mabel. [*Seated with a moonbeam in her lap.*] What would Joanna have said if she had seen you just now?

Purdie. A wife should be incapable of jealousy.

Mabel. Joanna jealous? But has she any reason? Jack, tell me, who is the woman?

Purdie. [*Restraining himself by a mighty effort, for he wishes always to be true to* JOANNA.] Shall I, Mabel, shall I?

Mabel. [*Faltering, yet not wholly giving up the chase.*] I can't think who she is. Have I ever seen her?

Purdie. Every time you look in the mirror.

Mabel. [*With her head on one side.*] How odd, Jack; that can't be; when I look in a mirror I see only myself.

Purdie. [*Gloating.*] How adorably innocent you are, Mabel. Joanna would have guessed at once.

[*Slowly his meaning comes to her, and she is appalled.*]

Mabel. Not that!

Purdie. [*Aflame.*] Shall I tell you now?

Mabel. [*Palpitating exquisitely.*] I don't know, I am not sure. Jack, try not to say it, but if you feel you must, say it in such a way that it would not hurt the feelings of Joanna if she happened to be passing by, as she nearly always is.

[*A little moan from* JOANNA'S *tree is unnoticed.*]

Purdie. I would rather not say it at all than that way. [*He is touchingly anxious that she should know him as he really is.*] I don't know, Mabel, whether you have noticed that I am not like other men. [*He goes deeply into the very structure of his being.*] All my life I have been a soul that has had to walk alone. Even as a child I had no hope that it would be otherwise. I distinctly remember, when I was six, thinking how unlike other children I was. Before

I was twelve I suffered from terrible self-depreciation; I do so still. I suppose there never was a man who had a more lowly opinion of himself.

Mabel. Jack, you who are so universally admired!

Purdie. That doesn't help; I remain my own judge. I am afraid I am a dark spirit, Mabel. Yes, yes, my dear, let me leave nothing untold, however it may damage me in your eyes. Your eyes! I cannot remember a time when I did not think of Love as a great consuming passion; I visualized it, Mabel, as perhaps few have done, but always as the abounding joy that could come to others but never to me. I expected too much of women: I suppose I was touched to finer issues than most. That has been my tragedy.

Mabel. Then you met Joanna.

Purdie. Then I met Joanna. Yes! Foolishly, as I now see, I thought she would understand that I was far too deep a nature really to mean the little things I sometimes said to her. I suppose a man was never placed in such a position before. What was I to do? Remember, I was always certain that the ideal love could never come to me. Whatever the circumstances, I was convinced that my soul must walk alone.

Mabel. Joanna, how could you?

Purdie. [*Firmly.*] Not a word against her, Mabel; if blame there is, the blame is mine.

Mabel. And so you married her.

Purdie. And so I married her.

Mabel. Out of pity.

Purdie. I felt it was a man's part. I was such a child in worldly matters that it was pleasant to me to have the right to pay a woman's bills; I enjoyed seeing her garments lying about on my chairs. In time that exultation wore off. But I was not unhappy, I didn't expect much, I was always so sure that no woman could ever plumb the well of my emotions.

Mabel. Then you met me.

Purdie. Then I met you.

Mabel. Too late—never—forever—forever—never. They are the saddest words in the English tongue.

Purdie. At the time I thought a still sadder word was Joanna.

Mabel. What was it you saw in me that made you love me?

Purdie. [*Plumbing the well of his emotions.*] I think it was the feeling that you are so like myself.

Mabel. [*With great eyes.*] Have you noticed that, Jack? Sometimes it has almost terrified me.

Purdie. We think the same thoughts; we are not two, Mabel; we are one. Your hair ——

Mabel. Joanna knows you admire it, and for a week she did hers in the same way.

Purdie. I never noticed.

Mabel. That was why she gave it up. And it didn't really suit her. [*Ruminating.*] I can't think of a good way of doing dear Joanna's hair. What is that you are muttering to yourself, Jack? Don't keep anything from me.

Purdie. I was repeating a poem I have written: it is in two words, "Mabel Purdie." May I teach it to you, sweet: say "Mabel Purdie" to me.

Mabel. [*Timidly covering his mouth with her little hand.*] If I were to say it, Jack, I should be false to Joanna: never ask me to be that. Let us go on.

Purdie. [*Merciless in his passion.*] Say it, Mabel, say it. See I write it on the ground with your sunshade.

Mabel. If it could be! Jack, I'll whisper it to you.

[*She is whispering it as they wander, not two but one, farther into the forest, ardently believing in themselves; they are not hypocrites. The somewhat bedraggled figure of* JOANNA *follows them, and the nightingale resumes his love-song. "That's all you know, you bird!" thinks* JOANNA *cynically. The nightingale, however, is not singing for them nor for her, but for another pair he has espied below. They are racing, the prize to be for the one who first finds the spot where the easel was put up last night. The* HOBBLEDEHOY *is sure to be the winner, for she is less laden, and the* FATHER *loses time by singing as he comes. Also she is all legs and she started ahead. Brambles adhere to her, one boot has been in the water and she has as many freckles as there are stars in heaven. She is as lovely as you think she is, and she is aged the moment when you like your daughter best. A hoot of triumph from her brings her* FATHER *to the spot.*]

Margaret. Daddy, Daddy. I have won. Here is the place. Crack-in-my-eye-Tommy!

[*He comes. Crack-in-the-eye-Tommy, this engaging fellow in tweeds, is* MR. DEARTH, *ablaze in happiness and health and a daughter. He finishes his song, picked up in the Latin Quarter.*]

Dearth. Yes, that is the tree I stuck my easel under last night, and behold the blessed moon behaving more gorgeously than ever. I am sorry to have kept you waiting, old moon; but you ought to know by now how time passes. Now, keep still, while I hand you down to posterity.

[*The easel is erected,* MARGARET *helping by getting in the way.*]

Margaret. [*Critical, as an artist's daughter should be.*] The moon is rather pale tonight, isn't she?

Dearth. Comes of keeping late hours.

Margaret. [*Showing off.*] Daddy, watch me, look at me. Please, sweet moon, a pleasant expression. No, no, not as if you were sitting for it; that is too professional. That is better; thank you. Now keep it. That is the sort of thing you say to them, Dad.

Dearth. [*Quickly at work.*] I oughtn't to have brought you out so late; you should be tucked up in your cosy bed at home.

Margaret. [*Pursuing a squirrel that isn't there.*] With the pillow anyhow.

Dearth. Except in its proper place.

Margaret. [*Wetting the other foot.*] And the sheet over my face.

Dearth. Where it oughtn't to be.

Margaret. [*More or less upside down.*] And Daddy tiptoeing in to take it off.

Dearth. Which is more than you deserve.

Margaret. [*In a tree.*] Then why does he stand so long at the door? And before he has gone she bursts out laughing, for she has been awake all the time.

Dearth. That's about it. What a life! But I oughtn't to have brought you here. Best to have the sheet over you when the moon is about; moonlight is bad for little daughters.

Margaret. [*Pelting him with nuts.*] I can't sleep when the moon's at the full; she keeps calling to me to get up. Perhaps I am *her* daughter too.

Dearth. Gad, you look it tonight.

Margaret. Do I? Then can't you paint me into the picture as well as Mamma? You could call it "A Mother and Daughter" or simply "Two Ladies," if the moon thinks that calling me her daughter would make her seem too old.

Dearth. O matre pulchra filia pulchrior. That means, "O Moon—more beautiful than any twopenny-halfpenny daughter."

Margaret. [*Emerging in an unexpected place.*] Daddy, do you really prefer her?

Dearth. 'Sh! She's not a patch on you; it's the sort of thing we say to our sitters to keep them in good humor. [*He surveys ruefully a great stain on her frock.*] I wish to heaven, Margaret, we were not both so fond of apple-tart. And what's this?

[*Catching hold of her skirt.*]

Margaret. [*Unnecessarily.*] It's a tear.

Dearth. I should think it is a tear.

Margaret. That boy at the farm did it. He kept calling Snubs after me, but I got him down and kicked him in the stomach. He is rather a jolly boy.

Dearth. He sounds it. Ye Gods, what a night!

Margaret. [*Considering the picture.*] And what a moon! Dad, she is not quite so fine as that.

Dearth. 'Sh! I have touched her up.

Margaret. Dad, Dad—what a funny man!

[*She has seen* MR. COADE *with whistle, enlivening the wood. He pirouettes round them and departs to add to the happiness of others.* MARGARET *gives an excellent imitation of him at which her father shakes his head, then reprehensibly joins in the dance. Her mood changes, she clings to him.*]

Margaret. Hold me tight, Daddy, I'm frightened. I think they want to take you away from me.

Dearth. Who, gosling?

Margaret. I don't know. It's too lovely, Daddy; I won't be able to keep hold of it.

Dearth. What is?

Margaret. The world—everything—and you, Daddy, most of all. Things that are too beautiful can't last.

Dearth. [*Who knows it.*] Now, how did you find that out?

Margaret. [*Still in his arms.*] I don't know, Daddy, am I sometimes stranger than other people's daughters?

Dearth. More of a madcap, perhaps.

Margaret. [*Solemnly.*] Do you think I am sometimes too full of gladness?

Dearth. My sweetheart, you do sometimes run over with it. [*He is at his easel again.*]

Margaret. [*Persisting.*] To be very gay, dearest dear, is so near to being very sad.

Dearth. [*Who knows it.*] How did you find that out, child?

Margaret. I don't know. From something in me that's afraid. [*Unexpectedly.*] Daddy, what is a "might-have-been"?

Dearth. A might-have-been? They are ghosts, Margaret. I daresay I "might have been" a great swell of a painter, instead of just this uncommonly happy nobody. Or again, I might have been a worthless idle waster of a fellow.

Margaret. [*Laughing.*] You!

Dearth. Who knows? Some little kink in me might have set me off on the wrong road. And that poor soul I might so easily have been might have had no Margaret. My word, I'm sorry for him.

Margaret. So am I. [*She conceives a

funny picture.] The poor old Daddy, wandering about the world without me!

Dearth. And there are other "might-have-beens"—lovely ones, but intangible. Shades, Margaret, made of sad folk's thoughts.

Margaret. [*Jiggling about.*] I am so glad I am not a shade. How awful it would be, Daddy, to wake up and find one wasn't alive.

Dearth. It would, dear.

Margaret. Daddy, wouldn't it be awful! I think men need daughters.

Dearth. They do.

Margaret. Especially artists.

Dearth. Yes, especially artists.

Margaret. Especially artists.

Dearth. Especially artists.

Margaret. [*Covering herself with leaves and kicking them off.*] Fame is not everything.

Dearth. Fame is rot; daughters are the thing.

Margaret. Daughters are the thing.

Dearth. Daughters are the thing.

Margaret. I wonder if sons would be even nicer?

Dearth. Not a patch on daughters. The awful thing about a son is that never, never —at least, from the day he goes to school— can you tell him that you rather like him. By the time he is ten you can't even take him on your knee. Sons are not worth having, Margaret. Signed, W. Dearth.

Margaret. But if you were a mother, Dad, I daresay he would let you do it.

Dearth. Think so?

Margaret. I mean when no one was looking. Sons are not so bad. Signed, M. Dearth. But I'm glad you prefer daughters. [*She works her way toward him on her knees, making the tear larger.*] At what age are we nicest, Daddy? [*She has constantly to repeat her questions, he is so engaged with his moon.*] Hie, Daddy, at what age are we nicest? Daddy, hie, hie, at what age are we nicest?

Dearth. Eh? That's a poser. I think you were nicest when you were two and knew your alphabet up to G but fell over at H. No, you were best when you were half-past three; or just before you struck six; or in the mumps year, when I asked you in the early morning how you were and you said solemnly, "I haven't tried yet."

Margaret. [*Awestruck.*] Did I?

Dearth. Such was your answer. [*Struggling with the momentous question.*] But I am not sure that chicken-pox doesn't beat mumps. Oh Lord, I'm all wrong. The nicest time in a father's life is the year before she puts up her hair.

Margaret. [*Topheavy with pride in herself.*] I suppose that is a splendid time. But there's a nicer year coming to you. Daddy, there is a nicer year coming to you.

Dearth. Is there, darling?

Margaret. Daddy, the year she does put up her hair!

Dearth. [*With arrested brush.*] Puts it up forever? You know, I am afraid that when the day for that comes I shan't be able to stand it. It will be too exciting. My poor heart, Margaret.

Margaret. [*Rushing at him.*] No, no, it will be lucky you, for it isn't to be a bit like that. I am to be a girl and woman, day about, for the first year. You will never know which I am till you look at my hair. And even then you won't know, for if it is down I shall put it up, and if it is up I shall put it down. And so my Daddy will gradually get used to the idea.

Dearth. [*Wryly.*] I see you have been thinking it out.

Margaret. [*Gleaming.*] I have been doing more than that. Shut your eyes, Dad, and I shall give you a glimpse into the future.

Dearth. I don't know that I want that: the present is so good.

Margaret. Shut your eyes, please.

Dearth. No, Margaret.

Margaret. Please, Daddy.

Dearth. Oh, all right. They are shut.

Margaret. Don't open them till I tell you. What finger is that?

Dearth. The dirty one.

Margaret. [*On her knees among the leaves.*] Daddy, now I am putting up my hair. I have got such a darling of a mirror. It is such a darling mirror I've got, Dad. Dad, don't look. I shall tell you about it. It is a little pool of water. I wish we could take it home and hang it up. Of course the moment my hair is up there will be other changes also; for instance, I shall talk quite differently.

Dearth. Pooh. Where are my matches, dear?

Margaret. Top pocket, waistcoat.

Dearth. [*Trying to light his pipe in darkness.*] You were meaning to frighten me just now.

Margaret. No. I am just preparing you. You see, darling, I can't call you Dad when my hair is up. I think I shall call you Parent. [*He growls.*] Parent dear, do you remember the days when your Margaret was a slip of a girl, and sat on your knee? How foolish we were, Parent, in those distant days.

Dearth. Shut up, Margaret.

Margaret. Now I must be more distant to you; more like a boy who could not sit on your knee any more.

Dearth. See here, I want to go on painting. Shall I look now?

Margaret. I am not quite sure whether I want you to. It makes such a difference. Perhaps you won't know me. Even the pool is looking a little scared. [*The change in her voice makes him open his eyes quickly. She confronts him shyly.*] What do you think? Will I do?

Dearth. Stand still, dear, and let me look my fill. The Margaret that is to be.

Margaret. [*The change in his voice falling clammy on her.*] You'll see me often enough, Daddy, like this, so you don't need to look your fill. You are looking as long as if this were to be the only time.

Dearth. [*With an odd tremor.*] Was I? Surely it isn't to be that.

Margaret. Be gay, Dad. [*Bumping into him and round him and over him.*] You will be sick of Margaret with her hair up before you are done with her.

Dearth. I expect so.

Margaret. Shut up, Daddy. [*She waggles her head, and down comes her hair.*] Daddy, I know what you are thinking of. You are thinking what a handful she is going to be.

Dearth. Well, I guess she is.

Margaret. [*Surveying him from another angle.*] Now you are thinking about—about my being in love some day.

Dearth. [*With unnecessary warmth.*] Rot!

Margaret. [*Reassuringly.*] I won't, you know; no, never. Oh, I have quite decided, so don't be afraid. [*Disordering his hair.*] Will you hate him at first, Daddy? Daddy, will you hate him? Will you hate him, Daddy?

Dearth. [*At work.*] Whom?

Margaret. Well, if there was?

Dearth. If there was what, darling?

Margaret. You know the kind of thing I mean, quite well. Would you hate him at first?

Dearth. I hope not. I should want to strangle him, but I wouldn't hate him.

Margaret. *I* would. That is to say, if I liked him.

Dearth. If you liked him how could you hate him?

Margaret. For daring!

Dearth. Daring what?

Margaret. You know. [*Sighing.*] But of course I shall have no say in the matter. You will do it all. You do everything for me.

Dearth. [*With a groan.*] I can't help it.

Margaret. You will even write my love-letters, if I ever have any to write, which I won't.

Dearth. [*Ashamed.*] Surely to goodness, Margaret, I will leave you alone to do that!

Margaret. Not you; you will try to, but you won't be able.

Dearth. [*In a hopeless attempt at self-defence.*] I want you, you see, to do everything exquisitely. I do wish I could leave you to do things a little more for yourself. I suppose it's owing to my having had to be father and mother both. I knew nothing practically about the bringing up of children, and of course I couldn't trust you to a nurse.

Margaret. [*Severely.*] Not you; so sure you could do it better yourself. That's you all over. Daddy, do you remember how you taught me to balance a biscuit on my nose, like a puppy?

Dearth. [*Sadly.*] Did I?

Margaret. You called me Rover.

Dearth. I deny that.

Margaret. And when you said "snap" I caught the biscuit in my mouth.

Dearth. Horrible!

Margaret. [*Gleaming.*] Daddy, I can do it still! [*Putting a biscuit on her nose.*] Here is the last of my supper. Say "snap," Daddy.

Dearth. Not I.

Margaret. Say "snap," please.

Dearth. I refuse.

Margaret. Daddy!

Dearth. Snap. [*She catches the biscuit in her mouth.*] Let that be the last time, Margaret.

Margaret. Except just once more. I don't mean now, but when my hair is really up. If I should ever have a—a Margaret of my own, come in and see me, Daddy, in my white bed, and say "snap"—and I'll have the biscuit ready.

Dearth. [*Turning away his head.*] Right-o.

Margaret. Dad, if I ever should marry, not that I will but if I should—at the marriage ceremony will you let me be the one who says, "I do"?

Dearth. I suppose I deserve this.

Margaret. [*Coaxingly.*] You think I'm pretty, don't you, Dad, whatever other people say?

Dearth. Not so bad.

Margaret. I *know* I have nice ears.

Dearth. They are all right now, but I had to work on them for months.

Margaret. You don't mean to say that you did my *ears*?

Dearth. Rather!

Margaret. [*Grown humble.*] My dimple is my own.

Dearth. I am glad you think so. I wore out the point of my little finger over that dimple.

Margaret. Even my dimple! Have I anything that is really mine? A bit of my nose or anything?

Dearth. When you were a babe you had a laugh that was all your own.

Margaret. Haven't I it now?

Dearth. It's gone. [*He looks ruefully at her.*] I'll tell you how it went. We were fishing in a stream—that is to say, I was wading and you were sitting on my shoulders holding the rod. We didn't catch anything. Somehow or another—I can't think how I did it—you irritated me, and I answered you sharply.

Margaret. [*Gasping.*] I can't believe that.

Dearth. Yes, it sounds extraordinary, but I did. It gave you a shock, and, for the moment, the world no longer seemed a safe place to you; your faith in me had always made it safe till then. You were suddenly not even sure of your bread and butter, and a frightened tear came to your eyes. I was in a nice state about it, I can tell you.

[*He is in a nice state about it still.*]

Margaret. Silly! [*Bewildered.*] But what has that to do with my laugh, Daddy?

Dearth. The laugh that children are born with lasts just so long as they have perfect faith. To think that it was I who robbed you of yours!

Margaret. Don't, dear. I am sure the laugh just went off with the tear to comfort it, and they have been playing about that stream ever since. They have quite forgotten us, so why should we remember them? Cheeky little beasts! Shall I tell you my farthest back recollection? [*In some awe.*] I remember the first time I saw the stars. I had never seen night, and then I saw it and the stars together. Crack-in-my-eye-Tommy, it isn't every one who can boast of such a lovely, lovely recollection for their earliest, is it?

Dearth. I was determined your earliest should be a good one.

Margaret. [*Blankly.*] Do you mean to say you planned it?

Dearth. Rather! Most people's earliest recollection is of some trivial thing; how they cut their finger, or lost a piece of string. I was resolved my Margaret's should be something bigger. I was poor, but I could give her the stars.

Margaret. [*Clutching him round the legs.*] Oh, how you love me, Daddikins.

Dearth. Yes, I do, rather.

[*A vagrant woman has wandered in their direction, one whom the shrill winds of life have lashed and bled; here and there ragged graces still cling to her, and unruly passion smoulders, but she, once a dear fierce rebel with eyes of storm, is now first of all a whimperer. She and they meet as strangers.*]

Margaret. [*Nicely, as becomes an artist's daughter.*] Good evening.

Alice. Good evening, Missy; evening, Mister.

Dearth. [*Seeing that her eyes search the ground.*] Lost anything?

Alice. Sometimes when the tourists have had their sandwiches there are bits left over, and they squeeze them between the roots to keep the place tidy. I am looking for bits.

Dearth. You don't tell me you are as hungry as that?

Alice. [*With spirit.*] Try me.

[*Strange that he should not know that once loved husky voice.*]

Margaret. [*Rushing at her father and feeling all his pockets.*] Daddy, that was my last biscuit!

Dearth. We must think of something else.

Margaret. [*Taking her hand.*] Yes, wait a bit, we are sure to think of something. Daddy, think of something.

Alice. [*Sharply.*] Your father doesn't like you to touch the likes of me.

Margaret. Oh yes, he does. [*Defiantly.*] And if he didn't, I'd do it all the same. This is a bit of *myself,* Daddy.

Dearth. That is all you know.

Alice. [*Whining.*] You needn't be angry with her, Mister; I'm all right.

Dearth. I am not angry with her; I am very sorry for you.

Alice. [*Flaring.*] If I had my rights, I would be as good as you—and better.

Dearth. I daresay.

Alice. I have had men-servants and a motor-car.

Dearth. Margaret and I never rose to that.

Margaret. [*Stung.*] I have been in a taxi several times, and Dad often gets telegrams.

Dearth. Margaret!

Margaret. I'm sorry I boasted.

Alice. That's nothing. I have a town house—at least I had . . . At any rate he said there was a town house.

Margaret. [*Interested.*] Fancy his not knowing for certain.

Alice. The Honorable Mrs. Finch-Fallowe—that's who I am.

Margaret. [*Cordially.*] It's a lovely name.

Alice. Curse him.

Margaret. Don't you like him?

Dearth. We won't go into that. I have nothing to do with your past, but I wish we had some food to offer you.

Alice. You haven't a flask?

Dearth. No, I don't take anything myself. But let me see. . . .

Margaret. [*Sparkling.*] I know! You said we had five pounds. [*To the needy one.*] Would you like five pounds?

Dearth. Darling, don't be stupid; we haven't paid our bill at the inn.

Alice. [*With bravado.*] All right; I never asked you for anything.

Dearth. Don't take me up in that way: I have had my ups and downs myself. Here is ten bob and welcome.

[*He surreptitiously slips a coin into* MARGARET'S *hand.*]

Margaret. And I have half a crown. It is quite easy for us. Dad will be getting another fiver any day. You can't think how exciting it is when the fiver comes in; we dance and then we run out and buy chops.

Dearth. Margaret!

Alice. It's kind of you. I'm richer this minute than I have been for many a day.

Dearth. It's nothing; I am sure you would do the same for us.

Alice. I wish I was as sure.

Dearth. Of course you would. Glad to be of any help. Get some victuals as quickly as you can. Best of wishes, ma'am, and may your luck change.

Alice. Same to you, and may yours go on.

Margaret. Good-night.

Alice. What is her name, Mister?

Dearth. [*Who has returned to his easel.*] Margaret.

Alice. Margaret. You drew something good out of the lucky bag when you got her, Mister.

Dearth. Yes.

Alice. Take care of her; they are easily lost. [*She shuffles away.*]

Dearth. Poor soul. I expect she has had a rough time, and that some man is to blame for it—partly, at any rate. [*Restless.*] That woman rather affects me, Margaret; I don't know why. Didn't you like her husky voice? [*He goes on painting.*] I say, Margaret, we lucky ones, let's swear always to be kind to people who are down on their luck, and then when we are kind let's be a little kinder.

Margaret. [*Gleefully.*] Yes, let's.

Dearth. Margaret, always feel sorry for the failures, the ones who are always failures —especially in my sort of calling. Wouldn't it be lovely, to turn them on the thirty-ninth year of failure into glittering successes?

Margaret. Topping.

Dearth. Topping.

Margaret. Oh, topping. How could we do it, Dad?

Dearth. By letter. "To poor old Tom Broken Heart, Top Attic, Garret Chambers, S.E.—DEAR SIR,—His Majesty has been graciously pleased to purchase your superb picture of Marlow Ferry."

Margaret. "*P.S.*—I am sending the money in a sack so as you can hear it chink."

Dearth. What could we do for our friend who passed just now? I can't get her out of my head.

Margaret. You have made me forget her. [*Plaintively.*] Dad, I didn't like it.

Dearth. Didn't like what, dear?

Margaret. [*Shuddering.*] I didn't like her saying that about your losing me.

Dearth. [*The one thing of which he is sure.*] I shan't lose you.

Margaret. [*Hugging his arm.*] It would be hard for me if you lost me, but it would be worse for you. I don't know how I know that, but I do know it. What would you do without me?

Dearth. [*Almost sharply.*] Don't talk like that, dear. It is wicked and stupid, and naughty. Somehow that poor woman—I won't paint any more tonight.

Margaret. Let's get out of the wood; it frightens me.

Dearth. And you loved it a moment ago. Hullo! [*He had seen a distant blurred light in the wood, apparently from a window.*] I hadn't noticed there was a house there.

Margaret. [*Tingling.*] Daddy, I feel sure there wasn't a house there!

Dearth. Goose. It is just that we didn't look: our old way of letting the world go hang; so interested in ourselves. Nice behavior for people who have been boasting about what they would do for other people. Now I see what I ought to do.

Margaret. Let's get out of the wood.

Dearth. Yes, but my idea first. It is to rouse these people and get food from them for the husky one.

Margaret. [*Clinging to him.*] She is too far away now.

Dearth. I can overtake her.

Margaret. [*In a frenzy.*] Don't go into that house, Daddy! I don't know why it is, but I am afraid of that house!

[*He waggles a reproving finger at her.*]

Dearth. There is a kiss for each moment until I come back. [*She wipes them from her face.*] Oh, naughty, go and stand in the corner. [*She stands against a tree but she stamps her foot.*] Who has got a nasty temper! [*She tries hard not to smile, but she smiles and he smiles, and they make comic faces at each other, as they have done in similar circumstances since she first opened her eyes.*] I shall be back before you can count a hundred.

[*He goes off humming his song so that she may still hear him when he is lost to sight; all just as so often before. She tries dutifully to count her hundred, but the wood grows dark and soon she is afraid again. She runs from tree to tree calling to her Daddy. We begin to lose her among the shadows.*]

Margaret. [*Out of the impalpable that is carrying her away.*] Daddy, come back; I don't want to be a might-have-been.

ACT III

LOB'S *room has gone very dark as it sits up awaiting the possible return of the adventurers. The curtains are drawn, so that no light comes from outside.*

[*There is a tapping on the window, and anon two intruders are stealing about the floor, with muffled cries when they meet unexpectedly. They find the switch and are revealed as* PURDIE *and his* MABEL. *Something has happened to them as they emerged from the wood, but it is so superficial that neither notices it: they are again in the evening dress in which they had left the house. But they are still being led by that strange humor of the blood.*]

Mabel. [*Looking around her curiously.*] A pretty little room; I wonder who is the owner?

Purdie. It doesn't matter; the great thing is that we have escaped Joanna.

Mabel. Jack, look, a man!

[*The term may not be happily chosen, but the person indicated is* LOB *curled up on his chair by a dead fire. The last look on his face before he fell asleep having been a leery one, it is still there.*]

Purdie. He is asleep.

Mabel. Do you know him?

Purdie. Not I. Excuse me, sir, Hi!

[*No shaking, however, wakens the sleeper.*]

Mabel. Darling, how extraordinary.

Purdie. [*Always considerate.*] After all, precious, have we any right to wake up a stranger, just to tell him that we are runaways hiding in his house?

Mabel. [*Who comes of a good family.*] I think he would expect it of us.

Purdie. [*After trying again.*] There is no budging him.

Mabel. [*Appeased.*] At any rate, we have done the civil thing. [*She has now time to regard the room more attentively, including the tray of coffee cups which* MATEY *had left on the table in a not unimportant moment of his history.*] There have evidently been people here, but they haven't drunk their coffee. Ugh! cold as a deserted egg in a bird's nest. Jack, if you were a clever detective you could construct those people out of their neglected coffee cups. I wonder who they are and what has spirited them away?

Purdie. Perhaps they have only gone to bed. Ought we to knock them up?

Mabel. [*After considering what her mother would have done.*] I think not, dear. I suppose we have run away, Jack—meaning to?

Purdie. [*With the sturdiness that weaker vessels adore.*] Irrevocably. Mabel, if the dog-like devotion of a lifetime. . . . [*He becomes conscious that something has happened to* LOB'S *leer. It has not left his face but it has shifted.*] He is not shamming, do you think?

Mabel. Shake him again.

Purdie. [*After shaking him.*] It's all right. Mabel, if the dog-like devotion of a lifetime . . .

Mabel. Poor little Joanna! Still, if a woman insists on being a pendulum round a man's neck . . .

Purdie. Do give me a chance, Mabel. If the dog-like devotion of a lifetime . . . [JOANNA *comes through the curtains so inopportunely that for the moment he is almost pettish.*] May I say, this is just a little too much, Joanna!

Joanna. [*Unconscious as they of her return to her dinner gown.*] So, sweet husband, your soul is still walking alone, is it?

Mabel. [*Who hates coarseness of any kind.*] How can you sneak about in this way, Joanna? Have you no pride?

Joanna. [*Dashing away a tear.*] Please to address me as Mrs. Purdie, madam. [*She sees* LOB.] Who is this man?

Purdie. We don't know; and there is no waking him. You can try, if you like.

[*Failing to rouse him* JOANNA *makes a third at table. They are all a little inconsequential, as if there were still some moonshine in their hair.*]

Joanna. You were saying something about the devotion of a lifetime; please go on.

Purdie. [*Diffidently.*] I don't like to before you, Joanna.

Joanna. [*Becoming coarse again.*] Oh, don't mind me.

Purdie. [*Looking like a note of interrogation.*] I should certainly like to say it.

Mabel. [*Loftily.*] And I shall be proud to hear it.

Purdie. I should have liked to spare you this, Joanna; you wouldn't put your hands over your ears?

Joanna. [*Alas!*] No, sir.

Mabel. Fie, Joanna. Surely a wife's natural delicacy . . .

Purdie. [*Severely.*] As you take it in that spirit, Joanna, I can proceed with a clear conscience. If the dog-like devotion of a lifetime——

[*He reels a little, staring at* LOB, *over whose face the leer has been wandering like an insect.*]

Mabel. Did he move?

Purdie. It isn't that. I am feeling—very funny. Did one of you tap me just now on the forehead?

[*Their hands also have gone to their foreheads.*]

Mabel. I think I have been in this room before.

Purdie. [*Flinching.*] There is something coming rushing back to me.

Mabel. I seem to know that coffee set. If I do, the lid of the milk jug is chipped. It is!

Joanna. I can't remember this man's name; but I am sure it begins with L.

Mabel. Lob.

Purdie. Lob.

Joanna. Lob.

Purdie. Mabel, your dress?

Mabel. [*Beholding it.*] How on earth . . . ?

Joanna. My dress! [*To* PURDIE.] You were in knickerbockers in the wood.

Purdie. And so I am now. [*He sees he is not.*] Where did I change? The wood! Let me think. The wood . . . the wood, certainly. But the wood wasn't the wood.

Joanna. [*Revolving like one in pursuit.*] My head is going round.

Mabel. Lob's wood! I remember it all. We were here. We did go.

Purdie. So we did. But how could . . . ? where was . . . ?

Joanna. And who was . . . ?

Mabel. And what was . . . ?

Purdie. [*Even in this supreme hour a man.*] Don't let go. Hold on to what we were doing, or we shall lose grip of ourselves. Devotion. Something about devotion. Hold on to devotion. "If the dog-like devotion of a lifetime . . ." Which of you was I saying that to?

Mabel. To me.

Purdie. Are you sure?

Mabel. [*Shakily.*] I am not quite sure.

Purdie. [*Anxiously.*] Joanna, what do you think? [*With a sudden increase of uneasiness.*] Which of you is my wife?

Joanna. [*Without enthusiasm.*] I am. No, I am not. It is Mabel who is your wife!

Mabel. Me?

Purdie. [*With a curious gulp.*] Why, of course you are, Mabel!

Mabel. I believe I am!

Purdie. And yet how can it be? I was running away with you.

Joanna. [*Solving that problem.*] You don't need to do it now.

Purdie. The wood. Hold on to the wood. The wood is what explains it. Yes, I see the whole thing. [*He gazes at* LOB.] You infernal old rascal! Let us try to think it out. Don't any one speak for a moment. Think first. Love . . . Hold on to love. [*He gets another tap.*] I say, I believe I am not a deeply passionate chap at all; I believe I am just . . . a philanderer!

Mabel. It is what you are.

Joanna. [*More magnanimous.*] Mabel, what about ourselves?

Purdie. [*To whom it is truly a nauseous draught.*] I didn't know. Just a philanderer! [*The soul of him would like at this instant to creep into another body.*] And if people don't change, I suppose we shall begin all over again now.

Joanna. [*The practical.*] I daresay; but not with each other. I may philander again, but not with you.

[*They look on themselves without approval, always a sorry occupation. The man feels it most because he has admired himself most, or perhaps partly for some better reason.*]

Purdie. [*Saying good-by to an old friend.*] John Purdie, John Purdie, the fine fellow I used to think you! [*When he is able to look them in the face again.*] The wood has taught me one thing, at any rate.

Mabel. [*Dismally.*] What, Jack?

Purdie. That it isn't accident that shapes our lives.

Joanna. No, it's Fate.

Purdie. [*The truth running through him, seeking for a permanent home in him, willing to give him still another chance, loth to desert him.*] It's not Fate, Joanna. Fate is something outside us. What really plays the dickens with us is something in ourselves. Something that makes us go on doing the same sort of fool things, however many chances we get.

Mabel. Something in ourselves?

Purdie. [*Shivering.*] Something we are born with.

Joanna. Can't we cut out the beastly thing?

Purdie. Depends, I expect, on how long we have pampered him. We can at least control him if we try hard enough. But I have for the moment an abominably clear perception that the likes of me never really tries. Forgive me, Joanna—no, Mabel—both of you. [*He is a shamed man.*] It isn't very pleasant to discover that one is a rotter. I suppose I shall get used to it.

Joanna. I could forgive anybody anything tonight. [*Candidly.*] It is so lovely not to be married to you, Jack.

Purdie. [*Spiritless.*] I can understand that. I do feel small.

Joanna. [*The true friend.*] You will soon swell up again.

Purdie. [*For whom, alas, we need not weep.*] That is the appalling thing. But at present, at any rate, I am a rag at your feet, Joanna—no, at yours, Mabel. Are you going to pick me up? I don't advise it.

Mabel. I don't know whether I want to, Jack. To begin with, which of us is it your lonely soul is in search of?

Joanna. Which of us is the fluid one, or the fluider one?

Mabel. Are you and I one? Or are you and Joanna one? Or are the three of us two?

Joanna. He wants you to whisper in his ear, Mabel, the entrancing poem, "Mabel Purdie." Do it, Jack; there will be nothing wrong in it now.

Purdie. Rub it in.

Mabel. When I meet Joanna's successor ——

Purdie. [*Quailing.*] No, no, Mabel, none of that. At least credit me with having my eyes open at last. There will be no more of this. I swear it by all that is——

Joanna. [*In her excellent imitation of a sheep.*] Baa-a, he is off again.

Purdie. Oh Lord, so I am.

Mabel. Don't, Joanna.

Purdie. [*His mind still illumined.*] She is quite right—I was. In my present state of depression—which won't last—I feel there is something in me that will make me go on being the same ass, however many chances I get. I haven't the stuff in me to take warning. My whole being is corroded. Shakespeare knew what he was talking about—

"The fault, dear Brutus, is not in our stars,
But in ourselves, that we are underlings."

Joanna. For "dear Brutus" we are to read "dear audience," I suppose?

Purdie. You have it.

Joanna. Meaning that we have the power to shape ourselves?

Purdie. We have the power right enough.

Joanna. But isn't that rather splendid?

Purdie. For those who have the grit in them, yes. [*Still seeing with a strange clearness through the chink the hammer has made.*] And they are not the dismal chappies; they are the ones with the thin bright faces. [*He sits lugubriously by his wife and is sorry for the first time that she has not married a better man.*] I am afraid there is not much fight in me, Mabel, but we shall see. If you catch me at it again, have the goodness to whisper to me in passing, "Lob's Wood." That may cure me for the time being.

Mabel. [*Still certain that she loved him once but not so sure why.*] Perhaps I will . . . as long as I care to bother, Jack. It depends on you how long that is to be.

Joanna. [*To break an awkward pause.*] I feel that there is hope in that as well as a warning. Perhaps the wood may prove to have been useful after all. [*This brighter view of the situation meets with no immediate response. With her next suggestion she reaches harbor.*] You know, we are not people worth being sorrowful about—so let us laugh.

[*The ladies succeed in laughing, though not prettily; but the man has been too much shaken.*]

Joanna. [*In the middle of her laugh.*] We have forgotten the others! I wonder what is happening to them?

Purdie. [*Reviving.*] Yes, what about them? Have *they* changed?

Mabel. I didn't see any of them in the wood.

Joanna. Perhaps we did see them without knowing them; we didn't know Lob.

Purdie. [*Daunted.*] That's true.

Joanna. Won't it be delicious to be here to watch them when they come back, and see them waking up—or whatever it was we did?

Purdie. What was it we did? I think something tapped me on the forehead.

Mabel. [*Blanching.*] How do we know the others *will* come back?

Joanna. [*Infected.*] We don't know. How awful!

Mabel. Listen!

Purdie. I distinctly hear some one on the stairs.

Mabel. It will be Matey.

Purdie. [*The chink beginning to close.*] Be cautious both of you; don't tell him we have had any . . . odd experiences.

[*It is, however,* MRS. COADE *who comes down-stairs in a dressing-gown and carrying a candle and her husband's muffler.*]

Mrs. Coade. So you are back at last. A nice house, I must say. Where is Coady?

Purdie. [*Taken aback.*] Coady! Did he go into the wood, too?

Mrs. Coade. [*Placidly.*] I suppose so. I have been down several times to look for him.

Mabel. Coady, too!

Joanna. [*Seeing visions.*] I wonder . . . Oh, how dreadful!

Mrs. Coade. What is dreadful, Joanna?

Joanna. [*Airily.*] Nothing. I was just wondering what he is doing.

Mrs. Coade. Doing? What should he be doing? Did anything odd happen to you in the wood?

Purdie. [*Taking command.*] No, no, nothing.

Joanna. We just strolled about, and came back. [*That subject being exhausted she points to* LOB.] Have you noticed him?

Mrs. Coade. Oh, yes; he has been like that all the time. A sort of stupor, I think; and sometimes the strangest grin comes over his face.

Purdie. [*Wincing.*] Grin?

Mrs. Coade. Just as if he were seeing amusing things in his sleep.

Purdie. [*Guardedly.*] I daresay he is. Oughtn't we to get Matey to him?

Mrs. Coade. Matey has gone too.

Purdie. Wha-at!

Mrs. Coade. At all events he is not in the house.

Joanna. [*Unguardedly.*] Matey! I wonder who is with him.

Mrs. Coade. Must somebody be with him?

Joanna. Oh, no, not at all.

[*They are simultaneously aware that some one outside has reached the window.*]

Mrs. Coade. I hope it is Coady.

[*The other ladies are too fond of her to share this wish.*]

Mabel. Oh, I hope not.

Mrs. Coade. [*Blissfully.*] Why, Mrs. Purdie?

Joanna. [*Coaxingly.*] Dear Mrs. Coade, whoever he is, and whatever he does, I beg you not to be surprised. We feel that though we had no unusual experiences in the wood, others may not have been so fortunate.

Mabel. And be cautious, you dear, what you say to them before they come to.

Mrs. Coade. "Come to?" You puzzle me. And Coady didn't have his muffler.

[*Let it be recorded that in their distress for this old lady they forget their own misadventures.* PURDIE *takes a step toward the curtains in a vague desire to shield her;—and gets a rich reward; he has seen the coming addition to their circle.*]

Purdie. [*Elated and pitiless.*] It is Matey!

[*A butler intrudes who still thinks he is wrapped in fur.*]

Joanna. [*Encouragingly.*] Do come in.

Matey. With apologies, ladies and gents. . . . May I ask who is host?

Purdie. [*Splashing in the temperature that suits him best.*] A very reasonable request. Third on the left.

Matey. [*Advancing upon* LOB.] Merely to ask, sir, if you can direct me to my hotel? [*The sleeper's only response is a slight quiver in one leg.*] The gentleman seems to be reposing.

Mrs. Coade. It is Lob.

Matey. What is lob, ma'am?

Mrs. Coade. [*Pleasingly curious.*] Surely you haven't forgotten?

Purdie. [*Overriding her.*] Anything we can do for you, sir? Just give it a name.

Joanna. [*In the same friendly spirit.*] I hope you are not alone: do say you have some lady friends with you.

Matey. [*With an emphasis on his leading word.*] My wife is with me.

Joanna. His wife! . . . [*With commendation.*] You *have* been quick!

Mrs. Coade. I didn't know you were married.

Matey. Why should you, madam? You talk as if you knew me.

Mrs. Coade. Good gracious, do you really think I don't?

Purdie. [*Indicating delicately that she is

subject to a certain softening.] Sit down, won't you, my dear sir, and make yourself comfy.

Matey. [*Accustomed of late to such deferential treatment.*] Thank you. But my wife . . .

Joanna. [*Hospitably.*] Yes, bring her in; we are simply dying to make her acquaintance.

Matey. You are very good; I am much obliged.

Mabel. [*As he goes out.*] Who can she be?

Joanna. [*Leaping.*] Who, who, who!

Mrs. Coade. But what an extraordinary wood! He doesn't seem to know who he is at all.

Mabel. [*Soothingly.*] Don't worry about that, Coady darling. He will know soon enough.

Joanna. [*Again finding the bright side.*] And so will the little wife! By the way, whoever she is, I hope she is fond of butlers.

Mabel. [*Who has peeped.*] It is Lady Caroline!

Joanna. [*Leaping again.*] Oh, joy, joy! And she was so sure she couldn't take the wrong turning!

[Lady Caroline *is evidently still sure of it.*]

Matey. May I present my wife—Lady Caroline Matey.

Mabel. [*Glowing.*] How do you do?

Purdie. Your servant, Lady Caroline.

Mrs. Coade. Lady Caroline Matey! You?

Lady Caroline. [*Without an* r *in her.*] Charmed, I'm sure.

Joanna. [*Neatly.*] Very pleased to meet any wife of Mr. Matey.

Purdie. [*Taking the floor.*] Allow me. The Duchess of Candelabra. The Ladies Helena and Matilda M'Nab. I am the Lord Chancellor.

Mabel. I have wanted so long to make your acquaintance.

Lady Caroline. Charmed.

Joanna. [*Gracefully.*] These informal meetings are so delightful, don't you think?

Lady Caroline. Yes, indeed.

Matey. [*The introductions being thus pleasantly concluded.*] And your friend by the fire?

Purdie. I will introduce you to him when you wake up—I mean when he wakes up.

Matey. Perhaps I ought to have said that I am *James* Matey.

Lady Caroline. [*The happy creature.*] *The* James Matey.

Matey. A name not, perhaps, unknown in the world of finance.

Joanna. Finance? Oh, so you did take that clerkship in the City!

Matey. [*A little stiffly.*] I began as a clerk in the City, certainly; and I am not ashamed to admit it.

Mrs. Coade. [*Still groping.*] Fancy that, now. And did it save you?

Matey. Save me, madam?

Joanna. Excuse us—we ask odd questions in this house; we only mean, did that keep you honest? Or are you still a pilferer?

Lady Caroline. [*An outraged swan.*] Husband mine, what does she mean?

Joanna. No offence; I mean a pilferer on a large scale.

Matey. [*Remembering certain newspaper jealousy.*] If you are referring to that Labrador business—or the Working Women's Bank. . . .

Purdie. [*After the manner of one who has caught a fly.*] O-ho, got him!

Joanna. [*Bowing.*] Yes, those are what I meant.

Matey. [*Stoutly.*] There was nothing proved.

Joanna. [*Like one calling a meeting.*] Mabel, Jack, here is another of us! You have gone just the same way again, my friend. [*Ecstatically.*] There is more in it, you see, than taking the wrong turning; you would always take the wrong turning. [*The only fitting comment.*] Tra-la-la!

Lady Caroline. If you are casting any aspersions on my husband, allow me to say that a prouder wife than I does not today exist.

Mrs. Coade. [*Who finds herself the only clearheaded one.*] My dear, do be careful.

Mabel. So long as you are satisfied, dear Lady Caroline. But I thought you shrank from all blood that was not blue.

Lady Caroline. You thought? Why should you think about me? I beg to assure you that I adore my Jim. [*She seeks his arm, but her* Jim *has encounered the tray containing coffee cups and a cake, and his hands close on it with a certain intimacy.*] Whatever are you doing, Jim?

Matey. I don't understand it, Caroliny; but somehow I feel at home with this in my hands.

Mabel. "Caroliny!"

Mrs. Coade. Look at me well; don't you remember me?

Matey. [*Musing.*] I don't remember you; but I seem to associate you with hard-boiled eggs. [*With conviction.*] You like your eggs hard-boiled.

Purdie. Hold on to hard-boiled eggs! She used to tip you especially to see to them. [MATEY's *hand goes to his pocket.*] Yes, that was the pocket.

Lady Caroline. [*With distaste.*] Tip!

Matey. [*Without distaste.*] Tip!

Purdie. Jolly word, isn't it?

Matey. [*Raising the tray.*] It seems to set me thinking.

Lady Caroline. [*Feeling the tap of the hammer.*] Why is my work-basket in this house?

Mrs. Coade. You are living here, you know.

Lady Caroline. That is what a person feels. But when did I come? It is very odd, but one feels one ought to say when did one go.

Purdie. She is coming to with a wush!

Matey. [*Under the hammer.*] Mr. . . . Purdie!

Lady Caroline. Mrs. Coade!

Matey. The Guv-nor! My clothes!

Lady Caroline. One is in evening dress!

Joanna. [*Charmed to explain.*] You will understand clearly in a minute, Caroliny. You didn't really take that clerkship, Jim; you went into domestic service; but in the essentials you haven't altered.

Purdie. [*Pleasantly.*] I'll have my shaving water at 7.30 sharp, Matey.

Matey. [*Mechanically.*] Very good, sir.

Lady Caroline. Sir? Midsummer Eve! The wood!

Purdie. Yes, hold on to the wood.

Matey. You are . . . you are . . . you are Lady Caroline Laney!

Lady Caroline. It is Matey, the butler!

Mabel. You seemed quite happy with him, you know, Lady Caroline.

Joanna. [*Nicely.*] We won't tell.

Lady Caroline. [*Subsiding.*] Caroline Matey! And I seemed to like it! How horrible!

Mrs. Coade. [*Expressing a general sentiment.*] It is rather difficult to see what we should do next.

Matey. [*Tentatively.*] Perhaps if I were to go downstairs?

Purdie. It would be conferring a personal favor on us all.

[*Thus encouraged* MATEY *and his tray resume friendly relations with the pantry.*]

Lady Caroline. [*With itching fingers as she glares at* LOB.] It is all that wretch's doing.

[*A quiver from* LOB's *right leg acknowledges the compliment. The gay music of a pipe is heard from outside.*]

Joanna. [*Peeping.*] Coady!

Mrs. Coade. Coady! Why is he so happy?

Joanna. [*Troubled.*] Dear, hold my hand.

Mrs. Coade. [*Suddenly trembling.*] Won't he know me?

Purdie. [*Abashed by that soft face.*] Mrs. Coade, I'm sorry. It didn't so much matter about the likes of us, but for your sake I wish Coady hadn't gone out.

Mrs. Coade. We that have been happily married this thirty years.

Coade. [*Popping in buoyantly.*] May I intrude? My name is Coade. The fact is I was playing about in the wood on a whistle, and I saw your light.

Mrs. Coade. [*The only one with the nerve to answer.*] Playing about in the wood with a whistle!

Coade. [*With mild dignity.*] And why not, madam?

Mrs. Coade. Madam! Don't you know me?

Coade. I don't know you. . . . [*Reflecting.*] But I wish I did.

Mrs. Coade. Do you? Why?

Coade. If I may say so, you have a very soft, lovable face.

[*Several persons breathe again.*]

Mrs. Coade. [*Inquisitorially.*] Who was with you, playing whistles in the wood?

[*The breathing ceases.*]

Coade. No one was with me.

[*And is resumed.*]

Mrs. Coade. No . . . lady?

Coade. Certainly not. [*Then he spoils it.*] I am a bachelor.

Mrs. Coade. A bachelor!

Joanna. Don't give way, dear; it might be much worse.

Mrs. Coade. A bachelor! And you are sure you never spoke to me before? Do think.

Coade. Not to my knowledge. Never . . except in dreams.

Mabel. [*Taking a risk.*] What did you say to her in dreams?

Coade. I said, "My dear." [*This when uttered surprises him.*] Odd!

Joanna. The darling man!

Mrs. Coade. [*Wavering.*] How could you say such things to an old woman?

Coade. [*Thinking it out.*] Old? I didn't think of you as old. No, no, young—with the morning dew on your face—coming across a lawn—in a black and green dress—and carrying such a pretty parasol.

Mrs. Coade. [*Thrilling.*] That was how he first met me! He used to love me in black and green; and it *was* a pretty parasol. Look, I am old. . . . So it can't be the same woman.

Coade. [*Blinking.*] Old? Yes, I suppose so. But it is the same soft, lovable face, and the same kind, beaming smile that children could warm their hands at.

Mrs. Coade. He always liked my smile.

Purdie. So do we all.

Coade. [*To himself.*] Emma!

Mrs. Coade. He hasn't forgotten my name!

Coade. It is sad that we didn't meet long ago. I think I have been waiting for you. I suppose we have met too late? You couldn't overlook my being an old fellow, could you, eh?

Joanna. How lovely; he is going to propose to her again. Coady, you happy thing, he is wanting the same soft face after thirty years!

Mrs. Coade. [*Undoubtedly hopeful.*] We mustn't be too sure, but I think that is it. [*Primly.*] What is it exactly that you want, Mr. Coade?

Coade. [*Under a lucky star.*] I want to have the right to hold the parasol over you. Won't you be my wife, my dear, and so give my long dream of you a happy ending?

Mrs. Coade. [*Preening.*] Kisses are not called for at our age, Coady, but here is a muffler for your old neck.

Coade. My muffler; I have missed it. [*It is, however, to his forehead that his hand goes. Immediately thereafter he misses his sylvan attire.*] Why . . . why what . . . who . . . how is this?

Purdie. [*Nervously.*] He is coming to.

Coade. [*Reeling and righting himself.*] Lob! [*The leg indicates that he has got it.*] Bless me, Coady, I went into that wood!

Mrs. Coade. And without your muffler, you that are so subject to chills. What are you feeling for in your pocket?

Coade. The whistle. It is a whistle I—Gone! of course it is. It's rather a pity, but . . . [*Anxious.*] Have I been saying awful things to you?

Mabel. You have been making her so proud. It is a compliment to our whole sex. You had a second chance, and it is her, again!

Coade. Of course it is. [*Crestfallen.*] But I see I was just the same nice old lazy Coady as before; and I had thought that if I had a second chance, I could do things. I have often said to you, Coady, that it was owing to my being cursed with a competency that I didn't write my great book. But I had no competency this time, and I haven't written a word.

Purdie. [*Bitterly enough.*] That needn't make you feel lonely in this house.

Mrs. Coade. [*In a small voice.*] You seem to have been quite happy as an old bachelor, dear.

Coade. I am surprised at myself, Emma, but I fear I was.

Mrs. Coade. [*With melancholy perspicacity.*] I wonder if what it means is that you don't especially need even me. I wonder if it means that you are just the sort of amiable creature that would be happy anywhere, and anyhow?

Coade. Oh dear, can it be as bad as that?

Joanna. [*A ministering angel she.*] Certainly not. It is a romance, and I won't have it looked upon as anything else.

Mrs. Coade. Thank you, Joanna. You will try not to miss that whistle, Coady?

Coade. [*Getting the footstool for her.*] You are all I need.

Mrs. Coade. Yes; but I am not so sure as I used to be that it is a great compliment.

Joanna. Coady, behave.

[*There is a knock on the window.*]

Purdie. [*Peeping.*] Mrs. Dearth! [*His spirits revive.*] She is alone. Who would have expected that of *her*?

Mabel. She is a wild one, Jack, but I sometimes thought rather a dear; I do hope she has got off cheaply.

[ALICE *comes to them in her dinner gown.*]

Purdie. [*The irrepressible.*] Pleased to see you, stranger.

Alice. [*Prepared for ejection.*] I was afraid such an unceremonious entry might startle you.

Purdie. Not a bit.

Alice. [*Defiant.*] I usually enter a house by the front door.

Purdie. I have heard that such is the swagger way.

Alice. [*Simpering.*] So stupid of me. I lost myself in the wood . . . and . . .

Joanna. [*Genially.*] Of course you did. But never mind that; do tell us your name.

Lady Caroline. [*Emerging again.*] Yes, yes, your name.

Alice. Of course, I am the Honorable Mrs. Finch-Fallowe.

Lady Caroline. Of course, of course!

Purdie. I hope Mr. Finch-Fallowe is very well? We don't know him personally, but may we have the pleasure of seeing him bob up presently?

Alice. No, I am not sure where he is.

Lady Caroline. [*With point.*] I wonder if the dear clever police know?

Alice. [*Imprudently.*] No, they don't. [*It is a very secondary matter to her. This woman of calamitous fires hears and sees her tormentors chiefly as the probable owners of the cake which is standing on that tray.*] So awkward, I gave my sandwiches to a poor girl and her father whom I met in the wood, and now . . . isn't it a nuisance—I am quite hungry. [*So far with a mincing bravado.*] May I?

[*Without waiting for consent she falls to upon the cake, looking over it like one ready to fight them for it.*]

Purdie. [*Sobered again.*] Poor soul.

Lady Caroline. We are so anxious to know whether you met a friend of ours in the wood —a Mr. Dearth. Perhaps you know him, too?

Alice. Dearth? I don't know any Dearth.

Mrs. Coade. Oh, dear, what a wood!

Lady Caroline. He is quite a front door sort of man; knocks and rings, you know.

Purdie. Don't worry her.

Alice. [*Gnawing.*] I meet so many; you see I go out a great deal. I have visiting-cards—printed ones.

Lady Caroline. How very distingué. Perhaps Mr. Dearth has painted your portrait; he is an artist.

Alice. Very likely; they all want to paint me. I daresay that is the man to whom I gave my sandwiches.

Mrs. Coade. But I thought you said he had a daughter?

Alice. Such a pretty girl; I gave her half a crown.

Coade. A daughter? That can't be Dearth.

Purdie. [*Darkly.*] Don't be too sure. Was the man you speak of a rather chop-fallen, gone-too-seed sort of person?

Alice. No, I thought him such a jolly, attractive man.

Coade. Dearth jolly, attractive! oh no. Did he say anything about his wife?

Lady Caroline. Yes, do try to remember if he mentioned her.

Alice. [*Snapping.*] No, he didn't.

Purdie. He was far from jolly in her time.

Alice. [*With an archness for which the cake is responsible.*] Perhaps that was the lady's fault.

[*The last of the adventurers draws nigh, carolling a French song as he comes.*]

Coade. Dearth's voice. He sounds quite merry!

Joanna. [*Protecting.*] Alice, you poor thing.

Purdie. This is going to be horrible.

[*A clear-eyed man of lusty gait comes in.*]

Dearth. I am sorry to bounce in on you in this way, but really I have an excuse. I am a painter of sorts, and . . .

[*He sees he has brought some strange discomfort here.*]

Mrs. Coade. I must say, Mr. Dearth, I am delighted to see you looking so well. Like a new man, isn't he?

[*No one dares to answer.*]

Dearth. I am certainly very well, if you care to know. But did I tell you my name?

Joanna. [*For some one has to speak.*] No, but—but we have an instinct in this house.

Dearth. Well, it doesn't matter. Here is the situation; my daughter and I have just met in the wood a poor woman famishing for want of food. We were as happy as grigs ourselves, and the sight of her distress rather cut us up. Can you give me something for her? Why are you looking so startled? [*Seeing the remains of the cake.*] May I have this? [*A shrinking movement from one of them draws his attention, and he recognizes in her the woman of whom he has been speaking. He sees her in fine clothing and he grows stern.*] I feel I can't be mistaken; it was you I met in the wood. Have you been playing some trick on me? [*To the others.*] It was for her I wanted the food.

Alice. [*Her hand guarding the place where his gift lies.*] Have you come to take back the money you gave me?

Dearth. Your dress! You were almost in rags when I saw you outside.

Alice. [*Frightened as she discovers how she is now attired.*] I don't . . . understand . . .

Coade. [*Gravely enough.*] For that matter, Dearth, I daresay you were different in the wood, too.

[DEARTH *sees his own clothing.*]

Dearth. What . . . !

Alice. [*Frightened.*] Where am I? [*To* MRS. COADE.] I seem to know you . . . do I?

Mrs. Coade. [*Motherly.*] Yes, you do; hold my hand, and you will soon remember all about it.

Joanna. I am afraid, Mr. Dearth, it is harder for you than for the rest of us.

Purdie. [*Looking away.*] I wish I could help you, but I can't; I am a rotter.

Mabel. We are awfully sorry. Don't you remember . . . Midsummer Eve?

Dearth. [*Controlling himself.*] Midsummer Eve? This room. Yes, this room. . . . You . . . was it you? . . . were going out to look for something. . . . The tree of knowledge, wasn't it? Somebody wanted me to go, too. . . . Who was that? A lady, I think. . . . Why did she ask me to go? What was I doing here? I was smoking a cigar. . . . I laid it down, there. . . . [*He finds the cigar.*] Who was the lady?

Alice. [*Feebly.*] Something about a second chance.

Mrs. Coade. Yes, you poor dear, you thought you could make so much of it.

Dearth. A lady who didn't like me—— [*With conviction.*] She had good reasons, too—but what were they . . . ?

Alice. A little old man! He did it. What did he do? [*The hammer is raised.*]

Dearth. I am . . . it is coming back—I am not the man I thought myself.

Alice. I am not Mrs. Finch-Fallowe. Who am I?

Dearth. [*Staring at her.*] You were that lady.

Alice. It is you—my husband!

[*She is overcome.*]

Mrs. Coade. My dear, you are much better off, so far as I can see, than if you were Mrs. Finch-Fallowe.

Alice. [*With passionate knowledge.*] Yes, yes indeed! [*Generously.*] But he isn't.

Dearth. Alice! . . . I—— [*He tries to smile.*] I didn't know you when I was in the wood with Margaret. She . . . she . . . Margaret . . . [*The hammer falls.*] O my God! [*He buries his face in his hands.*]

Alice. I wish—I wish——

[*She presses his shoulder fiercely and then stalks out by the door.*]

Purdie. [*To* LOB, *after a time.*] You old ruffian.

Dearth. No, I am rather fond of him, our lonely, friendly little host. Lob, I thank thee for that hour.

[*The seedy-looking fellow passes from the scene.*]

Coade. Did you see that his hand is shaking again?

Purdie. The watery eye has come back.

Joanna. And yet they are both quite nice people.

Purdie. [*Finding the tragedy of it.*] We are all quite nice people.

Mabel. If she were not such a savage!

Purdie. I daresay there is nothing the matter with her except that she would always choose the wrong man, good man or bad man, but the wrong man for her.

Coade. We can't change.

Mabel. Jack says the brave ones can.

Joanna. "The ones with the thin bright faces."

Mabel. Then there is hope for you and me, Jack.

Purdie. [*Ignobly.*] I don't expect so.

Joanna. [*Wandering about the room, like one renewing acquaintance with it after returning from a journey.*] Hadn't we better go to bed? It must be getting late.

Purdie. Hold on to bed! [*They all brighten.*]

Matey. [*Entering.*] Breakfast is quite ready. [*They exclaim.*]

Lady Caroline. My watch has stopped.

Joanna. And mine. Just as well perhaps!

Mabel. There is a smell of coffee.

[*The gloom continues to lift.*]

Coade. Come along, Coady; I do hope you have not been tiring your foot.

Mrs. Coade. I shall give it a good rest tomorrow, dear.

Matey. I have given your egg six minutes, ma'am.

[*They set forth once more upon the eternal round. The curious* JOANNA *remains behind.*]

Joanna. A strange experiment, Matey; does it ever have any permanent effect?

Matey. [*On whom it has had none.*] So far as I know, not often, miss; but, I believe, once in a while. [*There is hope in this for the brave ones. If we could wait long enough we might see the* DEARTHS *breasting their way into the light.*] He could tell you.

[*The elusive person thus referred to kicks responsively, meaning perhaps that none of the others will change till there is a tap from another hammer. But when* MATEY *goes to rout him from his chair he is no longer there. His disappearance is no shock to* MATEY, *who shrugs his shoulders and opens the windows to let in the glory of a summer morning. The garden has returned, and our queer little hero is busy at work among his flowers. A lark is rising.*]

JUNO AND THE PAYCOCK*

By

SEAN O'CASEY

THE PLAYS OF SEAN O'CASEY GAVE TO the Abbey Theater, Dublin, a new claim to universal attention. The great creative work of W. B. Yeats, Lady Gregory, and J. M. Synge during the first decade of the century had not been productive of large results in the years following. A profusion of good plays by other authors, however, were being produced under the leadership of W. B. Yeats, Lady Gregory, and Lennox Robinson. Suddenly there emerged from the terrors of the Black and Tan régime a series of vital plays, appealing to a public far beyond the city of Dublin. Some one had been watching the recent scenes of fratricidal fury with the impartial penetration of the true dramatist. For several years a tall slender figure in a trench coat, with cap pulled over his eyes, had become familiar to those who sat in the pit of the old theater. This attire, suggesting the gunman, was, in reality, that of the gentlest of men, whose knowledge of life and whose literary genius, suspected by none, were to bring that playhouse again to the attention of the world. Eight times he had laid his manuscripts before the directorate without results. Because of his persistence rather than for any faith in his dramatic power, these mentors finally decided to produce *The Shadow of a Gunman.* In this as in his later and better known plays, partisanship and political murder were exposed with the large-minded detachment of a pacifist that held humanity and truth above the animosity of patriotism. But so vital was the picture presented, and so appealing the wit and humor, that he at once captivated the audience from whom a riot had been expected. His plays are a daring blend of unrestrained humor and downright horror—but the sharp contrasts are life's and not the contrived theatricalities of sensational drama. Scenes from the city streets had projected themselves on the stage through the personality of this acute observer.

He had, in fact, been as conspicuous on the streets as in the pit—always alone, watching, listening, making notes. He was from the slums and wholly unschooled. He was fifteen before he learned by his own effort to read and write. Although he has read widely, he insists that education is a drawback to a dramatist, and that a knowledge of formal dramatic technique is a danger. His formlessness, however, is not without the suggestion of dramaturgy. Whether used consciously or not, old stage tricks are at times too apparent. There is artless vigor in abundance, and much beauty of thought and feeling. By the natural and undisciplined reflection of life, he produces the illusion of the carelessness and formlessness of nature, which, with such naturalists as Hauptmann, Gorki, and even Chekhov, are the effects of careful arrangement and purposeful art.

Juno and the Paycock was a veritable triumph. Its success in Dublin was followed by notable productions in London and New York. *The Plough and the Stars,* still more undisciplined and approaching epic grandeur of conception, placed O'Casey high among modern dramatists. *The Silver Tassie,* a pacifist play of noble conception, is less consistent in mood, and less effective theatrically. *Within the Gates,* a curious blend of realism and abstraction, was at once baffling and fascinating to audiences as a devastating satire of modern civilization.

Production

The vigorous realism of the Abbey Theater has too long been famous as an influence upon the world theater to need emphasis. It has set an example of folk acting at its best. It has responded subtly to the gentle idealism of Yeats, the sly, homely humor of Lady Gregory and Lennox Robinson, and the war cry, drunkenness, and rush of O'Casey. It must, however, be seen to be rightly understood, for it differs in its Celtic color and harmony from the humdrum realism of the English-speaking stage. The Abbey Theater company that brought *Juno and the Paycock* and *The Plough and the Stars* to New York in 1927-1928 gave performances that were notable in that great year in our theater. Padraic Colum attributes the success of the Abbey artists not to management, organization, or even to a progressive spirit, all of which are secondary in its work; but rather to poetic vision, the spirit of cooperation and improvisation, and, above all, to effective diction. "A play has to be talked into existence," he says, "and good plays are plays that are talked into existence entertainingly, beautifully. Those who began to write for the National Theater Society had one great point in their favor—they had an instinctive feeling for speech . . . Frank Fay (one of two brothers who led the first company of Abbey actors) labored with them to bring out everything that was fine in speech. . . . He established a tradition that is one of the very great assets of the Abbey Theater."

For discussion of the history and accomplishment of the Irish Theatre, see the prefaces to *Riders to the Sea* and *Hyacinth Halvey*.

SEAN O'CASEY

Born 1884, Dublin.
A common laborer. Self-educated.
War service in France.
1918, *History of the Citizen Army,* his first publication.
Wrote essays on labor problems, and political ballads.
1926, Awarded Hawthornden Prize.

PLAYS

1923 *The Shadow of a Gunman.* 1923 *Cathleen Listens In.* 1924 *Nannie's Night Out.* 1924 *Juno and the Paycock.* 1926 *The Plough and the Stars.* 1927 *The Silver Tassie.* 1933 *Within the Gates.* 1934 *The End of the Beginning.* 1934 *A Pound on Demand.* 1940 *The Star Turns Red.* 1940 *Purple Dust.*

WRITING ABOUT THE DRAMA

The Flying Wasp, 1937.

JUNO AND THE PAYCOCK

The Characters in the Play

"CAPTAIN" JACK BOYLE. JUNO BOYLE, *his wife.* JOHNNY BOYLE } *their* MARY BOYLE } *children.* "JOXER" DALY. MRS. MAISIE MADIGAN. "NEEDLE" NUGENT, *a tailor.* MRS. TANCRED.	*Residents in the Tenement.*	JERRY DEVINE. CHARLIE BENTHAM, *a school teacher.* AN IRREGULAR MOBILIZER. TWO IRREGULARS. A COAL-BLOCK VENDOR. A SEWING MACHINE MAN. TWO FURNITURE REMOVAL MEN. TWO NEIGHBORS.

SCENE

ACT I.—*The living apartment of a two-roomed tenancy of the Boyle family, in a tenement house in Dublin.*
ACT II.—*The same.*
ACT III.—*The same.*

A few days elapse between Acts I and II, and two months between Acts II and III.

During Act III, the curtain is lowered for a few minutes to denote the lapse of one hour.

Period of the play, 1922.

ACT I

The living room of a two-room tenancy occupied by the BOYLE *family in a tenement house in Dublin. Left, a door leading to another part of the house; left of door a window looking into the street; at back a dresser; farther to right at back, a window looking into the back of the house. Between the window and the dresser is a picture of the Virgin; below the picture, on a bracket, is a crimson bowl in which a floating votive light is burning. Farther to the right is a small bed partly concealed by cretonne hangings strung on a twine. To the right is the fireplace; near the fireplace is a door leading to the other room. Beside the fireplace is a box containing coal. On the mantelshelf is an alarm clock lying on its face. In a corner near the window looking into the back is a galvanized bath. A table and some chairs. On the table are breakfast things for one. A teapot is on the hob and a frying-pan stands inside the fender. There are a few books on the dresser and one on the table. Leaning against the dresser is a long-handled shovel—the kind invariably used by laborers when turning concrete or mixing mortar.*

[JOHNNY BOYLE *is sitting crouched beside the fire.* MARY *with her jumper off—it is lying on the back of a chair—is arranging her hair before a tiny mirror perched on the table. Beside the mirror is stretched out the morning paper, which she looks at when she isn't gazing into the mirror. She is a well-made and good-looking girl of twenty-two. Two forces are working in her mind—one, through the circumstances of her life, pulling her back; the other, through the influence of books she has read, pushing her forward. The opposing forces are apparent in her speech and her manners, both of which are degraded by her environment, and improved by her acquaintance—slight though it be—with literature. The time is early forenoon.*]

Mary. [*Looking at the paper.*] On a little by-road, out beyant Finglas, he was found.

[MRS. BOYLE *enters by door on right;*

she has been shopping and carries a small parcel in her hand. She is forty-five years of age, and twenty years ago she must have been a pretty woman; but her face has now assumed that look which ultimately settles down upon the faces of the women of the working-class: a look of listless monotony and harassed anxiety, blending with an expression of mechanical resistance. Were circumstances favorable, she would probably be a handsome, active, and clever woman.]

Mrs. Boyle. Isn't he come in yet?

Mary. No, mother.

Mrs. Boyle. Oh, he'll come in when he likes; struttin' about the town like a paycock with Joxer, I suppose. I hear all about Mrs. Tancred's son is in this mornin's paper.

Mary. The full details are in it this mornin'; seven wounds he had—one entherin' the neck, with an exit wound beneath the left shoulder-blade; another in the left breast penethratin' the heart, an' . . .

Johnny. [*Springing up from the fire.*] Oh, quit that readin', for God's sake! Are yous losin' all your feelin's? It'll soon be that none of yous'll read anythin' that's not about butcherin' !

[*He goes quickly into the room on left.*]

Mary. He's gettin' very sensitive, all of a sudden!

Mrs. Boyle. I'll read it myself, Mary, by an' by, when I come home. Everybody's sayin' that he was a die-hard—thanks be to God that Johnny had nothin' to do with him this long time. . . . [*Opening the parcel and taking out some sausages, which she places on a plate.*] Ah, then, if that father o' yours doesn't come in soon for his breakfast, he may go without any; I'll not wait much longer for him.

Mary. Can't you let him get it himself when he comes in?

Mrs. Boyle. Yes, an' let him bring in Joxer Daly along with him? Ay, that's what he'd like, an' that's what he's waitin' for—till he thinks I'm gone to work, an' then sail in with the boul' Joxer, to burn all the coal an' dhrink all the tea in the place, to show them what a good Samaritan he is! But I'll stop here till he comes in, if I have to wait till tomorrow mornin'.

Voice of Johnny. [*Inside.*] Mother!

Mrs. Boyle. Yis?

Voice of Johnny. Bring us in a dhrink o' wather.

Mrs. Boyle. Bring in that fella a dhrink o' wather, for God's sake, Mary.

Mary. Isn't he big an' able enough to come out an' get it himself?

Mrs. Boyle. If you weren't well yourself you'd like somebody to bring you in a dhrink o' wather.

[*She brings in drink and returns.*]

Mrs. Boyle. Isn't it terrible to have to be waitin' this way! You'd think he was bringin' twenty poun's a week into the house the way he's going on. He wore out the Health Insurance long ago, he's afther wearin' out the unemployment dole, an', now, he's thryin' to wear out me! An' constantly singin', no less, when he ought always to be on his knees offerin' up a Novena for a job!

Mary. [*Tying a ribbon fillet-wise around her head.*] I don't like this ribbon, ma; I think I'll wear the green—it looks betther than the blue.

Mrs. Boyle. Ah, wear whatever ribbon you like, girl, only don't be botherin' me. I don't know what a girl on strike wants to be wearin' a ribbon round her head for or silk stockin's on her legs either; it's wearin' them things that make the employers think they're givin' yous too much money.

Mary. The hour is past now when we'll ask the employers' permission to wear what we like.

Mrs. Boyle. I don't know why you wanted to walk out for Jennie Claffey; up to this you never had a good word for her.

Mary. What's the use of belongin' to a Trades Union if you won't stand up for your principles? Why did they sack her? It was a clear case of victimization. We couldn't let her walk the streets, could we?

Mrs. Boyle. No, of course yous couldn't—yous wanted to keep her company. Wan victim wasn't enough. When the employers sacrifice wan victim, the Trades Unions go wan betther be sacrificin' a hundred.

Mary. It doesn't matther what you say, ma—a principle's a principle.

Mrs. Boyle. Yis; an' when I go into oul' Murphy's tomorrow, an' he gets to know that, instead o' payin' all, I'm goin' to borry more, what'll he say when I tell him a principle's a principle? What'll we do if he refuses to give us any more on tick?

Mary. He daren't refuse—if he does, can't you tell him he's paid?

Mrs. Boyle. It's lookin' as if he was paid, whether he refuses or no.

[JOHNNY *appears at the door on left. He can be plainly seen now; he is a thin delicate fellow, something younger than* MARY. *He has evidently gone through a rough time. His face is pale and drawn; there is a tremulous look of in-*

definite fear in his eyes. The left sleeve of his coat is empty, and he walks with a slight halt.]

Johnny. I was lyin' down; I thought yous were gone. Oul' Simon Mackay is thrampin' about like a horse over me head, an' I can't sleep with him—they're like thunder-claps in me brain! The curse o'—God forgive me for goin' to curse!

Mrs. Boyle. There, now; go back an' lie down agan, an' I'll bring you in a nice cup o' tay.

Johnny. Tay, tay, tay! You're always thinkin' o' tay. If a man was dyin', you'd thry to make him swally a cup o' tay!

[*He goes back.*]

Mrs. Boyle. I don't know what's goin' to be done with him. The bullet he got in the hip in Easter Week was bad enough, but the bomb that shatthered his arm in the fight in O'Connell Street put the finishin' touch on him. I knew he was makin' a fool of himself. God knows I went down on me bended knees to him not to go agen the Free State.

Mary. He stuck to his principles, an', no matther how you may argue, ma, a principle's a principle.

Voice of Johnny. Is Mary goin' to stay here?

Mary. No, I'm not goin' to stay here; you can't expect me to be always at your beck an' call, can you?

Voice of Johnny. I won't stop here be meself!

Mrs. Boyle. Amn't I nicely handicapped with the whole o' yous! I don't know what any o' yous ud do without your ma. [*To* JOHNNY.] Your father'll be here in a minute, an' if you want anythin', he'll get it for you.

Johnny. I hate assin' him for anythin'. . . . He hates to be assed to stir. . . . Is the light lightin' before the picture o' the Virgin?

Mrs. Boyle. Yis, yis! The wan inside to St. Anthony isn't enough, but he must have another wan to the Virgin here!

[JERRY DEVINE *enters hastily. He is about twenty-five, well set, active, and earnest. He is a type, becoming very common now in the Labor Movement, of a mind knowing enough to make the mass of his associates, who know less, a power, and too little to broaden that power for the benefit of all.* MARY *seizes her jumper and runs hastily into room left.*]

Jerry. [*Breathless.*] Where's the Captain, Mrs. Boyle; where's the Captain?

Mrs. Boyle. You may well ass a body that: he's wherever Joxer Daly is—dhrinkin' in some snug or another.

Jerry. Father Farrell is just afther stoppin' to tell me to run up an' get him to go to the new job that's goin' on in Rathmines; his cousin is foreman o' the job, an' Father Farrell was speakin' to him about poor Johnny an' his father bein' idle so long, an' the foreman told Father Farrell to send the Captain up an' he'd give him a start—I wondher where I'd find him?

Mrs. Boyle. You'll find he's ayther in Ryan's or Foley's.

Jerry. I'll run around to Ryan's—I know it's a great house o' Joxer's.

[*He rushes out.*]

Mrs. Boyle. [*Piteously.*] There now, he'll miss that job, or I know for what! If he gets win' o' the word, he'll not come back till evenin', so that it'll be too late. There'll never be any good got out o' him so long as he goes with that shouldher-shruggin' Joxer. I killin' meself workin', an' he sthruttin' about from mornin' till night like a paycock!

[*The steps of two persons are heard coming up a flight of stairs. They are the footsteps of* CAPTAIN BOYLE *and* JOXER. CAPTAIN BOYLE *is singing in a deep, sonorous, self-honoring voice.*]

The Captain. Sweet Spirit, hear me prayer! Hear . . . oh . . . hear . . . me prayer . . . hear, oh, hear . . . oh, he . . . ar . . . oh, he . . . ar . . . me . . . pray . . . er!

Joxer. [*Outside.*] Ah, that's a darlin' song, a daaarlin' song!

Mrs. Boyle. [*Viciously.*] Sweet spirit hear his prayer! Ah, then, I'll take me solemn affeydavey, it's not for a job he's prayin'!

[*She sits down on the bed so that the cretonne hangings hide her from the view of those entering.*

THE CAPTAIN *comes slowly in. He is a man of about sixty; stout, gray-haired, and stocky. His neck is short, and his head looks like a stone ball that one sometimes sees on top of a gate-post. His cheeks, reddish-purple, are puffed out, as if he were always repressing an almost irrepressible ejaculation. On his upper lip is a crisp, tightly cropped moustache; he carries himself with the upper part of his body slightly thrown back, and his stomach slightly thrust forward. His walk is a slow, consequential strut. His clothes are dingy, and he wears a faded seaman's cap with a glazed peak.*]

Boyle. [*To* JOXER, *who is still outside.*]

Come on, come on in, Joxer; she's gone out long ago, man. If there's nothing else to be got, we'll furrage out a cup o' tay, anyway. It's the only bit I get in comfort when she's away. 'Tisn't Juno should be her pet name at all, but Deirdre of the Sorras, for she's always grousin'.

[JOXER *steps cautiously into the room. He may be younger than* THE CAPTAIN, *but he looks a lot older. His face is like a bundle of crinkled paper; his eyes have a cunning twinkle; he is spare and loosely built; he has a habit of constantly shrugging his shoulders with a peculiar twitching movement, meant to be ingratiating. His face is invariably ornamented with a grin.*]

Joxer. It's a terrible thing to be tied to a woman that's always grousin'. I don't know how you stick it—it ud put years on me. It's a good job she has to be so ofen away, for [*with a shrug*] when the cat's away, the mice can play!

Boyle. [*With a commanding and complacent gesture.*] Pull over to the fire, Joxer, an' we'll have a cup o' tay in a minute.

Joxer. Ah, a cup o' tay's a darlin' thing, a daaarlin' thing—the cup that cheers but doesn't . . .

[JOXER'S *rhapsody is cut short by the sight of* JUNO *coming forward and confronting the two cronies. Both are stupefied.*]

Mrs. Boyle. [*With sweet irony—poking the fire, and turning her head to glare at* JOXER.] Pull over to the fire, Joxer Daly, an' we'll have a cup o' tay in a minute! Are you sure, now, you wouldn't like an egg?

Joxer. I can't stop, Mrs. Boyle; I'm in a desperate hurry, a desperate hurry.

Mrs. Boyle. Pull over to the fire, Joxer Daly; people is always far more comfortabler here than they are in their own place.

[JOXER *makes hastily for the door.* BOYLE *stirs to follow him; thinks of something to relieve the situation—stops, and says suddenly:*]

Boyle. Joxer!

Joxer. [*At door ready to bolt.*] Yis?

Boyle. You know the foreman o' that job that's goin' on down in Killesther, don't you, Joxer?

Joxer. [*Puzzled.*] Foreman—Killesther?

Boyle. [*With a meaning look.*] He's a butty o' yours, isn't he?

Joxer. [*The truth dawning on him.*] The foreman at Killesther—oh yis, yis. He's an oul' butty o' mine—oh, he's a darlin' man, a daarlin' man.

Boyle. Oh, then, it's a sure thing. It's a pity we didn't go down at breakfast firs thing this mornin'—we might ha' been work ing now; but you didn't know it then.

Joxer. [*With a shrug.*] It's betther late than never.

Boyle. It's nearly time we got a start anyhow; I'm fed up knockin' round, doin nothin'. He promised you—gave you the straight tip?

Joxer. Yis. "Come down on the blow o dinner," says he, "an I'll start you, an' any friend you like to brin' with you." Ah, says I, you're a darlin' man, a daarlin' man.

Boyle. Well, it couldn't come at a betther time—we're a long time waitin' for it.

Joxer. Indeed we were; but it's a long lane that has no turnin'.

Boyle. The blow up for dinner is at one —wait till I see what time it 'tis.

[*He goes over to the mantelpiece, and gingerly lifts the clock.*]

Mrs. Boyle. Min' now, how you go on fiddlin' with that clock—you know the least little thing sets it asthray.

Boyle. The job couldn't come at a betther time; I'm feelin' in great fettle, Joxer. I'd hardly believe I ever had a pain in me legs, an' last week I was nearly crippled with them.

Joxer. That's betther an' betther; ah, God never shut wan door but he opened another!

Boyle. It's only eleven o'clock; we've lashins o' time. I'll slip on me oul' moleskins afther breakfast an' we can saunther down at our ayse. [*Putting his hand on the shovel.*] I think, Joxer, we'd better bring our shovels?

Joxer. Yis, Captain, yis; it's betther to go fully prepared an' ready for all eventualities. You bring your long-tailed shovel, an' I'll bring me navvy. We mighten' want them, an', then agen, we might: for want of a nail the shoe was lost, for want of a shoe the horse was lost, an' for want of a horse the man was lost—aw, that's a darlin' proverb, a daarlin' . . .

[*As* JOXER *is finishing his sentence,* MRS. BOYLE *approaches the door and* JOXER *retreats hurriedly. She shuts the door with a bang.*]

Boyle. [*Suggestively.*] We won't be long pullin' ourselves together agen when I'm working for a few weeks.

[MRS. BOYLE *takes no notice.*]

Boyle. The foreman on the job is an oul' butty o' Joxer's; I have an idea that I know him meself. [*Silence.*] . . . There's a button off the back o' me moleskin trousers. . . . If you leave out a needle an' thread I'll sew it on meself. . . . Thanks be to God, the pains in me legs is gone, anyhow!

Mrs. Boyle. [*With a burst.*] Look here, Mr. Jacky Boyle, them yarns won't go down with Juno. I know you an' Joxer Daly of an oul' date, an', if you think you're able to come it over me with them fairy tales, you're in the wrong shop.

Boyle. [*Coughing subduedly to relieve the tenseness of the situation.*] U-u-u-ugh.

Mrs. Boyle. Butty o' Joxer's! Oh, you'll do a lot o' good as long as you continue to be a butty o' Joxer's!

Boyle. U-u-u-ugh.

Mrs. Boyle. Shovel! Ah, then, me boyo, you'd do far more work with a knife an' fork than ever you'll do with a shovel! If there was e'er a genuine job goin' you'd be dh'other way about—not able to lift your arms with the pains in your legs! Your poor wife slavin' to keep the bit in your mouth, an' you gallivantin' about all the day like a paycock!

Boyle. It ud be betther for a man to be dead, betther for a man to be dead.

Mrs. Boyle. [*Ignoring the interruption.*] Everybody callin' you "Captain," an' you only wanst on the wather, in an oul' collier from here to Liverpool, when anybody, to listen or look at you, ud take you for a second Christo For Columbus!

Boyle. Are you never goin' to give us a rest?

Mrs. Boyle. Oh, you're never tired o' lookin' for a rest.

Boyle. D'ye want to dhrive me out o' the house?

Mrs. Boyle. It ud be easier to dhrive you out o' the house than to dhrive you into a job. Here, sit down an' take your breakfast —it may be the last you'll get, for I don't know where the next is goin' to come from.

Boyle. If I get this job we'll be all right.

Mrs. Boyle. Did you see Jerry Devine?

Boyle. [*Testily.*] No, I didn't see him.

Mrs. Boyle. No, but you seen Joxer. Well, he was here lookin' for you.

Boyle. Well, let him look!

Mrs. Boyle. Oh, indeed, he may well look, for it ud be hard for him to see you, an' you stuck in Ryan's snug.

Boyle. I wasn't in Ryan's snug—I don't go into Ryan's.

Mrs. Boyle. Oh, is there a mad dog there? Well, if you weren't in Ryan's you were in Foley's.

Boyle. I'm telling you for the last three weeks I haven't tasted a dhrop of intoxicatin' liquor. I wasn't in ayther wan snug or dh'other—I could swear that on a prayer-book—I'm as innocent as the child unborn!

Mrs. Boyle. Well, if you'd been in for your breakfast you'd ha' seen him.

Boyle. [*Suspiciously.*] What does he want me for?

Mrs. Boyle. He'll be back any minute an' then you'll soon know.

Boyle. I'll dhrop out an' see if I can meet him.

Mrs. Boyle. You'll sit down an' take your breakfast, an' let me go to me work, for I'm an hour late already waitin' for you.

Boyle. You needn't ha' waited, for I'll take no breakfast—I've a little spirit left in me still!

Mrs. Boyle. Are you goin' to have your breakfast—yes or no?

Boyle. [*Too proud to yield.*] I'll have no breakfast—yous can keep your breakfast. [*Plaintively.*] I'll knock out a bit somewhere, never fear.

Mrs. Boyle. Nobody's goin' to coax you —don't think that.

[*She vigorously replaces the pan and the sausages in the press.*]

Boyle. I've a little spirit left in me still.

[JERRY DEVINE *enters hastily.*]

Jerry. Oh, here you are at last! I've been searchin' for you everywhere. The foreman in Foley's told me you hadn't left the snug with Joxer ten minutes before I went in.

Mrs. Boyle. An' he swearin' on the holy prayer-book that he wasn't in no snug!

Boyle. [*To* JERRY.] What business is it o' yours whether I was in a snug or no? What do you want to be gallopin' about afther me for? Is a man not to be allowed to leave his house for a minute without havin' a pack o' spies, pimps, an' informers cantherin' at his heels?

Jerry. Oh, you're takin' a wrong view of it, Mr. Boyle; I simply was anxious to do you a good turn. I have a message for you from Father Farrell: he says that if you go to the job that's on in Rathmines, an' ask for Foreman Mangan, you'll get a start.

Boyle. That's all right, but I don't want the motions of me body to be watched the way an asthronomer ud watch a star. If you're folleyin' Mary aself, you've no pereeogative to be folleyin' me. [*Suddenly catching his thigh.*] U-ugh, I'm afther gettin' a terrible twinge in me right leg!

Mrs. Boyle. Oh, it won't be very long now till it travels into your left wan. It's miraculous that whenever he scents a job in front of him, his legs begin to fail him! Then, me bucko, if you lose this chance, you may go an' furrage for yourself!

Jerry. This job'll last for some time too

Captain, an' as soon as the foundations are in, it'll be cushy enough.

Boyle. Won't it be a climbin' job? How d'ye expect me to be able to go up a ladder with these legs? An', if I get up aself, how am I goin' to get down agen?

Mrs. Boyle. [*Viciously.*] Get wan o' the laborers to carry you down in a hod! You can't climb a laddher, but you can skip like a goat into a snug!

Jerry. I wouldn't let meself be let down that easy, Mr. Boyle; a little exercise, now, might do you all the good in the world.

Boyle. It's a doctor you should have been, Devine—maybe you know more about the pains in me legs than meself that has them?

Jerry. [*Irritated.*] Oh, I know nothin' about the pains in your legs; I've brought the message that Father Farrell gave me, an' that's all I can do.

Mrs. Boyle. Here, sit down an' take your breakfast, an' go an' get ready; an' don't be actin' as if you couldn't pull a wing out of a dead bee.

Boyle. I want no breakfast, I tell you; it ud choke me afther all that's been said. I've a little spirit left in me still.

Mrs. Boyle. Well, let's see your spirit, then, an' go in at wanst an' put on your moleskin trousers!

Boyle. [*Moving toward the door on left.*] It ud be betther for a man to be dead! U-ugh! There's another twinge in me other leg! Nobody but meself knows the sufferin' I'm goin' through with the pains in these legs o' mine!

[*He goes into the room on left as* MARY *comes out with her hat in her hand.*]

Mrs. Boyle. I'll have to push off now, for I'm terrible late already, but I was determined to stay an' hunt that Joxer this time.

[*She goes off.*]

Jerry. Are you going out, Mary?

Mary. It looks like it when I'm putting on my hat, doesn't it?

Jerry. The bitther word agen, Mary.

Mary. You won't allow me to be friendly with you; if I thry, you deliberately misundherstand it.

Jerry. I didn't always misundherstand it; you were ofen delighted to have the arms of Jerry around you.

Mary. If you go on talkin' like this, Jerry Devine, you'll make me hate you!

Jerry. Well, let it be either a weddin' or a wake! Listen, Mary, I'm standin' for the Secretaryship of our Union. There's only one opposin' me; I'm popular with all the men, an' a good speaker—all are sayin' that I'll get elected.

Mary. Well?

Jerry. The job's worth three hundred an' fifty pounds a year, Mary. You an' I could live nice an' cosily on that; it would lift you out o' this place an' . . .

Mary. I haven't time to listen to you now —I have to go.

[*She is going out when* JERRY *bars the way.*]

Jerry. [*Appealingly.*] Mary, what's come over you with me for the last few weeks? You hardly speak to me, an' then only a word with a face o' bittherness on it. Have you forgotten, Mary, all the happy evenin's that were as sweet as the scented hawthorn that sheltered the sides o' the road as we sauntered through the country?

Mary. That's all over now. When you get your new job, Jerry, you won't be long findin' a girl far betther than I am for your sweetheart.

Jerry. Never, never, Mary! No matther what happens you'll always be the same to me.

Mary. I must be off; please let me go, Jerry.

Jerry. I'll go a bit o' the way with you.

Mary. You needn't, thanks; I want to be by meself.

Jerry. [*Catching her arm.*] You're goin' to meet another fella; you've clicked with some one else, me lady!

Mary. That's no concern o' yours, Jerry Devine; let me go.

Jerry. I saw yous comin' out o' the Cornflower Dance Class, an' you hangin' on his arm—a thin, lanky strip of a Mickey Dazzler, with a walkin'-stick an' gloves!

Voice of Johnny. [*Loudly.*] What are you doin' there—pullin' about everything!

Voice of Boyle. [*Loudly and viciously.*] I'm puttin' on me moleskin trousers!

Mary. You're hurtin' me arm! Let me go, or I'll scream, an' then you'll have the oul' fella out on top of us!

Jerry. Don't be so hard on a fella, Mary, don't be so hard.

Boyle. [*Appearing at the door.*] What's the meanin' of all this hillabaloo?

Mary. Let me go, let me go!

Boyle. D'ye hear me—what's all this hillabaloo about?

Jerry. [*Plaintively.*] Will you not give us one kind word, one kind word, Mary?

Boyle. D'ye hear me talkin' to yous? What's all this hillabaloo for?

Jerry. Let me kiss your hand, your little, tiny, white hand!

Boyle. Your little, tiny, white hand—are you takin' leave o' your senses, man?

[MARY *breaks away and rushes out.*]

Boyle. This is nice goin's on in front of her father!

Jerry. Ah, dhry up, for God's sake!

[*He follows* MARY.]

Boyle. Chiselurs don't care a damn now about their parents, they're bringin' their fathers' gray hairs down with sorra to the grave, an' laughin' at it, laughin' at it. Ah, I suppose it's just the same everywhere—the whole worl's in a state o' chassis! [*He sits by the fire.*] Breakfast! Well, they can keep their breakfast for me. Not if they went down on their bended knees would I take it—I'll show them I've a little spirit left in me still! [*He goes over to the press, takes out a plate and looks at it.*] Sassige! Well, let her keep her sassige. [*He returns to the fire, takes up the teapot and gives it a gentle shake.*] The tea's wet right enough.

[*A pause; he rises, goes to the press, takes out the sausage, puts it on the pan, and puts both on the fire. He attends the sausage with a fork.*]

Boyle. [*Singing:*]

When the robins nest agen,
And the flowers are in bloom,
When the Springtime's sunny smile seems to banish all sorrow an' gloom;
Then me bonny blue-ey'd lad, if me heart be true till then—
He's promised he'll come back to me,
When the robins nest agen!

[*He lifts his head at the high note, and then drops his eyes to the pan.*]

Boyle. [*Singing:*]

When the . . .

[*Steps are heard approaching; he whips the pan off the fire and puts it under the bed, then sits down at the fire. The door opens and a* BEARDED MAN *looking in says:*]

You don't happen to want a sewin' machine?

Boyle. [*Furiously.*] No, I don't want e'er a sewin' machine!

[*He returns the pan to the fire, and commences to sing again.*]

Boyle. [*Singing:*]

When the robins nest agen,
And the flowers they are in bloom,
He's . . .

[*A thundering knock is heard at the street door.*]

Boyle. There's a terrible tatherarah—that's a stranger—that's nobody belongin' to the house. [*Another loud knock.*]

Joxer. [*Sticking his head in at the door.*] Did ye hear them tatherarahs?

Boyle. Well, Joxer, I'm not deaf.

Johnny. [*Appearing in his shirt and trousers at the door on left; his face is anxious and his voice is tremulous.*] Who's that at the door; who's that at the door? Who gave that knock—d' yous hear me—are yous deaf or dhrunk or what?

Boyle. [*To* JOHNNY.] How the hell do I know who 'tis? Joxer, stick your head out o' the window an' see.

Joxer. An' mebbe get a bullet in the kisser? Ah, none o' them thricks for Joxer! It's betther to be a coward than a corpse!

Boyle. [*Looking cautiously out of the window.*] It's a fella in a thrench coat.

Johnny. Holy Mary, Mother o' God, I . . .

Boyle. He's goin' away—he must ha' got tired knockin'.

[JOHNNY *returns to the room on left.*]

Boyle. Sit down an' have a cup o' tay, Joxer.

Joxer. I'm afraid the missus ud pop in on us agen before we'd know where we are. Somethin's tellin' me to go at wanst.

Boyle. Don't be superstitious, man; we're Dublin men, an' not boyos that's only afther comin' up from the bog o' Allen—though if she did come in, right enough, we'd be caught like rats in a thrap.

Joxer. An' you know the sort she is—she wouldn't listen to reason—an' wanse bitten twice shy.

Boyle. [*Going over to the window at back.*] If the worst came to the worst, you could dart out here, Joxer; it's only a dhrop of a few feet to the roof of the return room, an' the first minute she goes into dh'other room, I'll give you the bend, an' you can slip in an' away.

Joxer. [*Yielding to the temptation.*] Ah, I won't stop very long anyhow. [*Picking up a book from the table.*] Whose is the buk?

Boyle. Aw, one o' Mary's; she's always readin' lately—nothin' but thrash, too. There's one I was lookin' at dh'other day: three stories, *The Doll's House, Ghosts,* an' *The Wild Duck*—buks only fit for chiselurs!

Joxer. Didja ever rade *Elizabeth, or Th' Exile o' Sibayria* . . . ah, it's a darlin' story, a daarlin' story!

Boyle. You eat your sassige, an' never min' *Th' Exile o' Sibayria.*

[*Both sit down;* BOYLE *fills out tea, pours gravy on* JOXER'S *plate, and keeps the sausage for himself.*]

Joxer. What are you wearin' your moleskin trousers for?

Boyle. I have to go to a job, Joxer. Just afther you'd gone. Devine kem runnin' in to tell us that Father Farrell said if I went down to the job that's goin' on in Rathmines I'd get a start.

Joxer. Be the holy, that's good news!

Boyle. How is it good news? I wondher if you were in my condition, would you call it good news?

Joxer. I thought . . .

Boyle. You thought! You think too sudden sometimes, Joxer. D'ye know, I'm hardly able to crawl with the pains in me legs!

Joxer. Yis, yis; I forgot the pains in your legs. I know you can do nothin' while they're at you.

Boyle. You forgot; I don't think any of yous realize the state I'm in with the pains in me legs. What ud happen if I had to carry a bag o' cement?

Joxer. Ah, any man havin' the like of them pains 'id be down an' out, down an' out.

Boyle. I wouldn't mind if he had said it to meself; but, no, oh no, he rushes in an' shouts it out in front o' Juno, an' you know what Juno is, Joxer. We all know Devine knows a little more than the rest of us, but he doesn't act as if he did; he's a good boy, sober, able to talk an' all that, but still . . .

Joxer. Oh ay; able to argufy, but still . . .

Boyle. If he's runnin' afther Mary, aself, he's not goin' to be runnin' afther me. Captain Boyle's able to take care of himself. Afther all, I'm not gettin' brought up on Virol. I never heard him usin' a curse; I don't believe he was ever dhrunk in his life—sure he's not like a Christian at all!

Joxer. You're afther takin' the word out o' me mouth—afther all, a Christian's natural, but he's unnatural.

Boyle. His oul' fella was just the same—a Wicklow man.

Joxer. A Wicklow man! That explains the whole thing. I've met many a Wicklow man in me time, but I never met wan that was any good.

Boyle. "Father Farrell," says he, "sent me down to tell you." Father Farrell! . . . D'ye know, Joxer, I never like to be beholden to any o' the clergy.

Joxer. It's dangerous, right enough.

Boyle. If they do anything for you, they'd want you to be livin' in the Chapel. . . . I'm goin' to tell you somethin', Joxer, that I wouldn't tell to anybody else—the clergy always had too much power over the people in this unfortunate country.

Joxer. You could sing that if you had an air to it!

Boyle. [*Becoming enthusiastic.*] Didn't they prevent the people in '47 from seizin' the corn, an' they starvin'; didn't they down Parnell; didn't they say that hell wasn't hot enough nor eternity long enough to punish the Fenians? We don't forget, we don't forget them things, Joxer. If they've taken everything else from us, Joxer, they've left us our memory.

Joxer. [*Emotionally.*] For mem'ry's the only friend that grief can call its own, that grief . . . can . . . call . . . its own!

Boyle. Father Farrell's beginnin' to take a great intherest in Captain Boyle; because of what Johnny did for his country, says he to me wan day. It's a curious way to reward Johnny be makin' his poor oul' father work. But, that's what the clergy want, Joxer—work, work, work for me an' you; havin' us mulin' from mornin' till night, so that they may be in betther fettle when they come hoppin' round for their dues! Job! Well, let him give his job to wan of his hymn-singin', prayer-spoutin', craw-thumpin' Confraternity men!

[*The voice of a* COAL-BLOCK VENDOR *is heard chanting in the street.*]

Voice of Coal Vendor. Blocks . . . coal-blocks! Blocks . . . coal-blocks!

Joxer. God be with the young days when you were steppin' the deck of a manly ship, with the win' blowin' a hurricane through the masts, an' the only sound you'd hear was, "Port your helm!" an' the only answer, "Port it is, sir!"

Boyle. Them was days, Joxer, them was days. Nothin' was too hot or too heavy for me then. Sailin' from the Gulf o' Mexico to the Antanartic Ocean. I seen things, I seen things, Joxer, that no mortal man should speak about that knows his Catechism. Ofen, an' ofen, when I was fixed to the wheel with a marlinspike, an' the win's blowin' fierce an' the waves lashin' an' lashin', till you'd think every minute was goin' to be your last, an' it blowed, an' blowed—blew is the right word, Joxer, but blowed is what the sailors use. . . .

Joxer. Aw, it's a darlin' word, a daarlin' word.

Boyle. An', as it blowed an' blowed, I ofen looked up at the sky an' assed meself the question—what is the stars, what is the stars?

Voice of Coal Vendor. Any blocks, coal-blocks; blocks, coal-blocks!

Joxer. Ah, that's the question, that's the question—what is the stars?

Boyle. An' then, I'd have another look, an' I'd ass meself—what is the moon?

Joxer. Ah, that's the question—what is the moon, what is the moon?

[*Rapid steps are heard coming toward the door.* BOYLE *makes desperate efforts to hide everything;* JOXER *rushes to the window in a frantic effort to get out;* BOYLE *begins to innocently lilt—"Oh, me darlin' Jennie, I will be thrue to thee," when the door is opened, and the black face of the* COAL VENDOR *appears.*]

The Coal Vendor. D'yes want any blocks?

Boyle. [*With a roar.*] No, we don't want any blocks!

Joxer. [*Coming back with a sigh of relief.*] That's afther puttin' the heart across me—I could ha' sworn it was Juno. I'd betther be goin', Captain; you couldn't tell the minute Juno'd hop in on us.

Boyle. Let her hop in; we may as well have it out first as at last. I've made up me mind—I'm not goin' to do only what she damn well likes.

Joxer. Them sentiments does you credit, Captain; I don't like to say anything as between man an' wife, but I say as a butty, as a butty, Captain, that you've stuck it too long, an' that it's about time you showed a little spunk.

How can a man die betther than facin' fearful odds,
For th' ashes of his fathers an' the temples of his gods.

Boyle. She has her rights—there's no one denyin' it, but haven't I me rights too?

Joxer. Of course you have—the sacred rights o' man!

Boyle. Today, Joxer, there's goin' to be issued a proclamation be me, establishin' an independent Republic, an' Juno'll have to take an oath of allegiance.

Joxer. Be firm, be firm, Captain; the first few minutes'll be the worst:—if you gently touch a nettle it'll sting you for your pains; grasp it like a lad of mettle, an' as soft as silk remains!

Voice of Juno. [*Outside.*] Can't stop, Mrs. Madigan—I haven't a minute!

Joxer. [*Flying out of the window.*] Holy God, here she is!

Boyle. [*Packing the things away with a rush in the press.*] I knew that fella ud stop till she was in on top of us!

[*He sits down by the fire.*]

[JUNO *enters hastily; she is flurried and excited.*]

Juno. Oh, you're in—you must have been only afther comin' in?

Boyle. No, I never went out.

Juno. It's curious, then, you never heard the knockin'.

[*She puts her coat and hat on bed.*]

Boyle. Knockin'? Of course I heard the knockin'.

Juno. An' why didn't you open the door, then? I suppose you were so busy with Joxer that you hadn't time.

Boyle. I haven't seen Joxer since I seen him before. Joxer! What ud bring Joxer here?

Juno. D'ye mean to tell me that the pair of yous wasn't collogin' together here when me back was turned?

Boyle. What ud we be collogin' together about? I have somethin' else to think of besides collogin' with Joxer. I can swear on all the holy prayer-books . . .

Mrs. Boyle. That you weren't in no snug! Go on in at wanst now, an' take off that moleskin trousers o' yours, an' put on a collar an' tie to smarten yourself up a bit. There's a visitor comin' with Mary in a minute, an' he has great news for you.

Boyle. A job, I suppose; let us get wan first before we start lookin' for another.

Mrs. Boyle. That's the thing that's able to put the win' up you. Well, it's no job, but news that'll give you the chance o' your life.

Boyle. What's all the mysthery about?

Mrs. Boyle. G'win an' take off the moleskin trousers when you're told!

[BOYLE *goes into room on left.*]

[MRS. BOYLE *tidies up the room, puts the shovel under the bed, and goes to the press.*]

Mrs. Boyle. Oh, God bless us, looka the way everything's thrun about! Oh, Joxer was here, Joxer was here!

[MARY *enters with* CHARLIE BENTHAM; *he is a young man of twenty-five, tall, good-looking, with a very high opinion of himself generally. He is dressed in a brown coat, brown knee-breeches, gray stockings, a brown sweater, with a deep blue tie; he carries gloves and a walking-stick.*]

Mrs. Boyle. [*Fussing round.*] Come in, Mr. Bentham; sit down, Mr. Bentham, in this chair; it's more comfortabler than that, Mr. Bentham. Himself'll be here in a minute; he's just takin' off his trousers.

Mary. Mother!

Bentham. Please don't put yourself to any trouble, Mrs. Boyle—I'm quite all right here, thank you.

Mrs. Boyle. An' to think of you knowin' Mary, an' she knowin' the news you had for us, an' wouldn't let on; but it's all the more welcomer now, for we were on our last lap!

Voice of Johnny. [*Inside.*] What are you kickin' up all the racket for?

Boyle. [*Roughly.*] I'm takin' off me moleskin trousers!

Johnny. Can't you do it, then, without lettin' th' whole house know you're takin' off your trousers? What d'ye want puttin' them on an' takin' them off again?

Boyle. Will you let me alone, will you let me alone? Am I never goin' to be done thryin' to please th' whole o' yous?

Mrs. Boyle. [*To* BENTHAM.] You must excuse th' state o' th' place, Mr. Bentham; th' minute I turn me back that man o' mine always makes a litther o' th' place, a litther o' th' place.

Bentham. Don't worry, Mrs. Boyle; it's all right, I assure . . .

Boyle. [*Inside.*] Where's me braces; where in th' name o' God did I leave me braces? . . . Ay, did you see where I put me braces?

Johnny. [*Inside, calling out.*] Ma, will you come in here an' take da away ou' o' this or he'll drive me mad.

Mrs. Boyle. [*Going toward door.*] Dear, dear, dear, that man'll be lookin' for somethin' on th' day o' Judgment. [*Looking into room and calling to* BOYLE.] Look at your braces, man, hangin' round your neck!

Boyle. [*Inside.*] Aw, Holy God!

Mrs. Boyle. [*Calling.*] Johnny, Johnny, come out here for a minute.

Johnny. Oh, leave Johnny alone, an' don't be annoyin' him!

Mrs. Boyle. Come on, Johnny, till I inthroduce you to Mr. Bentham. [*To* BENTHAM.] Me son, Mr. Bentham; he's afther goin' through the mill. He was only a chiselur of a Boy Scout in Easter Week, when he got hit in the hip; and his arm was blew off in the fight in O'Connell Street. [JOHNNY *comes in.*] Here he is, Mr. Bentham; Mr. Bentham, Johnny. None can deny he done his bit for Irelan', if that's going to do him any good.

Johnny. [*Boastfully.*] I'd do it agen, ma, I'd do it agen; for a principle's a principle.

Mrs. Boyle. Ah, you lost your best principle, me boy, when you lost your arm; them's the only sort o' principles that's any good to a workin' man.

Johnny. Ireland only half free'll never be at peace while she has a son left to pull a trigger.

Mrs. Boyle. To be sure, to be sure—no bread's a lot betther than half a loaf. [*Calling loudly in to* BOYLE.] Will you hurry up there?

[BOYLE *enters in his best trousers, which aren't too good, and looks very uncomfortable in his collar and tie.*]

Mrs. Boyle. This is me husband; Mr. Boyle, Mr. Bentham.

Bentham. Ah, very glad to know you, Mr. Boyle. How are you?

Boyle. Ah, I'm not too well at all; I suffer terrible with pains in me legs. Juno can tell you there what . . .

Mrs. Boyle. You won't have many pains in your legs when you hear what Mr. Bentham has to tell you.

Bentham. Juno! What an interesting name! It reminds one of Homer's glorious story of ancient gods and heroes.

Boyle. Yis, doesn't it? You see, Juno was born an' christened in June; I met her in June; we were married in June, an' Johnny was born in June, so wan day I says to her, "You should ha' been called Juno," an' the name stuck to her ever since.

Mrs. Boyle. Here, we can talk o' them things agen; let Mr. Bentham say what he has to say now.

Bentham. Well, Mr. Boyle, I suppose you'll remember a Mr. Ellison of Santry—he's a relative of yours, I think.

Boyle. [*Viciously.*] Is it that prognosticator an' procrastinator! Of course I remember him.

Bentham. Well, he's dead, Mr. Boyle . . .

Boyle. Sorra many'll go into mournin' for him.

Mrs. Boyle. Wait till you hear what Mr. Bentham has to say, an' then, maybe, you'll change your opinion.

Bentham. A week before he died he sent for me to write his will for him. He told me that there were two only that he wished to leave his property to: his second cousin, Michael Finnegan of Santry; and John Boyle, his first cousin of Dublin.

Boyle. [*Excitedly.*] Me, is it me, me?

Bentham. You, Mr. Boyle; I'll read a copy of the will that I have here with me, which has been duly filed in the Court of Probate.

[*He takes a paper from his pocket and reads:*]

6th February, 1922.

This is the last Will and Testament of William Ellison, of Santry, in the County of Dublin. I hereby order and wish my property to be sold and divided as follows:—

£20 to the St. Vincent De Paul Society.

£60 for Masses for the repose of my soul (5s. for Each Mass).

The rest of my property to be divided between my first and second cousins.

I hereby appoint Timothy Buckly, of

Santry, and Hugh Brierly, of Coolock, to be my Executors.

[*Signed*] WILLIAM ELLISON.
HUGH BRIERLY.
TIMOTHY BUCKLY.
CHARLES BENTHAM, N.T.

Boyle. [*Eagerly.*] An' how much'll be comin' out of it, Mr. Bentham?

Bentham. The Executors told me that half of the property would be anything between £1500 and £2000.

Mary. A fortune, father, a fortune!

Johnny. We'll be able to get out o' this place now, an' go somewhere we're not known.

Mrs. Boyle. You won't have to trouble about a job for a while, Jack.

Boyle. [*Fervently.*] I'll never doubt the goodness o' God agen.

Bentham. I congratulate you, Mr. Boyle. [*They shake hands.*]

Boyle. An' now, Mr. Bentham, you'll have to have a wet.

Bentham. A wet?

Boyle. A wet—a jar—a boul!

Mrs. Boyle. Jack, you're speakin' to Mr. Bentham, an' not to Joxer.

Boyle. [*Solemnly.*] Juno . . . Mary . . . Johnny . . . we'll have to go into mournin' at wanst. . . . I never expected that poor Bill ud die so sudden. . . . Well, we all have to die some day . . . you, Juno, today . . . an' me, maybe tomorrow. . . . It's sad, but it can't be helped. . . . Requiescat in pace . . . or usin' our oul' tongue like St. Patrick or St. Briget, Guh sayeree jeea ayera!

Mary. Oh, father, that's not Rest in Peace; that's God save Ireland.

Boyle. U-u-ugh, it's all the same—isn't it a prayer? . . . Juno, I'm done with Joxer; he's nothin' but a prognosticator an' a . . .

Joxer. [*Climbing angrily through the window and bounding into the room.*] You're done with Joxer, are you? Maybe you thought I'd stop on the roof all the night for you! Joxer out on the roof with the win' blowin' through him was nothin' to you an' your friend with the collar an' tie!

Mrs. Boyle. What in the name o' God brought you out on the roof; what were you doin' there?

Joxer. [*Ironically.*] I was dhreamin' I was standin' on the bridge of a ship, an' she sailin' the Antartic Ocean, an' it blowed, an' blowed, an' I lookin' up at the sky an' sayin', what is the stars, what is the stars?

Mrs. Boyle. [*Opening the door and standing at it.*] Here, get ou' o' this, Joxer Daly; I was always thinkin' you had a slate off.

Joxer. [*Moving to the door.*] I have to laugh every time I look at the deep sea sailor; an' a row on a river ud make him sea-sick!

Boyle. Get ou' o' this before I take the law into me own hands!

Joxer. [*Going out.*] Say aw rewaeawr, but not good-by. Lookin' for work, an' prayin' to God he won't get it. [*He goes.*]

Mrs. Boyle. I'm tired tellin' you what Joxer was; maybe now you see yourself the kind he is.

Boyle. He'll never blow the froth off a pint o' mine agen, that's a sure thing. Johnny . . . Mary . . . you're to keep yourselves to yourselves for the future. Juno, I'm done with Joxer. . . . I'm a new man from this out. . . .

[*Clasping* JUNO's *hand, and singing emotionally:*]

Oh, me darlin' Juno, I will be thrue to thee;
Me own, me darlin' Juno, you're all the world to me.

CURTAIN

ACT II

SCENE: *The same, but the furniture is more plentiful and of a vulgar nature. A glaringly upholstered arm-chair and lounge; cheap pictures and photos everywhere. Every available spot is ornamented with huge vases filled with artificial flowers. Crossed festoons of colored paper chains stretch from end to end of ceiling. On the table is an old attaché case. It is about six in the evening, and two days after the First Act.*

[BOYLE, *in his shirt sleeves, is voluptuously stretched on the sofa; he is smoking a clay pipe. He is half asleep. A lamp is lighted on the table. After a few moments' pause the voice of* JOXER *is heard singing softly outside at the door—"Me pipe I'll smoke, as I dhrive me moke—are you there, Mor . . . ee . . . ar . . . i . . . teee!"*]

Boyle. [*Leaping up, takes a pen in his hand and busies himself with papers.*] Come along, Joxer, me son, come along.

Joxer. [*Putting his head in.*] Are you be yourself?

Boyle. Come on, come on; that doesn't matther; I'm masther now, an' I'm going to remain masther. [JOXER *comes in.*]

Joxer. How d'ye feel now, as a man o' money?

Boyle. [*Solemnly.*] It's a responsibility, Joxer, a great responsibility.

Joxer. I suppose 'tis now, though you wouldn't think it.

Boyle. Joxer, han' me over that attackey case on the table there. [JOXER *hands the case.*] Ever since the Will was passed I've run hundhreds o' dockyments through me han's—I tell you, you have to keep your wits about you.

[*He busies himself with papers.*]

Joxer. Well, I won't disturb you; I'll dhrop in when . . .

Boyle. [*Hastily.*] It's all right, Joxer, this is the last one to be signed today. [*He signs a paper, puts it into the case, which he shuts with a snap, and sits back pompously in the chair.*] Now, Joxer, you want to see me; I'm at your service—what can I do for you, me man?

Joxer. I've just dhropped in with the £3:5s. that Mrs. Madigan riz on the blankets an' table for you, an' she says you're to be in no hurry payin' it back.

Boyle. She won't be long without it; I expect the first cheque for a couple o' hundhred any day. There's the five bob for yourself—go on, take it, man; it'll not be the last you'll get from the Captain. Now an' agen we have our differ, but we're there together all the time.

Joxer. Me for you, an' you for me, like the two Musketeers.

Boyle. Father Farrell stopped me today an' tole me how glad he was I fell in for the money.

Joxer. He'll be stoppin' you ofen enough now; I suppose it was "Mr." Boyle with him?

Boyle. He shuk me be the han'. . . .

Joxer. [*Ironically.*] I met with Napper Tandy, an' he shuk me by the han'!

Boyle. You're seldom asthray, Joxer, but you're wrong shipped this time. What you're sayin' of Father Farrell is very near to blasfeemey. I don't like any one to talk disrespectful of Father Farrell.

Joxer. You're takin' me up wrong, Captain; I wouldn't let a word be said agen Father Farrell—the heart o' the rowl, that's what he is; I always said he was a darlin' man, a daarlin' man.

Boyle. Comin' up the stairs who did I meet but that bummer, Nugent. "I seen you talkin' to Father Farrell," says he, with a grin on him. "He'll be folleyin' you," says he, "like a Guardian Angel from this out"—all the time the oul' grin on him, Joxer.

Joxer. I never seen him yet but he had that oul' grin on him!

Boyle. "Mr. Nugent," says I, "Father Farrell is a man o' the people, an', as far as I know the History o' me country, the priests was always in the van of the fight for Irelan's freedom."

Joxer. [*Fervently:*]

Who was it led the van, Soggart Aroon?
Since the fight first bega.., Soggart Aroon?

Boyle. "Who are you tellin'?" says he. "Didn't they let down the Fenians, an' didn't they do in Parnell? An' now . . . ." "You ought to be ashamed o' yourself," says I, interruptin' him, "not to know the History o' your country." An' I left him gawkin' where he was.

Joxer. Where ignorance 's bliss 'tis folly to be wise; I wondher did he ever read the Story o' Irelan'.

Boyle. Be J. L. Sullivan? Don't you know he didn't.

Joxer. Ah, it's a darlin' buk, a daarlin' buk!

Boyle. You'd betther be goin', now, Joxer; his Majesty Bentham 'll be here any minute now.

Joxer. Be the way things is lookin', it'll be a match between him an' Mary. She's thrun over Jerry altogether. Well, I hope it will, for he's a darlin' man.

Boyle. I'm glad you think so—I don't. [*Irritably.*] What's darlin' about him?

Joxer. [*Nonplussed.*] I only seen him twiced; if you want to know me, come an' live with me.

Boyle. He's too ignified for me—to hear him talk you'd think he knew as much as a Boney's Oraculum. He's given up his job as teacher, an' is goin' to become a solicitor in Dublin—he's been studyin' law. I suppose he thinks I'll set him up, but he's wrong shipped. An' th' other fella—Jerry's as bad. The two o' them ud give you a pain in your face, listenin' to them; Jerry believin' in nothin', an' Bentham believin' in everythin'. One that says all is God an' no man; an' th' other that says all is man an' no God!

Joxer. Well, I'll be off now.

Boyle. Don't forget to dhrop down afther a while; we'll have a quiet jar, an' a song or two.

Joxer. Never fear.

Boyle. An' tell Mrs. Madigan that I hope

we'll have the pleasure of her organization at our little entertainment.

Joxer. Righto; we'll come down together.

[*He goes out.*]

[JOHNNY *comes from room on left, and sits down moodily at the fire.* BOYLE *looks at him for a few moments, and shakes his head. He fills his pipe.*]

Voice of Juno. [*At the door.*] Open the door, Jack; this thing has me nearly kilt with the weight.

[BOYLE *opens the door.* JUNO *enters carrying the box of a gramophone, followed by* MARY *carrying the horn, and some parcels.* JUNO *leaves the box on the table and flops into a chair.*]

Juno. Carrvin' that from Henry Street was no joke.

Boyle. U-u-ugh, that's a grand lookin' insthrument—how much was it?

Juno. Pound down, an' five to be paid at two shillin's a week.

Boyle. That's reasonable enough.

Juno. I'm afraid we're runnin' into too much debt; first the furniture, an' now this.

Boyle. The whole lot won't be much out of £2000.

Mary. I don't know what you wanted a gramophone for—I know Charlie hates them; he says they're destructive of real music.

Boyle. Desthructive of music—that fella ud give you a pain in your face. All a gramophone wants is to be properly played; its thrue wondher is only felt when everythin's quiet—what a gramophone wants is dead silence!

Mary. But, father, Jerry says the same; afther all, you can only appreciate music when your ear is properly trained.

Boyle. That's another fella ud give you a pain in your face. Properly thrained! I suppose you couldn't appreciate football unless your fut was properly thrained.

Mrs. Boyle. [*To* MARY.] Go on in ower that an' dress, or Charlie 'll be in on you, an' tea nor nothin' 'll be ready.

[MARY *goes into room left.*]

Mrs. Boyle. [*Arranging table for tea.*] You didn't look at our new gramophone, Johnny?

Johnny. 'Tisn't gramophones I'm thinking of.

Mrs. Boyle. An' what is it you're thinkin' of, allanna?

Johnny. Nothin', nothin', nothin'.

Mrs. Boyle. Sure, you must be thinkin' of somethin'; it's yourself that has yourself the way y'are; sleepin' wan night in me sisther's, an' the nex' in your father's brother's—you'll get no rest goin' on that way.

Johnny. I can rest nowhere, nowhere, nowhere.

Mrs. Boyle. Sure, you're not thryin' to rest anywhere.

Johnny. Let me alone, let me alone, let me alone, for God's sake.

[*A knock at street door.*]

Mrs. Boyle. [*In a flutter.*] Here he is; here's Mr. Bentham!

Boyle. Well, there's room for him; it's a pity there's not a brass band to play him in.

Mrs. Boyle. We'll han' the tea round, an' not be clusthered round the table, as if we never seen nothin'.

[*Steps are heard approaching, and* JUNO, *opening the door, allows* BENTHAM *to enter.*]

Juno. Give your hat an' stick to Jack, there . . . sit down, Mr. Bentham. . . . No, not there . . . in th' easy chair be the fire. . . . There, that's betther. Mary'll be out to you in a minute.

Boyle. [*Solemnly.*] I seen be the paper this mornin' that Consols was down half per cent. That's serious, min' you, an' shows the whole counthry's in a state o' chassis.

Mrs. Boyle. What's Consols, Jack?

Boyle. Consols? Oh, Consols is—oh, there's no use tellin' women what Consols is —th' wouldn't undherstand.

Bentham. It's just as you were saying, Mr. Boyle . . .

[MARY *enters charmingly dressed.*]

Bentham. Oh, good evening, Mary; how pretty you're looking!

Mary. [*Archly.*] Am I?

Boyle. We were just talkin' when you kem in, Mary. I was tellin' Mr. Bentham that the whole counthry's in a state o' chassis.

Mary. [*To* BENTHAM.] Would you prefer the green or the blue ribbon round me hair, Charlie?

Mrs. Boyle. Mary, your father's speakin'.

Boyle. [*Rapidly.*] I was jus' tellin' Mr. Bentham that the whole counthry's in a state o' chassis.

Mary. I'm sure you're frettin', da, whether it is or no.

Mrs. Boyle. With all our churches an' religions, the worl's not a bit the betther.

Boyle. [*With a commanding gesture.*] Tay!

[MARY *and* MRS. BOYLE *dispense the tea.*]

Mrs. Boyle. An' Irelan's takin' a leaf out o' the worl's buk; when we got the makin' of our own laws I thought we'd never stop to look behind us, but instead of that we never stopped to look before us! If the people ud folley up their religion betther there'd be a betther chance for us—what do you think, Mr. Bentham?

Bentham. I'm afraid I can't venture to express an opinion on that point, Mrs. Boyle; dogma has no attraction for me.

Mrs. Boyle. I forgot you didn't hold with us: what's this you said you were?

Bentham. A Theosophist, Mrs. Boyle.

Mrs. Boyle. An' what in the name o' God's a Theosophist?

Boyle. A Theosophist, Juno, 's a—tell her, Mr. Bentham, tell her.

Bentham. It's hard to explain in a few words: Theosophy's founded on The Vedas, the religious books of the East. Its central theme is the existence of an all-pervading Spirit—the Life-Breath. Nothing really exists but this one Universal Life-Breath. And whatever even seems to exist separately from this Life-Breath, doesn't really exist at all. It is all vital force in man, in all animals, and in all vegetation. This Life-Breath is called the Prawna.

Mrs. Boyle. The Prawna! What a comical name!

Boyle. Prawna; yis, the Prawna. [*Blowing gently through his lips.*] That's the Prawna!

Mrs. Boyle. Whist, whist, Jack.

Bentham. The happiness of man depends upon his sympathy with this Spirit. Men who have reached a high state of excellence are called Yogi. Some men become Yogi in a short time; it may take others millions of years.

Boyle. Yogi! I seen hundhreds of them in the streets o' San Francisco.

Bentham. It is said by these Yogi that, if we practice certain mental exercises, we would have powers denied to others—for instance, the faculty of seeing things that happen miles and miles away.

Mrs. Boyle. I wouldn't care to meddle with that sort o' belief; it's a very curious religion, altogether.

Boyle. What's curious about it? Isn't all religions curious? If they weren't you wouldn't get any one to believe them. But religions is passin' away—they've had their day like everything else. Take the real Dublin people, f'rinstance: they know more about Charlie Chaplin an' Tommy Mix than they do about SS. Peter an' Paul!

Mrs. Boyle. You don't believe in ghosts, Mr. Bentham?

Mary. Don't you know he doesn't, mother?

Bentham. I don't know that, Mary. Scientists are begining to think that what we call ghosts are sometimes seen by persons of a certain nature. They say that sensational actions, such as the killing of a person, demand great energy, and that that energy lingers in the place where the action occurred. People may live in the place and see nothing, when some one may come along whose personality has some peculiar connection with the energy of the place, and, in a flash, the person sees the whole affair.

Johnny. [*Rising swiftly, pale and affected.*] What sort o' talk is this to be goin' on with? Is there nothin' betther to be talkin' about but the killin' o' people? My God, isn't it bad enough for these things to happen without talkin' about them!

[*He hurriedly goes into the room on left.*]

Bentham. Oh, I'm very sorry, Mrs. Boyle; I never thought . . .

Mrs. Boyle. [*Apologetically.*] Never mind, Mr. Bentham, he's very touchy . . .

[*A frightened scream is heard from* JOHNNY *inside.*]

Mrs. Boyle. Mother of God, what's that?

[*He rushes out again, his face pale, his lips twitching, his limbs trembling.*]

Johnny. Shut the door, shut the door, quick, for God's sake! Great God, have mercy on me! Blessed Mother o' God, shelther me, shelther your son!

Mrs. Boyle. [*Catching him in her arms.*] What's wrong with you? What ails you? Sit down, sit down, here, on the bed . . . there now . . . there now.

Mary. Johnny, Johnny, what ails you?

Johnny. I seen him, I seen him . . . kneelin' in front o' the statue . . . merciful Jesus, have pity on me!

Mrs. Boyle. [*To* BOYLE.] Get him a glass o' whisky . . . quick, man, an' don't stand gawkin'. [BOYLE *gets the whisky.*]

Johnny. Sit here, sit here, mother . . . between me an' the door.

Mrs. Boyle. I'll sit beside you as long as you like, only tell me what was it came across you at all?

Johnny. [*After taking some drink.*] I seen him. . . . I seen Robbie Tancred kneelin' down before the statue . . . an' the red light shinin' on him . . . an' when I went in . . . he turned an' looked at me . . . an' I seen the woun's bleedin' in his breast. . . . Oh, why did he look at me like that? . . . it wasn't my fault that he was done in. . . . Mother o' God, keep him away from me!

Mrs. Boyle. There, there, child, you've imagined it all. There was nothin' there at all—it was the red light you seen, an' the talk we had, put all the rest into your head. Here, dhrink more o' this—it'll do you good. . . . An', now, stretch yourself down on the bed for a little. [*To* BOYLE.] Go in, Jack, an' show him it was only in his own head it was.

Boyle. [*Making no move.*] E-e-e-e-eh; it's all nonsense; it was only a shadda he saw.

Mary. Mother o' God, he made me heart lep!

Bentham. It was simply due to an overwrought imagination—we all get that way at times.

Mrs. Boyle. There, dear, lie down in the bed, an' I'll put the quilt across you . . . e-e-e-eh, that's it . . . you'll be as right as the mail in a few minutes.

Johnny. Mother, go into the room an' see if the light's lightin' before the statue.

Mrs. Boyle. [*To* BOYLE.] Jack, run in, an' see if the light's lightin' before the statue.

Boyle. [*To* MARY.] Mary, slip in an' see if the light's lightin' before the statue.

[MARY *hesitates to go in.*]

Bentham. It's all right; Mary, I'll go.

[*He goes into the room; remains for a few moments, and returns.*]

Bentham. Everything's just as it was—the light burning bravely before the statue.

Boyle. Of course; I knew it was all nonsense. [*A knock at the door.*]

Boyle. [*Going to open the door.*] E-e-e-e-eh.

[*He opens it, and* JOXER, *followed by* MRS. MADIGAN, *enters.* MRS. MADIGAN *is a strong, dapper little woman of about forty-five; her face is almost always a widespread smile of complacency. She is a woman who, in manner at least, can mourn with them that mourn, and rejoice with them that do rejoice. When she is feeling comfortable, she is inclined to be reminiscent; when others say anything, or following a statement made by herself, she has a habit of putting her head a little to one side, and nodding it rapidly several times in succession, like a bird pecking at a hard berry. Indeed, she has a good deal of the bird in her, but the bird instinct is by no means a melodious one. She is ignorant, vulgar, and forward, but her heart is generous withal. For instance, she would help a neighbor's sick child; she would probably kill the child, but her intentions would be to cure it; she would be more at home helping a drayman to lift a fallen horse. She is dressed in a rather soiled gray dress and a vivid purple blouse; in her hair is a huge comb, ornamented with huge colored beads. She enters with a gliding step, beaming smile, and nodding head.* BOYLE *receives them effusively.*]

Boyle. Come on in, Mrs. Madigan; come on in; I was afraid you weren't comin'. . . . [*Slyly.*] There's some people able to dhress, ay, Joxer?

Joxer. Fair as the blossoms that bloom in the May, an' sweet as the scent of the new mown hay. . . . Ah, well she may wear them.

Mrs. Madigan. [*Looking at* MARY.] I know some as are as sweet as the blossoms that bloom in the May—oh, no names, no pack dhrill!

Boyle. An', now, I'll inthroduce the pair o' yous to Mary's intended: Mr. Bentham, this is Mrs. Madigan, an oul' back-parlor neighbor, that, if she could help it at all, ud never see a body shuk!

Bentham. [*Rising, and tentatively shaking the hand of* MRS. MADIGAN.] I'm sure, it's a great pleasure to know you, Mrs. Madigan.

Mrs. Madigan. An' I'm goin' to tell you, Mr. Bentham, you're goin' to get as nice a bit o' skirt in Mary, there, as ever you seen in your puff. Not like some of the dhressed up dolls that's knockin' about lookin' for men when it's a skelpin' they want. I remember as well as I remember yestherday, the day she was born—of a Tuesday, the 25th o' June, in the year 1901, at thirty-three minutes past wan in the day be Foley's clock, the pub at the corner o' the street. A cowld day it was too, for the season o' the year; an' I remember sayin' to Joxer, there, who I met comin' up th' stairs, that the new arrival in Boyle's ud grow up a hardy chiselur if it lived, an' that she'd be somethin' one o' these days that nobody suspected, an' so signs on it, here she is today, goin' to be married to a young man lookin' as if he'd be fit to commensurate in any position in life it ud please God to call him!

Boyle. [*Effusively.*] Sit down, Mrs. Madigan, sit down, me oul' sport. [*To* BENTHAM.] This is Joxer Daly, Past Chief Ranger of the Dear Little Shamrock Branch of the Irish National Foresters, an oul' front-top neighbor, that never despaired, even in the darkest days of Ireland's sorra.

Joxer. Nil desperandum, Captain, nil desperandum.

Boyle. Sit down, Joxer, sit down. The two of us was ofen in a tight corner.

Mrs. Boyle. Ay, in Foley's snug!

Joxer. An' we kem out of it flyin', we kem out of it flyin', Captain.

Boyle. An', now, for a dhrink—I know yous won't refuse an oul' friend.

Mrs. Madigan. [*To* JUNO.] Is Johnny not well, Mrs. . . .

Mrs. Boyle. [*Warningly.*] S-s-s-sh.

Mrs. Madigan. Oh, the poor darlin'.

Boyle. Well, Mrs. Madigan, is it tea or what?

Mrs. Madigan. Well, speakin' for meself, I jus' had me tea a minute ago, an' I'm afraid to dhrink any more—I'm never the same when I dhrink too much tay. Thanks, all the same, Mr. Boyle.

Boyle. Well, what about a bottle o' stout or a dhrop o' whisky?

Mrs. Madigan. A bottle o' stout ud be a little too heavy for me stummock afther me tay. . . . A-a-ah, I'll thry the ball o' malt.

[BOYLE *prepares the whisky.*]

Mrs. Madigan. There's nothin' like a ball o' malt occasional like—too much of it isn't good. [*To* BOYLE, *who is adding water.*] Ah, God, Johnny, don't put too much wather on it! [*She drinks.*] I suppose yous'll be lavin' this place.

Boyle. I'm looking for a place near the sea; I'd like the place that you might say was me cradle, to be me grave as well. The sea is always callin' me.

Joxer. She is callin', callin', callin', in the win' an' on the sea.

Bolye. Another dhrop o' whisky, Mrs. Madigan?

Mrs. Madigan. Well, now, it ud be hard to refuse seein' the suspicious times that's in it.

Boyle. [*With a commanding gesture.*] Song! . . . Juno . . . Mary . . . "Home to Our Mount'ins"!

Mrs. Madigan. [*Enthusiastically.*] Hear, hear!

Joxer. Oh, that's a darlin' song, a daarlin' song!

Mary. [*Bashfully.*] Ah, no, da; I'm not in a singin' humor.

Mrs. Madigan. Gawn with you, child, an' you only goin' to be married; I remember as well as I remember yestherday—it was on a lovely August evenin', exactly, accordin' to date, fifteen years ago, come the Tuesday folleyin' the nex' that's comin' on, when me own man (the Lord be good to him) an' me was sittin' shy together in a doty little nook on a counthry road, adjacent to The Stiles. "That'll scratch your lovely, little white neck," says he, ketchin' hould of a danglin' bramble branch, holdin' clusters of the loveliest flowers you ever seen, an' breakin' it off, so that his arm fell, accidental like, roun' me waist; an' as I felt it tightenin', an' tightenin', an' tightenin', I thought me buzzum was every minute goin' to burst out into a roystherin' song about

The little green leaves that was shakin' on the threes,
The gallivantin' butterflies, an' buzzin' o' the bees!

Boyle. Ordher for the song!

Juno. Come on, Mary—we'll do our best.

[JUNO *and* MARY *stand up, and choosing a suitable position, sing simply "Home to Our Mountains."*
They bow to company, and return to their places.]

Boyle. [*Emotionally, at the end of song.*] Lull . . . me . . . to . . . rest!

Joxer. [*Clapping his hands.*] Bravo, bravo! Darlin' girulls, darlin' girulls!

Mrs. Madigan. Juno, I never seen you in betther form.

Bentham. Very nicely rendered indeed.

Mrs. Madigan. A noble call, a noble call!

Mrs. Boyle. What about yourself, Mrs. Madigan?

[*After some coaxing,* MRS. MADIGAN *rises, and in a quavering voice sings the following verse.*]

If I were a blackbird I'd whistle and sing;
I'd follow the ship that my thrue love was in;
An' on the top riggin', I'd there build me nest,
An' at night I would sleep on me Willie's white breast!

[*Becoming husky, amid applause, she sits down.*]

Mrs. Madigan. Ah, me voice is too husky now, Juno; though I remember the time when Maisie Madigan could sing like a nightingale at matin' time. I remember as well as I remember yestherday, at a party given to celebrate the comin' of the first chiselur to Annie an' Benny Jimeson—who was the barber, yous may remember, in Henrietta Street, that, afther Easter Week, hung out a green, white an' orange pole; an', then, when the Tans started their Jazz dancin', whipped it in agen, an' stuck out a red, white, an' blue wan instead, givin' as an excuse that a barber's pole was strictly non-political—singin' "An' You'll Remember Me," with the top notes quiverin' in a dead hush of pethrified attention, folleyed by a clappin' o' han's that shuk the tumblers on the table, an' capped be Jimeson, the barber, sayin' that it was the best rendherin' of "You'll Remember Me" he ever heard in his natural!

Boyle. [*Peremptorily.*] Ordher for Joxer's song!

Joxer. Ah, no, I couldn't; don't ass me, Captain.

Boyle. Joxer's song, Joxer's song—give us wan of your shut-eyed wans.

[JOXER *settles himself in his chair; takes a drink; clears his throat, solemnly closes his eyes, and begins to sing in a very querulous voice.*]

She is far from the lan' where her young hero sleeps,
An' lovers around her are sighing
[*He hesitates.*]
An' lovers around her are sighin' . . . sighin' . . . sighin' . . . [*A pause.*]

Boyle. [*Imitating* JOXER.]
And lovers around her are sighing!
What's the use of you thryin' to sing the song if you don't know it?

Mary. Thry another one, Mr. Daly—maybe you'd be more fortunate.

Mrs. Madigan. Gawn, Joxer, thry another wan.

Joxer. [*Starting again.*]
I have heard the mavis singin' his love song to the morn;
I have seen the dew-dhrop clingin' to the rose jus' newly born; but . . . but . . . [*frantically*] to the rose jus' newly born . . . newly born . . . born.

Johnny. Mother, put on the gramophone, for God's sake, an' stop Joxer's bawlin'.

Boyle. [*Commandingly.*] Gramophone! . . . I hate to see fellas thryin' to do what they're not able to do.

[BOYLE *arranges the gramophone, and is about to start it, when voices are heard of persons descending the stairs.*]

Mrs. Boyle. [*Warningly.*] Whisht, Jack, don't put it on, don't put it on yet; this must be poor Mrs. Tancred comin' down to go to the hospital—I forgot all about them bringin' the body to the church tonight. Open the door, Mary, an' give them a bit o' light.

[MARY *opens the door, and* MRS. TANCRED*—a very old woman, obviously shaken by the death of her son—appears, accompanied by several* NEIGHBORS. *The first few phrases are spoken before they appear.*]

First Neighbor. It's a sad journey we're goin' on, but God's good, an' the Republicans won't be always down.

Mrs. Tancred. Ah, what good is that to me now? Whether they're up or down—it won't bring me darlin' boy from the grave.

Mrs. Boyle. Come in an' have a hot cup o' tay, Mrs. Tancred, before you go.

Mrs. Tancred. Ah, I can take nothin' now, Mrs. Boyle—I won't be long afther him.

First Neighbor. Still an' all, he died a noble death, an' we'll bury him like a king.

Mrs. Tancred. An' I'll go on livin' like a pauper. Ah, what's the pains I suffered bringin' him into the world to carry him to his cradle, to the pains I'm sufferin' now, carryin' him out o' the world to bring him to his grave!

Mary. It would be better for you not to go at all, Mrs. Tancred, but to stay at home beside the fire with some o' the neighbors.

Mrs. Tancred. I seen the first of him, an' I'll see the last of him.

Mrs. Boyle. You'd want a shawl, Mrs. Tancred; it's a cowld night, an' the win's blowin' sharp.

Mrs. Madigan. [*Rushing out.*] I've a shawl above.

Mrs. Tancred. Me home is gone, now; he was me only child, an' to think that he was lyin' for a whole night stretched out on the side of a lonely counthry lane, with his head, his darlin' head, that I ofen kissed an' fondled, half hidden in the wather of a runnin' brook. An' I'm told he was the leadher of the ambush where me nex' door neighbor, Mrs. Mannin', lost her Free State soldier son. An' now here's the two of us oul' women, standin' one on each side of a scales o' sorra, balanced be the bodies of our two dead darlin' sons. [MRS. MADIGAN *returns, and wraps a shawl around her.*] God bless you, Mrs. Madigan. . . . [*She moves slowly toward the door.*] Mother o' God, Mother o' God, have pity on the pair of us! . . . O Blessed Virgin, where were you when me darlin' son was riddled with bullets, when me darlin' son was riddled with bullets! . . . Sacred Heart of the Crucified Jesus, take away our hearts o' stone . . . an' give us hearts o' flesh! . . . Take away this murdherin' hate . . . an' give us Thine own eternal love!

[*They pass out of the room.*]

Mrs. Boyle. [*Explanatorily to* BENTHAM.] That was Mrs. Tancred of the two-pair back; her son was found, e'er yestherday, lyin' out beyant Finglas riddled with bullets. A die-hard he was, be all accounts. He was a nice quiet boy, but lattherly he went to hell, with his Republic first, an' Republic last, an' Republic over all. He ofen took tea with us here, in the oul' days; an' Johnny, there, an' him used to be always together.

Johnny. Am I always to be havin' to tell you that he was no friend o' mine? I never cared for him, an' he could never stick me. It's because he was Commandant of the Battalion that I was Quarther-Masther of, that we were friends.

Mrs. Boyle. He's gone, now—the Lord be good to him! God help his poor oul' creature of a mother, for no matther whose friend or enemy he was, he was her poor son.

Bentham. The whole thing is terrible, Mrs. Boyle; but the only way to deal with a mad dog is to destroy him.

Mrs. Boyle. An' to think of me forgettin' about him bein' brought to the church tonight, an' we singin' an' all, but it was well we hadn't the gramophone goin', anyhow.

Boyle. Even if we had aself, we've nothin' to do with these things, one way or t'other. That's the Government's business, an' let them do what we're payin' them for doin'.

Mrs. Boyle. I'd like to know how a body's not to mind these things; look at the way they're afther leavin' the people in this very house. Hasn't the whole house, nearly, been massacreed? There's young Mrs. Dougherty's husband with his leg off; Mrs. Travers that had her son blew up be a mine in Inchegeela, in County Cork; Mrs. Mannin' that lost wan of her sons in an ambush a few weeks ago, an' now, poor Mrs. Tancred's only child gone West with his body made a collandher of. Sure, if it's not our business, I don't know whose business it is.

Boyle. Here, there, that's enough about them things; they don't affect us, an' we needn't give a damn. If they want a wake, well, let them have a wake. When I was a sailor, I was always resigned to meet with a wathery grave; an', if they want to be soldiers, well, there's no use o' them squealin' when they meet a soldier's fate.

Joxer. Let me like a soldier fall—me breast expandin' to th' ball!

Mrs. Boyle. In wan way, she deserves all she got; for lately, she let th' die-hards make an open house of th' place; an' for th' last couple of months, either when th' sun was risin', or when th' sun was settin', you had C.I.D. men burstin' into your room, assin' you where were you born, where were you christened, where were you married, an' where would you be buried!

Johnny. For God's sake, let us have no more o' this talk.

Mrs. Madigan. What about Mr. Boyle's song before we start th' gramophone?

Mary. [*Getting her hat, and putting it on.*] Mother, Charlie and I are goin' out for a little shtroll.

Mrs. Boyle. All right, darlin'.

Bentham. [*Going out with* MARY.] We won't be long away, Mrs. Boyle.

Mrs. Madigan. Gwan, Captain, gwan.

Boyle. E-e-e-e-eh, I'd want to have a few more jars in me, before I'd be in fettle for singin'.

Joxer. Give us that poem you writ t'other day. [*To the rest.*] Aw, it's a darlin' poem, a daarlin' poem.

Mrs. Boyle. God bless us, is he startin' to write poetry?

Boyle. [*Rising to his feet.*] E-e-e-e-eh. [*He recites in an emotional, consequential manner the following verses:*]

Shawn an' I were friends, sir, to me he was all in all.
His work was very heavy and his wages were very small.
None betther on th' beach as Docker, I'll go bail,
'Tis now I'm feelin' lonely, for today he lies in jail.
He was not what some call pious—seldom at church or prayer;
For the greatest scoundrels I know, sir, goes every Sunday there.
Fond of his pint—well, rather, but hated the Boss by creed
But never refused a copper to comfort a pal in need.
E-e-e-e-eh. [*He sits down.*]

Mrs. Madigan. Grand, grand; you should folley that up, you should folley that up.

Joxer. It's a daarlin' poem!

Boyle. [*Delightedly.*] E-e-e-e-eh.

Johnny. Are yous goin' to put on th' gramophone tonight, or are yous not?

Mrs. Boyle. Gwan, Jack, put on a record.

Mrs. Madigan. Gwan, Captain, gwan.

Boyle. Well, yous'll want to keep a dead silence.

[*He sets a record, starts the machine, and it begins to play "If you're Irish, come into the Parlor." As the tune is in full blare, the door is suddenly opened by a brisk, little bald-headed man, dressed circumspectly in a black suit; he glares fiercely at all in the room; he is* "NEEDLE" NUGENT, *a tailor. He carries his hat in his hand.*]

Nugent. [*Loudly, above the noise of the gramophone.*] Are yous goin' to have that thing bawlin' an' the funeral of Mrs. Tancred's son passin' the house? Have none of yous any respect for the Irish people's National regard for the dead?

[BOYLE *stops the gramophone.*]

Mrs. Boyle. Maybe, Needle Nugent, it's nearly time we had a little less respect for the dead, an' a little more regard for the livin'.

Mrs. Madigan. We don't want you, Mr. Nugent, to teach us what we learned at our mother's knee. You don't look yourself as if you were dyin' of grief; if y'ass Maisie Madigan anything, I'd call you a real thrue die-hard an' live-soft Republican, attendin' Republican funerals in the day, an' stoppin' up half the night makin' suits for the Civic Guards! [*Persons are heard running down to the street, some saying, "Here it is, here it is."* NUGENT *withdraws, and the rest, except* JOHNNY, *go to the window looking into the street, and look out. Sounds of a crowd coming nearer are heard; portion are singing.*]

To Jesus' Heart all burning
With fervent love for men,
My heart with fondest yearning
Shall raise its joyful strain.
While ages course along,
Blest be with loudest song,
The Sacred Heart of Jesus
By every heart and tongue.

Mrs. Boyle. Here's the hearse, here's the hearse!

Boyle. There's t'oul' mother walkin' behin' the coffin.

Mrs. Madigan. You can hardly see the coffin with the wreaths.

Joxer. Oh, it's a darlin' funeral, a daarlin' funeral!

Mrs. Madigan. We'd have a betther view from the street.

Boyle. Yes—this place ud give you a crick in your neck.

[*They leave the room, and go down.* JOHNNY *sits moodily by the fire.*]

[*A* YOUNG MAN *enters; he looks at* JOHNNY *for a moment.*]

The Young Man. Quarther-Masther Boyle.

Johnny. [*With a start.*] The Mobilizer!

The Young Man. You're not at the funeral?

Johnny. I'm not well.

The Young Man. I'm glad I've found you; you were stoppin' at your aunt's; I called there but you'd gone. I've to give you an ordher to attend a Battalion Staff meetin' the night afther tomorrow.

Johnny. Where?

The Young Man. I don't know; you're to meet me at the Pillar at eight o'clock; then we're to go to a place I'll be told of tonight; there we'll meet a mothor that'll bring us to the meeting. They think you might be able to know somethin' about them that gave the bend where Commandant Tancred was shelterin'.

Johnny. I'm not goin', then. I know nothin' about Tancred.

The Young Man. [*At the door.*] You'd betther come for your own sake—remember your oath.

Johnny. [*Passionately.*] I won't go! Haven't I done enough for Ireland! I've lost me arm, an' me hip's desthroyed so that I'll never be able to walk right agen! Good God, haven't I done enough for Ireland?

The Young Man. Boyle, no man can do enough for Ireland! [*He goes.*]

[*Faintly in the distance the crowd is heard saying:*]

Hail, Mary, full of grace, the Lord is with Thee;
Blessed art Thou amongst women, and blessed, etc.

CURTAIN

ACT III

SCENE: *The same as Act II. It is about half-past six on a November evening; a bright fire is burning in the grate.*

[MARY, *dressed to go out, is sitting on a chair by the fire, leaning forward, her hands under her chin, her elbows on her knees. A look of dejection, mingled with uncertain anxiety, is on her face. A lamp, turned low, is lighted on the table. The votive light under the picture of the Virgin gleams more redly than ever.* MRS. BOYLE *is putting on her hat and coat. It is two months later.*]

Mrs. Boyle. An' has Bentham never even written to you since—not one line for the past month?

Mary. [*Tonelessly.*] Not even a line, mother.

Mrs. Boyle. That's very curious. . . . What came between the two of yous at all? To leave you so sudden, an' yous so great together. . . . To go away t' England, an' not to even leave you his address. . . . The way he was always bringin' you to dances, I thought he was mad afther you. Are you sure you said nothin' to him?

Mary. No, mother—at least nothing that could possibly explain his givin' me up.

Mrs. Boyle. You know you're a bit hasty at times, Mary, an' say things you shouldn't say.

Mary. I never said to him what I shouldn't say, I'm sure of that.

Mrs. Boyle. How are you sure of it?

Mary. Because I love him with all my heart and soul, mother. Why, I don't know; I often thought to myself that he wasn't the man poor Jerry was, but I couldn't help loving him, all the same.

Mrs. Boyle. But you shouldn't be frettin' the way you are: when a woman loses a man, she never knows what she's afther losin', to be sure; but, then, she never knows what she's afther gainin', either. You're not the one girl of a month ago—you look like one pinin' away. It's long ago I had a right to bring you to the doctor, instead of waitin' till tonight.

Mary. There's no necessity, really, mother, to go to the doctor; nothing serious is wrong with me—I'm run down and disappointed, that's all.

Mrs. Boyle. I'll not wait another minute; I don't like the look of you at all. . . . I'm afraid we made a mistake in throwin' over poor Jerry. . . . He'd have been betther for you than that Bentham.

Mary. Mother, the best man for a woman is the one for whom she has the most love, and Charlie had it all.

Mrs. Boyle. Well, there's one thing to be said for him—he couldn't have been thinkin' of the money, or he wouldn't ha' left you . . . it must ha' been somethin' else.

Mary. [*Wearily*.] I don't know . . . I don't know, mother . . . only I think. . . .

Mrs. Boyle. What d'ye think?

Mary. I imagine . . . he thought . . . we weren't . . . good enough for him.

Mrs. Boyle. An' what was he himself, only a school teacher? Though I don't blame him for fightin' shy of people like that Joxer fella an' that oul' Madigan wan—nice sort o' people for your father to inthroduce to a man like Mr. Bentham. You might have told me all about this before now, Mary; I don't know why you like to hide everything from your mother; you knew Bentham, an' I'd ha' known nothin' about it if it hadn't bin for the Will; an' it was only today, afther long coaxin', that you let out that he'd left you.

Mary. It would have been useless to tell you—you wouldn't understand.

Mrs. Boyle. [*Hurt*.] Maybe not. . . . Maybe I wouldn't understand. . . . Well, we'll be off now. [*She goes over to door left, and speaks to* BOYLE *inside*.] We're goin' now to the doctor's. Are you goin' to get up this evenin'?

Boyle. [*From inside*.] The pains in me legs is terrible! It's me should be poppin' off to the doctor instead o' Mary, the way I feel.

Mrs. Boyle. Sorra mend you! A nice way you were in last night—carried in in a frog's march, dead to the world. If that's the way you'll go on when you get the money, it'll be the grave for you, an asylum for me, and the Poorhouse for Johnny.

Boyle. I thought you were goin'?

Mrs. Boyle. That's what has you as you are—you can't bear to be spoken to. Knowin' the way we are, up to our ears in debt, it's a wondher you wouldn't ha' got up to go to th' solicitor's an' see if we could ha' been gettin' a little o' the money even.

Boyle. [*Shouting*.] I can't be goin' up there night, noon, an' mornin', can I? He can't give the money till he gets it, can he? I can't get blood out of a turnip, can I?

Mrs. Boyle. It's nearly two months since we heard of the Will, an' the money seems as far off as ever. . . . I suppose you know we owe twenty poun's to oul' Murphy?

Boyle. I've a faint recollection of you tellin' me that before.

Mrs. Boyle. Well, you'll go over to the shop yourself for the things in future—I'll face him no more.

Boyle. I thought you said you were goin'?

Mrs. Boyle. I'm goin' now; come on, Mary.

Boyle. Ey, Juno, ey!

Mrs. Boyle. Well, what d'ye want now?

Boyle. Is there e'er a bottle o' stout left?

Mrs. Boyle. There's two o' them here still.

Boyle. Show us in one o' them an' leave t'other there till I get up. An' throw us in the paper that's on the table, an' the bottle o' Sloan's Liniment that's in th' drawer.

Mrs. Boyle. [*Getting the liniment and the stout*.] What paper is it you want—the *Messenger?*

Boyle. *Messenger! The News o' the World!*

[MRS. BOYLE *brings in the things asked for and comes out again*.]

Mrs. Boyle. [*At door*.] Mind the candle, now, an' don't burn the house over our heads. I left t'other bottle o' stout on the table.

[*She puts bottle of stout on table. She goes out with* MARY. *A cork is heard popping inside.*

A pause; then outside the door is heard the voice of JOXER *lilting softly: "Me pipe I'll smoke, as I dhrive me moke . . . are you . . . there . . . More . . . ee . . . aar . . . i . . . tee!" A gentle knock is heard and, after a pause, the door opens,* and JOXER, *followed by* NUGENT, *enters*.]

Joxer. Be God, they must be all out; I

was thinkin' there was somethin' up when he didn't answer the signal. We seen Juno an' Mary goin', but I didn't see him, an' it's very seldom he escapes me.

Nugent. He's not goin' to escape me—he's not goin' to be let go to the fair altogether.

Joxer. Sure, the house couldn't hould them lately; an' he goin' about like a mastherpiece of the Free State counthry; forgettin' their friends; forgettin' God—wouldn't even lift his hat passin' a chapel! Sure they were bound to get a dhrop! An' you really think there's no money comin' to him afther all?

Nugent. Not as much as a red rex, man; I've been a bit anxious this long time over me money, an' I went up to the solicitor's to find out all I could—ah, man, they were goin' to throw me down the stairs. They toul' me that the oul' cock himself had the stairs worn away comin' up afther it, an' they black in the face tellin' him he'd get nothin'. Some way or another that the Will is writ he won't be entitled to get as much as a make!

Joxer. Ah, I thought there was somethin' curious about the whole thing; I've bin havin' sthrange dhreams for the last couple o' weeks. An' I notice that that Bentham fella doesn't be comin' here now—there must be somethin' on the mat there too. Anyhow, who, in the name o' God, ud leave anythin' to that oul' bummer? Sure it ud be unnatural. An' the way Juno an' him's been throwin' their weight about for the last few months! Ah, him that goes a borrowin' goes a sorrowin'!

Nugent. Well, he's not goin' to throw his weight about in the suit I made for him much longer. I'm tellin' you seven poun's aren't to be found growin' on the bushes these days.

Joxer. An' there isn't hardly a neighbor in the whole street that hasn't lent him money on the strength of what he was goin' to get, but they're after backing the wrong horse. Wasn't it a mercy o' God that I'd nothin' to give him! The softy I am, you know, I'd ha' lent him me last juice! I must have had somebody's good prayers. Ah, afther all, an honest man's the noblest work o' God! [BOYLE *coughs inside.*]

Joxer. Whisht, damn it, he must be inside in bed.

Nugent. Inside o' bed or outside of it he's goin' to pay me for that suit, or give it back—he'll not climb up my back as easily as he thinks.

Joxer. Gwan in at wanst, man, an' get it off him, an' don't be a fool.

Nugent. [*Going to door left, opening it and looking in.*] Ah, don't disturb yourself, Mr. Boyle; I hope you're not sick?

Boyle. Th' oul' legs, Mr. Nugent, th' oul' legs.

Nugent. I just called over to see if you could let me have anything off the suit?

Boyle. E-e-e-eh, how much is this it is?

Nugent. It's the same as it was at the start—seven poun's.

Boyle. I'm glad you kem, Mr. Nugent; I want a good heavy top-coat—Irish frieze, if you have it. How much would a top-coat like that be now?

Nugent. About six poun's.

Boyle. Six poun's—six an' seven, six an' seven is thirteen—that'll be thirteen poun's I'll owe you.

[JOXER *slips the bottle of stout that is on the table into his pocket.* NUGENT *rushes into the room, and returns with suit on his arm; he pauses at the door.*]

Nugent. You'll owe me no thirteen poun's. Maybe you think you're betther able to owe it than pay it!

Boyle. [*Frantically.*] Here, come back to hell ower that—where're you goin' with them clothes o' mine?

Nugent. Where am I goin' with them clothes o' yours? Well, I like your damn cheek!

Boyle. Here, what am I goin' to dhress meself in when I'm goin' out?

Nugent. What do I care what you dhress yourself in? You can put yourself in a bolsther cover, if you like.

[*He goes toward the other door, followed by* JOXER.]

Joxer. What'll he dhress himself in! Gentleman Jack an' his frieze coat!

[*They go out.*]

Boyle. [*Inside.*] Ey, Nugent, ey, Mr. Nugent, Mr. Nugent!

[*After a pause* BOYLE *enters hastily, buttoning the braces of his moleskin trousers; his coat and vest are on his arm; he throws these on a chair and hurries to the door on right.*]

Boyle. Ey, Mr. Nugent, Mr. Nugent!

Joxer. [*Meeting him at the door.*] What's up, what's wrong, Captain?

Boyle. Nugent's been here an' took away me suit—the only things I had to go out in!

Joxer. Tuk your suit—for God's sake! An' what were you doin' while he was takin' them?

Boyle. I was in bed when he stole in like a thief in the night, an' before I knew even what he was thinkin' of, he whipped them from the chair, an' was off like a redshank!

Joxer. An' what, in the name of God, did he do that for?

Boyle. What did he do it for? How the hell do I know what he done it for? Jealousy an' spite, I suppose.

Joxer. Did he not say what he done it for?

Boyle. Amn't I afther tellin' you that he had them whipped up an' was gone before I could open me mouth?

Joxer. That was a very sudden thing to do; there mus' be somethin' behin' it. Did he hear anythin', I wondher?

Boyle. Did he hear anythin'?—you talk very queer, Joxer—what could he hear?

Joxer. About you not gettin' the money, in some way or t'other?

Boyle. An' what ud prevent me from gettin' th' money?

Joxer. That's jus' what I was thinkin'—what ud prevent you from gettin' the money—nothin', as far as I can see.

Boyle. [*Looking round for bottle of stout with an exclamation.*] Aw, holy God!

Joxer. What's up, Jack?

Boyle. He must have afther lifted the bottle o' stout that Juno left on the table!

Joxer. [*Horrified.*] Ah, no, ah, no! He wouldn't be afther doin' that, now.

Boyle. An' who done it then? Juno left a bottle o' stout here, an' it's gone—it didn't walk, did it?

Joxer. Oh, that's shockin'; ah, man's inhumanity to man makes countless thousands mourn!

Mrs. Madigan. [*Appearing at the door.*] I hope I'm not disturbin' you in any discussion on your forthcomin' legacy—if I may use the word—an' that you'll let me have a barny for a minute or two with you, Mr. Boyle.

Boyle. [*Uneasily.*] To be sure, Mrs. Madigan—an oul' friend's always welcome.

Joxer. Come in the evenin', come in th' mornin'; come when you're assed, or come without warnin', Mrs. Madigan.

Boyle. Sit down, Mrs. Madigan.

Mrs. Madigan. [*Ominously.*] Th' few words I have to say can be said standin'. Puttin' aside all formularies, I suppose you remember me lendin' you some time ago three poun's that I raised on blankets an' furniture in me uncle's?

Boyle. I remember it well. I have it recorded in me book—three poun's five shillin's from Maisie Madigan, raised on articles pawned; an', item: fourpence, given to make up the price of a pint, on th' principle that no bird ever flew on wan wing; all to be repaid at par, when the ship comes home.

Mrs. Madigan. Well, ever since I shoved in the blankets I've been perishing with th' cowld, an' I've decided, if I'll be too hot in th' nex' world aself, I'm not goin' to be too cowld in this wan; an' consequently, I want me three poun's, if you please.

Boyle. This is a very sudden demand, Mrs. Madigan, an' can't be met; but I'm willin' to give you a receipt in full, in full.

Mrs. Madigan. Come on, out with th' money, an' don't be jack-actin'.

Boyle. You can't get blood out of a turnip, can you?

Mrs. Madigan. [*Rushing over and shaking him.*] Gimme me money, y'oul' reprobate, or I'll shake the worth of it out of you!

Boyle. Ey, houl' on, there; houl' on, there! You'll wait for your money now, me lassie!

Mrs. Madigan. [*Looking around the room and seeing the gramophone.*] I'll wait for it, will I? Well, I'll not wait long; if I can't get th' cash, I'll get th' worth of it.

[*She catches up the gramophone.*]

Boyle. Ey, ey, there, wher'r you goin' with that?

Mrs. Madigan. I'm goin' to th' pawn to get me three quid five shillin's; I'll brin' you th' ticket, an' then you can do what you like, me bucko.

Boyle. You can't touch that, you can't touch that! It's not my property, an' it's not ped for yet!

Mrs. Madigan. So much th' betther. It'll be an ayse to me conscience, for I'm takin' what doesn't belong to you. You're not goin' to be swankin' it like a paycock with Maisie Madigan's money—I'll pull some o' th' gorgeous feathers out o' your tail!

[*She goes off with the gramophone.*]

Boyle. What's th' world comin' to at all? I ass you, Joxer Daly, is there any morality left anywhere?

Joxer. I wouldn't ha' believed it, only I seen it with me own two eyes. I didn't think Maisie Madigan was that sort of a woman; she has either a sup taken, or she's heard somethin'.

Boyle. Heard somethin'—about what, if it's not any harm to ass you?

Joxer. She must ha' heard some rumor or other that you weren't goin' to get th' money.

Boyle. Who says I'm not goin' to get th' money?

Joxer. Sure, I know—I was only sayin'.

Boyle. Only sayin' what?

Joxer. Nothin'.

Boyle. You were goin' to say somethin', don't be a twisther.

Joxer. [*Angrily.*] Who's a twisther?

Boyle. Why don't you speak your mind, then?

Joxer. You never twisted yourself—no, you wouldn't know how!

Boyle. Did you ever know me to twist; did you ever know me to twist?

Joxer. [*Fiercely.*] Did you ever do anythin' else? Sure, you can't believe a word that comes out o' your mouth.

Boyle. Here, get out, ower o' this; I always knew you were a prognosticator an' a procrastinator!

Joxer. [*Going out as* JOHNNY *comes in.*] The anchor's weighed, farewell, re . . . mem . . . ber . . . me. Jacky Boyle, Esquire, infernal rogue an' damned liar!

Johnny. Joxer an' you at it agen?—when are you goin' to have a little respect for yourself, an' not be always makin' a show of us all?

Boyle. Are you goin' to lecture me now?

Johnny. Is mother back from the doctor yet, with Mary?

[MRS. BOYLE *enters; it is apparent from the serious look on her face that something has happened. She takes off her hat and coat without a word and puts them by. She then sits down near the fire, and there is a few moments' pause.*]

Boyle. Well, what did the doctor say about Mary?

Mrs. Boyle. [*In an earnest manner and with suppressed agitation.*] Sit down here, Jack; I've something to say to you . . . about Mary.

Boyle. [*Awed by her manners.*] About . . . Mary?

Mrs. Boyle. Close that door there and sit down here.

Boyle. [*Closing the door.*] More throuble in our native land, is it? [*He sits down.*] Well, what is it?

Mrs. Boyle. It's about Mary.

Boyle. Well, what about Mary—there's nothin' wrong with her, is there?

Mrs. Boyle. I'm sorry to say there's a gradle wrong with her.

Boyle. A gradle wrong with her! [*Peevishly.*] First Johnny an' now Mary; is the whole house goin' to become an hospital! It's not consumption, is it?

Mrs. Boyle. No . . . it's not consumption . . . it's worse.

Johnny. Worse! Well, we'll have to get her into some place ower this, there's no one here to mind her.

Mrs. Boyle. We'll all have to mind her now. You might as well know now, Johnny, as another time. [*To* BOYLE.] D'ye know what the doctor said to me about her, Jack?

Boyle. How ud I know—I wasn't there, was I?

Mrs. Boyle. He told me to get her married at wanst.

Boyle. Married at wanst! An' why did he say the like o' that?

Mrs. Boyle. Because Mary's goin' to have a baby in a short time.

Boyle. Goin' to have a baby!—my God, what'll Bentham say when he hears that?

Mrs. Boyle. Are you blind, man, that you can't see that it was Bentham that has done this wrong to her?

Boyle. [*Passionately.*] Then he'll marry her, he'll have to marry her!

Mrs. Boyle. You know he's gone to England, an' God knows where he is now.

Boyle. I'll folley him, I'll folley him, an' bring him back, an' make him do her justice. The scoundrel, I might ha' known what he was, with his yogees an' his prawna!

Mrs. Boyle. We'll have to keep it quiet till we see what we can do.

Boyle. Oh, isn't this a nice thing to come on top o' me, an' the state I'm in! A pretty show I'll be to Joxer an' to that oul' wan, Madigan! Amn't I afther goin' through enough without havin' to go through this!

Mrs. Boyle. What you an' I'll have to go through'll be nothin' to what poor Mary'll have to go through; for you an' me is middlin' old, an' most of our years is spent; but Mary'll have maybe forty years to face an' handle, an' every wan of them'll be tainted with a bitther memory.

Boyle. Where is she? Where is she till I tell her off? I'm tellin' you when I'm done with her she'll be a sorry girl!

Mrs. Boyle. I left her in me sisther's till I came to speak to you. You'll say nothin' to her, Jack; ever since she left school she's earned her livin', an' your fatherly care never throubled the poor girl.

Boyle. Gwan, take her part agen her father! But I'll let you see whether I'll say nothin' to her or no! Her an' her readin'! That's more o' th' blasted nonsense that has the house fallin' down on top of us! What did th' likes of her, born in a tenement house, want with readin'? Her readin's afther bringin' her to a nice pass—oh, it's madnin', madnin', madnin'!

Mrs. Boyle. When she comes back say nothin' to her, Jack, or she'll leave this place.

Boyle. Leave this place! Ay, she'll leave this place, an' quick too!

Mrs. Boyle. If Mary goes, I'll go with her.

Boyle. Well, go with her! Well, go, th' pair o' yous! I lived before I seen yous, an' I can live when yous are gone. Isn't this a nice thing to come rollin' in on top o' me afther all your prayin' to St. Anthony an' The Little Flower? An' she's a child o' Mary, too—I wonder what'll the nuns think of her now? An' it'll be bellows'd all over th' disthrict before you could say Jack Robinson; an' whenever I'm seen they'll whisper, "That's th' father of Mary Boyle that had th' kid be th' swank she used to go with; d'ye know, d'ye know?" To be sure they'll know—more about it than I will meself!

Johnny. She should be dhriven out o' th' house she's brought disgrace on!

Mrs. Boyle. Hush, you, Johnny. We needn't let it be bellows'd all over the place; all we've got to do is to leave this place quietly an' go somewhere where we're not known, an' nobody'll be th' wiser.

Boyle. You're talkin' like a two-year-oul', woman. Where'll we get a place ou' o' this?—places aren't that easily got.

Mrs. Boyle. But, Jack, when we get the money . . .

Boyle. Money—what money?

Mrs. Boyle. Why, oul' Ellison's money, of course.

Boyle. There's no money comin' from oul' Ellison, or any one else. Since you've heard of wan throuble, you might as well hear of another. There's no money comin' to us at all—the Will's a washout!

Mrs. Boyle. What are you sayin', man—no money?

Johnny. How could it be a washout?

Boyle. The boyo that's afther doin' it to Mary done it to me as well. The thick made out the Will wrong; he said in th' Will, only first cousin an' second cousin, instead of mentionin' our names, an' now any one that thinks he's a first cousin or second cousin t'oul' Ellison can claim the money as well as me, an' they're springin' up in hundreds, an' comin' from America an' Australia, thinkin' to get their whack out of it, while all the time the lawyers is gobblin' it up, till there's not as much as ud buy a stockin' for your lovely daughter's baby!

Mrs. Boyle. I don't believe it, I don't believe it, I don't believe it!

Johnny. Why did you say nothin' about this before?

Mrs. Boyle. You're not serious, Jack; you're not serious!

Boyle. I'm tellin' you the scholar, Bentham, made a banjax o' th' Will; instead o' sayin', "th' rest o' me property to be divided between me first cousin, Jack Boyle, an' me second cousin, Mick Finnegan, o' Santhry," he writ down only, "me first an' second cousins," an' the world an' his wife are afther th' property now.

Mrs. Boyle. Now I know why Bentham left poor Mary in th' lurch; I can see it all now—oh, is there not even a middlin' honest man left in th' world?

Johnny. [*To* BOYLE.] An' you let us run into debt, an' you borreyed money from everybody to fill yourself with beer! An' now, you tell us the whole thing's a washout! Oh, if it's thrue, I'm done with you, for you're worse than me sisther Mary!

Boyle. You hole your tongue, d'ye hear? I'll not take any lip from you. Go an' get Bentham if you want satisfaction for all that's afther happenin' us.

Johnny. I won't hole me tongue, I won't hole me tongue! I'll tell you what I think of you, father an' all as you are . . . you . . .

Mrs. Boyle. Johnny, Johnny, Johnny, for God's sake, be quiet!

Johnny. I'll not be quiet, I'll not be quiet; he's a nice father, isn't he? Is it any wondher Mary went asthray, when . . .

Mrs. Boyle. Johnny, Johnny, for my sake be quiet—for your mother's sake!

Boyle. I'm goin' out to have a few dhrinks with th' last few makes I have, an' tell that lassie o' yours not to be here when I come back; for if I lay me eyes on her, I'll lay me han's on her, an' if I lay me han's on her, I won't be accountable for me actions!

Johnny. Take care somebody doesn't lay his han's on you—y'oul' . . .

Mrs. Boyle. Johnny, Johnny!

Boyle. [*At the door, about to go out.*] Oh, a nice son, an' a nicer daughter, I have. [*Calling loudly upstairs.*] Joxer, Joxer, are you there?

Joxer. [*From a distance.*] I'm here, More . . . ee . . . aar . . . i . . . tee!

Boyle. I'm goin' down to Foley's—are you comin'?

Joxer. Come with you? With that sweet call me heart is stirred; I'm only waiting for the word, an' I'll be with you, like a bird!

[BOYLE *and* JOXER *pass the door going out.*]

Johnny. [*Throwing himself on the bed.*] I've a nice sisther, an' a nice father, there's no bettin' on it. I wish to God a bullet or a bomb had whipped me ou' o' this long ago! Not one o' yous, not one o' yous have any thought for me!

Mrs. Boyle. [*With passionate remon-*

strance.] If you don't whisht, Johnny, you'll drive me mad. Who has kep' th' home together for the past few years—only me. An' who'll have to bear th' biggest part o' this throuble but me—but whinin' an' whingin' isn't goin' to do any good.

Johnny. You're to blame yourself for a gradle of it—givin' him his own way in everything, an' never assin' to check him, no matther what he done. Why didn't you look afther th' money? why . . .

[*There is a knock at the door;* MRS. BOYLE *opens it;* JOHNNY *rises on his elbow to look and listen; two* MEN *enter.*]

First Man. We've been sent up be th' Manager of the Hibernian Furnishing Co., Mrs. Boyle, to take back the furniture that was got a while ago.

Mrs. Boyle. Yous'll touch nothin' here—how do I know who yous are?

First Man. [*Showing a paper.*] There's the ordher, ma'am. [*Reading.*] A chest o' drawers, a table, wan easy an' two ordinary chairs; wan mirror; wan chestherfield divan, an' a wardrobe an' two vases. [*To his* COMRADE.] Come on, Bill, it's afther knockin'-off time already.

Johnny. For God's sake, mother, run down to Foley's an' bring father back, or we'll be left without a stick.

[*The* MEN *carry out the table.*]

Mrs. Boyle. What good would it be? You heard what he said before he went out.

Johnny. Can't you thry? He ought to be here, an' the like of this goin' on.

[MRS. BOYLE *puts a shawl around her, as* MARY *enters.*]

Mary. What's up, mother? I met men carryin' away the table, an' everybody's talking about us not gettin' the money after all.

Mrs. Boyle. Everythin's gone wrong, Mary, everythin'. We're not gettin' a penny out o' the Will, not a penny—I'll tell you all when I come back; I'm goin' for your father. [*She runs out.*]

Johnny. [*To* MARY, *who has sat down by the fire.*] It's a wondher you're not ashamed to show your face here, afther what has happened.

[JERRY *enters slowly; there is a look of earnest hope on his face. He looks at* MARY *for a few moments.*]

Jerry. [*Softly*] Mary!

[MARY *does not answer.*]

Jerry. Mary, I want to speak to you for a few moments, may I?

[MARY *remains silent;* JOHNNY *goes slowly into room on left.*]

Jerry. Your mother has told me everything, Mary, and I have come to you. . . . I have come to tell you, Mary, that my love for you is greater and deeper than ever. . . .

Mary. [*With a sob.*] Oh, Jerry, Jerry, say no more; all that is over now; anything like that is impossible now!

Jerry. Impossible! Why do you talk like that, Mary?

Mary. After all that has happened.

Jerry. What does it matter what has happened? We are young enough to be able to forget all those things. [*He catches her hand.*] Mary, Mary, I am pleading for your love. With Labor, Mary, humanity is above everything; we are the Leaders in the fight for a new life. I want to forget Bentham, I want to forget that you left me—even for a while.

Mary. Oh, Jerry, Jerry, you haven't the bitter word of scorn for me after all.

Jerry. [*Passionately.*] Scorn! I love you, love you, Mary!

Mary. [*Rising, and looking him in the eyes.*] Even though . . .

Jerry. Even though you threw me over for another man; even though you gave me many a bitter word!

Mary. Yes, yes, I know; but you love me, even though . . . even though . . . I'm . . . goin' . . . goin' . . . [*He looks at her questioningly, and fear gathers in his eyes.*] Ah, I was thinkin' so. . . . You don't know everything!

Jerry. [*Poignantly.*] Surely to God, Mary, you don't mean that . . . that . . . that . . .

Mary. Now you know all, Jerry; now you know all!

Jerry. My God, Mary, have you fallen as low as that?

Mary. Yes, Jerry, as you say, I have fallen as low as that.

Jerry. I didn't mean it that way, Mary . . . it came on me so sudden, that I didn't mind what I was sayin'. . . . I never expected this—your mother never told me. . . . I'm sorry . . . God knows, I'm sorry for you, Mary.

Mary. Let us say no more, Jerry; I don't blame you for thinkin' it's terrible. . . . I suppose it is. . . . Everybody'll think the same. . . . It's only as I expected—your humanity is just as narrow as the humanity of the others.

Jerry. I'm sorry, all the same. . . . I shouldn't have troubled you. . . . I wouldn't if I'd known. . . . If I can do anything for you . . . Mary . . . I will.

[*He turns to go, and halts at the door.*]

Mary. Do you remember, Jerry, the verses you read when you gave the lecture in the Socialist Rooms some time ago, on Humanity's Strife with Nature?

Jerry. The verses—no; I don't remember them.

Mary. I do. They're runnin' in me head now—

An' we felt the power that fashion'd
All the lovely things we saw,
That created all the murmur
Of an everlasting law,
Was a hand of force an' beauty,
With an eagle's tearin' claw.

Then we saw our globe of beauty
Was an ugly thing as well,
A hymn divine whose chorus
Was an agonizin' yell;
Like the story of a demon,
That an angel had to tell.

Like a glowin' picture by a
Hand unsteady, brought to ruin;
Like her craters, if their deadness
Could give life unto the moon;
Like the agonizing horror
Of a violin out of tune.

[*There is a pause, and* DEVINE *goes slowly out.*]

Johnny. [*Returning.*] Is he gone?

Mary. Yes.

[*The two* MEN *re-enter.*]

First Man. We can't wait any longer for t'oul' fella—sorry, Miss, but we have to live as well as th' nex' man.

[*They carry out some things.*]

Johnny. Oh, isn't this terrible! . . . I suppose you told him everything . . . . Couldn't you have waited for a few days? . . . He'd have stopped th' takin' of the things, if you'd kep' your mouth shut. Are you burnin' to tell every one of the shame you've brought on us?

Mary. [*Snatching up her hat and coat.*] Oh, this is unbearable! [*She rushes out.*]

First Man. [*Re-entering.*] We'll take the chest o' drawers next—it's the heaviest.

[*The votive light flickers for a moment, and goes out.*]

Johnny. [*In a cry of fear.*] Mother o' God, the light's afther goin' out!

First Man. You put the win' up me the way you bawled that time. The oil's all gone, that's all.

Johnny. [*With an agonizing cry.*] Mother o' God, there's a shot I'm afther gettin'!

First Man. What's wrong with you, man? Is it a fit you're takin'?

Johnny. I'm afther feelin' a pain in me breast, like the tearin' by of a bullet!

First Man. He's goin' mad—it's a wondher they'd leave a chap like that here be himself.

[*Two* IRREGULARS *enter swiftly; they carry revolvers; one goes over to* JOHNNY; *the other covers the two* FURNITURE MEN.]

First Irregular. [*To the* MEN, *quietly and incisively.*] Who are you—what are yous doin' here?—quick!

First Man. Removin' furniture that's not paid for.

Irregular. Get over to the other end of the room an' turn your faces to the wall—quick.

[*The two* MEN *turn their faces to the wall, with their hands up.*]

Second Irregular. [*To* JOHNNY.] Come on, Sean Boyle, you're wanted; some of us have a word to say to you.

Johnny. I'm sick, I can't—what do you want with me?

Second Irregular. Come on, come on; we've a distance to go, an' haven't much time—come on.

Johnny. I'm an oul' comrade—yous wouldn't shoot an oul' comrade.

Second Irregular. Poor Tancred was an oul' comrade o' yours, but you didn't think o' that when you gave him away to the gang that sent him to his grave. But we've no time to waste; come on—here, Dermot, ketch his arm. [*To* JOHNNY.] Have you your beads?

Johnny. Me beads! Why do you ass me that, why do you ass me that?

Second Irregular. Go on, go on, march!

Johnny. Are yous goin' to do in a comrade?—look at me arm, I lost it for Ireland.

Second Irregular. Commandant Tancred lost his life for Ireland.

Johnny. Sacred Heart of Jesus, have mercy on me! Mother o' God, pray for me—be with me now in the agonies o' death! . . . Hail, Mary, full o' grace . . . the Lord is . . . with Thee.

[*They drag out* JOHNNY BOYLE, *and the curtain falls. When it rises again most of the furniture is gone.* MARY *and* MRS. BOYLE, *one on each side, are sitting in a darkened room, by the fire; it is an hour later.*]

Mrs. Boyle. I'll not wait much longer . . . what did they bring him away in the mothor for? Nugent says he thinks they had guns . . . is me throubles never goin' to be over? . . . If anything ud happen to poor Johnny, I think I'd lose me mind. . . . I'll go to the

Police Station; surely they ought to be able to do somethin'.

[*Below is heard the sound of voices.*]

Mrs. Boyle. Whisht, is that something? Maybe it's your father, though when I left him in Foley's he was hardly able to lift his head. Whisht!

[*A knock at the door, and the voice of* MRS. MADIGAN, *speaking very softly.*]

Mrs. Boyle, Mrs. Boyle.

[MRS. BOYLE *opens the door.*]

Mrs. Madigan. Oh, Mrs. Boyle, God an' His Blessed Mother be with you this night!

Mrs. Boyle. [*Calmly.*] What is it, Mrs. Madigan? It's Johnny—something about Johnny.

Mrs. Madigan. God send it's not, God send it's not Johnny!

Mrs. Boyle. Don't keep me waitin', Mrs. Madigan; I've gone through so much lately that I feel able for anything.

Mrs. Madigan. Two polismen below wantin' you.

Mrs. Boyle. Wantin' me; an' why do they want me?

Mrs. Madigan. Some poor fella's been found, an' they think it's, it's . . .

Mrs. Boyle. Johnny, Johnny!

Mary. [*With her arms round her mother.*] Oh, mother, mother, me poor, darlin' mother.

Mrs. Boyle. Hush, hush, darlin'; you'll shortly have your own throuble to bear. [*To* MRS. MADIGAN.] An' why do the polis think it's Johnny, Mrs. Madigan?

Mrs. Madigan. Because one o' the doctors knew him when he was attendin' with his poor arm.

Mrs. Boyle. Oh, it's thrue, then, it's Johnny, it's me son, me own son!

Mary. Oh, it's thrue, it's thrue what Jerry Devine says—there isn't a God, there isn't a God; if there was, He wouldn't let these things happen!

Mrs. Boyle. Mary, Mary, you mustn't say them things. We'll want all the help we can get from God an' His Blessed Mother now! These things have nothin' to do with the Will o' God. Ah, what can God do agen the stupidity o' men!

Mrs. Madigan. The polis want you to go with them to the hospital to see the poor body—they're waitin' below.

Mrs. Boyle. We'll go. Come, Mary, an' we'll never come back here agen. Let your father furrage for himself now; I've done all I could an' it was all no use—he'll be hopeless till the end of his days. I've got a little room in me sisther's where we'll stop till your throuble is over, an' then we'll work together for the sake of the baby.

Mary. My poor little child that'll have no father!

Mrs. Boyle. It'll have what's far betther—it'll have two mothers.

[*A rough voice shouting from below.*]

Are yous goin' to keep us waitin' for yous all night?

Mrs. Madigan. [*Going to the door, and shouting down.*] Take your hour, there, take your hour! If yous are in such a hurry, skip off, then, for nobody wants you here—if they did, yous wouldn't be found. For you're the same as yous were undher the British Government—never where yous are wanted! As far as I can see, the Polis as Polis, in this city, is Null an' Void!

Mrs. Boyle. We'll go, Mary, we'll go; you to see your poor dead brother, an' me to see my poor dead son!

Mary. I dhread it, mother, I dhread it!

Mrs. Boyle. I forgot, Mary, I forgot; your poor oul' selfish mother was only thinkin' of herself. No, no, you mustn't come—it wouldn't be good for you. You go on to me sisther's an' I'll face th' ordeal meself. Maybe I didn't feel sorry enough for Mrs. Tancred when her poor son was found as Johnny's been found now—because he was a Die-hard! Ah, why didn't I remember that then he wasn't a Die-hard or a Stater, but only a poor dead son! It's well I remember all that she said—an' it's my turn to say it now: What was the pain I suffered, Johnny, bringin' you into the world to carry you to your cradle to the pains I'll suffer carryin' you out o' the world to bring you to your grave! Mother o' God, Mother o' God, have pity on us all! Blessed Virgin, where were you when me darlin' son was riddled with bullets, when me darlin' son was riddled with bullets? Sacred Heart o' Jesus, take away our hearts o' stone, and give us hearts o' flesh! Take away this murdherin' hate, an' give us Thine own eternal love!

[*They all go slowly out.*]

[*There is a pause; then a sound of shuffling steps on the stairs outside. The door opens and* BOYLE *and* JOXER, *both of them very drunk, enter.*]

Boyle. I'm able to go no farther. . . . Two polis, ey . . . what were they doin' here, I wondher? . . . Up to no good, anyhow . . . an' Juno an' that lovely daughter o' mine with them. [*Taking a sixpence from his pocket and looking at it.*] Wan single, solithary tanner left out of all I borreyed. . . . [*He lets it fall.*] The last o' the Mohicans. . . . The blinds is down, Joxer, the blinds is down!

Joxer. [*Walking unsteadily across the*

room, and anchoring at the bed.] Put all . . . your throubles . . . in your oul' kit bag . . . an' smile . . . smile . . . smile!

Boyle. The counthry'll have to steady itself . . . it's goin' . . . to hell. . . . Where'r all . . . the chairs . . . gone to . . . steady itself, Joxer. . . . Chairs'll . . . have to . . . . . . steady themselves. . . . No matther . . . what any one may . . . say. . . . Irelan' sober . . . is Irelan' . . . free.

Joxer. [*Stretching himself on the bed.*] Chains . . . an' . . . slaveree . . . that's a darlin' motto . . . a daaarlin' . . . motto!

Boyle. If th' worst comes . . . to th' worse . . . I can join a . . . flyin' . . . column. . . . I done . . . me bit . . . in Easther Week . . . had no business . . . to . . . be . . . there . . . but Captain Boyle's Captain Boyle!

Joxer. Breathes there a man with soul . . . so . . . de . . . ad . . . this . . . me . . . o . . . wn, me nat . . . ive l . . . an'!

Boyle. [*Subsiding into a sitting posture on the floor.*] Commandant Kelly died . . . in them . . . arms . . . Joxer. . . . Tell me Volunteer Butties . . . says he . . . that . . . I died for . . . Irelan'!

Joxer. D'jever rade Willie . . . Reilly . . . an' his . . . own . . . Colleen . . . Bawn? It's a darlin' story, a daarlin' story!

Boyle. I'm telling you . . . Joxer . . . th' whole worl's . . . in a terr . . . ible state o' . . . chassis!

AMERICAN PLAYS

AMERICAN PLAYS

The Emperor Jones	O'Neill
Processional	Lawson
Beggar on Horseback	Kaufman and Connelly
The Silver Cord	Howard
"The Hairy Ape"	O'Neill
Street Scene	Rice
Hotel Universe	Barry
Elizabeth the Queen	Anderson
Abe Lincoln in Illinois	Sherwood

THE EMPEROR JONES*

By
EUGENE O'NEILL

EUGENE O'NEILL'S FATHER WAS JAMES O'Neill, an actor of considerable reputation, particularly for the leading rôle in *The Count of Monte Cristo*. James O'Neill's family used to tour with him while Eugene was a child, so that he early learned the ways of the theater. After one year at Princeton, he began wandering: hunting gold in Honduras, holding small clerkships for American firms in South America, working as muletender on a cattle-ship and as able seaman on a trans-Atlantic liner, with intervals of return to his father's company as player of small parts. He had been a reporter on a New London paper for a short time when he was ordered to a sanatorium for tuberculosis. While there he decided to become a writer.

After six months in the sanatorium he spent a year or so in writing and reading plays—especially Strindberg's, he says. Then he went to Harvard to study for one year under Professor George Pierce Baker in the famous 47 playwriting course. His first publication was *Thirst and Other One-Act Plays* in 1914, but no play of his was staged until 1916, when an amateur group under the leadership of George Cram Cook produced *Bound East for Cardiff* at the Wharf Theater in Provincetown. There and in New York the Provincetown Players, as they came to call themselves, first staged almost all of O'Neill's one-act plays. They also first performed *The Emperor Jones* in 1920, though earlier in the same year, *Beyond the Horizon,* O'Neill's first full-length play to be produced, had been staged by a commercial manager. O'Neill probably owes a great deal, however, to the Provincetown Players and through them to the Little Theater movement they represented.

Of the plays O'Neill wrote before 1918, though many were full-length, only the one-act plays have ever seen the stage, or been published. Since 1919, he has written only longer plays. Though fewer than half of the longer plays produced since 1920 have been successes, either commercially or with the critics, O'Neill has now, by his energy, his experimenting spirit, his sincerity, and his control of the instrument of the theater, won position as the most important American playwright and as a world figure. He has thrice won the Pulitzer Prize: in 1920 with *Beyond the Horizon*; in 1922 with *Anna Christie*; in 1928 with *Strange Interlude*. And in 1936 he was awarded the Nobel Prize in literature.

From 1923 to 1927 O'Neill was associated with Kenneth Macgowan and Robert Edmund Jones in the management of the Greenwich Village Theatre, where several of his plays were produced.

The Emperor Jones was the first long play to show O'Neill as experimenter. Through the greater part of the play it is practically a dramatic monologue revealing successive stages in Jones's fear. This dramatization of the mental processes, derived from Strindberg, is sometimes called Expressionism, though O'Neill disowns the label. The success of the play—it ran for over a year in New York, and has been often revived—no doubt prepared the way for the experiments that have so often appeared in the American theater since, and especially prepared the way for the sympathetic and serious use of negroes as dramatic characters.

During the first run of *The Emperor Jones* in 1920, and also during its revival in 1926, the noted negro actor, Charles Gilpin, played the leading rôle. The first production was directed by George Cram Cook, and the scenic designer was Cleon Throckmorton. It was noteworthy as one of the first instances of the use in this country of the plaster sky-dome as a substitute for the old canvas cyclorama, a device which gave extraordinarily successful outdoor effects. The play has been often produced abroad, as have also *Anna Christie, The Hairy Ape,* and *Desire Under the Elms.*

O'Neill has described the genesis of the play in an interview in the New York *World:*

"The idea of *The Emperor Jones* came from an old circus man I knew. This man told me a story current in Hayti concerning the late President Sam. This was to the effect that Sam had said they'd never get him with a lead bullet; that he would get himself first with a silver one. . . . This notion about the silver bullet struck me, and I made a note of the story. About six months later I got the idea of the woods, but I couldn't see how it could be done on the stage, and I passed it up again. A year elapsed. One day I was reading of the religious feasts in the Congo and the uses to which the drum is put there: how it starts at a normal pulse and is slowly intensified until the heart-beat of every one present corresponds to the frenzied beat of the drum. There was an idea and an experiment. How would this sort of thing work on an audience in a theater? The effect of the tropical forest on the human imagination was honestly come by. It was the result of my own experience while prospecting for gold in Spanish Honduras."

EUGENE O'NEILL

Born 1888, New York City. Son of the actor, James O'Neill.

1906–1907, Princeton University.

1909–1911, Wanderings and various occupations in Central and South America, in the United States, and at sea.

1911–1912, Actor, and reporter on *The Telegraph,* New London, Conn. Also contributed verse.

1913–1914, Illness and convalescence. Wrote his first play (*The Web*).

1914–1915, At Harvard University studied playwriting under Prof. G. P. Baker (English 47).

1916, *Bound East for Cardiff* given at the Wharf Theatre, Provincetown.

1920–1921, *Beyond the Horizon* (Pulitzer Prize), *The Emperor Jones,* and *Anna Christie* (Pulitzer Prize), his first Broadway successes.

1927, *Marco Millions,* his first play to be produced by the New York Theatre Guild.

1928, Awarded the Pulitzer Prize (third time) for *Strange Interlude.*

1936, Awarded Nobel Prize for literature.

PLAYS

1914 *Thirst and Other One-Act Plays* (published). (Contains *Thirst, The Web, Warnings, Fog,* and *Recklessness.*) 1916 *Bound East for Cardiff.* 1916 *Before Breakfast.* 1917 *The Sniper* (not published). 1917 *In the Zone.* 1917 *The Long Voyage Home.* 1917 *Ile.* 1918 *The Rope.* 1918 *Where the Cross Is Made.* 1918 *The Moon of the Caribbees.* 1919 *The Dreamy Kid.* 1920 *Beyond the Horizon.* 1920 *Chris Christopherson* (rewritten as *Anna Christie*). 1920 *Exorcism* (not published). 1920 *The Emperor Jones.* 1920 *Diff'rent.* 1921 *Gold.* 1921 *Anna Christie.* 1921 *The Straw.* 1922 *The First Man.* 1922 *The Hairy Ape.* 1924 *Welded.* 1924 *The Ancient Mariner* (not published). 1924 *All God's Chillun Got Wings.* 1924 *Desire Under the Elms.* 1924 *S. S. Glencairn* (*The Moon of the Caribbees, The Long Voyage Home, In the Zone, Bound East for Car-*

diff, presented together as full-length play). 1925 *The Fountain.* 1926 *The Great God Brown.* 1927 *Marco Millions.* 1927 *Lazarus Laughed.* 1928 *Strange Interlude.* 1929 *Dynamo.* 1931 *Mourning Becomes Electra.* 1933 *Ah, Wilderness!* 1934 *Days without End.*

WRITINGS ABOUT THE DRAMA

Letter to the New York *Times,* 11 April 1920. (About *Beyond the Horizon*). Letter to the New York newspapers, 13, 14 February 1926 (about *The Great God Brown*). See also letters and notes in Barrett H. Clark's *Eugene O'Neill,* 1929.

THE EMPEROR JONES

Characters

BRUTUS JONES, *Emperor.*
HENRY SMITHERS, *A Cockney Trader.*
AN OLD NATIVE WOMAN.
LEM, *A Native Chief.*
SOLDIERS, *Adherents of Lem.*
The Little Formless Fears; Jeff; The Negro Convicts; The Prison Guard; The Planters; The Auctioneer; The Slaves; The Congo Witch-Doctor; The Crocodile God.

The action of the play takes place on an island in the West Indies as yet not self-determined by White Marines. The form of native government is, for the time being, an Empire.

SCENES

I.—*In the palace of the Emperor Jones. Afternoon.*
II.—*The edge of the Great Forest. Dusk.*
III.—*In the Forest. Night.*
IV.—*In the Forest. Night.*
V.—*In the Forest. Night.*
VI.—*In the Forest. Night.*
VII.—*In the Forest. Night.*
VIII.—*Same as Scene Two—the edge of the Great Forest. Dawn.*

SCENE ONE

The audience chamber in the palace of the Emperor—a spacious, high-ceilinged room with bare, white-washed walls. The floor is of white tiles. In the rear, to the left of center, a wide archway giving out on a portico with white pillars. The palace is evidently situated on high ground, for beyond the portico nothing can be seen but a vista of distant hills, their summits crowned with thick groves of palm trees. In the right wall, center, a smaller arched doorway leading to the living quarters of the palace. The room is bare of furniture with the exception of one huge chair made of uncut wood which stands at center, its back to rear. This is very apparently the Emperor's throne. It is painted a dazzling, eye-smiting scarlet. There is a brilliant orange cushion on the seat and another smaller one is placed on the floor to serve as a footstool. Strips of matting, dyed scarlet, lead from the foot of the throne to the two entrances.

It is late afternoon, but the sunlight still blazes yellowly beyond the portico and there is an oppressive burden of exhausting heat in the air.

[*As the curtain rises, a native* NEGRO WOMAN *sneaks in cautiously from the entrance on the right. She is very old, dressed in cheap calico, bare-footed, a red bandana handkerchief covering all but a few stray wisps of white hair. A bundle bound in colored cloth is carried over her shoulder on the end of a stick. She hesitates beside the doorway, peering back as if in extreme dread of being discovered. Then she begins to glide noiselessly, a step at a time, toward the doorway in the rear. At this moment* SMITHERS *appears beneath the portico.* SMITHERS *is a tall, stoop-shouldered man about forty. His bald head, perched on a long neck with an enormous Adam's apple, looks like an egg. The tropics have tanned his naturally pasty face with its small, sharp features to a sickly yellow, and native rum has painted his pointed nose to a startling red. His little, washy-blue eyes are red-rimmed and dart about him like a ferret's. His ex-*

pression is one of unscrupulous meanness, cowardly and dangerous. He is dressed in a worn riding suit of dirty white drill, puttees, spurs, and wears a white cork helmet. A cartridge belt with an automatic revolver is around his waist. He carries a riding whip in his hand. He sees the WOMAN *and stops to watch her suspiciously. Then, making up his mind, he steps quickly on tiptoe into the room. The* WOMAN, *looking back over her shoulder continually, does not see him until it is too late. When she does* SMITHERS *springs forward and grabs her firmly by the shoulder. She struggles to get away, fiercely but silently.*]

Smithers. [*Tightening his grasp—roughly.*] Easy! None o' that, me birdie. You can't wriggle out, now I got me 'ooks on yer.

Woman. [*Seeing the uselessness of struggling, gives way to frantic terror, and sinks to the ground, embracing his knees supplicatingly.*] No tell him! No tell him, Mister!

Smithers. [*With great curiosity.*] Tell 'im? [*Then scornfully.*] Oh, you mean 'is bloomin' Majesty. What's the gaime, any'ow? What are you sneakin' away for? Been stealin' a bit, I s'pose.

[*He taps her bundle with his riding whip significantly.*]

Woman. [*Shaking her head vehemently.*] No, me no steal.

Smithers. Bloody liar! But tell me what's up. There's somethin' funny goin' on. I smelled it in the air first thing I got up this mornin'. You blacks are up to some devilment. This palace of 'is is like a bleedin' tomb. Where's all the 'ands? [*The* WOMAN *keeps sullenly silent.* SMITHERS *raises his whip threateningly.*] Ow, yer won't, won't yer? I'll show yer what's what.

Woman. [*Coweringly.*] I tell, Mister. You no hit. They go—all go.

[*She makes a sweeping gesture toward the hills in the distance.*]

Smithers. Run away—to the 'ills?

Woman. Yes, Mister. Him Emperor—Great Father. [*She touches her forehead to the floor with a quick mechanical jerk.*] Him sleep after eat. Then they go—all go. Me old woman. Me left only. Now me go too.

Smithers. [*His astonishment giving way to an immense, mean satisfaction.*] Ow! So that's the ticket! Well, I know bloody well wot's in the air—when they runs orf to the 'ills. The tom-tom'll be thumping out there bloomin' soon. [*With extreme vindictiveness.*] And I'm bloody glad of it, for one! Serve 'im right! Puttin' on airs, the stinkin' nigger! 'Is Majesty! Gawd blimey! I only 'opes I'm there when they takes 'im out to shoot 'im. [*Suddenly.*] 'E's still 'ere all right, ain't 'e?

Woman. Him sleep.

Smithers. 'E's bound to find out soon as 'e wakes up. 'E's cunnin' enough to know when 'is time's come. [*He goes to the doorway on right and whistles shrilly with his fingers in his mouth. The* OLD WOMAN *springs to her feet and runs out of the doorway, rear.* SMITHERS *goes after her, reaching for his revolver.*] Stop or I'll shoot. [*Then stopping—indifferently.*] Pop orf then, if yer like, yer black cow.

[*He stands in the doorway, looking after her.* JONES *enters from the right. He is a tall, powerfully built, full-blooded negro of middle age. His features are typically negroid, yet there is something decidedly distinctive about his face—an underlying strength of will, a hardy, self-reliant confidence in himself that inspires respect. His eyes are alive with a keen, cunning intelligence. In manner he is shrewd, suspicious, evasive. He wears a light blue uniform coat, sprayed with brass buttons, heavy gold chevrons on his shoulders, gold braid on the collar, cuffs, etc. His pants are bright red with a light blue stripe down the side. Patent-leather laced boots with brass spurs, and a belt with a long-barreled, pearl-handled revolver in a holster complete his make up. Yet there is something not altogether ridiculous about his grandeur. He has a way of carrying it off.*]

Jones. [*Not seeing anyone—greatly irritated and blinking sleepily—shouts:*] Who dare whistle dat way in my palace? Who dare wake up de Emperor? I'll git de hide frayled off some o' you niggers sho'!

Smithers. [*Showing himself—in a manner half-afraid and half-defiant.*] It was me whistled to yer. [*As* JONES *frowns angrily.*] I got news for yer.

Jones. [*Putting on his suavest manner, which fails to cover up his contempt for the white man.*] Oh, it's you, Mister Smithers. [*He sits down on his throne with easy dignity.*] What news you got to tell me?

Smithers. [*Coming close to enjoy his discomfiture.*] Don't yer notice nothin' funny today?

Jones. [*Coldly.*] Funny? No. I ain't perceived nothin' of de kind!

Smithers. Then yer ain't so foxy as I thought yer was. Where's all your court? [*Sarcastically.*] The Generals and the Cabinet Ministers and all?

Jones. [*Imperturbably.*] Where dey mostly runs to minute I closes my eyes—drinkin' rum and talkin' big down in de town. [*Sarcastically.*] How come you don't know that? Ain't you sousin' with 'em most every day?

Smithers. [*Stung but pretending indifference—with a wink:*] That's part of the day's work. I got ter—ain't I—in my business?

Jones. [*Contemptuously.*] Yo' business!

Smithers. [*Imprudently enraged.*] Gawd blimey, you was glad enough for me ter take yer in on it when you landed here first. You didn't 'ave no 'igh and mighty airs in them days!

Jones. [*His hand going to his revolver like a flash—menacingly:*] Talk polite, white man! Talk polite, you heah me! I'm boss heah now, is you fergettin'?

[*The Cockney seems about to challenge this last statement with the facts, but something in the other's eyes holds and cows him.*]

Smithers. [*In a cowardly whine.*] No 'arm meant, old top.

Jones. [*Condescendingly.*] I accepts yo' apology. [*Lets his hand fall from his revolver.*] No use'n you rakin' up ole times. What I was den is one thing. What I is now's another. You didn't let me in on yo' crooked work out o' no kind feelin's dat time. I done de dirty work fo' you—and most o' de brain work, too, fo' dat matter—and I was wu'th money to you, dat's de reason.

Smithers. Well, blimey, I give yer a start, didn't I?—when no one else would. I wasn't afraid to 'ire you like the rest was—'count of the story about your breakin' jail back in the States.

Jones. No, you didn't have no s'cuse to look down on me fo' dat. You been in jail you'self more'n once.

Smithers. [*Furiously.*] It's a lie! [*Then, trying to pass it off by an attempt at scorn.*] Garn! Who told yer that fairy tale?

Jones. Dey's some tings I ain't got to be tole. I kin see 'em in folk's eyes. [*Then, after a pause—meditatively.*] Yes, you sho' give me a start. And it didn't take long from dat time to git dese fool, woods' niggers right where I wanted dem. [*With pride.*] From stowaway to Emperor in two years! Dat's goin' some!

Smithers. [*With curiosity.*] And I bet you got yer pile o' money 'id safe some place.

Jones. [*With satisfaction.*] I sho' has! And it's in a foreign bank where no pusson don't ever git it out but me, no matter what come. You didn't s'pose I was holdin' down dis Emperor job for de glory in it, did you? Sho'! De fuss and glory part of it, dat's only to turn de heads o' de low-flung, bush niggers dat's here. Dey wants de big circus show for deir money. I gives it to 'em an' I gits de money. [*With a grin.*] De long green, dat's me every time. [*Then, rebukingly:*] But you ain't got no kick agin me, Smithers. I'se paid you back all you done for me many times. Ain't I pertected you and winked at all de crooked tradin' you been doin' right out in de broad day? Sho' I has—and me makin' laws to stop it at de same time! [*He chuckles.*]

Smithers. [*Grinning.*] But, meanin' no 'arm, you been grabbin' right and left yourself, ain't yer? Look at the taxes you've put on 'em! Blimey! You've squeezed 'em dry!

Jones. [*Chuckling.*] No, dey ain't *all* dry yet. I'se still heah, ain't I?

Smithers. [*Smiling at his secret thought.*] They're dry right now, you'll find out. [*Changing the subject abruptly.*] And as for me breakin' laws, you've broke 'em all yerself just as fast as yer made 'em.

Jones. Ain't I de Emperor? De laws don't go for him. [*Judicially.*] You heah what I tells you, Smithers. Dere's little stealin' like you does, and dere's big stealin' like I does. For de little stealin' dey gits you in jail soon or late. For de big stealin' dey makes you Emperor and puts you in de Hall o' Fame when you croaks. [*Reminiscently.*] If dey's one thing I learns in ten years on de Pullman ca's listenin' to de white quality talk, it's dat same fact. And when I gits a chance to use it I winds up Emperor in two years.

Smithers. [*Unable to repress the genuine admiration of the small fry for the large.*] Yes, yer turned the bleedin' trick, all right. Blimey, I never seen a bloke 'as 'ad the bloomin' luck you 'as.

Jones. [*Severely.*] Luck? What you mean—luck?

Smithers. I suppose you'll say as that swank about the silver bullet ain't luck—and that was what first got the fool blacks on yer side the time of the revolution, wasn't it?

Jones. [*With a laugh.*] Oh, dat silver bullet! Sho' was luck! But I makes dat luck, you heah? I loads de dice! Yessuh! When dat murderin' nigger ole Lem hired to kill me takes aim ten feet away and his gun misses fire and I shoots him dead, what you heah me say?

Smithers. You said yer'd got a charm so's no lead bullet'd kill yer. You was so strong only a silver bullet could kill yer, you told 'em. Blimey, wasn't that swank for yer—and plain, fat-'eaded luck?

Jones. [*Proudly.*] I got brains and I uses 'em quick. Dat ain't luck.

Smithers. Yer know they wasn't 'ardly liable to get no silver bullets. And it was luck 'e didn't 'it you that time.

Jones. [*Laughing.*] And dere all dem fool bush niggers was kneelin' down and bumpin' deir heads on de ground like I was a miracle out o' de Bible. Oh Lawd, from dat time on I has dem all eatin' out of my hand. I cracks de whip and dey jumps through.

Smithers. [*With a sniff.*] Yankee bluff done it.

Jones. Ain't a man's talkin' big what makes him big—long as he makes folks believe it? Sho', I talks large when I ain't got nothin' to back it up, but I ain't talkin' wild just de same. I knows I kin fool 'em—I *knows* it—and dat's backin' enough fo' my game. And ain't I got to learn deir lingo and teach some of dem English befo' I kin talk to 'em? Ain't dat wuk? You ain't never learned ary word er it, Smithers, in de ten years you been heah, dough you knows it's money in you' pocket tradin' wid 'em if you does. But you'se too shiftless to take de trouble.

Smithers. [*Flushing.*] Never mind about me. What's this I've 'eard about yer really 'avin' a silver bullet molded for yourself?

Jones. It's playin' out my bluff. I has de silver bullet molded and I tells 'em when de time comes I kills myself wid it. I tells 'em dat's 'cause I'm de on'y man in de world big enuff to git me. No use'n deir tryin'. And dey falls down and bumps deir heads. [*He laughs.*] I does dat so's I kin take a walk in peace widout no jealous nigger gunnin' at me from behind de trees.

Smithers. [*Astonished.*] Then you 'ad it made—'onest?

Jones. Sho' did. Heah she be. [*He takes out his revolver, breaks it, and takes the silver bullet out of one chamber.*] Five lead an' dis silver baby at de last. Don't she shine pretty?

[*He holds it in his hand, looking at it admiringly, as if strangely fascinated.*]

Smithers. Let me see.

[*Reaches out his hand for it.*]

Jones. [*Harshly.*] Keep yo' hands whar dey b'long, white man.

[*He replaces it in the chamber and puts the revolver back on his hip.*]

Smithers. [*Snarling.*] Gawd blimey! Think I'm a bleedin' thief, you would.

Jones. No, 'tain't dat. I knows you'se scared to steal from me. On'y I ain't 'lowin' nary a body to touch dis baby. She's my rabbit's foot.

Smithers. [*Sneering.*] A bloomin' charm, wot? [*Venomously.*] Well, you'll need all the bloody charms you 'as before long, s' 'elp me!

Jones. [*Judicially.*] Oh, I'se good for six months yit 'fore dey gits sick o' my game. Den, when I sees trouble comin', I makes my getaway.

Smithers. Ho! You got it all planned, ain't yer?

Jones. I ain't no fool. I knows dis Emperor's time is sho't. Dat why I make hay when de sun shine. Was you thinkin' I'se aimin' to hold down dis job for life? No, suh! What good is gittin' money if you stays back in dis raggedy country? I wants action when I spends. And when I sees dese niggers gittin' up deir nerve to tu'n me out, and I'se got all de money in sight, I resigns on de spot and beats it quick.

Smithers. Where to?

Jones. None o' yo' business.

Smithers. Not back to the bloody States, I'll lay my oath.

Jones. [*Suspiciously.*] Why don't I? [*Then, with an easy laugh.*] You mean 'count of dat story 'bout me breakin' from jail back dere? Dat's all talk.

Smithers. [*Skeptically.*] Ho, yes!

Jones. [*Sharply.*] You ain't 'sinuatin' I'se a liar, is you?

Smithers. [*Hastily.*] No, Gawd strike me! I was only thinkin' o' the bloody lies you told the blacks 'ere about killin' white men in the States.

Jones. [*Angered.*] How come dey're lies?

Smithers. You'd 'ave been in jail if you 'ad, wouldn't yer then? [*With venom.*] And from what I've 'eard, it ain't 'ealthy for a black to kill a white man in the States. They burns 'em in oil, don't they?

Jones. [*With cool deadliness.*] You mean lynchin' 'd scare me? Well, I tells you, Smithers, maybe I does kill one white man back dere. Maybe I does. And maybe I kills another right heah 'fore long if he don't look out.

Smithers. [*Trying to force a laugh.*] I was on'y spoofin' yer. Can't yer take a joke? And you was just sayin' you'd never been in jail.

Jones. [*In the same tone—slightly boastful.*] Maybe I goes to jail dere for gettin' in an argument wid razors ovah a crap game.

Maybe I gits twenty years when dat colored man die. Maybe I gits in 'nother argument wid de prison guard was overseer ovah us when we're wukin' de road. Maybe he hits me wid a whip and I splits his head wid a shovel and runs away and files de chain off my leg and gits away safe. Maybe I does all dat an' maybe I don't. It's a story I tells you so's you knows I'se de kind of man dat if you evah repeats one word of it, I ends you' stealin' on dis yearth mighty damn quick!

Smithers. [*Terrified.*] Think I'd peach on yer? Not me! Ain't I always been yer friend?

Jones. [*Suddenly relaxing.*] Sho' you has —and you better be.

Smithers. [*Recovering his composure— and with it his malice.*] And just to show yer I'm yer friend, I'll tell yer that bit o' news I was goin' to.

Jones. Go ahead! Shoot de piece. Must be bad news from de happy way you look.

Smithers. [*Warningly.*] Maybe it's gettin' time for you to resign—with that bloomin' silver bullet, wot?

[*He finishes with a mocking grin.*]

Jones. [*Puzzled.*] What's dat you say? Talk plain.

Smithers. Ain't noticed any of the guards or servants about the place today, I 'aven't.

Jones. [*Carelessly.*] Dey're all out in de garden sleepin' under de trees. When I sleeps, dey sneaks a sleep, too, and I pretends I never suspicions it. All I got to do is to ring de bell and dey come flyin', makin' a bluff dey was wukin' all de time.

Smithers. [*In the same mocking tone.*] Ring the bell now an' you'll bloody well see what I means.

Jones. [*Startled to alertness, but preserving the same careless tone.*] Sho' I rings.

[*He reaches below the throne and pulls out a big common dinner bell which is painted the same vivid scarlet as the throne. He rings this vigorously—then stops to listen. Then he goes to both doors, rings again, and looks out.*]

Smithers. [*Watching him with malicious satisfaction, after a pause—mockingly.*] The bloody ship is sinkin' an' the bleedin' rats 'as slung their 'ooks.

Jones. [*In a sudden fit of anger flings the bell clattering into a corner.*] Low-flung, woods' niggers! [*Then catching* SMITHERS' *eye on him, he controls himself and suddenly bursts into a low chuckling laugh.*] Reckon I overplays my hand dis once! A man can't take de pot on a bob-tailed flush all de time. Was I sayin' I'd sit in six months mo'? Well, I'se changed my mind den. I cashes in and resigns de job of Emperor right dis minute.

Smithers. [*With real admiration.*] Blimey, but you're a cool bird, and no mistake.

Jones. No use'n fussin'. When I knows de game's up I kisses it good-by widout no long waits. Dey've all run off to de hills, ain't dey?

Smithers. Yes—every bleedin' man jack of 'em.

Jones. Den de revolution is at de post. And de Emperor better git his feet smokin' up de trail.

[*He starts for the door in rear.*]

Smithers. Goin' out to look for your 'orse? Yer won't find any. They steals the 'orses first thing. Mine was gone when I went for 'im this mornin'. That's wot first give me a suspicion of wot was up.

Jones. [*Alarmed for a second, scratches his head, then philosophically:*] Well, den, I hoofs it. Feet, do yo' duty. [*He pulls out a gold watch and looks at it.*] Three-thuty. Sundown's at six-thuty or dereabouts. [*Puts his watch back—with cool confidence:*] I got plenty o' time to make it easy.

Smithers. Don't be so bloomin' sure of it. They'll be after you 'ot and 'eavy. Ole Lem is at the bottom o' this business an' 'e 'ates you like 'ell. 'E'd rather do for you than eat 'is dinner, 'e would!

Jones. [*Scornfully.*] Dat fool no-count nigger! Does you think I'se scared o' him? I stands him on his thick head more'n once befo' dis, and I does it again if he comes in n. way—— [*Fiercely.*] And dis time I leave him a dead nigger fo' sho'!

Smithers. You'll 'ave to cut through the big forest—an' these blacks 'ere can sniff and follow a trail in the dark like 'ounds. You'd 'ave to 'ustle to get through that forest in twelve hours even if you knew all the bloomin' trails like a native.

Jones. [*With indignant scorn.*] Look-a-heah, white man! Does you think I'se a natural-bo'n fool? Give me credit fo' havin' some sense, fo' Lawd's sake! Don't you s'pose I'se looked ahead and made sho' of all de chances? I'se gone out in dat big forest, pretendin' to hunt, so many times dat I knows it high an' low like a book. I could go through on dem trails wid my eyes shut. [*With great contempt.*] Think dese ign'rent bush niggers, dat ain't got brains enuff to know deir own names even, can catch Brutus Jones? Huh, I s'pects not! Not on yo' life! Why, man, de white men went after me wid bloodhounds where I come from an' I jes' laughs at 'em. It's a shame to fool dese black trash around heah, dey're so easy. You watch me, man. I'll make dem look sick, I will. I'll be 'cross de plain to de edge of de forest by time dark comes. Once in de woods in de night, dey got a swell chance o' findin' dis baby! Dawn tomorrow I'll be out at de oder side and on de coast whar dat French gunboat is stayin'. She picks me up, takes me to Martinique when she go dar, and dere I is safe wid a mighty big bankroll in my jeans. It's easy as rollin' off a log.

Smithers. [*Maliciously.*] But s'posin' somethin' 'appens wrong an' they do nab yer?

Jones. [*Decisively.*] Dey don't—dat's de answer.

Smithers. But, just for argyment's sake—what'd you do?

Jones. [*Frowning.*] I'se got five lead bullets in dis gun good enuff fo' common bush niggers—and after dat I got de silver bullet left to cheat 'em out o' gittin' me.

Smithers. [*Jeeringly.*] Ho, I was fergettin' that silver bullet. You'll bump yourself orf in style, won't yer? Blimey!

Jones. [*Gloomily.*] You kin bet yo' whole roll on one thing, white man. Dis baby plays out his string to de end and when he quits, he quits wid a bang de way he ought. Silver bullet ain't none too good for him when he go, dat's a fac'! [*Then shaking off his nervousness—with a confident laugh.*] Sho'! What is I talkin' about? Ain't come to dat yit and I never will—not wid trash niggers like dese yere. [*Boastfully.*] Silver bullet bring me luck, anyway. I kin outguess, outrun, outfight, an' outplay de whole lot o' dem all ovah de board any time o' de day er night! You watch me!

[*From the distant hills comes the faint, steady thump of a tom-tom, low and vibrating. It starts at a rate exactly corresponding to normal pulse beat—72 to the minute—and continues at a gradually accelerating rate from this point uninterruptedly to the very end of the play.*]

Jones. [*Starts at the sound. A strange look of apprehension creeps into his face for a moment as he listens. Then he asks, with an attempt to regain his most casual manner:*] What's dat drum beatin' fo'?

Smithers. [*With a mean grin.*] For you. That means the bleedin' ceremony 'as started. I've 'eard it before and I knows.

Jones. Cer'mony? What cer'mony?

Smithers. The blacks is 'oldin' a bloody meetin', 'avin' a war dance, gettin' their courage worked up b'fore they starts after you.

Jones. Let dem! Dey'll sho' need it!

Smithers. And they're there 'oldin' their 'eathen religious service—makin' no end of devil spells and charms to 'elp 'em against your silver bullet. [*He guffaws loudly.*] Blimey, but they're balmy as 'ell!

Jones. [*A tiny bit awed and shaken in spite of himself.*] Huh! Takes more'n dat to scare dis chicken!

Smithers. [*Scenting the other's feeling—maliciously:*] Ternight when it's pitch black in the forest, they'll 'ave their pet devils and ghosts 'oundin' after you. You'll find yer bloody 'air'll be standin' on end before termorrow mornin'. [*Seriously.*] It's a bleedin' queer place, that stinkin' forest, even in daylight. Yer don't know what might 'appen in there, it's that rotten still. Always sends the cold shivers down my back minute I gets in it.

Jones. [*With a contemptuous sniff.*] I ain't no chicken-liver like you is. Trees an' me, we'se friends, and dar's a full moon comin' bring me light. And let dem po' niggers make all de fool spells dey'se a min' to. Does yo' s'pect I'se silly enuff to b'lieve in ghosts an' ha'nts an' all dat ole woman's talk? G'long, white man! You ain't talkin' to me. [*With a chuckle.*] Doesn't you know dey's got to do wid a man was member in good standin' o' de Baptist Church? Sho', I was dat when I was porter on de Pullmans, befo' I gits into my little trouble. Let dem try deir heathen tricks. De Baptist Church done pertect me and land dem all in hell. [*Then, with more confident satisfaction:*] And I'se got little silver bullet o' my own, don't forgit!

Smithers. Ho! You 'aven't give much 'eed to your Baptist Church since you been down 'ere. I've 'eard myself you 'ad turned yer coat an' was takin' up with their blarsted witch-doctors, or whatever the 'ell yer calls the swine.

Jones. [*Vehemently.*] I pretends to! Sho' I pretends! Dat's part o' my game from de fust. If I finds out dem niggers believes dat black is white, den I yells it out louder 'n deir loudest. It don't git me nothin' to do missionary work for de Baptist Church. I'se after de coin, an' I lays my Jesus on de shelf for de time bein'. [*Stops abruptly to look at his watch—alertly:*] But I ain't got de time to waste on no more fool talk wid you. I'se gwine away from heah dis secon'. [*He reaches in under the throne and pulls out an expensive Panama hat with a bright multicolored band and sets it jauntily on his head.*] So long, white man! [*With a grin.*] See you in jail sometime, maybe!

Smithers. Not me, you won't. Well, I wouldn't be in yer bloody boots for no bloomin' money, but 'ere's wishin' yer luck just the same.

Jones. [*Contemptuously.*] You're de frightenedest man evah I see! I tells you I'se safe's 'f I was in New York City. It takes dem niggers from now to dark to git up de nerve to start somethin'. By dat time, I'se got a head start dey never kotch up wid.

Smithers. [*Maliciously.*] Give my regards to any ghosts yer meet up with.

Jones. [*Grinning.*] If dat ghost got money, I'll tell him never ha'nt you less'n he wants to lose it.

Smithers. [*Flattered.*] Garn! [*Then, curiously.*] Ain't yer takin' no luggage with yer?

Jones. I travels light when I wants to move fast. And I got tinned grub buried on de edge o' de forest. [*Boastfully.*] Now say dat I don't look ahead an' use my brains! [*With a wide, liberal gesture:*] I will all dat's left in de palace to you—and you better grab all you kin sneak away wid befo' dey gits here.

Smithers. [*Gratefully.*] Righto — and thanks ter yer. [*As* JONES *walks toward the door in rear—cautioningly:*] Say! Look 'ere, you ain't goin' out that way, are yer?

Jones. Does you think I'd slink out de back door like a common nigger? I'se Emperor yit, ain't I? And de Emperor Jones leaves de way he comes, and dat black trash don't dare stop him—not yit, leastways. [*He stops for a moment in the doorway, listening to the far-off but insistent beat of the tom-tom.*] Listen to dat roll-call, will you? Must be mighty big drum carry dat far. [*Then with a laugh.*] Well, if dey ain't no whole brass band to see me off, I sho' got de drum part of it. So long, white man.

[*He puts his hands in his pockets and with studied carelessness, whistling a tune, he saunters out of the doorway and off to the left.*]

Smithers. [*Looks after him with a puzzled admiration.*] 'E's got 'is bloomin' nerve with 'im, s'elp me! [*Then angrily.*] Ho—the bleedin' nigger—puttin' on 'is bloody airs! I 'opes they nabs 'im an' gives 'im what's what!

CURTAIN

SCENE TWO

The end of the plain where the Great Forest begins. The foreground is sandy, level ground dotted by a few stones and clumps of stunted bushes cowering close against the earth to escape the buffeting of the trade wind. In the rear the forest is a wall of darkness dividing the world. Only when the eye becomes accustomed to the gloom can the outlines of separate trunks of the nearest trees be made out, enormous pillars of deeper blackness. A somber monotone of wind lost in the leaves moans in the air. Yet this sound serves but to intensify the impression of the forest's relentless immobility, to form a background throwing into relief its brooding, implacable silence.

[JONES *enters from the left, walking rapidly. He stops as he nears the edge of the forest, looks around him quickly, peering into the dark as if searching for some familiar landmark. Then, apparently satisfied that he is where he ought to be, he throws himself on the ground, dog-tired.*]

Jones. Well, heah I is. In de nick o' time, oo! Little mo' an' it'd be blacker'n de ace of spades heahabouts. [*He pulls a bandana handkerchief from his hip pocket and mops off his perspiring face.*] Sho'! Gimme air! I'se tuckered out sho' 'nuff. Dat soft Emperor job ain't no trainin' fo' a long hike ovah dat plain in de brilin' sun. [*Then with a chuckle.*] Cheer up, nigger, de worst is yet to come. [*He lifts his head and stares at the forest. His chuckle peters out abruptly. In a tone of awe.*] My goodness, look at dem woods, will you? Dat no-count Smithers said dey'd be black an' he sho' called de turn. [*Turning away from them quickly and looking down at his feet, he snatches at a chance to change the subject—solicitously:*] Feet, you is holdin' up yo' end fine an' I sutinly hopes you ain't blisterin' none. It's time you git a rest. [*He takes off his shoes, his eyes studiously avoiding the forest. He feels of the soles of his feet gingerly.*] You is still in de pink—on'y a little mite feverish. Cool yo'selfs. Remember you done got a long journey yit befo' you. [*He sits in a weary attitude, listening to the rhythmic beating of the tom-tom. He grumbles in a loud tone to cover up a growing uneasiness.*] Bush niggers! Wonder dey wouldn't git sick o' beatin' dat drum. Sound louder, seem like. I wonder if dey's startin' after me? [*He scrambles to his feet, looking back across the plain.*] Couldn't see dem now, nohow, if dey was hundred feet away. [*Then shaking himself like a wet dog to get rid of these depressing thoughts.*] Sho', dey's miles an' miles behind. What you gittin' fidgety about? [*But he sits down and begins to lace up his shoes in great haste, all the time muttering reassuringly:*] You know what? Yo' belly is empty, dat's what's de matter wid you. Come time to eat! Wid nothin' but wind on yo' stomach, o' course you feels jiggedy. Well, we eats right heah an' now soon's I gits these pesky shoes laced up. [*He finishes lacing up his shoes.*] Dere! Now le's see! [*Gets on his hands and knees and searches the ground around him with his eyes.*] White stone, white stone, where is you? [*He sees the first white stone and crawls to it—with satisfaction.*] Heah you is! I knowed dis was de right place. Box of grub, come to me. [*He turns over the stone and feels in under it—in a tone of dismay:*] Ain't heah! Gorry, is I in de right place or isn't I? Dere's 'nother stone. Guess dat's it. [*He scrambles to the next stone and turns it over.*] Ain't heah, neither! Grub, whar is you? Ain't heah. Gorry, has I got to go hungry into dem woods—all de night? [*While he is talking he scrambles from one stone to another, turning them over in frantic haste. Finally, he jumps to his feet excitedly.*] Is I lost de place? Must have! But how dat happen when I was followin' de trail across de plain in broad daylight? [*Almost plaintively:*] I'se hungry, I is! I gotta git my feed. Whar's my strength gonna come from if I doesn't? Gorry, I gotta find dat grub high an' low somehow! Why it come dark so quick like dat? Can't see nothin'. [*He scratches a match on his trousers and peers about him. The rate of the beat of the far-off tom-tom increases perceptibly as he does so. He mutters in a bewildered voice:*] How come all dese white stones come heah when I only remembers one? [*Suddenly, with a frightened gasp, he flings the match on the ground and stamps on it.*] Nigger, is you gone crazy mad? Is you lightin' matches to show dem whar you is? Fo' Lawd's sake, use yo' haid. Gorry, I'se got to be careful! [*He stares at the plain behind him apprehensively, his hand on his revolver.*] But how come all dese white stones? And whar's dat tin box o' grub I hid all wrapped up in oilcloth?

[*While his back is turned, the* LITTLE FORMLESS FEARS *creep out from the deeper blackness of the forest. They are black, shapeless, only their glittering little eyes can be seen. If they have any describable form at all it is that of a grubworm about the size of a creeping child. They move noiselessly, but with deliberate, painful effort, striving to raise themselves on end, failing and sinking prone again.* JONES *turns about to face the forest. He stares up at the tops of the trees, seeking vainly to discover his whereabouts by their conformation.*]

Jones. Can't tell nothin' from dem trees! Gorry, nothin' 'round heah looks like I evah seed it befo'. I'se done lost de place sho' 'nuff! [*With mournful foreboding:*] It's mighty queer! It's mighty queer! [*With sudden forced defiance—in an angry tone:*] Woods, is you tryin' to put somethin' ovah on me?

[*From the* FORMLESS CREATURES *on the ground in front of him comes a tiny gale of low, mocking laughter like a rustling of leaves. They squirm upward toward him in twisted attitudes.* JONES *looks down, leaps backward with a yell of terror, yanking out his revolver as he does so—in a quavering voice:*]

Jones. What's dat? Who's dar? What is you? Git away from me befo' I shoots you up! You don't?——

[*He fires. There is a flash, a loud report, then silence broken only by the far-off, quickened throb of the tom-tom. The* FORMLESS CREATURES *have scurried back into the forest.* JONES *remains fixed in his position, listening intently. The sound of the shot, the reassuring feel of the revolver in his hand, have somewhat restored his shaken nerve. He addresses himself with renewed confidence.*]

Jones. Dey're gone. Dat shot fix 'em. Dey was only little animals—little wild pigs, I reckon. Dey've maybe rooted out yo' grub an' eat it. Sho', you fool nigger, what you think dey is—ha'nts? [*Excitedly:*] Gorry, you give de game away when you fire dat shot. Dem niggers heah dat fo' su'tin! Time you beat it in de woods widout no long waits. [*He starts for the forest—hesitates before the plunge—then urging himself in with manful resolution:*] Git in, nigger! What you skeered at? Ain't nothin' dere but de trees! Git in!

[*He plunges boldly into the forest.*]

SCENE THREE

In the forest. The moon has just risen. Its beams, drifting through the canopy of leaves, make a barely perceptible, suffused, eerie glow. A dense, low wall of underbrush and creepers is in the nearer foreground, fencing in a small triangular clearing. Beyond this is the massed blackness of the forest like an encompassing barrier. A path is dimly discerned leading down to the clearing from left, rear, and winding away from it again toward the right. As the scene opens, nothing can be distinctly made out. Except for the beating of the tom-tom, which is a trifle louder and quicker than at the close of the previous scene, there is silence, broken every few seconds by a queer, clicking sound.

[*Then gradually the figure of the negro,* JEFF, *can be discerned crouching on his haunches at the rear of the triangle. He is middle-aged, thin, brown in color, is dressed in a Pullman porter's uniform and cap. He is throwing a pair of dice on the ground before him, picking them up, shaking them, casting them out with the regular, rigid, mechanical movements of an automaton. The heavy, plodding footsteps of some one approaching along the trail from the left are heard and* JONES'S *voice, pitched on a slightly higher key and strained in a cheery effort to overcome its own tremors.*]

Jones. De moon's rizen. Does you heah dat, nigger? You gits more light from dis out. No mo' buttin' yo' fool head again' de trunks an' scratchin' de hide off yo' legs in de bushes. Now you sees whar yo'se gwine. So cheer up! From now on you has a snap. [*He steps just to the rear of the triangular clearing and mops off his face on his sleeve. He has lost his Panama hat. His face is scratched, his brilliant uniform shows several large rents.*] What time's it gittin' to be, I wonder? I dassent light no match to find out. Phoo'. It's wa'm an' dat's a fac'! [*Wearily.*] How long I been makin' tracks in dese woods? Must be hours an' hours. Seems like fo'evah! Yit can't be, when de moon's jes' riz. Dis am a long night fo' yo', yo' Majesty! [*With a mournful chuckle:*] Majesty! Der ain't much majesty 'bout dis baby now. [*With attempted cheerfulness:*] Never min'. It's all part o' de game. Dis night come to an end like everything else. And when you gits dar safe and has dat bank-roll in yo' hands, you laughs at all dis. [*He starts to whistle but checks himself abruptly.*] What yo' whistlin' for, you po' dope! Want all de worl' to heah you? [*He stops talking to listen.*] Heah dat ole drum? Sho' gits nearer from de sound. Dey's packin' it along wid 'em. Time fo' me to move. [*He takes a step forward, then stops—worriedly:*] What's dat odder queer clickety sound I heah? Dere it is! Sound close! Sound like—sound like—— Fo' God sake, sound like some nigger was shootin' crap! [*Frightenedly:*] I better beat it quick when I gits dem notions. [*He walks quickly into the clear space—then stands transfixed as he sees* JEFF*—in a terrified gasp:*] Who dar? Who dat? Is dat you, Jeff? [*Starting toward the other, forgetful for a moment of his surroundings and really believing it is a living man that he sees —in a tone of happy relief:*] Jeff! I'se sho' mighty glad to see you! Dey tol' me you done died from dat razor cut I gives you. [*Stopping, suddenly, bewilderedly.*] But how you come to be heah, nigger? [*He stares fascinatedly at the other, who continues his mechanical play with the dice.* JONES'S *eyes begin to roll wildly. He stutters:*] Ain't you gwine—look up—can't you speak to me? Is you—is you—a ha'nt? [*He jerks out his revolver in a frenzy of terrified rage.*] Nigger, I kills you dead once. Has I got to kill you ag'in? You take it den. [*He fires. When the smoke clears away* JEFF *has disappeared.* JONES *stands trembling—then with a certain reassurance:*] He's gone, anyway. Ha'nt or not ha'nt, dat shot fix him. [*The beat of the far-off tom-tom is perceptibly louder and more rapid.* JONES *becomes conscious of it —with a start, looking back over his shoulder:*] Dey's gittin' near! Dey's comin' fast! And heah I is shootin' shots to let 'em know jes' whar I is! Oh, Gorry, I'se got to run!

[*Forgetting the path, he plunges wildly into the underbrush in the rear and disappears in the shadow.*]

SCENE FOUR

In the forest. A wide dirt road runs diagonally from right, front, to left, rear. Rising sheer on both sides the forest walls it in. The moon is now up. Under its light the road glimmers ghastly and unreal. It is as if the forest had stood aside momentarily to let the road pass through and accomplish its veiled purpose. This done, the forest will fold in upon itself again and the road will be no more.

[JONES *stumbles in from the forest on the right. His uniform is ragged and torn. He looks about him with numbed surprise when he sees the road, his eyes blinking in the bright moonlight. He flops down exhaustedly and pants heavily for a while. Then with sudden anger.*]

Jones. I'm meltin' wid heat! Runnin' an' runnin' an' runnin'! Damn dis heah coat! Like a straitjacket! [*He tears off his coat and flings it away from him, revealing himself stripped to the waist.*] Dere! Dat's better! Now I kin breathe! [*Looking down at his feet, the spurs catch his eye.*] And to hell wid dese high-fangled spurs. Dey're what's been a-trippin' me up an' breakin' my neck. [*He unstraps them and flings them away disgustedly.*] Dere! I gits rid o' dem frippety Emperor trappin's an' I travels lighter. Lawd! I'se tired! [*After a pause, listening to the insistent beat of the tom-tom in the distance.*] I must 'a' put some distance between myself an' dem—runnin' like dat—and yit—dat damn drum sounds jes' de same—nearer, even. Well, I guess I a'most holds my lead, anyhow. Dey won't never catch up. [*With a sigh.*] If on'y my fool legs stands up. Oh, I'se sorry I evah went in for dis. Dat Emperor job is sho' hard to shake. [*He looks around him suspiciously.*] How'd dis road evah git heah? Good level road, too. I never remembers seein' it befo'. [*Shaking his head apprehensively.*] Dese woods is sho' full o' de queerest things at night. [*With a sudden terror.*] Lawd God, don't let me see no more o' dem ha'nts! Dey gits my goat! [*Then trying to talk himself into confidence.*] Ha'nts! You fool nigger, dey ain't no such things! Don't de Baptist parson tell you dat many time? Is you civilized, or is you like dese ign'rent black niggers heah? Sho'! Dat was all in yo' own head. Wasn't nothin' dere. Wasn't no Jeff! Know what? You jus' get seein' dem things 'cause yo' belly's empty and you's sick wid hunger inside. Hunger 'fects yo' head and yo' eyes. Any fool know dat. [*Then pleading fervently:*] But bless God, I don't come across no more o' dem, whatever dey is! [*Then cautiously:*] Rest! Don't talk! Rest! You needs it. Den you gits on yo' way again. [*Looking at the moon.*] Night's half gone a'most. You hits de coast in de mawnin'! Den you's all safe.

[*From the right forward a small gang of* NEGROES *enter. They are dressed in striped convict suits, their heads are shaven, one leg drags limpingly, shackled to a heavy ball and chain. Some carry picks, the others shovels. They are followed by a* WHITE MAN *dressed in the uniform of a prison guard. A Winchester rifle is slung across his shoulders and he carries a heavy whip. At a signal from the* GUARD *they stop on the road opposite where* JONES *is sitting.* JONES, *who has been staring up at the sky, unmindful of their noiseless approach, suddenly looks down and sees them. His eyes pop out, he tries to get to his feet and fly, but sinks back, too numbed by fright to move. His voice catches in a choking prayer.*]

Jones. Lawd Jesus!

[*The* PRISON GUARD *cracks his whip—noiselessly—and at that signal all the convicts start to work on the road. They swing their picks, they shovel, but not a sound comes from their labor. Their movements, like those of* JEFF *in the preceding scene, are those of automatons—rigid, slow, and mechanical. The* PRISON GUARD *points sternly at* JONES *with his whip, motions him to take his place among the other shovelers.* JONES *gets to his feet in a hypnotized stupor. He mumbles subserviently:*]

Jones. Yes, suh! Yes, suh! I'se comin'.

[*As he shuffles, dragging one foot, over to his place, he curses under his breath with rage and hatred.*]

Jones. God damn yo' soul, I gits even wid you yit, sometime.

[*As if there were a shovel in his hands he goes through weary, mechanical gestures of digging up dirt, and throwing it to the roadside. Suddenly, the* GUARD *approaches him angrily, threateningly. He raises his whip and lashes* JONES *viciously across the shoulders with it.* JONES *winces with pain and cowers ab-*

jectly. The Guard *turns his back on him and walks away contemptuously. Instantly* Jones *straightens up. With arms upraised as if his shovel were a club in his hands he springs murderously at the unsuspecting* Guard. *In the act of crashing down his shovel on the white man's skull,* Jones *suddenly becomes aware that his hands are empty. He cries despairingly:*]

Jones. Whar's my shovel? Gimme my shovel 'til I splits his damn head! [*Appealing to his fellow convicts:*] Gimme a shovel, one o' you, fo' God's sake!

[*They stand fixed in motionless attitudes, their eyes on the ground. The* Guard *seems to wait expectantly, his back turned to the attacker.* Jones *bellows with baffled, terrified rage, tugging frantically at his revolver.*]

Jones. I kills you, you white debil, if it's de last thing I evah does! Ghost or debil, I kills you agin!

[*He frees the revolver and fires point blank at the* Guard's *back. Instantly the walls of the forest close in from both sides, the road and the figures of the convict gang are blotted out in an enshrouding darkness. The only sounds are a crashing in the underbrush as* Jones *leaps away in mad flight and the throbbing of the tom-tom, still far distant, but increased in volume of sound and rapidity of beat.*]

SCENE FIVE

A large circular clearing, enclosed by the serried ranks of gigantic trunks of tall trees whose tops are lost to view. In the center is a big dead stump worn by time into a curious resemblance to an auction block. The moon floods the clearing with a clear light.

[Jones *forces his way in through the forest on the left. He looks wildly about the clearing with hunted, fearful glances. His pants are in tatters, his shoes cut and misshapen, flapping about his feet. He slinks cautiously to the stump in the center and sits down in a tense position, ready for instant flight. Then he holds his head in his hands and rocks back and forth, moaning to himself miserably.*]

Jones. Oh, Lawd, Lawd! Oh, Lawd, Lawd! [*Suddenly he throws himself on his knees and raises his clasped hands to the sky—in a voice of agonized pleading.*] Lawd Jesus, heah my prayer! I'se a po' sinner, a po' sinner! I knows I done wrong, I knows it! When I cotches Jeff cheatin' wid loaded dice my anger overcomes me and I kills him dead! Lawd, I done wrong! When dat guard hits me wid de whip, my anger overcomes me, and I kills him dead. Lawd, I done wrong! And down heah whar dese fool bush niggers raises me up to the seat o' de mighty, I steals all I could grab. Lawd, I done wrong! I knows it! I'se sorry! Forgive me, Lawd! Forgive dis po' sinner! [*Then beseeching terrifiedly.*] And keep dem away, Lawd! Keep dem away from me! And stop dat drum soundin' in my ears! Dat begin to sound ha'nted, too. [*He gets to his feet, evidently slightly reassured by his prayer—with attempted confidence:*] De Lawd'll preserve me from dem ha'nts after dis. [*Sits down on the stump again.*] I ain't skeered o' real men. Let dem come. But dem odders—— [*He shudders—then looks down at his feet, working his toes inside the shoes—with a groan:*] Oh, my po' feet! Dem shoes ain't no use no more 'ceptin' to hurt. I'se better off widout dem. [*He unlaces them and pulls them off—holds the wrecks of the shoes in his hands and regards them mournfully.*] You was real, A-one patin' leather, too. Look at you now. Emperor, you'se gittin' mighty low!

[*He sighs dejectedly and remains with bowed shoulders, staring down at the shoes in his hands as if reluctant to throw them away. While his attention is thus occupied, a crowd of figures silently enter the clearing from all sides. All are dressed in Southern costumes of the period of the fifties of the last century. There are middle-aged men who are evidently well-to-do planters. There is one spruce, authoritative individual—the* Auctioneer. *There is a crowd of curious spectators, chiefly young belles and dandies who have come to the slave-market for diversion. All exchange courtly greetings in dumb show and chat silently together. There is something stiff, rigid, unreal, marionettish about their movements. They group themselves about the stump. Finally a batch of*

SLAVES *is led in from the left by an attendant—three men of different ages, two women, one with a baby in her arms, nursing. They are placed to the left of the stump, beside* JONES.

The white planters look them over appraisingly as if they were cattle, and exchange judgments on each. The dandies point with their fingers and make witty remarks. The belles titter bewitchingly. All this in silence save for the ominous throb of the tom-tom. The AUCTIONEER *holds up his hand, taking his place at the stump. The groups strain forward attentively. He touches* JONES *on the shoulder peremptorily, motioning for him to stand on the stump—the auction block.* JONES *looks up, sees the figures on all sides, looks wildly for some opening to escape, sees none, screams and leaps madly to the top of the stump to get as far away from them as possible. He stands there, cowering, paralyzed with horror. The* AUCTIONEER *begins his silent spiel. He points to* JONES, *appeals to the planters to see for themselves. Here is a good field hand, sound in wind and limb as they can see. Very strong still in spite of his being middle-aged. Look at that back. Look at those shoulders. Look at the muscles in his arms and his sturdy legs. Capable of any amount of hard labor. Moreover, of a good disposition, intelligent and tractable. Will any gentleman start the bidding? The* PLANTERS *raise their fingers, make their bids. They are apparently all eager to possess* JONES. *The bidding is lively, the crowd interested. While this has been going on,* JONES *has been seized by the courage of desperation. He dares to look down and around him. Over his face abject terror gives way to mystification, to gradual realization—stutteringly.*]

Jones. What you all doin', white folks? What's all dis? What you all lookin' at me fo'? What you doin' wid me, anyhow? [*Suddenly convulsed with raging hatred and fear.*] Is dis a auction? Is you sellin' me like dey uster befo' de war? [*Jerking out his revolver just as the* AUCTIONEER *knocks him down to one of the planters—glaring from him to the purchaser.*] And *you* sells me? And *you* buys me? I shows you I'se a free nigger, damn yo' souls!

[*He fires at the* AUCTIONEER *and at the* PLANTER *with such rapidity that the two shots are almost simultaneous. As if this were a signal the walls of the forest fold in. Only blackness remains and silence broken by* JONES *as he rushes off, crying with fear—and by the quickened, ever louder beat of the tom-tom.*]

SCENE SIX

A cleared space in the forest. The limbs of the trees meet over it, forming a low ceiling about five feet from the ground. The interlocked ropes of creepers reaching upward to entwine the tree trunks give an arched appearance to the sides. The space thus enclosed is like the dark, noisome hold of some ancient vessel. The moonlight is almost completely shut out and only a vague, wan light filters through.

[*There is the noise of some one approaching from the left, stumbling and crawling through the undergrowth.* JONES'S *voice is heard between chattering moans.*]

Jones. Oh, Lawd, what I gwine do now? Ain't got no bullet left on'y de silver one. If mo' o' dem ha'nts come after me, how I gwine skeer dem away? Oh, Lawd, on'y de silver one left—an' I gotta save dat fo' luck. If I shoots dat one I'm a goner sho'! Lawd, it's black heah! Whar's de moon? Oh, Lawd, don't dis night evah come to an end? [*By the sounds, he is feeling his way cautiously forward.*] Dere! Dis feels like a clear space. I gotta lie down an' rest. I don't care if dem niggers does cotch me. I gotta rest.

[*He is well forward now where his figure can be dimly made out. His pants have been so torn away that what is left of them is no better than a breech cloth. He flings himself full length, face downward on the ground, panting with exhaustion. Gradually it seems to grow lighter in the enclosed space and two rows of seated* FIGURES *can be seen behind* JONES. *They are sitting in crumpled, despairing attitudes, hunched, facing one another with their backs touching the forest walls as if they were shackled to them. All are negroes, naked save for loin cloths. At first they are silent and motionless. Then they begin to sway slowly forward toward each and back again in unison, as if they were laxly letting themselves follow the long roll of a ship at sea. At the same time, a low, melancholy murmur rises among them, increasing gradually by rhythmic degrees which seem to be directed and controlled by the throb of the tom-tom in the distance, to a long, tremulous wail of despair that reaches a certain pitch, unbearably acute, then falls by slow gradations of tone into silence and is taken up again.* JONES *starts, looks up, sees the* FIGURES, *and throws himself down again to shut out the sight. A shudder of terror shakes his whole body as the wail rises up about him again. But the next time, his voice, as if under some uncanny compulsion, starts with the others. As their chorus lifts he rises to a sitting posture similar to the others, swaying back and forth. His voice reaches the highest pitch of sorrow, of desolation. The light fades out, the other voices cease, and only darkness is left.* JONES *can be heard scrambling to his feet and running off, his voice sinking down the scale and receding as he moves farther and farther away in the forest. The tom-tom beats louder, quicker, with a more insistent, triumphant pulsation.*]

SCENE SEVEN

The foot of a gigantic tree by the edge of a great river. A rough structure of boulders, like an altar, is by the tree. The raised river bank is in the nearer background. Beyond this the surface of the river spreads out, brilliant and unruffled in the moonlight, blotted out and merged into a veil of bluish mist in the distance.

[JONES'S *voice is heard from the left rising and falling in the long, despairing wail of the chained slaves, to the rhythmic beat of the tom-tom. As his voice sinks into silence, he enters the open space. The expression of his face is fixed and stony, his eyes have an obsessed glare, he moves with a strange deliberation, like a sleepwalker, or one in a trance. He looks around at the tree, the rough stone altar, the moonlit surface of the river beyond, and passes his hand over his head with a vague gesture of puzzled bewilderment. Then, as if in obedience to some obscure impulse, he sinks into a kneeling, devotional posture before the altar. Then he seems to come to himself partly, to have an uncertain realization of what he is doing, for he straightens up and stares about him horrifiedly—in an incoherent mumble:*]

Jones. What—what is I doin'? What is—dis place? Seems like I know dat tree—an' dem stones—an' de river. I remember—seems like I been heah befo'. [*Tremblingly:*] Oh, Gorry, I'se skeered in dis place! I'se skeered. Oh, Lawd, pertect dis sinner!

[*Crawling away from the altar, he cowers close to the ground, his face hidden, his shoulders heaving with sobs of hysterical fright. From behind the trunk of the tree, as if he had sprung out of it, the figure of the* CONGO WITCH-DOCTOR *appears. He is wizened and old, naked except for the fur of some small animal tied about his waist, its bushy tail hanging down in front. His body is stained all over a bright red. Antelope horns are on each side of his head, branching upward. In one hand he carries a bone rattle, in the other a charm stick with a bunch of white cockatoo feathers tied to the end. A great number of glass beads and bone ornaments are about his neck, ears, wrists, and ankles. He struts noiselessly with a queer prancing step to a position in the clear ground between* JONES *and the altar. Then with a preliminary, summoning stamp of his foot on the earth, he begins to dance and to chant. As if in response to his summons the beating of the tom-tom grows to a fierce, exultant boom whose throbs seem to fill the air with vibrating rhythm.* JONES *looks up, starts to spring to his feet, reaches a half-kneeling, half-squatting position and remains rigidly fixed there, paralyzed with awed fascination by this new apparition. The* WITCH-DOCTOR *sways, stamping with his foot, his bone rattle clicking the time. His voice rises and falls in a weird, monotonous croon, without articulate word divisions. Gradually his dance becomes clearly one of a narrative in pantomime, his croon is an incantation, a charm to allay the fierceness of some implacable deity demanding sacrifice. He flees, he is pursued by devils, he hides, he flees again. Ever wilder and wilder becomes his flight, nearer and nearer draws the pursuing evil, more and more the spirit of terror gains possession of him. His croon, rising to intensity, is punctuated by shrill cries.* JONES *has become completely hypnotized. His voice joins in the incantation, in the cries, he beats time with his hands and sways his body to and fro from the waist. The whole spirit and meaning of the dance have entered into him, have become his spirit. Finally the theme of the pantomime halts on a howl of despair, and is taken up again in a note of savage hope. There is a salvation. The forces of evil demand sacrifice. They must be appeased. The* WITCH-DOCTOR *points with his wand to the sacred tree, to the river beyond, to the altar, and finally to* JONES *with a ferocious command.* JONES *seems to sense the meaning of this. It is he who must offer himself for sacrifice. He beats his forehead abjectly to the ground, moaning hysterically.*]

Jones. Mercy, Oh Lawd! Mercy! Mercy on dis po' sinner!

[*The* WITCH-DOCTOR *springs to the river bank. He stretches out his arms and calls to some god within its depths. Then he starts backward slowly, his arms remaining out. A huge head of a crocodile appears over the bank and its eyes, glittering greenly, fasten upon* JONES. *He stares into them fascinatedly. The* WITCH-DOCTOR *prances up to him, touches him with his wand, motions with hideous command toward the waiting monster.* JONES *squirms on his belly nearer and nearer, moaning continually.*]

Jones. Mercy, Lawd! Mercy!

[*The crocodile heaves more of his enormous hulk on to the land.* JONES *squirms toward him. The* WITCH-DOCTOR'S *voice shrills out in furious exultation, the tom-tom beats madly.* JONES *cries out in a fierce, exhausted spasm of anguished pleading.*]

Jones. Lawd, save me! Lawd Jesus, heah my prayer!

[*Immediately, in answer to his prayer, comes the thought of the one bullet left him. He snatches at his hip, shouting defiantly.*]

Jones. De silver bullet! You don't git me yit!

[*He fires at the green eyes in front of him. The head of the crocodile sinks back behind the river bank, the* WITCH-DOCTOR *springs behind the sacred tree and disappears.* JONES *lies with his face to the ground, his arms outstretched, whimpering with fear as the throb of the tom-tom fills the silence about him with a somber pulsation, a baffled but revengeful power.*]

SCENE EIGHT

Dawn. Same as Scene Two, the dividing line of forest and plain. The nearest tree trunks are dimly revealed but the forest behind them is still a mass of glooming shadow. The tom-tom seems on the very spot, so loud and continuously vibrating are its beats.

[LEM *enters from the left, followed by a small squad of his* SOLDIERS, *and by the Cockney trader,* SMITHERS. LEM *is a heavy-set, ape-faced old savage of the extreme African type, dressed only in a loin cloth. A revolver and cartridge belt are about his waist. His soldiers are in different degrees of rag-concealed nakedness. All wear broad palm-leaf hats. Each one carries a rifle.* SMITHERS *is the same as in Scene One. One of the soldiers, evidently a tracker, is peering about keenly on the ground. He points to the spot where* JONES *entered the forest.* LEM *and* SMITHERS *come to look.*]

Smithers. [*After a glance, turns away in disgust.*] That's where 'e went in right enough. Much good it'll do yer. 'E's miles orf by this an' safe to the Coast, damn 's 'ide! I tole yer yer'd lose 'im, didn't I?—wastin' the 'ole bloomin' night beatin' yer bloody drum and castin' yer silly spells! Gawd blimey, wot a pack!

Lem. [*Gutturally.*] We cotch him.

[*He makes a motion to his* SOLDIERS, *who squat down on their haunches in a semi-circle.*]

Smithers. [*Exasperatedly.*] Well, ain't yer goin' in an' 'unt 'im in the woods? What the 'ell's the good of waitin'?

Lem. [*Imperturbably—squatting down himself.*] We cotch him.

Smithers. [*Turning away from him contemptuously.*] Aw! Garn! 'E's a better man than the lot o' you put together. I 'ates the sight o' 'im but I'll say that for 'im.

[*A sound comes from the forest. The* SOLDIERS *jump to their feet, cocking their rifles alertly.* LEM *remains sitting with an imperturbable expression, but listening intently. He makes a quick signal with his hand. His followers creep quickly into the forest, scattering so that each enters at a different spot.*]

Smithers. You ain't thinkin' that would be 'im, I 'ope?

Lem. [*Calmly.*] We cotch him.

Smithers. Blarsted fat 'eads! [*Then, after a second's thought—wonderingly:*] Still an' all, it might 'appen. If 'e lost 'is bloody way in these stinkin' woods, 'e'd likely turn in a circle without 'is knowin' it.

Lem. [*Peremptorily.*] Sssh! [*The reports of several rifles sound from the forest, followed a second later by savage, exultant yells. The beating of the tom-tom abruptly ceases.* LEM *looks up at the white man with a grin of satisfaction.*] We cotch him. Him dead.

Smithers. [*With a snarl.*] 'Ow d'yer know it's 'im an' 'ow d'yer know 'e's dead?

Lem. My mens, dey got um silver bullets. Lead bullet no kill him. He got um strong charm. I cook um money, make um silver bullet, make um strong charm, too.

Smithers. [*Astonished.*] So that's wot you was up to all night, wot? You was scared to put after 'im till you'd molded silver bullets, eh?

Lem. [*Simply stating a fact.*] Yes. Him got strong charm. Lead no good.

Smithers. [*Slapping his thigh and guffawing.*] Haw-haw! If yer don't beat all 'ell! [*Then recovering himself—scornfully:*] I'll bet yer it ain't 'im they shot at all, yer bleedin' loony!

Lem. [*Calmly.*] Dey come bring him now. [*The* SOLDIERS *come out of the forest, carrying* JONES'S *limp body. He is dead. They carry him to* LEM, *who examines his body with great satisfaction.* SMITHERS *leans over his shoulder—in a tone of frightened awe.*] Well, they did for yer right enough, Jonesey, me lad! Dead as a 'erring! [*Mockingly:*] Where's yer 'igh an' mighty airs now, yer bloomin' Majesty? [*Then with a grin:*] Silver bullets! Gawd blimey, but yer died in the 'eighth o' style, any'ow!

CURTAIN

PROCESSIONAL*

By

JOHN HOWARD LAWSON

MR. LAWSON SAYS, IN THE PREFACE TO *Processional:*

"I have endeavored to create a method which shall express the American scene in native idiom, a method as far removed from the older realism as the facile mood of Expressionism. It is apparent that this new technique is essentially vaudevillesque in character—a development, a molding to my own uses, of the rich vitality of the two-a-day and the musical extravaganza.

"This is not an abstract theory. I have built upon this ground for the very practical reason that it seems to me the only ground on which to build. The legitimate theater seems without warmth or richness of method. It is only in the fields of vaudeville and revue that a native craftsmanship exists. Here, at least, a shining if somewhat distorted mirror is held up to our American nature. Here the national consciousness finds at least a partial reflection of itself in the mammy melody, the song-and-dance act, and the curtain of real pearls. Here the concern is with a direct contact, an immediate emotional response across the footlights."

The degree to which *Processional* is in debt to vaudeville becomes obvious on a reading of the play. The characters tend to become vaudeville stereotypes: for instance, Cohen, the Jewish low comedian; Rastus, the negro comedian; the Sheriff, the hard-boiled officer of the law; Phillpots, the smart city feller and brash journalist. The scenes are always on the point of breaking up into song-and-dance or tumbling acts—if any emotion rises in them it is purposely made so brittle that it can be broken into burlesque. The play has little more plot than a vaudeville bill, and it could go on forever as well as not. The jazz wedding at the end is obviously there to give an appearance of finality, and perhaps because weddings at the end are "native." The constant intrusion of music into the action is again vaudevillian. On the surface, then, Mr. Lawson has been successful in attaining his aims.

But the theory implies that he is closer to fact because of his technique; that he is, in fact, more realistic than anybody else. Mr. Lawson says that he can find vaudeville characters on every street corner, whereas the so-called realistic characters he sees on the stage he never meets in life. In other words, in vaudeville Mr. Lawson finds not only good theater, but also representation of reality.

The question raised by this is, of course, a philosophical one, too complicated for adequate discussion here. But it may be asked if the test of reality in the theater is not, after all, the acceptance by the audience of the characters and situations as real. Would many audiences nowadays find much likeness between their own experience and the experience of Mr. Lawson's people? Don't we still recognize the "older realism" as reality in the theater, admitting the possibility that in time we will see more truth in Mr. Lawson's work than in, say, Galsworthy's?

Processional was produced in 1925 by the Theatre Guild, and ran for ninety-six performances. By the critics it was very well received. Miss June Walker and Mr. George Abbott played the leading rôles, and the production was directed by Mr. Philip Moeller. Mordecai Gorelik designed the settings.

From 1927 to 1929 Mr. Lawson was associated with the New Playwrights' Theatre, a group composed also of Em Jo Basshe, Paul Sifton, and Michael Gold, whose aim was to reform the older commercial theater by staging their own radical plays. They failed to win public support.

Processional was revived in 1937 by the Federal Theatre and ran for 81 performances.

JOHN HOWARD LAWSON

Born 1894, New York City.
1914, Williams College.
Writer of scenarios and dialogue for talking moving pictures.

PLAYS

1915 *Standards.* 1917 *Servant-Master-Lover.* 1923 *Roger Bloomer.* 1925 *Processional.* 1926 *Nirvana.* 1927 *Loud Speaker.* 1928 *The International (musical).* 1932 *Success Story.* 1934 *The Pure in Heart.* 1934 *Gentlewoman.* 1937 *Marching Song.*

WRITINGS ABOUT THE DRAMA

Preface to *Processional*, 1925. *Theory and Technique of Playwriting*, 1936. Preface to *The Pure in Heart* and *Gentlewoman*, 1934.

SCREENWRITING

1929 *Dynamite.* 1930 *The Sea Bat.* 1930 *Our Blushing Brides.* 1930 *Ship from Shanghai.* 1931 *Bachelor Apartment.* 1934 *Success at Any Price.* 1934 *Goodbye Love.* 1934 *Treasure Island.* 1935 *Party Wire.* 1938 *Blockade.* 1938 *Algiers.* 1939 *They Shall Have Music.*

PROCESSIONAL

Characters

Boob Elkins.
Isaac Cohen.
Sadie Cohen.
Jake Psinski.
Pop Pratt.
MacCarthy } *Soldiers.*
Bill }
Phillpots.
The Sheriff.
A Man in a Silk Hat.
Old Maggie.
Mrs. Euphemia Stewart Flimmins.
Dynamite Jim.
Rastus.
Slop.
Smith.
First Soldier.
Second Soldier.
Third Soldier.
Fourth Soldier.

Place: Outskirts of a large town in the West Virginia coal fields during a strike.
Time: The present.

ACT I

On the Fourth of July

A drop curtain, like those used in the older vaudeville theaters, represents a town street painted with brick buildings, signs of Central Hotel, Palace Movie, Quick Lunch, etc. *In center of curtain is the door of Cohen's General Store, with show window painted on curtain and this sign:* Isaac Cohen the Cut-Rate Store, Green-Grocer, Antiseptic Barber, Kosher Delicatessen, Mining Tools. *Above the door a small practicable window in the curtain. The tone is that of the usual vaudeville drop, except that it is more startlingly crude, vigorous in color contrast, blaringly American.*

A broad, uniform row of steps leads up to the stage. Stage and auditorium brilliantly lighted.

[*Down the aisle of the theater comes a newsboy selling papers, shouting as he comes.* Boob Elkins *is a thin, pimply lad of sixteen, with bright eyes and a hoarse voice.*]

Boob. Extry! Extry! Trouble in West Virginia! Charleston paper! Jazzin' up the big strike! [*By this time he is on the stage, still shouting:*] Extry! Extry!

[Cohen *sticks his head out from square window in curtain. A middle-aged merchant with a lisp that makes his caressing voice a little ridiculous. A kindly man, puzzled and worried by the violent labor dispute going on around him. The vaudeville type of Yiddish figure. He has just gotten out of bed, his sleepy head surmounted by an absurd nightcap.*]

Cohen. Say, just lay one on the doorstep, will you? Here's a nickel.

[*He throws the coin.* Boob *catches it adroitly.* Boob *throws newspaper on doorstep. The head above disappears.*]

Boob. [*Shouting.*] Extry! Soldiers an' miners clash! Threats thrill throngs!

[*He exits left.*]

[*Enter right* Sadie Cohen, *a sallow-faced girl of seventeen, all dressed up in white with short skirts and frills calculated to fill out her childish figure. Her hair in two neat pigtails. Sometimes she sticks her finger in her mouth. She often stands on one leg and giggles.*]

Sadie. [*As she runs in breathless with news.*] Popper . . . Popper. . . . [*She stands on one leg for a minute waiting, then louder:*] Hey . . . Popper!

[Cohen *sticks his head out of square window again with nightcap as before.*]

Cohen. Well, who's dead now?

Sadie. Nobuddy yet, but they're gonna kill lots a' people, oo . . . lots a' people!

Cohen. Come indoors then, you li'l devil

you, before you get shot. Can't I get no sleep on a holiday?

Sadie. They got a lot a' soldiers an' they got martial law.

Cohen. Never heard of him.

Sadie. [*More and more breathless.*] The Governor a' West Virginia has made a big paper sayin' it's martial law an' everybuddy can be kilt. . . . an' the soldiers has taken the mines an' the strikers has got music an' they're marchin' an' they're marchin' . . .

Cohen. Is that a fact? There it is for the Fourth a' July. . . . Coal dust an' blood . . . oi, there's no money in it! I'll be right down; come indoors, Sadie.

[*He disappears from window.*]

[THE JAZZ MINERS *come through the audience playing the jazz march which forms a background throughout the play,* "Yankee Doodle Blues." *The band is a group of nine men in tattered blue overalls, playing on an incongruous assortment of instruments ranging from Jew's harps to bassoons. These do not keep time or tune very well but the effect is lively. The men are rugged types, hardened mine workers of the mountain region.* THE JAZZ BAND: (1) *The leader,* SLOP, *is thin, with a long, glum face, playing on an old-fashioned flute.* (2) JAKE PSINSKI, *a Pole, with fiery wild eyes and a starved face, blows a long trumpet.* (3) RASTUS JOLLY *is a Negro, his torn overalls hung up by a string over his muscular back. He plays a banjo and sings most of the time for good measure.* (4) *A big* SOILED MAN *with a beard, which looks as if chickens might roost in it, manipulates the slide trombone.* (5) *He is followed by a little, middle-aged, anæmic man who makes a ghostly effort to manage a badly dented French horn. The feeble player of this feeble instrument is known as* FELIX. (6) ALEXANDER GORE, *a man of the hayseed type, straw-colored hair and beard, red face, red bandana handkerchief tied around his scrawny neck, blows on the big bassoon.* (7) DAGO JOE, *a sleek, greasy Italian, has an accordion.* (8) WAYNE WHIFFLEHAGEN, *a man with a curious face, plays a harmonica. His face looks twisted as if seen in a distorted mirror.* (9) SMITH, *young and serious, brings up the rear with the big drum banging methodically. This group makes its noisy irruption into the theater, marches around the stage and lines up still playing.* SLOP, *the glum man with the flute, stands a step below leading them waving his arms.* SADIE *stands on one leg at edge of stage.**]

Slop. [*Pointing flute at* PSINSKI, *shouts angrily.*] Hey . . . you! [*The band stops in a straggling manner.* SLOP *approaches* PSINSKI *angrily.*] You with the face, what you trying to hog it all for?

Psinski. [*Taking* SLOP *by the arm.*] My friend, we make the jazz today for the glory of the working class.

Smith. [*Bored.*] Speech . . . speech . . .

Psinski. Each man make the big noise what he can.

[PSINSKI *is evidently a man of education, slight foreign accent.*]

Dago Joe. [*Pleased.*] Sure, maka da beeg noise!

Slop. Aw, say it with flowers—I'm a musician, that's what I am; I can sing too, that's my nature. This bunch a' tin-horn mechanics is rotten!

[*He sits down on top step wearily.* SADIE *walks in front of the* JAZZ BAND, *looking curiously at instruments, finger in mouth.*]

Gore. [*Poking* SMITH.] Who's the skirt?

Smith. Store-keeper's daughter.

Wayne. She's a li'l lady, y' know what I mean.

Smith. A clean, square li'l girl.

[*Seeing that there is a halt,* RASTUS *has seated himself on steps at extreme left, lazily twanging banjo.*]

Slop. I wish Jim Flimmins was here; he's the guy got music inside him comes out natural like the foam off beer.

Smith. Well, Jim's in jail, where we'll all be before long.

Rastus. No, sir!

Psinski. We do not go to jail, we got rights, we are class-conscious workmen——

Gore. [*Scratching himself uncomfortably.*] I ain't conscious a' nuthin' except an itch an' a thirst.

Slop. Now, if Jim was here, he'd blow a horn like it would make the cows shimmy.

Sadie. [*Who has been listening to the conversation, eager and scared.*] I can shimmy!

Rastus. Wanna join the coal town jazz, kid? Wanna step along in the big peerade with us guys?

Sadie. I'd be scared.

Gore. [*Offering* SADIE *his bassoon.*] Wanna play, kid?

Sadie. [*Looks down it.*] What's in it?

Gore. Noise.

* Note: The arrangement of instruments used by the Jazz Band can be modified according to the necessities of production.

[SADIE *turns to* SOILED MAN *with the trombone, who is pulling it in and out sadly.*]

Sadie. I like this one 'cause it slides so funny.

Wayne. Aw, give it to her. [SOILED MAN *looks puzzled, wipes the mouthpiece carefully and hands it to her.*] Gentlemen, lemme introduce Miss Sadie Cohen, about to tickle the slide trombone.

[SADIE *tries to play, when* COHEN *reappears at window in his undershirt.*]

Cohen. Sadie, what's that in your hand?

Sadie. Look, Pop.

Cohen. Lay it down.

Wayne. Just a slide trombone——

Cohen. Oi, a lot a' musical rippers, they don't mean you no good with their slide trombones! Get in the house for once, will you? I'm comin' down.

[*He disappears from window.*]

Sadie. [*Giving back the trombone.*] I don't do nuthin' I hadn't oughter, but Popper's always got the blues; he's always scoldin'.

[*Down aisle of theater comes* POP PRATT, *hobbling on a stick, a typical Civil War veteran, wizened and unbelievably old in his tattered blue uniform. He has one wooden leg. He carries a faded American flag.*]

Pop Pratt. [*Calling as he comes, in a plaintive, cracked voice.*] Hey, boys, wait for me; I wanna march along in this procession——

Wayne. He can't march, he ain't a member a' the Union.

Pop Pratt. What's that?

Wayne. A back number.

Smith. A hot sketch.

Slop. You ain't in, that's all; you're out.

Pop Pratt. Tiy the other ear. I don't hear very good.

Slop. You tell him.

[SADIE *sits down at foot of steps center, practically in the audience, looking up at group of men.*]

Wayne. [*To* POP PRATT.] Where you goin' with a face like the newspapers was writ on it?

Smith. What's eatin' you, old man?

Gore. [*Pulling him the other way.*] What for you wave the old flag?

[RASTUS *continues throughout to twang banjo in lazy accompaniment to scene, now and then breaking into song.*]

Rastus. [*Sings.*]

"He's got them Yankee Doodle Blues . . .
He's ninety an' he's spry,
With them never-say-die,
Them historic blues . . . Yankee Doodle Blues . . ."

Pop Pratt. I'm a-celebratin' the forty-four states.

Smith. There's forty-eight states now.

Pop Pratt. Eh?

Smith. [*Loudly, pointing to flag.*] Them stars is states, stars in that flag.

Pop Pratt. Oh . . . [*Scratching head.*] I quit countin' year Amanda died: Mandy died in '93 . . . now it don't seem like she could be dead, her with her yaller curls.

Wayne. I bet you seen lots of 'em die.

Pop Pratt. [*Not heeding him, pounds stick on ground and chuckles.*] That girl was a devil . . . yes, sir. Yaller-haired girls die quicker—they uses their strength dancin'.

Wayne. Ain't that the cat's knuckles? Ninety years a' drums a-rattlin', he's seen wars an' deaths an' the makin' a' states an' yet he won't die.

Rastus. [*Continues his accompaniment.*]

"He's got them Yankee Doodle . . .
Yes, sir . . . Blues."

Pop Pratt. They don't make girls the same no more, ain't got the same shape now. I seen shapes change——

Psinski. [*Pushing the others aside importantly.*] This is somethin' you ain't never seen, this is industrial, savvy—there's men marchin', men in a sweat an' their flag is the black smoke in the sky, 'cause they dig coal from the ground——

[PRATT *has not heard a word.*]

Slop. Save your hot air; he ain't your kind.

Smith. Listen, then.

[*He cocks the old man's hand over his ear, then he beats a lively volley on the drum.*]

Pop Pratt. [*Puts his hat on and salutes.*] I hear the drums a-rattlin' across Gettysburg.

Wayne. Don't it beat hell the way they walk aroun' rememberin'?

[RASTUS *sings low as* PRATT *continues.*]

Pop Pratt. [*Looking very much alive.*] Yes, friends, in them days sinful pride leaped up an' we fought our brothers, American blood to water American earth. . . . [*Tapping wooden leg with stick.*] That's what my flesh done; fertilizer. My leg went to make the flowers grow on Gettysburg. We fought our brothers, we did. . . .

Psinski. [*Shouts at* PRATT.] All men are brothers!

Pop Pratt. [*Turning and wiggling his finger in his ear.*] Try the other ear.

[COHEN, *dressed, has come out of store,*

carrying a large wooden board which he sets up beside door, on it written in big letters, HEADQUARTERS FOR GUNS—WHOLESALE PRICES. *He pushes through the men to* SADIE, *who stands up.*]

Cohen. Sadie . . . Sadie. . . . Did I tell you to get in the house, or are you deaf already, is it?

Sadie. I wanna hear the music, Pop.

Cohen. Ain't you got a swell victrola? Didn't I tell you them fellers mean you no good? [*Turning to the* JAZZ BAND.] Get away from the front a' my store an' leave my daughter alone.

Smith. We ain't said a word to her.

Wayne. She's just been settin' there, an' that's the truth.

Cohen. [*His arm affectionately around his daughter.*] A child raised for sassiety, understand . . . a flower, I am here to say it, a rosebud, a tulip, a forget-me-not, a regular Madonis! . . . What else? A lady. . . . Have I spoken? [JAZZ BAND *is impressed.* COHEN *looks them over.*] Oi, what a bunch this is!

Psinski. This is the Industrial Jazz chosen for their music talent, every mother's son.

Pop Pratt. [*Coming between them, trying to hear.*] What's that?

Cohen. [*Peering down the bassoon.*] Have you got a bomb in that thing?

Psinski. [*Catching* COHEN *by arm and swinging him around.*] Bourgeois!

Cohen. You dirty foreigner.

Smith. [*Swinging* COHEN *around the other way.*] Who the hell's a foreigner? What are you yourself?

Cohen. What's your name?

Smith. Smith.

Cohen. Mine's Cohen, you an' me is Americans, shake. [SMITH *turns away from him.* COHEN *shakes his own hand.*] It's just the same by me—half a' these birds can't even talk in U. S. A.

Dago Joe. Me savvy all linguagio, sail on da sea, walk on da land, see all da place, me clever wop, speaka Sensen wid Chinese girl, speaka Spearmint wid Eskimo girl, see all da place!

Slop. Line up, boys, it's your turn to show 'em.

Felix. Peerade——

Wayne. March——

Smith. Procession——

Slop. An' for Christ's sake, sugar it!

Cohen. [*As* JAZZ BAND *forms in line.*] Play the music, make a little music, murder an' starve—rights . . . rights . . . wave the flag an' play a little jazz. . . .

[*Music starts with a bang and they march off right, led by* SLOP. *Music continues in distance off stage.* PRATT, COHEN, *and* SADIE *remain.*]

Pop Pratt. [*Hand cocked over ear.*] Why don't them boys make a noise, eh . . . music, eh?

Cohen. You got luck an' you don't know it. Come on, Sadie.

[*He exits into shop.* SADIE *is at door of shop when* BOOB *returns, still shouting.*]

Boob. Extry! Extry! Threats thrill throngs!

Pop Pratt. Here y'are, boy.

[PRATT *buys a paper.* BOOB *turns to* SADIE.]

Boob. Hello, Sadie.

Sadie. Good mornin'.

Boob. Give us a kiss, will you?

Sadie. [*Pointing to* PRATT.] Hush, the old man.

Boob. When you gonna give me the other garter off your leg?

Sadie. I can't . . . I got nuthin' to keep my stockings up.

Boob. I'll give you a new pair with diamond buckles.

Sadie. You're kiddin', you ain't got the money——

Boob. I'd steal for you! Give us a kiss for the Fourth a' July.

Sadie. I don't want to.

Boob. [*Produces a pile of firecrackers from pocket.*] I'll give you a firecracker if you do.

Sadie. [*Hesitating, finger in mouth.*] Well . . . no, I don't want to.

Boob. I thought you was my girl.

Sadie. I ain't nobuddy's girl. I'm free, I'm a suffragette, I don't care!

[*She goes into shop.*]

Boob. Aw, listen, Sadie.

[*He follows her into shop, but only for an instant; then he is projected out head first, falling on the ground.* COHEN *appears in door.*]

Cohen. Out an' stay out, a boy that's no good, a thief, a loafer, I don't want to soil the hands on you again. [COHEN *disappears.* BOOB *picks himself up, produces firecracker, lights it and throws it into shop. A small explosion is heard inside.* COHEN'S *head appears at door.*] That's how boys learn to be gunmen an' murderers. You will end in a big jail.

[*He disappears again.* PRATT *limps forward.*]

Pop Pratt. What's a' matter here?

Boob. You're dead an' buried an' you don't know it. [*He waves a pack of firecrackers.*]

Pop Pratt. What you doin' with them things?

Boob. [*Hopping around.*] Celebratin' my country 'tis of thee . . . it makes people dance! [*He lights the pack, throws it under* PRATT *and runs off, shouting.*] Extry! Threats thrill throngs!

[BOOB *has gone. The firecrackers explode with bangs and puffs of smoke. The old man loses his balance, waves stick wildly and then goes flat on the ground. Enter on either side of stage simultaneously a* SOLDIER *fully armed. The* SOLDIERS *stand at either side, worried as if they were attacking an enemy trench.* MACCARTHY, *muscular and grizzled, hard-boiled, with dirty red hair, whispers loudly.*]

MacCarthy. D'ye hear it, Bill?

Bill. [*A young city boy, tough, but easily frightened.*] I heard shootin'.

[*They approach* PRATT *on the ground.*]

MacCarthy. They've done for the old man.

Pop Pratt. [*Angrily.*] Help me up, bloomin' fools!

MacCarthy. Where'd it get you?

Pop Pratt. My ear—— [MACCARTHY *and* BILL *look at each other.*] Louder.

MacCarthy. [*Shouts.*] What was it?

Pop Pratt. Rheumatism.

MacCarthy. He ain't hurt.

[*They help him up.*]

Bill. Handle him careful, he's a veteran.

MacCarthy. No, he ain't. Where's his American Legion button?

Bill. Sh . . . the other war . . . the Civil . . .

[COHEN *comes out of shop with a bunch of American flags on a stand which he hangs by the door, on it a sign,* "YOUR COUNTRY'S FLAG. SPECIAL SALE." *He bustles forward.*]

Cohen. Good mornin', gentlemen, nice mornin', can I sell you anything?

Bill. Say, you remind me of Second Avenue.

Cohen. A New York boy?

Bill. No, Jersey City.

Cohen. Keep your eye out, Sammy, this is a tough place.

MacCarthy. That's the bunk, tie it outside.

Cohen. They got what they call industrial warfare here——

MacCarthy. [*Slapping chest.*] We been in a real war; what about the Argonne?

Cohen. Well, what about it?

MacCarthy. Ever hear of Chateau Thierry? There was blood in the woods that day, a stinkin' lot a' blood.

Bill. Shut your head, I cough up every time I think a' that.

MacCarthy. Uncle Sam's gonna keep order here. Any guy doubts it goes underground with lead in him, that's the law an' order program, savvy, 'cause the place is lousy with foreigners that don't understand American freedom——

[*Enter* PSINSKI, *a bullet wound in shoulder, shirt torn open shows a red scar.*]

Bill. What's a' matter with him?

Psinski. Some guy didn't like the music —just a flesh wound, it's nuthin'.

MacCarthy. Hurry up, Bill, we better go look. [*Turning to* COHEN.] Send the old man home, he'll get hurt. Come on, Bill.

Bill. [*Whining as they go.*] I don't half like it.

[*Exit* MACCARTHY *and* BILL. *Off stage the recurrent rhythm of marching feet and music.*]

Psinski. [*Center.*] Hear them feet a-shufflin' . . . the feet go clippety-clop an' the music make a splash like dynamite!

Cohen. [*To* POP PRATT.] Better go home, Pop; looks like trouble here.

Pop Pratt. [*Listening intently.*] What's that about beer?

Cohen. [*Shouting angrily in* PRATT'S *ear.*] Trouble, disorder, riots, fighting . . .

[*Enter* PHILLPOTS, *young, amiable, brisk, neat made-to-order clothes, straw hat, nasal voice, folding kodak slung over shoulder, a very* George M. Cohan *sort of newspaper man.*]

Phillpots. Who said trouble? Riots, masses, poisonous gas, I'm for it!

Pop Pratt. [*To* COHEN.] Did you say there was gonna be another war?

Phillpots. Sure, why not?

Cohen. Stranger here?

Phillpots. I belong everywhere.

Cohen. Well, you look like you thought you was a devil with the women.

Phillpots. Confidentially, I am.

Cohen. A newspaper feller!

Psinski. Treat him good, he owns us all, the guy that holds the wires . . . he laughs, he makes death, he telegraphs——

Cohen. Umph!

Phillpots. That's me, Hiram, the History Kid. [*Inside the house* SADIE *has started the phonograph, a nasal voice singing.*] "There's no land so grand as my land from California to Manhattan Isle." [PHILLPOTS *continues to speak.*] Say, I've covered the map—steamers, trams, aeroplanes, camels, round and round in the path of war and all the time

I had . . . [*The phonograph goes on.*] "Make me lose those . . . Yankee Doodle Blues." [PHILLPOTS *joins in, singing.*]

"I had those, yes I had those . . .
Yankee Doodle Blues . . ."

[*The phonograph starts again at the beginning,* SADIE *dances out of store clapping her hands.*]

Sadie. I was makin' music an' I heard a voice that answered, heard a stranger's voice.

[PHILLPOTS *and* SADIE *look at each other smiling, stepping in time to the music.*]

Phillpots. Is this my dance?

[*He and* SADIE *dance.* POP PRATT *delighted, pounds stick and jigs in a circle.*]

Cohen. Here . . . here! [*He tries to stop them. The first time he fails, but on next round succeeds in separating them.*] Enough is too much, young man. That's my daughter an' you ain't been introduced.

Phillpots. She sure knows how to dance.

Cohen. She goes out now an' then to a social party where they dance genteel with a fox-trot an' a rabbit run, but no fightin' or pushin'—a social time would you believe it.

[*The phonograph ends in a cracked wheeze.*]

Phillpots. Are you one of the debutantes here?

Sadie. No, sir, I'm a good girl.

Phillpots. You can't kid me, little girl, my mother was Jewish . . .

Cohen. Welcome.

Phillpots. And my father was Irish.

Cohen. [*Suspiciously.*] Oh ho, is that so?

Phillpots. Yes, sir.

Sadie. What you doin' in coal town, stranger?

Phillpots. What sort of a place is this?

Cohen. Oh, there you ask somethin'. It's rotten! Look at me: I come up here from Charleston when the mines opened. It looked like a million dollars, an' I tumble into a valley where Death lives.

Psinski. Go up that big hill, see all the graves a' men died sweatin' in the mines, little stones standin' like an army; but there on the other side a' town a temple built by a rich man with statues an' all—but go look at them graves!

Phillpots. I don't care about the dead ones, but the live ones!——

Cohen. A live town, a coal center, ain't it? . . . [*He points to the picture on curtain.*] With a movie palace an' a rotary club an' a Ku Klux Klan—but out here on the outskirts a' town the hell a' coal begins, all these little black valleys full up with mines.

Phillpots. Out of this the soul of America rises in a pillar of smoke. It warms the heart of the U. S. A. all right.

Sadie. [*Stands on one leg looking at* PHILLPOTS, *gaping with admiration.*] Ain't he got the silver tongue, though?

Phillpots. Little girl, rose of the coal dust with olive skin, were you born of smoke?

Cohen. Not on your life, she ain't; I'm here to say it, an' don't you go give her no such ideas. What a place for a girl among all these foreigners an' rippers!

Sadie. What's a ripper, Pop?

Cohen. A feller pulls the clothes off your back.

Sadie. Oo . . . I'd like that!

Cohen. Innocent, ain't it? She's all I got in the world, I got money saved to send her to correspondence school, some swell place; y'know what I mean?

Psinski. [*Comes up to* PHILLPOTS, *looks him over thoughtfully.*] Looking for trouble, are you?

Phillpots. If I don't find it I'll make it. What do I care for guns! I'm going to raise the lid off this strike, make it a national issue, put it on the front page, put it before Congress, put it——

[*While he has been speaking, all his hearers have suddenly taken to cover, made signs of fright and disappeared.* PSINSKI *to left, followed by* POP PRATT, COHEN, *and* SADIE *into shop.* SADIE *peeks out once and retires as a big, dangerous-looking man enters right.* CONNOR, *the* SHERIFF, *carries two large pistols, dressed in half* Buffalo Bill *style, high boots, black whiskers, a very big badge on his chest. He twirls the pistols in each hand in a way to terrify any onlooker.* PHILLPOTS *sees him and his voice dies.*]

Sheriff. [*Roaring.*] Out a' my path, stranger! [PHILLPOTS *dives into* COHEN'S *store.* SHERIFF *walks up and down dangerously, trying to intimidate the audience. Enter right a tall* MAN IN A SILK HAT *and immaculate afternoon clothes, white kid gloves, followed by* BILL *and* MACCARTHY *marching stiffly, guns on shoulder.* SHERIFF *swings fiercely on the newcomer. His manner immediately changes to cringing civility. He salutes.*] Yes, sir.

Man in Silk Hat. [*Has a deep, ringing voice.*] I wish to announce . . . [*He clears his throat.*] Sheriff, I have arranged to have the strictest coöperation between your deputies and the army. The Colonel is sending his men out on police duty.

Sheriff and two Soldiers. [*In chorus.*] Yes, sir, yes, sir.

Man in Silk Hat. Another point, Sheriff. I am informed loose women are hanging around the camp making propositions to the soldiers. People take advantage of these periods of disorder to commit nuisances. [*Off stage the distant discord of the* JAZZ BAND *is heard again like a derisive echo.*] What's that?

MacCarthy. It's them musical miners.

Bill. It's that strikers' jazz.

Man in Silk Hat. Gratuitous effrontery ——

[*A shot off stage, and the silk hat flies off into wings, disclosing a shiny bald head.*]

MacCarthy. What was that?

Bill. Where was it?

Sheriff. You get the hat, you chase whoever done it.

[*The* SOLDIERS *hurry off, one on either side.*]

Man in Silk Hat. [*Clapping hands to head.*] Did it hit my head? . . . No, no, I think not.

Sheriff. [*Cheerfully.*] Why sure, that's nuthin'.

Man in Silk Hat. [*Muttering.*] I wish to announce. . . . [*Looking at watch.*] That is, I think I'll just be going, Sheriff, I have a meeting. . . .

[*He is so nervous that he leaves watch hanging on its gold chain.* BILL *returns with silk hat and a handsome gray wig.*]

Bill. I found this, too.

Sheriff. Excuse me.

[*He takes wig and brushes it. It is very dusty.* MAN IN SILK HAT *claps it sideways on head.*]

Man in Silk Hat. Yes, I have a meeting. . . . Law and order, Sheriff. . . .

[*He hurries off nervously.* PHILLPOTS *runs out of* COHEN'S *shop.*]

Phillpots. Who was that?

Sheriff. That's the President a' the Law an' Order League. [PHILLPOTS *laughs.* SHERIFF *produces both guns.*] Do you prefer to be tarred an' feathered or run out on a rail?

Phillpots. Don't make me laugh!

Sheriff. You're under martial law. We can investigate, search, enter an' strip you.

Phillpots. Oh, Sheriff!

Sheriff. [*To* BILL.] Search him, boy.

Phillpots. Don't search me. Here it is.

[*He produces large silver flask and hands it to* SHERIFF, *who smells it and takes a long drink.*]

Sheriff. [*With manner of a connoisseur.*] Not bad.

Phillpots. Johnnie Walker. [*He takes a drink himself.*] I want to get to know you better, Sheriff.

Sheriff. [*Pointing to camera.*] What you doin' with that picture machine?

Phillpots. Do you a big service, put your physiognomy on the front page in fourteen cities, badge and all.

[*He takes out handkerchief and polishes the* SHERIFF'S *badge.*]

Sheriff. [*At once becoming very civil.*] That's different. What paper do you represent?

Phillpots. The best. . . .

[*He unfolds copy of New York* Evening Journal. *The soldiers salute.*]

Sheriff. The open hand to friends an' a short gun for strangers. Shake. [*They shake hands.*] They call me the Big Sheriff with the Big Heart.

Phillpots. [*Opening camera.*] Good, now look pleasant, point your gun—not at me, point it at him.

[*He indicates* BILL. SHERIFF *has struck a very funny attitude. As* PHILLPOTS *is about to take the picture,* MACCARTHY *drags in* PSINSKI.]

MacCarthy. [*Roughly.*] I found this, Sheriff. I think mebbe he shot the silk hat.

[*He throws* PSINSKI *down in front of* SHERIFF, *who, with great presence of mind, strikes an even better attitude, glowering on the man at his feet.*]

Sheriff. Go right ahead with the picture.

Phillpots. [*Smiling.*] Oh, Sheriff. [*He clicks camera and comes forward.*] What's this man done?

MacCarthy. He took a pot shot at the Law an' Order League.

Psinski. [*Starting to get up.*] It's a lie, I got no gun, I do not shoot!

Sheriff. Go on, speak up.

Psinski. I believe in the brotherhood of man.

Sheriff. Knock him down, boys.

MacCarthy. [*Bored.*] All right.

[*He does so, using butt end of rifle expertly.*]

Phillpots. Say, is this legal?

Sheriff. Certainly. [SHERIFF *produces large pair of spectacles and sheaf of legal-looking papers with the air of a magician taking rabbits out of a hat.*] Search him, boys, in the name a' the Law. [BILL *proceeds to investigate* PSINSKI'S *pockets.* SHERIFF *fingers papers, reading.*] "Search an' Entry" . . . no that's not it. . . . "Summary action . . . can be applied to any person who talks, speaks, addresses, writes, advertises, states by word a' mouth by posted notice or placard"—well, you see how it is, we can make anythin' legal here!

Bill. [*Producing things from* PSINSKI'S *pockets.*] Here's a queer-lookin' book.

Psinski. That's the Rubáiyát of Omar Khayyám.

Sheriff. [*Taking it.*] One a' them Armenian Bolcheviks. We keep it for evidence.

Psinski. [*To the soldiers.*] You soldiers are workmen, too, what for you come here to shoot down your brothers?

MacCarthy. Hear him, Sheriff?

Bill. [*Holding up objects he finds on* PSINSKI.] One dime . . . first naturalization papers in state of Colorado . . . a letter in Chinee . . .

Psinski. That's Polish.

Sheriff. Well, it's good evidence, 'cause no one can read it.

[BILL *passes a picture to* MACCARTHY.]

MacCarthy. Here's a picture of an old girl.

Phillpots. [*Looking over* MACCARTHY'S *shoulder.*] That would be his mother.

Bill. [*Scratching his head.*] Even this dirty Pole got a mother, don't it beat all?

MacCarthy. Looks like the mother of all time.

Psinski. [*Fiercely.*] Gimme the picture!

Bill. That's all, Sheriff, except he's tattooed all over with crescents an' crosses.

Sheriff. I reckon he ain't worth hangin'.

[*Off stage the distant tooting of the* JAZZ BAND *breaks in again.*]

MacCarthy. There's that noise, Sheriff.

Sheriff. Them guys are at it again . . . well, I guess we better break it up.

Psinski. The music goes on.

Sheriff. That ain't music. I guess I know music when I hear it.

Psinski. It goes on, while there's a man left, they blow them horns!

Sheriff. [*To soldiers.*] Come on, boys, we'll see about that. [*To* PSINSKI.] You know what's healthy for you, better leave town in just about two hours, get me . . . I know your kind, this ain't a health resort for Bolcheviki—where's that music?

[*The persistent rhythm of the* JAZZ BAND *off stage grows louder. The men begin to sway in spite of themselves.*]

Bill. It's here.

MacCarthy. [*Pointing the other way.*] It's there.

Bill. Here an' there.

MacCarthy. It's everywhere.

Sheriff. [*To* PHILLPOTS.] You tell the world we keep order here.

[*Exit* SHERIFF *with* BILL *and* MACCARTHY. *The off-stage music dies down gradually.*]

Phillpots. [*Coming to* PSINSKI *with friendly interest.*] Are you going to get out of town?

Psinski. No.

Phillpots. Why not? What's going to happen? I want the news.

Psinski. People in a sweat marchin' under a lot a' flags—it is news that?

Phillpots. No, they're always doing it.

Psinski. An' fellers like you always lookin' on.

Phillpots. [*Waving newspaper.*] That's my job.

Psinski. You got a newspaper soul.

Phillpots. Never mind about my soul.

Psinski. City feller, ain't you?

Phillpots. Well, in a way.

Psinski. A fool that walks on asphalt among electric lights, what can you know about people born in the dark, a lonely bitter people in the mountains, an' to them come a stream of mystic foreigners—the Pole, the Greek, the Italian——

Phillpots. That's all right, but they all turn into Americans.

Psinski. They turn into dirt, the earth is their mother an' she calls em'.

[*Enter* OLD MAGGIE, *hobbling along energetically, a bent hag's body and bruised, wrinkled face.*]

Phillpots. There's Mother Earth now.

Psinski. That's Old Maggie that they call the daughter a' God 'cause she tells every one they're goin' to hell. Say, Maggie, tell us about God. Does He wear a silk hat, does He smoke a big cigar?

Old Maggie. [*Simply.*] No, he don't, but the lightnin' is his sword.

Psinski. Don't that beat hell?

Old Maggie. Yes, it beats hell.

Psinski. God, don't frighten me!

Old Maggie. There's a black time comin', I'm old an' my eyes is sore, but I can see things yet.

Psinski. What you see?

Old Maggie. Ruins an' a Bible as big as a baseball field spread over the ruins to cover 'em like a mustard plaster.

Psinski. Some say she can read the future in clouds an' the inside a' dead cows——

Old Maggie. Fools!

Psinski. [*To* OLD MAGGIE.] Don't you see a new light comin', a new sun risin'?

Phillpots. What's that?

Psinski. The Proletariat.

Phillpots. You don't expect me to fall for that bunk.

Psinski. I could convince you, you got some intelligence, come with me, I'll take you to a workers' meetin', show you the serious side.

Old Maggie. Fools, fools!

Phillpots. The old woman is wiser than you are.

Old Maggie. I ain't so all-fired proud. I just walk in the fields a-diggin' roots.

Phillpots. Are you alone in the world?

Old Maggie. Ain't we all alone, walkin' wherever we walk?

Phillpots. No, no, I mean family, men folks?

Old Maggie. There's been men I reared, but some died in the stinkin' mines, some choked off the coal dust, others kilt in some war a long ways off . . . only Jim's left an' he ain't so much, sittin' in the jail-house.

Psinski. She's got a daughter she lives with an' one grandson, Jim Flimmins, in jail——

Phillpots. On account of the strike?

Psinski. For the Proletariat——

Old Maggie. [*Screaming.*] I'll go mad hearin' them words!

Psinski. She don't know what it's all about, she just lives by boilin' up things that cure fever an' make dreams.

Phillpots. A witch.

Old Maggie. [*Standing huddled in her shawl, center.*] I known this soil since I was yaller-haired. I raised men out of it an' buried 'em. Why wouldn't I know what the green grass hides!

Psinski. Hides graves, that's what.

Old Maggie. An' flowers spring where the flesh rots.

Psinski. [*To* PHILLPOTS.] Come with me, I'll convince you, show you the tent colonies, show you where they live in pigsties an' barns. . . .

[*He and* PHILLPOTS *exit together,* PSINSKI *talking eagerly.*]

Old Maggie. [*Alone, pulling shawl closer around her.*] Fools . . . well, I'll be gettin' on. [*The lights fade,* OLD MAGGIE *in a blue spotlight huddled in shawl, shaking her head.*] There's a black time comin' . . .

[*Blackness covers her. In the dark a single blare of discordant music.*]

CURTAIN

ACT TWO

THE SAME EVENING

SCENE 1. DYNAMITE JIM

A dark curtain in which is a square window with bars five feet above the ground. From the window a red glow. Pale light and a shaft of moonlight center. An oblong box, evidently a coffin, lying on ground under window center.

[*Enter* MRS. FLIMMINS *and* OLD MAGGIE *left.* MRS. FLIMMINS *is a woman under forty, tall and bony in her loose dress. She has an odd, regal beauty, lines of age beginning to appear in her lean, noble face. Her hair is frowsy. A sugary, cracked voice, from which tense emotion flashes now and then like sparks.*]

Mrs. Flimmins. Come on, it's late, you walk so slowly.

Old Maggie. Can't no wise help it, dearie.

Mrs. Flimmins. This is his window . . . Jim . . . Jim . . . [JIM FLIMMINS *appears behind bars at window, a tall man with rough-hewn face and muscles like granite. He stares fixedly through the bars.*] It's your mammy, Jim. Are you all right?

Jim. Who's there with you?

Mrs. Flimmins. It's your granny I brung to see you.

Old Maggie. I hope you got peace, Jim.

Jim. All I need is a chew a' tobacco.

Mrs. Flimmins. Mebbe I can bring you tobacco tomorrow.

Old Maggie. You'd oughter pray!

Jim. I sit here watchin' the rats. A rat is a friendly kind a' animal, got a funny way a' scratchin' behind the ear, different from a dawg, ever notice it?

Mrs. Flimmins. You reckon they'll let you out?

Jim. They want me to rot here—but mebbe I'll take these bars an' twist 'em like wire in my two hands.

Old Maggie. Better set still an' pray, Jimmie.

Mrs. Flimmins. They got soldiers here thick as flies, soldiers come from Washington train after train, they got guns with knives on the end, they'd stick you like a pig.

Jim. If I had some shootin' irons an' a

bottle a' hooch I'd fight the army with one hand tied behind my back.

Old Maggie. You couldn't no wise hold a gun an' a bottle with one hand tied.

Mrs. Flimmins. He shoots his face but he don't mean nuthin', there's no harm in Jimmie.

Old Maggie. It's sinful pride, God help him.

Mrs. Flimmins. There may be trouble to-night, they been paradin' roun' an' threatenin' an' talkin' big.

Jim. I'd like to be in a fight.

Mrs. Flimmins. Never mind, Jim, when the strike's over they'll let you out an' we'll go to Philadelphia or New York.

Jim. Where do you reckon to git money for that?

Mrs. Flimmins. I'll manage.

Jim. When you an' the old girl ain't got no food for your face nor a roof in the rain.

Mrs. Flimmins. We're right comfortable, Jim, in that old barn on Mullins' hill.

Jim. A pigsty, that's what it is.

Mrs. Flimmins. I cleaned it up kind a' neat.

Jim. Rain comes in, don't it?

Mrs. Flimmins. There's cracks where the sun shines through an' the moon——

Jim. That's no place for a man's mother.

Old Maggie. Home is where the heart is.

Jim. God help us!

Mrs. Flimmins. Some day you'll be rich in New York, Jim.

Jim. I won't never see New York, I won't never see nuthin' but these dirty walls no bigger'n the sides of a grave.

Old Maggie. I brung men an' wimmin into the world till my old sides was sore, an' they died, exceptin' only you . . . you stand there lookin' out into the night.

Mrs. Flimmins. It don't do no good to cry about it. I'll get you tobacco tomorrow, Jim.

Jim. Mebbe I won't be here tomorrow.

Mrs. Flimmins. What you mean?

Jim. I dunno, never mind.

Mrs. Flimmins. What you so hot about?

Old Maggie. Better pray, Jim.

Mrs. Flimmins. Go home, Ma, an' pray yourself, I got errands to do.

Old Maggie. You better come home with me, Euphemia.

Mrs. Flimmins. I got other business——

Old Maggie. I'm afraid.

Mrs. Flimmins. You ain't scared a' the dark, are you?

Old Maggie. T'ain't that, it's people makin' mischief in the night, monkey-doin's, sin an' capers . . . they call Yoohoo, Yoohoo in the shadows—why ain't men got nuthin' better to do but kill an' drink an' chase wimmin folk?

Mrs. Flimmins. They've always done that.

Old Maggie. What makes 'em do it?

Mrs. Flimmins. The moon, I guess.

Jim. Yes, an' corn liquor.

Old Maggie. An' if they get to fightin' . . .

Mrs. Flimmins. You just head straight for home an' nobuddy will touch you. Toddle along, Ma.

Old Maggie. Don't be late like you been these last nights. I don't like to think a' you out alone.

Mrs. Flimmins. Oh, I guess I can take care a' myself.

Old Maggie. [*As she goes.*] I'm goin' then, but try to come home quick, Euphemia.

[OLD MAGGIE *exits.*]

Mrs. Flimmins. [*Starts to leave, and turns back.*] Good night, Jim.

Jim. Good night, Ma.

Mrs. Flimmins. Your granny's a terror. She's too old, always talkin'.

Jim. She'll die soon.

Mrs. Flimmins. Might be better.

[*Exit* MRS. FLIMMINS. JIM *makes sure no one is outside his window, then he starts to file at the bars, a regular grating noise. Enter left* RASTUS *with his banjo, singing. The rasping sound stops.*]

Rastus. [*Stands against the curtain crooning the unvarying blues tune.*]

"I got them Bow Wow Blues
'Cause they treats me like a dawg . . ."

[*He howls like a dog.*]

Jim. Who's there?

Rastus. [*Continuing to thrum banjo.*] One lonesome nigger, Boss, wid a heart full a' care an' desecration.

Jim. What you doin' roun' this jail?

Rastus. I wants to get in, wants to lay me on a prison bed.

Jim. What's a' matter?

Rastus. Ma woman done me wrong, she went to Alabama wid a Pullman porter man.

Jim. Always wimmin; hell with wimmin!

Rastus. Was it a woman put you in the jail-house, brudder?

Jim. No, it was like this . . . a bunch a' soldiers a-comin' down a road, with a big flag——

Rastus. [*Strumming banjo.*]

"Wid dem Yankee Doodle Blues . . ."

Jim. Me standin' in the road, can you picture it?—"Come on," they says—— [*He shakes his fist.*] So I come on an' they lowers the flag in my face. I was lousy with liquor, understan', first thing I knows I was in the flag like a net on a fish spittin' an' kickin' under them stars an' stripes, down in the mud. I seen black, couldn't see nuthin' else. I tore the guts out a' them stars I did—but it weren't wavin' in the sky that's the point. I says, "Hell, Judge," I says; but the Judge says, "Silence," he says——

Rastus. [*Singing.*]

"An' now you got those, yes, you got
those Yankee Doodle Blues . . ."

Jim. That's how I got in but you ain't heard yet how I'm gonna get out.

Rastus. You ain't a' gonna get out.

[JIM *reaches one arm through bars and grabs* RASTUS *in iron grip.*]

Jim. Ain't I, nigger?

Rastus. No, you ain't——

Jim. [*Shaking him.*] Wait'll you see me walkin' free.

Rastus. Leggo me.

Jim. Ain't I gonna get out?

Rastus. Mebbe you is. [*Shaking himself free from* JIM'S *grip.*] Say, brudder, you got that strangle grip. [*He exits left. His voice off stage singing:*]

"I got no girl neither white nor black
Ma woman's gonna hell in Alabama
An' she ain't acomin' back . . ."

[JIM *starts methodically to file again. Then, with a mighty effort of his arms he twists out two of the bars. With the movement of a cat he reaches the ground in one jump. He looks around ready to run. He pulls a piece of sacking out of the coffin and hides in coffin, throwing sacking over himself, as* BILL *and* MACCARTHY *enter right.*]

Bill. [*Whining.*] I don't half like it . . . that bunch a' miners is drunk an' you can't tell what they do next.

MacCarthy. They got no guns.

Bill. Mebbe they got guns hid somewheres, just waitin' for a sign to raise the lid off hell.

MacCarthy. No, no, these guys is good guys, y'know wot I mean, I was talkin' to one a' these miners.

Bill. What'd he say?

MacCarthy. A good guy, said his name was Smith, he gimme a drink. I reckon if them an' us could get together with some booze there wouldn't be no more strike.

Bill. Mebbe that's so——

MacCarthy. [*Seeing broken bars of window.*] Look a' that window, some guy has broke jail!

Bill. Hello inside, who's there?

MacCarthy. A man busted loose.

Bill. Where would he be?

MacCarthy. [*Knocks coffin with gun.*] What's this?

Bill. Just a box for some feller rotted in prison. What'll we do?

MacCarthy. Get the Sheriff. I'll go roun' the house this way. Make it snappy, now. [*He goes off right.* BILL *runs off left.* MACCARTHY'S *voice off stage right.*] Help! Man busted loose. . . .

[*Enter* RASTUS, *left, lounging along the wall of prison. Confused noise of voices and shouting off stage.*]

Rastus. Say, brudder, lonesome brudder in the jail-house . . .

[*He looks around to see the figure with sacking rise from coffin.*]

Jim. Yes.

Rastus. [*Trembles and goes down on his knees.*] I'm a good nigger an' I done no wrong, I paid ma dues an' I done no wrong, I kilt ma mother-in-law but I done no wrong. . . .

[JIM *ducks down again. Enter left* BILL *with* SHERIFF.]

Sheriff. What's that nigger doin'?

Bill. He's prayin' to his black God.

Sheriff. Get up, you.

Rastus. I can't right well 'cause ma laigs says no.

Sheriff. You see anybuddy?

Rastus. Ain't seen nobuddy livin'.

[*Enter* MACCARTHY *right.*]

MacCarthy. Who was it, Sheriff?

Sheriff. Jim Flimmins is out.

MacCarthy. Say, what sort a' guy was this?

Sheriff. Dynamite Jim, that's what he is.

Bill. Dynamite?

Sheriff. A rip-roarin' son of a gun, a guntotin' son of a bitch.

Bill. Is he a wobbly?

Sheriff. He ain't a Democrat, that's all I aim to know about a man.

MacCarthy. We'll get him dead or alive.

Sheriff. It would do my heart sweet to see six feet a' him layin' here.

[*Off stage distant blowing of discordant horns. The* JAZZ BAND *is at it again. It sounds slow and funereal.*]

MacCarthy. What's that?

Bill. It's them.

MacCarthy. At it again.

Sheriff. They call that music.

Bill. Sounds drunk.

Sheriff. They got away from us this mornin', hid down in a mine. I reckon we'll make Dynamite Jim dance to that music.

MacCarthy. Them fellers don't mean no

harm, Sheriff, they just like to jazz her up same as any man.

Sheriff. I make my jazz with a gun, understan'.

MacCarthy. Bill an' me will go hunt for this bird.

Bill. I don't half like it.

Sheriff. You boys go down the road there under the hill; keep a watch to each side. I'll give the alarm an' then I'll join you.

MacCarthy. Come on, Bill.

Sheriff. Y'know how coal gas is, one spark can set a whole mine to blazin'!

[SHERIFF *exits right,* BILL *and* MACCARTHY *left.* RASTUS *rises from ground still trembling.* JIM, *stepping out of coffin, taps* RASTUS *on shoulder.* RASTUS *tries to move away but his legs are rooted to the ground. He tickles banjo nervously.*]

Rastus. Seems like somethin' ghost-like jus' brushed ma shoulder.

Jim. Come with me.

Rastus. I ain't so friendly wid the ghosts.

Jim. I ain't a ghost . . . yet.

Rastus. Ain't you?

[*Enter* PSINSKI *right.*]

Psinski. So, you used the file I give you.

Jim. Thanks . . . thanks. . . .

Psinski. Now you are free, be a man, don't let 'em get you.

Jim. Pretty near tuk me. "Who's there?" they says. I pretty near says, "No one," I says—but I kept my jaw shut tight.

Psinski. If they catch you they string you up.

Jim. Help me then.

Psinski. You an' me is pals; stick with me an' you will be safe.

Jim. That's a go.

Psinski. [*To* RASTUS.] You help us.

Rastus. I ain't helpin' nobuddy.

Jim. If I could get home to my ma she'd mebbe hide me.

Psinski. Don't be a fool; that's the first place they look.

Jim. What do we do then?

Psinski. Y'know that big stone house on the hill that a rich man built?

Jim. The Labor Temple?

Psinski. Nobuddy'd ever go look there; we go hide in that.

Jim. Them soldiers is wantin' me.

Psinski. Which way they go?

Jim. That there road under the hill, but they wouldn't never think a' goin' up to the top a' the hill.

Psinski. Surely no: what's this?

[*He points at coffin.*]

Rastus. We all know what that is.

Psinski. Who's it for?

Rastus. Ma name ain't writ on it.

Jim. [*Pulling coffin forward.*] I'll get in this; you an' him carry this, understan', up the hill to that stone house.

Rastus. Come again?

Psinski. Carry it, you an' me.

Rastus. I ain't gonna carry no coffin.

Jim. You're gonna come, understan'?

Psinski. If anybody sees us they won't ever say a word.

Rastus. I ain't comin'.

Jim. [*Grabbing him, firmly.*] You is, or I wring your neck!

Rastus. [*Weakening.*] I might be.

Psinski. If you was in trouble, you'd want help. What you scared of?

Rastus. I ain't scared, just thoughtful, that's all.

Jim. Come on then. [*Gets in coffin.*]

Psinski. [*To* RASTUS.] Come on.

Jim. If you meet any one, make 'em take off their hats.

[*Off stage ghostly music continues a funereal sound, slow and painful rendering of the Bow Wow Blues converted to a funeral march. They start to move slowly with coffin. Lights go out. Stage is black.*]

Rastus' voice. Ain't it dark, though?

Jim's voice. Keep right on movin'.

Rastus. What's that?

Jim. That's me.

Rastus. I thought somebuddy else was you.

Psinski. Come on, everything's all right.

Rastus. Where are we now?

Psinski. Never mind.

[*In total darkness the distant music sounds dimly. Then two other men's voices take the place of those of* PSINSKI *and* RASTUS.]

SCENE 2. THE LABOR TEMPLE

[*In the dark, men's voices.*]

Bill's voice. Oh, God, if we only had some light.

MacCarthy's voice. What you doin'?

Bill. Never mind.

MacCarthy. A man's got no chance against black night; might as well look for a cross-eyed canary in an African jungle.

Bill. What's that about a cross-eyed canary? [*No answer.* BILL *calls out loudly.*] Help, help. [*Pause.*] Oh, God, where's that moon?

[*Stage lights up as the moon comes out.*

Drop curtain represents a marble temple with columns and two slightly grotesque statues painted on the canvas. A large door in this temple center. Elaborately carved inscriptions across top and under statues. Behind it the shadowy blue of the sky. Then a bright spot of moonlight falls front center.

Music stops. BILL *and* MACCARTHY *at edge of stage right.*]

MacCarthy. Who called for help? . . . Hey, Bill . . . Bill . . .

Bill. Must a' walked off this way.

MacCarthy. Weren't it dark jus' then?

Bill. I don't like the dark.

MacCarthy. We got the ole moon now.

Bill. Wonder where the feller went to.

MacCarthy. They say he eats the stuff.

Bill. What?

MacCarthy. Dynamite.

Bill. What's this place?

MacCarthy. We're way up the hill.

Bill. Is this a church? [*He approaches it, examining lettering on wall.*] Got writin' on it. "To the Spirit of American Industry, Coal . . . Steel . . . Oil . . ."

MacCarthy. Banana Oil!

Bill. One a' these here statues is Capital an' the other one is Labor. "American Manhood" it says.

MacCarthy. Don't kid me.

Bill. This is a queer place; let's beat it.

MacCarthy. Here's the Sheriff.

[*Enter* SHERIFF. *He stalks boldly into bright ray of light center.*]

Sheriff. Well, boys. [*They come to either side of him.*] Seen anybuddy?

Bill. Them trees throw funny shadows.

MacCarthy. What's this white house here?

Sheriff. That's no White House, that's the Labor Temple. Darius Swindleweight that was Governor a' West Virginia in 1908, he built that.

Bill. I'll say he got himself a swell house.

Sheriff. A farmer, a hard guy he was, too, that found coal where he plowed, so he figgered he'd like a swell white monument-like, to what coal could do. Now let's us get busy: you boys look over that side a' the hill, I got a posse beatin' through the woods.

MacCarthy. We'll look over the whole damn place.

Bill. I don't half like it.

MacCarthy. My friend's a little scared, Sheriff.

Bill. I seen some eyes lookin' out from them dirty shadows.

MacCarthy. Cats.

Bill. [*Relieved.*] Cats.

Sheriff. You're a soldier, ain't you?

Bill. Yes, but I can't help it. Say, I just think I'll put the bayonet in my gun, might be handy if I meet this dynamite child face to face, wouldn't like to hurt him but . . .

[*He puts bayonet in gun.*]

MacCarthy. Aw, you don't need that.

Bill. Can't tell. . . .

Sheriff. You got whistles, ain't you? If anythin' happens, whistle.

MacCarthy. Rely on us.

[*The three exit,* SHERIFF *right,* MACCARTHY *and* BILL *left. Off stage a distant note of derisive music. Then enter right* PHILLPOTS *and* SADIE *walking leisurely admiring the moonlight. They stop center. Off stage sound of languorous jazz continues.*]

Phillpots. It's not often I get a chance to go walking with a pretty girl and the moon shining.

Sadie. I shouldn't a' come. I stole the key off'n Popper's vest. Popper would kill me if he knew I was out.

Phillpots. Don't you worry, little girl. I shouldn't be here either, ought to be studying this strike.

Sadie. What do you care about the strike?

Phillpots. Are you interested in the labor question?

Sadie. Only when they get to shootin'; then it makes thrills up an' down your spine.

Phillpots. There's a good deal of shooting going on in town, but it's all serene here.

Sadie. Oh, it's quiet up here! Folks often comes along this hill to talk . . . an' . . . well, you know, talk—— [*Approaching him flirtatiously.*] You think kind a' slow for a city boy.

Phillpots. I don't get you, kid.

Sadie. Oh, talk . . . an' spoon . . .

Phillpots. Well, is that so?

Sadie. I don't even know your name.

Phillpots. Call me Mr. Zip.

Sadie. Ain't the moonlight silvery shivery?

Phillpots. You've caught a little of it in each eye, just a streak of moon!

Sadie. You got a jimjam line a' talk, Mr. Zip . . . Zip . . . Zip!

Phillpots. Sadie Cohen——

Sadie. Call me Desdemona . . . why do you laugh?

Phillpots. A great big black man killed her. Is that what will happen to you, little Desdemona, daughter of the smoke?

Sadie. Say, you're a real gent.

Phillpots. Yes, that's my trouble.

Sadie. If you want me, try an' catch me!

[*She suddenly runs off left.*]

Phillpots. [*Annoyed, muttering.*] Oh,

they're all the same. Now I'll break a leg on one of these tree stumps!

[*He follows her left. Off stage the jazz rhythm changes completely, becomes funeral blues. Enter* RASTUS *and* PSINSKI *right carrying the coffin. They stop center.*]

Rastus. Say, is this coffin made a' lead?

Psinski. Sure, lead to keep the dead from dancin' in the cold ground.

[*They set down the coffin left rear in shadows.*]

Rastus. Why don' we throw the box in a river an' be done wid it?

Jim. [*His head appears in coffin.*] Don't throw me in no river.

Psinski. This is the place I was talkin' about.

Jim. Sure there's nobuddy aroun'?

Rastus. That voice out a' the ghost-box gimme nervous indigestion.

Psinski. You black fellers is always afraid.

Rastus. I dunno; it just comes on.

Psinski. Guess it's in the blood; I can see your ancestors . . .

Rastus. [*Trembling.*] Where? Where?

Psinski. A people that ain't had a fair chance——

Rastus. Hush yo' mouth; some day we git a chance.

Psinski. Sure you will, the whole future belongs to you.

Rastus. A black future: mebbe the coons'll be kings, mebbe yet you see a black President 'a the United States——

Psinski. Sure . . . sure . . .

Rastus. A cultured nigger wid a good speakin' an' singin' voice!

Jim. [*Standing up.*] What's them ghost noises?

Psinski. We ain't alone here, there's voices somewheres.

Jim. If I could get in a good fight I wouldn't mind so much.

Psinski. Sit tight, the time ain't come for an open fight, you understand?

Jim. Not so much.

Psinski. You're a workman.

Jim. If I knew what it was about, I'd take a gun an' fight the world.

Rastus. Who, you?

Jim. Me alone.

Rastus. I don' so much mind a daylight fight wid a razor——

Psinski. Wait an' learn. You must hide here. [PSINSKI *turns to door of monument. From within comes noise of a woman singing raucously.*]

"Runnin' Wild. . . . Lost control. . . .
Runnin' Wild. . . . Mighty bold. . . ."

Psinski. There's some one inside there.

Jim. Who in hell would be in that place this time a' night? [*Men's rough laughter heard from rear inside the monument.*] Some fellers drunk in there.

Psinski. Huh, I hear men's voices.

Jim. I could do with a short swig a' liquor myself.

Psinski. It's probably soldiers.

Jim. We better get away from here quick.

Psinski. Can't now; may be other soldiers in any a' them shadows: lay low.

Rastus. Oh, Lawd!

Psinski. What's a' matter now?

Rastus. Red-hot ghost jus' passed through me.

Jim. If I had some shootin' irons!

Psinski. Stay right here; lay low, I'm goin' round, see what we can do.

Rastus. Don't bestir yourself, I'll go see. [*He exits hurriedly.*]

Psinski. He won't stop till he hits Kelly's Pool Parlor. [*Whispering to* JIM.] Some one comin' . . . lay quiet . . . I'll be back. . . .

[*Exit* PSINSKI *left.* JIM *lies down out of sight covered with sacking as* BILL *and* MACCARTHY *reënter right.*]

MacCarthy. I ain't gonna worry no more about chasin' nobuddy. The Sheriff's gone in the woods, let him worry. . . . I'd like to get a drink in me, y'know what I mean.

Bill. But we're on duty——

MacCarthy. That's the bunk, tie it outside. When officers ain't aroun' one man's as good as another.

Bill. I hear funny noises.

MacCarthy. It's them drunks playin' music. The soldiers is drunk an' the miners is drunk!

Bill. I don't see so much harm in it.

MacCarthy. No harm . . . it ain't a crime to play music, not yet it ain't—let's go see them miners . . . when a guy's as stewed as them he's everybuddy's friend. This is a good town.

Bill. It's a tough place.

MacCarthy. [*Strutting up and down.*] Well, I'm tough, ain't I? [BILL *nods sadly.*] What's the use a' bein' in the army excep' it leaves a guy free sometimes to raise cain when he feels it comin' on?

Bill. What's it get you?

MacCarthy. I like the life, makes me feel proud.

Bill. I had enough, I have, what are we here for? Shoot down other Americans; ain't they as good as we are?

MacCarthy. Can that talk, a soldier's got no right to think.

Bill. Makes you think, this stuff.

MacCarthy. Better write a letter to Congress.

Bill. They gassed me in the Argonne, they jailed me for bein' drunk in Haiti, got sick off'n a woman in Texas, I got a weak stomach —it's salute an' shoulder arms an' they kick you aroun'——

MacCarthy. That's seein' the world with Uncle Sam.

Bill. I don' wanna march no more in no dust, I don' wanna carry no flag, I ain't a pack-horse, I'm a man!

MacCarthy. Stand back while we see who's this.

[*They stand aside right as* FIRST SOLDIER *enters left doing a clog step.*]

Bill. It's one a' the boys.

MacCarthy. Hey feller, where you goin'?

First Soldier. [*Still doing a little dance.*] I'm off duty.

MacCarthy. [*To* BILL.] Y'see, he's full a' corn liquor.

First Soldier. Why shouldn't I be?

Bill. Listen, you ain't seen a dynamite-eatin' baby that busted out a' jail tonight?

First Soldier. [*Dancing.*] Ain't seen nuthin' but my own shadow, but I gotta date with frien's. She ain't so much in the face, but the shape!

[*He exits into monument center.*]

MacCarthy. He's gone inside that monument.

Bill. [*Reading from front of monument.*] "Labor . . . Industry . . . American Manhood." [*Scratching head.*] No, I don' understand it at all.

[*Enter a* SECOND SOLDIER *in a great hurry.*]

MacCarthy. Hey, you!

Second Soldier. [*Staccato.*] Good-by . . . don't stop me. . . . I'll be back. . . . Just gotta finish a piece a' business.

Bill. What business?

Second Soldier. Monkey business. . . . There's a skirt in there!

[*He starts toward door of monument.*]

MacCarthy. Say, I'm in on that.

Bill. [*Urgently.*] Listen to me, you fellers is all wrong, you should be ashamed a' yourselves.

MacCarthy. You'd oughter be a preacher, you ought!

Bill. No, 'tain't that, but I had experience, an' I love my mother.

[*Enter a* THIRD SOLDIER, *a big bulk of a man chewing tobacco.*]

MacCarthy. Hello, Hank.

Third Soldier. Jus' goin' to see a party a' frien's.

Bill. You boys has got the wrong dope: don't you know ev'ry time you drink an' cut loose, you do wrong to your mother? Each guy got a mother livin' or dead, ain't he?

MacCarthy. Dead ones don't count.

Bill. Even in hell a guy's mother's what made him out a' flesh an' sorrow, ain't she?

Second Soldier. [*Touched, sings.*]
"You are a wonderful mother . . .
Dear old mother a' mine. . . ."

MacCarthy. Banana Oil! One woman's just like another, jus' a bag a' bones!

Bill. Are you callin' my mother a bag a' bones? I'll fix you for that!

[*He tries to attack* MACCARTHY. SECOND *and* THIRD SOLDIERS *hold them back.*]

Second Soldier. Now, that's enough.

Third Soldier. You're pals, ain't you?

Bill. [*Shamefacedly.*] Sure, he's my buddy.

Second Soldier. Shake, then . . . pals got no cause to fight over wimmin.

MacCarthy. Aw, s'all right, I was jus' thinkin' a' my Ma an' how the ole man threw her out a' the house—good reason he had too!

Second Soldier. [*Continues to sing.*]
"Wonderful mother a' mine. . . ."

Third Soldier. Boys, we'd oughter be better men than we are. . . . I'm gonna take the pledge.

Bill. Why don't you take the pledge tonight?

Third Soldier. No, sir, tomorrow mornin'. . . . I'll feel like it then.

[*He goes hastily through door center.*]

Second Soldier. [*Still singing about his mother.*]
"You'll hold a spot down deep in
my heart
Till the stars no longer shine. . . ."

[*From inside the house raucous singing of "Runnin' Wild. . . . Lost control. . . ." breaks in on him. He hesitates, then, abruptly:*]

See you later, boys!

[*He exits center, joining in the chorus of "Running Wild" as he goes, and his voice is heard backstage still singing.*]

Bill. [*Querulously.*] They must a' cooked up a big party in there.

MacCarthy. Sure . . . there's a whole crowd in there, I should kiss a cross-eyed canary if there ain't.

[*Enter* PHILLPOTS *right.*]

Phillpots. Good evening, where's the fight?

MacCarthy. What fight? Booze fightin's about all you'll see aroun' here.

[*Chorus off stage singing.*]
"Runnin' Wild. . . . Lost control. . . .
Runnin' Wild. . . ."

Phillpots. What's that noise?

MacCarthy. They got a woman in there.

Phillpots. They have, have they?

MacCarthy. Can you imagine some girl, jus' a spring chicken, tender an' soft, with come-over-here in her eyes, an' kiss-me written on her lips—can you picture it?

Phillpots. Oh, yes, that's what I think about.

MacCarthy. Well, there's no such animal, not here there ain't, so me for a drink! [*He exits center.*]

Bill. They're all alike exceptin' me! I had experience, I gotta weak stomach.

Phillpots. Quite a philosopher, aren't you?

Bill. Aw, bunk!

Phillpots. I expected a big fight and I find you all boozing together.

Bill. A man only knows one thing: his mother's a good woman an' every other girl is a bum!

Phillpots. But maybe somebody's mother is in there.

Bill. Bunk! Strike, bunk! Army, bunk! Wimmin, bunk!

Phillpots. Oh, I'm an artist at bunk myself, but sometimes it gets me!

Bill. Is that so?

Phillpots. I'm a serious thinker, I am . . . sometimes I get to thinking, what's it mean?

Bill. Hear them drunks an' that woman singin'!

Phillpots. We don't know who it is, without eyes, without a face, to us she's just a voice, a kind of a song that's behind change and politics . . . hear it! [*The raucous woman's singing goes on, above the low hum of men's voices.*] The jazz melody of a bad woman in a small town, nobody's listened to that or told it.

Bill. Everythin' means somethin' if you can only figger it out.

Phillpots. Soldiers pass and a woman dances for them, laughs for them——

Bill. Gets their wads off 'em.

Phillpots. It's history, that is——

Bill. Aw, don't kid me.

Phillpots. Men have made religions out of women and this is how they treat her, a mother image——

Bill. What?

Phillpots. A dream . . . it might be a temple in Greece, they come to her to worship, it might be where the Chinese carved fairy-tales in stone——

Bill. Are you cuckoo?

Phillpots. Thinking, that's all, something I can't explain—it might be in some old Hindoo twilight, where men crowd around the perfumed body of a woman, without eyes, without a face—oh, it makes me sick!

Bill. You got wimmin on your mind, ain't you?

Phillpots. Guess I'll be getting down to the telegraph office. Good night.

Bill. Hey, buddy! [PHILLPOTS *turns.*] About wimmin . . . don't let it get you, boy, like it got me—they ain't worth it.

[PHILLPOTS *exits left.* BILL *disappears right.* JIM *rises from coffin.*]

Jim. [*Stretching.*] A woman, huh! God, I could use her . . . hot dawg! But it looks like this gimme my chance for a getaway. . . . Been lyin' in jail thinkin' about flesh an' bones till it drives you crazy . . . drives you . . . mebbe it ain't flesh an' bones, mebbe some kind a' meanin' in it. . . . [*Clenching his hands.*] Gawd, send me a woman!

[*Enter* SADIE *left. She comes center.*]

Sadie. Stick with me, Moon, help me find my way, 'cause I'm scared! [*She looks up and sees* JIM; *backing away from him.*] Oo . . . [JIM *seizes her roughly.*] Leggo me, leggo——

Jim. I heard your voice like callin'!

Sadie. I'll kick you, I'll slap your face.

Jim. Go on, I like it.

Sadie. I'll bite—oo, ain't you strong?

Jim. Bust your bones I'm so strong——

[*Enter* BILL *right.*]

Bill. Who are you? Are you the guy? . . . Yep, that's who you'd be, Dynamite, huh?

Jim. Mebbe so, mebbe not.

Bill. [*Points gun at* JIM.] Well, we'll see about that. I got you now, hands up.

Jim. [*Releasing* SADIE.] All right, baby, excuse me, kid, run home.

Sadie. [*Approaching* BILL.] Don't hurt him, please don't——

Jim. [*Between his teeth.*] I'll fix him! [BILL *is trembling a little.* JIM *approaches him calmly.*] You're one hell of a soldier.

Bill. Don't you come no nearer; I'll shoot.

Jim. Scared, ain't you?

Bill. Well, you know how a feller feels.

Jim. You guys is no good, ain't fit for an army.

Bill. I don' wanna be in no army.

Jim. Throw away your gun, then, an' fight like a man, huh?

Bill. I can't, I gotta kill you an' I don' want to!

Jim. One a' us has got to kill the other

Bill. Hands up or I knock you down——

Jim. [*Shouting.*] Come on then!

[JIM *lunges unexpectedly. They struggle.* SADIE *crouches at side.* JIM *wrenches the soldier's gun from his hands and* BILL *falls to ground. As he starts to rise viciously,* JIM, *gun in hand, jabs the bayonet down on the fallen body and wrenches it out. The soldier quivers and lies still.* SADIE *has watched intently. Now she faces* JIM.]

Sadie. I seen it go through him! [*A sob shakes her whole body. Beating against* JIM *with her fists.*] Oh, I hate you, you beast! I wanna kill you. . . .

[JIM *stands stolidly paying no attention to her. She runs off, crying hysterically.*]

Jim. [*Bends over soldier.*] He's gettin' cold . . . went through him . . . must feel funny to be stuck through . . . they'll hang me now; s'all right to talk but I never kilt a guy before. . . . [*From rear comes a sound of drunken laughter.*] That's for me, they're comin' for me . . . "hands up or I knock you down" was the last words he said. What curse makes a feller do them things? Gettin' cold, his soul's gone up in the sky, his soul's a-sittin' in the moon; he had a mother too. . . . I want my mammy's arms 'cause I done a black thing, oh, mammy, help me now!

[JIM *bends over the dead body muttering and praying. Again drunken laughter.*]

CURTAIN

ACT III

THE NEXT DAY

SCENE 1. MOTHER AND SON

A dilapidated barn which has been made roughly into a place in which to live. A wide opening rear without a door through which sunlight streams in. Sunlight also filters through cracks in the dilapidated walls. Straw is stuffed in the cracks. One broken table center and two broken chairs. A lamp with red cloth shade on the table. One or two boxes scattered about. Right of door a tin washstand with pitcher and basin. Also a rusty stove. Pair of rickety wooden stairs without a banister goes up the right hand wall with a landing and a door at the top. Rusty farm machinery in shadowy corners.

[*Left front, an iron bed, and right front a torn mattress lies on the floor. Both of these are occupied, figures huddled under bedclothes.* OLD MAGGIE *occupies the bed and* MRS. FLIMMINS *sleeps on mattress on floor. But only the outlines of the human forms are visible, their heads being under the covers.*

Enter JIM *and* PSINSKI, *their clothes torn, evidently escaping.* JIM *carries gun. They anxiously watch the sunlit door through which they have come.*]

Jim. [*Muttering.*] Home sweet home!

Psinski. We ain't safe here.

Jim. [*Looking at the beds, shouts suddenly.*] For Gawd's sweet sake, wake up!

Old Maggie. I had a dream an' it turned to steel against my belly!

Jim. Home to mommer an' all the folks is under the blankets sleepin' . . . [*He shouts again, hoarsely.*] Wake up!

[MRS. FLIMMINS *has risen from the mattress on the floor, gaunt in her frowsy nightgown.*]

Mrs. Flimmins. It's the boy, it's Jim! [JIM *laughs, she comes to him.*] You ain't hurt, are you?

Jim. I ain't exactly hurt.

Psinski. They're after us, that's all.

Mrs. Flimmins. Who's this?

Psinski. I'm an organizer here; the Sheriff's got my number.

Jim. Meet my pal . . . Jake, meet my mother that made me.

Psinski. They want to string us up.

Old Maggie. [*Crying softly.*] God deserts us an' the walls fall around our heads.

Mrs. Flimmins. [*Standing by the old woman.*] It's Jim, Ma, open your eyes an' look.

Psinski. We run in the dark, we hide, yet it is a beginning, we start something that make a noise an' a smell everywheres——

Mrs. Flimmins. Mostly smell——

Jim. [*Scratching himself, uncomfortably.*] Cut out that ghost talk, it's mornin', li'l birds is singin' in the trees.

[*Off stage a distant regular tread of feet is heard, monotonous, frightening.*]

Psinski. Hear them feet!

Mrs. Flimmins. Sounds like a train a-shufflin' along.

Psinski. More soldiers comin' off a train,

comin' from the station, comin' to clean the town——

Jim. That's for me, they're comin' for me, comin' to take me from my mammy's arms.

Psinski. What's a' matter, it's only shoe leather.

Mrs. Flimmins. It's a bad dream.

Jim. I know that feelin', sometimes I feel 'em in my sleep, guys bearin' down on me more'n you could count, with their bloody feet swingin' wide . . .

Psinski. Left, right . . . left, right . . .

Jim. Some day it'll come.

Mrs. Flimmins. What?

Jim. All them feet come to the door marchin' heavy, left, right, an' our ears'll bust. . . .

[*He sits down on bed, his head in his hands. The sound of marching feet dies down gradually.*]

Mrs. Flimmins. [*Her hand on his shoulder.*] Ain't no dreams no more. We gotta save your skin alive now!

Psinski. He'll be strung up if they get him.

Jim. I stuck a feller through.

Mrs. Flimmins. You what?

Jim. [*Vaguely, after a moment's hesitation.*] Killed . . . had to . . .

Mrs. Flimmins. Nobuddy's a-gonna touch him with me here.

Psinski. Ain't they?

Mrs. Flimmins. [*Quietly.*] No, I'm his Ma . . . ain't cryin', are you, Jimmie?

Jim. Dunno, you burn the strength right out a' me.

Mrs. Flimmins. Never no harm in Jimmie. Didn't I fix up this barn real sweet? I had a nice bedroom ready for you up them stairs, Jim, where the hay loft was.

Jim. Six feet a' ground'll do me now.

Psinski. What'll we do? [MRS. FLIMMINS *pulls open a trap door center in floor.*] What's that?

Mrs. Flimmins. A kind a' hole where nobuddy knows. Quick, both a' you go down.

Jim. It's dark there.

Psinski. We can talk. [*At door rear, excitedly.*] There's some one pickin' their way across the field here, looks like a silk hat.

Jim. Go down first.

[PSINSKI *nods and starts down.*]

Mrs. Flimmins. I'll bring you a candle, you stay there mebbe a week, mebbe . . .

Psinski. [*As he goes.*] Good! In this place I will explain the worker's place in history, the Proletariat. . . .

[*He disappears still talking.*]

Jim. Gimme the gun.

[*His mother hands it to him. He brandishes gun and disappears below.* MRS. FLIMMINS *shuts trap and rises, goes to door rear, then turns to the old woman.*]

Mrs. Flimmins. We must act like nuthin' was happenin'. Come on, take your clothes, we'll dress upstairs.

[*They take bundles of clothes and start up rickety stairs.*]

Old Maggie. What is it, are they comin' to take him away?

Mrs. Flimmins. They won't touch him.

Old Maggie. Why did he bust loose? Didn't he know you can't break law?

Mrs. Flimmins. He's heard too much a' this fool talk about the Proletariat.

Old Maggie. It makes a buzzin' in your ears, what is it? Proletariat! It burns in your mouth.

[*They exit at top of stairs.* PHILLPOTS *and* MAN IN SILK HAT *appear rear and walk up and down in sunlit doorway without entering.* PHILLPOTS *is dapper and amused as usual.* SILK HAT MAN *carries a newspaper.*]

Man in Silk Hat. Law and Order, that's the slogan today.

Phillpots. You sure this is the place?

Man in Silk Hat. Alleged to be headquarters of these gangsters.

Phillpots. I don't see anything.

Man in Silk Hat. Exactly, that's what makes it dangerous.

Phillpots. I'll tell the world——

Man in Silk Hat. That's just what you're here for. [*Tapping newspapers.*] But emphasize the law and order side, don't send out these sensational reports.

Phillpots. Sensational? I haven't begun yet.

Man in Silk Hat. The stock market will have a bad flurry this morning.

Phillpots. Guess I understand news values. . . . [*He opens papers, reads thoughtfully.*] "Plague Decimates China" . . . "Names Ape as Co-respondent in Sensational Divorce" . . . "Ireland" . . . there's a green place . . . "Man Stung on Head by Wasp Dies Immediately" . . . "Italian Woman Has Six Children at Once" . . . and they grow up to be stung on the head . . . that's news for you and this is the center of it where coal is made, because coal is power and power drives——

Man in Silk Hat. Remember the stock market!

Phillpots. I should worry!

Man in Silk Hat. Stock and bonds should be the main concern of a newspaper writer.

Phillpots. Look out for me then, I'm going to make a panic before I finish.

Man in Silk Hat. What do you mean? [PHILLPOTS *hands him a telegram which he reads.*] "Keep the wires hot . . . signed . . . William Randolph Hearst!" Well?

Phillpots. My job depends on getting a political sensation out of this.

Man in Silk Hat. There's no politics here.

Phillpots. Don't make me laugh, the threads of this strike go all over the country and you're the man that holds some of the strings. I'll stick to you like Mesopotamia fever.

Man in Silk Hat. Is this a threat?

[*Enter the* SHERIFF.]

Sheriff. I'm right sartain some of 'em is hid here.

Phillpots. Well, what are you going to do about it?

Sheriff. [*Pointing at* PHILLPOTS.] I don' trust him, sir, he's laughin' in his sleeve.

Phillpots. Just among gentlemen, there's no use deceiving ourselves, this strike is a comic opera. Look at the Sheriff you've got!

Sheriff. [*With dignity.*] Are you kiddin' me?

Phillpots. You bet your sweet life I'm here to kid everybody. I'm the guy with the typewriter and I know what I know; it's to laugh!

Man in Silk Hat. Is this the place, Sheriff?

Sheriff. Yes, sir, an' I got the soldiers waitin' near.

Man in Silk Hat. Good, where?

Sheriff. Over this way.

Man in Silk Hat. I don't like the atmosphere of this place. I'd feel safer with the soldiers.

Sheriff. This way, sir.

[*The three men disappear from doorway.* MRS. FLIMMINS, *dressed, comes downstairs, looks around, takes a candle from shelf, goes to trap door, taps once and speaks in whisper.*]

Mrs. Flimmins. Jimmie, darlin' . . .

[SADIE COHEN, *dressed in crude red, dashes in rear breathless.*]

Sadie. Ma'am . . .

Mrs. Flimmins. [*Rises hastily.*] What is it?

Sadie. They're after him, they got the soldiers waitin' there.

Mrs. Flimmins. What do you care?

Sadie. Your son, they're comin' to get him.

Mrs. Flimmins. I dunno what you mean.

Sadie. [*Desperately.*] Yes, you do, you gotta listen to me. It's about your son an' I want him——

Mrs. Flimmins. [*Pursuing her threateningly.*] What you want with him, little snip of a girl, don't you know nuthin'? Was you born yesterday, are you a week old, has you been washed yet after bein' born?

Sadie. Ma'am, ma'am——

[*But* MRS. FLIMMINS *goes on inscrutably.*]

Mrs. Flimmins. Has they sung to you in the cradle, has they whipped your backside——? [*She stops for breath.*]

Sadie. I seen him las' night, lemme tell you——

Mrs. Flimmins. Is it important?

Sadie. Yes'm, it's a message.

Mrs. Flimmins. Quiet, stand back there, hold your tongue.

[SADIE *stands in shadow by stairs as* SHERIFF *appears in doorway.*]

Sheriff. Mornin', ma'am.

Mrs. Flimmins. Mornin'. [MAN IN SILK HAT *and* PHILLPOTS *appear behind* SHERIFF. *Two soldiers lounge by the open doorway.*] What you men want in my house?

Phillpots. Do you live here?

Mrs. Flimmins. We had a nice home till the company threw us out. The furniture got lost in a coupla' big rains. [*Turning calmly to* SILK HAT MAN.] Nice mornin', ain't it? Have a seat, Sheriff.

Sheriff. The men we want ain't far from here an' we'll get 'em if we have to burn the house down.

Man in Silk Hat. Tell her the facts, Sheriff.

Mrs. Flimmins. Have you time to take a cup a' tea?

Sheriff. You got a son, ain't you? [*She nods gravely.*] Well, he's a leader a' these bums . . . James Baldwin Flimmins.

Mrs. Flimmins. He ain't never had the brain to lead nuthin' excep' a bottle to his mouth before this.

Sheriff. [*Produces spectacles and pile of legal papers, reading.*] "Conspirin' against the peace an' dignity a' the United States, ambush, lyin' in wait, assaultin', beatin', bruisin', an' killin' an officer a' the law——"

[SHERIFF'S *chair falls to pieces and he goes heavily to the ground.*]

Phillpots. Oh, Sheriff!

Mrs. Flimmins. Oh, I'm so sorry, I knew that chair weren't so strong, did it hurt you?

[PHILLPOTS *laughs,* SILK HAT MAN *looks very grave,* PHILLPOTS *helps the* SHERIFF *up.*]

Sheriff. [*Approaching* MRS. FLIMMINS

angrily.] You done that a' purpose. Wait till we lay hands on your son!

Mrs. Flimmins. They all come home to their mothers soon or later, don't they? Wanna see him? [*She produces a little locket around her neck and snaps it open in* SHERIFF's *face.*] Two year old, with gold curls.

Sheriff. Aw, hell.

Mrs. Flimmins. Now he's walked with a gun an' taken life. Funny how they grow up! an' me always dreamin'—then he was old enough to work an' there was a war an' away with the flags flyin'—talk about a dream that turns to steel against your belly!

Phillpots. Lived long in these parts?

Sheriff. Descended from original settlers.

Mrs. Flimmins. That's the Baldwins an' the Flimmins.

Phillpots. American Protestants?

Mrs. Flimmins. Church people, we been in these mountains a hundred years.

Phillpots. You fight the soil a hundred years and this is the end in a shack tumbling around your ears.

Man in Silk Hat. American stock, but there must be something rotten in it——

Mrs. Flimmins. [*Flaring up.*] Rotten yourself! Who made this strike? You did! Beatin' down the men till all the manhood in 'em was jus' liquor an' anger. You own the roads, you own the houses, you own the sky overhead—look at yourself in the glass. . . .

Phillpots. A man, monkey glands and all.

Mrs. Flimmins. I only wish it was you he'd kilt.

Sheriff. [*Looking at* MRS. FLIMMINS *admiringly.*] She's got that red fire in the eye herself.

Mrs. Flimmins. We're against outsiders here, we're a free people an' we're against soldiers——

Sheriff. That's the mountain way.

Mrs. Flimmins. Anyway, you're my kind, Sheriff, lemme speak to you alone, p'raps it would help——

[*They are interrupted by* BOOB, *who runs in closely pursued by* COHEN, *who is puffing like a seal. They irrupt into the scene wildly.* BOOB *breaks through the group center, then circles the stage, then runs down steps front to center aisle.*]

Cohen. [*Exhaustedly.*] Stop thief.

Sheriff. [*Producing both guns.*] Come here, kid.

[BOOB *slowly comes up steps to* SHERIFF, *who collars him.*]

Phillpots. What's the boy done?

Cohen. A thief, a thief, there's twenty dollars in his mouth.

Mrs. Flimmins. That's a great deal a' money.

Cohen. He sneaked into my store, he picked a twenty out a' the cash register, but I heard the bell. I seen him put it in his mouth!

Phillpots. Well, turn him up and shake him.

[BOOB *keeps his jaw tight closed.*]

Sheriff. Open your mouth or I'll knock your jaw out.

[BOOB *opens his mouth wide.*]

Phillpots. He's swallowed it.

Cohen. [*Plunges hand in* BOOB's *mouth.*] Ouch, he bit my hand.

Sheriff. Well, the money's inside him.

Cohen. Have you got a hammer?

Mrs. Flimmins. Good for him; anybuddy fools the law I'm right with 'em!

Man in Silk Hat. [*Fuming.*] This is really of no consequence.

[SADIE *comes forward from stairs.*]

Cohen. What you doin' here, Sadie?

Sadie. Never mind.

Phillpots. Good morning, Miss Cohen.

[SADIE *giggles.*]

Cohen. [*Pointing at* BOOB.] A thief. I always knew it, and we caught him now.

Boob. You got nuthin' on me. Who says I tuk it? Where is it? I'm too slick for you, see! Wait an' see who's United States Senator ten years from now, that's where a guy goes that can swaller coin!

Mrs. Flimmins. [*Laughing harshly.*] G'wan, kid, talk up.

Sadie. Ain't that swell, to be a reg'lar crook!

Mrs. Flimmins. [*To* SHERIFF.] There you are, take the kid to jail an' don't bother me no more, you see for yourself there's nuthin' you want in my house.

Sheriff. I ain't so sure.

Cohen. How do we know what else he stole? Better search him.

Man in Silk Hat. A very reasonable idea.

Sheriff. All right. [*To* COHEN.] You hold him. [SHERIFF *puts hand in one of* BOOB's *pockets.*] Marbles. [*Music plays off stage while the* SHERIFF *continues to produce articles from* BOOB's *pockets.*] Hold him tighter, will you? Jack knife . . . cigarette butt.

Cohen. What's that?

Sheriff. It's a cent.

Cohen. Put it back; he may need it.

Sheriff. Chewing gum.

Cohen. Ugh, it's been used.

[SHERIFF *produces from* BOOB's *inside breast pocket a girl's fancy garter with big pink flower on it.*]

Phillpots. The woman in the case.

Cohen. Did I tell you he was a ripper, or didn't I?

Boob. I guess I know about wimmin.

[*One of* SADIE'S *stockings is down almost to her ankles. She starts to sneak toward the door.*]

Man in Silk Hat. Look.

[*Everybody stares at* SADIE, *who giggles, embarrassed.*]

Cohen. [*Gazing tragically at bare leg.*] Do I see what I see or am I blind already?

[SADIE *clutches desperately at stocking.*]

Sheriff. Pull up your skirts. [*She hesitates.*] Up higher.

Phillpots. Oh, Sheriff!

[*They see garter on other leg, it is unmistakably the same.*]

Boob. Sure, it's her garter. Why wouldn't she give me her garter, she's my girl, ain't she? [SADIE *giggles.*]

Cohen. My daughter ain't frien's with no crook.

Boob. Her an' me is gonna go dance on Broadway together.

Sadie. [*Nods.*] We been practicin' them fancy steps; wanna see, Pop?

Cohen. [*Pulling her away from* BOOB.] No, I seen too much already: take the boy to jail, Sheriff; I make the complaint on him.

Sheriff. [*Nods and calls to the* SOLDIERS *lounging by the door.*] Boys!

Sadie. Don't you touch him!

Phillpots. Now really, Miss Cohen——

Sadie. Don't nobuddy touch me, neither, 'cause I got my own idea.

Cohen. [*Persuasively.*] Lemme hear an idea out a' my child's face before I bust it!

[SADIE *and* BOOB *dance side by side like a vaudeville team, and off stage music grows louder.*]

Boob. Her an' me will go to New York an' Philadelphia, ain't it the truth, Sadie?

Sadie. Well, I wouldn't care so much about Philadelphia.

Man in Silk Hat. [*Muttering.*] Disgraceful . . . disgraceful. . .

Cohen. [*Gives* SADIE *a resounding thwack.*] I'll fix you——

[SADIE *hides from* COHEN *behind* MRS. FLIMMINS.]

Sadie. Don't let him spank me no more, it hurts too much.

Mrs. Flimmins. [*To* COHEN.] If I was you I'd go easy on this.

[*Off-stage music stops.*]

Man in Silk Hat. None of this is of the slightest interest to me. My advice would be to send children of this type to the house of correction, but there are more serious matters in hand . . . h'm . . . the immediate capture of this criminal; that's your duty, Sheriff; you know where to reach me if you need me. Law and order, Sheriff!

[*He exits rear,* PHILLPOTS *follows him.*]

Phillpots. I'm going to stick right with you till you tell me all I want to know.

[*Exit* PHILLPOTS.]

Sheriff. I wouldn't arrest the kid if I was you.

Cohen. I make the complaint on him. Take him before I lay a hand on him myself.

Sheriff. Oh, all right. [*Calls to* SOLDIERS, *who have again retired to doorway.*] Hey, one of youse guys come here.

[*As the* SOLDIER *comes forward, he comes face to face with* MRS. FLIMMINS. *He surveys her in evident surprise.*]

Sheriff. What's a' matter?

Mrs. Flimmins. You don't know me.

Soldier. No, but you look like a dame that gimme a good time las' night.

Sheriff. Is that so?

Soldier. I was drunk when I seen her before.

Mrs. Flimmins. Bums.

Soldier. Who's a bum?

Sheriff. The lady's right, there's no argument.

Soldier. Well, I ain't startin' no argument.

[SHERIFF, *holding* BOOB *firmly by arm, passes him to* SOLDIER.]

Sheriff. Here's a package for you; take him to the coop, shove him in anywhere there's room.

Soldier. Pretty crowded now, but I guess he might fit in that closet under the stairs. [*The* SOLDIER *picks up* BOOB *by back of trousers and carries him off kicking.* SOLDIER *sings as he goes.*]

"When them lovin' arms is waitin'
When them lovin' lips is hot."

Sheriff. [*To* COHEN.] Now, take your daughter home an' there's an end a' it.

Cohen. [*To* SADIE.] Now for you.

Sadie. [*Hysterically.*] No, no, don't touch me.

Mrs. Flimmins. You better go with your father.

Sadie. Never goin' home, never! I'm goin' away, gonna find a lotta men to gimme kisses an' diamonds!

[*She dances wildly center.*]

Mrs. Flimmins. [*Comes to* COHEN *quietly.*] If I was you I'd leave her alone; I know them kind, lemme talk to her.

Sadie. I won't go home.

Mrs. Flimmins. [*To* COHEN.] Go away what she needs is common sense.

Cohen. You promise to send her home later?

Mrs. Flimmins. Sure, she'll come herself, don't you worry.

Cohen. I don't understand it at all.

[SADIE *laughs and continues to dance.*]

Mrs. Flimmins. None of us can understand; it's like walkin' in a mist with shoutin' an' strange words.

Cohen. Sadie . . . [MRS. FLIMMINS *motions to him.*] I'll go, then. . . . [*Wiping a tear from each eye.*] Didn't I raise her good, didn't I, with sugar candy an' a good lickin' on Saturdays?

[*He exits, head bent.* SHERIFF *looks on thoughtfully sitting on bed.*]

Sadie. [*Suddenly serious, comes to* MRS. FLIMMINS.] Y'see, I don't really mean all that; I ain't so bad, but he wants to lick me all the time, I can't stand it.

Mrs. Flimmins. You don't know what you mean; you're a shallow little dancin' fool.

Sadie. I'm not, you wait an' see.

Mrs. Flimmins. Keep still, I'm not thinkin' a' you at all. [*She goes to* SHERIFF.] Why don't you go?

Sheriff. I'm gonna set right here till I get your son.

Mrs. Flimmins. What then?

Sheriff. Then I reckon he'll hang on Lone Mountain, danglin' till he turns green with big birds peckin' at him all the time.

Mrs. Flimmins. [*Turns from him, then turns back with determination.*] Gimme a minute to explain, lemme talk to you.

Sheriff. Always ready to listen to a lady.

[MRS. FLIMMINS *picks up empty pail near door.*]

Mrs. Flimmins. [*To* SADIE.] Wait here an' don't you stir till I come back.

Sadie. Yes'm.

Mrs. Flimmins. Walk with me to the well, Sheriff; I'll tell you what I think can help. . . .

[*They go out together rear,* MRS. FLIMMINS *talking earnestly.* SADIE *goes to trap door and taps three times. She jumps back as trap door opens and* JIM *stands waist-high in opening carrying his gun.*]

Jim. I thought you was my mother.

Sadie. [*Scared.*] Stay back, stay back! I didn't think you was really there. [JIM *laughs and rises.*] Don't, don't; some one'll see you, there's soldiers all roun', Sheriff's jus' outside——

Jim. Is he alone?

Sadie. With your mother.

Jim. I got a mind to kill that Sheriff—one more or less, what's it matter?

Sadie. You must go back down.

Jim. No, gotta breathe, that feller talks his head off, mebbe I could make a run for it!

Sadie. Soldiers is right in sight: your Ma's tryin' to fix it. She thinks I'm a dumb-bell, but I ain't; I gotta message. The men are waitin' down a mine, mebbe they come out an' help you, anyways they gimme this paper for you.

[*She takes ragged slip of paper from dress.* JIM *scans it carefully.*]

Jim. Ahuh.

Sadie. What's it say?

Jim. I can't read.

Sadie. [*Takes it and reads.*] "Hail the chief; we will strike when the iron is hot."

Jim. What's it mean?

Sadie. They heard you busted loose, they heard about stickin' the soldier, you're a hero they says——

Jim. [*Spitting thoughtfully.*] I ain't so much.

Sadie. Mebbe they help you, they got pitchforks an' knives an' flags——

Jim. [*In a whisper.*] That dress is like a flag!

Sadie. Don't shout at me, they'll hear.

Jim. I ain't shoutin'.

Sadie. Yes, you are, inside you're beatin' like a drum, a drum that says, "Come here, come here!"

Jim. Go 'way then.

Sadie. Why?

Jim. [*Shaking her.*] 'Cause I don' wanna hurt you an' I feel like layin' my hands on somethin'——

[*He pushes her away from him.*]

Sadie. You're like you was las' night when you kilt him.

[*She runs out rear scared.* JIM *hides under stairs as* POP PRATT *enters rear hobbling energetically.*]

Pop Pratt. [*Calling loudly.*] Hallo . . . hallo . . . [*He pounds stick on floor.*] Anybuddy here?

[OLD MAGGIE *comes out on landing above.*]

Old Maggie. What you want?

Pop Pratt. Figgered I'd drop in keep you comp'ny for awhile. Heard there was a peck a' trouble up this way.

Old Maggie. What you heard don't matter; don't hang roun', we don't need you.

Pop Pratt. Eh? [MAGGIE *motions angrily toward door.* PRATT *at foot of stairs turns and looks out.*] Yep, li'l breeze blowin', looks like fixin' for one a' them thunder showers, but I don't mind the thunder so much now I can't hear nuthin'.

Old Maggie. You must go 'way, don't you hear?

Pop Pratt. [*Nodding head.*] All right, let's set awhile an' keep comp'ny bein' as us is the old folks that knows the meanin' a' things . . . what's a' matter, Maggie? You gotta funny look in the eyes.

Old Maggie. Look at me then.

Pop Pratt. A face full a' jimjam mem'ries: remember, Maggie, the day Abraham Lincoln stood on the hill yonder with his arms wavin' an' his voice like a taste a' bitter almonds in the wind!

Old Maggie. It's all diff'rent now.

Pop Pratt. You an' me walked on that hill when your hair was yaller an' the moon was bright on your hair——

Old Maggie. Don't talk like that, you old scarecrow!

Pop Pratt. Eh? What's a' matter with you, Maggie? Your jaws move but nuthin' comes out.

Old Maggie. I'm thinkin' have I brung men into the world, am I a mother a' drunken bums? That's the Proletariat!

Pop Pratt. What's that, one a' them new-fangled things for the bowels?

Old Maggie. Fools . . . fools . . .

[*She exits above.* MRS. FLIMMINS *and* SHERIFF *return rear.* SHERIFF *is carrying pail full of water.*]

Mrs. Flimmins. I tell you, I could raise the money.

Sheriff. [*Indicating* POP PRATT.] Easy now, look who's here.

Mrs. Flimmins. He can't hear nuthin'.

Sheriff. He sees a lot.

Mrs. Flimmins. [*To* POP PRATT.] Get out.

Pop Pratt. I jus' stepped in for a minute. . . . [*As she pushes him toward door.*] But yep . . . mebbe I'll jus' be goin'.

[POP PRATT *exits rear.*]

Mrs. Flimmins. [*Turns eagerly to* SHERIFF.] I'll give you money.

Sheriff. I thought you was dead busted, boilin' up roots to eat.

Mrs. Flimmins. But wimmin always got ways a' raisin' money.

Sheriff. [*Looking her over critically.*] Huh! Where'll I set this pail?

Mrs. Flimmins. You'll help Jim? I'll have the money in cash by tonight.

Sheriff. I'll say you got a way with you, ma'am.

Mrs. Flimmins. I'd do anythin' for my son.

Sheriff. An' supposin' I says, "'No, let 'im hang!'"?

Mrs. Flimmins. [*Flaring up angrily.*] You won't get him; my son's stronger'n you, mebbe he'll take you by the neck, throttle you, shake you——

Sheriff. Don't you fret, ma'am, I know this game.

Mrs. Flimmins. What game?

Sheriff. Man-huntin'.

Mrs. Flimmins. [*Suddenly becoming gracious, smiles blandly.*] Try woman-huntin', it's better.

Sheriff. I figgered you was one a' them prayin' kind, hot for God.

Mrs. Flimmins. I am, I'm prayin' God right this minute.

Sheriff. You sure look handsome shinin' like that.

Mrs. Flimmins. Soften your heart, Sheriff; let a little love-light in your heart. I'd do anythin' for a big man like you.

Sheriff. Would you now?

Mrs. Flimmins. Help a lone woman that's so weak with nuthin' but prayer to guide her.

Sheriff. I'll drop in tonight. P'raps you an' me could take a li'l walk when the moon's out.

Mrs. Flimmins. Guide me with your hand, Sheriff. I got lovin' ways when I——

[*Enter* MACCARTHY *rear.*]

MacCarthy. [*Angry and excited.*] Look a' here, Sheriff, I'm in on this; have you caught the guy yet?

Sheriff. What guy?

MacCarthy. He done in my buddy; I want 'im that's all, want to wring his dirty neck personally.

Sheriff. Don't get excited.

MacCarthy. I'm all broke up 'cause he done in my buddy.

Sheriff. We gotta go at this very quietly.

MacCarthy. [*Looking fixedly at* MRS. FLIMMINS.] Who's she? I seen you before somewheres.

Mrs. Flimmins. Why not? I got more right in coal town 'n you have.

MacCarthy. [*Scratching head.*] Then you sure are diff'rent from las' night.

Sheriff. What you mean?

MacCarthy. Aw, she's just sweaty now, but supposin' . . . just supposin' at night with flower water on her hair an' her voice like music playin' . . . can you picture it?

Mrs. Flimmins. Is this house a street like you all come in to look me over? You want me to lay down for the army to walk over my body?

MacCarthy. You ain't the same, an' yet . . . [*Turning to* SHERIFF.] She ain't so young but she got somethin' in her makes a ringin' in your ears.

Sheriff. Then you mean . . . ? [SHERIFF *and* MACCARTHY *whisper together.* MACCARTHY *laughs.*] She was up with all them soldiers?

MacCarthy. In that marble house.

Sheriff. Drinkin' with 'em?

MacCarthy. Gettin' their wads off 'em.

Mrs. Flimmins. [*Interrupting tensely*.] No . . . no . . .

Sheriff. Mebbe you're right.

MacCarthy. Oh, boy, I know it.

Sheriff. She told me she had lovin' ways . . . an' it's my idea she got her son hid here. Well, if she's that kind . . . .

MacCarthy. If the guy that stuck my buddy is hid here I'm gonna lay my hands on him an' then . . . then . . . [MRS. FLIMMINS *instinctively goes and stands over trap door center*. MACCARTHY *listens for a moment thoughtfully*.] Sheriff, I hear a kind a' scratchin' like a rat somewheres. Let's have a look a' this floor.

Mrs. Flimmins. [*Screaming*.] No, there's nuthin' there!

MacCarthy. [*Over the trap*.] Looks like a kind a' trap. [MRS. FLIMMINS *tries fiercely to keep them away from the trap*.] Pull her away.

[SHERIFF *pulls her roughly off*.]

Mrs. Flimmins. Listen . . . listen; it's true, I'll give you anythin', it was me with them soldiers, I got money hid away, I done it for my son, I'm a bad woman!

MacCarthy. What'd I tell you?

Mrs. Flimmins. Go away, only go away, I'll give you money . . . anythin' . . .

[MACCARTHY *has opened the trap*.]

MacCarthy. Guess we can bring home the bacon.

Sheriff. Come out, I got my gun on you. This ain't the one we want; but step out, you're under arrest.

[PSINSKI *comes out*. SHERIFF *peers down*.]

Psinski. The jail-house is better'n that hole.

Sheriff. Nuthin' else down there, but we got one Bolchevik rat.

MacCarthy. What we do with him?

Sheriff. Hand him over to some people that treat him good! You know!

[*He shuts trap door*.]

MacCarthy. The other one must be somewheres, an' we'll find him.

Psinski. I protest—you can't arrest me without a warrant.

MacCarthy. My Gawd, did you hear that, Sheriff? [*He sticks* PSINSKI *violently with gun*.] Tar an' feathers is what this bird needs.

Sheriff. Bring him along.

Psinski. I don't care what you do to me, but the workers'll lick you yet.

Sheriff. Treat him rough, we been too easy with these guys.

MacCarthy. That's right, they don't appreciate kindness.

[*Exit* SHERIFF *and* MACCARTHY, *the latter pulling* PSINSKI *along*.]

Mrs. Flimmins. [*Alone*.] Jimmy, where are you?

[JIM *comes forward, stands beside her white with anger, gun in hand*.]

Mrs. Flimmins. Jimmie, go down there an' don't come up no more.

Jim. [*Blankly*.] What?

Mrs. Flimmins. Down, quick.

Jim. I can't, Ma, till I get my strength back.

Mrs. Flimmins. You mean?

Jim. You know what I mean!

Mrs. Flimmins. What's it matter? It's safe for you now, they won't never look down there again.

Jim. They called my mammy a bad name. Suppose I gotta kill ev'ry guy calls you that.

Mrs. Flimmins. But what if it's true? Ain't you proud of it? It's for you, it's the money; we ain't been eatin' so much here, but I put away my little pile, watched it grow.

Jim. A guy's sweet mother!

Mrs. Flimmins. Waitin' for you till we could go away to New York, where people live, where we'd go to church——

Jim. What do I care now?

Mrs. Flimmins. [*Passionately*.] You're my son, mine . . . this ain't goin' on, I'm gonna learn you, an' make you a man——

Jim. I'm learnin' what ain't in the Bible

Mrs. Flimmins. Oh, you don't know what I'm feelin' inside me.

Jim. It's rot, it's decay, there's worms in us.

Mrs. Flimmins. No, Jim, we're all right.

Jim. Every guy's had my mammy's arms!

Mrs. Flimmins. We're up against somethin' we don't understan'—somethin' black—takes a man's muscle an' a woman's flesh.

Jim. All right, I'm gonna find out what that is!

Mrs. Flimmins. If we could get away from here—New York, a big city.

[OLD MAGGIE *comes out at top of stairs above, stands on landing unnoticed by the two intent figures*.]

Jim. So's you can get more men, huh? So's you can walk on a big main street givin' the glad eye to ev'ry stranger?

Mrs. Flimmins. Don't, Jim.

Jim. Dirty sin, rottin' inside us.

Mrs. Flimmins. If I search my heart,

mebbe somewhere in me there was the flesh cryin'.

Jim. It's in our blood.

Mrs. Flimmins. We're good blood, Jim, proud, pioneers.

Jim. Well, them pioneers was sons a' bitches.

Mrs. Flimmins. They dug in the ground.

Jim. They got the sinful dirt a' the earth in 'em. All right, let the earth have its way, then; my blood's ready to spread on the ground!

Mrs. Flimmins. [*Clinging to him.*] Jim, your father was a decent man.

Jim. Every guy's my father now, I shake ev'ry guy by the hand.

Mrs. Flimmins. We're all right; there's somethin' inside us, somethin' stirrin'——

Jim. Hell stirrin'!

Mrs. Flimmins. No, no, somethin' good, like when you pray till it burns.

Jim. I got a feelin' that burns my stomach.

Mrs. Flimmins. Las' night you kilt a man.

Jim. That's nuthin', but somethin' soft come into me, somethin' I hadn't known; what can a guy do when he's got that thing in his stomach stronger'n liquor?

Mrs. Flimmins. Go down there, Jim, an' wait.

Jim. Nuthin' to do but die.

Mrs. Flimmins. You needn't die, now I've known how to save you.

Jim. Yes, an' you're proud about it, ain't you?

Mrs. Flimmins. [*Trying desperately to calm him and explain.*] Las' night I was proud, 'cause my body's strong enough to drive men even when I'm old like walkin' in a mist.

Jim. What do I care now?

Mrs. Flimmins. Gimme that gun.

Jim. Get away from me, don' touch me! If you touch me, I'll curse you to hell!

Mrs. Flimmins. All right, sometimes mothers an' sons is a cursin' matter.

Jim. I'm goin' out an' fight, ain't kilt enough yet.

Mrs. Flimmins. If there's more fightin' to do, I'll do it. Gimme that gun.

Jim. [*Fiercely.*] Stand back!

[OLD MAGGIE *suddenly doubles up as if with a cramp, and rolls straight from top of stairs to bottom, where she lies in a heap.*]

Mrs. Flimmins. [*Screaming.*] Your granny, Jim, she heard the truth an' fell like a stone. [*Bending over* OLD MAGGIE.] She ain't hurt.

Jim. What do I care? I'm ready now. To the ash-pile with all of you!

Mrs. Flimmins. [*Clinging to him.*] Jim, I'm your Ma. Whatever I done, I done for you; you gotta stay with me now.

Jim. [*Waving gun.*] I'm through, I'm free now. Goddam this house, I'll fight alone! [*Holds up his gun and shouts in sunlit doorway.*] Let hell loose!

[*Darkness covers the stage.*]

EVENING OF THE SAME DAY

SCENE 2. WHAT HAPPENED TO SADIE

A mine entrance. Drop curtain represents a criss-cross of bars and derricks against a dirty yellow background. The black opening of the mine right. Fading gray light.

[*A noise of shooting and shouting off stage. There is rhythmic frightened music at intervals throughout this scene. A single shot rings out. Enter* PHILLPOTS *right.*]

Phillpots. Just missed me! Say, I didn't bargain for this; it's a real fight now . . . who goes there?

[COHEN *appears left, dishevelled and worried.*]

Cohen. What's a' matter?

Phillpots. The matter? You may well ask! The miners came out from where they were hiding and they're sniping from behind every tree. [*A shot off stage.*]

Cohen. Ouch!

Phillpots. [*Supporting him.*] Are you hurt?

Cohen. I ain't had time to look.

Phillpots. The soldiers are driving the strikers into the mountains, they'll soon capture the man they want—hear that?

Cohen. Oi, oi . . . .

Phillpots. You'd better go back home and put your head in a pillow.

Cohen. [*Pitifully.*] Where is she, what's happened to her?

Phillpots. Who?

Cohen. My daughter Sadie, who else is there?

Phillpots. You mean she's gone?

Cohen. I can't find her nowheres, all day she is gone.

Phillpots. [*Preoccupied, looking off stage.*] From what she said, maybe she's gone to New York.

Cohen. Fightin' everywheres, how do I know somebuddy won't hurt my little girl?

Phillpots. Well, she's nowhere around here,

that's sure, and you'd better look out for yourself.

Cohen. What do I care for myself? I will give her yet a weddin' dress with bells on it, I will find her if I have to walk to New York lookin' for her——

Phillpots. A wandering Jew!

Cohen. A Jew yes, an' all of a sudden the curse a' the race rises up an' slaps you in the face . . . but wait, in the end we'll beat you all; a people cursed but with wisdom in the heart, a lawful people livin' in the law ever since Moses, we win in the end!

Phillpots. You don't all do so badly right now.

Cohen. Say what you like, but your children's children will be shoutin' oi, oi, because we conquer . . . Sadie . . . Sadie . . .

[COHEN *goes away muttering.*]

Phillpots. [*Alone.*] No more shots . . . guess it's almost over, guess the miners are licked, guess they caught the one they wanted. [*A shot off stage.* PHILLPOTS *turns.*] It's a girl, somebody shot at a girl!

[SADIE *stumbles in, her clothes torn, spattered with mud, her hair loose.*]

Sadie. [*Forlornly.*] Mister . . .

Phillpots. Sadie Cohen . . . [*Holding her arm.*] This way, keep out of sight.

Sadie. Have they kilt him yet? Jim Flimmins, the man they're huntin' for?

Phillpots. I am informed that they'll have him any minute now. He started things going, he ran through Main Street shooting off a gun, but they'll get him now.

Sadie. Sweet God . . . Mister, where you goin' to, Mister?

Phillpots. I'm going to get out of this before somebody shoots me by mistake, I've got the biggest story of my life; now I'm called back to New York and the quicker I get there the better.

Sadie. What's that light there?

Phillpots. A burning cross, can you beat that? The Ku Klux Klan has got into the fight now. They must have come up by train loads from Charleston.

Sadie. I'm so tired!

Phillpots. Where have you been? Why are your clothes torn?

Sadie. I tuk to the open country, I climbed a mountain an' I got all tore, but I was scared alone with the moon an' the stars. I thought I'd go roun' the world but it looked kind a' big.

Phillpots. Better go back to home sweet home.

Sadie. [*With passion in her childish voice.*] Never no more!

[*An exchange of shots nearby.*]

Phillpots. Hear that, aren't you scared?

Sadie. [*With a little giggle.*] Not so much, it tickles my spine.

Phillpots. I must take you home, take you to a safe place.

Sadie. Never goin' home!

Phillpots. What do you expect to do then?

Sadie. You take me to New York with you.

Phillpots. What?

Sadie. [*Fiercely, coming close to him.*] Take me away anywheres.

Phillpots. [*Shakes his head and speaks very gently.*] Little girl, haven't you learned your lesson yet?

Sadie. I ain't done nuthin' yet.

Phillpots. Don't you see the impossibility of running wild? I'm sorry for you, but——

Sadie. Then take me to New York.

Phillpots. I'd look pretty bringing you to New York.

Sadie. You gotta take me with you.

Phillpots. What?

Sadie. 'Cause I had a dream an' God come to me in a dream an' said, "Go to New York an' get a job in the movies——"

Phillpots. [*Shocked.*] God said that?

Sadie. I think it was God.

Phillpots. You were mistaken.

Sadie. I gotta get away from this dirty valley, gotta see pleasures an' palaces.

Phillpots. Look at me. I've gone round and round looking for the news that's blown on the four winds.

Sadie. [*In a pitiful little singsong voice.*] Take me away from here anywheres wherever the winds blow.

Phillpots. No, I'm a careful man.

Sadie. You liked me yesterday.

Phillpots. Kidding, that's all. I'm just a poor fish who tries to make his way by kidding people.

Sadie. Were you kiddin'?

Phillpots. Yes.

Sadie. Well, even if you were . . . somewhere there's sweet flowers an' violins playin' them waltzes . . . that's love music . . . an' champagne . . .

Phillpots. [*Doubtfully.*] Perhaps.

Sadie. An' barrels full a' real diamonds.

Phillpots. Is that all you want?

Sadie. I want all the love in the world an' then some, an' then I wanna dance on my toes!

Phillpots. [*Softly.*] Desdemona, flower of the smoke, you'll get what's coming to you; I can't help it.

Sadie. I'd call you my sugar-popper.

Phillpots. My heart's breaking and you can't mend it.

Sadie. Go 'way from me then. I thought you was straight goods an' you're a fake.

Phillpots. Be a good little girl.

Sadie. I ain't a good li'l girl, I won't be, I ain't.

Phillpots. Listen, Sadie——

Sadie. Lemme alone, then, can't you, I need a man, not a dummy.

Phillpots. Sorry.

Sadie. Beat it then, what you so sad about?

Phillpots. Being a good middle-class man, I'm sorry for everybody, but I never know what to do about it. [*He laughs again.*] Shooting is all round us now. Look here, I've got to get you out of this.

Sadie. You don't care if I get kilt.

Phillpots. We've got to get across that field there and back into town. I'll see if there's a safe way. You stick right here where they can't see you, understand? I'll be right back. I'll see if there's a safe way.

[*Exit* PHILLPOTS *right.* SADIE, *alone, calls after him.*]

Sadie. Mebbe I won't be here when you come back. . . . [*Pause. She is frightened, uncertain. Shouts and shooting off stage. She kneels down pounding her little clenched fists against the ground.*] Oh, God, what'll I do? Sweet God, where'll I go? Lemme go roun' the world, lemme ride in an aeroplane, lemme put smelly stuff on my hair——

[JIM *appears, shouting as he comes.*]

Jim. You ain't got me yet, not yet you ain't!

[*He almost stumbles over* SADIE, *stops short abruptly.*]

Sadie. I thought you was kilt!

Jim. Not yet, but soon.

Sadie. They're lookin' for you everywheres.

Jim. I give 'em the slip. They want me; if they knew I was here they'd be closin' in on me—catch me like a rat.

Sadie. What you gonna do?

Jim. Die like a good guy.

Sadie. All them soldiers with guns——

Jim. All right . . . I'll get one good laugh on 'em! [SADIE *makes a wild dash to run away from him; he catches her.*] Nobuddy can get away from here now.

Sadie. [*Struggling with him.*] Lemme go——

Jim. [*Still holding her.*] I'm the guy stands alone against everybuddy . . . me myself, understan'!

Sadie. That's awful!

Jim. Afraid a' me? You seen me kill a man.

Sadie. I don't care.

Jim. I kilt others since then, I hid in the ground an' then I went out with a gun, I walk like a ghost, you smell the cold groun'?

[*Shouting and shots off stage.*]

Sadie. What you gonna do?

Jim. A black thing.

Sadie. I don't know what you mean.

Jim. You an' me, huh?

Sadie. What you mean?

Jim. You'll find out quick.

Sadie. No, I'm goin' away somewheres.

Jim. I can't go with you, gotta date pretty soon.

Sadie. Who with?

Jim. Coupla' hundred soldiers an' the gents a' the Ku Klux Klan—ain't you proud be with a guy got frien's like that? [*Noise and confused shouting come closer.*] Them soldiers is lookin' for me everywheres.

Sadie. I don't like this.

Jim. What you want, huh?

Sadie. Lemme go——

Jim. Tell me what you want?

Sadie. Oh, diamonds an' silks an' a job in the movies . . . I got a hunch——

Jim. [*Squeezing her arms, lifts her off the ground.*] Me too, I got a drivin' hunch!

Sadie. You're so strong!

Jim. You know what you want, huh? I can fix you so you won't want nuthin' . . . afraid now? I curse the mommer that made me! Wimmin is all bums, you squeeze 'em, you bust 'em, an' you got nuthin'. I used to be scared a' wimmin, but not now—— [*A terrible determination in his voice.*] Not since today!

Sadie. I'll be your sweet mommer!

Jim. Then I curse you, too!

Sadie. Me, why you could lift me in your arms . . . if you want to.

Jim. Mebbe I want to. [*He lifts her up.*] I can lift you higher'n that.

Sadie. Go on . . . hold me higher . . .

[*He lifts her high in his arms; she giggles wildly.*]

Jim. I raise you high to the moon, I steal a barrel full a' diamonds for you, reach up an' pick a bunch a' stars.

Sadie. You're kiddin'.

Jim. I ain't kiddin' . . . [*Still holding her in his arms.*] Listen, feet . . . comin' closer, ghost feet . . .

Sadie. I see shadows movin' everywheres.

Jim. Comin' closer but not so quick; they think there's a crowd here with guns, soldiers behind every tree: they got me here like a rat in a hole, no chance to get away.

Sadie. You must hide.

Jim. They'll find me quick enough. Let them soldiers come. They'll get me in a minute, but you're comin' with me.

Sadie. Where?

Jim. [*Indicating the mine entrance.*] Down there.

Sadie. Bluffin', that's all you are; ev'rybuddy kids me!

Jim. I don' bluff, not me; I'll fix you, I will . . .

Sadie. No, no, I don' wanna, lemme go——

Jim. Let them soldiers come, I'll have my way first.

[*He carries her down into the mine. Absolute darkness.*]

SCENE 3. THE MAN HUNT

[*Voices of* SOLDIERS *shout in blackness from either side of stage.*]

First Voice. Have they got him yet?

Second Voice. No, he got away.

First Voice. While we was waitin' for him at the front a' the mine he sneaked out like a mole through a hole at the back.

Second Voice. He done wrong to a girl.

First Voice. There he goes across the fields there.

Second Voice. Get him.

First Voice. Get him.

[*Shouting grows in volume, with drum beats and rapid rhythm of music. Then gradually revealed an open space suffused with ghostly light, across which stands a railing of heavy iron bars nine feet high, grim and foreboding against a wan sky.* JIM *crosses from left to right, his arms gesticulating wildly. Then* MACCARTHY *and other menacing figures, some with guns, others with torches, cross following him.* SOLDIERS *come down through audience shouting as they come and join in the pursuit.* MAN IN SILK HAT *appears in an upper box with a megaphone through which he shouts like an announcer at a race.*]

Man in Silk Hat. Jim Flimmins has escaped! This man is an enemy of society, a beast. He killed men, he attacked a woman, sinner, moral leper, society must be justified! They're off, the Man Hunt! Round and round men are unchained against him! [JIM, *alone this time, his arms gesticulating wildly, crosses from right to left.*] Stop him . . . he's in the field . . . hunted he runs . . . Halt! . . . Shoot! . . . The Man Hunt! [JIM *climbs grotesquely up the iron railing.*] He climbs the big fence. . . . Stop him! Over the fence he's safe, he's up to the top, over the fence he's free in the woods! [JIM *has reached the top of the fence.* MAN IN SILK HAT *shouts louder.*] No. . . . No. . . . [*In trying to get over,* JIM *has got caught by the back of his trousers on the point of one of the iron bars, where he hangs in mid-air, hanging downward, arms and legs sprawling.*] Caught by the pants, caught on the fence, he hangs like a rag on a railing; he hangs like a flag, a human flag, with arms and legs that wave in the wind, the flag of defeat, torn by the East wind, the North wind. . . . They've got him now!

[*A flashlight is turned on* JIM *where he hangs sprawling in the air, a figure of grotesque defeat. Points of guns bristle in a circle round him on the edge of the light. Blare of music.*]

CURTAIN

ACT FOUR

SIX MONTHS LATER

THE JAZZ WEDDING

A hilltop above the town. It is just before dawn. Trees and bushes are outlined blackly against the sky.

[*Enter* MRS. FLIMMINS *and* SADIE.]

Mrs. Flimmins. Come on, child, no use cryin'.

Sadie. Ain't cryin', I'm laughin'.

Mrs. Flimmins. Sounds the same.

Sadie. Jus' thinkin', where do we go from here? [MRS. FLIMMINS *is silent.*] Look . . . look, you can see it plain.

Mrs. Flimmins. They've driven us out, it's burnin' up an' that's an end a' it. We was real cosy in that barn.

Sadie. Yes, ma'am.

Mrs. Flimmins. Burn up mem'ries.

Sadie. It's an end a' us.

Mrs. Flimmins. Not yet it ain't . . . but I dunno where to turn. . . . The Sheriff's one a' the Klan himself. If we go into town he'll catch us an' hand us over to 'em.

Sadie. We got to go somewheres.

Mrs. Flimmins. How'd you know we have?

Mebbe they save us the trouble—I tell you they hate us all.

Sadie. Why should they hurt us?

Mrs. Flimmins. They burned the shack, ain't they?

Sadie. But why . . . I don't see why . . .

Mrs. Flimmins. Don't keep askin' why like your brain was full a' soap bubbles.

Sadie. Yes, ma'am——

Mrs. Flimmins. Don't "yes" me like that, if you hadn't said yes when you shouldn't you wouldn't be in this pickle now.

Sadie. I didn't say nuthin', it jus' happened.

Mrs. Flimmins. [*With a harsh laugh.*] I know my son, I know his way.

Sadie. I don't care.

Mrs. Flimmins. Carryin' a baby inside you without a name.

Sadie. [*Laughing softly.*] I don't care.

Mrs. Flimmins. You'll care when the Klan get you an' punish you for bein' bad.

Sadie. They're after you too, they call you bad names, kids throw stones at you!

Mrs. Flimmins. I'm diff'rent. I *know* what I do, I ain't a little sap-head fool like you.

Sadie. If I was somewheres else where people didn't know.

Mrs. Flimmins. Mebbe they'll put you on a train after they get through with you.

Sadie. The men in sheets?

Mrs. Flimmins. We got no money to get away, all the men that might help us has left the country.

Sadie. There's my Pop.

Mrs. Flimmins. He threw you out.

Sadie. He might help us now.

Mrs. Flimmins. He can't: what they won't do to him! A Jew storekeeper is what these people eat for breakfast, wait an' see!

Sadie. They mustn't touch me till it's born, they must let me alone till it's born. [MRS. FLIMMINS *laughs harshly.*] I want it, I want it.

Mrs. Flimmins. What makes wimmin do it?

Sadie. [*Crooning half to herself.*] Kind a' feelin' stealin' over you.

Mrs. Flimmins. Aw, shut up, don't sing to yourself like that. I'm sick a' hearin' you sing an' say you don't care. I'm sorry I tuk you in.

Sadie. You've treated me white all right.

Mrs. Flimmins. Well, it ain't for you, don't think that; it's for Jim an' what he done to you.

Sadie. A guy as strong as an ox, a guy that burned like liquor!

Mrs. Flimmins. He wouldn't accept things, wanted to fight all the time; so they strung him to a sour apple tree——

Sadie. Don't talk about it, don't——

Mrs. Flimmins. I ain't done hopin'.

Sadie. He's mine as well as yours, now.

Mrs. Flimmins. Don't you say that: you think he'd care if he come back now walkin' free? He'd call you a fool an' laugh it off.

Sadie. He won't come back.

Mrs. Flimmins. They never found the body . . . strung to that tree it was, an' it jus' disappeared.

Sadie. He's gone six months now.

Mrs. Flimmins. I got a feelin' perhaps he'll come back. . . . Pray hard, pray with all you got in you, and mebbe he'll come. [*Funereal music off stage.*] I hear those Kluxers.

Sadie. They're after us, they want us.

Mrs. Flimmins. Come this way.

[*As they move right an enormously tall man appears rear, in Ku Klux regalia, looking eight feet high. He smokes a large cigar from which come colored sparks when he puffs it. The* KING KLEAGLE *is, of course, another incarnation of the* MAN IN THE SILK HAT. MRS. FLIMMINS *and* SADIE *hide in shadows right. Funereal music grows louder, and a strange double procession comes down the aisles of the theater. These are the* KLAN *members, in robes, masks and full regalia, the man at the head of one line carrying a cross, at the head of the other line an American flag. They assemble about the commanding figure of the* KING KLEAGLE *center. He motions right; two members of the* KLAN *hurry off, and reappear dragging* SADIE *and* MRS. FLIMMINS, *whom they throw roughly to ground at front of stage.*]

Mrs. Flimmins. Leggo me, leggo. . . .

King Kleagle. You will await judgment in your turn.

[*The* KLANSMEN *point accusing fingers at the two women.*]

Mrs. Flimmins. Judgment! You cowards! You're a bunch a' old wimmin yourselves! [SADIE *screams.*] Let that little girl alone, she done nuthin' to you——

[*The* KING KLEAGLE *motions to have* MRS. FLIMMINS *removed. She is dragged away right, and* SADIE *remains on her knees front center.*]

King Kleagle. [*In a deep false voice sounding as if it came from heaven.*] Kleagles, wizards, goblins, gathered in this Kloncilium!

[*They all face the* KING KLEAGLE *with arms outstretched and the whole group chants in answer.*]

Responsive Chant. Glory . . . glory . . . Halleluiah. . . .

King Kleagle. We gather this night to protect morals. [*The group grumble and grunt ominously.*] Native-born Americans, Patriotic Protestants, regular citizens.

Responsive Chant. Glory . . . glory . . .

King Kleagle. Have you taken the oath to exterminate foreigners?

Responsive Chant. God's will be done!

King Kleagle. Are the tar and feathers ready?

Responsive Chant. God's will be done!

King Kleagle. Are the guns and knives on hand?

Responsive Chant. [*Very loud.*] God's will be done!

King Kleagle. Clean up the dirty foreigners, make 'em kiss the flag! Skin the Jews, lynch the niggers, make 'em kiss the flag!

Responsive Chant. [*Quite breathless and with a good deal of grunting.*] Halleluiah . . . Halleluiah . . .

King Kleagle. Order. [*Silence.*] I wish to announce, entire Congress of the United States joined the Ku Klux Klan last night.

Responsive Chant. [*The whole crowd point finger directly at audience and shout.*] Halleluiah!

King Kleagle. We gather in holy judgment, moral judgment. . . . First case! Name?

[WHITE FIGURES *in circle sway and* CHORUS *answers.*]

Responsive Chant. Sadie Cohen . . . Sadie Cohen, Sadie Cohen . . .

[SADIE *seeing them sway sways too, standing on one leg and then on the other.*]

King Kleagle. For six months she has embarrassed the community by her appearance and manners.

First Goblin. [*Stepping forward.*] Look at her dance, look at her sway.

Sadie. I can't help it.

[*They all begin to sway more emphatically.*]

Second Goblin. [*Stepping out.*] She's a Jazz kid.

First Goblin. Got a Jazz bug.

King Kleagle. It's outrageous!

First Goblin. It's contagious!

Low Chanting. Glory . . . glory . . .

King Kleagle. Look at her condition! It's unfortunate.

First Goblin. It's contortionate!.

King Kleagle. It's disreputable.

Sadie. [*Waving arms.*] Ghosts . . . ghosts, go away. . . .

[*And she tries to find a way out of the circle, but they surround her, swaying.* KING KLEAGLE *looms above her importantly.*]

King Kleagle. Outraged womanhood!

A Voice. Halleluiah . . .

[*Hushed by his companions.*]

King Kleagle. We'll teach her to be outraged, we'll lash the devil out of her.

Sadie. I'm a-walkin' in the dark, I ain't goin' home no more; my father cried an' swore. . . . [*Half sings in crooning voice.*] He sighed an' he cried an' he pretty near died. . . .

[*She weaves in and out among the* MASKED FIGURES.]

Responsive Chant. [*Picking up the refrain of a well-known song.*] "For the loss of her honor and her pride!" [*They all suddenly point at* SADIE *and shout.*] Shame!

Sadie. I ain't ashamed, I'm glad. [*Sudden silence. All the members of the* KLAN *stop stock still.*] I'm the glad girl, I don't care.

[KING KLEAGLE *stretches out his arms, touching flag and cross on either side of him. Both light up, the cross outlined in electricity, and a red, white and blue cluster on flag pole.* SADIE, *scared, sinks down on knees center.*]

King Kleagle. She's walking in the dark, the cross and the flag will save her, we must give her Christian punishment.

[*They all kneel.*]

Responsive Chant. [*In a whisper.*] " 'Cause she's walkin' in the dark!"

[PHILLPOTS *enters right, pushes the kneeling men out of his path so that they all fall on top of one another and stands protectingly by* SADIE.]

Phillpots. You will, will you? A lot of men picking on one little girl! Take a fellow your own size. [*Looking up at* KING KLEAGLE, *who towers above him.*] Come on, who's going to fight me?

[*But the* FIGURES *only go on chanting around him.*]

Responsive Chant.

"There's a black time comin' . . .
A-walkin' in the dark . . ."

King Kleagle. Back, back! You don't know what you're doing.

Phillpots. I know, all right, King Klux, I don't care if there's a thousand of you cowards! You attack a woman because it's easier——

King Kleagle. We protect morals.

[*Cheers from the* KLANSMEN.]

Phillpots. This little girl——

Sadie. I'm all right, Mister; they can't hurt me no worse.

Phillpots. I'm here to help you, little girl. I'm right with you.

[*He takes hold of* KING KLEAGLE, *who towers above him, and they circle round as if dancing.* SADIE *grabs* PHILLPOTS *to protect him and a little* GOBLIN *grabs* SADIE *to pull her away. In this way the four circle, swaying. One by one the other* MASKED FIGURES *take hold of the turning group while chanting goes on.*]

Responsive Chant.

"'Cause she's walkin' in the dark,
There's a black time comin' . . ."

King Kleagle. [*Raising both arms.*] Stop! [*Silence.*] We will give her the proper punishment, following which we will ride her out of town.

Responsive Chant. Halleluiah . . .

Phillpots. Now, look here——

King Kleagle. [*Roaring at him.*] Back! Back! And you may be glad that we don't skin you alive! March on, Klansmen! The Cross and the Flag and the world's eyes on us!

[*The* KLANSMEN *are now grouped in a compact crowd at edge of stage,* SADIE *amongst them. They withdraw, chanting softly.*]

Responsive Chant. [*As they go.*]

"There's a black time comin' . . .
A-walkin' in the dark . . ."

Phillpots. [*Trying to hold them back.*] Look here, don't take her with you, don't —— [*The* KLANSMEN *disappear.* PHILLPOTS *alone.*] I must get help . . . why, one of them's coming back! [*One of the* KLANSMEN *reappears right, dragging* SADIE *roughly.* PHILLPOTS *confronts him.*] Let go of her, leave her alone!

[*The* FIGURE *tears off its mask. It is* COHEN.]

Cohen. [*Gesticulating in his most Jewish manner.*] She was give into my care an' I got charge of her, ain't it?

Sadie. Popper!

Cohen. Look at her, my little daughter, a girl that don't know nuthin'!

Sadie. Look at yourself, you ain't so much in that nightgown.

Cohen. That's why I done myself up in fancy dress, to save my girl; the first one a' them devils touched her, he'd got a butcher knife in the head.

[*He shows a knife under his robe.*]

Sadie. Nobuddy can hurt me now. Nobuddy can touch me now.

Cohen. Listen, Sadie, for the last time I argue with you.

Sadie. [*Disregarding her father, turns eagerly to* PHILLPOTS.] Have you been a long ways off, Mister?

Phillpots. I went all around, to Tokio and Rome . . . but I was haunted——

Sadie. What?

Phillpots. Haunted, Sadie Cohen, by a dream of a little girl.

Sadie. [*Smiling.*] What did she want?

Phillpots. Love and champagne and a barrel of real diamonds.

Sadie. Ain't that the cat's earmuffs, though! What did she get?

Phillpots. She got tears in her eyes and a weight on her heart: what are you going to do?

Sadie. Don't worry about me, I ain't really alone.

Cohen. Look at her only, there it is for a girl I relied on, a girl I made a dream for.

Phillpots. Perhaps she made her own dream.

Sadie. When he's born, I'm gonna go to New York an' be a bad woman.

Cohen. There it is for a father's tears. She used to have her hair in a braid. She's a nightmare with her hair wild.

Phillpots. [*To* SADIE.] Better listen to reason.

Sadie. Ain't no reason in things, jus' a feelin' stealin' over you that tells you what to do, jus' a kind a' jazz——

Cohen. Ouch, jazz! Ain't I acted right, what have I done, where have I failed?

Sadie. [*Laughing and singing.*] I'm gonna raise my kid . . . sing to him . . . show him the moon . . .

Cohen. She's got a jazz itch. No use speakin' to you, Sadie, while you got such an itch.

Sadie. I don' wanna talk to you, I know what I must do! I'm a-gonna raise my kid. . . .

[*She runs away from* COHEN, *who tries to catch her. She exits.*]

Cohen. [*Following her.*] Listen, only listen. . . .

Phillpots. Really, Miss Cohen, my advice would be . . .

[PHILLPOTS *and* COHEN *follow* SADIE *off. Enter right a member of the* KLAN *running.* PSINSKI *appears left, carrying a gun with a ragged red flag tied to the muzzle.*]

Psinski. [*Shouting as he comes.*] Come on, men, we ain't afraid a' them white devils! [PSINSKI *sees the* KLANSMAN.] Stop or I shoot! [*The* GOBLIN *trembles visibly under his robe.* PSINSKI *seizes him, throws him on ground center.*] One a' you I got anyways.

Show me the face, Ku Klux, before I finish you!

[*Slowly figure on ground lifts hood and mask, revealing the black face of* RASTUS *scared so that eyes pop out of his head.*]

Rastus. [*Chants tragically.*]

"I ain't done nuthin' to nobuddy no time,
I ain't here to stay, I'm just a-goin' away
With them doggone Bow Wow Blues . . ."

Psinski. You can't belong to the Klan.

Rastus. How come? Anybuddy owns a sheet can belong. I reckoned it was safer——

[PSINSKI'S MEN *appear in a compact mass behind him rear. Confused shouting.*]

Psinski. You ain't fit to associate with class-conscious workmen.

Rastus. I'se willin' to withdraw.

[RASTUS *picks up skirts and runs left.*]

Psinski. [*Shouts.*] I'm with you, men! Come on!

[*He raises gun above head and leads* MEN *across through shadows rear. They carry flags, pitchforks, knives. Shouting grows to a crescendo. Then sudden silence.*

The scene begins to brighten. Enter JIM *in tattered clothes, feeling his way with a cane. He is evidently blind.*]

Jim. Can't find nuthin' . . . help . . . who's there? [*Noise of shouting off stage.*] Where am I? [*Swinging around with cane.*] Help, I say. Goddam, why do they leave me alone like this? Who's there?

[SADIE *runs in, gives a little gasp. Pause.*]

Sadie. [*Breathless.*] He's come.

Jim. Who's that, what voice is that?

Sadie. Your ma told me I should pray hard.

Jim. My ma?

Sadie. She must be right, 'cause I prayed like a steam engine an' you're here.

Jim. Damned if I know what you mean.

Sadie. Come over here an' then you'll know.

Jim. [*Waving cane in front of him.*] Can't . . . Can't find nuthin'.

Sadie. You can't see?

Jim. When the Klan strung me to that tree, they stuck things in my eyes, things to burn, won't never see no more.

Sadie. Oh . . . but you come . . . even like this, don't matter, you come.

[*Noise of shouting and fighting off stage.*]

Jim. What's that?

Sadie. The men, they're fightin' down there.

Jim. Where's that crazy Pole gone to?

Sadie. He's down there with the men.

Jim. I come with a bunch a' fellers, but I lost 'em all.

Sadie. [*Coming nearer to him.*] Don't matter. I'll lead you.

Jim. Why in hell should you?

Sadie. I knew you'd come.

Jim. [*Sullenly.*] Then take me to my mother. That's what I come for, get my mother out a' coal town, don't give a blue damn for anythin' else, I says, excep' my mother's waitin'! [*Shouts.*] Where is she?

Sadie. [*Frightened.*] Hush . . . quiet.

Jim. We went to the shack, me an' the bunch that come with me——

Sadie. Jus' too late, they burnt it down tonight.

Jim. I smelt the smoke.

Sadie. The Klan got everythin' their own way now.

Jim. I need my mammy's arms.

Sadie. They got her, now.

Jim. Where? Let me at 'em.

Sadie. Hush, be quiet.

Jim. Gotta find her, get her out a' this.

Sadie. We'll fool them men in sheets. We'll get away. [*She laughs excitedly.*] Some men have gone to help your ma, we better wait here—don't you know me?

Jim. [*Shaking head.*] Got a voice like a bell ringin'. I dunno no one with a voice like that.

Sadie. Who'd you think I am?

Jim. Some tall dame with hair all gold laughin' in the sun.

Sadie. [*Softly.*] I'm here for you.

Jim. [*Reaching out his arms.*] Hell then, lemme touch you——

Sadie. [*Backing away.*] No, no . . . who am I?

Jim. Voice of a li'l bell . . .

Sadie. Go on . . . go on . . .

Jim. Wearin' clothes all silk an' hair that smells a' pink roses.

Sadie. I'm here for you.

Jim. Where are you?

Sadie. [*Comes close to him. Whispers, trembling.*] Here.

[JIM *takes hold of her, fingers her shoulders brutally, her arms, her face, her hair.*]

Jim. I got you now, I got you—— [*Abruptly, as he recognizes her.*] Li'l girl with them funny eyes, li'l Sadie Cohen.

Sadie. Don't call me that; call me your daisy, call me Desdemona, call me funny names.

Jim. But your voice ain't the same, what's

happened? [*She laughs.*] Bells . . . I hear somethin' stirrin' in your voice.

Sadie. Somethin' stirrin' in me I come to meet you——

Jim. What you bring me so early in the mornin'?

Sadie. Hush . . . somethin' to sing to, somethin' to be born.

[*Enter* MRS. FLIMMINS *left.*]

Mrs. Flimmins. Jim . . . Jim . . . [*He starts wildly toward the voice. She clings to him.*] Can't you see me?

Jim. No.

Mrs. Flimmins. Jim . . .

Jim. I come to take you away from here.

Mrs. Flimmins. Your eyes, Jim, your eyes . . .

Sadie. They stuck things in his eyes.

Mrs. Flimmins. It's me must take you away, lead you . . .

Sadie. How can we get away from the Klan?

Mrs. Flimmins. A li'l crowd a' them Klan men had me in a circle askin' me questions, then a bunch a' other fellers come an' one man told me to run.

Jim. Jake Psinski done that. That's my pal Jake.

Sadie. Where are they now?

Jim. The Klan?

Mrs. Flimmins. We're on the hill an' they're all around us, but the men are fightin' 'em.

Jim. Smells like mornin'.

Mrs. Flimmins. How'd you get here, Jim? You ain't broke the law again?

Jim. No, I know 'bout the law now.

Mrs. Flimmins. It's law what you do you can't undo no ways.

Jim. I've been thinkin' 'bout that six months now, thinkin' how us folks got blood boilin' inside us, an' someways we can walk through hell in an asbestos skin.

Sadie. Me too, I know that now.

Jim. Are you laughin' or cryin'?

Sadie. It's nuthin,' I just' keep singin' to myself.

Mrs. Flimmins. [*Bitterly.*] She's one a' us kind now. [*Enter* PHILLPOTS *left.*]

Phillpots. [*Seeing* JIM.] So you're here again!

Mrs. Flimmins. What are them Kluxers doin'?

Phillpots. Guess it's turned into something of a fight, but the Klan's too strong for them. They're all around us—see the lights.

Jim. [*Mutters between his teeth.*] If I had my sight——

Phillpots. They told me you were done for six months ago, strung to a tree——

Jim. Farmer come an' cut me down, put me in a bed, hid me till I could walk; then I walked to Charleston feelin' my way with a stick. They set me in the jail down to Charleston; then the Judge says, there's no what you call evidence, he says. I jus' kep' my jaw shut tight an' they threw me out on my ear; they says can't do no harm no more, a guy without eyes is nuthin', the curse ain't on him no more. . . . [JIM *shouts triumphantly.*] The curse is lifted, let 'im walk!

Mrs. Flimmins. [*Tensely.*] A woman has tuk the curse off you, that's what.

Jim. You mean you?

Mrs. Flimmins. [*Indicating* SADIE.] I mean her, she carries the curse you give her.

Sadie. [*Singing softly.*]

"I'm a-gonna raise my kid,
I'm a-gonna sing to him soft . . ."

Jim. [*Roughly.*] What you laugh for, what you sing for?

Sadie. It's all for you, Jim.

Phillpots. Little Desdemona bearing a burden, little Desdemona from the black monster's hand!

Jim. I ain't so black.

Phillpots. It's not you; the black monster upon her is coal, rising upon her in a pillar of smoke.

Mrs. Flimmins. I tried to make her see reason but she wouldn't.

Sadie. They says to me, there's ways a' fixin' it. I dunno how . . . but not me, I'm a-gonna raise my kid, I'm wise now!

Jim. What's bein' wise?

Sadie. It's a sickness in the stomach.

Jim. Does it kick?

Sadie. Sometimes it kicks.

Mrs. Flimmins. T'aint worth it.

Sadie. It's my turn now, I'm ready——

Mrs. Flimmins. To make men. You poor fools, you think, you fight, an' make trouble, but rebellions come out a' our stomachs!

Phillpots. As a member of the good old middle class, I consider this conversation very irregular and I would suggest marriage.

Jim. [*Thoughtfully.*] I wouldn't care. [*Pause.*]

Sadie. I wouldn't care.

Mrs. Flimmins. None of us would care.

Phillpots. It will set you right with the community. They don't care about a killing or two, but this is a serious matter.

Mrs. Flimmins. I guess it's what the law would ask.

Sadie. When can we get married?

Jim. Right away!

[*Enter* COHEN *with Ku Klux uniform wrapped in a bundle.*]

Cohen. I'm through, I resign from this lodge, it's no good.

[*He throws the bundle away.*]

Phillpots. Come here, Mr. Cohen, you're just in time.

Cohen. [*To* JIM.] There you are, loafer . . . crow . . . jail-bird!

Jim. What's eatin' him?

Cohen. My daughter——

Mrs. Flimmins. [*Interrupting him harshly.*] That's just a joke, too. He's gonna marry her.

Cohen. Married, you say? Married, is it? That's another thing again.

Mrs. Flimmins. Can't you laugh, old man? Back up an' laugh like me, mebbe you an' me get married too!

Cohen. [*Turning from her sadly.*] I don't understand it at all.

[*A sound of raucous music off stage.*]

Mrs. Flimmins. What's that?

Jim. It's my pals, it's them musical miners. . . . [*Triumphantly.*] They're comin', I say, they're comin'!

[*Everybody turns to left as* JAZZ BAND *enters playing violently, led by* PSINSKI, *still carrying his gun. They line up across stage. Only* RASTUS *is not among them. The music stops in straggling manner. Other* MINERS *appear, still carrying guns and knives.*]

Phillpots. Where are the night riders?

Psinski. They all went away 'cause it's mornin'. Night riders don't work in daylight.

[*He is swaying a little, speaks thickly. The stage has become brightly illuminated.*]

Phillpots. Psinski, I believe you're drunk!

Psinski. [*Thickly.*] What of it?

Phillpots. [*Smiling.*] You, the revolutionist, the idealist, turned to whisky at last.

Psinski. Go on, make a joke a' me, it's all hopeless.

Phillpots. That's the Russian in you speaking.

Psinski. I ain't a Russian, I'm a Pole, an' it's all hopeless.

Smith. You're in America now, boy.

Phillpots. Land of optimists.

Psinski. [*Thickly.*] I'll speak to these Americans.

Smith. Speech . . . speech . . .

Psinski. [*Climbs uncertainly on to a soap box left, trying to find words.*] Comrades . . . we been fightin' like in a fog . . . [*Pointing to* JIM.] This guy lost his eyes . . . I speak in a fog a' thoughts now . . . in ten years, in fifty years, mebbe it will be clear . . . we got ideals, them guys in sheets got ideals, I am drunk with ideals . . . here's a girl gotta baby will be a workman in twenty years. Ask her what it means . . . I am tired!

Sadie. I carry a gravestone inside me, but I don't care; I'm a-gonna raise my kid. . . .

Psinski. [*Bitterly.*] An' his name shall be called Wonderful!

Responsive Chant. [*Of miners swaying in a row behind.*] "Wonderful . . . wonderful . . ."

Psinski. Mebbe that child will stand on the last barricade wavin' a red flag in the face a' all time! An' behind him will come marchin' a lot a' ghosts, all the soldiers that died at Bunker Hill an' on the Marne marchin' to be free——

Phillpots. [*Calmly.*] Bunk!

Psinski. [*Flustered, steps down.*] Sure, ev'rything's bunk, so I wanna die, why won't some fool shoot me? [*He throws down his gun. Stands forlornly center.*] Any guy will shoot me, I'll shake his hand, call him brother!

[MAN IN SILK HAT *appears suddenly, pushing his way through the crowd importantly.*]

Man in Silk Hat. [*Shaking* PSINSKI *warmly by hand.*] Give me your hand, my friend, I greet you. My friends, I bring good tidings. I'm glad you men have come, I am instructed to meet you half way.

Psinski. Is this half way?

Man in Silk Hat. We want to open up the mines, make concessions, boom business, sign contracts, all that sort of thing!

[*The* MEN *cheer and wave arms in perfunctory manner.*]

Psinski. [*Dazed.*] You mean, the strike is over an' you agree?

Man in Silk Hat. Yes, indeed, I may say a lasting agreement, everybody fully pardoned.

Jim. Pardoned?

Man in Silk Hat. [*A little flustered, but shaking him warmly by hand.*] My friend, this is indeed a pleasure. . . .

Psinski. The Klan? Where is the Klan?

Man in Silk Hat. Disbanded! All around you, you see the shining faces of loyal workmen!

[*He makes a grandiose gesture.*]

Phillpots. [*To* PSINSKI.] The laugh is always on you.

Man in Silk Hat. If you'll just come with me and sign the documents, the motion picture machines are ready for the ceremony.

Psinski. Ceremony?

Man in Silk Hat. [*Muttering as he leads way to right.*] Of course . . . by all means.

[*He meets* SHERIFF *at extreme right. He*

motions PSINSKI *off right and turns to the* SHERIFF.]

Sheriff. What's the meanin' a' this, sir?

Man in Silk Hat. [*In a low voice.*] The moral effect . . . can't afford further trouble . . . publicity value . . . dollars and cents.

Sheriff. What are your orders, sir?

Man in Silk Hat. Make a list of the marked men and we'll get them in their beds to-night! [*Turning suavely to group on stage.*] My friends, we have each other's confidence.

[*Exit* MAN IN SILK HAT *right.*]

Phillpots. Just a minute, Sheriff. [*Leading* SHERIFF *to* JIM.] This gives you your chance for a wedding.

Jim. Howdy, Sheriff. . . . Can you fix me up with a marriage license right off?

Sheriff. [*Produces his enormous sheaf of legal papers and starts thumbing them over industriously.*] Might be somethin' here that would do. [*He adjusts his glasses.*] If it ain't a weddin', it's a lynchin'—lemme see, war, insurrection an' riot—no, that won't hardly do.

Jim. Never mind, marry us right away quick, Sheriff.

Sheriff. [*Finding another paper.*] I'll have to fix you up with a dawg license. I'll revise it a little.

Man in Silk Hat. [*Appears suddenly in an upper box, with bright spotlight on him, and announces in best oratorical style:*] Gentlemen, I wish to announce that this is Mother's Day! I have here a telegram from Calvin C. Coolidge stating that all men are brothers.

[*He holds up the telegram. Applause from men on stage.*]

Phillpots. [*Picks up a megaphone at edge of stage right and announces through it as if addressing a huge crowd.*] Gentlemen, Industrial Peace has come! [*Turning to* SADIE *and* JIM.] Cemented in this marriage! A pact, a compact, an agreement, a document! The nation is rejoicing! There's going to be coal to keep 'em warm!

[*Enter* RASTUS, *left. Standing at edge of stage he begins to sing, softly twanging banjo.*]

Rastus.

" 'Cause there's no land so grand as my land
From California to Manhattan Isle,
North an' South, my sunny sky land,
I love every mile . . ."

[*All sway and sing.* PHILLPOTS *continues to announce.*]

Phillpots. Kindly turn to the financial page, wait till the market opens, all for Wall Street!

[SHERIFF *goes around shaking hands with everybody.* PHILLPOTS *puts away his megaphone. The crowd gather around* RASTUS *and join in the singing, in the manner of a college glee club.*]

Rastus and Chorus. [*Loudly.*]

"Yankee Doodle . . . that melody
Keeps on ringin' in my ear,
Yankee Doodle . . . that melody
Makes me stand right up an' cheer,
I'm comin', U. S. A., I'll say,
I love you . . .
Make me lose those . . . Yankee Doodle Blues . . ."

[*The* SHERIFF *is preparing for the marriage ceremony.* JIM *raises his arms and shouts.*]

Jim. Come on aroun', fellers that dig in the earth, make a cloud aroun', a cloud a' men like coal dust, a whirlwind makin' music——

[*The men, chanting softly, crowd around the marriage group, and jazz music continues.*]

Cohen. She ain't my Yiddisher Rose no more.

Phillpots. She's an American Beauty now.

Cohen. [*Wipes a tear from each eye.*] Babies they will have an' babies . . .

Phillpots. And their children's children will be shouting oi, oi!

Cohen. We should break a bottle over the bride's head!

[*Swaying and dancing to the music, the* SHERIFF *is performing the wedding ceremony with* MRS. FLIMMINS *and* COHEN *on either side of* SADIE *and* JIM.]

Sheriff. An' I hereby pronounce you——

Jim. [*Interrupting him.*] Sheriff, has it got a red seal on it?

Sheriff. No, I didn't have no seal.

Jim. Put my blood on it, put a drop a' blood on it.

Sheriff. Shut your mug till I finish.

Jim. Wait, got a knife? [SHERIFF, *annoyed, takes a knife from* COHEN *and hands it to* JIM. *In dead silence,* JIM *holds out his arm, pricks it and with awful ceremony lets a drop fall on the paper.*] There's blood, now go on. [*Singing and music start again with a blare of sound.* MRS. FLIMMINS, COHEN, SADIE *and* JIM *embrace one another dancing. The whole crowd forms a compact, swaying group behind them.* OLD MAGGIE *and* POP PRATT *appear and hobble forward doing an old-fashioned jig. Again a silence breaks the rhythm, and* JIM *shouts:*] Shake a leg, Ma!

Mrs. Flimmins. [*Harshly.*] We can dance with our hearts breakin'.

Jim. Everybuddy shake a leg.

Mrs. Flimmins. I can dance too, I can dance as well as any old fool.

[*She raises her skirts, revealing a bright red petticoat, and dances wildly. The violent rhythm grows in volume.*]

Smith. [*Shouts with megaphone.*] Join the Procession!

[*Down the aisle of theater comes* BOOB *with newspapers.*]

Boob. [*Shouting as he comes.*] Extry! Extry! Big peace!

Phillpots. [*At top of steps front.*] Here kid, I'll buy those papers. [*He takes them and starts tearing them, throwing them around.*] Here, boys, here's confetti, there's where the news belongs!

[JIM *stands center, smiling blandly.* SADIE *at a little distance from him swaying wildly, while the whole crowd marches around them, the* JAZZ BAND *and all the other characters. Then the Procession marches down through the audience. With an increasing noise and rhythm, the Procession disappears at rear of theater. Then there is silence.* JIM *and* SADIE *alone on stage.*

Sadie. They're gone, we're alone.

Jim. [*Feeling his way toward her.*] Where are you now?

Sadie. [*Swaying and singing softly.*] I'm a-gonna raise my kid, sing to him soft . . .

CURTAIN

BEGGAR ON HORSEBACK *

By

GEORGE S. KAUFMAN *and* MARC CONNELLY

IN 1923, WINTHROP AMES, HAVING BOUGHT the American rights to a satirical German play, *Hans Sonnenstössers Höllenfahrt,* by Paul Apel, chose George S. Kaufman and Marc Connelly to adapt it for the American stage. They had already distinguished themselves as writers of comedy by their earlier collaborations.

In outline of the story, and in method, *Beggar on Horseback* follows Apel's play closely. *Hans Sonnenstössers Höllenfahrt* (Johnny Sunstormer's Trip to Hell), first produced in 1911, concerns a composer who dreams himself married into a family of Philistines, having been tempted by the same considerations as in the American play. Likewise, he murders them in his dream. But *Beggar on Horseback* aims so distinctly at satire on America and Americans that it is obvious Kaufman and Connelly have made an almost new play. They have added and re-arranged episodes, inserted the pantomime in Part II, which was suggested by Mr. Ames, and satirized the cheap tabloid newspaper most cleverly. Deems Taylor composed the incidental music for the play and the pantomime.

Beggar on Horseback was first presented in New York under Mr. Ames's direction on February 12, 1924, and ran through the season. It had a short run in revival the next year. It was also successfully produced in London in 1925. It is probably the best example in English of the use for consistently comic purposes of the freer technique known as Expressionism. It does both the things that Expressionism attempts: reveal the "behind-life" of the central character, and synthesize and symbolize group-habits, group-moralities, and group-mentalities in the briefest possible action and dialogue.

Mr. Kaufman and Mr. Connelly have not collaborated since the year of *Beggar on Horseback.* But in the subsequent years Mr. Kaufman, though almost always collaborating, has become known as perhaps the most successful theater man of our time, both as writer and director. He is credited with great ability in giving dramatic ideas wit, brightness, and topical effectiveness.

Mr. Connelly's work for the theater has been more scanty, but his *The Green Pastures* is undoubtedly one of the great monuments of American dramatic art.

GEORGE S. KAUFMAN

Born 1889, Pittsburgh, Pa.
Educated in the public schools.
Play-doctor, stage-director, and journalist.
1932, Awarded Pulitzer Prize for *Of Thee I Sing.*
1937, Awarded Pulitzer Prize for *You Can't Take It With You.*

PLAYS

1918 *Among Those Present* (with Larry Evans and Walter Percival). 1918 *Someone in the House* (with Larry Evans and Walter Percival). 1919 *Jacques Duval* (adapted from the German of Hans Müller). 1921 *Dulcy* (with Marc Connelly). 1922 *To the Ladies* (with Marc Connelly). 1922 *Merton of the Movies* (with Marc Connelly, adapted from story by Harry Leon Wilson.) 1923 *Helen of Troy, New York* (musical comedy, with Marc Connelly). 1923 *The Deep Tangled Wildwood* (with Marc Connelly). 1924 *Beggar on Horseback* (with Marc Connelly). 1924 *Be Yourself* (musical comedy, with Marc Connelly). 1924 *Minick* (with Edna Ferber, dramatization of her *Old Man Minick*). 1925 *The Butter and Egg Man.* 1925 *The Cocoanuts* (musical comedy). 1926 *If Men Played Cards as Women Do.* 1926 *The Good Fellow* (with Herman J. Mankiewicz). 1927 *The Royal Family* (with Edna Ferber). 1927 *Strike Up the Band* (musical comedy with Morrie Ryskind). 1928 *Animal Crackers* (musical comedy, with Morrie Ryskind). 1929 *The Channel Road* (with Alexander Woollcott). 1929 *June Moon* (with Ring Lardner). 1930 *Once in a Lifetime* (with Moss Hart). 1931 *Of Thee I Sing* (musical comedy, with Morrie Ryskind). 1932 *Dinner at Eight* (with Edna Ferber). 1933 *Let 'Em Eat Cake* (musical comedy, with Morrie Ryskind). 1933 *The Dark Tower* (with Alexander Woollcott). 1934 *Merrily We Roll Along* (with Moss Hart). 1935 *First Lady* (with Katharine Dayton). 1936 *Stage Door* (with Edna Ferber). 1936 *You Can't Take It With You* (with Moss Hart). 1937 *I'd Rather Be Right* (musical comedy, with Moss Hart). 1938 *The Fabulous Invalid* (with Moss Hart). 1939 *The American Way* (with Moss Hart). 1939 *The Man Who Came to Dinner* (with Moss Hart). 1940 *George Washington Slept Here* (with Moss Hart).

SCREENWRITING

1930 *Royal Family of Broadway.* 1930 *Animal Crackers.* 1930 *Not So Dumb.* 1931 *June Moon.* 1932 *Once in a Lifetime.* 1933 *Dinner at Eight.* 1933 *Roman Scandals.* 1934 *Elmer and Elsie.* 1934 *The Man with Two Faces.* 1935 *A Night at the Opera.* 1935 *Riffraff.*

MARC CONNELLY

Born 1890, McKeesport, Pa.
Educated at Trinity Hall, Washington, Pa.
1930, Awarded Pulitzer Prize for *The Green Pastures.*
Journalist.

PLAYS

1921 *Dulcy* (with George S. Kaufman). 1922 *To the Ladies* (with George S. Kaufman). 1922 *Merton of the Movies* (with George S. Kaufman, adapted from story by Harry Leon Wilson). 1923 *Helen of Troy, New York* (musical comedy, with George S. Kaufman). 1923 *The Deep Tangled Wildwood* (with George S. Kaufman). 1924 *Beggar on Horseback* (with George S. Kaufman). 1924 *Be Yourself* (musical comedy, with George S. Kaufman). 1926 *The Wisdom Tooth.* 1927 *The Wild Man of Borneo* (with Herman J. Mankiewicz). 1930 *The Green Pastures* (adapted from Roark Bradford's *Ol' Man Adam and His Chillun*). 1934 *The Farmer Takes a Wife* (with Frank K. Elser, adapted from novel *Rome Haul* by Walter D. Edmonds). 1938 *Everywhere I Roam* (with Arnold Sundgaard). 1941 *The Mole on Lincoln's Cheek* (radio drama).

SCREENWRITING

1930 *Not So Dumb.* 1933 *Cradle Song.* 1934 *Elmer and Elsie.* 1935 *The Farmer Takes a Wife.* 1936 *The Green Pastures.* 1937 *Captains Courageous.*

BEGGAR ON HORSEBACK

PART I

The scene is NEIL MCRAE'S *apartment in a comfortable, run-down, and not very expensive building. It is plainly an artist's room, and furnished with as many good-looking things as the occupant could afford—which are not many. The most luxurious piece of furniture in the room is a grand piano, which* NEIL *has probably hung on to with no little difficulty. It stands well down left. Down right is an easy chair—the only chair in the room that even suggests comfort —and against the rear wall is* NEIL'S *desk. In front of the desk is a swivel chair, and two or three other chairs, stiff-backed, stand around the room. At the left of the stage, near the piano, is a window, hung with chintz curtains that have seen better days—curtains which come to life here and there in great splotches of red. Some of the same stuff hangs in a center doorway—a doorway that leads to* NEIL'S *bedroom and thence to a "kitchenette." The door into the apartment is at the right—somewhere beyond it is the elevator, and one needs only a look at the room to know that it is an elevator that requires four minutes to ascend the three floors.*

[*The time is about four-thirty of a Spring afternoon. The curtain rises on the room and nothing more; then, after a second, there comes a knock on the door. The knock is repeated, then the knob is cautiously turned and the door slowly opens.* DR. ALBERT RICE, *a young man of thirty or so, peers inquiringly into the room through the widening crack, sees no one, and enters.*]

Albert. Neil! [*There is no answer; he observes the room. Slightly to his surprise, he sees a sewing basket on the piano.*] Are you married? [*He goes up to the bedroom entrance and peers into the semi-darkness.*] Neil!

[CYNTHIA MASON, *who seems to be about twenty-five, appears suddenly in the doorway at right. There is a moment of uncertainty as she and the doctor confront each other.*]

Cynthia. Are you looking for Mr. McRae?

Albert. Yes. The door was open.

Cynthia. [*Disturbed.*] Really? Was it wide open?

Albert. It was closed, but it wasn't locked.

Cynthia. Oh! [*There is a pause of uncertainty.*] Was Mr. McRae expecting you?

Albert. No—I just got in from Chicago. Neil and I are old friends. My name is Rice.

Cynthia. Oh! You're not *Doctor* Rice?

Albert. Yes.

Cynthia. [*Laughing.*] I'm so relieved! My name is Cynthia Mason, Doctor Rice. I know a great deal about *you.* [*They shake hands.*]

Albert. Of course, Neil never writes letters, so you've been concealed from me. You didn't know him a few months ago, did you, when I left New York?

Cynthia. No, only since he moved here. I live across the hall.

Albert. Oh, I see.

Cynthia. [*Looking around.*] There's that work basket. [*She takes it from the piano, then faces the doctor again.*] I hope you'll forgive me, when I tell you why I lingered.

Albert. You're forgiven.

Cynthia. Night before last we had burglars.

Albert. Really?

Cynthia. Not on this floor—the apartment below. The poor man lost three or four suits of clothes, so——

Albert. [*With an understanding smile.*] So Neil leaves his door unlocked.

Cynthia. Probably since early this morning. Though I'm afraid the burglar who took Neil's clothes wouldn't do very well.

Albert. [*With a look around the room.*] No, I suppose not.

Cynthia. [*A pause; she turns, with an air of finality.*] Well, he'll be here soon.

Albert. You're not going?

Cynthia. I must. Neil has some people coming to tea.

Albert. [*Bent on holding her.*] Well—now, how do you know I'm *not* the burglar?

Cynthia. Because I don't believe there are such things as gentlemen burglars.

[*She drops a half curtsy; turns again toward the door.*]

Albert. Oh, wait! What did Neil tell you about me?

Cynthia. Let me see. He said you were extremely brilliant. But too versatile.

Albert. Brilliant, yes. But versatile—on the contrary, I'm going to become a specialist.

Cynthia. Sometimes I wonder what's happened to all the young men who used to become just doctors.

Albert. They all died of starvation.

[*There is a pause;* CYNTHIA *looks at her watch.*]

Cynthia. I don't know why Neil isn't here.

Albert. You don't expect *him* to be prompt, do you?

Cynthia. But he has some people coming. You may know them—their name is Cady.

Albert. Cady? Not the Cadys from Livingston?

Cynthia. Yes—*do* you know them?

Albert. I'm not sure—I think I used to. You know, I lived in Livingston myself, a long time ago.

Cynthia. So Neil told me.

Albert. [*Puzzled.*] The Cadys? What are *they* coming for?

Cynthia. Miss Cady is Neil's pupil.

Albert. You mean he's giving her music lessons?

Cynthia. He is.

Albert. But he's not a teacher. [*He waits for a denial.*] *Is* he?

Cynthia. He *must* do something.

Albert. [*With a sigh.*] Things aren't any better with him, then?

Cynthia. Well, he isn't ready to retire.

Albert. [*With a shake of the head.*] I suppose he'll always go on this way. He's so —utterly improvident, so——

Cynthia. [*Rallying to his defense.*] Well —he's really improved in that way. He may surprise you.

Albert. He certainly would.

Cynthia. He's saving money! [*Her tone changes.*] But the trouble is—he's working so hard to get it.

Albert. You mean giving music lessons?

Cynthia. Worse. You've got to talk to him —he won't listen to me. He's been sitting up night after night——

Neil. [*Heard in the hallway.*] Halloo! [*He kicks open the door and enters. He is carrying a pile of books, and on top of the pile a music portfolio. He sees* ALBERT; *dumps the books abruptly into the easy chair.*] Albert! Well, I'll be damned!

[*Tosses his hat into the bedroom; seizes* ALBERT'S *hand.*]

Albert. Mr. McRae, I believe?

Neil. Where did you come from? Chicago?

Albert. This morning. Of course, you never told me you'd moved. How are you?

Neil. Never felt better! Gosh, I'm glad you're back! You've met Cynthia?

Cynthia. Well, we've been talking. I thought I'd caught the burglar.

Neil. Did you find him in here? [*To* ALBERT.] How did you get in?

Albert. [*Elaborately.*] First I turned the knob of the door——

Cynthia. And, as you hadn't locked it, he had no difficulty in entering. [*She turns to the books in the easy chair.*] What are these?

Neil. Why—just some books.

Cynthia. [*Takes one up.*] "Life of Charles I." Neil!

Neil. Well—I used to be very interested in history, and especially——

Cynthia. [*Severely.*] The truth, Neil!

Neil. I—I bought them, that's all.

Cynthia. Oh, Neil. After your promise!

Neil. Well—— [*To* ALBERT.] Just take a look at this binding.

Albert. [*Giving no encouragement.*] Yes. I see it.

Cynthia. [*Determined.*] Neil, where did you get them?

Neil. [*Still to* ALBERT.] There was a burglary downstairs, and this fellow lost all his clothes.

Cynthia. [*Resigned.*] And you bought these books from him.

Neil. Well—ah——

Cynthia. You work at these terrible orchestrations to *make* a little money, and then —did you go to bed at all last night?

Neil. Of course I did.

Cynthia. Doctor, you *will* talk to him, won't you? [*She takes up her work basket.*] I'm sure he hasn't been sleeping—he hasn't been doing *anything* he should.

[*She is heading for the door.*]

Neil. You're not going.

Cynthia. I am. You have people coming to tea, remember.

Neil. Good heavens, what time is it?

Cynthia. Nearly five. I suppose you have everything ready?

Neil. Why, yes—I've got—that is, I think —— [*He smiles helplessly.*] Be a darling and help me, will you?

Cynthia. Are you sure you have everything? [*Knowing well that he hasn't.*]

Neil. I think so.

Cynthia. He thinks so.

[*This to* ALBERT, *with a smile, as she goes through the bedroom doorway.*]

Albert. She's charming, Neil.

Neil. Isn't she? [*He moves his portfolio from the chair to the desk.*] She's a designer in one of the big dressmaking firms. Did she tell you how we met?

Albert. No.

Neil. She lives across the hall. [*He raises his voice for* CYNTHIA'S *benefit.*] She thinks she can play the piano.

Cynthia. [*In the kitchen.*] I can!

Neil. You cannot! [*To* ALBERT.] One night I knocked on her door and asked her to stop. She did. We've been great pals ever since. [*Calling to* CYNTHIA.] Can I help you, Cynthia?

Cynthia. No, nor any one else. [*She returns.*] Do you remember when you last had any tea?

Neil. The other day.

Cynthia. You have three leaves left.

[*She exhibits them.*]

Neil. [*Inspects them.*] Four!

Cynthia. And did you know that your toast machine was burnt out?

Neil. Oh, yes—I forgot. But I'm sure there's some tea—I remember—no, I used the last of it early this morning. I'll run right out——

[*He is about to start.*]

Cynthia. [*Holding him.*] Neil!

Neil. What?

Cynthia. Then you *were* up all night?

Neil. Why—not exactly.

Cynthia. [*To the* DOCTOR.] He's been sitting up making orchestrations for a cheap little music publisher. Neil, it's like copying bad paintings. Doctor, you must make him stop.

Neil. Well—I'll go out and get some tea.

Cynthia. No! You stay and talk to the Doctor. I'll bring everything over from my place. [*Again she picks up the basket.*]

Neil. I can't let you do that. Let me help.

Cynthia. I will not. [*She goes.*]

Neil. [*More to himself than to* ALBERT.] I could have sworn I had everything.

Albert. She'll take care of things. [*He is near the window.*] Come over here and let me see you.

Neil. Now, you're not going to fuss over me just because I've been doing some work.

Albert. No. But I want to look at you.

[*An orchestra, in a restaurant across the street, strikes up a jazz tune. It comes faintly through the window.*]

Neil. Good Lord, that again!

Albert. What?

Neil. That damned cabaret orchestra across the street. It begins at five every afternoon.

Albert. You *are* nervous, aren't you?

Neil. Huh? No. I just don't like that music.

Albert. Did you work all night?

Neil. Some of it.

Albert. It's bad business, Neil. [*He feels for his pulse.*] How many Cadys are coming to tea?

Neil. Oh, did Cynthia tell you? You remember the Cadys?

Albert. Vaguely. I don't suppose they'd know me. Do they live here now?

Neil. They moved East a few months ago. Gladys is my one and only music pupil.

Albert. [*Watch in hand.*] Rich, I suppose?

Neil. Lord, yes. Millions.

Albert. What did he make it in?

[*He puts away the watch.*]

Neil. Funny—I don't even know. Manufactures something.

Albert. [*Trying to remember.*] Just the one daughter, isn't there?

Neil. Yes. [*Adds, as an afterthought.*] There's a brother.

Albert. [*Recalls him, apparently none too pleasantly.*] I remember him.

Neil. I *had* to ask them. For heaven's sake, stay and help out.

Albert. [*With a laugh.*] Well, I'll stay a little while. [*Feels for his pipe.*]

Neil. Try to get away. [ALBERT *laughs, lightly.*] Well, what's the verdict on *me*?

Albert. You're just a little tired, that's all. Sort of nervous.

Neil. Nonsense.

Albert. Got any tobacco?

Neil. Right there on the desk.

Albert. [*Fooling with the tobacco jar; unable to open it.*] Have you been writing *anything* of your own?

Neil. Well, no—only snatches of things. I'm going to get back at it soon, though.

Albert. That's good. [*The jar in hand.*] How do you open this thing?

Neil. [*Takes up a paper knife from the piano—a knife of ivory, scimitar-shaped, and with a long black tassel hanging from it.*] I use this. Give it to me.

[ALBERT *hands it over;* NEIL *opens and returns it, all without a word.*]

Albert. [*Filling his pipe.*] How old is the daughter now?

Neil. Gladys?

Albert. Yes.

Neil. Twenty-two or three—I don't know. Why?

Albert. How soon will they be here?

[*He puts the knife back on the piano.*]

Neil. Any minute, I guess. Why all the questions?

Albert. I just wondered. [*Takes a medical case from his pocket and shakes out a pill.*] I want you to take one of these before they come, and another one later on.

Neil. Good heavens, there's nothing the matter with me.

Albert. I know there isn't.

Neil. What'll they do—make me sleep?

Albert. They'll quiet you.

Neil. But I don't dare go to sleep. In the first place the Cadys are coming, and——

[CYNTHIA *reënters. She is now hatless, and carries a folded tablecloth.*]

Cynthia. I hope you scolded him.

[*She goes to the desk and begins to spread the cloth.*]

Albert. Not enough, I'm afraid. [*Pill in hand.*] Do you think you have a glass of water left?

Neil. [*Starting.*] Oh, of course.

Albert. No, no, I can find it.

[*He goes into the bedroom.*]

Cynthia. [*With a glance at the portfolio.*] You didn't let them give you more to do?

Neil. Why, hardly any. It's all right.

Cynthia. It *isn't* all right. Oh, I wouldn't mind if it were something decent! But it's perfectly sickening to think of your genius being choked to death in this way!

Neil. I'll work on the symphony soon, honestly.

Cynthia. And then make up for it by mere hackwork. I wish some one would subsidize you.

Neil. That would be nice.

[ALBERT *comes back with the glass of water.*]

Albert. Here you are!

[*Gives* NEIL *pill and glass.*]

Neil. Oh, all right. But there's nothing the matter with me. [*He takes the pill.*]

Albert. How was it?

Neil. I've tasted better. [*The orchestra across the street is heard in another outburst of jazz.*] Would you believe that people actually enjoy that? Wait! I've got one here that will be next month's national anthem. [*Searches for it in portfolio.*] There aren't any words to it yet, but it's going to be called "Sweet Mamma."

Cynthia. Don't, Neil. Play Doctor Rice the second movement of your symphony.

Neil. Want to hear it?

Albert. You bet. [*He indicates the pipe.*] Do you mind?

Cynthia. Not at all.

Neil. She calls it the second movement because there isn't any first.

Cynthia. [*Finding it.*] Here!

[*She spreads the manuscript on the rack.*]

Neil. You understand this is just a movement. It's—— [*He sees a place that needs correction.*] Oh! [*Starts fishing for a pencil.*] Of course I never have a pencil. [CYNTHIA *gets one from his left vest pocket and hands it to him.*] Oh, thanks! [*He makes the correction.*] It's just a sketch. Not finished, you know.

Cynthia. But it's going to be—and soon.

[NEIL *starts to play, but is not far into it when the 'phone rings.*]

Neil. [*Stops playing.*] I'll bet that's the Cadys. [*Goes to the 'phone.*] Hello! [*To* CYNTHIA.] It is. Downstairs. . . . Send them right up, Jerry.

Cynthia. Good heavens, I'll have to bring the tea things in.

Neil. Why not?

Cynthia. They don't want to meet me.

Neil. Don't be foolish.

Cynthia. Well—I won't stay.

[*She goes.*]

Neil. I suppose I ought to clear things up a bit.

Albert. [*With a glance at the books in the easy chair.*] If you expect them to sit down.

[NEIL *carries the books into his bedroom. He returns, counts the chairs, then tests a spindly-legged one that stands center.*]

Neil. I hope nobody heavy sits in this.

[*Voices are heard in the hall, and* MR. *and* MRS. CADY, HOMER, *and* GLADYS *appear at the open door.* MRS. CADY *enters first, then* GLADYS, *then* MR. CADY, *and* HOMER. *Together they make up an average Middle West family. They have no marked external characteristics except that* HOMER *is wearing a violent yellow tie.*]

Mrs. Cady. Why, Neil!

Neil. How are you, Mrs. Cady? Gladys.

Mrs. Cady. After all these years!

Gladys. Hello, Neil!

Cady. Well, well, Neil, my boy!

Neil. Hello, Mr. Cady!

Homer. Hello, there!

Neil. How are you, Homer?

Homer. Not so good.

Neil. [*Feeling keenly his position as host.*] Ah—this is Doctor Rice. Mr. and Mrs. Cady, and—Miss Cady and—Cady.

[*His voice trails off. There are the indistinct greetings that follow an introduction.*]

Mrs. Cady. Doctor, did you say?

Albert. Yes, ma'am.

Mrs. Cady. Homer, here's a doctor.

Homer. Yes?

Mrs. Cady. Homer's had a good deal of trouble from time to time. Sit here, Homer—in this easy chair.

[HOMER *takes the only easy chair.*]

Neil. [*Delinquent.*] Oh, yes—sit down, everybody. I'm sorry I—ah——

Mrs. Cady. Oh, that's all right. We'll just settle ourselves.

[*She sits in the swivel chair at the desk.*]

Neil. [*Stirring up conversation.*] Ah—Doctor Rice comes from Livingston, too.

Mrs. Cady. Really?

Cady. That so?

Albert. Oh, a long time ago. We moved away when I was very young.

Mrs. Cady. I wonder if I—[*there is a sneeze from* HOMER]—— Are you all right, Homer?

Homer. Yes.

[*Something in his tone says that he is as all right as possible, considering where he is.*]

Mrs. Cady. [*Blandly finishing.*] —knew your people?

Homer. I don't remember them.

[*You gather that* ALBERT *just couldn't have had any people.*]

Cady. [*At the telephone.*] Mind if I use this?

Neil. Oh, no, of course not.

Cady. Thanks. I left the office a little early. [*Takes the receiver off.*]

Mrs. Cady. [*Bent on placing the* DOCTOR.] Let me see. *Old* Mrs. Rice——

Cady. Cortlandt 8262.

Mrs. Cady. I guess you're not the same.

[*There is a half-query in her voice.*]

Albert. Well, as a matter of fact, I moved away just after you came there.

Mrs. Cady. Oh, I see.

Gladys. [*Producing a box of candy.*] I brought you some candy for your tea, Neil.

Neil. Oh, thanks. [*To* MRS. CADY, *who is teetering in the desk chair.*] There's another chair if——

Mrs. Cady. No, I like this. Feels like my rocking-chair at home.

[*She sways back and forth.*]

Gladys. Mother's favorite chair is her rocker.

Mrs. Cady. There's nothing like an old-fashioned rocking-chair.

Cady. [*At the 'phone.*] Let me talk to Burgess.

Mrs. Cady. Mr. Cady says I'm chair-bound. Just joking, you know. [*She explains elaborately to* ALBERT.] Mr. Cady. Says I'm chair-bound.

Albert. [*Just the news he was waiting for.*] Oh, yes.

SIMULTANEOUSLY

Mrs. Cady. Let me see: there were two families of Rice out there, and I remember that one of them came here, just before we left. [*She finishes in a sibilant whisper, having been shushed by her* HUSBAND.]	*Cady.* Burgess? Any word from 653? . . . Hush, Mother. . . . Well, I'll tell you what to do. We ought to send a tracer. . . . That's right. . . . Well, I'll tell you what to do—if you don't hear by six o'clock send a tracer. That's all. [CADY *hangs up; turns to* NEIL.]

Cady. Much obliged. When I get a foot away from a telephone I'm lost. [*He starts for the weak chair;* NEIL *makes a movement.*] What is it?

Neil. That chair isn't very strong.

Cady. Oh, I'll be careful.

Neil. [*Not exactly at ease.*] We're going to have some—tea and things—pretty soon now.

Cady. [*Has taken out a cigar.*] Match?

Neil. [*Starting.*] How's that?

Cady. Match.

Neil. Oh, yes! Right here.

[NEIL *lights his cigar.*]

Gladys. [*Taking in the room.*] See, Mama, isn't it cute?

Mrs. Cady. Yes, indeed.

Gladys. There's the piano over there.

Mrs. Cady. Oh, yes. [*Everybody looks at the piano.*] Neil must play something for us.

[*It is Remark No.* 80 *and purely perfunctory.*]

Cady. It's certainly very nice. We've been hearing quite a bit about you, Neil.

Neil. Is that so?

Cady. Hear you've become quite a musician since you went away from Livingston.

Neil. Oh, I don't know.

Cady. Well, Gladys has been telling us so. So we thought we'd come and find out for ourselves. Gave up a golf game to do it, too. Play golf?

Neil. No, I don't.

Cady. Play golf, Doctor?

Albert. I'm sorry.

Cady. Well, everybody ought to. Great exercise. Keeps a man fit for business. I'd make Homer do it, if he wasn't so delicate.

[HOMER *shifts in his seat.*]

Mrs. Cady. Comfortable, Homer?

Homer. [*Carelessly.*] Um-hum.

[CYNTHIA *comes in with the tea things.*]

Neil. Oh, here we are! I—I want you to meet Miss Mason. She's brought the things over from her place.

Mrs. Cady. Oh, I see.

Neil. [*Beginning again the weary round of introductions.*] Mrs. Cady and—of course you know Gladys—

Gladys. Yes.

Cynthia. How are you, Miss Cady?

Neil. And Mr. Cady and—another Mr. Cady. [HOMER *does not rise. Mumbled greetings are exchanged.*] Miss Mason lives —just across the hall.

Mrs. Cady. Yes, so Gladys has told us. Are you a musician too, Miss Mason?

Cynthia. No, I'm not, Mrs. Cady.

Mrs. Cady. [*Turning to her* HUSBAND.] Don't she make you think of Elizabeth Merkle, Fred?

Cady. Well—I see what you mean.

Homer. [*Ever the dissenter.*] She don't me.

Mrs. Cady. Of course Elizabeth's dark, but there's something about the shape of the face. [*To* NEIL.] *You* knew the Merkles, Neil. Mr. Merkle had the skating rink.

Neil. Oh, yes. Elizabeth was a little girl when I knew her.

Mrs. Cady. She's twenty-two or three. Twenty-three, isn't she, Fred?

Cady. Yes, I guess so.

Homer. Lizzie Merkle's crazy. She's going to marry Lou Carmichael.

Gladys. Oh, did Grandma say when it was to be?

Mrs. Cady. No, I don't think they know themselves. You knew Lou, didn't you, Neil? [CYNTHIA *is serving tea.*]

Neil. Did they live over on Pine Street?

Mrs. Cady. I think they did.

Homer. No, they didn't.

Gladys. Hush up! They did. They lived next door to Doctor Endicott.

Homer. They did not. They've always lived on Mead Avenue.

Gladys. Well, I guess I ought to know. Didn't I go and meet his sister once? Remember that tall girl, Mama?

Homer. You're crazy.

Mrs. Cady. Lou used to take Gladys to dances a lot.

Gladys. He was a wonderful dancer!

[*She giggles.*]

Mrs. Cady. He was with the telephone company.

Homer. [*Scornfully.*] Charlie Ferris nearly beat him up.

Mrs. Cady. Remember when he and Charlie Ferris were crazy about Gladys? This girl's had more boys crazy about her, Neil.

[CYNTHIA *gives tea to* CADY.]

Gladys. Oh, I never cared for either of them.

Homer. You never let them *think* so.

Gladys. [*Smugly.*] Homer!

Homer. [*To* NEIL, *unpleasantly, as he passes tea to him.*] No, thanks. Tea always sits on me.

Cady. Say, I hear your Uncle James is dead, Neil. Leave you anything?

Neil. No—Uncle James never had anything.

Cady. Too bad. He was a fine man. Everybody was sorry when he moved to Boston.

Mrs. Cady. He was nice. [*To* CYNTHIA.] We used to sing together in Sunday School when we were children.

Neil. I remember you sang in the choir.

Gladys. Mama still sings, when she lets herself go.

Homer. We call her Galli-Curci.

Mrs. Cady. [*Genially.*] They're always joking me about my voice. But I do love old hymns. Your father was a good singer, too, Neil.

Neil. I guess he was a better lawyer.

Cady. Yes, everybody had a great deal of respect for John McRae.

Mrs. Cady. He was a beautiful character.

Cady. He'd give his money away to everybody. Afraid he never made very much, though. Lawyers don't, as a rule. Neil, did you know that when I was a young man I studied law—right in the same office with your father?

Neil. No? Did you?

Cady. Yes, sir. Had it all figured out to be a judge—Judge Cady—till I found out what was the most a judge could make.

[*Puts his tea down, almost untasted.*]

Cynthia. Too strong?

Cady. No. I'm not much of a tea drinker.

Mrs. Cady. I guess Gladys and I are the tea drinkers in our family. We have it every afternoon.

[NEIL *is opening the candy box.*]

Gladys. Neil's going to come up and have some with us next week. Tuesday.

Neil. Candy?

[MRS. CADY *takes a piece; so does* MR. CADY.]

Mrs. Cady. That's nice. We'll have some people in. I want you to see the new house. My, I don't know what the folks would say back in Livingston if they could see it. Remember our house in Livingston, Neil?

Neil. Yes, indeed.

[*He passes the candy box to* HOMER, *who waves it disdainfully aside.*]

Mrs. Cady. [*Trying to be bantering.*] You ought to. You were there enough. Every afternoon, pretty near. Neil and Gladys would play together and I'd go out in the kitchen and make candy for them.

[*She rocks.*]

Gladys. Oh, yes! Wasn't it fun, Neil?

Mrs. Cady. We always saved some pieces for Mr. Cady. All the Cadys are fond of candy. Aren't they, Fred?

[*She taps his knee.*]

Cady. [*Munching.*] Guess that's right, Mother.

Homer. I'm not.

Mrs. Cady. Except Homer. [*She resumes, largely to herself.*] All the Cadys eat candy.

Cynthia. And now—if you'll excuse me.

[*Rises.*]

Neil. Oh, you're not going?

[HOMER *doesn't rise with the other* MEN.]

Cynthia. I'm afraid I must.

Cady. That's too bad.

Mrs. Cady. Well, I hope we meet again.

Cynthia. I just ran in for a moment to be temporary hostess.

Gladys. Good-bye, Miss Mason.

Cynthia. [*To* ALBERT.] I hope I'll see you again. [*Shakes his hand.*]

Albert. Oh, I'll be back in a few weeks.

[*There are further good-byes.* CYNTHIA *goes.*]

Mrs. Cady. [*Looking after her.*] She *is* like Elizabeth.

Cady. [*Noisily.*] Well—how are things generally, Neil? Making a lot of money out of your music?

Neil. No—with music you don't make a great deal of money.

Cady. I don't know about that. It's just like any other business. Maybe you're not giving them what they want.

Mrs. Cady. I guess Neil's doing his best, aren't you, Neil?

Cady. We've all got to please the public. Eh, Doctor?

Albert. Oh, yes.

Cady. I've got to in my business. Of course, I don't claim to know anything about music, but I think I represent about the average viewpoint. Now, what I like is a good lively tune—something with a little snap to it. As I understand it, though, you sort of go in for—highbrow music.

Neil. It isn't exactly that.

Cady. Well, there's no money in it. You know what happened to your father.

Mrs. Cady. Had to scrape all his life. [*Turns to* ALBERT.] Neil's father. Had to scrape all his life.

Cady. A young fellow's got to look out for his future, I claim—got to save up a little money.

Neil. [*Puzzled.*] Yes, sir.

Mrs. Cady. [*Helping along what is clearly a prearranged conversation.*] In some *business,* Mr. Cady means.

Cady. Yes. Now you take—well, my business, for example. We've always got an opening for—a bright young fellow.

Neil. You mean—*me*—in your business?

Cady. Well, I just mentioned that for example.

Neil. I—I'm afraid I wouldn't be much good in business, Mr. Cady.

Mrs. Cady. Of course you'd be good.

Neil. I did work once in an office, and I guess I wasn't—very——

Cady. That's all right. You'd learn. The idea is you'd be making money. Some day you'd maybe have a nice interest in the firm. 'Tain't as though you couldn't write a little music now and then in your spare time, and we'd be sort of all together.

[*The jazz orchestra is heard again—this time louder.*]

Mrs. Cady. Just like one big family.

Gladys. [*Singing and swaying to the tune.*] Oh, they're playing "The Frog's Party." [*To* NEIL.] Come on and dance!

Neil. I'm sorry, but I don't dance.

Gladys. Oh, so you don't—but I'm going to make you learn. I know a wonderful teacher. [*Turns to* ALBERT.] Dance, Doctor?

Albert. A little.

[GLADYS *and* ALBERT *take a few turns about the room.* MRS. CADY *hums the tune, not knowing the words.*]

Cady. Great song! A man I played golf with yesterday tells me that for the first six months of the fiscal year that song'll make a hundred thousand dollars. Write something like that and you're fixed. That's music.

Homer. We got it on the radio last night.

Albert. [*Politely.*] You don't say?

Gladys. [*Near the piano.*] Oh, Neil!

[*The three remaining* CADYS *are grouped with* ALBERT.]

SIMULTANEOUSLY

Gladys. [*Holds up a piece of music, as* NEIL *crosses to her.*] What's this?

Neil. Just something I'm working on.

Gladys. [*Sotto voce.*] I want to talk to you.

Neil. Oh!

Gladys. Don't you want to talk to me?

Neil. Oh, yes.

Gladys. Neil.

[*Points to a small photograph on piano.*]

Neil. Yes.

Gladys. [*Takes up the picture.*] Can I have one of these?

Neil. I'm afraid I haven't got another.

Gladys. This was in the Musical Courier, wasn't it?

Neil. Why, yes.

Gladys. I saw it. You're pretty well known, Neil. I'm proud of you. I wish I could have this one. Only I wish it were of you alone, instead of you and this other girl, whoever she is.

[*Puts picture back.*]

Neil. It's just a girl I met one summer.

[*A pause.*]

Gladys. Neil?

Neil. Well?

Gladys. Do you like me better than you do Miss Mason?

Neil. Well, I think she's awfully nice.

Gladys. Don't you think I'm nice, too?

Neil. Yes, of course.

Gladys. Because, I think *you* are. You know that, don't you, Neil?

Neil. [*Nearly choking.*] I'm—glad.

Gladys. So, of course, I want *you* to think *I* am.

Neil. I—do.

Gladys. [*Suddenly.*] Oh! That reminds me.

[*Fishes in her handbag.*]

Neil. What is it?

Gladys. [*Bringing out four or five small samples of colored cloths.*] I knew I wanted to ask you something. Which do you like best?

Neil. Why, they're all very nice.

Gladys. But don't you like one best?

Neil. I don't know. They're all sort of—ah —why——

Gladys. Because I'd like to get the one you'd like. [NEIL *is puzzled. She spreads the samples on his arm.*] They're samples, silly! I'm going from here to the dressmaker's to pick one out.

Neil. Oh, I see.

[*He removes the samples.*]

Gladys. [*Pouting.*] Of course if you don't care what I wear, why, all right.

Neil. [*Not enthusiastic.*] I do care.

Gladys. [*Eager again.*] Well, which one would you rather see me in? The blue?

Neil. Yes, that would be nice.

Gladys. I like the pink one myself.

Cady. Couple of hundred miles away, wasn't it?

Homer. Three hundred.

Cady. Think of that!

Albert. It's wonderful.

Mrs. Cady. I was going to ask you, Doctor, if you're related to those other Rices. There were two daughters, I think.

Albert. No, I haven't any relatives left there.

Cady. Live in New York, now, I suppose?

Albert. No, Chicago. I'm just here for a flying visit.

Cady. Chicago? Don't say! Well, that's a good town.

Homer. Chicago a good town? Huh!

Mrs. Cady. It would be nice if you could come up and see us, too, Doctor.

Albert. Thank you, but I'm going back soon.

Mrs. Cady. Well, do come if you can. Any day after Thursday. Both our butlers are leaving, and I can't get any new ones to come until after the holiday. But we always like to have people from Livingston drop in. I always say if you don't keep in touch with your old home town, why your old home town won't keep in touch with you.

Homer. I never want to go back there.

Cady. Well, I don't know as I do, either.

Mrs. Cady. Listen to that man. And to think he was president of the Board of Trade there for five mortal years.

Cady. [*Thoughtfully, to* ALBERT.] You know, I think I've got you placed now. Was your father E. J. Rice, in the lumber business?

Albert. No, he was an architect.

Mrs. Cady. An architect—you don't say? Put up buildings, did he?

Albert. Yes, a few.

Mrs. Cady. Put up any buildings in Livingston?

Albert. Why, yes.

Cady. Not the First National?

Albert. No, he designed the Mechanics' Building, right next door.

Cady. You don't say!

Mrs. Cady. Well, that's a nice building, too.

Homer. I remember it.

Mrs. Cady. Mr. Cady had his offices in the First National Building.

Albert. Is that so?

Cady. I guess there's been quite a building boom since you were there. That whole block is pretty solid now.

Albert. Really?

Mrs. Cady. My, yes. You wouldn't know the place.

Cady. Yes, sir! I guess there's been a good many million dollars invested there in the last five years.

Albert. You don't say!

Mrs. Cady. Mr. Cady put up a building himself.

Albert. That so?

Cady. Just a warehouse. Of course we still have a plant there ——

Homer. [*Heard by himself.*] It's half past, Pop. [*Rises.*]

Cady. Yes, I guess we'll have to be going. [*Rises.*]

Mrs. Cady. Ready, Gladys? [*Rises.*]

Gladys. Yes, Mama.

[*Starts, then turns back to* NEIL.]

SIMULTANEOUSLY

<table>
<tr>
<td>

Gladys. [*Suddenly, to* NEIL.] Oh, Neil!

Neil. Yes.

Gladys. I won't go home for dinner — if you don't want me to.

Neil. Well, I did sort of think I'd do some work——

Gladys. I'll go with *you* to a new restaurant I just heard about! I'll tell you what! I'll only be at the dressmaker's a few minutes. Then you can meet me.

Neil. Well, I don't know exactly how I'll be fixed.

Gladys. I'll telephone you the minute I'm finished.

Neil. But, Gladys, I'm going to be tied up, I'm afraid, and ——

Gladys. Well, anyway, I'll 'phone.

</td>
<td>

Mrs. Cady. Well, now, don't forget, Doctor! Come and see us, if you can.

Albert. Thank you.

Cady. Or have a round of golf with me some time. Play golf?

Albert. I'm sorry, I don't.

Cady. I remember—I asked you before.

Homer. [*Impatient.*] Oh, come on!

Mrs. Cady. Just a second, Homer. Gladys is talking.

Homer. She's always talking.

Mrs. Cady. [*To* ALBERT, *with a laugh.*] Just like a brother, isn't he?

Cady. Well, good-by, Doctor.

Albert. Good-by, Mr. Cady.

</td>
</tr>
</table>

Cady. Come on, Gladys.

Gladys. All right. [*To* NEIL.] I'll telephone you from the dressmaker's when I'm through.

Mrs. Cady. And, Neil—you're coming Tuesday, remember.

Neil. Oh, thanks. I'm sorry I couldn't have had a nicer party for you.

Mrs. Cady. It was elegant. Only next time we come, you must play something for us.

Neil. I'll ring for the elevator.

Mrs. Cady. Oh, that's nice. Come on, Homer.

[NEIL, MR. CADY, *and* MRS. CADY *pass into the hall.*]

Gladys. Good-by, Doctor.

Albert. Good-by, Miss Cady.

[GLADYS *follows them out;* HOMER *lingers with the* DOCTOR.]

Homer. What about him? Do you know him well?

[*He takes out a box of powders.*]

Albert. Who? Neil?

Homer. Yeh. Is he all right?

Albert. Why?

Homer. Well, I just like to know things about a possible brother-in-law.

Albert. I see.

Homer. Gladys is nutty about him. Thinks he's artistic, my God! And did you hear the old man? Just because his father was John McRae!

[*Puts the powder on his tongue—takes a glass of water.*]

Mrs. Cady. [*In the hall.*] Hurry, Homer!

Homer. [*Calling.*] All right! [*He swallows the words, drinking at the same time.*] So long. Well, I hope it don't happen.

[*He strolls out.*]

Albert. So long.

[*The voices of the departing* GUESTS *are heard in the hall.* NEIL *returns; looks back into the hall.*]

Neil. What was all that about?

Albert. Oh, nothing in particular.

Neil. How did you like the Cadys?

Albert. Seem to be all right. They must be richer than mud. Did you hear Mrs. Cady on her "butlers"?

Neil. No.

Albert. I never heard of anybody having more than one butler before, but the Cadys seem to have 'em in pairs.

Neil. [*Laughing.*] I haven't been to their house yet. I'm going next week, though. [*His glance going to the door.*] Say! Homer's a dirty dog, isn't he?

Albert. [*Thoughtfully.*] Neil, I want to talk to you.

Neil. Good Lord, again?

Albert. In the first place, I want you to go to bed.

Neil. At half past five o'clock?

Albert. You haven't slept for days.

Neil. But I can't go to bed now. I've got work to do. [*A second pause.*] You don't mean I'm sick?

Albert. No, but you need rest. I want you to put on your dressing gown and lie down for a while. And then take another one of these.

[*Produces the pills.*]

Neil. But I can't afford to go to sleep. I told you that. I've got work to do.

Albert. You can't work tonight.

Neil. I must.

Albert. On those orchestrations?

Neil. Yes. [*A pause.*]

Albert. Neil?

Neil. What?

Albert. I want to talk to you about something else.

Neil. Good heavens!

Albert. All right, but—somebody has to. [NEIL *looks up, sensing something important.*] What are you going to do about your work?

Neil. Huh?

Albert. Your *real* work, I mean? How much have you done since I went away?

Neil. Well, what you heard. And Miss Mason and I are working out a little pantomime together. It's going to be a lot of fun——

Albert. How much of it is written?

Neil. A lot. About half, I guess.

Albert. About half a movement of a symphony and about half a pantomime.

Neil. I still have to eat.

Albert. But Neil, don't you see—you're wasting your genius!

Neil. Genius, my hat!

Albert. You're wasting the best years you'll ever have doing odd jobs just to keep alive. You've got to be free to write.

Neil. Well, maybe some day I'll write a popular song and make a million.

Albert. If you ever did you'd either burn it or sell it for ten dollars. You'll never make any money, Neil. You know that as well as I do.

Neil. Then what's the answer? Are you going to subsidize me?

Albert. I wish to God I could! But there's no reason why you shouldn't subsidize yourself.

Neil. What do you mean?

Albert. I mean the Cadys.

Neil. What are you talking—oh, don't be foolish!

Albert. Why is it foolish?

Neil. Gladys would never—why, you're crazy!

Albert. Am I? Think back. How did she behave this afternoon? And Papa Cady? "Nice little share in the business?" And—well, I know what I'm talking about.

Neil. You mean you're seriously advising me to ask Gladys Cady to marry me?

Albert. That's exactly what I'm doing. She's a nice girl, and pretty. You'd have comfort and money and time——

Neil. [*Interrupting, with growing excitement.*] Well, what about me? Do you think money and music and time would make up for everything else? No, sir! I'd rather keep on living right here—just as I am now—all my life long.

Albert. Now, now! Don't get temperamental! If you'll just——

[CYNTHIA *opens the door.*]

Cynthia. May a poor girl call for her dishes?

Neil. I'm sorry—I should have brought them over.

Cynthia. [*Detecting a note in his voice.*] Neil, there's nothing the matter?

Albert. I've been trying to persuade him to rest. [*To* NEIL.] Won't you go in and —get ready?

Neil. I—I can't now.

Cynthia. Neil, please. [*A pause.*]

Neil. All right. But don't go away. I want to talk to you.

[*He goes into the bedroom.*]

Cynthia. He *is* difficult.

Albert. Yes, he is.

Cynthia. I'm glad you've taken charge of him.

[*She is collecting the tea dishes.*]

Albert. He'll be all right. Just needs sleep, that's all. I'm not worrying about him physically so much as—well, spiritually.

Cynthia. I know. I've been worrying about it for weeks.

Albert. You do see his genius, don't you?

Cynthia. Oh, yes! He has it, if any one ever had.

Albert. And this hack-work—it must be killing his spirit.

Cynthia. When I think of his keeping on, year after year! And he's such a babe-in-arms about practical things. He *does* so need——[*She hesitates.*] We must do something, mustn't we?

Albert. Yes, we must. [*A pause.*] There *is* a possible way out, you know.

[*A pause.*]

Cynthia. [*Slowly.*] Yes, I know.

[*A longer pause.*]

Albert. It's the only way, I'm afraid.

Cynthia. Oh, I've been thinking about it ever since she began coming here! You really *do* think it's the right thing for him? The wisest?

Albert. I'm sure of it.

Cynthia. But could he be happy?

Albert. That's the only way he *can* be happy, permanently—if he's free to write his music. That's the most important thing, in the end.

Cynthia. It seems—and yet I'm afraid you're right.

Albert. We only hurt people by being sentimental about them. That's one of the first things a doctor learns. Let's put this through. Will you?

Cynthia. Oh, I couldn't.

Albert. You can do more than I can. You'll be here, and I've got to go away. And anyway, a woman can always do more than a man about this sort of thing. [*Holds out his hand to her.*] For Neil's sake. [*He takes a step away from her as he hears* NEIL *returning.* NEIL *comes back, wearing a dressing gown.*] That's right! Now!

Neil. Of all the rot! Putting a grown man to bed at half past five!

Albert. Who ever accused you of being a grown man? Here! [*Produces a pill.*] Be brave. One swallow and it's over.

Neil Oh, all right—give it to me.

Albert. Here! [NEIL *takes it.*] And another before you go to bed. I'll put them here. [*He takes up his hat.*]

Neil. You're going?

Albert. Got to—dining uptown. [*Taps* NEIL *lightly with his gloves as he passes.*] I'll look in in the morning. You'll be all right then. Good-night, Miss Mason.

Cynthia. Good-by, Doctor.

[ALBERT *goes.*]

Neil. [*To* CYNTHIA, *who is gathering the last of her dishes.*] He's been talking to you about me, hasn't he?

Cynthia. Why—you and other things. [*Not looking up.*]

Neil. What did he say?

Cynthia. Don't you wish you knew—curiosity!

Neil. I *do* know. I know exactly. He said the same thing to me. He said I was a failure—practically. That I'd have to depend on other people all my life.

Cynthia. Neil, you're just exciting yourself. You're tired, and you know he wants you to——

Neil. No, wait! We've got to talk about this, you and I. He said more than that. He said that I ought to ask Gladys Cady to marry me. [*A pause.*] Well! You don't seem—surprised.

Cynthia. No, I'm not.

Neil. Don't you even think it's—funny, a little bit?

Cynthia. No.

Neil. Cynthia! [*Looks at her for a moment and then with a cry.*] Oh, Cynthia—dear! [*Takes her hand.*]

Cynthia. Don't, Neil!—*Please* don't!

Neil. But Cynthia, don't you know—without my telling you—that I love only you and no one else?

Cynthia. Oh, Neil, please! [*Then, with an attempt at lightness.*] This is so sudden!

Neil. [*Hurt.*] Oh, Cynthia, please don't!

Cynthia. Oh, please don't *you*!

Neil. You know I love you, Cynthia! Of course you know; you couldn't help knowing! I thought maybe you—don't you, at all, Cynthia?

Cynthia. [*Regaining control of herself.*] Neil, let me tell you something. I *have* seen that you were growing to care for me, and I've—I've tried to think what I ought to do about it.

Neil. Do about it! What can you do about it if——

Cynthia. You can do lots of things—if you're practical and sensible.

Neil. Oh, my dear!

Cynthia. I said to myself, I think he's beginning to care about me more than he ought to, considering how we're both situated, and that nothing could come of it. And if I stay here I mightn't be sensible either. So, I'm going away.

Neil. What!

Cynthia. I'm going to move uptown and live with Helen Noland. I'm going tomorrow.

Neil. Cynthia—do you mean that you don't care about me at all?

Cynthia. Oh, yes, I do, Neil. I care about you very much. I think you're a great artist.

Neil. Artist! [*He turns away from her.*]

Cynthia. And I think it would be the greatest possible misfortune for your music for you to go on this way, living from hand to mouth. So—when Doctor Rice suggested that you marry Miss Cady, it seemed to me a very sensible thing to do.

Neil. [*Faces her again.*] Cynthia—do you know what you're talking about?

Cynthia. Perfectly.

Neil. You can't mean that, music or no music, I ought to marry Gladys?

Cynthia. I think you ought to do just that for the sake of your music.

Neil. [*Hurt.*] Oh! You're like Albert! You think my music is the only thing about me that's worth while!

[*He again turns away.*]

Cynthia. Oh, Neil!

Neil. [*Continuing.*] It never *was* me that you cared about—only the music.

Cynthia. I want you to be happy, Neil.

Neil. [*Laughs mirthlessly.*] I certainly got it all wrong, didn't I? [*A pause.*] Well, good-by, Cynthia.

Cynthia. Oh, Neil! Don't say good-by like that.

Neil. What other way is there? You're all being so sensible and practical. I might as well be practical and sensible too. [CYNTHIA *starts to speak, chokes up, goes out—stifling her tears. After a moment* NEIL *turns and sees that she is gone.*] My music! [*Then, less viciously.*] My music! [*The 'phone bell rings.* NEIL *looks toward it—plainly,* GLADYS *has finished at the dressmaker's. For a second he hesitates; then he makes up his mind and strides to the 'phone. There is grim determination in his voice, from the opening greeting.*] Hello, Gladys!

Gladys. [*Over the 'phone.*] Hello, Neil!

Neil. Well, is the fitting over?

[*He stifles a yawn; the pills are beginning to work.*]

Gladys. Yes, but it wasn't a fitting.

Neil. Well, whatever it was.

Gladys. I took the pink one.

Neil. The pink one. That's fine.

Gladys. Oh, you don't care which at all!

Neil. Of course I care which.

Gladys. Can you meet me?

Neil. Well, I don't think I can do that.

Gladys. What?

Neil. I say I can't go out. The doctor says I must stay in for a while.

Gladys. Oh, my goodness! Are you sick?

Neil. Oh, no. Just tired. Really, that's all. I have to—sleep for about an hour.

[*He is growing momentarily more listless.*]

Gladys. Oh, dear!

Neil. Well, why don't you come up here instead?

Gladys. Shall I?

Neil. Of course.

Gladys. Why?

Neil. Well, there's something I want to say to you, to ask you—something we all want to—I mean something I want to ask you——

Gladys. I wish I knew!

Neil. Maybe you do know. We thought—that is, I thought—how would you like to marry a great composer?

[*The receiver nearly falls from his grip.*]

Gladys. Oh, darling! Do you mean it?

Neil. Sure I mean it.

Gladys. Of course I'll marry you!

Neil. Would you, honestly?

Gladys. Yes, indeed!

Neil. Well, that's fine. We'll show them, won't we?

Gladys. Who?

Neil. Oh, everybody.

Gladys. Can I tell them?

Neil. Yes, tell them all. Homer and——

Gladys. Oh, darling, I'm so happy!

Neil. [*His tone dull.*] Well, I'm happy, too.

Gladys. Let me hear you say "Sweetheart."

Neil. Do I have to say it?

Gladys. Of course.

Neil. [*Barely audible.*] Sweetheart.

Gladys. Go ahead.

Neil. Didn't you hear it?

Gladys. No.

Neil. [*Viciously.*] Sweetheart!

Gladys. Do you love me?

Neil. Of course I do.

Gladys. Well, I'll come over in about an hour.

Neil. All right. [*A sleepy pause.*] In about an hour. You come, and—I'll sleep for an hour. I'll— sleep. [*He tries to replace the receiver, but is too sleepy. It dangles from its cord.* NEIL *rouses himself from the chair with difficulty.*] And that's that! [*Across the street the jazz orchestra begins again to play "The Frog's Party." It seems louder than before—already* NEIL'S *imagination is causing it to swell. He wheels toward the window.*] Now go ahead and play! [*He staggers to the easy chair and drops into it.*] Play the wedding march, damn you! Play the wedding march!

[*The tune resolves itself into a jazzy version of Lohengrin's Wedding March. At the same time* NEIL *finally collapses into the chair, and the lights of the room begin to go down. As it grows dark the music swells. Then, after a moment, it begins to grow light again—but it is no longer* NEIL'S *room. It is a railway station, with the arch of Track 37 prominently visible, and other arches flanking it at the side. A muddled train schedule is printed on the station walls, with strange towns that never existed.* NEIL'S *piano, however, has remained where it was, and so has his easy chair. Then, down the aisles of the lighted theater, there comes suddenly a double wedding* PROCESSION. *One section is headed by* MR. CADY *and* GLADYS—MR. CADY *in golf knickers and socks, knitted vest, and frock coat, with a silk hat prominently on his arm.* GLADYS *is the gorgeously attired bride, bearing proudly a bouquet that consists entirely of banknotes. Behind them stream four* USHERS—*spats, frock coats, and high hats, to say nothing of huge bridal veils, draped over their heads. If you could peer beneath their veils, however, you would find that all four of them look just alike. The* PROCESSION *that comes down the other aisle is headed by* MRS. CADY *and* HOMER. MRS. CADY *wears a grotesque exaggeration of the dress that* NEIL *has seen her in, and* HOMER'S *yellow tie has assumed tremendous proportions. Behind* MRS. CADY *and* HOMER *are four* BANDSMEN. *Like the* USHERS, *they all look alike, all wearing bridal veils, through which they play their instruments.*

At the foot of the stage the PROCESSIONS *halt; the music stops.* ALBERT *appears from nowhere in particular; he has turned into a minister.*]

Gladys. Oh, Neil!

Neil. [*In his sleep.*] Huh?

[ALBERT *gently rouses him.*]

Albert. Neil! Did you forget that you were being married today?

Neil. Oh! Why—I'm afraid I did. [*He looks wonderingly at the railway station, then turns and sees* GLADYS.] Oh, hello, Gladys! I'm sorry.

[*The two* PROCESSIONS *stream up on to the stage. The* USHERS *and the* BANDSMEN *line up behind the* CADY *family.*]

Gladys. Neil. I want you to meet my ushers. They're all boys I used to know pretty well. [*As* GLADYS *begins the introductions the entire thing turns into a rhythmic chant, to an orchestral accompaniment.*] This is Alf and this is Georgie.

Neil. Glad to meet you!

Alf. Glad to meet you!

Gladys. This is Steve.

Neil. I'm glad to meet you!

Gladys. This is Fatty.

Neil. How d'you do?

Gladys. This is Lou.

Lou. I'm glad to meet you!

Neil. Glad to meet you!

Lou. Glad to meet you!

Gladys. And this last is Cousin Harry.

Harry. Glad to meet you!

Neil. How d'you do?

Cady. Hurry up, now! Let's get at it!

Albert. Take this man to be your husband?

[*A* TRAINMAN, *in uniform, enters through the gates of the railway station.*]

Trainman. Wolverine, for Monte Carlo!

Albert. Have and hold him . . .

Gladys. Yes, I do!

[*They all begin to rise and fall on their toes, to the beat of the music.*]

Albert. All your worldly goods and chattels. . . .

[*A* TRAINBOY, *carrying the usual magazines, chocolates, etc., comes through the gates.*]

Trainboy. Latest magazines and papers!

Mrs. Cady. Going off to leave her mama!

Homer. Say, it's cold here! Ah, ker-choo!

[*The* USHERS *begin to march around* GLADYS *and* NEIL, *faster and faster.*]

Cady. Train pulls out in just a minute!

Albert. Both for richer and for richer. . . .

Trainman. Pasadena, Paris, London!

Albert. Better, worser . . .

Gladys. Sure I will!

Cady. Special car Appolinaris!

[GLADYS *is kissing the* USHERS *as they march.*]

Trainboy. Nothing sold after the train leaves!

Mrs. Cady. Don't know *what* I'll do without her!

Trainman. Show your tickets!

Homer. Ma, keep still!

Cady. Get aboard! I'll tip the preacher!

Trainman. Right this way, please! Right this way, please!

Trainboy. Huyler's chocolates and bonbons!

Mrs. Cady. Oh, my baby!

Homer. Oh, good Lord!

Trainman. Lenox, Palm Beach, Narragansett!

Albert. I pronounce you—got the ring, Neil?

All the Ushers. Bet he's lost it! Bet he's lost it!

Gladys. Here's another!

Trainman. All aboard! [*The* PROCESSION *starts through the gates*—ALBERT *and* CADY *first, then the rest of the* CADYS, *then the* USHERS *and the* BANDSMEN. *As they all file through the* USHERS *continue the chant, calling out in unison:*]

Well, good-by! Congratulations!
Good-by, Gladys! Good-by, Gladys!
Send us back a picture postal!
Hope you're happy!
Well, good-by!

[GLADYS *tosses her bouquet back to them; the* USHERS *scramble for the banknotes. As the last of the procession disappears through the doors the lights die down. A moment later they come up again, revealing a row of white marble columns, with crimson curtains hung between them.* NEIL'S *piano, however, is still incongruously in the left corner, and his easy chair stands at the right. Immediately* NEIL *and* GLADYS *enter through side curtains.* NEIL *is still wearing his bathrobe—a somewhat sad spectacle amid all this grandeur.* GLADYS *is no longer in bridal costume, but wears a pleated dress—an exaggeration of the dress that she has worn in real life, with great pleats several inches thick.*]

Gladys. We're married, Neil!

Neil. Yes.

Gladys. I'm your little bride.

Neil. My little bride.

Gladys. [*Giggles.*] Isn't it all just too wonderful? [*Runs into his arms.*] This is our beautiful home—see! [*The curtains behind the front columns part, revealing a magnificent interior consisting entirely of more marble columns and velvet curtains.*] You're going to have everything you've always needed! Mama and Papa both say so!

Neil. Oh! Do they?

Gladys. Yes, indeed! You just wait—they'll be here any minute!

Neil. They're coming here?

Gladys. Of course they are! There're a lot of people coming—all coming to see our beautiful new home! Wait a minute—I'll show you! [*Calls.*] Butlers! [*Two* BUTLERS *appear. They are exactly alike.*] Announce somebody!

The Two Butlers. Mrs. Cady and her chair and knitting!

[MRS. CADY *enters with a rocking-chair attached to her. She begins knitting immediately. The two* BUTLERS *depart.*]

Mrs. Cady. Two little lovebirds! Gladys and Neil! Gladys and Neil! Are they happy? Oh, my dear, you never *saw* any one so happy! I was saying to Mr. Cady, "Well, Mr. Cady, what do you think of your little daughter now? [*She sits.*] How's this for a happy family?" And Mr. Cady says to me, "Well, I never would have believed it." And I says to Mr. Cady, and Mr. Cady says to me, and I says to Mr. Cady, and Mr. Cady says to me, and I says——

Neil. Stop! [MRS. CADY *stops.*] So—so you're my wife's mother?

Gladys. Why, of course she is! I think she's a pretty nice mother-in-law, don't you? Most people don't like their mothers-in-law, but I think *she's* pretty nice.

Neil. But is *she* going to be—always——

Gladys. Yes, indeed! Won't it be lovely? And that isn't all! [*Calls.*] Butlers!

[*Four* BUTLERS *enter.*]

The Four Butlers. Mr. Cady, her father!

[MR. CADY *enters. He is in complete golf attire, and there is a telephone attached to his chest. As he enters the* BUTLERS *depart.*]

Cady. [*Into the telephone.*] Yep! Yep! Hullo! Well, I'll tell you what to do! Sell eighteen holes and buy all the water hazards. Yep! Yep! Hullo! Well, I'll tell you what to do! I expect caddies will go up any time now. How's the eighth hole this morning? Uh-huh. Well, sell it in three. Yes, sir. That's fine. Yep! Yep! Hullo! Well, I'll tell you what to do! Buy——

Neil. No, no! [CADY *stops; looks at* NEIL.] You must stop—both of you! Do you know me?

Cady. My son! My new son! Well, Neil, how's the nice music and everything? Making a lot of money?

Neil. Are we all going to live together?

Gladys. Yes, indeed, darling.

Cady. Yes, indeed.

Mrs. Cady. Yes, indeed.

Gladys. And that isn't all. [*Six* BUTLERS *enter. Of course they are all alike.*] I've *another* surprise for you!

The Six Butlers. Her brother, Homer. He makes me sick.

First Butler. I don't think *he's* sick at all.

[*The* BUTLERS *go.* HOMER *enters—the yellow tie is bigger than ever.*]

Homer. Oh, there you are, you dirty dog! I'm on to you! You married her just because Dad's got a lot of money, and you think you're going to have a cinch. But if you think you're going to get all of Dad's money, you're mistaken, because I'm going to get my share and don't you forget it.

[*He makes straight for the easy chair, sits in it, and sneezes.*]

Mrs. Cady. Now, Homer! Homer's sick.

Cady. Yes, he's sick.

Gladys. It's all right, dearest.

Neil. It isn't all right. I don't want the money. All I want to do is write my music. That's what I want to do—work. Do you think I'll be able to?

Gladys. Why, of course you will, dear. We've just had this whole room done over for you to work in.

Mrs. Cady. It's awfully pretty, Neil.

Cady. Cost a lot of money, too. [*His 'phone rings.*] Hello! . . . No—wrong number! [*He hangs up.*]

Gladys. Don't you just love it, Neil, keeping house together? Say "Sweetheart!"

Neil. [*Automatically.*] Sweetheart.

Gladys. And next week we're going to have everything done over in some *other* color. Here are the samples—the samples. [*She produces another set of samples, larger than those used in real life.*] Now which color would you like? It's going to be whichever color you like.

Neil. Why, any one.

[*He removes the samples from his arm.*]

Homer. Make him pick one! Make him pick it!

Gladys. Here, I'll tell you! You stop in and get them matched! Get some of this one, and some of that one, and maybe some of the other one—on your way home from business tomorrow. It'll give you something to do.

Neil. Am I going to business tomorrow?

Cady. Yes, sir! Start right in at the bottom and work up. Learn all the ins and outs. Lots of people think the ins and outs don't amount to anything; but you can't get anywhere in business without them.

Neil. But if I have to go to business to

morrow I'd like to work on my symphony now—if you'll only go.

Homer. Huh! The symphony!

Gladys. That old thing!

Cady. That's no good!

Mrs. Cady. I wouldn't have it in the house!

Neil. But it is good—and I've got to finish it.

Cady. Highbrow music—that's what it is.

Neil. Well, then, I'll work on the pantomime—that's not so highbrow.

[*He goes to the piano.*]

Mrs. Cady. For my part, I like hymns. There's nothing like the old familiar hymns.

[*She sings—"Blessed Be the Tie that Binds."*]

Gladys. Anyhow, you can't work now. It's tea time!

Mrs. Cady. [*To the tune of the hymn.*] Yes, tea time! It's tea time! It's tea time!

Cady. So it is. [*Into his 'phone.*] Hello! . . . Don't disturb me now—I'm busy. . . . Tea!

Cady. Quite a crowd coming this afternoon.

Mrs. Cady. Yes, coming to meet Neil! Yes, Gladys and Neil! Gladys and Neil!

Gladys. Now, Neil, you be nice to everybody. I want you to make a nice impression. [*Eight* BUTLERS *enter.*]

The Eight Butlers. A friend of her family's.

[*The* BUTLERS *go. No one enters, but apparently the* CADYS *see some one. They greet the invisible guest.*]

Gladys. How do you do?

Cady. How do you do?

[*They bring her down to* MRS. CADY.]

Mrs. Cady. How do you do? Oh, what a nice new ear trumpet!

Gladys. I'm so glad you were able to come!

[NEIL *peers, trying his best to see what it is all about.*]

Mrs. Cady. Well, it's wonderful to see you again!

Gladys. Doesn't she look well, Mama?

Mrs. Cady. You're the picture of health! No one would ever say *you* had an operation. I say—no one would ever say you had an operation. Yes, it always does it if you were heavy before. Oh, was it a year ago? Well, tempus does fugit, as Homer says. You remember Homer?

Homer. I said hello.

Mrs. Cady. Homer's sick.

Gladys. Oh, Neil! I want you to meet an old friend of Mama's. She's deaf. You'll have to talk loud. [*Ten* BUTLERS *enter.*]

The Ten Butlers. Another friend of the family's! [*The* BUTLERS *go.*]

Gladys. [*Greeting the newcomer.*] How do you do?

Cady. How do you do?

Gladys. So glad to see you again. And little Hattie! Oh, look, Mama!

[CADY *and* GLADYS *bend over, as though greeting a child.*]

Mrs. Cady. Why, if it isn't little Hattie! Look, Gladys! Isn't she cunning?

Gladys. Isn't she? Those cute little curls! Do you want to meet your great big cousin Neilie? Neil, darling, this is your little cousin Hattie. Isn't she a big girl? Say something cute to her.

[GLADYS *turns away from* NEIL *and he passes his foot over the spot where the child is supposed to be. Twelve* BUTLERS *enter.*]

The Twelve Butlers. A great many other friends of the family.

First Butler. And all pretty terrible, if you ask me. [*They go.*]

Cady. Hello, Alf! You remember Mrs. Cady?

Homer. Hello, Fatty.

Mrs. Cady. How do you do?

Cady. Say, I called you up a couple times but couldn't get any answer.

Gladys. Why, how do you do, Alf? I'm awfully glad you were able to come. Oh, Neil! I want you to meet an old friend of Papa's. He's known me ever since I was—how high? Yes, but you couldn't lift me now.

[*The invisible guest tries to lift her and fails. She giggles.* BUTLERS *enter with imaginary trays.*]

Mrs. Cady. And now we'll have some nice tea to drink.

Homer. [*Probably to* FATTY.] He married Gladys for her money.

Mrs. Cady. And then Neil will play for us.

Gladys. Oh, hello! Haven't seen you in a long time! No, I guess I wasn't engaged then.

[*It is a Babel. The* CADYS *are all speaking together, moving around and greeting guests.* NEIL *moves through it all, walking through guests, passing his hands through the* BUTLERS' *trays—bewildered.*]

Cady. Oh, hello, Ralph. I want you to meet my new son-in-law. Neil, this is Mr. Umn.

Gladys. Oh, have you been out to California? Did it rain much?

Cady. Yes, he's going to be very valuable to me in business, too.

Homer. I'll bet he's rotten.

Cady. But, after all, there's nothing like business. It'll all be his when I retire—his and Homer's, his and Homer's.

[*Slaps* NEIL *on back. The following four speeches are spoken simultaneously.*]

Mrs. Cady. Well, Miss Mmm, you know Mmm, don't you? He's a cousin of John's who knew Francis very well. She's Ted's aunt. Yes. It's such a long time since you've been to see us. Gladys is always saying: "Mama, why is it Mrs. Mmm doesn't come and visit us, or why don't we go out and see her?" and all like that. You know Mrs. Mmm, don't you? You've become very plump, or you've become very thin. You don't mind my not getting up, do you? Mr. Cady always says I'm chair-bound. But that's his way of making a joke. He's always making a joke. You know Neil, of course. Would you like to have Neil play for us? Would you like to have Neil play for us? Neil, play for us.

Homer. Look at him, the dirty dog! He married her for her money all right, but if he thinks he's going to get it he's got another think coming. Pop's going to put him in the business! Huh! He thinks he's going to get the business, too. Well, I'll show him—the dirty dog! He isn't going to get the business away from me—not while I'm alive and kicking. All because he's a musician. Yes, he thinks he plays the piano. Well—let him play it and see if I care. I dare him to play it. Go on and play for us.

Mr. Cady. Well, well, well! You know Judge Mmm of course. Old man, I want you to meet the Judge. Yes, they've got a very beautiful home here. Would you like a cocktail, eh? Yes, sir! Well, Judge, how's everything been going? Say, you know Mr. Mmm, don't you? How are you? How have you been all these years? Have a cocktail—that's the boy. Yes, she's a big girl now. Grown up—married. That's her husband there. That's the one I bought for her. Very talented. I'll get him to play. Neil, we'd like to hear you play. Come on, Neil, play something on the piano.

Gladys. Oh, how do you do, Aunt Gertrude? You know Willie, of course. Willie, you remember Aunt Gertrude. Aunt Gertrude, you remember Willie. Yes, this is our beautiful home. My husband's very talented. No, you didn't interrupt him a bit. He's awfully glad you came. He wasn't going to do anything this afternoon. Anyway, we always have tea. And if it isn't tea, it's something else. We're always having such a good time, Neil and I. Yes, that's my husband there. He plays the piano beautifully. Shall I get him to play? I think he would if I ask him. Oh, Neil, darling, play something. Please, Neil! Neil, for my sake, you'll play, won't you?

[MR. *and* MRS. CADY, GLADYS, *and* HOMER *reach the "Come on and play" lines simultaneously.*]

The Cadys. Play something for us. Play something for us! Play something for us!

Neil. [*In quiet desperation.*] All right [*Crosses to piano, seats himself and turns on them.*] I'll play, but I'll play what I want to—and I don't think you'll like it.

[*He plays—music that is soft and flowing, and reminiscent of* CYNTHIA. *The lights fade on the* CADYS *and their reception; the curtains fall. Through the window by the piano comes* CYNTHIA.]

Neil. [*As he continues playing.*] Cynthia! I thought that would bring you—I hoped so.

Cynthia. Of course, Neil, dear.

Neil. Cynthia, it was a mistake! I'm terribly unhappy!

Cynthia. I'm so sorry, Neil. Because I want you to be happy, always.

Neil. But I can't be happy with these people. I should have married you, Cynthia. I wanted to, you remember? But you wouldn't. And now it's too late.

Cynthia. Yes, it's too late. And I'm sorry, too.

Neil. I don't want you to be sorry, Cynthia. I don't want you to regret anything. It was all my own fault.

[NEIL'S *music turns to jazz as he plays.*]

Cynthia. Oh, Neil, don't let your music do that!

[*She begins to draw back into the window.*]

Neil. [*Desperately, as the music becomes more and more jazzy.*] I can't help it! It's these people. I'm trying—but I can't help it. [CYNTHIA'S *image begins to fade.*] No—no! Don't leave me, Cynthia! I need you! Don't leave me with these people. They don't understand! They never can understand!

[*But* CYNTHIA *is gone now.* NEIL *ends the jazz music with a treble crash, and buries his head on the keyboard. Immediately* MR. CADY *enters—his hat on and a morning newspaper in his hand.*]

Cady. [*As he passes.*] Hurry up, Neil! Mustn't be late for business. [*An* ELEVATOR MAN, *the same who was the* TRAINMAN *during the wedding scene, enters from the other side and meets* MR. CADY *at center.*] Good morning, Jerry.

Elevator Man. Good morning, Mr. Cady. Express going up! Watch your step!

[NEIL *looks up. There is no elevator, but this time even* NEIL *is persuaded, and he believes that he sees it. Four* BUSINESS MEN, *all with hats and newspapers, and all looking just alike, enter one at a time and step into the imaginary elevator.*]

Cady. [*To the first of them.*] Good morning! Made it in twenty-eight minutes this morning!

First Business Man. Good morning! I got the eight-six this morning!

Second Business Man. Good morning! I missed the seven-forty-three.

Third Business Man. Good morning! I always take the nine-two.

Fourth Business Man. Good morning. I thought you were on the eight-sixteen.

[NEIL *gets into the car; the* MEN *huddle together.*]

Starter. [*Clicking his signal.*] All right! Twentieth floor first stop!

Cady. No, sir, I wouldn't sell under a million five! No, sir, a million five! Oh, good morning, Neil!

Neil. Well, I'm starting.

Cady. Good boy, Neil! I want you to meet some of my associates. This is my son-in-law, gentlemen. Just bought him for my daughter. Mr. Canoo, statistical department.

First Business Man. Four out!

[*As* MR. CADY *thus introduces him, the* FIRST BUSINESS MAN *walks out of the elevator, and goes off, paying no attention to* NEIL, *who nods at his retreating back.*]

Cady. Mr. Deloo, traffic department.

Second Business Man. Five out! [*He goes.*]

Cady. Mr. Meloo, tax department!

Third Business Man. Six out! [*He goes.*]

Cady. Mr. Beloo, general department.

Fourth Business Man. Eight out. [*He goes.*]

Cady. Well, well, Neil, starting in to work? You'll like it. You'll learn the ins and outs in no time. Hey! Wait a minute. I said nine out! [*He goes.*]

Neil. Excuse me, Jerry! Can you tell me where I can learn the Ins and Outs?

Starter. Ins and Outs Department! Room three hundred and thirty-three and one-third. Try and find it. [*He goes.*]

Neil. Thank you. [*The curtains between the marble columns at right part. A small office is disclosed.* MISS HEY, *a stenographer, is typing at a small desk behind a railing.*] I beg your pardon.

Miss Hey. Well?

Neil. I want a pencil.

Miss Hey. [*Still typing.*] What is it?

Neil. I want a pencil.

Miss Hey. Who sent you?

Neil. I don't know. But I have to have a pencil. I worked in a place like this once before. I had a great deal of difficulty getting a pencil then, I remember.

Miss Hey. It's just as hard to get one here.

Neil. I thought it would be. I suppose there's a lot of red tape to go through.

Miss Hey. [*Turning toward him.*] Yes. Now as I understand it, you want a pencil.

Neil. That's right.

Miss Hey. Of course, you've filled out a requisition?

Neil. No, I haven't. A piece of paper, isn't it? [*She hands him a tremendous sheet of paper. It is about twenty by thirty inches. He studies it.*] What I want is a pencil. There's a place for that to be put in, I suppose?

Miss Hey. [*Wearily.*] Yes—where it says: "The undersigned wishes a pencil to do some work with." How old are you?

Neil. Thirty-two.

Miss Hey. [*Taking the paper away.*] That's the wrong form. [*She gives him another—a blue one this time.*] Parents living?

Neil. No.

Miss Hey. What did you do with your last pencil?

Neil. I didn't have any.

Miss Hey. Did you have any before that?

Neil. I don't think I ever had any. [*He indicates the form.*] Is that all right?

Miss Hey. It isn't as regular as we like, but I guess it'll do.

Neil. What do I do now? Go to some one else, don't I?

Miss Hey. Oh, yes. Sometimes you travel for days.

Neil. Are we all crazy?

Miss Hey. Yes. [*She resumes typing.*] You might try Room E—right down the corridor.

[*The curtains close over her, and the curtains at the left simultaneously open, revealing another office, just like the first. Another stenographer,* Miss You, *is at work on a typewriter.* Neil *approaches her, requisition in hand.*]

Neil. Is this Room E?

Miss You. [*Mechanically.*] Did you have an appointment?

Neil. No—you don't understand. I'm trying to get a pencil.

Miss You. Well, what do you want to see him about?

Neil. [*Handing over the requisition.*] It's this. Somebody has to sign it.

Miss You. [*Takes requisition.*] Oh! [*Looks at it.*] Mr. Bippy! The man is here to see about getting a pencil or something.

Neil. It *is* a pencil.

Miss You. Did you see Mr. Schlink?

Neil. Yes.

Miss You. Mr. Woodge?

Neil. Yes.

Miss You. Mr. Meglup?

Neil. Yes.

Miss You. What did *they* say?

Neil. Why, they seemed to think it would be all right.

Miss You. [*Calls again.*] Oh, Mr. Bippy! [*To* Neil.] Belong to the Employees' Mutual Mutual?

Neil. Oh, yes.

Miss You. Cady Golf and Building Fund?

Neil. Yes.

Miss You. Well—all right.

[*She stamps the requisition with an elaborate machine, which rings a bell as it works. She hands the paper back to* Neil.]

Neil. Oh, thanks. Do I get a pencil now?

Miss You. Oh, no! It has to be O.K.'d by the President. All requisitions have to be O.K.'d by the President.

Neil. Is he around here some place?

Miss You. Oh, no! He's in a big office. Just keep going until you find a great big office.

Neil. Where?

Miss You. Oh, somewhere in the new building. Mr. Bippy!

[Neil *turns away. The curtains close.*]

Neil. The new building. A big office.

[*The center curtains open, revealing a larger office.* Mr. Cady, *seated at a long table, is dictating, in alternate sentences, to* Miss You, Miss Hey, *and to a dictaphone which stands before him.*

Neil *tries to attract* Miss Hey's *attention.*]

SIMULTANEOUSLY

Neil. [*To* Miss You.] I beg your pardon. . . . [*To* Miss Hey.] I beg your pardon . . . would you mind if I—is this the President's office? Excuse me. . . . Excuse me.

Miss Hey. [*To* Neil.] Well, what is it?

Neil. I want to see the President.

Miss Hey. What do you want to see him about?

Cady. [*Dictating.*] And so beg to state—yours of the 19th instant—hoping to receive your valued order — yours received and would say — our Mr. Mmm will call on you—*in re* our No. 2160—yours sincerely—annual sales convention—beg to state—beg to state—beg to state—pursuant to your instructions of the 13th ultimo — F.O.B. our factory—beg to state—beg to state—beg to state — as per your terms and specifications — would say — would say—

[*By this time, hearing* Neil's *voice,* Cady *turns.*]

Cady. Well, Neil!

Neil. Here I am—at work!

Cady. Yes, sir! Business! Big business!

Neil. Yes. Big business. What business are we in?

Cady. Widgets. We're in the widget business.

Neil. The widget business?

Cady. Yes, sir! I suppose I'm the biggest manufacturer in the world of overhead and underground A-erial widgets. Miss You!

Miss You. Yes, sir.

Cady. Let's hear what our business was during the first six months of the fiscal year. [*To* Neil.] The annual report.

Miss You. [*Reading.*] "The turnover in the widget industry last year was greater than ever. If placed alongside the Woolworth Building it would stretch to the moon. The operating expenses alone would furnish every man, woman and child in the United States, China, and similar places with enough to last for eighteen and one-half years, if laid end to end."

Cady. How's that?

Neil. It's wonderful!

Cady. And wait for September 17th!

Neil. Why?

Cady. That's to be National Widget Week! The whole country!

Neil. That's fine, but what I came up about——

Cady. Never mind that now—we've got more important things. Conferences, mostly.

[*To* MISS HEY *and* MISS YOU.] Any good conferences on for today?

Miss Hey and Miss You. [*Together.*] One at 3:19 this afternoon. [*They go.*]

Cady. That's fine! Ever been to a conference, Neil?

Neil. No, but I've heard a lot about them.

Cady. They're great! You make speeches and decide things, and nobody can get in while they're going on.

[MISS YOU *and* MISS HEY *reënter excitedly.*]

Miss You and Miss Hey. All ready! They're going to start the conference, the conference, the conference!

[*They rush out.*]

Cady. Fine! Come right in, gentlemen! [*Half a dozen* BUSINESS MEN *enter. They wear clothes that suggest fatness and prosperity. They walk in stiffly, in a line, repeating the phrases "Overhead," "Turnover," "Annual Report," "Overhead," "Turnover," "Annual Report." They sit, in stiff poses.*] We are going to have a conference! [*Calls off.*] Bolt the doors, out there! Gentlemen —this is our annual quarterly meeting. [*He drops a gold piece in front of each* MAN.] I want to introduce a young man who has been showing great promise in our factory. I don't know what he will have to say to you——

Neil. I know what to say! [*Rises.*] I remember now—I know exactly what to say!

Cady. Gentlemen, Mr. Neil McRae!

[*As* NEIL *rises to speak the* MEN *all fall into mechanical positions, reminiscent of the board of directors' pictures in the advertisements.* NEIL *pounds the table occasionally during his speech, but there is no sound.*]

Neil. I know you must be surprised to see so young a man stand up before you, but I have *trained* myself to occupy the position I am now in. I have learned my facts. That is how I happen to own my own home. It simply took up my spare time in the evenings. Then, one day, the head of the factory came through the room where I happened to be working on a very difficult piece of machinery. "Who is that?" he asked the foreman. "He seems to be brighter than the others." "Not at all," answered the foreman. "He has simply applied himself and I think we must raise his pay, if we want to hold him." A few weeks later I was able to solve in five minutes a problem that had puzzled the best brains in our organization. I am now the head of my department, and my old foreman is working under me.

[NEIL *sits; there is applause; the* MEN *lean over and shake his hand, congratulating him.*]

Business Men. Wonderful! Wonderful!

Cady. I knew he could do it! Gentlemen, he has saved us millions!

First Business Man. Why, he is going to be the biggest man in the organization.

Others. Yes! The very biggest!

First Business Man. What do you say to signing up with us for ten years at half a million dollars a year?

Second Business Man. And becoming sales manager?

Cady. How about a bonus?

First Business Man. Yes, a bonus!

Second Business Man. Here's my check for one hundred thousand dollars!

Cady. And here's mine! Two hundred thousand dollars.

First Business Man. And mine for one hundred thousand!

Other Business Men. And mine—one hundred and fifty thousand dollars!

Neil. Oh, thank you, thank you! [*He looks at the checks; they are of various-colored paper—pink, blue, yellow.*] It's an awful lot of money, isn't it?

Cady. A million dollars!

Neil. A million dollars!

Cady. Well, gentlemen, that was a dandy conference!

First Business Man. One of the best!

Cady. Let's have another!

Second Business Man. Yes, another.

[CADY *hands out gold pieces again as the curtains close in.* NEIL, *however, has stepped out of the scene and stands facing the audience. Curtains fall behind him.*]

Neil. Just think, a million dollars. [*He looks at the checks in his hand, but they have turned into samples of colored cloth.*] Blue and pink and yellow. Blue and yellow and pink. I was to match them. *I* know! I was to match them for——

Gladys. [*Heard in the distance.*] Oh, Neil!

Neil. For Gladys! [*Then, mechanically.*] Sweetheart!

[GLADYS, *resplendent in evening dress and wrap, joins him.*]

Gladys. Did you have a hard day at the office, Neil?

Neil. Here they are. It's a million dollars —I think.

Gladys. Oh, good! I always knew you'd be a big success, Neil.

Neil. [*Dully.*] But I'm not doing what I want to do. My music—I want to write my music.

Gladys. Oh, not now! It's time to go somewhere! We're going to dance!

Neil. No, no! I've got to write my music. I want to go home now!

Gladys. Oh, nobody ever goes home. We're going to go and dance!

Neil. But we've got to eat dinner first!

Gladys. Of course! We're going to eat right here!

Neil. In this restaurant again? But we were here last night, and the night before. You don't want to come here every night, do you?

Gladys. Why, of course I do! Suppose it *is* expensive, you can afford it now! And nobody comes here but the best people! We'll come here every night from now on! They have the nicest little lamps on the tables!

[*A* CHECK-ROOM BOY *enters from one side and a* HEADWAITER *from the other. A second glance reveals the fact that the* HEADWAITER *is* ALBERT. *The* CHECK BOY *takes* GLADYS'S *wrap and* NEIL'S *bathrobe.*]

Albert. Bon soir. [*Holds up two fingers.*] How many, please?

Neil. Two.

Albert. Two?

Neil. [*Counts them.*] Two.

Albert. Two?

Neil. Why, hello, Albert!

Albert. Hello, Neil!

Neil. Oh, yes! You were a waiter at college, weren't you? You know Gladys?

Gladys. Of course.

[ALBERT *and* GLADYS *shake hands. Then* ALBERT *immediately becomes again the formal waiter.*]

Albert. How many, please?

Neil. Two.

Albert. Two?

Neil. [*Looks around to see if a third has mysteriously appeared.*] Yes—two.

Albert. I will see if I can find you a table. [*He consults his chart.*] All our reserved tables are reserved. [*The center curtains part, revealing a gaudy cabaret interior. In the center, at the rear, is a window, set in a frame of wrought iron. There is a single table, set with much fancy glassware and two table lamps of the sort so dear to* GLADYS'S *heart. As this scene is revealed an unseen orchestra strikes up the jazz tune, "The Frog's Party."*] Ah! Right this way, please! Here is a nice one—right by the window! [*He seats them with an elaborate flourish simultaneously uttering the meaningless ritual of headwaiters everywhere.*] Yes, Madame! Yes, sir!

[*A* CIGARETTE GIRL, *Spanish in attire, enters and circles around the table.*]

Girl. Cigars and cigarettes! Cigars and cigarettes!

[ALBERT *presents the menu, a huge affair, to* NEIL.]

Gladys. See, Neil? Isn't it wonderful? [*She sways to the music.*] Order! He's waiting! Hurry up—you've got to order!

Neil. [*Scanning the card.*] I—I can't decide right away.

Gladys. Oh, that music! I can't stand it any longer! [*She rises and seizes* ALBERT.] Dance?

[*She whirls around the table with him, to the accompaniment of the jazz tune and the* CIGARETTE GIRL'S *chorus of "cigars, cigarettes."*]

Albert. [*When the dance is over.*] Perhaps Madame would care for some Bordelaise à la Bordelaise, or some Bordelaise à la Bordelaise, or some Bordelaise à la Bordelaise.

Gladys. Why, yes—I'd like that!

Albert. And what will Monsieur have?

Neil. [*Studying card.*] What *is* Bordelaise à la Bordelaise?

Albert. Very nice, sir.

Neil. Yes, I know, but what is it?

Albert. It's served in a little round dish —very nice.

Neil. Can't I find out what it is?

Albert. I'll see if anybody knows, sir.

[*He turns his back.*]

Gladys. Neil!

Neil. Well?

Gladys. People don't do that—making a scene in a restaurant!

Neil. I only want to know what it is.

Gladys. But you must pretend that you *do* know! *That's* the thing!

[ALBERT *turns back to* NEIL.]

Albert. I'm sorry, sir—nobody knows.

Neil. It doesn't matter. I'll take it.

Albert. Yes, sir. Thank you, sir.

[*Four* WAITERS *enter with dishes.*]

Gladys. Oh, here's dinner!

[*The* WAITERS *circle the table, clanking the lids of their dishes as they exhibit the food. They go slowly at first, then faster and faster, in time to the constantly accelerating music.*]

Neil. [*Springing up.*] Stop! I can't stand it! [*The* WAITERS *halt in their tracks; the music stops.*] Is it going to be like this always?

Gladys. What?

Neil. Our life!

[ALBERT *dismisses the* WAITERS.]

Gladys. Why, I think it's wonderful! You're going ahead being a big success in

Papa's office, and every night we'll go out and dance! You'll have to learn!

Neil. I won't dance! I don't want to dance! I wouldn't ever have had to dance if I hadn't married you! [*It gives him a thought.*] If I hadn't married you——

Gladys. Well, I don't care whether you dance or not. *I'm* going to! Albert—— [*She rises and seizes* ALBERT; *they dance off.*] If you hadn't married me you'd have starved to death—starved to death—starved to death——

[*Her voice dies down in the distance as she and* ALBERT *dance off to the accompaniment of the jazz tune. As* NEIL *starts the next speech the jazz tune slowly changes into the* CYNTHIAN *theme, and at the same time the gaudy cabaret changes into a sunny cottage.*]

Neil. I don't think so. I might have been poor, but we'd both have work to do. It's a small house, I know, but the sun finds it the first thing every morning. And flowers live longer in our windows than anywhere else, because she cares for them so.

[*The wrought-iron window has turned into a simple thing of chintzes; chintz curtains appear in the doorways, and a box of jonquils takes its place at the foot of the window. The table no longer contains restaurant silver and electric lamps, but is simply furnished with a few breakfast things, with a vase of jonquils to keep them company. The place is flooded with sunlight.*]

Neil. [*Calling.*] Cynthia!

Cynthia. [*Off.*] I'm coming!

Neil. Are you coming, or must I use force?

Cynthia. It's the toast machine. You sit down and begin.

Neil. As though I ever begin without you! Besides, I have something beautiful for you. [CYNTHIA *enters, bringing a tray laden with breakfast.*] See what I've done!

Cynthia. What?

Neil. Nothing at all! Merely created an utterly beautiful morning!

Cynthia. You did? I started it an hour ago.

Neil. Perhaps; but see those little powder-puff clouds? *They* weren't there ten minutes ago.

Cynthia. They *are* nice, darling. I didn't think you were so clever.

Neil. And wait till you see the sunset I'm planning.

Cynthia. You can't beat last night's. What a scarlet!

Neil. It blushed because we flattered it so. [*A pause.*]

Cynthia. Darling.

Neil. What?

Cynthia. A letter.

[*They stare at the envelope corner.*]

Neil. Didn't you dare open it?

Cynthia. No. But let's be brave. [*They hold hands and take a long breath.*] Now—one, two, three! [*They tear the letter open; read it in silence.*] Do you believe it?

[*The voice is ecstatic.*]

Neil. No! Do you?

Cynthia. Darling!

Neil. Darling!

Cynthia. But it *must* be real—it's typewritten.

Cynthia and Neil. [*Reading in unison.*] "Your symphony will be played by our orchestra on December the tenth."

Neil. Darling!

Cynthia. Darling! They'll applaud and applaud! You'll have to come out and bow!

Neil. I won't!

Cynthia. You'll have to have a new dress suit!

Neil. And you'll have to have a new evening dress—yellow chiffon, too. I can do their damned orchestrations now. I can do a hundred of them between now and October.

Cynthia. No, you won't!

Neil. But, my youngest child, we must continue to eat.

Cynthia. But, my dear, we're extremely wealthy. Have you seen my new housekeeping book?

Neil. No.

Cynthia. Look! I ruled every one of those columns myself.

Neil. [*Rises.*] Oh! Sit down!

Cynthia. That's why my middle finger is all red. [NEIL *kisses her finger.*] This is serious. This is finance. Listen! [*Reading from book.*] "To Mrs. Neil McRae—debtor. Ninety-seven dozen eggs from the little red hen at seventy-nine a dozen—ninety-seven, seventy-nine. Four hundred and forty-six quarts of milk from the little dun cow at sixty-four—four hundred and sixty-four. Thirty-six pots of jonquils sold Mr. Frost, the florist, at thirty-six, sixty-six—six sixty-six, sixty-six." And there's the total!

Neil. But, Cynthia, that can't be right; it's impossible!

Cynthia. Add it up for yourself.

Neil. Sixty-three and eight are forty-two ——

Cynthia. Neil, you may be one of the minor gods, but you can't add. [*Takes pencil.*] There! Look!

Neil. But that means——

Cynthia. It means we're billionaires—that's all.

Neil. We have a hundred and seventy-seven dollars and—seventy-seven cents?

Cythia. [*Nods.*] And we can keep on just as we have been doing.

Neil. Cynthia, do you suppose *any* two people *ever?* [*He kisses her.*]

Cynthia. No, I don't believe *any* two people *ever.*

[*The voice of* GLADYS *comes out of the distance, faintly.*]

Gladys. Oh, Ne-il!

Cynthia. What is it, dear?

Neil. I thought I heard some one calling.

Cynthia. You did that last night at tea time. I'm frightened.

Neil. You mustn't be—there are no fears in this house.

Gladys. [*Louder this time—the same old call.*] Oh, Ne-il!

Neil. Cynthia, it's calling me!

Cynthia. What?

Neil. I don't know. I must go to it.

[*He steps out of the cottage.*]

Cynthia. I'll go along!

[*Her voice grows weaker as* GLADYS'S *gets stronger.*]

Neil. You can't, my dear! It's too absurd.

[*The curtains close on the cottage; the jazz begins again.*]

Gladys. Oh, Ne-il!

Cynthia. [*Faintly.*] O-o-o-h!

Neil. Yes, what is it?

Gladys. Oh, Neil!

[GLADYS *enters—so do the* CHECK BOY, *the* CIGARETTE GIRL, ALBERT, *and the four* WAITERS. *They stand in a line with outstretched palms.*]

Neil. Yes, what is it?

[GLADYS, *as she speaks, dances with each* WAITER *in turn.*]

Gladys. Come on, sweetheart! We're going home now! Tip the waiters! Tip the waiters!

Neil. For heaven's sake, stop that dancing!

Gladys. I should say not! Tip the waiters! Tip them big! Tip them big!

[*She dances off with the last of the* WAITERS. NEIL *hands out large bundles of money to the* WAITERS, *then as he proceeds along the line, he comes suddenly to* ALBERT.]

Neil. Albert! [*The music stops.*] You got me into this! You've got to tell me how I'm going to get out of it!

Albert. What's the matter?

Neil. I can't stand it! I can't live with Gladys any longer. What am I going to dc about her?

Albert. Why, that's easy.

Neil. What do you mean?

Albert. Just kill her—that's all.

Neil. Kill her?

Albert. Of course. It's simple and practical.

Neil. Do you know, I never thought of that? I'm not very practical, am I?

Albert. No, you're not.

Neil. Of course, I wouldn't like to do it unless it were absolutely necessary.

Albert. Still, it's worth thinking about.

[*He leaves him with this thought.*]

Neil. Yes, it is.

[*The music starts;* GLADYS *and the* WAITER *dance on again.*]

Gladys. We're going home now! Tip the waiters! Did you tip them all? We're going home! Mama and Papa will be there, and Homer!

[*The* WAITERS *are now gone, and the curtains reopen on the Cady home of pillars.* HOMER *is working a radio set;* MR. CADY *is playing golf with an imaginary ball;* MRS. CADY *rocks, knits, and sings. All is pandemonium.*]

Cady. Fore! Everybody, fore!

Homer. I've got the radio fixed! Listen!

Radio. Stock market reports! Stock market reports! [*Ad infinitum.*]

Gladys. Oh, Neil! Isn't it nice to be in our own home again?

[*She leaps into his lap.*]

Mrs. Cady. [*Singing.*] "Bringing in the sheaves! Bringing in the sheaves!"

Cady. Give me the niblick! Give me the niblick!

Neil. I wish you'd all keep still.

Gladys. What, darling? Wait! Wait! [*Every one subsides.*] I hear them! The dancing teachers! The dancing teachers! *Now* you'll learn to dance.

Neil. I won't, I tell you!

Gladys. Oh, yes, you will! Here they are! The dancing teachers! Come in, dancing teachers! Now you'll learn to dance!

[*Six* DANCING TEACHERS *enter — exquisite gentlemen, one like another.*]

Neil. Gladys, I won't!

Gladys. You've got to! Look! Aren't they wonderful? Here he is—my husband! You're to teach him to dance!

Leader of the Dancing Teachers. Ah!

[*He circles around* NEIL, *about to pounce.*]

Neil. Gladys, I warn you! If you go ahead with this, you'll be sorry!

Gladys. Teach him to dance! Teach him to dance!

Leader. [*Advancing upon* NEIL.] You've got to dance! We teach the world to dance! We make it dance. [*He seizes him.*] We've got him.

Gladys. Now you'll learn to dance!

Leader. Now watch me! One foot out and one foot in! One foot out and one foot in!

Gladys. He's learning to dance! He's learning to dance!

All the Dancing Teachers. [*Forcing* NEIL'S *arms, shoulders and feet.*] One foot out and one foot in! One foot out and one foot in! Now your shoulder, now your elbow! Now your shoulder, now your elbow! One foot out and one foot in! One foot out and one foot in. Now your shoulder——

Neil. [*Tears himself loose.*] No! No! I tell you! Get out! All of you! [*They fall back.*] Get out, every one of you! I won't learn to dance!

[*They have disappeared.*]

Gladys. Neil!

Neil. [*The* CADYS *meantime unconcernedly continue their customary occupations, but in subdued tones.*] Thank God! Now I'm going to write!

Gladys. Neil, do you realize how you're behaving?

Neil. I do! I won't go on with this any longer! If this is to be our life together then I can't stand it! I won't! That's all—I won't!

Gladys. Neil! After all I've done for you! After all Papa's done for you!

Neil. Done for me? You've ruined me, that's all! You've given me a lot of money that I didn't want, and you won't let me do the one thing I want to do! Well, now I'm going to write my music! I'm going to finish my symphony!

Gladys. Oh, no, you're not! [*Crosses quickly to the piano and tears up the manuscript.*] There's your old symphony! Now, what have you got to say?

Neil. You tore it up! It was the only reason I married you, and you tore it up! All right—there's only one thing to do!

[*He takes up the paper knife from the piano—it is about twice the size that it was when the audience last saw it.*]

Gladys. Neil, Neil! What are you going to do?

Neil. I'm going to kill you!

[*She stands looking at him, transfixed. He stabs her, and she falls dead.*]

Mrs. Cady. [*Quietly.*] Now you've done it!

Neil. It was her fault! She killed my work!

Mrs. Cady. She was a sweet girl. The police will get you.

[*She sings "Bringing in the Sheaves."*]

Neil. Stop that singing!

Mrs. Cady. I won't!

Neil. And stop that damned knitting!

Mrs. Cady. I won't! "Rock of Ages, cleft for me."

[NEIL *stabs her. She dies, falling over backward, chair and all.*]

Cady. [*Blandly continuing his golf game.*] This is outrageous! The idea of killing a man's daughter and wife! I'm ashamed of you!

Neil. You're to blame, too! Just as much as the others! Look!

Cady. What is it?

Neil. You're dead, too.

Cady. Oh! [MR. CADY *dies.*]

Neil. Thank God, they're out of the way! Peace! I can work at last!

The Radio. Stock market reports! Stock market reports!

Homer. [*Coming from behind the radio machine.*] Is that so? I guess you forgot all about *me,* didn't you?

Neil. Forget you? Indeed I didn't! Homer, my boy! [*He stabs him;* HOMER *crumples up on the floor.*] I guess that ends that! Free! Free!

Homer. [*Sitting up.*] *Free nothing!* We'll sue you for this, you dirty dog!

[*He falls dead again.*]

Neil. It won't do you any good! Not when they know why I did it! Not when I show them what you killed! Not when I play them my music!

[*Half a dozen* NEWSPAPER REPORTERS *enter. They are dressed alike and look alike; each has a pencil expectantly poised over a piece of paper.*]

The Reporters. [*Speaking one at a time, as they surround* NEIL.] The *Times!* The *World!* The *Post!* The *Globe!* The *Sun!* The *News!* The *Times!* The *World!* The *Post!* The *Globe!* The *Sun!* The *News!*

Neil. [*Indulging in a gesture with the paper knife.*] Gentlemen, this is purely a family affair. I don't think I should say anything at this time, but do come to my trial.

The Reporters. [*Again speaking one at a time.*] A statement! A statement! A statement! A statement! A statement! A statement!

Neil. Well, gentlemen, it's a long story.

[*Instantly a dozen* NEWSBOYS *rush down the aisles of the theatre, crying, "Extra!*

Extra! All about the murders!" The din is terrific. Simultaneously the theatre lights up; the audience turns for a second to look at the NEWSBOYS, *and in that second the curtain falls. The* NEWSBOYS *pass out copies of* The Morning-Evening, *containing a full account of the quadruple murder.*]

END OF PART I

PART II

The scene is now a courtroom. Against curtains of black stand three major objects of red—the same red that appeared fitfully in NEIL'S *chintz curtains, and again as draperies for the pillars in the Cady home. Squarely in the center is a block of twelve seats mounted on a platform. They are designed, obviously, for the jury, but instead of being the customary jurors' chairs they are of the kind found in theatres.* NEIL'S *piano and easy chair, of course, remain in their accustomed places. At the right, also vividly red, is the judge's bench, and against it leans a frame of photographs, of the sort that you see in theatre lobbies. The pictures show* MR. CADY *in various costumes and poses. The witness's box is at the left, and beside it is a* TICKET-TAKER'S *box, presided over by the ubiquitous* JERRY. *Near him is a* HAT-CHECK BOY *recognizable as the same youth who took* NEIL'S *robe in the restaurant, and who also sold chocolates during the wedding ceremony. A couple of* USHERS, *girls, stand chatting beside the jury box.* NEIL, *of course, is also present, walking up and down somewhat nervously, and consulting his watch. The* JURORS *are beginning to arrive as the curtain ascends—three or four are streaming in. To* NEIL'S *surprise they all turn out to be* DANCING TEACHERS.

Ticket-taker. [*As the curtain ascends.*] Oyez! Oyez! Oyez!

[*He takes the tickets of the* JURORS, *returns the stubs, and drops the remainder into his box.*]

Check Boy. Check your coat! Check your coat!

First Juror. I guess we're early.

Neil. Excuse me, but are you some of the jurors?

Second Juror. We certainly are.

Neil. But—but you're dancing teachers, aren't you?

First Juror. Best in the world.

Neil. Are you going to try me? My music?

First Juror. That's what.

Neil. But it doesn't seem fair. I'm afraid you'll be prejudiced against something really good.

[*The* SECOND *and* THIRD JURORS *meet and automatically shake hands.*]

Second Juror. Hello, Ed!

Third Juror. Hello, Ed!

Second Juror. Well, you old son-of-a-gun!

Third Juror. Well, you old son-of-a-gun!

Second Juror. Glad to see you!

Third Juror. Glad to see you.

[*They put their hands in their pockets simultaneously.*]

Second Juror. Fine! How's every little thing?

Third Juror. Fine! How's every little thing?

Second Juror. Well, glad I saw you!

Third Juror. Well, glad I saw you!

Second Juror. Good-by, Ed!

Third Juror. Good-by, Ed!

First Juror. [*At the frame of photographs.*] Say, who's this?

Neil. That's the judge. It's the opening night of my trial, you know. That's the way he appeared in several famous cases.

Second Juror. [*Joining them and pointing to a picture.*] Oh, yes! That's the way he looked in the Watkins trial. He was terrible good. Did you see it?

[*A fourth* JUROR *is shown to a first-row seat by an* USHER.]

First Juror. No, I was out of town. [*Points to another picture.*] There he is in the Ferguson case! Gosh, he was good in that!

Neil. Yes, I heard he was.

Second Juror. Was he funny?

First Juror. Funny? He had that courtroom roaring half the time.

Second Juror. I don't know another judge in the country who can deliver a charge to a jury like he can. Pathos, comedy, everything.

First Juror. They say this will be the best trial he's ever done. I hear they were sold out last Monday.

[*More* JURORS *are entering.*]

Ticket-taker. Tickets, please!

Hat-check Boy. Coats checked! Check your coat!

[*The* Third Juror *presents his ticket stub to an usher.*]

Usher. Other aisle, please!

[*He crosses to the other side of the jury box and presents the stub to the other* Usher.]

Usher. Other aisle, please!

[*He returns to the* First Usher.]

Usher. Right this way!

[*She indicates a seat in the middle of the box.*]

Third Juror. [*Looking at the stub.*] Ain't this an aisle seat?

First Usher. No, sir. Fourth seat in.

Third Juror. After paying all that money to a speculator!

[*He takes his seat in the middle of the back row.*]

Fourth Juror. There ought to be a law against them.

[*Other* Jurors *are being seated.*]

Neil. [*At the footlights, catches the attention of the* Orchestra Leader.] Now, the overture to the trial, please.

[*The orchestra plays the overture—a few bars of cheap musical comedy strains, the modulation from one tune to another being most elaborate. As the orchestra plays, more* Jurors *are seated, leaving empty only the seat next the* Judge's *bench for the* Foreman, *and another in the middle of the first row. The* Jurors *look at their programs, talk, adjust opera glasses, etc. As the overture ends,* Albert *enters, a camera slung over his shoulder.*]

Neil. Why, hello, Albert!

Albert. Hello, Neil!

Neil. What are you doing here?

Albert. I'm covering the trial.

Neil. "Covering" it? For a newspaper?

Albert. [*Nods.*] I'm a reporter on the *Illustrated.*

Neil. Oh, yes! You used to write, didn't you?

Albert. I understand they're going to try some of your music?

Neil. Yes. You'll give it a fair criticism, won't you—in the paper?

Albert. In what paper?

Neil. Why, your paper.

Albert. The *Illustrated*? We don't use any writing. It's an *illustrated* paper. Didn't you ever see it—in the subway?

Neil. Of course! I remember—just pictures. But how do people know what they are?

Albert. Oh, we always have a few simple words, saying what the picture is about. A good many of our subscribers can read, and they tell the others.

[*A* Candy Seller *appears. He has the usual tray of chocolates and peppermints seen in the theatres.*]

Candy Seller. Chocolates and bon-bons! Fresh chocolates and bon-bons! Assorted chocolates!

First Juror. [*Leaning out of the jury box.*] Here you are.

[*Buys a box of candy. The* Candy Seller *goes out again. There is a sudden burst of activity in the jury box.*]

Neil. What's all that?

Albert. They are getting ready to elect a foreman for the jury.

[*There is something like a cheer from the jury box. At one end a sign appears, reading: JONES FOR FOREMAN. At the other side: SMITH FOR FOREMAN. The* First Juror *rises to speak. He receives hearty applause.*]

First Juror. Mr. Chairman and ladies and gentlemen of the Fifth Jury District: I don't think anybody here has to be told at this late date that Harry J. Smith, retired, is the logical man for foreman of this grand jury. I guess everybody here knows Mr. Smith's record. You have all known him since childhood. He is an old Eighth Ward boy and will give the jury a business administration.

Other Jurors. Hooray!

[*The* First Juror *sits. The* Second Juror *immediately demands attention.*]

Second Juror. Mr. Chairman and ladies and gentlemen of the Fifth Jury District: I don't think anybody here has to be told at this late date that Thomas A. Jones, retired, is the logical man for foreman of this grand jury. I guess everybody here knows Mr. Jones's record. You have all known him since childhood. He is an old Eighth Ward boy and will give the jury a business administration.

Voice. What about Ireland?

[*There are cries of "Throw him out!"* Neil *holds up a hand for silence.*]

Neil. Wait! [*He goes into the witness box.*] Ladies and gentlemen of the Fifth Jury District: I know it is late to be putting forward a new candidate for foreman of this grand jury, but this is my trial, and it is my music that you're going to hear. Both of the candidates who are now up before you are good dancers, but it is only fair that there should be some one on the jury who knows good music.

Jurors. Hooray!

Neil. Therefore, when the light on the

Times Building swings on tonight, I want it to be a steady red light, which will show that we have elected the Hon. Albert Rice, of Chicago, a man of the people, for the people, and by the people, and the Stars and Stripes forever in the good old U. S. A.!

Jurors. Hooray!

[*Almost immediately a red light shines across the group, and the orchestra strikes up Sousa's march, "Stars and Stripes." The* JURORS, *cheering, march around the jury box, carrying American flags, banners, noise-makers, etc. There are cries of "Rice Wins! Hoorah for Rice!"* ALBERT, *still mindful of the fact that he has been sent to get the news, makes ready his camera and calls on the crowd to halt.*]

Albert. Hold it, please!

[*They stop—there is a scurrying to get into the photograph.* ALBERT *snaps them.*]

Neil. Hold it! [*He takes the camera and* ALBERT *automatically prepares to have his own picture taken. One of the* USHERS *tries to slip into the picture, but* NEIL *waves her aside. He snaps* ALBERT.] Will they be out soon?

Albert. Soon? They are out! [*He pulls a copy of the* Illustrated *from his pocket—a newspaper covered with a front page crowded with photographs, but entirely blank elsewhere.*] I brought one with me.

Neil. They're on the front page.

Albert. Sure! We put everything on the front page. [*He points.*] There's a picture of the judge delivering his charge.

Neil. But he hasn't delivered it yet.

Albert. Well, we have to get things quick. Our readers expect it.

[ALBERT *takes his place in the jury box. The other* JURORS *lean over and shake his hand.*]

Neil. The Hon. Albert Rice assumes office as thousands cheer.

[*He waits for the cheer—it does not come. He motions to the* JURY. *They clap their hands perfunctorily.*]

Albert. Thank you, gentlemen.

Ticket Taker. [*Announcing.*] His Honor, the Judge!

[*Every one rises. The orchestra begins the Soldiers' Chorus from "Faust." The* JUDGE *enters. He is* MR. CADY, *his golf suit handsomely covered by an enormous red robe. He also wears an enormous* JUDGE'S *wig. He throws away all dignity, however, by lifting the skirts of his gown and skipping into view. The music ends on a long note in the brasses, such as attends the finish of an acrobat's trick.* CADY *curtsies toward the jury box in response to unanimous applause, and blows a kiss. He goes up to his chair and holds the pose of a satisfied actor as he waits for another burst of applause to subside.*]

Cady. [*At last—to* NEIL.] Got a match?

Neil. What?

Cady. Got a match?

Neil. Oh, yes! [*He strikes a match. Although several feet away from the cigar, the cigar lights.* MR. CADY *and* JURY *are about to sit when* NEIL *hisses:*] Look out!

Cady. What is it?

Neil. That chair. It isn't very strong, you know.

Cady. Oh, I'll be careful.

[*He sits. The* JURORS *sit.*]

Ticket Taker. Oyez! Oyez! Oyez!

[*The final* JUROR *enters and presents his ticket.*]

Cady. Ladies and gentlemen, I——

Neil. [*Noticing the tardy* JUROR.] Just a minute! He's late. [*To the* JUROR.] Can't you people ever be on time?

[*The tardy* JUROR *gives his seat check to an* USHER, *who starts to lead him to his place, in the middle of the second row, but finds somebody already in it.*]

Cady. [*Blandly.*] Ladies and gentlemen, I declare the court——

[*The confusion makes him break off again.*]

Usher. [*Leaning far over.*] May I see your check, please?

Cady. I declare the Court——

Usher. May I see your check?

Juror. [*Searching his pockets.*] I had it here some place. Ah!

[*Gives stub to the* USHER. *The* USHER *examines the ticket stub.*]

Usher. Oh, you belong in the row ahead. This gentleman has a ticket for this seat.

[*People in both rows have to stand up while the exchange is made. It is a good deal of trouble, to put it mildly.*]

Neil. [*To* CADY.] All right now. I'm sorry.

Cady. I declare the court to be in session. [*There is a round of applause.* CADY *bows.*] The business of the day is the trial of Neil Wadsworth McRae for murder. [*There is more applause.* NEIL *is finally compelled to bow.* CADY *again addresses* NEIL *confidentially.*] Am I right?

Neil. Yes. And don't forget, I'm going to play my symphony. That was the reason I did it, you know.

Cady. Yes, I remember. [*He is quite con-*

versational.] Now, the first thing to be done, I should say, is to have the prosecuting attorney make a sort of general charge. [*To* NEIL.] What do you think?

Neil. I guess that's right. How about it, Albert?

Albert. [*Looking up from his program.*] Yes, that's right.

[NEIL *nods to the* TICKET-TAKER.]

Ticket-taker. [*Announcing:*] The prosecuting attorney!

[HOMER *enters to the tune of "Tammany." He wears a long black robe. He receives a hearty round of applause, with a few hisses.*]

Neil. Oh, it's you!

Homer. [*Quietly.*] I'll get you now, you dirty dog!

Neil. I think not.

Cady. Come, come, we can't be all day at this. I've got to get back to the office. Now, just what were these murders all about?

Homer. [*Reads from document. As* HOMER *begins to read* USHER *and* CHECK BOY *begin a whispered conversation that soon dominates the scene.*]

SIMULTANEOUSLY

Homer. "On such and such a blank date, the defendant, Neil Wadsworth McRae, did brutally murder, maim, assault, destroy, stab, injure, kill and cause the death of Gladys Virginia Cady, his wife; Mr. Cady, her father; Mrs. Cady, her mother, and Homer Cady, her brother, destroying one and all of the aforesaid Gladys Virginia Cady, his wife; Mr. Cady, her father; Mrs. Cady, her mother, and Homer Cady, her brother—by the use of a large paper knife, of bone manufacture and curious design, a picture of which appeared in the newspapers at the time." [*Hands the newspaper containing the picture to* CADY.]	*Usher.* Did you sell much candy? *Check Boy.* Sure—enough to buy a couple seats for the movies. *Usher.* Oh, let's see the one up the street! *Check Boy.* Oh, that's punk! You always want to see the sad ones. *Usher.* I hate comedies. *Check Boy.* Well, I hate sad ones. *Neil.* Quiet, please; some of us would like to hear the show! [*They grudgingly leave the room.*]

Cady. Yes, I saw it. A great, big, long one. Exhibit A.

[*He hands it to the* FOREMAN.]

Albert. Exhibit A!

[*Passes it to the other* JURORS. *The other* JURORS *repeat "Exhibit A," passing the newspaper from one to another.*]

Homer. Having caused the death of the aforesaid and aforementioned people, I therefore call upon the Court to punish said Neil Wadsworth MacRae in one of two ways prescribed by law—death or hard labor for life, whichever they do in this state.

Cady. [*Realizing that maybe it's serious after all.*] Oh, no! Is that so?

Neil. [*Lightly.*] Just wait!

Cady. [*To* HOMER.] Yes. Just wait, please.

First Juror. [*Leans toward his neighbor, with open program, and reads from it, as though confiding a bit of real news.*] Say, this courtroom, with every seat occupied, can be emptied in less than three minutes.

Cady. Silence in the court. [*A pause.*]

Homer. The State rests.

[*He sits in the easy chair and is immediately seized with a fit of coughing.* MRS. CADY *instantly appears behind* HOMER; *she has her knitting, but no chair.*]

Mrs. Cady. Are you all right, Homer?

Homer. I guess so.

Mrs. Cady. [*To the* JURY.] Homer's sick. He was always delicate. But he was a good boy, though. When Homer wanted to be he was as good a boy as you'd find in a month of Sundays. There was no reason on earth why Neil shouldn't have allowed him to live, just like a lot of other people are allowed to live. [*The* JURORS *applaud her.*]

Cady. You are his mother?

Mrs. Cady. Yes, sir.

[CADY *shakes her hand, sympathetically.*]

Cady. You were also a victim, I believe?

Mrs. Cady. That's right. [CADY *shakes her hand again.*] You heard how he did it? With a paper knife.

Cady. Oh, yes! You see, we're trying him today.

Mrs. Cady. For the murders?

Cady. Yes.

Mrs. Cady. Oh, I beg your pardon! [*Begins to back away in confusion.*] I wouldn't have intruded, if I'd known.

Neil. Wait a minute! I'd like to have Mrs. Cady take the stand, please.

Mrs. Cady. [*Flustered.*] Who? Me?

Neil. If you don't mind.

Homer. What! Going to make her take the stand? A mother?

[*There are hisses from the* JURY.]

Neil. Over here, please! [*Leads her to the witness box.*] Do you swear to tell the truth—the truth—and—the truth?

Mrs. Cady. Yes.

Neil. You can't tell the truth unless you raise your hand, you know.

Mrs. Cady. No?

Neil. No. [*She puts up her hand.*] You're Mrs. Cady, aren't you?

Mrs. Cady. Yes. [*To* MR. CADY.] Is that right, Fred?

Cady. Yes—that's all right.

Neil. [*Suddenly wheeling on* MRS. CADY.] Now, then. [MRS. CADY *jumps.*] Where were you on Friday, June third?

Mrs. Cady. Knitting.

[*She suits the action to the word.*]

Neil. But you used to sing in the choir, didn't you?

Mrs. Cady. Oh, yes. [*Sings.*] "Just as I am, without one plea."

[*The* JURORS *stand and join in.* CADY *stops smoking for a moment and also sings a bar or two.*]

Cady. [*Suddenly rapping for order.*] Silence in the court!

Neil. [*Waves a warning finger at* MRS. CADY, *as though to intimate that another question is about to come.*] Prove an alibi!

Homer. I object, Your Honor!

Cady. Objection sustained and overruled! [*To* MRS. CADY.] Answer the question!

[NEIL *smiles mockingly at* HOMER.]

Mrs. Cady. What was it?

Neil. Prove an alibi!

Mrs. Cady. What kind?

Neil. [*To* CADY.] I didn't know there were different kinds.

Cady. Oh, yes—there are several kinds of alibis.

Neil. Then prove any kind.

Homer. Your Honor, I object!

Cady. You object?

Homer. Yes! [*He goes to* NEIL *and looks sinisterly at him.*] I object to his looks!

Neil. Why, what's the matter with them?

Cady. [*It is apparently a point of great import.*] An objection has been raised to the prisoner's looks. [*Looks at* NEIL *carefully.*] H'm! Have you anything to say?

Neil. Sir?

Cady. [*Quite casual.*] Have you anything to say about your looks?

Neil. Why—I think they're all right.

[*There is a weighty pause.*]

Cady. This is a serious question. [*He removes his wig. The* JURY *breaks out in chatter;* CADY *raps.*] Order, please! Now, the prisoner thinks that his looks are all right.

Homer. But he can't prove it!

Cady. [*To* NEIL.] *Can* you prove it?

Neil. Why——

[*Here's an awful situation.*]

Cady. You see, this is a court of law. Everything has to be proved.

Neil. Well, well—can't the jury tell by looking?

[NEIL *looks toward the* JURY, *which peers at him closely, but is puzzled. The* JURORS *shake their heads, uncertain.*]

Cady. You see, it's illegal for a jury to know anything until it's been instructed. Now, as I understand it, the point is that you think your looks are all right?

Neil. Yes.

Cady. But you can't prove it?

Neil. [*If he can only have a moment's peace in which to think it over!*] Oh, Lord! [*One of the* JURORS *is noisily unwrapping a candy box.*] Quiet! Good heavens—how can I think if they're going to—— Your Honor, they *must* be quiet!

Cady. Quiet!

The Juror. But it's candy!

[*It is a big box full and it is passed up to the* JUDGE.]

Cady. Oh, really?

[GLADYS *enters in a brilliant dinner gown and an ornate cloak.*]

Gladys. Oh, candy! [*She crosses to the* JUDGE'S *stand and begins rifling the box.*] Hello, Neil! I didn't meant to interrupt! I just ran in to get the boys! We're going dancing! [*Some of the* JURORS *rise; one or two even begin climbing over the railing to join her.*] There's a big new place opening tonight and they're going to take me there! Got some money, papa?

Cady. Ten thousand enough?

[*He gives her a handful of bills.*]

Gladys. Oh, thanks. Come on, boys!

[*The* JURORS *make further gestures toward going.*]

Neil. No, wait. [*All movement is suspended.*] You mean you want to take—*them*—away with you?

Gladys. Of course!

Neil. But—but I'm being tried for the murders. And if you take the jury away——

Gladys. I'm sorry, Neil, but I couldn't miss the opening, could I? Are you ready?

[*The* JURORS *step toward her.*]

Neil. No, no! [*Again the* JURORS *halt.* NEIL *appeals to* CADY.] She can't do that, can she?

Cady. [*Who has been eating so much candy he has had little time for the trial's new aspect.*] What?

Neil. Take the jury away, right in the middle of things?

Cady. [*Licking his fingers.*] She can, if it's habeas corpus.

Neil. [*Not at all sure.*] Well—is it?

Cady. [*He licks his fingers.*] It's beginning to look that way.

Neil. But it isn't fair! They've got to hear my music. I know what I'll do. [*He faces* CADY.] I'll take it to a higher court!

Cady. [*Just a bit hurt.*] Oh, don't you like this court?

Neil. It isn't that. It's a good court, I guess, and the people are lovely, but——

Cady. About how high a one would you want?

Neil. I'd want the highest I could get.

Cady. All right. [JUDGE CADY *slowly goes up in the air, as his stand grows two or three feet higher.*] Is this high enough for you?

Neil. I guess so. Is this the superior court?

Cady. Oh, yes. Much superior. And more up-to-date. We send out all our verdicts by radio.

Neil. She can't take them away with her now, can she—in this court?

Cady. Oh, no! You see, in a higher court the lower court is reversed.

Neil. Good!

[*The* JURORS *resume their old positions.*]

Gladys. Oh, the devil! Well, then, I'll take Albert. He's only the foreman.

[*She grabs* ALBERT *by the hand and leads him out of the courtroom.*]

Cady. [*Sucks a sticky thumb.*] Well, are the rest of you ready to bring in a verdict? All in favor will say——

Neil. No, wait! I'm not through—you haven't heard the music yet.

Cady. Oh, that's right! You're going to play for us.

Neil. Of course. That's why I killed them, you know—on account of the music. I want to prove that I was justified. Listen! [*He goes to the piano.*] You won't blame me when you've heard the music. [*He strikes a chord.*] This is a symphony in C Minor. [*He starts to play. The result is disconnected, meaningless. There is a budding hissing from the* JURORS. NEIL, *with a cry, jumps to his feet, holding up the torn sheet of music. He finds it almost impossible to speak.*] She destroyed it! She tore it up, and now I can't play it! Cynthia! Cynthia!

[CYNTHIA *appears at the piano. She is calm and sympathetic, as always.*]

Cynthia. Yes, dear?

Neil. Cynthia, she tore up the symphony! I can't remember it, and they're waiting for me to play!

Cynthia. You still have the pantomime, haven't you?

Neil. Yes.

Cynthia. Then play that for them instead. [*She finds the pantomime music.*] They'll think it's better, anyhow.

[*Puts the music before him.*]

Neil. But it isn't finished.

Cynthia. Well, now you *can* finish it.

Neil. Can I?

Cynthia. Of course. It'll be all right, dear —you'll see.

Neil. You—you think we ought to do it?

Cynthia. Of course.

Neil. All right. [*He faces his inquisitors.*] Ladies and gentlemen, instead of the symphony, we're going to play a little pantomime, called "A Kiss in Xanadu"—written by Cynthia Mason and Neil McRae. We'll need quite a lot of room, so if you don't mind clearing the court—— [*The Judge's dais and the witness box disappear. The jury box, too, moves into blackness.*] The scene is the royal palace in Xanadu. It's a night in June—one of those spring nights that you find only in Xanadu. Now, if you're all ready—music! [*The music of the pantomime begins.*] Cynthia, we ought to have a window to show what kind of night it is.

[*In the distance a great open window appears. Beyond a moonlit balustrade are flowers and trees and stars.*]

Cynthia. It's coming!

Neil. Thanks! The scene is the bedchamber of the Prince and Princess. On the right is the bed of the Princess and on the left is the bed of the Prince.

[*Two fairy-tale beds appear from the darkness. They are canopied in pink. Above them are flower-draped testers that rise to golden points.* NEIL *and* CYNTHIA *seat themselves at the piano and the pantomime begins.*

A LORD OF THE BEDCHAMBER *and a* LADY OF THE BEDCHAMBER *enter and bow to each other ostentatiously. They are followed into the room by two small black* PAGES, *carrying tiny bed tables. The one for the* PRINCESS' *bed bears a small lamp with a dainty shade. The* PRINCE'S *has a candle and shade, and a small phonograph. As the* LORD *and* LADY *examine the room the* PAGES *go out and return with a pillow, which is placed at the foot of the* PRINCESS' *bed; and a costumer, which is for the convenience of the* PRINCE. *The* ATTENDANTS *convince themselves there are no intruders under the beds and depart. A clock strikes nine.*

The PRINCESS *enters. She is very beautiful, but very bored. The lovely night lures her to the window. She goes out on the little balcony and sighs. She is a married Princess. She returns to the bedchamber and snappishly commands the* LADY *to undress her. Nothing to do but go to bed! The* LADY *draws the curtains and leaves.*

The PRINCE *enters with his* LORD. *He would like to be a Gay Dog Prince and he twirls his mustache bravely. He, too, would like to find romance again, but here he is—a married Prince! A* PAGE *puts his royal dressing gown and crown on the costumer. The* LORD *attaches curlers to the royal mustache and leaves the* PRINCE. *The* PRINCE *turns on the phonograph and tries to do his Nightly Dozen. But the night outside distracts him. He goes to the window. It is too much for him. A second attempt to exercise is abandoned. He will go out to adventure. If he turns the royal dressing gown inside out it should make a rather good disguise. He does so. The lining of the crown makes a serviceable cap. He tiptoes to the other bed. The* PRINCESS *is asleep. He draws the canopy across his own bed and steals out the window.*]

Cynthia. But the Princess wants to go adventuring, too, I know! Let's have the moon wake her!

Neil. Yes! Come on, moon! [*The moon obligingly sends its beams across the bed of the* PRINCESS.] Thank you!

[*The pantomime proceeds. The* PRINCESS' *head pops through the draperies. It is such a beautiful night! She observes the closed canopy of her lord's bed. He is asleep—the dull, conventional husband. She goes to the window. What a night! Romance lies out there. She hesitates. She decides. Frightened, but determined, she takes a cover from her bed. An excellent shawl it makes! But something is wrong. She stands undecided, her hands touching her lovely hair. The music stops.*]

Neil. We skipped a place here. We've got to disguise the Princess. She mustn't be recognized, either, you know.

Cynthia. Of course not. I have it! Let her put on her lamp-shade for a bonnet!

Neil. And she can use the Prince's candle-shade for a mask!

[*The music starts again and the* PRINCESS *dons the lamp-shade and puts two finger holes through the candle-shade. She is very happy and goes out to the trees and stars. There is darkness—and here we are in a public park in Xanadu. There are a good many flowery bushes to be seen, but they are not noticed by the* PRINCE, *who sits, depressed, on a park bench, under a street lamp. A* POLICEMAN, *a* LAMPLIGHTER *and two small* ATTENDANTS *enter on patrol, and sedately go about their business. The* PRINCESS *comes into the park. A* MAN, *a romantic-looking man, even if he is masked by that upturned coat collar! A* GIRL, *a charming girl, even if she is holding a small mask before her eyes! She skips away, but returns. She drops her handkerchief. She quietly and politely sneezes. He springs to her aid with her handkerchief. She sits beside him on the bench. He plucks a rose from the bush behind them and offers it timidly. She tosses it away. The light in the lamp is much too bright. A mighty puff from the* PRINCE *and it goes out. But the* WATCH *returns. The lamp is relighted. The* PRINCE *and the* PRINCESS *sit a little closer. He offers another rose. This time she accepts it. But that lamp! He has a permanent solution. He breaks the lamp in two. Masks are not needed in the darkness, but the moon comes up. He waves it away. She kisses him. A clock strikes five. The sun rises. The adventure is over. She runs away. He calls, but she does not answer. He picks up the rose she spurned. His grief is covered by considerate darkness.*

Once more it is the royal bedchamber. The PRINCESS *creeps into the room and into bed. The* PRINCE *steals in a moment later. He goes to the* PRINCESS' *bed. Still asleep! He goes to his bed. The clock strikes eight. The* LORD *and* LADY *arrive. The* PAGES *fetch a breakfast table. The royal pair are awakened. They sit down to eat. She starts to pour her husband's coffee. Oh, yes, she had forgotten! She rises and offers a cheek to be kissed. He mechanically obliges. They sit down again. But they cannot eat. The music of the night is still with them. They steal wistful looks at the window. The* PRINCESS *looks at the rose He gave her. The* PRINCE *looks at the one She first refused. The flowers are stealthily put away. The* PRINCE *and the* PRINCESS *unfold their napkins. It is the humdrum life once more.*

The curtain falls, slowly. Then, slowly, the footlights go down, plunging the auditorium into complete darkness. Immediately we hear the verdict from the vastly Superior Court—sent out, as JUDGE CADY *had said, by radio. It comes, through magnifiers, from the rear of the auditorium, and takes the form of loud and derisive laughter, punctuated by cries of "Rotten!" "No good!" "Highbrow!" "Terrible!" In the darkness the curtain again rises. Seated cross-legged on* NEIL'S *piano, still in the red wig and with a red light playing on him, is* JUDGE CADY. *As always, he is smoking a cigar.* NEIL *sits facing him on the piano stool.*]

Cady. [*To the invisible* VOICES.] Silence! [*The* VOICES *stop.*] Now, was that what you wanted to show us?

Neil. Yes, sir.

Cady. Well, of course we don't want to hurt your feelings, Neil, but I'm afraid it's a little bit highbrow. Don't you think so?

Neil. No, sir. Not very.

Cady. Well, I don't think it's what they want. [*To the unseen* JURORS.] How about it?

[*A single* VOICE *comes over the radio. It says, "Rotten!"*]

Cady. Are you ready to bring in a verdict?

First Juror's Voice. Yes, I move we bring in a verdict!

Second Juror's Voice. I second the motion!

First Juror's Voice. It is moved and seconded that we bring in a verdict. Remarks? [*A pause.*] All those in favor say "Aye."

Chorus of Voices. "Aye."

First Juror's Voice. Opposed—"No"? [*Pause.*] The motion is carried.

Cady. Well, what sort of a verdict do you want to bring in? There are several kinds of verdicts.

First Juror's Voice. I move we bring in a verdict of guilty!

Second Juror's Voice. I second that motion!

First Juror's Voice. It is moved and seconded that we bring in a verdict of guilty. Remarks? All those in favor say "Aye."

Chorus of Voices. Aye!

First Juror's Voice. Opposed—"No"? [*Pause.*] Well, I guess the motion's carried.

Cady. See, Neil? I told you so.

Neil. Well—well, what are you going to do with me?

Cady. This thing of using the imagination has got to stop. We're going to make you work in the right way. You see, your talents belong to us now, and we're going to use every bit of them. We're going to make you the most wonderful song writer that ever lived.

Neil. But I can't write that kind of music! You know I can't!

Cady. You can do it by our system. You are sentenced to be at the Cady Consolidated Art Factory at eight o'clock tomorrow morning!

Neil. Art factory?

Cady. At eight o'clock tomorrow morning!

[*The lights slowly dim and fade out, and instantly there is a burst of noise. Pianos are playing discordantly; there is the sound of machinery in the distance; a* VOICE *is singing a jazz tune, and other* VOICES *are heard in loud declamation. The lights go up again on a tier of four cells. In the first a* MAN *is dictating to a* STENOGRAPHER; *in the second* NEIL *is working away at a piano, while a* YOUTH *in a belted coat and a straw hat atilt on his head sings to the accompaniment of* NEIL'S *music; in the third cell an* ARTIST *works before an easel, and in the fourth a* YOUNG MAN *is loudly reciting poetry, apparently moved to do so by the posturings of two other* YOUTHS *who are in the cell with him. After a moment of this pandemonium a* GUIDE *enters, followed by three* VISITORS. *All four are* DANCING TEACHERS, *so far as outward appearances go, but they are marked apart by the fact that the* GUIDE *wears an official-looking cap, and the* VISITORS *carry umbrellas and open Baedekers. The* GUIDE *raises his voice for silence; a gong sounds somewhere, and all activity ceases. The* FIGURES *in the cages come down to the bars and stand waiting.*]

Guide. Now this, gentlemen, is the manufacturing department. In this studio [*He indicates the first.*] we have Walter Carp Smith, the world's greatest novelist——

Novelist. [*More or less routine.*] How are you?

Guide. [*Passing to the second cage.*] In this studio, Neil McRae, the world's greatest composer!

Neil. [*Listlessly.*] How are you?

Guide. [*At the third cage.*] In this one, Finley Jamison, the world's greatest magazine artist!

Artist. How are you?

Guide. [*At the fourth cage.*] And in this, James Lee Wrex, the world's greatest poet!

Poet. How are you?

Guide. [*Indicating the unseen cages beyond.*] The studios beyond are devoted to science and religion. Mr. Cady was the first person in the world to put religion up in ten-cent packages, selling direct to the consumer.

First Visitor. You don't say so!

Guide. He also prides himself on having the largest output of literature and music in the world. He's going to open two more plants the first of the month. Now, would you like to see how these men work?

First Visitor. Yes, indeed! [*Goes toward the first cage.*] Did you say this was the novelist?

Guide. The world's greatest. Author of more than two thousand published works.

First Visitor. What an imagination!

Guide. Yes, sir, none at all. Now if you're ready, I'll show you how he works. Go!

Novelist. [*Begins at once to dictate from a book in his hand.*] "Something closely resembling a tear fell from the old patrician's cheek. 'Margaret,' he cried, 'the people of the West have learned to love you, too.' 'Jackie boy,' she whispered. 'They have made you governor after all.' Far off on the—the——" [*He hesitates; the* STENOGRAPHER *takes up the story.*]

Stenographer. "—desert, the caravan faded away. Night took them in its arms and a great hush fell on the forest. The two lovers——"

Guide. Stop! [*He turns to the* VISITORS.] There you are!

First Visitor. Was *she* writing it?

Guide. Oh, no! Sometimes she gets a little ahead of him, that's all.

First Visitor. Isn't he wonderful!

Guide. Forty-five minutes after he finishes a novel we have it printed and assembled and on its way to the movie men.

First Visitor. May we talk to him?

Guide. Certainly.

First Visitor. [*To the* NOVELIST.] I've enjoyed your novels very much.

Novelist. Thank you.

First Visitor. I see you're writing a new one.

Novelist. Of course. I'm under contract.

First Visitor. What's that?

[*Indicating the book in the* NOVELIST'S *hand.*]

Novelist. It's my last one.

First Visitor. But weren't you just dictating from it, for your new one?

Novelist. Yes. They like it that way.

Guide. Under the old system they wrote it all new each time. Here—let the gentleman have it as a souvenir.

First Visitor. [*Reading the title.*] "Eternal Love." What's your new one called?

Novelist. "Love Eternal."

Guide. Don't forget—you're lecturing at three o'clock at Wanamaker's.

Second Visitor. Say, will you show us how the artist works?

Guide. Certainly. What will you have—a cover or an advertisement?

Second Visitor. What's the difference?

Guide. There isn't any.

Second Visitor. Well, then, I'll take an advertisement.

Guide. All right. Go! [*The* ARTIST *draws without looking at the canvas. He hands it to the* GUIDE, *who hands it to the* VISITOR. *The canvas is blank.*] There you are!

Second Visitor. What beautiful eyes!

Third Visitor. Wonderful!

Guide. Do you want to talk to him?

Second Visitor. Oh, thanks. I suppose it'll be used on a magazine?

Artist. Oh, yes—thousands.

Second Visitor. Must be worth five or six hundred dollars.

Artist. [*Bored to death.*] Thirty-five hundred.

First Visitor. You don't say so!

Guide. And here, gentlemen, is our poet. His "Jolly Jingles" are printed in three million newspapers a day.

First Visitor. [*Pointing to the* MEN *in back.*] Who are those men?

Guide. Those are his models. He is the only poet in the world who works from living models. That's why all his poetry is so true, so human. He'll show you. Go!

Poet. I will now write a friendship poem. [*Motions to his* MODELS.] Friendliness No. 3, please. "Friendship." [*The* MODELS *strike a pose, hands clasped. The* POET *recites.*]

"Good-by, old pal; hello, old pal; the greatest pal I ever knew.
A dog's your finest friend, my lad, when all the world is blue."

Second Visitor. Ain't it human?

Guide. And here, gentlemen, is Mr. Neil McRae, America's foremost composer.

First Visitor. Who's that in back?

Guide. That's his lyric writer. You will now see how they work. What kind of a song will it be, McRae?

Neil. A pathetic. [*Sits at the piano.*]

Guide. A pathetic. Go! [NEIL *plays.*]

Singer. [*In a horrible voice.*]

"You've broken my heart like you broke my heart,
So why should you break it again?"

[NEIL *comes to the bars again.*]

Guide. That will sell one and one-half million.

Second Visitor. I suppose you write other kinds of songs, too?

Neil. Oh, yes—mammies, sweeties, and fruit songs. The ideas are brought from the inspiration department every hour on the hour. After I turn them into music they are taken to the purifying department, and then to the testing and finishing rooms. They are then packed for shipment.

First Visitor. A wonderful system!

Third Visitor. I should say so!

Second Visitor. Do you work all the time?

Neil. No, the night shift comes on at eight.

First Visitor. How long have you been here?

Neil. For years and years.

Second Visitor. Say, will you write another song for us—just as a souvenir?

Neil. [*Desperately.*] Oh, why don't you all go away?

Guide. What's that? What was that? You get busy there and write another song!

Neil. No! I've been writing forever—I'm tired of it.

Guide. Do you want me to call Mr. Cady?

Neil. I don't care! I don't care what you do!

Guide. I'll give you one more chance.

Neil. No! I won't!

Guide. All right, then! Mr. Cady! Mr. Cady!

[*The* GUIDE *rushes out. The* VISITORS *slink away. A gong sounds. Those in the cages huddle in fear.* MR. CADY *appears behind the cages. He carries a large snake-whip.*]

Cady. What's the matter here?

Guide. McRae says he won't go on!

Cady. He won't, eh? Well, we'll see about that!

Neil. I can't go on! I'm tired!

Cady. What's that got to do with it? You've got to go on!

Neil. I *can't,* I tell you. I *can't* keep on at this sort of thing.

Cady. You know your sentence, don't you? You've got to work our way until you die.

Neil. [*Dully.*] Yes, I know.

Cady. We own you now. The family. The family owns you. [*He falls into rhythmic measure.*]

"You take our money and you live our life;
We own you, we own you.
You take our money and you live our life;
We own you, we own you.
You take our money and you live our way;
We pay the piper and we tell him what to play.
You sold your soul and you can't get away;
We own you, we own you."

[*The* CADY *family and others enter at back, and weave back and forth, joining in the chant, reaching through the bars at* NEIL.]

Neil. Until I die! I can be free from you if I die! I *can* die! You can't keep me from it! That's how I can get away from you! Open the door! Open the door! [*He shakes the door on the audience's side of the cage. It opens.*] It was never locked! [*He steps out and closes the door.* CYNTHIA *enters.*] Cynthia, Cynthia, I'm free! I can die! [*Those in the background disappear.*] Cynthia, how are we going to do it?

Cynthia. We'll go to an executioner. I know a good one. You mustn't be afraid. It won't hurt. [*An* EXECUTIONER *appears, masked, with a black robe and a huge paper knife.*] See—it's Jerry!

Jerry. Hello, Mr. McRae.

[*Takes off his mask and cap.*]

Neil. Oh, hello, Jerry! You're going to do it, are you?

Jerry. Sure.

[*Feels the edge of his knife.*

Neil. Oh, that's good.

Cynthia. Do we have to wait long?

Jerry. No—you're next.

Neil. Oughtn't we to have a block?

Cynthia. [*Moving the armchair.*] We'll use this. It'll be more comfortable.

Neil. Oh! And you'll stay with me?

Cynthia. Always. [*She stands beside him.*] But it won't hurt. [ALBERT *enters, wearing a short medical apron and jacket.*] Albert will give you a pill.

Neil. Oh, yes! Hello, Albert!

Albert. Hello, Neil! Got a glass of water?

Cynthia. [*Glass of water in hand.*] We're ready, Doctor.

[ALBERT *goes to the chair; tests its strength.*]

Albert. [*To the* EXECUTIONER.] Is the light all right?

[*The cabaret orchestra is heard in the distance.*]

Jerry. I think so.

Neil. There's that music again.

Albert. You're nervous, that's all. Here!

[NEIL *swallows a pill.*]

Cynthia. Now it can't possibly hurt you.

Albert. [*Motions* NEIL *to the chair.*] Here we are! [NEIL *sits.*] That's it—way back. [*To* JERRY.] Right?

Neil. Shall I take off my collar?

Albert. Oh, no. There's room, I think.

Neil. Just a once-through, please.

Albert. Of course. It'll be all over in a minute.

Neil. Cynthia!

Cynthia. Yes.

Neil. I was afraid you'd gone.

Cynthia. No, dear. [JERRY *taps his knife on floor.*] Are you ready, Neil?

Neil. Yes, except for that music. Charles the First didn't have any music.

[*The lights begin to fade.*]

Cynthia. He's ready, Doctor.

Neil. Don't go away, Cynthia!

Albert. All ready.

[JERRY *taps the knife again on the floor.*]

Neil. Good-by! I'll see you soon.

Cynthia. Are you comfortable?

Neil. Yes. You'll be with me always, won't you, Cynthia?

[*There is darkness, save for a cloudy, moving light on* NEIL.]

Cynthia. Always.

Albert. All right.

Neil. Cynthia, are you there?

Cynthia. Yes, darling.

[*There is a hum of* VOICES. *Presently one can discern several chanting, "You take our money and you lead our life."* MRS. CADY *is heard saying, "Homer's sick."* MR. CADY *is apparently telephoning somewhere. He is shouting, "Well, I'll tell you what to do!"* HOMER'S *voice repeats, "You dirty dog!"* GLADYS *shrilly calls out, "He's learning to dance!" The* VOICES *become a chant, finally unintelligible. The lights slowly go up again. We are back in* NEIL'S *apartment. He is asleep in his chair. It is sunset. There is a knock, a real knock, on the door.*]

Neil. [*Half asleep.*] Yes?

[CYNTHIA *enters.*]

Cynthia. Is anything the matter, Neil? I thought I heard you talking.

Neil. It didn't hurt. Was it a success?

Cynthia. Neil, are you all right?

Neil. [*Takes her hand.*] I need you, Cynthia!

Cynthia. Oh, Neil, do you? Are you sure you do? I—I couldn't stay away, Neil. I tried to, but I couldn't. Because I need you, too. I just couldn't give you up to any one else on earth.

Neil. Cynthia, dear.

Cynthia. It wouldn't have worked, Neil—with those people. Don't you know it wouldn't?

Neil. I think I do.

Cynthia. I've been sitting out on a bench in the square, trying to think out what it would mean—what it would do to you.

Neil. I know. Widgets.

Cynthia. That would be worse for you than any amount of poverty.

Neil. Poverty in our cottage.

Cynthia. Did you think of a cottage, too?

Neil. Of course—I lived there.

Cynthia. We could manage. I know quite a lot about raising chickens.

Neil. [*Reminiscently.*] A little red hen and a little dun cow.

Cynthia. Yes, we might have a cow. Have you been thinking about it, too? [*Rises.*]

Neil. Well—let's say dreaming. [*He rises and goes to the desk.*] It was terrible, Cynthia—do you know, I dreamed I was married to *her?*

Cynthia. To Gladys?

Neil. When I thought you didn't care, I was hurt and angry. And I dreamed she telephoned—— [*Sees the receiver off the hook.*] My God! Did she telephone? Oh, Cynthia, it's real! I *did* do it! I did!

Cynthia. Did what?

Neil. I did ask her to marry me!

Cynthia. Neil! You didn't! And she—accepted you?

Neil. Yes.

Cynthia. Oh, Neil.

[*A knock at the door.* JERRY *puts his head in. He wears a uniform somewhat like the one that accompanied him through the dream.*]

Jerry. It's me, Jerry. I've been ringing your 'phone for the last five minutes. Yeh, I thought so—you left it off the hook again. [NEIL *replaces the receiver.*] The young lady that came before was waiting, so I brought her right up.

Gladys. [*In the doorway.*] It's me, Neil—may I come in? [*Enters.*] Oh, hello again, Miss Mason!

Cynthia. I—I forgot my tea things.

[*Half choking, she takes up her tray of tea things and goes out.*]

Gladys. Well, here we are. Isn't it exciting! We're engaged.

Neil. Yes.

Gladys. Did you have a good nap?

Neil. Yes, thank you.

Gladys. [*Obviously something on her mind.*] Do you love me a lot, Neil? Enough to do me a great big favor?

Neil. What?

Gladys. It's a big one, and maybe you won't want to do it.

Neil. What is it?

Gladys. Well, it's this way. Coming back from the dressmaker's, I met Walter Craig. I told you about him, didn't I? He's a boy that sort of used to like me.

Neil. Oh, yes.

Gladys. Now, mind you, Neil, you can say "No" to this if you want to, but—he said, "What are you doing tonight?" Now, you won't be angry, Neil?

Neil. No, no.

Gladys. Well, then he said he didn't know any other girl in New York, and would I sort of play around with him this week. So all I wondered was—well—you know how a fellow is—if he thinks a girl's engaged, why, he won't come near her at all. Now mind, you don't have to do it—and I won't be a bit hurt if you don't, but what I thought was—if we could start being engaged, say, a week from today—you wouldn't mind, would you, Neil? Of course, next week, after we *are* engaged, we'll just go everywhere together.

Neil. I see.

Gladys. I know a dozen people, pretty near, that'll give big parties for us. It's an awful lot of fun, being engaged.

Neil. Is it? I'm afraid I wouldn't fit in with that sort of thing.

Gladys. Why, half the fun of being engaged is--well——

Neil. Gladys, just what is your idea of being engaged?

Gladys. Why—I've just been telling you. [NEIL *smiles.*] What's the matter?

Neil. Well, it's just that your idea of an engagement is different from mine.

Gladys. What is yours?

Neil. I think I'd want to be somewhere alone, just the two of us, where we could talk.

Gladys. Talk about what?

Neil. [*With a meaning look.*] I don't know.

Gladys. You don't mean you'd *always* be like that, do you? I mean, when you're married?

Neil. I might.

Gladys. Well, where would I come in? Do you mean you'd expect *me* to sit around *every* evening and—just talk? I did think you'd be willing to—play around the way other people do.

Neil. I see.

Gladys. But, of course, if you wouldn't—well—why—there doesn't seem to be much sense in our being engaged, does there?

Neil. It's to be just as you say, Gladys.

Gladys. Well, I don't think we're exactly suited to each other—if you think it over. Honestly, I don't. Do you?

Neil. No, Gladys.

Gladys. I noticed the difference the minute I saw Walter again! I can kind of let myself go with Walter. You're sure you don't think I'm a quitter?

Neil. I think you're all right.

Gladys. And we'll still be friends, won't we? I've always thought you were nice, Neil. [*She gives a sigh.*] It's a sort of a relief, isn't it?

Neil. Yes, it is—rather.

Gladys. Well, good-by. I've got to go, because I left Walter downstairs.

[*She departs.*]

Neil. Oh! [*Laughs. Starts to call out.*] Cyn——

[*Looks across the hall, crosses to the piano and begins to play the music of the pantomime. After a moment* CYNTHIA *comes slowly into the room.*]

Cynthia. [*Hesitatingly.*] Want me, Neil?

Neil. Do I want you?

[*He continues playing as he hears her approaching.*]

CURTAIN

THE SILVER CORD*

By

SIDNEY HOWARD

MR. HOWARD, IN THE PREFACE TO *Lucky Sam McCarver,* published in 1926, makes an interesting statement of his dramatic credo. He says:

"For me, the actor is the only theatrical element who matters. . . . Of all those concerned in the production of a play, only the actor utilizes his talents to their fullest. . . . And the dramatist—what, after all, is he but a vicarious actor who happens to write well enough to be useful to real actors? . . . Very few men of literary genius have written plays. . . . The drama does not spring from a literary impulse but from a love of the brave, ephemeral, beautiful art of acting. . . . The real merit of any play lies in the depth and scope of its acting parts far more than in its story or writing or idea content. . . ."

Mr. Howard's main interest in the construction of his plays, to judge from this preface, would seem the lifelikeness of his characters. He objected to "theatrical simplification of the motives" of the characters. He seemed, in fact, to be a realist of the Chekhov school.

But the list of plays in which he had a hand show him an eclectic. He has written romantic melodrama, drawing-room comedy, satirical drama, adapted at least one problem play, and one "well-made" play, besides following the path of sober realism. He was consistent, however, in all the plays he did by and of himself, in keeping his eye on character.

Sidney Howard won the Pulitzer prize for 1924 with *They Knew What They Wanted,* which was produced by the Theatre Guild. That organization in 1926 presented two of his plays within a month: *Ned McCobb's Daughter* and *The Silver Cord,* both successfully. Later, Mr. Howard's talents were given largely to the motion pictures, where he became among the most highly regarded screen writers.

Though Mr. Howard's greatest skill lay in adaptation, such plays as *The Silver Cord* and *Yellow Jack* established his powers as an originator. And even to an adaptation he could bring fresh force. The published version of *Dodsworth* contains most interesting comments by Mr. Howard and the novelist, Mr. Lewis, on Mr. Howard's work. Mr. Howard is apologetic and modest. He says, "To attempt (to dramatize) such a book as *Dodsworth* is to invite the reproaches of the literate and to spend the balance of one's days heartsick over one's sins of omission." But he tells how he had learned in writing for motion pictures the trick of "equivalents," that is, inventing scenes not in the original but faithful to its characters and theme. By neat use of such "equivalents," he made a play for which Mr. Lewis, in the same volume, has only praise. He says Mr. Howard "rendered the spirit of the novel by forgetting the letter." Thus Mr. Howard, even in adaptation, deserved the title of creator.

He acknowledged that he was fortunate in the casting of his plays, especially in *Ned McCobb's Daughter,* whose leading rôle was played by his wife, Miss Clare Eames, and in *The Silver Cord,* in which Laura Hope Crews played Mrs. Phelps.

In 1938 Mr. Howard shared in the organization of the Playwrights' Company, with S. N. Behrman, Maxwell Anderson, Robert E. Sherwood, and Elmer Rice to produce plays written by each of them. Mr. Howard, however, had not been able to contribute a play before his sudden death in 1939. His last work to appear publicly was the motion picture *Gone With the Wind.*

SIDNEY HOWARD

Born 1891, Oakland, California.
1915, University of California.
1915–1916, Harvard University (English 47).
War service as ambulance driver and aviator.
1925, Awarded Pulitzer Prize for *They Knew What They Wanted.*
Writer of sociological articles, short stories, verse.
Died 1939.

PLAYS

1921 *Swords.* 1922 *S.S. Tenacity* (adapted from the French of Charles Vildrac). 1923 *Casanova* (adapted from the Spanish of Lorenzo de Azertis). 1923 *Sancho Panza* (adapted from the Hungarian of Melchior Lengyel). 1924 *Bewitched* (with Edward Sheldon.) 1924 *They Knew What They Wanted.* 1924 *Lexington,* a pageant drama. 1925 *Michel Auclair* (adapted from the French of Charles Vildrac). 1925 *Lucky Sam McCarver.* 1925 *The Last Night of Don Juan* (adapted from the French of Edmond Rostand). 1925 *Morals* (with Charles Recht, adapted from the German of Ludwig Thoma). 1926 *Ned McCobb's Daughter.* 1926 *The Silver Cord.* 1928 *Salvation* (with Charles MacArthur). 1928 *Olympia* (adapted from the Hungarian of Ferenc Molnar). 1928 *Yellowjack* (produced 1934). 1929 *Half Gods.* 1930 *Marseilles* (adapted from the French of Marcel Pagnol). 1932 *The Late Christopher Bean* (adapted from the French of René Fauchois). 1933 *Alien Corn.* 1934 *Dodsworth* (adapted from the novel by Sinclair Lewis). 1934 *Ode to Liberty* (adapted from the French of Michel Duran). 1935 *Paths of Glory* (adapted from the novel by Humphrey Cobb). 1937 *The Ghost of Yankee Doodle.*

WRITING ABOUT THE DRAMA

Preface to *Lucky Sam McCarver,* 1926. *A Postscript on Dramatization,* preface to *Dodsworth,* 1934.

SCREENWRITING

1929 *Bulldog Drummond.* 1930 *A Lady to Love.* 1930 *Condemned.* 1931 *Raffles.* 1931 *The Greeks Had a Word for It.* 1931 *Arrowsmith.* 1931 *Free Love.* 1933 *The Silver Cord.* 1933 *Her Sweetheart Christopher Bean.* 1936 *Dodsworth.* 1939 *Gone With the Wind.*

THE SILVER CORD

Characters

MRS. PHELPS.
DAVID, *her son.*
ROBERT, *her younger son.*
CHRISTINA, *David's wife.*
HESTER, *Robert's fiancée.*
MAID (*Mute*).

THE SCENES

The action occurs in the present day in Mrs. Phelps's house, which is situated in one of the more mature residential developments of an eastern American city.
First in the living-room on Sunday afternoon.
Then in the living-room again, early that same evening.
Then in David's bedroom, later that same evening.
Then in the living-room, the Monday morning after.

ACT ONE

A living-room, built and decorated in the best manner of 1905, and cluttered with the souvenirs of maternal love, European travel, and an orthodox enthusiasm for the arts. There is a vast quantity of Braun Clement and Arundel Society reproduction of the Renaissance Italian masters. The piano features Grieg, Sibelius, and MacDowell. A door gives on a spacious hallway. Windows look out over a snow-covered garden.

[*The rise of the curtain discloses* HESTER *lost in the rotogravure sections of the Sunday papers. She is a lovely, frail phantom of a girl with a look of recent illness about her. She wears the simplest and most charming of house frocks. The doorbell rings. There is the least sound of commotion in the hall.* HESTER *looks up. In a moment, the doors open and* DAVID *enters. He is a personable young man, well enough dressed, and a gentleman. He belongs to the somewhat stolid or unimaginative type which is generally characterized, in this country, as "steady." His smile is slow and wide, his speech slow and to the point. His principal quality is a rare and most charming amiability, but he is clearly lacking in many of the more sophisticated perceptions and he is clearly of a conventional bent in his attitude toward life. The door, as he leaves it open, shows* CHRISTINA, *in the act of shedding her fur coat with the assistance of the* MAID. *She, as* DAVID'S *wife, presents something of a contrast to her husband. She is tall, slender, grave, honest, shy, intelligent, most trusting, and, when need be, courageous. She has a scientist's detachment and curiosity, and these serve oddly to emphasize a very individual womanliness which is far removed from the accepted feminine. One suspects that, where* DAVID *is stubborn, she is open-minded; where he is blind, she is amazingly clear-sighted. That is the difference which makes one the complement of the other. The common quality which brought them together in the holy bonds of matrimony is their mutual candor.* DAVID *is incapable of subtlety;* CHRISTINA *will not bother with it. The result is congeniality. So much for* DAVID *and* CHRISTINA. HESTER *rises.*]

Hester. Hello!

David. Eh? . . . Oh, I beg your pardon! The maid said there wasn't anybody home.

Hester. You're David, aren't you? [*She advances to meet him.*] I'm Hester.

David. You're not! [*He goes quickly toward her and shakes hands as* CHRISTINA *enters.*] Well! [*He turns; smiling broadly to* CHRISTINA.] Look, Chris! Here's Hester, who's going to marry my brother Rob.

Christina. [*With the most charming warmth.*] Isn't she lovely!

Hester. Oh, I think you're dears, both of you! [*The two* WOMEN *kiss.*] Aren't you hours ahead of time?

Christina. We caught the one o'clock instead of whatever the other was.

David. Where are Mother and Rob?

Hester. Your mother's drinking tea at . . . aren't there some people named Donohue?

David. Great friends of Mother's. Why aren't you there?

Hester. Not allowed. I'm having a breakdown.

Christina. Why don't you telephone her, Dave? She'll want to know that you're here.

David. She'll find out soon enough. Where's Rob?

Hester. Gone skating.

David. [*Turns to the window.*] On the pond? No. There's no one on the pond.

Hester. Somewhere else, then.

Christina. [*Hovering over the fire.*] Dave, do you suppose I could get some tea? I'm half frozen.

David. Of course you can. I'll order it. [*To* HESTER.] What's the maid's name?

Hester. Delia.

David. Delia. It used to be Hannah and before that it was Stacia, who got married to our old coachman, Fred. Well, it's not so bad to be home again!

[ROBERT *enters, very much dressed for skating, and carrying his skates.* ROBERT *only faintly suggests his brother. He is more volatile and stammers slightly.*]

Robert. [*A shout.*] Dave!

David. Hello, Robert! [*They shake hands vigorously.*] We were just wondering when you'd come in and Hester said . . .

Hester. [*Speaking at the same time.*] Wasn't it lucky I was here to receive them?

Robert. [*As he shakes* CHRISTINA's *hand.*] I think this is simply magnificent! [*As he strips off his skating things.*] How did you get here so soon? We weren't expecting you for . . .

David. We caught the one o'clock.

Christina. Just.

David. We thought it would be fun to surprise you.

Robert. Mother'll drop dead in her tracks.

David. How *is* she?

Robert. Oh, she's in fine form . . . [*To* CHRISTINA.] You'll adore her.

Christina. I'm sure I shall.

Robert. She *is* marvelous, isn't she, Hester?

Hester. She is indeed. . . . Perfectly marvelous!

David. Mother's immense. And I'm glad, for Chris's sake, that things worked out this way. First Chris sees the old house. Then she meets Hester. Then Rob comes breezing in, full of health. And, last of all, Mother comes.

Robert. It's like a play. I always want things to be like a play. Don't you, Hester?

Hester. I dunno. Why?

Robert. Don't you, Christina? [*But he does not wait for an answer—a habit with him in his better-humored moments.*] You have to tell us you like this old house, you know. Mother and I wouldn't change it for the world.

Christina. [*Smiling as she looks around her.*] How about that tea, Dave?

David. Excuse me, Chris! I forgot. . . .

Christina. [*To* ROBERT.] I've been here three minutes and I'm ordering food already!

Robert. Well, let me "do the honors."

David. Honors, hell! Isn't Julia still in the kitchen?

Robert. Sure she is.

David. Well, I *must* see Julia!

[*He goes.*]

Robert. [*To* CHRISTINA.] Julia'll drop dead, too. I expect half the town'll be dropping dead. Dave's always been the Greek god around this place, you know.

Hester. He should be.

Robert. I can remember the time I didn't think so.

[*A door slams. In the hall,* MRS. PHELPS *is heard talking, excitedly.*]

Mrs. Phelps. Those bags! Have they come, Delia?

Hester. Here's your mother now.

Christina. So soon? How nice!

[MRS. PHELPS *enters. She is pretty, distinguished, stoutish, soft, disarming, and, in short, has everything one could possibly ask, including a real gift for looking years younger than her age, which is well past fifty. She boasts a reasonable amount of conventional culture, no great amount of intellect, a superabundant vitality, perfect health, and a prattling spirit. At the moment she is still wearing her hat and furs and she looks wildly about her.*]

Mrs. Phelps. Dave! Dave, boy! Where are you, Dave? Where are you? It's Mother, Dave! [*She does not see him in the room and she is already turning back to the hall without a word or a look for anybody else.*] Where are you, Dave? Come here this minute! Don't you hear me, Dave? It's Mother! [*Then* DAVID *appears in the hall.*] Oh, Dave!

David. [*A little abashed by the vigor of this welcome.*] Hello, Mother.

Mrs. Phelps. Dave, is it really you?

David. Guess it must be, Mother.

Mrs. Phelps. Dave, dear!

[*She envelops as much of him as she can possibly reach.*]

David. [*Prying loose.*] Well! Glad to see us, Mother?

Mrs. Phelps. Glad!

David. You certainly seem to be glad. . . . But you haven't spoken to . . .

[CHRISTINA, *at his look, steps forward.*]

Mrs. Phelps. [*Still not seeing her.*] To think I wasn't here!

David. We're ahead of time, you know. Christina . . .

Mrs. Phelps. I must have known somehow. Something just made me put down my cup and rush home. But you're not looking badly. You *are* well, aren't you? I do believe you've put on weight. You must be careful, though, not to take cold this weather. Was the crossing awfully rough? Were you seasick? You haven't been working too hard, have you, Dave, boy?

Christina. [*Unable to stand on one foot any longer.*] He hasn't been working at all. Not for weeks!

Mrs. Phelps. [*She turns at the sound of the strange voice.*] Eh? Oh!

David. I've been trying to make you take notice of Christina, Mother.

Mrs. Phelps. [*With the utmost warmth.*] Oh, my dear Christina, I *am* sorry! [*She kisses* CHRISTINA *on both cheeks.*] Seeing this big boy again quite took me off my feet. Let me look at *you,* now. Why, Dave, she's splendid. Perfectly splendid! I always knew Dave would choose only the best. Didn't I always say so, Dave, boy? [*Which takes her back to* DAVID.] Dave, you *have* been working too hard. I don't like those circles under your eyes.

David. Nonsense, Mother!

Christina. I think he looks pretty well.

Mrs. Phelps. But only pretty well. I can't help worrying about these big boys of mine. [*Her emotion stops her. She turns gallantly to* ROBERT.] Did you skate, Rob?

Robert. As a matter of fact, I couldn't. They've been cutting ice on the pond and it's full of holes.

Mrs. Phelps. I must have signs put up tomorrow. Remember that, everybody. If any of you do go out in this freezing cold, don't take the short cut across the pond. . . . Dave, boy, this is too good to be true. After two whole years away and five, nearly six months married. [*The* MAID *brings tea.*]

David. Here's tea.

Mrs. Phelps. Sit down here beside me, dear, dear Christina. And, Dave boy, sit over there where I can see you. Just take my furs, Delia, so I can do my duty in comfort. My boy, my boy, you don't know . . . you don't know how happy I am to have you home again! Just hand me my salts, will you, Robin? This excitement has laid me out. Christina, my dear, how do you take your tea?

[*She sits at the table.* ROBIN *has fetched her bottle of "Crown Lavender" from somewhere. She motions him to put it down and proceeds to pour tea.*]

Christina. Just tea, please. As it comes and nothing in it.

Mrs. Phelps. A real tea drinker! I hope my tea stands the test. [*She passes* CHRISTINA *her cup and ceases to take any notice of her whatsoever.*] Tea, Dave, boy?

David. Please, Mother.

Mrs. Phelps. The same old way?

David. Yes.

Mrs. Phelps. Tea, Robin?

[*She hands* DAVID *his cup.*]

Robert. [*Busy passing sandwiches and such.*] As usual, please.

Mrs. Phelps. [*Very absent-minded about the salts.*] Who do you suppose was asking after you yesterday, Dave, boy? Old George, the doorman, down at the bank. You remember old George? He's so thrilled about your coming back! And Mrs. Donohue's so thrilled! Such a sweet woman! You know, I'm afraid he's drinking again. You must run right over early tomorrow morning and let her have a look at you. I must have some people in to meet you. Some very nice new people who've come here since you went away. Named Clay. He used to be a publisher in Boston, but he gave it up because he says nobody really cares about good books any more. Of course, this house has been a real godsend to him. I must give a big dinner for you, Dave, and ask all our old friends. I do need your cool head, too, in my business. Robin does his best, but he isn't really a business man. You remember the American Telephone I bought? Mr. Curtin, at the bank, advises me to sell and take my profit, but I don't think so. What do you think, Dave, boy?

Hester. May I have a cup, please, Mrs. Phelps?

Mrs. Phelps. Hester, my dear, how forgetful of me! How will you have it?

Hester. As usual.

Mrs. Phelps. Let me see, that's cream and sugar?

Hester. Only cream. No sugar.

Mrs. Phelps. Of course. Robin, will you give Hester her tea?

Robert. [*As he gives* HESTER *the cup.*] You see, we have to take a back seat now.

Mrs. Phelps. A back seat, Robin?

Robert. I'm only warning Hester. She's got to know what to expect in this family when Dave's around.

David. Oh, shut up, Rob!

Mrs. Phelps. [*Smiling.*] My two beaux! My two jealous beaux!

Robert. Oh, well! Dave's out in the great world now and I'm still the same old homebody I always was. Look at him, Mother!

Mrs. Phelps. [*Looking.*] Oh, my boy, my boy, if you knew what it means to me to see all my plans and hopes for you fulfilled. I've dreamed of your being an architect ever since . . . ever since . . .

Robert. Ever since he first showed an interest in his blocks.

Mrs. Phelps. I have those blocks still, Dave. Do you remember them?

David. Do I remember those blocks!

Mrs. Phelps. [*Solemnly.*] You must never forget them, because it's quite true what Robin says, and, some day, when you have children of your own, I shall show them the foundation stones of their father's great career. If I have one gift it's the ability to see what people have in them and to bring it out. I saw what David had in him, even then. And I brought it out.

[*She smiles benignly. There is a brief pause. A quizzical frown contracts* CHRISTINA'S *brow.*]

Christina. It seems a risky business.

Mrs. Phelps. [*Turning with that same start which* CHRISTINA'S *voice caused before.*] What seems a risky business?

Christina. The way families have of doing that.

Mrs. Phelps. [*Setting her tea-cup down a little too deliberately.*] What could be more natural?

Hester. [*Coming to* CHRISTINA'S *rescue from an abyss of boredom.*] I see what Christina means. From blocks to architecture *is* a long guess. You might very easily have guessed wrong, you know. I had some rabbits, once, and I loved 'em. Suppose my family had seen what I had in me, then, and brought me up to be a lion tamer?

Mrs. Phelps. [*Offended.*] Really, Hester!

Hester. Isn't that just what happens to most of us? Christina's job doesn't sound like the kind parents usually pick out for a girl, though.

Robert. I'll say it doesn't.

Christina. My parents did pick it out, though. I'm just like the rest.

Hester. Well, it only goes to prove what I was saying. Christina might have been a homebody instead of a scientist. I might have been a lion tamer. If only our parents hadn't had ideas about us!

David. One guess is as good as another. I dare say I wanted to be a fireman. What do little girls want to be?

Hester. Queens.

Christina. Wouldn't it be a pleasant world with nothing but queens and firemen in it!

Robert. I guess Mother knew. She always does know.

Hester. What I say about children is this: Have 'em. Love 'em. And then leave 'em be.

Christina. [*Amused.*] I'm not sure that isn't a very profound remark.

Mrs. Phelps. [*She makes up her mind to investigate this daughter-in-law more closely and, with sudden briskness, takes back the conversation.*] Why don't you two great things take the bags upstairs out of the hall?

David. That's an idea.

Mrs. Phelps. Dear Christina's in the little front room, and, Dave, you're in the back in your old room.

David. [*Surprised.*] I say, Mother . . . can't we . . .

Hester. Don't they want to be together, Mrs. Phelps? Let me move out of the guest room and then . . .

Mrs. Phelps. Indeed, I'll do nothing of the sort. Hester's here for a rest and I won't upset her. Dave can be perfectly comfortable in his old room and so can Christina in front, and it won't hurt them a bit.

Christina. Of course not. . . .

Hester. But, Mrs. Phelps . . .

Mrs. Phelps. Not another word, my dear. [*To* CHRISTINA.] This child has danced herself into a decline and she's got to be taken care of.

David. Right!

Robert. Come along, Dave.

Mrs. Phelps. Go and supervise, Hester, and leave me to . . . to visit with my new daughter.

[DAVE *and* ROB *go,* HESTER *following.*]

Hester. [*As she goes.*] But really, David, I might just as well move. I didn't think. And if you and Christina . . .

Mrs. Phelps. [*A broad smile to* CHRISTINA.] Now, my dear, let me give you another cup of tea.

Christina. Thank you.

Mrs. Phelps. And take your hat off so

that I can really see you. I've never seen a lady scientist before.

Christina. I hope I'm not so very different from other women.

Mrs. Phelps. I've quite got over being afraid of you.

Christina. Afraid of me, Mrs. Phelps?

Mrs. Phelps. Can't you understand that? My big boy sends me a curt cable to say that he's marrying a charming and talented research geologist.

Christina. Biologist.

Mrs. Phelps. Biologist. It did sound just the least bit in the world improbable.

Christina. Yes. . . . I can see that.

Mrs. Phelps. Now that I know you, though, I'm very proud to have you for a daughter. Every woman wants a daughter, you know!

Christina. You're being very nice to me, Mrs. Phelps.

Mrs. Phelps. It isn't at all hard to be nice to you, my dear. Tell me about your tour. You went to Sicily?

Christina. We did, indeed.

Mrs. Phelps. Sicily, the home of . . . [*she gives herself up to Sicilian emotion*] . . . of all those great ancient . . . poets and . . . poets. To think of your taking my boy to Sicily, where I'd always planned to take him! I've never been, you see. How many opportunities we miss! That's what we're always saying of dead people, isn't it? Though, of course, I shouldn't think of calling David dead merely because he's got married. I do hope you read "Glorious Apollo" before you went to Venice. When I read it, I felt that I had made a new friend. I always make such close friends of my books and, you know, there's no friend like a really good book. And there's nothing like a good historical novel to make a city vivid and interesting. They do bring things back to one. "Glorious Apollo"! What a despicable character that man Byron was! Though I dare say he couldn't have been as bad as he was painted. People do exaggerate so. Especially writers. Do you know "The Little Flowers of St. Francis"?

Christina. I'm afraid not. Are they exaggerated?

Mrs. Phelps. Well, of course, they're really fairy tales. Only to one with a profoundly religious point of view . . . and, if there's one thing I pride myself on it *is* my profoundly religious point of view . . . I always keep the "Little Flowers" on the table beside my bed. And read *in* them, you know? I quite brought Robin up on them. Dave never took to them. Though Dave loved his regular fairy tales. His Grimm and his Hans Christian. You read, I hope?

Christina. I can. I sometimes have to.

Mrs. Phelps. Oh, my dear, I only meant that I think it's so important, for David's happiness, that you should be what *I* call "a reader." Both my boys learned their classics at their mother's knee. Their Scott and their Thackeray. *And* their Dickens. Lighter things too, of course. "Treasure Island" and "Little Lord Fauntleroy." And you went to Prague, too. Dave wrote me from Prague. Such interesting letters Dave writes! I wondered why you stayed so long in Prague.

Christina. It's a charming city, and an architect's paradise. Dave and I thought he ought to look at something besides cathedrals and temples. . . . There *is* domestic architecture, you know.

Mrs. Phelps. Yes. I suppose there is.

Christina. People *do* want houses. I'm inclined to think houses are more interesting than churches nowadays.

Mrs. Phelps. Oh, nowadays! I'm afraid I've very little use for nowadays. I've always thought it a pity that Dave and Rob couldn't have grown up in Italy in the Renaissance and known such men as . . . well, as Cellini.

Christina. I'm not sure Cellini would have been the ideal companion for a growing boy.

Mrs. Phelps. No? Well, perhaps not. I must certainly take in Prague my next trip abroad. It's really been very hard for me to stay home these last two years. But I said to myself: Dave must have his fling. I don't like mothers who keep their sons tied to their apron strings. I said: Dave will come home to me a complete man. Though I didn't actually look for his bringing you with him, my dear, and coming home a married man. Still . . . so I stayed home with Robin. And I was glad to. I'm not sure I haven't sometimes neglected Robin for David. Given myself too much to the one, not enough to the other. The first-born, you know. We mothers are human, however much we may try not to be. Tell me, Christina, you think David *is* well, don't you?

Christina. Yes, perfectly.

Mrs. Phelps. He didn't seem quite himself just now.

Christina. Perhaps he was embarrassed.

Mrs. Phelps. With me? His own mother?

Christina. Wouldn't I have accounted for it?

Mrs. Phelps. How silly of me not to remember that! Tell me what your plans are —if you have any plans, which I hope you haven't, because I've been making so many for you, such perfect ones.

Christina. Well, as a matter of fact, we haven't many, but what we have are pretty definite.

Mrs. Phelps. Really! Are they, really? What are they?

Christina. Well, we're going to live in New York, of course.

Mrs. Phelps. Why "New York, of course"? It seems to me that you might choose a pleasanter place to live than New York.

Christina. No doubt of that, Mrs. Phelps. But it does seem a good place for Dave to work and . . .

Mrs. Phelps. Oh, I can't agree with you!

Christina. I shouldn't have thought there could be two ways about New York for Dave any more than for me.

Mrs. Phelps. For you?

Christina. It's where my appointment is.

Mrs. Phelps. Your appointment?

Christina. At the Rockefeller Institute.

Mrs. Phelps. So that's what takes Dave and you to New York? Your geology.

Christina. Partly. Only it isn't geology. It's biology.

Mrs. Phelps. Of course. Geology's about rocks, isn't it?

Christina. Largely.

Mrs. Phelps. And biology?

Christina. Well—about Life.

Mrs. Phelps. [*Getting it clear.*] So you're a student of Life, my dear. I do wish David had called you that instead of the other.

Christina. I understand how you felt, Mrs. Phelps. I hope you don't hold my job against me.

Mrs. Phelps. [*With deep feeling.*] My dearest Christina, I don't! Oh, if you thought that, I should be heart-broken. You've made my darling David happy, my dear, and for that I'm prepared to love everything about you. Even your job. Do you smoke?

Christina. Yes, thank you. May I?

Mrs. Phelps. Please. And I shall, too . . . [*They light cigarettes.*] Don't you like my lighter?

Christina. It's sweet. And very handy, I should think.

Mrs. Phelps. A friend sent it me from London. Let me give it to you.

Christina. Oh, no.

Mrs. Phelps. Please? I've not had a chance yet to give my new daughter anything. My dearest Christina . . . please?

Christina. Thank you. I shall always keep it and use it.

Mrs. Phelps. I like the little ceremonial gift. . . . Now, about your job . . .

Christina. My job?

Mrs. Phelps. As you call it. I don't like to say "profession," because that has such a sinister sound for a woman. And then science is hardly a profession, is it? Rather more of a hobby. You're planning to continue?

Christina. With my job? Oh, yes.

Mrs. Phelps. Just as though you hadn't married, I mean?

Christina. I have to, don't I? To earn my right to call myself a biologist . . .

Mrs. Phelps. Do people call you that?

Christina. I guess they call me "doctor."

Mrs. Phelps. You're *not* a doctor?

Christina. Technically, I am.

Mrs. Phelps. Oh, I can never agree with you that women make good doctors!

Christina. We shan't have to argue that point. I've no intention of practicing.

Mrs. Phelps. Not at all? Above all, not on David?

Christina. I shouldn't think of it.

Mrs. Phelps. I remember hearing that doctors never do practice on their own families. I remember that when our doctor here had a baby . . . of course, his wife had the baby . . . he called in quite an outsider to deliver the child. I remember how that struck me at the time. Tell me more about yourself, my dear. When Dave cabled me about meeting you and marrying you so suddenly . . .

Christina. It wasn't so sudden, Mrs. Phelps. I spent a good six or seven months turning him down flat.

Mrs. Phelps. [*Offended.*] Indeed?

Christina. Dave and I met in Rome last winter. Then he came to Heidelberg where I was working and I accepted him. . . . I'd never given him the least encouragement before.

Mrs. Phelps. [*As before.*] Indeed?

Christina. We were married straight off . . . and went to Sicily.

Mrs. Phelps. I didn't know about the preliminaries. Dave never told me. And now you're taking him off to New York!

Christina. Please don't put it that way.

Mrs. Phelps. I'm stating a fact, my dear girl. After all, you *have* got your—[*she gets it right this time*]—biology to think of.

Christina. You can't blame me for that, dear Mrs. Phelps, so long as I think of Dave's work, too.

Mrs. Phelps. No. . . . So long as you do that. . . . How did you come to select your career?

Christina. My father was a doctor. I grew up in his hospital. Everything followed quite naturally.

Mrs. Phelps. Your father—is he living?

Christina. He died two years ago. Tragically, but rather splendidly.

Mrs. Phelps. How?

Christina. He'd been experimenting for years on infantile paralysis and . . .

Mrs. Phelps. And he died of that? [CHRISTINA *nods rather solemnly.*] Is your mother living?

Christina. Oh, yes; at home.

Mrs. Phelps. At home?

Christina. In Omaha.

Mrs. Phelps. [*Meditatively.*] Omaha . . .

Christina. Yes.

Mrs. Phelps. H'm . . . And you'll go on with your father's experiments?

Christina. Oh, no! That's not at all in my line.

Mrs. Phelps. What *is* your line?

Christina. It's hard to say. I did some rather hard work this last year at Heidelberg on the embryos of chickens. In the egg, you know.

Mrs. Phelps. For heaven's sake, what for?

Christina. Trying to find out something about what makes growth stop.

Mrs. Phelps. Why . . . ?

Christina. Curiosity, I guess. Now I'm admitting what low people we scientists are. I think that curiosity's all we have. And a little training.

Mrs. Phelps. Does David follow your work?

Christina. No. And I don't expect him to.

Mrs. Phelps. Quite right. David wouldn't be appealed to by rotten eggs. . . . Not that he couldn't understand them if they did appeal to him.

Christina. Of course.

Mrs. Phelps. Isn't the Rockefeller Institute one of those places where they practice vivisection?

Christina. One of many. Yes. . . .

Mrs. Phelps. Have you . . .

Christina. What?

Mrs. Phelps. Experimented on animals?

Christina. Isn't it a part of my job? Dave understands that. You must try to understand it.

Mrs. Phelps. Very well, I shall try, my dear. Now you must listen to me and try to understand me. . . . Look at me. What do you see? Simply—David's mother. I can't say of you that you're simply David's wife, because, clearly, you're many things beside that. But I am simply his mother. . . . I think, as I talk to you, that I belong to a dead age. I wonder if you think that? In my day, we considered a girl immensely courageous and independent who taught school or gave music lessons. Nowadays, girls sell real estate and become scientists and think nothing of it. Give us our due, Christina. We weren't entirely bustles and smelling salts, we girls who did not go into the world. We made a great profession which I fear may be in some danger of vanishing from the face of the earth. We made a profession of motherhood. That may sound old-fashioned to you. Believe me, it had its value. I was trained to be a wife that I might become a mother. [CHRISTINA *is about to protest.* MRS. PHELPS *stops her.*] Your father died of his investigations of a dangerous disease. You called that splendid of him, didn't you? Would you say less of us who gave our lives to being mothers? Mothers of sons, particularly. Listen to me, Christina. David was five, Rob only a little baby, when my husband died. I'd been married six years, not so very happily. I was pretty, as a girl, too. Very pretty. [*This thought holds her for a second.*] For twenty-four years, since my husband died, I've given all my life, all my strength to Dave and Rob. They've been my life and my job. They've taken the place of husband and friends both, for me. Where do I stand, now? Rob is marrying. David is married already. This is the end of my life and my job. . . . Oh, I'm not asking for credit or praise. I'm asking for something more substantial. I'm asking you, my dear, dear Christina, not to take all my boy's heart. Leave me, I beg you, a little, little part of it. I've earned that much. I'm not sure I couldn't say that you owe me that much—as David's mother. I believe I've deserved it. Don't you think I have?

Christina. [*Deeply moved.*] My dear, dear Mrs. Phelps!

Mrs. Phelps. It's agreed then, isn't it, that I'm not to be shut out?

Christina. Of course you're not!

Mrs. Phelps. Not by you, Christina. Nor by your work?

Christina. No! No!

Mrs. Phelps. Nor by anything?

Christina. You must know that I should never come between a mother and her son. You must know that I appreciate what you've done for Dave and all you've always been and meant to him. You *must* know that!

Mrs. Phelps. Christina, my dear, you're a very disarming person. You are indeed. I've known you ten minutes and unloaded my whole heart to you.

Christina. I'm proud that you trust me.

Mrs. Phelps. [*Patting her hand.*] Thank you, my dear. And now . . . now that you know how I feel . . . now you won't go to New York, will you? You won't take Dave to New York?

Christina. [*Drawing back in alarm.*] But, Mrs. Phelps!

Mrs. Phelps. Because that *would* be coming between mother and son as you just now said. That could mean only one thing—crowding me out, setting me aside, robbing me. . . .

Christina. [*Completely baffled.*] You're quite mistaken, Mrs. Phelps! You've no reason to think any such thing!

Mrs. Phelps. Well, it's nice of you to reassure me, and we don't have to worry about it for some time yet. You'll have plenty of time to see how carefully I've worked everything out for David—and for you, too, my dear. You've a nice, long visit ahead and . . .

Christina. I only wish we *had* a nice long visit, Mrs. Phelps.

Mrs. Phelps. What do you mean?

Christina. I start work at the Institute a week from tomorrow.

Mrs. Phelps. [*Staggered.*] What *are* you saying, child?

Christina. We didn't even bring our trunks up, you know.

Mrs. Phelps. [*Recovering herself.*] I'll not hear of it! A week of David after two years without him? What *are* you thinking of? Don't you realize that David has practically been my sole companion for nearly twenty-five years?

Christina. You've had Robert, too.

Mrs. Phelps. I'm not thinking so much of Robert, now. He isn't threatened as David is.

Christina. Threatened, Mrs. Phelps?

Mrs. Phelps. I don't want to see David's career sacrificed.

Christina. But, I'm not planning to sacrifice it.

Mrs. Phelps. You make the word sound disagreeable. I admire your work, Christina, but I am very clearly of the impression that it may easily obliterate David's work.

Christina. I don't see any conflict.

Mrs. Phelps. Aren't you taking him to New York, which he simply loathes? To live in a stuffy tenement . . . well, an apartment. . . . they're the same thing . . . without proper heat or sunshine or food? I told you I'd made plans. I've arranged everything for David's best interest. I can't believe that a girl of your intelligence won't realize how good my arrangements are. I happen to own a very large tract of land here. A very beautiful tract, most desirable for residences. To the north of the Country Club, just beside the links. Hilly and wooded. You can see it, off there to the left of the pond. I've had many offers for it, most advantageous offers. But I've held on to it, ever since Dave chose his profession. Pleasant Valley, it's called. I shall change the name to Phelps Manor and open it. David will have charge. David will lay out the streets, design the gateways, build the houses and make his fortune, his reputation, and his place in the world out of it.

Christina. [*Pause, then:*] Don't you mean his place in this part of the world, Mrs. Phelps?

Mrs. Phelps. [*Positively.*] As well this as any. With me to back him, he's certain of a proper start here, and there can't be any doubt about the outcome. His success is assured here and his happiness and prosperity with it. And yours, too. Don't you see that?

Christina. It certainly sounds safe enough.

Mrs. Phelps. I knew you'd see. Furthermore, he's never happy in New York.

Christina. Happiness is very important. Only different people have different ideas of it.

Mrs. Phelps. David's always had my ideas. And they're very sound ones.

Christina. [*Politely.*] I'm sure of it. But perhaps they aren't sound for David. I mean, from what I know of him. . . .

Mrs. Phelps. I'm David's mother, my dear. I know him better than you do.

Christina. I wonder!

Mrs. Phelps. Oh, I do! And I know how little New York has to offer. I know the competition there. I know what the struggle would be. Look at the choice. On the one hand, obscurity, a desk in some other man's office, years of hack work and discouragement. On the other, immediate prominence, unquestionable success . . .

Christina. With his mother behind him.

Mrs. Phelps. Who better?

Christina. Oh, I see the difference!

Mrs. Phelps. Yes, don't you? And as to your work, my dear, I'm sure we can keep you busy and contented.

Christina. [*Smiling in spite of herself.*] How will you do that?

Mrs. Phelps. Well, it's hard to say, offhand. But if we really set our minds to it . . . I know! I'm the chairman of our hospital here, and I have a great deal of influence with the doctors. We've a beautiful laboratory. You couldn't ask for anything nicer or cleaner or more comfortable than that laboratory. You do your work in a laboratory, I suppose?

Christina. Usually.

Mrs. Phelps. I'll take you down in the morning and introduce you to Doctor McClintock, homeopathic, but very agreeable, and he'll show you our laboratory. We've just got in a new microscope, too. Oh, a very fine one! One the High School didn't want any more. You'll simply love our laboratory. Oh, you will! It has a splendid new sink with hot and cold running water and quite a good gas stove because it's also the nurses' washroom and diet kitchen. And you'll be allowed to putter around as much as you like whenever it isn't in use by the nurses or the real doctors. I can arrange everything perfectly, my dear. I'm certain that, when you see our laboratory, you'll sit right down and write to Mr. Rockefeller, who, I'm told, is a very kind old man at heart and won't misunderstand in the least, that you've found an opening here that's ever so much more desirable than his old Institute, where you won't be obliged to cut up cats and dogs. You will think it over, won't you? Going to New York, I mean—taking Dave to New York and ruining all his prospects?

Christina. [*After a pause, in all sincere kindliness.*] Mrs. Phelps, the third time I refused Dave, he asked me for a reason. I told him I couldn't throw myself away on a big frog in a small puddle.

Mrs. Phelps. You don't mean that you want him to be a small frog, a mere polliwog, in a great ocean like New York?

Christina. I'm afraid that's what I do mean. And when he came back at me three months later with some real sketches and a great deal more humility and with a real job in a real architect's office . . .

Mrs. Phelps. Has David a job? In New York?

Christina. A chance, anyway. With Michaels.

Mrs. Phelps. Michaels?

Christina. He's a big man. And he's interested in Dave.

Mrs. Phelps. I don't approve at all. I think it's madness.

Christina. You may be right. But isn't it best left to Dave and me?

Mrs. Phelps. [*Deeply hurt at the implication.*] My dear Christina, if you think I'm trying to interfere, you're quite mistaken. You're very unfair. . . . Only tell me what makes you so sure Dave can succeed in New York.

Christina. I haven't given a thought to whether he'll succeed or not. That depends on his own talent, doesn't it? As to how much he makes, or how we get on, at first, I don't think that matters either . . . so long as Dave stands really on his own feet.

Mrs. Phelps. Oh, Christina, be honest with yourself. You *are* sacrificing David!

Christina. How?

Mrs. Phelps. By thinking only of yourself, of course.

Christina. Won't you believe that I'm thinking of both of us?

Mrs. Phelps. How can I? It's too bad of you, really. It means [*in despair*]—it means that it's all been for nothing!

Christina. What has?

Mrs. Phelps. [*Crescendo, as she walks about.*] All, all that I've done for David and given up for him and meant to him!

Christina. How can you say that?

Mrs. Phelps. I did so want to be friendly with David's wife. If you knew how I've wished and dreamed and prayed for that!

Christina. [*Rising, herself.*] But can't we be friends?

Mrs. Phelps. Some day you'll have a child of your own and then you may know what I mean, if . . .

Christina. If what?

Mrs. Phelps. [*The last volley.*] If you don't sacrifice your child, too, to this work of yours.

Christina. [*Deeply distressed.*] Mrs. Phelps, I wish you wouldn't feel like that. It makes me feel that I've got off on a very wrong foot here. [ROBERT *enters.*]

Robert. Christina!

Christina. Yes?

Robert. Dave says, if you want a bath before dinner, you'd better be quick about it.

Christina. I didn't know it was so late. Thanks. [*She goes to* MRS. PHELPS.] You'll see that I do understand, dear Mrs. Phelps. You'll see that it all comes straight somehow and turns out for the best. Life takes care of such things. All we have to do is to keep out of life's way and make the best of things as *healthily* as possible.

Mrs. Phelps. You think I'm selfish.

Christina. Oh, no! I don't think anything of the sort!

Mrs. Phelps. Because if there's one thing I pride myself on—I may have many faults, but I am not selfish. I haven't a selfish hair in my head.

Christina. I tell you, I understand.

[*She kisses her quickly and goes out.*]

Robert. [*Looking curiously after* CHRISTINA.] Mother!

Mrs. Phelps. [*Wildly.*] Oh Robin! I'm so lonely! So lonely!

Robert. [*Startled.*] Mother!

Mrs. Phelps. I'm afraid I'm a dreadful coward!

Robert. You, Mother?

Mrs. Phelps. I ought to have been prepared to lose my two great, splendid sons. I've told myself over and over again that the time would come; and now that it *has* come, I can't face it! She's taking Dave away to New York, away from me, away from all the wonderful plans I've made for him here!

Robert. Well, if Dave's fool enough to go!

Mrs. Phelps. I shouldn't do to any woman on earth what she's doing to me!

Robert. Of course you wouldn't. But then, Christina isn't your sort, is she?

Mrs. Phelps. You've noticed that too?

Robert. Who *is* your sort, Mother? . . . Oh, it's a wonderful gift you've given us.

Mrs. Phelps. What's that, Robin?

Robert. A wonderful ideal of womanhood. You know what I mean.

Mrs. Phelps. No. What?

Robert. Your own marvelous self, Mother!

Mrs. Phelps. Dave didn't stop to think of any such ideal, did he?

Robert. Oh, Dave!

Mrs. Phelps. Perhaps I shouldn't be hurt. But you can't know what it is to be a mother. I nearly died when Dave was born. Hours and hours I suffered for him, trapped in agony. He was a twelve-pound baby, you know. If I could be sure of his happiness!

Robert. You mustn't ask too much.

Mrs. Phelps. You're right. No mother should expect any woman to love her son as she loves him.

Robert. Your sons don't expect any woman to love them as you do.

Mrs. Phelps. Oh, Robin! Is that how you feel?

Robert. I think it must be. [*She looks at him, watching him think it all out.*] It's a funny business, isn't it? After a woman like you has suffered the tortures of the damned bringing us into the world, and worked like a slave to help us grow up in it, we can't wait to cut loose and give up the one thing we can be sure of! And for what? To run every known risk of disillusion and disappointment.

Mrs. Phelps. [*Struck by this.*] What *is* the one thing you can be sure of, Robin?

Robert. You are. Don't you know that? Why can't we leave well enough alone?

Mrs. Phelps. Presently you'll be going too, Rob.

Robert. Yes . . . I know I shall. . . . But nothing will ever come between us, Mother.

Mrs. Phelps. Come over here by the fire, Robin, and let's forget all these unpleasant things. [*She goes to sit by the fire.*] Let's have a real old-time talk about nothing at all. Sit down. [*He sits as directed on a stool at her feet.*] Head in my lap! [*He obeys.*] So! This has shown me something I've always suspected. That you are *my son.* David takes after his father.

Robert. Mother!

Mrs. Phelps. Tell me, Robin, what you meant just now when you said that about the one thing you can be sure of. Did you mean that you've had dark thoughts about *your* future?

Robert. I must have meant something of the sort.

Mrs. Phelps. H'm. . . . It was dear of you, my great Robin, to say what you did about my being your ideal. You know my dream has always been to see my two boys married and settled down. But happily! Happily! Has Hester come to any decision about where she wants to spend her honeymoon?

Robert. Abroad.

Mrs. Phelps. Nothing more definite than just "abroad"?

Robert. No. She doesn't care where we go.

Mrs. Phelps. That seems very odd to me. I took such an interest in my honeymoon. Why, your father and I had every day of it planned weeks before we were married. . . . Hester hasn't picked out her flat silver yet, either, has she?

Robert. I don't think so.

Mrs. Phelps. I can't understand it!

Robert. What?

Mrs. Phelps. Her indifference. It rather shocks me. [*She notices that* ROBERT *is shocked, too.*] But I suppose I'm old-fashioned. Like this room. You must give me a little of your time and taste, Robin, before you're married, and advise me about doing this room over.

Robert. [*Eagerly.*] Have you come to that at last?

Mrs. Phelps. I'm afraid so. How's Hester planning to do your new home?

Robert. [*His spirits subsiding at once.*] Oh, I don't know.

Mrs. Phelps. You don't mean to say she hasn't made *any* plans?

Robert. I've been trying to get her interested in house-hunting.

Mrs. Phelps. And she doesn't care about that either?

Robert. She says anything will suit her.

Mrs. Phelps. Does she, indeed! Most girls . . . most *normal* girls, that is, look forward so to having their homes to receive their friends in.

Robert. She leaves it all to me. She says

I know much more about such things than she does.

Mrs. Phelps. How little she understands my poor Robin, who ought never to be bothered!

Robert. Oh, well!

Mrs. Phelps. Do you happen to know if Hester *has* many friends? I mean, many men friends? Did she have lots of suitors besides you?

Robert. I dare say she had loads.

Mrs. Phelps. Do you *know* that she had?

Robert. She never told me so. Why?

Mrs. Phelps. I was wondering. She's been out two years. One does wonder how much a girl has been sought after. But, then, why should she have bothered with others when she thought she could land you? You are rather a catch, you know.

Robert. I, Mother?

Mrs. Phelps. Any girl would set her cap for you.

Robert. I don't believe Hester did that.

Mrs. Phelps. My dear, I wasn't saying that she did! But why shouldn't she? Only . . .

Robert. Only what?

Mrs. Phelps. I can't help wondering if Hester's feeling for you is as strong as you think it is. [ROBERT *wonders, too.*] I've been wondering for some time, Robin. I've hesitated to speak to you about it. But after what you've just told me . . .

Robert. Well, it's too late to worry now.

Mrs. Phelps. I can't help worrying, though. Marriage is such an important step and you're such a sensitive, shrinking character. It would be too terrible if you had to go through what you were just speaking of —the disillusionment and disappointment. . . . I'm only trying to find out what it is that's come between you two young people.

Robert. Nothing has, Mother. Hester isn't you, that's all!

Mrs. Phelps. Nonsense, Robin! . . . It isn't that awful woman I was so worried about when you were at Harvard?

Robert. I'm not raising a second crop of wild oats.

Mrs. Phelps. Then it *must* be that risk you were speaking of! Oh why do boys run that risk! Why will they break away!

Robert. I wish I knew!

Mrs. Phelps. Perhaps your trouble is that—[*a pause. Then, very low:*] that you don't love Hester.

Robert. Oh, love! I must love her or I wouldn't have asked her to marry me. I guess she loves me in her way. Is her way enough? I'll find that out in time. A man ought to marry.

Mrs. Phelps. [*A little more positively.*] You *don't* love Hester, and it isn't fair to her!

Robert. Yes, I do love her! Only I wonder if I'm the marrying kind. Failing the possibility of marrying you. I mean your double.

Mrs. Phelps. [*Always increasing.*] You don't love Hester.

Robert. I do, I tell you! Who could help loving her? I mean . . . good God, what do I mean?

Mrs. Phelps. Either you don't love Hester or Hester doesn't love you.

Robert. She does love me.

Mrs. Phelps. She may say she does, but I haven't seen her showing it.

Robert. Mother!

Mrs. Phelps. You don't love Hester and Hester doesn't love you. It's as simple as that, Robin, and you're making a very grave mistake to go on with this. These things may be painful but they're better faced before than after. Children come after, Robin, and then it's too late! Think, Robin! Think before it's too late! And remember, the happiness of three people is at stake!

Robert. Hester's and mine and . . .

Mrs. Phelps. And mine! And mine! . . . Only, I was wrong to say that! You must put my fate out of your mind, just as Dave has done. Let Dave find out for himself what he's done. She won't be able to hold him. She won't have time for a home and children. She won't take any more interest in him than Hester takes in you. But you, Robin, *you* can still be saved! I want to save you from throwing yourself away as Dave has. You will face the facts, won't you?

Robert. You mean . . . I'm to . . . to break with Hester?

Mrs. Phelps. You will be a man?

Robert. [*Pause, then:*] Well . . . I'll . . . I'll—I'll try, Mother.

Mrs. Phelps. [*Pause, then:*] When?

Robert. Well . . . the . . . the first chance I get.

Mrs. Phelps. [*Trying not to appear eager.*] Tonight? . . . You'll have your chance tonight, Robin. I'll see that you get it. Promise me to take it?

Robert. [*Pause.*] All right. . . . If you think I'd better. . . . All right. . . .

Mrs. Phelps. Oh, thank God for this confidence between us! Thank God I've saved my boy one more tumble! You'll see it won't be so bad to put up with your mother a little longer! You'll see I've still plenty to give you and to do for you!

Robert. My blessed, blessed mother!

Mrs. Phelps. [*Unable to repress her triumph.*] And I won't have to be lonely now! I won't have to be lonely!

Robert. No, Mother! No!

[*He takes her in his arms.*]

Mrs. Phelps. Kiss me.

[*He does; on the lips, fervently.* DAVID *comes in dressed for dinner.*]

David. Hello! That's a pretty picture! Chris'll be down in a minute.

Robert. Where's Hester?

David. In Chris's room. I heard them giggling in there. Isn't it grand they've hit it off so well?

Robert. [*Meeting his mother's eyes.*] Isn't it? I'll make a cocktail. [*He goes.*]

David. You like Christina, don't you, Mother?

Mrs. Phelps. Didn't you know I should?

David. Sure I did! After all, I couldn't have gone far wrong on a wife, could I? I mean, having you for a mother would make most girls look pretty cheesy. I waited a long time. And all the time I was waiting for Chris! You'll see how wonderful Chris is. Why, she gets better every day. I don't know how I ever pulled it off. I swear I don't. I certainly had luck.

Mrs. Phelps. You're happy?

David. You bet I'm happy!

Mrs. Phelps. You're not going to let your happiness crowd me out entirely, are you, Dave, boy?

David. [*Amiably irritated.*] Oh, Mother! Lay off!

[ROBERT *returns with shaker and cocktail glasses.*]

Robert. This is just a preliminary, Mother. We both need it, before we dress.

Mrs. Phelps. Perhaps we do.

David. Shan't we call Chris and Hester?

Mrs. Phelps. No! Just we three!

Robert. It'll never be we three any more. I heard them coming as I crossed the hall.

[*He pours the cocktails into the glasses and goes about passing them.*]

Mrs. Phelps. My two boys! My big one and my little one!

David. [*Calls out.*] Hurry up, Chris!

Mrs. Phelps. If I can keep the little corner Christina doesn't need, Dave . . . that's all I ask. . . .

David. Don't worry, Mother. [CHRISTINA *and* HESTER *enter. They are both dressed appropriately for the evening.* CHRISTINA *is particularly lovely.*] Here we are!

Christina. Thank you, Robert.

[*They sip their cocktails.*]

David. Chris!

Christina. Yes?

David. Let's tell Mother.

Christina. Now? In front of everybody?

David. It won't hurt 'em to hear.

Christina. I don't mind, if they don't.

Robert. Mind what?

David. It'll make Mother so happy.

Mrs. Phelps. What will?

David. A surprise Chris and I have got to spring on you!

Mrs. Phelps. How nice! What is it?

Christina. [*A smiling pause—then:*] In about four months I'm going to have a baby.

Hester. Oh, Christina, how wonderful!

Robert. Are you really!

David. Isn't that a grand surprise, Mother?

Mrs. Phelps. [*Recovering as from a body blow.*] Of course . . . David. I'm very glad, my dear. Very glad. . . . Have you a napkin there, Robin? I've spilled my cocktail all over my dress.

CURTAIN

ACT TWO

THE FIRST SCENE

The living-room again. It is the same evening, after supper. The lamps are lighted.

[MRS. PHELPS, HESTER, CHRISTINA, DAVID, *and* ROB *are all present.* CHRISTINA, HESTER, *and* DAVID *are dressed as we saw them at the end of the first act.* ROB *wears his dinner coat and his mother has changed to a simple evening dress. They have only just finished their coffee and* MRS. PHELPS *is busily showing a collection of photographs which she has in a great Indian basket beside her chair.*]

Christina. What were you doing in the sailor suit, Dave?

David. Dancing the hornpipe, I believe.

Mrs. Phelps. [*Fondly.*] That was at Miss Briggs's dancing school. Do you remember Miss Briggs, David?

David. Do I! The hornpipe must have been something special, Mother.

Mrs. Phelps. I see that I've marked it "Masonic Temple, April 6th, 1904."

David. It must have been special. They don't usually dance hornpipes in Masonic Temples.

Christina. Did Miss Briggs teach you to be graceful, Dave?

David. She did indeed. As a boy I was a gazelle. But I got over it.

Christina. I'm just as glad. I've known one or two adult gazelles.

Mrs. Phelps. Both David and Robin danced beautifully.

David. I haven't thought of Miss Briggs for years. I remember her so well. She seemed so old to me. She must have been old, too. A good deal older than God. She looked it, in spite of her red hair and her castanets. Spain, she used to say, is the land of the dance.

Mrs. Phelps. She had all the nicest children.

David. Castanets and Spanish shawls . . . *and* a police whistle. She blew the whistle at the boys for running and sliding. God knows what dances she taught us. Very different from the steps you indulge in, Hester, with your low modern tastes.

Hester. Running and sliding sounds very pleasant.

David. We thought that up for ourselves.

Mrs. Phelps. How long ago that all seems! [*She shows another photograph.*] This is David when he was ten weeks old.

Christina. Oh, David!

Hester. Let me see. [CHRISTINA *shows her.*] What a darling baby! Did they always sit them in shells in those days?

Mrs. Phelps. [*Just a little coldly.*] It was a fashion like any other.

Christina. David on the half shell!

Hester. Have you ever noticed how much all babies look like Chief Justice Taft?

Mrs. Phelps. [*She takes the photograph back in ill-concealed irritation.*] David was a beautiful child.

David. I didn't always sit in shells. Mother's got one of me on a white fur rug.

Mrs. Phelps. It hangs over my bed to this day.

Christina. In the nude?

David. No. In an undershirt.

[HESTER *giggles.*]

Mrs. Phelps. Fashions change.

Christina. I suppose they must. David wouldn't think of being photographed in his undershirt, now. Let me see the picture again, Mrs. Phelps.

Mrs. Phelps. I think that's enough for this evening.

[*She rises, in great dignity, to put the photographs aside.*]

Christina. Dear Mrs. Phelps, please don't be angry. We were only teasing David. They're awfully interesting pictures.

Mrs. Phelps. Only interesting to me, I'm afraid.

Christina. Not at all. I loved them. Do show me some more, Mrs. Phelps. Are there many more?

Mrs. Phelps. [*Still stern about them.*] Dave and Robin were photographed twice every month until they were twelve years old.

Hester. [*Calculating rapidly.*] Good Lord! That makes over two hundred and fifty of each!

Mrs. Phelps. I never counted. I used to study their photographs, month by month, just as I did their weight. I wasn't satisfied to watch only their bodies grow. I wanted a record of the development of their little minds and souls as well. I could compare the expression of Dave's eyes, for instance, at nine, with their expression at eight and a half, and see the increased depth. And I was never disappointed.

Hester. I knew a mother once who called her son her "beautiful black swan."

Mrs. Phelps. I should never have called either of my sons by such a name!

Robert. I can remember when you used to call us your Arab steeds!

Mrs. Phelps. [*Furious.*] Only in fun. Will you put them away, Robin?

[ROBERT *takes the photographs.*]

Robert. Sure you don't want to go through the rest, Mother?

Mrs. Phelps. I'm afraid of boring Christina. Christina has other interests, of course. Higher interests than her husband. Higher even than children, I suspect.

[*There is an abashed, awful pause, at this.* CHRISTINA *looks hurt and baffled.* HESTER *is horrified.* DAVID, *puzzled, rises and goes to the window.* ROBERT *smiles to himself as he stows the photographs away.*]

Hester. [*Breaking out.*] Well, of all the . . .

[CHRISTINA, *catching her eye, stops her.*]

Mrs. Phelps. [*Polite, but dangerous.*] What was it you were about to say, Hester?

Hester. [*Recovering herself none too expertly.*] I was just looking at Christina's dress. I was just going to say: "Well, of all the lovely dresses I ever saw, that's the loveliest."

Christina. It *is* nice, isn't it? I got it in Paris. From Poiret. Dave made me.

Mrs. Phelps. [*As she studies the dress.*] I've a little woman right here in town who does well enough for me. I know who that dress *would* look well on! Dave, you remember Clara Judd? Such an exquisite figure, Clara had, and such distinction! That dress *wants* distinction and a figure. You might wear it, too, Hester.

[*There is another painful pause.* CHRISTINA *is really crushed.*]

David. [*Desperately snatching for a change of subject.*] Look, Chris! The moon's up. You can see the kids coasting down the long hill.

Christina. [*Joining him at the window gratefully.*] If I weren't all dressed up, I'd join them!

Hester. Don't you love coasting?

Christina. [*She nods.*] Once last winter we had a big snowfall at Heidelberg. I'd been all day in the laboratory, I remember, straining my eyes out at a scarlet fever culture for our bacteriology man. Krauss, his name was. They called him "The Demon of the Neckar." The theory was that he used to walk along the river bank, thinking up cruel things to say to his students. I never knew such a terrifying man. . . . Well, this day I'm talking about, I came out of Krauss's laboratory into the snow. Into Grimm's fairy tales, as Dave knows, because Dave's seen Heidelberg. Another bacteriologist, a dear boy from Marburg, came with me. We looked at the snow and we wanted to coast. . . . We found a small boy with a very large sled and we rented it, *with* the boy, who wouldn't trust us not to steal it. We certainly coasted. We got so ardent, we took the funicular up the Schlossberg and coasted down from there. The lights came out along the Neckar and the snow turned the colors and colors snow *can* turn and still we coasted. . . . Presently, we had an accident. A bob turned over in front of us with an old man on it. We couldn't stop and so we just hit the bob and the old man and you know how that is when you're going fast! . . . We picked ourselves up—or, rather, dug ourselves out—and went to see if we'd hurt the old fellow and, God save us, it was Krauss himself! . . . I don't mind telling you our hearts sank. We stood there petrified. But we needn't have worried. Krauss didn't mind. He smiled the sweetest smile —you'd *never* have suspected he had it in him!—and touched his cap like a little boy and apologized for his clumsiness. "My age hasn't improved my skill," he said. . . . I could have kissed him. I wasn't quite sure how he'd have taken that; so, instead, I asked him to join us. He was delighted. We kept it up for another hour, we two students and the great god Krauss. "Jugend ist Trunkenheit ohne Wein!" * he said. I dare say he was quoting a poem. . . . He couldn't have been a day under seventy. Three months later, he died of an inoperable internal tumor. In his notes, they found an observation he had written on his condition that very day we coasted. Think of a man who could write observations on his approaching death and then go off to coast afterwards! It's what life can be and should be. It's the difference between life and self.

Mrs. Phelps. H'm! . . .

Hester. I think that's the most marvelous story I've ever heard!

Robert. Isn't it marvelous?

Hester. I wish I'd known such a man!

Christina. Do you remember the night *we* coasted in Heidelberg, Dave?

David. Do I? [*To his mother.*] Chris means the night she accepted me!

Mrs. Phelps. Does she really?

David. [*Dashed and giving it up.*] Yeah. . . . Let's go outside and watch the kids, Chris. It'll do us good.

Christina. [*Seeing his point.*] Right! I'd love to! [*They go.*]

Mrs. Phelps. I'm beginning to wonder if Christina's studies at Heidelberg haven't made her just the least little bit in the world pro-German.

Hester. Mrs. Phelps, how *can* you say such a thing! [HESTER *looks from* ROBERT *to his mother in amazement.* MRS. PHELPS *sits down at the piano and begins to play the easier portions of one of Chopin's nocturnes.*] I think that was simply inspiring!

Mrs. Phelps. I can't play Chopin if you interrupt me, Hester.

Hester. I'm sorry. I simply can't get Christina out of my mind.

Mrs. Phelps. What do you mean?

Hester. I mean that I think she's the most perfect person I've ever seen.

Mrs. Phelps. Do you really? Which way did they go, Robin?

Robert. [*At the window.*] Down the front.

Mrs. Phelps. Can you see them?

Robert. They're just standing in the road. Now they're moving down under the trees.

* "Youth is drunkenness without wine." From Goethe's *Westöstlicher Divan.*

Mrs. Phelps. But they can't even *see* the long hill from the trees.

Robert. They're not looking at the long hill.

Mrs. Phelps. What *are* they looking at?

Robert. Each other. It's quite a romantic picture. Now she's put her head on his shoulder. His arm is around her waist. . . .

Mrs. Phelps. Faugh! Call them in!

[*Her irritation produces a discord in the nocturne.* ROBERT *moves to go.*]

Hester. Oh, don't, Rob! It's the first chance they've had to be alone together.

Mrs. Phelps. They can be alone without David's catching pneumonia, can't they? She drags him out of doors at night in freezing weather to spoon in the road like a couple of mill hands! I should think she might have some consideration for her husband's health, let alone for my feelings.

Hester. [*A little hotly.*] In the first place, it was David who dragged *her* out. In the second, they *are* in love and *do* want to be alone. In the third, I don't see any reason for worrying over the health of any man who looks as husky as David does. And in the fourth, if there *is* any worrying to be done, let me remind you that it's Christina and *not* David who is going to have a baby. [MRS. PHELPS *breaks off her playing in the middle of a phrase.*] I'm sorry if I've shocked you, but the truth is, you've both shocked me.

Robert. How have we shocked you?

Hester. By not being a great deal more thrilled over Christina's baby. When I drank my cocktail to it before dinner, neither of you drank yours. When I wanted to talk about it during dinner, you both changed the subject. You haven't mentioned that baby since dinner, except once, and that was catty! You've known about that baby for over two hours and you aren't excited about it yet! Not what *I* call excited.

Mrs. Phelps. If you'll forgive my saying so, Hester, I'm not sure that an unborn baby is quite the most suitable subject for . . .

Hester. I'm blessed if I see anything bad form about a baby!

Robert. No more does Mother—after it's born.

Hester. I can't wait for that. I *love* thinking about them. And wondering what they're going to be—I mean, boy or girl. Why, we had bets up on my sister's baby for months before he was born.

Mrs. Phelps. I'm not ashamed to be old-fashioned.

Hester. You ought to be. This is going to be a very remarkable baby. There aren't many born with such parents. And I intend to go right on talking about it with any one who'll listen to me. Christina doesn't mind. She's just as interested as I am. I've already made her promise to have my sister's obstetrician.

Mrs. Phelps. Really, Hester!

Hester. I'd go to the ends of the earth for that man. Christina's baby has put me in a very maternal frame of mind.

Mrs. Phelps. Maternal!

Hester. What I say is: I'm as good as married. I might as well make the best of my opportunities to get used to the idea. Because I intend to have as many babies as possible.

Mrs. Phelps. [*Glancing at* ROBERT.] Is that why you're marrying Rob, Hester?

Hester. What better reason could I have? I'm sorry if I've shocked you, but, as I said before, you've shocked me, and that's that.

[*Coolly,* MRS. PHELPS *goes for the coffee tray. Her eyes meet* ROBERT'S *and there is no mistaking the intention of the look they give him. Then, without a word, she leaves* ROBERT *and* HESTER *alone together.*]

Robert. [*Starting after her.*] Mother! . . . Hester didn't mean. . . . Oh. . . . [*He turns back to* HESTER.] Hester, how could you?

Hester. I don't know. . . . But I don't care if I did!

Robert. It doesn't make things any easier for me.

Hester. Oh, Rob, dear, I *am* sorry!

Robert. You've got Mother all ruffled and upset. Now we'll have to smooth her down and have all kinds of explanations and everything. Really, it was too bad of you.

Hester. I know. I lost my temper. . . . You understand, don't you?

Robert. I understand that you're a guest in Mother's house.

Hester. Is that *all* you understand? Oh, Rob!

Robert. I'm sorry, Hester. But, for the moment, I'm thinking of Mother.

Hester. I see. . . . I'll apologize.

Robert. That's up to you.

Hester. I suppose she'll never forgive me. It isn't this, though.

Robert. This?

Hester. The scene I made.

Robert. What do you mean?

Hester. I don't know. . . . Some mothers like the girls their sons marry.

Robert. Doesn't that depend on the girls?

Hester. Not entirely.

Robert. You mustn't be unjust to Mother.

Hester. Rob, I'm a little tired of hearing about your mother. . . . [*Suddenly penitent again.*] Oh, I didn't mean to say that! I didn't mean it a bit! I'm sorry, Rob. . . . Now I'm apologizing to you. Don't you hear me?

Robert. Yes, I hear you. What then?

Hester. Oh, what difference does it make? I'm not marrying your mother! I'm marrying you. And I love you, Rob! I love you!

Robert. Yes, my dear.

Hester. I'll never be bad again.

Robert. I'm willing to take your word for it.

Hester. You'd better be. Oh, you *are* angry with me, Rob!

Robert. No. I'm not.

Hester. You're a queer one.

Robert. Think so? How?

Hester. As a lover. I've never seen another like you.

Robert. Haven't you? [*A thought strikes him.*] Tell me something, Hester.

Hester. What?

Robert. Have you had many?

Hester. Many what?

Robert. Lovers.

Hester. Oh, Robert, what a thing to say to a lady!

Robert. You know what I mean.

Hester. I'm not quite sure I want to answer.

Robert. I'm not asking for their names.

Hester. Oh, I shouldn't mind that . . . the truth is . . . I don't know . . .

Robert. You must.

Hester. I don't really. I used to think . . . oh, quite often . . . that one of my beaux was coming to the point . . . but . . .

Robert. Yes?

Hester. But none of them ever did.

Robert. That surprises me. Why not?

Hester. I don't think it was entirely lack of allure, Rob.

Robert. Of course it wasn't!

Hester. *I* think it was because I always laughed.

Robert. You didn't laugh at me.

Hester. You looked foolish enough, now that I think of it.

Robert. Yes. I dare say. . . . So I *was* the only one.

Hester. Say the only one I didn't laugh at, please. You make me sound so undesirable.

Robert. I didn't mean to. Tell me, Hester . . .

Hester. Anything.

Robert. Have you thought what it will mean to be my wife?

Hester. A very pleasant life.

Robert. For you?

Hester. I certainly hope so.

Robert. I don't know that I quite share your enthusiasm for children.

Hester. You will.

Robert. They don't exactly help a career, you know.

Hester. Have you got a career?

Robert. I fully intend to have one.

Hester. I'm glad to hear it.

Robert. I've got just as much talent as Dave has.

Hester. What kind of talent?

Robert. I haven't decided. I can draw pretty well. I'm not a bad musician. I might decide to compose. I might even write. I've often thought of it. And children, you see . . .

Hester. I don't know much about careers, but Lincoln had children and adored 'em, and if you can do half as well as he did . . .

Robert. Then my preferences aren't to be considered?

Hester. You just leave things to me. If we're poor, I'll cook and scrub floors. I'll bring up our children. I'll take care of you whether we live in New York or Kamchatka. This business is up to me, Rob! Don't let it worry you.

Robert. [*Crushed.*] I only wanted to make sure you understood my point of view.

Hester. If I don't, I shall; so let's cut this short. [*She goes a little huffily to the window,* ROBERT *watching her uneasily.*] Hello!

Robert. What is it?

Hester. There goes your mother down the road.

Robert. [*He joins her.*] So it is! What can she be doing?

Hester. She's fetching her darling David in out of the cold. I knew she would.

Robert. Hester, would you mind not speaking that way of Mother?

Hester. Can't she leave them alone for a minute?

Robert. She's the worrying kind.

Hester. Oh, rot!

Robert. Evidently you're bent on making things as difficult as possible for me.

Hester. I'm sorry you feel that.

[*A long irritable pause, then:*]

Robert. Hester?

Hester. Yes?

Robert. Have you thought any more about our honeymoon?

Hester. Didn't we decide to go abroad?

Robert. Abroad's a pretty general term.

You were to think *where* you wanted to be taken.

Hester. I left that to you.

Robert. You said you "didn't care."

Hester. I don't.

Robert. Nor where we live after . . . nor how.

Hester. I don't . . . I don't . . . I want to live with *you.* [*Suddenly warming.*] What's the use of this, Rob?

Robert. We've never talked seriously about our marriage before.

Hester. What is there to say about it?

Robert. A great deal.

Hester. I don't agree. Marriages are things of feeling. They'd better *not* be talked about.

Robert. Real marriages can stand discussion!

Hester. Rob!

Robert. What?

Hester. That wasn't nice.

Robert. Wasn't it?

Hester. [*Suddenly frightened.*] What's the matter, Rob? I'll talk as seriously as you please. Do I love you? Yes. Am I going to make you a good wife? I hope so, though I *am* only twenty and may make mistakes. Are you going to be happy with me? I hope that, too, but you'll have to answer it for yourself.

Robert. I can't answer it.

Hester. Why can't you?

Robert. Because I'm not sure of it.

Hester. Aren't you, Rob?

Robert. These things are better faced before than after.

Hester. What is it you're trying to say?

Robert. If only we could be sure!

Hester. [*Stunned.*] So that's it!

Robert. Are you so sure you want to marry me?

Hester. How can I be—now?

Robert. Marriage is such a serious thing. You don't realize how serious.

Hester. Don't I?

Robert. No. . . . I hope you won't think harshly of me. . . . And, mind you, I haven't said I wanted to break things off. . . . I only want . . .

Hester. Please, Rob!

Robert. No. You've got to hear me out.

Hester. I've heard enough, thank you!

Robert. I'm only trying to look at this thing . . .

Hester. Seriously. . . . I know. . . .

Robert. Because, after all, the happiness of three people is affected by it.

Hester. Three?

Robert. As Mother said, before dinner.

Hester. So you talked this over with your mother?

Robert. Isn't that natural?

Hester. Is your mother the third?

Robert. Wouldn't she be?

Hester. Yes, I suppose she would. . . . I think you might tell me what else she had to say.

Robert. It was all wise and kind. You may be as hard as you like on me, but you mustn't be hard on poor, splendid, lonely Mother.

Hester. [*Savage—under her breath.*] So she's lonely, too!

Robert. You *will* twist my meaning!

Hester. You *said* "lonely."

Robert. Perhaps I did. But Mother didn't. You know, she never talks about herself.

Hester. I see. What else did she say about us?

Robert. Well, you haven't been very interested in planning our future. She notices such things.

Hester. What else?

Robert. She sees through people, you know.

Hester. Through me?

Robert. She thought, as I must say I do, that we didn't love each other quite enough to . . . at least, she thought we ought to think very carefully before we . . .

Hester. [*Gripping his two arms with all her strength, she stops him.*] If you really want to be free . . . if you really want that, Rob, it's all right. It's perfectly all right. . . . I'll set you free. . . . Don't worry. . . . Only you've got to say so. You've *got* to. . . . Answer me, Rob. *Do* you want to be rid of me? [*There is a pause.* ROBERT *cannot hold her gaze and his eyes fall. She takes the blow.*] I guess that's answer enough. [*She draws a little back from him and pulls the engagement ring from her finger.*] Here's your ring.

Robert. Hester! Don't do anything you'll be sorry for afterwards! Don't, please! I can't take it yet!

Hester. [*Without any sign of emotion, she drops it on a table.*] I shall have an easier time of it, if you keep away from me. I want to save my face . . . if I can.

Robert. Hester, please!

Hester. All right, if you won't go, I will.

Robert. I'm sorry. Of course I'll go.

Hester. And take your ring with you.

[*He goes to the table, picks up the ring, pockets it, and has just got to the door when* HESTER *breaks into furious, hysterical sobbing. Her sobs rack her and seem, at the same time, to strike* ROBERT *like the blows of a whip.*]

Robert. For God's sake, Hester. . . . [*She drops into a chair and sits, staring straight before her, shaken by her sobs of outraged fury and wretchedness.*] Mother! Christina! Come here! Hester . . . [CHRISTINA *appears in the door.* MRS. PHELPS *follows her.* DAVID *appears.* ROBERT *returns to* HESTER.] Can't you pull yourself together?

[*She motions him away.*]

Christina. What's the matter?

Robert. It's Hester. Can't you stop her?

Mrs. Phelps. Good heavens, Robin! What's wrong with the child?

Robert. She's . . . upset . . . you see, I was just . . . you know . . .

Mrs. Phelps. I see! . . . She's taking it badly.

[HESTER'S *sobs only increase.*]

Christina. Hester, stop it!

Hester. I'm all right. . . . I can't . . . I . . . Christina . . . please . . .

Christina. Open a window, Dave. . . . Haven't you any smelling salts in the house, Mrs. Phelps?

[MRS. PHELPS *goes for them where she left them at tea-time.*]

Hester. Tell Rob to go away! Tell Rob to go away!

Christina. Never mind Rob! . . . Get me some aromatic spirits, one of you! Hurry up! [ROBERT *goes.*]

Mrs. Phelps. Here are my salts.

Christina. [*Peremptorily.*] Hester! [*She holds the salts for* HESTER *to smell.*] Now, stop it! Stop it, do you hear me?

Hester. I'm trying to stop. If you'd only send these awful people out! Take me away, Christina! Take me back to New York! I've got to get away from here. I can't face them! I can't! I can't!

Christina. Now, *stop* it!

David. [*Comes forward from a window.*] Here's some snow in my handkerchief. Rub it on her wrists and temples.

Christina. Thanks, Dave.

[*She applies it.* HESTER, *by dint of great effort, gradually overcomes her sobs.* ROBERT *returns with a tumbler partly filled with a milky solution of aromatic spirits.*]

Mrs. Phelps. [*Speaking at the same time, in unfeigned wonderment to* DAVID.] Really, I do wonder at what happens to girls nowadays! When I was Hester's age I danced less and saved a little of my strength for self-control.

Robert. [*Speaking through.*] Here, Dave. Take this.

[DAVID *takes it.* ROBERT *goes again.* DAVID *gives the tumbler to* CHRISTINA.]

Christina. Good! Can you drink this now, Hester?

Hester. Thank you, Christina. I'm all right now. It was only . . .

Christina. Never mind what it was. Drink this. [HESTER *drinks it.*] There, now. That's better. Just sit still and relax.

David. What on earth brought it on?

Mrs. Phelps. [*Shrugging her shoulders.*] Rob and she must have had a falling out.

David. No ordinary one. . . . Rob! He's gone. . . . That's funny.

Mrs. Phelps. He'd naturally be distressed.

Hester. I'm really all right, now, Christina . . . and frightfully ashamed. . . .

Mrs. Phelps. You'd better see how Rob is, Dave. His nerves are none too stout. Such scenes aren't good for him.

Hester. [*In a high, strained voice.*] No, isn't that so, Mrs. Phelps?

Mrs. Phelps. Did you speak to me, Hester?

Hester. Take the smelling salts to Rob with my love. . . . Oh God, Christina!

Christina. Now, never *mind,* Hester. You'll go to pieces again.

Hester. But I've got to mind! And I'm all right! It won't hurt me. . . . I wish you'd go, David.

Christina. Yes, Dave, do. I'll come up in a jiffy.

Mrs. Phelps. When Hester's quieted down. [*To* DAVID.] We'd better both go and see how Rob is. [*She is just going.*]

Hester. Mrs. Phelps. There's something I want to ask you before we part.

Mrs. Phelps. Tomorrow, my dear girl. . . .

Hester. There isn't going to be any tomorrow.

Mrs. Phelps. What?

Hester. Rob has just broken our engagement.

Mrs. Phelps. Not really!

Christina. [*Staggered.*] Hester, what do you mean?

Hester. I mean what I say. Rob's just broken our engagement.

[CHRISTINA *motions to* DAVE *to go. He obeys.*]

Mrs. Phelps. I'm immensely distressed, of course.

Hester. [*Shaking her head doggedly.*] He talked it all over with you before dinner. He told me that much, so it won't do you the least bit of good to pretend to be surprised.

Mrs. Phelps. Aren't you forgetting yourself, Hester?

Hester. You made him do it. Why did you make him do it, Mrs. Phelps?

[CHRISTINA, *amazed, draws back to observe the pair of them.*]

Mrs. Phelps. [*Perfect dignity.*] I don't intend to stand here, Hester, and allow any hysterical girl to be rude to me.

Hester. [*Driving on querulously.*] I'm not being rude! All I want to know is why you talked Rob into jilting me. Will you answer me, please?

Mrs. Phelps. Such things may be painful, my dear girl, but they're far less painful before than after.

Hester. He quoted that much.

Christina. What's the good of this, Hester?

Hester. I'm only trying to make her tell me why she did it.

Mrs. Phelps. But, Hester! Really! This is absurd!

Hester. You've got to! You've got to explain!

Mrs. Phelps. I had nothing to do with Robin's change of heart.

Hester. You must have had, Mrs. Phelps, and I'm demanding an explanation of why you talked Rob into . . .

Mrs. Phelps. Isn't it enough that he found out in time that you weren't the wife for him?

Hester. That isn't the truth!

Christina. Hester, darling!

Hester. Can you tell me what he meant when he said that the happiness of *three* people was at stake?

Mrs. Phelps. He must have been thinking of your happiness as well as his own and mine.

Hester. What about your loneliness?

Mrs. Phelps. This *is* contemptible of you!

Christina. Really, Hester, this *can't* do any good!

Hester. I'm going to make her admit that she made Rob . . .

Mrs. Phelps. [*Exploding.*] Very well, then, since you insist! I did advise my son to break with you. Do you want to know why?

Hester. Yes.

Mrs. Phelps. Because of your indifference. . . .

Hester. Oh!

Mrs. Phelps. Because he came to me to say that you neither love him nor make any pretense of loving him . . .

Hester. Rob said that?

Mrs. Phelps. He even said that you must have misconstrued his friendship and that he never wanted to marry you . . .

Hester. No!

Mrs. Phelps. And I told him to risk anything . . . . anything, rather than such an appalling marriage . . .

Hester. I don't believe a word of it!

Mrs. Phelps. You may believe it or not!

Christina. Mrs. Phelps, you had really better let me handle this.

Mrs. Phelps. Willingly.

Hester. Do you believe I took advantage of Rob, Christina?

Christina. Of course not!

Mrs. Phelps. So, you take her side, Christina!

Christina. I don't believe *that,* Mrs. Phelps.

Mrs. Phelps. [*She realizes that she has gone too far.*] No? Well, perhaps . . .

Christina. Whatever Robert may think, I can't believe that he said . . .

Mrs. Phelps. [*Frightened.*] Perhaps he didn't say quite that, in so many words . . . but he certainly meant . . .

Hester. I'm going. I'm going now. Right this minute.

Mrs. Phelps. There's a train at nine in the morning. It gets you to New York at twelve. I shall have the car for you at eight-thirty.

Hester. May I have the car now, please, Mrs. Phelps?

Mrs. Phelps. There's no train tonight.

Hester. It doesn't matter. I won't stay here. Not another minute. I'll go to the hotel in town.

Mrs. Phelps. You'll do nothing of the sort!

Hester. You see if I don't!

Mrs. Phelps. You've got to think of appearances!

Hester. Appearances are your concern. Yours and Rob's. I'm going to the hotel. I don't care what people say! I don't care about anything. I won't stay here!

Mrs. Phelps. Can't you talk to her, Christina? Surely you see . . . for all our sakes!

Hester. If you won't let me have the car, I'll call a taxi. . . .

[*She plunges toward the telephone.*]

Mrs. Phelps. I forbid you!

Hester. [*Seizing the instrument.*] I want a taxi . . . a taxi. . . . What *is* the number? . . . Well, give it to me. . . . Locust 4000? Give me Locust 4000!

[MRS. PHELPS *hesitates an instant, then, with terrible coolness, steps forward and jerks the telephone cord from the wall. Except for a startled exclamation, very low, from* CHRISTINA, *there is not a sound.* HESTER *hangs up the receiver and sets down the dead instrument.*]

Mrs. Phelps. [*After an interminable silence.*] You are the only person in the world who has ever forced me to do an undignified thing. I shall not forget it.

[*She goes nobly.*]

Hester. [*Weakly, turning to* CHRISTINA.] Christina, it isn't true what she said. . . . He did. . . . He did want to marry me! Really, he did! He did!

Christina. Of course he did, darling!

Hester. I won't stay! I won't stay under that woman's roof!

Christina. Hester, darling!

Hester. I'll walk to town!

Christina. Don't, Hester!

Hester. That wasn't true, what she said!

Christina. Of course not!

Hester. I still love him. . . . Let me go, Christina, I'll walk . . .

Christina. You can't, at this time of night! It wouldn't be safe!

Hester. I don't care! I won't stay!

Christina. There! There! You'll come to bed now, won't you!

Hester. No! No! I can't! I'd rather die! I'll walk to town.

Christina. You'll force me to come with you, Hester. I can't let you go alone.

Hester. I won't stay another minute!

Christina. Do you want to make me walk with you? Think, Hester! Think what I told you before dinner? Do you want to make me walk all that way in the cold?

Hester. [*Awed by this.*] Oh, your baby! I didn't mean to forget your baby! Oh, Christina, you mustn't stay, either! This is a dreadful house! You've got to get your baby away from this house, Christina! Awful things happen here!

Christina. Hester, darling! Won't you please be sensible and come up to bed?

Hester. [*Speaking at the same time as her nerves begin to go again.*] Awful things, Christina. . . . You'll see if you don't come away! You'll see! . . . She'll do the same thing to you that she's done to me! You'll see! You'll see!

CURTAIN

THE SECOND SCENE

The curtain rises again, as soon as possible, upon DAVID'S *little bedroom, untouched since the day when* DAVID *went away to Harvard and scorned to take his prep-school trophies and souvenirs with him. The furniture is rather more than simple. The bed is single. There is a dresser. There are only a couple of chairs. The curtains at the single window have been freshly laundered and put back in their old state by* MRS. PHELPS *in a spirit of maternal archæology. Insignificant loving cups, won at tennis, stand about the dresser. No pennants, no banners. There might be some tennis rackets, golf sticks, crossed skis, a pair of snow-shoes, class photographs and framed diplomas. There must also be a fairly important reproduction of Velasquez' Don Balthazar Carlos on horseback, selected by* MRS. PHELPS *as* DAVID'S *favorite Old Master. A final touch is* DAVID'S *baby pillow.*

[DAVID *stands in his pajamas and socks, about to enter upon the last stages of his preparations to retire for the night. The room has been strewn with clothing during the preliminary stages. Now he is in the ambulatory state of mind. A series of crosses and circumnavigations produces several empty packs of cigarettes from several pockets, corners of the suitcase, etc. This frustration brings on baffled scratchings of the head and legs. Then he gives up the cigarette problem, turns again to the suitcase, spills out several dirty shirts and, finally, apparently from the very bottom, extracts a dressing-gown, a pair of slippers, a tooth-brush and some tooth-paste. He sheds the socks, dons the slippers and dressing-gown and sallies forth with brush and paste to do up his teeth in the bathroom. He goes by the door which gives on the hall at the head of the stairs.*

After he has been gone a few seconds, a tiny scratching sound is heard on the other side of the other door to the room and that is opened from without. We see the scratcher at work conveying the impression that a wee mousie wants to come in. The wee mousie is none other than MRS. PHELPS, *all smiles in her best negligee, the most effective garment she wears in the course of the entire play, carrying the largest eider-down comforter ever seen on any stage. The smile fades a little when she discovers that the room is empty. Then its untidiness catches her eye and she shakes her head reprovingly, as who should say: "What creatures these big boys are!" She goes to work at once, true mother that she is, to pick things up. She loves her work and puts her whole heart into it. The trousers are neatly hung over the back of the chair, the coat and waistcoat hung over them. The shirts, socks, and underwear are folded and laid chastely on the seat. One or two of the garments receive devout maternal kisses and hugs. Then she goes to the bed, lifts off the suitcase, pushes it underneath, adjusts the eiderdown, smooths the pillow and kisses that. Last, all smiles again, she sits, carefully disposing her laces and ribbons, to await* DAVID'S *return. She yearns for it and she has not long to wait.*

DAVID *returns. His mother's beaming smile, as he opens the door, arouses his usual distaste for filial sentimentality. It is intensified, now—and very ill-concealed—by the hour, his costume, and recent events. He hesitates in the doorway.*]

Mrs. Phelps. Why do you look so startled? It's only Mother!

David. [*Laconic.*] Hello, Mother!

Mrs. Phelps. I came in to ask if you needed anything and . . .

David. Not a thing, thanks.

Mrs. Phelps. And to warn you against opening the window in this weather. Oh, and I brought you that extra cover. I've been picking up after you, too!

David. [*Looking gloomily about.*] You needn't have troubled.

Mrs. Phelps. It took me back to the old days when I used to tuck you up in that same little bed . . .

David. [*A strong hint.*] Yeah. . . . I'm just turning in, Mother.

Mrs. Phelps. [*Regardless.*] . . . And then sit in this very chair and talk over all my problems with you. I feel that I must talk to my big boy tonight. . . . I must get acquainted with my Dave again.

David. [*An even stronger hint.*] We're not exactly strangers, are we? And besides, it's getting late.

Mrs. Phelps. [*Even more persistent.*] It was always in these late hours that we had our talks in the old days when we were still comrades. Oh, are those days gone forever? Don't you remember how we used to play that we had an imaginary kingdom where we were king and queen?

David. [*Moribund.*] Did we? I wish Chris 'ud come up.

Mrs. Phelps. [*A frown, and she speaks quickly.*] Have you noticed, Dave, boy, that your room is just as you left it? I've made a little shrine of it. The same curtains, the same . . .

David. [*Breaking in.*] I suppose Chris is still trying to get Hester quiet?

Mrs. Phelps. I suppose so. . . . And every day I dusted in here myself and every night I prayed in here for . . .

David. [*A little too dryly for good manners.*] Thanks.

Mrs. Phelps. [*Reproachfully.*] Oh, David, you can't get that horrid scene downstairs out of your mind!

David. No.

Mrs. Phelps. Try! I need my big boy so! Because I'm facing the gravest problem of my life, Dave. And you've got to help me.

David. What is it?

Mrs. Phelps. Is it true that I'm of no more use to my two sons?

David. Whatever put such an idea in your head?

Mrs. Phelps. You did.

David. [*Shocked.*] I?

Mrs. Phelps. [*Nodding.*] You weren't really glad to see me this afternoon.

David. [*In all sincerity.*] I was. . . . I was delighted!

Mrs. Phelps. [*Bravely stopping him.*] Not glad as I was to see you. I noticed, Dave! . . . And that made me wonder whether this scientific age—because it is a scientific age, Dave—isn't making more than one boy forget that the bond between mother and son is the strongest bond on earth. . . .

David. [*Not quite sure of the superlative.*] Well, it's certainly strong.

Mrs. Phelps. Do you realize how sinful any boy would be to want to loosen it?

David. Sure I realize that!

Mrs. Phelps. I see so many poor mothers, no less deserving of love and loyalty than I, neglected and discarded by their children, set aside for other interests.

David. What interests?

Mrs. Phelps. All kinds of things. . . . Wives. . . .

David. [*Shying.*] Nonsense, Mother!

Mrs. Phelps. The Chinese never set any relationship above their filial piety. They'd be the greatest people on earth if only they'd stop smoking opium.

David. You haven't any kick, have you? I mean: Rob and I haven't let you down?

Mrs. Phelps. Not yet, Dave. But, you know the old saying?

David. What old saying?

Mrs. Phelps. That a boy's mother is his best friend.

David. Oh! Bet I do!

Mrs. Phelps. Do you think of *your* mother as *your* best friend?

David. None better, certainly.

Mrs. Phelps. None better! H'm! You *can* say, though, that you haven't entirely outgrown me?

David. Of course I haven't! Why, I'd hate to have you think that just because I'm a grown man, I . . .

Mrs. Phelps. No son is ever a grown man to his mother! [*A knock at the door.*] Who can that be at this hour?

David. I hope it's Chris.

[*He starts for the door.*]

Mrs. Phelps. [*Freezing suddenly as she rises.*] Dave!

David. [*Turning.*] What?

Mrs. Phelps. Wait. . . . I mustn't intrude. . . . Good-night. . . .

David. [*Calling out.*] Just a minute! [*To his mother, politely.*] You wouldn't be intruding!

Mrs. Phelps. Not on you, I know. But . . .

David. Not on Chris either!

Mrs. Phelps. I know best. Kiss me good-night.

David. Good-night, Mother.

[*He kisses her cheek.*]

Mrs. Phelps. [*A quick hug.*] God bless my big boy!

[*She goes as she came.* DAVID'S *look, as he watches her door close behind her, is baffled. He goes quickly to the other door.* ROBERT *is standing outside.*]

David. For Pete's sake, Rob! I thought it was Chris! . . . Why didn't you walk in?

Robert. I thought Mother was in here.

David. She was. She just went to bed.

Robert. [*Entering.*] She must have thought it was Chris, too!

David. How do you mean?

Robert. I shouldn't rush things if I were you.

David. Maybe you're right. Women are too deep for me.

Robert. I came in for a smoke. I had to talk to you. I've been sitting in my room wondering what you think of all this.

David. [*Cigarette business.*] I don't think much and that's the truth!

Robert. Good God, Dave, can't you be a little easier on me? Didn't you ever feel any doubts when you were engaged? Were you always so sure of Christina that you . . .

David. The first time I asked Chris to marry me, she made it perfectly clear that, as far as she was concerned, I was to consider myself dripping wet. After that I was too damned scared I wouldn't get her to think whether she loved me or not.

Robert. [*Darkly.*] And I never had one comfortable moment from the time Hester accepted me.

David. Oh, being in love's like everything else. You've got to put some guts in it.

Robert. [*Bitter anger.*] You think I haven't got any guts. You want to make me look like a callous cad! All right, I'll *be* a cad. I don't care what people think about me! But I'll tell you one thing! I'm damned if I'm going to let you turn Mother against me!

David. Do *what?*

Robert. You heard me!

David. My God, haven't you outgrown that old stuff yet?

Robert. I know from experience what to expect when you and Mother get together. I used to listen at that door, night after night, night after night, while you and Mother sat in here and talked me over. Then I'd watch for the change in her next morning at breakfast when I hadn't slept a wink all night. The way you used to own the earth at those breakfasts! Well, if you try any of that old stuff tonight, I'll lose the only prop I've got left.

David. Isn't it about time you let go of Mother's apronstrings?

Robert. You would say that! You don't realize that I'm desperate.

David. Desperate, hell! You're crazy! Mother's gone to bed and . . . [*The wee mousie scratches at the door again.*] What's that?

Mrs. Phelps. [*Entering.*] It's only Mother. Are my two beaux quarreling? Jealous, jealous Robin! What's the matter?

David. Nothing.

Mrs. Phelps. A fine man is a frank man, David! Do you think I didn't hear every word you said? Surely you must know that Hester wasn't worthy of your brother?

David. Wasn't she? Well, let's not talk any more about it.

Mrs. Phelps. Oh, but we must. For all our sakes, we must clear the air. *I* have always taken the stand that my boys could do absolutely no wrong and that is the proper stand for a mother to take. Didn't I always side with you in your school scrapes? Even against the masters? Even when you were clearly in the wrong? Of course, I did! And I shall not permit one word of criticism against your brother now. Loyalty, Dave! Loyalty! Come, now! Tell Mother all about it!

David. But if you overheard every word we said!

Mrs. Phelps. "Overheard," David? Am I given to eavesdropping?

David. I didn't say so.

Mrs. Phelps. I simply want to make sure I didn't miss anything while I was in my bath.

David. I don't understand him. I'm sorry for Hester, that's all.

Robert. We're all sorry for Hester.

David. I don't think it's your place to be too sorry.

Robert. Let's drop it, Mother.

Mrs. Phelps. No. I've got to know what's on Dave's mind. My whole life may hang on it. What is it, Dave? [*Carefully sounding.*] If Robin's not to blame, perhaps I am?

Robert. [*Horrified.*] Mother!

David. What's the use of getting so worked up over nothing?

Mrs. Phelps. Nothing! Can you say "nothing" after what *we* were talking about a few minutes ago?

David. [*Cornered.*] I only think . . .

Mrs. Phelps. What?

David. Well, that you've both handed Hester a somewhat dirty deal. And Chris must think so, too!

Mrs. Phelps. [*Wary.*] Indeed! And how, please?

David. Well, it comes of what Chris calls "mythologizing."

Mrs. Phelps. [*Frightened.*] Does Christina discuss our family affairs already?

David. No. It's one of her old ideas about people in general. You mythologize Rob into a little tin god. Rob thinks he is a little tin god. Along comes Hester and falls in love with the real Rob. She never heard of your little tin god Rob. She doesn't deliver the incense and tom-toms. That makes you and Rob sore and the whole works go to hell. That's mythologizing. Believe me, it can make plenty of trouble.

Mrs. Phelps. [*Relieved that the criticism is so general.*] If that's all I'm to blame for, I don't know that I can object. Expecting the best of every one is, at least, a worthy fault. Still, if I may venture an older woman's opinion on one of Christina's ideas?

David. I wish to God I hadn't started this.

Mrs. Phelps. So do I. But perhaps you'll tell me what Christina would say to the true reason for Robin's break with Hester?

David. What is the true reason?

Mrs. Phelps. Do you want to tell him, Robin?

Robert. [*Inspired.*] I broke with Hester because of an ideal, the ideal of womankind Mother gave us both by being the great woman that she is. *I* knew *I* couldn't be happy with any woman who fell short of her.

Mrs. Phelps. What becomes of your "dirty deal" now, David?

David. But I'm not going against that ideal, Mother. That's another thing.

Robert. You couldn't have troubled much about it when you married!

Mrs. Phelps. You shouldn't have said that, Robin. I haven't had Christina's advantages. I wasn't given a German education.

David. Now, don't take this out on Chris, Mother.

Mrs. Phelps. I think I know a little of a mother's duty toward her daughter-in-law. Good-night, Robin. I must talk with your brother alone, now. And before you quarrel again, stop to think that you are all I have, you two, and try to consider me. It isn't much to ask and it won't be for long. You both know what the doctors think about my heart! Doctor McClintock tells me I may go at any moment. [*Pause, then:*] Good night, Robin.

Robert. [*Frightened.*] Good night, Mother.

Mrs. Phelps. You may come into my room later, if you like. I may need you to comfort me after . . . [*She waves her hand. He leaves. She has never taken her eyes off* DAVID. *When the door closes behind* ROBERT, *she speaks.*] David, in this moment, when your brother and I most needed your loyalty, you have hurt me more than I have ever been hurt in my life before, even by your father.

David. I never meant to hurt you.

Mrs. Phelps. [*Working it up.*] You have been wicked, David! Wicked! Wicked!

David. How?

Mrs. Phelps. You have shown me too clearly that what I most dreaded has already come to pass!

David. What, Mother?

Mrs. Phelps. You *have* loosened the bond between us. You *have* discarded me.

David. [*Horrified.*] But I haven't done any such thing!

Mrs. Phelps. Don't say any more! Act upon your treachery, if you will, but don't, please, don't say another thing. Remember!

"The brave man does it with a sword,
The coward with a word!"

[*And she sweeps out, slamming her door after her.*]

David. [*Speaking through her door.*] But I didn't mean anything. . . . Won't you let me explain? . . . I didn't know what I was talking about!

[*There is no answer. He rattles the door. It is locked. He comes away, swearing softly under his breath. Then, manfully, he takes refuge in sulks. He kicks off his slippers and throws his dressing-gown aside. He lights a cigarette and flounces into bed, snatching up a book or magazine en route. Just as he is settled, his mother's door opens again very slowly.* MRS. PHELPS *presents a tear-stained face to view and comes in.*]

Mrs. Phelps. Smoking in bed, Dave, boy?

David. [*Starting up.*] Eh?

Mrs. Phelps. It's only Mother. . . . No, don't get up. . . . Let me sit here as I used to in the old days.

David. [*Sitting up.*] Mother, I didn't mean . . .

Mrs. Phelps. Never mind. I was wrong to be hurt.

David. But you had me all wrong. I mean . . . you and I . . . We're just the same as we always were. . . . Believe me, we are. . . . Why, if anything came to spoil things between us . . .

Mrs. Phelps. [*The first objective conquered.*] That's what I wanted you to say! Now talk to me about Christina.

David. [*Taken aback without knowing why.*] Huh?

Mrs. Phelps. Give me your hand in mine and tell me all about her.

David. [*Obeying rather reluctantly.*] What is there to tell?

Mrs. Phelps. Well, for one thing, tell me you think she's going to like me!

David. [*Warmly.*] She does already!

Mrs. Phelps. Doesn't think I'm an old-fashioned frump?

David. I should say not! How could she?

Mrs. Phelps. She's such a modern young lady. So lovely, but so very up-to-date. You must tell me everything I can do to win her to me. And I'll do it. Though I'm afraid of her, Dave.

David. [*Amused.*] Afraid of Chris? Why?

Mrs. Phelps. She's so much cleverer than I am. She makes me realize that I'm just a timid old lady of the old school.

David. [*Nice indignation.*] You old!

Mrs. Phelps. [*Archly, so brave about it.*] Yes, I am!

David. Well, you and Chris are going to be the best friends ever.

Mrs. Phelps. You *are* happy, aren't you?

David. You bet I am!

Mrs. Phelps. Really happy?

David. Couldn't be happier!

Mrs. Phelps. I'm so glad! And I thank God that when your hour struck it didn't strike falsely, as it did for Robin. Because any one can see the difference between Christina and Hester. Of course, that's a little the difference between you and Rob. You know what I've always said. You are *my* son. Robert takes after his father. But you mustn't be impatient with Christina if she seems, at first, a little slow, a little resentful of our family. We've always been so close, we three. She's bound to feel a little out of it, at first. A little jealous . . .

David. Not Chris!

Mrs. Phelps. Oh, come now, Dave! I'm sure she's perfect, but you mustn't try to tell me she isn't human. Young wives are sure to be a little bit possessive and exacting and . . . selfish at first.

David. We needn't worry about that.

Mrs. Phelps. No. . . . At first I thought Christina was going to be hard and cold. I didn't expect her to have our sense of humor and I don't believe she has much of that. But we've more than we need already. If only she will learn to care for me as I care for her, we can be so happy, all four of us together, can't we?

David. You bet we can!

Mrs. Phelps. [*Dreamily.*] Building our houses in Phelps Manor. . . . Deciding to put an Italian Villa here and a little bungalow there. . . . [*As* DAVID *grows restive.*] But the important thing for you, Dave, boy, is a sense of proportion about your marriage. I'm going to lecture you, now, for your own good. If, at first, Christina does seem a little exacting or unreasonable, particularly about us, remember that she has to adjust herself to a whole new world here, a very different world from her friends in Omaha. And you must never be impatient with her. Because, if you are, I shall take her side against you.

David. You *are* a great woman, Mother!

Mrs. Phelps. You're the great one! How many boys of your age let their wives undermine all their old associations and loosen all their old ties!

David. Chris wouldn't try that!

Mrs. Phelps. She might not *want* to. But jealous girls think things that aren't so and say things that aren't true. Morbid things.

David. Morbid things? Chris?

Mrs. Phelps. Only you won't pay too much attention or take her too seriously. I know that, because you would no more let any one strike at me than I would let any one strike at you.

David. But Chris wouldn't . . .

Mrs. Phelps. As I said to Christina this afternoon: "Christina," I said, "I cannot allow you to sacrifice David!"

David. Chris sacrifice me! How?

Mrs. Phelps. Why, by taking you away from your magnificent opportunity here

David. Oh!

Mrs. Phelps. Be master in your own house. Meet her selfishness with firmness, her jealousy with fairness and her . . . her exaggerations with a grain of salt. . . .

David. What exaggerations?

Mrs. Phelps. Well, you know . . . a girl . . . a young wife, like Christina . . *might* possibly make the mistake of . . . well, of taking sides . . . in what happened downstairs, for instance . . . and without fully understanding. . . . You can see how fatal *that* would be. . . . But, if you face the facts always, Dave, boy, and nothing *but* the facts, your marriage will be a happy one. And, when you want advice, come to your mother always.

David. Thanks.

Mrs. Phelps. Now, isn't your mother your best friend?

David. You bet you are, Mummy!

Mrs. Phelps. How long it is since you've called me that! Bless you, my dear, dear boy!

[*She leans over to seal her triumph with a kiss.* CHRISTINA'S *entrance follows so closely upon her knock that the picture is still undisturbed for her to see. She has changed her dress for a very simple negligee. Her mood is dangerous.*]

Christina. Oh, I beg your pardon!

Mrs. Phelps. [*So sweetly, after the very briefest pause.*] Come in, Christina. I was only saying good-night to Dave. Nothing private! You're one of the family now. You must feel free to come and go as you like in the house.

Christina. Thank you.

Mrs. Phelps. We can accustom ourselves to it, can't we, Dave?

David. Yeah. . . .

Christina. Dave and I have got so used to sharing the same room, I came in here quite naturally and . . .

Mrs. Phelps. Here's your dressing-gown, Dave, boy. We won't look while you slip it on.

[*Confusedly* DAVE *gets out of bed and robes himself.* CHRISTINA'S *eyes meet his mother's.* CHRISTINA'S *eyes have the least flash of scorn in them,* MRS. PHELPS' *the least quaver of fear. In that glance, the two women agree on undying enmity.*]

David. You can . . . you can look now.

Christina. Are you quite sure *I* may, Mrs. Phelps?

Mrs. Phelps. Whatever else you may have taken from me, Christina, you can *not* take from me the joy of feeling my son here, once more, in his old room, beside me.

Christina. [*Marking up the first score.*] I haven't meant to take anything from you, Mrs. Phelps.

Mrs. Phelps. [*So sweetly again.*] You know I was only joking. [*She is routed, though.*] Good-night. [*The two women kiss.*] Don't keep Dave up too late. He's very tired. [*She pats* DAVE, *as she passes him on her way to her door.*] You must be tired, too, Christina. How *is* Hester, now?

Christina. Quite all right, thank you.

Mrs. Phelps. Thank *you*!

[*She blows a kiss to* DAVID *from the door and goes.* CHRISTINA *stands motionless.* DAVID *reaches for a cigarette.*]

David. You look pretty stern, Chris.

Christina. Do I?

David. You've been a brick.

Christina. Thanks.

David. Hester *is* all right, isn't she?

Christina. Yes, poor youngster! I shouldn't be surprised if she were really in luck, Dave.

David. You may be right. But it isn't exactly up to me to say so, is it?

[*He lights his cigarette. Her eyes burn him up.*]

Christina. Dave. . . .

David. Yes?

Christina. Whom do you love?

David. You. Why?

Christina. I wondered, that's all. I want to be kissed.

David. That's easy.

[*He takes her in his arms.*]

Christina. Such a tired girl, Dave. . . . I want to be held on to and made much of. . . . I want to feel all safe and warm. . . . I want you to tell me that you're in love with me and that you enjoy being in love with me. Because just loving isn't enough and it's being in love that really matters. . . . Will you tell me all that, please, Dave?

David. [*Hugging her.*] Darling!

Christina. You haven't kissed me yet.

David. [*Complying, a trifle absent-mindedly.*] There!

Christina. [*As she draws back from him.*] That isn't what I call making love in a big way.

David. [*Repeating the kiss with more energy.*] Is that better?

Christina. There's still something lacking.

. . . What's the matter? There's nobody watching us.

David. That's a funny thing to say.

Christina. You take me right back to my first beau in Germany. He never got very far, either. All the English he knew was "water closet."

David. Chris! Shame on you!

Christina. Shame on *you,* making me take to low jokes to amuse you. . . . I love you.

David. Darling, darling, Chris!

Christina. I love you! I love you! [*For a moment she clings to him wildly.*] I hate being so far from you tonight, Dave. 'Way off there at the other end of the hall!

David. I'm none too pleased myself. It's just one of Mother's fool ideas.

[*He lowers his voice whenever he mentions his mother.*]

Christina. She naturally wanted you near *her*!

David. That's it. [*His eyes fall beneath her steady gaze.*] We mustn't talk so loud. We'll keep Mother awake. She can hear every sound we make.

Christina. Let her hear! It'll do her good!

David. That's no way to talk, Chris!

Christina. Excuse me. I didn't mean to snap. I've been fearfully shaken up tonight.

David. I know you have.

Christina. And I'm awfully tired.

David. Poor girl!

Christina. Poor Hester! . . . I don't feel like going to bed yet. I want to talk. Do you mind?

David. Go to it.

Christina. I've never come up against anything like this before; I've heard of it, but I've never met it. I don't know what to do about it. And it scares me.

David. What does?

Christina. I don't know how to tell you. [*Then, with sudden force.*] But I've got to tell you, Dave. I've got to tell you. There are no two ways about that.

David. What are you driving at?

Christina. Well . . . [*But she changes her mind.*] May I ask you a question? Rather an intimate one?

David. If you must!

Christina. Being your wife, I thought I might.

David. Shoot!

Christina. Do you look on me as apart from all other women? I mean, do you think of all the women in the world and then think of me quite, quite differently? Do you, Dave?

David. I'll bite. Do I?

Christina. Please answer me. It's awfully important to me just now.

David. Of course I do. . . . Why is it so important just now?

Christina. Because that's how I feel about you and all the other men in the world. Because that's what being in love must mean and being properly and happily married. Two people, a man and a woman, together by themselves, miles and miles from everybody, from *everybody* else, glancing around, now and then, at all the rest of mankind, at *all* the rest, Dave, and saying: "Are you still there? And getting along all right? Sure there's nothing we can do to help?"

David. Only we do help, don't we?

Christina. Only really if we feel that way about one another. Only *by* feeling that way.

David. That's pretty deep! You do go off on the damnedest tacks!

Christina. Don't you see how that feeling between a man and a woman is what keeps life going?

David. Is it?

Christina. What else could be strong enough?

David. Perhaps you're right. [*Then, unaccountably, he shies.*] But what's the idea in getting so worked up about it?

Christina. Because it matters so much, Dave . . . just now . . . that you and I feel that way about each other and that we go on feeling that way and exclude everybody, *everybody* else. Tell me you think so, too?

David. Sure, I think so. . . . [*Then, again he shies from her inner meaning.*] You're getting the worst habit of working yourself up over nothing!

Christina. Do you realize, Dave, that the blackest sinner on earth is the man . . . or woman . . . who breaks in on that feeling? Or tampers with it in any way? Or perverts it?

David. If you say so, I'll say he is.

Christina. He!

David. Huh?

Christina. Never mind. . . . Your brother didn't feel that way about poor Hester, did he?

David. Rob always was a funny egg.

Christina. Your mother calls him Robin! "Tweet! Tweet! What does the Birdie say?"

David. From all I can gather, Hester didn't feel much of *any* way about him.

Christina. I know better than that. . . . I've had that child on my hands for the past hour. I've learned an awful lot, Dave. About her, and *from* her.

David. Look here, Chris. . . . Don't you get mixed up in this business, will you?

Christina. I wonder if I'm not mixed up in it already.

David. Well, don't "take sides."

Christina. I wonder if I can help taking sides.

David. It's none of our business.

Christina. I wish I were sure of that. [*Baffled, she again shifts her approach.*] Poor little Hester goes tomorrow morning. How long are we staying?

Dave. Oh, I dunno.

Christina. A week?

David. We can't do less, can we?

Christina. Can't we?

David. Don't you want to? [*There is another pause before* CHRISTINA *shakes her head.* DAVID *frowns.*] You see what comes of taking things so hard? I'm just as distressed over what's happened as you are. Maybe more. But I certainly don't want to run away. It wouldn't be right. Mother'd never understand. I'd feel like a bum going off and leaving her in the lurch after this. Think what Rob's put her through today and what she'll have to go through with Hester's family and all her friends and everybody else before she's done!

Christina. She seems to be bearing up.

David. You can't be sure with Mother.

Christina. Can't you?

David. She's so damned game.

Christina. Is she?

David. Can't you see that? And, anyway, I've got to look around.

Christina. What at? The houses in Phelps Manor?

David. I know how you feel, Chris, about Mother's helping hand. But I can't be *throwing* away opportunities, now, can I? With the baby coming?

Christina. [*Gravely.*] No, Dave. Of course, you can't. Neither can I.

David. How do you mean?

Christina. Forgotten all about *my* opportunities, haven't you?

David. What opportunities?

Christina. My appointment.

David. Didn't Mother say she could scare up something for you here?

Christina. She thought she might "scare up" a place where I could "putter around" and keep myself "happy and contented" when the "real doctors" weren't working.

David. She didn't mean anything unkind, Chris. Just give Mother a chance and . . . What are you crying for?

Christina. [*Hotly untruthful.*] I'm not crying.

David. You are!

Christina. I can't help it. . . .

David. But what's the matter?

Christina. It doesn't look as if I'm to have much of a show for my eight years of hard work, does it?

David. Mother and I'll dope out something. I couldn't leave her now. You know that. And anyway, I've got to stay till I get my shirts washed. I've only got two left.

Christina. Then we stay, of course.

David. And I must say, Chris, that I don't think you're quite playing ball to judge my home and my family entirely on what you've seen tonight. Besides, the whole purpose of this visit was to bring you and Mother together and to show Mother that a lady scientist mayn't be as bad as she sounds. Because you and Mother have just got to hit it off, you know.

Christina. Have we?

David. You're apt to be impatient, Chris, and I'm afraid you're intolerant.

Christina. Those are bad faults in a scientist.

David. They're bad faults in anybody. . . . Now, you just give me time and you'll see how things straighten out.

Christina. Aren't you satisfied with the way our meeting has come off?

David. There's no use pretending it was ideal. I believe in facing the facts always. But don't you worry. Mother gets on *my* nerves sometimes. You just have to remember what a hard life she's had.

Christina. How has it been hard?

David. Oh, lots of ways. My father wasn't much, you know.

Christina. I didn't know. You've never mentioned him.

David. He died when I was five.

Christina. What was the matter with him? Women or drink?

David. Nothing like that. He just didn't amount to much.

Christina. Made a lot of money, didn't he?

David. Lots.

Christina. And left your mother rich. What other troubles has she had?

David. Well, her health.

Christina. It doesn't seem so bad.

David. It is, though. Heart. And I wish I could tell you half of what she's gone through for Rob and me.

Christina. Go on and tell me. I'd like to hear.

David. I've heard her say she was born without a selfish hair in her head.

Christina. No!

David. And that's about true. Why, I've seen her nurse Rob through one thing after another when she'd admit to me that she was twice as sick as he was. I've seen her come in here from taking care of him and she'd be half fainting with her bad heart, but there'd be nothing doing when I'd beg her to get him a nurse. She said we were her job and she just wouldn't give in. And the way she always took interest in everything we did. Why, when she used to come up to school, all the boys went just crazy about her.

Christina. I'm sure they did. [*But she turns the inquiry into more significant channels.*] How did your girl friends get on with her?

David. Oh, they loved her, too! Mother used to give us dances here.

Christina. Did she invite the girls you were in love with?

David. I never fell in love! Not really. Not till I met you.

Christina. Darling! [*She smiles rather absently.*] What was the name of the one your mother thought could wear my dress?

David. Clara Judd?

Christina. Weren't you sweet on Clara?

David. I dunno. What made you ask that?

Christina. Just something in the way your mother spoke of her this evening. It came back to me. Weren't you?

David. Mother thought so.

Christina. Used to pester you about Clara, didn't she?

David. She was afraid I was going to marry Clara.

Christina. I see. Anything wrong with her?

David. With Clara? No. Damn nice girl. You'll meet her.

Christina. Then why didn't your mother want you to marry her?

David. Thought I was too young.

Christina. When was it?

David. Summer after the war.

Christina. You weren't so young, were you?

David. You know Mother.

Christina. How about your brother? Did he used to fall in love a great deal?

David. I don't know that I'd call it "in love."

Christina. Why not?

David. It's the family skeleton. She was a chorus girl, my dear. She cost Mother twelve thousand berries.

Christina. That must have been jolly! Was she the only one or were there others?

David. There were plenty of others. Only they didn't have lawyers.

Christina. And then Hester?

David. Right.

Christina. Well, that's all very interesting.

David. What are you trying to prove?

Christina. An idea this affair of Hester's put into my head. And I must say, it fits in rather extraordinarily.

David. What does?

Christina. Your being too young to marry after the war and Robert's taking to wild women. . . . And you had to be three thousand miles from home to fall in love with me! Never mind. . . . That's enough of that! Now let me tell *you* something. Only you must promise not to get mad.

David. I won't get mad.

Christina. Promise?

David. Promise.

Christina. [*A deep breath, then:*] Shirts or no shirts, we've got to get out of here tomorrow.

David. [*As though she had stuck him with a pin.*] Now, Chris! Haven't we been over all that?

Christina. Yes. But not to the bottom of it.

David. What more is there to say?

Christina. [*With sudden violence.*] That a defenseless, trusting little girl has been cruelly treated! We've got to "take sides" with her, Dave!

David. What's the matter with Hester's own family? This is their business, not ours!

Christina. We owe it to ourselves to *make* it our business.

David. I don't see it.

Christina. Why don't you see it? What have you put over your eyes that keeps you from seeing it? Do you dare answer that?

David. Dare? What do you mean?

Christina. "Face the facts," Dave! "Face the facts!"

David. Rot! You're making a mountain out of a mole-hill!

Christina. Cruelty to children isn't a mole-hill!

David. You're exaggerating! Hester's engagement isn't the first that was ever broken.

Christina. Think how it was broken and by whom!

David. You just said she was in luck to be rid of Rob. I'll grant you that. I haven't any more use for Rob than you have.

Christina. Who stands behind Rob?

David. I don't know what you mean.

Christina. Don't you?

David. No.

Christina. All right, I'll tell you.

David. [*Quickly.*] You needn't. . . . Are you trying to pick a fight with me?

Christina. On the contrary. I'm asking you to stand by me. [*Her eyes corner him.*]

David. I won't go away and leave Mother in the lurch.

Christina. You see? You do know what I mean!

David. I don't! I'm just telling you I won't let Mother down.

Christina. You'd rather stand by your mother than by the right, wouldn't you?

David. Oh, the right?

Christina. Isn't Hester the right?

David. [*Cornered again.*] I can't help it if she is. I won't let Mother down.

Christina. You'll let *me* down.

David. Oh, Chris! It's late. Come on. Let's turn in.

Christina. You'd rather stand by your mother than by me, wouldn't you?

David. No, I wouldn't. I tell you Hester's none of our business.

Christina. You'll admit *this* is?

David. What is?

Christina. This! . . . Who comes first with you? Your mother or me?

David. Now what's the good of putting things that way?

Christina. That's what things come to! If your mother and I ever quarreled about anything, if it ever came up to you to choose between sticking by me and sticking by her, which would you stick by?

David. I'd . . . I'd try to do the right thing. . . .

Christina. That isn't an answer. That's another evasion.

David. But why ask such a question?

Christina. Because I love you. Because I've got to find out if you love me. And I'm afraid . . . I'm afraid. . . .

David. Why?

Christina. Because you won't see the facts behind all this. I'm trying to tell you what they are and you won't listen. You can't even hear me.

David. I *can* hear you. And a worse line of hooey I've never listened to in my life.

Christina. [*Gravely, but with steadily increasing fervor.*] Have you ever thought what it would be like to be trapped in a submarine in an accident? I've learned tonight what that kind of panic would be like. I'm in that kind of panic now, this minute. I've been through the most awful experience of my life tonight. And I've been through it alone. I'm still going through it alone. It's pretty awful to have to face such things alone. . . . No, don't interrupt me. I've got to get this off my chest. Ever since we've been married I've been coming across queer rifts in your feeling for me, like arid places in your heart. Such vast ones, too! I mean, you'll be my perfect lover one day, and the next I'll find myself floundering in sand, and alone, and you nowhere to be seen. We've never been really married, Dave. Only now and then, for a little while at a time, between your retirements into your arid places. . . . I used to wonder what you did there. At first, I thought you did your work there. But you don't. Your work's in my part of your heart, what there is of my part. Then I decided the other was just No-Man's Land. And I thought: little by little, I'll encroach upon it and pour my love upon it, like water on the western desert, and make it flower here and bear fruit there. I thought: then he'll be all alive, all free and all himself; not partly dead and tied and blind; not partly some one else—or nothing. You see, our marriage and your architecture were suffering from the same thing. They only worked a little of the time. I meant them both to work all the time. I meant you to work all the time and to win your way, *all* your way, Dave, to complete manhood. And that's a good deal farther than you've got so far. . . . Then we came here and this happened with Hester and your brother and you just stepped aside and did nothing about it! You went to bed. You did worse than that. You retired into your private wastes and sat tight. . . . I've shown you what you should do and you won't see it. I've called to you to come out to me, and you won't come. So now I've discovered what keeps you. Your mother keeps you. It isn't No-Man's Land at all. It's your mother's land. Arid, sterile, and your mother's! You won't let me get in there. Worse than that, you won't let life get in there! Or she won't! . . . That's what I'm afraid of, Dave—your mother's hold on you. And that's what's kept me from getting anywhere with you, all these months. I've seen what she can do with Robert. And what she's done to Hester. I can't help wondering what she may not do with you and to me and to the baby. That's why I'm asking you to take a stand on this business of Hester's, Dave. You'll never find the right any clearer than it is here. It's a kind of test case for me. Don't you see? What you decide about this is what you may, eventually, be expected to decide about . . . about our marriage.

David. [*A pause, then, with sullen violence.*] No! I'm damned if I see!

Christina. [*Breaking.*] Then I can't hope for much, can I? . . . I feel awfully like a lost soul, right now. . . . Oh, my God, what am I going to do! What am I going to do!

David. I hope you're going to behave. You ought to be ashamed. Just as I was bringing Mother around to you and . . .

Christina. [*Violently.*] You'd better think a little about bringing me around to your mother!

David. Chris!

Christina. Why should your mother and I get on?

David. Because you should, that's why. Because she's an older woman and my mother. And you know, just as well as I do . . .

Christina. I know a great deal better than you that your mother dislikes me fully as much as I dislike her. You're wasting your time trying to bring your mother and me together, because we won't be brought. You say you believe in facing the facts. Well, let's see you face that one!

David. I've never heard anything so outrageous. When you know what Mother means to me and what . . .

Christina. [*Desperate.*] Your mother! Your mother! Always your mother! She's got you back! Dave, her big boy, who ran off and got married! She's got you back!

David. I won't stand for any more of this. A man's mother is his mother.

Christina. [*Crescendo.*] And what's his wife, may I ask? Or doesn't she count?

David. This is morbid rot! She warned me you'd be jealous of her!

Christina. Did she?

David. But I never expected anything like this!

Christina. What's going to become of me?

David. I won't stand for any more. . . .

Christina. Hester's escaped, but I'm caught! I can't go back and be the old Christina again. She's done for. And Christina, your wife, doesn't even exist! That's the fact I've got to face! I'm going to have a baby by a man who belongs to another woman!

David. Damn it, Chris! Do you want Mother to hear you?

Christina. Do I not?

[MRS. PHELPS *stands in her door, white, but steady.*]

David. [*Turning, sees her.*] Oh . . . You *did* hear!

Mrs. Phelps. How could I help hearing every word that Christina said?

David. Oh, this is awful!

Mrs. Phelps. We know, now, where we stand, all three of us.

David. Chris, can't you tell her you didn't mean it?

Mrs. Phelps. [*Heroic sarcasm.*] Christina isn't one to say things she doesn't mean. And I have no intention of defending myself.

David. Mother, please! . . . Chris, you'd better beat it.

Mrs. Phelps. I ask her to stay. She has made me afraid ever to be alone with you again. She must have made you afraid to be alone with me.

David. Nonsense, Mother! She hasn't done anything of the sort. You'd better go, Chris. It's the least that you can do after what you've said.

Christina. The very least. I belong with Hester now. [*She goes quickly.*]

David. [*Turning wildly to his mother.*] I'll straighten everything out in the morning. I swear I will!

Mrs. Phelps. [*A very different, very noble tone.*] This is an old story, Dave, boy, and I'm on Christina's side just as I said I should be.

David. I can't have you talking like that, Mother!

Mrs. Phelps. I accept my fate. You have your own life to live with the woman you have chosen. No boy could have given me back the love I gave you. Go to Christina! Make your life with her! No bond binds you to me any longer.

David. That isn't true!

Mrs. Phelps. I'm not complaining. I'm only sorry for one thing. I'm only sorry to see you throw away your chance here, your great chance!

David. But I haven't thrown it away. I'll stay here and work for you, if you want me to.

Mrs. Phelps. Christina won't let you. You know that!

David. She's my wife, isn't she?

Mrs. Phelps. Think what that means, Dave! Think what that means!

David. And you're my mother. I'm thinking what that means, too!

Mrs. Phelps. Then it *isn't* good-by? Then I've still got my big boy, after all?

David. You bet you've got him!

Mrs. Phelps. [*Triumph.*] Oh, Dave! Dave! Dave!

David. Now, Mummy! [*But a sound downstairs distracts him.*] Hello! What's that? [*She listens, too.*]

Mrs. Phelps. Heavens, it isn't a fire, is it?

David. Wait . . . I'll see. . . .

[*He opens the door into the hall and stands listening.*]

Christina. [*Off stage and below.*] I went into her room and she wasn't there and then I looked for her and I found the dining-room window open.

Robert. [*Off stage and below.*] What do you think has happened?

Christina. [*Off stage and below.*] I don't like to imagine things, but . . .

Robert. [*Off stage and below.*] Hester, where are you?

Christina. [*Off stage and below.*] She's got away! I tell you, she's got away! I shouldn't have left her. . . .

David. [*Speaking during the above.*] What?

Mrs. Phelps. It's Christina and Robert.

David. Something's happened to Hester.

Mrs. Phelps. No!

David. Chris! What's going on?

Robert. [*Off stage.*] Hester! Where are you, Hester?

Christina. [*Appearing in the hall.*] Hester's got away, Dave. Out by the dining-room window. You'll have to get dressed and find her. She can't get to town tonight in this cold.

David. All right. We'll have a look.

Mrs. Phelps. The little fool! Let her go, Dave!

Christina. But, Mrs. Phelps, she isn't properly dressed. She didn't even take her coat. . . .

Robert. [*Still calling off stage and below.*] Hester! Where are you, Hester? Hester! . . . Oh, my God!

[CHRISTINA *has walked to the window to look out. She utters an inarticulate scream.*]

David. What is it, Chris?

Mrs. Phelps. Good heavens!

Christina. [*Strangled with horror.*] It's the pond! The holes in the pond! Quick, Dave, for heaven's sake!

David. What? . . . Oh! . . .

[*He runs out as* CHRISTINA *opens the window.*]

Mrs. Phelps. Dave! . . . [*To* CHRISTINA.] What is it you say?

Robert. [*Off stage and below.*] Dave! For God's sake! Hold on, Hester! Don't struggle! [DAVID'S *shouts join his.*]

Christina. [*As she collapses on the bed.*] The pond! . . . I can't look. . . .

Mrs. Phelps. Oh, I've no patience with people who have hysterics!

Christina. Mrs. Phelps, the girl's drowning!

Mrs. Phelps. Oh, no! . . . Not that! [*She, too, goes to the window, but recoils in horror from what she sees.*] They'll save her, won't they? They must . . . they must save her. . . . If only . . . [*Then a new fear overwhelms her.*] If only those two boys don't catch pneumonia! [*And she leaps to the window to call after her sons as they race, shouting, across the snow.*] Robin, you're not dressed! Dave, get your coat! Are you crazy? Do you *want* to catch pneumonia?

CURTAIN

ACT THREE

The living-room again, and the next morning.

[MRS. PHELPS *is wearing a simple house dress and busily fixing a great many flowers which she takes from boxes strewn about the stage. After she has been so occupied for a few seconds,* ROBERT *enters.*]

Robert. The doctor's gone.

Mrs. Phelps. [*Surprised.*] Without seeing me?

Robert. It seems so.

Mrs. Phelps. Doesn't that seem very strange to you, Robin? Of course, I thought it best not to go up to Hester's room with him. In view of the perfectly unreasonable attitude she's taken toward me. But I should have supposed, naturally, that he'd have made his report to me.

Robert. He says she may as well go today. He says traveling won't be as bad for her as staying here.

Mrs. Phelps. Did he say that to you?

Robert. I couldn't face him. *They* told him the whole story.

Mrs. Phelps. Christina and Hester? [ROBERT *nods.*] I might have known they would. . . . And he listened to them and never so much as asked for me?

Robert. What of it?

Mrs. Phelps. He'll never enter this house again!

Robert. So *he* said! He also said there's nothing the matter with your heart and never has been anything the matter with it. He said it would take a stick of dynamite to kill you.

Mrs. Phelps. Damned homeopath!

Robert. And that isn't the worst.

Mrs. Phelps. What more?

Robert. He said that I'd always been a rotter.

Mrs. Phelps. Oh?

Robert. And that I couldn't have been anything else—with such a mother.

[*There is venom in this last.* MRS. PHELPS's *lips stiffen under it.*]

Mrs. Phelps. I think you might have spared me that, Robin.

Robert. I didn't mean to be nasty.

Mrs. Phelps. No. Still, there are things one doesn't repeat to sensitive people. [*But a dark foreboding will not be downed.*] Somehow, though, I can't help feeling that . . .

[*She does not say what she sees in the future.*]

Robert. Neither can I.

[*She looks at him in quick fear. Then she returns to her flowers with a shrug.*]

Mrs. Phelps. Oh, well! There can't have been much wrong with the girl if she's able to go this morning.

Robert. Thank God for that. [*Then, with level-eyed cruelty:*] It might have been serious, though, after what you did to the telephone. Because we couldn't have reached a soul, you know. And without Christina in the house . . .

Mrs. Phelps. How was I to know the little fool wanted to drown herself?

Robert. [*Shuddering.*] For heaven's sake, don't put it that way.

Mrs. Phelps. How do *you* put it?

Robert. She tried to get away, that's all. And she got lost in the dark and . . .

Mrs. Phelps. I tell you, she tried to kill herself. I've always suspected there was insanity in her family. She had a brother who was an aviator in the war. Everybody knows that aviators are lunatics. Her own conduct has never been what I should call normal. Everything points to insanity. That's another reason why you shouldn't have married her. Because we've never had any of that in our family. Except your father's Bright's disease. I shall certainly tell every one that Hester is insane.

Robert. Perhaps that *will* make things simpler.

Mrs. Phelps. As to the telephone, it's the only thing I've ever done to be ashamed of, and I said as much when I did it. She made me angry with her wanton attacks on you.

Robert. I didn't hear any wanton attacks.

Mrs. Phelps. Where were you?

Robert. Out there in the hall.

Mrs. Phelps. You couldn't have heard the things she muttered under her breath.

Robert. [*An incredulous sneer.*] No! [*There is a pause, sullen on his part, troubled on hers.*] We're just like Macbeth and Lady Macbeth, aren't we?

Mrs. Phelps. For heaven's sake, how?

Robert. We've got into a mess we can't ever get out of. We'll have to get in deeper and deeper until *we* go mad and . . .

Mrs. Phelps. Don't be ridiculous.

Robert. I'm sorry, Mother, but I can't help regretting.

Mrs. Phelps. Regretting what?

Robert. [*Low.*] Hester.

Mrs. Phelps. Nonsense, Robin! I tell you . . .

Robert. What do you know about it? Do you understand me any better than Hester did?

Mrs. Phelps. How *can* you, Robin? I not understand you? Haven't I always told you that however David may take after his father, you are *my* son?

Robert. What's that got to do with it?

Mrs. Phelps. Robin!

Robert. If I wasn't sure that I *loved* Hester, how on earth can I be sure that I *didn't* love her? I don't know this minute whether I loved her or not. I only know that I'll regret losing her all my life long. [*A movement of exasperation from his mother stops him. Then he concludes:*] Maybe Dave's right about me. Maybe I *am* too weak to love any one.

Mrs. Phelps. [*Frightened—to herself.*] Dave didn't say *that!*

Robert. He said I hadn't any guts.

Mrs. Phelps. Ugh! That horrible word! No, Robin. You must put all such thoughts aside.

Robert. I suppose I'll have to take your word for it. [*Then with sudden, cold fury:*] But I won't next time!

Mrs. Phelps. Robin! You're not holding *me* responsible?

Robert. Who put the idea in my head? Who persuaded me? Who made me promise?

Mrs. Phelps. Are you implying that *I* came between you?

Robert. Well, if you didn't, who did?

Mrs. Phelps. Robin! You ought to be ashamed!

Robert. Think so?

Mrs. Phelps. That *you* should turn on me! Some day you'll regret this. It won't be Hester, but *this* that you'll regret. . . . When it's too late.

[*And from force of habit her hand steals to her heart.*]

Robert. I dare say I've got a life full of regrets ahead of me.

[*He walks sullenly to the window.*]

Mrs. Phelps. You frighten me, Robin! I don't know you like this.

Robert. Don't you?

[*There is a pause.* MRS. PHELPS *stares at him in growing horror. He looks out of the window.*]

Mrs. Phelps. No.

Robert. [*Looking out, his back to her.*] That's too bad. . . . There's Dave putting up danger signs all around the pond! Isn't it like him! After it's too late. [*She turns away from him and dully goes on with her flowers, carrying a bowl of them over to the piano.* ROBERT *watches her coldly. Then a sudden frown contracts his brow and he moves toward her.*] Mother!

Mrs. Phelps. What?

Robert. Don't put those flowers there! They're too low!

Mrs. Phelps. Fix them yourself.

Robert. [*Changing them with a jar of something else.*] Isn't that better?

Mrs. Phelps. Much. What an eye you have!

Robert. Perhaps I'll develop it some day.

Mrs. Phelps. Would you like to?

Robert. I've got to do something.

Mrs. Phelps. [*Darkly.*] I quite agree. Every young man should have some expression.

[*Then, suddenly and involuntarily, the boy reverts and is a child again.*]

Robert. What are we going to do, Mother?

Mrs. Phelps. [*Low.*] Do?

Robert. What are we going to do, you and I? We're in the same boat, you know.

Mrs. Phelps. [*Lower.*] I don't know what you mean.

Robert. Well, what am I going to do, then? I can't stay here and face people after this!

Mrs. Phelps. What will there be to face?

Robert. [*Crescendo.*] You know as well as I do. This story'll be all over this damn town. And Hester's people aren't going to keep quiet in New York. Her brothers go everywhere I go. My friends will begin cutting me in the street.

Mrs. Phelps. If we say she's insane?

Robert. What difference will that make?

Mrs. Phelps. [*Very low.*] The *Paris* sails on Saturday.

Robert. [*Pause, then, tremulously.*] What of it?

Mrs. Phelps. We might go to Washington to hurry our passports.

Robert. Could we get passage, though?

Mrs. Phelps. [*Slowly.*] I've already wired for it. This morning.

Robert. I see. . . . Then we're to sneak away like two guilty fugitives!

Mrs. Phelps. [*Avoiding his eye.*] Sh! Don't say such things!

[DAVID *enters, his cheeks stung crimson by the cold.*]

David. Phew, it's cold! The pond'll be frozen again by tomorrow if this keeps up. What's the doc say about Hester?

Robert. She's leaving us today.

David. I'm glad she's well enough.

Mrs. Phelps. There never was anything the matter with her.

David. It's easy to see, Mother, that you don't often bathe in that pond in zero weather.

Mrs. Phelps. I hope I have more self-control. Robin, will you see, please, that the car is ready for Hester?

Robert. Yes. [*He goes.*]

David. Anybody seen Chris?

Mrs. Phelps. Not I.

David. No. I suppose not. . . . What's the idea in the floral display?

Mrs. Phelps. I felt I had to have flowers about me.

David. That sounds pretty Green Hattish. . . . It has a festive look, too. I don't see what there is to celebrate.

Mrs. Phelps. [*Noble tragédienne that she is.*] Last night, at a single blow, beauty was stricken out of my life. I can't live without beauty, Dave. You must know that. So I went to the florist this morning and bought these. They comfort me . . . a little.

David. [*That worried look again.*] I've been thinking, Mother, that maybe, all things considered, after last night, it will be as well for me to take Chris away on Wednesday, say.

Mrs. Phelps. If you like.

David. We can come back later. After things have cooled down.

Mrs. Phelps. Later, I hope, and often.

David. Time does make things easier, doesn't it?

Mrs. Phelps. They say so.

David. When scientists get these wild ideas and fly off the handle, they're just as embarrassed afterwards as any one else would be.

Mrs. Phelps. Naturally.

David. And then Hester's running away and the telephone being busted and all. . . .

Mrs. Phelps. I quite understand.

David. I knew you would.

Mrs. Phelps. [*The boxes and papers all stowed away, she sits down to business.*]

What I'm wondering now, though, is what I'm to do with Robin. And I'm afraid you've got to help me with him.

David. I'll do anything I can.

Mrs. Phelps. If I were well and able to stand the things I used to stand before my heart went back on me—because it *has* gone back on me—and before my blood pressure got so high . . . I shouldn't trouble you. But as I am, and with Robin on the verge of a complete breakdown . . .

David. But Rob isn't . . .

Mrs. Phelps. Oh, yes, he is, Dave! He said things to me before you came in that no son of mine would dream of saying unless he had something the matter with him. I've got to get him away.

David. Send him abroad.

Mrs. Phelps. I don't think he ought to go alone. He can't face things alone. He's like his father, in that. You're *my* son, you know. That's why I always turn to you.

David. Why not go with him?

Mrs. Phelps. Because I'm really not well enough in case anything should happen. . . . And I don't know what to do. Oh, Dave, boy, do you think . . .

David. What?

Mrs. Phelps. That Christina could spare you for a little? Just a few weeks? Just long enough to get Rob and me settled in some restful place? Do you think she would?

David. There's no need of that!

Mrs. Phelps. Of course, I'd love to have Christina, too. Only I'm afraid that *would* be asking too much. I mean, making her put off her work when she's so set on it.

David. But Rob isn't going to give you any trouble.

Mrs. Phelps. Do you think I'd ask such a sacrifice of you . . . and Christina, if I weren't sure it's absolutely necessary? Oh, I'm not thinking of myself. I no longer matter. Except that I shouldn't want to die abroad with only Robin there, in his present condition.

David. Don't talk that way, Mother!

Mrs. Phelps. Why not? I'm not asking you to be sorry for me. It's Robin I'm thinking of. Because we haven't done all that we should for Robin. And now that I'm old . . . and sick . . . dying . . .

[*She breaks down.*]

David. You're not, Mother!

Mrs. Phelps. [*Weeping hysterically.*] I can't cope with him. He'll slip back again to drinking and fast women . . .

David. Get hold of yourself, Mother!

Mrs. Phelps. [*More hysterical.*] And when I think of what I might have done for him and realize that it's too late, that I haven't any more time . . . only a few months . . . or weeks . . . I don't know . . . I . . .

[*She really becomes quite faint.*]

David. [*Snatching her hand in terror.*] Mother, what's the matter? Are you ill?

Mrs. Phelps. [*Recovering by inches as she gasps for breath.*] No! It's nothing . . . I . . . Just give me a minute . . . Don't call any one . . . I'll be all right. . . . There! . . . That's better!

David. You scared me to death.

Mrs. Phelps. I scare myself sometimes. You see I do need *somebody's* help.

David. Yes, I see you do.

Mrs. Phelps. And so I thought: well, since Dave *is* going to build my houses in Phelps Manor. . . . You're not going to disappoint me there, I hope?

David. Oh, no!

Mrs. Phelps. Well, then, you won't want to start in that New York office.

David. Why not?

Mrs. Phelps. When you'll be leaving so soon to begin here? They wouldn't want you.

David. I hadn't thought of that.

Mrs. Phelps. And so I thought: well, he can't begin here until April, anyway, and that leaves him with two idle months on his hands when he might be drawing plans and getting ideas abroad. Think it over, Dave boy.

David. You certainly are a great planner, Mother.

Mrs. Phelps. I make such good plans!

David. When would you be sailing?

Mrs. Phelps. Well, . . . I *had* thought . . . vaguely . . . of sailing on the *Paris* . . . Saturday . . .

David. Good Lord! Give a man time to think! I want to do the right thing, but I couldn't leave Chris. . . . Not with the baby coming, you know.

Mrs. Phelps. But you'll be home in plenty of time for that.

David. That may all be, but, just the same, I wouldn't feel right to leave her.

[Robert *returns.*]

Mrs. Phelps. I've just been telling Dave about our wonderful plans, Robin, and he's so enthusiastic! I shouldn't wonder if he came along with us.

[*A sign to* David *to play up.*]

Robert. What *are* the plans?

Mrs. Phelps. Why, your going abroad to study interior decorating, of course.

[Robert *looks surprised.*]

David. Oh, is Rob going to do that?

Robert. Any objections?

David. I think it's just the job for you. Painting rosebuds on bathtubs.

Robert. I can make your houses look like something after you've finished with them.

Mrs. Phelps. [*Ecstatically.*] My two boys in partnership! Oh, that's always been my dream! Oh, how simply things come straight when people are willing to coöperate and make little sacrifices! If there's one thing I pride myself on, it's my willingness to make little sacrifices. Here we are, we three, a moment ago all at odds with life and with each other; now united and of a single mind . . .

David. This is all very fine. But don't you forget that I've got to talk to Christina . . .

[*But* CHRISTINA *has opened the door upon his very words. She is dressed as she was when she first came to the house. She wears her hat and her fur coat and carries her bag in her hand.*]

Christina. [*Speaking as she enters.*] Well, now's your chance, Dave. What have you got to talk to me about?

David. [*Staring at her.*] What's the idea, Chris?

Christina. [*Setting the bag down by the door.*] I'm going away with Hester. Are you coming, too?

David. [*staggered.*] Now?

Christina. In a few minutes. I came down ahead. No, don't go, Mrs. Phelps. And won't you stay, too, Robert? I think it's best that we should thrash this question out together, here and now, for good and all.

Mrs. Phelps. What question, Christina?

Christina. The David question, Mrs. Phelps. Whether David is going on from this point as your son or as my husband.

Robert. What?

Christina. Isn't that the issue?

[*She asks the question less of* DAVID *than of* MRS. PHELPS, *who turns to her sons in terror.*]

Mrs. Phelps. I can't go through this a second time!

David. [*Quieting her with a gesture.*] No one expects you to. . . . [*To* CHRISTINA, *pleading, almost pathetically.*] You're not going to begin all that again, Chris?

Christina. I'm afraid I am.

David. But just as I was getting everything all straightened out . . .

Christina. Were you doing that?

David. If only you'll leave things be, they'll be all right. You may believe it or not . . .

Christina. I can't believe it and I can't leave things be. Oh, I'd walk out without a word, even loving you as I do, if I thought this state of affairs made any one of you happy.

Robert. What state of affairs?

Christina. The state of affairs you've all been living in and suffering from, for so long.

Mrs. Phelps. You might let us judge our own happiness.

Christina. I might, if you had any. But you haven't.

Robert. You're quite sure of that?

Christina. Quite, Robert. You're all of you perfectly miserable! Am I wrong?

Mrs. Phelps. Christina! Please!

Robert. Thank you for being sorry for us!

Christina. You give me such good reason, Robert. Such awfully good reason! Because you're not really bad people, you know. You're just wrong, all wrong, terribly, pitifully, all of you, and you're trapped . . .

Mrs. Phelps. What we say in anger, we sometimes regret, Christina. . . .

Christina. Oh, I'm not angry. I was, but I've got over it. I rather fancy myself, now, as a sort of scientific Nemesis. I mean to strip this house and to show it up for what it really is. I mean to show you up, Mrs. Phelps. Then Dave can use his own judgment.

Mrs. Phelps. [*Blank terror at this attack.*] Oh! Dave, I . . .

David. Now, Mother! Chris! Haven't you any consideration for our feelings? Are they nothing to you?

Christina. I'm trying to save my love, my home, my husband, and my baby's father. Are they nothing to you?

David. But surely I can be both a good son and a good husband!

Christina. Not if your mother knows it, you can't!

Mrs. Phelps. [*A last desperate snatch at dignity.*] If you'll excuse me, I'd rather not stay to be insulted again. [*She is going.*]

Christina. You'll probably lose him if you don't stay, Mrs. Phelps! [MRS. PHELPS *stays.* CHRISTINA *turns to* DAVID.] No, Dave. There's no good in any more pretending. Your mother won't allow you to divide your affections and I refuse to go on living with you on any basis she will allow.

Mrs. Phelps. I cannot see that this is necessary.

Christina. It's a question a great many young wives leave unsettled, Mrs. Phelps. I'm not going to make that mistake. [*Back to* DAVE *again.*] You see, Dave, I'm not beating about the bush. I'm not persuading you or wasting any time on tact. Do you want your chance or don't you? Because, if you don't, I'll have to get over being in love with you as best I can and . . .

David. I wish you wouldn't talk this way, Chris!

Christina. Are you coming with me? On the understanding that, for the present, until your affections are definitely settled on your wife and child, you avoid your mother's society entirely. Well? What do you say?

David. I don't know what to say.

Christina. You never do, Dave darling.

David. I'm too shocked. I've never been so shocked in my life.

Christina. [*A glance at her wrist watch.*] Just take your time and think before you speak.

David. I don't mean that I don't know what to say about taking my chance, as you call it. I can answer that by reminding you of your duty to me. I can answer that by calling all this what I called it last night. Morbid rot! But I *am* shocked at your talking this way about my mother and to her face, too!

Christina. Is that your answer?

David. No, it isn't! But a man's mother *is* his mother.

Christina. So you said last night. I'm not impressed. An embryological accident is no grounds for honor. Neither is a painful confinement, for I understand, Mrs. Phelps, that you're very proud of the way you bore your children. I know all about the legend of yourself as a great woman that you've built up these thirty years for your sons to worship. It hasn't taken me long to see that you're not fit to be any one's mother.

David. Chris!

Robert. [*Speaking at the same time.*] See here, now!

Mrs. Phelps. Let her go on! Let her go on! She will explain that or retract it!

Christina. I'm only too glad to explain. It's just what I've been leading up to. And I'll begin by saying that if my baby ever feels about me as your sons feel about you, I hope that somebody will take a little enameled pistol and shoot me, because I'll deserve it.

Mrs. Phelps. [*Going again.*] I've been insulted once too often.

Christina. I don't mean to insult you. I'm being as scientific and impersonal as possible.

Robert. Good God!

Christina. [*Regardless.*] Speaking of insults, though, what explanation can *you* offer *me* for your rudeness to me as a guest in your house?

Mrs. Phelps. I have not been rude to you.

Christina. You have been appallingly rude. Second question: Why do you resent the fact that I am going to have a baby?

Mrs. Phelps. I don't resent it.

Christina. Then why are you so churlish about it?

Mrs. Phelps. Your indelicacy about it would have . . .

Christina. That's another evasion. You're afraid that baby will give me another and stronger hold on David and you mean to separate David and me if it's humanly possible.

Mrs. Phelps. I do not! I do not!

Christina. Did you or did you not bend every effort to separate Hester and Robert?

Mrs. Phelps. I most certainly did not!

Christina. Then how do you account for the deliberate and brutal lies you told Hester about Robert? Because she did lie to Hester about you, Robert. She told Hester that you never wanted to marry her.

Robert. [*Aghast.*] Mother, you didn't!

Mrs. Phelps. Of course I didn't!

Christina. [*Joan of Arc raising the siege of Orleans.*] I heard her. And I heard her call both of you back, last night, when you ran out to save Hester from drowning. I heard her call you back from saving a drowning girl for fear of your catching cold. I heard her. I heard her.

David. [*Shaken.*] You shouldn't have called us, Mother!

Christina. Can she deny that her one idea is to keep her sons dependent on her? Can she deny that she opposes any move that either one of you makes toward independence? Can she deny that she is outraged by your natural impulses toward other women?

Mrs. Phelps. [*Furious.*] I deny all of it!

Christina. You may deny it until you're black in the face; every accusation I make is true! You belong to a type that's very common in this country, Mrs. Phelps—a type of self-centered, self-pitying, son-devouring tigress, with unmentionable proclivities suppressed on the side.

David. Chris!

Christina. I'm not at all sure it wouldn't be a good idea, just as an example to the rest of the tribe, to hang one of your kind every now and then!

Robert. Really!

Christina. Oh, there are normal mothers around; mothers who *want* their children to be men and women and take care of themselves; mothers who are people, too, and don't have to be afraid of loneliness after they've outlived their motherhood; mothers who can look on their children as people and enjoy them as people and not be forever holding on to them and pawing them and fussing about their health and singing them lullabies and tucking them up as though they were everlasting babies. But you're *not* one of the normal ones, Mrs. Phelps! Look at your sons, if you don't believe me. You've destroyed Robert. You've swallowed him up until there's nothing left of him but an effete make-believe. Now he's gone melancholy mad and disgraced himself. And Dave! Poor Dave! The best he can do is dodge the more desperate kinds of unhappiness by pretending! How he survived at all is beyond me. If you're choking a bit on David, now, that's my fault, because you'd have swallowed him up, too, if I hadn't come along to save him! Talk about cannibals! You and your kind beat any cannibals I've ever heard of! And what makes you doubly deadly and dangerous is that people admire you and your kind. They actually admire you! You professional mothers! . . . You see, I'm taking this differently from that poor child upstairs. She's luckier than I am, too. She isn't married to one of your sons. Do you remember what she said about children yesterday? "Have 'em. Love 'em. And leave 'em be."

Mrs. Phelps. You are entitled to your opinions, Christina, just as I am to mine and David is to his. I only hope that he sees the kind of woman he's married. I hope he sees the sordidness, the hardness, the nastiness she offers him for his life.

Christina. [*An involuntary cry of pain.*] I'm not nasty! I'm not!

Mrs. Phelps. What have you to offer David?

Christina. A hard time. A chance to work on his own. A chance to *be* on his own. Very little money on which to share with me the burden of raising his child. The pleasure of my society. The solace of my love. The enjoyment of my body. To which I have reason to believe he is not indifferent.

Mrs. Phelps. [*Revolted.*] Ugh!

Christina. Can you offer so much?

Mrs. Phelps. I offer a mother's love. Or perhaps you scoff at that?

Christina. Not if it's kept within bounds. I hope my baby loves me. I'm practically certain I'm going to love my baby. But within bounds.

Mrs. Phelps. And what do you mean by within bounds?

Christina. To love my baby with as much and as deep respect as I hope my baby will feel for me if I deserve its respect. To love my baby unpossessingly; above all, unromantically.

Mrs. Phelps. I suppose that's biology! You don't know the difference between good and evil!

Christina. As a biologist, though, I do know the difference between life and death. And I know sterility when I see it. I doubt if evil is any more than a fancy name for sterility. And sterility, of course, is what you offer Dave. Sterility for his mind as well as for his body. That's your professional mother's stock in trade. Only we've been over that, haven't we? Well, Dave! How about it?

Robert. I think this has gone far enough!

Mrs. Phelps. No! This woman has got to answer me one question.

Christina. Willingly. What is it?

Mrs. Phelps. How old were you when you married?

Christina. The same age I am now. Twenty-nine.

Mrs. Phelps. I was twenty.

Christina. Just Hester's age.

Mrs. Phelps. [*Riding over her.*] I was twenty and my husband was fifteen years older than I. Oh, thirty-five isn't old, but he was a widower, too, and an invalid. Every one told me I'd made a great match. And I thought I had. But before we'd been married a week, I saw my illusions shattered. I knew at the end of a week how miserable and empty my marriage was. He was good to me. He made very few demands on me. But he never dreamed of bringing the least atom of happiness into my life. Or of romance. . . . Only a woman who has lived without romance knows how to value it. . . . That isn't true of my life either. I didn't live without romance. I found it . . . and I'm proud to have found it where you say it doesn't belong . . . in motherhood. I found it in my two babies. In Dave first and in Robin four years later. I found it in doing for them myself all those things which, nowadays, nurses and governesses are hired to do. To spare mothers! I never asked to be spared. . . . Their father died. The night he died, Robin had croup and I had to make the final choice between my duties. I stayed with Robin. You, with your modern ideas and your science, Christina, would you have chosen differently? I knew the difference between life and death that night. And I've known it for every step of the way I battled for Robin's health, every step as I taught Dave his gentleness and his generosity. . . .

If I made my mistakes, and I'm only human . . . I'm sorry for them. But I can point to my two sons and say that my mistakes could not have been serious ones. . . . Think! I was a widow, rich, and very pretty, at twenty-five. Think what that means! But I had found my duty and I never swerved from it. . . . There was one man in particular. A fine man. But I resisted. I knew that second marriage was not for me. Not when I had my sons. I put them first, always. . . . I shall not stoop to answer any of the foulnesses you have charged me with. They are beneath my dignity as a woman and my contempt as a mother. No, there is one I cannot leave unanswered. That word "sterility." Sterility is what I offer David, you say. I wonder, is sterility David's word for all he has had of me these thirty years? Let him answer that for himself. All my life I have saved to launch my two boys on their careers, saved in vision as well as in money. I don't offer my sons a love half dedicated to selfish, personal ambition. I don't offer them careers limited by the demands of other careers. I offer David a clear field ahead and a complete love to sustain him, a mother's love, until a real marriage, a suitable marriage may be possible for him. And I do *not* deny that I would cut off my right hand and burn the sight out of my eyes to rid my son of you! . . . That is how I answer your impersonal science, Christina.

Christina. [*Before either of the boys can speak.*] I see! . . . Well. . . . It's a very plausible and effective answer. And I'm sure you mean it and I believe it's sincere. But it *is* the answer of a woman whose husband let her down pretty hard and who turned for satisfaction to her sons. . . . I'm almost sorry I can't say more for it, but I can't. . . . [*She turns from* Mrs. Phelps *to the two sons.*] It's a pity she didn't marry again. Things would have been so much better for both of you if she had. [*Then, with an increasing force, to* David.] But the fact remains, Dave, that she did separate you and me last night and that she separated us because she couldn't bear the thought of our sleeping together. [*They flinch at this, but she downs them.*] And she couldn't bear that because she refuses to believe that you're a grown man and capable of desiring a woman. And that's because, grown man that you are, down, down in the depths of her, she still wants to suckle you at her breast!

David. [*A cry of horror.*] Chris!

Robert. [*At the same time.*] Good God!

Mrs. Phelps. [*At the same time.*] No!

Christina. You find that picture revolting, do you? Well, so it is. . . . I can't wait any longer for your answer, Dave.

David. I don't think you've any sense of decency left in you. Of all the filthy, vile . . .

Christina. I'm sorry you feel that way.

David. How else *can* I feel?

Christina. Is that your answer?

David. I want to do the right thing, but . . .

Christina. Remember me, won't you, on Mother's Day! [*Then she calls out.*] Are you ready, Hester?

David. You make things mighty hard, Chris, for a man who knows what fair play is and gratitude and all those other things I naturally feel for my mother.

Christina. Do I?

David. What do you expect me to say?

Christina. I don't know. I've never known. That's been the thrill of it. [Hester, *dressed for her journey, appears in the door and stands beside* Christina. Christina's *arm encircles the younger girl's shoulders.*] It's time, Hester.

Hester. Isn't David coming with us?

Christina. I'm afraid not.

Hester. Oh, Christina!

Christina. Sssh! Never mind. It can't be helped.

Robert. [*Breaking out.*] Hester! Hester! Couldn't we try again? Couldn't you . . .

Hester. What?

Robert. I mean . . . what are you going to do . . . now?

Hester. I don't know. [*Then a smile comes through.*] Yes, I do, too, know. I'm going to marry an orphan.

Christina. [*A long look at* David.] Good-by, Dave.

David. [*Desperately pleading.*] Chris, you can't! It isn't fair to me!

Christina. [*Still looking at him.*] I'm sorry it's come to this. . . . It might easily have been so . . .

[*Her voice chokes with crying. She picks up her bag where she put it down beside the door and goes quickly out.* Hester, *with a reproachful glance at* David, *follows her.* David *stands rigid.* Mrs. Phelps *watches him.* Robert *covers his face with his hands. Then the front door slams and* David *comes suddenly to life.*]

David. [*A frantic cry.*] Chris! [*He turns excitedly to his mother.*] I'm sorry, Mother, but I guess I'll have to go.

Mrs. Phelps. [*Reeling.*] No, Dave! No! No!

David. I guess she's right.

Mrs. Phelps. Oh, no! You mustn't say that! You mustn't say that!

David. [*Holding her off from him.*] I can't help it. She said we were trapped. We *are* trapped. I'm trapped.

Mrs. Phelps. [*Absolutely beyond herself.*] No! No! She isn't right! She can't be right! I won't believe it!

David. [*Breaking loose from her.*] I can't help that!

Mrs. Phelps. [*Speaking at the same time.*] For God's sake, Dave, don't go with her! Not with that awful woman, Dave! That wicked woman! For God's sake don't leave me for her, Dave! [*She turns wildly to* ROBERT.] You know it isn't true, Robin! You know it was vile, what she said! Tell him! Tell him! [*But he is gone.*] Dave! My boy! My boy! My boy! Oh, my God! Dave! She isn't right! She isn't, Dave! Dave! Dave! [*The front door slams a second time. An awful pause, then:*] He's gone.

Robert. [*Uncovering his face.*] Who? Dave?

Mrs. Phelps. Can you see them from the window?

Robert. [*Looking out.*] Yes. . . . They're talking. . . . Now he's kissed her and taken the suitcase. . . . Now he's helping Hester . . . Hester into the car. . . . Now he's getting in. . . . Now they're starting.

Mrs. Phelps. I loved him too much. I've been too happy. Troubles had to come. I must be brave. I must bear my troubles bravely.

Robert. [*Turning to her.*] Poor Mother!

Mrs. Phelps. I must remember that I still have one of my great sons. I must keep my mind on that.

Robert. [*A step or two toward her.*] That's right, Mother.

Mrs. Phelps. And we'll go abroad, my great Robin and I, and stay as long as ever we please.

Robert. [*As he kneels beside her.*] Yes, Mother.

Mrs. Phelps. [*Her voice growing stronger as that deeply religious point of view of hers comes to her rescue.*] And you must remember what David, in his blindness, has forgotten. That mother love suffereth long and is kind; envieth not, is not puffed up, is not easily provoked; beareth all things; believeth all things; hopeth all things; endureth all things. . . . At least, I think *my* love does?

Robert. [*Engulfed forever.*] Yes, Mother.

CURTAIN

"THE HAIRY APE"*

[A Comedy of Ancient and Modern Life in Eight Scenes]

By

EUGENE O'NEILL

EUGENE O'NEILL † IS NOT ONLY AMERica's outstanding playwright; he is also chief of her dramatic rebels. But his rebellion is not against institutions or individuals; it is the more radical one aimed at spiritual slavery and effete convention. He is the dramatic apostle of a new vitality for man and art. His plays are a prologue to the great emancipation—the freeing of the human spirit. His leading characters are recruited from the ranks of those who, perhaps like himself, are the victims of a hypocritical civilization that represses and tortures the soul, while it romantically proclaims its liberty. Enmeshed in a confusion of restraints and taboos, social, religious, and moral, they contend with tragic futility for self-expression. Even their goals of happiness are illusory. For most of them there is only defeat. But in the struggle each achieves a symbolic grandeur that is O'Neill's chief contribution to our theater.

Man's good, he seems to say, is in courageous striving, if only he is true to his instinctive faith in his own spiritual value against the assaults of man-made conventions. In such strife he finds joy. When reproached for not writing happier plays, he replied in his master Strindberg's vein:

"Sure I'll write about happiness if I can happen to meet up with that luxury, and find it sufficiently dramatic and in harmony with any deep rhythm in life. But happiness is a word. What does it mean? Exaltation; an intensified feeling of the significant worth of man's being and becoming? Well, if it means that—and not a mere smirking contentment with one's lot—I know there is more of it in one real tragedy than in all the happy-ending plays ever written. It's merely present-day judgment to think of tragedy as unhappy!"

O'Neill came to this rebellion from a sousing in the romantic sentimentality of the theater. As son of a great romantic actor he early acquired a loathing for the stuff of his father's dramas, in several of which, like the *Count of Monte Cristo,* he had to act for his bread. He was soon at work on a series of short plays, the stark realism of which shocked his father and seemed unsuited to the polite theater of that day. Since O'Neill knew seamen, as no other dramatist has ever known them, he made them his usual dramatic material, presenting them frankly as he had observed them. One of these sea plays, *Bound East for Cardiff,* he offered to the newly organized Wharf Theatre at Provincetown, where he was summering. The company gave it in their second bill. It was surprisingly successful. From that afternoon in 1916 until the early twenties, they and O'Neill worked together in that now historic campaign of the Provincetown Players to create a new American drama to replace a staling convention.

Even in the earlier sketches there was the kernel of the later O'Neill. With all his bluntness and fidelity to life went the poet's vision of a deeper meaning than surfaces alone could convey. Many of his characters were impelled by some purpose beyond themselves, some vision of happiness toward which they struggled—often blindly, always tragically. In the death ravings of a seaman in *Bound East for Cardiff* there are fragments of such meaning.

But, above all, O'Neill is an instinctive dramatist and master of theatrical effect. As restive in the limitations of the theater as in those imposed upon the mind, he has sought fresh forms of presentation for what he calls "the behind life." In *Emperor Jones* he threw off entirely the theater conventions

† For biographical data and play list see *The Emperor Jones,* p. 832 f.

that he had so far respected and gave direct *expression* to the negro's thoughts and fears in rhythmic monologues and symbolic hallucinations. In *"The Hairy Ape,"* which soon followed, he adopted the method of abstraction, another aspect of Expressionism,‡ although he disclaims any attempt to model his work on that of the German dramatists Wedekind, Kaiser, and Toller, who first used this style. Unlike them O'Neill kept his human symbols as real in speech and action as possible, while making them the epitome of the classes they represent and their conflict allegorical rather than actual. Yank is an abstraction of all labor in its attempt to win recognition. His tragedy—failing "to belong"—is itself a symbol of the plight of the emergent worker. His likeness to *Le Penseur* further emphasizes this symbolism.

In the staging of the play at the Provincetown Theatre in 1923 and in many later revivals, these abstract values have been pointed by unrealistic scenes and rhythmic or mechanized movements, especially of the stokers and the church paraders.

This avoidance of what O'Neill calls "the banality of surfaces" began a long series of experiments, each differing from the rest, to give his characters meaning beyond the possibility of the realist theater. Masks in *The Great God Brown* and *Lazarus Laughed,* asides in *Strange Interlude,* and dual personality in *Days Without End* are devices that have most tellingly served his purpose. He now has plans for thirty or more plays. Many of them, it is rumored, will be linked in a great epic cycle. Whether he will persist in experimentation or return to the normality of *Mourning Becomes Electra* and *Ah, Wilderness!* is a question of much concern to his public and to the art of our theater.

‡ For a discussion of this term see preface to *Man and the Masses,* p. 448.

"THE HAIRY APE"

Characters

ROBERT SMITH, "YANK."
PADDY.
LONG.
MILDRED DOUGLAS.
HER AUNT.
SECOND ENGINEER.
A GUARD.
A SECRETARY OF AN ORGANIZATION.
STOKERS, LADIES, GENTLEMEN, ETC.

SCENES

I.—*The firemen's forecastle of an ocean liner—an hour after sailing from New York.*
II.—*Section of promenade deck, two days out—morning.*
III.—*The stockade. A few minutes later.*
IV.—*Same as Scene I. Half an hour later.*
V.—*Fifth Avenue, New York. Three weeks later.*
VI.—*An island near the city. The next night.*
VII.—*In the city. About a month later.*
VIII.—*In the city. Twilight of the next day.*

TIME—*The Modern.*

SCENE ONE

The firemen's forecastle of a transatlantic liner an hour after sailing from New York for the voyage across. Tiers of narrow, steel bunks, three deep, on all sides. An entrance in rear. Benches on the floor before the bunks. The room is crowded with men, shouting, cursing, laughing, singing—a confused, inchoate uproar swelling into a sort of unity, a meaning—the bewildered, furious, baffled defiance of a beast in a cage. Nearly all the men are drunk. Many bottles are passed from hand to hand. All are dressed in dungaree pants, heavy ugly shoes. Some wear singlets, but the majority are stripped to the waist.

The treatment of this scene, or of any other scene in the play, should by no means be naturalistic. The effect sought after is a cramped space in the bowels of a ship, imprisoned by white steel. The lines of bunks, the uprights supporting them, cross each other like the steel framework of a cage. The ceiling crushes down upon the men's heads. They cannot stand upright. This accentuates the natural stooping posture which shoveling coal and the resultant over-development of back and shoulder muscles have given them. The men themselves should resemble those pictures in which the appearance of Neanderthal Man is guessed at. All are hairy-chested, with long arms of tremendous power, and low, receding brows above their small, fierce, resentful eyes. All the civilized white races are represented, but except for the slight differentiation in color of hair, skin, eyes, all these men are alike.

[*The curtain rises on a tumult of sound.* YANK *is seated in the foreground. He seems broader, fiercer, more truculent, more powerful, more sure of himself than the rest. They respect his superior strength—the grudging respect of fear. Then, too, he represents to them a self-expression, the very last word in what they are, their most highly developed individual.*]

Voices. Gif me trink dere, you!
'Ave a wet!
Salute!
Gesundheit!
Skoal!
Drunk as a lord, God stiffen you!
Here's how!
Luck!
Pass back that bottle, damn you!

Pourin' it down his neck!
Ho, Groggy! Where the devil have you been?
La Touraine.
I hit him smash in yaw, py Gott!
Jenkins—the First—he's a rotten swine——
And the coppers nabbed him—and I run——
I like peer better. It don't pig head gif you.
A slut, I'm sayin'! She robbed me aslape——
To hell with 'em all!
You're a bloody liar!
Say dot again! [*Commotion. Two men about to fight are pulled apart.*]
No scrappin' now!
Tonight——
See who's the best man!
Bloody Dutchman!
Tonight on the for'ard square.
I'll bet on Dutchy.
He packa da wallop, I tella you!
Shut up, Wop!
No fightin', maties. We're all chums, ain't we?

[*A voice starts bawling a song.*]

"Beer, beer, glorious beer!
Fill yourselves right up to here."

Yank. [*For the first time seeming to take notice of the uproar about him, turns around threateningly—in a tone of contemptuous authority.*] Choke off dat noise! Where d'yuh get dat beer stuff? Beer, hell! Beer's for goils—and Dutchmen. Me for somep'n wit a kick to it! Gimme a drink, one of youse guys. [*Several bottles are eagerly offered. He takes a tremendous gulp at one of them; then, keeping the bottle in his hand, glares belligerently at the* OWNER, *who hastens to acquiesce in this robbery by saying:*] All righto, Yank. Keep it and have another.

[YANK *contemptuously turns his back on the crowd again. For a second there is an embarrassed silence. Then:*]

Voices. We must be passing the Hook.
She's beginning to roll to it.
Six days in hell—and then Southampton.
Py Yesus, I vish somepody take my first vatch for me!
Gittin' seasick, Square-head?
Drink up and forget it!
What's in your bottle?
Gin.
Dot's nigger trink.
Absinthe? It's doped. You'll go off your chump, Froggy!
Cochon!
Whisky, that's the ticket!
Where's Paddy?
Going asleep.
Sing us that whisky song, Paddy.

[*They all turn to an old, wizened* IRISHMAN *who is dozing, very drunk, on the benches forward. His face is extremely monkey-like with all the sad, patient pathos of that animal in his small eyes.*]

Singa da song, Caruso Pat!
He's getting old. The drink is too much for him.
He's too drunk.

Paddy. [*Blinking about him, starts to his feet resentfully, swaying, holding on to the edge of a bunk.*] I'm never too drunk to sing. 'Tis only when I'm dead to the world I'd be wishful to sing at all. [*With a sort of sad contempt.*] "Whisky Johnny," ye want? A chanty, ye want? Now that's a queer wish from the ugly like of you, God help you. But no matther.

[*He starts to sing in a thin, nasal, doleful tone.*]

Oh, whisky is the life of man!
Whisky! O Johnny! [*They all join in on this.*]
Oh, whisky is the life of man!
Whisky for my Johnny! [*Again chorus.*]
Oh, whisky drove my old man mad!
Whisky! O Johnny!
Oh, whisky drove my old man mad!
Whisky for my Johnny!

Yank. [*Again turning around scornfully.*] Aw hell! Nix on dat old sailing ship stuff! All dat bull's dead, see? And you're dead, too, yuh damned old Harp, on'y yuh don't know it. Take it easy, see? Give us a rest. Nix on de loud noise. [*With a cynical grin.*] Can't youse see I'm tryin' to t'ink?

All. [*Repeating the word after him, as one, with the same cynical amused mockery.*] Think!

[*The chorused word has a brazen metallic quality as if their throats were phonograph horns. It is followed by a general uproar of hard, barking laughter.*]

Voices. Don't be cracking your head wit ut, Yank.
You gat headache, py yingo!
One thing about it—it rhymes with drink!
Ha, ha, ha!
Drink, don't think!
Drink, don't think!
Drink, don't think!

[*A whole chorus of voices has taken up this refrain, stamping on the floor, pounding on the benches with fists.*]

Yank. [*Taking a gulp from his bottle—good-naturedly:*] Aw right. Can de noise. I got yuh de foist time.

[*The uproar subsides. A very drunken sentimental* TENOR *begins to sing.*]

"Far away in Canada,
Far across the sea,
There's a lass who fondly waits
Making a home for me——"

Yank. [*Fiercely contemptuous.*] Shut up, yuh lousy boob! Where d'yuh get dat tripe? Home? Home, hell! I'll make a home for yuh! I'll knock yuh dead. Home! T'hell wit home! Where d'yuh get dat tripe? Dis is home, see? What d'yuh want wit home? [*Proudly.*] I runned away from mine when I was a kid. On'y too glad to beat it, dat was me. Home was lickings for me, dat's all. But yuh can bet your shoit no one ain't never licked me since! Wanter try it, any of youse? Huh! I guess not. [*In a more placated but still contemptuous tone.*] Goils waitin' for yuh, huh? Aw, hell! Dat's all tripe. Dey don't wait for no one. Dey'd double-cross yuh for a nickel. Dey're all tarts, get me? Treat 'em rough, dat's me. To hell wit 'em. Tarts, dat's what, de whole bunch of 'em.

Long. [*Very drunk, jumps on a bench excitedly, gesticulating with a bottle in his hand.*] Listen 'ere, Comrades! Yank 'ere is right. 'E says this 'ere stinkin' ship is our 'ome. And 'e says as 'ome is 'ell. And 'e's right! This is 'ell. We lives in 'ell, Comrades—and right enough we'll die in it. [*Raging.*] And who's ter blame, I arsks yer. We ain't. We wasn't born this rotten way. All men is born free and ekal. That's in the bleedin' Bible, maties. But what d'they care for the Bible—them lazy, bloated swine what travels first cabin? Them's the ones. They dragged us down 'til we're on'y wage slaves in the bowels of a bloody ship, sweatin', burnin' up, eatin' coal dust! Hit's them's ter blame—the damned Capitalist clarss!

[*There had been a gradual murmur of contemptuous resentment rising among the* MEN *until now he is interrupted by a storm of catcalls, hisses, boos, hard laughter.*]

Voices. Turn it off!
Shut up!
Sit down!
Closa da face!
Tamn fool! [*Etc.*]

Yank. [*Standing up and glaring at* LONG.] Sit down before I knock yuh down! [LONG *makes haste to efface himself.* YANK *goes on contemptuously.*] De Bible, huh? De Cap'tlist class, huh? Aw, nix on dat Salvation Army-Socialist bull. Git a soapbox! Hire a hall! Come and be saved, huh? Jerk us to Jesus, huh? Aw g'wan! I've listened to lots of guys like you, see? Yuh're all wrong. Wanter know what I t'ink? Yuh ain't no good for no one. Yuh're de bunk. Yuh ain't got no noive, get me? Yuh're yellow, dat's what. Yellow, dat's you. Say! What's dem slobs in de foist cabin got to do wit us? We're better men dan dey are, ain't we? Sure! One of us guys could clean up de whole mob wit one mit. Put one of 'em down here for one watch in de stokehole, what'd happen? Dey'd carry him off on a stretcher. Dem boids don't amount to nothin'. Dey're just baggage. Who makes dis old tub run? Ain't it us guys? Well den, we belong, don't we? We belong and dey don't. Dat's all. [*A loud chorus of approval.* YANK *goes on.*] As for dis bein' hell—aw, nuts! Yuh lost your noive, dat's what. Dis is a man's job, get me? It belongs. It runs dis tub. No stiffs need apply. But yuh're a stiff, see? Yuh're yellow, dat's you.

Voices. [*With a great hard pride in them.*]
Righto!
A man's job!
Talk is cheap, Long.
He never could hold up his end.
Divil take him!
Yank's right. We make it go.
Py Gott, Yank say right ting!
We don't need no one cryin' over us.
Makin' speeches.
Throw him out!
Yellow!
Chuck him overboard!
I'll break his jaw for him!

[*They crowd around* LONG *threateningly.*]

Yank. [*Half good-natured again—contemptuously.*] Aw, take it easy. Leave him alone. He ain't woith a punch. Drink up. Here's how, whoever owns dis.

[*He takes a long swallow from his bottle. All drink with him. In a flash all is hilarious amiability again, back-slapping, loud talk, etc.*]

Paddy. [*Who has been sitting in a blinking, melancholy daze—suddenly cries out in a voice full of old sorrow.*] We belong to this, you're saying? We make the ship to go, you're saying? Yerra then, that Almighty God have pity on us! [*His voice runs into the wail of a keen; he rocks back and forth on his bench. The men stare at him, startled and impressed in spite of themselves.*] Oh, to be back in the fine days of my youth, ochone! Oh, there was fine beautiful ships them days—clippers wid tall masts touching the sky—fine strong men in them—men that was sons of the sea as if 'twas the mother that bore them. Oh, the clean skins of them, and the clear eyes, the straight backs and full chests of them! Brave men they was, and bold men surely! We'd be sailing out, bound down round the Horn maybe. We'd be making sail in the dawn, with a fair breeze, singing a chanty song wid no care to it. And astern the land would be sinking low and dying out, but we'd give it no heed but a laugh, and never a look behind. For the day that was, was enough, for we was free men—and I'm thinking 'tis only slaves do be giving heed to the day that's gone or the day to come—until they're old like me. [*With a sort of religious exaltation.*] Oh, to be scudding south again wid the power of the Trade Wind driving her on steady through the nights and the days! Full sail on her! Nights and days! Nights when the foam of the wake would be flaming wid fire, when the sky'd be blazing and winking wid stars. Or the full of the moon maybe. Then you'd see her driving through the gray night, her sails stretching aloft all silver and white, not a sound on the deck, the lot of us dreaming dreams, till you'd believe 'twas no real ship at all you was on but a ghost ship like the *Flying Dutchman* they says does be roaming the seas forevermore widout touching a port. And there was the days, too. A warm sun on the clean decks. Sun warming the blood of you, and wind over the miles of shiny green ocean like strong drink to your lungs. Work—aye, hard work—but who'd mind that at all? Sure, you worked under the sky and 'twas work wid skill and daring to it. And wid the day done, in the dog watch, smoking me pipe at ease, the lookout would be raising land maybe, and we'd see the mountains of South Americy wid the red fire of the setting sun painting their white tops and the clouds floating by them! [*His tone of exaltation ceases. He goes on mournfully.*] Yerra, what's the use of talking? 'Tis a dead man's whisper. [*To* YANK *resentfully.*] 'Twas them days a ship was part of the sea, and a man was part of a ship, and the sea joined all together and made it one. [*Scornfully.*] Is it one wid this you'd be, Yank—black smoke from the funnels smudging the sea, smudging the decks—the bloody engines pounding and throbbing and shaking—wid divil a sight of sun or a breath of clean air—choking our lungs wid coal dust—breaking our backs and hearts in the hell of the stokehole—feeding the bloody furnace—feeding our lives along wid the coal, I'm thinking—caged in by steel from a sight of the sky like bloody apes in the zoo! [*With a harsh laugh.*] Ho-ho, divil mend you! Is it to belong to that you're wishing? Is it a flesh and blood wheel of the engines you'd be?

Yank. [*Who has been listening with a contemptuous sneer, barks out the answer.*] Sure ting! Dat's me. What about it?

Paddy. [*As if to himself—with great sorrow:*] Me time is past due. That a great wave wid sun in the heart of it may sweep me over the side sometime I'd be dreaming of the days that's gone!

Yank. Aw, yuh crazy Mick! [*He springs to his feet and advances on* PADDY *threateningly—then stops, fighting some queer struggle within himself—lets his hands fall to his sides—contemptuously:*] Aw, take it easy. Yuh're aw right, at dat. Yuh're bugs, dat's all—nutty as a cuckoo. All dat tripe yuh been pullin'—Aw, dat's all right. On'y it's dead, get me? Yuh don't belong no more, see. Yuh don't get de stuff. Yuh're too old. [*Disgustedly.*] But aw say, come up for air onct in a while, can't yuh? See what's happened since yuh croaked. [*He suddenly bursts forth vehemently, growing more and more excited.*] Say! Sure! Sure I meant it! What de hell— Say, lemme talk! Hey! Hey, you old Harp! Hey, youse guys! Say, listen to me—wait a moment—I gotter talk, see? I belong and he don't. He's dead but I'm livin'. Listen to me! Sure I'm part of de engines! Why de hell not! Dey move, don't they? Dey're speed, ain't dey? Dey smash trou, don't dey? Twenty-five knots a hour! Dat's goin' some! Dat's new stuff! Dat belongs! But him, he's too old. He gets dizzy. Say, listen. All dat crazy tripe about nights and days; all dat crazy tripe about stars and moons; all dat crazy tripe about suns and winds, fresh air and de rest of it—Aw hell, dat's all a dope dream! Hittin' de pipe of de past, dat's what he's doin'. He's old and don't belong no more. But me, I'm young! I'm in de pink! I move wit it! It, get me! I mean de ting dat's de guts of all dis. It ploughs trou all de tripe he's been sayin'. It blows dat up! It knocks dat dead! It slams dat offen de face of de oith! It, get me! De engines and de coal and de smoke and all de rest of it! He can't breathe and swallow coal dust, but I kin, see? Dat's fresh air for me! Dat's food for me! I'm new, get me? Hell in de stokehole? Sure! It takes a man to work in hell. Hell, sure, dat's my fav'rite climate. I eat it up! I git fat on it! It's me makes it hot! It's me makes it roar! It's me makes it move! Sure, on'y for me everything stops. It all goes dead, get me? De noise and smoke and all de engines movin' de woild, dey stop. Dere ain't nothin' no more! Dat's what I'm sayin'. Everyting else dat makes de woild move, somep'n makes it move. It can't move witout somep'n else, see? Den yuh get down to me. I'm at de bottom, get me! Dere ain't nothin' foither. I'm de end! I'm de start! I start somep'n and de woild moves! It—dat's me!—de new dat's moiderin' de old! I'm de ting in coal dat makes it boin; I'm steam and oil for de engines; I'm de ting in noise dat makes yuh hear it; I'm smoke and express trains and steamers and factory whistles; I'm de ting in gold dat makes it money! And I'm what makes iron into steel! Steel, dat stands for de whole ting! And I'm steel—steel—steel! I'm de muscles in steel, de punch behind it! [*As he says this he pounds with his fist against the steel bunks. All the* MEN, *roused to a pitch of frenzied self-glorification by his speech, do likewise. There is a deafening metallic roar, through which* YANK'S *voice can be heard bellowing:*] Slaves, hell! We run de whole woiks. All de rich guys dat tink dey're somep'n, dey ain't nothin'! Dey don't belong. But us guys, we're in de move, we're at de bottom, de whole ting is us! [PADDY *from the start of* YANK'S *speech has been taking one gulp after another from his bottle, at first frightenedly, as if he were afraid to listen, then desperately, as if to drown his senses, but finally has achieved complete indifferent, even amused, drunkenness.* YANK *sees his lips moving. He quells the uproar with a shout.*] Hey, youse guys, take it easy! Wait a moment! De nutty Harp is sayin' somep'n.

Paddy. [*Is heard now—throws his head back with a mocking burst of laughter.*] Ho-ho-ho-ho-ho——

Yank. [*Drawing back his fist, with a snarl.*] Aw! Look out who yuh're givin' the bark!

Paddy. [*Begins to sing the "Miller of Dee" with enormous good nature.*]

"I care for nobody, no, not I,
And nobody cares for me."

Yank. [*Good-natured himself in a flash, interrupts* PADDY *with a slap on the bare back like a report.*] Dat's de stuff! Now yuh're gettin' wise to somep'n. Care for nobody, dat's de dope! To hell wit 'em all! And nix on nobody else carin'. I kin care for myself, get me! [*Eight bells sound, muffled, vibrating through the steel walls as if some enormous brazen gong were imbedded in the heart of the ship. All the men jump up mechanically, file through the door silently, close upon each other's heels in what is very like a prisoners' lock-step.* YANK *slaps* PADDY *on the back.*] Our watch, yuh old Harp! [*Mockingly.*] Come on down in hell. Eat up de coal dust. Drink in de heat. It's it, see! Act like yuh liked it, yuh better—or croak yuhself.

Paddy. [*With jovial defiance.*] To the divil wid it! I'll not report this watch. Let thim log me and be damned. I'm no slave the like of you. I'll be settin' here at me ease, and drinking, and thinking, and dreaming dreams.

Yank. [*Contemptuously.*] Tinkin' and dreamin', what'll that get yuh? What's tinkin' got to do wit it? We move, don't we? Speed, ain't it? Fog, dat's all you stand for. But we drive trou dat, don't we? We split dat up and smash trou—twenty-five knots a hour! [*Turns his back on* PADDY *scornfully.*] Aw, yuh make me sick! Yuh don't belong!

[*He strides out the door in rear.* PADDY *hums to himself, blinking drowsily.*]

CURTAIN

SCENE TWO

Two days out. A section of the promenade deck.

[MILDRED DOUGLAS *and her* AUNT *are discovered reclining in deck chairs. The former is a girl of twenty, slender, delicate, with a pale, pretty face marred by a self-conscious expression of disdainful superiority. She looks fretful, nervous, and discontented, bored by her own anemia. Her* AUNT *is a pompous and proud—and fat—old lady. She is a type even to the point of a double chin and lorgnettes. She is dressed pretentiously, as if afraid her face alone would never indicate her position in life.* MILDRED *is dressed all in white.*

The impression to be conveyed by this scene is one of the beautiful, vivid life of the sea all about—sunshine on the deck in a great flood, the fresh sea wind blowing across it. In the midst of this, these two incongruous, artificial figures, inert and disharmonious, the elder like a gray lump of dough touched up with rouge, the younger looking as if the vitality of her stock had been sapped before she was conceived, so that she is the expression not of its life energy but merely of the artificialities that energy had won for itself in the spending.]

Mildred. [*Looking up with affected dreaminess.*] How the black smoke swirls back against the sky! Is it not beautiful?

Aunt. [*Without looking up.*] I dislike smoke of any kind.

Mildred. My great-grandmother smoked a pipe—a clay pipe.

Aunt. [*Ruffling.*] Vulgar!

Mildred. She was too distant a relative to be vulgar. Time mellows pipes.

Aunt. [*Pretending boredom but irritated.*] Did the sociology you took up at college teach you that—to play the ghoul on every possible occasion, excavating old bones? Why not let your great-grandmother rest in her grave?

Mildred. [*Dreamily.*] With her pipe beside her—puffing in Paradise.

Aunt. [*With spite.*] Yes, you are a natural born ghoul. You are even getting to look like one, my dear.

Mildred. [*In a passionless tone.*] I detest you, Aunt. [*Looking at her critically.*] Do you know what you remind me of? Of a cold pork pudding against a background of linoleum tablecloth in the kitchen of a—but the possibilities are wearisome.

[*She closes her eyes.*]

Aunt. [*With a bitter laugh.*] Merci for your candor. But since I am and must be your chaperon—in appearance, at least—let us patch up some sort of armed truce. For my part you are quite free to indulge any pose of eccentricity that beguiles you—as long as you observe the amenities——

Mildred. [*Drawling.*] The inanities?

Aunt. [*Going on as if she hadn't heard.*] After exhausting the morbid thrills of social service work on New York's East Side—how they must have hated you, by the way, the poor that you made so much poorer in their own eyes!—you are now bent on making your slumming international. Well, I hope Whitechapel will provide the needed nerve tonic. Do not ask me to chaperon you there, however. I told your father I would not. I loathe deformity. We will hire an army of detectives and you may investigate everything—they allow you to see.

Mildred. [*Protesting with a trace of genuine earnestness.*] Please do not mock at my attempts to discover how the other half lives. Give me credit for some sort of groping sincerity in that at least. I would like to help them. I would like to be some use in the world. Is it my fault I don't know how? I would like to be sincere, to touch life somewhere. [*With weary bitterness.*] But I'm afraid I have neither the vitality nor integrity. All that was burnt out in our stock before I was born. Grandfather's blast furnaces, flaming to the sky, melting steel, making millions—then father keeping those home fires burning, making more millions—and little me at the tail-end of it all. I'm a waste product in the Bessemer process—like the millions. Or rather, I inherit the acquired trait of the by-product, wealth, but none of the energy, none of the strength of the steel that made it. I am sired by gold and dammed by it, as they say at the race track—damned in more ways than one.

[*She laughs mirthlessly.*]

Aunt. [*Unimpressed—superciliously:*] You seem to be going in for sincerity today. It isn't becoming to you, really—except as an obvious pose. Be as artificial as you are, I advise. There's a sort of sincerity in that, you know. And, after all, you must confess you like that better.

Mildred. [*Again affected and bored.*] Yes, I suppose I do. Pardon me for my outburst. When a leopard complains of its spots, it must sound rather grotesque. [*In a mocking tone.*] Purr, little leopard. Purr, scratch, tear, kill, gorge yourself and be happy—only stay in the jungle where your spots are camouflage. In a cage they make you conspicuous.

Aunt. I don't know what you are talking about.

Mildred. It would be rude to talk about anything to you. Let's just talk. [*She looks at her wrist watch.*] Well, thank goodness, it's about time for them to come for me. That ought to give me a new thrill, Aunt.

Aunt. [*Affectedly troubled.*] You don't mean to say you're really going? The dirt—the heat must be frightful——

Mildred. Grandfather started as a puddler. I should have inherited an immunity to heat that would make a salamander shiver. It will be fun to put it to the test.

Aunt. But don't you have to have the captain's—or someone's—permission to visit the stokehole?

Mildred. [*With a triumphant smile.*] I have it—both his and the chief engineer's. Oh, they didn't want to at first, in spite of my social service credentials. They didn't seem a bit anxious that I should investigate how the other half lives and works on a ship. So I had to tell them that my father, the president of Nazareth Steel, chairman of the board of directors of this line, had told me it would be all right.

Aunt. He didn't.

Mildred. How naïve age makes one! But I said he did, Aunt. I even said he had given me a letter to them—which I had lost. And they were afraid to take the chance that I might be lying. [*Excitedly.*] So it's ho! for the stokehole. The second engineer is to escort me. [*Looking at her watch again.*] It's time. And here he comes, I think.

[*The* SECOND ENGINEER *enters. He is a husky, fine-looking man of thirty-five or so. He stops before the two and tips his cap, visibly embarrassed and ill-at-ease.*]

Second Engineer. Miss Douglas?

Mildred. Yes. [*Throwing off her rugs and getting to her feet.*] Are we all ready to start?

Second Engineer. In just a second, ma'am. I'm waiting for the Fourth. He's coming along.

Mildred. [*With a scornful smile.*] You don't care to shoulder this responsibility alone, is that it?

Second Engineer. [*Forcing a smile.*] Two are better than one. [*Disturbed by her eyes, glances out to sea—blurts out:*] A fine day we're having.

Mildred. Is it?

Second Engineer. A nice warm breeze——

Mildred. It feels cold to me.

Second Engineer. But it's hot enough in the sun——

Mildred. Not hot enough for me. I don't like Nature. I was never athletic.

Second Engineer. [*Forcing a smile.*] Well, you'll find it hot enough where you're going.

Mildred. Do you mean hell?

Second Engineer. [*Flabbergasted, decides to laugh.*] Ho-ho! No, I mean the stokehole.

Mildred. My grandfather was a puddler. He played with boiling steel.

Second Engineer. [*All at sea—uneasily:*] Is that so? Hum, you'll excuse me, ma'am, but are you intending to wear that dress?

Mildred. Why not?

Second Engineer. You'll likely rub against oil and dirt. It can't be helped.

Mildred. It doesn't matter. I have lots of white dresses.

Second Engineer. I have an old coat you might throw over——

Mildred. I have fifty dresses like this. I will throw this one into the sea when I come back. That ought to wash it clean, don't you think?

Second Engineer. [*Doggedly.*] There's ladders to climb down that are none too clean—and dark alleyways——

Mildred. I will wear this very dress and none other.

Second Engineer. No offense meant. It's none of my business. I was only warning you——

Mildred. Warning? That sounds thrilling.

Second Engineer. [*Looking down the deck—with a sigh of relief:*] There's the Fourth now. He's waiting for us. If you'll come——

Mildred. Go on. I'll follow you. [*He goes.* MILDRED *turns a mocking smile on her* AUNT.] An oaf—but a handsome, virile oaf.

Aunt. [*Scornfully.*] Poser!

Mildred. Take care. He said there were dark alleyways——

Aunt. [*In the same tone.*] Poser!

Mildred. [*Biting her lips angrily.*] You are right. But would that my millions were not so anemically chaste!

Aunt. Yes, for a fresh pose I have no doubt you would drag the name of Douglas in the gutter!

Mildred. From which it sprang. Good-by, Aunt. Don't pray too hard that I may fall into the fiery furnace.

Aunt. Poser!

Mildred. [*Viciously.*] Old hag!

[*She slaps her* AUNT *insultingly across the face and walks off, laughing gaily.*]

Aunt. [*Screams after her:*] I said poser!

CURTAIN

SCENE THREE

The stokehole. In the rear, the dimly-outlined bulks of the furnaces and boilers. High overhead one hanging electric bulb sheds just enough light through the murky air laden with coal dust to pile up masses of shadows everywhere. A line of men, stripped to the waist, is before the furnace doors. They bend over, looking neither to right nor left, handling their shovels as if they were part of their bodies, with a strange, awkward, swinging rhythm. They use the shovels to throw open the furnace doors. Then from these fiery round holes in the black a flood of terrific light and heat pours full upon the men who are outlined in silhouette in the crouching, inhuman attitudes of chained gorillas. The men shovel with a rhythmic motion, swinging as on a pivot from the coal which lies in heaps on the floor behind to hurl it into the flaming mouths before them. There is a tumult of noise—the brazen clang of the furnace doors as they are flung open or slammed shut, the grating, teeth-gritting grind of steel against steel, and of crunching coal. This clash of sounds stuns one's ears with its rending dissonance. But there is order in it, rhythm, a mechanical, regulated recurrence, a tempo. And rising above all, making the air hum with the quiver of liberated energy, the roar of leaping flames in the furnaces, the monotonous throbbing beat of the engines.

[*As the curtain rises, the furnace doors are shut. The* MEN *are taking a breathing spell. One or two are arranging the coal behind them, pulling it into more accessible heaps. The others can be dimly made out leaning on their shovels in relaxed attitudes of exhaustion.*]

Paddy. [*From somewhere in the line—plaintively:*] Yerra, will this divil's own watch nivir end? Me back is broke. I'm destroyed entirely.

Yank. [*From the center of the line—with exuberant scorn:*] Aw, yuh make me sick! Lie down and croak, why don't yuh? Always beefin', dat's you! Say, dis is a cinch! Dis was made for me! It's my meat, get me! [*A whistle is blown—a thin, shrill note from somewhere overhead in the darkness.* YANK *curses without resentment.*] Dere's de damn engineer crackin' de whip. He tinks we're loafin'.

Paddy. [*Vindictively.*] God stiffen him!

Yank. [*In an exultant tone of command.*] Come on, youse guys! Git into de game! She's gittin' hungry! Pile some grub in her. Trow it into her belly! Come on now, all cf youse! Open her up!

[*At this last all the* MEN, *who have followed his movements of getting into position, throw open their furnace doors with a deafening clang. The fiery light floods over their shoulders as they bend round for the coal. Rivulets of sooty sweat have traced maps on their backs. The enlarged muscles form bunches of high light and shadow.*]

Yank. [*Chanting a count as he shovels without seeming effort.*] One-two-three—— [*His voice rising exultantly in the joy of battle.*] Dat's de stuff! Let her have it! All togedder now! Sling it into her! Let her ride! Shoot de piece now! Call de toin on her! Drive her into it! Feel her move! Watch her smoke! Speed, dat's her middle name! Give her coal, youse guys! Coal, dat's her booze! Drink it up, baby! Let's see yuh sprint! Dig in and gain a lap! Dere she go-o-es.

[*This last in the chanting formula of the gallery gods at the six-day bike race. He slams his furnace door shut. The others do likewise with as much unison as their wearied bodies will permit. The effect is of one fiery eye after another being blotted out with a series of accompanying bangs.*]

Paddy. [*Groaning.*] Me back is broke. I'm bate out—bate——

[*There is a pause. Then the inexorable whistle sounds again from the dim regions above the electric light. There is a growl of cursing rage from all sides.*]

Yank. [*Shaking his fist upward—contemptuously.*] Take it easy dere, you! Who d'yuh tink's runnin' dis game, me or you? When I git ready, we move. Not before! When I git ready, get me!

Voices. [*Approvingly.*] That's the stuff!
Yank tal him, py golly!
Yank ain't affeerd.
Goot poy, Yank!
Give him hell!
Tell 'im 'e's a bloody swine!
Bloody slave-driver!

Yank. [*Contemptuously.*] He ain't got no noive. He's yellow, get me? All de engineers is yellow. Dey got streaks a mile wide. Aw, to hell wit him! Let's move, youse guys. We had a rest. Come on, she needs it! Give her pep! It ain't for him. Him and his whistle, dey don't belong. But we belong, see! We gotter feed de baby! Come on!

[*He turns and flings his furnace door open. They all follow his lead. At this instant the* SECOND *and* FOURTH ENGINEERS *enter from the darkness on the left with* MILDRED *between them. She starts, turns paler, her pose is crumbling, she shivers with fright in spite of the blazing heat, but forces herself to leave the* ENGINEERS *and take a few steps nearer the men. She is right behind* YANK. *All this happens quickly while the men have their backs turned.*]

Yank. Come on, youse guys!

[*He is turning to get coal when the whistle sounds again in a peremptory, irritating note. This drives* YANK *into a sudden fury. While the other* MEN *have turned full around and stopped dumbfounded by the spectacle of* MILDRED *standing there in her white dress,* YANK *does not turn far enough to see her. Besides, his head is thrown back, he blinks upward through the murk trying to find the owner of the whistle, he brandishes his shovel murderously over his head in one hand, pounding on his chest, gorilla-like, with the other, shouting.*]

Yank. Toin off dat whistle! Come down outa dere, yuh yellow, brass-buttoned, Belfast bum, yuh! Come down and I'll knock yer brains out! Yuh lousy, stinkin', yellow mut of a Catholic-moiderin' bastard! Come down and I'll moider yuh! Pullin' dat whistle on me, huh? I'll show yuh! I'll crash yer skull in! I'll drive yer teet' down yer troat! I'll slam yer nose trou de back of yer head! I'll cut yer guts out for a nickel, yuh lousy boob, yuh dirty, crummy, muck-eatin' son of a——

[*Suddenly he becomes conscious of all the other* MEN *staring at something directly behind his back. He whirls defensively with a snarling, murderous growl, crouching to spring, his lips drawn back over his teeth, his small eyes gleaming ferociously. He sees* MILDRED, *like a white apparition in the full light from the open furnace doors. He glares into her eyes, turned to stone. As for her, during his speech she has listened, paralyzed with horror, terror, her whole personality crushed, beaten in, collapsed, by the terrific impact of this unknown, abysmal brutality, naked and shameless. As she looks at his gorilla face, as his eyes bore into hers, she utters a low, choking cry and shrinks away from him, putting both hands up before her eyes to shut out the sight of his face, to protect her own. This startles* YANK *to a reaction. His mouth falls open, his eyes grow bewildered.*]

Mildred. [*About to faint—to the* ENGINEERS, *who now have her one by each arm —whimperingly:*] Take me away! Oh, the filthy beast!

[*She faints. They carry her quickly back, disappearing in the darkness at the left, rear. An iron door clangs shut. Rage and bewildered fury rush back on* YANK. *He feels himself insulted in some unknown fashion in the very heart of his pride. He roars.*]

Yank. God damn yuh!

[*And hurls his shovel after them at the door which has just closed. It hits the steel bulkhead with a clang and falls clattering on the steel floor. From overhead the whistle sounds again in a long, angry, insistent command.*]

CURTAIN

SCENE FOUR

The firemen's forecastle. YANK'S *watch has just come off duty and had dinner. Their faces and bodies shine from a soap and water scrubbing but around their eyes, where a hasty dousing does not touch, the coal dust sticks like black make-up, giving them a queer, sinister expression.*

[YANK *has not washed either face or body. He stands out in contrast to them, a blackened, brooding figure. He is seated forward on a bench in the exact attitude of Rodin's "The Thinker." The others, most of them smoking pipes, are staring at* YANK *half-apprehensively, as if fearing an outburst; half-amusedly, as if they saw a joke somewhere that tickled them.*]

Voices. He ain't ate nothin'.
Py golly, a fallar gat to gat grub in him.
Divil a lie.
Yank feeda da fire, no feeda da face.
Ha-ha.
He ain't even washed hisself.
He's forgot.
Hey, Yank, you forgot to wash.

Yank. [*Sullenly.*] Forgot nothin'! To hell wit washin'.

Voices. It'll stick to you.
It'll get under your skin.
Give yer the bleedin' itch, that's wot.
It makes spots on you—like a leopard.
Like a piebald nigger, you mean.
Better wash up, Yank.
You sleep better.
Wash up, Yank.
Wash up! Wash up!

Yank. [*Resentfully.*] Aw say, youse guys. Lemme alone. Can't youse see I'm tryin' to tink?

All. [*Repeating the word after him, as one, with cynical mockery.*] Think!

[*The word has a brazen, metallic qual-*

ity as if their throats were phonograph horns. It is followed by a chorus of hard, barking laughter.]

Yank. [*Springing to his feet and glaring at them belligerently.*] Yes, tink! Tink, dat's what I said! What about it?

[*They are silent, puzzled by his sudden resentment at what used to be one of his jokes.* YANK *sits down again in the same attitude of "The Thinker."*]

Voices. Leave him alone.
He's got a grouch on.
Why wouldn't he?

Paddy. [*With a wink at the others.*] Sure I know what's the matther. 'Tis aisy to see. He's fallen in love, I'm telling you.

All. [*Repeating the word after him, as one, with cynical mockery.*] Love!

[*The word has a brazen, metallic quality as if their throats were phonograph horns. It is followed by a chorus of hard, barking laughter.*]

Yank. [*With a contemptuous snort.*] Love, hell! Hate, dat's what. I've fallen in hate, get me?

Paddy. [*Philosophically.*] 'Twould take a wise man to tell one from the other. [*With a bitter, ironical scorn, increasing as he goes on.*] But I'm telling you it's love that's in it. Sure what else but love for us poor bastes in the stokehole would be bringing a fine lady, dressed like a white quane, down a mile of ladders and steps to be havin' a look at us?

[*A growl of anger goes up from all sides.*]

Long. [*Jumping on a bench—hecticly:*] Hinsultin' us! Hinsultin' us, the bloody cow! And them bloody engineers! What right 'as they got to be exhibitin' us 's if we was bleedin' monkeys in a menagerie? Did we sign for hinsults to our dignity as 'onest workers? Is that in the ship's articles? You kin bloody well bet it ain't! But I knows why they done it. I arsked a deck steward 'oo she was and 'e told me. 'Er old man's a bleedin' millionaire, a bloody Capitalist! 'E's got enuf bloody gold to sink this bleedin' ship! 'E makes arf the bloody steel in the world! 'E owns this bloody boat! And you and me, Comrades, we're 'is slaves! And the skipper and mates and engineers, they're 'is slaves! And she's 'is bloody daughter and we're all 'er slaves, too! And she gives 'er orders as 'ow she wants to see the bloody animals below decks and down they takes 'er!

[*There is a roar of rage from all sides.*]

Yank. [*Blinking at him bewilderedly.*] Say! Wait a moment! Is all dat straight goods?

Long. Straight as string! The bleedin' steward as waits on 'em, 'e told me about 'er. And what're we goin' ter do, I arsks yer? 'Ave we got ter swaller 'er hinsults like dogs? It ain't in the ship's articles. I tell yer we got a case. We kin go to law——

Yank. [*With abysmal contempt.*] Hell! Law!

All. [*Repeating the word after him, as one, with cynical mockery.*] Law!

[*The word has a brazen metallic quality as if their throats were phonograph horns. It is followed by a chorus of hard, barking laughter.*]

Long. [*Feeling the ground slipping from under his feet—desperately:*] As voters and citizens we kin force the bloody governments——

Yank. [*With abysmal contempt.*] Hell! Governments!

All. [*Repeating the word after him, as one, with cynical mockery.*] Governments!

[*The word has a brazen metallic quality as if their throats were phonograph horns. It is followed by a chorus of hard, barking laughter.*]

Long. [*Hysterically.*] We're free and equal in the sight of God——

Yank. [*With abysmal contempt.*] Hell! God!

All. [*Repeating the word after him, as one, with cynical mockery.*] God!

[*The word has a brazen metallic quality as if their throats were phonograph horns. It is followed by a chorus of hard, barking laughter.*]

Yank. [*Witheringly.*] Aw, join de Salvation Army!

All. Sit down! Shut up! Damn fool! Sea-lawyer!

[LONG *slinks back out of sight.*]

Paddy. [*Continuing the trend of his thoughts as if he had never been interrupted —bitterly:*] And there she was standing behind us, and the Second pointing at us like a man you'd hear in a circus would be saying: In this cage is a queerer kind of baboon than ever you'd find in darkest Africy. We roast them in their own sweat—and be damned if you won't hear some of thim saying they like it!

[*He glances scornfully at* YANK.]

Yank. [*With a bewildered uncertain growl.*] Aw!

Paddy. And there was Yank roarin' curses and turning round wid his shovel to brain her—and she looked at him, and him at her——

Yank. [*Slowly.*] She was all white. I tought she was a ghost. Sure.

Paddy. [*With heavy, biting sarcasm.*] 'Twas love at first sight, divil a doubt of it! If you'd seen the endearin' look on her pale mug when she shriveled away with her hands over her eyes to shut out the sight of him! Sure, 'twas as if she'd seen a great hairy ape escaped from the Zoo!

Yank. [*Stung—with a growl of rage:*] Aw!

Paddy. And the loving way Yank heaved his shovel at the skull of her, only she was out the door! [*A grin breaking over his face.*] 'Twas touching, I'm telling you! It put the touch of home, swate home in the stokehole.

[*There is a roar of laughter from all.*]

Yank. [*Glaring at* PADDY *menacingly.*] Aw, choke dat off, see!

Paddy. [*Not heeding him—to the others:*] And her grabbin' at the Second's arm for protection. [*With a grotesque imitation of a woman's voice.*] Kiss me, Engineer dear, for it's dark down here and me old man's in Wall Street making money; Hug me tight, darlin', for I'm afeerd in the dark and me mother's on deck makin' eyes at the skipper!

[*Another roar of laughter.*]

Yank. [*Threateningly.*] Say! What yuh tryin' to do, kid me, yuh old Harp?

Paddy. Divil a bit! Ain't I wishin' myself you'd brained her?

Yank. [*Fiercely.*] I'll brain her! I'll brain her yet, wait 'n' see! [*Coming over to* PADDY*—slowly:*] Say, is dat what she called me—a hairy ape?

Paddy. She looked it at you if she didn't say the word itself.

Yank. [*Grinning horribly.*] Hairy ape, huh? Sure! Dat's de way she looked at me, aw right. Hairy ape! So dat's me, huh? [*Bursting into rage—as if she were still in front of him.*] Yuh skinny tart! Yuh white-faced bum, yuh! I'll show yuh who's a ape! [*Turning to the others, bewilderment seizing him again.*] Say, youse guys. I was bawlin' him out for pullin' de whistle on us. You heard me. And den I seen youse lookin' at somep'n and I tought he'd sneaked down to come up in back of me, and I hopped round to knock him dead wit de shovel. And dere she was wit de light on her! Christ, yuh coulda pushed me over wit a finger! I was scared, get me? Sure! I tought she was a ghost, see? She was all in white like dey wrap around stiffs. You seen her. Kin yuh blame me? She didn't belong, dat's what. And den when I come to and seen it was a real skoit and seen de way she was lookin' at me—like Paddy said—Christ, I was sore, get me? I don't stand for dat stuff from nobody. And I flung de shovel—on'y she'd beat it. [*Furiously.*] I wished it'd banged her! I wished it'd knocked her block off!

Long. And be 'anged for murder or 'lectrocuted? She ain't bleedin' well worth it.

Yank. I don't give a damn what! I'd be square wit her, wouldn't I? Tink I wanter let her put somep'n over on me? Tink I'm goin' to let her git away wit dat stuff? Yuh don't know me! No one ain't never put nothin' over on me and got away wit it, see! —not dat kind of stuff—no guy and no skoit neither! I'll fix her! Maybe she'll come down again——

Voice. No chance, Yank. You scared her out of a year's growth.

Yank. I scared her? Why de hell should I scare her? Who de hell is she? Ain't she de same as me? Hairy ape, huh? [*With his old confident bravado.*] I'll show her I'm better'n her, if she on'y knew it. I belong and she don't, see! I move and she's dead! Twenty-five knots a hour, dat's me! Dat carries her but I make dat. She's on'y baggage. Sure! [*Again bewilderedly.*] But, Christ, she was funny lookin'! Did yuh pipe her hands? White and skinny. Yuh could see de bones through 'em. And her mush, dat was dead white, too. And her eyes, dey was like dey'd seen a ghost. Me, dat was! Sure! Hairy ape! Ghost, huh? Look at dat arm! [*He extends his right arm, swelling out the great muscles.*] I coulda took her wit dat, wit just my little finger even, and broke her in two. [*Again bewilderedly.*] Say, who is dat skoit, huh? What is she? What's she come from? Who made her? Who give her de noive to look at me like dat? Dis ting's got my goat right. I don't get her. She's new to me. What does a skoit like her mean, huh? She don't belong, get me! I can't see her. [*With growing anger.*] But one ting I'm wise to, aw right, aw right! Youse all kin bet your shoits I'll git even wit her. I'll show her if she tinks she— She grinds de organ and I'm on de string, huh? I'll fix her! Let her come down again and I'll fling her in de furnace! She'll move den! She won't shiver at nothin', den! Speed, dat'll be her! She'll belong den!

[*He grins horribly.*]

Paddy. She'll never come. She's had her belly-full, I'm telling you. She'll be in bed now, I'm thinking, wid ten doctors and nurses feedin' her salts to clean the fear out of her.

Yank. [*Enraged.*] Yuh tink I made her sick, too, do yuh? Just lookin' at me, huh?

Hairy ape, huh? [*In a frenzy of rage.*] I'll fix her! I'll tell her where to git off! She'll git down on her knees and take it back or I'll bust de face offen her! [*Shaking one fist upward and beating on his chest with the other.*] I'll find yuh! I'm comin', d'yuh hear? I'll fix yuh, God damn yuh!

[*He makes a rush for the door.*]

Voices. Stop him!
He'll get shot!
He'll murder her!
Trip him up!
Hold him!
He's gone crazy!
Gott, he's strong!
Hold him down!
Look out for a kick!
Pin his arms!

[*They have all piled on him and, after a fierce struggle, by sheer weight of numbers have borne him to the floor just inside the door.*]

Paddy. [*Who has remained detached.*] Kape him down till he's cooled off. [*Scornfully.*] Yerra, Yank, you're a great fool. Is it payin' attention at all you are to the like of that skinny sow widout one drop of rale blood in her?

Yank. [*Frenziedly, from the bottom of the heap.*] She done me doit! She done me doit, didn't she? I'll git square wit her! I'll get her some way! Git offen me, youse guys! Lemme up! I'll show her who's a ape!

CURTAIN

SCENE FIVE

Three weeks later. A corner of Fifth Avenue in the Fifties on a fine Sunday morning. A general atmosphere of clean, well-tidied, wide street; a flood of mellow, tempered sunshine; gentle, genteel breezes. In the rear, the show windows of two shops, a jewelry establishment on the corner, a furrier's next to it. Here the adornments of extreme wealth are tantalizingly displayed. The jeweler's window is gaudy with glittering diamonds, emeralds, rubies, pearls, etc.. fashioned in ornate tiaras, crowns, necklaces, collars, etc. From each piece hangs an enormous tag from which a dollar sign and numerals in intermittent electric lights wink out the incredible prices. The same in the furrier's. Rich furs of all varieties hang there bathed in a downpour of artificial light. The general effect is of a background of magnificence cheapened and made grotesque by commercialism, a background in tawdry disharmony with the clear light and sunshine on the street itself.

[*Up the side street* YANK *and* LONG *come swaggering.* LONG *is dressed in shore clothes, wears a black Windsor tie, cloth cap.* YANK *is in his dirty dungarees. A fireman's cap with black peak is cocked defiantly on the side of his head. He has not shaved for days and around his fierce, resentful eyes—as around those of* LONG *to a lesser degree—the black smudge of coal dust still sticks like make-up. They hesitate and stand together at the corner, swaggering, looking about them with a forced, defiant contempt.*]

Long. [*Indicating it all with an oratorical gesture.*] Well, 'ere we are. Fif' Avenoo. This 'ere's their bleedin' private lane, as yer might say. [*Bitterly.*] We're trespassers 'ere. Proletarians keep orf the grass!

Yank. [*Dully.*] I don't see no grass, yuh boob. [*Staring at the sidewalk.*] Clean, ain't it? Yuh could eat a fried egg offen it. The white wings got some job sweepin' dis up. [*Looking up and down the avenue—surlily:*] Where's all de white-collar stiffs yuh said was here—and de skoits—*her* kind?

Long. In church, blarst 'em! Arskin' Jesus to give 'em more money.

Yank. Choich, huh? I useter go to choich onct—sure—when I was a kid. Me old man and woman, dey made me. Dey never went demselves, dough. Always got too big a head on Sunday mornin', dat was dem. [*With a grin.*] Dey was scrappers for fair, bot' of dem. On Satiday nights when dey bot' got a skinful dey could put up a bout oughter been staged at de Garden. When dey got trough dere wasn't a chair or table wit a leg under it. Or else dey bot' jumped on me for somep'n. Dat was where I loined to take punishment. [*With a grin and a swagger.*] I'm a chip offen de old block, get me?

Long. Did yer old man follow the sea?

Yank. Naw. Worked along shore. I runned away when me old lady croaked wit de tremens. I helped at truckin' and in de market. Den I shipped in de stokehole. Sure. Dat belongs. De rest was nothin'. [*Looking around him.*] I ain't never seen dis before. De Brooklyn waterfront, dat was where I was dragged up. [*Taking a deep breath.*] Dis ain't so bad at dat, huh?

Long. Not bad? Well, we pays for it wiv our bloody sweat, if yer wants to know!

Yank. [*With sudden angry disgust.*] Aw, hell! I don't see no one, see—like her. All dis gives me a pain. It don't belong. Say, ain't dere a back room around dis dump? Let's go shoot a ball. All dis is too clean and quiet and dolled-up, get me? It gives me a pain.

Long. Wait and yer'll bloody well see——

Yank. I don't wait for no one. I keep on de move. Say, what yuh drag me up here for, anyway? Tryin' to kid me, yuh simp, yuh?

Long. Yer wants to get back at 'er, don't yer? That's what yer been sayin' every bloomin' hour since she hinsulted yer.

Yank. [*Vehemently.*] Sure ting I do! Didn't I try to get even wit her in Southampton? Didn't I sneak on de deck and wait for her by de gangplank? I was goin' to spit in her pale mug, see! Sure, right in her pop-eyes! Dat woulda made me even, see? But no chanct. Dere was a whole army of plainclothes bulls around. Dey spotted me and gimme de bum's rush. I never seen her. But I'll git square wit her yet, you watch! [*Furiously.*] De lousy tart! She tinks she kin get away wit moider—but not wit me! I'll fix her! I'll tink of a way!

Long. [*As disgusted as he dares to be.*] Ain't that why I brought yer up 'ere—to show yer? Yer been lookin' at this 'ere 'ole affair wrong. Yer been actin' an' talkin' 's if it was all a bleedin' personal matter between yer and that bloody cow. I wants to convince yer she was on'y a representative of 'er clarss. I wants to awaken yer bloody clarss consciousness. Then yer'll see it's 'er clarss ye've got to fight, not 'er alone. There's a 'ole mob of 'em like 'er, Gawd blind 'em!

Yank. [*Spitting on his hands—belligerently:*] De more de merrier when I gits started. Bring on de gang!

Long. Yer'll see 'em in arf a mo', when that church lets out. [*He turns and sees the window display in the two stores for the first time.*] Blimey! Look at that, will yer? [*They both walk back and stand looking in the jeweler's.* LONG *flies into a fury.*] Just look at this 'ere bloomin' mess! Just look at it! Look at the bleedin' prices on 'em—more'n our 'ole bloody stokehole makes in ten voyages sweatin' in 'ell! And they—'er and 'er bloody clarss—buys 'em for toys to dangle on 'em! One of these 'ere would buy scoff for a starvin' family for a year!

Yank. Aw, cut de sob stuff! T' hell wit de starvin' family! Yuh'll be passin' de hat to me next. [*With naïve admiration.*] Say, dem tings is pretty, huh? Bet yuh dey'd hock for a piece of change aw right. [*Then turning away, bored.*] But, aw hell, what good are dey? Let her have 'em. Dey don't belong no more'n she does. [*With a gesture of sweeping the jeweler's into oblivion.*] All dat don't count, get me?

Long. [*Who has moved to the furrier's—indignantly:*] And I s'pose this 'ere don't count neither—skins of poor, 'armless animals slaughtered so as 'er and 'ers can keep their bleedin' noses warm!

Yank. [*Who has been staring at something inside—with queer excitement:*] Take a slant at dat! Give it de once-over! Monkey fur—two t'ousand bucks! [*Bewilderedly.*] Is dat straight goods—monkey fur? What de hell——?

Long. [*Bitterly.*] It's straight enuf. [*With grim humor.*] They wouldn't bloody well pay that for a 'airy ape's skin—no, nor for the 'ole livin' ape with all 'is 'ead, and body, and soul thrown in!

Yank. [*Clenching his fists, his face growing pale with rage as if the skin in the window were a personal insult.*] Trowin' it up in my face! Christ! I'll fix her!

Long. [*Excitedly.*] Church is out. 'Ere they come, the bleedin' swine. [*After a glance at* YANK'S *lowering face—uneasily:*] Easy goes, Comrade. Keep yer bloomin' temper. Remember force defeats itself. It ain't our weapon. We must impress our demands through peaceful means—the votes of the on-marching proletarians of the bloody world!

Yank. [*With abysmal contempt.*] Votes, hell! Votes is a joke, see? Votes for women! Let dem do it!

Long. [*Still more uneasily.*] Calm, now. Treat 'em wiv the proper contempt. Observe the bleedin' parasites but 'old yer 'orses.

Yank. [*Angrily.*] Git away from me! Yuh're yellow, dat's what. Force, dat's me! De punch, dat's me every time, see!

[*The* CROWD *from church enter from the right, sauntering slowly and affectedly, their heads held stiffly up, looking neither to right nor left, talking in toneless, simpering voices. The* WOMEN *are rouged, calcimined, dyed, over-dressed to the nth degree. The* MEN *are in Prince Alberts, high hats, spats, canes, etc. A procession of gaudy marionettes, yet with something of the relentless horror of Frankensteins in their detached, mechanical unawareness.*]

Voices. Dear Doctor Caiaphas! He is so sincere!

What was the sermon? I dozed off.

About the radicals, my dear—and the false doctrines that are being preached.

We must organize a hundred per cent American bazaar.

And let everyone contribute one one-hundredth per cent of their income tax.

What an original idea!

We can devote the proceeds to rehabilitating the veil of the temple.

But that has been done so many times.

Yank. [*Glaring from one to the other of them—with an insulting snort of scorn:*] Huh! Huh!

[*Without seeming to see him, they make wide detours to avoid the spot where he stands in the middle of the sidewalk.*]

Long. [*Frightenedly.*] Keep yer bloomin' mouth shut, I tells yer.

Yank. [*Viciously.*] G'wan! Tell it to Sweeney! [*He swaggers away and deliberately lurches into a top-hatted* GENTLEMAN, *then glares at him pugnaciously.*] Say, who d'yuh tink yuh're bumpin'? Tink yuh own de oith?

Gentleman. [*Coldly and affectedly.*] I beg your pardon.

[*He has not looked at* YANK *and passes on without a glance, leaving him bewildered.*]

Long. [*Rushing up and grabbing* YANK'S *arm.*] 'Ere! Come away! This wasn't what I meant. Yer'll 'ave the bloody coppers down on us.

Yank. [*Savagely—giving him a push that sends him sprawling.*] G'wan!

Long. [*Picks himself up—hysterically:*] I'll pop orf then. This ain't what I meant. And whatever 'appens, yer can't blame me.

[*He slinks off left.*]

Yank. T' hell wit youse! [*He approaches a* LADY*—with a vicious grin and a smirking wink:*] Hello, Kiddo. How's every little ting? Got anything on for tonight? I know an old boiler down to de docks we kin crawl into. [*The* LADY *stalks by without a look, without a change of pace.* YANK *turns to others—insultingly.*] Holy smokes, what a mug! Go hide yuhself before de horses shy at yuh. Gee, pipe de heinie on dat one! Say, youse, yuh look like de stoin of a ferry-boat. Paint and powder! All dolled up to kill! Yuh look like stiffs laid out for de boneyard! Aw, g'wan, de lot of youse! Yuh give me de eye-ache. Yuh don't belong, get me! Look at me, why don't youse dare? I belong, dat's me! [*Pointing to a skyscraper across the street which is in process of construction—with bravado:*] See dat building goin' up dere? See de steel work? Steel, dat's me! Youse guys live on it and tink yuh're somep'n. But I'm *in* it, see! I'm de hoistin' engine dat makes it go up! I'm it—de inside and bottom of it! Sure! I'm steel and steam and smoke and de rest of it! It moves—speed—twenty-five stories up—and me at de top and bottom—movin'! Youse simps don't move. Yuh're on'y dolls I winds up to see 'm spin. Yuh're de garbage, get me—de leavins—de ashes we dump over de side! Now, what 'a' yuh gotta say? [*But as they seem neither to see nor hear him, he flies into a fury.*] Bums! Pigs! Tarts! Bitches! [*He turns in a rage on the* MEN, *bumping viciously into them but not jarring them the least bit. Rather it is he who recoils after each collision. He keeps growling.*] Git off de oith! G'wan, yuh bum! Look where yuh're goin', can't yuh? Git outa here! Fight, why don't yuh? Put up yer mits! Don't be a dog! Fight or I'll knock yuh dead! [*But, without seeming to see him, they all answer with mechanical affected politeness:*] I beg your pardon.

[*Then, at a cry from one of the* WOMEN, *they all scurry to the furrier's window.*]

The Woman. [*Ecstatically, with a gasp of delight.*] Monkey fur! [*The whole crowd of* MEN *and* WOMEN *chorus after her in the same tone of affected delight.*] Monkey fur!

Yank. [*With a jerk of his head back on his shoulders, as if he had received a punch full in the face—raging:*] I see yuh, all in white! I see yuh, yuh white-faced tart, yuh! Hairy ape, huh? I'll hairy ape yuh!

[*He bends down and grips at the street curbing as if to pluck it out and hurl it. Foiled in this, snarling with passion, he leaps to the lamp-post on the corner and tries to pull it up for a club. Just at that moment a bus is heard rumbling up. A fat, high-hatted, spatted* GENTLEMAN *runs out from the side street. He calls out plaintively:*]

Gentleman. Bus! Bus! Stop there!

[*And runs full tilt into the bending, straining* YANK, *who is bowled off his balance.*]

Yank. [*Seeing a fight—with a roar of joy as he springs to his feet:*] At last! Bus, huh? I'll bust yuh!

[*He lets drive a terrific swing, his fist landing full on the fat* GENTLEMAN'S *face. But the* GENTLEMAN *stands unmoved as if nothing had happened.*]

Gentleman. I beg your pardon. [*Then irritably.*] You have made me lose my bus. [*He claps his hands and begins to scream:*] Officer! Officer!

[*Many police whistles shrill out on the instant and a whole platoon of* POLICEMEN *rush in on* YANK *from all sides. He tries to fight but is clubbed to the pavement and fallen upon. The* CROWD *at the window have not moved or noticed this disturbance. The clanging gong of the patrol wagon approaches with a clamoring din.*]

CURTAIN

SCENE SIX

Night of the following day. A row of cells in the prison on Blackwell's Island. The cells extend back diagonally from right front to left rear. They do not stop, but disappear in the dark background as if they ran on, numberless, into infinity. One electric bulb from the low ceiling of the narrow corridor sheds its light through the heavy steel bars of the cell at the extreme front and reveals part of the interior.

[YANK *can be seen within, crouched on the edge of his cot in the attitude of Rodin's "The Thinker." His face is spotted with black and blue bruises. A blood-stained bandage is wrapped around his head.*]

Yank. [*Suddenly starting as if awakening from a dream, reaches out and shakes the bars—aloud to himself, wonderingly:*] Steel. Dis is de Zoo, huh?

[*A burst of hard, barking laughter comes from the unseen* OCCUPANTS *of the cells, runs back down the tier, and abruptly ceases.*]

Voices. [*Mockingly.*] The Zoo? That's a new name for this coop—a damn good name!

Steel, eh? You said a mouthful. This is the old iron house.

Who is that boob talkin'?

He's the bloke they brung in out of his head. The bulls had beat him up fierce.

Yank. [*Dully.*] I musta been dreamin'. I tought I was in a cage at de Zoo—but de apes don't talk, do dey?

Voices. [*With mocking laughter.*] You're in a cage aw right.

A coop!

A pen!

A sty!

A kennel!

[*Hard laughter—a pause.*]

Say, guy! Who are you? No, never mind lying. What are you?

Yes, tell us your sad story. What's your game?

What did they jug yuh for?

Yank. [*Dully.*] I was a fireman—stokin' on de liners. [*Then with sudden rage, rattling his cell bars.*] I'm a hairy ape, get me? And I'll bust youse all in de jaw if yuh don't lay off kiddin' me.

Voices. Huh! You're a hard boiled duck, ain't youse!

When you spit, it bounces!

[*Laughter.*]

Aw, can it. He's a regular guy. Ain't you? What did he say he was—a ape?

Yank. [*Defiantly.*] Sure ting! Ain't dat what youse all are—apes?

[*A silence. Then a furious rattling of bars from down the corridor.*]

A Voice. [*Thick with rage.*] I'll show yuh who's a ape, yuh bum!

Voices. Ssshh! Nix!

Can de noise!

Piano!

You'll have the guard down on us!

Yank. [*Scornfully.*] De guard? Yuh mean de keeper, don't yuh?

[*Angry exclamations from all the cells.*]

Voice. [*Placatingly.*] Aw, don't pay no attention to him. He's off his nut from the beatin'-up he got. Say, you guy! We're waitin' to hear what they landed you for—or ain't yuh tellin'?

Yank. Sure, I'll tell youse. Sure! Why de hell not? On'y—youse won't get me. Nobody gets me but me, see? I started to tell de Judge and all he says was: "Toity days to tink it over." Tink it over! Christ, dat's all I been doin' for weeks! [*After a pause.*] I was tryin' to git even wit someone, see? —someone dat done me doit.

Voices. [*Cynically.*] De old stuff, I bet. Your goil, huh?

Give yuh the double-cross, huh?

That's them every time!

Did yuh beat up de odder guy?

Yank. [*Disgustedly.*] Aw, yuh're all

wrong! Sure dere was a skoit in it—but not what youse mean, not dat old tripe. Dis was a new kind of skoit. She was dolled up all in white—in de stokehole. I tought she was a ghost. Sure. [*A pause.*]

Voices. [*Whispering.*] Gee, he's still nutty.
Let him rave. It's fun listenin'.

Yank. [*Unheeding — groping in his thoughts.*] Her hands—dey was skinny and white like dey wasn't real but painted on somep'n. Dere was a million miles from me to her—twenty-five knots a hour. She was like some dead ting de cat brung in. Sure, dat's what. She didn't belong. She belonged in de window of a toy store, or on de top of a garbage can, see! Sure! [*He breaks out angrily.*] But would yuh believe it, she had de noive to do me doit. She lamped me like she was seein' somep'n broke loose from de menagerie. Christ, yuh'd oughter seen her eyes! [*He rattles the bars of his cell furiously.*] But I'll get back at her yet, you watch! And if I can't find her I'll take it out on de gang she runs wit. I'm wise to where dey hangs out now. I'll show her who belongs! I'll show her who's in de move and who ain't. You watch my smoke!

Voices. [*Serious and joking.*] Dat's de talkin'!
Take her for all she's got!
What was this dame, anyway? Who was she, eh?

Yank. I dunno. First cabin stiff. Her old man's a millionaire, dey says—name of Douglas.

Voices. Douglas? That's the president of the Steel Trust, I bet.
Sure. I seen his mug in de papers.
He's filthy with dough.

Voice. Hey, feller, take a tip from me. If you want to get back at that dame, you better join the Wobblies. You'll get some action then.

Yank. Wobblies? What de hell's dat?

Voice. Ain't you ever heard of the I. W. W.?

Yank. Naw. What is it?

Voice. A gang of blokes—a tough gang. I been readin' about 'em today in the paper. The guard give me the *Sunday Times.* There's a long spiel about 'em. It's from a speech made in the Senate by a guy named Senator Queen. [*He is in the cell next to* YANK'S. *There is a rustling of paper.*] Wait'll I see if I got light enough and I'll read you. Listen. [*He reads:*] "There is a menace existing in this country today which threatens the vitals of our fair Republic—as foul a menace against the very life-blood of the American Eagle as was the foul conspiracy of Catiline against the eagles of ancient Rome!"

Voice. [*Disgustedly.*] Aw, hell! Tell him to salt de tail of dat eagle!

Voice. [*Reading:*] "I refer to that devil's brew of rascals, jailbirds, murderers, and cutthroats who libel all honest working men by calling themselves the Industrial Workers of the World; but in the light of their nefarious plots, I call them the Industrious *Wreckers* of the World!"

Yank. [*With vengeful satisfaction.*] Wreckers, dat's de right dope! Dat belongs! Me for dem!

Voice. Ssshh! [*Reading:*] "This fiendish organization is a foul ulcer on the fair body of our Democracy——"

Voice. Democracy, hell! Give him the boid, fellers—the raspberry! [*They do.*]

Voice. Ssshh! [*Reading:*] "Like Cato I say to this Senate, the I. W. W. must be destroyed! For they represent an ever-present dagger pointed at the heart of the greatest nation the world has ever known, where all men are born free and equal, with equal opportunities to all, where the Founding Fathers have guaranteed to each one happiness, where Truth, Honor, Liberty, Justice, and the Brotherhood of Man are a religion absorbed with one's mother milk, taught at our father's knee, sealed, signed, and stamped in the glorious Constitution of these United States!"

[*A perfect storm of hisses, catcalls, boos, and hard laughter.*]

Voices. [*Scornfully.*] Hurrah for de Fort' of July!
Pass de hat!
Liberty!
Justice!
Honor!
Opportunity!
Brotherhood!

All. [*With abysmal scorn.*] Aw, hell!

Voice. Give the Queen Senator guy the bark! All togedder now—one—two—three ——

[*A terrific chorus of barking and yapping.*]

Guard. [*From a distance.*] Quiet there, youse—or I'll git the hose.

[*The noise subsides.*]

Yank. [*With growling rage.*] I'd like to catch dat senator guy alone for a second. I'd loin him some trute!

Voice. Ssshh! Here's where he gits down to cases on the Wobblies. [*Reads:*] "They plot with fire in one hand and dynamite in the other. They stop not before murder to gain their ends, nor at the outraging of defenseless womanhood. They would tear down society, put the lowest scum in the seats of the mighty, turn Almighty God's revealed plan for the world topsy-turvy, and make of our sweet and lovely civilization a shambles, a desolation where man, God's masterpiece, would soon degenerate back to the ape!"

Voice. [*To* YANK.] Hey, you guy. There's your ape stuff again.

Yank. [*With a growl of fury.*] I got him. So dey blow up tings, do they? Dey turn tings round, do dey? Hey, lend me dat paper, will yuh?

Voice. Sure. Give it to him. On'y keep it to yourself, see? We don't wanter listen to no more of that slop.

Voice. Here you are. Hide it under your mattress.

Yank. [*Reaching out.*] Tanks. I can't read much but I kin manage. [*He sits, the paper in the hand at his side, in the attitude of Rodin's "The Thinker." A pause. Several snores from down the corridor. Suddenly* YANK *jumps to his feet with a furious groan as if some appalling thought had crashed on him—bewilderedly.*] Sure—her old man—president of de Steel Trust—makes half de steel in de world—steel—where I thought I belonged—drivin' trou—movin'—in dat—to make *her*—and cage me in for her to spit on! Christ! [*He shakes the bars of his cell door till the whole tier trembles. Irritated, protesting exclamations from those awakened or trying to get to sleep.*] He made dis—dis cage! Steel! *It* don't belong, dat's what! Cages, cells, locks, bolts, bars—dat's what it means!—holdin' me down with him at de top! But I'll drive trou! Fire, dat melts it! I'll be fire—under de heap—fire dat never goes out—hot as hell—breakin' out in de night——

[*While he has been saying this last he has shaken his cell door to a clanging accompaniment. As he comes to the "breakin' out" he seizes one bar with both hands and, putting his two feet up against the others so that his position is parallel to the floor like a monkey's, he gives a great wrench backwards. The bar bends like a licorice stick under his tremendous strength. Just at this moment the* PRISON GUARD *rushes in, dragging a hose behind him.*]

Guard. [*Angrily.*] I'll loin youse bums to wake me up! [*Sees* YANK.] Hello, it's you, huh? Got the D. Ts., hey? Well, I'll cure 'em. I'll drown your snakes for yuh! [*Noticing the bar.*] Hell, look at dat bar bended! On'y a bug is strong enough for dat!

Yank. [*Glaring at him.*] Or a hairy ape, yuh big yellow bum! Look out! Here I come!

[*He grabs another bar.*]

Guard. [*Scared now—yelling off left.*] Toin de hose on, Ben!—full pressure! And call de others—and a straitjacket!

[*The curtain is falling. As it hides* YANK *from view, there is a splattering smash as the stream of water hits the steel of* YANK'*s cell.*]

CURTAIN

SCENE SEVEN

Nearly a month later. An I. W. W. local near the waterfront, showing the interior of a front room on the ground floor, and the street outside. Moonlight on the narrow street, buildings massed in black shadow. The interior of the room, which is general assembly room, office, and reading room, resembles some dingy settlement boys' club. A desk and high stool are in one corner. A table with paper, stacks of pamphlets, chairs about it, is at center. The whole is decidedly cheap, banal, commonplace, and unmysterious as a room could well be. [*The* SECRETARY *is perched on the stool making entries in a large ledger. An eye shade casts his face into shadows. Eight or ten* MEN, LONGSHOREMEN, IRON WORKERS, *and the like, are grouped about the table. Two are playing checkers. One is writing a letter. Most of them are smoking pipes. A big signboard is on the wall at the rear, "Industrial Workers of the World—Local No. 57."* YANK *comes down the street outside. He is dressed as in Scene Five. He moves cautiously, mysteriously. He comes to a point opposite the door; tiptoes softly up to it, listens, is impressed by the silence within, knocks carefully, as if he were guessing at the password to some secret rite. Listens. No answer.*

Knocks again a bit louder. No answer. Knocks impatiently, much louder.]

Secretary. [*Turning around on his stool.*] What the hell is that—someone knocking? [*Shouts:*] Come in, why don't you?

[*All the* MEN *in the room look up.* YANK *opens the door slowly, gingerly, as if afraid of an ambush. He looks around for the secret doors, mystery, is taken aback by the commonplaceness of the room and the* MEN *in it, thinks he may have gotten in the wrong place, then sees the signboard on the wall and is reassured.*]

Yank. [*Blurts out:*] Hello.

Men. [*Reservedly.*] Hello.

Yank. [*More easily.*] I thought I'd bumped into de wrong dump.

Secretary. [*Scrutinizing him carefully.*] Maybe you have. Are you a member?

Yank. Naw, not yet. Dat's what I come for—to join.

Secretary. That's easy. What's your job —longshore?

Yank. Naw. Fireman—stoker on de liners.

Secretary. [*With satisfaction.*] Welcome to our city. Glad to know you people are waking up at last. We haven't got many members in your line.

Yank. Naw. Dey're all dead to de woild.

Secretary. Well, you can help to wake 'em. What's your name? I'll make out your card.

Yank. [*Confused.*] Name? Lemme tink.

Secretary. [*Sharply.*] Don't you know your own name?

Yank. Sure; but I been just Yank for so long—Bob, dat's it—Bob Smith.

Secretary. [*Writing.*] Robert Smith. [*Fills out the rest of card.*] Here you are. Cost you half a dollar.

Yank. Is dat all—four bits? Dat's easy.

[*Gives the* SECRETARY *the money.*]

Secretary. [*Throwing it in drawer.*] Thanks. Well, make yourself at home. No introductions needed. There's literature on the table. Take some of those pamphlets with you to distribute aboard ship. They may bring results. Sow the seed, only go about it right. Don't get caught and fired. We got plenty out of work. What we need is men who can hold their jobs—and work for us at the same time.

Yank. Sure.

[*But he still stands, embarrassed and uneasy.*]

Secretary. [*Looking at him—curiously:*] What did you knock for? Think we had a coon in uniform to open doors?

Yank. Naw. I tought it was locked—and dat yuh'd wanter give me the once-over trou a peep-hole or somep'n to see if I was right.

Secretary. [*Alert and suspicious but with an easy laugh.*] Think we were running a crap game? That door is never locked. What put that in your nut?

Yank. [*With a knowing grin, convinced that this is all camouflage, a part of the secrecy.*] Dis burg is full of bulls, ain't it?

Secretary. [*Sharply.*] What have the cops got to do with us? We're breaking no laws.

Yank. [*With a knowing wink.*] Sure. Youse wouldn't for woilds. Sure. I'm wise to dat.

Secretary. You seem to be wise to a lot of stuff none of us knows about.

Yank. [*With another wink.*] Aw, dat's aw right, see? [*Then made a bit resentful by the suspicious glances from all sides.*] Aw, can it! Youse needn't put me trou de toid degree. Can't youse see I belong? Sure! I'm reg'lar. I'll stick, get me? I'll shoot de woiks for youse. Dat's why I wanted to join in.

Secretary. [*Breezily, feeling him out.*] That's the right spirit. Only are you sure you understand what you've joined? It's all plain and above board; still, some guys get a wrong slant on us. [*Sharply.*] What's your notion of the purpose of the I. W. W.?

Yank. Aw, I know all about it.

Secretary. [*Sarcastically.*] Well, give us some of your valuable information.

Yank. [*Cunningly.*] I know enough not to speak outa my toin. [*Then resentfully again.*] Aw, say! I'm reg'lar. I'm wise to de game. I know yuh got to watch your step wit a stranger. For all youse know, I might be a plain-clothes dick, or somep'n, dat's what yuh're thinkin', huh? Aw, forget it! I belong, see? Ask any guy down to de docks if I don't.

Secretary. Who said you didn't?

Yank. After I'm 'nitiated, I'll show yuh.

Secretary. [*Astounded.*] Initiated? There's no initiation.

Yank. [*Disappointed.*] Ain't there no password—no grip nor nothin'?

Secretary. What'd you think this is—the Elks—or the Black Hand?

Yank. De Elks, hell! De Black Hand, dey're a lot of yellow backstickin' Ginees. Naw. Dis is a man's gang, ain't it?

Secretary. You said it! That's why we stand on two feet in the open. We got no secrets.

Yank. [*Surprised but admiringly.*] Yuh mean to say yuh always run wide open—like dis?

Secretary. Exactly.

Yank. Den yuh sure got your noive wit youse!

Secretary. [*Sharply.*] Just what was it made you want to join us? Come out with that straight.

Yank. Yuh call me? Well, I got noive, too! Here's my hand. Yuh wanter blow tings up, don't yuh? Well, dat's me! I belong!

Secretary. [*With pretended carelessness.*] You mean change the unequal conditions of society by legitimate direct action—or with dynamite?

Yank. Dynamite! Blow it offen de oith —steel—all de cages—all de factories, steamers, buildings, jails—de Steel Trust and all dat makes it go.

Secretary. So—that's your idea, eh? And did you have any special job in that line you wanted to propose to us?

[*He makes a sign to the* MEN, *who get up cautiously one by one and group behind* YANK.]

Yank. [*Boldly.*] Sure, I'll come out wit it. I'll show youse I'm one of de gang. Dere's dat millionaire guy, Douglas——

Secretary. President of the Steel Trust, you mean? Do you want to assassinate him?

Yank. Naw, dat don't get yuh nothin'. I mean blow up de factory, de woiks, where he makes de steel. Dat's what I'm after—to blow up de steel, knock all de steel in de woild up to de moon. Dat'll fix tings! [*Eagerly, with a touch of bravado.*] I'll do it by me lonesome! I'll show yuh! Tell me where his woiks is, how to git there, all de dope. Gimme de stuff, de old butter—and watch me do de rest! Watch de smoke and see it move! I don't give a damn if dey nab me—long as it's done! I'll soive life for it—and give 'em de laugh! [*Half to himself.*] And I'll write her a letter and tell her de hairy ape done it. Dat'll square tings.

Secretary. [*Stepping away from* YANK.] Very interesting.

[*He gives a signal. The* MEN, *huskies all, throw themselves on* YANK *and before he knows it they have his legs and arms pinioned. But he is too flabbergasted to make a struggle, anyway. They feel him over for weapons.*]

Man. No gat, no knife. Shall we give him what's what and put the boots to him?

Secretary. No. He isn't worth the trouble we'd get into. He's too stupid. [*He comes closer and laughs mockingly in* YANK'S *face.*] Ho-ho! By God, this is the biggest joke they've put up on us yet. Hey, you Joke! Who sent you—Burns or Pinkerton? No, by God, you're such a bonehead I'll bet you're in the Secret Service! Well, you dirty spy, you rotten agent provocator, you can go back and tell whatever skunk is paying you blood-money for betraying your brothers that he's wasting his coin. You couldn't catch a cold. And tell him that all he'll ever get on us, or ever has got, is just his own sneaking plots that he's framed up to put us in jail. We are what our manifesto says we are, neither more nor less—and we'll give him a copy of that any time he calls. And as for you—— [*He glares scornfully at* YANK, *who is sunk in an oblivious stupor.*] Oh, hell, what's the use of talking? You're a brainless ape.

Yank. [*Aroused by the word to fierce but futile struggles.*] What's dat, yuh Sheeny bum, yuh!

Secretary. Throw him out, boys.

[*In spite of his struggles, this is done with gusto and éclat. Propelled by several parting kicks,* YANK *lands sprawling in the middle of the narrow cobbled street. With a growl he starts to get up and storm the closed door, but stops bewildered by the confusion in his brain, pathetically impotent. He sits there, brooding, in as near to the attitude of Rodin's "Thinker" as he can get in his position.*]

Yank. [*Bitterly.*] So dem boids don't tink I belong, neider. Aw, to hell wit 'em! Dey're in de wrong pew—de same old bull—soapboxes and Salvation Army—no guts! Cut out an hour offen de job a day and make me happy! Gimme a dollar more a day and make me happy! Tree squares a day, and cauliflowers in de front yard—ekal rights—a woman and kids—a lousy vote—and I'm all fixed for Jesus, huh? Aw, hell! What does dat get yuh? Dis ting's in your inside, but it ain't your belly. Feedin' your face—sinkers and coffee—dat don't touch it. It's way down—at de bottom. Yuh can't grab it, and yuh can't stop it. It moves, and everything moves. It stops and de whole woild stops. Dat's me now—I don't tick, see?—I'm a busted Ingersoll, dat's what. Steel was me, and I owned de woild. Now I ain't steel, and de woild owns me. Aw, hell! I can't see—it's all dark, get me? It's all wrong! [*He turns a bitter mocking face up like an ape gibbering at the moon.*] Say, youse up dere, Man in de Moon, yuh look so wise, gimme de answer, huh? Slip me de inside dope, de information right from de stable—where do I get off at, huh?

A Policeman. [*Who has come up the street*

in time to hear this last—with grim humor:] You'll get off at the station, you boob, if you don't get up out of that and keep movin'.

Yank. [*Looking up at him—with a hard, bitter laugh:*] Sure! Lock me up! Put me in a cage! Dat's de on'y answer yuh know. G'wan, lock me up!

Policeman. What you been doin'?

Yank. Enuf to gimme life for! I was born, see? Sure, dat's de charge. Write it in de blotter. I was born, get me?

Policeman. [*Jocosely.*] God pity your old woman! [*Then matter-of-fact.*] But I've no time for kidding. You're soused. I'd run you in but it's too long a walk to the station. Come on now, get up, or I'll fan your ears with this club. Beat it now!

[*He hauls* YANK *to his feet.*]

Yank. [*In a vague mocking tone.*] Say, where do I go from here?

Policeman. [*Giving him a push—with a grin, indifferently:*] Go to hell.

CURTAIN

SCENE EIGHT

Twilight of the next day. The monkey house at the Zoo. One spot of clear gray light falls on the front of one cage so that the interior can be seen. The other cages are vague, shrouded in shadow from which chatterings pitched in a conversational tone can be heard. On the one cage a sign from which the word "gorilla" stands out. The gigantic ANIMAL *himself is seen squatting on his haunches on a bench in much the same attitude as Rodin's "Thinker."*

[YANK *enters from the left. Immediately a chorus of angry chattering and screeching breaks out. The* GORILLA *turns his eyes but makes no sound or move.*]

Yank. [*With a hard, bitter laugh.*] Welcome to your city, huh? Hail, hail, de gang's all here! [*At the sound of his voice the chattering dies away into an attentive silence.* YANK *walks up to the* GORILLA'S *cage and, leaning over the railing, stares in at its occupant, who stares back at him, silent and motionless. There is a pause of dead stillness. Then* YANK *begins to talk in a friendly confidential tone, half-mockingly, but with a deep undercurrent of sympathy.*] Say, yuh're some hard-lookin' guy, ain't yuh? I seen lots of tough nuts dat de gang called gorillas, but yuh're de foist real one I ever seen. Some chest yuh got, and shoulders, and dem arms and mits! I bet yuh got a punch in eider fist dat'd knock 'em all silly! [*This with genuine admiration. The* GORILLA, *as if he understood, stands upright, swelling out his chest and pounding on it with his fist.* YANK *grins sympathetically.*] Sure, I get yuh. Yuh challenge de whole woild, huh? Yuh got what I was sayin' even if yuh muffed de woids. [*Then bitterness creeping in.*] And why wouldn't yuh get me? Ain't we both members of de same club—de Hairy Apes? [*They stare at each other—a pause —then* YANK *goes on slowly and bitterly.*] So yuh're what she seen when she looked at me, de white-faced tart! I was you to her, get me? On'y outa de cage—broke out—free to moider her, see? Sure! Dat's what she tought. She wasn't wise dat I was in a cage, too—worser'n yours—sure—a damn sight—'cause you got some chanct to bust loose—but me—— [*He grows confused.*] Aw, hell! It's wrong, ain't it? [*A pause.*] I s'pose yuh wanter know what I'm doin' here, huh? I been warmin' a bench down to de Battery—ever since last night. Sure. I seen de sun come up. Dat was pretty, too—all red and pink and green. I was lookin' at de skyscrapers—steel—and all de ships comin' in, sailin' out, all over de oith—and dey was steel, too. De sun was warm, dey wasn't no clouds, and dere was a breeze blowin'. Sure, it was great stuff. I got it aw right—what Paddy said about dat bein' de right dope—on'y I couldn't get *in* it, see? I couldn't belong in dat. It was over my head. And I kept tinkin'—and den I beat it up here to see what youse was like. And I waited till dey was all gone to git yuh alone. Say, how d'yuh feel sittin' in dat pen all de time, havin' to stand for 'em comin' and starin' at yuh—de white-faced, skinny tarts and de boobs what marry 'em—makin' fun of yuh, laughin' at yuh, gittin' scared of yuh—damn 'em! [*He pounds on the rail with his fist. The* GORILLA *rattles the bars of his cage and snarls. All the other monkeys set up an angry chattering in the darkness.* YANK *goes on excitedly.*] Sure! Dat's de way it hits me, too. On'y yuh're lucky, see? Yuh don't belong wit 'em and yuh know it. But me, I belong wit 'em—but I don't, see?

Dey don't belong wit me, dat's what. Get me? Tinkin' is hard—— [*He passes one hand across his forehead with a painful gesture. The* GORILLA *growls impatiently.* YANK *goes on gropingly.*] It's dis way, what I'm drivin' at. Youse can sit and dope dream in de past, green woods, de jungle, and de rest of it. Den yuh belong and dey don't. Den yuh kin laugh at 'em, see? Yuh're de champ of de woild. But me—I ain't got no past to tink in, nor nothin' dat's comin', on'y what's now—and dat don't belong. Sure, you're de best off! Yuh can't tink, can yuh? Yuh can't talk neider. But I kin make a bluff at talkin' and tinkin'—a'most git away wit it—a'most!—and dat's where de joker comes in. [*He laughs.*] I ain't on oith and I ain't in heaven, get me? I'm in de middle tryin' to separate 'em, takin' all de woist punches from bot' of 'em. Maybe dat's what dey call hell, huh? But you, yuh're at de bottom. You belong! Sure! Yuh're de on'y one in de woild dat does, yuh lucky stiff! [*The* GORILLA *growls proudly.*] And dat's why dey gotter put yuh in a cage, see? [*The* GORILLA *roars angrily.*] Sure! Yuh get me. It beats it when you try to tink it or talk it—it's way down—deep—behind—you 'n' me we feel it. Sure! Bot' members of dis club! [*He laughs—then in a savage tone:*] What de hell! T' hell wit it! A little action, dat's our meat! Dat belongs! Knock 'em down and keep bustin' 'em till dey croaks yuh wit a gat—wit steel! Sure! Are yuh game? Dey've looked at youse, ain't dey—in a cage? Wanter git even? Wanter wind up like a sport 'stead of croakin' slow in dere? [*The* GORILLA *roars an emphatic affirmative.* YANK *goes on with a sort of furious exaltation.*] Sure! Yuh're reg'lar. Yuh'll stick to de finish! Me 'n' you, huh?—bot' members of this club! We'll put up one last star bout dat'll knock 'em offen deir seats! Dey'll have to make de cages stronger after we're trou! [*The* GORILLA *is straining at his bars, growling, hopping from one foot to the other.* YANK *takes a jimmy from under his coat and forces the lock on the cage door. He throws this open.*] Pardon from de governor! Step out and shake hands! I'll take yuh for a walk down Fif' Avenoo. We'll knock 'em offen de oith and croak wit de band playin'. Come on, Brother. [*The* GORILLA *scrambles gingerly out of his cage. Goes to* YANK *and stands looking at him.* YANK *keeps his mocking tone—holds out his hand.*] Shake—de secret grip of our order. [*Something, the tone of mockery, perhaps, suddenly enrages the* ANIMAL. *With a spring he wraps his huge arms around* YANK *in a murderous hug. There is a crackling snap of crushed ribs—a gasping cry, still mocking, from* YANK.] Hey, I didn't say kiss me! [*The* GORILLA *lets the crushed body slip to the floor; stands over it uncertainly, considering; then picks it up, throws it in the cage, shuts the door, and shuffles off menacingly into the darkness at left. A great uproar of frightened chattering and whimpering comes from the other cages. Then* YANK *moves, groaning, opening his eyes, and there is silence. He mutters painfully:*] Say—dey oughter match him—wit Zybszko. He got me, aw right. I'm trou. Even him didn't tink I belonged. [*Then, with sudden passionate despair.*] Christ, where do I get off at? Where do I fit in? [*Checking himself as suddenly.*] Aw, what de hell! No squawkin', see! No quittin', get me! Croak wit your boots on! [*He grabs hold of the bars of the cage and hauls himself painfully to his feet—looks around him bewilderedly—forces a mocking laugh.*] In de cage, huh? [*In the strident tones of a circus barker.*] Ladies and gents, step forward and take a slant at de one and only—[*His voice weakening*]—one and original—Hairy Ape from de wilds of——

[*He slips in a heap on the floor and dies. The monkeys set up a chattering, whimpering wail. And, perhaps, the Hairy Ape at last belongs.*]

CURTAIN

STREET SCENE *

By

ELMER L. RICE

SIGNIFICANT OF THE TENDENCIES IN OUR theater is the fact that Elmer L. Rice (Reizenstein), one of the most experimental and propagandist of American playwrights, achieved his greatest success without the least suggestion of futurism and with hardly more propaganda than is inevitable in any serious depiction of life. Such a success was his photographic *Street Scene* in 1929, six years after he had given the New York stage its first experience of uncompromising Expressionism in *The Adding Machine.*

A New Yorker from birth, Mr. Rice has been an acute observer of city life and its soul-destroying forces. He has found a career devoted to the dramatic expression of his notings to be more satisfying than the legal one for which he was trained with high honors. He has sometimes worked alone and sometimes in collaboration, as when he devised with Philip Barry the ingenious but flimsy mystery play, *Cock Robin.*

Whether experimenting with technical expedients, as when he introduced the flashback in *On Trial* (1914), with Expressionism, or with more conventional forms of tragedy (*The Subway,* 1929), comedy (*Wake Up, Jonathan,* 1921), melodrama (*Counsellor-at-law,* 1931), or farce (*See Naples and Die,* 1929), Rice's distinctive excellencies remain the same: vivid objectivity in marshalling realistic detail and a commanding sense of stage effect, both of which he displays with an easy profusion that is breath-taking, as in *Counsellor-at-law,* if not bewildering, as in *We, the People.* Less convincing was his experiment in the strange patriotic fantasy called *American Landscape* (1939). Although *Two on an Island* (1940) was in Rice's better style, it lacked dramatic interest. *Flight to the West* (1940) still shows him stronger in stage effect than in dramatic coherence.

Through this technical brilliance there appear, however, a sympathetic and often beautiful portrayal of human nature and a prophetic vision of better social relations than those he puts crassly on the stage. At his best, as in *Street Scene,* he lets the objects of his dislike condemn themselves, and he permits his dreams of a better world to suggest themselves, as in life, through appropriate characters. Less admirable, at times, is his over-emphatic denunciation and propaganda, as in *We, the People* (1933), which was received with a broadside of caustic criticism.

The staging of *Street Scene,* which had been refused by most of the Broadway producers, was finally undertaken by William A. Brady. The direction was entrusted to the author himself. So carefully were all its "minute brush strokes," as Rice called them, reproduced, and so perfect was Jo Mielziner's solidly constructed brown-front New York tenement house filling the stage, that the audience was hardly aware that they were in a theater and not actually gazing through the window of a house opposite upon a stream of life made fascinating by its vivid variety and its symbolism as a cross-section of a false-face civilization.

ELMER RICE

Born 1892, New York City.
1912, LL.B., New York Law School.
1914, His first play, *On Trial.* Abandoned law for the career of dramatist.

1929, Awarded the Pulitzer Prize for *Street Scene.*
1930, Novel: *A Voyage to Purilia* (satire on the motion pictures).
1935–1937, Regional director, Federal Theater Project.
1937, Novel: *Imperial City.*

PLAYS

1914 *On Trial.* 1917 *The House of the Free* (published in *Morningside Plays*). 1917 *The Iron Cross.* 1919 *For the Defence.* 1921 *Wake Up, Jonathan* (with Hatcher Hughes). 1922 *It Is the Law* (with Hayden Talbot). 1923 *The Adding Machine.* 1924 *The Mongrel* (adapted from the German). 1924 *Close Harmony,* also titled *The Lady Next Door* (with Dorothy Parker). 1927 *Cock Robin* (with Philip Barry). 1929 *Street Scene.* 1929 *See Naples and Die.* 1929 *The Subway.* 1929 *Life Is Real.* 1929 *The Blue Hawaiian.* 1931 *The Left Bank.* 1931 *Counsellor-at-law.* 1932 *Black Sheep.* 1932 *The House in Blind Alley.* 1933 *We, the People.* 1934 *The Passing of Chow-Chow.* 1934 *Three Plays without Words* (*Landscape with Figures; Rus in Urbe; Exterior*), copyrighted in 1924 under the title, *Sidewalks of New York.* 1934 *Judgment Day.* 1934 *Between Two Worlds.* 1935 *Not for Children.* 1939 *American Landscape.* 1940 *Two on an Island.* 1940 *Flight to the West.*

WRITINGS ABOUT THE DRAMA

Theatre in Russia, New York Times, August 28, 1932, IX, 1:6; and September 4, 1932, IX, 1:8. *Letter on his relation to the theatre, New York Times,* February 12, 1933, III, 3:1. *People's Art Theatre, New York Times,* October 8, 1933, X, 1:6. *Farewell to Broadway, New York Times,* November 11, 1934, IX, 1:3 and 2:2, 3; November 18, IX, 2:1, 2. *About the Pulitzer Prize, New York Times,* December 20, 1935, 29:6.

STREET SCENE

Characters

(In the Order of Their First Appearance)

ABRAHAM KAPLAN.
GRETA FIORENTINO.
EMMA JONES.
OLGA OLSEN.
WILLIE MAURRANT.
ANNA MAURRANT.
DANIEL BUCHANAN.
FRANK MAURRANT.
GEORGE JONES.
STEVE SANKEY.
AGNES CUSHING.
CARL OLSEN.
SHIRLEY KAPLAN.
FILIPPO FIORENTINO.
ALICE SIMPSON.
LAURA HILDEBRAND.
MARY HILDEBRAND.
CHARLIE HILDEBRAND.
SAMUEL KAPLAN.
ROSE MAURRANT.
HARRY EASTER.
MAE JONES.
DICK MCGANN.
VINCENT JONES.
DR. JOHN WILSON.
OFFICER HARRY MURPHY.
A MILKMAN.
A LETTER-CARRIER.
AN ICE-MAN.
TWO COLLEGE GIRLS.
A MUSIC STUDENT.
MARSHALL JAMES HENRY.
FRED CULLEN.
AN OLD-CLOTHES MAN.
AN INTERNE.
AN AMBULANCE DRIVER.
A FURNITURE MOVER.
TWO NURSE-MAIDS.
POLICEMEN.
TWO APARTMENT HUNTERS.
PASSERS-BY.

ACT ONE

SCENE.—*The exterior of a "walk-up" apartment-house, in a mean quarter of New York. It is of ugly brownstone and was built in the '90's. Between the pavement of large, gray flagstones and the front of the house, is a deep and narrow "areaway," guarded by a rusted, ornamental iron railing. At the right, a steep flight of rotting wooden steps leads down to the cellar and to the janitor's apartment, the windows of which are just visible above the street level. Spanning the areaway is a "stoop" of four shallow, stone steps, flanked on either side by a curved stone balustrade. Beyond the broad fourth step, another step leads to the double wooden outer doors of the house; and as these are open, the vestibule, and the wide, heavy glass-panelled entrance door beyond are visible. Above the outer doors is a glass fanlight, upon which appears the half-obliterated house number. At the left side of the doorway is a sign which reads: "Flat To Let. 6 Rooms. Steam Heat."*

On either side of the stoop are the two narrow windows of the ground-floor apartments. In one of the windows, at the left, is a sign bearing the legend: "Prof. Filippo Fiorentino. Music for all occasions. Also instruction." Above are the six narrow windows of the first-floor apartments, and above that, the stone sills of the second-floor windows can just be seen.

To the left of the house, part of the adjoining building is visible: the motor entrance to a storage warehouse. Crude boarding across the large driveway and rough planks across the sidewalk and curb indicate that an excavation is in progress. On the boarding is painted in rude lettering: "Keep Out"; and at the curb is a small barrel bearing a sign with the words: "Street Closed." To the wall of the warehouse is affixed a brass plate, bearing the name: "Patrick

Mulcahy Storage Warehouse Co., Inc." To the right of the house, scaffolding and a wooden sidewalk indicate that the house next door is being demolished. On the scaffolding is a large, wooden sign reading: "Manhattan House-Wrecking Corp." In the close foreground, below the level of the curb, is a mere suggestion of the street.

At rise, the house is seen in the white glare of an arc-light, which is just off-stage to the right. The windows in the janitor's apartment are lighted, as are also those of the ground-floor apartment, at the right, and the two windows at the extreme left of the first-floor. A dim, red light is affixed to the boarding of the excavation at the left.

[*In the lighted ground-floor window, at the right of the doorway,* ABRAHAM KAPLAN *is seated in a rocking-chair, reading a Yiddish newspaper. He is a Russian Jew, well past sixty: clean-shaven, thick gray hair, hooked nose, horn-rimmed spectacles. To the left of the doorway,* GRETA FIORENTINO *is leaning out of the window. She is forty, blonde, ruddy-faced, and stout. She wears a wrapper of light, flowered material and a large pillow supports her left arm and her ample, uncorseted bosom. In her right hand is a folding paper fan, which she waves languidly.*

Throughout the act and, indeed, throughout the play, there is constant noise. The noises of the city rise, fall, intermingle: the distant roar of "L" trains, automobile sirens, and the whistles of boats on the river; the rattle of trucks and the indeterminate clanking of metals; fire-engines, ambulances, musical instruments, a radio, dogs barking and human voices calling, quarrelling, and screaming with laughter. The noises are subdued and in the background, but they never wholly cease.

A moment after the rise of the curtain, an elderly man enters at the right and walks into the house, exchanging a nod with MRS. FIORENTINO. A MAN, *munching peanuts, crosses the stage from left to right.*]

A Voice. [*Off-stage.*] Char-lie!

[EMMA JONES *appears at the left. She is middle-aged, tall, and rather bony She carries a small parcel.*]

Mrs. Fiorentino. [*She speaks with a faint German accent.*] Good evening, Mrs. Jones.

Mrs. Jones. [*Stopping beneath* MRS. FIORENTINO'S *window.*] Good evenin', Mrs. F. Well, I hope it's hot enough for you.

Mrs. Fiorentino. Ain't it joost awful? When I was through with the dishes, you could take my clothes and joost wring them out.

Mrs. Jones. Me, too. I ain't got a dry stitch on me.

Mrs. Fiorentino. I took off my shoes and my corset and made myself nice and comfortable, and tonight before I go to bed, I take a nice bath.

Mrs. Jones. The trouble with a bath is, by the time you're all through, you're as hot as when you started. [*As* OLGA OLSEN, *a thin, anemic Scandinavian, with untidy fair hair, comes up the cellar steps and onto the sidewalk.*] Good evenin', Mrs. Olsen. Awful hot, ain't it?

Mrs. Olsen. [*Coming over to the front of the stoop.*] Yust awful. Mrs. Forentiner, my hoosban' say vill you put de garbage on de doom-vaider?

Mrs. Fiorentino. Oh, sure, sure! I didn't hear him vistle. [*As* MRS. JONES *starts to cross to the stoop.*] Don't go 'vay, Mrs. Jones. [*She disappears from the window.*]

Mrs. Olsen. [*Pushing back some wisps of hair.*] I tank is more cooler in de cellar.

Mrs. Jones. [*Sitting on the stoop and fanning herself with her parcel.*] Phew! I'm just about ready to pass out.

Mrs. Olsen. My baby is crying, crying all day.

Mrs. Jones. Yeah, I often say they mind the heat more'n we do. It's the same with dogs. My Queenie has jes' been layin' aroun' all day.

Mrs. Olsen. The baby get new teet'. It hurt her.

Mrs. Jones. Don't tell me! If you was to know what I went t'roo with my Vincent. Half the time he used to have convulsions.

[WILLIE MAURRANT, *a disorderly boy of twelve, appears at the left, on roller skates. He stops at the left of the stoop and takes hold of the railing with both hands.*]

Willie. [*Raising his head and bawling.*] Hey, ma!

Mrs. Jones. [*Disapprovingly.*] If you want your mother, why don't you go upstairs, instead o' yellin' like that?

Willie. [*Without paying the slightest attention to her, bawls louder.*] Hey, ma!

Mrs. Maurrant. [*Appearing at one of the lighted first-floor windows.*] What do you want, Willie?

[*She is a fair woman of forty, who looks*

her age, but is by no means unattractive.]

Willie. Gimme a dime, will ya? I wanna git a cone.

Mrs. Maurrant. [*To* MRS. OLSEN *and* MRS. JONES.] Good evening.

Mrs. Olsen and Mrs. Jones. Good evenin', Mrs. Maurrant.

Mrs. Maurrant. [*To* WILLIE.] How many cones did you have today, already?

Willie. [*Belligerently.*] I'm hot! All de other guys is havin' cones. Come on, gimme a dime.

Mrs. Maurrant. Well, it's the last one.

[*She disappears.*]

Mrs. Jones. You certainly don't talk very nice to your mother. [*To* MRS. OLSEN.] I'd like to hear one o' mine talkin' that way to me!

Mrs. Maurrant. [*Appearing at the windows.*] Remember, this is the last one.

Willie. Aw right. T'row it down.

[MRS. FIORENTINO *reappears and leans out of the window again.*]

Mrs. Maurrant. Catch it!

[*She throws out a twist of newspaper.* WILLIE *scrambles for it, hastily extracts the dime, drops the newspaper on the pavement and skates off, at the left.*]

Mrs. Fiorentino. [*Twisting her neck upwards.*] Good evening, Mrs. Maurrant.

Mrs. Maurrant. Good evening, Mrs. Fiorentino. [*Calling after* WILLIE.] And don't come home too late, Willie!

[*But* WILLIE *is already out of earshot.*]

Mrs. Fiorentino. Why don't you come down and be sociable?

Mrs. Maurrant. I'm keeping some supper warm for my husband. [*A slight pause.*] Well, maybe I will for just a minute.

[*She leaves the window. The lights in her apartment go out.*]

Mrs. Fiorentino. She has her troubles with dot Willie.

Mrs. Jones. I guess it don't bother her much. [*Significantly.*] She's got her mind on other things.

Mrs. Olsen. [*Looking about cautiously and coming over to the left of the stoop between the two women.*] He vas comin' again today to see her.

Mrs. Jones. [*Rising excitedly, and leaning over the balustrade.*] Who—Sankey?

Mrs. Olsen. [*Nodding.*] Yes.

Mrs. Fiorentino. Are you sure, Mrs. Olsen?

Mrs. Olsen. I seen him. I vas doostin' de halls.

Mrs. Fiorentino. Dot's terrible!

Mrs. Jones. Wouldn't you think a woman her age, with a grown-up daughter——!

Mrs. Olsen. Two times already dis veek, I see him here.

Mrs. Jones. I seen him, meself, one day last week. He was comin' out o' the house, jest as I was comin' in wit' de dog. "Good mornin', Mrs. Jones," he says to me, as if butter wouldn't melt in his mouth. "Good mornin'," says I, lookin' him straight in the eye— [*Breaking off suddenly, as the vestibule door opens.*] Be careful, she's comin'.

[MRS. MAURRANT *comes out of the house and stops, for a moment, on the top step.*]

Mrs. Maurrant. Goodness, ain't it hot? I think it's really cooler upstairs.

[*She comes down the steps to the sidewalk.*]

Mrs. Jones. Yeah, jes' what I was sayin', meself. I feel like a wet dish-rag.

Mrs. Maurrant. I would have liked to go to the Park concert tonight, if Rose had got home in time. I don't get much chance to go to concerts. My husband don't care for music. But Rose is more like me—just crazy about it.

Mrs. Jones. Ain't she home yet?

Mrs. Maurrant. No. I think maybe she had to work overtime.

Mrs. Jones. Well, all mine ever comes home for is to sleep.

Mrs. Fiorentino. The young girls nowadays——!

Mrs. Olsen. My sister was writin' me in Schweden is same t'ing——

Mrs. Jones. It ain't only the young ones, either.

[*A baby is heard crying in the cellar.*]

Olsen's Voice. [*From the cellar.*] Ol-ga!

[*A* MAN, *in a dinner jacket and straw hat, appears at the left, whistling a jazz tune. He crosses the stage and goes off at the right.*]

Mrs. Olsen. [*Hurrying to the right.*] I betcha the baby, she's cryin' again.

Olsen's Voice. Ol-ga!

Mrs. Olsen. Yes. I come right away.

[*She goes down the cellar steps.*]

Mrs. Jones. What them foreigners don't know about bringin' up babies would fill a book.

Mrs. Fiorentino. [*A little huffily.*] Foreigners know joost as much as other people, Mrs. Jones. My mother had eight children and she brought up seven.

Mrs. Jones. [*Tactfully.*] Well, I'm not sayin' anythin' about the Joimans. The Joimans is different—more like the Irish. What I'm talkin' about is all them squareheads an'

Polacks—[*with a glance in* KAPLAN's *direction*]—an' Jews.

Buchanan's Voice. [*From a third story window.*] Good evening, ladies.

The Women. [*In unison, looking upward.*] Oh, good evening, Mr. Buchanan.

Buchanan's Voice. Well, is it hot enough for you?

Mrs. Jones. I'll say!

Buchanan's Voice. I was just saying to my wife, it's not the heat I mind as much as it is the humidity.

Mrs. Jones. Yeah, that's it! Makes everything stick to you.

Mrs. Maurrant. How's your wife feeling in this weather?

Buchanan's Voice. She don't complain about the weather. But she's afraid to go out of the house. Thinks maybe she couldn't get back in time, in case—you know.

Mrs. Jones. [*To the other women.*] I was the same way with my Vincent—afraid to take a step. But with Mae, I was up an' out till the very last minute.

Mrs. Fiorentino. [*Craning her neck upward.*] Mr. Buchanan, do you think she would eat some nice minestrone—good Italian vegetable soup?

Buchanan's Voice. Why, much obliged, Mrs. F., but I really can't get her to eat a thing.

Mrs. Jones. [*Rising and looking upward.*] Tell her she ought to keep up her strength. She's got two to feed, you know.

Buchanan's Voice. Excuse me, she's calling.

Mrs. Jones. [*Crossing to the railing, at the left of* MRS. FIORENTINO.] You'd think it was him that was havin' the baby.

Mrs. Maurrant. She's such a puny little thing.

Mrs. Fiorentino. [*With a sigh.*] Well, that's the way it goes. The little skinny ones have them and the big strong ones don't.

Mrs. Maurrant. Don't take it that way, Mrs. Fiorentino. You're a young woman yet.

Mrs. Fiorentino. [*Shaking her head.*] Oh, well!

Mrs. Jones. My aunt, Mrs. Barclay, was forty-two—— [*Breaking off.*] Oh, good evenin', Mr. Maurrant!

[FRANK MAURRANT *appears at the left, with his coat on his arm. He is a tall, powerfully-built man of forty-five, with a rugged, grim face.*]

Mrs. Fiorentino. Good evening, Mr. Maurrant.

Maurrant. 'Evenin'. [*He goes to the stoop and seats himself, mopping his face.*] Some baby of a day!

Mrs. Maurrant. Have you been working all this while, Frank?

Maurrant. I'll say I've been workin'. Dress-rehearsin' since twelve o'clock, with lights—in this weather. An' to-morra I gotta go to Stamford for the try-out.

Mrs. Maurrant. Oh, you're going to Stamford tomorrow?

Maurrant. Yeah, the whole crew's goin'. [*Looking at her.*] What about it?

Mrs. Maurrant. Why, nothing. Oh, I've got some cabbage and potatoes on the stove for you.

Maurrant. I just had a plate o' beans at the Coffee Pot. All I want is a good wash. I been sweatin' like a horse all day.

[*He rises and goes up the steps.*]

Mrs. Fiorentino. My husband, too; he's sweating terrible.

Mrs. Jones. Mine don't. There's some people that just naturally do, and then there's others that don't.

Maurrant. [*To* MRS. MAURRANT.] Is anybody upstairs?

Mrs. Maurrant. No. Willie's off playing with the boys. I can't keep him home.

Maurrant. What about Rose?

Mrs. Maurrant. I think maybe she's working overtime.

Maurrant. I never heard o' nobody workin' nights in a real-estate office.

Mrs. Maurrant. I thought maybe on account of the office being closed tomorrow—— [*To the others.*] Mr. Jacobson, the head of the firm, died Tuesday, and tomorrow's the funeral, so I thought maybe——

Mrs. Jones. Yeah. Leave it to the Jews not to lose a workin' day, without makin' up for it.

Maurrant. [*To* MRS. MAURRANT.] She shouldn't be stayin' out nights without us knowin' where she is.

Mrs. Maurrant. She didn't say a word about not coming home.

Maurrant. That's what I'm sayin', ain't it? It's a mother's place to know what her daughter's doin'.

Mrs. Fiorentino. [*Soothingly.*] Things are different nowadays, Mr. Maurrant, from what they used to be.

Maurrant. Not in my family, they're not goin' to be no different. Not so long as I got somethin' to say.

A Girl's Voice. [*Off-stage.*] Red Rover! Red Rover! Let Freddie come over!

[GEORGE JONES, *a short, rather plump, red-faced man, cigar in mouth, comes out of the house, as* MAURRANT *enters the vestibule.*]

Jones. Hello, Mr. Maurrant.

Maurrant. [*Curtly.*] 'Evenin'.

[*He enters the house.* JONES *looks after him in surprise for a moment.* MRS. MAURRANT *seats herself on the stoop.*]

Jones. Good evenin', ladies.

Mrs. Fiorentino and Mrs. Maurrant. Good evening, Mr. Jones.

Jones. [*Seating himself on the left balustrade.*] What's the matter with your hubby, Mrs. Maurrant? Guess he's feelin' the heat, huh?

Mrs. Maurrant. He's been working till just now and I guess he's a little tired.

Mrs. Jones. Men are all alike. They're all easy to get along with, so long as everythin's goin' the way they want it to. But once it don't—good night!

Mrs. Fiorentino. Yes, dot's true, Mrs. Jones.

Jones. Yeah, an' what about the women?

Mrs. Maurrant. I guess it's just the same with the women. I often think it's a shame that people don't get along better together. People ought to be able to live together in peace and quiet, without making each other miserable.

Mrs. Jones. The way I look at it, you get married for better or worse, an' if it turns out to be worse, why all you can do is make the best of it.

Mrs. Maurrant. I think the trouble is people don't make allowances. They don't realize that everybody wants a kind word now and then. After all, we're all human, and we can't just go along by ourselves, all the time, without ever getting a kind word.

[*While she is speaking,* STEVE SANKEY *appears at the right. He is in the early thirties, and is prematurely bald. He is rather flashily dressed, in a patently cheap, light-gray suit and a straw hat with a plaid band. As he appears,* MRS. JONES *and* MRS. FIORENTINO *exchange a swift, significant look.*]

Sankey. [*Stopping at the right of the stoop and removing his hat.*] Good evening, folks! Is it hot enough for you?

The Others. Good evening.

Mrs. Maurrant. [*Self-consciously.*] Good evening, Mr. Sankey.

[*Throughout the scene,* MRS. MAURRANT *and* SANKEY *try vainly to avoid looking at each other.*]

Sankey. I don't know when we've had a day like this. Hottest June fifteenth in forty-one years. It was up to ninety-four at three P. M.

Jones. Six dead in Chicago. An' no relief in sight, the evenin' paper says.

[MAURRANT *appears at the window of his apartment and stands there, looking out.*]

Mrs. Fiorentino. It's joost awful!

Sankey. Well, it's good for the milk business. You know the old saying, it's an ill wind that blows nobody any good.

Mrs. Maurrant. Yes. You hardly get the milk in the morning, before it turns sour.

Mrs. Jones. I'm just after pourin' half-a-bottle down the sink.

[MAURRANT *leaves the window.*]

Mrs. Fiorentino. You shouldn't throw it away. You should make—what do you call it?—schmier-käs'.

Sankey. Oh, I know what you mean—pot-cheese. My wife makes it, too, once in a while.

Mrs. Maurrant. Is your wife all right again, Mr. Sankey? You were telling me last time, she had a cold.

[MRS. JONES *and* MRS. FIORENTINO *exchange another look.*]

Sankey. Was I? Oh, sure, sure. That was a couple weeks ago. Yes, sure, she's all right again. That didn't amount to anything much.

Mrs. Jones. You got a family, too, ain't you?

Sankey. Yes. Yes, I have. Two little girls. Well, I got to be going along. [*He goes to the left of the stoop and stops again.*] I told my wife I'd go down to the drug-store and get her some nice cold ginger-ale. You want something to cool you off in this kind of weather.

Mrs. Jones. [*As* SANKEY *passes her.*] If you ask me, all that gassy stuff don't do you a bit of good.

Sankey. I guess you're right, at that. Still it cools you off. Well, good-night, folks. See you all again.

[*He strolls off, at the left, with affected nonchalance; but when he is almost out of sight, he casts a swift look back at* MRS. MAURRANT. *A dowdy* WOMAN, *wheeling a dilapidated baby carriage, appears at the left, and crosses the stage.*]

Jones. What's his name—Sankey?

Mrs. Jones. Yeah—Mr. Sankey.

Mrs. Maurrant. He's the collector for the milk company.

[AGNES CUSHING *comes out of the house. She is a thin, dried-up woman, past fifty.*]

Miss Cushing. [*Coming down the steps.*] Good evening.

The Others. Good evening, Miss Cushing.

Mrs. Maurrant. How is your mother today, Miss Cushing?

Miss Cushing. [*Passing at the left of the stoop.*] Why, she complains of the heat. But I'm afraid it's really her heart. She's seventy-two, you know. I'm just going down to the corner to get her a little ice-cream.

[*As she goes off at the left,* OLSEN, *the janitor, a lanky Swede, struggles up the cellar steps with a large, covered, tin garbage-barrel. The others look around in annoyance as he bangs the garbage-barrel upon the pavement.*]

Olsen. Phew! Hot!

[*He mops his face and neck with a dingy handkerchief, then lights his pipe and leans against the railing.*]

Mrs. Jones. [*Significantly, as she crosses to the center of the stoop and sits.*] Between you and I, I don't think her mother's got long for this world. Once the heart starts goin' back on you——!

Mrs. Fiorentino. It's too bad.

Mrs. Maurrant. Poor soul! She'll have nothing at all when her mother dies. She's just spent her whole life looking after her mother.

Mrs. Jones. It's no more than her duty, is it?

Mrs. Fiorentino. You could not expect that she should neglect her mother.

A Voice. [*Off-stage.*] Char-lie!

Mrs. Maurrant. It's not a matter of neglecting. Only—it seems as if a person should get more out of life than just looking after somebody else.

Mrs. Jones. Well, I hope to tell you, after all I've done for mine, I expect 'em to look after me in my old age.

Mrs. Maurrant. I don't know. It seems to me you might as well not live at all, as the way she does. [*Rising, with affected casualness.*] I don't know what's become of Willie. I think I'd better walk down to the corner and look for him. My husband don't like it if he stays out late.

[*She goes off at the left. They all watch her, in dead silence, until she is out of earshot. Then the storm breaks.*]

Mrs. Jones. [*Rising excitedly.*] Didja get that? Goin' to look for Willie! Can ya beat it?

Mrs. Fiorentino. It's joost terrible.

Jones. You think she's just goin' out lookin' for this guy Sankey?

Mrs. Jones. [*Scornfully.*] Ain't men the limit? What do you think he come walkin' by here for? [*Mincingly.*] Just strolled by to get the wife a little ginger-ale! A fat lot he cares whether his wife has ginger-ale!

Mrs. Fiorentino. Two little girls he's got, too!

Jones. Yeah, that ain't right—a bird like that, wit' a wife an' two kids of his own.

Mrs. Fiorentino. The way he stands there and looks and looks at her!

Mrs. Jones. An' what about the looks she was givin' him? [*Seating herself again.*] You'd think he was the Prince of Wales, instead of a milk-collector. And didja get the crack about not seein' him for two weeks?

Mrs. Fiorentino. And joost today he was upstairs, Mrs. Olsen says.

[OLSEN *approaches the stoop and removes his pipe from his mouth.*]

Olsen. [*Pointing upwards.*] Some day, her hoosban' is killing him.

[*He replaces his pipe and goes back to his former position.*]

Mrs. Fiorentino. Dot would be terrible!

Jones. He's li'ble to, at that. You know, he's got a wicked look in his eye, dat baby has.

Mrs. Jones. Well, it's no more than he deserves, the little rabbit—goin' around breakin' up peoples' homes. [*Mockingly.*] Good evenin', folks! Jes' like Whozis on the radio.

Jones. D'ya think Maurrant is wise to what's goin' on?

Mrs. Jones. Well, if he ain't, there must be somethin' the matter with him. But you never can tell about men. They're as blind as bats. An' what I always say is, in a case like that, the husband or the wife is always the last one to find out.

[MISS CUSHING, *carrying a small paper bag, hurries on, at the left, in a state of great excitement.*]

Miss Cushing. [*Breathlessly, as she comes up the left of the stoop.*] Say, what do you think? I just saw them together—the two of them!

Mrs. Jones. [*Rising excitedly.*] What did I tell you?

Mrs. Fiorentino. Where did you see them, Miss Cushing?

Miss Cushing. Why, right next door, in the entrance to the warehouse. They were standing right close together. And he had his hands up on her shoulders. It's awful, isn't it?

Jones. Looks to me like this thing is gettin' pretty serious.

Mrs. Jones. You didn't notice if they was kissin' or anythin', did you?

Miss Cushing. Well, to tell you the truth, Mrs. Jones, I was so ashamed for her that I hardly looked at all.

Jones. [*Sotto voce, as the house door opens.*] Look out! Maurrant's comin'.

[*A conspirator's silence falls upon them*

as MAURRANT, *pipe in mouth, comes out of the house.*]

Miss Cushing. [*Tremulously.*] Good evening, Mr. Maurrant.

Maurrant. [*On the top step.*] 'Evenin'. [*To the others.*] What's become of me wife?

Mrs. Jones. Why, she said she was goin' around the corner to look for Willie.

Maurrant. [*Grunts.*] Oh.

Mrs. Jones. They need a lot of lookin' after when they're that age.

[*A momentary silence.*]

Miss Cushing. Well, I think I'd better get back to my mother.

[*She goes up the steps.*]

Mrs. Jones, Mrs. Fiorentino, and Jones. Good night, Miss Cushing.

Miss Cushing. Good night. [*As she passes* MAURRANT.] Good night, Mr. Maurrant.

Maurrant. 'Night.

[*She looks at him swiftly, and goes into the vestibule.*]

A Boy's Voice. [*Off-stage.*] Red Rover! Red Rover! Let Mary come over!

[*As* MISS CUSHING *enters the house,* SHIRLEY KAPLAN *appears at the ground-floor window, at the extreme right, with a glass of steaming tea in her hand. She is a dark, unattractive Jewess, past thirty. She wears a light house-dress.* KAPLAN *goes on reading.*]

Shirley. [*To the neighbors outside; she speaks with the faintest trace of accent.*] Good evening.

The Others. [*Not very cordially.*] Good evenin'.

Shirley. It's been a terrible day, hasn't it?

Jones and Mrs. Jones. Yeah.

Shirley. [*Going to the other window.*] Papa, here's your tea. Haven't you finished your paper yet? It makes it so hot, with the lights on.

Kaplan. [*Lowering his newspaper.*] Oll right! Oll right! Put it out! Put it out! There is anahoo notting to read in de papers. Notting but deevorce, skendal, and moiders.

[*He speaks with a strong accent, over-emphatically, and with much gesticulation. He puts his paper away, removes his glasses, and starts to drink his tea.*]

Shirley. There doesn't seem to be a breath of air anywhere.

[*No one answers.* SHIRLEY *goes away from the window and puts out the lights.*]

Mrs. Jones. [*Sotto voce.*] You wouldn't think anybody would want to read that Hebrew writin', would ya? I don't see how they make head or tail out of it, meself.

Jones. I guess if you learn it when you're a kid——

Mrs. Jones. [*Suddenly.*] Well, will you look at your hubby, Mrs. F.! He's sure got his hands full!

[*She looks toward the left, greatly amused.* SHIRLEY *reappears at the window at the extreme right, and seats herself on the sill.*]

Mrs. Fiorentino. [*Leaning far out.*] Joost look at him! [*Calling.*] Lippo, be careful you don't drop any!

Lippo. [*Off-stage.*] 'Allo, Margherita!

[*They all watch in amusement, as* FILIPPO FIORENTINO, *a fat Italian, with thick black hair and moustache, comes on at the left. He is clutching a violin in his left arm and balancing five ice-cream cones in his right hand.*]

Lippo. [*Shouting.*] Who wants da ice-cream cone? Nice fresha ice-cream cone!

Mrs. Fiorentino. Lippo, you will drop them!

Mrs. Jones. [*Going up to him.*] Here, gimme your violin.

[*She relieves him of the violin and he shifts two of the cones to his left hand.*]

Lippo. [*As* MRS. JONES *hands the violin to* MRS. FIORENTINO.] T'ank you, Meeses Jones. 'Ere's for you a nica, fresha ice-cream cone.

[MRS. FIORENTINO *puts the violin on a chair behind her.*]

Mrs. Jones. [*Taking a cone.*] Why thank you very much, Mr. F.

Lippo. [*Going up to the window.*] Meeses Fiorentino, 'ere's for you a nica, fresha ice-cream cone.

Mrs. Fiorentino. [*Taking the cone.*] It makes me too fat.

Lippo. Ah, no! Five, ten poun' more, nobody can tell da deef!

[*He laughs aloud at his own joke and crosses to the stoop.*]

Mrs. Jones. [*Enjoying her cone.*] Ain't he a sketch, though?

Lippo. Meester Jones, you eata da cone, ha?

Jones. Why, yeah, I will at that. Thanks. Thanks.

Lippo. Meester Maurrant?

Maurrant. Naw; I got me pipe.

Lippo. You lika better da pipe den da ice-cream? [*Crossing the stoop.*] Meessa Kaplan, nica, fresha cone, yes?

Shirley. No, thanks. I really don't want any.

Lippo. Meesta Kaplan, yes?

Kaplan. [*Waving his hand.*] No, no! Tenks, tenks!

Mrs. Jones. [*To* JONES.] You oughta pay Mr. F. for the cones.

Jones. [*Reluctantly reaching into his pocket.*] Why, sure.

Lippo. [*Excitedly.*] Ah, no, no! I don' taka da mon'. I'm treata da whole crowd. I deedn' know was gona be such a biga crowd or I bringa doz'. [*Crossing to* OLSEN.] Meester Olsen, you lika da cone, ha?

Olsen. Sure. Much oblige'.

[*He takes the pipe from his mouth and stolidly licks the cone.*]

Lippo. [*Seating himself on the stoop, with a long sigh of relaxation.*] Aaah! [*He tastes the cone and smacking his lips, looks about for approval.*] Ees tasta good, ha?

Jones. [*His mouth full.*] You betcha!

Mrs. Jones. It cools you off a little.

Lippo. Sure. Dassa right. Cool you off. [*He pulls at his clothing and sits on the stoop.*] I'ma wat, wat—like I jus come outa da bad-tub. Eees 'ota like hal in da Park. Two, t'ree, t'ousan' people, everybody sweatin'—ees smal lika menageria.

[*While he is speaking,* ALICE SIMPSON, *a tall, spare spinster, appears at the right. She goes up the steps, enters the vestibule, and is about to push one of the buttons on the side wall.*]

Mrs. Jones. [*Sotto voce.*] She's from the Charities. [*Coming over to the stoop and calling into the vestibule.*] If you're lookin' for Mrs. Hildebrand, she ain't home yet.

Miss Simpson. [*Coming to the doorway.*] Do you know when she'll be back?

Mrs. Jones. Well, she oughta be here by now. She jus' went aroun' to the Livingston. That's the pitcher-theayter.

Miss Simpson. [*Outraged.*] You mean she's gone to a moving-picture show?

Olsen. [*Calmly.*] She's comin' now.

Lippo. [*Rising to his feet and calling vehemently.*] Mees Hil'brand! Hurry up! Hurry up! Ees a lady here.

[*He motions violently to her to hurry.* LAURA HILDEBRAND *appears at the right, with her two children,* CHARLIE *and* MARY. *She is a small, rather young woman, with a manner of perpetual bewilderment. Both children are chewing gum, and* MARY *comes on skipping a rope and chanting: "Apple, peach, pear, plum, banana."* CHARLIE *carefully avoids all the cracks in the sidewalk.*]

Miss Simpson. [*Coming out on the steps.*] Well, good evening, Mrs. Hildebrand!

Mrs. Hildebrand. [*Flustered.*] Good evening, Miss Simpson.

Miss Simpson. Where have you been?—to a moving-picture show?

Mrs. Hildebrand. Yes, ma'am.

Miss Simpson. And where did you get the money?

Mrs. Hildebrand. It was only seventy-five cents.

Miss Simpson. Seventy-five cents is a lot, when you're being dispossessed and dependent upon charity. I suppose it came out of the money I gave you to buy groceries with.

Mrs. Hildebrand. We always went, Thursday nights, to the pictures when my husband was home.

Miss Simpson. Yes, but your husband isn't home. And as far as anybody knows, he has no intention of coming home.

Kaplan. [*Leaning forward out of his window.*] Ees dis your conception of cherity?

Shirley. Papa, why do you interfere?

Miss Simpson. [*To* KAPLAN.] You'll please be good enough to mind your own business.

Kaplan. You should go home and read in your Bible de life of Christ.

Mrs. Jones. [*To* MRS. FIORENTINO.] Will you listen to who's talkin' about Christ!

Miss Simpson. [*Turning her back on* KAPLAN *and speaking to* MRS. HILDEBRAND.] You may as well understand right now that nobody's going to give you any money to spend on moving-picture shows.

Lippo. Ah, wotsa da matter, lady? [*He thrusts his hand into his pocket and takes out a fistful of coins.*] 'Ere, you taka da mon', you go to da pitcha ever' night. [*He forces the coins into* MRS. HILDEBRAND'S *hand.*] An' here's for da bambini.

[*He gives each child a nickel.*]

Mrs. Fiorentino. [*To* MRS. JONES.] Dot's why we never have money.

Mrs. Hildebrand. [*Bewildered.*] I really oughtn't to take it.

Lippo. Sure! Sure! I got plenta mon'.

Miss Simpson. [*Disgustedly.*] We'd better go inside. I can't talk to you here, with all these people.

Mrs. Hildebrand. [*Meekly.*] Yes, ma'am.

[*She follows* MISS SIMPSON *into the house, her children clinging to her.*]

Mrs. Jones. Wouldn't she give you a pain?

Lippo. I tella you da whola troub'. She's a don' gotta nobody to sleepa wit'.

[*The* MEN *laugh.*]

Mrs. Jones. [*To* MRS. FIORENTINO.] Ain't he the limit!

Mrs. Fiorentino. [*Greatly pleased.*] Tt!

Lippo. Somebody go sleepa wit' her, she's alla right. Meester Jones, 'ow 'bout you?

[SHIRLEY, *embarrassed, leaves the window.*]

Jones. [*With a sheepish grin.*] Naw, I guess not.

Lippo. Wot'sa matter? You 'fraid you' wife, ha? Meester Maurrant, how 'bout you?

[MAURRANT *emits a short laugh.*]

Mrs. Fiorentino. [*Delighted.*] Lippo, you're joost awful.

Lippo. [*Enjoying himself hugely.*] Alla ri'. Ahma gonna go myself!

[*He laughs boisterously. The others laugh too.*]

Mrs. Jones. [*Suddenly.*] Here's your wife now, Mr. Maurrant.

[*A sudden silence falls upon them all, as* MRS. MAURRANT *approaches at the left. A swift glance appraises her of* MAURRANT'S *presence.*]

Lippo. 'Allo, Meeses Maurrant. Why you don' come to da concerto?

Mrs. Maurrant. Well, I was waiting for Rose, but she didn't get home. [*To* MAURRANT, *as she starts to go up the steps.*] Is she home yet, Frank?

Maurrant. No, she ain't. Where you been all this while?

Mrs. Maurrant. Why, I've been out looking for Willie.

Maurrant. I'll give him a good fannin', when I get hold of him.

Mrs. Maurrant. Ah, don't whip him, Frank, please don't. All boys are wild like that, when they're that age.

Jones. Sure! My boy Vincent was the same way. An' look at him today—drivin' his own taxi an' makin' a good livin'.

Lippo. [*Leaning on the balustrade.*] Ees jussa same t'ing wit' me. W'en Ahm twelva year, I run away—I don' never see my parent again.

Maurrant. That's all right about that. But it ain't gonna be that way in my family.

Mrs. Maurrant. [*As* MISS SIMPSON *comes out of the house.*] Look out, Frank. Let the lady pass.

Miss Simpson. Excuse me.

[*They make way for her, as she comes down the steps.* MRS. MAURRANT *seats herself on the stoop.*]

Lippo. Meeses Hil'brand, she gotta de tougha luck, ha? Tomorra, dey gonna t'row 'er out in da street, ha?

Miss Simpson. [*Stopping at the right of the stoop and turning toward him.*] Yes, they are. And if she has any place to sleep, it will only be because the Charities find her a place. And you'd be doing her a much more neighborly act, if you helped her to realize the value of money, instead of encouraging her to throw it away.

Lippo. [*With a deprecatory shrug.*] Ah, lady, no! I give 'er coupla dollar, maka 'er feel good, maka me feel good—dat don' 'urt nobody.

[SHIRLEY *reappears at the window.*]

Miss Simpson. Yes it does. It's bad for her character.

Kaplan. [*Throwing away his cigarette and laughing aloud.*] Ha! You mek me leff!

Miss Simpson. [*Turning, angrily.*] Nobody's asking your opinion.

Kaplan. Dot's oll right. I'm taling you wit'out esking. You hoid maybe already dot poem:

"Orgenized cherity, measured and iced,
In der name of a kushus, stetistical
Christ."

Miss Simpson. [*Fiercely.*] All the same, you Jews are the first to run to the Charities.

[*She strides angrily off at the right.* LIPPO, *affecting a mincing gait, pretends to follow her.*]

Kaplan. [*Leaning out of the window.*] Come back and I'll tal you somet'ing will maybe do good your kerecter.

Mrs. Fiorentino. Lippo!

Mrs. Jones. [*Highly amused.*] Look at him, will ya?

Lippo. [*Laughing and waving his hand.*] Gooda-bye, lady!

[*He comes back to the stoop.*]

Kaplan. [*To the others.*] Dey toin out in de street a mudder vit' two children, and dis female comes and preaches to her bourgeois morelity.

Mrs. Jones. [*To* MRS. FIORENTINO.] He's shootin' off his face again.

Shirley. Papa, it's time to go to bed!

Kaplan. [*Irritably.*] Lat me alone, Shoiley. [*Rising and addressing the others.*] Dees cherities are notting but anudder dewise for popperizing de verking-klesses. W'en de lendlords steal from de verkers a million dollars, dey give to de Cherities a t'ousand.

Maurrant. Yeah! Well, who's puttin' her out on the street? What about the lan'lord here? He's a Jew, ain't he?

Mrs. Jones. I'll say he's a Jew! Isaac Cohen!

Kaplan. Jews oder not Jews—wot has dis got to do vit' de quastion? I'm not toking releegion, I'm toking economics. So long as de ke*pit*alist klesses——

Maurrant. [*Interrupting.*] I'm talkin' about if you don't pay your rent, you gotta move.

Mrs. Maurrant. It doesn't seem right, though, to put a poor woman out of her home.

Mrs. Fiorentino. And for her husband to run away—dot vos not right either.

Lippo. I betcha 'e's got 'nudder woman. He find a nice blonda chicken, 'e run away.

Mrs. Jones. There ought to be a law against women goin' around, stealin' other women's husbands.

Mrs. Fiorentino. Yes, dot's right, Mrs. Jones.

Maurrant. Well, what I'm sayin' is, it ain't the landlord's fault.

Kaplan. Eet's de folt of our economic system. So long as de institution of private property exeests, de verkers will be at de moicy of de property-owning klesses.

Maurrant. That's a lot o' bushwa! I'm a woikin' man, see? I been payin' dues for twenty-two years in the Stage-Hands Union. If we're not gettin' what we want, we call a strike, see?—and then we get it.

Lippo. Sure! Ees same wit' me. We gotta Musician Union. We getta pay for da rehears', we getta pay for da overtime——

Shirley. That's all right when you belong to a strong union. But when a union is weak, like the Teachers' Union, it doesn't do you any good.

Mrs. Jones. [*To* MRS. FIORENTINO.] Can y' imagine that?—teachers belongin' to a union!

Kaplan. [*Impatiently.*] Oll dese unions eccomplish notting wotever. Oll dis does not toch de fondamental problem. So long as de tuls of industry are in de hands of de ke*pit*alist klesses, ve vill hev exploitation and sloms and——

Maurrant. T' hell wit' all dat hooey! I'm makin' a good livin' an' I'm not doin' any kickin'.

Olsen. [*Removing his pipe from his mouth.*] Ve got prosperity, dis country.

Jones. You said somethin'!

Kaplan. Sure, for de reech is planty prosperity! Mister Morgan rides in his yacht and upstairs dey toin a woman vit' two children in de street.

Maurrant. And if you was to elect a Socialist president tomorra, it would be the same thing.

Mrs. Fiorentino. Yes, dot's right, Mr. Maurrant.

Jones. You're right!

Kaplan. Who's toking about electing presidents? Ve must put de tuls of industry in de hends of de vorking-klesses and dis ken be accomplished only by a sushal revolution!

Maurrant. Yeah? Well, we don't want no revolutions in this country, see?

[*General chorus of assent.*]

Mrs. Jones. I know all about that stuff—teachin' kids there ain't no Gawd an' that their gran'fathers was monkeys.

Jones. [*Rising, angrily.*] Free love, like they got in Russia, huh?

[KAPLAN *makes a gesture of impatient disgust, and sinks back into his chair.*]

Maurrant. There's too goddam many o' you Bolshevikis runnin' aroun' loose. If you don't like the way things is run here, why in hell don't you go back where you came from?

Shirley. Everybody has a right to his own opinion, Mr. Maurrant.

Maurrant. Not if they're against law and order, they ain't. We don't want no foreigners comin' in, tellin' us how to run things.

Mrs. Fiorentino. It's nothing wrong to be a foreigner. Many good people are foreigners.

Lippo. Sure! Looka Eetalians. Looka Cristoforo Colombo! 'E'sa firs' man discov' America—'e's Eetalian, jussa like me.

Maurrant. I'm not sayin' anythin' about that——

Olsen. [*Removing his pipe.*] Firs' man is Leif Ericsson.

Lippo. [*Excitedly, going toward* OLSEN.] Wassa dat?

Olsen. Firs' man is Leif Ericsson.

Lippo. No! No! Colombo! Cristoforo Colomb'—'e'sa firs' man discov' America—ever'body knowa dat!

[*He looks about appealingly.*]

Mrs. Jones. Why, sure, everybody knows that.

Jones. Every kid learns that in school.

Shirley. Ericsson was really the first discoverer——

Lippo. [*Yelling.*] No! Colomb!

Shirley. But Columbus was the first to open America to settlement.

Lippo. [*Happily, as he goes back to the stoop.*] Sure, dassa wot Ahm say—Colomb' is firs'.

Olsen. Firs' man is Leif Ericsson.

[LIPPO *taps his forehead significantly.*]

Lippo. Looka wot Eetalian do for America—'e build bridge, 'e build railroad, 'e build subway, 'e dig sewer. Wit'out Eetalian, ees no America.

Jones. Like I heard a feller sayin': the Eye-talians built New York, the Irish run it, an' the Jews own it. [*Laughter.*]

Mrs. Fiorentino. [*Convulsed.*] Oh! Dot's funny!

Jones. [*Pleased with his success.*] Yep; the Jews own it all right.

Maurrant. Yeah, an' they're the ones that's doin' all the kickin'.

Shirley. It's no disgrace to be a Jew, Mr. Maurrant.

Maurrant. I'm not sayin' it is. All I'm sayin' is, what we need in this country is a little more respect for law an' order. Look at what's happenin' to people's homes, with all this divorce an' one thing an' another. Young girls goin' around smokin' cigarettes an' their skirts up around their necks. An' a lot o' long-haired guys talkin' about free love an' birth control an' breakin' up decent people's homes. I tell you it's time somethin' was done to put the fear o' God into people!

Mrs. Jones. Good for you, Mr. Maurrant!

Jones. You're damn right.

Mrs. Fiorentino. Dot's right, Mr. Maurrant!

Mrs. Maurrant. Sometimes, I think maybe they're only trying to get something out of life.

Maurrant. Get somethin', huh? Somethin' they oughtn't to have, is that it?

Mrs. Maurrant. No; I was only thinking——

Maurrant. Yeah, you were only thinkin', huh?

Kaplan. [*Rising to his feet again.*] De femily is primerily an economic institution.

Mrs. Jones. [*To* MRS. FIORENTINO.] He's in again.

Kaplan. W'en priwate property is ebolished, de femily will no longer hev eny reason to exeest.

Shirley. Can't you keep quiet, papa?

Maurrant. [*Belligerently.*] Yeah? Is that so? No reason to exist, huh? Well, it's gonna exist, see? Children respectin' their parents an' doin' what they're told, get me? An' husbands an' wives, lovin' an' honorin' each other, like they said they would, when they was spliced—an' any dirty sheeny that says different is li'ble to get his head busted open, see?

Mrs. Maurrant. [*Springing to her feet.*] Frank!

Shirley. [*Trying to restrain* KAPLAN.] Papa!

Kaplan. Oll right! I should argue vit' a low-kless gengster.

Maurrant. [*Raging.*] Who's a gangster? Why, you goddam——!

[*He makes for the balustrade.*]

Mrs. Maurrant. [*Seizing his arm.*] Frank!

Jones. [*Seizing the other arm.*] Hey! Wait a minute! Wait a minute!

Maurrant. Lemme go!

Shirley. [*Interposing herself.*] You should be ashamed to talk like that to an old man!

[*She slams down the window.*]

Maurrant. Yeah? [*To* MRS. MAURRANT *and* JONES.] All right, lemme go! I ain't gonna do nothin'.

[*They release him.* SHIRLEY *expostulates with* KAPLAN *and leads him away from the window.*]

Mrs. Jones. [*Who has run over to the right of the stoop.*] Maybe if somebody handed him one, he'd shut up with his talk for a while.

Lippo. 'E talka lika dat een Eetaly, Mussolini's gonna geeve 'eem da castor-oil.

Mrs. Jones. [*Laughing.*] Yeah? Say, that's a funny idea!

[*Still chuckling, she goes back to the railing at the left of the stoop.*]

Jones. No kiddin', is that what they do?

Mrs. Fiorentino. Yes, dot's true. My husband read it to me in the Italian paper.

Mrs. Maurrant. Why must people always be hurting and injuring each other? Why can't they live together in peace?

Maurrant. [*Mockingly.*] Live in peace! You're always talkin' about livin' in peace!

Mrs. Maurrant. Well, it's true, Frank. Why can't people just as well be kind to each other?

Maurrant. Then let 'im go live with his own kind.

Jones. [*Coming down the steps.*] Yeah, that's what I say. [*As* MRS. JONES *laughs aloud.*] What's eatin' you?

Mrs. Jones. I was just thinkin' about the castor-oil.

[MAURRANT *seats himself on the right balustrade.*]

Lippo. Sure, 'esa funny fell', Mussolini. [*Doubling up in mock pain.*] 'E geeve 'em da pain in da belly, dey no can talk. [*Suddenly.*] Look! 'Eresa da boy. 'Esa walk along da street an' reada da book. Datsa da whola troub': reada too much book.

[*While* LIPPO *is speaking,* SAMUEL KAPLAN *appears at the left. He is twenty-one, slender, with dark, unruly hair and a sensitive, mobile face. He is hatless, and his coat is slung over one shoulder. He walks along slowly, absorbed in a book. As he approaches the stoop,* SHIRLEY, *in a kimono, appears at the closed window, opens it, and is about to go away again, when she sees* SAM.]

Shirley. [*Calling.*] Sam!

Sam. [*Looking up.*] Hello, Shirley.

Shirley. Are you coming in?

Sam. No, not yet. It's too hot to go to bed.

Shirley. Well, I'm tired. And papa's going to bed, too. So don't make a noise when you come in.

Sam. I won't.

Shirley. Good night.

Sam. Good night.

[SHIRLEY *goes away from the window*.]

Sam. [*To the others, as he seats himself on the curb to the right of the stoop*.] Good evening!

Several. 'Evening.

Lippo. [*Approaching* SAM.] 'Ow you lika da concerto? I see you sittin' in da fronta seat.

Sam. I didn't like it. Why don't they play some real music, instead of all those Italian organ-grinder's tunes?

Lippo. [*Excitedly*.] Wotsa da matter? You don't lika de Verdi?

Sam. No, I don't. It's not music!

Lippo. Wot you call music—da Tschaikov', ha?

[*He hums derisively a few bars from the first movement of the "Symphonie Pathétique*."]

Sam. Yes, Tschaikovsky—and Beethoven. Music that comes from the soul.

Mrs. Maurrant. The one I like is——

[*She hums the opening bars of Mendelssohn's "Spring Song*."]

Lippo. Dotsa da Spreeng Song from da Mendelson.

Mrs. Maurrant. Yes! I love that.

[*She goes on humming softly*.]

Mrs. Fiorentino. And the walzer von Johann Strauss.

[*She hums the "Wienerwald Waltz*."]

Mrs. Jones. Well, gimme a good jazz band, every time.

Lippo. [*Protesting*.] Ah no! Ees not music, da jazz. Ees breaka your ear.

[*He imitates the discordant blaring of a saxophone*.]

Jones. [*Bored*.] Well, I guess I'll be on me way.

Mrs. Jones. Where are *you* goin'?

Jones. Just around to Callahan's to shoot a little pool. Are you comin' along, Mr. Maurrant?

Maurrant. I'm gonna wait awhile.

[*A* MAN, *with a club-foot, appears at the right and crosses the stage*.]

Mrs. Jones. [*As* JONES *goes toward the right*.] Don't be comin' home lit, at all hours o' the mornin'.

Jones. [*Over his shoulder*.] Aw, lay off dat stuff! I'll be back in a half-an-hour.

[*He goes off at the right*.]

A Voice. [*Off-stage*.] Char-lie!

Mrs. Jones. Him an' his pool! Tomorra he won't be fit to go to work again.

Sam. [*Who has been awaiting a chance to interrupt*.] When you hear Beethoven, it expresses the struggles and emotions of the human soul.

Lippo. [*Waving him aside*.] Ah, ees no good, da Beethoven. Ees alla time sad, sad. Ees wanna maka you cry. I don' wanna cry, I wanna laugh. Eetalian music ees make you 'appy. Ees make you feel good.

[*He sings several bars of "Donna è mobile*."]

Mrs. Maurrant. [*Applauding*.] Yes, I like that, too.

Lippo. Ah, ees bew-tiful! Ees maka you feela fine. Ees maka you wanna dance.

[*He executes several dance steps*.]

Mrs. Fiorentino. [*Rising*.] Vait, Lippo, I vill give you music.

[*She goes away from the window. The lights go on, in the Fiorentino apartment*.]

Lippo. [*Calling after her*.] Playa Puccini, Margherita! [*He hums an air from "Madame Butterfly." Then as* MRS. FIORENTINO *begins to play the waltz from "La Bohème" on the piano*.] Ah! La Bohème! Bew-tiful! Who'sa gonna dance wit' me? Meeses Maurrant, 'ow 'bout you?

Mrs. Maurrant. [*With an embarrassed laugh*.] Well, I don't know.

[*She looks timidly at* MAURRANT, *who gives no sign*.]

Lippo. Ah, come on! Dansa wit' me!

[*He takes her by the hand*.]

Mrs. Maurrant. Well, all right, I will.

Lippo. Sure, we hava nica dance.

[*They begin to dance on the sidewalk*.]

Lippo. [*To* MAURRANT.] Your wife ees dansa swell.

Mrs. Maurrant. [*Laughing*.] Oh, go on, Mr. Fiorentino! But I always loved to dance!

[*They dance on.* SANKEY *appears, at the left, carrying a paper bag, from which the neck of a ginger-ale bottle protrudes.* MAURRANT *sees him and rises*.]

Mrs. Jones. [*Following* MAURRANT'S *stare and seeing* SANKEY.] Look out! You're blockin' traffic!

Sankey. [*Stopping at the left of the stoop*.] I see you're having a little dance.

[MRS. MAURRANT *sees him and stops dancing.* LIPPO *leans against the right balustrade, panting. The music goes on*.]

Sankey. Say, go right ahead. Don't let me stop you.

Mrs. Maurrant. Oh, that's all right. I guess we've danced about enough.

[*She goes up the steps, ill at ease.*]

Sankey. It's a pretty hot night for dancing.

Mrs. Maurrant. Yes, it is.

Sankey. [*Going toward the right.*] Well, I got to be going along. Good night, folks.

The Others. [*Except* MAURRANT.] Good night.

Lippo. [*As he seats himself at the left of the stoop.*] Stoppa da music, Margherita!

[*The music stops.*]

[SANKEY *goes off at the right.* MRS. MAURRANT *goes quickly up the steps.*]

Maurrant. [*Stopping her.*] Who's that bird?

Mrs. Maurrant. Why, that's Mr. Sankey. He's the milk-collector.

Maurrant. Oh, he is, is he? Well, what's he hangin' around here for?

Mrs. Maurrant. Well, he lives just down the block somewhere.

Mrs. Jones. He's just been down to the drug-store, gettin' some ginger-ale for his wife.

Maurrant. Yeah? Well, what I want to know is, why ain't Rose home yet?

Mrs. Maurrant. I told you, Frank——

Maurrant. I know all about what you told me. What I'm sayin' is, you oughta be lookin' after your kids, instead of doin' so much dancin'.

Mrs. Maurrant. Why, it's the first time I've danced in I don't know when.

Maurrant. That's all right about that. But I want 'em home, instead o' battin' around the streets, hear me?

[*While he is speaking,* WILLIE *appears sobbing at the left, his clothes torn and his face scratched. He is carrying his skates.*]

Mrs. Maurrant. [*Coming down the steps.*] Why, Willie, what's the matter? [*Reproachfully, as* WILLIE *comes up to her, sniffling.*] Have you been fighting again?

Willie. [*With a burst of indignation.*] Well, dat big bum ain't gonna say dat to me. I'll knock da stuffin's out o' him, dat's what I'll do!

Maurrant. [*Tensely, as he comes down the steps.*] Who's been sayin' things to you?

Willie. Dat big bum, Joe Connolly, dat's who! [*Blubbering.*] I'll knock his goddam eye out, next time!

Mrs. Maurrant. Willie!

Maurrant. [*Seizing* WILLIE'S *arm.*] Shut up your swearin', do you hear?—or I'll give you somethin' to bawl for. What did he say to you, huh? What did he say to you?

Willie. [*Struggling.*] Ow! Leggo my arm!

Mrs. Maurrant. What difference does it make what a little street-loafer like that says?

Maurrant. Nobody's askin' you! [*To* WILLIE.] What did he say? [*He and* MRS. MAURRANT *exchange a swift involuntary look; then* MAURRANT *releases the boy.*] G'wan up to bed now, an' don't let me hear no more out o' you. [*Raising his hand.*] G'wan now. Beat it!

[WILLIE *ducks past* MAURRANT *and hurries up the steps and into the vestibule.*]

Mrs. Maurrant. Wait; Willie, I'll go with you. [*She goes up the steps, then stops and turns.*] Are you coming up, Frank?

Maurrant. No I ain't. I'm goin' around to Callahan's for a drink, an' if Rose ain't home when I get back, there's gonna be trouble.

[*Without another glance or word, he goes off at the right.* MRS. MAURRANT *looks after him for a moment with a troubled expression.*]

Mrs. Maurrant. [*Entering the vestibule.*] Well, good night, all.

The Others. Good night.

[SAM *rises. As* MRS. MAURRANT *and* WILLIE *enter the house,* MRS. FIORENTINO *reappears at the window.*]

Mrs. Fiorentino. Lippo!

[*She sees that something is wrong.*]

Mrs. Jones. Say, you missed it all!

[SAM, *about to go up the steps, stops at the right of the stoop.*]

Mrs. Fiorentino. [*Eagerly.*] Vat?

Mrs. Jones. [*Volubly.*] Well, they were dancin', see? An' who should come along but Sankey!

Mrs. Fiorentino. Tt!

[*A light appears in the* MAURRANT *apartment.*]

Mrs. Jones. Well, there was the three o' them—Mr. Maurrant lookin' at Sankey as if he was ready to kill him, an' Mrs. Maurrant as white as a sheet, an' Sankey as innocent as the babe unborn.

Mrs. Fiorentino. Did he say something?

Mrs. Jones. No, not till after Sankey was gone. Then he wanted to know who he was an' what he was doin' here. "He's the milk-collector," she says.

Mrs. Fiorentino. It's joost awful.

Mrs. Jones. Oh, an' then Willie comes home.

Lippo. Da boy tella 'eem 'is mamma ees a whore an' Weelie leeck 'im.

Mrs. Jones. Well, an' what else is she?

Sam. [*Unable longer to restrain himself.*] Stop it! Stop it! Can't you let her alone?

Have you no hearts? Why do you tear her to pieces like a pack of wolves? It's cruel, cruel!

[*He chokes back a sob, then dashes abruptly into the house.*]

Lippo. [*Rising to his feet and yelling after him.*] Wotsa matter you?

Mrs. Jones. Well, listen to him, will you! He must be goin' off his nut, too.

Lippo. Eesa reada too mucha book. Ees bad for you.

Mrs. Fiorentino. I think he is loving the girl.

Mrs. Jones. Yeah? Well, that's all the Maurrants need is to have their daughter get hooked up wit' a Jew. It's a fine house to be livin' in, ain't it, between the Maurrants upstairs, an' that bunch o' crazy Jews down here.

[*A* GIRL *appears at the left, glancing apprehensively, over her shoulder, at a* MAN *who is walking down the street behind her. They cross the stage and go off at the right.*]

Mrs. Jones. [*As* MRS. OLSEN *comes up the cellar steps and over to the stoop.*] Well, good night.

Mrs. Fiorentino. Good night, Mrs. Jones.

Lippo. Goo' night, Meeses Jones.

Mrs. Jones. Wait a minute, Mrs. Olsen. I'll go with you.

[MRS. JONES *and* MRS. OLSEN *enter the house.* OLSEN *yawns mightily, knocks the ashes from his pipe, and goes down the cellar steps.* WILLIE MAURRANT *leans out of the window and spits into the areaway. Then he leaves the window and turns out the light. A* POLICEMAN *appears, at the right, and strolls across the stage.*]

Lippo. [*Who has gone up the steps.*] Margherita, eef I ever ketcha you sleepin' wit' da meelkaman, Ahm gonna breaka your neck.

Mrs. Fiorentino. [*Yawning.*] Stop your foolishness, Lippo, and come to bed!

[LIPPO *laughs and enters the house.* MRS. FIORENTINO *takes the pillow off the window-sill, closes the window, and starts to pull down the shade.* ROSE MAURRANT *and* HARRY EASTER *appear at the left.* ROSE *is a pretty girl of twenty, cheaply but rather tastefully dressed.* EASTER *is about thirty-five, good-looking, and obviously prosperous.*]

Mrs. Fiorentino. Good evening, Miss Maurrant

Rose. [*As they pass the window.*] Oh, good evening, Mrs. Fiorentino.

[ROSE *and* EASTER *cross to the stoop.* MRS. FIORENTINO *looks at them a moment, then pulls down the shade and turns out the lights.*]

Rose. [*Stopping at the foot of the steps.*] Well, this is where I live, Mr. Easter. [*She extends her hand.*] I've had a lovely time.

Easter. [*Taking her hand.*] Why, you're not going to leave me like this, are you? I've hardly had a chance to talk to you.

Rose. [*Laughing.*] We've been doing nothing but talking since six o'clock.

[*She tries gently to extricate her hand.*]

Easter. [*Still holding it.*] No, we haven't. We've been eating and dancing. And now, just when I want to talk to you—[*He puts his other arm around her.*] Rose——

Rose. [*Rather nervously.*] Please don't, Mr. Easter. Please let go. I think there's somebody coming.

[*She frees herself as the house-door opens and* MRS. OLSEN *appears in the vestibule. They stand in silence, as* MRS. OLSEN *puts the door off the latch, tries it to see that it is locked, dims the light in the vestibule and comes out on the stoop.*]

Mrs. Olsen. [*As she comes down the steps.*] Goot evening, Miss Maurrant.

[*She darts a swift look at* EASTER *and crosses to the cellar steps.*]

Rose. Good evening, Mrs. Olsen. How's the baby?

Mrs. Olsen. She vas cryin' all the time. I tank she vas gettin' new teet'.

Rose. Oh, the poor little thing! What a shame!

Mrs. Olsen. [*As she goes down the steps.*] Yes, ma'am. Goot night, Miss Maurrant.

Rose. Good night, Mrs. Olsen. [*To* EASTER.] She's got the cutest little baby you ever saw.

Easter. [*Rather peevishly.*] Yeah? That's great. [*Taking* ROSE'S *hand again.*] Rose, listen——

Rose. I've really got to go upstairs now, Mr. Easter. It's awfully late.

Easter. Well, can't I come up with you for a minute?

Rose. [*Positively.*] No, of course not!

Easter. Why not?

Rose. Why, we'd wake everybody up. Anyhow, my father wouldn't like it.

Easter. Aren't you old enough to do what you like?

Rose. It's not that. Only I think when you're living with people, there's no use doing things you know they don't like. [*Embarrassed.*] Anyhow, there's only the front room and my little brother sleeps there. So good night, Mr. Easter.

Easter. [*Taking both her hands.*] Rose—I'm crazy about you.

Rose. Please let me go now.

Easter. Kiss me good-night.

Rose. No.

Easter. Why not, h'm?

Rose. I don't want to.

Easter. Just one kiss.

Rose. No.

Easter. Yes!

[*He takes her in his arms and kisses her.* ROSE *frees herself and goes to the right of the stoop.*]

Rose. [*Her bosom heaving.*] It wasn't nice of you to do that.

Easter. [*Going over to her.*] Why not? Didn't you like it? H'm?

Rose. Oh, it's not that.

Easter. Then what is it, h'm?

Rose. [*Turning and facing him.*] You know very well what it is. You've got a wife, haven't you?

Easter. What of it? I tell you I'm clean off my nut about you.

Rose. [*Nervously, as the house-door opens.*] Look out! Somebody's coming.

[EASTER *goes to the other side of the stoop and they fall into a self-conscious silence, as* MRS. JONES *comes out of the house, leading an ill-conditioned dog.*]

Mrs. Jones. [*As she comes down the steps.*] Oh, good evenin'.

[*She stares at* EASTER, *then goes toward the right.*]

Rose. Good evening, Mrs. Jones. It's been a terrible day, hasn't it?

Mrs. Jones. Yeah. Awful. [*Stopping.*] I think your father's been kinda worried about you.

Rose. Oh, has he?

Mrs. Jones. Yeah. Well, I gotta give Queenie her exercise. Good night.

[*She stares at* EASTER *again, then goes off at right.*]

Rose. Good night, Mrs. Jones. [*To* EASTER.] I'll soon have all the neighbors talking about me.

Easter. [*Going over to her again.*] What can they say, h'm?—that they saw you saying good night to somebody on the front door-step?

Rose. They can say worse than that—and what's more, they will, too.

Easter. Well, why not snap out of it all?

Rose. Out of what?

Easter. [*Indicating the house.*] This! The whole business. Living in a dirty old tenement like this; working all day in a real-estate office for a measly twenty-five a week. You're not going to try to tell me you like living this way, are you?

Rose. No, I can't say that I like it especially. But maybe it won't always be this way. Anyhow, I guess I'm not so much better than anybody else.

Easter. [*Taking her hand.*] Do you know what's the matter with you? You're not wise to yourself. Why, you've got just about everything, you have. You've got looks and personality and a bean on your shoulders—there's nothing you haven't got. You've got It, I tell you.

Rose. You shouldn't keep looking at me, all the time, at the office. The other girls are beginning to pass hints about it.

Easter. [*Releasing her hand, genuinely perturbed.*] Is that a fact? You see, that shows you! I never even knew I was looking at you. I guess I just can't keep my eyes off you. Well, we've got to do something about it.

Rose. [*Nervously snapping the clasp of her handbag.*] I guess the only thing for me to do is to look for another job.

Easter. Yes, that's what I've been thinking, too. [*As she is about to demur.*] Wait a minute, honey! I've been doing a little thinking and I've got it all doped out. The first thing you do is throw up your job, see?

Rose. But——

Easter. Then you find yourself a nice, cozy little apartment somewhere. [*As she is about to interrupt him again.*] Just a minute, now! Then you get yourself a job on the stage.

Rose. How could I get a job on the stage?

Easter. Why, as easy as walking around the block. I've got three or four friends in the show-business. Ever hear of Harry Porkins?

Rose. No.

Easter. Well, he's the boy that put on Mademoiselle Marie last year. He's an old pal of mine, and all I'd have to say to him is: [*Putting his arm around her shoulder.*] "Harry, here's a little girl I'm interested in," and he'd sign you up in a minute.

Rose. I don't think I'd be any good on the stage.

Easter. Why, what are you talking about, sweetheart? There's a dozen girls, right now, with their names up in electric lights, that haven't got half your stuff. All you got to do is go about it in the right way—put up a little front, see? Why, half the game is nothing but bluff. Get yourself a classy little apartment, and fill it up with trick furniture, see? Then you doll yourself up in a flock of Paris clothes and you throw a couple or three parties and you're all set. [*Taking her arm.*] Wouldn't you *like* to be on Broadway?

Rose. I don't believe I ever could be.

Easter. Isn't it worth trying? What have you got here, h'm? This is no kind of a racket for a girl like you. [*Taking her hand.*] You do like me a little, don't you?

Rose. I don't know if I do or not.

Easter. Why, sure you do. And once you get to know me better, you'd like me even more. I'm no Valentino, but I'm not a bad scout. Why, think of all the good times we could have together—you with a little apartment and all. And maybe we could get us a little car——

Rose. And what about your wife?

Easter. [*Letting go her hand.*] The way I figure it is, she doesn't have to know anything about it. She stays up there in Bronxville, and there are lots of times when business keeps me in New York. Then, in the Summer, she goes to the mountains. Matter of fact, she's going next week and won't be back until September.

Rose. [*Shaking her head and going toward the stoop.*] I don't think it's the way I'd want things to be.

Easter. Why, there's nothing really wrong about it.

Rose. Maybe there isn't. But it's just the way I feel about it, I guess.

Easter. Why, you'd get over that in no time. There's lots of girls——

Rose. Yes, I know there are. But you've been telling me all along I'm different.

Easter. Sure you're different. You're in a class by yourself. Why, sweetheart——

[*He tries to take her in his arms.*]

Rose. [*Pushing him away.*] No. And you mustn't call me sweetheart.

Easter. Why not?

Rose. Because I'm not your sweetheart.

Easter. I want you to be——

[*A sudden yell of pain is heard from upstairs. They both look up, greatly startled.*]

Easter. My God, what's that—a murder?

Rose. It must be poor Mrs. Buchanan. She's expecting a baby.

Easter. Why does she yell like that? God, I thought somebody was being killed.

Rose. The poor thing! [*With sudden impatience she starts up the steps.*] I've got to go now. Good night.

Easter. [*Taking her hand.*] But, Rose——

Rose. [*Freeing her hand quickly.*] No, I've got to go. [*Suddenly.*] Look, there's my father. There'll only be an argument, if he sees you.

Easter. All right, I'll go.

[*He goes toward the left, as* MAURRANT *appears at the right.*]

Rose. [*Going up to the top step.*] Good night.

Easter. Good night.

[*He goes off at the left.* ROSE *begins searching in her hand-bag for her latch-key.*]

Rose. [*As* MAURRANT *approaches.*] Hello, pop.

Maurrant. [*Stopping at the foot of the steps.*] Who was that you was talkin' to?

Rose. That's Mr. Easter. He's the manager of the office.

Maurrant. What's he doin' here? You been out wi' him?

Rose. Yes, he took me out to dinner.

Maurrant. Oh, he did, huh?

Rose. Yes, I had to stay late to get out some letters. You see, pop, the office is closed tomorrow, on account of Mr. Jacobson's funeral——

Maurrant. Yeah, I know all about that. This is a hell of a time to be gettin' home from dinner.

Rose. Well, we danced afterwards.

Maurrant. Oh, you danced, huh? With a little pettin' on the side, is that it?

Rose. [*Rather angrily, as she seats herself on the left balustrade.*] I don't see why you can never talk to me in a nice way.

Maurrant. So you're startin' to go on pettin' parties, are you?

Rose. Who said I was on a petting party?

Maurrant. I suppose he didn't kiss you or nothin', huh?

Rose. No, he didn't! And if he did——

Maurrant. It's your own business, is that it? [*Going up the steps.*] Well, I'm gonna make it my business, see? Is this bird married? [ROSE *does not answer.*] I thought so! They're all alike, them guys—all after the one thing. Well, get this straight. No married men ain't gonna come nosin' around my family, get me?

Rose. [*Rising agitatedly as the house-door opens.*] Be quiet, pop! There's somebody coming.

Maurrant. I don't care!

[BUCHANAN *hurries out of the house. He is a small and pasty young man—a typical "white-collar slave." He has hastily put on his coat and trousers over his pajamas and his bare feet are in slippers.*]

Buchanan. [*As he comes down the steps.*] I think the baby's coming!

Rose. [*Solicitously.*] Can I do anything, Mr. Buchanan?

Buchanan. [*As he hurries toward the left.*] No, I'm just going to phone for the doctor.

Rose. [*Coming down the steps.*] Let me do it, and you go back to your wife.

Buchanan. Well, if you wouldn't mind. It's Doctor John Wilson. [*Handing her a slip of paper.*] Here's his number. And the other number is her sister, Mrs. Thomas. And here's two nickels. Tell them both to come right away. She's got terrible pains. [*Another scream from upstairs.*] Listen to her! I better go back.

[*He dashes up the steps and into the house.*]

Rose. Oh, the poor woman! Pop, tell ma to go up to her. Hurry!

Maurrant. Aw, all right.

[*He follows* BUCHANAN *into the house.* ROSE *hurries off at the left, just as* MAE JONES *and* DICK MCGANN *appear.* MAE *is a vulgar shopgirl of twenty-one;* DICK, *a vacuous youth of about the same age.* MAE *is wearing* DICK'S *straw hat and they are both quite drunk.*]

Mae. [To ROSE.] Hello, Rose. What's your hurry?

Rose. [*Without stopping.*] It's Mrs. Buchanan. I've got to phone to the doctor.

[*She hurries off.*]

Dick. [*As they approach the stoop.*] Say, who's your little friend?

Mae. Oh, that's Rose Maurrant. She lives in the house.

Dick. She's kinda cute, ain't she?

Mae. [*Seating herself on the stoop.*] Say, accordin' to you, anythin' in a skirt is kinda cute—providin' the skirt is short enough.

Dick. Yeah, but they ain't any of 'em as cute as you, Mae.

Mae. [*Yawning and scratching her leg.*] Yeah?

Dick. Honest, I mean it. How 'bout a little kiss?

[*He puts his arms about her and plants a long kiss upon her lips. She submits with an air of intense boredom.*]

Dick. [*Removing his lips.*] Say, you might show a little en-thoo-siasm.

Mae. [*Rouging her lips.*] Say, you seem to think I oughta hang out a flag every time some bozo decides to wipe off his mouth on me.

Dick. De trouble wit' you is you need another little snifter.

[*He reaches for his flask.*]

Mae. Nope! I can't swaller any more o' that rotten gin o' yours.

Dick. Why, it ain't no worse. I don't mind it no more since I had that brass linin' put in me stomach. Well, happy days!

[*He takes a long drink.*]

Mae. [*Rising indignantly.*] Hey, for God's sake, what are you doin'—emptyin' the flask?

Dick. [*Removing the flask from his lips.*] I t'ought you didn't want none.

Mae. Can't you take a joke?

[*She snatches the flask from him and drains it, kicking out at* DICK, *to prevent his taking it from her.*]

Dick. [*Snatching the empty flask.*] Say, you wanna watch your step, baby, or you're li'ble to go right up in a puff o' smoke.

Mae. [*Whistling.*] Phew! Boy! I feel like a t'ree alarm fire! Say, what de hell do dey make dat stuff out of?

Dick. T'ree parts dynamite an' one part army-mule. Dey use it for blastin' out West.

Mae. [*Bursting raucously into a jazz tune.*] Da-da-da-da-dee! Da-da-da-da-dee!

[*She executes some dance steps.*]

Dick. Say, shut up, will ya? You'll be wakin' the whole neighborhood.

Mae. [*Boisterously.*] What the hell do I care? Da-da-da-da-dee! Da-da-da-da-dee! [*Suddenly amorous, as she turns an unsteady pirouette.*] Kiss me, kid!

Dick. I'll say!

[*They lock in a long embrace.* SAM, *coatless, his shirt-collar open, appears at the window, watches the pair for a moment, and then turns away, obviously disgusted. They do not see him.*]

Dick. [*Taking* MAE'S *arm.*] Come on!

Mae. Wait a minute! Where y' goin'?

Dick. Come on, I'm tellin' ya! Fred Hennessy gimme de key to his apartment. Dere won't be nobody dere.

Mae. [*Protesting feebly.*] I oughta go home. [*Her hand to her head.*] Oh, baby! Say, nail down dat sidewalk, will ya?

Dick. Come on!

[ROSE *appears at the left.*]

Mae. Sweet papa! [*She kisses* DICK *noisily; then bursts into song again.*] Da-da-da-da-dee! Da-da-da-da-dee! [*As they pass* ROSE.] Hello, Rose. How's de milkman?

Dick. [*Raising his hat with drunken politeness.*] Goo' night, sweetheart.

[*They go off at the left,* MAE'S *snatches of song dying away in the distance.* ROSE *stands still, for a moment, choking back her mortification.*]

Buchanan's Voice. Miss Maurrant, did you get them?

Rose. [*Looking up.*] Why yes, I did. The doctor will be here right away. And Mrs. Thomas said it would take her about an hour.

[VINCENT JONES *appears at the right and stops near the stoop. He is a typical New York taxicab driver, in a cap.* ROSE *does not see him.*]

Buchanan's Voice. She's got terrible pains. Your mother's up here with her. [MRS. BUCHANAN *is heard calling faintly.*] I think she's calling me.

[ROSE *goes toward the stoop and sees* VINCENT.]

Vincent. Hello, Rosie.

Rose. Good evening.

[*She tries to pass, but he blocks her way.*]

Vincent. What's your hurry?

Rose. It's late.

Vincent. You don' wanna go to bed, yet. Come on, I'll take you for a ride in me hack.

[*He puts his arm about her.*]

Rose. Please let me pass.

[SAM *appears at the window. They do not see him.*]

Vincent. [*Enjoying* ROSE's *struggle to escape.*] You got a lot o' stren'th, ain't you? Say, do you know you're gettin' fat?

[*He passes one hand over her body.*]

Rose. Let me go, you big tough.

Sam. [*Simultaneously.*] Take your hands off her!

[*He climbs quickly out of the window and onto the stoop.* VINCENT, *surprised, releases* ROSE *and steps to the sidewalk.* ROSE *goes up the steps.* SAM, *trembling with excitement and fear, stands on the top step.* VINCENT *glowers up at him.*]

Vincent. Well, look who's here! [*Mockingly.*] Haster gesehn de fish in de Bowery? [*Menacingly.*] What de hell do you want?

Sam. [*Chokingly.*] You keep your hands off her!

Vincent. Yeah? [*Sawing the air with his hands.*] Oi, Jakie! [*He suddenly lunges forward, seizes* SAM's *arm, pulls him violently by the right hand down the steps and swings him about, so that they stand face to face, to the left of the stoop.* ROSE *comes down between them.*] Now what o' ya got t' say?

Rose. Let him alone!

Sam. [*Inarticulately.*] If you touch her again——

Vincent. [*Mockingly.*] If I touch her again——! [*Savagely.*] Aw, shut up, you little kike bastard!

[*He brushes* ROSE *aside and putting his open hand against* SAM's *face, sends him sprawling to the pavement.*]

Rose. [*Her fists clenched.*] You big coward.

Vincent. [*Standing over* SAM.] Get up, why don't you?

Rose. [*Crossing to* SAM.] If you hit him again, I'll call my father.

Vincent. [*As* MRS. JONES *and the dog appear at the right.*] Gee, don't frighten me like dat. I got a weak heart.

[*He is sobered, nevertheless.* SAM *picks himself up.*]

Vincent. [*As* MRS. JONES *approaches.*] Hello, ma.

Mrs. Jones. [*With maternal pride.*] Hello, Vincent. What's goin' on here?

Vincent. Oh, just a little friendly argument. Ikey Finkelstein don't like me to say good evenin' to his girl friend.

Rose. You'd better keep your hands to yourself hereafter.

Vincent. Is dat so? Who said so, huh?

Mrs. Jones. Come on, Vincent. Come on upstairs. I saved some stew for you.

Vincent. All right, I'm comin'. [*To* ROSE.] Good night, dearie.

[*He makes a feint at* SAM, *who starts back in terror.* VINCENT *laughs.*]

Mrs. Jones. Aw, let 'im alone, Vincent.

Vincent. [*As he goes up the steps.*] Who's touchin' him? A little cockroach like dat ain't woit' my time. [*To* ROSE.] Some sheik you picked out for yourself!

[*He enters the vestibule and opens the door with his latchkey.*]

Mrs. Jones. [*Going up the steps.*] You seem to have plenty of admirers, Miss Maurrant. [*Pausing on the top step.*] But I guess you come by it natural.

[ROSE *does not reply.* MRS. JONES *follows* VINCENT *into the house.* ROSE *averts her head to keep back the tears.* SAM *stands facing the house, his whole body quivering with emotion. Suddenly he raises his arms, his fists clenched.*]

Sam. [*Hysterically, as he rushes to the foot of the stoop.*] The dirty bum! I'll kill him!

Rose. [*Turning and going to him.*] It's all right, Sam. Never mind.

Sam. [*Sobbing.*] I'll kill him! I'll kill him!

[*He throws himself on the stoop and, burying his head in his arms, sobs hysterically.* ROSE *sits beside him and puts her arm about him.*]

Rose. It'll all right, Sam. Everything's all right. Why should you pay any attention to a big tough like that? [SAM *does not answer.* ROSE *caresses his hair and he grows calmer.*] He's nothing but a loafer; you know that. What do you care what he says?

Sam. [*Without raising his head.*] I'm a coward.

Rose. Why no, you're not, Sam.

Sam. Yes, I am. I'm a coward.

Rose. Why, he's not worth your little finger, Sam. You wait and see. Ten years from now, he'll still be driving a taxi and you —why, you'll be so far above him, you won't even remember he's alive.

Sam. I'll never be anything.

Rose. Why, don't talk like that, Sam. A boy with your brains and ability. Graduating from college with honors and all that! Why, if I were half as smart as you, I'd be just so proud of myself!

Sam. What's the good of having brains, if nobody ever looks at you—if nobody knows you exist?

Rose. [*Gently.*] I know you exist, Sam.

Sam. It wouldn't take much to make you forget me.

Rose. I'm not so sure about that. Why do you say that, Sam?

Sam. Because I know. It's different with you. You have beauty—people look at you —you have a place in the world——

Rose. I don't know. It's not always so easy, being a girl—I often wish I were a man. It seems to me that when you're a man, it's so much easier to sort of—be yourself, to kind of be the way you feel. But when you're a girl, it's different. It doesn't seem to matter what you are, or what you're thinking or feeling—all that men seem to care about is just the one thing. And when you're sort of trying to find out just where you're at, it makes it hard. Do you see what I mean? [*Hesitantly.*] Sam, there's something I want to ask you—— [*She stops.*]

Sam. [*Turning to her.*] What is it, Rose?

Rose. I wouldn't dream of asking anybody but you. [*With a great effort.*] Sam, do you think it's true—what they're saying about my mother?

[SAM *averts his head, without answering.*]

Rose. [*Wretchedly.*] I guess it is, isn't it?

Sam. [*Agitatedly.*] They were talking here, before—I couldn't stand it any more! [*He clasps his head and, springing to his feet, goes to the right of the stoop.*] Oh, God, why do we go on living in this sewer?

Rose. [*Appealingly.*] What can I do, Sam? [SAM *makes a helpless gesture.*] You see, my father means well enough, and all that, but he's always been sort of strict and—I don't know—sort of making you freeze up, when you really wanted to be nice and loving. That's the whole trouble, I guess; my mother never had anybody to really love her. She's sort of gay and happy-like—you know, she likes having a good time and all that. But my father is different. Only—the way things are now—everybody talking and making remarks, all the neighbors spying and whispering—it sort of makes me feel—— [*She shudders.*] I don't know——!

Sam. [*Coming over to her again.*] I wish I could help you, Rose.

Rose. You do help me, Sam—just by being nice and sympathetic and talking things over with me. There's so few people you can really talk to, do you know what I mean? Sometimes, I get the feeling that I'm all alone in the world and that——

[*A scream of pain from* MRS. BUCHANAN.]

Rose. [*Springing to her feet.*] Oh, just listen to her!

Sam. Oh, God!

Rose. The poor thing! She must be having terrible pains.

Sam. That's all there is in life—nothing but pain. From before we're born, until we die! Everywhere you look, oppression and cruelty! If it doesn't come from Nature, it comes from humanity—humanity trampling on itself and tearing at its own throat. The whole world is nothing but a blood-stained arena, filled with misery and suffering. It's too high a price to pay for life—life isn't worth it!

[*He seats himself despairingly on the stoop.*]

Rose. [*Putting her hand on his shoulder.*] Oh, I don't know, Sam. I feel blue and discouraged sometimes, too. And I get a sort of feeling of, oh, what's the use. Like last night. I hardly slept all night, on account of the heat and on account of thinking about—well, all sorts of things. And this morning, when I got up, I felt so miserable. Well, all of a sudden, I decided I'd walk to the office. And when I got to the Park, everything looked so green and fresh, that I got a kind of feeling of, well, maybe it's not so bad, after all. And then, what do you think?—all of a sudden, I saw a big lilac-bush, with some flowers still on it. It made me think about the poem you said for me—remember?—the one about the lilacs.

Sam. [*Quoting.*]

"When lilacs last in the dooryard bloom'd
And the great star early droop'd in the western sky in the night,
I mourn'd and yet shall mourn, with ever-returning Spring."

[*He repeats the last line.*]

I mourn'd and yet shall mourn, with ever-returning Spring? Yes!

Rose. No, not that part. I mean the part about the farmhouse. Say it for me, Sam.

[*She sits at his feet.*]

Sam.
"In the door-yard, fronting an old farm-house, near the white-washed palings,
Stands the lilac-bush, tall-growing, with heart-shaped leaves of rich green,
With many a pointed blossom, rising delicate, with the perfume strong I love,
With every leaf a miracle—and from this bush in the door-yard,
With delicate-color'd blossoms and heart-shaped leaves of rich green,
A sprig with its flower I break."

Rose. [*Eagerly.*] Yes, that's it! That's just what I felt like doing—breaking off a little bunch of the flowers. But then I thought, maybe a policeman or somebody would see me, and then I'd get into trouble; so I didn't.

Buchanan's Voice. Miss Maurrant! Miss Maurrant!

[SAM *and* ROSE *spring to their feet and look up.*]

Rose. Yes?

Buchanan's Voice. Do you mind phoning to the doctor again? She's getting worse.

Rose. Yes, sure I will. [*She starts to go.*] Wait! Maybe this is the doctor now.

Buchanan's Voice. [*Excitedly as* DR. WILSON *appears at the left.*] Yes, that's him. Mrs. Maurrant! Tell her the doctor's here! Doctor, I guess you're none too soon.

Dr. Wilson. [*A seedy, middle-aged man in a crumpled Panama.*] Plenty of time. Just don't get excited.

[*He throws away his cigarette and enters the vestibule. The mechanical clicking of the door-latch is heard as* DR. WILSON *goes into the house.*]

Rose. I hope she won't have to suffer much longer.

Maurrant. [*Appearing at the window, in his undershirt.*] Rose!

Rose. [*Rather startled.*] Yes, pop, I'll be right up.

Maurrant. Well, don't be makin' me call you again, d'ya hear?

Rose. I'm coming right away.

[MAURRANT *leaves the window.*]

Rose. I'd better go up now, Sam.

Sam. Do you have to go to bed when you're told, like a child?

Rose. I know, Sam, but there's so much wrangling goes on all the time, as it is, what's the use of having any more? Good night, Sam. There was something I wanted to talk to you about, but it will have to be another time.

[*She holds out her hand.* SAM *takes it and holds it in his.*]

Sam. [*Trembling and rising to his feet.*] Rose, will you kiss me?

Rose. [*Simply.*] Why, of course I will, Sam.

[*She offers him her lips. He clasps her in a fervent embrace, to which she submits but does not respond.*]

Rose. [*Freeing herself gently.*] Don't be discouraged about things, Sam. You wait and see—you're going to do big things some day. I've got lots of confidence in you.

Sam. [*Turning away his head.*] I wonder if you really have, Rose?

Rose. Why, of course, I have! And don't forget it! Good night. I hope it won't be too hot to sleep.

Sam. Good night, Rose.

[*He watches her, as she opens the door with her latch-key and goes into the house. Then he goes to the stoop and seating himself, falls into a reverie. A* POLICEMAN *appears at the right and strolls across, but* SAM *is oblivious to him. In the distance, a home-comer sings drunkenly. A light appears in the* MAURRANT *hall-bedroom, and a moment later* ROSE *comes to the window and leans out.*]

Rose. [*Calling softly.*] Hoo-hoo! Sam! [SAM *looks up, then rises.*] Good night, Sam.

[*She wafts him a kiss.*]

Sam. [*With deep feeling.*] Good night, Rose dear.

[*She smiles at him. Then she pulls down the shade.* SAM *looks up for a moment, then resumes his seat. A scream from* MRS. BUCHANAN *makes him shudder. A deep rhythmic snoring emanates from the* FIORENTINO *apartment. A steamboat whistle is heard. The snoring in the* FIORENTINO *apartment continues.* SAM *raises his clenched hands to heaven. A distant clock begins to strike twelve.* SAM'S *arms and head drop forward.*]

THE CURTAIN FALLS SLOWLY

ACT TWO

Daybreak, the next morning. It is still quite dark and comparatively quiet. The rhythmic snoring in the FIORENTINO *apartment is still heard, and now and then a distant "L" train or speeding automobile.*

[*A moment after the rise of the curtain,* JONES *appears, at the right, on his way home from the speakeasy. He reels slightly, but negotiates the steps and entrance-door without too much difficulty. It grows lighter—and noisier. The street-light goes out. The* OLSEN *baby begins to cry. An alarm clock rings. A dog barks. A canary begins to sing. Voices are heard in the distance. They die out and other voices are heard. The house-door opens and* DR. WILSON *comes out, passing* JONES *at the top of the stoop.* DR. WILSON *stands on the steps and yawns the yawn of an overtired man. Then he lights a cigarette and goes toward the left.*]

Buchanan's Voice. Doctor!

Dr. Wilson. [*Stopping and looking up.*] Well?

Buchanan's Voice. What if she does wake up?

Dr. Wilson. [*Sharply.*] She won't, I've told you! She's too exhausted. The best thing you can do is lie down and get some sleep yourself.

[*As he goes off at the left,* MAE *and* DICK *appear. They walk slowly and listlessly and far apart.*]

Dick. [*As they reach the stoop.*] Well, goo' night.

Mae. [*With a yawn, as she finds her latch-key.*] Goo' night. [*Going up the steps and looking toward the* FIORENTINO *apartment.*] Aw, shut up, you wop!

Dick. [*His dignity wounded.*] How 'bout kissin' me good night?

Mae. [*Venomously, from the top step.*] For God's sake, ain't you had enough kissin' for one night!

[*She enters the vestibule and puts the key in the lock. The ringing of an alarm clock is heard.*]

Dick. [*Raising his voice.*] Well, say, if that's the way you feel about it——

Mae. Aw, go to hell!

[*She enters the house. The alarm clock has stopped ringing.*]

Dick. You dirty little tart!

[*He stands muttering to himself for a moment, then goes off at the right, passing the* POLICEMAN, *who looks at him suspiciously. The sounds of a Swedish quarrel are heard from the janitor's apartment. The baby is still crying. As the* POLICEMAN *goes left, a* MILKMAN *appears, whistling and carrying a rack of full milk-bottles.*]

The Policeman. Hello, Louie.

[*The snoring in the* FIORENTINO *apartment stops.*]

The Milkman. Hello, Harry. Goin' to be another scorcher.

The Policeman. You said it.

[*He goes off at the left.*]

[THE MILKMAN *crosses to the cellar steps.* MAE *appears, at the hall bedroom window of the* JONES *apartment, and removes her dress over her head.* THE MILKMAN, *about to go down the steps, sees her and stops to watch.* MAE, *about to slip out of her step-in, sees him, throws him an angry look and pulls down the shade.* THE MILKMAN *grins and goes down the cellar steps.* CHARLIE HILDEBRAND *comes out of the house. He is chewing gum and as he comes out to the top of the stoop, he scatters the wrappings of the stick of gum on the stoop. Then he jumps down the four steps of the stoop in one jump, and goes off at the left, pulling the chewing-gum out in a long ribbon, and carefully avoiding all the cracks in the pavement. A* YOUNG WORKMAN, *carrying a kit of tools and a tin lunch-box, appears at the left, extinguishes the red light on the excavation, and opening the door, goes in. A* TRAMP *comes on at the right and shuffles across. He sees a cigar butt on the pavement, picks it up and pockets it, as he exits at the left.* ROSE, *in her nightgown, appears at the window, yawns slightly and disappears. It is daylight now. The baby stops crying.* MRS. OLSEN *comes up the cellar steps. She goes up the stoop, turns out the light in the vestibule, and takes the door off the latch.* THE MILKMAN *comes up the cellar steps, his tray laden with empty bottles and goes off, whistling, at the left.* SAM, *coatless, a book in his hand, appears at the window. He looks out for a moment, then climbs out on the stoop, looks up at* ROSE'S *window, then seats himself and begins to read.* WILLIE *comes out of the house.*]

Willie. [*Chanting, as he comes down the steps.*] Fat, Fat, the water-rat, Fifty bullets in his hat.

Sam. Hello, Willie. Is Rose up yet?

Willie. [*Without stopping or looking at him.*] Yeah. I don't know. I guess so.

[*He turns a somersault and goes off at left, continuing his chanting.* SAM *glances up at* ROSE'S *window again, then resumes his book.* MRS. JONES *and her dog come out of the house.*]

Mrs. Jones. [*Haughtily, as she comes down the steps.*] Mornin'.

Sam. [*Scarcely looking up from his book.*] Good morning.

[MRS. JONES *and the dog go off at the right. A middle-aged* WORKMAN, *carrying a large coil of wire, appears at the left and goes to the door of the excavation.* MRS. OLSEN *comes out of the house and exits into the basement.*]

The Workman. [*Calling.*] You down there, Eddie?

A Voice. [*From the depths.*] Yeah!

The Workman. All right!

[*He climbs down into the excavation.* ROSE *comes to window and pulls up the shade.* WILLIE *and* CHARLIE *can be heard, offstage left, engaged in an earnest conversation.*]

Charlie. [*Offstage.*] He could not!

Willie. [*Offstage.*] He could so!

[*They appear at left. Each has under his arm a paper-bag, from which a loaf of bread protrudes.*]

Charlie. I'll betcha he couldn't.

Willie. I'll betcha he could.

Charlie. I'll betcha a million dollars he couldn't.

Willie. I'll betcha five million dollars he could. Hold that! [*He hands* CHARLIE *his loaf of bread and turns a cart-wheel.*] Bet you can't do it.

Charlie. Bet I can.

[*He puts both loaves of bread on the pavement, attempts a cart-wheel and fails.*]

Willie. [*Laughing raucously.*] Haw-haw! Told you you couldn't!

Charlie. Can you do this?

[*He turns a back somersault.*]

Willie. Sure—easy! [*He turns a back somersault. They pick up their loaves again.* WILLIE'S *drops out of the bag, but he dusts it with his hand and replaces it.*] How many steps can you jump up?

Charlie. Three.

[*He jumps up three steps.*]

Willie. I can do four.

Charlie. Let's see you.

[WILLIE, *the bread under his arm, jumps up the four steps, undisturbed by* SAM'S *presence. He drops the bread, and is about to replace it in the bag, but gets a better idea. He inflates the bag and explodes it with a blow of his fist.* CHARLIE *looks on, in admiration and envy.*]

Rose. [*Appearing at the window.*] Willie, we're waiting for the bread.

Willie. [*Holding it up.*] All right! Cantcha see I got it?

[*He enters the house, followed by* CHARLIE.]

Sam. [*Rising.*] Hello, Rose.

Rose. Hello, Sam.

Sam. Come down.

Rose. I haven't had breakfast yet. [*Calling into the room.*] Yes! He's on his way up.

Miss Cushing. [*Coming out of the house.*] Good morning.

[*She looks inquiringly from* SAM *to* ROSE.]

Sam. [*Impatiently.*] Good morning.

[*A middle-aged* NUN *appears at the right, accompanied by a scrawny* CHILD *of about fourteen. They walk across the stage.*]

Rose. Good morning, Miss Cushing.

[MISS CUSHING *goes off, at the left, glancing back at* ROSE *and* SAM.]

Rose. I'm going to Mr. Jacobson's funeral. [*Calling into the room.*] Yes, I'm coming. [*To* SAM.] Breakfast's ready. I'll be down as soon as the dishes are done.

[*She disappears.* SAM *looks up at the window for a moment, then begins to read again.* MRS. FIORENTINO *appears at the window, at the extreme left, with a double armful of bedding, which she deposits upon the window-sill. Then she goes away again.*]

Shirley. [*Appearing at the window.*] Sam, breakfast is ready.

Sam. I don't want any breakfast.

Shirley. What do you mean, you don't want any breakfast? What kind of a business is that, not to eat breakfast?

Sam. Do I have to eat breakfast, if I don't want to?

Shirley. You've got your head so full of that Rose Maurrant upstairs that you don't want to eat or sleep or anything any more.

Sam. If I don't feel like eating, why should I eat? [*Bursting out.*] You're always telling me: "Eat!" "Don't eat!" "Get up!" "Go to bed!" I know what I want to do, without being told.

Shirley. I don't see. just when you're

graduating from college, why you want to get mixed up with a little batzimer like that!

Sam. It's always the same thing over again with you. You never can get over your race prejudice. I've told you a hundred times that the Jews are no better than anybody else.

Shirley. I'm not talking about that! Look at the kind of family she comes from. What's her father? Nothing but an illiterate roughneck. And her mother——

Sam. [*Indignantly.*] Are you starting, too?

Kaplan's Voice. Shoi-ley!

Shirley. Wait a minute, papa's calling. [*Into the room.*] All right, papa! [*To* SAM.] Come in, Sam, or papa will be making long speeches again.

Sam. [*Impatiently.*] All right! All right! I'll come.

[*A young* SHOPGIRL, *smiling to herself, appears at the right and walks across the stage.* SAM *rises and goes into the house.* SHIRLEY *leaves the window.* BUCHANAN, *emerging from the house, collarless and unshaven, encounters* SAM *in the vestibule.*]

Buchanan. [*Eagerly.*] Good morning!

Sam. [*Abruptly.*] Good morning.

[*He enters the house.* BUCHANAN *looks back at him, then comes down the steps.* MRS. FIORENTINO *raises the drawn shade and opens the window.*]

Mrs. Fiorentino. Good morning, Mr. Buchanan.

Buchanan. Oh, good morning, Mrs. Fiorentino. [*Going over to the left balustrade.*] I guess you know that the baby came last night, don't you?

Mrs. Fiorentino. No! I did not hear a word about it.

Buchanan. Why, I thought she'd wake up the whole neighborhood, the way she was yelling. Three-thirty this morning the baby came. I been up the whole night.

[*An old* LETTER-CARRIER, *coatless, appears at the right.*]

Mrs. Fiorentino. A boy, is it?

Buchanan. No, it's a little girl. I guess we'll call her Mary, after my mother.

Letter-Carrier. [*Going up the steps.*] Mornin'.

Mrs. Fiorentino. Good morning. Any letters for me?

Letter-Carrier. [*From the top of the steps.*] No, not a thing.

Buchanan. [*Turning toward him.*] I was just telling Mrs. Fiorentino, I had a little addition to my family last night.

Letter-Carrier. Your first, is it?

Buchanan. [*Hastening to explain.*] Well, we've only been married a little over a year.

Letter-Carrier. Well, I've had seven, an' I'm still luggin' a mail-bag at sixty-two.

[*He goes into the vestibule and puts the mail into the letter-boxes.*]

Mrs. Fiorentino. How is your wife?

Buchanan. Well, she had a pretty hard time of it. Her sister's up there with her. And Mrs. Maurrant was up, nearly all night. I don't know what we'd have done without her.

Letter-Carrier. [*Coming down the steps.*] It don't pay to let 'em have their own way too much. That's where I made my mistake.

[*As the* LETTER-CARRIER *goes off at the left,* LIPPO *appears at the window behind his wife, and tickles her.*]

Mrs. Fiorentino. [*Startled.*] Lippo!

Buchanan. Morning. I was just telling your wife——

Mrs. Fiorentino. Lippo, what do you think? Mr. Buchanan has a little girl!

Lippo. Ah, dotsa fine! Margherita, why you don' have da baby, ha?

Mrs. Fiorentino. [*Abruptly.*] I must go and make the coffee.

[*She goes away from the window.* OLSEN *comes half-way up the steps and leans against the railing, smoking his pipe.*]

A Voice. [*Offstage left.*] Oh-h! Corn! Sweet corn!

Lippo. Eees funny t'ing. You gotta de leetle, skeeny wife and she's hava da baby. My Margherita, she's beeg an' fat an' she no can hava da baby.

Buchanan. Well, that's the way o' the world, I guess.

[*As he goes off, at the left, an* ICE-MAN *appears, trundling a three-wheeled cart, filled with ice.*]

Lippo. Buon giorno, Mike.

Mike. Buon giorno, signore. Come sta?

Lippo. Benissimo. Fa molto caldo ancora, oggi.

Mike. Si, si, signore. Bisognera abbastanza ghiaccio. Twen'y fi' cent, ha?

Lippo. No, no, è troppo.

Mike. Twen'y cent? Eesa melta fas'.

Lippo. Alla right. Gimme twen'y cent.

Mike. Si, si, signore. Sure.

[*As he wheels the cart to the cellar-entrance and begins to chop a block of ice, a* MAN *in shirt-sleeves strides in from the left and stops at the curb, as though seeing someone in a house across the street.*]

The Man. [*Angrily.*] Well, what about it? We've been waiting a half an hour!

A Voice. I'll be right over!

The Man. Yeah? Well, make it snappy!

[*He strides off at the left, muttering angrily.* ROSE *comes out of the house and stands in the doorway, looking for* SAM. *Then she comes out on the stoop and peers into the* KAPLAN *apartment. As she turns away, she sees* LIPPO.]

Rose. [*Crossing to the left of the stoop.*] Good morning.

Lippo. Gooda mornin', Meesa Maurrant.

[MIKE *goes down into the cellar, with a chunk of ice.*]

Rose. It's awful hot again, isn't it?

Lippo. You don' like?

Rose. I don't sleep very well, when it's so hot.

Lippo. No? Ahm sleepa fine. Een Eetaly, where Ahm born, is much more 'ot like 'ere. Een summer, ees too 'ot for workin'. Ees too 'ot only for sleepin'. W'en Ahm leetla boy, Ahm sleepa, sleepa, whola day. I don't wear no clo's—nawthin' only leetle short pair pants. I lay down on groun' under da lemon-tree, Ahm sleepa whola day.

Rose. Under a lemon-tree! That must have been nice.

Lippo. Ees smella sweet, lemon-tree. Where Ahm born ees t'ousan' lemon-tree. Lemon an' olive an' arancia.

Rose. Oh, that must be lovely!

Lippo. Ah, ees bew-tiful! Ees most bewtiful place in whole worl'. You hear about Sorrent', ha?

Rose. No, I don't think I ever did.

Lippo. [*Incredulously.*] You never hear about Sorrent'?

Rose. No, I don't know much about geography. Is it a big place?

Lippo. Ees not vera beeg—but ever'body know Sorrent'. Sorrento gentile! La bella Sorrento! You hear about Napoli—Baia di Napoli?

Rose. Oh yes, the Bay of Naples! Is it near there?

Lippo. Sure, ees on Bay of Napoli. Ees bew-tiful! Ees alla blue. Sky blue, water blue, sun ees shine alla time.

Rose. Oh, how lovely.

[MIKE *comes up the cellar-steps, chops another block of ice, and goes down the cellar-steps with it.*]

Lippo. An' ees Vesuvio, too. You hear about Vesuvio?—ees beeg volcano.

Rose. Oh yes, sure. I saw a picture once, called "The Last Days of Pompeii," and it showed Mount Vesuvius, with smoke coming out of the top.

Lippo. Da's right. An' night-time, ees fire come out, maka da sky red.

Rose. Didn't it frighten you?

Lippo. Ah no, ees nawthin' to be afraid. Ees jus' volcano.

Rose. I'd love to go to Italy. It must be awfully pretty. But I don't suppose I ever will.

Lippo. W'y sure! Some day you gonna marry reech fella; 'e's take you Eetaly—ever'where.

Rose. I guess there's not much chance of that. Rich fellows aren't going around looking for girls like me to marry. Anyhow, I don't think money is everything, do you?

Lippo. Ees good to hava money. Da's w'y Ahm come to America. Een Eetaly, ees bewtiful, but ees no money. 'Ere ees not bewtiful, but ees plenty money. Ees better to 'ave money.

[*An elderly* MAN, *in the gray uniform of a special officer, comes out of the house, filling his pipe from a tobacco-box.*]

The Man. Good mornin'.

Rose. Good morning, Mr. Callahan. [THE MAN *drops the empty tobacco-tin on the sidewalk and goes off slowly at the left.*] I don't think I'd be happy, just marrying a man with money, if I didn't care for him, too.

Lippo. [*Laughing.*] Wotsa matter, ha? You lova da leetla kike, ha?

Rose. Why no, I don't. I don't love anybody—at least, I don't think I do. But it's not on account of his being a Jew.

Lippo. No, ees no good—Jew. 'E's only t'ink about money, money—alla time money.

Rose. But Sam isn't like that, a bit. He's only interested in poetry and things like that.

[*The* ICE-MAN *comes up out of the cellar and trundles off his cart at the right.*]

Mrs. Fiorentino. [*Calling.*] Lippo! Breakfast!

Lippo. [*Calling.*] Alla right, Margherita! [*To* ROSE.] You marry fella wit' lot o' money. Ees much better.

[*He goes away from the window as* MISS CUSHING *appears at the left, carrying a paper bag.*]

Rose. How's your mother today, Miss Cushing?

Miss Cushing. She's not feeling so good today.

Rose. It's too bad she's not feeling well.

Miss Cushing. I'm afraid it's her heart. At her age, you know——!

[*As she enters the house, two* COLLEGE GIRLS *of nineteen appear at the right.*]

First Girl. [*As they appear.*] I don't understand it.

Second Girl. Convex is this way; and concave is this way.

First Girl. That I know.

Second Girl. When you're near-sighted, they give you convex glasses, and when you're far-sighted, they give you concave.

First Girl. That I didn't know.

Second Girl. Of course, you know it. Didn't we have it in psychology?

First Girl. [*As they disappear at the left.*] I don't remember.

[WILLIE *comes out of the house on his way to school. He is hatless, and carries his books under his arm.*]

Rose. [*Intercepting him at the top of the stoop.*] Why, Willie, the way you look! Your collar's all open.

Willie. I know it! De button came off.

Rose. Why didn't you ask ma to sew it on for you?

Willie. She ain't dere. She's up at Buchanan's.

Rose. Well, wait till I see if I have a pin.

[*She searches in her hand-bag.*]

Willie. [*Starting down the steps.*] Aw, it's all right de way it is.

Rose. [*Following him to the sidewalk.*] No, it isn't. You can't go to school like that. [*Producing a safety-pin.*] Now, hold still while I fix it.

Willie. [*Squirming.*] Aw, fer de love o' Mike——!

Rose. You'll get stuck, if you don't hold still. There, that looks better now. And you didn't comb your hair, either.

Willie. [*Trying to escape.*] Say, lemme alone, cantcha?

Rose. [*Taking a comb out of her hand-bag and combing his hair.*] You can't go to school looking like a little street-loafer.

Willie. Aw, you gimme a pain in de——

Rose. You're getting big enough to comb your own hair, without being told. There! Now you look very nice.

Willie. So's your old man!

[*He runs toward the left kicking the empty tobacco tin ahead of him, then stops, turns, and deliberately rumples his hair.*]

Rose. [*Indignantly, as* WILLIE *runs off.*] Why, Willie!

[MRS. JONES *and the dog appear at right.* OLSEN *knocks the ashes out of his pipe and goes down into the cellar.* MRS. MAURRANT *comes out of the house.*]

Rose. Hello, ma.

Mrs. Jones. [*At the steps.*] Good mornin'.

Rose and Mrs. Maurrant. Good morning, Mrs. Jones.

Mrs. Jones. How's little Mrs. Buchanan gettin' on?

Mrs. Maurrant. Well, she's sleeping now, poor thing. She was so worn out she just went off into a sound sleep. I really didn't think, last night, she'd have the strength to pull through it.

Mrs. Jones. Well, it's somethin' we all got to go through. I been through enough with mine, I hope to tell you. Not that they didn't turn out all right.

Mrs. Maurrant. I wouldn't give up having mine for anything in the world.

Mrs. Jones. Well, after all, what more does any woman want than watchin' her kids grow up an' a husband to look out for her?

Mrs. Maurrant. Yes, that's true.

Mrs. Jones. Yes, and the world would be a whole lot better off, if there was more that lived up to it. [*Starting up the steps.*] Well, I gotta get my Mae up out o' bed. Gawd knows what time she got in this mornin'. [*She enters the vestibule, then stops and turns.*] If you don't mind my bein' so bold, Mrs. Maurrant—an' I don't mind sayin' it in front of your daughter, either—I'd think twice before I'd let any child o' mine bring a Jew into the family.

Rose. [*With a show of temper.*] I don't see what it has to do with you, Mrs. Jones.

Mrs. Jones. There's no need to get huffy about it. I'm only advisin' you for your own good. I'm sure it don't make no difference to me what you do. Come on, Queenie.

[*She goes into the house.*]

Rose. Well, of all the nerve I ever heard in my life——! She and those wonderful children of hers!

Mrs. Maurrant. [*Coming half way down the steps.*] The best way is not to pay any attention to her. There's lots of people like that in the world—they never seem to be happy, unless they're making trouble for somebody. Did Willie go to school?

Rose. Yes, he did. It's awful the way he goes around, looking like a little tough. And the language he uses, too.

Mrs. Maurrant. I know. I just don't seem able to manage him any more.

Rose. I sometimes wonder if it wouldn't be better for us all, if we moved out to the suburbs somewhere—you know, some place in Jersey or Staten Island.

Mrs. Maurrant. I don't think pop would do it. [*As* MAURRANT *comes out the house, carrying a much-battered satchel.*] Are you leaving now, Frank?

Maurrant. [*From the top of the stoop.*] Looks like it, don't it? Where you been all this while?

Mrs. Maurrant. Why, you know where I've been, Frank—up to Mrs. Buchanan's.

Maurrant. Yeah? An' where you goin' now?

Mrs. Maurrant. Just around to Kraus's to get a chicken. I thought I'd make her some chicken-soup, to give her strength.

Maurrant. Say, how about lookin' after your own home an' lettin' the Buchanans look after theirs?

Mrs. Maurrant. All I'm trying to do is to be a little neighborly. It's the least anybody can do, with the poor thing hardly able to lift her hand.

Maurrant. That's all right about that! [*Coming down the steps.*] A woman's got a right to stay in her own home, lookin' after her husband an' children.

Mrs. Maurrant. [*Going toward him.*] What else have I been doing all these years, I'd like to know?

Maurrant. Well, just see that you don't forget it, that's all—or there's li'ble to be trouble.

Mrs. Maurrant. [*Putting her hand on his arm.*] All right, Frank. Don't say any more, please. When will you be back—tomorrow?

Maurrant. I don't know when I'll be back. Whenever I'm t'roo wit' me work—that's when. What are you so anxious to know for, huh?

Mrs. Maurrant. Why, I just asked, that's all.

Maurrant. Oh, you just asked, huh? Just in case somebody wanted to come aroun' callin', is that it?

Mrs. Maurrant. No, it isn't. It isn't anything of the kind. You got no right to talk to me like that in front of my own daughter. You got no right. No, you haven't!

[*She turns away and hurries off abruptly at the left.*]

Rose. Ma!

[*She starts to run after her mother.*]

Maurrant. [*Imperiously.*] Come back here, you! [Rose *hesitates.*] Come back, hear me? [Rose *turns and comes slowly back.*] You stay right here.

[*He puts down his satchel and takes a flask from his pocket.*]

Rose. Why do you talk to her like that?

Maurrant. Nobody's askin' you.

Rose. If you were only a little nicer to her, maybe everything would be different.

Maurrant. Yeah? Where's she got any kick comin'? Ain't I always been a good husband to her? Ain't I always looked after her? [*He takes a drink.*]

Rose. It's not that, pop. It's somebody to be sort of nice to her that she wants—sort of nice and gentle, the way she is to you. That's all it is.

Maurrant. [*Turning to her.*] So she's got you headed the same way, has she? Goin' out nights with married men, huh?

Rose. You don't need to worry about me, pop. I can take care of myself, all right.

Maurrant. No daughter o' mine ain't gonna go that way. I seen too many o' those kind around the theayter.

Rose. Things are different nowadays, pop. I guess maybe you don't realize that. Girls aren't the way they used to be—sort of soft and helpless. A girl nowadays knows how to look out for herself. But not her, pop; she needs somebody to look after her.

Maurrant. Aw, can all that talk! You been listenin' to them Bolshevikis, that's the trouble. But I'm gonna keep you straight, by God, or I'll know the reason why.

Rose. I guess I've got a right to think about things for myself.

Maurrant. Yeah? Well, don't let me ketch that other bozo comin' around here, either—that's all I got to say.

Rose. [*Hesitantly, going up to him.*] Pop, listen—couldn't we get a little house somewhere—Queens or somewhere like that?

Maurrant. What's the idea?

Rose. Well, I don't know. I sort of thought it would be nice for all of us. And maybe if ma had a nice little home and some real nice neighbors—do you see what I mean?

Maurrant. This place suits me all right.

Rose. You can get some real nice little houses that don't cost such an awful lot. And I wouldn't mind helping to pay for it. And once we had it all fixed up——

Maurrant. Forget it! I don' know when I'll be back. [*As he starts to go right.*] An' remember what I tol' you, hear?

Mrs. Jones. [*Appearing at her window with a tin dust-pan.*] Good mornin', Mr. Maurrant. You off on a little trip?

Maurrant. [*Curtly.*] Yeah.

[*He goes off.* Mrs. Jones *empties the dust-pan out of the window and goes away.* Kaplan *comes out of the house, a bundle of newspapers under his arm. He walks slowly and painfully, with the aid of a heavy stick.*]

Kaplan. [*At the foot of the steps.*] Vy do you look so sed, h'm?

Rose. [*Turning and sitting on the right balustrade.*] Oh, good morning, Mr. Kaplan.

Kaplan. A young girl, like you, should not look so sed.

Rose. I'm not sad, especially, only——

Kaplan. You got troubles, h'm?

Rose. I don't know. It's just sort of everything.

Kaplan. Velt-schmerz you got, h'm? Vit' my boy Sem is de same t'ing. Dees vay you feel only ven you are young. Ven you gat old like me, you tink only: "Moch longer I von't be here."

Rose. Why should things be the way they are, Mr. Kaplan? Why must people always be fighting and having troubles, instead of just sort of being happy together?

Kaplan. My dear young leddy, ef I could enser dis quastion, I would be de greatest benefactor thet de verld hes ever known. Dees is somet'ing, vich all de philosophers hev been unable to enser. De ones thet believe in God, say de davil is responsible; and de ones thet don't believe in God, say 'uman nature is responsible. It is my opinion thet most unheppiness can be traced to economic cosses and thet——

[CHARLIE *and* MARY HILDEBRAND *have come out of the house, carrying their school-books.*]

Mary. Hello.

Rose. Hello, Mary. Hello, Charlie.

Charlie. Hello.

Mary. [*Chattily, as they reach the sidewalk.*] We're going to be dispossessed today.

Rose. What a shame!

Mary. Yes, ma'am. My father went away and so we couldn't pay the rent.

Charlie. [*Tugging at her arm.*] Aw, come on, Mary.

Rose. Have you another place to live, Mary?

Mary. No ma'am. But Miss Simpson, from the Charities, says she'll find us a place. She says we must learn to be less extravagant.

Charlie. Come ahead, will you?

Mary. I'm going to school now. Good-by.

Rose. Good-by.

[*The* CHILDREN *go off at the left.*]

Kaplan. More trobles!

Rose. I know. Isn't it awful to think of them being turned out in the street like that?

Kaplan. In a ciwilized verld, soch t'ings could not heppen.

Rose. You mean if there were different laws?

Kaplan. Not laws! We got already too many laws. Ve must hev ection, not laws. De verking-klesses must t'row off de yoke of ke*pit*alism, and ebolish wage-slavery.

Rose. But wouldn't people still be unkind to each other and fight and quarrel among themselves?

Kaplan. My dear young leddy, so long as ve keep men in slevery, dey vill behave like sleves. But wance ve establish a verld based upon 'uman needs and not upon 'uman greed——

Rose. You mean people will begin being nice to each other and making allowances and all?

Kaplan. All dees vill come. Wot ve hev now is a wicious soicle. On de one hend, ve hev a rotten economic system——

Rose. Excuse me, here's my mother.

[*She goes toward the left as* MRS. MAURRANT *approaches, a paper package in her hand.* KAPLAN *goes off at the right.*]

Mrs. Maurrant. [*As* ROSE *comes up to her.*] Did he go?

[*They stop on the pavement, at the left of the stoop.*]

Rose. Yes.

Mrs. Maurrant. I got a little chicken, to make Mrs. Buchanan some soup.

Rose. He had a flask with him, ma. I hope he doesn't start drinking.

Mrs. Maurrant. What did he say—anything?

Rose. No, only the way he always talks. I tried to talk to him about buying a house somewheres, but he wouldn't listen.

Mrs. Maurrant. No, I knew he wouldn't.

Rose. It doesn't seem to be any use trying to get him to listen to anything.

Mrs. Maurrant. It's always been that way. I've always tried to be a good wife to him, Rose. But it never seemed to make any difference to him.

Rose. I know, ma.

Mrs. Maurrant. And I've tried to be a good mother, too.

Rose. I know, ma. I know just the way you feel about it.

Mrs. Maurrant. [*Appealingly.*] Do you, Rose?

Rose. Yes, ma, I do. Honest I do.

Mrs. Maurrant. I've always tried to make a nice home for him and to do what's right. But it doesn't seem to be any use.

Rose. I know, ma. [*Hesitantly.*] But it's on account of—— [*She stops.*]

Mrs. Maurrant. Are you going to start, too? Are you going to start like all the others?

[*She turns away and bursts into tears.*]

Rose. [*Fondling her.*] Don't, ma. Please don't.

Mrs. Maurrant. I thought you'd be the one that would feel different.

Rose. I do, ma—really I do.

Mrs. Maurrant. What's the good of being alive, if you can't get a little something out of life? You might just as well be dead.

Rose. Look out, ma. Somebody's coming.

[*A smartly-dressed* GIRL, *with one side of her face covered with cotton and adhesive tape, appears at the left and crosses the stage. At the same time,* JONES *comes out of the house.* ROSE *and* MRS. MAURRANT *stand in awkward silence, as he comes down the stoop and approaches them.*]

Jones. Well, is it hot enough for you today?

Rose. It's awful, isn't it?

Jones. [*As he goes toward the left.*] You said it. Still along about January, we'll all be wishin' we had a little o' this weather.

[*He exits.* MRS. MAURRANT *goes toward the stoop.*]

Rose. Ma, listen. If I say something, will you listen to me?

Mrs. Maurrant. Yes, sure I will, Rose. I'll listen to anything you say, only——

Rose. Well, what I was thinking was, if he didn't come around here so much, maybe. Do you see what I mean, ma?

Mrs. Maurrant. [*Constrainedly.*] Yes, Rose.

Rose. [*Putting her arm around her.*] It's on account of all that's going around—everybody in the whole house. You see what I mean, don't you, ma?

Mrs. Maurrant. Every person in the world has to have somebody to talk to. You can't live without somebody to talk to. I'm not saying that I can't talk to you, Rose, but you're only a young girl and it's not the same thing.

Rose. It's only on account of pop. I'm scared of what he's likely to do, if he starts drinking.

Mrs. Maurrant. Well, I'll see, Rose. Sometimes I think I'd be better off if I was dead.

Rose. If there was only something I could do.

Mrs. Maurrant. There isn't anything anybody could do. It's just the way things are, that's all.

[BUCHANAN *appears at the left. They turn and face him as he approaches.*]

Mrs. Maurrant. Oh, Mr. Buchanan, I got a little chicken, so that I could make her some good, nourishing soup.

Buchanan. Well, say, you got to let me pay you for it.

Mrs. Maurrant. Oh, never mind about that. We'll have the chicken for supper tonight. Did you have her medicine made up?

Buchanan. Yes, I got it right here. I called up the office and they told me not to come down today.

Mrs. Maurrant. Well, that's very nice. It'll be a comfort to her to have you around.

Buchanan. Yes, that's what I thought, too. Well, I'd better be getting upstairs.

[*He goes up the steps.*]

Mrs. Maurrant. I'll be up later, with the soup.

Buchanan. Well, thanks. [*Stopping at the top of the stoop and turning to her.*] You've been a mighty good neighbor, Mrs. Maurrant.

[*He enters the house.*]

Mrs. Maurrant. He's an awful nice young feller—so nice and gentle. And he's always trying to be so helpful. It makes you feel sort of sorry for him.

[SHIRLEY *comes out of the house, carrying a large wicker bag, which contains her lunch and school-books. She takes a post-card out of the mail-box.*]

Mrs. Maurrant. [*Going up the steps.*] Well, I'd better go and start this chicken. Are you coming home for lunch, Rose?

Rose. Yes. I'll be back as soon as the funeral's over.

Mrs. Maurrant. Oh, all right. [*As she sees* SHIRLEY.] Good morning.

Shirley. [*Coming out of the vestibule, reading the post-card.*] Good morning.

Rose. Good morning.

[MRS. MAURRANT *goes into the house. The shade of* MAE'S *window flies up and she is seen, for an instant, dressed only in her step-in. She yawns noisily and turns away from the window.*]

Rose. [*Seating herself on the stoop.*] It's another awful day, isn't it?

Shirley. Yes, and when you have to keep forty children quiet—! Well, thank goodness, in two weeks, school closes. Otherwise, I think I'd go crazy.

Rose. Well, you get a nice long vacation, anyhow.

Shirley. Not much vacation for me. I'm taking Summer courses at Teachers' College. [*She looks at* ROSE *a moment, hesitates, and then comes down the steps.*] Miss Maurrant, if you don't mind, I want to talk to you about my brother Sam.

Rose. Why certainly, Miss Kaplan.

Shirley. I guess you know he's only finishing college this month——

Rose. Yes, of course, I do.

Shirley. Then he has to go three years to law-school and pass the bar examination, before he can be a full-fledged lawyer.

Rose. Yes, it takes a long time.

Shirley. A long time and lots of money. And before a young lawyer begins to make his own living, that takes a long time, too. It will be ten years, maybe, before he's making enough to support himself and a family.

[*Looking away.*] Then it's time enough for him to think about marriage.

Rose. You don't mean me and Sam, Miss Kaplan?

Shirley. Yes, that's just what I mean.

Rose. Why, we're just good friends, that's all.

Shirley. I know how it is with a boy like Sam, Miss Maurrant. He thinks he's a man already; but he's nothing but a boy. If you're such a good friend, you shouldn't take his mind away from his work.

Rose. But I haven't meant to, Miss Kaplan—honest I haven't.

Shirley. I've had to work hard enough to get him as far as he is. And I have my father to take care of, too. The few dollars he makes, writing for the radical papers, don't even pay the rent. Believe me, every dollar I make goes.

Rose. I know. Sam's often told me how much he owes to you.

Shirley. He doesn't owe me anything. I don't care about the money. Only he should be thinking about his work and not about other things.

Rose. Yes, he should be thinking about his work. But don't you think there are other things in the world, too, besides just work?

Shirley. Don't you think I know that? I know that just as well as you do. Maybe you think I'm only an old-maid schoolteacher, without any feelings.

Rose. Oh, I don't—really I don't!

Shirley. [*Turning her head away.*] Maybe I'm not a movie vamp, with dimples—but I could have had my chances, too. Only, I wanted to give Sam an education.

Rose. I haven't tried to vamp Sam, honestly I haven't. We just seemed sort of naturally to like each other.

Shirley. Why must you pick out Sam? You could get other fellows. Anyhow, it's much better to marry with your own kind. When you marry outside your own people, nothing good ever comes of it. You can't mix oil and water.

Rose. I don't know. I think if people really care about each other——

Shirley. He's nothing but a baby. He sees a pretty face and, right away, he forgets about everything else.

Rose. [*With a flash of temper.*] I know I haven't as much brains as Sam, or as you, either, if that's what you mean.

Shirley. [*Contritely, going toward her.*] I didn't mean to hurt your feelings. I haven't got anything against you. Only, he's all I've got in the world. What else have I got to live for?

Sam. [*Appearing at the extreme right window, with a cup of coffee and a piece of coffee-cake.*] Hello, Rose.

Rose. Hello, Sam.

Shirley. [*In a low tone.*] Please don't tell him what I said.

[SAM *goes to the other window.*]

Rose. Oh no, I won't.

[SHIRLEY *hurries off at the left.*]

Rose. [*Rising and turning toward Sam.*] Sam——

Sam. [*Holding out the coffee-cake.*] Want some coffee-cake?

Rose. No. [*Going up the steps.*] Sam, there's something I want to ask you, before I forget. Is there any special way you have to act in a synagogue?

Sam. [*Eating throughout.*] In a synagogue?

Rose. Yes. The funeral I'm going to is in a synagogue, and I thought there might be some special thing you have to do. Like in church, you know, a girl is always supposed to keep her hat on.

Sam. I don't know. I've never in my life been in a synagogue.

Rose. Didn't you ever go to Sunday-school, or anything like that?

Sam. No.

Rose. That's funny. I thought everybody went once in a while. How about when your mother died?

Sam. She was cremated. My parents were always rationalists.

Rose. Didn't they believe in God or anything?

Sam. What do you mean by God?

Rose. [*Puzzled.*] Well—you know what I mean. What anybody means—God. Somebody that sort of loves us and looks after us, when we're in trouble.

Sam. [*Sitting on the window-sill.*] That's nothing but superstition—the lies that people tell themselves, because reality is too terrible for them to face.

Rose. But, Sam, don't you think it's better to believe in something that makes you a little happy, than not to believe in anything and be miserable all the time?

Sam. There's no such thing as happiness. That's an illusion, like all the rest.

Rose. Then, what's the use of living?

Sam. [*Brushing the last crumbs off his hands.*] Yes, what is the use?

Rose. Why, you oughtn't to talk like that, Sam—a person with all the talent and brains that you've got. I know things aren't just the way you want them to be. But they aren't for anybody. They aren't for me, either.

Sam. Then, why don't we get out of it together?

Rose. I don't see just how we could do that, Sam.

Sam. It would be easy enough—ten cents' worth of carbolic acid.

Rose. Why, Sam, you don't mean kill ourselves!

Sam. Is your life so precious to you that you want to cling to it?

Rose. Well, yes. I guess it is.

Sam. Why? Why? What is there in life to compensate for the pain of living?

Rose. There's a lot. Just being alive—breathing and walking around. Just looking at the faces of people you like and hearing them laugh. And seeing the pretty things in the store-windows. And rough-housing with your kid brother. And—oh, I don't know—listening to a good band, and dancing—Oh, I'd hate to die! [*Earnestly.*] Sam, promise you won't talk about killing yourself, any more.

Sam. What difference would it make to you, if I did?

Rose. Don't talk like that, Sam! You're the best friend I've ever had.

[*She puts her hand on his.*]

Sam. I can't think of anything but you.

Rose. There's something I want to ask your advice about, Sam. It's about what I started to tell you about, last night. A man I know wants to put me on the stage.

Sam. [*Releasing her hand and drawing back.*] What man?

Rose. A man that works in the office. He knows a manager and he says he'll help me get started. You see, what I thought was, that if I could only get out of here and have a decent place to live and make a lot of money, maybe everything would be different, not only for me, but for ma and pop and Willie.

Sam. But don't you know what he wants, this man?

Rose. Nobody gives you anything for nothing, Sam. If you don't pay for things in one way, you do it another.

Sam. Rose, for God's sake, you mustn't!

[VINCENT JONES *comes out of the house.*]

Rose. [*Seeing* VINCENT *in the vestibule.*] Look out, Sam, here's that tough from upstairs.

[*She goes over to the left of the stoop.*]

Vincent. [*In the doorway.*] Hello, Rosie. Been here all night, talkin' to the little yid?

[ROSE *does not answer.*]

Vincent. [*Turning to* SAM.] Hello, motzers! Shake!

[*He leans over the balustrade and seizes* SAM's *hand in a crushing grip.*]

Sam. [*Writhing with pain.*] Let me go!

Rose. Let him alone!

[VINCENT *gives* SAM's *hand another vicious squeeze and then releases him.* SAM *cowers back in the window, nursing his hand.*]

Vincent. [*Waving his hand about in mock pain.*] Jesus, what a grip dat little kike's got! I'd hate to get into a mix-up wit' him. [*To* ROSE.] Got a date tonight, kid?

Rose. Yes, I have.

Vincent. Yeah? Gee, ain't dat too bad? I'll give you two dollars, if you let me snap your garter.

Rose. Shut up, you!

[VINCENT *laughs.* SAM *makes an inarticulate sound.*]

Vincent. [*Threateningly.*] Whadja say? I tought I hoid you say sumpin.

[*He makes a threatening gesture.* SAM *shrinks back.*]

Vincent. [*With a loud laugh, as he goes down the steps.*] Fightin' Kaplan, de pride o' Jerusalem! [*He looks at them both, then laughs again.*] Fer cryin' out loud!

[*He goes off at the left.*]

Rose. Oh, if there was only some way of getting out of here. [SAM *puts the back of his hand to his forehead and turns away.*] I sometimes think I'd just like to run away.

Sam. [*Without turning.*] Yes!

Rose. Anywhere — it wouldn't matter where—just to get out of this.

Sam. [*Turning.*] Why shouldn't we do it?

Rose. [*Rather startled, coming over to the right balustrade.*] Would you go with me, Sam?

Sam. Yes—anywhere.

Rose. I've heard that people are much nicer and friendlier, when you get outside of New York. There's not so much of a mad rush, other places. And being alone, you could sort of work things out for yourself. [*Suddenly.*] Only, what would you do, Sam?

Sam. I could get a job, too.

Rose. And give up your law-work?

Sam. I'd give up everything, to be with you.

Rose. No. I wouldn't let you do that, Sam. It's different with me——

[EASTER *appears at the right.*]

Easter. [*Stopping at the right of the stoop.*] Good morning, Miss Maurrant.

[*Startled,* ROSE *turns and sees him, for the first time.*]

Rose. [*None too pleased.*] Oh, good morning, Mr. Easter. What brings you in this neighborhood?

Easter. [*Not very plausibly.*] Well, I just happened to have a little business right around the corner. So, I thought as long as you were going to the funeral, we might just as well go together.

Rose. Well, I hardly expected to see you around here. [*An awkward pause.*] Oh, I'd like you to meet my friend, Mr. Kaplan.

Easter. How do you do, Mr. Kaplan? Glad to know you.

[SAM *murmurs something inaudible. An awkward silence.*]

Rose. [*To* SAM.] Mr. Easter is the manager of the office.

[SAM *does not reply. Another silence.*]

Rose. [*To* EASTER.] It's awful hot again, isn't it?

Easter. Worse than yesterday. [*Approaching the stoop.*] Tell you what I was thinking. I was thinking that after the funeral, we might take a run down to the beach, somewhere, and cool off a little.

Rose. I can't today. I've got a lot of things I want to do.

Easter. Oh, you can do 'em some other day.

Rose. No, really, I can't. [*Looking at her watch.*] Well, I guess it's time we got started. [*She comes down the steps.*]

Easter. Yes, it is. We'll pick up a cab at the corner.

[MRS. MAURRANT *appears at her window, looks out, and sees* ROSE *and* EASTER.]

Rose. Why, I thought I'd walk. It's not far.

Easter. Too hot today for any walking.

Rose. [*Starting to go toward the left.*] Not if you keep in the shade.

Easter. Much more comfortable taking a cab.

Rose. I'd rather walk.

Easter. Well, whatever you say. Good morning, Mr. Kaplan. Glad to have met you.

[SAM *murmurs an inaudible reply.*]

Rose. Good-by, Sam, I'll see you later.

[SAM *does not answer.* ROSE *and* EASTER *go toward the left, in silence.* SAM *watches them intently, trembling with jealousy.* MRS. MAURRANT, *surprised and disturbed, watches* ROSE *and* EASTER.]

Rose. [*To* EASTER, *as they disappear.*] It's a lucky thing my father wasn't around.

[SAM *suddenly turns and disappears into the house.* MRS. MAURRANT *remains at the window, looking out with obvious expectancy.*]

A Distant Voice. [*Off-stage left.*] *Straw*-berries! Straw-*berries!*

[*An anemic* GIRL *of eighteen, with a music-roll under her arm, appears at the left. She enters the house and pushes one of the buttons in the vestibule, then goes to the entrance-door and waits. A moment later* MRS. FIORENTINO *appears hastily at the window, and whisks away the bed-clothes. After another moment the latch clicks and the* GIRL *enters the house.*]

The Voice. [*A little nearer.*] *Oh-h! Straw*-berries! Straw-*berries!*

[SANKEY *appears at the right. He carries a pencil behind his ear, wears a round cap with a metal name-plate and a stiff visor, and carries a large black-covered bill-holder. He and* MRS. MAURRANT *see each other and both become tense with excitement.* MRS. MAURRANT *beckons to him and he comes over to the railing under her window.*]

Mrs. Maurrant. [*In a low, tense voice.*] Come up.

Sankey. [*Looking about nervously.*] Now?

Mrs. Maurrant. Yes. I got to talk to you.

Sankey. Is it all right?

Mrs. Maurrant. Yes. He's gone to Stamford.

Sankey. How about later?

Mrs. Maurrant. No. Rose'll be home in an hour. She's not working today.

Sankey. All right.

[*He looks about again, then goes quickly toward the steps.* SAM *appears at the entrance-door. He is about to step out, when he sees* SANKEY. *He stops and looks at him.* SANKEY *sees* SAM, *hesitates a moment, then goes quickly into the house. Meanwhile,* MRS. MAURRANT *has closed both windows and pulled down the shades.* SAM *takes a periodical out of the mail-box, then comes out of the house and down the steps. He looks up at the* MAURRANT *windows, sees the drawn shades, and looks about in perturbed perplexity, not knowing what to do. At length, he sits down on the steps of the stoop, tears the wrapper off the periodical*—The Nation—*and begins to read. The girl in* LIPPO'S *apartment begins playing the piano. This continues throughout the scene. Two untidy and rather coarse-looking* MEN *appear at the left and approach the stoop:* JAMES HENRY, *a city-marshal, and* FRED CULLEN, *his assistant. They stop in front of the house.* SAM *pays no attention to them.*]

The Marshal. [*Crossing to the left of the stoop, and taking a paper from his pocket.*] Dis is it. [*To* SAM.] Hildebrand live here?

Sam. [*Startled.*] What?

The Marshal. I'm askin' you if Hildebrand lives here.

Sam. Yes. Fourth floor.

The Marshal. Better give de janitor a buzz, Fred.

[FRED *goes up the steps and rings the janitor's bell, then leans over the left balustrade.*]

Fred. [*Bawling.*] Hey, janitor.

Olsen. [*Below.*] Vell?

Fred. Come on out a minute. [*As* OLSEN *appears below.*] We got a warrant for Hildebrand.

Olsen. Fourt' floor—Hildebrand.

Fred. Yeah, I know. We got a warrant for her.

The Marshal. I'm City Marshal Henry. We got a dispossess warrant.

Olsen. [*Coming up the steps.*] Oh, sure. You gonna put 'em out?

The Marshal. Yeah, dat's it. Has she got anybody to take de foinicher away?

Olsen. [*With a shrug.*] I don't know.

The Marshal. Well, we'll have t' dump it on de sidewalk, den. Go ahead, Fred.

[*They enter the house.* OLSEN *leans his elbows on the coping, and smokes his pipe.* SAM *sits on the steps, deep in troubled thought. A* GROCERY-BOY, *with a full basket, appears at the right, and goes down the cellar-steps.* MAE JONES *comes out of the house. She stands on the top step, yawns noisily, and goes off at left. She and* SAM *do not pay the slightest attention to each other.*]

A Voice. [*A little nearer.*] *Straw*-berries! Straw-*berries!*

[MRS. OLSEN *comes up the cellar-steps with a heavy pail of water.* OLSEN *leans forward to make room for her. She staggers over to the stoop, almost dropping the pail, and goes up the steps into the vestibule.* OLSEN *yawns and goes down into the cellar.* MRS. JONES *appears at the window, her hair wet and stringy, a towel pinned about her shoulders, and leans out to dry her hair.*]

An Old-Clothes Man. [*Appearing at left.*] I kesh ko! I kesh ko!

[*He wears a battered derby and carries a folded newspaper under his arm.* MRS. OLSEN, *on her knees, begins washing up the vestibule.* FRED *comes out of the house, carrying a worn chair and a large gilt-framed picture, which he deposits on the sidewalk, against the railing to the left of the stoop.*]

An Old-Clothes Man. [*As if to someone across the street.*] Kesh ko? [*To* SAM.] Any old klose, mister?

[SAM *pays no attention to him.* FRED *re-enters the house.*]

The Old-Clothes Man. [*To* MRS. JONES.] Any ol' klose, leddy?

Mrs. Jones. Naw, nawthin'.

The Old-Clothes Man. Hets? Shoes? Ol' stockings?

Mrs. Jones. Nawthin', I tell you.

[*As the* OLD-CLOTHES MAN *goes off at the right,* MAURRANT *appears, still carrying his satchel.*]

Mrs. Jones. Why, hello, Mr. Maurrant. [MAURRANT *looks up without replying and comes over to the stoop.*] I thought you was off to Stamford.

Maurrant. I changed me——

[*He stops, to the right of the stoop, and looks up at the drawn shades of his apartment.* SAM *rises, slowly and rigidly, his eyes glued in fascination upon* MAURRANT. MAURRANT'S *movements take on a lithe and cat-like quality. Then, slowly and deliberately, he goes toward the steps, his back arched, like a tiger ready to spring.*]

Sam. [*Suddenly blocking the steps.*] No! No! For God's sake——!

Maurrant. [*Raging.*] Out o' me way, you goddam little rat!

[*He flings* SAM *violently aside, almost knocking him down.* MRS. OLSEN, *terrified, rises and shrinks into a corner as* MAURRANT *with swift stealthiness enters the house.* MRS. JONES *leans out to see what is wrong.* SAM *rushes down the steps and stands under the* MAURRANT *windows. The* MARSHAL *comes out of the house, carrying a wash-boiler filled with pots.*]

Sam. [*Hysterically.*] Mrs. Maurrant! Mrs. Maurrant!

Mrs. Jones. What's the matter?

[*The* MARSHAL *puts the wash-boiler on the balustrade and looks on in amazement.*]

Sam. [*To* MRS. JONES.] Quick! Run and tell her! Quick!

Mrs. Jones. What is it? [*Suddenly.*] Oh, Gawd, is he in there?

[*She leaves the window hastily.*]

Sam. Yes! Mrs. Maurrant! Mrs. Maurrant!

[*A scream of terror is heard from the* MAURRANT *apartment.*]

Mrs. Maurrant's Voice. Frank! Frank!

[*Two shots are heard, in quick succession, and then a heavy fall.* MRS. OLSEN *runs out of the vestibule and down into the cellar.* SANKEY'S *voice is heard, inarticulate with fear. Then one of the shades shoots up, and* SANKEY *appears at the window, coatless, his face deformed by terror. He tries to open the window, but succeeds only in shattering the pane with his elbow.* MAURRANT *appears behind him and pulls him away from the window. Then another shot is heard.*]

The Marshal. For Chris' sake, what's happenin'? Get an ambulance, you!

[*He pushes* SAM *toward the left, then hurries off at the right. As* SAM *runs off, a* CROWD *begins to form.* OLSEN *comes up from the cellar, followed by the* GROCERY-BOY. *The two* WORKMEN *come up out of the excavation.*

Two or three of the WORKMEN *from the demolished building run on at the right.*]

A Workman. What's happening?

A Man. What is it? A murder?

[*Still others join the crowd: A* HUCKSTER, *a* JANITOR *from a neighboring house, a* MULATTO GIRL, *six or eight* WOMEN *of the neighborhood, some in street-dresses, others in house-dresses or dingy wrappers.* LIPPO'S PUPIL *appears at the window, badly frightened. The* CROWD *surges about uncertainly, not knowing what has happened, and buzzing with questions which nobody can answer. While the* CROWD *is still forming,* FRED, *the* MARSHAL'S *assistant, appears at the broken window.*]

Fred. [*Excitedly.*] Grab dat boid! He's comin' down!

A Workman. What boid?

A Man. Here he is, now!

[*The* CROWD *murmurs with excitement and surges about the stoop as the house-door opens and* MAURRANT *appears.* His *coat is open and his shirt is torn almost to shreds. His face, hands, and clothing are covered with blood. He stands in the door-way for a moment, surveying the* CROWD, *his eyes glaring.*]

Fred. Grab him! Don't let him get away!

[*As the* CROWD *makes a concerted movement toward* MAURRANT, *he whips out an automatic revolver and levels it. The* CROWD *shrinks back. Some of the* WOMEN *scream.*]

Maurrant. Git back! Git back, all o' you!

[*The* CROWD *falls back toward the left to make way for him. With his back to the balustrade, he comes quickly down the steps, and still leveling his revolver at the* CROWD, *retreats backwards to the cellar steps. A* MAN, *approaching at the right, comes stealthily up behind him, but* MAURRANT *senses his presence in time, wheels quickly, menaces the* MAN *with his revolver, then rushes down the cellar steps. While all this is happening, the other shade in the* MAURRANT *apartment flies up and* MISS CUSHING *opens the window and leans out.*]

Miss Cushing. Hurry up! Get an ambulance!

[*No one pays any attention to her, as they are all watching* MAURRANT. *As* MAURRANT *runs down the cellar steps, the* CROWD *surges forward to the railing on both sides of the stoop and leans over. A scream from* MRS. OLSEN *is heard from the basement.* FRED *goes away from the window.*]

Miss Cushing. Get an ambulance, somebody!

[*Unable to attract anyone's attention, she leaves the window.*]

Olsen. Olga!

[*He hurries down the cellar steps.*]

A Man. [*Calling.*] Here's a cop! [*The* CROWD *looks to the right.*] Hey! Hurry up!

[*A* POLICEMAN *runs on from the right.*]

The Policeman. Where is he?

Voices in the Crowd. He's down the cellar! He ran down the cellar! He went down the steps!

The Policeman. Get out of the way!

[*The* POLICEMAN *and two* MEN *in the crowd go down the cellar steps.*]

Voices in the Crowd. Watch yourself! Look out, he's got a gun! He's a big guy with his shirt torn!

[*The rest of the* CROWD *peers over the railing.*]

Miss Cushing. [*Leaning out of* ROSE'S *window.*] Hey, don't you hear me? Get an ambulance!

Another Man. [*Looking up.*] What's de matter? You want de ambulance?

Miss Cushing. Yes! Right away!

Another Man. [*To the* GROCERY-BOY.] Run aroun' de corner to de horspital, Johnny, an' tell 'em to send de ambulance!

The Grocery-Boy. Sure!

Miss Cushing. Run!

[*The* GROCERY-BOY *runs off swiftly at the left.* MISS CUSHING *leaves the window. Meanwhile, as the* POLICEMAN *and the two* MEN *have gone down the cellar steps, the* MARSHAL *has run on from the right, panting.*]

The Marshal. [*As the* GROCERY-BOY *runs off.*] Did dey git 'm?

A Man. He beat it down de cellar.

A Workman. De cop's gone after him.

The Marshal. Why de hell didn' you stop 'im?

[FRED *comes out of the house.*]

A Workman. He had a gun.

Fred. Did somebody go for de ambulance?

A Man. Yeah. De kid went.

A Woman. It's only aroun' de corner.

Another Man. Dey'll be here, right away.

[*The* CROWD *moves over toward* FRED.]

The Marshal. [*Pushing his way through the crowd and up the steps.*] What de hell happened, Fred?

Fred. [*As the* CROWD *moves toward the stoop.*] It's a moider. Dis boid's wife an' some other guy. Jesus, you oughta see de blood.

[*Another* POLICEMAN *runs up at the left, closely followed by* SAM.]

Fred. Upstairs, officer! Dere's two of 'em got shot.

The Policeman. [*Elbowing his way through the* CROWD.] Look out o' the way, youse! [*He goes up the stoop and crosses to the door.*] Where's de guy dat did it?

Voices in the Crowd. Down de cellar! He beat it down de steps!

Fred. Dere's another cop after 'im. You better look after dem upstairs. Foist floor.

Sam. [*Agonized.*] Are they dead?

[*No one pays any attention to him.*]

The Marshal. [*Stopping the* POLICEMAN, *and exhibiting his badge.*] I'm City Marshal Henry. Kin I do anythin'?

Policeman. Don' let anybody in or out! hear?

The Marshal. Yeah, sure!

[*The* POLICEMAN *exits quickly into the house.*]

Sam. Are they dead?

[*No one notices him. The* MARSHAL *takes up his position in the doorway.*]

Buchanan. [*Appearing at the* MAURRANT *window.*] Where's the ambulance?

The Marshal. It'll be here right away. Dere's a cop on his way up.

Sam. Mr. Buchanan! Mr. Buchanan! Are they dead?

[*But* BUCHANAN *has already disappeared. The two* MEN *who followed the first* POLICEMAN *into the cellar now come up the steps. The* CROWD *moves over to the railing at the right.*]

The Marshal. Did you get him, boys?

One of the Men. He must be hidin' somewheres. De cop's lookin' for 'im.

Another Man. Somebody better call de resoives.

[SAM *runs up the steps and tries to enter the house.*]

The Marshal. [*Seizing him roughly.*] You can't get in now! Get back dere!

[*He pushes* SAM *back into the* CROWD *at the foot of the steps.*]

The Policeman. [*Appearing at the* MAURRANT *window.*] Hey, call up headquarters an' tell 'em to send the resoives. Make it quick!

[*He goes away from the window.*]

The Marshal. You go, Fred.

Fred. Sure!

A Man. Dere's a phone in de warehouse.

[*An ambulance bell is heard at the left, as* FRED *goes quickly toward the left. Another* SPECTATOR *hurries on and joins the* CROWD.]

Voices in the Crowd. Dere it is! Dere's de ambulance now! Here dey come!

[*The* CROWD *moves over toward the left.*]

A Man. Dey won't be able to git past.

The Policeman. [*Reappearing at the window.*] Is dat de ambulance?

The Marshal. Yeah.

[BUCHANAN *and* MRS. JONES *crowd to the window, behind the* POLICEMAN, *and, at the other window,* LIPPO, MISS CUSHING, *and* MRS. HILDEBRAND *appear. A* HOSPITAL INTERNE *and an* AMBULANCE-DRIVER *comes on at the left.*]

The Policeman. Hurry up, Doc! She's still breathin'.

The Interne. [*Forcing his way through the* CROWD.] All right! Better bring the stretcher, Harry.

The Ambulance-Driver. Yes, sir.

[*He hurries off at the left. The* INTERNE *goes quickly into the house. The* CROWD *attempts to follow, several of its members going up the steps.*]

The Marshal. [*Pushing them back.*] Keep back, now! Back off de stoop, everybody!

[*The* CROWD *forms a compact mass about the foot of the steps. The persons at the* MAURRANT *windows have disappeared.* FRED *hurries on at the left.*]

Fred. [*Pushing his way through the* CROWD *and up the steps.*] I got 'em. Dey'll be right up. Anudder cop jes' wen' in t'roo de warehouse cellar.

The Marshal. Dey'll git 'im all right. [*Looking at his watch.*] Better git busy wit' dat foinicher, Fred. We got two udder jobs today.

Fred. Yeah, sure, Jimmy.

[*He enters the house. The* AMBULANCE-

DRIVER *appears at the left, carrying a canvas stretcher.*]

The Ambulance-Driver. Get out o' the way!

The Marshal. Git back, can't youse? What de hell's de matter wit' youse?

[*He comes down the steps and violently pushes the* CROWD *back. The* AMBULANCE-DRIVER *enters the house.*]

The Policeman. [*At the window.*] Are dey bringin' dat stretcher?

The Marshal. On de way up! [*To the* CROWD.] Keep back!

[*The* POLICEMAN *leaves the window.* LIPPO'S PUPIL, *her music-roll under her arm, appears timidly in the doorway.*]

The Marshal. [*Grabbing her arm roughly.*] Where you goin'?

The Girl. [*Nervously.*] I'm going home.

The Marshal. Home? Where do you live?

The Girl. Ninety-first Street.

The Marshal. What are you doin' here?

The Girl. I just came for a music-lesson, that's all.

The Marshal. Yeah? Well, you can't go now.

The Girl. [*Beginning to whimper.*] I want to go home.

The Marshal. You can't go now. Nobody can't leave de house now.

The Policeman. [*Coming out of the house.*] Who's dis kid?

The Marshal. Says she come here to take a music-lesson an' she wants to go home.

The Policeman. [*To the* GIRL.] Do you know anythin' about this killin'?

The Girl. No, I don't. I just heard some shooting, that's all. My mother will be worried, if I don't come home.

The Policeman. Well, you can't go now. Get inside dere, out o' de way. Dey'll be bringin' her down in a minute.

[*He pushes the* GIRL *inside the house and comes down the steps.*]

The Policeman. Come on, git back from dem steps! Back now, all o' youse!

[*He and the* MARSHAL *push the* CROWD *back to the right of the stoop, leaving the steps and the sidewalk in front of them clear. Then he goes up the steps again.*]

The Marshal. What did he do? Shoot two of 'em?

The Policeman. I'll say he did! His wife an' her sweetie. A guy named Sankey. He was dead when I got up dere.

The Marshal. I seen him tryin' to climb out t'roo de winder. An' dis guy grabs 'im an' pulls 'im back.

The Interne. [*From the* MAURRANT *window.*] Officer! Come on up!

[*He leaves the window, as the* POLICEMAN *exits into the house. Suddenly* SAM *utters an exclamation of anguish and, pushing his way out of the crowd, hurries over to the left.*]

The Marshal. Hey, you! Where you goin'?

[SAM *ignores him and hurries on.*]

A Woman. Look! There's the Maurrant girl!

Another Woman. Who?

A Woman. It's her dauhgter.

[*The* CROWD *murmurs excitedly, as* ROSE *comes on quickly at the left.*]

Rose. What's the matter, Sam? What's the ambulance for? Did anybody get hurt?

Sam. Go away, Rose. Go away.

Rose. Who is it, Sam? What's the matter? Is it my mother? It's not my mother, is it? [*Clinging to him.*] Sam, is it?

Sam. There's been an accident. Go away, Rose. [*He tries to force her away.*]

Rose. Tell me what's happened! Tell me!

Miss Cushing. [*Appearing at the window.*] They're bringing her down!

Rose. [*With a cry.*] It *is* my mother!

Miss Cushing. [*Seeing her.*] Oh, my God, there's Rose!

[MRS. FIORENTINO, MRS. JONES, MRS. HILDEBRAND, LIPPO, *and* BUCHANAN *crowd to the* MAURRANT *windows.*]

Sam. Rose! Go away!

[*She pays no attention to him, but stands watching the door, transfixed. The* INTERNE *comes briskly out of the house.*]

The Interne. [*To the* MARSHAL.] Hold the door open, will you?

[*He comes down the steps.*]

The Marshal. Sure, doc!

[*He hurries into the vestibule.*]

The Interne. [*To the* CROWD.] Keep back, now!

Rose. [*Seizing the* INTERNE'S *arm.*] Doctor! Is she dead?

The Interne. Who are you? Her daughter?

Rose. Yes, sir. I'm her daughter.

The Interne. She's pretty badly hurt. Step aside, now!

[*They step aside, as the* AMBULANCE-DRIVER *and the* POLICEMAN *come out of the house, carrying* MRS. MAURRANT *on the stretcher. There is a low murmur from the crowd.*]

The Ambulance-Driver. Easy, now.

The Policeman. All right.

[*They come down the steps and go toward the left.*]

Rose. [*Running forward and gripping the side of the stretcher.*] Mother! Mother!

Mrs. Maurrant. [*Opening her eyes, feebly.*] Rose!

[*She tries to lift her hand, but it falls back.*]

The Interne. [*Pulling* ROSE *back.*] You mustn't talk to her now.

[SAM *takes her about the shoulders. They and the* INTERNE *follow the stretcher off at the left. The* CROWD *swarms after them.* FRED *comes out of the house, carrying one end of an iron bedstead.*]

CURTAIN

ACT THREE

Mid-afternoon of the same day. At the left of the stoop is a large roll of bedding. Before the rise of the curtain, and continuing faintly thereafter, a woman can be heard singing scales.

[OLSEN, *pipe in mouth, is leaning against the railing. Two* MEN, *furniture-movers, appear at the left.*]

One of the Men. [*Picking up the bedding.*] All right. Dat's all, Charlie!

[*The* MEN *exit left. A* POLICEMAN *comes out of the house, carrying the blood-stained dress of* MRS. MAURRANT, *and* SANKEY'S *coat, cap, and bill-holder. He comes down the steps, and exits at the right. At the left, two young* NURSE-MAIDS, *in smart uniforms, appear, each wheeling a de-luxe baby-carriage.*]

First Nurse-Maid. [*Seeing the house-number.*] This must be the place, right here—346.

[*They stop, under the* MAURRANT *windows.*]

Second Nurse-Maid. Yes, I guess it is.

First Nurse-Maid. Yes, this is it, all right. [*Looking up.*] Must be right up there, on the first floor, see?

Second Nurse-Maid. Yes, sure. [*Excitedly.*] Say, look! You can see where the glass is out of the window. That's where this feller What's-his-name tried to climb out.

First Nurse-Maid. Oh, yes, I see it! Say, what do you know about that!

Second Nurse-Maid. [*Taking a pink tabloid newspaper from under the hood of the baby-buggy.*] Wait! There's a picture of it somewhere. [*Turning the pages.*] Here it is. [*They excitedly examine it together, as she reads:*] "Composograph showing Sankey, scantily clad, in a last vain attempt to escape the vengeance of the jealousy-crazed husband whose home he had destroyed." And there's Maurrant pulling him back. And Mrs. Maurrant trying to get the pistol away from him, see? Look at the blood running down her face, will you?

First Nurse-Maid. It's worse than awful! Can you *imagine* what those two must have felt like, when he walked in on them like that?

Second Nurse-Maid. Well, he just happened to be one of the ones that find out! Believe me, there's lots and lots of husbands that don't know the half of what goes on uptown, while they're down-town making a living.

First Nurse-Maid. Say, you're not telling me, are you? If I was to spill all I know, there'd be many a happy home busted up. I wonder if they caught him.

Second Nurse-Maid. [*As her* BABY *begins a thin wailing.*] Oh, God, he's in again! [*To the unseen* BABY.] Shut up a little while, can't you? [*She shakes the carriage.*]

A Policeman. [*Appearing at the* MAURRANT *windows, a tabloid in his hand.*] Keep movin', ladies. No loiterin' aroun' here.

First Nurse-Maid. [*Eagerly.*] Say, have they caught him yet?

The Policeman. Why, ain't you hoid? He was last seen flyin' over Nova Scotia, on his way to Paris.

First Nurse-Maid. Who are you trying to string, anyhow?

Second Nurse-Maid. [*Coquettishly.*] Say, will you let us come up and look around?

The Policeman. Why, sure, sure! Bring de babies, too. De commissioner is soivin' tea up here at four-thoity.

Second Nurse-Maid. You're awful smart, aren't you?

The Policeman. Yeah, that's why dey put me on de entertainment committee. I'm Handsome Harry Moiphy, de boy comedian o' Brooklyn.

First Nurse-Maid. [*Looking at her watch.*] Oh, say, I ought to be getting back. [*Turning her carriage.*] Clarice darling would throw a duck-fit, if she knew I brought her precious dumplings to a neighborhood like this.

Second Nurse-Maid. [*Turning her carriage.*] There's not so much to see, anyhow. It's nothing but a cheap common dump.

[*They go toward the left.*]

The Policeman. Over de river, goils. See you in de funny paper.

Second Nurse-Maid. Don't you get so fresh.

The Policeman. Drop in again, when you're in de neighborhood. An' tell Mrs. Vanderbilt Harry was askin' for her.

[*As the* NURSE-MAIDS *go off at the left,* EASTER *hurries on at the right, several folded newspapers under his arm.*]

Easter. [*To the* POLICEMAN, *going to the left of the stoop.*] Is Miss Maurrant up there, officer?

The Policeman. No. There ain't nobody up here but me.

Easter. You don't happen to know where she is, do you?

The Policeman. No, I don't. Are you a reporter?

Easter. Who, me? I'm just a friend of hers. I've got to see her.

The Policeman. Well, I ain't seen her since she went off to the horspital this mornin'. She ain't been back since.

[*He starts to leave the window.*]

Easter. Oh, officer!

The Policeman. Yeah?

Easter. Have they caught him yet?

The Policeman. Naw, not yet. But we'll get 'im, all right!

[*He leaves the window.* EASTER *remains at the left of the stoop, uncertain whether to go or not.* MRS. JONES *appears, at the right, carrying several newspapers.*]

Mrs. Jones. [*To* OLSEN.] Have they caught him yet?

Olsen. [*Shaking his head.*] No.

Mrs. Jones. I been down at Police Headquarters all this while—[*Breaking off, as she notices* EASTER.] Say, what's he want here?

[OLSEN *shrugs his shoulders.*]

Easter. [*Approaching them.*] Pardon me, but maybe you can tell me where I can find Miss Maurrant? [OLSEN *shakes his head.*]

Mrs. Jones. Why no, I can't. I jus' this minute got back from Police Headquarters. Maybe she's aroun' at the horspital.

Easter. No, I just came from there.

Mrs. Jones. Well, I really couldn't say where she is. Was there somethin' special you wanted to see her about?

Easter. I'm a friend of hers——

Mrs. Jones. Yeah, I noticed you talkin' to her last night, when I took the dog out. [*Staring at him.*] Well, I guess she'll need all the friends she's got now. Imagine a thing like this happenin' right here in this house, at ten o'clock in the mornin'! Everythin' goin' on just as usual, and then, all of a sudden, before you know it, there's two people murdered.

Olsen. I tal everybody some day he kill her.

Mrs. Jones. Well, I ain't sayin' it's right to kill anybody, but if anybody had a reason, he certainly had. You oughta heard some o' the questions they was askin' me down at the Police. I could feel myself gettin' redder an' redder. "Say," I says, "how do you expect me to know things like that?" [*Suddenly, as she looks left.*] Here's Rose, now!

Easter. Where?

[*He turns quickly and hurries to the left, as* ROSE *appears, carrying four or five packages.*]

Mrs. Jones. [*To* OLSEN.] He seems to take a pretty friendly interest in her.

[OLSEN *nods.*]

Rose. [*Anxiously, as she comes up to* EASTER *at the left of the stoop.*] Have they caught him yet?

Easter. Why no, they haven't. I just asked the officer upstairs.

Rose. Oh, I hope he got away! If they get him, there's no telling what they'll do to him. And what would be the good of that? He never would have done it, if he'd been in his right mind.

Easter. I only heard about it a little while ago. So I went right around to the hospital. But they said you'd left.

Rose. [*Going to the steps.*] She never opened her eyes again. They did everything they could for her, but it didn't help.

Easter. Here, let me take your bundles.

Rose. No, it's all right. I think I'll just sit down for a minute.

[*She sits on the stoop and puts the packages beside her.*]

Easter. Can't I get you something? A drink or something?

Rose. No, I'm all right. It's so hot. [*She puts her hand to her head.*] And all those people asking me a lot of questions.

Mrs. Jones. [*Approaching the stoop.*] Are you feelin' dizzy or anythin'?

Rose. No, I'll be all right in a minute.

Mrs. Jones. Well, I was gonna say, if you want to go up to my flat an' lay down for a minute——

Rose. No, thanks; I don't want to lie down. I've got to go upstairs to get some things.

Easter. Why, say, you don't want to go up there!

Rose. I've got to; there's some things I need.

Easter. Well, let me get them for you. Or this lady here.

Mrs. Jones. Yeah, sure. The place is a sight up there. You're li'ble to go into a faint or somethin'.

Rose. I guess nothing can be any worse than what's happened already. [*Indicating the bundles.*] I got to change my dress. I bought a white dress for her. And white silk stockings. I want her to look pretty.

Mrs. Jones. Yeah, white is the nicest.

Rose. She looks so quiet and natural. You'd think she was asleep.

Mrs. Jones. It was the same way with my mother. You'd of thought she was gonna get up the next minute. [*Starting to go up the steps.*] Well, I gotta go up an' get me some lunch. Between everythin' happenin' an' goin' down to Police Headquarters an' all, I ain't had a bite to eat since breakfast. [*Stopping on the top step, and looking from* ROSE *to* EASTER.] Well, you certainly never know, when you get up in the mornin', what the day is gonna bring. [*She enters the house.*]

Rose. [*Rising.*] Well, I'd better be going up, too. There's a lot of things to attend to.

Easter. You better let me come up with you.

Rose. Why thanks, Mr. Easter. But I'd rather go alone, if you don't mind.

Easter. But, listen here—you can't go through all this alone—a kid like you. That's why I came around. I knew you'd be needing a helping hand.

Rose. That's awfully nice of you, Mr. Easter. But I don't need any help, honest I don't. [*She opens one of the packages.*]

Easter. Why, you can't handle everything yourself! What about a place to live and all that?

Rose. [*Taking a rosette of black crape out of the package.*] Well, I don't exactly know, yet. I'll have to find some place where Willie and I can live. I'd like it to be some place where he wouldn't be running around the streets all the time. You see, there's nobody but me to look out for him now.

[OLSEN *crosses to the cellar.* MRS. JONES *appears at her window and furtively peeps out at* ROSE *and* EASTER.]

Rose. [*As she sees that* OLSEN *is about to descend the cellar steps.*] Oh, Mr. Olsen!

Olsen. [*Stopping.*] Yes, ma'am.

Rose. Would you mind lending me a hammer and some tacks? I want to put up this crape.

Olsen. Yes, ma'am; I bring 'em right away.

[*He goes down into the cellar.* MRS. JONES *leaves the window.*]

Easter. [*Insistently.*] But why won't you let me help you out?

Rose. It's terribly nice of you, Mr. Easter. But I'll be able to manage alone, really I will. It isn't as if I wasn't young and strong and able to take care of myself. But as it is, I'd sort of rather not be under obligations.

Easter. Why, you wouldn't be under any obligations. I just mean it in a friendly way, that's all.

Rose. You've been very nice to me and all that, Mr. Easter. But—well, I've been sort of thinking things over—you know, about what we talked about last night and all. And I honestly don't think I'd care about going on the stage.

Easter. Say, you've got me all wrong, Rose! Just forget all about that, will you? I just want to help you out, that's all. [*Taking a step toward her.*] I think you're one swell kid, and I want to do something for you. I'm not trying to put anything over on you.

[SHIRLEY *appears, at the left, carrying her school-bag, from which a newspaper protrudes.*]

Rose. Well, that's nice and friendly of you, Mr. Easter. And if I ever do need any help——

Shirley. [*Catching sight of* ROSE.] Rose! You poor thing! [*She runs up to* ROSE *and throws her arms about her.*] It's terrible—terrible!

Rose. Yes, it is. But I sort of had a feeling all along that something terrible was going to happen.

[OLSEN *comes up the steps, with a hammer and a box of tacks.*]

Shirley. How could he do such a thing! I couldn't believe it when I read it.

Rose. He was out of his mind when he did it. Oh, I only hope he got away. [*As* OLSEN *approaches.*] Oh, thanks, Mr. Olsen.

Olsen. I do it.

Rose. [*Giving him the crape.*] Oh, would you, please? Right up there, I think.

[*She indicates the left of the doorway.*]

Olsen. [*Going up the steps.*] Sure.

Rose. [*Going to* EASTER *and extending her hand.*] Thanks for coming around, Mr. Easter. I don't know when I'll be able to get back to the office.

Easter. Why, that's all right about that. Only, in the meantime, I wish——

Rose. If I need any help, I'll let you know.

[*With a tone of finality in her voice.*] Good-by.

Easter. All right; but don't forget. [*He hesitates, then decides to go.*] Well, good-by.

[*He goes off at left.*]

Rose. I've got to go up and get some things that Willie and I need. Sam went to call for him at school and take him around to my aunt's. You see, I didn't want him coming back here. He's only a little kid, after all.

Shirley. Oh, it's such a terrible thing! I can't believe it yet.

Olsen. [*Holding up the crape.*] Dis vay?

Rose. Yes, like that. [*Hesitantly, as she picks up her bundles.*] Miss Kaplan, it's sort of silly of me, I guess. But I'm kind of afraid to go up there alone. I wonder if you'd mind coming up with me.

[OLSEN *tacks up the crape.*]

Shirley. Anything I can do for you, poor child!

[*She and* ROSE *go up the steps.*]

Rose. Thanks ever so much. [*To* OLSEN.] Thanks, Mr. Olsen. It's awfully nice of you.

[*She and* SHIRLEY *enter the house.* OLSEN *exits down the cellar steps.* KAPLAN *appears at his window, and seating himself, begins to read a newspaper. An undersized* MAN *and a tall, athletic* WOMAN *appear at the right. They are dressed for tennis, and carry tennis-rackets.*]

Man. [*As they cross.*] He *would* say that.

Woman. So I just looked at him for a moment, without saying anything. And then I said: "My dear boy," I said. "What do you expect anyhow, in this day and age?" I said, "Why even Frankl has to do a black bathroom occasionally," I said.

Man. [*As they disappear at the left.*] Exactly! And what did he say to that?

[BUCHANAN *comes out of the house, and, seeing* KAPLAN *at the window, stops at the right balustrade.*]

Buchanan. Well, there's been *some* excitement around here today.

Kaplan. [*Looking up from his paper.*] Dees is a terrible t'ing vich hes heppened.

Buchanan. I'll say it is! You know, the way I look at it, he didn't have a right to kill the both of them like that. Of course I'm not saying what she did was right, either.

Kaplan. How ken ve call ourselves ciwilized, ven ve see thet sax jealousy hes de power to avaken in us de primitive pessions of de sevege?

Buchanan. [*Rather bewildered by this.*] Yes, that's true, too. Of course, you can't expect a man to stand by and see his home broken up. But murdering them, like that, is going a little too far. Well, I got to go and phone the doctor. This thing's given my wife a kind of a *re*lapse. She thought a lot of Mrs. Maurrant.

[*He goes down the steps, and off at the left, as* LIPPO *appears at the right.*]

Lippo. [*Stopping in front of* KAPLAN'S *window.*] Dey don' ketcha Maurrant, ha?

Kaplan. I hevn't hoid anyt'ing foider.

Lippo. He'sa gonna gat da 'lectrica-chair, ha?

Kaplan. De blood-lust of our enlightened population must be setisfied! De Chreestian state will kerry out to de last letter de Mosaic law.

Lippo. Eef Ahm ketcha my wife sleepin' wit' 'nudder man, Ahm gonna keela 'er, too.

[SAM *hurries on at the left.*]

Kaplan. So you t'ink thet merriage should give to de hosband de power of life and det' and thet——

Sam. [*Going up the steps.*] Papa, is there any news of Maurrant?

Kaplan. I hev heard notting.

Sam. The police are going to make me testify against him. What can I do, papa?

Kaplan. You ken do notting.

Sam. How can I send a man to the electric-chair? How can I? I tried to stop him, papa. I tried to warn her— [*He stops short, as several shots are heard off-stage at the left.*] What's that?

Lippo. [*Excitedly.*] Dey finda 'im!

[*He runs off at the left, followed by* SAM. KAPLAN *leans out of the window. At the same moment,* MRS. JONES *leans out of her window and, a moment later,* MRS. FIORENTINO *out of hers. In the* MAURRANT *apartment, the* POLICEMAN *leans out and* ROSE *and* SHIRLEY *appear in the hall bedroom window.* ROSE *is wearing a mourning-dress.* OLSEN *comes up the cellar steps and runs off at the left.* MRS. OLSEN *comes up the steps. Several* MEN *and* WOMEN *appear at the right, and run off at the left.*]

Rose. [*Agitatedly.*] Is that him?

The Policeman. Must be!

[*Voices are heard shouting in the distance, and then another shot. The* POLICEMAN *leaves the window.*]

Rose. Oh, God! They wouldn't shoot him, would they? [*She leaves the window.*]

Shirley. [*Following her.*] Rose!

[*Two or three more* PERSONS *appear at the right and run off at the left. The* POLICEMAN *runs out of the house, as* BUCHANAN *appears at the left.*]

Buchanan. [*Excitedly.*] They got him!

[*The* POLICEMAN *runs off at the left.* SHIRLEY *reappears at the* MAURRANT *window.*]

Mrs. Jones. [*Calling.*] Have they got him?

Buchanan. Yes! He was hiding in the furnace, down at 322. [*As* ROSE *comes out of the house.*] They found him, Miss Maurrant!

Rose. [*Her hand to her heart.*] Oh! Is he hurt?

Buchanan. I don't know. He fired at the cops and they fired back at him. I was just passing the house when it happened.

Mrs. Jones. [*Leaning far out.*] Here they come!

[*She leaves the window. The low murmur of the approaching* CROWD *can be heard, off-stage left.*]

Rose. Where? [*She comes down the stoop and looks off at the left.*] Oh!

[*She covers her eyes and turns away.*]

Mrs. Fiorentino. You better come inside.

Shirley. Come up, Rose.

Buchanan. Yes, you better.

[*He takes her by the arm.*]

Rose. [*Resisting.*] No. No. Please let me alone. I want to see him.

[*She leans against the railing. Meanwhile, the murmur and tramp of the approaching* CROWD *has grown nearer and nearer.*]

Mrs. Fiorentino. Look at him, vill you!

[MISS CUSHING *comes out of the house and stands on the stoop, followed a moment later by* MRS. JONES. MAURRANT *appears at the left, between two policemen. Behind him a third* POLICEMAN *holds back a swarming* CROWD, *which includes* SAM *and* LIPPO. MAURRANT'S *clothes are torn, and his right arm is in a crude sling. Sweat, blood, and grime have made him almost unrecognizable. The* POLICEMEN, *too, show evidences of a struggle.*]

Rose. [*Running forward.*] Pop! Are you hurt?

Maurrant. [*Seeing her for the first time.*] Rose!

One of the Policemen. [*To whom* MAURRANT *is manacled.*] Keep back, miss!

Maurrant. It's me daughter! Fer Chris' sake, boys, lemme talk to me daughter! Maybe I'll never be seein' her again!

First Policeman. Give 'im a woid wit' her.

[*He is the* OFFICER *who was on duty in the* MAURRANT *apartment.*]

Second Policeman. [*After a moment's hesitation.*] Well, all right. [*Savagely to* MAURRANT.] But don't try to pull nothin', hear?

[*There is a forward movement in the* CROWD.]

First Policeman. [*To the* CROWD.] Keep back, youse!

Maurrant. Rose! You're wearin' a black dress, Rose!

Rose. Oh, pop, why did you do it? Why did you?

Maurrant. I must o' been out o' me head, Rose. Did she say anythin'?

Rose. She never opened her eyes again.

Maurrant. I'd been drinkin', Rose—see what I mean?—an' all the talk that was goin' around. I just went clean off me nut, that's all.

Rose. What'll they do to you, pop?

Maurrant. It's the chair for me, I guess. But I don't care—let 'em give me the chair. I deserve it all right. But it's her I'm thinkin' of, Rose—the way she looked at me. I oughtn't to done it, Rose.

Rose. She was always so good and sweet.

Maurrant. Don't I know it? I ain't no murderer—you ought to be the one to know that, Rose. I just went out o' me head, that's all it was.

Second Policeman. All right, that's all now. Come on!

Maurrant. Gimme a minute, can't you? She's me daughter. Gimme a chance, can't you? What's gonna happen to you, Rose?

Rose. I'll be all right, pop. You don't need to worry about me.

Maurrant. I ain't been a very good father, have I?

Rose. Don't worry about that, pop.

Maurrant. It ain't that I ain't meant to be. It's just the way things happened to turn out, that's all. Keep your eye on Willie, Rose. Don't let Willie grow up to be a murderer, like his pop.

Rose. I'm going to do all I can for him, pop.

Maurrant. You're a good girl, Rose. You was always a good girl.

Rose. [*Breaking down.*] Oh, pop!

[*She throws her arms about his neck and buries her head against him.* MAURRANT *sobs hoarsely.*]

First Policeman. [*Gently.*] Come on now, miss.

[*He and* SAM *take* ROSE *from* MAURRANT.]

Second Policeman. All right. Come on, Charlie.

[*They go toward the right, the* CROWD *swarming behind them. Straggling along at the very end of the* CROWD *is an un-*

kempt WOMAN, *wheeling a ramshackle baby-carriage.* MRS. JONES *and* MISS CUSHING *fall in with the* CROWD. ROSE *gradually recovers her self-control, and stands at the stoop with* SAM *beside her. The others watch the receding* CROWD *for a moment. Then* KAPLAN *and* MRS. FIORENTINO *leave their windows. The* FIRST POLICEMAN *enters the house, followed by* LIPPO. MRS. OLSEN *goes to the cellar.* SHIRLEY *looks down at* ROSE *and* SAM *for a moment, then abruptly leaves the window.*]

Sam. [*Taking* ROSE *by the arm.*] Rose, you better come inside.

Rose. No, I'm all right again, Sam—honestly I am. [*Trying to regain her self-composure.*] What about Willie, Sam?

Sam. I told him an accident had happened.

Rose. It's better to break it to him that way. But I'll have to tell him, I guess. He'd only find it out himself tomorrow, with the papers all full of it. I saw Mrs. Sankey down at Police Headquarters. It's terrible for her, with two little children.

Shirley. [*Appearing at the* MAURRANT *window, a covered pot in her hand.*] Rose!

Rose. [*Looking up.*] Yes, Miss Kaplan?

Shirley. There's a chicken here that I found on the gas-stove.

Rose. A chicken?

Shirley. Yes. The policeman says he smelt it cooking this morning, so he turned out the gas.

Rose. Oh, I remember, now. My mother said she was going to make some soup for poor Mrs. Buchanan, upstairs.

Shirley. It won't keep long in this weather.

Rose. No. I really think Mrs. Buchanan ought to have the good of it.

Shirley. All right. I'll take it up to her.

Rose. Thanks ever so much, Miss Kaplan. [SHIRLEY *leaves the window.*] It's only a few hours ago that she was standing right here, telling me about the chicken. And then she went upstairs, and the next I saw of her, they were carrying her out. [*Abruptly, as she starts to go up the steps.*] Well, I've got to go up and get my things.

Sam. I must talk to you! What are you going to do, Rose?

Rose. Well, I haven't really had any time to do much thinking. But I really think the best thing I could do, would be to get out of New York. You know, like we were saying this morning—how things might be different, if you only had a chance to breathe and spread out a little. Only when I said it, I never dreamt it would be this way.

Sam. If you go, I'll go with you.

Rose. But, Sam dear——

Sam. I don't care anything about my career. It's you—you—I care about. Do you think I can stay here, stifling to death, in this slum, and never seeing you? Do you think my life means anything to me without you?

Rose. But, Sam, we've got to be practical about it. How would we manage?

Sam. I don't care what I do. I'll be a day-laborer; I'll dig sewers—anything. [*Taking her passionately in his arms.*] Rose, don't leave me!

Rose. I like you so much, Sam. I like you better than anybody I know.

Sam. I love you, Rose. Let me go with you!

Rose. It would be so nice to be with you. You're different from anybody I know. But I'm just wondering how it would work out.

Sam. If we have each other, that's the vital thing, isn't it? What else matters but that?

Rose. Lots of things, Sam. There's lots of things to be considered. Suppose something was to happen—well, suppose I was to have a baby, say. That sometimes happens, even when you don't want it to. What would we do, then? We'd be tied down then, for life, just like all the other people around here. They all start out loving each other and thinking that everything is going to be fine—and before you know, they find out they haven't got anything and they wish they could do it all over again—only it's too late.

Sam. It's to escape all that, that we must be together. It's only because we love each other and belong to each other, that we can find the strength to escape.

Rose. [*Shaking her head.*] No, Sam.

Sam. Why do you say no?

Rose. It's what you said just now—about people belonging to each other. I don't think people ought to belong to anybody but themselves. I was thinking that if my mother had really belonged to herself, and that if my father had really belonged to himself, it never would have happened. It was only because they were always depending on somebody else for what they ought to have had inside themselves. Do you see what I mean, Sam? That's why I don't want to belong to anybody, and why I don't want anybody to belong to me.

Sam. You want to go through life alone?—never loving anyone, never having anyone love you?

Rose. Why, of course not, Sam! I want love more than anything else in the world. But loving and belonging aren't the same thing. [*Putting her arms about him.*] Sam, dear, listen. If we say good-by now, it doesn't mean that it has to be forever. Maybe some day, when we're older and wiser, things will be different. Don't look as if it was the end of the world, Sam!

Sam. It *is* the end of my world.

Rose. It isn't, Sam! If you'd only believe in yourself a little more, things wouldn't look nearly so bad. Because once you're sure of yourself, the things that happen to you aren't so important. The way I look at it, it's not what you do that matters so much; it's what you are. [*Warmly.*] I'm so fond of you, Sam. And I've got such a lot of confidence in you. [*Impulsively.*] Give me a nice kiss!

[SAM *takes her in his arms and kisses her passionately. A gawky* GIRL *of seventeen—one of* LIPPO'S *pupils, appears at the left, and looks at them, scandalized. Then she goes into the vestibule and rings the bell. The door clicks and she enters the house, as* SHIRLEY *comes out, carrying a wicker suit-case.* SHIRLEY *looks at* SAM *and* ROSE.]

Rose. [*To* SHIRLEY.] I was just telling Sam that I think I'll soon be going away from New York.

[SAM *looks at her for a moment, in agony, then goes abruptly into the house.*]

Shirley. I put your things in this suit-case. [*She comes down to the pavement. The* GIRL, *in the* FIORENTINO *apartment, begins tuning her violin.*]

Rose. [*Taking the suit-case.*] You've been awfully nice to me. Don't worry about Sam, Miss Kaplan. Everything will be all right with him.

Shirley. I hope so.

[*From the* FIORENTINO *apartment come the strains of Dvorák's "Humoresque," jerkily played on a violin.*]

Rose. Oh, I just know it will! [*Extending her hand.*] Good-by, Miss Kaplan.

Shirley. Good-by, Rose. [*Impulsively.*] You're a sweet girl!

[*She hugs and kisses her.*]

Rose. I hope I'll see you again.

Shirley. [*Crying.*] I hope so, Rose.

[ROSE *takes up the suit-case and goes off at the left.* SHIRLEY *stands watching her.*]

Kaplan. [*Re-appearing at his window.*] Shoiley, vot's de metter again vit Sem? He's crying on de bed.

Shirley. Let him alone, papa, can't you? [*She turns and enters the house.* KAPLAN *sighs and, seating himself at the window, opens a newspaper. A shabby, middle-aged* COUPLE *appear at the right, and approach the stoop.*]

The Man. [*Reading the To Let sign.*] Here's a place. Six rooms. Want to take a look at it?

[A GROUP OF CHILDREN *off-stage left begin singing "The Farmer in the Dell." This continues until after the curtain is down.*]

The Woman. All right. No harm lookin'. Ring for the janitor. [THE MAN *goes up the stoop and rings the* JANITOR'S *bell.*] Somebody must o' just died.

The Man. Yeah, maybe that's why they're movin' out. [*Wiping his face with a handkerchief.*] Phoo! Seems to be gettin' hotter every minute.

[MRS. FIORENTINO *seats herself at her window, a sewing-basket in her lap.* MRS. JONES *and* MISS CUSHING *appear at the right, busily engaged in conversation.*]

Miss Cushing. The poor little thing!

Mrs. Jones. [*As they go up the steps.*] Well, you never can tell with them quiet ones. It wouldn't surprise me a bit, if she turned out the same way as her mother. She's got a gentleman friend that I guess ain't hangin' around for nothin'. I seen him late last night, and this afternoon, when I come home from the police——

[*She is still talking, as they enter the house.* MRS. OLSEN *comes up the cellar steps. A* SAILOR *appears at the left with two* GIRLS, *an arm about the waist of each. They stroll slowly across.*]

CURTAIN

HOTEL UNIVERSE*

By

PHILIP BARRY

PROBABLY THE PEOPLE PHILIP BARRY knows best have means; they are leisurely, cultivated, traveled, worldly. At least, these are the people he writes about most easily. The characters of his early plays had one great ideal, the attainment of freedom, freedom for self-expression, a highly individualistic liberty. This is the theme of *You and I,* of *Paris Bound,* of *Holiday.* These plays met admirably the temper of the nineteen-twenties, and were very successful, being brightly written, affording excellent acting opportunities, and presenting agreeable people in not very disturbing situations.

But Mr. Barry is a Catholic, and probably a sincere one. As early in his career as 1927 his *John,* a play about John the Baptist, showed that he wished to be more than "smart." *John* failed commercially, of course, but with *Hotel Universe* and the plays after it Mr. Barry indicated that he believes freedom is not enough, is not even very much. The people in *Hotel Universe* are free, but one of them says of their life, "it couldn't be any worse than it is," though "we are the lucky ones." The gay freedom which seems to give such full life gives only the hysterical longing for death.

Similarly, in *Tomorrow and Tomorrow,* the wife rejects freedom with her lover; in *The Animal Kingdom,* the hero accepts the bond of obligation to his past. And in *The Joyous Season* Mr. Barry plainly upholds the superiority of the religious life to the worldly, the life of duty and obedience to the life of egoism.

Bright Star concerns a man whose sense of guilt for his past prevents his loving his pure and wholesome wife. But Mr. Barry faces moral and philosophical problems most squarely in *Here Come the Clowns.* That deeply moving and brilliant play's central character has suffered, and suffers during the play, as many and harsh afflictions as Job suffered at God's hands. He tries to ask God why evil exists, and finally answers himself that God gave man free will, and man too often chooses evil instead of good

Taking this frank position as a moralist rather than as an entertainer had its risks for Mr. Barry, notably the risk that he would lose his audience. It cannot be said that Mr. Barry has escaped that loss. After *The Animal Kingdom* he had no commercial success until *The Philadelphia Story,* which returned to the mood of *Holiday.* But Mr. Barry's contribution to the American stage, both in gay drawing-room comedy and in more serious work, already establishes his high position. He is a very skilful writer, especially of amusing dialogue; he knows the theater, and he has things to say.

Though *Hotel Universe* leans heavily on Freud—in Lily's and Pat's Oedipus complexes, for instance, in many of the characters' yearning for a return to childhood, in the power ascribed to the dream life—the play cannot accurately be described as psychoanalytic. Mr. Barry uses to build his characters only such Freudian concepts as would easily be understood by a lay audience, and certainly avoids the psychological determinism found in such a Freudian dramatist as Lenormand, for instance.

That *Hotel Universe* is fundamentally a cheerful and optimistic play, in spite of the distressing state of most of its characters during it, may be seen by a comparison with the British Barrie's *Dear Brutus,* a play of similar theme. The power of Stephen in *Hotel Universe* is very like the power of Lob in *Dear Brutus,* but it is very much less cruel, very much more hopeful. Stephen apparently believes, as Lob does not believe, that the other life that envelops this life is kind; it can be invoked for our health, and not merely to show us helpless. The people of *Dear Brutus* end, but the people of *Hotel Universe,* we are told, begin.

PHILIP BARRY

Born 1896, Rochester, N. Y.
1919, A. B., Yale University.
1919–1922, studied playwriting at Harvard under Professor Baker.

PLAYS

1921 *A Punch for Judy*. 1922 *You and I*. 1924 *The Youngest* (also called *Poor Richard* and *God Bless Our Home*). 1925 *In a Garden*. 1926 *White Wings*. 1927 *John*. 1927 *Paris Bound*. 1928 *Cock Robin* (with Elmer Rice). 1928 *Holiday*. 1930 *Hotel Universe*. 1931 *Tomorrow and Tomorrow*. 1932 *The Animal Kingdom*. 1934 *The Joyous Season*. 1935 *Bright Star*. 1936 *Spring Dance* (adapted from play by Eleanor Golden and Eloise Barrangon). 1938 *Here Come the Clowns* (adapted from the author's novel, *War in Heaven*). 1939 *The Philadelphia Story*. 1941 *Liberty Jones*.

HOTEL UNIVERSE

Characters

Stephen Field.
Ann Field.
Pat Farley.
Lily Malone.
Tom Ames.
Hope Ames.
Norman Rose.
Alice Kendall.
Felix.

ACTION AND SCENE

The action of the play is continuous, and takes place in the course of about two hours, upon the terrace of a house in the south of France, near Toulon. The time is an evening in early July, last summer.

The Terrace is like a spacious, out-door room, irregularly paved with flags of gray stone. The house itself forms one wall on the left, a wall from which two screened doors open—the first from a hall, the second from a sitting-room. Down left, against this wall, a flight of outside stairs, guarded by a slender iron railing, mounts to a balcony.

The other entrance is at the right down from the garden by stone steps. A three-foot wall follows the back and left sides of the terrace just to where the row of small cypresses, which screens the garden terrace, begins. Over and beyond the wall nothing is visible: sea meets sky without a line to mark the meeting. There, the angle of the terrace is like a wedge into space.

Down right, a small but ancient fig-tree in full leaf rises from the pavement. There is a large fan-back chair beneath it. Upon the wall at back, there are two folding-cushions. A small upright piano stands against the wall of the house. Near it, there is a table, upon which stand a carafe of brandy, a bottle of Cointreau, a bottle of champagne, and glasses. A few straw and wicker chairs and a sofa complete the furniture. It is about nine o'clock in the evening, and still quite light.

[Ann Field *sits at a small table at left, a silver coffee-service before her. She is about twenty-eight, and lovely. Near her, taking their coffee, sit* Tom *and* Hope Ames, Lily Malone, *and* Norman Rose. *On the other side of the terrace, half asleep upon a cushion with a coffee-cup beside her,* Alice Kendall *reclines. She is twenty-six, very smart, and rather pretty.* Pat Farley *is at the piano. He is thirty-two, medium tall, slight, likable looking.* Norman Rose *is the handsomest of the men, and about thirty-eight.* Tom Ames *is forty, of amiable good looks.* Hope, *his wife, is four years younger, in full bloom.* Lily Malone *is small, slight, and thirty. Without a feature to remark upon, she is able to impart to her small, impudent face a certain prettiness. All are browned by the sun and wear light summer clothes. The women, except* Lily, *who is in a linen day-dress, wear simple evening-dress. The men are in flannels.*]

Pat. —And this is a cheerful number from the heart of Old Provence: "Le Roy a fait battre Tambour." Yvette Guilbert used to do it.

[*He plays and sings the song, with its threatening, repeated refrain "Rat-a-plan, rat-a-plan, rat-a-plan-plan-plan-plan."*]

Tom. [*At the conclusion.*] Sad.

Hope. Oh, isn't it!

Lily. Lovely, though.

Alice. But Ann said to play something gay.

Pat. Yes? How gay, Ann—very gay? [*He looks at* Ann. *She meets his eyes for a moment, then averts her head sharply.*] Well, here's how the monks tried to be gay at Easter. It's Gregorian—eleventh century—rejoice, rejoice—— God, how gay! [*He begins to intone the chant: "Halleluiah! Halleluiah!"*]—Can't you see the lines of them, shuffling along, heads down, hands in sleeves, rejoicing, rejoicing?

[*He continues to sing "Halleluiah! Halleluiah!" Suddenly* ANN *rises.*]

Ann. Pat!

[*But he goes on singing.* ANN *mounts the steps to the balcony and goes into the house.* HOPE *rises and goes to* PAT.]

Hope. Pat——

Pat. What?

Hope. Quit it!

Pat. Why?

Hope. Why must we take our nerves out on Ann?

Pat. "Nerves" did you say?

Hope. You heard what I said. And you've been the worst. Knowing what you used to be to her, I suppose the torture's great fun.

Pat. Go away, Hope.

Hope. —Then why do you suppose she suddenly leaves us this way?

Pat. It's her own house, isn't it?

Hope. Yes—and a fine time we've been giving her in it! The wonder to me is that she's endured our bad manners as long as she has.

Tom. Oh come now, darling——

Hope. I mean it! All we've done for three mortal days has been to sit around and make bitter cracks about anything we could put our tongues to.—Don't you realize that we're the first Americans she's seen since she's been here? She begged us to come. It meant so much to her to have us. And now, on our very last night with her, we still behave like —Oh, I'm so ashamed!

[*She returns to her chair.*]

Tom. What do you want us to do, Hope?

Norman. Yes, what shall we?

Hope. I don't know—something—anything but what we have been. It must be horrible for her, living here. She had a right to expect we'd bring some breath of life with us. And what have we given her?

Pat. Say it: the breath of death.

Lily. [*To* HOPE.] You know the reason for our so-called "nerves," don't you?

Tom. [*Quickly.*] Now don't start that, Lily. We agreed when we left Antibes not to speak of that again.

Norman. Yes—Ann's got enough to depress her without adding the sad story of a person she never knew or heard of.

Lily. Nobody's going to burden Ann with it. The point is, what it did to us. Every time I close my eyes I see him: a bright, sweet, utterly unimaginative boy of twenty-six——

Hope. Don't——

Lily. —standing up there, brown as a berry in a pair of blue swimming-pants on the highest rock over the sea, and—— Pat, did you really hear him say that?

Pat. Of course I did. He said, "Look, Farley, I'm off for Africa!"

Tom. It was the most beautiful dive I've ever seen.

Alice. He couldn't have meant it. I'm sure it was an accident.

Pat. Accident nothing. It was suicide.

Lily. Just five minutes before, I was rubbing his back with oil. He asked me to. He couldn't reach between the shoulders.

Pat. Little mother——

Lily. Shut up.

Hope. He had a daisy behind his ear, the way a grocer-boy wears a pencil——

Tom. And didn't look silly, either.

Lily. Not he!

Norman. Of course there must have been some reason for what he did.

Hope. Please, let's not talk about it any more. It isn't safe to dwell on things like that. It makes you morbid.

Tom. There was something grand about the way he did it.

Lily. He laughed up at me—the way his teeth gleamed from the water!—Did he have unusually white teeth?

Pat. —Brushed them night and morning. Promised nurse he would.

Hope. Pat——

Pat. Oh, what the hell—you all make me sick. None of us gave a hang for him. We scarcely knew him.

Tom. We do now.

Pat. A neat job, I call it—no body to dispose of. You know, it's the devil getting a body out of France. The export duty's enormous. And I think there's a luxury-tax.—Do I offend you? Sorry.

Lily. Why did he do it? Why did he *do* it?

Pat. He'd just had enough, that's all. Eleven o'clock in the morning, up on a rock in the blazing sun—— [*He looks away, his eyes narrowing.*] "I'm off for Africa" and that's all. Lord, it's magnificent. It's scored for drums, that. [*He sings again.*] "Rat-a-plan, rat-a-plan, rat-a-plan, plan, plan."

Tom. Look here, if we don't get that boy off our minds——

Lily. I know. There's something contagious about it. It's like having been in a room with a person with——

Hope. Lily——

Lily. All right.

Tom. No one is to mention it again. We're here on this visit to dispense cheer to Ann, aren't we? Isn't that why we came? Well, then——

Lily. Hopeless, hopeless, hopeless. — As cheer-makers I'd sell the lot of us at a nickel a pound, on the hoof.

Tom. We can keep the ball in the air until we go, at any rate.

Hope. We've simply got to. Think of her —buried down here for three years in this fake, rootless country, dying of homesickness with a half-mad father——

Alice. I saw him, you know.

Hope. You did?

Norman. When?

Tom. Where, Alice?

Alice. It must have been him. Last night I woke up and couldn't get back to sleep again. I thought I heard someone down here, so I came out on the balcony. It was a funny light. Everything was—I don't know —awfully pale. For instance, that fig-tree didn't seem to have any color.

Tom. Where was he? Here?

Alice. Yes. At least there was a man— quite a nice-looking man, with gray hair. He was all in white. He was standing here at the wall, looking out over. The light-house was lit, and every now and then it would light him all up.

Pat. [*Unimpressed.*] Was there a very bright star in the sky?

Alice. I didn't notice.

Lily. You ought to look out for those things, Alice, you really ought.

Alice. I can see it all so distinctly, even to the way a button on his coat caught the light and a lace on his shoe that was untied and dragged along after him.

Pat. Then what did he do—ride off on a unicorn?

Alice. No, he just went up there into the garden, the rooster after him.

Hope. The what?

Alice. Didn't I tell you? He had a white rooster with him.—After a while I heard it crow, quite far away.

Hope. It must have been dawn then——

Alice. No—it was nowhere near it.

Lily. Well, it must have been dawn somewhere——

Pat. It usually is——

Tom. You dreamed all that, Alice.

Alice. I saw it.

Pat. —While we're here he's staying down at the what-do-you-call-it—the little house— the bastide. I imagine he's sicker than he thinks. A fine end for one of the foremost electrical experts in the country, eh? A swell finish for the only first-rate physicist we've ever had.

Alice. But hasn't he always been a little— you-know?

Pat. He never seemed so to me.—Who'll have a drink? [*He refills his glass.*]

Norman. But when was it he began to crack?

Pat. Only about five or six years ago.— This is a noble brandy.

Tom. I heard something about his haranguing a crowd in Central Park once——

Pat. He can't take people casually—that was part of his trouble. He's supposed to have some kind of power over them. Somebody said it's because he always seems so close to death.—It tastes like cucumbers.

Lily. I've never known anyone to seem further from it than that boy standing there on that rock, and——

Hope. Lily!

Lily. Oh, all right.—Only I never have— not anyone.

Pat. Finally Ann had to bring him here, where he doesn't see anyone but her, and seems to be all right. It's a swell deal for Ann. [*His tone changes.*] So we thought we'd come and put on a show for her, did we? We thought we'd remind her of what a big, gay, exciting life exists outside these walls—rub a little salt in, just so she'd be really content to stay on here—is that it?

Tom. Lord, you can be a louse.

Pat. You bet I can.—If Ann has any illusions about what goes on in the great big, wonderful world back home, *I* haven't.

[*He goes to the wall and sits there, looking out.*]

Hope. Just the same, Pat——

Pat. —Oh, go ahead. Do as you like. Be bright, be merry.

[*A silence.* Lily *looks about her.*]

Lily. I'm not happy in this old place. It's too violent, it's too dramatic. I know I'm an actress but hang it, I'm on a holiday. You get a sense of things being born all the time. They come bursting out of the ground. There's too much raw life about.

Tom. The house used to be a small hotel —the Hotel de l'Univers, it was called. I heard a tale or two about it down at the port today. It had been deserted for quite a while before Ann and her father took it.

Hope. Deserted? Why?

Tom. The boatman said things began to happen. [Pat *laughs.*]

Pat. The man in 608 had a nightmare, and the lady in 609 rang for ice-water.

Alice. Things! What things?

Tom. The idea seemed to be that people began to resemble other people and the place itself other places. And time went sort of funny. Their pasts kept cropping up.

Lily. —Excuse me, friends, but *I'm* taking the nightboat for Albany.

Tom. I'm only telling you what I heard at the port.

Norman. There may be something in it.—When *I* stepped out on this terrace the other night, it was for all the world like the Grand Central the first time I saw it, when I was fifteen. I don't mean just the way it looked. I mean——

Lily. I know—and now it's a hill-top in New Hampshire. We played Concord once. I used to climb out my window at night when Father had drunk enough to sleep—and up it, and lie on my back there.

[*She closes her eyes.*]

Tom. Maybe what you call the "raw life" here makes people children again.—Lord, I remember the way Under the Piano became as many places in as many moments: a boat to London, and then London. An airship, and a grocery-store. A circus-tent, and 'way down cellar.—And it was—for the moment it really was.

[*A silence. Then:*]

Hope. Tom, I wonder how the children are? I'm worried. I think I'll cable.

[*Another silence. Then:*]

Lily. Dear, dear Father—how I miss him.

Alice. Oh, she's got her father on the brain. Every theater we went to in Paris, she did nothing but talk about how he used to play——

Lily. That's enough, Alice.

Alice. Of course we're sorry he's dead, but why we should be bored with endless accounts of his——

Lily. I say it's enough!

Tom. This is pleasant.

Hope. I tell you, you're all in a state.

Pat. I don't doubt that the people who used to come here were, too. Lord knows it's on the edge of the world.

[HOPE *glances toward the house.*]

Hope. Here she is. Now for Heaven's sake——

[ANN *comes in from the house.*]

Ann. —That was foolish of me. Please don't mind. [*She goes to the coffee-table.*] More coffee, anyone?

Tom. I will.

Hope. Me too. It's so delicious.

Ann. It took me two years to discover why French coffee was so vile.

Hope. I could have told you. They load it full of chicory.

Ann. But the real trouble is in the roasting. They roast it black, till it looks like shoe-buttons.

Norman. That was the spirit that won the War.

Tom. [*Reflectively.*] —When I was a child, I used to have a pair of button-shoes that I wore Sundays.

Lily. [*To* NORMAN.] Has there been a war? I've been away——

Tom. I don't think they make them any more.

Ann. —So what did I do, but buy a roasting-machine of my own. It makes a very fine smell of a morning. More, Pat?

[PAT *turns.*]

Pat. Thanks, I'll take another brandy.

Tom. So will Tom. I like my good things together.

[PAT *fills two glasses for them and returns to the wall with his.*]

Hope. It stays light so late, doesn't it?

Ann. Wasn't the beach a glory today? Wasn't it? Oh, I love that beach! It's my mother.—Why do you go? Why don't you all stay on with me? I'll be good to you——

Lily. If we could——

Ann. You're really splendid, you know. You are so splendid!

Lily. Don't make me cry, Ann.

Ann. You? [*She laughs.*] Imagine! [*And turns to* PAT.] What *are* you doing there, Pat?

Pat. Me? Oh, just looking——

Ann. But I thought you didn't like views.

Pat. This isn't a view. For a view you've got to have a horizon. There's not a sign of one out there. The sea meets the sky without a line to mark the meeting. The dome begins under your feet. The arc's perfect.

Ann. But I want to see your face. I'm fond of your lean, brown face—— [*He turns to her.*] That's better!—Pat, you're older. [*He turns away again.*]—But I like you better older!

Lily. [*After a slight pause.*] It's fantastic, this terrace. It just hangs here. Some day it'll float off in space—and anchor there, like an island in time.—I'm full of whimsies tonight. I need a good dose at bedtime.

Ann. Lily, why do you spoil everything you say?

Lily. Do I?

Ann. Yes. What are you afraid of?

Lily. Oh—these people's gibes.

Ann. I don't understand it.

Lily. Ah, Ann—come on home with us! We do need you so.

Hope. Yes, Ann! To Paris tonight—sail with us Wednesday. Just as a farewell-present. Oh, do!

Ann. What a grand idea!—Tied up in a box—ribbons! Lovely!

Hope. Isn't it even possible?

[ANN *laughs.*]

Ann. No, dear, it's not—not possibly possible.

[LILY *picks up a book and begins to read it.*]

Hope. But surely you could leave your father for a month, say. You could get a good nurse in Marseilles or Toulon, and——

Ann. Father doesn't need a nurse.

Hope. I'm sorry. I'm stupid.

Ann. No, you're not. You're sweet. You're all sweet. But I'm like that tilleul tree—um, smell it!—I live here.

Norman. Three years is quite a while in one place——

Ann. Not here. Ever since we came my sense of time's been confined to music.

[PAT *lights a cigarette.*]

Pat. —Look, everyone: there's nothing travels so fast as light—thirty million miles a minute. But by the time they see this match on Orion we'll all have been dead fifty years, maybe more.

[FELIX, *a French butler of about fifty, in a white summer uniform, comes in from the house.*]

Ann. [*Laughing.*] There's a modest man! He thinks they're hanging out of windows on Orion, to see him light a little match! [*She turns to* FELIX.]—Oui, Félix?

Felix. [*To* PAT.] Pardon, Monsieur——

Pat. Oui?

Felix. Il est neuf heure juste, Monsieur.

Pat. Bon. Merci.

[FELIX *traverses the terrace and goes out into the garden.*]

Alice. —And why was that, may I ask?

Pat. We've got to leave before eleven. I told him to let me know every half-hour from nine until then.

Ann. That was perfectly dear of you, Pat. That will help. [*A moment. Then impulsively.*] Oh, I don't see why you at least can't stay on! I want you to. Pat—stay——

Pat. I wish I could, but I've got dates with mountains.

[TOM *pours himself a glass of champagne.*]

Tom. If you had any sense at all you'd know you ought to train for mountain-climbing.

Pat. I feel pretty good, thanks.—Oh, by the way, would you mail some letters for me in New York?

Tom. Sure.

[PAT *from a book on the wall takes several small envelopes and one large one and gives them to* TOM.]

Tom. —The big one's got no address.

Pat. There are four or five others inside it. I thought they'd be easier to carry.

[TOM *puts the envelopes in his pocket, the large one with difficulty.*]

Tom. You were wrong.

[LILY *slams her book shut and tosses it upon the sofa.*]

Lily. —Another blonde heroine who won't take her milk, and Mama will throw up.

[*There is a silence, which* ALICE *finally breaks.*]

Alice. —Did I tell you?—I saw the most amusing boat this afternoon: all white, with sienna sails, and a thin white prow——

[*Another silence.*]

Tom. —Gondolas are built in a rather curious way. You know how they seem to pivot—well——

[*But he relapses into silence.*]

Hope. The air's so heavy—give me a glass of water, someone.

[TOM *gives her his glass of champagne.* HOPE *takes a swallow, and chokes.*]

Hope. This isn't water.

Tom. The water in France isn't safe. It's full of Frenchmen.

Pat. —And sometimes an American, who swims out too far.

[LILY *turns on him angrily.*]

Lily. Oh damn you, Pat! Shut your trap, will you?

Norman. [*Quickly.*] How long is the drive to Toulon?

Tom. Fifty minutes, Mr. Rose.

Hope. [*Reflectively.*] —Bags to be packed.

Ann. No, no—please—there's all the time in the world!

[*Another brief silence. Then* PAT *speaks.*]

Pat. It was funny motoring over here. We passed the old Hotel Beau-Site in Cannes. Lord, how it took me back. I had an English tutor there, named Briggs, when I was twelve. He fell in love with my mother.

Alice. What did she do? Fire him?

Pat. Heavens, no.—Mother?

[NORMAN *starts a record on a portable gramophone which stands upon the wall—it is the "Nailla" of Delibes.*]

Lily. Dear God, not that again. If you knew what that tune does to me.

[NORMAN *promptly turns it off and returns to his chair. Silence is again about to descend upon them, but* HOPE *will not have it.*]

Hope. Seriously, Ann—how did you know we were at Antibes?

Ann. I told you: I had a hunch.

[TOM'S *elbow catches on the bulky envelope protruding from his coat pocket. Unnoticed by* PAT, *he takes it out, opens it and extracts four smaller envelopes from it.*]

Hope. I know you said that. But seriously——

Ann. I have them, I tell you!—It's not my first one about Pat, is it, Pat?—Do you remember my cable to London once, years ago?

Pat. What? Oh yes—yes, sure.

Ann. I got a feeling that he was in some kind of trouble, so I cabled.—But what the trouble was, I never knew.

[TOM *is distributing the letters in his inside pockets and his wallet.*]

Lily. [*To* PAT.] Don't tell me anything's ever gone against *you,* darling. I couldn't bear it.

Ann. —I asked you about it once before, didn't I?

Pat. Did you?

Ann. Yes. Don't you know what you said?

Pat. What?

[*Now* TOM *has but one letter without a place for it. He reads the address upon it, starts slightly, frowns, and looks from it to* PAT, *and back again.*]

Ann. You said: "I'll tell you that the day before I die."

Pat. All right. That still goes.

Norman. It sounds ominous.

Ann. Doesn't it!

[TOM *taps the letter reflectively. Then:*]

Tom. [*Suddenly.*] Pat—this letter——

[PAT *turns swiftly, goes to him, and takes it from his hand.*]

Pat. Oh—oh, that—I'll tell you about that later.

Tom. I think you'd better.

[LILY *is watching* ANN.]

Lily. —I wish I was like Ann.—Ann, I do wish I was like you. I feel so inadequate near you.

[ANN *laughs and blows her a kiss.*]

Ann. Darling! You're famous—I'm nobody. I do nothing but read of your triumphs.

Lily. —The triumph of trash. You can have my public, if you'll give me your heart.

Ann. But you have it already!

Lily. I'd like to think that.

Tom. You may.

Lily. I want to play Cordelia in *King Lear.*

Norman. Cordelia! You?

Lily. —And Booth turns a handspring in his grave. All right, but somehow that part fascinates me. Whenever I think of it I go absolutely cold. And still I know that if ever I have the guts to do Cordelia, my life will be a different thing.

Pat. Then why not try it? I'll back you, Lily.

Lily. [*In fright.*] No! No! I wouldn't dare. [*Then she laughs.*]—No. I start my farewell tour any day now. I'm going to play the Styx instead.—That's a joke, the *river* Styx.

Norman. Everybody laugh.

[LILY *springs up.*]

Lily. Norman, there are times when I can't stand this damned Jewish superiority of yours, and this is one of them.

Norman. Really? I'm so sorry.

Lily. —The way you look down from your eminence of three thousand years—honestly, who do you think you are, some Disraeli?

Norman. He was later, wasn't he?

Lily. [*To the others.*] You see?

Norman. Besides, I've always considered him enormously overrated.

Lily. I wouldn't mind so much if it made you happy. But you're one of the most wretched men I know.

Tom. Go on—bankers are always happy.

Alice. Norman's more than a banker. He's a financial genius. My uncle says so.

[ANN *laughs.*]

Ann. There, Norman! Now are you happy? [*A moment. Then:*]

Norman. No. —I'll tell you, Ann: here's how I see my life——

Lily. Tune in on Norman Rose Hour.

Norman. —There are several angles to it: When a man decides he wants to accumulate a fortune——

Tom. It's going to be a speech.

Pat. —I can't speak to Mr. Morgan just now. Tell him I'll call him back.

Tom. —Nine-thirty A. M. The great Norman Rose enters his office——

[*He goes to the table.*]

Lily. [*In three tones of voice.*] Good morning, Mr. Rose. Good morning, Mr. Rose! Good morning, Mr. Rose!

[TOM *grunts, seats himself at the table and contemplates the bottles and glasses.*]

Tom. I see my desk is piled with work again.

Lily. You must learn to depute the smaller duties to underlings, Mr. Rose.

Tom. I have to think of my stockholders. [LILY *knocks three times upon her book.* TOM *turns.*] Who's there?

Lily. It's me, Mr. Rose. Little Lily Malone. You know *me.*

Tom. [*Wearily.*] Come in, come in!

[LILY *enters the great man's office.*]

Lily. —A gentleman to see you, sir.

Tom. I don't like gentlemen. It's ladies I like.—Come closer, Miss Malone.

[LILY *stiffens.*]

Lily. —A Mr. Patrick Farley. Morgan and Company. Sleighs and Violins Mended.

Tom. Show him in.

Lily. —Mr. Rose will see you now, Mr. Farley. [PAT *comes in,* LILY *announces him.*] Mr. Farley, Mr. Rose.—I know you'll like each other.

[LILY *retires.* TOM *indicates a chair.* PAT *seats himself.*]

Tom. Well, Farley, what is it?

Pat. It's—just about everything, Doctor. I feel awful.

Tom. Your Chemistry is down. C-minus.

Pat. Yes, sir.

Tom. Your Physics is down. D.

Pat. Yes, sir.

Tom. Your English is down.

Pat. Yes, sir. I can keep everything down now, sir.

Tom. You were not so good as that last night, Farley.

Pat. I think you are forgetting your place, Rose. Please remember that my grandfather kept slaves, and your grandfather was one of them.

Tom. Yes, and a good one!

Pat. [*Sneering.*] —Pride of race, eh?

Tom. If you like.

Pat. And if I don't?

Tom. Farley, I am a busy man.

Pat. Just so. And that is why I want to ask you a question:—That shipment of earmarked gold for Sweden——

Tom. My God.

Pat. Don't temporize, Mr. Rose. He is my God as well as yours.

Tom. But I must have a moment to myself, to think. [*Suddenly.*] I know what! I'll telephone about it!

[*He takes a long spoon from the table and holds the handle to his ear.*]

Pat. —That was the old Norman Rose speaking. That was the Norman Rose we once knew, and loved.

[TOM *speaks into the other end of the spoon.*]

Tom. Get me Equitable Trust. [*Then to* PAT.] What ever became of your Aunt Jessie Sprague?

Pat. None of that now! Don't try to get me off on sex.

Tom. [*To the telephone.*] Hello?

Pat. Say this to him first: Say, "What *is* ear-marked gold?"

[TOM *nods and waits a moment. Then:*]

Tom. Hello, is that you, Trust? Yes. This is Norman Rose speaking—the old Norman Rose. Listen now, Eq—about that gold for Sweden—Sweden, yes.—Look here, old man, maybe you can tell me: what *is* ear-marked gold? [PAT *nods approvingly. There is a silence.* TOM *holds his hands over the end of the spoon and turns to* PAT.]—He's bluffing. [*Another moment, then again to the spoon:*] Oh it *is,* is it? That's what it is, is it? Well, let me tell *you* something: you're not a big enough man to bluff Norman Rose. No sir!—Well, it's your *business* to know! [*To* PAT.]—Still bluffing. [*To the telephone.*] All right, all right—that's all right with me! But if you think you can—Hello! Hello, are you there? Hello—hello —— [*He puts down the spoon and turns to* PAT.] He's gone. He's hung up, the big bluffer.

[PAT *fixes him with his eye.*]

Pat. It's you who are bluffing, Rose. [*He points his finger at him.*] What *is* earmarked gold?

Tom. [*Confused.*] I—why, it's—I'm not sure, but I *think* it's——

Pat. We have no place here for men who are not sure.

Tom. Don't be hard on me, boy.

Pat. I'll give you two alternatives.

Tom. Make it three.

Pat. I'll give you three alternatives.

Tom. Four.

Pat. Four and a half.

Tom. Five. Five twenty-five!

[PAT'S *fist descends upon the table.*]

Pat. Sold!—To the gentleman in the straw hat, for five twenty-five!

Tom. But who—who are you?

[PAT *rises, opens his coat, and points to his badge.*]

Pat. The Chairman of your Board of Directors. [TOM *covers his face.* PAT *speaks quietly.*] Good afternoon, Mr. Rose. [TOM *rises, and makes one mute gesture of appeal.*] Good afternoon, Mr. Rose.

[TOM *hulks out of his office, a broken man.* PAT *seats himself at the table and pours a drink.*]

Norman. [*Laughing.*] All right! I'll resign!

Hope. Silly—they are so silly.

Ann. It was lovely! Do another——

Hope. No, they mustn't. I'm always afraid they'll slip over the line and turn into the people they're pretending to be.

Lily. It would be grand just to let yourself go some time. I wonder what would happen?

Hope. I hate to think.

Lily. It couldn't be any worse than it is. [*She closes her eyes.*] Hopeless, hopeless——

Norman. What?

Lily. Hopeless.

Pat. [*Humming.*] Rat-a-plan, rat-a-plan, rat-a-plan-plan-plan.

Norman. [*To* LILY.] But while there's life, my dear——

Lily. —There's the rent to pay.

Pat. —And what's the big premium on life, I'd like to know?

Norman. Well, it does look like all we've got.

Pat. There was a great big war, Pet, and we survived it. We're living on borrowed time.

Tom. Lost: one battalion.

Pat. We're not lost. Our schedule is different, that's all.—What I mean is, we'll have had the works at forty instead of eighty.

Norman. I've got a theory people expect too much from life.

Ann. But you can't! That's one thing that's not possible!

Lily. Then why is everyone so disappointed in it?

Ann. Because all they concern themselves with are its probabilities. Think of the things that might happen, can happen, do happen! The possibilities!

Lily. There might be a ray of hope in that. Who, for instance, would ever have thought that the little back-stage rat I was, would spend a week-end with the King of Spain? —Not that I enjoyed it.

Alice. —Snob.

Ann. [*Laughing.*] You might spend a week-end with yourself some time, Lily. You just might have a lovely time.

Lily. I'd bore myself stiff. I'd get to showing myself card-tricks.

Tom. A person's got to look for disillusionment all the way along. It's the price paid by everyone who uses his head for anything but a hat-rack.

Ann. But Tom! What do you want with illusions in the first place?

Lily. Oh—just to make himself feel important. That's why he quit his business with such a great big gesture.

Tom. I quit publishing because it seemed ridiculous to devote my life to bringing out books about life.

Lily. Exactly—and how important the gesture made you feel. Sure. That's what we're all after—and that's all we're after.

Ann. You know, Lily, you're so completely debunked, there's very little of you left.

Lily. I tell you, to beat this game you've got to be born rich and healthy, and preferably a Farley—with Pat's private slant that nothing matters a damn anyway.

Pat. Is that my slant?

Lily. Isn't it?

Ann. It wasn't when I knew him.

Pat. People change, they say.

Ann. It breaks my heart to have you change, Pat.

[PAT *glances at her, then looks away.* ALICE *stretches upon her cushion.*]

Alice. Oh, you all think too much. Why don't you be like me?

Lily. Need you ask, dear?

Alice. I know that when I die, I die. But in the meantime I hope to keep my days and nights fairly full.

Lily. Of what?

Alice. I may not be as clever as you, Lily, but I'm a whole lot happier.

[*She yawns luxuriously.*]

Lily. I have a cat that is, too.

Alice. I love cats. Cats have the right idea.

Pat. They also have kittens.

[NORMAN *clears his throat.*]

Norman. It all resolves itself into the fundamental problem of the location of Man in the Universe.

Pat. Really? Is that all?

Tom. Oh Lord, how can anyone believe he matters any, when he knows that in a few years he'll be dead and done with?

Ann. You honestly think that *this* is all there is, then?

Tom. This what?

Ann. This life.

Tom. Why, of course. Don't you?

[ANN *laughs.*]

Ann. Oh no, no, *no!* Of course not! Not possibly.

[*They all look at her in astonishment. Even* ALICE *raises herself upon her elbow on the cushion.* LILY *murmurs.*]

Lily. —She's marvellous. She's really marvellous.

Tom. Chemistry is chemistry, Ann.

Ann. [*Still laughing.*] Heavens, Tom, is that as far as you've got?

Lily. There's always the next step. Look: you see that nice little white scar there?

[*She holds one hand out for her to see, wrist upward.* ANN *is serious in a moment.*]

Ann. Lily—what do you mean?

Hope. Lily! You didn't!

Lily. —Didn't I, though.—At last a real use for old razor-blades.

Hope. But when?

Lily. Oh—about a year ago. I forget, exactly.

Hope. But my dear—*why*?

Lily. I just got sick of myself. [*She apologizes.*]—It wasn't very successful. I know too much. I made the tourniquet myself.

Pat. That's right, Actress, do your stuff. God's out front tonight.

Lily. —Will you tell the Kind Gentleman I enjoyed his little piece, but found no part in it for me?

Tom. Don't talk that way, Lily.

Lily. Why not?

Tom. It's blasphemy. I was born a Catholic, and I don't like it.

[LILY *stares at him, finds him quite serious.*]

Lily. "Blasph—"? I haven't heard that word in years. Say another.

Norman. I thought you'd given up your religion?

Tom. So I have. But all the same, the only real dope on life I ever got was from an old priest at school. I'd like to see that old fellow again. He was a nice old fellow. Father Francis, his name was.

Ann. There's been a great space left in you, Tom. It will take some filling.

Tom. And with what?

Lily. They say cyanide is quite satisfactory.

Hope. Don't, Lily——

Lily. Why? Don't tell me *you've* never thought of it. [HOPE *is about to reply, but does not.*] Ha-ha! Caught you——

Tom. Darling—you haven't really——

Hope. Well, haven't you?

Tom. I know, but——

Hope. Is it anyone's special privilege? Am I not worthy?

[LILY *laughs, and turns to* ALICE.]

Lily. Alice? [ALICE *sits up.*]

Alice. Yes, dear?

Lily. No, there'd be no point in it for you—it would be too little change.—But what about you, Norman? Do you ever yearn out windows? [NORMAN *smiles.*]

Norman. I can't say I've ever seriously contemplated it, no.

Lily. Then go on and contemplate it.

[*A brief pause. Then:*]

Norman. Well, I wouldn't do anything positive—but if I knew I could save my life by changing from this chair to that one, I doubt if I'd move.

[*Again* LILY *laughs.* ANN *is gazing at them in amazement.*]

Lily. This is grand! [*To* ANN.] I suppose we can count you out, though.

Ann. [*Briefly.*] Yes. I'm out.

Lily. —And as for you, Patrick? How long since *your* last confession?

Pat. I'm sorry to disappoint you, but it's never crossed my mind.

Lily. And if I were you, I'd take precious good care it never did.

Pat. Thanks. You're kind. I'll remember.

Lily. —Because I don't think it would cross yours. I think it would stick there. [*She looks about her. Then, to* ANN:] Four out of six. Not a bad average, is it?

Tom. Pat, why was that letter addressed to me? [PAT *smiles.*]

Pat. Suppose my foot should slip on an Alp?

Tom. Do you expect it to?

Pat. Not particularly, but there's always the hope.

Tom. You're not usually so foresighted.

Pat. But this time I am.

Tom. —I don't like it. May I read it now?

Pat. It would make me feel a little foolish. It's signed, "Oceans of love, Patrick."

Ann. What letter are you talking about?

Pat. One that he——

Alice. [*Suddenly.*] Oh, good Lord——

Hope. What's the matter?

Alice. Suddenly I had the most abominable chill.

Lily. On a night like this?

Alice. What a fool I am, really.

[NORMAN *wraps a thin beach-blanket about her.*]

Lily. [*Sweetly.*] Please dear, let *me* say that.

Norman. I wouldn't give two francs for any of our nervous systems.

Hope. It's probably too much sun and too little sleep for a week.

[PAT *pours himself another brandy.*]

Pat. —And the grape—the grape and the grain.

[*And drains the glass. Again silence descends upon them.* HOPE *finally breaks it.*]

Hope. Is it always so heavenly here, Ann?

Ann. —Except for some overcast nights in the Autumn with no moon, no stars. Then there's such blackness as you wouldn't believe.—Only the light from the lighthouse on the Ile de Port-Cros, crossing the terrace here—like the finger of God, Father says.

[*It has got darker, but the atmosphere*

possesses a luminous quality that imparts a strange definiteness of outline to the objects and the people upon the terrace. Again, silence. Then:]

Lily. I'm sad.—I could cry.—I am crying.—Oh, behave yourself.

[*Suddenly* ANN *stands bolt upright, rigid*.]

Hope. What is it?

Ann. Wait a minute.

Hope. Honestly, Ann, I do wish——

Ann. Wait! [*For a moment they wait, silent, tense. Then from the distance is heard one muffled report*.]—There. It's all right. Don't worry.

Hope. But what on earth *was* it?

Ann. It's Father. He's at the bastide. Sometimes he fires a sunset-gun. I get to expect it.

Alice. [*Awed*.] He won't do it again tonight, will he?

Ann. I said a sunset-gun. It sets only once a day as a rule. [*There is a silence. She rises, abruptly*.] Well, why shouldn't he, if he likes? I think it's splendid of him! [*A moment. Then she laughs shortly*.] Sorry! [*Waits another moment, and continues*.]—I imagine he'd seem a trifle strange to you, but to me it's a pretty grand sort of strangeness. I believe he is a very wise man.

Tom. I don't doubt it.

Ann. I don't always understand him, but that's my fault. I understand better than I used to, and some time I hope to understand all. So I just try to follow him wherever his mind leads. I've been beautiful places there with him.

Tom. [*After a pause*.] I unearthed a marble tablet in the lower garden today. It was in Latin and said: "To Semptronius who, at age 12, danced here, and pleased."

Ann. But how charming that is!—Can't you see him?—Semptronius——

[TOM *rises. All at once he is as excited as a child*.]

Tom. I'd like to dance here, too. [*To* PAT.] Will you play? And would anyone mind?

Hope. —Now that's what I mean! Really, we're not acting at all sensibly, don't you realize it?

[TOM *looks at her, and returns to the wall*.]

Tom. —Ten years ago I wouldn't even have asked. It's a rotten feeling, knowing your youth's gone—knowing that all the brave things you once dreamed of doing, somehow just won't get done.

Pat. [*As a small boy would say it*.] I wanna go out to the South Seas like Father Damien!

Tom. [*Soberly*.] I did, at that.

Alice. Who is Father Damien?

Tom. [*Reciting*.] Father Damien was a noble priest who went to the South Seas to help the lepers and got it himself.

Hope. Sometimes I don't know his voice from little Tommy's.

[*Suddenly* TOM *stands up upon the wall*.]

Tom. Look, Mummy! Look where *I* am!

Hope. Get down, Tom, you'll fall.

Tom. Don't punish me, Mummy.—Reason with me.

Hope. —Acting like that! I don't know where you think you are.

[TOM *descends from the wall*.]

Tom. —Under the piano. [*He moves away from them, toward the table*.]—Under the apple tree—[*He seats himself cross-legged beside the table, whistling a tune softly through his teeth and trying to wrench the top from a wooden champagne-stick. A moment, then he calls, as a small boy would:*] Hey, Pat! Pat! C'mon over!

[PAT *comes forward to him*.]

Pat. Hello, Tom.

Tom. Hello, yourself.

Pat. Where're the other fellows?

Tom. How should I know? I got better things to do than follow *them* all over everywheres.

[*He examines his stick with interest.* PAT *seats himself on the ground beside him*.]

Hope. Don't, Tom.—Make them stop, Ann. They go too far with it.

[*But* ANN *is silent, watching them intently*.]

Pat. —Gosh, I feel good, don't you?

Tom. I feel all right.

Pat. —But don't you ever feel—gosh, I don't know—*good*?

Tom. You don't feel very good when you've got things the matter with you, like I have.

Pat. What have you got? [*No answer*.] Aw, come on, Tom—is it really bad?

[TOM'S *head bends lower over his stick*.]

Tom. It's awful.

Pat. Aw gosh, I'm sorry—tell me, Tom——

[*A moment, then:*]

Tom. Will you promise never so long as you live—[PAT *nods eagerly*.]—I think I've got something, Pat.

Pat. What?

Tom. I think I got the leprosy.

Pat. [*Appalled*.] You've—? Gosh, Tom, why do you think that?

Tom. I read a book last night about Father Damien in the South Seas and he got the leprosy and I think I've got it.

Pat. How—how do you suppose you ever ——

Tom. I gave a old woman a dime the other day, and she went and kissed my hand, and I think it must of been her that gave it to me.

Pat. But didn't you wash or anything?

Tom. I couldn't till I got home. And it takes awful fast. Look at that——

[*He shows his wrist.*]

Pat. Where?

[*He almost touches* TOM's *wrist—but draws his hand back, fearfully.*]

Tom. Doesn't it look sort of—white to you?

Pat. It does, sort of.

Tom. —And scaly? That's the way it starts. My foot's the same way. I could tell for sure by putting it in hot water.

Pat. Hot water?

Tom. If you've got it, you don't feel anything, not even the water, even. Father Damien didn't. That's the way he knew.

[NORMAN *is drawn over to them. He, too, has begun whistling softly. His tune is "Pony Boy."*]

Pat. Oh, he was prob'ly just a crazy ole priest.—H'lo, Norman.

[TOM *scowls.* NORMAN *gestures "Hello," and goes on whistling, hands in pockets.*]

Tom. A *what,* did you say?

Pat. Well, there *are* crazy priests. Anyways, I bet there have been, some time.

Tom. Never. Never one. God wouldn't let there be.

Norman. What about Theo-philus?

Tom. Who?

Norman. Theo-philus.

Tom. What did he do that was so crazy?

Norman. Just burnt the library at Alexandria, that's all.

Tom. I never heard of it.

Pat. I did. Alexander the Great built it, quite a long time ago, to please his vanity.

Norman. [*Reciting.*] —And Theo-philus was a crazy Christian monk that burnt up the library which was the greatest in the whole world and which history tells us contained over seventy thousand volumes.

Tom. Well, if he did, I bet he had some good reason. I bet they were impure books, or something.

Norman. He was crazy.

Tom. I bet he knew they were good and lashivious and he just burnt 'em to the honor and glory of God.

Norman. He was crazy.

Pat. [*Pointedly.*] Of course you'd say so, anyway. I guess you'd say any Christian holy man of God was crazy.

Norman. I wouldn't either. [*A moment.*] *Why* would I?

Pat. I suppose you think we didn't notice you didn't eat that ham-sandwich the other day and asked for a sardine.

Norman. I wanted a sardine. I like sardines better. I like their taste better.

Pat. Yes, you do!

Tom. [*To* PAT.] —Anyone says sardines taste better'n ham says so for some good alterior reason, you bet.

Norman. You know what *you* are, don't you?

Tom. What?

Norman. Cath'lic! Cath'lic!

Tom. [*Soberly.*] I am a Catholic. Yes. I am proud to be a Catholic.

Norman. Yes—well, before *I'd* go to confession and things——

Tom. You know why?—You wouldn't get the chance. They wouldn't let you in. See, Mr. Jew?

Pat. You are a Jew, aren't you?

[NORMAN *raises his head proudly.*]

Norman. Of course I am. What about it?

Tom. You crucified our Lord, that's what about it.

Norman. Oh, no I didn't.

Pat. Who did, then?

Norman. The Roman soldiers. See?

Pat. Oh, you think you know everything. All you do is sit around and read books, little Ikey.

Norman. I'm not an Ikey! Don't you call me that!

Tom. [*To* PAT.] —You're just as bad as he is. A heretic's what *you* are— Protestant-dog-sit-on-a-log-and-eat-meat-on-*Friday!*

Pat. I'll eat anything I like any day I like—see? *And* ham.

Tom. It's all right now, only wait'll you die. Just wait'll then.

Pat. [*To* NORMAN.] Pooh, "when I die." That's what the priest tells him——

Tom. Well, just let me tell *you*: when I grow up maybe *I'm* going to be a priest. See? Maybe I've got a vacation right this minute. See?

Pat. A what?

Tom. A vacation—a call.

[PAT *looks at him in wonder.*]

Pat. Gosh.

Tom. [*Closer to him.*] Just think that over, Mr. Fresh.—And when you hear of me going out to the South Seas and places like Father Dami——

[*Awestruck, he remembers his malady. In fear he peers at his wrist again.*]

Pat. Is it any worse?

Tom. I think it's spread a little.

Pat. Listen——

Tom. What——

Pat. I know a fellow's got a doctor-book. Only he won't lend it. You got to look at it at his house. Shall we——?

Tom. All right. [*A moment. Then:*] Pat——

Pat. What?

Tom. What would you do if *you* had the —the you-know?

Pat. [*After thought.*] I'd kill myself.

Tom. You couldn't. You'd go straight to hell. And the tortures of the you-know are as nothing to the tortures of hell.

Pat. Just the same I'd do it, though. I certainly wouldn't go around with the lepr —[TOM *claps his hand over his mouth.*] Let go!

Tom. —You promised! [*To* NORMAN.] —You get out. Get out, now!—If you know what's good for you——

[NORMAN *leaves them.* PAT *struggles.*]

Pat. Let go! I'm—I can't breathe. Let go——!

[*Still* TOM *holds him.* PAT *struggles harder. He begins to beat at him with his fists. Finally freeing himself, he goes at him violently.* TOM *retaliates. They go up and down the terrace, advancing, retreating, clinching, separating, raining blows upon each other in dead earnest.* HOPE *suddenly realizes that they are no longer playing, and cries:*]

Hope. Stop it! [*But they go on. She begins to strike at* PAT.] Stop! Stop it, do you hear me? [*She turns imploringly to* NORMAN.] Norman!

[NORMAN *goes to* TOM.]

Norman. Come on, now—that's enough! [*He holds his arms from behind.*] What's got into you two?

[HOPE *stands between* PAT *and* TOM, *protecting* TOM. *They are gasping for breath, glaring at each other.* TOM *lurches forward once more.*]

Hope. Stop, Tom!—How often must I tell you—[*Then she takes him in her arms.*] Oh, didn't I beg you not to?

[ANN *goes to* PAT.]

Ann. Pat—Pat, dear——

[PAT *stares at her blankly for a moment, then suddenly slumps down into a chair.*]

Pat. I'm—I don't know——

[NORMAN *releases* TOM, *who stares first at* HOPE, *then at* PAT, *amazement growing in his eyes.*]

Alice. Well, of all the——

Ann. Wait!—Are you all right, Pat?

Pat. [*Weakly.*] Sure.

[HOPE *covers her face.*]

Hope. Oh, I'm scared—I'm so scared.

Ann. Of what, Hope—of seeing life burst the walls of the little room we try to keep it in?

[*Suddenly* TOM *turns upon her.*]

Tom. Well, Ann—if you know so much, what's the answer to the whole works?

Ann. If I could tell you——

Hope. [*Gently.*] Tom—listen——

Tom. [*Suddenly savage.*] I say, what's the answer? I want to know! [*He averts his head, sharply.*] God help me, I've got to know!

Ann. —But I can't tell you!—I don't know how.—Oh my dears—what is to become of you? How can I let you go to rove the world like ghosts this way? You're so pitiful, and I love you so!

[FELIX *comes in from the garden.*]

Felix. [*To* ANN.] Pardon, Mademoiselle ——

Ann. Oui? Qu'est-ce-que c'est?

Felix. C'est le père de Mademoiselle qui fait demander si elle a besoin de lui.

Ann. Où est-il?

Felix. A la bastide, Mademoiselle.

[*A moment.* ANN *looks about her, at the others. Then:*]

Ann. I'll go to him.

[*She turns and goes out, up the garden steps.* FELIX *turns to* PAT.]

Felix. Pardon, Monsieur—il est neuf heures-et-demi, Monsieur.

Pat. Merci.

[FELIX *bows and goes out into the house, taking the coffee-service with him. There is a long silence, then* LILY *collects herself and speaks.*]

Lily. What did he say to Ann?

Alice. Her father sent to ask if she needed him. She's gone to him.

Hope. Needed him!—For what, I wonder.

[*Another pause.* LILY *ventures hopefully:*]

Lily. It is not generally known that polo was invented by Chinese women.—An interesting fact, is it not? [*No one replies.*]—Nope.

Norman. [*Reflectively.*] —I'd like to go all alone to Andorra.

Alice. Where's that?

Norman. I don't know.

Alice. Then what do you want to go for?

Norman. No Federal Reserve—no "giant mergers."—Time to think—Lord, time to think!

Lily. About what?

Norman. Lily, I'm sorrier for you than for anyone I know.

Lily. I don't want your pity, Mr. Rose. I just want your money.

Norman. [*Pondering.*] When I was working in that fur shop on Twenty-third street, I was a free man. [*A moment. Then he rises abruptly.*] I think I'll go in and pack.

[*And goes out into the house.*]

Tom. Of course *I* think the trouble with Norman is, he's caught and he knows it. He'd like to retire now, but he can't. Too much depends on him.

[PAT *laughs shortly.*]

Pat. —All looking for the answer, when there isn't any answer. [*A moment.*]—Unless maybe it's "Off for Africa."

Hope. —That will do, Pat. Don't even start it.

Alice. I still don't see why men like you three can't enjoy life.

Lily. Promise me something, dear——

Alice. What?

Lily. —When you die, leave your head to the Rockefeller Institute. It's a little gem.

[ALICE *rises and moves toward the house.*]

Alice. Oh, you're always so bright——

Lily. I know. Isn't it the devil?

Alice. If you weren't, *au fond,* such a common little piece——

Lily. —*N'est-ce pas?* [*To the others.*]—She thinks in French.

[*At the door* ALICE *turns and contemplates them.*]

Alice. Honestly, it's all so boring——

[*And goes out.*]

Lily. The trouble with that girl is complete lack of vitamins A to Z.

Hope. Do you suppose Norman is really in love with her?

Lily. I don't know. Anyhow, there's a chink in that fine Semitic pride of his. It would never risk a refusal.

Hope. But surely if she cared for him ——

Lily. She doesn't—too much effort.

[*A pause.* TOM *rises.*]

Tom. Oh Lord, if only I'd died at fifteen.

Pat. Maybe you did.

Hope. It's been a ghastly week all around. No wonder we're depressed.

[TOM *looks at her.*]

Tom. Hope, sometimes I feel I don't know you at all. [*He mounts the steps to the house.*] —And we're supposed to be the lucky ones! We're the ones who've got the world by the top of the head.—I'll let you know when I'm packed, Hope.

[*And goes out.*]

Hope. I'm coming now. [*To* PAT *and* LILY.]—He came abroad this time to study the origins of Ecclesiastical Precedence in Rome. He got as far as Antibes. He gets vaguer all the time. I'm so worried about him I can't see straight.

Pat. Of course *I* think Tom's trouble is having too much time on his hands.

Hope. But it's his time to himself he always said he wanted! That would solve everything. And now that he's got it, *it's* not enough. I wish to heaven we were home with the children and he was still rushing madly for the 8:22. He cursed it, but it kept him going.

Pat. You're just travel-worn, that's all. Why not let him make his crusades for Truth by himself?

Hope. —And get sent for the first day he's lonely? That's what's always happened. —Except once, just once, when he did go to Canada for a month. [*She rises.*] He accomplished two things toward his soul's salvation there—two great things.

Pat. What?

Hope. —He grew a red beard and learned to whistle through his teeth. [*She moves toward the stairs.*]—Talk about children! He's the worst one I've got. Oh, if you *knew* how I want to stay home with my *real* babies!

[*And goes into the house.*]

Lily. —Which is the answer, of course, to Hope.

Pat. What is?

Lily. She's so peaceful, so normal. She's all home and babies.

Pat. That's not a bad thing to be.

Lily. It's a grand thing to be.—And so is it to be the fine, free, roving soul that Tom might. It's the combination that's wrong. Of course *I* think the real trouble with them both is—[*Suddenly she stops, and laughs.*] Do you realize what we've been doing?

Pat. What?

Lily. —When I go in, what will you say about me?—The trouble with Lily is what? What's wrong with Lily?

Pat. Is there anything?

Lily. Plenty. But Pat——

Pat. What?

Lily. I think we've been good for each other, don't you?

Pat. I suppose so.

Lily. You lie, you don't!

[PAT *looks at her mildly.*]

Pat. Don't be violent, Lily.

[LILY *groans.*]

Lily. —Now he's going to turn gent on me again. That's the catch with you: you were born a gent and you can't get over it.

Pat. I think I've done pretty well.

Lily. Oh, you do, do you ? Well, listen to me——

Pat. Lily, I'm sunk.—And low, deep, full fathom five.

[*She looks at him curiously. There is a silence. Then she speaks in a different tone.*]

Lily. Have a drink.

Pat. No, thanks.

Lily. Pat, when I first knew you, your spine had turned to jelly——

Pat. Yes?

Lily. Yes. And your slant was all wrong. You'd been expecting too much of something —I don't know what—and hadn't got it. You were a mass of sobs.

Pat. That's a pretty picture.

Lily. It was you.—I'd knocked around enough, man and boy, to know what people really are. I taught you to expect nothing, didn't I?

Pat. Yes. [*She raises her glass.*]

Lily. —And what a dandy little mother's-helper *this* is—— [*She drinks.*]

Pat. Yes.

Lily. —And that there's no de-lousing station big enough to pass the whole world through.

Pat. That's right.

Lily. Well—have a drink.

[*But he decides not to.*]

Pat. —I suppose they're good things to have learned.

Lily. I've changed your slant, haven't I?

Pat. Something has.

Lily. You've done a lot for me, too. How is it I don't fall in love with you, I wonder——

Pat. I don't know. Have you tried very hard?

Lily. Awfully hard.

Pat. I'm sorry. Maybe I'm just not your type.

Lily. Would you like to be?

Pat. I never gave it much thought.

Lily. Don't I attract you at all, Pat?

Pat. You might, if I thought about it.

Lily. Think about it. [*He does so. They look intently into each other's eyes.*] Have you thought?

Pat. Um.

Lily. What's the answer?

Pat. I'm attracted.

Lily. Much?

Pat. Quite a lot.

Lily. Would you mind kissing me, Pat?

Pat. On the contrary.

Lily. Then do, please. [*He kisses her. She clings to him briefly, then turns away.*] Oh, it's so awful——

Pat. Thanks! [*Then:*] What is?

Lily. I don't feel anything. I don't feel anything at all.

Pat. No. I thought not.

[*She turns quickly.*]

Lily. You knew about me?

Pat. I imagined.

Lily. Don't get me wrong, Pat. I'm not one of the girls, either.

Pat. I never supposed you were.

Lily. I just—don't feel anything for anyone.

Pat. Some people have all the luck.

Lily. Oh, no—don't say that! I want to, so much—[*A moment.*] It seems to me—dimly—way back somewhere, I loved someone terribly. I don't know who—my father, maybe.

Pat. There you go about your father again.

Lily. —All I know is, that since, there's been nothing.

Pat. Maybe that did the trick, Lily.

Lily. How?

Pat. Maybe that's all you get.

Lily. You're a wise guy, in a way.

Pat. You think?

Lily. [*Touching his forehead.*] —The Farley brow, eight months gone with Minerva. Where do you get all your dope?

Pat. The ravens feed me.

Lily. Oh, hell—nothing happens any more.

Pat. Buck up, Lily. Something will before you know it.

Lily. A broken neck would be welcome.

Pat. Give things a chance. Don't try so hard for them.

Lily. All right, teacher.—Have another drink?

Pat. Later—when the night wears on a bit.

Lily. Yes—and won't it, though——

[ALICE *appears on the balcony.*]

Alice. [*Lowly.*] Listen, you two——

[LILY *puts on her humorless smile.*]

Lily. Yes, Angel? [*To* PAT.] Reach me my Winchester, will you?

Alice. Honestly, I've got the queerest feeling.

Lily. I told you a week ago you swallow too fast.

Alice. —I don't suppose we could decently leave *before* eleven——

Pat. No, I don't suppose we could.

Alice. I was afraid we couldn't. [*She moves toward the doorway, but sways against the railing. She exclaims weakly:*] Oh—come up here a minute, someone—will you? I feel awful.

Lily. Right away, dear.

[ALICE *goes out, into the house again.*]

Pat. You'd better go. She may be ill.

[LILY *is looking off into the garden.*]

Lily. Ann's coming back. One thing, Pat——

Pat. What?

Lily. [*As she moves to follow* ALICE.] If I were you, I'd be careful tonight.

Pat. About what?

Lily. About Ann. You may not know it, but you're still the world to that girl.

Pat. You're talking tripe, Lily.

Lily. Just the same, I'd be careful. [PAT *turns abruptly and looks out over the wall.* FELIX *has come out upon the balcony, with three or four small candle-lamps, unlighted, which he arranges upon the balcony wall.* ANN *comes in from the garden.*] Ann—do you suppose your maid could give me a hand with my things?

Ann. But of course! She's in my room. Call her.

[LILY *mounts the steps.* FELIX *takes out his watch.*]

Lily. —And it isn't tripe, my Patrick.

[*From far in the distance beyond the wall a small pencil of light is cast. It performs an arc in space, sweeping across the terrace, flooding over the upper wall of the house and disappearing again in the garden above.*]

Felix. Pardon, Monsieur—il manque dix-sept minutes de dix heures, Monsieur.

Pat. [*Without turning.*] Bon.

[FELIX *goes into the house.*]

Lily. [*At the top of the steps.*] What happens when you forget to wind him up?

[*She goes into the house by the other door.* ANN *stands silently watching* PAT *until the door has closed behind* LILY. *Then suddenly, swiftly, she goes to him, takes him by the shoulders and turns him about, facing her.*]

Pat. Oh hello, Ann.

[*From the distance piano-music begins to be heard.*]

Ann. [*Lowly, intensely.*] I won't have it, Pat. I just will not have it!

Pat. It?—What's that you won't have?

Ann. Something's burning you up. Tell me what it is!

Pat. I'm afraid you're imagining things. Where's the music from?

Ann. René Mayer has a house up the road. It's always full of musicians.—You've got to listen to me. I——

Pat. Have you heard Sandy Patch's new song? [*He moves toward the piano.*]—It's called "Drunk and Disorderly." It goes like this——

Ann. Don't, Pat—we haven't time——

Pat. Then let's get the others down, shall we?—And enjoy what there is left.

[*He makes a move toward the house. Her hand upon his arm stops him.*]

Ann. Wait!

[*She looks away, to control herself, her hand still upon his arm.*]

Pat. I'm all right, my dear. Really I am.

Ann. We've known each other quite a few years, now——

Pat. We have, haven't we? I feel pretty spry, though, don't you?

Ann. We've always been able to talk.

Pat. They say I could talk when I was only——

[*Her hand tightens upon his arm.*]

Ann. —Which we've always done directly, and honestly.

Pat. Yes?

Ann. Shan't we now?

Pat. If you like. Why not?

Ann. When you leave tonight I shan't see you again for at least a year—maybe more——

Pat. Oh—before I forget——

[*From his pocket, in a fold of tissue-paper, he brings a very simple and fine ruby pendant, and gives it to her.*]

Ann. What is it?

Pat. It was Mother's. I'm sure she'd want you to have it. I know I do.

Ann. Beautiful——

Pat. I think so.

Ann. But Pat—it's priceless——

Pat. So was she. So is Ann.

Ann. Oh, thank you for it! Put it on for me—[*He catches it around her throat. She turns again, facing him, then stands for a moment with her forehead against his breast.*] Pat—my dear Pat——

Pat. Things don't go the way we'd like them to, Ann.

[*A moment, then she leaves him.*]

Ann. —You've been dodging around corners, to get away from me.

Pat. I didn't know it.

Ann. I won't bite you, Pat.—What's been happening to you these past three years? I'm still a little interested.

Pat. It's been pretty much the same sort of life, thanks.

Ann. What are you doing with all that money?

Pat. Oh—spending some of it—giving away quite a lot of it. It's an awful pile to make a dent in.

Ann. You never found the job we used to talk so much about——

[PAT *smiles.*]

Pat. How well she knows me.

Ann. There are only two people in this world who are really important to me—you and Father.

Pat. I'm—Thanks, Ann. That's good to know.

Ann. I've been able to help him a little——

Pat. I should think you had.

Ann. I'd give the eyes right out of my head, if I could help you. [*He lifts her hand to his lips, kisses it, and turns away.*] Oh Pat, *Pat*—whatever has happened to you?

Pat. Myself.

Ann. —Don't you go telling yourself you're no good! You're the best there is.

Pat. You don't know.

Ann. Oh, yes I do!

Pat. Anyhow, let's not get solemn about——

Ann. —And what do you suppose it means to me to know that a person I love as I love you is breaking up into little pieces over something I've no share in?

Pat. But Ann—you don't love me any more.

Ann. I do, though. I've never got over it—never. I love you with all my heart. [*A silence. She smiles uncertainly.*]—I don't suppose by any chance you love me back——

Pat. [*With difficulty.*] There's something in the way. Nothing can ever come of you and me now. There's something in the——

[*He turns away, with an exclamation.*]

Ann. Tell me.

Pat. I can't.

Ann. —You'll be shocked to hear I'm living with you in my mind. I've taught myself to dream about you nearly every night. That gives me—rights.

Pat. Ah, Ann—let it go—please let it go.

Ann. I can't. I simply can't.—You've always been a life-and-death person. You take things terribly hard. I'm sure it's not as hopeless as it seems. [*But he does not answer.*]—Do you remember the first time we met, on the Westbury Road?—me lost, with a sprained ankle, and you——

Pat. —When I forget anything about you and me——

Ann. I wish we could get back there. I wish we could start from the Westbury Road again.

Pat. —But we can't.

Ann. —Such a dear, serious boy you were. All the time you were in college you used to come to me with your little troubles——

[*He laughs.*]

Pat. —Would I row on the Crew?—I didn't make the Dramatic Club.—What if they passed me up on Tap Day?—Poor Ann——

Ann. I was important to you then——

Pat. You still are.

Ann. Come to me now with your big trouble, Pat.

Pat. I'm just a flop, darling.

Ann. It's a little soon to decide that, don't you think?

Pat. I told you my schedule was different.

Ann. Pat, whatever happened, happened four years ago. You came from a year in England, and you were changed. It was a girl, wasn't it? I saw her picture in your study. What was it—wouldn't she have you?

[PAT *smiles.*]

Pat. I forget. What did she look like?

Ann. Very young, quite English, very fair. A lovely face—pretty, oh, so pretty.

Pat. Funny—I've forgotten.

Ann. I haven't.—Then you went over again the next winter—for how long was it?

Pat. I don't know—three weeks——

Ann. That's when I had my hunch about you. It wasn't long after you'd sailed. I was walking up Madison Avenue and in a florist's window I saw a lot of hawthorn blossoms——

[PAT *starts slightly.*]

Pat. Hawthorn——

Ann. Yes. They were lovely, and I was going in to get some when all at once I began to feel terribly queer. It was as if the bottom had dropped out of everything. I knew it had something to do with you, and I love you and I just went on home without them.

Pat. I don't get it at all.

Ann. Nor do I.—But the next morning I passed the same shop and saw that the hawthorn was gone. Somehow, that was terrible. I couldn't get warm again all day. I love you and I had to cable you.

Pat. I don't get it.

Ann. I've never known such a change in a person, as in you when you came back. Suddenly you were as hard as nails, and so bitter. I hated leaving you that way when I came here with Father. But I was sure you'd get through it somehow, back to yourself. Now I see that you haven't. I see that it's worse than it ever was, it's destroying you. Oh, Pat—it can't be just some fool of a girl who wouldn't have you.—What has done it?

Pat. Honestly, Ann—it's all so long ago.

Ann. But I've *got* to know. Tell me!

[PAT *shakes his head.*]

Pat. It's all too ridiculous. Really. I never even think of it any more.

Ann. Whether you do or not, it's got you still. Something awful's got you. Tell me—it will help to tell me. Ah, *please*—because I love you——

Pat. I would if I could. I want to. I simply can't.

Ann. I'll find out!

Pat. All right, Ann.

Ann. —But can't you *accept* it, somehow? Can't you take life whole—all of it—for what it is, and be glad of it? Why do you have to go at it with a tin box of paints, daubing it up pretty? You're grown-up, now. —Why, my dear! What have I said? What is there in that, to hurt you so?

Pat. Listen: you can have your marvellous life. I'm not taking any.

Ann. What are you talking about?

Pat. —The lot of you—clutching, grabbing at some little satisfaction that lasts a day or two—a swell business.

Ann. You dare talk to me about my life like that!

Pat. Yours—theirs—anyone's——

Ann. Oh, you're horrible——

[PAT *looks at her intently.*]

Pat. So you're the last to go. You fail me too——

Ann. [*A cry.*] —You?—And who are you, that you shouldn't be failed some time?

Pat. I don't know, Ann. I've often wondered. [*Again he moves to the wall and stands looking out over it, the light from the lighthouse breaking over his head.* ANN *sinks into a corner of the sofa. From the distance, the piano-music begins to be heard more clearly. For a long time they are silent. Then* PAT *speaks. His voice is one of wonder, almost of fright.*]—They're right about this place—it *is* so, you-know—it's really so——

Ann. What is?

Pat. —Like other places—like another place——

Ann. Where?

Pat. —A house my mother had in Florida, four years ago, when I came back from England——

Ann. That was the second time——

Pat. Yes. It was in March. I came straight down here from New York—I mean straight down there. Mother was in the patio all alone, having coffee—[*Still he looks out over the wall, without turning.*]—I had so much to tell her—I'll never forget it—I thought if only I could talk to some one who——

[ANN *speaks softly.*]

Ann. Hello, Son. It's good to have you back.

Pat. —Could talk to someone who might, just might, have some little faint idea of what I——

Ann. Hello, Son. It's good to have you back. [*A moment. Then:*]

Pat. [*A murmur.*] Hello, Mother. It's good to be back.

[*He comes forward to her, slowly.*]

Ann. I didn't expect you quite so soon.

Pat. I know.

[*He sinks down upon a cushion on the floor beside her. The eyes of both are straight ahead, not looking at each other.*]

Ann. You're looking tired.

Pat. It was a rotten trip. [*He goes on in a low voice, almost mechanically.*] —I think I'll stay a while this time.

Ann. I'm glad.

Pat. It seems like a pleasant place.

Ann. It's peaceful.

Pat. That's good.

Ann. Ah, Pat—what is it, dear? I've worried so about you.

Pat. Yes. I suppose.

Ann. I've wanted to ask, but——

Pat. I know. I just couldn't talk.

Ann. Are you so very much in love?

Pat. Yes.

Ann. Tell me about her. Who is she?

Pat. Oh, it's all over now.

Ann. Over?

Pat. Yes.

Ann. But are you sure?

Pat. I'm certain. [*A moment. Then:*]

Ann. Who was she, then?

Pat. —Mary Carr—the niece of one of my dons at Cambridge. [*A moment. His voice hardens.*]—Cambridge—another of Father's fake ideas. Finish me off, eh? Turn me into the little gentleman. Every inch a Farley—God!

Ann. Hush, Pat——

Pat. —Be good at everything. Shine! Always shine! And if you can't, don't play.—I can still hear his voice.

Ann. —Mary Carr, I've seen her photograph. She's very lovely.

Pat. Yes.

Ann. —And young.

Pat. She was eighteen in November. [*A pause. Then suddenly:*] God, that is young. Father was right *there,* at least.

Ann. What happened when he went over to you last year——

Pat. I cabled I wanted to get married. He cabled me to wait, he was coming. I waited. He came. He talked me out of it. [*Bitterly.*]—She wasn't suitable.

Ann. But that wasn't *your* reason——

Pat. I tell you I let him talk me out of it!

Ann. You agreed to put it off, that's all.

Pat. Yes—that's what I told myself—and that's what I told Mary.—That's what the little swine I was grunted at Mary—just put it off a while, that's all. But somehow the point missed Mary—somehow she didn't get me.—She just stopped talking in the middle of a word, and went into the house. And I took a train, and sailed with *him.* He was ill then—or said he was—we couldn't wait a day.

Ann. [*Hesitantly, after a pause.*] You—I suppose you and she—you'd been a good deal to each other.

Pat. We'd been everything.

Ann. I see.

Pat. —But there wasn't to be a baby, if that's what you mean—[*Again the bitter voice returns.*] Wise boy, young Farley. *He* knows his way around!

Ann. But you wrote her. Surely you wrote her.

Pat. All the time, but I never had one little word from her. A dozen times I'd have gone over, but how could I with Father dying and then all that tangle settling the estate? [*He concludes, lowly:*]—It was a year and three months since I'd seen her, when I'd sailed. I didn't even wire—I was afraid she'd run away somewhere.

Ann. But she hadn't, had she?

Pat. No.

Ann. She was there——

Pat. She was there.

[*A moment. Then:*]

Ann. —And she just won't have you.

[*Her hand reaches to comfort him. He turns to her.*]

Pat. Mother, she just won't have me. [*Suddenly he stares at her.*] You're not—oh, damn you, Ann——

[*He rises, and leaves her. She follows him.*]

Ann. All right! But tell me. You've got to finish now! [*In another voice.*]—Surely it isn't hopeless. Surely you can——

Pat. But it is, you see.

Ann. I don't believe it. Where is she now?

Pat. Down in the ground.

Ann. Pat—she isn't—?

Pat. She is, though—as a doornail.

Ann. Oh, my poor boy——

Pat. My poor Mary.

Ann. But listen to me—listen——!

Pat. No. *You* do. [*He points his finger at her, and speaks.*] Three days before I came, she walked out under a tree where—she'd walked out under a hawthorn-tree at the end of a very sweet lane we knew, and stood there and shot herself.

Ann. Pat—Pat——

[*He moves away from her.*]

Pat. You wanted to know, didn't you?

[*She looks at him. Then:*]

Ann. —So I lose you to a dead girl.

Pat. I've lost myself to her.

Ann. You loved me first.

Pat. But she died—[*He goes to the piano and seats himself, running his fingers silently over the keys.*]—If only I could get back to her somehow. If I could just let her know I did come back.

Ann. How much of it is losing her—and how much the loss of yourself?

Pat. I don't understand that.

Ann. —You used to have a fair opinion of Pat Farley. That was essential to you—that *was* you.

Pat. All I know is that nothing's been any good to me since. I'm licked, Ann.

Ann. Well, what are you going to do about it?

[*Unnoticed by them* STEPHEN FIELD *has appeared at the top of the garden-steps, where he stands, a figure in white, watching them. He is about fifty-eight, slight in build, gray-haired, with a face uncommonly strong, fine, and sensitive, lined and worn as it is, gray, too, as it is.*]

Pat. What is there to?

Ann. [*Suddenly, sharply.*] Pat!

Pat. [*Without turning.*] What?

Ann. You said you'd tell me this the day before you died——

[*As she reaches the word, he strikes a chord and drowns it.*]

Pat. —But I changed my mind, didn't I? —And told you now! [*He turns toward the house, and calls:*] What'll I play? Call your tunes, gents—almost closing-time!

Ann. —And the letter to Tom—. Oh my dear—what is it?

Pat. Don't be a fool.

[*A moment, then* STEPHEN *speaks:*]

Stephen. Pat——

Pat. [*Without turning.*] What do you want?

[*He is completely unnerved now.*]

Stephen. I wouldn't do it, if I were you.

Pat. Do what?

Stephen. I really wouldn't. Things may change.

[*He speaks with a clear, incisive strength.*]

Pat. —Change? How? Who wants things changed? [*He turns, stares at him a moment, then rises.*] Oh, how do you do, Mr. Field? How are you? —Everything's fine with me. Everything is——

Stephen. —And yet I wouldn't do it. I wouldn't go from here to those high places —to that strange accident. I really wouldn't.

[PAT *laughs shortly.*]

Pat. Honestly!—If you think just because a fellow's planned a trip to climb an Alp or two——

[ANN *takes his shoulders in her hands, turns him about and gazes into his eyes.*]

Ann. Pat!

Pat. I don't know what he's talking about. [*To* STEPHEN.] I don't know what you're talking about. You're beyond me. I can't follow all this——

Ann. Oh, my poor Sweet, why do you want to do it? [*She shakes his shoulders.*] *Why?*

Pat. Why not?—Maybe you can tell me that!—Why not?—I should have three years ago, but I was too yellow then. [*Still she stares. Another silence, then he pulls away from her mumbling:*]—All right. Don't worry about me. It's all right. Small brainstorm, that's all—Over now——

Ann. Promise it!

[*He gestures vaguely.*]

Stephen. It is not so easy. He is in love with death.

[PAT *turns to him and sings, beating time with his finger.*]

Pat. —Rat-a-plan, rat-a-plan, rat-a-plan-plan-plan-plan— [*He stops on the high note, holds out his arms, and cries:*] Yes!

[*And goes to the point of the wall, where he stands with his back to them.*]

Ann. Father—Pat's mine—I can't lose Pat!

[FELIX *comes out upon the balcony, watch in hand.* STEPHEN *descends the steps and comes upon the terrace.*]

Stephen. I know, dear. [*He is watching the house.*] —But let us take it quietly. Let us take it very quietly——

Felix. [*To* PAT.] Pardon, Monsieur—il est dix heures, juste.

[PAT *does not reply.* FELIX *goes out.*]

Stephen. —Here are your other friends.

[TOM *and* HOPE *enter.*]

Tom. [*To* HOPE, *on the balcony.*] —No, no—what's the good of talking?

Hope. Well maybe if you'd——

[*She sees* STEPHEN, *and stops.*]

Ann. This—these are Tom and Hope Ames.—My Father, Hope.

Hope. How do you do, Mr. Field?

Tom. How do you do, sir?

[STEPHEN *murmurs a greeting.* LILY *enters from the house.*]

Lily. —I gave Alice a bromide, and she's sleeping like a log. She's——

[*She sees* STEPHEN *and stops.*]

Stephen. What a beautiful color you all are. You look like savages. People don't realize that the sun here in the Midi is——

Tom. Didn't I meet you once with Father Francis at St. Luke's?

Stephen. I'm afraid not.

Tom. Perhaps it's just that your voice reminds me of him.

[LILY, *eyes wide, stands staring at* STEPHEN.]

Stephen. [*To* HOPE.] What do you think of our little retreat here?

Hope. It's lovely. The days have gone so quickly.

Stephen. —Quickly—so quickly. [*To* LILY.]—Why do you stare at me so?

Lily. Why I—I'm terribly sorry. I——

Stephen. But what is it?

Lily. It's just that you're so like my own father——

Stephen. Yes?

Lily. He was an actor in a touring-company. He died years ago in Cleveland. He wanted me to be a dancer. I used to dance for him, often. It was a great pleasure to him. I mean to say——

Stephen. [*Gently.*] I am sure it was.

[NORMAN *comes in from the house.*]

Lily. [*In a burst.*] —He was superb! He was so kind, so loving. He was the most beautiful man I've ever—! [*She stops suddenly, then continues:*]—But he deserted my mother, you know. He was simply foul to her.—Hell, I suppose he was just a ham actor—yes, and a drunkard, to boot. [*Again she stops.*]—What am I spilling all this for? What's biting me now?

[STEPHEN *turns inquiringly to* ANN.]

Ann. —Lily Malone, Father.

Stephen. Poor child. [*To* NORMAN.]—And this?

Norman. [*Advancing.*] I'm Norman Rose, sir.

[*They shake hands.*]

Stephen. I understand that you must leave us soon.

Norman. I'm afraid we must, sir.—At eleven, to be exact.

Stephen. That is unfortunate. [*Again he smiles.*] Well—let us set the hour-glass on its side, and ask the Old Gentleman to put his sickle by, and sit down with us and rest a moment. [*He seats himself.*] Before you go I want you all to see my bed of white phlox in the lower garden. In the moonlight it is white as white was never. I have banked the petunias near it——

Hope. [*Delightedly.*] But *I* did that at home!

[STEPHEN *is watching the balcony.* ALICE *has appeared upon it.*]

Stephen. The odor at night is so sweet, so pungent—cinnamon and gunpowder.—And is this Alice?

[ALICE *comes down the stairway without touching the railing, eyes far away, walking as in a dream.* ANN *rises.*]

Ann. Yes——

Lily. Go back to bed, you foolish girl.

[ALICE *approaches them, unseeing.*]

Ann. —This is my father.—Alice Kendall, Father.

Stephen. How do you do, my dear?

[*But she does not regard him.*]

Norman. She's——!

Ann. Father, what is it?

Stephen. Sh! Be gentle with her——

Hope. Oh, I don't like it!

Lily. I told you about that time she walked out into the hall, in Paris.

[ANN *goes to* ALICE.]

Ann. —There, dear, it's all right. Just be quiet—quiet——

[PAT *is watching her, fascinated.*]

Pat. Take her back. It's horrible——

[*Swiftly, directly* ALICE *walks to the angle of the wall.*]

Hope. Norman—don't let her hurt herself!

[NORMAN *and* ANN *have followed her.*]

Ann. Alice—*Alice*——

[ALICE *turns to her. In a moment her eyes uncloud.*]

Alice. —But hello, my dear. They didn't tell me you were coming down. Divine house, isn't it?

[*She speaks as if she were reading aloud.*]

Ann. Listen to me a moment, dear——

Alice. They're right. There's nothing like May in England. Who's on the party, do you know?

Ann. Oh—lots of people. But Alice, listen——

Alice. Any extra men?

Ann. I think so.

[PAT *goes to the wall and stands there with his back to them.*]

Alice. I like this Norman person——

Ann. Yes, he's very nice. But——

[ALICE *laughs shrilly.*]

Alice. I know!—But not too nice! [*Her voice lowers, confidentially.*] My dear, he burns me up. He looks so strong—so strong. I'll bet he'd give a girl a roll for her money, don't you? [*A moment. Then to herself, with real feeling:*]—Why can't he tell?—Why doesn't he know the way I ache for him?

Pat. Take her back, take her *back*——

Alice. —Which one shall I wear?—I think the blue one, with the ruffle down the front——

[*She unfastens a shoulder-clasp, and steps out of her dress.*]

Hope. But she mustn't——!

[ANN *turns to* NORMAN *with a helpless gesture.*]

Norman. I'll speak to her.—Alice!

[ALICE *whispers:*]

Alice. Who's that?—Is that you, Norman?

Norman. Hello, Alice——

Alice. It was naughty of you to bring me here, you know it was— [*She leans toward him.*] What did you tell the clerk at the desk?

Norman. Why, I just said that——

Alice. Oh, I'm a pretty girl! [*She extends her arms.* NORMAN *takes one of her hands in his.*] Why does no one want me? What are they afraid of?

Norman. Maybe they do. [*He turns to the others, painfully.*] I love this girl. I've been crazy about her for years.

Stephen. Humble yourself before her beauty, sir.

Alice. Come—there are people in the next room. I can hear them. They may come in— [*Suddenly she drags her hand from his and cries in terror:*]—Ann—Ann! [ANN *goes to her swiftly.*]—This man's—been following me everywhere——

Ann. It's all right, darling, he won't hurt you. He's a nice man.

[ALICE *begins to whimper.*]

Alice. Is he? [*She turns to* NORMAN, *fearfully.*] Are you? [*He nods, speechless. She darts a glance at* ANN *and huddles herself in her arms.*]—But look at me—out on the street like this. Where's my little jacket? I want my little jacket——

[NORMAN *wraps a thin beach-blanket about her, and gives her her dress.*]

Norman. Here you are, dear.

[*He leads her gently to the steps. She looks up at him with a smile of child-like trust.*]

Alice. You *are* a nice man——

[*They mount the steps. There is a si-*

lence until they have gone out into the house.]

Lily. She seemed to be so many places all at once.

Stephen. Sleep has freed her from time and space. One day sleep's sister will free her further. [*He hums a measure of a song, laughs softly, and concludes:*]—And near the white phlox I have a dappled pink variety which I developed by crossing a strain of crimson——

Tom. [*An appeal.*] Mr. Field—What's the—? Mr. Field——!

Stephen. —Yes. It does bewilder one at first. I know. I too used to believe life had one aspect only. I was so sure that sleep and dreaming was—well, sleep and dreaming. And of course I knew that with death it was all over——

Pat. Well?

Stephen. Well, now I know I was mistaken.

Pat. How?

Stephen. I have found out a simple thing: that in existence there are three estates. There is this life of chairs and tables, of getting up and sitting down. There is the life one lives in one's imagining, in which one wishes, dreams, remembers. There is the life past death, which in itself contains the others. The three estates are one. We dwell now in this one, now in that—but in whichever we may be, breezes from the others still blow upon us.

Pat. I'm sorry, I don't follow you.

Stephen. There are no words for it. It is a sense, a knowing. It may come upon you in a field one day, or as you turn a corner, or one fine morning, as you stoop to lace your shoe. [*A brief pause.*]—Or even as it came on me.

Tom. How was that, sir?

Stephen. Here on this terrace.

Ann. Father——

Stephen. I know, dear.

Pat. —So life does go on, does it?

Stephen. Oh, yes. Of course.

Pat. How, for instance?

[STEPHEN *smiles.*]

Stephen. —As it was in the beginning, is now, and ever shall be——

Pat. —World without end, eh?

Stephen. Without end.

Pat. Hah! That'd be a good joke.

Lily. Look out, Pat.

[NORMAN *comes out again upon the balcony and stands there, watching them.*]

Stephen. —Let us be bold and change the "world" to "universe."—A fine night, isn't it? [*His gesture includes the sky.*]—There is the space we one day shall inhabit, with all our memories and all our dreams. I ask you to admire this, gentlemen——

Lily. It's not always so fine, is it?

Stephen. But I ask you to admire that, too! [*To* PAT.] If one could but once see his life whole, present and past together in one living instant, he would not wish to leave it before his time—oh no!

Pat. I know my time.

Stephen. I thought I knew mine once. My mind was quite made up, that night. Nothing was to deter me.—But the light from the Ile de Port-Cros described its arc as it does now. [*He stands erect.*] It stopped me, held me.—How long I stood here, I don't know. But when I was aware again——

Ann. Father——

Tom. —What had happened to you? [HOPE *goes to him and tries to draw him away from the wall, murmuring "Tom—Tom!" but he does not answer and will not come.*] Say what had happened!

[*The terrace, in a brief space, has become flooded with moonlight. There is a silence. Then* STEPHEN *begins to speak again, this time more softly, gently, coaxingly.*]

Stephen. I had walked back in time. It is a very interesting excursion. You merely lift your foot, place it so, and there you are —or are you? One thinks one is going forward and one finds instead the remembered touch of water somewhere—the odor of geranium—sight of a blowing curtain—the faint sound of snow—the taste of apples. One finds the pattern of his life, traced with the dreadful clarity of dream. Then he knows that all that comes in remains—nothing is lost—all is important.

Ann. [*A small voice.*] Father——

Stephen. Are you afraid?

[*A moment. Then:*]

Ann. No.

Hope. [*In a whisper.*] But I am, I am! Tom—Tom, listen——

[TOM *does not stir.* HOPE *leaves him.*]

Stephen. Here is the moon at last, you see?—Here is our day's reflection, hung in space. [*He hums another measure and again laughs softly.*] Space is an endless sea, and time the waves that swell within it, advancing and retreating. Now and again the waves are still and one may venture any way one wishes. [*A moment.*] They seem to be still now—quite still. So which way would you go—where would you travel?

[*A silence. Then* TOM *moves into the angle of the wall.*]

Tom. To what I was——

[*Another silence.* LILY *moves toward* STEPHEN.]

Lily. To him I love——

Norman. [*After a moment.*] Wherever I should go——

[*He turns and goes into the house again.*]

Hope. Nowhere. I'm happy as I am—or would be, if Tom were——

[*A silence. Then:*]

Pat. [*A murmur.*] To Mary—Mary——

Ann. [*A cry:*] No, no!—To the Westbury Road! [PAT *hums softly.*]

Pat. —Rat-a-plan-plan-plan-plan.

Stephen. [*To* LILY.] Listen: there is a turning. All things are turned to a roundness. Wherever there is an end, from it springs the beginning.

Pat. [*Barely audible.*] —Ta-plan-plan-plan-plan.

[LILY *moves to the garden steps and out, following the movement of* STEPHEN'S *hand.* TOM *turns and gazes at* HOPE *with a curious expression.*]

Hope. What's the matter with you?

Stephen. Pat—Ann—it was not so long ago. Was it so long ago?

[ANN *shakes her head hopelessly, and moves toward the garden, mounts the steps and goes out. Slowly* PAT *crosses the terrace in the opposite direction, and enters the house.*]

Hope. [*To* TOM.] What are you staring at?

[TOM *smiles, but does not reply.* STEPHEN *turns to* TOM *and* HOPE.]

Stephen. And for us—shall we see my white phlox, first?

Hope. Oh, Mr. Field—you mustn't let them go on like this! It's so frightening. [*She turns and sees* TOM *still staring at her.*] Tom's looking at me in the queerest way.—It's as if he didn't know me.

Stephen. Possibly you have changed.

Hope. I——?

Stephen. —In his eyes. Perhaps you have one child too many.

Hope. I don't know what you mean.

Stephen. It may be that he sees you not as a mother, but as a woman that he loves. I should not discourage that.

[TOM *goes to* HOPE *and gently turns her about, facing him. He looks at her with a curious smile.*]

Hope. Tom, what's the matter with you, anyhow? [*His answer is to take her in his arms and kiss her. She frees herself.*] Honestly, I don't know what you're thinking of! What on earth has— [*He takes her face in his hands and kisses her again. She averts her head.*] I can't imagine what's come over you. I want to talk to Mr. Field. [*To* STEPHEN.] It seems to me that you're all— [TOM *comes to her again, takes both her hands in his and smiles into her eyes.*] I'm not fooling. I really mean it.

Pat. [*From the house.*] Mary? *Mary!*

Hope. [*To* STEPHEN.] Who's he calling? —I tell you it isn't good for people to let themselves go that way— [TOM *draws her into his arms, and holds her there.*] It's a form of self-indulgence.—Stop, Tom! It's a — [*Again* TOM *kisses her.*] Tom, will you let me *go!*

[*He opens his arms suddenly and she is freed, almost falling. She recovers herself and turns once more, with dignity, to* STEPHEN.]

Pat. [*From the house.*] Mary! Where are you?

Hope. The things that are happening here tonight aren't natural, and what's not natural must be wrong.

Stephen. To me they are more natural than nature.

Hope. Of course I don't pretend to follow *your* extraordinary— [*From behind her,* TOM *is taking the hair pins from her hair. She stamps her foot in exasperation.*] Honestly! This is *too* much! [*To* STEPHEN.] I hope you realize that goings on of this sort are not at all usual with us.

Stephen. I think that is a pity.

[*Tenderly, lovingly,* TOM *kisses the back of her neck.*]

Hope. Tom—don't be an utter fool! [*To* STEPHEN.] —To me, life is a very simple thing——

Stephen. Is it?

Hope. One has one's home, one's children, and one's husband——

Stephen. Or has one's home and children only?

[HOPE *looks at him, startled.* TOM *returns to the wall.*]

Hope. You mean you think that to me Tom's just another——?

Stephen. What do *you* think?

[HOPE *turns to* TOM.]

Hope. Tom, darling—*surely* you must know that I——

[LILY'S *voice is heard from the garden, calling as a little girl would.*]

Lily. Good-by, Pa! Good-by!—Come right home after, won't you, Pa?

Hope. [*To* STEPHEN.] You see? That's Lily. Oh I know she'll hurt herself! [*To* TOM.] Now you stay right here, won't you?

Please, Tom—like a good boy. [*She hurries off to the garden, calling:*] Lily! Wait, dear!

[*A moment, then* TOM *speaks from the depths of his wretchedness:*]

Tom. Oh, Father Francis—can't a fellow do anything without it's being sinful?

[STEPHEN *goes to a chair and seats himself.*]

Stephen. What have you to tell me?

Tom. So much. I know it's after hours. I know you're tired, but——

Stephen. Come——

[TOM *comes, head down, hands clasped. He kneels beside* STEPHEN'S *chair and makes the Sign of the Cross.*]

Tom. Bless me, Father, for I have sinned. It is about three months ago since my last confession. Since then, I accuse myself of the following sins: Father, I've cursed and sworn and taken the name of the Lord in vain. I've neglected my morning prayers and missed Mass once, and been distracted during Mass seven times——

Stephen. Yes—but what is really wrong?

Tom. I've been drunk, and had immodest thoughts, and eaten meat on an Ember-Day, and committed acts of impurity four times——

Stephen. But what is really wrong?

[TOM *chokes.*]

Tom. Oh, Father Francis—I don't believe any more! Nothing's got any meaning for me. I look around me, and nothing means anything at all—and I want it to! It must—it's got to—or I'll, or I'll——

Stephen. Your childhood faith is gone——

Tom. It wasn't true.

Stephen. Are you so sure?

Tom. Yes, and it meant so much to me. I even thought I ought to be a priest, but I lost my faith.

Stephen. Perhaps in order that you need not be one.

Tom. I know I've got no soul—nobody has.

Stephen. Look closer.

Tom. I have. It isn't there. There isn't any. There never was.

Stephen. At some time there is a soul born to every *body*—and like it, subject to many ills. But the soul's life is the only life there is, so the world is peopled with the living and with the dead. We know the living. Sometimes the dead deceive us.

Tom. You mean that maybe mine is——?

Stephen. No. The dead do not deceive me.—I mean that birth is painful. The infant suffers too.

Tom. It's awful—I can't stand it. Let me be damned!

Stephen. No.

Tom. But now I'm nothing—let me be *something*!

Stephen. Now you begin to be.

Tom. I keep wanting to do great things—too great for what I am——

Stephen. There are many men who would go to the ends of the earth for God——

Tom. I would! I keep starting to——

Stephen. —And cannot get through their own gardens.

Tom. Oh, don't! I'm such a weak soul——

Stephen. —Such a human being.

Tom. Something always stops me, always——

Stephen. Your own humanity.—But there are strong souls who never leave their gardens. Their strength is not in the doing, but in the wish to do. There is no strength anywhere, but in the wish. Once realized, it has spent itself, and must be born again.

Tom. But I don't know what I'm here at all for——

Stephen. To suffer and to rejoice. To gain, to lose. To love, and to be rejected. To be young and middle-aged and old. To know life as it happens, and then to say, "This is it."

Tom. Yes—but who *am* I? And what shall *I* be when it's over?

Stephen. You are the sum of all your possibilities, all your desires—each faint impression, each small experience——

Tom. —But when it's *over*?

Stephen. You will be what your spirit wants and takes of them. Life is a wish. Wishing is never over.

[*A brief silence.* TOM *rises to his feet.*]

Tom. —Then everything about me *has* a meaning!—Everything I see and feel and think and do—dream, even!

[STEPHEN *closes his hand over* TOM'S.]

Stephen. Great heaven, yes!

Tom. I've got a feeling that I'm dreaming now.

Stephen. It may be.

Pat. [*From the house.*] Mary!

Tom. —But Father Francis—are you ill?

Stephen. Why?

Tom. You look awfully white—and your hand—it was as cold as ice. I'm afraid I've been a strain for you. Good Lord, Father—you do look white. Here—take this—[*He goes to the table and pours a glass of brandy.* STEPHEN *goes to the fan-back chair in the shadow in the corner of the terrace.* TOM *turns with the glass.*] This will fix you. This—why, where are you, Father? [*He looks about him.*] Confound it, where's he gone to? He looked sick— [*He calls.*] Father Francis!

[STEPHEN *does not answer.* TOM *moves toward the house, with the brandy. As he reaches the steps,* NORMAN *darts out with a small, white fur-rug in his hands.*]

Norman. One minute, Mister!

Tom. What do you want? Have you seen Father Francis?

Norman. [*In a moderate Jewish accent.*] How'd you like to buy a nice fur neck-piece?

Tom. Don't be a fool.

Norman. —Make a present to your lady-friend, eh? You can have it cheap——

Tom. No, thanks. Let me by—I'm in a hurry.

Norman. All right—I resign—I quit!—I'll get a job as runner in a bank. In five years I'll be rich—I'll be the biggest man in Wall Street! [*Again he offers the rug.*] Look—five dollars—it's worthy fifty——

[TOM *tries to pass him.*]

Tom. Oh, for God's sake, Norman—Father Francis is ill——

Norman. I'll have money, power—that's what makes you happy—that's the life! [*Again, the rug.*] Look: it's a bargain. Buy it. An inside tip: the National City's taken half the issue at 91, and Pritchard, Ames is bidding for another hundred thousand at——

Tom. [*Suddenly.*] I know—the bastide!

Norman. Don't you call me that, you leper! [TOM *pulls away from him.*]

Tom. Get away, I'm not fooling. Let me by!

[*He crosses the terrace quickly, and goes up the garden steps and out.*]

Norman. But what a bargain! [*He shrugs.*] I should care. [*Then he turns and speaks to the empty chair in front of him.*] Look here, Mr. Sterner—I resign—I'm through!

Stephen. [*From the corner of the terrace, hidden in his chair.*] When I've given you such a fine opportunity, when I have even ——?

Norman. Oh, I'll pay you back!—But I'm quitting, see? I've got better things to do than this. I'll educate myself. I'll——

Stephen. So ambitious, eh? Ah, you're all alike, you young people.—And next you marry a Gentile girl, I suppose, and have her despise you—ruin you.

Norman. Oh no!—Say, am I such a fool as that? Marry a *schiksa*—me? Whose uncle is a rabbi—? I guess not! But what I'll do is get an honest job—yes! "White fox"—this cat-fur! I'm sick of it—I'm through. I'll get up in the world. You watch me! Have educated people for my friends——

Stephen. May you be happy with them.

Norman. —Happy and strong and rich and honest! Watch me! [*He offers the despised rug to another unseen client, is refused, and shrugs again.*] No?—*I* should care!

[*And re-enters the house, whistling. For a moment* STEPHEN *is alone upon the terrace.* PAT'S *voice is heard from the house, in growing alarm:*]

Pat. —Aren't you here?—It's me—it's Pat, Mary!

[STEPHEN *passes his hand over his brow.*]

Stephen. My head—my head. [*A moment. Then:*] —But this is very strange. What is this mist that closes in around me? This is a winter mist, and it is summer. Wait a bit, you, I am not ready yet!

[*The distant music changes to "L'Enfant et ses Sortilèges" from Ravel's ballet "Five o'Clock."* LILY, *her hair flying about her shoulders, runs down the steps from the garden. She is crossing in the direction of the house, when the music stops her. She listens intently for a moment, then with a swift motion slips the belt from her dress and drops it upon a chair. Her appearance has changed to that of a girl of thirteen. She begins to rise up and down upon her toes, in a formal movement of ballet-practice. Her breath becomes a little short. Frowning, she bends and feels her instep.* STEPHEN *rises from his chair, and turns to her. She exclaims in joy:*]

Lily. Pa! Oh Pa, you *did* come right home!

[*She runs and kisses him. He strokes her head.*]

Stephen. Well, well, well—and how has my little sprite endured her prison?

[*He speaks in the eloquent voice of an old-fashioned actor.*]

Lily. Prison? Oh, I've been all right. I like it here. I think it's a nice hotel—nicer than the one in Harrisburg was, much nicer, warmer.—Pa, were you good tonight?

Stephen. I was splendid.

[*He seats himself in another chair, facing her.*]

Lily. How many curtain-calls were there?

Stephen. Alas, none. But I was magnificent.

Lily. I wish I'd gone. I wish you'd of let me. Could I maybe come tomorrow aft?

Stephen. Say "afternoon," child. Do not clip your words.

Lily. "Afternoon."—But could I?

Stephen. We shall see. [*With a gesture.*] Fix me my drink— [LILY *goes to the table and makes a brandy-and-soda.*]—And one for yourself.

Lily. I—I don't want any.

Stephen. And one for yourself, I said!—'Twill do you good.

Lily. Just a little one, then—it makes me feel so funny.

[STEPHEN's *manner begins to change.*]

Stephen. I like you funny.

Lily. Can I put sugar in it?

Stephen. Put anything you like in it. Put salt in it.

Lily. Oh—I wouldn't like that!

[*She brings him the glass, and a small one for herself. He seizes her glass and tastes it.*]

Stephen. Water!

Lily. [*In fright.*] But Pa, I——

Stephen. —Your mother's daughter, eh? Lying, deceiving——

Lily. I'm not! I just didn't want——

Stephen. [*The actor.*] Whose child are you, eh? Are you my child, at all?

Lily. Oh yes, yes! Pa—I *am* your child! Truly I am!

Stephen. Then obey me—without question, without equivocation. [*He drains his glass and gives it to her.*] Fill them both.

Lily. All right. I'll put some in—I'll put a lot in.

[*Again she goes to the table with the glasses, refills them and returns to him.*]

Stephen. Let me taste— [*He tastes her glass, and gives it back to her.*] That's better. You are your old man's daughter. Give me a kiss——

[*She kisses his cheek. He takes a swallow from his glass and she does likewise.*]

Lily. —But you aren't an old man! You aren't old at all. And look, Pa: I don't ever lie to you. I love you too much to. I just can't tell you how much I— [*She strikes a posture, and declaims:*]

"Then poor Cordelia!
And yet, not so; since, I am sure, my love's
More richer than my tongue. . . .
Good my lord,
You have begot me, bred me, loved me: I
Return those duties back as are right fit:
Obey you, love you, and most honor you.
. . ."

Stephen. "Pray, do not mock me.
I am a very foolish, fond old man,
Fourscore and upward, not an hour more nor less;
And to deal plainly,
I fear I am not in my perfect mind. . . .
Do not laugh at me;
For, as I am a man, I think this lady
To be my child Cordelia.

Lily. "And so I am, I am."

Stephen. Not bad, not half bad. You get the feeling well enough, but you lack voice. You need filling out everywhere. You're thin all over. I don't like you thin.—What did you do while I was playing?

Lily. Well, you know how it snowed——

Stephen. Yes?

[*She is sipping from her glass.*]

Lily. Well, I got a whole shoe-box full off the window-sill and I was making a little girl out of it, only as fast as I made her she melted.

Stephen. What else?

Lily. Well, I did my toe-exercises.

Stephen. For how long?

Lily. A whole hour.—Well, almost a whole hour.

Stephen. You're lying to me.

Lily. Oh no, Pa!

Stephen. Don't you ever lie to me.

Lily. Oh, no.

Stephen. If you do, I'll treat you the way I did your mother.

Lily, Pa! You wouldn't ever leave me!

Stephen. Just let me catch you lying once.

Lily. But I never, never!

Stephen. See that you don't.

Lily. I don't know what I'd do if ever you should leave me——

Stephen. —Pick up with some cheap tout, most likely, and go off with him.

[LILY *turns her innocent eyes upon him.*]

Lily. What?

Stephen. Never mind. [*She passes her hand vaguely over her eyes.*]—What ails you?

Lily. It's—beginning to feel, in my head.

Stephen. Drink it down.

Lily. I can't. My throat won't turn over any more. And—and things are going round——

Stephen. Then start the music and go around with them. [*She giggles.*]

Lily. Oh, that's funny! That's so funny. You're such a funny man.

Stephen. Stop laughing.

Lily. I—I can't stop.

Stephen. Go start the music— [*Struggling hard to control her hysterics,* LILY *starts the gramophone. Again, it is the "Nailla" of Delibes. He follows the introductory bars with his hand, as if conducting an orchestra.*] Now then——

[*With difficulty, she empties her glass, and begins to dance haltingly.*]

Lily. [*An appeal.*] Oh, Pa——

Stephen. What?

Lily. I don't want to.

Stephen. Why not?

Lily. My foot hurts. I hurt my foot practicing.

Stephen. If you'd done it right, you wouldn't have hurt it. Go on and dance.

Lily. I can't, truly I can't.

Stephen. Is a man to have no amusement when he comes home of nights after playing his heart out to silly fools who don't know art from turnips? Come on—get going.

Lily. [*Almost in tears.*] Pa—this isn't like you. This isn't my you at all. My you tells me stories about queens and palaces and you hold me on your knee and rock me off to sleep and you tuck me in at night and say God love you, little daughter. That's what *you* do.

Stephen. Oh I do, do I? And how often? In my tender moments twice a year.—Not like me, is it? I'll show you what's like me. Will you dance?

Lily. Oh yes, yes. See? I'm dancing——

[*Again she begins to dance, this time more haltingly. He stands over her.*]

Stephen. Faster!—Wasn't Burbage amused when he came home? Wasn't Barrett and wasn't Booth? Is it too much to ask, eh?

Lily. Oh no, Pa! See me, Pa?

Stephen. That's better.

[*She goes on, as well as she is able. At length:*]

Lily. [*Panting.*] —My hurt foot—it won't go up any more——

Stephen. No? Try it.

[HOPE *appears at the top of the garden-steps, where she stands unseen by them, watching them in horror.*]

Lily. But I *am* trying!—Is it all right if I just—? [*Again she tries to rise upon her toes, and cannot. She attempts a pitiful* pas seul, *fails in it, falls to the floor. Then, all at once she turns into a raging fury and screams:*] God damn! Hell! [*He laughs.*]

Stephen. Good!

Lily. Oh, I hate you. I hate you. I don't *love* you any more!

Stephen. Splendid! Go on—more!

[*She rises to her feet and confronts him, trembling with rage.*]

Lily. You're a dirty drunk! You left my mother when she was sick. You can't act. You're just a super, that's all you are. You can't act any!

[*Laughing, he holds his arms out to her.*]

Stephen. Come here. Give us a kiss.

Lily. No. You smell of whisky and nasty grease-paint. You're dirty—I hate you! I won't stay with you any longer—I'll run away, that's what I'll do.

Pat. [*From the house.*] Mary! I've come back. Where are you?

[STEPHEN'S *voice changes back to his own voice. Suddenly he seems very tired.*]

Stephen. —Then go quickly. Go very quickly. See—there is the door. It is open. Go in, and up the stairs, and to your room.

[*She gazes at him for a moment, then turns and walks directly to the steps and into the house. Again* STEPHEN *sinks into a chair, his hand over his eyes. There is a slight pause, and* HOPE *comes down from the garden.*]

Hope. Oh, that was terrible! Why did you do it?

Stephen. I—? I did nothing. Tell me what happened——

Hope. You know perfectly well what happened!— And she adored him. She— [*She turns and follows* LILY *into the house, calling:*] Lily!

[STEPHEN *is alone. He rises from his chair with effort, and moves toward the garden-steps. He stiffens suddenly, then exclaims in wonder:*]

Stephen. What's this? [*Another moment. Then, more sharply:*] Come now! What is it? [*He slumps against the wall, and plucks at his left arm, which has gone limp, then tries to raise his right hand to his head, and cannot.*]—Cerebral hemorrhage, is that it? That's very interesting, I'm sure. The left side is quite numb—the lesion must be in the right lobe, in the Area of—God, when we crack we crack, don't we? [*A moment. Then summoning his remaining strength:*] —But I am not ready, yet! [*He makes his way to the fan-back chair in the corner of the terrace and slowly lets himself into it. He calls:*] Pat! Ann! [*Another moment.*] There—there's the pulse—it is quite hard, quite stringy—[*Again he calls:*] Ann!—But the breathing is regular, Doctor—difficult, but regular.—I say, not yet! I'll go, but in my proper time.—Curious there is no pain—only a sense of— [*He catches his breath.*] No pain, did I say? [*And collects his strength for a final cry:*] Ann!

[*And sinks lower into his chair. From the distance piano-music begins to be heard again. It is a popular waltz of ten years ago. A moment, then* ANN *comes down the steps from the garden. She is limping. As she crosses the terrace she murmurs to herself:*]

Ann. Poor dear—poor darling—what can I do for him? [*As she reaches the sofa her ankle gives way under her and she sinks down upon the floor, exclaiming:*] Ouch—*ouch*—oh, where *is* that road?

[PAT *comes in from the house, calling softly:*]

Pat. Mary! Where are you, Mary?

Ann. Ouch—ouch——

[PAT *hesitates a moment, then comes up to her.*]

Pat. Excuse me. Is there anything the ——? [ANN *starts in alarm.*]

Ann. —Oh!

Pat. I'm all right. I'm harmless.—But I was just wandering around here and I saw you from across the field and I thought something might be the matter, and——

Ann. —There is. Plenty.

Pat. What? Can I help?

Ann. Well, for one thing, I've probably broken my ankle. And for another, I'm lost. And for another—no, I'm not sure you can.

Pat. Does your ankle hurt?

Ann. Oh no, it feels wonderful. They do, you know.—Ouch!

Pat. Maybe if I could get a car up into this field for you——

Ann. Have you got one that climbs fences?

Pat. What are you lost from?

Ann. The Westbury Road.

[*A breeze brings the music closer.*]

Pat. That's easy.

Ann. It hasn't been.

Pat. You're practically on it. It's just over there——

Ann. No!

Pat. Honest.

Ann. Then what's that music I've been hearing. Isn't it the Club?

Pat. No. It's from a party I'm at.

Ann. At?

Pat. Well, one I got away from.

Ann. Whose?

Pat. Mine. At my house.

Ann. I'm impressed. Why wasn't *I* asked?

Pat. You would have been.—Where do you live?

Ann. I'm staying down here with some people named Ames. But I got the wanders and had to walk.

Pat. So did I.—Tom and Hope Ames?

Ann. That's right.

Pat. They said they couldn't come.

Ann. Maybe they don't like parties. Or maybe they didn't want people to see me. In the Spring I get freckled.—Oh, this *damned* ankle!

Pat. Quit talking about your ankle. What's your name?

Ann. Ann Field. What's yours?

Pat. Don't laugh——

Ann. No.

Pat. Patrick—[*She laughs.*] You said you wouldn't.

Ann. But I've always wanted to know one!—What was it you said to Mike?

Pat. That's not very new, you know.—My last name's Farley.

Ann. —Not one of the great, enormous, important, rich ones!

Pat. Well——

Ann. —Please, forget everything I've said. You're beautiful. You'll get me home all right.

Pat. I'm—er—I came down for the spring holidays, and I thought I'd swing a little party, and——

Ann. Why, bless his heart, he's embarrassed! Lovely!

Pat. Oh, go to hell.

Ann. You're sweet. I think you're really sweet. [PAT *seats himself beside her.*]

Pat. Foolish to stay indoors a night like this. Foolish to sleep even.—You've got awfully pretty hands.

Ann. Thanks. My eyes are nice, too. They don't cross, or anything.

Pat. Say—you come right back at a fellow, don't you?

Ann. Do I?

Pat. —Ever read a poem called "Pale hands I loved beside the Shal-i-mar"?

Ann. [*Suspiciously.*] What about it?

Pat. I just wondered. Didn't you like it?

Ann. I thought it was awful.

Pat. Why?

Ann. I don't know. I just did.

Pat. You're a funny girl. Maybe you don't like poetry.

Ann. —Maybe I do! [*He laughs.*] I like the way you laugh.

Pat. I'll hire me a couple of expert ticklers. [*And then they both laugh.*]

Ann. You have awfully white teeth, haven't you? [*Suddenly* PAT *frowns.*]

Pat. —What?

Ann. I said, you have——

Pat. [*Slowly.*] I know—I'm trying to think: there was someone with white teeth that gleamed from the water—Oh, never mind. [*Another moment. Then:*]—Funny, our meeting like this. I suppose that's the way good things happen.

Ann. Maybe.—I wish you'd brought a crutch, though, or a wheel-chair.

[*He eyes her reflectively.*]

Pat. How much do you weigh?

Ann. Something fairly serious—or I did. Tonight I've walked a good deal of it off.

Pat. We've got to do something about moving you.

Ann. I hoped you'd get around to that.

Pat. That is, eventually. There's lots of time.—Say, are you moody?

Ann. Maybe.—Am I ?

Pat. Because I am. That's why I got to walking tonight. I had something on my mind.

Ann. So had I.

Pat. Really? What?

Ann. My father.

Pat. Is he—is he sick?

Ann. I don't know.—What is it that worried you?

Pat. [*A moment.*] —Well, you see, at Christmas I came down with the Copes——

Ann. Are they like the measles?

[PAT *laughs, and explains:*]

Pat. —Down *here,* with Johnny and Nora Cope. Well, one night we were coming home quite late from somewheres and we stopped in at the dog-wagon in the village to get— [*He stops suddenly and stares at her.*] Jeerusalem! I believe you're her!

Ann. "She," you should say.—Who?

Pat. [*Overcome with awe.*] Good Lord Almighty——

Ann. I wonder if it's the same dog-wagon I know.

Pat. Of course!—But this is—Gosh! Do you know what this means to me?

Ann. I'm trying awfully hard to follow, but——

Pat. [*Still staring.*] I had a Western, with a lot of onions, and we got up to go and there was a girl there sitting at the counter with a couple of other people and a great big glass of milk and she looked up as I went by, and——

[ANN *smiles.*]

Ann. I did, didn't I?

Pat. [*Excitedly.*] Yes!—and the milk had made a little white rim along your upper lip and——

Ann. [*Distressed.*] Oh dear——

Pat. It was beautiful.—And ever since, I've seen your face the whole time, in my mind, and I could never find you. It's been terrible.—And now—Oh Lord!—Imagine!

[ANN *smiles.*]

Ann. Well—here I am.

Pat. It's just miraculous, that's all, it's miraculous. Gosh, I don't know what to say. You know this isn't like the usual—there's something terribly right about it.—Ever since that night I've been longing to—Jeez, I thought I'd go crazy if I couldn't find you —been longing to take your face in my hands like this, and——

[*He takes her face between his hands.*]

Ann. Wait. Let me look at you.

[*She looks.*]

Pat. I'm not much on looks——

Ann. Shhh! [*She looks a longer time.*] Why—it's the queerest thing. I think I——

Pat. —And to kiss that lovely mouth that had the white rim along the top of it——

Ann. But somehow—I don't think you'd better—yet——

Pat. No, I suppose not.—But I don't see why! [*A moment. Still they gaze at each other. Then:*] Look: do you ever get a feeling that you—oh, Lord—that you know all about it?

Ann. Sometimes.

Pat. I do now! I've never felt alive before! Everything's as clear as— [*Suddenly, directly.*] Look: I'll be at the Ames's for lunch tomorrow. Tell 'em I like steak.

[ANN *laughs.*]

Ann. I like *you!*

Pat. —As much as I like steak?

Ann. How much do you like steak?

Pat. I'm crazy for it. I dream about it. Well——?

[*Again* ANN *laughs, and rises.*]

Ann. Come on.

[*He catches her hand in his.*]

Pat. Ah, Ann—tell me, Ann!

Ann. No, no! This is ridiculous. It's——

[*She frees herself.*]

Pat. Oh, please! Tell me—do you like me?

[*A moment. Then:*]

Ann. Yes.

Pat. Much?

Ann. A lot. Terribly!

[*For* PAT *this is almost too much to bear.*]

Pat. Gosh, I'm glad.

Ann. I hope I'll be.—Come on—shall we?

Pat. Look: You've got to come up to the Spring Dance with me, and the ball games, and the boat races—I row Number Seven—and—oh, Ann——

Ann. What, Pat?

Pat. It's wonderful.

Ann. It is, it is.—Do come—come on——

[*They go on another step or two, toward the garden-steps, where again her ankle gives way. He catches her in his arms. She recovers herself and, still in his arms, turns and looks at him. For a long moment their eyes hold them together. At length they kiss. For an instant* ANN *clings to him, then leaves him.*] Pat—Pat—we're crazy.

Pat. No!

Ann. [*Breathlessly.*] Come on—— We must——

[*She takes his hand. He turns.*]

Pat. First, let's look back at our meadow.

[ANN *frowns, half puzzled, half in alarm. Then:*]

Ann. [*Suddenly, sharply.*] No! That's wrong!

[*He had not said that. The spell is breaking.*]

Pat. What is? [*He takes a deep breath.*] —Um! Doesn't it smell good, though! What is it? Hawthorn?

Ann. No!

Pat. [*Slowly, from very far away.*] But I—I guess they're right. I guess there's nothing like May in England—— [*Suddenly he stops, releasing her hand. His face becomes troubled. He looks at the house, frowning.*] What's that house?

Ann. [*A sudden cry:*] Don't think, Pat! Don't think at all! Come with me——

Pat. —But there's something I've got to do in this house.

Ann. No!

Pat. Yes. And I can't think what. And it's terribly important. I've waited too long. It's got to be done at once. It's getting late. —I know!—I've got to pack a bag. It's late. I've got to get that bag packed. I've got to pack a bag and catch a boat and go to England.

[ANN *is still at the garden-steps. His eyes have not left the house.*]

Ann. Stay with me, Pat! I'll lose you there!

Pat. I tell you she's waiting, and it's getting late.

[*Again he moves toward the house.*]

Ann. Oh, why must I always lose you?

[*She goes up the garden-steps and out.* PAT *advances further toward the house, but* STEPHEN *rises.*]

Stephen. Pat!

[PAT *halts, turns slowly, looks at him, then goes to him.*]

Pat. Why—why, how do you do, Mr. Carr? I feel as if I'd been away for—I came across the fields and down the lane—the hawthorn's early, isn't it? I didn't wire. I thought I'd surprise her. How has she been?

Stephen. You cannot surprise her.

Pat. You mean she had a hunch that I was——? But where is she, then? I've been calling her all over everywhere. [STEPHEN *does not reply. Suddenly* PAT *becomes alarmed.*] Say, what is this—a joke? Because if it is—yes, and what about my letters? Why didn't she answer them? Did you and Father fix it so she wouldn't get them? I've been almost crazy. I've been—where is she? She's here—I know she's here——[*He calls:*] Ann! [*Then feeling something wrong, whispers:*] Mary. [*Then, more confidently:*] It's Pat, Mary! [*He turns again to* STEPHEN.]—And you needn't think we're going to stay on with people who fixed it up to separate us, either. Not for one minute. I'm going to take her with me this very night, and——

Stephen. That is too soon.

Pat. It's not. Haven't we waited years already? We'll be wanting to get married right away. Tomorrow, most likely—or the next day——

Stephen. —Too soon.

Pat. Look here, Mr. Carr—— [*Then correcting himself.*] Mr. Field—I know you're a sick man. But Ann's got her whole life ahead of her. You can't take it from her. You've taken too much of it already. I don't hold with those old ideas. Ann and I are in love, and if you don't grant that that's the most important thing, it's time you did. I'm sorry to have to put it this way, but I've got to speak as I feel. I'll certainly never expect a child of mine to—to——

Stephen. —To what?

Pat. —To give her whole life up to me, and I don't think you should.

Stephen. I see.

Pat. You let her bring you here, away from all the——

Stephen. —She has needed me as much these last three years as I have needed her.

Pat. That may be. But——

Stephen. Wait! [*He looks at* PAT *intently, then speaks with a slow emphasis.*] —But now she does not need me any longer.

Pat. What are you looking like that for? What do you mean? [*Then suddenly, wildly:*] She's not! That's not true—you're lying. It's not possible—it can't be! She's here—I know she's here. [*Again he calls:*] Ann! Ann!

Stephen. She does not come.

Pat. Ann, dear! It's Pat, Ann!

Stephen. And still she does not come.

Pat. Oh, don't keep saying that! She's here—I can feel her all about me. [*He wheels about and looks around him.*] What kind of a deal is this, anyway? What am I doing—dreaming? [*Then one last despairing cry:*] Ann! [*And a long silence. Finally:*]—Because she thought I wasn't coming back—— [*Another moment. Then, in anguish:*]—I can't believe—but how?—*how* did she? She couldn't have hurt that sweet place at her temple, that lovely breast. What has death to do with her?

Stephen. —With anyone.

Pat. But I did come back! I wasn't the swine she thought me. I did come—she must know that. I'm sure she knows it!

Stephen. So then, you have your picture back——

Pat. My picture?

Stephen. The one you love so—your picture of yourself. Now your pet illusion is whole again, and all is well, eh?

Pat. I don't know what you're——

Stephen. You built your whole life upon an illusion—and it went—and still you want it back—from death, even!

Pat. I don't know what you're talking about.

Stephen. Your idea of your own perfection.

Pat. That's not true——

Stephen. No?—You came back, yes—but in your own time. A swine? Indeed you are!—But what brought you? How much of it was the self-contempt you felt for having left her?

Pat. None of it.

Stephen. —And how much your love of her, your want of her?

Pat. All!

Stephen. Which is it you can't live with, now? Which is it that spoils your picture?

Pat. Oh, be still about my picture! You're talking about a spoiled boy, stuffed with what he thought were fine ideals. Fakes, all of them! I've left that boy behind. I've got no picture any more. I know I'm what I am —myself!

Stephen. Then can you face yourself—say good-by to your last illusion, and come through alive?

Pat. Go—will you?

Stephen. If you cannot—what else is there for you? [*A moment. Then:*]

Pat. [*To himself.*] —Off to Africa.

Stephen. Well——?

[PAT *moves toward the garden-steps.*]

Pat. Off to——! [*But half way up the steps, he stops. When he speaks, it is with a fine, saving scorn.*]—One big last shining gesture, eh? Watching myself go by. Another pretty picture: "He died for love." [*He raises his head.*] No!—That's for the weak ones. I stay.

Stephen. [*A murmur.*] That's right, that's right.

[*He leaves him, and moves painfully toward his corner.*]

Pat. But I want her so. Ann—Ann——

[FELIX *comes in from house.*]

Felix. Pardon, Monsieur—je regrette que j'avais laissé passer l'heure. Maintenant, il est onze heures moins douze. Je regrette beaucoup, Monsieur. C'est ma faute.

[PAT *does not reply.* FELIX *goes out. A moment, then* ANN'S *voice is heard softly, from the garden:*]

Ann. Pat?

Pat. [*A cry of joy.*] Ann! [*In an instant he is up the garden-steps and out.*] I'll find you this time. Ann!

[STEPHEN *gropes for his chair in the corner and seats himself.*]

Stephen. —All right, you. Very well—I am ready. This ends, and that begins.—Oh, so you'd like to end it, would you? All of it, eh? [*He half rises, gasping for breath.*] Well, you can't!—I tell you—you cannot! [*Gasping.*] I tell you——!

[*There is a slight shuffling sound, as he slumps into death. A moment. Then* TOM *comes in from the garden with the brandy-glass, as* FELIX *enters from the house and crosses the terrace toward him, with three traveling-bags.*]

Felix. Pardon, Monsieur——

[*He goes up the garden-steps and out.* HOPE *comes in from the house. She is dressed to leave. She sees* TOM *and goes to him quickly.*]

Hope. Tom, Tom——

Tom. —I beg your pardon, but have you by any chance seen an old priest called Father—— [*Then he recognizes her.*] Why, why, hello, Hope——

Hope. —Who, did you say?

Tom. Why—I don't know—— [*He frowns at the brandy-glass.*] I thought I—I had this for someone—who was it? I was taking it to him, to—Lord *I* don't know—— [*He looks at her closer.*]—How are the children?

[LILY *comes in from the house, also dressed for departure.*]

Hope. —The children—that's good, that is!—Do you realize that that's just what you've been acting like?

Tom. [*To himself.*] —Under the piano. Under the——

[ALICE *comes down the stairs from the balcony. She wears a coat and carries a small traveling-bag.*]

Alice. Listen: could anyone tell me what's got into the Rose man?

Hope. Not Norman, too!

Alice. —I opened my door into the hall, and there he was, stretched on the floor outside it, fast asleep on a fur rug. [*She looks back over her shoulder.*]—And now he's——

[NORMAN *appears upon the balcony, the fur rug still over his arm.*]

Norman. [*Heartily.*] Well, everyone—how goes it?

Tom. What's that you've got?

Norman. How'd you like to——? [*He stops and frowns at the rug.*] Why, it's a ——[*His accent leaves him.*] Damned if I know.

[*He drops it, and cleans his fastidious hands of it.*]

Tom. Was it a bargain?

[NORMAN *looks at him sharply.*]

Norman. —Am I right in believing that some pretty funny business went on here tonight?

[*All look troubled, eyeing one another furtively, trying to figure out how much the other remembers, how much one remembers oneself.*]

Lily. [*Finally.*] Well, I don't know if you'd call it funny—but suddenly everything seems possible.—It's like beginning all over again. [ALICE *stretches upon her cushion.*]

Alice. I hope I didn't miss anything. I had a delicious nap.

Lily. —And did you dream?

Alice. Dream?—I should say not. I was too dead. [*Another silence. All stare in front of them. Finally* ALICE *speaks again, this time as if from a distance.*] Did I tell you?—Once when I was in England staying with the Potters, they had a—— [*Then suddenly, with an air of discovery.*]—Why, Norman! That was where I met you, wasn't it?

Norman. Yes.

Alice. —Strange. [*Again silence. Then:*]

Tom. At school the big idea used to be to sneak off in the afternoons and smoke real tobacco in real pipes.—Lord, how big that made us feel.

Norman. [*After another moment.*] —I often wonder what happened to old Morris Sterner. He gave me my first real job.—Once he told me that——

[*But he relapses into silence, which* LILY *at length breaks.*]

Lily. It's fantastic, this terrace. It just hangs here. Some day it will float off into space, and anchor there, like an island in time.

Hope. Don't!

Alice. Don't what?

Hope. Please, everyone make sense. It must be nearly time to leave.

Tom. Hope—— [*She turns to him.*] Would you mind awfully if I don't sail with you?

Hope. Why?

Tom. I want to go off somewhere by myself for a while. I think at last I've really got a line on something that may be the answer for me.

Hope. [*Unconvinced.*] Yes?

Tom. —In a way it's a kind of faith, in place of the old one—maybe it's the same. Anyhow, I want to work it out.

Hope. Sweet Tom.

[PAT *and* ANN *are nearing the terrace from the garden.* PAT'S *voice is heard.*]

Pat. There's so much I'd have gone without——

[*They come in, her hand in his, and stand together upon the garden-steps.*]

Tom. [*To* HOPE.] —I don't know how long it will take—but if I send for you——

[HOPE *smiles.*]

Hope. Don't come——

Tom. Don't come.

[*Now everyone is talking in concert.*]

Pat. —Without so many good, quiet things——

Tom. I'm excited about this, Hope.

Hope. So am I, Tom—if you do it.

Pat. [*To* ANN.] I want to sit with the wife I love, and read books, and look at maps——

Lily. You won't believe me when I tell you——

Alice. What?

Lily. Next year I'm going to play Cordelia in King Lear.

Pat. —And fish trout-streams with my boys, and take my daughter walking——

Hope. —What time is it, Norman? Oughtn't we be starting?

Norman. I'm not going to Paris.

[ALICE *glances at him in alarm.*]

Hope. Really!—And who was it who simply had to be home by the tenth for a corporation meeting?

Norman. They can meet without me. They can whistle for me. I'll be in Andorra.

Pat. [*To* ANN.] —And build a house and mend a fence, and be tired of a good day's work, and sleep——

[*Now they have come down the steps and joined the others.* ALICE *moves toward* NORMAN.]

Alice. Norman——

Norman. What, Alice?

Alice. I'll miss you.—Take me with you!

[NORMAN *starts forward.*]

Norman. You'd come?

Alice. Just ask me.

Norman. Alice——

Alice. —Darling.

Norman. *That's* the way to see Andorra!

[ALICE *and* NORMAN *keep on gazing at*

each other as if they could never look their fill.]

Tom. [*Suddenly.*] Now I know how it happened! [*To* ANN.] Where's your father?

[LILY *rises quickly, and stares toward* STEPHEN'S *chair, which conceals him from their view.*]

Ann. He must have gone down to the bastide.—Why?

Tom. Hotel Universe!—*He'll* know.

Ann. What?

Tom. Don't you know the story?

Ann. Oh—you mean about René Mayer's house——

Tom. I mean about this house——

Ann. You must be mixed, Tom. This was built in nineteen-twelve by a man from Lyons.

[*A moment.* TOM *gazes at her. Then:*]

Tom. Are you sure?

Ann. Oh, yes. Father leased it from him.

[LILY *starts back from* STEPHEN'S *chair with a sudden cry.*]

Lily. Pa!

Hope. Don't, Lily—please don't again——

Lily. Pat—Pat!. [*He goes to her.*]

Pat. What is it, Lily?

Lily. [*A moan.*] —I don't know, I don't know——

Ann. Lily—darling——

Lily. —I feel as if all that held me together had suddenly let go.

[*She begins to cry softly.*]

Ann. Lily—darling—don't!

Lily. It's all right—I'll be all right——

[FELIX *re-enters from the garden and goes to* PAT.]

Felix. Pardon, Monsieur—il est onze heures juste, Monsieur.

[HOPE *jumps up.*]

Hope. Eleven! We've got to fly!

[*They all talk together.*]

Alice. We'll probably be late at that.

Norman. Oh, no—not if we hurry.

Tom. You can make good time on these roads at night.

Felix. [*To* ANN.] Pardon, Mademoiselle, les valises sont dans les voitures.

Ann. —Your bags are all in.

Tom. Where's yours, Pat? Are you ready?

Lily. No! *You've* got to stay! Do you understand that?—You've got to stay!

Pat. Why yes, of course.—I'm not going.

[ANN *glances at him quickly.*]

Ann. Pat!

Pat. I'm staying, Ann.

Tom. Now there's a good idea!

Hope. I had a hunch Pat was no mountain-climber!

Norman. That's the stuff, Pat.

[HOPE *goes to* ANN *and kisses her.* ALICE *slips her arm through* NORMAN'S.]

Hope. Good-by, Ann.

Ann. Good-by, dear.

Tom. Good-by, Pat. Take it easy for a while.

Pat. Yes. Good-by, Tom.

Lily. Hurry, *hurry!*

[TOM *kisses* ANN.]

Tom. Good-by and thanks, Ann.—Say good-by to your father for me.

Hope. Yes.

Norman. Yes!

[TOM *frowns.*]

Tom. Say to him, that——

Lily. *Hurry, hurry!*

Tom. —Say good-by to him.

Norman. Do you want to come with us, Tom?

[TOM *turns upon the garden-steps.*]

Tom. To Andorra? Why, it sounds like a good idea.

Hope. No, no! Alone! You've got to go alone!

Tom. But Hope—you know what a friendly soul I am. You know how I need company.

Hope. [*To the others.*] What can you do with him?

[*They go out.* NORMAN *and* ALICE *mount the steps, calling over their shoulders:*]

Norman and Alice. Good-by! Thanks! Good-by! [PAT, ANN, *and* LILY *are left.*]

Lily. You two—you're for each other, aren't you?

Pat. I hope so.

Ann. Then we are.

Lily. [*To* ANN.] Your father—remember what he said? It does go on. [ANN *looks at her.*] Wherever we may be—breezes from the other fields still blow upon us——

Ann. Why, yes. Why do you——?

Lily. I think that's good to know. God love him. God love you. Good-by——

[*She mounts the steps, pauses for one brief instant to glance down at* STEPHEN, *then goes out into the garden.* PAT *and* ANN *are left alone.* ANN *touches his cheek.*]

Ann. Dear love.

Pat. I want to make love to you for years. Oh, it's a life, Ann!

Ann. I know, dear—don't I know! [*She murmurs.*] —Thank you, Father.

Pat. Yes—thanks! [*In the distance, far off in the garden, a cock crows hoarsely.* PAT *starts.*] What's that? What time is it?

Ann. Hush, darling, never mind.—It's just an old white rooster—one of Father's pets—his clock he calls him.

Pat. It must be dawn somewhere.

Ann. But of course, dear—always!

Pat. Wherever there is an end, he said——

Ann. —From it the beginning springs.

[*She stares straight in front of her, her apprehension growing in her eyes. Slowly, fearfully, her head turns in the direction of* STEPHEN. *Silence. Then again the cock exults.*]

CURTAIN

ELIZABETH THE QUEEN *

By

MAXWELL ANDERSON

MAXWELL ANDERSON HAS COME TO stand in the American theater for lofty rhetoric adapted to lofty themes. He has been attracted to historical or semi-historical subjects from the beginning of his playwriting career, as in *First Flight,* about young Andrew Jackson, or *The Buccaneer,* about Henry Morgan. To these plays of history, beginning with *Elizabeth the Queen,* and continuing through *Mary of Scotland, Valley Forge, The Wingless Victory, The Masque of Kings, Journey to Jerusalem,* he has fitted an easy, flowing, eminently speakable form of verse. He has even dared use this verse for such plays of contemporary life as *Winterset* and *High Tor.* Mr. Anderson, it is clear, regards writing for the stage as a high art, capable of employing not merely the bare and broken half-utterances of naturalistic dialogue, but the highest resources of our speech.

He says, in his *Prelude to Poetry in the Theatre:*

"The best prose in the world is inferior on the stage to the best poetry. . . . Prose is the language of information and poetry the language of emotion . . . Under the strain of an emotion the ordinary prose of our stage breaks down into inarticulateness, just as it does in life. . . . It is incumbent on the dramatist to be a poet, and incumbent on the poet to be prophet, dreamer and interpreter of the racial dream. . . .

"When I wrote my first play, *White Desert,* I wrote it in verse because I was weary of plays in prose that never lifted from the ground. It failed, and I did not come back to verse again until I had discovered that poetic tragedy had never been successfully written about its own place and time. . . . With this admonition in mind I wrote *Elizabeth the Queen* and a succession of historical plays in verse . . . and found myself immediately labeled a historical and romantic playwright, two terms I found equally distasteful."

Mr. Anderson is justified by the record in denying the label "historical and romantic." Of the plays in his list, fewer than half are historical, though perhaps more could be counted as romantic. But if he is not an historical and romantic playwright, what is he?

He says the dramatist must be a prophet and interpreter of the racial dream. Prophet of what? What is the racial dream? It is difficult to find out from Mr. Anderson's work the answers to these questions. Perhaps Mr. Anderson would say that he has at least told what the racial dream is not. It is not political chicanery (*Both Your Houses*), or commercialism (*High Tor* and *The Star-Wagon*), or injustice (*Gods of the Lightning* and *Winterset*), or Puritanism (*The Wingless Victory*). But these negatives scarcely define a racial dream. The racial dream can not be expressed, either, in such plays of purely personal bearing as *Gypsy*, or *Saturday's Children.* Probably, whether he likes it or not, Mr. Anderson comes closer to giving us his vision of the racial dream in plays like *Elizabeth the Queen* or *Journey to Jerusalem* than he does in his more topical works. In the historical plays the re-creation of the past by the imagination permits the poetry to reach more directly to the unconscious, racial mind; in them, as in no play of our own time, we are made free to dream.

Elizabeth the Queen was first performed by the Theatre Guild in 1930, with Alfred Lunt as Essex and Lynn Fontanne as Elizabeth. The settings were designed by Lee Simonson, who has described his production of the play most interestingly in *The Stage Is Set.*

In 1938 Mr. Anderson joined with Elmer Rice, S. N. Behrman, Robert Sherwood, and Sidney Howard in forming the Playwright's Company to produce the plays written by members of the group.

MAXWELL ANDERSON

Born 1888, Atlantic, Pennsylvania.
1911, B. A., University of North Dakota.
1914, M. A., Leland Stanford, Jr., University.
Teacher and Journalist to 1924.
1933, *Both Your Houses* wins Pulitzer Prize.
1936, *Winterset* wins New York Drama Critics' Prize.
1937, *High Tor* wins New York Drama Critics' Prize.

PLAYS

1923 *White Desert.* 1924 *What Price Glory* (with Laurence Stallings). 1925 *Outside Looking In.* 1925 *First Flight* (with Laurence Stallings). 1925 *The Buccaneer* (with Laurence Stallings). 1927 *Saturday's Children.* 1928 *Gods of the Lightning* (with Harold Hickerson). 1929 *Gypsy.* 1930 *Elizabeth the Queen.* 1932 *The Sea-Wife.* 1932 *Night over Taos.* 1933 *Both Your Houses.* 1933 *Mary of Scotland.* 1934 *Valley Forge.* 1935 *Winterset.* 1936 *The Wingless Victory.* 1937 *High Tor.* 1937 *The Masque of Kings.* 1937 *The Feast of Ortolans* (a radio drama). 1937 *The Star-Wagon.* 1938 *Second Overture* (a radio drama). 1938 *Knickerbocker Holiday* (musical comedy). 1939 *Key Largo.* 1940 *Journey to Jerusalem.*

WRITINGS ABOUT THE DRAMA

Prelude to Poetry in the Theatre—Preface to *Winterset*, 1935. *The Politics of 'Knickerbocker Holiday,'* 1938. Both the preceding reprinted in *The Essence of Tragedy*, 1939. Preface to *Journey to Jerusalem*, 1940.

ELIZABETH THE QUEEN

Characters

In the Order of Appearance

SIR WALTER RALEIGH.
PENELOPE GRAY.
A CAPTAIN.
SIR ROBERT CECIL.
LORD ESSEX.
FRANCIS BACON.
QUEEN ELIZABETH.
LORD BURGHLEY.
LORD HOWARD.
THE FOOL.
CAPTAIN ARMIN.
MARY.
ELLEN.
TRESSA.
MARVEL.
A COURIER.
A HERALD.
BURBAGE.
HEMMINGS.
FALSTAFF.
PRINCE HENRY.
GADSHILL.
PETO.
POINS.
} *Players in the scene from Henry IV*
ALSO GUARDS, MEN-AT-ARMS, MAIDS-IN-WAITING, AND OTHERS.

ACT ONE

SCENE I

SCENE.—*An entrance hall before a council chamber in the palace at Whitehall.*
[*The entrance to the council room is closed and four* GUARDS *with halberds stand at either side. A small door at the left of the entrance is also shut. It is early morning. The* GUARDS *stand immobile.*]

First Guard. The sun's out again, and it's guineas to pounds the earl comes back this morning.

Second Guard. I'll be glad of it, for one. You get nothing but black looks about the court when he's away.

First Guard. You'll get little else now he's back, my bully. They quarrelled too far for mending, this time.

Third Guard. Tut! They quarrel no more than the cock with the hen. The earl's been sick.

First Guard. Sick of the queen's displeasure. It's a disease a favorite can die of, and many have.

Fourth Guard. He's no sicker of her displeasure than she of his, if a man may judge. Once the earl's gone there's no dancing, no plays, no feasting . . . nothing to do nights but sleep. The very scullery-maids grow cold, and go to bed alone—like the queen.

First Guard. There are some even a scullery-maid would seldom kiss, save in moments of great excitement. Poor Wat looks forward to feast nights.

Fourth Guard. I've had my luck.

First Guard. You've had what was coming to you. Mucklemouth Jean, of the back kitchen.

Fourth Guard. You'd have been glad of her yourself if you could have had her.

First Guard. Consider, man. She may not have been true. When she wouldn't play with you, mayhap she was playing with somebody else. And if the queen could live without her Earl of Essex, it may have been because Sir Walter had a new suit of silver armor.

Third Guard. And there's a handsome man.

Fourth Guard. God defend me from speaking lightly of the queen!

First Guard. Eh? God defend you? Let no man accuse me of speaking lightly of the queen, nor of any other woman . . . unless she be a light woman, in which case, God defend me, I will speak lightly of her if I choose.

Third Guard. What say you of the queen?

First Guard. Of the queen? I say she is well-known to be the virgin queen; I say no more.

Second Guard. But do you think she is a virgin?

First Guard. She has doubtless been a virgin, bully, for all women have been virgins, but the question is: First, when . . . and, second, where?

Second Guard. Where?

First Guard. Where, bully, where?

Third Guard. Would you not say, in the proper place?

First Guard. No. I would not say in the proper place. Because it is hard to say if there is a proper place wherein to be a virgin . . . unless it be in church, and, God defend me, I do not go to church.

Second Guard. You do not go to church?

First Guard. No, for my sins, I do not go to church . . . or, if you like, I do not go to church for my sins.

Second Guard. Does it follow that the church is a proper place for virgins?

First Guard. It does. Did I not tell you I do not go there for my sins?

Fourth Guard. They say the queen's getting to be an old woman; but I swear she looks younger than my wife, whom I married a young thing, six years come Easter.

Third Guard. It would age a girl fast, just the look of you.

First Guard. As for the queen, powder and paint account for some of it. To say nothing of the earl. A young lover will do much for a lady's face.

Fourth Guard. Now God defend me . . .

First Guard. Aye, aye . . . God defend poor Wat.

[*A* NOBLEMAN *enters in silver armor. It is* SIR WALTER RALEIGH, *no other.*]

Raleigh. Has the queen come forth yet?

First Guard. No, Sir Walter.

Raleigh. The Earl of Essex . . . is he here?

First Guard. No, my lord.

Raleigh. When he comes send me word. I shall be in the north corridor. [*He turns.*]

First Guard. Good, my lord.

[PENELOPE GRAY *comes in from the right, passing through.*]

Raleigh. [*Meeting her.*] Greetings, lady, from my heart.

Penelope. Good morrow, lord, from my soul.

Raleigh. I take my oath in your face that you are rushing to the window to witness the arrival of my lord of Essex.

Penelope. And in your teeth I swear I am on no such errand . . . but only to see the sun-rise.

Raleigh. The sun has been up this hour, my dear.

Penelope. The more reason to hurry, gracious knight.

Raleigh. Do you think to pull the bag over my head so easily, Penelope? On a day when the earl returns every petticoat in the palace is hung with an eye to pleasing him. Yours not the least.

Penelope. I deny him thrice.

Raleigh. I relinquish you, lady. Run, run to the window! He will be here and you will miss him!

Penelope. Is there a lady would run from Sir Walter in his silver suiting? Since the sun is up . . . I have no errand.

Raleigh. Is there no limit to a woman's deception, wench? Would you go so far as to appear pleased if I kissed you?

Penelope. And no deception. [*He kisses her.*] I call the Gods to witness . . . did I not blush prettily?

Raleigh. And meant it not at all. Tell me, did the queen send you to look out the casement for news of her Essex, or did you come at the prompting of your heart?

Penelope. Shall I tell you the truth?

Raleigh. Verily.

Penelope. The truth is I cannot answer.

Raleigh. Both, then?

Penelope. Both or one or neither.

Raleigh. Fie on the baggage.

Penelope. Is it not a virtue to be close-mouthed in the queen's service?

Raleigh. If you kept the rest of your person as close as your mouth what a paragon of virtue you would be!

Penelope. Indeed, my lord, I am.

Raleigh. Indeed, my lady? Have there not been certain deeds on dark nights?

Penelope. Sh! Under the rose.

Raleigh. Meaning under covers . . .

Penelope. Fie on my lord, to make me out a strumpet!

Raleigh. It is my manner of wooing, fair maid! I woo by suggestion of images . . .

Penelope. Like small boys on the closet wall . . .

Raleigh. Like a soldier . . .

Penelope. Aye, a veteran . . . of encounters . . .

Raleigh. I will have you yet, my love; I will take lessons from this earl . . .

Penelope. Take this lesson from me, my lord: You must learn to desire what you would have. Much wanting makes many a maid a wanton. You want me not . . . nor I you. You wear your silver for a queen.

[*A* CAPTAIN *enters from the left.*]

Captain. Good-morrow, Sir Walter. Is the queen still under canopy?

Raleigh. I know not.

Captain. The earl is here and would see her.

Raleigh. Bid him hurry if he wishes to find her abed as usual.

Penelope. She is dressed and stirring, captain, and awaits my lord.

Raleigh. And many another fair maid awaits him likewise, captain. Take him that message from me. Run, girl, run. Tell the queen.

[*The* CAPTAIN *goes out left.*]

Penelope. [*Going.*] You make yourself so easily disliked.

[*She goes right.* CECIL *enters, passing her.*]

Cecil. He is here?

Raleigh. So. The heavenly boy, clad in the regalia of the sun, even now extracts his gallant foot from his golden stirrup and makes shift to descend from his heaving charger. Acclamation lifts in every voice, tears well to every eye . . . with the exception of mine, perhaps, and yours, I hope . . .

Cecil. I am at a pass to welcome him, myself. This Elizabeth of ours can be difficult on her good days . . . and there have been no good ones lately.

[*Two* MEN-AT-ARMS *enter with silver armor in their arms.*]

Raleigh. And what is all this, sirrah?

First Man. Armor, my lord.

Raleigh. For whom?

First Man. We know not.

Raleigh. Now by the ten thousand holy names! Am I mistaken, Robert, or is this armor much like my own?

Cecil. Very like, I should say. Is it sterling?

Raleigh. And the self-same pattern. Has the earl gone lunatic?

Cecil. He means to outshine you, perhaps.

Raleigh. Has it come to this? Do I set the style for Essex?
That would be a mad trick, to dress himself like me!

[BACON *appears in the doorway at right.*]

What do you know of this, Sir Francis?

Bacon. Greeks, my lord, bearing gifts.

Raleigh. To hell with your Greeks! The devil damn him!
This is some blackguardry!

[*Two more* MEN-AT-ARMS *enter, carrying armor.*]

There's more of it! Good God, it comes in bales!
I say, who's to wear this, sirrah? Who is it for?

[ESSEX *enters from corridor between the two files of soldiers, pushing them aside as he does so, and crosses to right of* RALEIGH, *speaking as he enters.*]

Essex. Their name is legion, Sir Walter. Happily met!
Felicitations on your effulgence, sir!
You're more splendid than I had imagined. News came of your silver
Even in my retreat! I was ill, and I swear it cured me!
You should have heard the compliments I've heard
Passed on you! Sir Walter's in silver! The world's outdone,
They said—the moon out-mooned. He gleams down every corridor
And every head's turned after him. The queen
Herself has admired it—the design—the workmanship!
There's nothing like it this side of Heaven's streets.
And I said to myself—the great man—this is what we have needed——
More silver everywhere—oceans of silver!
Sir Walter has set the style, the world will follow.
So I sent for the silver-smiths, and by their sweat
Here's for you, lads, tailored to every man's measure——
Shall Raleigh wear silver alone? Why, no,
The whole court shall go argent!

Raleigh. Take care, my lord.
I bear insults badly.

Essex. And where are you insulted?
For the queen's service you buy you a silver armor.
In the queen's service I buy you a dozen more.
A gift, my friends, each man to own his own,
As you own yours. What insult?

Raleigh. Have your laugh,
Let the queen and court laugh with you! Since you are envious
You may have my suit. I had not thought even Essex
Bore so petty a mind.

Essex. I misunderstood you
Perhaps, Sir Walter. I had supposed you donned
Silver for our queen, but I was mistaken . . .
Keep these all for yourself. The men shall have others . . .
Some duller color.

Raleigh. I have borne much from you
Out of regard for the queen, my lord of Essex.

Essex. And I from you.
By God . . .

Cecil. You have forgotten, Sir Walter,
A certain appointment . . .

Raleigh. And you will bear more, by Heaven! . . .
Cecil. He is going to the queen,
Remember. And we have an errand.
Essex. You presume to protect me,
Master Secretary?
Cecil. I protect you both, and our mistress.
There can be no quarreling here.
Raleigh. That's very true. Let us go.
[CECIL *and* RALEIGH *go out right.*]
Bacon. And this armor? What becomes of it?
Essex. I have given it.
Would you have me take it back?
Bacon. There has seldom been
A man so little wise, so headstrong, but he
Could sometimes see how necessary it is
To keep friends and not make enemies at court.
But you . . . God knows.
Essex. Let him make friends with me.
He may need friends himself.
[*To the* GUARDS.] These are your armors.
Keep them, wear them, sell them, whatever you like . . .
Or your captain directs you.
First Guard. We thank you.
[*They retire to examine the armor.*]
Bacon. You are going to the queen?
Essex. Yes. God help us both!
Bacon. Then hear me a moment. . . .
Essex. Speak, schoolmaster,
I knew it was coming. You've been quiet too long.
Bacon. Listen to me this once, and listen this once
To purpose, my lord, or it may hardly be worth
My while ever to give you advice again
Or for you to take it. You have enough on your hands
Without quarrelling with Raleigh. You have quarrelled with the queen
Against my judgment. . . .
Essex. God and the devil! Can a man
Quarrel on order or avoid a quarrel at will?
Bacon. Why certainly, if he knows his way.
Essex. Not I.
Bacon. You quarrelled with her, because she wished to keep peace.
And you wanted war. . . .
Essex. We are at war with Spain!
But such a silly, frightened, womanish war
As only a woman would fight. . . .
Bacon. She is a woman and fights a womanish war;
But ask yourself one question and answer it
Honestly, dear Essex, and perhaps you will see then
Why I speak sharply. You are my friend and patron.
Where you gain I gain . . . where you lose I lose . . .
And I see you riding straight to a fall today . . .
And I'd rather your neck weren't broken.
Essex. Ask myself
What question?
Bacon. Ask yourself what you want:
To retain the favor of the queen, remain
Her favorite, keep all that goes with this;
Or set yourself against her and trust your fortune
To popular favor?
Essex. I'll not answer that.
Bacon. Then . . . I have done.
Essex. Forgive me, dear friend, forgive me,
I have been ill, and this silly jackanapes
Of a Raleigh angers me with his silver mountings
Till I forget who's my friend. You know my answer
In regard to the queen. I must keep her favor.
Only it makes me mad to see all this . . .
This utter mismanagement, when a man's hand and brain
Are needed and cannot be used.
Bacon. Let me answer for you;
You are not forthright with yourself. The queen
Fights wars with tergiversation and ambiguities . . .
You wish to complete your record as general,
Crush Spain, subdue Ireland, make a name like Cæsar's,
Climb to the pinnacle of fame. Take care.
You are too popular already. You have
Won at Cadiz, caught the people's hearts,
Caught their voices till the streets ring your name
Whenever you pass. You are loved better than
The queen. That is your danger. She will not suffer
A subject to eclipse her; she cannot suffer it.
Make no mistake. She will not.
Essex. And I must wait,
Bite my nails in a corner, let her lose to Spain,
Keep myself back for policy?
Bacon. Even so.

Essex. I come of better blood than Elizabeth.
My name was among the earls around King John
Under the oak.* What the nobles have taught a king
A noble may teach a queen.

Bacon. You talk treason and death.
The old order is dead, and you and your house will die
With it if you cannot learn.

Essex. So said King John
Under the oak, or wherever he was standing,
And little he got by it, as you may recall.
What the devil's a king but a man, or a queen but a woman?

Bacon. King John is dead; this is Elizabeth,
Queen in her own right, daughter of a haughty line.
There is one man in all her kingdom she fears
And that man's yourself, and she has good reason to fear you.
You're a man not easily governed, a natural rebel,
Moreover, a general, popular and acclaimed,
And, last, she loves you, which makes you the more to be feared,
Whether you love her or not.

Essex. I do love her! I do!

Bacon. My lord, a man as young as you——

Essex. If she were my mother's kitchen hag,
Toothless and wooden-legged, she'd make all others
Colorless.

Bacon. You play dangerously there, my lord.

Essex. I've never yet loved or hated
For policy nor a purpose. I tell you she's a witch——
And has a witch's brain. I love her, I fear her,
I hate her, I adore her——

Bacon. That side of it you must know
For yourself.

Essex. I will walk softly—here is my hand.
Distress yourself no more—I can carry myself.

Bacon. Only count not too much on the loves of queens.

Essex. I'll remember.

[CECIL *and* RALEIGH *reappear in the doorway at the right.* RALEIGH *is wearing ordinary armor and carries his silver suit.* ESSEX *looks at him, biting his lip.*]

Sir Walter, take care of your health!

Raleigh. My health, sir?

Essex. [*Going out.*] Wearing no silver, in this chilly weather.

Raleigh. [*Tossing his silver armor into the pile.*] Put that with the others.

First Guard. Are we to wear them, sir?

Raleigh. No. Melt them down and sell the silver. And thus see for yourself how soon a fool is parted from his money. Take station in the outer hall and carry this trash with you.

First Guard. Yes, sir.

[*The* GUARDS *go out right carrying the armor.*]

Raleigh. [*To* BACON.] And you, sir, you are his friend. . . .

Bacon. And yours, Sir Walter. . . .

Raleigh. It's the first I've heard of it, but if you're mine too, so much the better. Carry this news to him: his suits go to the melting-pot.

Bacon. Willingly, my lord, if I see him.
You have done quite properly.

Raleigh. I do not ask your commendation!

Bacon. No, but you have it.

[*He bows low and goes out to left.*]

Raleigh. There's the viper under our flower, this Francis.
He should be on the winning side.

Cecil. He will be yet . . .
Like all wise men. For myself, I no longer
Stomach Lord Essex. Every word he speaks
Makes me feel queasy.

Raleigh. Then why put up with him?

Cecil. The queen, my friend, the queen. What she wants she will have,
And she must have her earl.

Raleigh. Which does she love more,
Her earl or her kingdom?

Cecil. Yes, which? I have wondered.

Raleigh. Then you're less sapient
Than I've always thought you, Cecil. She loves her kingdom
More than all men, and always will. If he could
Be made to look like a rebel, which he's close to being . . .
And she could be made to believe it, which is harder,
You'd be first man in the council.

Cecil. And you would be? . . .

Raleigh. Wherever I turn he's stood
Square in my way! My life long here at court

* Essex refers to the signing of the Magna Carta, 1215.

He's snatched honor and favor from before my eyes
Till his voice and walk and aspect make me writhe . . .
There's a fatality in it!

Cecil. If he could be sent from England . . . we might have a chance
To come between them.

Raleigh. Would she let him go?

Cecil. No . . . but if he could be teased
And stung about his generalship till he was
Too angry to reflect. . . . Suppose you were proposed
As general for the next Spanish raid?

Raleigh. He would see it,
And so would she.

Cecil. Then if you were named
For the expedition to Ireland?

Raleigh. No, I thank you.
He'd let me go, and I'd be sunk in a bog
This next three hundred years. I've seen enough
Good men try to conquer Ireland.

Cecil. Then how would this be?
We name three men for Ireland of his own supporters;
He will oppose them, not wishing his party weakened
At the court. Then we ask what he suggests
And hint at his name for leader. . . .

Raleigh. Good so far.

Cecil. He will be angry and hint at your name; you will offer
To go if he will.

Raleigh. No. Not to Ireland.

Cecil. Yes!
Do you think he'd let you go with him and share
The military glory? It will go hard,
Having once brought up his name, if we do not manage
To ship him alone to Dublin.

Raleigh. We can try it, then,
Always remembering that no matter what
Is said . . . no matter what I say or you . . .
I do not go. You must get me out of that,
By Christ, for I know Ireland.

Cecil. I will. Be easy.

Raleigh. When is the council?

Cecil. At nine.

Raleigh. You'll make these suggestions?

Cecil. If you'll play up to them.

Raleigh. Count on me. I must look after
These silver soldiers.

Cecil. At nine then.

Raleigh. Count on me.

[*They go out in opposite directions.*]

CURTAIN

SCENE II

SCENE.—*The queen's study, which adjoins her bed-chambers and the council hall. It is a severe little room, with chairs, a desk, and a few books, huge and leather-bound.*

[PENELOPE *comes in from the bed-chamber and looks out through a curtain opposite. She returns to the chamber, then re-enters to wait.* ESSEX *enters.*]

Penelope. [*Rising.*] Good-morrow, my lord.

Essex. Good-morrow, Penelope. Have I kept the queen?

Penelope. If so, would I acknowledge it?

Essex. I commend me to your discretion.

Penelope. Only to my discretion?

Essex. Take her what message you will . . . only let it be that I am here.

Penelope. May I have one moment, my lord? She is not quite ready.

Essex. As many as you like. What is it, my dear?

Penelope. Do you love the queen?

Essex. Is that a fair question, as between maid and man?

Penelope. An honest question.

Essex. Then I will answer honestly. Yes, my dear.

Penelope. Dearly?

Essex. Yes.

Penelope. I would you loved someone who loved you better.

Essex. Meaning . . . whom?

Penelope. Meaning . . . no one. Myself, perhaps. That's no one. Or . . . anyone who loved you better.

Essex. Does she not love me, sweet?

Penelope. She loves you, loves you not, loves you, loves you not. . . .

Essex. And why do you tell me this?

Penelope. Because I am afraid.

Essex. For me?

Penelope. I have heard her when she thought she was alone, walk up and down her room soundlessly, night long, cursing you . . . cursing you because she must love you and could not help herself . . . swearing to be even with you for this love she scorns to bear you. My lord, you anger her too much.

Essex. But is this not common to lovers?

Penelope. No, I have never cursed you. And I have good cause.

Essex. But if I were your lover, you would, sweet. So thank God I am not.

Penelope. I must go and tell her you are here. [*She lifts her face to be kissed.*] Good-by.

Essex. Good-by, my dear. [*He kisses her.*] And thank you.

Penelope. Will you beware of her?

Essex. Lover, beware your lover, might well be an old maxim. I will beware.

Penelope. For I am afraid.

[*A* MAID-IN-WAITING *appears in the doorway.*]

Maid. Her Majesty is ready.

Penelope. I will tell her my lord is here.

[*She runs out hastily.* ELIZABETH *enters, signing imperiously to the* MAID, *who disappears. There is a moment's silence.*]

Elizabeth. When we met last it was, as I remember,
Ill-met by moonlight, sir.

Essex. Well-met by day,
My queen.

Elizabeth. I had hardly hoped to see you again,
My lord of Essex, after what was vowed
Forever when you left.

Essex. You are unkind
To remind me.

Elizabeth. I think I also used
The word forever, and meant it as much, at least . . .
Therefore, no apology. Only my Penelope
Passed me just now in the door with eyes and lips
That looked the softer for kissing. I'm not sure
But I'm inopportune.

Essex. She's a crazy child.

Elizabeth. A child! That's for me, too, no doubt! These children
Have their little ways with each other!

Essex. Must we begin
With charges and counter-charges, when you know. . . .

Elizabeth. Do I indeed? . . .
You have been gone a week, at this Wanstock of yours . . .
And a week's a long time at court. You forget that I
Must live and draw breath whether I see you or not . . .
And there are other men and women, oh yes, all fully
Equipped for loving and being loved! Penelope . . .
You find Penelope charming. And as for me
There's always Mountjoy . . . or Sir Walter . . . the handsome,
Sir Walter, the silver-plated . . .

Essex. He'll wear no more
Silver at your door.

Elizabeth. What have you done . . . come, tell me.
I knew this silver would draw fire. What happened?

Essex. Nothing . . . but the fashion's gone out.

Elizabeth. No, but tell me!

Essex. He happened to be in the way
When the upstairs pot was emptied.
He's gone to change his clothes.

Elizabeth. You shall not be allowed
To do this to him . . .

Essex. [*Moving toward her.*] You shall not be allowed
To mock me, my queen. [*He kisses her.*]

Elizabeth. Isn't it strange how one man's kiss can grow
To be like any other's . . . or a woman's
To be like any woman's?

Essex. Not yours for me,
No, and not mine for you, you lying villain,
You villain and queen, you double-tongued seductress,
You bitch of brass!

Elizabeth. Silver, my dear. Let me be
A bitch of silver. It reminds me of Raleigh.

Essex. Damn you!

Elizabeth. Damn you and double-damn you for a damner!
Come some day when I'm in the mood. What day's this? . . .
Thursday? Try next Wednesday . . . or any Wednesday
Later on in the summer . . . Any summer
Will do. Why are you still here?

Essex. Oh, God, if I could but walk out that door
And stay away!

Elizabeth. It's not locked.

Essex. But I'd come back!
Where do you think I've been this last week? Trying,
Trying not to be here! But you see, I am here.

Elizabeth. Yes, I see.

Essex. Why did you plague me without a word?

Elizabeth. Why did you not come?

Essex. You are a queen, my queen. You had proscribed me.
Sent formal word I'd not be admitted if I came.

Elizabeth. I may have meant it at the time.

Essex. I think I have a demon, and you are it!

Elizabeth. If ever a mocking devil tortured a woman

You're my devil and torture me! Let us part and quickly,
Or there'll be worse to come. Go.

Essex. I tell you I will not.

Elizabeth. Come to me, my Essex. Let us be kind
For a moment. I will be kind. You need not be.
You are young and strangely winning and strangely sweet.
My heart goes out to you wherever you are.
And something in me has drawn you. But this same thing
That draws us together hurts and blinds us until
We strike at one another. This has gone on
A long while. It grows worse with the years. It will end badly.
Go, my dear, and do not see me again.

Essex. All this
Is what I said when last I went away.
Yet here I am.

Elizabeth. Love someone else, my dear.
I will forgive you.

Essex. You mean you would try to forgive me.

Elizabeth. Aye, but I would.

Essex. What would you have to forgive?
I have tried to love others. It's empty as ashes.

Elizabeth. What others?

Essex. No one.

Elizabeth. What others?

Essex. Everyone.

Elizabeth. Everyone?

Essex. That too has been your triumph! What is a cry
Of love in the night, when I am sick and angry
And care not? I would rather hear your mocking laughter——
Your laughter—mocking at me—defying me
Ever to be happy—with another.

Elizabeth. You have done this to me?

Essex. You have done this to me! You've made it all empty
Away from you! And with you too!

Elizabeth. And me—what of me while you were gone?

Essex. If we
Must quarrel when we meet, why then, for God's sake,
Let us quarrel. At least we can quarrel together.

Elizabeth. I think if we are to love we must love and be silent——
For when we speak——

Essex. I'll be silent then.
And you shall speak——

Elizabeth. [*Her finger to her lips.*] Hush!

Essex. If you would sometimes heed me ——

Elizabeth. Hush!

Essex. Only sometimes—only when I'm right. If you would
Say to yourself that even your lover might be
Right sometimes, instead of flying instantly
Into opposition as soon as I propose
A shift in policy!

Elizabeth. But you were wrong! You were wrong!
A campaign into Spain's pure madness, and to strike at Flanders
At the same moment . . . think of the drain in men
And the drain on the treasury, and the risks we'd run
Of being unable to follow success or failure
For lack of troops and money . . . !

Essex. [*Letting his arms fall.*] But why lack money . . .
And why lack men? There's no richer country in Europe
In men or money than England! It's this same ancient
Unprofitable niggardliness that pinches pennies
And wastes a world of treasure! You could have all Spain,
And Spain's dominions in the new world, an empire
Of untold wealth . . . and you forgo them because
You fear to lay new taxes!

Elizabeth. I have tried that . . .
And never yet has a warlike expedition
Brought me back what it cost!

Essex. You've tried half-measures . . .
Raids on the Spanish coast, a few horsemen sent
Into Flanders and out again, always defeating
Yourself by trying too little! What I plead for
Is to be bold once, just once, give the gods a chance
To be kind to us . . . walk through this cobweb Philip
And take his lazy cities with a storm
Of troops and ships!
If we are to trifle we might better sit
At home forever, and rot!

Elizabeth. Here we sit then,
And rot, as you put it.

Essex. I'm sorry. . . .

Elizabeth. It seems to me
We rot to some purpose here. I have kept the peace
And kept my people happy and prosperous.

Essex. And at what a price . . .
What a cowardly price!

Elizabeth. I am no coward, either.
It requires more courage not to fight than to fight
When one is surrounded by hasty hot-heads, urging
Campaigns in all directions.

Essex. Think of the name
You will leave. . . . They will set you down in histories
As the weasel queen who fought and ran away,
Who struck one stroke, preferably in the back,
And then turned and ran. . . .

Elizabeth. Is it my fame you think of,
Or your own, my lord? Have you not built your name
High enough? I gave you your chance at Cadiz,
And you took it, and now there's no name in all England
Like yours to the common people. When we ride in the streets
Together, it's Essex they cheer and not their queen.
What more would you have?

Essex. Is it for fear of me
And this hollow cheering you hold me back from Spain?

Elizabeth. It's because I believe in peace, and have no faith
In wars or what wars win.

Essex. You do not fear me?

Elizabeth. Yes, and I fear you, too! You believe yourself
Fitter to be king than I to be queen! You are flattered
By this crying of your name by fools! You trust me no more
Than you'd trust . . . Penelope . . . or any other woman
To be in power! You believe you'd rule England better
Because you're a man!

Essex. That last is true. I would.
And that doesn't mean I don't love you . . . remember that.
I love you, my queen, madly, beyond all measure,
But that's not to say I cannot see where you fail
As sovereign here, and see that why you fail
When you do is merely because a woman cannot
Act and think like a man.

Elizabeth. Act and think like a man . . . !
Why should I
Think like a man when a woman's thinking's wiser?
What do you plan? To depose me, take over the kingdom?

Essex. [*Smiling.*] You are a touchy queen.

Elizabeth. I had bad bringing up.
I was never sure who my mother was going to be
Next day, and it shook my nerves.

Essex. You're your father's daughter,
I'll swear to that. I can tell by your inconstancy.

Elizabeth. I wish you had need
To fear for me . . . or at any rate that I'd never
Let you see how much I'm yours.

Essex. But why?

Elizabeth. Tell me, my dear,
Do you tire of me . . . do I wear upon you a little?

Essex. Never.

Elizabeth. But you'd have to say that, you can see . . .
You'd have to say it, because you wouldn't hurt me,
And because I'm your queen. And so I'll never know
Until everyone else has known and is laughing at me,
When I've lost you. Wait, let me say this, please . . . When the time
Does come, and I seem old to you, and you love
Someone else, tell me, tell me the first . . .

Essex. You are not old! I will not have you old!

Elizabeth. Will you do that, in all kindness, in memory
Of great love past? No. You could not, could not.
It's not in a man to be kind that way, nor in
A woman to take it kindly. I think I'd kill you,
In a first blind rage.

Essex. Kill me when I can say it.

Elizabeth. Love, will you let me
Say one more thing that will hurt you?

Essex. Anything.

Elizabeth. Your blood's on fire to lead a new command
Now that you've won so handsomely in Spain,
And when I need a general anywhere
You'll ask to go. Don't ask it . . . and don't go.
You're better here in London.

Essex. Was this all you wanted? [*Stepping back.*]
To make me promise this?

Elizabeth. [*Softly.*] Not for myself,
I swear it, not because I think you reckless
With men and money, though I do think that.

Not because you might return in too much triumph
And take my kingdom from me, which I can imagine,
And not because I want to keep you here
And hate to risk you, though that's also true . . .
But rather . . . and for this you must forgive me . . .
Because you're more a poet than general . . .
And I fear you might fail, and lose what you have gained,
If you went again.

Essex. God's death! Whom would you send?

Elizabeth. I asked you not to be angry.

Essex. Not to be angry!
How do you judge a leader except by whether
He wins or loses? Was it by chance, do you think,
That I took Cadiz?

Elizabeth. Very well. You shall go.
Go if you will. Only I love you, and I say
What would be wiser.

Essex. You choose the one thing I must have
And ask me not to ask it! No. Forgive me.

Elizabeth. I'll not say it again.

Essex. But if I'm more poet than
General, why poets make better generals
Than generals do, on occasion.

Elizabeth. You've proved it so.
On more than one occasion.

[*A clock strikes. She rises.*]

There's the chime.
The council's waiting, and we shall hear about Ireland,
If Cecil has his way. One thing remember,
You must not go to Ireland.

Essex. No. That's a war
I'm content to miss.

Elizabeth. Thank God for that much then. I've been afraid
Ireland might tempt you. And one more thing remember . . .
I'll have to oppose you in the council on
The Spanish hostages. . . . You'll have your way . . .
But I'll have to oppose you, lest they think it's your kingdom. . . .
Will you understand . . . ?

Essex. I'll play my part perfectly.

[*He kisses her hand, then her lips.*]

Elizabeth. Now what can come between us, out of heaven or hell,
Or Spain or England?

Essex. Nothing . . . never again.

CURTAIN

SCENE III

SCENE.—*The same as Scene I, save that the doors to the council room have been thrown back, revealing a chair of state for the* QUEEN, *and beneath it a table at which her* COUNCILLORS *sit.*

[*The* GUARDS *are placed at left and right. The* QUEEN *sits in her chair* RALEIGH, CECIL, ESSEX, BURGHLEY, HOWARD, *and one or two others are at the table. The queen's* JESTER *sits cross-legged on a mat.* BURGHLEY *is speaking.*]

Burghley. It is quite true we shall have an enemy
In Spain while Philip lives and his state has power
To wage war on us, but there is little he can do
Against an island as well walled as ours.
He has tried his best, and failed. My lord of Essex
Says it costs more to fight Spain every year
In this chronic fashion than it would to throw
A challenge down, raid the Escurial
And sack the empire. With this the weight of the council
Disagrees, and we may hold it settled
That our tactics continue defensive till the queen
Rule otherwise.

Elizabeth. You'll wait some time for that.

Burghley. But in the matter
Of the Spanish ransoms it appears to me
Lord Essex has right on his side. The English soldiers
Who brought their prisoners home from the last raid
Deserve their prize money. By immemorial custom
The ransom belongs to the taker of the prisoner
And not to the state.

Elizabeth. That I intend to change,
That same immemorial custom. I thought you had been
Informed, Lord Burghley, that it was my will
That the Spanish ransoms be paid to the treasury.

Burghley. But my lord of Essex . . .

Elizabeth. My lord of Essex does not speak for me.
I was told this expedition into Spain
Would be paid for in booty. The cost, so far,

Has not been made up; and since there are Spanish nobles
To be ransomed, I think they should pay it.

Essex. Your Majesty,
I do not speak for myself . . . I took no prizes . . .
But only to redeem my word. I assured
My followers that they would have for their own
Whatever ransoms they earned.

Elizabeth. And by what right
Did you make this promise?

Essex. By this same ancient custom
Of which Lord Burghley speaks. A custom so well
Established there's not a soldier anywhere
But takes it for granted.

Elizabeth. Your word is pledged?

Essex. It is.

Elizabeth. [*Smiling.*] And if the state should confiscate these ransoms
You would make them good to the captors?

Essex. No. To speak frankly . . .
[*He smiles.*]
No.

Elizabeth. Then the issues lies between the queen
And her soldiers . . . and your lordship need feel no
Concern in the matter.

Essex. When I made these promises
I spoke for Your Majesty . . . or believed I did.

Elizabeth. Master Cecil, advise us: am I as queen
Bound by Lord Essex's promise?

Cecil. No, my liege;
It is well known a regent may repudiate
Treaty or word of a subject officer.
The throne is not bound.

Essex. If it comes to repudiation,
The throne can, of course, repudiate what it likes.
But not without breaking faith.

Elizabeth. I fear we are wrong, Sir Robert;
And what has been promised for me and in my name
By my own officer, my delegate in the field,
I must perform. The men may have their ransoms.
The state will take its loss; for this one time
Only, and this the last. In the future a prisoner
Is held in the name of the state, and whatever price
Is on his head belongs to the crown. Our action
Here is made no precedent. What further
Business is there before us?

Cecil. There is one perpetual
Subject, Your Majesty, which we take up
Time after time, and always leave unsettled,
But which has come to a place where we must act
On way or another. Tyrone's rebellion in Ulster
Is no longer a smouldering coal, but a running fire
Spreading north to south. We must conquer Ireland
Finally now, or give over what we have won.
Ireland's not Spain.

Elizabeth. I grant you.

The Fool. I also grant you.

Elizabeth. Be quiet, fool.

The Fool. Be quiet, fool.
[*He slaps his own mouth.*]

Elizabeth. Lord Burghley,
You shall speak first. What's to be done in Ireland?

Burghley. If my son is right, and I believe him to be,
We can bide our time no longer there. They have
Some help from Spain, and will have more, no doubt,
And the central provinces are rising. We must
Stamp out this fire or lose the island.

Elizabeth. This means
Men, money, ships?

Burghley. Yes, madam.

Cecil. And more than that . . .
A leader.

Elizabeth. What leader?

Cecil. A Lord Protector
Of Ireland who can carry sword and fire
From one end of the bogs to the other, and have English law
On Irish rebels till there are no rebels.
We've governed Ireland with our left hand, so far,
And our hold is slipping. The man who goes there now
Must be one fitted to master any field . . .
The best we have.

Elizabeth. What man? Name one.

Cecil. We should send,
Unless I am wrong, a proved and able general,
Of no less rank, say, than Lord Howard here,
Lord Essex, Sir Walter Raleigh, Knollys, or Mountjoy . . .
This is no slight matter, to keep or lose the island.

Elizabeth. I grant you that also.

The Fool. I also grant you. Be quiet,
Fool! [*He slaps his mouth.*]

Elizabeth. I ask you for one and you name a dozen, Sir Robert.

Raleigh. Why should one go alone, if it comes
To that? Why not two expeditions, one
To Dublin, one into Ulster, meeting half-way?
Elizabeth. Are there two who could work together?
Cecil. Knollys and Mountjoy.
They are friends and of one house.
Essex. Yes, of my house.
Elizabeth. Essex, whom would you name?
Essex. Why, since Lord Cecil
Feels free to name my followers, I shall feel free
To name one or two of his. . . .
Elizabeth. In other words,
You would rather Knollys and Mountjoy did not go?
Essex. I would rather they stayed in England, as Sir Robert knows.
I have need of them here. But I will spare one of them
If Lord Cecil will let Sir Francis Vere go with him.
Elizabeth. Let Vere and Knollys go.
Cecil. Lord Essex names
Sir Francis Vere because he knows full well
I cannot spare him, my liege.
Elizabeth. Is this appointment
To wait for all our private bickerings?
Can we send no man of worth to Ireland, merely
Because to do so would weaken some house or party
Here at court?
The Fool. Your Majesty has said . . .
Elizabeth. Be quiet. . . .
The Fool. Fool!
Elizabeth. Be quiet!
The Fool. Fool!
Elizabeth. Be quiet!
[*The* Fool *forms the word "fool" with his lips, but makes no sound.*]
Cecil. [*Rising.*] I hope I betray no secret, Sir Walter,
If I tell the council that I spoke with you
Before the session, and asked you if you would go
Into Ireland if the queen requested it . . . and that you said
Yes, should the queen desire it.
Burghley. That would answer.
Cecil. But I believe, and Sir Walter believes, there should be
More than one hand in this . . . that if he goes
Lord Essex should go with him.
Elizabeth. With him?
Essex. In what
Capacity?
Cecil. Leading an equal command. Two generals
Of coeval power, landing north and south
And meeting to crush Tyrone.
Essex. Would you set up
Two Lord Protectors?
Cecil. It was my thought that we name
Raleigh as Lord Protector.
Essex. And I under him?
Cecil. Since the Azores adventure
Which my Lord Essex led, and which came off
A iittle lamer than could be wished, but in which
Sir Walter showed to very great advantage,
It has seemed to me that Raleigh should receive
First place if he served in this.
Essex. [*Rising.*] This is deliberate,
An insult planned!
Cecil. It is no insult, my lord,
But plain truth. I speak for the good of the state.
Essex. You lie! You have never spoken here or elsewhere
For any cause but your own!
Elizabeth. No more of this!
Essex. The good of the state! Good God!
Am I to swallow this from a clerk, a pen-pusher . . .
To be told I may have second place, for the good of the state?
Cecil. Were you not wrong at the Azores?
Essex. No, by God!
And you know it!
Elizabeth. Whoever makes you angry has won
Already, Essex!
Essex. They have planned this!
Cecil. I say no more.
Raleigh will go to Ireland as Lord Protector
And go alone, if the queen asks it of him,
And since you will not go.
Essex. I have not said
I would not go. But if I were to go I would go
Alone, as Lord Protector!
Elizabeth. That you will not.
I have some word in this.
Essex. If this pet rat
Lord Cecil wishes to know my mind about him,
And it seems he does, he shall have it! How he first crept
Into favor here I know not, but the palace is riddled
With his spying and burrowing and crawling underground!
He has filled the court with his rat friends, very gentle,

White, squeaking, courteous folk, who show their teeth
Only when cornered; who smile at you, speak you fair
And spend their nights gnawing the floors and chairs
Out from under us all!
Elizabeth. My lord!
Essex. I am
Not the gnawing kind, nor will I speak fair
To those who don't mean me well . . . no, nor to those
To whom I mean no good! I say frankly here,
Yes, to their faces, that Cecil and Walter Raleigh
Have made themselves my enemies because
They cannot brook greatness or power in any but
Themselves! And I say this to them . . . and to the world. . . .
I, too, have been ambitious, as all men are
Who bear a noble mind, but if I rise
It will be by my own effort, and not by dragging
Better men down through intrigue! I admit
Sir Walter Raleigh's skill as a general
And Cecil's statecraft! I could work with them freely
And cheerfully, but every time I turn
My back they draw their knives! When Cecil left England
I guarded his interests as I would my own
Because he asked me to . . . but when I left,
And left my affairs in his hands . . . on my return
I found my plans and my friends out in the rain
Along with the London beggars!
Cecil. I did my best. . . .
Essex. Aye . . . the best for yourself! For the good of the state!
Raleigh. If Lord Essex wishes
To say he is my enemy, very well . . .
He is my enemy.
Essex. But you were mine first. . . .
And I call the gods to witness you would be my friend
Still, if I'd had my way! I take it hard
That here, in the queen's council, where there should be
Magnanimous minds if anywhere, there is still
No trust or friendship!
Elizabeth. I take it hard that you
Should quarrel before me.
Essex. Would you have us quarrel
Behind your back? It suits them all too well
To quarrel in secret and knife men down in the dark!
Burghley. This is fantastic, my lord. There has been no knifing.
Let us come to a decision. We were discussing
The Irish protectorate.
Cecil. And as for Ireland,
I am willing to leave that in Lord Essex' hands
To do as he decides.
Essex. Send your Sir Walter
To Ireland as Protector! And be damned to it!
Cecil. As the queen wishes.
It is a task both difficult and dangerous.
I cannot blame Lord Essex for refusing
To risk his fame there.
Essex. There speaks the white rat again!
Yet even a rat should know I have never refused
A task out of fear! I said I would not go
As second in command!
Cecil. Then would you go
As Lord Protector?
Elizabeth. You have named your man . . .
Sir Walter Raleigh.
Raleigh. I'll go if Essex goes.
Essex. What! Is our Raleigh
Afraid to go alone?
Raleigh. I don't care for it . . .
And neither does our Essex!
Essex. Why, what is this
That hangs over Ireland? Is it haunted, this Ireland?
Is it a kind of hell where men are damned
If they set foot on it? I've never seen the place,
But if it's a country like other countries, with people
Like other people in it, it's nothing to be
Afraid of, more than France or Wales or Flanders
Or anywhere else!
Cecil. We hear you say so.
Essex. If I
Am challenged to go to Ireland, then, Christ, I'll go!
Give me what men and horse I need, and put me
In absolute charge, and if I fail to bring
This Tyrone's head back with me, and put the rebellion
To sleep forever, take my sword from me
And break it . . . I'll never use it again!
Elizabeth. Will you listen . . . ?
Essex. They've challenged me!
Elizabeth. If you volunteer
To go to Ireland there is none to stop you.
You are first soldier here, first in acclaim

And in achievement, but since the decision lies
With yourself alone, reflect a little.
Essex. My queen,
I can see that Raleigh and Cecil have set themselves
To bait me into Ireland! They know and I know
That Ireland has been deadly to any captain
Who risked his fortunes there; moreover, once
I'm gone they think to strip me here at home,
Ruin me both ways! And I say to them: "Try it!"
There are men who are greater than Ireland or their chicane. . . .
Since this is a challenge I go, and go alone,
And return victorious, and, by God, more of a problem
To Cecils and Raleighs than when I went!
[*The* FOOL *rises and approaches* ESSEX *from behind.*]
Burghley. If Essex
Will go, it solves our problem, Your Majesty.
We could hardly refuse that offer.
Elizabeth. No.
Essex. I will go,
And I will return! Mark me!
The Fool. [*Touching* ESSEX.] My lord! my lord!
Essex. [*Turning suddenly with an instinctive motion that sweeps the* FOOL *to the floor.*] Take your hands off me! You touch me for a fool?
[*He helps the* FOOL *up.*]
Get up!
The Fool. Do not go to Ireland!
Essex. [*Impatiently.*] You too?
The Fool. Because, my lord, I come from Ireland.
All the best fools come from Ireland, but only
A very great fool will go there.
Essex. Faugh!
The Fool. It's not too late yet!
Elizabeth. Break up the council, my lords.
We meet tomorrow.
Burghley. And this is decided?
Essex. Yes.
Elizabeth. Yes, if you wish it. Go now.
[*The* COUNCIL *rises when the queen does and files out silently, leaving* ESSEX *and* ELIZABETH.]
You should have had
The fool's brain and he yours! You would have bettered
By the exchange.
Essex. I thank you kindly, lady.
Elizabeth. What malicious star
Danced in my sky when you were born, I wonder?
Essex. What malicious star danced in the sky
Of Ireland, you should ask.
Elizabeth. Oh, my dear,
You are a child in council. I saw them start
To draw you into this, and tried to warn you . . .
But it was no use.
Essex. They drew me into nothing.
I saw their purpose and topped it with my own.
Let them believe they've sunk me.
Elizabeth. You will withdraw.
I'll countermand this.
Essex. And give them the laugh on me?
I'll have the laugh on them yet.
Elizabeth. Better they should laugh
A little now than laugh at you forever.
Essex. And why not win in Ireland?
Elizabeth. No man wins there.
You're so dazzled
With the chance to lead an army you'd follow the devil
In an assault on heaven.
Essex. No, but I'd lead him.
Heaven is always taken by storm. That's one thing
The devil doesn't know. Ireland is only
A country, and this is superstition.
Elizabeth. I know.
You were quite right. I thought so as you said it.
Only somehow here in my breast something constricts . . .
Is it the heart grows heavy? I must let you go . . .
And I'll never see you again.
Essex. Mistrust all these
Forebodings. When they prove correct we remember them,
But when they're wrong we forget them. They mean nothing.
Remember this when I'm back and all turns out well . . .
That you felt all would turn out badly.
Elizabeth. Oh, my love,
Come touch me, tell me all will happen well.
Essex. And so it will.
Elizabeth. Do you want to go?
Essex. Why yes . . .
And no. I've said I would and I will.
Elizabeth. It's not yet
Too late. There are no announcements made, no orders

Given. If you win, that will divide us . . .
And if you lose, that will divide us too.

Essex. I'll win, and it will not divide us. Is it so hard
To believe in me?

Elizabeth. No . . . I'll believe in you . . .
And even forgive you if you need it. Here.
My father gave me this ring . . . and told me if ever
He lost his temper with me, to bring it to him
And he'd forgive me. And so it saved my life . . .
Long after, when he'd forgotten, long after, when
One time he was angry.

Essex. Darling, if ever
You're angry rings won't help.

Elizabeth. Yes, but it would.
I'd think of you as you are now, and it would.
Take it.

Essex. I have no pledge from you. I'll take it
To remember you in absence.

Elizabeth. Take it for a better reason. Take it because
The years are long, and full of sharp, wearing days
That wear out what we are and what we have been
And change us into people we do not know,
Living among strangers. Lest you and I who love
Should wake some morning strangers and enemies
In an alien world, far off; take my ring, my lover.

Essex. You fear
You will not always love me?

Elizabeth. No, that you
Will not love me, and will not let me love you. [*She puts the ring on his finger.**]

CURTAIN

ACT TWO

Scene I

Scene.—*The queen's study.*

[Penelope *is sitting reading. The* Fool *enters. She does not see him.*]

The Fool. Sh! Make no noise.

Penelope. What do you mean?

The Fool. Silence! Quiet!

Penelope. I am silent, fool.

The Fool. You silent? And even as you say it you are talking!

Penelope. You began it.

The Fool. Began what?

Penelope. Talking.

The Fool. Oh, no. Talking began long before my time. It was a woman began it.

Penelope. Her name?

The Fool. Penelope, I should judge.

Penelope. Fool.

The Fool. [*Looking away.*] No, for with this same Penelope began also beauty and courage and tenderness and faith . . . all that a man could desire or a woman offer . . . and all that this early Penelope began has a later Penelope completed.

Penelope. [*Rising.*] It lacked only this . . . that the court fool should make love to me.

The Fool. I am sorry to have been laggard. But truly I have never found you alone before.

Penelope. How lucky I've been!

The Fool. Are you angered?

Penelope. At what?

The Fool. At my loving you.

Penelope. I've learned to bear nearly everything.

The Fool. A lover's absence?

Penelope. Among other things.

The Fool. The presence of suitors undesired?

Penelope. That, too.

The Fool. I am not a suitor, my lady. I ask nothing. I know where your heart lies. It is with my Lord Essex in Ireland. I do not love you.

Penelope. Good.

The Fool. I lied to you. I do love you.

Penelope. I am sorry.

The Fool. You will not laugh at me?

Penelope. No.

The Fool. Then there is yet some divinity in the world . . . while a woman can still be sorry for one who loves her without return.

Penelope. A woman is sadly aware that when a man loves her it makes a fool of him.

* The ring story appeared first in a frankly fictional publication, *circa* 1640. There is no evidence of its truth.

The Fool. And if a fool should love a woman . . . would it not make a man of him?

Penelope. No, but doubly a fool, I fear.

The Fool. And the women . . . how of the women?

Penelope. They have been fools, too.

The Fool. The more fool I, I tried to save Lord Essex from Ireland . . . but he needs must go . . . the more fool he.

Penelope. Let us not talk of that.

The Fool. May I kiss you?

Penelope. No.

The Fool. Your hand?

Penelope. Yes. [*He kisses her hand.*]

The Fool. I thank you.

[*She touches his fool's cap gently with her hand.*]

Penelope. The more fool you, poor boy.

[ROBERT CECIL *enters from the left.*]

Cecil. This is hardly a seemly pastime, Mistress Gray.

Penelope. And are you now the judge of what is seemly, Sir Robert?

Cecil. [*To the* FOOL.] Be off with you! [*To* PENELOPE.] The queen is expecting Master Bacon here? [*The* FOOL *goes.*]

Penelope. I am set to wait for him.

Cecil. You will not be needed.

Penelope. Excellent.

[*She goes out right, passing* RALEIGH, *who enters.*]

Cecil. This Bacon keeps himself close. I have been unable to speak with him. She has this news?

Raleigh. Yes.

Cecil. She believes it?

Raleigh. Burghley himself believes it.

Cecil. Then she does.

Raleigh. Beyond question.

[*The curtains part at the left and* BACON *enters.*]

Cecil. Good morrow, Master Bacon.

Bacon. And to you, my lords.

Cecil. I have sent everywhere for you, sir, this three hours . . . and perhaps it was not altogether by accident that I could not find you.

Bacon. I was not at home. You must forgive me.

Cecil. You are here to see the queen?

Bacon. [*Bowing.*] The queen has also been good enough to send for me.

Cecil. It was my wish to speak with you first . . . and it is my opinion that it will be the better for all of us, if I do so now . . . late as it is.

Bacon. I am but barely on time, gentlemen.

Cecil. You need answer one question only. You have been in correspondence with Lord Essex in Ireland?

Bacon. Perhaps.

Cecil. The queen has this morning received news warning her that Lord Essex is allied with the Irish rebels and is even now leading his army back to England to usurp her throne. Had you heard this?

Bacon. No.

Cecil. Do you credit it?

Bacon. It is your own scheme, I believe.

Cecil. That Essex should rebel against the queen?

Bacon. Even so.

Raleigh. You accuse us of treason?

Bacon. If the queen were aware of certain matters she would herself accuse you of treason.

Cecil. What matters?

Bacon. I prefer that the queen should question me.

Cecil. Look to yourself, Master Bacon. If you intend to accuse any man of the suppression of letters written by Essex to the queen, or of the suppression of letters sent by the queen to Essex, you will be unable to prove these assertions and you will argue yourself very neatly into the Tower.

Bacon. My lord . . . I had no such business in mind.

Raleigh. Then what? . . .

Bacon. I hope I can keep my own counsel. The truth is, my lords, you are desperate men. You have overreached yourselves, and if wind of it gets to the royal ears you are done.

Raleigh. We shall drag a few down with us if we are done, though, and you the first.

Cecil. You have but a poor estimate of me, Master Bacon. If you go in to the queen and reveal to her that her letters to Essex have not reached him . . . as you mean to do . . . the queen will then send for me, and I will send for Lord Essex' last letter to you, containing a plan for the capture of the city of London. It will interest you to know that I have read that letter and you are learned enough in the law to realize in what light you will stand as a witness should the queen see it.

Bacon. I think it is true, though, that if I go down I shall also drag a few with me, including those here present.

Cecil. I am not so sure of that either. I am not unready for that contingency. But to be frank with you, it would be easier for both you and us if you were on our side.

Bacon. You must expect a man to side with his friends.

Cecil. And a man's friends . . . who are

they? Those who can help him to what he wants.

Bacon. Not always.

Cecil. When he is wise. You have served Lord Essex well and I believe he has made you promises. But the moment Essex enters England in rebellion, he is doomed, and his friends with him.

Bacon. One word from the queen to him . . . one word from him to the queen . . . one word from me, revealing that their letters have been intercepted, and there can be no talk of rebellion. There has been some underhand traffic with the couriers between here and Ireland. Their letters have been lost, you have induced the queen to promulgate arbitrary orders . . . and since they are both proud, you have bred distrust in her and defiance in him. Your machinations have been so direct, so childish, so simple . . . and so simply exposed . . . that I wonder at you!

Cecil. My friend, a child could trip him. Not so simple as your own. I have news this morning that Lord Essex has already landed in England and set up his standard here. He is a rebel, and when a man is once a rebel, do you think there will be any careful inquiry into how he happened to become one?

Bacon. Essex in England!

Cecil. In England.

Raleigh. And has neglected to disband his army.*

Cecil. You speak of explanations between the queen and Essex. Unless you betray us there will be no explanations. They are at war and will never meet again.

Bacon. That is, if your plan succeed.

Cecil. [*Standing aside.*] Very well, then. Go in. You have chosen your master. I have done with you.

Bacon. [*Not moving.*] And if I say nothing?

Cecil. Then . . . whatever you have been promised, whatever you have desired, that you shall have. There is no place in the courts you could not fill. You shall have your choice. If you need excuse, no one should know better than you that this Essex is a danger to the state, a danger to the queen, a danger to liberty.

Bacon. If I need excuse I shall find one for myself.

[*There is a pause. Then the curtain parts to the right and* PENELOPE *enters. She holds the curtain back.*]

Penelope. Yes, Your Majesty; he is here.

* Essex did not actually return to England in force. There was an interval between his coming from Ireland and his rebellion.

Elizabeth. Why was I not told? [*She enters.*] Is this an ante-chamber, Sir Robert? Am I never to look out of my room without seeing you?

Cecil. Your pardon, Your Majesty. I was just going.

Elizabeth. Then go. You need not pause to explain why you came. I am weary of your face!

Cecil. Yes, Your Majesty.

[CECIL *and* RALEIGH *bow and depart.*]

Elizabeth. I have heard that you are a shrewd man, Master Bacon.

Bacon. Flattery, Majesty, flattery.

Elizabeth. I have heard it,
And in a sort I believe it. Tell me one thing . . .
Are you Cecil's friend?

Bacon. I have never been.

Elizabeth. He is a shrewd man; he's
A man to make a friend of if you'd stand well
In the court, sir.

Bacon. It may be so.

Elizabeth. Why are you not
His friend then?

Bacon. We are not on the same side.

Elizabeth. You follow Lord Essex?

Bacon. Since I have known him.

Elizabeth. There's
A dangerous man to follow.

Bacon. Lord Essex?

Elizabeth. Lord Essex.

Bacon. I am sorry, madam,
If I have displeased you.

Elizabeth. You have displeased me.

Bacon. I repeat then . . .
I am sorry.

Elizabeth. You will change, then? You will forget
This Essex of yours?

Bacon. If you ask it . . . if there is reason . . .

Elizabeth. Well, there is reason! He has taken up arms
Against me in Ireland.

Bacon. You are sure of this?

Elizabeth. I have reports. Is it so hard to believe?

Bacon. Without proofs, it is.

Elizabeth. I have proof.

Bacon. May I ask of what sort?

Elizabeth. Proof good enough. You know the punishment
For treason? From what I have heard
Of late both you and Essex should remember
That punishment.

Bacon. Madam, for myself I have
No need to fear, and if Lord Essex has
I am more than mistaken in him.

Elizabeth. I am very sorry
That I must do this . . . but all friends of Essex
Go straightway to the Tower. I have sent for you
To give you a last chance to change your mind
Before this blow falls. Are you still his friend?
Bacon. Yes, Majesty.
Elizabeth. I am sorry for it.
Bacon. That is all?
Elizabeth. Why, no. You do not believe me?
Bacon. I do not.
Elizabeth. And why?
Bacon. I neither believe our Essex a rebel
Nor that you believe so. If you intended to place me
In the Tower . . . I would be in the Tower . . . and no talk about it.
Elizabeth. You are shrewd indeed.
Bacon. I am Essex' friend.
Elizabeth. If that
Were true . . . if I could speak to you . . . if there were only
The sound of one honest voice!
. . . I must rule England,
And they say he is rebel to me . . . and day and night,
Waking, sleeping, in council, there is still always
One thing crying out in me over and again . . .
Waking and sleeping I hear it crying: He cannot,
Cannot fail me! But I have written him my love
And he has not answered. What you know of this
Answer me truly, truly . . . bitter or not,
And you shall not lose!
Bacon. He has not answered?
Elizabeth. No.
Bacon. If I
Knew why I would know much. Have you angered him . . .
Sent arbitrary orders?
Elizabeth. I have ordered him to disband
His forces and return. I have cut off
Revenue and supplies.
Bacon. But this was rash . . .
To send a popular leader out with an army
And then check him suddenly, heap disgrace upon him . . .
He has great pride.
Elizabeth. [*Getting up.*] He has rebelled then?
I wrote him lovingly.
Bacon. And he answered? . . .
Elizabeth. Nothing.
Bacon. That could not be excused.
Elizabeth. And it cannot be. It's true. It will not be!
Bacon. Dear queen, I fear
I have turned you against him!
Elizabeth. No, no! I needed that!
Bacon. And if there were something wrong . . .
Some misunderstanding? . . .
Elizabeth. No, no . . . don't try comfort now . . .
He had my letters. That could not go wrong.
Did he not have my letters?
Bacon. Could it be otherwise?
Elizabeth. You would know that. You would know if he had not.
You've had word from him?
Bacon. Yes.
Elizabeth. He has written you,
But not me! Or are you traitor to him also? . . .
I think you are! I think you lie to me! I am
Encompassed by lies! I think you, too, betray him . . .
But subtly, with infinite craft, making me believe
First that you would not wrong him! No, no . . . I'm gone mad
Pacing my room, pacing the room of my mind.
They say a woman's mind is an airless room,
Sunless and airless, where she must walk alone
Saying he loves me, loves me, loves me not,
And has never loved me. The world goes by, all shadows,
And there are voices, all echoes till he speaks . . .
And there's no light till his presence makes a light
There in that room. But I am a queen. Where I walk
Is a hall of torture, where the curious gods bring all
Their racks and gyves, and stretch me there to writhe
Till I cry out. They watch me with eyes of iron
Waiting to hear what I cry! I am crying now . . .
Listen, you gods of iron! He never loved me . . .
He wanted my kingdom only . . .
Loose me and let me go! I am yet a queen . . .
That I have! That he will not take from me.
I shall be queen, and walk his room no more.
He thought to break me down by not answering . . .

Break me until I'd say, I'm all yours . . . what I am
And have, all yours! That I will never, never,
Never say. I'm not broken yet.

Bacon. Nor will be, Majesty.

Elizabeth. We must not follow him.
We must forget him, break him as he would break us,
Bow that bright head . . . I shall be as I was.
See him no more, my friend.
He walks on quicksand. Avoid him.

Bacon. Yes, my queen.

Elizabeth. Go, my friend.
You have done well. I trust you.

Bacon. I thank Your Majesty.

[*He goes out.* ELIZABETH *claps her hands twice. After a moment* CAPTAIN ARMIN *enters.*]

Elizabeth. Captain Armin, keep a watch on Master Bacon,
On his house and on his correspondence.
I wish to know all he knows.

Armin. Yes, Your Majesty.

Elizabeth. Wait. I have found you true of word,
And sure of hand. Moreover, you can keep counsel—

[ARMIN *bows. She beckons him to come to her. He does so.*]

What we say now is forever secret between us—
Between us two—not one other.

Armin. I'll hold it so.

Elizabeth. It is reported there is an army risen
Against me——

Armin. God forbid!

Elizabeth. It is so reported. The rebellion I speak of's the force
Lord Essex has brought back with him from Ireland.
I wish to make this preparation for it: Whatever orders
You receive from your superiors, whatever broils
Occur, he is to have free access to my presence.

Armin. There would be danger to your person, madam.

Elizabeth. I will risk that.

Armin. You would be hostage if he were in command.

Elizabeth. Be ready for danger—and if need be, death.

Armin. Yes, Majesty.

[*He goes out.* ELIZABETH *stands motionless for a moment. There is a sudden burst of girls' laughter in an adjoining room, and the* FOOL *runs in with a garment in his hand. Three* GIRLS *run after him, the foremost tripping him so that he falls in a corner and is instantly pounced upon by all three.*]

Mary. [*Entering.*] Thief! Thief! Stop thief!

Ellen. Kill the slobber thief! Fall on him!

Tressa. Can a maid not keep a silk smock?

The Fool. Help! Salvage! Men-at-arms to the rescue! I am boarded by pirates!

[*They tickle him.*]

Ellen. Tear it from him! He will exhibit it!

Tressa. No, no! Don't tear it!

The Fool. If you sit on me in that fashion, darling, you will regret it. There will be issue!

Ellen. What issue?

The Fool. Twins! Seven or eight!

[ELLEN *slaps him.*]

Mary. Rise! Rise quickly! The queen is here. Rise!

[*They all get up in confusion.*]

Tressa. We are sorry, Your Majesty.

[ELIZABETH *looks at them without seeing them, and goes out to her bedroom.*]

Ellen. What is it? She seemed not to see.

Mary. It's not like her not to strike us.

Tressa. We'll be whipped.

The Fool. No, no. She strikes instantly or not at all.

Tressa. Give me that.

[*She snatches her smock from the* FOOL.]

Mary. Come. [*They tiptoe out.*]

CURTAIN

SCENE II

SCENE.—*The interior of* ESSEX' *tent on the coast of England.*

[ESSEX *sits in the light of a candle, reading dispatches. A* GUARD *stands in the shadow.* MARVEL, *an aide, enters.*]

Marvel. There is a courier from the queen, my lord.

Essex. At last, then.

Marvel. You will see him at once?

Essex. Yes . . . Wait. Bring him in and stay here while I read the dispatches. If I give orders to torture or kill him, show no surprise. You understand?

Marvel. You will not torture him?

Essex. Am I not tortured? And you, too, sirrah. You will remember?

The Guard. Yes, my lord.

Essex. Good.

[MARVEL *goes out*. ESSEX *rises and stands out of the light, waiting*. MARVEL *enters with the* COURIER, *who falls on his knee before* ESSEX.]

The Courier. My lord of Essex?

Essex. Yes.

Courier. Dispatches from the queen.

Essex. When did you leave London?

Courier. Four days ago, my lord. We were delayed.

Essex. What delayed you?

Courier. Robbers.

Essex. And they took what from you?

Courier. Our horses and money.

Essex. And the letters? . . .

Courier. Were returned to me untouched.

Essex. When did this happen?

Courier. This side of the ford. There were four armed men against us two.

Essex. Give me the letters. [*The* COURIER *does so*. ESSEX *reads briefly*.] This is all?

Courier. Yes, my lord.

Essex. You are sure you have lost nothing?

Courier. Indeed yes, my lord. There was but one missive and the seal was returned unbroken. The cut-throats told us they cared the less about our letters for they could not read.

Essex. You are a clever liar, sirrah, and you are the third liar who has come that same road to me from London. You are the third liar to tell this same tale. You shall pay for being the third.

Courier. My lord, I have not lied to you.

Essex. Take his weapons from him, lieutenant. [MARVEL *obeys*.] Set him against the post there. Not so gently. He shall lose his ears first and then his lying tongue.

Courier. Your lordship does not mean this?

Essex. And why not? We shall then cut him in pieces . . . but gradually, with infinite delicacy.

[MARVEL *approaches the* COURIER *with a knife*. *The* GUARD *holds him*.]

Courier. No, no, no, no! Oh, God! Oh, my lord! My lord!

Essex. What are you waiting for?

Marvel. We must tie him to the pole first, sir.

Essex. Then tie him!

Courier. No, no . . . oh, God, no! What do you want of me? I swear to you I haven't lied to you! I swear . . . ugh!

[*He is choked*.]

Essex. Let him speak. What do you swear?

Courier. My lord, I have not lied . . . I speak truth . . .

Essex. Tie him up.

Courier. Let me speak . . . I can . . . ugh . . .

Essex. Silence him. We know too well what you have done, sirrah. We need no evidence of that. What we ask is that you tell us who set you on . . . and your accomplices. Tell us this and I want no more of you. You shall have your freedom . . . and this . . . [*He tosses a clinking bag at his feet*.] Speak.

Courier. My lord, if I knew . . .

Essex. Bind him. Truss him up and cut him open. Dispense with these niceties. Have you no knife? [*He is bound*.] We have heard enough! Take out his tongue!

[*They approach him. He becomes calm*.]

Courier. My lord, I am not a coward, though it may seem to you
I am, for I have cried out . . . but I cried out
Not so much for pain or fear of pain
But to know this was Lord Essex, whom I have loved
And who tortures innocent men.

Essex. Come, silence him!

Courier. Come then. I am innocent. If my Lord Essex
Is as I have believed him, he will not hurt me;
If he will hurt me, then he is not as I
And many thousands believe him, who have loved him,
And I shall not mind much dying.

[*A pause*.]

Essex. Let him go.

[*They unbind the* COURIER.]

I thought my letters had been tampered with.
You'd tell me if it were so.

Courier. My honored lord,
By all the faith I have, and most of it's yours,
I'd rather serve you well and lose in doing it
Than serve you badly and gain. If something I've done
Has crossed you or worked you ill I'm enough punished
Only knowing it.

Essex. This letter came
From the queen's hands?

Courier. It is as I received it
From the queen's hands.

Essex. There was no other?

Courier. No other.

Essex. Take this and go.

[*He tosses the bag to the* COURIER.]

Courier. I have brought misfortune . . .

Essex. You bring good news. We break camp tomorrow for London . . . Go . . . take that news with you. They'll welcome you outside. Remain with my guard and return with us. [*The* COURIER *goes out.*]

Marvel. We march tomorrow?

Essex. Yes.

Marvel. Under orders?

Essex. No. [*He reads.*]

"Lord Essex is required to disperse his men
And return to the capital straightway on his own
Recognizance, to give himself up."

Marvel. And nothing with this?

Essex. Give out the necessary orders, we shall
Move at daybreak.

Marvel. Yes, my lord.

Essex. And it is
As well it falls out this way! By right of name
And power and popular voice this is my kingdom . . .
This England under my feet, more mine than hers,
As she shall learn. It is quite as well.

Marvel. There is no man
But will think so. There is victory in your path,
My lord. The London citizens will rise
At the first breath of your name.

Essex. Yes . . . that I'm sure of.

Marvel. And with London in your hands . . . well . . . it's your world then . . .
As far as you like.

Essex. And I am glad for England.
She has lain fallow in fear too long! Her hills
Shall have a spring of victory. Goodnight.

Marvel. Goodnight.

Essex. And for this order, I received it not. [*He tears the paper.*]

CURTAIN

SCENE III

SCENE.—*The council hall of Act I is cleared here for a court assembly.*

[*Those who attended the council are present, save for* ESSEX, *also the* FOOL, ELLEN, MARY, TRESSA, PENELOPE, BACON, *and other* LORDS- AND LADIES-IN-WAITING. BURGHLEY *and* CECIL *are standing to one side in earnest talk. Across from them a group made up of* RALEIGH, BACON, *the* FOOL, *and a number of others.*]

Burghley. These players should be put down with an iron hand. They have neither conscience nor morals. They will make any display for money. In my young days they were allowed only interludes and instructive entertainment. The queen has been too lax . . .

Cecil. Have you seen this play of Richard II?

Burghley. I see no plays.

Cecil. It's high treason. Richard is deposed in it. High treason.

Bacon. Treason to depose a king? Not if you succeed.

Cecil. No, but treason to teach treason.

Bacon. What is treason?

Raleigh. Said jesting Pilate.

Cecil. Is it not treason to depose a king?

Raleigh. What if it makes a king of you?

The Fool. It would then be treason not to have done it.

Bacon. The Fool is a Jesuit.

The Fool. In truth, he was deposed. It is treason to all his successors to deny it.

Bacon. An excellent Jesuit.

The Fool. What? I a Jesuit? Jesu!

Penelope. And a wit.

Bacon. Bad.

Penelope. Very bad.

Raleigh. Unutterably bad. What? Jesu-wit! Poisonous. Shall we allow this?

Penelope. I am guilty. I surrender.

Raleigh. What did you do with the body?

Penelope. There was none. I did eat my words.

Raleigh. A cannibal, a monster, a word-swallower!

The Fool. A man-eater.

Penelope. Nay, nay!

Bacon. Do you eat your men with butter or salt?

Penelope. With salt if they are buttery and with butter if they are salty.

Raleigh. Ready then. Here comes a salty man to be buttered.

Penelope. A butter-in.

The Fool. A salt-butter.

Bacon. A cheese . . . a whole cheese.

Tressa. Full of holes, holey.

Ellen. Pitted.

Penelope. What? Am I pitted against a cheese?

Raleigh. Let but this cheese roll into your pit, Lady . . . and you are answered.

Penelope. No . . . you are answered. You are answered no.

Burghley. [*To* CECIL.] There can be no doubt the Essex faction sent money to the actors to purchase a performance of Richard It is an old play; it would draw no public.

Cecil. The actors are then accessory.

Burghley. Think you so?

Cecil. They could hardly be unaware of the purposes of the Essex party.

Bacon. It is so certain that Essex has a purpose?

Cecil. He has led his army into London.

Bacon. The men live in London. Moreover, the order to disperse on landing may not have been received. Such things have happened.

Cecil. Yes?

Bacon. Aye, indeed.

Cecil. [*To* BURGHLEY.] You are to see these actors?

Burghley. They are sending spokesmen today.

The Fool. Let them put on the play for us.

Tressa. Yes . . . the deposition scene. It may convince us. We may all turn rebel.

Burghley. Tut!

The Fool. Tut? What does this mean . . . this tut?

Burghley. Will you learn manners, sirrah? In my young days there was no such loose speaking about the court.

The Fool. There was no tutting, neither.

Penelope. You are mistaken. There used to be tutting parties. They all brought their tutting.

The Fool. Fie on you! Also pooh on you!

Penelope. Yes . . . there were fieing and poohing parties also.

Raleigh. True, true. Well I remember the old days when all the young people would get together and try which could make the greatest pooh.

Tressa. There was such laughter and jesting!

Raleigh. Ah, yes, at the old Tut, Fie and Pooh Tavern! It's torn down now, but what a place it was!

The Fool. The game went out of fashion, alas, when it was discovered that a virgin could always pooh farther than anybody else.

Tressa. Tut!

Mary. Fie!

Ellen. Pooh!

The Fool. I beg pardon. I had forgotten there were virgins present.

Penelope. We are all virgins.

Raleigh. The proof then, quickly. Show me.

Penelope. It is nothing that can be seen, my lord.

Raleigh. They say seeing is believing.

Penelope. Virginity is rather a state of mind.

Ellen. Nay . . . a state of preservation.

The Fool. I have seen these preserved virgins.

Raleigh. You have seen them?

The Fool. Seen them? I've been bothered by them. The whole court used to be driven indoors by them regularly on our progress through Middlesex.

Raleigh. They are worse at night, I believe? Middlesex . . . Middlesex . . .

Penelope. Change the subject, gentles. This virginity begins to wear thin.

The Fool. It has worn clear through, and a great hole appears in the center.

Penelope. A hole in your wit.

Raleigh. His Jesuit.

Penelope. His half-wit.

[*A* HERALD *enters and speaks to* CECIL.]

The Herald. My lord, there are two fellows here who ask for audience with the queen.

Cecil. Who are they?

Herald. Players, my lord.

Cecil. Tell them to wait. The queen will see them presently.

[*The* HERALD *goes out.*]

Burghley. To my mind it was one of these same players writ the ballad that was posted up at St. Paul's.

Cecil. No, no . . . the man has been discovered . . . and will have his ears cropped for it.

Burghley. But he could not have written it . . . he was but an instrument. The actors are too devilish ingenious at writing ballads. I cannot put it out of my mind they are all treasonous scoundrels.

Raleigh. Is this the ballad on the Earl's return?

Cecil. Aye . . . "When England needeth
victories
She calleth Essex on . . ."
And more to the same purpose. What I cannot understand is that the queen should take no steps to put the city in a posture of defense. Essex draws near with his army . . . and we swing the gates as usual.

Bacon. Is that a symptom of danger . . . that an English general should return with his army to the English capital?

Cecil. Are you not aware that Essex' house in the Strand is a camp brimming full of armed nobles going and coming?

The Fool. It is much more likely to be brimming with drunken nobles going and coming brim full.

Cecil. Be quiet!

The Fool. Fool. [CECIL *lays a hand on his sword angrily. The* FOOL *points to his own breast and repeats:*] Fool.

[CECIL *turns away. There is a rustling among those present. Several rise. At the rear the* QUEEN *appears silently, two*

LADIES *following her. She comes forward without speaking, her eyes seeking for someone. She fixes on* LORD BURGHLEY.]

The Queen. Is it true, then, my dear Burghley, that you have taken to attending the Theatre?

Burghley. No, madam.

The Queen. It was not you, then, who forbade the performances of Richard II without asking my advice?

Burghley. It was, madam.

The Queen. On what ground?

Burghley. Your Majesty, the play is treasonous. It shows the deposition of a king, and its performance was procured by rebels.

The Queen. Rebels? What rebels?

Burghley. I know not, madam. I have sent for the players to discover that.

The Queen. You have sent for them?

Burghley. Aye, madam . . . and they are here.

The Queen. They will laugh at you, dear Burghley.

Burghley. Others have laughed at me, Majesty.

The Queen. They will laugh at you, sir, and you will deserve it. Is my kingdom so shaky that we dare not listen to a true history? Are my people so easily led that the sight of a king deposed in play will send them running hither to pull the queen out of her chair? Have we not passion plays in every little town showing the murder of our Lord? You are nervous, Lord Burghley. Let these children play their plays.

Cecil. Your Majesty, I very much fear they are not children, and that they mean to do harm.

The Queen. Then let them. Let them do all the harm they can. Are we too stupid to see that to prohibit a rebellious play is to proclaim our fear of rebellion? Who is there here who fears a rebellion against me? I do not.

Cecil. It is dangerous to let these mutterings grow, dear queen.

Elizabeth. It is dangerous to touch them. Let them mutter, if they will. Let them cry out . . . let them run the streets, these children! When they have worn themselves weary running and crying "Up with Essex!" "Down with Elizabeth!" and got themselves drunk on mutual pledges, they will go to bed and sleep soundly and wake up wiser. Let me speak to these players. Bring them to me.

Burghley. Here, madam?

Elizabeth. Here.

Cecil. Majestas, adsunt legati de curia Galliæ. Placetne eos recipere antequam . . .

The Queen. Cras illos recipiam.

Cecil. Sed maxime præstat . . .

The Queen. Si bene mihi videbitur, cras redituros recipiam! *
Nay, I can bang you in Latin too!

[CECIL *goes out.* ELIZABETH *sits and turns to the* FOOL.]

You, sirrah . . . I hear that you have fallen in love. Do you wish to be whipped?

The Fool. I would rather have been whipped, madam; much rather.

Elizabeth. Why?

The Fool. It would hurt less.

Elizabeth. Good. You shall be whipped.

The Fool. Madam, if you can whip it out of me I will give you my lucky shilling.

Elizabeth. You shall be whipped and keep your shilling.

The Fool. You would better take it, madam queen.

Elizabeth. Your shilling?

The Fool. Yes, madam queen, to buy another whip with for yourself. Nay, you had perhaps better buy several. But in truth, dear queen, I have not fallen in love, only a pretty little strumpet has fallen in love with me and I beg leave that we be allowed to marry.

Elizabeth. Is she of the court?

The Fool. Yes, madam.

Elizabeth. What, are there strumpets at court?

The Fool. Oh, they are all strumpets here at court. Some are here because they are strumpets and some are strumpets because they are here, but strumpets they all are.

Elizabeth. Which is it you wish to marry?

The Fool. It is not that I wish to marry her, madam, but she wishes to marry me. [*Walking about to choose, finally pointing to* TRESSA.] This one, Majesty.

Tressa. [*Leaping at him.*] Scoundrel! . . .

The Fool. [*Pointing to* ELLEN.] No, no . . . I mean this one.

Ellen. You dog! You . . .

[*The* FOOL *passes* PENELOPE *by.*]

The Fool. [*Pointing to* MARY.] Or that one . . .

Mary. What!

The Fool. I feel sure it was one of them, Majesty . . . but it was dark at the time . . . and in truth I gave her my word of honor in the dark that I would make an honest

* "Your Majesty, the French ambassadors are here. Would it please you to receive them before . . ."
"I will receive them tomorrow."
"But it is of the highest importance . . ."
"If it seems well to me, I will receive them when they come back tomorrow."

woman of her by daylight. It is thus that most marriages are made.

Elizabeth. How, fool?

The Fool. In the dark, my lady. Quite in the dark.

Elizabeth. [*To a* SOLDIER.] Take this fool, captain, and put him in the dark for three days with but little bread and water. I have a distaste for this fooling.

The Fool. No, no, madam.

Elizabeth. I am tired of your strumpets! And let him not see his lady Penelope meanwhile. You will be sure of that, mistress?

Penelope. I have no desire to see him.

Elizabeth. Whom do you desire to see?

Penelope. No one, your Majesty.

Elizabeth. You lie! This Mistress Gray, take her too! Let her have bread and water!

[*She looks at* PENELOPE *with hatred.*]

Penelope. Your Majesty . . . what is this?

Elizabeth. I am weary to death of you! I am weary of all men and women, but more of you than any! You have written. You have had letters! I say, take her out of my sight! [*The soldiers start to take out* PENELOPE *and the* FOOL.] Whip them first, whip them both! [*The two are taken to the door.*] Nay, leave them here, leave them, knaves . . . leave them! Damn you, do you hear me? You are too quick to obey orders! You like this whipping too well, sirrah! You have an itch for laying on! You beef-witted bastards! And now let us have entertainment, gentle lords! Let us be merry! The players are here! Let us have a play!

[*A* HERALD *runs in to the* QUEEN *without ceremony, calling out as he comes:*]

The Herald. Your Majesty, Your Majesty! Lord Scroop sends me from the city to tell you there is a rising in London! There is a mob rising in the city!

Elizabeth. What . . . is this one of the players? Are you playing Richard II for us?

The Herald. No, no, Your Majesty! A great number of people came through Fleet Street . . . and they have sacked a grocer's and broken into a wine-merchant's cellar! It is said they will break into Fleet Prison and set all free. . . .

Elizabeth. Not they. If they've broken into a wine-cellar they'll get no farther. We're a marvellous people, we English, but we cannot hold liquor. Now if they were Scotch one might worry. What are they saying, these wine drinkers?

The Herald. I cannot tell you that, Your Majesty.

Elizabeth. Are they not crying "Up with Essex!" "Down with Elizabeth!"?

The Herald. Yes, madam!

Elizabeth. Why surely. What else would they be crying? "Up with Essex!" Viva! "Down with Elizabeth!" A bas! The queen is dead, long live the king! If I were there I would cry it myself! It has a marvellous ring! "Up with Essex!" "Down with Elizabeth!"

Burghley. What are we to do, madam?

Elizabeth. [*To the* HERALD.] What is the Lord Mayor doing about this?

The Herald. Nothing, Madam.

Elizabeth. How like a Lord Mayor and how sensible. That's the first principle of government. Never do anything. Let the others make all the mistakes.

Cecil. But madam . . . there are five hundred of the royal guard at the Tower. . . .

Elizabeth. Let the mayor of London look out for his people. If he allows them to run up and down breaking into wine-cellars, it's his own affair.

Burghley. But if it spreads to the palace, Majesty?

Elizabeth. Why yes . . . let them bring their revolution here to me. I should be amused to see it. They are children, Burghley, drunken children. Would you fire on children?

Burghley. Then let me go into London, madam . . .

Elizabeth. And call out the gard and put down these traitors with powder and ball? No! They are to be allowed to get quite drunk and then go to sleep. Where are these players?

[CECIL *enters with* BURBAGE *and* HEMMINGS.*]

Cecil. Here, madam.

Elizabeth. Ah, yes, bold Burbage and handsome Hemmings. Well, my masters, I understand that you have come to me to have your noses slit and your thumbs branded? Is it so?

Burbage. Only if unavoidable, Your Majesty.

Elizabeth. You have put on a play, I believe?

Burbage. Many, Your Majesty.

Elizabeth. You have revived the old play of Richard II, including in it the deposition scene which was censored on its first presentation, and you have done this to foster treasonous projects.

Burbage. No, Your Majesty, I swear it.

* Richard Burbage and John Hemmings were members of Shakespeare's company. Burbage was its leading actor in romantic parts. He was stout, but he probably never acted Falstaff, which rôle was played by Thomas Pope. Hemmings was prominent in the business affairs of the Globe Theatre and was a sponsor of the collection of Shakespeare's plays, the First Folio of 1623.

Elizabeth. You have not played this play?

Burbage. But not to foster treason, that I swear.

Elizabeth. If you played Richard with that pot-belly it was treason indeed. Then for what purpose?

Burbage. To make money.

Elizabeth. On an old play?

Burbage. We were paid in advance . . .

Elizabeth. By whom?

Burbage. By Lord Southampton.†

Burghley. You see? A friend of Essex

Elizabeth. You have much too handsome a nose for slitting, Master Hemmings, yet you say nothing.

Hemmings. There is only this to say, Your Majesty . . . that we knew nothing of any traitorous intent in the matter . . . and that, had we known of such intent, we would not have given the performance.

Elizabeth. I think you are all traitorous knaves and rascals, as a matter of fact, in league with Essex and Southampton—and the smoothest liars in Christendom. Is there something in this?

Hemmings. No, madam.

Elizabeth. You know Essex and Southampton?

Hemmings. We know Lord Southampton.

Elizabeth. How much were you paid for the revival of Richard?

Hemmings. Three pounds, Your Majesty.*

Elizabeth. No more?

Hemmings. No more.

Elizabeth. Play it again this afternoon, masters, play it at my request this afternoon, and you shall have ten pounds for it. Lord Cecil, pay Master Burbage ten pounds from the royal exchequer for one performance of Richard. And let it stand in the record.

Cecil. Yes, madam.

Elizabeth. [*To* HEMMINGS.] And tell Lord Southampton when you see him that I paid ten to his three. Will you tell him?

Hemmings. Yes, Your Majesty.

Elizabeth. And when you have all this treason out of your systems be ready to play Sir John Falstaff for me at the end of the week. I should like to see your Falstaff again, sir.

Burbage. Yes, Your Majesty.

Elizabeth. You may go.

[BURBAGE *and* HEMMINGS *go out.*]

Cecil. [*Waiting till they are gone.*] You are mad, Your Majesty! This is a rebellion, and you play into their hands. The outer court is thronging with messengers from the city! Half the town is in uprising!

Elizabeth. I know.

Cecil. Madam . . .

Elizabeth. Little man, little man, let me alone.

Cecil. This much I must tell you. Lord Essex has been seen with an armed force in the city.

Elizabeth. Lord Essex?

Cecil. With an army. Where he is now no one can say.

Elizabeth. And if one were to guess?

Cecil. He is on his way hither.

Elizabeth. So I think. I shall be glad to see him. Let him bring his revolution here. How long think you it will last after I have looked on it?

Burghley. Madam, the palace is unprotected from the waterside. The guard must be drawn up.

Elizabeth. With your permission, my lord, I would rather not.

Cecil. I took the liberty of ordering a guard posted along the river.

[*A door is opened without and a sudden snarl of angry voices breaks in on the conference.*]

The Voices. "Who has given these orders?"
"Back there . . . back!"
"Not the queen, by God!"
"The queen . . . the queen! Defend the queen!"
"An Essex!"
"Hold your mouth!"
"Stand back, fellow!"

Essex. [*Outside.*] I say the queen will see me! Stand back!

[*There is a clank of armor in the hallway and* ESSEX *appears in the doorway,* SOLDIERS *following him.*]

Elizabeth. You come with a file of soldiers at your back, my lord of Essex.

Essex. Do I need them, Your Majesty?

Elizabeth. No.

Essex. Then be off with you. Follow my orders. [SOLDIERS *go out.*] They told me you would not see me.

Elizabeth. They were wrong. I will see you. It seems you are in rebellion,
My good lord. Enter and state your grievance,
If you have grievance. For myself, I have
A great affection for rebels, being one myself
Much of the time.

Essex. I am no rebel, Your Majesty . . .
But, newly arrived from Ireland, and bearing news

† Southampton, the most conspicuous of Essex' co-plotters, actually had no part in the plans for the play's revival.

* The actual payment was forty shillings.

Of your subjects there, I venture to come to see you,
No more.

Elizabeth. And your army? . . . You have an army with you?

Essex. I have brought my men home to London.

Elizabeth. You received
My orders, no doubt, directing you to disband?

Essex. I believed them to be mistaken. To disband on the coast
And leave my expedition there, seemed strange,
And dangerous to the country. An army turned loose
Becomes a mob.

Elizabeth. And you tell me this! You are informed in these matters
But I am not!

Essex. Indeed, that is quite true . . .
I do know about armies . . . and you do not.

Elizabeth. Oh, yes . . .
Oh, indeed. And who paid them then? I believe
Your supplies were cut off?

Essex. I have paid them.

Elizabeth. They are then
In your service?

Essex. In my service and therefore
Devoted yours.

Elizabeth. And Ireland? How of Ireland?

Essex. I could have conquered Ireland had you given me time.
I left it worse than I found it.

Elizabeth. An honest answer,
At any rate.

Essex. Why should I lie? The fault,
If any, was yours. To conquer Ireland requires
More than the months you gave me. Years, perhaps.

Elizabeth. You were engaged in subduing the rebels, then,
When I summoned you home?

Essex. Just so.

Elizabeth. You were not, by chance,
Joined with the rebels?

Essex. Never.

Elizabeth. You held no parleys
With our friend Tyrone?

Essex. I did. They were part of my plan.

Elizabeth. Your plans! Your plans! Why did you write me nothing
Of these your plans? Am I a witch to find out
What happens on the far side of the Irish Sea
Without being told?

Essex. I wrote you . . .

Elizabeth. Masterly letters.
Brief, to the point, wasting no words, in short,
Nothing.

Essex. I know not what Your Majesty means
By that. I wrote you fully, and in answer
Received no reply.

Elizabeth. You wrote me?

Essex. Many times.

Elizabeth. And had no letters from me?

Essex. None.

Elizabeth. Before God.
If the couriers were tampered with there shall be
Some necks stretched here! My lords, I wish to speak
With Lord Essex here alone! Leave us.

Cecil. Dear queen,
Do you think it safe . . .

Elizabeth. Leave us!

[BURGHLEY *makes a sign and the stage is silently emptied save for the* QUEEN *and* ESSEX. *A pause.*]

What did you write me?

Essex. I wrote you my love—for I thought you loved me then—
And then I pled with you not to bring me home
In the midst of my mission—and then at last angrily—
For I had not heard—but always to say I loved you—
Always.

Elizabeth. But is this true?

Essex. Would I lie?

Elizabeth. Some one
Has lied and will pay with his life if this is true!—
Before God and hell—some one will pay for this.

Essex. What did you write me?

Elizabeth. I wrote—my love——
God keep you safe—I know not—and then, not hearing,
I wrote God knows what madness—as to a rebel——
Thinking you no longer mine—faithless!
Thinking——

Essex. I would I had known—I was in torment——
I—forgive me——

Elizabeth. You should never have gone away.
God, how I've hated you!——

Essex. No!

Elizabeth. Planned to put you to torture!

Essex. I have been in torture!

[*He steps toward her.*]

Elizabeth. Not yet—I can't breathe yet—
I can't breathe——
Or think or believe——
Essex. Nor I.
Elizabeth. Can we ever——
Believe again? Can it be as it used to be?
Essex. We can make it so.
Elizabeth. Come, kill me if you will. Put your arms round me——
If you love me. Do you still love me?
Essex. Yes.
Elizabeth. Yes, yes——
If this were false, then, then truly—then I should die.
I thought because I was older—you see—some one else——
Essex. No one—never a breath——
Elizabeth. Is it all, all as before?
Essex. We have not changed.
Elizabeth. No. Yes, a little, perhaps.
They have changed us a little.
Essex. Not I. I have not changed.
Elizabeth. Can I trust you now?
Essex. Sweet, think back, all those months,
All those hideous months! No word, no love.
And then word did come, it was to make me prisoner!
Christ, I have pride!
And though I came here in defiance, I came truly to find you
Who have been lost from me.
Elizabeth. Do you ask forgiveness?
It is all forgiven.
Essex. Then, why then, hell's vanished—
And here's heaven risen out of it, a heaven of years
In the midst of desolate centuries.
Elizabeth. We have so few years.
Let us make them doubly sweet, these years we have,
Be gracious with each other, sway a little
To left or right if we must to stay together—
Never distrust each other—nay, distrust
All others, when they whisper. Let us make this our pact
Now, for the fates are desperate to part us
And the very gods envy this happiness
We pluck out of loss and death.
Essex. If two stand shoulder to shoulder against the gods,
Happy together, the gods themselves are helpless
Against them, while they stand so.
Elizabeth. Love, I will be
Your servant. Command me. What would you have?
Essex. Why nothing——
Elizabeth. Take this my world, my present in your hands!
You shall stand back of my chair and together we
Shall build an England to make the old world wonder
And the new world worship!—What is this doubt in your brow?
Essex. I am troubled to be dishonest. I have brought my army
Here to the palace—and though it's all true that we've said——
No letters—utter agony over long months——
It is something in myself that has made me do this,
Not Cecil—nor anyone. No one but myself.
The rest is all excuse.
Elizabeth. Speak what you will.
Essex. If you had but shown anger I could have spoken
Easily. It's not easy now, but speak I must!
Oh, I've thought much about this
On lonely marches and in distant tents,
Thinking of you and me. I say this now
Without rancor—in all friendliness and love——
The throne is yours by right of descent and by
Possession—but if this were a freer time,
And there were election, I should carry the country before me,
And this being true, and we being equal in love,
Should we not be equal in power as well?
Elizabeth. We are equal.
I have made you so.
Essex. Yes, but still it's all yours——
Yours to grant me now or take away.
Elizabeth. How could this well be otherwise?
Essex. Am I not—and I say this too in all love—
As worthy to be king as you to be queen?
Must you be sovereign alone?
Elizabeth. You are young in policy,
My Essex, if you do not see that if I
Should grant high place to you now it would show ill to the kingdom——
It would be believed that you had forced this on me,
Would be called a revolution. It would undermine
All confidence. What is built up for years
In people's minds blows away like thistledown
When such things get abroad.
Essex. But is this your reason
Or have you another? Would you trust me as king?
Elizabeth. No.

Essex. And are you still reluctant to give up
Your prerogatives?
Elizabeth. Yes.
Essex. Then now, when the country is mine, the court in my hands,
You my prisoner, I must send my men away,
Disband my army, give back your kingdom to you,
And know I have been king for a moment only
And never will be again?
Elizabeth. I am your prisoner?
Essex. The palace and the city are in my hands.
This England is mine now for the taking * ——
Elizabeth. This is your friendship! This is your love!
Essex. As water finds its level, so power goes
To him who can use it, and soon or late the name
Of king follows where power is.
Elizabeth. Oh, my Essex,
You are a child in war as you are in council.
Why all this talk of power? No army opposed you
When your troops came the road from Ireland. No guard was set
To stop your entrance with your thousand halberds.
Shall I tell you why? Because I wished to keep
A semblance of peace between us. And for that,
I am your prisoner!
Essex. Yes. My dear prisoner.
Elizabeth. Now I do know at least
What it was you wanted. You wanted my kingdom. You have it.
Make the best of it. And so shall I.
What are your plans?
Essex. I have none.
Elizabeth. The Tower, the block——
You could hardly take a queen prisoner and have no thought
Of her destiny. I am my mother's daughter,
I too can walk the path my mother walked.
Essex. These are heroics. You know you are free as air.
Elizabeth. If I do as you ask.
Essex. Is it so hard to share your power with your love?
I could have all—and I offer to share with you.

* Actually, Essex's rebellion failed to draw many adherents, and, without attempting to capture the Queen, he withdrew to his London house to await arrest.

Elizabeth. Let's have no more pretending.
I'd have given all—but you came with an army, demanding——
In short, you don't love—nor trust me—no—nor want me——
Essex. God knows I have wanted you. I have wanted power——
Believed myself fitted to hold it—but not without you.
Elizabeth. If you had wanted me would you rise and strike
At me with an army? Never, never! You'd have come
To me quietly, and we'd have talked of it together
As lovers should—and we'd both have our way——
And no one the wiser. But now, to take the palace,
Hold me prisoner—no—what you wanted you've taken——
And that is all you shall have. This is your kingdom——
But I—I am not yours.
Essex. But I am yours
And have been.
Elizabeth. Who will believe that? Not the world,
No, and not I. I'd rather go to the Tower
Than share my place on terms like these. Put me where I
Will do least harm.
Essex. I cannot, could not, will not.
Elizabeth. If I could have given freely—
But not now. Not surrendering. Not to a victor.
Essex. I am no victor if I lose you. The only gift
That I could take from you is that we are equals.
Elizabeth. Yes, but not now.
Essex. I ask one word from you.
Give me this word—this one word—and these soldiers
Shall leave, and you shall be free.
Elizabeth. I'll believe that
When it happens.
Essex. I'll believe you when you promise.
Elizabeth. Then you have my promise.
You shall share the realm with me. As I am queen,
I promise it.
Essex. Then this is my answer.
[*He kisses her, then calls:*]
Marvel!—Marvel! [MARVEL *enters.*]
Carry out the order of release. Dismiss my guard——
Return the palace into the queen's hands.
Retire with all our forces to the Strand.

Release all prisoners. Release the queen's guard
And send them to their stations.
[MARVEL *goes out.*]
The palace will be
Returned as quickly as taken. This is our last quarrel.

Elizabeth. Yes—our last.

Marvel's Voice. [*Off-stage.*] Form for retire!

Another Voice. Form for retire!

A More Distant Voice. Form for retire!

A Voice. [*In the distance.*] Ready to march!

Another Voice. Ready to march!

Another. All ready!

Another. Ready, captain!

[MARVEL *enters.*]

Marvel. The order is obeyed, my lord.

Essex. Follow your men.

Marvel. Yes, my lord. [*He goes out.*]

Essex. It is as I planned. They are leaving the palace.
Now let us talk no more of this tonight——
Let us forget this matter of thrones and kingdoms
And be but you and me for a while.

Elizabeth. [*Immobile.*] Yes—yes——
Let us forget. Have you kept your word indeed?

Essex. I have kept my word.

Elizabeth. If I clapped my hands
Would my guard come now—or yours?

Essex. Yours only. Shall I call them?

Elizabeth. No—I'll call them. [*She claps her hands four times.* CAPTAIN ARMIN *appears in the entrance followed by four* BEEF-EATERS *with halberds. They stand at attention in the entrance.*]
To be sure I have a guard
Once more. [*To the* CAPTAIN.]
The palace has been returned? It is in
Our hands?

Captain. Yes, Majesty.

Elizabeth. I have ruled England a long time, my Essex,
And I have found that he who would rule must be
Quite friendless, without mercy, without love.
Arrest Lord Essex!
Arrest Lord Essex! Take him to the Tower
And keep him safe.

Essex. Is this a jest?

Elizabeth. I never
Jest when I play for kingdoms, my lord of Essex.

Essex. I trusted you.

Elizabeth. I trusted you,
And learned from you that no one can be trusted.
I will remember that.

Essex. Lest that should be all
You ever have to remember, Your Majesty,
Take care what you do.

Elizabeth. I shall take care.

[ESSEX *unsheathes his sword, breaks it across his knee, flings it at the foot of the throne, turns and walks out between the two files of* GUARDS.]

CURTAIN

ACT THREE

SCENE.—*The queen's apartments in the Tower,* a square and heavy room, long and with a raised stone platform, at one end of which stands a regal chair. It is dawn, the light filtering in coldly.*

[ELLEN *stands in the doorway at the left, weeping, with one arm before her face. The* FOOL, *who has been sleeping wrapped in the draperies of the queen's chair, uncoils himself from among them and rolls over to rub his eyes.* TRESSA *hurries in.*]

Tressa. Come back quickly, dear, quickly! She's sorry she hurt you. She'll have no one else read to her.

Ellen. [*Weeping.*] I can't read now. I'm —I don't mind if she strikes me—only—it wasn't my fault—— We're all so weary.

Tressa. She's sorry——

The Fool. [*Waking.*] One, two—there should be three.

[MARY *comes to the door.*]

Mary. [*Very low.*] Ellen——

The Fool. Three.

Mary. Ellen! She wants you at once.

[ELLEN *runs out.*]

The Fool. Where am I?

Mary. Yes—and what are you doing there?

The Fool. Trying to sleep.

Mary. Sleep? In the Tower?

The Fool. Come and help me. I have heard that you are perfect at lying down. [MARY *and* TRESSA *go out. The* FOOL *looks*

* Essex was executed 25 February 1601. The Queen did not go to the Tower.

about him sleepily, then remembers something and hunts for it under a chair. When he extracts it it proves to be a roasted bird on a wooden platter, covered with leaves. He examines it, then replaces a large leaf over it. PENELOPE, *fully dressed, comes in from the rear.*] Penelope?

Penelope. Yes?

The Fool. Have you slept?

Penelope. No.

The Fool. Then you should break your fast. You are hungry?

Penelope. No. I can't eat.

The Fool. [*Showing his capon.*] Look.

Penelope. What's that?

The Fool. Breakfast. I brought it from Whitehall.

Penelope. Eat it then.

[*She sits on a step disconsolately.*]

The Fool. You won't have any?

Penelope. No.

The Fool. [*Pushing the food away.*] I'm not hungry either.

Penelope. Eat it, poor fool.

The Fool. I don't want it. I brought it for you.

Penelope. I know. But eat it.

[*She wipes her eyes.*]

The Fool. Why should you weep?

Penelope. God knows. He never wept for me.

The Fool. The earl's not dead yet, remember.

Penelope. No.

The Fool. And she'll never let it happen.

Penelope. The clock's struck five. He's to die at six.

The Fool. Why has she not sent to him?

Penelope. She has. We were awake all night. She has sent messages but he's not answered. She's been waiting for word from him. But he's as silent as if he wanted to die.

The Fool. Will she let them kill him if he says nothing?

Penelope. She's a strange woman. She wants him to beg her pardon . . . or something like that.

The Fool. Would you beg her pardon if you were he?

Penelope. No.

The Fool. Then he won't. For I think he's as proud as you.

Penelope. He has not said a word or sent a message since his arrest.

The Fool. And the queen has not slept?

Penelope. No.

The Fool. Nor you?

Penelope. No.

The Fool. God help these women.

Penelope. She says she gave him a ring once. If he ever wanted forgiveness he was to send the ring. And he sits there stubbornly with the ring on his finger. Oh, God, will nothing happen?

[*The* FOOL *has absent-mindedly pulled the capon toward him again, and begins to eat.* ELIZABETH *emerges from the rear.*]

Elizabeth. Penelope?

Penelope. Yes.

Elizabeth. Have the players come?

Penelope. Not yet.

[*The* FOOL *has pushed the food guiltily behind him.*]

Elizabeth. These cheating grooms! I'll have them carbonadoed for this dallying! I shall go mad here! Bring me the little book of prayers . . . from the window-sill. No . . . leave it. The gods of men are sillier than their kings and queens . . . and emptier and more powerless. There is no god but death, no god but death! [*She sees the food the* FOOL *has been hiding.*] Gnaw your bones somewhere else! [*The* FOOL *goes out left.*] Come here, my dear. I heard the clock strike five.

Penelope. Yes. I heard it.

[*They sit together on the steps, and* PENELOPE *puts her arm round* ELIZABETH.]

Elizabeth. Do you love him well, my dear?

Penelope. Yes, Your Majesty.

[ELIZABETH *bows her head wearily on* PENELOPE.]

Elizabeth. I love him. He has never loved me.

Penelope. Yes, yes. He does love you. I've been madly jealous of you.

Elizabeth. Of me? Poor child.

Penelope. But he loved you . . . and never me at all.

Elizabeth. How do you know?

Penelope. He told me.

Elizabeth. What did he say?

Penelope. He said, "I love her dearly." I wanted him for myself, and I warned him against you. He laughed at me. He said, "I love her very dearly."

Elizabeth. You tell me this because you want to save him.

Penelope. No, dear queen. It's true.

Elizabeth. This is the end of me, dear. This is the end.
It comes late. I've been a long while learning,
But I've learned it now. Life is bitter. Nobody

Dies happy, queen or no. Will he speak, think you?
Will he send to me?

Penelope. No. Not now.

Elizabeth. You see,
This is the end of me. Oh, I shall live,
I shall walk about and give orders . . . a horrible while . . .
A horrible old hag.

Penelope. You must send for him.
He's proud as you are, and you have the upper hand.
He'll say nothing. You must send for him, bring him here.

[*The chimes ring the quarter hour.*]

Elizabeth. Not yet. Not yet. [*She rises.*]
Where are the players? I sent
For the players hours ago! They shall pay for this,
The insolent servants! Mary . . . Tressa, God's head!
I'm bestially served! Ellen!

[ELLEN *looks in, partly dressed.*]

Find out if the players
Are here? And be quick.

Ellen. Yes, madam. [*She disappears.*]

Elizabeth. Where's my fool?

The Fool. [*Looking in with a bone in his hand.*] Here, madam.

Elizabeth. Where are you when I need you?
Look at the oaf! Say nothing! You're funny enough
The way you are with your capon in your mouth!
Eat! Eat! Let me see you!

The Fool. I don't seem to be hungry!

Elizabeth. Eat, I say!

The Fool. Yes, madam. [*He tries to eat.*]

Elizabeth. Now wipe your fingers.
Here, take my napkin, child. Come here! You're disgusting!

[*She gives him a kerchief.*]

Can you not clean your face?

The Fool. With this?

Elizabeth. Aye, with that.

[*She takes his bone and throws it.*]

Why do you make mouths at it? It's clean.

The Fool. Yes, madam!

[*He begins to wipe his mouth, then starts to cry; and, sitting down on the steps, sobs heavily, his head in his hands.*]

Elizabeth. What is it now? What good's a fool that cries
When you need comfort? What's the matter?

The Fool. Please,
I don't know. You aren't like the queen.

Elizabeth. I am
The queen, though.

Tressa. [*Looking in.*] The players, madam.

Elizabeth. Bring them here.

Penelope. The time's grown short. Will you send for him?

Elizabeth. Wait . . . he may come.

Penelope. No, no. He won't. You'll let it go too long
Watching the players.

Elizabeth. Let them come in.

[TRESSA *is seen at the doorway with the* ACTORS.]

Penelope. You should eat
A little something first.

Elizabeth. No, no. Bring them in.

[*The* ACTORS *enter.*]

Come in, my masters, let us have a play . . .
Let us have revels and amusements quickly . . .
If ever you played play now. This is my bad
Quarter of an hour.*

Penelope. Please, please . . .

Elizabeth. Quick! Quick . . .
You are late, sirs . . . never mind . . . some scene from Falstaff . . .
The one where he lies to the prince about running away
And the prince catches him . . .

Hemmings. Where, Majesty?

Elizabeth. There, anywhere. Come, sit down. Sit down.

[*The* GIRLS *and the* FOOL *group about her.*]

Begin, Falstaff! "I call thee coward! I'll see thee
Damned ere I call thee coward!"

Falstaff. I call thee coward! I'll see thee damned ere I call thee coward: but I would give a thousand pound I could run as fast as thou canst.

Prince Henry. What's the matter?

Falstaff. What's the matter! there be four of us here have ta'en a thousand pound this day morning.

Prince Henry. Where is it, Jack? where is it?

Falstaff. Where is it! taken from us it is: a hundred upon poor four of us.

Prince Henry. What, fought ye with them all?

Falstaff. All! I know not what ye call all; but if I fought not with fifty of them, I am a bunch of radish: if there were not two or three and fifty upon poor old Jack, then am I no two-legged creature.

Elizabeth. Come, come . . . this is not to

* A play was performed before the Queen by Shakespeare's company 24 February 1601. What play is not known.

the purpose . . . I had thought this witty . . . [*The* PLAYERS *pause.*] Play! Play!

Prince Henry. Pray God, you have not murdered some of them.

Falstaff. Nay, that's past praying for: I have peppered two of them; two I am sure I have paid, . . . two rogues in buckram suits. I tell thee what, Hal, . . . if I tell thee a lie, spit in my face, call me horse. Thou knowest my old ward . . . here I lay, and thus I bore my point. Four rogues in buckram let drive at me . . .

Price Henry. What, four? thou saidst but two even now.

Falstaff. Four, Hal; I told thee four.

Poins. Ay, ay, he said four.

Falstaff. These four came all a-front, and mainly thrust at me. I made me no more ado but took all their seven points in my target, thus.

[*The* QUEEN *walks from place to place, restlessly.*]

Prince Henry. Seven? why, there were but four even now.

Falstaff. In buckram?

Poins. Aye, four in buckram suits.

Falstaff. Seven, by these hilts, or I am a villain else.

Prince Henry. Pr'ythee, let him alone; we shall have more anon.

Falstaff. Dost thou hear me, Hal?

Prince Henry. Ay, and mark thee too, Jack.

Elizabeth. Aye, aye . . . we are listening . . . Play!

Falstaff. Do so, for it is worth the listening to. These nine in buckram that I told thee of . . .

Prince Henry. So, two more already.

Falstaff. Began to give me ground: but I followed me close, came in foot and hand; and with a thought seven of the eleven I paid.

Prince Henry. O monstrous! eleven buckram men grown out of two!

Falstaff. But, as the devil would have it, three misbegotten knaves in Kendal green came at my back and let drive at me . . . for it was so dark, Hal, that thou couldst not see thy hand.

Prince Henry. These lies are like the father that begets them . . . gross as a mountain, open, palpable. Why, thou clay-brained guts, thou knotty-pated fool, thou whoreson, obscene, greasy tallow-ketch . . .

Falstaff. What, art thou mad? art thou mad? is not the truth the truth?

Prince Henry. Why, how couldst thou know these men in Kendal green, when it was so dark thou couldst not see thy hand? come, tell us your reason: what sayest thou to this?

Poins. Come, your reason, Jack . . . your reason.

Falstaff. What, upon compulsion? Give you a reason on compulsion! if reasons were as plenty as blackberries I would give no man a reason on compulsion, I.

Prince Henry. I'll be no longer guilty of this sin; this sanguine coward, this bed-presser, this horse back-breaker, this huge hill of flesh . . .

Falstaff. Away, you starveling, you elf-skin, you dried neat's tongue . . . O for breath to utter what is like thee! . . . you tailor's yard, you sheath, you bowcase, you vile standing-tuck . . .

Prince Henry. Well, breathe awhile, and then to it again: and when thou hast tired thyself in base comparisons, hear me speak but this.

Poins. Mark, Jack.

Prince Henry. We two saw you four set on four; you bound them, and were masters of their wealth. . . . Mark now, how a plain tale shall put you down. . . . Then did we two set on you four; and, with a word, outfaced you from your prize, and have it: yes, and can show it you here in the house: . . . and, Falstaff, you carried your guts away as nimbly, with as quick dexterity, and roared for mercy, and still ran and roared, as ever I heard bull-calf. What a slave art thou, to hack thy sword as thou hast done, and then say it was in fight! What trick, what device, what starting-hole canst thou now find out to hide thee from this open and apparent shame?

Poins. Come, let's hear, Jack; what trick hast thou now?

Falstaff. By the Lord, I knew ye as well as He that made ye. Why, hear ye, my masters: was it for me to kill the heir-apparent? Should I turn upon the true prince? Why, thou knowest I am as valiant as Hercules: but beware instinct; the lion will not touch the true prince. Instinct is a great matter; I was a coward on instinct. I shall think the better of myself and thee during my life; I for a valiant lion, and thou for a true prince. But, by the Lord, lads, I am glad you have the money. What, shall we be merry? Shall we have a play extempore?

Elizabeth. My God, my God . . . can not one forget for a moment?
Who are these strangers? What is this interlude?
Go! Go! It's a vile play and you play it vilely!

Go! By my God, will no one deliver me from this torment? [*The* PLAYERS *start out.*]
Take your trappings and go!
[*They leave. The chimes strike.*]
Again . . . the half-hour . . . [CECIL *enters.*]
Yes? [*To* PENELOPE.]
Was I not wise to wait? He has spoken first! Yes?

Cecil. Your Majesty, a citizen rabble has gathered
To protest the execution of Essex. The captain
Begs permission to use your guard. There's no other
Force at hand to disperse them.

Elizabeth. It's your day, Cecil.
I daresay you know that. The snake-in-the-grass
Endures, and those who are noble, free of soul,
Valiant and admirable . . . they go down in the prime,
Always they go down . . .

Cecil. Madam, the guard
Is needed at once . . .

Elizabeth. Aye . . . the snake-mind is best . . .
One by one you out-last them. To the end
Of time it will be so . . . the rats inherit the earth.
Take my guard. Take it. I thought you brought word from . . .
Go, call Lord Essex for me
From his cell . . . and bring him hither! I'll wait no longer!

Cecil. Lord Essex is prepared for execution.
The priest has been sent to him.

Elizabeth. Bring him here, I say,
And now . . . at once!
[CECIL *bows and goes out.*]
Go out from me, all of you,
All save Penelope. Go quickly, quickly . . .
All . . . [*They leave.*]
Penelope, bring my robe, the one
Laid out . . . [PENELOPE *goes.* ELIZABETH *seats herself in the royal chair.* PENELOPE *returns with the robe.*]
Look here in my face, Penelope. He's so young,
And I'm old, girl, I'm old. It shows in my eyes.
Dear, you're so young. Do not be here when he comes . . .
Do you mind? You'll look so young.

Penelope. Yes, madam . . . but you . . .
You're beautiful.

Elizabeth. Beautiful still? But I was once . . . I was . . .
You'd not believe it now.

Penelope. Oh, yes . . .
You're always beautiful. You've always been.

Elizabeth. Thank you,
My dear. Go now. He'll come.

Penelope. Yes.
[*She goes out to the rear. After a moment* ESSEX *enters from the left with a* GUARD. *The* GUARD *leaves him and steps out.* ESSEX *is dressed in black and is very pale.*]

Essex. You sent for me?
Or so they said.

Elizabeth. Yes.

Essex. It would have been kinder
To leave me with my thoughts till the axe came down
And ended them. You spoil me for death.

Elizabeth. Are you
So set on dying?

Essex. I can't say I care for it.
This blood that beats in us has a way of wanting
To keep right on. But if one is to die
It's well to go straight toward it.

Elizabeth. You must have known
I never meant you to die.

Essex. I am under sentence
From Your Majesty's courts. There's no appeal that I know of.
I am found guilty of treason on good evidence,
And cannot deny it. This treason, I believe,
Is punishable with death.

Elizabeth. God knows I am proud . . .
And bitter, too . . . bitter at you with much cause,
But I have sent for you. I've taken the first step
That way. Do not make me take the next!

Essex. The next is to the scaffold. It's only a step
Now, and I've made ready.

Elizabeth. Aye, you are bitter,
Too; we have let it go late; we've both
Waited for the other. But it was I who spoke
First . . . Will you make me tell you first how much
I've longed for you? It's hard for me.

Essex. My dear,
You can tell me so gracefully, for you
Have nothing to gain or lose by me . . . but I
Have life and love to gain, and I find it less
Than fitting to speak like a lover, lest you suppose
I do it to save my head.

Elizabeth. It's true that you never

Loved me, isn't it? You were ambitious, and I
Loved you, and it was the nearest way to power,
And you took the nearest way? No, no . . . one moment . . .
This is an hour for truth, if there's ever truth . . .
I'm older than you . . . but a queen; it was natural
You'd flatter me, speak me fair, and I believed you.
I'm sorry I believed you. Sorry for you
More than for me.
Essex. Why, yes . . . that's true enough.
Now may I go? This dying sticks in my mind,
And makes me poor company, I fear.
Elizabeth. It was true.
It was true then?
Essex. If you wish to make me tell you
What you well know, how much I used to love you,
How much I have longed for you, very well, I will say it.
That's a small victory to win over me now,
But take it with the rest.
Elizabeth. You did love me?
Essex. Yes.
Elizabeth. And love me still?
Essex. Yes. You should know that, I think.
Elizabeth. You kept my ring. You never sent my ring.
I've been waiting for it.
Essex. You may have it back.
If you have use for it . . . I had thought to wear it
As far as my grave, but, take it.
Elizabeth. I'd have forgiven
All that had passed, at any hour, day or night,
Since I last saw you. I have waited late at night
Thinking, tonight the ring will come, he will never
Hold out against me so long, but the nights went by
Somehow, like the days, and it never came,
Till the last day came, and here it is the last morning
And the chimes beating out the hours.
Essex. Dear, if I'd known . . .
But I could not have sent it.
Elizabeth. Why?
Essex. If I'd tried
To hold you to a promise you could not keep
And you had refused me, I should have died much more
Unhappy than I am now.
Elizabeth. I'd have kept my promise.
I'd keep it now.
Essex. If I offered you this ring?
Elizabeth. Yes . . . even now.
Essex. You would pardon me, set me free
Cede back my estates to me, love me as before,
Give me my place in the state?
Elizabeth. All as it was.
Essex. And what would happen to your throne?
Elizabeth. My throne?
Nothing.
Essex. Yes, for I'd take it from you.
Elizabeth. Again? You'd play that game again?
Essex. The games one plays
Are not the games one chooses always. I
Am still a popular idol of a sort.
There are mutterings over my imprisonment,
Even as it is . . . and if you should set me free
And confess your weakness by overlooking treason
And setting me up in power once more, the storm
That broke last time would be nothing to the storm
That would break over you then. As for myself,
I played for power and lost, but if I had
Another chance I think I'd play and win.
Elizabeth. Why do you say this?
Essex. I say it because it's true.
I have loved you, love you now, but I know myself.
If I were to win you over and take my place
As it used to be, it would gall me. I have a weakness
For being first wherever I am. I refuse
To take pardon from you without warning you
Of this. And when you know it, pardon becomes
Impossible.
Elizabeth. You do this for me?
Essex. Why, yes,
But not altogether. Partly for England, too.
I've lost conceit of myself a little. A life
In prison's very quiet. It leads to thinking.
You govern England better than I should.
I'd lead her into wars, make a great name,
Perhaps, like Henry Fifth and leave a legacy
Of debts and bloodshed after me. You will leave
Peace, happiness, something secure. A woman governs
Better than a man, being a natural coward.
A coward rules best.
Elizabeth. Still bitter.
Essex. Perhaps a little.

It's a bitter belief to swallow, but I believe it.
You were right all the time.
[The chimes ring three-quarters.]
And now, if you'll pardon me,
I have an appointment near-by with a headsman.
He comes sharp on the hour.

Elizabeth. You have an hour yet.
It's but struck five.

Essex. It struck five some time since.

Elizabeth. It cannot go this way!

Essex. Aye, but it has.
It has and will. There's no way out. I've thought of it
Every way. Speak frankly. Could you forgive me
And keep your throne?

Elizabeth. No.

Essex. Are you ready to give
Your crown up to me?

Elizabeth. No. It's all I have. [*She rises.*]
Why, who am I
To stand here paltering with a rebel noble!
I am Elizabeth, daughter of a king,
The queen of England, and you are my subject!
What does this mean, you standing here eye to eye
With me, your liege? You whom I made, and gave
All that you have, you, an upstart, defying
Me to grant pardon, lest you should sweep me from power
And take my place from me? I tell you if Christ his blood
Ran streaming from the heavens for a sign
That I should hold my hand you'd die for this,
You pretender to a throne upon which you have
No claim, you pretender to a heart, who have been
Hollow and heartless and faithless to the end!

Essex. If we'd met some other how we might have been happy . . .
But there's been an empire between us! I am to die . . .
Let us say that . . . let us begin with that . . .
For then I can tell you that if there'd been no empire
We could have been great lovers. If even now
You were not queen and I were not pretender,
That god who searches heaven and earth and hell
For two who are perfect lovers, could end his search
With you and me. Remember . . . I am to die . . .
And so I can tell you truly, out of all the earth
That I'm to leave, there's nothing I'm very loath
To leave save you. Yet if I live I'll be
Your death or you'll be mine.

Elizabeth. Give me the ring.

Essex. No.

Elizabeth. Give me the ring. I'd rather you killed me
Than I killed you.

Essex. It's better for me as it is
Than that I should live and batten my fame and fortune
On the woman I love. I've thought of it all. It's better
To die young and unblemished than to live long and rule,
And rule not well.

Elizabeth. Aye, I should know that.

Essex. Is it not?

Elizabeth. Yes.

Essex. Good-by, then.

Elizabeth. Oh, then I'm old, I'm old!
I could be young with you, but now I'm old.
I know now how it will be without you. The sun
Will be empty and circle round an empty earth . . .
And I will be queen of emptiness and death. . . .
Why could you not have loved me enough to give me
Your love and let me keep as I was?

Essex. I know not.
I only know I could not. I must go.

Elizabeth. [*Frozen.*] Yes.
[*He goes to the door.*]
Lord Essex! [*He turns.*]
Take my kingdom. It is yours!
[ESSEX, *as if not hearing, bows and goes on.* PENELOPE *runs in, meeting him.*]

Penelope. My lord! She has forgiven you?

Essex. Good-by, my dear. [*He kisses her.*]

Penelope. No, no! She loves you! Go to her. [ESSEX *goes out.*]
Run to her! She waits you still! See, if you turn
She waits you still! Dear queen, would you let him go?
He goes to his death! Send, send after him!
[*The queen lifts her head and shows a face so stricken that* PENELOPE, *who has gone to her, says no more. The clock strikes six.* ELIZABETH *bows her head on* PENELOPE'S *knees, her hands over her ears.*]

CURTAIN

ABE LINCOLN IN ILLINOIS*

[*A Play in Twelve Scenes*]

By

ROBERT EMMET SHERWOOD

"ABE LINCOLN IN ILLINOIS" IS NOT MERELY our theater's best portrait of Lincoln. It is its author's most mature and satisfying play. For the first time in his writing for the stage, form and substance are blended in it with the convincing artistry that marks the full-grown playwright.

This advance is due not alone to the greatness of the subject, or to increased technical facility, both of which are evident. It has resulted rather from the gradual awakening of the disillusioned intellectual, with a negative philosophy, to a live sense of the positive ideals that alone can save a bewildered humanity, and incidentally its drama.

Sherwood's thought experience has been that of most sensitive minds of the post-war generation. In the preface to *There Shall Be No Night* Mr. Sherwood makes plain the steps leading to his change from futile pacifism to belligerency in defence of human liberty. Lincoln, he admits, made him fully aware that even a great pacifist, when right principles are threatened by war, can put no reliance in appeasement. In this connection Mr. Sherwood writes of Lincoln:

"He had to face the issue of appeasement or war. He faced it. . . . It did mean war—and for Lincoln four years of anguish and then violent death. But it saved the Union."

The uncompromising attitude that led Lincoln to war has become Mr. Sherwood's own. In the phrases searchingly selected and spliced with the perceptiveness of a portrait artist who delineates more than surfaces, Sherwood speaks with Lincoln; and nowhere more movingly than when his hero faces this centralizing issue:

"I am not preaching civil war. All I am trying to do—now, and as long as I live—is to state and restate the fundamental virtues of our democracy. . . .

"I believe most seriously that the perpetuation of these virtues is endangered . . . by those who echo Judge Douglas in shouting, 'Leave it [slavery] alone!' This is the complacent policy of indifference to evil and that policy I cannot but hate."

And the same thought intensified is put into the President's words of farewell:

"We gained democracy, and now there is the question whether it is fit to survive. Perhaps we shall come to the dreadful day of awakening, and the dream is ended. . . . Let us believe that it is not true!"

Such impassioned positiveness contrasts refreshingly with the defeatist sentiments of *The Petrified Forest* or the mere war abhorrence of *Idiot's Delight*. It rises to whiter heat in *There Shall Be No Night*. In that play with less artistry than in *Abe Lincoln* the incidents of the plot become a mere vehicle for its overpowering eloquence. In *Abe Lincoln* a finely woven play pattern exhibits the character in a moving struggle with himself as he gropes from inquiring irresponsibility toward strong conviction and finally to the assumption of the world's weightiest responsibility, for which a fate—mysterious to himself—seems to destine him. Grandly has Mr. Sherwood charted this course, and even more grandly has he ended it at the point where Lincoln leaves the security of his beloved Springfield to meet the tragic destiny that he vaguely senses and the audience knows. This masterstroke in selection and arrangement is one of the most daring and distinguished in modern drama.

But the portrait pattern is hardly more vivid or significant than the treatment of the background against which it is projected. The epic quality of the Lincoln life is sharply defined in the scenes, both varied and symbolic, which Sherwood has constructed to explain and develop it. In them the loyalties and conflicts of democracy, like forge and anvil, beat out a life whose own vision and humorous tolerance make it the perfect material for the process. From it that life emerges not so much the representative of America as its substance and symbol. This epic significance is further touchingly suggested at the heart of the play in a scene wholly Mr. Sherwood's own—that of the prairie (Sc. VII). Imaginatively it conjures back the moment in the Lincoln life that has eluded the most searching of his biographers —the moment of his awakening to the call of destiny. It is Fortinbras to a sluggish Hamlet: Gethsemane to a divine spirit. The suffering and fortitude of his pioneer friends open to him the vista of the hazardous way to a great end, which from that moment must be his way—the way of every worthy American.

We print after the play the dramatist's documentation of the episodes, not to attest the sincerity of his work, but rather to emphasize the skill with which he has fused his materials into convincing dramatic form.

The play was first presented at the National Theatre in Washington on October 3, 1938, and its long run in New York at the Plymouth Theatre began on October 15. It was produced by the Playwrights' Company, an organization of which the author and his celebrated fellow dramatists, Maxwell Anderson, S. N. Behrman, Sidney Howard, and Elmer Rice were the members. The play was staged under the direction of Elmer Rice and its sets were designed by Jo Mielziner. Raymond Massey was Lincoln. The success of the play has been outstanding among the brilliant productions of this auspicious league of playwrights, a cooperative effort almost unprecedented in theater history.

ROBERT EMMET SHERWOOD

Born 1896, New Rochelle, New York.
1914–1917, Harvard University (editor of *The Lampoon*).
1917–1919, War service with the Canadian "Black Watch."
1919–1920, Dramatic editor of *Vanity Fair.*
1920–1928, Co-editor and editor of *Life,* and motion picture editor of *Life* and *The New York Herald.*
1927, *The Road to Rome,* his first play.
1931, A novel: *The Virtuous Knight.* His increasing success as a dramatist has led him to devote his time chiefly to the theater.
1936, Awarded Pulitzer Prize for *Idiot's Delight.*
1939, Awarded Pulitzer Prize for *Abe Lincoln in Illinois.*

PLAYS

1927 *The Road to Rome.* 1927 *The Love Nest.* 1928 *The Queen's Husband.* 1929 *Waterloo Bridge.* 1930 *This Is New York.* 1931 *Reunion in Vienna.* 1932 *The Unending Crusade.* 1933 *Acropolis* (produced in England). 1935 *The Petrified Forest.* 1936 *Idiot's Delight.* 1936 *Tovarich* (adapted from the French of Jacques Deval). 1938 *Abe Lincoln in Illinois.* 1940 *There Shall Be No Night.*

SCREENWRITING

1929 *The Road to Rome.* 1931 *Reunion in Vienna.* 1931 *Waterloo Bridge.* 1931 *The Royal Bed.* 1932 *Cock of the Air.* 1932 *Two Kinds of Women.* 1933 *Roman Scandals.* 1935 *The Scarlet Pimpernel.* 1936 *The Petrified Forest.* 1936 *The Ghost Goes West.* 1937 *Thunder in the City.* 1938 *The Adventures of Marco Polo.* 1939 *Idiot's Delight.* 1940 *Abe Lincoln in Illinois.* 1940 *Rebecca.*

ABE LINCOLN IN ILLINOIS

Characters

MENTOR GRAHAM.
ABE LINCOLN.
ANN RUTLEDGE.
BEN MATTLING.
JUDGE BOWLING GREEN.
NINIAN EDWARDS.
JOSHUA SPEED.
TRUM COGDAL.
JACK ARMSTRONG.
BAB.
FEARGUS.
JASP.
SETH GALE.
NANCY GREEN.
WILLIAM HERNDON.
ELIZABETH EDWARDS.
MARY TODD.
THE EDWARDS' MAID.
JIMMY GALE.
AGGIE GALE.
GOBEY.
STEPHEN A. DOUGLAS.
WILLIE LINCOLN.
TAD LINCOLN.
ROBERT LINCOLN.
THE LINCOLNS' MAID.
CRIMMIN.
BARRICK.
STURVESON.
JED.
KAVANAGH.
MAJOR.

SOLDIERS, RAILROAD MEN, TOWNSPEOPLE.

ACT ONE: In and about New Salem, Illinois, in the 1830's.

SCENE I.—*Mentor Graham's cabin near New Salem, Illinois.*
SCENE II.—*The Rutledge Tavern, New Salem.*
SCENE III.—*Bowling Green's house near New Salem.*

ACT TWO: In and about Springfield, Illinois, in the 1840's.

SCENE IV.—*Law office of Stuart and Lincoln on the second floor of the Court House in Springfield, Illinois.*
SCENE V.—*Parlor of the Edwards house in Springfield.*
SCENE VI.—*Again the law office.*
SCENE VII.—*On the prairie, near New Salem.*
SCENE VIII.—*Again the parlor of the Edwards house.*

ACT THREE: In Springfield, 1858–61.

SCENE IX.—*A speakers' platform in an Illinois town.*
SCENE X.—*Parlor of the Lincolns' home.*
SCENE XI.—*Lincoln campaign headquarters in the Illinois State House.*
SCENE XII.—*The yards of the railroad station at Springfield.*

ACT I

SCENE I

MENTOR GRAHAM'S *cabin near New Salem, Illinois. Late at night.*

There is one rude table, piled with books and papers. Over it hangs an oil lamp, the only source of light.

[*At one side of the table sits* MENTOR GRAHAM, *a sharp but patient schoolteacher.*

Across from him is ABE LINCOLN—*young, gaunt, tired but intent, dressed in the ragged clothes of a backwoodsman. He speaks with the drawl of southern Indiana—an accent which is more Kentuckian than Middle-Western.*

MENTOR *is leaning on the table.* ABE'S *chair is tilted back, so that his face is out of the light.* MENTOR *turns a page in a grammar book.*]

Mentor. The Moods. [MENTOR *closes the book and looks at* ABE.] Every one of us has many moods. You yourself have more than your share of them, Abe. They express the various aspects of your character. So it is with the English language—and you must try to consider this language as if it were a living person, who may be awkward and stumbling, or pompous and pretentious, or simple and direct. Name me the five moods.

Abe. The Indicative, Imperative, Potential, Subjunctive, and Infinitive.

Mentor. And what do they signify?

Abe. The Indicative Mood is the easy one. It just indicates a thing—like "He loves," "He is loved"—or, when you put it in the form of a question, "Does he love?" or "Is he loved?" The Imperative Mood is used for commanding, like "Get out and be damned to you."

Mentor. [*Smiling.*] Is that the best example you can think of?

Abe. Well—you can put it in the Bible way—"Go thou in peace." But it's still imperative.

Mentor. The mood derives its name from the implication of command. But you can use it in a very different sense—in the form of the humblest supplication.

Abe. Like "Give us this day our daily bread and forgive us our trespasses."

Mentor. [*Reaching for a newspaper in mess on the table.*] I want you to read this—it's a speech delivered by Mr. Webster before the United States Senate. A fine document, and a perfect usage of the Imperative Mood in its hortatory sense. Here it is. Read this—down here.

[*He leans back to listen.*]

Abe. [*Takes paper, leans forward into the lights and reads:*] "Sir," the Senator continued, in the rich deep tones of the historic church bells of his native Boston, "Sir—I have not allowed myself to look beyond the Union, to see what might be hidden in the dark recess behind. While the Union lasts . . ."

[ABE *has been reading in a monotone, without inflection.*]

Mentor. [*Testily.*] Don't read it off as if it were an inventory of Denton Offut's groceries. Imagine that *you're* making the speech before the Senate, with the fate of your country at stake. Put your own life into it!

Abe. I couldn't use words as long as Dan'l Webster.

Mentor. That's what you're here for—to learn! Go ahead.

Abe. [*Reading slowly, gravely.*] "While the Union lasts, we have high prospects spread out before us, for us and our children. Beyond that, I seek not to penetrate the veil. God grant that in my day, at least, the curtain may not rise."

Mentor. Notice the use of verbs from here on.

Abe. [*Reads:*] "When my eyes shall be turned to behold for the last time the sun in heaven, may I not see him shining on the broken and dishonored fragments of a once glorious Union; on States dissevered, discordant, belligerent; on a land rent with civil feuds, or drenched, it may be, in fraternal blood! Let their last feeble glance rather behold the glorious ensign of the republic, now known and honored throughout the earth, not a single star of it obscured, bearing for its motto no such miserable interrogatory . . ." [*He stumbles over the pronunciation.*]

Mentor. Interrogatory.

Abe. [*Continuing.*] ". . . interrogatory as 'What is all this worth?' Nor, those other words of delusion and folly, 'Liberty first and Union afterwards'; but everywhere, spread all over in characters of living light, that other sentiment, dear to every true American heart—Liberty and Union . . ."

Mentor. Emphasize the "*and.*"

Abe. "Liberty *and* Union, now and forever, one and inseparable!" [*He puts the paper back on the table.*] He must have had 'em up on their feet cheering with *that*, all right.

Mentor. Some cheered, and some spat, depending on which section they came from.

Abe. What was he talking about?

Mentor. It was in the debate over the right of any state to secede from the Union. Hayne had pleaded South Carolina's cause—pleaded it ably. He said that just as we have liberty as individuals—so have we liberty as states—to go as we please. Which means, if we don't like the Union, as expressed by the will of its majority, then we can leave it, and set up a new nation, or many nations—so that this continent might be as divided as Europe. But Webster answered him all right. He proved that without Union, we'd have precious little liberty left. Now—go on with the Potential Mood.

Abe. That signifies possibility—usually of an unpleasant nature. Like, "If I ever get out of debt, I will probably get right back in again."

Mentor. [*Smiles.*] Why did you select that example, Abe?

Abe. Well—it just happens to be the thought that's always heaviest on my mind.

Mentor. Is the store in trouble again?

Abe. [*Calmly.*] Yes. Berry's drunk all the whiskey we ought to have sold, and we're going to have to shut up any day now. I guess I'm my father's own son. Give me a steady job, and I'll fail at it.

Mentor. You haven't been a failure here, Abe. There isn't a manjack in this community that isn't fond of you and anxious to help you get ahead.

Abe. [*With some bitterness.*] I know—just like you, Mentor, sitting up late nights, to give me learning, out of the goodness of your heart. And now, Josh Speed and Judge Green and some of the others I owe money to want to get me the job of post-master, thinking that maybe I can handle *that,* since there's only one mail comes in a week. I've got friends, all right—the best friends. But they can't change my luck, or maybe it's just my nature.

Mentor. What you want to do is get out of New Salem. This poor little forgotten town will never give any one any opportunity.

Abe. Yes—I've thought about moving, think about it all the time. My family have always been movers, shifting about, never knowing what they were looking for, and whatever it was, never finding it. My old father ambled from Virginia, to one place after another in Kentucky, where I was born, and then into Indiana, and then here in Illinois. About all I can remember of when I was a boy was hitching up, and then unhitching, and then hitching up again.

Mentor. Then get up and go, Abe. Make a new place for yourself in a new world.

Abe. As a matter of fact, Seth Gale and me have been talking a lot about moving—out to Kansas or Nebraska territory. But—wherever I go—it'll be the same story—more friends, more debts.

Mentor. Well, Abe—just bear in mind that there are always two professions open to people who fail at everything else: there's school-teaching, and there's politics.

Abe. Then I'll choose school-teaching. You go into politics, and you may get elected.

Mentor. Yes—there's always that possibility.

Abe. And if you get elected, you've got to go to the city. I don't want none of that.

Mentor. What did I say about two negatives?

Abe. I meant, any of that.

Mentor. What's your objection to cities, Abe? Have you ever seen one?

Abe. Sure. I've been down river twice to New Orleans. And, do you know, every minute of the time I was there, I was scared?

Mentor. Scared of what, Abe?

Abe. Well—it sounds kind of foolish—I was scared of people.

Mentor. [*Laughs.*] Did you imagine they'd rob you of all your gold and jewels?

Abe. [*Serious.*] No. I was scared they'd kill me.

Mentor. [*Also serious.*] Why? Why should they want to kill you?

Abe. I don't know.

Mentor. [*After a moment.*] You think a lot about death, don't you?

Abe. I've had to, because it has always seemed to be so close to me—always—as far back as I can remember. When I was no higher than this table, we buried my mother. The milksick got her, poor creature. I helped Paw make the coffin—whittled the pegs for it with my own jackknife. We buried her in a timber clearing beside my grandmother, old Betsy Sparrow. I used to go there often and look at the place—used to watch the deer running over her grave with their little feet. I never could kill a deer after that. One time I catched hell from Paw because when he was taking aim I knocked his gun up. And I always compare the looks of those deer with the looks of men—like the men in New Orleans—that you could see had murder in their hearts.

Mentor. [*After a moment.*] You're a hopeless mess of inconsistency, Abe Lincoln.

Abe. How do you mean, Mentor?

Mentor. I've never seen any one who is so friendly and at the same time so misanthropic.

Abe. What's that?

Mentor. A misanthrope is one who distrusts men and avoids their society.

Abe. Well—maybe that's how I am. Oh—I like people, well enough—when you consider 'em one by one. But they seem to look different when they're put into crowds, or mobs, or armies. But I came here to listen to you, and then I do all the talking.

Mentor. Go right on, Abe. I'll correct you when you say things like "catched hell."

Abe. [*Grins.*] I know. Whenever I get talking about Paw, I sort of fall back into his language. But—you've got your own school to teach tomorrow. I'll get along. [*He stands up.*]

Mentor. Wait a minute. . . . [*He is fishing about among the papers. He takes out a copy of an English magazine.*] There's just one more thing I want to show you. It's a poem. [*He finds the place in the magazine.*] Here it is. You read it, Abe. [*He hands* ABE *the magazine.*]

[ABE *seats himself on the edge of the table, and holds the magazine under the light.*]

Abe. [*Reads:*] " 'On Death,' written at the age of nineteen by the late John Keats:
'Can death be sleep, when life is but a dream,
And scenes of bliss pass as a phantom by?
The transient [*he hesitates on that word*] pleasures as a vision seem,
And yet we think the greatest pain's to die.
[*He moves closer to the light.*]
How strange it is that man on earth should roam,
And lead a life of woe, but not forsake
His rugged path—nor dare he view alone
His future doom—which is but to awake.' "
[*He looks at* MENTOR.] That sure is good, Mentor. It's *fine!* [*He is reading it again, to himself, when the lights fade.*]

SCENE II

The Rutledge Tavern, New Salem. Noon on the Fourth of July.

It is a large room, with log walls, but with curtains on the windows and pictures on the walls to give it an air of dressiness. The pictures include likenesses of all the Presidents from Washington to Jackson, and there is also a picture (evidently used for campaign purposes) of Henry Clay.

At the left is a door leading to the kitchen. At the back, toward the right, is the main entrance, which is open. The sun is shining brightly.

The furniture of the room consists of two tables, two benches, and various chairs and stools.

[BEN MATTLING *is seated on a bench at the rear of the room. He is an ancient, paunchy, watery-eyed veteran of the Revolution, and he wears a cocked hat and the tattered but absurd semblance of a Colonial uniform.* JUDGE BOWLING GREEN *and* NINIAN EDWARDS *come in, followed by* JOSHUA SPEED. BOWLING *is elderly, fat, gentle.* NINIAN *is young, tall, handsome, prosperous.* JOSH *is quiet, mild, solid, thoughtful, well-dressed.*]

Bowling. [*As they come in.*] This is the Rutledge Tavern, Mr. Edwards. It's not precisely a gilded palace of refreshment.

Ninian. Make no apologies, Judge Green. As long as the whiskey is wet.

[JOSH *has crossed to the door at the left. He calls off:*]

Josh. Miss Rutledge.

Ann. [*Appearing at the door.*] Yes, Mr. Speed?

Josh. Have you seen Abe Lincoln?

Ann. No. He's probably down at the foot races. [*She goes back into the kitchen.* JOSH *turns to* BOWLING.]

Josh. I'll find Abe and bring him here.

Ninian. Remember, Josh, we've got to be back in Springfield before sundown.

[JOSH *has gone out.*]

Bowling. [*To* MATTLING.] Ah, good day, Uncle Ben. Have a seat, Mr. Edwards.

[*They cross to the table at the right.*]

Ben. Good day to you, Bowling.

[ANN *comes in from the kitchen.*]

Ann. Hello, Judge Green.

Bowling. Good morning, Ann. We'd be grateful for a bottle of your father's best whiskey.

Ann. Yes, Judge. [*She starts to go off.*]

Ben. [*Stopping her.*] And git me another mug of that Barbadoes rum.

Ann. I'm sorry, Mr. Mattling, but I've given you one already and you know my father said you weren't to have any more till you paid for . . .

Ben. Yes, wench—I know what your father said. But if a veteran of the Revolutionary War is to be denied so much as credit, then this country has forgot its gratitude to them that made it.

Bowling. Bring him the rum, Ann. I'll be happy to pay for it.

[TRUM COGDAL *comes in. He is elderly, pernicketty.*]

Ben. [*Reluctantly.*] I have to say thank you, Judge.

Trum. Ann, bring me a pot of Sebago tea.

Ann. Mr. Cogdal.

[*She goes out at the left.* TRUM *sits down at the table.*]

Bowling. Don't say a word, Ben.

Trum. Well, Mr. Edwards—what's your impression of our great and enterprising metropolis?

Ninian. Distinctly favorable, Mr. Cogdal. I could not fail to be impressed by the beauty of your location, here on this hilltop, in the midst of the prairie land.

Trum. Well, we're on the highroad to the West—and when we get the rag, tag, and bobtail cleaned out of here, we'll grow. Yes, sir—we'll grow!

Ninian. [*Politely.*] I'm sure of it.

[ANN *has returned with the whiskey, rum and tea.*]

Bowling. Thank you, Ann.

Ann. Has the mud-wagon come in yet?

Trum. No. I been waiting for it.

Bowling. Not by any chance expecting a letter, are you, Ann?

Ann. Oh, no—who'd be writing to *me,* I'd like to know?

Bowling. Well—you never can tell what might happen on the Fourth of July. [*He and* NINIAN *lift their glasses.*] But I beg to wish you all happiness, my dear. And let me tell you that Mr. Edwards here is a married man, so you can keep those lively eyes to yourself.

Ann. [*Giggles.*] Oh, Judge Green—you're just joking me!

[*She goes to the kitchen.*]

Ninian. A mighty pretty girl.

Trum. Comes of good stock, too.

Ninian. With the scarcity of females in these parts, it's a wonder some one hasn't snapped her up.

Bowling. Some one has. The poor girl promised herself to a man who called himself McNiel—it turned out his real name's McNamar. Made some money out here and then left town, saying he'd return soon. She's still waiting for him. But your time is short, Mr. Edwards; so if you tell us just what it is you want in New Salem, we'll do our utmost to . . .

Ninian. I'm sure you gentlemen know what I want.

Trum. Naturally, you want votes. Well you've got mine. Anything to frustrate that tyrant, Andy Jackson. [*He shakes a finger at the picture of* ANDREW JACKSON.]

Ninian. I assure you that I yield to none in my admiration for the character of our venerable president, but when he goes to the extent of ruining our banking structure, destroying faith in our currency and even driving sovereign states to the point of secession —then, gentlemen, it is time to call a halt.

Bowling. We got two more years of him—if the old man lives that long. You can't make headway against his popularity.

Ninian. But we can start now to drive out his minions here in the government of the state of Illinois. We have a great battle cry: "End the reign of Andrew Jackson."

[JACK ARMSTRONG *and three others of the Clary's Grove boys have come in during this speech. The others are named* BAB, FEARGUS *and* JASP. *They are the town bullies—boisterous, good-natured but tough.*]

Jack. [*Going to the door at the left.*] Miss Rutledge!

Ann. [*Appearing in the doorway.*] What do *you* want, Jack Armstrong?

Jack. Your humble pardon, Miss Rutledge, and we will trouble you for a keg of liquor.

Bab. And we'll be glad to have it quick, because we're powerful dry.

Ann. You get out of here—you get out of here right now—you low *scum*!

Jack. I believe I said a keg of liquor. Did you hear me say it, boys?

Feargus. That's how it sounded to me, Jack.

Jasp. Come along with it, Annie——

Ann. If my father were here, he'd take a gun to you, just as he would to a pack of prairie wolves.

Jack. If your Paw was here, he'd be scareder than you. 'Cause he knows we're the wildcats of Clary's Grove, worse'n any old wolves, and we're a-howlin', and a-spittin' for drink. So get the whiskey, Miss Annie, and save your poor old Paw a lot of expenses for damages to his property.

[ANN *goes.*]

Trum. [*In an undertone to* NINIAN.] That's the rag, tag, and bobtail I was . . .

Jack. And what are you mumblin' about, old measely-weasely Trum Cogdal—with your cup of tea on the Fourth of July?

Bab. He's a cotton-mouthed traitor and I think we'd better whip him for it.

Feargus. [*At the same time.*] Squeeze that air tea outen him, Jack.

Jasp. [*Shouting.*] Come on you, Annie, with that liquor!

Jack. And you, too, old fat-pot Judge Bowling Green that sends honest men to prison—and who's the stranger? Looks kind of damn elegant for New Salem.

Bowling. This is Mr. Ninian Edwards of Springfield, Jack—and for the Lord's sake, shut up, and sit down, and behave yourselves.

Jack. Ninian Edwards, eh! The Governor's son, I presume. Well—well!

Ninian. [*Amiably.*] You've placed me.

Jack. No wonder you've got a New Orleans suit of clothes and a gold fob and a silver-headed cane. I reckon you can buy the best of everything with that steamin' old pirate land-grabber for a Paw. I guess them fancy pockets of yourn are pretty well stuffed with the money your Paw stole from us taxpayers—eh, Mr. Edwards?

Bab. Let's take it offen him, Jack.

Feargus. Let's give him a lickin', Jack.

Jack. [*Still to* NINIAN.] What you come here for anyway? Lookin' for a fight? Because if that's what you're a-cravin', I'm your man—wrasslin', clawin', bitin', and tearin'.

Ann. [*Coming in.*] Jack Armstrong, here's your liquor! Drink it and go away.

[ANN *carries four mugs.*]

Jasp. He told you to bring a keg!

Jack. [*Contemplating the mugs.*] One little noggin apiece? Why—that ain't enough to fill a hollow tooth! Get the keg, Annie.

Feargus. Perhaps she can't tote it. I'll get it, Jack.

[*He goes out into the kitchen.*]

Ann. [*Desperate.*] Aren't there any of you men can do anything to protect decent people from these ruffians?

Ninian. I'll be glad to do whatever I . . . [*He starts to rise.*]

Bowling. [*Restraining him.*] I'd be rather careful, Mr. Edwards.

Jack. That's right, Mr. Edwards. You be careful. Listen to the old Squire. He's got a round pot but a level head. He's seen the Clary's Grove boys in action, and he can tell you you might get that silver-headed cane rammed down your gullet. Hey, Bab—you tell him what we did to Hank Spears and Gus Hocheimer. Just tell him!

Bab. Jack nailed the two of 'em up in a barr'l and sent 'em rollin' down Salem hill and it jumped the bank and fotched up in the river and when we opened up the barr'l they wasn't inclined to move much.

Jack. Of course, it'd take a bigger barr'l to hold you and your friend here, Squire, but I'd do it for you and I'd do it for any by God rapscallions and sons of thieves that come here a-preachin' treachery and disunion and pisenin' the name of Old Hickory, the people's friend.

[FEARGUS *returns with the keg.*]

Ben. Kill him, boys! You're the only *real* Americans we got left!

Ninian. [*Rising.*] If you gentlemen will step outside, I'll be glad to accommodate you with the fight you seem to be spoiling for.

Trum. You're committing suicide, Mr. Edwards.

Jack. Oh, no—he ain't. We ain't killers—we're just bone crushers. After a few months, you'll be as good as new, which ain't saying much. You bring that keg, Feargus.

[*They are about to go when* ABE *appears in the door. He now is slightly more respectably dressed, wearing a battered claw-hammer coat and pants that have been "foxed" with buckskin. He carries the mail. Behind him is* JOSH SPEED.]

Abe. The mud-wagon's in! Hello, Jack. Hello, boys. Ain't you fellers drunk yet? Hello, Miss Ann. Got a letter for you. [*There is a marked shyness in his attitude toward* ANN.]

Ann. Thank you, Abe.

[*She snatches the letter and runs out with it.*]

Ben. Abe, there's goin' to be a fight!

Ninian. [*To* JACK.] Well—come on, if you're coming.

Jack. All right, boys.

Abe. Fight? Who—and why?

Jack. This is the son of Ninian Edwards, Abe. Come from Springfield lookin' for a little crotch hoist and I'm aimin' to oblige.

[ABE *looks* NINIAN *over.*]

Bowling. Put a stop to it, Abe. It'd be next door to murder.

Jack. You shut your trap, Pot Green. Murder's too good for any goose-livered enemy of Andy Jackson. Come on, boys!

Abe. Wait a minute, boys. Jack, have you forgotten what day it is?

Jack. No, I ain't! But I reckon the Fourth is as good a day as any to whip a politician!

Abe. [*Amiably.*] Well, if you've just got to fight, Jack, you shouldn't give preference to strangers. Being postmaster of this thriving town, I can rate as a politician, myself, so you'd better try a fall with me—[*He thrusts* JACK *aside and turns to* NINIAN.] And as for you, sir, I haven't the pleasure of your acquaintance; but my name's Lincoln, and I'd like to shake hands with a brave man.

Ninian. [*Shaking hands with* ABE.] I'm greatly pleased to know you, Mr. Lincoln.

Abe. You should be. Because I come here just in time to save you quite some embarrassment, not to mention injury. Oh, got a couple of letters for you, Bowling. And here's your *Cincinnati Journal,* Trum.

Jack. Look here, Abe—you're steppin' into something that ain't none of your business. This is a private matter of patriotic honor . . .

Abe. Everything in this town is my business, Jack. It's the only kind of business I've got. And besides—I saw Hannah down by the grove and she says to tell you to come on to the picnic and that means *now* or she'll give the cake away to the Straders children and you and the boys'll go hungry. So get moving.

Feargus. [*To* JACK.] Are you goin' to let Abe talk you out of it?

Abe. Sure he is. [*He turns to* TRUM.] Say, Trum—if you ain't using that *Journal* for a while, would you let me have a read?

Trum. By all means, Abe. Here you are. [*He tosses the paper to* ABE.]

Abe. Thanks. [*He turns again to* JACK.]

You'd better hurry, Jack, or *you'll* get a beating from Hannah.

[*He starts to take the wrapper off, as he goes over to a chair at the left.* JACK *looks at* ABE *for a moment, then laughs.*]

Jack. [*To* NINIAN.] All right! Abe Lincoln's saved your hide. I'll consent to callin' off the fight just because he's a friend of mine.

Abe. [*As he sits.*] And also because I'm the only one around here you can't lick.

Jack. But I just want to tell you, Mr. Ninian Edwards, Junior, that the next time you come around here a-spreadin' pisen and . . .

Abe. Go on, Jack. Hannah's waiting.

Jack. [*Walking over to* ABE.] I'm going, Abe. But I warn you—you'd better stop this foolishness of readin'—readin'—readin', mornin', noon, and night, or you'll be gettin' soft and you won't be the same fightin' man you are now—and it would break my heart to see you licked by anybody, includin' me! [*He laughs, slaps* ABE *on the back, then turns to go.*] Glad to have met you, Mr. Edwards.

[*He goes out, followed by* BAB *and* JASP. FEARGUS *picks up the keg and starts after them.*]

Ninian. [*To* JACK.] It's been a pleasure.

Abe. Where'd you get that keg, Feargus?

Feargus. [*Nervously.*] Jack told me to take it outen Mis' Rutledge's kitchen and I . . .

Abe. Well—put it down. . . . If you see Seth Gale, tell him I've got a letter for him.

Feargus. I'll tell him, Abe.

[FEARGUS *puts down the keg and goes.* JOSH SPEED *laughs and comes up to the table.*]

Josh. Congratulations, Ninian. I shouldn't have enjoyed taking you home to Mrs. Edwards after those boys had done with you.

Ninian. [*Grinning.*] I was aware of the certain consequences, Josh. [*He turns to* ABE.] I'm deeply in your debt, Mr. Lincoln.

Abe. Never mind any thanks, Mr. Edwards. Jack Armstrong talks big but he means well.

Ninian. Won't you join us in a drink?

Abe. No, thank you.

[*He's reading the paper.* BOWLING *fills the glasses.*]

Bowling. *I'm* going to have another! I don't mind telling you, I'm still trembling. [*He hands a glass to* NINIAN, *then drinks himself.*]

Trum. You see, Mr. Edwards. It's that very kind of lawlessness that's holding our town back.

Ninian. You'll find the same element in the capital of our nation, and everywhere else, these days. [*He sits down and drinks.*]

Abe. Say, Bowling! It says here that there was a riot in Lyons, France. [*He reads.*] "A mob of men, deprived of employment when textile factories installed the new sewing machines, re-enacted scenes of the Reign of Terror in the streets of this prosperous industrial center. The mobs were suppressed only when the military forces of His French Majesty took a firm hand. The rioters carried banners inscribed with the incendiary words, 'We will live working or die fighting!'" [ABE *looks at the group at the right.*] That's Revolution!

Bowling. Maybe, but it's a long way off from New Salem.

Josh. Put the paper down, Abe. We want to talk to you.

Abe. Me? What about? [*He looks curiously at* JOSH, BOWLING, *and* NINIAN.]

Josh. I brought Mr. Edwards here for the sole purpose of meeting you—and with his permission, I shall tell you why.

Ninian. Go right ahead, Josh.

[*All are looking intently at* ABE.]

Josh. Abe—how would you like to run for the State Assembly?

Abe. When?

Josh. Now—for the election in the fall.

Abe. Why?

Ninian. Mr. Lincoln, I've known you for only a few minutes, but that's long enough to make me agree with Josh Speed that you're precisely the type of man we want. The whole Whig organization will support your candidacy.

Abe. This was all your idea, Josh?

Josh. [*Smiling.*] Oh, no, Abe—you're the people's choice!

Trum. What do *you* think of it, Bowling?

Bowling. [*Heartily.*] I think it's as fine a notion as I ever heard. Why, Abe—I can hear you making speeches, right and left, taking your stand on all the issues—secession, Texas, the National Bank crisis, abolitionism—it'll be more fun than we ever had in our lives!

Abe. [*Rising.*] Isn't anybody going to ask what *I* think?

Josh. [*Laughs.*] All right, Abe—*I'll* ask you.

Abe. [*After a moment's pause.*] It's a comical notion, all right—and I don't know if I can give you an answer to it offhand. But my first, hasty impression is that I don't think much of it.

Bowling. Don't overlook the fact that, if elected, your salary would be three whole dollars a day.

Abe. That's fine money. No doubt of that. And I see what you have in mind, Bowling. I owe you a considerable sum of money; and if I stayed in the legislature for, say, twenty years I'd be able to pay off—let me see—two dollars and a half a day. . . . [*He is figuring it up on his fingers.*]

Bowling. I'm not thinking about the debts, Abe.

Abe. I know you ain't, Bowling. But I've got to. And so should you, Mr. Edwards. The Whig party is the party of sound money and God save the National Bank, ain't it?

Ninian. Why, yes—among other things. . . .

Abe. Well, then—how would it look if you put forward a candidate who has demonstrated no earning power but who has run up the impressive total of fifteen hundred dollars of debts?

Bowling. [*To* NINIAN.] I can tell you something about those debts. Abe started a grocery store in partnership with an unfortunate young man named Berry. Their stock included whiskey, and Berry started tapping the keg until he had consumed all the liquid assets. So the store went bankrupt—and Abe voluntarily assumed all the obligations. That may help to explain to you, Mr. Edwards, why we think pretty highly of him around here.

Ninian. It's a sentiment with which I concur most heartily.

Abe. I thank you one and all for your kind tributes, but don't overdo them, or I'll begin to think that three dollars a day ain't enough!

Josh. What's the one thing that you want most, Abe? You want to learn. This will give you your chance to get at a good library, to associate with the finest lawyers in the State.

Abe. I've got a copy of Blackstone already. Found it in an old junk barrel. And how can I tell that the finest lawyers would welcome association with *me*?

Ninian. You needn't worry about that. I saw how you dealt with those ruffians. You quite obviously know how to handle men.

Abe. I can handle the Clary's Grove boys because I can outwrassle them—but I can't go around Sangamon County throwing *all* the voters.

Bowling. [*Laughing.*] I'll take a chance on that, Abe.

Abe. [*To* NINIAN.] Besides—how do you know that my political views would agree with yours? How do you know I wouldn't say the wrong thing?

Ninian. What *are* your political leanings, Mr. Lincoln?

Abe. They're all toward staying out. . . . What sort of leanings did you want?

Ninian. We have a need for good conservative men to counteract all the radical firebrands that have swept over this country in the wake of Andrew Jackson. We've got to get this country back to first principles!

Abe. Well—I'm conservative, all right. If I got into the legislature you'd never catch me starting any movements for reform or progress. I'm pretty certain I wouldn't even have the nerve to open my mouth.

Josh. [*Laughs.*] I told you, Ninian—he's just the type of candidate you're looking for.

[NINIAN *laughs too, and rises.*]

Ninian. [*Crossing toward* ABE.] The fact is, Mr. Lincoln, we want to spike the rumor that ours is the party of the more privileged classes. That is why we seek men of the plain people for candidates. As postmaster, you're in an excellent position to establish contacts. While delivering letters, you can also deliver speeches and campaign literature, with which our headquarters will keep you supplied.

Abe. Would you supply me with a suit of store clothes? A candidate mustn't look *too* plain.

Ninian. [*Smiling.*] I think even that could be arranged, eh, Judge?

Bowling. I think so.

Ninian. [*Pompously.*] So—think it over, Mr. Lincoln, and realize that this is opportunity unlimited in scope. Just consider what it means to be starting up the ladder in a nation which is now expanding southward, across the vast area of Texas; and westward, to the Empire of the Californias on the Pacific Ocean. We're becoming a continent, Mr. Lincoln—and all that we need is men! [*He looks at his watch.*] And now, gentlemen, if you will excuse me—I must put in an appearance at the torch-light procession in Springfield this evening, so I shall have to be moving on. Good-by, Mr. Lincoln. This meeting has been a happy one for me.

Abe. [*Shaking hands.*] Good-by, Mr. Edwards. Good luck in the campaign.

Ninian. And the same to you.

[*All at the right have risen and are starting to go, except* BEN MATTLING, *who is still sitting at the back, drinking.*]

Abe. Here's your paper, Trum.

Trum. Go ahead and finish it, Abe. I won't be looking at it yet awhile.

Abe. Thanks, Trum. I'll leave it at your house.

[TRUM *and* NINIAN *have gone.*]

Bowling. I'll see you later, Abe. Tell Ann I'll be back to pay for the liquor.

Abe. I'll tell her, Bowling.

[BOWLING *goes.* JOSH *is looking at* ABE, *who, after a moment, turns to him.*]

Abe. I'm surprised at you, Josh. I thought you were my friend.

Josh. I know, Abe. But Ninian Edwards asked me is there anybody in that God-forsaken town of New Salem that stands a chance of getting votes, and the only one I could think of was you. I can see you're embarrassed by this—and you're annoyed. But—whether you like it or not—you've got to grow; and here's your chance to get a little scrap of importance.

Abe. Am I the kind that wants importance?

Josh. You'll deny it, Abe—but you've got a funny kind of vanity—which is the same as saying you've got some pride—and it's badly in need of nourishment. So, if you'll agree to this—I don't think you'll be sorry for it or feel that I've betrayed you.

Abe. [*Grins.*] Oh—I won't hold it against you, Josh. [*He walks away and looks out the door.*] But that Mr. Ninian Edwards—he's rich and he's prominent and he's got a high-class education. Politics to him is just a kind of game. And maybe I'd like it if I could play it *his* way. [*He turns to* JOSH.] But when you get to reading Blackstone, not to mention the Bible, you can't help feeling maybe there's some serious responsibility in the giving of laws—and maybe there's something more important in the business of government than just getting the Whig Party back into power.

[SETH GALE *comes in. He is a young, husky frontiersman, with flashes of the sun of Western empire in his eyes.*]

Seth. Hey, Abe—Feargus said you've got a letter for me.

Abe. [*Fishing in his mail pouch.*] Yes.

Seth. Hello, Mr. Speed.

Josh. How are you, Mr. Gale?

Abe. Here you are, Seth.

[*He hands him a letter.* SETH *takes it to the right, sits down and starts to read.*]

Josh. I've got to get home to Springfield, Abe, but I'll be down again in a week or so.

Abe. I'll be here, Josh.

[JOSH *goes.* ABE *sits down again at the right, picks up his paper, but doesn't read it.* BEN *stands up and comes down a bit unsteadily.*]

Ben. [*Angrily.*] Are you going to do it, Abe? Are you goin' to let them make you into a *candidate*?

Abe. I ain't had time to think about it yet.

Ben. Well—I tell you to stop thinkin' before it's too late. Don't let 'em get you. Don't let 'em put you in a store suit that's the uniform of degradation in this miserable country. You're an honest man, Abe Lincoln. You're a good-for-nothin', debt-ridden loafer—but you're an honest man. And you have no place in that den of thieves that's called gov'ment. They'll corrupt you as they've corrupted the whole damn United States. Look at Washington, look at Jefferson, and John Adams—[*He points grandly to the pictures.*]—where are they today? Dead! And everything they stood for and fought for and *won*—that's dead too.

[ANN *comes in to collect the mugs from the table at the left.* ABE *looks at her.*]

Why—we'd be better off if we was all black niggers held in the bonds of slavery. *They* get fed—*they* get looked after when they're old and sick. [ANN *goes.*] But *you* don't care—you ain't listenin' to me, neither . . .

[*He starts slowly toward the door.*]

Abe. Of course I'm listening, Ben.

Ben. No, you ain't. *I* know. You're goin' to the assembly and join the wolves who're feedin' off the carcass of Liberty. [*He goes out.*]

Abe. You needn't worry. I'm not going.

[ANN *comes in. She crosses to the right to pick up the glasses. She seems extremely subdued.* ABE *looks at her, curiously.*]

Abe. Bowling Green said to tell you he'd be back later, to pay you what he owes.

Ann. [*Curtly.*] That's all right.

[ANN *puts the glasses and bottle on a tray and picks it up.* ABE *jumps to his feet.*]

Abe. Here, Ann. Let me take that.

Ann. [*Irritably.*] No—leave it alone! I can carry it! [*She starts across to the left.*]

Abe. Excuse me, Ann. . . .

Ann. [*Stopping.*] Well?

Abe. Would you come back after you're finished with that? I—I'd like to talk to you.

[SETH *has finished the letter. Its contents seem to have depressed him.*]

Ann. All right. I'll talk to you—if you want.

[*She goes out.* SETH *crosses toward* ABE, *who, during the subsequent dia-*

logue, is continually looking toward the kitchen.]

Seth. Abe . . . Abe—I got a letter from my folks back in Maryland. It means—I guess I've got to give up the dream we had of moving out into Nebraska territory.

Abe. What's happened, Seth?

Seth. [*Despondently.*] Well—for one thing, the old man's took sick, and he's pretty feeble.

Abe. I'm sorry to hear that.

Seth. So am I. They've sent for me to come back and work the farm. Measly little thirty-six acres—sandy soil. I tell you, Abe, it's a bitter disappointment to me, when I had my heart all set on going out into the West. And the worst of it is—I'm letting *you* down on it, too.

Abe. [*With a glance toward the kitchen.*] Don't think about that, Seth. Maybe I won't be able to move for a while myself. And when your father gets to feeling better, you'll come back . . .

Seth. He won't get to feeling better. Not at his age. I'll be stuck there, just like he was. I'll be pushed in and cramped all the rest of my life, till the malaria gets me, too. . . . Well—there's no use crying about it. If I've got to go back East, I've got to go. [ANN *comes back.*] I'll tell you good-by, Abe, before I leave.

[*He goes.* ABE *turns and looks at* ANN, *and she at him.*]

Ann. Well—what is it, Abe?

Abe. [*Rising.*] I just thought—you might like to talk to me.

Ann. [*Sharply.*] What about?

Abe. That letter you got from New York State.

Ann. What do *you* know about that letter?

Abe. I'm the postmaster. I know more than I ought to about people's private affairs. I couldn't help seeing that that was the handwriting of Mr. McNiel. And I couldn't help seeing, from the look on your face, that the bad news you've been afraid of has come.

[ANN *looks at him with surprise. He is a lot more observant than she had thought.*]

Ann. Whatever the letter said, it's no concern of yours, Abe.

Abe. I know that, Ann. But—it appears to me that you've been crying—and it makes me sad to think that something could have hurt you. The thing is—I think quite a lot of you—always have—ever since I first came here, and met you. I wouldn't mention it, only when you're distressed about something it's a comfort sometimes to find a pair of ears to pour your troubles into—and the Lord knows my ears are big enough to hold a lot.

[*Her attitude of hostility softens and she rewards him with a tender smile.*]

Ann. You're a Christian gentleman, Abe Lincoln. [*She sits down.*]

Abe. No, I ain't. I'm a plain, common sucker with a shirt-tail so short I can't sit on it.

Ann. [*Laughs.*] Well—sit down, anyway, Abe—here, by me.

Abe. Why—it'd be a pleasure. [*He crosses and sits near her.*]

Ann. You can always say something to make a person laugh, can't you?

Abe. Well—I don't even have to *say* anything. A person just has to *look* at me.

Ann. You're right about that letter, Abe. It's the first I've heard from him in months—and now he says he's delayed by family troubles and doesn't know when he'll be able to get to New Salem again. By which he probably means—never.

Abe. I wouldn't say that, Ann.

Ann. I would. [*She looks at him.*] I reckon you think I'm a silly fool for ever having promised myself to Mr. McNiel.

Abe. I think no such thing. I liked him myself, and still do, and whatever reasons he had for changing his name I'm sure were honorable. He's a smart man, and a handsome one—and I—I wouldn't blame any girl for—loving him.

Ann. [*Too emphatically.*] I guess I don't love him, Abe. I guess I couldn't love anybody that was as—as faithless as that.

Abe. [*Trying to appear unconcerned.*] Well, then. There's nothing to fret about. Now—poor Seth Gale—he got some *really* bad news. His father's sick and he has to give up his dream which was to go and settle out West.

Ann. [*Looks at him.*] I don't believe you know much about females, Abe.

Abe. Probably I don't—although I certainly spend enough time thinking about 'em.

Ann. You're a big man, and you can lick anybody, and you can't understand the feelings of somebody who is weak. But—I'm a female, and I can't help thinking what they'll be saying about me—all the old gossips, all over town. They'll make it out that he deserted me; I'm a rejected woman. They'll give me their sympathy to my face, but they'll snigger at me behind my back.

[*She rises and crosses toward the right.*]

Abe. Yes—that's just about what they would do. But—would you let *them* disturb you?

Ann. [*Rising.*] I told you—it's just weakness—it's just vanity. It's something you couldn't understand, Abe.

[*She has crossed to the window and is staring out.* ABE *twists in his chair to look at her.*]

Abe. Maybe I can understand it, Ann. I've got a kind of vanity myself. Josh Speed said so, and he's right. . . . It's—it's nothing but vanity that's kept me from declaring my inclinations toward you.

[*She turns, amazed, and looks at him.*]

You see, I don't like to be sniggered at, either. I know what I am—and I know what I look like—and I know that I've got nothing to offer any girl that I'd be in love with.

Ann. Are you saying that you're in love with me, Abe?

Abe. [*With deep earnestness.*] Yes—I am saying that. [*He stands up, facing her. She looks intently into his eyes.*] I've been loving you—a long time—with all my heart. You see, Ann—you're a particularly fine girl. You've got sense, and you've got bravery—those are two things that I admire particularly. And you're powerful good to look at, too. So—it's only natural I should have a great regard for you. But—I don't mean to worry you about it, Ann. I only mentioned it because—if you would do me the honor of keeping company with me for a while, it might shut the old gossips' mouths. They'd figure you'd chucked McNiel for—for someone else. Even me.

Ann. [*Going to him.*] I thought I knew you pretty well, Abe. But I didn't.

Abe. [*Worried.*] Why do you say that? Do you consider I was too forward, in speaking out as I did?

Ann. [*Gravely.*] No, Abe. . . . I've always thought a lot of you—the way I thought you were. But—the idea of love between you and me—I can't say how I feel about that, because now you're like some other person, that I'm meeting for the first time.

Abe. [*Quietly.*] I'm not expecting you to feel anything for me. I'd never dream of expecting such a thing.

Ann. I know that, Abe. You'd be willing to give everything you have and never expect anything in return. Maybe you're different in that way from any man I've ever heard of. And I can tell you this much—now, and truthfully—if I ever do love you, I'll be happy about it—and lucky, to be loving a good, decent man. . . . If you just give me time—to think about it. . . .

Abe. [*Unable to believe his eyes and ears.*] You mean—if you took time—you might get in your heart something like the feeling I have for you?

Ann. [*With great tenderness.*] I don't know, Abe. [*She clutches his lapel.*] But I do know that you're a man who could fill any one's heart—yes, fill it and warm it and make it glad to be living.

[ABE *covers her hand with his.*]

Abe. Ann—I've always tried hard to believe what the orators tell us—that this is a land of equal opportunity for all. But I've never been able to credit it, any more than I could agree that God made all men in his own image. But—if I could win you, Ann—I'd be willing to disbelieve everything I've ever seen with my own eyes, and have faith in everything wonderful that I've ever read in poetry books. [*Both are silent for a moment. Then* ANN *turns away.*] But—I'm not asking you to say anything now. And I won't ask you until the day comes when I know I've got a right to. [*He turns and walks quickly toward the door, picking up his mail pouch.*]

Ann. Abe! Where are you going?

Abe. I'm going to find Bowling Green and tell him a good joke. [*He grins. He is standing in the doorway.*]

Ann. A *joke*? What about?

Abe. I'm going to tell him that I'm a candidate for the assembly of the State of Illinois. [*He goes.*]

[*The light fades.*]

SCENE III

Bowling Green's house near New Salem.

It is a small room, but the walls are lined with books and family pictures. In the center is a table with a lamp on it. Another light—a candle in a glass globe—is on a bureau at the right. There are comfortable chairs on either side of the table, and a sofa at the left.

At the back, toward the left, is the front door. A rifle is leaning against the wall by the door. There is another door in the right wall. Toward the right, at the back, is a ladder fixed against the wall leading up through an opening to the attic.

It is late in the evening, a year or so after Scene II. A storm is raging outside.

[BOWLING *is reading aloud from a sort of pamphlet. His comfortable wife,* NANCY, *is listening and sewing.*]

Bowling. "And how much more interesting did the spectacle become when, starting into full life and animation, as a simultaneous call for 'Pickwick' burst from his followers, that illustrious man slowly mounted into the Windsor chair, on which he had been previously seated, and addressed the club himself had founded."

[BOWLING *chuckles.* NANCY *laughs.*]

Nancy. He sounds precisely like *you,* Bowling.

[*There is a knock at the door.*]

Nancy. [*Nervous.*] That's not Abe's knock. Who can it be?

Bowling. [*Rising.*] We don't know yet, my dear.

Nancy. It's a strange hour for any one to be calling. You'd better have that gun ready.

[BOWLING *unbolts and opens the door. It is* JOSH SPEED.]

Bowling. Why—Josh Speed!

Josh. Good evening, Bowling.

Bowling. We haven't seen you in a coon's age.

Nancy. Good evening, Mr. Speed.

Josh. Good evening, Mrs. Green. And I beg you to forgive me for this untimely intrusion.

Nancy. We're delighted to see you. Take your wrap off.

Josh. Thank you. I've just come down from Springfield. I heard Abe Lincoln was in town and I was told I might find him here.

Bowling. He's been sleeping here, up in the attic.

Nancy. But he's out at the Rutledge Farm, tending poor little Ann.

Josh. Miss Rutledge? What's the matter with her?

Nancy. She's been taken with the brain sickness. It's the most shocking thing. People have been dying from it right and left.

Bowling. But Ann's young. She'll pull through, all right. Sit down, Josh.

Josh. Thank you.

[*He sits.* BOWLING *places the pamphlet on the top of the bookcase and stands there, filling his pipe.*]

Nancy. I suppose you know that Abe came rushing down from Vandalia the moment he heard she was taken. He's deeply in love with her.

Bowling. Now, Nancy—don't exaggerate.

[JOSH *is listening to all this, intently.*]

Josh. So Abe is in love. I wondered what has been the matter with him lately.

Nancy. Why, it's written all over his poor, homely face.

Josh. The last time I saw him, he seemed pretty moody. But when I asked him what was wrong, he said it was his liver.

Bowling. [*Laughing.*] That sounds more likely. Has he been getting on well in the Assembly?

Josh. No. He has just been sitting there —drawing his three dollars a day—and taking no apparent interest in the proceedings. Do you fancy that Miss Rutledge cares anything for him?

Nancy. Indeed she does! She broke her promise to that Mr. McNiel because of her feelings for Abe!

Josh. Has he any notion of marrying her?

Nancy. It's the only notion of his life right now. And the sooner they are married, the better for both of them.

Bowling. [*Seating himself.*] Better for her, perhaps—but the worse for him.

Nancy. [*Finishing her sewing.*] And why? The Rutledges are fine people, superior in every way to those riff-raff Hankses and Lincolns that are Abe's family!

Bowling. I think you feel as I do, Josh. Abe has his own way to go and—sweet and pretty as Ann undoubtedly is—she'd only be a hindrance to him.

Josh. I guess it wouldn't matter much if she could give him a little of the happiness he's never had.

Nancy. [*Rising.*] That's just it! I think as much of Abe as you do, Bowling. But we can't deny that he's a poor man, and he's failed in trade, and he's been in the legislature for a year without accomplishing a blessed thing . . . [*She goes to the bookcase to put her sewing-basket away.*]

Bowling. He could go to Springfield and set up a law practice and make a good thing of it. Ninian Edwards would help him to get started. And he'd soon forget little Ann. He has just happened to fasten on her his own romantic ideal of what's beautiful and unattainable. Let him ever attain her, and she'd break his heart.

Nancy. [*Seating herself.*] Do you agree with Bowling on that, Mr. Speed?

Josh. [*Sadly.*] I can't say, Mrs. Green. I've abandoned the attempt to predict anything about Abe Lincoln. The first time I ever saw him was when he was piloting that steamboat, the *Talisman.* You remember how she ran into trouble at the dam. I had a valuable load of goods aboard for my father's store, and I was sure that steamboat, goods, and all were a total loss. But Abe got her through. It was a great piece of work. I thought, "Here is a reliable man." So I cultivated his acquaintance, believing, in my conceit, that I could help him to fame and fortune. I soon learned differently. I found out that he has plenty of strength and courage in his body—but in his mind he's a hopeless hypochondriac. He can split rails, push a plough, crack jokes, all day—and then sit up all night reading "Hamlet" and brooding over his own fancied resemblance to that melancholy prince. Maybe he's a great philosopher—maybe he's a great fool. I don't know what he is.

Bowling. [*Laughs.*] Well—if only Ann had sense enough to see all the things *you* saw, Josh, she'd be so terrified of him she'd run all the way back to York State and find McNiel. At least, *he's* not complicated.

Nancy. [*With deeper emotion.*] You're talking about Abe Lincoln as if he were some problem that you found in a book, and it's interesting to try to figure it out. Well—maybe he is a problem—but he's also a man, and a miserable one. And what do you do for his misery? You laugh at his comical jokes and you vote for him on election day and give him board and lodging when he needs it. But all that doesn't give a scrap of satisfaction to Abe's soul—and never will. Because the one thing he needs is a woman with the will to face life for him.

Bowling. You think he's afraid to face it himself?

Nancy. He is! He listens too much to the whispers that he heard in the forest where he grew up, and where he always goes now when he wants to be alone. They're the whispers of the women behind him—his dead mother—and *her* mother, who was no better than she should be. He's got that awful fear on him, of not knowing what the whispers mean, or where they're directing him. And none of your back-slapping will knock that fear out of him. Only a woman can free him—a woman who loves him truly, and believes in him. . . .

[*There is a knock on the door.*]

Bowling. That's Abe now. [*He gets up and opens it.*]

[ABE *is there, bareheaded, wet by the storm. He now wears a fairly respectable dark suit of clothes. He looks older and grimmer.*]

Bowling. Why, hello, Abe! We've been sitting up waiting for you. Come on in out of the wet!

[ABE *comes in.* BOWLING *shuts the door behind him.*]

Nancy. We were reading "The Posthumous Papers of the Pickwick Club" when Mr. Speed came in.

Abe. Hello, Josh. Glad to see you.

Josh. Hello, Abe.

[ABE *turns to* NANCY.]

Abe. Nancy . . .

Nancy. Yes, Abe?

Abe. She's dead.

Bowling. Ann? She's dead?

Abe. Yes. Tonight the fever suddenly got worse. They couldn't seem to do anything for it.

[NANCY *gives* BOWLING *a swift look, then goes quickly to* ABE *and takes his hand.*]

Nancy. Oh, Abe—I'm so sorry. She was such a dear little girl. Every one who knew her will join in mourning for her.

Abe. I know they will. But it won't do any good. She's dead.

Bowling. Sit down, Abe, and rest yourself.

Abe. No—I'm not fit company for anybody. I'd better be going.

[*He turns toward the door.*]

Josh. [*Stopping him.*] No, you don't, Abe. You'll stay right here.

Bowling. You better do what Josh tells you.

Nancy. Come here, Abe. Please sit down. [ABE *looks from one to the other, then obediently goes to a chair and sits.*] Your bed is ready for you upstairs when you want it.

Abe. [*Dully.*] You're the best friends I've got in the world, and it seems a pretty poor way to reward you for all that you've given me, to come here now, and inflict you with a corpse.

Bowling. This is your home, Abe. This is where you're loved.

Abe. Yes, that's right. And I love you, Bowling and Nancy. But I loved her more than everything else that I've ever known.

Nancy. I know you did, Abe. I know it.

Abe. I used to think it was better to be alone. I was always most contented when I was alone. I had queer notions that if you got too close to people, you could see the truth about them, that behind the surface they're all insane, and they could see the same in you. And then—when I saw her, I knew there could be beauty and purity in people—like the purity you sometimes see in the sky at night. When I took hold of her hand and held it, all fear, all doubt, went out of me. I believed in God. I'd have been glad to work for her until I die, to get for her everything out of life that she wanted. If she thought I could do it, then I could. That was my belief. . . . And then I had to stand there, as helpless as a twig in a whirlpool; I had to stand there and watch her die. And her father and mother were there, too, praying to God for her soul. "The Lord giveth, and the Lord taketh away, blessed be the name of the Lord!" That's what they kept on saying. But I couldn't pray with them. I couldn't give any devotion to one who has the power of death, and uses it. [*He has stood up, and is speaking with more passion.*] I'm making a poor exhibition of myself—and I'm sorry—but—I can't stand it. I can't live with myself any longer. I've got to die and be with her again, or I'll go crazy! [*He goes to the door and opens it. The storm continues.*] I can't bear to think of her out there alone!

[NANCY *looks at* BOWLING *with frantic appeal. He goes to* ABE, *who is standing in the doorway, looking out.*]

Bowling. [*With great tenderness.*] Abe . . . I want you to go upstairs and see if you can't get some sleep. . . . Please, Abe—as a special favor to Nancy and me.

Abe. [*After a moment.*] All right, Bowling. [*He turns and goes to the ladder.*]

Nancy. Here's a light for you, dear Abe. [*She hands him the candle.*]

Abe. Thank you, Nancy. . . . Good night. [*He goes up the ladder into the attic.*]

[*They all look up after him.*]

Nancy. [*Tearful.*] Poor, lonely soul.

[BOWLING *cautions her to be quiet.*]

Josh. Keep him here with you, Mrs. Green. Don't let him out of your sight.

Bowling. We won't, Josh.

Josh. Good night. [*He picks up his hat and cloak and goes.*]

Bowling. Good night, Josh. [*He closes and bolts the door, then comes down to the table and picks up the lamp.*]

[NANCY *looks up once more, then goes out at the right.* BOWLING *follows her out, carrying the lamp with him. He closes the door behind him, so that the only light on the stage is the beam from the attic.*]

CURTAIN

ACT II

SCENE IV

Law office of Stuart and Lincoln on the second floor of the Court House in Springfield, Illinois. A sunny summer's afternoon, some five years after the preceding scene.

The room is small, with two windows and one door, upstage, which leads to the hall and staircase.

At the right is a table and chair, at the left an old desk, littered with papers. At the back is a ramshackle bed, with a buffalo robe thrown over it. Below the windows are some rough shelves, sagging with law books. There is an old wood stove.

On the wall above the desk is hung an American flag, with 26 stars. Between the windows is an election poster, for Harrison and Tyler, with a list of Electors, the last of whom is Ab'm Lincoln, of Sangamon.

[BILLY HERNDON *is working at the table. He is young, slight, serious-minded, smouldering. He looks up as* ABE *comes in.* ABE *wears a battered plug hat, a light alpaca coat, and carries an ancient, threadbare carpet-bag. He is evidently not in a talkative mood. His boots are caked in mud. He is only thirty-one years old, but his youth was buried with Ann Rutledge.*

He leaves the office door open, and lettered on it we see the number 4, and the firm's name—Stuart & Lincoln, Attorneys & Counsellors at Law.]

Billy. How de do, Mr. Lincoln? Glad to see you back.

Abe. Good day, Billy. [*He sets down the carpet-bag, takes off his hat and puts it on his desk.*]

Billy. How was it on the circuit, Mr. Lincoln?

Abe. About as usual.

Billy. Have you been keeping in good health?

Abe. Not particularly. But Doc Henry dosed me enough to keep me going.

[*He sits down at the desk and starts looking at letters and papers that have accumulated during his absence. He takes little interest in them, pigeonholing some letters unopened.*]

Billy. Did you have occasion to make any political speeches?

Abe. Oh—they got me up on the stump a couple of times. Ran into Stephen Douglas —he was out campaigning, of course—and we had some argument in public.

Billy. [*Greatly interested.*] That's good! What issues did you and Mr. Douglas discuss?

Abe. Now—don't get excited, Billy. We weren't taking it serious. There was no blood shed. . . . What's the news here?

Billy. Judge Stuart wrote that he arrived safely in Washington and the campaign there is getting almost as hot as the weather. Mrs. Fraim stopped in to say she couldn't possibly pay your fee for a while.

Abe. I should hope not. I ought to be paying her, seeing as I defended her poor husband and he hanged.

[BILLY *hands him a letter and watches him intently while he reads it.*]

Billy. That was left here by hand, and I promised to call it especially to your attention. It's from the Elijah P. Lovejoy League of Freemen. They want you to speak at an Abolitionist rally next Thursday evening. It'll be a very important affair.

Abe. [*Reflectively.*] It's funny, Billy—I was thinking about Lovejoy the other day—trying to figure what it is in a man that makes him glad to be a martyr. I was on the boat coming from Quincy to Alton, and there was a gentleman on board with twelve Negroes. He was shipping them down to Vicksburg for sale—had 'em chained six and six together. Each of them had a small iron clevis around his wrist, and this was chained to the main chain, so that those Negroes were strung together precisely like fish on a trotline. I gathered they were being separated forever from their homes—mothers, fathers, wives, children—whatever families the poor creatures had got—going to be whipped into perpetual slavery, and no questions asked. It was quite a shocking sight.

Billy. [*Excited.*] Then you will give a speech at the Lovejoy rally?

Abe. [*Wearily.*] I doubt it. That Freemen's League is a pack of hell-roaring fanatics. Talk reason to them and they scorn you for being a mealy-mouth. Let 'em make their own noise.

[ABE *has opened a letter. He starts to read it.*

BILLY *looks at him with resentful disappointment, but he knows too well that any argument would be futile. He resumes his work. After a moment,* BOWLING GREEN *comes in, followed by* JOSH SPEED.]

Bowling. Are we interrupting the majesty of the Law?

Abe. [*Heartily.*] Bowling! [*He jumps up and grasps* BOWLING'S *hand.*] How are you, Bowling?

Bowling. Tolerably well, Abe—and glad to see you.

Abe. This is Billy Herndon—Squire Green, of New Salem. Hello, Josh.

Josh. Hello, Abe.

Billy. [*Shaking hands with* BOWLING.] I'm proud to know you, sir. Mr. Lincoln speaks of you constantly.

Bowling. Thank you, Mr. Herndon. Are you a lawyer, too?

Billy. [*Seriously.*] I hope to be, sir. I'm serving here as a clerk in Judge Stuart's absence.

Bowling. So now you're teaching others, Abe?

Abe. Just providing a bad example.

Bowling. I can believe it. Look at the mess on that desk. Shameful!

Abe. Give me another year of law practice and I'll need a warehouse for the overflow. . . . But—sit yourself down, Bowling, and tell me what brings you to Springfield.

[BOWLING *sits.* JOSH *has sat on the couch, smoking his pipe.* BILLY *is again at the table.*]

Bowling. I've been up to Lake Michigan —fishing—came in today on the steam-cars —scared me out of a year's growth. But how are you doing, Abe? Josh says you're still broke, but you're a great social success.

Abe. True—on both counts. I'm greatly in demand at all the more elegant functions. You remember Ninian Edwards?

Bowling. Of course.

Abe. Well, sir—I'm a guest at his mansion regularly. He's got a house so big you could race horses in the parlor. And his wife is one of the Todd family from Kentucky. Very high-grade people. They spell their name with two D's—which is pretty impressive when you consider that one was enough for God.

Josh. Tell Bowling whom you met over in Rochester.

Abe. The President of the United States!

Bowling. You don't tell me so!

Abe. Do you see that hand?

[*He holds out his right hand, palm upward.*]

Bowling. Yes—I see it.

Abe. It has shaken the hand of Martin Van Buren!

Bowling. [*Laughing.*] Was the President properly respectful to you, Abe?

Abe. Indeed he was! He said to me, "We've been hearing great things of you in Washington." I found out later he'd said the same thing to every other cross-roads politician he'd met. [*He laughs.*] But Billy Herndon there is pretty disgusted with me for associating with the wrong kind of people. Billy's a firebrand—a real, radical abolitionist—and he can't stand anybody who keeps his mouth shut and abides by the Constitution. If he had his way, the whole Union would be set on fire and we'd all be burned to a crisp. Eh, Billy?

Billy. [*Grimly.*] Yes, Mr. Lincoln. And if you'll permit me to say so, I think you'd be of more use to your fellow-men if you allowed some of the same incendiary impulses to come out in you.

Abe. You see, Bowling? He wants me to get down into the blood-soaked arena and grapple with all the lions of injustice and oppression.

Bowling. Mr. Herndon—my profound compliments.

Billy. [*Rising and taking his hat.*] Thank you, sir. [*He shakes hands with* BOWLING, *then turns to* ABE.] I have the writ prepared in the Willcox case. I'll take it down to the Clerk of Court to be attested.

Abe. All right, Billy.

Billy. [*To* BOWLING.] Squire Green—Mr. Lincoln regards you and Mr. Speed as the best friends he has on earth, and I should like to beg you, in his presence, for God's sake drag him out of this stagnant pool in which he's rapidly drowning himself. Good day, sir—good day, Mr. Speed.

Josh. Good day, Billy. [BILLY *has gone.*]

Bowling. That's a bright young man, Abe. Seems to have a good grasp of things.

Abe. [*Looking after* BILLY.] He's going downstairs to the Clerk's office, but he took his hat. Which means that before he comes back to work, he'll have paid a little visit to the Chenery House saloon.

Bowling. Does the boy drink?

Abe. Yes. He's got great fires in him, but he's putting 'em out fast. . . . Now—tell me about New Salem.

[*He leans against the wall near the window.*]

Bowling. Practically nothing of it left.

Abe. How's that blessed wife of yours?

Bowling. Nancy's busier than ever, and more than ever concerned about your innermost thoughts and yearnings. In fact, she instructed me expressly to ask what on earth is the matter with you?

Abe. [*Laughs.*] You can tell her there's nothing the matter. I've been able to pay off my debts to the extent of some seven cents on the dollar, and I'm sound of skin and skeleton.

Bowling. But why don't we hear more from you and of you?

Abe. Josh can tell you. I've been busy.

Bowling. What at?

Abe. I'm a candidate.

Josh. [*Pointing to the poster.*] Haven't you noticed his name? It's here—at the bottom of the list of Electors on the Whig ticket.

Abe. Yes, sir—if old Tippecanoe wins next fall, I'll be a member of the Electoral College.

Bowling. The Electoral College! And is that the best you can do?

Abe. Yes—in the limited time at my disposal. I had a letter from Seth Gale—remember—he used to live in New Salem and was always aiming to move West. He's settled down in Maryland now and has a wife and a son. He says that back East they're powerful worried about the annexation of Texas.

Bowling. They have reason to be. It would probably mean extending slavery through all the territories, from Kansas and Nebraska right out to Oregon and California. That would give the South absolute rule of the country—and God help the rest of us in the free states.

Josh. It's an ugly situation, all right. It's got the seeds in it of nothing more nor less than civil war.

Abe. Well, if so, it'll be the abolitionists' own fault. They know where this trouble might lead, and yet they go right on agitating. They ought to be locked up for disturbing the peace, all of them.

Bowling. I thought you were opposed to slavery, Abe. Have you changed your mind about it?

Abe. [*Ambles over to the couch and sprawls on it.*] No. I am opposed to slavery. But I'm even more opposed to going to war. And, on top of that, I know what you're getting at, both of you. [*He speaks to them with the utmost good nature.*] You're following Billy Herndon's lead—troubling your kind hearts with concerns about me and when am I going to amount to something. Is that it?

Bowling. Oh, no, Abe. Far be it from me to interfere in your life.

Josh. Or me, either. If we happen to feel that, so far, you've been a big disappointment to us, we'll surely keep it to ourselves.

Abe. [*Laughs.*] I'm afraid you'll have to do what I've had to do—which is, learn to accept me for what I am. I'm no fighting man. I found that out when I went through the Black Hawk War, and was terrified that I might have to fire a shot at an Indian. Fortunately, the Indians felt the same way, so I never saw one of them. Now, I know plenty of men who like to fight; they're willing to kill, and not scared of being killed. All right. Let them attend to the battles that have to be fought.

Bowling. Peaceable men have sometimes been of service to their country.

Abe. They may have been peaceable when they started, but they didn't remain so long after they'd become mixed in the great brawl of politics. [*He sits up.*] Suppose I ran for Congress and got elected. I'd be right in the thick of that ugly situation you were speaking of. One day I might have to cast my vote on the terrible issue of war or peace. It might be war with Mexico over Texas; or war with England over Oregon; or even war with our own people across the Ohio River. What attitude would I take in deciding which way to vote? "The Liberal attitude," of course. And what is the Liberal attitude? To go to war, for a tract of land, or a moral principle? Or to avoid war at all costs? No, sir. The place for me is in the Electoral College, where all I have to do is vote for the President whom everybody else elected four months previous.

Bowling. Well, Abe—you were always an artful dodger—and maybe you'll be able to go on to the end of your days avoiding the clutch of your own conscience.

[NINIAN EDWARDS *comes in. He is a little stouter and more prosperous.*]

Abe-Josh. Hello, Ninian.

Ninian. Hello. I saw Billy Herndon at the Chenery House and he said you were back from the circuit. [*He sees* BOWLING.] Why—it's my good friend Squire Green. How de do?—and welcome to Springfield.

[*He shakes hands with* BOWLING.]

Bowling. Thank you, Mr. Edwards.

Ninian. I just called in, Abe, to tell you you must dine with us. And, Squire, Mrs. Edwards would be honored to receive you, if your engagements will permit—and you, too, Josh.

Josh. Delighted!

Ninian. We're proudly exhibiting my sister-in-law, Miss Mary Todd, who has just come from Kentucky to grace our home. She's a very gay young lady—speaks French like a native, recites poetry at the drop of a hat, and knows the names and habits of all the flowers. I've asked Steve Douglas and some of the other eligibles to meet her, so you boys had better get in early.

Bowling. My compliments to Mrs. Edwards, but my own poor wife awaits me impatiently, I hope.

Ninian. I appreciate your motives, Squire, and applaud them. You'll be along presently, Abe?

Abe. I wouldn't be surprised.

Ninian. Good. You'll meet a delightful young lady. And I'd better warn you she's going to survey the whole field of matrimonial prospects and select the one who promises the most. So you'd better be on your guard, Abe, unless you're prepared to lose your standing as a free man.

Abe. I thank you for the warning, Ninian.

Ninian. Good day to you, Squire. See you later, Josh. [*He goes out.*]

Abe. There, Bowling—you see how things are with me. Hardly a day goes by but what I'm invited to meet some eager young female who has all the graces, including an ability to speak the language of diplomacy.

Bowling. I'm sorry, Abe, that I shan't be able to hear you carrying on a flirtation in French.

[ABE *looks at him, curiously.*]

Abe. I'm not pretending with you, Bowling—or you, Josh. I couldn't fool you any better than I can fool myself. I know what you're thinking about me, and I think so, too. Only I'm not so merciful in considering my own shortcomings, or so ready to forgive them, as you are. But—you talk about civil war—there seems to be one going on inside me all the time. Both sides are right and both are wrong and equal in strength. I'd like to be able to rise superior to the struggle—but—it says in the Bible that a house divided against itself cannot stand, so I reckon there's not much hope. One of these days, I'll just split asunder, and part company with myself—and it'll be a good riddance from both points of view. However—come on. [*He takes his hat.*] You've got to get back to Nancy, and Josh and I have got to make a good impression upon Miss Mary Todd, of Kentucky. [*He waves them to the door. As they go out, the light fades.*]

SCENE V

Parlor of the Edwards house in Springfield. An evening in November, some six months after the preceding scene.

There is a fireplace at the right, a heavily curtained bay window at the left, a door at the back leading into the front hall.

At the right, by the fireplace, are a small couch and an easy chair. There is an-

other couch at the left, and a table and chairs at the back. There are family portraits on the walls. It is all moderately elegant.

[NINIAN *is standing before the fire, in conversation with* ELIZABETH, *his wife. She is high-bred, ladylike—excessively so. She is, at the moment, in a state of some agitation.*]

Elizabeth. I cannot believe it! It is an outrageous reflection on my sister's good sense.

Ninian. I'm not so sure of that. Mary has known Abe for several months, and she has had plenty of chance to observe him closely.

Elizabeth. She has been entertained by him, as we all have. But she has been far more attentive to Edwin Webb and Stephen Douglas and many others who are distinctly eligible.

Ninian. Isn't it remotely possible that she sees more in Abe than you do?

Elizabeth. Nonsense! Mr. Lincoln's chief virtue is that he hides no part of his simple soul from any one. He's a most amiable creature, to be sure; but as the husband of a high-bred, high-spirited young lady . . .

Ninian. Quite so, Elizabeth. Mary *is* high-spirited! That is just why she set her cap for him.

[ELIZABETH *looks at him sharply, then laughs.*]

Elizabeth. You're making fun of me, Ninian. You're deliberately provoking me into becoming excited about nothing.

Ninian. No, Elizabeth—I am merely trying to prepare you for a rude shock. You think Abe Lincoln would be overjoyed to capture an elegant, cultivated girl, daughter of the President of the Bank of Kentucky, descendant of a long line of English gentlemen. Well, you are mistaken . . .

[MARY TODD *comes in. She is twenty-two—short, pretty, remarkably sharp. She stops short in the doorway, and her suspecting eyes dart from* ELIZABETH *to* NINIAN.]

Mary. What were you two talking about?

Ninian. I was telling your sister about the new song the boys are singing:

"What is the great commotion, motion,
Our country through?
It is the ball a-rolling on
For Tippecanoe and Tyler, too—for Tippecanoe . . ."

Mary. [*With a rather grim smile.*] I compliment you for thinking quickly, Ninian. But you were talking about *me!* [*She looks at* ELIZABETH, *who quails a little before her sister's determination.*] Weren't you?

Elizabeth. Yes, Mary, we were.

Mary. And quite seriously, I gather.

Ninian. I'm afraid that our dear Elizabeth has become unduly alarmed . . .

Elizabeth. [*Snapping at him.*] Let me say what I have to say! [*She turns to* MARY.] Mary—you must tell me the truth. Are you—have you ever given one moment's serious thought to the possibility of marriage with Abraham Lincoln? [MARY *looks at each of them, her eyes flashing.*] I promise you, Mary, that to me such a notion is too far beyond the bounds of credibility to be . . .

Mary. But Ninian has raised the horrid subject, hasn't he? He has brought the evil scandal out into the open, and we must face it, fearlessly. Let us do so at once, by all means. I shall answer you, Elizabeth: I have given more than one moment's thought to the possibility you mentioned—and I have decided that I shall be Mrs. Lincoln [*She seats herself on the couch.* NINIAN *is about to say, "I told you so," but thinks better of it.* ELIZABETH *can only gasp and gape.*] I have examined, carefully, the qualifications of all the young gentlemen, and some of the old ones, in this neighborhood. Those of Mr. Lincoln seem to me superior to all others, and he is my choice.

Elizabeth. Do you expect me to congratulate you upon this amazing selection?

Mary. No! I ask for no congratulations, nor condolences, either.

Elizabeth. [*Turning away.*] Then I shall offer none.

Ninian. Forgive me for prying, Mary—but have you as yet communicated your decision to the gentleman himself?

Mary. [*With a slight smile at* NINIAN.] Not yet. But he is coming to call this evening, and he will ask humbly for my hand in marriage; and, after I have displayed the proper amount of surprise and confusion, I shall murmur, timidly, "Yes!"

Elizabeth. [*Pitiful.*] You make a brave jest of it, Mary. But as for me, I am deeply and painfully shocked. I don't know what to say to you. But I urge you, I beg you, as your elder sister, responsible to our father and our dead mother for your welfare . . .

Mary. [*With a certain tenderness.*] I can assure you, Elizabeth—it is useless to beg or command. I have made up my mind.

Ninian. I admire your courage, Mary, but I should like . . .

Elizabeth. I think, Ninian, that this is a matter for discussion solely between my sister and myself!

Mary. No! I want to hear what Ninian has to say. [*To* Ninian.] What is it?

Ninian. I only wondered if I might ask you another question.

Mary. [*Calmly.*] You may.

Ninian. Understand, my dear—I'm not quarreling with you. My affection for Abe is eternal—but—I'm curious to know—what is it about him that makes you choose him for a husband?

Mary. [*Betraying her first sign of uncertainty.*] I should like to give you a plain, simple answer, Ninian. But I cannot.

Elizabeth. [*Jumping at this.*] Of course you cannot! You're rushing blindly into this. You have no conception of what it will mean to your future.

Mary. You're wrong about that, Elizabeth. This is not the result of wild, tempestuous infatuation. I have not been swept off my feet. Mr. Lincoln is a Westerner, but that is his only point of resemblance to Young Lochinvar. I simply feel that of all the men I've ever known, he is the one whose life and destiny I want most to share.

Elizabeth. Haven't you sense enough to know you could never be happy with him? His breeding—his background—his manner—his whole point of view . . .?

Mary. [*Gravely.*] I could not be content with a "happy" marriage in the accepted sense of the word. I have no craving for comfort and security.

Elizabeth. And have you a craving for the kind of life you would lead? A miserable cabin, without a servant, without a stitch of clothing that is fit for exhibition in decent society?

Mary. [*Raising her voice.*] I have not yet tried poverty, so I cannot say how I should take to it. But I might well prefer it to anything I have previously known—so long as there is forever before me the chance for high adventure—so long as I can know that I am always going forward, with my husband, along a road that leads across the horizon. [*This last is said with a sort of mad intensity.*]

Elizabeth. And how far do you think you will go with any one like Abe Lincoln, who is lazy and shiftless and prefers to stop constantly along the way to tell jokes?

Mary. [*Rising; furious.*] He will *not* stop, if I am strong enough to make him go on! And I am strong! I know what *you* expect of me. You want me to do precisely as you have done—and marry a man like Ninian—and I know many, that are *just* like him! But with all due respect to my dear brother-in-law—I don't want that—and I won't have it! Never! You live in a house with a fence around it—presumably to prevent the common herd from gaining access to your sacred precincts—but really to prevent you, yourselves, from escaping from your own narrow lives. In Abraham Lincoln I see a man who has split rails for other men's fences, but who will never build one around himself!

Elizabeth. What are you *saying,* Mary? You are talking with a degree of irresponsibility that is not far from sheer madness . . .

Mary. [*Scornfully.*] I imagine it does seem like insanity to you! You married a man who was settled and established in the world, with a comfortable inheritance, and no problems to face. And you've never made a move to change your condition, or improve it. You consider it couldn't be improved. To you, all this represents perfection. But it doesn't to me! I want the chance to *shape* a new life, for myself, and for my husband. Is that irresponsibility?

[*A* Maid *appears.*]

Maid. Mr. Lincoln, ma'am.

Elizabeth. He's here.

Mary. [*Firmly.*] I shall see him!

Maid. Will you step in, Mr. Lincoln?

[Abe *comes in, wearing a new suit, his hair nearly neat.*]

Abe. Good evening, Mrs. Edwards. Good evening, Miss Todd. Ninian, good evening.

Elizabeth. Good evening.

Mary. Good evening, Mr. Lincoln. [*She sits on the couch at the left.*]

Ninian. Glad to see you, Abe.

[Abe *sees that there is electricity in the atmosphere of this parlor. He tries hard to be affably casual.*]

Abe. I'm afraid I'm a little late in arriving, but I ran into an old friend of mine, wife of Jack Armstrong, the champion rowdy of New Salem. I believe you have some recollection of him, Ninian.

Ninian. [*Smiling.*] I most certainly have. What's he been up to now?

Abe. [*Stands in front of the fireplace.*] Oh, he's all right, but Hannah, his wife, is in fearful trouble because her son Duff is up for murder and she wants me to defend him. I went over to the jail to interview the boy and he looks pretty tolerably guilty to me. But I used to give him lessons in the game of marbles while his mother foxed my pants for me. [*He turns to* Elizabeth.] That means, she sewed buckskin around the legs of my pants so I wouldn't tear 'em to shreds going through underbrush when I was surveying. Well—in view of old times, I felt I had to take the case and do what I can to obstruct the orderly processes of justice.

Ninian. [*Laughs, with some relief.*] And the boy will be acquitted. I tell you, Abe—this country would be law-abiding and peaceful if it weren't for you lawyers. But—if you will excuse Elizabeth and me, we must hear the children's prayers and see them safely abed.

Abe. Why—I'd be glad to hear their prayers, too.

Ninian. Oh, no! You'd only keep them up till all hours with your stories. Come along, Elizabeth.

[ELIZABETH *doesn't want to go, but doesn't know what to do to prevent it.*]

Abe. [*To* ELIZABETH.] Kiss them good night, for me.

Ninian. We'd better not tell them you're in the house, or they'll be furious.

Elizabeth. [*Making one last attempt.*] Mary! Won't you come with us and say good night to the children?

Ninian. No, my dear. Leave Mary here—to keep Abe entertained. [*He guides* ELIZABETH *out, following her.*]

Mary. [*With a little laugh.*] I don't blame Ninian for keeping you away from those children. They all adore you.

Abe. Well—I always seemed to get along well with children. Probably it's because they never want to take me seriously.

Mary. You understand them—that's the important thing . . . But—do sit down, Mr. Lincoln. [*She indicates that he is to sit next to her.*]

Abe. Thank you—I will.

[*He starts to cross to the couch to sit beside* MARY. *She looks at him with melting eyes. The lights fade.*]

SCENE VI

Again the Law Office. It is afternoon of New Year's Day, a few weeks after the preceding scene.

[ABE *is sitting, slumped in his chair, staring at his desk. He has his hat and overcoat on. A muffler is hanging about his neck, untied.*

JOSH SPEED *is half-sitting on the table at the right. He is reading a long letter, with most serious attention. At length he finishes it, refolds it very carefully, stares at the floor.*]

Abe. Have you finished it, Josh?

Josh. Yes.

Abe. Well—do you think it's all right?

Josh. No, Abe—I don't. [ABE *turns slowly and looks at him.*] I think the sending of this letter would be a most grave mistake—and that is putting it mildly and charitably.

Abe. Have I stated the case too crudely?

[ABE *is evidently in a serious state of distress, although he is making a tremendous effort to disguise it by speaking in what he intends to be a coldly impersonal tone. He is struggling mightily to hold himself back from the brink of nervous collapse.*]

Josh. No—I have no quarrel with your choice of words. None whatever. If anything, the phraseology is too correct. But your method of doing it, Abe! It's brutal, it's heartless, it's so unworthy of you that I—I'm at a loss to understand how you ever thought you could do it this way.

Abe. I've done the same thing before with a woman to whom I seemed to have become attached. She approved of my action.

Josh. This is a different woman. [*He walks over to the window, then turns again toward* ABE.] You cannot seem to accept the fact that women are human beings, too, as variable as we are. You act on the assumption that they're all the same one—and that one is a completely unearthly being of your own conception. This letter isn't written to Mary Todd—it's written to yourself. Every line of it is intended to provide salve for your own conscience.

Abe. [*Rising; coldly.*] Do I understand that you will not deliver it for me?

Josh. No, Abe—I shall not.

Abe. [*Angrily.*] Then some one else will!

Josh. [*Scornfully.*] Yes. You could give it to the minister, to hand to the bride when he arrives for the ceremony. But—I hope, Abe, you won't send it till you're feeling a little calmer in your mind. . . .

Abe. [*Vehemently, turning to* JOSH.] How can I ever be calm in my mind until this thing is settled, and out of the way, once and for all? Have you got eyes in your head, Josh? Can't you see that I'm desperate?

Josh. I can see that plainly, Abe. I think your situation is more desperate even than you imagine, and I believe you should have the benefit of some really intelligent medical advice.

Abe. [*Seating himself at* BILLY'S *table.*] The trouble with me isn't anything that a doctor can cure.

Josh. There's a good man named Dr. Drake, who makes a specialty of treating people who get into a state of mind like yours, Abe . . .

Abe. [*Utterly miserable.*] So that's how you've figured it! I've done what I've threatened to do many times before: I've gone crazy. Well—you know me better than most men, Josh—and perhaps you're not far off right. I just feel that I've got to the end of my rope, and I must let go, and drop—and where I'll land, I don't know, and whether I'll survive the fall, I don't know that either. . . . But—this I *do* know: I've got to get out of this thing—I can't go through with it—I've got to have my release!

[JOSH *has turned to the window. Suddenly he turns back, toward* ABE.]

Josh. Ninian Edwards is coming up. Why not show this letter to him and ask for his opinion. . . .

Abe. [*Interrupting, with desperation.*] No, no! Don't say a word of any of this to him! Put that letter in your pocket. I can't bear to discuss this business with him, now.

[JOSH *puts the letter in his pocket and crosses to the couch.*]

Josh. Hello, Ninian.

Ninian. [*Heartily, from off.*] Hello, Josh! Happy New Year! [NINIAN *comes in. He wears a handsome, fur-trimmed great-coat, and carries two silver-headed canes, one of them in a baize bag, which he lays down on the table at the right.*]

Ninian. And Happy New Year, Abe—in fact, the happiest of your whole life!

Abe. Thank you, Ninian. And Happy New Year to you.

Ninian. [*Opening his coat.*] That didn't sound much as if you meant it. [*He goes to the stove to warm his hands.*] However, you can be forgiven today, Abe. I suppose you're inclined to be just a wee bit nervous. [*He chuckles and winks at* JOSH.] God—but it's cold in here! Don't you ever light this stove?

Abe. The fire's all laid. Go ahead and light it, if you want.

Ninian. [*Striking a match.*] You certainly are in one of your less amiable moods today. [*He lights the stove.*]

Josh. Abe's been feeling a little under the weather.

Ninian. So it seems. He looks to me as if he'd been to a funeral.

Abe. That's where I have been.

Ninian. [*Disbelieving.*] What? A funeral on your wedding day?

Josh. They buried Abe's oldest friend, Bowling Green, this morning.

Ninian. [*Shocked.*] Oh—I'm mighty sorry to hear that, Abe. And—I hope you'll forgive me for—not having known about it.

Abe. Of course, Ninian.

Ninian. But I'm glad you were there, Abe, at the funeral. It must have been a great comfort to his family.

Abe. I wasn't any comfort to any one. They asked me to deliver an oration, a eulogy of the deceased—and I tried—and I couldn't say a thing. Why do they expect you to strew a lot of flowery phrases over anything so horrible as a dead body? Do they think that Bowling Green's soul needs quotations to give it peace? All that mattered to me was that he was a good, just man—and I loved him—and he's dead.

Ninian. Why didn't you say that, Abe?

Abe. [*Rising.*] I told you—they wanted an oration.

Ninian. Well, Abe—I think Bowling himself would be the first to ask you to put your sadness aside in the prospect of your own happiness, and Mary's—and I'm only sorry that our old friend didn't live to see you two fine people married. [*He is making a gallant attempt to assume a more cheerily nuptial tone.*] I've made all the arrangements with the Reverend Dresser, and Elizabeth is preparing a bang-up dinner—so you can be sure the whole affair will be carried off handsomely and painlessly.

[BILLY HERNDON *comes in. He carries a bottle in his coat pocket, and is already more than a little drunk and sullen, but abnormally articulate.*]

Ah, Billy—Happy New Year!

Billy. The same to you, Mr. Edwards. [*He puts the bottle down on the table and takes his coat off.*]

Ninian. I brought you a wedding present, Abe. Thought you'd like to make a brave show when you first walk out with your bride. It came from the same place in Louisville where I bought mine.

[*He picks up one of the canes and hands it proudly to* ABE, *who takes it and inspects it gravely.*]

Abe. It's very fine, Ninian. And I thank you. [*He takes the cane over to his desk and seats himself.*]

Ninian. Well—I'll frankly confess that in getting it for you, I was influenced somewhat by consideration for Mary and her desire for keeping up appearances. And in that connection—I know you'll forgive me, Josh, and you, too, Billy, if I say something of a somewhat personal nature.

Billy. [*Truculent.*] If you want me to leave you, I shall be glad to. . . .

Ninian. No, please, Billy—I merely want to speak a word or two as another of Abe's friends; it's my last chance before the ceremony. Of course, the fact that the bride is my sister-in-law gives me a little added responsibility in wishing to promote the success of this marriage. [*He crosses to* ABE.] And a success it will be, Abe . . . if only you will bear in mind one thing: you must keep a tight rein on her ambition. My wife tells me that even as a child, she had delusions of grandeur—she predicted to one and all that the man she would marry would be President of the United States. [*He turns to* JOSH.] You know how it is—every boy in the country plans some day to be President, and every little girl plans to marry him. [*Again to* ABE:] But Mary is one who hasn't entirely lost those youthful delusions. So I urge you to beware. Don't let her talk you into any gallant crusades or wild goose chases. Let her learn to be satisfied with the estate to which God hath brought her. With which, I shall conclude my pre-nuptial sermon. [*He buttons his coat.*] I shall see you all at the house at five o'clock, and I want you to make sure that Abe is looking his prettiest.

Josh. Good-by, Ninian.

[NINIAN *goes out.* ABE *turns again to the desk and stares at nothing.* BILLY *takes the bottle and a cup from his desk and pours himself a stiff drink. He raises the cup toward* ABE.]

Billy. [*Huskily.*] Mr. Lincoln, I beg leave to drink to your health and happiness . . . and to that of the lady who will become your wife.

[ABE *makes no response.* BILLY *drinks it down, then puts the cup back on the table.*]

You don't want to accept my toast because you think it wasn't sincere. And I'll admit I've made it plain that I've regretted the step you've taken. I thought that in this marriage, you were lowering yourself—you were trading your honor for some exalted family connections. . . . I wish to apologize for so thinking. . . .

Abe. No apologies required, Billy.

Billy. I doubt that Miss Todd and I will ever get along well together. But I'm now convinced that our aims are the same—particularly since I've heard the warnings delivered by her brother-in-law. [*A note of scorn colors his allusion to* NINIAN.] If she really is ambitious for you—if she will never stop driving you, goading you—then I say, God bless her, and give her strength!

[*He has said all this with* ABE'S *back to him.* BILLY *pours himself another drink, nearly emptying the large bottle.* ABE *turns and looks at him.*]

Abe. Have you had all of that bottle today?

Billy. This bottle? Yes—I have.

Josh. And why not? It's New Year's Day!

Billy. [*Looking at* JOSH.] Thank you, Mr. Speed. Thank you for the defense. And I hope you will permit me to propose one more toast. [*He takes a step toward* ABE.] To the President of the United States, and Mrs. Lincoln! [*He drinks.*]

Abe. [*Grimly.*] I think we can do without any more toasts, Billy.

Billy. Very well! That's the last one—until after the wedding. And then, no doubt, the Edwards will serve us with the costliest champagne. And, in case you're apprehensive, I shall be on my best behavior in that distinguished gathering!

Abe. There is not going to be a wedding. [BILLY *stares at him, and then looks at* JOSH, *and then again at* ABE.] I have a letter that I want you to deliver to Miss Todd.

Billy. What letter? What is it?

Abe. Give it to him, Josh. [JOSH *takes the letter out of his pocket, and puts it in the stove.* ABE *jumps up.*] You have no right to do that!

Josh. I know I haven't! But it's done. [ABE *is staring at* JOSH.] And don't look at me as if you were planning to break my neck. Of course you could do it, Abe—but you won't. [JOSH *turns to* BILLY.] In that letter, Mr. Lincoln asked Miss Todd for his release. He told her that he had made a mistake in his previous protestations of affection for her, and so he couldn't go through with a marriage which could only lead to endless pain and misery for them both.

Abe. [*Deeply distressed.*] If that isn't the truth, what is?

Josh. I'm not disputing the truth of it. I'm only asking you to tell her so, to her face, in the manner of a man.

Abe. It would be a more cruel way. It would hurt her more deeply. For I couldn't help blurting it *all* out—all the terrible things I didn't say in that letter. [*He is speaking with passion.*] I'd have to tell her that I have hatred for her infernal ambition—that I don't want to be ridden and driven, upward and onward through life, with her whip lashing me, and her spurs digging into me! If her poor soul craves importance in life, then let her marry Stephen Douglas. He's ambitious, too. . . . I want only to be left alone! [*He sits down again and leans on the table.*]

Josh. [*Bitterly.*] Very well, then—tell her all that! It will be more gracious to admit that you're afraid of her, instead of letting her down flat with the statement that your ardor, such as it was, has cooled.

[BILLY *has been seething with a desire to get into this conversation. Now, with a momentary silence, he plunges.*]

Billy. May I say something?

Abe. I doubt that you're in much of a condition to contribute. . . .

Josh. What is it, Billy?

Billy. [*Hotly.*] It's just this. Mr. Lincoln, you're not abandoning Miss Mary Todd. No! You're only using her as a living sacrifice, offering her up, in the hope that you will thus gain forgiveness of the gods for your failure to do your own great duty!

Abe. [*Smouldering.*] Yes! My own great duty. Every one feels called upon to remind me of it, but no one can tell me what it is.

Billy. [*Almost tearful.*] I can tell you! I can tell you what is the duty of every man who calls himself an American! It is to perpetuate those truths which were once held to be self-evident: that all men are created equal—that they are endowed with certain inalienable rights—that among these are the right to life, liberty, and the pursuit of happiness.

Abe. [*Angrily.*] And are those rights denied to *me?*

Billy. Could you ever enjoy them while your mind is full of the awful knowledge that two million of your fellow beings in this country are slaves? Can you take any satisfaction from looking at that flag above your desk, when you know that ten of its stars represent states which are willing to destroy the Union—rather than yield their property rights in the flesh and blood of those slaves? And what of all the States of the future? All the territories of the West—clear out to the Pacific Ocean? Will they be the homes of free men? Are you answering *that* question to your own satisfaction? That is your flag, Mr. Lincoln, and you're proud of it. But what are you doing to save it from being ripped into shreds?

[ABE *jumps to his feet, towers over* BILLY *and speaks with temper restrained, but with great passion.*]

Abe. I'm minding my own business—that's what I'm doing! And there'd be no threat to the Union if others would do the same. And as to slavery—I'm sick and tired of this righteous talk about it. When you know more about law, you'll know that those property rights you mentioned are guaranteed by the Constitution. And if the Union can't stand on the Constitution, then let it fall!

Billy. The hell with the Constitution! This is a matter of the rights of living men to freedom—and those came before the Constitution! When the Law denies those rights, then the Law is wrong, and it must be changed, if not by moral protest, then by force! There's no course of action that isn't justified in the defense of freedom! And don't dare to tell me that any one in the world knows that better than you do, Mr. Lincoln. You, who honor the memory of Elijah Lovejoy and every other man who ever died for that very ideal!

Abe. [*Turning away from him.*] Yes—I honor them—and envy them—because they could believe that their ideals are *worth* dying for. [*He turns to* JOSH *and speaks with infinite weariness.*] All right, Josh—I'll go up now and talk to Mary—and then I'm going away. . . .

Josh. Where, Abe?

Abe. [*Dully.*] I don't know.

[*He goes out and closes the door after him. After a moment,* BILLY *rushes to the door, opens it, and shouts after* ABE.]

Billy. You're quitting, Mr. Lincoln! As surely as there's a God in Heaven, He knows that you're running away from your obligations to Him, and to your fellow-men, and your own immortal soul!

Josh. [*Drawing* BILLY *away from the door.*] Billy—Billy—leave him alone. He's a sick man.

Billy. [*Sitting down at the table.*] What can we do for him, Mr. Speed? What can we do? [BILLY *is now actually in tears.*]

Josh. I don't know, Billy. [*He goes to the window and looks out.*] He'll be in such a state of emotional upheaval, he'll want to go away by himself, for a long time. Just as he did after the death of poor little Ann Rutledge. He'll go out and wander on the prairies, trying to grope his way back into the wilderness from which he came. There's nothing we can do for him, Billy. He'll have to do it for himself.

Billy. [*Fervently.*] May God be with him!

[*The lights fade.*]

SCENE VII

On the prairie, near New Salem. It is a clear, cool, moonlit evening, nearly two years after the preceding scene.

In the foreground is a campfire. Around it are packing cases, blanket rolls and one ancient trunk. In the background is a covered wagon, standing at an angle, so that the opening at the back of it is visible to the audience.

[SETH GALE *is standing by the fire, holding his seven-year-old son,* JIMMY, *in his arms. The boy is wrapped up in a blanket.*]

Jimmy. I don't want to be near the fire, Paw. I'm burning up. Won't you take the blanket offen me, Paw?

Seth. No, son. You're better off if you keep yourself covered.

Jimmy. I want some water, Paw. Can't I have some water?

Seth. Yes! Keep quiet, Jimmy! Gobey's getting the water for you now.

[*He looks off to the right, and sees* JACK ARMSTRONG *coming.*]

Hello, Jack, I was afraid you'd got lost.

Jack. [*Coming in.*] I couldn't get lost anywhere's around New Salem. How's the boy?

Seth. [*With a cautionary look at* JACK.] He—he's a little bit thirsty. Did you find Abe?

Jack. Yes—it took me some time because he'd wandered off—went out to the old cemetery across the river to visit Ann Rutledge's grave.

Seth. Is he coming here?

Jack. He said he'd better go get Doc Chandler who lives on the Winchester Road. He'll be along in a while. [*He comes up to* JIMMY.] How you feelin', Jimmy?

Jimmy. I'm burning . . .

[AGGIE *appears, sees* JACK.]

Aggie. Oh—I'm glad you're back, Mr. Armstrong.

Jack. There'll be a doctor here soon, Mrs. Gale.

Aggie. Thank God for that! Bring him into the wagon, Seth. I got a nice, soft bed all ready for him.

Seth. You hear that, Jimmy? Your ma's fixed a place where you can rest comfortable.

[AGGIE *retreats into the wagon.*]

Jimmy. When'll Gobey come back? I'm thirsty. When'll he bring the water?

Seth. Right away, son. You can trust Gobey to get your water. [*He hands* JIMMY *into the wagon.*]

Jack. He's worse, ain't he?

Seth. [*In a despairing tone.*] Yes. The fever's been raging something fierce since you left. It'll sure be a relief when Abe gets here. He can always do something to put confidence in you.

Jack. How long since you've seen Abe, Seth?

Seth. Haven't laid eyes on him since I left here—eight—nine years ago. We've corresponded some.

Jack. Well—you may be surprised when you see him. He's changed plenty since he went to Springfield. He climbed up pretty high in the world, but he appears to have slipped down lately. He ain't much like his old comical self.

Seth. Well, I guess we all got to change. [*He starts up, hearing* GOBEY *return.*] Aggie! [GOBEY, *a Negro, comes in from the left, carrying a bucket of water.* AGGIE *appears from the wagon.*] Here's Gobey with the water.

Gobey. Yes, Miss Aggie. Here you are. [*He hands it up.*]

Aggie. Thanks, Gobey. [*She goes back into the wagon.*]

Gobey. How's Jimmy now, Mr. Seth?

Seth. About the same.

Gobey. [*Shaking his head.*] I'll get some more water for the cooking. [*He picks up a kettle and a pot and goes.*]

Seth. [*To* JACK.] It was a bad thing to have happen, all right—the boy getting sick—when we were on an expedition like this. No doctor—no way of caring for him.

Jack. How long you been on the road, Seth?

Seth. More than three months. Had a terrible time in the Pennsylvania Mountains, fearful rains and every stream flooded. I can tell you, there was more than one occasion when I wanted to turn back and give up the whole idea. But—when you get started—you just can't turn . . . [*He is looking off right.*] Say! Is that Abe coming now?

Jack. [*Rising.*] Yep. That's him.

Seth. [*Delighted*] My God, look at him! Store clothes and a plug hat! Hello—Abe!

Abe. Hello, Seth. [*He comes on and shakes hands, warmly.*] I'm awful glad to see you again, Seth.

Seth. And me, too, Abe.

Abe. It did my heart good when I heard you were on your way West. Where's your boy?

Seth. He's in there—in the wagon. . . .

[AGGIE *has appeared from the wagon.*]

Aggie. Is that the doctor?

Seth. No, Aggie—this is the man I was telling you about I wanted so much to see. This is Mr. Abe Lincoln—my wife, Mrs. Gale.

Abe. Pleased to meet you, Mrs. Gale.

Aggie. Pleased to meet you, Mr. Lincoln.

Abe. Doc Chandler wasn't home. They said he was expected over at the Boger farm at midnight. I'll go there then and fetch him.

Seth. It'll be a friendly act, Abe.

Aggie. We'll be in your debt, Mr. Lincoln.

Abe. In the meantime, Mrs. Gale, I'd like to do whatever I can. . . .

Seth. There's nothing to do, Abe. The

boy's got the swamp fever, and we're just trying to keep him quiet.

Aggie. [*Desperately.*] There's just one thing I would wish—is—is there any kind of a preacher around this God-forsaken place?

Seth. [*Worried.*] Preacher?

Abe. Do you know of any, Jack?

Jack. No. There ain't a preacher within twenty miles of New Salem now.

Aggie. Well—I only thought if there was, we might get him here to say a prayer for Jimmy.

[*She goes back into the wagon.* SETH *looks after her with great alarm.*]

Seth. She wants a preacher. That looks as if she'd given up, don't it?

Jack. It'd probably just comfort her.

Abe. Is your boy very sick, Seth?

Seth. Yes—he is.

Jack. Why don't *you* speak a prayer, Abe? You could always think of somethin' to say.

Abe. I'm afraid I'm not much of a hand at praying. I couldn't think of a blessed thing that would be of any comfort.

Seth. Never mind. It's just a—a religious idea of Aggie's. Sit down, Abe.

Abe. [*Looking at the wagon.*] So you've got your dream at last, Seth. You're doing what you and I used to talk about—you're moving.

Seth. Yes, Abe. We got crowded out of Maryland. The city grew up right over our farm. So—we're headed for a place where there's more room. I wrote you—about four months back—to tell you we were starting out, and I'd like to meet up with you here. I thought it was just possible you might consider joining in this trip.

Abe. It took a long time for your letter to catch up with me, Seth. I've just been drifting—down around Indiana and Kentucky where I used to live. [*He sits down on a box.*] Do you aim to settle in Nebraska?

Seth. No, we're not going to stop there. We're going right across the continent—all the way to Oregon.

Abe. [*Deeply impressed.*] Oregon?

Jack. Sure. That's where they're all headin' for now.

Seth. We're making first for a place called Westport Landing—that's in Kansas right on the frontier—where they outfit the wagon trains for the far West. You join up there with a lot of others who are like-minded, so you've got company when you're crossing the plains and the mountains.

Abe. It's staggering—to think of the distance you're going. And you'll be taking the frontier along with you.

Seth. It may seem like a fool-hardy thing to do—but we heard too many tales of the black earth out there, and the balance of rainfall and sunshine.

Jack. Why don't you go with them, Abe? That country out west is gettin' settled fast. Why—last week alone, I counted more than two hundred wagons went past here—people from all over—Pennsylvania, Connecticut, Vermont—all full of jubilation at the notion of gettin' land. By God, I'm goin' too, soon as I can get me a wagon. They'll need men like me to fight the Indians for 'em—and they'll need men with brains, like you, Abe, to tell 'em how to keep the peace.

Abe. [*Looking off.*] It's a temptation to go, I can't deny that.

Jack. Then what's stoppin' you from doin' it? You said yourself you've just been driftin'.

Abe. Maybe that's it—maybe I've been drifting too long. . . . [*He changes the subject.*] Is it just the three of you, Seth?

Seth. That's all. The three of us and Gobey, the nigger.

Abe. Is he your slave?

Seth. Gobey? Hell, no! He's a free man! My father freed his father twenty years ago. But we've had to be mighty careful about Gobey. You see, where we come from, folks are pretty uncertain how they feel about the slave question, and lots of good free niggers get snaked over the line into Virginia and then sold down river before you know it. And when you try to go to court and assert their legal rights, you're beaten at every turn by the damned, dirty shyster lawyers. That's why we've been keeping well up in free territory on this trip.

Abe. Do you think it will be free in Oregon?

Seth. Of course it will! It's got to . . .

Abe. [*Bitterly.*] Oh no, it hasn't, Seth. Not with the politicians in Washington selling out the whole West piece by piece to the slave traders.

Seth. [*Vehemently.*] That territory has got to be free! If this country ain't strong enough to protect its citizens from slavery, then we'll cut loose from it and join with Canada. Or, better yet, we'll make a *new* country out there in the far west.

Abe. [*Gravely.*] A new country?

Seth. Why not?

Abe. I was just thinking—old Mentor Graham once said to me that some day the United States might be divided up into many hostile countries, like Europe.

Seth. Well—let it be! Understand—I love this country and I'd fight for it. And I guess George Washington and the rest of them loved England and fought for it when they were young—but they didn't hesitate to cut loose when the government failed to play fair and square with 'em. . . .

Jack. By God, if Andy Jackson was back in the White House, he'd run out them traitors with a horsewhip!

Abe. It'd be a bad day for us Americans, Seth, if we lost you, and your wife, and your son.

Seth. [*Breaking.*] My son!—Oh—I've been talking big—but it's empty talk. If he dies—there won't be enough spirit left in us to push on any further. What's the use of working for a future when you know there won't be anybody growing up to enjoy it. Excuse me, Abe—but I'm feeling pretty scared.

Abe. [*Suddenly rises.*] You mustn't be scared, Seth. I know I'm a poor one to be telling you that—because I've been scared all my life. But—seeing you now—and thinking of the big thing you've set out to do—well, it's made me feel pretty small. It's made me feel that I've got to do something, too, to keep you and your kind in the United States of America. You mustn't quit, Seth! Don't let anything beat you—don't you ever give up!

[AGGIE *comes out of the wagon. She is very frightened.*]

Aggie. Seth!

Seth. What is it, Aggie?

Aggie. He's worse, Seth! He's moaning in his sleep, and he's gasping for breath. . . .

[*She is crying.* SETH *takes her in his arms.*]

Seth. Never mind, honey. Never mind. When the doctor gets here, he'll fix him up in no time. It's all right, honey. He'll get well.

Abe. If you wish me to, Mrs. Gale—I'll try to speak a prayer.

[*They look at him.*]

Jack. That's the way to talk, Abe!

Seth. We'd be grateful for anything you might say, Abe.

[ABE *takes his hat off. As he starts speaking,* GOBEY *comes in from the left and stops reverently to listen.*]

Abe. Oh God, the father of all living, I ask you to look with gentle mercy upon this little boy who is here, lying sick in this covered wagon. His people are travelling far, to seek a new home in the wilderness, to do your work, God, to make this earth a good place for your children to live in. They can see clearly where they're going, and they're not afraid to face all the perils that lie along the way. I humbly beg you not to take their child from them. Grant him the freedom of life. Do not condemn him to the imprisonment of death. Do not deny him his birthright. Let him know the sight of great plains and high mountains, of green valleys and wide rivers. For this little boy is an American, and these things belong to him, and he to them. Spare him, that he too may strive for the ideal for which his fathers have labored, so faithfully and for so long. Spare him and give him his fathers' strength—give us all strength, O God, to do the work that is before us. I ask you this favor, in the name of *your* son, Jesus Christ, who died upon the Cross to set men free. Amen.

Gobey. [*With fervor.*] Amen!

Seth and Aggie. [*Murmuring.*] Amen!

[ABE *puts his hat on.*]

Abe. It's getting near midnight. I'll go over to the Boger farm and get the doctor. [*He goes out.*]

Seth. Thank you, Abe.

Aggie. Thank you—thank you, Mr. Lincoln.

Gobey. God bless you, Mr. Lincoln!

[*The lights fade quickly.*]

SCENE VIII

Again the parlor of the Edwards house. A few days after preceding scene.

[MARY *is seated, reading a book. After a moment, the* MAID *enters.*]

Maid. Miss Mary—Mr. Lincoln is here.

Mary. Mr. Lincoln! [*She sits still a moment in an effort to control her emotions, then sharply closes the book and rises.*]

Maid. Will you see him, Miss Mary?

Mary. Yes—in one moment.

[*The* MAID *goes off.* MARY *turns, drops her book on the sofa, then moves over toward the right, struggling desperately to compose herself. At the fireplace, she stops and turns to face* ABE *as he enters.*]

I'm glad to see you again, Mr. Lincoln.

[*There is considerable constraint between them. He is grimly determined to come to the point with the fewest possible words; she is making a gallant, well-bred attempt to observe the social amenities.*]

Abe. Thank you, Mary. You may well wonder why I have thrust myself on your mercy in this manner.

Mary. [*Quickly.*] I'm sure you're always welcome in Ninian's house.

Abe. After my behavior at our last meeting here, I have not been welcome company for myself.

Mary. You've been through a severe illness. Joshua Speed has kept us informed of it. We've been greatly concerned.

Abe. It is most kind of you.

Mary. But you're restored to health now—you'll return to your work, and no doubt you'll be running for the assembly again—or perhaps you have larger plans?

Abe. I have no plans, Mary. [*He seems to brace himself.*] But I wish to tell you that I am sorry for the things that I said on that unhappy occasion which was to have been our wedding day.

Mary. You need not say anything about that, Mr. Lincoln. Whatever happened then, it was my own fault.

Abe. [*Disturbed by this unforeseen avowal.*] *Your* fault! It was my miserable cowardice . . .

Mary. I was blinded by my own self-confidence! I—I loved you. [*For a moment her firm voice falters, but she immediately masters that tendency toward weakness.*] And I believed I could make you love me. I believed we might achieve a real communion of spirit, and the fire of my determination would burn in you. You would become a man and a leader of men! But you didn't wish that. [*She turns away.*] I knew you had strength—but I did not know you would use it, all of it, to resist your own magnificent destiny.

Abe. [*Deliberately.*] It is true, Mary—you once had faith in me which I was far from deserving. But the time has come, at last, when I wish to strive to deserve it. [Mary *looks at him sharply.*] When I behaved in that shameful manner toward you, I did so because I thought that our ways were separate and could never be otherwise. I've come to the conclusion that I was wrong. I believe that our destinies are together, for better or for worse, and I again presume to ask you to be my wife. I fully realize, Mary, that taking me back now would involve humiliation for you.

Mary. [*Flaring.*] I am not afraid of humiliation, if I know it will be wiped out by ultimate triumph! But there can be no triumph unless you yourself are sure. What was it that brought you to this change of heart and mind?

Abe. On the prairie, I met an old friend of mine who was moving West, with his wife and child, in a covered wagon. He asked me to go with him, and I was strongly tempted to do so. [*There is great sadness in his tone—but he seems to collect himself, and turns to her again, speaking with a sort of resignation.*] But then I knew that was not my direction. The way I must go is the way you have always wanted me to go.

Mary. And you will promise that never again will you falter, or turn to run away?

Abe. I promise, Mary—if you will have me—I shall devote myself for the rest of my days to trying—to do what is right—as God gives me power to see what is right.

[*She looks at him, trying to search him. She would like to torment him, for a while, with artful indecision. But she can not do it.*]

Mary. Very well, then—I shall be your wife. I shall fight by your side—till death do us part. [*She runs to him and clutches him.*] Abe! I love you—oh, I love you! Whatever becomes of the two of us, I'll die loving you! [*She is sobbing wildly on his shoulder.*]

[*Awkwardly, he lifts his hands and takes hold of her in a loose embrace. He is staring down at the carpet, over her shoulder.*]

CURTAIN

ACT III

SCENE IX

A speakers' platform in an Illinois town. It is a summer evening in the year 1858.

A light shines down on the speaker at the front of the platform.

[*At the back of the platform are three chairs. At the right sits* Judge Stephen A. Douglas—*at the left,* Abe, *who has his plug hat on and makes occasional notes on a piece of paper on his knee. The chair in the middle is for* Ninian, *acting as Moderator, who is now at the front of the platform.*]

Ninian. We have now heard the leading arguments from the two candidates for the high office of United States Senator from Illinois—Judge Stephen A. Douglas and Mr. Abraham Lincoln. A series of debates between these two eminent citizens of Illinois has focused upon our state the attention of the entire nation, for here are being discussed the vital issues which now affect the lives of all Americans and the whole future history of our beloved country. According to the usual custom of debate, each of the candidates will now speak in rebuttal. . . . Judge Douglas.

[NINIAN *retires and sits, as* DOUGLAS *comes forward. He is a brief but magnetic man, confident of his powers.*]

Douglas. My fellow citizens: My good friend, Mr. Lincoln, has addressed you with his usual artless sincerity, his pure, homely charm, his perennial native humor. He has even devoted a generously large portion of his address to most amiable remarks upon my fine qualities as a man, if not as a statesman. For which I express deepest gratitude. But—at the same time—I most earnestly beg you not to be deceived by his seeming innocence, his carefully cultivated spirit of good will. For in each of his little homilies lurk concealed weapons. Like Brutus, in Shakespeare's immortal tragedy, Mr. Lincoln is an honorable man. But, also like Brutus, he is an adept at the art of inserting daggers between an opponent's ribs, just when said opponent least expects it. Behold me, gentlemen—I am covered with scars. And yet—somehow or other—I am still upright. Perhaps because I am supported by that sturdy prop called "Truth." Truth—which, crushed to earth by the assassin's blades, doth rise again! Mr. Lincoln makes you laugh with his pungent anecdotes. Then he draws tears from your eyes with his dramatic pictures of the plight of the black slave labor in the South. Always, he guides you skilfully to the threshold of truth, but then, as you are about to cross it, diverts your attention elsewhere. For one thing—he never, by any mischance, makes reference to the condition of labor here in the North! Oh, no! Perhaps New England is so far beyond the bounds of his parochial ken that he does not know that tens of thousands of working men and women in the textile industry are now on STRIKE! And why are they on strike? Because from early morning to dark of night—fourteen hours a day—those "free" citizens must toil at shattering looms in soulless factories and never see the sun; and then, when their fearful day's work at last comes to its exhausted end, these ill-clad and undernourished laborers must trudge home to their foul abodes in tenements that are not fit habitations for rats! What kind of Liberty is this? And if Mr. Lincoln has not heard of conditions in Massachusetts—how has it escaped his attention that here in our own great state no wheels are now turning on that mighty railroad, the Illinois Central? Because its oppressed workers are also on STRIKE! Because they too demand a living wage! So it is throughout the North. Hungry men, marching through the streets in ragged order, promoting riots, because they are not paid enough to keep the flesh upon the bones of their babies! What kind of Liberty is *this?* And what kind of equality? Mr. Lincoln harps constantly on this subject of equality. He repeats over and over the argument used by Lovejoy and other abolitionists: to wit, that the Declaration of Independence having declared all men free and equal, by divine law, thus Negro equality is an inalienable right. Contrary to this absurd assumption stands the verdict of the Supreme Court, as it was clearly stated by Chief Justice Taney in the case of Dred Scott. The Negroes are established by this decision as an inferior race of beings, subjugated by the dominant race, enslaved and, therefore, *property*—like all other property! But Mr. Lincoln is inclined to dispute the constitutional authority of the Supreme Court. He has implied, if he did not say so outright, that the Dred Scott decision was a prejudiced one, which must be over-ruled by the voice of the people. Mr. Lincoln is a lawyer, and I presume, therefore, that he knows that when he seeks to destroy public confidence in the integrity, the inviolability of the Supreme Court, he is preaching *revolution!* He is attempting to stir up odium and rebellion in this country against the constituted authorities; he is stimulating the passions of men to resort to violence and to mobs, instead of to the law. He is setting brother against brother! There can be but one consequence of such inflammatory persuasion—and that is *Civil War!* He asks me to state my opinion of the Dred Scott decision, and I answer him unequivocally by saying, "I take the decisions of the Supreme Court as the law of the land, and I intend to obey them as such!" Nor will I be swayed from that position by all the rantings of all the fanatics who preach "racial equality," who ask us to vote, and eat, and sleep, and marry with Negroes! And I say further—Let each State mind its own business and leave its neighbors alone. If we will stand by that principle, then Mr. Lincoln will find that this great republic can exist forever divided into free and slave states. We can go on as we have done, increasing in wealth, in population, in power, until we shall be the admiration and the terror of the world! [*He glares at the audience, then turns, mopping his brow and resumes his seat.*]

Ninian. [*Rising.*] Mr. Lincoln.

[ABE *glances at his notes, takes his hat off, puts the notes in it, then rises slowly and comes forward. He speaks quietly, reasonably. His words come from an emotion so profound that it needs no advertisement.*]

Abe. Judge Douglas has paid tribute to my skill with the dagger. I thank him for that, but I must also admit that he can do more with that weapon than I can. He can keep ten daggers flashing in the air at one time. Fortunately, he's so good at it that none of the knives ever falls and hurts anybody. The Judge can condone slavery in the South and protest hotly against its extension to the North. He can crowd loyalty to the Union and defense of states' sovereignty into the same breath. Which reminds me—and I hope the Judge will allow me one more homely little anecdote, because I'd like to tell about a woman down in Kentucky. She came out of her cabin one day and found her husband grappling with a ferocious bear. It was a fight to the death, and the bear was winning. The struggling husband called to his wife, "For heaven's sake, *help* me!" The wife asked what could *she* do? Said the husband, "You could at least *say* something encouraging." But the wife didn't want to seem to be taking sides in this combat, so she just hollered, "Go it, husband—go it, bear!" Now, you heard the Judge make allusion to those who advocate voting and eating and marrying and sleeping with Negroes. Whether he meant me specifically, I do not know. If he did, I can say that just because I do not want a colored woman for a slave, I don't necessarily want her for a wife. I need not have her for either. I can just leave her alone. In some respects, she certainly is not my equal, any more than I am the Judge's equal, in some respects; but in her natural right to eat the bread she earns with her own hands without asking leave of some one else, she is my equal, and the equal of all others. And as to sleeping with Negroes—the Judge may be interested to know that the slave states have produced more than four hundred thousand mulattoes—and I don't think many of them are the children of abolitionists. That word "abolitionists" brings to mind New England, which also has been mentioned. I assure Judge Douglas that I have been there, and I have seen those cheerless brick prisons called factories, and the workers trudging silently home through the darkness. In those factories, cotton that was picked by black slaves is woven into cloth by white people who are separated from slavery by no more than fifty cents a day. As an American, I cannot be proud that such conditions exist. But—as an American—I can ask: would any of those striking workers in the North elect to change places with the slaves in the South? Will they not rather say, "The remedy is in *our* hands!" And, still as an American, I can say—thank God we live under a system by which men have the *right* to strike! I am not preaching rebellion. I don't have to. This country, with its institutions, belongs to the people who inhabit it. Whenever they shall grow weary of the existing government, they can exercise their constitutional right of amending it, or their revolutionary right to dismember or overthrow it. If the founding fathers gave us anything, they gave us that. And I am not preaching disrespect for the Supreme Court. I am only saying that the decisions of mortal men are often influenced by unjudicial bias—and the Supreme Court is composed of mortal men, most of whom, it so happens, come from the privileged class in the South. There is an old saying that judges are just as honest as other men, and not more so; and in case some of you are wondering who said that, it was Thomas Jefferson. [*He has half turned to* DOUGLAS.] The purpose of the Dred Scott decision is to make property, and nothing but property, of the Negro in all states of the Union. It is the old issue of property rights versus human rights—an issue that will continue in this country when these poor tongues of Judge Douglas and myself shall long have been silent. It is the eternal struggle between two principles. The one is the common right of humanity, and the other the divine right of kings. It is the same spirit that says, "You toil and work and earn bread, and I'll eat it." Whether those words come from the mouth of a king who bestrides his people and lives by the fruit of their labor, or from one race of men who seek to enslave another race, it is the same tyrannical principle. As a nation, we began by declaring, "All men are created equal." There was no mention of any exceptions to the rule in the Declaration of Independence. But we now practically read it, "All men are created equal except Negroes." If we accept this doctrine of race or class discrimination, what is to stop us from decreeing in the future that "All men are created equal except Negroes, foreigners, Catholics, Jews, or—just poor people?" That is the conclusion toward which the advocates of slavery are driving us. Many good citizens, North and South, agree with the Judge that we should accept that conclusion—don't stir up trouble—"Let each State mind its own business." That's the safer course, for the time being. But—I advise you to watch out! When you have enslaved any of your fellow beings, dehumanized him, denied him all claim to the dignity of manhood, placed him among the beasts, among the damned, are you quite sure that the demon you have thus created will not turn and rend *you?* When you begin qualifying freedom, watch out for the consequences to *you*! And I am not preaching civil war. All I am trying to do—now, and as long as I live—is to state and restate the fundamental virtues of our democracy, which have made us great, and which can make us greater. I believe most seriously that the perpetuation of those virtues is now endangered, not only by the honest proponents of slavery, but even more by those who echo Judge Douglas in shouting, "Leave it alone!" This is the complacent policy of indifference to evil, and that policy I cannot but hate. I hate it because of the monstrous injustice of slavery itself. I hate it because it deprives our republic of its just influence in the world; enables the enemies of free institutions everywhere to taunt us as hypocrites; causes the real friends of freedom to doubt our sincerity; and especially because it forces so many good men among ourselves into an open war with the very fundamentals of civil liberty, denying the good faith of the Declaration of Independence, and insisting that there is no right principle of action but *self-interest*. . . . In his final words tonight, the Judge said that we may be "the terror of the world." I don't think we want to be that. I think we would prefer to be the encouragement of the world, the proof that man is at last worthy to be free. But—we shall provide no such encouragement, unless we can establish our ability as a nation to live and grow. And we shall surely do neither if these states fail to remain *united*. There can be no distinction in the definitions of liberty as between one section and another, one race and another, one class and another. "A house divided against itself cannot stand." This government can not endure permanently, half slave and half free! [*He turns and goes back to his seat.*]

[*The lights fade.*]

SCENE X

Parlor of the Edwards home, now being used by the Lincolns. Afternoon of a day in the early Spring of 1860.

[ABE *is sitting on the couch at the right, with his seven-year-old son,* TAD, *on his lap. Sitting beside them is another son,* WILLIE, *aged nine. The eldest son,* ROBERT, *a young Harvard student of seventeen, is sitting by the window, importantly smoking a pipe and listening to the story* ABE *has been telling the children.* JOSHUA SPEED *is sitting at the left.*]

Abe. You must remember, Tad, the roads weren't much good then—mostly nothing more than trails—and it was hard to find my way in the darkness. . . .

Willie. Were you scared?

Abe. Yes—I was scared.

Willie. Of Indians?

Abe. No—there weren't any of them left around here. I was afraid I'd get lost, and the boy would die, and it would be all my fault. But, finally, I found the doctor. He was very tired, and wanted to go to bed, and he grumbled a lot, but I made him come along with me then and there.

Willie. Was the boy dead?

Abe. No, Willie. He wasn't dead. But he was pretty sick. The doctor gave him a lot of medicine.

Tad. Did it taste bad, Pa?

Abe. I presume it did. But it worked. I never saw those nice people again, but I've heard from them every so often. That little boy was your age, Tad, but now he's a grown man with a son almost as big as you are. He lives on a great big farm, in a valley with a river that runs right down from the tops of the snow mountains. . . .

[MARY *comes in.*]

Mary. Robert! You are smoking in my parlor!

Robert. [*Wearily.*] Yes, Mother. [*He rises.*]

Mary. I have told you that I shall not tolerate tobacco smoke in my parlor or, indeed, in any part of my house, and I mean to . . .

Abe. Come, come, Mary—you must be respectful to a Harvard man. Take it out to the woodshed, Bob.

Robert. Yes, Father.

Mary. And this will not happen again!

Robert. No, Mother. [*He goes out.*]

Abe. I was telling the boys a story about some pioneers I knew once.

Mary. It's time for you children to make ready for your supper.

[*The* CHILDREN *promptly get up to go.*]

Willie. But what happened after that, Pa?

Abe. Nothing. Everybody lived happily ever after. Now run along.

[WILLIE *and* TAD *run out.*]

Josh. What time *is* it, Mary?

Mary. It's nearly half past four. [*She is shaking the smoke out of the curtains.*]

Josh. Half past four, Abe. Those men will be here any minute.

Abe. [*Rising.*] Good Lord!

Mary. [*Turning sharply to* ABE.] What men?

Abe. Some men from the East. One of them's a political leader named Crimmin—and there's a Mr. Sturveson—he's a manufacturer—and . . .

Mary. [*Impressed.*] Henry D. Sturveson?

Abe. That's the one—and also the Reverend Dr. Barrick from Boston.

Mary. [*Sharply.*] What are they coming here for?

Abe. I don't precisely know—but I suspect that it's to see if I'm fit to be a candidate for President of the United States. [MARY *is, for the moment, speechless.*] I suppose they want to find out if we still live in a log cabin and keep pigs under the bed. . . .

Mary. [*In a fury.*] And you didn't *tell* me!

Abe. I'm sorry, Mary—the matter just slipped my . . .

Mary. You forgot to tell me that we're having the most important guests who ever crossed the threshold of my house!

Abe. They're not guests. They're only here on business.

Mary. [*Bitterly.*] Yes! Rather important business, it seems to me. They want to see us as we *are*—crude, sloppy, vulgar Western barbarians, living in a house that reeks of foul tobacco smoke.

Abe. We can explain about having a son at Harvard.

Mary. If I'd only *known*! If you had only given me a little time to prepare for them. Why didn't you put on your best suit? And those filthy old boots!

Abe. Well, Mary, I clean forgot. . . .

Mary. I declare, Abraham Lincoln, I believe you would have treated me with much more consideration if I had been your slave, instead of your wife! You have never, for one moment, stopped to think that perhaps I have some interests, some concerns, in the life we lead together. . . .

Abe. I'll try to clean up my boots a little, Mary.

[*He goes out, glad to escape from this painful scene.* MARY *looks after him. Her lip is quivering. She wants to avoid tears.*]

Mary. [*Seating herself; bitterly:*] You've seen it all, Joshua Speed. Every bit of it—courtship, if you could call it that, change of heart, change back again, and marriage, eighteen years of it. And you probably think just as all the others do—that I'm a bitter, nagging woman, and I've tried to kill his spirit, and drag him down to my level. . . .

[JOSH *rises and goes over to her.*]

Josh. [*Quietly.*] No, Mary. I think no such thing. Remember, I know Abe, too.

Mary. There never could have been another man such as he is! I've read about many that have gone up in the world, and all of them seemed to have to fight to assert themselves every inch of the way, against the opposition of their enemies and the lack of understanding in their own friends. But he's never had any of that. He's never had an enemy, and every one of his friends has always been completely confident in him. Even before I met him, I was told that he had a glorious future, and after I'd known him a day, I was sure of it myself. But he didn't believe it—or, if he did, secretly, he was so afraid of the prospect that he did all in his power to avoid it. He had some poem in his mind, about a life of woe, along a rugged path, that leads to some future doom, and it has been an obsession with him. All these years, I've tried and tried to stir him out of it, but all my efforts have been like so many puny waves, dashing against the Rock of Ages. And now, opportunity, the greatest opportunity, is coming here, to him, right into his own house. And what can I do about it? He *must* take it! He *must* see that this is what he was meant for! But I can't persuade him of it! I'm tired—I'm tired to death! [*The tears now come.*] I thought I could help to shape him, as I knew he should be, and I've succeeded in nothing—but in breaking myself. . . . [*She sobs bitterly.*]

[JOSH *sits down beside her and pats her hand.*]

Josh. [*Tenderly.*] I know, Mary. But—there's no reason in heaven and earth for you to reproach yourself. Whatever becomes of Abe Lincoln is in the hands of a God who controls the destinies of all of us, including lunatics, and saints. [ABE *comes back.*]

Abe. [*Looking down at his boots.*] I think they look all right now, Mary. [*He looks at* MARY, *who is now trying hard to control her emotion.*]

Mary. You can receive the gentlemen in here. I'll try to prepare some refreshment for them in the dining-room.

[*She goes out.* ABE *looks after her, miserably. There are a few moments of silence. At length,* ABE *speaks, in an offhand manner.*]

Abe. I presume these men *are* pretty influential.

Josh. They'll have quite a say in the delegations of three states that may swing the nomination away from Seward.

Abe. Suppose, by some miracle, or fluke, they did nominate me; do you think I'd stand a chance of winning the election?

Josh. An excellent chance, in my opinion. There'll be four candidates in the field, bumping each other, and opening up the track for a dark horse.

Abe. But the dark horse might run in the wrong direction.

Josh. Yes—you can always do that, Abe. I know *I* wouldn't care to bet two cents on you.

Abe. [*Grinning.*] It seems funny to be comparing it to a horse-race, with an old, spavined hack like me. But I've had some mighty energetic jockeys—Mentor Graham, Bowling Green, Bill Herndon, you, and Mary—most of all, Mary.

Josh. [*Looking at* Abe.] They don't count now, Abe. You threw 'em all, long ago. When you finally found yourself running against poor little Douglas, you got the bit between your teeth and went like greased lightning. You'd do the same thing to him again, if you could only decide to get started, which you probably won't . . . [*The doorbell jangles.* Josh *gets up.*]

Abe. I expect that's them now.

Josh. I'll go see if I can help Mary. [*He starts for the door but turns and looks at* Abe, *and speaks quietly.*] I'd just like to remind you, Abe—there are pretty nearly thirty million people in this country; most of 'em are common people, like you. They're in serious trouble, and they need somebody who understands 'em, as you do. So—when these gentlemen come in—try to be a *little* bit polite to them. [Abe *grins.* Josh *looks off.*] However—you won't listen to any advice from me.

[Josh *goes. The door is opened by a* Maid *and* Sturveson, Barrick, *and* Crimmin *come in.* Sturveson *is elderly, wealthy, and bland.* Barrick *is a soft Episcopalian dignitary.* Crimmin *is a shrewd, humorous fixer.*]

Abe. Come right in, gentlemen. Glad to see you again, Mr. Crimmin.

[*They shake hands.*]

Crimmin. How de do, Mr. Lincoln? This is Dr. Barrick of Boston, and Mr. Sturveson, of Philadelphia.

Dr. Barrick. Mr. Lincoln.

Sturveson. I'm honored, Mr. Lincoln.

Lincoln. Thank you, sir. Pray sit down, gentlemen.

Sturveson. Thank you. [*They sit.*]

Crimmin. Will Mrs. Lincoln seriously object if I light a seegar?

Lincoln. Go right ahead! I regret that Mrs. Lincoln is not here to receive you, but she will join us presently. [*He sits down.*]

Barrick. [*With great benignity.*] I am particularly anxious to meet Mrs. Lincoln, for I believe, with Mr. Longfellow, that "as unto the bow the cord is, so unto the man is woman."

Sturveson. [*Very graciously.*] And we are here dealing with a bow that is stout indeed. [Abe *bows slightly in acknowledgment of the compliment.*] And one with a reputation for shooting straight. So you'll forgive us, Mr. Lincoln, for coming directly to the point.

Abe. Yes, sir. I understand that you wish to inspect the prairie politician in his native lair, and here I am.

Sturveson. It is no secret that we are desperately in need of a candidate—one who is sound, conservative, safe—and clever enough to skate over the thin ice of the forthcoming campaign. Your friends—and there's an increasingly large number of them throughout the country—believe that you are the man.

Abe. Well, Mr. Sturveson, I can tell you that when first I was considered for political office—that was in New Salem, twenty-five years ago—I assured my sponsors of my conservatism. I have subsequently proved it, by never progressing anywhere.

Barrick. [*Smiling.*] Then you agree that you are the man we want?

Abe. I'm afraid I can't go quite that far in self-esteem, Dr. Barrick, especially when you have available a statesman and gentleman as eminent as Mr. Seward, who, I believe, is both ready and willing.

Sturveson. That's as may be. But please understand that this is not an inquisition. We merely wish to know you better, to gain a clearer idea of your theories on economics, religion, and national affairs, in general. To begin with—in one of your memorable debates with Senator Douglas, your opponent indulged in some of his usual demagoguery about industrial conditions in the North, and you replied shrewdly that whereas the slaves in the South . . .

Abe. Yes, I remember the occasion. I replied that I was thankful that laborers in free states have the right to strike. But that wasn't shrewdness, Mr. Sturveson. It was just the truth.

Sturveson. It has gained for you substantial support from the laboring classes, which is all to the good. But it has also caused a certain amount of alarm among business men, like myself.

Abe. I cannot enlarge on the subject. It seems obvious to me that this nation was founded on the supposition that men have the right to protest, violently if need be, against authority that is unjust or oppressive. [*He turns to* BARRICK.] The Boston Tea Party was a kind of strike. So was the Revolution itself. [*Again to* STURVESON.] So was Nicholas Biddle's attempt to organize the banks against the Jackson administration.

Sturveson. Which is all perfectly true—but—the days of anarchy are over. We face an unprecedented era of industrial expansion—mass production of every conceivable kind of goods—railroads and telegraph lines across the continent—all promoted and developed by private enterprise. In this great work, we must have a free hand, and a firm one, Mr. Lincoln. To put it bluntly, would you, if elected, place the interests of labor above those of capital?

Abe. I cannot answer that, bluntly, or any other way; because I cannot tell what I should do, if elected.

Sturveson. But you must have inclinations toward one side or the other. . . .

Abe. I think you know, Mr. Sturveson, that I am opposed to slavery.

Barrick. And we of New England applaud your sentiments! We deplore the inhumanity of our Southern friends in . . .

Abe. [*To* BARRICK.] There are more forms of slavery than that which is inflicted upon the Negroes in the South. I am opposed to all of them. [*He turns again to* STURVESON.] I believe in our democratic system—the just and generous system which opens the way to all—gives hope to all, and consequent energy and progress and improvement of condition to all, including employer and employee alike.

Barrick. We support your purpose, Mr. Lincoln, in steadfastly proclaiming the rights of men to resist unjust authority. But I am most anxious to know whether you admit One Authority to whom devotion is unquestioned?

Abe. I presume you refer to the Almighty?

Barrick. I do.

Abe. I think there has never been any doubt of my submission to His will.

Barrick. I'm afraid there is a great deal of doubt as to your devotion to His church.

Abe. I realize that, Doctor. They say I'm an atheist, because I've always refused to become a church member.

Barrick. What have been the grounds of your refusal?

Abe. I have found no churches suitable for my own form of worship. I could not give assent without mental reservations to the long, complicated statements of Christian doctrine which characterize their Articles of Belief and Confessions of Faith. But I can promise you, Dr. Barrick—I shall gladly join any church at any time if its sole qualification for membership is obedience to the Saviour's statement of Law and Gospel: "Thou shalt love the Lord thy God with all thy heart and with all thy soul and with all thy mind, and thou shalt love thy neighbor as thyself.". . . But—I beg you gentlemen to excuse me for a moment. I believe Mrs. Lincoln is preparing a slight collation, and I must see if I can help with it. . . .

Crimmin. Certainly, Mr. Lincoln.

[ABE *goes, closing the door behind him.* CRIMMIN *looks at the door, then turns to the others.*]

Well?

Barrick. The man is unquestionably an infidel. An idealist—in his curious, primitive way—but an infidel!

Sturveson. And a radical!

Crimmin. A radical? Forgive me, gentlemen, if I enjoy a quiet laugh at that.

Sturveson. Go ahead and enjoy yourself, Crimmin—but I did not like the way he evaded my direct question. I tell you, he's as unscrupulous a demagogue as Douglas. He's a rabble rouser!

Crimmin. Of course he is! As a dealer in humbug, he puts Barnum himself to shame.

Sturveson. Quite possibly—but he is not *safe*!

Crimmin. Not safe, eh? And what do you mean by that?

Sturveson. Just what I say. A man who devotes himself so whole-heartedly to currying favor with the mob develops the mob mentality. He becomes a preacher of discontent, of mass unrest. . . .

Crimmin. And what about Seward? If we put him up, he'll start right in demanding liberation of the slaves—and then there *will* be discontent and unrest! I ask you to believe me when I tell you that this Lincoln *is* safe—in economics and theology and every thing else. After all—what is the essential qualification that we demand of the candidate of our party? It is simply this: that he be able to get himself elected! And there is the man who can do that. [*He points off-stage.*]

Sturveson. [*Smiling.*] I should like to believe you!

Barrick. So say we all of us!

Crimmin. Then just keep faith in the eternal stupidity of the voters, which is what *he* will appeal to. In that uncouth rail splitter you may observe one of the smoothest, slickest politicians that ever hoodwinked a yokel mob! You complain that he evaded your questions. Of course he did, and did it perfectly! Ask him about the labor problem, and he replies, "I believe in democracy." Ask his views on religion, and he says, "Love thy neighbor as thyself." Now—you know you couldn't argue with that, either of you. I tell you, gentlemen, he's a vote-getter if I ever saw one. His very name is right—Abraham Lincoln! Honest Old Abe! He'll play the game with us now, and he'll go right on playing it when we get him into the White House. He'll do just what we tell him. . . .

Dr. Barrick. [*Cautioning him.*] Careful, Mr. Crimmin. . . . [ABE *returns.*]

Abe. If you gentlemen will step into the dining-room, Mrs. Lincoln would be pleased to serve you with a cup of tea.

Barrick. Thank you.

Sturveson. This is most gracious.

[*He and* BARRICK *move off toward the door.*]

Abe. Or perhaps something stronger for those who prefer it.

[STURVESON *and* BARRICK *go.* CRIMMIN *is looking for a place to throw his cigar.*]

Abe. [*Heartily.*] Bring your seegar with you, Mr. Crimmin!

Crimmin. Thank you—thank you.

[*He smiles at* ABE, *gives him a slap on the arm, and goes out,* ABE *following. The lights fade.*]

SCENE XI

Lincoln campaign headquarters in the Illinois State House. The evening of Election Day, November 6th, 1860.

It is a large room with a tall window opening out on to a wide balcony. There are doors upper right and upper left. At the left is a table littered with newspapers and clippings. There are many chairs about, and a liberal supply of spittoons. At the back is a huge chart of the thirty-three states, with their electoral votes, and a space opposite each side for the posting of bulletins. A short ladder gives access to Alabama and Arkansas at the top of the list.

On the wall at the left is an American flag. At the right is a map of the United States, on which each state is marked with a red, white, or blue flag.

[ABE *is sitting at the table, with his back to the audience, reading newspaper clippings. He wears his hat and has spectacles on.* MRS. LINCOLN *is sitting at the right of the table, her eyes darting nervously from* ABE, *to the chart, to the map. She wears her bonnet, tippet and muff.*

ROBERT LINCOLN *is standing near her, studying the map.* NINIAN EDWARDS *is sitting at the left of the table and* JOSH SPEED *is standing near the chart. They are both smoking cigars and watching the chart.*

The door at the left is open, and through it the clatter of telegraph instruments can be heard. The window is partly open, and we can hear band music from the square below, and frequent cheers from the assembled mob, who are watching the election returns flashed from a magic lantern on the State House balcony.

Every now and then, a telegraph operator named JED *comes in from the left and tacks a new bulletin up on the chart. Another man named* PHIL *is out on the balcony taking bulletins from* JED.]

Robert. What do those little flags mean, stuck into the map?

Josh. Red means the state is sure for us. White means doubtful. Blue means hopeless.

[ABE *tosses the clipping he has been reading on the table and picks up another.* JED *comes in and goes up to pin bulletins opposite Illinois, Maryland, and New York.*]

Ninian. [*Rising to look.*] Lincoln and Douglas neck and neck in Illinois.

[JOSH *and* ROBERT *crowd around the chart.*]

Josh. Maryland is going all for Breckenridge and Bell. Abe—you're nowhere in Maryland.

Mary. [*With intense anxiety.*] What of New York?

Jed. [*Crossing to the window.*] Say, Phil—when you're not getting bulletins, keep that window closed. We can't hear ourselves think.

Phil. All right. Only have to open 'er up again. [*He closes the window.*]

Mary. What does it say about New York? [JED *goes.*]

Ninian. Douglas a hundred and seventeen

thousand—Lincoln a hundred and six thousand.

Mary. [*Desperately, to* ABE.] He's winning from you in New York, Abe!

Josh. Not yet, Mary. These returns so far are mostly from the city, where Douglas is bound to run the strongest.

Abe. [*Interested in a clipping.*] I see the New York *Herald* says I've got the soul of a Uriah Heep encased in the body of a baboon. [*He puts the clipping aside and starts to read another.*]

Ninian. [*Who has resumed his seat.*] You'd better change that flag on Rhode Island from red to white, Bob. It looks doubtful to me.

[ROBERT, *glad of something to do, changes the flag as directed.*]

Mary. What does it look like in Pennsylvania, Ninian?

Ninian. There's nothing to worry about there, Mary. It's safe for Abe. In fact, you needn't worry at all.

Mary. [*Very tense.*] Yes. You've been saying that over and over again all evening. There's no need to worry. But how can we help worrying when every new bulletin shows Douglas ahead?

Josh. But every one of them shows Abe gaining.

Ninian. [*Mollifying.*] Just give them time to count all the votes in New York and then you'll be on your way to the White House.

Mary. Oh, why don't they hurry with it? Why don't those returns come in?

Abe. [*Preoccupied.*] They'll come in, soon enough.

[BILLY HERNDON *comes in from the right. He has been doing a lot of drinking but has hold of himself.*]

Billy. That mob down there is sickening! They cheer every bulletin that's flashed on the wall, whether the news is good or bad. And they cheer every picture of every candidate, including George Washington, with the same, fine, ignorant enthusiasm.

Josh. That's logical. They can't tell 'em apart.

Billy. [*To* ABE.] There are a whole lot of reporters down there. They want to know what will be your first official action after you're elected.

Ninian. What do you want us to tell 'em, Abe?

Abe. [*Still reading.*] Tell 'em I'm thinking of growing a beard.

Josh. A beard?

Ninian. [*Amused.*] Whatever put that idea into your mind?

Abe. [*Picking up another clipping.*] I had a letter the other day from some little girl. She said I ought to have whiskers, to give me more dignity. And I'll need it—if elected.

[JED *arrives with new bulletins.* BILLY, NINIAN, JOSH, *and* ROBERT *huddle around* JED, *watching him post the bulletins.*]

Mary. What do they say now?

[JED *goes to the window and gives some bulletins to* PHIL.]

Mary. Is there anything new from New York?

Ninian. Connecticut—Abe far in the lead. That's eleven safe electoral votes anyway. Missouri—Douglas thirty-five thousand—Bell thirty-three—Breckenridge sixteen—Lincoln, eight. . . .

[*Cheers from the crowd outside until* PHIL *closes the window.* JED *returns to the office at the left.*]

Mary. What are they cheering for?

Billy. They don't know!

Abe. [*With another clipping.*] The Chicago *Times* says, "Lincoln breaks down! Lincoln's heart fails him! His tongue fails him! His legs fail him! He fails all over! The people refuse to support him! They laugh at him! Douglas is champion of the people! Douglas skins the living dog!"

[*He tosses the clipping aside.* MARY *stands up.*]

Mary. [*Her voice is trembling.*] I can't stand it any longer!

Abe. Yes, my dear—I think you'd better go home. I'll be back before long.

Mary. [*Hysterical.*] I won't go home! You only want to be rid of me. That's what you've wanted ever since the day we were married—and before that. Anything to get me out of your sight, because you hate me! [*Turning to* JOSH, NINIAN, *and* BILLY.] And it's the same with all of you—all of his friends—you hate me—you wish I'd never come into his life.

Josh. No, Mary.

[ABE *has stood up, quickly, at the first storm signal. He himself is in a fearful state of nervous tension—in no mood to treat* MARY *with patient indulgence. He looks sharply at* NINIAN *and at the others.*]

Abe. Will you please step out for a moment?

Ninian. Certainly, Abe.

[*He and the others go into the telegraph office.* JOSH *gestures to* ROBERT *to go with them.* ROBERT *casts a black look at his mother and goes. . . .* ABE *turns on* MARY *with strange savagery.*]

Abe. Damn you! Damn you for taking

every opportunity you can to make a public fool of me—and yourself! It's bad enough, God knows, when you act like that in the privacy of our own home. But here—in front of people! You're not to do that again. Do you hear me? You're never to do that again!

[MARY *is so aghast at this outburst that her hysterical temper vanishes, giving way to blank terror.*]

Mary. [*In a faint, strained voice.*] Abe! You cursed at me. Do you realize what you did? You cursed at me.

[ABE *has the impulse to curse at her again, but with considerable effort, he controls it.*]

Abe. [*In a strained voice.*] I lost my temper, Mary. And I'm sorry for it. But I still think you should go home rather than endure the strain of this—this Death Watch.

[*She stares at him, uncomprehendingly, then turns and goes to the door.*]

Mary. [*At the door.*] This is the night I dreamed about, when I was a child, when I was an excited young girl, and all the gay young gentlemen of Springfield were courting me, and I fell in love with the least likely of them. This is the night when I'm waiting to hear that my husband has become President of the United States. And even if he does—it's ruined, for me. It's too late. . . .

[*She opens the door and goes out.* ABE *looks after her, anguished, then turns quickly, crosses to the door at the left and opens it.*]

Abe. [*Calling off.*] Bob!

[ROBERT *comes in.*]

Go with your mother.

Robert. Do I have to?

Abe. Yes! Hurry! Keep right with her till I get home.

[ROBERT *has gone.* ABE *turns to the window.* PHIL *opens it.*]

Phil. Do you think you're going to make it, Mr. Lincoln?

Abe. Oh—there's nothing to worry about.

Crowd Outside. [*Singing.*]

Old Abe Lincoln came out of the wilderness
Out of the wilderness
Out of the wilderness
Old Abe Lincoln came out of the wilderness
Down in Illinois!

[NINIAN, JOSH, BILLY, *and* JED *come in, the latter to post new bulletins. After* JED *has communicated these,* PHIL *again closes the window.* JED *goes.*]

Ninian. It looks like seventy-four electoral votes sure for you. Twenty-seven more probable. New York's will give you the election.

[ABE *walks around the room.* JOSH *has been looking at* ABE.]

Josh. Abe, could I get you a cup of coffee?

Abe. No, thanks, Josh.

Ninian. Getting nervous, Abe?

Abe. No. I'm just thinking what a blow it would be to Mrs. Lincoln if I should lose.

Ninian. And what about me? I have ten thousand dollars bet on you.

Billy. [*Scornfully.*] I'm afraid that the loss to the nation would be somewhat more serious than that.

Josh. How would you feel, Abe?

Abe. [*Sitting on the chair near the window.*] I guess I'd feel the greatest sense of relief of my life.

[JED *comes in with a news despatch.*]

Jed. Here's a news despatch. [*He hands it over and goes.*]

Ninian. [*Reads.*] "Shortly after nine o'clock this evening, Mr. August Belmont stated that Stephen A. Douglas has piled up a majority of fifty thousand votes in New York City and carried the state."

Billy. Mr. Belmont be damned!

[CRIMMIN *comes in, smoking a cigar, looking contented.*]

Crimmin. Good evening, Mr. Lincoln. Good evening, gentlemen—and how are you feeling *now*? [*They all greet him.*]

Ninian. Look at this, Crimmin.

[*He hands the despatch to* CRIMMIN.]

Crimmin. [*Smiles.*] Well—Belmont is going to fight to the last ditch, which is just what he's lying in now. I've been in Chicago and the outlook there is cloudless. In fact, Mr. Lincoln, I came down tonight to protect you from the office-seekers. They're lining up downstairs already. On the way in I counted four Ministers to Great Britain and eleven Secretaries of State.

[JED *has come in with more bulletins to put on the chart and then goes to the window to give* PHIL *the bulletins.*]

Billy. [*At the chart.*] There's a bulletin from New York! Douglas a hundred and eighty-three thousand—Lincoln a hundred and eighty-*one* thousand! [JED *goes.*]

Josh. Look out, Abe! You're catching up!

Crimmin. The next bulletin from New York will show you winning. Mark my words, Mr. Lincoln, this election is all wrapped up tightly in a neat bundle, ready for delivery on your doorstep tonight. We've fought the good fight, and we've won!

Abe. [*Pacing up and down the room.*] Yes—we've fought the good fight—in the dirtiest campaign in the history of corrupt politics. And if I have won, then I must cheerfully pay my political debts. All those who helped to nominate and elect me must be paid off. I have been gambled all around, bought and sold a hundred times. And now I must fill all the dishonest pledges made in my name.

Ninian. We realize all that, Abe—but the fact remains that you're winning. Why, you're even beating the coalition in Rhode Island!

Abe. I've got to step out for a moment.

[*He goes out at the right.*]

Ninian. [*Cheerfully.*] Poor Abe.

Crimmin. You gentlemen have all been close friends of our Candidate for a long time, so perhaps you could answer a question that's been puzzling me considerably. Can I possibly be correct in supposing that he doesn't want to win?

Josh. The answer is—yes.

Crimmin. [*Looking toward the right.*] Well—I can only say that, for me, this is all a refreshingly new experience.

Billy. [*Belligerently.*] Would *you* want to become President of the United States at this time? Haven't you been reading the newspapers lately?

Crimmin. Why, yes—I try to follow the events of the day.

Billy. [*In a rage.*] Don't you realize that they've raised ten thousand volunteers in South Carolina? They're arming them! The Governor has issued a proclamation saying that if Mr. Lincoln is elected, the State will secede tomorrow, and every other state south of the Dixon line will go with it. Can you see what that means? War! Civil War! And *he'll* have the whole terrible responsibility for it—a man who has never wanted anything in his life but to be let alone, in peace!

Ninian. Calm down, Billy. Go get yourself another drink. [JED *rushes in.*]

Jed. Mr. Edwards, here it is!

[*He hands a news despatch to* NINIAN, *then rushes to the window to attract* PHIL'S *attention and communicate the big news.*]

Ninian. [*Reads.*] "At 10:30 tonight the New York *Herald* conceded that Mr. Lincoln has carried the state by a majority of at least twenty-five thousand and has won the election!" [*He tosses the despatch in the air.*] He's won! He's won! Hurrah!

[*All on the stage shout, cheer, embrace, and slap each other.*]

Billy. God be praised! God be praised!

Crimmin. I knew it! I never had a doubt of it!

[JED *is on the balcony, shouting through a megaphone.*]

Jed. Lincoln is elected! Honest Old Abe is our next President!

[*A terrific cheer ascends from the crowd below.* ABE *returns. They rush at him.* BILLY *shakes hands with him, too deeply moved to speak.*]

Ninian. You've carried New York, Abe! You've won! Congratulations!

Crimmin. My congratulations, Mr. President. This is a mighty achievement for all of us. [JED *comes in and goes to* ABE.]

Jed. My very best, Mr. Lincoln!

Abe. [*Solemnly.*] Thank you—thank you all very much.

[*He comes to the left.* JOSH *is the last to shake his hand.*]

Josh. I congratulate you, Abe.

Abe. Thanks, Josh.

Ninian. Listen to them, Abe. Listen to that crazy, howling mob down there.

Crimmin. It's all for you, Mr. Lincoln.

Ninian. Abe, get out there and let 'em see you!

Abe. No. I don't want to go out there. I—I guess I'll be going on home, to tell Mary.

[*He starts toward the door. A short, stocky officer named* KAVANAGH *comes in from the right. He is followed by two* SOLDIERS.]

Crimmin. This is Captain Kavanagh, Mr. *President.*

Kavanagh. [*Salutes.*] I've been detailed to accompany you, Mr. Lincoln, in the event of your election.

Abe. I'm grateful, Captain. But I don't need you.

Kavanagh. I'm afraid you've got to have us, Mr. Lincoln. I don't like to be alarming, but I guess you know as well as I do what threats have been made.

Abe. [*Wearily.*] I see . . . Well—Good night, Josh—Ninian—Mr. Crimmin—Billy. Thank you for your good wishes.

[*He starts for the door. The others bid him good night, quietly.*]

Kavanagh. One moment, Sir. With your permission, I'll go first.

[*He goes out,* ABE *after him, the two other* SOLDIERS *follow. The light fades.*]

SCENE XII

The yards of the railroad station at Springfield. The date is February 11, 1861. At the right, at an angle toward the audience, is the back of a railroad car. From behind this, off to the upper left, runs a ramp. Flags and bunting are draped above.

In a row downstage are SOLDIERS, *with rifles and bayonets fixed, and packs on their backs, standing at ease. Off to the left is a large* CROWD, *whose excited murmuring can be heard.*

[KAVANAGH *is in the foreground. A* BRAKEMAN *with a lantern is inspecting the wheels of the car, at the left. A* WORKMAN *is at the right, polishing the rails of the car.* KAVANAGH *is pacing up and down, chewing a dead cigar. He looks at his watch. A swaggering* MAJOR *of militia comes down the ramp from the left.*]

Major. I want you men to form up against this ramp. [*To* KAVANAGH, *with a trace of scorn.*] You seem nervous, Mr. Kavanagh.

Kavanagh. Well—I am nervous. For three months I've been guarding the life of a man who doesn't give a damn what happens to him. I heard today that they're betting two to one in Richmond that he won't be alive to take the oath of office on March the 4th.

Major. I'd like to take some of that money. The State Militia is competent to protect the person of our Commander-in-Chief.

Kavanagh. I hope the United States Army is competent to help. But those Southerners are mighty good shots. And I strongly suggest that your men be commanded to keep watch through every window of every car, especially whenever the train stops—at a town, or a tank, or anywhere. And if any alarm is sounded, at any point along the line . . .

Major. [*A trifle haughty.*] There's no need to command my men to show courage in an emergency.

Kavanagh. No slur was intended, Major—but we must be prepared in advance for everything.

[*A brass band off to the left strikes up the campaign song, "Old Abe Lincoln came out of the wilderness." The crowd starts to sing it, more and more voices taking it up. A* CONDUCTOR *comes out of the car and looks at his watch. There is a commotion at the left as* NINIAN *and* ELIZABETH EDWARDS, *and* JOSH, BILLY, *and* CRIMMIN *come in and are stopped by the* SOLDIERS. *The* MAJOR *goes forward, bristling with importance.*]

Major. Stand back, there! Keep the crowd back there, you men!

Ninian. I'm Mr. Lincoln's brother-in-law.

Major. What's your name?

Kavanagh. I know him, Major. That's Mr. and Mrs. Edwards, and Mr. Speed and Mr. Herndon with them. I know them all. You can let them through.

Major. Very well. You can pass.

[*They come down to the right. The* MAJOR *goes off at the left.*]

Crimmin. How is the President feeling today? Happy?

Ninian. Just as gloomy as ever.

Billy. [*Emotionally.*] He came down to the office, and when I asked him what I should do about the sign, "Lincoln and Herndon," he said, "Let it hang there. Let our clients understand that this election makes no difference to the firm. If I live, I'll be back some time, and then we'll go right on practising just as if nothing had happened."

Elizabeth. He's always saying that—"If I live" . . .

[*A tremendous cheer starts and swells offstage at the left. The* MAJOR *comes on briskly.*]

Major [*To* KAVANAGH.] The President has arrived! [*To his men.*] Attention! [*The* MAJOR *strides down the platform and takes his position by the car, looking off to the left.*]

Kavanagh. [*To* NINIAN *and the others.*] Would you mind stepping back there? We want to keep this space clear for the President's party.

[*They move upstage, at the right. The cheering is now very loud.*]

Major. Present—Arms!

[*The* SOLDIERS *come to the Present. The* MAJOR *salutes. Preceded by* SOLDIERS *who are looking sharply to the right and left,* ABE *comes in from the left, along the platform. He will be fifty-two years old tomorrow. He wears a beard. Over his shoulders is his plaid shawl. In his right hand, he carries his carpet-bag; his left hand is leading* TAD. *Behind him are* MARY, ROBERT, *and* WILLIE, *and the* MAID. *All, except* MARY, *are also carrying bags. She carries a bunch of flowers. When they come to the car,* ABE *hands his bag up to the* CONDUCTOR, *then lifts* TAD *up.* MARY, ROBERT, WILLIE, *and the* MAID *get on board, while* ABE *steps over to talk to* NINIAN *and the others. During this, there is considerable commotion at the left, as the* CROWD *tries to surge forward.*]

Major. [*Rushing forward.*] Keep 'em back! Keep 'em back, men!

[*The* SOLDIERS *have broken their file on the platform and are in line, facing the*

CROWD. KAVANAGH *and his* MEN *are close to* ABE. *Each of them has his hand on his revolver, and is keeping a sharp lookout.*]

Kavanagh. Better get on board, Mr. President.

[ABE *climbs up on to the car's back platform. There is a great increase in the cheering when the* CROWD *sees him. They shout: "Speech! Speech! Give us a speech, Abe! Speech, Mr. President! Hurray for Old Abe!" etc. . . .* ABE *turns to the* CROWD, *takes his hat off and waves it with a half-hearted gesture. The cheering dies down.*]

Ninian. They want you to say something, Abe.

[*For a moment,* ABE *stands still, looking off to the left.*]

Abe. My dear friends—I have to say good-by to you. I am going now to Washington, with my new whiskers—of which I hope you approve.

[*The* CROWD *roars with laughter at that. More shouts of "Good Old Abe!" In its exuberant enthusiasm, the* CROWD *again surges forward, at and around the* SOLDIERS, *who shout, "Get back, there! Stand back, you!"*]

Abe. [*To the* MAJOR.] It's all right—let them come on. They're all old friends of mine.

[*The* MAJOR *allows his* MEN *to retreat so that they form a ring about the back of the car.* KAVANAGH *and his* MEN *are on the car's steps, watching. The* CROWD—*an assortment of townspeople, including some Negroes—fills the stage.*]

Abe. No one, not in my situation, can appreciate my feelings of sadness at this parting. To this place, and the kindness of you people, I owe everything. I have lived here a quarter of a century, and passed from a young to an old man. Here my children have been born and one is buried. I now leave, not knowing when or whether ever I may return. I am called upon to assume the Presidency at a time when eleven of our sovereign states have announced their intention to secede from the Union, when threats of war increase in fierceness from day to day. It is a grave duty which I now face. In preparing for it, I have tried to enquire: what great principle or ideal is it that has kept this Union so long together? And I believe that it was not the mere matter of separation of the colonies from the motherland, but that sentiment in the Declaration of Independence which gave liberty to the people of this country and hope to all the world. This sentiment was the fulfillment of an ancient dream, which men have held through all time, that they might one day shake off their chains and find freedom in the brotherhood of life. We gained democracy, and now there is the question whether it is fit to survive. Perhaps we have come to the dreadful day of awakening, and the dream is ended. If so, I am afraid it must be ended forever. I cannot believe that ever again will men have the opportunity we have had. Perhaps we should admit that, and concede that our ideals of liberty and equality are decadent and doomed. I have heard of an eastern monarch who once charged his wise men to invent him a sentence which would be true and appropriate in all times and situations. They presented him the words, "And this too shall pass away." That is a comforting thought in time of affliction—"And this too shall pass away." And yet—[*Suddenly he speaks with quiet but urgent authority.*] —let us believe that it is not true! Let us live to prove that we can cultivate the natural world that is about us, and the intellectual and moral world that is within us, so that we may secure an individual, social, and political prosperity, whose course shall be forward, and which, while the earth endures, shall not pass away. . . . I commend you to the care of the Almighty, as I hope that in your prayers you will remember me. . . . Good-by, my friends and neighbors.

[*He leans over the railing of the car platform to say good-by to* NINIAN, ELIZABETH, JOSH, BILLY, *and* CRIMMIN, *shaking each by the hand. The band off-stage strikes up "John Brown's Body." The cheering swells. The* CONDUCTOR *looks at his watch and speaks to the* MAJOR, *who gets on board the train. The* CROWD *on stage is shouting "Good-by, Abe," "Good-by, Mr. Lincoln," "Good luck, Abe," "We trust you, Mr. Lincoln."*

As the band swings into the refrain, "Glory, Glory Hallelujah," the CROWD *starts to sing, the number of voices increasing with each word.*

KAVANAGH *tries to speak to* ABE *but can't be heard. He touches* ABE'S *arm, and* ABE *turns on him quickly.*]

Kavanagh. Time to pull out, Mr. President. Better get inside the car.

[*These words cannot be heard by the audience in the general uproar of singing.* NINIAN, ELIZABETH, JOSH, *and*

BILLY *are up on the station platform. The* SOLDIERS *are starting to climb up on to the train.* ABE *gives one last wistful wave of his hat to the* CROWD, *then turns and goes into the car, followed by* KAVANAGH, *the* MAJOR, *and the* SOLDIERS. *The band reaches the last line of the song.*]

All. [*Singing.*] "His soul goes marching on."

[*The* BRAKEMAN, *downstage, is waving his lantern. The* CONDUCTOR *swings aboard. The* CROWD *is cheering, waving hats and handkerchiefs. The shrill screech of the engine whistle sounds from the right.*]

CURTAIN

THE SUBSTANCE OF "ABE LINCOLN IN ILLINOIS"

The purpose of these supplementary notes is to state the principal sources from which the material of this play and the conception of its various characters are derived; to attempt to tell what is the historical basis for each of the twelve scenes, and wherein and why I have departed from the recorded facts; to indicate the events which occurred between scenes; and also to give me an excuse for adding some information which I was unable, for one reason or another, to incorporate in the play's structure.

Not that I hope, in these notes, to establish a convincing case for myself as a learned biographer. The playwright's chief stock in trade is feelings, not facts. When he writes of a subject out of history, or out of today's news, he cannot be a scholarly recorder or a good reporter; he is, at best, an interpreter, with a certain facility for translating all that he has heard in a manner sufficiently dramatic to attract a crowd. He has been granted, by a tradition that goes back to the Kings of Thebes, considerable poetic license to distort and embellish the truth; and he generally takes advantage of far more license than he has been granted. The Cleopatra who actually existed may have borne no resemblance to the Cleopatra of Shakespeare's creation nor to the entirely different one of Shaw's, but no one now cares about that, even in Egypt.

However, in the case of a play about the development of the extraordinary character of Abraham Lincoln, a strict regard for the plain truth is more than obligatory; it is obviously desirable. His life as he lived it was a work of art, forming a veritable allegory of the growth of the democratic spirit, with its humble origins, its inward struggles, its seemingly timid policy of "live and let live" and "mind your own business," its slow awakening to the dreadful problems of reality, its battles with and conquest of those problems, its death at the hands of a crazed assassin, and its perpetual renewal caused by the perpetual human need for it. Furthermore, just as Lincoln's life needs no adornments of symbolism to make it pertinent, his character needs no romanticizing, no sentimentalizing, no dramatizing.

Lincoln's great achievement, most of which was accomplished by the echoes of his words, long after his death, was the solidification of the American ideal. But this is not a play about his achievement: it is, rather, a play about the solidification of Lincoln himself—a long, uncertain process, effected by influences some of which came from within his own reasoning mind, some from his surrounding circumstances, some from sources which we cannot comprehend. As many as possible of these influences are indicated in this play; the rest are left to the imagination of the audience, because they are beyond mine.

Like many others, I obtained my first instruction in Lincoln's life from Ida M. Tarbell, and in the events of his period from Albert Bushnell Hart, but it was not until I had read Carl Sandburg's *The Prairie Years* that I began to feel the curious quality of the complex man who, in his statement of the eternal aspirations of the human race, achieved a supreme triumph of simplicity. It was Sandburg who guided me back to the main sources of Lincoln lore, made me wish to know more of the forces, from without him and from within, which shaped this strange, gentle genius. *The Prairie Years* is an incomparable portrait of Lincoln and of the young, boisterous America in which he grew up. It is the work of a faithful historian who is also a major poet. Here is one sentence of Sandburg's: "So the woman, Nancy Hanks, died, thirty-six years old, a pioneer sacrifice, with memories of monotonous, endless everyday chores, of mystic Bible verses read over and over for their promises, and with memories of blue wistful hills and a summer when the crab-apple blossoms flamed white and she carried a boy-child into the world."

The Prairie Years is published by Harcourt, Brace and Co., who are now publishing the completion of Mr. Sandburg's great work, *The War Years.*

The best short biography of Lincoln, in its understanding of the inner man, is Nathaniel Wright Stephenson's. The two volumes by Albert J. Beveridge, which cover Lincoln's life up to the time of the Douglas debates, contain the most complete sifting of all the existing evidence. Beveridge gives the precise record of Lincoln's career, but refrains from speculation as to his character.

These books provided the main modern sources for this play. I have also had reference to the excellent biographies by W. E. Barton and Lord Charnwood; to studies of Mary Todd Lincoln by Carl Sandburg and W. A. Evans; to *Lincoln's Rise to Power,* by William Baringer; and (for all sorts of material) to the *Dictionary of American Biography,* especially the admirable article on Lincoln by James G. Randall. There are hundreds more books that I could mention, but I haven't read them; and there was John Drinkwater's beautiful play, which I saw several times and admired greatly.

The two original authors to whose works all students of this subject must ever return were Lincoln himself and the odd little enthusiast who was his law partner, William H. Herndon.

Lincoln's *Complete Works* were compiled by John G. Nicolay and John Hay and published in 1894. Herndon's letters and papers have come out gradually through the years —first in the Herndon and Weik biography (1889), then in Weik's *The Real Lincoln* (1922); and a new collection, Emanuel Hertz's *The Hidden Lincoln,* was published in 1938, after this play was written. Mr. Hertz's book is of enormous interest, although it contains some admittedly fantastic statements made by Herndon in his dotage when, broken in health and impoverished, he was trying desperately to think up something new and sensational to reveal about his mighty friend.

To Herndon we owe a debt of inestimable gratitude. Had it not been for him, only the most fragmentary knowledge of Lincoln's true character would have survived the bullet of John Wilkes Booth. Many revealing statements would never have been made or recorded, many all-important letters would have been lost. Lincoln would be today only the frozen saint of the statuary, and we should have but a small conception of his real greatness. He was, as Herndon said, "a shut-mouth man" when it came to discussing his own hidden emotions. Herndon himself was as close to Lincoln as any man could be for more than twenty years; but he confesses that during this long association he could do no more than guess at what was going on behind that resistant exterior. First as clerk and then as partner, from 1839 to 1861, Herndon shared the same small office with Lincoln; he was in intimate association with him through all the period of his law practice, his marriage to the ill-starred Mary Todd, his one unsuccessful term in Congress, the painfully deliberate arousing of his ambition, his reluctant enlistment in the national struggle, his debates with Douglas, his nomination and election to the Presidency. Immediately after Lincoln's death, Herndon devoted himself with all his energy and all his limited means to one task, which was the collection of every available scrap of evidence from those who had known Lincoln in the years before the nation took him and made him its most faithful servant. To gain a conception of the overwhelming importance of Herndon's accomplishment, you may read through the ten-volume biography written by Lincoln's secretaries, Nicolay and Hay, and you will find that while all the events, particularly those following Fort Sumter, are carefully chronicled, there is hardly one revealing word of the nature of Lincoln's tragic soul, of his relations with his wife and other women, of the doubts that hindered him and the fears that obsessed him.

Here is a passage from Herndon, as published for the first time by Mr. Hertz:

"This man, this long, tall, bony, homely, wiry, sad, gloomy man floated into our country in 1831, in a frail canoe down the north fork of the Sangamon River, friendless, penniless, powerless, and alone, begging for work in this city, ragged, struggling for the common necessaries of life. This man, this peculiar man, left us here in 1861 the President of the United States, backed by friends and power, by fame and all individual and national forces, and it is well to inquire into the how."

That was the mission of Herndon's life—inquiring into "the how" of "this peculiar man."

Herndon says further: "Mr. Lincoln was a kind of fatalist in some aspects of his philosophy, and skeptical in his religion. He was a sad man, a terribly gloomy one—a man of sorrow, if not of agony. This, his state, may have arisen from a defective physical organization, or it may have arisen from some fatalistic idea, that he was to die a sudden and terrible death. Some unknown power seemed to buzz about his consciousness, his being, his mind, that whispered in his ear: 'Look out for danger ahead!' . . . He has said to me more than once: 'Billy, I feel as if I shall meet with some terrible end.' He did not know what would strike him, nor when, nor where, nor how hard; he was a blind, intellectual Samson, strug gling and fighting in the dark against the fates. I say on my own personal observation that he felt this for years. Often and often I have resolved to make or get him to reveal the causes of his misery, but I had not the courage nor the impertinence to do it. . . . May I say that I have many times thoroughly sympathized with Mr. Lincoln in his intense sufferings; but I dared not obtrude into the sacred ground of his thoughts. . . ."

There was evidently only one man in all of Lincoln's life who was permitted to catch more than a glimpse of that sacred ground, and that one man was Joshua Speed. If Herndon was Lincoln's Fidus Achates, Speed was his Horatio. There is a remarkable statement of the relationship of Lincoln and Speed in *The Prairie Years:*

"Joshua Speed was a deep chested man of large sockets with broad measurement between the ears. A streak of lavender ran through him; he had spots soft as May violets. And he and Abraham Lincoln told each other their secrets about women. Lincoln too had tough physical shanks and large sockets, also a streak of lavender, and spots soft as May violets."

To Speed, Lincoln revealed aspects of his being that were never made visible to any other man, or any woman; and Speed would probably have taken these secrets with him to the grave had they not been pried out of him by Herndon.

Speed wrote to Herndon: "Mr. Lincoln was so unlike all the men I had ever known before or seen or known since that there is no one to whom I can compare him." Another of Speed's observations has exerted a profound influence on the conception of Lincoln that is given in this play: "He must believe he was right, and that he had truth and justice with him, or he was a weak man; but no man could be stronger if he thought he was right."

Over the statue in the Lincoln Memorial in Washington are the beautiful words, "In this Temple as in the hearts of the people for whom he saved the Union the memory of Abraham Lincoln is enshrined forever." And for those who stand in that temple, their spirit of reverence must be immeasurably increased by the knowledge that he was "a man of sorrow, if not of agony," "a peculiar man," and when not quite sure that he was right, "a weak man."

While I have made a steadfast effort to reflect the character of Lincoln as truthfully as I can, I have been less faithful in the portraits of the other historical characters who appear in this play, although I don't think I have done any grave injustice to the memory of any of them (except possibly Stephen A. Douglas, of whom more later). These other characters had to be used, for dramatic purposes, not as people important in themselves but as sources of light, each one being present only for the purpose of casting a beam to illumine some one of the innumerable facets of Lincoln's spirit.

I confess that I should like to have had a lot more time in this play for development of the character of Mary Todd Lincoln. She too was a very strange and pathetic person, but her rôle could be only that of a symbol of her husband's glorious, tragic destiny.

Her early letters reveal that, as a young girl, she had unusual intelligence, culture, perception, and humor. She was tremendously ambitious—snobbish, to a certain degree—and was courted by many young men of wealth, breeding, and excellent prospects, but she chose, against the opposition of her family, to marry a shabby, poverty-stricken, coarse, and generally shiftless lawyer, who could have had little to recommend him to the attention of a young lady. It is to be presumed that she loved him dearly and had abiding faith in him when there seemed scant reason for it.

She lived with him through eighteen years (preceding his election) which must have imposed an intolerable strain on her patience. She bore him four sons, suffered poverty and indignity and neglect. During most of this time, he apparently progressed nowhere. If he had his own plans or hopes for the future, it is evident that he communicated no substantial part of them to his wife.

When the wildest dream of her life at length came true, and Mrs. Lincoln entered the White House, she was freely snubbed by Eastern society; she was publicly deplored; she was even accused of treason because of her family connections with the Southern cause. One of her sons had died in Springfield, another died in Washington. She was beginning to be unmistakably insane. All through the night after the firing of the shot in Ford's Theatre she sat weeping, "uttering heartbroken exclamations," and when they finally told her that the end of Abraham Lincoln had come, she moaned, *"Oh my God, and I have given my husband to die!"*

I have put those words in italics because I think they contain a poignant revelation of character. It was as though, even in that moment of fierce, maniacal grief, she wanted above all else to assure herself, and posterity, "It was *I* who made him President!"

Five years later, her son Tad died. Her extravagance, which had always run to the purchase of frills and furbelows at the expense of adequate food for her own family, now ran to fantastic extremes; for instance, she bought dozens of pairs of window curtains which she carried about with her from one hotel to another. Ten years after her husband's death, attorneys for Robert Todd Lincoln, her sole surviving son, entered a court application which began, "The petition of Robert T. Lincoln would respectfully represent that his mother, Mary Lincoln, widow of Abraham Lincoln, deceased, a resident of Cook County, is insane, and that it would be for her benefit and for the safety of the community that she should be confined."

She was brought into court, and the application was granted. The County Clerk filed papers marked "Mary Lincoln, Lunatic." Before she was taken away, she tried to commit suicide. She was later released through the intervention of her brother-in-law, Ninian Edwards; and, in 1882, in his Springfield house, where she had met and married Abe Lincoln, she died. Buried with her was her wedding ring, inscribed "A.L. to Mary, Nov. 4, 1842. Love is Eternal."

In one of the Herndon letters in *The Hidden Lincoln* are these remarks:

"I say, Lincoln told her *he did not love her*. The world does not know her, Mrs. L's sufferings, her trials, and the causes of things. Sympathize with her. I shall never rob Mrs. Lincoln of her justice—justice due her. Poor woman! She will yet have her rewards."

Herndon wrote these sympathetic words in 1866, when Mrs. L. (who never liked him) had many sufferings and trials still before her. She has never received the rewards, at least upon this earth, to which he believed her entitled. Indeed, the voices of the scandal-mongers of Washington in her own day have only tended to increase in volume throughout the years. Of late, the domestic troubles of the Lincolns have received the attention of psychiatrists; these two unhappy people provide wonderful specimens for the Freudians to dissect. But, as Sandburg so perfectly expresses it, "Both gossip and science have little to guide them in effecting a true and searching explanation of the married life of a slow-going wilderness bear and a cultivated, tempestuous wildcat."

Just how far the bear would have gone without the wildcat is something we shall never know and don't need to worry about. To the student of history there should be no such word as "If."

I now go on to discussion of the various scenes as they come:

Scene I (1833)

In the summer of 1831, when Lincoln was twenty-two, he arrived in New Salem, Ill., a village of fifteen log cabins. An election was being held when he drifted into town. One of the election clerks was a fairly prosperous young Easterner, named John McNamar, who was engaged to be married to the local belle, Ann Rutledge, daughter of the proprietor of the tavern and the mill. The other clerk was Mentor Graham, the neighborhood school teacher. McNamar was ill, and a substitute had to be found, so Graham asked the uncouth stranger if he could read and write. Lincoln replied that he could and was promptly pressed into service to help record the votes—the start of his political career and of a friendship with Mentor Graham which meant much to him.

Lincoln boarded with Graham and that good man sat up nights, teaching him the rudiments of grammar and later of all manner of subjects, from Shakespeare to surveying. "I know of my own knowledge," wrote R. B. Rutledge (Ann's brother), "that Graham did more than all others to educate Lincoln."

Graham himself said of Abe, "He was the most studious, diligent strait forward young man in the pursuit of literature and a knowledge I have taught," and he added that all loved this pupil because he was one of "the most *companionable* persons you will ever see in this world." He also said that he had once had to talk Abe out of committing suicide.

In this first scene is reference to Lincoln's trips by flat-boat to New Orleans, and I have been asked why I did not make mention of his visit to the New Orleans slave market, his rage at the spectacle, and his oft-quoted remark, "Someday I shall hit this thing and hit it hard!" I left that out because I don't believe any of it. If Lincoln was determined at this early stage of his career to free the slaves there is no reliable evidence that he ever said so. Perhaps he did visit the slave market, and perhaps that horrid sight did start certain thoughts forming in his mind—but, if so, it was a long, long time before he was ready to utter them and act on them.

The reading of Keats's "On Death," which concludes this scene, is one demonstration of the use of the playwright's license, previously referred to. There is no record of Lincoln's having read this poem. It is in keeping, however, with his taste in verse. He naturally had a great fondness for the sombre, his favorite poem being the one which started,

"Oh, why should the spirit of mortal be proud?
Like a swift-fleeting meteor, a fast-flying cloud,
A flash of the lightning, a break of the wave,
He passes from life to his rest in the grave."

Scene 2 (1834)

Several of the characters in this scene—Ben Mattling, Trum Cogdal, Seth Gale, and the subordinate Clary's Grove boys—are imaginary. Mattling is introduced solely to show that Lincoln knew men who had fought in the Revolution, and Seth Gale because he will be of importance in a later scene.

Joshua Speed is introduced prematurely. He is an important character in the play, and therefore should become known to the audience this early. Actually, he and Lincoln did not meet until the latter moved to Springfield, some two or three years later. Speed was a merchant there, a man of good family and superior education, and he described the meeting in the following terms:

"He came into my store, set his saddle-bags on the counter, and enquired what the furniture for a single bedstead would cost. I took slate and pencil, made a calculation, and found the sum for furniture complete would amount to seventeen dollars in all. Said he: 'It is probably cheap enough; but I want to say that, cheap as it is, I have not the money to pay. But if you will credit me until Christmas, and my experiment here as a lawyer is a success, I will pay you then. If I fail in that, I will probably not pay you at all.' The tone of his voice was so melancholy that I felt for him. I looked up at him and I thought then, as I think now, that I never saw so gloomy and melancholy a face in my life. I said to him, 'So small a debt seems to affect you so deeply, I think I can suggest a plan by which you will be able to attain your end without incurring any debt. I have a very large room and a very large double bed in it, which you are perfectly welcome to share with me if you choose.' 'Where is your room?' he asked. 'Upstairs,' said I. . . . Without saying a word he took his saddle-bags on his arm, went upstairs, came down again, and with a face beaming with pleasure and smiles, exclaimed, 'Well, Speed, I'm moved.'"

Which odd story is evidence of one of the most remarkable elements in Lincoln's life: his astonishing gift for achieving immediate popularity. He was always able, and without any great expenditure of effort, to gain the devotion, trust, and enthusiastic support of almost any one he might meet. What has made him so peculiarly loved in retrospect must have stood out all over him and made him loved instantaneously. Of course, some of the tributes to his early charm, honesty, and high promise were made after he had come to glory, and so may be discounted; but there are many contemporary testimonials and there are the strange facts of his life to establish the paradox that whereas he spent his years, even his crowded years in the White House, in a state of miserable loneliness, he never wanted for friends.

There is a letter extant (in the Barrett collection) written by a settler in New Salem and dated September 17, 1835, which gives us a good picture of young Abe Lincoln: "The Post Master is very careless about leaving his office open and unlocked during the day—half the time I go in and get my papers, etc., without any one being there, as was the case yesterday. The letter was only marked 25, and even if he had been there and known it was double, he would not (have) charged me any more—luckily he is a very clever fellow and a particular friend of mine."

This was the overwhelming sentiment of the community; they were all "particular" friends of Abe's. When Lincoln was twenty-three years old, and only seven months after he had first come out of the wilderness to New Salem, he ran for the State Assembly. His first speech began, "Fellow Citizens, I presume you all know who I am—I am humble Abraham Lincoln." (Even then he was shrewdly emphasizing his humility; thirty years later *The New York Herald* compared him to Uriah Heep.) He continued, "My politics are short and sweet, like the old woman's dance," and concluded, with another display of diffidence, "If elected I shall be thankful; if not it will be all the same to me."

The vote of the citizens of New Salem for the stranger in their midst was as follows:

For Abraham Lincoln.	205
For his Opponent (whoever he was). .	3

Of course, this overwhelming majority may have been attributable in part to the presence at the polls of the Clary's Grove boys, ready to do violence to any one who dared to vote against their friend Abe. But, says Beveridge, his "local popularity was so great that their combative support was neither needed nor displayed."

Equally eloquent of his position in the hearts of his neighbors was his ability to run into debt and to be trusted for it. Although penniless, and with no prospects, he was in debt $1100 as a result of the collapse of the grocery store. He got in much deeper before he began to get out. Sandburg tells a story: "He was sued for ten dollars owing on his horse; a friend let him have the ten dollars; the horse was saved. He was sued again, and his horse, saddle, bridle, surveying instruments were taken away. James Short, a Sand Ridge farmer, heard about it; he liked Lincoln as a serious student, a pleasant joker, and a swift corn-husker; he had told people, when Lincoln worked for him, 'He husks two loads of corn to my one.' Short went to the auction, bought in the horse and outfit for $125.00, and gave them back to Lincoln, who said, 'Uncle Jimmy, I'll do as much for you some time.' "

Short was paid back some years later from the earnings of the law practice in Springfield. The last of the New Salem debts were settled, after seventeen years, with money saved during Lincoln's one term in Congress.

There were many James Shorts in Lincoln's life, glad to come forth with substantial expressions of their faith in him; none of them was ever disappointed.

Bowling Green was Justice of the Peace and leading citizen of New Salem. An immensely fat, hearty, and sympathetic man, he loved and appreciated Abe and was the first, undoubtedly, to stimulate his interest in the law. This new interest had an important effect on Lincoln's character. Said R. B. Rutledge, "I think that he never avoided men until he commenced the study of law." It was the first evidence of his abstraction, his tendency to misanthropy.

Ninian Edwards was one of the leaders of the early Illinois aristocracy. His father was appointed by President Madison as first Governor of the Territory and was later elected Governor of the State. He had also been Ambassador to Mexico. Thus, young Ninian enjoyed inherited prominence as well as wealth; and yet, when he and the unknown Lincoln campaigned on the same ticket for the State Assembly in 1836, Lincoln ran ahead of Edwards and all other candidates in the voting. Of Ninian Edwards, a contemporary (U. F. Linder) wrote: "He was naturally and constitutionally an aristocrat, and hated democracy . . . as the devil is said to hate holy water."

In the scene between Abe and Ann Rutledge occurs the line, "I'm a plain, common sucker with a shirt-tail so short I can't sit on it." It may interest the reader to know that this is the first line of the play which contains any of Lincoln's own words. The shirt-tail expression was one that he liked to quote from his father. The word "sucker" meant at that time a native of Illinois—like "Hoosier" of Indiana; the Barnum definition came into the American language later.

There is little in the available records to indicate that Lincoln's decision to run for the Assembly was influenced by his love for Ann Rutledge—although I don't think I'm stretching my license too far by suggesting this. There have been fabulous estimates of the effect of Ann Rutledge on Lincoln's entire life, but actually we know little. This whole affair has been so clouded by the mauve mists of romantic legend that it is impossible to say for sure whether Abe ever proposed marriage to Ann and, if so, whether he was ever accepted. She had been engaged to McNamar, whose real name turned out to be McNiel. His rôle bears some resemblances to the traditional one of the city slicker. He left New Salem, to go back East and collect his family, and he stayed away for so long that she naturally felt she must abandon hope of him and look elsewhere for consolation. Perhaps Abe provided it; perhaps she was inconsolable.

A short time after Ann's death McNamar returned to New Salem to prove the honorableness of his intentions and claim his bride. Years later, he said, "I never heard any person say that Mr. Lincoln addressed Miss Ann Rutledge in terms of courtship, neither her own family nor my own acquaintances otherwise. I heard simply from two prominent Gentlemen of my acquaintance and Personal friends that Mr. Lincoln was Grieved very much at her death."

From all the testimony of those who were in the neighborhood at the time we may draw the following conclusions about Ann Rutledge and her importance: she was an attractive girl; she inspired deep emotions in the heart and the imagination of Abraham Lincoln; and she died.

That is all that really matters: she died.

Scene 3 (1835)

The reading of *Pickwick,* with which this scene opens, is a slight anachronism, as publication of Dickens's first and greatest work did not start until 1836. More accurate is the reference in a speech of Speed's to Abe's absorption in "Hamlet." Lincoln read the tragedies of Shakespeare with consuming interest at this time, and memorized long passages. He also read Voltaire, and Tom Paine's *Age of Reason,* and Constantine de Volney's *Ruins,* a strange diet for a postmaster in a frontier village, though not so strange when you know what he was to be. When he was in the White House, he wrote to the actor James H. Hackett, "For one of my age I have seen very little of the drama. The first presentation of *Falstaff* I ever saw was yours here. . . . Perhaps the best compliment I can pay is to say, as I truly can, I am very anxious to see it again. Some of Shakespeare's plays I have never read; while others I have gone over perhaps as frequently as any unprofessional reader. Among the latter are 'Lear,' 'Richard III,' 'Henry VIII,' 'Hamlet,' and especially 'Macbeth.' I think nothing equals 'Macbeth.' It is wonderful. Unlike you gentlemen of the profession, I think the soliloquy in 'Hamlet' commencing 'Oh, my offense is rank,' surpasses that commencing 'To be or not to be.' But pardon the small attempt at criticism. I should like to hear you pronounce the opening speech of Richard III."

That soliloquy which Lincoln admired ends with the violent words:

"O wretched state! O bosom black as death!
O limed soul, that struggling to be free
Art more engaged! Help, angels! Make assay!
Bow, stubborn knees, and, heart with strings of steel,
Be soft as sinews of the new-born babe!
All may be well."

One can see him, sitting at the edge of the forest, reading excitedly, feeling some weird kinship with those turbulent, blood-stained, eternally self-questioning princes of old, struggling to understand them.

You may find a fine passage describing the effects of Ann Rutledge's death on Lincoln in Nathaniel Wright Stephenson's sensitive biography. Here is a quotation from it:

"The sunny Lincoln, the delight of Clary's Grove, had vanished. In his place was a desolated soul—a brother to dragons, in the terrible imagery of Job—a dweller in the dark places of affliction. It was his mother reborn in him. It was all the shadowiness of his mother's world; all that frantic reveling in the mysteries of woe to which, hitherto, her son had been an alien.

"To the simple minds of the villagers, with their hard-headed, practical way of keeping all things, especially love and grief, in the outer layer of consciousness, this revelation of an emotional terror was past understanding. Some of them, true to their type, pronounced him insane . . .

"In this crucial moment, when the real base of his character had been suddenly revealed—all the passionateness of the forest shadow, the unfathomable gloom laid so deep at the bottom of his soul—he was carried through his spiritual eclipse by the loving comprehension of two fine friends . . . two people who deserve to be remembered—Bowling Green and his wife . . .

"Ever after, at heart, he was to dwell alone, facing, silent, those inscrutable things which to the primitive mind are things of every day. Always, he was to have for his portion in his real self, the dimness of twilight, or at best, the night with its stars, 'never glad, confident morning again.'"

In this scene the only words that may have been said by Lincoln (and even their authenticity is doubtful) are, "I can't bear to think of her out there alone." His embittered remarks about the prayers of the Rutledges—"the Lord giveth and the Lord taketh away"—are not unjustifiable. I have mentioned his tastes in reading at this time, and he himself now wrote a tract on religion which, had it survived, might well have made his name anathema to all church-going people. It was mercifully burned by a friend named Samuel Hill, who was also a suitor for the hand of Ann Rutledge.

1835–1840

Some five years pass between Scenes 3 and 4. It was a time for Lincoln of considerable transformation, of a maturing process accelerated by contact with a new world. He changed from a backwoodsman into a townsman. Later he said that even before he was thirty years of age he was considered "an old man."

He left New Salem forever and moved to Springfield, where he entered law practice as partner of Judge John T. Stuart. He indulged in a romance (if such it could be called) with a Miss Mary Owens. Neither of them took it very seriously. More important to his career were his first meetings and clashes with "The Little Giant," Stephen A. Douglas, who had moved to Illinois from his native Vermont and was now serving in the Assembly with Lincoln and voting against him—though not on the issue which was to bring these two men into historic opposition in the great debates of 1858 and the Presidential campaign of 1860.

Lincoln made a speech at this time in which he said, "The subject heretofore and now to be discussed is the subtreasury scheme of the present administration, as a means of collecting, safe-keeping, transferring, and disbursing the revenues of the nation, as contrasted with a national bank for the same purposes. Mr. Douglas has said that we (the Whigs) have not dared to meet them (the Locos) in argument on this question. I protest against this assertion." Lincoln and Douglas became very heated on fiscal matters (these were the days of Andrew Jackson and his heir, Martin Van Buren), but there was not a word about slavery. Beveridge says, "although advertisements of runaway slaves were conspicuous in the Vandalia newspapers and appeared with increasing frequency, no one did or said anything about the matter." But, in Boston, William Lloyd Garrison had been shouting, "I am in earnest, I will not equivocate, I will not excuse, I will not retreat a single inch, and I WILL BE HEARD!" If Lincoln and Douglas did hear him, they probably agreed, over a drink (Douglas's), that he was a dangerous radical who should be suppressed. However, Lincoln collaborated with one Dan Stone on a resolution which declared that "the institution of slavery is founded on both injustice and bad policy, but that the promulgation of abolition doctrines tends rather to increase than abate its evils."

Lincoln's main activity at this time was in political manœuvring to promote the transfer of the State Capital from Vandalia to Springfield. He helped to accomplish that, by a display of considerable skill as a lobby trader, and the citizens of Springfield began to regard him as a favorite son.

Scene 4 (1840)

The speech in which Lincoln describes seeing the slaves on a river boat, chained together, is quoted almost verbatim from a letter he wrote to Joshua Speed's sister. The joke about the two d's in Todd was his own and typical of his humor, which, be it said, was not always animated by a spirit of malice toward none. It has often been said of him, "His wit was always kindly; he never hurt any one with his quips." I believe Lincoln would resent that.

Reference is made to the Black Hawk War, in which Lincoln led a company of New Salem volunteers, including Jack Armstrong as sergeant. That was in 1832. The company saw no action, but they did meet the author of *Thanatopsis,* William Cullen Bryant, who was making a tour of Illinois for *The New York Evening Post.* He described Lincoln as "a raw youth" of "quaint and pleasant talk." During this brief campaign Abe encountered for the first time the difficulties of leadership. With his little company, he came up to a fence and realized that he didn't know the correct military command for getting over it. He pondered the problem for a moment, then said, "The company will now fall out, and will immediately fall in again on the other side of the fence." This was the sum total of his military experience before he became Commander-in-Chief of the army and navy of the United States in the first great war fought under modern conditions.

In the fourth scene, Lincoln's speeches expressive of his reluctance to become involved in national affairs indicate a breadth of interest which he can hardly be said to have displayed at this time (1840). However, this happened to be the only place within the play's structure where he could reasonably express the point of view which was to be his when, a few years later, he served in Congress and gained great unpopularity by opposing the Mexican War. There again he was opposed by Douglas, who shouted for the war, quoting Frederick the Great, "Take possession first and negotiate afterward." Lincoln denounced the whole project as a land grab, which it was.

Scene 5 (1840)

One of the many people from whom Herndon obtained statements was Elizabeth Todd Edwards, wife of Ninian. Here is her description of the strange courtship of her sister by Abraham Lincoln:

"I have often happened in the room where they were sitting and Mary invariably led the conversation. Mr. Lincoln would sit at her side and listen. He scarcely said a word but gazed on her as if irresistibly drawn to her by some superior and unseen power. He could not maintain himself in a continued conversation with a lady reared as Mary was.

He was not educated and equipped mentally to make himself either interesting or attractive to the ladies. He was a good, honest, and sincere young man whose rugged manly qualities I admired; but to me he somehow seemed ill-constituted by nature and education to please such a woman as my sister. Mary was quick, gay, and in the social world somewhat brilliant. She loved show and power, and was the most ambitious woman I ever knew. She used to contend when a girl, to her friends in Kentucky, that she was destined to marry a President. I have heard her say that myself, and after mingling in society in Springfield she repeated the seemingly absurd and idle boast. Although Mr. Lincoln seemed to be attached to Mary, and fascinated by her wit and sagacity, yet I soon began to doubt whether they could always be so congenial. In a short time I told Mary my impression that they were not suited, or, as some persons who believe matches are made in heaven would say, not intended for each other."

Subsequent events proved Mrs. Edwards eminently correct in assuming that they were "not suited." But those who believe in the will of God, or those metaphysicians who believe in the existence of inexorable psychic forces, will maintain they most certainly were "intended."

Scene 6 (1841)

The episode of the burned letter in this scene is not an invention, as some who have seen this play have supposed. For some time before the date set for the wedding, Lincoln had been casting about desperately for a means of escape, and Mary Todd had attempted to transform him from the pursued to the pursuer by means of the ancient device of stimulating jealousy: she flirted conspicuously with other men, especially Douglas. This failed to have the desired effect on Lincoln; perhaps he didn't even notice what she was up to. He did what many other men have done in their cowardly but understandable desire to avoid a distasteful scene—he put his sentiments down on paper and gave that paper to a friend for delivery.

Of this letter, Joshua Speed has said: "In it he made a plain statement of his feelings, telling her that he had thought the matter over calmly and with deep deliberation, and now felt that he did not love her sufficiently to warrant her in marrying him. This letter he desired me to deliver. Upon my declining to do so he threatened to intrust it to some other person's hand. . . . Thereupon I threw the unfortunate letter in the fire. 'Now,' I continued, 'if you have the courage of manhood, go to see Mary yourself; tell her, if you do not love her, the facts.' . . . Thus admonished, he buttoned his coat, and with a rather determined look started out to perform the serious duty."

There is plenty of testimony to the resultant state of Lincoln's mind. "Restless, gloomy, miserable, desperate, he seemed an object of pity," wrote Herndon. "Knives and razors, and every instrument that could be used for self-destruction were removed from his reach," said Speed. "Lincoln went as crazy as a loon," said Ninian Edwards. And Lincoln himself wrote to his law partner, Judge Stuart: "I have within the last few days, been making a most discreditable exhibition of myself in the way of hypochondriacism . . . I am now the most miserable man living. If what I feel were distributed to the whole human family, there would not be one cheerful face left on earth. Whether I shall ever be better, I cannot tell; I awfully forbode I shall not. To remain as I am is impossible; I must die or be better, it appears to me."

Reference is made in this scene to Doctor Daniel Drake, to whom Lincoln was recommended at that time. Lincoln did not go to Cincinnati to see him, but sent him a long letter, detailing all his symptoms. Most of this letter was read to Speed before it was posted, but there was one portion so personal that Lincoln wouldn't reveal it even to his trusted friend. Speed romantically believed that this unknown part of the confession might have related to the tragic loss of Ann Rutledge, but Speed was merely guessing. Herndon had another explanation. It is tantalizing to think that this letter does not survive today. Doctor Drake received it, and replied that he could not render an opinion without a personal examination. Perhaps Lincoln asked him to destroy the letter and he did so. He was one of the great leaders of his profession, founder of the Ohio Medical College, and a keen historian of pioneer days in the Middle West; it is a great shame that he could not have known Lincoln's letter was the most important historical document that ever came before his eyes.

The outburst of Herndon toward the end of this sixth scene is an imaginary interlude. Herndon was a hot-headed radical, devoted to the memory of the martyred Lovejoy, and he has confessed that he wanted many times to talk thus to Lincoln; but there is no indication that he ever had the courage to do so, even aided (as he so frequently was) by strong drink. However, there is every reason in the world to believe that Lincoln said such things to himself, again and again, with increasing fervor as the years went on, until the time came when he could no longer refrain from saying them out loud.

Scene 7 (1842)

Of all the twelve scenes, this one is the most completely fictitious, and the one which presented the greatest difficulty in the writing. It requires explanation.

It is obvious that, in the course of his life, Lincoln underwent an astonishing metamorphosis, from a man of doubt and indecision —even of indifference—to a man of passionate conviction and decisive action. This metamorphosis was not accomplished in one stroke, by one magnificent act of God. It was so slow and gradual that its progress was not visible to any one, even (in all likelihood) to Lincoln himself. What caused it?

Perhaps, in this play, I have exaggerated the fact that he was forever pushed forward by his wife and his friends. Certainly, they were always trying—they were expressing, however unconsciously, the need of the people of their shuddering country for a leader who was a man of the people—but for a long time he successfully resisted them. When he did go forward, it was entirely under his own steam. But what were the deep fires of wrath that produced that steam?

In this seventh scene, I had to try to suggest the answer to that question.

We know that Lincoln was always opposed to slavery in theory, but he was even more opposed to the stirring up of trouble—and he knew that in the slave question were stores of high explosive which, if ignited, could destroy the Union. He was not one to go examining those stores with lighted matches. He would never have lifted his finger, or raised his voice, to deprive the Southerners of their right to hold their own property. In so far as he was concerned. North and South could go on living together, harmoniously, half slave and half free. He vaguely hoped that, somehow or other. the slave problem would work itself out.

But—in these stirred, troubled years, the United States was refusing to remain as it had been, divided into North and South. The wheels of the covered wagons were beginning to cut long furrows across the plains beyond the Mississippi River. Lincoln could hear the rumble of those wagons. He crossed their trails many times, when he was out on the circuit, when he was travelling down to Kentucky to visit Josh Speed's family and recover from his "hypochondriacism." Settlers were pouring through Missouri and Iowa into Kansas and Nebraska; they were even starting to travel overland to the remote Pacific Coast. The Republic of Texas was hammering for admission to the Union.

Lincoln had frequent contact with the drivers of those covered wagons. In the very depths of his nature, in the very chemistry of his blood, he was one of them, a carrier of the progressive spirit that makes men restless and turns them into pioneers. So it was a personal matter to him when he heard increasingly hot arguments as to whether all this vast new territory of the West should be slave or free. This problem had been disposed of, temporarily, by the Missouri Compromise, which, in effect, extended the Mason-Dixon Line on into the West; but Stephen A. Douglas helped to shatter that Compromise, and the Supreme Court handed down the Dred Scott decision. It was then that Lincoln began to move.

Said Herndon: "The repeal of the Missouri Compromise acts roused Lincoln—waked him up to his new opportunities and he seized them."

Thus, it was not the mere fact of slavery which converted Lincoln into the leader of a militant cause: it was the question of its extension. If he was willing to let the South mind its own business, he was not willing to stand by in silence when it threatened to establish domination of the West. He knew that the West would not accept such domination, and would fight back. The West was being settled by rebellious men, like Osawatomie John Brown.

I have tried, all through this play, from the first scene on, to provide evidence of Lincoln's awareness of the West, of his feeling of kinship for those who were to be its first settlers, and the sense of responsibility which he ultimately had to them. To crystallize all this, to indicate that Lincoln had at length made up his own mind and the influences that forced him to do it, is the purpose of this symbolic seventh scene. The prayer which Lincoln gives for a sick boy is, in effect, a prayer for the survival of the United States of America.

Scene 8 (1842)

All that can be said about this brief scene is that it seemed necessary. The chronology of the play, which had been fairly orderly and correct throughout the first six scenes, was completely disrupted in the seventh, so that Lincoln's return to Mary Todd is merely expressive of his acceptance of his destiny. The suggestion that he had made up his mind before his marriage is, of course, ridiculous. It actually took him twelve more years of searching thought and observation, as will be shown.

(1843–1858)

Four sons were born to the Lincolns—Robert Todd, in 1843; Edward, 1846; William Wallace, 1850; and Thomas ("Tad") 1852. Edward died when he was four.

(It is known that Lincoln wanted to name his first son after Joshua Speed, but this wish was overruled by the majority in the home and the boy was named after his maternal grandfather who had been a captain in the War of 1812 and a bank president in Kentucky. Robert justified his name by following in the dainty footsteps of the Todds rather than the huge ones of the Lincolns. He was educated at Exeter and Harvard, served as Secretary of War under President Garfield, as Minister to London under President Harrison, became a successful corporation lawyer and president of the Pullman Company—in which capacity his hostility to the interests of labor indicated that he had not paid strict attention to the opinions of his father. He spent the last fifteen years of his life in retirement at his Vermont home, playing golf and saying "No" to all who begged him for access to the private papers which had come to him with his father's meager estate. Indeed, he decided to burn these papers and was restrained from doing so only by the timely intervention of Nicholas Murray Butler, who persuaded him at least to place them under seal in the Library of Congress. Robert Lincoln left orders that they shall not be opened until 1976, when a new series of biographies and plays about Abraham Lincoln may be written.)

Two years after his marriage, Lincoln revisited scenes of his youth in Indiana and was moved to write some mournful doggerel, in the mood of Gray's *Elegy*. Here are two of the twenty-four stanzas:

"I hear the lone survivors tell
  How naught from death could save,
Till every sound appears a knell
  And every spot a grave—

"I range the fields with pensive tread,
  I pace the hollow rooms;
And feel (companion of the dead)
  I'm living in the tombs—"

In 1846 he ran for Congress, without much enthusiasm, and was elected. A letter to Joshua Speed at this time indicated how marriage had parted these two friends: "You, no doubt, assign the suspension of our friendship to the true philosophic cause; though it must be confessed by both of us that this is rather a cold reason for allowing a friendship such as ours to die by degrees . . . Being elected to Congress, though I am very grateful to our friends for having done it, has not pleased me as much as I expected."

As has been said, Lincoln's one term in Congress was not a success. He breakfasted in the home of Daniel Webster, whose reply to Hayne had thrilled him when he was barely twenty-one, and he attracted the attention of Horace Greeley, who was then, in *The New York Tribune,* pointing with indignation at Congressmen who took too much for mileage from the taxpayers' pockets; Greeley said that Lincoln had taken $676.80 in excess of the proper mileage from Springfield to Washington.

On January 12, 1848, Lincoln gave a vibrant speech, attacking President Polk and the whole purpose of the Mexican War. This speech makes good reading today, embodying as it does the true spirit of his liberalism. It did not go well with his patriotic constituents. *The Illinois State Register* branded him as "a second Benedict Arnold," and he was not renominated. His political career seemed finished. But a singularly perceptive (though unfortunately anonymous) Washington correspondent of *The Baltimore Patriot*, hearing the homely man from Illinois speaking in Congress, wrote back to his paper, "Evidently there is music in that very tall Mr. Lincoln." Whoever this correspondent may have been, I hope he lived to know the Gettysburg Address, and to be proud of the sensitivity of his own ear.

A comment on Lincoln at this time was provided by Douglas: "Mr. Lincoln served with me in the Legislature in 1836, when we both retired, and he subsided, or became submerged, and he was lost sight of as a public man for some years. In 1846, when Wilmot introduced his celebrated proviso, and the abolition tornado swept over the country, Lincoln again turned up as a member of Congress from the Sangamon district. I was then in the Senate, and was glad to welcome my old friend and companion. Whilst in Congress he distinguished himself by his opposition to the Mexican War, taking the side of the common enemy against his own country; and when he returned home he found that the indignation of the people followed him everywhere, and he was again submerged or obliged to retire into private life, forgotten by his former friends." It must have been particularly galling to Douglas, whose whole career was one of unremitting and conspicuous activity, that his old friend and companion could not seem to remain submerged.

Lincoln joined in resolutions of sympathy with the cause of Hungarian freedom—"*Resolved,* That in the opinion of this meeting, the immediate acknowledgment of the independence of Hungary by our government is due from American freemen to their struggling brethren, to the general cause of republican liberty." (He was always deeply concerned with the struggle for freedom, wherever it might be.) A few years later he wrote a "Fragment on Government" and said: "Government is a combination of the people of a country to effect certain objects by joint effort. The best framed and best administered governments are necessarily expensive" . . . and a "Fragment on Slavery": "Advancement—improvement in condition—is the order in a society of equals. As labor is the common burden of our race, so the effort of some to shift their share of the burden onto the shoulders of others is the great durable curse of the race."

A philosophy was slowly developing, a philosophy relentless in its thoroughness. Lincoln had the soul of a poet, but he had the mind of a pure scientist, and these may be said to have been his laboratory years. He would not acknowledge that he had seen things at all until he had seen them whole, and all the implications beyond them. That is why people who hear words of his repeated in this play are surprised at their "timeliness." Joshua Speed has recorded, "I once remarked to him that his mind was a wonder to me; that impressions were made on it and never effaced. 'No,' he said, 'you are mistaken; I am slow to learn and slow to forget what I have learned. My mind is like a piece of steel—very hard to scratch anything on it, and almost impossible after you get it there to rub it out.' "

In 1854, Lincoln decided that he was ready to go. His speech at Peoria in that year was the first that gained him any degree of national prominence. Indeed, it established him as a member of "the liberal party throughout the world" (the words are his own). He said that it was our duty to that liberal party to save our Union; and "succeeding millions of free happy people, the world over, shall rise up and call us blessed." The Peoria address is one of the great, heroic documents of human history, for it proclaimed that Abraham Lincoln, of Sangamon County, Illinois, was no longer a weak, hesitant man who was not quite sure that he had truth and justice on his side.

Scene 9 (1858)

Douglas was running for re-election to the Senate and Lincoln was opposing him. Lincoln's opening gun in the campaign was his "House Divided" speech, which was considered so inflammatory, even by Lincoln's own supporters who read it in advance, that he was urged to tone it down; but the marks had been graven deep on that "piece of steel" and nothing could rub them out. Douglas answered this speech, many times, proclaiming in tones of thunder that Lincoln was preaching Civil War!

The people of Illinois were excited by this campaign—it was a good, hot one—and people in the East and the South were beginning to take note of it. In *The New York Tribune* Horace Greeley wrote, "We trust Messrs. Lincoln and Douglas will speak together at some of the most important widely accessible points throughout the State." Lincoln decided shrewdly to act upon this suggestion and sent a note to Douglas, "Will it be agreeable to make an arrangement for you and myself to divide time, and address the same audiences the present canvass?" Douglas didn't think much of the idea. "Between you and me," he told friends, "I do not feel that I want to go into this debate. The whole country knows me and has me measured. Lincoln is comparatively unknown . . . Should I win, I shall gain but little. I do not want to go into a debate with Lincoln." Perhaps the country didn't know Lincoln—but Douglas did!

Despite Douglas's accountable reluctance, public opinion demanded the debates and they were held. There were seven of them, and each lasted three or more hours. The crowds were huge and vociferous. They cheered and laughed uproariously, and when either of the contestants scored a particularly telling point, they shouted "Hit him again!" They did hit each other, and not always above the belt. Reading these many long speeches in cold print today you realize that their authors were not the usual senatorial candidates; they were men of genuine intellectual stature. Theirs were profound statements of political and social philosophy, full of reason and knowledge of history. When one considers the temper of audiences of voters today, one wonders how these Illinois crowds had the patience to sit through such lengthy discussions of abstruse problems and even to maintain fervent enthusiasm to the end; but one must remember that the Illinoisans of 1858 did not enjoy the boons now conferred by the radio and moving pictures, and for them political meetings were rare sources of entertainment.

Douglas's speech in this ninth scene is compounded of several of his utterances, especially those on the subject of the Supreme Court; but he never did hurl at Lincoln the scornful remarks about the state of striking labor in the North. Charges such as those were frequently made then, and Lincoln answered them, but they came from the more extreme partisans of the Southern cause. I am regretfully aware that this scene does much less than justice to Douglas. Unlike his great opponent, he was not at his best in a speech lasting only a few minutes. He needed (and took) hours.

Lincoln's reply is also a patchwork of quotations and paraphrases from various speeches given by him during the debates and before them and after them, and some of it is from his letters. For instance, the lines about the right to revolution are from the First Inaugural, those about the right to strike from a speech delivered in Hartford, Conn., when that state was suffering from shoemakers' strikes and Douglas was blaming it on sectional warfare. The passage toward the end of this speech about the policy of indifference, which Lincoln said, "I can not but hate," is from the Peoria speech. The last words, of course, are from the opening of the "House Divided" speech.

On the subject of racial discrimination and oppression Lincoln spoke and wrote voluminously and explicitly. He was concerned not only with the immediate problem of Negro slavery, but with the consequences of its continued existence and of the authority for its extension given by the Supreme Court in the Dred Scott decision. As has been said in these notes, he realized all the implications, and when, speaking of these implications, he warned, with terrible earnestness, "I advise you to watch out," he knew what he was saying. There was, in his time, an organization which called itself the American Party, but which was generally known as the Know-nothing Party. It was dedicated to the proposition that only Protestants of pure Anglo-Saxon blood should rule America, that all Catholics, Jews, and "foreigners" in general (including Germans) should be reduced to the status of Negroes. Lincoln wrote to Speed, "You inquire where I now stand. That is a disputed point . . . I am not a Know-nothing; that is certain. How could I be? How can any one who abhors the oppression of Negroes be in favor of degrading classes of white people? Our progress in degeneracy seems pretty rapid." Some of the words that followed in that same letter are quoted in this debate speech.

As to the Supreme Court, Lincoln assailed it angrily time and again for the Dred Scott decision. He accused it of prejudice, of error, of "following the election returns" (as did Mr. Dooley), even of falsehood and conspiracy. His remarks on that subject in this speech are mild compared to some of his more extended diatribes. I have included his quotation from Jefferson, which he used at least twice. He also quoted Jefferson as saying, of judges, "They have, with others, the same passion for party, for power, and the privilege of their corps."

Such sentiments as Lincoln expressed on the sacred subject of the Supreme Court would constitute political suicide for any candidate for national office today, but in this 1858 campaign he won the majority of the popular vote. However, the senatorial election had to be decided in the State Legislature and it was in Douglas's favor. This was no set-back for Lincoln. Every one knew that he had beaten his lusty opponent all hollow. He was not yet taken seriously as a Presidential possibility, but his lengthy shadow was beginning to be noticed far beyond the boundaries of Sangamon County.

To those unfamiliar with the life of Douglas, a few words about him may be interesting: he was honorable, able, and a fine patriot, and it is rather sad to reflect that he is known today only as a doormat for a greater man. As we have seen, his path and Lincoln's crossed and re-crossed throughout a period of twenty-five years. They had even courted the same girl. In 1860 their persistent rivalry was to reach its fantastic culmination, when they ran against each other for the Presidency. Douglas was beaten again, and finally, because his party was split three ways as a result of his own decent refusal to compromise with the more implacable proponents of slavery. After Lincoln's election, Douglas came to him and offered his services. They were accepted, and Douglas, together with Seward (another rival), helped Lincoln compose the First Inaugural Address. (There was ghost-writing in high places even then.) When that speech was delivered, at the Capitol in Washington, Douglas stood beside his old friend and adversary and held his plug hat. After the start of the Civil War, Douglas was again at Lincoln's side, giving support and counsel. Knowing that enthusiasm for the war and for the President was insufficient among many people in the Northwest, he volunteered to make a speaking tour through that territory and whip them up.

In the article on Douglas by Allen Johnson in the *Dictionary of American Biography* you may read a description of the Little Giant's last stand:

"On April 25, he made a remarkable speech to his own people in the Capitol at Springfield. Fifty years later, men who had been his political opponents could not speak of it without emotion . . . His great sonorous voice reverberated through the chamber until it seemed to shake the building, stirring men and women to a frenzy of excitement. In a few weeks that great voice was still. Stricken soon after with typhoid fever, he battled resolutely as ever with this last foe, but succumbed on June 3, 1861, his last words a message to his two boys bidding them to obey the laws and support the Constitution."

Americans should honor his memory.

Scene 10 (1860)

The three characters who enter this scene —Sturveson, Barrick, and Crimmin—are of course apocryphal and not based on any of Lincoln's contemporaries. Their purpose in the play, obviously, is to represent the world into which the crossroads politician was being drawn.

Lincoln's views on religion, as expressed in his reply to Doctor Barrick, are taken from F. B. Carpenter's *Six Months at the White House with Abraham Lincoln.* Mrs. Lincoln once said of her husband, "He never joined a church, but he was still a religious man. But it was a kind of poetry in his nature, and he never was a technical Christian." That was as good a way as any of accounting for the manifold, unfathomable mysteries in Abraham Lincoln: "It was a kind of poetry in his nature." That is why Sandburg is the perfect biographer.

Later on, in Washington, Lincoln attended regularly the Presbyterian Church, but never joined it. Stephenson has written, "His religion flowered in his later temper. It did not, to be sure, overcome his melancholy. That was too deeply laid. Furthermore, we fail to discover in the surviving evidences any certainty that it was a glad phase of religion. Neither the ecstatic joy of the wild women, which his mother had, nor the placid joy of the ritualist, which he did not understand, nor those other variants of the joy of faith, were included in his portion. It was a lofty but grave religion. . . ." In fact, a form of religion inherited from his forebears of Puritan New England but qualified by his own eternal doubts and broadened by his own essential liberalism. If he knew any form of spiritual gladness, it was what has been called by another descendant of the Puritans, Mr. Justice Oliver Wendell Holmes, "the secret isolated joy of the thinker."

Lincoln's most vigorous statements on the relationship of capital and labor were made in an address delivered to a gathering of Wisconsin farmers at the State Fair in Milwaukee on September 30th, 1859, and he repeated these statements and enlarged upon them in his Message to Congress in December, 1861. Near the beginning of the Milwaukee speech you may find a paragraph which is a superb example of his humor and his artful method of winning the attention and affection of a crowd of strangers. He said, "I presume I am not expected to employ the time assigned me in the mere flattery of the farmers as a class. My opinion of them is that, in proportion to numbers, they are neither better nor worse than other people. In the nature of things they are more numerous than any other class; and I believe there really are more attempts at flattering them than any other, the reason of which I can not perceive, unless it be that they can cast more votes than any other. On reflection, I am not quite sure that there is not cause of suspicion against you in selecting me, in some sort a politician and in no sort a farmer, to address you." (A year later, in the Presidential election, he carried Wisconsin by a handsome majority.)

This tenth scene (and I have mentioned this point before in these notes) may seem to overemphasize Lincoln's shrinking from great responsibility, suggesting again that he never sought public office for himself, but was always being thrust into it by others. Such was not my intention in writing the play, but it is evidently the impression that has been conveyed to many.

It is true that Lincoln's friends always displayed more confidence in him than he did in himself, and that his *persona* (to employ just one word out of psychoanalysis) was that of a man who is reluctant to advance, indifferent to fame and fortune. Nevertheless, it is a mistake to assume that he never pulled any strings on his own behalf. He pulled many, and he did it with consummate skill. He was, in fact, one of the most artful campaigners that ever lived. When he could finally make up his mind that he wanted office and that he was fitted for it he went about the getting of it in a manner that was infinitely crafty. I don't know just when the Presidential bee entered his bonnet, but it was probably a lot earlier than any one knew at the time. He wrote a great number of letters to influential men, choosing his words carefully so as not to commit himself but still managing to suggest that he might be available. All of these letters ended with strict injunctions to secrecy—"burn this," etc.—but fortunately his orders were not always obeyed. In politics, as in everything else (except perhaps his humor), he was a profoundly subtle man. But—in politics, as in everything else, he was a bewilderingly contradictory one.

He worked hard, if silently, to win the Republican nomination. He sent $100 to a Kansas friend to help him get to the Chicago Convention, and he enclosed many instructions with the money. Others of his friends, such as Judge David Davis, Orville H. Browning, Judge Stephen T. Logan, Norman B. Judd and Leonard Swett, many of whom had known him since the New Salem days, were in Chicago working furiously, bargaining, trading, playing off such masters of the craft as Thurlow Weed and Horace Greeley against one another, preparing one of the most astounding coups in the history of political chicanery. While the Convention was in session, Lincoln was in Springfield, playing handball and (according to Herndon) steadying his nerves with an occasional glass of beer. But he was in close touch with his own shock troops at the front.

Nobody of any prominence in the highest councils of the party thought that Lincoln had the remotest chance of winning the nomination. Seward was far in the lead, and certainly deserved to win. But Lincoln's strategy had been brilliantly prepared, and his lieutenants were not too heavily burdened with the scruples that have wrecked many a political boom. The crisis came during the night before the first ballot was taken. Judge Davis and the others were sweating and struggling to win various delegations, notably Pennsylvania's, by munificent offers of jobs. It was at that crucial moment that Lincoln let them down.

Whether his conscience triumphed over his political ambition, or his nerve failed him, he suddenly shrank back and refused to go through with the disreputable business. Davis telegraphed him that they could make a deal to capture the Pennsylvania delegates if Lincoln would promise the office of Secretary of the Treasury to that dubious politician, Governor Simon Cameron. Lincoln replied, "I authorize no bargains and will be bound by none." Later, at literally the eleventh hour, he sent a messenger to Chicago with a heavily underlined message, "Make no contracts that will bind me."

This strange reneging by their candidate caused consternation among the frantic men in Lincoln headquarters. Jesse K. Dubois said, "Damn Lincoln!" Judge Davis, more practically, said, "Lincoln ain't here, and don't know what we have to meet, so we will go ahead, as if we hadn't heard from him, and he must ratify it!"

So the corrupt bargains were made, and Lincoln gained the nomination, and he did ratify it—although with a bitterness that found expression in these words (which are quoted in the next scene): "They have gambled me all around, bought and sold me a hundred times. I can not begin to fill the pledges made in my name."

Cameron became Secretary of War in a cabinet which ranks amongst the worst that have ever sat about a White House table.

Nevertheless, if Lincoln played ball with the boys before he became President, he stopped it afterward. He provided many stunning surprises for those (including the estimable Seward) who thought he would be malleable, tractable, and take orders. There is probably no other Chief Executive in our history who so thoroughly deserved the term Chief. Lincoln came to rule with an iron hand, taking but little advice and no orders from any one. In this way he gained the hatred and the attempted insubordination of those who had thought he would be easily bossed, but he gained the admiration and the invaluable friendship of Seward.

A memorandum which Lincoln read to his Cabinet in the last year of the Civil War is eloquent: "I must myself be the judge how long to retain in and when to remove any of you from his position. It would greatly pain me to discover any of you endeavoring to procure another's removal, or in any way to prejudice him before the public . . . My wish is that on this subject no remark be made nor question asked by any of you, here or elsewhere, now or hereafter."

Thus the humble Illinois sucker. Eight hours after his death, leaders of the Republican Party gathered and discussed plans "to get rid of the last vestige of Lincolnism." (You will find a fine description of this in Claude G. Bowers' powerful, shocking book, *The Tragic Era.*) At that meeting of political gangsters the horrors of the Reconstruction Period were gleefully plotted. One of those present was George Washington Julian, chairman of the Committee of Public Lands in the House of Representatives, and it is to his long unpublished diary that we are indebted for the knowledge that among his associates "the hostility for Lincoln's policy of conciliation and contempt for his weakness" were "undisguised" and that "his death is a Godsend to our cause."

The boys in the back room were grateful to John Wilkes Booth for killing that one, solitary, strong man whose policy was based on the belief that "a just and lasting peace" might be achieved "with malice toward none; with charity for all."

Any one who doubts that Lincoln was absolute ruler of the United States of America during four years of emergency has only to contemplate the chaotic orgy of corruption which followed his death. Andrew Johnson turned out to be an honorable man, but neither he nor Seward nor any one else in the administration had the personal power of control which went to the grave with Lincoln.

However—I'm straying far from this play.

Scene 11 (1860)

The Presidential election which was held on November 6, 1860, was the most terrific in its excitement in our history. Not that there was any particular uncertainty as to the count of the votes, for Lincoln's election was virtually assured; but the country knew that these ballots could start fires of hatred which might never be put out. As was said at the time, Southern patriots were working to gain victory in this election, but they would not accept defeat!

As the nation went to the polls that day, Lincoln could read in the newspapers that Governor Gist of South Carolina had recommended the use of all available means for arming every man in the State between the ages of eighteen and forty-five, urging the need for such drastic action because, as he told the Legislature, "of the probability of the election to the Presidency of a sectional candidate by a party committed to the support of measures which if carried out will inevitably destroy our equality in the Union, and ultimately reduce the Southern States to mere provinces of a consolidated despotism."

These sentiments were wildly cheered throughout the South, and other States were preparing to take similar measures. Small wonder that Lincoln was moved to say that "the task before me is greater than that which rested on Washington."

It is worth remembering that no man ever assumed the Presidency with so little of experience in public life to guide him. All other Presidents down to the present day had gained some substantial prominence as statesmen, soldiers, or, at least, as vote-getters, before receiving nomination to the highest office. Even those Vice-Presidents who acceded through death—Tyler, Johnson, Arthur, Theodore Roosevelt, and Coolidge—had far more in their records to recommend them than did Lincoln, who had served only in the State Assembly when he was in his twenties and one inconspicuous term in Congress when he was in his thirties, and had never done anything to reveal any degree of executive ability. But he faced the greatest task of them all. He had reason for nervousness on November 6, 1860.

In this eleventh scene is one speech that has been much criticized and deplored by good people who revere Lincoln's memory and who cannot believe that he ever cursed at his wife. There is certainly overwhelming evidence of the fact that, in the years in the White House, he treated the obstreperous Mrs. Lincoln with unfailing courtesy and tender considerateness. This was his public behavior and, so far as any one can know, his private behavior, as well.

Nevertheless, I did not feel that this play concerning a part of the tragedy of Lincoln's life would be complete in its attempted honesty if I did not include the admission that, on occasion, his monumental patience snapped. That it did, before the move from Springfield, there can be no doubt. Usually he met her tirades with stony silence, or abrupt departure, or with laughter (the most infuriating response of all). But Herndon records that at least once, when she had run him out of the house and was chasing him down Eighth Street, and they approached some churchgoers, he turned on her, picked her up, spanked her, and thrust her back into the house, saying, "There, now, stay in the house and don't be a damned fool before the people."

Feeling that one such outburst from Lincoln to his wife was necessary, I placed it in this scene on Election Night, considering that this was the most appropriate moment, with the nerves of both so severely strained.

In this eleventh scene is reference to the letter from a little girl suggesting that Lincoln should grow a beard. Her name was Grace Bedell, of New York, and Lincoln's reply to her, written two weeks before the election, was as follows:

"My dear little Miss: Your very agreeable letter of the 15th is received. I regret the necessity of saying I have no daughter. I have three sons—one seventeen, one nine, and one seven years of age. They, with their mother, constitute my whole family. As to the whiskers, having never worn any, do you not think people would call it a piece of silly affectation if I were to begin it now? Your very sincere well-wisher, A. Lincoln."

In the election, Lincoln received about 40 per cent of the popular vote, Douglas about 30 per cent, and the rest divided between Breckenridge and Bell. In the Electoral College, Lincoln had 180 votes to 123 for the other three.

Scene 12 (1861)

There is no exaggeration in the suggestion that Lincoln's life was constantly threatened after his election, or that he himself was unresponsive to the attempts to guard him from assassination. He knew that there were many brave, desperate men determined to prevent him from taking the oath of office on March 4th, but he protested against bodyguards by saying, "What's the use of putting up a gap when the fence is down all around?" He did send Thomas S. Mather, Adjutant-General of Illinois, to Washington to sound out General Winfield Scott, a Virginian, on his loyalty to the new administration. Scott, who was known as "Old Fuss and Feathers," sent back these words: "Say to him that, when once here, I shall consider myself responsible for his safety. If necessary I'll plant cannon at both ends of Pennsylvania Avenue, and if any show their hands or even venture to raise a finger, I'll blow them to hell." On his journey East Lincoln was warned to keep out of the free city of Baltimore, and a plot was discovered to blow up his train. He was compelled to travel from Harrisburg to Washington in strictest secrecy, so that he literally slunk into the capital.

The farewell speech from the train platform in this final scene, like the Douglas debate speech, is a blend of several of Lincoln's utterances, starting with the moving words he actually delivered to his neighbors on this occasion. The lines about the "sentiment in the Declaration of Independence," were from his speech in Independence Hall, in Philadelphia, on Washington's Birthday, eleven days later. The mystic lines about the Eastern monarch and his wise men were from the address given to farmers in Milwaukee a year and a half previously.

There is, in this farewell speech, one group of words which seems to me a particularly fine example of Lincoln's poetry: "not knowing when or whether ever I may return." That strange and beautiful construction is comparable to "The world will little note nor long remember . . ." in the Gettysburg address.

The play ends with words written by Thomas Brigham Bishop (not, as many people suppose, by Julia Ward Howe): "His soul goes marching on." They referred originally to John Brown, whose body lay a-mouldering in the grave when the first regiments marched off to war in 1861; but they express now the most important of all facts about Abraham Lincoln—the fact that, by the eternal nature of the truths that he uttered, he can never die.

In these notes I have quoted many authorities on his life, and I shall now quote from an article, published in the *Locomotive Engineers Journal,* which provides stirring testimony to the extent of his influence upon men of good will the world over. It was written by the late B. Charney Vladeck shortly after he first came to this country, a Jewish refugee from oppression in Tsarist Russia. Vladeck had been a member of the Bolshevist Party, had voted at the meeting which had elected Lenin their leader, and had served in prison for his revolutionary activities. He then emigrated to America, a man whose heart was filled with bitterness—and he learned here that those illusive words, liberty and equality, may have profound meaning. He became a good and useful American citizen, and in the last year of his life was chosen leader of the coalition of liberal Republicans, Democrats, and Labor Party members of the Council of the City of New York.

"One of my first and most memorable lessons in Americanization," he wrote, "was

Lincoln's Gettysburg address. When I read it and reread it and learned it by heart, struck by its noble clearness and sweeping faith in America, I felt as if the whole past of this country had been lit up by a row of warm and beautiful lights; as if some unknown friend had taken me by the hand on a dark and uncertain road, saying gently: 'Don't doubt and don't despair. This country has a soul and a purpose and, if you so wish, you may love it without regrets' . . .

"On the winding highway of American history I picture Lincoln as a sad but gentle landscape, permeated with the beauty of eternity. I ennobled myself by trying to understand him, and I am grateful to America for making him possible."

Here, in these glowing words from one who had been a deeply skeptical alien, is the essence of what we like to call "Americanization," but which is actually just what Lincoln meant it to be: liberation. Those who study Lincoln most closely know that he was no chauvinistic flag-waver—and may God forgive the loud-mouthed Fourth of July orators who wave the American flag boastfully in his name. The reason that he lives today, and still inspires so many men everywhere with the will to shake off their chains and find freedom and opportunity in the brotherhood of life, is that he was essentially a citizen of the world. In a letter from the White House, he wrote: "The strongest bond of human sympathy, outside of the family relation, should be one uniting all working people, of all nations, and tongues, and kindreds." He was never parochial, never nationalistic; he was never heard to utter thanks for that providential accident of geography which gave us the protection of the Atlantic Ocean. In his recorded speeches and letters, from his earliest frontier days, he spoke not as a representative of any one community, any one faith or class, but as a member of the whole human race. He was forever conscious of the obligation of all Americans to their brethren in all other lands—to "the Liberal party throughout the world"—to make the democratic spirit live and grow.

In the speech that he gave in Independence Hall, ten days before his first Inaugural, he said: "I have often enquired of myself what great principle or idea it was that kept this Confederacy so long together. It was not the mere matter of separation of the colonies from the motherland, but that sentiment in the Declaration of Independence which gave liberty not alone to the people of this country, but hope to all the world, for all future time." And he added: "If this country can not be saved without giving up that principle, I would rather be assassinated on this spot than surrender it."

In his first Message to Congress, when he was discussing most soberly the results of the firing on Fort Sumter, he said: "This issue embraces more than the fate of these United States. It presents to the whole family of man the question whether a constitutional republic or democracy—a government of the people by the same people—can or cannot maintain its territorial integrity against its own domestic foes."

Four years later, at his second Inaugural, in the last weeks of his life, he repeated Christ's words, "Woe unto the world because of offenses! for it must needs be that offenses come; but woe to that man by whom the offense cometh!"

APPENDIX

BIBLIOGRAPHY OF GENERAL WORKS

BIBLIOGRAPHIES OF INDIVIDUAL DRAMATISTS

REFERENCES TO ILLUSTRATIONS OF THE PLAYS

BIBLIOGRAPHY

GENERAL

Aleksieev, Konstantin S. (Stanislavsky, Constantin). *My Life in Art*. 1924.
Anderson, John. *The American Theatre*. 1938.
Archer, William. *Playmaking*. 1912.
Archer, William. *The Old Drama and the New*. 1923.
Bab, Julius. *Das Theater der Gegenwart*. 1928.
Bahr, Hermann. *Expressionism*. 1925.
Baker, George Pierce. *Dramatic Technique*. 1918.
Bakshy, Alexander. *The Path of the Modern Russian Stage*. 1918.
Balmforth, Ramsden. *The Problem Play*. 1928.
Beerbohm, Max. *Around Theatres*. 1928.
Bishop, George W. *Barry Jackson and the London Theatre*. 1933.
Block, Anita (Cahn). *The Changing World in Plays and Theatre*. 1939.
Brady, William A. *Showman*. 1937.
Brown, John Mason. *The Art of Playgoing*. 1936.
Brown, John Mason. *Upstage*. 1930.
Brown, John Mason. *The Modern Theatre in Revolt*. 1929.
Burris-Meyer, Homer, and Cole, E. C. *Scenery for the Theatre*. 1938.
Byrne, Dawson. *The Story of Ireland's National Theatre*. 1929.
Carpenter, Bruce. *The Way of the Drama*. 1929.
Carter, Huntley. *The New Theatre and Cinema of Soviet Russia*. 1924.
Carter, Jean, and Ogden, J. *Everyman's Drama*. 1938.
Chandler, Frank W. *Modern Continental Playwrights*. 1931.
Charques, Richard D. *Footnotes to the Theatre*. 1938.
Cheney, Sheldon. *Stage Decoration*. 1928.
Cheney, Sheldon. *The Art Theatre*. 1917, 1925.
Cheney, Sheldon. *The Theatre*. 1929.
Clark, Barrett H. *European Theories of the Drama*. 1918.
Clark, Barrett H. *An Hour of American Drama*. 1930.
Clark, Barrett H. *A Study of the Modern Drama*. 1938.
Cogniat, Raymond. *Décors de Théâtre*. 1930.
Craig, Edward G. *On the Art of the Theatre*. 1911.
Craig, Edward G. *The Theatre—Advancing*. 1925.
Crawford, Mary C. *The Romance of the American Theatre*. 1925.
Dana, Henry W. L. *Handbook on Soviet Drama* (bibliography). 1938.
Deutsch, Helen and Hanau, S. *The Provincetown*. 1931.
Dickinson, Thomas H., ed. *The Theatre in a Changing Europe*. 1937.
Dickinson, Thomas H. *Playwrights of the New American Theatre*. 1925.
Dickinson, Thomas H. *An Outline of Contemporary Drama*. 1927.
Dolman, John. *Art of Play Production*. 1928.
Downs, Harold, ed. *Theatre and Stage*. 1934.
Dubech, Lucien. *Histoire Générale Illustrée du Théâtre*. 5 vols. 1931–1934.
Drew, Elizabeth. *Discovering Drama*. 1937.
Dukes, Ashley. *Drama*. 1926.
Dukes, Ashley. *The Youngest Drama*. 1924.
Eaton, Walter P. *The Theatre Guild*. 1929.
Eaton, Walter P. *The Drama in English*. 1930.
Ellehauge, Martin. *Striking Figures Among Modern English Dramatists*. 1931.
Ellis-Fermor, Una M. *The Irish Dramatic Movement*. 1939.
Fay, William G. and Carswell, C. *The Fays of the Abbey Theatre*. 1935.
Fischel, Oskar. *Das Moderne Bühnenbild*. 1923.
Flanagan, Hallie. *Arena*. 1940.
Flexner, Eleanor. *American Playwrights, 1918–1938*. 1938.
Freedley, George, and Reeves, J. A. *History of the Theatre*. 1941.
Fuchs, Theodore. *Stage Lighting*. 1929.
Gamble, William B. *The Development of Scenic Art and Stage Machinery* (bibliography). 1928.
Gassner, John. *Masters of the Drama*. 1940.
Goldberg, Isaac. *The Drama of Transition*. 1922.
Gorelik, Mordecai, *New Theatres for Old*. 1941.
Granville-Barker, Harley. *The Study of Drama*. 1935.
Gregor, Joseph, and Fülöp-Miller, R. *The Russian Theatre*. 1930.
Gregor, Joseph, and Fülöp-Miller, R. *Das Amerikanische Theater und Kino*. 1931.
Hale, Edward E., Jr. *Dramatists of Today*. 1911.
Harris, Mark. *The Case for Tragedy*. 1932.
Hartman, John G. *The Development of American Social Comedy*. 1939.
Heffner, Hubert C.; Selden, S.; and Sellman, H. D. *Modern Theatre Practice*. 1939.
Henderson, Archibald. *European Dramatists*. 1926.
Hewitt, Barnard. *Art and Craft of Play Production*. 1940.
Houghton, Norris. *Moscow Rehearsals*. 1936.
Hughes, Glenn. *The Story of the Theatre*. 1928.
Hume, Samuel J., and Fuerst, W. R. *Twentieth Century Stage Decoration*. 1929.
Huneker, James G. *Iconoclasts*. 1905.
Isaacs, Edith J. R., ed. *Theatre*. 1927.

Isaacs, Edith J. R., ed. *Architecture for the New Theatre.* 1935.
Jones, Robert E. *Drawings for the Theatre.* 1925.
Komisarjevsky, Theodore, and Simonson, L. *Settings and Costumes of the Modern Stage.* 1933.
Krutch, Joseph W. *The American Drama Since 1918.* 1939.
Lawson, John H. *Theory and Technique of Playwriting.* 1936.
Lewisohn, Ludwig. *The Modern Drama.* 1915.
Lewisohn, Ludwig. *The Drama and the Stage.* 1922.
Littlewood, Samuel R. *Dramatic Criticism.* 1939.
McCleery, Albert, and Glick C. *Curtains Going Up.* 1939.
Macgowan, Kenneth. *Footlights Across America.* 1929.
Macgowan, Kenneth. *American Playwrights of Today.* 1929.
Macgowan, Kenneth, and Jones, R. E. *Continental Stagecraft.* 1924.
Mackay, Constance D. *The Little Theatre in the United States.* 1917.
Malone, Andrew E. *The Irish Drama.* 1929.
Mantle, Robert Burns. *Contemporary American Playwrights.* 1938.
Mantle, Robert Burns. *American Playwrights of Today.* 1929.
Mantle, Robert Burns, ed. *The Best Plays of 1909–1919, 1919–1920,* and subsequent years.
Marriott, James W. *Modern Drama.* 1934.
Miller, Anna I. *The Independent Theatre in Europe.* 1931.
Moderwell, Hiram K. *The Theatre of Today.* 1927.
Morgan, Arthur E. *Tendencies of Modern English Drama.* 1924.
Morley, Malcolm. *The Theatre.* 1935.
Moses, Montrose J. *The American Dramatist.* 1925.
Moses, Montrose J., and Brown, J. M. *The American Theatre as Seen by Its Critics, 1752–1934.* 1934.
Moussinac, Leon. *Tendances Nouvelles du Théâtre.* 1931.
Moussinac, Leon. *The New Movement in the Theatre.* 1931.
Nathan, George J. *The House of Satan.* 1926.
Nathan, George J. *The Morning after the First Night.* 1938.
Nemirovich-Danchenko, Vladimir I. *My Life in the Russian Theatre.* 1936.
Nicoll, Allardyce. *The Theory of Drama.* 1931.
Nicoll, Allardyce. *The Development of the Theatre.* 1927, 1937.
Nicoll, Allardyce. *The English Theatre.* 1936.
Nicoll, Allardyce. *Film and Theatre.* 1936.
Oenslager, Donald. *Scenery Then and Now.* 1936.
O'Hara, Frank H. *Today in American Drama.* 1939.
O'Hara, Frank H., and Bro, M. H. *A Handbook of Drama.* 1938.
Pelizzi, Camillo. *English Drama.* 1935.
Pfister, Oskar R. *Expressionism in Art.* 1922.
Phelps, William L. *Essays on Modern Dramatists.* 1921.
Quinn, Arthur H. *A History of American Drama.* 1936.
Sayler, Oliver M. *The Russian Theatre.* 1922.
Sayler, Oliver M. *Our American Theatre.* 1923.
Sayler, Oliver M. *Revolt in the Arts.* 1930.
Sayler, Oliver M. *Max Reinhardt and His Theatre.* 1924.
Selden, Samuel. *The Stage in Action.* 1941.
Shaw, George Bernard. *Dramatic Opinions and Essays.* 1906, 1928.
Sheringham, George. *Designs for the Theatre.* 1927.
Simonson, Lee. *The Stage Is Set.* 1932.
Simonson, Lee. *Theatre Art.* 1934.
Skinner, Richard Dana. *Our Changing Theatre.* 1931.
Smith, Hugh A. *Main Currents of Modern French Drama.* 1925.
Sobel, Bernard, ed. *Theatre Handbook and Digest of Plays.* 1940.
Stevens, Thomas W. *The Theatre from Athens to Broadway.* 1932.
Stanislavsky. See above Aleksieev.
Stratton, Clarence. *Theatron.* 1928.
Stratton, Clarence. *Producing in Little Theatres.* 1921.
Strong, Leonard A. G. *Common Sense about Drama.* 1937.
Stuart, Donald C. *The Development of Dramatic Art.* 1928.
Sutton, Graham. *Some Contemporary Dramatists.* 1926.
Thorndike, Ashley H. *English Comedy.* 1929.
Thouless, Priscilla. *Modern Poetic Drama.* 1934.
Waxman, Samuel M. *Antoine and the Théâtre-Libre.* 1926.
Whitman, Willson. *Bread and Circuses, a Study of the Federal Theatre.* 1937.
Whitworth, Geoffrey A. *Theatre in Action.* 1938.
Young, Stark. *Theatre Practice.* 1926.
Young, Stark. *The Flower in Drama.* 1923.

Periodicals

Stage, N. Y. 1923–1939 (vols. 6–9 known as *Theatre Guild Magazine*).
Theatre Arts Monthly, N. Y. 1916ff.
Theatre Magazine, N. Y. 1900–1931.
Drama, Chicago. 1911–1931.
Dramatic Index. 1909ff.

Maxwell Anderson

Anderson, Maxwell. *The Essence of Tragedy.* 1939.
Block, Anita. *The Changing World in Plays and Theatre.* 1939.
Clark, Barrett H. *Maxwell Anderson, the Man and His Plays.* 1933.
Clark, Barrett H. *An Hour of American Drama.* 1930.
Flexner, Eleanor. *American Playwrights 1918–1938.* 1938.
Gassner, John. *Masters of the Drama.* 1940.
Krutch, Joseph W. *The American Drama since 1918.* 1939.
Mantle, Burns. *American Playwrights of Today.* 1929.

Mantle, Burns. *Contemporary American Playwrights.* 1938.
O'Hara, Frank H. *Today in American Drama.* 1939.
Quinn, Arthur H. *A History of American Drama.* 1936.
Skinner, Richard D. *Our Changing Theatre.* 1931.

LEONID ANDREYEV

Chandler, Frank W. *Modern Continental Playwrights.* 1931.
Dickinson, Thomas H., ed. *The Theatre in a Changing Europe.* 1937.
Gassner, John. *Masters of the Drama.* 1940.
Gorki, Maxim. (Pyeshkov, Alexei M.) *Reminiscences of Andreyev.* 1928.
Gorki, Maxim. (Pyeshkov, Alexei M.) *Reminiscences of Tolstoy, Chekhov, and Andreyev.* 1934.
Kaun, Alexander. *Leonid Andreyev.* 1924.
Kommisarjevsky, Theodore. *Myself and the Theatre.* 1930.
Meader, Clarence L., and Scott, F. N. Preface to *Plays by Leonid Andreyev.* 1915.
Mirsky, Dimitry S. *Contemporary Russian Literature.* 1926.
Moderwell, Hiram K. *The Theatre of Today.* 1927.
Wiener, Leo. *The Contemporary Drama of Russia.* 1924.

SIR JAMES MATTHEW BARRIE

Cunliffe, John W. *Modern English Playwrights.* 1927.
Darlington, William A. *J. M. Barrie.* 1938.
Ellehauge, Martin. *Striking Figures Among Modern English Dramatists.* 1931.
Frohman, Daniel. *Memories of a Manager.* 1911.
Gassner, John. *Masters of the Drama.* 1940.
Hammerton, Sir John A. *Barrie.* 1929.
Howe, Percival P. *Dramatic Portraits.* 1913.
Lewisohn, Ludwig. *The Drama and the Stage.* 1922.
Marcosson, Isaac F., and Frohman, D. *Charles Frohman, Manager and Man.* 1916.
Marriott, James W. *Modern Drama.* 1934.
Moderwell, Hiram K. *The Theatre of Today.* 1927.
Morgan, Arthur E. *Tendencies of Modern English Drama.* 1924.
Moult, Thomas. *Barrie.* 1928.
Pelizzi, Camillo. *English Drama.* 1935.
Phelps, William L. *Essays on Modern Dramatists.* 1921.
Roy, James A. *James Matthew Barrie.* 1937.
Scott, Dixon. *Men of Letters.* 1923.
Skinner, Richard D. *Our Changing Theatre.* 1931.
Walbrook, Henry M. *J. M. Barrie and the Theatre.* 1922.

PHILIP BARRY

Brown, John M. *Upstage.* 1930.
Clark, Barrett H. *An Hour of American Drama.* 1930.
Flexner, Eleanor. *American Playwrights 1918–1938.* 1938.
Gassner, John. *Masters of the Drama.* 1940.
Krutch, Joseph W. *The American Drama since 1918.* 1939.
Mantle, Burns. *American Playwrights of Today.* 1929.
Mantle, Burns. *Contemporary American Playwrights.* 1938.
Quinn, Arthur H. *A History of American Drama.* 1936.
Skinner, Richard D. *Our Changing Theatre.* 1931.

JACINTO BENAVENTE

Bell, Aubrey F. G. *Contemporary Spanish Literature.* 1925.
Chandler, Frank W. *Modern Continental Playwrights.* 1931.
Dickinson, Thomas H., ed. *The Theatre in a Changing Europe.* 1937.
Gassner, John. *Masters of the Drama.* 1940.
Goldberg, Isaac. *The Drama of Transition.* 1922.
Gregerson, Halfdan. *Ibsen and Spain.* 1936.
Starkie, Walter. *Jacinto Benavente.* 1924.
Turrell, Charles A. *Contemporary Spanish Drama.* 1919.
Underhill, John G. Prefaces to *Plays of Jacinto Benavente.* 1917-1924.
Warren, Leslie A. *Modern Spanish Literature.* 1929.

KAREL ČAPEK

Čapek, Karel. *How a Play is Produced.* 1928.
Chandler, Frank W. *Modern Continental Playwrights.* 1931.
Dickinson, Thomas H., ed. *The Theatre in a Changing Europe.* 1937.
Dukes, Ashley. *The Youngest Drama.* 1924.

ANTON CHEKHOV

Block, Anita. *The Changing World in Plays and Theatre.* 1939.
Chandler, Frank W. *Modern Continental Playwrights.* 1931.
Chekhov, Anton P. *Notebooks.* 1921.
Chekhov, Anton P. *Letters of Anton Tchekoff to His Family and Friends.* 1920.
Chekhov, Anton P. *Letters on the Short Story, the Drama, and Other Literary Topics.* 1924.
Dickinson, Thomas H., ed. *The Theatre in a Changing Europe.* 1937.
Fell, Marian. Preface to *Plays of Anton Tchekoff, First Series.* 1912.
Gassner, John. *Masters of the Drama.* 1940.
Gerhardi, William. *Anton Chekhov.* 1923.
Gorki, Maxim. *Reminiscences of Tolstoy, Chekhov, and Andreyev.* 1934.
Houghton, Norris. *Moscow Rehearsals.* 1936.
Koteliansky, Samuel S., and Tomlinson, P. *Life and Letters of Anton Tchekhov.* 1925.
Koteliansky, Samuel S. Preface to *The Wood Demon.* 1926.
Koteliansky, Samuel S. *Anton Tchekhov: Literary and Theatrical Reminiscences.* 1927.

Mirsky, Dimitry S. *Contemporary Russian Literature.* 1926.
Moderwell, Hiram K. *The Theatre of Today.* 1927.
Nemirovich-Danchenko, Vladimir. *My Life in the Russian Theatre.* 1936.
Perry, Henry T. E. *Masters of Dramatic Comedy.* 1939.
Sayler, Oliver M. *The Russian Theatre.* 1922.
Shestov, Leo. *Anton Tchekhov and Other Essays.* 1916.
Skinner, Richard D. *Our Changing Theatre.* 1931.
Stanislavsky, C. (Aleksieev) *My Life in Art.* 1924.
Toumanova, Nina A. *Anton Chekhov, the Voice of Twilight Russia.* 1937.
West, Julius. Preface to *Plays by Anton Tchekoff, Second Series.* 1916.
Wiener, Leo. *The Contemporary Drama of Russia.* 1924.

François De Curel

Antoine, André. *Mes Souvenirs sur le Théâtre-Libre.* 1921.
Chandler, Frank W. *The Contemporary Drama of France.* 1925.
Chandler, Frank W. *Modern Continental Playwrights.* 1931.
Clark, Barrett H. *Contemporary French Dramatists.* 1915.
Gassner, John. *Masters of the Drama.* 1940.
Lalou, René. *History of Contemporary French Literature.* 1924.
Lewisohn, Ludwig. *The Modern Drama.* 1915.
Moderwell, Hiram K. *The Theatre of Today.* 1927.
Smith, Hugh A. *Main Currents of Modern French Drama.* 1925.
Waxman, Samuel M. *Antoine and the Théâtre-Libre.* 1926.

John Galsworthy

Baker, George P. Introduction to *Representative Plays of John Galsworthy.* 1924.
Block, Anita. *The Changing World in Plays and Theatre.* 1939.
Coats, Robert H. *John Galsworthy as a Dramatic Artist.* 1926.
Ellehauge, Martin. *Striking Figures among Modern English Dramatists.* 1931.
Ervine, St. John. *Some Impressions of My Elders.* 1924.
Gassner, John. *Masters of the Drama.* 1940.
Guedalla, Philip. *A Gallery.* 1924.
Howe, Percival P. *Dramatic Portraits.* 1913.
Kaye-Smith, Sheila. *John Galsworthy.* 1916.
Landa, Myer J. *The Jew in Drama.* 1926.
Marriott, James W. *Modern Drama.* 1934.
Marrott, Harold V. *The Life and Letters of John Galsworthy.* 1936.
Moderwell, Hiram K. *The Theatre of Today.* 1927.
Morgan, Arthur E. *Tendencies of Modern English Drama.* 1924.
Pelizzi, Camillo. *English Drama.* 1935.
Phelps, William L. *Essays on Modern English Dramatists.* 1921.
Schalit, Leon. *John Galsworthy.* 1929.
Skinner, Richard D. *Our Changing Theatre.* 1931.

Maxim Gorki

Block, Anita. *The Changing World in Plays and Theatre.* 1939.
Chandler, Frank W. *Modern Continental Playwrights.* 1931.
Dickinson, Thomas H., ed. *The Theatre in a Changing Europe.* 1937.
Gassner, John. *Masters of the Drama.* 1940.
Gorki, Maxim. (Pyeshkov, Alexei M.) *My Childhood.* 1915.
Gorki, Maxim. *Reminiscences of My Youth.* 1924.
Gorki, Maxim. *My University Days.* 1923.
Gorki, Maxim. *In the World.* 1917.
Gorki, Maxim. *Fragments from My Diary.* 1924.
Harris, Frank. *Contemporary Portraits, 4th Series.* 1923.
Huneker, James G. *Iconoclasts.* 1928.
Kaun, Alexander. *Maxim Gorki and His Russia.* 1931.
Mirsky, Dimitry S. *Contemporary Russian Literature.* 1926.
Moderwell, Hiram K. *The Theatre of Today.* 1927.
Nemirovich-Danchenko, Vladimir. *My Life in the Russian Theatre.* 1936.
Skinner, Richard D. *Our Changing Theatre.* 1931.
Stanislavsky, C. (Aleksieev) *My Life in Art.* 1924.
Wiener, Leo. *The Contemporary Drama of Russia.* 1924.

Gerhart Hauptmann

Bertaux, Felix. *A Panorama of German Literature, 1871–1931.* 1935.
Block, Anita. *The Changing World in Plays and Theatre.* 1939.
Chandler, Frank W. *Modern Continental Playwrights.* 1931.
Dickinson, Thomas H., ed. *The Theatre in a Changing Europe.* 1937.
Eloesser, Arthur. *Modern German Literature.* 1933.
Gassner, John. *Masters of the Drama.* 1940.
Hale, Edward E., Jr. *Dramatists of Today.* 1911.
Huneker, James G. *Iconoclasts.* 1928.
Klenze, Camille von. *From Goethe to Hauptmann.* 1926.
Lessing, Otto E. *Masters in Modern German Literature.* 1912.
Lewisohn, Ludwig. *The Spirit of Modern German Literature.* 1916.
Lewisohn, Ludwig. *The Modern Drama.* 1915.

Sidney Howard

Brown, John M. *Upstage.* 1930.
Clark, Barrett H. *An Hour of American Drama.* 1930.
Flexner, Eleanor. *American Playwrights 1918–1938.* 1938.

Gassner, John. *Masters of the Drama.* 1940.
Krutch, Joseph W. *The American Drama since 1918.* 1939.
Mantle, Burns. *American Playwrights of Today.* 1929.
Mantle, Burns. *Contemporary American Playwrights.* 1938.
O'Hara, Frank H. *Today in American Drama.* 1939.
Skinner, Richard D. *Our Changing Theatre.* 1931.

Henrik Ibsen

Archer, William. Prefaces to his editions of Ibsen. 1891, 1908, 1912.
Block, Anita. *The Changing World in Plays and Theatre.* 1939.
Brandes, Georg. *Creative Spirits of the Nineteenth Century.* 1923.
Chandler, Frank W. *Modern Continental Playwrights.* 1931.
Dickinson, Thomas H., ed. *The Theatre in a Changing Europe.* 1937.
Eikeland, Peter J. *Ibsen Studies.* 1934.
Firkins, Ida T. E. *Henrik Ibsen: a Bibliography.* 1921.
Gassner, John. *Masters of the Drama.* 1940.
Gosse, Edmund. *Henrik Ibsen.* 1917.
Gregerson, Halfdan. *Ibsen and Spain.* 1936.
Henderson, Archibald. *European Dramatists.* 1926.
Huneker, James G. *Iconoclasts.* 1928. (First ed. 1905.)
Huneker, James G. *Egoists.* 1909.
Ibsen, Henrik. *From Ibsen's Workshop.* 1912.
Ibsen, Henrik. *Letters.* 1905.
Koht, Halvdan. *The Life of Henrik Ibsen.* 1931.
Krutch, Joseph W. *The American Drama since 1918.* 1939.
Lee, Josephine. *The Ibsen Secret.* 1907.
Marriott, James W. *Modern Drama.* 1934.
Roberts, Richard E. *Henrik Ibsen.* 1912.
Shaw, George B. *The Quintessence of Ibsenism.* 1913.
Skinner, Richard D. *Our Changing Theatre.* 1931.
Weigand, Hermann J. *The Modern Ibsen.* 1925.
Zucker, Adolf E. *Ibsen, the Master Builder.* 1929.

Kaufman and Connelly

Clark, Barrett H. *An Hour of American Drama.* 1930.
Dickinson, Thomas H. *Playwrights of the New American Theatre.* 1925.
Flexner, Eleanor. *American Playwrights 1918–1938.* 1938.
Gassner, John. *Masters of the Drama.* 1940.
Krutch, Joseph W. *The American Drama since 1918.* 1939.
Mantle, Burns. *American Playwrights of Today.* 1929.
Mantle, Burns. *Contemporary American Playwrights.* 1938.
O'Hara, Frank H. *Today in American Drama.* 1939.
Skinner, Richard D. *Our Changing Theatre.* 1931.

John Howard Lawson

Block, Anita. *The Changing World in Plays and Theatre.* 1939.
Dickinson, Thomas H. *Playwrights of the New American Theatre.* 1925.
Flexner, Eleanor. *American Playwrights 1918–1938.* 1938.
Gassner, John. *Masters of the Drama.* 1940.
Krutch, Joseph W. *The American Drama since 1918.* 1939.
Mantle, Burns. *Contemporary American Playwrights.* 1938.
Skinner, Richard D. *Our Changing Theatre.* 1931.

Maurice Maeterlinck

Bithell, Jethro. *Life and Writings of Maurice Maeterlinck.* 1913.
Bithell, Jethro. *Contemporary Belgian Literature.* 1915.
Chandler, Frank W. *Modern Continental Playwrights.* 1931.
Chandler, Frank W. *The Contemporary Drama of France.* 1925.
Clark, Barrett H. *European Theories of the Drama.* 1925.
Clark, Macdonald. *Maurice Maeterlinck.* 1915.
Dickinson, Thomas H., ed. *The Theatre in a Changing Europe.* 1937.
Ellehauge, Martin. *Striking Figures among Modern English Dramatists.* 1931.
Flaccus, Louis W. *Artists and Thinkers.* 1916.
Gassner, John. *Masters of the Drama.* 1940.
Hale, Edward E., Jr. *Dramatists of Today.* 1911.
Harry, Gerard. *Maurice Maeterlinck.* 1910.
Hills, Elijah C. *Evolution of Maeterlinck's Dramatic Theory.* 1907.
Huneker, James G. *Iconoclasts.* 1928.
Jackson, Holbrook. *Maurice Maeterlinck.* 1910.
Leblanc, Georgette. *Souvenirs.* 1932.
Moderwell, Hiram K. *The Theatre of Today.* 1927.
Moses, Montrose J. *Maurice Maeterlinck.* 1911.
Phelps, William L. *Essays on Modern Dramatists.* 1921.
Smith, Hugh A. *Main Currents of Modern French Drama.* 1925.
Sturgis, G. F. *The Psychology of Maeterlinck.* 1914.
Taylor, Una. *Maurice Maeterlinck.* 1914.
Thomas, Edward. *Maurice Maeterlinck.* 1911.
Turquet-Milnes, Gladys. *Some Modern Belgian Writers.* 1917.

W. Somerset Maugham

Aldington, Richard. *W. Somerset Maugham.* 1939.
Bason, Frederick T. *William Somerset Maugham Bibliography.* 1931.
Block, Anita. *The Changing World in Plays and Theatre.* 1939.
Cordell, Richard A. *W. Somerset Maugham.* 1937.
Lewisohn, Ludwig. *The Drama and the Stage.* 1922.
Gassner, John. *Masters of the Drama.* 1940

Maugham, William S. *The Summing Up.* 1938.
McIver, Claude S. *William Somerset Maugham.* 1936.
Pelizzi, Camillo. *English Drama.* 1935.
Sawyer, Newell W. *The Comedy of Manners.* 1931.
Sutton, Graham. *Some Contemporary Dramatists.* 1926.

A. A. Milne

Cunliffe, John W. *Modern English Playwrights.* 1927.
Milne, Alan A. *Autobiography.* 1939.
Pelizzi, Camillo. *English Drama.* 1935.
Skinner, Richard D. *Our Changing Theatre.* 1931.
Sutton, Graham. *Some Contemporary Dramatists.* 1926.

Sean O'Casey

Byrne, Dawson. *The Story of Ireland's National Theatre.* 1929.
Gassner, John. *Masters of the Drama.* 1940.
Malone, Andrew E. *The Irish Drama.* 1929.
O'Casey, Sean. *The Flying Wasp.* 1937.
O'Casey, Sean. *I Knock at the Door.* 1939.
Pelizzi, Camillo. *English Drama.* 1935.
Robinson, Lennox, ed. *The Irish Theatre.* 1937.

Eugene O'Neill

Block, Anita. *The Changing World in Plays and Theatre.* 1939.
Brown, John M. *Upstage.* 1930.
Clark, Barrett H. *Eugene O'Neill.* 1929.
Clark, Barrett H. *An Hour of American Drama.* 1930.
Dickinson, Thomas H. *Playwrights of the New American Theatre.* 1925.
Eaton, Walter P. *The Drama in English.* 1930.
Flexner, Eleanor. *American Playwrights 1918–1938.* 1938.
Gassner, John. *Masters of the Drama.* 1940.
Geddes, Virgil. *The Melodramadness of Eugene O'Neill.* 1934.
Glaspell, Susan. *The Road to the Temple.* 1927.
Hamilton, Clayton. *Conversations on Contemporary Dramatists.* 1924.
Karsner, David. *Sixteen Authors to One.* 1928.
Krutch, Joseph W. *The American Drama since 1918.* 1939.
Mantle, Burns. *American Playwrights of Today.* 1929.
Mantle, Burns. *Contemporary American Playwrights.* 1938.
Mickle, Alan D. *Studies on Six Plays of Eugene O'Neill.* 1929.
Moses, Montrose J. *The American Dramatist.* 1925.
O'Hara, Frank H. *Today in American Drama.* 1939.
Pelizzi, Camillo. *English Drama.* 1935.
Sanborn, Ralph, and Clark, B. H. *A Bibliography of the Works of Eugene O'Neill.* 1931.
Sayler, Oliver M. *Our American Theatre.* 1923.
Sergeant, Elizabeth S. *Fire under the Andes.* 1927.
Skinner, Richard D. *Our Changing Theatre.* 1931.
Skinner, Richard D. *Eugene O'Neill.* 1935.
Sutton, Graham. *Some Contemporary Dramatists.* 1926.
Van Doren, Carl. *American and British Literature since 1890.* 1925.
Whipple, Thomas K. *Spokesmen.* 1928.
Winther, Sophus K. *Eugene O'Neill.* 1934.

Sir Arthur Wing Pinero

Clark, Barrett H. *European Theories of the Drama.* 1925.
Cunliffe, John W. *Modern English Playwrights.* 1927.
Dickinson, Thomas H. *The Contemporary Drama of England.* 1917.
Fyfe, Hamilton. *Sir Arthur Pinero's Plays and Players.* 1930.
Fyfe, Hamilton. *Arthur Pinero.* 1902.
Gassner, John. *Masters of the Drama.* 1940.
Hale, Edward E., Jr. *Dramatists of Today.* 1905.
Hamilton, Clayton. Preface to *The Social Plays of Arthur Wing Pinero.* 1917.
Howe, Percival P. *Dramatic Portraits.* 1913.
Landa, Myer J. *The Jew in Drama.* 1926.
Lewisohn, Ludwig. *The Modern Drama.* 1915.
Morgan, Arthur E. *Tendencies of Modern English Drama.* 1924.
Pelizzi, Camillo. *English Drama.* 1935.
Sawyer, Newell W. *Comedy of Manners.* 1931.

Luigi Pirandello

Chandler, Frank W. *Modern Continental Playwrights.* 1931.
Dickinson, Thomas H., ed. *The Theatre in a Changing Europe.* 1937.
Gassner, John. *Masters of the Drama.* 1940.
Livingston, Arthur. Prefaces to *Three Plays by Pirandello* and *Each in His Own Way and Other Plays.* 1922 and 1924.
MacClintock, Lander. *The Contemporary Drama of Italy.* 1923.
Nardelli, Frederico V. *L'Uomo Segreto.* 1932.
Palmer, John. *Studies in the Contemporary Theatre.* 1927.
Skinner, Richard D. *Our Changing Theatre.* 1931.
Starkie, Walter. *Luigi Pirandello.* 1937.
Vittorini, Domenico. *The Drama of Luigi Pirandello.* 1935.

Elmer Rice

Block, Anita. *The Changing World in Plays and Theatre.* 1939.
Clark, Barrett H. *An Hour of American Drama.* 1930.
Dickinson, Thomas H. *Playwrights of the New American Theatre.* 1925.
Gassner, John. *Master of the Drama.* 1940.
Krutch, Joseph W. *The American Drama since 1918.* 1939.
Mantle, Burns. *Contemporary American Playwrights.* 1938.
Moses, Montrose J. *The American Dramatist* 1925.
Pelizzi, Camillo. *English Drama.* 1935.
Skinner, Richard D. *Our Changing Theatre.* 1931

EDMOND ROSTAND

Chandler, Frank W. *Modern Continental Playwrights.* 1931.
Chandler, Frank W. *The Contemporary Drama of France.* 1925.
Chandler, Frank W. *Aspects of Modern Drama.* 1914.
Clark, Barrett H. *Contemporary French Drama.* 1915.
Cunliffe, John W., and de Bacourt, P. *French Literature of the Last Half-Century.* 1923.
Duclaux, Agnes M. F. *Twentieth Century French Writers.* 1919.
Eliot, Thomas S. *The Sacred Wood.* 1921.
Gassner, John. *Masters of the Drama.* 1940.
Hale, Edward E., Jr. *Dramatists of Today.* 1911.
Moderwell, Hiram K. *The Theatre of Today.* 1927.
Phelps, William L. *Essays on Modern Dramatists.* 1921.
Smith, Hugh A. *Main Currents of Modern French Drama.* 1925.

ARTHUR SCHNITZLER

Björkman, Edwin A. Introduction to *The Lonely Way,* etc. 1917.
Block, Anita. *The Changing World in Plays and Theatre.* 1939.
Chandler, Frank W. *Modern Continental Playwrights.* 1931.
Dukes, Ashley. *The Youngest Drama.* 1924.
Eloesser, Arthur. *Modern German Literature.* 1933.
Gassner, John. *Masters of the Drama.* 1940.
Lewisohn, Ludwig. *The Spirit of Modern German Literature.* 1916.
Lewisohn, Ludwig. *The Modern Drama.* 1915.
Liptzin, Solomon. *Arthur Schnitzler.* 1932.
Moderwell, Hiram K. *The Theatre of Today.* 1927.

AUGUST STRINDBERG

Björkman, Edwin A. Introductions to *Plays by August Strindberg.* 1912–1917.
Campbell, George A. *Strindberg.* 1933.
Chandler, Frank W. *Modern Continental Playwrights.* 1931.
Dickinson, Thomas H., ed. *The Theatre in a Changing Europe.* 1937.
Gassner, John. *Masters of the Drama.* 1940.
Henderson, Archibald. *European Dramatists.* 1916.
Huneker, James G. *Iconoclasts.* 1928. (First ed. 1905.)
Lewisohn, Ludwig. *The Modern Drama.* 1915.
Lind-af-Hageby, Lizzy. *August Strindberg, the Spirit of Revolt.* 1913.
Lind-af-Hageby, Lizzy. *August Strindberg.* 1928.
Macy, John A. *The Critical Game.* 1922.
McGill, Vivian J. *August Strindberg, the Bedevilled Viking.* 1930.
Moderwell, Hiram K. *The Theatre of Today.* 1927.
Uddgren, Carl G. *Strindberg the Man.* 1920.

HERMANN SUDERMANN

Chandler, Frank W. *Modern Continental Playwrights.* 1931.
Eloesser, Arthur. *Modern German Literature.* 1933.
Gassner, John. *Masters of the Drama.* 1940.
Hale, Edward E., Jr. *Dramatists of Today.* 1911.
Huneker, James G. *Iconoclasts.* 1928.
Lewisohn, Ludwig. *The Modern Drama.* 1915.

SYNGE, DUNSANY, AND LADY GREGORY

Bickley, Francis L. *Synge and the Irish Dramatic Movement.* 1912.
Bierstadt, Edward H. *Dunsany the Dramatist.* 1917.
Bourgeois, Maurice. *John Millington Synge and the Irish Theatre.* 1913.
Boyd, Ernest A. *Ireland's Literary Renaissance.* 1916.
Boyd, Ernest A. *The Contemporary Drama of Ireland.* 1917.
Byrne, Dawson. *The Story of Ireland's National Theatre.* 1929.
Corkery, Daniel. *Synge and Anglo-Irish Literature.* 1931.
Ellehauge, Martin. *Striking Figures among Modern English Dramatists.* 1931.
Ellis-Fermor, Una. *The Irish Dramatic Movement.* 1939.
Fay, William G. *The Fays of the Abbey Theatre.* 1935.
Gassner, John. *Masters of the Drama.* 1940.
Gregory, Augusta I. *Our Irish Theatre.* 1913.
Gwynn, Stephen, ed. *Scattering Branches.* 1940.
Howe, Percival P. *John Millington Synge.* 1912.
Malone, Andrew E. *The Irish Drama.* 1929.
Marriott, James W. *Modern Drama.* 1934.
Masefield, John. *John M. Synge.* 1915.
Miller, Anna I. *The Independent Theatre in Europe.* 1931.
Moore, George. *Hail and Farewell.* 1914.
Morgan, Arthur E. *Tendencies of Modern English Drama.* 1924.
Pelizzi, Camillo. *English Drama.* 1935.
Robinson, Lennox, ed. *The Irish Theatre.* 1939.
Synge, Samuel. *Letters to My Daughter.* 1932.
Weygandt, Cornelius. *Irish Plays and Playwrights.* 1912.
Yeats, William B. *Synge and the Ireland of His Time.* 1911.
Yeats, William B. *Plays and Controversies.* 1923.
Yeats, William B. *Autobiography.* 1938.

ERNST TOLLER

Block, Anita. *The Changing World in Plays and Theatre.* 1939.
Chandler, Frank W. *Modern Continental Playwrights.* 1931.
Dickinson, Thomas H., ed. *The Theatre in a Changing Europe.* 1937.
Gassner, John. *Masters of the Drama.* 1940.
Toller, Ernst. *Look Through the Bars.* 1937.

ILLUSTRATIONS TO THE PLAYS

NOTE: Figures following colons are page numbers in the indicated volumes.

ABE LINCOLN IN ILLINOIS

Theatre Arts. 22:700, 806, 849; 23:801.
Mantle: *The Best Plays of 1938–1939:* front.
New International Year Book 1938: 216.
Life. 31 Oct. '38: cover, 42, 45; 6 Feb. '39:29.
Stage. 16:Nov. 8; 15 Apr. 39:43; June 39: cover; Oct. 44.

BEGGAR ON HORSEBACK

Theatre Magazine. 39:May 13; 40:Oct. 29; 41: Jan. 32; 44:Nov. 43; 53:Feb. 49.
Theatre Arts. 10:644.
Drama. 21:Nov. 25.
Illustrated London News. 166 (1925):1001.
Gregor and Fülöp-Miller: *Das Amerikanische Theater:* No. 57.
Anderson: *American Theatre:* 210.
Stratton: *Theatron:* 101.
Mantle: *Best Plays of 1923–1924:* 182.
Komisarjevsky and Simonson: *Settings and Costumes for the Modern Stage:* 119.
Rotha: *Movie Parade:* 33.
Dolman: *Art of Play Production:* 78.
Freedley and Reeves: *History of the Theatre:* No. 372.

THE CHERRY ORCHARD

Theatre Arts. 4:204; 7:2, 32, 33, 34, 35; 16: 572; 17:924; 18:145, 611; 20:551, 951.
Drama. 13:136; 19:110.
Theatre Guild Magazine. 9:Oct. 15.
Illustrated London News. 183:694.
Stage. 10:Apr. 7.
Life. 29 May '39:70.
Sayler: *Russian Theatre:* 46, 47, 59.
Macgowan and Jones: *Continental Stagecraft:* 10.
Cheney: *Stage Decoration:* No. 42.
Hume and Fuerst: *Twentieth Century Stage Decoration:* No. 5.
Moderwell: *Theatre of Today:* 126.
Isaacs: *Theatre:* 4.
Moscow Art Theatre Plays. I.
Carter: *New Theatre of Soviet Russia:* 204.
Stanislavsky: *My Life in Art:* 420.
Cheney: *Theatre:* 507.
Bakshy: *Path of the Modern Russian Stage:* 25.
Lanchester: *Charles Laughton and I:* 132.
Encyclopaedia Britannica (14th edition): 22: 22.
Dubech: *Histoire Générale du Théâtre:* 5:387.
Gielgud: *Early Stages:* 88.
Freedley and Reeves: *History of the Theatre:* No. 295.

THE CIRCLE

Theatre Magazine. 34:319; 39:Jan. 21; 49: Mar. 57.
Theatre Arts. 22:397.
Illustrated London News. 158 (1922):478; 178 (1931):556.
L'Illustration. 172:704.

CYRANO DE BERGERAC

Theatre Magazine. 1:Dec. 48; 7:284; 9:85; 17: 106, 107; 39:Jan. 23; 48: Aug. 35; 49:Mar. 36.
Theatre Arts. 8:77, 118; 11:679; 15:616; 18: 610; 20:509; 23:678; 25:63.
L'Illustration. 187:476; 111:25, 27; 141:269; 178:323; 187:476.
McClure's. 35:524.
Hume and Fuerst: *Twentieth Century Stage Decoration:* No. 136.
Fischel: *Das Moderne Bühnenbild:* No. 89.
Anderson: *American Theatre:* 205, 231, 238.
Crawford: *Romance of the American Theatre:* 483.
Dubech: *Histoire Générale du Théâtre:* 3:238, 269; 5:177.
Wilstach: *Richard Mansfield:* 318, 322, 324.
Loraine: *Head Wind:* 258.
Smith: *Main Currents of Modern French Drama:* 103.
Fuchs: *Stage Lighting:* 471, 472, 473.
Gregor and Fülöp-Miller: *Das Amerikanische Theater:* No. 43, No. 90, No. 98.
Sayler: *Max Reinhardt and His Theatre:* 88.
Winter: *Life of Mansfield II:* 128, 136.
Hooker translation of play: front.

DEAR BRUTUS

Theatre Magazine. 29:81, 156.
Theatre Arts. 20:799.
Stratton: *Theatron:* 100.
Macgowan: *Footlights Across America:* 151.
Brown: *Letters to Mary:* 68.

A DOLL'S HOUSE

Theatre Magazine. 2:Aug. 3; 7:71, 218.
Theatre Arts. 10:217; 12:23, 221; 15:594; 20: 398, 951; 21:503; 22:84, 162, 240.
Illustrated London News. 138:720; 167:1214.
Theatre Guild Magazine. 7:June 32, 33.
Stage. 15:Oct. 73, Jan. 41, Feb. 55.
L'Illustration. 197:126.
Dubech: *Histoire Générale du Théâtre:* 5:409.
Hume and Fuerst. *Twentieth Century Stage Decoration:* No. 1.
Carter: *New Theatre of Soviet Russia:* 216.
Bab: *Theater der Gegenwart:* 50, 71.
Lugné-Poe: *Ibsen:* No. 17, 38.
Gorelik: *New Theatres for Old:* 52.

THE DREAM PLAY

Theatre Magazine. 51:Mar. 39.
Hume and Fuerst: *Twentieth Century Stage Decoration:* No. 210, No. 211.
Deutsch and Hanau: *The Provincetown:* 156.

ELIZABETH THE QUEEN

Theatre Magazine. 52:Nov. 27, Dec. 30; 53:Jan. cover, Feb. 28.
Theatre Arts. 14:902; 19:492; 20:861; 23:803.
Theatre Guild Magazine. 8:Nov. 10, Apr. 17.
Stage. 13:June 54.
Illustrated London News. 184 (1934):854.
Life. 1 Nov. 1937:109.
Mantle: *Best Plays of 1930–1931:* 34.

THE EMPEROR JONES

Theatre Magazine. 33:8; 41:May 53; 45:Jan. 11; 53:Feb. 51.
Theatre Arts. 5:11, 12; 6:43; 8:377, 378, 379, 399, 400; 10:117, 118; 13:492; 16:521, 607; 17:801, 531; 18:525; 22:881; 24:573.
Drama. 12:23.
Theatre Guild Magazine. 9:Nov. 13.
Illustrated London News. 167 (1925): 538; 184 (1934): 414.
Stage. 9:Sept. 23; 10:Dec. 19, Aug. 40; 13:July 66; 15:Apr. 80.
Isaacs: *Theatre:* 298.
Sayler: *American Theatre:* 93.
Gregor and Fülöp-Miller: *Das Amerikanische Theater:* No. 177, No. 178.
Saturday Review of Literature. 15 (1937):6.
Komisarjevsky and Simonson: *Settings and Costumes of the Modern Stage:* 128.
Stratton: *Producing in the Little Theatre:* 38.
Moussinac: *Tendances Nouvelles du Théâtre:* 18, 19.
Deutsch and Hanau: *The Provincetown:* 68, 145.
Stratton: *Theatron:* 241.
Hume and Fuerst: *Twentieth Century Stage Decoration:* No. 219.
Simonson: *Theatre Art:* No. 621.
Oenslager: *Scenery Then and Now:* at back.
Burris-Meyer and Cole: *Scenery for the Theatre:* 245.
Anderson: *American Theatre:* 260.
Rotha: *Movie Parade:* 92.
Heffner, *et al.*: *Modern Theatre Practice:* 161.
Freedley and Reeves: *History of the Theatre:* No. 330.

THE FOSSILS

Dubech: *Histoire Générale du Théâtre:* 5:157.

THE GLITTERING GATE

Theatre Arts. 1:173, 174; 8:509, 511, 624.
Drama. 20:244.
Gregor and Fülöp-Miller: *Das Amerikanische Theater:* No. 175, No. 176.
Anderson: *American Theatre:* 259.
Simonson: *Theatre Art:* 489.
Cheney: *Art Theatre* (1917 edition): 64.
Mackay: *Little Theatre in the United States:* 174.
Bierstadt: *Dunsany the Dramatist:* 26.

THE HAIRY APE

Theatre Magazine. 35:283; 36:80, 82, 153; 47:Feb. 13; 52:Oct. 50.
Theatre Arts. 6:183; 10:331; 12:654; 14:602; 18:554, 598; 20:559.
Drama. 12:330.
Theatre Guild Magazine. 7:Aug. 13; 9:Nov. 11.
New International Year Book, 1922:206.
Sayler: *Our American Theatre:* 39.
Simonson: *The Stage Is Set:* 522.
Deutsch and Hanau: *The Provincetown:* 81.
Komisarjevsky and Simonson: *Settings and Costumes of the Modern Stage:* 54, 88.
Theatre Arts Prints. Series I.

HEDDA GABLER

Theatre Magazine. 3:266; 7:219; 21:11; 27:349; 4:292; 36:141; 40:Aug. 5; 43:Apr. 14; 48:Dec. 53.
Theatre Arts. 16:345, 603; 20:398, 912; 18:231; 10:221.
Theatre Guild Magazine. 7:June 33, 34.
Stage. 10:Dec. 20; 11:Dec. 30.
Drama. 16:251.
Le Gallienne: *Civic Repertory Plays:* 5.
Lugné-Poe: *Ibsen:* No. 16, No. 40.
Woollcott: *Mrs. Fiske:* 46.

"HENRY IV"

Theatre Arts. 8:223; 15:729.
Illustrated London News. 164:1113.
Gregor and Fülöp-Miller: *Das Amerikanische Theater:* No. 255.
Anderson: *American Theatre:* 300.
Flanagan: *Shifting Scenes:* No. 3.
Sheringham: *Design in the Theatre:* No. 24, No. 25.

HE WHO GETS SLAPPED

Theatre Magazine. 35:141, 231; 38:Oct. 42; 36:229, 291; 41:Feb. 40.
Theatre Arts. 6:97, 303, 304; 14:352; 19:525; 20:883; 22:449.
Theatre Guild Magazine. 8:Oct. 23.
Illustrated London News. 171:978.
Drama. 12:194; 16:185; 18:150.
Theatre Guild edition of play: passim.
Eaton: *Theatre Guild:* 97.
Rotha: *Movie Parade:* 83.
Stratton: *Theatron:* 49.
Macgowan: *Footlights Across America:* 18.
Macgowan and Jones: *Continental Stagecraft:* 24.

HOTEL UNIVERSE

Theatre Magazine. 51:June 44.
McCleery and Glick: *Curtains Going Up:* 52.
Hewitt: *Art and Craft of Play Production:* 29.

HYACINTH HALVEY

Fay and Carswell: *Fays of the Abbey Theatre:* 164.

JUNO AND THE PAYCOCK

Theatre Magazine. 43:June 17.
Theatre Arts. 10:288; 11:791, 541; 16:569; 12:227; 9:397; 18:791; 24:154.
Drama. 18:68; 21:Feb. 34.

Justice

Theatre Magazine. 24:23, 77; 23:296, 297.
Stage. 10:Dec. 20; 14:Aug. 72.
Illustrated London News. 46 (1910):432.

Loyalties

Theatre Magazine. 36:370.
Illustrated London News. 160 (1922):386, 478; 181 (1932):338; 183 (1933):6.
Galsworthy: *Plays, 5th series:* 2, 20, 42, 56, 72.

Magda

Theatre Magazine. 2:Feb. 3; 49:May 15.
Illustrated London News. 108:783; 162:748.
Illustrirte Zeitung. 184:488.
Winter: *Wallet of Time* II: 354.
Modjeska: *Memories and Impressions:* 532.

Man and the Masses

Theatre Magazine. 39:Jan. 22, June 5; 52: Sept. 49.
Theatre Arts. 6:219–222; 8:361, 513; 15:536; 23:503.
Theatre Guild Magazine. 9:Oct. 32; 7:Oct. 31.
Isaacs: *Theatre:* 64.
Theatre Guild edition of play: passim.
Simonson: *Stage Is Set:* 512, 513.
Fischel: *Das Moderne Bühnenbild:* 119.
Gregor and Fülöp-Miller: *Das Amerikanische Theater:* No. 220, No. 222.
Moussinac: *Tendances Nouvelles du Théâtre:* 111–113.
Houghton: *Moscow Rehearsals:* 77.
Macgowan and Jones: *Continental Stagecraft:* 148–156.
Carter: *New Theatre of the Soviets:* 52.
Toller: *Look Through the Bars:* 212.
Anderson: *American Theatre:* 281, 284.
Hewitt: *Art and Craft of Play Production:* 171.
Gorelik: *New Theatres for Old:* 276.

Mid-Channel

Theatre Magazine. 11:73; 23:81.
Illustrated London News. 45 (1909):572.
Pinero: *Social Plays IV:* 294, 416, 470.

Mr. Pim Passes By

Theatre Magazine. 33:319, 328; 34:152, 154, 156, 158; 38:Aug. 29; 50:Nov. 51.
Illustrated London News. 156 (1920): 412.

Night's Lodging (The Lower Depths)

Theatre Magazine. 36:216; 37:Mar. 14.
Theatre Arts. 4:339; 7:32, 33, 34; 8:104; 14: 196; 18:299, 555; 19:878; 21:569; 24:482.
Drama. 13:128; 20:246.
L'Illustration. 126:272.
Theatre Guild Magazine. 9:Oct. 17, Nov. 18.
Encyclopaedia Britannica, 14th edition: 22:22.
Sayler: *Russian Theatre:* 66.
Hume and Fuerst: *Twentieth Century Stage Decoration:* No. 104.
Sayler: *Max Reinhardt and His Theatre:* 70, 71.
Carter: *New Theatre of Soviet Russia:* 212.
Stanislavsky: *My Life in Art:* 394.
Moscow Art Theatre Plays I.
Hughes: *Story of the Theatre:* 306.
Dubech: *Histoire Générale du Théâtre:* 5:392.
Nemirovich-Danchenko: *My Life in the Russian Theatre:* 234.
Freedley and Reeves: *History of the Theatre:* No. 288, 293.

The Passion Flower

Theatre Magazine. 31:183, 259.
Drama. 11:72.
Downs: *Theatre and Stage* I: 402.

Pélléas and Mélisande

Theatre Magazine. 7:174; 8:112, 113; 12:194, 195; 13:41, 77; 21:11; 39:Feb. 14.
Theatre Arts. 3:112, 183, 184, 185, 186; 8:151, 152, 595; 9:351; 23:359.
Stage. 14:Jan. 89.
L'Illustration. 136:153.
Gregor and Fülöp-Miller: *Das Amerikanische Theater und Kino:* No. 54, No. 154, No. 155.
Hume and Fuerst: *Twentieth Century Stage Decoration:* No. 204, No. 224, 225, No. 253.
Macgowan: *Theatre of Tomorrow:* front.
Cogniat: *Décors de Théâtre:* No. 62.
Jones: *Drawings for the Theatre:* No. 15.
Ridge: *Stage Lighting:* 167.
Leblanc: *Souvenirs:* 171.
Martin-Harvey: *Autobiography:* 388.
Anderson: *American Theatre:* 232.
Smith: *Main Currents of Modern French Drama:* 294.

Processional

Theatre Magazine. 41:Apr. 14.
Theatre Arts. 9:148; 18:592; 20:972.
Theatre Guild Magazine. 8:Feb. 42.
Drama. 15:101, 103, 109; 16:146.
Theatre Guild edition of play: passim.
Eaton: *Theatre Guild:* 160.
Gregor and Fülöp-Miller: *Das Amerikanische Theater:* No. 204, No. 209.
Anderson: *American Theatre:* 244, 276.
Freedley and Reeves: *History of the Theatre:* No. 382.

Riders to the Sea

Theatre Magazine: 46:July 45.
Theatre Arts. 16:569, 920; 24:482.
Drama. 15:106.

R. U. R.

Theatre Magazine. 37:Jan. 18.
Theatre Arts. 7:13; 8:29, 626, 627, 713; 9:256; 18:556.
Drama. 21:May 26.
Illustrated London News. 162:794.
Theatre Guild edition of play: passim.
Sayler: *American Theatre:* 263.
Cheney: *Stage Decoration:* No. 90.
Stratton: *Theatron:* 197.

Hume and Fuerst: *Twentieth Century Stage Decoration:* No. 158, No. 159.
Eaton: *Theatre Guild:* 113.
Simonson: *Theatre Art:* No. 193.
Freedley and Reeves: *History of the Theatre:* No. 334.

THE SILVER CORD

Theatre Magazine. 45:Mar. 19, 50.
Illustrated London News. 171 (1927):622.
Mantle: *Best Plays of 1926–1927:* 222.
McCleery and Glick: *Curtains Going Up:* 308.
Edition of play: 5, 51.

STREET SCENE

Theatre Magazine. 49:Apr. 26, 27; 50:Aug. 34, Sept. front.; 51:May 20.
Theatre Arts. 13:167; 15:255; 16:47; 18:555, 593; 23:479.
Illustrated London News. 180 (1932):12.
Stage. 16:1 May:56.
Dickinson: *Theatre in a Changing Europe:* 411.
Mantle: *Best Plays of 1928–1929:* 48.
Komisarjevsky and Simonson: *Settings and Costumes of the Modern Stage:* 121.
McCleery and Glick: *Curtains Going Up:* 52.

UNCLE VANYA

Theatre Magazine. 37:May 23; 43:June 21; 51: June 18, 19, 20, 45; 52:July 21, 43, Nov. 19.
Theatre Arts. 4:340; 14:456; 18:551.
Theatre Guild Magazine. 7:June 10, May 13; 9:Oct. 16.
Macgowan and Jones: *Continental Stagecraft:* 124.
Sayler: *The Russian Theatre:* 58.
Moscow Art Theatre Plays, vol. 1.
Nemirovich-Danchenko: *My Life in the Russian Theatre:* 200.
Bakshy: *Path of the Modern Russian Stage:* 17.
Whitworth: *Theatre in Action:* 42.
Hewitt: *Art and Craft of Play Production:* 239.

WHAT EVERY WOMAN KNOWS

Theatre Magazine. 9:17, 39, 65, 118, 119; 44: July 13; 49:May 49.
Theatre Arts. 16:727; 20:792, 800.
Illustrated London News. 43 (1908): 538.
Stage. 13:Sept. 50.
Drama. 17:9; 19:84.
Brown: *Letters to Mary:* 116.
Brady: *Showman:* 238.